BRITISH MUSEUM Dept. of printed books.

GENERAL CATALOGUE OF PRINTED BOOKS

Photolithographic edition
to 1955

Volume 30

BURGERM—BUTS

PUBLISHED BY
THE TRUSTEES OF THE BRITISH MUSEUM

LONDON 1965

Printed in England by
Balding + Mansell, London and Wisbech

BURGERMAN. Regenten of vertegenwoordigers der burgerij? Een praatje . . . opgedragen . . . in 1883 . . . door een Burgerman. pp. 31. *Nijmegen*, 1885. 8°. **8081. h. 4. (5.)**

BÜRGERMEISTER. *See* BUERGERMEISTER.

BÜRGERMEISTER. [For the German surname of this form:] *See* BUERGERMEISTER.

BURGERMEISTER (JOHANN STEPHAN) *See* GERMANY. [*Laws, etc.*—I.] Teutsches Corpus juris, publici & privati, oder Codex diplomaticus. Der teutschen Staats-, Lehen-, Burger- und peinlichen Rechten und Gewohnheiten, wie auch Process-Ordnungen an denen Kayserl. Reichs-, Hof-, Cammer- und Land-Gerichten, &c. . . . Collectore J. S. Burgermeistero. 1717. 4°. **229. h. 1, 2.**

—— *See* GERMANY. [*Laws, etc.*—II. *Knights.*] Codex diplomaticus equestris, cum continuatione, oder Reichs-Ritter-Archiv, mit dessen Fortsetzung . . . Curante J. S. Burgermeistero, *etc.* 1721. 4°. **229. h. 7–10.**

—— Bibliotheca equestris . . . Curante J. S. Burgermeistero, *etc.* 2 Tl. *Ulm*, 1720. 4°. **229. h. 3–6.**

—— Graven und Ritter-Saal, das ist Gründliche Vorstellung und Ausführung; welcher gestalt des H. Röm. Reichs Grafen, Herren und die andere Reichs-Ritterschafft bey des H. Röm. Reichs dreyen namhafften Veränderungen . . . gegen- und beyeinander gestanden, *rc.* Samt einem Anhang von 2. andern Discursen . . . 1. D. Joh. Ulrichs Pregitzers . . . über des Schilteri diatribam de prærogativa comitum, &c. Und 2. Wolffgangi de Gemmingen . . . de conjunctione antiqua comitum cum reliquis nobilibus immediatis . . . Collectore J. S. Burgermeistero. 2 pt. *Franckfurt*, 1721. 4°. **26. h. 24.**

—— *See* GERMANY.—*Nobility.* Adeliches Ritter-Feld . . . Nebst einem Vorbericht . . . darinnen Dr. Burgemeisters sogenannter Grafen- und Ritter-Saal summariter untersuchet ist. 1721. 4°. **9905. bbb. 26.**

—— Manuale equestre, oder Compendium der Reichs-ritterschaftlichen alt-hergebrachten Rechten, kayserlichen Privilegien und Freyheiten . . . Curante D. J. S. B. C. C. & U. [i.e. Domino Johanne Stephano Burgermeistero Consiliario Caesareo et Ulmensi], *etc.* 2 vol. 1720, 21. 8°. *See* C. et U., D. I. S. B. C. **26. h. 23.**

—— Status equestris Caesaris et Imperii Romano-Germanici, das ist: Dess unmittelbaren . . . Reichs-Adels . . . in Schwaben, Francken, und am Rhein-Strohm, ursprüngliche Im̃edietät, Prærogativen, Immunitäten, *etc.* pp. 735 [755]. *Ulm*, 1709. 4°. **26. h. 14.**

—— [Another edition.] Thesaurus iuris equestris publici et privati . . . Collectore J. S. Burgermeistero. 2 Tl. *Ulm*, 1718. 4°. **19. a. 13, 14.**

BURGERMEISTERUS (GABRIEL FRANCISCUS) Dissertationem hanc historico-juridicam, qua legitimatio per rescriptum principis Justiniano Imperatori tanquam auctori acque inventori vindicatur . . . exponit G. F. Burgermeisterus. *Praes.* C. H. Hillerus. pp. 46. *Tubingæ*, [1723.] 4°. **897. b. 6. (7.)**

BURGERMEISTERUS (JOHANNES STEPHANUS) *See* BURGERMEISTER (Johann Stephan)

BURGERS' CODE COMPANY. Burgers' Private Code System. pp. 17. *New York*, [1921.] 4°. **8764. d. 17.**

BURGERS (HEINRICH JACOB) *See* HEIJE (J. P.) De Gelaarsde kat . . . Ets-photogrammen door H. J. Burgers, *etc.* [1870.] 4°. **11556. k. 21.**

BURGERS (HENRI JOSEPH) Dissertation sur la ménorrhagie, *etc.* pp. 24. *Paris*, 1815. 4°. **1183. c. 14. (18.)**

BURGERS (JOACHIM) *See* HUNNIUS (H. U.) Dn. Helfrici Ulrici Hunnii . . . Encyclopedia juris universi, *etc.* [Edited by J. Burgers.] 1675. fol. **5510. f. 7.**

BURGERS (JOHANNES MARTINUS) *See* KÁRMÁN (Th*eodore* von) and BURGERS (J. M.) General Aerodynamic Theory, *etc.* 1935. 8°. **08770. d. 1.**

—— *See* SLIJPER (E. J.) De Vliegkunst in het dierenrijk. Door . . . E. J. Slijper . . . met medewerking van . . . J. M. Burgers. 1950. 8°. **7286. d. 33.**

—— Deformation and Flow. Monographs on the rheological behaviour of natural and synthetic products. Edited by J. M. Burgers . . . J. J. Hermans . . . G. W. Scott Blair. *North-Holland Publishing Co.: Amsterdam*, 1952– . 8°. W.P. B. **683.**

—— Grondslagen voor een nomenclatuur der deformaties. Door J. M. Burgers, R. N. J. Saal en C. B. Biezeno. pp. 44. *Amsterdam*, 1941. 8°. [*Verhandelingen der Nederlandsche Akademie van Wetenschappen.* Afd. Natuurkunde. sect. 1. dl. 18. no. 1.] **Ac.944/2.(a.)**

—— Mathematical Examples illustrating Relations occurring in the Theory of Turbulent Fluid Motion, *etc.* pp. 53. *Amsterdam*, 1939. 8°. [*Verhandelingen der Koninklijke Nederlandsche Akademie van Wetenschappen.* Afd natuurkunde. sectie 1. dl. 17. no. 2.] **Ac.944/2.(a.)**

—— On the Motion of Small Particles of Elongated Form suspended in a Viscous Liquid. 1938. *See* AMSTERDAM.—*Koninklijke Akademie van Wetenschappen.—Viscositeitscommissie.* First [*etc.*] Report on Viscosity and Plasticity. Second Report. 1935, *etc.* 8°. [*Verhandelingen der Koninklijke Akademie van Wetenschappen.* Afd. natuurkunde. sect. 1. dl. 16. no. 4.] **Ac.944/2.(a.)**

—— Over de verhouding tussen het entropiebegrip en de levensfuncties. pp. 39. *Amsterdam*, 1943. 8°. [*Verhandelingen der Nederlandsche Akademie van Wetenschappen.* Afd. Natuurkunde. sect. 1. dl. 18. no. 3.] **Ac.944/2.(a.)**

—— Trekken van de moderne Westerse wetenschap. pp. 24. *Amsterdam*, 1944. 8°. [*Mededeelingen der Nederlandsche Akademie van Wetenschappen.* Afd. Letterkunde. Nieuwe reeks. dl. 7. no. 5.] Ac. **944. (2.)**

BURGERS (JOHANNES MARTINUS) and **BLAIR** (GEORGE WILLIAM SCOTT)

—— Report on the Principles of Rheological Nomenclature. pp. 72. 1949. 8°. *See* INTERNATIONAL COUNCIL OF SCIENTIFIC UNIONS.—*Joint Committee on Rheology.* **8536. c. 14.**

BURGERS (JOHANNES MARTINUS) and **ZIJNEN** (BERNARD GERARD VAN DER HEGGE)

—— Preliminary Measurements of the Distribution of the Velocity of a Fluid in the Immediate Neighbourhood of a Plane, Smooth Surface . . . Mededeeling no. 5 uit het Laboratorium voor Aerodynamica en Hydrodynamica der Technische Hoogeschool te Delft. pp. 33. *Amsterdam*, 1924. 8°. [*Verhandelingen der Koninklijke Akademie van Wetenschappen te Amsterdam.* Afd. natuurkunde. sect. 1. dl. 13. no. 3.] **Ac.944/2.(a.)**

BURGERS (M.) *See* RUSS (Carl) *Dr.* [Der Wellensittich.] The Budgerigar . . . Translated by Dr. M. Burgers, *etc.* [1928.] 8°. **7286. aa. 41.**

BURGERS (MARIUS PHILIP OLIVIERA)

—— Die Mens Langenhoven . . . Dissertasie, *etc.* [With a portrait.] pp. 342. *Kaapstad*, 1939. 8°. **20014.** e. 5.

BURGERS (NICOLAUS) Anatomia Calixtina, h.e. Vindiciæ catholicæ, quas . . . pro asserendo S. Rom. Ecclesiae tribunali in fidei causis infallibili . . . contra Georgii Calixti . . . nov-antiquas impugnationes . . . solenni disceptatione indicit N. Burgers, *etc.* *Praes.* V. Ebermannus. pp. 47. *N. Heyll: Moguntiæ*, 1644. 4°. **3907.** bb. **17.** (**1.**)

BURGERS (OLIVIER) Sannie. Dramatisiering van " Die Wegraak van Sannie," van Eugène N. Marais. Deur O. Burgers. pp. 46. *Pretoria*, [1930.] 8°. **20001.** aa. **5.**

BURGERS (THOMAS FRANÇOIS) *President of the Transvaal. See* ENGELBRECHT (S. P.) Thomas François Burgers. 'n Lewenskets. 1933. 8°. **10760.** g. **32.**

—— *See* ENGELBRECHT (Stephanus P.) Thomas François Burgers. A biography. 1946. 8°. **010608.** e. **18.**

—— [For official documents issued by T. F. Burgers as President of the Transvaal:] *See* TRANSVAAL.

—— Schetsen uit die Transvaal . . . Opnuut uitgegee en van aantekeninge vorsien deur Dr. S. P. Engelbrecht, *etc.* [With a portrait.] pp. ix. 40. *Pretoria*, 1934. 8°. **20009.** h. **5.**

—— Tooneelen uit ons dorp . . . Met . . . portret van den onlangs overlenen schrijver, en een voorwoord van Theod. M. Tromp. pp. viii. 237. v. *'s-Gravenhage*, 1882. 8°. **12580.** n. **29.**

BURGERS (WILHELM GERARD) *See* HOUWINK (Roelof) Elasticity, Plasticity and Structure of Matter . . . With a chapter on the plasticity of crystals by . . . W. G. Burgers. 1937. 8°. **8710.** aaa. **18.**

—— *See* INTERNATIONAL CONFERENCE ON THE PHYSICS OF METALS. International Conference on the Physics of Metals. (Papers.) [Edited by W. G. Burgers and M. J. Druyvesteyn.] 1949. 8°. **07107.** w. **14.**

—— Plasticity of Crystals. *In:* HOUWINK (Roelof) Elasticity, Plasticity and Structure of Matter, *etc.* pp. 73–127. 1954. 8°. **8714.** cc. **15.**

BURGERSDICIUS (FRANCO) *See* BURGERSDIJCK.

BURGERSDIJCK (FRANCO) [For dissertations at which F. Burgersdijck acted as praeses:]

See BALFOUR (David) *M.D., the Elder.*
BERCKELIUS (H. W. F.)
CABELIAVIUS (S.)
DOORNYCK (P. J. F.)
HANECOPIUS (A.)
HOOLCK (C. G. van der)
JONGE (A. de)
LE COQ (P.)
OUDOUS (P.)
PISTORIUS (W.)
RHAMPIUS (C.)
SCHOONHOVIUS (A.)
STEYARDUS (P.)
SYLVIUS (Jacobus) *Harlem.*
VERTRECHT (J.)
VOGELSANG (J.)

—— *See* HEEREBOORD (A.) Adriani Heereboord . . . ἑρμηνεια logica, seu Explicatio . . . synops. logicæ Burgersdicianæ, *etc.* 1657. 8°. **1478.** cc. **50.**

—— *See* SACRO BOSCO (J. de) Sphæra . . . Operâ & studio F. Burgersdicii. 1647. 8°. **10006.** b. **32.**

—— Idea philosophiæ tum naturalis tum moralis, sive epitome compendiosa vtriusq; ex Aristotele excerpta & methodicè disposita . . . Editio tertia prioribus emendatior. 2 pt. *Excudebat Ioh. Lichfield, impensis Henrici Curteyne: Oxoniæ*, 1631. 12°. **1472.** a. **7.**

BURGERSDIJCK (FRANCO)

—— Idea philosophiæ tum moralis tum naturalis: sive Epitome compendiosa utriusque ex Aristotele excerpta, & methodicè disposita: a M. F. Burgersdicio . . . Editio quarta prioribus castigatior. (Franconis Burgersdici Idea philosophiæ naturalis: sive Methodus definitionum & controversiarum physicarum. Editio postrema.) 2 pt. *Excudebat Guilielmus Turner, impensis Henrici Curteyne: Oxonii*, 1637. 12°. **8407.** a. **53.**

—— Idea Philosophiæ, tum Moralis, tum Naturalis . . . Editio quarta, *etc.* (Idea Philosophiæ Naturalis. Editio postrema.) *Oxonii*, 1637. 12°. Mic. A. **587.** (**12.**)
MICROFILM *of a copy of the preceding in Cambridge University Library. Made by University Microfilms*, 1954.

—— Collegium physicum. In quo tota philosophia naturalis aliquot disputationibus perspicue & compendiose explicatur. Auctore & præside M. F. Burgersdicio, *etc.* (Disputationum physicarum prima—trigesima-secunda.) 34 pt. *Ex officina B. & A. Elzevir: Lugduni Batavorum*, 1632. 4°. **536.** h. **29.**

—— [Another copy.] MS. NOTES. **536.** d. **11.**
Imperfect; wanting the first leaf, containing the collective titlepage and a part of the list of contents.

—— Editio secunda, autoris manu aucta. pp. 353. *Ex officinâ Elziviriorum: Lugd. Batavorum*, 1642. 12°. **531.** a. **6.**

—— Disputatio physica prima (—decima-sexta), *etc. Praes.* F. Burgersdijck. 16 pt. *J. Cornelii: Lugduni Batavorum*, 1624. 4°. **534.** c. **36.**
(**1, 5, 6, 8, 10, 12, 13, 16, 18, 20, 22, 25–27, 30, 33.**)
Pt. 1 *and* 4 *are cropped.*

—— Disputationum physicarum prima (—decima-octava), *etc. Praes.* F. Burgersdijck. pt. 1, 2, 4–18. MS. NOTES. *Ex officina B. & A. Elzevir: Lugduni Batavorum*, 1627. 4°. **534.** c. **36.**
(**2, 3, 7, 9, 11, 14, 15, 17, 19, 21, 23, 24, 28, 29, 31, 32, 34.**)
Wanting " Disputationum physicarum tertia."

—— Idea philosophiæ moralis, ex Aristotele maxima parte excerpta, & methodice disposita, a M. F. Burgersdicio. pp. 348. *Ex officina Elzeviriana: Lugduni Batavorum*, 1623. 12°. **8406.** a. **3.** (**1.**)

—— Idea philosophiæ moralis, sive Compendiosa institutio . . . Editio postrema, multis in locis emendata. pp. 161 [261]. *Ex officina Elzeviriana: Lugd. Batav.* 1644. 12°. **8406.** a. **29.**

—— Idea philosophiæ naturalis, collecta et consignata, a F. Burgersdicio. pp. 110. MS. NOTES. *Apud B. & A. Elzevirium: Lugd. Batavorum*, 1622. 12°. **8406.** a. **3.** (**2.**)

—— Fr. Burgersdijcki Idea politica, cum annotationibus Georgii Hornii. pp. 225. *F. Lopez de Haro: Lugd. Batav.*, 1668. 12°. **8010.** a. **42.** (**1.**)
The titlepage is engraved.

—— Franconis Burgersdici Institutionum logicarum libri duo . . . ex Aristotelis præceptis novâ methodo ac modo formati, atque editi. Editio secunda, ab autore multis locis emendata. pp. 224 [424]. *Apud A. Commelinum: Lugduni Batavorum*, 1634. 8°. **8466.** aa. **21.** (**1.**)

—— [Another edition.] pp. 304. *Ex Academiæ celeberrimæ typographeo: Cantabrigiæ*, 1637. 8°. **8467.** aa. **3.** (**1.**)

—— Fr. Burgersdicii Institutionum Logicarum Libri duo, *etc. Cantabrigæ*, 1637. 8°. Mic. A. **587.** (**11.**)
MICROFILM *of a copy of the preceding in Cambridge University Library. Made by University Microfilms*, 1954.

BURGERSDIJCK (FRANCO)

—— [Another edition.] Fr. Burgersdicii Institutionum logicarum libri duo. (Institutionum logicarum synopsis, sive Rudimenta logica.) pp. 288. 62. *Ex officina Rogeri Daniel: Cantabrigiæ*, 1647. 8°. **720. a. 39.**

—— [Another edition.] pp. 288. 62. *Ex officina Rogeri Danielis: Londini*, 1651. 8°. **527. d. 16. (1.)**

—— [Another edition.] 2 pt. *Apud Joann. Field: Cantabrigiæ*, 1666. 12°. **8468. a. 1. (1, 2.)**

—— [Another edition.] pp. 357. *Apud Joann. Hayes: Cantabrigiæ*, 1680. 8°. **8463. aaa. 20. (2.)**

—— Franconis Burgersdici Institutionum logicarum synopsis, sive Rudimenta logica, *etc.* pp. 92. *Apud A. Commelinum: Lugduni Batavorum*, 1632. 8°. **8466. aa. 21. (2.)**

—— [Another edition.] pp. 67. *Ex Academiæ celeberrimæ typographeo: Cantabrigiæ*, 1637. 8°. **8467. aa. 3. (2.)**

—— *See* HEEREBOORD (A.) Ἑρμηνεία logica; seu Synopseos logicæ Burgersdicanæ explicatio, *etc.* 1658. 8°. **527. b. 15.**

—— —— 1663. 12°. **8468. a. 1. (3.)**

—— —— 1676. 8°. **527. d. 16. (2.)**

—— —— 1680. 8°. **8463. aaa. 20. (1.)**

—— Franconis Burgersdici Institutionum metaphysicarum libri II. Opus posthumum. Editio ultima, longè emendatior. [Edited by A. Heereboord.] pp. 370. *A. Vlaco: Hagae-Comitis*, 1657. 12°. **8464. a. 29.**

—— Editio ultima, longè emendatior. pp. 354. *Typis H. Hall, impensis Ric. Davis: Oxon.*, 1675. 12°. **527. a. 32.**

BURGERSDIJK ET NIERMANS. Bulletin mensuel de la librairie ancienne Burgersdijk & Niermans à Leyde, Hollande. no. 4. mars-avril, 1898. *Leyde*, [1898.] 8°. **11902. c. 36. (3.)**

—— Catalogue no. 47. Thèses de droit soutenues aux universités des Pays-Bas, 1700–1898. Avec table des matières. pp. 151. *Lugduni Batavorum*, 1898. 8°. **11903. g. 13.**

—— Philologie classique et archéologie. Catalogue de livres anciens et modernes aux prix marqués. no. 50. pp. 548. *Leyde*, 1912. 8°. **11908. c. 16.**

—— Théologie. Philosophie. Catalogue de livres anciens et modernes aux prix marqués. no. 48. pp. ii. 870. *Leyde*, 1900. 8°. **4999. ff. 25.**

BURGERSDIJK (LEENDERT ALEXANDER JOHANNES) *the Elder. See* AESCHYLUS. [*Works.—Dutch.*] De Treurspelen van Aeschylos en Sophokles, vertaald in de versmaat van het oorspronkelijke door Dr. L. A. J. Burgersdijk, *etc.* [1903.] 8°. **11707. h. 10.**

—— *See* AESCHYLUS. [*Agamemnon.—Greek and Dutch.*] Αἰσχύλου Ἀγαμέμνων . . . Vertaald door Dr. L. A. J. Burgersdijk. 1887. 4°. **11707. h. 25.**

—— *See* SHAKESPEARE (W.) [*Works.—Dutch.*] De Werken van William Shakespeare. Vertaald door L. A. J. Burgersdijk. [In verse.] 1886, *etc.* 8°. **11766. g. 20.**

—— —— [1895, *etc.*] 8°. **11766. d. 3.**

—— —— [1898.] 8°. **11765. dd. 6.**

BURGERSDIJK (LEENDERT ALEXANDER JOHANNES) *the Elder.*

—— *See* SHAKESPEARE (William) [*As You Like It.—Dutch.*] Elk wat wils . . . in de vertaling van Dr. L. A. J. Burgersdijk, *etc.* 1952. 8°. **011768. a. 19.**

—— *See* SHAKESPEARE (W.) [*Cymbeline.—Dutch.*] Cymbeline . . . Vertaald door Dr. L. A. J. Burgersdijk. 1878. 8°. **11763. df. 7. (2.)**

—— *See* SHAKESPEARE (W.) [*Hamlet.—Dutch.*] Hamlet, Prins van Denemarken . . . Vertaald en voor het hedendaagsch tooneel bewerkt door Dr. L. A. J. Burgerdijk. 1882. 8°. **11762. bb. 12.**

—— *See* SHAKESPEARE (W.) [*Macbeth.—Dutch.*] Macbeth . . . Vertaald door Dr. L. A. J. Burgersdijk. 1882. 8°. **11763. df. 7. (4.)**

—— *See* SHAKESPEARE (William) [*Midsummer Night's Dream.—Dutch.*] Een Midzomernachtdroom, in de vertaling van Dr. L. A. J. Burgersdijk, *etc.* 1952. 8°. **011768. a. 21.**

—— *See* SHAKESPEARE (William) [*Twelfth Night.—Dutch.*] Driekoningenavond . . . in de vertaling van Dr. L. A. J. Burgersdijk, *etc.* 1952. 8°. **011768. a. 20.**

—— *See* SHAKESPEARE (W.) [*Sonnets.—Dutch.*] Shakspere's Sonnetten. Vertaald door Dr. L. A. J. Burgersdijk. 1879. 8°. **11766. f. 1.**

—— Handleiding tot de beoefening der plantenkunde. (Natuurkundige leercursus ten gebruike der Koninklijke Akademie voor de Zee- en Landmagt.) pp. xxviii. 476. *Breda*, 1857. 8°. **7055. c. 49.**

—— Atlas van platen behoorende bij den Leercursus der natuurlijke historie. pl. xv. [*Breda*, 1857.] 4°. **7055. dd. 3.**

BURGERSDIJK (LEENDERT ALEXANDER JOHANNES) *the Younger. See* AESCHYLUS. [*Works.—Dutch.*] De Treurspelen van Aeschylos en Sophokles vertaald . . . door Dr. L. A. J. Burgersdijk . . . uitgegeven door Dr. L. A. J. Burgersdijk Jr. [1903.] 8°. **11707. h. 10.**

BURGERSTEIN (ALFRED) Die Transpiration der Pflanzen. Eine physiologische Monographie. pp. x. 283. *Jena*, 1904. 8°. **07031. f. 14.**

BURGERSTEIN (JOSEF) Franz Anton Graf von Thun-Hohenstein. Biographische Skizze. Mit einem Portrait in Holzschnitt. pp. 23. *Wien*, 1871. 8°. **10705. ff. 15.**

—— Spravedlivý trychtýř parlamentární výmluvnosti, *etc.* pp. 31. *ve Vídni*, 1861. 16°. **11826. a. 14.**

—— Veselé rozjímání o nejnovější Fejfalíkiádě: Über die "Königinhofer Handschrift" . . . Druhé vydání. pp. 32. *ve Vídni*, 1861. 16°. **11826. bb. 42. (3.)**

—— Žertóvné výpisky z tobolek starých študentů. Sebral a vydal J. Burgerstein . . . Druhé vydání. Svaz. 1, 2. *ve Vídni*, 1860, 62. 16°. **12350. aaa. 50.**

BURGERSTEIN (LEO) [Schulhygiene.] School Hygiene . . . Translated from the third edition by Beatrice L. Stevenson and Anna L. Osten, *etc.* [With plates.] pp. xix. 188. *G. G. Harrap & Co.: London*, 1916. 8°. **7404. ppp. 19.**

—— [Zur häuslichen Gesundheitspflege der Schuljugend.] On the Healthy Home Life of School Children. Notes for parents and guardians . . . Eleventh revised edition. Translated by R. T. Williamson. pp. 15. *John Heywood: Manchester*, [1909.] 8°. **07305. i. 41. (2.)**

BURGERSTEIN (Leo) and **NETOLITZKY** (Aug.)

—— Handbuch der Schulhygiene, *etc.* *Jena*, 1895. 8°. [*Handbuch der Hygiene.* Bd. 7. Abt. 1.] **7391.** dd. **9.**

BÜRGERT (Edward)

—— The Dependence of Part 1 of Cynewulf's Christ upon the Antiphonary . . . A dissertation, *etc.* pp. 102. *Washington*, 1921. 8°. **11871.** ee. **16.**

BÜRGERTHUM. *See* Buergerthum.

BURGERUS (Casparus) *See* Horst (Gregorius) *M.D., the Elder.* Gregor. Horstii . . . Disputationum medicarum viginti, *etc.* (Disputationum medicarum secunda. De elementis ac temperamentis. *Resp.* C. Burgerus.) 1609, *etc.* 8°. **1184.** a. **1.**

—— *See* Horst (Gregorius) *M.D., the Elder.* Disputationum medicarum prima [*etc.*], *etc.* (Disputationum medicarum secunda, de elementis et temperamentis, *etc.* *Resp.* C. Burgerus.—Disputationum medicarum decima tertia, de pulsibus, *etc.* *Resp.* C. Burgerus.) 1606, *etc.* 4°. **1179.** c. **3. (15, 26.)**

BURGERUS (Fridericus Augustus) De templo curia ad C. Suet. Tranqv. D. Octav. Caes. Aug. c. xxix et xxxv, exponit . . . F. A. Burgerus. pp. viii. *See* Green (G. S.) M. Georgii Sigismundi Greenii . . . Exercitationes philologicae, *etc.* pt. 29. 1744. 4°. **1087.** c. **43.**

BURGERUS (Joannes Gottlob) *Resp.* *See* Moller (C. G.) Dissertatio philologica de genuina vocum χαρακτηρ et ὑποστασις notione ad illustrandum locum Ebr. I. v. 3, *etc.* [1738.] 4°. **T. 2203. (15.)**

BURGERUS (Jobus Christianus) Dissertatio juridica de spurio herede instituto querelam inofficiosi testamenti fratri excluso non procreante, *etc.* *Praes.* G. Sturmius. pp. 36. *Vitembergæ*, [1733.] 4°. **897.** c. **6. (20.)**

BURGER VAN SCHOOREL (Dirk) *See* Schoorel.

BURGER-VILLINGEN (Robert) Die menschlichen Formengesetze als Schlüssel zur Rassenkunde. pp. 125. pl. xxiv. *Leipzig*, [1935.] 8°. **010006.** g. **28.**

BURGER-VRIEND. De Burger-vriend. Of gemeenzaame gesprekken, tusschen een' Utrechtsch burger-officier, met zijne twe rotsgezellen, Gozewijn, een' gegoeden burger, en Jan, een' werkman. pp. 32. [*Rotterdam?* 1785?] 8°. **934.** d. **12. (9.)**

BÜRGERWEHR-MARSCH. *See* Buergerwehr-Marsch.

BURGES (Anthony) *See* Burgesse.

BURGES (Arnold) The American Kennel and Sporting Field. pp. 201. *J. B. Ford & Co.: New York*, 1876. 4°. **7907.** f. **3.**

BURGES (Bartholomew) A Series of Indostan Letters . . . Containing a striking account of the manners & customs of the Gentoo Nations & of the Moguls & other Mahomedan tribes in Indostan, with other polemical East India tracts. pp. xxv. 168. *W. Ross: N. York*, [1790.] 12°. **10057.** a. **18.**
The titlepage is engraved.

—— A Short Account of the Solar System, and of Comets in general: with a particular account of the comet that will appear in 1789. [With a plate.] pp. 16. *B. Edes & Son: Boston*, 1789. 12°. **T. 421. (10.)**

BURGES (Cornelius) *See* England.—*Parliament.* [*Parliamentary Proceedings.*—II.] An Ordinance . . . inabling the Lord Maior . . . to seize . . . all the Houses . . . belonging to the Deane . . . and all other Officers belonging to the Cathedrall Church of Pauls . . . And for the paying Doctor Burges 400. pounds per annum for a publike lecture in the said Church, *etc.* [12 March 1644.] 1645. 4°. **E. 283. (2.)**

—— —— [1645.] 4°. **E. 40. (2.)**

—— *See* England.—*Church of England.—Archbishops and Bishops.* [*Appendix.*] An Apology for the ancient Right and Power of the Bishops to sit and vote in Parliaments . . . With an answer to the reasons maintained by Dr. Burgesse and many others against the votes of Bishops, *etc.* 1661. 4°. **1130.** f. **1.**

—— *See* Gauden (John) successively *Bishop of Exeter* and *of Worcester.* Antisacrilegus: or, a Defensative against the plausible pest or guilded poison of that nameless paper, supposed to be the plot of Dr. C. Burges, and his partners; which tempts the King's Majestie . . . to make good . . . to the purchasers of bishops, deans, and chapters lands, their illegal bargains for ninety nine years. 1660. 4°. **E. 1044. (10.)**

—— Another Sermon preached to the Honorable House of Commons . . . November the fifth, 1641, *etc.* pp. 65. *Printed by R. B. for P. Stephens & C. Meridith: London*, 1641. 4°. **1479.** aa. **16.**

—— Baptismall Regeneration of Elect Infants, professed by the Church of England, according to the Scriptures, the Primitiue Church, the present Reformed Churches, and many particular Divines apart. pp. 347. *I. L.* [*J. Lichfield*] *for Henry Curteyn: Oxford*, 1629. 4°. **4323.** c. **6.**

—— The Broken Title of Episcopall Inheritance. Or, a Discovery of the weake reply [by Gerard Langbaine] to the Humble Examination of the Answers to the Nine Reasons of the House of Commons, against the votes of Bishops in Parliament, *etc.* [By C. Burges.] [June 1641.] pp. 21. 1642. 4°. *See* England.—*Parliament.—House of Commons.* [*Proceedings.*—II. 1641.] **E. 140. (20.)**

—— A Case concerning the buying of Bishops Lands with the lawfulness thereof. And the difference between the contractors for sale of those lands, and the corporation of Wells: ordered, Anno. 1650. to be reported to the then Parliament, with the necessity thereof, since fallen on Dr Burges. pp. 80. *London*, 1659. 4°. **108.** g. **33.**

—— No Sacrilege nor Sinne to aliene or purchase the lands of Bishops, or others, whose offices are abolished. The second edition . . . By C. B. D.D. [i.e. C. Burges.] [A revised and enlarged version of "A Case concerning the buying of Bishops Lands."] pp. 188. 1659. 8°. *See* B., C., *D.D.* **108.** a. **61.**

—— [Another edition.] No Sacrilege nor Sin to alienate or purchase Cathedral Lands, as such . . . The third edition, revised, and abbreviated, for the service of the Parliament: with a postscript to Dr. Pearson (and his No Necessity of Reformation of the Publick Doctrine of the Church of England). pp. 69. *Printed by James Cottrel: London*, 1660. 4°. **698.** g. **14. (8.)**

—— —— 1660. 4°. **E. 764. (5.)**

—— *See* Gauden (John) successively *Bishop of Exeter* and *of Worcester.* Anti Baal-Berith: or, the binding of the Covenant and all Covenanters to their good Behaviours. By a just vindication of Dr. Gaudens Analysis . . . against the cacotomy of a nameless and shameless libeller the worthy Hyperaspistes of Dr. Burges . . . With an answer to that monstrous paradox, of No Sacriledge no Sin, to alienate Church lands, *etc.* 1661. 4°. **E. 1083. (5.)**

—— *See* Osborne (John) *a Lover of the Truth as it is in Jesus.* An Indictment against Tythes . . . To which are added, certain reasons taken out of Doctor Burgess his Case, concerning the buying of Bishops lands, *etc.* 1659. 4°. **E. 989. (29.)**

—— *See* Pearson (John) *Bishop of Chester.* An Answer to Dr. Burgess's Word by way of postscript; in vindication of, No Necessity of Reformation of the Publick Doctrine of the Church of England. 1709. 8°. [*Bibliotheca scriptorum Ecclesiæ Anglicanæ.* vol. 1.] **4105. c. 23.**

—— An Answer to Doctor Burgess his book, entituled, A Case concerning of buying Bishop Lands . . . By G. F. [i.e. George Fox.] 1659. 4°. *See* F., G. **4152. bb. 61.**

—— The Fire of the Sanctuarie newly vncovered, or, a Compleat tract of zeale. pp. 492. *Printed by G. Miller & R. Badger: London,* 1625. 12°. **4377. a. 11.**
Imperfect; wanting the frontispiece and pp. 433, 434.

—— The Whipper Whipt. Being a reply upon a scandalous pamphlet, called "The Whip:" abusing that excellent work of C. Burges . . . intituled, The Fire of the Sanctuary newly Discovered. [By Francis Quarles.] pp. 44. [*R. Royston: London,*] 1644. 4°. **E. 13. (16.)**

—— [Another copy.] **108. b. 58.**
Imperfect; wanting the leaf following the titlepage.

—— The First Sermon, preached to the Honourable House of Commons . . . at their Publique Fast. Novemb. 17. 1640, *etc.* pp. 80. *I. L. for P. Stephens & C. Meredith: London,* 1641. 4°. **E. 204. (8.)**
The dedication, which applies to both the sermons preached before the Commons on November 17, is signed by Burges and by Stephen Marshall, the author of the second sermon. Marshall's sermon was published separately.

—— [Another issue.] *London,* 1641. 4°. **4476. ee. 9. (7*.)**
Imperfect; wanting sig. A1–A4, *containing the titlepage and the dedication.*

—— [The First Sermon, preached to the Honourable House of Commons.] A Sermon Preached to the Honourable House of Commons . . . At their publique fast, Novem. 17. 1640 . . . The third edition revised and corrected by the author. pp. 48. *Printed by Iohn Legatt, for P. Stephens & C. Meredith: London,* 1641. 4°. **1481. aaa. 58.**

—— An Humble Examination of a Printed Abstract of the Answers [by John Williams, Archbishop of York] to nine reasons of the House of Commons against the votes of Bishops in Parliament, *etc.* [By C. Burges. June 1641.] pp. 77. 1641. 4°. *See* England.—*Parliament.—House of Commons.* [*Proceedings.*—ii. 1641.] **E. 164. (14.)**

—— *See* England.—*Parliament.—House of Commons.*—[*Proceedings.*—ii. 1641.] Episcopall Inheritance. Or a Reply to the Humble Examination of a Printed Abstract of the Answers to Nine Reasons of the House of Commons against the votes of Bishops in Parliament, *etc.* [By G. Langbaine.] 1641. 4°. **E. 132. (29.)**

—— The Necessity of Agreement with God: opened in a sermon to the . . . House of Peers . . . upon the 29th of October, 1645. being the monethly fast, *etc.* pp. 51. *G. Miller for Philemon Stephens: London,* 1645. 4°. **E. 307. (19.)**

—— A New Discovery of Personal Tithes: or the Tenth part of mens cleere gaines proued due both in conscience, and by the lawes of this kingdome. pp. 81. *I. L. for William Sheffard: London,* 1625. 12°. **4103. a. 9.**

—— No Sacrilege nor Sinne to aliene or purchase the lands of Bishops, *etc.* *See* supra: A Case concerning the buying of Bishops Lands.

—— Reasons shewing the Necessity of Reformation of the Publick 1. Doctrine, 2. Worship, 3. Rites and Ceremonies, 4. Church-Government, and Discipline . . . Humbly offered to the serious consideration of this present . . . Parliament. By divers Ministers of sundry counties in England. [Edited by C. Burges.] pp. 63. 1660. 4°. *See* England.—*Parliament.* [*Petitions, etc.*—1660.] **E. 764. (4.)**

—— [Another edition.] pp. 63. 1660. 4°. *See* England.—*Parliament.* [*Petitions, etc.*—1660.] **108. c. 37.**

—— The second edition, revised and enlarged. pp. 63. [1661?] 4°. *See* England.—*Parliament.* [*Petitions, etc.*—1660.] **698. g. 14. (9.)**

—— *See* England.—*Parliament.* [*Petitions, etc.*—1660.] A Defence of the Liturgy of the Church of England. Being an answer to the book . . . entituled Reasons shewing the Necessity of Reformation, *etc.* 1661. 12°. **E. 2106. (3.)**

—— *See* Pearson (John) *Bishop of Chester.* No Necessity of Reformation of the Publick Doctrine of the Church of England. [A reply to the petition edited by C. Burges.] 1660. 4°. **E. 1040. (7.)**

—— *See* S., H., *D.D.* Reasons shewing that there is no need of such a Reformation . . . as is pretended by Reasons offered to the serious consideration of this present parliament, *etc.* [An answer by Henry Savage to the petition edited by C. Burges.] 1660. 4°. **E. 1043. (7.)**

—— The Second Sermon, preached to the honourable House of Commons, April 30. 1645, *etc.* *See* infra: Two Sermons preached to the honourable House of Commons, *etc.*

—— Sion College, what it is, and doeth. Together with a vindication of that Society from the slanderous diffamations of two . . . satyres, the one called Sion College visited [by John Goodwin]: the other The Pulpit Incendiary [by John Price]. As also a little taste . . . of another young thing of Mr J. Goodwins . . . under the name of *Νεοφυτοπρεσβυτερος* . . . By C. B. [i.e. C. Burges], *etc.* pp. 31. 1648. 4°. *See* B., C., *a Member of Sion College.* **E. 444. (3.)**

—— *See* Goodwin (John) *Vicar of St. Stephen's, Coleman Street.* *Νεοφυτοπρεσβυτερος* . . . With a brief answer . . . to the frivolous exceptions made by C. B. [i.e. C. Burges] against Sion Colledge visited, in a late trifling pamphlet called, Sion Colledge what it is, *etc.* 1648. 4°. **E. 447. (27.)**

—— Two Sermons preached to the honourable House of Commons, at two publike fasts; the one, March 30. 1642. the other, April 30. 1645. The former, opening the

BURGES (CORNELIUS)

necessity and benefit of washing the heart. The later, discovering the vanity and mischief of an heart unwashed, *etc.* 2 pt. *J. R. for Phil. Stephens: London*, 1645. 4°. **E.138.(15.)** & **E. 280. (2.)**
The publisher's name does not occur in the imprint of pt. 2.

—— Two Sermons preached to the Honourable House of Commons, at two publike fasts; the one, March 30. 1642; the other, April 30. 1645, *etc.* 2 pt. *J. R. for Christopher Meredith: London*, 1645. 4°. **4474. d. 111.**
Leaves G2–H1 of pt. 1 are mutilated.

—— [For editions of "A Vindication of the Ministers of the Gospel in, and about London, from the unjust Aspersions cast upon their former Actings for the Parliament, *etc.*" signed by C. Burges and others:] *See* LONDON.—*Ministers.*

—— A Vindication of the Ministers of the Gospel, *etc.* pp. 11. *A. M. for Th. Underhill: London*, 1648. 4°. **E. 540. (11.)**

—— [A Vindication of the Ministers of the Gospel.] The Presbyterians Not Guilty of the Unjust Charge of being concern'd in the Murther of King Charles I. As appears by their abhorrence of the then proceedings against His Majesty: faithfully printed from the original copy, sign'd by fifty seven of the most eminent Presbyterian ministers then possess'd of the parish churches in and about the City of London. With a vindication of moderate Churchmen and Dissenters, from the aspersions cast upon them in the late addresses, &c. That they are men of republican and antimonarchical principles, *etc.* pp. 24. *A. Baldwin: London*, 1710. 8°. **698. g. 24. (1.)**

—— A Vindication of the Ministers of the Gospel, *etc.* *In*: A Sermon preach'd to a Congregation of Dissenters, on . . . the Anniversary of the Murther of K. Charles the First, *etc.* 1714. 8°. **10806. a. 32.**

BURGES (CYRIL TRAVERS) The Abstract Basis of Peace. pp. 24. *C. T. Burges: Staines*, [1939.] 8°. **8425. tt. 39.**

—— History Mnemonics System for Dates. [1948.] *s. sh.* fol. **14000. r. 24. (10.)**
Reproduced from typewriting.

—— History Rhymes for Preparatory Schools. *C. T. Burges: Staines*, [1938.] 4°. **11656. g. 1.**
Reproduced from typewriting.

—— Mental Evolution Bulletins. Numbers 1 and 2 [*etc.*]. *Staines*, 1939– . 4°. **8471. h. 15**
Typewritten.

BURGES (DANIEL) *Antiquary.* *See* BURGESS (Daniel) *the Younger.*

BURGES (DANIEL) *Priest, of Dublin.* *See* PARK (James) *Quaker.* The Way of God, and them that walk in it, vindicated . . Being an answer to a malicious pamphlet, entituled "A Caveat against the cheat of the Quakers chaff," written by D. Burges, *etc.* 1673. 4°. **4151. c. 92.**

BURGES (ELIZA SWANSON) *See* BURGES (George) *Vicar of Halvergate.* A Discourse occasioned by the Death of a beloved Child (E. S. Burges). 1802. 8°. **4905. dd. 10. (3.)**

BURGES (ELLEN) Vizcaya. Or, Life in the land of the Carlists at the outbreak of the Insurrection 1872–1873. With some account of the iron mines in the vicinity of Bilbao. Illustrated by a map and by eight original sketches. [Edited by E. Burges.] pp. viii. 198. *H. S. King & Co.: London*, 1874. 8°. **10160. aaa. 27.**

BURGES (ERNEST TRAVERS) The Deserted Lake. Or, the Dragon that could not eat fish . . . With illustrations by Dorothea T. Burges. pp. 27. *Longmans & Co.: London*, 1912. 4°. **012808. d. 38.**

BURGES (FRANCIS) Some Observations on the Use and Original of the noble Art and Mystery of Printing. 1745. *See* HARLEIAN MISCELLANY. The Harleian Miscellany, *etc.* vol. 3. 1744, *etc.* 4°. **185. a. 7.**

—— [Another edition.] 1809. *See* HARLEIAN MISCELLANY. The Harleian Miscellany, *etc.* vol. 3. 1808, *etc.* 4°. **2072.g.**

BURGES (GEORGE) *of Trinity College, Cambridge.* *See* AESCHYLUS. [*Supplices.—Greek.*] Αἰσχυλου . . . λειψανα . . . Supplices . . . recensui G. Burges, *etc.* 1821. 8°. **997. e. 9.**

—— *See* AESCHYLUS. [*Prometheus Vinctus.—Greek.*] The Prometheus, *etc.* [Edited by G. Burges.] 1831. 12°. **1211. h. 1.**

—— —— 1833. 12°. **11705. bbb. 3.**

—— *See* DEMOSTHENES. [*In Midiam.—English.*] Specimen of a Translation of Demosthenes, *etc.* [Part of the Oration against Midias translated by G. Burges.] [1842.] 8°. **G. 17055.**

—— *See* DEMOSTHENES. [*In Midiam.—English.*] The Midian Oration of Demosthenes, translated by G. Burges. 1842. 8°. **G. 17054.**

—— *See* DEMOSTHENES. [*Philippicae.—English.*] A Specimen of a new Translation of Demosthenes. By G. Burges . . . The First Philippic. [1842.] 8°. **11391. bb. 5.**

—— *See* EURIPIDES. [*Phoenissae.—Greek.*] Εὐριπιδου Φοινισσαι. Euripidis Phœnissæ. Cum notulis edidit G. Burges. 1809. 8°. **999. n. 9.**

—— *See* EURIPIDES. [*Troades.—Greek.*] Εὐριπιδου Τρῳαδες. Euripidis Troades . . . Studio G. Burges. 1807. 8°. **995. g. 20.**

—— *See* GREEK ANTHOLOGY. The Greek Anthology, as selected for the use of Westminster, Eton . . . Literally translated into English prose. Chiefly by G. Burges, *etc.* 1852. 8°. **2500. f. 6.**

—— *See* HERMESIANAX. Hermesianactis . . . fragmentum . . . Accedit G. Burgesii epistola critica. 1839. 8°. **1348. c. 23.**

—— *See* PLATO. [*Works.—Greek and Latin.*] Platonis et quæ vel Platonis esse feruntur, vel Platonica solent comitari scripta, Græce omnia, *etc.* [Edited by G. Burges.] 1826. 8°. **525. k. 1–11.**

—— *See* PLATO. [*Works.—English.*] The Works of Plato, *etc.* [vol. 3–6 translated by G. Burges.] 1848, *etc.* 8°. **2500. g. 6.**

—— *See* PLATO. [*Two or more Works.—Greek.*] Plato's Four Dialogues, the Crito, Hippias, Alcibiades, and Sisyphus with English notes and examination questions, *etc.* [Edited by G. Burges.] [1833.] 12°. **1211. h. 7.**

—— *See* PLATO. [*Respublica.—Greek.*] Πλατωνος Πολιτεια. Platonis Respublica, *etc.* [Edited by G. Burges.] 1825. 8°. **714. e. 1.**

—— *See* POPPO (E. F.) Poppo's Prolegomena on the Peculiarities of Thucydidean Phraseology, translated, abridged and criticized by G. Burges, *etc.* [1837.] 8°. **586. f. 24.**

—— *See* POPPO (E. F.) Poppo's Prolegomena, *etc.* [With thirteen leaves of translations in MS. intended for Burges's projected work "The Scholar's Album," and six leaves of additional remarks on Poppo.] [1837.] 8°. **G. 8246.**

BURGES (GEORGE) *of Trinity College, Cambridge.*

—— *See* SOPHOCLES. [*Philoctetes.—Greek.*] The Philoctetes of Sophocles with English notes . . . and examination questions . . . by G. Burges. 1833. 12°. **1211**. h. **11**.

—— Demosthenes and Lord Brougham! The Oration of Demosthenes upon the Crown, translated into English with notes!!! and the Greek text. By Henry Lord Brougham, *etc.* [A review by G. Burges cut from "The Times" of 21–28 March and 3, 4 April 1840, and mounted.] [1840.] 8°. *See* DEMOSTHENES. [*De Corona.—Appendix.*] **11391**. d. **14**.

—— Native Guano the best Antidote against the Future Fatal Effects of a Free Trade in Corn. pp. 44. *Effingham Wilson: London*, 1848. 8°. **1252**. c. **34**. (**4**.)

—— A Review of Lord Brougham's Translation of the Oration of Demosthenes on the Crown. Re-printed from "The Times" newspaper. [By G. Burges.] pp. 167. 1840. 12°. *See* DEMOSTHENES. [*De Corona.—Appendix.*] **834**. h. **31**. (**2**.)

—— The Son of Erin, or the Cause of the Greeks. A play, *etc.* pp. xii. 124. *John Miller: London*, 1823. 8°. T. **1065**. (**4**.)

BURGES (GEORGE) *Vicar of Halvergate.* *See* also CATO, *pseud.* [i.e. G. Burges.]

—— An Address to the Misguided Poor of the disturbed districts throughout this kingdom. pp. 40. *Rivingtons: London*, 1830. 12°. T. **1394**. (**7**.)

—— An Address to the People of Great Britain. pp. 24. *T. N. Longman: London*, 1798. 8°. **102**. g. **63**.

—— An Address to the Right Reverend Edward Stanley Lord Bishop of Norwich. [On his "Reply . . . to the Bishop of Exeter's Speech, upon moving his Resolutions on the system of National Education in Ireland."] pp. v. 86. *Wix: London; Matchett, Stevenson & Matchett: Norwich*, 1838. 8°. T. **2345**. (**2**.)

—— A Commentary on the Act for the Commutation of Tithes in England and Wales. pp. iv. 134. *J. G. & F. Rivington: London*, 1838. 12°. T. **2379**. (**4**.)

—— A Conservative Address to the Freeholders of the British Empire. pp. 45. *Rivingtons: London*, 1835. 8°. T. **1603**. (**3**.)

—— The Conservative Standard of the British Empire: erected in a time of trouble for all those who fear God and honour the king . . . Second edition. pp. iv. 244. *Whittaker & Co.; Rivingtons: London*, 1835. 8°. T. **1908**. (**1**.)

—— A Discourse delivered at West Walton . . . on Thursday, December 5, 1805, being the day appointed for a general thanksgiving. pp. 30. *John White: Wisbech*, 1806. 8°. **4473**. c. **11**. (**1**.)

—— A Discourse occasioned by the Death of a Beloved Child (Eliza Swanson Burges). pp. 25. *Charles Jacob: Peterborough*, 1802. 8°. **4905**. dd. **10**. (**3**.) "*Not sold.*"

—— A Letter to the . . . Bishop of Ely on the subject of a new and authoritative translation of the Holy Scriptures. pp. 42. *J. Jacob: Peterborough*, 1796. 8°. T. **736**. (**7**.)

—— A Letter to T. W. Coke, Esq. M.P. on the tendency of certain speeches delivered at the county meeting, in the Shire-Hall, Norwich, on Saturday, April 5, 1817 . . . The second edition, corrected and enlarged. pp. vi. 149. *Burks & Kinnebrook: Norwich*, 1817. 8°. **1102**. g. **20**. (**7**.)

BURGES (GEORGE) *Vicar of Halvergate*

—— Observations on the Rev. G. Burges's Letter to T. W. Coke, Esq. With remarks on the Rev. G. Glover's Answer. By a man of no party. pp. 68. *J. Stacy: Norwich*, [1817.] 8°. **1102**. g. **21**.

—— A Protestant Letter, addressed to a friend, on the concession of the Roman Catholic claims. pp. 95. *C. J. G. & F. Rivington: London*, 1830. 8°. T. **1290**. (**14**.)

—— Reflections on the Nature and Tendency of the present Spirit of the Times, in a letter to the freeholders of the County of Norfolk. pp. iv. 362. *Burks & Kinnebrook: Norwich*, 1819. 8°. **1117**. g. **10**.

—— The second edition, revised and enlarged. pp. viii. 341. *Burks & Kinnebrook: Norwich*, 1820. 8°. **8010**. d. **4**.

—— Remarks on a Commutation of the Tithe-System. pp. 45. *C. J. G. & F. Rivington: London*, 1831. 8°. T. **1352**. (**20**.)

—— Remarks on Mr. Wakefield's Enquiry into the Expediency and Propriety of Public or Social Worship. pp. 59. *J. Evans: London*, 1792. 8°. **4372**. g. **21**. (**1**.)

—— Remarks on the leading Arguments in favor of Catholic Emancipation. pp. vii. 97. *J. White: Wisbech*, 1812. 8°. **3942**. b. **9**.

—— The second edition, corrected. pp. vii. 89. *J. White: Wisbech*, 1813. 8°. **3940**. h. **4**. (**4**.)

—— Sixty-eight Reasons for opposing the Reform Bill now pending in Parliament. [By G. Burges.] pp. 41. 1832. 8°. *See* ENGLAND.—*Parliament.* [*Bills.*—II.] [1831. Dec. 12.] T. **1389**. (**6**.)

BURGES (JAMES) An Account of the Preparation and Management necessary to Inoculation. pp. viii. 44. *P. Vaillant: London*, 1754. 8°. T. **304**. (**5**.)

—— [Another copy.] T. **356**. (**3**.)

—— [Another copy.] **1174**. h. **37**.

BURGES, afterwards **LAMB** (*Sir* JAMES BLAND) *Bart.* *See* also ALFRED, *pseud.* [i.e. Sir J. B. Burges, afterwards Lamb.]

—— *See* BURGES (Mary A.) The Progress of the Pilgrim Good-Intent . . . With an introduction by Sir J. B. Burges. 1822. 12°. **4414**. d. **12**.

—— *See* CUMBERLAND (Richard) *LL.D., Dramatist.* The Exodiad, a poem. By the authors of Calvary (R. Cumberland) and Richard the First [i.e. Sir J. B. Burges]. 1807. 4°. **11642**. h. **25**.

—— *See* MASSINGER (Philip) Riches . . . a play . . . founded on Massinger's Comedy of the City Madam. By Sir J. B. Burges, Bart. 1810. 8°. **643**. g. **6**. (**11**.)

—— —— 1810. 8°. **11775**. g. **4**. (**2**.)

—— —— [1850?] 12°. [*Cumberland's British Theatre.* vol. 24.] **642**. a. **12**.

—— *See* MASSINGER (Philip) Riches; or, the Wife and brother. (Founded on Massinger's City Madam.) By Sir J. B. Burges, *etc.* [1886.] 8°. [*Dicks' Standard Plays.* no. 717.] **11770**. bbb. **4**.

—— Dramas. 2 vol. *Edward Kerby: London*, 1817. 8°. **11771**. f. **2**.

—— Selections from the Letters and Correspondence of Sir J. B. Burges . . . With notices of his life. Edited by James Hutton. pp. xi. 387. *John Murray: London,* 1885. 8°. **2410**. c. **3.**

—— The Birth and Triumph of Love: a poem. pp. vii. 58. *C. Roworth: London,* 1796. 4°. **644**. k. **24**. (**3**.)

—— [Another copy.] [With plates engraved from designs of H.R.H. the Princess Elizabeth.] **83**. k. **16**.
The plates were sold separately.

—— [Another edition.] pp. 56. *P. W. Tomkins: London,* 1822. 8°. **11641**. bb. **12**.
Imperfect; wanting the leaf containing stanzas 1–3 *of canto* 1, *which has been replaced by the leaf containing stanzas* 1–3 *of canto* 2.

—— [A reissue.] *R. Jennings; P. W. Tomkins: London,* 1823. 8°. **994**. k. **18**.

—— Considerations on the Law of Insolvency. With a proposal for a reform. pp. 391. *T. Cadell: London,* 1783. 8°. **227**. i. **9**. (**1**.)

—— The Dragon Knight. A poem, in twelve cantos. pp. vii. 342. *Longman & Co.: London,* 1818. 8°. **993**. i. **10**.

—— An Enquiry into the Cause of the Procrastination & Delay attributed to the Judicial Proceedings of the House of Lords and the Court of Chancery. pp. 133. *W. Reynolds: London,* 1824. 8°. T. **1087**. (**2**.)

—— Heroic Epistle from Serjeant Bradshaw, in the Shades, to John Dunning, Esq. [By Sir J. B. Burges, afterwards Lamb.] pp. 14. 1780. 4°. *See* BRADSHAW (John) *Lord President of the High Court of Justice.* **163**. m. **15**.

—— A Letter to the Earl of Effingham on his lately proposed Act of Insolvency. pp. 129. *T. Cadell: London,* 1783. 8°. **6405**. b. **9**.

—— Reasons in Favour of a new Translation of the Holy Scriptures. pp. v. 152. *Budd & Calkin: London,* 1819. 8°. **689**. d. **17**. (**1**.)

—— [Another copy.] **217**. i. **10**.

—— *See* TODD (Henry J.) A Vindication of our Authorized Translation . . . of the Bible . . . occasioned by certain objections made by Mr. J. Bellamy . . . and by Sir J. B. Burges, in his Reasons in favour of a new translation of the Holy Scriptures. 1819. 8°. **689**. d. **17**. (**2**.)

—— Richard the First: a poem. [By Sir J. B. Burges, afterwards Lamb.] [The proof sheets with MS. notes by C. Anstey.] pp. 660. [1800.] 8°. *See* RICHARD I., *King of England,* called *Cœur de Lion.* C. **28**. h. **11**.

—— [Another copy.] MS. NOTES [by W. Boscawen]. C. **28**. h. **9**.

—— [Another copy.] MS. NOTES [by R. Cumberland]. C. **28**. h. **10**.

—— [Another copy.] [With MS. notes by the author incorporating the corrections and emendations suggested by Anstey, Boscawen, Cumberland, Fitz-Gerald, Nares, Pye and Sotheby.] C. **28**. h. **12**.

—— Richard the First, a poem: in eighteen books. 2 vol. *C. Roworth: London,* 1801. 8°. **79**. f. **19**.
With a MS. letter from the author to Sir F. Barnard prefixed.

—— Songs, Duets, &c. in Tricks upon Travellers, a comic opera [by Sir J. B. Burges, afterwards Lamb] . . . Second edition. pp. 15. 1810. 8°. *See* TRICKS. **11779**. g. **89**.

BURGES (JOHN) *See* CLARK (Thomas) *of Sutton-Coldfield.* The Popes Deadly Wound . . . Published by Doctor Burges, *etc.* 1635. 12°. **3936**. a. **29**.

—— *See* WILCOX (Thomas) The Works of that late Divine . . . Thomas Wilcox, *etc.* [Edited by J. Burges.] 1624. fol. **3752**. f. **11**.

—— An Answer reioyned to that much applauded Pamphlet of a Namelesse Author, bearing this title: viz. A Reply to Dr Mortons Generall Defence of three Nocent Ceremonies, &c. the innocency and lawfulnesse whereof is againe in this reioynder vindicated. pp. 653. *Augustine Matthewes for Robert Milbourne: London,* 1631. 4°. **108**. b. **15**.

—— *See* AMES (William) *D.D.* A Fresh Suit against Human Ceremonies in God's Worship. Or, a Triplication unto D. Burgesse his rejoinder for D. Morton. 1633. 4°. **4135**. a. **3**.

—— A Briefe Answer vnto Certaine Reasons by way of an Apologie . . . by Mr Iohn Burges: wherin he laboureth to prooue, that hauing heretofore subscribed four times, and now refusing, as a thing vnlawfull, that he hath notwithstanding done lawfully in both. Written by William Couell. [With the text of the Apology.] pp. 160. *G. S. for Clement Knight: London,* 1606. 4°. **698**. f. **25**.

—— The Lawfulnes of Kneeling in the act of receiving the Lords Supper. Wherein, by the way, also, somewhat of the Crosse in Baptisme, *etc.* pp. 120. *Augustine Matthewes for Robert Milbourne: London,* 1631. 4°. **117**. g. **4**.

—— A Sermon preached before the late King James His Majesty, at Greenwich, the 19. of Iuly, 1604. Together with two letters in way of apology for his sermon, *etc.* pp. 29. *Printed by Thomas Brudenell: London,* 1642. 4°. **693**. f. **4**. (**7**.)

—— [Another copy.] E. **145**. (**5**.)

BURGES (JOHN HART) *See* JESUS CHRIST.—*Christ Church, West Hartlepool.* Plain Statement of Facts as to Christ Church, West Hartlepool. [On the conduct of R. W. Jackson towards the incumbent, J. H. Burges.] [1856.] 8°. **1414**. f. **44**. (**5**.)

BURGÈS (JULES) *See* BOURGÈS.

BURGES (MARY ANNE) The Progress of the Pilgrim Good-Intent, in Jacobinical times. [By M. A. Burges.] pp. viii. 190. 1800. 12°. *See* GOOD-INTENT, *Pilgrim.* **4414**. bbb. **28**.

—— The second edition. pp. viii. 191. 1800. 12°. *See* GOOD-INTENT, *Pilgrim.* **4411**. c. **13**.

—— The third edition. pp. viii. 191. 1800. 12°. *See* GOOD-INTENT, *Pilgrim.* **4416**. d. **1**.

—— [Another edition.] The third edition. pp. 199. 1801. 12°. *See* GOOD-INTENT, *Pilgrim.* **4414**. ccc. **23**.

—— The second American, from the fifth English edition. pp. 119. 1801. 12°. *See* GOOD-INTENT, *Pilgrim.* **4414**. dd. **15**.

—— The seventh edition. pp. viii. 191. 1801. 12°. *See* GOOD-INTENT, *Pilgrim.* **4416**. bbb. **18**.

—— The third American, from the fifth English edition. pp. 110. 1802. 12°. *See* GOOD-INTENT, *Pilgrim.* **4414**. bbb. **29**.

BURGES (Mary Anne)

—— The tenth edition. With an introduction, by Sir James Bland Burges. pp. xii. 191. *J. Hatchard & Son: London*, 1822. 12°. **4414**. d. **12**.

BURGES (Paul) The Three Worthy Butchers of the North. [A ballad.] B.L. *For P. Brooksby: London*, [1678 ?] *s. sh.* fol. C. **20**. f. **10**.

—— [Another edition.] B.L. *For P. Brooksby: London*, [1680 ?] *s. sh.* fol. C. **20**. f. **9**.

—— The Youth's Guide, *etc.* [A ballad. By P. Burges.] B.L. [1680 ?] *s. sh. obl.* fol. *See* Youth. C. **22**. f. **6**. **(216.)**

BURGES (Petrus Baptista) *See* Burgus.

BURGES (Tristam) *See* Bowen (Henry L.) Memoir of Tristam Burges; with selections from his speeches and writings. [With a portrait.] 1835. 8°. **1453**. d. **4**.

—— Address to the Rhode-Island Society for the Encouragement of Domestick Industry . . . October 17, 1821. pp. 29. *Mill & Hutchens: Providence*, 1822. 8°. **8246**. e. **9**.

—— Battle of Lake Erie. With notices of Commodore Elliot's conduct in that engagement. pp. 132. *B. B. Mussey: Boston*, 1839. 8°. **1446**. c. **17**.

—— *See* Cooper (James F.) The Battle of Lake Erie; or, Answers to Messrs. Burges, Duer and Mackenzie. 1843. 12°. **1446**. b. **8**.

—— Liberty, Glory and Union, or American Independence: an oration, *etc.* pp. 22. *Rhode Island American: Providence*, [1810.] 8°. **12301**. f. **5**. **(5.)**

—— An Oration. Delivered before the Rhode-Island Federal Adelphi . . . Sept. 9, 1831. pp. 36. *Weeden & Knowles: Providence*, 1831. 8°. **12301**. f. **46**. **(2.)**

—— An Oration, pronounced before the citizens of Providence, on the Fourth of July 1831, *etc.* pp. 32. *W. Marshall & Co.: Providence*, [1831.] 8°. **8177**. g. **30**.

—— Solitude and Society contrasted. An oration pronounced at the annual meeting of the Philological Society in Middleborough . . . 1797. *Carter & Wilkinson: Providence*, 1797. 8°. **8404**. e. **10**.
Imperfect; wanting all after p. 22.

—— Speech of Mr. Burges . . . delivered in the House of Representatives . . . April 21st, A.D. 1828, on the Tariff. pp. 90. *Way & Gideon: Washington*, 1828. 8°. **8246**. e. **10**.

—— Speech of Mr. Burges . . . on the motion to strike from the General Appropriation Bill the salary appropriated for the minister to Russia. Delivered in the House of Representatives . . . February 3, 1831. pp. 53. *Gales & Seaton: Washington*, 1831. 12°. **8177**. b. **8**.

—— The Speech of Tristam Burges, in the House of Representatives . . . May 10, 1830, on the bill for the more effectual collection of the duties on imports, *etc.* pp. 28. *Marshall & Hammond: Providence*, 1830. 8°. **8246**. e. **11**.

—— War, Necessary, Just and Beneficial: an oration, *etc.* pp. 8. [*B. Wheeler*:] *Providence*, 1799. 8°. **8176**. aaa. **41**. **(1.)**
Cropped.

BURGES (William) *See* Lucas (Charles) *Architect.* Deux architectes anglais. W. Burges . . . et R. P. Pullan, *etc.* 1886. 8°. **10601.d.18.(10.)**

BURGES (William)

—— *See* Scott (*Sir* George G.) Gleanings from Westminster Abbey . . . With appendices . . . by W. Burges, *etc.* 1861. 8°. **7820**. e. **29**.

—— —— 1863. 8°. **2261**. e. **7**.

—— The Architectural Designs of W. Burges, A.R.A. Details of stonework. Edited by Richard Popplewell Pullan. pp. 8. pl. 39. *B. T. Batsford: London*, 1887. fol. **7816**. g. **48**.

—— Architectural Drawings. pp. 29. pl. 75. *W. Clowes & Sons: London*, 1870. fol. **1730**. c. **17**.

—— Art and Religion. *See* Shipley (Orby) The Church and the World: essays, *etc.* 1868. 8°. **4108**. e. **62**.

—— Art applied to Industry. A series of lectures. pp. 120. *J. H. & J. Parker: Oxford & London*, 1865. 8°. **7943**. cc. **36**.

—— The Designs of William Burges, A.R.A. Edited by R. P. Pullan. pp. 9. pl. 23. [*B. T. Batsford: London*, 1886.] fol. **Cup.1249.b.18.**

—— The House of William Burges, A.R.A. Edited by R. P. Pullan. pp. 14. pl. 40. [*B. T. Batsford: London*, 1886.] fol. **7815**. f. **12**.

—— Iconographie de la Ragione, grande salle de l'Hôtel de Ville de Padoue. [With an introduction by A. N. Didron. With plates.] pp. 24. *Paris*, 1860. 4°. **7820**. g. **56**. **(4.)**

—— Law Courts Commission. Report to the Courts of Justice Commission. [The plans and specifications for the new Law Courts. With plates.] pp. 16. *G. E. Eyre & W. Spottiswoode: London*, 1867. fol. **1732**. d. **9**.

—— The Legend of Waltham Abbey, and the history of the church, founded by King Harold. pp. 15. *E. Littler: Waltham Abbey*, 1860. 8°. **4705**. cc. **14**. **(2.)**

—— Report on the Condition of the Eastern Part of King's College Chapel. pp. 7. [1874.] 4°. **7822**. d. **28**.

—— A Description of Mr. Burges' Models for the Adornment of St. Pauls now exhibited at the Royal Academy. pp. 19. *E. Stanford: London*, 1874. 8°. **7814**. bbb. **41**. **(4.)**

BURGES (William) and **DIDRON** (Adolphe Napoléon)

—— Venise. Iconographie des chapiteaux du Palais ducal. [With plates.] pp. 58. *Paris*, 1857. 4°. **7816**. b. **11**.

BURGES (Ynyr Henry) The Land Question in Ireland economically considered. 1869. *See* Practice. Practice with Science, *etc.* vol. 2. 1867, *etc.* 8°. **7078**. d. **25**.

BURGESIUS (Georgius) *See* Burges (George) *of Trinity College, Cambridge.*

BURGESS. The Burgess. *See* Scarborough.—*Scarborough Association for the Protection and Extension of Civil and Religious Liberty.*

—— City and Port of Bristol. Letters, essays, tracts, and other documents, illustrative of the municipal history of Bristol, and of the trade of its port. Written, collected, and arranged by a Burgess [i. e. J. B. Kington]. 13 pt. *W. Browne: Bristol*, 1836. 8°. **8247**. a. **38**.

BURGESS.

—— The Newcastle Freeman's Pocket Companion, containing a copious view of the charters granted to the town and county of the town of Newcastle upon Tyne. Including a particular account of the customs and privileges peculiar to the free burgesses of the said town. By a Burgess (Joseph Clark). 1808. 12°. *See* CLARK (Joseph) **10368**. cc. **50**.

—— Ten Objections to the Birmingham Corporation. By a Burgess. pp. 12. *T. Ragg & Co.: Birmingham,* [1839.] 12°. **08275**. df. **27**.

—— Thirty Letters on the Trade of Bristol, the Causes of its Decline and Means of its Revival. [Reprinted from the Bristol Mercury.] By a Burgess [i.e. J. B. Kington]. With notes; extracts from the evidence given before the Commissioners of Corporate Enquiry in this city; additional information relative to its commercial and municipal history; tables of all the local dues . . . and of the state of trade in Bristol during the last nine years. pp. vii. 346. *John Wright: Bristol,* 1834. 12°. **8247**. bb. **16**.

—— Town Moor Act, 1774. The Act of Parliament obtained in the year 1774, for confirming to resident freemen of Newcastle upon Tyne and their widows, their full right and benefit to the herbage of the Town Moor, Castle Leazes, and Nun's Moor. With a . . . detail of the . . . proceedings for obtaining a new Act. Together with a particular account of the speeches and resolutions of the Court of Guild, Michaelmas, 1811. By a Burgess [i.e. Joseph Clark]. pp. 34. *J. Marshall: Newcastle upon Tyne,* 1811. 12°. **10347**. d. **10**. (2.)

BURGESS HILL.

—— Burgess Hill. The official guide, *etc.* [With illustrations and maps.] pp. 40. *Ed. J. Burrow & Co.: Cheltenham & London,* [1951.] 8°. **010368**. w. **95**.

—— Burgess Hill and district, Sussex. The official guide, *etc.* [With illustrations.] pp. 28. *Century Press: London,* [1947.] 8°. **10359**. c. **25**.

—— Burgess Hill and Haywards Heath. An introduction to two charming Sussex towns, *etc.* pp. 19. *British Publishing Co.: Gloucester,* [1936.] 8°. **010352**. a. **21**.

International Bible Training Institute.

—— The International Review. An independent journal of evangelism and international affairs. *Burgess Hill,* 1950– . 8°. P.P. **728**. bbf.

—— *Savoy School.* The Savoyard. *London,* 1930– . 4°. P.P. **6139**. fk.

BURGESS ( ) A Reply to Mr. Burgess's Journey to Eden, &c. With an explanation of the two genealogical tables of Jesus Christ; in a short conversation between an Indian and a Briton. By the author of A Treatise on the Fall of Adam. pp. 31. *Printed for the Author: London,* 1818. 8°. T. **1005**. (**10**.)

BURGESS ( ) *Mrs.* The Oaks; or, the Beauties of Canterbury. A comedy, *etc.* pp. 7. 62. *Simmons & Kirkby: Canterbury,* 1780. 12°. **11777**. aa. **8**.

BURGESS (ALAN)

—— Come Live with Me. pp. 176. *Hutchinson & Co.: London,* [1945.] 8° NN. **35086**.

—— No Risks—No Romance. [With plates.] pp. 341. *Jonathan Cape: London,* 1941. 8°. **10497**. a. **60**.

BURGESS (ALAN)

—— Warwickshire . . . With a map. pp. viii. 312. pl. 49. *Robert Hale: London,* 1950. 8°. [*County Books Series.*] W.P. **1690/21**.

BURGESS (ALAN E.)

—— 16 mm. Projection from A to Z, *etc.* pp. 103. *Cinema Press: London,* [1952.] 8°. **8914**. bb. **6**.
With an errata slip.

BURGESS (ALBERT FRANKLIN) The Dispersion of the Gipsy Moth. [With a map.] pp. 62. pl. XVI. *Washington,* 1913. 8°. [*U.S. Department of Agriculture. Bureau of Entomology. Bulletin.* no. 119.] A.S. **814**.

BURGESS (ALBERT FRANKLIN) and **COLLINS** (CHARLES WALTER)

—— The Genus Calosoma. Including studies of seasonal histories, habits and economic importance of American species north of Mexico and of several introduced species. pp. 124. *Washington,* 1917. 8°. [*U.S.A. Department of Agriculture. Bulletin.* no. 417.] A.S. **800**.

BURGESS (ALBERT FRANKLIN) and **CROSSMAN** (SAMUEL SUTTON)

—— Imported Insect Enemies of the Gipsy Moth and the Brown-Tail Moth. pp. 147. pl. 6. *Washington,* 1929. 8°. [*U.S. Department of Agriculture. Technical Bulletin.* no. 86.] A.S. **800/2**.

BURGESS (ALEXANDER) *Bishop of the Protestant Episcopal Church in Quincy.* Memoir of the Life of the Right Reverend George Burgess . . . Edited by the Rev. A. Burgess. pp. 419. *Claxton, Remsen, & Haffelfinger: Philadelphia,* 1869. 8°. **4986**. cc. **92**.

BURGESS (ALEXANDER) *of Kennoway, Fifeshire. See* also POUTE, *of the Leven Saat Pans, pseud.* [i.e. A. Burgess.]

—— Faint, yet Pursuing. [An essay on the Sabbath.] [1849?] *See* PERIODICAL PUBLICATIONS.—*London.* The Working Man's Charter, *etc.* [1848, *etc.*] 8°. P.P. **723**.

—— "Poute"! Being poutry, poetry, and prose. [An enlarged edition of "The Book of Nettercaps."] pp. x. 125. *A. Westwood & Son: Cupar-Fife; J. Menzies & Co.: Edinburgh & Glasgow,* [1890.] 8°. **12330**. cc. **51**.
The earlier edition, entitled "The Book of Nettercaps," is entered under POUTE, *of the Leven Saat Pans, pseud.*

BURGESS (ALFRED THOMAS) The "Classified" Series of Science & Art Questions . . . Containing those set . . . during the years 1884 to 1893—inclusive—in hygiene. pp. 16. *A. T. Burgess: London,* [1894.] 8°. **7306**. e. **22**. (**12**.)

—— First Stage Agriculture. Being the elementary principles of agriculture scientifically explained, *etc.* pp. viii. 124. *J. Hughes & Co.: London,* 1893. 8°. **7077**. de. **38**.

—— "Sprigs and Sprays." Being original poems. (Subscribers' edition.) [With plates, including a portrait.] pp. 120. [*The Author:*] *London,* 1909. 8°. **011650**. f. **17**.

BURGESS (AMY VIOLET)

—— An Analysis of the Female Characters of Grillparzer's Dramas contrasted with those of Goethe's and Schiller's. *In:* Aberystwyth Studies. vol. 1. pp. 63–111. 1912. 8°. Ac. **1375**.

BURGESS (ANTHONY) *Vicar of Sutton Coldfield.* *See* BURGESSE.

BURGESS (ARCHIBALD) Baptism considered in relation to its Mode and Subjects, in a series of discourses. pp. 258. *Perkins & Marvin: Boston,* 1837. 8°. **4326.** aa. **16.**

BURGESS (ARTHUR) My Holy Place, *etc.* pp. vi. 26. *Theosophical Publishing House: [London,* 1918.] 16°. **8632.** a. **35.**

—— The Voice of the Beloved. pp. 59. *Simpkin, Marshall & Co.: London,* 1923. 8°. **8633.** aaa. **55.**

BURGESS (ARTHUR EDWARD) School Gardening. By A. E. Burgess . . . Poultry Keeping. By O. R. Stevenson . . . Cane and Raffa Basketry. By A. H. Crampton. [With plates.] pp. xv. 233. *New Era Publishing Co.: London,* 1931. 4°. [*Practical Instruction Handbooks.* Senior Series. vol. 3.] **7955.** bb. **45/6.**

BURGESS (ARTHUR JAMES WETHERALL) *See* CLARK (Atwood) Those Were the Days! Illustrated by A. J. W. Burgess. 1933. 8°. **2271.** d. **3.**

BURGESS (CECIL RITCHIE)

—— Meteorology for Seamen. [With illustrations and maps.] pp. xi. 252. *Brown, Son & Ferguson: Glasgow,* 1950. 8°. **8754.** bb. **38.**

BURGESS (CHARLES FREDERICK) Applied Electrochemistry and Metallurgy . . . Applied Electrochemistry by C. F. Burgess . . . Metallurgy by H. B. Pulsifer . . . and Benjamin B. Freud, *etc.* pp. 198. *American Technical Society: Chicago,* 1920. 8°. **8759.** b. **10.**

BURGESS (CHARLES HENRY)

—— Letters from Persia written by Charles and Edward Burgess, 1828–1855. Edited by Benjamin Schwartz. (Reprinted from the Bulletin of the New York Public Library.) [With plates, including a portrait.] pp. 125. *New York Public Library: New York,* 1942. 8°. **010920.** m. **35.**

BURGESS (CHARLES OWEN)

—— Metallic and Non-metallic Coatings for Gray Iron. [With illustrations.] pp. 67. ix. *Gray Iron Founders' Society: Cleveland,* [1951.] 8°. **07107.** tt. **11.**

—— Welding, Joining and Cutting of Gray Iron. pp. 37. iv. *Gray Iron Founders' Society: Cleveland,* [1951.] 8°. **07109.** m. **26.**

BURGESS (CHRISTOPHER VICTOR)

—— The Burgess Books. 4 pt. *University of London Press: London,* [1955.] 8°. **12838.** b. **51.**

—— Teacher's Book. pp. 32. *University of London Press: London,* [1955.] 8°. **12838.** b. **51a.**

—— More Plays for Large Classes. pp. 108. *University of London Press: London,* [1955.] 8°. **11785.** a. **4.**

—— Read, Write and Act Series. *Sir Isaac Pitman & Sons: London,* 1954– . 8°. W.P. c. **372.**

—— Short Plays for Large Classes. pp. 92. *University of London Press: London,* [1953.] 8°. **11784.** aaa. **63.**

—— The Time-Bomb. A story to read and a play to act. pp. vi. 25. *Sir Isaac Pitman & Sons: London,* 1954. 8°. [*Read, Write and Act Series.*] W.P. c. **372/3.**

BURGESS (CLARA AMY) The Sex Philosophy of a Bachelor Girl. pp. 68. *Advanced Thought Publishing Co.: Chicago,* [1920.] 8°. **08415.** e. **38.**

BURGESS (CORNELIUS) *See* BURGES.

BURGESS (D.) *A.M.* The Entertainer; or, Youth's delightful preceptor, containing a collection of . . . pieces . . . Collected from the most eminent authors . . . To which is prefixed, a Plan of Education, from the Chevalier Ramsay . . . By D. Burgess. pp. 329. *R. Taylor: Berwick,* 1759. 12°. **732.** a. **27.**

BURGESS (DANIEL) *the Elder.* *See* FLEMING (Robert) *the Elder.* The Confirming Work of Religion . . . Now published by D. Burgess. 1693. 8°. **852.** e. **14.** (**2.**)

—— *See* FLEMING (Robert) *the Elder.* The Fulfilling of the Scripture, *etc.* [With a preface by D. Burgess.] 1753. 8°. **4379.** aaa. **5.**

—— *See* HENRY (Matthew) *Nonconformist Minister.* A Sermon preach'd upon occasion of the funeral of the Reverend Mr. Daniel Burgess, *etc.* 1713. 8°. **225.** h. **18.** (**2.**)

—— *See* OWEN (John) *D.D.* Of Communion with God . . . With a preface by the late Rev. D. Burgess. 1859. 12°. **4404.** g. **32.**

—— *See* PORTER (Robert) *Minister of the Gospel in Nottinghamshire.* The Life of Mr. John Hieron . . . Published by D. Burgess. 1691. 4°. **490.** c. **31.** (**3.**)

—— Appellatio ad fratres exteros, in qâ controversiæ status inter Hierarchicos & Nonconformes Anglicanos . . . proponitur. Plurimorum J. Christi ministrorum hortatu . . . scripsit, emisitq: Christianus Catholicus [i.e. D. Burgess]. pp. 39. 1690. 4°. *See* APPELLATIO. **1470.** b. **6.**

—— Ἀποκαραδοκια κ' εὐχη ἡ χριστιανικη. Christians earnest expectation and longing for the glorious appearing of the great God and our Saviour Jesus Christ. Set forth in a discourse occasioned by the decease of . . . Mr. Noah Webb, *etc.* pp. 46. *For O. C.: [London ?]* 1675. 8°. **1418.** i. **51.**

—— Causa Dei: or Counsel to the rich of this world. To the highest part of the dust of the earth. To which is prefixed an humble address to the King's Majesty. pp. xvi. 128. *For Joseph Fox: London,* 1697. 8°. **852.** e. **15.**

—— Characters of a Godly Man. Both, as more and less grown in grace. pp. 128. *For Tho. Parkhurst: London,* 1691. 8°. **852.** e. **14.** (**1.**)

—— Christian Commemoration, and Imitation of Saints Departed; explicated, and pressed from Heb. 13. 7. Occasioned by the decease of the Reverend Mr. Henry Hurst. [With a prefatory letter by Richard Baxter.] pp. 120. *For Tho. Parkhurst: London,* 1691. 12°. **1418.** a. **3.**

—— The Church's Triumph over Death. A funeral-sermon preached upon the decease of blessed Mr. Robert Fleming. pp. 111. *J. D. for Tho. Parkhurst; A. Bell & J. Luntley: London,* 1694. 8°. **1417.** a. **24.**

—— [Another edition.] *See* FLEMING (Robert) *the Elder.* The Fulfilling of the Scripture Complete, *etc.* 1726. fol. **689.** g. **15.**

—— The Death and Rest, Resurrection and Blessed Portion of the Saints. In a discourse, on Dan. 12. 13. Together with the Work of the Redeemer, and the Work of the Redeemed. pp. 156. *For John Lawrence: London,* 1692. 12°. **1025.** b. **22.** (**2.**)

—— Directions for Daily Holy Living. *For Tho. Parkhurst: London,* 1690. *s. sh.* fol. **816.** m. **22.** (**25.**)

—— Foolish Talking and Jesting described and condemned. In a discourse on Ephes. 5. 4, *etc.* [With a portrait.] pp. 110. *For A. Bell & J. Luntley: London*, 1694. 8°. **693. d. 7. (2.)**

—— The Golden Snuffers: or, Christian reprovers, and reformers, characterized, cautioned, and encouraged. A sermon preach'd unto the Societies for Reformation of Manners, *etc.* pp. 80. MS. NOTE. *J. Darby for T. Parkhurst: London*, 1697. 8°. **4474. aa. 81.**

—— Proofs of God's Being, and of the Scriptures Divine Original. With twenty directions for the profitable reading of them. Being the sum of several sermons, desired by many hearers. *For T. Parkhurst: London*, 1697. 8°. **693. d. 7. (3.)**
Imperfect; wanting all after p. 16.

—— The second edition. pp. 23. *For Tho. Parkhurst: London*, 1698. 8°. **693. d. 7. (1.)**

—— Psalms, Hymns, and Spiritual Songs. By the late Reverend Mr. D. Burgess. [Edited by John Billingsley.] pp. viii. 312. 1714. 12°. *See* BIBLE.—*Psalms.—Selections.* [*English.*] **3436. bb. 31.**

—— [Another copy.] Psalms, Hymns, and Spiritual Songs. 1714. 12°. *See* BIBLE.—*Psalms.—Selections.* [*English.*] **03440. f. 36.**

—— Rules for Hearing the Word of God with certain and saving benefit . . . The fourth edition. pp. 24. *T. Field: London*, 1757. 12°. **4498. a. 19.**

—— The fifth edition. pp. 23. *Daniel Smith: Leeds*, 1771. 12°. **10347. de. 3. (2.)**

—— [Another copy.] **10347. de. 2. (3.)**

—— [Another edition.] pp. ix. 31–48. [*London*, 1800?] 8°. **4378. c. 1. (3.)**
An extract from a larger work.

—— Seasonable Words: the sum of a sermon preached on the late publick fast, January the 14th, 170$\frac{7}{8}$. pp. 36. *T. Parkhurst: London*, 1708. 8°. **4476. aaa. 25.**

—— The Way to Peace. A funeral sermon . . . preached upon the decease of . . . Elizabeth, Countess of Ranalagh. pp. 79. *J. D. for Jonathan Robinson & Brab. Ailmer: London*, 1695. 8°. **1418. f. 43.**
The titlepage is mutilated.

—— Wherein may we more hopefully attempt the Conversion of Younger People, than of others? *See* ANNESLEY (Samuel) *LL.D., Minister of St. Giles', Cripplegate.* Casuistical Morning-Exercises, *etc.* vol. 4. 1690. 4°. **858. k. 12.**

—— [Another edition.] 1844. *See* ANNESLEY (Samuel) *LL.D., Minister of St. Giles', Cripplegate.* The Morning Exercises at Cripplegate, *etc.* vol. 4. 1844, *etc.* 8°. **1356. h. 4.**

—— Dr. Burgis's Answer to Dr. Sacheverel's high flown Sermon [i.e. "The Perils of False Brethren, both in Church and State"], preach'd before the Lord Mayor, &c. . . . on the fifth of November, 1709. [An apocryphal work.] pp. 8. *T. White: London*, [1710?] 8°. **114. e. 35.**

—— [Another copy.] **E. 1989. (11.)**
Mutilated.

—— The Craftsmen: a sermon or paraphrase upon several verses of the 19th chapter of the Acts of the Apostles. Composed by the late D. Burgess, and intended to be preach'd by him in the high times, but prevented by the burning of his Meeting-House. [A Whig pamphlet. By Thomas Gordon.] pp. 38. *A. Moore: London*, 1720. 8°. **T. 1792. (13.)**

—— [Another edition.] pp. 25. *A. Moore: London*, 1721. 8°. **4475. a. 33.**

—— Seventh edition. pp. 27. *A. Moor: London*, 1732. 8°. **4475. de. 8. (11.)**

—— A new edition. pp. 47. *J. Thompson: Birmingham*, 1791. 8°. **4372. f. 9. (3.)**

—— The Life, Death and Character of Mr. Daniel Burgess . . . With a new elegy on his much lamented death. pp. 12. *Edw. Midwinter: London*, [1713.] 4°. **G. 2046.**

BURGESS (DANIEL) *the Younger.* A Letter to the Bishop of Salisbury [Gilbert Burnet], occasion'd by his son's [Thomas Burnet's] Letter to the Earl of Hallifax. Containing a fair state of the case of the late ministry, and a full answer to all Mr. Burnet's arguments for an impeachment. By a good friend to the late ministers [i.e. D. Burgess]. pp. 33. 1715. 8°. *See* BURNET (*Sir* Thomas) *one of the Justices of the Court of Common Pleas.* **8133. aaa. 13.**

—— A Short Account of the Roman Senate, and the manner of their proceedings. pp. 60. *J. Roberts: London*, 1729. 4°. **804. d. 17.**

—— [Another copy.] **E. 2019. (12.)**

BURGESS (EBENEZER) *See* SŪRYA-SIDDHĀNTA. Translation of the Sûrya-Siddhânta . . . with notes, and an appendix . . . by Rev. E. Burgess, *etc.* 1860. 8°. **14053. d. 5.**

—— —— 1935. 8°. **14055. c. 14.**

—— Dedham Pulpit: or, Sermons by the pastors of the First Church in Dedham, in the XVIIth and XVIIIth centuries; with a centennial discourse by the present pastor (E. Burgess). [Edited by E. Burgess.] pp. viii. 517. *Perkins & Marvin: Boston*, 1840. 8°. **4485. f. 115.**

—— A Sermon preached before the Auxiliary Education Society of Norfolk County, at their annual meeting . . . June 8, 1825. pp. 44. *Crocker & Brewster: Boston*, 1825. 8°. **4486. cc. 18. (6.)**

—— What is Truth? An inquiry concerning the antiquity and unity of the human race; with an examination of recent scientific speculations on those subjects. [The editor's preface signed: W.] pp. 424. *I. P. Warren: Boston*, [1871.] 8°. **10006. df. 27.**

—— [Another issue.] *Hodder & Stoughton: London*, 1871. 8°. **4379. dd. 5.**

BURGESS (EDWARD) *of Tabriz.*

—— Letters from Persia written by Charles and Edward Burgess, 1828–1855, *etc.* 1942. 8°. *See* BURGESS (Charles H.) **010920. m. 35.**

BURGESS (EDWARD) *Secretary to the Boston Society of Natural History.*

—— *See* NICHOLS (William R.) Report on a Peculiar Condition of the Water supplied to the City of Boston. 1875–76. By Prof. Nichols . . . Mr. Burgess. 1876. 8°. **8777. aa. 19. (12.)**

BURGESS (Edward) *Secretary to the Boston Society of Natural History.*

—— Contributions to the Anatomy of the Milk-Weed Butterfly, Danais Archippus, Fabr. pp. 16. pl. II. *See* Boston, *Mass.—Boston Society of Natural History.* Anniversary Memoirs, *etc.* 1880. 4°. Ac. **3042/12.**

—— English and American Yachts : illustrating and describing the most famous yachts now sailing in English and American waters . . . Illustrated with photogravure engravings. pp. 14. *Chapman & Hall: London,* 1888. *obl.* fol. **Cup.1246.b.29.**

BURGESS (Edward Loftie) A Vision of Ideal Bliss, *etc.* (An original poem.) pp. 8. *Arliss Andrews: London,* 1879. 8°. **11651. d. 26. (17.)**

BURGESS (Edward Sandford) Studies in the History and Variations of Asters. 2 pt.

I. History of pre-Clusian Botany in its relation to Aster. pp. xii. 447.
II. Species and Variations of Biotian Asters, with discussion of variability in aster. pp. xv. 419. pl. 13.

1902, 06. 8°. *See* New York.—*Torrey Botanical Club.* **7029. c. 35.**

BURGESS (Edwin) The Edwin Burgess Letters on Taxation. First published by " The Racine Advocate " . . . 1859–60. [With an introduction by Hyland Raymond and William S. Buffham, and a portrait.] pp. 35. *W. S. Buffham: Racine, Wis.,* [1912.] 8°. **08227. cc. 22. (5.)**

BURGESS (Elizabeth) Life and History of Betty Bolaine, late of Canterbury, a well known character for parsimony and vice . . . Interspersed with original poetry. [With a portrait.] pp. 67. *Printed for the Author: Canterbury,* 1805. 12°. **615. b. 28. (3.)**

—— Second edition. pp. 40. *Henry Ward: Canterbury,* 1832. 8°. **1414. f. 43. (3.)**

—— Third edition. pp. 31. *W. S. Grigg: Canterbury,* 1880. 8°. **10600. ff. 7. (1.)**

BURGESS (Ellen) Miss Hawkins: the Ocean Boarder. [Tales.] pp. 352. *W. & R. Chambers: London & Edinburgh,* 1933. 8°. **012614. aa. 15.**

BURGESS (Emily) Working Drawings for Wood Carvers. pl. XXIV. *Bemrose & Sons: London & Derby,* [1901.] 4°. **7875. v. 8.**

BURGESS (Eric) Poems of Embryo and Ego. pp. 64. *L. Williams & Co.: London,* 1933. 8°. **011641. df. 99.**

BURGESS (Eric) *F.R.A.S.*

—— Frontier to Space, *etc.* [With plates.] pp. xvi. 174. *Chapman & Hall: London,* 1955. 8°. **8713. de. 35.**

—— Rocket Propulsion. With an introduction to the idea of interplanetary travel. [With plates.] pp. 235. *Chapman & Hall: London,* 1952. 8°. **8774. aa. 5.**

—— Rocket Propulsion . . . Second edition, revised. pp. 235. *Chapman & Hall: London,* 1954. 8°. **08774. b. 11.**

BURGESS (Eric Alexander)

—— Accident to Adeline. pp. 223. *Michael Joseph: London,* 1952. 8°. **NNN. 2368.**

—— A Knife for Celeste. pp. 222. *Michael Joseph: London,* 1949. 8°. **NN. 39493.**

—— The Malice of Monday. pp. 271. *Michael Joseph: London,* 1950. 8°. **NNN. 314**

BURGESS (Ernest) The Book of Angela. pp. 205. *Quota Press: Belfast,* 1927. 8°. **012601. d. 8.**

BURGESS (Ernest Travers)

—— Industrial Work in Missions. pp. 4. *Society for Promoting Christian Knowledge: London,* 1908. 8°. [*Pan-Anglican Papers.* S.D. 2h.] **4108. cc. 35.**

BURGESS (Ernest Watson) *See* Chicago.—*University of Chicago.* The University of Chicago Sociological Series. (Editorial committee, E. Faris . . . E. W. Burgess.) 1927, *etc.* 8°. Ac. **2691. d/37.**

—— *See* Havighurst (Robert J.) The American Veteran back home . . . [By] R. J. Havighurst . . . E. W. Burgess. 1951. 8°. **8277. dd. 40.**

—— *See* Park (Robert E.) The City. By R. E. Park, E. W. Burgess, *etc.* 1925. 8°. Ac. **2691. d/34. (1.)**

—— *See* Park (Robert E.) and Burgess (E. W.) Introduction to the Science of Sociology. 1924. 8°. **08248. h. 51.**

—— An Open Letter to Governor Horner . . . and report to him entitled " The Next Step in the War on Crime—legalize gambling," *etc.* pp. 31. *Printed for private circulation: Chicago,* [1935.] 8°. **8435. i. 34.**

—— Personality and the Social Group. Edited by E. W. Burgess. pp. xii. 230. *Chicago,* 1929. 8°. [*University of Chicago Sociological Series.*] Ac. **2691. d/37. (9.)**

—— The Urban Community. Selected papers from the Proceedings of the American Sociological Society, 1925. Edited by E. W. Burgess. pp. xii. 268. *Chicago,* 1926. 8°. [*University of Chicago Studies in Urban Sociology.*] Ac. **2691. d/34. (3.)**

BURGESS (Ernest Watson) and **LOCKE** (Harvey James)

—— The Family. From institution to companionship. pp. xv. 800. *American Book Co.: New York,* [1945.] 8°. [*American Sociology Series.*] W.P. **3558/15.**

—— The Family . . . Second edition. pp. xiv. 729. *American Book Co.: New York,* [1953.] 8°. [*American Sociology Series.*] W.P. **3558/23.**

BURGESS (Ernest Watson) and **WALLIN** (Paul)

—— Courtship, Engagement and Marriage. By E. W. Burgess . . . and P. Wallin . . . with Gladys Denny Shultz. pp. 444. *J. B. Lippincott Co.: Philadelphia & New York,* [1954.] 8°. **8417. f. 25.**

—— Engagement and Marriage. pp. xii. 819. *J. B. Lippincott Co.: Chicago,* [1953.] 8°. Cup. **366. b. 14.**

BURGESS (Esther Margaret Rooke)

—— Cherry Becomes International. Illustrated by M. W. Whittington. pp. 166. *A. H. Stockwell: Ilfracombe,* 1946. 8°. **12830. aa. 55.**

—— Dalmira Wins Through. pp. 128. *London ; Dublin* printed, [1934.] 8°. [*Mellifont Press Juvenile Series.* no. 8.] W.P. **8641/8.**

—— The Girl Guide Book of Ideas. pp. vi. 180. *Brown, Son & Ferguson: Glasgow,* 1931. 8°. **07912. e. 67.**

—— The Girl Guide Book of Knowledge. pp. viii. 220. *Brown, Son & Ferguson: Glasgow,* 1933 [1932]. 8°. **12216. aa. 15.**

—— The Girl Guide Book of Recreation. pp. 266. *Brown, Son & Ferguson: Glasgow,* 1934. 8°. **7916. ee. 15.**

BURGESS (Esther Margaret Rooke)

—— The Girl Guide Omnibus Book of Ideas, etc. pp. x. 358. *Brown, Son & Ferguson: Glasgow*, 1951. 8°. **8833. a. 48.**

—— Hilary Follows Up; or, the Peridew tradition, *etc.* pp. 207. *Blackie & Son: London & Glasgow*, [1939.] 8°. **12824. a. 5.**

—— Hilary Follows Up . . . Edited and adapted by Geoffrey G. Bond. pp. 136. *Blackie & Son: London & Glasgow*, 1948. 8°. [*Life and Adventure Series.* Girls' section. no. 3.] W.P. **13289. b/3.**

—— [A reissue.] Hilary follows up, *etc.* *London & Glasgow*, [1954.] 8°. **12838. b. 34.**

—— Ready for Anything . . . Illustrated by M. W. Whittington. pp. 176. *Arthur H. Stockwell: Ilfracombe*, [1948.] 8°. **12827. e. 88.**

—— The Second Girl Guide Book of Ideas, *etc.* pp. vii. 229. *Brown, Son & Ferguson: Glasgow*, 1936. 8°. **07908. e. 17.**

—— The Third Girl Guide Book of Ideas. pp. x. 246. *Brown, Son & Ferguson: Glasgow*, 1940. 8°. **08820. a. 103.**

—— The Youth Club Book of Recreation. 186 games and competitions for the teen-ager . . . Illustrated by Jennetta Vise. pp. 287. *Brown, Son & Ferguson: Glasgow*, 1954. 8°. **7922. aa. 5.**

BURGESS (F. A.) Is Relativity True? If so, how true? pp. 112. *Lincoln Williams: London*, 1933. 8°. **8707. aaa. 34.**

BURGESS (Forsyth Francis Robert) Sporting Fire-Arms for Bush and Jungle . . . With illustrations by the author. pp. viii. 136. pl. vi. *W. H. Allen & Co.: London*, 1884. 8°. **7908. b. 41.**

BURGESS (Francis) *See* Bible.—*Psalms.—Selections.* [*English.*] The Plainchant Evening Psalter and Canticles. Edited by F. Burgess. 1916. 8°. **03089. e. 25.**

—— —— 1920. 8°. **03089. e. 30.**

—— Bizet's Carmen. [With musical notes.] pp. 45. *Alexander Moring: London*, 1905. 8°. [*Nights at the Opera.* no. 7.] **7897. p. 1/6.**

—— The Church and Modern Art, *etc.* (Reprinted from the official report of the Church Congress.) pp. 4. *Bemrose & Sons: Derby & London*, [1908.] 8°. **07807. i. 41. (5.)**

—— Gounod's Faust. [With musical notes.] pp. 49. *Alexander Moring: London*, 1905. 8°. [*Nights at the Opera.* no. 8.] **7897. p. 1/7.**

—— Handbooks of Church Music, under the general editorship of F. Burgess. no. 1–4. "*Musical Opinion*": *London*, 1919–25. 8° & 4°. **07899. ee. 47.** *No more published. No. 2 is of the second edition.*

—— Mozart's Don Giovanni. [With musical notes.] pp. 49. *Alexander Moring: London*, 1905. 8°. [*Nights at the Opera.* no. 9.] **7897. p. 1/8.**

—— [Another copy.] Mozart's Don Giovanni. *London*, 1905. 12°. Hirsch **3802.**

—— The Organ fifty years hence. A study of its development in the light of its past history and present tendencies. pp. 32. *William Reeves: London*, 1908. 8°. **7891.aa.40.**

BURGESS (Francis)

—— The Rudiments of Gregorian Music. [With musical notes.] pp. 24. *Wm. Reeves: London*, [1909.] 8°. **7898. k. 42.**

—— The Rudiments of Plainchant. [With musical notes.] pp. 40. "*Musical Opinion*": *London*, 1919. 8°. [*Handbooks of Church Music.* no. 1.] **07899. ee. 47/1.**

—— The Teaching and Accompaniment of Plainsong. [With musical notes.] pp. 83. *Novello & Co.: London*, [1914.] 8°. [*Handbooks for Musicians.*] **7893. s. 7/2.**

—— A Textbook of Plainsong and Gregorian Music. [With musical notes.] pp. vii. 128. *Vincent Music Co.: London*, [1906.] 8°. **7899. aaaa. 20.**

—— Verdi's Il Trovatore. [With musical notes.] pp. 56. *Alexander Moring: London*, 1906. 8°. [*Nights at the Opera.* no. 10.] **7897. p. 1/9.**

—— Verdi's Rigoletto. [With musical notes.] pp. 42. *Alexander Moring: London*, 1906. 8°. [*Nights at the Opera.* no. 11.] **7897. p. 1/10.**

BURGESS (Francis Guild) Little Beginnings, and other sermons to the boys and girls. pp. 158. *Francis Griffiths: London* 1913. 8°. **4466. g. 32.**

—— The Story of the Kingdom. Church history for the boys and girls, *etc.* pp. xii. 271. *Francis Griffiths: London*, 1914. 8°. **4535. b. 31.**

BURGESS (Frank)

—— The Cardinal on Trial. [An account of the trial of Cardinal Mindszenty.] pp. 16. *London*, [1949.] 8°. ["*Sword*" *Pamphlet.*] W.P. **455/8.**

BURGESS (Frank Gelett) *See* Periodical Publications.—*San Francisco.* The Lark. (G. Burgess, editor.) 1895, *etc.* 8°. P.P. **6343. ac.**

—— Are You a Bromide? or, the Sulphitic theory, *etc.* [Reprinted from "The Smart Set."] pp. 63. *B. W. Huebsch: New York*, 1906. 8°. **012316. de. 52.**

—— Blue Goops and Red. A manual of polite deportment for children . . . With illustrations. pp. 81. *F. A. Stokes Co.: New York*, 1909. 4°. **12812. bb. 18.**

—— The Burgess Nonsense Book. Being a complete collection of the humorous masterpieces of Gelett Burgess, Esq. . . . Adorned with . . . illustrations by the author, *etc.* pp. 239. *Simpkin, Marshall & Co.: London*, 1914. 8°. **012331. k. 39.**

—— Burgess Unabridged. A new dictionary of words you have always needed . . . With . . . illustrations by Herbert Roth. pp. xxiv. 119. *Simpkin, Marshall & Co.: London*, 1914. 8°. **12316. ff. 37.**

—— A Gage of Youth. Lyrics from "The Lark" and other poems. pp. viii. 56. *Small, Maynard & Co.: Boston*, 1901. 8°. **11688. aa. 49.**

—— Goop Tales alphabetically told . . . With numerous illustrations. pp. 106. *F. A. Stokes Co.: New York*, [1904.] 8°. **12812. b. 37.**

—— Goops and how to be them. A manual of manners for polite infants . . . With ninety drawings. *Methuen & Co.: London*, 1900. 8°. **12809. o. 21.**

—— The Heart Line . . . Illustrated by Lester Ralph. pp. 480. *Grant Richards: London*, 1908. 8°. **012626. aaa. 9.**

BURGESS (Frank Gelett)

—— The Lively City o' Ligg. A cycle of modern fairy tales for city children . . . With . . . illustrations by the author. pp. 219. *Methuen & Co.: London; printed in America,* 1900. 8º. **12809**. q. **23**.

—— Look Eleven Years Younger. [With plates.] pp. xix. 233. *Simon & Schuster: New York,* 1937. 8º. **08408**. h. **64**.

—— Love in a Hurry . . . Illustrated by R. M. Brinkerhoff. pp. 345. *Bobbs-Merrill Co.: Indianapolis,* [1913.] 8º. **12720**. b. **6**.

—— The Maxims of Noah. Derived from his experience with women both before and after the flood as given in counsel to his son Japhet . . . With illustrations and designs by Louis D. Fancher. pp. 119. *Simpkin, Marshall & Co.: London,* 1913. 8º. **012331**. g. **67**.

—— Mrs. Hope's Husband . . . Illustrated by Henry Raleigh. pp. 161. *Century Co.: New York,* 1917. 8º. **12702**. b. **1**.

—— More Goops and how not to be them, *etc.* *J. Wilson & Son: Cambridge* [*Mass.*], 1903. 4º. **12806**. h. **104**.

A slip bearing the imprint "London: Grant Richards" has been pasted on the titlepage.

—— The Romance of the Commonplace. [Essays.] pp. 152. *P. Elder & M. Shepard: San Francisco,* 1902. 8º. **012356**. h. **69**.

—— [Another edition.] pp. xiv. 344. *Bobbs-Merrill Co.: Indianapolis,* 1916. 8º. **012352**. de. **14**.

—— Too Good Looking. The romance of Flossidoodle Darlo. pp. 351. *Bobbs-Merrill Co.: Indianapolis, New York,* [1936.] 8º. A.N. **3068**.

—— Two O'Clock Courage. pp. 348. *Bobbs-Merrill Co.: Indianapolis,* [1934.] 8º. **12709**. h. **6**.

—— [Another edition.] pp. 387. *I. Nicholson & Watson: London,* 1934. 8º. A.N. **2175**.

—— Vivette, or the Memoirs of the Romance Association. Setting forth the diverting adventures of one Richard Redforth in the very pleasant city of Millamours, *etc.* pp. 152. *Copeland & Day: Boston,* 1897. 8º. **012706**. e. **34**.

—— The White Cat . . . With illustrations by Will Grefé. pp. 390. *Chapman & Hall: London,* 1908. 8º. **012627**. ccc. **18**.

—— Why Men Hate Women . . . Illustrations by Herb Roth. pp. 67. *Payson & Clarke: New York,* 1927. 8º. **08416**. aa. **17**.

—— [Another edition.] pp. 75. *Brentano's: London,* 1928. 8º. **08416**. aa. **22**.

BURGESS (Frederick H.) *See* Kauffmann (C.) and Kruse (U. J.) *pseud.* [Der Kopfarbeiter.] The Brainworkers' Handbook . . . Translated by F. H. Burgess & H. N. Casson. [1928.] 8º. **8403**. ee. **18**.

BURGESS (Frederick William) *See* Periodical Publications.—*London.* The Hardware Magazine. [Edited by F. W. Burgess.] 1907, *etc.* 4º. P.P. **1653**. h.

—— Chats on Household Curios . . . With 94 illustrations. pp. 360. *T. Fisher Unwin: London,* 1914. 8º. **07709**. aa. **10**.

BURGESS (Frederick William)

—— Chats on Old Coins . . . With 258 illustrations. pp. 393. *T. Fisher Unwin: London,* 1913. 8º. **7757**. aaa. **28**.

—— Chats on Old Copper and Brass . . . With frontispiece and illustrations from photographs and wash drawings. pp. 400. *T. Fisher Unwin: London,* 1914. 8º. **07805**. b. **12**.

—— Chats on Old Copper and Brass . . . Edited and revised by C. G. E. Bunt. pp. 183. pl. 46. *Ernest Benn: London,* 1954. 8º. **07813**. e. **25**.

—— The Home Connoisseur Series. [With plates.] 5 vol.

Antique Furniture, *etc.* pp. xi. 499. 1915.
Old Pottery and Porcelain, *etc.* pp. xvii. 426. 1916.
Antique Jewellery and Trinkets, *etc.* pp. xiii. 399. 1919.
Silver: Pewter: Sheffield Plate, *etc.* pp. xvi. 304. 1921.
Old Prints and Engravings, *etc.* pp. xii. 281. 1924.

G. Routledge & Sons: London, 1915–24. 8º. **07804**. aa. **6**.

—— The Practical Retail Draper. A complete guide for the drapery and allied trades. 5 vol. *Virtue & Co.: London,* [1912–14.] 8º. **8226**. tt. **2**.

BURGESS (G. Arthur) How the Canadian Soldiers might become Rich . . . Described in two open letters to Sir R. L. Borden, *etc.* pp. 7. *Carleton Place, Ont.,* [1919.] 8º. **08028**. de. **12**.

BURGESS (G. E. E.) Two Possible Developments of the Large Marine Diesel Engine. pp. 54. [*London,*] 1921. 8º. [*Association of Engineering and Shipbuilding Draughtsmen. Publications of the Technical Section.*] Ac. **4395**. (**14**.)

BURGESS (Gelett) *See* Burgess (Frank G.)

BURGESS (George) *Bishop of the Protestant Episcopal Church in Maine.* *See* Bible.—*Psalms.* [*English.—Miscellaneous Metrical Versions.*] The American Metrical Psalter. [The preface signed: G. B., i.e. G. Burgess.] 1864. 8º. **3090**. aaa. **31**.

—— *See* Burgess (Alexander) *Bishop of the Protestant Episcopal Church in Quincy.* Memoir of the Life of the Right Reverend George Burgess, *etc.* 1869. 8º. **4986**. cc. **92**.

—— *See* Doane (George W.) *Bishop of the Protestant Episcopal Church in New Jersey.* The Protest and Appeal of George Washington Doane . . . as aggrieved, by the Right Reverend W. Meade . . . the Right Reverend G. Burgess, *etc.* 1852. 8º. **4183**. bb. **85**. (**1**.)

—— *See* Doane (George W.) *Bishop of the Protestant Episcopal Church in New Jersey.* The Record of the Proceedings of the Court of Bishops, assembled for the trial of the Rt. Rev. G. W. Doane . . . upon a presentment made by the Rt. Rev. W. Meade . . . the Rt. Rev. G. Burgess. 1852. 8º. **5175**. d. **17**.

—— —— 1853. 8º. **4183**. bb. **85**. (**3**.)

—— *See* United States of America.—*Protestant Episcopal Church.* List of Persons admitted to the Order of Deacons in the Protestant Episcopal Church, in the United States of America from A.D. 1785 to A.D. 1857 . . . Prepared by . . . G. Burgess. 1875. 8º. **4744**. bbb. **2**.

—— Poems . . . With an introduction by the Bishop of Western New York (A. C. C. [i.e. Arthur Cleveland Coxe]). pp. viii. 276. *Brown & Gross: Hartford,* 1868. 8º. **11687**. d. **37**.

—— Adult Baptism. pp. 24. *Protestant Episcopal Society for the Promotion of Evangelical Knowledge: New-York,* [1854.] 12º. **4325**. aaa. **18**.

BURGESS (George) *Bishop of the Protestant Episcopal Church in Maine.*

—— Bishop Burgess' Contribution [to the Report of the Commission of Bishops appointed to consider and report upon the Memorial of sundry Presbyters]. *See* Potter (Alonzo) *Bishop of the Protestant Episcopal Church in Pennsylvania.* Memorial Papers, *etc.* 1857. 8°. **4745.** bb. **38.**

—— Education Sanctified by Prayer. A sermon preached at the consecration of St. Mark's Chapel, in Bishop's College, Lennoxville, *etc.* pp. 20. *John Lovell: Montreal,* 1857. 8°. **4486.** c. **28.** (**8.**)

—— The Gospel in its first Progress Westward. A sermon preached . . . at the consecration of the Rev. W. Ingraham Kip . . . as missionary Bishop of California. pp. 25. *Joel Munsell: Albany,* 1853. 8°. **4486.** d. **36.** (**12.**)

—— The Martyrdom of St. Peter and St. Paul; a poem. pp. 48. *Marshall, Brown & Co.: Providence,* 1834. 12°. **11687.** b. **11.**

—— The Modern Necromancy no Argument against the Gospel. *See* Potter (Alonzo) *Bishop of the Protestant Episcopal Church in Pennsylvania.* Lectures on the Evidences of Christianity, *etc.* 1855. 8°. **4016.** f. **42.**

—— Pages from the Ecclesiastical History of New England, during the century between 1740 and 1840. [By G. Burgess.] pp. 126. 1847. 12°. *See* New England. **4744.** d. **13.**

—— A Sermon, preached in Christ Church, Hartford, on the second Sunday after the Epiphany, 1840, being the Sunday after the loss, by fire, of the steamboat Lexington, in Long Island Sound. pp. 15. *L. Skinner: Hartford,* 1840. 8°. **4486.** cc. **16.** (**8.**)

—— Sermons on the Christian Life. pp. 316. *Herman Hooker: Philadelphia,* 1854. 12°. **4485.** c. **70.**

—— The Stranger in the Church. pp. 23. *Tract Committee of the Diocese of Massachusetts: Boston,* 1848. 12°. **4183.** aa. **23.**

—— Two Sermons preached at Christ Church, Hartford, on . . . October 24, 1847. pp. 24. *Brown & Parsons: Hartford,* 1847. 8°. **4486.** cc. **21.** (**15.**)

BURGESS (George) *of Durban.* Every Man's Wages: how to increase them permanently. A claim for the taxation of land value. pp. 47. *United Committee for the Taxation of Land Values: London; T. W. Griggs & Co: Durban,* [1922.] 8°. **08282.** b. **62.**

BURGESS (George Kimball) *See* Duhem (P. M. M.) [Thermodynamique et chimie.] Thermodynamics and Chemistry . . . Authorized translation by G. K. Burgess. 1903. 8°. **08909.** eee. **44.**

—— *See* Le Chatelier (H.) and Boudouard (O. L.) [Mesure des températures élevées.] High Temperature Measurements . . . Translated by G. K. Burgess, *etc.* 1901. 8°. **8716.** aa. **26.**

—— *See* Le Chatelier (H.) and Boudouard (O. L.) The Measurement of High Temperatures . . . By G. K. Burgess . . . and H. Le Chatelier . . . Third edition [of "High Temperature Measurements" by H. Le Chatelier and O. L. Boudouard], *etc.* 1912. 8°. **08715.** d. **16.**

—— Biographical Memoir Henry Marion Howe, 1848–1922. [With a portrait and a bibliography.] pp. 11. 1926. *See* Washington, *City of.—National Academy of Sciences.* Memoirs. vol. 21. 1884, *etc.* 4°. A.S. **940.**

BURGESS (Gilbert) *See* Hackman (James) The Love Letters of Mr. H. & Miss R. Edited by G. Burgess. 1895. 8°. **10921.** e. **22.**

BURGESS (Gladys) The Song of the Soul, and other poems. pp. 16. *A. H. Stockwell: London,* [1927.] 8°. **011644.** df. **114.**

BURGESS (Grace) A Plain Address on the Importance of Religion. Sixth edition. [With plates, including a portrait.] pp. 15. *Hickman & Stapledon: Henley,* 1835. 8°. **4411.** i. **44.** (**1.**)

BURGESS (Guy Francis de Moncy)

—— *See* Connolly (Cyril V.) The Missing Diplomats, *etc.* [On the disappearance in May, 1951 of G. de M. Burgess and D. D. Maclean. With a portrait.] 1952. 8°. **8140.** aaa. **64.**

—— *See* Mather (John S.) The Great Spy Scandal, *etc.* [On the disappearance of G. F. de M. Burgess and D. D. Maclean. With portraits.] 1955. 8°. **8140.** ff. **24.**

BURGESS (Harold Richard) *of Bray.*

—— *See* Periodical Publications.—*Barmouth.* The Welsh National Hunter Stud Book. [Edited by H. R. Burgess.] 1912. 8°. P.P. **2489.** zdt.

—— *See* Periodical Publications.—*Bray, Wicklow.* Official Hunting Guide . . . Edited by H. R. Burgess. 1924, *etc.* 8°. P.P. **2512.** lba.

—— *See* Periodical Publications.—*London.* The Agricultural Register (The Country Magazine and Agricultural Register) . . . Edited by H. R. Burgess. 1901. 8°. P.P. **2297.** ac.

—— *See* Periodical Publications.—*London.* The Imperial Cart Horse Stud Book (The Cart Horse Stud Book) . . . Edited . . . by H. R. Burgess. 1904, *etc.* 8°. P.P. **2489.** zdu.

—— *See* Periodical Publications.—*London.* The Imperial Harness Horse Stud Book (The Harness Horse Stud Book) . . . Edited . . . by H. R. Burgess. 1904, *etc.* 8°. P.P. **2489.** zdw.

—— *See* Periodical Publications.—*London.* The Imperial Hunter Stud Book . . . Edited by H. R. Burgess. 1904, *etc.* 8°. P.P. **2489.** zdf.

—— *See* Periodical Publications.—*London.* The Imperial Pony Stud Book (The Pony Stud Book). Edited . . . by H. R. Burgess. 1904, *etc.* 8°. P.P. **2489.** zdv.

BURGESS (Harold Richard) *Writer of Verse.*

—— [Miscellaneous works in verse.] 5 pt. [*H. R. Burgess: Liverpool,* 1941–43.] *obl.* 8°. **11656.** h. **37.**
Reproduced from manuscript.

BURGESS (Harry) My Musical Pilgrimage. An unconventional survey of music and musicians . . . Illustrated by autographed portraits. pp. viii. 149. *Simpkin, Marshall & Co.: London,* 1911. 8°. **7896.** ppp. **25.**

BURGESS (Henry) *of* 81 *Lombard Street.* A Letter to the Right Hon. George Canning, to explain in what manner the industry of the people, and the productions of the country, are connected with, and influenced by, internal bills of exchange, country bank notes and country bankers, Bank of England notes, and branch banks, *etc.* pp. iv. 139. *Harvey & Darton; J. Ridgway: London,* 1826. 8°. T. **1170.** (**2.**)

BURGESS (Henry) *of* 81 *Lombard Street.*

—— [Another copy.] A Letter to the Right Hon. George Canning, *etc. London*, 1826. 8°. **8220**. aa. **8**. (**6**.)

—— A Memorial, addressed to the Right Honorable Lord Viscount Goderich, on the fitness of the system of England,—of the country banks,—and of the branch banks of England,—to the wants of the people: and on the ample means of protection, which private bankers and the public have, against the monopoly of the Bank of England . . . Second edition. (Suggestions respecting the formation of a National Bank, *etc.*) pp. 53. *J. Ridgeway: London*, 1827. 8°. T. **1241**. (**2**.)

—— [Another edition.] pp. 25. 1828. *See* Periodical Publications.—*London*. The Pamphleteer, *etc.* vol. 28. 1813, *etc.* 8°. P.P. **3557**. w.

—— On the Establishment of an Extra Post, for the purpose of multiplying and improving the means of postage communications between the distant and important parts of the kingdom. [With a map.] pp. 23. *Printed for the Author: London*, 1819. 8°. **1391**. i. **15**.

—— A Petition to the Honourable the Commons House of Parliament, to render manifest the errors, the injustice, and the dangers, of the measures of Parliament respecting currency and bankers, *etc.* pp. 152. *J. Ridgway; J. M. Richardson: London*, 1829. 8°. **8229**. d. **23**. (**3**.)

—— A Plan for Obtaining a more speedy Postage Communication between London and the distant Parts of the Kingdom. [With a map.] pp. 60. *Printed for the Author: London*, 1819. 8°. **8247**. dd. **15**.

BURGESS (Henry) *Vicar of St. Andrew's, Whittlesey. See* Athanasius, *Saint, Patriarch of Alexandria.* [*Epistolae Festales.*] The Festal Epistles of S. Athanasius, *etc.* [Translated by H. Burgess.] 1854. 8°. **3628.de.1.**

—— *See* Ephraim, *Saint, the Syrian.* Select Metrical Hymns and Homilies . . . Translated . . . with an introduction and . . . notes, by the Rev. H. Burgess. 1853. 12°. **753**. c. **60**.

—— *See* Ephraim, *Saint, the Syrian.* The Repentance of Nineveh, a metrical homily . . . Translated . . . with an introduction and notes, by the Rev. H. Burgess. 1853. 12°. **3805**. a. **50**.

—— *See* Hincks (Edward) On Assyrian Verbs . . . Edited by the Rev. H. Burgess. [1856.] 8°. **12904**. cc. **25**. (**1**.)

—— *See* Kitto (John) A Cyclopædia of Biblical Literature . . . Revised by the Rev. H. Burgess, *etc.* 1856. 8°. **3126**. e. **29**.

—— *See* Periodical Publications.—London.—*The Clerical Journal.* The Clerical Journal Almanac . . . Edited by H. Burgess. [1856.] *s. sh.* fol. **1880**. d. **6**. (**113**.)

—— *See* Periodical Publications.—*London.* The Journal of Sacred Literature, *etc.* (New ser. vol. 6, 7; ser. 3. vol. 1–13 edited by H. Burgess. ser. 3. vol. 13 edited by H. Burgess and B. H. Cowper.) 1848, *etc.* 8°. P.P. **186**.

—— The Amateur Gardener's Year-Book, *etc.* pp. xi. 347. *A. & C. Black: Edinburgh*, 1854. 8°. **7055**. d. **6**.

—— The Art of Preaching, and the Composition of Sermons, with an introductory essay on the present position and influence of the pulpit of the Church of England, *etc.* pp. xv. 396. *Hamilton, Adams & Co.: London*, 1881. 8°. **4498**. f. **8**.

—— The Bible and Lord Shaftesbury: an examination of the positions of his Lordship respecting the Holy Scriptures, delivered at a public meeting of the Bible Society at Oxford . . . In a letter to John D. Macbride. pp. 48. *J. H. & J. Parker: Oxford & London*, 1856. 8°. **3149**. e. **48**. (**3**.)

BURGESS (Henry) *Vicar of St. Andrew's, Whittlesey.*

—— The Bible Translation Society of the Baptists shown to be uncalled for and injurious: in a series of letters to W. B. Gurney, Esq. By a Baptist [i.e. H. Burgess]. pp. 64. 1840. 8°. *See* Baptist. **3128**. d. **9**.

—— Disestablishment and Disendowment. The national Church of England defended against the attacks of social, religious, and political opponents, *etc.* pp. viii. 40. *Longmans & Co.: London*, 1875. 8°. **4109**. aaa. **24**.

—— The Duty of the State to its Infant Poor. A letter to Lord John Russell, occasioned by the recent disclosures respecting the infant poor at Tooting. pp. 15. *C. Cox: London*, 1849. 8°. **8275**. e. **15**.

—— Essays, Biblical and Ecclesiastical, relating chiefly to the Authority and Interpretation of Holy Scripture. pp. xv. 410. *Longmans & Co.: London*, 1873. 8°. **4379**. h. **14**.

—— Lectures on Infidelity, and the Evidences of Christianity, delivered at the Baptist Meeting House, Luton. pp. 200. *James Dinnis: London*, 1832. 12°. **1022**. a. **15**.

—— Maurice's Essays. A plea for the old theology . . . Reprinted from the Journal (of Sacred Literature), *etc.* pp. 22. *Blackader & Co.: London*, 1854. 8°. **4372**. g. **21**. (**3**.)

—— The Reformed Church of England in its principles and their legitimate development: a contribution to the settlement of existing controversies. pp. xvi. 334. *William Macintosh: London*, 1869. 8°. **4108**. bb. **72**.

—— Revision of Translations of the Holy Scriptures: an argument against objectors . . . Reprinted from the "Journal of Sacred Literature," *etc.* pp. 18. *J. H. & J. Parker: Oxford & London*, 1857. 8°. **3149**. e. **48**. (**5**.)

—— Truth or Orthodoxy; to which must we sacrifice? A friendly address to the Wesleyan Methodist preachers of Great Britain. pp. 23. *John Heaton: Leeds*, 1849. 8°. **4135**. c. **12**.

—— Testimonials on behalf of the Rev. Henry Burgess . . . in reference to the Rectorship of the Edinburgh Academy. pp. 25. *Walton & Mitchell: London*, 1854. 8°. **4906**. d. **8**.

BURGESS (Henry James)

—— If a Man Die. [On the Christian doctrine of immortality.] pp. 31. *Tyndale Press: London*, 1946. 8°. [*Books for the Sixth Former.*] W.P. **956/3**.

BURGESS (Henry James) and **PROUDLOVE** (David Bertram)

—— Watching unto Prayer. One hundred Bible readings on prayer. pp. 110. *Lutterworth Press: London & Redhill*, 1944. 8°. **3458**. aaa. **38**.

BURGESS (Henry Thomas) My Friends. A study in personal relations. pp. 48. *C. H. Kelly: London*, 1914. 12°. **04376**. de. **8**. (**4**.)

—— [Another copy.] **4224**. de. **51**.

—— 'Our Father.' Studies in the Lord's Prayer. [With a portrait.] pp. 287. *C. H. Kelly: London*, 1917. 8°. **4400**. p. **44**.

—— The Relation of the Children to the Church. pp. 31. *C. H. Kelly: London*, [1897.] 12°. **4418**. cc. **53**. (**1**.)

BURGESS (Henry W.) Eidodendron, Views of the general Character & Appearance of Trees, foreign & indigenous, connected with picturesque scenery. [With an introductory essay, entitled "Botanical Diversions. 1. Amœnitates quernеæ," by G. T. Burnett, and with a portrait.] pp. iii. ff. 26. pl. 54. *J. Dickinson: London*, 1827. fol. **1824**. e. **14**.

—— Studies of Trees. [Twelve plates.] *J. Dickinson; the Artist: London*, 1837. *obl.* fol. **1759**. a. **13**.

BURGESS (Herbert Smith) *See* Sinclair (Walter) and Wright (C. E. S.) A Dictionary of Naval Equivalents, *etc.* (The Dutch portion . . . by Lieut. Commander C. Mayers . . . and Paymaster Sub-Lieutenant H. S. Burgess.) 1912, *etc.* 4°. **8808**. cc. **13**.

BURGESS (Hilkiah) *See* Burgess (William) *of Fleet, near Holbeach*, and Burgess (H.) [Twelve views of churches in Lincolnshire and Cambridgeshire drawn and engraved by W. and H. Burgess.] 1800, *etc.* 4°. G. **4176**. (**3**.)

—— *See* Burgess (William) *of Fleet, near Holbeach*, and Burgess (H.) Subscribers to W. & H. Burges's View of Lincoln Cathedral. 1812. 12°. **797**. b. **32**.

BURGESS (I. G.)

—— The Trial of Edward Breton . . . William Jones . . . and William Mason . . . for a Conspiracy, to defraud Margaret Howlett and Sarah Hutton . . . under the pretence of compounding a charge of felony made against James Howlett, John Morris, and Samuel Barrett, *etc.* pp. 18. *Lufton Relfe: London*, 1821. 8°. **6497**. b. **22**.

BURGESS (Isaac) *See* Hervey (James) Letters . . . illustrative of the author's character, *etc.* [Edited by I. Burgess.] 1811. 8°. **88**. d. **19**.

BURGESS (Isaac Bronson) *See* Burton (Ernest De W.) and Mathews (S.) The Life of Christ . . . Adapted . . . by I. B. Burgess, *etc.* 1930. 8°. Ac. **2691**. d/**27**. (**35**.)

—— *See* Harper (William R.) and Burgess (I. B.) An Inductive Latin Method. [1888.] 8°. **12935**. cc. **35**.

—— A Teacher's Manual for the Life of Christ [i.e. for "The Life of Christ . . . Adapted from the life of Christ by Ernest D. Burton and S. Mathews, by I. B. Burgess"]. pp. ix. 29. *Chicago*, 1927. 8°. [*Chicago University Publications in Religious Education. Constructive Studies.*] Ac. **2691**. d/**27**. (**24**.)

BURGESS (J. A.)

—— *See* Davis (Walter Cochran) and Burgess (J. A.) Market Classes and Grades of Dressed Lamb and Mutton. 1927. 8°. [*U.S. Department of Agriculture. Department Bulletin.* no. 1470.] A.S. **800**.

—— *See* Davis (Walter C.) and Burgess (J. A.) Market Classes and Grades of Dressed Lamb and Mutton. 1942. 8°. [*U.S. Department of Agriculture. Department Bulletin.* no. 1470.] A.S. **800**.

BURGESS (J. G.) *See* Haselden (James) The Trial of James Haselden, Richard Dixon, and others, for a conspiracy to defraud R. Tattersall & E. Tattersall . . . By J. G. Burgess. [1827.] 8°. **6495**. c. **23**. (**8**.)

BURGESS (James) *Art Critic. See* Lives. The Lives of the most Eminent Modern Painters . . . (Extracted chiefly from a French author [i.e. from "Abrégé de la vie des plus fameux peintres," by A. J. Dezallier d'Argenville].) By J. B. [i.e. J. Burgess or J. Buckridge ?] 1754. 8°. **562***. a. **23**. (**2**.)

BURGESS (James) *Director-General of the Archaeological Survey of India. See* Bartholomew (John G.) Constable's Hand Gazetteer of India . . . Edited with additions by J. Burgess. 1898. 8°. **010057**. e. **58**.

—— *See* Buehler (J. G.) [Über die indische Secte der Jaina.] On the Indian Sect of the Jainas . . . Edited with an outline of Jaina mythology by J. Burgess. 1903. 8°. **4506**. b. **22**.

—— *See* Fergusson (James) *Architect.* History of Indian and Eastern Architecture . . . Revised and edited, with additions: Indian Architecture, by J. Burgess, *etc.* 1910. 8°. 2031.c.

—— *See* Fleet (John F.) Pâli, Sanskrit and Old Canarese Inscriptions from the Bombay Presidency . . . Prepared under the direction of J. Burgess. 1875. fol. **7701**. h. **16**.

—— *See* Fuehrer (A.) The Sharqî Architecture of Jaunpûr . . . Edited by J. Burgess. 1889. 4°. 1710.b.1/8.

—— *See* Gruenwedel (A.) Buddhist Art in India . . . Revised and enlarged by J. Burgess, *etc.* 1901. 8°. **07807**. l. **21**.

—— *See* India.—*Archaeological Survey.* Epigraphia Indica . . . Edited by J. Burgess, *etc.* 1892, *etc.* fol. 1710.b.1/9.

—— *See* Murray (John) *Publishing Firm.* [*Handbooks for Travellers.—India.*] A Handbook for Travellers in India, Burma and Ceylon, *etc.* [Revised by J. Burgess.] 1901. 8°. **10028**. ccc. **30**.

—— *See* Periodical Publications.—*Bombay.* The Indian Antiquary . . . Edited by J. Burgess. 1872, *etc.* 4°. 15011.c.1.

—— *See* Ranchhodji Amarji. Târikh-i-Sorath . . . Translated from the Persian. [Edited by J. Burgess.] 1882. 12°. **757**. bb. **1**.

—— *See* Sewell (Robert) *of the Madras Civil Service.* List of Monuments selected for Conservation in the Presidency of Madras in 1884, *etc.* [With an introduction by J. Burgess.] [1885.] fol. **7702**. k. **14**.

—— The Ancient Monuments, Temples and Sculptures of India. Illustrated in a series of reproductions of photographs in the India Office, Calcutta Museum, and other collections. With descriptive notes and references by J. Burgess. 2 pt. pp. 49. pl. 340. *W. Griggs & Sons: London*, 1897, [1910.] fol. **1705**. a. **22**.

—— The Buddhist Stûpas of Amarâvatî and Jaggayyapeṭa in the Kṛishṇâ District, Madras Presidency, surveyed in 1882 . . . With translations of the Aśoka inscriptions at Jaugada and Dhauli, by Georg Bühler. [With plates.] pp. ix. 131. *Trübner & Co.: London*, 1887. 4°. [*Archaeological Survey of India. New Imperial Series of Reports.* vol. 6. *Archaeological Survey of Southern India. Reports.* New series. vol. 1.] **1710**. b. **1/6**.

—— Cave Temples of Western India. *See* Fergusson (James) *Architect.* The Cave Temples of India. 1880. 8°. 7708.t.41.

—— The Chronology of Modern India for four hundred years from the close of the fifteenth century, A.D. 1494–1894. pp. vi. 483. *John Grant: Edinburgh*, 1913. 8°. **09057**. d. **35**.

—— The Gandhâra Sculptures. [With plates.] 1900. *See* Periodical Publications.—*London.* The Journal of Indian Art. vol. 8. [1884, *etc.*] fol. P.P. **1803**. kf.

BURGESS (JAMES) *Director-General of the Archaeological Survey of India.*

—— The Geography of India, *etc.* pp. 68. *T. Nelson & Sons: London*, 1871. 8°. [*Royal School Series.*]
12202. cc. **3/36.**

—— Lists of the Antiquarian Remains in the Bombay Presidency, with an appendix of inscriptions from Gujarât. pp. ix. 340. *Bombay*, 1885. 4°. [*Archæological Survey of Western India. Miscellaneous Publications.* no. 11.]
1710. a. **6.**

—— [Another edition.] Revised Lists of Antiquarian Remains in the Bombay Presidency and the Native States of Barodâ, Pâlanpur, Radhanpur, Kâthiawâd, Kachh, Kolhâpur, and the Southern Marâthâ Minor States . . . Revised by Henry Cousens. [With plates, including maps.] pp. iii. 398. *Bombay*, 1897. 4°. [*Archæological Survey of Western India. Reports.* vol. 8.]
1710.b.1/12.

—— Revised Lists of Antiquarian Remains in the Bombay Presidency . . . Originally compiled by J. Burgess . . . Revised by Henry Cousens. [With maps.] pp. iii. 398. *Bombay*, 1897. 4°. [*Archaeological Survey of India. New Imperial Series of Reports.* vol. 16. *Archaeological Survey of Western India. New series.* vol. 8.]
1710. b. **1/12.**

—— Lists of Remains (in the Ahmadnagar, Nasik, Puna, Thana, and Kaládgi Zillas). *See* SINCLAIR (William F.) Notes on the Antiquities of the Talukas of Parner, Sangamner, *etc.* 1877. 4°. [*Archæological Survey of Western India. Miscellaneous Publications.* no. 6.]
1710. a. **6.**

—— Memorandum on the Antiquities at Dabhoi, Ahmedabad, Thân, Junâgaḍh, Girnâr, and Dhank. [With plates.] pp. 38. xvii. *Bombay*, 1875. 4°. [*Archæological Survey of Western India. Miscellaneous Publications.* no. 2.]
1710. a. **6.**

—— Memorandum on the Buddhist Caves at Junnar, by J. Burgess . . . and Translations of three Inscriptions from Badâmî, Pattadkal, and Aiholli, by J. F. Fleet. pp. 15. *Bombay*, 1874. 4°. [*Archæological Survey of Western India. Miscellaneous Publications.* no. 1.]
1710. a. **6.**

—— Memorandum on the Remains at Gumli, Gop, and in Kachh, &c. pp. 27. *Bombay*, 1875. 4°. [*Archæological Survey of Western India. Miscellaneous Publications.* no. 3.]
1710. a. **6.**

—— The Muhammadan Architecture of Aḥmadâbâd . . . With . . . plates. 2 pt. *W. Griggs & Sons: London*, 1900, 05. 4°. [*Archaeological Survey of India. New Imperial Series of Reports.* vol. 24, 33. *Archæological Survey of Western India. Reports.* vol. 7, 8.]
1710. b. **1/19.**

Pt. 2 contains a combined index to this work and to "On the Muhammadan Architecture of Bharoch, Cambay, etc." by the same author.

—— Notes of a Visit to Gujarât, in December 1869 . . . Reprinted from the "Times of India." pp. 120. *Times of India: Bombay*, 1870. 12°.
10057. a. **1.**

—— Notes on the Amarāvati Stūpa. pp. 57. pl. XVII. *Madras*, 1882. 4°. [*Archæological Survey of Southern India. Reports.* Old series. Vol. 3.]
1710. a. **3.**

—— Notes on the Bauddha Rock-Temples of Ajaṇṭâ, their Paintings and Sculptures, and on the paintings of the Bagh caves, modern Bauddha mythology, &c. pp. iv. 111. pl. XXX. *Bombay*, 1879. 4°. [*Archæological Survey of Western India. Miscellaneous Publications.* no. 9.]
1710. a. **6.**

BURGESS (JAMES) *Director-General of the Archaeological Survey of India.*

—— On the Definite Integral $\frac{2}{\sqrt{\pi}}\int_0^t \epsilon^{-t^2}\,dt$, with extended tables of values. [An offprint from the Transactions of the Royal Society of Edinburgh.] pp. 65. *R. Grant & Son: Edinburgh*, 1898. 4°. **8532.** ff. **39.** (**1.**)

—— On the Muhammadan Architecture of Bharoch, Cambay, Ḍholkâ, Châmpânir, and Mahmudâbâd in Gujarât. pp. ii. 47. pl. LXXVII. 1896. 4°. *W. Griggs & Sons: London*, 1896. 4°. [*Archaeological Survey of India. New Imperial Series of Reports.* vol. 23. *Archæological Survey of Western India. New series.* vol. 6.]
1710. b. **1/19.**

A combined index to this work and to "The Muhammadan Architecture of Aḥmadâbâd" by the same author, appears in pt. 2 of the latter work.

—— Provisional Lists of Architectural and other Archæological Remains in Western India, including the Bombay Presidency, Sindh, Berar, Central Provinces and Haiderabad. pp. 60. *Bombay*, 1875. 4°. [*Archæological Survey of Western India. Miscellaneous Publications.* no. 4.]
1710. a. **6.**

—— Report of the First Season's Operations [of the Archæological Survey of Western India] in the Belgâm and Kaladgi Districts, January to May 1874. pp. viii. 45. pl. LVI. *India Museum: London*, 1874. 4°. [*Archaeological Survey of India. New Imperial Series of Reports.* vol. 1. *Archaeological Survey of Western India. New series.* vol. 1.]
1710. b. **1/1.**

—— Report on the Antiquities in the Bidar and Aurungâbâd Districts, in the territories of . . . the Nizam of Haiderâbâd, being the result of the third season's operations of the Archæological Survey of Western India, *etc.* pp. viii. 138. pl. LXVI. *W. H. Allen & Co.: London*, 1878. 4°. [*Archaeological Survey of India. New Imperial Series of Reports.* vol. 3. *Archaeological Survey of Western India. New series.* vol. 3.]
1710. b. **1/3.**

—— Report on the Antiquities of Kâṭhiâwâd and Kachh, being the result of the second season's operations of the Archæological Survey of Western India, *etc.* [With a map.] pp. x. 242. pl. LXXIV. 29. *India Museum: London*, 1876. 4°. [*Archaeological Survey of India. New Imperial Series of Reports.* vol. 2. *Archaeological Survey of Western India. Reports.* vol. 2.] **1710.** b. **1/2.**

—— Report on the Buddhist Cave Temples and their Inscriptions. Being part of the results of the fourth, fifth, and sixth seasons' operations of the Archæological Survey of Western India . . . Supplementary to the volume on "The Cave Temples of India. pp. x. 140. pl. LX. *Trübner & Co.: London*, 1883. 4°. [*Archaeological Survey of India. New Imperial Series of Reports.* vol. 4. *Archaeological Survey of Western India. New series.* vol. 4.]
1710. b. **1/4.**

—— Report on the Elurâ Cave Temples and the Brahmanical and Jaina Caves in Western India. Completing the results of the fifth, sixth, and seventh seasons' operations of the Archæological Survey . . . Supplementary to the volume on "The Cave Temples of India." pp. vii. 89. pl. L. *Trübner & Co.: London*, 1883. 4°. [*Archaeological Survey of India. New Imperial Series of Reports.* vol. 5. *Archaeological Survey of Western India. New series.* vol. 5.]
1710. b. **1/5.**

—— The Rock-Temples of Elephanta or Ghârâpurî . . . With photographic illustrations by D. H. Sykes. pp. 40. *D. H. Sykes & Co.; Thacker, Vining & Co.: Bombay*, 1871. *obl.* fol. **1702.** a. **13.**

BURGESS (James) *Director-General of the Archaeological Survey of India.*

—— The Rock Temples of Elurâ or Verul . . . With 12 photographs. pp. iv. 77. *Education Society's Press: Bombay*, 1877. 8°. **7708. a. 25.**

—— Tamil and Sanskrit Inscriptions, with some notes on village antiquities collected chiefly in the south of the Madras Presidency . . . With translations by S. M. Naṭêśa Śâstrî, Paṇḍit. pp. vi. 237. *Madras*, 1886. 4°. [*Archæological Survey of Southern India. Reports.* Old Series. Vol. 4.] **1710. a. 4.**

BURGESS (James) *Director-General of the Archaeological Survey of India*, and **BHAGAVĀN-LĀLA INDRĀJĪ.**

—— Inscriptions from the Cave-Temples of Western India, with descriptive notes, &c. [With plates.] pp. v. 114. *Bombay*, 1881. 4°. [*Archæological Survey of Western India. Miscellaneous Publications.* no. 10.] **1710. a. 6.**

BURGESS (James) *Director-General of the Archaeological Survey of India*, and **COUSENS** (Henry)

—— The Antiquities of the Town of Dabhoi in Gujarât. [With plates.] pp. 13. pl. xxii. *G. Waterston & Sons: Edinburgh*, 1888. fol. **1706. b. 2.**

—— The Architectural Antiquities of Northern Gujarât, more especially of the districts included in the Baroda State. [With a map.] pp. x. 118. pl. cxi. *Bernard Quaritch: London*, 1903. 4°. [*Archaeological Survey of India. New Imperial Series of Reports.* vol. 32. *Archaeological Survey of Western India. Reports.* vol. 9.] **1710. b. 1/24.**

BURGESS (James) *Minister of Haugh-Fold Chapel, near Whitworth, Lancashire.* Beelzebub driving and drowning his Hogs. A sermon, *etc.* pp. 34. *J. Buckland; E. & C. Dilly: London*, 1770. 8°. **4473. c. 7. (1.)**

—— [Another copy.] **4478. aaa. 121. (1.)**

—— [Another edition.] pp. 29. *M. Richardson: Manchester*, [1820?] 8°. **4410. i. 29. (4.)**

BURGESS (James) *of Droylsden.* Pictures of Social Life; being select poems. pp. vii. 140. *John Heywood: Manchester*, [1869.] 8°. **11648. ccc. 22.**

BURGESS (James) *Railway Guard. See* Pierce (William) *Grocer.* A Full Report of the Great Gold Robbery, *etc.* (Trial of Pierce, Burgess, and Tester.) [1856.] 8°. **6497.b.14.**

BURGESS (James) *Vicar of Great Maplestead.* A Sermon, preached on . . . March 9, 1796, being the day appointed for a general fast. pp 24. *F. & C. Rivington; R. Faulder: London*, 1796. 8°. **4475. aa. 14.**

BURGESS, afterwards **LAMB** (*Sir* James Bland) *Bart. See* Burges, afterwards Lamb.

BURGESS (James John) Flora of Moray, Vice County no. 95. Flowering & flowerless plants, including conifers, ferns, mosses, fungi and algae. Edited by J. J. Burgess. pp. xv. 104. "*Courant and Courier*": *Elgin*, 1935. 8°. **7029. pp. 1.**

—— [Another copy.] **07030. ff. 60.**

BURGESS (James John Haldane) Lowra Biglan's Mutch. A Shetland novelette. pp. 58. *The Leonards: Kirkwall*, 1896. 8°. **012628. e. 71.**

BURGESS (James John Haldane)

—— Rasmie's Büddie. Poems in the Shetlandic. pp. viii. 118. *T. & J. Manson: Lerwick*, 1891. 8°. **011653. k. 59.**

—— [Another edition.] pp. 134. *Alexander Gardner: Paisley*, 1892. 8°. **011653. l. 64.**

—— [Another edition.] pp. 129. *T. & J. Manson: Lerwick*, 1913. 8°. **011649. de. 10.**

—— Rasmie's Smaa Murr. *J. J. H. Burgess: Lerwick*, 1916. 8°. **012305. f. 32.**

—— Shetland Sketches and Poems, *etc.* pp. 128. *H. Morrison: Lerwick*, [1886.] 8°. **12316. f. 46.**

—— Some Shetland Folk. First group. [Tales.] pp. 163. *Thomas Mathewson: Lerwick*, 1902. 8°. **012638. aa. 46.** *No more published.*

—— Tang. A Shetland story. pp. 239. *Johnson & Greig: Lerwick*, 1898. 8°. **012623. g. 30.**

—— The Treasure of Don Andres. A Shetland romance of the Spanish Armada. pp. viii. 318. *Thomas Mathewson: Lerwick*, 1903. 8°. **012638. dd. 33.**

—— Up-Helli-Aa Song, 1897. *Lerwick*, 1897. 16°. **1865. c. 8. (30.)**

—— Second edition. *Thomas Mathewson: Lerwick*, 1905. 16°. **1865. c. 8. (30.)**

—— Third edition. *Thomas Mathewson: Lerwick*, 1907. 16°. **1865. c. 8. (30.)**

—— The Viking Path. A tale of the White Christ. pp. vi. 375. *W. Blackwood & Sons: Edinburgh & London*, 1894. 8°. **012629. ee. 42.**

—— Young Rasmie's Kit. A book of verse. pp. 94. *T. & J. Manson: Lerwick*, 1928. 8°. **011644. f. 27.**

BURGESS (James Rose) The Fellowcrafts' Charge, Lodge Canongate Kilwinning. (Charge in the second Degree.) pp. 10. *Privately printed: Edinr.*, [1902.] 16°. **4783. a. 53.**

BURGESS (James W.) A Practical Treatise on Coach-Building . . . With fifty-seven illustrations. pp. v. 188. *C. Lockwood & Co.: London*, 1881. 12°. **7956. aa. 3.**

BURGESS (John) *Artist. See* Aspa (R.) John Burgess . . . of the Society of Painters in Water-colours. [With plates, including a portrait.] [1925.] 8°. [*Walker's Quarterly.* no. 16.] **P.P. 1906. da.**

BURGESS (John) *Farmer, of Marsh-Chapel. See* Floyer (John G.) Report of the Proceedings in a Suit instituted . . . by J. G. Floyer, Esq. against Mr. J. Burgess, for the recovery of certain small tithes arising in the parish of Marsh-Chapel, *etc.* 1834. 8°. **1246. c. 13. (3.)**

BURGESS (John) *Presbyterian Minister, of New South Wales.* The Protestant Faith contrasted with the Roman Catholic Faith. pp. viii. 344. *Angus & Robertson: Sydney*, 1928. 8°. **3942. ee. 22.**

BURGESS (John) *Rector of Sutton Coldfield. See* Burges.

BURGESS (John) *Wesleyan Minister.* A Word to Wesleyan Methodists on the Extension of the Work of God, by the immediate appropriation of the surplus income of the chapels and other Wesleyan Trust property, and by the gradual liquidation and ultimate extinction of their existing debts; as shown in a narrative of the successful application of the plan on the Melton Mowbray Circuit. pp. 16. *Simpkin, Marshall & Co.: London*, [1845.] 8°. **1355. e. 9.**

BURGESS (John Cart) An Easy Introduction to Perspective, for the use of young persons . . . Second edition. pp. vii. 38. pl. x. *Printed for the Author: London,* 1819. 8º. **1422.** f. **19.**

—— An Easy Introduction to Perspective for the Use of Young Persons. Fourth edition. To which are now added: Useful Hints on Drawing and Painting, formerly published in a separate form. [With plates.] pp. vi. 50. *J. Souter: London,* 1828. 8º. **7870.** aa. **64.**

—— Sixth edition, revised . . . with new plates. pp. 39. pl. 6. *Printed for the Author: London,* 1835. 8º. **1422.** h. **19.**

—— A Practical Essay on the Art of Flower Painting . . . Together with . . . accounts of the lives and works of eminent flower painters. pp. xix. 130. *Printed for the Author: London,* 1811. 8º. **786.** h. **29.**

—— Useful Hints on Drawing & Painting; intended to facilitate the improvement of young persons. pp. vii. 54. *The Author: London,* 1818. 8º. **7807.** aaa. **9.** (**1.**)

BURGESS (John Harold) The Limit. An autograph album for globe-trotters. *J. H. Burgess: London,* [1924.] *obl.* 8º. **10026.** a. **24.**

BURGESS (John Harold Michael) *See* Parsons (Thomas) *of Clapham.* The Chronicles of Clapham . . . together with . . . an introduction & sundry additions by J. H. M. Burgess. 1929. 8º. **10349.** r. **11.**

BURGESS (John Hugh) Church and Dissent. pp. 15. *J. & C. Mozley: London,* [1865?] 12º. **4106.** aa. **11.**

BURGESS (John Lane) *See* Periodical Publications.—*London.* The Homing Fancier's Annual. Edited by J. L. Burgess. 1882, *etc.* 8º. **P.P. 2298.**

—— The Belgian Homing Pigeon. pp. 52. ii. *Hamilton, Adams & Co.: London; Keyworth & Everard: Cirencester,* [1881.] 8º. **7295.** b. **2.**

—— (Second edition.) pp. 79. *Kent & Co.: London; C. H. Savory: Cirencester,* [1882.] 8º. **7294.** aaa. **4.**

—— [Another copy.] **7293.** b. **13.**

BURGESS (John Sanderlain) *See* Howell (Leander D.) and Burgess (J. S.) Farm Prices of Cotton as related to its Grade and Staple Length, *etc.* 1936. 8º. [*U.S. Department of Agriculture. Technical Bulletin.* no. 493.] **A.S. 800/2.**

BURGESS (John Sanderlain) and **WEAVER** (Otis T.)

—— Expenses, Income and Dividends of Oklahoma and Texas Cooperative Cotton Gins. pp. vi. 62. *Washington,* 1940. 8º. [*U.S. Farm Credit Administration. Cooperative Research and Service Division. Bulletin.* no. 41.] **A.S. 929/6.**

BURGESS (John Stewart) *See* Gamble (Sidney D.) Peking. A social survey . . . By S. D. Gamble, assisted by J. S. Burgess, *etc.* [1921.] 8º. **010056.** f. **35.**

—— The Guilds of Peking, *etc.* [A thesis.] pp. 271. *New York,* 1928. 8º. **8230.** c. **38.**

—— [Another issue.] *New York,* 1928. 8º. [*Columbia University Studies in History, Economics and Public Law.* no. 308.] **Ac. 2688/2.**
Without the leaf bearing the author's Vita.

BURGESS (John William)

—— *See* Brown (Bernard E.) American Conservatives: the political thought of Francis Lieber and J. W. Burgess. 1951. 8º. [*Studies in History, Economics and Public Law.* no. 565.] **Ac. 2688/2.**

BURGESS (John William)

—— America's Relations to the Great War. pp. 209. *A. C. McClurg & Co.: Chicago,* 1916. 8º. **08027.** df. **53.**

—— The American University. When shall it be? Where shall it be? What shall it be? An essay. pp. 22. *Ginn, Heath & Co.: Boston,* 1884. 8º. **8365.** aa. **10.**

—— The Civil War and the Constitution, 1859–1865. 2 vol. *C. Scribner's Sons: New York,* 1901. 8º. [*American History Series.*] **9616.** p. **2/5.**

—— The European War of 1914: its causes, purposes and probable results. pp. 209. *A. C. McClurg & Co.: Chicago,* 1915. 8º. **08027.** d. **26.**

—— Der europäische Krieg, *etc.* (Übertragen von Max Iklé.) pp. v. 170. *Leipzig,* 1915. 8º. **08028.** ee. **5.**

—— The German View. [A letter to "The Springfield Republican."] *See* Wilkinson (Henry S.) Great Britain and Germany. 1914. 8º. **08028.** de. **93/4.**

—— The Middle Period, 1817–1858, *etc.* pp. xvi. 544. *C. Scribner's Sons: New York,* 1897. 8º. [*American History Series.*] **9616.** p. **2/4.**

—— Political Science and Comparative Constitutional Law. 2 vol. 1890, 91. 8º. *See* New York.—~~*Columbia College,*~~ afterwards *Columbia University.—Faculty of Political Science.* **8009.** f. **12.**

—— The Foundations of Political Science. [A revised edition of the chapters in "Political Science and Comparative Constitutional Law" relating to the Nation and the State.] pp. viii. 158. *Columbia University Press: New York,* 1933. 8º. **8005.** gg. **8.**

—— Recent Changes in American Constitutional Theory. pp. xi. 115. *Columbia University Press: New York,* 1923. 8º. **08176.** a. **1.**

—— Reminiscences of an American Scholar. The beginnings of Columbia University, *etc.* [With a portrait.] pp. viii. 430. *Columbia University Press: New York,* 1934. 8º. **10881.** ppp. **11.**

—— [Another copy.] **010886.** ee. **16.**

—— The Sanctity of Law: wherein does it consist? pp. ix. 335. *Ginn & Co.: Boston,* [1927.] 8º. **6004.** e. **30.**

—— [Another edition.] pp. vii. 345. *Harper & Bros.: New York & London,* 1928. 8º. **06004.** ee. **9.**

BURGESS (Joseph) *Clerk to the Governors and Guardians of the Parish of St. Mary, Newington.* Saint Mary, Newington, Surrey. The Local Act of Parliament, relating to the management & relief of the poor; the Walworth Common Inclosure Amendment Act; the Orders of the Poor Law Board: an account of the South Metropolitan District School; together with a history of the several charity estates belonging to the parish. Compiled by J. Burgess. [With plates and maps.] pp. 324. *M. Burgess: London,* 1859. 8º. **10350.** aaa. **13.**

BURGESS (Joseph) *Socialist.* British Agriculture versus Foreign Tributes, *etc.* [Incorporating selected chapters from "Merrie England," by Robert Blatchford.] pp. xxviii. 210. *Francis Johnson: London,* 1925. 8º. **08285.** de. **69.**

—— Homeland or Empire? pp. xiv. 169. *Homeland League Press: Bradford,* 1915. 8º. **08248.** c. **22.**

BURGESS (JOSEPH) *Socialist.*

—— "In Memory of My Wife." A volume of amatory and elegiac verse. [With a portrait.] pp. 89. *Simpkin, Marshall & Co.: London,* 1875. 8°. **11650. a. 47.**

—— John Burns: the Rise and Progress of a Right Honourable . . . Third edition. [With plates, including portraits.] pp. xxi. 201. *Reformers' Bookstall: Glasgow.* 1911. 8°. **10826.** de. **40.**

—— John Burns: the rise and progress of a Right Honourable. [With plates, including portraits.] pp. xxi. 201. *Reformers' Bookstall: Glasgow,* 1911. 8°. **10862.** a. **61.**

—— A Potential Poet? His autobiography and verse. [With a portrait.] pp. xvi. 301. 8. *Burgess Publications: Ilford,* [1927.] 8°. **011644.** df. **144.**

—— [Another copy.] **11655.** aa. **92.**

—— Will Lloyd George Supplant Ramsay MacDonald? *etc.* pp. 246. *Joseph Burgess: Ilford,* [1926.] 8°. **08139.** aa. **49.**

BURGESS (JOSEPH) *Wesleyan Minister. See* BURGESS (William P.) Memoirs of the Rev. Joseph Burgess, *etc.* 1842. 12°. **1372.** c. **14.**

BURGESS (JOSEPH BELL)

—— Introduction to the History of Philosophy. pp. xi. 631. *McGraw-Hill Book Co.: New York, London,* 1939. 8°. **08486.** d. **4.**

BURGESS (JOSEPH TOM) [Articles on the antiquities of Warwickshire, reprinted from periodicals.] 7 pt. [1872–77.] 8°. **7709.** c. **5.**

—— Angling: a practical guide to bottom fishing, trolling, spinning and fly-fishing. With a chapter on sea fishing. [With plates.] pp. viii. 182. *F. Warne & Co.: London,* [1867.] 8°. **7906.** aa. **10.**

—— [Another edition.] Angling and how to angle . . . Revised and brought down to date by R. B. Marston. With a special article on pike-fishing by A. J. Jardine, *etc.* pp. x. 212. *F. Warne & Co.: London & New York,* 1895. 8°. **07905.** ee. **2.**

—— Dominoes and how to play them, *etc.* [By J. T. Burgess.] pp. 64. 1877. 8°. *See* DOMINOES. **7913.** bbb. **18.**

—— Early Earthworks in Warwickshire. [Reprinted from the "Transactions of the Archæological Section of the Birmingham and Midland Institute."] pp. 11. *Josiah Allen: Birmingham,* [1872.] 4°. **7708.** f. **25.**
One of an edition of twelve copies.

—— A Few Notes on the Fortifications of Warwick, with transcriptions of the documents relating thereto and an account of the existing remains. pp. 29. *J. Glover: Leamington,* 1875. 8°. **7708.** aa. **44.** (2.)

—— A Handbook to the Cathedral of Worcester . . . With a complete list of the bishops, priors and deans from the earliest times to the present day . . . Illustrated, *etc.* pp. vii. 88. *N. May & Co.: London,* [1884.] 16°. **10352.** a. **22.**
The title on the binding is "Norman May's Guide to Worcester Cathedral."

—— Harry Hope's Holidays: what he saw, what he did, and what he learnt during a year's rambles in country places. [With plates.] pp. viii. 301. *G. Routledge & Sons: London,* [1871.] 8°. **12806.** e. **22.**

BURGESS (JOSEPH TOM)

—— Historic Warwickshire: its legendary lore, traditionary stories, and romantic episodes . . . With numerous illustrations. pp. xiii. 407. *Simpkin, Marshall & Co.: London,* [1876.] 8°. **12431.** cc. **1.**

—— Second edition. Edited and revised by Joseph Hill. [With a memoir and portrait of the author.] pp. xx. 304. *Midland Educational Co.: Birmingham; Simpkin Marshall & Co.: London,* [1892, 93.] 4°. **2367.** bb. **12.**
Published in parts.

—— Knots, Ties and Splices, *etc.* pp. viii. 101. *G. Routledge and Sons: London, New York,* [1884.] 8°. **8807.** b. **40.**

—— [Another edition.] Revised and rewritten by Commander J. Irving. pp. v. 122. *G. Routledge & Sons: London,* 1934. 8°. **8808.** e. **4.**

—— The Last Battle of the Roses. A paper on the battle of Bosworth Field . . . To which is added Saville's chronicle & Drayton's description of the battle, with map and other illustrations. pp. 22. *Arthur & Cunnew: Leamington,* 1872. 4°. **9505.** d. **9.**
The illustrations were never published.

—— Life Scenes and Social Sketches: a book for English hearths and homes . . . Illustrated by several engravings on wood. pp. xii. 155. *W. Kent & Co.: London,* [1862.] 8°. **12621.** a. **13.**

—— Old English Wild Flowers to be found by the wayside, fields, hedgerows, rivers, moorlands, meadows, mountains, and sea-shore . . . With numerous illustrations. pp. x. 291. *F. Warne & Co.: London,* 1868. 8°. **7032.** aa. **16.**

BURGESS (JOSHUA) *M.D.* The Medical and Legal Relations of Madness; showing a cellular theory of mind, and of nerve force, and also of vegetative vital force. pp. xi. 283. *John Churchill: London,* 1858. 8°. **7660.** e. **11.**

BURGESS (KENNETH FARWELL) *See* VANDERBLUE (Homer B.) and BURGESS (K. F.) Railroads, *etc.* 1923. 8°. **08235.** cc. **55.**

BURGESS (L. A.) With Drums Unmuffled. pp. 325. *Mills & Boon: London,* 1913. 8°. NN. **1050.**

BURGESS (LESLIE)

—— The Beverleys. [A novel.] pp. 256. *Hutchinson & Co.: London,* [1940.] 8°. NN. **31136.**

—— Hallowe'en. pp. 223. *Hutchinson & Co.: London & Melbourne,* [1941.] 8°. NN. **32585.**

—— Short Let. pp. 285. *Hutchinson & Co.: London,* [1938.] 8°. [*First Novel Library.* no. 71.] **12627.** p. **1/71.**

BURGESS (LUCY M.) The Child's Guide to Spiritualism. pp. 16. *Colby & Rich: Boston,* 1874. 8°. **8631.** aa. **3.**

BURGESS (M. J.) and **WHEELER** (RICHARD VERNON)

—— Flameproof Electrical Apparatus. Experiments on pressure development and release in oil-filled mining gear. pp. 18. *London,* 1940. 4°. [*British Electrical and Allied Industries Research Association. Technical Report.* Reference G/T 63.] W.P. **9138/382.**

BURGESS (MALCOLM WILLIAM) Warships To-day. pp. 141. pl. 15. *Oxford University Press: London,* 1936. 8°. [*Pageant of Progress.*] W.P. **11721/6.**

BURGESS (Marion Ardern)
—— A History of Burlington School. [With plates.] pp. 75. [c. 1940.] 8°. **08368.** cc. **56.**

BURGESS (Marjorie Agnes Lovell) Great Possessions. pp. 288. *Henry Walker: London,* [1927.] 8°. NN. **13288.**

—— A Popular Account of the Development of the Amateur Ciné Movement in Great Britain, *etc.* [With plates, including a portrait.] pp. xvi. 212. *Sampson Low & Co.: London,* [1932.] 8°. **8902.** c. **40.**

—— Provincial Interlude. pp. 224. *Alston Rivers: London,* [1932.] 8°. NN. **19584.**

BURGESS (May Ayres) The Measurement of Silent Reading. [A thesis.] pp. 163. [1921.] 8°. *See* New York.—*Russell Sage Foundation.—Department of Education.* **08311.** de. **61.**

BURGESS (Megan) Looking for Love, *etc.* pp. 64. *William Stevens: London,* [1938.] 8°. [*True Love Series.*] **12633.p.1/161.**

BURGESS (Mildred Mabel) The Care of Infants and Young Children in Health. pp. viii. 72. *H. K. Lewis: London,* 1910. 8°. **7580.** ff. **41.**

—— Second edition. pp. viii. 82. *H. K. Lewis: London,* 1912. 8°. **07580.** df. **8.**

—— Third edition. pp. vii. 76. *H. K. Lewis & Co.: London,* 1924. 8°. **07580.** ee. **42.**

—— Health . . . With . . . illustrations by Eleanor M. Cartwright. pp. viii. 175. *H. K. Lewis: London,* 1914. 8°. **7404.** pp. **22.**

BURGESS (Murray) An Alphabetical and Classified Catalogue of the Tasmanian Public Library and Reading Room. (Compiled by M. Burgess.) With the rules, regulations, and bye-laws. pp. 89. 1855. 8°. *See* Hobart Town.—*Tasmanian Public Library.* **11901.** aaa. **32.** (**4.**)

—— Alphabetical Catalogue of the Tasmanian Public Library and Reading Room [by M. Burgess], with the rules, regulations, and bye laws. pp. 82. 1862. 8°. *See* Hobart Town.—*Tasmanian Public Library.* **11901.** aaa. **32.** (**6.**)

BURGESS (Nathan G.) The Ambrotype Manual: a practical treatise on the art of taking positive photographs on glass, commonly known as ambrotypes . . . To which is added the practice of the negative process and positive photographs on paper . . . Third edition. pp. 184. *J. M. Fairchild & Co.: New York,* 1857. 12°. **1399.** c. **13.**

—— [Another edition.] The Photograph Manual, *etc.* (Eleventh edition.) pp. 251. *D. Appleton & Co.: New York, London,* 1863. 12°. **1399.** b. **6.**

BURGESS (Neil) *See* Barnard (Charles) and Burgess (N.) The County Fair, *etc.* [1922.] 8°. **011781.** g. **1/24.**

BURGESS (Otis Asa) What must I do to be saved? [A sermon. With a portrait.] *See* Moore (William T.) The Living Pulpit of the Christian Church, *etc.* 1868. 8°. **4478.** l. **1.**

BURGESS (Otto F.) *See* Vail (Roger) The Vail-Burgess Debate. A religio-educational discussion between O. F. Burgess . . . and R. Vail, *etc.* [1890.] 8°. **8304.** e. **22.** (**9.**)

BURGESS (*Mrs.* Palmer G.) Talks on New Chums for Young Canadians. For leaders of junior organizations. pp. 30. *Canadian Council of the Missionary Education Movement: [Toronto,* 1922.] 4°. **20054.** dd. **5.**

BURGESS (Peggie)
—— Man Lost. A play in one act. pp. 31. *London,* [1939.] 8°. [*French's Acting Edition.*] **11791.** t. **1/619.**

BURGESS (Perry)
—— Born of those Years. An autobiography. [With plates, including portraits.] pp. xii. 307. *Henry Holt & Co.: New York,* [1951.] 8°. **10889.** aaa. **32.**

—— Born of those Years. An autobiography. [With plates including a portrait.] pp. xiii. 306. *J. M. Dent & Sons. London,* 1952. 8°. **10889.** bb. **19**

—— Who Walk Alone. [The story of a leper.] pp. viii. 308. *H. Holt & Co.: New York,* [1940.] 8°. **10888.** h. **1.**

—— Who Walk Alone . . . Illustrated, *etc.* pp. 318. *J. M. Dent & Sons: London,* 1941. 8°. **10888.** f. **22.**

BURGESS (R. Henry) *See* Wilkie (G. B.) Nationalisation of Insurance . . . Edited by R. H. Burgess. [1931.] 8°. **08227.** a. **59.**

BURGESS (Ricardus) Disputatio medica quædam de mulierum infœcunditate complectens, *etc.* pp. 28. *Neill & Socii: Edinburgi,* 1814. 8°. **1184.** b. **20.** (**1.**)

—— [Another copy.] **1184.** b. **20.** (**2.**)

BURGESS (Richard) *Prebendary of St. Paul's.*

—— *See* Baggs (Charles M.) *Bishop of Pella.* A Letter addressed to the Rev. R. Burgess, *etc.* [In reference to his work entitled "Greece and the Levant," and other of his writings.] 1836. 8°. **3940.** f. **49.**

—— A City for the Pope; or, the Solution of the Roman Question. [With a plan.] pp. 17. *James Ridgway: London,* 1860. 8°. **8033.** b. **71.** (**2.**)

—— The Confessional. Two sermons, *etc.* pp. 47. *Seeleys: London,* 1852. 12°. **4107.** a. **18.**

—— Constantinople and Greek Christianity, *etc.* *See* London.—iii. *Young Men's Christian Association.* Lectures delivered before the Young Men's Christian Association . . . from November 1854, to February 1855. 1855. 8°. **4461.** d. **18.**

—— Description of the Circus on the Via Appia, near Rome; with some account of the Circensian Games. [With folding plates.] pp. vii. 111. *John Murray: London,* 1828. 8°. **7702.** aa. **29.**

—— Descrizione del Circo sulla Via Appia presso Roma . . . Tradotta . . . da Giuseppe Porta. Illustrata di piante dall'architetto Sig. Giuseppe Pardini. pp. 42. *Roma,* 1829. 8°. **899.** d. **7.** (**9.**)

—— Education of the Middle Classes. An address delivered at the opening of the East Islington Commercial School, in union with the Metropolitan Institution, *etc.* pp. 16. *Compton & Ritchie: London,* 1841. 8°. **8305.** bb. **25.**

—— Educational Statistics. A letter, addressed to J. C. Colquhoun. pp. 25. *J. Hatchard & Son: London,* 1838. 8°. T. **2327.** (**3.**)

—— An Enquiry into the State of the Church of England Congregations in France, Belgium, and Switzerland, made under the authority . . . of . . . the Lord Bishop of London in August, September, and October, of 1849. pp. 34. *F. & J. Rivington: London*, 1850. 8°. **4705. b. 32.**

—— Greece and the Levant; or, Diary of a summer's excursion in 1834, with epistolary supplements. [With a map.] 2 vol. *Longman & Co.: London*, 1835. 8°. **790. d. 2.**

—— The History of French Protestantism: its present condition and prospects. *See* ENGLAND.—*Young Men's Christian Association.* Twelve Lectures delivered . . . from November 1849, to February 1850. 1850. 8°. **4461. d. 13.**

—— Lecture . . . on the Present State and Aspect of Popery on the Continent. pp. 21. *R. Folthorp; C. A. Johnson: Brighton*, [1852.] 12°. [*Brighton Protestant Tracts.* no. 14.] **3940. aaa. 36. (1.)**

—— Lectures on the Insufficiency of Unrevealed Religion, and on the succeeding influence of Christianity, *etc.* pp. xxxviii. 308. *J. F. & G. Rivington: London*, 1832. 8°. **1021. h. 15.**

—— A Letter to the Parishioners of Upper Chelsea. pp. 30. *Jacques: Chelsea*, [1837.] 8°. **4108. d. 115. (3.)**
"*Not published.*"

—— A Letter to the Rev. John Morison . . . occasioned by his animadversions upon a circular lately addressed to the parishioners of Upper Chelsea, on the subject of new churches. pp. 20. *Davis & Porter: Chelsea*, 1836. 8°. **4473. f. 17. (3.)**

—— A Letter to the Rev. W. F. Hook . . . on his Proposed Plan for the Education of the People. pp. 32. *J. Hatchard & Son: London*, 1846. 8°. **1387. f. 50.**

—— Second edition. pp. 32. *J. Hatchard & Son: London*, 1846. 8°. **8308. d. 17.**

—— Metropolis Schools for the Poor. A letter to . . . the Lord Bishop of London . . . and his Lordship's answer to the same. pp. 16. 1846. 8°. *See* LONDON, *Diocese of.*—*London Diocesan Board of Education.* **4476. e. 11.**

—— National Education. A sermon preached . . . on behalf of the Islington Parochial Schools. pp. 24. *Hatchard & Son: London*, 1839. 8°. **4476. bb. 99. (13.)**

—— National Education, by Rates or Taxes. A letter addressed to . . . Sir George Grey, Bart, *etc.* pp. 16. *Seeley, Jackson, & Halliday; B. Seeley: London*, 1855. 8°. **8308. e. 14.**

—— The National Education Question practically considered; in a letter to . . . Sir James Graham, Bart., *etc.* pp. 40. *J. Hatchard & Son: London*, 1842. 8°. **1387. d. 26. (1.)**

—— National Prosperity Proportioned to True Religion. A sermon, *etc.* pp. 27. *William Fick: Geneva*, 1832. 8°. **4475. e. 17.**

—— National Schools and National School Teachers. A letter to . . . the Archbishop of Canterbury. pp. 33. *J. Hatchard & Son: London*, 1848. 8°. **8305. e. 8.**

—— The Nature and Object of Education. A sermon, preached . . . on behalf of the National Society. pp. 16. *J. Hatchard & Son; Davis & Porter: London*, 1838. 8°. **4473. h. 16. (3.)**

—— Observations on an "Appeal to the Members of the Society for Promoting Christian Knowledge, on doctrinal changes lately introduced into the series of tracts circulated under their authority." In a letter to the Rev. Dr. Russell. [Defending "The Doctrine of Justification briefly stated," by J. B. Sumner, Bishop of Chester, against the imputation of unorthodoxy.] pp. 31. *Seeley, Burnside & Seeley: London*, 1844. 8°. **4418. i. 32.**

—— On the Egyptian Obelisks in Rome, and Monoliths as Ornaments of Great Cities, read at the . . . meeting of the Royal Institute of British Architects, May 31st, 1858 . . . Followed by remarks on the application of the entasis to the obelisk, by John Bell, *etc.* [Reprinted from the "Transactions of the Royal Institute of British Architects." With a folding plate.] pp. 42. [1862.] 8°. **7704. b. 35. (4.)**

—— One Disease, one Remedy, *etc.* *See* MACKENZIE (William B.) Twelve Sermons preached at the Special Services for the Working Classes, Exeter Hall, *etc.* 1858. 8°. **4462. b. 35.**

—— Sermons prêchés à Exeter Hall, pendant l'été de 1858. (Un mal, un remède. Sermon prêché . . . par le Rév. R. Burgess . . . Traduit . . . par R. Cassignard.—Difficilement sauvé. Sermon prêché . . . par le Rév. W. B. Mackenzie . . . Traduit . . . par S. Bérard.) pp. 55. *Toulouse*, 1859. 12°. **4476. aa. 109. (11.)**

—— The Only "Way." A sermon, *etc.* 1859. *See* WESTMINSTER ABBEY SERMONS. Westminster Abbey Sermons for the Working Classes. ser. 2. 1858, *etc.* 8°. **4477. a. 127. (2.)**

—— The Remembrance of the Righteous. A sermon preached . . . on the twenty-third of July, 1843, being the Sunday immediately following the death of the Rev. Henry Blunt, *etc.* pp. 27. *J. Hatchard & Son: London*, 1843. 8°. **4905. e. 11.**

—— Sermon. [Preached at the eighth annual meeting of the Society for Promoting the Due Observance of the Lord's Day.] 1839. *See* LONDON.—III. *Society for Promoting the Due Observance of the Lord's Day.* The Third [*etc.*] Annual Report, *etc.* Eighth report. 1834, *etc.* 8°. **P.P. 1025. cd.**

—— A Sermon delivered in the English Chapel at Rome, on the tenth of April 1836. pp. 20. *William Fick: Geneva*, 1836. 8°. **4475. e. 18.**

—— Sermons for the Times. pp. 171. *Seeleys: London*, 1851. 12°. **4461. e. 6.**

—— The Sixth Biennial Letter to the Parishioners of Upper Chelsea. pp. 16. *Jacques & Robinson: Chelsea*, 1848. 8°. **4109. h. 14. (7.)**

—— The Topography and Antiquities of Rome; including the recent discoveries made about the Forum and the Via Sacra. [With plates and maps.] 2 vol. *Longman & Co.: London*, 1831. 8°. **574. h. 11.**

—— What may this System of National Education be? An inquiry, recommended to the clergy of the Established Church. pp. 32. *J. Hatchard & Son: London*, 1838. 8°. **T. 2327. (5.)**

—— What must I do to be saved? A sermon, *etc.* pp. 16. *Seeley, Jackson & Halliday; B. Seeley: London*, 1857. 12°. **4478. a. 126. (3.)**

—— [Another edition.] *See* LONDON.—III. *Exeter Hall.* Exeter-Hall Sermons for the Working Classes, *etc.* 1857. 8°. **4463. d. 13.**

BURGESS (RICHARD) *Prebendary of St. Paul's*, and **MONEY** (CHARLES FORBES SEPTIMUS)

—— Psalms and Hymns for Public Worship. Selected and arranged by the Rev. R. Burgess . . . and the Rev. C. F. S. Money . . . Sixth edition. 1861. 12°. *See* BIBLE.—*Psalms.—Selections.* [*English.*] **3433.** aaaa. **46.**

BURGESS (ROBERT) *M.Sc., Ph.D.*

—— *See* GALLOWAY (Leslie D.) and BURGESS (R.) Applied Mycology and Bacteriology. [1937.] 8°. W.P. **994/4.**

—— *See* GALLOWAY (Leslie D.) and BURGESS (R.) Applied Mycology and Bacteriology. [1940.] 8°. W.P. **994/5.**

—— *See* GALLOWAY (Leslie D.) and BURGESS (R.) Applied Mycology and Bacteriology, originally compiled by L. D. Galloway . . . and R. Burgess, *etc.* (Third edition.) 1950. 8°. W.P. **994/6.**

BURGESS (ROBERT) *Petty Officer Writer*, and **BLACKBURN** (ROLAND)

—— We Joined the Navy. Traditions, customs and nomenclature of the Royal Navy pp. vi. 124. *A. & C. Black: London*, 1943. 8°. **8809.** a. **23.**

BURGESS (ROBERT WILBUR) Introduction to the Mathematics of Statistics, *etc.* pp. viii. 304. *Houghton Mifflin Co.: Boston*, [1927.] 8°. **8507.** ccc. **20.**

—— [Another copy, with a different titlepage.] *G. G. Harrap & Co.: London; Cambridge, Mass.* printed, [1929.] 8°. **08531.** ee. **58.**

BURGESS (ROBERT WILLIAM)

—— Velocette Motor Cycles. A practical guide covering models from 1933 . . . With 67 illustrations. pp. 198. *C. Arthur Pearson: London*, 1952. 8°. [*Motor Cycle Maintenance and Repair Series.*] W.P. **13293/26.**

—— Velocette Motor Cycles. A practical guide covering models from 1933, *etc.* (Second edition.) [With illustrations.] pp. 200. *C. Arthur Pearson: London*, 1953. 8°. [*Motor Cycle Maintenance and Repair Series.*] W.P. **13293/38.**

BURGESS (RON)

—— Football—my Life, *etc.* [With plates, including portraits.] pp. 179. *Souvenir Press: London*, [1952.] 8°. **7920.** aaa. **80.**

BURGESS (RONALD E.)

—— *See* THOMAS (Horace A.) and BURGESS (R. E.) Survey of Existing Information and Data on Radio Noise over the Frequency Range 1–30 Mc/s. 1947. 8°. [*Department of Scientific and Industrial Research. Radio Research Special Report.* no. 18.] B.S. **38.** k/4.

—— Valve and Circuit Noise. A survey of existing knowledge and outstanding problems. [Prepared by R. E. Burgess and others.] pp. iv. 18. *London*, 1951. 8°. [*Department of Scientific and Industrial Research. Radio Research Special Report.* no. 20.] B.S. **38.** k/4.

BURGESS (SAMUEL WALTER) Historical Illustrations of the Origin and Progress of the Passions, and their influence on the conduct of mankind; with some subordinate sketches of human nature and human life. [By S. W. Burgess.] 2 vol. 1825. 8°. *See* ILLUSTRATIONS. **528.** k. **21.**

—— [Another edition.] 2 vol. *Longman & Co.: London*, 1828. 8°. **722.** h. **9.**

BURGESS (THOMAS) successively *Bishop of Saint David's* and *of Salisbury*. *See* also BRITANNICUS, *pseud.* [i.e. T. Burgess.]

—— *See* also PHILOPATRIS, *pseud.* [i.e. T. Burgess.]

—— *See* ARISTOTLE. [*Poetica.—Greek and Latin.*] Aristotelis De poetica liber . . . Illustravit T. Tyrwhitt. [Edited by T. Burgess.] 1794. 8°. **714.** d. **12.**

—— *See* ARISTOTLE. [*Doubtful or Supposititious Works.—Peplus.—Greek.*] *Ἀριστοτέλους Πεπλος, etc.* [Edited by T. Burgess.] 1798. 12°. **672.** a. **15.**

—— *See* BELSHAM (Thomas) A Letter to the Unitarian Christians in South Wales, occasioned by the animadversions of . . . the Lord Bishop of St. David's. To which are annexed 1. Letters . . . in reply to his Lordship's letters to the Unitarians. 2. A brief review of his Lordship's treatise, entitled "The Bible, and nothing but the Bible, the Religion of the Church of England." 3. An estimate of his Lordship's character and qualifications as a theological polemic. 1816. 8°. **4225.** c. **11.**

—— *See* BIBLE.—*Philippians.* [*Polyglott.*] Initia Paulina, sive introductio ad lectionem Pauli Epistolarum, *etc.* [Edited by T. Burgess.] 1804. 12°. **691.** a. **11.**

—— *See* BURTON (John) *D.D. Πενταλογια* . . . cui observationes, indicemque Græcum . . . adjecit T. Burgess. 1779. 8°. **165.** i. **9, 10.**

—— *See* CRITO, *Cantabrigiensis, pseud.* A Vindication of the Literary Character of Professor Porson, from the Animadversions of . . . Thomas Burgess . . . in various publications on 1 John v. 7. 1827. 8°. **1115.** i. 5.

—— *See* DAWES (Richard) *M.A., Master of the Grammar School, Newcastle-on-Tyne.* Ricardi Dawes Miscellanea critica . . . Curavit et appendicem adnotationis addidit T. Burgess. 1781. 8°. **672.** f. **21.**

—— —— 1800. 8°. **1088.** m. **26.**

—— *See* EPICTETUS. The Christianity of Stoicism: or, Selections from Arrian's Discourses of Epictetus: by the Bishop of St. David's. 1818. 8°. **722.** d. **50.**

—— —— 1822. 8°. **722.** c. **61.**

—— *See* EPICTETUS. Connexion between Sacred and Profane Literature, *etc.* (Epicteti Dissertationum . . . lib. II. cap. xvi.) [Edited with an introduction by T. Burgess.] 1835. 12°. **T. 1899. (18.)**

—— *See* ESTLIN (John P.) A Unitarian Christian's Statement and Defence of his Principles, with reference particularly to the charges of . . . the Lord Bishop of St. David's, *etc.* 1815. 8°. **701.** i. **16.** (3.)

—— *See* GIFFORD (James) *Rear Admiral.* The Remonstrance of a Unitarian, addressed to the Bishop of St. David's. 1818. 8°. **701.** i. **17.** (6.)

—— —— 1820. 8°. **4225.** bb. **28.**

—— *See* GRAVINA (G. V.) Jani Vincentii Gravinæ opuscula ad historiam litterariam, et studiorum rationem pertinentia, *etc.* [Edited by J. Burgess.] 1792. 8°. **832.** b. **4.**

—— *See* HARFORD (John S.) The Life of Thomas Burgess, *etc.* [With portraits and a bibliography.] 1840. 8°. **1126.** i. **37.**

—— *See* HOMER. [*Iliad.—Greek.*] *Προπαρασκευης Ὁμηρικης.* Pars altera. [A specimen of "Initia Homerica," containing bk. 3 of the Iliad, edited, with a paraphrase in Greek prose, by T. Burgess.] [1787.] 8°. **1103.** c. **4.** (4.)

BURGESS (THOMAS) successively *Bishop of Saint David's* and *of Salisbury*.

—— *See* HOMER. [*Iliad.—Greek.*] Initia Homerica, sive excerpta ex Iliade Homeri cum locorum omnium græca metaphrasi . . . Edidit T. Burgess. 1788. 8°. **995.** i. **2.**

—— *See* LEAR (Francis) *Dean of Salisbury.* Peace the Perfect and Assured Portion of the Believer: a sermon, delivered . . . March 5, 1837, being the Sunday following the interment of the Right Reverend Thomas Burgess, *etc.* 1837. 8°. **4903.** eee. **9. (7.)**

—— *See* MILTON (John) [*Prose Works.—Of True Religion, Heresy, etc.*] Protestant Union. A Treatise of True Religion, Heresy . . . To which is prefixed, a preface on Milton's religious principles, and unimpeachable sincerity. By T. Burgess. 1826. 8°. **845.** f. **23. (3.)**

—— *See* NELSON (Robert) *Esq.* A Review and Analysis of Bishop Bull's Exposition of the Doctrine of Justification, by R. Nelson . . . Extracted from his Life of Bishop Bull, *etc.* [Edited by T. Burgess.] 1827. 8°. **1117.** c. **9.**

—— *See* PALAEOROMAICA. A Supplement to Palæoromaica, with remarks on the strictures made on that work by the Bishop of St. David's [in "The Greek Original of the New Testament asserted, in answer to . . . Palæoromaica"], *etc.* 1824. 8°. **1017.** h. **5. (2.)**

—— *See* PERERIUS (B.) *Valentinus.* De Pauli Apostoli itinere in Hispaniam disputationes duæ. [Edited by T. Burgess.] 1819. 8°. **4805.** d. **22.**

—— *See* SHARP (Granville) *Philanthropist.* Remarks on the Uses of the Definitive Article in the Greek Text of the New Testament . . . To which is added a plain matter-of-fact argument for the divinity of Christ, by the editor. [Edited by T. Burgess.] 1798. 8°. **623.** e. **11.**

—— —— 1802. 12°. **623.** d. **1.**

—— —— 1803. 12°. **623.** d. **2.**

—— *See* SMITH (Elizabeth) *of Burnhall.* A Vocabulary, Hebrew, Arabic, and Persian, *etc.* [Edited by T. Burgess.] 1814. 8°. **12903.** b. **2.**

—— *See* TIPTAFT (William) A Letter to the Bishop of Salisbury . . . To which are added, three letters from the Bishop to Mr. Tiptaft, threatening him with legal proceedings for preaching in unconsecrated places, *etc.* 1834. 12°. **4108.** de. **28. (6.)**

—— *See* TRINITARIAN. An Examination of a Remonstrance addressed to the Bishop of St. David's . . . by Captain James Gifford. 1822. 8°. **1114.** k. **4.**

—— *See* TYRWHITT (Thomas) *F.R.S.* Thomae Tyrwhitti Conjecturae in Æschylum, Euripidem et Aristophanem, *etc.* [Edited by T. Burgess.] 1822. 8°. **631.** k. **23.**

—— Elementary Evidences of the Truth of Christianity; in a series of Easter catechisms, *etc.* pp. vi. 264. *F. C. & J. Rivington: London,* 1806. 12°. **852.** a. **2.**

—— Christ, and not Saint Peter, the Rock of the Christian Church; and Saint Paul, the Founder of the Church in Britain: a letter to the clergy of the Diocess of St. David's. —A Second Letter . . . on the Independence of the Ancient British Church on any Foreign Jurisdiction. *See* LONDON. —III. *Society for the Distribution of Tracts, etc.* The Churchman Armed against the Errors of the Time. vol. 2. 1814. 8°. **495.** f. **15.**

—— Tracts on the Origin and Independence of the Ancient British Church; on the supremacy of the Pope . . . and on the differences between the Churches of England and of Rome . . . Second edition, with additions. To which is prefixed a map, *etc.* pp. viii. 326. *F. C. & J. Rivington: London,* 1815. 8°. **3940.** h. **8. (2.)**

BURGESS (THOMAS) successively *Bishop of Saint David's* and *of Salisbury*.

—— [Another copy.] **210.** b. **6.**
Imperfect; wanting the map.

—— Tracts on the Divinity of Christ, and on the Repeal of the Statute against Blasphemy: containing I. The Bible, and nothing but the Bible. II. Evidence of the Divinity of Christ. III. A Brief Memorial. IV. Three Addresses to Unitarians, &c. To which is prefixed a preface containing strictures on the recent publications of Mr. Belsham and Dr. Carpenter; with an analysis of 1 John, v. 20, and a summary of the whole Epistle, as evidences of Christ's divinity. *J. Hatchard & Son: London,* 1820. 8°. **1120.** e. **7.**

—— Three Catechisms on the Principles of our Profession as Christians, as Members of the Church of England, and as Protestants; containing Easter Catechisms . . . The Church of England-Man's Catechism . . . The Protestant's Catechism . . . Fourth edition. To which is added a speech, on the principles of Popery, *etc.* pp. ix. 280. *J. Hatchard & Son: London,* 1823. 8°. **3938.** aaa. **7.**

—— An Introduction to the Controversy on the Disputed Verse of St. John, as revived by Mr. Gibbon: to which is added, Christian Theocracy; or, a second letter to Mrs. Joanna Baillie, on the doctrine of the Trinity. 2 pt. *W. B. Brodie & Co.: Salisbury,* 1835. 8°. **T. 2027. (8.)**

—— [Copper-plate copies of Hebrew letters and words, made by T. Burgess.] [1807.] *obl.* 12°. **829.** a. **35.**

—— [Another copy.] **T. 990. (6*.)**

—— Adnotationes Millii, auctæ et correctæ ex prolegominis suis, Wetstenii, Bengelii, et Sabaterii, ad I. Joann. v. 7. una cum duabus epistolis Richardi Bentleii et observationibus Joannis Seldeni, Christophori Matthiæ Pfaffii, Joannis Francisci Buddei, et Christiani Friderici Schmidii de eodem loco. Collectæ et editæ a T. Burgess. pp. vi. 295. *Typis Joannis Evans: Mariduni,* 1822. 8°. **690.** f. **12.**

"*Not published.*"

—— The Arabick Alphabet; or, an Easy introduction to the reading of Arabick. For the use of Hebrew students. pp. v. 20. *S. Hodgson: Newcastle,* 1809. 8°. **T. 990. (5.)**

—— Bagley; a descriptive poem. With the annotations of Scribberus Secundus: to which are prefixed, by the same, Prolegomena on the poetry of the present age. [By T. Burgess? or A. C. Schomberg?] pp. 72. 1777. 4°. *See* BAGLEY. **162.** m. **33.**

—— The Bible, and nothing but the Bible, the Religion of the Church of England: being an answer to the Letter of an Unitarian Lay Seceder [i.e. "A Letter to the Bishop of St. David's" by G. W. Meadley]: with notes and illustrations containing Schleusner's interpretation of passages of the New Testament relative to the established doctrines of Christianity: to which are added, a postscript on the anti-Socinianism of Newton and Locke: and a letter dedicatory to the Bishop of Gloucester on the Divinity and Atonement of Christ. pp. xxviii. 152. 27. *Jonathan Harris: Carmarthen,* 1815. 8°. **1114.** g. **13. (1.)**

—— A Second Letter to the Bishop of St. David's. By a Lay Seceder [i.e. G. W. Meadley]. [An answer to "The Bible, and nothing but the Bible, the Religion of the Church of England."] pp. 36. *R. Hunter: London,* 1816. 8°. **701.** i. **16. (9.)**

BURGESS (Thomas) successively *Bishop of Saint David's* and *of Salisbury*.

—— Bishops and Benefactors of St. Davids Vindicated from the Misrepresentations of a recent Publication [i.e. " An Historical Tour through Pembrokeshire " by Richard Fenton], in a charge delivered to the Chapter of St. Davids, at his primary visitation of the Cathedral Church . . . by the Right Rev. T. Burgess, *etc.* pp. xviii. 63. *J. Evans: Carmarthen,* 1812. 4°. **694**. h. **10**. (**9**.)

—— [Another copy.] **114**. b. **5**.

—— A Brief Memorial on the Repeal of so much of the Statute 9. and 10. William III. as relates to persons denying the doctrine of the Holy Trinity . . . To which is prefixed, a demonstration of the three great truths of Christianity, together with specimens of Unitarian rejection of Scripture and of all antiquity. [With special reference to the writings of Thomas Belsham.] pp. 86. *F. C. & J. Rivington; J. Hatchard: London,* 1814. 8°. **4225**. b. **12**.

—— A Charge delivered to the Clergy of the Diocese of Salisbury, at the primary visitation of the diocese in August 1826. (Justification by Faith only . . . In illustration and defence of Bishop Bull's Harmonia Apostolica. [An answer to " On Justification " by John Henry Browne.]) pp. xxxviii. 144. 20. *Brodie & Dowding: Salisbury,* [1828.] 8°. **4445**. cc. **9**.

—— [Another edition.] pp. xxxviii. 164. *C. & J. Rivington: London,* 1828. 8°. **1119**. e. **20**. (**3**.)

—— A Charge, delivered to the Clergy of the Diocese of Salisbury, in July and August, 1832. pp. 52. *W. B. Brodie & Co.: Salisbury,* 1832. 8°. T. **1440**. (**2**.)

—— Charity, the Bond of Peace and of all Virtues. A sermon preached before the Society of the Sons of the Clergy in the Diocese of Durham, *etc.* pp. 43. *L. Pennington: Durham,* 1803. 8°. **4475**. b. **28**.

—— Christ, and not Saint Peter, the Rock of the Christian Church; and St. Paul, the Founder of the Church in Britain: a letter to the clergy of the diocese of St. David's. pp. viii. 69. *J. Evans: Carmarthen,* 1812. 8°. **3939**. d. **13**.

—— Examination of certain Opinions, advanced by . . . Dr. Burgess . . . in two recent publications, entitled, Christ, and not Peter, the Rock, and Johannis Sulgeni Versus hexametri in laudem Sulgeni patris. [By John Lingard.] pp. 51. *O. Syers: Manchester,* 1813. 8°. **3940**. h. **6**. (**2**.)

—— Christian Theocracy: or, the Doctrine of the Trinity, and the ministration of the Holy Spirit, the leading and pervading doctrine of the New Testament . . . In a second Letter to Mrs. Joanna Baillie. pp. xii. 56. *W. B. Brodie & Co.: Salisbury,* 1834. 8°. T. **1484**. (**8**.)

—— [Another copy.] **4374**. d. **15**. (**11**.)

—— Considerations on the Abolition of Slavery and the Slave Trade, upon grounds of natural, religious, and political duty. pp. 166. *D. Prince & J. Cooke: Oxford,* 1789. 8°. **1118**. h. **5**. (**3**.)

—— [Another copy.] T. **700**. (**10**.)

—— [Another copy.] **682**. c. **21**. (**4**.)

—— Conspectus criticarum observationum (in scriptores græcos et latinos, ac locos antiquæ eruditionis edendarum una cum enarrationibus collationibusque veterum codicum MSSorum, et sylloge anecdotorum græcorum). pp. 15. [1788.] 8°. **687**. g. **34**. (**7**.)

—— [Another copy.] **1103**. c. **14**. (**6**.)

BURGESS (Thomas) successively *Bishop of Saint David's* and *of Salisbury*.

—— A Creed of Christian Evidences: with an introduction containing . . . proofs of the existence of the soul . . . and a conclusion on the Gospel way of salvation. pp. 14. *L. Pennington: Durham,* 1806. 12°. **4376**. de. **23**. (**2**.)

—— The Divinity of Christ proved from his own Declarations attested and interpreted by his living Witnesses, the Jews. A sermon, *etc.* pp. 47. *Clarendon Press: Oxford,* 1790. 4°. **682**. e. **24**. (**16**.)

—— [Another copy.] **694**. i. **2**. (**12**.)

—— [Another edition.] pp. 73. *F. & C. Rivington: London,* 1792. 8°. **4473**. f. **10**. (**6**.)

—— An Easter Catechism. 3 pt. *L. Pennington: Durham,* [1798,] 1802. 8°. **3504**. de. **48**. (**2**.)
Pt. 2 is of the second edition.

—— Ecclesiæ Christianæ primordia; sive episcoporum hierosolymitanorum series ac tempora, *etc.* [Compiled by T. Burgess.] pp. 16. *G. Walker: Dunelmiæ,* 1814. 8°. **4374**. d. **3**. (**5**.)

—— English Reformation and Papal Schism; or, the Grand schism of the sixteenth century, in this country, shewn to have been the separation of the Roman Catholics from the Church of England and Ireland, in a letter to . . . Lord Kenyon, on Mr. Wix's plan of union between the Churches of England and of Rome. To which is added, a postscript, in answer to Dr. Milner's Postcript. pp. xxvii. 63. *Rivingtons; Hatchard: London,* 1819. 8°. **701**. e. **26**. (**2**.)

—— *See* Wix (Samuel) A Letter to the Bishop of St. David's, occasioned by his Lordship's misconceptions and misrepresentations of a pamphlet, entitled: " Reflections concerning the Expediency of a Council of the Church of England and The Church of Rome being holden, &c." [An answer to " English Reformation and Papal Schism."] 1819. 8°. **701**. e. **26**. (**3**.)

—— An Essay on the Study of Antiquities. *See* infra: On the Study of Antiquities.

—— Evidence of the Divinity of Christ from the Literal Testimony of Scripture. *See* infra: Peculiar Privileges of the Christian Ministry.

—— First Principles of Christian Knowledge: consisting of I. An explanation of the more difficult terms and doctrines of the Church Catechism and Office of Confirmation; II. The Apostles' and Nicene Creeds exemplified and proved from the Scriptures. To which is prefixed an introduction on the duty of conforming to the Established Church, *etc.* pp. xvi. 116. *L. Pennington: Durham,* 1804. 12°. **3559**. aa. **28**.

—— The second edition. pp. xvi. 124. *F. C. & J. Rivington; J. Hatchard: London,* 1804. 12°. **3505**. c. **47**.

—— A Short Catechism on the Duty of Conforming to the Established Church, as good subjects and good Christians: being an abstract of a larger catechism on the same subject. The third edition. [From " First Principles of Christian Knowledge."] *See* England.—*Church of England.—Society for Promoting Christian Knowledge.* Religious Tracts, *etc.* vol. 3. 1807. 12°. **863**. l. **3**.

—— The fourth edition. pp. 23. *F. C. & J. Rivington: London,* 1808. 12°. **4139**. b. **20**.

—— The sixth edition. pp. 23. *F. C. & J. Rivington: London,* 1814. 8°. **3558**. b. **8**.

BURGESS (Thomas) successively *Bishop of Saint David's* and *of Salisbury.*

—— Ninth edition. pp. 16. *F. & J. Rivington: London,* 1850. 16°. **1353**. a. **37**. (**5**.)

—— Remarks on Religious Liberty, and the Duty of Nonconformity to Human Prescriptions in Religion; with an appendix, illustrating the beneficial influence of Dissent on the national interest: occasioned by the Bishop of Salisbury's "Catechism on the Duty of Conforming to the Established Church." pp. viii. 63. *B. J. Holdsworth: London,* 1828. 8°. **4135**. e. **7**. (**6**.)

—— The First Seven Epochs of the Ancient British Church: a sermon preached . . . on the second of July, 1812, at the anniversary meeting of the Society for promoting Christian Knowledge and Church Union, in the Diocese of St. David's. (The Lord Chancellor's Decretal Order, for the regulation of Mrs. Bevan's Charity Schools. [11 July 1807.]) pp. 43. *F. C. & J. Rivington: London,* 1813. 8°. **4707**. b. **8**.

—— [Another edition.] pp. 48. *F. C. & J. Rivington: London,* 1813. 4°. **4715**. e. **6**.

—— A Hebrew Primer. *See* infra: The Hebrew Reader.

—— The Hebrew Reader: or, a Practical introduction to the reading of the Hebrew Scriptures. 2 pt. *F. & C. Rivington: London,* 1808. 8°. **4374**. d. **4**. (**1**.)

—— [Another copy of pt. 1.] **621**. g. **14**. (**2**.)

—— [Another copy of pt. 2.] T. **990**. (**2**.)

—— [Another edition, without the sections of pt. 1 published separately as "A Hebrew Primer" and "Syllabarium Hebraicum." The preface signed: T. St. D., i.e. T. Burgess, Bishop of Saint David's.] pp. lii–lvi. 57–187. 1822, 23. 12°. *See* D. (T. St.) **825**. a. **16**.

—— A Hebrew Primer. To which are prefixed, the opinions of Melanchthon, Luther, and others, on the utility, necessity, and easiness of the study of the Hebrew language. [By T. Burgess. Extracted from "The Hebrew Reader," pt. 1.] pp. xii. 16. 1808. 12°. *See* Hebrew Primer. T. **990**. (**4**.)

—— The Hebrew Reader. Part I. Containing the Decalogue, and the first chapter of Genesis, in Hebrew and English, with the reading of the Hebrew in Roman letters. To which are prefixed, Testimonia de officio instituendi pueros in Hebraicis litteris. [Extracted from "The Hebrew Reader," pt. 1.] pp. viii. 29. *W. H. Lunn: London,* 1808. 12°. **621**. g. **14**. (**1**.)

—— Syllabarium Hebraicum: or, a Second step to the reading of Hebrew without points. [By T. Burgess. Extracted from "The Hebrew Reader," pt. 1.] pp. 28. 1808. 12°. *See* Hebrew Syllabary. T. **990**. (**3**.)

—— A Letter from the Bishop of Salisbury to the Duke of Wellington. Letter from the Rev. G. S. Faber, on the Coronation Oath. Observations of an eminent barrister, on the Danger of Popish Ministers. pp. 12. *R. Clay: London,* [1829.] 12°. **3938**. aaa. **2**. (**12**.)

—— [Another copy.] **3939**. aaa. **2**. (**19**.)

—— The Bishop of Salisbury's Letters to the Duke of Wellington, on the Catholic Question. [Another edition of the first letter from the preceding work, with the addition of a second letter.] pp. 7. *L. B. Seeley & Sons: London,* 1829. 8°. **3938**. e. **20**.

—— A Letter to the Bishop of Norwich, from the Bishop of Salisbury. [In reply to a letter by Henry Bathurst, Bishop of Norwich, published in the "St. James's Chronicle," concerning Catholic emancipation.] pp. 40. *W. B. Brodie & Co.: Salisbury,* 1830. 8°. T. **1290**. (**3**.)

—— [Another copy.] T. **2006**. (**14**.)
Imperfect; wanting the titlepage and all after p. 24.

—— The second edition. To which are added, two letters to . . . the Duke of Wellington; and a speech delivered . . . against the second reading of the Roman Catholic Relief Bill. pp. 75. *W. B. Brodie & Co.: Salisbury,* 1830. 8°. **3938**. e. **21**.

—— [Another issue of the appendix.] Appendix to the Second Edition of A Letter to the Bishop of Norwich from the Bishop of Salisbury. pp. 44–75. *W. B. Brodie & Co.: Salisbury,* [1830.] 8°. T. **1290**. (**4**.)

—— A Letter to the Clergy of the Diocese of St. David's, on a Passage of the Second Symbolum Antiochenum of the fourth century, as an Evidence of the Authenticity of 1 John v. 7. pp. 40. *F. & C. Rivington; J. Hatchard & Son: London,* 1825. 8°. **3266**. d. **20**.

—— [Another edition.] [With the addition of an advertisement, a postscript, and an appendix containing the text of the Symbolum Antiochenum in Greek, Latin, French and English, and of the Symbolum Sirmii in Greek. With a facsimile.] pp. x. 123. *F. & C. Rivington; J. Hatchard & Son: London,* 1825. 8°. **4224**. g. **2**.

—— A Letter to the Honourable and Right Reverend the Lord Bishop of Durham, on the Origin of the Pelasgi, and on the original Name and Pronunciation of the Æolic Digamma: in answer to Professor Marsh's Horæ Pelasgicæ. pp. 42. *J. Evans: Carmarthen,* 1815. 8°. **626**. g. **16**. (**4**.)

—— [Another copy.] **67**. b. **7**.

—— [Another copy.] T. **712**. (**8**.)
With this copy are bound up four unnumbered leaves, apparently containing part of a projected but unpublished "Continuation."

—— A Letter to the Reverend Thomas Beynon, Archdeacon of Cardigan, in reply to A Vindication of the Literary Character of Professor Porson, by Crito Cantabrigiensis: and in further proof of the authenticity of 1 John, v. 7. pp. lxxiv. 67. *Brodie & Dowding: Salisbury,* 1829. 8°. **1117**. f. **15**.

—— A Letter to the Right Honourable Lord Viscount Melbourne, on the Idolatry and Apostasy of the Church of Rome, *etc.* pp. 20. *J. Hearn: Salisbury; Rivingtons: London,* 1835. 8°. T. **1914**. (**5**.)

—— The Bishop of Salisbury's Letters to the Duke of Wellington, on the Catholic Question. *See* supra: A Letter from the Bishop of Salisbury to the Duke of Wellington.

—— Moral Annals of the Poor, and Middle Ranks of Society, in various situations, of good and bad conduct. [By T. Burgess.] 2 pt. 1793, 95. 8°. *See* Annals. **8404**. de. **30**.

—— [Another edition of pt. 1.] pp. iv. 44. 1795. 8°. *See* Annals. **8404**. dd. **18**.

—— Motives to the Study of Hebrew. [By T. Burgess.] pp. 46. 1809. 12°. *See* Hebrew Language. **12903**. a. **20**.

—— [Another copy.] T. **909**. (**6**.)

BURGESS (Thomas) successively *Bishop of Saint David's* and *of Salisbury.*

—— Second edition. pp. 149. *W. H. Lunn: London,* 1814. 12°. **63.** l. **4.**

—— Musei Oxoniensis litterarii conspectus et specimina. [Edited by T. Burgess.] 2 fasc. *J. Fletcher: Oxonii,* 1792, 97. 8°. **684.** e. **19.** (**1, 2.**)

—— [Another copy.] T. **953.** (**8.**) *Imperfect; wanting all after p. 48 of fasc. 2.*

—— Observationes in Sophoclis Œdipum Tyrannum, Œdipum Coloneum, Antigonam: Euripidis Phœnissas, Æschyli Septem contra Thebas. pp. 142. *E Typographeo Clarendoniano: Oxonii,* 1778. 8°. **995.** g. **21.** (**2.**)

—— Observations on Mr. Sharp's Biblical Criticisms. *See* Hoare (Prince) Memoirs of Granville Sharp, *etc.* 1820. 4°. **135.** b. **1.**

—— [Another edition.] *See* Hoare (Prince) Memoirs of Granville Sharp, *etc.* vol. 2. 1828. 8°. **10854.** f. **8.**

—— On the Importance and Difficulty of the Pastoral Office, and the Danger of rashly undertaking it. [Containing a summary of "De dignitate sacerdotii christiani" by G. I. Huntingford, Bishop of Gloucester, "Extracts from Bishop Bull's Discourse on the Importance and Difficulty of the Pastoral Office" and extracts from the Ordination Service. Edited by T. Burgess.] pp. 29. *J. Evans: Carmarthen,* [1811.] 8°. **4498.** c. **6.**

—— On the Study of Antiquities. *See* Oxford.—*University of Oxford.* [*Prize Poems and Essays.*] The Oxford English Prize Essays, *etc.* vol. I. 1836. 12°. **8364.** b. **39.**

—— [Another edition.] An Essay on the Study of Antiquities. The second edition, corrected and enlarged. pp. v. 142. 1782. 8°. *See* Essay. **277.** k. **7.**

—— Peculiar Privileges of the Christian Ministry considered in a charge delivered to the clergy of the Diocese of St. David's at the primary visitation of that diocese in the year 1804. pp. 36. *L. Pennington: Durham,* 1805. 4°. **694.** h. **10.** (**8.**)

—— The second edition. To which is added, an appendix on Mr. Sharp's rule for the interpretation of certain passages of the New Testament relative to the Divinity of Christ; and on right principles of interpretation. pp. xii. 63. *F. C. & J. Rivington: London,* 1810. 8°. **695.** g. **2.** (**5.**)

—— Evidence of the Divinity of Christ from the Literal Testimony of Scripture: containing a vindication of Mr. Sharp's rule from the objections of the Rev. Calvin Winstanley [in "A Vindication of certain Passages in the Common English Version of the New Testament"]; with observations on right principles of interpretation . . . The second edition [of the appendix to "Peculiar Privileges of the Christian Ministry"]. pp. xv. 42. *Rivingtons: London,* 1815. 8°. **4372.** f. **10.** (**2.**)

—— *See* Popkin (John) Observations on the Nature of the House of God . . . Occasioned by . . . the Lord Bishop of St. David's address to the clergy of that diocese, *etc.* [With reference to "Peculiar Privileges of the Christian Ministry considered in a charge delivered to the clergy of the diocese of St. David."] 1813. 8°. **4372.** i. **11.** (**2.**)

—— Popery Incapable of Union with a Protestant Church; and not a remedy for schism, nor an exemplar of unity, sanctity, or Christian verity: a letter in reply to the Rev. Samuel Wix [i.e. to "A Letter to the Bishop of St. David's"] . . . containing an examination of the subjects included in the Parliamentary declarations against popery; and a view of papal schisms, *etc.* pp. vi. 203. *J. Harris: Carmarthen,* 1820. 8°. **3938.** b. **7.**

—— *See* Wix (Samuel) Christian Union without the Abuses of Popery. A letter to . . . the Lord Bishop of St. David's, in reply to his Lordship's letter, entitled, "Popery Incapable of Union with a Protestant Church," &c. 1820. 8°. **4107.** b. **76.**

—— Primary Principles of Christianity and the Church. A charge delivered to the clergy of the diocese of Salisbury in the summer of 1829, *etc.* pp. 63. *W. B. Brodie & Co.: Salisbury,* 1829. 8°. T. **1374.** (**1.**)

—— The Protestant's Catechism, in which it is clearly proved, that the ancient British Church existed several centuries before popery had any footing in Great Britain, *etc.* [By T. Burgess.] pp. 52. 1817. 8°. *See* Protestant. **3940.** de. **1.** (**3.**)

—— [Another copy.] **3940.** de. **6.** (**1.**)

—— [Another edition.] The Protestant's Catechism on the Origin of Popery, and on the Grounds of the Roman Catholic Claims; to which are prefixed, the opinions of Milton, Locke, Hoadley, Blackstone, and Burke: with a postscript on the introduction of popery into Ireland, *etc.* pp. viii. 72. *Rivingtons: London,* 1818. 8°. **3938.** e. **18.**

—— Second edition. pp. xii. 48. *Rivingtons: London,* 1818. 12°. **3939.** b. **40.**

—— *See* Milner (John) The End of Religious Controversy . . . Addressed to . . . Dr. Burgess . . . in answer to his Lordship's "Protestant [*sic*] Catechism," *etc.* 1842. 12°. **3939.** a. **32.**

—— The End of Religious Controversy . . . Addressed to the . . . Lord Bishop of St. David's, in answer to his Lordship's Protestant's Catechism. By the Rev. J. M., D.D., F.S.A. [i.e. John Milner.] 1818. 8°. *See* M., J., *Rev., D.D., F.S.A.* **1119.** k. **5.**

—— Second edition, *etc.* 1819. 8°. *See* M., J., *Rev., D.D., F.S.A.* **1352.** k. **14.**

—— Fifth edition, *etc.* 1824. 8°. *See* M., J., *Rev., D.D., F.S.A.* **3940.** g. **6.**

—— Reasons why a New Translation of the Bible should not be published, without a previous statement and examination of all the material passages which may be supposed to be misinterpreted. [By T. Burgess.] pp. 16. 1816. 8°. *See* Bible.—*Appendix.* [*English.*] T. **736.** (**8.**)

—— Second edition. pp. 24. 1819. 8°. *See* Bible.—*Appendix.* [*English.*] **689.** d. **17.** (**3.**)

—— Reflections on the Judgement delivered by Sir John Nicholl against the Rev. J. W. Wickes (for refusing to read the Church burial service over the corpse of a child baptized by a Dissenting minister). [The preface signed: T. St. D., i.e. T. Burgess, Bishop of Saint David's.] pp. xxxii. 80. [1811.] 8°. *See* D. (T. St.) T. **1005.** (**4.**)

BURGESS (Thomas) successively *Bishop of Saint David's* and *of Salisbury*.

—— Remarks on Josephus's Account of Herod's Rebuilding of the Temple at Jerusalem; occasioned by a pamphlet [by Charles Hawtrey] lately published, entitled Evidence that the Relation of Josephus concerning Herod's having new built the Temple at Jerusalem is either false or misinterpreted. (Excerptum e Flavii Josephi Antiq. Jud. lib. xv. *Gr. & Lat.*—J. A. Ernesti De templo Herodis M. ad Aggaei cap. ii. 10. et Josephi A. I. xv. extr.) pp. iv. 58. 37. viii. *D. Prince & J. Cooke: Oxford*, 1788. 8°. **1103**. c. **8**. **(6.)**

—— [Another copy.] **1118**. h. **5**. **(1.)**

—— [Another copy.] **687**. g. **25**. **(1.)**

—— *See* Josephus (F.) [*Antiquitates Judaicae.—Appendix.*] A Continuation of the Evidence that the Relation of Josephus concerning Herod's having new built the Temple at Jerusalem is either false or misinterpreted. With some observations on Mr. Burgess's Remark's [*sic*], *etc.* 1789. 8°. **687**. g. **25**. **(3.)**

—— Remarks on the General Tenour of the New Testament, regarding the Nature and Dignity of Jesus Christ: addressed to Mrs. Joanna Baillie. [In reply to "A View of the General Tenour of the New Testament regarding the Nature and Dignity of Jesus Christ."] pp. 78. *W. B. Brodie & Co.: Salisbury*, 1831. **689**. c. **18**. **(2.)**

—— Remarks on the Scriptural Account of the Dimensions of Solomon's Temple: occasioned by the supplement to a pamphlet [by Charles Hawtrey] entitled Evidence that the Relation of Josephus concerning Herod's having new built the Temple at Jerusalem is either false or misinterpreted. By the author of Remarks on the Evidence [i.e. T. Burgess]. pp. 54. 1790. 8°. *See* Josephus (F.) [*Antiquitates Judaicae.—Appendix.*] **1118**. h. **5**. **(2.)**

—— [Another copy.] **687**. g. **25**. **(4.)**

—— Remarks on the Western Travels of Saint Paul, as an evidence of the truth of Christianity, and an argument of prescription against the Supremacy of the Pope and of the Church of Rome. To which are added Pererius's two dissertations on St. Paul's journey to Spain. [Occasioned by "An Essay on the Origin and Purity of the Primitive Church of the British Isles" by William Hales.] pp. 19. *Payne & Foss; Priestly: London*, 1820. 8°. **4805**. d. **8**.
Without the Dissertations of Pererius, which were published separately.

—— Rudiments of Hebrew Grammar . . . Second edition. pp. 147. *J. Priestley: London*, 1816. 12°. **63**. l. **5**.

—— The Salisbury Spelling-Book, for the use of Sunday Schools; with historical and moral extracts from the New Testament, and prayers . . . The second edition, corrected and enlarged. [By T. Burgess.] pp. xii. 132. 1786. 12°. *See* Salisbury Spelling-Book. **12983**. a. **53**.

—— The seventh edition. pp. 72. 1810. 12°. *See* Salisbury Spelling-Book. **12981**. a. **48**.

—— The Samaritan and Syriack Alphabets, with a praxis to each. [The advertisement signed: T. St. D., i.e. T. Burgess, Bishop of Saint David's.] pp. 24. 1814. 8°. *See* D. (T. St.) **12903**. aaa. **4**.

—— Scripture and Antiquity united in a Christian's Testimony, against the recent publications of Mr. Belsham and Dr. Carpenter. [Extracted from the preface to "Tracts on the Divinity of Christ."] To which is added, The Unitarian Catechised. pp. 54. *Carmarthen; J. Hatchard & Son: London*, 1820. 8°. **702**. h. **8**. **(8.)**

BURGESS (Thomas) successively *Bishop of Saint David's* and *of Salisbury*.

—— A Second Letter from the Bishop of St. David's to the Clergy of his Diocese; on the independence of the ancient British Church on any foreign jurisdiction: with a postscript on the testimony of Clemens Romanus. pp. 57. *J. Evans: Carmarthen*, 1812. 8°. **3938**. e. **19**.

—— A Selection of Tracts and Observations on 1 John v. 7. Part the first, consisting of Bishop Barlow's letter to Mr. Hunt . . . Bishop Smallbrooke's letter to Dr. Bentley; two anonymous letters to Dr. Bentley; with Dr. Bentley's answer; and extracts from Martin's Examination of Emlyn's Answer, relative to that letter; together with notes of Hammond and Whitby on the controverted verse; and Dr. Adam Clarke's account of the Montfort manuscript. [Edited by T. Burgess. With facsimiles.] pp. lxxii. 131. *Rivington: London*, 1824. 8°. **4224**. f. **5**.
No more published.

—— A Sermon, preached at the Anniversary of the Royal Humane Society . . . on . . . April 15, 1804 . . . To which is added, an appendix of miscellaneous observations on resuscitation. By the Society. pp. viii. 44. *F. & C. Rivington: London*, 1804. 8°. T. **195**. **(9.)**

—— [Another copy.] **1026**. f. **3**. **(8.)**

—— [Another copy.] **114**. b. **57**.

—— The third edition. pp. viii. 44. *F. & C. Rivington: London*, 1804. 8°. **1026**. h. **29**. **(7.)**

—— A Sermon preached before the Incorporated Society for the Propagation of the Gospel in Foreign Parts; at their anniversary meeting . . . on . . . February 19, 1808. pp. 74. *S. Brooke: London*, 1808. 4°. **694**. h. **6**. **(3.)**

—— A Sermon preached before the Lords, Spiritual and Temporal, in the Abbey-Church, Westminster, on . . . January 30, 1807. pp. 26. *F. C. & J. Rivington; J. Hatchard: London*, 1807. 4°. **694**. k. **13**. **(7.)**

—— [Another copy.] **114**. b. **58**.

—— A Short Catechism on the Duty of Conforming to the Established Church. *See* supra: First Principles of Christian Knowledge.

—— Syllabarium Hebraicum. *See* supra: The Hebrew Reader.

—— Three Letters to the Rev. Dr. Scholz . . . on the Contents of his Note, on 1 John, v., 7, in his Edition of the Greek Testament. pp. iv. 17. *Thomas King: Southampton*, 1837. 8°. **3266**. d. **21**.

—— The Truth to which Christ Came into the World to Bear Witness; and the testimony of Christ's contemporaries to His own declaration of His Divinity confirmed by His discourses, actions, and death: a sermon, *etc.* pp. viii. 35. *J. Evans: Carmarthen*, 1815. 8°. **4477**. aaa. **10**.

—— Vindication of the late Bishop of St. Asaph's Edition of the Lacedæmonian Decree, and of his List of Books for the use of the younger Clergy, from the strictures of R. P. Knight . . . and the Rev. H. Marsh. pp. 72. *G. Walker: Durham*, 1816. 8°. T. **712**. **(9.)**

—— [Another edition.] A Vindication of Bishop Cleaver's Edition of the Decretum Lacedæmoniorum contra Timotheum, from the strictures of R. P. Knight. [With facsimiles.] pp. viii. 77. *J. Nichols & Son: London*, [1821.] 8°. **12923**. d. **1**.

—— [Another copy.] G. **8108**. **(2.)**

BURGESS (THOMAS) successively *Bishop of Saint David's* and *of Salisbury*.

—— A Vindication of 1 John, v. 7. from the Objections of M. Griesbach: in which is given a new view of the external evidence, with Greek authorities for the authenticity of the verse, *etc.* [With a facsimile.] pp. xx. 70. *Rivingtons: London*, 1821. 8°. **4372**. h. **14**. (1.)

—— The second edition, to which are added, a preface in reply to the Quarterly Review, and a postscript, in answer to a recent publication entitled Palæoromaica. pp. xlii. 214. *Rivingtons: London*, 1823. 8°. **4224**. cc. **26**.

—— The Duty of Conforming to the Established Church as Good Subjects and Good Christians. By the Right Rev. T. Burgess . . . Extracted from his elementary works by the Rev. Henry Hutton. pp. vi. 36. *B. Dunn: South Molton*, 1846. 12°. **1354**. b. **44**.

—— A Letter to the Bishop of St. David's on some Extraordinary Passages, in a Charge, delivered to the clergy of his diocese, in September, 1813 [i.e. "A Charge on the Repeal of the Act against Blasphemy"]. By a Lay Seceder [i.e. George Wilson Meadley]. pp. 24. *J. Johnson & Co.: London*, 1814. 8°. **701**. i. **16**. (2.)

—— A Letter to the Right Rev. Thomas Burgess . . . Lord Bishop of St. David's. Containing remarks on his Lordship's Introduction to the Doctrine of the Trinity, and to the Athanasian Creed [in "Tracts of various writers on the Doctrine of the Holy Trinity," edited by T. Burgess]. By a Clergyman of the Church of England. Second edition, with additions, & corrections. pp. 98. *Rodwell & Martin: London*, 1817. 8°. **4227**. c. **2**. (8.)

—— A Letter to the Right Reverend the Lord Bishop of St. David's, concerning the Admission of Unqualified Persons into Holy Orders. Wherein are suggested, some Expedients for supplying the Church with a more learned clergy; especially where non-academics are usually ordained. pp. 46. *M. Cooper: London*, [1805?] 8°. **4107**. e. **13**.

—— A Postscript to the Second Edition of the Address to the Right Reverend the Lord Bishop of St. David's, occasioned by his Lordship's 'One Word to the Rev. Dr. Milner' [in "Three Words on General Thornton's Speech on the Declaration against Transubstantiation; and One Word on Dr. Milner's End of Religious Controversy"]. [Signed: J. M. D.D., i.e. John Milner.] 1819. 8°. *See* M., J., *D.D.* T. **1231**. (1.)

—— A Vindication of the End of Religious Controversy, from the exceptions of the Right Rev. Dr. T. Burgess . . . By the Rev. J. M., D.D. F.S.A. [i.e. John Milner.] 1822. 8°. *See* M., J., *Rev., D.D., F.S.A.* **3940**. e. **7**.

BURGESS (THOMAS) *Minister of Ebenezer Chapel, Deptford*. *See* HUNTINGTON (William) *S.S.* The Excellency of the Bible, *etc.* [Edited by T. Burgess.] 1819. 8°. **3756**. e. **6**. (6.)

—— The Peaceful End of the Upright. The substance of a sermon, occasioned by the death of the Rev. Wm Huntington, *etc.* pp. 30. *E. Huntington: London*, 1813. 8°. **4905**. e. **12**.

—— The Days of the Upright; and their Peaceful End: containing a short account of the peaceful end of the late Rev. T. Burgess, minister . . . at Ebenezer Chapel, King Street, Deptford. Also a brief statement of the unscriptural conduct of the trusts of that place. pp. 48. *Printed tor* [sic] *the Author: Deptford*, 1825. 8°. **4920**. d. **16**.

BURGESS (THOMAS) *Rev., of Saco, Maine*. Greeks in America. An account of their coming, progress, customs, living, and aspirations. With an historical introduction and the stories of some famous American-Greeks. [With plates.] pp. xiv. 256. *Sherman, French & Co.: Boston*, 1913. 8°. **08175**. cc. **2**.

BURGESS (THOMAS HENRY) *See* CAZENAVE (P. L. A.) Diseases of the Human Hair. From the French . . . With a description of an apparatus for fumigating the scalp. By T. H. Burgess. 1851. 16°. **1186**. a. **68**.

—— *See* CAZENAVE (P. L. A.) and SCHEDEL (H. E.) Manual of Diseases of the Skin. From the French . . . with notes and additions, by T. H. Burgess. 1842. 8°. **1187**. a. **34**.

—— —— 1854. 8°. **1188**. a. **21**.

—— Climate of Italy in relation to Pulmonary Consumption: with remarks on the influence of foreign climates upon invalids. pp. vii. 206. *Longman & Co.: London*, 1852. 12°. **1170**. h. **42**.

—— Das Clima von Italien und seine Heilwirkungen bei Lungenschwindsucht . . . Frei übersetzt und unter Berücksichtigung der für Lungenschwindsüchtige geeignetsten Aufenthaltsorte in Deutschland mit Zusätzen versehen von . . . Richard Hagen. pp. vi. 210. *Leipzig*, 1854. 8°. **7686**. a. **11**.

—— *See* BLOXAM (James M.) The Climate of the Island of Madeira, or the Errors & misrepresentations on this subject contained in a recent work on climate [i.e. "Climate of Italy in relation to Pulmonary Consumption"] by T. H. Burgess, *etc.* 1855. 8°. **7686**. d. **41**. (1.)

—— Eruptions of the Face and Hands: with the latest improvements in the treatment of diseases of the skin, *etc.* pp. xiv. 254. pl. IV. *Henry Renshaw: London*, 1849. 8°. **1187**. k. **22**.

—— The Physiology or Mechanism of Blushing; illustrative of the influence of mental emotion on the capillary circulation; with a general view of the sympathies, *etc.* pp. viii. 202. *John Churchill: London*, 1839. 8°. **783**. n. **8**.

BURGESS (THOMAS JOSEPH WORKMAN) A Historical Sketch of our Canadian Institutions for the Insane. 1898. *See* OTTAWA.—*Royal Society of Canada*. Proceedings and Transactions, *etc.* ser. 2. vol. 4. 1883, *etc.* 4°. Ac. **1883**.

BURGESS (THORNTON WALDO) The Bedtime Story-Books . . . Illustrated by Harrison Gady. *John Lane: London*, 1931– . 8°. **20054**. ee.

—— The Burgess Animal Book for Children . . . With illustrations by Louis Agassiz Fuertes. pp. xvii. 363. *Little, Brown & Co.: Boston*, 1920. 8°. **07207**. e. **35**.

—— The Burgess Bird Book for Children . . . With illustrations in color by Louis Agassiz Fuertes. pp. xvi. 351. *Little, Brown & Co.: Boston*, 1919. 8°. **7286**. g. **25**.

—— The Burgess Flower Book for Children . . . With illustrations. pp. xviii. 350. *Little, Brown & Co.: Boston*, 1923. 8°. **07030**. de. **18**.

—— The Burgess Seashore Book for Children . . . With illustrations by W. H. Southwick and George Sutton. pp. xiv. 336. *Little, Brown & Co.: Boston*, 1929. 8°. **07290**. e. **18**.

BURGESS (Thornton Waldo)

—— Green Forest Series . . . With illustrations by Harrison Cady. 4 vol. *Little, Brown & Co.: Boston*, 1921–23. 8°. **012809.** bbb. **13.**

—— [Another edition.] 4 vol. *John Lane: London*, 1933. 8°. **12819.** b. **37.**

—— Green Meadow Series . . . With illustrations by Harrison Cady. vol. 3, 4. *Little, Brown & Co.: Boston*, 1920. 8°. **012803.** d. **65.**
Imperfect; wanting vol. 1, 2.

—— [Another edition.] 4 vol. *John Lane: London*, [1934.] 8°. **12823.** a. **10.**

—— The Little Burgess Animal Book for Children . . . With illustrations by Louis Agassiz Fuertes. pp. 64. *Rand McNally & Co.: Chicago*, [1941.] 8°. **12822.** a. **43.**

—— The Little Burgess Bird Book for Children . . . With illustrations by Louis Agassiz Fuertes. pp. 64. *Rand McNally & Co.: Chicago*, [1941.] 8°. **12822.** a. **42.**

—— Smiling Pool Series . . . With illustrations by Harrison Cady. 4 vol. *Little, Brown & Co.: Boston*, 1924–27. 8°. **012808.** h. **66.**

—— Tales from the Storyteller's House . . . With illustrations by Lemuel Palmer. pp. 194. *John Lane: London; printed in U.S.A.*, [1938.] 8°. **12821.** bb. **25.**

—— Tommy and the Wishing Stone . . . With illustrations by Harrison Cady. pp. vii. 290. *Century Co.: New York*, 1915. 8°. **012807.** bb. **38.**

—— While the Story-Log Burns . . . With illustrations by Lemuel Palmer. pp. 194. *John Lane: London; printed in U.S.A.*, [1939.] 4°. **12825.** c. **4.**

BURGESS (Tom) *See* Burgess (Joseph T.)

BURGESS (Trevor)

—— The Mystery of the Missing Book. A school story. pp. 216. *Hutchinson & Co.: London*, 1950. 8°. **12833.** ff. **13.**

—— The Racing Wraith, *etc.* pp. 304. *Hutchinson & Co.: London*, [1953.] 8°. **12834.** i. **16.**

—— A Spy at Monks' Court. pp. 228. *Hutchinson & Co.: London*, [1954.] 8°. **12832.** a. **40.**

BURGESS (W.) *Temperance Advocate.* The Excelsior Melody Sheet, comprising new and selected temperance melodies, sung by W. Burgess. [*London*, 1868.] *s. sh.* fol. **1870.** d. **1.** **(47*.)**

BURGESS (W. C.) Six Discourses: containing lectures, expositions and discussions, relating to the Second Coming of Christ, *etc.* [Numbered 7–12.] 6 pt. *J. Heydon: Devonport*, [1848.] 12°. **4478.** aa. **118.** **(3.)**

—— A Discourse on the Danger of being Spoiled through Philosophy and Vain Deceit, *etc.* pp. 12. *E. Aunger: Devonport*, [1850.] 12°. **4478.** aaa. **9.**

—— A Discourse on the Importance of Contending for the Faith once delivered to the Saints, *etc.* pp. 12. *E. Aunger: Devonport*, [1850.] 12°. **4478.** aaa. **8.**

—— A Discourse on the "Kingdom of God," *etc.* pp. 12. *J. Heydon: Devonport*, [1848.] 12°. **4477.** aa. **14.**

BURGESS (W. C.)

—— Evidence from Scripture and History, and the signs of the present times, of the speedy personal coming of Christ to reign King over all the earth; contained in a sermon, *etc.* pp. 12. *J. Heydon: Devonport*, [1848.] 12°. **4477.** aa. **15.**

—— Farewell Discourses, *etc.* pp. 36. *E. Gilbert: Plymouth*, [1851.] 12°. **4478.** aa. **118.** **(4.)**

—— On the Parable of the Ten Virgins and the Midnight Cry applied to the present time: contained in a sermon, *etc.* pp. 12. *J. Heydon: Devonport*, [1848.] 8°. **4106.** cc. **2.** **(4.)**

—— Signs of the Times. Substance of a lecture delivered . . . in Exeter and other places, *etc.* *See* Jones (Henry) *of New York.* Modern Phenomena of the Heavens, *etc.* 1847. 12°. **3186.** aa. **25.**

BURGESS (W. H.) *A Governor of the Bethlehem Hospital.* Bethlem Hospital. A Letter to the President upon the state of the question as to the expediency of appointing a Resident Chaplain. From a Governor [i.e. W. H. Burgess]. [With a Postscript.] pp. 53. 1819. 4°. *See* London.—III. *Bethlehem Hospital.* **783.** l. **26.** **(2.)**

—— Bethlem Hospital. Chaplaincy Appointment. A second Postscript to a Letter to the President upon the state of this question. From a Governor [i.e. W. H. Burgess]. pp. 28. 1820. 4°. *See* London.—III. *Bethlehem Hospital.* **783.** l. **26.** **(3.)**

BURGESS (W. Orme) A Minister's Concern for the Spiritual Welfare of his Hearers: being the substance of a sermon preached in the Independent Chapel, Keswick, *etc.* pp. 18. *J. Allison: Penrith*, 1838. 8°. **4476.** f. **15.**

BURGESS (W. Starling) The Eternal Laughter, and other poems . . . With an introduction by Julian Hawthorne. With drawings by Edward Lyne & Edmund H. Garrett. ff. 60. *W. B. Clarke Co.: Boston, Mass.; C. D. Cazenove & Son: London*, 1903. 4°. **11688.** d. **37.**
Printed on one side of the leaf only.

BURGESS (Walter Herbert) John Robinson, pastor of the Pilgrim Fathers. A study of his life and times. [With plates.] pp. xii. 426. *Williams & Norgate: London*, 1920. 8°. **4908.** h. **4.**

—— John Smith the Se-Baptist, Thomas Helwys, and the first Baptist Church in England, with fresh light upon the Pilgrim Fathers' Church. pp. 363. *James Clarke & Co.: London*, 1911. 8°. **4715.** bbb. **9.**

—— The Story of Dean Row Chapel, Wilmslow, Cheshire. [With plates.] pp. 122. *Elsom & Co.: Hull*, 1924. 8°. **04715.** e. **17.**

BURGESS (Walter William) Bits of Old Chelsea. A series of forty-one etchings by W. W. Burgess . . . With letterpress description by Lionel Johnson and Richard Le Gallienne. pp. vii. 84. *Kegan Paul & Co.: London*, 1894. fol. **L.R.404.h.2.**

BURGESS (Warren Randolph) *See* Strong (Benjamin) Interpretations of Federal Reserve Policy . . . Edited by W. R. Burgess. 1930. 8°. **08176.** aa. **29.**

—— The Reserve Banks and the Money Market, *etc.* pp. xxi. 328. *Harper & Bros.: New York & London*, 1927. 8°. **08225.** aaa. **29.**

—— Revised edition. pp. xxv. 342. *Harper & Bros.: New York & London*, 1936. 8°. **8233.** b. **45.**

—— Trends of School Costs, *etc.* [A thesis.] pp. 142. 1920. 8°. *See* New York.—*Russell Sage Foundation.—Department of Education.* **8385.** aa. **9.**

BURGESS (WILLIAM) Great Exhibition, 1851. [A hymn.] *Billing & Son: London*, [1851.] *s. sh.* fol. **806. k. 16. (27.)**

BURGESS (WILLIAM) *Artist, of Dover.* Dover Castle, A.D. 1642. A series of eight views illustrative of the enterprize of Drake the Dover Merchant & his 12 companions in their successful surprize of the Castle on the night of the 1st of August 1642 . . . Painted by W. Burgess. Drawn on stone by W. Burgess. [With descriptive letterpress.] pp. 7. *W. Burgess: Dover*, 1847. fol. **Cup.652.m.39**

BURGESS (WILLIAM) *Emigration Agent.* Remarks on Bermuda, for the information of British Emigrants. pp. 14. *Bermuda*, [1842.] 8°. **10408. aa. 34. (1.)**

BURGESS (WILLIAM) *Minister of the Gospel.* The Bible the Book of God; or, a Summary view of the principal evidences of the inspiration of the Scriptures, *etc.* pp. 28. *J. Montgomery: Sheffield*, 1795. 12°. **4402. bbb. 42. (11.)**

BURGESS (WILLIAM) *of Fleet, near Holbeach,* and **BURGESS** (HILKIAH) [Twelve views of churches in Lincolnshire and Cambridgeshire; drawn and engraved by W. and H. Burgess.] *W. & H. Burgess: Fleet, Lincs.*, 1800–05. 4°. **G. 4176. (3.)**

—— Subscribers to W. & H. Burges's View of Lincoln Cathedral. *Wisbeach*, 1812. 12°. **797. b. 32.**

BURGESS (WILLIAM) *Vicar of Thorpe-le-Soken, Essex.* The Christian Believer's Consolation in his Afflictions. A sermon, preached . . . on occasion of the death of William Blackbone, *etc.* pp. vii. 35. *Swinborne, Walter & Taylor: Colchester*, [1831.] 8°. **4905. c. 77. (3.)**

—— The Nature and Necessity of Sober-Mindedness. A sermon preached . . . on occasion of the death of . . . J. Keymer, who was drowned while bathing, *etc.* pp. 32. *Swinborne & Walter: Colchester*, 1820. 8°. **4906. dd. 5.**

—— The Reciprocal Duties of a Minister and his People. Two Sermons, *etc.* pp. 32. *Swinborne & Walter: Colchester*, [1823.] 8°. **4473. g. 26. (12.)**

—— The Syrophœnician's Prayer. [A sermon.] *See* HOLLAND (Charles) *Rector of Petworth, Sussex.* The Scripture Expositor, *etc.* vol. 1. 1848. 12°. **3127. d. 16.**

BURGESS (WILLIAM) *Writer on Shakespeare.* The Bible in Shakspeare. A study of the relation of the works of William Shakspeare to the Bible. With numerous parallel passages, quotations, *etc.* pp. xiv. 288. *Winona Publishing Co.: Chicago*, [1903.] 8°. **11766. cc. 21.**

—— [Third edition.] pp. xiv. 288. *T. Y. Crowell Co.: New York*, [1903.] 8°. **11762. ee. 5.**

BURGESS (WILLIAM ANTHONY A.) High-Tension Switchgear. 1932. *See* KEMP (Philip) Electrical Machinery and Apparatus Manufacture, *etc.* vol. 7. 1931, *etc.* 8°. **08755. bb. 43.**

BURGESS (WILLIAM LESLIE) Diagnostic Value of the 'Vaccinia Variola' Flocculation Test. By W. L. Burgess, James Craigie, and W. J. Tulloch. pp. 43. *London*, 1929. 8°. [*Medical Research Council. Special Report Series.* no. 143.] **B.S. 25/8.**

BURGESS (WILLIAM PENINGTON) A Memoir of the late Mr. Hugh Phillips, of Treloweth, near Redruth. [By W. P. Burgess ?] pp. ii. 6–32. 1821. 12°. *See* PHILLIPS (Hugh) *Methodist Preacher.* **4804. aa. 23. (4.)**

BURGESS (WILLIAM PENINGTON)

—— Memoirs of the Rev. Joseph Burgess, formerly an officer in the Army, afterwards a Wesleyan Minister, comprising an account of his mother-in-law, Mrs. Penington and notices connected with the history of Methodism in various places. pp. viii. 136. *John Mason: London*, 1842. 12°. **1372. c. 14.**

—— Moses' Request, and God's Gracious Promise. 1851. *See* WESLEYAN METHODIST MINISTERS. Sermons by Wesleyan-Methodist Ministers. 1850, *etc.* 12°. **4461. f. 24.**

—— The Principles and Doctrines of Christianity examined in reference to their Tendency and Influence. In a series of essays. pp. viii. 187. *John Mason: London*, 1842. 12°. **1351. a. 14.**

—— Secret things and Things Revealed. *See* SERMONS. Sermons . . . By several Ministers of the Wesleyan-Methodist Connexion. 1832. 8°. **1024. k. 18.**

—— Sermons designed to illustrate the Doctrines, Experience, and Practice of Primitive Christianity. pp. 202. *J. Brokenshir: Truro*, 1823. 12°. **4461. c. 6.**

—— Wesleyan Hymnology; or, a Companion to the Wesleyan Hymn Book, *etc.* pp. x. 282. *Thomas Riley: London*, 1845. 18°. **3434. c. 30.**

—— Wesleyan Hymnology . . . Second edition, revised and corrected. pp. xii. 304. *John Snow: London*, 1846. 12°. **03440. df. 4.**

BURGESS (WILLIAM ROSCOE) Exsurgat Deus. A Critical Commentary on the Sixty-Eighth Psalm. [With the text.] pp. 29. 1875. 8°. *See* BIBLE.—*Psalms.—Selections.* [*English.—Single Psalms.*] **3089. f. 30.**

—— An Inquiry into the Relations of the Sin-Offering and Trespass-Offering to the Sacrifice of Christ. pp. xi. 108. *Bell & Daldy: London*, 1865. 8°. **4226. bbb. 9.**

—— An Investigation of a Common Aryan and Semitic Demonstrative Base. pp. xiii. 80. *Williams & Norgate: London & Edinburgh*, 1867. 8°. **12901. bb. 23.**

—— Michael Faraday. [With a portrait.] pp. 48. *London*, [1877.] 8°. **10826.a.2.**

—— Notes, chiefly critical and philological, on the Hebrew Psalms. 2 vol. *Williams & Norgate: London & Edinburgh*, 1879, 81. 8°. **3089. ff. 11.**

—— The Realm of Religion. pp. xv. 45. *Williams & Norgate: London & Edinburgh*, 1876. 8°. **4379. aaa. 13.**

—— The Relations of Language to Thought. pp. 73. *Williams & Norgate: London & Edinburgh*, 1869. 8°. **12901. bbb. 20.**

BURGESS (WILLIAM VALENTINE) The Billiard Marker. A story of slum and country life. pp. 348. *Sherratt & Hughes: London, Manchester*, 1908. 8°. **012625. aa. 42.**

—— Birds and Flowers in Fact and Fancy. pp. 340. *Sherratt & Hughes: London, Manchester*, 1907. 8°. **7002. de. 15.**

—— Cheshire Village Stories. pp. 244. *Sherratt & Hughes: London, Manchester*, 1906. 8°. **012633. dd. 41.**

—— One Hundred Sonnets. Prefaced by an essay on the sonnet's history and place in English verse. pp. xxv. 118. *Sherratt & Hughes: Manchester*, 1901. 8°. **011652. g. 105.**

BURGESS (WILSON) *See* CANDLER (John) and BURGESS (W.) Narrative of a recent visit to Brazil, *etc.* 1853. 8°. **10480. dd. 18.**

BURGESS (Yorke) Burgess Blue Book. Electrical formulas and electrical drawings, *etc.* ff. 108. *Burgess Engineering Co.: Chicago,* [1920.] 12°. **8758**. a. **31**.
Partly lithographed. Printed on one side of the leaf only.

BURGESSE (Anthony) A Treatise of Self-Judging, in order to the worthy receiving of the Lords Supper. Together with a Sermon of the generall Day of Judgement. 2 pt. *J. H. for T. Underhill & M. Keinton: London,* 1658. 12°. E. **1904**. (**1**.)

—— A Demonstration of the Day of Judgment, against Atheists & Hereticks . . . Preached at St. Pauls, May 11. 1656. pp. 70. *For T. Underhill: London,* 1657. 12°. E. **1715**. (**2**.)

—— The Difficulty of, and the Encouragements to a Reformation. A sermon preached before the Honourable House of Commons, at the Publike Fast, Septem. 27. 1643. pp. 28. *R. Bishop for Thomas Underhill: London,* 1643. 4°. **1482.aaa.22.(3.)**

—— [Another copy.] **E.71.(2.)**

—— [The Doctrine of Original Sin, asserted & vindicated against the old and new adversaries thereof . . . And practically improved for the benefit of the meanest capacities . . . In four parts. To which is added a digressive Epistle concerning Justification by Faith alone, *etc.*] pp. 555. *Abraham Miller for Thomas Underhill: London,* 1659. fol. **4425**. f. **16**.
Each part has a separate titlepage, dated 1658.
Imperfect; wanting the general title page.

—— Judgements Removed, where Judgement is Executed, or a Sermon preached to the Court Marshall in Lawrence Iury . . . the 5th of Septemb. 1644, *etc.* pp. 13. *M. Simmons for Thomas Underhill: London,* 1644. 4°. C. **55**. c. **22**. (**15**.)

—— The Magistrates Commission from Heaven. Declared in a Sermon preached in Laurence jury . . . the 28. day of Sept. 1644. at the Election of the Lord Major. pp. 20. *George Miller for Thomas Underhill: London,* 1644. 4°. E. **14**. (**18**.)

—— [Another issue.] *London,* 1644. 4°. **114**. b. **59**.

—— cxlv Expository Sermons upon the whole 17th Chapter of the Gospel according to St John: or, Christs Prayer before his Passion explicated and both practically and polemically improved. pp. 672. *Abraham Miller for Thomas Underhill: London,* 1656. fol. **3227**. h. **5**.

—— Paul's last Farewel, or a Sermon, preached at the Funerall of . . . Mr. Thomas Blake . . . With a funeral Oration made at Mr. Blakes death by Samuel Shaw, *etc.* pp. 24. *For Abel Roper: London,* 1658. 4°. E. **937**. (**1**.)

—— [Another copy.] **1415**. b. **41**.
Imperfect; wanting the Oration.

—— Publick Affections, pressed in a Sermon before the Honourable House of Commons . . . Upon the solemn day of Humiliation, Febr. 25. 1645. pp. 23. *J. Y.* [*James Young*] *for Thomas Underhill: London,* 1646. 4°. **1482.aaa.22.(6.)**

—— [Another copy.] E. **325**. (**5**.)

—— The Reformation of the Church to be endeavoured more then that of the Common-Wealth, declared, in a sermon, preached before the Right Honourable House of Lords at the publike Fast, August 27. 1645. pp. 27. *G. M.* [*George Miller*] *for T. Underhill: London,* 1645. 4°. **1482.aaa.22.(5.)**

—— [Another copy.] E. **298**. (**13**.)

—— [Another copy.] **693**. f. **4**. (**6**.)

BURGESSE (Anthony)

—— Romes Cruelty & Apostacie: declared in a Sermon preached on the fifth of November, 1644, before the Honourable House of Commons. pp. 21. *George Miller for Tho. Underhill: London,* 1645. **1482.aaa.22.(4.**

—— [Another copy.] E. **19**. (**16**.)

—— The Scripture Directory, for Church-officers and people. Or, A Practical Commentary upon the whole third Chapter of the first Epistle of St. Paul to the Corinthians. To which is annexed the Godly and the Natural Man's Choice, upon Psal. 4. vers. 6, 7, 8. 2 pt. *Abraham Miller for T. U.* [*Thomas Underhill*]*: London,* 1659. 4°. **3266**. f. **30**.
The latter work has two separate titlepages.

—— Spiritual Refining: or, a Treatise of grace and assurance . . . Being cxx sermons, *etc.* pp. 696. *A. Miller for Thomas Underhill: London,* 1652. fol. **4256**. h. **5**.

—— [Another edition.] Spirituall Refinings: in two parts. Delivered in clxi. sermons . . . The second edition. 2 pt. *J. Streater for T. U.* [*Thomas Underhill*]*: London,* 1658. fol. **4453**. g. **7**.

—— The True Doctrine of Iustification asserted, and vindicated, from the errors of Papists, Arminians, Socinians, and more especially Antinomians. In xxx lectures, preached at Lawrence-Iury, London. pp. 275. *Robert White for Thomas Underhil: London,* 1648. 4°. E. **429**. (**7**.)

—— The second edition corrected and revised. pp. 272. *A. Miller for Tho. Underhil: London,* 1651. 4°. **4478**. ee. **44**. (**1**.)

—— [Another copy.] The True Doctrine of Justification . . . The second edition, *etc.* *London,* 1651. 4°. 1482. aaa. 22. (2.)

—— The True Doctrine of Justification asserted & vindicated from the Errours of many, and more especially Papists and Socinians. Or, a Treatise of the Natural Righteousness of God, and Imputed Righteousness of Christ. (A Treatise of Justification. Part ii.) pp. 456. *For Thomas Underhill: London,* 1654. 4°. **4478**. ee. **44**. (**2**.)
A different work from the preceding, forming a continuation of it.

—— [Another copy.] E. **810**.

—— Vindiciæ Legis: or, a Vindication of the Morall Law and the Covenants, from the Errours of Papists, Arminians, Socinians, and more especially, Antinomians. In xxix. lectures, preached at Laurence-Jury, London. pp. 271. *James Young for T. Underhill: London,* 1646. 4°. E. **357**. (**3**.)

—— Vindiciæ Legis: or, a Vindication of the morall law and the covenants . . . The second edition, corrected and augmented. pp. 281. *James Young for Thomas Underhill: London,* 1647. 4°. **1482**. aaa. **22**. (**1**.)

—— *See* Towne (Robert) A Re-Assertion of Grace . . . In a modest reply to Mr. A. Burgesses Vindiciæ Legis, *etc.* 1654. 4°. **4256**. aaa. **43**.

BURGESSE (Cornelius) *D.D.* *See* Burges.

BURGESSE (John) *D.D.* *See* Burges.

BURGESSE (John) *of Bush Hill, Edmonton.* An Address to the Elders of the People call'd, Quakers. Being, an Essay to demonstrate it to be a religious, and a reasonable Duty to pay tythes and swear, *etc.* pp. 23. *J. Roberts: London,* 1728. 8°. **855**. f. **13**. (**4**.)

BURGES-SHORT (George) *See* Short.

BURGESSIUS (Thomas) successively *Bishop of Saint David's* and *of Salisbury*. *See* Burgess.

BURGESUS (Joannes) Disputatio inauguralis de cholera vera, *etc.* *T. Basson: Lugduni Batavorum*, 1611. 4°. **1185**. g. **1**. (**45**.)

BURGETT (Arthur Edward) The Cathedral Church of the Holy Trinity, Quebec. A brief description. [With illustrations.] *Quebec Telegraph Print: [Quebec*, 1908.] *obl.* 8°. **7820**. aa. **45**.

—— The Door of Heaven. A manual for Holy Communion. For young people, *etc.* pp. 55. 1914. 16°. *See* Liturgies. —*Church of England.*—*Common Prayer.*—*Communion Office.* [*English.*] **4326**. de. **11**.

—— A Short Service of Preparation for Holy Communion. pp. 15. *S.P.C.K.: London*, [1919.] 16°. **3476**. a. **19**.

BURGETUS (Ludovicus) *See* Bourget.

BURGEVIN (François) Considerations générales sur les soins que réclame l'état de la femme pendant et après l'accouchement naturel. Thèse, *etc.* pp. 24. *Paris*, 1821. 4°. **1183**. g. **2**. (**24**.)

BURGEVIN (Leslie Gale) A Little Farm: the Horatian concept of rural felicity in English literature. *See* Horatius Flaccus (Q.) [*Appendix.—Miscellanea.*] Horace. Three phases of his influence, *etc.* 1936. 8°. **20030**. ee. **51**.

BURGEZ (Charles Constant) De l'emploi du cautère actuel en chirurgie. pp. 39. *Paris*, 1853. 4°. [*Collection des Thèses soutenues à la Faculté de Médecine de Paris.* An 1853. tom. 3.] **7372**. f. **5**.

BURGFELD (Carl) Sechs Jahre aus Carl Burgfeld's Leben. . . . Von dem Verfasser des Pächter Martins [i.e. H. C. G. Demme]. pp. 286. *Leipzig*, 1793. 8°. **1204**. a. **15**.

BURGGALLER (Ernst Guenther) *See* Stuck (H.) and Burggaller (E. G.) [Das Autobuch.] Motoring Sport, *etc.* [1936.] 8°. **7916**. h. **36**.

BURGGRAAFF (   )

—— Catalogue de tableaux précieux des écoles flamande, hollandaise, allemande et française formant le cabinet de Mr Burggraaff . . . Par J. B. P. Lebrun, *etc.* pp. 19. ms. notes of prices. *Paris*, 1811. 8°. **7854**. cc. **37**. (**1**.)

—— [Another copy.] Catalogue de tableaux précieux des écoles flamande, hollandaise, allemande et française, formant le cabinet de Mr Burggraaff, *etc.* ms. notes of prices. *Paris*, 1811. 8°. **562**. e. **27**. (**7**.)

—— [Another copy.] Catalogue de tableaux précieux des écoles flamande, hollandaise, allemande et francaise, formant le cabinet de Mr Burggraaff, *etc.* ms. notes of prices. *Paris*, 1811. 8°. **562**. e. **22**. (**10**.)

BURGGRAEVE (Adolphe Pierre) *See* Belgians. Les Belges illustres, *etc.* (pt. 3. Par MM. A. Baron, Burggraeve, *etc.*) 1844, *etc.* 8°. **1321**. f. **2**, **3**.

—— *See* Ravoth (Friedrich) and Vocke (Friedrich) Chirurgische Klinik. Ein Handbuch der Chirurgie und Akiurgie . . . Mit Zugrundlegung von A. Burggraeve's Tableaux synoptiques de clinique chirurgicale. 1852. 8°. **783**. a. **36**.

BURGGRAEVE (Adolphe Pierre)

—— Œuvres médico-chirurgicales.

tom. 1. Études sur André Vésale, avec l'histoire de l'anatomie.
tom. 5. Le Génie de la chirurgie conservatrice.
tom. 6. Études sociales.

Paris ; Bruxelles [printed], 1862. 8°. **7305**. cc. **4**. *No more published.*

—— A la mer, ou Conseils pour la santé. 2e édition revue et condensée. pp. ii. 126. *Paris ; Bruxelles* [printed], 1877. 12°. **7404**. aaa. **41**.

—— L'Afrique centrale et le Congo indépendant belge. pp. 119. *Bruxelles*, 1889. 8°. **10097**. c. **24**.

—— Amélioration de l'espèce humaine, *etc.* pp. 316. *Paris ; Gand [printed]*, 1860. 12°. **7406**. aa. **18**.

—— Le Choléra indien considéré au point de vue de la médecine dosimétrique . . . Deuxième édition . . . mise au courant de la science, avec gravures par A. Heins. pp. viii. 723. *Paris*, 1885. 8°. **7560**. h. **10**.

—— Concours Guinard pour l'amélioration de la position matérielle et intellectuelle de la classe ouvrière en général et sans distinction. pp. xxiii. 411. *Gand*, 1886. 8°. **8276**. bb. **55**.

—— De l'épizootie actuelle et des moyens d'y remédier. pp. 31. *Bruxelles*, 1865. 8°. **7295**. bbb. **79**. (**1**.)

—— Études médico-économiques, *etc.* pp. xii. 527. *Paris ; Bruxelles* [printed], 1885. 8°. **7305**. g. **11**.

—— Études médico-philosophiques sur Joseph Guislain. [With a portrait.] pp. l. 452. *Bruxelles*, 1867. 8°. **7410**. e. **38**.

—— Études sur André Vésale, précédées d'une notice historique sur sa vie et ses écrits. [With a portrait.] pp. xxxiii. 439. *Gand*, 1841. 8°. **551**. d. **20**.

—— Études sur Hippocrate au point de vue de la méthode dosimétrique . . . Deuxième édition considérablement augmentée. pp. xxxvi. 765. *Paris*, 1893. 8°. **7383**. h. **14**.

—— Guide de médecine dosimétrique, ou Instructions pour l'Administration des médicaments simples à doses mathématiquement définies. pp. 132. *Paris ; Bruxelles* [printed], 1872. 16°. **7462**. a. **26**.

—— Hygiène thérapeutique des pays torrides fondée sur la médecine dosimétrique . . . Deuxième édition. pp. xii. 304. *Gand*, 1887. 8°. **7404**. c. **19**.

—— Livre d'or de la médecine dosimétrique. Par le docteur Ad. Burggraeve . . . avec la collaboration de M. E. Gras. pp. ccxxxv. 500. *Paris*, 1886. 8°. **7383**. g. **2**.

—— La Longévité humaine par la médecine dosimétrique . . . Deuxième édition, revue et augmentée. pp. xv. 368. *Bruxelles*, 1887. 8°. **7404**. c. **21**.

—— [Manuel de thérapeutique dosimétrique.] The New Handbook of Dosimetric Therapeutics ; or the Treatment of diseases by simple remedies . . . Translated from the French, and edited, by H. A. Allbutt. pp. xxxi. 208. *David Bogue: London*, 1882. 8°. **7461**. c. **10**.

—— Médecine atomistique, ou Nouvelle méthode de thérapeutique avec expériences thermométriques, *etc.* pp. x. 519. *Bruxelles*, 1870. 8°. **7461**. g. **11**.

—— La Médecine dosimétrique, ses fins et ses moyens, ou Discours et articles de fonds qui ont paru au Répertoire universel de médecine dosimétrique depuis sa fondation . . . 1871–1882. pp. viii. 598. *Paris ; Bruxelles* [printed] 1883. 8°. **7305**. g. **12**

BURGGRAEVE (Adolphe Pierre)

—— La Médecine dosimétrique contemporaine. Correspondances, consultations, *etc.*
Médecine humaine. sér. 1. 1871–1886. pp. iv. 559.
Médecine vétérinaire. sér. 1. 1871–1886. pp. viii. 439.
Bruxelles ; Paris, 1886. 8°. **7383**. g. **1**.
No more published.

—— Méthode atomistique. Résultats des expériences faites avec cette méthode. pp. 23. *Bruxelles*, 1868. 8°. **7321**. dd. **22**. (**4**.)

—— Monument à E. Jenner, ou Histoire générale de la vaccine à l'occasion du premier centenaire de son invention, *etc.* [With a portrait.] pp. xvi. 377. pl. vi. *Bruxelles*, 1875. fol. **1832**. c. **3**.

—— Nouvel organon ou instrument de médecine dosimétrique, fondé sur les faits cliniques consignés dans les dix premières années du Répertoire universel de médecine dosimétrique humaine et vétérinaire. 1871–1882. Partie humaine. pp. xxxv. 1354. *Bruxelles*, 1889. 4°. **7383**. r. **2**.

—— Précis de l'histoire de l'anatomie, comprenant l'examen comparatif des ouvrages des principaux anatomistes anciens et modernes. pp. viii. 503. *Gand*, 1840. 8°. **550**. b. **22**.

—— Projet d'une haute cour pour la collation des diplomes d'avocat et de médecin. pp. 32. *Bruxelles*, 1871. 8°. **5423**. dd. **18**.

—— Répertoire de médecine dosimétrique, *etc.* *Paris*, 1872. 8°. **7461**. h. **27**.
Imperfect ; wanting all except livr. 1.

—— La Société de Médecine de Gand et la médecine dosimétrique . . . 1834 à 1889. pp. cxxvi. 312. *Bruxelles*, 1890. fol. **7383**. l. **1**.

—— La Surveillance maternelle, ou hygiène thérapeutique de la première enfance d'après la méthode dosimétrique. pp. 155. *Gand*, 1887. 8°. **7581**. bbb. **22**.

BURGGRAF (Julius) *Pastor in Bremen.* Goethe und Schiller. Im Werden der Kraft. pp. 468. *Stuttgart*, 1902. 8°. **11853**. b. **24**.

—— Goethepredigten . . . Bearbeitet und herausgegeben von Karl Rösener . . . Mit der Selbstbiographie und dem Bilde Burggrafs. pp. viii. 364. *Giessen*, 1913. 8°. **4427**. i. **8**.

—— Schillers Frauengestalten. pp. xii. 490. *Stuttgart*, 1897. 8°. **011851**. g. **12**.

—— Theodor Hossbach. Zur Erinnerung an sein Leben und Wirken, *etc.* pp. viii. 200. *Berlin*, 1895. 8°. **10707**. ccc. **41**.

BURGGRAF (Julius) *Writer of Verse.* Das Brunnenbecken. Gedichte. pp. 74. *Leipzig*, [1931.] 8°. **11521**. ee. **46**.

BURGGRAFF (Johann Ernst) *See* Burggrav.

BURGGRAFF (Johann Philipp) *See* Burggrav.

BURGGRAFIUS (Joannes Philippus) *See* Burggrav (Johann P.)

BURGGRAV (Johann Ernst) *See* Beuther (D.) D. Beuthers vniuersal, vnd vollkommener Bericht, von der . . . Kunst der Alchymj . . . Sampt beygefügtem Gespräch, von Betrug vnd Irrweg, etlicher vnerfahrnen Laboranten . . . ex Bibliotheca chymica D. I. E. Burggrauii. 1631. 4°. **1033**. h. **35**.

BURGGRAV (Johann Ernst)

—— *See* Clodius (B.) Balduini Clodii . . . Officina Chymica . . . Jetzo publiciert vnd an Tag geben durch J. E. B. Medicum zu S. [i.e. J. E. Burggrav.] 1620. 4°. **1033**. h. **34**.

—— *See* Clodius (B.) Balduini Clodii . . . Officina Chymica . . . zusammen gezogen, und . . . an Tag gegeben, durch . . . J. E. Burggrauium, *etc.* 1733. 4°. **1033**. i. **9**. (**1**.)

—— *See* Drebbel (C. J.) Cornelii Drebbel . . . Tractatus de natura elementorum . . . in linguam Latinam translatus & in lucem emissus à I. E. Burggrauio. 1628. 8°. **1033**. d. **16**. (**6**.)

—— Ioan. Ernesti Burggravi Achilles πανοπλος redivivus, seu Panoplia physico-vulcania quâ in prœlio φιλοπλος in hostem educitur sacer et inviolabilis. Cui præmissa est Marcelli Vranckheim . . . ἐπικρισις στοχαστικη ad Achillem παννπεροπλομαχον. pp. 130. *Apud H. Laurentium: Amsterodami*, [1612.] 8°. **621**. b. **24**. (**1**.)

—— Biolychnium seu Lucerna, cum vita ejus, cui accensa est Mysticè, vivens jugiter; cum morte ejusdem expirans; omnesq; affectus graviores prodens. Huic accessit Cura Morborum Magnetica ex Theophr. Parac [i.e. Paracelsi] Mumia: itemq; omnium venenorum Alexipharmacum. Auctiora & emendatiora omnia curis secundis I. E. Burggravi. pp. 176. *V. D. Balck: Franekeræ*, 1611. 8°. **1033**. e. **8**.

—— [Another edition.] pp. 144. *Sumptibus W. Fitzer: [Frankfort,]* 1629. 8°. **1033**. f. **27**.

—— [A reissue.] Porro adjunctus est P. Ribolæ . . . Tractatus secretus de facultate metallorum germinatrice secundum Hermeticos. 2 pt. *Impensis G. Fitzeri: Francofurti*, 1630. 8°. **1032**. b. **24**.

—— [Another edition.] Lampadem vitæ & mortis omniumque graviorum in microcosmo παθων indicem; hoc est: biolychnium sive lucernam . . . antehâc quidem cura & studio J. E. B. [i.e. J. E. Burggravii] . . . traditam: nunc dilucidiori stylo se expositurum intimat G. F. MDCS. pp. 72. 1678. 12°. *See* B., J. E. **526**. a. **20**. (**3**.)

—— [Another copy.] **1036**. a. **33**.

—— Tractat von der Ungarischen Hauptschwachheit, auch andern Epidemischen gifftigen Fiebern, deroselben . . . Zufällen, sampt deren præservatifs vnd curatifs Mitteln. Widerumb publiciret vnd in Truck befürdert. pp. 110. *See* Clodius (B.) Fünff . . . Tractätlein, *etc.* 1640. 4°. **1143**. c. **31**.

BURGGRAV (Johann Philipp) *the Elder.* Disputatio . . . de malo sinensi aureo. *See* Valentini (M. B.) Michaelis Bernhardi Valentini . . . Aurifodina medica, *etc.* (Mantissæ exoticorum academicæ disp. vii.) 1723. fol. **444**. k. **16**.

—— [Another edition.] *See* Valentini (M. B.) Michaelis Bernhardi Valentini . . . Historia simplicium, *etc.* 1732. fol. **456**. f. **11**.

—— Johannis Philippi Burggravii . . . Jatrice ominum lethique curiosa; sive, De morte, ejusque præsensione ; physico medica commentatio. pp. 136. *Francofurti*, 1706. 8°. **784**. c. **28**.

—— Johannis Philippi Burggrafii . . . Libitina ovans fatis Hygieæ; seu de medicæ artis æque ac medicorum præcipuis fatis, dissertatio epistolica, *etc.* pp. 96. *Francofurti*, 1701. 8°. **1172**. e. **6**. (**10**.)

BURGGRAV (Johann Philipp) *the Younger.* *See* Conringius (H.) H. Conringii De habitus corporum germanicorum causis liber singularis. Annotationibus uberrimis dilucidavit J. P. Burggravius. 1727. 8°. **1194**. a. **16**.

—— *See* Helvetius (J. C. A.) Principia physico-medica . . . Præfatus est J. P. Burggravius. 1754. 4°. **537**. b. **28**.

—— D. Johann Philipp Burggrave des jüngern . . . auserlesene medicinische Fälle und Gutachten. pp. 356. *Frankfurt*, 1784. 8°. **1174**. h. **34**. (**1**.)

—— Joannis Philippi Burggravii . . . De aere aquis & locis urbis Francofurtanæ ad Moenum commentatio. Accedit disquisitio, de origine et indole animalculorum spermaticorum. pp. 180. *Francofurti*, 1751. 8°. **236**. k. **40**.

—— Joannis Philippi Burggravii, Jun. . . . De existentia spirituum nervosorum eorumque vera origine indole motu effectibus et affectibus in corpore humano vivo sano et ægro commentatio medica viro clarissimo Andr. Ottom. Goelicke inprimis opposita. [In reply to Goelicke's "Spiritus animalis ex foro medico relegatus."] pp. 93. *Francofurti*, 1725. 4°. **1166**. h. **17**. (**1**.)

—— [Another copy.] **781**. f. **25**.

—— *See* Goelicke (A. O.) Spiritus animalis ex foro medico juste relegatus, sive Vindiciæ disquisitionum physiologico-pathologicarum, commentationi medicae . . . J. P. Burggravii, Jun. . . . oppositæ, *etc.* 1728. 4°. **781**. f. **26**.

—— Dissertatio . . . de methodo medendi pro climatum diversitate varie instituenda, *etc.* pp. 23. *Lugduni Batavorum*, 1724. 4°. **1185**. h. **19**. (**7**.)

—— Jo. Philippi Burggravii, Jun. . . . Lexicon medicum universale, omnium verborum, præcipue vero rerum ad medicinam et disciplinas illi famulantes spectantium, explicationem systematicam exhibens, *etc.* tom. 1. A–B. coll. 1752. *Francofurti*, 1733. fol. **774**. n. **3**.

—— Spiritus nervosus immerens exul, pristinis laribus avitisque sedibus summo jure restitutus; ac ab iniquis imputationibus . . . A. O. Goelickii . . . denuo absolutus, *etc.* [In reply to Goelicke's "Spiritus animalis ex foro medico juste relegatus."] pp. 75. *Francofurti*, 1729. 4°. **549**. e. **5**. (**2**.)

—— [Another copy.] **781**. f. **24**.

—— *See* Goelicke (A. O.) Spiritus animalis merens exul justarumque imputationum plenissime convictus adversus . . . J. P. Burggravium, Jun., *etc.* [In reply to Burggrav's "Spiritus nervosus immerens exul pristinis laribus restitutus."] 1731. 4°. **525**. d. **21**. (**11**.)

—— *See* Gohl (J. D.) Insufficientia cerebri, ad sensum & motum animalis expenditur, meningumque ad illos indispensabilior usus assertus, adversus vagas intentationes J. P. Burggravii . . . ulterius argumentis ex scriptis dn. adversarii depromptis stabilitur. [In reply to Burggrav's "Spiritus nervosus immerens exul pristinis laribus restitutus."] 1732. 4°. **705**. d. **3**. (**2**.)

—— D. J. P. Burggravens des Jüngern, Vertheidigter Beweiss von der Würcklichkeit derer Nerven-Geister, denen Einwürffen Hrn. D. Ursini Wahrmunds entgegen gesetzt. [In reply to "Versuch patriotischer Gedancken, über den von Vorurtheilen krancken Verstand," written by J. D. Gohl under the pseudonym of Ursinus Wahrmund.] pp. 18. *Franckfurt*, 1727. 4°. **1166**. h. **17**. (**2**.)

BURGGRAVE (Johann Ernst) *See* Burggrav.

BURGGRAVE (Johann Philipp) *See* Burggrav.

BURGGRAVE (Justus Heinricus) Dissertatio . . . de motu velut magno ad longævitatem acquirendam remedio, *etc.* *Praes.* J. A. Fischer. pp. 16. *Erfordiæ*, [1723.] 4°. **7306**. g. **10**. (**6**.)

BURGGRAVIUS (Joannes Ernestus) *See* Burggrav (Johann E.)

BURGGRAVIUS (Joannes Philippus) *See* Burggrav (Johann P.)

BURGH, *Lincolnshire.—Museum.* Catalogue of the Valuable Collection of Carvings, Curiosities . . . China, Coins, &c. at the Burgh Museum, Lincolnshire, which will be sold by auction August 7 & 8, 1888. pp. 40. *J. Avery: Skegness*, [1888.] 8°. **7704**. aaa. **34**. (**3**.)

Saint Paul's Missionary College.

—— Report [by W. J. Oldfield] Addressed to the Lord Bishop of Lincoln . . . of an Enquiry as to the Advisability of Undertaking the Training of Men for Lay-Work in the Mission Field Abroad. Together with an Appendix containing the replies of Colonial and Missionary Bishops, and of others, *etc.* pp. 46. *Thomas Brakell: Liverpool*, 1893. 8°. **4768**. c. **57**. (**6**.)

BURGH, *Norfolk.* A Sermon, preached at the Parish Churches of Burgh, Thurlton & Thorpe, in the County of Norfolk, on the General Fast, February 25th 1795 . . . by the officiating minister [viz. William Boycott]. pp. 20. *I. D. Downes: Yarmouth*, [1795.] 8°. **4473**. c. **17**. (**1**.)

—— [Another copy.] **4473**. c. **10**. (**1**.)

—— A Transcript of the Register of the Parish of Burgh. [1563–1810.] Communicated by the Rev. E. T. Yates. 1884. *See* Norwich.—*Norfolk and Norwich Archaeological Society.* Norfolk Archæology, *etc.* vol. 9. 1847, *etc.* 8°. Ac. **5685**.

BURGH BOOKLETS. *See* Shaw (Gilbert)

BURGH CASTLE.

—— Burgh Castle, Suffolk. *London*, 1948. 8°. [*Ministry of Works. Ancient Monuments Inspectorate. Ancient Monuments and Historic Buildings. Leaflet Guides.*] B.S. **46/32**. (**49**.)

BURGH (A. H. H. van der) Gesantschappen door Zweden en Nederland wederzijds afgevaardigd gedurende de jaren 1592–1795. Chronologische lijsten opgemaakt uit de stukken in het Rijksarchief aanwezig, *etc.* pp. viii. 84. *'s-Gravenhage*, 1886. 8°. **10759**. k. **12**.

BURGH (Albert) and **VELTDRIEL** (Johan van) Донесенія посланниковъ Республики Соединенныхъ Нидерландовъ при русскомъ дворѣ. Отчетъ А. Бурха и І. фанъ Фелтдриля о посольствѣ ихъ въ Россію въ 1630 и 1631. гг. Съ приложеніемъ очерка сношеній Московскаго государства съ Республикою Соединенныхъ Нидерландовъ до 1631 г. Под редакціею В. А. Кордта. *Dutch & Russ.* pp. xii. cccxlvii. 243. 1902. 8°. [*Сборникъ Императорскаго Русскаго Историческаго Общества.* том. 116.] *See* Netherlands.—*United Provinces.* [*Miscellaneous Official Publications and Public Documents.*] Ac. **7886**.

BURGH (Albertus) *See* Franciscus, *de Hollandia, O.F.M.* [A. Burgh.]

BURGH (Allatson)

—— Anecdotes of Music, historical and biographical; in a series of letters from a gentleman to his daughter. 3 vol. *Longman & Co.: London*, 1814. 12°. **7889**. a. **22**.

—— [Another copy.] **7896**. a. **43**. *Imperfect; wanting the titlepage to vol.* 3.

—— [Another copy.] Anecdotes of Music, *etc.* *London*, 1814. 8°. Hirsch **5499**.

BURGH (Antonius van der) Disputatio medica inauguralis de pica, *etc.* *Apud A. Elzevier: Lugduni Batavorum*, 1684. 4°. **1185**. g. **16**. (**37**.)

—— Disputatio philosophica inauguralis de amore, *etc.* *Praes.* J. Perizonius. pp. 23. *Lugduni Batavorum*, 1707. 4°. **1386**. h. **37**.

BURGH (Benedict) *See* Aristotle. [*Doubtful or Suppositious Works.—Secreta Secretorum.—English.*] Lydgate and Burgh's Secrees of Old Philisoffres. A version of the 'Secreta Secretorum.' Edited . . . by R. Steele. 1894. 8°. [*Early English Text Society.* Extra series. 66.] Ac. **9926/38**.

—— *See* Cato (M. P.) *the Censor.* [*Supposititious Works.—Disticha de Moribus.—Latin and English.*] *Begin.* [fol. 2 *recto*:] Hic incipit paruus Chato. [fol. 3 *verso*:] Hic incipit magnus Chato. [With a paraphrase in English verse by B. Burgh.] [1481 ?] fol. IB. **55034**.

—— *See* Cato (M. P.) *the Censor.* [*Supposititious Works.—Disticha de moribus.—Latin and English.*] *Begin.* [fol. 2 *recto*:] Hic incipit paruus Chato, *etc.* [The text, with an English translation in verse by B. Burgh.] [1481 ?] fol. Mic. A. **125**. (**22**.)

—— —— 1558. 8°. G. **9792**.

—— —— 1906. 8°. **12207**. n. **35/6**.

—— *See* Governance. This present boke called the Gouernaunce of kynges and prync3, *etc.* [A verse translation by John Lydgate and an anonymous poet, possibly B. Burgh, of the "Secreta Secretorum" ascribed to Aristotle.] 1511. 4°. Mic. A. **708**. (**17**.)

BURGH (Benet) *See* Burgh (Benedict)

BURGH (Cornelius van der) Oratio de Baptistæ Mantuani dicto: Virtute decet non sanguine niti. pp. 16. *G. de Iager: Rotterdam*, 1676. 4°. **525**. e. **40**. (**3**.)

BURGH (Elias Codde van der) Disputatio medica de lycanthropia, *etc.* *Praes.* A. Deusingius. *Apud E. Agricolam: Groningæ*, 1654. 4°. **1185**. b. **13**. (**7**.)

BURGH (Hugh Nicholas) A Prologue, and other fragments in verse. pp. 65. *S. C. Mayle: London*, 1902. 8°. **011652**. m. **32**.

—— Unpainted Pictures, and other fragments in verse. *Elliot Stock: London*, 1899. 8°. **011651**. ee. **27**.

BURGH (Jacob van der) *See* Hooft (P.) Gedichten . . . verzamelt en uytgegeven door I. van der Burgh. 1636. 4°. **10663**. f. **1**. (**2**.)

—— —— 1644. 8°. **11556**. bb. **31**.

—— —— 1657, *etc.* 8°. **11555**. aa. **19**.

—— —— 1823. 12°. **1209**. a. **2–4**.

—— —— 1853. 16°. [*Klassiek letterkundig Panthéon.* no. 18, 19.] **12258**. aa.

BURGH (James) *See also* Neck (J. Vander) *pseud.* [i.e. J. Burgh.]

—— The Art of Speaking . . . [By J. Burgh.] The second edition with additions, &c. [Edited by Samuel Whyte.] pp. 376. 1763. 12°. *See* Art. C. **64**. dd. **16**.

—— The second edition. pp. 372. 1768. 8°. *See* Art. **11825**. dd. **34**.

—— The sixth edition. pp. 373. 1784. 8°. *See* Art. **11825**. dd. **35**.

—— The seventh edition. pp. 372. 1792. 8°. *See* Art. **11824**. d. **16**.

—— [Another edition.] pp. 322. 1795. 12°. *See* Art. **11824**. a. **24**.

—— Britain's Remembrancer: or, the Danger not over. Being some thoughts on the proper improvement of the present juncture. The character of this age and nation. A brief view, from history, of the effects of the vices which now prevail in Britain, upon the greatest empires and states of former times, *etc.* [By J. Burgh.] pp. 46. 1746. 8°. *See* England. [*Appendix.—Miscellaneous.*] **8133**. c. **9**.

—— [Another edition.] pp. 52. 1746. 8°. *See* England. [*Appendix.—Miscellaneous.*] **8133**. a. **19**.

—— The fourth edition. pp. 48. 1747. 8°. *See* England. [*Appendix.—Miscellaneous.*] T. **1112**. (**5**.)

—— The fifth edition. pp. 48. 1748. 8°. *See* England. [*Appendix.—Miscellaneous.*] **8132**. aa. **15**. (**5**.)

—— [Another edition.] With a preface by Mr. Thomas Boston, *etc.* 1792. 8°. [*Britannicus, pseud., i.e. Niel Douglas. A Monitory Address to Great Britain, etc.*] *See* England. [*Appendix.—Miscellaneous.*] **992**. k. **26**. (**2**.)

—— Crito, or, Essays on various subjects. [By J. Burgh.] 2 vol. 1766, 67. 8°. *See* Crito. **8407**. b. **30**.

—— The Dignity of Human Nature; or, a Brief account of the certain and established means for attaining the true end of our existence . . . By J. B. (James Burgh.) pp. xvi. 430. *J. & P. Knapton: London*, 1754. 4°. **528**. n. **5**.

—— A new edition. 2 vol. *J. Johnson & J. Payne; T. Cadell: London*, 1767. 8°. **232**. i. **16**, **17**.

—— A new edition. pp. xvi. 544. *C. Dilly: London*, 1794. 8°. **8404**. df. **11**.

—— An Hymn to the Creator of the World. The thoughts chiefly taken from Psal. civ. To which is added in Prose, An Idea of the Creator from his Works. [By J. Burgh.] pp. iii. 44. 1750. 8°. *See* Hymn. **117**. f. **63**.

—— Political Disquisitions: or, an Enquiry into public errors, defects, and abuses, *etc.* (By J. B. Gent. Author of the Dignity of Human Nature, and other tracts [i.e. J. Burgh].) 3 vol. 1774, 75. 8°. *See* B., J., *Gent.* **288**. e. **18–20**.

—— Thoughts on Education . . . By the author of Britain's Remembrancer [i.e. J. Burgh]. pp. 60. 1747. 8°. *See* Thoughts. T. **1614**. (**6**.)

—— Youth's Friendly Monitor: being a set of directions, prudential, moral, religious, and scientific . . . To which is prefixed, an account of the extraordinary proceedings of some persons, which occasioned the publication of this tract . . . Together with Theophilus, a character worthy of imitation. By the author of Britain's Remembrancer, *etc.* [The epistle to the reader signed: J. B., i.e. J. Burgh.] 2 pt. 1754. 12°. *See* B., J. **1133**. b. **12**. (**2**.)

BURGH (JAMES)

—— The second edition, corrected. pp. 60. 1754. 12°. *See* YOUTH. **8307. a. 8.**

BURGH (NICHOLAS) *See* BIBLE.—*Prophets.—Selections.* [*English.*] A Short Guide to the Reading of the Prophets . . . By N. Burgh. 1898. 8°. **3185.** df. **44.**

BURGH (NICHOLAS PROCTER) The Indicator Diagram practically considered. pp. xii. 164. *E. & F. N. Spon: London,* 1869. 8°. **8765.** bb. **29.**

—— Link-Motion and Expansion-Gear, practically considered, *etc.* pp. xvi. 232. pl. 72. *E. & F. N. Spon: London,* 1870. 4°. **08767.** dd. **6.**

—— The Manufacture of Sugar, and the machinery employed for colonial and home purposes. Read before the Society of Arts . . . April 4th, 1866. pp. 31. *Trubner & Co.: London,* [1866.] 8°. **7943.** bb. **50.** (**7.**)

—— Modern Marine Compound Engine. A large coloured diagram, showing front and end sectional elevations, plans, &c. With description. *J. Reynolds & Sons: London,* [1883.] 4°. **8805.** ff. **16.**

—— Modern Marine Engineering, *etc.* (Modern Marine Compound Engines, forming a supplement to Modern Marine Engineering.) 2 pt. pp. 410. pl. 54. *E. & F. N. Spon: London,* 1867, 73. 4°. **8765.** g. **11.**

—— Modern Screw-Propellers practically considered. Read before the Society of Arts . . . March 10th, 1869. pp. 39. *E. & F. N. Spon: London,* [1869.] 8°. **8766.** ee. **28.**

—— Pocket-book of Practical Rules for the Proportions of Modern Engines & Boilers for land and marine purposes. pp. 190. *E. & F. N. Spon: London,* 1864. *obl.* 12°. **8767.** de. **20.**

—— Second edition. pp. 250. *E. & F. N. Spon: London,* 1868. *obl.* 12°. **8767.** de. **19.**

—— Pocket-Book on Compound Engines. pp. vi. 285. *N. P. Burgh: London,* [1876.] *obl.* 8°. **8765.** a. **1.**

—— [A reissue.] *C. Wilson: London,* [1879.] *obl.* 8°. **8765.** aa. **14.**

—— Practical Illustrations of Modern Land and Marine Engines, showing in detail the improvements in high and low pressure, ordinary and surface condensation, *etc.* pl. 20. *E. & F. N. Spon: London,* 1864. fol. **1802.** d. **11.**

—— A Practical Treatise on Boilers and Boiler-Making, *etc.* pp. vii. 391. pl. 45. *E. & F. N. Spon: London,* 1873. 4°. **1806.** cc. **16.**

—— A Practical Treatise on Modern Screw-Propulsion, *etc.* pp. iv. 280. pl. 41. *E. & F. N. Spon: London,* 1869 [1868, 69]. 4°. **8766.** f. **5.** *Published in parts.*

—— A Practical Treatise on the Condensation of Steam, *etc.* pp. ix. 251. *E. & F. N. Spon: London,* 1871. 8°. **8764.** b. **9.**

—— The Slide Valve practically considered. pp. iv. 76. vii. *E. & F. N. Spon: London,* 1865. 8°. **8766.** aa. **24.**

—— The Slide Valve practically considered . . . Fifth edition. pp. viii. 121. *E. & F. N. Spon: London,* 1874. 8°. **08773.** aa. **17.**

BURGH (NICHOLAS PROCTER)

—— Eleventh edition. (With an appendix, bringing the information down to the present time.) pp. viii. 141. *W. Clowes & Sons: London,* 1884. 8°. **8767.** b. **31.**

—— A Treatise on Sugar Machinery: including the process of producing sugar from the cane, refining moist and loaf sugar, *etc.* pp. ii. 64. pl. 16. *E. & F. N. Spon: London,* 1863. 4°. **8765.** g. **8.**

—— W. R. Jackson's New Series of Educational Diagrams. (Designed, arranged & drawn by N. P. Burgh.) no. 1, 2. *W. R. Jackson: London,* [1863.] fol. **1801.** d. **2.** (**9, 10.**)

BURGH (PETRUS VAN DER) De incomprehensibilitate Dei. *See* VRIES (Gerard de) *Professor of Philosophy at Utrecht.* Meditationes philosophicæ de Deo, *etc.* (Exercitationis pneumaticæ pars decima-tertia.) 1682, *etc.* 4°. **480.** a. **5.**

BURGH (ROBERT FREDERIC)

—— *See* MORRIS (Earl H.) and BURGH (R. F.) Anasazi Basketry. Basket maker II through Pueblo III, *etc.* 1941. 4°. [*Carnegie Institution of Washington. Publication.* no. 533.] Ac. **1866.**

—— *See* MORRIS (Earl H.) and BURGH (R. F.) Basket Maker II Sites near Durango, *etc.* 1954. 4°. [*Carnegie Institution of Washington. Publication.* no. 604.] Ac. **1866.**

BURGH (ROBERT FREDERIC) and **SCOGGIN** (CHARLES R.)

—— The Archaeology of Castle Park Dinosaur National Monument, *etc.* [With plates.] pp. 102. *University of Colorado Press: Boulder,* 1948. 8°. [*University of Colorado Studies. Series in Anthropology.* no. 2.] Ac. **2691.** g/**2.** (**5.**)

BURGH (THOMAS) A Method to Determine the Areas of Right-Lined Figures Universally. Very useful for ascertaining the contents of any survey. pp. 33. *Dublin; Richard Wilkins: London,* 1724. 4°. **529.** k. **4.**

—— [Another copy.] **51.** e. **3.**

BURGH (THOMAS) *Baron Burgh.*

—— *See* DEVEREUX (Robert) *2nd Earl of Essex.* Opinions delivered by the Earl of Essex . . . Lord Burrough [and others] . . . on the Alarm of an Invasion from Spain in the year 1596, and the measures proper to be taken on that occasion. [1794?] 8°. **8135.** c. **18.**

BURGH (WALTER) *See* BIBLE.—*Psalms.—Selections.* [*English.*] An Arrangement of the most suitable Verses for Singing . . . By the Rev. W. Burgh. 1824. 12°. **1018.** k. **2.**

—— Hymns, Anthems, and Psalms, compiled by the Rev. W. Burgh, *etc.* pp. iv. 340. *A. & W. Watson: Dublin,* 1826. 12°. **844.** f. **11.** (**1.**)

BURGH, afterwards **DE BURGH** (WILLIAM) *See* BIBLE.—*Appendix.—Old Testament.—Concordances.* [*Hebrew.*] The Englishman's Hebrew and Chaldee Concordance of the Old Testament, *etc.* [Based on the unpublished work of W. Burgh. Edited by G. V. Wigram.] 1843. 8°. **3107.** de. **10.**

—— —— 1860. 8°. **2007.f.**

—— *See* BIBLE.—*Appendix.—New Testament.—Concordances.* [*Greek.*] The Englishman's Greek Concordance of the New Testament, *etc.* [By G. V. Wigram, assisted by W. Burgh.] 1839. 8°. **690.** e. **11.**

—— —— 1860. 8°. **2007.f.**

—— *See* CROSTHWAITE (J. C.) Observations on Nonconformity and Separation, in a letter to the Rev. W. Burgh. [In reply to Burgh's "Dissent from the Church of England, shewn to be unwarrantable, in a letter to a clergyman."] 1834. 8°. **T. 1506. (4.)**

—— *See* KELLY (Thomas) *Rev.* A Letter to the Rev. W. Burgh, in answer to his "Letter to a Clergyman" [i.e. "Dissent from the Church of England, shewn to be unwarrantable, in a letter to a clergyman"]. 1833. 12°. **4372. bb. 36. (2.)**

—— *See* MILLER (George) *D.D.* The Change of the Sabbath . . . With an appendix, animadverting on a tract by W. Burgh, A.B. [i.e. "The Scriptural Observance of the First Day of the Week."] 1829. 8°. **T. 1256. (8.)**

—— Antichrist. A discourse . . . With . . . an appendix, containing an answer to the sermon of the Rev. H. McNeile . . . bearing same title. pp. 48. *Printed for the Author: Dublin,* [1839.] 12°. **908. b. 1. (7.)**

—— The Apocalypse Unfulfilled; or, an Exposition of the Book of Revelation . . . [Lectures on ch. iv-xxii.] Second edition. pp. iv. 264. *R. M. Tims: Dublin,* 1833. 12°. **764. c. 23. (3.)**

—— [Another edition.] An Exposition of the Book of Revelation . . . Third edition [of "The Apocalypse Unfulfilled"]. [With eight additional lectures on ch. i–iii.] pp. 265. *R. M. Tims: Dublin,* 1834. 12°. **3187. bb. 36.**

—— Fifth edition, revised and improved. pp. xii. 432. *Hodges, Smith & Co.: Dublin,* 1857. 8°. **3186. a. 47.**

—— The Catechist: an exposition of the Church Catechism, in question and answer, *etc.* pp. x. 163. 1853. 8°. *See* LITURGIES.—*Church of England.—Common Prayer.—Catechism.* [*English.*] **3505. c. 7.**

—— The Christian Sabbath, considered as to its distinctive obligation and observance. pp. 19. *Rivingtons: London,* [1856.] 8°. **4355. e. 28.**

—— A Collection of Psalms and Hymns, used in the Chapel of the Dublin Female Penitentiary . . . Second edition, with an appendix. [The compiler's preface signed: W. B., i.e. W. Burgh.] pp. xv. 286. 1839. 32°. *See* B., W. **3438. df. 7.**

—— The Coming of the Day of God, in connexion with the first resurrection, the reign of Christ on earth, the restitution of all things . . . By an humble expectant of the promise [i.e. W. Burgh] . . . Second edition revised, with some additions. pp. 58. 1826. 8°. *See* COMING. **T. 1213. (2.)**

—— A Commentary on the Book of Psalms; critical, devotional, and prophetical: with the text of the Authorized Version, metrically arranged, according to the original Hebrew. 2 vol. pp. 1028. 1860 [1858–60]. 8°. *See* BIBLE.—*Psalms.* [*English.*] **3089. f. 21.**

—— Review of De Burgh on the Psalms. Extracted for private circulation from the Church of England Monthly Review, *etc.* *London,* 1860. 8°. **3090. cc. 38.**

—— A Compendium of Hebrew Grammar, designed to facilitate the study of the language, and simplify the system of the vowel-points. pp. viii. 68. *University Press: Dublin,* 1847. 8°. **825. i. 13.**

—— Discourses on the Life of Christ, or the Principal events in the personal history of the Redeemer. pp. viii. 276. *F. & J. Rivington: London,* 1849. 8°. **4805. c. 6.**

—— The Divinity of Christ, experimentally considered in four discourses. pp. viii. 101. *W. Curry, Jun., & Co.: Dublin,* 1836. 8°. **T. 2114. (1.)**

—— The Early Prophecies of a Redeemer; from the first promise to the prophecy of Moses: considered in six discourses, *etc.* pp. xi. 178. *University Press: Dublin,* 1854. 8°. **4255. c. 22.**

—— For the Festival of Easter. The Christian's life in Christ . . . Three discourses on Coloss. III. 1–4, the Epistle for Easter-Day. pp. 46. *M. Ogle & Son: Glasgow,* 1849. 8°. **4375. a. 15.**

—— Lectures on the Second Advent . . . With an introduction on the use of Unfulfilled Prophecy. pp. vii. 252. *R. M. Tims: Dublin,* 1832. 12°. **764. c. 23. (2.)**

—— Second edition, enlarged. pp. ix. 300. *W. Curry, Jun., & Co.: Dublin,* 1835. 8°. **695. b. 23. (1.)**

—— *See* CUNINGHAME (William) The Church of Rome the Apostasy . . . of St Paul's Prophecy . . . With an appendix, containing an examination of the Rev. W. Burgh's attempt to vindicate the Papacy [in his "Lectures on the Second Advent"], *etc.* 1833. 12°. **1114. c. 15.**

—— The Messianic Prophecies of Isaiah; the Donnellan Lecture for 1862, with appendixes and notes: being a sequel to "The Early Prophecies of a Redeemer," *etc.* pp. xiii. 252. *Hodges, Smith & Co.: Dublin,* 1863. 8°. **3166. cc. 41.**

—— New Marginal Readings and References, adapted to the Authorized Version of the Holy Scriptures, with occasional notes . . . The four Gospels, with a Harmony. A new and improved edition. pp. viii. 307. *W. Curry, Jun. & Co.; Grant & Bolton: Dublin,* 1844. 12°. **1107. b. 22.** *Pp.* 59, 60 *are mutilated.*

—— The One Catholic and Apostolic Church. A sermon, preached . . . October 28th, 1843, *etc.* pp. 24. *W. Curry, Jun., & Co.: Dublin,* 1844. 12°. **1358. b. 50.**

—— Partaking of Christ, in connexion with the Holy Communion. A sermon, *etc.* pp. 19. *Hodges, Smith & Co.: Dublin,* 1856. 8°. **4323. cc. 26. (1.)**

—— [Another copy.] **4323. c. 44.**

—— Six Discourses on the Nature and Influence of Faith. pp. xiii. 173. *W. Curry, Jun., & Co.: Dublin,* 1835. 8°. **695. b. 23. (2.)**

—— Tracts for the Church . . . First and second series. Second thousand. pp. 68. *R. M. Tims: Dublin,* 1838. 8°. **4422. h. 16. (8.)**

—— Truth Out of Place the Most Dangerous Error. Seven letters to a clergyman in reference to the controversy between Protestants and Romanists, occasioned by the late secessions to the Church of Rome. pp. viii. 122. *Madden & Oldham: Dublin,* 1858. 8°. **3940. b. 48.**

—— Second edition. pp. vi. 112. *Madden & Oldham: Dublin,* 1858. 8°. **3939. b. 54.**

BURGH (WILLIAM) *Esq.* William Burgh, Esquire, Appellant. Colthurst Langton, Gent. Respondent. The appellant's case. pp. 4. [*London,* 1724.] fol. **19. h. 2. (79.)**

—— William Burgh, Esq; Appellant. Colthurst Langton, Gent. Respondent. The respondents case. pp. 4. [*London,* 1724.] fol. **19. h. 2. (80.)**

BURGH (WILLIAM) *LL.D.* *See* MASON (William) *Poet.* Poems. (vol. 1. The English Garden . . . To which are added a commentary and notes by W. Burgh.) 1830, *etc.* 12°. **1465.** a. **29.**

—— *See* MASON (William) *Poet.* The English Garden . . . To which are added a commentary and notes by W. Burgh. 1783. 8°. **239.** i. **31.**

—— An Inquiry into the Belief of the Christians of the First Three Centuries respecting the One Godhead of the Father, Son, and Holy Ghost. Being a sequel to A Scriptural Confutation of the Rev. Mr. Lindsey's late Apology. pp. xi. 472. *Printed for the Author: York,* 1778. 8°. **4224.** d. **1.** (**2.**)

—— A Letter to the Reverend Theophilus Lindsey. [In reference to his " Apology." By W. Burgh ?] pp. 24. 1778. 8°. *See* LINDSEY (Theophilus) **4226.** bb. **25.**

—— A Scriptural Confutation of the Arguments against the One Godhead of the Father, Son, and Holy Ghost, produced by the Reverend Mr. Lindsey in his late Apology. By a Layman [i.e. W. Burgh]. pp. v. 244. 1774. 8°. *See* LAYMAN. **4105.** b. **13.** (**4.**)

—— [Another copy.] **1120.** d. **11.**

—— The second edition. pp. v. iv. 244. *Printed for the Author: York,* 1775. 8°. **479.** b. **22.** (**3.**)

—— The third edition. pp. iv. 244. *A. Leathley: Dublin,* 1775. 8°. **4225.** bb. **77.** (**2.**)

—— Third edition. pp. x. 274. *Printed for the Author: York,* 1779. 8°. **4224.** d. **1.** (**1.**)

—— *See* FISHER (Joseph) *Vicar of Drax, Yorkshire.* Remarks upon the Remarker [i.e. A. Temple] on a late publication by a Layman [i.e. " A Scriptural Confutation," by W. Burgh], *etc.* 1775. 8°. **4372.** f. **9.** (**2.**)

—— *See* LAYMAN. Remarks on a late publication, intitled, " A Scriptural Confutation of the Arguments against the One Godhead of the Father, Son, and Holy Ghost, produced by the Reverend Mr. Lindsey in his late Apology. By a Layman." In an address to the Author [i.e. W. Burgh]. By a member of the Church of Christ [i.e. Anthony Temple]. 1775. 8°. **4225.** d. **17.**

—— —— 1775. 8°. **4225.** d. **18.**

—— *See* LAYMAN. Theological Doubts . . . interspersed with a defence of the one personality of the Supreme Being ; from the attack of W. Burgh, Esq., in his " Scriptural Confutation," *etc.* 1841. 8°. **1120.** e. **27.**

BURGHAH (EDWARD) *See* BURGHALL.

BURGHALL (EDWARD) Providence Improved. A manuscript by Ed. Burghah—Burghall—the Puritanical Vicar of Acton. Begun in 1628, and ended 1663. *See* BARLOW (Thomas W.) Cheshire, *etc.* 1855. 8°. **10804.** c. **16.**

—— [Another edition.] *See* MALBON (Thomas) Memorials of the Civil War in Cheshire, *etc.* 1889. 8°. [*Record Society for Lancashire and Cheshire.* vol. 19.] Ac. **8121.**

BURGHARD (FRÉDÉRIC FRANÇOIS) *See* CHATELIN (Charles) and MARTEL (T. de) Wounds of the Skull and Brain . . . Edited with a preface by F. F. Burghard, *etc.* 1918. 8°. **07305.** ccc. **20.**

BURGHARD (FRÉDÉRIC FRANÇOIS)

—— *See* CHEYNE (*Sir* William) *Bart.*, and BURGHARD (F. F.) A Manual of Surgical Treatment. 1899, *etc.* 8°. **7481.** k. **8.**

—— —— 1904, *etc.* 8°. **7481.** dd. **2.**

—— —— 1912, *etc.* 8°. **7481.** dd. **11.**

—— *See* LERICHE (R.) The Treatment of Fractures . . . Edited, with a preface, by F. F. Burghard. 1918. 8°. **07305.** ccc. **8.**

—— *See* SENCERT (L.) Wounds of the Vessels . . . Edited with a preface by F. F. Burghard, *etc.* 1918. 8°. **07305.** ccc. **19.**

—— A System of Operative Surgery. By various authors. Edited by F. F. Burghard. 4 vol. *Oxford University Press ; Hodder & Stoughton: London,* 1909. 8°. [*Oxford Medical Publications.*] **20036.a.1/71.**

—— New edition. 5 vol. *Oxford University Press ; Hodder & Stoughton: London,* 1914. 8°. [*Oxford Medical Publications.*] **20036.a.1/529.**

BURGHARD (FRÉDÉRIC FRANÇOIS) and **KANAVEL** (ALLEN BUCKNER)

—— Oxford Loose-Leaf Surgery. By various authors. Edited by F. F. Burghard and A. B. Kanavel. 5 vol. *Oxford University Press: New York,* 1919, 20. 8°. [*Oxford Medical Publications.*] **20036.a.1/463.**

BURGHARD (HENRI) Essai sur Mahomet et la dogmatique du Coran. Thèse, *etc.* pp. 55. *Strasbourg,* 1862. 8°. **3678.** bb. **11.** (**8.**)

BURGHARDI (JOHANNES CHRISTIANUS) Dissertatio medica inauguralis de opio, *etc.* *Praes.* G. E. Hamberger. pp. 32. *Ienae,* [1749.] 4°. B. **28.** (**7.**)

BURGHARDT (C. F.) *See* BIBLE.—*Gospels.* [*Eskimo.—Labrador dialect.*] The Gospels according to St. Matthew, St. Mark, St. Luke, and St. John, *etc.* [Edited by C. F. Burghardt.] 1813. 12°. **842.** a. **13.**

BURGHARDT (CHARLES A.) Sewage and its purification. Paper, *etc.* pp. 18. *Biggs & Co.: London,* 1892. 8°. **8709.** c. **10.** (**10.**)

BURGHARDT (ERNESTUS GOTTHILF) Dissertatio inauguralis medica de fonticulis caute occludendis, *etc.* *Praes.* J. H. Schulze. pp. 32. *Halae Magdeburgicae,* [1741.] 4°. **7306.** f. **10.** (**29.**)

BURGHARDT (ERNST) *See* BURGHARDT (Johann E.)

BURGHARDT (GEORG THEODOR AUGUST) Johanna Gray. Ein Trauerspiel in fünf Aufzügen. [In verse.] pp. 214. *Bonn,* 1866. 12°. **11746.** aaa. **16.**

BURGHARDT (GOTTHARD) Fliegerwetterkunde. Meteorologisches Merkbuch, *etc.* pp. 131. pl. 8. *Berlin,* 1927. 8°. [*Bibliothek für Luftschiffahrt und Flugtechnik.* Bd. 26.] **08767.** d. **1/26.**

BURGHARDT (HENRY D.) Machine Tool Operation. 2 pt. *McGraw-Hill Book Co.: New York,* 1919, 22. 8°. **8764.** de. **6.**

—— [Another edition.] 2 pt. *McGraw-Hill Book Co.: New York & London,* [1936, 37.] 8°. **08769.** aa. **41.**

BURGHARDT (HENRY D.)

—— Machine Tool Operation. (Third edition.—Pt. 2. By H. D. Burghardt and Aaron Axelrod.) 2 pt. *McGraw-Hill Book Co.: New York & London*, [1941, 54.] 8°. **8774.** de. **8.**

—— [Another issue.] Machine Tool Operation . . . Third edition. pt. 2. *McGraw-Hill Publishing Co.: London; printed in U.S.A.*, 1954. 8°. **8774.** e. **35.**

—— Machine Tool Operation . . . By H. D. Burghardt and Aaron Axelrod . . . Fourth edition. (pt. 2. [By] H. D. Burghardt, A. Axelrod and James Anderson.) 2 pt. *McGraw-Hill Book Co.: New York*, [1953, 60.] 8°. 8778. f. 9.

—— [Another issue.] Machine Tool Operation . . . Fourth edition. *McGraw-Hill Publishing Co.: London; printed in U.S.A.*, 1953- . 8°. W.P. c. **439.**

—— [A reissue.] Machine Tool Operation . . . Fourth edition. (Third printing.) *McGraw-Hill Book Co.: New York*, [1955- .] 8°. **8774.** de. **50.**

BURGHARDT (JOHANN ERNST) **Über den Einfluss des Englischen auf das Anglonormannische. pp. xii. 109. *Halle*, 1906. 8°. [*Studien zur englischen Philologie.* Hft. 24.] 12981. f. 23.**

BURGHARDT (JOSEPH) Vademecum von Rohitsch-Sauerbrunn, mit drei lithographirten Tafeln . . . Herausgegeben von Dr. J. Burghardt. pp. 88. *Wien*, 1868. 8°. **7470.** ee. **5.**

BURGHARDT (OSWALD)

—— *See* also KLEN (Yu.) *pseud.* [i.e. O. Burhardt.]

—— *See* DICKENS (Charles) [*Oliver Twist.*] Олівер Твіст, *etc.* [With an introduction by O. Burhardt.] 1929. 8°. **012631.** s. **1.**

—— Die Gegenwartliteratur der Westukraine. *See* UKRAINIAN LITERATURE. Ukrainische Literatur im Dienste ihrer Nation, *etc.* [1938.] 8°. **11864.** b. **33.**

BURGHARDUS (FRANCISCUS) *See* BURCHARD (Franz) *pseud.* [i.e. A. Erstenberger.]

BURGHART (GOTTFRIED HEINRICH) *See* **MELLEN** (J. von) **Jacobi a Mellen . . . Series regum Hungariae e nummis aureis . . . ins Teutsche gebracht; mit Anmerckungen erläutert; bis auf unsre Zeiten fortgesetzet; und . . . ansehnlich vermehret, von D. G. H. Burghart. 1750. 4°. 812. e. 26.**

—— D. Gottfried Heinrich Burgharts . . . freundliches Schreiben an Herrn D. Balthasar Ludwig Tralles . . . worinnen die Nothwendigkeit und Nutzbarkeit des Aderlassens bey denen Blattern, durch mancherley Erfahrungen bestättiget wird. pp. 46. *Breslau*, 1736. 8°. 07305. i. 1. (1.)

—— D. Gottfried Heinrich Burgharts . . . historisch-physicalisch- und medicinische Abhandlung, von den warmen Bädern bey Land-Ecke . . . Mit Kupfern. pp. 456. *Breslau*, 1744. 4°. 7470. ff. 39. (1.)

—— Gothofr. Henr. Burgharti . . . Iter Sabothicum, das ist: ausführliche Beschreibung einiger An. 1733. und die folgenden Jahre auf den Zothen-Berg gethanen Reisen . . . Mit Kupffern. pp. 176. *Bresslau & Leipzig*, 1736. 8°. 10250. a. 51. (1.)

—— [Another copy.] **980.** c. **15.**

BURGHART (GOTTFRIED HEINRICH)

—— Medicorum Silesiacorum Satyræ, quæ varias observationes, casus, experimenta, tentamina, ex omni medicinæ ambitu petita exhibent. Specimen I (-VI). Cum figuris. [By G. H. Burghart.] 6 pt. 1736-38. 8°. *See* SILESIAN PHYSICIANS. **1169.** f. **10, 11.**

—— [Another copy.] **1169.** f. **12–14.**

—— Gottfried Heinrich Burgharts . . . Sendschreiben an einen guten Freund, betreffend einen zweyleibigen sonderbaren gestalten Mann Sigr. A. Martinelli, aus Cremona, und eine künstliche junge Posituрmacherin, desgleichen verschiedene andre in die Naturgeschichte Schlesiens und die Arzneykunst einschlagende lesenswürdige Sachen. Mit einem Kupfer. pp. 57. *Frankfurth a. d. O.*, 1752. 8°. **07305.** i. **9. (1.)**

BURGHART (GOTTLOB EHRENHOLDT) Dissertatio inauguralis medica de naturæ lucta cum morbo et medico, *etc. Praes.* M. Alberti. pp. 40. *Halæ Magdeburgicæ*, 1727. 4°. **1179.** f. **11. (14.)**

BURGHART (HERMANN) Die Volksschullehrer dürfen nicht Staatsdiener werden. Ein Ferienschriftchen. pp. 24. *Nordhausen*, 1848. 8°. **8305.** d. **49. (8.)**

BURGHARTUS (CHRISTOPHORUS GOTTEHR) De malo sic dicto hypochondriaco . . . disseret C. G. Burghartus, *etc. Praes.* C. Vater. pp. 36. *Wittenbergæ*, [1703.] 4°. T. **558. (16.)**

BURGHARTUS (GOTHOFREDUS HENRICUS) *See* BURGHART (Gottfried H.)

BURGHAUS (CONRAD JOHANN AUGUST VON) *Count.* Briefe eines schlesischen Grafen [i.e. C. J. A. von Burghaus] an einen kurländischen Edelmann, den Adel betreffend. Herausgegeben von Heinrich Würtzer. pp. 192. *Altona*, 1795. 8°. **1133.** a. **27.**

BURGHAUSEN (HANNS WILLHELM SYLVIUS VON) *Count. See* BURGHAUSS.

BURGHAUSER (GUSTAV) Germanische Nominalflexion auf vergleichender Grundlage. pp. 28. *Wien*, 1888. 8°. **12964.** d. **42.**

—— Die germanischen Endsilbenvocale und ihre Vertretung im Gotischen, Altwestnordischen, Angelsächsischen und Althochdeutschen . . . Sonderabdruck aus dem XII. Jahresberichte der deutschen Staatsrealschule in Prag-Karolinenthal. pp. 17. *Wien*, 1888. 8°. **12902.** i. **28.**

—— Indogermanische Praesensbildung im Germanischen. Ein Capitel vergleichender Grammatik. pp. 55. *Wien*, 1887. 8°. **12901.** i. **28. (6.)**

BURGHAUSS (HANNS WILLHELM SYLVIUS VON) *Count.* Die wesentliche Acten-Stücke des merkwürdigen Processes der Gräflich Burghausischen Agnaten gegen den Herrn Grafen von Burghausen auf Sulau, *etc.* pp. 126. [*Breslau*,] 1793. 4°. **5505.** d. **5.**

BURGHCLERE, HERBERT COULSTOUN, *Baron. See* GARDNER.

——, WINIFRED ANNE HENRIETTA CHRISTINA, *Baroness. See* GARDNER.

BURGHEIM (ALFRED) Der Kirchenbau des 18. Jahrhunderts im Nordelbischen . . . Mit einem Anhang von 132 Abbildungen, *etc.* 2 Tl. *Hamburg*, 1915. 8°. **7816.** pp. **17.**

BURGHEIM (JULIUS) Sammlung leicht auszuführender Grab-Monumente, aufgenommen auf den vorzüglichsten Kirchhöfen Deutschlands und Frankreichs. [Plates, with explanatory text.] *Bielefeld*, 1846. 4°. **1269.** f. **16.**

BURGHEIM (SALOMO HIRSCH) *See* HIRSCH BURGHEIM.

BURGHER ASSOCIATION. Burgher Association of Ceylon. *See* CEYLON.

BURGHER SECEDERS. Letters on the Burgher and Anti-Burgher Seceders, with remarks on the proposed union betwixt these numerous and respectable bodies. [Signed: R.] 1819. 8°. *See* R. **4175. bb. 84.**

BURGHER UNION. Burgher Union of Colombo. *See* COLOMBO.

BÜRGHER. [For the German surname of this form:] *See* BUERGHER.

BURGHERR (WILLI) Johannes Mahler, ein schweizerischer Dramatiker der Gegenreformation. pp. 166. *Bern,* 1925. 8°. **011805. k. 13.**

BURGHERS (MICHAEL) *See* HYDE (Thomas) Syntagma dissertationum . . . Cum appendice de lingua Sinensi aliisque linguis orientalibus una cum quamplurimis tabulis æneis [*sic*] quibus earum characteres exhibentur, *etc.* [The plates engraved by M. Burghers.] 1767. 4°. **14003. h. 15.**

BURGHERSDORP.—*Burghersdorp Club.* The Rules and Regulations of the Burghersdorp Club. pp. 8. *Argus Printing & Publishing Co.: Cape Town,* 1893. 8°. **10095. dd. 9.**

BURGHERSDORP CLUB. *See* BURGHERSDORP.

BURGHERSH. Burghersh, or the Pleasures of a country life. Illustrated, *etc.* pp. 90. *Partridge, Oakey & Co.: London,* 1855. 8°. **10351. e. 5.**

BURGHERSH, JOHN, *Lord.* *See* FANE (J.) *11th Earl of Westmorland.*

——, PRISCILLA ANNE WELLESLEY, *Lady.* *See* FANE (P. A. W.) *Countess of Westmorland.*

BURGHESIUS (CAESAR) Curationes quædam medicæ ad recentiorum mentem exaratæ. pp. 166. *Ticini Regii,* 1752. 8°. **7383*. b. 16. (3.)**

BURGHESIUS (CAMILLUS) *Cardinal.* *See* PAUL V., *Pope* [C. Borghese].

BURGHESIUS (DOMINICUS ANDREAS) [For decrees issued by D. A. Burghesius as Minister General of the Friars Minor Conventual:] *See* FRANCISCANS.

BURGHESIUS (JOANNES BAPTISTA) *Duke di Rignano.* *See* BORGHESE (Giovanni Battista)

BURGHESIUS (LUDOVICUS) *Senensis.* Ludouici Burghesi Senensis Repetitio sup legē primaȝ .ff. đ iud. [With woodcuts.] *Per Simeonem Nicolai: Saenis,* 1516. 4°. **5306. aa. 2.**

BURGHESIUS (MARCUS ANTONIUS) *Prince di Sulmona.* *See* BORGHESE (Marco Antonio)

BURGHILL.—*Hereford County and City Lunatic Asylum.* The First [*etc.*] Annual Report of the Committee of Visitors of the Hereford County & City Lunatic Asylum (Hereford County and City Mental Hospital) . . . for the year 1872 [*etc.*]. *Hereford,* 1873- . 8°. P.P. **2707. hk.**
Imperfect; wanting the reports for the years 1887, 1900, 1901, 1908, 1913, 1915.

BURGHILL (FRANCIS) [For Heraldic Visitations made by F. Burghill:] *See* ENGLAND.—*College of Arms.* [*Visitations.*]

BURGHILL (ROBERT) *See* BURHIL.

BURGHLEY, WILLIAM, *Baron.* *See* CECIL.

BURGHLEY HOUSE. A Guide to Burghley House, Northamptonshire, the seat of the Marquis of Exeter; containing a catalogue of all the paintings, antiquities, &c. With biographical notices of the artists. [By Thomas Blore. With plates.] pp. x. 292. *John Drakard: Stamford,* 1815. 8°. **578. e. 19.**

—— [Another copy.] **L.P.** **578. g. 11.**
With an additional titlepage, engraved.

—— [Another copy.] **L.P.** **191. a. 13.**

—— [Another copy.] **L.P.** G. **3479.**

—— [Another edition.] pp. 112. *J. Drakard: Stamford,* [1815 ?] 8°. **10358. ccc. 3.**
Without the biographical notices of the artists.

—— A History or Description, general and circumstantial, of Burghley House, the Seat of the Right Honourable the Earl of Exeter. [By J. Horn.] pp. vii. 205. *J. & W. Eddowes: Shrewsbury,* 1797. 8°. **578. e. 18.**

—— [Another copy.] **290. g. 46.**

BURGHLEY (FELTHAM) *pseud.* [i.e. CHARLES AUGUSTUS WARD.] England Subsists by Miracle. pp. 109. *James Blackwood: London,* 1859. 8°. **8138. df. 24.**

—— Preaching, Prosing, & Puseyism, with other Peas of the Pod. pp. 119. *J. F. Hope: London,* 1858. 8°. **4108. b. 94.**

—— Sir Edwin Gilderoy, a ballad. [With an introductory essay.] pp. cxix. 86. *John Chapman: London,* 1856. 8°. **11649. d. 25.**

—— Sonnets. pp. xli. 152. *Longman & Co.: London,* 1855. 16°. **11648. a. 14.**

—— The Sutherland Clearance: a ballad. pp. 14. *Archibald Sinclair: Glasgow,* 1860. 12°. **11650. cc. 13. (8.)**

BURGHOFF (HILGERUS) Elucidatio exemptionis et jurisdictionis sacri ordinis Cisterciensis, in qua summorum pontificum Bullæ . . . recentiorumque doctorum sententiæ circa Cisterciensium exemptionem & jurisdictionem . . . exponuntur, *etc.* pp. 229. *Ad Monasterium de Waldsassio,* 1729. 8°. **4071. aaa. 11.**

BURGHOLD (IDA) *See* LEOPOLD (J. C. F.) J. C. F. Leopold . . . sein Leben und sein Process wegen Ermordung der I. Burghold, *etc.* 1869. 8°. **1414. i. 28. (3.)**

BURGHOLD (JULIUS) *See* WAGNER (W. R.) [*Die Meistersinger von Nürnberg.*] Die Meistersinger von Nürnberg. Text mit den hauptsächlichsten Leitmotiven und einer Notentafel. Herausgegeben von Dr. J. Burghold. 1904. 8°. **11747. ee. 73.**

—— *See* WAGNER (W. R.) [*Parsifal.*] Parsifal . . . Herausgegeben von Dr. J. Burghold. [1897.] 8°. Hirsch **5668. (2.)**

—— *See* WAGNER (W. R.) [*Der Ring des Nibelungen.*] Das Rheingold . . . (Die Walküre.—Siegfried.—Götterdämmerung.) Herausgegeben von Dr. J. Burghold. [1897.] 8°. Hirsch **5669.**

—— Methodische Musik-Hermeneutik. (Sonderabdruck aus den Preussischen Jahrbüchern.) *Berlin,* 1920. 8°. Hirsch **5384.**

BURGHOLD (KARL SEELKOPF) *See* SEELKOPF-BURGHOLD (K.)

BURGHOLZER (JOSEPH) Heinrich Brauns Thatenleben und Schriften. Ein Beytrag zur baier'schen Schul- und Gelehrtengeschichte. Von einem dankbaren Zögling seines Zeitalters. [With a portrait.] pp. 67. *München*, 1793. 8°. **10704.** b. **35.** (**3.**)

—— Stadtgeschichte von München, als Wegweiser für Fremde und Reisende, *etc.* 2 Bdchn. pp. xlii. 519. *München*, 1796. 12°. **10231.** aa. **37.**

BURGHOLZHAUSEN (AUGUST FRIEDRICH MARSCHALL VON) *Count.* *See* MARSCHALL VON BURGHOLZHAUSEN.

BURGHOORN (ISAAC) *See* BURCHOORN.

BURGHOPE (GEORGE) Autarchy: or, the Art of self-government, in a moral essay, *etc.* [The epistle dedicatory signed: G. B., i.e. G. Burghope.] pp. 158. 1691. 8°. *See* B., G. **8406.** bbb. **34.**

—— [Another copy.] **1030.** f. **24.**

—— Ἀυταρχια, or the Art of self-government . . . The second edition, corrected. [The epistle dedicatory signed: G. B., i.e. G. Burghope.] pp. 130. 1713. 8°. *See* B., G. **1030.** d. **12.**

—— A Discourse of Religious Assemblies: wherein the nature and necessity of Divine Worship is explain'd and asserted, against negligence & prophaneness, *etc.* pp. 184. *For Tho. Bennet: London*, 1697. 8°. **3475.** a. **39.**

—— Spiritual Hymns upon Divine and Practical Subjects. *See* GROOME (John) The Golden Cordial, *etc.* 1705. 12°. **3457.** dd. **18.**

BURGHOPE (M.) The Government of the Passions. A sermon, *etc.* pp. 16. *J. Wyat: London*, 1701. 4°. **4474.** g. **11.**

BURGHT (RAYMOND VANDER)

—— Joseph François, peintre belge, émule de David, 1759–1851, *etc.* [With reproductions and the text of " Premier voiage en Italie et en Allemagne " and " Notes pour servir à mon second voiage," by J. François.] pp. 215. *Bruxelles*, 1948. 8°. **010665.** i. **110.**

BURGHT (WILHELMUS VAN DER) Disputatio theologica exhibens sacramentorum considerationem generaliorem. Prima et secunda, *etc.* *Praes.* B. de Moor. pp. 23. *Lugduni Batavorum*, 1750. 4°. T. **2189.** (**10.**)

BURGHWALLIS.

—— The Parish Register of Burghwallis, Yorks . . . Transcribed, edited and indexed by . . . C. E. Whiting. pp. vi. 82. *Leeds*, 1947. 8°. [*Publications of the Yorkshire Parish Register Society.* vol. 116.] Ac. **8136.**

BÜRGI ( ) [For the German surname of this form:] *See* BUERGI.

BÜRGIN ( ) [For the German surname of this form:] *See* BUERGIN.

BURGIN (CYRIL)

—— A Picture Book of Free Spanish Composition in Spanish. pp. 30. *Hachette: London*, [1953.] 8°. **12944.** g. **10.**

BURGIN (*Right Hon.* EDWARD LESLIE) Administration of Foreign Estates. Being the principles of private international law relating to the administration of the estates of deceased persons, *etc.* pp. xxiv. 271. *Stevens & Sons: London*, 1913. 8°. **6916.** e. **12.**

—— British Industry. Its problems and purpose. An address, *etc.* pp. 15. *Liberal National Organization: London*, 1944. 8°. **8290.** h. **6.**

BURGIN (*Right Hon.* EDWARD LESLIE) and **FLETCHER** (ERIC GEORGE MOLYNEUX)

—— The Students' Conflict of Laws. Being an introduction to the study of private international law, based on Dicey. pp. xvii. 336. *Stevens & Sons; Sweet & Maxwell: London*, 1928. 8°. **6916.** d. **18.**

—— Second edition. pp. xvi. 344. *Stevens & Sons; Sweet & Maxwell: London*, 1934. 8°. **2227.** d. **17.**

—— Third edition. pp. xvi. 347. *Stevens & Sons; Sweet & Maxwell: London*, 1937. 8°. **6915.** f. **22.**

BURGIN (GEORGE BROWN) All Things Come Round. pp. 288. *Hutchinson & Co.: London*, [1929.] 8°. NN. **15419.**

—— Allandale's Daughters. pp. 320. *Hutchinson & Co.: London*, [1928.] 8°. NN. **14620.**

—— The Belle of Santiago. pp. viii. 320. *Hutchinson & Co.: London*, 1911. 8°. **012618.** bb. **13.**

—— The Belles of Vaudroy. pp. 335. *Hutchinson & Co.: London*, 1906. 8°. **012633.** b. **13.**

—— The Bread of Tears. pp. 319. *John Long: London*, 1899. 8°. **012643.** h. **44.**

—— [Another edition.] pp. 156. *London*, [1906.] 8°. [*Newnes Sixpenny Novels.*] **012604.f.1/6.**

—— The Cattle Man. pp. viii. 246. *Grant Richards: London*, 1898. 8°. **012623.** ff. **31.**

—— [Another edition.] pp. 96. *Hodder & Stoughton: London*, [1914.] 8°. **012600.** b. **54.**

—— Cyrilla Seeks Herself. pp. 288. *Hutchinson & Co.: London*, [1922.] 8°. NN. **7976.**

—— The Dale of Dreams. pp. 284. *Hutchinson & Co.: London*, [1927.] 8°. NN. **13262.**

—— The Dance at the Four Corners. pp. 202. *J. W. Arrowsmith: Bristol*, [1894.] 8°. **012629.** de. **9.**

—— The Devil's Due. A romance. pp. 315. *Hutchinson & Co.: London*, 1905. 8°. **012631.** c. **50.**

—— Diana of Dreams. pp. viii. 329. *Hutchinson & Co.: London*, 1910. 8°. **012623.** b. **7.**

—— " Dickie Dilver." pp. 336. *Hutchinson & Co.: London*, 1912. 8°. NN. **16.**

—— The Duke's Stratagem. pp. 288. *Wright & Brown: London*, 1931. 8°. NN. **18130.**

—— The Duke's Twins. pp. 339. *Hutchinson & Co.: London*, 1914. 8°. NN. **2119.**

—— Eternal Justice. pp. 286. *Wright & Brown: London*, [1932.] 8°. NN. **19536.**

—— The Faithful Fool. pp. 302. *Books: London*, [1921.] 8°. [" *Sign of the Rose* " *Series.*] **012600.** bb. **3/10.**

—— Fanuela. pp. 304. *Hutchinson & Co.: London*, 1907. 8°. **012625.** aaa. **1.**

—— A Fateful Fraud. pp. 283. *Wright & Brown: London*, [1934.] 8°. NN. **22934.**

—— The Final Test. pp. 287. *Hutchinson & Co.: London*, [1928.] 8°. NN. **14237.**

—— Fleurette of Four Corners. pp. 288. *Hutchinson & Co.: London*, [1925.] 8°. NN. **10609.**

BURGIN (George Brown)

—— Flowers of Fire. pp. 287. *Eveleigh Nash: London,* 1908. 8°. **012625**. aaa. **2**.

—— The Forest Lure. A fantasy. pp. 280. *Hutchinson & Co.: London,* [1926.] 8°. NN. **12065**.

—— Fortune's Footballs. pp. viii. 255. *C. A. Pearson: London,* 1897. 8°. **012625**. l. **7**.

—— Galahad's Garden. pp. vii. 336. *Eveleigh Nash: London,* 1908. 8°. **012625**. aaa. **3**.

—— A Game of Hearts. A romance. pp. 348. *Hutchinson & Co.: London,* 1915. 8°. NN. **2917**.

—— Gascoigne's Ghost. pp. 241. *Neville Beeman: London,* [1896.] 8°. [*New Vagabond Library.* no. 1.] **012600**. e. **45/1**.

—— A Gentle Despot. pp. 248. *Hutchinson & Co.: London,* [1919.] 8°. NN. **5333**.

—— The Girl who Got Out. pp. viii. 315. *Hutchinson & Co.: London,* 1916. 8°. NN. **3830**.

—— A Goddess of Gray's Inn. pp. 311. *C. A. Pearson: London,* 1901. 8°. **012639**. aaa. **41**.

—— The Golden Penny. pp. 288. *Wright & Brown: London,* 1937. 8°. NN. **27237**.

—— The Greater Gain. pp. 307. *Hutchinson & Co.: London,* 1917. 8°. NN. **4477**.

—— The Hate that Lasts. pp. 287. *Hutchinson & Co.: London,* [1925.] 8°. NN. **11310**.

—— The Herb of Healing. A romance. pp. 347. *Hutchinson & Co.: London,* 1915. 8°. NN. **2618**.

—— The Hermit of Bonneville. pp. vii. 304. *Grant Richards: London,* 1904. 8°. **012630**. aa. **42**.

—— The Hermits of Gray's Inn. pp. 291. *C. A. Pearson: London,* 1899. 8°. **012642**. aaa. **3**.

—— His Lordship, and others. pp. 209. *Henry & Co.: London,* [1893.] 8°. [*Whitefriars Library of Wit and Humour.*] **012202**. g. **2/3**.

—— The Honour of Four Corners. pp. 288. *Wright & Brown: London,* 1934. 8°. NN. **21839**.

—— The House of Fiske. pp. 288. *Hutchinson & Co.: London,* [1927.] 8°. NN. **12538**.

—— The Hundredth Man. pp. 284. *Hutchinson & Co.: London,* [1927.] 8°. NN. **13292**.

—— The Hut by the River. pp. viii. 312. *Hutchinson & Co.: London,* 1916. 8°. NN. **3504**.

—— The Ills Men Do. pp. 287. *Wright & Brown: London,* 1937. 8°. NN. **28383**.

—— The Judge of the Four Corners. pp. 344. *A. D. Innes & Co.: London,* 1896. 8°. **012627**. h. **14**.

—— The King of Four Corners. pp. 321. *Hutchinson & Co.: London,* 1910. 8°. **012623**. b. **9**.

—— The Kiss. pp. 288. *Hutchinson & Co.: London,* [1924.] 8°. NN. **10433**.

—— The Ladies of the Manor. pp. viii. 317. *Grant Richards: London,* 1903. 8°. **012628**. b. **33**.

—— Lady Mary's Money. pp. 288. *Hutchinson & Co.: London,* 1918. 8°. NN. **4731**.

BURGIN (George Brown)

—— A Lady of Spain. pp. 334. *Hutchinson & Co.: London,* 1911. 8°. **012618**. bb. **14**.

—— The Land of Silence. pp. vii. 316. *Eveleigh Nash: London,* 1904. 8°. **012630**. dd. **27**.

—— The Lord of Little Langton. A modern romance. pp. 285. *Hutchinson & Co.: London,* [1924.] 8°. NN. **10902**.

—— Love and the Locusts. A romance. pp. 285. *Hutchinson & Co.: London,* [1922.] 8°. NN. **7553**.

—— The Love that Lasts. pp. 320. *Hodder & Stoughton: London,* [1913.] 8°. NN. **1127**.

—— The Man Behind. A Turkish romance. pp. 287. *Hutchinson & Co.: London,* [1923.] 8°. NN. **8867**.

—— The Man from Turkey. pp. 288. *Hutchinson & Co.: London,* [1921.] 8°. NN. **7247**.

—— The Man in the Corner. pp. 287. *Wright & Brown: London,* [1939.] 8°. NN. **29730**.

—— The Man who Died. A middle-class comedy. [A novel.] pp. 280. *R. A. Everett & Co.: London,* 1903. 8°. **012628**. d. **4**.

—— Manetta's Marriage. pp. 288. *Hutchinson & Co.: London,* [1922.] 8°. NN. **8304**.

—— Many Memories. [With a portrait.] pp. 288. *Hutchinson & Co.: London,* 1922. 8°. **010855**. b. **34**.

—— The Marble City. pp. 304. *Hutchinson & Co.: London,* 1905. 8°. **012630**. d. **44**.

—— Mariette's Lovers. pp. 287. *Hutchinson & Co.: London,* [1929.] 8°. NN. **14853**.

—— Memoirs of a Clubman. [With a portrait.] pp. 287. *Hutchinson & Co.: London,* [1921.] 8°. **010855**. dd. **16**.

—— More Memoirs, and some Travels. pp. xvii. 335. *Hutchinson & Co.: London,* 1922. 8°. **010855**. b. **32**.

—— Nitana. pp. 287. *Hutchinson & Co.: London,* [1928.] 8°. NN. **13729**.

—— "Old Man's" Marriage. pp. 304. *Grant Richards: London,* 1897. 8°. **012625**. de. **16**.

—— [Another edition.] pp. 128. *Hodder & Stoughton: London,* [1914.] 8°. **012600**. b. **30**.

—— One Traveller Returns. pp. 288. *Wright & Brown: London,* [1931.] 8°. NN. **18598**.

—— The Only World. pp. 301. *Hutchinson & Co.: London,* 1906. 8°. **012632**. c. **32**.

—— Out of the Swim. pp. 287. *Hutchinson & Co.: London,* [1930.] 8°. NN. **16179**.

—— Peggy the Pilgrim. pp. 332. *Hutchinson & Co.: London,* 1907. 8°. **012633**. dd. **34**.

—— The Person in the House. pp. 317. *Hurst & Blackett: London,* 1900. 8°. **012641**. c. **16**.

—— Pierrepont's Daughters. pp. 286. *Hutchinson & Co.: London,* [1935.] 8°. NN. **24761**.

—— Pilgrims of Circumstance. pp. 271. *Hutchinson & Co.: London,* 1920. 8°. NN. **6040**.

—— A Pious Fraud. pp. 288. *Wright & Brown: London,* 1938. 8°. NN. **29125**.

BURGIN (George Brown)

—— A Poor Millionaire. pp. 284. *Wright & Brown: London*, 1933. 8°. **NN. 19903.**

—— The Puller of Strings. An Ottawa Valley romance. pp. 311. *Hutchinson & Co.: London*, 1917. 8°. **NN. 4184.**

—— A Rubber Princess. pp. 285. *Hutchinson & Co.: London*, [1919.] 8°. **NN. 5598.**

—— Sally's Sweetheart. A novel. pp. 288. *Hutchinson & Co.: London*, [1923.] 8°. **NN. 9074.**

—— The "Second-Sighter's" Daughter, a romance. pp. 343. *Hutchinson & Co.: London*, 1913. 8°. **NN. 681.**

—— Settled out of Court. pp. viii. 324. *C. A. Pearson: London*, 1898. 8°. **012643.** ccc. **15.**

—— The Shutters of Silence. pp. 317. *John Long: London*, [1903.] 8°. **012638.** aa. **36.**

—— [Another edition.] pp. 345. *Eveleigh Nash: London*, 1904. 8°. [*Collection of Popular Novels.*] **012602.** de. **7/3.**

—— A Simple Savage. pp. viii. 343. *Hutchinson & Co.: London*, 1909. 8°. **012623.** b. **8.**

—— The Slaves of Allah. pp. 351. *Hutchinson & Co.: London*, 1909. 8°. **012624.** d. **22.**

—— Slaves of the Ring. pp. 288. *Hutchinson & Co.: London*, [1936.] 8°. **NN. 25638.**

—— Some More Memoirs . . . With nine illustrations. pp. 319. *Hutchinson & Co.: London*, [1924.] 8°. **010856.** f. **32.**

—— A Son of Mammon. pp. 295. *John Long: London*, [1901.] 8°. **012640.** d. **10.**

—— The Spending of the Pile. pp. 288. *Hutchinson & Co.: London*, [1924.] 8°. **NN. 9527.**

—— The Throw-Back. pp. viii. 252. *Hutchinson & Co.: London*, 1918. 8°. **NN. 5093.**

—— This Son of Adam. pp. 336. *Hutchinson & Co.: London*, 1910. 8°. **012623.** b. **10.**

—— The Tiger's Claw. pp. 320. *C. A. Pearson: London*, 1900. 8°. **012641.** aa. **33.**

—— Tomalyn's Quest. pp. 314. *Innes & Co.: London*, 1896. 8°. **012626.** e. **26.**

—— The Trickster. pp. viii. 276. *Stanley Paul & Co.: London*, 1909. 8°. **012626.** aaa. **10.**

—— Tuxter's Little Maid. pp. 320. *Cassell & Co.: London*, 1895. 8°. **012628.** i. **40.**

—— [Another edition.] pp. 148. *London*, [1906.] 8°. [*Newnes Sixpenny Novels.*] **012604.f.1/5.**

—— [Another edition.] pp. 320. *Cassell & Co.: London*, 1911. 8°. **012618.** bb. **11.**

—— Uncle Jeremy. pp. 288. *Hutchinson & Co.: London*, [1920.] 8°. **NN. 6572.**

—— Uncle Patterley's Money. pp. 288. *Wright & Brown: London*, [1936.] 8°. **NN. 25065.**

—— The Vagabond's Annual . . . [Tales by various authors.] Edited by G. B. Burgin. pp. 196. *Bristol*, 1893. 8°. [*Arrowsmith's Bristol Library.* vol. 55.] **12207.** g.

BURGIN (George Brown)

—— Varick's Legacy. pp. 335. *Hutchinson & Co.: London*, 1912. 8°. **NN. 180.**

—— The Vision of Balmaine. pp. viii. 331. *Hutchinson & Co.: London*, 1911. 8°. **012618.** bb. **12.**

—— The Way Out. pp. 295. *John Long: London*, 1900. 8°. **012641.** dd. **25.**

—— [Another edition.] pp. 126. *Hodder & Stoughton: London*, 1915. 8°. **012600.** c. **72.**

—— The Wheels of Fate. pp. 284. *Wright & Brown: London*, 1933. 8°. **NN. 20980.**

—— When Dreams Come True. pp. 288. *Wright & Brown: London*, [1932.] 8°. **NN. 19658.**

—— Which Woman ? pp. 344. *Eveleigh Nash: London*, 1907. 8°. **012634.** c. **24.**

—— Who Loses Pays. pp. 284. *Wright & Brown: London*, [1935.] 8°. **NN. 23691.**

—— A Wilful Woman. pp. 324. *John Long: London*, 1902. 8°. **012637.** c. **16.**

—— Within the Gates. A romance. pp. 336. *Hutchinson & Co.: London*, 1914. 8°. **NN. 1614.**

—— The Woman without a Heart. [With a portrait.] pp. x. 310. *Alexander-Ouseley: London*, 1930. 8°. **NN. 16624.**

—— A Woman's Way. pp. 344. *Hutchinson & Co.: London*, 1908. 8°. **012625.** aaa. **4.**

—— The Wrong Woman. pp. 284. *Wright & Brown: London*, 1932. 8°. **NN. 22659.**

—— Young Deloraine. pp. 288. *Hutchinson & Co.: London*, [1926.] 8°. **NN. 11646.**

—— The Young Labelle. pp. 283. *Hutchinson & Co.: London*, [1924.] 8°. **NN. 9931.**

BURGIN (Isabel) The Web of Circumstance, *etc.* pp. 288. *J. Clarke & Co.: London*, [1908.] 8°. **012625.** aaa. **5.**

BURGIN (*Right Hon.* Leslie) *See* Burgin (*Right Hon.* Edward L.)

BURGIN (Miron)

—— *See* Washington, *D.C.—American Council of Learned Societies.—Committee on Latin American Studies.* Handbook of Latin American Studies, *etc.* (vol. 6. [*etc.*]. Edited by M. Burgin.) 1936, *etc.* 8°. Ac. **2684.** d.

—— The Economic Aspects of Argentine Federalism, 1820–1852. pp. xiv. 304. *Harvard University Press: Cambridge, Mass.*, 1946. 8°. [*Harvard Economic Studies.* vol. 78.] Ac. **2692/11.**

—— [Another copy.] The Economic Aspects of Argentine Federalism 1820–1852. *Cambridge, Mass.*, 1946. 8°. **8218.** b. **47.**

BURGINE (Darby) Victorious Newes from Ireland, being a Battail fought by the Lord of Ormond, the nineteenth day of June [1642], to the losse of two thousand of the rebels, ten miles beyond Limbrick . . . As also a Letter that was sent from the . . . Earl of Warwick . . . to Master Iohn Pym, Esquire, and presented to both Houses of Parliament, July 6. 1642. pp. 7. *For Marmaduke Boat: London*, [1642.] 4°. **E. 154. (19.)**

BURGIO (Francesco) *See* Parthenotimus (Candidus) *pseud.* [i.e. F. Burgio.]

BURGIO (Niccolò Maria) Dissertazione critico-storica sulla patria di Sant' Alberto degli Abbati . . . Seconda edizione, corretta ed accresciuta dal medesimo autore, *etc.* pp. 156. *Trapani,* 1778. fol. **664.** g. **3.**

BURGIS (Daniel) *See* Burgess (Daniel) *the Elder.*

BURGIS (Edward Ambrose) The Annals of the Church from the death of Christ. [By E. A. Burgis.] 5 vol. 1737. 8°. *See* Annals. **488.** a. **1–4.**

BURGIS (Edwin) Perils to British Trade; how to avert them. pp. xii. 251. *S. Sonnenschein & Co.: London,* 1895. 8°. **08276.** ee. **4.**

—— Third edition. pp. xvi. 270. *S. Sonnenschein & Co.: London,* 1904. 8°. **08276.** e. **70.**

BURGIS (Edwin) and **JACKSON** (William V.)

—— Fiscal Lights searching the Industrial Question. pp. 91. *Sherratt & Hughes: London, Manchester,* 1913. 8°. **8228.** aaa. **47.**

BURGIS (Paul) *See* Burges.

BURGISS (Elizabeth) Strange and wonderful News from Yowel in Surry; giving a true and just account of one Elizabeth Burgiss, who was most strangely bewitched, *etc.* pp. 6. *For J. Clarke: London,* 1681. 4°. **8630.** d. **11.**

—— [Another copy.] **8631.** d. **41.**

BÜRGISSER ( ) [For the German surname of this form:] *See* Buergisser.

BURGIUS (Alexander) *Bishop of Borgo San Sepolcro.* A. Burgii . . . Oratio. Ad illustrissimos . . . Cardinales pro nouo Pontifice eligendo, *etc.* *Apud Iunctas: Florentiæ,* 1605. 4°. **113.** b. **7.**

BURGIUS (Annas) *See* Du Bourg (Anne)

BURGIUS (Joannes Fridericus) *See* Burg (Johann Friedrich)

BURGIUS (Petrus) Petri Burgii Electorum liber; quo varios juris locos illustrandi, conciliandi, sanandi ratio tentatur. *See* Otto (E.) Thesaurus juris Romani, *etc.* tom. 1. 1725, *etc.* fol. **499.** d. **2.**

—— [Another edition.] *See* Otto (E.) Thesaurus juris Romani, *etc.* tom. 1. 1733, *etc.* fol. **5206.** h. **1.**

—— [Another edition.] *See* Otto (E.) Thesaurus juris Romani, *etc.* tom. 1. 1741, *etc.* fol. **5254.** f. **8.**

BURGK (Engelbertus A) De quatuor virtutibus cardinalibus disputatio prima. *Praes.* J. Thomasius. *Typis J. Wittigau: Lipsiæ,* [1665.] 4°. **525.** e. **17.** (4.)

BURGK (Johannes Ludovicus) Dissertatio academica, de poenis quibusdam juris romani in Germaniam recipiendis, *etc.* *Praes.* H. E. Kestner. pp. 30. *Rintelii,* [1710.] 4°. **897.** d. **5.** (**5.**)

—— [Another copy.] **5512.a.4.**

BURGK (Max Schmid) *See* Schmid-Burgk.

BURGKHARDT (Johannes) Das Erzgebirge. Eine orometrisch-anthropogeographische Studie, *etc.* [With a map.] pp. 79. *Stuttgart,* 1888. 8°. [*Forschungen zur deutschen Landes- und Volkskunde.* Bd. 3. Hft. 3.] **10235.** de. **3.** (**3.**)

BURGKLEHNER (Matthias) *See* Rangger (L.) Matthias Burgklehner. Beiträge zur Biographie und Untersuchung zu seinen historischen und kartographischen Arbeiten. 1906, *etc.* 8°. [*Forschungen und Mitteilungen zur Geschichte Tirols und Vorarlbergs.* Jahrg. 3. Hft. 3; Jahrg. 4. Hft. 1.] Ac. **761.**

—— Thesaurus historiarum. 2 tom. *Apud Ioannem Agricolam, sumptibus Auctoris: Oeniponti,* 1602, 04. fol. C. **82.** f. **6.**
Tom. 2 has the imprint: " Apud Danielem Agricolam."

BÜRGKLY ( ) [For the German surname of this form:] *See* Buergkly.

BURGKMAIER (Hans) *See* Burgkmair.

BURGKMAIR (Hans) *the Elder.* *See* Bible.—*New Testament.* [*German.*] Das neu Testament. [With woodcuts by H. Burgkmair.] 1523. fol. **3041.** g. **11.**

—— *See* Burkhard (Arthur) Hans Burgkmair d. Ä., *etc.* [With reproductions.] [1934.] 4°. **7874.c.74.**

—— *See* Geiler (J.) *von Kaisersberg.* Das buch granatapfel, im latin genant Malogranatus, *etc.* [With woodcuts by H. Burgkmair.] 1510. fol. C. **64.** f. **13.**

—— *See* Geiler (J.) *von Kaisersberg.* Predigen teütsch vnd vil gutter leeren, *etc.* [With woodcuts, one signed: H. B. G., i.e. Hans Burgkmair.] 1510. fol. Dept. of Prints & Drawings.

—— *See* Haug (H.) Martin Schongauer et Hans Burgkmair. Étude sur une Vierge inconnue. 1938. 8°. **7852.** r. **49.**

—— *See* Kanzlei. Cantzley buchlin, *etc.* [With a woodcut, signed H. B., i.e. Hans Burgkmair.] 1528. 4°. Dept. of Prints & Drawings.

—— *See* Maximilian i., *Emperor of Germany.* Der Weiss Kunig; eine Erzehlung von den Thaten Kaiser Maximilian i. . . . nebst den von H. Burgmair dazu verfertigten Holzschnitten, *etc.* 1775. fol. **170.** k. **10.**

—— *See* Maximilian i., *Emperor of Germany.* Der Weisskunig, *etc.* [With reproductions of Hans Burgkmair's woodcuts.] 1888. fol. [*Jahrbuch der kunsthistorischen Sammlungen des Allerhöchsten Kaiserhauses.* Bd. 6.] **1765.** e.

—— *See* Riedrer (F.) Spiegel der waren Rhetoric, *etc.* [With woodcuts, attributed variously to Hans Burgkmair and Hans Weiditz.] 1535. fol. C. **48.** h. **8.**

—— *See* Schmid (Alfred) Forschungen über Hans Burgkmair, *etc.* 1888. 8°. **07807.** k. **1.** (**3.**)

—— *See* Waldauff (F.) Das Haller Heiltumbuch [by F. Waldauff] mit den Unika-Holzschnitten Hans Burgkmairs des Älteren. Von Josef Garber, *etc.* 1915. fol. [*Jahrbuch der Kunsthistorischen Sammlungen des Kaiserhauses.* Bd. 32. Hft. 6.] **1765.** e.

—— *See* Warnecke (F.) Rare Book-Plates . . . of the xvth and xvith centuries, by Albert Duerer, H. Burgmair, *etc.* 1894. 4°. **9903.** c. **33.**

—— *See* Woltmann (A. F. G. A.) Matthias Grünewald. H. B. Grien. Hans Burckmair. [1877.] 8°. [*Kunst und Künstler des Mittelalters.* Abt. 1. Bd. 1.] **2262.** f. **3.**

—— Die Genealogie des Kaisers Maximilian i. Von Simon Laschitzer. [Reproductions of a series of woodcuts by Hans Burgkmair from cod. 8018 of the K. K. Hofbibliothek, Vienna, with an introduction.] 1888. *See* Periodical Publications.—*Vienna.* Jahrbuch der kunsthistorischen Sammlungen des Allerhöchsten Kaiserhauses, *etc.* Bd. 7. 1883, *etc.* fol. **1765.** e.

BURGKMAIR (HANS) *the Elder.*

—— Die Heiligen aus der " Sipp-, Mag- und Schwägerschaft " des Kaisers Maximilian I. [The series of plates designed by Burgkmair, with an introduction by Simon Laschitzer.] 2 pt. 1886, 87. *See* PERIODICAL PUBLICATIONS.—*Vienna.* Jahrbuch der kunsthistorischen Sammlungen des Allerhöchsten Kaiserhauses, *etc.* Bd. 4, 5. 1883, *etc.* fol. **1765.** e.

—— H. Burgkmair's Leben und Leiden Christi. Deuotissime Meditationes de vita: beneficiis: et passiõe saluatoris Jesu chr̄i cū gratiarū actione. Augsburg bei Grimm & Wyrsung, 1520. *München,* 1887. 4°. **012202.** eee. **18.** *Part of the " Liebhaber-Bibliothek alter Illustratoren in Facsimile-Reproduction."*

—— Images de saints et saintes issus de la famille de l'empereur Maximilien I. En une suite de cent dix neuf planches gravées en bois par differens graveurs d'après les dessins de H. Burgmaier. pp. 11. pl. 119. *Vienne,* 1799. fol. **1266.** k. **15.**

—— Kaiser Maximilians I. Triumph. Le Triomphe de l'Empereur Maximilien I. En une suite de cent trente cinq planches gravées en bois d'après les desseins de H. Burgmair, accompagnées de l'ancienne description dictée par l'Empereur à son secrétaire Marc Treitzsaurwein. pp. 30. pl. 135. *J. Edwards: London; Vienne* [printed], 1796. fol. **1899.n.40.**

—— The Triumphs of the Emperor Maximilian I. by Burgmair. (Woodcuts designed by H. Burgmair.) Edited by Alfred Aspland. 3 vol. *Manchester,* 1873, 75. *obl.* fol. & 8°. [*Holbein Society's Fac-simile Reprints.*] Ac. **4660.** (**9.**)

BURGKMAIR (HANS) *the Younger.* Hans Burgkmaiers Turnier-Buch. [Reproductions in colour.] Herausgegeben von J. v. Hefner. pp. 35. *Frankfurt,* 1853. fol. **Dept.of Prints & Drawings.**

BURGKSTORFF (CHRISTOPHORUS ULRICUS À) Exercitatio de iudiciis reipublicæ Germanicæ, *etc. Praes.* H. Conringius. *Typis H. Mulleri: Helmestadii,* 1647. 4°. **897.** c. **3.** (**42.**)

BURGL (LUDWIG FRANZ) *See* OTT (F. A.) Darstellung der wahren Verhältnisse der . . . Aerzte in Bayern . . . nebst einem Anhange als Würdigung einer von Dr. L. F. Burgl geschriebenen Abhandlung über die Gebrechen des Medizinalwesens in Bayern. 1840. 8°. **7680.** a. **69.** (**2.**)

BURGLAR. In the Clutch of Circumstance. My own story. By a Burglar. pp. 271. *D. Appleton & Co.: New York, London,* 1922. 8°. **6055.** de. **29.**

BÜRGLEN, *Canton Uri. See* BUERGLEN.

BÜRGLEN ( ) [For the German surname of this form:] *See* BUERGLEN.

BURGLIN (FRANCISCUS JOSEPHUS) Dissertatio medica inauguralis de hæmaturia, *etc.* pp. 32. *Parisiis,* 1820. 4°. **1183.** f. **7.** (**8.**)

BÜRGLIN (FRANÇOIS JOSEPH) De la version. Thèse, *etc.* pp. 30. *Strasbourg,* 1852. 4°. [*Collection générale des dissertations de la Faculté de Médecine du Bas-Rhin.* sér. 2. tom. 15.] **7381.** d.*

BURGLON (NORA) Children of the Soil. A story of Scandinavia, *etc.* pp. 272. *Doubleday, Doran & Co.: Garden City, N.Y.,* 1932. 8°. **20053.** ff. **15.**

—— The Cuckoo Calls. A story of Finland, *etc.* pp. vii. 280. *J. C. Winston Co.: Philadelphia,* [1940.] 8°. **12815.** b. **9.**

BURGLON (NORA)

—— Deep Silver. A story of the cod banks . . . With illustrations by Peter Hurd. pp. vii. 264. *G. Routledge & Sons: London,* 1939. 8°. **12817.** b. **10.**

—— Lost Island, *etc.* pp. vii. 261. *J. C. Winston Co.: Philadelphia,* [1939.] 8°. **12824.** c. **20.**

BURGMAIER (HANS) *See* BURGKMAIR.

BURGMAIR (HANS) *See* BURGKMAIR.

BURGMANN (ARTHUR) Petroleum und Erdwachs. Darstellung der Gewinnung von Erdöl und Erdwachs . . . Mit besonderer Rücksichtnahme auf die aus Petroleum dargestellten Leuchtöle, deren Aufbewahrung und technische Prüfung, *etc.* pp. xvi. 232. *Wien,* 1880. 8°. **7106.** b. **20.**

BURGMANN (CHRISTOPHORUS FRIDERICUS) Dissertatio inauguralis medica de febre bullosa et pemphygo, *etc.* pp. 32. *Goettingae,* [1796.] 4°. T. **550.** (**35.**)

BURGMANN (ERNEST HENRY) *Bishop of Goulburn.*

—— The Education of an Australian. pp. 95. *Angus & Robertson: Sydney, London,* 1944. 8°. **4910.** b. **9.**

—— The Faith of an Anglican. pp. 57. *Angus & Robertson: Sydney, London,* 1943. 8°. **4109.** dd. **11.**

BURGMANN (JOACHIM HEINRICH) *Praes. See* BRUNNEMANNUS (C. A.) Dissertatio philologica ἀπέχει illud Christi Marci XIV. comm. XLI. a J. C. de Pauw . . . censura nupera vindicans, *etc.* [1735.] 4°. T. **2178.** (**13.**)

—— Dissertatio historico-ecclesiastica, de historiæ Mennoniticæ fontibus & subsidiis, *etc. Praes.* J. C. Burgmann. pp. 45. *Rostochii,* [1732.] 4°. **700.** h. **6.** (**10.**)

—— Predigt . . . über Matth. 5, 20–26. *See* WIGGERS (J. O. A.) Zeugnisse, *etc.* 1847. 8°. **4424.** bb. **37.**

BURGMANN (JOANNES CHRISTIANUS) *Praes. See* BURGMANN (J. H.) Dissertatio . . . de historiæ Mennoniticæ fontibus & subsidiis, *etc.* [1732.] 4°. **700.** h. **6.** (**10.**)

—— *Praes. See* BURGMANN (P. C.) Tentamen physicum de genesi sensionis, *etc.* [1722.] 4°. **537.** f. **31.** (**8.**)

—— *Praes. See* HILMERS (J. H.) Commentatio historico-ecclesiastica de Ubbone Philippi et Ubbonitis, *etc.* [1733.] 4°. **700.** h. **6.** (**11.**)

BURGMANN (JOHANN GEORG) Das Leben des weyland Magnifici, und Hochbenahmten Herrn, Herrn Johannis Burgmann, *etc. Greiffswald,* 1730. 4°. **010708.** e. **1.** (**4.**)

BURGMANN (JOHANN GUSTAV) *See* DUITSCH (S.) Kurtzgefasster Auszug aus der Bekehrungsgeschichte des ehemaligen Jüdischen Rabbinen S. Duitsch. Aus dem Holländischen übersetzt und mit einigen Anmerckungen begleitet von J. C. Burgmann. 1770. 8°. **1370.** b. **14.**

—— *See* DUITSCH (S.) A Short Account of the Wonderful Conversion to Christianity of Solomon Duitsch . . . Improved with a preface and remarks by . . . Mr. Burgmann, *etc.* 1771. 8°. **4886.** bb. **21.**

—— —— 1818. 12°. **4886.** a. **34.**

—— Das geseegnete Alter der Gerechten. Psalm XCII. 15, 16. Eine Predigt gehalten . . . 1772, als . . . Herr F. M. Ziegenhagen . . . Hofprediger bey der deutschen Hofcapelle in St. James, sein 50stes Amts-Jahr . . . vollendete. [With a portrait.] pp. 48. *J. Miller: London,* 1773. 8°. **4427.** b. **21.** (**1.**)

BURGMANN (JOHANN GUSTAV)

—— Die nöthigsten Wahrheiten, welche ein . . . Lehrer seiner . . . Gemeine vortragen soll, wurden in einer Anzugs-Predigt der Evangel. Luther. Savoy-Gemeinde zu London . . . vorgestellet, *etc.* pp. 32. *C. Heydinger: London,* 1768. 8°. **4427**. b. **21**. (5.)

—— Johann Gustav Burgmanns . . . pracktische Reden über den zweyten Artickel des christlichen Glaubens und dessen Erklärung von D. J. M. Luther. pp. xviii. 378. *Mülheim am Rhein,* [1780.] 8°. **3907**. aa. **16**.

—— Die vornehmsten Beweise von der Evangelischen Hauptlehre der allgemeinen Gnade Gottes in Jesu Christo, *etc.* pp. viii. 110. *C. Heydinger: London,* 1772. 8°. **4427**. b. **21**. (3.)

BURGMANN (PETRUS CHRISTOPHORUS) Dissertatio epistolica . . . de singulari tunicarum utriusque oculi expansione . . . 1729. *See* HALLER (A. von) *Baron.* Disputationes chirurgicae, *etc.* tom. 1. 1755, *etc.* 4°. **7481**. ff. **20**.

—— Petri Christophori Burgmanni . . . Succinctum hypotheseos Stahlianæ examen de anima rationali corpus humanum struente motusque vitales tam in statu sano quam morboso administrante. 2 pt. *Lipsiæ,* 1731, 35. 8°. **784**. c. **34, 35**.

—— Tentamen physicum de genesi sensionis. *Praes.* J. C. Burgmann. pp. 24. *Rostochii,* [1722.] 4°. **537**. f. **31**. (8.)

BURGMANNUS (JOACHIMUS HENRICUS) *See* BURGMANN (Joachim Heinrich)

BURGMANNUS (JOHANNES MARTINUS) *See* PERIODICAL PUBLICATIONS.—*Leipzig.* Nova literaria, *etc.* [Edited by J. M. Burgmannus.] [1727, *etc.*] 4°. **818**. h. **40**.

BURGMANNUS (NICOLAUS) Nicolai Burgmanni . . . Imperatorum et regum romanorum Spiræ sepultorum historiæ a Carolo M. ad Carolum IIII. Accedit anonymi ad easdem historias appendix ad Sigismundum Caes. Aug. E cod. MS. chartaceo Bibliothecæ Bavaricæ in lucem edidit A. F. Oefelius. *See* OEFELIUS (A. F.) Rerum boicarum scriptores, *etc.* tom. 1. 1763. fol. **168**. h. **10**.

BURGMANNUS (PETRUS CHRISTOPHORUS) *See* BURGMANN.

BURGMEISTER (PAULLUS) Dissertatio historico-politica de antiquissimo illo more, quo veteres reorum innocentiam culpamve per aquam ferventem ac frigidam probare solebant, *etc.* *Praes.* E. R. Roth. *Typis Hæred: C. B. Kühn: Ulmæ,* [1680.] 4°. **5511**. bbb. **27**. (4.)

BURGMUELLER (NORBERT) *See* ECKERT (Heinrich) *Writer on Music.* Norbert Burgmüller, *etc.* 1932. 8°. [*Veröffentlichungen des Musikwissenschaftlichen Institutes der Deutschen Universität in Prag.* Bd. 3.] Ac. **798**. dd.

BURGMÜLLER ( ) [For the German surname of this form :] *See* BURGMUELLER.

BURGO DE OSMA.—*Cathedral Church of.* Catálogo descriptivo de los Códices que se conservan en la Santa Iglesia Catedral de Burgo de Osma. [By Timoteo Rojo Orcajo.] [With plates.] pp. 305. *Madrid,* 1929. 8°. **011900**. c. **38**.

BURGO (ALESSANDRO) *Bishop of Catania.* *See* BURGOS.

BURGO (AUGUSTINUS GIBBON DE) *See* GIBBON.

BURGO (DIONYSIUS DE) *See* DIONYSIUS, *de Burgo Sancti Sepulchri.*

BURGO (DOMINICK DE) *R.C. Bishop of Elphin.* *See* BURKE.

BURGO (GIOVANNI BATTISTA DE) Conclusiones de lapidis philosophorum veritate et constructione, *etc.* *Praes.* B. de Brunis. pp. 38. *Apud Io: Antonij de Bonardis: Florentiæ,* 1654. 4°. **1148**. c. **5**.

—— Hydraulica, o sia trattato dell'acque minerali del Massino, S. Mauritio, Favera, Scultz, e Bormio, con la guerra della Valtellina del 1618. sin' al 1638. con altre curiosità. pp. 428. *Nelle stampe dell'Agnelli: Milano,* 1689. 12°. **659**. a. **38**.

—— [Another copy.] **233**. a. **38**.

—— [Another copy.] G. **7275**.

—— Viaggio di cinque anni in Asia, Africa, & Europa del Turco. [With plates.] 3 vol. *Nelle stampe dell'Agnelli: Milano,* [1686.] 12°. **1051**. c. **17–19**.

—— [Another copy.] G. **7272–74**.
Imperfect; wanting the frontispiece.

—— [Another edition, without plates.] 3 vol. *Nelle stampe dell'Agnelli: Milano,* [1686?] 12°. **1051**. c. **14–16**.
Vol. 3 *is a duplicate of vol.* 3 *of the preceding edition, without the plates.*

—— [Another copy of vol. 1.] **978**. b. **32**.

BURGO (JAIME DEL)

—— Al Borde de la Traición. Drama en tres actos y en prosa. pp. 133. *Pamplona,* 1936. 8°. **11729**. a. **1**.

—— Fuentes de la historia de España. Bibliografía de las Guerras Carlistas y de las luchas políticas del siglo XIX. Antecedente desde 1814 y apéndice hasta 1936. 3 tom. *Pamplona,* 1953–55. 8°. **2762**.cs.**1**.

BURGO (JOANNES DE) Pupilla Oculi oībus presbyteris precipue Anglicanis summe necessaria . . . In qua tractat de septē sacramentorum administratione. De decē preceptis decalogi ⁊ reliquis ecclesiasticorum officiis . . . Iāprimum accuratissime castigata atq; tersissime in lucē edita. [Edited by A. Agge.] G.L. ff. cxxxvi. *Impensis W. bretton; venūdatur Londoñ. apud bibliopolas in cimiterio Sancti Pauli: sub intersignio sāctissime ac indiuidue trinitatis; in alma Parisiorum academia opera wolffgāgi hopylii impressa,* 1510. 4°. **474**. c. **20**.

—— [Another copy.] **4498**. g. **15**.
Imperfect; wanting the last leaf bearing the printer's device.

—— [Another copy.] FEW MS. NOTES. **474**. c. **7**.

—— [Another edition.] G.L. *Per P. oliuier, impensis J. richardi: Rothomagi,* 1510. 4°. **845**. f. **11**.

—— [Another edition.] G.L. *Per J. pouchin, impensis F. regnault: Parrhisii,* 1514. 4°. **845**. k. **22**.

—— [Another edition.] G.L. ff. clxx. *Opa J. Knoblouchij impēsis P. Boetz: [Strasburg,]* 1514. 4°. **845**. k. **21**

—— [Another edition.] G.L. ff. clxx. *P̄lo J. Schotti sumptib⁹ J. Knoblouchi ⁊ P. Bōtz: [Strasburg,]* 1516. 4°. **845**. k. **23**
The date in the colophon is 1517.

—— [Another edition.] G.L. ff. clxx. MS. NOTES. *Opa J. Knoblouchij; impensis P. Bōtz: [Strasburg,]* 1518. 4°. **845**. k. **24**

—— [Another edition.] G.L. *Impensis F. Regnault: Parrhisij,* 1521. 8°. C. **66**. d. **11**.

BURGO (JOANNES BAPTISTA) *See* BURGO (Giovanni B. de)

BURGO (JOHANNES DE) *See* LEIPZIG.—*Academia Lipsiensis.* Rector Academiæ Lipsiensis ad exequias . . . Dni. Johannis de Burgo . . . cives academicos . . . invitat. [1667.] 4°. **1090.** l. **18.** (**13.**)

BURGO (JULIÁN DE APRAIZ Y SÁENZ DEL) *See* APRAIZ Y SÁENZ DEL BURGO.

BURGO (LUCA DE) *See* PACCIOLI (L.)

BURGO (LUCAS PACIOLUS DE) *See* PACCIOLI (L.)

BURGO (NICHOLAS DE) *See* NICHOLAS, *de Burgo, Franciscan.*

BURGO (THOMAS DE) *Bishop of Ossory.* *See* BURKE.

BURGOA (AGUSTIN DE) Eusquerasco Doctriñie otsandijoaco. Escolan lenao usetan san escu letrasco cartillatic ata, da gausa batsubetan barristaute. pp. 85. *Bilbon,* 1849. 8°. **886.** f. **28.**

BURGOA (FRANCISCO DE) Geografica Descripcion de la parte septentrional del polo artico de la America, y nueva Iglesia de las Indias occidentales, y sitio astronomico de esta provincia de Predicadores de Antequera valle de Oaxaca, *etc.* (De la vida y costumbres exemplares de el Padre Fr. Nicolas de Rojas.) 2 tom. ff. 423. 18. *I. Ruyz: Mexico,* 1674. fol. **10460.g.15.**
The running title reads "II Parte de la Historia de la provincia de Predicadores de Guaxaca" and is intended to connect this work with "Palestra historial" by the same author.

—— [Another edition.] 2 tom. *México,* 1934. 4°. [*Publicaciones del Archivo General de la Nación.* vol. 25.] **LAS.F.17/2.**

—— Palestra Historial. (Palestra historial de virtudes, y exemplares apostólicos. Fundada del zelo de insignes heroes de la sagrada orden de predicadores en este nuevo Mundo, *etc.*) [The editor's preface signed: R. L., i.e. Rafael López.] pp. xvi. 609. *México,* 1934. 4°. [*Publicaciones del Archivo General de la Nación.* vol. 24.] **LAS.F.17/2.**

BURGOINE (JOHN) *See* BURGOYNE.

BURGOLDENSIS (PHILIPPUS ANDREAS) *pseud.* [i.e. PHILIPPUS ANDREAS OLDENBURGERUS.] Notitia rerum illustrium imperii Romano-Germanici tripertita, sive Discursus juridico-politico-historici ad instrumentum sive tabulas pacis Osnabrugo-Monasteriensis . . . Editio secunda . . . cura et studio Warmundi von Friedberg. 3 pt. *Apud A. Verum: Freistadii,* 1669. 4°. **119.** b. **16.**

—— *See* IRENICUS (F.) *pseud.* Collegium juris publici Imperii Romano-Germanici in P. A. Burgoldensis discursus historico-juridico-politicos ad instrumentum pacis Cæsareo-Suecicum conscriptos, *etc.* 1670. 4°. **29.** a. **21.**

BURGON (JOHN WILLIAM) *Dean of Chichester.* *See* BIBLE.—*Gospels.* [*Greek.*] A Textual Commentary upon the Holy Gospels. Largely from the use of materials, and mainly on the text, left by the late J. W. Burgon, *etc.* 1899, *etc.* 8°. **03225.** ee. **7.**

—— *See* BIBLE.—*Gospels.* [*English.*] A Plain Commentary on the Four Holy Gospels, *etc.* [By J. W. Burgon.] 1855. 16°. **3227.** b. **2.**

—— *See* BIBLE.—*Appendix.* [*Pictorial Illustrations.*] The Picture Bible . . . By the Rev. H. J. Rose . . . and the Rev. J. W. Burgon. [1855.] fol. **742.** g. **9.**

—— *See* DERMOUT (J.) Disputatio theologica inauguralis, *etc.* MS. NOTES [by J. W. Burgon]. 1825. 8°. **1009.** c. **23.**

BURGON (JOHN WILLIAM) *Dean of Chichester.*

—— *See* GOULBURN (Edward M.) *Dean of Norwich.* John William Burgon . . . A biography, with extracts from his letters and early journals. 1892. 8°. **4920.** ee. **20.**

—— *See* LIDDELL (Henry G.) *Dean of Christchurch.* Correspondence between . . . H. G. Liddell . . . and Mr. Burgon, concerning a privilege of Convocation in respect of the nomination of select preachers. 1872. 8°. **8365.** bb. **2.** (**4.**)

—— *See* ROSE (Henry J.) *Archdeacon of Bedford,* and BURGON (J. W.) *Dean of Chichester.* Large Coloured Prints from Sacred Subjects, etc. [1867.] fol. **1881.** b. **25.**

—— *See* ROSE (Henry J.) *Archdeacon of Bedford,* and BURGON (J. W.) *Dean of Chichester.* Scripture Prints, *etc.* 1851, *etc.* 8°. **550.** d. **26.**

—— *See* SCOTT (*Sir* George G.) Personal and Professional Recollections . . . With an introduction by the Very Rev. J. W. Burgon, *etc.* 1879. 8°. **10856.** d. **15.**

—— *See* SHAW (Henry) *F.S.A.* The Arms of the Colleges of Oxford . . . With historical notices . . . by J. W. Burgon. 1855, *etc.* **9906.** h. **25.**

—— The Athanasian Creed to be retained in its integrity: and why. Being the substance of two sermons, *etc.* pp. 48. *J. Parker & Co.: Oxford & London,* 1872. 8°. **4479.** d. **3.** (**1.**)

—— Canon Robert Gregory: a letter of friendly remonstrance. pp. 80. *Longmans & Co.: London,* 1881. 8°. **4109.** h. **18.** (**5.**)

—— The Causes of the Corruption of the Traditional Text of the Holy Gospels. Being the sequel to The Traditional Text of the Holy Gospels . . . Arranged, completed, and edited by Edward Miller. pp. xiv. 290. *G. Bell & Sons: London,* 1896. 8°. **3226.** f. **29.**

—— A Century of Verses, in memory of the Reverend, the President of Magdalen College. [An elegy on the death of M. J. Routh.] *J. H. Parker: Oxford,* 1855. 4°. **11647.** e. **23.**

—— Christ Standing at the Door and Knocking. A sermon, *etc.* pp. 15. *J. H. & J. Parker: Oxford & London,* 1858. 8°. **4478.** a. **125.** (**9.**)

—— The Disestablishment of Religion in Oxford, the Betrayal of a Sacred Trust:—words of warning for the University. A sermon, *etc.* pp. 54. *Parker & Co.: Oxford & London,* [1881.] 8°. **4473.** f. **19.** (**25.**)

—— Disestablishment,—the Nation's Formal Rejection of God, and Denial of the Faith. A sermon, *etc.* pp. 32. *J. Parker & Co.: Oxford & London,* 1868. 8°. **4478.** b. **13.**

—— Divergent Ritual. Remarks on "The Address for Toleration": a letter to . . . the Lord Archbishop of Canterbury. pp. 8. *Rivingtons: London,* 1881. 8°. **4109.** h. **13.** (**16.**)

—— Dr. Temple's "Explanation" examined. pp. 20. *J. Parker & Co.: Oxford & London,* 1870. 8°. **4108.** b. **101.** (**14.**)

—— Home Missions and Sensational Religion: a sermon . . . also Humility—ad Clerum: a sermon, *etc.* pp. 36. *J. Parker & Co.: Oxford & London,* 1876. 8°. **4473.** b. **10.** (**23.**)

—— Inspiration and Interpretation: seven sermons preached before the University of Oxford with preliminary remarks: being an answer to a volume entitled "Essays and Reviews." pp. ccxxviii. 279. *J. H. & J. Parker: Oxford & London*, 1861. 8°. **4373. dd. 18.**

—— *See* Clissold (Augustus) Inspiration and Interpretation: being a review of seven sermons preached before the University of Oxford, by J. W. Burgon, *etc.* 1861, *etc.* 12°. **4327. d. 18.**

—— Jacob in Life and in Death. 1864. 8°. *See* L., H. R. Sermons preached during Lent, 1864, *etc.* 1864. 8°. **4464. aaa. 20.**

—— The Lambeth Conference and the Encyclical. A sermon, *etc.* pp. 19. *J. Parker & Co.: Oxford & London*, 1867. 8°. **4477. bb. 73. (19.)**

—— The Last Twelve Verses of the Gospel according to S. Mark, vindicated against recent critical objectors, and established . . . With facsimiles of Codex ℵ and Codex L. pp. xv. 334. *J. Parker & Co.: Oxford & London*, 1871. 8°. **3225. ee. 14.**

—— The Late Vicar of S. Mary's in Explanation. A few words on the lodging-house question. In a letter to the Vice-Chancellor of the University of Oxford. pp. 8. *J. Parker & Co.: Oxford*, 1876. 8°. **8304. d. 2. (10.)**

—— Letters from Rome to Friends in England. pp. xv. 420. *John Murray: London*, 1862. 8°. **10136. ccc. 21.**

—— The Life and Times of Sir Thomas Gresham; compiled chiefly from his correspondence . . . including notices of contemporaries. [With plates, including a portrait.] 2 vol. *Robert Jennings: London*, 1839. 8°. **1202. k. 2, 3.**

—— Lives of Twelve Good Men, *etc.* 2 vol. *John Murray: London*, 1888. 8°. **4902. g. 24.**

—— New edition, with portraits. pp. xxiv. 484. *John Murray: London*, 1891. 8°. **4902. g. 26.**

—— Dean Burgon's Memorandum. [On the ecclesiastical antiquities of the parish of Houghton Conquest in Bedfordshire. Extracted from the Houghton Conquest Parish Magazine. Edited by H. W. Macklin.] ms. notes. [1910.] 8°. **4707. ff. 5.**

—— Nehemiah, a Pattern to Builders: counsels on the recommencement of the academical year. A sermon, *etc.* pp. 23. *J. Parker & Co.: Oxford & London*, 1878. 8°. **4479. d. 2. (8.)**

—— The New Lectionary. A sermon, *etc.* [With a letter by E. B. Denison.] pp. 16. *J. Parker & Co.: Oxford & London*, 1872. 8°. **3476. f. 19.**

—— The New Lectionary examined. *See* Liturgies.—*Church of England.—Common Prayer.—Calendar and Lectionary.* [*Appendix.*] The New Lectionary examined . . . By C. Wordsworth . . . E. M. Goulburn . . . and J. W. Burgon. 1877. 8°. **3126. dd. 16. (12.)**

—— Ninety Short Sermons for Family Reading. By the author of A Plain Commentary on the Gospels [i.e. J. W. Burgon]. 2 pt. 1855. 8°. *See* Sermons. **4463. b. 37.**

—— Ninety-one Short Sermons for Family Reading: following the course of the Christian seasons. Second series. 2 vol. pp. xvi. vii. 784. *J. Parker & Co.: Oxford & London*, 1867. 8°. **4463. aa. 11.**

—— On a New Method of obtaining Representations of Coins. [Signed: J. W. B., i.e. J. W. Burgon.] [With a ms. letter from the author to Samuel Rogers.] pp. 3. [1841.] 8°. *See* B., J. W. **7756. de. 8. (2.)**

—— One Soweth and another Reapeth. A sermon . . . To which is prefixed some account of the special services for the working classes in North Bucks during the Lenten Ember Week, 1859. pp. 30. *J. H. & J. Parker: Oxford & London*, 1859. 8°. **4446. b. 16.**

—— The Oxford Diocesan Conference; and Romanizing within the Church of England: two sermons, *etc.* pp. 40. *J. Parker & Co.: Oxford & London*, 1873. 8°. **4109. b. 2. (7.)**

—— Second edition, corrected and enlarged. pp. 40. *J. Parker & Co.: Oxford & London*, 1873. 8°. **4109. b. 2. (6.)**

—— Oxford Reformers. A letter to Endemus and Ecdemus. By a Fellow of Oriel (J. W. Burgon). [In reply to "Common-Room Common-Places. By two Oxford Fellows."] pp. 19. *J. H. Parker: Oxford*, 1854. 8°. **8304. ff. 12. (2.)**

—— [Another copy.] **8364. d. 5.**

—— Petra, a prize poem, *etc.* pp. 29. *Francis Macpherson: Oxford*, 1845. 8°. **11601. ee. 33. (4.)**

—— Second edition. To which a few short poems are now added. pp. 62. *Francis Macpherson: Oxford*, 1846. 8°. **11645. h. 13.**

—— Plea for a Fifth Final School. A letter to the . . . Vice-Chancellor of the University of Oxford. pp. 27. *J. Parker & Co.: Oxford*, 1868. 8°. **8364. bb. 53. (12.)**

—— A Plea for the Study of Divinity in Oxford. pp. 56. *J. Parker & Co.: Oxford & London*, 1875. 8°. **8364. cc. 1. (7.)**

—— Poems, 1840 to 1878. pp. 147. *Macmillan & Co.: London*, 1885. 8°. **11641. bbb. 47.**

—— The Portrait of a Christian Gentleman. A memoir of Patrick Fraser Tytler, etc. pp. xii. 356. *John Murray: London*, 1859. 8°. **10826. c. 5.**

—— [Another copy.] The Portrait of a Christian Gentleman, *etc. London*, 1859. 8°. **10860. aa. 59. (1.)**

—— Second edition. pp. xii. 368. *John Murray: London*, 1859. 8°. **10856. a. 15.**

—— The Prayer Book, a devotional manual and guide. 1876. *See* Kempe (John E.) The St. James's Lectures, *etc.* ser. 2. 1875, *etc.* 8°. **4464. i. 1.**

—— [Another edition.] *See* Kempe (John E.) Companions for the Devout Life, *etc.* 1877. 8°. **4466. a. 12.**

—— Prophecy,—not "Forecast" . . . A sermon . . . With introductory remarks: being a reply to the Rev. Brownlow Maitland's "Argument from Prophecy." pp. 47. *J. Parker & Co.: Oxford & London*, 1880. 8°. **4478. h. 9. (10.)**

—— Protests of the Bishops against the Consecration of Dr. Temple to the See of Exeter: preceded by a letter to . . . John Jackson, D.D., Bishop of London. pp. 31. *J. Parker & Co.: Oxford & London*, 1870. 8°. **4108. b. 87.**

—— The Review of a Year. A sermon, *etc.* pp. 15. *J. Parker & Co.: Oxford & London*, 1871. 8°. **4478. h. 1.**

BURGON (John William) *Dean of Chichester.*

—— The Revision Revised. Three articles reprinted from the 'Quarterly Review.' I. The New Greek Text. II. The New English Version. III. Westcott and Hort's New Textual Theory. To which is added, a reply to Bishop Ellicott's pamphlet in defence of the revisers and their Greek text of the New Testament, *etc.* pp. xlii. 549. *John Murray: London,* 1883. 8°. **03128. k. 26.**

—— *See* Bible.—*Appendix.—New Testament.* [*Greek.*] The Revisers and the Greek Text of the New Testament, *etc.* [Chiefly in answer to the criticisms by J. W. Burgon, in the Quarterly Review, of the Greek Testament as revised by B. F. Westcott and F. J. A. Hort.] 1882. 8°. **3127. k. 25. (2.)**

—— The Roman Council. A sermon preached . . . Dec. 12, 1869; being the Sunday after the death of J. Parsons, Esq. pp. 12. *J. Parker & Co.: Oxford & London,* 1869. 8°. **4906. d. 9.**

—— The Servants of Scripture, *etc.* pp. x. 132. *S.P.C.K.: London,* 1878. 8°. **4420. bbb. 13.**

—— Some Remarks on Art, with reference to the studies of the University. In a letter addressed to the Rev. Richard Greswell. pp. 73. *Francis Macpherson: Oxford,* 1846. 8°. **7806.b.3.**

—— The Structure and Method of the Book of Common Prayer. (Two sermons.) pp. 32. *S.P.C.K.: London,* 1886. 8°. **4421. a. 14. (4.)**

—— To Educate Young Women like Young Men, and with Young Men,—a Thing Inexpedient and Immodest. A sermon, *etc.* pp. 32. *Parker & Co.: Oxford & London,* [1884.] 8°. **4473. bb. 17. (10.)**

—— The Traditional Text of the Holy Gospels vindicated and established . . . Arranged, completed, and edited by E. Miller. pp. xx. 317. *G. Bell & Sons: London,* 1896. 8°. **3226. f. 28.**

—— A Treatise on the Pastoral Office, addressed chiefly to candidates for holy orders, *etc.* pp. xxiv. 470. *Macmillan & Co.: London,* 1864. 8°. **4498. cc. 15.**

—— An Unitarian Reviser of our Authorized Version, intolerable: an earnest remonstrance and petition addressed to C. J. Ellicott, Bishop of Gloucester and Bristol. pp. 8. *J. Parker & Co.: Oxford & London,* 1872. 8°. **4372. g. 5. (2.)**

—— Woman's Place. A sermon, *etc.* pp. 12. *J. Parker & Co.: Oxford & London,* 1871. 8°. **8415. ee. 18.**

—— A Woman's Reply to a Sermon preached by the Rev. J. W. Burgon . . . on "Woman's Place"; with a general review of the "Woman's Question." pp. 16. *George Shrimpton: Oxford; Whittaker & Co.: London,* 1871. 8°. **8415. ee. 19.**

—— The Work of the Christian Builder tried by Fire. A sermon, *etc.* pp. 16. *J. H. & J. Parker: Oxford & London,* 1865. 8°. **4477. aaa. 11.**

—— Saint and Soubrette, or "Chops and Tomato Sauce!" A brief reply to Mr. Burgon's attack on the Oxford lodging-houses. pp. 8. *J. Vincent: Oxford,* 1876. 8°. **8365. bbb. 66. (2.)**

BURGON (Thomas) An Inquiry into the Motive which influenced the Ancients in their choice of the various representations which we find stamped on their money. pp. 35. *J. Wertheimer & Co.: London,* 1836. 8°. **7755. b. 12.**

With a MS. *letter from the author to Dawson Turner inserted.*

BURGON (Thomas)

—— Prefatory Remarks, and Index, to the first and second portions of the Greek, Roman, and mediæval Coins and Medals [in the collection of T. Thomas]. pp. xxii. [1844?] 8°. **S.C. 851.**

BURGONDIO (Orazio) *See* Burgundius (Horatius)

BURGONIONS. *See* Burgundians.

BURGONOVENSIS (Archangelus) *See* Arcangelo [Pozzo], *da Borgo-Nuovo.*

BURGONOVENSIS (Puteus Archangelus) *See* Arcangelo [Pozzo], *da Borgo-Nuovo.*

BURGO-NOVO (Archangelus de) *See* Arcangelo [Pozzo], *da Borgo-Nuovo.*

BURGONS LIMITED. Burgons Monthly Magazine. vol. 15. no. 4. Apr. 1904. *Manchester,* 1904. 4°. **1866. b. 13. (9.)**

BURGONS MONTHLY MAGAZINE. *See* Burgons Limited.

BURGOS.

OFFICIAL DOCUMENTS.

—— *Begin.* Don Diego de Vargas Manrique . . . Corregidor en esta ciudad de Burgos, *etc.* [Orders for combating the plague, dated 27 Aug. 1597, with a list of places put under quarantine, in accordance with a royal provision of 21. Aug. 1597. With the text.] [1597.] fol. *See* Spain.—Philip II., *King.* **Eg. MS. 356. ff. 296, 297.**

—— *Begin.* Don Diego de Vargas Manrique . . . Corregidor en esta ciudad de Burgos, *etc.* [A revised list of places put under quarantine on account of the plague. Dated: 1 Oct. 1597.] [*Burgos,* 1597.] *s. sh.* fol. **Eg. MS. 356. f. 295.**

—— Lista de los lugares que se tiene relacion estan tocados de mal contagioso y de peste: reformados otros que por la misericordia de Dios estan restituydos en sanidad, *etc.* [Issued by D. de Vargas Manrique as corregidor of Burgos, 3 Oct. 1597.] [*Burgos,* 1597.] *s. sh.* fol. **Eg. MS. 356. f. 300.**

—— *Begin.* Don Diego de Vargas Manrique . . . Corregidor en esta . . . ciudad de Burgos, *etc.* [A revised list of places put under quarantine on account of the plague. Dated: 13 Aug. 1598.] [*Burgos,* 1598.] *s. sh.* fol. **Eg. MS. 356. f. 301.**

—— Pregon de capitulos de buena gouernacion, en las ventas que se hizieren con libertad de Pragmatica y sin tassa, del Trigo, Cenada y Centeno, acordados y ordenados por la . . . ciudad de Burgos. [Aug. 17, 1598.] [*Burgos,* 1598.] *s. sh.* fol. **Eg. MS. 356. f. 129.**

MUNICIPAL INSTITUTIONS.

Consulado.

—— *See* infra: Universidad de la Contratación.

Estación Meteorológica.

—— Estación Meteorológica de Burgos. Resultados de las observaciones del año 1867. [The preface signed: José M. Otaño.] pp. x. 218. *Burgos,* 1868. fol. **8752. e. 14.**

Universidad de la Contratación.

—— Begin. Este es un Traslado . . . d'el original de las Ordenãças d'el Prior Cõsules, de la Vniuersidad de la Contratacion de . . . Burgos, *etc.* ff. 56. [1572.] fol. **503. h. 19.**

BURGOS.

—— Ordenanzas del Consulado de Burgos de 1538 . . . anotadas y precedidas de un bosquejo histórico del Consulado por el Dr. Eloy García de Quevedo y Concellón, *etc.* pp. 300. *Burgos*, 1905. 4°. **5384.** ff. **14.**

—— Real Cedula de Confirmacion, y nuevas Ordenanzas del Consulado, Universidad, y Casa de Contratacion de la ciudad de . . . Burgos, *etc.* ff. 42. *Madrid*, 1766. fol. T. **16*.** (**35.**)

MISCELLANEOUS INSTITUTIONS.

CATHEDRAL.

—— Cartulario de la Catedral de Burgos. [Edited by Luciano Serrano.] *See* SERRANO (L.) El Obispado de Burgos y Castilla Primitiva desde el Siglo V al XIII. tom. 3. 1935. 8°. **20010.** bb. **43.**

—— *Begin.* Muy poderoso señor. Auiendo mandado V. Alt. por sus Reales prouisiones de 3. de Diziembre del año passado, *etc.* [A report from the Dean and Chapter of the Cathedral Church of Burgos to the Royal Council on the administration of the benefactions of Pedro Fernandez Cerezo. Dated: 7 Jan. 1620.] 1620. fol. Eg. MS. **356.** ff. **396–407.**

—— Por las Santas Yglesias de Burgos, Siguença, Segouia, Osma, y Zamora. Con las santas Yglesias de Toledo, Seuilla, y . . . las demas Catedrales destos Reynos de Castilla y Leon. Sobre que se hagan verdaderos valores de todos los frutos y rētas eclesiasticas de los dichos Reynos, *etc.* [1616?] fol. **1322.** k. **14.** (**11.**) *Imperfect; wanting all after fol.* 20.

—— Album de la Catedral de Burgos. 72 vistas. *Madrid*, [1925.] *obl.* 8°. **7817.** aa. **30.**

—— Catálogo de los códices de la Catedral de Burgos. [Compiled by D. Mansilla.] pp. 205. pl. XVII. *Madrid*, 1952. 8°. **4999.** t. **11.**

—— Catedral de Burgos: septimo centenario de su fundación: 1221. (Burgos y la Provincia. [By Luis de Pablo Ibáñez.]) [With illustrations.] pp. xc. 143. *Burgos*, [1921.] 16°. **10162.** bb. **6.**

CONGREGACION DE NACIONALES DE LAS MONTAÑAS.

—— Constituciones, *etc.* pp. 39. [1752.] 4°. T. **1304.** (**3.**)

EXPOSICIÓN DE ARTE RETROSPECTIVO.

—— VII Centenario de la Catedral de Burgos, 1921. Catálogo general de la Exposición de Arte Retrospectivo, *etc.* [Edited with an introduction by Eloy García de Quevedo y Concellón.] pp. xxvii. 134. pl. XLVI. *Burgos*, 1926. fol. **7804.** v. **2.**

IGLESIA DE SAN LESMES.

—— *See* ADELELMUS, *Saint, Church of, at Burgos.*

MONASTERIO DE SAN AGUSTÍN.

—— Libro de los milagros del sancto Crucifixo, que esta en el monasterio de sant Agustin de la ciudad de Burgos. ff. 145. *Philippe de Iunta: Burgos*, 1574. 8°. C. **125.** a. **9.**

MUSEO ARQUEOLÓGICO PROVINCIAL.

—— Catalogo del Museo Arqueológico Provincial de Burgos. Por Matías Martínez Burgos. pp. 167. pl. LVII. *Cuerpo Facultativo de Archiveros, Bibliotecarios y Anticuarios: Madrid*, 1935. 8°. **07707.** e. **11.**

BURGOS.

REAL ACADEMIA MÉDICO-QUIRURGICA DE CASTILLA LA VIEJA.

—— Instruccion prophilactico-terapeutica del Colera-morbo Asiatico. pp. 27. *Valladolid*, [1834.] 4°. **7561.** d. **32.** (**3.**)

APPENDIX.

—— Burgos y su provincia. Fundacion, historia, monumentos . . . Artículos firmados por varios escritores antiguos y modernos, *etc.* tom. 1–3. *Vitoria*, 1898–1901. 8°. **10162.** dd. **19.**

BURGOS, *Diocese of. Begin.* Si los notables fueran verdaderos, dizen, la illacion, es evidente, *etc.* [On the jurisdiction of the Diocesans of Burgos.] MS. NOTES. [1720?] fol. **5107.** ff. **1.** (**23.**)

BURGOS, ALPHONSUS, *Bishop of.* [1435–1456.] *See* ALONSO, *de Cartagena, etc.*

——, FRANCISCO, *Bishop of.* [1550–1566.] *See* HURTADO DE MENDOZA Y BOBADILLA (F.) *Cardinal.*

——, JUAN, *Bishop of.* [1514–1524.] *See* RODRÍGUEZ DE FONSECA (J.) successively *Bishop of Badajos, of Cordova, etc.*

——, MAURICIUS, *Bishop of.* [1213–1238.] *See* MAURICIUS.

——, PAULUS, *Bishop of.* [1415–1435.] *See* PAULUS, *de Sancta Maria*, successively *Bishop of Carthagena* and *of Burgos.*

BURGOS (ALESSANDRO) *Bishop of Catania. See* ANGELERIUS (H.) Hippolyti Angelerii . . . De antiquitate urbis Atestinæ liber . . . cum animadversionibus & emendationibus F. Alexandri Burgos, *etc.* 1722. fol. [*GRAEVIUS* (*J. G.*) *Thesaurus antiquitatum et historiarum Italiæ.* tom. 7. pt. 1.] **L.R.302.a.2/7.**

—— F. Alexandri de Burgos . . . De ecclesiasticæ historiæ in theologia auctoritate atque usu præfatio, *etc.* pp. 29. *Perusiæ*, 1702. 8°. **658.** e. **20.** (**3.**)

—— [Another edition.] 1759. *See* SICILIAN AUTHORS. Opuscoli di autori siciliani. tom. 2. 1758, *etc.* 4°. **663.** g. **1.**

—— [Another edition.] 1790. *See* SICILIAN AUTHORS. Nuova raccolta di opuscoli di autori siciliani. tom. 3. 1788, *etc.* 4°. **96.** d. **2.**

—— Distinta relatione dello spauentoso eccidio cagionato da' terremoti . . . accaduto a' 9. & 11. gennaro 1693. nel regno di Sicilia . . . Cauata da vna lettera . . . scritta dal P. A. Burgos ad vn suo amico. *A. Epiro: Palermo; il Parrino: Napoli*, 1693. 4°. **444.** c. **41.** (**16.**)

—— [Another edition.] Sicilia piangente su le rovine delle sue più belle città atterrate da' tremuoti agli vndeci di gennaio dell'anno 1693 . . . Con l'aggiunta delle notizie fin' ora hauute dal regno delli danni caggionati da' tremuoti sudetti. 2 pt. *A. Epiro: Palermo*, 1693. 4°. **1057.** h. **26.** (**5.**)

—— Terræmotus siculus anni MDCXCII. (Ex italo latine vertit suasque curas adjecit S. Havercampus.) *See* CARRERA (P.) Petri Carreræ . . . Descriptio Ætnæ, *etc.* 1723. fol. [*GRAEVIUS* (*J. G.*) *Thesaurus antiquitatum et historiarum Italiæ, Neapolis, Siciliæ.* Sicilia. vol. 9.] **L.R.302.a.2/9.**

—— [Three eclogues.] *See* MOREI (M. G.) Arcadum carmina, *etc.* pt. 1. 1757, *etc.* 8°. **78.** c. **34.**

BURGOS (ANDRES DE) Relaciō verdadera del rebato q̄ dieron Quatrocientos y cincuēta Turcos en el almadraua de Zaara, *etc.* [A facsimile of the edition published at Seville in 1562.] [1880?] 4°. **899. f. 16. (12.)**

BURGOS (AUGUSTO DE) *Count de Rault y de Ramsault. See* HERRERA (G. A. de) Agricultura general . . . revisada por D. A. de Burgos. 1858. 8°. **7073. aa. 24.**

—— *See* PERIODICAL PUBLICATIONS.—*Madrid.* El Agricultor español . . . redactado por el Conde de Rault, *etc.* [1850, *etc.*] 8°. **P.P. 2226.**

—— *See* SUE (M. J. E.) Martin el Expósito . . . Version castellana por D. A. de Burgos. 1846, *etc.* 12°. **12515. ccc. 31.**

—— Blason de España. Libro de oro de su nobleza . . . Parte primera. Casa real y grandeza de España. [With plates.] 6 tom. *Madrid*, 1853–60. fol. **L.R.400.d.3.** *No more published.*

BURGOS (CARMEN DE) *See* BURGOS SEGUÍ.

BURGOS (DIEGO DE) Querella de la fe comēçada por diego de burgos y acabada . . . por dō pero fernādez de villegas. *See* DANTE ALIGHIERI. [*Divina Commedia.—Spanish.—Inferno.*] Con previlegio real: La traduciō del dante, *etc.* 1515. fol. **C. 56. f. 9.**

BURGOS (DIONYSIUS DE) *See* DIONYSIUS, *de Burgo Sancti Sepulchri.*

BURGOS (ERNESTO BONETTI) *See* BONETTI BURGOS.

BURGOS (FAUSTO) and **CATULLO** (MARÍA ELENA) Tejidos Incaicos y Criollos, *etc.* [With plates.] pp. 125. 1927. fol. *See* ARGENTINE REPUBLIC.—*Ministerio de Justicia, é Instrucción Pública.* **7742. r. 19.**

BURGOS (FRANCISCO CANTERA) *See* CANTERA BURGOS.

BURGOS (FRANCISCO JAVIER DE) Anales del Reinado de Dª Isabel II. Obra postuma. [With a life of the author, signed: A. P., and with plates, including a portrait.] 6 tom. *Madrid*, 1850, 51. 8°. **10632. d. 2.**

BURGOS (FRANCISCUS) Brief aus Sud-America. 1726. *See* JESUITS. [*Letters from Missions.*] Allerhand so lehr-als geist-reiche Brief, Schrifften und Reis-Beschreibungen, *etc.* Bd. 1. Tl. 4. no. 90. 1728, *etc.* fol. **4767. g. 3.**

BURGOS (FRANK GELETT) and **IRWIN** (WILL)

—— The Picaroons. A San Francisco night's entertainment. pp. vii. 272. *Chatto & Windus: London*, 1903. 8°. **012707. l. 62.**

—— [A reissue.] *London*, 1904. 8°. **012707. cc. 2.**

BURGOS (FRANKLIN MIESES) *See* MIESES BURGOS (F.)

BURGOS (J. F.) Dissertation sur la rage. Tribut académique, *etc.* pp. 40. *Montpellier*, an XI [1803]. 4°. **1180. e. 3. (7.)**

BURGOS (JAVIER DE) *Dramatist. See* BURGOS Y SARRAGOTI (Francisco J. de)

BURGOS (JAVIER DE) *Historian. See* BURGOS (Francisco J. de)

BURGOS (JEAN) *of Jarsy.*

—— Considérations générales et relatives à l'influence que présentent les révolutions des âges sur les maladies chroniques. Dissertation, *etc.* pp. 36. *Montpellier*, an VIII [1800]. 4°. **1180. d. 7. (12.)**

BURGOS (JOANNES BAPTISTA) Ioan. Baptistæ Burgos . . . Concio euangelica ad patres Concilii Tridentini . . . de quattuor extirpandarum omnium hæresum præcipuis remediis. *Apud C. Gryphium: Patauii*, 1563. 4°. **222. e. 22. (28.)**

BURGOS (JOSÉ CARRALERO Y) *See* CARRALERO Y BURGOS.

BURGOS (JUAN DE) Otro romāce del conde claros nueuamēte trobado por otra manera. G. L. [*Seville*, 1515?] 4°. **G. 11022. (4.)**

BURGOS (MATÍAS MARTÍNEZ DE) *See* MARTÍNEZ DE BURGOS.

BURGOS (MIGUEL DE)

—— Observaciones sobre el arte de la imprenta. Edición y notas por Antonio Rodríguez-Moñino. pp. 82. *Valencia*, 1947. 8°. **2715.c.9/2.** [*Gallardo. Colección de opusculos para bibliófilos.* no. 2.]

BURGOS (SIMON) [For official documents issued by S. Burgos as Secretary of State of the Department of War and Marine in the Republic of New Granada:] *See* NEW GRANADA, *Republic of.* [1831–1858.]—*Despacho de Guerra y Marina.*

BURGOS (VICENTE) *See* MEURICE (Paul) El Maestro de Primeras Letras. Drama . . . por D. V. Burgos y D. A. Carralon de Lara . . . basado sobre el de M. P. Maurice [*sic*], *etc.* 1861. 8°. **11725. h. 19.**

BURGOS (VICENTE DE) *See* VICENTE, *de Burgos.*

BURGOS DE PAZ (DIDACUS) *See* SALON DE PAZ (D.)

BURGOS DE PAZ (MARCUS) *See* SALON DE PAZ (M.)

BURGOS SEGUÍ (CARMEN DE)

—— *See* LEOPARDI (G.) *Count, the Poet.* [*Collections.—I. Prose and Verse.—Italian and Spanish.*] Giacomo Leopardi. Su vida y sus obras. [Edited, with a commentary, by C. de Burgos Seguí.] [1911.] 8°. **10633. bb. 24.**

—— *See* MATTACHICH-KEGLEVICH (G.) *Count.* Loca por razón de Estado. La Princesa Luisa de Bélgica. Memorias inéditas . . . Traducción y prólogo de C. de Burgos Seguí. 1904. 8°. **010708. e. 73.**

—— El Divorcio en España. pp. 142. *Madrid*, 1904. 8°. **5175. a. 5.**

—— Peregrinaciones . . . Epílogo por Ramón Gómez de la Serna. pp. 462. *Madrid*, 1916. 8°. **010106. e. 1.**

—— Quiero vivir mi vida. Novela . . . Prólogo del Dr. D. Gregorio Marañón. pp. 253. *Madrid*, 1931. 8°. **12488. s. 29.**

BURGOS Y MAZO (MANUEL DE)

—— De la república a ...? pp. 215. *Madrid*, 1931. 8°. **08042. b. 80.**

—— La Dictadura y los Constitucionalistas. 4 vol. *Madrid*, 1934. 8°. **08042. aa. 21.**

—— Vida Política Española. Páginas históricas de 1917. pp. 345. *Madrid*, [1918.] 8°. **9180. b. 25.**

BURGOS Y SARRAGOTI (FRANCISCO JAVIER DE)

—— *See* MESA ANDRÉS (J.) La Moza del Cantar. Drama . . . original de J. Mesa Andrés . . . y J. de Burgos, *etc.* 1924. 8°. **11726. h. 14.**

BURGOS Y SARRAGOTI (Francisco Javier de)
—— Colección completa de cuentos de Javier de Burgos, *etc.* [In verse.] pp. 191. *Madrid, Barcelona,* [1902.] 8°. **011451.** g. **34.**

—— Argumento del juguete cómico-lírico en un acto . . . en verso Caramelo, *etc.* pp. 16. *Sevilla,* [1884.] 8°. **11726.** aa. **11.** (**2.**)

—— Cádiz; episodio . . . dramático en dos actos . . . en verso . . . Cuarta edicion. pp. 104. *Madrid,* 1887. 8°. **11728.** bbb. **13.** (**8.**)

—— El Censo de Poblacion, sainete en un acto y en verso. pp. 33. *Madrid,* 1878. 8°. **11728.** bbb. **10.** (**10.**)

—— Trafalgar. Episodio nacional, lírico-dramático en dos actos . . . en verso, *etc.* pp. 82. *Madrid,* 1891. 8°. **11726.** e. **15.** (**8.**)

—— Argumento de Trafalgar, episodio nacional en dos actos, *etc.* (Los Alojados. Zarzuela en un acto.) [In verse.] pp. 16. *Sevilla,* [1891.] 8°. **11726.** aa. **11.** (**1.**)

—— Tres Visitas oportunas, comedia en un acto original y en verso. pp. 32. *Madrid,* 1875. 8°. **11728.** bbb. **6.** (**3.**)

BURGOWER (Johannes) Disputatio medica de ruminatione humana, *etc.* 1631. *See* Genathius (J. J.) Decas VII. disputationum medicarum select., *etc.* disp. 3. 1618, *etc.* 4°. **1179.** g. **4.** (**23.**)

BURGOYNE, BURBIDGES AND CO. Medico-Chemical Novelties. pp. 19. *London,* 1894. 8°. **7306.** e. **22.** (**13.**)

—— A Review of New Therapeutic Remedies and special preparations of recent introduction, by Burgoyne, Burbidges & Compy. pp. 62. *London,* 1894. 8°. **07305.** f. **17.** (**13.**)

BURGOYNE (*Sir* Alan Hughes) *See* Clowes (*Sir* William L.) and Burgoyne (*Sir* A. H.) Trafalgar Refought. [1905.] 8°. **012631.** dd. **46.**

—— —— [1907.] 8°. **012625.** aaa. **37.**

—— *See* London.—III. *Navy League.* The Navy League Annual . . . Edited by A. H. Burgoyne. 1907, *etc.* 8°. P.P. **2486.** uf.

—— *See* Periodical Publications.—*London.* Submarine Navigation . . . A scientific quarterly by A. H. Burgoyne. 1901. 8°. P.P. **1653.** d.

—— As the Spirit moved me. [Poems.] pp. 59. *A. L. Humphreys: London,* 1918. 8°. **011648.** eee. **85.**

—— Submarine Navigation, past and present . . . Illustrated. 2 vol. *Grant Richards: London; E. P. Dutton & Co.: New York,* 1903. 8°. **2248.** c. **16.**

—— The War Inevitable. [A novel.] pp. 313. *Francis Griffiths: London,* 1908. 8°. **12619.** ee. **6.**

—— What of the Navy? . . . With eight plates. pp. vi. 192. *Cassell & Co.: London,* 1913. 8°. **08806.** f. **42.**

BURGOYNE (Anne) *Lady.* *See* Whyle (Humphrey) A Sermon preach'd at the funeral of Anne Lady Burgoyne, *etc.* 1694. 4°. **4903.** ccc. **37.**

BURGOYNE (E. H.) The Graphic Theatrical Autograph Album. Edited by E. H. Burgoyne. 4 pt. *J. Gosnell & Co.: London,* [1877.] fol. **1874.** e. **1.**

BURGOYNE (Elizabeth)

—— Carmen Sylva, Queen and Woman. [With portraits.] pp. 320. *Eyre & Spottiswoode: London,* 1941. 8°. **10608.** dd. **10.**

BURGOYNE (Elizabeth)

—— Road Royal. pp. 288. *Stanley Paul & Co.: London,* [1935.] 8°. NN. **23549.**

—— Travail. pp. 255. *Stanley Paul & Co.: London,* [1934.] 8°. NN. **22017.**

BURGOYNE (Frank James) *See* Dudley (Robert) *Earl of Leicester.* History of Queen Elizabeth, Amy Robsart and the Earl of Leicester. Being a reprint of "Leycesters Commonwealth" . . . Edited by F. J. Burgoyne. 1904. 4°. **9512.** df. **11.**

—— *See* Northumberland Manuscript. Northumberland Manuscripts . . . Transcribed and edited with notes and introduction by F. J. Burgoyne. 1904. fol. MS. Facs. **194.**

—— Catalogue of the Books in the Tate Central Library, *etc.* pp. 270. 1893. 8°. *See* London.—II. *Borough Councils.—Lambeth.—Lambeth Public Libraries.* **11900.** dd. **74.**

—— Index-Catalogue of the Books in the Durning Lending Library, Kennington Cross. pp. 116. 1889. 8°. *See* London.—II. *Borough Councils.—Lambeth.—Lambeth Public Libraries.* **011904.** bb. **12.**

—— Library Construction, *etc.* pp. xx. 336. *George Allen: London,* 1897. 8°. [*Library Series.* vol. 2.] **011899.** h. **26.**

BURGOYNE (Frank James) and **BALLINGER** (*Sir* John)

—— Books for Village Libraries . . . With notes upon the organization and management of village libraries. By J. D. Brown. pp. vi. 42. *London,* 1895. 8°. [*Library Association Series.* no. 6.] Ac. **9115/7.**

BURGOYNE (George) The Universal Penny. *See* London.—III. *Bromley Literary Association.* The Bromley Prize Essays, *etc.* 1862. 12°. **11825.** aaa. **5.**

BURGOYNE (Gerald)

—— The Fife & Forfar Imperial Yeomanry and its predecessors. Compiled . . . from regimental and troop order books . . . and from an MS. history of the Regiment by Lieutenant Benson Freeman, R.N. pp. 103. *J. G. Innes: Cupar-Fife,* 1904. 8°. **8839.** aa. **55.**

BURGOYNE (*Right Hon.* John) *See* Batchelder (Samuel F.) Burgoyne and his Officers in Cambridge, 1777–1778. 1926. 8°. **010815.** i. **15.**

—— *See* Conway (*Hon.* Henry S.) Prologue and Epilogue to The Way to keep him . . . The epilogue written by . . . Lieut. Gen. Burgoyne, *etc.* [1787.] fol. **11707.** i. **13.**

—— *See* Deane (Charles) *of Cambridge, Massachusetts.* Lieutenant-General John Burgoyne and the Convention of Saratoga, *etc.* 1877. 8°. [*American Antiquarian Society. Report of the Council.* 1877.] Ac. **5798/15.**

—— *See* De Fonblanque (Edward B.) Political and Military Episodes . . . derived from the Life and Correspondence of the Right Hon. J. Burgoyne, *etc.* 1876. 8°. **10816.** cc. **2.**

—— *See* Digby (William) *Lieutenant.* The British Invasion from the North. The campaigns of Generals Carleton and Burgoyne from Canada, 1776, with the journal of Lieut. W. Digby, *etc.* 1887. 4°. **9605.** dd. **4.**

—— *See* Drake (Samuel A.) Burgoyne's Invasion of 1777, *etc.* 1889. 8°. **9605.** aaa. **8.**

BURGOYNE (*Right Hon.* JOHN)

—— *See* ENGLAND. [*Appendix.—History and Politics.*—II. 1779.] A Brief Examination of the Plan, and Conduct of the Northern Expedition in America, in 1777. And of the surrender of the army under the command of Lieutenant-General Burgoyne. 1779. 8°. **8132. e. 27.**

—— *See* HAYLEY (William) *Esq.* Three Plays: with a preface, including dramatic observations, of the late Lieutenant General Burgoyne. 1811. 8°. **1344. h. 9.**

—— *See* HUDLESTON (Francis J.) Gentleman Johnny Burgoyne, *etc.* [With portraits.] [1927.] 8°. **010815. g. 18.**

—— —— 1928. 8°. **010815. df. 28.**

—— *See* LINGUET (Simon N. H.) Reponse à un article des Annales politiques de Mr. Linguet, no. 17, concernant la défaite du Gen. Burgoyne en Amerique. 1778. 8°. **101. l. 53.**

—— *See* NEILSON (Charles G.) An Original, Compiled, and Corrected Account of Burgoyne's Campaign . . . 1777, *etc.* 1844. 12°. **1447. c. 30.**

—— *See* NICKERSON (Hoffman) The Turning Point of the Revolution; or, Burgoyne in America, *etc.* [With a portrait.] 1928. 8°. **9615. ccc. 19.**

—— *See* REVIEW. The Poetical Review . . . Being a satirical display of the literal characters of Mr. G * rr * ck . . . and Genl. B * * rg * * * e [i.e. J. Burgoyne], *etc.* [1780 ?] 8°. **644. k. 18. (12.)**

—— *See* SCOTT, afterwards SCOTT WARING (John) *Major.* The Speech of Major Scott in the House of Commons . . . May 21, 1790, on the complaint of General Burgoyne for a breach of privilege. [1790.] 8°. **8022. f. 13. (4.)**

—— *See* SEDAINE (M. J.) Richard Coeur de Lion, *etc.* [Translated by J. Burgoyne.] 1786. 8°. **839. d. 10. (3.)**

—— —— 1786. 12°. **640. h. 16. (1.)**

—— —— [1787 ?] 8°. **11777.c.92.**

—— *See* SEDAINE (M. J.) Richard Cœur de Lion . . . Translated . . . By Lieut. General Burgoyne, *etc.* 1795. 12°. [*Jones's British Theatre.* vol. 8.] 11784. g. 8/8.

—— —— 1804. 8°. **11775. g. 2. (7.)**

—— —— 1805. 8°. **11779. c. 82.**

—— —— 1806. 12°. **11779. a. 1. (1.)**

—— —— 1806. 8°. [*Cawthorn's Minor British Theatre.* vol. 5. no. 21.] **11770. e. 1.**

—— —— 1815. 12°. [INCHBALD (*E.*) *Mrs. A Collection of Farces.* vol. 6.] **1345. b. 14.**

—— —— 1815. 16°. [*London Theatre.* vol. 4.] **1344. a. 23.**

—— —— [1825 ?] 8°. **1343. f. 25. (1.)**

—— —— [1826.] 8°. [*London Stage.* vol. 3.] **2306. g. 4.**

—— —— 1872. 8°. [*British Drama. Illustrated.* vol. 12.] **11770. bbb. 16. (4.)**

—— *See* SEDAINE (M. J.) Songs, Chorusses, &c. of the historical romance of Richard Cœur de Lion, *etc.* [Translated by J. Burgoyne.] 1787. 8°. **643. h. 3. (6.)**

—— *See* STONE (William L.) *the Younger.* Ballads and Poems relating to the Burgoyne Campaign, *etc.* 1893. 4°. **11687. h. 34.**

BURGOYNE (*Right Hon.* JOHN)

—— *See* STONE (William L.) *the Younger.* The Campaign of Lieut. Gen. J. Burgoyne, *etc.* 1877. 12°. **9603. bb. 7.**

—— The Dramatic and Poetical Works of the late Lieut. Gen. J. Burgoyne; to which is prefixed, Memoirs of the author. 2 vol. *C. Whittingham: London,* 1808. 8°. **1344. h. 18, 19.**

—— The Dashing White Sergeant. [A song.] *See* ELEANOR. Fair Eleanor, *etc.* [1830 ?] *s. sh.* 4°. **11630. f. 7. (74.)**

—— The Dashing White Sergeant. [A song.] *See* CLAUDEY. Banks of the Claudey To-morrow, and The Dashing White Sergeant. [1850 ?] *s. sh.* 4°. **11630. f. 7. (41.)**

—— General Burgoyne's Account of the Battle. *See* PULSIFER (David) An Account of the Battle of Bunker Hill, *etc.* 1872. 16°. **9603. a. 9.**

—— The Heiress; a comedy, *etc.* [The dedication signed: J. Burgoyne.] pp. 112. *J. Debrett: London,* 1786. 8°. **643. e. 15. (4.)**

—— [Another copy.] **841. e. 62.**

—— [Another copy.] G. **18756. (1.)**

—— Second edition. pp. 112. *J. Debrett: London,* 1786. 8°. **161. g. 65.**

—— Third edition. pp. 112. *J. Debrett: London,* 1786. 8°. **11775. e. 2. (3.)**

—— Fifth edition. pp. 112. *J. Debrett: London,* 1786. 8°. **11777. d. 5.**

—— Ninth edition. pp. 76. *J. Debrett: London,* 1787. 8°. **11777. d. 6.**

—— The Heiress . . . as performed at the Theatre-Royal, Drury-Lane, *etc.* [With a titlepage dated 1794.] pp. 120. *In:* Jones's British Theatre. vol. 8. 1795. 12°. **11784.** g. **8/8.**

—— [Another edition.] pp. xi. 84. *Chamberlaine: Dublin,* [1801.] 12°. **640. h. 6. (6.)**

—— The Heiress, *etc.* pp. 88. *In:* Sharpe's British Theatre. vol. 5. 1804. 32°. **11784. ee. 3. (3.)**

—— [A reissue.] The Heiress, *etc.* *In:* INCHBALD (Elizabeth) The British Theatre, *etc.* vol. 22. 1808 [1816 ?]. 12°. **1345. a. 22.**

—— The Heiress . . . With remarks by Mrs. Inchbald. pp. 91. *Longman, Hurst, Rees, Orme, & Brown: London,* [1816 ?] 12°. **11778.** p. **10. (6.)**

—— [Another edition.] With remarks by Mrs. Inchbald. pp. 91. *Longman & Co.: London,* [1820 ?] 12°. **11777. a. 5. (4.)**

—— [Another edition.] [1826.] *See* LONDON STAGE. The London Stage, *etc.* vol. 3. [1824, *etc.*] 8°. **2306. g. 4.**

—— [Another edition.] 1871. *See* BRITISH DRAMA. The British Drama. Illustrated. vol. 7. 1864, *etc.* 8°. **11770. bbb. 12. (60.)**

—— [A reissue.] *London,* [1883 ?] 8°. [*Dicks' Standard Plays.* no. 164.] **11770. bbb. 4.**

—— L'Héritière. [Translated by A. F. Villemain.] 1822. *See* CHEFS-D'OEUVRE. Chefs-d'œuvre des théâtres étrangers, *etc.* tom. 3. 1822, *etc.* 8°. **1342. h. 3.**

—— Die Erbin . . . Übersetzt von Wilhelm Schenk. pp. 190. 1793. *See* GERMAN STAGE. Deutsche Schaubühne. Bd. 52. 1788, *etc.* 8°. **752. a. 1/52.**

BURGOYNE (*Right Hon.* John)

—— [Another edition.] pp. 190. 1803. *See* German Stage. Neueste Deutsche Schaubühne. Jahrg. 1. Bd. 1. 1803, *etc.* 8°. **11746. aa.**

—— A Letter from Lieut.-Gen. Burgoyne to his Constituents, upon his late Resignation; with the correspondences between the Secretaries of War and him, relative to his return to America. The fourth edition. pp. 37. *J. Almon: London,* 1779. 8°. **8135. e. 15.**

—— The fifth edition. pp. 37. *J. Almon: London,* 1779. 8°. **T. 987. (7.)**

—— [Another copy.] **103. c. 59.**

—— *See* Englishman. A Letter to Lieut.-Gen. Burgoyne on his Letter to his Constituents. 1779. 8°. **103. c. 70.**

—— A Reply to Lieut. Gen. Burgoyne's Letter to his Constituents. pp. 46. *J. Wilkie: London,* 1779. 8°. **103. c. 69.**

—— The second edition. pp. 46. *J. Wilkie: London,* 1779. 8°. **1103. g. 54.**

—— The Lord of the Manor, a comic opera, *etc.* [By J. Burgoyne.] pp. xxvi. 96. 1781. 8°. *See* Lord. **643. g. 6. (12.)**

—— [Another copy.] **1346. f. 19.**

—— The Lord of the Manor . . . as performed at the Theatre-Royal, Drury-Lane, *etc.* [With a titlepage dated 1794. With a portrait.] pp. 94. *In:* Jones's British Theatre. vol. 8. 1795. 12°. **11784. g. 8/8.**

—— [Another edition.] pp. 58. *London,* [1832?] 12°. [*Cumberland's British Theatre.* vol. 13.] **642. a. 7.**

—— The Lord of the Manor. An opera. Altered from General Burgoyne, by C. Dibdin, *etc.* pp. 60. *Whittingham & Arliss: London,* 1816. 16°. [*London Theatre.* vol. 21.] **1344. a. 28.**

—— [Another edition.] pp. 16. 1825. *See* London Stage. The London Stage, *etc.* vol. 2. [1824, *etc.*] 8°. **2306. g. 4.**

—— [Another edition.] 1864. *See* British Drama. The British Drama. Illustrated. vol. 2. 1864, *etc.* 8°. **11770. bbb. 10. (38.)**

—— [A reissue.] *London,* [1874?] 8°. [*Dicks' Standard Plays.* no. 48.] **11770. bbb. 4.**

—— Airs, Duets, Trios, &c. in The Lord of the Manor, *etc.* pp. 19. 1780. 8°. *See* Lord. **11777. g. 54.**

—— The Lord of the Manor. A song from that opera. [1785?] *s. sh.* 8°. *See* Lord. **11621. i. 11. (32.)**

—— Airs, Duets, Choruses, &c. &c. in . . . The Lord of the Manor, *etc.* pp. 23. MS. NOTES. [1812.] 8°. *See* Lord. **11602. ff. 32*. (24.)**

—— The Maid of the Oaks, *etc.* [By J. Burgoyne.] pp. 68. 1774. 8°. *See* Maid. **643. e. 6. (1.)**

—— A new edition. pp. 68. 1775. 8°. *See* Maid. **11777. g. 56.**

—— [Another edition.] 1776. 8°. [*Collection of New Plays.* vol. 2.] *See* Maid. **11770. b. 2.**

—— [Another edition.] pp. 41. 1788. 8°. *See* Maid. **643. g. 6. (13.)**

BURGOYNE (*Right Hon.* John)

—— The Maid of the Oaks. A new dramatic entertainment . . . as performed at the Theatre-Royal, Drury-Lane, *etc.* [With a titlepage dated 1794.] pp. 79. *In:* Jones's British Theatre. vol. 8. 1795. 12°. **11784. g. 8/8.**

—— [Another edition.] *See* British Drama. The Modern British Drama. vol. 5. 1811. 8°. **11783.bbb.41.**

—— [Another edition.] *See* Inchbald (Elizabeth) A Collection of Farces, *etc.* vol. 6. 1815. 12°. **1345. b. 14.**

—— Das Mädchen im Eichthale, *etc.* [Translated by J. C. Bock.] pp. 110. 1778. *See* Schroeder (F. U. L.) Hamburgisches Theater. Bd. 3. 1776, *etc.* 8°. **87. e. 3.**

—— The Maid of the Oaks. Altered into an after-piece of two acts, by a gentleman of the Theatre-Royal, Edinburgh. 1788. 12°. [*A Collection of the most esteemed Farces and Entertainments performed on the British Stage.* vol. 6.] *See* Maid. **1344. c. 11.**

—— [Another edition.] pp. 32. *Sherwood, Neely & Jones: London,* 1818. 12°. [*London Theatre.* vol. 25.] **1344. a. 29.**

—— [Another edition.] [1826.] *See* London Stage. The London Stage, *etc.* vol. 3. [1824, *etc.*] 8°. **2306. g. 4.**

—— [Another edition.] *See* Drama. The Acting Drama, *etc.* 1834. 8°. **2302. f. 1.**

—— [Another edition.] 1872. *See* British Drama. The British Drama. Illustrated. vol. 11. 1864, *etc.* 8°. **11770. bbb. 15. (12.)**

—— [A reissue.] *London,* [1877?] 8°. [*Dicks' Standard Plays.* no. 185.] **11770. bbb. 4.**

—— Songs, Chorusses, &c. in the pastoral entertainment of the Maid of the Oaks, *etc.* pp. 22. 1774. 8°. *See* Maid. **1346. f. 8.**

—— Orderly Book of Lieut. Gen. John Burgoyne from his entry into the State of New York until his surrender at Saratoga, 16th Oct., 1777 . . . Edited by E. B. O'Callaghan. [With plates.] pp. xxxiv. 221. *J. Munsell: Albany, N.Y.,* 1860. 4°. **8827. ff. 49.**

—— Richard Cœur de Lion . . . By General Burgoyne [or rather, translated and adapted by the Right Hon. J. Burgoyne from the work by J. M. Sedaine]. pp. 33. *In:* Sharpe's British Theatre. vol. 10. 1804. 32°. **11784. ee. 8. (4.)**

—— A State of the Expedition from Canada, as laid before the House of Commons by Lieutenant-General Burgoyne . . . with a collection of authentic documents, and an addition of many circumstances . . . Written and collected by himself, *etc.* pp. viii. 140. lix. pl. 7. *J. Almon: London,* 1780. 4°. **194. a. 19.**

—— The second edition. [With maps.] pp. ix. 191. cix. *J. Almon: London,* 1780. 8°. **1130. e. 32.**

—— A Supplement to the State of the Expedition from Canada, containing General Burgoyne's orders respecting the principal movements and operations of the army to the raising of the siege of Ticonderoga. pp. 26. *J. Robson: London,* 1780. 4°. **9007. h. 4. (1.)**

—— Remarks on General Burgoyne's State of the Expedition from Canada. pp. 59. *G. Wilkie: London,* 1780. 8°. **103. d. 24.**

BURGOYNE (*Right Hon.* JOHN)

—— The Substance of General Burgoyne's Speeches on Mr. Vyner's motion on the 26th of May, and upon Mr. Hartley's motion on the 28th of May, 1778. With an appendix, containing General Washington's letter to General Burgoyne, &c. pp. 42. *J. Almon: London*, 1778. 8°. **102.** g. **47.**

—— The third edition. pp. 42. *J. Almon: London*, 1778. 8°. **1061.** h. **30. (3.)**

—— Condolence: an elegiac epistle from Lieut. Gen. B-rg-yne [i.e. J. Burgoyne], captured at Saratoga, Oct. 17, 1777 to Lieut. Gen. Earl C-rnw-ll-is [i.e. Cornwallis], captured at York-Town, Oct. 17, 1781. With notes by the editor. [The whole written by Michael Dorset.] pp. 32. 1782. 4°. *See* B-RG-YNE, *Lieut. Gen.* **643.** k. **2. (6.)**

—— The second edition. pp. 32. 1782. 4°. *See* B-RG-YNE, *Lieut. Gen.* **11630.** e. **14. (7.)**

—— A Letter to General Burgoyne [blaming him for absenting himself from his army], *etc.* *See* ESSAY. An Essay on Modern Martyrs, *etc.* 1780. 8°. **1103.** g. **55.**

BURGOYNE (*Sir* JOHN) *See* BURGOYNE (*Sir* John F.) *Bart.*

BURGOYNE (JOHN CHARLES) Chronological Account of India: showing the principal events connected with the Mahomedan and European governments in India. pp. vii. 85. *W. H. Allen & Co.: London*, 1859. 8°. **9055.** b. **24.**

BURGOYNE (JOHN EDGAR GALBRAITH) *See* HENNINGS (Richard) Klein Heini . . . Edited by J. E. G. Burgoyne, *etc.* 1928. 8°. **12213.** a. **1/239.**

—— German Composition Book. By J. E. G. Burgoyne . . . In collaboration with Helmut Hamann. [With key.] 2 pt. *London*, 1933. 8°. [*Harrap's Modern Language Series.*] **12213.** a. **1/305.**

BURGOYNE (*Sir* JOHN FOX) *Bart.* *See* HEAD (*Sir* Francis B.) *Bart.* A Sketch of the Life and Death of the late Field-Marshal Sir John Burgoyne, Bart, *etc.* 1872. 8°. **10817.** aaa. **37.**

—— *See* WROTTESLEY (*Hon.* George) Life and Correspondence of Field Marshal Sir John Burgoyne, Bart. 1873. 8°. **10817.** dd. **7.**

—— Army Reform. pp. 30. *W. Skeffington: London*, 1857. 8°. **8828.** b. **60. (8.)**

—— Coast Defences, chiefly as applicable to the coast of Great Britain. *See* ENGLAND.—*Army.—Engineers.—Royal Engineers.* [*Works edited by the Royal Engineers.*] Papers, *etc.* New ser. vol. 1. 1851, *etc.* 8°. **P.P. 4050.** i.

—— Ireland in 1831. Letters, *etc.* [By Sir J. F. Burgoyne.] pp. 48. 1831. 8°. *See* IRELAND. [*Appendix.—Miscellaneous.*] **8831.** bb. **41. (2.)**

—— A Letter . . . to Dan[l] O'Connell, Esq., M.P. . . . on the City of Dublin Steam Packet Company's Bill. pp. 8. *J. Brimmer: London*, 1836. 8°. **08806.** f. **2. (1.)**

—— Memoranda on Blasting Rock. 1840. *See* ENGLAND.—*Army.—Engineers.—Royal Engineers.* [*Works edited by the Royal Engineers.*] Papers, *etc.* vol. 4. 1844, *etc.* 4°. **P.P. 4050.** i.

—— Memoranda on the Defence of Posts . . . Reprinted 1862. pp. 8. 1862. 8°. *See* ENGLAND.—*Army.—Engineers.—Royal Engineers.* [*Works edited by the Royal Engineers.—Textbooks, etc.*] **C.T. 283. (4.)**

BURGOYNE (*Sir* JOHN FOX) *Bart.*

—— The Military Opinions of General Sir J. F. Burgoyne, Bart. . . . Collected and edited by Captain the Honble George Wrottesley, *etc.* pp. vii. 479. *Richard Bentley: London*, 1859. 8°. **8828.** cc. **31.**

—— *See* B., A., *Capitaine d'État-Major.* Situation militaire de la Grande Bretagne, *etc.* [A critique of "The Military Opinions of General Sir J. F. Burgoyne."] 1860. 8°. **8828.** c. **53. (6.)**

—— Our Defensive Forces. pp. 24. *Smith, Elder & Co.: London*, 1869. 8°. **8824.** dd. **42. (9.)**

—— [Another copy.] **C.T. 283. (3.)**

—— Second edition, *etc.* pp. x. 24. *Smith, Elder & Co.: London*, 1869. 8°. **8824.** dd. **42. (10.)**

—— Third edition, *etc.* pp. viii. 24. *Smith, Elder & Co.: London*, 1870. 8°. **8826.** dd. **18.**

—— Remarks on the Maintenance of Macadamised Roads. [Signed: J. F. B., i.e. Sir John F. Burgoyne.] pp. 38. 1843. 8°. *See* B., J. F. **C.T. 228. (7.)**

—— Remarks on the Maintenance of Macadamised Roads, *etc.* pp. 45. 1849. 8°. *See* TASMANIA. [*Miscellaneous Official Publications.*] **8776.** bb. **21.**

—— [Another edition.] *See* LAW (Henry) *Civil Engineer.* Rudiments of the Art of Constructing and Repairing Common Roads, *etc.* 1861–2. 8°. **8768.** b. **10.**

—— [Another edition.] *See* MALLET (Robert) Rudimentary Papers on the Art of Constructing and Repairing Common Roads, *etc.* 1868. 12°. **8703.** cc. **30.**

—— Rudimentary Treatise on the Blasting and Quarrying of Stone for Building and other Purposes, *etc.* pp. vii. 106. *John Weale: London*, 1849. 12°. **8703.** a. **5.**

—— Sir John Burgoyne, a Sacrifice to "the slanders of a ribald press," his history and services described in a letter published in the Morning Chronicle of the 1st March, by an Englishman and Civilian . . . Second edition. pp. 14. *James Ridgway: London*, 1855. 8°. **8028.** c. **94. (1.)**

—— Sir John Burgoyne, a Sacrifice to "the slanders of a ribald press." Second letter to the Morning Chronicle . . . By an Englishman and Civilian. pp. 7. *James Ridgway: London*, 1855. 8°. **8028.** c. **94. (2.)**

—— Second edition. pp. 7. *James Ridgway: London*, 1855. 8°. **8028.** c. **14.**

BURGOYNE (*Sir* JOHN FOX) *Bart.*, and **HUTCHINSON** (CHARLES SCROPE)

—— On Quarrying Rock for Great Works as practised at Holyhead in the years 1850 and 1851. 1852. *See* ENGLAND.—*Army.—Engineers.—Royal Engineers.* [*Works edited by the Royal Engineers.*] Papers etc. New series. vol. 2. 1851, *etc.* 8°. **P.P. 4050.** i.

BURGOYNE (*Sir* JOHN MONTAGU) *Bart.* Regimental Records of the Bedfordshire Militia, from 1759 to 1884. pp. 123. *W. H. Allen & Co.: London*, 1884. 8°. **8829.** b. **13.**

—— A Short History of the Naval and Military Operations in Egypt from 1798 to 1802. pp. vii. 181. *Sampson Low & Co.: London*, 1885. 8°. **9061.** de. **12.**

BURGOYNE (LEON E.)

—— Ensign Ronan . . . Illustrations by Dirk Gringhuis. pp. viii. 184. *John C. Winston Co.: Philadelphia, Toronto,* [1955.] 8°. **12838. g. 27.**

—— Jack Davis, Forward . . . Illustrated by Dirk Gringhuis. pp. vii. 213. *John C. Winston Co.: Philadelphia, Toronto,* [1953.] 8°. **12732. e. 19.**

—— State Champs . . . Illustrated by Joseph Bolden. [A tale.] pp. vii. 210. *John C. Winston Co.: Philadelphia, Toronto,* [1951.] 8°. **12834. bb. 1.**

BURGOYNE (LORNA) *See* SHAKESPEARE (W.) [*Midsummer Night's Dream.*] The Play of Shakespeare, Midsummer Night's Dream. Illustrated by L. Burgoyne. 1919. fol. **11764. m. 18.**

BURGOYNE (MARY E.)

—— *See* BURGOYNE (Samuel R.) and BURGOYNE (M. E.) India Printing Book. 1954. *obl.* 8°. Cup. **1253. a. 61.**

BURGOYNE (MONTAGU) *See* BIBLE.—*Psalms.*—*Selections.* [*English.*] Select Portions of the Psalms, extracted from the Book of Common Prayer . . . by M. Burgoyne. 1827. 8°. **1411. k. 6.**

—— An Address to the Governors and Directors of the Public Charity Schools, pointing out some defects and suggesting remedies. pp. 42. *Rivington: London,* 1829. 8°. **T. 1296. (4.)**

—— Third edition, *etc.* pp. 32. *Rivington: London,* 1831. 8°. **8304. b. 6. (5.)**

—— A Letter from Montagu Burgoyne, Esquire . . . on the Present State of Public Affairs and the Representation of the County of Essex, *etc.* pp. 78. *Meggy & Chalk: Chelmsford,* 1808. 8°. **8142. c. 51.**

—— A Letter from Montagu Burgoyne . . . to his brother Churchwardens in the Diocese of Lincoln; giving a summary account of the prosecution, conviction, and deprivation of the Rev. Dr. Edward Drax Free, Rector of Sutton . . . With . . . hints on the seriousness of the oath taken by Churchwardens, *etc.* pp. 30. *Rivingtons; J. Hatchard: London,* 1830. 8°. **T. 1297. (2.)**

—— [Another copy.] A Letter . . . to his Brother Churchwardens, in the diocese of Lincoln, *etc. London,* 1830. 8°. **8364. bb. 61. (16.)**

—— A Letter from Montagu Burgoyne . . . to the Freeholders and Inhabitants of . . . Essex, on the present state of public affairs, and the pressing necessity of a reform in the Commons House of Parliament. pp. vii. 58. *Meggy & Chalk: Chelmsford,* 1809. 8°. **8138. de. 4. (10.)**

—— A Letter to the Churchwardens of the Diocese of Lincoln . . . with reference to a Letter addressed to them last year, on the subject of the prosecution and conviction of Dr. Free, *etc.* pp. 14. *Rivingtons: London,* 1831. 8°. **8135. bb. 16.**

—— A Letter to the Freeholders of Essex, occasioned by a Public Address to them, dated the 22nd of May, 1802, and signed Montagu Burgoyne. By a Brother Freeholder. pp. 14. *R. Carpenter: London,* [1802.] 8°. **8025.cc.13.**

—— A Letter to the Right Hon. Sturges Bourne . . . on the subject of the removal of the Irish by the 59th Geo. III. cap. XII sec. 33. pp. 54. *J. Shaw: London,* 1820. 8°. **1138. k. 10.**

BURGOYNE (MONTAGU)

—— A Letter to the Right Honorable the Lord Duncannon and the Lords Commissioners of his Majesty's Woods and Forests; shewing the necessity of the removal of the deer from the forests of Waltham and Hainault, and also of an enclosure of parts of these forests, *etc.* pp. 78. *Rivingtons: London,* 1831. 8°. **T. 1394. (17.)**

BURGOYNE (MONTAGUE) Proceedings of a General Court-Martial . . . for the Trial of Col. Montague Burgoyne . . . on charges preferred against him by Major Crosse and Captains Bund and Graham, etc. pp. ii. 310. xxvii. *J. Moore: Dublin,* 1800. 8°. **1132. f. 2.**

BURGOYNE (PETER) *pseud.* [i.e. PETER BURGOYNE RATTENBURY.]

—— The School of Mystery. Illustrated by David Morrow. pp. 206. *Blackie & Son: London & Glasgow,* [1954.] 8°. **12837. ff. 24.**

BURGOYNE (PHILIP ARTHUR)

—— Cursive Handwriting: its history, practice and application. pp. 60. pl. 2. *Dryad Press: Leicester,* 1955. 8°. **7947. c. 84.**

BURGOYNE (RODERICK HAMILTON) Historical Records of the 93rd Sutherland Highlanders, now the 2nd Battalion Princess Louise's Argyll and Sutherland Highlanders. pp. xvi. 430. *R. Bentley & Son: London,* 1883. 8°. **8829. k. 15.**

BURGOYNE (ROSE)

—— The Wish and the Way; or, Passages in the life of Rose Burgoyne. By the author of 'The Diamond Wreath' [i.e. Mary H. Holt, afterwards Meldrum]. pp. viii. 376. *W. Oliphant & Co.: Edinburgh,* 1871. 8°. **12804. h. 27.**

BURGOYNE (SAMUEL ROBERT)

—— India—Land of the Ladder. [With plates.] pp. 35. *Bible Churchmen's Missionary Society: London,* 1948. 8°. [*Field Surveys.* no. 1.] **4764.de.49/1.**

BURGOYNE (SAMUEL ROBERT) and **BURGOYNE** (MARY E.)

—— India Printing Book. *Bible Churchmen's Missionary Society: London,* 1954. *obl.* 8°. Cup. **1253. a. 61.**

BURGOYNE (SIDNEY J.) *See* BROWNE (Evelyn G.) Friendly Fellows. A few thoughts . . . by S. J. Burgoyne, put into verse by E. G. Browne. [1926.] 12°. **011686. dg. 39.**

BURGRÆD, *King of Mercia. See* HEYWOOD (Nathan) The Kingdom and Coins of Burgred. 1885. 8°. **7758.b.22.**

BURGRAEVE (ADOLPHE) *See* BURGGRAEVE.

BURGRAVIUS (ANGELUS) *Count. See* MARCHESE (M.) Accipiter panegyricus in laudem . . . A. Maggii. [Edited by Count A. Burgravius.] 1646. 4°. **4865. bbb. 28.**

BURGRAVIUS (JOANNES ERNESTUS) *See* BURGGRAV (Johann E.)

BURGRED, *King of Mercia. See* BURGRÆD.

BURG-SCHAUMBURG (PAUL) *See* SCHAUMBURG (P. E. B. R.)

BURG-SCHNEITHER (JOHANNA PETRONELLA VAN) *See* SALLY, *pseud.* [i.e. J. P. van Burg-Schneither.]

BURGSDORF (CARL FRIEDRICH WILHELM VON) Etwas gegen das "Etwas über die preussische Pferdezucht . . . Vom Dr. T. Renner." pp. 73. *Gumbinnen,* 1846. 8°. **775. i. 36. (3.)**

BURGSDORF (CARL FRIEDRICH WILHELM VON)

—— Versuch eines Beweises, dass die Pferderennen in England so wie sie jetzt bestehen, kein wesentliches Beförderungs-Mittel der bessern edlen Pferdezucht in Deutschland werden können. pp. 122. *Königsberg*, 1827. 8°. **779. g. 11.**

—— *See* BIEL (G. W. L. von) *Baron*. Einiges über edle Pferde . . . Veranlasst durch folgende Schriften: 1. Versuch eines Beweises, dass die Pferderennen in England . . . kein wesentliches Beförderungsmittel der . . . Pferdezucht in Deutschland werden können, von Herrn von Burgsdorf, *etc.* 1830. 8°. **1146. e. 19.**

BURGSDORF (CARL GOTTLOB VON) Lob- und Trauer-Rede, welche den 14ten Junii 1746 bey des . . . Herzogs Johann Adolphs . . . Exequien . . . gehalten worden. *See* JOHN ADOLPHUS, *Duke of Saxe-Weissenfels*. Hochverdientes Ehren- und Liebes-Denkmahl, *etc.* [1746.] fol. **10703. i. 10.**

BURGSDORF (CONRAD ALEXANDER MAGNUS VON) *See* SPANNAGEL (C.) Konrad von Burgsdorff, *etc.* 1903. 8°. [*Quellen und Untersuchungen zur Geschichte des Hauses Hohenzollern.* Bd. 5. Reihe 3. Hft. 3.] **9917. dd. 27.**

BURGSDORF (DIETRICH VON) *Bishop of Naumburg*. *See* BOCKSDORF (Theodericus von)

BURGSDORF (FRIEDRICH AUGUST LUDWIG VON) Anleitung zur sichern Erziehung und zweckmässigen Anpflanzung der einheimischen und fremden Holzarten; welche in Deutschland und unter ähnlichen Klima im Freyen fortkommen. [With plates.] 2 Tl. *Berlin*, 1787. 8°. **969. b. 31.**

—— Revidirte und vermehrte Auflage. 2 Tl. [*Berlin*,] 1795. 8°. **987. d. 26.**

—— Burgsdorfs Anviisning til at opelske indenlandske og udenlandske Træearter i det Frie. Oversat og omarbeidet . . . af Martin Gottlieb Schæffer . . . forsynet med Anmærkninger af Erik Viborg. Dl. 1. pp. 354. *Kiøbenhavn*, 1799. 8°. **988. f. 25.**
No more published.

—— Forsthandbuch. Allgemeiner theoretisch-praktischer Lehrbegriff sämtlicher Försterwissenschaften . . . Dritte verbesserte Auflage. Nebst . . . Tabellen, *etc.* pp. lvi. 793. *Frankfurt & Leipzig*, 1795. 8°. **970. b. 23.**

—— *See* REITTER (J. D.) and ABEL (G. F.) Abbildungen der hundert deutschen wilden Holz-Arten nach dem Numern-Verzeichnis im Forst-Handbuch von F. A. L. von Burgsdorf. Als eine Beilage zu diesem Werke, heraus gegeben . . . von I. D. Reitter . . . und G. F. Abel. 1790. 4°. **1253. g. 12.**

—— Versuch einer vollständigen Geschichte vorzüglicher Holzarten in systematischen Abhandlungen, *etc.* [With plates.] Tl. 1, Tl. 2. Bd. 1. *Berlin*, 1783, 87. 4°. **441. f. 9, 10.**
Imperfect; wanting Tl. 2. Bd. 2.

BURGSDORF (KONRAD ALEXANDER MAGNUS VON) *See* BURGSDORF (Conrad A. M. von)

BURGSDORFF (ALEXANDER VON) and **RECKLINGHAUSEN** (VON) Tafeln zur Flugbahnberechnung der Infanteriegeschosse. Nebst kurzer Anleitung zum Gebrauch der Tafeln. pp. vi. 213. *Berlin*, 1897. 8°. **8831. m. 25.**

BURGSDORFF (ALHARD VON) Das Westfälische Ulanen-Regiment Nr. 5 und seine Kriegsformationen im Weltkriege. Herausgegeben von A. v. Burgsdorff, *etc.* [With plates and maps.] pp. 408. *Oldenburg, Berlin*, 1930. 8°. [*Erinnerungsblätter deutscher Regimenter. Truppenteile des ehemaligen preussischen Kontingents.* Bd. 300.] **8836. e. 1/300.**

BURGSDORFF (CARL FRIEDRICH WILHELM VON) *See* BURGSDORF.

BURGSDORFF (HEDWIG VON) Lebenslauf der Frau Hedwig von Burgsdorff geborne von der Osten geb. 1613, gest. 1676. Von ihr selbst aufgesetzt. Herausgegeben von der von Burgsdorff'schen Familie, *etc.* pp. iv. 62. *Berlin*, 1873. 8°. **10602. h. 4. (3.)**

BURGSDORFF (KONRAD ALEXANDER MAGNUS VON) *See* BURGSDORF (Conrad A. M. von)

BURGSDORFF (WILHELM VON) Briefe an Brinkman, Henriette v. Finckenstein, Wilhelm v. Humboldt, Rahel, Friedrich Tieck, Ludwig Tieck und Wiesel. Herausgegeben von Alfons Fedor Cohn. pp. xv. 230. *Berlin*, 1907. 8°. [*Deutsche Literaturdenkmale des* 18. *und* 19. *Jahrhunderts*. no. 139.] **12253. bbb.**

BURGSDORF-SERPENTEN (CARL FRIEDRICH WILHELM VON) *See* BURGSDORF.

BURGSSUN (R. E.) Sang-Po—Lu-Lien-Yang. Chinesische Oper . . . Dichtung von R. E. Burgssun . . . Zweite Auflage. pp. 19. *Wien*, [1924.] 4°. **11747. h. 41.**

—— Sang-Po, el Don Juan de Oriente . . . Versión . . . en castellano, por José Lleonart. *Wien*, [1924.] 4°. **11747. h. 40.**

BURGST (HUIBERT GERARD NAHUYS VAN) *Baron*. *See* NAHUYS VAN BURGST.

BURGSTALLER (ANTOINE) *See* BURGSTHALER.

BURGSTALLER (FRIEDRICH)

—— *See* KORN (R.) and BURGSTALLER (F.) Papier- und Zellstoff-Prüfung, *etc.* 1944. 8°. **7947. c. 41.**

BURGSTALLER (SEPP)

—— Erblehre, Rassenkunde und Bevölkerungspolitik. 400 Zeichenskizzen für den Schulgebrauch. pp. 52. *Wien*, [1941.] *obl.* fol. Cup. **1247. aaa. 26.**

BURGSTHALER (ANTOINE) *See* JESUITS. [*Appendix.*] Missions-Unfug der Jesuiten. Dargelegt in den Predigten der P. Burgstaller. P. Damberger, *etc.* 1843. 8°. **1360. k. 16.**

BURGSTORFF (CONRADUS FRIDERICUS À) Dissertatio de officialibus Imperii Romano-Germanici, *etc.* *Praes.* H. Conringius. *Typis H. Mulleri: Helmestadii*, 1669. 4°. **835. e. 6. (13.)**

—— Exercitatio ethica de gradibus læsionum. *Praes.* H. Uffelmannus. *Typis H. Mulleri: Helmestadii*, 1669. 4°. **525. e. 42. (1.)**

BURGT (FRANCISCUS PETRUS VAN DE) De celebratione missarum. Fragmentum juris canonici, *etc.* pp. viii. 199. *Ultrajecti*, 1871. 8°. **5063. de. 4.**

—— De jubilaeo. SS. D. N. Pii PP. IX encyclicae Gravibus explanatio, rectoribus ecclesiarum et confessariis maxime dicata. [With the text.] pp. xvi. 103. *Ultrajecti*, 1875. 8°. **3900. g. 1. (9.)**

—— Tractatus de dispensationibus matrimonialibus, *etc.* pp. 144. *Bruxellis*, 1855. 12°. **5176. c. 19.**

—— Tractatus de matrimonio. pp. viii. 476. iv. *Sylvae Ducis*, 1859. 12°. **8415. h. 17.**

—— Editio secunda. pp. 483. *Ultrajecti*, 1875. 8°. **8415. h. 2.**

BURGT (J. M. M. VAN DER) Dictionna[ire] français-k[irundi] avec l'indication succincte de la signification swahili et allemande. Ouvrage illustré d'une carte, de . . . gravures . . . et augmenté d'une introduction et 196 articles ethnologiques sur l'Urundi et les Warundi. pp. cxix. 647. *Bois-le-Duc*, 1903. 8º. **12910**. v. **35**.
The titlepage and the two leaves following are mutilated.

—— Éléments d'une grammaire kirundi. (Supplément. Langue des Watwa, Kitwa = Pygmées.) pp. 108. 1902. *See* BERLIN.—*Friedrich-Wilhelms-Universität.—Seminar für orientalische Sprachen.* Mitteilungen, *etc.* Jahrg. 5. Abt. 3. 1898, *etc.* 8º. Ac. **8816**. b.

BURGTORF (F.) Wiesen- und Weidenbau. Praktische Anleitung zur Auswahl und Cultur der Wiesen- und Weidenpflanzen, nebst Berechnung der erforderlichen Samenmengen. pp. 139. *Berlin*, 1873. 8º. [*Thaer-Bibliothek.* Bd. 3.] **7078**. aaa. **3**.

BURGUERA GARCÍA (LUIS)

—— Política de trabajo. Conferencia pronunciada en el ciclo de mensajes políticos del segundo curso de "Adsum," revista oral del Departamento Provincial de Seminarios de Alicante, *etc.* [*Alicante*, 1954.] fol. **8042**. m. **10**.

BURGUERO (ALFONSO DANVILA Y) *See* DANVILA Y BURGUERO.

BURGUES MISSIESSY (ÉDOUARD JACQUES) *Count.* Installations des vaisseaux, *etc.* pp. xii. 403. pl. IX. an VI [1798]. 4º. *See* FRANCE.—*Ministère de la Marine et des Colonies.* **1397**. i. **19**.

—— *See* MATHIEU-MIRAMPAL (J. B. C.) Corps législatif. Conseil des Cinq-Cents. Discours . . . sur un ouvrage publié par le citoyen Missiessy [i.e. "Installations des vaisseaux"], *etc.* [1798.] 8º. F.R. **593**. (**11**.)

BURGUET (ADOLPHE ZÜND) *See* ZÜND-BURGUET.

BURGUET (GUSTAVE) Du diagnostic différentiel des tumeurs du creux poplité. pp. 53. *Paris*, 1854. 4º. [*Collection des thèses soutenues à la Faculté de Médecine de Paris.* An 1854. tom. 3.] **7372**. g. **3**.

BURGUET (HENRI) Dissertation sur la chlorose; thèse, *etc.* pp. 19. *Paris*, 1836. 4º. **1184**. g. **16**. (**9**.)

BURGUET (JEAN AUGUSTE) Réflexions sur la doctrine des crises; thèse, *etc.* pp. 39. *Paris*, 1817. 4º. **1183**. d. **11**. (**16**.)

BURGUET (LÉONARD) Dissertation sur la métro-péritonite puerpérale; thèse, *etc.* pp. 30. *Paris*, 1833. 4º. **1184**. f. **2**. (**30**.)

BURGUETE (RICARDO) Rectificaciones históricas. De Guadalete á Covadonga, y primer siglo de la reconquista de Asturias. Ensayo de un nuevo método de investigación, *etc.* pp. 321. pl. VI. *Madrid*, 1915. 8º. **9180**. bbb. **25**.

BURGUIÈRES (ÉDOUARD EDMOND) Des vices de conformation des orifices du cœur, *etc.* pp. 54. *Paris*, 1841. 4º. [*Collection des thèses soutenues à la Faculté de Médecine de Paris.* An 1841. tom. 3.] **7371**. c. **3**.

BURGUILLOS (ANTONIO PLANCHART) *See* PLANCHART BURGUILLOS.

BURGUILLOS (TOMÉ DE) *pseud.* [i.e. LOPE FELIX DE VEGA CARPIO.] Rimas humanas y diuinas, del Licenciado Tomé de Burguillos, no sacadas de blibioteca [*sic*] ninguna . . . sino de papeles de amigos y borradores suyos . . . Por Frey Lope Felix de Vega Carpio. ff. 160. *En la Imprenta del Reyno: Madrid*, 1634. 4º. **1064**. i. **7**.

BURGUILLOS (TOMÉ DE) *pseud.* [i.e. LOPE FELIX DE VEGA CARPIO.]

—— [Another copy.] **11450**. c. **47**.
Cropped.

—— [Another edition.] ff. 160. FEW MS. NOTES. *En la Imprenta Real: Madrid*, 1674. 4º. **11450**. e. **34**.

—— [Another edition.] pp. 6. 258. 1792. *See* LEONARDO Y ARGENSOLA (L.) Rimas. tom. 11. 1786, *etc.* 8º. **242.i.23.**

—— (Edición conmemorativa de la Fiesta del Libro del año MCMXXXV.) [A facsimile of the edition of 1634.] [1935.] 8º. *See* MADRID.—*Cámara Oficial del Libro.* **20010**. b. **20**.

—— Cancion. *See* LOPEZ DE SEDANO (J. J.) Parnaso Español, *etc.* tom. 1. 1768, *etc.* 8º. **242**. k. **28**.

—— La Gatomachia, poema epico burlesco. [1770.] *See* LOPEZ DE SEDANO (J. J.) Parnaso Español, *etc.* tom. 2. 1768, *etc.* 8º. **242**. k. **29**.

BURGUM PLEBIS. *See* PIEVE, *on the Aroccia.*

BURGUM (EDWIN BERRY)

—— Academic Freedom & New York University. The case of Professor Edwin Berry Burgum. pp. 80. *Committee for the Reinstatement of Professor Burgum: New York*, 1954. 8º. **08385**. m. **3**.

—— The Novel and the World's Dilemma. pp. 352. *Oxford University Press: New York*, 1947. 8º. **11868**. b. **5**.

BURGUM (HENRY) *See* GEORGE (William) *of Bristol.* The "Grateful Society" in 1767, and its president H. Burgum, *etc.* [1879.] 8º. C. **60**. m. **2**. (**4**.)

—— *See* PINE (William) An Answer to A Narrative of Facts . . . lately published by H. Burgum, as far as relates to the character of W. Pine. 1775. 12º. **1414**. b. **9**.

BURGUN (ACHILLE) Le Développement linguistique en Norvège depuis 1914. 2 pt. *Kristiania*, 1919, 21. 8º. [*Skrifter utgit av Videnskapsselskapet i Kristiania.* Hist.-fil. Klasse. 1917. no. 1; 1921. no. 5.] Ac. **1054/5**.

BURGUND (ELISABETH) Die Entwicklung der Theorie der französischen Schauspielkunst im 18. Jahrhundert bis zur Revolution. pp. 131. *Breslau*, 1931. 8º. **11822**. w. **26**.

BURGUNDESCH LEGENDE. *See* BURGUNDIAN LEGEND.

BURGUNDIA (ANTONIUS A) Linguæ vitia & remedia emblematice expressa. pp. 190. *Apud vidua Cobbaert: Antuerpiæ*, 1652. *obl.* 16º. **11408**. a. **24**.
The titlepage is engraved.

—— Mundi lapis lydius, siue vanitas per veritatē falsi accusata & conuicta. [With engravings by Andreas Pauli.] pp. 249. *Typis viduæ I. Cnobbari: Antuerp.*, 1639. 4º. **8405**. g. **12**.
The titlepage is engraved.

—— Des Wereldts proef-steen, ofte de ydelheydt door de waerheydt beschuldight ende overluyght van valscheydt . . . Met Neder-landtsche dichtē verlicht door Petrus Geschier. [With engravings by Andreas Pauli.] pp. 368. *Gedruckt by de Weduwe ende Erfgenamē van I. Cnobbaert: Antwerpen*, 1643. 4º. **11556**. cc. **24**.
The titlepage is engraved.

BURGUNDIA (Antonius a)

—— *See* Clemens (A. A.) Mundi lapis lydius . . . Versibus illustrabat A. A. Clemens. [Containing the engravings by Andreas Pauli illustrating Burgundia's "Mundi lapis lydius."] [1665?] 4°. **89. k. 4.**

BURGUNDIA (Jacobus a) *See* Bourgogne (Jacques de) *Seigneur de Falais et de Bredam.*

BURGUNDIA (Joannes de) *See* John, *de Bourdeaux.*

BURGUNDIA (Philippus a) *Bishop of Utrecht. See* Philip, *of Burgundy, Bishop of Utrecht.*

BURGUNDIA (Vincentius de) *See* Vincentius, *Bellovacensis.*

BURGUNDIAN. Décentralisation. Par un Bourguignon [i.e. Viscount F. H. de Sarcus]. pp. 37. *Dijon,* 1863. 8°. **8050. h. 39. (1.)**

—— Le Manuel du Bourguignon, ou recueil abrégé des titres qui servent à prouver les privilèges de la province. [By Viscount de Chastenay Saint-Georges.] pp. 80. [1788.] 8°. **F. 1264. (1.)**

—— Observations sur une brochure intitulée: "Le Manuel du Bourguignon." pp. 48. 1789. 8°. **F. 1264. (3.)**

BURGUNDIAN GENTLEMAN. Le Gentil-homme bourguignon. [A political tract.] pp. 12. *Paris,* 1615. 8°. **8050. b. 10. (3.)**

BURGUNDIAN LEGEND. Légende bourguignonne. Burgundesch Legende. [A poem.] Strasbourg, 1477.—Légende bourguignonne . . . Séconde edition. Augsbourg, 1477. [Facsimiles. With a French translation of the Strasburg edition.] *Ger. See* Picot (A. E.) and Stein (H.) Recueil de pièces historiques imprimées sous le règne de Louis xi., *etc.* 1923. 4°. **Ac. 8933. c.**

BURGUNDIAN POEMS. Poésies bourguignonnes inédites, accompagnées de quelques autres d'une grande rareté. *See* Mignard (T. J. A. P.) Histoire de l'idiome bourguignon, etc. 1856. 8°. **12953. f. 17.**

BURGUNDIANS. [For editions of the Lex Burgundionum:] *See* Burgundy. [*Laws and Public Documents.—Lex Burgundionum.*]

—— A true and perfecte Discourse of the ouerthrow of certaine companies of Burgonions both horse & foot men at Villefranche, a town scituate on the borders of Champaigne, vpon the riuer of Meuze, betweene Sunday at night & Munday morning being the 4. day of August 1597. together with the certaine number of how many are slaine and taken prisoners. Translated out of French into English, by W. P. [i.e. W. Peters? or W. Phillip?] 𝔅.𝔏. *Printed by E. Allde for Cuthbert Burbie: London,* [1597.] 4°. **C. 114. d. 5. (4.)**

BURGUNDIO, *Pisano. See* Buonamici (Francesco) *of Pisa.* Burgundio Pisano. 1908. 8°. [*Annali delle Università toscane.* tom. 28.] **Ac. 46.**

—— *See* Nemesius, *Bishop of Emesa.* Gregorii Nysseni—Nemesii Emeseni—περι φυσεως ἀνθρωπου liber a Burgundione in latinum translatus . . . Capitulum i. Cui epistola Burgundionis ad Fredericum i. imperatorem et indices omnium capitulorum praemittuntur, *etc.* 1891. 8°. **08467. i. 20.**

BURGUNDIONE, *Pisano. See* Burgundio, *Pisano.*

BURGUNDIONES. *See* Burgundians.

BURGUNDIUS (Horatius) [Poems.] 1756. *See* Morei (M. G.) Arcadum carmina, *etc.* 1757, *etc.* 8°. **78. c. 34, 35.**

BURGUNDIUS (Nicolaus) Nicolai Burgundi . . . Historia bavarica, sive Ludovicus iv. Imperator. pp. 180. *Iuxta exemplar impressum Ingolstadii anno* 1636 [*Amsterdam?* 1650?]. 4°. **1054. g. 26.**

—— [Another edition.] Iterum edidit, cum præfatione, Iustus Christophorus Böhmer. pp. 180. *Helmestadii,* 1705. 4°. **172. d. 14. (1.)**

—— Nicolai Burgundj . . . Historia belgica ab anno m.d.lviii. pp. 355. *Ex officina W. Ederi; apud I. Bayr: Ingolstadii,* 1633. 8°. **1193. k. 8.**

—— [Another edition.] Cum præfatione Nicolai Hieronymi Gundlingii. pp. 203. *Halæ Magdeburgicæ,* 1708. 4°. **172. d. 14. (2.)**

—— Nicolai Burgundii . . . Poëmata, *etc.* pp. 190. *Apud G. Lesteenum: Antuerpiæ,* 1621. 12°. **11409. a. 20.**

—— Soltani Solimanni Turcarum imperatoris horrendum facinus in proprium filium . . . Mustapham, anno Domini 1553. patratum. *See* Lonicerus (P.) Chronicorum Turcicorum . . . tomus primus [*etc.*]. tom. 1. 1578. fol. **434. i. 17.**

BURGUNDUS (Jacobus) *See* Bourgogne (Jacques de) *Seigneur de Falais et de Bredam.*

BURGUNDUS (Matthaeus) *See* Mathey (Jean B.) *Architect.*

BURGUNDUS (Nicolaus) *See* Burgundius.

BURGUNDUS (Petrus) *See* Estella (D. de) R.P. Fr. Didaci Stellæ . . . De contemnendis mundi vanitatibus libri tres. Recenter ex hispanica lingua in italicam traducti . . . iam verò ex italica in latinâm translati, à . . . P. Burgundo. 1585. 8°. **526. d. 1. (2.)**

—— —— 1603. 12°. **4399. bb. 73.**

BURGUNDUS (Vincentius) *See* Vincentius, *Bellovacensis.*

BURGUNDY.

Arrangement.

LAWS AND PUBLIC DOCUMENTS.

Lex Burgundionum.

—— Antiquæ Burgundionum leges. *See* Franks. Libelli seu decreta a Clodoveo, et Childeberto, & Clothario . . . ædita, *etc.* [1500?] 16°. **C. 28. a. 20.**

—— Lex Burgundionum. *See* Lindenbrog (F.) Codex legum antiquarum, *etc.* 1613. fol. **503. i. 1.**

—— Lex Burgundionum. *See* Georgisch (P.) Corpus juris Germanici antiqui, *etc.* 1738. 4°. **503. f. 7.**

—— Lex Burgundionum. 1741. *See* Bouquet (M.) Recueil des historiens des Gaules et de la France, *etc.* tom. 4. 1738, *etc.* fol. **Circ.8–9.b.**

BURGUNDY. [LAWS AND PUBLIC DOCUMENTS.—LEX BURGUNDIONUM.]

—— Lois des Bourguignons vulgairement nommées Loi Gombette, traduites pour la première fois par M. J.-F.-A. Peyré . . . Contenant la Loi salique et la Loi ripuaire. pp. 144. *Lyon*, 1855. 8°. **5405. c. 8.**

—— Leges Burgundionum. Edidit Ludovicus Rudolfus de Salis. pp. 188. *Hannoverae*, 1892. fol. [*Monumenta Germaniae historica*. Legum sectio I. tom. 2. pt. 1.] **2087.c.**

—— Gesetze der Burgunden. Herausgegeben von Franz Beyerle. *Lat. & Ger.* pp. xvi. 191. *Weimar*, 1936. 8°. [*Germanenrechte*. Bd. 10.] Ac. **2121.**

—— The Burgundian Code. Liber constitutionum sive lex Gundobada. Constitutiones extravagantes. Translated by Katherine Fischer. pp. xiii. 106. *University of Pennsylvania Press: Philadelphia*, 1949. 8°. [*University of Pennsylvania. Department of History. Translations and Reprints from the Original Sources of History.* ser. 3. vol. 5.] Ac. **2692.** p/5.

LATER COLLECTIONS.

—— Lescoustumes du pays de Bourgongne redigees par escript: visitees ordonnees et corrigees par les seigneurs tant des parlements que de lostel de trespuissant illustrissime prince Philippe iadis duc de Bourgongne . . . Auec les postilles de droit escript int[er]pretāt lesd coustumes, *etc.* (Corrigees ⁊ redigees par Maistre Hugues descousu.) 𝕲.𝕷. *Venundantur per Petrum Baleti ; imprimees par A. dury: Luduni*, 1516. 8°. **706. a. 17.**

—— La Coustume de Bourgongne, de nouueau commentée, abregée, et conferée avec toutes les autres coustumes de France par I. Bouuot. Auec vn autre petit commentaire sur la mesme Coustume escrit . . . par Hugues Descousu . . . Et vn troisiesme: y ioints quelques arrests dudit Parlement de Dijon. 5 pt. *Pour P. & I. Chouët: Geneue*, 1632. 4°. **5402. c. 2.**

—— La Coustume du duché de Bourgongne, enrichie des commentaires faicts sur son texte par les Srs Begat . . . & Depringle . . . et de plusieurs obseruations faictes par diuers aduocats de la Prouince [or rather by N. Canat], et plusieurs arrests . . . ensemble vn traicté des Mainmortes [by Philippe de Villeva] & des Censes faict par Monsieur Begat, et un traicté particulier faict par Monsieur Souuert, & autres. (Traicté et formulaire de practique, dressé par Estienne Bernard.) 2 pt. MS. NOTES. *Lyon ; P. Cusset: Châlon*, 1652. 4°. **5402. bb. 9. (1.)**

—— Coustumes generales du pays et duché de Bourgongne, auec les annotations de Monsieur Begat . . . & du Sieur Depringles . . . Reueuës, corrigées, & augmentées de plusieurs arrests, auxquelles on a adjoûté les notes de M. Charles du Moulin. [Edited by Jacques Auguste de Chevanes.] pp. 538. *La vefve de P. Cusset: Châlon*, 1665. 4°. **5402. bb. 9. (2.)**

—— Coutume generale des pays et duché de Bourgogne, avec le commentaire de Monsieur Taisand . . . A quoi on a joint les notes de Me Charles du Moulin & ses décisions sur des questions considerables, *etc.* pp. 872. *J. Ressayre: Dijon*, 1698. fol. **5406. k. 10.**

—— Coutume generale des pays et duché de Bourgogne, avec les observations de Messire François Bretagne . . . Celles de Me. Nicolas Perrier . . . sur le premier titre: des notes de Mes. de La Mare & Jehannin, & plusieurs arrêts rendus en interpretation de quelques articles, &c. pp. 635. *Dijon*, 1736. 4°. **5402. bb. 5.**

BURGUNDY. [LAWS AND PUBLIC DOCUMENTS.—LATER COLLECTIONS.]

—— Les Coutûmes du duché de Bourgogne. Avec les anciennes coutûmes, tant générales, que locales de la même province, non encore imprimées. Et les observations de M. Bouhier. 2 tom. *Dijon*, 1742, 46. fol. **503. k. 10, 11.**

—— Recueil des édits . . . & autres réglements émanés du Roi & de son Conseil, concernant l'administration des États de Bourgogne, des arrêts des Parlements, Chambres de Comptes, Cours des Aides, qui peuvent avoir quelque rapport aux objets de ladite administration, et des principaux décrets des États de ladite Province. Le tout disposé par ordre chronologique, & imprimé par ordre de MM. les Élus-généraux desdits États, *etc.* tom. 1. *Dijon*, 1784. 4°. **5423. h. 17.**
Imperfect; wanting tom. 2.

SINGLE LAWS.

—— ROBERT II., *Duke.* [1272–1306.] Le Mémorial de Robert II, duc de Bourgogne, 1273–1285. (Un document financier du XIIIe siècle.) [Compiled by Raoul de Beaune. Edited by Henri Jassemin.] pp. xxxii. 160. *Paris*, 1933. 8°. **08229. l. 16.**

—— PHILIP III., *Duke.* [1419–1467.] Merkwürdiger Versönbrief Philipp Herzogs von Burgund, Lothringen und den Niederlanden mit der Stadt Bremen vom Jahre 1446. Einladungsschrift zu Feier welche am 29. des Brachmonats . . . von der hiesigen teutschen Gesellschaft öffentlich augestellet werden soll, aufgesezt von Johann Philipp Cassel. pp. 16. *Bremen*, 1768. 4°. **573. k. 32. (6.)**

OFFICIAL BODIES.

ASSEMBLÉE DE LA NOBLESSE.

—— *Begin.* Les Gentilshommes de la province de Bourgogne, s'adressant au Bureau intermédiaire de Messieurs les Élus, *etc.* [A request that the king be petitioned to call the Estates of Burgundy. 29 Aug. 1788.] pp. 4. [1788.] 8°. **F.R. 25. (16.)**

—— Discours prononcé par l'un de MM. les secrétaires de la Noblesse, au nom de son ordre, à l'Assemblée des députés du Clergé de la Sainte-Chapelle de Dijon, & de ceux des corps & communautés du Tiers-État de cette ville . . . le 27 décembre 1788. (Extrait des registres du parlement de Dijon.) pp. 15. [1789.] 8°. R. **244. (1.)**

—— Protestation de la noblesse de Bourgogne. [31 Dec. 1788.] pp. 8. [1788.] 8°. **F.R. 25. (18.)**

—— Lettre de convocation adressée à chacun des députés aux États de Bourgogne, à l'effet de se rendre à Dijon le 14 février prochain, pour se trouver à l'assemblée générale indiquée au 15 dudit mois. [27 Jan. 1789.] pp. 4. [1789.] 8°. F.R. **25. (20.)**

—— [Another copy.] Lettre de convocation, adressée à chacun des députés aux États de Bourgogne, *etc.* [1789.] 8°. R. **244. (2.)**

—— Discours qui devoit être prononcé à l'Assemblée de la Noblesse de Bourgogne, le 15 février 1789. Par un membre de cette Assemblée. pp. 22. 1789. 8°. F. **89. (3.)**

CHAMBRE DES ÉLUS GÉNÉRAUX.

—— *See* infra: ÉTATS.

ÉTATS.

—— [Decrees relating to the administration of Burgundy.] *See* supra: LAWS AND PUBLIC DOCUMENTS. [*Later Collections.*] Receuil des édits, *etc.* 1784. 4°. **5423. h. 17.**

—— Remonstrances au Roy des deputez des trois estats de son Duche de Bourgoigne sur l'edict de la pacification, par ou se monstre qu'en vn Royaume deux religions ne se peuuent soustenir, & les maulx qui ordinairement aduiennent aux Roys & prouinces ou les heretiques sont permis & tolerez. ff. 16. *Par G. Silvius: Anuers,* 1563. 4°. **156. l. 3.**

—— Remonstrances faictes au Roy de France, par les deputez des trois Estats du Duché de Bourgoigne, sur l'Edict de la pacification des troubles du Royaume de France . . . Reueu corrigé & amplifié, *etc.* pp. 63. *Par G. Silvius: Anuers,* 1564. 8°. **8050. aaa. 13.**

—— Ad Burgundiae Comitia in litteratos munifica. [A poem. By J. B. de Santeul.] pp. 4. [*Dijon?* 1694.] 4°. **837. h. 6. (8.)**

Chambre des Élus Généraux.

—— Placet adressé au roi, par la Chambre des élus généraux de la province de Bourgogne, le 3 juin 1788. pp. 11. [1788.] 8°. **F. 864. (23.)**

MARÉCHAUSSÉE.

—— Mémoire pour la ci-devant compagnie de marechaussée [*sic*] de Bourgogne et Bresse. pp. 6. 8. *Paris,* 1791. 4°. **936. f. 17. (36.)**

PARLEMENT.

—— Registre des Parlements de Beaune et de Saint-Laurent-lès-Chalon, 1357–1380. Publié avec une introduction par Pierre Petot. pp. lxviii. 375. 1927. 8°. *See* PARIS.—*Société d'Histoire du Droit.* **Ac. 2112/3.**

—— Arrests notables du Parlement de Dijon, recueillis par M. François Perrier . . . avec des observations sur chaque question par Guillaume Raviot, *etc.* 2 tom. *Dijon,* 1738. fol. **21. f. 1, 2.**

—— Registres du Parlement de Dijon, de tout ce qui s'est passé pendant la Ligue. [31 Dec. 1588–23 July 1594.] pp. viii. 4–328. [1763.] 12°. **8052. bb. 18.**

—— Arrêtés et lettres au Roi des classes du Parlement séant à Dijon, Aix, Toulouse et Rouen, en faveur de celles séantes à Rennes & à Pau. pp. 37. 1765. 12°. **4091. bb. 35. (12.)**

—— Arrest de la Court de Parlement de Bourgõgne seant à Dijon, du XII. d'Aoust 1589. Par lequel defences sont faictes à tous Princes, Seigneurs & autres, de receuoir ny recognoistre pour Roy Henry de Nauarre, le fauoriser, ou luy bailler aide . . . à peine d'estre punis comme Heretiques & perturbateurs du repos public. pp. 3. *Par I. Pillehotte: Lyon,* 1589. 8°. **1192. g. 15. (3.)**

—— Extrait des registres du Parlement de Dijon. [Requiring the Superior of the Jesuits' College at Dijon to submit all regulations concerning the Society to the inspection of the Parlement. 8 March 1763.] pp. 8. [*Dijon,* 1763.] 12°. **4091. bb. 35. (6.)**

—— Arrest du Parlement de Bourgogne qui ordonne que l'imprimé intitulé, Mémoire présenté au Roi par deux magistrats du Parlement d'Aix, contre des arrêts & arrêtés de leur compagnie, sera lacéré & brûlé . . . Du 18 mars 1763, *etc.* pp. 4. *Dijon,* [1763.] 12°. **4091. bb. 35. (8.)**

—— Extrait des registres du Parlement de Dijon. Du 18 mars 1763. [Requiring the production of the title-deeds of Jesuit Colleges.] pp. 8. [*Dijon,* 1763.] 12°. **4091. bb. 35. (7.)**

—— Extrait des Registres du Parlement de Dijon, du 11 juillet 1763. [Suppressing the Society of Jesus within the jurisdiction of the Parlement.] pp. 15. *Dijon,* 1763. 12°. **4091. bb. 35. (9.)**

—— Très-humbles et très-respectueuses remontrances du Parlement séant à Dijon, au sujet de la déclaration du 21 novembre 1763. [19 Jan. 1764.] pp. 58. [1764.] 12°. **4091. bb. 35. (10.)**

—— Très-humbles et très-respectueuses remontrances du Parlement séant à Dijon, sur les mauvais traitemens faits au Parlement séant à Toulouse, à Grenoble, & à Rouen. [14 Feb. 1764.] pp. 15. [1764.] 12°. **4091. bb. 35. (11.)**

—— Arrêté du Parlement de Dijon . . . du lundi 10 septembre 1787. (Arrêté . . . du mercredi 12 septembre 1787.) [Requesting the king to recall the Parliament of Paris from Troyes.] pp. 7. 1787. 8°. **F.R. 4. (33.)**

—— Remontrances du Parlement de Dijon, sur l'usage des lettres de cachet. [Jan. ? 1788.] pp. 16. [1788.] 8°. **R. 23. (8.)**

—— Remontrances du Parlement de Dijon, du mois d'avril 1788, sur l'édit des vingtièmes. pp. 31. *Dijon,* 1788. 8°. **R. 23. (6.)**

—— Protestations du Parlement de Bourgogne. [A protest against the transference of the Parlement's powers to the grands-bailliages.] [4 June 1788.] pp. 18. [1788.] 8°. **F.R. 25. (15.)**

—— Extrait des Protestations du Parlement de Dijon, du 4 juin 1788. pp. 8. [*Dijon,*] 1788. 8°. **R. 23. (7.)**

—— Très-humbles et très-respectueuses remontrances qu'addressent au Roi . . . les gens tenant sa Cour de Parlement à Dijon, sur un arrêt du Conseil du 14 février dernier, concernant la Commission de Commandant en second donnée par sa Majesté au sieur de la Charce. [5 March 1789.] pp. 19. [1789.] 8°. **F. 4. (2.)**

Ordre des Avocats.

—— Discours de doléance prononcé à Monsieur le Premier Président du Parlement de Dijon, au nom de l'Ordre des Avocats, le 13 Juin 1788, contenant des protestations. pp. 4. [1788.] 8°. **F.R. 26. (29.)**

—— Protestations. [Signed by certain advocates of the Parlement, disclaiming responsibility for the "Projets de mandats & de cahiers pour les deputés du Tiers-État," published in March 1789.] pp. 8. [*Dijon,* 1789.] 8°. **R. 23. (9.)**

APPENDIX.

—— Avertissement à la noblesse et villes de Bourgongne tenans le party de la feinte union. Réimpression conforme à l'édition originale de 1594, publiée par Henri Chevreul. [A reply to Étienne Bernard's "Advis des Estats de Bourgogne aux Français."] pp. 28. *Paris,* 1886. 8°. **9004. h. 27. (7.)**

—— Costumes, mœurs et usages de la cour de Bourgogne sous le règne de Philippe III dit le Bon, 1455–1460. [Facsimiles of leaves from an illuminated manuscript entitled "L'Histoire de Girart, comte de Nevers, et de la belle Euriant, sa mie."] livr. 1–5. [1850?] fol. *See* GERARD, *Count de Nevers.* **1857. b. 2.**

BURGUNDY. [APPENDIX.]

—— De la Bourgogne, de ce qu'elle a été, de ce qu'elle est, & de ce qu'elle sera. pp. 36. [1788 ?] 8°. F.R. **25. (21.)**

—— *See* ESPRITS. Aux esprits impartiaux, car il s'en trouve toujours. [A reply to "De la Bourgogne, de ce qu'elle a été, de ce qu'elle est, et de ce qu'elle sera."] pp. 8. [1788.] 8°. **F. 37. (12.)**

—— Dissertation sur la representation en succession, suivant la coutume du duché de Bourgogne. Avec une explication de l'article 25. de la même coutume. pp. xii. 187. *Dijon*, 1734. 8°. **5424. aa. 1.**

—— Histoire secrète de Bourgogne. [By C. R. de Caumont de la Force.] 2 tom. pp. 536. *S. Benard: Paris*, 1694. 12°. **9210. b. 1.**

—— [Another edition.] 2 tom. *Paris*, 1710. 12°. **596. c. 30.**

—— The Secret History of Burgundy: or, the Amorous and political intrigues of Charles Duke of Burgundy and Louis XI. of France, *etc.* [A translation by G. Roussillon of "Histoire secrète de Bourgogne," by C. R. de Caumont de la Force.] pp. xii. 396. *J. Walthoe, Jun.; T. Woodward: London*, 1723. 12°. **12512. ccc. 24.**

—— Die geheime Geschichte von Burgund, nebst den Begebenheiten der Koeniginn von Navarra, Margaretha von Valois. [A translation of "Histoire secrète de Bourgogne" and of pt. 1. of "Histoire de Marguerite de Valois" by C. R. Caumont.] pp. 534. *Stockholm & Leipzig*, 1745. 8°. **1319. c. 24.**

—— Nueua Relacion de lo que ha sucedido en Borgoña, en la Campaña, del año de 1640. Con muy raros exemplares de la constant, y inuencible fidelidad de aquella Nacion, y su respuesta a los engaños y trampas con que tentaron los Franceses de alborotar, y apartarla de la obediencia de su Magestad. *I. Sanchez: Madrid*, 1641. fol. **593. h. 22. (81.)**

BURGUNDY, ADELAIDE, *Duchess of.* *See* MARY ADELAIDE [of Savoy], *Consort of Louis, Grandson of Louis XIV., Dauphin of France.*

——, CHARLES, *Duke of.* [1466–1477.] *See* CHARLES, *Duke of Burgundy*, called *the Bold.*

——, JOHN, *Duke of.* [1404–1419.] *See* JOHN, *Duke of Burgundy*, called *the Fearless.*

——, LOUIS, *Duke of.* *See* LOUIS, *Duke de Bourgogne, Dauphin of France.*

——, LOUIS JOSEPH XAVIER, *Duke of.* *See* LOUIS JOSEPH XAVIER [de Bourbon], *Duke de Bourgogne.*

——, MARY, *Duchess of.* [1477.] *See* MARY, *Duchess of Burgundy, Consort of Maximilian I., etc.*

——, MARY ADELAIDE, *Duchess of.* *See* MARY ADELAIDE [of Savoy], *Consort of Louis, Grandson of Louis XIV., Dauphin of France.*

—— PHILIP II., *Duke of.* [1363–1404.] *See* PHILIP II., called *the Bold, Duke of Burgundy.*

——, PHILIP III., *Duke of.* [1419–1467.] *See* PHILIP III., called *the Good, Duke of Burgundy.*

——, PHILIP OF, *Bishop of Utrecht.* *See* PHILIP, *of Burgundy, Bishop of Utrecht.*

——, ROBERT I., *Duke of.* [1032–1075.] *See* ROBERT I., *Duke of Burgundy.*

BURGUNDY,

——, ROBERT II., *Duke of.* [1272–1306.] *See* ROBERT II., *Duke of Burgundy.*

BURGUNDY, *Counts of.* *See* STOUFF (L.) Les Comtes de Bourgogne et leurs villes domaniales, *etc.* 1899. 8°. **010168. g. 13.**

—— Cartulaire des Comtes de Bourgogne, 1166–1321. [Edited by Jules Gauthier and, after his death, by Count Joseph de Sainte-Agathe and Roger de Lurion.] pp. xx. 507. *Besançon*, 1908. 8°. [*Mémoires et documents inédits pour servir à l'histoire de la Franche-Comté.* tom. 8.] **Ac. 282.**

BURGUNDY, *County of.* *See* FRANCHE-COMTÉ.

BURGUNDY, *Dukes of.* *See* BRUGIÈRE DE BARANTE (A. G. P.) *Baron.* Histoire des ducs de Bourgogne de la maison de Valois, *etc.* 1825, *etc.* 8°. **1058. h. 18.**

—— *See* CALMETTE (J. L. A.) Les Grands ducs de Bourgogne. 1949. 8°. **9906. a. 48.**

—— *See* CARTELLIERI (O.) Am Hofe der Herzöge von Burgund. Kulturhistorische Bilder. 1926. 8°. **010168. k. 23.**

—— *See* CARTELLIERI (O.) Beiträge zur Geschichte der Herzöge von Burgund. 1912, *etc.* 8°. [*Sitzungsberichte der Heidelberger Akademie der Wissenschaften.* Phil.-hist. Klasse. Jahrg. 1912. Abh. 11; Jahrg. 1913. Abh. 2, 9; Jahrg. 1914. Abh. 6.] **Ac. 892/2.**

—— *See* CARTELLIERI (O.) Geschichte der Herzöge von Burgund 1363–1477. 1910. 8°. **09210. g. 17.**

—— *See* CHEVILLARD (Jacques) *Genealogist.* Genealogie de Messeigneurs les princes ducs de Bourgogne, *etc.* [1700 ?] *s. sh.* fol. **1850. d. 4. (2.)**

—— *See* DUCHESNE (A.) Histoire genealogique des ducs de Bourgongne de la maison de France, *etc.* 1628. 4°. **138. b. 1.**

—— *See* FABERT(de) pseud. L'Histoire des ducs de Bourgogne. 1687. 12°. **9210. b. 20.**

—— —— 1689. 12°. **596. b. 28.**

—— *See* LAMEERE (E.) Le Grand conseil des ducs de Bourgogne de la maison de Valois, *etc.* 1900. 8°. **09225. h. 8.**

—— *See* MORILLOT (L.) *Abbe.* La Question des restes de Jean sans Peur. Caveaux, cercueils, ossements et épitaphes des ducs, duchesses et princesses de Bourgogne inhumés dans les caveaux de l'église de la Chartreuse à Dijon. [1905.] 4°. **10659. h. 17.**

—— *See* PETIT (E.) Ducs de Bourgogne de la maison de Valois. D'après des documents inédits. 1909. 8°. **10661. s. 16.**

—— *See* PETIT (E.) Histoire des ducs de Bourgogne de la race capétienne, avec des documents inédits et des pièces justificatives. 1885, *etc.* 8°. **09200. f. 3.**

—— Bibliothèque royale des ducs de Bourgogne. *See* BRUSSELS.—*Bibliothèque royale de Belgique.*

—— Inventaires mobiliers et extraits des comptes des ducs de Bourgogne de la maison de Valois, 1363–1477. Publiés par B. Prost. 2 tom. 1902–13. 8°. *See* FRANCE.—*Ministère de l'Instruction Publique, etc.* **07709. dd. 19.**

BURGUNDY, *Kings of.* Essai sur l'histoire des premiers rois de Bourgogne et sur l'origine des Bourguignons. [By B. Legoux de Gerland.] [With plates.] pp. xiv. 144. *Dijon,* 1770. 4°. **804.** e. **14.** (**1.**)

—— [Another copy.] **181.** b. **10.**

BURGUNDY-CRUYBECK, *House of.* *See* MOILON (J.) and CANAYE (J.) Abbregé et tableau genealogiques, comprenans . . . l'origine, les alliances, et lignées des deux entières maisons de Bourgongne-Cruybeck ; et de Bourgongne-Herlaer, *etc.* 1665. 12°. **9905.** a. **1.**

BURGUNDY-HERLAER, *House of.* *See* MOILON (J.) and CANAYE (J.) Abbregé et tableau genealogiques, comprenans . . . l'origine, les alliances, et lignées des deux entières maisons de Bourgongne-Cruybeck ; et de Bourgongne-Herlaer, *etc.* 1665. 12°. **9905.** a. **1.**

BURGUNDY (BILLY) Billy Burgundy's Letters. [By O. V. Limerick. With plates.] pp. 74. *J. F. Taylor & Co.: New York,* 1902. 8°. **12314.** aaaa. **18.**

BURGUS (HEINRICH VON) *See* HEINRICH, *von Burgus.*

BURGUS (PETRUS BAPTISTA) Petri Baptistæ Burgi . . . De bello suecico commentarii, quibus Gostaui Adulphi . . . in Germaniā expeditio usq; ad ipsius mortem comprehenditur, *etc.* pp. 272. *Apud H. Edelmannum: Leodii,* 1633. 4°. **153.** b. **5.**
The titlepage is engraved.

—— [Another edition.] Editio ultima castigatior. pp. 416. *Apud H. Edelmannum: Leodii,* 1639. 12°. **1193.** b. **3.**

—— [Another edition.] Petri Baptistæ Burgi . . . Mars sueco-germanicus, *etc.* pp. 334. *Ex officina A. Binghy: Coloniæ Agrippinæ,* 1641. 12°. **9327.** a. **19.**
With an additional titlepage, engraved, with an imprint reading " Antverpiæ, apud viduam et hæred. Io. Cnobbari et [sic]. "

—— [Another edition.] Petri Baptistæ Burgi . . . De bello suecico commentarii . . . Editio ultima figuris æneis adornata. pp. 424. *Apud H. Edelmannum: Leodii,* 1643. 8°. **1193.** b. **4.**
With an additional titlepage, engraved.

—— [Another edition.] Petri Baptistæ Burgi . . . Mars sueco-germanicus, *etc.* pp. 232. *Apud A. Binghium: Coloniæ Agrippinæ,* 1644. 12°. **1193.** b. **2.**

—— De dignitate Genuensis Reipublicæ disceptatio. pp. 102. *I. M. Farronus: Genuæ,* 1646. 4°. **660.** l. **7.**

—— Petri Baptistæ Burgi De dominio Ser^mæ Genuensis Reip. in mari Ligustico libri. II. pp. 257. *D. Marcianus: Romæ,* 1641. 4°. **661.** c. **9.**
The titlepage is engraved.

—— [Another copy.] **180.** h. **19.**

—— [Another edition.] *See* GERMANY. [*Appendix.—History and Politics.*—II.] Imperii Germanici ius ac possessio in Genua Ligustica eiusque ditionibus, *etc.* 1751. 4°. **8032.** i. **8.**

—— *See* GRASWINCKEL (D.) Thod. J. F. Graswinckelj . . . Maris liberi vindiciæ: adversus P. B. Burgum Ligustici maritimi dominii assertorem. 1652. 4°. **1374.** c. **23.**

—— *See* SELDEN (John) Joannis Seldeni Vindiciæ secundum integritatem existimationis suæ, per convitium de scriptione Maris clausi . . . læsæ in vindiciis maris liberi adversus P. B. Burgum, Ligustici maritimi dominii assertorem Hagæ Comitis . . . emissis. 1653. 4°. **1127.** h. **28.** (**7.**)

BURGUS (SIGISMUNDUS) Sigismundi Burgi . . . Cremonensium oratoris panaegyricus Leonardo Lauretano optimo humanissimoque principi Venetiis dictus . . . M.D. .III. .XII. Kld. Maii. *Per Bernardinum Venetum de Vitalibus: Venetiis,* 1503. 4°. **1342.** o. **19.**

BURGUY (   ) *Dramatist,* and **BORDIER** (FRÉDÉRIC) Roméo et Paméla. Comédie-vaudeville en un acte. pp. 52. *Paris,* 1874. 12°. **11739.** b. **35.** (**8.**)

BURGUY (GEORGES FRÉDÉRIC) *See* HERRIG (L.) and BURGUY (G. F.) La France littéraire, *etc.* 1870. 8°. **12236.** cc. **12.**

—— Grammaire de la langue d'oïl, ou grammaire des dialectes français aux XIIe et XIIIe siècles, suivie d'un glossaire, *etc.* 3 tom. *Berlin,* 1853–56. 8°. **1331.** g. **12.**

BURGUY (S.) Les Préludes, poésies . . . Avec une introduction par M. Charles de Franciosi. pp. 186. 3. *Lille,* 1860. 8°. **11481.** bb. **7.**

BURGWARDT (HEINRICH) *See* PESTALOZZI (J. H.) Heinrich Pestalozzi. Ein Buch für Eltern und Lehrer . . . Herausgegeben von H. Burgwardt. 1846. 12°. **8305.** b. **41.**

—— Morgenstimmen eines naturgemässen und volksthümlichen Sprach- und Schulunterrichts in niederdeutschen Volksschulen. pp. viii. 263. *Leipzig,* 1857. 8°. **8309.** d. **3.**

—— Der naturgemässe und instructive Sprachunterricht in Volksschulen gegenüber dem analytischen und . . . L. Kellner . . . als Berichterstatter und Kritiker im " Pädagogischen Jahresbericht " von 1859/60, *etc.* pp. viii. 128. *Wismar,* 1863. 8°. **12963.** dd. **14.**

BURGWART. Der Burgwart. Zeitschrift für Burgenkunde und das ganze mittelalterliche Befestigungswesen. *See* BERLIN.—*Vereinigung zur Erhaltung deutscher Burgen.*

BURGWEGER (THEODOR) Meta Bergmann. Ein Schauspiel in drei Akten. pp. 86. *Bad Salzungen,* [1912.] 8°. **11748.** de. **42.** (**2.**)

BURGWINDHEIM.

—— Bericht, von der wunderthätigen Krafft vnd heylsamen Wirckung, dess newlichst entstandenen Heyl-Bronnens, bey Burgwinnumbein Meil von Closter Ebrach, *etc.* [With a woodcut.] [1626 ?] *s. sh.* fol. Tab. **597.** d. **2.** (**14.**)

BURGWINNUMB. *See* BURGWINDHEIM.

BURGWYN (MEBANE HOLOMAN)

—— Lucky Mischief . . . Pictures by Gertrude Howe. pp. 246. *Oxford University Press: New York,* 1949. 8°. **12831.** c. **31.**

—— Moonflower. pp. 186. *J. B. Lippincott Co.: Philadelphia & New York,* 1954. 8°. **12825.** ee. **28.**

—— Penny Rose. pp. 223. *Oxford University Press: New York,* 1952. 8°. **12730.** d. **19.**

BURGWYN (WILLIAM HYSLOP SUMNER) *See* NORRIS (William H.) Digest of the Maryland Reports, *etc.* (vol. 21–45. By W. H. S. Burgwyn.) 1847, *etc.* 8°. **6699.** c. **7.**

BURHĀN (MUḤAMMAD ḤUSAIN IBN KHALAF) *Tabrīzī.*

—— Borhani Quaṭiu, a Dictionary, of the Persian Language, explained in Persian . . . With a short grammar prefixed . . . The whole arranged, carefully corrected, revised, and the text occasionally illustrated with Persian notes, by Thomas Roebuck. *Printed by Philip Pereira, at the Hindoostanee Press: Calcutta,* 1818. fol. **757.** l. **8.**

BURHĀN AḤMAD FĀRŪḲĪ.

—— Imam-i-Rabbani Mujaddid-i-Alf-i-Thani Shaikh Ahmad Sirhindi's Conception of Tawhid, *etc.* pp. xii. 192. *Sh. Muhammad Ashraf: Lahore*, 1940. 8°. **04504.** c. **14.**

BURHĀN AL-DĪN, *al-Zarnūjī.* Enchiridion studiosi, arabice conscriptum a Borhaneddino Alzernouchi cum duplici versione latina altera a Friderico Rostgaard . . . elaborata altera Abrahami Ecchellensis. Ex museo Rostgardiano edidit Hadrianus Relandus. (تعليم المتعلم طريق التعلم) *Arab. & Lat.* pp. 250. *Trajecti ad Rhenum*, 1709. 12°. **14540.** b. **2.**

—— [Another copy.] **14540.** b. **3.**

—— تعليم المتعلم طريق التعلم Borhân-ed-dîni Es-Sernûdji Enchiridion studiosi. Ad fidem editionis Relandianae nec non trium codd. Lipss. et duorum Berolinn. denuo arabice edidit, latine vertit, praecipuas lectt. varr. et scholia Ibn-Ismaëlis selecta ex cod. Lips. et Berolin. adjecit, textum et scholia vocalibus instruxit et lexico explanavit C. Caspari . . . Praefatus est Henricus Orthobius Fleischer. *Arab. & Lat.* pp. xiv. 82. 48. *Lipsiae*, 1838. 4°. **14540.** c. **1.**

—— Semita Sapientiae . . . nunc primum latini juris facta, ab Abrahamo Ecchellensi [from the Arabic of Burhān al-Dīn al-Zarnūjī], *etc.* 1646. 8°. *See* SEMITA. **722.** d. **8.** (**1.**)

BURHĀN AL-DĪN KĀMIL. Die Türken in der deutschen Literatur bis zum Barock und die Sultansgestalten in den Türkendramen Lohensteins. Inaugural-Dissertation, *etc.* pp. 59. *Kiel*, 1935. 8°. **11856.** f. **51.**

BURHĀN AL-DĪN KHĀN, *Kushkekī.* Каттаган и Бадахшан. Данные по географии страны, естественно-историческим условиям, населению, экономике и путям сообщения, с 34 картами. Перевод с персидского П. П. Введенского, Б. И. Долгополова . . . и Е. В. Левкиевского. Под редакцией . . . А. А. Семенова. pp. xiii. 248. *Ташкент*, 1926. 8°. [*Общество для изучения Таджикистана и иранских народностей за его пределами.* no. 2.] Ac. **1164.**

BURHĀN IBN ḤASAN. Tūzak-i-Wālājāhī of Burhān ibn Ḥasan. Translated . . . by S. Muḥammad Ḥusayn Nainar, *etc.* [With plates, including a portrait.] *Madras*, 1934, 39. 8°. [*Madras University Islamic Series.* no. 1, 4. 2 pt. **14003.s.2/1,4.**

BURHANS (DANIEL) The Scripture Doctrine of the Election of Jacob, and Rejection of Esau, considered. A sermon, *etc.* pp. 31. *O. Steele & Co.: New-Haven* [*Conn.*], 1811. 8°. **4486.** f. **25.**

—— Second edition, *etc.* pp. 31. *J. Adams: Boston*, 1828. 8°. **4486.** c. **33.** (**4.**)

—— A Sermon, preached at Waterbury . . . on the death of Mr. Asahel Lewis. Also, at Danbury . . . at the funeral of James Clark, Esq. pp. 22. *Oliver Steele: New-Haven* [*Conn.*], 1809. 8°. **4986.** cc. **16.**

BURHANS (ROBERT D.)

—— The First Special Service Force. A war history of the North Americans, 1942–1944. pp. xiii. 376. 1947. 8°. *See* UNITED STATES OF AMERICA.—*Army.*—*First Special Service Force.* **9101.** f. **94.**

BURHĀN SHEHĪDĪ.

—— Уйгурско-Китайско-Русский Словарь. pp. 827. [*Peking,*] 1953. 8°. **12912.** g. **72.**

BURHENNE (CARL) Werner Siemens als Sozialpolitiker, *etc.* [With plates, including a portrait.] pp. 119. *München*, 1932. 8°. **10709.** f. **20.**

BURHENNE (HEINRICH) *Geologist.*

—— Beitrag zur Kenntniss der Fauna der Tentaculitenschiefer im Lahngebiet mit besonderer Berücksichtigung der Schiefer von Leun unweit Braunfels, *etc.* pp. 56. pl. v. *Berlin*, 1899. 8°. [*Abhandlungen der Königlich Preussischen geologischen Landesanstalt.* Neue Folge. Hft. 29.] Ac. **3139.**

BURHENNE (HEINRICH) *Writer for Children.*

—— Das Mutterbüchlein. Den deutschen Müttern gewidmet. Ausgewählt von H. Burhenne. pp. 48. *Halle a. S.*, [1938.] 8°. **08416.** ee. **56.**
Hft. 42 *of* "*Marholds Jugendbücher.*"

BURHENNE (KARL) *See* BURHENNE (Carl)

BURHIL (ROBERT) *See* SMITH (Miles) *Bishop of Gloucester.* A Learned and Godly Sermon, *etc.* [With a dedicatory preface by Robert Burhil.] 1602. 8°. C. **12.** d. **18.** (**3.**)

—— De potestate regia et usurpatione papali, pro Tortura torti, contra Parallelum Andreæ Eudæmonioannis Cydonii Iesuitæ, responsio R. Burhilli. [A defence of Lancelot Andrewes's "Tortura torti."] pp. 291. *Excudebat Iosephus Barnesius: Oxoniæ*, 1613. 8°. **847.** k. **20.** (**2.**)

—— Pro Tortura torti contra Martinum Becanum Iesuitam, responsio R. Burhilli. [A defence of Lancelot Andrewes's "Tortura torti."] pp. 303. *Excudebat Robertus Barkerus: Londini*, 1611. 8°. **850.** b. **9.** (**2.**)

BURHILL CLUB. *See* WALTON-ON-THAMES.

BURHILLUS (ROBERTUS) *See* BURHIL (Robert)

BURHOP (ERIC HENRY STONELEY)

—— *See* MASSEY (Harrie S. W.) and BURHOP (E. H. S.) Electronic and Ionic Impact Phenomena. 1952. 8°. W.P. **2180**/**39.**

—— *See* MOON (Philip B.) and BURHOP (E. H. S.) Atomic Survey, *etc.* [1947.] 8°. **8426.** aa. **61.**

—— The Auger Effect and other radiationless transitions. pp. xiv. 188. pl. v. *University Press: Cambridge*, 1952. 8°. [*Cambridge Monographs on Physics.*] W.P. **13761**/**12.**

—— The Challenge of Atomic Energy. By E. H. S. Burhop, with the collaboration of John Hasted. pp. x. 137. *Lawrence & Wishart: London*, 1951. 8°. **8714.** aa. **3.**

BURHRED, *King of Mercia.* *See* BURGRÆD.

BURI (ERNST CARL LUDWIG YSENBURG VON) Das Intelligenzblatt. Ein Schauspiel in drey Aufzügen. [By E. C. L. Y. von Buri.] 1789. 8°. [*Deutsche Schaubühne.* Bd. 4.] *See* INTELLIGENZBLATT. **752.** a. **1**/**4.**

—— Ludwig Capet, oder der Königsmord. Ein bürgerliches Trauerspiel in vier Aufzügen. pp. 120. 1794. *See* GERMAN STAGE. Deutsche Schaubühne. Bd. 65. 1788, *etc.* 8°. **752.** a. **1**/**65.**

—— Marie Antonie von Oesterreich, Königinn in Frankreich. Ein Trauerspiel in vier Aufzügen. pp. 128. 1794. *See* GERMAN STAGE. Deutsche Schaubühne. Bd. 64. 1788, *etc.* 8°. **752.** a. **1**/**64.**

BURI (Ernst Carl Ludwig Ysenburg von)

—— Die Matrosen. Ein Schauspiel mit Gesang in zwey Aufzügen. [By E. C. L. Y. von Buri.] 1788. 8°. [*Deutsche Schaubühne.* Bd. 3.] *See* Matrosen. **752. a. 1/3.**

—— Die Stimme des Volkes; oder die Zerstörung der Bastille. Ein bürgerliches Trauerspiel in vier Aufzügen. pp. 174. *Neuwied*, 1791. 8°. **11746. df. 4.**

BURI (Friedrich Carl von) *See* Gudenus (V. F. de) Codex diplomaticus, *etc.* [tom. 4 continued by F. C. von Buri.] 1743, *etc.* 4°. **125. i. 4.**

—— Friderich Carl von Buri . . . ausführliche Abhandelung von denen Bauer-Gütern in Teutschland, *etc.* [With a portrait.] pp. 627. *Giessen*, 1769. 4°. **496. d. 21.**

—— Ausführliche Erläuterung des in Teutschland üblichen Lehen-Rechts, oder: Anmerckungen über Johannis Schilteri Institutiones juris feudalis Germanici & Longobardici, *etc.* pp. 1404. *Giessen*, 1732–38. 4°. **5551. f. 9.**

—— [Another edition.] [With a portrait.] 2 pt. *Giessen*, 1769. 4°. **5306. b. 1.**

—— Friedrich Carl Buri . . . behauptete Vorrechte derer alten Königlichen Bann-Forste, insbesondere des Reichslehenbaren Forst- und Wild-Banns zu der Drey-Eich . . . nebst einer Abhandlung von der Regalität derer Jagten in Teutschland, *etc.* [A reply to an answer published by the city of Frankfort to the "Gründlicher Bericht von dem uralten Reichs- und Königs-Forst zur Drey-Eichen" of J. A. Kopp.] 3 pt. *Franckfurt; Offenbach*, 1744, 42, 44. fol. **5505. g. 7.**

BURI (Fritz)

—— *See* Schweitzer (A.) Ehrfurcht vor dem Leben . . Eine Freundesgabe, *etc.* [The dedicatory letter signed: F. Buri.] [1955.] 8°. **012359. cc. 47.**

—— Angst und Religion. pp. 20. *Bern*, 1939. 8°. **04374. k. 25.**

—— Die Bedeutung der neutestamentlichen Eschatologie für die neuere protestantische Theologie. Ein Versuch zur Klärung des Problems der Eschatologie und zu einem neuen Verständnis ihres eigentlichen Anliegens. pp. vii. 191. *Zürich & Leipzig*, [1935.] 8°. **03226. g. 29.**

—— Clemens Alexandrinus und der paulinische Freiheitsbegriff. pp. 114. *Zürich & Leipzig*, [1939.] 8°. **20043. bb. 26.**

—— Kreuz und Ring. Die Kreuzestheologie des jungen Luther und die Lehre von der ewigen Wiederkunft in Nietzsches "Zarathustra." pp. 121. *Bern*, [1947.] 8°. **3909. b. 4.**

BURI (Henricus Gulielmus Antonius) *See* Gudenus (V. F. de) Codex diplomaticus, *etc.* [tom. 5. By H. W. A. Buri.] 1743, *etc.* 4°. **125. i. 4*.**

BURI (Ludwig Ysenburg von) *See* Buri (Ernst C. L. Y. von)

BURI (Max) *See* Trog (H.) Max Buri, *etc.* 1917. 4°. [*Neujahrsblatt der Zürcher Künstlergesellschaft.* 1917.] **Ac. 4557.**

—— *See* Widmer (J.) Der Schweizer Maler Max Buri. Werk und Wesen . . . Mit fünf Incavogravüren. 1919. 8°. **12216. d. 1/61.**

BURI (Maximilian von) Abhandlungen aus dem Strafrecht. pp. 222. *Stuttgart*, 1878. 8°. [*Der Gerichtssaal.* Bd. 29. Beilagehft.] **P.P. 1403. d.**

—— Beiträge zur Theorie des Strafrechts und zum Strafgesetzbuche. Gesammelte Abhandlungen. pp. vi. 484. *Leipzig*, 1894. 8°. **6055. cc. 6.**

—— Die Causalität und ihre strafrechtlichen Beziehungen. pp. 155. *Stuttgart*, 1885. 8°. [*Der Gerichtssaal.* Bd. 37. Beilagehft.] **P.P. 1403. d.**

—— Einheit und Mehrheit der Verbrechen. pp. 121. *Stuttgart*, 1879. 8°. [*Der Gerichtssaal.* Bd. 31. Beilagehft.] **P.P. 1403. d.**

—— Ueber Causalität und deren Verantwortung. pp. 154. *Leipzig*, 1873. 8°. **8469. b. 46.**

—— Zur Lehre von der Theilnahme an dem Verbrechen und der Begünstigung. pp. 105. *Giessen*, 1860. 8°. **5655. bbb. 8.**

BURI (Richard de) *See* Bury (Richard de) *Advocate.*

BURI (Richardus de) *Bishop of Durham.* *See* Aungerville (Ricardus d') *Bishop of Durham.*

BURI (Rudolf O.) Zur Anatomie des Flügels von Micropus melba und einigen anderen Coracornithes, zugleich Beitrag zur Kenntnis der systematischen Stellung der Cypselidae. [With plates.] 1900. *See* Jena.—*Medizinisch-naturwissenschaftliche Gesellschaft.* Jenaische Zeitschrift für Naturwissenschaft, *etc.* Bd. 33. Hft. 3, 4. 1874, *etc.* 8°. **Ac. 3760.**

BURI (Vincenzo) L'Unione della Chiesa Copta con Roma sotto Clemente VIII. pp. 164. *Roma*, 1931. 8°. [*Orientalia christiana.* no. 72.] **Ac. 2002. bb.**

BURIAL. Extramural Burial. The three schemes. I. The London Clergy Plan. II. The Board of Health or Erith Plan. III. The Woking Necropolis Plan. With general remarks. [By James Osborne.] pp. 35. *Effingham Wilson: London*, 1850. 8°. **7405. b. 9.**

—— On Burial, Death, and Resurrection. *Jane Jowett: Leeds*, [1855.] *s. sh.* 8°. **8705. f. 1. (1.)**

BURIAL CLUB. Burial Club.—Pat Brady. [Songs.] *Manchester*, [1850?] *s. sh.* 4°. **C. 116. i. 1. (172.)**

—— Burial Club.—The Pilot. [Songs.] [*London*, 1850?] *s. sh.* 4°. **C. 116. i. 1. (170.)**

—— [Another edition.] [*London*, 1850?] *s. sh.* 4°. **C. 116. i. 1. (171.)**

BURIAL REFORMER. *See* Periodical Publications.—*London.*

BURIALS QUESTION. The Burials Question. What is to be done? [Signed: H. B. R.] 1877. 8°. *See* R., H. B. **4109. h. 7. (13.)**

—— The Burials Question further examined, from a layman's point of view. Is there a grievance? pp. 19. *W. J. Johnson: London*, 1880. 8°. **4109. f. 22. (2.)**

BURIAN. *See* Bury Saint Edmunds.—*King Edward VI.'s School.*

BURIAN (Emil František)

—— F. F. Burian. [A note on his life and works.] *Ger.* pp. 2. [c. 1930.] *s. sh.* fol. **Hirsch 5132**
Reproduced from typewriting.

BURIAN (F. František) *See* Burian (E. F.)

BURIAN (HERMANN M.)

—— Fusional Movements. Role of peripheral retinal stimuli. (Reprinted from the Archives of Ophthalmology.) pp. 6. *Chicago*, [1939.] 8°. **7612. cc. 29.**

BURIAN (JOSEF JOHANN) Das Brod und das Wesen der Brodbereitung, *etc.* pp. 33. *Wien*, 1866. 8°. **7945. h. 34. (11.)**

—— Das Heeres-Verpflegswesen in technischer und technologischer Beziehung, mit einschlägiger Statistik und Handr Geographie, *etc.* pp. xii. 487. *Wien*, 1876. 8°. **8830. k. 3.**

BURIAN (MICHAELIS) Dissertatio historico-critica de duplici ingressu in Transsilvaniam Georgii Blandratæ, *etc.* pp. xxviii. 288. *Albo-Carolinæ*, 1806. 8°. **9314. aaa. 12.**

BURIAN (ORHAN)

—— *See* SHAKESPEARE (William) [*As You Like It.—Turkish.*] Beğendiğiniz ğibi [*sic*] . . . Orhan Burian tarafından tercüme edilmiştir. 1943. 8°. **14479. c. 19.**

—— *See* SHAKESPEARE (William) [*Othello.—Turkish.*] Othello . . . Orhan Burian tarafından tercüme edilmiştir. 1943. 8°. **14479. c. 13.**

—— *See* SHAKESPEARE (William) [*Timon of Athens.—Turkish.*] Atinalı Timon . . . Orhan Burian tarafından tercüme edilmiştir. 1944. 8°. **14479. c. 16.**

BURIAN (STEPHAN) *Count.* *See* BURIAN VON RAJECZ.

BURIAN (THOMAS) Ausführliches, theoretisch-practisches Lehrbuch der böhmischen Sprache für Deutsche, *etc.* pp. 500. *Prag & Königgrätz*, 1839. 8°. **12962. dd. 17.**

BURIÁNEK (FRANTIŠEK)

—— *See* GELLNER (F.) Z díla Františka Gellnera. (Uspořádal a úvod napsal F. Buriánek.) 1952. 8°. **12266. m. 9.**

—— *See* MAYER (R.) Dílo . . . K vydání připravil a úvodní studii napsal F. Buriánek. 1950. 8°. **12266. de. 7.**

—— Česká poesie. Vybor básní XIX. a XX. století. (Uspořádali F. Buriánek, F. Kautman [and others].) pp. 535. *Praha*, 1951. 8°. **11588. ff. 35.**

—— Petr Bezruč. pp. 30. *Praha*, 1952. 8°. **11871. e. 30.** *Knihovna Československé společnosti pro šíření politických a vědeckých znalostí.* sv. 13.

—— Proti buržoasní literární " vědě " Arne Nováka. pp. 27. *Praha*, 1952. 8°. **11870. e. 1.** *Knihova Socialistické akademie.* sv. 41.

BURIANI (RAFFAELLO) Versi giocosi bolognesi e italiani. pp. 240. *Bologna*, 1870. 8°. **11436. aaa. 49.**

BURIAN VON RAJECZ (STEPHAN) *Count.* Drei Jahre aus der Zeit meiner Amtsführung im Kriege. pp. 333. *Berlin*, 1923. 8°. **9082. cc. 34.**

—— [Drei Jahre aus der Zeit meiner Amtsführung im Kriege.] Austria in Dissolution . . . Translated by Brian Lunn. pp. 455. *Ernest Benn: London*, 1925. 8°. **09083. d. 61.**

BURIANYK (WILLIAM) A Short Cut to Musical Theory. With chart. pp. 24. *Music Chart Co.: Winnipeg*, [1932.] 8°. **07899. df. 27.**

BURIAT AUTONOMOUS SOVIET SOCIALIST REPUBLIC.

Buriat-Mongol Autonomous Soviet Socialist Republic, 1923–58.
Buriat Autonomous Soviet Socialist Republic, 1958–

—— 15 лет Бурят-Монгольской АССР. Политико-экономический сборник, посвященный празднованию 15-летнего юбилея БМАССР. pp. 101. *Улан-Удэ*, 1938. 8°. **8289.bb.27.**

Бурят-Монгольский Государственный Научно-Исследовательский Институт Культуры.

—— Русско–бурят-монгольский словарь. Под редакцией Ц. Б. Цыдендамбаева. Около 40000 слов. pp. 750. *Москва*, 1954. 4°. **012977. h. 4.**

Бурят-Монгольский Государственный Научно-Исследовательский Институт Языка, Литературы и Истории.

—— Библиография Бурят-Монголии за 1890–1936 гг. Составлена под руководством Н. В. Здобнова, *etc.* (Bibliography of Buryat-Mongolia, 1890–1936, *etc.*) [Published by the Academy of Sciences of the USSR.] *Москва, Ленинград*, 1946, 40– . 8°. W.P. **5883.**

Бурят-Монгольский Научно-Исследовательский Институт Культуры.

—— История Бурят-Монгольской (Бурятской) АССР. в двух томах. [Edited by P. T. Khaptaev and others. With plates and maps.] 2 том. *Улан-Удэ*, 1954–59. 8°. **9075. i. 11.**
Том 1 *is of the second edition.*

Союз Советских Писателей Бурят-Монголии.

—— Антология бурят-монгольской советской поэзии. [With biographical notes on the contributors.] Под редакцией Ц. Галсанова, В. Замятина и И. Ким. pp. 287. *Улан-Удэ*, 1950. 8°. Mon. **151.**

Центральный Комитетъ.—Государственный Научно-Изслѣдовательскій Институтъ Языка, Литературы и Исторіи.

—— История бурят-монгольского народа. От XVII в. до 60-х годов XIX в. Очерки. [By Th. A. Kudryavtsev. With a map.] pp. 242. *Москва, Ленинград*, 1940. 8°. Ac. **1129. f.**

BURIAT-MONGOL AUTONOMOUS SOVIET SOCIALIST REPUBLIC. *See* BURIAT AUTONOMOUS SOVIET SOCIALIST REPUBLIC.

BURIAT-MONGOLIA.

—— Библиография Бурят-Монголии за 1890–1936 гг., *etc.* *See* ZDOBNOV (N. V.)

—— Поэзия Советской Бурят-Монголии, *etc.* 1959. 8°. *See* TUMUNOV (Zh. T.) and SHERVINSKY (S.) Mon. **130.**

BURIAT MONGOLS.

—— Материалы для истории бурят-монголов. *Mong.* *Москва, Ленинград*, 1935– . 8°. [*Труды Института Востоковедения.* том. 8, 9, 12, *etc.*] Ac. **1125.** ik/2.

BURIATS.

—— Летописи селенгинских бурят. (Материалы для истории бурят-монголов. no. 3.) *Mong.* *Москва, Ленинград*, 1936– . 8°. [*Труды Института Востоковедения.* том. 12, *etc.*] Ac. **1125.** ik/2.

BURIATS.

—— Летописи хоринских бурят. (Материалы для истории бурят-монголов. no. 2.) *Mong.* *Москва, Ленинград,* 1935- . 8°. [*Труды Института Востоковедения.* том. 9.] Ac. **1125**. ik/2.

—— Летопись баргузинских бурят. Тексты и исследования. (Материалы для истории бурят-монголов. no. 1.) [With a Russian translation by Tsuideb Dzhab Sakharov of the Mongol text. Edited by A. I. Vostrikov and N. N. Poppe.] pp. 75. *Москва, Ленинград,* 1935. 8°. [*Труды Института Востоковедения.* том. 8.] Ac. **1125**. ik/2.

—— Сказанія Бурятъ, записанныя разными собирателями. Издано . . . Д. Г. Гомбоева. pp. ii. 159. *Иркутскъ,* 1890. 8°. [*Записки Восточно-Сибирскаго Отдѣла Императорскаго Русскаго Географическаго Общества по отдѣленію этнографіи.* том. 1. вып. 2.] Ac. **6130/9**.

BURIDAN (Jean Baptiste) *See* Vermandois. Les Coustumes generales du Baillage de Vermandois . . . Auec commentaires sur icelles . . . par Maistre I. B. Buridan, *etc.* 1630. 4°. **5402**. e. **11**.

—— —— 1728. fol. **1238**. k. 3, 4.

BURIDANUS (Joannes) *See* Aristotle. [*Ethica Nicomachea.—Latin.*] Textus ethicorū Aristotelis ad Nicomachum iuxta antiquā translationē cum familiarissimo cōmentario in eundem et cōpendiosis questionibus ac dubiis . . . ad mentem . . . Martini magistri et Iohannis buridani maiori pro parte decisis. [1500 ?] fol. IB. **40248**.

—— *See* Faral (E.) Jean Buridan. Notes sur les manuscrits, les éditions et le contenu de ses ouvrages. 1946. 8°. [*Archives d'histoire doctrinale et littéraire du moyen âge.* année 1946.] P.P. **4331**. abk.

—— *See* Faral (E.) Jean Buridan, maître ès arts de l'Université de Paris. 1949. 4°. [*Histoire littéraire de la France.* tom. 38. fasc. 2.] L.R. **48**. c.

—— In Metaphysicen Aristotelis. Quęstiões argutissimæ Magistri Ioannis Buridani in vltima prælectione ab ipso recognitæ & emissæ : ac ad archetypon diligenter repositæ, *etc.* G.L. ff. lxxvii. few ms. notes. *Impensis I. Badii Ascensii: [Paris,]* 1518. fol. **520**. h. **10**.

—— [Another copy.] IB. **42833**. (3.)

—— *Begin.* [fol. 2 *recto*:] Proemium Ioannis Buridani in Questiones super .x. libros Aris. ad Nicomachum. *End.* [fol. 266 *recto*:] Huc vsq₃ ꝓducte sunt questiones Buridani morales . . . q̄s Egidius delfus . . . imprimi curauit, *etc.* *Impressore vuolfgango hopyl: [Paris,]* decima quarta die Iulii, 1489. fol. IB. **40108**.
266 *leaves, the first blank,* 2–266 *numbered* ii–cclxiiii, lxv, lxiiii. *Sig.* a–z⁸ ⁊⁸ ꝯ⁸ A–G⁸ H¹⁰. *Double columns,* 51 *lines to a column.*

—— [Another edition.] Questiones Ioannis buridani super decem libros ethicorū aristotelis ad nicomachum. (Quas Egidius Delfus cū annotatiōib⁹ in margine adiectis, emēdatius imprimi curauit.) G.L. ff. ccxiiii. *Venundātur a Pōceto le preux: parrhisiis,* 1513. fol. C. **81**. d. **2**. (1.)

—— Acutissimi philosophi reuerendi Magistri Iohānis buridani subtilissime questiones super octo phisicorum libros Aristotelis diligēter recognite & reuise a magistro Iohanne dullaert de gandauo antea nusq̄ impresse. G.L. ff. cxxi. *Opera P. ledru ; impensis D. roce: parhisiis,* 1509. fol. **520**. g. **4**.

BURIDANUS (Joannes)

—— Quaestiones super libris quattuor De caelo et mundo. Edited by Ernest Addison Moody. pp. xxxv. 274. *Cambridge, Mass.,* 1942. 8°. [*Mediaeval Academy of America. Publication.* no. 40.] **Ac.2684/2.(40.)**

—— Questiones Iohannis buridani super octo libros politicorum Aristotelis . . . correcte & emendate necnon singulis in marginibus annotate. [Edited by Guillermus Baterel.] ff. cxv. *Opera N. depratis ; expensis I. petit : parisius,* 1513. fol. C. **81**. d. **2**. (**2**.)

—— [Another edition.] pp. 431. *Excudebat Guilielmus Turner : Oxoniæ,* 1640. 4°. **523**. g. **53**.

—— Sophismata buridani. G.L. *p felicē balligault: parisius,* ex die. xx. Nouembris, 1493. 4°. IA. **40502**.
54 *leaves. Sig.* a–f⁸ g⁶. *Double columns,* 41 *lines to a column.*

BURIED. Buried Alone. A story. By a new writer [i.e. Charles W. Wood]. pp. 313. *Tinsley Bros.: London,* 1869. 8°. **12622**. bbb. **1**.

BURIEL (Andres Marcos) *See* Burriel.

BURIGENUS, *Doctor de Kornis, pseud.* *See* Waldensians. Apologia veræ doctrinæ, eorum qui vulgo appellantur Waldenses . . . qui retinuerunt Iohannis Hus doctrinam . . . Oblata D. Georgio Marchioni Brandebur. anno m.dxxxii . . . Ex Bohemico exemplari translata . . . per Burigenum Doctorem de Kornis. 1616. 8°. [*Lydius* (*B.*) *Waldensia, etc.* tom. 1.] **692**. a. **14**.

BURIGNI (Jean Levesque de) *See* Levesque de Burigny.

BURIGNY (Jean Levesque de) *See* Levesque de Burigny.

BURIGOZZO (Giovanni Marco) Cronaca di Milano . . . dall'anno 1500 sino al 1544. 1842. *See* Italian Historical Archives. Archivio storico italiano, *etc.* tom. 3. 1842, *etc.* 8°. P.P. **3557**. a.

BURIKS (A.) Democratisch Gemeentebeheer. Een verhandeling over Commission Government in Amerikaansche steden. pp. vii. 363. *'s-Gravenhage,* 1918. 8°. **08175**. dd. 4.

BURIKS (Agatha Anna)

—— *Περι τυχης.* De ontwikkeling van het begrip tyche tot aan de Romeinse tijd, hoofdzakelijk in de philosophie. Proefschrift, *etc.* [With summaries in French and English.] pp. 143. *Leiden,* [1948.] 8°. **4506**. ee. **48**.

BURILEANU (Costantino N.) I Romeni di Albania, *etc.* [With plates.] pp. xxiv. 396. *Bologna,* 1912. fol. **10125**. g. **23**.

BURILL (Ives Marie Paul Jean) La Marquise de Sévigné, docteur en médecine, honoris causa, *etc.* [With a portrait.] pp. 140. *Paris,* [1932.] 8°. **10656**. i. **24**.

BURILL (Paul) De l'ivrognerie et des moyens de la combattre. pp. 86. *Paris,* 1872. 4°. [*Collection des thèses soutenues à la Faculté de Médecine de Paris.* An 1872. tom. 3.] **7373**. n. 9.

BURÍN (Antonio Gallego y) *See* Gallego y Burín.

BURIN (Antonio Sendras y) *See* Sendras y Burin.

BURIN (Ivan)

—— *See* Osinin (D. N.) and Burin (I.) Горло ле, майко хайдушка, *etc.* [1953.] 8°. **11588**. bbb. **39**.

BURIN (Ivan)

—— Ботев и народния поетичен гений. Литературно-критически изследвания. pp. 298. *София*, [1954.] 8°. **11871.** b. **38.**

—— Огньовете на Бузлуджа. pp. 118. [*Sofia*,] 1953. 8°. **11588.** i. **37.**

—— По неравни профили. Пътят на Пеню Генчев. Очерк. [With a portrait.] pp. 114. *София*, 1950. 8°. **8236.** de. **30.**
Герои на труда. no. 5.

BURIN (L. P. A.) Dissertation sur le cancer de la lèvre inférieure. Thèse, *etc.* pp. 19. *Montpellier*, 1836. 4°. **1181.** g. **16.** (**23.**)

BURIN (Pierre) Response à une epistre [by G. Papon] commenceamt [*sic*] Seigneur Eluide, où est traitté des massacres faits en France, en l'an 1572. pp. 40. *Par M. Cousin: Basle*, 1574. 8°. **1080.** c. **9.** (**2.**)

—— [Another edition.] pp. 45. *Par M. Cousin: Basle*, 1574. 8°. **285.** a. **32.** (**10.**)

BURIN (Roland Michel) *Marquis de la Gallissonnière.* *See* Barrin.

BURINA (Fran Lukarević) *See* Lukarević (F.)

BURIN D'AISSARD (Guillaume Marie) De la nature de l'hystérie, *etc.* pp. 29. *Paris*, 1841. 4°. [*Collection des thèses soutenues à la Faculté de Médecine de Paris.* An 1841. tom. 3.] **7371.** c. **3.**

BURIN-D'AISSARD (L. M.) Dissertation sur l'empyème. pp. 24. *Paris*, 1812. 4°. **1182.** i. **1.** (**15.**)

BURIN-DESROZIERS (Joseph Guillaume) Faculté de Droit de Paris. Thèse pour la licence, *etc.* (Jus romanum. De in diem addictione, *etc.*—Droit français. De la résolution et de la rescision du contrat de vente.) pp. 40. *Paris*, 1859. 8°. **5406.** b. **10.** (**22.**)

BURIN DU BUISSON (A. M. B.) *See* Magnes-Lahens ( ) Du sesquichlorure de fer liquide. Réponse . . . à M. Burin du Buisson. 1861. 8°. **8906.** aaa. **50.** (**10.**)

—— De la présence du manganèse dans le sang et de sa valeur en thérapeutique. pp. 20. *Paris, Lyon*, 1854. 8°. **7420.** bb. **33.** (**4.**)

—— Mémoire sur l'existence du manganèse dans le sang humain, sur son role dans l'économie animale et sur la préparation de quelques nouveaux produits pharmaceutiques de fer et de manganèse. (Extrait de la Revue médicale.) pp. 55. *Lyon*, 1852. 8°. **7406.** b. **14.**

—— [Quelques mots sur l'acide lactique.] Remarks on Lactic Acid and Alkaline Lactates, their action in the animal economy, and especially in the process of digestion. *See* Petrequin (T. J. E.) On the Use of Alkaline Lactates in the Treatment of Functional Diseases of the Digestive Organs, *etc.* 1864. 8°. **7461.** cc. **49.** (**5.**)

—— Traité de l'action thérapeutique du perchlorure de fer, *etc.* pp. 392. *Paris*, 1860. 8°. **7461.** g. **12.**

BURINGER (Bernardus) Serta moralia a concionatoribus diebus dominicis populo e cathedra exhibenda ex floribus Sacræ Scripturæ, sententiis SS. Patrum . . . contexta per . . . Bernardum Buringer. 2 vol. *Francofurti*, 1717. 4°. **4423.** dd. **12.**

BURINGH (P.)

—— Over de bodemgesteldheid rondom Wageningen. With a summary: Soil conditions in the environments of Wageningen. [With maps.] pp. 131. pl. 3. *'s-Gravenhage*, 1951. 8°. [*Bodemkartering van Nederland.* dl. 9.] **S. 625.** b/**6.**

BURINGTON (Richard Stevens) and **TORRANCE** (Charles Chapman)

—— Higher Mathematics. With applications to science and engineering. pp. xiii. 844. *McGraw-Hill Book Co.: New York & London*, 1939. 8°. **08535.** b. **25.**

BURINSKY (Zakhar) Поэзія. [An ode.] pp. 13. *Москва*, 1802. 8°. **011586.** c. **89.**

BURION (Amédée) Rosa Bordas, sa biographie [by L. Vidal]. Appréciations de la presse, études littéraires, épilogue. Documents rassemblés et coordonnés par A. Burion. [With a portrait.] pp. 32. *Paris*, 1870. 8°. **10602.** h. **6.** (**3.**)

BURIOT, afterwards **BURIOT-DARSILES** (Henri) *See* Eucken (R. C.) Les Grands courants de la pensée contemporaine . . . Traduit de l'allemand sur la quatrième édition par H. Buriot . . . et G. H. Luquet, *etc.* 1911. 8°. **08461.** h. **57.**

—— *See* West (Julius) La Municipalisation du gaz et ses résultats dans le Royaume-Uni. (Traduit par H. Buriot.) 1911. 8°. **08229.** i. **8.**

—— Maguelone, petite île—grand passé. Suivi d'un guide du touriste . . . Illustrations. pp. 206. *Montpellier*, 1937. 8°. **10167.** de. **41.**

BURIOT, afterwards **BURIOT-DARSILES** (Henri) and **DÉNIER** (Marc)

—— Essai de répertoire des ex-libris, anciens et nouveaux, intéressant le Bourbonnais. pp. ii. 46. *Paris*, 1930. 8°. **11901.** pp. **11.**

BURIOT, afterwards **BURIOT-DARSILES** (Henri) and **LOCQUIN** (Jean)

—— Le Musée de Moulins. pp. 86. 1915. *See* Periodical Publications.—*Nevers.* Les Cahiers nivernais et du Centre, *etc.* Numéro hors série. 1909, *etc.* 8°. **P.P. 4382.** ec.

BURIRHAT.—*Agricultural Station.*

—— Annual Report of the Burirhat Agricultural Station for the year 1911-1912 (1912-13). *Calcutta*, 1913. 8°. **I.S.** be. **241/8.**
Previously issued as part of the "Annual Report of the Agricultural Stations in Eastern Bengal and Assam," and subsequently as part of the "Annual Reports of the Expert Officers of the Department of Agriculture, Bengal."

BURISCH (Ingo) Englands Haltung in der bosnichen Annexionskrise. pp. 76. *Halle*, 1935. 8°. **08028.** cc. **21.**

BURIUS (Guilielmus) Brevis romanorum pontificum notitia, paucis declarans, qui ecclesiae ritus a quibus instituti, vel quid notabile sub singulis actum . . . Accedit Onomasticon, quo voces obscuriores in Officio Ecclesiastico, Missali, Breviario, ac Martyrologio Romano, & hac notitia, huic inde occurrentes, etymologice explicantur. pp. 296. 110. *Apud J. Jaye: Mechliniae*, 1675. 8°. **4855.** a. **9.**

—— [Another edition.] pp. 576. *Augustæ-Vindel.*, 1727. 12°. **4855.** a. **10.**

BURIUS (GUILIELMUS)

—— [Another edition.] [Edited by H. de Blanchis.] pp. 610. *Patavii*, 1747. 12°. **4855**. de. **1**.

—— [Another edition.] pp. 610. *Venetiis*, 1757. 12°. **4855**. aaa. **5**.

—— Strena poetica serenissimo atque invictissimo princi[p]i nostro Archiduci Leopoldo . . . nonnulla, ante, sub, & post adventum eius nuper in Belgium, carmine complectens, *etc*. pp. 7. *Apud G. Schovartium: Bruxellæ*, 1647. 4°. **1481**. aaa. **43**. (**8**.)

BURIUS (JOHANNES) Micae historico-chronologicae evangelico-pannonicae σκιαγραφικως collectae et adumbratae opella vigilaci diutina J. Burii . . . Ex autographo posoniensi edidit Paulus Lichner. pp. xvii. 220. *Posonii*, 1864. 8°. **4695**. cc. **14**.

BURIUS (WILHELMUS) *See* BURIUS (Guilelmus)

BÜRJA (　　) [For the German surname of this form :] *See* BUERJA.

BURJA (ABEL) *See* BUERJA.

BURJAKOW (H. VON MORAWIEW) *See* MURAV'EV BURYAKOV (H.)

BURJAM (FRITZ DANIEL CHRISTIAN)

—— Den Produktiva aktiviteten i dess förhållande till konjunkturutvecklingen. pp. 283. *Helsingfors*, 1914. 8°. [*Skrifter utgivna av Economiska Samfundet i Finland*. no. 3.] Ac. **2345**.

BURJAN, *z Kornic*. *See* SOBEK (B.) *z Kornic*.

BÜRK (　　)

—— [For the German surname of this form :] *See* BUERK.

BURK (AUGUST) Die Pädagogik des Isokrates als Grundlegung des humanistischen Bildungsideals, im Vergleich mit den zeitgenössischen und den modernen Theorien dargestellt, *etc*. pp. viii. 231. *Würzburg*, 1923. 8°. [*Studien zur Geschichte und Kultur des Altertums*. Bd. 12. Hft. 3, 4.] Ac. **2026/9**.

BURK (CARL) Geschichte der christlichen Kirche bis zu ihrer Pflanzung auf deutschem Boden. pp. viii. 337. *Stuttgart*, 1885. 8°. **4531**. aaa. **11**.

—— Martin Luther. pp. viii. 342. *Stuttgart*, 1883. 8°. **4888**. b. **34**.

—— Predigt zum Schluss des Jahres 1866, *etc*. pp. 14. *Schw. Hall*, 1867. 8°. **4423**. aaa. **2**. (**3**.)

BURK (CAROLINE FREAR) *See* BURK (Frederic L.) Self-Instruction Arithmetic . . . Edited by C. F. Burk. [1929.] 8° & *obl*. fol. **8530**. ff. **39** & i. **36**.

BURK (CASSIE) A Study of the Influence of some Factors in Style of Composition on the Interest, Comprehension, and Rate of Reading of Fourth-Grade Pupils . . . [A thesis.] Reprinted from the Journal of Experimental Education, *etc*. [*Minneapolis*, 1936.] 4°. **08385**. i. **25**. *Reproduced from typewriting*.

BURK (E. I.) *See* BIBLE.—*Mark*. [*Lega*.] Misagu misoga anga bwazisanzagazo Marko Mutundwa. [Translated by E. I. Burk.] 1934. 8°. **03068**. k. **67**.

BURK (FREDERIC LISTER) Self-Instruction Arithmetic . . . Edited by Caroline F. Burk. 9 pt.

Common Fractions. 6 pt.
Decimal Fractions. 3 pt.

Rand, McNally & Co.: New York, [1929.] 8° & *obl*. fol. **8530**. ff. **39**. & i. **36**.

Imperfect; wanting the parts dealing with addition, subtraction, multiplication and division.

BURK (JOHANN ALBRECHT) Gebet- und Lieder-Buch zum Privat-Gebrauch für Kinder und für junge Christen reiferen Alters. Aus den besten Schriftstellern und Dichtern gesammelt. pp. lxii. 274. *Tübingen*, 1775. 8°. **3425**. bb. **29**.

BURK (JOHANN CHRISTIAN FRIEDRICH) *See* BENGEL (J. A.) Dr. Johann Albrecht Bengel's . . . hinterlassene Predigten . . . Gesammelt und herausgegeben von M. J. C. F. Burk, *etc*. 1839. 8°. **1113**. e. **32**.

—— *See* BENGEL (J. A.) Dr. Johann Albrecht Bengel's literarischer Briefwechsel . . . Mitgetheilt von M. J. C. F. Burk. 1836. 8°. **10920**. dd. **21**.

—— *See* BIBLE.—*Revelation*. [*German*.] Erklärte Offenbarung Johannis . . . Nebst einem Anhange bisher noch ungedruckter apocalyptischer Briefe Bengels, mitgetheilt von Pfarrer Burk. 1834. 8°. **3186**. bbb. **32**.

—— *See* BIBLE.—*Revelation*. [*German*.] Dr. Joh. Albrecht Bengels sechzig erbauliche Reden über die Offenbarung Johannis . . . Mit einer Vorrede von M. J. C. F. Burk, *etc*. 1837. 8°. **3186**. bb. **59**.

—— *See* PERIODICAL PUBLICATIONS.—*Stuttgart*. Süddeutscher Schul-Bote . . . (Jahrg. 1–5.) In Verbindung mit . . . Stadtpfarrer Burk . . . und andern herausgegeben von Pfarrer Stotz. 1836, *etc*. 4°. P.P. **1200**. ae.

—— Dr. Johann Albrecht Bengel's Leben und Wirken, meist nach handschriftlichen Materialien bearbeitet. . . . Mit Bengel's Bildniss. Zweite Auflage. pp. xii. 579. *Stuttgart*, 1832. 8°. **1372**. g. **6**.

—— A Memoir of the Life and Writings of John Albert Bengel . . . Compiled principally from original manuscripts . . . Translated . . . by Robert Francis Walker. pp. xii. 533. *William Ball: London*, 1837. 8°. **1124**. f. **27**.

—— Christian Biography. Life of John Albert Bengel, Prelate in Würtemburg. (Abridged from " A Memoir of the Life and Writings of John Albert Bengel . . . compiled . . . by the Rev. J. C. F. Burk . . . Translated . . . by Robert Francis Walker.") pp. 144. *R.T.S.: London*, [1840.] 12°. **4419**. g. **20**.

—— *See* BERGQUIST (C. R. E.) Johan Albrecht Bengels Lif och verksamhet efter J. C. F. Burk, och O. Wächter, *etc*. 1871. 8°. **4887**. aaa. **45**.

BURK (JOHN DALY) *See* CAMPBELL (Charles) *of Petersburg, Va*. Some Materials to serve for a brief Memoir of John Daly Burk, *etc*. 1868. 8°. **10882**. i. **20**.

—— Bunker-Hill; or, the Death of General Warren: an historic tragedy in five acts, *etc*. [In verse.] pp. 55. MS. NOTES. *T. Greenleaf: New-York*, 1797. 12°. **11791**. b. **36**.

—— [Another edition.] [Reprinted from the edition published by the Dunlap Society in 1891.] pp. 45. *Tarrytown*, 1931. 4°. [*Magazine of History*. Extra no. 168.] P.P. **3437**. bab.

BURK (JOHN DALY)

—— The History of Virginia, from its first settlement to the commencement of the Revolution. 3 vol. *Dickson & Pescud: Petersburg, Va.*, 1822. 8°. **1447. h. 1.**

BURK (JOHN JUNIUS) *See* CAMPBELL (Charles) *of Petersburg, Va.* Some Materials to serve for a brief Memoir of John Daly Burk . . . With a sketch of the life and character of Judge J. J. Burk, *etc.* 1868. 8°. **10882. i. 20.**

BURK (JOHN NAGLEE) *See* HALE (Philip) *Writer on Music.* Philip Hale's Boston Symphony Programme Notes . . . Edited by J. N. Burk. 1935. 8°. **07899. df. 31.**

—— *See* WAGNER (W. R.) [*Letters.*] Letters of Richard Wagner. The Burrell collection . . . Edited with notes by J. N. Burk. 1951. 8°. **10922. d. 28.**

—— Clara Schumann. A romantic biography. [With plates, including portraits.] pp. ix. 438. *Random House: New York*, [1940.] 8°. **010703. h. 76.**

—— The Life and Works of Beethoven. (Second printing.) [With a portrait.] pp. viii. 483. *Random House: New York*, [1943?] 8°. **7890. b. 19.**

BURK (JUNIA AGNES) *See* CAMPBELL (Charles) *of Petersburg, Va.* Some Materials [largely contributed by J. A. Burk] to serve for a brief Memoir of John Daly Burk, *etc.* 1868. 8°. **10882. i. 20.**

BURK (L. B.)

—— Market Classes and Grades of Lambs and Sheep. By L. B. Burk . . . C. E. Gibbons . . . and M. T. Foster. (Revised.) pp. 35. *Washington*, 1940. 8°. [*U.S. Department of Agriculture. Circular.* no. 383.] **A.S. 804/2.**

BURK (L. B.) and WHALIN (CHARLES VIVION)

—— Market Classes and Grades of Livestock. pp. 30. *Washington*, 1942. 8°. [*U.S. Department of Agriculture. Department Bulletin.* no. 1360.] **A.S. 800.**

BURK (MARCUS PH.) Eine Reihe römischer Kaiser nach einem höchstseltenen Kunstalterthum welches aus illuminierten Handzeichnungen und geschriebenen teutschen Reimen vom Jahr 1544 besteht, beschrieben und mit . . . Erläuterungen herausgegeben von B. [i.e. M. P. Burk.] [With a transcription of the verses of Sebastian Wild.] pp. 56. 1791. 4°. *See* B. **11515. d. 1.**

BURK (MARGUERITE C.)

—— *See* CLARK (Faith) Nutritive Value of the per capita food supply, 1909–45. By F. Clark . . . M. C. Burk. 1947. 4°. [*U.S. Department of Agriculture. Miscellaneous Publication.* no. 616.] **A.S. 802/5.**

BURK (PHILIP DAVID) *See* BENGEL (J. A.) D. Io. Alberti Bengelii Apparatus criticus ad Novum Testamentum . . . Editio secunda . . . aucta et emendata . . . curante P. D. Burkio. 1763. 4°. **673. g. 2.**

—— Philippi Davidis Burkii Gnomon in duodecim Prophetas Minores, in quo ex nativa verborum vi simplicitas profunditas, concinnitas, salubritas sensuum cœlestium indicatur. Cum præfatione B. Jo. Alberti Bengelii. pp. 675. *Heilbronnæ*, 1753. 4°. **1007. c. 13.**

—— [Another copy.] **671. f. 2.**

—— Gnomon Psalmorum, in quo ex nativa verborum vi simplicitas, profunditas, concinnitas, salubritas sensuum cœlestium indicatur, *etc.* 2 tom. pp. 1428. *Stutgardiæ*, 1760. 8°. **3090. d. 3.**

BURK (PHILIPP DAVID) Ph. Dav. Burk's Rechtfertigung und Versicherung. In geordnetem Auszuge neu herausgegeben von Ernst Kern. pp. viii. 181. *Stuttgart*, 1854. 8°. **4255. d. 13.**

—— Phil. Dav. Burk's Sammlungen zur Pastoral-Theologie. Neu herausgegeben von Victor Friedrich Oehler, *etc.* pp. xvi. 602. *Stuttgart*, 1867. 8°. **4499. d. 10.**

BURK (RICKARD) *See* BURKE.

BURK (ROBERT EMMETT) and GRUMMITT (OLIVER JOSEPH)

—— Advances in Nuclear Chemistry and Theoretical Organic Chemistry. Editors: R. E. Burk . . . O. Grummitt. (Second printing.) pp. 165. 1946. 8°. *See* CLEVELAND, *Ohio.—Western Reserve University.* **8896. f. 6.**

—— Frontiers in Chemistry. (Edited by R. E. Burk and Oliver Grummitt.)

vol. 5. Chemical Architecture. pp. 202. 1948.
vol. 6. High Molecular Weight Organic Compounds. pp. 330. 1949.
vol. 7. Recent Advances in Analytical Chemistry. pp. 209. 1949.
vol. 8. Frontiers in Colloid Chemistry. pp. 157. 1950.

Interscience Publishers: New York, 1948– . 8°. **W.P. 666.**
Imperfect; wanting vol. 1–4.

BURK (SAMUEL L. H.)

—— *See* BENGE (Eugene J.) Manual of Job Evaluation . . . [By] E. J. Benge . . . S. L. H. Burk, *etc.* 1941. 8°. **8287. c. 66.**

BURK (WALTHER) Der versunkene Herrgott. Roman. pp. 292. *Berlin*, 1914. 8°. [*Grote'sche Sammlung von Werken zeitgenössischer Schriftsteller.* Bd. 118.] **12255.a.1/118.**

BURKA (SAMUEL MOSES) Hypersensitizing Commercial Panchromatic Plates. A dissertation, *etc.* p. 24. *Baltimore*, 1919. 8°. **8904. b. 29.**

BURKAMP (WILHELM) Die Entwicklung des Substanzbegriffs bei Ostwald. pp. 118. *Leipzig*, 1913. 8°. **8462. k. 17.**

—— Wirklichkeit und Sinn. 2 Bd. *Berlin*, 1938. 8°. **8471. g. 4.**

BURKARD, *Probst von Ursberg.* *See* BURCHARDUS, *Urspergensis.*

BURKARD (CHRISTIANUS BERNARDUS JOSEPHUS) Dissertatio inauguralis medica de remediis in febribus intermittentibus cortici peruviano substitutis, *etc.* pp. 20. *Argentorati*, 1808. 4°. [*Collection générale des dissertations de l'École spéciale de Médecine de Strasbourg.* vol. 13.] **7381*.b.**

BURKARD (JOHANN GEORG) Sammlung vermischter Gedichte. pp. 190. *Gotha*, 1789. 8°. **11525. de. 13.**

BURKARD (JOSEPH) *See* SPENCE (Joseph) [Polymetis.] Von der Übereinstimmung der Werke der Dichter mit den Werken der Künstler, nach dem Englischen des Herrn Spence, von J. Burkard. 1773, *etc.* 8°. **11805. d. 34.**

—— Auf den Tod der Erzherzoginn Theresia von Oesterreich. [In verse.] *Wien*, 1770. 8°. **11517. df. 9. (3.)**

BURKARD (JOSEPH)

—— Der Triumph Theresiens als Ihre kaiserl. königl. apostol. Majestät nach beglückter Genesung das erstemal öffentlich erschien. [In verse.] *Wien*, 1767. 8°.
11521. ee. 25. (1.)

BURKARD (JULES THÉODORE) Épopée des Zouaves. 4e Zouaves et Zouaves de la Garde . . . Illustrations de Paul de Sémant, *etc.* 2 tom. *Paris*, [1897.] 8°.
8825. bb. 42.

BURKARD (LISBERT) Manual of Plain Chant. A text-book for the singer and organist. pp. vii. 55. *J. Fischer & Bro.: New York*, [1906.] 8°. **7898. s. 5.**

BURKARDT (AUGUST) August Burkardts Anleitung zur Bücherkunde in allen Wissenschaften. Grundlage zu einer auserlesenen Bibliothek in allen Fächern. pp. 391. *Bern; Leipzig*, 1797. 8°. **11904. bbb. 17.**

BURKARDT (JOSEPH VINCENS) Staats-Wissenschafts-Lehre, mit Rücksicht auf die gegenwärtige Zeit. pp. xiv. 614. *Leipzig*, 1821. 8°. **1027. l. 21.**

BURKARDT (LUDWIG JULIUS MICHAEL) Rückbildung und Neubildung im Eierstock unbegatteter Weibchen der Rana esculenta. Inaugural-Dissertation . . . Sonder-Abdruck aus dem Archiv für mikroskopische Anatomie, *etc.* pp. 35. *Bonn*, [1911.] 8°. **07207. i. 8. (2.)**

BURKARDUS. [For Saints, Sovereigns and Princes of Sovereign Houses of this name:] *See* BURCHARD.

BURKARDUS, *a Benedictine Monk of Saint Gall.* Burkhardi monachi S. Galli Liber de casibus Monasterii S. Galli in Alamannia. *See* GOLDAST (M.) Alamannicarum rerum scriptores, *etc.* tom. 1. 1606. fol. **591. g. 13.**

—— [Another edition.] (Goldasti glossæ in Burkhardi casus.) *See* GOLDAST (M.) Rerum Alamannicarum scriptores, *etc.* tom. 1. 1730. fol. **169. g. 1.**

BURKARDUS, *de Hallis.* *See* BURCARDUS.

BURKARDUS (JOANNES) *Master of the Ceremonies of the Papal Chapel.* *See* BURCHARDUS (J.) *Bishop of Cività Castellana and Orte.*

BURKART, *von Hohenfels.* *See* SYDOW (M.) Burkart von Hohenfels und seine Lieder, *etc.* 1901. 8°.
11853. ee. 23.

BURKART ( ) *Bürgermeister in Constanz.* Ueber die Auffindung des Platzes, auf welchem Johannes Huss und Hieronimus von Prag verbrennt wurden. pp. 18. [*Constance?*] 1828. 8°. **1371. h. 31. (1.)**

BURKART (ADOLF) *See* EHRENFORTH (F.) and BURKART (A.) Geschichte des Reserve-Jäger-Bataillons Nr. 17, *etc.* 1926. 8°. **8836. e. 1/174.**

BURKART (ARTURO)

—— Estudio del género de Compuestas Chaptalia, con especial referencia a las especies argentinas. [With plates.] 1944. *See* PERIODICAL PUBLICATIONS.—*Buenos Ayres.* Darwiniana, *etc.* tom. 6. no. 4. 1922, *etc.* 8°.
P.P. **3862.** cgb.

—— Estudios sistemáticos sobre las leguminosas-hedisareas de la República Argentina y regiones adyacentes. [With plates.] 1939. *See* PERIODICAL PUBLICATIONS.—*Buenos Ayres.* Darwiniana, *etc.* tom. 3. no. 2. 1922, *etc.* 8°.
P.P. **3862.** cgb.

BURKART (CARL JOSEF) Die Bühnenbearbeitungen des Don Carlos von Schiller—Jambenfassung. Inaugural-Dissertation, *etc.* pp. 54. *Bruchsal*, 1933. 8°.
11857. aa. 16.

BURKART (EUGEN ADRIAN) Stephen Hawes' "The Pastime of Pleasure" . . . Critical introduction to a proposed new edition of the text. Inaugural dissertation, *etc.* pp. 60. *T. Wohlleben: London*, 1899. 8°.
011840. aaa. 66.

BURKART (F.) *Dr.* Richard Wagner's Meistersinger in dramatischer, sprachlicher und musikalischer Hinsicht kritisch beleuchtet. pp. 31. *Wiesbaden*, 1880. 8°.
11840. c. 39.

BURKART (FRANZ) Franz Burkarts . . . ohnmassgebliche Gedanken über die zur Einrichtung des Armenwesens im Fürstenthume Bamberg von Sr. Hochfürstlichen Gnaden . . . am Ende des Jahrs 1787 aufgestellten Preisfragen. pp. 140. *Bamberg*, 1790. 8°. [*Ueber das Armenwesen im Fürstenthume Bamberg.* pt. 1.] **8285. bb. 35.**

BURKART (FRITZ) Die fünf grossen englischen Depositen-Banken—the Big Five. pp. xi. 188. *Basel*, 1925. 8°.
08225. c. 16.

BURKART (J.) *of Magden.* *See* KELLER (Augustin) *Landammann.* Augustin Keller in seinen Reden und Bekenntnissen . . . Herausgegeben von J. Burkart. [1906.] 8°. **012301. f. 39.**

BURKART (JOSEPH) *Königl. Preuss. Ober-Bergamts-Secretair.* *See* NOEGGERATH (J. J.) and BURKART (J.) Der Bau der Erdrinde nach dem heutigen Standpunkte der Geognosie, *etc.* 1838. fol. **557*. i. 31.**

—— Aufenthalt und Reisen in Mexico in den Jahren 1825 bis 1834 . . . Mit einem Vorworte von Dr. J. Nöggerath. [With plates.] 2 Bd. *Stuttgart*, 1836. 8°. **1050. k. 23.**

BURKART (JOSEPH) *Practischer Arzt in Stuttgart.* Die Sterblichkeitsverhältnisse Stuttgarts im neunzehnten Jahrhundert und ihre Beziehung zu den Fragen der öffentlichen Gesundheitspflege. pp. 79. *Stuttgart*, 1875. 8°. **7305. c. 4. (8.)**

BURKART (RUDOLPH) Die chronische Morphiumvergiftung in Folge subkutaner Morphiuminjektionen und deren Behandlung. pp. 30. *Bonn*, 1877. 8°.
7306. c. 14. (10.)

—— Die chronische Morphiumvergiftung und deren Behandlung durch allmählige Entziehung des Morphium, *etc.* pp. vii. 184. *Bonn*, 1880. 8°. **7620. f. 3.**

—— Ueber Mastdarmstenosen. Inaugural-Dissertation, *etc.* pp. 43. *Bonn*, 1869. 8°. **7385.*d. (4.)**

—— Ueber Wesen und Behandlung der chronischen Morphiumvergiftung. pp. 42. *Leipzig*, 1884. 8°. [*Sammlung klinischer Vorträge. Innere Medizin.* no. 83.]
7441. g.

—— Weitere Mittheilungen über die chronische Morphiumvergiftung in Folge subkutaner Morphiuminjektionen und deren Behandlung. pp. 34. *Bonn*, 1878. 8°.
7306. c. 14. (16.)

—— Zur Behandlung schwerer Formen von Hysterie und Neurasthenie. pp. 48. *Leipzig*, 1884. 8°. [*Sammlung klinischer Vorträge. Gynäkologie.* no. 68.] **7441. g.**

BURKART (W.) *of Brünn.*

—— Burkart's Sammlung der wichtigsten europäischer Nutzhölzer in charakteristischen Schnitten, ausgeführt von F. M. Podany in Wien. Mit einem erläuternden Text. pp. 75. pl. 40. 1880. 8°. *See* VIENNA.—*Technologisches Gewerbe-Museum.*
7073. ee. 10.

BURKART (WALO)

—— Crestaulta. Eine bronzezeitliche Hügelsiedlung bei Surin im Lugnez, *etc.* pp. viii. 74. pl. XXIII. VIII. *Basel,* 1946. 4°. [*Monographien zur Ur- und Frühgeschichte der Schweiz.* Bd. 5.] **Ac. 5362/2.**

BURKAT (LEONARD)

—— *See* MUNCH (C.) [Je suis chef d'orchestre.] I am a Conductor. Translated by L. Burkat. 1955. 8°. **7900.** de. **50.**

BURKE PUBLISHING COMPANY. Burke's Company Tables, 1922(-26). A ten years' summary of the balance sheets of the leading public companies. vol. 1-6. *Burke Publishing Co.: London,* [1922-26.] 4°. **8232. h. 19.**
Two editions were issued in 1922. *Subsequently incorporated in "Wheeler's Company Tables," which are entered under* WHEELER (*Arthur*) AND CO.

—— Burke's Playtime Books. [Children's games with stories.] *Burke Publishing Co.: London,* [1953- .] *obl.* fol. W.P. c. **859.**

BURKE'S HANDBOOK. Burke's Handbook to the Most Excellent Order of the British Empire. *See* THORPE (Arthur W.)

BURKE'S HELP YOURSELF SERIES. *See* HELP YOURSELF SERIES.

BURKE'S LOOSE-LEAF WAR LEGISLATION. *See* ENGLAND. [*Laws and Statutes.*—IV. *Emergency Legislation.*]

BURKE'S WHO'S WHO IN SPORT. Burke's Who's Who in Sport, and Sporting Records. *See* DIRECTORIES.—*Sport.*

BURKE, *Mr.* Mr. Burke's Nieces. By the author of "May Cunningham's Trial" [i.e. E. A. Hart], *etc.* pp. viii. 205. *Cassell & Co.: London,* [1883.] 8°. **12805. o. 11.**

BURKE ( ) *Countess. See* BOURK (de) *Countess.*

BURKE ( ) *Miss.* Songs, Duets, Choruses, &c. in The Ward of the Castle. A comic opera, in two acts [by Miss Burke], *etc.* pp. 22. 1793. 8°. *See* WARD. **11602. ff. 32. (11.)**

BURKE ( ) *Rev.* The Quack-Doctor. A poem [by Rev. — Burke ?] As originally spoke at the Free Grammar School in Manchester. With notes . . . To which is added a Declamation [in Latin], spoke at the same time . . . December 13, 1744. pp. 15. 1745. 4°. *See* QUACK-DOCTOR. **11633. cc. 18.**

BURKE (AEDANUS) An Address to the Freemen of the State of South-Carolina . . . By Cassius. Supposed to be written by Ædanus Burke, *etc.* pp. 32. *Robert Bell: Philadelphia,* 1783. 8°. **8177. e. 11.**

—— Considerations on the Society or Order of Cincinnati; lately instituted by the Major-Generals, Brigadier-Generals, and other officers of the American Army . . . Addressed to the people of South Carolina, and their representatives. By Cassius. Supposed to be written by Ædanus Burke, *etc.* pp. 16. *Robert Bell: Philadelphia,* 1783. 8°. **8175. aa. 32.**

BURKE (AGNES)

—— *See* CRAIG (Gerald S.) and BURKE (A.) We Find Out, *etc.* [1940.] 8°. **08710.bb.59/5.**

BURKE (ANDREW) Burke's Descriptive Guide; or, the Visitor's Companion to Niagara Falls: its strange and wonderful localities. By an old resident. pp. 106. *Andrew Burke: Buffalo,* [1854.] 12°. **10411. a. 25.**

BURKE (ANNA CHRISTIAN) *See* GAUDICHOT-MASSON (A. M. B.) Celebrated Children of all Ages and Nations . . . Translated . . . by Mrs. L. Burke. 1853. 8°. **10604. c. 13.**

—— *See* GAUDICHOT-MASSON (A. M. B.) Celebrated Children . . . Translated . . . by Mrs. L. Burke, *etc.* 1856. 8°. **10603. aa. 30.**

—— *See* MEULAN, afterwards GUIZOT (E. C. P. de) Moral Tales . . . Translated . . . by Mrs. L. Burke. 1852. 8°. **12510. c. 32.**

—— *See* MEULAN, afterwards GUIZOT (E. C. P. de) Popular Tales . . . Translated . . . by Mrs. L. Burke. 1854. 8° **12512. c. 23.**

—— The Illustrated Language of Flowers. pp. 95. *G. Routledge & Co.: London, New York,* 1856. 16°. **723. b. 48.**

—— [Another edition.] The Miniature Language of Flowers . . . With illustrations. pp. 95. *Routledge, Warne & Routledge: London,* 1864. 32°. **7075. a. 17.**
With an additional titlepage, lithographed.

—— [Another edition.] The Coloured Language of Flowers. pp. 128. *G. Routledge & Sons: London, New York,* [1886.] 16°. **7032. aa. 7.**

—— [Another edition.] The Language of Flowers. pp. 64. *G. Routledge & Sons: London,* [1920.] 16°. **07029. ff. 16.**

BURKE (ARTHUR EDWARD)

—— Architectural and Building Trades Dictionary. [By] A. E. Burke . . . J. Ralph Dalzell . . . Gilbert Townsend . . . Edited by Pearl Jenison, *etc.* pp. 377. *American Technical Society: Chicago,* 1950. 8°. **07822. g. 32.**
Part of the "Books of the Building Trade Series." A slip bearing the imprint "Technical Press: London" has been pasted below the original imprint.

—— Architectural Lettering for Plans and Ornamental Design. By A. E. Burke . . . with the collaboration of Truman C. Buss. pp. xi. 187. *American Technical Society: Chicago,* 1953. 4°. **7869. t. 22.**
A slip bearing the imprint "Technical Press: London" has been pasted over the original imprint.

BURKE (ARTHUR MEREDYTH) *See* SAINT MARGARET, *Westminster, Parish of.* Memorials of St. Margaret's Church, Westminster. The Parish Registers, 1539-1660. Edited, with introduction and notes, by A. M. Burke, *etc.* 1914. 8°. **4707. h. 8.**

—— Indexes to the Ancient Testamentary Records of Westminster . . . With map. pp. xiv. 104. *Eyre & Spottiswoode: London,* 1913. 8°. **2099.g.**

—— Key to the Ancient Parish Registers of England and Wales. [With a supplement. With facsimiles.] 2 pt. *Sackville Press: London,* 1908, 09. fol.
The imprint of the supplement reads: "Printed for the Author by Eyre & Spottiswoode." **BB.0.b.11.**

—— [Another copy.] **9914. cc. 11.**

—— The Prominent Families of the United States of America. Edited by A. M. Burke. vol. 1. pp. 510. *Sackville Press: London,* [1909.] fol. **9915. r. 11.**
No more published.

BURKE (Arvid James) *See* Cyr (Frank W.) Paying for our Public Schools. [By] F. W. Cyr . . . A. J. Burke, *etc.* 1938. 8°. **8314.bb.1/6.**

—— Defensible Spending for Public Schools, *etc.* pp. xviii. 379. *Columbia University Press: New York,* 1943. 8°. **8385.** dd. **31.**

—— Financing the Public Schools in the United States. pp. xv. 584. *Harper & Bros.: New York,* [1951.] 8°. [*Exploration Series in Education.*] W.P. **4065/2.**

BURKE (Ashworth Peter) *See* Burke (*Sir* John B.) A Genealogical and Heraldic History of the Colonial Gentry, *etc.* (vol. 2 edited by A. P. Burke.) 1891, *etc.* 8°. **2098.a.**

—— *See* Burke (*Sir* John B.) A Genealogical and Heraldic History of the Landed Gentry of Great Britain & Ireland. By Sir B. Burke . . . Edited by his sons, *etc.* [The editor's preface signed: A. P. Burke.] 1894. 8°. **2409.** g. **4.**

—— —— 1898. 8°. **2409.** g. **5.**

—— —— 1900, *etc.* 8°. **2409.** g. **6.**

—— —— 1906. 8°. **2409.** g. **7.**

—— *See* Burke (*Sir* John B.) A Genealogical and Heraldic History of the Landed Gentry of Ireland. By Sir B. Burke . . . Edited by his son (A. P. Burke), *etc.* 1899. 8°. **2409.** d. **2.**

—— —— 1904. 8°. **2409.** d. **3.**

—— *See* Periodical Publications.—*London.* A General and Heraldic Dictionary of the Peerage and Baronetage of the United Kingdom, *etc.* [Sixty-second—seventy-ninth editions edited by A. P. Burke.] 1826, *etc.* 8° P.P. **2505.** ac. & **2098.d.**

—— Family Records. pp. xi. 709. *Harrison & Sons: London,* 1897. 8°. **2098.a.**

—— [Another copy.] **9905.** s. **6.**

BURKE (Barbara) *pseud.* [i.e. Oona Howard Ball.] Barbara goes to Oxford . . . With sixteen illustrations. pp. vii. 293. *Methuen & Co.: London,* 1907. 8°. **012634.** dd. **4.**

BURKE (*Sir* Bernard) *See* Burke (*Sir* John B.)

BURKE (Billie) [Mary William Ethelbert Appleton Burke.]

—— With a Feather on my Nose. By Billie Burke with Cameron Shipp, *etc.* [An autobiography. With plates, including portraits.] pp. x. 236. *Peter Davies: London,* 1950. 8°. **10862.** aa. **45.**

BURKE (Catherine) *See* Catherine [Burke], *de Saint-Thomas, Ursuline.*

BURKE (Charles) *of Camberwell.* History of the Camberwell Catholic Mission, 1860–1910. [With illustrations.] pp. 32. *Salesian Press: London,* [1910.] 8°. **4530.** eee. **16.** (**5.**)

BURKE (Charles) *Writer of Plays.* Rip van Winkle; a legend of the Catskills. A romantic drama, in two acts. Adapted from Washington Irving's Sketch Book by C. Burke. pp. 27. *Samuel French: New York,* [1868 ?] 12°. **11791.** cc. **25.** (**5.**)

—— [Another edition.] pp. 14. *London,* [1883 ?] 8°. [*Dicks' Standard Plays.* no. 340.] **11770.** bbb. **4.**

BURKE (Charles Bell) *See* Rossetti (Christina G.) Selected Poems . . . Edited with introduction and notes by C. B. Burke. 1913. 8°. **12199.a.1/102.**

BURKE (Christian) The Flowering of the Almond-Tree, and other poems. pp. ix. 145. *Blackwood & Sons: Edinburgh & London,* 1896. 4°. **11652.** dd. **1.**

—— "Given to Hospitality." pp. 61. *S.P.C.K.: London,* 1896. 8°. **4429.** a. **123.**

—— In a Difficult Position. pp. 160. *R.T.S.: London,* [1895.] 8°. **4429.** g. **11.**

—— Jim: a story of child-life. pp. 64. *Blackie & Son: London,* [1887.] 16°. **12806.** n. **25.**

—— Roses and Lilies of Christendom; or, Sketches of the lives of some of the saintly women of the first thirteen centuries. pp. xii. 330. *G. Routledge & Sons: London,* 1889 [1888]. 8°. **4829.** aaa. **35.**

BURKE (Coralie Evelyn) Child Study and Education, *etc.* pp. xxvii. 184. *Browne & Nolan: Dublin,* 1908. 8°. **8311.** eee. **5.**

—— Daily Readings for a Month. Compiled by Mrs. W. A. Burke. pp. iv. 91. *Catholic Truth Society: London,* 1900. 16°. **3940.** a. **35.**

—— The Structure of Life . . . With a preface by Rev. William Barry . . . Second edition. pp. xxxi. 243. *Art & Book Co.: London,* 1899. 8°. **8410.** f. **45.**

—— The Value of Life, *etc.* pp. 243. *Catholic Truth Society: London,* 1897. 12°. **4399.** aaaa. **33.**
The titlepage is a cancel.

BURKE (Dan) Van Gogh. A play in six scenes. pp. 80. *Constable & Co.: London,* 1938. 8°. **011781.** k. **38.**

BURKE (Dominick) *R.C. Bishop of Elphin.* Ad SS. D. N. Innocentium Papam xii. Libellus supplex Ecclesiasticorum Hibernorum exulum . . . de præsenti Acatholicorum molimine ad Catholicam religionem in Hibernia extirpandam, *etc.* [By D. Burke.] [1697.] 8°. *See* Ireland.—*Clergy, Roman Catholic.* G. **5503.**

BURKE (Dorothy Williams) Youth and Crime. A study of the prevalence and treatment of delinquency among boys over juvenile-court age in Chicago. pp. v. 205. *Washington,* 1930. 8°. [*U.S. Children's Bureau. Publication.* no. 196.] A.S. **79.**

BURKE (Eddie)

—— The Ups and Downs of the Jamaican Boy, Newsy Wapps, *etc.* bk. 4, 5. *The Herald: Kingston,* 1948. 8°. **12833.** bb. **7.**

BURKE (Edgar)

—— *See* Bergman (Ray) Trout . . . Fly plates in full colour painted by Dr. Edgar Burke. [1950.] 4°. W.P. **1156/15.**

BURKE (Edmund) *Bishop of Zion.* *See* O'Brien (Cornelius) *Archbishop of Halifax, N.S.* Memoirs of the Rt. Rev. Edmund Burke, Bishop of Zion, *etc.* [With a portrait.] 1894. 8°. **4956.** bbb. **14.**

—— Remarks on a Pamphlet [by Thomas MacCulloch] entitled. Popery condemned by Scripture and the Fathers. [Signed: E. B. V.G.Q., i.e. Edmund Burke, Vicar-General of Quebec.] pp. 403. ms. note [by the author]. 1809. 8°. *See* B., E., *V.G.Q.* **3936.** h. **3.**

BURKE (EDMUND) *Bishop of Zion.*

—— Remarks on the Rev. Mr. Stanser's Examination of the Rev. Mr. Burke's Letter of instruction to the C. M. [i.e. Catholic Missionaries] of Nova Scotia. Together with a reply to the Rev. Mr. Cochran's fifth and last letter to Mr. B. published in the Nova-Scotia Gazette; as also a short review of his former letters and the replies which were made. [The postscript signed: E. B. V.G., i.e. E. Burke, Vicar-General.] 2 vol. 1805. 8°. *See* B., E., *V.G.* **3938. d. 69.**

—— A Treatise on the First Principles of Christianity, in which all difficulties stated by ancient and modern sceptics, are dispassionately discussed. [The dedication signed: E. B., V.G. Que., i.e. Edmund Burke, Vicar-General of Quebec.] (Continuation of the First Principles, *etc.*) 2 pt. FEW MS. NOTES. 1808, 10. 8°. *See* B., E., *V.G. Que.* **4033. cc. 48.**

BURKE (EDMUND) *Member of the U.S. House of Representatives.* [For reports issued by E. Burke as Commissioner of Patents:] *See* UNITED STATES OF AMERICA.—*Patent Office.*

—— The Protective System considered in connection with the Present Tariff, in a series of twelve essays, originally published in the Washington Union, *etc.* pp. 40. *J. & G. S. Gideon: Washington,* 1846. 8°. **8246. e. 13.**

—— Speech. (In the House of Representatives, June 13, 1840, on the Independent Treasury Bill.) pp. 16. [*Washington,* 1840.] 8°. **8226. e. 18.**

—— Speech . . . in reply to the attack of Mr. Arnold, of Tennessee, upon the State of New Hampshire. Delivered in the House of Representatives, December 28, 1841. pp. 4. [*Washington,* 1841.] 8°. **8177. cc. 49. (11.)**

—— Speech . . . on the Tariff Bill: delivered in the House of Representatives, July 8, 1842. pp. 15. *Globe Office: Washington,* 1842. 8°. **8246. e. 12.**

—— [Another copy.] **8177. cc. 49. (12.)**

BURKE (EDMUND) *Novelist.* A Cluster of Shamrocks [and other stories]. pp. vii. 312. *Lynwood & Co.: London,* 1912. 8°. NN. **2509.**

BURKE (EDMUND) *of Kinvarra.* Musings in the Village Haunts; or, Early poems, including sketches from Irish peasant life, *etc.* pp. 196. *M. Talbot: Ennis,* 1856. 8°. **11645. e. 51.**

BURKE (*Right Hon.* EDMUND)

ARRANGEMENT.

WORKS.

—— The Works of the Right Honourable Edmund Burke. [vol. 4–8 edited until 1808 by Walker King, Bishop of Rochester, and French Laurence, and afterwards by W. King alone.] 8 vol. *J. Dodsley: London,* 1792–1827. 4°. **91. e. 8–15.**

Vol. 4–8 were published by F. C. & J. Rivington.

BURKE (*Right Hon.* EDMUND) [WORKS.]

—— A new edition. [Edited until 1808 by W. King, Bishop of Rochester, and F. Laurence, and afterwards by W. King alone.] 16 vol. *F. & C. Rivington: London,* 1803–27. 8°. **12272. d. 8.**

—— A new edition. vol. 1–12. *F. C. & J. Rivington: London,* 1808–13. 8°. **12268. d. 7.**

Vol. 9–12 are duplicates of vol. 9–12 of the preceding.

—— The Works of the Right Honourable Edmund Burke. With a portrait, and life of the author. 8 vol. *Thomas M'Lean: London,* 1823. 8°. **12272. g. 1.**

—— The Works of the Right Hon. Edmund Burke, with a biographical and critical introduction, and portrait after Sir Joshua Reynolds. 2 vol. *Holdsworth & Ball: London,* 1834. 8°. [by Henry Rogers] **522. k. 13, 14.**

—— The Works of the Right Hon. Edmund Burke, with a biographical and critical introduction, by Henry Rogers, and portrait after Sir Joshua Reynolds. 2 vol. *Samuel Holdsworth: London,* 1837. 8°. **12269. h. 8.**

—— The Works of Edmund Burke. 9 vol. *C. C. Little & J. Brown: Boston,* 1839. 8°. **1341. m. 7–15.**

—— The Works and Correspondence of the Right Honourable Edmund Burke. A new edition. (vol. 1, 2. Correspondence. Edited by Charles William, Earl Fitzwilliam, and Sir Richard Bourke.) [With a portrait.] 8 vol. *F. & J. Rivington: London,* 1852. 8°. **12272. e. 3.**

—— The Works of the Right Honourable Edmund Burke. 8 vol. *London,* 1854–89, 57. [*Bohn's British Classics.*] **2500. c. 3.**

A made-up set. Vol. 3 & 5 are of a later issue, were published by G. Bell & Sons and bear the series title, "Bohn's Standard Library."

—— The Works of the Right Honorable Edmund Burke. Revised edition. [With a portrait.] 12 vol. *Little, Brown & Co.: Boston,* 1865–67. 8°. **12273. cc. 4.**

—— The Works of the Right Honourable Edmund Burke. [With introductions by W. Willis, F. W. Raffety, and F. H. Willis.] 6 vol. *Oxford University Press: London,* 1906, 07. 8°. [*World's Classics.*] **012209. df. 47.**

SMALLER COLLECTIONS.

—— The Political Tracts and Speeches of Edmund Burke. pp. 440. *Wm. Wilson: Dublin,* 1777. 8°. **8135. dd. 1.**

—— Select Works. Edited with introduction and notes by E. J. Payne. 2 vol.

vol. 1. Thoughts on the Present Discontents. The Two Speeches on America.
vol. 2. Reflections on the Revolution in France.

Oxford, 1874, 75. 8°. [*Clarendon Press Series.*] **12205. m. 21.**

—— Essays . . . comprising Reflections on Revolution in France, On the Sublime and Beautiful, Abridgment of English History, and Speech on the Law of Libel. pp. 343. *Ward, Lock & Co.: London,* [1876.] 8°. **12269. df. 3.**

—— Select Works. Edited . . . by E. J. Payne . . . New edition, with additions and corrections. 3 vol.

vol. 1. Thoughts on the Present Discontents. The Two Speeches on America.
vol. 2. Reflections on the Revolution in France.
vol. 3. Four Letters on the Proposals for Peace with the Regicide Directory of France.

Oxford, 1876–78. 8°. [*Clarendon Press Series.*] **12205. n. 49.**

Vol. 1 and 2 only are of the new edition. Previous edition 1874, 75.

—— Letters, Speeches and Tracts on Irish Affairs . . . Collected and arranged by Matthew Arnold. With a preface. pp. xiii. 439. *Macmillan & Co.: London,* 1881. 8°. **2238**. bb. **1**.

—— On Conciliation with America, and Two Letters to Gentlemen of Bristol on Trade with Ireland . . . With an introduction by Vincent Scully. pp. 67. *M. H. Gill & Son: Dublin,* 1882. 8°. **8176**. aaa. **42**. (**2**.)

—— Two Speeches on Conciliation with America and Two Letters on Irish Questions . . . With an introduction by Henry Morley. pp. 284. *G. Routledge & Sons: London,* 1886. 8°. [*Morley's Universal Library.*] **12204.gg.1/38.**

—— Thoughts on the Present Discontents, and Speeches (on the Middlesex election, the power of juries, the duration of parliaments, and parliamentary reform). [Edited by Henry Morley.] pp. 192. *London,* 1886. 8°. [*Cassell's National Library.* vol. 18.] **12208.bb.15/18.**

—— Burke's Speeches on American Taxation, on Conciliation with America, and Letter to the Sheriffs of Bristol. Edited with introduction and notes by F. G. Selby. pp. xlviii. 328. *Macmillan & Co.: London,* 1895. 8°. **12301**. bb. **32**.

—— Select Works. Edited . . . by E. J. Payne . . . New edition, with additions and corrections. 3 vol. *Oxford,* 1897, 98, 92. 8°. [*Clarendon Press Series.*] **2320**. e. **16**.
Previous edition 1876–78.

—— Thoughts on the Present Discontents and Speeches . . . With an introduction by Henry Morley. pp. 192. *London,* 1904. 8°. [*Cassell's National Library.* New series. vol. 51.] **012209.ff.1/51.**
A reissue of the edition published in 1886.

—— Thoughts on the Cause of the Present Discontents. Together with Observations on a late Publication intituled 'The Present State of the Nation.' pp. vii. 256. *G. Routledge & Sons: London,* [1905.] 8°. [*New Universal Library.*] **12204**. p. **2/33**.
With a half-title reading "The Works of Edmund Burke. I." No more published.

—— Selections from Edmund Burke. Edited with notes and introduction by Bliss Perry. pp. xxvi. 298. *G. Bell & Sons: London,* 1908. 8°. [*English Readings.*] **12271**. w. **7/8**.

—— Burke's Speeches and Letters on American Affairs. (Introduction by Hugh Law.) pp. xiii. 295. *J. M. Dent & Co.: London; E. P. Dutton & Co.: New York,* [1908.] 8°. [*Everyman's Library.*] **12206.p.1/144.**

—— Reflections on the French Revolution & other essays. (With an introduction by A. J. Grieve.) pp. xv. 361. *J. M. Dent & Sons: London; E. P. Dutton & Co.: New York,* [1910.] 8°. [*Everyman's Library.*] **12206.p.1/322.**

—— Edmund Burke. Selections from his political writings and speeches. [With an introduction signed: J. B., i.e. John Buchan, Baron Tweedsmuir.] pp. 476. [*London,* 1911.] 8°. [*Nelson's Classics.* no. 73.] **012206**. f. **38**.

—— Select Works. Edited with introduction and notes by E. J. Payne. (Reprint from the first volume of the edition of Select Works by the late E. J. Payne, containing Thoughts on the Cause of the Present Discontents, the Speech on American Taxation, and the Speech on Conciliation with the Colonies.) 3 vol. pp. lxii. lxii. lxii. 328. *Clarendon Press: Oxford,* 1912. 8°. **012273**. df. **4**.

—— A Letter to the Sheriffs of Bristol. A Speech at Bristol on Parliamentary Conduct. A Letter to a Noble Lord. Edited by W. Murison. pp. xxix. 312. *University Press: Cambridge,* 1920. 8°. [*Pitt Press Series.*] **2322**. bb. **29**.

—— Edmund Burke. Selections from his political writings and speeches. pp. 476. *T. Nelson & Sons:* [*London,* 1925.] 8°. **12628**. de. **47**.
A reissue of the edition of 1911.

—— Conciliation with America. (I. Speech in Parliament.—II. Address to the British Colonists in North America.) pp. 115. *T. Nelson & Sons: London,* 1937. 8°. [*Masterpieces of English.* vol. 19.] **12275.aaa.9/19.**

—— Reflections on the French Revolution [and other essays]. pp. xv. 361. *J. M. Dent & Sons: London; E. P. Dutton & Co.: New York,* 1953. 8°. [*Everyman's Library.* no. 460.] **12206**. p. **1/831**.
A reissue of the edition of 1910.

—— Speeches and Letters on American Affairs. Introduction by Very Rev. Canon Peter McKevitt. pp. xii. 287. *J. M. Dent & Sons: London; E. P. Dutton & Co.: New York,* 1955. 8°. [*Everyman's Library.* no. 340.] **12206**. p. **1/931**.
A reissue of the edition of [1908].

LETTERS.

—— [Letters to James Barry.] *See* BARRY (James) *R.A.* The Works of James Barry, *etc.* vol. 1. 1809. 4°. **561***. d. **9**.

—— [Letters to the Earl of Charlemont.] *See* HARDY (Francis) Memoirs of the Political and Private Life of James Caulfeild, Earl of Charlemont. 1810. 4°. **614**. l. **29**.

—— [Another edition.] *See* HARDY (Francis) Memoirs of the Political and Private Life of James Caulfeild, Earl of Charlemont, *etc.* vol. 2. 1812. 8°. **615**. g. **11**.

—— [Two letters to William Richardson on the dramatic characters of Shakespeare.] *See* RICHARDSON (William) *Professor of Humanity, etc.* Essays on Shakespeare's Dramatic Characters, *etc.* 1812. 8°. **81**. d. **10**.

—— [A reissue.] *See* RICHARDSON (William) *Professor of Humanity, etc.* Essays on Shakespeare's Dramatic Characters, *etc.* 1818. 8°. **11762**. bbb. **7**.

—— [Five letters to Richard Burke, with a letter to Henry Grattan.] *See* THERRY (Roger) A Letter to the Right Hon. George Canning, *etc.* 1826. 8°. T. **1004**. (**3**.)

—— [Another edition.] *See* THERRY (Roger) A Letter to the Right Hon. George Canning, *etc.* 1827. 8°. **8138**. b. **94**. (**3**.)

—— The Epistolary Correspondence of the Right Hon. Edmund Burke and Dr. French Laurence. Published from the original manuscripts. pp. xxvii. 305. *C. & J. Rivington: London,* 1827. 8°. **1086**. g. **22**.

—— Correspondence of the Right Honourable Edmund Burke; between the year 1744, and the period of his decease, in 1797. Edited by Charles William, Earl Fitzwilliam and Lieutenant-General Sir Richard Bourke. [With a portrait.] 4 vol. *F. & J. Rivington: London,* 1844. 8°. **2410**. e. **1**.

—— [Another copy.] G. **2104**.

—— Letters from Edmund Burke to Richard Shackleton. *See* Leadbeater (Mary) The Leadbeater Papers, *etc.* vol. 2. 1862. 8°. **10826. aa. 8.**

—— [Another edition.] *See* Leadbeater (Mary) The Leadbeater Papers, *etc.* 1862. 8°. **10826. aa. 7.**

—— [Letters to Sir Philip Francis.] *See* Parkes (Joseph) Memoirs of Sir Philip Francis, *etc.* vol. 2. 1867. 8°. **10815. cc. 5.**

—— Correspondence of Edmund Burke & William Windham, with other illustrative letters from the Windham Papers in the British Museum. Edited by J. P. Gilson. pp. xx. 254. 1910. 4°. *See* London.—iii. *Roxburghe Club.* **C. 101. e. 16.**

—— Letters . . . A selection. Edited, with an introduction, by Harold J. Laski. pp. xvi. 430. *Oxford University Press: London,* 1922. 12°. [*World's Classics.*] **012209. df. 140.**

—— Correspondence between Burke and Shackleton relating to the description of Burke which appeared in the London Evening Post, 14th and 17th April, 1770. *See* Samuels (Arthur P. I.) The Early Life, Correspondence and Writings of the Rt. Hon. Edmund Burke, *etc.* 1923. 8°. **010856. dd. 14.**

—— [A letter to Henry Flood, dated 18 May 1765, dealing with the relationship between Burke and W. G. Hamilton.] *See* R., T. Original Letters . . . to the Right Hon. Henry Flood, *etc.* 1820. 4°. **831. k. 23.**

—— Lettre . . . sur les affaires de France et des Pays-Bas, adressée à M. le vicomte de Rivarol. Traduite de l'anglais. (Replique à la lettre précédente.) pp. 27. *Paris,* [1791?] 8°. **F. 1582. (9.)**

—— [Another copy.] **R. 76. (3.)**

SPEECHES.

Two or more Speeches.

—— Mr. Edmund Burke's Speeches at his Arrival at Bristol and at the Conclusion of the Poll. [13 Oct., 3 Nov. 1774.] pp. 16. *J. Wilkie: London,* 1774. 4°. **T. 1148. (7.)**

—— The second edition. pp. 31. *J. Dodsley: London,* 1775. 8°. **T. 1148. (8.)**

—— The Speeches of the Right Honourable Edmund Burke, in the House of Commons, and in Westminster Hall. 4 vol. *Longman & Co.; J. Ridgway: London,* 1816. 8°. **1205. e. 1–4.**

—— [Selected speeches.] *See* Pitt (William) *Earl of Chatham.* Celebrated Speeches of Chatham, Burke, *etc.* 1841. 8°. **1205. d. 14.**

—— The Speeches of the Right Hon. Edmund Burke. *Aylott & Jones: London,* 1847. 8°. [*Modern Orator.* vol. 1.] **1205. k. 7.**

—— The Speeches of the Right Hon. Edmund Burke, with memoir and historical introductions. By James Burke. pp. 456. *James Duffy: Dublin,* 1854. 8°. **1205. f. 6.**

—— Edmund Burke's Reden On American Taxation und On Conciliation with America. Zum Schulgebrauch mit einer Einleitung und Anmerkungen versehen von Dr. J. C. A. Winkelmann. *Eng.* pp. iv. 203. *Gotha,* 1864. 8°. **8175. aa. 31.**

—— Burke's Speeches on America. With introduction and notes by C. E. Vaughan. pp. xxiv. 154. *Percival & Co.: London,* 1893. 8°. [*English Classics for Schools.*] **12201. df. 1/3.**

—— [A reissue.] *Rivingtons: London,* [1898.] 8°. [*English Classics for Schools.*] **12201. df. 1/48.**

—— Speeches on America. [Edited by C. B. Hawkins. With a portrait.] pp. xvi. 234. *J. M. Dent & Co.: London,* 1906. 8°. [*Temple Classics.*] **012200.de.8/127.**

—— Speeches on America. (Edited by W. H. D. Rouse.) pp. 127. 1906. 8°. [*Blackie's English School Texts.*] **012208. e. 22/9.**

—— Speeches on American Taxation and Conciliation with America. Edited by Arthur D. Innes. pp. xxxiii. 200. *University Press: Cambridge,* 1906. 8°. [*Pitt Press Series.*] **2322. dd. 60.**

—— Speeches on America. Edited by A. J. F. Collins . . . With an introduction by F. J. C. Hearnshaw. pp. xxxv. 149. *W. B. Clive: London,* [1913.] 8°. **12301. bb. 37.**

—— [A reissue.] Speeches on American Taxation and Conciliation with America. Edited by Arthur D. Innes. pp. xxxiii. 200. *University Press: Cambridge,* 1916. 8°. [*Pitt Press Series.*] **2322. de. 190.**
A reissue of the edition of 1906.

—— [A summary in French of Burke's speeches of 6 & 11 May 1791.] *See* Willon, *le Pleureur, pseud.* Lettre de Willon le Pleureur . . . aux orateurs des révolutions . . . Contenant les derniers discours de M. Burke sur la Révolution française. 1791. 8°. **F. 364. (9.)**

Single Speeches.

1774.

—— Speech . . . on American Taxation, April 19, 1774. pp. iv. 57. *J. Dodsley: London,* 1775. 4°. **834. i. 22.**

—— The second edition. pp. 96. *J. Dodsley: London,* 1775. 8°. **E. 2241. (6.)**

—— [Another copy, with a different titlepage.] **T. 683. (9.)**

—— The third edition. pp. 96. *J. Dodsley: London,* 1775. 8°. **1197. h. 15. (4.)**

—— [Another copy.] Speech . . . on American Taxation, April 19, 1774. The third edition. ms notes [by Jeremy Bentham]. *London,* 1775. 8°. **08138. dd. 50. (6.)**

—— The fourth edition. pp. 96. *J. Dodsley: London,* 1775. 8°. **T. 1148. (9.)**

—— [Another edition.] pp. 51. *W. Pine: Bristol,* [1777?] 8°. **8175. aa. 30.**

—— The fourth edition. pp. 96. *J. Dodsley: London,* 1783. 8°. **G. 13552. (3.)**
A different edition from that of 1775 *described as* "*the fourth edition.*"

—— [Another edition.] Edited with introduction and notes by James Hugh Moffatt. pp. xxxvi. 88. *Ginn & Co: Boston,* [1905.] 8°. [*Standard English Classics.*] **012203. f. 39/1.**

—— *See* Constitutio, *pseud.* A Letter to Edmund Burke, Esq; controverting the principles of American government, laid down in his lately published speech on American taxation, *etc.* 1775. 8°. **102. f. 31.**

—— An Answer to the Printed Speech of Edmund Burke, Esq; spoken in the House of Commons, April 19, 1774, *etc.* [By John Shebbeare.] pp. iv. 222. *T. Evans; J. Bew: London,* 1775. 8°. **102. f. 74.**

—— The second edition. pp. iv. 222. *T. Evans; J. Bew: London,* 1776. 8°. **8135. bb. 17.**

1775.

—— Speech of Edmund Burke, Esq. on moving his resolutions for conciliation with the Colonies, March 22, 1775. The second edition. pp. 107. *J. Dodsley: London,* 1775. 8°. **E. 2241. (7.)**

—— The third edition. pp. 107. *J. Dodsley: London,* 1784. 8°. **G. 13552. (5.)**

—— [Another edition.] *See* ADAMS (Charles K.) Representative British Orations, *etc.* vol. 1. 1884. 16°. **12301. cc. 3.**

—— [Another edition, with the addition of a version in shorthand.] *See* ADAMS (Charles K.) Representative British Orations, *etc.* vol. 1. 1887, *etc.* 8°. **12991. bb. 61.**

—— [Another edition.] Speech on Conciliation with America . . . Edited by William MacDonald. pp. 164. *American Book Co.: New York,* [1904.] 8°. [*Gateway Series of English Texts.*] **12269. ee. 32/2.**

—— [Another edition.] Edited with introduction and notes by Sidney Carleton Newsom. [With a portrait.] pp. xxxviii. 124. *New York,* 1909. 8°. [*Macmillan's Pocket American and English Classics.*] **12199.a.1/44.**

—— [Another edition.] Edited, with introduction and notes, by F. G. Selby. pp. xxxv. 127. *Macmillan & Co.: London,* 1912. 8°. **8132. aa. 41.**

—— [Another edition.] Edited with introduction and notes by John Morrison. pp. xv. 127. *London,* 1912. 8°. [*Bell's English Classics.*] **012272. aaaa. 1/26.**

—— *See* PERCIVAL (H. M.) Notes on "Conciliation with the Colonies," *etc.* 1898. 8°. **5319. a. 32.**

—— *See* SHEBBEARE (John) An Essay on the Origin . . . of National Society . . . To which is added an appendix on the excellent and admirable in Mr Burke's second printed speech of the 22d of March, 1775. 1776. 8°. **100. l. 18.**

—— —— 1776. 8°. **8175. dd. 1. (1.)**

—— *See* TUCKER (Josiah) *Dean of Gloucester.* A Letter to Edmund Burke, Esq. . . . in answer to his printed speech, said to be spoken in the House of Commons on the twenty-second of March, 1775. 1775. 8°. **T. 683. (7.)**

—— —— 1775. 8°. **522. g. 5. (3.)**

1779.

—— [Speech delivered by Burke on 15 Dec. 1779 on giving notice of his intention to propose a plan of public economy.] *See* ENGLAND.—*Parliament.—House of Commons.* [*Proceedings.*—II.] Substance of the Speeches made . . . the 15th of December, 1779, *etc.* 1779. 8°. **8132. de. 3. (5.)**

1780.

—— Speech . . . on presenting to the House of Commons—on the 11th. of February, 1780—a plan for the better security of the independence of Parliament and the oeconomical reformation of the civil and other establishments. pp. 95. *J. Dodsley: London,* 1780. 8°. **T. 1127. (8.)**

—— [Another copy.] **T. 318. (2.)**

—— [Another copy.] **679. c. 4. (3.)**

—— Speech . . . on presenting to the House of Commons—on the 11th of February, 1780—a plan for the better security of the independence of Parliament . . . The third edition. pp. 95. *J. Dodsley: London,* 1780. 8°. **12305.k.38.(4.)**

—— [Another copy.] Speech . . . on presenting to the House of Commons—on the 11th of February, 1780—a plan for the better security of the independence of Parliament . . . The third edition. MS. notes [by Jeremy Bentham]. *London,* 1780. 8°. **08138. dd. 50. (4.)**

—— [Another copy.] **8132.df.10.(3.)**
Imperfect; wanting the last leaf.

—— The fourth edition. pp. 95. *J. Dodsley: London,* 1780. 8°. **8133. e. 7.**

—— A new edition. pp. 95. *J. Dodsley: London,* 1780. 8°. **8133. e. 6.**

—— A new edition. pp. 76. *J. Dodsley: London,* 1780. 8°. **1027. b. 24. (3.)**

—— [Another copy.] **G. 13552. (4.)**

—— *See* BENTHAM (Jeremy) [*Single Works.*] Defence of Economy, against the late Mr. Burke. [A criticism of the proposals in Burke's speech of 11 Feb. 1780.] 1817. 8°. **6025. bb. 6. (3.)**

—— *See* TOMLINSON (Lovel) Mr. E—— B——'s Answer to his own Speech of the 11th of February, 1780. With Mr. F——'s animadversions thereon, *etc.* [A satire on Edmund Burke and Charles James Fox.] 1780. 8°. **103. d. 32.**

—— The Constitution, or a Full answer to Mr. Edmund Burke's anti-constitutional plan of reform. Addressed to the Honourable the Speaker of the House of Commons. By a lover and strenuous supporter of the constitution. pp. 119. *W. Nicoll: London,* 1781. 8°. **523. f. 33.**

—— [Another copy.] MS. NOTES. **110. e. 51.**

—— A Speech of Edmund Burke, Esq. at the Guildhall in Bristol, previous to the late election in that city, upon certain points relative to his parliamentary conduct. [6 Sept. 1780.] pp. 68. *J. Dodsley: London,* 1780. 8°. **8135. d. 81. (1.)**

—— [Another copy.] A Speech of Edmund Burke, Esq. at the Guildhall, in Bristol . . . upon certain points relative to his parliamentary conduct. MS. NOTES [by Jeremy Bentham]. *London,* 1780. 8°. **08138. dd. 50. (2.)**

—— The second edition. pp. 68. *J. Dodsley: London,* 1780. 8°. **T. 1127. (9.)**

—— [Another copy.] **T. 179. (8.)**

—— The third edition. pp. 68. *J. Dodsley: London,* 1780. 8°. **1093. i. 19.**

—— [Another edition.] pp. 80. MS. NOTES. *R. Marchbank: Dublin,* 1780. 8°. **8133. b. 23.**

—— The fifth edition. pp. 68. *J. Dodsley: London,* 1782. 8°. **G. 13553. (4.)**

—— [Another edition.] *See* REILY (Hugh) The Impartial History of Ireland, *etc.* 1787. 12°. **1325. a. 5.**

—— [Another edition.] *See* CURRAN (*Right Hon.* John P.) Speeches, *etc.* vol. 2. 1809. 8°. **1205. k. 18.**

—— [An extract from Burke's speech of 6 Sept. 1780.] *See* MONTAGU (Basil) Enquiries respecting the Insolvent Debtor's Bill, *etc.* 1815. 8°. **6147.bb.38.**

—— [Another edition.] *See* MONTAGU (Basil) Enquiries respecting the Insolvent Debtors' Bill, *etc.* 1816. 8°. **T. 2055. (7.)**

1783.

—— Mr. Burke's Speech, on the 1st December 1783, upon the question for the Speaker's leaving the chair, in order for the House to resolve itself into a committee on Mr. Fox's East India Bill. pp. 105. *J. Dodsley: London,* 1784. 8°. **08139.ccc.44.(1.)**

—— [Another copy.] **8022. b. 18.**
Wanting the half-title.

—— [Another edition.] pp. 105. *L. White: Dublin,* 1784. 8°. **8132. df. 4. (6.)**

—— *See* SCOTT, afterwards SCOTT WARING (John) A Letter to the Right Honourable Edmund Burke, Paymaster General of His Majesty's Forces. [With reference to his support of Fox's East India Bill.] 1783. 8°. **8022. bbb. 7.**

—— *See* SCOTT, afterwards SCOTT WARING (John) A Reply to Mr. Burke's Speech of the first of December, 1783, on Mr. Fox's East-India Bill. 1784. 8°. **T. 128. (6.)**

—— Letters to the Rt. Hon. Edmund Burke. [With special reference to Burke's speech of 1 Dec. 1783.] By J. S. [i.e. John Scott, afterwards Scott Waring.] 1783. 8°. *See* S., J. **T. 703. (1.)**

—— [Another copy.] **T. 128. (2.)**

—— Observations on Mr. Burke's Speech on Mr. Fox's India Bill, in an address to that gentleman. pp. 44. *Printed for the Author: London,* 1784. 8°. **E. 2146. (7.)**

1784.

—— A Representation to His Majesty (on the Speech from the Throne), moved in the House of Commons by the Right Honourable Edmund Burke and seconded by the Right Honourable William Windham, on Monday, June 14, 1784, and negatived. With a preface and notes. pp. iii. 31. *J. Debrett: London,* 1784. 4°. **793. l. 40. (10.)**

—— A Representation to His Majesty, moved in the House of Commons by . . . Edmund Burke, *etc.* pp. 52. *Luke White; Patt. Byrne: Dublin,* 1784. 8°. **8140. e. 20.**

—— [Another copy.] **T. 661. (4.)**
Imperfect; wanting the half-title.

—— A new edition. pp. 81. *J. Debrett: London,* 1785. 8°. **8132. e. 14.**

—— [Another copy.] **103. e. 26.**

—— [Another copy.] **G. 13553. (5.)**

—— Speech . . . on Reform, delivered in the House of Commons, 1782 [or rather 16 June 1784]. To which are added some extracts from the speech of the late Right Honble. William Windham on Mr. Curwen's Reform Bill, 1809. pp. 32. *C. J. G. & F. Rivington: London,* 1831. 8°. **8135. d. 11.**

1785.

—— Mr. Burke's Speech on the Motion made for Papers relative to the directions for charging the Nabob of Arcot's private debts to Europeans, on the revenues of the Carnatic. February 28th, 1785. With an appendix, containing several documents. pp. xi. 98. 93. *J. Dodsley: London,* 1785. 8°. **12305.k.38.(5.)**

—— [Another copy.] **G. 13553. (6.)**

—— [Another edition.] pp. xi. 98. 93. *P. Byrne: Dublin,* 1785. 8°. **8022. bb. 43.**

1788.

—— Speech of the Rt. Hon. Edmund Burke, manager for the House of Commons, in opening the Impeachment, 15 February, 1788. *See* HASTINGS (*Right Hon.* Warren) *Governor-General of India.* Speeches of the Managers and Counsel in the Trial of Warren Hastings, *etc.* vol. 1. 1859. 8°. **8022. e. 6.**

—— *See* SCOTT, afterwards SCOTT WARING (John) Major Scott's Charge against the Right Honourable Edmund Burke, February 6, 1789. [With special reference to Burke's speech in opening the impeachment of Warren Hastings.] 1789. 8°. **8135. c. 82.**

1789.

—— Speech . . . in opening the sixth article of the charge, relating to presents; 21 April, 1789. *See* HASTINGS (*Right Hon.* Warren) *Governor-General of India.* Speeches of the Managers and Counsel in the Trial of Warren Hastings, *etc.* vol. 2. 1859. 8°. **8022. e. 6.**

—— [Speech on the motion for the abolition of the slave trade, 12 May 1789.] *See* ENGLAND.—*Parliament.—House of Commons.* [*Proceedings.*—II.] The Speeches of Mr. Wilberforce, Lord Penrhyn, *etc.* 1789. 8°. **8155. c. 74.**

1790.

—— Substance of the Speech of the Right Honourable Edmund Burke in the Debate on the Army Estimates in the House of Commons, on Tuesday the 9th day of February, 1790. Comprehending a discussion of the present situation of affairs in France. pp. 36. *J. Debrett: London,* 1790. 8° **C.115.e.3.(4.)**

—— [Another copy.] **8135. c. 11.**

—— The fourth edition. pp. 36. *J. Debrett: London,* 1790. 8°. **G. 13553. (7.)**

—— Sur la révolution arrivée en France. Ouvrage traduit de l'anglois par . . . le B. de B * * *. [An abridgment of Burke's speech of 9 Feb. 1790.] pp. 21. *Londres,* 1790. 8°. **F. 1263. (1.)**

—— Discours . . . sur la situation actuelle de la France, prononcé . . . dans la Chambre des Communes d'Angleterre, le 9 février 1790, lors du fameux débat sur les estimations de l'armée. Traduit littéralement de l'anglois, & dédié à l'Assemblée nationale. [A free adaptation.] pp. 28. [*Paris,* 1790.] 8°. **F. 557. (5.)**

—— [Another copy.] **R. 75. (1.)**

—— [Another edition.] pp. 27. [*Paris,* 1790.] 8°. **8050. d. 62. (17.)**

—— [Another edition.] pp. 15. [*Paris,* 1790.] 8°. **R. 75. (2.)**

BURKE (*Right Hon.* EDMUND) [SPEECHES.—SINGLE SPEECHES.]

—— *See* DESTUTT DE TRACY (A. L. C.) *Count.* M. de Tracy à M. Burke. [In reply to Burke's speech of 9 Feb. 1790.] [1790.] 8º. F. **1582**. (**6**.)

—— *See* STANHOPE (Charles) *Earl Stanhope.* A Letter to the Right Honourable Edmund Burke . . . Containing a short answer to his late speech [of 9 Feb. 1790] on the French Revolution, *etc.* 1790. 8º. E. **2160**. (**1**.)

—— —— 1790. 8º. **1103**. g. **58**. (**4**.)

—— *See* STANHOPE (Charles) *Earl Stanhope.* Lettre . . . au très honorable Edmond Burke contenant une courte réponse à son dernier discours sur la Révolution de France. 1790. 8º. F. **561**. (**13**.)

—— —— [1790 ?] 8º. F. **582**. (**9**.)

—— *See* STANHOPE (Charles) *Earl Stanhope.* Apologie de la révolution française . . . ou Lettre au très-honorable Edmund Burke, servant de réplique à son discours . . . contre la révolution française, *etc.* 1791. 8º. **1481**. c. **3**.

—— Observations sur le discours de M. Burk, au sujet de la Revolution française. pp. 17. [*Paris*, 1790.] 8º. R. **75**. (**3**.)

1791.

—— [Speech in the House of Commons, 6 May 1791, on the French Revolution. Translated into French.] *See* ENGLAND.—*Parliament.*—*House of Commons.* [*Proceedings.* —II.] Discours improvisés, par MM. Burke et Fox, et autres membres de la Chambre des Communes, *etc.* 1791. 8º. R. **76**. (**2**.)

1794.

—— Substance of the Speech of the Right Honourable Edmund Burke in the House of Commons, on Friday the 23d day of May, 1794, in answer to certain observations on the Report of the Committee of Managers, representing that report to have been a libel on the judges. pp. 26. *J. Debrett: London*, 1794. 8º. E. **2165**. (**5**.)

—— Speech . . . in general reply on the several charges; 28 May, 1794. *See* HASTINGS (*Right Hon.* Warren) *Governor-General of India.* Speeches of the Managers and Counsel in the Trial of Warren Hastings, *etc.* vol. 4. 1859. 8º. **8022**. e. **6**.

SINGLE WORKS.

APPEAL FROM THE NEW TO THE OLD WHIGS.

—— An Appeal from the New, to the Old Whigs, in consequence of some late discussions in Parliament, relative to the Reflections on the French Revolution. pp. 139. *J. Dodsley: London*, 1791. 8º. **8135**. c. **90**.

—— [Another copy.] **110**. e. **58**.

—— [Another copy.] C.115.e.3.(5.)

—— The third edition. pp. 143. *J. Dodsley: London*, 1791. 8º. **8133**. d. **5**.

—— [Another copy.] G. **13554**. (**3**.)

—— The fourth edition. pp. 144. *J. Dodsley: London*, 1791. 8º. **8135**. dd. **44**.

—— [Another copy.] An Appeal from the New to the Old Whigs . . . The fourth edition. *London*, 1791. 8º. **8051**. de. **50**. (**3**.)

BURKE (*Right Hon.* EDMUND) [SINGLE WORKS.]

—— [Another edition.] pp. 141. *M. Mills: Dublin*, 1791. 8º. **8135**. cc. **56**. (**1**.)

Appendix.

—— *See* BELSHAM (William) *Historian.* Examination of an Appeal from the New to the Old Whigs, *etc.* 1792. 8º. T. **1120**. (**11**.)

—— *See* BOOTHBY (*Sir* Brooke) *Bart.* Observations on the Appeal from the New to the Old Whigs, *etc.* 1792. 8º. **8132**. ee. **22**.

—— *See* ROUS (George) A Letter to the Right Honourable Edmund Burke . . . in reply to his Appeal from the New to the Old Whigs. [1791.] 8º. **8133**. cc. **10**.

ARTICLES OF CHARGE AGAINST WARREN HASTINGS.

—— [For editions of the articles of charge against Warren Hastings, which were drawn up by Burke with the assistance of others:] *See* HASTINGS (*Right Hon.* Warren)

ESSAY TOWARDS AN ABRIDGMENT OF ENGLISH HISTORY.

—— An Essay towards an Abridgment of the English History. pp. 1–48. [*London*, 1757.] 4º. T. **922**. (**8**.)
Sig. B–G. "*This Essay, which was never finished, was begun by Mr. Burke for Mr. Dodsley, among whose books in quire it was found by Mr. Nichol . . . and by whom it was given to me.*" MS. *note by Dr. Charles Burney*, 1799.

LETTER FROM A DISTINGUISHED ENGLISH COMMONER TO A PEER OF IRELAND.

—— *See* infra : LETTER TO SIR HERCULES LANGRISHE.

LETTER FROM A GENTLEMAN IN THE ENGLISH HOUSE OF COMMONS.

—— A Letter from a Gentleman in the English House of Commons [i.e. E. Burke], in vindication of his conduct with regard to the affairs of Ireland, addressed to a member of the Irish Parliament (T. B., Esq. [i.e. Thomas Burgh.]). pp. 58. 1780. 8º. *See* B., T., *Esq.* **116**. g. **37**.

—— [Another edition.] A Letter from Edmund Burke, Esq. in vindication of his conduct with regard to the affairs of Ireland. Addressed to Thomas Burgh, Esq. Member of Parliament for Athy. pp. 58. *P. Byrne: Dublin*, 1780. 8º. **8145**. dd. **5**.

—— A Letter from Edmund Burke, Esq. in vindication of his conduct, with regard to the affairs of Ireland, addressed to Thomas Burgh . . . Second edition. pp. 58. MS. NOTES [by Jeremy Bentham]. *J. Bew: London*, 1781. 8º. **08138**. dd. **50**. (**3**.)

LETTER TO A MEMBER OF THE NATIONAL ASSEMBLY.

—— A Letter from Mr. Burke, to a Member of the National Assembly; in answer to some objections to his book on French affairs. pp. 74. MS. NOTES. *J. Dodsley: London*, 1791. 8º. **8050**. e. **13**.

—— The second edition. pp. 74. *J. Dodsley: London*, 1791. 8º. **935**. i. **9**.

—— [Another copy.] B. **722**. (**4**.)

—— The third edition. pp. 74. *J. Dodsley: London*, 1791. 8º. **8050**. e. **14**.

BURKE (*Right Hon.* EDMUND) [SINGLE WORKS.—LETTER TO A MEMBER OF THE NATIONAL ASSEMBLY.]

—— The fourth edition. pp. 74. *J. Dodsley: London,* 1791. 8°. **8050.** e. **15.**

—— [Another copy.] G. **13554.** (**2.**)

—— A Letter . . . to a Member of the National Assembly . . The fifth edition. pp. 74. *J. Dodsley: London,* 1791. 8° **8051.** de. **50.** (**2.**)

—— [Another edition.] pp. 60. *William Porter: Dublin,* 1791. 8°. **8052.** ccc. **16.**

—— Lettre de M. Burke, à un membre de l'Assemblée nationale de France. pp. 99. [*Paris,*] M.DCCCXI [1791]. 8° F. **1582.** (**8.**)

—— [Another edition.] pp. 99. [*Paris,*] M.DCCCXI [1791]. 8°. R. **75.** (**11.**)

—— [Another edition.] Suite des Réflexions sur la Révolution de France par le Right Honourable Edmund Burke, en forme d'une nouvelle lettre à un membre de l'Assemblée nationale de France qui lui avoit écrit au sujet de la première. Traduction de l'anglois. pp. 116. *Paris,* 1792. 8°. **9220.** c. **25.**

—— Lettera del signor Burke a un membro dell'Assemblea nazionale . . . Tradotta . . . da Benedetto Crispi sulla quarta edizione. pp. 104. *Ferrara,* 1793. 8°. **899.** c. **18.** (**2.**)

Appendix.

—— *See* LALLY TOLLENDAL (T. G. de) *Marquis.* Lettre écrite au très-honorable Edmund Burke, *etc.* [With reference to Burke's " Letter to a Member of the National Assembly."] [1791.] 8°. F. **332.** (**3.**)

—— *See* LALLY TOLLENDAL (T. G. de) *Marquis.* Seconde lettre de M. de Lally-Tolendal à M. Burke. [With reference to Burke's " Letter to a Member of the National Assembly."] 1792. 8°. R. **77.** (**12.**)

—— *See* LOFFT (Capel) *the Elder.* Remarks on the Letter of Mr. Burke to a Member of the National Assembly, *etc.* 1791. 8°. **8135.** c. **55.**

LETTER TO A NOBLE LORD.

—— A Letter from the Right Honourable Edmund Burke to a Noble Lord, on the attacks made upon him and his pension, in the House of Lords, by the Duke of Bedford and the Earl of Lauderdale, early in the present sessions of Parliament. pp. 80. *J. Owen; F. & C. Rivington: London,* 1796. 8°. E. **2169.** (**6.**)

—— (Second edition.) pp. 80. *J. Owen; F. & C. Rivington: London,* 1796. 8°. **8133.** e. **8.**

—— [Another edition.] The second edition. pp. 32. *T. Williams: London,* 1796. 8°. T. **1094.** (**13.**)

—— (The third edition.) pp. 80. *J. Owen; F. & C. Rivington: London,* 1796. 8°. **8132.** df. **11.** (**1.**)

—— (The fourth edition.) pp. 80. *J. Owen; F. & C. Rivington: London,* 1796. 8°. E. **2067.** (**1.**)

—— [Another edition.] The fourth edition. pp. 32. *T. Williams: London,* 1796. 8°. **8133.** e. **9.**

—— (The fifth edition.) pp. 80. *J. Owen; F. & C. Rivington: London,* 1796. 8°. **8133.** e. **10.**

—— (The sixth edition.) pp. 80. *J. Owen; F. & C. Rivington: London,* 1796. 8°. **8132.** df. **11.** (**2.**)

BURKE (*Right Hon.* EDMUND) [SINGLE WORKS.—LETTER TO A NOBLE LORD.]

—— (The seventh edition.) pp. 80. *J. Owen; F. & C. Rivington: London,* 1796. 8°. T. **1094.** (**12.**)

—— (The eighth edition.) pp. 80. *J. Owen; F. & C. Rivington: London,* 1796. 8°. **8132.** df. **11.** (**3.**)

—— (The eleventh edition.) pp. 80. *J. Owen; F. & C. Rivington: London,* 1796. 8°. **8135.** f. **4.**

—— (The thirteenth edition.) pp. 80 *J. Owen; F. & C. Rivington: London,* 1796. 8°. E. **2067.** (**2.**)

—— [Another copy.] T. **137.** (**1.**)
Imperfect; wanting the half-title and all after p. 78.

—— First American edition, with a preface by Peter Porcupine [i.e. William Cobbett]. pp. iv. 58. *B. Davies, etc.: Philadelphia,* [1796.] 8°. **8133.** bb. **9.**

—— New edition. pp. 59. *C. J. G. & F. Rivington: London,* 1831. 8°. **8132.** df. **11.** (**4.**)

—— [Another edition.] pp. 50. *Thomas Clark: Edinburgh,* 1837. 8°. [*Cabinet Library of Scarce and Celebrated Tracts.* no. 8.] **1153.** i. **2.** (**2.**)

—— [Another copy.] **8132.** de. **3.** (**14.**)

—— [Another edition.] *See* BAUMANN (Arthur A.) Burke: the founder of Conservatism, *etc.* 1929. 8°. **08139.** a. **91.**

—— Lettre du très-honorable Edmond Burke à un noble Lord, sur les attaques dirigées contre lui dans la Chambre des Pairs, par le duc de Bedfort et le comte de Lauderdale . . . Traduite sur la sixième édition de Londres. (Lettre à la noblesse française.—De la vie politique, de la fuite et de la capture de M. La Fayette. [By Antoine Rivarol.]) pp. 111. [*Paris,* 1796.] 8°. F. **1582.** (**1.**)

—— Edmund Burke's Rechtfertigung seines politischen Lebens. Gegen einen Angriff des Herzogs von Bedford und des Grafen Lauderdale bei Gelegenheit einer ihm verliehenen Pension. Uebersetzt mit einer Vorrede und einigen Anmerkungen von Friedrich Gentz. pp. xxxiv. 156. *Berlin,* 1796. 8°. **8133.** a. **2.**

Appendix.

—— *See* ADAIR (*Right Hon. Sir* Robert) Part of a Letter . . . to the Right Honourable Charles James Fox; occasioned by Mr. Burke's mention of Lord Keppel in a recent publication [i.e. " A Letter to a Noble Lord "]. 1796. 8°. **1102.** i. **39.**

—— *See* BROWNE (M. C.) A Leaf out of Burke's Book: being an epistle to that Right Honourable Gentleman in reply to his Letter to a Noble Lord, *etc.* 1796. 8°. E. **2067.** (**5.**)

—— —— 1796. 8°. **8139.** b. **15.** (**4.**)

—— *See* MACLEOD (Allan) A Warm Reply to Mr. Burke's Letter [i.e. " A Letter to a Noble Lord "]. 1796. 8°. **8132.** df. **11.** (**5.**)

—— *See* MILES (William A.) Political Writer. A Letter to Henry Duncombe, Esq. . . . on the subject of the very extraordinary pamphlet, lately addressed by Mr. Burke, to a Noble Lord. 1796. 8°. E. **2067.** (**4.**)

—— —— 1796. 8°. E. **2169.** (**7.**)

—— —— 1796. 8°. **8132.** df. **9.** (**5.**)

BURKE (*Right Hon.* EDMUND) [SINGLE WORKS.—LETTER TO A NOBLE LORD.]

—— *See* NEALE (George) *Rev.* A Letter to the Right Honourable Edmund Burke, in answer to a letter respecting the Duke of Bedford and the Earl of Lauderdale: to which is appended some anticipation of Mr. Burke's Thoughts on a Regicide Peace. 1796. 8°. **1414. e. 65. (3.)**

—— *See* SARPEDON, *pseud.* A Letter to Mr. Miles, occasioned by his late scurrilous attack on Mr. Burke, *etc.* [With special reference to "A Letter to a Noble Lord."] 1796. 8°. **103. e. 55**

—— *See* SIMKIN, *Redivivus, pseud.* Simkin Redivivus to Simon: a satirical and poetical epistle, describing Edmund Burke's Letter to a Noble Lord in defence of his pension, *etc.* 1796. 8°. **T. 1057. (9.)**

—— *See* STREET (Thomas G.) A Vindication of the Duke of Bedford's Attack upon Mr. Burke's Pension: in reply to a Letter . . . to a Noble Lord. 1796. 8°. **103. e. 59.**

—— *See* THELWALL (John) *Lecturer.* Sober Reflections on the Seditious and Inflammatory Letter of the Right Hon. Edmund Burke to a Noble Lord, *etc.* 1796. 8°. **E. 2067. (3.)**

—— —— 1796. 8°. **12270. pp. 4. (1.)**

—— *See* TOWNSHEND (Thomas) *of Gray's Inn.* A Summary Defence of the Right. Hon. Edmund Burke, *etc.* [With special reference to "A Letter to a Noble Lord."] 1796. 8°. **103. e. 56.**

—— *See* WAKEFIELD (Gilbert) Unitarian. A Reply to the Letter of Edmund Burke, Esq., to a Noble Lord. 1796. 8°. **8132. df. 11. (6.)**

—— —— 1796. 8°. **8132. df. 3. (5.)**

—— A General Reply to the several Answerers, &c. of a Letter written to a Noble Lord by the Right Honourable Edmund Burke. pp. 79. *Allen & West: London,* 1796. 8°. **8135. a. 26.**

—— Remarks on Conversations occasioned by Mr. Burke's Letter [i.e. "A Letter to a Noble Lord"]. In a letter to a Professor on the Continent. [By — Beckett.] pp. 31. *George Cawthorne: London,* 1796. 8°. **8133. e. 12.**

—— Strictures on Mr. Burke's Letter to a Noble Lord, on the attacks made upon him and his pension, in the House of Lords, by the Duke of Bedford and Lord Lauderdale. pp. 15. *D. I. Eaton: London,* 1796. 8°. **8133. e. 11.**

LETTER TO SIR HERCULES LANGRISHE.

—— A Letter . . . to Sir Hercules Langrishe, Bart., M.P., on the subject of Roman Catholics of Ireland, and the propriety of admitting them to the elective franchise, *etc.* pp. 88. *J. Debrett: London,* 1792. 8°. **3942. b. 10.**

—— The second edition, corrected. pp. 88. *J. Debrett: London,* 1792. 8°. **8145. d. 9.**

—— [Another copy.] A Letter . . . to Sir Hercules Langrishe . . . on the subject of Roman Catholics of Ireland . . . The second edition, corrected. *London,* 1792. 8°. C.T. **64. (2.)**

—— [Another edition.] pp. iv. 27. *P. Byrne: Dublin,* 1792. 8°. **E. 2163. (3.)**

BURKE (*Right Hon.* EDMUND) [SINGLE WORKS.]

—— A Letter from a Distinguished English Commoner, to a Peer in Ireland, on the Repeal of a Part of the Penal Laws against the Irish Catholics. (Extract from Mr. Burke's Letter to Sir Hercules Langrishe. A reprint of the original Dublin edition.) [Edited by Hugh C. Clifford.] pp. viii. 29. *P. Keating: London,* 1785 [1824]. 12°. **8146. aaa. 7. (1.)**

LETTER TO THE DUKE OF PORTLAND.

—— *See* infra: OBSERVATIONS ON THE CONDUCT OF THE MINORITY.

LETTER TO THE SHERIFFS OF BRISTOL.

—— A Letter from Edmund Burke, Esq., one of the Representatives in Parliament for the City of Bristol, to John Farr and John Harris, Esqrs., sheriffs of that city, on the affairs of America. pp. 75. *J. Dodsley: London,* 1777. 8°. **1061. h. 23. (3.)**

—— [Another copy.] **679. c. 4. (1.)**

—— The second edition. pp. 75. *J. Dodsley: London,* 1777. 8°. **T. 1050. (6.)**

—— [Another copy.] **E. 2230. (2.)**

—— The third edition. pp. 75. *J. Dodsley: London,* 1777. 8°. **8007. bb. 7.**

—— The fourth edition. pp. 79. *J. Dodsley: London,* 1777. 8°. **G. 13553. (1.)**

—— [Another edition.] pp. 79. *William Pine: Bristol,* 1777. 8°. **8175. b. 17.**

—— [Another edition.] pp. 55. *W. Whitestone, etc.: Dublin,* 1777. 8°. **8145. bbb. 7. (1.)**

Appendix.

—— *See* BERTIE (Willoughby) *Earl of Abingdon.* Thoughts on the Letter of Edmund Burke, Esq., to the Sheriffs of Bristol, on the affairs of America. [1777.] 8°. **523. g. 19. (3.)**

—— —— [1777.] 8°. **E. 2230. (3.)**

—— —— [1777?] 8°. **679.c.4.(2.)**

—— *See* BERTIE (Willoughby) *Earl of Abingdon.* Thoughts on the Letter of Edmund Burke, Esq; to the Sheriffs of Bristol . . . The second edition. [1777.] 8°. **12305. k. 38. (3.)**

—— *See* BERTIE (Willoughby) *Earl of Abingdon.* Thoughts on the Letter of Edmund Burke, *etc.* 1780. 8°. **08139. ccc. 35.**

—— *See* BERTIE (Willoughby) *Earl of Abingdon.* Second Thoughts: or, Observations upon Lord Abingdon's Thoughts on a Letter of Edmund Burke Esq., to the Sheriffs of Bristol. By the author of the Answer to Mr. Burke's Letter [i.e. George Chalmers]. 1777. 8°. **103. c. 43.**

—— *See* CARTWRIGHT (John) *Major.* A Letter to the Earl of Abingdon, discussing a position . . . contained in his Lordship's Thoughts on the Letter of Edmund Burke, Esq., to the Sheriffs of Bristol. 1778. 8°. **E. 2230. (4.)**

—— *See* TOPHAM (Edward) *Major.* An Address to Edmund Burke, Esq., on his late Letter [to the Sheriffs of Bristol] relative to the affairs of America. 1777. 4°. **102. g. 43.**

—— An Answer from the Electors of Bristol to the Letter of Edmund Burke, Esq. on teh [*sic*] Affairs of America. [By George Chalmers.] pp. 85. 5. *T. Cadell: London*, 1777. 8°. **T. 1050. (8.)**

—— [Another copy.] **1061. h. 23. (5.)**

—— An Answer to the Letter of Edmund Burke, Esq., one of the representatives of the city of Bristol, to the sheriffs of that city. pp. 60. *T. Cadell: London*, 1777. 8°. **T. 1050. (7.)**

—— [Another copy.] **1061. h. 23. (4.)**

—— [Another copy.] **103. c. 29.**

—— The second edition. [The preface signed: H. C.] 1777. 8°. *See* C., H. **8177. aa. 13.**

OBSERVATIONS ON A LATE STATE OF THE NATION.

—— Observations on a late State of the Nation. [A reply by Burke to a pamphlet by William Knox, assisted by George Grenville, entitled, "The Present State of the Nation."] pp. 97. 1769. 4°. *See* ENGLAND. [*Appendix.—Trade and Commerce.*] **1103. k. 81.**

—— The second edition. pp. 155. 1769. 8°. *See* ENGLAND. [*Appendix.—Trade and Commerce.*] **1093. e. 79.**

—— [Another copy.] **08218. b. 15. (2.)**

—— [Another copy.] **522. g. 14.**

—— [Another copy.] **1102. h. 10. (6.)**

—— [Another copy.] **102. e. 51.**

—— The fourth edition. pp. 155. 1769. 8°. *See* ENGLAND. [*Appendix.—Trade and Commerce.*] **T. 1117. (2.)**

—— [Another copy.] Observations on a late State of the Nation. The fourth edition. [By E. Burke.] MS. NOTES [by Jeremy Bentham]. 1769. 8°. *See* ENGLAND. [*Appendix.—Trade and Commerce.*] **08138. dd. 50. (1.)**

—— [Another copy.] **G. 16249. (2.)**

—— [Another edition.] pp. 114. 1769. 8°. *See* ENGLAND. [*Appendix.—Trade and Commerce.*] **T. 698. (2.)**

—— The fifth edition. pp. 155. 1782. 8°. *See* ENGLAND. [*Appendix.—Trade and Commerce.*] **G. 13552. (2.)**

—— Burke's Observations on a Late Publication entitled the Present State of the Nation. By [i.e. translated by] L. N. Wild. (The Chancellor's Prize for Latin Prose Composition, 1935.) *Lat. & Eng.* pp. 15. *Basil Blackwell: Oxford*, 1935. 8°. **20003. e. 58.**

Appendix.

—— *See* ENGLAND. [*Appendix.—Trade and Commerce.*] An Appendix to The Present State of the Nation. Containing a reply to the Observations [by Edmund Burke] on that pamphlet. [By William Knox.] 1769. 8°. **T. 698. (3.)**

—— —— 1769. 8°. **8145. cc. 22.**

OBSERVATIONS ON THE CONDUCT OF THE MINORITY.

—— A Letter . . . to his Grace the Duke of Portland, on the Conduct of the Minority in Parliament. Containing fifty-four articles of impeachment against the Rt. Hon. C. J. Fox. From the original copy, in the possession of the noble Duke. pp. 94. *Printed for the Editor: London*, 1797. 8°. **E. 2171. (4.)**

—— [Another copy.] **G. 13556. (1.)**

—— [Another copy.] **8135. c. 13.**
With a MS. copy of an answer by Sir Robert Adair, published in the "Morning Herald," 15 Feb. 1797.

—— Two Letters on the Conduct of our Domestick Parties with regard to French Politicks; including "Observations on the Conduct of the Minority in the Session of M.DCC.XCIII." [The authorised edition of the "Observations" and the "Letter to ******* *******, Esquire. Occasioned by the account given in a newspaper of the speech made in the House of Lords, by **** of ******* in the debate concerning Lord Fitzwilliam, 1795."] pp. lxxii. 127. *F. & C. Rivington: London*, 1797. 8°. **E. 2087. (2.)**

—— [Another copy.] **G. 13555. (1.)**

PHILOSOPHICAL ENQUIRY INTO THE ORIGIN OF OUR IDEAS OF THE SUBLIME AND BEAUTIFUL.

—— A Philosophical Enquiry into the Origin of our Ideas of the Sublime and Beautiful. [By E. Burke.] pp. viii. 184. 1757. 8°. *See* ENQUIRY. **11805. ccc. 17.**

—— The second edition. With an introductory discourse concerning taste, and several other additions. pp. ix. 342. 1759. 8°. *See* ENQUIRY. **C.108.d.23.**

—— The third edition, *etc.* pp. ix. 342. 1761. 8°. *See* ENQUIRY. **1421. g. 5.**

—— A Philosophical Enquiry into the Origin of our Ideas of the Sublime and Beautiful. The fourth edition . . . To which is added, A Vindication of Natural Society, after the manner of a late noble writer, by the same author [i.e. E. Burke]. 2 pt. 1766. 12°. *See* ENQUIRY. **8408. de. 34.**

—— The seventh edition, *etc.* pp. ix. 342. 1773. 8°. *See* ENQUIRY. **1091. b. 19.**

—— [Another copy.] **G. 19457.**

—— The eighth edition, *etc.* pp. ix. 342. 1776. 8°. *See* ENQUIRY. **31. a. 4.**

—— The ninth edition, *etc.* pp. ix. 342. 1782. 8°. *See* ENQUIRY. **1476. bb. 17.**

—— A new edition. pp. ix. 342. 1787. 8°. *See* ENQUIRY. **818. g. 1.**

—— A new edition. pp. x. 291. 1792. 8°. *See* ENQUIRY. **8403. h. 14.**

—— The Sublime and Beautiful, *etc.* pp. vi. 194. *Oxford*, 1796. 8°. **011824. g. 12.**

—— A Philosophical Inquiry into the Origin of our Ideas of the Sublime and Beautiful . . . A new edition. [With a portrait.] pp. xix. 273. *F. & C. Rivington: London*, 1801. 8°. **11805. e. 40.**
Imperfect; wanting pp. xv, xvi.

—— A Philosophical Inquiry into the Origin of our Ideas of the Sublime and Beautiful . . . Tegg's miniature edition. pp. viii. 172. *T. Tegg: London*, 1810. 12°. **011852. ff. 19.**

—— [Another edition.] pp. 97. *Printed for the Proprietors: London*, 1818. 8°. [*First Class of the Course of Education pursued at the Universities of Cambridge and Oxford.* vol. 3.] **8364. f. 14.**

—— [Another edition.] pp. xvi. 262. *Thomas M'Lean: London*, 1823. 8°. **11805. aaa. 16.**

—— [Another edition.] To which is added a Treatise on the Sublime, by Dionysius Longinus. pp. xiv. 200. *N. Hailes, etc.: London*, 1824. 8°. **11850. a. 4.**

BURKE (*Right Hon.* EDMUND) [SINGLE WORKS.—PHILOSOPHICAL ENQUIRY INTO THE ORIGIN OF OUR IDEAS OF THE SUBLIME AND BEAUTIFUL.]

—— A Philosophical Inquiry, *etc.* pp. viii. 158. *Printed by C. & C. Whittingham: Chiswick; sold by Thomas Tegg: London,* 1825. 8°. **8475. a. 1.**
Whittingham's Cabinet Library. no. 54. *With an additional titlepage, engraved, reading "Burke on the Sublime and Beautiful."*

—— [Another copy.] A Philosophical Inquiry into the Origin of our Ideas of the Sublime and Beautiful, *etc.* *Chiswick,* 1825. 8°. Hirsch **5385.**

—— [A reissue.] A Philosophical Inquiry into the Origin of our Ideas of the Sublime and Beautiful, *etc.* *London,* 1825. 12°. **11871. a. 5.**

—— Burke's Philosophical Inquiry into the Origin of our Ideas of the Sublime and Beautiful, *etc.* pp. iv. 172. *J. F. Dove: London,* 1827. 12°. **11867. a 21.**

—— An Essay on the Sublime and Beautiful. (Edited by Henry Morley.) pp. 192. *London,* 1887. 8°. [*Cassell's National Library.* vol. 88.] **12208.bb.15/88.**

—— A Philosophical Inquiry into the Origin of our Ideas of the Sublime and Beautiful . . . With a biographical introduction [signed: E. B., i.e. Edward Bell]. pp. xxiii. 133. *G. Bell & Sons: London,* 1889. 8°. [*Bohn's Select Library.*] **2502. k. 4.**

—— An Essay on the Sublime and Beautiful . . . With an introduction by Henry Morley. pp. 192. *London,* 1905. 8°. [*Cassell's National Library.* New ser. vol. 67.] **012209.ff.1/67.**

—— Recherches philosophiques sur l'origine des idées que nous avons du beau & du sublime, précédées d'une dissertation sur le goût. Traduites . . . par l'abbé D.. F...... [i.e. Des François.] 2 tom. *Londres; Hocheveau: Paris,* 1765. 8°. **528. e. 35.**

—— Recherche philosophique sur l'origine de nos idées du sublime et du beau . . . Traduit . . . sur la septième édition, avec un précis de la vie de l'auteur, par E. Lagentie de Lavaïsse. pp. xxxix. 22–323. *Paris,* 1803. 8°. **1086. e. 34.**

—— Burkes philosophische Untersuchungen über den Ursprung unsrer Begriffe vom Erhabnen und Schönen. Nach der fünften englischen Ausgabe. [Translated by Christian Garve.] pp. 302. *Riga,* 1773. 8°. **8464. b. 3.**

—— Indagacion Filosófica sobre el Orígen de nuestras Ideas acerca de lo Sublime e lo Bello . . . Traducida . . . por Don Juan de la Dehesa. pp. 242. *Alcalá,* 1807. 4°. **8462. c. 16.**

Appendix.

—— *See* GENTLEMAN. A Letter from a Gentleman [i.e. Fr. Plumer] to his Nephew at Oxford. [Criticising Burke's "Philosophical Enquiry into the Origin of our Ideas of the Sublime and Beautiful."] 1772. 8°. **12355. f. 14. (4.)**

—— *See* PRICE (*Sir* Uvedale) *Bart.* A Dialogue on . . . the Picturesque and the Beautiful . . . Prefaced by an introductory essay on beauty, with remarks on the ideas of . . . Mr. Burke upon that subject. 1801. 8°. **11825. g. 4.**

BURKE (*Right Hon.* EDMUND) [SINGLE WORKS.—PHILOSOPHICAL ENQUIRY INTO THE ORIGIN OF OUR IDEAS OF THE SUBLIME AND BEAUTIFUL.]

—— *See* WALKER (Alexander) *Physiologist.* Beauty; illustrated chiefly by an analysis and classification of beauty in woman. Preceded by a critical view of the general hypotheses respecting beauty, by Hume . . . Burke, *etc.* 1836. 8°. **783. n. 22.**

—— —— 1852. 8°. **C. 31. k. 6.**

—— —— 1892. 8°. **7858. gg. 10.**

REFLECTIONS ON THE REVOLUTION IN FRANCE.

—— Reflections on the Revolution in France and on the proceedings in certain societies in London relative to that event. In a letter intended to have been sent to a gentleman in Paris. pp. iv. 356. *J. Dodsley: London,* 1790. 8°. **1059. i. 24.**

—— [Another copy.] **C.115.e.3.(1.)**

—— The second edition. pp. iv. 356. *J. Dodsley: London,* 1790. 8°. **08052.de.6.**

—— [Another copy.] **286.f.12.**

—— Reflections on the Revolution in France . . . The third edition. pp. iv. 364. *J. Dodsley: London,* 1790. 8°. **08052. c. 69.**

—— The fourth edition. pp. iv. 364. *J. Dodsley: London,* 1790. 8°. **8050. cc. 23.**

—— Reflections on the Revolution in France . . . The fifth edition. pp. iv. 364. *J. Dodsley: London,* 1790. 8°. **08052. c. 73.**

—— [Another edition.] pp. iv. 356. *W. Watson, etc.: Dublin,* 1790. 8°. **8006. c. 40. (1.)**

—— Reflections on the Revolution in France, and on the proceedings in certain societies in London, relative to that event. In a letter intended to have been sent to a gentleman in Paris . . . The seventh edition. pp. iv. 364. *J. Dodsley: London,* 1790. 8°. **08052. c. 87.**

—— The eighth edition. pp. iv. 356. *William Porter: Dublin,* 1791. 8°. **1389. e. 11.**

—— Reflections on the Revolution in France . . . The ninth edition. pp. iv. 364. *J. Dodsley: London,* 1791. 8°. **8052. k. 20.**

—— The eleventh edition. pp. iv. 364. *J. Dodsley: London,* 1791. 8°. **G. 13554. (1.)**

—— Reflections on the Revolution in France . . . The twelfth edition. pp. iv. 364. *J. Dodsley: London,* 1793. 8°. **8051. de. 50. (1.)**

—— A new edition. [With alterations by the editor, who signs the "advertisement": S. J.] pp. iv. 158. *J. Parsons: London,* 1793. 8°. **8135. a. 25.**

—— [Another copy.] **8005. df. 31. (2.)**

—— A new edition. pp. 246. *John Bell: London,* 1814. 12°. **8052. aaa. 23.**

—— [Another edition.] 2 vol. *John Sharpe: London,* 1820. 12°. [*British Prose Writers.* vol. 21.] **12271. de. 1.**
With an additional titlepage to each volume, engraved.

—— [Another edition.] pp. 286. *Charles Daly: London,* [1830?] 16°. **8135. a. 1.**
With an additional titlepage, engraved.

—— New edition, with a short biographical notice. pp. 280. *Rivingtons: London,* 1868. 8°. **8135. aa. 9.**

—— [Another edition.] pp. 239. *Seeley, Jackson & Halliday: London,* 1872 [1871]. 16°. **8050. a. 9.**

—— [Another edition.] Edited, with introduction and notes, by F. G. Selby. pp. lxxxi. 484. *Macmillan & Co.: London & New York,* 1890. 8°. **8050. bb. 19.**

—— [Another edition.] With an introduction by George Sampson. pp. xxvi. 314. *London,* [1900.] 8°. [*Scott Library.* vol. 110.] **012208.ee.2/41.**

—— Reflections on the French Revolution. [With "The Substance of Mr. Burke's Speech, in the debate on the Army Estimates . . . the 9th day of February, 1790," and with an introduction by Sir Sidney Lee.] pp. xiv. 200. *London,* 1905. 8°. [*Methuen's Standard Library.*] **012203. f. 33/5.**

With a half-title reading "Select Works of Edmund Burke. Volume 1."

—— [Another edition.] Edited with introduction and notes by A. J. Grieve. pp. xii. 275. *London,* 1910. 8°. [*Dent's Temple Series of English Texts.*] **12274.df.10/19.**

—— [Another edition.] Edited by H. P. Adams. pp. xxxvi. 283. *W. B. Clive: London,* [1910.] 8°. [*Tutorial Series.*] **12205. c. 97.**

—— [Another edition.] Edited by W. Alison Phillips . . . and Catherine Beatrice Phillips. pp. liv. 311. *University Press: Cambridge,* 1912. 8°. [*Pitt Press Series.*] **2322. bb. 14.**

—— Burke's Reflections on the Revolution in France. With introduction, notes, & appendices by J. H. Boardman . . . Third edition. pp. xvi. 288. *Normal Press: London,* [1912.] 8°. [*Normal Tutorial Series.*] **012201. dd. 1/39.**

—— Reflections on the French Revolution . . . Second edition. pp. xiv. 200. *Methuen & Co.: London,* 1923. 8°. **9226. b. 34.**

Previous edition 1905.

—— Reflections on the Revolution in France. Edited by H. P. Adams . . . Second edition. pp. xxxvi. 283. *W. B. Clive: London,* [1927.] 8°. **08052. a. 66.**
Previous edition, published in the "Tutorial Series," 1910.

—— Reflections on the French Revolution. Edited by W. Alison Phillips . . . and Catherine Beatrice Phillips. pp. liv. 311. *University Press: Cambridge,* 1929. 8°. [*Pitt Press Series.*] **2322. de. 169.**
A reissue of the edition of 1912.

—— Réflexions sur la Révolution de France, et sur les procédés de certaines sociétés à Londres relatifs à cet événement . . . Traduit . . . sur la troisième édition [by — Dupont] . . . Seconde édition, revue corrigée & augmentée, *etc.* (Lettre de M. Burke à son traducteur.) pp. viii. 536. 8. 8. *Paris; Londres,* [1790.] 8°. **283. h. 16.**

—— Troisième édition, *etc.* pp. viii. 8. 536. 8. *Paris; Londres,* [1790.] 8°. **522. g. 31.**

—— Réflexions sur la Révolution française. Traduites . . . par Jacques d'Anglejan et précédées d'une introduction du même. Nouvelle édition conforme à l'original. pp. xxviii. 418. *Paris,* 1912. 8°. **09231. ee. 20.**

BURKE (*Right Hon.* EDMUND) [SINGLE WORKS.—REFLECTIONS ON THE REVOLUTION IN FRANCE.]

—— Betrachtungen über die französische Revolution. Nach dem Englischen . . . neu-bearbeitet, mit einer Einleitung, Anmerkungen, politischen Abhandlungen, und einem critischen Verzeichniss der in England über diese Revolution erschienen Schriften, von Friedrich Gentz. 2 Tl. *Berlin,* 1793. 8°. **9210. c. 34.**

—— [Another copy.] **1389. e. 8.**

—— Reflexiones sobre la Revolucion de Francia . . . Nueva edicion, corregida y revisada con esmero, por J. A. A * * *, Caballero de la Legion de Honor. Traducida al castellano. pp. 256. *México,* 1826. 8°. **8051. dd. 30.**

—— [Selections, chiefly from the "Reflections on the Revolution in France."] *See* BRITISH WRITERS. A Comparative Display of the Different Opinions of . . . British Writers on the subject of the French Revolution. 1793. 8°. **8051. g. 13.**

—— [Another edition.] *See* BRITISH WRITERS. A Comparative Display of the Different Opinions of . . . British Writers on the subject of the French Revolution, *etc.* 1811. 8°. **8008. f. 14.**

—— Extract from Reflections on the French Revolution. *See* LONDON.—III. *Society for the Distribution of Tracts, etc.* The Churchman armed, *etc.* vol. 1. 1814. 8°. **495. f. 14.**

—— Liberation tested by Philosophy and Experience. In "Reflections on the French Revolution," *etc.* [The dedication signed: Christian English.] pp. 16. *Rivingtons: London,* [1861.] 8°. **08012.h.17.**

—— Burke's Reflections on the French Revolution. [An abridgment.] With introduction and notes by C. E. Vaughan. pp. xvi. 144. *Percival & Co.: London,* 1892. 8°. [*English Classics for Schools.*] **12201. df. 1/1.**

—— [A reissue.] Selections from Burke's Reflections on the French Revolution, *etc.* *London,* 1893. 8°. [*English Classics for Schools.*] **12201. df. 1/2.**

—— Réflexions sur la révolution de France, et sur les procédés de certaines sociétés, relatifs à cette révolution. Extrait du livre de M. Burke, troisième édition, imprimée à Londres. pp. 36. *Londres; Paris,* 1790. 8°. **R. 75. (8.)**

Appendix.

—— *See* BOOTHBY (*Sir* Brooke) *Bart.* A Letter to the Right Honourable Edmund Burke. [Criticising his "Reflections on the Revolution in France."] 1791. 8°. **E. 2160. (8.)**

—— —— 1791. 8°. **T. 1120. (10.)**

—— *See* BOUSFIELD (Benjamin) Observations on the Right Hon. Edmund Burke's Pamphlet on the subject of the French Revolution. 1791. 8°. **8135. c. 6.**

—— *See* CHRISTIE (Thomas) *of Montrose.* Letters on the Revolution of France . . . occasioned by the publications of the Right Hon. E. Burke . . . and A. de Calonne, *etc.* 1791. 8°. **1059. h. 1.**

—— *See* COOPER (Samuel) *D.D.* The First Principles of Civil and Ecclesiastical Government, delineated in letters to Dr. Priestley, occasioned by his to Mr. Burke. 1791. 8°. **958. k. 1.**

BURKE (*Right Hon.* EDMUND) [SINGLE WORKS.—REFLECTIONS ON THE REVOLUTION IN FRANCE.—*Appendix.*]

—— *See* DUPONT (Gaetan P. M.) An answer to the Reflections of . . . Edmund Burke, *etc.* 1791. 8º. **08052. bb. 48.**

—— *See* DUPONT (Gaetan P. M.) Answer to the Reflections of . . . Edmund Burke, *etc.* 1791. 8º. **8145. de. 43.**

—— *See* FRANCE.—*Assemblée Nationale.—Appendix.* [1789–1792.] A Letter to a Member of the National Assembly, containing . . . strictures on the political doctrines of Mr. Burke, *etc.* [With special reference to "Reflections on the Revolution in France."] 1791. 8º. **8135. c. 43.**

—— *See* GEORGE IV., *King of Great Britain and Ireland.* [*Appendix.*] Lessons to a Young Prince . . . With the addition of a lesson on the mode of studying and profiting by Reflections on the French Revolution, by the Right Honourable E. Burke. [By David Williams.] 1790. 8º. **8135. bb. 48.**

—— —— 1791. 8º. **8135. cc. 58. (1.)**

—— —— 1791. 8º. **8135. c. 33.**

—— —— 1791. 8º. **1102. i. 14.**

—— *See* GOOLD (Thomas) A Vindication of the Right Hon. Edmund Burke's Reflections on the Revolution in France, *etc.* 1791. 8º. **08052. c. 85.**

—— *See* HUBERT, *Old, pseud.* An Address to the Hon. Edmund Burke. From the Swinish Multitude. [With reference to a passage in the "Reflections on the Revolution in France."] 1793. 8º. **8135. b. 3. (6.)**

—— *See* LOFFT (Capel) *the Elder.* Remarks on the Letter of the Rt. Hon. Edmund Burke concerning the Revolution in France, *etc.* 1790. 8º. **T. 1102. (2.)**

—— *See* LOFFT (Capel) *the Elder.* Remarks on the Letter of the Rt. Hon. Edmund Burke concerning the Revolution in France . . . Second edition, with . . . remarks on Mr. Burke's Letter to a Member of the National Assembly. 1791. 8º. **8050. e. 32.**

—— *See* MACKINTOSH (*Right Hon. Sir* James) Vindiciae Gallicae. Defence of the French Revolution . . . against the accusations of the Right Hon. Edmund Burke, *etc.* 1791. 8º. **8006. c. 40. (2.)**

—— —— 1791. 8º. **8050. dd. 28.**

—— —— 1791. 8º. **1059. i. 25.**

—— —— 1837. 12º. **8050. b. 37.**

—— *See* MACKINTOSH (*Right Hon. Sir* James) Apologie de la Révolution française . . . en réponse aux attaques d'Edmund Burke, *etc.* 1792. 8º. **R. 76. (8.)**

—— [For editions of Thomas Paine's "Rights of Man: being an answer to Mr. Burke's attack on the French Revolution":] *See* PAINE (Thomas) *Political Writer.* [*Rights of Man.*]

—— *See* PAINE (Thomas) *Political Writer.* [*Rights of Man.—Appendix.*] Paine and Burke contrasted . . . With some observations on the Rights of Man, by T. Paine, and Burke, on the French Revolution, *etc.* [1792.] 8º. **C.115.e.3.(3.)**

—— *See* PRIESTLEY (Joseph) *LL.D.* Letters to the Right Honourable Edmund Burke, occasioned by his Reflections on the Revolution in France, etc. 1791. 8º. **T. 88. (2.)**

—— —— 1791. 8º. **8050. dd. 35.**

—— —— 1791. 8º. **8050. cc. 38.**

—— —— 1791. 8º. **8050. d. 52.**

—— *See* PRIESTLEY (Joseph) *LL.D.* Lettres au très-honorable Edmund Burke, au sujet de ses Réflexions sur la révolution de France, *etc.* 1791. 8º. **R. 75. (9.)**

—— *See* PRIESTLEY (Joseph) *LL.D.* An Answer to Dr. Priestley's Letters to the Right Honourable Edmund Burke. In a letter to the author, *etc.* 1791. 8º. **8132. df. 10. (6.)**

—— *See* ROUS (George) Thoughts on Government: occasioned by Mr. Burke's Reflections, *etc.* 1791. 8º. **8135. ccc. 2. (2.)**

—— *See* SCHEPELERN (V. E.) Burke's "Reflections" og den franske revolutions statsopfattelse. 1950. 8º. [*Studier fra sprog- og oldtidsforskning.* no. 216.] **Ac. 9877/2.**

—— *See* SCOTT, afterwards SCOTT WARING (John) A Letter from Major Scott to the Right Honourable Edmund Burke. [Criticising his "Reflections on the Revolution in France."] 1791. 8º. **E. 2160. (7.)**

—— *See* SECRETAN (P.) Réflexions sur les gouvernemens, pour servir de suite à l'ouvrage de Mr. Burke sur la révolution en France, *etc.* 1792. 8º. **E. 2068. (3.)**

—— *See* SHARPE (J.) *of Sheffield.* A Rhapsody to E * * * * * B * * * * Esq. . . . Ornamented with a humorous print of "The Swinish Multitude." [Satirical verses, with special reference to a passage in Burke's "Reflections on the Revolution in France."] 1792. 8º. [*DAMM (Benjamin) An Address to the Public.*] **8007. bbb. 10.**

—— *See* STONE (Francis) *Rector of Cold Norton.* An Examination of the Right Hon. Edmund Burke's Reflections on the Revolution in France, *etc.* 1792. 8º. **8051. ccc. 30.**

—— *See* TATHAM (Edward) Letters to the Right Honourable Edmund Burke. [With special reference to his "Reflections on the Revolution in France."] 1791. 8º. **1103. g. 58. (5.)**

—— *See* TOWERS (Joseph) Thoughts on the Commencement of a New Parliament. With an appendix, containing remarks on the letter of the Right Hon. Edmund Burke, on the Revolution in France. 1790. 8º. **8135. bb. 75.**

—— —— 1791. 8º. **8145. dd. 71.**

—— *See* WOOLSEY (Robert) Reflections upon Reflections . . . In two letters to the Right Hon. Edmund Burke in answer to his pamphlet [i.e. "Reflections on the Revolution in France"]. 1790. 8º. **8135. ccc. 2. (1.)**

—— An Address, in verse, to the Author of the Poetical and Philosophical Essay on the French Revolution [addressed to the Right Hon. Edmund Burke by John Courtenay]. pp. 12. *J. Owen: London,* 1793. 4º. **11630. d. 17. (17.)**

—— Burke's Address to the "Swinish Multitude." [Satirical verses. By Thomas Spence.] *Printed for T. Spence: London,* [1793.] 8º. **1389. c. 12. (2.)**

—— [Another edition.] [*London,* 1830?] *s. sh.* fol. **806. k. 16. (119.)**

—— Correspondance entre un Genevois refugié à Paris, & un officier aux Gardes, domicilié dans cette ville, dans laquelle on réfute l'ouvrage de M. Burk sur la révolution de France. pp. 8. [*Geneva,* 1791.] 8º. **R. 76. (1.)**

BURKE (*Right Hon.* EDMUND) [SINGLE WORKS.—REFLECTIONS ON THE REVOLUTION IN FRANCE.—*Appendix.*]

—— Courte réponse aux Réflexions de M. Burke sur la Révolution de France . . . Par un Anglois, témoin de la Révolution. pp. 32. *Paris*, 1791. 8°. **R. 76. (4.)**

—— A Letter to the Right Hon. Edmund Burke, Esq., from a Dissenting Country Attorney; in defence of his civil profession and religious dissent. [In answer to "Reflections on the Revolution in France."] pp. 150. *John Thompson: Birmingham*, 1791. 8°. **8138. df. 10. (3.)**

—— A Letter to the Right Hon. Edmund Burke, in reply to his "Reflections on the Revolution in France, &c." By a Member of the Revolution Society [i.e. John Scott, afterwards Scott Waring]. pp. iv. 55. *John Stockdale: London*, 1790. 8°. **T. 1102. (4.)**

—— A Letter to the Right Hon. Edmund Burke, in reply to his "Reflections on the Revolution in France, &c." By a Member of the Revolution Society [i.e. John Scott, afterwards Scott Waring]. pp. iv. 55. *J. Sheppard, etc.: Dublin*, 1791. 8°. **8146. ee. 27.**

—— Observations on the Reflections of the Right Hon. Edmund Burke, on the Revolution in France, in a letter to the Right Hon. the Earl of Stanhope. [By Catherine Macaulay, afterwards Graham.] pp. 95. *C. Dilly: London*, 1790. 8°. **T. 88. (3.)**

—— A Poetical and Philosophical Essay on the French Revolution. [By John Courtenay.] Addressed to the Right Hon. Edmund Burke [in reply to his "Reflections on the Revolution in France"]. pp. vi. 39. *J. Ridgway: London*, 1793. 4°. **816. k. 4. (6.)**

—— Second edition. pp. vi. 39. *J. Ridgway: London*, 1793. 4°. **11630. d. 17. (16.)**

—— Strictures on the Letter of the Right Hon. Mr. Burke on the Revolution in France. pp. 173. *H. Gardiner: London*, 1791. 8°. **8132. ee. 10. (1.)**

—— Temperate Comments upon Intemperate Reflections: or, a Review of Mr. Burke's letter [i.e. his "Reflections on the Revolution in France]. pp. 67. *J. Walter: London*, 1791. 8°. **T. 1102. (5.)**

—— The second edition. pp. 70. *J. Walter: London*, 1791. 8°. **8133. bb. 11. (7.)**

—— Thoughts on Government, occasioned by Mr. Burke's Reflections, &c. In a letter to a friend. [By George Rous.] pp. iv. 48. *J. Debrett: London*, 1790. 8°. **E. 2160. (3.)**

—— A Vindication of the Right Honorable Edmund Burke's Reflections on the Revolution in France, in answer to all his opponents. pp. 143. *J. Debrett: London*, 1791. 8°. **8050. d. 9.**

—— [Another copy.] **8135. cc. 55. (4.)**

—— A Vindication of the Rights of Men, in a letter to the Right Honorable Edmund Burke occasioned by his Reflections on the Revolution in France. [By Mary Wollstonecraft, afterwards Godwin.] pp. iv. 150. *J. Johnson: London*, 1790. 8°. **T. 1102. (3.)**

REPORTS FROM THE SELECT COMMITTEE ON THE ADMINISTRATION OF JUSTICE IN THE PROVINCES OF BENGAL, BAHAR AND ORISSA.

—— [For editions of the reports of this committee, issued in 1782, 83, for the compilation of which Burke was largely responsible:] *See* ENGLAND.—*Parliament.—House of Commons.* [*Proceedings.*—II.]

BURKE (*Right Hon.* EDMUND) [SINGLE WORKS.]

Appendix.

—— *See* DETECTOR. A Letter to the Rt. Hon. Edmund Burke, on the subject of his late charges against the Governor-General of Bengal. [With special reference to certain of the reports from the Select Committee.] 1783. 8°. **8022. b. 28.**

—— *See* SCOTT, afterwards SCOTT WARING (John) *Major.* Two Letters to the Rt. Hon. Edmund Burke, in reply to the Insinuations and palpable Misrepresentations, in . . . the Ninth Report from the Select Committee, *etc.* 1783. 8°. **08139. d. 107. (1.)**

—— *See* SCOTT, afterwards SCOTT WARING (John) Two Letters to the Rt. Hon. Edmund Burke, in reply to . . . a pamphlet, entitled The Ninth Report from the Select Committee, *etc.* 1783. 8°. **T. 128. (3, 4.)**

—— A Letter to Edmund Burke, Esq; on the latter part of the late report of the Select Committee on the State of Justice in Bengal [i.e. the first report, here attributed to Burke]. With some curious particulars . . . concerning the forgery committed by Maha Rajah Nundcomar Bahadar . . . Together with some remarks on the conduct of the majority of the civil government at that time in Fort William, Bengal, *etc.* [By Joseph Price.] pp. 100. 20. 70. *Printed for the Author: London*, 1782. 8°. **8023. ee. 16. (1.)**

—— [Another edition.] pp. 227. *London*, 1783. 8°. **959. e. 4. (1.)**

—— [Another copy.] **112. d. 44. (1.)**

—— A Second Letter to the Right Honourable Edmund Burke, Esq. on the subject of the Evidence referred to in the Second Report of the Select Committee . . . With a compleat refutation of every paragraph of the letter of Mr. Philip Francis, *etc.* [By Joseph Price.] pp. 65. *London*, 1783. 8°. **959. e. 4. (2.)**

—— [Another copy.] **112. d. 44. (2.)**

—— A Third Letter to the Right Honourable Edmund Burke, Esq., on the subject of the evidence contained in the Reports of the Select Committee of the House of Commons. With an introductory preface. [By Joseph Price.] pp. 39. 70. *Printed for the Author: London*, 1782. 8°. **E. 2102. (1.)**

—— [Another edition.] pp. 52. 95. *London*, 1783. 8°. **959. e. 4. (3.)**

—— [Another copy.] **112. d. 44. (3.)**

—— A Letter to the Rt. Hon. Edmund Burke, in reply to the insinuations in the Ninth Report of the Select Committee, which affect the character of Mr. Hastings. By J. S. [i.e. John Scott, afterwards Scott-Waring.] 1783. 8°. *See* S., J. **E. 2144. (5.)**

THIRD LETTER ON THE PROPOSALS FOR PEACE WITH THE REGICIDE DIRECTORY.

—— *See* infra: THOUGHTS ON THE PROSPECT OF A REGICIDE PEACE.

THOUGHTS AND DETAILS ON SCARCITY.

—— Thoughts and Details on Scarcity, originally presented to the Right Hon. William Pitt, in the month of November, 1795. pp. xvi. 48. *F. & C. Rivington: London*, 1800. 8°. **713. f. 14. (2.)**

—— [Another issue.] Thoughts and Details on Scarcity, *etc.* *London*, 1800. 8°. **08218. bb. 29. (6.)**

THOUGHTS ON THE CAUSE OF THE PRESENT DISCONTENTS.

—— Thoughts on the Cause of the Present Discontents. [By E. Burke.] pp. 61. 1770. 4°. *See* THOUGHTS. **T. 921. (2.)**

—— [Another copy.] **102. f. 3.**

—— The second edition. pp. 118. 1770. 8°. *See* THOUGHTS. **8138. b. 85.**

—— The third edition. pp. 118. 1770. 8°. *See* THOUGHTS. **T. 1117. (9.)**

—— [Another copy.] Thoughts on the Cause of the Present Discontents. The third edition. [By E. Burke.] MS. NOTES [by Jeremy Bentham]. 1770. 8°. *See* THOUGHTS. **08138.** dd. **50.** (5.)

—— The fourth edition. pp. 118. 1770. 8°. *See* THOUGHTS. **8132. d. 62.**

—— The fifth edition. pp. 118. 1775. 8°. *See* THOUGHTS. **T. 1118. (4.)**

—— The sixth edition. pp. 118. 1784. 8°. *See* THOUGHTS. **G. 13552. (1.)**

—— Burke's Thoughts on the Cause of the Present Discontents. Edited, with introduction and notes, by F. G. Selby. pp. xix. 172. *Macmillan & Co.: London,* 1902. 8°. **8138. aaa. 29.**

—— [Another edition.] With introduction, notes, and appendices. By J. H. Boardman. pp. 184. *Normal Correspondence College Press: London,* [1904.] 8°. [*Normal Tutorial Series.*] **12201. d. 31/116.**

—— [Another edition.] Edited by W. Murison. pp. xxxviii. 163. *University Press: Cambridge,* 1913. 8°. [*Pitt Press Series.*] **2322. bb. 16.**

—— Thoughts on the Cause of the Present Discontents. Edited by W. Murison. pp. xxxviii. 163. *University Press: Cambridge,* 1930. 8°. [*Pitt Press Series.*] **2322.** de. **170.**

A reissue of the edition of 1913.

—— Upon Party. By the Right Hon. Edmund Burke and Lord John Russell. [Passages extracted from Burke's "Thoughts on the Cause of the Present Discontents," and Earl Russell's "Life of Lord William Russell."] Edited by Charles Purton Cooper . . . Second edition. pp. x. 58. *William Pickering: London,* 1850. 8°. **8138.** df. **18.**

—— [Another copy.] **8138.** bb. **2.** (2.)

—— [Another copy.] **8009.** c. **30.** (1.)

Appendix.

—— *See* MACAULAY, afterwards GRAHAM (Catharine) Observations on a Pamphlet [by E. Burke], entitled, Thoughts on the Cause of the Present Discontents. 1770. 4°. **8139.** ff. **101.**

THOUGHTS ON THE PROSPECT OF A REGICIDE PEACE.

—— Thoughts on the Prospect of a Regicide Peace, in a series of letters. pp. iv. 131. *J. Owen: London,* 1796. 8°. **8135.** c. **86.**

The right of publication of this work was withdrawn from Owen by the author before its issue. It was subsequently published by F. and C. Rivington under the title "Two Letters addressed to a Member of the present Parliament," etc., having been to some extent rewritten.

—— [Another copy.] **T. 1122. (4.)**

—— [Another copy.] **E. 2066. (1.)**

—— Two Letters addressed to a Member of the Present Parliament, on the Proposals for Peace with the Regicide Directory of France. pp. 188. *F. & C. Rivington: London,* 1796. 8°. **E. 2170. (2.)**

—— [Another edition.] pp. 188. *F. & C. Rivington: London,* 1796. 8°. **8132.** df. **10.** (5.)

—— (Sixth edition.) pp. 188. *F. & C. Rivington: London,* 1796. 8°. **8010.** c. **10.**

—— (Seventh edition.) pp. 188. *F. & C. Rivington: London,* 1796. 8°. **8135.** c. **12.**

—— Two Letters addressed to a Member of the Present Parliament, on the proposals for peace, *etc.* (Ninth edition.) pp. 188. *F. & C. Rivington: London,* 1796. 8°. **08139.** ccc. **49.**

—— (Tenth edition.) pp. 193. *F. & C. Rivington: London,* 1796. 8°. **8050.** e. **16.**

—— (Eleventh edition.) pp. 193. *F. & C. Rivington: London,* 1796. 8°. **E. 2066. (2.)**

—— [Another copy.] **G. 13556. (2.)**

—— Burke's Letters on a Regicide Peace. Letters I. and II. With introduction and notes by H. G. Keene. pp. xxxviii. 176. *London,* 1893. 8°. [*Bell's English Classics.*] **012272.** aaaa. **1/7.**

—— Lettres d'Edmond Burke à un membre de la Chambre de Communes du Parlement d'Angleterre, sur les négociations de paix ouvertes avec le Directoire. [A translation of the first two letters, by J. G. Peltier.] pp. vi. 212. *Paris,* [1796.] 8°. **F. 559. (1.)**

—— On the Proposals for Peace with the Regicide Directory of France. Letter I. Edited by F. J. C. Hearnshaw. pp. xxxvi. 95. *W. B. Clive: London,* [1906.] 8°. [*University Tutorial Series.*] **12205. e. 76.**

—— A Third Letter to a Member of the present Parliament, on the Proposals for Peace with the Regicide Directory of France. pp. vi. 165. *F. & C. Rivington: London,* 1797. 8°. **E. 2087. (1.)**

—— (Second edition.) pp. vi. 165. *F. & C. Rivington London,* 1797. 8°. **8132.** df. **10.** (11.

—— [Another edition.] pp. xii. 165. *F. & C. Rivington London,* 1797. 8°. **G. 13556.** (3.

Appendix.

—— *See* FRANCE. [*Appendix.—History and Politics.—Miscellaneous.*] Thoughts on a Peace with France; with observations on Mr. Burke's Two Letters on Proposals fo Peace with the Regicide Directory. 1796. 8°. **8135.** c. **41**

—— *See* SIMPKIN, *the Second, pseud.* Letters from Simkin the Second to his brother Simon, in Wales, *etc.* [Verse satirising Burke's "Thoughts on the Prospect of a Regicid Peace."] 1796. 8°. **992. h. 23.** (3.

BURKE (*Right Hon.* Edmund) [Single Works.—Thoughts on the Prospect of a Regicide Peace.]

—— *See* Thelwall (John) *Lecturer.* The Rights of Nature . . . A series of letters . . . occasioned by the recent effusions of the Right Honourable Edmund Burke (Letters on the Prospect of a Regicide Peace). 1796. 8°. **12270**. pp. **5**. **(1.)**

—— *See* Tyro, *pseud.* The Retort Politic on Master Burke, or a Few words, en passant, occasioned by his Two Letters on a Regicide Peace, *etc.* 1796. 8°. **8139**. b. **17**. **(3.)**

—— *See* Waddington (Samuel F.) Remarks on Mr. Burke's Two Letters "on the Proposals for Peace with the Regicide Directory of France." 1796. 8°. E. **2066**. **(3.)**

—— *See* Williams (William) *of Gray's Inn.* A Reply to Mr. Burke's Two Letters on the Proposals for Peace with the Regicide Directory of France. 1796. 8°. **1103**. k. **77**.

—— *See* Williams (William) *of Gray's Inn.* Rights of the People . . . With a few anticipating strictures upon Mr. Burke's long promised Letters against a Regicide Peace. 1796. 8°. **1103**. i. **26**.

—— *See* Workman (James) *of the Middle Temple.* A Letter to His Grace the Duke of Portland, being a defence of the conduct of His Majesty's ministers, in sending an ambassador to treat for peace with the French Directory, against the attack made upon that measure by the Right Hon. Edmund Burke, *etc.* 1797. 8°. **8135**. ccc. **26**.

—— *See* Workman (James) *of the Middle Temple.* Political Essays relative to the War of the French Revolution; viz. . . . A Letter to the Duke of Portland, being an answer to the Two Letters of the late Right Honorable Edmund Burke against treating for peace with the French Republic, *etc.* 1801. 8°. **8175**. a. **73**.

—— Strictures on Mr. Burke's Two Letters, addressed to a Member of the present Parliament [on the proposals for peace with the regicide Directory]. [By Ralph Broome.] pt. 1. pp. 79. *G. G. J. & J. Robinson: London,* 1796. 8°. **8133**. bb. **14**.

Three Memorials on French Affairs.

—— Three Memorials on French Affairs. Written in the years 1791, 1792 and 1793. (Hints for a Memorial to be delivered to Monsieur de M.M.—Thoughts on French Affairs.—Heads for Consideration on the Present State of Affairs.—Remarks on the Policy of the Allies.) pp. xxxi. *4. 199. *F. & C. Rivington: London,* 1797. 8°. E. **2066**. **(5.)**

—— [Another copy.] G. **13555**. **(2.)**

Two Letters on the Conduct of our Domestick Parties.

—— *See* supra: Observations on the Conduct of the Minority.

Two Letters on the Proposals for Peace with the Regicide Directory.

—— *See* supra: Thoughts on the Prospect of a Regicide Peace.

Two Letters to Gentlemen in Bristol.

—— Two Letters . . . to Gentlemen in the City of Bristol, on the Bills depending in Parliament relative to the trade in Ireland. pp. 32. *J. Dodsley: London,* 1778. 8°. T. **771**. **(1.)**

BURKE (*Right Hon.* Edmund) [Single Works.]

—— [Another copy.] Two Letters . . . to Gentlemen in the City of Bristol, on the Bills depending in Parliament relative to the trade of Ireland. MS. notes [by Jeremy Bentham]. *London,* 1778. 8°. **08138**. dd. **50**. **(8.)**

—— [Another copy.] E. **2231**. **(5.)**

—— The second edition. pp. 32. *J. Dodsley: London,* 1778. 8°. G. **13553**. **(2.)**

Vindication of Natural Society.

—— A Vindication of Natural Society: or, a View of the miseries and evils arising to mankind from every species of artificial society. In a letter to Lord * * * *. By a late noble writer. [By E. Burke. A satirical imitation of the style of Henry St. John, Viscount Bolingbroke.] pp. 106. 1756. 8°. *See* Vindication. **8005**. d. **40**.

—— [Another copy.] **521**. g. **5**.

—— [Another copy.] E. **2210**. **(2.)**

—— [Another edition.] 1761. 8°. [*Fugitive Pieces.* vol 2.] *See* Vindication. **12352**. ee. **21**.

—— [Another edition.] 1762. 8°. [*Fugitive Pieces.* vol. 2.] *See* Vindication. **12268**. aaa. **11**.

—— [Another edition.] 1765. 8°. [*Fugitive Pieces.* vol. 2.] *See* Vindication. **12352**. f. **17**.

—— A Vindication of Natural Society . . . [By E. Burke.] The third edition, with a new preface. pp. x. 94. *See* supra: A Philosophical Enquiry into the Origin of our Ideas of the Sublime and Beautiful, *etc.* 1766. 12°. **8408**. de. **34**.

—— [Another edition.] 1771. 8°. [*Fugitive Pieces.* vol. 2.] *See* Vindication. **12315**. bb. **40**.

—— The third edition. pp. xiv. 106. 1780. 8°. *See* Vindication. G. **13553**. **(3.)**

—— A new edition. pp. viii. 62. *Oxford,* 1796. 8°. **8005**. c. **10**.

—— The Inherent Evils of all State Governments demonstrated; being a reprint of . . . "A Vindication of Natural Society." With notes and an appendix, *etc.* pp. vi. 66. *Holyoake & Co.: London,* 1858. 8°. **8005**. c. **11**.

—— A Vindication of Natural Society. pp. 60. *A. C. Fifield: London,* 1905. 8°. [*Simple Life Series.* no. 22.] **012203**. e. **7/22**.

MISCELLANEA.

—— Extracts from Mr. Burke's Table-Talk, at Crewe Hall. Written down by Mrs. Crewe. pp. 62. [1862.] *See* London.—iii. *Philobiblon Society.* Bibliographical and Historical Miscellanies. (Miscellanies of the Philobiblon Society.) vol. 7. 1854, *etc.* 8°. Ac. **9120**.

—— Heads of Objections to be enquired into before it will be advisable to take Paul Benfield, Esq. again into the Company's Service. Delivered to the General Court of the East India Company by Edmund Burke, Esquire. (Mr. Benfield's Answers.) pp. 13. [*London,* 1780.] 4°. **583**. h. **10**. **(4.)**

—— The Minute Book, and notes. [The text of the Minute Book of the Trinity College Debating Club, for April–July 1747. Written by E. Burke. With a facsimile.] 1923. 8°. [SAMUELS (*Arthur P. I.*) *The Early Life . . . of the Rt. Hon. Edmund Burke, etc.*] See DUBLIN.—*University of Dublin.—Trinity College.—Debating Club.* **010856. dd. 14.**

SELECTIONS AND EXTRACTS.

—— [Selections and extracts from Burke's speeches attacking Lord North.] *See* FOX (*Right Hon.* Charles J.) The Beauties of Fox, North and Burke, selected from their speeches, *etc.* 1784. 8°. **1416. g. 19.**

—— [Another edition.] *See* FOX (*Right Hon.* Charles J.) The Beauties and Deformities of Fox, North and Burke . . . With a frontispiece of . . . Burke, *etc.* 1784. 8°. **8135. a. 53.**

—— [Another edition.] *See* FOX (*Right Hon.* Charles J.) The Beauties and Deformities of Fox, North and Burke, *etc.* 1784. 8°. **12301. b. 14.**

—— Pearls cast before Swine, by Edmund Burke. [Extracts.] Scraped together by Old Hubert [i.e. — Parkinson]. pp. 8. *D. I. Eaton: London,* [1793 ?] 8°. **8135. b. 3. (4.)**

—— The Beauties of the late Right Hon. Edmund Burke, selected from the writings, &c. of that extraordinary man . . . To which is prefixed a sketch of the life, with some original anecdotes of Mr. Burke. [By Charles H. Wilson.] 2 vol. pp. vi. cxxxvi. 499. *W. West: London,* 1798. 8°. **632. i. 22.**

—— Opinions on Reform. [Extracts, compiled by T. H. Burke.] pp. 48. *C. J. G. & F. Rivington: London,* 1831. 8°. **8006. b. 7.**

—— The Wisdom and Genius of the Right Hon. Edmund Burke, illustrated in a series of extracts from his writings and speeches; with a summary of his life: by Peter Burke. pp. li. 426. *Edward Moxon: London,* 1845. 12°. **1205. d. 13.**

With an additional titlepage, engraved.

—— Edmund Burke: being first principles selected from his writings. With an introductory essay by Robert Montgomery. pp. xxxii. 416. *G. Routledge & Co.: London,* 1853. 8°. **1205. b. 7.**

—— Extracts from Burke's Earlier Writings With notes by the Rev. C. E. Moberly. pp. xv. 107. *Whittaker & Co.: London,* 1873. 8°. **12273. b. 3.**

—— The Wisdom of Edmund Burke. Extracts from his speeches and writings, selected and arranged by Edward Alloway Pankhurst. pp. xi. 250. *John Murray: London,* 1886. 8°. **12270. bb. 28.**

—— Selections from the Speeches and Writings of Edmund Burke. pp. xxxi. 416. *G. Routledge & Sons: London,* 1893. 8°. [*Sir John Lubbock's Hundred Books.* no. 52.] **012207.1.1/52.**

—— Edmund Burke. [Selections.] By T. Dundas Pillans. pp. xix. 68. *Orient Press: London,* [1905.] 8°. [*Wisdom of the West Series.*] **12204. r. 4/1.**

—— Selections from Burke. pp. 47. *Edward Arnold: London,* [1905.] 8°. [*Arnold Prose Books.* bk. 10.] **12270. de. 15/10.**

—— Selections from the Speeches and Writings of Edmund Burke. With biographical introduction by Hannaford Bennett. pp. 160. *London,* 1907. 8°. [*John Long's Carlton Classics.*] **12204. p. 11/31.**

—— Maxims and Reflections of Burke. Selected and edited by F. W. Raffety. [With a portrait.] pp. xii. 152. *T. S. Clark & Co.: London,* [1909.] 8°. **012305. h. 30.**

—— Edmund Burke. Selections. With essays by Hazlitt, Arnold, & others. With an introduction and notes by A. M. D. Hughes. [With a portrait.] pp. xvi. 192. *Oxford,* 1921. 8°. [*Clarendon Series of English Literature.*] **W.P. 6807/4.**

—— Edmund Burke. Selected prose, edited and introduced by Sir Philip Magnus. pp. 99. *Falcon Press London,* 1948. 8°. [*Falcon Prose Classics.*] **W.P.13287/6.**

WORKS EDITED OR WITH CONTRIBUTIONS BY BURKE.

—— *See* AMERICA. An Account of the European Settlements in America, *etc.* [By W. Burke. Revised by E. Burke.] 1757. 8°. **279. h. 29, 30.**

—— —— 1758. 8°. **1061. d. 11, 12.**

—— —— 1762. 8°. **10408. a. 3.**

—— —— 1765. 8°. **10408. d. 3.**

—— —— 1770. 8°. **10412. bb. 22.**

—— —— 1777. 8°. **10480. e. 3.**

—— *See* BRISSOT (J. P.) called BRISSOT DE WARVILLE. J. P. Brissot . . . to his Constituents . . . Translated from the French [by W. Burke], *etc.* [The translation revised and the preface written by E. Burke.] 1794. 8°. **1059. i. 29. (1.)**

—— *See* PATRIOT. A Patriot's Letter to the Duke of Dorset written in the year 1731. With a dedication [by E. Burke ?] to the Cork-Surgeon of the year 1749. 1749. 8°. **E. 2091. (7.)**

—— [For editions of the "Annual Register," which until 1791 was edited and largely written by Burke:] *See* PERIODICAL PUBLICATIONS.—*London.*

—— *See* VALENS, *pseud.* The Letters of Valens, *etc.* [By William Burke, assisted by Edmund and Richard Burke ?] 1777. 8°. **E. 2230. (1.)**

WORKS WITH MS. NOTES BY BURKE.

—— *See* ENGLAND.—*Parliament.—House of Commons.* [*Proceedings.—II.*] First(—Sixth) Report from the Committee of Secrecy appointed to enquire into the causes of the War in the Carnatic, &c. FEW MS. NOTES [by E. Burke]. 1787, *etc.* fol. **749. d. 1.**

—— *See* POWNALL (Thomas) The Administration of the Colonies, *etc.* MS. NOTES [by E. Burke]. 1768. 8°. **C. 60. i. 9.**

DOUBTFUL OR SUPPOSITITIOUS WORKS.

—— [Five articles, by E. Burke? reprinted from "The Censor."] *See* LUCAS (Charles) *M.P.* The Political Constitutions of Great Britain and Ireland, *etc.* 1751. 8°. **288. c. 33.**

—— [Another edition, abridged.] *See* SAMUELS (Arthur P. I.) The Early Life, Correspondence and Writings of the Rt. Hon. Edmund Burke, *etc.* 1923. 8°. **010856. dd. 14.**

—— Discours de M. Burke sur la monnoie de papier, et sur le systême des assignats de France. pp. 27. [*Paris ?*] 1790. 8°. **F. 210. (10.)**

—— [Another copy.] **R. 75. (7.)**

BURKE (*Right Hon.* EDMUND) [DOUBTFUL OR SUPPOSITITIOUS WORKS.]

—— *See* AMERICA, *North.* The Comparative Importance of our Acquisitions from France in America. With remarks on a pamphlet [by E. Burke?] intitled, An Examination of the Commercial Principles of the late Negotiation in 1761. 1762. 8°. **104. i. 4.**

—— A Free Briton's Advice to the Free Citizens of Dublin. [Signed: Helvidius Priscus.] 3 no. 1748. 8°. *See* PRISCUS (Helvidius) *pseud.* [i.e. *Right Hon.* E. Burke?] **8145. b. 96.**

—— [Another edition.] *See* SAMUELS (Arthur P. I.) The Early Life, Correspondence and Writings of the Rt. Hon. Edmund Burke, *etc.* 1923. 8°. **010856. dd. 14.**

—— A Letter to the Citizens of Dublin. [A reply to "The Cork Surgeon's Antidote," by "Anthony Litten," i.e. Sir Richard Cox, 2nd Bart. By E. Burke?] pp. 20. 1749. 8°. *See* DUBLIN. **8145. b. 30.**

—— The third edition. pp. 20. 1749. 8°. *See* DUBLIN. **E. 2091. (8.)**

—— [Another edition.] *See* SAMUELS (Arthur P. I.) The Early Life, Correspondence and Writings of the Rt. Hon. Edmund Burke, *etc.* 1923. 8°. **010856. dd. 14.**

—— A Second Letter to the Citizens of Dublin. To which is prefixed; a Letter to a Member of Parliament, *etc.* [By E. Burke?] pp. 25. 1749. 8°. *See* DUBLIN. **E. 2091. (8*.)**

—— [Another edition.] *See* SAMUELS (Arthur P. I.) The Early Life, Correspondence and Writings of the Rt. Hon. Edmund Burke, *etc.* 1923. 8°. **010856. dd. 14.**

—— Lettre de M. Burke, membre de la Chambre des Communes d'Angleterre, au traducteur de son Discours sur la situation actuelle de la France, *etc.* pp. 39. *Paris,* [1790.] 8°. **F. 1582. (2.)**

—— Lettre de M. Burke, membre du parlement d'Angleterre, aux François. pp. 28. *Londres* [*Paris?*], 1790. 8°. **F. 1582. (7.)**

—— [Another copy.] **R. 75. (4.)**

—— Lucubrations philosophiques du célèbre Burke, sur divers objets de politique. Traduites de l'Anglois. No. I. Décadence de la monarchie françoise. Précédées d'une réponse à la note importante de M. Cérutti, sur M. Burke. pp. 42. [*Paris,*] 1790. 8°. **F. 1582. (3.)**

—— [Another copy.] **F. 393. (16.)**

—— [Another copy.] **R. 75. (5)**

—— Suite des Lucubrations de M. Burke sur divers objets de politique. Traduites de l'anglais. Jugement de l'Europe sur les suites de la Révolution française. Alliance de la liberté avec la monarchie. pp. 32. [*Paris,*] 1790. 8°. **F. 1582. (4.)**

—— [Another copy.] **R. 75. (6.)**

—— The Naked Truth; or Lucas and La Touche set forth in their proper colours. pp. 16. 1749. 8°. *See* RHECTOR (Philo) *pseud.* [i.e. *Right Hon.* E. Burke?] **8145. aaa. 107.**

—— [Another edition.] *See* SAMUELS (Arthur P. I.) The Early Life, Correspondence and Writings of the Rt. Hon. Edmund Burke, *etc.* 1923. 8°. **010856. dd. 14.**

—— The Reformer. [A reprint of no. 1–8, 10–13 of the edition of 1748; being the numbers attributed to Burke.] 1923. 8°. [SAMUELS (*Arthur P. I.*) *The Early Life . . . of the Rt. Hon. Edmund Burke, etc.*] *See* PERIODICAL PUBLICATIONS.—*Dublin.* **010856. dd. 14.**

BURKE (*Right Hon.* EDMUND) [DOUBTFUL OR SUPPOSITITIOUS WORKS.]

—— A Reply to the Treasury Pamphlet [by the Right Hon. George Rose], entitled: "The Proposed System of Trade with Ireland explained." [By T. L. O'Beirne? or E. Burke?] pp. 90. 1785. 8°. *See* IRELAND. [*Appendix.—II. Miscellaneous.*] **1102. h. 14. (2.)**

—— [Another copy.] **111. d. 44.**

—— [Another copy.] **117. i. 2.**

—— *See* IRELAND. [*Appendix.—II. Miscellaneous.*] An Answer to the Reply to the supposed Treasury Pamphlet. 1785. 8°. **1102. h. 14. (3.)**

—— A Second Letter to the Citizens of Dublin. *See* supra: A Letter to the Citizens of Dublin.

—— Suite des Lucubrations de M. Burke sur divers objets de politique. *See* supra: Lucubrations philosophiques, *etc.*

—— Traduction d'un article inseré dans l'Evening Mail—Malle du Soir—de Londres, du lundi au mercredi 19 sept. 1792. [Advocating a subscription on behalf of the exiled clergy of France.] (Cette adresse est attribuée à Mr. Edmond Burke.) pp. 4. [*London,* 1792.] 8°. **4406. g. 2. (54.)**

APPENDIX.

—— *See* ALBION, *pseud.* Four Pleasant Epistles, written for the entertainment and gratification of four unpleasant characters, viz. a very exalted subject in His Majesty's dominions [i.e. George, Prince of Wales], the most unpatriotic man alive [i.e. C. J. Fox], the most artful man alive [i.e. R. B. Sheridan], and Second Childhood [i.e. E. Burke]. 1789. 4°. **8135. k. 2.**

—— *See* B—, E., *D.D.* The Honor of the University of Oxford defended, against the illiberal aspersions of E — d B — e, Esq. [i.e. Edmund Burke], *etc.* [1781?] 8°. **103. d. 45.**

—— *See* BARKER (Edmund H.) The Claims of Sir Philip Francis to the authorship of Junius's Letters disproved . . . Observations on the conduct, character, and style of the writings of the late Right Hon. Edmund Burke, *etc.* 1828. 12°. **713. d. 8.**

—— *See* BARKER (Sir Ernest) *University of Cambridge.* Burke and Bristol, *etc.* 1931. 8°. **10823. a. 7.**

—— *See* BARRY (Liam) Our Legacy from Burke, *etc.* 1952. 8°. **11869. aa. 15.**

—— *See* BATCHELDER (James L.) The Genius of Edmund Burke. 1866. 12°. **10817. aaa. 25.**

—— *See* BAUMANN (Arthur A.) Burke: the founder of Conservatism, *etc.* 1929. 8°. **08139. a. 91.**

—— *See* BEST (George) *of Spa-Fields, Clerkenwell.* A Letter of Thanks, on behalf of those who profess the Gospel, of all denominations, to the Right Hon. Edmund Burke, *etc.* 1792. 8°. **T. 88. (1.)**

—— *See* BISSET (Robert) The Life of Edmund Burke, *etc.* [With a portrait.] 1798. 8°. **614. i. 2.**

—— —— 1800. 8°. **1452. h. 7.**

—— *See* BRAUNE (F.) Edmund Burke in Deutschland, *etc.* 1917. 8°. **09009. ff. 2/50.**

—— *See* B — RKE, *Begum.* Begum B — rke to Begum Bow, *etc.* [A satire on E. Burke.] 1789. 4°. **11630. c. 11. (9.)**

BURKE (*Right Hon.* EDMUND) [APPENDIX.]

—— *See* BROOKE (Benjamin F.) Edmund Burke: a literary essay, *etc.* 1896. 8°. **10803. d. 2. (12.)**

—— *See* BRYANT (Donald C.) Edmund Burke and his Literary Friends. 1939. 8°. [*Washington University Studies.* New ser. Language and literature. no. 9.] **Ac.2691.o/1.(2.)**

—— *See* BURKE (Peter) The Public and Domestic Life of the Right Hon. Edmund Burke. 1853. 8°. **741. b. 23.**

—— *See* BUTLER (*Sir* George G. G.) *K.B.E.* The Tory Tradition. Bolingbroke, Burke, *etc.* 1914. 8°. **8139. c. 26.**

—— *See* BUTLER (Henry M.) *Master of Trinity College, Cambridge.* The Character of Edmund Burke, *etc.* [1854.] 8°. **10803. bb. 29. (1.)**

—— *See* CAPADOSE (I.) Edmund Burke. Overzigt van het leven en de schriften van een antirevolutionair staatsman. 1857. 8°. **10817. cc. 21. (3.)**

—— *See* CHADWICK (George A.) *Bishop of Derry and Raphoe.* Edmund Burke. 1902. 8°. [*Peplographia Dublinensis.*] **4478. g. 11.**

—— *See* CLACK (Franklin H.) The Character of Edmund Burke, *etc.* 1845. 8°. **10826. dd. 11. (1.)**

—— *See* COBBAN (Alfred) Edmund Burke and the Revolt against the Eighteenth Century, *etc.* 1929. 8°. **08007. de. 71.**

—— *See* COOPER (Thomas) *M.D., etc.* A Reply to Mr. Burke's Invective against Mr. Cooper and Mr. Watt, in the House of Commons, on the 30th of April, 1792. 1792. 8°. **8138. aaa. 34.**

—— —— 1792. 8°. **1102. f. 4. (6.)**

—— —— 1792. 8°. **8135. bb. 5. (4.)**

—— *See* COPELAND (Thomas W.) Edmund Burke. Six essays. 1950. 8°. **10862. c. 22.**

—— *See* CROLY (George) B.C. A Memoir of the Political Life of the Right Honourable Edmund Burke, *etc.* 1840. 8°. **1202. d. 23.**

—— *See* DRUMMOND (William H.) *D.D.* One is your Master —even Christ. A discourse, containing a refutation of certain high-church principles, held by the celebrated Edmund Burke, *etc.* 1831. 8°. **T. 1509. (1.)**

—— *See* EINAUDI (M.) The British Background of Burke's Political Philosophy, *etc.* 1934. 8°. **08008. b. 36.**

—— *See* EINAUDI (M.) Edmondo Burke e l'indirizzo storico nelle scienze politiche. 1930. 8°. [*R. Università di Torino. Memorie dell'Istituto Giuridico.* ser. 2. mem. 7.] **Ac. 2308.**

—— *See* FITZROY (Augustus H.) *Duke of Grafton.* A Letter to the Duke of Grafton . . . To which is annexed a complete exculpation of M. de la Fayette from the charges indecently urged against him by Mr. Burke in the House of Commons, on the 17th March, 1794. [By W. A. Miles.] 1794. 8°. **8052. dd. 20.**

—— *See* FRIEND. A New Friend on an Old Subject. [A defence of Burke's views on the French Revolution.] 1791. 8°. **8052. dd. 24.**

—— *See* FRY (Alfred A.) A Lecture on the Writings and Literary and Personal Character of the Right Hon. Edmund Burke, *etc.* 1838. 8°. **1203. d. 8. (3.)**

BURKE (*Right Hon.* EDMUND) [APPENDIX.]

—— *See* GIBSON (William) *Vicar-Apostolic of Northern England.* An Account of a Conversation between the Rt. Hon. Edm. Burke and the Rt. Rev. Dr. Gibson. 1819. 8°. **4431. bb. 5. (12.)**

—— *See* GRIERSON (*Sir* Herbert J. C.) Edmund Burke. 1914. 8°. [*Cambridge History of English Literature.* vol. 11.] **18870.g.1.**

—— *See* HAGBERG (K. H.) Burke, Metternich, Disraeli. 1931. 8°. **010603. dd. 19.**

—— *See* HARDINGE (George) *M.P.* A Series of Letters to the Right Honorable Edmund Burke, in which are contained enquiries into the constitutional existence of an impeachment against Mr. Hastings. [With special reference to Burke's speeches in the House of Commons, 17 & 23 Dec., 1790.] 1791. 8°. **517. k. 20. (4.)**

—— —— 1791. 8°. **514. c. 6.**

—— *See* JUNIUS, *pseud.* [*Author of the "Letters."*] The Genuine Letters of Junius. To which are prefixed anecdotes of the author [who is here assumed to be Burke]. 1771. 8°. **8007. bbb. 22.**

—— *See* JUNIUS, *pseud.* [*Author of the "Letters."*] [*Appendix.*] Junius proved to be Burke, *etc.* 1826. 8°. **T. 1167. (13.)**

—— *See* LASKI (Harold J.) Edmund Burke. An address delivered on the occasion of the bi-centenary of the foundation of Burke's "Club," *etc.* 1947. 8°. **10860. b. 45.**

—— *See* LENNOX (Richmond) Edmund Burke und sein politisches Arbeitsfeld in den Jahren 1760 bis 1790, *etc.* 1923. 8°. **010856. cc. 21.**

—— *See* MACCORMICK (Charles) Memoirs of the Right Honourable Edmund Burke, *etc.* 1797. 4°. **614. l. 24.**

—— ——1798. 4°. **10825. f. 18.**

—— *See* MACCUNN (John) The Political Philosophy of Burke. 1913. 8°. **08139. a. 2.**

—— *See* MACKNIGHT (Thomas) History of the Life and Times of Edmund Burke. 1858, *etc.* 8°. **2406. c. 6.**

—— *See* MAGNUS (*Sir* Philip M.) *Bart.* Edmund Burke. A life. [With portraits.] 1939. 8°. **10859. c. 6.**

—— *See* MEUSEL (F.) Edmund Burke und die französische Revolution, *etc.* 1913. 8°. **8051. dd. 43.**

—— *See* MILES (William A.) A Letter to the Duke of Grafton . . . Including a complete exculpation of M. de la Fayette from the charges indecently urged against him by Mr. Burke, *etc.* 1794. 8°. **1103. i. 15.**

—— *See* MONTGOMERY (Hugh de F.) Gladstone and Burke. 1886. 8°. **8146. f. 23. (4.)**

—— *See* MORLEY (John) *Viscount Morley of Blackburn.* Burke. 1879. 8°. **2326. b. 6.**

—— —— 1888. 8°. **10815. aaa. 24.**

—— *See* MORLEY (John) *Viscount Morley of Blackburn.* Edmund Burke: a historical study. 1867. 8°. **2406. c. 5.**

—— *See* MURRAY (Robert H.) Edmund Burke. A biography. [With a portrait.] 1931. 8°. **10823. c. 10.**

—— *See* NAPIER (*Right Hon. Sir* Joseph) *Bart.* Edmund Burke: a lecture, *etc.* 1863. 8°. [*Lectures delivered before the Dublin Young Men's Christian Association.*] **4463. d. 12.**

—— *See* NEWMAN (Bertram) Edmund Burke. [With a portrait.] 1927. 8°. **010826**. f. **51**

—— *See* NICOLL (Henry J.) Great Orators. Burke, Fox, *etc.* 1880. 8°. **10815**. aaa. **25**.

—— *See* O'BRIEN (William) *M.P. for Cork.* Edmund Burke as an Irishman. 1924. 8°. **010856**. b. **12**.

—— —— 1926. 8°. **010855**. b. **53**.

—— *See* OLIVER (Robert T.) Four who spoke out. Burke, Fox, Sheridan, Pitt. [1946.] 8°. **10804**. s. **2**.

—— *See* ONEIROPHILOS, *pseud.* Gynomachia; or, a Contest between two old ladies in the service of a celebrated orator. [A satirical poem on Burke.] [1789.] 4°. **78**. g. **9**.

—— *See* OPPENHEIMER (F. von) *Baron.* Montaigne. Edmund Burke und die französische Revolution, *etc.* 1928. 8°. **010603**. h. **10**.

—— *See* OPZOOMER (C. W.) Conservatismus und Reform. Eine Abhandlung über Edmund Burke's Politik, *etc.* 1852. 8°. **8008**. c. **37**. (**4**.)

—— *See* OSBORN (Annie M.) Rousseau and Burke. A study of the idea of liberty in eighteenth century political thought. 1940. 8°. **08004**. f. **20**.

—— *See* P., J. B. Lettre à l'Assemblée nationale de France: par un de ses membres, actuellement à Londres. [On the attitude of Burke to the Revolution.] 1791. 8°. R. **75**. (**12**.)

—— *See* PANKHURST (Edward A.) Edmund Burke. A study of life and character. 1886. 8°. **10815**. b. **77**.

—— *See* PILLANS (T. D.) Edmund Burke: apostle of justice and liberty. 1905. 8°. **010817**. h. **48**.

—— *See* PRIOR (*Sir* James) Memoir of the Life and Character of the Right Hon. Edmund Burke, *etc.* [With a portrait and a bibliography.] 1824. 8°. **614**. i. **3**.

—— —— 1826. 8°. **614**. i. **4, 5**.

—— —— 1854. 8°. **2500**. d. **2**.

—— *See* REYNOLDS (Ernest E.) Edmund Burke, Christian statesman. [With a portrait.] 1948 [1949]. 8°. W.P. **1294/6**.

—— *See* ROBERTSON (James B.) Lectures on the Life, Writings and Times of Edmund Burke. [1869.] 8°. **10854**. bbb. **24**.

—— *See* ROCHE (John) *President of the Royal Physical Society of Edinburgh.* An Inquiry concerning the Author of the Letters of Junius; in which it is proved . . . that they were written by the late Right Hon. E. Burke. 1813. 8°. **8005**. dd. **30**.

—— *See* ROUGANE (C.) Plaintes à Monsieur Burke, sur sa lettre à M. l'archevêque d'Aix. [1791.] 8°. F.R. **142**. (**10**.)

—— *See* SAMUELS (Arthur P. I.) The Early Life, Correspondence and Writings of the Rt. Hon. Edmund Burke, *etc.* [With a portrait.] 1923. 8°. **010856**. dd. **14**.

—— *See* SCHAEDEL (O.) Edmund Burke. 1898. 8°. **10816**. df. **6**.

—— *See* SCHEPELERN (V. E.) Edmund Burke, Friedrich Gentz, Adam Müller. Et Bidrag til Revolutions- og Napoleonstidens politiske Idéhistorie. 1953. 8°. **8011**. c. **65**.

BURKE (*Right Hon.* EDMUND) [APPENDIX.]

—— *See* SPINELLI (N.) The Political Life of Edmund Burke. 1908. 8°. **10816**. d. **27**.

—— *See* THERRY (Roger) A Letter to the Right Hon. George Canning, *etc.* (Reminiscences of the Right Hon. Edmund Burke and his son, &c.) 1826. 8°. T. **1004**. (**3**.)

—— —— 1827. 8°. **8138**. b. **94**. (**3**.)

—— *See* TIMBS (John) Anecdote Biography. William Pitt, Earl of Chatham, and Edmund Burke. [With a portrait.] 1860. 8°. **10816**. df. **21**.

—— *See* VALLE (E.) La Mente di Edmondo Burke. Brano della storia parlamentare inglese, *etc.* 1870. 8°. **8132**. eee. **3**.

—— *See* VEṆĪ-PRASĀDA, *of the University of Allahabad.* Edmund Burke on Indian Governance. 1944. 8°. [*University of Allahabad Studies.* 1944. Politics Section.] **14005**. n. **1**.

—— *See* WEARE (George E.) Edmund Burke's Connection with Bristol, from 1774 till 1780; with a prefatory memoir of Burke. 1894. 8°. **10815**. e. **17**.

—— *See* WECTER (Dixon) Edmund Burke and his Kinsmen, *etc.* 1939. 8°. [*University of Colorado Studies.* ser. B. vol. 1. no. 1.] Ac. **2691**. g/**2**. (**2**.)

—— *See* WEST (Jane) An Elegy on the Death of the Right Honourable Edmund Burke. 1797. 4°. **11633**. g. **40**.

—— *See* WILLIS (William) *County Court Judge.* Edmund Burke: the story of his life, *etc.* 1889. 8°. **10603**. dd. **4**. (**12**.)

—— *See* YOUNG (George M.) Burke, *etc.* [1944.] 8°. [*Annual Lecture on a Master Mind, Henriette Hertz Trust,* 1943.] Ac. **1186/9**.

—— The Beauties of Burke! or, Ignorance triumphant. [A satire.] pp. 12. *Printed for the Author: London,* 1797. 12°. E. **2067**. (**6**.)

—— Catalogue of the Library of the late Right Hon. Edmund Burke, the Library of the late Sir M. B. Clare, M.D., some articles from Gibbon's Library, etc. . . . which will be sold by auction, *etc.* pp. 74. *W. Nicol: London,* [1833.] 8°. S.C. E. **49**. (**1**.)
Interleaved. With the names of the purchasers and the prices inserted in MS.

—— A Catalogue of the Very Valuable Collection of Highly Interesting Antique Statues, Bustos, and Other Marbles, and capital Italian pictures, collected at Rome, with the the assistance and advice of . . . Cavaceppi, by William Lloyd, Esq., and subsequently the property of the Rt. Hon. Edmund Burke, now brought from his seat, Butler's Court, near Beaconsfield, Bucks., together with a few prints and drawings . . . which will be sold by auction, *etc.* pp. 8. [*London,* 1812.] 4°. **555**. c. **38**. (**2**.)
With some of the prices marked in MS.

—— A Defence of the Political and Parliamentary Conduct of the Right Honourable Edmund Burke. [A satire.] pp. 35. *D. I. Eaton: London,* 1794. 8°. T. **134**. (**2**.)

—— [Another copy.] E. **2167**. (**5**.)

—— Edmund Burke. A sketch of his life and his services to India. pp. 55. *G. A. Natesan & Co.: Madras,* [1912.] 8°. [" *Friends of India* " *Series.*] **010803**. de. **37/1**.

BURKE (*Right Hon.* EDMUND) [APPENDIX.]

—— A Letter to Edmund Burke, Esq., by birth an Irishman, by adoption an Englishman, containing some reflections on patriotism, party-spirit, and the union of free nations. With observations upon the means on which Ireland relies for obtaining political independence. pp. 37. *William Hallhead: Dublin*, 1780. 8°. **E. 2099. (12.)**

—— The Life, Death, and Wonderful Atchievements of Edmund Burke. A new ballad. By the author of the Wrongs of Africa [i.e. William Roscoe]. pp. 8. [*Edinburgh*,] 1792. 12°. **1078. l. 17.**

—— [Another edition.] pp. 8. [*Edinburgh?* 1792?] 12°. **11621. b. 30. (23.)**

—— [Another edition.] [*London?* 1800?] *s. sh.* 4°. **806. k. 16. (118.)**

—— Remarks on the Posthumous Works of the late Right Hon. Edmund Burke; and on the preface published by his executors, the Doctors French Laurence and Walker King. pp. 65. *J. Debrett: London*, 1797. 8°. **8135. ccc. 10.**

BURKE (EDMUND H.)

—— Archery Handbook. [With illustrations, including a portrait.] pp. 144. *Fawcett Publications: Greenwich, Conn.*, [1954.] 8°. **7921. i. 8.**
Fawcett Book. no. 221.

BURKE (EDMUND J.) Political Economy. Designed for use in Catholic colleges, high schools, and academies. pp. xvi. 479. *American Book Co.: New York*, [1913.] 8°. **08207. f. 51.**

BURKE (EDMUND N.)

—— *See* VILLAGE LIFE. Village Life in the West Indies, and How to Improve It. Adapted by E. N. Burke from "Village Life and How to Improve It," Sheldon Press, London, *etc.* [1945.] 8°. **W.P.3306/10.**

—— *See* VILLAGE LIFE. Village Life in the West Indies and how to improve it. Adapted by E. N. Burke, *etc.* [1951.] 8°. W.P. **3306/10a.**

—— Speaking together and enjoying it! pp. 69. *Jamaica Welfare: Kingston*, [1951.] 8°. [*Caribbean Home Library Series.* no. 33.] W.P. **3306/33.**

—— Working together. A handbook of projects for groups. [With illustrations.] pp. 38. *Jamaica Social Welfare Commission: Kingston*, [1951.] 8°. [*Caribbean Home Library Series.* no. 29.] W.P. **3306/29.**

BURKE (EDMUND TYTLER)

—— The Modern Treatment of Venereal Diseases. pp. 105. *John Bale Medical Publications: London*, [1942.] 8°. **7642. b. 12.**

—— Scourges of To-day. Venereal disease, cancer, tuberculosis, alcoholism, *etc.* pp. xiii. 166. *Faber & Gwyer: London*, 1926. 8°. [*Modern Health Books.*] **7383. d. 28/8.**

—— Treatment of Venereal Disease in General Practice. [With plates.] pp. 162. *Faber & Gwyer: London*, 1927. 8°. **07640. de. 62.**

—— Tropical Tips for Troops, or How to keep fit in the tropics, *etc.* pp. xii. 63. *William Heinemann: London*, 1941. 8°. **7385. aa. 5.**

BURKE (EDMUND TYTLER)

—— Tropical Tips for Troops . . . Second edition, enlarged. pp. x. 74. *William Heinemann Medical Books: London*, 1942. 8°. **7392. aa. 8.**

—— Venereal Diseases, *etc.* pp. xv. 549. pl. vi. *H. K. Lewis & Co.: London*, 1940. 8°. **07641. f. 42.**

—— The Venereal Problem, *etc.* pp. 208. *Henry Kimpton: London*, 1919. 8°. **07640. de. 25.**

BURKE (EDWARD) *pseud.* [i.e. WINIFRED BOGGS.] *See* also BOGGS (Winifred)

—— Bachelors' Buttons. The candid confessions of a shy bachelor. pp. vi. 399. *Herbert Jenkins: London*, 1913 [1912]. 8°. **NN. 416.**

—— The Bewildered Benedict. The story of a superfluous uncle. pp. vi. 386. *Herbert Jenkins: London*, 1914 [1913]. 8°. **NN. 1426.**

—— Getting rid of Uncle, *etc.* (Popular and revised edition of "A Bewildered Benedict.") pp. 320. *Herbert Jenkins: London*, 1924. 8°. **012637. bbb. 15.**

—— My Wife. pp. 315. *Herbert Jenkins: London*, 1917 [1916]. 8°. **NN. 3964.**

—— The Spinster Aunt. pp. 308. *Herbert Jenkins: London*, 1922. 8°. **NN. 7628.**

BURKE (EDWARD H.) Enamelled Cane Craft and Basketry. pp. 54. *Sir I. Pitman & Sons: London*, 1936. 8°. **7941. ppp. 7.**

BURKE (EDWARD PLUNKETT) Sir Edward Coke. [By E. P. Burke.] pp. 32. 1833. 8°. [*Lives of Eminent Persons.*] *See* COKE (*Sir* Edward) *Lord Chief Justice of the Court of King's Bench.* **737. d. 9.**

BURKE (EDWIN) This Thing called Love. A comedy in three acts. pp. 104. *New York, London*, [1929.] 8°. [*French's Standard Library Edition.*] **011781. g. 1/231.**

BURKE (EMILY MARIA) Ancient Civilisations. 3 vol.

1. The Shining East, *etc.* pp. 166. [1915.]
2. The Violet Crown and the Seven Hills, *etc.* pp. 177. [1919.]
3. The Old Order and the New, *etc.* pp. 184. [1921.]

Ralph, Holland & Co.: London, [1915–21.] 8°. **07704. df. 38.**

—— [A reissue of no. 2.] *T. Werner Laurie: London*, [1920.] 8°. **9025. bbb. 31.**

—— The Hornsey County School. A review of its first twenty-five years of educational work, 1904–1929. [With plates.] pp. 99. *Macaire, Mould & Co.: London*, 1930. 8°. **08364. de. 40.**

BURKE (FIELDING) *pseud.* [i.e. OLIVE TILFORD DARGAN.] *See* also DARGAN (Olive T.)

—— Call Home the Heart. A novel. pp. 432. *Longmans & Co.: London; printed in U.S.A.*, 1932. 8°. **A.N. 1408.**

—— [Another issue.] *London; printed in U.S.A.*, 1932. 8°. **12708. i. 3.**

—— A Stone Came Rolling. A novel. pp. 412. *Longmans & Co.: New York, Toronto*, 1935. 8°. **A.N. 2830.**

BURKE (FRANCES) *See* BUTLER (William) *Attorney.* Wm. Butler, Appel[nt]. John Burke Esq; and Frances his wife, Resp[nts] et e con . . . The case of the said J. Burke, and Frances his wife, Respondents, *etc.* [1719.] fol. **19. h. 1. (123.)**

BURKE (FRANCES)

—— *See* BUTLER (William) *Attorney.* William Butler, Appellant. John Bourke, and Frances his wife, Respondents. The Appellant's case. [1719.] fol. **19. h. 1. (122.)**

BURKE (FREDERICK H.)

—— In Africa with Blackboard and Chalk. The ABC of Salvation, *etc.* *Christian Publishing Co.: Johannesburg,* [1944.] 8°. **4194. b. 15.**

—— Ozayo emhlabeni. pp. 56. *Nelspruit,* 1945. 8°. **12912. e. 21.**

—— Ozayo emhlabeni. pp. 56. *Nelspruit,* [1946.] 8°. **12912. e. 22.**

—— Ukuchasiselwa kwevangeli ngemifanekiso . . . Evangelistic chalk talks, *etc.* pp. 66. *Nelspruit,* [c. 1950.] 8°. **4384. d. 4.**

BURKE (GERALD) *See* EYRE (Edward) *of Leitrim.* Edward Eyre, Dennis Daly, and Nicholas Darcy, Esqs. Appellants. Gerald Burke, Esq; Respondent. The case of the appellant. [1724.] fol. **19. h. 2. (137.)**

—— *See* EYRE (Edward) *of Leitrim.* Edward Eyre, Nicholas Darcy, and Dennis Daly, Esqs; Appellants. Gerald Burke, Esq; Respondent. The respondent's case. [1724.] fol. **19. h. 2. (138.)**

—— Detraction Refuted, being a vindication of Gerald Burke, Esq; fr[om] divers calumnies spread ab[out by] his enemies. [Written by himself.] pp. iv. 43. *Edward Waters: Dublin,* [1740.] 4°. **1414. c. 59.**
The titlepage is slightly mutilated.

BURKE (H. H.) Black Diamonds; or, the Gospel in a colliery district. By H. H. B. [i.e. H. H. Burke.] With a preface by the Rev. J. B. Owen. pp. xii. 297. 1861. 8°. *See* B., H. H. **4193. c. 45.**

BURKE (HARRY) Harry Burke. A story of the Fifth Commandment. By the author of "Nellie and Alice," *etc.* pp. 61. *S.P.C.K.: London,* [1866.] 16°. **4416. aa. 17.**

BURKE (HARRY EUGENE) *See* DOANE (Rennie W.) Forest Insects . . . By R. W. Doane . . . H. E. Burke. 1936. 8°. **W.P. 10970/5.**

BURKE (HARRY M.)

—— *See* KIPHUTH (Robert J. H.) and BURKE (H. M.) Basic Swimming. 1951. 8°. **7919. f. 20.**

BURKE (HARRY ROSECRANS)

—— *See* HERNDON (William H.) Lincoln and Ann Rutledge. . . . Introduction by H. R. Burke. 1945. 12°. **11923. c. 1.**

—— Visitation at Thatchcot. A symposium of little journeys to the home of Trovillion Private Press. By H. R. Burke and F. A. Behymer. pp. 22. *Trovillion Private Press: Herrin, Ill.,* 1944. 12° **Cup.510.n.7.**

BURKE (HELEN)

—— The Albatross Cookery Book. [By H. Burke.] pp. 47. [1937.] 8°. **7949. l. 11.**

—— Economy Supplement to the Albatross Cookery Book. pp. 24. [1940?] 8°. **7949. l. 11a.**
See ALBATROSS COOKERY BOOK.

—— Christmas Fare 1944 (1945), *etc.* 2 pt. [*British Commercial Gas Association: London,* 1944, 45.] 8°. **7947. aaa. 52.**

BURKE (HELEN)

—— Helen Burke's Cookery Book. pp. 292. *Shaylor: London,* 1930. 8°. **07941.pp.52.**

—— New edition. pp. 292. *G. Routledge & Sons: London,* 1933. 8°. **7942. t. 6.**

—— The New Albatross Recipe Book. pp. 32. *Spillers: London,* [1951.] 8°. **7949. l. 12.**

—— Training Margaret. A book for every mistress, maid, bride and bride-to-be, *etc.* pp. 175. *Hutchinson & Co.: London,* [1937.] 8°. **7944. ppp. 16.**

—— War Time Cakes. pp. 16. *Todd Publishing Co.: London,* [1943.] 8°. **7946. df. 49.**

—— War-Time Kitchen. pp. 128. *Hutchinson & Co.: London,* [1943.] 8°. **7946. df. 26.**

BURKE (HENRY) *See* COLLIS (Robert) *Curate of the Chapel of Ease, Innisrush.* A Sermon, preached on occasion of the death of Mr. Henry Burke, *etc.* 1822. 8°. **4920. d. 11.**

BURKE (*Sir* HENRY FARNHAM) *K.C.V.O.* *See* MAIRE (Henry) afterwards LAWSON (*Sir* H.) Genealogical Collections illustrating the History of Roman Catholic Families of England . . . Edited by J. J. Howard . . . H. F. Burke, *etc.* 1887, *etc.* fol. **1861. d. 14.**

—— *See* THEYDON MOUNT. Theydon Mount: its Lords and Rectors . . . Edited by J. J. Howard and H. F. Burke, *etc.* [1894.] 4°. **9906. g. 4.**

—— A Descriptive Catalogue of Manorial Rolls belonging to Sir H. F. Burke . . . By E. Margaret Thompson. 2 pt. *London,* 1922, 23. 4°. [*Manorial Society's Publications.* no. 11, 12.] **Ac. 8115. e.**

—— The Historical Record of the Coronation of their Majesties King George the Fifth and Queen Mary, 1911. [With plates.] pp. 264. *McCorquodale & Co.: London,* [1911.] 4°. **C. 64. i. 7.**

—— The Historical Record of the Coronation of their Most Excellent Majesties King Edward VII. and Queen Alexandra solemnized in the Abbey Church of Westminster on Saturday the ninth day of August in the year of Our Lord 1902. [With plates by Byam Shaw.] pp. 86. lxviii. *Harrison & Sons: London,* 1904. fol. **K.T.C. 113. a.**
Privately printed.

—— History of the Family of Bonython of Bonython in the Duchy of Cornwall. pp. 34. *Harrison & Sons: London,* 1926. 8°. **9907. f. 34.**

—— Pedigree and Quarterings of De Trafford. Compiled from the records of the Heralds College, Record Office, probate registries, *etc.* [With a plate.] pp. 22. *Privately printed: London,* 1890. 4°. **09915. k. 18.**

—— Pedigree of the Family of Darwin. Compiled by H. F. Burke. [With plates, including portraits.] pp. 23. 1888. 8°. **09915. v. 17.**
One of an edition of sixty copies, privately printed.

BURKE (J. F.) *Translator.*

—— *See* MAGNONE (G.) [La Face W des Drus.] The West Face . . . Translated . . . by J. F. Burke. 1955. 8°. **7922. g. 8.**

BURKE (JACK)

—— The Natural Way to Better Golf . . . Illustrations by Norman Todhunter. pp. 151. *Constable: London,* 1955. 8°. **7922. c. 6.**

BURKE (Jackson)

—— Prelum to Albion. A history of the development of the hand press from Gutenberg to Morris. pp. 24. *Press of M. L. & J. Burke: San Francisco,* 1940. 8°. **7946.** e. **1.**

BURKE (James) *Barrister-at-Law.*

—— *See* Burke (*Right Hon.* Edmund) [*Speeches.—Two or more Speeches.*] The Speeches of the Right Hon. Edmund Burke, with memoir and historical introductions, by J. Burke. 1854. 8°. **1205.** f. **6.**

—— *See* Lingard (John) *D.D.* Abridgment of the History of England, by John Lingard D.D., with continuation from 1688 to the reign of Queen Victoria. Adapted for the use of schools by J. Burke. 1855. 8°. **9505.** aaa. **11.**

—— *See* Moore (Thomas) *Poet.* Travels of an Irish Gentleman in Search of a Religion . . . With a biographical and literary introduction by J. Burke. 1853. 8°. **4416.** g. **23.**

—— *See* Periodical Publications.—*York.* The Lamp; a weekly catholic journal of literature, *etc.* [vol. 8 edited by J. Burke and T. L. Bradley; new series by J. Burke and T. E. Bradley.] [1850, *etc.*] 4°. P.P. **262.** d.

—— An Explanatory Abridgment of the Land Law Act, 1881. pp. 32. *J. Duffy & Sons: Dublin,* 1881. 8°. **8146.** aaa. **4.** **(3.)**

—— Gems from Catholic Poets, with a biographical & literary introduction. [With illustrations.] pp. 128. *Catholic Publishing & Bookselling Co.: London,* 1859. 8°. **11603.** c. **5.**

—— The Life of Thomas Moore, *etc.* pp. xii. 240. *James Duffy: Dublin,* 1852. 12°. **10854.** a. **7.**

—— Centenary edition. pp. 256. *J. Duffy & Sons: Dublin,* [1879.] 16°. **10855.** aa. **6.**

—— The Practice of the Court for Relief of Insolvent Debtors in Ireland, in town and country cases. With an appendix, containing the Act 3rd & 4th Vic., ch. 107, complete, with a key, also abstracts of other acts, rules, forms and costs. To which are added, those portions of the Civil Bill Act of 1851, relating to insolvent debtors . . . Second edition. pp. ix. 257. *Hodges & Smith: Dublin,* 1852. 12°. **6503.** a. **19.**

—— 12 & 13 Victoriæ, Cap. 77. An Act further to facilitate the sale and transfer of incumbered estates in Ireland, with an introductory analysis, and a copious index. By J. Burke. pp. 108. *Hodges & Smith: Dublin,* 1849. 12°. **6503.** a. **17.**

—— Second edition, with the Commissioners' rules, forms, and directions. pp. 76. *Hodges & Smith: Dublin,* 1849. 12°. **6503.** a. **18.**

BURKE (James) *Biographer of William Burke.*

—— My Father in China. pp. 288. *Michael Joseph: London,* 1945. 8°. **4910.** b. **16.**

BURKE (James Henry) Days in the East. A poem. pp. iv. 115. *Smith, Elder & Co.: London,* 1842. 8°. **1466.** f. **3.**

—— India Salt. Scinde versus Cheshire, Calcutta, and Bombay. With an illustrative map. pp. 31. *Smith, Elder & Co.: London,* 1847. 8°. **1252.** c. **31.**

BURKE (James L.) *Engineer.*

—— *See* Wilson (Wilbur M.) and Burke (J. L.) Rate of Propagation of Fatigue Cracks in 12-Inch by ¾-Inch Steel Plates with Severe Geometrical Stress-Raisers, *etc.* 1947. 8°. [*University of Illinois. Engineering Experiment Station. Bulletin Series.* no. 371.] Ac. **2692.** u/4.

BURKE (James Lester) *See* Cash (Martin) The Adventures of Martin Cash . . . Edited by J. L. Burke. 1870. 8°. **10827.** bbb. **22.**

BURKE (James Saint George) *See* Robins (George) Report of the Trial of the Cause of George Robins versus Burke and Grubb, *etc.* 1845. 8°. **6583.** cc. **23.**

—— An Account of the Proceedings of the Great Western Railway Company, in the Session of 1835. [By J. St. George Burke.] pp. 24. [1835.] 8°. *See* Great Western Railway Company. **08235.** c. **60.** **(6.)**

—— The Advantages and Profits of the Southampton Railway Analysed. [By J. St. George Burke.] pp. 58. 1834. 8°. *See* London and Southampton Railway. **08235.** c. **60.** **(1.)**

—— Great Western Railway. Case of the promoters of the Bill [of 1835]. [By J. St. George Burke.] pp. 20. [1835?] 8°. *See* Great Western Railway Company. **08235.** c. **60.** **(5.)**

—— Speech of J. St. George Burke . . . in opening the case of the promoters of the Great Eastern Northern Junction Railway Bill . . . before the Select Committee of the House of Commons, May 4, 1864. pp. 72. *Harrison & Sons: London,* 1864. 8°. **08235.** c. **7.** **(4.)**

BURKE (James Wakefield)

—— The Big Rape. [A novel.] pp. 282. *Farrar, Straus & Young: New York,* [1952.] 8°. **Cup.800.a.8.**

BURKE (Joan Violet) Little Thoughts. In verse. pp. 12. *A. H. Stockwell: London,* [1934.] 8°. **011641.** ee. **105.**

BURKE (John) *Baron Burke of Castle Connell.* *See* Bourke.

BURKE (John) *Colonel.* *See* Bourke (John) *Earl of Clanricarde.*

BURKE (John) *Dean, University College, Dublin.*

—— The Ceremony of Consecration of a Bishop-Elect according to the Roman Pontifical. By the Rev. John Burke . . . [With the Latin text.] With translations from Latin into English by the Rev. John Ryan. pp. 44. 1939. 8°. *See* Liturgies.—*Latin Rite.—Pontificals.—* i. [*Abridgments and Extracts.*] **3407.** c. **106.**

BURKE (John) *Director of Moss Litter & Peat Industries, Ltd.* Moss Peat and its Products. pp. 32. *Moss Litter & Peat Industries Ltd.: London,* [1895.] 8°. **07031.** de. **1.** **(14.)**

BURKE (John) *Earl of Clanricarde.* *See* Bourke.

BURKE (John) *Esq.* *See* Butler (William) *Attorney.* Wm. Butler, Appel^nt^. John Burke Esq; and Frances his wife, Resp^nts^. et e con . . . The case of the said J. Burke, and Frances his wife, Respondents, *etc.* [1719.] fol. **19.** h. **1.** **(123.)**

—— *See* Butler (William) *Attorney.* William Butler, Appellant. John Bourke, and Frances his Wife, Respondents. The Appellant's case. [1719.] fol. **19.** h. **1.** **(122.)**

BURKE (John) *Genealogist.* *See* Periodical Publications.—*London.* The Patrician. Edited by J. Burke [May 1846—March 1848]. 1846, *etc.* 8°. P.P. **3868.**

—— A Genealogical and Heraldic History of the Commoners of Great Britain and Ireland, enjoying territorial possessions or high official rank, *etc.* 4 vol. *Henry Colburn: London,* 1833–38. 8°. **2409.** e. **1.**

—— [A reissue.] ms. notes. *London,* 1836, 35–38. 8°. **9906.** d. **5.**

Vol. 1 *only is a reissue; vol.* 2, 4 *are duplicates and vol.* 3 *is another issue of the corresponding volumes in the edition of* 1833–38.

BURKE (JOHN) *Genealogist.*

—— [A reissue.] A Genealogical and Heraldic History of the Landed Gentry; or, Commons of Great Britain and Ireland . . . Small paper edition. *London,* 1837, 38. 8°. **9907.** c. **10.**

Vol. 1–3 *are reissues, vol.* 4 *is a duplicate, of the corresponding volumes in the edition of* 1833–38. *The edition of* 1846, 49 *is entered under* BURKE *(John) and* BURKE *(Sir John B.). Subsequent editions are entered under* BURKE *(Sir John B.).*

—— *See* ORMEROD (George) Index to the Pedigree [i.e. Pedigrees] in Burke's Commoners . . . prepared . . . in 1840. 1907. 8°. **9902.** ccc. **31.**

—— A General and Heraldic Dictionary of the Peerage and Baronetage of the United Kingdom. [First, fourth, fifth editions.] By J. Burke. 1826–37. 8°.
[Continued as:]
A Genealogical and Heraldic Dictionary of the Peerage and Baronetage of the British Empire. (Ninth, tenth edition. By J. Burke and J. B. Burke; Twelfth—sixty-eighth edition by J. B. Burke; Sixty-ninth—95th edition by Sir B. Burke and A. P. Burke; 96th—98th edition by Sir B. Burke; 99th [*etc.*] edition. Editor, L. G. Pine.) 1839– . 8°. *See* PERIODICAL PUBLICATIONS.—*London.* P.P. **2505.** ac. & **2098.** d.

—— [Another copy of the first edition.] MS. NOTES [by F. Broderip]. **9905.** b. **36.**

—— A General and Heraldic Dictionary of the Peerages of England, Ireland, and Scotland, extinct, dormant, and in abeyance . . . England. pp. viii. 631. *H. Colburn & R. Bentley: London,* 1831. 8°. **9902.** cc. **24.**
No more of this edition published.

—— [Another edition.] A Genealogical and Heraldic Dictionary of the Peerages of England, Ireland, and Scotland, extinct, dormant, and in abeyance . . . By J. Burke . . . and John Bernard Burke [i.e. written by J. Burke, and edited by Sir J. B. Burke] . . . Second edition. pp. vi. 795. *Henry Colburn: London,* 1840. 8°. **9917.** ccc. **42.**
With an additional titlepage, lithographed.

—— Third edition. pp. viii. 795. *Henry Colburn: London,* 1846. 8°. **1328.** c. **26.**
A later edition, entitled " A Genealogical History of the Dormant, Abeyant, Forfeited and Extinct Peerages of the British Empire," is entered under BURKE *(Sir John B.).*

—— The Official Kalendar for 1831 . . . By J. Burke. 1831. 8°. *See* PERIODICAL PUBLICATIONS.—*London.* **808.** k. **10.**

—— The Portrait Gallery of Distinguished Females, including beauties of the Courts of George IV. and William IV. With memoirs by J. Burke, *etc.* 2 vol. *Edward Bull: London,* 1833. 4°. **2409.** d. **1.**

BURKE (JOHN) *Genealogist,* and **BURKE** (*Sir* JOHN BERNARD)

—— Encyclopædia of Heraldry, *etc. See* infra: A General Armory of England, Scotland, and Ireland.

—— A Genealogical and Heraldic Dictionary of the Landed Gentry of Great Britain and Ireland, *etc.* [With a " supplementary volume."] 3 vol. *Henry Colburn: London,* 1846, 49 [1843–49]. 8°. **2409.** f. **1.**
Published in parts. Vol. 1 *has an additional titlepage, bearing the date* 1843. *The supplementary volume has an additional titlepage, bearing the date* 1848. *Previous editions are entered under* BURKE *(John) Genealogist.*

BURKE (JOHN) *Genealogist,* and **BURKE** (*Sir* JOHN BERNARD)

—— [Another copy.] MS. NOTES [by J. G. Nichols]. **9905.** e. **30.**
Interleaved and bound in 8 *vol. Imperfect; wanting the titlepages issued on the completion of vol.* 1 *and* 3, *and dated respectively* 1846 *and* 1849.

—— [A reissue.] *London,* 1846–49. 8°. **9907.** cc. **15.**
Subsequent editions are entered under BURKE *(Sir John B.).*

—— A Genealogical and Heraldic Dictionary of the Landed Gentry of Great Britain & Ireland . . . Vol. III. Supplement, corrigenda, and general index. 2 pt. 1850, 53 [1847–52]. *See* BURKE (*Sir* John B.) A Genealogical and Heraldic Dictionary of the Landed Gentry of Great Britain & Ireland, *etc.* 1850, *etc.* 8°. **2409.** f. **2.**

—— A Genealogical and Heraldic History of the Extinct and Dormant Baronetcies of England. pp. 599. *Scott, Webster & Geary: London,* 1838. 8°. **9907.** aa. **4.**

—— Second edition. pp. 637. *Scott, Webster & Geary: London,* 1841. 8°. **1328.** e. **27.**

—— [A reissue.] *J. R. Smith: London,* 1844. 8° **2098.d.**

—— [Another copy.] **09917.** b. **16.**

—— A General Armory of England, Scotland, and Ireland. [With a " correcting sheet " and supplement.] *Edward Churton: London,* 1842. 8°. **605.** f. **11.**

—— [Another edition.] Encyclopædia of Heraldry, or General Armory of England, Scotland, and Ireland . . . Third edition, with a supplement. MS. NOTES [by J. G. Nichols]. *H. G. Bohn: London,* 1844. 8°. L.R. **33.** b. **11.**
Interleaved and bound in 3 *vol.*

—— [Another edition.] Encyclopædia of Heraldry, or General Armory of England, Scotland, and Ireland . . . Third edition, with a supplement. *H. G. Bohn: London,* 1847. 8°. **9902.** g. **2.**
Later editions, entitled " The General Armory of England, Scotland, Ireland, and Wales " are entered under BURKE *(Sir John B.).*

—— Heraldic Illustrations, comprising the armorial bearings of the principal families of the Empire; with pedigrees and annotations. pl. CXLVI. *E. Churton: London,* 1845. 8°. **09915.** d. **17.**

—— Heraldic Illustrations, with annotations. By J. B. Burke [or rather, a reissue of the work by J. Burke and Sir J. B. Burke]. 3 vol. 1853. 8°. *See* BURKE (*Sir* John B.) **9918.n.3.**

—— *See* BURKE (*Sir* John B.) Illuminated Supplement to the Heraldic Illustrations. With annotations. 1851. 8°. **1328.** h. **8.**

—— —— 1856. 8°. **9918.n.3.**

—— The Knightage of Great Britain and Ireland. [By J. Burke and Sir J. B. Burke.] pp. xv. 221. 1841. 12°. *See* ENGLAND.—*Knights.* **607.** c. **18.**

—— The Royal Families of England, Scotland, and Wales, with their descendants, sovereigns and subjects. 2 vol. *E. Churton: London,* 1847, 51. 8°. **9915.** c. **22.**
Each volume has an additional titlepage dated respectively 1848 *and* 1849. *A later abridgment is entered under* BURKE *(Sir John B.).*

BURKE (JOHN) *Genealogist,* and **BURKE** (*Sir* JOHN BERNARD)

—— *See* FANE (A. G. C.) A Complete Index to the Family Names in Burke's Royal Families of England, Scotland and Wales, *etc.* 1932. 8°. **09917**. de. **12**.

BURKE (JOHN) *Historical Writer.*

—— Chronological Records of Great Britain, from the Demise of King George II. to the Coronation of His Majesty King George IV. 1825. *See* HUME (David) *the Historian.* [*History of England.*] The History of England, *etc.* vol. 6. 1825, *etc.* 8°. **09504**. h. **31**.

BURKE (JOHN) *M.D.* *See* TISSOT (S. A. A. D.) A Letter . . . to Dr. Zimmerman on the Morbus Niger . . . Translated . . . by J. Burke. 1776. 8°. **T. 312. (4.)**

BURKE (JOHN) *Novelist.* Carrigaholt: a tale of eighty years ago. pp. 77. *Hodges, Figgis & Co.: Dublin,* 1885 [1884]. 8°. **12623**. h. **15**.

BURKE (JOHN) *of Gray's Inn.* Observations on Precedents and Authorities in Law. pp. viii. 26. 1836. *See* PALMER (John) *Solicitor.* Tracts on Law, *etc.* 1836, *etc.* 8°. **713**. d. **21**.

BURKE (JOHN) *Poet.* *See* RUBEK (Sennoia) *pseud.* [i.e J. Burke.]

BURKE (JOHN) *Roman Catholic Priest.* *See* GORDON (James E.) Substance of the Controversy between Mr. Gordon . . . and the Rev. J. Burke . . . on the Christian rule of faith, and the idolatrous worship of the Church of Rome, *etc.* 1829. 8°. **3939**. e. **38**.

BURKE (*Sir* JOHN) *Bart.*

—— Indenture of Release from Sir John Burke Bart. to Arthur Nugent Junr. Esquire, *etc.* [Dated 1836, with letter attached, dated 1835. Transcribed by John H. Harvey.] ff. 4. 1941. 4°. **9915**. t. **24**.
Reproduced from typewriting.

BURKE (JOHN BENJAMIN BUTLER) The Emergence of Life. Being a treatise on mathematical philosophy and symbolic logic by which a new theory of space and time is evolved. pp. viii. 396. *Oxford University Press: London,* 1931. 8°. **8710**. aaa. **5**.

—— The Mystery of Life. pp. 159. *E. Mathews & Marrot: London,* 1931. 8°. [*Library of New Ideas.* no. 5.] **012209.bb.6/5.**

—— The Origin of Life. Its physical basis and definition. pp. xiv. 351. *Chapman & Hall: London,* 1906. 8°. **7405**. h. **1**.

BURKE (*Sir* JOHN BERNARD) *See* BATTLE ABBEY. The Roll of Battle Abbey, annotated. By J. B. Burke. 1848. 16°. **1328**. a. **13**.

—— *See* BURKE (John) *Genealogist.* A Genealogical and Heraldic Dictionary of the Peerages of England, Ireland, & Scotland, extinct, dormant, & in abeyance . . . By J. Burke . . . and J. B. Burke [i.e. written by J. Burke, and edited by Sir J. B. Burke], *etc.* 1840. 8°. **9917**. ccc. **42**.

—— —— 1846. 8°. **1328**. c. **26**.

—— *See* BURKE (John) *Genealogist,* and BURKE (*Sir* J. B.) A Genealogical and Heraldic Dictionary of the Landed Gentry of Great Britain and Ireland, *etc.* 1846, *etc.* 8°. **2409**. f. **1**.

BURKE (*Sir* JOHN BERNARD)

—— *See* BURKE (John) *Genealogist,* and BURKE (*Sir* J. B.) A Genealogical and Heraldic History of the Extinct and Dormant Baronetcies of England. 1838. 8°. **9907**. aa. **4**.

—— —— 1841. 8°. **1328**. e. **27**.

—— *See* BURKE (John) *Genealogist,* and BURKE (*Sir* J. B.) A General Armory of England, Scotland, and Ireland. 1842. 8°. **605**. f. **11**.

—— —— 1844. 8°. L.R. **33**. b. **11**.

—— *See* BURKE (John) *Genealogist,* and BURKE (*Sir* J. B.) Heraldic Illustrations, comprising the armorial bearings of the principal families of the Empire, *etc.* 1845. 8°. **09915**. d. **17**.

—— *See* BURKE (John) *Genealogist,* and BURKE (*Sir* J. B.) The Royal Families of England, Scotland, and Wales, *etc.* 1847, *etc.* 8°. **9915**. c. **22**.

—— *See* ENGLAND.—*Knights.* The Knightage of Great Britain and Ireland. [By J. Burke and Sir J. B. Burke.] 1841. 12°. **607**. c. **18**.

—— *See* FISHER (Denis O. C.) and BURKE (*Sir* J. B.) The Pedigree and Arms of the Glovers, of Mount Glover, *etc.* 1858. 8°. **9916**. aaa. **6**. (**1**.)

—— *See* HOWARD (George W. F.) *Earl of Carlisle.* Lines on a Withered Tree in the Viceregal Grounds . . . Imitated in Latin, Greek, French, German, Italian, Spanish and Portuguese. [Edited by Sir J. B. Burke.] 1870. 8°. **11647**. aa. **35**.

—— *See* PERIODICAL PUBLICATIONS.—*London.* A General and Heraldic Dictionary of the Peerage and Baronetage of the United Kingdom (A Genealogical and Heraldic Dictionary of the Peerage and Baronetage of the British Empire), *etc.* (Ninth, tenth edition by J. Burke and J. B. Burke; Twelfth—sixty-eighth edition by J. B. Burke; Sixty-ninth—95th edition by Sir B. Burke and A. P. Burke; 96th—98th edition by Sir B. Burke.) 1826, *etc.* 8°. P.P. **2505**. ac. & **2098**. d.

—— *See* PERIODICAL PUBLICATIONS.—*London.* The Patrician, *etc.* [April–Oct. 1848 edited by J. B. Burke.] 1846, *etc.* 8°. P.P. **3868**.

—— *See* PERIODICAL PUBLICATIONS.—*London.* The St. James's Magazine, and Heraldic and Historical Register. Edited by J. B. Burke. 1850. 8°. P.P. **3869**.

—— Anecdotes of the Aristocracy, and Episodes in Ancestral Story. 2 vol. *Henry Colburn: London,* 1849. 8°. **1327**. b. **29**.

—— Second series, *etc.* 2 vol. *E. Churton: London,* 1850. 12°. **1327**. b. **30**.

—— The Romance of the Aristocracy: or, Anecdotes and records of distinguished families . . . New and revised edition, *etc.* [Selections from "Anecdotes of the Aristocracy."] 3 vol. *For Henry Colburn by his successors Hurst & Blackett: London,* 1855. 8°. **2400**. b. **14**.

—— [Another copy.] **9903**. bb. **31**.

—— Authorized Arms of the Gentry of Great Britain and Ireland. *See* infra: A Selection of Arms authorized by the Laws of Heraldry.

—— The Book of Orders of Knighthood and Decorations of Honour of all nations, comprising an historical account of each order . . . With lists of the knights and companions of each British order. Embellished with facsimile coloured illustrations of the insignia of the various orders. pp. vii. 411. pl. 100. *Hurst & Blackett: London*, 1858. 8°. **09917.df.28.**

—— The Book of Precedence. The peers, baronets, and knights, and the companions of the several orders of knighthood, placed according to their relative rank, *etc.* pp. 88. *Harrison: London*, 1881. 8°. **9905. f. 15.**

—— Burke's Distinguished Families of America, *etc.* *See* infra: Burke's Genealogical and Heraldic History of the Landed Gentry.

—— Family Romance; or, Episodes in the domestic annals of the aristocracy, *etc.* 2 vol. *Hurst & Blackett: London*, 1853. 12°. **1328. e. 28.**

—— Third edition. pp. vi. 341. *Hurst & Blackett: London*, 1860. 8°. **2400. a. 6.**

—— A Genealogical and Heraldic Dictionary of the Landed Gentry of Great Britain & Ireland, for 1850, *etc.* (vol. 3. Supplement, Corrigenda, and General Index. By John Burke and J. B. Burke.) 3 vol. *Henry Colburn: London*, 1850–53 [1847–52]. 8°. **2409. f. 2.**
Published in parts. Previous editions are entered under BURKE *(John) Genealogist, and* BURKE *(Sir J. B.).*

—— [Another edition.] [With a portrait.] pp. 1404. *Harrison: London*, 1858 [1855–58]. 8°. **2409. f. 3.**
Published in parts. With an additional titlepage bearing the imprint "Published for Henry Colburn, by his successors, Hurst and Blackett, 1855."

—— Fourth edition. [With an "Essay on the Position of the British Gentry" by John Hamilton Gray.] 2 pt. pp. xviii. 1759. *Harrison: London*, 1862, 63. 8°. **2409. f. 4.**

—— Fourth edition. Revised and enlarged. pp. xviii. 1747. *Harrison: London*, 1868. 8°. **2409. f. 5.**

—— Fifth edition. 2 vol. pp. iii. 1600. *Harrison: London*, 1871. 8°. **2409. f. 6.**

—— [Another copy.] **9916. f. 1.**
Imperfect; wanting pp. 699, 700.

—— Fifth edition, with supplement and addenda. 2 vol. pp. iii. 1600. ii. 100. *Harrison: London*, 1875. 8°. **2409. f. 7.**

—— Sixth edition. 2 vol. pp. 1836. *Harrison: London*, 1879. 8°. **2409. g. 1.**

—— [Another copy.] **9917. g. 3.**

—— Sixth edition, with supplement. 2 vol. pp. 1894. *Harrison: London*, 1882. 8°. **2409. g. 2.**

—— Seventh edition. 2 vol. pp. 2078. *Harrison & Sons: London*, 1886. 8°. **2409. g. 3.**

—— [Another copy.] **9917. f. 5.**
Imperfect; wanting pp. 1909–14.

—— Eighth edition. [Edited by Ashworth P. Burke.] 2 vol. pp. xxviii. 2308. *Harrison: London*, 1894. 8°. **2409. g. 4.**

—— Ninth edition. [Edited by Ashworth P. Burke.] 2 vol. pp. xiv. 1665. 495. *Harrison & Sons: London*, 1898. 8°. **2409. g. 5.**

—— [Another edition.] A Genealogical and Heraldic History of the Landed Gentry of Great Britain . . . Edited by Ashworth P. Burke . . . Tenth edition. pp. viii. 1777. *Harrison & Sons: London*, 1900. 8°. **2409. g. 6.**
That part of the work relating to Ireland was omitted from this and subsequent editions and published separately as "A Genealogical and Heraldic History of the Landed Gentry of Ireland."

—— Eleventh edition. [Edited by Ashworth P. Burke.] pp. x. 1882. *Harrison & Sons: London*, 1906. 8°. **2409. g. 7.**

—— [Another copy.] **9916. f. 2.**
Imperfect; wanting pp. 1737, 38.

—— Twelfth edition. Revised by A. C. Fox-Davies. pp. viii. 2102. *Harrison & Sons: London*, 1914. 8°. **2409. f. 8.**

—— [Another copy.] **9907. h. 3.**

—— [Another edition.] Edited by A. Winton Thorpe. Thirteenth edition. pp. ii. 1963. *Burke Publishing Co.: London*, 1921. 8°. **9907. h. 12.**

—— [Another copy.] **9907. cc. 4.**

—— Fourteenth edition. pp. x. 1963. *Burke Publishing Co.: London*, 1925. 8°. **9907. pp. 16.**

—— [Another edition.] Burke's Genealogical and Heraldic History of the Landed Gentry . . . Centenary, 15th, edition. Edited by H. Pirie-Gordon. [With Irish Supplement.] pp. lxxiv. 2756. *Shaw Publishing Co.: London*, 1937 [1936]. 8°. **9918.ee.7.**

—— Burke's Genealogical and Heraldic History of the Landed Gentry . . . Edited by L. G. Pine . . . Seventeenth edition. pp. clxxviii. 2840. pl. LIII. *Burke's Peerage: London*, 1952. 8°. **2098.d.**

—— [Another copy.] Burke's Genealogical and Heraldic History of the Landed Gentry . . . Seventeenth edition. *London*, 1952. 8°. **9904. w. 15.**

—— Burke's Genealogical and Heraldic History of the Landed Gentry, including American families with British ancestry, *etc.* pp. xviii. 3058. pl. LIV. *Burke's Peerage: London*, 1939. 8°. **9915. t. 15.**

—— Burke's Distinguished Families of America. *etc.* *London*, [1947.] 8°. **2101.e.**
A reissue of the American section of "Burke's Genealogical and Heraldic History of the Landed Gentry."

—— A Genealogical and Heraldic History of the Landed Gentry of Ireland. By Sir Bernard Burke . . . Edited by his son (A. P. Burke). 9th edition. With supplement. pp. liv. 495. *Harrison & Sons: London*, 1899. 8°. **2409. d. 2.**
A reissue of that part of the ninth edition of "A Genealogical and Heraldic History of the Landed Gentry of Great Britain & Ireland" relating to Ireland, with a supplement.

—— [Another edition.] Edited by Ashworth P. Burke . . . Tenth edition. pp. 673. *Harrison & Sons: London*, 1904 [1903]. 8°. **2409. d. 3.**

—— New edition. Revised by A. C. Fox-Davies. pp. iv. 786. *Harrison & Sons: London*, 1912. 8° **9902.v.5.**

—— [Another copy.] **9906. v. 13.**

—— A Genealogical and Heraldic History of the Colonial Gentry, *etc.* (Vol. 2 edited by Ashworth P. Burke.) 2 vol. pp. xxiii. iii. 876. *Harrison & Sons: London,* 1891, 95. 8°. **2098.a.**

—— [Another copy.] A Genealogical and Heraldic History of the Colonial Gentry, *etc. London,* 1891, 95. 8°. 9918. c. 4.

—— A Genealogical and Heraldic History of the Landed Gentry of Great Britain. *See* supra: A Genealogical and Heraldic Dictionary of the Landed Gentry of Great Britain & Ireland

—— A Genealogical and Heraldic History of the Landed Gentry of Ireland. *See* supra: A Genealogical and Heraldic Dictionary of the Landed Gentry of Great Britain & Ireland.

—— A Genealogical History of the Dormant, Abeyant, Forfeited, and Extinct Peerages of the British Empire . . . New edition [of " A General and Heraldic Dictionary of the Peerages . . . extinct, dormant, and in abeyance " by John Burke]. pp. x. 636. *Harrison: London,* 1866. 8°. 9915. pp. 34.

—— [Another copy.] **9918.f.15.**

—— A Genealogical History of the Dormant, Abeyant, Forfeited and Extinct Peerages of the British Empire . . . New edition [of " A General and Heraldic Dictionary of the Peerages . . . extinct, dormant, and in abeyance " by John Burke]. pp. ix. 642. *Harrison: London,* 1883. 8°. **2098.d.**

—— [Another copy.] **9906. dd. 19.**

—— A Genealogical History of the House of Gwysaney. pp. 73. *Privately printed: London,* 1847. fol. **9902. l. 13.**

—— The General Armory of England, Scotland, Ireland, and Wales; comprising a registry of armorial bearings from the earliest to the present time. [An enlarged edition of " A General Armory of England, Scotland, and Ireland," by John Burke and Sir J. B. Burke.] pp. lxxii. 1185. *Harrison: London,* 1878. 8°. **9917. g. 4.**

—— [Another edition.] With a supplement. pp. lxxix. 1185. *Harrison: London,* 1883. 8°. **09915. t. 3.**

—— [Another issue.] *London,* 1884. 8°. **2102.d.**

—— [Another copy.] **9917. f. 2.**

—— Heraldic Illustrations, with annotations. By J. B. Burke [or rather, a reissue of the work by J. Burke and Sir J. B. Burke]. 3 vol. *Hurst & Blackett: London,* 1853. 8°. **9918.n.3.**

—— The Historic Lands of England. [With plates.] pp. xxxii. 170. *E. Churton: London,* 1848. 8°. **1303. m. 12.**

—— Illuminated Supplement to the Heraldic Illustrations [of John Burke and Sir J. B. Burke] with annotations. pl. XVI. *E. Churton: London,* 1851. 8°. **1328. h. 8.**

—— [Another edition.] Illuminated Heraldic Illustrations, with annotations. pl. XVI. *Hurst & Blackett: London,* 1856. 8°. **9918.n.3.**
Bound up with vol. 3 *of " Heraldic Illustrations."*

—— A Pedigree of O'Sullivan Beare, *etc. See* AMORY (Thomas C.) Materials for a History of the Family of John Sullivan, *etc.* 1893. 8°. **9902. dd. 9.**

—— The Rise of Great Families, other essays, and stories pp. iv. 371. *Longmans & Co.: London,* 1873 [1872]. 8°. **2400. b. 13**

—— Reminiscences, Ancestral, Anecdotal and Historic . . A remodelled and revised edition of "The Rise of Grea Families and other essays." pp. iv. 380. *Longmans & Co. London,* [1882.] 8°. **2400. b. 2**

—— The Romance of the Aristocracy, *etc. See* supra: Anec dotes of the Aristocracy, *etc.*

—— Royal Descents and Pedigrees of Founders' Kin. 2 pt. *Harrison: London,* 1858 [1855, 58]. **9917. g. 21**
With an additional titlepage bearing the imprint "Hurst & Blackett: London, 1855."

—— The Royal Families of England, Scotland, and Wales with pedigrees of royal descents in illustration. [A abridgment of the work of the same title by John Burk and Sir J. B. Burke.] *Harrison: London,* 1876. 8°. **2400. g. 1**

—— The Royal Families of England, Scotland, and Wale . . . Pedigree, no. 16 continued down to William Ray mond Croft Murray, *etc.* [1904.] *s. sh.* fol. **1860. d. 1. (106.**

—— A Selection of Arms authorized by the Laws of Heraldry With annotations by Sir B. Burke. pp. iv. 244. pl. XXXIV *Harrison: London,* 1860 [1858–60]. 8°. **9915. aa. 3**
Published in parts. The title on the wrappers read "Authorized Arms of the Gentry of Great Britain an Ireland."

—— The Sovereigns of England from the Norman Conquest in rhyme. [The preface signed: J. B. B. i.e. Sir J. B Burke.] pp. 19. [1876.] 8°. *See* B., J. B. **11652. df. 2**

—— Vicissitudes of Families, and other essays. pp. vi. 437. *Longman & Co.: London,* 1859. 8°. **9917. d. 19**

—— Third edition. pp. vi. 437. *Longman & Co.: London* 1859. 8°. **9917. d. 20**

—— Fifth edition. pp. vi. 437. *Longman & Co.: London* 1861. 8°. **9917. d. 21**

—— A Second Series of Vicissitudes of Families. pp. 438. *Longman & Co.: London,* 1860. 8°. **9917. d. 35**

—— Second edition. pp. iv. 436. *Longman & Co.: London* 1861. 8°. **9917. d. 22**

—— Third series. pp. xix. 444. *Longman & Co.: London* 1863. 8°. **9917. d. 36**

—— Remodelled edition [of ser. 1–3], *etc.* 2 vol. *Longmans & Co.: London,* 1869. 8°. **9917. ccc. 40**

—— New edition, *etc.* 2 vol. *Longmans & Co.: London* 1883. 8°. **2400. b. 3**

—— A Visitation of the Seats and Arms of the Noblemen an Gentlemen of Great Britain. [With plates.] 2 vol. *Colburn & Co.: London,* 1852, 53. 8°. **2100.b.**
Vol. 2 *was published by Hurst & Blackett.*

—— [Another copy.] **9904. p. 1**

—— [Another copy.] **9903. p. 9**

—— Second series. [With plates.] 2 vol. *Hurst & Blackett: London,* 1854, 55. 8°. **2100.b.**

—— [Another copy.] **9904. p. 2**

—— [Another copy.] **9903. p. 10**

BURKE (JOHN BUTLER) *See* BURKE (John Benjamin B.)

BURKE (JOHN FLORENCE) Outlines of the Industrial History of Ireland. pp. vii. x. 282. *Dublin*, [1928.] 8°. [*Browne & Nolan's Intermediate School Series.*] **8230.a.67.**

—— Outlines of the Industrial History of Ireland . . . Revised with chapter VII added by Michael J. Cryan . . . and Michael J. Kennedy. pp. xx. 379. *Browne & Nolan*: [*Dublin*, 1940.] 8°. **8222. aa. 13.**

BURKE (JOHN FREDERICK)

—— Another Chorus. [A novel.] pp. 254. *Werner Laurie: London*, 1949. 8°. **NN. 40029.**

—— Chastity House. pp. 221. *Werner Laurie: London*, [1952.] 8°. **NNN. 3498.**

—— The Outward Walls. pp. 231. *Werner Laurie: London*, [1952.] 8°. **NNN. 2501.**

BURKE (JOHN FREDERICK) *See* also BURKE (Jonathan) *pseud.* [i.e. J. F. Burke.]

—— Swift Summer. pp. 228. *Werner Laurie: London*, [1949.] 8°. **NN. 39352.**

—— These Haunted Streets. The sentimental education of Michael Peregrine. pp. 223. *Werner Laurie: London*, [1950.] 8°. **NNN. 1355.**

BURKE (JOHN FRENCH) British Husbandry; exhibiting the farming practice in various parts of the United Kingdom. [By J. F. Burke.] 3 vol. 1834–40. 8°. *See* ENGLAND. [*Appendix.—Agriculture.*] **737. e. 1–3.**

—— [A reissue of "British Husbandry," vol. 3.] Husbandry: volume the third, *etc.* [By J. F. Burke.] [c. 1850.] 8°. [*Library of Useful Knowledge. Farmers' Series.*] *See* ENGLAND. [*Appendix.—Agriculture.*] **07295. pp. 42. (2.)**

—— Darstellung der Landwirtschaft Grossbritanniens in ihrem gegenwärtigen Zustande. Nach dem Englischen bearbeitet von Dr. A. G. Schweitzer. [A translation of "British Husbandry" by J. F. Burke.] 2 Bd. 1839, 40. 8°. *See* ENGLAND. [*Appendix.—Agriculture.*] **7076. bb. 1.**

—— The Dispensing Chemist's and Medical Pupil's Assistant; containing Latin directions, with their translations, for every species of medical prescription, *etc.* pp. viii. 112. *Robert Baldwin: London*, 1844. 8°. **777. b. 43.**

—— Farming for Ladies; or, a Guide to the poultry-yard, the dairy and piggery. By the author of "British Husbandry" [i.e. J. F. Burke]. pp. xviii. 511. 1844. 8°. *See* FARMING. **1252. b. 39.**

—— On Land-Drainage, Subsoil-Ploughing, and Irrigation. By the author of "British Husbandry" [i.e. J. F. Burke]. pp. 46. 1841. 8°. *See* LAND-DRAINAGE. **727. e. 19. (2.)**

—— Remarks on the Treatment of Fractures of the Lower Extremities without the aid of Splints. With cases. pp. 39. *S. Highley: London*, 1837. 8°. **T. 2398. (5.)**

BURKE (JOHN J.) *M.R.S.A.I.*

—— The Last Resting Places of Notable Irishmen. pp. 32. *A. H. Stockwell: London*, [1940.] 8°. **10858. a. 26.**

BURKE (JOHN J.) *of Watertown Arsenal Laboratory.*

—— *See* ABKOWITZ (Stanley) Titanium in Industry . . . [By] S. Abkowitz . . . J. J. Burke, *etc.* [1955.] 8°. **7112. bb. 11.**

BURKE (JOHN JAMES) *A.F.I.A., A.I.I.S.*

—— Business Principles and Practice. Secondary commercial course . . . Third edition. pp. 251. *Angus & Robertson: Sydney, London*, 1947. 8°. **8234. ee. 78.**

—— Company Law for Accountancy Students. pp. x. 252. *Angus & Robertson: Sydney, London*, 1947. 8°. **6378. b. 18.**

BURKE (JOHN JAMES) *Rev.*

—— *See* ANGER (J.) [Le Corps mystique.] The Doctrine of the Mystical Body of Christ . . . Translated . . . by . . . J. J. Burke, *etc.* 1932. 8°. **4223. cc. 22.**

—— *See* CLAUDEL (P. L. C. M.) [*Single Works.*] [Le Chemin de la Croix.] "Stations of the Cross." [The translation by J. J. Burke.] 1927. 8°. [*Ecclesiastical Review.* vol. 77.] **P.P. 875.**

—— *See* DUPERRAY (J.) Christ in the Christian Life . . . From the French . . . by J. J. Burke. 1927. 8°. **03265. e. 84**

—— The Armor of Light. Short sermons on the Epistles for every Sunday in the year. pp. ix. 224. *B. Herder Book Co.: St. Louis & London*, 1925. 8°. **4473. dd. 8.**

BURKE (JOHN M.) called ARIZONA JOHN. "Buffalo Bill" from Prairie to Palace. An authentic history of the Wild West. With sketches . . . and anecdotes of "Buffalo Bill" (W. F. Cody), *etc.* [With portraits.] pp. 275. *Rand, McNally & Co.: Chicago & New York*, 1893. 8°. **10883. bb. 30.**

—— Buffalo Bill's Wild West. America's national entertainment. [An illustrated pamphlet.] [1887.] 8°. **10408. g. 25.**

BURKE (JOHN MACDONALD)

—— *See* ENCYCLOPAEDIAS. The Encyclopædia of Forms and Precedents, *etc.* (Supplement. Edited by J. M. Lightwood and J. Burke.) 1925, *etc.* 8°. **6126.p.1a.**

—— *See* ENGLAND. [*Laws & Statutes.*—II.] The Complete Statutes of England, *etc.* (Revising editors: J. Burke, G. E. Hart.) 1929, *etc.* 8°. **W.P. 14725.**

—— *See* ENGLAND. [*Laws and Statutes.*—II.] Current Law Consolidation . . . General editor: J. Burke, *etc.* 1952, *etc.* 8°. **W.P. A. 620.**

—— *See* ENGLAND. [*Laws and Statutes.*—IV. *Emergency Legislation.*] Loose-Leaf War Legislation. Edited by J. Burke. 1939, *etc.* 8°. **6429. m. 2.**

—— *See* ENGLAND. [*Laws and Statutes.*—IV. *Income Tax.*] "Current Law" Income Tax Acts Service . . . General editor J. Burke, *etc.* 1952. 8°. **6429. g. 32.**

—— *See* LEWIN (Thomas) *Barrister-at-Law.* Lewin's Practical Treatise on the Law of Trusts, *etc.* (Third, Fourth, Cumulative Supplement by J. Burke.) 1939, *etc.* 8° **6355. t. 15. c.**

—— *See* STROUD (Frederick) The Judicial Dictionary, *etc.* (Supplement, 1930–1946. By J. Burke.) 1903, *etc.* 8°. **6192.d.8.& 2016.f.**

BURKE (JOHN MACDONALD)

—— *See* STROUD (Frederick) Stroud's Judicial Dictionary of Words and Phrases . . . General editor: J. Burke, *etc.* 1952, *etc.* 8°. **2016.f.**

—— Courts Emergency Powers. pp. iv. 148. *Sweet & Maxwell: London,* 1943. 8°. **6192.** b. **3.**

—— Courts Emergency Powers . . . Second edition. pp. iv. 121. *Sweet & Maxwell: London,* 1943. 8°. **6147.** b. **13.**

—— Current Law. Index to the law for 1946. pp. 60. *Sweet & Maxwell; Stevens & Sons: London,* [1947.] 8°. **6429.** aa. **28.**

—— Loose-Leaf Encyclopædia of War Damage and Compensation. Edited by J. Burke. [With supplements.] [1941– .] 8°. *See* ENGLAND. [*Laws and Statutes.—* IV. *War Damage.*] W.P. **12182.**

—— Planning and Compensation Reports. Editor: John Burke, *etc.* *Sweet & Maxwell: London,* 1950– . 8°. W.P. **13010.**

—— Rights & Powers of the Home Guard, *etc.* pp. 16. *Hamish Hamilton: London,* 1940. 8°. **6875.** d. **44.**

—— War Damage Guide. pp. x. 148. *Sweet & Maxwell: London,* 1943. 8°. **6307.** aa. **22.**

BURKE (JOHN MACDONALD) and **ALLSOP** (PETER HENRY BRUCE)

—— The Common Law Library . . . General editors: J. Burke and P. Allsop. *Sweet & Maxwell: London,* 1955– . 8°. W.P. D. **89.**

BURKE (JOHN WILLIAM) Life of Robert Emmett . . . with his speeches, &c. Also, an appendix, containing valuable portions of Irish history . . . Third edition. pp. viii. 300. *Courtenay & Wienges: Charleston,* 1852. 12°. **10815.** a. **49.**

BURKE (JONATHAN) *pseud.* [i.e. JOHN FREDERICK BURKE.] *See* also BURKE (John F.)

—— Alien Landscapes. Science fiction stories. pp. 160. *Museum Press: London,* 1955. 8°. NNN. **6605.** *One of the "Books of the Future."*

—— Pattern of Shadows. [A novel.] pp. 128. *Museum Press: London,* 1954. 8°. NNN. **5811.** *One of the "Books of the Future."*

BURKE (JOSEPH) *M.D.*

—— *See* SCHMIDT (Rudolf) *Professor of Medicine in the University of Innsbruck.* [Interne Klinik der bösartigen Neubildungen der Bauchorgane.] Diagnosis of the Malignant Tumors of the Abdominal Viscera . . . English version by J. Burke. [1913.] 8°. **7620.** g. **18.**

BURKE (JOSEPH) *Writer on Art.*

—— *See* HOGARTH (William) The Analysis of Beauty . . . Edited with an introduction by J. Burke. 1955. 8°. **7801.** c. **45.**

—— Hogarth and Reynolds. A contrast in English art theory. pp. 27. *Oxford University Press: London,* 1943. 8°. [*William Henry Charlton Memorial Lecture.* 1941.] Ac. **2671.** g/2.

BURKE (JOSEPH ELDRID)

—— *See* SEYBOLT (Alan U.) and BURKE (J. E.) Procedures in Experimental Metallurgy. [1953.] 8°. **7112.** c. **5.**

BURKE (JOSEPHINE MARY)

—— St. Margaret of Scotland. pp. 60. *Blackie & Son: London & Glasgow,* 1951. 8°. [*Troubadour Plays.*] W.P. **1969/26.**

BURKE (KATHARINE ALICE) *See* THOMSEN (H. P. J. J.) Thermochemistry . . . Translated . . . by K. A. Burke. 1908. 8°. **08909.** d. **9.**

BURKE (KATHLEEN)

—— Homage to Patricia. pp. 282. *Herbert Jenkins: London,* 1940. 8°. NN. **31406.**

—— How Blew the Wind? pp. 256. *John Long: London,* [1939.] 8°. NN. **30881.**

—— The Living Way. pp. 286. *Andrew Melrose: London,* 1937. 8°. NN. **28389.**

—— Love, Dance a Jig. pp. 256. *John Long: London,* 1938. 8°. NN. **29570.**

—— Love Wore a Cloak. pp. 252. *Herbert Jenkins: London,* 1941. 8°. NN. **32998.**

—— Splendid Surrender. pp. 287. *Andrew Melrose: London,* [1937.] 8°. NN. **26875.**

—— The White Road to Verdun. pp. 127. *Hodder & Stoughton: London,* 1916. 8°. **09082.** aa. **64.**

BURKE (KENNETH DUVA)

—— *See* LUDWIG (Emil) Genius and Character . . . Translated by K. Burke. [1927.] 8°. **010603.** g. **14.**

—— —— 1927. 8°. **010603.** aaa. **15.**

—— Attitudes toward History. 2 vol. *New Republic: New York,* 1937. 8°. **09008.** a. **7.**

—— Counter-Statement. pp. xi. 268. *Harcourt, Brace & Co.: New York,* [1931.] 8°. **11855.** aa. **2.**

—— A Grammar of Motives. [On the basic forms of thought exemplified in the attributing of motives.] pp. xxiii. 530. *Prentice-Hall: New York,* 1945. 8°. **8472.** cc. **15.**

—— Permanence and Change. An anatomy of purpose. pp. 351. *New Republic: New York,* 1935. 8°. **08466.** de. **31.**

—— The Philosophy of Literary Form. Studies in symbolic action. pp. xvi. 455. *Louisiana State University Press:* [*Baton Rouge,*] 1941. 8°. **11864.** d. **21.**

—— A Rhetoric of Motives. pp. xv. 340. *Prentice-Hall. New York,* 1950. 8°. **11804.** f. **5.**

—— [Another copy.] **8473.** ff. **31.**

BURKE (LEDA) *pseud.* [i.e. DAVID GARNETT.] *See* also GARNETT (D.)

—— Dope-Darling. pp. 128. *T. Werner Laurie: London,* [1919.] 8°. **012624.** de. **68.**

BURKE (LUKE) *See* PERIODICAL PUBLICATIONS.—*London.* The Ethnological Journal; a magazine of ethnography, phrenology & archæology, *etc.* (Edited by L. Burke.) 1848, *etc.* 8°. P.P. **3862.** a.

—— *See* PERIODICAL PUBLICATIONS.—*London.* The Ethnological Journal: a monthly record of ethnological research and criticism. (Edited by L. Burke.) 1865, *etc.* 8°. P.P. **3862.** aa.

BURKE (Luke)

—— *See* Periodical Publications.—*London.* The Future. A monthly journal of research and criticism in the physical and historical sciences. (Edited by L. Burke.) 1860, *etc.* 8°. P.P. **3862.**

BURKE (*Mrs.* Luke) *See* Burke (Anna C.)

BURKE, afterwards SMITH (Margaret E. D.) Builders of Nations; new light on the duties of motherhood. pp. 92. *Greening & Co.: London,* 1911. 8°. **08415.** df. **19.**

—— [Another edition.] The Service of Motherhood. pp. xiv. 169. *Heath Cranton: London,* 1927. 8°. **08416.** aa. **14.**

BURKE (Mary) A New Method of Teaching Writing to Infants. pp. 12. *G. Philip & Son: London; Philip, Son & Nephew: Liverpool,* [1909.] *obl.* 8°. **7942.** a. **27.**

BURKE (Mary William Ethelbert Appleton) *See* Burke (Billie) [M.W.E.A. Burke.]

BURKE (Merle)

—— United States History. The growth of our land . . . Illustrated. pp. ix. 502. *American Technical Society: Chicago,* 1951. 8°. **9551.** w. **8.**
A slip bearing the imprint "Technical Press: Kingston Hill" has been pasted below the original imprint.

BURKE (Michael) *Earl of Clanricarde. See* Bourke.

BURKE (Michael Courtenay) The Summons: Ireland's anti-Communist anthem, and other poems. pp. 63. *Talbot Press: Dublin & Cork,* 1936. 8°. **11655.** c. **6.**

BURKE (Milo Darwin) Brick for Street Pavements. An account of tests made of bricks and paving blocks, with a brief discussion of street pavements and the method of constructing them. New edition, with a paper on country roads, *etc.* pp. 108. *R. Clarke & Co.: Cincinnati,* 1894. 8°. **8768.** cc. **39.**

BURKE (Nicholas) *See* Burke (Thomas N. A.)

BURKE (Noel Hawley Michael) and **MILLER** (Emanuel) Child Mental Hygiene—its history, methods and problems . . . From the British Journal of Medical Psychology. *University Press: Cambridge,* [1931.] 8°. **8305.** f. **45.**

BURKE (Norah) *See* Burke (Redmond St. G.) and Burke (N.) Jungle Days, *etc.* 1935. 8°. **07908.** f. **16.**

—— The Awakened Heart. pp. 190. *G. G. Swan: London,* 1944. 8°. NN. **34476.**

—— Dark Road. pp. 287. *Stanley Paul & Co.: London,* [1933.] 8°. NN. **21355.**

—— Dreams come true. pp. 111. *Gerald G. Swan: London,* [1948.] 8°. **012646.** c. **13.**

—— Gold Temple Bells. pp. 192. *Gerald G. Swan: London,* 1949. 8°. NN. **39985.**

—— Hazelwood. A romance. pp. 224. *Hodder & Stoughton: London,* 1953. 8°. NNN. **4118.**

—— Merry England. pp. 288. *Stanley Paul & Co.: London,* [1934.] 8°. NN. **23156.**

—— The Scarlet Vampire. pp. 288. *Stanley Paul & Co.: London,* [1936.] 8°. NN. **25795.**

BURKE (Oliver Joseph) The Abbey of Ross, its history and details. [With plates.] pp. vi. 80. *E. Ponsonby: Dublin,* 1868. 8°. **010390.** e. **33.**

—— Second edition. pp. vi. 80. *E. Ponsonby: Dublin,* 1869. 8°. **10390.** bbb. **2.**

—— New edition. pp. 86. *M. H. Gill & Son: Dublin & Waterford,* 1908. 8°. **10390.** df. **28.**

—— Anecdotes of the Connaught Circuit. From its foundation in 1604 to close upon the present time. [With portraits.] pp. xxiv. 357. *Hodges, Figgis & Co.: Dublin,* 1885. 8°. **6006.** h. **5.**

—— The History of the Catholic Archbishops of Tuam. From the foundation of the see to the death of the Most Rev. John MacHale, D.D. a.d. 1881. pp. 416. *Hodges, Figgis & Co.: Dublin,* 1882. 8°. **4735.** b. **7.**

—— The History of the Lord Chancellors of Ireland, from a.d. 1186 to a.d. 1874. [With plates.] pp. xvii. 378. *E. Ponsonby: Dublin,* 1879. 8°. **2407.** d. **3.**

—— The South Isles of Aran, County Galway. pp. x. 112. *Kegan Paul & Co.: London,* 1887. 8°. **10390.** bbb. **18.**

BURKE (Oliver Wallis)

—— *See* United States of America.—*Committee on Butadiene Specifications and Methods of Analyses.* Light Hydrocarbon Analysis . . . Edited by O. W. Burke . . . C. E. Starr, *etc.* 1951. 8°. **08909.** p. **9.**

BURKE (P. J.) *Dramatist,* and **OTHER** (A. N.) *pseud.* The New T.D. A farcical drama, in three acts. pp. 72. *Talbot Press: Dublin & Cork,* [1938.] 8°. **11792.** a. **108.**

BURKE (Peter) *See* Burke (*Right Hon.* Edmund) [*Selections and Extracts.*] The Wisdom and Genius of the Right Hon. Edmund Burke, illustrated in a series of extracts from his writings and speeches; with a summary of his life: by P. Burke. 1845. 12°. **1205.** d. **13.**

—— *See* England. [*Laws, etc.*—iv. *Debtors.*] The Three Statutes forming the New Law for the Relief of Insolvent Debtors, in the Court of Bankruptcy, analysed, simplified and arranged; with the Acts themselves, and an index. By P. Burke. 1844. 12°. **1380.** c. **9.**

—— *See* Godson (Richard) A Supplement to Godson's Practical Treatise on the Law of Patents for Inventions, and of Copyright . . . [Revised edition.] By P. Burke. 1851. 8°. **516.** c. **29.**

—— Celebrated Naval and Military Trials. pp. 399. *W. H. Allen & Co.: London,* 1866. 8°. **6875.** aa. **37.**

—— Celebrated Trials connected with the Aristocracy in the relations of private life. pp. v. 505. *W. Benning & Co.: London,* 1849. 8°. **1132.** e. **46.**

—— Celebrated Trials connected with the Upper Classes of Society, in the relations of private life. pp. viii. 520. *W. Benning & Co.: London,* 1851. 8°. **1132.** e. **51.**

—— The Complete Book of the New County Courts, containing the Small Debts Act, 9 & 10 Vict. c. 95, explained; together with the Judges' Rules of Practice and Forms; and also, a list of the circuits . . . Second edition. pp. 264. *W. Benning & Co.: London,* 1847. 12°. **1382.** c. **10.**

—— The Copyright Law and the Press. An essay, to shew the necessity of an immediate amendment of the copyright law upon the removal of the stamp duty from newspapers. pp. 11. *Sampson Low & Son: London,* 1855. 8°. **8140.aa.53.(7.)**

BURKE (PETER)

—— The Criminal Law, and its Sentences, in Treasons, Felonies, and Misdemeanors. pp. xi. 242. *J. Richards & Co.: Dublin,* 1842. 16°. **1381. a. 3.**

—— [Another edition.] With an addendum including all statutable alterations and additions down to the present time. pp. xii. 276. *Owen Richards: London,* 1844. 16°. **1379. a. 1.**

—— An Explanatory Analysis of the Protection of Inventions' Act, the 14 Vict. c. 8, for preventing the piracy of inventions during their exhibition in 1851, with the Act itself, and also a summary in French . . . The whole being a further supplement to the last edition of Godson and Burke's Practical Treatise on the Law of Patents and Copyright. pp. 19. *W. Benning & Co.: London,* 1851. 8°. **6375. c. 35. (3.)**

—— Faversham et Cantorbéry. Discours, *etc.* (Extrait du Bulletin de la Société des Antiquaires de Normandie.) pp. 30. *Caen,* 1868. 8°. **10360. c. 28. (7.)**

—— The Law of International Copyright between England and France, in literature, the drama, music, and the fine arts, analysed and explained; with the Convention, the Orders in Council, and the recent Acts of Parliament on the subject, *etc.* (Loi internationale entre l'Angleterre et la France, *etc.*) *Eng. & Fr.* pp. xi. 158. *Sampson Low & Son: London,* 1852. 12°. **1128. d. 27.**

—— The Patent Law Amendment Act, the 15 & 16 Vict. c. 83., and the Patent Law generally as affected by that Statute, analysed and explained, *etc.* pp. 50. *W. G. Benning & Co.: London,* 1852. 8°. **6375. d. 3.**

—— [Another edition.] pp. 54. *W. G. Benning & Co.: London,* 1853. 8°. **6376. e. 2.**

—— The Public and Domestic Life of the Right Hon. Edmund Burke. [With illustrations, including portraits.] pp. xvi. 315. *Ingram, Cooke & Co.: London,* 1853. 8°. [*National Illustrated Library.* vol. 31.] **741. b. 23.**

—— The Romance of the Forum, or, Narratives, scenes, and anecdotes from courts of justice, *etc.* 2 vol. *Colburn & Co.: London,* 1852. 12°. **6056. b. 19.**

—— [Another edition.] pp. ix. 341. *Hurst & Blackett: London,* [1861.] 8°. **6056. b. 21.**

—— The Romance of the Forum . . . Second series, *etc.* 2 vol. *Hurst & Blackett: London,* 1854. 8°. **6056. b. 20.**

—— A Treatise on the Law of Copyright in literature, the drama, music, engraving, and sculpture; and also in designs for ornamenting articles of manufacture: including the recent Statutes on the subject. pp. xii. 128. *J. Richards & Co.: London,* 1842. 12°. **1130. d. 44.**

BURKE (PETER JOSEPH) The Royal Register, Genealogical and Historic, for 1831. By P. J. Burke. 1831. 12°. *See* PERIODICAL PUBLICATIONS.—*London.* **606. b. 18.**

BURKE (REDMOND SAINT GEORGE) and **BURKE** (NORAH) Jungle Days. A book of big-game hunting . . . With thirty-two illustrations [including a portrait], *etc.* pp. 288. *Stanley Paul & Co.: London,* 1935. 8°. **07908. f. 16.**

BURKE (RICHARD) *Clerk of the Waterford Poor Law Union.* [A volume of cuttings from newspapers with a title in MS. reading "Trial Conviction and Execution of R. Burke . . . for the poisoning of his wife. Summer Assizes 1862 . . . Together with the report of the Coroner's Inquest, the Convict's memorial and the articles which appeared in the local newspapers," etc.] [1862.] 8°. **6495. e. 2.**

BURKE (RICHARD) *Novelist.*

—— Barbary Freight. pp. 281. *G. P. Putnam's Sons: New York,* [1943.] 8°. **12724. dd. 10.**

—— Barbary Freight. pp. 192. *T. V. Boardman & Co.: London, New York,* 1945. 8°. **12728. aa. 29.**

—— Chinese Red. pp. 248. *G. P. Putnam's Sons: New York,* [1942.] 8°. **12725. bbb. 7.**

—— The Dead Take No Bows. pp. 238. *Houghton Mifflin Co.: Boston,* 1941. 8°. **12723. a. 8.**

—— The Frightened Pigeon. pp. 184. *Jarrolds: London,* [1946.] 8°. **NN. 36609.**

—— The Red Gate. pp. 225. *Ziff-Davis Publishing Co.: Chicago,* 1947. 8°. **12726. b. 58**

—— Reluctant Hussy. pp. 224. *Jarrolds: London,* 1947. 8°. **NN. 38133.**

—— Sinister Street, *etc.* pp. 199. *Ziff-Davis Publishing Co.: Chicago,* [1948.] 8°. **12726. b. 64.**

BURKE (RICHARD) *of Sudbury, Massachusetts. See* BOUTELLE (John A.) The Burke and Alvord Memorial. A genealogical account of the descendants of R. Burke of Sudbury, Mass., *etc.* 1864. 8°. **9914. i. 37.**

BURKE (RICHARD) *Recorder of Bristol. See* VALENS, *pseud.* The Letters of Valens, *etc.* [By William Burke, with the assistance of Edmund and R. Burke?] pp. xv. 160. 1777. 8°. **E. 2230. (1.)**

—— A Charge delivered to the Grand-Jury at a Sessions of Oyer and Terminer and General Gaol Delivery for the City and County of Bristol . . . the 6th of April, 1793 . . To which is added, the address of the Grand-Jury presented to the Recorder, at the close of the Sessions. pp. 27. *J. Rudhall: Bristol,* 1793. 8°. **113. i. 21**

BURKE (RICHARD) *Son of the Right Hon. Edmund Burke. See* THERRY (Roger) *Puisne Judge of the Supreme Court of New South Wales.* A Letter to the Right Hon. George Canning . . . To which are annexed . . . Reminiscences (of E. Burke and his son), *etc.* 1826. 8°. **T. 1004. (3.)**

—— A Letter from Richard Burke, Esq. to ***** ***** Esq. of Cork. In which the legality and propriety of the meeting recommended in Mr. Byrne's circular letter are discussed; together with some observations on a measure proposed by a friend to be substituted in the place of the Catholic Committee. pp. 46. *P. Byrne: Dublin,* 1792. 8°. **8146. b. 50**

BURKE (RICHARD WILLIAM) Pernicious Malaria, or 'Surra' in animals. pp. vi. 77. *D. V. Kristnan & Co. Bellary,* 1900. 8°. **07291. g. 13**

BURKE (RICKARD) R. Burke, Gent. and Elizabeth his Wife . . . appellants. Christopher O'Brien Esq; respondent et e contra. The first appellant's case. pp. 3. [*London,* 1724.] fol. **19. h. 2. (133.)**

—— R. Burk and Elizabeth his Wife, appellants. Christopher O'Brien Esq; respondent. et e contra. The case of the respondent, *etc.* pp. 4. [*London,* 1725.] fol. **19. h. 2. (134.)**

—— Rickard Burk, Plaintif, Richard Morgan, Defendant in error. The case of the plaintif in error. pp. 3. [*London,* 1717.] fol. **19. h. 1. (26.)**

BURKE (RICKARD)

—— R. Burke, Plaintiff in error. Richard Morgan, lessee of Henry Blake. Defendant in error. [The defendant's case.] pp. 3. [*London*, 1717.] fol. **19. h. 1. (27.)**

BURKE (ROBERT BELLE) *See* BACON (Roger) [*Opus Majus.*] The Opus Majus of Roger Bacon. A translation by R. B. Burke. 1928. 8°. **08460. i. 16.**

—— *See* BIEL (G.) Treatise on the Power and Utility of Moneys . . . Done into English by R. B. Burke, *etc.* 1930. 4°. **08206. e. 16.**

—— *See* GOULLET (R.) Compendium on the Magnificence, Dignity, and Excellence of the University of Paris . . . Done into English by R. B. Burke, *etc.* 1928. 8°. **08355. ff. 42.**

BURKE (ROBERT EUGENE)

—— Olson's New Deal for California. [With a portrait.] pp. 279. *University of California Press: Berkeley & Los Angeles*, 1953. 8°. **8175. dd. 3.**

BURKE (ROBERT O'HARA) *See* BOURNE (George) *Australian Traveller.* Bourne's Journal of Landsborough's Expedition from Carpentaria in search of Burke and Wills. 1862. 8°. **10491.d.30.(9.)**

—— *See* CHAPALAY (L.) L'Australie. Récit d'un voyage . . . à travers le continent australien par Burke, Wills, *etc.* [Including " Fragments retrouvés des notes prises par M. Burke."] 1864. 8°. **10491. aaa. 16.**

—— *See* CLUNE (Frank) Dig, *etc.* [A narrative of the expedition made into Central Australia in 1860 by R. O'H. Burke and W. J. Wills.] 1937. 8°. **10493. df. 7.**

—— *See* DAVIS (John) *of Adelaide.* Tracks of McKinlay . . . With an introductory view of the . . . Australian explorations of . . . Burke and Wills, *etc.* 1863. 8°. **10492. e. 3.**

—— *See* JACKSON (Andrew) *Ensign.* Robert O'Hara Burke and the Australian Exploring Expedition of 1860. 1862. 8°. **10491. d. 26.**

—— *See* VICTORIA, *Australia.—Commission of Inquiry into the Burke and Wills Exploring Expedition.* Supplementary Pamphlet to the Burke and Wills Exploring Expedition: containing the evidence taken before the Commission of Inquiry, *etc.* 1861. 8°. **10491. ee. 4. (2.)**

—— Burke and his Companions. The Victorian Expedition; from its origin to the return from Carpentaria; and the death of Burke, Wills, and Gray, from starvation; with Burke's and Wills' Journals, King's Narrative, Howitt's Diary, &c., &c. pp. xvi. 176. *Herald Office: Melbourne*, [1861.] 16°. **10492. a. 17.**

—— The Burke and Wills Exploring Expedition: an account of the crossing the continent of Australia, from Cooper's Creek to Carpentaria, with biographical sketches of R. O'H. Burke and William John Wills. [With extracts from their journals, and portraits.] pp. iv. 36. *Wilson & Mackinnon: Melbourne*, 1861. 8°. **10492. bbb. 35.**

BURKE (S. HUBERT) Historical Portraits of the Tudor Dynasty and the Reformation Period. 4 vol. *John Hodges: London*, 1879–83. 8°. **9512. c. 12.**

—— Ireland Sixty Years Ago. Being an account of a visit to Ireland by . . . King George IV. in the year 1821. pp. 32. *John Hodges: London*, 1885. 8°. **9510. ccc. 14.**

—— Men and Women as they appeared in the far-off time. pp. viii. 199. *Burns & Oates: London*, [1884.] 8°. **7709. aaa. 10.**

BURKE (S. HUBERT)

—— The Men and Women of the English Reformation, from the days of Wolsey to the death of Cranmer. 2 vol. *R. Washbourne: London*, 1870, 71. 8°. **4902. bbb. 26.**

—— The Monastic Houses of England; their accusers and defenders . . . By S. H. B. [i.e. S. H. Burke.] pp. vii. 61. 1869. 8°. *See* B., S. H. **4071. aaa. 7.**

—— The Rise and Progress of Father Mathew's Temperance Mission. pp. 20. *S. W. Black: London*, 1885. 8°. **8436. aaa. 48. (15.)**

BURKE (SARAH J.) *See* BARNUM (Phineas T.) and BURKE (S. J.) P. T. Barnum's Circus, *etc.* 1888. 4°. **7955. f. 26.**

—— *See* BARNUM (Phineas T.) and BURKE (S. J.) P. T. Barnum's Museum, *etc.* 1888. 4°. **7955. f. 25.**

BURKE (SEAMUS) The Foundations of Peace . . . With an introduction by Darrell Figgis. pp. xi. 172. *Maunsel & Co.: Dublin & London*, 1920. 8°. **8425. p. 50.**

BURKE (SIMON)

—— Death is the Pay-Off. [A novel.] pp. 125. *Scion: London*, [1950.] 8°. **12651. f. 33.**

BURKE (T. A.) *See* LAMAR (John B.) Polly Peablossom's Wedding; and other tales . . . Edited by T. A. Burke. 1851. 8°. **12314. c. 17.**

BURKE (THOMAS) *Bishop of Ossory.* *See* LITURGIES.—*Latin Rite.—Combined Offices.*—IV. *Officia Propria.—Ireland.* Officia propria sanctorum Hiberniæ . . . Procurante A. R. P. T. de Burgo, *etc.* 1751. 12°. **1018. g. 9.**

—— A Catechism Moral and Controversial . . . To which is annexed . . . a practical method of preparing for sacramental confession . . . By T . . . s M . . . s B . . . ke O.P. [The dedication signed: Thomas de Burgo.] pp. 416. *Lisbon*, 1752. 8°. **3505. df. 2.**

—— Hibernia Dominicana. Sive historia provinciæ Hiberniæ ordinis praedicatorum, *etc.* (Supplementum.) pp. xvi. 949. *Ex typographia Metternichiana: Coloniæ Agrippinæ* [*James Stokes: Kilkenny?*], 1762. 4°. **700. k. 30.**

—— [Another copy, with a different titlepage.] **G. 5785.**

—— Ossorien. Parocchialis, *etc.* [Papers and correspondence relating to the ecclesiastical cause between T. Burke and Patrick Molloy, Parish Priest of St. Mary's, Kilkenny.] MS. ADDITIONS. 9 pt. *Typis Bernabò: [Rome,]* 1761, 62. 8°. **5107. e. 23.**

BURKE (THOMAS) *of Eltham.*

—— *See* DE QUINCEY (Thomas) The Ecstasies of Thomas De Quincey. Chosen by T. Burke. 1928. 8°. **012352. d. 13.**

—— *See* ENGLAND. [*Appendix.—Descriptions, Travels and Topography.*] Introducing Britain. [By] K. Johnstone, T. Burke, *etc.* 1938. 8°. **2366. aa. 31.**

—— *See* GERMANY.—*Army.* [*Appendix.*] The German Army from Within. By a British Officer who has served in it. [Edited by T. Burke.] 1914. 8°. **08821. a. 32.**

—— *See* HAYS (Margaret G.) and BURKE (T.) Kiddie Land, *etc.* [1913.] 8°. **11647. g. 56.**

—— Abduction. A story of Limehouse. pp. 286. *Herbert Jenkins: London*, 1939. 8°. **NN. 30549.**

BURKE (THOMAS) *of Eltham.*

—— An Artist's Day Book. A treasury of good counsel from the great masters in the arts for their disciples. Edited by T. Burke. pp. xii. 155. *Herbert & Daniel: London*, [1911.] 8°. **12352. de. 40.**

—— Life and Art, *etc.* [A new edition of part of "An Artist's Day Book."] pp. 61. *Jonathan Cape: London*, 1921. 8°. **12298. a. 2.**

—— Truth and Beauty, *etc.* [A new edition of part of "An Artist's Day Book."] pp. 63. *Jonathan Cape: London*, 1921. 8°. **12298. a. 3.**

—— The Beauty of England. [With plates.] pp. 367. *G. G. Harrap & Co.: London*, 1933. 8°. **010352. bb. 12.**

—— Billy and Beryl in Chinatown, *etc.* pp. 95. *G. G. Harrap & Co.: London*, 1935. 8°. **20055. e. 17.**

—— Billy and Beryl in Old London, *etc.* pp. 93. *G. G. Harrap & Co.: London*, 1936. 8°. **010349. aa. 40.**

—— Billy and Beryl in Soho, *etc.* pp. 92. *G. G. Harrap & Co.: London*, 1936. 8°. **20059. c. 31.**

—— The Book of the Inn . . . Selected and edited by T. Burke. pp. xxiii. 401. *Constable & Co.: London*, 1927. 8°. **12298. aa. 24.**

—— The Bloomsbury Wonder. pp. 102. *Mandrake Press: London*, 1929. 16°. **012600. i. 11.**

—— Broken Blossoms. *See* infra : Limehouse Nights.

—— The Charm of England. An anthology compiled and edited by T. Burke. pp. 179. *Truslove & Hanson: London*, [1914.] 8°. **12354. ccc. 33.**

—— The Charm of the West Country. An anthology compiled and edited by T. Burke. (The Childe of Bristow. A poem by John Lydgate.) pp. xvi. 244. *J. W. Arrowsmith: Bristol; Simpkin, Marshall & Co.: London*, 1913. 8°. **12271. p. 16.**

—— Children in Verse. Fifty songs of playful childhood, collected and edited by T. Burke. With illustrations . . . by Honor C. Appleton. pp. x. 135. *Duckworth & Co.: London*, 1913. 8°. **11646. i. 12.**

—— City of Encounters. A London divertissement. pp. 372. *Constable & Co.: London*, 1932. 8°. **NN. 18898.**

—— The Contented Mind. An anthology of optimism. Edited by T. Burke. pp. 159. *Truslove & Hanson: London*, [1914.] 8°. **8411. k. 27.**

—— Dark Nights. pp. 154. *Herbert Jenkins: London*, [1944.] 8°. **NN. 34851.**

—— Dinner is Served! or, Eating round the world in London, *etc.* pp. 75. *G. Routledge & Sons: London*, 1937. 8°. **010349. aa. 41.**

—— East of Mansion House. [Tales.] pp. 269. *Cassell & Co.: London*, 1928. 8°. **NN. 13732.**

—— The English and their Country. [With illustrations.] pp. 30. *Published for the British Council by Longmans, Green & Co.: London*, [1945.] 8°. [*The British People—how they live and work.*] **010360. pp. 1/11.**

—— Englezi i njihova zemlja. Od Tomasa Berka. [With illustrations.] pp. 30. [1948.] 8°. *See* ENGLAND.—*British Council.* **10359. c. 31.**

BURKE (THOMAS) *of Eltham.*

—— [The English and their Country.] England: Natur og Folk. pp. 30. [1946.] 8°. *See* ENGLAND.—*British Council.* **010358. pp. 28.**

—— Les Anglais chez eux. [A translation of "The English and their Country."] pp. 30. [1946.] 8°. *See* ENGLAND.—*British Council.* **010352. bbb. 75.**

—— Anglia i Anglicy. Przekład Marii Danilewiczowej. pp. 30. [1946.] 8°. *See* ENGLAND.—*British Council.* **010358. pp. 25.**

—— The English Inn. pp. xi. 175. *Longmans & Co.: London*, 1930. 8°. [*English Heritage Series.*] **W.P. 9008/6.**

—— (Illustrated edition.) pp. xii. 186. *Longmans & Co.: London*, 1931. 8°. **010360. b. 39.**

—— English Inns . . . With 8 plates in colour and 24 illustrations in black & white. pp. 47. *William Collins: London*, 1943. 8°. [*Britain in Pictures. The British People in Pictures.*] **W.P. 10933/1. (44.)**

—— English Inns. *See* TURNER (Walter J.) The Englishman's Country, *etc.* 1945. 8°. **W.P. 10933/1. (89.**

—— The English Inn. (Revised.) [With plates.] pp. 189. *Herbert Jenkins: London*, 1947. 8°. [*Country Books.*] **W.P. 1574/3.**

—— English Night-Life. From Norman curfew to present black-out . . . Illustrated from prints, paintings, drawings and photographs. pp. ix. 150. *B. T. Batsford: London*, 1941. 8°. **10353. b. 56.**

—— The English Townsman, as he was and as he is. [With plates.] pp. vii. 151. *B. T. Batsford: London*, 1946. 8°. **10359. bb. 24.**

—— Thomas Burke. [Essays.] pp. 63. *G. G. Harrap & Co.: London*, 1928. 8°. [*Essays of To-day and Yesterday.*] **012330. k. 72/22.**

—— The Flower of Life. [A novel.] pp. 132. *Constable & Co.: London*, 1929. 8°. **012604. bb. 48.**

—— Life and Art. *See* supra : An Artist's Day Book, *etc.*

—— Limehouse Nights. Tales of Chinatown. pp. 311. *Grant Richards: London*, 1917. 8°. **012626. b. 44.**

—— Limehouse Nights. Illustrated by Mahlon Blaine. (New edition.) pp. 277. *Robert M. McBride & Co.: New York*, [1926.] 8°. **12653. b. 12.**

—— [A reissue.] pp. 252. *Readers Library Publishing Co.: London*, [1928.] 8°. **012603. f. 52.**

—— [Another edition.] pp. 252. [*London*, 1938.] 8°. [*Daily Express Fiction Library.*] **W.P. 7451/9.**

—— Broken Blossoms. A selection of stories from "Limehouse Nights." pp. 15–184. *Grant Richards: London*, 1920. 8°. **012603. f. 5.**

—— Living in Bloomsbury. pp. 361. *G. Allen & Unwin: London*, 1939. 8°. **12359. g. 9.**

—— London in My Time. pp. 256. *Rich & Cowan: London*, 1934. 8°. **010348. ff. 18.**

—— London Lamps. A book of songs. pp. 47. *Grant Richards: London*, 1917. 8°. **011649. ff. 15.**

—— The London Spy. A book of town travels. pp. 318. *Thornton Butterworth: London*, 1922. 8°. **010349. g. 44.**

—— (Popular edition.) pp. 318. *Thornton Butterworth: London*, 1925. 8°. **010349.** aa. **7.**

—— The Maid's Head, Norwich. [With illustrations.] pp. 10. *True Temperance Association: London*, [1931.] 8°. [*Some British Inns.* no. 8.] W.P. **4891/8.**

—— Murder at Elstree; or, Mr. Thurtell and his gig. pp. 177 *Longmans & Co.: London*, 1936. 8°. **12626.** w. **14.**

—— Murder at Elstree; or, Mr. Thurtell and his gig. pp. 190. *Readers Library Publishing Co.: London*, [1940.] 8°. [*New Chevron Series.* no. 99.] **012206.ee.1/99.**

—— Night Pieces. Eighteen tales. pp. 311. *Constable & Co.: London*, 1935. 8°. NN. **24550.**

—— Nights in Town. A London autobiography. pp. 410. *G. Allen & Unwin: London*, 1915. 8°. **10349.** t. **6.**

—— (Cheap edition.) pp. 287. *G. Allen & Unwin: London*, 1925. 8°. **010349.** a. **10.**

—— An Old London Alehouse: the Anchor, at Bankside. [With illustrations.] pp. 8. *True Temperance Association: London*, [1932.] 8°. [*Some British Inns.* no. 13.] W.P. **4891/13.**

—— Out and About. A note-book of London in war-time. pp. 142. *G. Allen & Unwin: London*, 1919. 8°. **012352.** e. **64.**

—— The Outer Circle. Rambles in remote London. pp. 221. *G. Allen & Unwin: London*, 1921. 8°. **012350.** g. **29.**

—— The Pleasantries of Old Quong. pp. vii. 279. *Constable & Co.: London*, 1931. 8°. NN. **17539.**

—— The Real East End . . . The lithographs by Pearl Binder. pp. vii. 163. *Constable & Co.: London*, 1932. 8°. **010349.** cc. **22.**

—— The Small People. A little book of verse about children for their elders. Chosen, edited & arranged by T. Burke. pp. xx. 219. *Chapman & Hall: London*, 1910. 8°. **11604.** bb. **15.**

—— Son of London. [Autobiographical reminiscences.] pp. 223. *Herbert Jenkins: London*, [1946.] 8°. **10861.** de. **3.**

—— The Song Book of Quong Lee of Limehouse. pp. 40. *G. Allen & Unwin: London*, 1920. 8°. **011648.** df. **105.**

—— The Streets of London through the centuries . . . Illustrated from prints, paintings, drawings and photographs. pp. viii. 152. *B. T. Batsford: London*, 1940. 8° **010349.** pp. **1.**

—— The Streets of London through the Centuries . . . Illustrated, *etc.* (Fourth edition.) pp. viii. 152. *B. T. Batsford: London*, 1949. 8°. **010349.** pp. **44.**

—— The Sun in Splendour. pp. 341. *Constable & Co: London*, 1927. 8°. NN. **12742.**

—— Travel in England. From pilgrim and pack-horse to light car and plane. [With plates.] pp. vi. 154. *B. T. Batsford: London*, 1942 [1943]. 8°. **010358.** m. **26.**

—— [A reissue.] Travel in England, *etc.* *London*, 1949. 8°. **010368.** pp. **8.**

—— Truth and Beauty. *See* supra: An Artist's Day Book, *etc.*

—— Twinkletoes. A tale of Chinatown. (Reprinted.) pp. 213. *Grant Richards: London*, 1917. 8°. NN. **4679.**

—— [Another edition.] pp. 250. *Readers Library Publishing Co.: London*, [1927.] 8°. **012601.** bbb. **9.**

—— Vagabond Minstrel. The adventures of Thomas Dermody. pp. 345. *Longmans & Co.: London*, 1936. 8°. NN. **26148.**

—— Victorian Grotesque. pp. 254. *Herbert Jenkins: London*, 1941. 8°. NN. **32644.**

—— Whispering Windows. Tales of the waterside. pp. 309. *Grant Richards: London*, 1921. 8°. NN. **7016.**

—— Why Bring That Up? [On book-collecting. With a bibliography of T. Burke's writings.] *See* GAWSWORTH (John) *pseud.* Ten Contemporaries . . . Second series, *etc.* 1933. 8°. **011903.** a. **61.**

—— Will Someone lead me to a Pub? Being a note upon certain of the taverns, old and new, of London, *etc.* (Illustrated by Frederick Carter.) pp. 84. *G. Routledge & Sons: London*, 1936. 8°. **010349.** b. **15.**

—— The Wind and the Rain. A book of confessions. pp. 288. *Thornton Butterworth: London*, 1924. 8°. NN. **10228.**

—— [Another copy.] **F.P.** **012603.** bb. **1.**

—— The Winsome Wench. The story of a London inn, 1825–1900. [A novel.] pp. 307. *G. Routledge & Sons: London*, 1938. 8°. NN. **28532.**

—— The Best Stories of Thomas Burke. Selected, with a foreword, by John Gawsworth. pp. 256. *Phoenix House: London*, 1950. 8°. NNN. **87.**

BURKE (THOMAS) *of Liverpool?* Catholic History of Liverpool. pp. 284. *C. Tinling & Co: Liverpool*, 1910. 8°. **4571.eee.7.**

BURKE (*Hon.* THOMAS) *See* BOURKE (John) *9th Earl of Clanricarde.* The Right Honourable John, Earl of Clanricard, and Michael, Lord Dunkellin . . . Appellants. The Honourable Colonel Thomas Bourke, and Hellen, Countess Dowager of Clanricarde . . . Respondents. The Appellants Case. [1717.] fol. **19.** h. **1.** **(42.)**

—— *See* BOURKE (John) *9th Earl of Clanricarde.* The R^t^ Honble John Earl of Clanrickard, and Michael, Lord Dunkellin . . . Appell^ts^. Thomas Bourke, Esq; and the Right Honble Hellen Countess Dowager of Clanrickard . . . Respond^ts^. The Respondents Case. [1717.] fol. **19.** h. **1.** **(43.)**

BURKE (THOMAS F.) *Fenian.* *See* CHAMNEY (William G.) "The Fenian Conspiracy." Report of the trials of T. F. Burke and others, *etc.* 1869. 8°. **6495.** f. **3.**

BURKE (THOMAS HENRY) *See* AINSLIE (Henry) Man's Wrath no Instrument of God's Righteous Retribution. A sermon preached . . . on receiving intelligence of the assassinations [of Lord F. Cavendish and T. H. Burke] in Dublin. [1882.] 8°. **4473.** g. **14.** **(5.)**

—— *See* IRELAND.—Spencer (John Poyntz) *Earl Spencer, Lieutenant-General.* A Proclamation, *etc.* [Offering a reward for information leading to the arrest of persons harbouring the murderers of Lord Frederick Cavendish and T. H. Burke.] [1882.] fol. C.S. A. **26/15.** **(1.)**

BURKE (Thomas Nicholas Anthony)

—— *See* Cassidy (James F.) The Great Father Tom Burke. [With a portrait.] 1947. 8°. **4957**. b. **11**.

—— *See* Fitz-Patrick (William J.) The Life of the Very Rev. T. N. Burke. 1885. 8°. **4956. f. 7.**

—— —— 1894. 8°. **4956. aaa. 23.**

—— *See* Humanitas, *pseud.* Is God the First Cause? Being also a brief reply to Father Burke's 'locomotive engine' theory of science and revealed religion, *etc.* 1883. 8°. **4018. b. 17.**

—— English Misrule in Ireland. A course of lectures . . . in reply to James Anthony Froude . . . With an appendix, containing a review of the so-called "Bull" of Adrian iv., by the Most Rev. P. H. Moran . . . and "an Analysis of the Rebellion of 1641," by Mathew Carey. [With a portrait.] pp. 324. *Lynch, Cole & Meehan: New York,* 1873. 12°. **8145. de. 14.**

—— [Another edition.] Ireland's Case stated in reply to Mr. Froude. pp. 238. *P. M. Haverty: New York,* 1873. 8°. **8145. de. 15.**

—— Froude's Crusade. Lecture by the Very Rev. T. N. Burke . . . Subject—"Mr. Froude's Last Words." Also lecture by Wendell Phillips . . . Subject—"Review of Froude." With a sketch of the life and labours of Father Burke. [Edited by James W. O'Brien.] pp. 3–8, 37–52, 76–80. *J. W. O'Brien: New York,* 1872. 8°. **8145. ee. 25.**

The title on the wrapper reads "Final Answer of the Very Rev. T. N. Burke . . . to Mr. James Anthony Froude." The pagination is that of the enlarged edition of the same year, in which the omitted portions first appeared.

—— [Another edition.] Froude's Crusade—Both sides. Lectures by Very Rev. T. N. Burke . . . John Mitchel, Wendell Phillips, and Mr. James Anthony Froude, in summing up the controversy, *etc.* [Edited by J. W. O'Brien.] pp. 80. 1872. 8°. *See* Froude (James A.) **8145. ee. 26.**

—— Lectures on Faith & Fatherland. pp. 284. *Cameron & Ferguson: Glasgow & London,* [1874.] 8°. **8145. aa. 8.**

—— Father Burke's Oration. [The oration delivered on occasion of the removal of the remains of D. O'Connell to Glasnevin.] *See* O'Connell (Daniel) Popular Life of Daniel O'Connell, *etc.* [1875.] 8°. **10815. aaa. 1.**

—— St. Ignatius and the Jesuits. A sermon, *etc.* pp. 34. *Burns & Oates: London,* 1880. 8°. **4473. g. 7. (16.)**

—— The Inner Life of Father Thomas Burke, O. P. By a Dominican Friar of the English Province. pp. 108. *Burns & Oates: London,* [1894.] 8°. **4956. aaa. 22.**

BURKE (Thomas Travers)

—— *See* Ossian. Dar-thula: a poem . . . translated . . . By T. T. Burke. 1820. 8°. **11658**. h. **28**.

—— *See* Ossian. Fingal . . With notes. By T. T. Burke. 1844. 12°. **11661**. b. **5**.

—— *See* Ossian. Ossian; his principal poems, translated into English verse [by T. T. Burke and others], *etc.* 1858. 12°. **11595. c. 33.**

—— *See* Ossian. Temora . . . versified from Macpherson's prose translation of the Poems of Ossian. By T. T. Burke. 1818. 8°. **1064**. l. **17**. **(1, 2.)**

BURKE (Thomas Travers)

—— The Accoucheur's Vademecum: or, Modern guide to the practice of midwifery. pp. xlviii. 450. *Simpkin, Marshall & Co.: London,* 1840. 8°. **1177. b. 41.**

BURKE (Trude)

—— The Wild Stranger . . . Illustrated by Paul Brown. [A story for children.] pp. 129. *Henry Holt & Co.: New York,* [1953.] 8°. **012826**. aa. **34**.

BURKE (Ulick) *Marquis of Clanricarde. See* Bourke.

BURKE (Ulick) *Writer of Verse.* Donegal Rhymes. pp. vii. 31. *Claude Stacey: London,* [1927.] 8°. **011645. h. 137.**

BURKE (Ulick John) The Boy's Walton. A discourse on fishing . . . With illustrations. pp. 174. *M. Ward & Co.: London,* 1878. 8°. **7908. aaaa. 11.**

—— Couleur de Rose. A novel. 2 vol. *W. Sonnenschein & Co.: London,* 1884. 8°. **12636. r. 3.**

BURKE (Ulick Ralph) *See* Borrow (George H.) [*The Bible in Spain.*] The Bible in Spain . . . A new edition . . . by U. R. Burke, *etc.* 1896. 8°. **10161. bb. 23.**

—— —— 1899. 8°. **2342. d. 1.**

—— —— 1907. 8°. **010160. e. 60.**

—— *See* Cervantes Saavedra (M. de) [*Don Quixote.—Spanish and English.—Extracts.*] Sancho Panza's Proverbs, and others which occur in Don Quixote; with a literal English translation, notes, and an introduction by U. R. Burke. 1872. 8°. Cerv. **65.**

—— —— 1877. 8°. **12304**. cc. **7**.

—— —— 1892. 8°. Cerv. **74**.

—— Beating the Air. [A novel.] 3 vol. *Chapman & Hall: London,* 1879. 8°. **12640. e. 2.**

—— Business and Pleasure in Brazil. By U. R. Burke and R. Staples Jr. pp. iv. 148. *Field & Tuer: London; Scribner & Welford: New York,* [1886.] 8°. **10481**. ee. **16**.

—— The Great Captain; an eventful chapter in Spanish history. [A biography of Gonzalo Fernandez de Cordova y Aguilar.] pp. 176. *S.P.C.K.: London,* [1877.] 8°. **4419**. cc. **30**.

—— A Handbook of Sewage Utilization. pp. vi. 60. *E. & F. N. Spon: London & New York,* 1872. 8°. **8776. aaa. 50.**

—— Second edition . . . enlarged. pp. xxiii. 84. *E. & F. N. Spon: London & New York,* 1873. 8°. **8775**. aaaa. **8**.

—— A History of Spain from the earliest times to the death of Ferdinand the Catholic. 2 vol. *Longmans & Co.: London,* 1895. 8°. **9180**. eee. **2**.

—— Second edition, edited, with additional notes and an introduction, by M. A. S. Hume. 2 vol. *Longmans & Co.: London,* 1900. 8°. **2388. a. 12.**

—— A Life of Benito Juarez, Constitutional President of Mexico. pp. x. 384. *Remington & Co.: London,* 1894. 8°. **10883**. c. **20**.

—— Loyal and Lawless. A novel. 2 vol. *Chapman & Hall: London,* 1880. 8°. **12641**. i. **5**.

BURKE (Victor) Revision of the Fishes of the Family Liparidae. pp. xii. 204. *Washington,* 1930. 8°. [*U.S. National Museum. Bulletin.* 150.] Ac. **1875/13.**

BURKE (W.) *Writer of Verse.*

—— Poems. pp. 16. *A. H. Stockwell: Ilfracombe,* [1943.] 8°. **11656**. n. **69**.

BURKE (*Mrs.* W.) Adela Northington, a novel, *etc.* [By Mrs. W. Burke.] 3 vol. 1796. 12°. *See* NORTHINGTON (Adela) N. **2321**.

—— Ela, ou les Illusions du cœur. Traduit de l'anglois. [A translation of "Ela; or, the Delusions of the heart," by Mrs. W. Burke.] pp. 211. 1788. 12°. *See* ELA. **12808**. r. **15**.

—— Émilie Fairville, ou la Philosophie du sentiment. Par l'auteur d'Ela [i.e. Mrs. W. Burke] . . . Traduit de l'anglais, par J. B. Sanchamau. 2 pt. 1789. 12°. *See* FAIRVILLE (Émilie) **12808**. u. **30**.

BURKE (W. S.) *Editor of "The Indian Field." See* SHAW (Vero K.) and HAYES (M. H.) Dogs for Hot Climates . . . Second edition, revised and brought up to date by W. S. Burke. 1908. 16°. **07293**. ee. **11**.

—— *See* THOMAS (Henry S.) Tank Fishing in India . . . Edited by W. S. Burke, *etc.* 1927. 8°. **7915**. p. **26**.

—— The Indian Field Shikar Book . . . Fourth edition. pp. ii. 406. v. *"Indian Field Office": Calcutta,* 1908. *obl.* 8°. **07905**. de. **12**.

—— Fifth edition. pp. iv. 585. *Thacker, Spink & Co.: Calcutta & Simla,* 1920. *obl.* 8°. **7911**. **aa**. **26**.

BURKE (W. S.) *of Galway.* Quelques propositions sur la rage; thèse, *etc.* pp. 11. *Paris,* 1835. 4°. **1184**. f. **18**. (**4**.)

BURKE (W. S.) *of the Bengal Cyclists' Association.* Cycling in Bengal, a guide to practical tours . . . The official handbook of the Bengal Cyclists Association. [With a map.] pp. 98. xi. *W. Newman & Co.: Calcutta,* 1898. 8°. **10058**. de. **17**.

BURKE (WILBERT E.) *See* CHAPMAN (William J.) and BURKE (W. E.) Twentieth Century Cyclists' Record and Road Guide of Ontario, *etc.* 1901. 8°. **10470**. aa. **65**.

BURKE (WILLIAM) *Author of "South American Independence."* Additional Reasons, for our immediately emancipating Spanish America, deduced from the . . . present crisis: and containing valuable information, respecting the late important events, both at Buenos Ayres, and in the Caraccas: as well as with respect to the present disposition and views of the Spanish Americans: being intended as a supplement to "South American Independence" . . . Second edition, enlarged. (Letter to the Spanish Americans, by D. Juan Pablo Viscardo y Guzman, *etc.*—Letters and proclamations by General Miranda.) pp. xxxvi. 132. *J. Ridgway: London,* 1808. 8°. **8175**. b. **18**.

—— [Another copy.] **1446**. h. **14**.
Imperfect; wanting the half-title.

—— The Armed Briton; or, the Invaders vanquished; a play, in four acts. pp. 60. *J. T. Hughes: London,* 1806. 8°. **841**. f. **10**.

—— [Another copy.] **161**. g. **66**.

—— History of the Campaign of 1805 in Germany, Italy, the Tyrol, &c. pp. viii. 299. *James Ridgway: London,* 1806. 8°. **1311**. g. **4**.

—— South American Independence: or, the Emancipation of South America, the glory and interest of England. pp. vi. 82. *J. Ridgway: London,* 1807. 8°. **8179**. b. **65**. (**1**.)

BURKE (WILLIAM) *Hydropathic Doctor.* The Mineral Springs of Western Virginia: with remarks on their use, and the diseases to which they are applicable. [With an illustration and a map.] pp. 391. *Wiley & Putnam: New-York,* 1842. 12°. **1170**. e. **5**.

—— The second edition . . . To which are added a notice of the Fauquier White Sulphur Spring, and a chapter on taverns, also, a review of a pamphlet published by Dr. J. J. Moorman [i.e. "A Brief Notice of a portion of a work by W. Burke, entitled 'The Mineral Springs of Western Virginia.'"] pp. 394. *Wiley & Putnam: New York,* 1846. 12°. **1170**. e. **7**.

BURKE (WILLIAM) *Missionary.*

—— *See* BURKE (James) *Biographer of William Burke.* My Father in China. 1945. 8°. **4910**. b. **16**.

BURKE (WILLIAM) *Murderer. See* ADAM (Hargrave L.) Burke and Hare. The story of a terrible partnership. [1936.] 8°. **6059.aaa.9/6.**

—— *See* ADAM (Hargrave L.) Burke and Hare. The story of a terrible partnership. [1948.] 8°. **6059**. a. **11**.

—— *See* MACGREGOR (George) *F.S.A., Scot.* The History of Burke and Hare, *etc.* 1884. 8°. **6495**. f. **11**.

—— *See* WAUCH (Mansie) Mansie Waugh's Dream concerning the execution of Burke, *etc.* [1829.] fol. **840**. m. **34**. (**34**.)

—— *See* WRETCH, *pseud.* Wretch's Illustrations of Shakespeare, *etc.* [Coloured prints, with parodies on quotations from Shakespeare, satirizing W. Burke and others.] [1829.] fol. **1764**. a. **16**. (**1**.)

—— Burke and Hare. Edited by William Roughead. [With plates.] pp. x. 280. *W. Hodge & Co.: Edinburgh & London,* 1921. 8°. [*Notable British Trials.*] **6496**. d. **1/2**.

—— [Another edition.] [With illustrations and a bibliography.] pp. xi. 412. *W. Hodge & Co.: Edinburgh & London,* 1921. 8°. **6056**. y. **10**.

—— Burke and Hare. Edited by William Roughead. (New and enlarged general edition.) [With plates.] pp. xi. 412. *William Hodge & Co.: London,* 1948. 8°. [*Notable British Trials.*] **6496**. d. **1/54**.

—— A Correct Account of the Life, Confession, and Execution of Willm. Burke, who was executed at Edinburgh on Wednesday, 28 Jan. 1829. pp. 8. *G. Caldwell: Paisley,* [1829.] 8°. **11621**. aaa. **1**. (**9**.)

—— Horrible Discovery. The life and trial of Burke and his associates, the Edinburgh murdere [*sic*], who slaughtered their victims for sale. pp. 4. *W. Mason, for B. Hopner:* [*London,* 1828.] 8°. **6495**. bb. **2**. (**12**.)

—— Trial of William Burke and Helen M'Dougal, before the High Court of Justiciary, at Edinburgh . . . December 24. 1828, for the murder of Margery Campbell, or Docherty. Taken in short hand by Mr. John Macnee . . . With . . . portraits, *etc.* (Supplement to the Trial of William Burke & Helen M'Dougal, containing the whole legal proceedings against William Hare, in order to bring him to trial for the murder of James Wilson, or Daft Jamie. With an appendix of curious and interesting information, regarding the late West-port murders. Illustrated by a . . . print of Mrs. Hare, *etc.*) [Edited by Charles Kirkpatrick Sharpe.] 3 pt. *Robert Buchanan: Edinburgh,* 1829. 8°. **1245**. c. **29**.

BURKE (William) *Murderer.*

—— The Trial of William Burke & Helen M'Dougal for the Horrible Murder of Margery Campbell, for the purpose of disposing of her body for dissection. pp. 8. *G. Smeeton: London,* [1828.] 8°. **6495.** bb. **2. (11.)**

BURKE (William) *of the Secretary of State's Office. See* Barry (James) *R.A.* The Works of James Barry . . . containing his correspondence from France and Italy with Mr. Burke [and with W. Burke], *etc.* 1809. 4°. **561*.** d. **9, 10.**

—— *See* Brissot (J. P.) called Brissot de Warville. J. P. Brissot . . . to his Constituents . . . Translated from the French [by W. Burke]. With a preface and occasional notes by the translator. 1794. 8°. **1059.** i. **29. (1.)**

—— *See* Symons (Jelinger C.) William Burke the Author of Junius, *etc.* 1859. 8°. **8007.** b. **35.**

—— An Account of the European Settlements in America; with maps of North and South America. [By W. Burke. Revised by Edmund Burke.] 2 vol. 1757. 8°. *See* America. **279.** h. **29, 30.**

—— Second edition. 2 vol. 1758. 8°. *See* America. **1061.** d. **11, 12.**

—— Fourth edition, *etc.* 2 vol. 1762. 12° *See* America. **10408.** a. **3.**

—— Fourth edition, *etc.* 2 vol. 1765. 8°. *See* America. **10408.** d. **3.**

—— The fifth edition, *etc.* 2 vol. 1770. 8°. *See* America. **10412.bb.22.**

—— Sixth edition, *etc.* 2 vol. 1777. 8°. *See* America. **10480.** e. **3.**

—— [Another edition.] *See* Burke (*Right Hon.* Edmund) The Works of Edmund Burke. vol. 9. 1839. 8°. **1341.** m. **15.**

—— An Examination of the Commercial Principles of the Late Negotiations between Great Britain and France in 1761: in which the system of that negotiation with regard to our colonies and commerce is considered. [By W. Burke.] pp. 100. 1762. 8°. *See* England. [*Appendix.—History and Politics.*—ii. 1761.] **E. 2221. (4.)**

—— [Another copy.] ms. notes. **104.** i. **3.**

—— An Examination of the Commercial Principles of the late Negotiation between Great Britain and France . . . [By W. Burke.] The second edition. pp. 108. 1762. 8°. *See* England. [*Appendix.—History and Politics.*—ii. 1761.] **08139.** d. **104. (1.)**

—— The Letters of Valens . . . With corrections, explanatory notes, and a preface, by the author. [By W. Burke, assisted by Edmund and Richard Burke?] pp. ii. xv. 160. 1777. 8°. *See* Valens, *pseud.* **E. 2230. (1.)**

—— [Another copy.] The Letters of Valens, *etc.* [By W. Burke, assisted by Edmund and Richard Burke?] ms. notes [by Jeremy Bentham]. 1777. 8°. *See* Valens, *pseud.* **08138.** dd. **50. (7.)**

—— Remarks on the Letter address'd to Two Great Men [by John Douglas, successively Bishop of Carlisle and of Salisbury]. In a letter to the author of that piece. [Variously attributed to Charles Townshend and W. Burke.] pp. 64. [1760.] 8°. *See* Letter. **1093.** b. **37.**

—— [Another copy.] **E. 2213. (4.)**

BURKE (William) *of the Secretary of State's Office.*

—— The second edition. pp. 64. [1760.] 8°. *See* Letter. **102.** d. **67.**

—— The third edition, corrected. pp. 72. [1760.] 8°. *See* Letter. **08139.b.55.**

—— [Another copy.] **899.** c. **22. (3.)**

BURKE (William) *Philological Writer.* The Greek-English Derivative Dictionary: showing, in English characters, the Greek originals of such words in the English language as are derived from the Greek, *etc.* *J. Johnson: London,* 1806. 12°. **12985.** aa. **28. (2.)**

BURKE (William) *Surgeon.* A Popular Compendium of Anatomy: or, a Concise and clear description of the human body . . . Containing also an essay on suspended animation . . . Second edition. pp. xii. 261. *Highley & Son: London,* 1813. 12°. **1405.** d. **10.**

BURKE (William Alvord) *See* Boutelle (John A.) The Burke and Alvord Memorial, *etc.* [With a preface by W. A. Burke.] 1864. 8°. **9914.** i. **37.**

BURKE (*Mrs.* William Anthony) *See* Burke (Coralie E.)

BURKE (William E.) Federal Finances, or, the Income of the United States. pp. 263. *J. F. Schulte & Co.: Chicago,* [1891.] 8°. **08227.** de. **11.**

BURKE (William Jeremiah)

—— The Literature of Slang, *etc.* (Reprinted from the Bulletin of the New York Public Library.) pp. vii. 180. *New York Public Library: New York,* 1939. 8°. **11924.** d. **10.**

—— Rudolph Ackermann, Promoter of the Arts and Sciences. With a selected list of his publications in the New York Public Library. (Reprinted from the Bulletin of the New York Public Library.) [With plates, including a portrait.] pp. 36. *New York,* 1935. 8°. **010822.** i. **27.**

BURKE (William Jerry) *See* Burke (William Jeremiah)

BURKE (William Maxwell) History and Functions of Central Labor Unions. pp. 125. *Macmillan Co.: New York; P. S. King & Son: London,* 1899. 8°. [*Studies in History, Economics and Public Law.* vol. 12. no. 1.] **Ac. 2688/2.**

BURKE (William P.) *Rev.* History of Clonmel. [With illustrations.] pp. v. 523. *For the Clonmel Library Committee: Waterford,* 1907. 8°. **10390.** h. **23.**

—— The Irish Priests in the Penal Times, 1660–1760. From the State Papers in H.M. Record Offices, Dublin and London, the Bodleian Library, and the British Museum. pp. vii. 491. *Printed for the Author: Waterford,* 1914. 8°. **4735.** e. **17.**

BURKE (William Patrick) "Señor Burky." The adventurous life-story of W. P. Burke. [With a portrait.] pp. 270. *G. G. Harrap & Co.: London,* 1935. 8°. **010822.** e. **19.**

BURKE (William Willard) Administration of Private Social Service Agencies. A topical bibliography, *etc.* pp. viii. 41. *University Press: Chicago,* 1927. 8°. **11916.** b. **3.**

BURKE (WILLIAM WILLARD)

—— The Illinois Board of Charities as a State Supervisory Authority for the Care of the Mentally Diseased. A part of a dissertation submitted . . . August, 1934. [Typescript.] pp. 94. *Chicago*, 1946. Mic. A. **35.**
MICROFILM. *Issued by the University of Chicago Library Dept. of Photographic Reproduction.*

BURKE (WINIFRED) *See* WELLS, afterwards BURKE.

BURKE-GAFFNEY (JOHN JOSEPH) *See* GAFFNEY (J. J. B.)

BURKE-GAFFNEY (T. N.) *See* GAFFNEY.

BURKENHARE, *pseud.* The Flunkey, and the British Flunkeyage, being a companion to Burke's Peerage. By Burkenhare. pp. 48. *G. Vickers: London*, 1848. 16°. **012314. e. 22. (2.)**

BURKERSRODA (von) *Major.* Die Sachsen in Russland. Ein Beitrag zur Geschichte des russischen Feldzugs im Jahre 1812, besonders im Bezug auf das Schicksal der Königl. Sächsischen Truppen-Abtheilung bei der grossen französischen Armee. Aus dem Nachlasse des . . . Majors von Burkersroda, *etc.* pp. iv. 64. *Naumburg*, 1846. 8°. **9079. aa. 41.**

BURKERSRODE (JOHANNES) Anweisung zu dem Testheft für die Feststellung der Gutbegabten des 4. Schuljahres. Bearbeitet von J. Burkersrode und Mitarbeitern. pp. 67. 1933. 8°. *See* LEIPZIG.—*Institut des Leipziger Lehrervereins.* **8358. d. 45.**

BURKERT (GEORG) Gottfried Benjamin Hancke. Ein schlesischer Spät-Barockdichter. Inaugural-Dissertation, *etc.* pp. vi. 63. *Breslau*, 1933. 8°. **11856. ff. 29.**

BURKERT (OTTO) *See* KOTHE (G.) and FORCHHAMMER (T.) Führer durch die Orgel-Literatur . . . Vollständig neubearbeitet und bedeutend erweitert von O. Burkert. 1909. 8°. **7895. p. 4.**

—— Erläuterung der Disposition und musikalische Wertung des Werkes [i.e. of the giant organ in Breslau]. *In:* WALCKER (P.) Die Riesenorgel von Breslau. [1914.] 8°. Hirsch **1700.**

BURKERT (PAUL)

—— Weisser Kampf. Eigene Erlebnisse in Grönland. Mit . . . Aufnahmen, *etc.* pp. 79. *Berlin*, [1938.] 8°. **010460. k. 11.**

BURKES (LUDWIG) Mein Dörfchen. Gedichte. pp. 16. [*Schwerin*, 1867.] 16°. **11528. aaa. 11.**

BURKET (LESTER WILLIAM)

—— Oral Medicine. Diagnosis, treatment . . . With a section on Oral Aspects of Aviation Medicine by Alvin Goldhush, *etc.* pp. xxvii. 674. *J. B. Lippincott Co.: Philadelphia*, [1946.] 8° **7612. cc. 3.**

—— Oral Medicine . . . With a chapter on oral cancer by S. Gordon Castigliano . . . Second edition. pp. xxiii. 575. pl. 10. *J. B. Lippincott Co.: Philadelphia*, [1952.] 8°. **07611. k. 68.**

BURKETT (CHARLES) *See* SCHOLAS (William) An Authentic Account of the Trials . . . of the five Malefactors [C. Burkett and others], who were executed . . . for the divers robberies they had committed, *etc.* [1770.] 4°. **1132. k. 42.**

BURKETT (CHARLES WILLIAM) *See* HUNT (Thomas F.) and BURKETT (C. W.) Farm Animals, *etc.* 1914. 8°. **07207. e. 28.**

BURKETT (CHARLES WILLIAM)

—— *See* HUNT (Thomas F.) and BURKETT (C. W.) Soils and Crops, *etc.* 1913. 8°. **07073. f. 12.**

—— Agriculture for Beginners. By C. W. Burkett and Frank Lincoln Stevens and Daniel Harvey Hill. pp. xii. 267. *Ginn & Co.: Boston & London*, 1903. 8°. **07077. g. 45.**

—— Revised edition. pp. x. 355. *Ginn & Co.: Boston*, [1914.] 8°. **07077. g. 90.**

—— Country Life Education Series. Edited by C. W. Burkett. 9 vol. *Ginn & Co.: Boston*, [1906–20.] 8°. **07294. gg. 1.**

—— First Principles of Feeding Farm Animals, *etc.* pp. xvi. 336. *Orange Judd Co.: New York; Kegan Paul & Co.: London*, 1912. 8°. **7294. ccc. 5.**

—— Soils: their properties, improvement, management, and the problems of crop growing and crop feeding . . . Illustrated. pp. x. 303. *Orange Judd Co.: New York*, 1907. 8°. **07077. h. 42.**

BURKETT (CHARLES WILLIAM) and **POE** (CLARENCE HAMILTON)

—— Cotton. A practical manual of its culture, harvesting, marketing, manufactures and by-products . . . Illustrated from photographs. pp. ix. 331. *Doubleday, Page & Co.: London; New York* printed, 1906. 8°. [*Farm Library.*] **07076. l. 44/4**

—— [Another edition.] pp. ix. 331. *A. Constable & Co.: London*, 1906. 8°. **07076. k. 34.**

BURKETT (CHARLES WILLIAM) and **SWARTZEL** (KARL DALE)

—— Farm Arithmetic . . . Illustrated. pp. xiii. 280. *Orange Judd Co.: New York, Kegan Paul & Co.: London*, 1913. 8°. **8503. ccc. 36.**

BURKEY (LLOYD A.)

—— *See* SANDERS (George P.) General Procedure for Manufacturing Swiss Cheese. By G. P. Sanders, L. A. Burkey. 1950. 8°. [*U.S. Department of Agriculture. Circular.* no. 851.] A.S. **804/2.**

BURKH (AL'BERT) *See* BURGH.

BURKHALTER (JOSEF)

—— *See* GOTTHELF (J.) *pseud.* Mir wei eis uf Lützelflüh. Jeremias Gotthelfs Briefwechsel mit Amtsrichter Burkhalter. 1941. 8°. **10923. aa. 6.**

—— Amtsrichter Burkhalter und seine Briefe an Jeremias Gotthelf. Herausgegeben von G. Joss, *etc.* pp. xlvii. 86. *Bern*, 1899. 8°. **010910. b. 27.**

BURKHANOV (SHUKUR)

—— *See* OLIDOR (O.) Шукур Бурханов. [With portraits.] 1952. 8°. **11797. a. 109.**

BURKHARD. Burkhard und Amadine. Eine H x ı ballade von Jahre 1775. [By C. F. Sander ?] pp. 56. [*Hamburg*,] 1783. 8°. **11522. ccc. 15. (2.)**

BURKHARD, *Family of, of Basle.* *See* HEMMINGER (Z.) Historischer Entwurf des Burckhardischen Stamm-Baums, *etc.* 1715. 4°. **9903. bb. 10.**

BURKHARD (ARTHUR)

—— *See* CARDUCCI (G. A. G.) [*Selections.*] Twenty four Sonnets . . . Translated . . . by A. Burkhard. 1947. 8°. **11436. r. 24.**

—— *See* GRILLPARZER (F.) [Ein Bruderzwist in Habsburg.] Family Strife in Hapsburg . . . Translated by A. Burkhard. 1940. 8°. **11749. c. 21.**

—— *See* GRILLPARZER (F.) The Golden Fleece . . . Translated by A. Burkhard. 1942. 8°. **11749. c. 27.**

—— *See* GRILLPARZER (F.) The Jewess of Toledo. Esther. Dramas . . . Translated by A. Burkhard. 1953. 8°. **11749. c. 22.**

—— *See* GRILLPARZER (F.) Sappho . . . Translated by A. Burkhard. 1953. 8°. **11749. c. 25.**

—— *See* GRILLPARZER (F.) [Ein treuer Diener seines Herrn.] A Faithful Servant of his Master . . . Translated by A. Burkhard. 1941. 8°. **11749. c. 20.**

BURKHARD (ARTHUR) *See* KUHN (Charles L.) A Catalogue of German Paintings of the Middle Ages and Renaissance in American Collections . . . With an introduction to German painting by A. Burkhard. 1936. fol. **Ac. 2692. bp.**

—— Conrad Ferdinand Meyer: the style and the man. pp. ix. 225. *Harvard University Press: Cambridge, Mass.*, 1932. 8°. **20016. h. 20.**

—— Hans Burgkmair d. Ä . . . Mit 118 Abbildungen. pp. 203. *Leipzig*, [1934.] 4°. **7874. c. 74.**
Part of the series "Deutsche Meister."

—— Matthias Grünewald. Personality and accomplishment. [With reproductions and a bibliography.] pp. x. 123. pl. 100. *Harvard University Press: Cambridge, Mass.*, 1936. 8°. **7863. r. 21.**

BURKHARD (AUG.) Burkhard's Tables and Code, *etc.* *Hamilton, Adams & Co.: London; J. Dale & Co.: Bradford*, [1894.] 8°. **8548. b. 34.**

BURKHARD (C.) *Königl. bayr. Gymnasial-Professor.* Agrippina, des M. Agrippa Tochter, August's Enkelin, in Germanien, im Orient und in Rom. Drei Vorlesungen . . . Mit einer artistischen Beilage. pp. 100. *Augsburg*, 1846. 8°. **10605. d. 21.**

BURKHARD (C.) *Professor at the Gymnasium at Bayreuth.* Ueber das richtige Verhältniss in Anwendung der sogenannten künstlichen oder käuflichen Düngemittel zu den natürlichen, insbesondere dem Stallmist. Vortrag, *etc.* pp. 30. *Bayreuth*, 1863. 8°. **7076. aaa. 68. (3.)**

BURKHARD (CARL FRIEDRICH) Die Nomina der Kâçmîrî-Sprache. [1888.] *See* MUNICH.—*Königliche Akademie der Wissenschaften.* Sitzungsberichte der philosophisch-philologischen und historischen Classe, *etc.* 1888. Bd. 1. 1871, *etc.* 8°. **Ac. 713/8.**

BURKHARD (CAROLUS IMMANUEL) *See* NEMESIUS, *Bishop of Emesa.* Gregorii Nysseni—Nemesii Emeseni—περι φυσεως ἀνθρωπου liber a Burgundione in latinum translatus . . . Nunc primum ex libris manuscriptis edidit et apparatu critico instruxit C. I. Burkhard, *etc.* 1891. 8°. **08467. i. 20.**

—— *See* NEMESIUS, *Bishop of Emesa.* Nemesii Episcopi Premnon physicon, sive περι φυσεως ἀνθρωπου liber a N. Alfano . . . in latinum translatus. Recognovit C. Burkhard. 1917. 8°. **2049. d. 27.**

BURKHARD (FRANZ) Burg Eppstein. Denkschrift zur sechshundertsten Wiederkehr der Stadtwerdung Eppstein i. Taunus . . . Eine baugeschichtliche Abhandlung. [With illustrations.] pp. 74. *Frankfurt*, [1918.] 8°. **07816. k. 50.**

BURKHARD (JOHANN ANDREAS CHRISTIAN) Kurzer und gründlicher Unterricht im Generalbasse, *etc.* (Tl. 2. Kurze und gründliche Anleitung zum Orgelspiele, *etc.*) 2 Tl. *Ulm*, [1825, 29.] 4°. **7897. f. 13. (1.)**

—— Neuestes vollständiges musikalisches Wörterbuch, *etc.* pp. vi. 382. *Ulm*, 1832. 8°. **1042. f. 19.**

BURKHARD (JOHANN BALTHASAR) J. B. Burcardi . . . De assensu dissertatio philosophica. 1747. *See* PERIODICAL PUBLICATIONS.—*Zurich.* Museum Helveticum, *etc.* pt. 4. 1746, *etc.* 8°. **248. c. 26.**

—— J. B. Burchardi . . . De Judæis corruptionis Vet. Test. falso insimulatis dissertatio, *etc.* 1734. *See* GERDES (D.) Miscellanea Duisburgensia, *etc.* tom. 2. fasc. 1. [1732, *etc.*] 8°. **851. g. 2.**

—— J. B. Burcardi . . . Oratio de criminibus Josepho Patriarchæ à Morgano impactis, *etc.* 1746. *See* PERIODICAL PUBLICATIONS.—*Zurich.* Museum Helveticum, *etc.* pt. 3. 1746, *etc.* 8°. **248. c. 26.**

BURKHARD (JOHANN DANIEL) Dissertatio de duobus codicibus MSS. V. T. Bibliothecae Publicae Norimbergensis cum specimine variae lectionis ex quatuor codicibus MSS. V. T., *etc.* *Praes.* J. A. M. Nagel. pp. 28. *Altorfii*, [1769.] 4°. **1110. e. 28. (3.)**

BURKHARD (JOHANN GOTTLIEB) Vollständige Geschichte der Methodisten in England, aus glaubwürdigen Quellen. Nebst den Lebensbeschreibungen ihrer beyden Stifter, des Herrn Johann Wesley und George Whitefield. 2 Tl. *Nürnberg*, 1795. 8°. **4135. aa. 20.**

BURKHARD (KARL FRIEDRICH) *See* BURKHARD (Carl F.)

BURKHARD (OSCAR CARL)

—— *See* UYS (P. H. de V.) 'n Taal- en leesboek vir Duitsleerlinge van sekondêre en hoërskole. (Verwerking van Lernen Sie Deutsch! deur O. C. Burkhard.) 1944. 8°. **12964. n. 11.**

—— Lesen Sie Deutsch! . . . Illustrated. pp. ix. 166. xxii. *London*, 1936. 8°. [*Harrap's Modern Language Series.*] **12213. a. 1/376.**

—— Readings in Medical German. pp. xviii. 242. lxxxvi. *London*, 1937. 8°. [*Harrap's Modern Language Series.*] **12213. a. 1/393.**

—— Sprechen Sie Deutsch! . . . Illustrated. pp. xxi. 235. xxiv. *London*, 1935. 8°. [*Harrap's Modern Language Series.*] **12213. a. 1/333.**

—— [A reissue.] Sprechen Sie Deutsch! *etc.* *London*, 1952. 8°. **12965. aa. 21.**

BURKHARD (OSCAR CARL) and **DOWNS** (LYNWOOD G.)

—— Schreiben sie Deutsch! pp. x. 236. lvi. *London*, 1940. 8°. [*Harrap's Modern Language Series.*] **12213. a. 1/440.**

BURKHARD (PAUL) Die Stellung des christlichen Predigtamtes in der Gegenwart. Predigt, *etc.* pp. 16. *Zürich*, 1861. 8°. **4424. aa. 7.**

BURKHARD (WERNER) Grimmelshausen. Erlösung und barocker Geist. pp. 154. *Frankfurt*, 1929. 8°. [*Deutsche Forschungen.* Hft. 22.] **12213.ff.1/22**

BURKHARD (Wilhelm) Finanzentscheidungen. Eine Sammlung der wichtigsten Entscheidungen . . . über Fragen des Finanzrechts und der Finanzverwaltung in Bayern, *etc.* pp. viii. 930. *Würzburg,* 1888. 8°. **08229.** e. **6.**

BURKHARDSBERG (Wilhelm) Vorarbeiten zur Familienchronik. Herausgegeben von W. Burkhardsberg. 5 Hft. *München,* 1911–17. 8°. **9906.** a. **41.**

BURKHARDT (Abel) Christus in Gethsemane. Predigt am Palmsonntag, *etc. See* Basle.—*Evangelische Missions-Gesellschaft.* Dein Reich komme. Eine Sammlung kirchlicher Zeugnisse, *etc.* 1865. 8°. **4426.** bb. **6.**

BURKHARDT (Bruno) Gesetz betreffend die Bekämpfung gemeingefährlicher Krankheiten. Vom 30. Juli 1900. Text-Ausgabe mit Anmerkungen . . . von Dr. Burkhardt. pp. 121. *Berlin,* 1900. 16°. [*Guttentag'sche Sammlung deutscher Reichsgesetze.* no. 56.] **2227.** b. **56.**

BURKHARDT (Carl August Hugo) *See* Brandenburg. [*Collections of Laws and other Public Documents.*] Das funfft merckisch Buech des Churfuersten Albrecht Achilles . . . Herausgegeben von Dr. C. A. H. Burkhardt. 1857. 8°. **9914.** aa. **17.**

—— *See* Goethe (Catharina E.) Briefe von Goethes Mutter an die Herzogin Anna Amalia. Herausgegeben von C. A. H. Burkhardt. 1885. 8°. [*Schriften der Goethe-Gesellschaft.* Bd. 1.] Ac. **9422.**

—— *See* Goethe (J. W. von) [*Letters.—German.*] Goethe's Briefe an Philipp Seidel . . . Mit einer Einleitung von Dr. C. A. H. Burkhardt. 1893. 8°. **010910.** c. **3.** (**5.**)

—— *See* Goethe (J. W. von) [*Letters.—German.*] Goethes Briefe an Philipp Seidel. Mit einer Einleitung von Dr. C. A. H. Burkhardt, *etc.* 1909. 4°. **10923.** b. **26.**

—— *See* Luther (M.) [*Collections of Letters.*] Dr. Martin Luther's Briefwechsel. Mit vielen unbekannten Briefen . . . Herausgegeben von Dr. C. A. H. Burkhardt. 1866. 8°. **3905.** h. **7.**

—— *See* Mueller (Theodor A. H. F. von) Goethe's Unterhaltungen mit dem Kanzler Friedrich v. Müller. Herausgegeben von C. A. H. Burkhardt. 1870. 8°. **10708.** e. **36.**

—— —— 1898. 8°. **010707.** ee. **58.**

—— *See* Saxony, *Electorate of.—Landtag.* Ernestinische Landtagsakten . . . Bearbeitet von Dr. C. A. H. Burkhardt. 1902. 8°. [*Thüringische Geschichtsquellen.* Neue Folge. Bd. 5.] **9366.** ee. **1.**

—— *See* Sibylla, *Consort of John Frederick, Elector of Saxony.* Briefe der Herzogin Sibylla von Jülich-Cleve-Berg . . . herausgegeben von Dr. C. A. H. Burkhardt, *etc.* [1868.] 8°. **10921.** f. **15.**

—— Correcturen und Zusätze zu Quellenschriften für Hohenzollrische Geschichte. I. Das kaiserliche Buch des Markgrafen Albrecht Achilles herausgegeben von Dr. Constantin Höfler. pp. vi. 31. *Jena,* 1861. 8°. **9385.** e. **11.**

—— Die Gefangenschaft Johann Friedrichs des Grossmüthigen und das Schloss zur "Fröhlichen Wiederkunft," *etc.* pp. viii. 76. *Weimar,* 1863. 8°. **10703.** e. **20.** (**4.**)

—— Geschichte der sächsischen Kirchen- und Schulvisitationen von 1524 bis 1545, *etc.* pp. xxviii. 347. *Leipzig,* 1879. 8°. **4661.** ee. **33.**

—— Goethe und der Komponist Ph. Chr. Kayser . . . Mit Bild und Compositionen Kaysers. pp. viii. 79. *Leipzig,* 1879. 8°. **11825.** o. **13.** (**2.**)

BURKHARDT (Carl August Hugo)

—— [Another copy.] Goethe und der Komponist Ph. Chr. Kayser, *etc.* *Leipzig,* 1879. 8°. Hirsch **3424.**

—— Goethe's Verhältniss zu Philipp Seidel, *etc.* [Extracted from "Im neuen Reich."] [1871.] 8°. **011840.** g. **45.** (**19.**)

—— Das Grabmal der Corona Schroeter in Ilmenau. *In:* Schroeter (C. E. W.) Fünf Volkslieder, *etc.* [1902.] 4°. Hirsch M. **521.**

—— Hand- und Adressbuch der deutschen Archive im Gebiete des deutschen Reiches, der österreich-ungarischen Monarchie, der russischen Ostseeprovinzen und der deutschen Schweiz, *etc.* pp. viii. 208. *Leipzig,* 1875. 8°. **011899.a.4.**

—— Zweite, stark vermehrte Auflage. 2 Tl. *Leipzig,* 1887. 8°. **011900.** e. **16.** & de. **12.**

—— Der historische Hans Kohlhase und Heinrich von Kleist's Michael Kohlhaas, *etc.* pp. 59. *Leipzig,* 1864. 8°. **10707.** dd. **38.** (**9.**)

—— Das Repertoire des Weimarischen Theaters unter Goethes Leitung, 1791–1817. Bearbeitet und herausgegeben von Dr. C. A. H. Burkhardt. pp. xl. 152. *Hamburg & Leipzig,* 1891. 8°. [*Theatergeschichtliche Forschungen.* no. 1.] **011795.** i. **55/1.**

—— Repertorium zu Wieland's deutschem Merkur. 2 Tl. *Weimar,* 1872. *obl.* fol. Cup. **1247.** m. **4.** *Lithographed.*

—— Urkundenbuch der Stadt Arnstadt 704–1495 . . . herausgegeben von Dr. C. A. H. Burkhardt. pp. x. 503. *Jena,* 1883. 8°. [*Thüringische Geschichtsquellen.* Neue Folge. Bd. 1.] **9366.** ee. **1.**

BURKHARDT (Ernst Hugo Bruno) Ueber das runde Magengeschwür. Medicinische Inaugural-Dissertation, *etc.* pp. 28. *Halle,* [1872.] 8°. **7386.c.16.(5.)**

BURKHARDT (Eve) *See* Bliss (Adam) *pseud.* [i.e. R. F. Burkhardt and E. Burkhardt.]

—— *See* also Eden (Rob) *pseud.* [i.e. R. F. Burkhardt and E. Burkhardt.]

BURKHARDT (Felix) *See* Czuber (E.) Die statistischen Forschungsmethoden . . . Herausgegeben von F. Burkhardt, *etc.* 1938. 8°. **08535.** bb. **15.**

BURKHARDT (Frederick Henry)

—— *See* Herder (J. G. von) [Gott.] God, Some Conversations. A translation with a critical introduction and notes by F. H. Burkhardt. 1940. 8°. **04373.** ee. **11.**

BURKHARDT (Guido) *See* Zinzendorf (N. L. von) *Count.* Geistliche Gedichte . . . Herausgegeben von H. Bauer und G. Burkhardt. 1900. 8°. **011528.** k. **103.**

—— Die Brüdergemeine . . . Im Auftrag der Unitäts-Ältesten-Konferenz bearbeitet. 2 Tl. 1893, 97. 8°. *See* United Brethren.—*Unitäts-Ältesten-Konferenz.* **4662.** b. **11.**

—— Das geistliche Lied in seiner geschichtlichen Entwickelung bis auf die Gegenwart, vom Standpunkt der Brüdergemeine aus betrachtet . . . Ein Vortrag, *etc.* pp. 35. *Königsfeld ; Stuttgart* [printed], 1879. 8°. **3910.** ee. **7.** (**18.**)

—— Zinzendorf und die Brüdergemeine. pp. 177. *Gotha,* 1866. 8°. **4887.** b. **15.**

BURKHARDT (Gustav Emil) Handbuch der klassischen Mythologie nach genetischen Grundsätzen . . . Erste Abtheilung: Griechische Mythologie. Erster Band. Die Mythologie des Homer und Hesiod. pp. xiv. 435. *Leipzig*, 1844. 8°. **1363**. g. **3**.
No more published.

—— Praktische Anleitung zu einem gründlichen Schulstudium, als Vorbereitung auf die akademischen Studien. (Marci Antonii Mureti Institutio puerilis, seu Disticha de moribus, *etc.* [With a German verse translation.]) pp. 155. *Lützen*, 1846. 8°. **8307**. g. **3**. **(1.)**

BURKHARDT (H.) *of the Goethe-Gesellschaft.* *See* Burkhardt (C. A. H.)

BURKHARDT (Hans) Musik. pp. 83. *Heidelberg*, [1920.] 8°. [*Die Auskunft.* Hft. 2.] **12208**. cc. **4/2**.

BURKHARDT (Heinrich) Analysis. Redigiert von H. Burkhardt . . . W. Wirtinger . . . und R. Fricke (und E. Hilb). 3 Tl. *Leipzig*, 1898–1921. 8°. [*Encyklopädie der mathematischen Wissenschaften.* Bd. 2.] **08532**. h. **1**.

—— Funktionentheoretische Vorlesungen. 2 Tl.

Tl. 1. Einführung in die Theorie der analytischen Functionen einer complexen Veränderlichen, *etc.* pp. xii. 213.
Tl. 2. Elliptische Functionen, *etc.* pp. xvi. 373.

Leipzig, 1897, 99. 8°. **08533**. i. **34**.

—— [Another edition.]

Bd. 1. Hft. 1. Algebraische Analysis, *etc.* pp. xii. 195.
Bd. 1. Hft. 2. Einführung in die Theorie der analytischen Functionen einer komplexen Veränderlichen . . . Zweite, durchgesehene und teilweise umgearbeitete Auflage, *etc.* pp. xii. 227.

Leipzig, 1903. 8°. **08533**. h. **56**.
Imperfect; wanting Bd. 2, "*Elliptische Funktionen.*"

—— [Another edition.]

Bd. 1. Hft. 1. Algebraische Analysis . . . Zweite, durchgesehene und vermehrte Auflage, *etc.* pp. xii. 199.

Leipzig, 1908. 8°. **08533**. i. **57**.
Imperfect; wanting Bd. 1. *Hft.* 2. *Bd.* 2 *was not published in this edition.*

—— [Another edition.] Neu herausgegeben von Dr. Georg Faber.

Bd. 1. Hft. 2. Einführung in die Theorie der analytischen Functionen einer komplexen Veränderlichen. Fünfte umgearbeitete Auflage, *etc.* pp. x. 286.
Bd. 2. Elliptische Funktionen. Dritte . . . umgearbeitete Auflage, *etc.* pp. xvi. 444.

Leipzig, 1921, 20. **08533**. i. **56**.
Imperfect; wanting Bd. 1. *Hft.* 1.

—— Theory of Functions of a Complex Variable . . . Authorized translation from the fourth German edition with the addition of figures and exercises, by S. E. Rasor. pp. xiii. 432. *D. C. Heath & Co.: London*, [1914.] 8°. **8503**. f. **14**.

BURKHARDT (Heinz) *See* Burkhardt (Willy H.)

BURKHARDT (Helene) Studien zu Paul Hervieu als Romancier und als Dramatiker. pp. 244. *Zürich*, 1917. 8°. **011853**. s. **22**.

BURKHARDT (Horst)

—— Experimentelle Untersuchung der Fresnel'schen Beugungserscheinungen am Spalt, *etc.* pp. 26. *München*, 1954. 4°. [*Abhandlungen der Bayerischen Akademie der Wissenschaften.* Math.-naturw. Klasse. Neue Folge. Hft. 64.] Ac. **713/4**.

BURKHARDT (Hugo) *See* Burkhardt (Ernst H. B.)

BURKHARDT (Johann Gottlieb) *See* Burckhardt.

BURKHARDT (Johanna) Das Erlebnis der Wirklichkeit und seine künstlerische Gestaltung in Joseph Conrads Werk. Inaugural-Dissertation, *etc.* pp. v. 108. *Marburg*, 1935. 8°. **11857**. b. **15**.

BURKHARDT (Johannes) and **KUESTERMANN** (Otto) Beschreibende Darstellung der älteren Bau- und Kunstdenkmäler des Kreises Merseburg. Unter Mitwirkung von Dr. th. Heinrich Otte . . . bearbeitet von Dr. J. Burkhardt . . . und O. Küstermann, *etc.* pp. viii. 271. *Halle*, 1883. 8°. [*Beschreibende Darstellung der älteren Bau- und Kunstdenkmäler der Provinz Sachsen.* Hft. 8.] Ac. **7161/3**.

BURKHARDT (Martha) Rapperswil die Rosenstadt, erzählt aus ihrer . . . Vergangenheit, sowie von ihrem . . . Leben der Gegenwart zu hundert Zeichnungen von M. Burkhardt. pp. 155. *Zürich & Leipzig*, [1921.] 4°. **10196**. i. **18**.

BURKHARDT (Max)

—— Johannes Brahms. Ein Führer durch seine Werke mit einer einleitenden Biographie, zahlreichen Notenbeispielen, sowie . . . einem Uberblick [*sic*] über die Brahmsliteratur. [With plates, including portraits.] pp. 223. *Berlin*, [1912.] 8°. Hirsch **2715**.

BURKHARDT (Otto) Die Einführung der Reformation in den reussischen Ländern, zugleich ein Beitrag zur Kirchengeschichte dieser Länder. pp. 45. *Leipzig*, 1894. 8°. **4530**. ee. **28**. **(3.)**

BURKHARDT (Paul) Die Landschaft in Carl Spittelers "Olympischem Frühling." Eine kritisch-aesthetische Untersuchung vornehmlich unter dem Gesichtspunkt des Laokoon-Problems. pp. 181. *Zürich*, 1919. 8°. **11825**. k. **37**.

BURKHARDT (Robert) Chronik der Insel Usedom, *etc.* [With plates.] 3 pt. *Swinemünde*, 1909–12. 8°. **10230**. ccc. **38**.

—— Die Jagd nach Vineta. Ein Ueberblick—und eine Antwort. [An account of the attempts to identify the site, with an answer to Richard Hennig's work "Wo lag Vineta?"] pp. 84. *Swinemünde*, 1935. 8°. **07707**. eee. **40**.

BURKHARDT (Robert Ferdinand) *See* Bliss (Adam) *pseud.* [i.e. R. F. Burkhardt and E. Burkhardt.]

—— *See* also Eden (Rob) *pseud.* [i.e. R. F. Burkhardt and E. Burkhardt.]

BURKHARDT (Werner) and **VOIGT** (Hans Joachim) Signal: Jot—Dora! Der Schicksalsruf der Hochseeflotte, *etc.* [With plates.] pp. viii. 184. *Berlin*, 1938. 8°. **9087**. a. **2**.

BURKHARDT (Willy Heinz) Natur und Heimat bei Francis Jammes. Inaugural-Dissertation, *etc.* pp. v. 119. *Würzburg*, 1937. 8°. **11859**. ee. **18**.

—— Über Verlagerung raümlicher Gestalten. pp. 158. 1934. *See* Krueger (Felix) Neue psychologische Studien. Bd. 7. 1926, *etc.* 8° **8473.f.1/38.**

BURKHARDUS, *a Benedictine Monk of Saint Gall.* *See* Burkardus.

BURKHARDUS (Henricus) and **LOCHERUS** (Henricus) Specimen philosophiæ naturalis ad usum vitæ applicandæ expositum, in meditationibus de frigore, *etc. Praes.* J. Gesner. pp. 19. *Tiguri*, 1734. 4°. B. **64**. (**6**.)

BURKHARDUS (Joannes Daniel) *See* Burkhard (Johann D.)

BURKHART (Erwin)

—— Goslars Dachschieferbergbau von seinen Anfängen bis zur Gegenwart. [With a map.] pp. 272. *Goslar*, 1938. 8°. [*Beiträge zur Geschichte der Reichsbauernstadt Goslar.* Hft. 11.] **10240**. ccc. **8/9**.

BURKHART (Georg Albert) Friedrich Herlin-Forschungen, *etc.* pp. 130. pl. 11. *Erlangen*, 1912. 8°. [*Beiträge zur fränkischen Kunstgeschichte.* Hft. 2.] **7813.aaa.23/2.**

BURKHART (Harvey Jacob) Care of the Mouth and Teeth. pp. iv. 45. *Funk & Wagnalls Co.: New York & London*, 1928. 8°. [*National Health Series.*] W.P. **7825/21.**

BURKHART (Roy Abram)

—— *See* Hayward (Percy R.) and Burkhart (R. A.) Young People's Method in the Church. [1933.] 8°. **04192**. d. **1/83**.

—— From Friendship to Marriage. A guide to youth, *etc.* pp. x. 161. *Harper & Bros.: New York & London*, 1937. 8°. **08416**. l. **9**.

—— Guiding Individual Growth. A discussion of personal counseling in religious education. pp. 205. *Abingdon Press: New York*, [1935.] 8°. [*Abingdon Religious Education Texts.*] **04192**. d. **1/85**.

—— How the Church Grows, *etc.* pp. xiii. 210. *Harper & Bros.: New York & London*, [1947.] 8°. **4381**. eee. **70**.

—— The Secret of a Happy Marriage. A guide for a man and woman in marriage and the family. pp. 75. *Harper & Bros.: New York*, [1949.] 16°. **8417**. e. 42.

—— The Secret of Life. pp. 118. *Harper & Bros.: New York*, [1950.] 8°. **4397**. f. **26**.

BURKHEAD (Henry) A Tragedy of Cola's Furie, or Lirenda's Miserie. [In verse.] pp. 61. *Printed [by Thomas Bourke] at Kilkenny*, 1645; *to be sold at the signe of the white Swanne: Kilkenny*, 1646. 4°. C. **21**. c. **54**.

BURKHEISER (Carl) Grenzen des Staatskredits. pp. 102. *Berlin*, 1937. 8°. **8288**. aaa. **16**.

BURKHEISER (Karl) *See* Burkheiser (Carl)

BURKHOLDER (Lewis J.) A Brief History of the Mennonites in Ontario . . . Written and compiled under the direction of the Mennonite Conference of Ontario by L. J. Burkholder. pp. 358. 1935. 8°. *See* Ontario.—*Mennonite Conference of Ontario.* **20031**. b. **10**.

BURKHOLDER (Mabel Grace) Before the White Man Came. Indian legends and stories, *etc.* pp. 317. *McClelland & Stewart: Toronto*, [1923.] 8°. **012403**. e. 5.

—— A Pageant of Bethlehem in four scenes. pp. 8. [*Mount Hamilton, Ont.*, 1922.] 8°. **20018**. f. **50**.

—— A Prince in Egypt. [A play.] pp. 16. [*Mount Hamilton, Ont.*, 1922.] 8°. **20019**. bbb. **50**.

BURKHOLDER (Mabel Grace)

—— The Ten Virgins. In one scene. pp. 7. [*Mount Hamilton, Ont.*, 1922.] 8°. **11780**. aa. **28**.

BURKHOLDER (Paul Rufus) *See* Jensen (P. B.) [Die Wuchsstofftheorie.] Growth Hormones in Plants . . . Translated and revised by G. S. Avery, Jr., and P. R. Burkholder, *etc.* 1936. 8°. **7030**. p. **30**.

BURKHOLDER (Walter H.) A Bacterial Blight of Iris. (Reprinted from Phytopathology.) [1937.] 8°. **7028**. s. **27**.

—— The Bacterial Diseases of the Bean. A comparative study. pp. 88. pl. vi. *Ithaca, N.Y.*, 1930. 8°. [*Cornell University Agricultural Experiment Station. Memoir.* 127.] Ac. **2692**. h/2.

—— A Bacterial Leaf Spot of Geranium. (Reprinted from Phytopathology.) [1937.] 8°. **7028**. s. **28**.

—— Diseases, and Insect and other Pests, of the Field Bean in New York. [By] W. H. Burkholder and I. M. Hawley. (Revised.) [Two essays.] pp. 40. *Ithaca*, 1929. 8°. [*Cornell Extension Bulletin.* no. 58.] Ac. **2692**. ha/2.

—— Diseases, and Insect and other Pests, of the Field Bean in New York. [By] W. H. Burkholder and C. R. Crosby. (Revised.) [A new edition of W. H. Burkholder's essay, with an essay by C. R. Crosby replacing that by I. M. Hawley.] pp. 38. *Ithaca*, 1932. 8°. [*Cornell Extension Bulletin.* no. 58.] Ac. **2692**. ha/2.

—— [Another edition.] pp. 38. *Ithaca*, 1935. 8°. [*Cornell Extension Bulletin.* no. 58.] Ac. **2692**. ha/2.

—— Serological Reactions for the Determination of Bacterial Plant Pathogens. (Reprinted from Phytopathology.) pp. 3. [1937.] 8°. **7028**. s. **32**.

BÜRKI ( ) [For the German surname of this form:] *See* Buerki.

BURKILL (Harold J.)

—— British Gall Mites, *etc.* [*London*,] 1930. 8°. [" *London Naturalist* " *Reprints.* no. 9.] **Ac.3652.b/2.**

BURKILL (Isaac Henry)

—— *See* Finlow (Robert S.) and Burkill (I. H.) The Inheritance of Red Colour, and the Regularity of Self-Fertilisation, in Corchorus Capsularis, Linn., the Common Jute Plant. 1912. 4°. [*Memoirs of the Department of Agriculture in India.* Botanical series. vol. 4. no. 4.] I.S. **356**. (**2**.)

—— *See* Prain (*Sir* David) and Burkill (I. H.) An Account of the Genus Dioscorea in the East. 1936, *etc.* fol. [*Annals of the Royal Botanic Garden, Calcutta.* vol. 14.] **1820**. f.

—— The Botanic Gardens, Singapore. Illustrated guide. pp. 67. *Waterlow & Sons: London*, [1925?] *obl.* 8°. **7030**. e. **42**.

—— The Botany of the Abor Expedition. [With a map.] 2 pt. pp. 420. pl. x. *Calcutta*, 1924, 25. 8°. [*Records of the Botanical Survey of India.* vol. 10. no. 1, 2.] **7028**. r.

—— A Dictionary of the Economic Products of the Malay Peninsula. By I. H. Burkill . . . With contributions by William Birtwistle . . . Frederick W. Foxworthy . . . J. B. Scrivenor . . . and J. G. Watson . . . Published on behalf of the Governments of the Straits Settlements and Federated Malay States. 2 vol. pp. xi. 2402. 1935. 8°. *See* Straits Settlements. [Miscellaneous Official Publications.] **07076**. dd. **29**.

BURKILL (Isaac Henry)

—— Gossypium Obtusifolium, Roxburgh. pp. 10. *Calcutta*, 1906. 8°. [*Memoirs of the Department of Agriculture in India.* Botanical series. vol. 1. no. 4.] I.S. **356. (2.)**

—— Habits of Man and the Origins of the Cultivated Plants of the Old World. (The Hooker Lecture.) *In:* Proceedings of the Linnean Society of London. vol. 164. pt. 1. pp. 12–42. 1953. 8°. Ac. **3020/2.**

—— A List of Oriental Vernacular Names of the Genus Dioscorea. [With maps.] *Singapore*, 1924. 8°. [*Gardens' Bulletin, Straits Settlements.* vol. 3. no. 4–6.] P.P. **2312.** k.

—— Notes from a Journey to Nepal. [With a map.] *Calcutta*, 1910. 8°. [*Records of the Botanical Survey of India.* vol. 4. no. 4.] **7028.** r.

—— A Working List of the Flowering Plants of Baluchistan. pp. 136. *Superintendent Government Printing: Calcutta*, 1909. 8°. **7031.** v. **17.**

BURKILL (John) Bolton Illustrated: a series of views of the scenery around Bolton Abbey . . . from drawings made on the spot by J. Burkill . . . With original sonnets [by R. W. Hamilton], and notes descriptive and historical, *etc. J. Hogarth: London*, 1848. fol. **1782.** e. **6.**

—— The Pictorial Beauties of Mona. A selection of drawings from the romantic scenery of the Isle of Man . . . First series. *John Mylrea: Douglas*, 1857. fol. Maps **13.** f. **19.**

Lithographed. No more published.

BURKILL (John Charles)

—— The Lebesgue Integral. pp. viii. 87. *University Press: Cambridge*, 1951. 8°. [*Cambridge Tracts in Mathematics and Mathematical Physics.* no. 40.] **08534.** f. **1/40.**

BURKINSHAW (J. B.) Philips' Landscape Drawing Studies. From original drawings by J. B. Burkinshaw. *G. Philip & Son: London*, [1875.] *obl.* fol. **1755.** a. **12.**

BURKINSHAW (S.) Easy Landscapes. *London*, [1872.] *obl.* 4°. [*Philip's Series of Drawing Books.*] **7855.** aa. **25.**

—— Simple Studies in Straight Line and Perspective. *London*, [1872.] *obl.* 4°. [*Philip's Series of Drawing Books.*] **7855.** aa. **25.**

BURKIT (William) *See* Burkitt.

BURKITT (Charles Gray) *See* Weissenborn (E. W.) Weissenborn's Homeric Life. Translated and adapted to the needs of American students by G. C. Scoggin . . . and C. G. Burkitt, *etc.* 1903. 8°. **14003.** m. **3.**

BURKITT (Edward Herbert) A Short History of the Worshipful Company of Curriers, *etc.* [With plates.] pp. 72. [1906.] 8°. *See* London.—II. *Livery Companies.—Curriers.* **8248.** b. **18.**

—— Revised edition, *etc.* pp. 75. 1923. 8°. *See* London.—II. *Livery Companies.—Curriers.* **8248.** ccc. **8.**

BURKITT (Francis Crawford) *See* Bardesan. The Hymn of Bardaisan rendered into English by F. C. Burkitt. 1899. 8°. **753.** a. **56.**

BURKITT (Francis Crawford)

—— *See* Bible.—*Kings.—Selections.* [*Greek.*] Fragments of the Books of Kings according to the translation of Aquila . . . Edited . . . by F. C. Burkitt, *etc.* 1897. 4°. **L.9.f.12.**

—— *See* Bible. — *Ecclesiastes.* — *Selections.* [*English.*] Ecclesiastes rendered into English verse by F. C. Burkitt. 1918. 8°. **3050.** b. **41.**

—— —— 1922. 8°. **03051.** k. **17.**

—— *See* Bible.—*Gospels.* [*Polyglott.*] Evangelion da-Mepharreshe: the Curetonian version of the four Gospels, with the readings of the Sinai palimpsest and the early Syriac patristic evidence, edited, collected and arranged (with literal translations of text and variants) by F. C. Burkitt. 1904. 4°. **753.** i. **23.**

—— *See* Bible.—*Gospels.* [*Syriac.*] The Four Gospels in Syriac, transcribed from the Sinaitic palimpsest . . . by the late R. L. Bensly . . . and by F. C. Burkitt, *etc.* 1894. 4°. **753.** k. **43.**

—— *See* Bible.—*Gospels.—Selections.* [*Greek.*] The Biblical Text of Clement of Alexandria in the four Gospels and the Acts of the Apostles . . . With an introduction by F. C. Burkitt. 1899. 8°. [*Texts and Studies.* vol. 5. no. 5.] **03605.h.21/5.**

—— *See* Ephraim, *Saint, the Syrian.* S. Ephraim's Prose Refutations . . . published by C. W. Mitchell (and completed by A. A. Bevan and F. C. Burkitt). 1912, *etc.* 8°. **14005.** e. **5.**

—— *See* Ephraim, *Saint, the Syrian.* S. Ephraim's Quotations from the Gospel. Collected and arranged by F. C. Burkitt. 1901. 8°. [*Texts and Studies.* vol. 7. no. 2.] **03605.h.21/7.**

—— *See* Euphemia, *Saint and Martyr.* Euphemia and the Goth, with the Acts of Martyrdom of the Confessors of Edessa. Edited and examined by F. C. Burkitt. 1913. 8°. **14005.** e. **8.**

—— *See* Francis [Bernardoni], *of Assisi, Saint.* The Song of Brother Sun, in English rime. [Translated by F. C. Burkitt.] [1926.] 8°. **011645.** h. **45.**

—— *See* Gwilliam (George H.) Biblical and Patristic Relics of the Palestinian Syriac Literature . . . Edited by G. H. Gwilliam . . . F. C. Burkitt, *etc.* 1896. 4°. **12204.** f. **11/9.**

—— *See* Tichonius, *Afer.* The Book of Rules of Tyconius. Newly edited . . . by F. C. Burkitt. 1894. 8°. [*Texts and Studies.* vol. 3. no. 1.] **03605.h.21/3.**

—— *See* Vollers (C.) The Modern Egyptian Dialect of Arabic . . . Translated by F. C. Burkitt. 1895. 8°. **012904.** ee. **8.**

—— The Ancient Versions of the New Testament. *See* Henson (Herbert H.) successively *Bishop of Hereford* and *of Durham.* Criticism of the New Testament, *etc.* 1902. 8°. **03225.** e. **9.**

—— Christian Beginnings. Three lectures. [With special reference to " The Beginnings of Christianity," edited by F. J. F. Jackson and K. Lake.] pp. 152. *University of London Press: London*, 1924. 8°. **03226.** e. **35.**

—— Christian Worship. *See* Church. The Church of Today, *etc.* 1930. 8°. **2210.** bb. **8/3.**

—— Church & Gnosis. A study of Christian thought and speculation in the second century. The Morse lectures for 1931. pp. ix. 153. *University Press: Cambridge*, 1932. 8°. **3622.** aa. **27.**

—— Claude Montefiore. An appreciation. *See* Montefiore (Claude G.) Speculum Religionis, *etc.* 1929. 8°. 04504. i. 58.

—— The Earliest Sources for the Life of Jesus. pp. 122. *Constable & Co.: London,* 1910. 8°. [*Modern Religious Problems.*] 4017. dg. 48/1.

—— New and revised edition. pp. 130. *Constable & Co.: London,* 1922. 8°. 03226. e. 5.

—— Early Christianity outside the Roman Empire. Two lectures delivered at Trinity College, Dublin. pp. 89. *University Press: Cambridge,* 1899. 8°. 2214. aa. 2.

—— Early Eastern Christianity. St. Margaret's lectures, 1904, on the Syriac-speaking Church. [With plates.] pp. viii. 228. *John Murray: London,* 1904. 8°. 2214. aa. 1.

—— The Early Syriac Lectionary System . . . From the Proceedings of the British Academy, *etc.* [With a translation of British Museum Additional ms. 14528, ff. 152–191.] pp. 38. *Oxford University Press: London,* [1923.] 8°. 3478. h. 35.

—— Eucharist and Sacrifice. (Reprinted from "The Interpreter.") pp. 23. *W. Heffer & Sons: Cambridge,* 1921. 8°. 4325. dd. 9.

—— (Second edition.) pp. 26. *W. Heffer & Sons: Cambridge,* 1927. 8°. 4323. e. 14.

—— "The Failure of Liberal Christianity," and "Some Thoughts on the Athanasian Creed." Two addresses. pp. 40. *Bowes & Bowes: Cambridge,* 1910. 8°. 4107. de. 37. (1.)

—— Some Thoughts on the Athanasian Creed. [An abridgment.] pp. 12. *S.P.C.K.: London,* 1916. 16°. 03504. ee. 22.

—— The Gospel History and its Transmission. pp. viii. 359. *T. & T. Clark: Edinburgh,* 1906. 8°. 03225. ee. 23.

—— Third edition. pp. xviii. 365. *T. & T. Clark: Edinburgh,* 1911. 8°. 03225. ee. 45.

—— How to Teach the Bible. pp. 4. *Society for Promoting Christian Knowledge: London,* 1908. 8°. [*Pan-Anglican Papers.* S.B. 26.] 4108. cc. 35.

—— Jesus Christ. An historical outline. pp. viii. 90. *Blackie & Son: London & Glasgow,* 1932. 8°. 4227. d. 19.

—— Jewish and Christian Apocalypses. pp. vi. 80. *Oxford University Press: London,* 1914. 8°. [*Schweich Lectures.* 1913.] Ac. 1186/2.

—— Notes upon some Agreements between the Sinai Palimpsest and the Textus Receptus in St. Mark's Gospel. *See* Hutton (Edward A.) An Atlas of Textual Criticism, *etc.* 1911. 8°. 03225. df. 72.

—— The Old Latin and the Itala. With an appendix containing the text of the S. Gallen palimpsest of Jeremiah. pp. viii. 96. *University Press: Cambridge,* 1896. 8°. [*Texts and Studies.* vol. 4. no. 3.] 03605.h.21/4.

—— Pagan Philosophy and the Christian Church.—The Christian Church in the East. [With additions by J. M. Creed.] 1939. *See* Bury (John B.) Cambridge Ancient History, *etc.* vol. 12. 1923, *etc.* 8°.
[Latest edition.] 2070.e-f
[Earlier editions.] 09004. de.

—— Petra and Palmyra. *See* Palestine. Palestine in General History. 1929. 8°. [*Schweich Lectures.* 1926.] Ac. 1186/2.

—— Pistis Sophia and the Coptic Language. (Extract from The Journal of Theological Studies.) [1926.] 8°. 07705. b. 11

—— The Religion of the Manichees. Donnellan lectures for 1924. [With plates.] pp. viii. 129. *University Press: Cambridge,* 1925. 8°. 04530. de. 17.

—— Robert Henry Charles, 1855–1931. From the Proceedings of the British Academy, *etc.* pp. 11. *Humphrey Milford: London,* [1932.] 8°. 10854. g. 33.

—— Setheus. (Extract from The Journal of Theological Studies.) *Oxford,* [1935.] 8°. 07705. b. 15.

—— Some Thoughts on the Athanasian Creed. *See* supra: "The Failure of Liberal Christianity," *etc.*

—— The Syriac Forms of New Testament Proper Names . . . From the Proceedings of the British Academy, *etc.* pp. 32. *Oxford University Press: London,* [1912.] 8°. 03129. i. 3. (4.)

—— Twenty-Five Years of Theological Study. A lecture delivered at the University of Manchester . . . Together with "The commemoration of the twenty-fifth anniversary of the establishment of the Theological Faculty in the University of Manchester, with some reference to its origins and history," by R. G. Parsons . . . Reprinted from "The Bulletin of the John Rylands Library." pp. 24. *Manchester University Press: Manchester,* 1930. 8°. 20017. k. 10.

—— Two Lectures on the Gospels. pp. 94. *Macmillan & Co.: London, New York,* 1901. 8°. 03225. df. 12.

—— Francis Crawford Burkitt, 1864–1935. [A biographical memoir. By J. F. Bethune-Baker.] From the Proceedings of the British Academy, *etc.* pp. 42. *Humphrey Milford: London,* [1937.] 8°. 010821. i. 2.

BURKITT (Francis Crawford) and **NEWSOM** (George Ernest)

—— The Layman's Library. Edited by F. C. Burkitt . . . and the Rev. G. E. Newsom. 6 vol. *Longmans & Co.: London,* 1914, 15. 8°. 3624. a. 5.

BURKITT (Francis George) The Bible and the Evolution Theories. pp. 16. *C. A. Hammond: London,* [1928.] 8°. 03126. df. 47.

—— Brief Remarks on Eternal Life in its Various Aspects. pp. 14. *Central Bible Truth Depot: London; W. M. Roberts: Leicester,* [1925.] 8°. 4255. ee. 45.

—— A Brief Outline of Coming Events. From the present period to the end of time, as set forth in the prophetic scriptures. [Signed: F. G. B., i.e. F. G. Burkitt.] pp. 31. 1901. 8°. *See* B., F. G. 03128. g. 41. (4.)

—— "Behold He Cometh." An outline of prophetic truth from the present period to the end of time. (New and revised edition [of "A Brief Outline of Coming Events"].) pp. 69. *C. A. Hammond: London,* 1926. 8°. 03187. e. 42.

BURKITT (Francis George)

—— Christ our Sacrifice and Priest; being brief notes on the Epistle to the Hebrews. pp. 45. *James Carter: London*, [1907.] 8°. 4373. df. 6. (6.)

—— A Few Remarks on Eternal Life. [Signed: F. G. B., i.e. F. G. Burkitt ?] pp. 8. [1895.] 8°. *See* B., F. G. 4371. bb. 9. (6.)

—— A Few Remarks on Recent Doctrines contained in "Notes of Readings" held in the United States and Canada, revised by F. E. R. [i.e. F. E. Raven.] [Signed: F. G. B., i.e. F. G. Burkitt ?] pp. 16. [1900.] 8°. *See* B., F. G. 4373. df. 6. (2.)

—— Third edition. pp. 31. 1905. 8°. *See* B., F. G. 4377. de. 13. (4.)

—— A Message of Life. [Five religious essays. The first, second, fourth and fifth signed: F. G. B., i.e. F. G. Burkitt ?, the third signed: C. H. M.] pp. 15. [1906.] 8°. *See* B., F. G. 04420. h. 8. (3.)

—— Plain Papers for Young Christians. ser. 1. pp. 16. *James Carter: London*, [1908.] 8°. 04420. ee. 55.

—— Plain Papers on the Future State and Eternal Punishment. [Signed: F. G. B., i.e. F. G. Burkitt ?] pp. 40. 1903. 8°. *See* B., F. G. 04420. g. 54. (1.)

—— Tables of Logarithms and Decimals adapted to business and statistical calculations. Compiled by F. G. Burkitt. pp. 23. *Simpkin, Marshall & Co.: London*, [1903.] 8°. 08548. e. 8.

BURKITT (Frederick Evelyn)

—— *See* Co-Respondent. The Co-Respondent. By the author of "The Terror by Night" [i.e. Gertrude C. S. Saben and F. E. Burkitt]. [1912.] 8°. 012618. cc. 3.

—— *See* Saben (Gregory) *pseud.* [i.e. G. C. S. Saben and F. E. Burkitt.]

BURKITT (Henry John) Great Truths Simply Explained, in the form of instructions for confirmation, *etc.* pp. 120. *Marshall, Morgan & Scott: London, Edinburgh*, [1936.] 8°. 4324. e. 62.

—— The History of The Queen's, Royal West Surrey Regiment, in the form of a lantern lecture, *etc.* [With plates.] pp. 96. *A. C. Curtis & Co.: Guildford & Godalming*, 1917. 8°. 08821. aaa. 4.

—— The Story of Stoughton. By pen and camera. [Reprinted from the Stoughton parish magazine.] pp. 45. *Biddle & Shippam: Guildford*, 1910. 8°. 010368. de. 28.

BURKITT (Henry Lemuel) *See* Burkitt (Lemuel) and Read (J.) A Concise History of the Kehukee Baptist Association . . . Revised and improved by H. L. Burkitt. 1850. 8°. 4745. aa. 11.

BURKITT (James) The Golden Altar. An exposition of Hebrews xiii. 10, 11. pp. 16. *Elliot Stock: London*, 1903. 8°. 4474. d. 118. (6.)

—— Religious Controversy. An address delivered in Trinity College, Dublin . . . at the opening of the nineteenth session of the College Theological Society, *etc.* pp. 19. *Hodges, Smith & Co.: Dublin*, 1856. 8°. 4376. cc. 5.

BURKITT (Judith) *See* Hextal (William) A Due Preparation for Death and Eternity, considered and recommended. A funeral discourse . . . on occasion of the . . . death of Mrs. J. Burkitt, *etc.* 1753. 8°. 1416. d. 53.

BURKITT (Kenneth Frank Philip)

—— *See* Cooke (Herbert J.) Biology. By H. J. Cooke . . . K. F. P. Burkitt, *etc.* 1949. 8°. 7007. aa. 31.

BURKITT (Lemuel) and READ (Jesse) A Concise History of the Kehukee Baptist Association, from its original rise down to 1803 . . . Revised and improved by Henry L. Burkitt. (Appendix. Biography of Elder Lemuel Burkitt and his family, by Dr. Wm. P. A. Hail.) pp. 351. *Lippincott, Grambo & Co.: Philadelphia*, 1850. 8°. 4745. aa. 11.

BURKITT (Miles Crawford) *See* Breuil (H.) and Burkitt (M. C.) Rock Paintings of Southern Andalusia, *etc.* 1929. fol. 7709. pp. 21.

—— The Old Stone Age, *etc.* pp. xiv. 254. pl. viii. *University Press: Cambridge*, 1933. 8°. 07704. de. 51.

—— The Old Stone Age . . . Second edition. pp. xiv. 254. pl. viii. *University Press: Cambridge*, 1949. 8°. 07708. aa. 11.

—— Our Early Ancestors. An introductory study of mesolithic, neolithic and copper age cultures in Europe and adjacent regions. [With illustrations.] pp. xii. 243. *University Press: Cambridge*, 1926. 8°. 010007. e. 19.

—— Our Forerunners. A study of palæolithic man's civilisations in Western Europe and the Mediterranean basin. pp. 227. *Williams & Norgate: London*, [1924.] 8°. [*Home University Library.*] 12199. p. 1/114.

—— Pensées sur la vie. pp. 8. *Rouen*, 1918. 8°. 8460. ee. 60.

—— Prehistory. A study of early cultures in Europe and the Mediterranean basin, *etc.* [With illustrations.] pp. xix. 438. *University Press: Cambridge*, 1921. 8°. 010007. h. 9.

—— Second edition. pp. xxiii. 438. *University Press: Cambridge*, 1925. 8°. 10007. i. 36.

—— South Africa's Past in Stone & Paint. pp. xiv. 183. pl. viii. *University Press: Cambridge*, 1928. 8°. 010006. f. 24.

BURKITT (Robert) *Anthropologist.* *See* Káal (T.) The Hills and the Corn . . . Translated . . . by R. Burkitt. 1920. 8°. [*University of Pennsylvania. University Museum Anthropological Publications.* vol. 8. no. 2.] Ac. 2692. q/3.

BURKITT (Robert) *Farmer.* Burkitt's Observations on the Inland Navigation, draining of loughs, making entrances into ports and a bridge over the ferry of Wexford, and the benefits to be had by sowing of cole-seed. pp. 8. *Sarah Cotter: Dublin*, 1755. 8°. 8246. bbb. 2.

BURKITT (Roland Wilks)

—— *See* Gregory (Joseph R.) Under the Sun. A memoir of Dr. R. W. Burkitt, *etc.* [With portraits.] [c. 1950.] 8°. 10863. f. 73.

—— The Settlement of Sins, willy-nilly, *etc.* pp. 54. *S. Martin & Co.: London*, [1930.] 8°. 4370. de. 1.

BURKITT (W. M.) *See* Liturgies.—*Church of England.* —*Common Prayer.* The Book of Common Prayer . . . With notes and annotations (by the Revd W. M. Burkitt). 1833. 8°. 3408. d. 21.

—— —— 1839. 8°. 3407.d.25.(1.)

BURKITT (WILLIAM) *See* BIBLE. [*English.*] The Holy Bible . . . Illustrated with annotations . . . selected from the works of Stackhouse, Burkitt, *etc.* 1806, *etc.* fol. **L.15.e.5.**

—— *See* BIBLE. [*English.*] The Royal Standard Devotional Family Bible . . . With moral . . . observations . . . chiefly compiled from the writings of Gill . . . Burkitt, *etc.* [1815?] 4°. **L.8.d.4.**

—— *See* BIBLE.—*New Testament.* [*English.*] The New Testament . . . With critical and explanatory notes . . . from the writings and sermons of . . . Grotius . . . Burkitt, *etc.* 1736. fol. **L.15.b.4.**

—— *See* BIBLE.—*New Testament.* [*English.*] The New Testament . . . with observations and practical instructions, being an abridgement of the . . . work of . . . the Rev. Mr. W. Burkitt, *etc.* 1806. 4°. **5.** e. **5, 6.**

—— *See* LITURGIES.—*Church of England.—Common Prayer.* The Complete Family Prayer Book . . . Elucidated with . . . notes . . . selected from the works of the late Rev. Mr. Burkitt, *etc.* 1775. 4°. **3407.** e. **13.**

—— *See* MAC KEON (Hugh) An Inquiry into the Birth-Place . . . of the Reverend W. Gurnall . . . To which is added, A Biographical Sketch of the Reverend W. Burkitt, *etc.* 1830. 12°. **4905.** aa. **8.**

—— *See* PARKHURST (Nathaniel) The Life of the Reverend Mr. W. Burkitt . . . To which is added, a funeral sermon, preached a week after his burial, *etc.* 1704. 8°. **1416.** a. **21.**

—— The Poor Man's Help, and Young Man's Guide . . . Unto which is added Principles of Religion . . . with Forms of Prayer for Families and Single Persons, also, Divine Hymns . . . The tenth edition [of "The Poor Man's Help"], with additions. pp. 184. *J. Laurence: London,* 1712. 12°. **4403.** bbb. **19.**

—— The twelfth edition, with additions. pp. 184. *J. Laurence: London,* 1715. 12°. **4404.** d. **1.**

—— The twentieth edition, with additions. pp. 184. *D. Midwinter & A. Ward: London,* 1732. 12°. **875.** a. **8.**

—— [Another edition.] An Help and Guide to Christian Families . . . With Forms of Prayer . . . Also Divine Hymns . . . The twenty seventh edition, with additions. *R. Ware: London,* 1749 [1757]. 12°. **4410.** b. **9.**
The titlepages of "Family Instructions: or Principles of religion, etc.," and of "Forms of Prayer for Families, etc." bear the date 1757.

—— [Another copy, with a different titlepage.] The Poor Man's Help, and Young Man's Guide . . . The thirtieth edition, with additions. pp. viii. 184. *R. Ware: London,* 1757. 12°. **4403.** aaa. **4.**

—— [Another edition.] An Help and Guide to Christian Families . . . The thirty-third edition, with additions. pp. viii. 184. *J. Rivington: London,* 1767. 12°. **4406.** aaa. **19.**

—— The thirty-sixth edition, with additions. pp. viii. 184. *J. F. & C. Rivington: London,* 1787. 12°. **4405.** bbb. **34.**

—— The thirty-eighth edition, with additions. pp. viii. 184. *F. & C. Rivington: London,* 1802. 12°. **4407.** aaa. **17.**

—— [Another edition.] pp. xi. 204. *J. Agg: Evesham,* 1814. 12°. **1018.** f. **14.**

BURKITT (WILLIAM)

—— The forty-third edition, with additions. pp. xii. 204. *F. C. & J. Rivington: London,* 1818. 12°. **4413.** bb. **4.**

—— The forty-fourth edition, with additions. pp. iv. 152. *F. C. & J. Rivington: London,* 1822. 12°. **3476.** c. **41.**

—— The forty-fifth edition, with additions. pp. iv. 148. *C. & J. Rivington: London,* 1824. 12°. **4405.** ccc. **20.**

—— New edition, *etc.* pp. iv. 111. *J. G. & F. Rivington: London,* 1835. 12°. **863.** h. **29.** (1.)

—— An Argumentative and Practical Discourse of Infant-Baptism . . . The third edition. pp. 67. *Tho. Parkhurst: London,* 1702. 8°. **4325.** aa. **15.**

—— The fourth edition. pp. 68. *J. Lawrence: London,* 1712. 8°. **4325.** c. **14.**

—— [Another edition.] Plain Words about Infant Baptism . . . Edited by Rev. J. H. Hobart De Mille. pp. 121. *H. B. Durand: New York,* 1864. 12°. **4326.** aa. **17.**

—— *See* KEACH (Benjamin) The Rector Rectified . . . Being a sober answer to a late pamphlet, entituled, An Argumentative and Practical Discourse of Infant-Baptism; published by Mr. W. Burkit, *etc.* 1692. 8°. **4323.** a. **30.**

—— Expository Notes, and Practical Observations on the four Holy Evangelists (on the remaining part of the New Testament) . . . wherein the sacred text is at large recited, the sence [*sic*] explained, doubts resolved . . . seeming contradictions reconciled, *etc.* 2 pt. 1700. fol. *See* BIBLE.—*New Testament.* [*English.*] **L.15.h.6.**

—— Expository Notes, with Practical Observations, on the New-Testament . . . The third edition. [With a portrait.] 1707. fol. *See* BIBLE.—*New Testament.* [*English.*] **3125.** f. **15.**

—— The sixth edition, carefully corrected. 1716. fol. *See* BIBLE.—*New Testament.* [*English.*] **L.16.c.8.**

—— The seventh edition, carefully corrected. 1719. fol. *See* BIBLE.—*New Testament.* [*English.*] **L.15.d.5.**

—— [Another copy.] **L.15.d.8.**

—— The eighth edition, carefully corrected. 1724. fol. *See* BIBLE.—*New Testament.* [*English.*] **L.16.g.9.**

—— The ninth edition, carefully corrected. 1729. fol. *See* BIBLE.—*New Testament.* [*English.*] **L.17.h.1.**

—— Expository Notes with Practical Observations on the New Testament . . . By W. Burkitt. The tenth edition carefully corrected. [With a portrait.] 1734. fol. *See* BIBLE.—*New Testament.* [*English.*] L.R. **300.** bbb. **9.**

—— The eleventh edition, carefully corrected. 1739. fol. *See* BIBLE.—*New Testament.* [*English.*] **L.17.c.9.**

—— The twelfth edition, carefully corrected. 1749. fol. *See* BIBLE.—*New Testament.* [*English.*] **L.12.e.10.**

—— The fourteenth edition, carefully corrected. pp. vii. 878. 1753. fol. *See* BIBLE.—*New Testament.* [*English.*] **L.15.b.6.**

—— The fifteenth edition, carefully corrected. pp. viii. 878. 1760. fol. *See* BIBLE.—*New Testament.* [*English.*] **L.16.g.8.**

—— The sixteenth edition, carefully corrected. pp. viii. 878. pl. LXXVII. 1765. fol. *See* BIBLE.—*New Testament.* [*English.*] **L.14.g.2.**

BURKITT (William)

—— The seventeenth edition, carefully corrected. pp. viii. 578. pl. lxxvii. 1772. fol. *See* Bible.—*New Testament.* [*English.*] 3. e. 2.

—— [Another edition.] pp. v. 1178. 1789. 4°. *See* Bible.—*New Testament.* [*English.*] **3051.** eee. **8.**

—— Expository Notes, with Practical Observations, on the New Testament . . . By the Rev. W. Burkitt . . . To this edition will be added, the life of the author, *etc.* [With plates, including a portrait.] 1810. 4°. *See* Bible.—*New Testament.* [*English.*] 3054. d. 3

—— New edition, carefully revised and collected. pp. 998. 1814. 4°. *See* Bible.—*New Testament.* [*English.*] **3226.** g. **8.**

—— Expository Notes, with Practical Observations, on the New Testament . . . By W. Burkitt. [With plates, including a portrait.] pp. 990. 1818. fol. *See* Bible.—*New Testament.* [*English.*] **3054.** dd. **4.**

—— Nod[au] Eglurhaol, gyda sylwadau ymarferol ar Destament Newydd . . . yn yr hwn y mae y testyn cyssegredig wedi ei argraffu yn gyflawn, yr ystyr hefyd yn cael ei egluro . . . Wedi ei gyfieithu gan Josiah Thomas Jones. pp. 882. 1835. 4°. *See* Bible.—*New Testament.* [*Welsh.*] **3103.** e. **17.**

—— Family Instruction: or, Principles of religion, necessary to be known by family governors, and needful to be taught their children and servants, for preparing both themselves and theirs, to receive the Holy Communion with benefit, *etc.* pp. 32. *Tho. Parkhurst: London,* 1704. 8°. **3506.** c. **15.**

—— The Peoples Zeal Provok't to an Holy Emulation, by the . . . example of their dead minister: or, a Seasonable memento to the parishioners of Lavenham . . . Being a sermon preached to that people, soon after the . . . enterrment of their Reverend . . . Minister Mr. William Gurnall, *etc.* pp. 28. *M. W. for Ralph Smith: London,* 1680. 4°. **1416.** h. **37.**

—— [Another copy.] **114.** f. **30.**

—— [Another edition.] [With a preface by Robert Ainslie.] pp. viii. iv. 10–26. *Richard Baynes: London,* 1829. 8°. **4905.** d. **9.**

—— The Poor Man's Help, and Young Mans Guide: containing i. Doctrinal instructions for the right informing of his judgment. ii. Practical directions for the general course of his life. iii. Particular advices for the well-managing of every day . . . The second edition. pp. 80. *For Tho. Parkhurst: London,* 1694. 8°. **4403.** d. **33.** *Imperfect; wanting pp.* 27–30.

—— The third edition. pp. 119. *For Tho. Parkhurst: London,* 1697. 8°. **4399.** aa. **11.**

—— The sixth edition. pp. 76. *T. Parkhurst: London,* 1705. 8°. **694.** c. **31.** (**3.**) *Cropped.*

—— The Poor Man's Help, and Young Man's Guide . . . The twenty fourth edition, with additions. pp. 184. *D. Midwinter, etc.: London,* 1741. 12°. **03440.** cc. 36.

—— Drych anffaeledig; neu Frywyd santaidd a rhinweddol yr Arglwydd Iesu Grist . . . wedi ei gasglu yn ofalus gan y Parch. W. Burkitt . . . cyhoeddedig yn bresennol, yn Gymmraeg, gan J. T. Jones. pp. 8. *J. T. Jones: Caernarfon,* 1833. 8°. **4460.** h. **8.** (**4.**)

BURKITT (William)

—— Memoirs of the Life of the Rev. William Burkitt, *etc.* [An abridged and altered version of the life of W. Burkitt by Nathaniel Parkhurst.] pp. 16. *John Pytt: Glocester,* [1780?] 8°. **4906.** bb. **10.**

BURKITT (William T.) The Coming Day. A story of inevitable social and industrial progress. pp. 96. *Drane's: London,* [1913.] 8°. **08275.** df. **14.**

BURKIUS (Philippus David) *See* Burke (Philip D.)

BÜRKLE ( ) [For the German surname of this form:] *See* Buerkle.

BÜRKLEIN ( ) [For the German surname of this form:] *See* Buerklein.

BÜRKLEN ( ) [For the German surname of this form:] *See* Buerklen.

BURKLEY (Francis Joseph) The Faded Frontier. [Episodes in the early history of Omaha. With illustrations.] pp. 436. *Burkley Envelope & Printing Co.: Omaha,* [1935.] 8°. **9615.** pp. **16.**

BÜRKLI ( ) [For the German surname of this form:] *See* Buerkli.

BÜRKLIN ( ) [For the German surname of this form:] *See* Buerklin.

BURKMAN (Ella Benedict)

—— Leaflets from Ravenhurst. [Poems.] pp. 89. *Branwell Co.: New York,* 1927. 8°. **11689.** b. **15.**

BURKMAN (John) *See* Wagner (Glendolin D.) Old Neutriment. [J. Burkman's account of his service under General G. A. Custer, compiled by G. D. Wagner. With portraits.] [1934.] 8°. **10890.e.14.**

BÜRKNER ( ) [For the German surname of this form:] *See* Buerkner.

BURKO (I.)

—— *See* England. [*Appendix.—Miscellaneous.*] Інформатор про Англію. Переглянув: І. Бурко. [1946?] 8°. **10359.** a. **30.**

BURKOV (A. D.) Законодательство о наемном труде в сельском и лесном хозяйстве. Составил А. Д. Бурков. pp. 151. iv. [*Nizhny-Novgorod,*] 1926. 8°. **08286.** c. **31.**

BURKOV (B.)

—— Морально-политическое единство советского общества. pp. 54. *Москва,* 1951. 8°. **8095.** l. **45.**

BURKS (Allison L.)

—— Tight Rope. [A novel.] pp. 191. *William Heinemann: London, Toronto,* 1947. 8°. NN. **37134.**

BURKS (Ardath Walter)

—— *See* Linebarger (Paul M. A.) Far Eastern Governments and Politics . . . [By] P. M. A. Linebarger . . . A. W. Burks. [1954.] 8°. **08023.** dd. **87.**

BURKS (Arthur J.)

—— *See* Underhill (Vera B.) and Burks (A. J.) Creating Hooked Rugs, *etc.* [1951.] 4°. **7744.** gg. **30**

BURKS (Arthur J.)

—— The Great Mirror. [A tale.] pp. 127. *Gerald G. Swan: London,* [1952.] 8°. **012642.** n. **212.** *The author's name appears only on the cover.*

BURKS (Arthur J.) Here Are My People. [Reminiscences.] pp. v. 314. *Funk & Wagnalls Co.: New York & London,* 1934. 8°. **10881**. ppp. **13**.

—— Land of Checkerboard Families. pp. vi. 278. *Coward-McCann: New York,* [1932.] 8°. **12709**. m. **15**.

BURKS (Arthur J.) *Lt. Col., United States Marine Corps Reserve.*

—— *See* Smith (Marion Funk) Teaching the Slow Learning Child. By M. F. Smith, in collaboration with A. J. Burks. [1954.] 8°. **8306**. dd. **56**.

—— *See* Wilson (William H.) *Writer on Poultry,* and Burks (A. J.) The Chicken and the Egg. [1955.] 8°. **07295**. eee. **89**.

BURKS (Arthur Walter)

—— *See* Peirce (Charles S. S.) Collected Papers of Charles Sanders Peirce, *etc.* (vol. 7, 8. Edited by A. W. Burks.) 1931, *etc.* 8°. **8470**. l. **62**.

—— Icon, Index and Symbol . . . Reprinted from Philosophy and Phenomenological Research, *etc.* (A dissertation.) [On Charles Sanders Peirce's classifications of signs.] [1949.] 8°. **8473**. pp. **19**.

—— Peirce's Conception of Logic as a Normative Science . . . Reprinted from the Philosophical Review, *etc.* [1943.] 8°. **8467**. h. **38**.

—— Peirce's Theory of Abduction. (Reprinted from Philosophy of Science.) [1946.] 8°. **8467**. h. **37**.

BURKS (Barbara Stoddard)

—— *See* Jones (Mary C.) and Burks (B. S.) Personality Development in Childhood, *etc.* 1936. 8°. [*Monographs of the Society for Research in Child Development.* no. 4.] Ac. **3866**. b.

—— The Promise of Youth. Follow-up studies of a thousand gifted children. [By] B. S. Burks, Dortha Williams Jensen, Lewis M. Terman, *etc.* [With a chart.] pp. xiv. 508. *Stanford University Press: Stamford University; G. G. Harrap & Co.: London,* 1930. 8°. [*Genetic Studies of Genius.* vol. 3.] **8478.d.18/3.**

BURKS (Barnard De Witt)

—— The North American Parasitic Wasps of the Genus Tetrastichus—a Contribution to Biological Control of Insect Pests. *Washington,* 1943. 8°. [*Proceedings of the United States National Museum.* vol. 93. no. 3170.] Ac. **1875**/**12**.

—— Revision of the Chalcid-Flies of the Tribe Chalcidini in America North of Mexico. *Washington,* 1940. 8°. [*Proceedings of the United States National Museum.* no. 3082.] Ac. **1875**/**12**.

BURKS (Edward C.) *See* Virginia, *State of.* [*Public Documents.*] The Code of Virginia, *etc.* [Revised by E. C. Burks and others.] 1887, *etc.* 8°. **A.S.v.46/7.**

BURKS (Frances Williston) Barbara's Philippine Journey, *etc.* pp. 199. *World Book Co.: Yonkers-on-Hudson & Manila,* 1913. 8°. **012704**. cc. **11**.

BURKS (Frances Williston) and **BURKS** (Jesse Desmaux)

—— Health and the School. A round table, *etc.* pp. xviii. 393. *D. Appleton & Co.: New York, Chicago,* [1913.] 8°. **7390**. df. **37**.

BURKS (Jesse Desmaux) *See* Burks (Frances W.) and Burks (J. D.) Health and the School, *etc.* [1913.] 8°. **7390**. df. **37**.

BURKS (Joseph) Affidavit. [A sworn statement by J. Burks on the severity of the treatment of prisoners in the House of Correction, Cold-bath-fields, and a denial that he had expressed a regret for his statements on the subject. With an account of his imprisonment.] pp. 4. [1798.] 4°. **6144**. k. **1**. (**2**.)

BURKS (Martin Parks) Notes on the Property Rights of Married Women in Virginia. pp. viii. 87. *J. P. Bell Co.: Lynchburg,* 1893. 8°. **06616**. df. **19**.

BURKSER (Evgen Samoilovich) Солоні озера та лимани України. Гідрохімічний нарис, *etc.* [With a summary in French.] pp. 348. iii. *у Києві,* 1928. 8°. [*Всеукраїнська Академія Наук. Труди фіз.-мат. відділу.* том. 8. вип. 1.] Ac. **1101**. h/**2**.

—— Труды конференции по проблеме Сиваша. 1938 г. (Ответственный редактор Е. С. Бурксер.) pp. 152. 1940. 8°. *See* Kiev.—*Українська Академія Наук.—Інститут Геології.* **7110**. c. **9**.

BURKY (Charles A.)

—— *See* Frueh (J.) [Geographie der Schweiz.] Géographie de la Suisse . . . Traduction française de C. Burky. 1937, *etc.* 8°. **2060.ee.**

—— La Politique du commerce extérieur. *See* Switzerland. La Suisse et l'autarcie, *etc.* 1939. 8°. Ac. **2297**. c.

BURLA. Saynete nuevo intitulado : La Burla del Miserable. Por D. V. M. y M. de R. 1816. 4°. *See* M. y M. de R., D.V. **11726**. cc. **33**.

—— Sainete. La Burla del Posadero, y Castigo de la Estafa, *etc. Madrid,* 1804. 4°. **1342**. f. **5**. (**120**.)

—— [Another edition.] Saynete nuevo, intitulado: La Burla del Posadero, *etc.* [*Madrid,*] 1804. 4°. **1342**. f. **5**. (**121**.)

—— [Another copy.] [*Coleccion de Saynetes, etc.* tom. 1. no. 7.] **11725**. c. **21**.

—— [Another edition.] pp. 8. *Barcelona,* 1858. 4°. **11726**. g. **11**. (**23**.)

—— Saynete intitulado: La Burla del Pintor Ciego, *etc.* pp. 12. *Madrid,* 1800. 4°. **1342**. f. **5**. (**119**.)

BURLA (Jacob Hai) *See* Luria (I ben S.) ספר שבחי הארי״ [Edited by J. H. Burla.] [1876.] 12°. **1967**. c. **21**.

BURLABER (J.) *Baron.*

—— L'Ami des aristocrates. [Signed : J. Burlaber, ci-devant Baron.] pp. 8. [1790?] 8°. R. **197**. (**13**.)

BURLACCHINI (Burlacchino) Ragionamento sopra la peste dell' anno MDLXXVI, *etc.* pp. 420. *Appresso B. Sermartelli: Firenze,* 1577. 8°. **1167**. c. **5**. (**2**.)
Pp. 1, 2, 7–10 *and* 13–18 *are slightly mutilated.*

BURLACE (John Binmore) *See* Ward (Rowland) Rowland Ward's Records of Big Game . . . Edited by R. Lydekker . . . and J. B. Burlace. 1914. 4°. **7204**. d. **19**.

—— —— 1922. 4°. **7208**. g. **28**.

—— —— 1928. 4°. **7204**. cc. **5**.

—— —— 1935. 4°. **07207**. k. **58**.

BURLACE (JOHN BINMORE)

—— *See* WARD (Rowland) Rowland Ward's Sportsman's Handbook . . . Edited by J. B. Burlace, *etc.* 1923. 8°. **7205**. df. **16**.

BURLACEY (MILES) The King of France his Message to the Queene of England: presented to Her Majesty by Colonell Goring, at the Hague . . . in answer to her Letter sent to the French King at Paris . . . Wherein is declared what forces are raising in Flanders . . . for the assistance of the Malignant Party against the Parliament in England . . . Sent from M. Burlacey at the Hague . . . to a Merchant in London . . . Also the Parliaments Instructions to Sir Edward Rodes and Captaine Hotham, *etc.* pp. 6. *For T. Wright: London*, 1642. 4°. E. **129**. (**24**.)

—— [Another copy.] G. **3805**. (**14**.)

BURLACHENKO (A. P.)

—— Театральный Ленинград. Справочник. Театр, музыка, цирк, эстрада, *etc.* (Ответственный редактор— А. П. Бурлаченко.) pp. 524. 1948. 8°.
See LENINGRAD.—*Дирекция Театральных Касс.* **11797**. a. **83**.

BURLADOR. Saynete nuevo intitulado: El Burlador Burlado, *etc.* [By R. F. de la Cruz Cano y Olmedilla.] pp. 12. *Valencia*, 1816. 4°. **1342**. f. **5**. (**23**.)

—— [Another copy.] **11726**. h. **3**. (**14**.)
Imperfect; wanting pp. 5–8 which are replaced by pp. 5–8 of "El Novio Rifado" by the same author.

BURLAEUS (GUALTERUS) *See* BURLEY (Walter)

BURLAGE (HENRY MATTHEW)

—— Fundamental Principles and Processes of Pharmacy. By H. M. Burlage . . . Joseph B. Burt . . . Charles O. Lee . . . L. Wait Rising. pp. xiii. 615. *New York & London*, 1944. 8°. [*McGraw-Hill Publications in Pharmacy.*] W.P. **9344/7**.

—— Fundamental Principles and Processes of Pharmacy. By H. M. Burlage . . . J. B. Burt . . . C. O. Lee . . . and L. W. Rising . . . Second edition. pp. xiv. 651. *McGraw-Hill Book Co.: New York*, 1949. 8°. [*McGraw-Hill Publications in Pharmacy.*] W.P. **9344/7a**.

—— Introduction to Pharmacy. A revision of Fundamental Principles and Processes of Pharmacy. [By] H. M. Burlage . . . editor . . . Joseph B. Burt . . . Charles O. Lee . . . L. Wait Rising . . . Third edition. pp. xii. 710. *McGraw-Hill Book Co.: New York*, 1954. 8°. **7511**. e. **2**.

—— Laboratory Manual for Principles and Processes of Pharmacy. H. M. Burlage, editor . . . Joseph B. Burt . . . L. Wait Rising. pp. xix. 271. *McGraw-Hill Book Co.: New York, London*, 1946. 4°. **7509**. k. **24**.

—— Laboratory Manual for Principles and Processes of Pharmacy. H. M. Burlage, editor . . . Joseph B. Burt . . . L. Wait Rising . . . Second edition. pp. xvii. 271. *McGraw-Hill Book Co.: New York*, 1949. 4°. **07509**. l. **34**.

BURLAGE (JOSEPHUS HENRICUS) Verleden en heden. Een lied, *etc.* pp. 8. *Amsterdam*, 1863. 8°. **11555**. cc. **46**. (**7**.)

BURLAK-KOMMUNIST. Бурлак-коммунист. *See* RUSSIA.—*Всероссiискiй Союзъ Рабочихъ Воднаго Транспорта.*

BURLAMACCHI (CESARE NICOLÒ) *See* BOSSUET (J. B.) successively *Bishop of Condom* and *of Meaux*. [*Miscellaneous Writings.*] Massime e riflessioni . . . sopra la commedia, tradotte in lingua toscana da un sacerdote lucchese [i.e. C. N. Burlamacchi]. 1773. 8°. **11824**. de. **4**. (**1**.)

BURLAMACCHI (ENRICO) Orazione panegirica in lode di S. Agostino detto in Napoli nel giorno della sua festa nella Chiesa de' P.P. Agostiniani degli Studj. pp. 15. *Venezia*, 1715. 4°. **4424**. dd. **4**. (**8**.)

BURLAMACCHI (FEDERIGO) *See* CATHARINE [Benencasa], *of Sienna, Saint.* L'Opere della . . . santa Caterina da Siena, *etc.* (tom. 2, 3. L'Epistole . . . Aggiuntevi nuovamente le annotazioni del padre F. Burlamacchi.) 1707, *etc.* 4°. **663**. c. **10, 11**.

—— *See* CATHARINE [Benencasa], *of Sienna, Saint.* Epistole . . . Colle annotazioni del P. F. Burlamacchi. 1842, *etc.* 8°. **1223**. g. **6**.

BURLAMACCHI (FILIPPO) *See* BURLAMACCHI (Pacifico)

BURLAMACCHI (FRANCESCO) *See* BONARI (R.) Francesco Burlamacchi, *etc.* 1874. 8°. **10631**. ee. **20**.

—— *See* GUERRAZZI (F. D.) Vita di Francesco Burlamacchi. 1868. 8°. **10631**. aaa. **2**.

—— *See* MINUTOLI (C.) Francesco Burlamacchi. Storia lucchese del secolo XVI. 1844. 8°. **10631**. c. **30**.

—— *See* REUMONT (A. von) Francesco Burlamacchi. Episode lucchesischer Geschichten. 1849. 8°. [*Historisches Taschenbuch.* Neue Folge. Jahrg. 10.] P.P. **3625**.

BURLAMACCHI (L.) *Marchioness.* Luca della Robbia. [With plates, including a portrait.] pp. xiv. 126. *G. Bell & Sons: London*, 1900. 8°. [*Great Masters in Painting and Sculpture.*] **2263**. d. **22**.

BURLAMACCHI (PACIFICO) Incomincia la Vita del M. R. P. F. Girolamo Savonarola, *etc.* *See* BALUZE (E.) Stephani Baluzii . . . Miscellanea, *etc.* tom. 1. Appendix. 1761, *etc.* fol. **13**. e. **9**.

—— [Another edition.] Vita del P. F. Girolamo Savonarola . . . Riveduta poco dopo ed aggiunta dal P. F. Timoteo Botonio. [With a preface by Federigo Vincenzo di Poggio.] pp. 227. *Lucca*, 1761. 8°. **4867**. aaaa. **42**.

—— [Another edition.] Con la giunta del catalogo delle opere scritte dal Savonarola & una lettera apologetica di esse [both by F. V. de Poggio]. Nuova edizione. [With the corrections and additions of Timoteo Bottoni, and with a portrait.] pp. cxix. 220. *Lucca*, 1764. 8°. **663**. b. **22**.

—— [Another edition.] La Vita con alcuni scritti del padre F. Girolamo Savonarola, *etc.* (Notizie su la vita e su gli studi del padre Fra Girolamo Savonarola scritte da Girolamo Tiraboschi.) [Edited by Bartolommeo Gamba. With a portrait.] pp. 240. *Milano*, 1847. 8°. **4867**. a. **12**.

—— [Another edition.] La Vita del beato Ieronimo Savonarola, scritta da un anonimo del sec. XVI e già attribuita a Fra Pacifico Burlamacchi. Pubblicata secondo il codice ginoriano a cura del Principe Piero Ginori Conti. [With an introduction by Marquis Roberto Ridolfi and with portraits.] pp. xxiii. 284. *Firenze*, 1937. fol. **20088**. b. **32**.

BURLAMAQUI (Frederico Leopoldo Cesar) Memoria analytica á cerca do commercio d'escravos e á cerca dos malles da escravidão domestica. Por F. L. C. B. [i.e. F. L. C. Burlamaqui.] pp. xi. 142. 1837. 8°. *See* B., F. L. C. **8155**. c. **7**.

BURLAMAQUI (Jean Jacques)

—— *See* Borgeaud (C.) La Publication des " Principes du droit politique " de Burlamaqui. 1938. 8°. **8011**. c. **38**.

—— *See* Gagnebin (B.) Burlamaqui et le droit naturel. [With portraits.] [1944.] 8°. **6003**. bb. **25**.

—— *See* Harvey (Ray F.) Jean Jacques Burlamaqui. A liberal tradition in American constitutionalism. [With a bibliography, and with a portrait.] 1937. 8°. **20033**. ff. **6**.

—— Principes du droit naturel et politique . . . Nouvelle édition revuë & corrigée. (Supplément. i. Éloge historique de Mr. Burlamaqui. [By L. Baulacre.] ii. Jugement sur l'ouvrage de Mr. Burlamaqui, par Mr. le professeur Hubner, avec ses remarques sur l'opinion de l'auteur touchant les loix de simple permission. iii. Lettre de l'auteur sur le mariage, *etc.*) 3 tom. *Geneve & Coppenhague*, 1764. 12°. **502**. a. **14–16**.

—— [Another edition.] Principes du droit de la nature et des gens . . . avec la suite du Droit de la nature . . . le tout . . . augmenté par M. le professeur de Félice. Nouvelle édition, revue, corrigée et augmentée d'une table générale analytique . . . par M. Dupin. (Lettre de M. Burlamaqui sur le mariage, *etc.*) 5 tom. *Paris*, 1820, 21. 8°. **501**. d. **21–25**.

—— The Principles of Natural and Politic Law . . . Translated . . . by Mr. Nugent. The second edition, revised and corrected. 2 vol. *J. Nourse: London*, 1763. 8°. **6005**. bb. **12**.

—— [Another edition.] Translated from the Latin original. pp. iv. 397. *Military Classics: Oxford & London*, 1817. 8°. [*First Class of the Course of Education pursued at the Universities of Cambridge & Oxford, etc.* vol. 1.] **8364**. f. **14**.

—— [Another edition.] From the seventh London edition. (Nugent's translation of the first, second and third parts of Burlamaqui's . . . treatise. With . . . modifications.) pp. xii. 283. *J. H. Riley & Co.: Columbus, Ohio*, 1859. 8°. **6025**. c. **10**.

—— Principes du droit naturel. pp. xxxx. 548. *Genève*, 1748. 12°. **502**. e. **12**.

—— Nouvelle édition. pp. xxiv. 352. *Amsterdam*, 1751. 4°. **15**. a. **2**.

—— The Principles of Natural Law . . . Translated . . . by Mr. Nugent. pp. xvi. 312. *J. Nourse: London*, 1748. 8°. **502**. e. **13**.

—— Burlemaqui's Principles of Natural Law. Translated by Mr. Nugent. With questions for examination. By a graduate of the University [of Dublin]. pp. xxii. 190. *T. V. Morris: Dublin*, 1838. 12°. **06004**. e. **12**.

—— Burlamaqui's Natural Law. Catechetically arranged by L. Badham. pp. 55. *J. J. Ekens: Dublin*, 1838. 12°. **6005**. a. **15**.

—— Principes du droit politique. [By J. J. Burlamaqui.] 2 tom. 1751. 8°. *See* Principes. **6055**. a. **56**.

BURLAMAQUI (Jean Jacques)

—— [Another edition.] pp. vi. 305. 1754. 4°. *See* Principes. **15**. a. **3**.

—— The Principles of Politic Law: being a sequel to the Principles of Natural Law . . . Translated . . . by Mr. Nugent. pp. 372. *J. Nourse: London*, 1752. 8°. **502**. e. **14**.

—— Élémens du droit naturel . . . Ouvrage posthume, publié complet pour la première fois. pp. lxxxiv. 364. *Lausanne*, 1775. 8°. **6006**. aaa. **4**.
Pt. 2 & 3 of this work contain the text elsewhere described as " La suite du Droit de la nature."

—— Elementos de Derecho Natural . . . Traducidos del latin al frances por Barbeyrac, y al castellano por D. M. B. Garcia Suelto. pp. [xxxiv.] 314. *Caracas*, 1826. 8°. **6005**. aaa. **22**.

BURLAMAQUI KOPKE (Carlos)

—— Antologia da poesia brasileira moderna, 1922–1947. Seleção e introdução de Carlos Burlamaqui Kopke. pp. 324. [*São Paulo*,] 1953. 8°. **11454**. b. **28**.
Clube de poesia de São Paulo. Coleção " Documentos." vol. 1.

BURLAND (Charles) The Ship Captain's Medical Guide. Edited by C. Burland. (Fifteenth edition.) [Originally compiled by Harry Leach.] pp. xii. 214. 1912. 8°. *See* England.—*Board of Trade.—Naval Department.* **B.S.43/106.**

—— Sixteenth edition. pp. 172. 1918. 8°. *See* England.—*Board of Trade.—Naval Department.* **B.S.43/106.**

—— [Another edition.] pp. viii. 183. 1921. 8°. *See* England.—*Board of Trade.—Naval Department.* **B.B.43/106.**

BURLAND (Cottie Arthur)

—— *See* Fawcett (Raymond) How did they live? *etc.* [The text of the last three parts prepared by C. G. E. Bunt, C. A. Burland.] [1951, *etc.*] 8°. **9088**. k. **30**.

—— *See* Hooper (James T.) The Art of Primitive Peoples. By J. T. Hooper and C. A. Burland, *etc.* 1953. 8°. **7813**. l. **41**.

—— Art and Life in Ancient Mexico, *etc.* [With illustrations.] pp. 111. *Bruno Cassirer: Oxford*, 1948. 4°. **7711**. dd. **7**.

—— The Four Directions of Time. An account of page one of Codex Fejervary Mayer, a pre-Columbian manuscript. [With a reproduction.] *Museum of Navajo Ceremonial Art: Santa Fe, N.M.*, 1950. 4°. **7870**. m. **7**.

—— Magic Books from Mexico. With an introduction and notes on the plates by C. A. Burland. pp. 30. pl. 16. *Penguin Books: Harmondsworth*, 1953. 8°. [*King Penguin Books.* no. 64.] **12208**. a. **4/64**.

BURLAND (Jeffrey Hale) The Metric System, etc. [A chart.] *Canadian Metric Bureau: Montreal*, 1901. *obl.* fol. **8548**. dd. **53**.

BURLAND (John Burland Harris) Amy Robsart. The Newdigate poem, 1893. pp. 22. *A. T. Shrimpton & Son: Oxford*, 1893. 16°. **11601**. d. **32**. **(1.)**

—— Baldragon. pp. viii. 318. *Chapman & Hall: London*, 1914. 8°. NN. **2313**.

—— The Black Motor-Car, *etc.* pp. viii. 364. *E. Grant Richards: London*, 1906. 8°. **012632**. ccc. **21**.

BURLAND (JOHN BURLAND HARRIS)

—— The Broken Law. pp. viii. 363. *E. Grant Richards: London,* 1906. 8º. **012633. c. 48.**

—— The Brown Book. pp. 254 *John Long: London,* 1923. 8º. **NN. 9278.**

—— The Curse of Cloud. pp. viii. 342. *Chapman & Hall: London,* 1914. 8º. **NN. 1812.**

—— [Another edition.] pp. 251. *George Newnes: London,* [1919.] 8º. **012603. de. 48.**

—— Dacobra, or the White Priests of Ahriman. pp. 315. *R. A. Everett & Co.: London,* 1903. 8º. **012638. dd. 19.**

—— The Disc. pp. 318. *Greening & Co.: London,* 1909. 8º. **012623. b. 12.**

—— Dr. Silex, *etc.* pp. 344. *Ward, Lock & Co.: London,* 1905. 8º. **012631. aa. 42.**

—— The Financier. A novel . . . Illustrations by C. Grunwald. pp. 320. *Greening & Co.: London,* 1906. 8º. **012632. dd. 46.**

—— Popular edition. pp. 128. *Greening & Co.: London,* 1907. 8º. **012624. l. 96.**

—— The Gold Worshippers. A tale. pp. viii. 312. *Greening & Co.: London,* 1907. 8º. **012634. a. 11.**

—— [Another edition.] pp. 174. *The Proprietors: London,* [1914.] 8º. [*Fiction Lover's Library.* no. 12.] **12649. aaa. 1/12.**

—— The Grey Cat. pp. 316. *Chapman & Hall: London,* 1913. 8º. **NN. 1318.**

—— [Another edition.] pp. 250. *George Newnes: London,* [1919.] 8º. **012603. de. 42.**

—— The Hidden Hour. pp. 311. *John Long: London,* 1925. 8º. **NN. 10363.**

—— Popular edition. pp. 254. *John Long: London,* 1926. 8º. **012604. b. 22.**

—— The House of the Soul. pp. 303. *Chapman & Hall: London,* 1909. 8º. **012624. d. 23.**

—— Life's Golden Web. pp. 252. *George Newnes: London,* [1912.] 8º. **012631. cc. 26.**

—— Lord of Irongray. A novel. pp. 365. *Greening & Co.: London,* 1911. 8º. **012618. bb. 15.**

—— [Another edition.] pp. 158. *London,* [1914.] 8º. [*Hutchinson's Sixpenny Novels.*] **012600. b. 1/4.**

—— Love the Criminal. pp. viii. 327. *Greening & Co.: London,* 1907. 8º. **012625. aaa. 6.**

—— The Poison League. pp. 376. *J. Bale & Co.: London,* [1921.] 8º. **NN. 7006.**

—— The Red Moon. pp. 254. *John Long: London,* 1923. 8º. **NN. 8821.**

—— Popular edition. pp. 254. *John Long: London,* 1926. 8º. **012641. de. 33.**

—— The Secret of Enoch Seal. pp. 314. *Chapman & Hall: London,* 1910. 8º. **012623. b. 11.**

—— [Another edition.] pp. 158. *London,* [1914.] 8º. [*Hutchinson's Sixpenny Novels.*] **012600. b. 1/5.**

—— The Shadow of Malreward. pp. 411. *Chapman & Hall: London,* 1911. 8º. **012618. bb. 16.**

—— [Another edition.] pp. 158. *London,* [1914.] 8º. [*Hutchinson's Sixpenny Novels.*] **012600. b. 1/6.**

BURLAND (JOHN BURLAND HARRIS)

—— Sunk Island. pp. 316. *George Newnes: London,* [1911.] 8º. **012631. cc. 6.**

—— [A reissue.] *London,* [1915.] 8º. **12621. de. 30.**

—— [A reissue.] *London,* [1917.] 8º. [*Newnes' Trench Library.*] **012643. f. 46/12.**

—— The Torhaven Mystery. pp. 316. *Chapman & Hall: London,* 1910. 8º. **012623. b. 13.**

—— [Another edition.] pp. 254. *George Newnes: London,* [1919.] 8º. **012603. de. 46.**

—— The White Rook. pp. 227. *Chapman & Hall: London,* 1917. 8º. **NN. 4450.**

—— [Another edition.] (Abridged.) pp. 128. *London,* [1921.] 8º. [*Newnes Sevenpenny Novels.* no. 26.] **12645. a. 1/26.**

—— Workers in Darkness. pp. 323. *Greening & Co.: London,* 1908. 8º. **012625. aaa. 7.**

BURLANDO (FRANCIS) *See* SEMERIA (G. B.) Sketches of the Life of the Very Rev. Felix de Andreis, *etc.* [Translated by F. Burlando.] 1861. 8º. **4986. bb. 31.**

BURLANDT (LOUIS) Symphonien der Stille. Psychologische Nüancen des Alltags. pp. 94. *Berlin,* 1933. 8º. **12356. p. 25.**

BURLAT (HUGUES) Remarques des blasphemes, erreurs, et impostures contenus au liure du ministre Loque, de n'agueres publié sous tiltre des Abus de la Messe. ff. 299. *Par C. de Monstr'oeil & I. Richer: Paris,* 1598. 8º. **1018. c. 17. (2.)**

—— Response à la declaration publiee par les ministres souz le nom de Fabrice Bascourt: soy disant Curé de S. Germain d'Orleans, touchant les causes de son changement de Religion, addressee aux habitans d'Orleans. Auec les lettres nouuellement receuës dudict Bascourt, apres auoir publiquement recogneu sa faute en l'Eglise Metropolitaine d'Aux, le jour de Noël 1603. pp. 67. *I. de la Place: Paris,* 1604. 8º. **3900. aa. 10.**

—— Responce au liuret intitulé, Sommaire des raisons que rendent ceux qui ne veulent participer à la Messe: & pareillement aux Sonnets adioustez audict Sommaire [by Jean de l'Espine] . . . Seconde edition. ff. 42. *Par I. Richer: Paris,* 1596. 8º. **1018. c. 17. (1.)**

BURLAUD (C. P. A.) Étude sur les tumeurs fibro-plastiques du tissu cellulaire, *etc.* pp. 87. *Paris,* 1868. 4º. [*Collection des thèses soutenues à la Faculté de Médecine de Paris.* An 1868. tom. 2.] **7373. i. 6.**

BURLE (E.)

—— Essai historique sur le développement de la notion de droit naturel dans l'antiquité grecque. Thèse, *etc.* pp. xv. 632. *Trévoux,* 1908. 8º. **6006. h. 26.**
Imperfect; wanting pp. 631 *and* 632, *which are supplied in typescript.*

BURLE (M. F.)

—— *See* STEWART (William) *B.Sc.*, and BURLE (M. F.) The Application of Jet Propulsion to Helicopters. *London,* 1950. fol. [*Aeronautical Research Council. Current Papers.* no. 8.] B.S. **62/32.**

BURLEFER (STEPHANUS) *See* BRULEFER.

BURLEIGH, ROBERT, *Lord. See* BALFOUR (R.) *4th Lord Balfour of Burleigh.*

——, WILLIAM, *Baron. See* CECIL (W.) *Baron Burghley.*

BURLEIGH JOURNAL.

—— The Burleigh Journal. *See* WALLIS AND LINNELL LTD. The House of Burleigh.

BURLEIGH LIBRARY. The Burleigh Library. 9 vol. *Bliss & Sands: London*, 1896. 8°. **12201**. e. **2**.

BURLEIGH, *Family of*. *See* BURLEIGH (Charles) The Genealogy of the Burley or Burleigh family of America. 1880. 8°. **9914**. i. **7**.

BURLEIGH ( ) Burleigh's Universal Cable Condenser. For use in connection with all numerical codes of less than 150,000 code words. [1907.] 4°. **1805**. aa. **13**. (**1**.)

BURLEIGH (AVERIL) *See* EVERETT (Leolyn L.) Thistledown . . . Illustrated by A. Burleigh. 1927. 8°. **011644**. df. **156**.

—— *See* KEATS (J.) The Poems of John Keats. With twenty-four illustrations in colour by A. Burleigh. [1911.] 8°. **012207**. i. **17/6**.

BURLEIGH (BENNET) An Address on Old-Age Pensions, *etc.* pp. 21. *Political Committee of the National Liberal Club: London*, [1908.] 8°. **08286**. h. **9**. (**10**.)

—— Desert Warfare. Being the chronicle of the Eastern Soudan Campaign . . . with official maps. pp. xi. 320. *Chapman & Hall: London*, 1884. 8°. **9060**. ccc. **26**.

—— Empire of the East; or, Japan and Russia at war, 1904–5. [With illustrations and maps.] pp. xii. 458. *Chapman & Hall: London*, 1905. 8°. **09055**. b. **11**.

—— Khartoum Campaign, 1898; or, the Re-conquest of the Soudan . . . With maps . . . and . . . illustrations. pp. xii. 340. *Chapman & Hall: London*, 1899. 8°. **9060**. dd. **13**.

—— The Natal Campaign . . . With illustrations and maps. pp. viii. 418. *Chapman & Hall: London*, 1900. 8°. **09061**. a. **5**.

—— Sirdar and Khalifa; or, the Re-conquest of the Soudan, 1898 . . . With portraits . . . illustrations, maps, *etc.* pp. xiv. 305. *Chapman & Hall: London*, 1898. 8°. **9060**. d. **16**.

—— Two Campaigns. Madagascar and Ashantee . . . Illustrated. pp. x. 555. *T. F. Unwin: London*, 1897. 8°. **9060**. ccc. **4**.

BURLEIGH (BERTHA BENNET) An Artist at the Zoo. Drawings and text by B. B. Burleigh. *Collins: London*, [1934.] 4°. **7202**. f. **11**.

—— Circus. Written and illustrated by B. B. Burleigh. *Collins: London*, 1937. fol. **11795**. tt. **68**.

BURLEIGH (CELIA) *See* BURLEIGH (William H.) Poems by W. H. Burleigh. With a sketch of his life. By C. Burleigh. 1871. 8°. **11688**. cc. **31**.

BURLEIGH (CHARLES) The Genealogies of the Burley or Burleigh Family of America. pp. 200. *B. Thurston & Co.: Portland [Maine]*, 1880. 8°. **9914**. i. **7**.

BURLEIGH (CHARLES CALISTUS) *See* THOMPSON (George) *M.P.* Discussion on American Slavery . . . With an appendix [by C. C. Burleigh]. 1836. 8°. **8156**. ee. **40**.

—— No Slave Hunting in the Old Bay State. Speech . . . at the Annual Meeting of the Massachusetts A.S. Society, *etc.* pp. 32. *Massachusetts A.S. Society: Boston*, 1859. 16°. **8156**. a. **16**.

BURLEIGH (CHARLES CALISTUS)

—— Reception of George Thompson in Great Britain. Compiled from various British publications. pp. xvi. 238. *I. Knapp: Boston*, 1836. 12°. **8157**. bb. **7**.

—— Thoughts on the Death Penalty. pp. 144. *Merrihew & Thompson: Philadelphia*, 1845. 12°. **6055**. aaa. **6**.

—— *See* LEWIS (Tayler) An Essay on the Ground and Reason of Punishment . . . With an appendix, containing a review of Burleigh on the Death Penalty. 1846. 8°. **1384**. b. **5**.

BURLEIGH (CONSTANCE) Etiquette Up to Date. pp. xv. 236. *T. Werner Laurie: London*, [1925.] 8°. **08408**. de. **36**.

—— A Fettered Life. pp. 128. *Mellifont Press: London; Dublin* printed, [1940.] 8°. **012646**. aa. **37**.

—— A Woman's Honour. pp. 128. *Mellifont Press: London; Dublin* printed, [1939.] 8°. **12643.y.9.**

BURLEIGH (DOUGLAS HENRY) *See* ROBERTSON (P. W.) and BURLEIGH (D. H.) Qualitative Analysis, *etc.* 1920. 8°. **8908**. aaa. **45**.

BURLEIGH (ELLEN) *See* CHAPPELL (Jennie) Three Brave Women . . . Mrs. Burleigh of Cape Horn, *etc.* [1920.] 8°. **4804**. cc. **31**.

BURLEIGH (ELMER) Only a Slip. pp. 63. *T. Nelson & Sons: London*, 1886. 8°. **12811**. a. **28**.

—— Owen's Hobby; or, Strength in weakness. A tale. pp. 416. *T. Nelson & Sons: London*, 1881. 8°. **12808**. d. **34**.

—— [A reissue.] *London & Edinburgh*, [1906.] 8°. **12813**. y. **20**.

BURLEIGH (FLORENCE A.) Her Sister's Rival, *etc.* pp. 64. *London*, 1934. 8°. [*Newnes' 2d. Novels.*] W.P. **5816/12**.

—— Twice Told Fairy Tales. pp. 139. *Drane's: London*, [1923.] 8°. **12801**. bb. **56**.

BURLEIGH (FLORENCE S. HOWARD)

—— The Applewood Mystery. pp. 96. *Fiction House: London*, [1942.] 8°. [*Piccadilly Novels.* no. 191.] **012643**. r. **1/191**.

—— Dreams at Dusk. *Fiction House: London*, [1939.] 8°. [*Piccadilly Novels.* no. 131.] **012643**. r. **1/131**.

—— House of Dreams. *Fiction House: London*, [1939.] 8°. [*Piccadilly Novels.* no. 112.] **012643**. r. **1/112**.

—— Love Decides. *Fiction House: London*, [1938.] 8°. [*Piccadilly Novels.* no. 98.] **012643**. r. **1/98**.

—— Love decides, *etc.* pp. 128. *Fiction House: London*, [1954.] 8°. **12654**. ee. **23**.

BURLEIGH (FRANCIS) [For the "Authorised Version" of 1611, of which Gen.—2 Kings was translated by F. Burleigh and others:] *See* BIBLE. [*English.* 1611, *etc.*]

BURLEIGH (HILARY)

—— Her Hour of Temptation. pp. 128. *London*, [1937.] 8°. [*Pearson's Big Threepennies.* no. 51.] **012632.n.1/51.**

30-9

BURLEIGH (HILARY)

—— Murder at Maison Manche. pp. 207. *Hurst & Blackett: London,* [1948.] 8°. **NN. 38266.**

BURLEIGH (JAMES)

—— Olde Tyme Dances. pp. 15. *Danceland Publications: [London,* 1944.] 8°. **7917.** dc. **61.**

BURLEIGH (JOHN) *Captain. See* BURLEY.

BURLEIGH (JOHN) *Minister of Ednam.* Ednam and its Indwellers. pp. viii. 212. *Fraser, Asher & Co.: Glasgow & Dalbeattie,* 1912. 8°. **010370.** e. **64.**

—— Forming the Line. An experiment. [Tales of the history of Glasgow.] pp. 193. *Alexander Gardner: Paisley,* 1922. 8°. **010370.** eee. **78.**

BURLEIGH (JOHN HENDERSON SEAFORTH)

—— *See* AUGUSTINE, *Saint, Bishop of Hippo.* [*Two or more Works.—English.*] Augustine: Earlier Writings. Selected and translated with introductions by J. H. S. Burleigh. 1953. 8°. W.P. B. **296/6.**

—— The Church—What is it? pp. 32. *Edinburgh,* 1937. 8°. [*Church of Scotland Booklets.* no. 9.] W.P. **4468/9.**

—— The City of God. A study of St. Augustine's philosophy, *etc.* (Based upon the Croall Lectures delivered in New College, Edinburgh.) pp. 226. *Nisbet & Co.: London,* 1949. 8°. **3670.** b. **47.**

BURLEIGH (JOSEPH BARTLETT) The American Manual; containing a brief outline of the origin and progress of political power, and the laws of nations; a commentary on the constitution of the United States of North America, and a lucid exposition of the duties and responsibilities of voters, jurors and civil magistrates; with questions, definitions and marginal exercises, *etc.* pp. 318. 55. *Grigg, Elliot & Co.: Philadelphia,* 1848. 12°. **8005.** d. **11.**

—— The Child's Little Thinker, a practical spelling book, containing . . . lessons in pronouncing, spelling, reading, thinking and composing, *etc.* pp. 77. *Lippincott, Grambo & Co.: Philadelphia,* 1852. 16°. **12982.** aaa. **8.**

—— The Legislative Guide, containing all the rules for conducting business in Congress; Jefferson's Manual; and the Citizens' Manual . . . with copious notes and marginal references. [Containing a lithographed copy of the Constitution of the United States of America, and a reprint of the original Articles of Confederation.] pp. 287. 30. *Lippincott, Grambo & Co.: Philadelphia,* 1852. 8°. **8005.** d. **12.**

BURLEIGH (LOUISE) The Story of the Theater, *etc.* pp. 69. *Harper & Bros.: New York & London,* 1929. 8°. [*City and Country Series.*] **012208.b.2/9.**

BURLEIGH (LUCIAN) The Descent from the Cross. A poem. pp. 16. *Case, Tiffany & Burnham: Hartford,* 1841. 8°. **11687.** h. **30.** (**1.**)

BURLEIGH (THOMAS DEARBORN)

—— *See* PETERS (Harold S.) and BURLEIGH (T. D.) The Birds of Newfoundland, *etc.* 1951. 8°. C.S. E. **437.**

BURLEIGH (WALTER) *See* BURLEY.

BURLEIGH (WILLIAM HENRY) Poems. pp. 248. *J. M. M'Kim: Philadelphia,* 1841. 12°. **1466.** c. **23.**

BURLEIGH (WILLIAM HENRY)

—— [Another edition.] With a sketch of his life. By Celia Burleigh. pp. xlv. 306. *Hurd & Houghton: New York,* 1871. 8°. **11688.** cc. **31.**

BÜRLEIN (   ) [For the German surname of this form:] *See* BUERLEIN.

BURLEIUS (GUALTERUS) *See* BURLEY (Walter)

BURLEMAQUI (JEAN JACQUES) *See* BURLAMAQUI.

BURLEND (EDWARD) Amy Thornton; or, the Curate's daughter. pp. 382. *Simpkin, Marshall & Co.: London,* [1862.] 8°. **12632.** ccc. **9.**

—— A Catechism of English History, *etc.* pp. 89. *Simpkin & Marshall: London; David Green: Leeds,* 1855. 12°. **807.** a. **38.**

—— [Another copy.] **807.** a. **37.**

BURLEND (REBECCA) A True Picture of Emigration: or, Fourteen years in the interior of North America, *etc.* [By R. Burlend.] pp. 62. [1848.] 8°. *See* PICTURE. **010409.** eee. **4.**

—— [Another edition.] Edited by Milo Milton Quaife. pp. xxxi. 167. *R. R. Donnelley & Sons Co.: Chicago,* 1936. 8°. **010409.** e. **39.**

BURLEND (THOMAS HAROLD) First Book of Zoology. pp. vi. 159. *Macmillan & Co.: London,* 1911. 8°. [*First Books of Science.*] **8707.** de. **1/5.**

—— [Another edition.] Adapted for Canadian schools by George A. Cornish. pp. v. 180. *Toronto,* 1915. 8°. [*Macmillan's Canadian School Series.*] **012209.aaa.4/2.**

BURLE RÉAL DE CURBAN (BALTHASAR DE) *See* RÉAL DE CURBAN (G. de) La Science du gouvernement, *etc.* [Edited by B. de Burle Réal de Curban.] 1761, *etc.* 4°. **1389.** k. **1.**

BURLES (EDWARD) Grammatica Burlesa: or, a New English Grammar made Plaine and Easie for Teacher & Scholar, and profitable to Gentlemen for the recovery of what they have lost by discontinuance from their studies. [A Latin grammar in English, based largely on "A Short Introduction of Grammar" and the "Brevissima Institutio."] pp. 394. *T. N. for Humphrey Moseley: London,* 1652. 12°. **E. 1270.**

BURLESCO (CYMON) *pseud.* A Letter of Condolence to His Most Gracious Majesty on the death of his Royal Consort. [In verse.] pp. 19. *J. Turner: London,* 1821. 8°. **1103.** g. **69.**

BURLESON (ADELE STEINER) Every Politician and his Wife, *etc.* pp. xii. 177. *Dorrance & Co.: Philadelphia,* [1921.] 8°. **012601.** cc. **24.**

BURLESON (ALBERT SIDNEY) *See* UNITED STATES OF AMERICA.—*Post Office.* Postal Laws and Regulations . . . Revised and edited . . . under the direction of A. S. Burleson. 1913. 8°. **A.S.390.(8.)**

BURLESON (GRETCHEN LYON)

—— A Pliocene Pinniped from the San Diego Formation of Southern California. *University of California Press: Berkeley & Los Angeles,* 1948. 8°. [*University of California Publications in Zoölogy.* vol. 47. no. 10.] Ac. **2689.** g/**28.**

One of thirty copies printed on 100% rag paper.

BURLESQUE. Burlesque of Compulsory Early Closing Act. A forecast of it. *W. J. Massey: London,* [1905.] *s. sh.* 4°. **1865.** c. **19.** (**12.**)

BURLET (Claudius) *Praes.* *See* Du Bois (Joannes B.) *M.D.* Quæstio medica . . . An gracilibus pomaceum vino salubrius? [1725.] 4°. **1182**. e. **3**. (**133**.)

—— *Praes.* *See* Mongin (J. B.) Quæstio medica . . . Tutiorne intemperantia in potione, quàm in esca? [1706.] 4°. **1182**. e. **3**. (**60**.)

—— Quæstio medica . . . An alterum circuitûs sanguinis organum, pulmo? *Praes.* L. de Vaux. pp. 4. *F. Muguet: Parisiis,* [1690.] 4°. **1182**. e. **2**. (**59**.)

BURLET (Herman Maximilian de)

—— *See* Weber (Max W. C.) Die Säugetiere . . . Zweite Auflage, *etc.* (Unter Mitwirkung von O. Abel und H. M. de Burlet.) 1927, *etc.* 8°. **7205**. dd. **20**.

BURLET (Joseph) Le Culte de Dieu, de la Sainte Vierge et des Saints en Savoie avant la Révolution. Essais de géographie hagiologique. (Inventaire hagiologique de la Savoie.—Quelques anciens calendriers liturgiques en usage dans la Savoie.) [With a map.] pp. 350. 1922. 8°. [*Académie des Sciences, Belles-Lettres et Arts de Savoie. Documents.* vol. 9.] *See* Liturgies.—*Latin Rite.*—*Martyrologies.*—II. *Savoy.* Ac. **34**/2.

—— La Savoie avant le christianisme, *etc.* pp. v. 407. *Chambéry,* 1901. 8°. **07703**. ee. **9**.

BURLET (Lucien de) Au Canada. De Paris à Vancouver. Notes d'hier et d'aujourd'hui. Deuxième édition. pp. 286. *Paris,* [1910.] 8°. **10470**. ppp. **5**.

BURLET (Philibert) Du spiritisme considéré comme cause d'aliénation mentale. pp. 57. *Lyon,* 1863. 8°. **8630**. cc. **30**. (**2**.)

—— Du tétanos intermittent et de la périodicité dans les névroses. Thèse, *etc.* pp. 56. *Montpellier,* 1872. 4°. **7379**. i. **1**. (**16**.)

BURLETIO (Marino) *See* Barletius (Marinus)

BURLETT (Christianus Fredericus de) Dissertatio juridica inauguralis qua Benthami de utili doctrina dijudicatur, *etc.* pp. xii. 103. *Amstelaedami,* 1829. 8°. **6005**. aaa. **23**.

BURLEUS (Gualterus) *See* Burley (Walter)

BURLEW (John Swalm)

—— Algal Culture from Laboratory to Pilot Plant. Edited by J. S. Burlew. pp. ix. 357. *Washington,* 1953. 8°. [*Carnegie Institution of Washington Publication.* no. 600.] Ac. **1866**.

BURLEY-IN-WHARFEDALE.—*District Nursing Association.* Report . . . for 1914. pp. 15. *Burley-in-Wharfedale,* [1915.] 8°. **07688**. df. **42**.

BURLEY-ON-THE-HILL. Sketch and plan of a wash-pit for sheep at the Earl of Winchilsea's, Burley, near Oakham, Rutland. [Two plates, with descriptive letter-press.] [1800?] *obl.* fol. **1251.1.18.**

—— [Another copy.] B. **266**. (**8**.)
In this copy the sketch is coloured.

BURLEY, *Family of.* *See* Burleigh (Charles) The Genealogies of the Burley or Burleigh Family of America. 1880. 8°. **9914**. i. **7**.

BURLEY (Alfred Cunningham) Spurgeon and his Friends, *etc.* [With plates, including portraits.] pp. 180. *Epworth Press: London,* 1933. 8°. **2216**. a. **13**.

BURLEY (George Harry Cook)

—— The History of King Edward's School, Stourbridge. (A paper given to the Stourbridge and District Historical and Archaeological Society.) pp. 14. [1948.] 8°. **8369**. b. **16**.

BURLEY (George William) Lathes: their construction and operation . . . With two hundred illustrations. pp. xi. 231. *Scott, Greenwood & Son: London,* 1915. 8°. [*Broadway Series of Engineering Handbooks.* vol. 14.] **8763**. de. **1**/**17**.

—— Second revised edition. pp. xi. 231. *Scott, Greenwood & Son: London,* 1923. 8°. [*Broadway Series of Engineering Handbooks.* vol. 14.] **8763**. de. **1**/**36**.

—— Machine and Fitting Shop Practice. 2 vol. *Scott, Greenwood & Son: London,* 1918, 19. 8°. [*Broadway Series of Engineering Handbooks.* vol. 28, 29.] **8763**. de. **1**/**27**.

—— The Principles and Practice of Toothed Gear Wheel Cutting, *etc.* pp. viii. 460. *Scott, Greenwood & Son: London,* 1922. 8°. **08768**. b. **31**.

—— The Testing of Machine Tools, *etc.* pp. viii. 231. *Scott, Greenwood & Son: London,* 1915. 8°. [*Broadway Series of Engineering Handbooks.* vol. 18.] **8763**. de. **1**/**18**.

BURLEY (James) *See* Taylor (Richard V.) *Headmaster of Wheatley Senior School, Doncaster,* and Burley (J.) Golden Mean Arithmetics, *etc.* 1938, *etc.* 8°. W.P. **12665**.

BURLEY (John) *Captain.* *See* Wight, *Isle of.* A declaration from the Isle of Wyght . . . concerning the King: and the triall of Captain Burley, upon high treason about the late Muteny in the said isle, *etc.* 1648. 4°. E. **423**. (**17**.)

—— A Designe by Captain Barley, and others, to surprize Carisbrook Castle, in the Isle of Wight, where his Majesty now is. With the proceedings of Colonel Hammond against them . . . Also some proceedings in Parliament, concerning the King . . . for the security of his person. pp. 5. *Printed by Robert Ibbitson: London,* 1648. 4°. E. **421**. (**24**.)

—— [Another copy.] **103**. a. **61**

—— Captaine Burley his Speech at the Place of Execution at Winchester, where he was hang'd, drawn, and quartered, for endeavouring to raise forces to take away the King from the Isle of Wyght: also a letter from his Majesties court at Carisbrook-Castle; and a great rising in the city of Worcester; certified by a letter to a member of the House of Commons. pp. 6. *Printed by Robert Ibbitson: London,* 1648. 4°. E. **425**. (**19**.)

—— The Relation of the unjust proceedings against Captaine Burley at Winchester and of his magnanimous and Christian suffering. pp. 23. [*London,*] 1648. 8°. E. **1182**. (**9**.)

—— A True and Brief Relation of the Araignment, Condemnation, and Suffering, of Captaine John Burleigh, who was drawn, hang'd, and quartered at Winton. pp. 6. [*London,*] 1648. 4°. E. **426**. (**1**.)

BURLEY (John) *Dramatist.* Tom Trouble. A play in four acts. pp. 54. *Hendersons: London,* 1920. 8°. **11775**. f. **86**

BURLEY (John) *of Bayswater.* Lines on Roslin Castle, Chapel and Linn, Edinburghshire, N.B. pp. 16. *For private circulation: London,* [1866?] 16°. **11649**. cc. **18**. (**4**.)

BURLEY (JOHN) *of Bayswater.*

—— Our Landlord's Tale. "The Milverton Ghost." A legend of Warwick. [In verse.] pp. 15. *For private circulation: [London,* 1867.] 16°. **11647. a. 82. (9.)**

BURLEY (JOHN M.) First Aid to the Disabled Locomotive, Engine, Air Brake and Air Signal . . . A catechism concerning breaks and failures that are liable to occur. How to prevent some and to locate and repair others. pp. 200. [*The Author: State Line, Pa.,*] 1907. 8°. **8767. ee. 40.**

BURLEY (NANCY E.)

—— Cookery. A practical course for post-primary schools. pp. 216. *Whitcombe & Tombs: Christchurch,* 1955. 8°. **7950. f. 12**

BURLEY (ORIN EVERETT)

—— The Consumers' Cooperative as a Distributive Agency. pp. xiv. 338. *McGraw-Hill Book Co.: New York & London,* 1939. 8°. **08286. k. 41.**

BURLEY (R. W.) *See* WELLOCH (M. J.) and BURLEY (R. W.) The Storytime Readers. [1934.] 8°. **12980. i. 27.**

BURLEY (RAYMOND FOSS)

—— A Report on Pacific Coastwise Shipping. With special reference to the San Francisco Bay Ports Area. Prepared . . . by R. F. Burley, *etc.* 1953. 4°. *See* CALIFORNIA.—*San Francisco Bay Ports Commission.* A.S. c. 6/16.

BURLEY (ROSE) Betrayed by her Friend, *etc.* pp. 64. *William Stevens: London,* [1936.] 8°. [*True Love Series.*] **12633.p.1/47.**

—— Her Rich Rival. pp. 48. *C. Tinling & Co.: Liverpool,* [1941.] 8°. [*Women's 2½d Novels.* no. 7.] **012643. s. 1/7.**

—— Love shall Reign, *etc.* pp. 64. *William Stevens: London,* [1936.] 8°. [*True Love Series.*] **12633.p.1/44.**

—— Love's Loyalty, *etc.* pp. 64. *William Stevens: London,* [1938.] 8°. [*True Love Series.*] **12633.p.1/134.**

—— When Money Killed Love, *etc.* pp. 64. *William Stevens: London,* [1936.] 8°. [*True Love Series.*] **12633.p.1/56.**

BURLEY (SYLVESTER W.) Burley's United States Centennial Gazetteer and Guide. *See* KIDDER (Charles H.)

BURLEY (THEODORE LE GAY) Playhouses and Players of East Anglia . . . Illustrated. pp. xi. 180. *Jarrold & Sons: Norwich,* 1928. 8°. **011805. h. 44.**

BURLEY (WALTER) [De vita ac moribus philosophorum.] *Begin.* [fol. 1 *recto:*] Presētis opusculi tabula Iuxta Alphabeti ordinē, *etc.* [fol. 15 *recto:*] Liber de vita ac morib⁹ ph'oꝝ poetarūq̧ veteꝝ. Ex multis libris tractus. necnō breuit' ꝛ cōpendiose ꝑ venerabilē viꝝ mgr̄m walterum Burley ꝯpilat⁹ Incipit Felicit'. **G.L.** [*Ulrich Zel: Cologne,* 1470?] 4°. **G. 8956.**
112 *leaves, without signatures.* 27 *lines to a page.*

—— [De vita ac moribus philosophorum.] *Begin.* [fol. 1 *recto:*] [A]Bstinentie exemplūū [*sic*] Plato, *etc.* [fol. 13 *recto:*] Incipit Pulcher tractat⁹ collcūs. ꝑ venerabilem doctorē Walterū burley Anglicū De vita phoꝝ, *etc.* *End.* [fol. 98 *verso:*] Et sic finitur perpulcher tractatus ꝯtinens vitā mores: ac elegātissima phylozophoꝝ dcā: simul et gesta, *etc.* **G.L.** *Per me Arnoldū ter hornē: [Cologne,]* 1472. 4°. **IA. 3120.**
98 *leaves, without signatures.* 27 *lines to the page.*

BURLEY (WALTER)

—— *Begin.* [fol. 1 *verso:* [A]Naximander. vi., *etc.*] [fol. 2 *recto:*] Incipit liber de vita et moribus philosophorū: *End.* [fol. 52 *recto:*] Walteri burley anglici in vitas philosophorum. Cernitur hic finis, *etc.* **G.L.** MS. NOTES. [*Cologne,* 1472?] fol. **G. 8978.**
58 *leaves, without signatures. Double columns,* 38 *lines to a column. Imperfect; wanting the first leaf.*

—— *Begin.* [fol. 2 *recto:*] Incipit tabula scd'm ordinem alphabeti in vitas ph'oꝝ, *etc.* [fol. 8 *recto:*] Incipit libellus deuita & moribꝰ ph'oꝝ & poetaꝝ. [By W. Burley.] **G.L.** [1472?] fol. *See* VITA. **C. 14. b. 7. (2.)**

—— [Another copy.] **G. 8977.**

—— *Begin.* [fol. 2 *recto:*] Incipit tabula scd'm ordinem alphabeti ī vitas philosophorum *etc.* [fol. 8 *recto:*] Incipit libellus de vita ꝛ moribꝰ ph'oꝝ et poetaꝝ. [By W. Burley.] **G.L.** 1477. fol. *See* VITA. **IB. 7154.**

—— [Another copy.] **167. d. 7.**

—— *Begin.* [fol. 2 *recto:*] Incipit tabula ſm ordinem alphabeti in vitas philosophoꝝ, *etc.* [fol. 7 *recto:*] Incipit libell⁹ d' vita et moribꝰ philosophoꝝ et poetaꝝ. [By W. Burley.] **G.L.** 1479. fol. *See* VITA. **IB. 7636.**

—— *Begin.* [fol. 1 *recto:*] Presentis opusculi tabula iuxta alphabeti ordinē, *etc.* [fol. 15 *recto:*] Liber de vita ac moribus ph'orum. poetarūq̧ veteꝝ ex multis libris tractus: necnō breuiter ꝛ ꝯpendiose ꝑ venerabilem virum mgr̄m walteꝝ burley ꝯpilatus: incipit feliciter. **G.L.** *per Conradū de homborch: [Cologne,* 1479.] 8°. **C. 5. a. 6.**
112 *leaves. Sig.* [*⁸ **⁶] a–l⁸ m¹⁰. 27 *lines to a page.*

—— *Begin.* [fol. 2 *recto:*] Incipit tabula secundum ordinem alphabeti ī vitas philosophorum, *etc.* [fol. 8 *verso:*] Incipit libellus de vita ꝛ moribus philosophoꝝ ꝛ poetarū. [By W. Burley.] **G.L.** [1480?] 4°. *See* VITA. **IA. 49244.**

—— [Another copy.] **IA. 49245.**

—— De vita philosophorum. [By W. Burley.] **G.L.** [1485?] fol. *See* VITA. **IB. 3585.**

—— *Begin.* [fol. 2 *recto:*] Incipit libellus de vita et moribus philosophorum et poetarū. [By W. Burley.] **G.L.** [1490?] 4°. *See* VITA. **I.A.50178.**

—— Vita omnium philosophorū & poetarum cū auctoritatibus & sētentiis aureis eorundem annexis. [By W. Burley. With a woodcut.] [1505?] 4°. *See* VITA. **523. i. 11.**

—— [Another edition.] [1510?] 4°. **523. i. 12.**

—— Vita philosophoꝝ et poetarū cū auctoritatibus et sentētiis aureis eorundē annexis. [By W. Burley.] **G.L.** ff. li[i]. 1510. 4°. *See* VITA. **10603. cc. 2.**

—— [Another edition.] **G.L.** [1515?] 8°. *See* VITA. **525. b. 32.**

—— [Another edition.] [1515?] 4°. *See* VITA. **10606. b. 32.**

—— Gualteri Burlaei Liber de vita et moribus philosophorum, mit einer altspanischen Übersetzung der Eskurialbibliothek. Herausgegeben von Hermann Kunst. pp. 441. *Tübingen,* 1886. 8°. [*Bibliothek des litterarischen Vereins in Stuttgart.* no. 177.] **Ac. 8963.**

—— Das buch von dem leben vnd sitten der heydnischen maister. [The "De vita ac moribus philosophorum" of Walter Burley.] *End.* [fol. 160 *recto:*] Hie endet sich daz buch der leben, der natürlichen maister, mit jren

BURLEY (Walter)

züchten: leeren, vnd sprüchen der sitten auss jren bůchern aussgezogen. Vnnd hÿejnn durch Anthoni sorgen . . . auss dem latein in teütsch geschriben vnd gemachet, *etc.* [fol. 161 *recto*:] HIenach volget das register, *etc.* ff. clx. 1490. 4°. *See* Buch. **IA. 6046.**

—— [Expositio in Physica Aristotelis.] *Begin.* [fol. 1 *recto*:] Quoniam quidem intelligere ⁊ scire ꝯtingit circa oēs sciētias quaꝝ sunt principia cause, *etc.* [fol. 275 *verso*:] Clarissimi expositoris Gualteri burlei ĩ octo uolumina diui Arił. de physico auditu expositio finit, *etc.* **G. L.** *Thomas ex capitaneis de asula ⁊ magister Bonus de frantia. Padue,* die decimo octauo Iulii, 1476. vfol. **IC. 29952.**
276 *leaves. Sig.* a10 b8 c6 d8 e4 f10 g–i8 k4 l6 m6 n–r8 s6 t6 u6 x6 y8 z8 ⁊8 ꝯ4 ꝝ4 ; .a–.c8 .d6.e6 .f8 .g6 .h4 ; :a8 [:b8 :c8] :d–:f6. *Double columns,* 66 *lines to a column.*

—— Berleus super octo libros Phisicorum. [With the text. Edited by N. Vernia.] **G. L.** ff. 267. 1501. fol. *See* Aristotle. [*Physica.—Latin.*] **520. k. 7. (1.)**

—— Gualterii Burlæi . . . Super Aristotelis libros, de physica auscultatione lucidissima commentaria. Cum noua veterique interpretatione, *etc.* coll. 1116. 1609. fol. *See* Aristotle. [*Physica.—Latin.*] **520. l. 18.**

—— [Expositio super Artem veterem Porphyrii et Aristotelis.] *Begun.* [fol. 1 *recto*:] Preclarissimi uiri gualterij burlei . . . sup artem ueterem porphyrij ⁊ aristotelis expositio siue scriptū feliciter incipit. *End.* [fol. 118 *recto*:] Gualterij āglici sr̄ uiřib9 pdicam̄tis. sex pncipiis. ⁊ phyrmēijs Ari. op9 emēdatū p . . . Symonē alexādrinū . . . felicit' explicit. **G. L.** copious ms. notes. *p xpoforū arnoldū: venetijs,* [1476?] fol. **IB. 19997.**
118 *leaves. Sig.* a–o8p6. *Double columns,* 49 *lines to a column.*

—— *Begin.* [fol. 2 *recto*:] Preclarissimi viri Gualterii Burlei . . . sup artem vetereȝ Porphyrii ⁊ Aristotelis expositio siue scriptum feliciter incipit, *etc.* [With the text.] **G. L.** 1481. fol. *See* Aristotle. [*Organon.—Two or more Parts.—Latin.*] **IB. 21550.**

—— *Begin.* [fol. 2 *recto*:] Preclarissimi viri Gualterij Burlei . . . super artem veterem Porphyrij ⁊ Aristotelis expositio siue scriptum feliciter incipit. *End.* [fol. 91 *verso*:] Explicit scriptū preclarissimi viri Gualterij Burlei . . . in artem veterem Porphyrii ⁊ Aristotelis Per . . . Fratrem Mattheum cāpagnam de cherio . . . ab infinitis fere erroribꝰ . . . absolutum. q etiā magister . . . qões eiusdem Burlei super ꝓlogo porphyrij cnrauit [*sic*] adiungere, *etc.* [With the text.] **G. L.** 1492. fol. *See* Aristotle. [*Organon.—Two or more Parts.—Latin.*] **IB. 21948.**

—— Burlei super artem veterem Porphirii et Aristotelis. [With the text.] **G. L.** 1497. fol. *See* Aristotle. [*Organon.—Two or more Parts.—Latin.*] **IB. 24589.**

—— [Scriptum super libros Ethicorum Aristotelis.] *Begin.* [fol. 2 *recto*:] Gualteri Burlei super libros Ethycorum Aristotelis scriptum feliciter incipit. [With the text.] **G. L.** 1481. fol. *See* Aristotle. [*Ethica Nicomachea.—Latin.*] **IB. 21170.**

—— Expositio Gualteri Burlei super decem Libros Ethicorum Aristotelis. [With the text.] **G. L.** 1500. fol. *See* Aristotle. [*Ethica Nicomachea.—Latin.*] **IB. 24667.**

—— [Scriptum super libros Posteriorum Analyticorum Aristotelis.] *Begin.* [fol. 1 *recto*:] Scriptū excellētissimi doctoris mgrī galteri burlei super libro posteriorum aristoteł feliciter incipit. **G. L.** [*Johannes Herbort: Padua,* 1477.] fol. **IB. 29937.**
12 *leaves. Sig.* a6 b6. *Double columns,* 39 *lines to a column.*

BURLEY (Walter)

—— [Another edition.] *See* Aristotle. [*Organon.—Posteriora Analytica.—Latin.*] Commentaria Roberti Linconiensis in libros posterioꝝ Aristotelis, *etc.* 1494. fol. **IB. 22914.**

—— [Another edition.] *See* Aristotle. [*Organon.—Posteriora Analytica.—Latin.*] Commentaria Roberti Linconiēsis in libros posteriorum Aristotelis, *etc.* 1497. fol. **IB. 24587.**

—— [Another edition.] *See* Aristotle. [*Organon.—Posteriora Analytica.—Latin.*] Habes accuratissime lector Aristotelis posteriorum opus, *etc.* 1514. fol. **519. h. 22.**

—— [Another edition.] *See* Aristotle. [*Organon.—Posteriora Analytica.—Latin.*] Aristo. Posteriorum libri, *etc.* 1552. fol. **519. h. 23.**

BURLFORD (Thomas Rugby) American Hatred and British Folly. pp. 75. *T. R. Burlford: London,* [1911.] 8°. **8176. f. 21.**

—— Britannia's Awakening. Britain in 1922. pp. 56. *"Marshalsea Press": London,* [1912.] 8°. **12315. l. 25. (3.)**

BURLIFER (Stephanus) *See* Brulefer.

BURLIN. Burlin der Diener, Vater, und Schwiegervater in einer Person. Ein Lustspiel in fünf Aufzügen. [By Carl Franz Romanus.] *Wienn,* 1763. 8°. [*Neue Sammlung von Schauspielen welche auf der Kaiserlich Königlich privil. deutschen Schaubühne zu Wien aufgeführet werden.* Bd. 2.] **11747. g. 1.**
A later edition, entitled "Crispin als Kammerdiener," and bearing the author's name, is entered under Romanus *(C. F.).*

BURLIN (Natalie) *See* Curtis, afterwards Burlin.

BURLING (Arthur Hart)

—— *See* Burling (Judith) and Burling (A. H.) Chinese Art. [1954.] 8°. **7813. i. 22.**

BURLING (Beverly Burdette) *See* Consoliver (Earl L.) Automotive Electricity . . . Revised by B. B. Burling, *etc.* 1932. 8°. **08755. aaa. 58.**

BURLING (Judith) and **BURLING** (Arthur Hart)

—— Chinese Art. [With illustrations and a bibliography.] pp. 384. *Thames & Hudson: London; Cornwall, N.Y.* printed, [1954.] 8°. **7813. i. 22.**

BURLING (Lancaster A.) *See* Burling (Lancaster D.)

BURLING (Lancaster Demorest) Our Earth: some chapters in its history. (Scientific Group, T.S. in England.) pp. 28. [*Theosophical Society:*] *London,* [1923.] 8°. **07105. i. 10.**

BURLING (Temple)

—— *See* Rennie (Thomas A. C.) Vocational Rehabilitation of Psychiatric Patients. [By] T. A. C. Rennie . . . T. Burling, *etc.* 1950. 8°. **7661. a. 20.**

BURLINGAME (Anne Elizabeth) The Battle of the Books in its Historical Setting, *etc.* [A thesis.] pp. x. 227. *B. W. Huebsch: New York,* 1920. 8°. **011851. aaa. 46.**

—— Condorcet. The torch bearer of the French Revolution. pp. ii. 249. *Stratford Co.: Boston,* [1930.] 8°. **10655. de. 26.**

BURLINGAME (ANSON) *See* APPLETON (William) *of Boston, Mass.* Read this before you vote! To the voters of the Fifth District [Boston]. Appleton, and Burlingame: Which shall be your Representative? [1861.] 8°. **8176. g. 2. (2.)**

—— *See* GUMPACH (J. von) The Burlingame Mission: a political disclosure, *etc.* 1872. 8°. **8023. dd. 2.**

—— *See* WILLIAMS (Frederick W.) Anson Burlingame and the first Chinese mission to foreign powers. 1912. 8°. **10883. d. 21.**

—— Defence of Massachusetts. Speech . . . in the United States House of Representatives, June 21, 1856. pp. 33. *Printed for private distribution: Cambridge* [*Mass.*], 1856. 8°. **8156. d. 5.**

—— Speech of Hon. Anson Burlingame, candidate for Congress, to the Electors of the fifth Congressional District, at the Free Democratic meeting in Faneuil Hall, October 13, 1852, *etc.* pp. 8. *Boston,* 1852. 8°. **8177. f. 26.**

—— [Another issue.] *See* BUCKINGHAM (Joseph T.) Speeches, *etc.* 1852. 8°. **8177. g. 28.**

BURLINGAME (EDWARD LIVERMORE) *See* WAGNER (W. R.) [*Selections.*] Art Life and Theories of Richard Wagner. Selected . . . and translated by E. L. Burlingame, *etc.* 1875. 12°. **7897. e. 8.**

—— Current Discussion. A collection from the chief English essays on questions of the time. Edited by E. L. Burlingame. 2 vol. *G. P. Putnam's Sons: New York,* 1878. 8°. **12273. f. 12.**

BURLINGAME (EUGENE WATSON) *See* BUDDHAGHOSA Buddhist Legends, translated . . . by E. W. Burlingame. 1921. 8°. **14003. l. 3.**

—— Buddhist Parables. Translated from the original Pāli. pp. xxix. 348. *Yale University Press: New Haven,* 1922. 8°. **014098. cc. 16.**

—— The Grateful Elephant, and other stories (selected from Buddhist Parables). Translated from the Pāli by E. W. Burlingame. With illustrations by Dorothy Lathrop. pp. xxxv. 172. *Yale University Press: New Haven,* 1923. 4°. **14099. a. 14.**

BURLINGAME (HARDIN J.) Herrmann the Magician. His life; his secrets . . . Illustrated. [The life and secrets of Carl and Alexander Herrmann.] pp. 298. *Laird & Lee: Chicago,* [1897.] 8°. **10706. d. 41.**

—— Leaves from Conjurers' Scrap Books; or, Modern magicians and their works. pp. 274. *Donohue, Henneberry & Co.: Chicago,* 1891. 8°. **7913. ee. 26.**

BURLINGAME (LEONAS LANCELOT) General Biology. By L. L. Burlingame . . . Harold Heath . . . Ernest Gale Martin . . . and George James Peirce. pp. xxix. 568. *Jonathan Cape: London; printed in U.S.A.,* [1923.] 8°. **7001. eee. 34.**

—— Heredity and Social Problems. pp. xi. 369. *New York & London,* 1940. 8°. [*McGraw-Hill Publications in the Zoological Sciences.*] **W.P. 3430/49.**

BURLINGAME (PAUL L.) *See* LONG (Joseph A.) and BURLINGAME (P. L.) The Development of the External Form of the Rat, *etc.* 1938. 8°. [*University of California Publications in Zoölogy.* vol. 43. no. 8.] **Ac. 2689. g/28.**

BURLINGAME (ROGER) *See* BURLINGAME (William R.)

BURLINGAME (WILLIAM ROGER)

—— Backgrounds of Power. The human story of mass production. pp. x. 372. *Charles Scribner's Sons: London, New York; printed in the U.S.A.,* 1949. 8°. **8286. c. 79.**

—— Engines of Democracy. Inventions and society in mature America. [With plates.] pp. xviii. 606. *C. Scribner's Sons: New York, London,* 1940. 8°. **8713. b. 11.**

—— General Billy Mitchell, champion of air defense. [With plates, including portraits.] pp. ix. 212. *McGraw-Hill Book Co.: New York,* [1952.] 8°. [*They made America.*] **W.P. B. 19/7.**

—— The Heir. pp. 412. *Cassell & Co.: London,* 1930. 8°. **A.N. 698.**

—— High Thursday. pp. 334. *C. Scribner's Sons: New York,* 1928. 8°. **12713. c. 25.**

—— Inventors behind the Inventor. [With plates.] pp. 211. *Harcourt, Brace & Co.: New York,* [1947.] 8°. **10604. p. 8.**

—— March of the Iron Men. A social history of union through invention. [With plates and a bibliography.] pp. xvi. 500. *C. Scribner's Sons: New York, London,* 1938. 8°. **08286. eee. 15.**

—— Mosquitoes in the Big Ditch. The story of the Panama Canal . . . Illustrated by Helen Damrosch Tee-Van. pp. ix. 177. *John C. Winston Co.: Philadelphia, Toronto,* [1952.] 8°. [*Winston Adventure Books.*] **W.P. A. 269/6.**

—— Of Making Many Books. A hundred years of reading, writing and publishing, *etc.* pp. xii. 347. *Charles Scribner's Sons: New York,* 1946. 8°. **11867. cc. 7.**

—— Susan Shane. A story of success. pp. 411. *C. Scribner's Sons: New York,* 1926. 8°. **12711. aa. 17.**

—— [Another edition.] pp. 362. *William Heinemann: London,* 1927. 8°. **12713. a. 12.**

—— Three Bags Full. pp. 637. *Jonathan Cape: London; printed in U.S.A.,* 1937. 8°. **012600. d. 53.**

BURLINGAME (WILLIAM ROGER) and **STEVENS** (ALDEN)

—— Victory without Peace. pp. 335. *Harcourt, Brace & Co.: New York,* [1944.] 8°. **9087. a. 32.**

BURLINGHAM (   )

—— *See* HEERMANN (J.) [*Begin.*
Ach Jesu! dessen Treu, im Himmel und auf Erden,
Durch keines Menschen Mund kann gnug gepriesen werden.]
The Precious Name of Jesus. A hymn . . . From the German, *etc.* [Translated by Miss — Burlingham.] [c. 1870.] 32°. **03440. dg. 47.**

BURLINGHAM (A. H.) *See* HEADLEY (Phineas C.) The Reaper and the Harvest . . . With an introduction by . . . A. H. Burlingham. 1884. 8°. **4985. dd. 12.**

—— —— [1885.] 8°. **4907. bbb. 10.**

—— *See* HERVEY (George W.) The Story of Baptist Missions . . . With an introduction by . . . A. H. Burlingham. 1886. 8°. **4766. ee. 5.**

BURLINGHAM (CHARLES CULP) Heidelberg and the Universities of America. [Letters and articles reprinted from " The Times " and " Nature " on the refusal of the English Universities to participate in the celebration of the 550th anniversary of the University of Heidelberg. Edited by C. C. Burlingham, James Byrne, Samuel Seabury and Henry L. Stimson.] pp. v. 61. *Viking Press: New York,* 1936. 8°. **8358.** ccc. **34.**

BURLINGHAM (DOROTHY)

—— Twins. A study of three pairs of identical twins. With 30 charts. pp. x. 94. *Imago Publishing Co.: London,* 1952. 8°. **08366.** ppp. **40.**

BURLINGHAM (DOROTHY) and **FREUD** (ANNA)

—— Infants without Families. The case for and against residential nurseries. pp. 108. *G. Allen & Unwin: London,* 1943. 8°. **8312.** a. **51.**

—— Enfants sans famille . . . Traduit . . . par Anne Berman. pp. vii. 128. *Paris,* 1949. 8°. **08311.** b. **60.**
Part of the " Nouvelle encyclopédie pedagogique."

—— [Infants without Families.] Anstaltskinder. pp. 138. *Imago Publishing Co.: London,* 1950. 8°. **08311.** c. **83.**

—— Barn utan familj. (Översättning: Gustav Gustafson.) pp. 124. *Stockholm,* 1948. 8°. **08308.** aa. **16.**

—— Young Children in War-Time. A year's work in a residential war nursery. pp. 81. *G. Allen & Unwin: London,* 1942. 12°. **08367.** aa. **18.**

—— [Young Children in War-Time.] Kriegskinder. Jahresbericht des Kriegskinderheims Hampstead Nurseries. pp. 82. *Imago Publishing Co.: London,* 1949. 8°. **08368.** aa. **19.**

BURLINGHAM (FREDERICK) How to become an Alpinist . . . Illustrated with sixty-three photographs by the author. [With a portrait.] pp. xii. 218. *T. Werner Laurie: London,* [1914.] 8°. **7904.** aaa. **22.**

BURLINGHAM (ROBERT)

—— The Odyssey of Modern Drug Research. (Pharmaceutical manufacture; its science and economics.) [On the work of the Upjohn Company. With illustrations including portraits.] pp. 124. *Upjohn Co.: Kalamazoo,* 1951. 4°. **08909.** p. **3.**

BURLINGHAM (RUSSELL)

—— Forrest Reid: a portrait and a study, *etc.* [With a portrait and a bibliography.] pp. 259. *Faber & Faber: London,* 1953. 8°. **11869.** cc. **25.**

BURLINGHAME (MAXCY WHIPPLE) Ministerial Support. A sermon. *See* WILLIAMS (A. D.) *Baptist Minister.* The Rhode Island Free-Will Baptist Pulpit. 1852. 12°. **4985.** b. **29.**

BURLINGTON. The Burlington: a high class monthly magazine, *etc.* *See* PERIODICAL PUBLICATIONS.—*London.*

BURLINGTON, *New Jersey.—Burlington College.* Burlington College. Address of the Trustees; prospectus of the preparatory school. pp. 16. *Burlington,* 1846. 8°. **8304.** aaa. **16.** (**2.**)

—— Sixth edition. pp. 36. *Burlington,* 1848. 12°. **8366.** aaa. **1.** (**1.**)

—— Seventh edition. (Appendix. A word or two with parents.) pp. 84. *Burlington,* 1848. 12°. **8366.** aaa. **1.** (**2.**)

BURLINGTON, *New Jersey.—Burlington College.*

—— Proceedings of the Fourth of July, 1850, at Burlington College. pp. 39. *Burlington,* 1850. 8°. **8365.** ee. **28.** (**3.**)

Court.

—— The Burlington Court Book. A record of Quaker jurisprudence in West New Jersey, 1680–1709. Edited by H. Clay Reed . . . and George J. Miller. pp. lv. 372. *American Historical Association: Washington,* 1944. 4°. [*American Legal Records.* vol. 5.] Ac. **8504/18.**

—— *New Jersey Society for Promoting the Abolition of Slavery.* The Constitution of the New Jersey Society, for promoting the abolition of slavery: to which is annexed, Extracts from a law of New-Jersey passed the 2d March, 1786, and Supplement to the same, passed the 26th November, 1788. pp. 14. *Burlington,* 1793. 8°. **8176.** a. **14.**

—— *Saint Mary's Hall.* The Way of the Church with Children; together with the Catalogue and Prospectus of St. Mary's Hall. Summer Term, MDCCCXLVIII. pp. 24. *Burlington,* 1848. 12°. **8365.** c. **90.**

—— Nurture: together with the Catalogue and Prospectus of St. Mary's Hall.—Winter Term, MDCCCXLVIII–IX. (Appendix. A word or two with parents.) pp. 44. *Burlington,* 1849. 12°. **8365.** c. **91.**

—— St. Mary's Hall: Register: fifteenth year. pp. 31. *Burlington,* 1852. 12°. **8365.** c. **92.**

—— Notices of St. Mary's Hall. pp. 11. [*Burlington?* 1837?] 8°. **8366.** c. **13.**

—— *Society of Friends.* Stephen Grellet. (Testimony of Burlington Monthly Meeting concerning S. Grellet.) [With an obituary notice reprinted from the " Burlington American."] pp. 16. [*Burlington,*] 1856. 8°. **4920.** g. **20.**

—— [Another edition.] A Testimony concerning Stephen Grellet, *etc.* [With notes.] pp. 31. ix. *Harrison Penney: Darlington,* 1856. 16°. **4920.** a. **5.**

BURLINGTON, *Vermont.—Fletcher Free Library.*

—— Fifth (Thirty-fifth) Annual Report of the Trustees of the Fletcher Free Library. 2 pt. *Burlington, Vt.,* 1879, 1909. 8°. A.R. **988.**

—— Bulletin. vol. 2. no. 1. [*Burlington,*] 1909. 8°. **11909.** p. **28.**

—— *University of Vermont,* afterwards *University of Vermont and State Agricultural College.* Catalogue of the Officers and Students of the University of Vermont . . . October, 1823. pp. 7. [*Burlington,* 1823.] 8°. **8366.** d. **4.**

—— Catalogue of the Officers and Students of the University of Vermont . . . November—1834. pp. 14. *Burlington,* 1834. 8°. **8366.** d. **5.**

—— Catalogue of the Officers and Students of the University of Vermont. November—1835. pp. 16. *Burlington,* 1835. 8°. **8366.** d. **5*.**

—— Catalogue of the Officers and Students of the University of Vermont . . . October—1839. pp. 10. *Burlington,* [1839.] 8°. **8365.** c. **3.**

—— Catalogus Senatus Academici, et eorum qui munera et officia gesserunt, quive alicujus gradus laurea donati sunt, in Universitate Viridimontana. pp. 29. *Burlingtoniæ,* 1843. 8°. **8365.** d. **29.** (**10.**)

BURLINGTON, *Vermont.—Fletcher Free Library.*

—— Catalogue of the Corporation, Officers and Students of the University of Vermont. October—1844. pp. 16. [*Burlington*, 1844.] 8°. **8365**. c. **63**.

—— A Catalogue of the Corporation, Officers, and Students of the University of Vermont. October—1849. pp. 16. *Burlington*, 1849. 8°. **8365**. cc. **2**. (**25**.)

—— A Catalogue of the Officers and Students of the University of Vermont and State Agricultural College. With a statement of the several Courses of Instruction. 1866–7. *Burlington*, 1866. 8°. **8366**. cc. **35**. (**10**.)

—— Catalogue of the University of Vermont and State Agricultural College . . . 1899–1900. pp. 126. *Burlington*, 1899. 8°. **08366**. de. **30**.

—— General Catalogue of the University of Vermont and State Agricultural College . . . 1791–1900. pp. 258. *Burlington*, 1901. 8°. **8385**. f. **11**.

—— The Billings Library, the gift to the University of Vermont of Frederick Billings. [A series of 17 plates, with a prospectus of the series.] *Boston*, [1894.] fol. **1887**. b. **50**.

—— Catalogue of the Library of George Perkins Marsh. (By H. L. Koopman.) pp. viii. 742. *Burlington*, 1892. 8°. **11915.i.5.**

—— Bibliography of G. P. Marsh. Compiled by H. L. Koopman. [Extracted from the Catalogue of the Marsh Collection.] pp. 24. *Burlington*, 1892. 8°. **011900**. ee. **5**. (**16**.)

—— Centennial Addresses delivered at Commencement 1891 and 1892. By R. D. Benedict and J. E. Goodrich. 2 pt. [*Burlington*, 1892.] 8°. **8366**. de. **36**.

—— Studies in Tolerance of New England Forest Trees. XII. Effect of thinning in plantations on some of the physical factors of the site and on the development of young northern White Pine—Pinus strobus L.—and Scotch Pine—Pinus silvestris L. By W. R. Adams. pp. 156. *Burlington*, 1935. 8°. Ac. **3511**. b.
Bulletin 390 *of the Vermont Agricultural Experiment Station.*

BURLINGTON, *Yorkshire.* *See* BRIDLINGTON.

BURLINGTON, RICHARD, *Earl of.* *See* BOYLE.

BURLINGTON ALMANACK. *See* EPHEMERIDES. New-Jersey. The Burlington Almanack, *etc.*

BURLINGTON ARCADE. Burlington Arcade: being a discourse on shopping for the élite. [Signed: H. J. B.] 1925. 12°. *See* B., H. J. **010349**. de. **26**.

BURLINGTON ART MINIATURES. The Burlington Art Miniatures. 20 vol. *Fine Arts Publishing Co.: London*, 1909. 8°. **7875**. pp. **1**.

BURLINGTON BAY. Burlington Bay.-(Tartar Tongue. A parody on the Tartar Drum.—Mary le Moor.) [Songs.] *J. Catnach:* [*London*, 1830?] *s. sh.* 4°. C. **116**. i. **1**. (**173**.)

BURLINGTON CHARITY SCHOOL. *See* LONDON.—III.

BURLINGTON COMPENDIUM. Instructions for the 50 Indoor Games contained in the Burlington Compendium. pp. 14. [1904.] 8°. **7907**. ee. **36**. (**2**.)

BURLINGTON FINE ARTS CLUB. *See* LONDON.—III.

BURLINGTON GAZETTE. *See* PERIODICAL PUBLICATIONS.—*London.* The Burlington Magazine.

BURLINGTON HOUSE. *See* LONDON.—III.

—— Burlington House. A magazine and critic of the Royal Academy, *etc.* *See* PERIODICAL PUBLICATIONS.—*London.*

BURLINGTON LIBRARY. The Burlington Library. 7 vol. *Chapman & Hall: London*, [1910–12.] 8°. **012207**. i. **17**

BURLINGTON MAGAZINE. *See* PERIODICAL PUBLICATIONS.—*London.*

BURLINGTON QUAY. *See* BRIDLINGTON QUAY.

BURLINGTON (CHARLES) *See* BRITISH TRAVELLER. The Modern Universal British Traveller; or, a New, complete, and accurate tour through England, Wales, and Scotland . . . The articles respecting England by C. Burlington, *etc.* 1779. fol. **10348**. l. **6**.

BURLINGTON (JOSEPH) *See* WHITEHAVEN.—*Whitehaven Scientific Association.* The Annual Journal, *etc.* [no. 9–15 edited by J. Burlington.] 1899, *etc.* 8°. Ac. **1197**

BURLINSON (HARRISON) and **SIMPSON** (WILLIAM HENRY) The Iron Shipbuilders', Engineers', and Iron Merchants' Guide & Assistant, containing the calculated weights of upwards of 150,000 different sizes of iron plates. Carefully compiled, and thoroughly revised. pp. 219. *McCorquodale & Co.: London*, 1865. *obl.* 4°. **7945**. e. **26**.

—— [A reissue.] *C. Lockwood & Co.: London*, 1886. *obl.* fol. **8548**. de. **2**

BURLISON (CLEMENT) *See* HENDERSON (William) *F.R.H.S.* My Life as an Angler . . . With . . . woodcuts engraved . . . from drawings by C. Burlison, *etc.* 1879. 8° **7907**. g. **11**

BURLISON (WILLIAM LEONIDAS) and **ALLYN** (ORR MILTON) Yields of Winter Grains in Illinois. *Urbana*, 1917. 8°. [*University of Illinois. Agricultural Experiment Station. Bulletin.* no. 201.] **A.S.i.22/2.**

BURLITON (ZORZ) *pseud.* [i.e. GEMINIANO MEGNANI.] *See* MEGNANI (G.)

BURLIUK (DAVID DAVIDOVICH) *See* BURLYUK.

BURLIUK (NICHOLAS)

—— *See* DREIER (Katherine S.) Burliuk . . . Part I. Russia In collaboration with N. Burliuk, *etc.* 1944. 4°. **7866**. ppp. **35**

BURLON DE LA BUSBAQUERIE (HONORÉ FIACRE) *pseud.* [i.e. PIERRE FRANÇOIS GUYOT DESFONTAINES.] *See* also GUYOT DESFONTAINES (P. F.)

—— *See* DESGROUAIS (   )
Lettre à M. Burlon de la Busbaquerie . . . Pour servir de réponse au jugement que cet infidèle journaliste a porté d'une première critique de la traduction de Virgile par M. l'abbé Des Fontaines, *etc.* [1745.] 12°. **011824**. de. **13**. (**5**.)

—— *See* PERIODICAL PUBLICATIONS.—*Avignon.* Jugemens sur quelques ouvrages nouveaux. [Written in part by P. F. Guyot Desfontaines, under the pseudonym Burlon de la Busbaquerie.] 1744, *etc.* 12°. **264**. i. **22–32**

BURLOUD (ALBERT) La Pensée d'après les recherches expérimentales de H.-J. Watt, de Messer et de Bühler. pp. 192. *Paris*, 1927. 8°. **08465**. i. **18**.

BURLOUD (Albert)

—— Principes d'une psychologie des tendances. pp. 430. *Paris*, 1938. 8°. **8471.** ee. **5.**

—— Psychologie de la sensibilité. pp. 223. *Paris*, 1954. 8°. **8469.** de. **42.**
Collection Armand Colin. Section de philosophie. no. 293.

BURLS (George Arthur) *See* Clerk (Dugald) The Gas, Petrol, and Oil Engine, *etc.* (vol. 2 by D. Clerk and G. A. Burls.) 1909, *etc.* 8°. **08767.** d. **35.**

—— Aero Engines . . . With 76 illustrations: with a general introductory account of the theory of the internal-combustion engine, *etc.* pp. x. 196. *C. Griffin & Co.: London*, 1915. 8°. **08768.** d. **44.**

—— Third edition, *etc.* pp. x. 196. *C. Griffin & Co.: London*, 1916. 8°. **08768.** c. **41.**

—— Tenth edition, enlarged, *etc.* pp. x. 196. *C. Griffin & Co.: London*, 1918. 8°. **08768.** dd. **26.**

—— Cost of Power Production by Internal-Combustion Engines. pp. 56. *Blackie & Son: London*, 1924. 4°. **8763.** ccc. **25.**

BURLS (Robert) A Brief Review of the Plan and Operations of the Essex Congregational Union for promoting the knowledge of the Gospel in the county of Essex and its vicinity. With an appendix containing biographical notices of the principal founders and supporters of the society. pp. 153. *P. H. Youngman: Maldon*, 1848. 8°. **4707.** aa. **29.**

—— [Another copy.] **4139.** aa. **35.**

—— Paul's Voyage to Rome, considered in connexion with his faith. 1832. *See* British Preacher. The British Preacher, *etc.* vol. 3. no. 22. 1831, *etc.* 8°. **1024.** k. **13.**

BURLS (William)

—— *See* Payne (Ernest A.) The Excellent Mr. Burls, *etc.* [1951.] 8°. **10804.** m. **34/4.**

BURLTON (Charles H. B.) *See* Bible.—*Revelation.* [*English.*] A Metrical Version of the Revelations. By C. H. B. Burlton. 1900. 8°. **3187.** aa. **74.**

—— —— [1903.] 8°. **03187.** df. **28.**

—— Old Friends with New Faces. [A poem. With "Twelve translations from the French."] pp. 72. *Selwyn & Blount: London*, 1925. 8°. **011644.** e. **8.**

BURLTON (Gladys) Retail Selling, *etc.* pp. 192. *Jonathan Cape: London*, 1927. 8°. **08246.** ff. **19.**

—— Warehouse Selling, *etc.* pp. 111. *Burlton Institute: London*, [1940.] 8°. **08230.** a. **47.**

BURLTON (William) A Few Brief Comments on Sir Charles Napier's Letter to Sir J. Hobhouse, "On the Baggage of the Indian Army." pp. 57. *Smith, Elder & Co.: London*, 1829. 8°. **1398.** d. **41.**

—— *See* MacMurdo (*Sir* William M. S.) Sir Charles Napier's Indian Baggage-Corps. Reply to Lieut.-Col. Burlton's attack. 1850. 8°. **8825.** d. **4.**

BURLTON-BENNET (John Robert) *See* Bennet.

BURLUGUAY (Jean)

—— Toillette de M. l'Archevesque de Sens, ou réponse au Factum des Filles Sainte Catherine lés Provins, contre les Pères Cordeliers. [By J. Burluguay.] pp. 83. 1669. 12°. *See* Provins.—*Monastère de Sainte Catherine.* **4071.** aa. **18.**

BURLUREAUX (Charles) *See* Voisin (A. F.) and Burlureaux (C.) De la mélancolie dans ses rapports avec la paralysie générale, *etc.* 1880. 4°. **7660.** dd. **7.**

—— Considérations sur le siége, la nature, les causes, de la folie paralytique. pp. 92. *Paris*, 1874. 4°. [*Collection des thèses soutenues à la Faculté de Médecine de Paris.* An 1874. tom. 3.] **7374.** a. **8.**

—— La Pratique de l'antisepsie dans les maladies contagieuses et en particulier dans la tuberculose, *etc.* pp. 274. *Paris*, 1892. 12°. **7460.** aa. **4.**

—— Traité pratique de psychothérapie. pp. viii. 447. *Paris*, 1914. 8°. **7409.** ee. **25.**

BURLUREAUX (F.) Essai clinique sur les ulcères syphilitiques. Thèse, *etc.* pp. 31. *Montpellier*, 1843. 4°. **1182.** c. **17.** (**27.**)

BURLUREAUX (Philippe) De la compression sous le point de vue thérapeutique. Thèse, *etc.* pp. 31. *Montpellier*, 1843. 4°. **1182.** c. **19.** (**4.**)

BURLYUK (David Davidovich)

—— *See* Dreier (Katherine S.) Burliuk, *etc.* [With reproductions and portraits.] 1944. 4°. **7866.** ppp. **35.**

BURM (David) Breue ristretto de' capitoli della pace generale stabilita nella città di Ratisbona il dì 13. ottobre, 1630. pp. 8. *L'Herede del Benacci: Fiorenza & Bologna*, 1630. 4°. T. **42*.** (**6.**)

—— [Another edition.] pp. 8. *P. Nesti: Firenze*, 1630. 4°. **1193.** m. **1.** (**28.**)

BURMA.

ARRANGEMENT.

CONSTITUTIONS.

—— The Constitution of the Union of Burma. pp. 67. *Rangoon*, 1947. 8°. I.S. bu. **202.**

LAWS.—I. GENERAL COLLECTIONS.

—— The British Burma Code: consisting of the regulations and local acts in force in British Burma. pp. vi. 189. 1877. 8°. *See* India.—*Legislative Department.* I.S. **364/2.**

—— The British Burma Manual; or, a collection of departmental rules, orders and notifications in force in the Province of British Burma; together with the treaties concluded with the Kingdoms of Ava and Siam. Compiled and arranged by Captain C. B. Cooke. vol. 1 corrected up to the 31st December, 1878. pp. lxxviii. 784. *Thacker, Spink & Co.: Calcutta*, 1879. 8°. **5319.** ee. **11.**
No more published.

—— The Burma Code, containing the Bengal Regulations, the local acts of the Governor-General in Council and the regulations under 33 Victoria, Cap. 3, in force in Lower and Upper Burma, with chronological tables and an appendix. pp. x. 504. 1889. 8º. *See* INDIA.—*Legislative Department.* I.S. **364/16.**

—— The Burma Rules Manual: a collection of local rules and orders made under enactments applying to Burma. pp. iii. iv. clxxix. 372. xxxix. xviii. *Rangoon,* 1893. 8º. I.S. BU. **108/4.**

—— Second edition. [With supplement.] 2 pt. *Rangoon,* 1897. 8º. I.S. BU. **108/5.**

—— The Burma Code. Third edition. pp. xi. 648. 1899. 8º. *See* INDIA.—*Legislative Department.* I.S. **364/24.**

—— A Collection of the Acts passed by the Lieutenant-Governor of Burma in Council in the year 1898(–1915 to 1919). 6 pt. *Rangoon,* 1900–21. 8º.
[Continued as:]
A Collection of the Acts passed by the Local Legislature of Burma in the years 1920 to 1923 [*etc.*]. *Rangoon,* 1924– . 8º. I.S. BU. **124.**

—— Local Rules and Orders made under Enactments applying to Burma, *etc.* 2 vol. *Rangoon,* 1903. 8º. I.S. BU. **108/6.**

—— Local Rules and Orders made under Enactments applying to Burma, *etc.* 2 vol. *Rangoon,* 1908 [1909], 09. 8º. I.S. BU. **108/7.**

—— The Burma Code. Fourth edition. pp. xvi. 741. 1910. 8º. *See* INDIA.—*Legislative Department.* I.S. **364/34.**

—— Local Rules and Orders made under Enactments applying to Burma, *etc.* 2 vol. *Rangoon,* 1915. 8º. I.S. BU. **108/8.**

—— The Burma Boundaries Act, 1880 (Act v of 1880), and the Burma Laws Act, 1898 (Act no. XIII of 1898). As amended up to date. With . . . rulings and . . . notes by D. J. Daniel. pp. iii. 27. 35. *Rangoon,* 1922. 8º. **5310.** g. **17.**
Vol. 4 & 5 of the Burma Local Laws series.

—— The Burma Code . . . Fifth edition. 2 vol. pp. cix. 10. 1035. v. *Rangoon,* 1924. 8º. I.S. BU. **108/2.**

—— The Burma Code. 2 vol. *Calcutta,* [1943, 44.] 4º. I.S. BU. **108/3.**

LAWS.—II. COLLECTIONS OF LAWS ON SPECIAL SUBJECTS.

Civil Defence.

—— The Burma Air Raid Precautions General Lighting Restrictions Order . . . and the Burma Air Raid Warning Order. pp. 21. *Rangoon,* 1941. fol. I.S. BU. **29/6.**

Civil Service.

—— Burma Government Servants'—Secretary of State's Services—Conduct Rules, 1938, and subsidiary rules issued thereunder, *etc.* pp. 8. *Rangoon,* 1941. 8º. I.S. BU. **7/6.**

Land Revenue.

—— The Upper Burma Land Revenue Manual, containing the Upper Burma Land and Revenue Regulation, 1889, the Land Improvement Loans Act, 1883, the Agriculturist's Loans Act, 1884, and the rules, notifications, and orders thereunder, in force in Upper Burma. Corrected up to the 6th August 1900. pp. v. 316. x. *Rangoon,* 1900. 8º. I.S. BU. **142/2.**

—— The Lower Burma Land Revenue Manual, containing the Lower Burma Land and Revenue Act, 1876, the Lower Burma Fisheries Act, 1875, the Land Improvement Loans Act, 1883, the Agriculturist's Loans Act, 1884, the Revenue Recovery Act, 1890, and the rules, notifications, and orders thereunder in force in Lower Burma. Corrected up to the 31st May 1901. pp. iii. 362. *Rangoon,* 1901. 8º. I.S. BU. **142/3.**

—— The Upper Burma Land Revenue Manual . . . Corrected up to the 15th August 1905. pp. ii. 253. *Rangoon,* 1905. 8º. I.S. BU. **142/19.**

—— The Lower Burma Land Revenue Manual, 1906, *etc.* pp. ii. iii. 239. *Rangoon,* 1907. 8º. I.S. BU. **142/22.**

—— The Lower Burma Land Revenue Manual, 1911, *etc.* pp. viii. 327. *Rangoon,* 1911. 8º. I.S. BU. **142/23.**

—— The Upper Burma Land Revenue Manual, 1911: containing the Upper Burma Land and Revenue Regulation, 1889 . . . the rules, notifications, directions and forms in force thereunder, certain orders supplementary to them and the Revenue Recovery Act, 1890, *etc.* pp. ii. 309. *Rangoon,* 1911. 8º. I.S. BU. **142/20.**

—— The Lower Burma Land Revenue Manual, 1911: containing the Lower Burma Land and Revenue Act, 1876 . . . the rules, notifications, directions and forms in force thereunder, and certain acts and orders supplementary to them, *etc.* pp. viii. 327. *Rangoon,* 1915. 8º. I.S. BU. **142/24.**

—— The Lower Burma Land Revenue Manual, 1911 . . . Corrected up to the 1st April 1927. pp. x. 351. *Rangoon,* 1927. 8º. I.S. BU. **142/25.**

—— The Upper Burma Land Revenue Manual, 1911 . . . Corrected up to the 1st April 1927. pp. ii. 325. *Rangoon,* 1927. 8º. I.S. BU. **142/21.**

LAWS.—IV. SEPARATE LAWS.

—— [For editions of Acts of the Indian legislature applicable to Burma:] *See* INDIA. [*Laws.*—IV.]

—— The Burma Gambling Act, 1899. By D. J. Daniel . . . Second edition. pp. vii. 128. *Burma Art Press: Rangoon,* 1923. 8º. **5318.** e. **24.**
Burma Local Laws Series. vol. 1.

—— The Motor Spirit—Duties—Act, 1917, an extract from the Indian Finance Act, 1922, and the orders and notifications issued thereunder, corrected so as to include the amendments made under the Adaptation of Laws Order. pp. 17. *Rangoon,* 1939. 8º. I.S. BU. **105/87.** (2.)

TREATIES.

—— Exchanges of Notes between His Majesty's Government in the United Kingdom and the Government of Burma, and the National Government of the Republic of China concerning the Burma-Yunnan Boundary. Chungking, 18th June, 1941, *etc.* *Eng. & Chin.* [With maps.] pp. 17. 1947. 8º. [*England. Foreign Office. Treaty Series.* 1947. no. 80.] See ENGLAND. [*Treaties, etc.*—II. George VI. 1936–1952.] B.S. **14/137.**

—— Burma. Treaty between the Government of the United Kingdom and the Provisional Government of Burma, with annex and exchange of notes. London, 17th October, 1947, *etc.* pp. 12. [1947.] 8º. *See* ENGLAND. [*Treaties, etc.*—II. George VI. 1936–52.] B.S. **101/3.**

—— Agreement between the Government of the United Kingdom and the Provisional Government of Burma concerning certain Jurisdictional and Fiscal Immunities to be accorded to Personnel of the United Kingdom Forces in Burma. Rangoon, 4th January, 1948, *etc.* pp. 5. pp. 5. 1948. 8º. *See* ENGLAND. [*Treaties, etc.*—II. George VI. 1936–1952.] B.S. **14/127. (81.)**

—— Treaty between the Government of the United Kingdom and the Provisional Government of Burma regarding the Recognition of Burmese Independence and Related Matters. With exchange of notes and annex. London, 17th October, 1947. Ratifications exchanged at Rangoon, 4th January, 1948, *etc.* pp. 12. 1948. 8º. [*England. Foreign Office. Treaty Series.* 1948. no. 16.] *See* ENGLAND. [*Treaties, etc.*—II. George VI. 1936–1952.] B.S. **14/137.**

—— Agreement between the Government of the United Kingdom of Great Britain and Northern Ireland and the Government of the Union of Burma for the Avoidance of Double Taxation and the Prevention of Fiscal Evasion with Respect to Taxes on Income. Rangoon, 13th March, 1950, *etc.* pp. 9. 1950. 8º. *See* ENGLAND.—*Treaties, etc.*—II. George VI. [1936– .] B.S. **14/127. (8.)**

—— Agreement between the Government of Mauritius and the Government of the Union of Burma . . . for the Supply of Rice during the years 1954, 1955, 1956 and 1957. pp. 16. 1954. 8º. *See* MAURITIUS, *Island of.* [*Miscellaneous Official Publications.*] C.S. D. **399/10.**

MISCELLANEOUS PUBLIC DOCUMENTS.

—— A Collection of Papers on Settlement Questions in Upper Burma, with an explanatory note. 2 vol. *Rangoon,* 1899, 1904. 8º. I.S. BU. **129.**

—— Selected Correspondence of Letters issued from and received in the Office of the Commissioner, Tenasserim Division, for the years 1825-26 to 1842-43. pp. 280. *Rangoon,* 1928 [1929]. fol. I.S. BU. **26/7.**

—— Memoranda submitted to the Statutory Commission by the Government of Burma. pp. 590. [*Rangoon,*] 1930. 8º. I.S. BU. **119/19.**

—— Howard-Nixon Memorandum. Revised and additional figures for Annexures A to O as placed before the Tribunal appointed to advise on the Formulation of a Financial Settlement between India and Burma, *etc.* pp. 23. [*Rangoon,*] 1935. fol. I.S. BU. **101/21.**

—— Convention between His Majesty in respect of the United Kingdom and the Emperor of Japan regarding Trade and Commerce between Burma and Japan, with Protocol of Signature. London, June 7, 1937, *etc.* pp. 7. *Rangoon,* 1937. 8º. I.S. BU. **146/7.**

—— *Begin.* The Letters Patent constituting the Office of Governor of Burma; the Royal Commission appointing . . . Sir Archibald Douglas Cochrane . . . to be Governor of Burma; and the instructions issued . . . to the Governor of Burma, *etc.* pp. 11. [*Rangoon,*] 1937. fol. I.S. BU. **101/20.**

—— [Texts of various Orders in Council relating to Burma made 1937–1940, issued as press communiqués.] 12 pt. [*Rangoon,*] 1937–40. fol. I.S. BU. **29/7.**

—— Commercial Agreement between the Government of Burma and the Government of the Union of South Africa. Rangoon and Pretoria, November 14th, 1938. pp. 4. *Rangoon,* 1939. 8º. I.S. BU. **108/9.**

MISCELLANEOUS OFFICIAL PUBLICATIONS.

—— [Reports on Archaeological Work done in Burma by Dr. Emil Forchhammer.] 5 pt. [*Rangoon,* 1889–91.] fol. **7701.** c. **1.** (**1.**)

—— Agricultural Leaflets. 2 vol. *Rangoon,* 1927. 8º. I.S. BU. **114/18.**

—— Agriculture in Burma. A collection of papers written by Government Officials for the Royal Commission on Agriculture, 1926–28. [With maps.] pp. iv. 189. *Rangoon,* 1927. 8º. I.S. BU. **114/19.**

—— Annual Financial Statement of the Government of Burma for the year 1937-38 [*etc.*]. [*Rangoon,*] 1937– . 8º. I.S. BU. **111/4.**

—— Annual Financial Statement of the Shan States Federation for the year 1937–38. pp. 43. *Rangoon,* 1937. 8º. I.S. BU. **186.**

—— Annual Report (Report) of the Working of Co-operative Credit Societies (of the Co-operative Societies Act) in Burma for the year 1905-06 [*etc.*]. *Rangoon,* 1906– . fol. & 8º. I.S. BU. **11** & **170.**

—— Annual Report (Report) on the Administration of Province of British Burmah (Lower Burma) for the year 1861-62(–1886-87). 26 pt. [*Calcutta ;*] *Rangoon,* [1862–88.] fol. & 8º. I.S. BU. **1** & **119.**
The Report on Lower Burma for 1885-86 *includes the Report on Upper Burma for* 1886.

—— Annual Report on the Working of the Factories Act, 1934, in Burma for the year 1935 [*etc.*]. *Rangoon,* 1936– . 8º. I.S. BU. **152/6.**

—— Annual Report on the Working of the Indian Factories Act, 1911, in Burma for the year 1912(–34). 23 pt. *Rangoon,* 1913–35. fol. & 8º. I.S. BU. **15/2** & **152/2.**

—— Annual Report on the Working of the Mines Act in Burma for the year 1937. pp. 14. *Rangoon,* 1938. 8º. I.S. BU. **125/9.**

—— Archæological Notes on Mandalay. By Taw Sein Ko. [With maps.] pp. 39. *Rangoon,* 1917. 8º. **07704.** de. **9.**

—— [Another edition.] pp. 37. *Rangoon,* 1924. 8º. **7702.** a. **40.**

—— Archæological Notes on Pagan. By Taw Sein Ko. [With a map.] pp. 40. *Rangoon,* 1917. 8º. **07704.** de. **8.**

—— A Brief Description of the Method of assessing Land Revenue in Burma and of the Work of the Settlement and Land Records Departments. pp. 18. *Rangoon,* 1937. 8º. I.S. BU. **142/26.**

—— British Burma. Education Report (Report on Public Instruction in Lower Burma) 1867-68(–1889-90). 23 pt. *Maulmain, Rangoon,* 1868–90. 8° & fol. I.S. BU. **116/4** & **50.**

—— British Burma. Revenue Report (Reports on the Revenue Administration of Lower Burma) for 1867-68 (–1887-88). 21 pt. *Maulmain, Rangoon,* 1869–88. 8° & fol. I.S. BU. **142** & **30.**

—— British Burma. Vaccination Report 1867–68(–1871-72). 5 pt. *Rangoon,* [1868]–73. 8°. I.S. BU. **145/2.**

—— The British Burma Gazetteer, *etc.* [With photographs.] 2 vol. *Rangoon,* 1880, 79. 8°. **10057.** df. **26.**

—— Budget Estimates of Expenditure on Burma Defence Services, Army and Royal Navy, for the year 1937-1938 [*etc.*] and of connected receipts. *Rangoon,* 1937– . 8°. I.S. BU. **111/9.**

—— The Burma Carbide of Calcium Rules, 1937. pp. 17. *Rangoon,* 1938. 8°. I.S. BU. **117.**

—— The Burma District Office Manual. pp. 121. vii. *Rangoon,* 1901. 8°. I.S. BU. **119/10.**

—— (Second edition.) pp. viii. 176. *Rangoon,* 1905. 8°. I.S. BU. **119/35.**

—— The Burma District Office Manual. Third edition. pp. 10. 2. iv. 176. xxxvi. *Rangoon,* 1915. 8°. I.S. BU. **119/36.**

—— Burma Gazetteer. *Rangoon,* 1913, 07– . 8° & fol. I.S. BU. **147.**

The B volumes, containing statistics, are in various editions. Some of them are entitled: Census Tables.

—— [Another edition.] *Rangoon,* 1935– . 8°. I.S. BU. **147/3.**

—— The Burma Government Servants' Conduct Rules, 1940. pp. 11. *Rangoon,* 1941. 8°. I.S. BU. **177/3.**

—— Burma Handbook. [With maps.] pp. i. 126. *Simla,* 1944. 8°. I.S. BU. **179.**

—— Burma Inspection Manual. (For the use of Commissioners in inspecting the offices of Deputy Commissioners.) pp. 2. ii. 62. *Rangoon,* 1898. 8°. I.S. BU. **119/15.**

—— The Burma Laws List: a list of unrepealed statutes, acts, and regulations and rules and notifications thereunder in force in Burma. Fourth edition. pp. vii. 503. xxix. 7. *Rangoon,* 1892. 8°. I.S. BU. **108.**

—— Fifth edition. 3 pt. *Rangoon,* 1897. 8°. I.S. BU. **108/3.**

—— The Burma Legislative Manual. pp. 126. xvii. *Rangoon,* 1910. 8°. I.S. BU. **136/2.**

—— The Burma Medical Manual: containing rules for the management of charitable hospitals and dispensaries and for the guidance of medical officers under the Government of Burma. pp. 47. cxxx. *Rangoon,* 1898. 8°. I.S. BU. **141/5.**

—— The Chin Hills Manual, *etc.* pp. 3. 40. *Rangoon,* 1915. 8°. I.S. BU. **119/16.**

—— [Another edition.] pp. 4. 56. *Rangoon,* 1927. 8°. I.S. BU. **119/43.**

—— Circulars of the Local Administration. Issued during th years 1888–1896. pp. xlviii. 459. xii. *Rangoon* 1897. 8°. I.S. BU. **119/4**

—— Collection of Reports on the Kadonbaw Forest Reserve Colonisation Scheme in the Hanthawaddy District during the five years 1914 to 1919. [With maps.] pp. 87. *Rangoon,* 1920. fol. I.S. BU. **23.**

—— Collection of Reports on the Yandoon Island Colonisatio Scheme in the Ma-Ubin District, during the years 1912 t 1922. pp. 86. *Rangoon,* 1923. fol. I.S. BU. **23/3**

—— Collection of Reports on the Yitkangyi Forest Reserve Colonisation Scheme in the Hanthawaddy District, during the three years 1916 to 1918. pp. 99. *Rangoon,* 1920. fol. I.S. BU. **23/2**

—— Compilation on Tenancy Matters. By J. P. Hardiman pp. vi. 139. ii. *Rangoon,* 1913. fol. I.S. BU. **38/3**

—— Completion Report. Kalaw water supply. [By F. A Clift. With plans.] pp. 10. *Rangoon,* 1918. fol. I.S. BU. **53/27**

—— Consolidated Burma Land and Revenue Rules, wit an exhibition in parallel columns of the rules fro which they are derived. (Draft.) pp. 175. [*Rangoon,*] 1912. fol. I.S. BU. **37/**

—— Conspectus of Operations for an Increase of Wolfra Output in the Tavoy District during the year 191 [With maps.] pp. 38. [*Rangoon,*] 1918. fol. I.S. BU. **47/1**

—— Contracts relating to Burma Railways System, *e* pp. xxvi. 98. 22. *Rangoon,* 1916. fol. I.S. BU. **64/**

—— Co-operation in Four Indian Provinces. The Punja the Central Provinces, Bombay and Madras. Report of tour made in December 1921 and January 1922. B Maung Maung Bya . . . Maung Po Sa . . . Maung Se . . . Maung Ba Maung. pp. 49. *Rangoon,* 1922. 8°. I.S. BU. **170/**

—— Correspondence for the years 1825-26 to 1842–48 [rather, 1842-43] in the Office of the Commissione Tenasserim Division, *etc.* [A calendar.] pp. 100. *Rangoon,* 1929. fol. I.S. BU. **26/**

—— Digest of the Government of Burma Act (1935). Con piled by Arthur Eggar. pp. iii. 123. vi. *Rangoo* 1937. 8°. I.S. BU. **124/**

—— Divisional Reports (Report, Resolution on the Report on the working of the Indian Factories Act in Low Burma for the year 1898 (1900, 1909, 1910, 1911). 5 pt *Rangoon,* 1899–1912. fol. I.S. BU. **1**

—— The Economics of the Central Chin Tribes by H. N. Stevenson, *etc.* [With plates.] pp. xv. 200. *Tim of India Press: Bombay,* [1943.] 8°. I.S. BU. **1**

—— Effect of Legislation by the Lieutenant-Governor Burma in Council, *etc.* (Effect of Legislation by t Burma Legislature.) [For the years 1898, etc.] *Rangoon,* 1902– . 8°. I.S. BU. **13**

Imperfect; wanting the parts for the years 1923–32.

—— Elementary Hand-book of the Burmese Language. Taw Sein Ko. pp. ii. vi. 121. *Rangoon,* 1898. 8°. **14302.** h. **3**

—— An Elementary Manual of Silviculture for the use of the Burma Forest School, Pyinmana. Compiled by G. S. Shirley. pp. ii. 111. vii. *Rangoon*, 1929 [1930]. 8°. I.S. BU. **151/30.**

—— Epidemic Diseases Act, 1897 [India Act III of 1897], as subsequently amended and regulations and rules [of the Government of Burma] thereunder and under other enactments concerning epidemic diseases. pp. 11. *Rangoon*, 1937. 8°. I.S. BU. **145/20.**

—— Exploitation of Junglewoods in Burma. Reports on selected forests. By J. Lafon. [With maps.] pp. 78. *Rangoon*, 1921. fol. I.S. BU. **21/84.**

—— Extracts from the Burma Census Report and Tables of 1921 relating to Languages and Races. (By Mr. L. F. Taylor.) pp. 58. [*Rangoon*,] 1923. fol. I.S. BU. **10/3.**

—— The Family Law of the Chinese. By P. G. von Möllendorff. Translated . . . by Mrs. S. M. Broadbent. pp. 43. *Rangoon*, 1920 [1921]. 8°. **5309.** d. **2.**

—— [Another edition.] pp. 43. *Rangoon*, 1925. 8°. **5318.** dd. **16.**

—— The Ficus elastica in Burma Proper, or, a Narrative of my journey in search of it: a descriptive account of its habits of growth and the process followed by the Kakhyens in the preparation of caoutchouc. Accompanied by a map . . . By G. W. Strettell. pp. 3. 222. v. ii. *Rangoon*, 1876. 4°. **10058.** f. **2.**

—— Fishery Settlement Report, 1929. [By A. M. Bown.] pp. 119. *Rangoon*, 1929. fol. I.S. BU. **16/2.**

—— Forest Administration in the Arakan Forest Division from the 1st July 1902 to the 30th June 1915. By A. H. M. Barrington . . . With appendices and map. pp. ii. 227. *Rangoon*, 1917 [1918]. fol. I.S. BU. **18/3.**

—— Fundamental Rules made by the Secretary of State in Council under Section 96-B of the Government of India Act. Corrected up to the 1st November 1926 (up to the 1st March 1928). 2 pt. *Rangoon*, 1927, 28. fol. I.S. BU. **7/3.**

—— Fundamental Rules made by the Secretary of State in Council under Section 96-B of the Government of India Act. Corrected up to the 31st March 1937, *etc.* pp. 31. *Rangoon*, 1939. fol. I.S. BU. **101/22.**

—— Gazetteer of Upper Burma and the Shan States . . . Compiled from official papers by J. George Scott . . . assisted by J. P. Hardiman. [With plates.] 2 pt. *Rangoon*, 1900, 10. 8°. **010055.** i. **13.**
Pt. 1 *is in two vol. and pt.* 2 *in three vol.*

—— The General Orders of the Warden, Burma Oil-Fields. Revised 1937. pp. 23. *Rangoon*, 1937. 8°. I.S. BU. **125.**

—— Geological Report on the Water Supply of Bassein. By P. Leicester. [With a map.] pp. 14. *Rangoon*, 1931. fol. I.S. BU. **100/15.**

—— The Geology and Underground Water of Rangoon. With special reference to tube-wells. By P. Leicester. [With maps.] pp. 78. *Rangoon*, 1932. fol. I.S. BU. **49/5.**

—— Glossary of Vernacular Terms relating to Irrigation, Embankments and Waterways in Burma. pp. 25. *Rangoon*, 1941. 8°. **12906.** s. **26.**

—— Government Dockyard, Rangoon. Report [by Messrs. Price, Waterhouse & Co.] on costing and accounting system in force with recommendations as to improvements therein. pp. 34. *Rangoon*, 1922. fol. I.S. BU. **48/5.**

—— Government of Burma. Rules of Executive Business. Dated Rangoon, the 16th April 1923. pp. 12. [*Rangoon*,] 1924. 8°. I.S. BU. **119/21.**

—— Gradation and Distribution List of the Offices of the Accountant-General, Burma, and Commissioner of Paper Currency, Rangoon, as it stood on the 1st February 1901 (1st May 1904). 2 pt. *Rangoon*, 1901, 04. 8°. I.S. BU. **133.**

—— The Grasses of Burma. By D. Rhind. pp. 99. *Simla*, 1945. 8°. **7035.** e. **18.**

—— A Guide to the Borers of Commercial Timber in Burma. By P. F. Garthwaite. pp. vi. 33. pl. IX. *Rangoon*, 1940. 8°. I.S. BU. **151/32.**

—— Handbook for Burmese Midwives. By Miss I. Sexton *etc.* pp. 36. *Rangoon*, 1909. 8°. I.S. BU. **141/11.**

—— [Another edition.] pp. ii. 59. *Rangoon*, 1918. 8°. I.S. BU. **141/21.**

—— A Hand-Book of Agriculture for Burma. pp. iv. 87. *Rangoon*, 1910. 8°. I.S. BU. **114/21.**

—— A Handbook of Co-operative Credit for Burma. By A. E. English. pp. 206. *Rangoon*, 1911. 8°. I.S. BU. **170/3.**

—— [Another edition.] A Hand-book of Co-operation for Burma . . . 1914. pp. 2. 158. *Rangoon*, 1915. 8°. I.S. BU. **170/7.**

—— [Another edition.] pp. 174. xii. *Rangoon*, 1920. 8°. I.S. BU. **170/8.**

—— Hints on the Preservation of Health for the Guidance of Officers in Burma. (By H. S. Middleton-West.) pp. ii. 15. *Rangoon*, 1926. 8°. I.S. BU. **145/18.**

—— History of Services of Gazetted and other Officers in Burma. *Rangoon*, 1896– . 8°. I.S. BU. **131/2.**
Imperfect; wanting vol. 2 *of* 1896–99; *vol.* 1 *of* 1903; *vol.* 2 *of* 1908; 1924, 27, 32; *vol.* 2 *of* 1934–35.

—— Imperial Commerce. Six lectures on commercial subjects delivered in Rangoon during the months of May to October 1922 under the auspices of the Standing Committee on the Imperial Idea. By Edmund Horswell. pp. ii. 80. iii. *Rangoon*, 1924. 8°. I.S. BU. **146/5.**

—— Imperialism in Modern History. Six lectures. By D. G. E. Hall. pp. 83. *Rangoon*, 1923. 8°. I.S. BU. **105/83.**

—— The Indian Civil Service Family Pension Fund Rules. (Statutory Rules and Orders [of Great Britain] 1937 no. 1217.) pp. 29. *Rangoon*, 1938. 8°. I.S. BU. **124/13.**

—— Indo-Burma Connection Railway, Coast Route . . . Report and estimates, 1915. [By George Richards. With maps.] 4 pt. *Rangoon*, 1915, 16. fol. I.S. BU. **64.**

—— Information supplied for the Simla Anti-Malarial Conference of 1909. By Colonel W. G. King. pp. 28. *Rangoon*, 1909. fol. I.S. BU. **13/6.**

—— Insect Pests of Burma. By C. C. Ghosh. pp. ii. 216. xv. pl. LXXXVII. *Rangoon*, 1940. 8°. I.S. BU. **114/28.**

—— Investigation of Irrigation Works in the Magwe District. [By B. M. Samuelson. With maps.] pp. 8. 39. *Rangoon*, 1910. fol. I.S. BU. **53/23.**

—— Investigation of Malaria at Kyaukpyu. [By N. P. O'G. Lalor. With charts and maps.] pp. 32. *Rangoon*, 1912. fol. I.S. BU. **13/7.**

—— Investigation of Malaria in the District of Katha. [By N. P. O'G. Lalor. With charts and maps.] pp. iii. 18. *Rangoon*, 1913. fol. I.S. BU. **13/9.**

—— The Kachin Hills Manual, 1898. pp. 24. *Rangoon*, 1898. 8°. I.S. BU. **119/8.**

—— Land Records Administration Report (Report on the Lands Records Administration of Burma) for the year ending 30th June 1902 [*etc.*]. *Rangoon*, 1902– . fol. & 8°. I.S. BU. **8/6** & **129/2.**

—— List of Ancient Monuments in Burma. 8 pt. *Rangoon*, 1916. 8°. **07702.** d. **22.**

—— Amended List of Ancient Monuments in Burma. 8 pt. *Rangoon*, 1921. 8°. **07702.** d. **49.**

—— List of Industrial Establishments in Burma, 1929 [*etc.*]. *Rangoon*, 1931– . 8°. I.S. BU. **117/19.**

—— List of Objects of Antiquarian and Archæological Interest in British Burma. pp. 39. *Rangoon*, 1884. 8°. **7708.** cc. **40.**

—— List of Objects of Antiquarian and Archæological Interest in Upper Burma. pp. 22. *Rangoon*, 1901. fol. I.S. BU. **6/5.**

—— List of Objects of Antiquarian Interest in Lower Burma. I. Arakan. pp. 9. *Rangoon*, 1891. fol. I.S. BU. **6/7.**

—— List of Protected Monuments in the Burma Circle. Corrected up to the 30th September, 1925. pp. 6. [*Rangoon*,] 1926. fol. I.S. BU. **6/6.**

—— Lists of Firms registered under the Burma Registration of Business Names Act, 1920. pp. xxvii. 348. [*Rangoon*,] 1927. 8°. I.S. BU. **103/16.**

—— Local Government Circulars issued from the General Secretariat, 1888–1908. 2 vol. *Rangoon*, 1909. 8°. I.S. BU. **119/28.**

—— Local Government Circulars issued from the General Secretariat, 1888 to the 31st March 1915. 2 vol. *Rangoon*, 1916. 8°. I.S. BU. **119/29.**

—— Logarithmic and other Tables for Schools. pp. 35. *Rangoon*, 1938. 8°. I.S. BU. **116/25.**

—— Lower Burma Railways. Reconnaissance surveys. 2′ 6″ gauge. Moulmein-Victoria Point Railway. Report and estimates. [By Malcolm T. Porter. With maps.] pp. 44. *Rangoon*, 1913. fol. I.S. BU. **64/3.**

—— Mandalay Municipality. Hand-book containing the rules, notifications, directions, and orders made under the Burma Municipal Act, no. III of 1898, and the Vaccination Act, XIII of 1880, with an index and a map of Mandalay . . . Corrected up to 1st June 1901. ff. 68. pp. iv. *Rangoon*, 1901. 8°. **5311.** l. 3.

—— The Mineral Deposits of Burma. By E. L. G. Clegg [With a map.] pp. 45. [*Rangoon*,] 1939. fol. I.S. BU. **101/2**

—— The Mineral Deposits of Burma. By G. de P. Cotter. [With a map.] pp. 53. *Rangoon*, 1924. 8°. I.S. BU. **117/13.**

—— Miscellaneous Rulings, etc., affecting the Shan States and Karenni. pp. 8. *Rangoon*, 1909. 8°. I.S. BU. **119/20.**

—— Monograph on Ivory Carving in Burma. By H. S. Pratt pp. 6. *Rangoon*, 1901. 8°. I.S. BU. **120/6**

—— A Monograph on Tanning and Working in Leather in the Province of Burma. By E. J. Colston. [With plates.] pp. ii. 69. *Rangoon*, 1903 [1904]. 8°. I.S. BU. **120/8**

—— The Motor Spirit Duties Act, 1917, II of 1917, an extract from the Indian Finance Act, 1922, XII of 1922, and the Orders and Notifications issued thereunder. pp. 19. *Rangoon*, 1933. 8°. I.S. BU. **105/87**
A later edition is entered above under [*Laws and Regulations.*]

—— Narrative Completion Report on the Lashio Water-Works. By Mr. G. T. I. Oliver. [With maps.] pp. 6. *Rangoon*, 1908. fol. I.S. BU. **53/25.**

—— Narrative Completion Report on the Rangoon Cantonment Water Supply. [By Frederick W. Vyall. With maps.] pp. 5. [*Rangoon*, 1908.] fol. I.S. BU. **49/3**

—— Nomenclature of Diseases in Burmese. By Lieut.-Col. R. H. Castor. pp. x. 54. *Rangoon*, 1922. 8°. I.S. BU. **149/11.**

—— Note by Mr. B. M. Samuelson . . . on Mr. Gordon's Gauging of the Discharge of the Irrawaddy River in 1872-73 and 1875 [detailed in his "Report on the Irrawaddy River"], and also on the effect of double embanking the river from Saiktha to Yandoon. [With maps.] pp. 40. pl. 7 *Rangoon*, 1914. fol. I.S. BU. **53/13**

—— Note on Bye-Productions from the Manufacture of Salt in the Amherst District. By Mr. E. G. Robertson. pp. 6. *Rangoon*, 1920. fol. I.S. BU. **46/6.**

—— Note on Mr. Gordon's Discharge Scales for the Irrawaddy River at Saiktha in 1872–73 and 1875 [in his "Report on the Irrawaddy River"]. By B. M. Samuelson. pp. 7. *Rangoon*, 1879. fol. I.S. BU. **53/1[illegible]**

—— A Note on Rubber Cultivation in the Amherst District. By Mr. W. S. Todd. pp. 16. *Rangoon*, 1906. fol. I.S. BU. **47/8.**

—— [Another edition.] pp. 16. *Rangoon*, 1910. fol. I.S. BU. **47/11.**

—— Note on Teaching of Decimal Fractions. By P. B. Quinlan. pp. 15. *Rangoon*, 1932. 8°. I.S. BU. **116/8**

—— Note on the Co-operative Movement in Burma. By Mr. M. L. Darling, *etc.* pp. ii. 22. *Rangoon*, 1937. fol. I.S. BU. **11/2.**

—— A Note on the Fisheries of the Inle Lake, Southern Shan States. By Dr. N. Annandale. pp. 10. *Rangoon*, 1917. fol. I.S. BU. **16/4**

—— Note on the Irrawaddy River, with reference to the feasibility of double embanking in the upper delta from Tullokmaw to Yandoon. By B. M. Samuelson. pp. 7. 138. *Rangoon*, 1915. fol. I.S. BU. **53/16.**

—— A Note on the Palaungs of the Kodaung Hill Tracts of the Mong Mit State. By A. A. Cameron. [With a map.] pp. 61. *Rangoon*, 1912. 8°. **10007.** t. **26.**

—— Note on the Present Condition of Survey Schools in Burma, and the Measures required for their Improvement. By R. E. V. Arbuthnot. pp. 34. *Rangoon*, 1919. fol. I.S. BU. **34/3.**

—— Note on the Salt Boiling Industry in Burma. By R. M. Thurley. pp. 28. *Rangoon*, 1908. fol. I.S. BU. **46/5.**

—— Note on the Salt Industry and Salt Revenue. pp. 8. [*Rangoon*,] 1924. 8°. I.S. BU. **120/9.**

—— Notes and Statistics in four parts . . . corrected up to 1st May 1890, *etc.* pp. iii. 189. *Rangoon*, 1890. 8°. I.S. BU. **119/3.**

—— Third edition . . . corrected up to 1st April 1893. [With a map.] pp. 3. 274. *Rangoon*, 1893. 8°. I.S. BU. **119/26.**

—— Notes for the use of Teachers of General Science. By D. H. Peacock . . . and F. J. Meggitt. pp. ii. 131. iv. *Rangoon*, 1937. 8°. I.S. BU. **116/24.**

—— Notes on British and French Light Houses. By O. F. Wheeler Cuffe. [With plates.] pp. ii. ii. 120. vi. *Rangoon*, 1910. fol. I.S. BU. **39/2.**

—— Notes on Sanitary Organization and Development in Burma. pp. 32. *Rangoon*, 1915. 8°. I.S. BU. **145/16.**

—— Notes on the Aneroid Barometer, for the use of travellers and others in determining the relative heights of places in Southern India . . . By Major B. R. Branfill. pp. 13. *Rangoon*, 1902. fol. I.S. BU. **34/5.**

—— [Notes on the Early History and Geography of British Burma. By Em. Forchhammer.] 2 pt. [*Rangoon*, 1884.] 8°. **5319.** c. **14.** (**1.**)
Imperfect ; wanting the titlepage of pt. 1.

—— Notes on the Early History and Geography of British Burma. By Em. Forchhammer . . . I. The Shwe Dagon Pagoda. pp. 18. *Rangoon*, 1891. 8°. I.S. BU. **147/2.**

—— Notes on the Effect of Plague Driving, etc., in the Pegu Division on human mortality during the plague seasons 1909-10 and 1910-11. By Captain W. F. Brayne. [With charts.] pp. ii. 52. *Rangoon*, 1911, fol. I.S. BU. **13/4.**

—— Notes on the Languages and Dialects spoken in British Burma. [Letters from E. Forchhammer and others.] pp. 20. *Rangoon*, 1884. 8°. **5319.** c. **14.** (**2.**)

—— Notes on the Mineral Resources of Upper Burma. By Dr. Fritz Noetling. [With plates.] 2 pt. *Rangoon*, 1893. fol. I.S. BU. **47/7.**

—— Notes on the Twante Canal, 1932, and other papers. pp. iii. 71. *Rangoon*, 1933. fol. I.S. BU. **53/19.**

—— Nyaunggyat Dam Project, 1927. [With maps.] pp. ix. 139. 4. iv. *Maymyo*, 1928. fol. I.S. BU. **53/21.**

—— On the Preservation of Health. For the guidance of young officers on their arrival in India. By J. T. Calvert. pp. 2. 23. *Rangoon*, 1921. 8°. I.S. BU. **145/19.**

—— The Origin and Causes of the Burma Rebellion, 1930–32, *etc.* pp. 44. *Rangoon*, 1934. fol. I.S. BU. **100/38.**

—— Paper on the "Alguada Reef Lighthouse." By Mr. O. F. W. Cuffe. [With plates.] pp. 23. *Rangoon*, 1913. fol. I.S. BU. **39/3.**

—— A Paper read by U Tin Gyi . . . at the Annual General Meeting of the Burma Economic Society on the 23rd July 1936. (Reconstruction of Co-operative Societies in Burma.) pp. 13. *Rangoon*, 1937. 8°. I.S. BU. **170/9.**

—— The Pocket Criminal Index. An aid to the tracing of criminals wanted by the police. By C. W. B. Anderson. pp. 18. *Rangoon*, 1909. 8°. I.S. BU. **115/8.**

—— A Pocket Guide to Burma. pp. 56. [1945.] 16°. **010058.** s. **5.**

—— Portable Tramways and Timber Skidding Machines in the Pegu Circle, Burma, 1914–1916. By F. A. Leete. pp. 17. *Rangoon*, 1916. fol. I.S. BU. **21/87.**

—— Preliminary Report on the Administration of Upper Burma in 1887–88. pp. iii. 46. *Rangoon*, 1888. fol. I.S. BU. **1/3.**

—— Proceedings of the First Burma Forest Conference held at Maymyo between the 13th and 20th June 1910. With appendices. pp. 100. *Rangoon*, 1910. fol. I.S. BU. **18/5.**

—— The Quarterly Civil List for Burma. no. 96, *etc.* *Rangoon*, 1894– . 8°. I.S. BU. **131/3.**
Imperfect ; wanting no. 98–101, 105, 114, 130, 134, 136–139, 154–204, 206–236.

—— Railway Audit Code, *etc.* pp. 29. *Rangoon*, 1937. 8°. I.S. BU. **185/3.**

—— The Rangoon Hackney Carriage Rules, 1918, as amended up to the 1st August 1939. pp. 13. [*Rangoon*,] 1939. 8°. I.S. BU. **124/14.**

—— Rangoon Water Supply and Hydro-Electric Scheme. Geological report on the Lewa-Pyagawpu Area. By P. Leicester. [With a map.] pp. 24. pl. 13. *Rangoon*, 1928. 8°. I.S. BU. **169/5.**

—— Register of Higher Grade Pleaders of the Subordinate Courts of Burma. Corrected up to June, 1937 [*etc.*]. *Rangoon*, 1937– . fol. I.S. BU. **91/2.**

—— Register of Lower Grade Pleaders of the Subordinate Courts of Burma. Corrected up to June 1937 [*etc.*]. *Rangoon*, 1937– . fol. I.S. BU. **91.**

—— Registrar, Co-operative Societies' Office Code. pp. vi. 79. *Rangoon*, 1924. 8°. I.S. BU. **170/2.**

—— Report by V. D. Kothare . . . on the Tidal and Hydraulic Investigations on the Twante Canal, 1927–28. pp. 3. 31. pl. 12. 9. *Rangoon*, 1929. fol. I.S. BU. **53/19.**

—— Report of a Tour to visit various University and College Buildings in India. By Mr. Seton-Morris . . . and Mr. Hunter. [With plans.] pp. 12. *Rangoon*, 1915. fol. I.S. BU. **100/37.**

—— Report of an Enquiry into the Standard and Cost of Living of the Working Classes in Rangoon. By J. J. Bennison. [With plates.] pp. v. 221. *Rangoon*, 1928. 8°. I.S. BU. **103/15.**

—— Report of Inquiry into the Condition of Agricultural Tenants and Labourers. By T. Couper. pp. iii. 4. 69. *Rangoon*, 1924. 8°. I.S. BU. **114/22.**

—— Report of the Delegation of the British Social Hygiene Council, Inc., to the Government of Burma (on the question of venereal disease). pp. 76. *Rangoon*, 1927. 8°. I.S. BU. **149/10.**

—— Report of the Investigation on the Pollution of the Rangoon River Water, 1933–34. By G. C. Moitra. [With a map.] pp. 21. *Rangoon*, 1938. 8°. I.S. BU. **177/2.**

—— Report of the Revision Settlement of the Bassein District. Together with the original settlement of certain areas in the Yegyi, Thabaung, Bassein West and Ngaputaw townships. Season 1935–39. By U Maung Maung Gyi. [With maps.] pp. 14. 23. vii. 300. *Rangoon*, 1941. fol. I.S. BU. **36/62.**

—— Report of the Settlement Operations in the Mandalay District, season 1892–93. [By Maxwell Laurie.] Accompanied with maps. 21 pt. *Rangoon*, 1894. fol. I.S. BU. **35/8.**

—— Report on a Preliminary Survey of the Salt Industry in the Shwebo and Sagaing Districts. By Mr. E. G. Robertson. pp. 27. *Rangoon*, 1923. fol. I.S. BU. **46/7.**

—— Report on a Visit to some Salt Workings in the Shwebo and Sagaing Districts, Upper Burma. By F. W. Walker. [With a map.] pp. 4. *Rangoon*, 1923. fol. I.S. BU. **46/8.**

—— Report on Development of Industries in Burma. By Mr. A. P. Morris. pp. 21. [*Rangoon*,] 1920. fol. I.S. BU. **47/15.**

—— Report on Forest Administration in the Federated Shan States for the year ending 31st March 1923. pp. 21. *Rangoon*, 1923. fol. I.S. BU. **18/2.**

—— Report on Local Allowances and Special Rates of Travelling Allowances in Burma. By L. J. MacCallum. pp. ii. 42. xxvi. *Rangoon*, 1920. fol. I.S. BU. **7/2.**

—— Report (Annual Report) on Lock Hospitals in British Burma (Lower Burma), for the year 1873(1875–1886). 13 pt. [*Rangoon*, 1875–87.] fol. I.S. BU. **27/2.**

—— Report on Matters in connection with Suburban Development. By C. F. Grant. [With maps.] pp. 2. 35. *Rangoon*, 1915. fol. I.S. BU. **48/4.**

—— [Another edition.] pp. ii. 35. *Rangoon*, 1921. fol. I.S. BU. **48/6.**

—— Report on Municipal Administration in Burma (Review of Municipal Administration in Burma except Rangoon) during the year 1891-92(–1927-28). 36 pt. *Rangoon*, 1892–1929. fol. & 8°. I.S. BU. **41/4 & 150/5.**

—— Report on Municipal Administration in Upper Burma during the year 1888-89(–1890-91). 3 pt. *Rangoon*, 1889–91. fol. I.S. BU. **41/2.**

—— Report on Prome Plague Drive. By Captain W. F. Brayne. [With charts and a map.] pp. 34. *Rangoon*, 1910. fol. I.S. BU. **13/3.**

—— Report on Public Instruction in Upper Burma for the year 1889-90. pp. ii. 2. 15. xiv. *Rangoon*, 1890. fol. I.S. BU. **51.**

—— Report on Revision Settlement Operations in the Bassein District, season 1897-98(1898-99), *etc.* [By James Mackenna. With maps.] 2 pt. *Rangoon*, 1899, 1900. fol. I.S. BU. **35/12.**

—— Report on Revision Settlement Operations in the Henzada Distrcit [*sic*], season 1899-1900 (1900–1901). Accompanied by maps. [By James Mackenna.] 2 pt. *Rangoon*, 1901, 02. fol. I.S. BU. **35/56.**

—— Report on Revision Settlement Operations in the Myaungmya District. Season 1897-98. Accompanied by maps. [By William Edward Lowry.] pp. ii. 41. lxxiii. 2. 5. 2. 5. 3. *Rangoon*, 1899. fol. I.S. BU. **35/14.**

—— Report on the Administration of Burma during 1887-88 [*etc.*]. *Rangoon*, 1888– . fol. & 8°. I.S. BU. **1/2 & 119/44.**

—— Report on the Administration of the Chin Hills for the year 1894-95 (for the year ended 30th June 1914–1923). *Rangoon*, 1895–1923. fol. & 8°. I.S. BU. **1/6.**

—— Report on the Administration of the Shan States (of the Shan and Karenni States) for the year 1894-95 (for the year ended the 30th June 1912–1923). *Rangoon*, 1895–1924. fol. & 8°. I.S. BU. **1/9.**

—— Report on the Burma Government Stand at the British Industries Fair, 1939. London—20th February to 3rd March. By U Myat Tun. pp. 9. *Rangoon*, 1939. fol. I.S. BU. **101.**

—— Report on the Burma Soap-Sand Industry. [By Arthur P. Morris.] pp. 14. *Rangoon*, 1918. fol. I.S. BU. **47/12.**

—— Report on the Census of British Burma. Taken in August 1872. *Rangoon*, 1875. fol. I.S. BU. **10/1.**

—— Report on the Census of British Burma. Taken on the 17th February 1881. [With a map.] pp. v. 96. 2. ccxii. 86. *Rangoon*, 1881. fol. I.S. BU. **10/2.**

—— Report on the Completion of the Moulmein Water Works Scheme. [By P. N. Sen.] pp. 5. ff. 6–14. pl. 6. *Rangoon*, 1910. fol. I.S. BU. **53/28.**

—— Report on the Cultivation of Cotton in British Burma for the year 1880-81(1881-82). 2 pt. *Rangoon*, 1881, 82. fol. I.S. BU. **46.**

—— Report on the Enquiry regarding Rents of Government Land in Rangoon. By Maung Shwe Zan Aung. pp. 65. [*Rangoon*,] 1910. fol. I.S. BU. **33/4.**

—— Report on the Ferries on the Mali Hka between Nonghkai Village in the Putao District, and the Mali Hka-N'Mai Hka confluence in the Myitkyina District. [By William A. Hertz. With a map.] pp. 7. [*Rangoon*,] 1916. fol. I.S. BU. **53/20.**

—— Report on the Fisheries in the Henzada District for the year 1886. Accompanied by maps. pp. 37. *Rangoon*, 1886. fol. I.S. BU. **16.**

—— Report on the Garden Classification, Tavoy District, during the years 1897-98 and 1898-99. [By Alfred B. Pritchard. With maps.] pp. 5. 4. 2. 3. *Rangoon*, 1899. fol. I.S. BU. **36/3.**

—— Report on the Goitre and General Medical Survey, Chin Hills, January to April 1940. By Major R. L. Raymond, I.M.S., Dr. U Ohn Pe and Dr. Howya Chinpaw. [With maps and plates.] pp. ii. 101. xv. *Rangoon*, 1940. 8°. I.S. BU. **149/20.**

—— Report on the Hydrometric Survey of the Myitmaka River and its Tributaries. By U Tun Tin . . . Also Review of the report by . . . C. C. Mackintosh. [With graphs.] pp. iv. 56. *Rangoon*, 1937. fol.
I.S. BU. **101/5.**

—— Report on the Irrawaddy River . . . By R. Gordon. 4 pt. *Rangoon*, 1879. fol. I.S. BU. **53/6.**

—— Report on the Leprosy Survey of Henzada District, conducted by U Tha Din. [With a map.] pp. 6. *Rangoon*, 1941. 8°. I.S. BU. **149/23.**

—— Report on the Leprosy Survey of Sagaing District, conducted by U Tha Din. [With a map.] pp. 5. *Rangoon*, 1941. 8°. I.S. BU. **149/21.**

—— Report on the Leprosy Survey of Thaton District, conducted by U Tha Din. [With a map.] pp. 5. *Rangoon*, 1941. 8°. I.S. BU. **149/24.**

—— Report on the Leprosy Survey of Yamethin District, conducted by U Tha Din. [With a map.] pp. 12. *Rangoon*, 1941. 8°. I.S. BU. **149/22.**

—— Report on the Light Houses for 1870(-1900-1901). 28 pt. *Rangoon*, 1871-1901. 8° & fol. I.S. BU. **127 & 39.**
Imperfect; wanting the four reports previous to 1870 *and the* 6*th and* 15*th reports.*

—— Report on the Manufacture of Paper and Paper Pulp in Burma . . . By R. W. Sindall. [With a map.] pp. 32. *Rangoon*, 1906. fol. I.S. BU. **47/9.**

—— Report on the Mosquito Survey of Rangoon. By G. G. Jolly. [With maps and graphs.] pp. 54. *Rangoon*, 1933. fol. I.S. BU. **98/3.**

—— Report on the Oil-Fields of Twingoung and Beme, *etc.* [By Fritz Noetling. With a map.] pp. 30. xxv. *Rangoon*, 1889. fol. I.S. BU. **47.**

—— Report on the Organization and Methods employed for Plague Prevention in the Meiktila Division, 1909. By Captain E. A. Walker. pp. 7. *Rangoon*, 1910. fol.
I.S. BU. **13/2.**

—— Report on the Original Settlement of the Mamauk Tract in the Kawa Township of the Pegu District, season 1924-25. [By Robert C. Barber.] pp. ii. 3. 23. *Rangoon*, 1926. fol. I.S. BU. **36/52.**

—— Report on the Petroleum Industry in Upper Burma from the end of the last century up to the beginning of 1891 . . . By Dr. Fritz Noetling. [With plates.] pp. ii. 72. *Rangoon*, 1892. fol. I.S. BU. **47/6.**

—— Report on the Plague Preventive Scheme in the Irrawaddy Division for the year 1911-12. By Capt. S. C. Chuckerbutty. pp. ii. 31. *Rangoon*, 1912. fol.
I.S. BU. **13.**

—— Report on the Position of Lac Industry in Burma. By M. Rangaswami. pp. 18. *Rangoon*, 1941. fol.
I.S. BU. **101/3.**

—— Report on the Prevention of Crime and the Treatment of the Criminal in the Province of Burma. By Alexander Paterson. pp. 6. 94. *Rangoon*, 1926. 8°.
I.S. BU. **115/4.**

—— [Another edition.] pp. vi. 94. *Rangoon*, 1927. 8°.
I.S. BU. **115/5.**

—— Report on the Progress of Arakan under British Rule. From 1826 to 1875. pp. 53. 21. xvi. *Rangoon*, 1876. 8°.
I.S. BU. **119/2.**

—— Report on the Progress of Cotton Work in Burma, for the year 1938-39. pp. 11. *Rangoon*, 1939. 8°.
I.S. BU. **118/23.**

—— Report on the Progress of Education in Irrawaddy Circle during the quinquennium 1912-13 to 1916-17. pp. 6. *Rangoon*, 1917. fol. I.S. BU. **51/3.**

—— Report on the Prospecting Operations, Mergui District, 1891-92. pp. 5. 4. 6. *Rangoon*, 1892. fol.
I.S. BU. **47/4.**

—— Report on the Rat Flea Survey of Rangoon Port Area, conducted by the Director with the Staff of the Bacteriological Section, Harcourt Butler Institute of Public Health, Rangoon, during 1938. [With a map.] pp. 21. *Rangoon*, 1939. 8°. I.S. BU. **149/26.**

—— Report on the Rent Settlement Operations in the Yandoon Island Colonisation Areas of the Ma-ubin District, season 1925-26. By R. C. Barber. [With a map.] pp. 3. 17. *Rangoon*, 1927. fol. I.S. BU. **36/47.**

—— Report on the Revision Settlement of the Amherst District, season 1930-33. By B. O. Binns. [With maps.] pp. 16. viii. 324. 9. 2. 9. 2. pl. III. *Rangoon*, 1934. fol. I.S. BU. **36/61.**

—— Report on the Revision Settlement Operations in the Akyab District, season 1901-1902(1902-1903). [By William E. Lowry. With maps.] 2 pt. *Rangoon*, 1903. fol. I.S. BU. **35/55.**
The date in the colophon of the report for 1902-1903 *is* 1904.

—— Report on the Revision Settlement Operations in the Prome District, season 1900-1901. [By William E. Lowry. With maps.] pp. 3. 7. ii. 142. 17. 2. *Rangoon*, 1902. fol. I.S. BU. **35/59.**

—— Report on the Sanitary Condition of Schools and School Hostels in Burma. pp. 2. 18. *Rangoon*, 1916. fol.
I.S. BU. **55/4.**

—— Report on the Second Settlement of the Toungoo District, November 1910—October 1913. [By S. A. Smyth. With maps.] pp. 7. 7. 15. vii. 207. 6. 9. *Rangoon*, 1914 [1915]. fol. I.S. BU. **36/27.**

—— Report on the Settlement of the Karen Hills Subdivision for the year 1884-85. [By Thomas M. Jenkins. With a map.] pp. 3. 2. 2. 8. viii. *Rangoon*, 1885. fol.
I.S. BU. **35/70.**

—— Report on the Settlement Operations in the Akyab District. Season 1885-86 (1886-87, 1887-88). Accompanied by maps. [By H. Adamson.] 3 pt. *Rangoon*, 1887, 88. fol. I.S. BU. **34.**

—— Report on the Settlement Operations in the Bassein and Thôngwa Districts. Season 1888-89. [By Henry M. S. Mathews.] Accompanied by maps. pp. ii. 3. 4. 6. 2. 31. xlvi. *Rangoon*, 1890. fol. I.S. BU. **35/3.**

—— Report on the Settlement Operations in the Myaungmya and Thongwa Districts, season 1902-1903. [By James Mackenna. With maps.] pp. 3. 3. 3. 118. 8. 3. *Rangoon*, 1903. fol. I.S. BU. **35/62.**

—— Report on the Suspension of Grants in the Hanthawaddy District. [By C. M. Webb.] pp. 2. 23. *Rangoon,* 1910. fol. I.S. BU. **36/45.**

—— Report on the System of Municipal Administration of the City of Bombay with suggestions for its adoption in Rangoon. By Gavin Scott. pp. ii. ii. 73. *Rangoon,* 1916. fol. I.S. BU. **49.**

—— Report on the Thabeitkyin Stone Tract. By U Khin Maung Gyi. pp. 7. *Rangoon,* 1938. 8º. I.S. BU. **125/10.**

—— Report on the Third Settlement of the Tharrawaddy District. Season 1913–15. By J. L. McCallum. [With maps.] pp. 2. 2. 14. vii. 148. 4. 4. 2. *Rangoon,* 1916 [1918]. fol. I.S. BU. **36/29.**

—— Report on the Trade of the Chiengmai District for the year 1894. [By W. J. Archer.] pp. 9. *Rangoon,* 1895. fol. I.S. BU. **63.**

—— Report on the Training Colleges of Scotland, and a comparison with the work of training in Burma. pp. 27. 47. *Rangoon,* 1905. fol. I.S. BU. **51/7.**

—— Report on the Working of the Municipalities of British Burma (Lower Burma), for 1876-77–1890-91. 15 pt. [*Rangoon,* 1878]–91. fol. I.S. BU. **41.**
The title is taken from the Report for 1878-79.

—— Report on the Working of the Revised Arrangements for the Vend of Opium in Lower Burma, during the year ended 31st March 1904 (during the year 1906-07, 1907-08). 3 pt. *Rangoon,* 1904–09. fol. I.S. BU. **46/2.**
Imperfect ; wanting the reports for 1904-05, 1905-06.

—— Report on Tin-Mining in Perak and in Burma. By Mr. W. T. Hall . . . and Preliminary Sketch of the Mining Industry of Perak and Burma. By Mr. T. W. H. Hughes. pp. 26. xxi. 3. *Rangoon,* 1889. fol. I.S. BU. **47/3.**

—— Report on Tin-Mining in the Protected Malay States of Perak and Selangor. By Mr. R. Parry. pp. 5. 33. xxxviii. *Rangoon,* 1898. fol. I.S. BU. **47/5.**

—— Report on Visit to Hydro-Electric Installations in Switzerland, July-August 1920. By J. M. B. Stuart. pp. 8. pl. 21. *Rangoon,* 1921. fol. I.S. BU. **17.**

—— Report to the Government of Burma on the Pearl Oyster Fisheries of the Mergui Archipelago and Moskos Islands. By R. N. Rudmose Brown . . . and Jas. J. Simpson. [With a map.] pp. 27. *Rangoon,* 1907. fol. I.S. BU. **16/3.**

—— Reports (Annual Report) on Public Instruction in Burma for the year 1890-91 [*etc.*]. *Rangoon,* 1891– . fol. & 8º. I.S. BU. **51/2** & **116/2.**
Beginning with the year 1896-97, *the Annual Report is replaced every five years by a Quinquennial Report.*

—— Reports on the Cocos Islands. By Captain Butterfield . . . Mr. G. F. S. Christie . . . and Mr. E. V. Ellis. [With a map.] pp. 20. *Rangoon,* 1913. fol. I.S. BU. **100/35.**

—— Reports (Report) on the North-Eastern Frontier, for the year 1894-95 (for the year ended 30th June 1914–1923). *Rangoon,* 1895–1923. fol. & 8º. I.S. BU. **1/7.**

—— Reprint from Dalrymple's Oriental Repertory, 1791–7, of portions relating to Burma. [Edited by Godfrey E. Harvey. With maps.] pp. ix. 260. *Rangoon,* 1926. 8º. **010055. d. 43.**

—— Review of Forest Administration in Burma (including the Federated Shan States), during the five years 1909-10 to 1913-14(–1929-1934). *Rangoon,* 1916–35. fol. & 8º. I.S. BU. **18/6.** & **151/14**
Wanting the Review for 1914/15 *to* 1918/19.

—— Rules and Regulations concerning the Training and Appoinment of Public Health Inspectors in Burma. pp. 24. *Rangoon,* 1931. 8º. I.S. BU. **145/13**

—— Rules and Regulations for the Election of Representatives of Burma on the Council of State and the Legislative Assembly. pp. 68. *Rangoon,* 1920. 8º. I.S. BU. **136/4**

—— Rules for the Election and Nomination of Members to the Burma Legislative Council, for the qualification of electors and members, the constitution of constituencies and the final decision of doubts and disputes as to the validity of elections. pp. ii. 36. [*Rangoon,*] 1925. fol. I.S. BU. **32/2**

—— Rules for the Election and Nomination of Members to the Burma Legislative Council, for the qualification of electors and members, the constitution of constituencies and the final decision of doubts and disputes as to the validity of elections, and the Burma Electoral Regulations. Corrected up to the 5th September 1928 (30th June 1935). 2 pt. *Rangoon,* 1928, 35. fol. I.S. BU. **32/3**

—— Rules for the Medical Inspection of Vessels and instructions for the guidance of masters of vessels detained under those Rules, *etc.* pp. 24. *Rangoon,* 1926. 8º. I.S. BU. **145/15**

—— Rules for the Medical Inspection of Vessels, framed under Section 6, subsection (1), clause (p) of the Ports Act and Orders and Instructions issued thereunder, *etc.* pp. 27. [*Rangoon,* 1939.] 8º. I.S. BU. **149/27**

—— Rules for the Proper Enforcement of the Vaccination Act, 1880, XIII of 1880, within the notified area of Kyaikla[illegible] Town. pp. 6. *Rangoon,* 1905. 8º. I.S. BU. **145/11.**

—— Rules for the Proper Enforcement of the Vaccination Act, 1880, XIII of 1880, within the notified area of Nyaungu. pp. 4. *Rangoon,* 1905. 8º. I.S. BU. **145/21**

—— Schedule of Differential Customs-Duties, leviable under the provisions of paragraph 6, part III, of the India and Burma, Trade Regulation, Order, 1937. For the year ending 31st December 1939. pp. 17. *Rangoon,* 1939. fol. I.S. BU. **14/10**

—— Season and Crop Report of Burma for the year ending 30th June 1902 [*etc.*]. *Rangoon,* 1902– . fol. & 8º. I.S. BU. **8/5** & **114/4.**
Imperfect ; wanting the report for the year ending June 1920.

—— Services of Gazetted Officers in Burma. (History of Services of Officers holding substantive gazetted appointments in Burma.) no. 13, 15–17. *Rangoon,* 1891–95. 8º. I.S. BU. **131.**

—— Shan States Manual, *etc.* pp. vii. 4. 84. *Rangoon,* 1901. 8º. I.S. BU. **119/7.**

—— [Another edition.] pp. xvi. 209. viii. *Rangoon,* 1910. 8º. I.S. BU. **119/31.**

—— [Another edition.] pp. iv. ix. 241. *Rangoon,* 1925. 8º. I.S. BU. **119/32**

—— [Another edition.] Corrected up to the 31st January 1932. pp. v. viii. 374. *Rangoon,* 1933. 8º. I.S. BU. **119/25.**

—— Silk in Burma. By J. P. Hardiman. [With plates.] pp. 57. *Rangoon*, 1901. 8°. I.S. BU. **120/7.**

—— Souvenir of the Memorial Ceremony for the Men who died in Captivity at Work on the Burma-Siam Railway, 1942–45, held at Thanbyuzayat, Burma, on December 18th, 1946. pp. 16. [*Rangoon*,] 1947. *obl.* 8°. I.S. BU. **197/8.**

—— Spleen Census Report for Burma, with malarial map of the province and a preliminary note of black water fever. [By N. P. O'Gorman Lalor. With a map.] pp. 9. *Rangoon*, 1912. fol. I.S. BU. **13/8.**

—— Statistical Report of Province Amherst. [By J. P. Briggs.] pp. 7. [*Calcutta*, 1857.] fol. I.S. BU. **26. (1.)**

—— Statistical Report of the Martaban Province. [By H. Bernmore.] pp. 3. [*Calcutta*, 1858.] fol. I.S. BU. **26. (2.)**

—— Statistical Report of the Mergui Province. [By E. M. Ryan.] pp. 10. [*Calcutta*, 1858.] fol. I.S. BU. **26. (3.)**

—— Statistical Tables relating to Excise and Opium in the Province of Burma. Compiled from the Annual Excise Administration Reports. pp. 57. *Rangoon*, 1940. fol. I.S. BU. **14/3. (2.)**

—— [Statistics of Lock-Hospitals in Burma for 1887 and 1888.] 2 pt. [*Rangoon*, 1888, 89.] fol. I.S. BU. **27/4.**

—— The Strength and Elasticity of some of the most common Burmese Timbers and Size of Scantlings deduced from first principles. By H. L. Holman-Hunt. pp. 34. pl. XI. *Rangoon*, 1916. fol. I.S. BU. **46/9.**

—— A Summary of a Report on Tin Mining in the Tavoy District, Burma. By John J. A. Page. pp. 7. *Rangoon*, 1910. fol. I.S. BU. **47/14.**

—— Table of Drainage Areas, from 1 acre to 2,000 square miles, calculated up to $M^{\frac{3}{4}}$ in which M = drainage area in square miles. By R. C. Anderson. pp. 8. *Rangoon*, 1902. fol. I.S. BU. **53/24.**

—— Tables for the Transliteration of Burmese into English, with lists showing the names, in English and Burmese, of the divisions, townships and circles of British Burma, *etc.* pp. 65. *Government Press: Rangoon*, 1884. 8°. **14302.** i. 4. **(2.)**

—— [Another edition.] pp. xviii. 202. *Supdt., Government Printing: Rangoon*, 1896. 8°. **14302.** k. 4. **(1.)**

—— [Another edition.] pp. xviii. 202. *Supdt., Government Printing: Rangoon*, 1898. 8°. **14302.** k. 4. **(2.)**

—— Tables for the Transliteration of Shan Names into English. pp. 12. *Rangoon*, 1891. 8°. **11103.** f. **2. (1.)**

—— [Another edition.] pp. 13. *Rangoon*, 1900. 8°. **11103.** f. **2. (2.)**

—— A Text Book of Botany for use at the Burma Forest School, Pyinmana. By A. Long. pp. v. 65. 21. *Rangoon*, 1930. 8°. I.S. BU. **151/29.**

—— Tin Mining in Mergui District. By T. W. H. Hughes. [With a map.] pp. 17. *Rangoon*, 1889. fol. I.S. BU. **47/2.**

—— Translation of a Digest of the Burmese Buddhist Law concerning Inheritance and Marriage; being a collection of texts from thirty-six dhammathats, compared and arranged under the supervision of U Gaung, *etc.* 2 vol. *Rangoon*, 1902, 05. 8°. **14300.** ggg. **23.**

—— Water-supply. British Infantry Cantonments, Maymyo. [By G. T. I. Oliver. With maps.] pp. 3. pl. 5. [*Rangoon*,] 1909. fol. I.S. BU. **53/26.**

—— Ye-u Canal Project. Completion report of construction estimate. [With a map.] pp. 28. *Rangoon*, 1927. fol. I.S BU. **53/35.**

—— Ye-u Canal Project, 1904. [With a map.] pp. 77. *Rangoon*, 1905. fol. I.S. BU. **53/33.**

LEGISLATIVE BODIES.

COUNCIL OF THE LIEUTENANT-GOVERNOR.

—— *See* infra: LEGISLATIVE COUNCIL. [1897–1922.]

LEGISLATIVE COUNCIL. [1897–1922.]

—— Abstract of the Proceedings of the Council of the Lieutenant-Governor of Burma, assembled for the purpose of making Laws and Regulations under the provisions of the Indian Councils Act, 1861 (Government of India Act). [Nov. 1897—Nov. 1922.] pp. 1094. [*Rangoon*,] 1900–22. fol. I.S. BU. **32.**
Published in parts.

LEGISLATIVE COUNCIL. [1923–1936.]

—— Burma Legislative Council Proceedings, *etc.* 32 vol. *Rangoon*, 1923–36. 8°. I.S. BU. **124/3.**

—— Burma Legislative Council Manual. 4 pt. [*Rangoon*,] 1923, 24. 8°. I.S. BU. **136/6.**

—— [Another edition.] 2 vol. pp. 19. 418. 5. xxxiv. *Rangoon*, 1926. 8°. I.S. BU. **136/7.**

—— Rules and Standing Orders, 1933. pp. 29. [*Rangoon*,] 1933. 8°. I.S. BU. **136/5.**

Committee on Public Accounts.

—— Proceedings of the first (third) Meeting, *etc.* 2 pt. [*Rangoon*,] 1924, 25. 8°. I.S. BU. **124/5.**

Finance Committee.

—— Proceedings of the first six (of the seventh, eighth and ninth) Meetings May–October, 1923 (November 1923—February 1934). 2 pt. [*Rangoon*,] 1923 [1923, 24]. 8°. I.S. BU. **124/4.**

LEGISLATURE. [1937–41.]

—— Joint Meeting of the Senate and the House of Representatives. Monday, the 29th August, 1938 (Tuesday, the 18th February, 1941). 2 pt. *Rangoon*, 1938, 41. 8°. I.S. BU. **124/12.**

Fiscal Committee.

—— Interim Report on Local Taxation. pp. 15. *Rangoon*, 1940. 8°. I.S. BU. **113/22.**

House of Representatives.

—— Burma Legislature. Proceedings of the first [*etc.*] House of Representatives, *etc.* *Rangoon*, 1937– . 8°. I.S. BU. **124/10.**

—— The House of Representatives Electoral Rules. pp. 57 *Rangoon*, 1940. 8°. I.S. BU. **121**

—— Manual of Business and Procedure . . . 1939. pp. ii. 396. xxxi. *Rangoon*, 1939. 8°. I.S. BU. **124/16.**

Senate.

—— Burma Legislature. Proceedings of the first [*etc.*] Senate, *etc. Rangoon*, 1937– . 8°. I.S. BU. **124/9.**

—— Manual of Business and Procedure . . . 1938. pp. ii. 314. xxxi. *Rangoon*, 1938. 8°. I.S. BU. **124/15.**

—— Corrections and Amendments. Pamphlet no. 1. [*Rangoon*,] 1938. *s. sh.* 8°. I.S. BU. **124/15.**

DEPARTMENTS OF STATE AND PUBLIC INSTITUTIONS.

Accounts Department.

—— The Burmah Ready Reckoner. By B. N. Sen, *etc.* pp. 235. *Rangoon*, 1906. 8°. I.S. BU. **135/5.**

—— Third edition, revised, *etc.* pp. 274. *Rangoon*, 1925. 8°. I.S. BU. **135/6.**

—— Fourth edition, revised and improved . . . by B. K. Sen Gupta. pp. 265. *Rangoon*, 1934. 8°. I.S. BU. **135/7.**

—— The Burma Travelling Allowance Manual . . . Second edition. pp. ii. ii. 40. *Rangoon*, 1897. 8°. I.S. BU. **107/10.**

—— (Third edition.) pp. 2. ii. 57. *Rangoon*, 1901. 8°. I.S. BU. **107/6.**

—— Fifth edition. pp. iii. ii. 80. *Rangoon*, 1908. 8°. I.S. BU. **107/8.**

—— Compilation of the Fundamental Rules made by the Secretary of State in Council under Section 96B of the Government of India Act, including Orders, etc., issued by the Secretary of State, Government o [*sic*] India, Auditor-General, etc., and the Subsidiary Rules made by the Governor in Council acting with Ministers, including Orders, etc., issued by the Government of Burma. [With lists of corrections.] *Rangoon*, 1931– . 8°. I.S. BU. **119/18.**

—— District Cess and District Funds and the Burma Steam-Boiler Inspection Fund. [Report for the year 1908-09.] pp. 3. *Rangoon*, 1909. fol. I.S. BU. **28/2.**

—— Gradation List of the Office of the Accountant-General, Burma, including the Outside Audit, Commercial Audit, Customs Audit and Public Works branches as it stood on 1st April 1937 [*etc.*]. *Rangoon*, 1937– . 8°. I.S. BU. **133/2.**

—— List of Government Promissory Notes in the Custody of the Accountant-General, Burma, and the Comptroller and Auditor-General, Calcutta, on the 31st December 1906, deposited under Article 164, Volume 1, Civil Account Code. pp. 7. [*Rangoon*,] 1907. fol. I.S. BU. **30/4.**

—— List of Major and Minor Heads of Account of Receipts and Disbursements of the Government of Burma and the Federal Fund of the Federated Shan States, *etc.* pp. 43. *Rangoon*, 1939. 8°. I.S. BU. **113/21.**

Agricultural Department.

—— *See* infra : Department of Agriculture.

Archaeological Department.

—— Epigraphia Birmanica. Being lithic and other inscriptions of Burma, *etc. Rangoon*, 1919– . 4°. **14302.** c. **9.**

—— A List of Inscriptions found in Burma . . . Compiled and edited by Chas. Duroiselle. *Rangoon*, 1921. fol. pt.1. pp. vii. 216. **7006.dd.8.**

—— Publications of the Archæological Department, Burma.

no. 1. Index inscriptionum Birmanicarum. vol. 1. pp. 10. 1900.
no. 2. List of Pagodas at Pagan under the custody of Government. [With maps.] *Eng. & Burm.* 2 pt. 1901.

Rangoon, 1900, 01. fol. I.S. BU. **6/2.**

—— Report on Archæological Work in Burma (Report of the Superintendent, Archæological Survey, Burma), *etc.* [1901-02–1925-26.] 25 pt. *Rangoon*, 1902–26. fol. & 8°. I.S. BU. **6.** & **164/2.**

Reports from 1948 *onward, issued in Burmese, are placed in the Department of Oriental Printed Books and Manuscripts.*

Archaeological Survey.

—— *See* supra : Archaeological Department.

Audit Department.

—— *See* supra : Accounts Department.

Burma Allowance Committee.

—— Report of the Burma Allowance Committee, with the appendices. pp. 2. 92. 212. *Rangoon*, 1911. fol. I.S. BU. **7.**

Burma Currency Board.

—— Report of the Burma Currency Board for the Period 1st April, 1947, to 30th September, 1948 — 30 June 1952. *London*, [1949–52.] fol. I.S. BU. **88.**

Burma Defence Council.

—— The Rangoon Civil Evacuation Scheme. (Synopsis for publication.) pp. 40. [*Rangoon*,] 1941. 8°. I.S. BU. **101/4.**

Burma Educational Syndicate.

—— Rules for the Guidance of Examiners. Extracted from the general rules for examinations conducted by the Burma Educational Syndicate. [*Rangoon*,] 1923. *s. sh.* fol. I.S. BU. **51/5.**

Burma Forest Committee.

—— Report of the Burma Forest Committee, 1925. pp. 38 *Rangoon*, 1926. fol. I.S. BU. **18/7.**

Burma Frontier Force.

—— The Half-Yearly Burma Frontier Force List. *Rangoon*, 1937– . 8°. I.S. BU. **153/6.**

—— Report on the Administration of the Burma Frontier Force for the year 1937. pp. 20. *Rangoon*, 1939. 8°. I.S. BU. **153/7.**

Burma Medical Examination Board.

—— Calendar for 1917-18. pp. 61. *Rangoon*, 1918. 8°. I.S. BU. **145/7.**

Burma Police Enquiry Committee, 1924.

—— Report of the Burma Police Enquiry Committee, 1924. pp. 187. *Rangoon*, 1924. fol. I.S. BU. **42/4.**

BURMA. [DEPARTMENTS OF STATE AND PUBLIC INSTITUTIONS.]

BURMA POSTS AND TELEGRAPHS DEPARTMENT.

—— *See* infra: POSTS AND TELEGRAPHS DEPARTMENT.

BURMA PUBLIC HEALTH DEPARTMENT RE-ORGANIZATION COMMITTEE.

—— Report of the Burma Public Health Department Re-organization Committee. pp. 41. *Rangoon*, 1930. 8°. I.S. BU. **141/9.**

BURMA REFORMS COMMITTEE.

—— Report and Appendices. [With "Record of Evidence."] 4 pt. *Rangoon*, 1921, 22. fol. I.S. BU. **73.**

BURMA RETRENCHMENT COMMITTEE, 1923.

—— Report of the Burma Retrenchment Committee. pp. viii. 107. *Rangoon*, 1923. 8°. I.S. BU. **150/8.**

BURMA RETRENCHMENT COMMITTEE, 1934.

—— Report of the Burma Retrenchment Committee, 1934. pp. 245. *Rangoon*, 1934. fol. I.S. BU. **30/5.**

BURMA SECRETARIAT.

—— Burma Secretariat. Office Code. pp. iii. 128. xx. xv. *Rangoon*, 1902. 8°. I.S. BU. **119/9.**

—— Secretariat Circulars, 1888–1901, *etc.* pp. lxxv. 374. xi. *Rangoon*, 1901. 8°. I.S. BU. **119/27.**

BURMA UNIVERSITY COMMITTEE.

—— Interim Report of the Burma University Committee. pp. 53. *Rangoon*, 1918. fol. I.S. BU. **51/6.**

CENTRAL (JAIL) REVISORY BOARD.

—— Hand Book of Instructions for the guidance of Superintendents of Jails and District Magistrates, *etc.* pp. 17. *Rangoon*, 1941. 8°. I.S. BU. **115/9.**

CHIEF COURT OF LOWER BURMA.

—— *See* infra: COURTS OF JUSTICE.

CIVIL MEDICAL DEPARTMENT.

—— Circulars issued by the Inspector-General of Civil Hospitals, Burma, for the years 1908 to 1912, *etc.* pp. xxii. 189. xix. *Rangoon*, 1913. 8°. I.S. BU. **141/3.**

—— Circulars issued by the Inspector-General of Civil Hospitals, Burma, during the years 1908 to 1918, *etc.* pp. 2. vi-xl. 440. xxv. *Rangoon*, 1920. 8°. I.S. BU. **141/19.**

—— Report of the Chemical Examiner and Bacteriologist (Report of the Chemical Examiner) to the Government of Burma for the year 1911 [*etc.*]. *Rangoon*, 1912– . fol. & 8°. I.S. BU. **9 & 171.**

—— Rules of Office Procedure. Office of Inspector-General of Civil Hospitals, Burma. pp. 14. *Rangoon*, 1906. 8°. I.S. BU. **141/6.**
Interleaved.

CIVIL VETERINARY DEPARTMENT.

—— Bulletin no. 1 [*etc.*], 1928 [*etc.*]. *Rangoon*, 1929– . 8°. I.S. BU. **168/2.**

—— Reports on the Investigation of Diseases of Elephants. By G. Pfaff . . . With pamphlets on the injection of animals and the preparation of blood smears, issued by the Veterinary Department, Burma. [With plates.] pp. 91. ii. *Rangoon*, 1940. 8°. I.S. BU. **168/4.**

BURMA. [DEPARTMENTS OF STATE AND PUBLIC INSTITUTIONS.]

COMMERCE AND INDUSTRIES DEPARTMENT.

—— *See* infra: DEPARTMENT OF COMMERCE AND INDUSTRY.

COMMISSION OF INQUIRY TO EXAMINE THE QUESTION OF INDIAN IMMIGRATION INTO BURMA.

—— Report on Indian Immigration. By James Baxter. [With tables and maps.] pp. vii. 192. *Rangoon*, 1941. fol. I.S. BU. **24.**

COMMITTEE APPOINTED TO ASCERTAIN AND ADVISE HOW THE IMPERIAL IDEA MAY BE INCULCATED AND FOSTERED IN SCHOOLS AND COLLEGES IN BURMA.

—— Report of the Committee appointed to ascertain and advise how the Imperial Idea may be inculcated and fostered in Schools and Colleges in Burma. pp. vii. 94. *Rangoon*, 1917. fol. I.S. BU. **100/36.**

COMMITTEE APPOINTED TO CONSIDER THE TREATMENT OF JUVENILE DELINQUENCY IN BURMA.

—— Report of the Committee appointed to consider the Treatment of Juvenile Delinquency, *etc.* [With a map.] pp. vi. 132. *Rangoon*, 1928. 8°. I.S. BU. **115/6.**

COMMITTEE APPOINTED TO EXAMINE THE LAND REVENUE SYSTEM.

—— Report of the Committee appointed to examine the Land Revenue System of Burma. 2 vol. *Rangoon*, 1922. 8°. I.S. BU. **129/16.**

COMMITTEE APPOINTED TO INVESTIGATE THE ALLEGED HARDSHIPS CAUSED BY THE COMPULSORY VACCINATION OF LABOURERS ARRIVING IN RANGOON BY SEA.

—— Report, *etc.* pp. 7. 152. *Rangoon*, 1918. fol. I.S. BU. **57/2.**

COMMITTEE OF ENQUIRY INTO THE INDIGENOUS SYSTEM OF MEDICINE.

—— Report of the Committee of Enquiry into the Indigenous System of Medicine. pp. 49. *Rangoon*, 1931. 8°. I.S. BU. **141/8.**

COMMITTEE ON CO-OPERATION IN BURMA.

—— Report of the Committee on Co-operation in Burma, 1928-29. pp. v. 8. 164. *Rangoon*, 1929. 8°. I.S. BU. **170/4.**

COMMITTEE ON EXPENDITURE ON THE PUBLIC SERVICES.

—— Report . . . 1939–40. 2 pt. pp. ii. 299. *Rangoon*, 1940, 41. 8°. I.S. BU. **182/5.**

COMMITTEE ON MUNICIPAL TAXATION.

—— Report on the Committee on Municipal Taxation appointed on the 31st March 1921. pp. 5. 68. *Rangoon*, 1922. fol. I.S. BU. **41/3.**

COURTS OF JUSTICE.

Chief Court of Lower Burma.

—— *Library.* Chief Court Library Catalogue, 1903. I. Index of Authors. ff. 58. *Rangoon*, 1903. 8°. **11908. e. 25.**
Printed on one side of the leaf only.

—— Chief Court Library Catalogue, 1904. ff. 76. *Rangoon*, 1904. 8°. **011900. c. 51.**
Printed on one side of the leaf only.

Court of the Judicial Commissioner, British Burma.

—— *See* infra: *Court of the Judicial Commissioner, Lower Burma.*

Court of the Judicial Commissioner, Lower Burma.

—— Notes on Buddhist Law. By the Judicial Commissioner, British Burma [i.e. Sir John Jardine, K.C.I.E.]. [In part edited by E. Forchhammer.] 8 pt. *Rangoon,* 1882, 83. 8°. **5319.** c. **14.** (3.)

—— Selected Judgments and Rulings of the Court of the Judicial Commissioner, and of the Special Court, Lower Burma. Volume 1. For the period extending from 1872–1892 . . . Compiled by Frederick Ripley. pp. vii. 662. xlviii [lxviii]. *Rangoon,* 1893. 8°. I.S. BU. **110.**

No more published.

Court of the Judicial Commissioner, Upper Burma.

—— The Upper Burma Rulings, 1897–1901. Volume I. Criminal, *etc.* pp. iii. iv. 393. xxiii. *Rangoon,* 1903. 8°. I.S. BU. **137.**

District Court of Rangoon.

—— Select Decisions of the District Court of Rangoon, during the years 1859 & 1860. Major T. P. Sparks, Judicial Deputy Commissioner. pp. ii. 164. *Rangoon,* 1862. 8°. **5319.** bb. **28.**

High Court.

—— The Burma Companies Rules, 1940, being the rules published by the High Court of Judicature at Rangoon under section 246 of the Burma Companies Act. pp. 121. [*Rangoon,* 1940.] 8°. **05318.** e. **41.**

—— The Indian Law Reports . . . Rangoon series, containing cases determined by the High Court at Rangoon and by the Judicial Committee of the Privy Council on appeal from that Court, *etc.* *Rangoon,* 1923– . 8°. P.P. **1351.** ap.

—— Rules relating to the Qualifications and Admission of Advocates and Pleaders in Burma, *etc.* pp. 22. *Rangoon,* 1937. 8°. I.S. BU. **137/2.**

—— *Library.* Catalogue of the High Court Library, Rangoon, *etc.* 2 vol. *Rangoon,* 1924. 8°. **011900.** c. **52.**

CRIMINAL INVESTIGATION DEPARTMENT.

—— *See* infra: POLICE DEPARTMENT.

CUSTOMS DEPARTMENT.

—— Audit Manual. Rangoon Custom House. ff. 2. 4. 58. 2. 2. 2. 2. [*Rangoon,* 1936.] fol. I.S. BU. **14/9.** *Reproduced from typewriting.*

—— Customs Rules and Regulations relating to the War. For departmental use only. Corrected up to the 18th September 1915. pp. ii. 45. *Rangoon,* 1915. fol. I.S. BU. **14/2.**

Interleaved.

—— Second edition. Corrected up to the 31st May 1916. pp. iii. 100. *Rangoon,* 1916. fol. I.S. BU. **14/5.** *Interleaved.*

—— Third edition. Corrected up to the 15th May 1917. [Without the appendices. With addenda.] pp. ii. 49. *Rangoon,* 1917. fol. I.S. BU. **14/6.** *Interleaved.*

—— Fourth edition. Corrected up to the 15th September 1918. pp. iii. 54. *Rangoon,* 1918. fol. I.S. BU. **14/7.**

—— Customs Tariff Guide, *etc.* 16 pt. *Rangoon,* 1906–24. 8°. I.S. BU. **138/3.**

—— Gradation List of Customs Establishment in Burma as it stood on the 1st April 1937 [*etc.*]. *Rangoon,* 1937– . 8°. I.S. BU. **138/14.**

DEPARTMENT OF AGRICULTURE.

—— Agricultural Surveys. *Rangoon,* 1910– . fol. & 8°. I.S. BU. **8/3.**

—— Bulletin no. 1 [*etc.*]. *Rangoon,* 1909– . 8°. I.S. BU. **118.**

Imperfect; wanting no. 2, 18.

—— Proceedings of the sixth (—ninth) Half-Yearly Conference of the Agricultural Department held . . . December 1914(—August 1916). 4 pt. *Rangoon,* 1915, 16. 8°. I.S. BU. **114/7.**

—— Report of the first(—seventh) Agricultural and Co-operative Conference, Burma, held at Mandalay . . . 1911 (–1923). *Rangoon,* 1911–23. 8°. I.S. BU. **118/3.**

—— Report on the Operations of the Department of Agriculture, Burma, for the year ending the 30th June 1907 [*etc.*]. *Rangoon,* 1907– . fol. & 8°. I.S. BU. **8/2** & **114/3.**

Markets Section.

—— Development of Standards. Quantity. pp. 10. *Rangoon,* 1940. 8°. I.S. BU. **114/27.** *Markets Section Bulletin.* no. 6.

DEPARTMENT OF AGRICULTURE AND FORESTS.

Forest Enquiry Committee.

—— Report of the Forest Enquiry Committee, 1937. [With a map.] pp. iv. 28. *Rangoon,* 1937. fol. I.S. BU. **18/11.**

DEPARTMENT OF COMMERCE AND INDUSTRY.

—— Burma Customs Tariff, first [*etc.*] issue. *Rangoon,* 1938– . 4°. I.S. BU. **60/4.**

—— Extracts from the India and Burma—Transitory Provisions—Order, 1937, *etc.* [*Rangoon,*] 1937. *s. sh.* fol. I.S. BU. **29/5.**

—— History of Services of the Gazetted and other Officers of the Burma Posts and Telegraphs Department, *etc.* pp. 58. ii. *Rangoon,* 1939. 8°. I.S. BU. **148/11.** *A later edition, published by the Government of Burma Labour Department, is entered thereunder.*

—— The Merchant Shipping—Registrars of British Ships in Burma—Order, 1937, *etc.* [*Rangoon,*] 1937. *s. sh.* fol. I.S. BU. **65/3.**

—— The Merchant Shipping—Registration of Burma Government Ships—Order, 1937, *etc.* pp. 2. [*Rangoon,*] 1937. *s. sh.* fol. I.S. BU. **65/2.**

URMA. [DEPARTMENTS OF STATE AND PUBLIC INSTITUTIONS.]

— Particulars of Local Certificates which have been issued in Burma under the Indian Steam Ships Act, VII, and Inland Steam Vessels Act, VI of 1884, during the year 1900. pp. 8. *Rangoon*, 1901. fol. I.S. BU. **65.**

— Report of the Oil-Fields Labour Enquiry Committee. pp. iii. 123. *Rangoon*, 1941. 8°. I.S. BU. **182/3.**

DEPARTMENT OF LAND RECORDS AND AGRICULTURE.

— Circulars of the Director of the Department of Land Records and Agriculture, Burma, issued from August 1888 to October 1899. pp. 2. lxxiv. 255. xvi. *Rangoon*, 1899. 8°. I.S. BU. **114/2.**

DEPARTMENT OF LANDS AND REVENUE.

— Report of the Rangoon Development Trust Enquiry Committee, 1941. pp. ii. 69. *Rangoon*, 1941. 8°. I.S. BU. **182/2.**

DEPARTMENT OF PUBLIC HEALTH.

— The Burma Public Health Inspectors' Guide. pp. 16. [*Rangoon*,] 1940. 8°. I.S. BU. **145/13.**

— Notes for the use of Vaccinators. By Major J. Entrican . . . (Third edition.) Revised by Lieut.-Col. G. Jolly. pp. 46. *Rangoon*, 1934. 8°. **I.S.BU.145/12.(2.)**

— Pamphlet of Advice on Hygiene and the Framing of Sanitary Bye-Laws, for the Guidance of Rural Councils, *etc.* pp. ii. ii. 43. iii. *Rangoon*, 1925. 8°. I.S. BU. **145/17.**

DEPARTMENT OF WAR SUPPLIES AND ECONOMIC WARFARE.

— Control of Iron and Steel, Machinery and Millwork, *etc.* pp. 32. *Rangoon*, 1941. 8°. I.S. BU. **87/2.**

— Notification . . . Newsprint Control Order, 1941. pp. 3. *Rangoon*, 1941. fol. I.S. BU. **87.**

DIRECTORATE OF INFORMATION.

— *See* infra: MINISTRY OF INFORMATION.

ECONOMIC PLANNING BOARD.

— Two-Year Plan of Economic Development for Burma. [With diagrams.] pp. 55. *Rangoon*, 1948. 8°. I.S. BU. **225.**

EDUCATION DEPARTMENT.

— Departmental Instructions. 2 vol. *Rangoon*, 1915. 8°. I.S. BU. **116/5.**

— Educational Rules for Anglo-Vernacular and European Schools. *Rangoon*, 1920– . 8°. I.S. BU. **116/10.**
Various editions.

— Notes to Drawing and Art Masters on the New Curriculum. pp. 15. [*Rangoon*,] 1922. fol. I.S. BU. **51/4.**

— Report on the Sinking Funds constituted for the Repayment of Loans raised in the Open Market by the Municipal Corporation of the City of Rangoon for the year 1937-38. pp. 6. [*Rangoon*,] 1937. fol. I.S. BU. **45/2.**

— The Vernacular Education Code, 1932, *etc.* pp. iii. 63. *Rangoon*, 1932. 8°. I.S. BU. **116/19.**

BURMA. [DEPARTMENTS OF STATE AND PUBLIC INSTITUTIONS.]

Burma Text-Book Enquiry Committee.

—— Report of the Burma Text-Book Enquiry Committee, 1940. pp. 26. [*Rangoon*,] 1941. 8°. I.S. BU. **116/27.**

Committee on Technical and Vocational Education.

—— Report of the Committee on Technical and Vocational Education, 1927. [With plates.] pp. xxv. 228. *Rangoon*, 1928. 8°. I.S. BU. **116/18.**

University Act Enquiry Committee.

—— University Act Enquiry Committee Report. pp. 43. [*Rangoon*,] 1937. fol. I.S. BU. **51/9.**

Vernacular Education Committee.

—— Report of the Vernacular Education Committee. pp. 98. *Rangoon*, 1924. 8°. I.S. BU. **116/14.**

EXCISE DEPARTMENT.

—— British Burma. Excise Report (Report on the Excise Department of Lower Burma), 1867-68(–1888-89). 22 pt. *Maulmain, Rangoon*, 1869–89. 8° & fol. I.S. BU. **140 & 14.**
The report for 1888-89 *contains a "Note on the Excise Administration of Upper Burma."*

—— Report on the Excise Department of Burma for the year 1889-90 [*etc.*]. *Rangoon*, 1890– . fol. & 8°. I.S. BU. **14/8 & 140/3.**
Imperfect; wanting the reports for 1926-27 *and* 1928-29.

—— Report on the Working of the Revised Arrangements for the Vend of Opium in Upper Burma, during the years 1905-06 and 1906-07 (during the year 1907-08). 2 pt. *Rangoon*, 1908, 09. fol. I.S. BU. **46/3.**

FINANCE DEPARTMENT.

—— Annual Report (Note) on the Working of the Income-Tax Act, II of 1886, in Burma, *etc.* [1888-89–1917-18.] 42 pt. *Rangoon*, 1889–1918. fol. I.S. BU. **28.**
Beginning with the year 1901-02 *the "Annual Report" or "Note" is replaced every third year by a triennial "Report." Imperfect; wanting the reports for* 1893-94 & 1894-95.

—— Annual Review of the Working of the Treasuries in Burma for the year 1922-23. pp. 22. *Rangoon*, 1923. fol. I.S. BU. **30/2.**

—— The Burma District Office Manual. Reprint. [A reprint of the third edition of 1915, incorporating Correction Lists 1–33.] pp. iv. 235. *Rangoon*, 1934. 8°. I.S. BU. **119/37.**

—— The Burma Subdivisional and Township Office Manual. ff. 53. *Rangoon*, 1903. 8°. I.S. BU. **119/14.**

—— Second edition. pp. 53. *Rangoon*, 1904. 8°. I.S. BU. **119/38.**

—— Third edition. pp. ii. 74. *Rangoon*, 1910. 8°. I.S. BU. **119/39.**

—— Third edition, reprint. pp. ii. 57. xii. *Rangoon*, 1926. 8°. I.S. BU. **119/40.**

—— Third edition, reprint. pp. ii. 57. xii. *Rangoon*, 1927. 8°. I.S. BU. **119/41.**

—— Fourth edition. pp. ii. 60. xiii. *Rangoon*, 1928. 8°. I.S. BU. **119/42.**

BURMA. [DEPARTMENTS OF STATE AND PUBLIC INSTITUTIONS.]

—— Finance Accounts, 1937–38, and the Audit Report. pp. 158. *Rangoon*, 1939. 8°. I.S. BU. **111/10.**

—— Note on the Working of the Income-Tax Act, VII of 1918, in Burma for the year 1918-19(–1921-22). 5 pt. *Rangoon*, 1919–22. fol. I.S. BU. **28/8.**
The report for 1919-20 *is replaced by a triennial report bearing the title* "*Report on the Working of the Income Tax Act, II of* 1886, *and Indian Income Tax Act, VII of* 1918, *in Burma for the triennuum* 1917-18 *to* 1919-20."

—— Report on the Land Revenue Administration of Burma during the 15 months ended 30th June 1902 [*etc.*]. *Rangoon*, 1902– . fol. & 8°. I.S. BU. **37** & **129/3.**

—— Report on the Revenue Administration of Burma for the year 1888-89(–1900-1901). *Rangoon*, 1889–1901. fol. I.S. BU. **30/6.**
Imperfect ; wanting the report for 1894-95.

FLOODS ENQUIRY COMMITTEE.

—— *See* infra : PUBLIC WORKS DEPARTMENT.

FOREST DEPARTMENT.

—— Burma Forest Bulletin. *Rangoon*, 1921– . 8° & fol. I.S. BU. **151/8** & **18/12.**

—— Departmental Instructions for Forest Officers in Burma. Third edition, *etc.* pp. xii. 397. *Rangoon*, 1936. 8°. I.S. BU. **151/31.**

—— Forest Settlement Officer's Report on the Mayu Forest Reserve. [By Francis C. Owens. With a map.] pp. 55. [*Rangoon*, 1922.] fol. I.S. BU. **21/78.**

—— History of the Wegyi Boom and Depôt, Prome Forest Division, Burma. [By F. A. Leete. With plates.] pp. 29. *Rangoon*, 1916. fol. I.S. BU. **21/92.**

—— Inspection Note on Teak Fellings and Extraction in the Nawin Forests, Prome Division, under the 15 year lease dating from 1908-09 held by Messrs. Steel Bros. & Co., Ltd. By F. A. Leete, *etc.* pp. 30. *Rangoon*, 1915. fol. I.S. BU. **19/3.**

—— List of Useful Timbers other than Teak found commonly in the Tenasserim Forest Circle. pp. 5. [*Rangoon*, 1907.] fol. I.S. BU. **47/13.**

—— Note on a Tour of Inspection in the South Tenasserim Forest Division in January and February 1919. With map. By C. G. Rogers, *etc.* pp. 23. *Rangoon*, 1919. fol. I.S. BU. **19.**

—— Note on a Tour of Inspection through the Kamase, Yitkangyi and Alangon Reserves in the Pegu Forest Division, Tenasserim Circle, Lower Burma in January and February 1916. By C. G. Rogers. [With maps.] pp. 11. *Rangoon*, 1916. fol. I.S. BU. **21/79.**

—— Note on a Visit to the Sundarbans Forest Division, Bengal and suggestions for the Irrawaddy Delta. By Mr. A. W. Moodie. [With a map.] pp. 26. *Rangoon*, 1921. fol. I.S. BU. **21/77.**

—— Note on Departmental Extraction of Teak in Prome, Zigon and Tharrawaddy Divisions Pegu Circle, Lower Burma. By H. W. H. Watson, *etc.* pp. 18. *Rangoon*, 1917. fol. I.S. BU. **21/82.**

—— Note on the Inspection in December 1918 of the River Training Works on the Myitmaka and its Tributaries in the Prome, Zigôn and Tharrawaddy Divisions, Pegu Circle Lower Burma, undertaken in the dry season of 1917-18 and arrangements for working teak logs down the Myitmaka and its tributaries to Rangoon. By C. G. Rogers *etc.* [With maps.] pp. 34. *Rangoon*, 1919. fol. I.S. BU. **21/90**

—— Note on the Inspection of the Training Works of the Myitmaka and some of its Tributaries in the Prome Zigôn and Tharrawaddy Divisions, Pegu Circle, Lower Burma, undertaken in the dry seasons of 1913-14 and 1914-15. By C. G. Rogers. [With a map.] pp. 15. *Rangoon*, 1915. fol. I.S. BU. **53/18**

—— A Note on the Pegu Yoma Forests. By H. W. A. Watson. [With maps.] pp. ii. 109. *Rangoon*, 1923. fol. I.S. BU. **21/80.**

—— A Note on the Position of the Province as regards the Preparation and Revision of Working Plans. By H. W. A. Watson. pp. 39. *Rangoon*, 1921. fol. I.S. BU. **18/8.**

—— Observations on the Germination and Behaviour of Tree Seedlings, with special reference to taungya plantations. By H. R. Blanford. ff. 51. *Rangoon*, 1920. fol. I.S. BU. **21/85.**
Printed on one side of the leaf only.

—— Progress Report of Forest Administration in British Burma (Lower Burma) for 1876-77(–1891-92). 6 pt. [*Calcutta* ;] *Rangoon*, 1878–93. fol. I.S. BU. **18.**
Imperfect ; wanting the reports for 1879-80–1881-82 *and* 1883-84–1889-90.

—— Progress Report on Forest Administration in Upper Burma for 1890-91(1891-92) . . . With a review by the Chief Commissioner, and the orders of the Government of India. 2 pt. *Rangoon*, 1891, 93. fol. I.S. BU. **18/9.**

—— Progress Reports on Forest Administration (Report on Forest Administration) in Burma for the year 1893-94 [*etc.*]. *Rangoon*, 1895– . fol. & 8°. I.S. BU. **18/10** & **151/7.**

—— A Report and Valuation Survey of the Ngawun Reserved Forest, South Tenasserim Division. By Mr. Taw Ky Saing. pp. 21. *Rangoon*, 1923. fol. I.S. BU. **19/4**

—— Report on Boom and Mechanical Appliances for getting Teak Logs out of the Schwele Stream at Chaunggwa, Prome Division. By C. G. Rogers. [With maps.] pp. 53 *Rangoon*, 1913. fol. I.S. BU. **21/91**
Imperfect ; wanting pp. 31–43.

—— Report on the Pyinkadoh Forests of Arakan . . By W. Schlich. pp. 35. xiv. *Rangoon*, 1870. fol. **7074.** m. **12**

—— River Training Works in 1914 and 1915 for the Floating of Teak down the Myitmaka and its Tributaries in the Prome, Zigôn and Tharrawaddy Forest Divisions. By F. A. Leete . . . and B. M. Samuelson. [With plates, including maps.] pp. ii. 4. 40. 31. 51. *Rangoon* 1916. fol. I.S. BU. **21/89**

—— Rules to Regulate the Course of Instruction at, Admission to, and Discipline at, the Vernacular Forest School, Tharrawaddy, Burma. pp. 6. [*Rangoon*,] 1904. fol. I.S. BU. **19/2.**

BURMA. [DEPARTMENTS OF STATE AND PUBLIC INSTITUTIONS.]

—— Scheme for Girdling over the Teak Forests not under Working Plans, east of the Dawnas, Thaungyin Division. Period 1931–32 to 1944–45. [With a map.] pp. 3. *Rangoon*, 1932. fol. I.S. BU. **21/93.**

—— Standing Orders for the Commercial Accounts of the Utilization Forest Circle, Burma, *etc.* pp. 18. *Rangoon*, 1929. fol. I.S. BU. **18/4.**

—— Zigon Division. Note on the Floating of Timber in the Myitmaka and its Branches during the Rains 1914. By F. A. Leete. [With a map.] pp. 18. *Rangoon*, 1915. fol. I.S. BU. **21/75.**

Utilization Circle.

—— History and Activities of the Timber Research Branch. By E. Q. O'Brien-Smith. pp. 17. *Simla*, [1944.] 8°. I.S. BU. **151/33.**

FOREST ENQUIRY COMMITTEE.

—— *See* supra: DEPARTMENT OF AGRICULTURE AND FORESTS.

FRONTIER AREAS COMMITTEE OF ENQUIRY.

—— *See* ENGLAND.—*Burma Office.—Frontier Areas Committee of Enquiry.*

GOVERNMENT EXPERIMENTAL SALT FACTORY.

—— *See* PANGA.

HIGH COURT.

—— *See* supra: COURTS OF JUSTICE.

HOME DEPARTMENT.

—— British Burma . . . Annual Report on Criminal and Civil Justice (Civil and Criminal Justice) in the Courts of the Recorders and in the Small Cause Courts of Rangoon and Maulmain during 1868 (1869). 2 pt. *Rangoon*, 1869, 70. 8°. I.S. BU. **139/3.**

—— The Government of Burma—High Court Judges—Order, 1937. pp. 4. [*Rangoon*,] 1937. fol. I.S. BU. **29/3.**

—— Report of the Secretariat Incident Enquiry Committee. [With plates.] pp. 44. *Rangoon*, 1939. 8°. I.S. BU. **182.**

Bribery and Corruption Enquiry Committee.

—— Report of the Bribery and Corruption Enquiry Committee, 1940. pp. 62. *Rangoon*, 1941. 8°. I.S. BU. **176.**

INTELLIGENCE BRANCH.

—— Report on a Tour through the Trans-Salween Shan States. By . . . C. Ainslie . . . Season 1892-93. [With maps.] *Rangoon*, 1893. fol. I.S. BU. **75. (1.)**

—— Report on the Kaukkwe Police Column Operations during the Cold Season of 1892-93, together with appendix, including routes, sketches, &c. By . . . E. F. Cooke-Hurle. [With maps.] *Rangoon*, 1893. fol. I.S. BU. **75. (3.)**

—— Report on the Operations in the Chin Hills during the Cold Season of 1892-93, together with appendix containing routes, sketches, &c. By . . . R. Baker. [With maps.] *Rangoon*, 1893. fol. I.S. BU. **75. (2.)**

BURMA. [DEPARTMENTS OF STATE AND PUBLIC INSTITUTIONS.]

Library.

—— List of Books and Reports in Library, Intelligence Branch, Burma. Mandalay, the 1st December, 1892. pp. 8. *Rangoon*, 1893. fol. **11908. i. 3. (2.)**

JUDICIAL DEPARTMENT.

—— British Burma Civil Justice Report (Report on Civil Justice). 1867(–1869). 3 pt. *Rangoon*, 1868–70. 8°. I.S. BU. **139/2.**

—— British Burma. Criminal Justice Report (Report on Criminal Justice). 1867(–1869). 3 pt. *Rangoon*, [1868]–70. 8°. I.S. BU. **139.**

—— British Burma . . . Report on Criminal and Civil Justice (Report on Civil and Criminal Justice in British Burma) for 1870(–1876). 6 pt. *Rangoon*, 1872–77. 8°. I.S. BU. **139/4.**
Imperfect; wanting the report for 1872.

—— The Civil Justice Report (of British Burma—of Lower Burma) for the year 1877(–1889). *Rangoon*, 1879–90. fol. I.S. BU. **12/6.**

—— Motor Vehicles Manual; containing the Indian Motor Vehicles Act, 1914, VIII of 1914, and rules thereunder. Corrected up to 1st June 1935. pp. 86. *Rangoon*, 1935. 8°. I.S. BU. **123.**

—— Notification. Rangoon, the 8th September 1937. (The Government of Burma—Adaptation of Laws—Supplementary Order, 1937.) [*Rangoon*,] 1937. *s. sh.* fol. I.S. BU. **29/2.**

—— Report on the Criminal Justice of British Burma (The Criminal Justice Report of Lower Burma) for the year 1877(–1889). 13 pt. *Rangoon*, 1878–90. fol. I.S. BU. **12/5.**

—— Reports on Civil Justice (Report on the Administration of Civil Justice) in Burma for the year 1890 [*etc.*]. *Rangoon*, 1891– . fol. & 8°. I.S. BU. **12/8 & 139/5.**
Imperfect; wanting the report for 1902.

—— Reports on Criminal Justice (Report on the Administration of Criminal Justice) in Burma for the year 1890 [*etc.*]. *Rangoon*, 1891– . fol. & 8°. I.S. BU. **12/9 & 139/6.**

LABOUR DEPARTMENT.

—— History of Services of the Gazetted and other Officers of the Burma Posts and Telegraphs Department, *etc.* pp. 47. ii. *Rangoon*, 1941. 8°. I.S. BU. **148/11. (2.)**
An earlier edition, published by the Government of Burma Department of Commerce and Industry, is entered thereunder.

LINGUISTIC SURVEY.

—— Linguistic Survey of Burma. Preparatory stage or linguistic census. pp. xiii. 67. *Rangoon*, 1917. fol. I.S. BU. **10/4.**

MARINE AND COMMERCE DEPARTMENT.

—— *See* supra: DEPARTMENT OF COMMERCE AND INDUSTRY.

MEDICAL DEPARTMENT.

—— *See* supra: CIVIL MEDICAL DEPARTMENT.

BURMA. [DEPARTMENTS OF STATE AND PUBLIC INSTITUTIONS.]

METEOROLOGICAL DEPARTMENT.

—— Report on the Administration of the Meteorological Department, Burma, 1937–41. pp. 18. *Rangoon,* 1941. 8°. I.S. BU. **172/2.**

—— Burma Monthly Weather Review. Jan. 1938—Sept. 1940. *Rangoon,* 1938–40. fol. I.S. BU. **72.**

—— Meteorological Organization for Airmen. M.O.A. Pamphlet, 1939. pp. 33. *Rangoon,* 1940. 8°. I.S. BU. **172.**

MINISTRY OF INFORMATION.

—— A Brief Review of Disturbances in Burma. [*Rangoon,*] 1949– . 8°. I.S. BU. **215/4.**

—— Broadcast Speech by the Hon'ble Prime Minister on 23rd August 1948. pp. 8. [*Rangoon,* 1948.] 8°. I.S. BU. **215/11.**

—— Buddhist Mission to Burma. A short note by Dr. S. Paranavitana. pp. 6. [*Rangoon,*] 1950. 8°. I.S. BU. **197/9.**

—— Burma. *Rangoon,* 1950– . 4°. I.S. BU. **215/4.**

—— Burma and the Insurrections. [With maps.] pp. 63. [*Rangoon,*] 1949. 8°. I.S. BU. **197.**

—— Burma in 1948. Facts and figures. pp. 12. [*Rangoon,*] 1949. 8°. I.S. BU. **215/3.**

—— Burma Independence Celebrations. [With illustrations.] pp. 42. [*Rangoon,* 1948.] 8°. I.S. BU. **215/2.**

—— Burma National Flag. (State Seal.) [*Rangoon,* 1950?] *obl.* 8°. I.S. BU. **215/5.**

—— Burma Weekly Bulletin. no. 100, *etc.* Week ending 14 Jan. 1950, *etc. Rangoon,* 1950– . fol. I.S. BU. **215/13.**

Reproduced from typewriting.

—— Burma's Fight for Freedom. Independence Commemoration. [With illustrations.] pp. 119. [*Rangoon,* 1948.] 8°. I.S. BU. **215.**

—— Burma's Freedom. The first anniversary. [With illustrations.] pp. 61. *Rangoon,* 1949. 8°. I.S. BU. **215/8.**

—— Events relating to the Karen rising. pp. 9. [*Rangoon,*] 1949. 8°. I.S. BU. **215/6.**
Burma Facts and Figures. no. 4.

—— Factories in Burma. pp. 8. [*Rangoon,*] 1949. 8°. I.S. BU. **215/7.**
Burma Facts and Figures. no. 2.

—— The Four Pledges. [Speeches by the Burmese Prime Minister and others.] pp. 15. [*Rangoon,*] 1949. 8°. I.S. BU. **215/12.**

—— From Peace to Stability . . . Translation of selected speeches by the Hon'ble Thakin Nu, Prime Minister . . . from 15th August 1949 to 20th April 1951. pp. iii. 218. *Rangoon,* 1951. 8°. I.S. BU. **215/15.**

—— KNDO Insurrection—Second edition. pp. 59. [*Rangoon,*] 1949. 8°. I.S. BU. **197/6.**

BURMA. [DEPARTMENTS OF STATE AND PUBLIC INSTITUTIONS.]

—— Shwedagon, the sacred shrine. [By Aung Than. With plates.] pp. 32. [*Rangoon,*] 1949. 8°. I.S. BU. **197/7.**

—— Summary of the Hon'ble Prime Minister's Speech delivered in Parliament on 3rd October 1950 in support of "Buddha Sasana Organization Act." pp. 4. *Rangoon,* 1950. 8°. I.S. BU. **197/11.**

—— Translation of the Hon'ble Prime Minister's Speech delivered at the Conference of Civil and Military Officers on Friday, the 5th August 1949. pp. 8. *Rangoon,* 1949. 8°. I.S. BU. **197/3.**

—— Translation of the Hon'ble Prime Minister's Speech delivered at the Karen New Year Day Celebration on the 19th December 1949. pp. 8. *Rangoon,* 1949. 8°. I.S. BU. **197/4.**

—— Translation of the Speech delivered by the Hon'ble Thakin Nu, Prime Minister of the Union of Burma, in Parliament on the 5th September 1950, calling for the House to approve the Government's statement of 8th July 1950 supporting the United Nations Resolution on Korea. pp. 13. *Rangoon,* 1950. 8°. I.S. BU. **197/12.**

—— United Nations Day Speech at the Rotary Club lunch at the Strand Hotel, Rangoon on 24th October, 1950, on "Burma and the U N" read by the Acting Hon'ble Minister for Foreign Affairs. pp. 15. *Rangoon,* 1950. 8°. I.S. BU. **197/10.**

MUNICIPAL DEPARTMENT.

—— Report of the Rangoon Development Committee, August 1917, and Report on the Reclamation of Rangoon Town Lands for the year 1916-17. With Joint resolution of the local government. [With maps and plans.] pp. x. 49. *Rangoon,* 1917. fol. I.S. BU. **33/6.**

—— [Another edition.] pp. xi. 42. *Rangoon,* 1921. fol. I.S. BU. **33/7.**

—— Report on the Reclamation of Rangoon Town Lands, for the year 1908-09(–1919-20). 10 pt. *Rangoon,* [1909–21.] fol. I.S. BU. **33/2.**
The report for 1916-17 *was published with the* "*Report of the Rangoon Development Committee, August* 1917."

—— Reports of the Suburban Development Committee, Rangoon, and the Departmental Committee on Town Planning, Burma, with resolution of the local government. [With maps.] pp. ix. ii. 135. *Rangoon,* 1917. fol. I.S. BU. **48.**

—— Reports of the Suburban Development Committee, Rangoon, and the Departmental Committee on Town Planning, Burma, with resolution of the local government. pp. viii. ii. 129. *Rangoon,* 1921. fol. I.S. BU. **48/3.**

OFFICE OF INSPECTOR-GENERAL OF CIVIL HOSPITALS.

—— *See* supra: CIVIL MEDICAL DEPARTMENT.

OFFICE OF THE ACCOUNTANT-GENERAL.

—— *See* supra: ACCOUNTS DEPARTMENT.

OFFICE OF THE COMMISSIONER OF INCOME-TAX.

—— Report on the Working of the Income-Tax Act, XI of 1922, in Burma for the year 1922-23. (Annual Report and Returns of the Income-Tax Department, Burma, 1923-24.) 2 pt. *Rangoon,* 1923, 24. 8° & fol. I.S. BU. **28/5.**

BURMA. [DEPARTMENTS OF STATE AND PUBLIC INSTITUTIONS.]

OFFICE OF THE COMMISSIONER OF SETTLEMENTS AND LAND RECORDS.

—— Burma Civil Budget Estimates for the year 1908-09. (Departments of Survey and Settlement, Land Records, Survey Schools and Inland Trade Registration.) pp. 23. [*Rangoon*,] 1908. fol. I.S. BU. **28/3.**

—— Manual relating to the Registration of the External Land Trade of Burma. pp. ii. 63. *Rangoon*, 1913. 8°. I.S. BU. **146/4.**

Central Settlement Library.

—— Catalogue of the Central Settlement Library, *etc.* pp. 2. 62. *Rangoon*, 1924. 8°. **011900. d. 32.**

Statistical Department.

—— Statistical Bulletins published by the Statistical Department of the Office of the Commissioner of Settlements and Land Records. 3 pt. *Rangoon*, 1924, 23. 8°. I.S. BU. **129/4.**

OFFICE OF THE COMPTROLLER OF POSTS AND TELEGRAPHS ACCOUNTS.

—— Gradation List of the Office of the Comptroller of Posts and Telegraphs Accounts . . . Corrected up to 1st July 1937. pp. 21. *Rangoon*, 1937. 8°. I.S. BU. **148/10.**

OFFICE OF THE FINANCIAL COMMISSIONER.

—— *See* supra: FINANCE DEPARTMENT.

OFFICE OF THE NAUTICAL ADVISER.

—— Office Manual of the Office of the Nautical Adviser to the Government of Burma. pp. 144. *Rangoon*, 1936. 8°. I.S. BU. **154/15.**

PAPER CURRENCY DEPARTMENT.

—— Report on the Resource and Currency Operations in the Province of Burma for the year 1915-16(–1919-20). 5 pt. *Rangoon*, 1916–20. fol. I.S. BU. **30/3.**

POLICE COMMITTEE.

—— Summary of the Views of Witnesses examined by the Members of the Police Committee, Burma, *etc.* pp. ii. 52. ix. *Rangoon*, 1902. fol. I.S. BU. **42/3.**

POLICE DEPARTMENT.

—— The Abridged Law Manual for Sub-Inspectors of Police, Burma, *etc.* pp. 391. *Rangoon*, 1926. 8°. I.S. BU. **143/29.**

—— The Burma Police Manual, containing orders and rules made for the Burma Police . . . Compiled by A. St. J. Ingle . . . Second edition. 2 vol. *Rangoon*, 1899. 8°. I.S. BU. **143/4.**

Vol. 2 is of the 1st edition.

—— [Another edition of vol. 1.] Third edition. pp. ii. vii. 514. lxiv. c. *Rangoon*, 1913. 8°. I.S. BU. **143/21.**

No more of this edition published.

—— Fourth edition. pp. ii. vi. 353. l. lxx. *Rangoon*, 1926. 8°. I.S. BU. **143/22.**
This edition does not contain the material previously published as vol. 2.

—— The Burma Police Training School Manual, *etc.* pp. 46. *Rangoon*, 1939. 8°. I.S. BU. **143/35.**

BURMA. [DEPARTMENTS OF STATE AND PUBLIC INSTITUTIONS.]

—— Criminal Investigation Department Manual . . . Second edition. pt. 1, 2, 4. *Rangoon*, 1923, 22. 8°. I.S. BU. **143/6.**

Imperfect; wanting pt. 3.

—— [Another edition of pt. 1.] pp. 131. *Rangoon*, 1925. 8°. I.S. BU. **143/23.**

—— [Another edition of pt. 1.] pp. 134. *Rangoon*, 1929. 8°. I.S. BU. **143/25.**

—— District Police Office Manual. pp. 43. *Rangoon*, 1918. 8°. I.S. BU. **143/9.**

—— The District Police Office Manual . . . Second edition. pp. iii. 212. *Rangoon*, 1926. 8°. I.S. BU. **143/30.**

—— The Drill and Musketry Manual for the Use of the Burma Civil Police, 1931 . . . Third edition. pp. ii. iv. 214. *Rangoon*, 1932. 8°. I.S. BU. **143/33.**

—— Drill Manual for the use of the Burma Police. pp. xii. 3. 135. *Rangoon*, 1909. 16°. I.S. BU. **143/8.**

—— Drill Manual for the use of the Burma Police. pp. ix. iii. 160. *Rangoon*, 1913. 16°. I.S. BU. **143/31.**

—— The Drill Manual for the use of the Burma Police, 1926 . . . Second edition. pp. iii. 119. *Rangoon*, 1926. 8°. I.S. BU. **143/32.**

—— Manual for the Military Police, containing orders and rules for the Burma Military Police . . . Compiled by Major H. Parkin, *etc.* pp. 2. 127. xv. *Rangoon*, 1901. 8°. I.S. BU. **143/3.**

—— Burma Military Police Manual, containing orders and rules made for the Burma Military Police with the sanction of the Lieutenant-Governor of Burma . . . Second edition. Revised and brought up to date. pp. ii. ii. 271. xxxi. *Rangoon*, 1914. 8°. I.S. BU. **143/26.**

—— Manual for the Burma Military Police. Corrected up to the 31st December 1930. (Third edition.) pp. x. 328. xli. *Rangoon*, 1931. 8°. I.S. BU. **143/27.**

—— Manual of Preventive Law, *etc.* pp. 79. *Rangoon*, 1925. 8°. I.S. BU. **143/17.**

—— Second edition, *etc.* pp. ii. 122. *Rangoon*, 1927. 8°. I.S. BU. **143/28.**

—— Police Duty at Air-Raid Incidents. By Sergeant C. E. Turner. pp. 14. *Rangoon*, 1941. 8°. I.S. BU. **143/34.**

—— Police Report, British Burma (Report on the Police Administration of Lower Burma), 1867(–1887). 20 pt. *Maulmain, Rangoon*, 1868–88. 8° & fol. I.S. BU. **143 & 42.**
Imperfect; wanting the report for 1871.

—— Police Supply and Clothing Manual for Burma, containing orders and rules for the guidance of officers of civil and military police, *etc.* pp. 123. xvi. *Rangoon*, 1908. 8°. I.S. BU. **143/5.**

—— Second edition. pp. 143. *Rangoon*, 1925. 8°. I.S. BU. **143/24.**

—— The Railway Police Manual, containing orders and rules made for the Railway Police. pp. 92. *Rangoon*, 1925. 8°. I.S. BU. **143/16.**

—— Report of the Crime Enquiry Committee, 1923. (Resolution on the Report of the Crime Enquiry Committee.) 2 pt. *Maymyo*, 1923. fol. I.S. BU. **12/7.**

BURMA. [DEPARTMENTS OF STATE AND PUBLIC INSTITUTIONS.]

—— Report on the Police Administration of Burma for the year 1888 [*etc.*]. *Rangoon*, 1889– . fol. & 8°.
I.S. BU. **43 & 143/7.**

—— Report on the Police Administration of Upper Burma for the year 1887. [With Report of the Police Supply and Clothing Department for the year 1887–88]. pp. v. 5. 36. 70. *Rangoon*, 1888. fol. I.S. BU. **42/2.**

POLITICAL DEPARTMENT.

Political Department.

—— Report on the Administration of the Hill Tracts, Northern Arakan, 1871–72. pp. v. 66. *Rangoon*, 1872. 8°. I.S. BU. **119/45.**

POSTS AND TELEGRAPHS DEPARTMENT.

—— Annual Report for the year 1937–38. (Report on the working of the Burma Posts and Telegraphs Department, 1939–40.) 2 pt. *Rangoon*, 1939, 41. 8°. I.S. BU. **148/9.**

—— Detailed Statements in support of Demands for Grants for the year 1937-38 [*etc.*]. *Rangoon*, 1937– . 8°.
I.S. BU. **148/8.**

—— History of Services of the Gazetted and other Officers of the Burma Posts and Telegraphs Department, *etc.* pp. 58. ii. 1939. 8°. *See* supra: *Department of Commerce and Industry.* I.S. BU. **148/11.**

—— History of Services of the Gazetted and other Officers of the Burma Posts and Telegraphs Department, *etc.* pp. 47. ii. 1941. 8°. *See* supra: *Labour Department.*
I.S. BU. **148/11.** (2.)

PRISON DEPARTMENT.

—— A Note on Ankylostoma Infection and Ankylostomiasis in the Mandalay Central Jail. By Captain P. K. Tarapore. pp. 13. *Rangoon*, 1912. fol. I.S. BU. **13/10.**

—— Report on Cases of Oedema at Myingyan and Prevalence of Intestinal Parasites in Bassein Jail. By Lieutenant-Colonel R. H. Castor. pp. 5. *Rangoon*, 1913. fol.
I.S. BU. **13/11.**

PROVINCIAL BANKING ENQUIRY COMMITTEE.

—— Report of the Burma Provincial Banking Enquiry Committee, 1929-30. *Rangoon*, 1930. 8°. I.S. BU. **111/8.** *Imperfect; wanting vol.* 1.

PUBLIC RELATIONS DEPARTMENT.

—— Health Notes for Government Officials. By Colonel M. L. Treston. pp. 64. *Simla*, [1946?] 8°.
I.S. BU. **149/25.**

—— A Simple Key to One Hundred Common Trees of Burma. Compiled by C. B. Smales. (Second edition.) pp. viii. 26. *Simla*, 1945. 8°. **7081.** a. 5.

—— Wild Life Protection in Burma. By H. C. Smith. (Burma's Decreasing Wild Life. By D'Arcy Weatherbe.) pp. 15. *Simla*, [1945?] 8°. I.S. BU. **183.**

PUBLIC SERVICE COMMISSION.

—— Pamphlet of the Competitive Examination for Recruitment to Burma Civil Service, Class I, and Burma Audit and Accounts Service, Class I, held in January 1938. Rules, syllabus, question papers, results and précis of reports of examiners. pp. 62. *Rangoon*, 1938. fol.
I.S. BU. **7/4.**

BURMA. [DEPARTMENTS OF STATE AND PUBLIC INSTITUTIONS.]

—— Pamphlet of the Competitive Examination for Recruitment to the Burma Police, Class I, held in September 1937. Rules, etc., question papers, results and precis of reports of examiners. pp. 25. *Rangoon*, 1938. fol. I.S. BU. **7/5**

PUBLIC WORKS DEPARTMENT.

—— Classified List and Distribution Return of Establishment, Buildings and Roads Branch . . . Corrected up to the 31st December 1922(—31st December 1923). 3 pt. *Rangoon*, 1923, 24. 8°. I.S. BU. **132/2.**

—— Classified List and Distribution Return of Establishment, Irrigation Branch . . . Corrected up to the 30th June 1923. pp. ii. 26. iii. *Rangoon*, 1923. 8°.
I.S. BU. **132/3.**

—— Embankment Report of the Bassein Division (of the Bassein and Henzada Divisions) for 1899-1900(1900-1901—from 1st April 1902 to 31st October 1902). [With maps.] *Rangoon*, 1900–03. fol. I.S. BU. **53/3**

—— Embankment Report of the Myaungmya and Henzada Divisions from 1st November 1902 to 31st October 1903. [With plates.] pp. 11. *Rangoon*, 1904. fol.
I.S. BU. **53/4**

—— Handbook of Public Works Department Circulars. Revised edition 1934 . . . embodying all corrections issued up to the 1st of August 1937. pp. xliv. 266. *Rangoon*, 1937. 8°. I.S. BU. **155/19**

—— List of Circuit, Rest, and Shelter Houses, and Inspection and Dâk Bungalows in Upper and Lower Burma, 1900 (1923, 1928). (List of Circuit Houses, Circuit-Rooms, Dak Bungalows, Public Works Department Inspection Bungalows, District Bungalows and Forest and other Rest Houses in Burma, 1933 [1938].) 5 pt. *Rangoon*, 1901–38. fol. I.S. BU. **52/5–52/5.** (5.

—— Môn Canals Project, 1900. pp. 2. 3. 109. *Rangoon*, 1901. fol. I.S. BU. **53/31**

—— Môn Canals Project. Revised estimate. [With a map.] pp. 6. 88. *Rangoon*, 1910. fol. I.S. BU. **53/32.**

—— Note on the Breaching of the Nyaungyan-Minhla Tank on September 11th, 1910. By J. M. B. Stuart. [With a map.] pp. 31. *Rangoon*, 1914. fol. I.S. BU. **53/9**

—— Note on the Protective Embankments in the Irrawaddy Delta, 1862–1912. By Mr. C. G. Barnett, *etc.* [With a map.] pp. 142. *Rangoon*, 1914. fol. I.S. BU. **53/14**

—— Pegu-Syriam Railway Survey, 1901–02. Metre-gauge 67 miles. Reconnaissance report and abstract of cost. [By A. R. Lilley.] pp. 6. *Rangoon*, 1902. fol.
I.S. BU. **64/4**

—— Report on the Embankments on the Left Bank of the Irrawaddy. [By O. C. Lees.] pp. 21. *Rangoon*, 1907. fol. I.S. BU. **53/10**

—— Report on the Survey of the Village Embankments on the East Bank of the Irrawaddy between Apyauk and Aingtalok, 1910. [By John N. List.] pp. 2. 8. *Rangoon*, 1910. fol. I.S. BU. **53/11**

—— Report on the Survey Operations carried out in the Delta Circle . . . for the season 1922-23. [With maps.] pp. 25. [*Rangoon*,] 1923. fol. I.S. BU. **53/8**

—— Report on the Waterways in the Irrawaddy Delta. [By B. M. Samuelson. With maps.] pp. 24. pl. 2. *Rangoon*, 1915. fol. I.S. BU. **53/15.**

—— Roads: their construction and maintenance. pp. 62. *Rangoon*, 1903. 8°. I.S. BU. **103/7.**

—— Southern Shan States Railway Project, 1901–1902. 2′ 6″ gauge. 112.2 miles. [By A. R. Lilley.] pp. 79. *Rangoon*, 1903. fol. I.S. BU. **64/5.**

—— Unauthorised Embankments on the East Bank of the Irrawaddy River in the Upper Delta. By J. P. Candy. pp. iii. 64. *Rangoon*, 1931. fol. I.S. BU. **53/30.**

—— Ye-u Canal Project. Revised estimate. 1908. pp. 22. [*Rangoon*,] 1909. fol. I.S. BU. **53/34.**

Committee appointed to advise on Measures which should be taken to improve the Salween River south of Moulmein for Navigation Purposes.

—— Report of the Committee . . . dated the 10th December 1906. [With maps.] pp. 6. pl. 2. *Rangoon*, 1907. fol. I.S. BU. **53/17.**

Embankment Division.

—— Embankment Report for the year 1st June 1920 to 31st May 1921. pp. 20. *Rangoon*, 1921. fol. I.S. BU. **53/7.**

Floods Enquiry Committee.

—— Report of the Floods Enquiry Committee, 1924–25. [With plans.] 2 pt. pp. iv. 308. pl. 30. *Rangoon*. 1927. fol. I.S. BU. **53/22.**

Irrigation Branch.

—— Completion Report and Schedules of the Salin Canal Remodelling Project. [By W. L. Roseveare. With a map.] pp. 35. *Rangoon*, 1937. fol. I.S. BU. **53/36.**

Secretariat Library.

—— Alphabetical List of Books in the Library of the Burma Public Works Secretariat. pp. 71. 8. 13. *Rangoon*, 1893. fol. **11908.** i. **3.** (**1.**)

—— Catalogue of Books, Periodicals, and Reports, etc. in the Burma P. W. Sectt. Library. pp. ii. 233. [*Rangoon*,] 1909. fol. **11901.** ppp. **22.**

—— Catalogue of Books in the Burma Public Works Secretariat Library, 1924. [*Rangoon*,] 1924. fol. **11901.** ppp. **21.**

Interleaved.

Public Works Secretariat.—*Library.*

—— *See* supra: Public Works Department.—*Secretariat Library.*

Rangoon Foreshore Committee.

—— Report of the Rangoon Foreshore Committee, 1909. pp. iv. 4. 317. *Rangoon*, 1910. fol. I.S. BU. **48/2.**

Rangoon Traffic Enquiry Committee.

—— Report of the Rangoon Traffic Enquiry Committee, 1925. [With plans.] pp. 32. *Rangoon*, 1925. fol. I.S. BU. **49/2.**

Reforms Office.

—— The Burma Electoral Rules and Regulations. pp. 42. [*Rangoon*, 1923.] 8°. I.S. BU. **136/3.**

Rice Export-Trade Enquiry Committee.

—— Report of the Rice Export-Trade Enquiry Committee. pp. ii. ii. 115. *Rangoon*, 1937. 8°. I.S. BU. **117/16.**

Sanitary Department.

—— Reports on Plague Operations carried out in Shwebo, Sagaing and Lower Chindwin Districts during the early months of 1914. pp. 10. *Rangoon*, 1915. fol. I.S. BU. **13/5.**

State Colonies Department.

—— Report on the State Colonies Department, Burma, for the year ending 30th June 1939. pp. 28. *Rangoon*, 1940. 8°. **I.S.BU.114/24.**

Text-Book Committee.

—— List of Geographical Names of which the Burmese Orthography has been authorized by the Text-Book Committee. pp. 50. *Rangoon*, 1895. 8°. **14302.** i. **7.** (**1.**)

—— List of Terms used in Arithmetic, Algebra and Geometry of which the Burmese equivalents have been authorized by the Text-Book Committee. pp. 20. *Rangoon*, 1895. 8°. **14302.** i. **7.** (**2.**)

Vernacular and Vocational Education Reorganization Committee.

—— Report of the Vernacular and Vocational Education Reorganization Committee, 1936. pp. viii. ii. xxiii. 456. *Rangoon*, 1936. 8°. I.S. BU. **116/23.**

Veterinary Department.

—— *See* supra: Civil Veterinary Department.

Village Administration Committee.

—— Report of the Village Administration Committee, 1941. pp. 34. *Rangoon*, 1941. 8°. I.S. BU. **182/4.**

Women's Auxiliary Service (Burma).

—— The Wasbies. The story of the Women's Auxiliary Service (Burma). [With illustrations.] pp. 79. *War Facts Press: London*, [1947.] 8°. **9059.** c. **33.**

MISCELLANEOUS INSTITUTIONS AND SOCIETIES.

Burmah Baptist Missionary Convention.

—— Seventh (eighth) Annual Report of the Burmah Baptist Missionary Convention. Including reports of the stations and statistics for the year 1871-2 (1872-3), *etc.* 2 pt. *Rangoon*, 1873. 12°. **4192.** c. **1.**

Khālsā Diwan.

—— Farewell Address of Sir Reginald Craddock . . . to the Burma Sikhs . . . Comments by the executive committee of the Khalsa Diwan Burma. 14th April 1923. pp. 11. *Panthic Press: Amritsar*, 1923. 8°. **012301.** eee. **58.**

Union of Burma Buddha Sāsana Council.

—— Chattha Sangayana. The Sixth Great Council, a joint undertaking of all the Buddhist countries of the world, to be held in Burma, commencing . . . May 1954 . . . terminating . . . May 1956, *etc.* [A prospectus issued by the Buddha Sāsana Council.] pp. 11. [1953?] 8°. *See* Buddhists.—*Chattha Sangayana.* **4508.** cc. **1.**

—— The Light of the Dhamma. vol. 1. no. 2, *etc.* Jan. 1953, *etc.* *Rangoon*, 1953– . 4°. P.P. **636.** coh.

—— The Sangāyanā Monthly Bulletin. vol. 1. no. 2, *etc.* June 1953, *etc.* *Rangoon*, 1953– . fol. & 8°. P.P. **636.** coi.

—— Sangāyanā Souvenir. [With plates.] pp. 63. *Rangoon*, 1954. 8°. **4508.** dd. **7.**

APPENDIX.

—— An Account of the Burman Empire and the kingdom of Assam, *etc.* pp. 155. *Calcutta*, 1839. 8°. **1298.** i. **9.**

—— An Account of the Burman Empire . . . A Description of different tribes inhabiting in and around that dominion; and a Narrative of the late military and political operations in the Burmese Empire, with some account of the present condition of the country, its manners, customs and inhabitants. By Henry G. Bell. [With a map.] pp. 116. 87. *D'Rozario & Co.: Calcutta*, 1852. 8°. **10057.** aaa. **24.**
The " Narrative " only is by Henry G. Bell.

—— The All-English Aid to the " Tales and Legends of Ancient Burma " . . . Book of meanings, by an experienced English teacher. pp. iv. 50. *British Burma Press: Rangoon*, 1916. 8°. **12984.** ee. **47.**

—— Burma. [A periodical.] *See* BURMA.—*Ministry of Information.*

—— Бирма. Индонезия. 1955. 8°. *See* TOLOKONNIKOV (A.) W.P. **527/1.**

—— Burma. Political, Social and Economic Background . . . Prepared for the British Commonwealth Relations Conference 1945. pp. 5. 1945. fol. **8155.** h. **40.**
Reproduced from typewriting.

—— Burma and its People. pp. 32. *T. Woolmer: London*, [1888.] 8°. **10058.** a. **36.** (2.)

—— Burma and the Burmese. Compiled from Shway Yoe, Hunter . . . and others. [With illustrations.] pp. 50. *Christian Literature Society: Madras*, 1892. 4°. **010055.** g. **10.** (2.)

—— Burma, the Foremost Country. A timely discourse. To which is added, John Bull's neighbour squaring up; or, how the Frenchman sought to win an empire in the East . . . By the author of " Our Burmese Wars and Relations with Burma " [i.e. William F. B. Laurie], *etc.* pp. xxviii. 146. *W. H. Allen & Co.: London*, 1884. 8°. **10058.** bbb. **3.**

—— A Christian Hermit in Burma, and other tales. Illustrated. pp. 85. *S.P.G.: Westminster*, 1914. 8°. **04419.** de. **36.**

—— A Concise Geography of Burma for Middle Schools. [By Maung Kyī.] pp. 40. *Burma School Book Co.: Moulmein*, 1913. 8°. **10055.** b. **39.**

—— The Glass Palace Chronicle of the Kings of Burma. Translated by Pe Maung Tin and G. H. Luce. pp. xxiii. 179. *London*, 1923. 8°. [*Burma Research Society. Text Publication Fund.*] **14302.** bbb. **3.**

—— Looking at Burma. By Kathleen McKellen, G. W. Rowland [and others], *etc.* [With plates.] pp. 24. *Bible Churchmen's Missionary Society: London*, 1953. 8°. [*Look on the Field Series.*] **4768.a.97/1.**

—— The Recent Sufferings of the American Missionaries in the Burman Empire, during the late war: with their signal deliverance by being conveyed to the British Camp, *etc.* pp. 129. *Waugh & Innes: Edinburgh*, 1827. 12°. **1124.** a. **29.**

—— Return to Burma. Letters from missionaries and Burmese Christians tell of the sufferings and courage of the Church under Japanese invasion. pp. 32. *S. P. G. Westminster*, 1946. 8°. **9056.** aa. **55.**

—— Songs of Burma. By R. L. C. 1926. 8°. *See* C. R. L. **11654.** a. **61.**

—— The Voice of Young Burma. The reproduction of the articles published by the Publicity Bureau of the University Boycotters. pp. 212. *New Burma Press Rangoon*, [1922.] 8°. **8355.** aaa. **66.**

BURMA FOREST BULLETIN. *See* BURMA.—*Forest Department.*

BURMA GOVERNMENT MEDICAL SCHOOL. *See* RANGOON.

BURMA MEDICAL EXAMINATION BOARD. *See* BURMA.

BURMA MONTHLY WEATHER REVIEW. *See* BURMA.—*Meteorological Department.*

BURMA OFFICE. *See* ENGLAND.

BURMA PAMPHLETS.

—— Burma Pamphlets. *Longmans & Co.: London; Calcutta* printed, 1943– . 8°. **010058.m.29.**

BURMA POCKET ALMANAC AND DIRECTORY. *See* EPHEMERIDES.

BURMA RESEARCH SOCIETY. *See* RANGOON.

BURMA RICE.

—— Burma Rice. With 6 illustrations and 1 map. pp. 32. *Longmans & Co.: London; Calcutta* printed, 1944. 8°. [*Burma Pamphlets.* no. 4.] **010058.m.29/4.**

BURMA SOCIETY. *See* LONDON.—III.

BURMA STATE RAILWAY VOLUNTEER RIFLES. *See* INDIA.—*Army.*—*Infantry.*—*Rangoon and Irrawaddy State Railway Volunteer Rifles, etc.*

BURMA WEEKLY BULLETIN. *See* BURMA.—*Ministry of Information.*

BURMA (JOHN HARMON)

—— Spanish-Speaking Groups in the United States. pp. ix. 214. *Duke University Press:* [*Durham, N.C.*,] 1954. 8°. [*Duke University Press Sociological Series.*] W.P. **11900/9.**

BURMA (JOHN HARMON) and **DE POISTER** (W. MARSHON)

—— Workbook in Introductory Sociology. pp. vii. 196. *Prentice-Hall: New York*, 1955. 4°. **8295.** i. **3.**

BURMAH. *See* BURMA.

BURMAH BAPTIST MISSIONARY CONVENTION. *See* BURMA.

BURMAH BIBLE AND TRACT SOCIETY. *See* RANGOON.

BURMAH PRODUCE. Calculations for Burmah Produce. pp. 110. *Carter & Bromley: London*, 1858. 4°. **8247. b. 54.**

BURMAHS. *See* BURMESE.

BURMAN EMPIRE. *See* BURMA.

BURMAN SLAVE GIRL. *See* BURMESE SLAVE GIRL.

BURMAN, *Family of.* *See* BURMAN-BECKER (J. G.) Nachrichten von dem Geschlechte Burman. [With a genealogical table.] 1831. 8°. **1327. b. 21.**

BURMAN, *Family of, of Warwickshire.*

—— *See* BURMAN (John) *of Shirley, Warwickshire.* The Burman Chronicle, *etc.* 1940. 8°. **09915. r. 7.**

—— *See* BURMAN (*Sir* John B.) The Burman Family of Warwickshire. [With a genealogical table.] 1916. 8°. **9903. g. 40.**

BURMAN (ABRAHAMUS L.) Disputatio de apotheosi, *etc.* *Praes.* Johannes Columbus. pp. 101. *N. Wankijff: Holmiæ,* [1683.] 12°. **604. a. 24.**

BURMAN (ANATOLY) The Tragedy of Nijinsky. By A. Bourman . . . in collaboration with D. Lyman. [With plates, including portraits.] pp. 320. *R. Hale & Co.: London,* 1937. 8°. **10796. c. 7.**

BURMAN (BEN LUCIEN)

—— Blow for a Landing . . . Illustrations by Alice Caddy. pp. 335. *Lutterworth Press: London & Redhill,* 1948. 8°. **12729. ee. 4.**

—— The Four Lives of Mundy Tolliver . . . Line drawings by Alice Caddy. pp. 262. *Vallentine, Mitchell & Co.: London,* 1955. 8°. NNN. **7131.**

—— Miracle on the Congo. Report from the Free French front. [With maps.] pp. 153. *John Day Co.: New York,* [1942.] 8°. **9101. e. 31.**

—— [A reissue.] Miracle on the Congo, *etc.* *Macmillan & Co.: London,* 1943. 8°. **09231. h. 32.**

—— Rooster Crows for a Day . . . Sketches by Alice Caddy. pp. 301. *Lutterworth Press: London & Redhill,* 1948. 8°. **12730. a. 12.**

—— Steamboat round the Bend. pp. vii. 280. *T. Nelson & Sons: London,* 1936. 8°. [*Nelson Novels.*] **012604.p.1/20.**

—— Then there's Cripple Creek. pp. 285. *Thornton Butterworth: London,* 1930. 8°. A.N. **263.**

BURMAN (C. J.) *See* BURMAN (Johan J.) Anteckningar, *etc.* [Edited by C. J. Burman.] 1865. 8°. **9435. dd. 12.**

BURMAN (CASPAR) *See* PETRONIUS ARBITER (T.) Titi Petronii Arbitri Satyricon quæ supersunt . . . curante P. Burmanno, *etc.* [With a preface by C. Burman.] 1743. 4°. **833. k. 14.**

—— *See* UTRECHT. Utrechtsche jaarboeken van de vyftiende eeuw . . . T'zamen gestelt door Mr K. Burman. 1750. 8°. **10271. cc. 1.**

—— Hadrianus VI. sive Analecta historica de Hadriano sexto Trajectino, Papa Romano. Collegit, edidit, et notas adjecit C. Burmannus. [With plates, including a portrait.] pp. 541. *Trajecti ad Rhenum,* 1727. 4°. **484. c. 23.**

—— [Another copy.] **207. c. 13.**

BURMAN (CASPAR)

—— Trajectum eruditum, virorum doctrina inlustrium, qui in urbe Trajecto, et regione Trajectensi nati sunt, sive ibi habitarunt, vitas, fata, et scripta exhibens. pp. 469. *Trajecti ad Rhenum,* 1738. 4°. **119. b. 18.**

—— [A reissue.] *Trajecti ad Rhenum,* 1750. 4°. **819. g. 12*.**

BURMAN (CHARLES) *See* ASHMOLE (Elias) Memoirs of the Life of that learned Antiquary Elias Ashmole . . . Publish'd by C. Burman. 1717. 12°. **615. a. 11.**

—— *See* ASHMOLE (Elias) The Lives of those Eminent Antiquaries Elias Ashmole . . . and Mr. William Lilly . . . Containing . . . the life of Elias Ashmole . . . by way of diary. With several occasional letters, by [i.e. edited by] C. Burman. 1774. 8°. **275. h. 23.**

BURMAN (CHARLES CLARK) *See* ALNWICK. The Registers of the Parish Church of Alnwick. Baptisms (1645–69). Transcribed . . . by C. C. Burman. [1902, *etc.*] 8°. **9903. aa. 20.**

—— An Account of the Art of Typography, as practised in Alnwick from 1781 to 1815, with bibliographical notes of all the publications during that period. pp. 72. *Alnwick & County Gazette: Alnwick,* 1896. 8°. **11902. d. 46.**

BURMAN (CONNY) *See* BURMAN (Johan F. C.)

BURMAN (DEBAJYOTI) *See* DEVA-JYOTI VARMAN.

BURMAN (ELLEN ELIZABETH) Poetical Remains of Ellen Elizabeth Burman, with a brief memoir by the Rev. William Bruce. pp. 114. *Seeley, Jackson, & Halliday: London,* 1862. 8°. **11644. aaa. 38.**

BURMAN (ERIC) *Praes.* *See* LÖFGRÖN (A.) Dissertatio musica de basso fundamentali, *etc.* [1728.] 8°. **7898. e. 11.**

BURMAN (ERIK OLOF)

—— Hegels rättsfilosofi. Offentliga föreläsningar vid Upsala Universitet . . . Stenografiskt upptecknade och utgivna av Ernst Andersson Akmar. pp. 112. *Uppsala,* 1939. 8°. **8471. ff. 30.**

—— Om den nyare italienska filosofien. pp. 174. *Upsala,* 1879. 8°. [*Upsala Universitets årsskrift.* 1879.] Ac. **1075/6.**

—— Om Kants kunskapslära. pp. 92. *Upsala,* 1884. 8°. [*Upsala Universitets årsskrift.* 1884.] Ac. **1075/6.**

—— Om Schleiermachers kritik af Kants och Fichtes sedeläror. [With a summary in German.] pp. 283. ii. *Upsala,* 1894. 8°. [*Skrifter utgifna af Humanistiska Vetenskapssamfundet i Upsala.* bd. 3. no. 3.] Ac. **1078.**

—— Die Transcendentalphilosophie Fichte's und Schelling's dargestellt und erläutert. pp. 388. *Upsala,* 1891. 8°. [*Skrifter utgifna af Humanistiska Vetenskapssamfundet i Upsala.* bd. 1. no. 4.] Ac. **1078.**

—— Festskrift tillägnad E. O. Burman på hans 65-års dag, den 7 Oktober 1910. [With a portrait.] pp. 307. *Uppsala,* 1910. 8°. **8460. l. 6.**

BURMAN (FRANCIS) *See* BURMANNUS (Franciscus) *the Younger.*

BURMAN (FRANÇOIS) *See* BURMANNUS (Franciscus) *the Elder.*

BURMAN (FRANS) *See* BURMANNUS (Franciscus)

BURMAN (GERARDUS H.) Disputatio ethica inauguralis de principiis actionum humanarum, *etc.* *I. Alberti: Franekeræ*, 1647. 4°. **8409. d. 44. (2.)**

BURMAN (HERMAN JOSEPH) *See* IMPERATORI (Charles J.) and BURMAN (H. J.) Diseases of the Nose and Throat, *etc.* [1935.] 8°. **7611. ppp. 9.**

—— *See* IMPERATORI (Charles J.) and BURMAN (H. J.) Diseases of the Nose and Throat, *etc.* [1947.] 8°. **7612. d. 10.**

BURMAN (IVY D.) Bright Gleams through the Shadows. [Poems.] pp. 8. *A. H. Stockwell: London*, [1930.] 8°. **011644. g. 138.**

BURMAN (JAMES)

—— Statute Laws of the Isle of Man, promulgated since the year 1848: with an appendix containing the additional bye-laws for the regulation and government of towns; rules of the Court of Chancery respecting insolvent debtors, &c. By J. Burman. pp. vi. 278. 1853. 8°. *See* MAN, *Isle of.* [*Laws.*—I. *General Collections.*] C.S. A. **17/2. (2.)**

BURMAN (JAN) *See* BURMANNUS (Joannes)

BURMAN (JOHAN FREDRIK CONSTANTIN) *See* also CONNY, *pseud.* [i.e. J. F. C. Burman.]

—— Minnen . . . Med 80 illustrationer, *etc.* pp. 274. *Stockholm*, 1904. 8°. **10761. eee. 40.**

BURMAN (JOHAN JAKOB) Anteckningar, förda under tiden från år 1785 till år 1816 jemte relation om Savolaks-brigadens operationer under 1808 och 1809 års krig, *etc.* [Edited by C. J. Burman.] 2 afdl. *Stockholm*, 1865. 8°. **9435. dd. 12.**

—— Berättelse om femte brigadens af finska arméen krigs-rörelser och operationer i Savolaks, Karelen, Öster- och Westerbotten åren 1808 och 1809 . . . Redigerad och utgifven af R. A. Renvall. Med sex kartor. pp. iv. 112. *Helsingfors*, 1858. 8°. [*Societas Scientiarum Fennica. Bidrag till kännedom om Finlands natur och folk, etc.* Hft. 2.] Ac. **1094/4.**

BURMAN (JOHAN JAKOB) and **KNORRING** (ERIC OSCAR VON)

—— Ett hundra års minne. Minnesbilder. [With plates.] pp. 127. iv. *Stockholm*, 1909. 8°. **8821. c. 23.**

BURMAN (JOHANNES) *See* BURMANNUS (Joannes)

BURMAN (JOHN) *M.A.* *See* PLOT (Robert) The Natural History of Oxford-shire, *etc.* [The publisher's note to the reader signed: J. B., M.A., i.e. J. Burman.] 1705. fol. **434. h. 25.**

BURMAN (JOHN) *of Shirley, Warwickshire.*

—— The Burman Chronicle. The story of a Warwickshire family. [With plates, including a portrait.] pp. 99. *Cornish Bros.: Birmingham*, 1940. 8°. **09915. r. 7.**

—— Gleanings from Warwickshire History. [With genealogical tables.] pp. 118. *Cornish Bros.: Birmingham*, 1933. 8°. **010360. aa. 111.**

—— In the Forest of Arden. [With plates.] pp. 124. *Cornish Bros.: Birmingham*, 1948. 8°. **10359. aa. 93.**

BURMAN (JOHN) *of Shirley, Warwickshire.*

—— Old Warwickshire Families and Houses. pp. 117. *Cornish Bros.: Birmingham*, 1934. 8°. **9917. cc. 42.**

—— Shirley and its Church. [With illustrations.] pp. 27. *British Publishing Co.: Gloucester*, [1947.] 8°. **07822. aaa. 49.**

—— Solihull and its School. [With plates.] pp. 90. *Cornish Bros.: Birmingham*, 1939. 8°. **08366. p. 13.**

—— The Story of Tanworth-in-Arden, Warwickshire. [With plates, and a map.] pp. ii. 184. *Burman, Cooper & Co.: Birmingham*, 1930. 8°. **010360. dd. 41.**

—— Warwickshire People and Places. pp. 112. *Cornish Bros.: Birmingham*, 1936. 8°. **010352. aaa. 69.**

BURMAN (*Sir* JOHN BEDFORD) The Burman Family of Warwickshire. [With plates and a genealogical table.] pp. iv. 88. *Printed for private circulation: Birmingham*, 1916. 8°. **9903. g. 40.**

BURMAN (KASPER) *See* BURMAN (Caspar)

BURMAN (M. E.)

—— *See* BAKANOV (N. A.) Справочник по крахмало-поточному производству. Под редакцией . . . М. Е. Бурмана. [By M. E. Burman and others.] 1952. 8°. **08218. aa. 16.**

BURMAN (MAURICE)

—— Cymbal Set-Ups. [With illustrations.] pp. 23. *John E. Dallas & Sons: London*, [1951.] *obl.* 8°. **7900. m. 5.**

BURMAN (MICHAEL SAMUEL) and **SINBERG** (SAMUEL EDWARD)

—— Injury of the Xiphoid. pp. xii. 92. *Columbia University Press: New York*, 1952. 8°. **07482. bb. 45.**

BURMAN (NIKOLAAS LAURENS) *See* BURMANNUS (Nicolaus Laurentius)

BURMAN (PIETER) *See* BURMANNUS (Petrus)

BURMAN (REGINALD)

—— Baston Church Chest. [Description by R. Burman.] [1953.] 4°. *See* BASTON.—*Parish Church of Saint John the Baptist.* **3479. c. 22.**

BURMAN (T.)

—— 1939 Reflections. In verse. pp. 7. *A. H. Stockwell: London*, [1939.] 8°. **11656. i. 13.**

BURMAN (WILFRED ALFRED)

—— Church Work amongst the Aborigines in Christendom. Indian missions in the province of Rupert's Land. A survey of their condition and prospects. pp. 4. *Society for Promoting Christian Knowledge: London*, 1908. 8°. [*Pan Anglican Papers.* S.E. 4g.] **4108. cc. 35**

BURMAN (WINIFRED)

—— *See* WILLIAMSON (C.) *Teacher of Domestic Subjects*, and MULCASTER (E. C.) The New Housecraft Book for Girls . . . revised by W. Burman. 1950. 8°. **7949. eee. 36**

—— Housecraft. By W. Burman . . . M. Pleydell-Bouverie . . . and M. I. Urquhart. [With illustrations.] pp. v. 154 *Macmillan & Co.: London*, 1954. 8°. **7950. b. 3**

BURMAN (WINIFRED)

—— Ourselves and our Homes. [With plates.] pp. 250. *Blackie & Son: London & Glasgow*, 1951. 8°. 7949. l. 18.

—— Talk plus Chalk. A handbook for teachers. pp. 115. *H. V. Capsey: London*, 1943. 8°. 08311. a. 66.

BURMAN-BECKER (GOTTFRIED) *See* BECKETT (Francis) Altertavler i Danmark fra den senere Middelalder, *etc.* [Edited by G. Burman-Becker.] 1895. 4°, *etc.* 1758. a. 6 & d. 1.

BURMAN-BECKER (JOHANN GOTTFRIED) *See also* GOTTFRIEDSEN (Johann) *pseud.* [i.e. J. G. Burman-Becker.]

—— *See* MONRAD (J.) Etatsraad Johan Monrad's og Notarius publicus Rasmus Æreboe's Autobiographier, udgivne . . . ved Dr. J. G. Burman Becker. 1862. 8°. 10761. aa. 14.

—— Forsøg til en Beskrivelse af og Efterretninger om vævede Tapeter og andre mærkelige Vægdecorationer i Danmark . . . Anden forøgede Udgave. pp. 60. *Kjøbenhavn*, 1878. 8°. 7943. aa. 33.

—— Nachrichten von dem Geschlechte Becker. [With a genealogical table.] pp. 13. *Kopenhagen*, 1831. 8°. 1327. b. 24.

—— Nachrichten von dem Geschlechte Burman. [With a genealogical table.] pp. 20. *Kopenhagen*, 1831. 8° 1327. b. 21.

BURMANIA (REYNKEN VAN) *See* AERSSEN (F. van) *Heer van Sommeldijk.* Verbaal van de Ambassade van Aerssen, Joachimi en Burmania naar Engeland. 1625. 1867. 8°. [*Werken uitgegeven door het Historisch Genootschap gevestigd te Utrecht.* Nieuwe reeks. no. 10.] Ac. 7510/7.

BURMANIA (STEPHANUS DE) *pseud.* [i.e. GEORGE RATALLER DOUBLETH.] Mare belli Anglicani injustissimè Belgis illati Helena. pp. 42. [*The Hague?*] 1652. 4°. 1127. h. 28. (2.)

—— De Zee is de Helena waerom de Enghelse den onrechtveerdighen oorloch de Vereenichde Nederlantse Provintien aendoen . . . Int Nederduyts overgeset door A. V. [i.e. Adrien Vlacq.] pp. 24. *A. Vlack: 's Graven-Hage*, M.D.LII [1652]. 4°. 8122. ee. 4. (54.)

BURMANIA (WILLEM FREDERIK SCHRATENBACH A) Wil. Fr. Schratenbach a Burmania Tractatus juris publici federati Belgii de jure comitiorum Frisicorum. pp. 232. *Franequeræ*, 1751. 8°. 5695. a. 20.

BURMANN (CASPAR) *See* BURMAN.

BURMANN (FRANS) *See* BURMANNUS (Franciscus)

BURMANN (GOTTLOB WILHELM) Auswahl einiger vermischter Gedichte. pp. 198. *Berlin & Leipzig*, 1783. 8°. 11526. df. 30. (5.)

—— Einige Gedichte ohne den Buchstaben R. . . . Neueste . . . durchgesehne, und . . . vermehrte Ausgabe. pp. xiv. 64. *Berlin*, 1796. 16°. 11526. de. 28.

—— Etwas. Nebst einem Anhange. pp. 47. *Berlin*, [1773.] 8°. 11522. df. 4. (4.)

—— Fabeln und Erzählungen. pp. 96. *Frankfurt a. d. Oder*, 1771. 8°. 11526. df. 20.

—— Für Litteratur und Herz. Eine Wochenschrift. pp. 422. [1775.] 8°. *See* PERIODICAL PUBLICATIONS.—*Berlin.* P.P. 4606. k.

BURMANN (GOTTLOB WILHELM)

—— Lieder in drey Büchern. pp. 152. *Berlin*, 1774. 8°. 11525. de. 12.

—— Ziethen. Dem nachstrebendem Sohne gewidmet. *Berlin*, 1786. 4°. 11525. g. 3. (1.)

BURMANN (HANS)

—— *See* KAUFMANN (G.) and BURMANN (F.) Handbuch des gesamten Jugendrechts . . . Herausgegeben von G. Kauffmann . . . und H. Burmann. [1939, *etc.*] 8°. 5607. aa. 30.

BURMANN (J. G. CAROLUS) De poetis comoediae Atticae antiquae, qui commemorantur ab Aristophane. pp. 36. *Berolini*, 1868. 8°. 11705. g. 16. (6.)

—— [Another copy.] 11313. p. 7. (2.)

BURMANN (JOANNES) *See* BURMANNUS.

BURMANN (NICOLAUS LORENZ) *See* BURMANNUS (N. Laurentius)

BURMANN (PETER) *See* BURMANNUS (Petrus)

BURMANN (PIETER) *See* BURMANNUS (Petrus)

BURMANN (SIGFREDO) *See* MARTÍNEZ SIERRA (G.) Un Teatro de Arte in España, *etc.* [With designs by S. Burmann.] 1926. fol. L.R. 262. c. 5.

BURMANNUS (CASPARUS) *See* BURMAN (Caspar)

BURMANNUS (FRANCISCUS) *the Elder.* *See* DESCARTES (R.) Entretien avec Burman, *etc.* (Responsiones Renati Des Cartes ad quasdam difficultates ex meditationibus ejus, etc. ab ipso haustæ. Per Burmannum.) 1937. 8°. 8471. b. 13.

—— *See* GRAEVIUS (J. G.) Joannis Georgii Grævii Oratio funebris in obitum viri perquam reverendi et celeberrimi Francisci Burmanni, *etc.* 1679. 4°. 835. g. 17. (11.)

—— *Praes.* *See* LULLIUS (J.) Disputationum theologicarum de œconomia fœderum Dei, decima-octava, de lapsu Adami prima, *etc.* 1667. 4°. 4255. b. 50.

—— Francisci Burmanni . . . Belgica afflicta, sive Oratio de calamitatibus communis patriæ, præcipue vero Ultrajectinæ provinciæ, *etc.* pp. 52. *Apud C. J. Noenardum: Trajecti ad Rhenum*, 1673. 4°. 1055. g. 19. (7.)

—— *Praes.* Disputationum theologicarum analyticarum, de prophetiis V. T. prima(—vicesima sexta), *etc.* 26 pt. *M. a Dreunen: Ultrajecti*, 1676–79. 4°. 3165. ccc. 27.

—— Francisci Burmanni Exercitationum academicarum pars prior (posterior). [Edited by Adam van Halen.] 2 pt. *R. à Doesburgh: Roterodami*, 1688. 4°. 3705. b. 5.

—— Francisci Burmanni . . . Oratio de causis Belgicæ afflictæ, *etc.* pp. 44. *Apud C. J. Noenardum: Trajecti ad Rhenum*, 1674. 4°. 1055. g. 19. (6.)

—— Francisci Burmanni Oratio inauguralis de collegiis theologicis & philosophicis, *etc.* pp. 51. *Apud J. Elsevirium: Lugduni Batavorum*, 1661. 4°. 491. b. 16. (3.)

—— Francisci Burmanni . . . Oratio inauguralis de doctrina Christiana, *etc.* pp. 78. *M. à Dreunen: Ultrajecti*, 1662. 4°. 835. f. 21. (4.)

—— [Another copy.] 491. b. 30.

BURMANNUS (FRANCISCUS) *the Elder*.

—— Francisci Burmanni . . . Synopsis theologiæ, & specia-tim œconomiæ fœderum Dei, ab initio sæculorum usque ad consummationem eorum . . . (Consilium de studio theologico feliciter instituendo.) Editio ultima indicibus multò locupletioribus quàm antea exornata. [With a portrait.] 2 tom. *Apud J. Wolters: Amstelædami*, 1699. 4º. **1335. k. 7.**

—— Epicedia in obitum D. Francisci Burmanni. *C. Noenart: Ultrajecti*, 1679. 4º. **837. f. 32.**

BURMANNUS (FRANCISCUS) *the Younger*. *See* DRAKENBORCH (A.) Arnoldi Drakenborch Oratio funebris in obitum viri celeberrimi Francisci Burmanni, *etc.* 1719. 4º. **T. 947. (7.)**

—— —— 1722. 8º. [KAPP (*J. E.*) *Clarissimorum virorum orationes selectae, etc.* pt. 3.] **236. a. 6.**

—— *See* GOEREE (W.) D'Algemeene bouwkunde . . . In desen laatsten druk vermeerderd met een voorberigt tegens den Brief van . . . J. H. Koccejus, agter't Hoogste Goed der Spinosisten, door der Hr. F. Burmannus uitgegeven. 1705. 8º. **7814. b. 19.**

—— Burmannorum pietas, gratissimæ beati parentis memoriæ communi nomine exhibita . . . Adjiciuntur mutuæ Cl. Limburgii & F. Burmanni epistolæ. 2 pt. *Trajecti ad Rhenum*, 1700. 8º. **4885. a. 7.**

—— Francisci Burmanni . . . Itineris Anglicani acta diurna, quæ nunc primum edidit, præfatus est notisque illustravit Abrahamus Capadose. pp. xx. 79. *Amstelædami*, 1828. 8º. **1430. d. 3.**

—— Visit to Cambridge . . . 1702. [An extract translated from the Itineris anglicani acta diurna.] *See* MAYOR (John E. B.) Cambridge under Queen Anne, *etc.* 1911. 8º. **08365. e. 19.**

—— Oratio de persecutione Diocletianea, *etc.* *See* KAPP (J. E.) Clarissimorum virorum orationes selectae, *etc.* pt. 1. 1722. 8º. **236. a. 5.**

—— Theologus: sive, De iis quae ad verum et consummatum theologum requiruntur, oratio inauguralis, *etc.* pp. 75. *Trajecti ad Rhenum*, 1715. 4º. **3559. c. 8.**

BURMANNUS (FRANCISCUS PETRUS) Carmina juvenilia. *See* HOEUFFT (J. H.) Jacobi Henrici Hoeufft et Francisci Petri Burmanni Carmina juvenilia. 1778. 8º. **11408. d. 13.**

BURMANNUS (JACOBUS FABRICIUS) Carmen seculare, ad decorandum centesimum Academiae Ultrajectinae natalem. [*Utrecht*, 1736.] 4º. **T. 717. (9.)**

BURMANNUS (JOANNES) *See* PLUMIER (C.) Plantarum Americanarum fasciculus primus(—decimus) . . . Primum edidit . . . descriptionibus, & observationibus . . . illustravit J. Burmannus. 1755, *etc.* fol. **447. k. 11.**

—— *See* WEINMANN (J. W.) Duidelyke vertoning eeniger duizend . . . bomen, stammen, kruiden . . . nevens een register, *etc.* (Nu in het Nederduitsch door een vornaam Kender . . . vertaalt, en opgeheldert door J. Burmannus.) 1736, *etc.* fol. **725. l. 16–23.**

—— Dissertatio medica inauguralis de χυλοποιησι, sive alimentorum in chylum mutatione, *etc.* pp. 39. *Lugduni Batavorum*, 1728. 4º. **1185. i. 4. (3.)**

—— Flora Malabarica, sive Index in omnes tomos horti Malabarici [i.e. the Hortus Indicus Malabaricus of H. A. van Rheede tot Draakestein], *etc.* (Index alter in omnes tomos Herbarii Amboinensis Cl. G. E. Rumphii, *etc.*) 2 pt. *Amstelædami*, 1769. fol. **449. l. 13. (2.)**

BURMANNUS (JOANNES)

—— Joannis Burmanni . . . Rariorum Africanarum plantarum, ad vivum delineatarum, iconibus ac descriptionibus illustratarum decas prima(—decima). [With a portrait.] pp. viii. 268. pl. c. *Amstelædami*, 1738, 39. 4º. **35. f. 18.**

—— [Another copy.] **447. e. 4.**
Imperfect; wanting the titlepages of decades 7 *and* 8.

—— Thesaurus Zeylanicus, exhibens plantas in insula Zeylana nascentes, *etc.* (Catalogi duo plantarum Africanarum, *etc.*) [With a portrait.] pp. 235. 33. pl. 110. MS. NOTES. *Amstelædami*, 1737. 4º. **447. e. 3.**

—— [Another copy.] **35. e. 14.**

—— Wachendorfia. [With a plate.] pp. 4. *Amstelædami*, 1757. fol. **450. l. 5. (2.)**

—— [Another edition.] pp. xii. pl. III. *Geræ*, 1771. 4º. **444. e. 2.**

BURMANNUS (NICOLAUS LAURENTIUS) Nicolai Laurentii Burmanni Flora Indica: cui accedit series zoophytorum Indicorum, nec non prodromus florae Capensis. pp. 241. 28. pl. 67. *Lugduni Batavorum, Amstelædami*, 1768. 4º. **448. f. 10.**

—— [Another copy.] **36. d. 21.**

—— Specimen botanicum de geraniis, *etc.* (De medulla radicis ad florem pertingente disserit C. C. Schmidel.) pp. 52. pl. II. *Lugduni Batavorum*, 1759. 4º. **B. 7. (2.)**

BURMANNUS (PETRUS) *the Elder*. *See* also NORICUS (Favoritus) *pseud.* [i.e. P. Burmannus.]

—— [For dissertations at which P. Burmannus acted as praeses:]
See ALPHEN (G. van) DRAKENBORCH (A.)
DOUGLASS (William) *M.D.* NEVETT (T.)

—— *See* BUCHANAN (George) *the Humanist*. [*Works*.] Georgii Buchanani . . . opera omnia . . . Cum . . . præfatione P. Burmanni, *etc.* 1725. 4º. **632. k. 3, 4.**

—— *See* CALPURNIUS FLACCUS. Calpurnii Flacci excerptae decem rhethorum minorum . . . Curante P. Burmanno. 1825. 8º. [*M. Fab. Quintiliani opera*. vol. 6.] **1087. k. 6.**

—— *See* CLAUDIANUS (C.) Claudii Claudiani opera, quæ exstant, omnia . . . Cum notis . . . ineditis P. Burmanni, *etc.* [Edited by P. Burmannus the younger from materials left by P. Burmannus the elder.] 1760. 4º. **833. i. 3.**

—— *See* CUNAEUS (P.) Petri Cunæi . . . et doctorum virorum ad eumdem epistolæ . . . Nunc primum editæ curâ P. Burmanni. 1725. 8º. **1084. l. 15.**

—— *See* FRONTINUS (S. J.) Sexti Julii Frontini . . . quae exstant, *etc.* MS. NOTES [by P. Burmannus]. 1661. 8º. **C. 45. c. 27.**

—— *See* GRAEVIUS (J. G.) Thesaurus antiquitatum et historiarum Italiae, Neapolis, Siciliae . . . Cum praefationibus P. Burmanni, *etc.* 1704, *etc.* fol. **L.R.302.a.2.**

—— *See* GRAEVIUS (J. G.) Catalogus omnium librorum qui in thesauro antiquitatum & historiarum Italiæ . . . J. G. Grævii ex consilio & cum præfationibus P. Burmanni . . . reperiuntur. 1725. 12º. **810. g. 1. (2.)**

BURMANNUS (PETRUS) *the Elder.*

—— *See* GRATIUS, *Faliscus.* Gratii Falisci Cynegeticon et M. Aurelii Olympii Nemesiani Cynegeticon . . . Cum notis selectis Titii, Barthii . . . et P. Burmanni integris. 1775. 8°. **988**. f. **14**.

—— —— 1788. 8°. [*M. Manilii Astronomicôn libri v, etc.*] **1001**. b. **12**.

—— *See* GRUTERUS (J.) Inscriptiones antiquae totius orbis Romani, *etc.* [With a preface by P. Burmannus.] 1707. fol. **1705**. b. **8**.

—— *See* GUDIUS (M.) Marquardi Gudii et doctorum virorum ad eum epistolae . . . Curante P. Burmanno. 1697. 4°. **636**. k. **14**.

—— *See* HORATIUS FLACCUS (Q.) [*Works.—Latin.*] Q. Horatius Flaccus. Accedunt J. Rutgersii lectiones Venusinæ. [Edited by P. Burmannus.] 1699. 12°. **11352.a.40.**

—— —— 1713. 12°. **166**. k. **3**.

—— *See* LUCANUS (M. A.) [*Pharsalia.—Latin.*] M. Annæi Lucani Pharsalia, cum commentario P. Burmanni. 1740. 4°. **11385**. k. **29**.

—— *See* MELA (P.) Pomponii Melæ de situ orbis libri tres . . . Cum . . . notis . . . H. Barbari . . . P. Burmanni, *etc.* 1807, *etc.* 8°. **569**. d. **9–15**.

—— *See* OVIDIUS NASO (P.) [*Works.—Latin.*] P. Ovidii Nasonis operum tom. I(–III). P. Burmannus ad fidem veterum exemplarium castigavit. 1713. 12°. **1001**. a. **17**.

—— —— 1727. 4°. **681**. d. **6**.

—— —— 1820, *etc.* 8°. **11305**. h. **9**.

—— —— 1825, *etc.* 8°. **999**. l. **3**.

—— *See* OVIDIUS NASO (P.) [*Two or more Works.—Latin.*] Publii Ovidii Nasonis Tristium libri v, Ex Ponto libri IIII. Ex recensione P. Burmanni, *etc.* 1772. 8°. **1001**. h. **23**.

—— *See* OVIDIUS NASO (P.) [*Epistolae Heroïdum.—Latin.*] Publii Ovidii Nasonis Heroides, ex editione P. Burmanni. 1789. 8°. **76**. a. **23**.

—— —— 1829, *etc.* 8°. **11385**. d. **13**.

—— *See* PERIODICAL PUBLICATIONS.—*London.* Miscellaneæ observationes criticæ in auctores veteres et recentiores, *etc.* [Edited by P. Burmannus and J. P. d'Orville.] 1732, *etc.* 8°. P.P. **4945**.

—— *See* PERSIUS FLACCUS (A.) [*Latin.*] Auli Persii Flacci Satirarum liber, *etc.* MS. NOTES [by P. Burmannus, in the autograph of T. Combe]. 1647. 8°. **1349**. a. **24**.

—— *See* PETRONIUS ARBITER (T.) [*Latin.*] Titi Petronii Arbitri Satyricon quæ supersunt . . . Curante P. Burmanno. 1709. 4°. **834**. k. **6**.

—— —— 1743. 4°. **833**. k. **14**.

—— *See* PETRONIUS ARBITER (T.) [*Appendix.*] Chrestomathia Petronio-Burmanniana sive cornu-copiæ observationum . . . quas P. Burmannus congessit in Petronium Arbitrum, *etc.* [An attack on P. Burmannus's edition of Petronius attributed to Verburgius and T. Hemsterhuys.] 1734. 4°. **1079**. m. **4**.

BURMANNUS (PETRUS) *the Elder.*

—— *See* PHAEDRUS. [*Latin.*] Phædri . . . Fabularum Æsopiarum libri v. . . . Curante P. Burmanno. 1698. 8°. **999**. ee. **2**.

—— —— 1708. 8°. **637**. i. **15**.

—— —— 1718. 8°. **637**. i. **16**.

—— —— 1719. 12°. **637**. b. **22**.

—— —— 1727. 4°. **638**. k. **3**.

—— —— 1728. 8°. C. **72**. c. **1**.

—— —— 1745. 8°. **166**. n. **7**.

—— —— 1751. 8°. **166**. k. **34**.

—— —— 1767. 12°. **1163**. a. **13**.

—— —— 1779, *etc.* 8°. **51**. k. **11**.

—— *See* PHILELEUTHERUS, *Lipsiensis, pseud.* Emendationes in Menandri et Philemonis reliquias ex nupera editione J. Clerici, *etc.* [With a preface by P. Burmannus.] 1710. 8°. **998**. i. **17**.

—— *See* PRISCIANUS. Prisciani Periegesis . . . cui accedunt ejusdem Carmen de ponderibus et mensuris et Epitome phænomenon . . . Recensuit et notis integris . . . J. Caesarii . . . P. Burmanni in Carmen de pond. et mensuris . . . illustravit J. C. W. 1825. 8°. [*Bibliotheca classica Latina.* vol. 137.] **11305**. m. **5**.

—— *See* QUINTILIANUS (M. F.) M. Fabii Quinctiliani de institutione oratoria libri duodecim . . . emendati per P. Burmannum, *etc.* (M. F. Quinctiliani ut ferunt Declamationes . . . et Calpurnii Flacci Declamationes . . . curante P. Burmanno.) 1720. 4°. **836**. k. **6–8**.

—— *See* QUINTILIANUS (M. F.) M. Fabii Quinctiliani de institutione oratoria libri duodecim, summa cura recogniti & emendati per P. Burmannum, *etc.* 1736. 8°. **236**. h. **9, 10**.

—— *See* RUDDIMAN (Thomas) Audi alteram partem . . . With an appendix containing some critical remarks on Mr. Burman's philological notes in his edition of Buchanan's Works. 1756. 8°. **600**. g. **25**. (**2**.)

—— *See* SCHACHT (H. O.) Oratio funebris in obitum viri doctissimi et celeberrimi Petri Burmanni, *etc.* 1741. 4°. T. **656**. (**1**.)

—— —— 1742. 8°. **11824**. aaa. **25**. (**2**.)

—— *See* SUETONIUS TRANQUILLUS (C.) [*Works.*] C. Suetonius Tranquillus . . . Curante P. Burmanno, *etc.* 1736. 4°. **588**. h. **3**.

—— *See* THEOCRITUS. [*Greek and Latin.*] Θεοκριτου τα εὑρισκομενα, *etc.* MS. NOTES [by P. Burmannus]. 1699. 8°. C. **45**. c. **19**.

—— *See* TROGUS POMPEIUS. [*Latin.*] Justini Historiae Philippicae . . . Variantes lectiones adjecit P. Burmannus. 1722. 12°. **9039**. a. **12**.

—— —— 1757. 8°. **9040**. c. **23**.

—— —— 1827, *etc.* 8°. **1305**. c. **5**.

—— *See* VALERIUS FLACCUS (C.) C. Valerii Flacci . . Argonautica, *etc.* [Edited by P. Burmannus.] 1702. 12°. **166**. k. **30**

—— —— 1724. 4°. **833**. i. **12**.

—— —— 1781. 8°. **166**. f. **23, 24**.

—— *See* VALOIS (H. de) *Seigneur d'Orcé.* Henrici Valesii . . . Emendationum libri quinque et de critica libri duo. . . . Edente P. Burmanno . . . qui praefationem, notas, & indices adjecit. 1740. 4°. **631. k. 14.**

—— *See* VELLEIUS PATERCULUS (M.) C. Velleii Paterculi quæ supersunt ex Historiæ Romanæ voluminibus duobus . . . Curante P. Burmanno. 1719. 8°. **196. a. 2.**

—— —— 1744. 8°. **58. l. 1.**

—— —— 1752. 8°. **803. b. 13.**

—— *See* VIRGILIUS MARO (P.) [*Works.*] P. Virgilii Maronis opera . . . Animadversiones . . . addidit P. Burmannus, *etc.* 1746. 4°. **11355. h. 2.**

—— —— 1778. fol. **72. l. 12.**

—— *See* VIRGILIUS MARO (P.) [*Minor Poems.—Culex.*] P. Virgilii Maronis Culex . . . commentariis integris J. Scaligeri, Burmanni, *etc.* 1817. 12°. **11355. a. 31.**

—— Petri Burmanni Orationes antea sparsim editae et ineditis auctae. Adcedit carminum adpendix. [Edited by Nicolaus Bondt.] pp. 459. *Hagæ Comitis,* 1759. 4°. **835. k. 18.**

—— Petri Burmanni Vectigalia populi Romani, et *Ζευς Καταιβατης* sive Jupiter Fulgerator, in Cyrrhestarum nummis, curis secundis illustrata. pp. 346. *Leidae,* 1734. 4°. **143.d.13.**

—— Petri Burmanni Epistolae ad Ant. Magliabechium. *See* TARGIONI TOZZETTI (G.) Clarorum Belgarum ad Ant. Magliabechium . . . epistolae, *etc.* tom. 2. 1745. 8°. **1082. f. 1.**

—— Petri Burmanni Antiquitatum Romanarum brevis descriptio. Passim emendavit ac supplevit et notulas subjecit Fridericus Volgangus Reizius. pp. 82. *Lipsiae,* 1792. 8°. **575. c. 33.**

—— Petri Burmanni Batesteinum, in concione Academica celebratum. pp. 37. *Leidæ,* [1738.] 4°. **T. 1055. (12.)**

—— Petri Burmanni Carmen elegiacum, auctoribus . . . Academiæ Batavæ . . . curatoribus et urbis consulibus, in celeberrima panegyri, quæ ad decorandum Academiæ centesimum et quinquagesimum natalem . . . convenerat, dictum. [*Leyden,*] 1725. 4°. **T. 656. (4.)**

—— [Another edition.] [*Leyden,*] 1725. fol. **643. m. 13. (22.)**

—— *See* TREYTELIUS (J. N.) Celeusma Nehalenniæ Zelandicæ, ad abstergendam inhumanitatis labem, nomini Zelandico aspersam a . . . P. Burmanno . . . in Carmine seculari, ad decorandum III. Acad. Lugd. Bat. natalem publice recitato. 1725. 4°. **11408. f. 43.**

—— Catalogus rarissimorum & præstantissimorum librorum, qui in thesauris romano, græco, italico, & siculo [of J. G. Graevius] continentur, *etc.* pp. 88. *Leidae,* 1725. 8°. **810. g. 1. (3.)**

—— [Another copy.] **274. e. 35.**

—— Petri Burmanni de vectigalibus populi romani dissertatio. pp. 259. *Trajecti ad Rhenum,* 1714. 8°. **590. a. 25.**

—— [Another copy.] **590. a. 26.**

—— [Another edition.] *See* POLENI (G.) *Marquis.* Utriusque thesauri . . . supplementa, *etc.* vol. 1. 1737. fol. **1489.1.7.**

—— Dialogus I. inter Spudaeum et Gorallum. [By P. Burmannus.] pp. 15. [1705?] 4°. *See* SPUDAEUS. **715. d. 29.**

—— Elegia in acerbum funus . . . Ioannis de Weede, *etc.* pp. 8. [*Utrecht,* 1710?] 4°. **T. 947. (9.)**

—— Petri Burmanni Epistola ad Claudium Capperonnerium . . . de nova ejus M. Fabii Quinctiliani de institutione oratoria editione. pp. 102. *Leidæ,* 1726. 4°. **836. k. 15.**

—— *See* OGIER, *the Dane, pseud.* Holger Danske's Brev til Buurman. [Relative to a passage in his " Epistola ad Capperonnerium."] [1727?] 8°. **11565. c. 47. (2.)**

—— Le Gazettier menteur ou Mr. Le Clerc convaincu de mensonge de & [*sic*] calomnie. [In reply to J. Le Clerc's attack on his edition of Petronius Arbiter.] pp. 246. *Utrecht,* 1710. 12°. **1088. b. 11. (1.)**

—— Peter Burmann's macaronisches Gedicht über das Tabackrauchen . . . Herausgegeben von F. W. Genthe. pp. 7. *Eisleben,* 1846. 12°. **11408. c. 82. (3.)**

—— Petri Burmanni Oratio de auspicatissima terra marique anni CIↃ IↃCCVI. Batavorum & foederatorum militia, & praeclaris a communi hoste reportatis victoriis, *etc.* pp. 45. *Trajecti ad Rhenum,* 1706. fol. **835. l. 7. (10.)**

—— [Another copy.] **T. 656. (2.)**

—— [Another edition.] *See* KAPP (J. E.) Clarissimorum virorum orationes selectae, *etc.* pt. 2. 1722. 8°. **236. a. 6**

—— Petri Burmanni Oratio de eloquentia & poëtice, *etc.* pp. 48. *F. Halma: Trajecti ad Rhenum,* 1696. 4°. **836. f. 21. (10.)**

—— [Another copy.] **835. f. 21. (3.)**

—— Petri Burmanni Oratio de publici humanioris disciplinae professoris proprio officio et munere, *etc.* pp. 80. *Lugduni Batavorum,* 1715. 4°. **T. 717. (1.)**

—— [Another copy.] **731. e. 5. (27.)**

—— [Another copy.] **835. f. 21. (8.)**

—— [Another copy.] **T. 656. (9.)**
Imperfect; wanting the titlepage.

—— Petri Burmanni Oratio funebris in obitum viri celeberrimi Hermanni von Halen, *etc.* pp. 37. *Trajecti ad Rhenum,* [1701.] 4°. **T. 656. (7.)**

—— [Another copy.] **835. g. 17. (14.)**

—— [Another edition.] *See* KAPP (J. E.) Clarissimorum virorum orationes selectae, *etc.* pt. 3. 1722. 8°. **236. a. 6**

—— Petri Burmanni Oratio funebris in obitum viri clarissimi Joannis Georgii Græyii, *etc.* (Amicorum carmina in obitum . . . J. G. Grævii.) pp. 57. *Trajecti ad Rhenum* 1703. 4°. **1415. h. 6**

—— [Another copy.] **835. f. 21. (5.)**

—— [Another copy.] **835. g. 17. (16.)**

—— [Another edition.] *See* GRAEVIUS (J. G.) Jo. Georgii Grævii Præfationes et epistolæ CXX., *etc.* 1707. 8°. **1084. i. 1**

—— [Another edition.] *See* GRAEVIUS (J. G.) Jo. Georgii Grævii Præfationes et epistolæ CXX., *etc.* 1713. 8°. **1084. i. 20**

BURMANNUS (PETRUS) *the Elder.*

—— [Another edition.] *See* GRAEVIUS (J. G.) Johannis Georgii Græevii Orationes quas Ultrajecti habuit. 1717. 8°. **1090. l. 11.**

—— [Another edition.] *See* FROTSCHER (C. H.) Eloquentium virorum narrationes, *etc.* vol. 1. 1826. 8°. **10707. ccc. 25.**

—— Petri Burmanni Oratio in humanitatis studia, *etc.* pp. 61. *Lugduni Batavorum*, 1720. 4°. T. **656. (11.)**

—— [Another copy.] T. **717. (2.)**

—— [Another copy.] **835. f. 21. (6.)**

—— [Another edition.] *See* KAPP (J. E.) Clarissimorum virorum orationes selectæ, *etc.* 1722. 8°. **236. a. 5.**

—— An Oration . . . against the Studies of Humanity. Shewing, that the learned languages . . . are not only useless, but also dangerous to the studies of law, physick, philosophy, and above all of divinity . . . Translated into English, and the original annext. pp. 91. *J. W.: London*, 1721. 12°. **8307. aa. 29.**

—— The second edition. pp. 91. *J. W.: London*, 1722. 8°. **1090. c. 6. (2.)**

—— Pieter Burmans Redenvoering over de beschaafde letteroeffening . . . Vertaald door Jan van Leene. pp. 44. *Utrecht*, 1720. 4°. **3908. e. 10. (59.)**

—— Petri Burmanni Oratio in obitum viri illustrissimi Everardi de Weede, *etc.* pp. 40. *Trajecti ad Rhenum*, 1702. 4°. **835. g. 17. (15.)**

—— [Another copy.] **835. f. 20. (11.)**

—— [Another edition.] *See* KAPP (J. E.) Clarissimorum virorum orationes selectae, *etc.* pt. 3. 1722. 8°. **236. a. 6.**

—— Petri Burmanni Oratio in obitum viri optimi . . . Jani Broukhusii, *etc.* pp. 28. *Lugduni Batavorum*, [1708.] 4°. T. **656. (8.)**

—— [Another copy.] **835. h. 19. (4.)**

—— Petri Burmanni Oratio pro comœdia, *etc.* pp. 36. *Trajecti ad Rhenum*, 1711. 4°. **731. f. 5. (19.)**

—— [Another copy.] T. **656. (10.)**

—— Petri Burmanni Oratio pro pigritia, *etc.* pp. 23. [*Utrecht?*] 1702. 4°. **8406. f. 42.**

—— [Another edition.] pp. 23. [*Utrecht?*] 1702. 4°. **8406. f. 43.**

—— Petri Burmanni Poëmatum libri quatuor. Nunc primum in lucem editi. Curante Petro Burmanno juniore. pp. 427. *Amstelædami*, 1746. 4°. **837. i. 13.**

—— Poetae Latini minores, sive Gratii Falisci Cynegeticon, M. Aurelii Olympii Nemesiani Cynegeticon, et ejusdem Eclogae IV., T. Calpurnii Siculi Eclogae VII., Claudii Rutilii Numatiani Iter, Q. Serenus Samonicus de medicina, Vindicianus sive Marcellus de medicina, Q. Rhemnius Fannius Palaemon de ponderibus & mensuris, et Sulpiciae Satyra. Cum integris doctorum virorum notis, & quorumdam excerptis, curante P. Burmanno, qui & suas adjecit adnotationes. 2 tom. *Leidae*, 1731. 4°. **655. b. 18, 19.**
With an additional titlepage, engraved.

—— [Another copy.] **54. f. 11.**

—— [Another copy.] **L.P.** G. **10025, 26.**

BURMANNUS (PETRUS) *the Elder.*

—— Poetae Latini minores, ex editione P. Burmanni fideliter expressi. [The texts only, without the critical apparatus.] pp. 151. *In aedibus academicis excudebant R. & A. Foulis: Glasguae*, 1752. 8°. **166. c. 16.**

—— [Another copy.] G. **9835.**

—— Petri Burmanni Pro literatoribus et grammaticis oratio, *etc.* pp. 75. *Leidae*, [1732.] 4°. T. **656. (6.)**

—— [Another copy.] **835. f. 21. (9.)**

—— Petri Burmanni Somnium, sive iter in Arcadiam novam, *etc.* [In verse.] [*Utrecht*, 1710.] 4°. **731. f. 5. (18.)**

—— [Another copy.] T. **656. (5.)**

—— [Another copy.] T. **717. (3.)**

—— [Another edition.] *Berolini*, 1740. 8°. **11824. aaa. 32. (1.)**

—— Sylloges epistolarum a viris illustribus scriptarum tomi quinque, collecti et digesti per P. Burmannum. 5 tom. *Leidae*, 1727. 4°. **636.k.16–20.**

—— [Another copy.] **87. h. 9–13.**

—— Petri Burmanni Ζευς καταιβατης, sive Jupiter Fulgerator in Cyrrhestarum nummis, *etc.* pp. 122. *Trajecti Batavorum*, 1700. 4°. **7757. a. 12. (3.)**

—— Bibliotheca Burmanniana, sive Catalogus librorum instructissimæ bibliothecæ viri summi D. Petri Burmanni . . . Quorum publica fiet auctio . . . die lunæ 26. Februarii . . . 1742. pp. 344. FEW MS. NOTES OF PRICES. *Lugduni in Batavis*, 1742. 8°. **820. d. 2.**
Interleaved.

—— Burmanniana, sive Calumniarum Petri Burmanni in collegas & populares specimen. pp. 20. *Amstelodami*, 1710. 12°. **1088. b. 11. (2.)**

BURMANNUS (PETRUS) *the Younger.* *See* AGRICOLA (A.) Sapientia hyperborealis . . . Cum notis anonymi [i.e. P. Burmannus and C. A. Duker], *etc.* 1733. 8°. **1088. l. 6. (2.)**

—— *See* ARISTOPHANES. [*Works.—Greek and Latin.*] Aristophanis Comœdiæ undecim. Curante P. Burmanno, *etc.* 1760. 4°. **653. c. 4, 5.**

—— *See* BURMANNUS (Petrus) *the Elder.* Petri Burmanni Poëmatum libri quatuor. Nunc primum in lucem editi. Curante P. Burmanno juniore. 1746. 4°. **837. i. 13.**

—— *See* CICERO (M. T.) [*Doubtful and Supposititious Works.—Rhetorica ad C. Herennium.*] Ciceronis, vel incerti auctoris, Rhetoricorum ad Herennium libri quatuor, et de inventione libri duo . . . Curante P. Burmanno qui . . . de auctore Rhetoricorum ad Herennium disseruit. 1761. 8°. **57. h. 7.**

—— *See* CLAUDIANUS (C.) Claudii Claudiani opera quæ exstant, omnia . . . Subjungitur Lactantii Elegia de Phœnice . . . cum . . . adnotationibus P. Burmanni secundi. [Edited by P. Burmannus the younger from materials left by P. Burmannus the elder.] 1760. 4°. **833. i. 3.**

—— —— 1819. 12°. **832. a. 13.**

—— —— 1821. 8°. **11388. dd. 2.**

—— *See* EUGENIUS III., *Saint, Bishop of Toledo.* Beati Eugenii . . . opuscula, *etc.* MS. NOTES [by P. Burmannus]. 1619. 8°. **11409. c. 19.**

—— *See* HEEMSKERK (Willem van) *Burgomaster of Amsterdam.* Zamenspraak in het ryk der dooden, tusschen . . . Willem Heemskerk . . . en Jonkheer Johan Derk Baron van der Capellen tot de Poll, met Johan van Oldenbarnevelt . . . en P. Burmannus. [1787.] 8°. **934. e. 16. (6.)**

—— *See* HEINSIUS (N.) Nicolai Heinsii . . . Adversariorum libri IV . . . Curante P. Burmanno . . . qui præfationem & commentarium de vita N. Heinsii adjecit. 1742. 4°. **631. k. 15.**

—— *See* KLOTZ (C. A.) Christiani Adolphi Klotzii Anti Burmannus, *etc.* 1761. 4°. **836. i. 6. (1.)**

—— *See* KLOTZ (C. A.) Funus Petri Burmanni Secundi, *etc.* 1762. 4°. **1476. d. 4.**

—— *See* LOTICHIUS (P.) *Secundus.* Petri Lotichii . . . Poëmata omnia . . . Recensuit, notis & praefatione instruxit P. Burmannus. 1754. 4°. **11408. g. 22.**

—— —— 1773. 8°. **11408. aaa. 59. (1.)**

—— —— [1842.] 16°. **11409. aa. 20.**

—— *See* LUCANUS (M. A.) [*Pharsalia.—Latin.*] M. Annaei Lucani Pharsalia, *etc.* COPIOUS MS. NOTES [a few being by P. Burmannus]. 1740. 4°. **11385. k. 29.**

—— *See* ORVILLE (J. P. d') Jacobi Philippi D'Orville Sicula . . . Edidit et commentarium ad numismata sicula . . . adjecit P. Burmannus. 1764. fol. **181. i. 11.**

—— *See* PROPERTIUS (S.) Sex. Aurelii Propertii Elegiarum libri IV. Cum commentario perpetuo P. Burmanni, *etc.* 1780. 4°. **655. b. 17.**

—— *See* SALOMON III. [Ramschwag], *Bishop of Constance.* [fol. 2 *recto*:] Epistola prelibatica in sequentis operis commendationem, *etc. Begin.* [*ibid.* col. 2:] Salemonis ecclesie Constantiensis epi glosse, &c. FEW MS. NOTES [by P. Burmannus]. [1475?] fol. **167. g. 3, 4.**

—— *See* SECUNDUS (J.) Ioannis Nicolaii Secundi . . . opera omnia, emendatius et cum notis adhuc ineditis P. Burmanni, *etc.* 1821. 8°. **1461. d. 25.**

—— *See* VIRGILIUS MARO (P.) [*Works.—Latin.*] P. Virgilii Maronis opera . . . Editionis curam suscepit P. Burmannus junior, *etc.* 1746. 4°. **11355. h. 2.**

—— —— 1774. 8°. **11355. bbb. 3.**

—— *See* WERNICKE (J. E.) Priapeia . . . Recensuit notasque J. Scaligeri . . . P. Burmanni . . . addidit J. Æ. Wernicke. 1853. 8°. **11375. c. 43.**

—— *See* WILLIAM IV., *Prince of Orange, Stadholder of the Netherlands.* Zamenspraken gehouden in het ryk der dooden tusschen Willem Carel Hendrik Friso . . . Mr Jan Hop . . . en Mr Pieter Burman. [1782.] 8°. **934. e. 16. (2.)**

—— Analectorum Belgicorum pars prima (secunda). [Edited by P. Burmannus.] 2 vol. *Lugduni Batavorum,* 1772. 8°. **1055. g. 9.**

—— Anthologia veterum Latinorum epigrammatum et poëmatum. Sive Catalecta poëtarum Latinorum . . . Primum à Josepho Scaligero, Petro Pithoeo . . . aliisque, colligi incepta. Nunc autem ingenti ineditorum accessione locupletata . . . & nonnullis virorum doctorum notis excerptis illustrata, cura P. Burmanni . . . qui perpetuas adnotationes adjecit. 2 tom. *Amstelaedami,* 1759, 73. 4°. **833. k. 4, 5.**

—— [Another copy.] **671. k. 5, 6.**

—— [Another copy.] **54. f. 13.**

—— [Another edition.] Editionem Burmannianam digessit et auxit Henricus Meyerus. 2 tom. *Lipsiæ,* 1835. 8°. **011388.b.14.**

—— Petri Burmanni . . . Antiklotzius. pp. 136. *Amstelædami,* 1762. 4°. **836. i. 6. (2.)**

—— *See* SAXE (C.) Christopheri Saxi Epistola ad Petrum Burmannum. [Refuting the charges brought against him in the "Antiklotzius" of P. Burmannus.] 1762. 4°. **616. k. 15. (4.)**

—— Dissertatio literario-juridica inauguralis de jure aureorum annulorum, *etc.* pp. 25. *Trajecti ad Rhenum,* 1734. 4°. **T. 50*. (1.)**

—— [Another edition.] 1752. *See* GORI (A. F.) Symbolae litterariae, *etc.* vol. 6. 1751, *etc.* 8°. **657. a. 7.**

—— [Another edition.] 1770. *See* OELRICHS (G.) Thesauri dissertationum juridicarum . . . volumen I(–III), *etc.* vol. 2. 1769, *etc.* 4°. **6006. g. 1.**

—— Petri Burmanni . . . Epistola ad fratrem Franciscum Burmannum . . . de scriniis literariis ex Museo Burmanniano a Christophero quodam Saxe . . . subreptis. pp. 30. [*Amsterdam?* 1761?] 4°. **616. k. 15. (1.)**
With MS. *verses in Dutch on the same subject inserted at the end.*

—— *See* SAXE (C.) Christopheri Saxii Iusta depulsio immanis calumniarum atrocitatis, qua . . . scripta ad fratrem theologum epistola grassatus est P. Burman, *etc.* 1761. 4°. **616. k. 15. (3.)**

—— Genethliacon filiolo Francisco Petro Burmanno, felici puerperio conjugis carissimae Dorotheae Albertinae Six in lucem edito d. XXIII. Junii CIↃ IↃ CCLVI. [*Amsterdam?* 1756.] 4°. **616. k. 15. (2.)**

—— Petri Burmanni . . . Oratio de Maecenatibus doctis, validissimis musarum præsidiis, *etc.* pp. 66. *Amstelaedami,* 1763. 4°. **T. 48*. (17.)**

—— Petri Burmanni . . . Oratio funebris in obitum viri celeberrimi Jacobi Philippi d'Orville, *etc.* pp. 61. *Amstelædami,* 1751. 4°. **835. h. 20. (3.)**

—— Petri Burmanni . . . Oratio funebris in obitum viri clarissimi Cornelii Sieben, *etc.* pp. 46. *Amstelaedami,* 1743. 4°. **T. 947. (14.)**

—— Petri Burmanni . . . Oratio inauguralis de enthusiasmo poetico, *etc.* pp. 58. *Amstelaedami,* 1742. 4°. **T. 717. (14.)**

—— [Another copy.] **T. 948. (2.)**

—— [Another copy.] **T. 48*. (10.)**
Imperfect; wanting all after p. 56.

—— Intreéreden . . . over de poetische verrukking . . . in Nederduitsche vaerzen nagevolgt door Dirk Smits. pp. 77. *Rotterdam,* 1743. 4°. **C. 69. f. 7. (2.)**

—— Petri Burmanni . . . Oratio inauguralis pro criticis, *etc.* pp. 52. *Franequeræ,* 1736. 4°. **T. 48*. (5.)**

—— Petri Burmanni . . . Specimen novae editionis Anthologiae Latinae, et animadversionum ad epigrammata et catalecta veterum poëtarum Latinorum prodromus. pp. 51. *Amstelaedami,* 1747. 4°. **638. k. 4. (3.)**

BURMANNUS (Petrus) *the Younger.*

—— Bibliotheca Burmanniana, sive Catalogus librorum instructissimæ bibliothecæ viri celeberrimi, Petri Burmanni secundi . . . quorum publica fiet auctio . . . die lunæ 27 Septembris . . . 1779. (Catalogus codicum manuscriptorum.—Catalogue d'une belle collection de tableaux, *etc.*) 3 pt. *Lugduni Batavorum,* 1779. 8°. **11903.** c. **19.**

BURMANTOV (Evgeny Ivanovich) Смерть Уара—последний царевич. Исторический роман в трех частях. pp. 391. *Москва,* 1929. 8°. **12590.** r. **31.**

BURMAR, *pseud.*

—— The Smith Slayer. By " Burmar." pp. 284. *Wells, Gardner & Co.: London,* [1939.] 8°. NN. **31276.**

BURMEISTER (C. C. H.) Ueber die Sprache der früher in Meklenburg wohnenden Obodriten-Wenden. pp. 40. *Rostock,* 1840. 8°. **1332.** a. **43.**

BURMEISTER (C. E. J.) De fabula quæ de Niobe ejusque liberis agit . . . Commentatio . . . praemio ornata. pp. 94. *Vismariae,* 1836. 8°. **833.** e. **13.**

BURMEISTER (Carl Hermann Conrad) *See* Alton (Johann S. E. d') and Burmeister (C. H. C.) Der Fossile Gavial von Boll in Würtemberg, *etc.* 1854. fol. **1824.** d. **11.**

—— *See* Nitzsch (C. L.) System der Pterylographie von C. L. Nitzsch. Nach seinen handschriftlich aufbewahrten Untersuchungen verfasst von H. Burmeister. 1840. 4°. **7284.** f. **12.**

—— *See* Petermann (A. H.) Die süd-amerikanischen Republiken, Argentina, Chile, Paraguay und Uruguay . . . Nebst einem geographisch-statistischen Compendium von Prof. Dr H. Burmeister. 1878. 4°. [*Petermann's Geographische Mittheilungen.* Ergänzungshft. 39.] P.P. **3946.**

—— *See* Wagner (Andreas J.) Abweisung der von Herrn Professor H. Burmeister zu Gunsten des geologisch-vulkanistischen Fortschrittes und zu Ungunsten der mosaischen Schöpfungsurkunden vorgebrachten Behauptungen, *etc.* 1845. 8°. **1254.** f. **21.**

—— Beiträge zur näheren Kenntniss der Gattung Tarsius . . . Nebst einem helminthologischen Anhange von Dr. Creplin, *etc.* pp. x. 140. pl. 7. *Berlin,* 1846. 4°. **1258.** k. **19.**

—— Beiträge zur Naturgeschichte der Rankenfüsser—Cirripedia . . . Mit zwei Kupfertafeln. pp. viii. 60. *Berlin,* 1834. 4°. **7298.** e. **9.**

—— Bemerkungen über Zeuglodon cetoides Owen's, Basilosaurus Harlan's, Hydrarchos Koch's . . . Aus dem Iuniheft der Allgem. Lit. Zeit., *etc.* [With a plate.] coll. 28. *Halle,* 1847. 4°. **7203.** ee. **12.**

—— Bericht über ein Skelet von Machaerodus im Staats-Museum zu Buenos-Aires . . . Aus den Abhandlungen der Naturforschenden Gesellschaft zu Halle . . . besonders abgedruckt. [With a plate.] pp. 18. *Halle,* 1867. 4°. **7203.** ee. **13.**

—— Beschreibung der Macrauchenia patachonica Owen . . . Nach A. Bravard's Zeichnungen und den im Museo zu Buenos Aires vorhandenen Resten entworfen . . . Aus den Abhandlungen der Naturforschenden Gesellschaft zu Halle . . . besonders abgedruckt. pp. 40. pl. 3. *Halle,* 1864. 4°. **7105.** e. **12.**

BURMEISTER (Carl Hermann Conrad)

—— Los Caballos fósiles de la Pampa Argentina, *etc.* (Die fossilen Pferde der Pampasformation, *etc.*) [With plates and with a supplement.] *Span. & Ger.* 2 pt. *Buenos Aires,* 1875, 89. fol. **1824.** e. **2.**

—— De insectorum systemate naturali. Dissertatio inauguralis, *etc.* pp. 40. *Halis,* [1829.] 8°. **730.** g. **20.** (**1.**)

—— Erläuterungen zur Fauna Brasiliens enthaltend Abbildungen und ausführliche Beschreibungen neuer oder ungenügend bekannter Thier-Arten . . . Mit xxxii Tafeln. pp. viii. 115. *Berlin,* 1856. fol. **1821.** d. **4.**

—— Genera insectorum. Iconibus illustravit et descripsit H. Burmeister . . . Volumen i. Rhynchota. *Berolini,* 1838–46. 8°. **1258.** f. **13.**
Published in parts. No more published.

—— Geologische Bilder zur Geschichte der Erde und ihrer Bewohner. Zweite Auflage. 2 Bd. *Leipzig,* 1855. 8°. **7108.** aa. **13.**

—— Geschichte der Schöpfung. Eine Darstellung des Entwickelungsganges der Erde und ihrer Bewohner . . . Zweite vermehrte Auflage. pp. x. 574. *Leipzig,* 1845. 8°. **1254.** f. **3.**

—— Sechste Auflage. Mit dem Bildniss des Verfassers. pp. viii. 608. *Leipzig,* 1856. 8°. **7108.** bb. **14.**

—— Grundriss der Naturgeschichte, *etc.* pp. viii. 184. *Berlin,* 1833. 8°. **7206.** c. **10.**

—— Fünfte Auflage. pp. viii. 190. *Berlin,* 1845. 8°. **7207.** d. **6.**

—— Achte Auflage. pp. viii. 196. *Berlin,* 1852. 8°. **7003.** b. **4.**

—— *See* Katzfey (J.) Leitfaden zur Naturbeschreibung. Nach dem Grundrisse von Dr. Burmeister bearbeitet. [1864.] 8°. **7206.** bb. **33.**

—— Habsburg oder Hohenzollern. Wem gebührt die Hegemonie in Deutschland? [Signed: H. B., i.e. C. H. C. Burmeister.] pp. 30. 1848. 8°. *See* B., H. **8072.** d. **7.**

—— Handbuch der Entomologie. 5 Bd. *Berlin,* 1832–55. 8°. **1258.** f. **1–7.**

—— Abbildungen nebst deren Erklärung zum ersten Theile des Handbuchs der Entomologie. pp. 22. pl. 16. [*Berlin,* 1832.] 4°. **1258.** i. **21.**

—— A Manual of Entomology, translated [from Bd. 1 of " Handbuch der Entomologie "] . . . by W. E. Shuckard . . . With additions by the author, and original notes and plates by the translator. pp. xii. 654. pl. 32. *Edward Churton: London,* 1836. 8°. **975.** h. **12.**

—— Handbuch der Naturgeschichte. Zum Gebrauch bei Vorlesungen. pp. xxvi. 858. *Berlin,* 1837. 8°. **7005.** e. **10.**

—— Die Labyrinthodonten aus dem bunten Sandstein von Bernburg, zoologisch geschildert. (Abt. 3. Die Labyrinthodonten aus dem Saarbrücker Steinkohlengebirge.) [With plates.] Abt. 1, 3. *Berlin,* 1849. 4°. **1253.** i. **28.**
No more published.

—— Landschaftliche Bilder Brasiliens und Portraits einiger Urvölker; als Atlas zu seiner Reise durch die Provinzen von Rio de Janeiro und Minas geraës entworfen und herausgegeben von Dr. H. Burmeister. pp. 7. pl. xi. *Berlin,* 1853. *obl.* fol. **14001.** c. **14.**

BURMEISTER (Carl Hermann Conrad)

—— Lehrbuch der Naturgeschichte. pp. x. 594. *Halle*, 1830. 8°. **7005**. e. **9**.

—— Neue Beobachtungen an Macrauchenia Patachonica. 1885. *See* Germany.—*Academia Caesarea Naturae Curiosorum*. Nova acta, *etc*. Bd. 47. 1757, *etc*. 4°. Ac. **2871**.

—— Die Organisation der Trilobiten, aus ihren lebenden Verwandten entwickelt; nebst einer systematischen Uebersicht aller zeither beschriebenen Arten, *etc*. pp. xii. 147. pl. vi. *Berlin*, 1843. 4°. **1254**. k. **4**.

—— The Organization of Trilobites deduced from their living affinities . . . Edited from the German by Professor Bell and Professor E. Forbes. pp. x. 136. pl. vi. 1846. 4°. *See* London.—iii. *Ray Society*. Ac. **3023/27**.

—— [Physikalische Beschreibung der Argentinischen Republik.] Description physique de la République Argentine d'après des observations personnelles et étrangères . . . Traduite . . . par E. Maupas. (tom. 2; tom. 3. pt. 1. Traduite par E. Maupas avec le concours de E. Daireaux.) tom. 1, 2; tom. 3. pt. 1; tom. 5. pt. 1. *Paris*, 1876–79. 8°. **10480**. eee. **2**.
No more published.

—— Atlas. Deuxième section. Mammifères. (Cinquième section. Seconde partie. Lépidoptères.) 1881, 79–86. 4° & fol. **1820**. c. **20** & **1819**. d. **2**.
Wanting the first section of plates. No more published.

—— Reise durch die La Plata-Staaten, mit besonderer Rücksicht auf die physische Beschaffenheit und den Culturzustand der Argentinischen Republik, *etc*. [With maps.] 2 Bd. *Halle*, 1861. 8°. **010480**. ee. **1**.

—— Reise nach Brasilien, durch die Provinzen von Rio de Janeiro und Minas geraës. Mit besonderer Rücksicht auf die Naturgeschichte der Gold- und Diamantendistricte . . . Mit einer Karte. pp. vii. 608. *Berlin*, 1853. 8°. **10481**. e. **6**.

—— Systematische Uebersicht der Sphingidæ Brasiliens. pp. 17. *Halle*, 1856. 4°. **7296**. e. **6**.

—— Systematische Uebersicht der Thiere Brasiliens, welche während einer Reise durch die Provinzen von Rio de Janeiro und Minas geraës gesammelt oder beobachtet wurden, *etc*. Tl. 1–3. *Berlin*, 1854–56. 8°. **7205**. cc. **7**.
No more published.

—— Ueber die Ohrenrobben der Ostküste Süd-Amerika's. [Extracted from the "Zeitschrift für gesammte Naturwissenschaften."] [1868.] 8°. **7284**. b. **22**.

—— Untersuchungen über die Flügeltypen der Coleopteren. [With a plate.] Abt. 1. pp. 16. *Halle*, 1855. 8°. **7296**. e. **5**.
No more published.

—— Verzeichniss der im zoologischen Museum der Universität Halle-Wittenberg aufgestellten Säugethiere, Vögel und Amphibien. pp. 84. 1850. 8°. *See* Halle, *an der Saale.—Academia Fridericiana.—Zoologisches Museum*. **1256**. g. **24**. (**1**.)

—— Zoologischer Hand-Atlas zum Schulgebrauch und Selbstunterricht, *etc*. *Berlin*, 1835 [1835–43]. fol. **1487.1.20.**
Published in parts.

—— Zoonomische Briefe. Allgemeine Darstellung der thierischen Organisation. 2 Tl. *Leipzig*, 1856. 8°. **7205**. cc. **8**.

BURMEISTER (Carl Hermann Conrad)

—— Zur Naturgeschichte der Gattung Calandra, nebst Beschreibung einer neuen Art, Calandra Sommeri, *etc*. [With a plate.] pp. 24. *Berlin*, 1837. 4°. **446**. f. **19**.

—— Memoria de la Comisión del Monumento a Burmeister. [With portraits and a bibliography.] pp. 78. *Buenos Aires*, 1903. fol. **010708**. l. **10**.

BURMEISTER (Carlos Germán Conrado) *See* Burmeister (Carl Hermann Conrad)

BURMEISTER (Ernst) Gegenerklärung und Bitte an die kirchliche Conferenz in Mecklenburg-Schwerin. pp. 15. *Parchim*, 1877. 8°. **3910**. ee. **7**. (**3**.)

—— Luther eine Säule der Auctorität, in seinem persönlichen Vorbilde und durch die Reformationslehre vom Gesetz historisch begründet . . . i. Luther, gegenüber der Auctorität seines Vaters. pp. v. 20. *Stettin*, 1892. 8°. **3910**. dd. **47**.
No more published.

—— Das Wort zur Tages-Ordnung verweigert von einer kirchlichen Conferenz. pp. 26. *Parchim*, 1876. 8°. **3910**. ee. **8**. (**3**.)

—— *See* Brackebusch (Ludwig) *Pastor zu Herzfeld*. Zur Vorgeschichte der kirchlichen Conferenz in Bützow, *etc*. [Against E. Burmeister's "Das Wort zur Tages-Ordnung verweigert, *etc*."] 1877. 8°. **3910**. ee. **8**. (**5**.)

BURMEISTER (Eva)

—— Forty-five in the Family. The story of a home for children. pp. xvi. 247. *Columbia University Press*: *New York*, 1949. 8°. **08385**. df. **23**

—— Roofs for the Family. Building a center for the care of children. (With drawings by the author.) [An account of the building of Lakeside Children's Center, Milwaukee.] pp. 203. *Columbia University Press*: *New York*, 1954. 8°. **8290**. b. **13**

BURMEISTER (Federico) *See* Bettfreund (C.) Flora Argentina. Recolección y descripción de plantas vivas por C. Bettfreund. Dibujadas del natural y litografiadas por F. Burmeister. [1898, *etc*.] 8°. **07031**. k. **25**

BURMEISTER (Fridericus) De fontibus Vellei Paterculi. pp. 83. *Berlin*, 1894. 8°. [*Berliner Studien für classische Philologie*. Bd. 15. Hft. 1.] P.P. **4991**. e

BURMEISTER (Georg) *See* Burmeisterus (Georgius)

BURMEISTER (German) *See* Burmeister (Carl Hermann C.)

BURMEISTER (Gustav)

—— *See* Gobbert (F.) Verzeichniss sämmtlicher amtlich ausgegebenen Briefmarken der Staaten des Deutschen Bundes . . . Herausgegeben von G. Burmeister. 1891. 8°. Crawford **779**. (**10**.)

BURMEISTER (Hermann) *See* Burmeister (Carl H. C.)

BURMEISTER (Joachim) *See* Burmeisterus (I.)

BURMEISTER (Johann) *See* Burmeisterus (Joannes)

BURMEISTER (Karl Hermann Konrad) *See* Burmeister (Carl H. Conrad)

BURMEISTER (Karoline Wilhelmine) *See* Pierso (K. W.)

BURMEISTER (LUDWIG PETER AUGUST) *See* LYSER (J. P. T.) *pseud.* [i.e. L. P. A. Burmeister.]

BURMEISTER (MARCUS) *See* BURMEISTERUS.

BURMEISTER (OTTO) Nachdichtungen und Buehneneinrichtungen von Shakespeare's Merchant of Venice. pp. 142. *Rostock,* 1902. 8°. **11764. f. 14.**

BURMEISTER (OTTO) *Professor.*

—— Die Ganzheitsmethode. Methodische Einführung in "Unsere Fibel." Von Dr. O. Baumeister . . . Rudolf Krüger . . . Adolf Plagemann . . . Zweite Auflage. pp. 61. 20. *Langensalza,* 1938. 8°. **8312. aa. 76.**

BURMEISTER (PARIL) *See* PERIODICAL PUBLICATIONS.—*Copenhagen.* Theori og Praxis. Et Tidsskrift for anvendt Videnskab . . . redigeret af P. Burmeister. 1869, *etc.* 8°. **P.P. 1487. d.**

BURMEISTER (THEODOR) Beiträge zur Histogenese der acuten Nierenentzündungen . . . (Aus dem pathologischen Institut der Universität Rostock.) Mit einer Tafel. pp. 64. *Berlin,* 1894. 8°. **07306. g. 14. (2.)**

BURMEISTER (WERNER) *Dr. phil.*

—— Wandmalerei in Mecklenburg bis 1400. [With plates.] 1925. *See* SCHWERIN.—*Verein für mecklenburgische Geschichte und Altertumskunde.* Jahrbücher, *etc.* Jahrg. 89. 1836, *etc.* 8°. **Ac. 7165.**

—— Die westfälischen Dome: Paderborn, Soest, Osnabrück, Minden, Münster. Aufgenommen von Walter Hege, beschrieben von W. Burmeister. pp. 88. pl. 120. *Berlin,* 1936. 4°. **L.R. 293. d. 9.**

BURMEISTER-NORBURG (   ) *Dr. See* CAVLING (H.) Dänisch-Westindien . . . Deutsch von Dr. Burmeister-Norburg. 1902. 8°. [*Kreuz und Quer durchs Leben.* no. 2.] **010708. ee. 86.**

BURMEISTERUS (GEORGIUS) *Resp.* Disputatio XII . . . De cœna Domini. 1611. *See* FRANTZE (W.) Augustanæ confessionis articuli fidei XXI, et articuli abusuum VII, *etc.* 1611, *etc.* 4°. **1353. e. 2.**

BURMEISTERUS (IOACHIMUS)

—— *See* BRUCAEUS (H.) Musica theorica Henrici Brucæi . . . Edita operâ et impensis M. Ioachimi Burmeisteri. 1609. 4°. **Hirsch I. 92.**

—— Musica poetica, Rostock 1606. Faksimile-Nachdruck herausgegeben von Martin Ruhnke. pp. 76. *Kassel & Basel,* 1955. 4°. [*Documenta musicologica.* Reihe 1. no. 10.] **W.P. 11059. (a.) 10.**

BURMEISTERUS (JOANNES) Joan. Burmeisteri . . . Martialis renati, parodiarum sacrarum pars prima (—ultima) . . . Quibus obposita M. Val. Martialis Epigrammata. 3 pt. 1612. 12°. *See* MARTIALIS (M. V.) [*Latin.*] **11405. de. 3.**

BURMEISTERUS (MARCUS) *Resp. See* GODELMANN (J. G.) Disputatio de magis, veneficis, maleficis et lamiis, *etc.* 1584. 4°. **8630. e. 50.**

BURMESE. *See* also BURMESE LANGUAGE.

—— Catechismus pro Barmunis eorum lingua primisque nunc litterarum typis excusus. Addita etiam Latina interpretatione opera clericorum regularium S. Paulli in regno Avae missionariorum. 4 pt. *Romæ,* 1785, 86. 8°. **849. l. 20.**

BURMESE.

—— Narrative of the Captivity of an Officer who fell into the hands of the Burmāhs during the late war. [By Richard Bennett.] pp. ii. 145. *Male Asylum Press: Madras,* 1827. 8°. **10057. bb. 37.**

BURMESE ALMANAC. *See* EPHEMERIDES.

BURMESE ALPHABET.

—— [For editions of "Alphabetum Barmanum" issued by the Congregatio de Propaganda Fide:] *See* ROME, *Church of. Congregatio de Propaganda Fide.*

BURMESE IMPERIAL STATE CARRIAGE. The Rath; or Burmese Imperial State Carriage, and Throne . . . captured in the present Indian war, which is now exhibiting as drawn by elephants, at the Egyptian Hall, Piccadilly. Fifth edition, enlarged. [With a plate.] pp. 32. *Printed for the Proprietors: London,* 1826. 8°. **817. b. 35. (6.)**

—— [Another edition of pp. 1–10.] The Rath; or Burmese Imperial State Carriage, and Throne . . . Sixth edition. pp. 8. *Printed for the Proprietors: London,* 1827. 8°. **7957. aaaa. 6.**

BURMESE LANGUAGE.

—— Tables for the Transliteration of Burmese into English, with lists showing the names, in English and Burmese, of the divisions, townships and circles of British Burma, *etc.* pp. 65. 1884. 8°. *See* BURMA. [*Miscellaneous Public Documents, etc.*] **14302. i. 4. (2.)**

—— [Another edition.] pp. xviii. 202. 1896. 8°. *See* BURMA. [*Miscellaneous Public Documents, etc.*] **14302. k. 4. (1.)**

—— [Another edition.] pp. xviii. 202. 1898. 8°. *See* BURMA. [*Miscellaneous Public Documents.*] **14302. k. 4. (2.)**

BURMESE LIFE. Burmese Life and Scenes. *See* RANGOON. Views depicting the principal features of interest in Rangoon, *etc.* [1924.] *obl.* 8°. **10057. p. 18.**

BURMESE, MALÁYU AND T'HÁI LANGUAGES.

—— A Comparative Vocabulary of the Barma, Maláyu and T'hái Languages. [By John Leyden.] pp. lv. ii. 239. *Mission Press: Scrampore,* 1810. 8°. **12904. cc. 12.**

BURMESE SLAVE GIRL. The Burman Slave Girl. pp. 32. *R.T.S.: London,* [1830?] 16°. **864. a. 27. (4.)**

BURMESE SPELLING BOOK. Burmese Spelling Book. *Maulmian* [sic], 1852. 12°. **12910. a. 10.**

BURMESTER (A.) Ueber den Einflusz der Metapher auf die Entwicklung der Sprache. *See* BARMEN.—*Realschule.* Jahresbericht, *etc.* 1863. 4°. **12901. k. 36. (1.)**

BURMESTER (ARNOLD C.) *See* FORBES (Urquhart A.) and BURMESTER (A. C.) Our Roman Highways. 1904. 8°. **07707. eee. 7.**

BURMESTER (EDGAR) Thomas Taeglichsbeck, 1799–1867, und seine Instrumentalkompositionen. Ein Beitrag zur Geschichte der Instrumentalmusik des 19. Jahrhunderts. Inaugural-Dissertation, *etc.* [With plates, including portraits, and with musical notes.] pp. 162. *Würzburg,* 1936. 8°. **7898. d. 14.**

BURMESTER (Frances G.) A Bavarian Village Player. pp. 317. *Greening & Co.: London*, 1911. 8°. **012618**. bb. **17**.

—— Clemency Shafto. pp. 321. *Smith, Elder & Co.: London*, 1906. 8°. **012633**. c. **3**.

—— Davina. pp. 350. *Smith, Elder & Co.: London*, 1909. 8°. **012623**. b. **14**.

—— The Dogs of War. pp. 284. *William Heinemann: London*, 1916. 8°. NN **3997**.

—— John Lott's Alice. pp. viii. 414. *Grant Richards: London*, 1902. 8°. **012639**. d. **27**.

—— A November Cry. pp. 352. *Smith, Elder & Co.: London*, 1904. 8°. **012630**. a. **11**.

BURMESTER (Heinrich) Hans Höltig. 'ne Geschicht ut plattdütschen Lann'. pp. 241. *Berlin*, [1886.] 8°. **12555**. i. **25**.

—— Harten Leina. En Speigel vör Land un Lüd. Mit einer Einleitung von Karl Theodor Gaedertz. Zweite Auflage. 2 Tl. *Berlin*, [1884.] 8°. **12551**. bbb. **33**.

BURMESTER (Joannes Joachimus) Consultatio medica super morbo spastico, adiecta observationum biga de mortibus subitaneis ex pectoris et cordis vitiis. Dissertatio inauguralis, *etc.* pp. 44. *Goettingae*, [1791.] 4°. **T. 572**. **(28.)**

BURMESTER (Johann Friedrich) Beiträge zur Kirchengeschichte des Herzogthums Lauenburg, *etc.* pp. xiv. 234. *Ratzeburg*, 1832. 8°. **4661**. aa. **25**.

BURMESTER (Johann Heinrich) *Praes.* *See* Hellman (P.) Dissertatio . . . nonnullas antiquissimi cultus lunaris reliquias . . . exhibens, *etc.* [1754.] 4°. **278**. e. **39**. **(9.)**

BURMESTER (Ludwig) Elemente einer Theorie der Isophoten . . . Inaugural-Dissertation, *etc.* pp. 62. *Göttingen*, 1865. 8°. **8716**. bbb. **45**. **(3.)**

—— Lehrbuch der Kinematik . . . Erster Band. Die ebene Bewegung. Mit einem Atlas, *etc.* 2 pt. pp. xx. 941. pl. lvii. *Leipzig*, 1888. 8°. **1803**. b. **8**.
No more published.

—— Theorie und Darstellung der Beleuchtung gesetzmässig gestalteter Flächen, *etc.* pp. xvi. 368. *Leipzig*, 1871. 8°. **8533**. cc. **25**.

—— Atlas, *etc.* pl. 14. *obl.* fol. **1803**. c. **14**.

BURMESTER (Luis Germán)

—— Historia Americana, *etc.* *Buenos Aires*, 1939– . 8°. W.P. **7855**.

BURMESTER (Mary Alice) *See* Cook (Sherburne F.) and Burmester (M. A.) Laboratory Manual in Elementary Human Physiology. 1935. 8°. **7406**. ppp. **14**.

—— *See* Lawson (Chester A.) Laboratory Studies in Biology, *etc.* [By C. A. Lawson, M. A. Burmester and others.] 1955. 4°. W.P. **58/7**.

BURMESTER (Oswald Hugh Ewart) *See* Bible.—*Psalms.* [*Coptic.*] Psalterii versio Memphitica . . . Réédition . . . par O. H. E. Burmester, *etc.* 1925. 8°. **17000**. b. **1**.

—— *See* Cyril iii., called Ibn Laklak, 75*th Patriarch of Alexandria*. The Canons of Cyril iii . . . By O. H. E. Khs-Burmester. 1949, *etc.* 8°. [*Bulletin de la Société d'Archéologie Copte.* tom 12, *etc.*] Ac. **13**. f.

BURMESTER (Oswald Hugh Ewart)

—— *See* Liturgies.—*Lesser Eastern Rites.*—*Coptic Rite.*—*Katameros.* Le Lectionnaire de la Semaine sainte. Texte copte édité avec traduction française . . . par O. H. E. Burmester. 1933, 4°. [*Patrologia orientalis.* tom. 24.] **2005**. a.

—— *See* Philippou (Loïzos) Paphos, *etc.* [By L. Philippou in collaboration with O. H. E. Burmester.] 1948. 8°. **10127**. ff. **49**.

—— The Baptismal Rite of the Coptic Church. A critical study. *In:* Bulletin de la Société d'Archéologie Copte. tom. 11. pp. 27–86. 1947. 8°. Ac. **13**. f.

—— A Guide to the Monasteries of the Wadi 'n-Natrun. pp. 40. pl. xxxii. *Société d'Archéologie Copte: Le Caire*, 1954. 8°. **010077**. l. **20**.

—— The Ṭurūḥāt of the Saints, *etc.* [With extracts from the text.] *In:* Bulletin de la Société d'Archéologie Copte. tom. 4, 5. 1938, 39. 8°. Ac. **13**. f.

BURMESTER (Theophilus Andreas) De usu vini medico. Dissertatio inauguralis, *etc.* pp. 28. *Gottingae*, [1797.] 8°. **7386**. b. **(13.)**

—— [Another copy.] **T. 616**. **(26.)**

BURMESTER (Willy) Fünfzig Jahre Künstlerleben. [With portraits and facsimiles.] pp. 213. *Berlin*, [1926.] 8°. **010704**. de. **71**.

BURMINGHAM. *See* Birmingham.

BURMISTER (Donald Martin)

—— A Study of the Physical Characteristics of Soils, with special reference to earth structures. [A thesis.] pp. 63. *New York*, 1938. 8°. **07076**. cc. **35**.

BURMISTROV (F. L.)

—— *See* Itskov (N. Ya.) and Turova (A. D.) Скополия гималайския, *etc.* [By F. L. Burmistrov and others.] 1953. 8°. **7036**. b. **22**.

BURMISTROV (N. S.)

—— Как планируется себестоимость промышленной продукции. pp. 93. *Москва*, 1954. 8°. **8208**. ff. **17**.

BURMISTRZ. Burmistrz. [By — Vergis? Containing strictures on the laws and administration of Poland in dialogue form.] pp. 97. [*Warsaw?* 1790.] 8°. **8276**. aa. **16**. **(2.)**

BURMOV (Aleksandăr K.)

—— *See* Botev (Kh.) Съчинения, *etc.* (Под редакцията на А. Бурмов и С. Божков.) 1950, *etc.* 8°. W.P. B. **332**.

—— *See* Botev (Kh.) Стихотворения. Редакция и коментаръ отъ А. Бурмовъ. 1946. 8°. **11587**. a. **68**.

—— *See* Karavelov (L. S.) and Botev (Kh.) Знаеш ли ти кои сме? . . . Редакция и коментар от А. Бурмов. 1947. 8°. **08028**. aaa. **51**.

—— *See* Sofia.—*Историческо Дружество.* Исторически преглед. (Гл. редактор проф. А. Бурмов.) 1945, *etc.* 8°. Ac. **1137**. d.

—— Български революцоненъ централенъ комитетъ, 1868–1876. pp. 195. *София*, 1943. 8°. **09136**. a. **15**.

BURMOV (ALEKSANDĂR K.)

—— История на България през времето на Шишмановци, 1323–1396 г. . . . La Bulgarie sous le règne des Chichmanes, *etc.* (Résumé.) *София*, 1947– . 8°. [*Годишник на Софийския Университет. Историко-филологически факултет.* том. 43. no. 10, *etc.*] Ac. **1137**. (**1.**)

—— Христо Ботевъ презъ погледа на съвременницитѣ си. Спомени, впечатления и изказвания на Ботеви другари и съвременници. pp. 383. *София*, 1945. 8°. **10797**. ee. **74**.

BURMOV (TEODOR ST.) Българо-гръцката църковна разпра, 1867 до 1870. [1898.] *See* BULGARIA.—*Министерство на Народното Просвѣщение.* Сборникъ, *etc.* кн. 15. 1889, *etc.* 8°. **11900.p.1/15.**

—— Българо-Гръцката църковна распря, *etc.* pp. iv. 620. 7. 1902. 8°. *See* BULGARIA.—[*Churches, etc.*]—*Българска Црква.—Свети Синодъ.* **3926**. dd. **2**.

BURN, *the Violer.* *See* BURNE (Nicol)

BURN SIDE. The Burn Side, to which is added, The Braes of Balquhither, The Miller, The Rantin' Highlandman and The Turtle Dove. [Songs.] pp. 8. *R. Hutcheson & Co.: Glasgow*, [1815?] 12°. **11621**. b. **22**. (**4.**)

BURN'S COMMERCIAL DIARY. *See* EPHEMERIDES.

BURN'S COMMERCIAL GLANCE. *See* PERIODICAL PUBLICATIONS.—*Manchester.*

BURN ( ) *Mrs.* The Contrast; or, the Shepherd of Bentham Hill. pp. 251. *W. P. Kennedy: Edinburgh*, [1863.] 12°. **4416**. aa. **18**.

—— The Road to Glory. pp. 140. *W. P. Kennedy: Edinburgh*, 1860. 12°. **4414**. c. **23**.

BURN (A.) *Teacher of the Mathematics in Tarporley, Cheshire.* *See* BURNS (Arthur)

BURN (ANDREW) *Major-General.* The Christian Officer's Panoply: containing arguments in favour of a Divine Revelation. By a Marine Officer [i.e. A. Burn]. With a recommendation of the work by Sir Richard Hill, Bart. pp. xiv. 232. 1789. 8°. *See* CHRISTIAN OFFICER. **1019**. e. **28**.

—— [Another edition.] The Christian Officer's Complete Armour . . . Second edition. pp. xii. 232. *Mathews & Leigh: London*, 1806. 12°. **4016**. a. **11**.

—— Fourth edition. pp. xvi. 187. *Samuel Leigh: London*, 1818. 12°. **1115**. b. **7**.

—— Memoirs of the Life of the late Major-General Andrew Burn . . . collected from his journals: with copious extracts from his principal works on religious subjects. [Edited by John Allen, of Hackney. With a preface by Olinthus Gregory, J. Handfield and J. Dyer. With a portrait.] 2 vol. *W. Winchester & Son: London*, 1815. 12°. **615**. e. **7**.

—— Second edition. pp. xx. 291. *W. Winchester & Son: London*, 1816. 8°. **10817**. bbb. **15**.

—— An Abridged Memoir of Major General Andrew Burn, *etc.* pp. 37. *Edmond Barber: Cork*, 1821. 12°. **4906**. b. **61**. (**1.**)

—— The Life of Major-Gen. Andrew Burn, of the Royal Marines. (Abridgment.) pp. 144. *R.T.S.: London*, [1832.] 12°. [*Christian Biography.*] **864**. f. **11/25**.

BURN (ANDREW) *Major-General.*

—— A Remarkable Dream. [Extracted from "Memoirs of the Life of the late Major-General Burn."] *J. Groom: Birmingham*, [1855?] *s. sh.* 8°. **4422**. h. **36**. (**39.**)

—— Resurrection of the Two Witnesses, exhibited in the formation and great success of the British and Foreign Bible Society; being a paraphrase on the eleventh chapter of the Revelation. pp. 32. *W. Richardson: Greenwich*, [1812?] 8°. **3129**. e. **63**.

—— The second edition, enlarged. pp. 43. *W. Richardson: Greenwich*, [1813?] 8°. **3185**. bb. **45**.

—— A Second Address to the People of Great Britain: containing a new, and most powerful argument to abstain from the use of West India sugar. By an eye witness to the facts related [i.e. A. Burn]. pp. 11. 1792. 8°. *See* ENGLAND. [*Appendix.—History and Politics.*—II. 1791.] **10368**. e. **1**. (**2.**)

—— The second edition, enlarged. pp. 12. *M. Gurney: London*, 1792. 8°. **8157**. aaa. **9**.

—— Who Fares Best, the Christian or the Man of the World? or, the Advantages of a life of real piety to a life of fashionable dissipation. By a Marine Officer [i.e. A. Burn]. pp. v. 62. 1789. 8°. *See* CHRISTIAN. **701**. e. **30**. (**2.**)

—— Second edition. pp. vii. 64. 1792. 8°. *See* CHRISTIAN. **4408**. f. **5**.

—— Fourth edition. pp. 88. *G. H. Huttmann: Calcutta*, 1828. 8°. **4404**. cc. **5**.

—— The fourth edition. With a preface by Olinthus Gregory. pp. 64. *Edward Suter: London*, 1832. 8°. T. **1362**. (**8.**)

BURN (ANDREW) *Missionary to Sindh.* *See* BIBLE.—*New Testament.* [*Sindhi.*] نئون عهدنامو الخ [Translated by A. Burn and others.] [1890.] 8°. **14164**. a. **49**.

—— *See* BIBLE.—*Gospels.* [*Sindhi.*] خداوند يسوع مسيح تنه جو انجيل [The Gospels and Acts, edited by A. Burn.] [1870.] 4°. **14164**. a. **48**.

—— *See* BIBLE.—*Mark.* [*Sindhi.*] خداوند يسوع مسيح تهنجو انجيل ناهيل مرقس جو [Translated by A. Burn, assisted by A. Matchett.] [1868.] 8°. **14164**. a. **46**. (**3.**)

—— *See* BIBLE.—*John, Gospel of.* [*Sindhi.*] ਅੰਜੀਲ ਈਸਾ ਮਸੀਹ ਜੋ ॥ [Translated by A. Burn.] [1859.] *obl.* 8°. **14164**. a. **45**.

—— —— [1869.] 8°. **14164.a.46.(5.)**

—— *See* BIBLE.—*Acts.* [*Sindhi.*] خداوند يسوع مسيح تهنجو انجيل رسولن جاكم [The Acts of the Apostles edited by A. Burn.] [1870.] 8°. **14164**. a. **46**. (**6.**)

BURN (ANDREW EWBANK) *Dean of Salisbury.* *See* ANDREWES (Lancelot) successively *Bishop of Chichester, of Ely* and *of Winchester.* The Preces Privatae of Lancelot Andrewes . . . Edited with an introduction by A. E. Burn. 1908. 8°. **03605**. de. **2/27**.

—— *See* NICETAS, *Saint, Bishop of Remesiana.* Niceta of Remesiana: his life and works. By A. E. Burn. 1905. 8°. **3622**. df. **2**.

BURN (Andrew Ewbank) *Dean of Salisbury.*

—— *See* Wilson (Thomas) *Bishop of Sodor and Man.* Sacra Privata . . . Edited, with an introduction, by A. E. Burn. 1903. 8°. **03605. de. 2/18.**

—— *See* Zahn (T.) The Apostles' Creed . . . Translated by C. S. Burn and A. E. Burn. 1899. 8°. **3506. ee. 32.**

—— *See* Zahn (T.) [Brot und Salz aus Gottes Wort.] Bread and Salt from the Word of God . . . Translated by C. S. Burn and A. E. Burn. 1905. 8°. **4466. l. 1/6.**

—— The Apostles' Creed. pp. 120. *Rivingtons: London,* 1906. 8°. [*Oxford Church Text Books.*] **03605. de. 1/5.**

—— The Athanasian Creed. pp. 114. *Rivingtons: London,* 1912. 8°. [*Oxford Church Text Books.*] **03605. de. 1/29.**

—— The Athanasian Creed and its early commentaries. [With the texts.] pp. xcix. 68. 1896. 8°. [*Texts & Studies.* vol. 4. no. 1.] *See* Athanasian Creed. [*Latin.*] **03605.h.21/4.**

—— The Council of Nicaea. A memorial for its sixteenth centenary, *etc.* pp. xi. 146. *S.P.C.K.: London,* 1925. 8°. **04530. de. 20.**

—— The Crown of Thorns. Meditations for Lent, Holy Week and Easter Day. pp. 173. *Edward Arnold: London,* 1911. 8°. **4223. df. 34.**

—— Facsimiles of the Creeds from early manuscripts. Edited by A. E. Burn . . . With palaeographical notes by the late Dr. Ludwig Traube. (Supplementary note on Cod. Colon. 212. By C. H. Turner.) pp. viii. 53. pl. xxiv. *London,* 1909. 4°. [*Henry Bradshaw Society. Publications.* no. 36.] Ac. **9929/28.**

—— The Hymn Te Deum, and its author [here said to be St. Nicetas]. [With plates.] pp. 86. *Faith Press: London,* 1926. 8°. **4830. aa. 28.**

—— An Introduction to the Creeds and to the Te Deum. pp. xiv. 323. *Methuen & Co.: London,* 1899. 8°. **3506. g. 4.**

—— New Light on the Second Epistle to the Corinthians. A paper read before the Chester Clerical Society. pp. 23. *Phillipson & Golder: Chester,* 1913. 8°. **03129. f. 40. (4.)**

—— The Nicene Creed. pp. 118. *Rivingtons: London,* 1909. 8°. [*Oxford Church Text Books.*] **03605. de. 1/1.**

—— S. Eustathius of Antioch. pp. 26. *Faith Press: London,* 1926. 8°. [*Nicæan Lecture.* no. 1.] **4830. bb. 3/1.**

BURN (Andrew Robert) *See* Finett (*Sir* John) Sir John Finet, his byll. [Edited by A. R. Burn.] [1936.] 8°. **010822. f. 56.**

—— Agricola and Roman Britain. pp. x. 182. *English Universities Press: London,* 1953. 8°. [*Teach Yourself History.*] W.P. **1030/29.**

—— Alexander the Great and the Hellenistic Empire. [With a portrait and maps.] pp. xiii. 297. *Hodder & Stoughton for the English Universities Press: London,* 1947. 8°. [*Teach Yourself History Library.*] W.P. **1030/14.**

—— The Government of the Roman Empire from Augustus to the Antonines. pp. 19. *George Philip & Son: London,* 1952. 8°. [*Historical Association. General Series.* no. 21.] W.P. **3175/21.**

BURN (Andrew Robert)

—— Hic breve vivitur. A study of the expectation of life in the Roman Empire. *In:* Past & Present. no. 4. pp. 2–31. 1953. 8°. P.P. **5939.** bex.

—— Minoans, Philistines and Greeks. B.C. 1400–900. [With maps.] pp. xv. 273. pl. xvi. *Kegan Paul & Co.: London,* 1930. 8°. [*The History of Civilization.*] **09009. e. 1/49.**

—— The Modern Greeks. [With plates.] pp. vii. 55. *T. Nelson & Sons: London,* 1944. 8°. **010127. a. 13.**

—— Pericles and Athens. pp. xxv. 253. *Hodder & Stoughton for the English Universities Press: London,* 1948. 8°. [*Teach yourself History.*] W.P. **1030/18.**

—— The Romans in Britain. An anthology of inscriptions, with translations and a running commentary. [With plates.] pp. 228. *Basil Blackwell: Oxford,* 1932. 8°. **07709. aa. 18.**

—— The World of Hesiod. A study of the Greek middle ages, c. 900–700 B.C. pp. xv. 263. *Kegan Paul & Co.: London,* 1936. 8°. [*The History of Civilization.*] **09009. e. 1/61.**

BURN (Bruno) Codes, Cartels, National Planning. The road to economic stability. By B. Burn . . . in collaboration with S. Flink. pp. x. 413. *McGraw-Hill Book Co.: New York & London,* 1934. 8°. **08285. i. 24.**

BURN (C. S.) *See* Zahn (T.) The Apostles' Creed . . . Translated by C. S. Burn and A. E. Burn. 1899. 8°. **3506. ee. 32.**

—— *See* Zahn (T.) [Brot und Salz aus Gottes Wort.] Bread and Salt from the Word of God . . . Translated by C. S. Burn and A. E. Burn. 1905. 8°. **4466. l. 1/6.**

BURN (Charles) On the Construction of Breakwaters, for harbours similarly situated as the one at Dover. pp. 34. pl. 4. *John Weale: London,* 1859. 8°. **8776. a. 63. (4.)**

—— On the Construction of Horse Railways for Branch Lines in England and the Colonies. [With plates.] pp. 59. *John Weale: London,* 1860. 8°. **8235. c. 92. (9.)**

—— Second edition, revised and enlarged. pp. 81. pl. 8. *John Weale: London,* 1860. 8°. **8776. b. 3.**

BURN (David) The Chivalry of the Mercantile Marine illustrated by some remarkable passages in the life of Captain John Lennon. pp. 32. *Jenkin Thomas: Plymouth,* 1841. 8°. **1414. c. 67.**

—— [Another copy.] **1414. f. 56. (1.)**

—— Plays, and Fugitive Pieces, in verse. 2 vol. pp. 434. *William Pratt: Hobart Town,* 1842. 8°. **1344. k. 26.**

—— Vindication of Van Diemen's Land; in a cursory glance at their colonists as they are, not as they have been represented to be. [A criticism of views expressed by Archbishop Whately.] pp. 79. *J. W. Southgate: London,* 1840. 8°. **8154. bb. 31. (1.)**

BURN (David)

—— Narrative of the Overland Journey of Sir John and Lady Franklin and party from Hobart Town to Macquarie Harbour, 1842 . . . Edited, with an introduction, notes and commentary by George Mackaness . . . With . . . illustrations [including portraits]. pp. 72. *D. S. Ford: Sydney,* 1955. 8°. [*Australian Historical Monographs.* no. 32.] W.P. A. **268/11.**
Privately printed.

BURN (David Bryce) Notes on Transport and on Camel Corps. [With plates.] pp. 318. 1887. 8°. *See* England.—*War Office.—Intelligence Division.* **8829. b. 22.**

BURN (David William Murray) *See* also Marsyas, *pseud.* [i.e. D. W. M. Burn.]

—— Cantilenosae Nugae, being vol. i. of the poetical works of D. W. M. Burn. pp. viii. 200. *D. W. M. Burn: Oamaru,* 1891. 8°. **011653. m. 5.**

—— [Another copy.] **011653. m. 32.**

BURN (Dennis H.) *Begin.* Preface. The following pages, *etc.* [A specimen of "an improved and simple form of subject catalogue or index."] [*London,* 1879.] 4°. **11903. g. 4.**

Lithographed throughout.

BURN (Dixon) How, and What are we to Preach? A letter . . . to Mr. J. E. Cracknell; or, Mr. B. B. Wale reviewed; and the views holden by Mr. Philpot, Mr. Foreman, and Mr. James Wells, briefly considered. pp. 12. *James Paul; Caryl Book Society: London,* [1864.] 8°. **4498. ee. 19.**

BURN (Duncan Lyall)

—— The Economic History of Steelmaking, 1867–1939. A study in competition. pp. x. 548. *University Press: Cambridge,* 1940. 8°. **8232. g. 44.**

BURN (Edward) *See* Laicus. Letter to a Layman, on his Remarks on the Rev. Edward Burn. [1819.] 8°. **8135. cc. 6. (12.)**

—— *See* Priestley (Joseph) *LL.D.* Familiar Letters, *etc.* (Also letters to the Rev. E. Burn, in answer to his on the infallibility of the Apostolic testimony concerning the person of Christ, *etc.*) 1790. 8°. **698. i. 21.**

—— Letters to the Rev. Dr. Priestley, on the infallibility of the apostolic testimony, concerning the Person of Christ. pp. 32. *J. Johnson: London,* [1790.] 8°. **04227. aa. 32.**

—— Letters to the Rev. Dr. Priestley, in vindication of those already addressed to him, on the infallibility of the apostlic testimony, concerning the Person of Christ. [A reply to Joseph Priestley's "Letters to the Rev. E. Burn."] pp. 71. *E. Piercy: Birmingham; Rivington: London,* [1790.] 8°. **04227. aa. 33.**

—— A Reply to the Reverend Dr. Priestley's Appeal to the Public on the Subject of the late Riots at Birmingham, in vindication of the clergy and other respectable inhabitants of the town. pp. xvi. 125. *T. Pearson: Birmingham,* 1792. 8°. **1414. h. 26. (3.)**

—— *See* Edwards (John) *Unitarian Minister.* Letters to the British Nation . . . Occasioned by the appearance of a pamphlet, intitled 'A Reply to the Rev. Dr. Priestley's Appeal to the Public on the Subject of the Riots at Birmingham' . . . having in its title-page the signature of the Rev. E. Burn. [1791.] 8°. **8132. bb. 5.**

—— Serious Hints: respectfully addressed to the consideration of the clergy, at this momentous crisis: in a sermon preached before the University of Oxford, *etc.* pp. 28. *Printed for the Author: Birmingham,* 1798. 8°. **4477. cc. 54. (1.)**

—— A Sermon occasioned by the death of the late Miss Elizabeth Hutchinson . . . With an appendix containing a short memoir of her life, etc. Together with letters written by the deceased, *etc.* pp. 62. *Grafton & Reddell: Birmingham,* 1800. 8°. **4466. k. 11. (4.)**

BURN (Edward)

—— A Sermon preached at the Parish Church of St. Andrew . . . Blackfriars . . . before the Society for Missions, *etc.* 1806. *See* England.—*Church of England.—Church Missionary Society.* Proceedings, *etc.* vol. 2. 1801, *etc.* 8°. **P.P. 935.**

—— A Sermon preached before the Society, at Christ Church, Newgate Street . . . May 2, 1822. 1822. *See* London.—iii. *Prayer-Book and Homily Society.* Proceedings, *etc.* 1821–1822. 1819, *etc.* 8°. **P.P. 926. i.**

—— A Word for my King, my Country, and my God; being the substance of a discourse lately addressed to the Congregation of St. Mary's, Birmingham. pp. 23. *Beilby & Knotts: Birmingham,* [1819.] 8°. **4480. f. 23.**

—— A Word for My King, My Country, and My God; being the substance of a discourse lately addressed to the Congregation of St. Mary's, Birmingham . . . Second edition. pp. 23. *Beilby & Knotts: Birmingham,* [1819.] 8°. **4475. bb. 25.**

—— Fourth edition. pp. 23. *Beilby & Knotts: Birmingham,* [1819.] 8°. **4463. d. 4.**

—— Fifth edition. pp. 23. *Beilby & Knotts: Birmingham,* [1819.] 8°. **8135. cc. 6. (11.)**

—— Sixth edition. pp. 23. *Beilby & Knotts: Birmingham,* [1819.] 8°. **4473. g. 26. (9.)**

—— *See* Layman. Letter ii. to the Rev. Edward Burn. [With reference to Burn's sermon: "A Word for My King, My Country, and My God."] [1819.] 8°. **8133. cc. 26.**

BURN (Ernest William)

—— A Mathematical Handbook for Sixth Forms. pp. 164. *G. G. Harrap & Co.: London,* 1939. 8°. **08535. aa. 47.**

—— A Mathematical Handbook for Sixth Forms . . . New edition revised. pp. 162. *George G. Harrap & Co.: London,* 1947. 8°. **08535. aa. 81.**

BURN (Francis H.) *Son of Henry E. Burn.* *See* Burn (Henry E.) Lays of a Lifetime. [Selected by F. H. Burn.] 1934. 8°. **11654. bb. 13.**

BURN (Francis Henry) *See* Periodical Publications.—*London.* St. John's Quarterly Literary Magazine. Edited by F. H. Burn. 1899. 8°. **1866. a. 6. (13.)**

BURN (Francis W.) A Commercial Guide to the Court Practice in Debt Recovery, *etc.* pp. 39. *The Author: Manchester,* [1886.] 8°. **6146. d. 8. (7.)**

BURN (George) Modern Science. What is the duty of the clergy in relation to it? pp. 31. *S.P.C.K.: London,* 1880. 8°. **4420.g.3.**

BURN (George Francis) First Stage Practical Plane and Solid Geometry, *etc.* pp. viii. 240. *University Tutorial Press: London,* 1903. 8°. [*Organized Science Series.*] **8768. a. 14.**

—— Third impression, second edition. pp. viii. 263. *University Tutorial Press: London,* 1904. 8°. [*Organized Science Series.*] **8768. a. 14.**

—— Eighth impression, third edition. pp. viii. 282. *University Tutorial Press: London,* 1911. 8°. [*Organized Science Series.*] **8768. a. 14.**

BURN (George Francis)

—— Helps to the Solutions of the Examination Papers in the Honours Stage of Practical, Plane and Solid Geometry, for the years 1887 and 1890, set by the Department of Science and Art. pp. 12. *Charles Greening: Bradford,* [1891.] 8°. **8530.** bbb. **27.** (5.)

BURN (Henry Edward) Lays of a Lifetime. [Selected by Francis H. Burn. With a portrait.] pp. 96. *F. H. Burn: London,* 1934. 8°. **11654.** bb. **13.**

BURN (I.) *P. Pro G. M. Glasgow.*

—— An Historical Sketch of the Independent Order of Oddfellows M. U. pp. 180. *A. Heywood: Manchester,* [1845?] 12°. **4786.** df. **26.**
The titlepage is engraved.

BURN (Irene) The Border Line. pp. x. 323. *Chapman & Hall: London,* 1916. 8°. NN. **3370.**

—— Generous Gods. pp. 277. *W. H. Eaton: Leek; Simpkin, Marshall & Co.: London,* 1908. 8°. **012625.** aaa. **8.**

—— The Unforgiving Minute. A novel. pp. 317. *T. Fisher Unwin: London, Leipsic,* 1913. 8°. NN. **1128.**

—— The Unknown Steersman. pp. 314. *T. Fisher Unwin: London,* 1912. 8°. **012618.** bb. **18.**

BURN (J. W.) *See* Bible.—*Old Testament.—Appendix.* [*Miscellaneous.*] The Preacher's Complete Homiletical Commentary on the Old Testament, *etc.* (A Homiletic Commentary on the Book of Psalms . . . On Psalms cx–cxx. By J. W. Burn.) 1879, *etc.* 8°. **3165.** ee. **5.**

BURN (Jacob Henry) *See* Amory (Thomas) *Author of "John Buncle."* The Life of John Buncle, Esq., *etc.* [Edited by J. H. Burn.] 1825. 8°. N. **296, 297.**

—— Catalogue of a Collection of Early Newspapers and Essayists, formed by the late John Thomas Hope, and presented to the Bodleian Library by the late Rev. Frederick William Hope. pp. 178. 1865. 8°. *See* Oxford.—*University of Oxford.—Bodleian Library.* **11925.e.4.**

—— A Descriptive Catalogue of the London Traders, Tavern, and Coffee-House Tokens current in the seventeenth century; presented to the Corporation Library by Henry Benjamin Hanbury Beaufoy. [With plates, including a portrait of Beaufoy.] pp. xlvii. 237. 1853. 8°. *See* London.—ii. *Corporation of the City.—Library.* **7755.** d. **4.**

—— Second edition. pp. xcv. 287. 1855. 8°. *See* London.—ii. *Corporation of the City.—Library.* **7755.** c. **36.**

—— Memoir on the Roettiers. [Reprinted from "The Numismatic Chronicle."] pp. 32. [1841.] 8°. **811.** i. **15.**

—— Scarce Early Coin-Sale Catalogues, now on sale, at the prices affixed, by J. H. Burn, *etc.* pp. 12. [*London,* 1844.] 8°. **7807.** d. **6.** (25.)

BURN (James) *Minister of the Gospel at Forgan in Fife.* Sermons, selected from the manuscripts of the late James Burn. pp. 411. *R. T. Miller: Dundee,* 1805. 8°. **4455.** d. **4.**

BURN (James) *of South Shields.* The History of the Great Pyramid—Dead Yet Speaketh. [With plates, including a portrait.] pp. 169. [*South Shields,* 1937.] 8°. **8634.** ff. **1.**

BURN (James) *W.S.* The Pooll [*sic*] Doody. A new song, *etc.* [By J. Burn.] [1820?] *s. sh.* fol. *See* Doody (Poll) **11602.** h. **14.** (10.)

BURN (James Dawson) The Autobiography of a Beggar Boy, *etc.* [By J. D. Burn.] pp. vi. 200. 1855. 8°. *See* Autobiography. **10826.** a. **6.**

—— Second edition. pp. xi. 200. 1856. 12°. *See* Autobiography. **10826.** a. **7.**

—— Third edition. pp. xi. 200. 1856. 8°. *See* Autobiography. **10826.** a. **8.**

—— Fourth edition. pp. vii. 200. 1859. 8°. *See* Autobiography. **10856.** a. **9.**

—— James Burn; the "beggar boy." An autobiography, *etc.* pp. xi. 651. *Hodder & Stoughton: London,* 1882. 8°. **10827.** bb. **13.**

—— Commercial Enterprise and Social Progress; or Gleanings in London . . . By the author of "The Autobiography of a Beggar Boy" [i.e. J. B. Burn]. pp. 195. 1858. 8°. *See* Enterprise. **8247.** e. **30.**

—— A Glimpse at the Social Condition of the Working Classes during the early part of the present century . . . By the author of "The Autobiography of a Beggar Boy" [i.e. J. D. Burn]. pp. 156. *See* Glimpse. **8282.** aa. **39.**

—— Three Years among the Working Classes of the United States during the War. By the author of "The Autobiography of a Beggar-Boy" [i.e. J. D. Burn]. pp. xvi. 309. 1865. 8°. *See* United States of America. [*Appendix.—Descriptions, Travels and Topography.*] **8276.** bb. **48.**

BURN (John) *of Glasgow.* A Practical Grammar of the English Language, *etc.* pp. xv. 203. *Archibald M'Lean: Glasgow,* 1766. 12°. **626.** a. **13.** (1.)

—— The eighth edition. To which is added an appendix containing instructions for writing English, by another hand. pp. xx. 268. *J. & A. Duncan: Glasgow,* 1802. 12°. **1212.** h. **19.**

BURN (John) *Son of Dr. Richard Burn.* *See* Burn (Richard) *LL.D.* The Justice of the Peace, and Parish Officer . . . Continued to the present time by J. Burn, *etc.* 1788. 8°. **516.** f. **15–18.**

—— —— 1793. 8°. **516.** g. **1–4.**

—— —— 1797. 8°. **516.** g. **5–8.**

—— —— 1800. 8°. **228.** i. **21–24.**

—— *See* Burn (Richard) *LL.D.* A New Law Dictionary . . . Continued to the present time by J. Burn. 1792. 8°. **507.d.18,19.**

—— An Appendix to the seventeenth edition of Dr. Burn's Justice of the Peace, and Parish Officer, containing all the Acts of Parliament and adjudged cases which relate to the office of a justice of the peace, from 32 Geo. iii. to the present time. pp. 206. *T. Cadell Jun. & W. Davis; J. Butterworth: London,* 1795. 8°. **516.** d. **18.** (3.)

BURN (John Henry) *See* Alexander (William) successively *Bishop of Derry and Raphoe* and *Archbishop of Armagh.* Thoughts & Counsels of many Years . . . Selected and arranged by J. H. Burn. 1902. 8°. **3751.** aa. **24.**

—— *See* Bible. [*English.*] The Churchman's Bible. General editor: J. H. Burn. 1899, *etc.* 8°. **03107.** e. **2.**

—— *See* BODY (George) The Soul's Pilgrimage. Devotional readings . . . Selected and arranged by J. H. Burn. 1901. 16°. **4399**. b. **18**.

—— *See* CARPENTER (William B.) *Bishop of Ripon.* Aids to Practical Religion . . . Edited by J. H. Burn. 1902. 8°. **4401**. l. **41**.

—— *See* CREIGHTON (Mandell) successively *Bishop of Peterborough* and *of London.* Counsels for Churchpeople . . . Selected and arranged by J. H. Burn. 1901. 8°. **4109**. de. **10**.

—— *See* FARRAR (Frederick W.) *Dean of Canterbury.* The Life of Christian Service. A book of devotional thoughts from the writings of F. W. Farrar . . . Selected and arranged by J. H. Burn. 1900. 8°. **4402**. g. **41**.

—— *See* GENT (George W.) Papers and Essays . . . Edited by the Rev. J. H. Burn, *etc.* 1899. 8°. **4429**. cc. **21**.

—— *See* HOLLAND (Henry S.) Helps to Faith and Practice. From the writings of H. Scott Holland . . . Selected and arranged by J. H. Burn. 1900. 8°. **4402**. o. **14**.

—— *See* LITTLE (William J. K.) Our Reasonable Service. Spiritual thoughts . . . Selected and arranged by J. H. Burn. [1901.] 8°. **4399**. cc. **44**.

—— *See* TAYLOR (Tom) *Dramatist.* Storm at Midnight . . . Edited by the Rev. J. H. Burn. 1893. 4°. **11602**. gg. **32**. **(7.)**

—— *See* TEMPLE (Frederick) successively *Bishop of Exeter* and *of London,* and *Archbishop of Canterbury.* Helps to Godly Living . . . Selected and arranged . . . by J. H. Burn. 1899. 8°. **4399**. c. **33**.

—— *See* WILKINSON (George H.) successively *Bishop of Truro, of Saint Andrews, etc.* For Quiet Moments. Devotional readings . . . Selected and arranged by J. H. Burn. 1900. 8°. **3456**. ddd. **28**.

—— Bibliography of the Organ. *See* DICTIONARY. Dictionary of Organs and Organists, *etc.* 1921. 8°. **7895**. c. **57**.

—— Children's Answers, shrewd, witty, nonsensical and pathetic. Collected by J. H. Burn. pp. viii. 267. *A. Treherne & Co.: London,* 1905. 8°. **12314**. de. **49**.

—— New and enlarged edition. pp. ix. 282. *A. Treherne & Co.: London,* 1906. 8°. **12316**. r. **3**.

—— The Church's Outlook for the Twentieth Century: a series of handbooks on current ecclesiastical problems. General editor: J. H. Burn. 4 vol. *Elliot Stock: London,* 1902, 03 [1901–03]. 8°. **4109**. ee. **47**.

—— The Churchman's Library. Edited by J. H. Burn. 10 vol. *Methuen & Co.: London,* 1898 [1897–1902]. 8°. **4108**. df. **32**.

—— The Churchman's Pulpit: being sermons and addresses for the Sundays, festivals and holy days of the Christian year. Edited by the Rev. J. H. Burn. 28 vol. *Francis Griffiths: London,* 1911–15. 8°. **4461**. m. **1**.

—— The Churchman's Treasury of Song, gathered from the Christian poetry of all ages. pp. xx. 427. *Methuen & Co.: London,* 1907. 8°. **11604**. e. **33**.

—— Conflict and Conquest. A course of seventeen addresses . . . Edited by J. H. Burn. pp. 413. *Skeffington & Son: London,* [1929.] 8°. **04478**. h. **67**.

BURN (JOHN HENRY)

—— A Day Book from the Saints and Fathers. Edited by J. H. Burn. pp. 339. *Methuen & Co.: London,* 1904. 8°. [*Library of Devotion.*] **03605**. de. **2/20**.

—— The Divine Garner. A second series of harvest homilies. Edited by J. H. Burn. pp. 126. *Skeffington & Son: London,* [1929.] 8°. **04478**. df. **103**.

—— Divine Worship. Sermon, *etc.* pp. 12. *St. Giles' Printing Co.: Edinburgh,* [1889.] 8°. **4479**. aaa. **46**. **(11.)**

—— Doctrine and Duty. Sermons . . . Edited by J. H. Burn. pp. 288. *Skeffington & Son: London,* [1926.] 8°. **04478**. f. **59**.

—— Edmund Schulze's English Organs. [Reprinted from 'The Rotunda.''] [1934.] 4°. **7891**. c. **12**. (**2**.)

—— Edmund Schulze's Exhibition Organ. (Reprinted from The Organ.) pp. 4. [1930.] 4°. **7891**. c. **12**. (**1**.)

—— The Expositor's Library. Edited by the Rev. J. H. Burn. 12 vol. *Francis Griffiths: London,* 1912. 8°. **03107**. g. **8**.

—— From Cross to Crown. A course of fifteen addresses for Holy Week and Easter Day. Edited by J. H. Burn. pp. 143. *Skeffington & Son: London,* [1928.] 8°. **04478**. ee. **51**.

—— God Controls All. A sermon, *etc.* pp. 10. *"Royal Gazette" Office: Hamilton, Bermuda,* 1884. 8°. **4479**. aaa. **46**. **(6.)**

—— Handbooks of English Church History. General editor: J. H. Burn. 6 vol. *Methuen & Co.: London,* 1909, 10. 8°. **4705**. de. **39**.

—— A Homiletical Commentary on the Gospel according to St. Mark. pp. 673. *Funk & Wagnalls Co.: New York,* 1896. 8°. [*The Preacher's Complete Homiletical Commentary on the New Testament, etc.*] **03126**. g. **9**.

—— The Ladder of Lent. A course of seventeen addresses . . . Edited by J. H. Burn. pp. 140. *Skeffington & Son: London,* [1930.] 8°. **04478**. g. **56**.

—— Laity in Council. Essays on ecclesiastical and social problems. By lay members of the Anglican communion. [Edited by J. H. Burn.] pp. 334. *Wells Gardner & Co.: London,* [1901.] 8°. **4109**. f. **31**.

—— A Manual of Consolation from the Saints and the Fathers. Compiled and arranged by J. H. Burn. pp. vii. 280. *Methuen & Co.: London,* 1902. 8°. [*Library of Devotion.*] **03605**. de. **2/14**.

—— The Mother's Book of Song. [Compiled by J. H. Burn.] With illustrations by Charles Robinson. pp. xv. 216. *Wells Gardner & Co.: London,* [1902.] 8°. **011651**. eee. **99**.

—— A Pastoral Letter to the Congregation of St. Drostane's, Deer. pp. 7. [*Privately printed:*] *Peterhead,* [1888.] 4°. **4446**. h. **2**. **(3.)**

—— Preachers in Council. A collection of illustrations and anecdotes . . . Edited by J. H. Burn. vol. 1. pp. 288. *Skeffington & Son: London,* [1931.] 8°. **20032**. a. **48**. *No more published.*

—— Pulpit Preparation. A series of sermons by various divines . . . Edited by J. H. Burn. 2 vol. *Skeffington & Son: London,* [1925, 26.] 8°. **4465**. de. **12**.

BURN (John Henry)

—— A Reasonable Faith . . . Sermons by various divines for Sundays throughout the Christian year. Edited by J. H. Burn. pp. 284. *Skeffington & Son: London,* [1928.] 8°. **04478. ee. 70.**

—— Sermon preached in the Parish Church of Poslingford . . . at a Memorial Service for the late Captain J. F. Mackain, *etc.* pp. 8. [1914.] 12°. **4463. de. 7.**

—— Sermons for Matins . . . Edited by J. H. Burn, *etc.* 2 vol. *Skeffington & Son: London,* [1927, 28.] 8°. **04478. ee. 55.**

—— Short Addresses after Evensong . . . Edited by J. H. Burn. 2 vol. *Skeffington & Son: London,* [1929, 30.] 8°. **04478. i. 23.**

—— Sunday by Sunday. A series of fifty-three sermons . . . Edited by J. H. Burn. pp. 288. *Skeffington & Son: London,* [1930.] 8°. **04478. g. 47.**

—— Through Penitence to Peace. A course of twelve addresses . . . Edited by J. H. Burn. pp. 141. *Skeffington & Son: London,* [1927.] 8°. **04478. df. 71.**

—— Twenty Harvest Homilies. Edited by J. H. Burn. pp. 126. *Skeffington & Son: London,* [1927.] 8°. **04478. df. 75.**

—— The Upward Path. Addresses for Lent and Easter. Edited by J. H. Burn. pp. 110. *Skeffington & Son: London,* [1932.] 8°. **04478. i. 43.**

BURN (John Ilderton)

—— Case of the Right Hon. Alexander Earl of Stirling and Dovan, respecting his Lordship's title to Nova Scotia, and other territorial possessions in North America: containing a narrative of the proceedings taken on his Lordship's behalf for the restitution of the property, with observations thereon. pp. ii. 92. *Hatchard & Son: London,* 1833. 8°. **10863. b. 35.**

—— Familiar Letters on Population, Emigration, Home Colonization, &c. &c. pp. viii. 255. *Hatchard & Son: London,* 1832. 12°. **1027. a. 13.**

—— The second edition. pp. liv. 255. *J. W. Parker: London,* 1841. 12°. **8207. aa. 33.**

BURN (John Lancelot)

—— Public Health Services . . . Official handbook, second edition. pp. 26. [1940.] 8°. *See* Barnsley.—*Town Council.* **7391. v. 22.**

—— Recent Advances in Public Health, *etc.* pp. viii. 409. *J. & A. Churchill: London,* 1947. 8°. [*Recent Advances Series.*] **7442. p. 1/116.**

BURN (John Southerden) *See* English. Livre des Anglois, à Genève. With a few biographical notes by J. S. Burn. 1831. 8°. **T. 1395. (9.)**

—— The Fleet Registers. Comprising the history of Fleet marriages, and some account of the parsons and marriage-house keepers; with extracts from the registers: to which are added notices of the May Fair, Mint, and Savoy Chapels, and an appendix relating to parochial registration. pp. vi. 121. *Rivingtons: London,* 1833. 8°. **577. c. 11.**

—— Second edition. pp. x. 154. *Rivingtons: London,* 1834. 8°. **2228. c. 2.**

BURN (John Southerden)

—— The High Commission. Notices of the court and its proceedings. pp. vi. 92. *J. R. Smith: London,* 1865. 8°. **4707. bb. 4.**

—— A History of Henley-on-Thames, in the County of Oxford. [With plates.] pp. viii. 362. *Longman & Co.: London,* 1861. 4°. **10350. d. 16.**

—— The History of the French, Walloon, Dutch, and other Foreign Protestant Refugees settled in England, from the reign of Henry viii. to the revocation of the Edict of Nantes, *etc.* pp. viii. 284. *Longman & Co.: London,* 1846. 8°. **2212. b. 9.**

—— The Marriage and Registration Acts—6 & 7 Will. iv. Cap. 85 and 86—with instructions, forms, and practical directions, *etc.* pp. 144. *Henry Butterworth: London,* 1836. 12°. **516. b. 33.**

—— A Plea for Parish Registers. pp. 4. [*The Author: Henley-on-Thames,* 1867?] 4°. **1897. c. 19. (17*.)**

—— Registrum Ecclesiæ Parochialis. The History of Parish Registers in England, also of the Registers of Scotland, Ireland, the East and West Indies . . . With observations on Bishops' Transcripts and the provisions of the Act of the 52d. George iii. cap. 146. pp. viii. 246. *Edward Suter: London,* 1829. 8°. **819. e. 5.**

—— Second edition. pp. vii. 296. *J. R. Smith: London,* 1862. 8°. **2228. e. 4.**

—— The Star Chamber. Notices of the court and its proceedings; with a few additional notes of the High Commission. pp. viii. 199. *J. T. Smith: London,* 1870. 8°. **6145. bb. 11.**

BURN (*Sir* Joseph) *K.B.E.* Mechanization of Accounts and Records, *etc.* [Reprinted from "The Accountant."] pp. 32. *Efficiency Magazine: London,* [1933.] 8°. [*Up-to-Date Bulletins for Business Men.* no. 35.] **W.P. 78/35.**

—— Stock Exchange Investments in Theory and Practice, with chapters on the constitution and operations of the Bank of England and the national and local debts of the United Kingdom. A course of lectures. pp. vii. 322. 1909. 8°. *See* London.—iii. *Institute of Actuaries.* **08227. b. 7.**

—— Vital Statistics Explained. Some practical suggestions, *etc.* pp. x. 140. *Constable & Co.: London,* 1914. 8°. [*Chadwick Library.*] **12211.r.3/1.**

BURN (*Sir* Joseph) *K.B.E.*, and **BROWN** (Edward Harold)

—— Elements of Finite Differences, also solutions to questions set for part i. of the examinations of the Institute of Actuaries. pp. 259. *C. & E. Layton: London,* 1902. 8°. **8506. dd. 13.**

—— Second edition. pp. 289. *C. & E. Layton: London,* 1915. 8°. **8507. g. 21.**

BURN (Joshua Harold)

—— *See* Whitla (*Sir* William) Whitla's Pharmacy, Materia Medica and Therapeutics . . . Revised by J. H. Burn . . . and E. R. Withell, *etc.* 1939. 8°. **07510. e. 57.**

—— *See* Whitla (*Sir* William) Whitla's Pharmacy Materia Medica and Therapeutics. Fourteenth edition. Revised by J. H. Burn, *etc.* 1943. 8°. **7511. aa. 9.**

BURN (Joshua Harold)

—— The Background of Therapeutics. pp. vi. 367. *Oxford University Press: London,* 1948. 8°. [*Oxford Medical Publications.*] **20036.** a. **1/737.**

—— Biological Standardization. By J. H. Burn . . . D. J. Finney . . . and L. G. Goodwin . . . Second edition. pp. x. 440. *Oxford University Press: London,* 1950. 8°. [*Oxford Medical Publications.*] **20036.** a. **1/772.**

—— Biological Standardization. pp. xviii. 288. *Oxford University Press: London,* 1937. 8°. [*Oxford Medical Publications.*] **20036.a.1/594.**

—— The Formation of Adrenaline in the Body. pp. 19. *Nottingham,* [1951.] 8°. [*Sir Jesse Boot Foundation Lecture.* no. 24.] Ac. **2673.** b/**2.**

—— Lecture Notes on Pharmacology. pp. viii. 128. *Blackwell Scientific Publications: Oxford,* 1948. 8°. **07510.** f. **56.**

—— Methods of Biological Assay, *etc.* pp. xvii. 126. *Oxford University Press: London,* 1928. 8°. [*Oxford Medical Publications.*] **20036.a.1/338.**

—— Practical Pharmacology . . . Illustrations by E. M. Vaughan Williams. pp. viii. 72. *Blackwell Scientific Publications: Oxford,* 1952. 8°. **7509.** dd. **35.**

—— Recent Advances in Materia Medica, *etc.* pp. x. 224. *J. & A. Churchill: London,* 1932 [1931]. 8°. [*Recent Advances Series.*] **7442.** p. **1/42.**

BURN (Joshua Harold) and **DALE** (*Sir* Henry Hallett)

—— Reports on Biological Standards. I. On the Physiological Standardization of Extracts of the Posterior Lobe of the Pituitary Body. pp. 24. *London,* 1922. 8°. [*Medical Research Council. Special Report Series.* no. 69.] B.S. **25/8.**

BURN (Lambton)

—— "Down Ramps!" Saga of the Eighth Armada . . . from Tobruk, 1941 to Kiel, 1945. [With plates.] pp. x. 262. *Carroll & Nicholson: London,* 1947. 8°. **09101.** e. **27.**

BURN (Louis) Workshop Gauges and Measuring Appliances, *etc.* pp. ix. 154. *Sir I. Pitman & Sons: London,* 1924. 8°. **8764.** de. **39.**

BURN (Mary) *See* Herbert (George) *the Poet.* Gathered Rosemary from the Poems of George Herbert . . . Edited by M. Burn, *etc.* [1911.] 8°. **04402.** fff. **1/32.**

—— The Pearl Divers. Pictures from the life & work of Prebendary Carlile and the Church Army. Edited by M. Burn. pp. 221. *Marshall Bros.: London,* 1920. 8°. **4193.** b. **84.**

BURN (Michael) *See* Bradley (Arthur P.) and Burn (M.) Wheels take Wings, *etc.* 1933. 8°. **7916.** d. **2.**

—— Childhood at Oriol, *etc.* pp. 325. *Rupert Hart-Davis: London,* 1951. 8°. NNN. **2165.**

—— The Flying Castle . . . Illustrated by Richard Macdonald. [Poems.] pp. 38. *Rupert Hart-Davis: London,* 1954. 8°. **11659.** cc. **27.**

—— The Labyrinth of Europe. [With maps.] pp. xi. 307. *Methuen & Co.: London,* 1939. 8°. **08028.** cc. **73.**

BURN (Michael)

—— The Midnight Diary, *etc.* pp. 254. *Rupert Hart-Davis: London,* 1952. 8°. NNN. **3028.**

—— The Modern Everyman. A play in one act. pp. x. 63. *Rupert Hart-Davis: London,* 1948. 8°. **11783.** aaa. **114.**

—— Poems to Mary. pp. 78. *Rupert Hart-Davis: London,* 1953. 8°. **11659.** b. **61.**

—— Yes, Farewell. [A novel.] pp. 432. *Jonathan Cape: London,* 1946. 8°. NN. **35923.**

BURN (Nicol) *See* Burne.

BURN (Pelham)

—— Peace—is it Impossible?, *etc.* [With portraits.] pp. 236. *Century Press: London,* 1949. 8°. **08425.** g. **65.**

BURN (Peter) Poems. pp. xii. 288. *J. R. Smith: London; Geo. Coward: Carlisle,* 1871. 8°. **11649.** ee. **6.**

—— [Another edition.] pp. xvi. 389. *Bemrose & Sons: London; G. & T. Coward: Carlisle,* 1885. 8°. **11653.** e. **46.**

—— Complete revised edition. [With a portrait.] pp. xv. 395. *Bemrose & Sons: London; G. & T. Coward: Carlisle,* 1900. 8°. **011651.** eee. **64.**

—— English Border Ballads. pp. viii. 121. *G. & T. Coward: Carlisle; Bemrose & Sons: London,* 1874. 8°. **11652.** e. **30.**

—— Night, and other poems. pp. viii. 98. *Elliot Stock: London,* 1867. 8°. **11647.** de. **3.**

—— Rosenthal: a North Country story. pp. vii. 374. *Bemrose & Sons: London; G. & T. Coward: Carlisle,* 1891. 8°. **012634.** i. **48.**

—— Voices of Nature: or Moral and instructive lessons, chiefly derived from natural objects. [Poems.] pp. viii. 86. *Francis Oliver: Hull,* 1860. 8°. **11643.** b. **2.**

BURN (Richard) *LL.D.* *See* Blackstone (*Sir* William) *One of the Justices of the Court of Common Pleas.* [*Commentaries on the Laws of England.*] Commentaries on the Laws of England . . . Continued to the present time by R. Burn. 1783. 8°. **507.** b. **13–16.**

—— —— 1787. 8°. **507.** b. **21–24.**

—— —— 1791. 8°. **507.** c. **1–4.**

—— *See* Nicolson (Joseph) and Burn (R.) The History and Antiquities of the Counties of Westmorland and Cumberland. 1777. 4°. **578.** i. **30.**

—— *See* Sayer (W.) Sayer's History of Westmoreland, containing the substance of all the remarkable events recorded by Burn & Nicolson, *etc.* 1847. 8°. **10352.h.2.**

—— A Digest of the Militia Laws. pp. viii. 88. *A. Millar: London,* 1760. 8°. E. **2218.** (**2.**)

—— Ecclesiastical Law. 2 vol. *A. Millar: London,* 1763, 65. 4°. **517.** l. **13, 14.**

—— The second edition. 4 vol. *A. Millar; T. Cadell: London,* 1767. 8°. **517.** i. **5–8.**

—— The third edition. 4 vol. *T. Cadell: London,* 1775. 8°. **517.** i. **9–12.**

—— The fourth edition. 4 vol. *T. Cadell: London,* 1781. 8°. **517.** i. **13–16.**

—— The fifth edition. 4 vol. *T. Cadell: London*, 1788. 8°. **16**. a. **2–5**.

—— The sixth edition; with notes and references by Simon Fraser. 4 vol. *T. Cadell & W. Davies; J. Butterworth: London*, 1797. 8°. **517**. i. **17–20**.

—— The seventh edition, corrected, *etc.* 4 vol. *T. Cadell & W. Davies: London*, 1809. 8°. **5155**. aaa. **91**.

—— The eighth edition, corrected; with considerable additions by Robert Philip Tyrwhitt. 4 vol. *T. Cadell: London*, 1824. 8°. **517**. i. **21–24**.

—— The ninth edition, corrected; with considerable additions . . . by Robert Phillimore. 4 vol. *S. Sweet: London*, 1842. 8°. **5155**. f. **2**.

—— The History of the Poor Laws: with observations. pp. 295. *A. Millar: London*, 1764. 8°. **516**. d. **4**.

—— An Examination of the Alterations in the Poor's Laws, proposed by Dr. Burn [in his " History of the Poor Laws "], and a refutation of his objections to workhouses . . . Together with observations upon the bill lately offered to Parliament for " the better relief and employment of the poor," *etc.* pp. 34. *T. Becket & P. A. De Hondt: London*, 1766. 8°. **6429**. de. **14**.

—— The Justice of the Peace and Parish Officer. 2 vol. *A. Millar:* [*London*,] 1755. 8°. **883**. l. **15**.

—— The second edition, *etc.* 2 vol. *A. Millar:* [*London*,] 1756. 8°. **516**. f. **1**, **2**.

—— The third edition. pp. xvii. 775. *A. Millar:* [*London*,] 1756. fol. **516**. m. **4**.

—— The Justice of the Peace, and Parish Officer . . . The fourth edition, *etc.* vol. 1. pp. xxiv. 520. *A. Millar:* [*London*,] 1757. 8°. **6283**. bb. **7**.
Imperfect; wanting vol. 2 *and* 3.

—— The Justice of the Peace . . . The eighth edition. 2 vol. *A. Millar: London*, 1764. 4°. **6193**. dd. **2**.

—— The tenth edition. 4 vol. *A. Millar: London*, 1766. 8°. **6282**. bbb. **3**.

—— The eleventh edition. 4 vol. *T. Cadell: London*, 1770, 69, 70. 8°. **6281**. e. **2**.

—— The thirteenth edition. 4 vol. *T. Cadell: London*, 1776. 8°. **516**. f. **3–6**.

—— The fourteenth edition, *etc.* 4 vol. *T. Cadell: London*, 1780. 8°. **516**. f. **7–10**.

—— The fifteenth edition, *etc.* 4 vol. *T. Cadell: London*, 1785. 8°. **516**. f. **11–14**.

—— [Another edition.] Continued . . . by John Burn . . . The sixteenth edition, *etc.* 4 vol. *T. Cadell: London*, 1788. 8°. **516**. f. **15–18**.

—— The seventeenth edition, *etc.* 4 vol. *T. Cadell: London*, 1793. 8°. **516**. g. **1–4**.

—— The eighteenth edition, corrected, and considerably enlarged, *etc.* 4 vol. *T. Cadell & W. Davies; J. Butterworth: London*, 1797. 8°. **516**. g. **5–8**.

—— The nineteenth edition, corrected, and considerably enlarged, *etc.* 4 vol. *T. Cadell & W. Davies; J. Butterworth: London*, 1800. 8°. **228**. i. **21–24**.

—— [Another copy.] The Justice of the Peace, and Parish Officer, *etc.* *London*, 1800. 8°. **6147**. b. **12**.

—— [Another edition.] Continued to the present time by William Woodfall . . . The twentieth edition, corrected and considerably enlarged. 4 vol. *T. Cadell & W. Davies: London*, 1805. 8°. **6282**. bbb. **4**

—— The twenty-first edition: with many corrections additions, and improvements, by the late Charles Durnford . . . and continued by John King, *etc.* 5 vol. *T. Cadell & W. Davies: London*, 1810. 8°. **1382**. h. **1**

—— The Justice of the Peace, and Parish Officer . . . The twenty-second edition: with many corrections, additions and improvements, by John King, *etc.* 5 vol. *T. Cadell & W. Davies: London*, 1814. 8°. **6283**. bb. **3**

—— The twenty third edition; with corrections, additions and improvements . . . By George Chetwynd. (A Supplement to the twenty third edition, by George Chetwynd.) 6 vol. *T. Cadell: London*, 1820, 23. 8°. **516**. g. **9–13** & **19**

—— The twenty fourth edition: with corrections, additions and improvements . . . By Sir George Chetwynd. 5 vol. *T. Cadell: London*, 1825. 8°. **516**. g. **14–18**

—— The twenty fifth edition: with corrections and addition . . . By George Wharton Marriott. 5 vol. *T. Cadell London*, 1830. 8°. **516**. h. **1–5**

—— The twenty sixth edition, corrected and greatly enlarge . . . The titles " Excise and Customs," " Poor " an " Taxes " by J. Chitty . . . The rest of the work b Thomas Chitty. 6 vol. *S. Sweet: London*, 1831. 8°. **516**. h. **6–11**

—— A new edition; with corrections and additions . . Vol. III.—Criminal law—and vol. IV.—Poor—by Thoma D'Oyly . . . The rest of the work by Edward Vaugha Williams. 5 vol. *T. Cadell: London*, 1836. 8°. **516**. i. **1–5**

—— The twenty-eighth edition, corrected and greatl enlarged . . . The titles " Excise and Customs," " Poor, and " Taxes " by J. Chitty . . . The title " Poor " als very carefully edited by Montague B. Bere . . . and th rest of the work by Thomas Chitty. 6 vol. *S. Sweet London*, 1837. 8°. **516**. i. **6–11**

—— The twenty-ninth edition, corrected and greatly enlarge . . . The title " Poor " by Mr. Commissioner Bere . . the rest of the work by Thomas Chitty. 6 vol. *Sweet London*, 1845. 8°. **6282**. c.

—— The thirtieth edition . . . Edited except the volum of " Poor," by J. B. Maule. (vol. 1 by T. Sirell Pritchar vol. 2 by S. B. Bristowe. vol. 3 by L. W. Cave. vol. by J. E. Davis. vol. 5 by J. B. Maule.) 5 vol. *H. Swee London*, 1869. 8°. **6281**. i.

—— Burn's Abridgment, or, the American Justice; contai ing the whole practice, authority and duty of Justices the Peace . . . adapted to the present situation of t United States. The second edition. [By Eliphalet Ladd pp. viii. 484. *Eliphalet Ladd: Dover, New-Hampshir* 1792. 8°. **6615**. b.

—— Le Juge à Paix, et officier de paroisse, pour la Provinc de Quebec. Extrait de R. Burn . . . Traduit par Jo F. Perrault. pp. 561. *Montreal*, 1789. 8°. **1384**. d. **2**
Imperfect; wanting the index after sig. Aaaa 1.

—— *See* Burn (John) *Son of Dr. Richard Burn.* A Appendix to the seventeenth edition of Dr. Burn' Justice of the Peace, and Parish Officer, *etc.* 1795. 8°. **516**. d. **18**. (**3**.

BURN (Richard) *LL.D.*

—— *See* Clapham (Samuel) A Collection of the Several Points of Sessions' Law . . . contained in Burn and Williams on the Office of a Justice, *etc.* 1818. 8°. **516.** e. **4.**

—— *See* Keane (David D.) Magistrates' Statutes. Supplement to Burn's Justice of the Peace, *etc.* 1849, *etc.* **6282.** c. **6.**

—— *See* Parker (James) *Justice of the Peace for Middlesex County, New Jersey.* Conductor Generalis . . . Compiled chiefly from Burn's Justice, *etc.* 1764. 8°. **6281.** cc. **17.**

—— —— 1788. 8°. **6281.** cc. **18.**

—— —— 1794. 8°. **6617.** c. **6.**

—— *See* Rastall (William D.), afterwards Dickinson (W.) The Justice Law of the last five Years, viz. from 1813 to 1817 . . . being supplementary to the several treatises on the office and duties of a Justice of the Peace, by Burn, Williams, and Dickinson, *etc.* 1818. 8°. **516.** e. **5.**

—— *See* Saunders (Thomas W.) Supplement to Burn's Justice of the Peace and Parish Officer, *etc.* 1848. 8°. **6281.** d. **25.**

—— —— 1849. 8°. **6281.** d. **26.**

—— —— 1851. 8°. **6281.** d. **27.**

—— *See* United States of America.—*Justices of the Peace.* The Complete Justice of the Peace, containing extracts from Burn's Justice, *etc.* 1806. 8°. **6625.** c. **23.**

—— *See* Williams (Edward) *Barrister-at-Law.* Precedents of Warrants, Convictions, and other Proceedings, before Justices of the Peace . . . containing none that are to be met with in Dr. Burn's Justice, to which this publication is offered as a supplement of practical forms, *etc.* 1801. 8°. **227.** i. **6.**

—— *See* Wise (Edward) *Barrister-at-Law.* Chitty's Burn's Justice of the Peace and Parish Officer. Supplement to the twenty-ninth edition, *etc.* 1852. 8°. **6282.** c. **5.**

—— A New Law Dictionary . . . continued to the present time by John Burn. [With a portrait.] 2 vol. *T. Cadell: London,* 1792. 8°. **507.** d. **18, 19.**

—— Observations on the Bill intended to be offered to Parliament for the better relief and employment of the poor: in a letter to a Member of Parliament. pp. 52. *T. Cadell: London,* 1776. 8°. T. **790.** **(7.)**

—— [Another copy.] **104.** n. **11.**

—— Sermons on Practical Subjects: extracted chiefly from the works of divines of the last century. 4 vol. *T. Cadell: London,* 1774. 8°. **227.** g. **12–15.**

BURN (Richard) *of Manchester.* *See* Periodical Publications.—*Manchester.* Burn's Commercial Glance. 1845. fol. Tab. **597.** c. **(57.)**

—— A Few Original Ideas of a Manchester Man [i.e. R. Burn?] respecting our Bad Trade & Government Interference. pp. 32. [1876.] 8°. *See* Manchester Man. **08229.** a. **57.**

—— The Present and Long-continued Stagnation of Trade: its causes, effects, and cure. Being a sequel to An Inquiry into the Commercial Position of Great Britain, &c. By a Manchester Man (R. Burn). Revised and enlarged edition. pp. 39. *John Heywood: Manchester,* [1870.] 8°. **8245.** bbb. **4.**

BURN (Richard) *of Manchester.*

—— Statistics of the Cotton Trade arranged in a tabular form; also a chronological history of the various inventions, improvements, etc., etc. pp. xvi. ff. 34. *Simpkin, Marshall & Co.: London,* [1847.] 8°. **1400.** g. **13.**
Printed on one side of the leaf only.

BURN (*Sir* Richard)

—— *See* Carré de Chambon (B.) The Travels of the Abbé Carré in India and the Near East . . . Edited by Sir C. Fawcett with the assistance of Sir R. Burn. 1947, *etc.* 8°. **Ac.6172/142.**

—— *See* Chatterjee (*Sir* Atul C.), *G.C.I.E., K.C.S.I.* and Burn (*Sir* R.) British Contributions to Indian Studies, *etc.* 1943. 8°. **11865.** b. **39.**

—— *See* Ḥāmid 'Alī Khān. *Begin:* Sir, I am asked to give my opinion about the question of securing adequate representation of Musalmans on District and Municipal Boards, *etc.* [A letter in answer to one sent by Sir R. Burn to the Commissioners of Divisions of the United Provinces of Agra and Oudh.] 1911. fol. **8022.** i. **5.**

—— *See* India. The Imperial Gazetteer of India, *etc.* [Edited by Sir R. Burn and others.] 1907, *etc.* 8°. **2059.** b.

—— Humāyūn.—Jahāngīr.—Shāh Jahān. 1937. *See* India. Cambridge History of India. vol. 4. 1922, *etc.* 8°. W.P. **5616.**

—— The Mughul Period. Planned by . . . Sir Wolseley Haig . . . Edited by Sir R. Burn. [With maps.] pp. xxvi. 670. pl. lviii. *Cambridge,* 1937. 8°. [*Cambridge History of India.* vol. 4.] W.P. **5616.**

—— The National Congress and Early Political Literature.—The Reforms of 1909.—Political Movements, 1909–1917.—The Reforms of 1919. *See* Dodwell (Henry H.) The Indian Empire, 1858–1918, *etc.* 1932. 8°. [*Cambridge History of the British Empire.* vol. 5.] **2090.a.**

—— The Place of Coins in the Study of Indian History . . . Reprinted from the Hindustan Review, *etc.* pp. 10. *Allahabad,* 1905. 8°. **7757.** d. **28.** **(2.)**

BURN (Robert) *Colonel, R.A.* A Naval and Military Technical Dictionary of the French Language; with explanations of the various terms in English. pp. 178. *E. Jones: Woolwich,* 1842. 12°. **12953.** bb. **36.**

—— [Another edition.] In two parts: French-English, and English-French, *etc.* 2 pt. *John Murray: London,* 1852. 8°. **2276.** d. **23.**

—— Third edition. 2 pt. *John Murray: London,* 1854, 63. 8°. **12980.** cc. **8.**
Pt. 2 is of the fourth edition.

BURN (Robert) *Fellow and Tutor of Trinity College, Cambridge.* God our Refuge. A sermon preached . . . the Sunday after the death of the Rev. Adam Sedgwick. pp. 15. *Deighton, Bell & Co.: Cambridge,* 1873. 8°. **4479.** cc. **2.** **(2.)**

—— On the Course of Reading for the Classical Tripos. *See* Seeley (*Sir* John R.) *K.C.M.G.* The Student's Guide to the University of Cambridge. 1863. 8°. **8364.** a. **21.**

—— [Another edition.] *See* Seeley (*Sir* John R.) *K.C.M.G.* The Student's Guide to the University of Cambridge, *etc.* 1866. 8°. **8364.** a. **22.**

BURN (ROBERT) *Fellow and Tutor of Trinity College, Cambridge.*

—— [Another edition.] The Classical Tripos. *See* S., J. R. The Student's Guide to the University of Cambridge, *etc.* 1874. 8°. **8364. aa. 34.**

—— [Another edition.] pp. 48. *Deighton, Bell & Co.: Cambridge,* 1880. 8°. [*Student's Guide to the University of Cambridge.* pt. 3.] **8364. a. 58.**

—— [Another edition.] pp. 50. *Deighton, Bell & Co.: Cambridge,* 1891. 8°. [*Student's Guide to the University of Cambridge.* pt. 3.] **8364. a. 59.**

—— A Reply to Mr. J. H. Parker's Criticisms on "Rome and the Campagna." pp. 16. *Deighton, Bell & Co.: Cambridge,* 1872. 8°. **010136. e. 1.**

—— Roman Literature in relation to Roman Art . . . With illustrations. pp. x. 315. *Macmillan & Co.: London,* 1888. 8°. **7807. g. 27.**

—— Rome and the Campagna. An historical and topographical description of the site, buildings and neighbourhood of Ancient Rome. With 85 illustrations by Jewitt, and 25 maps and plans. (Appendix on the most important recent excavations in Rome.) pp. lxxxiii. 483. *Deighton, Bell & Co.: Cambridge; Bell & Daldy: London,* 1871, 76. 4°. **10131. h. 23.**

—— Old Rome: a handbook to the ruins of the City and the Campagna . . . Being an epitome of 'Rome and the Campagna.' [With illustrations and maps.] pp. xii. 266. *G. Bell & Sons: London; Deighton, Bell & Co.: Cambridge,* 1880 [1879]. 8°. **7705.c.43.**

—— [Another edition.] pp. xiii. 292. *G. Bell & Sons: London,* 1895. 8°. [*Bohn's Illustrated Library.*] **2502. e. 1.**

—— *See* PARKER (John H.) *C.B.* Old Rome, by R. Burn . . . and the Architectural History of the City of Rome, abridged from Parker's "Archæology of Rome," compared and contrasted, *etc.* [1882.] 8°. **7706. aaa. 34. (3.)**

BURN (ROBERT) *Missionary. See* BIBLE.—*New Testament.* [*Malay.*] . . . سورة تستمنت بهارو The New Testament. [Revised edition by C. H. Thompson and R. Burn.] 1831. 8°. **14620. ee. 14.**

BURN (ROBERT SCOTT) *See* DONALDSON (John) *Professor of Botany.* Suburban Farming . . . With considerable additions . . . by R. S. Burn, *etc.* 1877. 8°. **7074. d. 12.**

—— *See* PERIODICAL PUBLICATIONS.—*Edinburgh.* Year Book of Agricultural Facts for 1859. Edited by R. S. Burn. 1860, *etc.* 8°. **P.P. 2284.**

—— *See* SLIGHT (James) and BURN (R. S.) The Book of Farm Implements & Machines, *etc.* 1858. 8°. **7076. d. 44.**

—— *See* STEPHENS (Henry) *F.R.S.E., etc.,* and BURN (R. S.) The Book of Farm Buildings, *etc.* 1861. 8°. **07073. e. 4.**

—— *See* YOUATT (William) The Complete Grazier . . . enlarged . . . by R. S. Burn. 1864. 8°. **07077. l. 12.**

—— —— 1877. 8°. **7074. ccc. 14.**

BURN (ROBERT SCOTT)

—— The Architectural Designer's Guide; or Builder's practical assistant, being a series of finished and working drawings . . . of windows, doors, cornices, mouldings . . . with examples of . . . domestic and street architecture in plans, elevations, and sections, *etc.* [By R. S. Burn.] pt. 1–26. [1853-59.] 4°. *See* DESIGNER. **1261. c. 17.**

—— Architectural Drawing in Outline. 3 bk. *London & Edinburgh,* 1854. *obl.* 4°. [*Chamber's Educational Course. Drawing and Perspective, etc.*] **1899.ccc.30.**

—— The Book of Architectural Design. A guide to the planning and decoration of domestic structures in the various modern styles . . . Edited by R. S. Burn . . . The designs prepared by Edward S. Eyland. 2 pt. pl. XXXVI. *W. & R. Chambers: London & Edinburgh,* 1861, 62. 4°. **7816. b. 14.**

—— Building Construction; showing the employment of brick, stone, and slate, in the practical construction of buildings. 2 vol. pp. 135. pl. XIX. *London & Glasgow,* 1873, 74. 8°. [*Collins' Elementary Science Series.*] **8708. aaa. 16.**

—— Building Construction; showing the employment of brickwork and masonry, in the practical construction of buildings. 2 vol. pp. 198. pl. XXXVIII. *London & Glasgow,* 1876. 8° & 4°. [*Collins' Advanced Science Series.*] **8708. aa. 9 & 8707. l. 2.**

—— Building Construction, showing the employment of timber, lead and iron work, in the practical construction of buildings. 2 vol. pp. 256. pl. LX. *London & Glasgow,* 1876, 77. 8° & 4°. [*Collins' Advanced Science Series.*] **8708. aa. 10 & 8707. l. 4.**

—— Building Construction; showing the employment of timber, lead, and iron work, in the practical construction of buildings. 2 vol. pp. 136. pl. XX. *London & Glasgow,* 1874. 8°. [*Collins' Elementary Science Series.*] **8708. aaa. 17.**
A different work from the preceding.

—— The Carpenter and Joiner . . . By various experts and authorities. Edited and arranged by R. S. Burn, *etc.* pp. viii. 280. pl. L. *Ward, Lock & Co.: London,* 1892. 8°. **7817. e. 22.**

—— The Colonist's and Emigrant's Hand Book of the Mechanical Arts. pp. viii. 130. *W. Blackwood & Sons: Edinburgh & London,* 1854. 8°. **8765. d. 17.**

—— Conservatories, their Arrangement and Construction. With practical observations and suggestions explanatory of the details of green houses and hot houses . . . Edited by R. S. Burn. 8 pt. pl. XVIII. *George Hebert: London,* 1852, 53. 4°. **7028. f. 5.**
The titlepage is lithographed.

—— Glossary of Technical Terms employed in the practical construction of buildings and in the fitting and construction of machinery, *etc.* pp. 12. pl. x. *W. & R. Chambers: London & Edinburgh,* 1860. 4°. **7816. c. 7. (2.)**

—— The Grammar of House Planning: hints on arranging and modifying plans . . . By an M.S.A. and M.R.A.S. [i.e. R. S. Burn], *etc.* pp. x. 190. pl. XXXI. 1866. 8°. *See* GRAMMAR. **7815. aa. 20.**

BURN (Robert Scott)

—— The Handbook of Object Teaching, consisting of essays descriptive of the sciences, machines, and industrial processes illustrated in the book of large sheet drawings, by R. S. Burn . . . assisted by various authors and artists. pp. viii. 520. pl. xxv. *A. Fullarton & Co.: Edinburgh, London,* [1868.] 8°. **1803. a. 34.**

—— [Plates.] pl. xl. [1868.] fol. **1803. e. 3.**
Published in parts.

—— Handbook of the Mechanical Arts . . . Second edition. pp. iv. 324. *W. Blackwood & Sons: Edinburgh & London,* 1860. 8°. **8765. b. 30.**

—— Handy Hints on the internal arrangement, and the sanitary contrivances, of cottages and villas. By the author of " The Grammar of House Planning " [i.e. R. S. Burn]. *See* Bogue (James W.) Domestic Architecture, *etc. obl.* 4°. **1732. a. 22.**

—— Hints for Farmers, and Useful Information for Agricultural Students. pp. v. 171. *Routledge & Co.: London,* 1861. 8°. **7076. a. 7.**

—— The Illustrated London Architectural, Engineering, and Mechanical Drawing Book. pp. 151. *Ingram, Cooke & Co.: London,* 1853. 12°. **7820. d. 10.**

—— Tenth edition, revised and corrected, *etc.* pp. 155. *Ward, Lock & Co.: London,* 1893. 8°. **7855. c. 53.**

—— The Illustrated London Drawing Book, *etc.* pp. 146. [*Ingram, Cooke & Co.:*] *London,* 1852. 8°. **7855. e. 31.**

—— The Illustrated Drawing Book . . . Third edition, revised [of " The Illustrated London Drawing Book "]. pp. 143. *Ward & Lock: London,* 1856. 8°. **7855. e. 30.**

—— New edition. Revised, corrected and enlarged, *etc.* pp. 186. *Ward, Lock & Co.: London,* 1893. 8°. **7855. c. 54.**

—— The Illustrated London Practical Geometry, and its application to architectural drawing, *etc.* pp. iii. 77. *Ingram, Cooke & Co.: London,* 1853. 12°. **8531. c. 27.**

—— Illustrations of Carpentry and Framing; being drawings to scale, of roofs, partitions, floors, joints, *etc.* 2 ser. *W. & R. Chambers: London & Edinburgh,* 1859. 4°. **7816. b. 13.**

—— Illustrations of Joinery. (Companion work to Illustrations of Carpentry.) Being drawings of moulding, architraves, *etc.* pp. 8. pl. xiv. *W. & R. Chambers: London & Edinburgh,* 1859. 4°. **1269. g. 32.**

—— Second series. pp. 2. pl. xviii. *W. & R. Chambers: London & Edinburgh,* 1861. 4°. **7816. c. 7. (3.)**

—— Illustrations of Machine and Mill Gearing, *etc.* pl. vii. *George Hebert: London,* [1856.] 4°. **8766. e. 25. (2.)**

—— Illustrations of Mechanical Movements and Machines, *etc.* pp. 12. pl. xi. *W. & R. Chambers: London & Edinburgh,* 1861. 4°. **8766. e. 25. (6.)**

—— Isometrical Drawing. 2 bk. *London,* 1855. *obl.* 4°. [*Chambers's Educational Course. Drawing and Perspective, etc.*] **1899.ccc.30.**

—— The Lessons of My Farm; a book for amateur agriculturists; being an introduction to farm practice, in the culture of crops, the feeding of cattle, *etc.* pp. xvi. 334. *Lockwood & Co.: London,* 1862. 8°. **7073. aa. 7.**

BURN (Robert Scott)

—— Systematic Small Farming; or, the Lessons of my farm, *etc.* [An enlarged edition of " The Lessons of My Farm."] pp. xiv. 386. *C. Lockwood & Co.: London,* 1886. 8°. **07077. g. 62.**

—— Mechanics and Mechanism: being elementary lessons and examples for the use of schools, students, and artisans. pp. viii. 113. *Ingram, Cooke & Co.: London,* 1853. 8°. **8765. c. 7.**

—— Third and revised edition. pp. 125. *Ward & Lock: London,* 1858. 8°. **8766. c. 18.**

—— Seventh edition, revised and enlarged. pp. 141. *Ward, Lock & Co.: London,* 1892. 8°. **8767. c. 38.**

—— Model Designs for Mansions, Villas, Dwelling-Houses, Cottages, Gates, and Stables . . . with hints on sanitary construction, and an Essay on dwellings for the working classes, *etc.* [With plates.] 4 pt. *George Hebert: London,* 1853. 4°. **7815. c. 5.**
Published in parts. The " Essay on dwellings for the working classes " has the imprint " W. Blackwood & Sons: Edinburgh & London."

—— (Cheap edition.) [With supplementary parts: " Cottage Accommodation for our Labourers " and " Conservatories. Their arrangement and construction." With plates.] 10 pt. *W. & R. Chambers: London & Edinburgh,* 1860 [1859, 60]. 4°. **7820. i. 14.**

—— Modern Mechanical Engineering and Machine Making: a series of working drawings and practical designs; including numerous examples from the Paris and Havre International Exhibitions, with papers on technical subjects, *etc.* pp. 280. pl. lxiii. *A. Fullarton & Co.: Edinburgh & London,* [1869?] fol. **1804. c. 21.**

—— The New Guide to Carpentry, General Farming, and Joinery. Edited by R. S. Burn, *etc.* [With plates.] pp. viii. 364. *A. Fullarton & Co.: Edinburgh, London,* [1868–72.] 4°. **7816. e. 3.**
Published in parts.

—— The New Guide to Masonry, Bricklaying and Plastering theoretical and practical. Edited by R. S. Burn, *etc.* [With plates.] pp. xi. 440. pl. 133. *A. Fullarton & Co.: Edinburgh, London,* [1868–72.] 4°. A-ZAA. **7816. e. 16.**
Published in parts.

—— Notes of an Agricultural Tour in Belgium, Holland, & the Rhine, *etc.* pp. x. 241. *Longman & Co.: London,* 1862. 8°. **7075. cc. 10.**

—— On the Arrangement, Construction, and Fittings of School-Houses. pp. 27. pl. vi. *W. Blackwood & Sons: Edinburgh & London,* 1856. 4°. **7815. c. 6.**

—— The Ornamental Draughtsman and Designer . . . By several practical draughtsmen and designers. Arranged by R. S. Burn, *etc.* pp. viii. 142. pl. xxxvii. *Ward, Lock & Co.: London,* 1892. 8°. **7854. d. 40.**

—— Ornamental Drawing, and Architectural Design, with notes, historical and practical . . . Fourteenth thousand. pp. 124. *Ward, Lock & Tyler: London,* 1857. 8°. **7820. e. 13.**

—— Outlines of Farm Management and the Organization of Farm Labour, *etc.* pp. viii. 272. *C. Lockwood & Co.: London,* 1880. 12°. **7078. b. 64.**

BURN (ROBERT SCOTT)

—— Outlines of Landed Estates Management, *etc.* pp. vi. 252. *C. Lockwood & Co.: London,* 1877. 12°. **7074.** bbb. **8.**

—— Second edition. pp. ix. 252. *C. Lockwood & Co.: London,* 1880. 12°. **07077.** e. **19.**

—— Outlines of Modern Farming, *etc.* 5 vol. *Virtue Bros. & Co.: London,* 1863–65. 12°. **8703.** c. **50.**

—— The seventh edition. 5 vol. *C. Lockwood & Son: London,* 1889–1904. 8°. **07077.** e. **13.**
Vol. 2 and 5 are of the sixth, and vol. 4 of the eighth edition.

—— Practical Architecture, as applied to Farm Buildings . . . Reprinted from "The Country." pp. 204. *London,* [1878.] 8°. **7820.** bbb. **10.**

—— The Practical Directory for the Improvement of Landed Property, rural and suburban, and the economic cultivation of its farms, *etc.* pp. xviii. 608. pl. 77. *William Paterson: Edinburgh,* 1881. 4°. **7073.** f. **2.**

—— Practical Ventilation as applied to Public, Domestic, and Agricultural Structures, *etc.* pp. xiii. 208. *W. Blackwood & Sons: Edinburgh & London,* 1850. 8°. **1400.** f. **15.**

—— Profitable Pig Keeping. Dealing with their treatment in health and disease, *etc.* pp. 44. *Cable Printing & Publishing Co.: London,* [1899.] 12°. [*Cable Series of Farm and Household Books.* no. 4.] **07944.** g. **81.**

—— Sanitary Science: as applied to the healthy construction of houses in town and country. pp. v. 264. *W. Collins, Sons & Co.: Glasgow & London,* 1872. 8°. **7814.** aa. **5.**

—— The Steam Engine, its history and mechanism, *etc.* pp. viii. 189. *H. Ingram & Co.: London,* 1854. 8°. **8765.** b. **31.**

—— Second edition, *etc.* pp. 142. *Ward & Lock: London,* 1857. 8°. **8768.** bbb. **30.**

—— Eighth and enlarged edition, *etc.* pp. vi. 184. *Ward, Lock & Co.: London,* 1894. 8°. **8768.** cc. **34.**

—— Robert Scott Burn, das Nothwendige und Wesentliche zur Kenntniss der Dampfmaschinen . . . Nach dem Englischen frei und allgemein verständlich bearbeitet von Dr. Carl Hartmann. pp. xiv. 193. pl. XIII. *Weimar,* 1855. 8°. [*Neuer Schauplatz der Künste.* Bd. 224.] **896.** dd. **90.**

—— The Steam Engine User. Being practical descriptions and illustrations of the stationary steam engine in its various forms . . . By various writers. Edited and arranged by R. S. Burn, *etc.* pp. xii. 402. *Ward, Lock & Co.: London,* 1894. 8°. **8767.** cc. **29.**

—— Systematic Small Farming. *See* supra: The Lessons of My Farm.

—— The Technical Student's Introduction to Mechanics . . . By various writers. Edited by R. S. Burn, *etc.* pp. xvi. 544. *Ward, Lock & Co.: London,* 1892. 8°. **8767.** f. **23.**

—— Working Drawings & Designs in Architecture and Building; with essays on various subjects . . . By Edward S. Eyland . . . Francis Lightbody . . . and R. S. Burn, general editor. [With plates.] *A. Fullarton & Co.: Edinburgh & London,* [1863–68.] fol. **1731.** c. **12.**
Published in parts.

BURN (ROBERT SCOTT)

—— Working Drawings & Designs in Engineering, Architecture, Building, & Machine-Making; with essays on various subjects . . . By Francis Lightbody . . . Edward S. Eyland . . . and R. S. Burn, general editor. pl. LXXII. *A. Fullarton & Co.: Edinburgh & London,* [1864–68.] fol. **1801.** b. **16.**
Published in parts.

—— Working Drawings & Designs in Mechanical Engineering & Machine-Making; with essays on various subjects . . . by W. Walker . . . Francis Lightbody . . . A. B. Brown . . . Robert Davis . . . and R. S. Burn, general editor. [With plates.] *A. Fullarton & Co.: Edinburgh & London,* [1864–68.] fol. **1801.** b. **17.**
Published in parts.

—— Working Drawings and Details of Steam Engines for the use of practical mechanics and students. Example number one, Horizontal High-Pressure Engine, *etc.* pp. 2. pl. IV. *George Hebert: London,* [1856.] 4°. **8766.** e. **25.** (3.)

BURN (SAMUEL) A Humble Companion to the Pilgrim's Progress: being a series of discourses on that great allegory. Originally delivered in Oakes Chapel, Huddersfield, *etc.* pp. viii. 412. *Hodder & Stoughton: London,* 1874. 8°. **4414.** ee. **32.**

BURN (THOMAS) Harry's Heroism. pp. iv. 92. *Elliot Stock: London,* 1884. 8°. **12805.** t. **14.**

BURN (WALTER ADAM) Claims against the Military; or, the Requisitioning of supplies, etc., under martial law during the South African War . . . To which is added the full text of the Hague Convention . . . in the original French with an English translation. pp. 74. *J. C. Juta & Co.: Cape Town,* 1903. 8°. **06955.** de. **9.**

BURN (WALTER ADAM) and **RAYMOND** (WILLIAM THOMAS)

—— A Manual of the Law regulating the Volunteer Forces, including the Volunteer Acts 1863 & 1869, *etc.* pp. xii. 80. *Stevens & Sons: London,* 1882. 8°. **6875.** aa. **17.**

BURN (WILLIAM LAURENCE)

—— The British West Indies. pp. 196. *Hutchinson's University Library: London,* 1951. 8°. [*Hutchinson's University Library. British Empire History.*] W.P. **1413/53.**

—— Emancipation and Apprenticeship in the British West Indies. pp. 398. *Jonathan Cape: London,* 1937. 8°. **20031.** d. **31.**

—— Policy and Opinion in Imperial Affairs. pp. 16. *Nottingham,* [1952.] 8°. [*Cust Foundation Lecture.* no. 25.] W.P. **5679/20.**

BURNABY (ANDREW) *Archdeacon of Leicester.* Six Occasional Sermons upon the following subjects. Viz. Sermon I. The Necessity of religious principles. Sermon II. The Degrees of charity due to men of different religious persuasions. Sermon III. The Maintenance due to the Ministers of the Gospel. Sermon IV. The Nature of subscription to articles of religion. Sermon V. Of Things belonging to the peace and welfare of nations. Sermon VI. Of moral advantages to be derived from travelling in Italy. pp. 124. *London,* 1777. 8°. **111.** f. **10.**

BURNABY (Andrew) *Archdeacon of Leicester.*

—— Occasional Sermons and Charges. pp. xii. 462. *J. Delahoy: Deptford*, 1805. 8°. **1026**. k. **2**.

—— The Blessings enjoyed by Englishmen, a motive for their repentance: a sermon preached in Greenwich Church, on the 19th of April, 1793. The day appointed for a general fast, *etc.* pp. 21. *T. Payne: London*, 1793. 4°. **694**. i. **10**. (**7**.)

—— A Charge delivered to the Clergy of the Archdeaconry of Leicester, by the Rev. A. Burnaby . . . at his visitation, held on the 5th, 6th, and 7th of May, 1801. pp. 23. *T. Payne: London*, [1801.] 8°. **695**. g. **2**. (**7**.)

—— Journal of a Tour to Corsica, in the year 1766 . . . With a series of original letters from General Paoli to the author, referring to the principal events which have taken place in that island, from 1766 to 1802, *etc.* pp. 172. *Luke Hansard: London*, 1804. 4°. **180**. h. **6**.

—— A Sermon on the Nature of Subscription to Articles of Religion, *etc.* pp. 28. *T. Payne: London*, 1774. 8°. **695**. g. **14**. (**9**.)

—— A Sermon preached before the Honourable House of Commons . . . on Wednesday, February 21, 1781 . . . being the day appointed for a general fast. pp. 24. *T. Payne & Son: London*, 1781. 4°. **694**. i. **9**. (**10**.)

—— A Sermon preached in Greenwich Church, on Thursday, July 29, 1784; the day appointed for a general thanksgiving, *etc.* pp. 23. *T. Payne & Son: London*, 1784. 4°. **694**. h. **8**. (**4**.)

—— A Sermon preached in Greenwich Church, on Thursday, April 23d, 1789; the day appointed for a general thanksgiving on account of His Majesty's happy recovery, *etc.* pp. 20. *T. Payne & Sons: London*, 1789. 4°. **694**. k. **9**. (**8**.)

—— A Sermon preached in Greenwich Church, on Sunday, November 4, 1792. pp. 13. *T. Payne: London*, 1793. 4°. **114**. b. **60**.

—— The Sin and Danger of Schism, considered in a charge —intended to be delivered to the clergy of the Archdeaconry of Leicester, at the summer visitation in 1811. pp. 23. *T. Payne; F. C. & J. Rivington: London*, 1811. 8°. **695**. g. **2**. (**8**.)

—— Travels through the Middle Settlements in North-America, in the years 1759 and 1760. With observations upon the state of the colonies. pp. viii. 106. *T. Payne: London*, 1775. 4°. T. **3**. (**5**.)

—— [Another copy.] **601**. i. **6**. (**2**.)

—— [Another copy.] **147**. d. **20**.

—— [Another copy.] **104**. i. **53**.

—— The second edition. pp. xvi. 198. *T. Payne: London*, 1775. 8°. **792**. e. **8**.

—— [Another copy.] G. **15765**. (**1**.)

—— Edition the third; revised, corrected, and greatly enlarged, by the author. pp. xix. 209. *T. Payne: London*, 1798. 4°. **10410**. f. **18**.

—— [Another edition.] 1812. *See* Pinkerton (John) *Antiquary.* A General Collection of . . . Voyages and Travels, *etc.* vol. 13. 1808, *etc.* 4°. L.R. **80**. c. **1**.

—— [Another edition.] Reprinted from the third edition of 1798. With introduction and notes by Rufus Rockwell Wilson. pp. 265. *A. Wessels Co.: New York*, 1904. 8°. **010883**. g. **25**.

BURNABY (Andrew) *Archdeacon of Leicester.*

—— Two Charges, delivered to the Clergy, of the Archdeaconry of Leicester, in the years . . . 1786 and 1787. pp. vii. 38. *T. Payne & Son: London*, 1787. 8°. **695**. g. **2**. (**6**.)

BURNABY (Andrew) *Rector of Ashfordby.* School Hours; or, a Collection of exercises and prize poems, composed by the young gentlemen under the tuition of the Reverend A. Burnaby, *etc.* pp. 181. *Simpkin & Marshall: London*, 1823. 8°. **12355**. aa. **39**.

BURNABY (Anthony) An Essay upon the Excising of Malt: as also the present case of tallies consider'd. pp. 85. *Printed for the Author: London*, 1696. 8°. T. **1814**. (**4**.)

—— [Another copy.] **517**. e. **2**. (**1**.)

—— [Another copy.] **288**. b. **25**.

—— Two Proposals, humbly offer'd to the Honourable House of Commons . . . I. That a duty be laid on malt, in the stead of the present duty on beer and ale . . . II. That a duty be laid on malt, and the present duty on beer and ale be continued. To which is annex'd an accompt, what . . . the frauds of brewers do amount to, *etc.* pp. 26. *London*, 1696. 4°. T. **1788**. (**4**.)

BURNABY (C. A.) Harold's Friends; or, the New rector of Greythorpe. pp. 192. *R.T.S.: London*, [1890.] 8°. **4419**. g. **8**.

—— [Another edition.] pp. 186. *R.T.S.: London*, [1903.] 8°. **04429**. ff. **70**.

—— Our Story. pp. 32. [*R.T.S.: London*, 1906.] 8°. [*Bouverie Series of Penny Stories.* no. 22.] **4430**. ee. **18**.

—— Tom Larkins, or, the Boy who was no good. pp. 127. *R.T.S.*: [*London*, 1887.] 8°. **4420**. h. **40**.

BURNABY (Charles) [For editions of "The Ladies Visiting Day," "The Modish Husband," "The Reform'd Wife" and "Love Betray'd," sometimes attributed to C. Burnaby but more probably by William Burnaby:] *See* Burnaby (William)

BURNABY (Edwyn Andrew) A Letter to the Cabinet Ministers, suggesting a mode to relieve, in part, the distresses of the Empire, and to make its income and expenditure balance, *etc.* pp. 35. *J. Hatchard: London*, 1817. 8°. B. **516**. (**11**.)

BURNABY (Edwyn Sherard) An Account of the Right Flank Company of the 3rd Battalion Grenadier Guards defending the right of the British position, and subsequently the colours of the Battalion . . . at the battle of Inkermann, 5th November, 1854. (Various returns and states of the 3rd Battalion Grenadier Guards, during the eastern campaign, 1854, 1855, 1856.) [The editor's preface signed: E. S. B., i.e. E. S. Burnaby.] 2 pt. 1857. 8°. *See* B., E. S. **9077**. eee. **31**. (**4**.)

—— A Few Short Demonstrations on the Advantage of employing a British-European Legion in India. Prepared for the Honble East India Company, *etc.* [With a map.] 3 pt. *Staunton & Son:* [*London*,] 1857. fol. **8010**. i. **3**.

—— John Bryant: or, the Stag-Hunt. A true tale. By E. S. B. [i.e. E. S. Burnaby?] pp. 16. [1869.] 8°. [*Homely Tales for Homely Readers.* no. 4.] *See* B., E. S. **4418**. ee. **85**

BURNABY, afterwards **MAIN**, afterwards **LE BLOND** (ELIZABETH ALICE FRANCES) *See* CHARLOTTE AMELIA, *Consort of Anthony, Count of Aldenburg.* The Autobiography of Charlotte Amélie, Princess of Aldenburg . . . Translated . . . and edited by her descendant, Mrs. A. Le Blond. 1913. 8°. **010662**. d. **14**.

—— *See* LYAUTEY (L. H. G.) [Lettres du Tonquin et de Madagascar.] Intimate Letters from Tonquin . . . Translated by Mrs. A. Le Blond, *etc.* 1932. 8°. **10906**. g. **13**.

—— *See* MAECKEL (O. V.) The Dunkelgraf Mystery. By O. V. Maeckel. With the collaboration of Mrs. A. Le Blond, *etc.* [1929.] 8°. **10235**. cc. **32**.

—— *See* TRIGGS (Henry I.) The Art of Garden Design in Italy. Illustrated by . . . twenty-eight plates from photographs by Mrs. A. Le Blond. 1906. fol. Tab. **700**. b. **4**.

—— Adventures on the Roof of the World . . . Illustrated. pp. xvi. 333. *T. Fisher Unwin: London,* 1904. 8°. **10196**. ee. **19**.

—— [Another edition.] pp. 382. *London,* [1916.] 8°. [*Nelson's Shilling Library.*] **12204**. d. **17/117**.

—— Charlotte Sophie Countess Bentinck. Her life and times, 1715–1800 . . . With 72 illustrations, *etc.* 2 vol. *Hutchinson & Co.: London,* 1912. 8°. **010706**. g. **34**.

—— Cities and Sights of Spain. A handbook for tourists . . . With numerous illustrations from photographs by the author. [With a map.] pp. xv. 214. *G. Bell & Sons: London,* 1899. 8°. **10160**. bbb. **26**.

—— (Revised re-issue.) pp. xv. 214. *G. Bell & Sons: London,* 1904. 8°. **2362**. b. **7**.

—— Day in, Day out . . . [An autobiography.] With twenty-nine illustrations [including portraits]. pp. 264. *John Lane: London,* 1928. 8°. **010855**. f. **21**.

—— The High Alps in Winter; or, Mountaineering in search of health. [With plates, including a portrait.] pp. xvii. 204. *Sampson Low & Co.: London,* 1883. 8°. **10196**. bbb. **13**.

—— High Life and Towers of Silence. [With plates.] pp. xii. 195. *Sampson Low & Co.: London,* 1886. 8°. **10196**. bb. **8**.

—— Hints on Snow Photography . . . With illustrations. pp. 14. *Sampson Low & Co.: London,* [1895.] 8°. **8909**. cc. **11**.

—— Mountaineering in the Land of the Midnight Sun . . . With 71 illustrations and map. pp. xii. 304. *T. Fisher Unwin: London, Leipsic,* 1908. 8°. **10281**. e. **18**.

—— My Home in the Alps. pp. vi. 131. *Sampson Low & Co.: London,* 1892. 8°. **10196**. cc. **7**.

—— The Old Gardens of Italy. How to visit them. By Mrs. A. Le Blond. With illustrations from her photographs. pp. xiii. 172. *John Lane: London, New York,* 1912. 8°. **10151**. c. **37**.

—— (Second edition, revised.) pp. xiii. 172. *John Lane: London,* 1926. 8°. **10136**. d. **27**.

—— The Story of an Alpine Winter. pp. vii. 289. *G. Bell & Sons: London,* 1907. 8°. **12803**. r. **24**.

BURNABY, afterwards **MAIN**, afterwards **LE BLOND** (ELIZABETH ALICE FRANCES)

—— True Tales of Mountain Adventure for non-climbers young and old. [With plates, including portraits.] pp. xvi. 299. *T. Fisher Unwin: London,* 1903. 8°. **10196**. ee. **17**.

—— [Another edition.] pp. 383. *London,* [1915.] 8°. [*Nelson's Shilling Library.*] **12204**. d. **17/110**.

BURNABY (EVELYN HENRY VILLEBOIS) Memories of Famous Trials. [With plates, including a portrait.] pp. xix. 240. *Sisley's: London,* 1907. 8°. **6495**. d. **14**.

—— Second impression. pp. xix. 240. *Sisley's: London,* 1907. 8°. **6055**. de. **25**.

—— [Another edition.] pp. xvi. 232. *Sisley's: London,* [1909.] 8°. **6496**. aa. **36**.

—— A Ride from Land's End to John o' Groats. pp. xxii. 146. *Sampson Low & Co.: London,* 1893. 8°. **10351**. e. **42**.

BURNABY (*Mrs.* FRED.) *See* BURNABY, afterwards MAIN, afterwards LE BLOND (Elizabeth A. F.)

BURNABY (FREDERICK GUSTAVUS) *See* DUFF (Louis B.) Burnaby. [With a portrait.] 1926. 8°. **10816**. e. **28**

—— *See* MANN (R. K.) The Life, Adventures, and Politica[l] Opinions of Frederick Gustavus Burnaby. 1882. 8°. **10816**. bb. **4**

—— *See* WARE (James R.) and MANN (R. K.) The Life and Times of Colonel Fred. Burnaby. [With a portrait.] [1885.] 8°. **10816**. c. **28**.

—— *See* WRIGHT (Thomas) *of Olney.* The Life of Colonel Fred Burnaby, *etc.* [With portraits.] 1908. 8°. **10816**. de. **9**.

—— On Horseback through Asia Minor . . . With portrait and maps. 2 vol. *Sampson Low & Co.: London,* 1877. 8°. **2356**. d. **3**.

—— Our Radicals. A tale of love and politics . . . Edited, with preface, by . . . J. Percival Hughes. [With a facsimile.] 2 vol. *R. Bentley & Son: London,* 1886. 8°. **12619**. l. **16**.

—— New edition. pp. xxiv. 315. *R. Bentley & Son: London,* 1886. 8°. **12618**. n. **3**.

—— The Practical Instruction of Staff Officers in Foreign Armies . . . From the Journal of the Royal United Service Institution, *etc.* [With maps.] pp. 46. *W. Mitchell & Co.: London,* [1872.] 8°. **8829**. e. **42**. **(2.)**

—— A Ride across the Channel, and other adventures in the air. [With a map.] pp. 128. *Sampson Low & Co.: London,* 1882. 8°. **8755**. bbb. **18**.

—— A Ride to Khiva: travels and adventures in Central Asia . . . With maps and an appendix . . . Third edition. pp. xviii. 487. *Cassell & Co.: London,* 1876. 8°. **10076**. ee. **4**.

—— Eleventh edition. pp. xviii. 487. *Cassell & Co.: London,* 1877. 8°. **2356**. b. **18**.

—— (People's edition.) pp. 56. *Cassell & Co.: London,* [1882.] fol. **10077**. l. **4**.

—— Cheap edition. pp. 398. *Cassell & Co.: London,* [1884.] 8°. **10076**. bbb. **2**.

BURNABY (Frederick Gustavus)

—— New edition, *etc.* pp. xiv. 334. *Cassell & Co.: London,* 1895. 8°. **10076. aa. 8.**

—— [Another edition.] pp. 126. *Cassell & Co.: London,* 1905. 8°. **010075.** e. **5.**

—— *See* Burnand (*Sir* Francis C.) The Ride to Khiva, *etc.* [A parody of " A Ride to Khiva."] 1877. 8°. **12314.** g. **19.**

—— —— 1879. 8°. **12314.** g. **11.**

BURNABY (H. M.) Three Monologues, *etc.* pp. 4. *Cavendish Music Co.: London,* [1929.] 4°. **11778.** h. **28.**

BURNABY (Hugh) *See* Margueritte (V.) [La Garçonne.] The Bachelor Girl . . . Translated by H. Burnaby. 1923. 8°. **012547.** a. **53.**

BURNABY (John)

—— *See* Augustine, *Saint, Bishop of Hippo.* [*Two or more Works.—English.*] Augustine: Later Works. Selected and translated with introductions by J. Burnaby. 1955. 8°. W.P. b. **296/8.**

—— Amor Dei. A study of the religion of St. Augustine. The Hulsean lectures for 1938. pp. xi. 338. *Hodder & Stoughton: London,* 1938. 8°. **3622.** e. **23.**

—— Christian Words and Christian Meanings. pp. 160. *Hodder & Stoughton: London,* 1955. 8°. **4382.** de. **58.**

—— Education, Religion, Learning and Research. An inaugural lecture. pp. 25. *Cambridge University Press: London, New York,* [1953.] 8°. **12302.** a. **43.**

—— Is the Bible inspired? pp. 120. *Gerald Duckworth & Co.: London,* 1949. 8°. [*Colet Library of Modern Christian Thought and Teaching.* no. 9.] W.P. **13184/9.**

BURNABY (Nigel) *pseud.* [i.e. Harold Picton Ellett.] The Clue of the Green-Eyed Girl. pp. 319. *Ward, Lock & Co.: London & Melbourne,* 1935. 8°. NN. **23769.**

—— The Forest Mystery. A novel. pp. 320. *Ward, Lock & Co.: London & Melbourne,* 1934. 8°. NN. **22112.**

—— The Secret of Matchams. pp. 312. *Ward, Lock & Co.: London & Melbourne,* 1934. 8°. NN. **23270.**

—— Two Deaths for a Penny. pp. 320. *Ward, Lock & Co.: London & Melbourne,* 1935. 8°. NN. **24990.**

BURNABY (Robert Beaumont) *See* Ovidius Naso (P.) [*Selections.—Latin.*] Elegiac Selections from Ovid. By R. B. Burnaby. 1905. 8°. **11304.** bb. **25/15.**

BURNABY (Sherrard Beaumont) Elements of the Jewish and Muhammadan Calendars, with rules and tables and explanatory notes on the Julian and Gregorian calendars. pp. xv. 554. *G. Bell & Sons: London,* 1901. 8°. **8563.** e. **17.**

BURNABY (T. F. A.) *See* Newark.—*Magnus Song School.* The Ordinance and Foundation of the Schools of Grammar and Song at Newark-upon-Trent . . . Prepared by T. F. A. Burnaby, *etc.* 1855. 8°. **8364.** aaa. **62.** (**1.**)

BURNABY (Thomas) A Sermon preached in St. George's Church, Leicester . . . on . . . February 18th, 1827; being the day on which it was opened for divine worship, *etc.* pp. 20. *C. & J. Rivington: London; Combe: Leicester,* 1827. 8°. T. **1204.** (**2.**)

BURNABY (William) *See* Petronius Arbiter (T.) The Satyr of Titus Petronius Arbiter . . . Made English by Mr. Burnaby . . . and another hand. 1694. 8°. **11306.** b. **27.**

—— —— 1708. 8°. **11306.** d. **4.**

—— —— [1923.] 8°. **012201.** b. **1/18.**

—— The Dramatic Works of William Burnaby. Edited by F. E. Budd. pp. 469. *Eric Partridge: London,* 1931. 8°. **11771.** g. **14.**

—— The Ladies Visiting-Day. A comedy . . . With the addition of a new scene. By the author of The Reformed Wife [i.e. W. Burnaby?]. pp. 52. 1701. 4°. *See* Ladies. **83.** a. **8.** (**3.**)

—— Second edition. pp. 68. 1708. 4°. *See* Ladies. **642.** k. **39.**

—— Love Betray'd; or, the Agreable disapointment. A comedy . . . By the author of The Ladies Visiting Day [i.e. W. Burnaby?]. pp. 61. 1703. 4°. *See* Love. **83.** a. **8.** (**1.**)

—— The Modish Husband: a comedy . . . By the author of The Ladies Visiting Day [i.e. W. Burnaby?]. pp. 68. 1702. 4°. *See* Husband. **11775.** d. **23.**

—— [Another copy.] **83.** a. **8.** (**2.**)

—— The Reform'd Wife. A comedy, *etc.* [By W. Burnaby?] pp. 45. 1700. 4°. *See* Wife. **644.** d. **37.**

—— [Another copy.] **643.** i. **58.** (**9.**)

—— Second edition, with the addition of a new scene. pp. 45. 1700. 4°. *See* Wife. **83.** a. **8.** (**4.**)

—— [Another copy.] **642.** k. **40.**

BURNACINI (Giovanni) *See* Biach-Schiffmann (F.) Giovanni und Ludovico Burnacini, *etc.* [With a portrait.] 1931. 8°. **11795.** r. **13.**

BURNACINI (Lodovico Ottavio) *See* Biach-Schiffmann (F.) Giovanni und Ludovico Burnacini, *etc.* [With a portrait.] 1931. 8°. **11795.** r. **13.**

—— Maschere. [Plates. With explanatory text by Joseph Gregor.] pp. 13. pl. xx. [1925.] 8° & 4°. [*Denkmäler des Theaters.* Portfolio 1.] Dept. of Prints & Drawings.

BURNAM (Curtis Field) *M.D.* *See* Kelly (Howard A.) and Burnam (C. F.) Diseases of the Kidneys, *etc.* 1914. 8°. **07640.** f. **16.**

—— —— [1922.] 8°. **7640.** k. **22.**

BURNAM (Curtis Field) *of Yale College.* *See* Hollister (G. H.) A Poem by Gideon Hiram Hollister; and the Valedictory Oration, by C. F. Burnam, pronounced before the senior class in Yale College, *etc.* 1840. 8°. **11686.** f. **20.**

BURNAM (ELIZABETH) *See* BURNAM (Robert) A Remonstrance, or, a Necessitated Vindication of Robert Burnam against two false scandalous libells, malitiously scattered in the name of E. Burnam his wife, *etc.* 1645. 4°. E. **322**. (**17**.)

BURNAM (JOHN MILLER)

—— *See* LUCCA.—*Cathedral Church.—Biblioteca Capitolare.* A Classical Technology. Edited from Codex Lucensis 490 by J. M. Burnam. [1920.] 8°. **07942**. d. **65**.

—— *See* MADRID CODEX A 16. Recipes from Codex Matritensis A 16 . . . By J. M. Burnam. [1912.] 8°. Dept. of Manuscripts.

—— *See* MADRID CODEX A 113. A Brief Catalonian Medical Text. By J. M. Burnam. [Text, with an introduction.] [1913.] 8°. Dept. of Manuscripts.

—— The Early Gold and Silver Manuscripts. (Reprinted from Classical Philology.) [*Chicago*, 1911.] 8°. Dept. of Manuscripts.

—— Miscellanea Hispanica . . . Reprinted . . . from Modern Philology, *etc.* [*New York*, 1914.] 8°. Dept. of Manuscripts.

—— Palæographia Iberica. Fac-similés de manuscrits espagnols et portugais, IXe–XVe siècles, avec notices et transcriptions par J. M. Burnam. 3 fasc. pp. 228. pl. LX. *Paris*, [1912–25.] fol. MS. Facs. **187**.

BURNAM (ROBERT) A Remonstrance, or, a Necessitated Vindication of Robert Burnam against two false scandalous libels, malitiously scattered in the name of Elizabeth Burnam his wife . . . or, the Plaine mans declaration against conjugall separation, wherein . . . you may lively behold the vast difference betweene a good wife and one transcendently bad, *etc.* pp. 15. *Thomas Paine: London*, 1645. 4°. E. **322**. (**17**.)

BURNAND (   ) *See* FABRICIUS (Johann A.) [Hydrotheologie.] Theologie de l'eau, *etc.* [Translated by — Burnand.] 1741. 8°. **858**. b. **16**.

BURNAND (AUG.) Le Colonel Henry Bouquet, vainqueur des Peaux-Rouges de l'Ohio. (Extrait de la Revue historique vaudoise.) 1909. *See* SWISS SOLDIERS. Soldats suisses au service étranger, *etc.* 1908, *etc.* 8°. **08821**. e. **1/2**.

BURNAND (EUGÈNE) *See* BIBLE.—*Gospels.—Selections.* [*English.*] The Parables. Illustrated by E. Burnand, *etc.* 1910. fol. **L.R.404.e.6.**

—— *See* BIBLE.—*Gospels.—Selections.* [*French.*] Les Paraboles, illustrées par E. Burnand, *etc.* 1917. 4°. **3227**. h. **18**.

—— *See* BURNAND (R.) Eugène Burnand: l'homme, l'artiste et son œuvre, *etc.* [With plates, including a portrait.] 1926. 8°. **7859**. c. **25**.

—— *See* DAUDET (A.) Contes choisis . . . Avec sept eaux-fortes par E. Burnand. 1883. 8°. **12517**. k. **24**.

—— *See* FRANCIS [Bernardoni], *of Assisi, Saint.* The Little Flowers of Saint Francis . . . With thirty drawings by E. Burnand. 1919. 4°. L.R. **30**. b. **16**.

—— *See* GRELLET (M. V.) Eugène Burnand . . . Ouvrage illustré d'un portrait . . . et de 17 reproductions des œuvres de l'artiste, *etc.* [1921.] *obl.* 8°. **10704**. bbb. **34**.

BURNAND (EUGÈNE)

—— *See* MISTRAL (F.) Mireille. Poème provençal . . . Avec 25 eaux-fortes . . . par E. Burnand, *etc.* 1884. 4°. **1869**. d. **1**.

—— —— 1891. 8°. **11498**. k. **15**.

—— *See* SAND (George) *pseud.* François le Champi. Dessins et aquarelles de E. Burnand. 1888. 8°. **012547**. g. **6**.

BURNAND (EUGÈNE ROBERT)

—— *See* CLOUZOT (E.) Catalogue des publications et des manuscrits composant la collection Nadar à la bibliothèque. [By E. Clouzot, G. Henriot and R. Burnand.] 1913. 8°. [*Bulletin de la Bibliothèque et des Travaux Historiques de la Ville.* fasc. 6.] **11908**. e. **38/6**.

—— *See* PARIS.—*Palais National des Arts.—Exposition "Chefs-d'œuvre de l'Art français."* Chefs-d'œuvre de l'art français, *etc.* (Les notices rédigées par R. Burnand.) 1937. 4°. **7866**. s. **7**.

—— Bazaine. pp. 253. *Paris*, 1939. 8°. **10655**. k. **25**.

—— La Cour des Valois. pp. 256. [*Paris*,] 1938. 8°. **09200**. de. **20**.

—— Le Duc d'Aumale et son temps. pp. 251. *Paris*, 1949. 8°. **10661**. w. **36**.

—— L'Étrange baronne de Feuchères. *In:* Les Œuvres libres. Nouvelle série. no. 42. pp. 199–228. 1949. 8°. **12208**. ee. **267**.

—— L'Hôtel Royal des Invalides, 1670–1789. [With illustrations.] pp. xxiii. 295. *Paris, Nancy*, 1913. 8°. **010171**. m. **2**.

—— Napoléon III et les siens. pp. 383. [*Paris*,] 1948. 8°. **10656**. gg. **51**.
Part of a series entitled " L'Histoire anecdotique."

—— Vie et mort de la Marquise de Brinvilliers. pp. 224. *Paris*, [1931.] 8°. **10655**. de. **4**.

—— La Vie quotidienne en France de 1870 à 1900. pp. 305. *Paris*, 1947. 8°. **010171**. pp. **23**.

BURNAND (*Sir* FRANCIS COWLEY) *See* BISSON (A.) and BURNAND (*Sir* F. C.) Captain Thérèse, *etc.* [1890.] 8°. **11779**. c. **21**. (**1**.)

—— —— [1890.] 8°. **906**. i. **9**. (**1**.)

—— *See* BLOOMFIELD (Robert) Poet. The Horkey, *etc.* [Edited by Sir F. C. Burnand.] 1882. 8°. **12810**. d. **5**.

—— *See* BROUGH (William) Dramatist. Beeton's Book of Burlesques . . . By W. Brough and F. C. Burnand. 1865. 8°. **11781**. aaa. **29**.

—— *See* CHIVOT (H.) and DURU (A.) La Cigale . . . English libretto by Messrs. F. C. Burnand, & G. A. Beckett. [1890.] 8°. **11740**. de. **3**. (**3**.)

—— *See* CLEMENS (Samuel L.) [*Single Works.*] Mark Twain's Nightmare . . . With tales . . . by Mark Twain, F. C. Burnand, *etc.* [1878.] 8°. **12314**. g. **12**.

—— *See* HARTE (Francis B.) Bret Harte's Great Deadwood Mystery; with tales . . . by F. C. Burnand, *etc.* [1879.] 8°. **12315. ccc. 23.**

—— *See* HOOD (Thomas) *the Elder.* Poems . . . With an introduction by Sir F. C. Burnand. 1907. 8°. **012209.fff.1/42.**

—— *See* MORTON (John M.) and BURNAND (*Sir* F. C.) Cox and Box, *etc.* [1874.] 12°. [*Lacy's Acting Edition.* vol. 99. no. 1475.] **2304. g. 17.**

—— *See* PERIODICAL PUBLICATIONS.—*London.* The Catholic Who's Who & Year-Book . . . Edited by Sir F. C. Burnand. [1908, *etc.*] 8°. **P.P.2484.da.& Ref.336.**

—— *See* PERIODICAL PUBLICATIONS.—*London.* Punch, *etc.* [1880–1906 edited by Sir F. C. Burnand.] 1841, *etc.* 4°. **P.P. 5270.**

—— *See* PERIODICAL PUBLICATIONS.—London.—*Punch.* Poems from Punch. 1841–1884. With introduction by Sir F. C. Burnand. 1908. 8°. **11603. dd. 14.**

—— *See* WILLIAMS (Montagu S.) and BURNAND (*Sir* F. C.) "B. B." An original farce, *etc.* [1860.] 12°. [*Lacy's Acting Edition.* vol. 45. no. 668.] **2304. e. 19.**

—— *See* WILLIAMS (Montagu S.) and BURNAND (*Sir* F. C.) Carte de Visite, *etc.* [1863.] 12°. [*Lacy's Acting Edition.* vol. 57. no. 845.] **2304. f. 2.**

—— *See* WILLIAMS (Montagu S.) and BURNAND (*Sir* F. C.) The Isle of St. Tropez, *etc.* [1862.] 12°. [*Lacy's Acting Edition.* vol. 52. no. 767.] **2304. e. 26.**

—— *See* WILLIAMS (Montagu S.) and BURNAND (*Sir* F. C.) The Turkish Bath, *etc.* [1864.] 12°. [*Lacy's Acting Edition.* vol. 51. no. 754.] **2304. e. 25.**

—— "Our Novel Shilling Series." 4 vol.

One-and-Three! By—that distinguished French novelist —Fictor Nogo. pp. viii. 112. 1878.
Strapmore! A romance by Weeder. pp. viii. 114. 1878.
What's the Odds? or, the Dumb jockey of Jeddington. pp. viii. 94. 1879.
Gone Wrong. A new novel. By Miss Rhody Dendron. pp. vi. 99. 1881.

Bradbury, Agnew & Co.: London, 1878–81. 8°. *Imperfect; wanting* "Chikkin Hazard" **12314. g. 38.**

—— Sir Dagobert and the Dragon.—Beautiful Helen. *See* PLAYS. Short Plays for Drawing-Room Performance, *etc.* 1890. 8°. **11781. df. 37.**

—— Happy Thoughts (More Happy Thoughts) . . . With illustrations from "Punch." pp. 425. *Bradbury, Agnew & Co.: London,* 1890. 8°. **012314. i. 41.**

—— Some Old Friends . . . With illustrations from "Punch." [Containing "Strapmore," "The Beadle," "One-and-Three," "Injyable Ingia," "Across the Keep it dark Continent."] pp. 416. *Bradbury, Agnew & Co.: London,* 1892. 8°. **12331. k. 2.**

—— The "A.D.C." Being personal reminiscences of the University Amateur Dramatic Club, Cambridge. pp. xvi. 267. *Chapman & Hall: London,* 1880 [1879]. 8°. **11794. e. 29.**

—— Acis and Galatea; or, the Nimble nymph, and the terrible troglodyte! An extravaganza. pp. 47. *London,* [1863.] 12°. [*Lacy's Acting Edition.* vol. 58. no. 860.] **2304. f. 3.**

—— "Airey" Annie. Travestie on Mrs. Campbell Praed's play of "Ariane," *etc.* pp. 24. *Bradbury, Agnew & Co.: London,* [1888.] 8°. **11779. aaa. 15. (10.)**

—— Alonzo the Brave; or, Faust and the fair Imogene. A tragical, comical . . . burlesque, *etc.* pp. 34. *London,* [1863.] 12°. [*Lacy's Acting Edition.* vol. 58. no. 864.] **2304. f. 3.**

—— A grand new and original burlesque, entitled Antony and Cleopatra; or, His-tory and Her-story in a modern nilo-metre. pp. 40. *Strand Printing & Publishing Co.: London,* 1866. 12°. **011781. k. 27.**

—— Betsy. Comedy, in three acts. [Adapted from "Bébé" by E. de Najac and A. Hennequin.] pp. 56. *London,* [1888.] 12°. [*Lacy's Acting Edition.* vol. 128. no. 1916.] **2304. h. 19.**

—— Bishop Colenso utterly refuted by Lord Dundreary. With a short memoir and a few notes by . . . F. C. Burnand [or rather, written by him]. pp. 8. 1862. 8°. *See* DUNDREARY, *Lord.* **3155. cc. 54.**

—— A new and original burlesque, entitled the latest edition of Black-Eyed Susan; or, the Little bill that was taken up. [With "Opinions of the Press."] pp. 44. 14. *Strand Printing & Publishing Co.: London,* 1867. 12°. **11783. a. 14. (3.)**

—— The latest edition of Black-eyed Susan; or, the Little bill that was taken up. An original burlesque. pp. 44. *London,* [1868.] 12°. [*Lacy's Acting Edition.* vol. 77. no. 1150.] **2304. f. 22.**

—— The Comic Business. A fragment from a harlequinade. (Illustrated by Thomas D. D. A. Kerr. From the burlesque drawing-room pantomime called "Boadicea the Beautiful, or, Harlequin Julius Cæsar and the Delightful Druid." By F. C. Burnand.) [*Perry & Co.: London,* 1943.] *obl.* 8°. **011781. h. 158.**

—— An original comic opera in two acts, entitled: The Chieftain, *etc.* pp. vi. 55. *Boosey & Co.: London,* [1895.] 8°. **11781. h. 22. (4.)**

—— Cupid and Psyche; or, Beautiful as a butterfly. A new and original extravaganza. pp. 36. *London,* [1865,] 12°. [*Lacy's Acting Edition.* vol. 64. no. 956.] **2304. f. 9.**

—— Deadman's Point; or, the Lighthouse on the Carn Ruth. A drama in four acts, *etc.* pp. 44. *London,* 1871. 12°. [*Lacy's Acting Edition.* vol. 92. no. 1372.] **2304. g. 10.**

—— The Deal Boatman. A serio-comic drama, in two acts. pp. 34. *London,* [1864.] 12°. [*Lacy's Acting Edition.* vol. 60. no. 888.] **2304. f. 5.**

—— Dido. A tragical, classical, and original burlesque, in one act. [In verse.] pp. 38. *London,* [1860.] 12°. [*Lacy's Acting Edition.* vol. 44. no. 655.] **2304. e. 18.**

—— Fair Rosamond; or, the Maze, the maid, and the monarch! An entirely new, but historically true version of the ancient strange story. [In verse.] pp. 43. *London,* [1862.] 12°. [*Lacy's Acting Edition.* vol. 55. no. 813.] **2304. e. 29.**

—— A Fairy Dream . . . Fifteen illustrations in colours by George Cruickshank. pp. 32. *London*, 1881. fol. [*Father Christmas*. 1881.] **1865**. b. **22**.

—— Faust and Loose. [In verse.] pp. 29. *Bradbury, Agnew & Co.: London*, [1886.] 8°. **11778**. e. **6**. (**2**.)

—— Faust and Marguerite. An entirely new original travestie, in one act. [In verse.] pp. 42. *London*, [1865.] 12°. [*Lacy's Acting Edition*. vol. 63. no. 935.] **2304**. f. **8**.

—— The Fox's Frolic; or, a Day with the Topsy Turvy Hunt. Pictured by Harry B. Neilson. [1917.] *obl.* fol. **11646**. p. **13**.

—— [A reissue.] *Collins: Glasgow*, [1935.] *obl.* fol. **20100**. a. **4**.

—— A grand new and original burlesque, entitled: Der Freischutz; or, a Good cast for a piece. [In verse.] pp. 55. *Merser & Gardner: London*, [1870?] 12°. **11778**. a. **7**. (**2**.)

—— An entirely new oriental piece of magnificence . . . entitled, The Great Eastern; or, a Harem-Scarum tale of a great moor and a little game. [In verse.] *See* SWEETS. Mixed Sweets, *etc.* [1867.] 8°. **12352**. cc. **6**.

—— Happy-Thought Hall . . . Illustrated by the author. pp. xii. 227. *Bradbury, Evans & Co.: London*, 1872. 8°. **12331**. bbb. **30**.

—— [Another edition.] pp. xii. 227. *Bradbury, Agnew & Co.: London*, [1883.] 8°. **12316**. h. **45**.

—— Happy Thoughts . . . Tenth thousand. pp. xvi. 303. *Bradbury, Evans & Co.: London*, 1868. 8°. [*Handy-Volume Series*. no. 4.] **12205**. cc. **15**.

—— [Another edition.] pp. 244. *Bradbury, Agnew & Co.: London*, 1904. 8°. **12314**. aaaa. **37**.

—— [Another edition.] pp. 251. *Bradbury, Agnew & Co.: London*, [1915.] 8°. **012330**. e. **88**.

—— [Another edition.] pp. xx. 285. *Methuen & Co.: London*, 1930. 8°. **012352**. dd. **14**.

—— [A reissue.] Happy Thoughts, *etc.* *Peter Nevill: London & New York*, 1954. 8°. **12330**. s. **45**.

—— A Day with the Harriers. An extract from "Happy Thoughts" . . . Illustrated by W. J. Hodgson. pp. 21. *Hildesheimer & Faulkner*: [*London*, 1884.] *obl.* 8°. **12330**. g. **42**.

—— "Happy Thoughts" Birthday Book. Selected and arranged from Mr. Punch's pages by Rosie Burnand. Illustrated. [A selection from Sir F. C. Burnand's "Happy Thoughts." With a portrait.] pp. 251. [1888.] 16°. *See* BURNAND (Rosie) **12270**. aaaa. **7**.

—— The latest edition of Helen; or, Taken from the Greek. A burlesque, *etc.* [In verse.] pp. 40. *London*, [1868.] 12°. [*Lacy's Acting Edition*. vol. 77. no. 1152.] **2304**. f. **22**.

—— How to get out of Newgate. By one who has done it, and can do it again. [By Sir F. C. Burnand.] pp. 32. [1873.] 8°. *See* LONDON.—III. *Newgate*. **12331**. aaaa. **10**.

—— "Humbug!" A comedy, in two acts. pp. 38. *London*, [1868.] 12°. [*Lacy's Acting Edition*. vol. 79. no. 1175.] **2304**. f. **24**.

—— Humbug Rhymes . . . Pictures by Winifred Burnand. *Sisley's & the Globe Press: London*, [1908.] *obl.* 8°. **12809**. p. **3**.

—— In for a Holyday, an original farce, in one act. pp. 17 *London*, [1856.] 12°. [*Lacy's Acting Edition*. vol. 26 no. 387.] **2304**. d. **30**

—— The Incompleat Angler. After Master Izaak Walton Edited by F. C. Burnand . . . and illustrated by Harry Furness. pp. x. 94. *Bradbury, Agnew & Co.: London* 1887. 8°. **12305**. f. **44**

—— [Another copy.] The Incompleat Angler, *etc.* *London* 1887. 8°. **12332**. b. **53**

—— Ixion; or, the Man at the wheel. An original extravaganza. [In verse.] pp. 44. *London*, [1864.] 12°. [*Lacy' Acting Edition*. vol. 60. no. 889.] **2304**. f. **5**

—— King of the Merrows; or, the Prince and the piper A fairy extravaganza. Written by F. C. Burnand . . from an original plot constructed by J. Palgrave Simpson pp. 48. *London*, [1862.] 12°. [*Lacy's Acting Edition* vol. 53. no. 790.] **2304**. e. **27**

—— Lord Lovel and Lady Nancy Bell; or, the Boundin brigand of the Bakumboilum. A thrillingly-interestin and tragically-startling burlesque. [In verse.] pp. 22. *London*, [1857.] 12°. [*Lacy's Acting Edition*. vol. 3(no. 443.] **2304**. e.

—— Madame Berliot's Ball; or, the Chalet in the valley. comic drama, in two acts, *etc.* pp. 36. *London*, [1864.] 12 [*Lacy's Acting Edition*. vol. 61. no. 906.] **2304**. f.

—— Mary Turner; or, the Wicious willin and wictorio wirtue! An entirely new and original burlesque, in o act. [In verse.] pp. 38. *London*, [1868.] 12°. *Lacy Acting Edition*. vol. 78. no. 1158.] **2304**. f. **2**

—— Mokeanna! A treble temptation, *etc.* pp. 270. *Bradbury, Agnew & Co.: London*, 1873. 8°. **12331**. aaaa. **4**

—— More Happy Thoughts . . . Second edition. pp. xvi. 297. *Bradbury, Evans & Co.: London*, 1871. [*Handy-Volume Series*. no. 10.] **12205**. cc.

—— My Health. pp. xv. 290. *Bradbury, Evans & C London*, 1872. 8°. **12314**. b.

—— My Time and What I've done with it. An au biography. Compiled from the diary, notes, and perso recollections of Cecil Colvin, *etc.* [A novel.] pp. xii. 4 *Macmillan & Co.: London*, 1874. 8°. **12638**. d.

—— A new and revised edition. With a portrait of t author. pp. xii. 447. *Burns & Oates: London New York*, [1890.] 8°. **012632**. i.

—— The New History of Sandford and Merton . . . W seventy-six illustrations by Linley Sambourne. pp. xvi. 268. *Bradbury, Evans & Co.: London*, 1872. **12803**. e.

—— [Another edition.] pp. xi. 216. *Bradbury, Agnew & C London*, [1892.] 8°. **012314**. f.

—— A New Light thrown across the Keep it quite Darkest Africa, *etc.* (Sixth edition.) [A burlesque of "In Darkest Africa" by Sir H. M. Stanley.] pp. 176. *Trischler & Co.: London,* [1891.] 8°. **012314. e. 48.**

—— No Rose without a Thorn. *See* SOCIETY NOVELETTES. Society Novelettes, *etc.* vol. 1. 1883. 8°. **12643. m. 1.**

—— Occasional Happy Thoughts. 2 vol.

1. About Buying a Horse.—The Story of my Legal Examination.—My Aunt's great Police Case.—Our Representative Man. pp. xii. 291.
2. Round About My Garden.—The Incomplete Angler.—Our Representative. pp. xii. 308.

Bradbury, Agnew & Co.: London, 1875, 76. 8°. **12316. aaa. 33.**

—— Out of Town. pp. 346. *Bradbury, Evans & Co.: London,* 1868. 8°. [*Handy-Volume Series.* no. 6.] **12205. cc. 17.**

—— Paris; or, Vive Lemprière, an original burlesque. pp. 48. *Strand Printing & Publishing Co.: London,* 1866. 12°. **11783. a. 14. (2.)**

—— Paris; or, Vive Lemprière, an original burlesque. [In verse.] pp. 52. *London,* [1869.] 12°. [*Lacy's Acting Edition.* vol. 84. no. 1250.] **2304. g. 2.**

—— Patient Penelope; or, the Return of Ulysses. A burlesque, in one act. [In verse.] pp. 24. *London,* [1864.] 12°. [*Lacy's Acting Edition.* vol. 61. no. 902.] **2304. f. 6.**

—— "Pickwick." A dramatic cantata in one act, *etc.* [Based on an incident in Dickens's novel.] pp. 29. *Boosey & Co.: London,* [1889.] 8°. **11779. bb. 21. (2.)**

—— Pirithoüs, the son of Ixion. A new and original extravaganza. [In verse.] pp. 46. *London,* [1866.] 12°. [*Lacy's Acting Edition.* vol. 65. no. 974.] **2304. f. 10.**

—— Present Pastimes of Merrie England, interpreted from ancient MSS. and annotated by F. C. Burnand: with illustrations drawn from yᵉ quicke by J. E. Rogers, *etc.* pp. 32. *Cassell & Co.: London,* [1872.] 4°. **1871. c. 24.**

—— Proof; or, a Celebrated case. A drama in a prologue and three acts. Adapted to the English stage. pp. 52. *London, New York,* [1893.] 12°. [*French's Acting Edition.* vol. 133. no. 1990.] **2304. h. 24.**

—— *See* WILLIAMS (Henry L.) Proof: a celebrated case. Founded . . . on the celebrated drama by F. C. Burnand, *etc.* [1878.] 4°. **12612. i. 2. (1.)**

—— Proof Positive. A comedy. pp. 53. *Privately printed for the author:* [*London,* 1870?] 12°. **11783. a. 14. (6.)**

—— Quite at Home . . . With illustrations from "Punch." pp. 416. *Bradbury, Agnew & Co.: London,* 1890. 8°. **012314. i. 42.**

—— Rather at Sea . . . With illustrations from "Punch." pp. 417. *Bradbury, Agnew & Co.: London,* 1890. 8°. **012314. i. 31.**

—— The Episode of the Pilot. (Reprinted from F. C. Burnand's "Rather at Sea.") *See* WAGNER (Leopold) XX Stories by XX Tellers, *etc.* 1895. 8°.
C.132.g.63.

—— The Real Adventures of Robinson Crusoe . . . [A burlesque of Defoe's romance.] With fifty-six illustrations by Linley Sambourne. pp. xiii. 214. *Bradbury, Agnew & Co.: London,* 1893. 8°. **012314. g. 6.**

—— Records and Reminiscences, personal and general . . . With numerous illustrations [including portraits] and facsimile letters. 2 vol. *Methuen & Co.: London,* 1904 [1903]. 8°. **10855. cc. 19.**

—— Fourth and cheaper edition, revised. pp. xiv. 462. *Methuen & Co.: London,* 1905. 8°. **10855. b. 30.**

—— Records and Reminiscences, *etc.* [Abridged by E. V. Lucas.] pp. 254. *London,* 1917. 8°. [*Methuen's Shilling Books.* no. 234.] **012202. bb. 1/46.**

—— The Ride to Khiva . . . Second edition. [A burlesque of "A Ride to Khiva" by F. G. Burnaby.] pp. x. 113. *Bradbury, Agnew & Co.: London,* 1877. 8°. **12314. g. 19.**

—— The Ride to Khiva and to K. Bul, communicated by submarine K-Bul. pp. xvi. 96. *Bradbury, Agnew & Co.: London,* 1879 [1878]. 8°. **12314. g. 11.**

—— Robin Hood; or, the Forester's fate! An extravaganza. [In verse.] pp. 40. *London,* [1863.] 12°. [*Lacy's Acting Edition.* vol. 57. no. 841.] **2304. f. 2.**

—— Romance under Difficulties. An original farce in one act. pp. 16. *London,* [1856.] 12°. [*Lacy's Acting Edition.* vol. 26. no. 388.] **2304. d. 30.**

—— The Royal Rabbit; or, the Fairy Evanessa and the dolls of Dort. With sixteen illustrations in colour by George Cruickshank. pp. 36. *London,* 1880. fol. [*Father Christmas.* 1880.] **1865. b. 22.**

—— Rumplestiltskin; or, the Woman at the wheel! An extravaganza in one act. pp. 51. *T. H. Lacy: London,* [1864?] 12°. **11783. a. 13. (1.)**

—— Rumplestiltskin; or, the Woman at the wheel! An extravaganza, in one act. pp. 50. *London,* [1865.] 12°. [*Lacy's Acting Edition.* vol. 62. no. 923.] **2304. f. 7.**

—— The Siege of Seringapatam; or, the Maiden of Mesopotamia. A hippodramatic spectacle in three scenes & one grand act. Written . . . specially for the fête given . . . in aid of the funds of the Hospital for Incurables, 1863. pp. 8. *London,* [1863.] 8°. [*Lacy's Sensation Series.*] **11781. df. 30. (1.)**

—— Sir George and a Dragon; or, "We are seven." A burlesque extravaganza, *etc.* pp. 48. *Arthur Swanborough: London,* [c. 1870.] 12°. **11783. bb. 46.**

—— Snowdrop; or, the Seven mannikins and the magic mirror. An entirely new original burlesque extravaganza. pp. 42. *London,* [1865.] 12°. [*Lacy's Acting Edition.* vol. 64. no. 951.] **2304. f. 9.**

—— Sporting Intelligence Extraordinary! A match is arranged to come off at the Royal Olympic Theatre . . . between the Unknown and the Seneca Indian, Deerfoot. A farce, in one act. pp. 16. *London,* [1862.] 12°. [*Lacy's Acting Edition.* vol. 53. no. 789.] **2304. e. 27.**

BURNAND (*Sir* FRANCIS COWLEY)

—— Tracks for Tourists; or, the Continental companion: being a handbook with foot-notes for pedestrians; and a guide to the principal mounts for equestrians . . . Reprinted from the pages of "Punch," with copious notes, emendations . . . The tours illustrated with carica-tours by Charles Keene. pp. xii. 110. *Bradbury & Evans: London*, 1864. 8°. **12350**. aaa. **22**.

—— Ulysses; or, the Iron-clad warrior and the little tug of war. An entirely original burlesque. [In verse.] pp. 38. *London*, [1866.] 12°. [*Lacy's Acting Edition*. vol. 66. no. 980.] **2304**. f. **11**.

—— Venus and Adonis; or, the Two rivals & the small boar. Being a full, true, and particular account, adapted to the requirements of the present age of an ancient mythological piece of scandal. pp. 50. *London*, [1865.] 12°. [*Lacy's Acting Edition*. vol. 62. no. 922.] **2304**. f. **7**.

—— Very Much Abroad . . . With illustrations from "Punch." pp. 436. *Bradbury, Agnew & Co.: London*, 1890. 8°. **12331**. i. **11**.

—— Villikins and his Dinah. A tragico-comico-burlesque in one act. [In verse.] pp. 21. *London*, [1856.] 12°. [*Lacy's Acting Edition*. vol. 54. no. 796.] **2304**. e. **28**.

—— The White Cat! Or, Prince Lardi-Dardi & the radiant Rosetta. A fairy burlesque extravaganza. [In verse.] pp. 33. *London*, [1871.] 12°. [*Lacy's Acting Edition*. vol. 90. no. 1339.] **2304**. g. **8**.

—— New edition, especially written for the Holborn, of The White Fawn; or, the Loves of Prince Buttercup and the Princess Daisy. An entirely new spectacular extravaganza. *London*, [1868.] 12°. [*Lacy's Acting Edition*. vol. 79. no. 1176.] **2304**. f. **24**.

—— Windsor Castle. An original opera-burlesque, in one act, *etc*. [In verse.] pp. 48. *London*, [1866.] 12°. [*Lacy's Acting Edition*. vol. 67. no. 992.] **2304**. f. **12**.

—— The Z.Z.G., or Zig Zag Guide round and about the bold and beautiful Kentish coast . . . Illustrated by Phil May. pp. viii. 188. *A. & C. Black: London*, 1897. 8°. **10352**. g. **28**.

BURNAND (*Sir* FRANCIS COWLEY) and **A'BECKETT** (ARTHUR WILLIAM)

—— The Doom of St. Querec. A Xmas legend . . . Illustrated by C. Green and S. J. Gregory. pp. 100. *Bradbury, Agnew & Co.: London*, [1875.] 8°. **012634**. m. **56**.

—— The Shadow Witness . . . Illustrated by C. Green. pp. 102. *Bradbury, Agnew & Co.: London*, [1877.] 4°. **12620**. g. **3**.

BURNAND (*Sir* FRANCIS COWLEY) and **WILLIAMS** (MONTAGU STEPHEN)

—— Easy Shaving. A farce, in one act. pp. 18. *London*, [1864.] 12°. [*Lacy's Acting Edition*. vol. 60. no. 891.] **2304**. f. **5**.

—— [Another edition.] pp. 17. *New York*, [1869.] 8°. [*De Witt's Acting Plays*. no. 47.] **11791**. ccc. 4. (**47**.)

BURNAND (GEORGE) **AND CO.** Loans redeemable a par by drawings. 1870. Compiled by Geo. Burnan & Co. (Second edition.) *London*, [1870.] *s. sh.* fol. **1880**. d. **2**. (**74**.

BURNAND (RENÉ)

—— L'Étonnante histoire des Girardet, artistes suisses [With plates, including portraits.] pp. 299. *Neuchâtel* 1940. 4°. **7869**. b. **27**

—— Eugène Burnand: l'homme, l'artist et son œuvre. Avec 8 planches en couleurs et 7 en noi *etc*. [With a portrait.] pp. 372. *Paris*, 1926. 8°. **7859**. c. **2**

—— Promenades égyptiennes. Avec vingt-quatre illustra tions en hors-texte. pp. 136. *Neuchâtel, Paris; [printe in Belgium*, 1938.] 8°. **010093**. de. **7**

—— Une Ville sur la montagne. [A description of life in tuberculosis sanatorium.] pp. 210. *Neuchâtel, Pari* 1938. 8°. **7679**. a. **5**

BURNAND (ROBERT) *See* BURNAND (Eugène R.)

BURNAND (ROSIE) "Happy Thoughts" Birthday Book Selected and arranged from Mr. Punch's pages by R Burnand. Illustrated. [A selection from Sir F. C Burnand's "Happy Thoughts." With a portrait.] pp. 251. *Bradbury, Agnew & Co.: London*, [1888.] 16° **12270**. aaaa.

BURNAND (TONY)

—— *See* OGRIZEK (D.) and RUFENACHT (J. G.) La Suisse Texte de T. Burnand, *etc*. [1947.] 16°. **10196**. l. **1**

—— En pêchant la truite, *etc*. pp. 174. *Paris*, 1933. 8°. **7916**. ee. **1**

—— Grosse bête et petit gibier. pp. 222. *Paris*, 1937. 8° **07908**. i.

—— Pêches de partout et ailleurs. pp. 237. *Paris* 1948. 8°. **07908**. i. **3**

BURNAND (TONY) and **OBERTHÜR** (JOSEPH)

—— Toute la Camargue . . . Cent cinquante illustrations de J. Oberthür, *etc*. 2 tom. *Paris*, 1938. 8°. **010171**. m. **7**

BURNAND (TONY) and **RITZ** (CHARLES C.)

—— A la mouche. Méthodes et matériel modernes pour l pêche à la mouche . . . La théorie solunaire de J. A Knight . . . Dessins de Henri Jaloux, *etc*. pp. 347. *Paris*, 1939. 8°. **7915**. s. **3**

BURNAND (WILLIAM ERNEST) Life's Spectrum. Eco nomics, science, metaphysics. pp. 87. *S W. C. Leng & Co.: Sheffield*, 1935. 8°. **8230**. f.

BURNAP (FRANCIS) Lecture before the Temperanc Society, at Saint Catharines, Upper Canada . . . Secon edition. pp. 24. *H. Leavenworth: [Saint Catharines* 1837. 8°. **8435**. d. **66**. (**3**

BURNAP (GEORGE) Parks. Their design, equipment an use . . . With . . . 163 illustrations, *etc*. pp. 327. *J. B. Lippincott Co.: Philadelphia & London*, 1916. 8 **7815**. s.

BURNAP (GEORGE WASHINGTON) Miscellaneous Writin . . . Collected and revised by the author. pp. 343. *John Murphy: Baltimore*, 1845. 8°. **12296**. c.

BURNAP (George Washington)

—— The Atonement, *etc.* pp. 24. *J. Munroe & Co.: Boston*, 1844. 12°. **4255**. dd. **13**.

—— Charges of Unbelief, *etc.* pp. 20. *W. Crosby & H. P. Nichols: Boston*, 1848. 12°. **4418**. f. **18**.

—— Church and State: or, the Privileges and duties of an American citizen. A discourse, *etc.* pp. 24. *J. D. Toy: Baltimore*, 1844. 8°. **4486**. e. **52**. (**1**.)

—— Commemorative Discourse, delivered in the First Independent Church of Baltimore . . . on the occasion of the decease of the Rev. F. W. P. Greenwood. pp. 16. *John Murphy: Baltimore*, [1843.] 8°. **4486**. cc. **20**. (**8**.)

—— A Discourse on the Principles involved in the Pusey Controversy. pp. 24. *J. D. Toy: Baltimore*, 1844. 8°. **4486**. h. **34**.

—— The Duties of the Citizen Soldier. A discourse, delivered in the First Independent Church in Baltimore . . . before the Maryland Cadets, *etc.* pp. 20. *John Murphy: Baltimore*, [1844.] 8°. **4486**. e. **48**. (**14**.)

—— Life of Leonard Calvert, First Governor of Maryland. 1846. *See* Sparks (Jared) The Library of American Biography . . . Second series. vol. 9. 1844, *etc.* 8°. **10883**. df. **8**.

—— Memoir of Henry Augustus Ingalls . . . With selections from his writings. [With a portrait.] pp. 210. *J. Munroe & Co.: Boston*, 1846. 12°. **1453**. b. **7**.

—— Origin and Causes of Democracy in America: a discourse . . . delivered in Baltimore, before the Maryland Historical Society, *etc.* pp. 29. *J. D. Toy: [Baltimore*, 1853.] 8°. **8175**. bb. **62**. (**7**.)

—— The Position of Unitarianism defined. A discourse, delivered at the re-opening of the First Independent Church of Baltimore, *etc.* pp. 31. *J. D. Toy: Baltimore*, 1848. 8°. **4486**. d. **36**. (**10**.)

—— The Professions: an oration, delivered before the literary societies of Marshall College, Mercersburg, Pennsylvania, at their anniversary, September 27, 1842. pp. 31. *John Murphy: Baltimore*, [1842.] 8°. **8305**. d. **48**. (**4**.)

—— The Sphere and Duties of Woman. A course of lectures . . . Second edition, corrected and enlarged. pp. 326. *John Murphy: Baltimore*, 1848. 12°. **8415**. d. **31**.

—— Theology and Religion, *etc.* pp. 17. *W. Crosby & H. P. Nichols: Boston*, 1846. 12°. **4485**. aa. **21**.

—— Unitarian Christianity Expounded and Defended. A discourse, *etc.* *See* Charleston, *South Carolina.—Unitarian Church.* The Old and the New, *etc.* 1854. 8°. **4183**. e. **48**.

—— The Uses and Abuses of War. A discourse delivered before the Ancient and Hon. Artillery Company of Boston, *etc.* pp. 31. *Wright & Hasty: Boston*, 1854. 8°. **4486**. e. **52**. (**16**.)

BURNAP (Jacob) A Discourse delivered . . . at the Funeral of the Rev. Joseph Kidder . . . with a summary history of the Church of Christ in Dunstable. By Rev. E. P. Sperry. pp. 24. *Richard Boylston: Amherst*, 1819. 8°. **4985**. cc. **4**.

BURNAP (Jacob)

—— A Sermon preached . . . before His Excellency the Governor, the Honorable Council, Senate, and House of Representatives of the State of New Hampshire. pp. 23. *George Hough: Concord*, 1801. 8°. **4485**. e. **12**.

BURNAP (Uzziah C.) Bible Servitude. A sermon delivered . . . on the day of annual thanksgiving, *etc.* pp. 20. *A. E. Newton & A. O. Ordway: Lowell*, 1843. 8°. **4486**. cc. **20**. (**9**.)

—— Priestcraft Exposed. A lecture delivered in Chester, April 9, 1830, being the annual fast; together with an essay on the clergy of the United States. pp. 28. *J. C. Allen: Windsor* [*Vt.*], 1830. 8°. **4487**. e. **6**. (**11**.)

BURNARD (Alexander) *See* Burnard (David A.)

BURNARD (David Alexander)

—— Harmony and Composition for the Student and the Potential Composer. pp. x. 233. *Angus & Robertson: Sydney, London*, 1950. 8°. **7900**. g. **5**.

BURNARD (Edwin) Too Late, a play in five acts. pp. 67. *Ballard: London*, 1886. 8°. **11779**. aaa. **11**. (**6**.)

BURNARD (Grafton) Where the Sun turns. A novel. pp. 288. *Stanley Paul & Co.: London*, [1935.] 8°. NN. **23368**.

BURNARD (John) Manual of Devotion, compiled from the Book of Common Prayer and other sources. pp. viii. 100. *J. Vincent: Oxford*, 1849. 32°. **3455**. b. **21**.

BURNARD (Robert) The Acquisition of the Forest of Dartmoor as a County Park. pp. 10. *W. Brendon & Son: Plymouth*, 1894. 8°. **8282**. ff. **9**. (**18**.)

—— Dartmoor Pictorial Records. 4 vol. *W. Brendon & Son: Plymouth*, 1890–94. 8°. **010358**. f. **12**.
Printed for private circulation.

—— Recent Dredging in Cattewater . . . Reprinted from the Transactions of the Plymouth Institution, *etc.* pp. 16. [1887.] 8°. **8768**. i. **8**. (**5**.)

BURNASHEV (S. N.) Новые матеріалы для жизнеописанія и дѣятельности С. Д. Бурнашева, бывшаго в Грузіи съ 1783 по 1787 г. Собралъ и издалъ съ приложеніемъ картъ, портретовъ и факсимиле С. Н. Бурнашевъ. Подъ редакціей . . . А. А. Цагарели. pp. iv. 64. *С.-Петербургъ*, 1901. 8°. **010790**. i. **27**.

BURNASHEV (Stepan Danilovich) *See* Burnashev (S. N.) Новые матеріалы для жизнеописанія С. Д. Бурнашева, *etc.* 1901. 8°. **010790**. i. **27**.

BURNASHEV (Vladimir Petrovich) Изъ воспоминаній Петербургскаго старожила. [Signed: " В. Б.," i.e. V. P. Burnashev.] 1872. 8°. [*Памятники новой Русской исторіи.* том. 2.] *See* B., V. **9455**. e. **22**.

BURNAT (A. J. Daniel) Disputatio de gravitate, *etc.* pp. 16. 1719. *See* Crousaz (J. P. de) Systhematis physici disputatio prima [*etc.*]. pt. 40. 1707, *etc.* 4°. **536**. f. **25**. (**7**.)

BURNAT (Émile) Autobiographie, publiée avec une étude sur le botaniste et son œuvre, des souvenirs et documents divers par John Briquet et François Cavillier. [With a portrait.] pp. vii. 185. *Genève*, 1922. 8°. **10656**. cc. **1**.

BURNAT (ÉMILE)

—— Flore des Alpes maritimes ou Catalogue raisonné des plantes qui croissent spontanément dans la chaîne des Alpes maritimes, *etc.* 6 vol. *Genève & Bâle,* 1892–1917. 8°. **07031**. i. **2**.

BURNAT (ÉMILE) and **GREMLI** (AUGUST)

—— Catalogue raisonné des Hieracium des Alpes maritimes, *etc.* pp. xxxv. 84. *Genève,* [1883.] 8°. **7033**. g. **23**.

—— Observations sur quelques roses de l'Italie. pp. 52. *Genève & Bâle,* 1886. 8°. **07028**. h. **1**. (**7**.)

—— Les Roses des Alpes maritimes, études, *etc.* pp. 136. *Genève,* 1879. 8°. **7033**. cc. **9**.

BURNAT (EUGÈNE) Lelio Socin. pp. 96. *Vevey,* 1894. 8°. **4864**. d. **27**.

BURNAT (JEAN)

—— Boires et déboires de Giacomo Serpoletti. Suite burlesque. *In:* Les Œuvres libres. Nouvelle série. no. 97. pp. 33–84. 1954. 8°. **12208**. ee. **322**.

—— Le Cœur en feu. Nouvelle. *In:* Les Œuvres libres. Nouvelle série. no. 84. pp. 29–70. 1953. 8°. **12208**. ee. **309**.

BURNAT (*Sir* THOMAS) *See* BURNET (*Sir* T.) *M.D.*

BURNATHUS (GILBERTUS) *See* BURNET (Gilbert) *Professor at Montauban.*

BURNATOVICH (OLEKSA) Українська ідеольоґія революційної доби. pp. 118. *Львів, Відень; Відень* [printed], 1922. 8°. **8095**. df. **40**.

BURNAT-PROVINS (MARGUERITE) *See* MALO (H.) Marguerite Burnat-Provins . . . Biographie . . . illustrée d'un portrait, *etc.* 1920. 8°. **10657**. aa. **34**.

—— Le Chant du verdier. pp. 128. *Paris,* 1922. 16°. **012356**. g. **31**.

—— Contes en vingt lignes. pp. 96. *Saint-Raphaël,* 1922. 8°. **012547**. cc. **13**.

—— Heures d'automne. (Poèmes en prose.) pp. 94. *Paris,* 1921. 16°. **012354**. df. **58**.

—— Le Livre pour toi . . . Vingt-neuvième édition. pp. 201. *Paris,* [1921.] 8°. **012350**. ff. **81**.

—— Petits tableaux valaisans. [With illustrations.] pp. 192. *Vevey,* 1903. *obl.* 8°. **1787**. a. **1**.

—— Poèmes de la soif. 2 tom. *Paris,* [1921.] 16°. **012354**. df. **46**.
Tom. 2 bears the title "Poèmes du Scorpion."

—— Poèmes troubles. pp. 159. *Paris,* 1920. 12°. **12350**. a. **60**.

—— Près du rouge-gorge. pp. 204. *Lille,* 1937. 8°. **012551**. n. **11**.

—— Le Voile. Roman. pp. 252. *Paris,* 1929. 8°. **12515**. tt. **4**.

—— Vous. pp. 144. *Paris,* 1919. 8°. **012352**. de. **67**.

BURNAY (EDUARDO) Elogio historico do Dr Agostinho Vicente Lourenço lido na sessão publica da Academia Real das Sciencias de Lisboa, *etc.* pp. 41. *Lisboa,* 1893. 4°. **10632**. h. **20**.

BURNAY (JEAN)

—— Notes biographiques sur Mgr. Brigot . . . Reprinted from the Journal of the Thailand Research Society, *etc.* [1941.] 8°. **20039**. c. **6**.

—— Notes siamoises . . . Extrait du Bulletin de l'École Française d'Extrême-Orient, *etc.* pp. 4. 1938. 8°. **12906**. i. **31**.

BURNBLUM (L. G.) *See* LABICHE (E. M.) [*Works written in Collaboration.*] La Poudre aux yeux . . . With explanatory notes by L. G. Burnblum. 1888. 8°. **12954**. de. **39**

—— —— 1896. 8°. **11740**. aa. **52/17**

BURNBY (JOHN) *Attorney at Canterbury.*

—— An Historical Description of the Cathedral and Metropolitical Church of Christ, Canterbury: containing an account of its antiquities, *etc.* [By J. Burnby.] pp. 105 1772. 8°. *See* CANTERBURY.—*Canterbury Cathedral* [*Appendix.*] **579**. c. **3**. (**1**.

—— [Another copy.] **578**. f. **18**

—— The second edition, greatly enlarged, with a preface containing observations on the Gothic architecture, and an historical account of the Archbishops of Canterbury from Augustin to the present time. Together with an elegy, written by the Rev. John Duncombe. pp. viii. 15[6] 1783. 8°. *See* CANTERBURY.—*Cathedral Church.* [*Appendix.*] **578**. f. **2**[1]

—— [Another copy.] T. **1098**. (**1**

—— [Another copy.] **297**. k. [5]

—— The Kentish Cricketers: a poem . . . Being a reply t[o] . . . a parody on the Ballad of Chevy Chace intituled Surry Triumphant: or, the Kentish Men's defeat. pp. 2[3] MS. NOTES. *T. Smith & Son: Canterbury,* 1773. 4°. **1346**. k. **36**. (**2**

—— Summer Amusement: or, Miscellaneous poems: inscribed to the frequenters of Margate, Ramsgate, *et[c.]* pp. 94. *J. Dodsley: London,* 1772. 8°. **11641**. bbb. **4**[0]

—— Thoughts on the Freedom of Election. pp. 16. *T. Fisher: Rochester,* 1785. 8°. E. **2150**. (**2***

BURNBY (JOHN) *Prior of Durham.* *See* EBCHESTE[R] (William) The Obituary Roll of W. Ebchester and J. Burnby, Priors of Durham, *etc.* 1856. 8°. Ac. **8045/2**

BURNCE (FRANCES)

—— *See* ABRAHAM BEN SHĀLŌM. Deep Furrows . . . Translated by F. Burnce. [1937.] 8°. **010077**. f. **6**

BURNDEPT LTD. Monthly News Bulletin. no. 1– May–Aug. 1934. *London,* 1934. fol.
Reproduced from typewriting.
[Continued as:]
The Minstrel. The official organ of Burndept Limited. vol. 1. no. 5, *etc.* Sept. 1934, *etc.* *London,* 1934– . 4°. P.P. **1607**. d

BURNE (ADA E.) Verses, grave and gay. pp. 78. *T[he] Author: Chester,* 1928. 8°. **011644**. ee. **7**

BURNE (Alfred Higgins) *See* also Basilisk, *pseud.* [i.e. A. H. Burne.]

—— The Art of War on Land. Illustrated by campaigns and battles of all ages . . . With 23 maps and 11 diagrams. pp. xi. 227. *Methuen & Co.: London,* 1944. 8°. **8838.** aa. **21.**

—— The Art of War on Land, *etc.* (Second edition.) pp. xi. 227. *Methuen & Co.: London,* 1950. 8°. **8839.** b. **63.**

—— The Battlefields of England . . . With 32 maps and 9 panoramas. pp. xviii. 315. *Methuen & Co.: London,* 1950. 8°. **9507.** aa. **5.**

—— The Battlefields of England, *etc.* (Second edition.) pp. xviii. 315. *Methuen & Co.: London,* 1951. 8°. **9507.** aa. **14.**

—— The Crecy War. A military history of the Hundred Years War from 1337 to the peace of Bretigny, 1360. [With plates and maps.] pp. 366. *Eyre & Spottiswoode: London,* 1955. 8°. **09073.** h. **3.**

—— Lee, Grant and Sherman. A study in leadership in the 1864–65 campaign. [With portraits and maps.] pp. xv. 216. pl. 23. *Gale & Polden: Aldershot,* 1938. 8°. **9605.** pp. **6.**

—— Lee, Grant and Sherman. A study in leadership in the 1864–65 campaign, *etc.* [With portraits and maps.] pp. xxiii. 216. *C. Scribner's Sons: New York,* 1939. 8°. **10887.** g. **15.**

—— The Liao-Yang Campaign . . . Illustrated with maps. pp. xvii. 125. *William Clowes: London,* 1936. 8°. **9058.** f. **19.**

—— Mesopotamia: the last phase, *etc.* [With maps.] pp. xi. 124. *Gale & Polden: Aldershot,* 1936. 8°. **9058.** e. **2.**

—— Second edition. pp. xii. 124. *Gale & Polden: Aldershot,* [1938.] 8°. **09079.** d. **24.**

—— More Battlefields of England . . . With 18 maps, *etc.* pp. xv. 216. *Methuen & Co.: London,* 1952. 8°. **9501.** aa. **6.**

—— The Noble Duke of York. The military life of Frederick, Duke of York and Albany. [With plates, including portraits.] pp. 350. *Staples Press: London, New York,* 1949. 8°. **010807.** h. **31.**

—— Policing the Saar. [Containing " The International Force in the Saar " by A. H. Burne and " The Saar Plebiscite " by Sarah Wambaugh.] pp. 31. *London,* 1936. 8°. [*New Commonwealth Pamphlets.* ser. A. no. 8.] W.P. **2742.**

—— The Royal Artillery Mess, Woolwich, and its surroundings. [With illustrations.] pp. 248. *W. H. Barrell: Portsmouth,* 1935. 8°. **8820.** df. **20.**

—— The Woolwich Mess. An abridgement and revision of " The Royal Artillery Mess, Woolwich, and its Surroundings." [With plates.] pp. 94. *Gale & Polden: Aldershot,* 1954. 8°. **8838.** aa. **53.**

—— Some Pages from the History of " Q " Battery, R.H.A., in the Great War . . . By A. H. B. [i.e. A. H. Burne.] With 2 plates and 3 maps. pp. 51. 1922. 8°. *See* B., A. H. **09084.** aaa. **27.**

30-13

BURNE (Alfred Higgins)

—— Strategy as exemplified in the Second World War. A strategical examination of the land operations . . . The Lees Knowles Lectures for 1946. pp. 89. *University Press: Cambridge,* 1946. 8°. **8839.** aa. **43.**

—— The Woolwich Mess. *See* supra: The Royal Artillery Mess, Woolwich.

BURNE (C. S.) *Political Writer.* Papers for the People. 4 pt. *Central Committee, Patriotic Organizations: London; W. H. Robinson & Co.: Walsall,* 1914, 15. 8°. **08027.** ff. **35.**

BURNE (Charles Richard Newdigate) With the Naval Brigade in Natal, 1899–1900. Journal of active service kept during the relief of Ladysmith and subsequent operations in northern Natal and the Transvaal, *etc.* [With illustrations and a map.] pp. ix. 156. *Edward Arnold: London,* 1902. 8°. **09061.** b. **30.**

BURNE (Charlotte Sophia) The Handbook of Folklore. New edition, revised and enlarged. By C. S. Burne. [Retaining only certain passages from the original edition by Sir George L. Gomme.] pp. x. 364. 1914. 8°. *See* London.—iii. *Folk-Lore Society.* Ac. **9938/28.**

—— Shropshire Folk-Lore . . . Edited by C. S. Burne from the collections of Georgina F. Jackson. pp. xiv. 663. *Trübner & Co.: London,* 1883. 8°. **12450.** g. **21.**

BURNE (Evelyn) *pseud.* [i.e. Ethel Bourne.] Storm-beaten and Weary. A novel. pp. 399. *Griffith, Farran & Co.: London,* 1887. 8°. **012633.** f. **31.**

BURNE (F. S. Janet) Sybil's Dutch Dolls . . . Illustrated. pp. 174. *Field & Tuer: London,* 1887. 8°. **12806.** s. **36.**

BURNE (F. S. Janet) and **MILES** (Helen J. A.)

—— Tiles from Dame Marjorie's Chimney-Corner, and China from her Cupboard. [Verses, with illustrations.] *Wells Gardner & Co.: London,* [1886.] *obl.* 8°. **12811.** a. **42.**

BURNE (Frances Caroline) Margaret's Marriage; or, Lights and shadows on the hills. [A tale.] pp. 58. *Griffith & Farran: London,* 1890. 8°. **012631.** e. **70.**

BURNE (George Henry Poyntz)

—— *See* Bible.—*Song of Solomon.* [*English.*] The Song of Songs; an attempt to produce a rhyming paraphrase, *etc.* [By G. H. P. Burne.] [1910?] 4°. **3054.** d. **10.**

—— [An unfinished account of the travels in Greece of the author and his wife.] [1910?] fol. **10127.** k. **2.** *Typewritten.*

—— The Leicestershire Militia in South Africa. [With illustrations.] pp. vii. 116. *Clarke & Satchell: Leicester,* [1902?] *obl.* 8°. Cup. **1252.** a. **91.**

—— Who wrote the Plays and Poems known as " The Works of Shakespeare "? An undelivered lecture. By G. H. P. B. [i.e. G. H. P. Burne.] pp. 48. 1908. 8°. *See* B., G. H. P. **011765.** gg. **47. (3.)**

BURNE (Harry) Harry Burne, and other stories. pp. 64. *T. Nelson & Sons: London,* [1877?] 16°. [*Home Library for Little Readers.*] **4422.** cc. **23.**

BURNE (Henry Thomas) Apostolic Consolation: a few considerations, affectionately offered to the attention of the sorrowing Christian. pp. 47. *James Nisbet: London,* 1831. 16°. **764.** i. **14.** (**25.**)

—— Brief Remarks on the Mistatements [*sic*], &c. in the last pamphlet of the Rev. R. Meek, on "The True Nature of our Lord's Humanity," &c. pp. 20. *A. Douglas: London,* 1833. 12°. **764.** i. **14.** (**27.**)

—— The Present Mourner marked against Evil Times. A sermon, *etc.* pp. 29. *L. B. Seeley & Sons: London,* 1829. 8°. **4476.** bb. **101.** (**5.**)

—— [Another copy.] **764.** i. **14.** (**24.**)

—— The Scripture Doctrine of the Person and Humanity of our Divine Redeemer, the Lord Jesus Christ. With some remarks on a publication by the Rev. R. Meek [entitled "The Sinless Humanity of Christ, vindicated against the Irving heresy"]. pp. xvii. 42. *A. Douglas: London,* 1833. 12°. **764.** i. **14.** (**26.**)

—— *See* Meek (Robert) The True Nature of our Lord's Humanity and Atonement; stated in reply to the misrepresentations . . . of the Rev. H. T. Burne, on "The Scripture Doctrine of the Person . . . of our Divine Redeemer," *etc.* 1833. 12°. T. **1456.** (4.)

BURNE (James) *See* Man. The Man of Nature. Translated from the French by J. Burne. [A translation of "L'Élève de la Nature," by G. Guillard de Beaurieu.] 1773. 12°. **12510.** cc. **7.**

BURNE (John) An Oration on the Principles of the Practice of Medicine, delivered before the Medical Society of London, *etc.* pp. 25. *Longman & Co.: London,* 1828. 4°. **07305.** k. **3.** (**10.**)

—— A Practical Treatise on the Typhus or Adynamic Fever. pp. xvi. 248. *Longman & Co.: London,* 1828. 8°. **1168.** l. **21.**

—— A Treatise on the Causes and Consequences of Habitual Constipation. pp. xv. 257. *Longman & Co.: London,* 1840. 8°. **1190.** l. 4.

BURNE (John Butler) Parson and Peasant: some chapters of their natural history. pp. viii. 260. *Methuen & Co.: London,* 1891. 8°. **012357.** e. 4.

BURNE (Kathleen E.)

—— *See* Andrew, *Father, S.D.C.* [H. E. Hardy.] The Life and Letters of Father Andrew, S.D.C. Edited and compiled by K. E. Burne. 1948. 8°. **10922.** aa. **24.**

—— *See* Andrew, *Father, S.D.C.* [H. E. Hardy.] Prayers from Father Andrew. Edited by K. E. Burne. 1950. 16°. **3458.** a. **89.**

—— *See* Andrew, *Father, S.D.C.* [H. E. Hardy.] The Wisdom of Father Andrew. An anthology from his writings. Compiled by K. E. Burne, *etc.* 1949. 16°. **4400.** l. **60.**

BURNE (Margaret) The Bullyns. [A novel.] pp. viii. 343. *John Murray: London,* 1923. 8°. NN. **9161.**

—— The Fledglings. [A novel.] pp. 276. *John Murray: London,* 1922. 8°. NN. **8234.**

BURNE (Newdigate) Our Position in the One Brotherhood. [The prefatory note signed: N. B., i.e. Newdigate Burne.] pp. 14. [1886.] 8°. *See* B., N. **764.** i. **14.** (**20.**)

—— Albury. Death of Mr. Newdigate Burne. [A newspaper cutting.] [1895.] *s. sh.* 8°. **764.** i. **14.** (**22.**)

BURNE (Nicol) *Professor of Philosophy at St. Andrews* The Disputation concerning the Controuersit Headdi of Religion, haldin in the Realme of Scotland, the zeir o God ane thousand, fyue hundreth fourscoir zeiris. Betuix The prætendit Ministeris of the deformed Kirk in Scot land. And, N. Burne Professor of philosophie in S Leonardis college, *etc.* ff. 190. *Parise,* 1581. 8°. **699.** b. **5**

—— [Another copy.] G. **972**

—— [Another edition.] *See* Law (Thomas G.) Catholi Tractates of the Sixteenth Century, *etc.* 1901. 8° Ac. **9943/2C**

—— Extract from one of the numerous Libels raised by th Catholics against . . . John Knox. [Taken from chap. 2 of the "Disputation."] *See* Extracts. Extracts, *et* [1829?] 8°. **1325.** d. **3.** (4

BURNE (Nicol) *the Violer.* A Delectable New Balla intituled, Leader-Haughs and Yarow. (The words Burn the violer.) 𝔅.𝔏. [*London?* 1690?] *s. sh.* fol. Rox. ii. **57**

—— [Another edition.] [*Edinburgh?* 1700?] *s. sh.* fol. Rox. iii. **72**

BURNE (*Sir* Owen Tudor) *G.C.I.E.* Clyde and Strat nairn. [An account of the part taken in the India Mutiny operations by Lord Clyde and Lord Strathnair With portraits and a map.] pp. 194. *Clarendon Press Oxford,* 1891. 8°. [*Rulers of India.*] **10603.** dd. **1**

—— The Holy Eucharist. Rough notes. [By Sir O. Burne.] pp. 10. [1890?] 8°. *See* Lord's Supper. **764.** i. **14.** (**23**

—— Memories. [With plates, including a portrait.] pp. ix. 343. *Edward Arnold: London,* 1907. 8°. **10817.** eee.

BURNE (Peter) The Concordance of Scripture and Scienc Illustrated, with reference to the temperance cause . . With a prefatory letter by Dr Lees, on the philosophy an philology of the question. pp. 116. *A. Hall & Co. London; J. M. Burton: Ipswich,* 1847. 8°. **8435.** d. **2**

BURNE (Richard Higgins)

—— *See* Fraser (Francis C.) Handbook of R. H. Burne Cetacean Dissections. 1952. 4°. **07209.** dd.

—— *See* London.—iii. *Britis Museum.—British Antarctic ("Terra Nova") Expedi tion,* 1910. Natural History Report. (vol. 2. no. 10 Mollusca. Part iv.—Anatomy of Pelecypoda. By R. H Burne.) 1914, *etc.* 4°. **7006.w.1/2.**

—— Descriptive and Illustrated Catalogue of the Physio logical Series of Comparative Anatomy contained in th Museum . . . Vol. iii. Second edition. pp. xiii. 391. 1907. 8°. *See* London.—iii. *Royal College of Surgeons.* Ac. **3836/12**

BURNE (Richard Vernon Higgins) A History of th Parish of Upton-cum-Chalvey, Buckinghamshire, com monly known as Slough. pp. 98. *Charles Luff: Slough* 1913. 8°. **4535.** f. 9. (6

BURNE (Sambrooke Arthur Higgins)

—— *See* Parrott (Richard) *of Bignall End.* An Account who hath enjoyed the severall estates in the parish Audley, *etc.* [Edited with an introduction by S. A. H Burne.] 1947. 8°. [*Collections for a History of Stafford shire.* 1944.] Ac. **5704**

BURNE (Sambrooke Arthur Higgins)

—— *See* Stafford.—*North Staffordshire Field Club.* Jubilee Volume . . . Edited by S. A. H. Burne . . . J. T. Stobbs, *etc.* 1916. 8°. Ac. **3007**. g/2.

—— *See* Stafford, *County of.—Quarter Sessions.* The Staffordshire Quarter Sessions Rolls . . . Edited by S. A. H. Burne. 1931, *etc.* 8°. [*Collections for a History of Staffordshire.* 1929, 30, 32, 35, *etc.*] Ac. **5704**.

—— *See* Tunstall, *Staffordshire, Manor of.* Court Rolls of the Manor of Tunstall. [Edited by S. A. H. Burne.] 1925, *etc.* 8°. [*North Staffordshire Field Club. Transactions, etc.* vol. 59–66, *etc.*] Ac. **3007**. g.

—— The Partition of Cheadle Grange, with some notes on the descent of the manor. Compiled from documents in the William Salt Library by S. A. H. Burne. *In:* Collections for a History of Staffordshire, *etc.* 1947. pp. 47–67. 1948. 8°. Ac. **5704**.

BURNEIUS (Carolus) *See* Burney (Charles) *D.D.*

BURNE-JONES (*Sir* Edward Coley) *Bart.* *See* Jones.

BURNE-JONES (Georgiana) *Lady.* *See* Jones.

BURNE-JONES (*Sir* Philip) *Bart.* *See* Jones.

BURNEL (A.) *of Nice.* Nice. pp. iv. 235. *Nice,* 1857. 8°. **10132**. aa. **10**.

BURNEL (Étienne Laurent Pierre) Burnel, agent particulier du Directoire exécutif aux colonies orientales à tous ceux qui ont lu l'adresse de l'Assemblée coloniale de l'Isle-de-France. [Refuting charges respecting his conduct in the Isle of France.] pp. 4. [*Paris,* 1796.] 8°. F. **704**. (8.)

BURNEL (Henry) *See* Burnell.

BURNEL (Rebecca) Light in Darkness. An essay on the piety which by remembring the many days of darkness, will change them into a marvellous light. With a notable example of it, in . . . Mrs. Rebeckah Burnel, in the seventeenth year of her age: meeting her death, with uncommon triumphs over it. [By Cotton Mather.] pp. 20. *Nath. Belknap: Boston,* 1724. 8°. **4985**. a. **49**.

BURNELL (Arthur) Some Thoughts on Socialism. pp. 24. *Elliot Stock: London,* 1895. 8°. **08282**. g. **4**. (2.)

BURNELL (Arthur Coke) *See* Beschi (C. G.) Clavis humaniorum litterarum sublimioris tamulici idiomatis, *etc.* [Edited by A. C. Burnell.] 1876. 8°. **14172**. f. **17**.

—— *See* Bible.—*Matthew.—Selections.* [*Polyglott.*] Specimens of S. Indian Dialects . . . collected by A. C. Burnell, *etc.* 1873, *etc.* 16°. **14137**. a. **74**.

—— *See* Bible.—*Matthew.—Selections.* [*Marathi.—Konkani dialect.*] The Parables of the Sower, etc. . . . Translated . . . into the Konkani . . . With an introductory note on this dialect [signed: A. B., i.e. A. C. Burnell]. 1872. 16°. **14137**. a. **76**.

—— *See* Brāhmaṇas.—*Talavakārabrāhmaṇa.* A Legend from the Talavakāra or Jaiminīya Brāhmaṇa . . . by A. C. Burnell. 1878. 16°. **14007**. b. **3**.

—— *See* Linschoten (J. H. van) The Voyage of John Huyghen van Linschoten to the East Indies . . . Edited, the first volume by the late A. C. Burnell . . . the second volume by Mr. P. A. Tiele. 1885, *etc.* 8°. Ac. **6172/59**.

BURNELL (Arthur Coke)

—— *See* Mādhava, *Son of Māyaṇa.* Dâya-Vibhâga . . . translated . . . by A. C. Burnell. 1868. 8°. **14039**. b. **4**.

—— *See* Manu. The Ordinances of Manu. Translated . . . With an introduction, by . . . A. C. Burnell, *etc.* 1884. 8°. **2318**. g. **19**.

—— *See* Yule (*Sir* Henry) *K.C.S.I.*, and Burnell (A. C.) Hobson-Jobson: being a glossary of Anglo-Indian colloquial words, *etc.* 1886. 8°. **12906**. r. **28**.

—— —— 1903. 8°. **2058.g.**

—— A Classified Index to the Sanskrit mss. in the Palace at Tanjore. Prepared for the Madras Government. pp. xii. 239. 1880 [1879, 80]. 4°. *See* Tanjore.—*Sarasvatī Mahall Library.* **14096**. f. **10**.

—— Elements of South Indian Palæography from the fourth to the seventeenth century a.d. Being an introduction to the study of South-Indian inscriptions and mss. [With plates.] pp. viii. 98. *Basel Mission Press: Mangalore; Trübner & Co.: London,* 1874. 4°. **7705**. ee. **1**.

—— Second enlarged and improved edition. pp. xii. 147. *Trübner & Co.: London,* 1878. 4°. **14058**. c. **13**.

—— On the Aindra School of Sanskrit Grammarians, their place in the Sanskrit and subordinate literatures. pp. viii. 120. *Basel Mission Book & Tract Depository: Mangalore,* 1875. 8°. **12907**. eee. **32**.

—— [Another copy.] On the Aindra School of Sanskrit Grammarians, *etc.* *Mangalore,* 1875. 8°. **14092**. b. **31**.

—— A Tentative List of Books and some mss. relating to the History of the Portuguese in India Proper. pp. vi. 133. *Basel Mission Press: Mangalore,* 1880. 4°. C. **55**. c. **35**.
One of fifteen copies privately printed.

BURNELL (Charles) The Johnsons, by a Friend of the Family, *etc.* [A novel.] pp. 155. *C. Brooks & Co.: London,* 1880. 8°. **12643**. a. **18**.

BURNELL (Ethel Myra)

—— Fragments of Thought. pp. 16. *A. H. Stockwell: Ilfracombe,* [1944.] 8°. **11657**. ee. **2**.

BURNELL (Frederic Spencer) Australia versus Germany. The story of the taking of German New Guinea . . . Illustrated with photographs. pp. 254. *G. Allen & Unwin: London,* 1915. 8°. **9082**. e. **26**.

—— Rome . . . With illustrations. pp. vii. 303. *E. Arnold & Co.: London,* 1930. 8°. **010151**. df. **39**.

—— A Sallet of Songs. pp. 127. *Holden & Hardingham: London,* 1920. 8°. **011648**. h. **39**.

—— Wanderings in Greece. [With plates.] pp. 253. *E. Arnold & Co.: London,* 1931. 8°. **10127**. df. **9**.

BURNELL (George Rowdon) *See* Periodical Publications.—*London.* The Annual Retrospect of Engineering and Architecture . . . Edited by G. R. Burnell. 1862. 8°. P.P. **1736**.

—— *See* Periodical Publications.—*London.* The Builder's and Contractor's Price-Book, *etc.* (1861–73 revised by G. R. Burnell.) 1856, *etc.* 12°. P.P. **2491**. ca.

BURNELL (GEORGE ROWDON)

—— *See* SWINDELL (John G.) Rudimentary Treatise on Wells and Well-Sinking. By J. G. Swindell . . . and G. R. Burnell, *etc.* 1883. 12°. **8703. c. 1.**

—— *See* WEALE (John) The Theory, Practice and Architecture of Bridges, etc. (Supplement . . . Edited by G. R. Burnell.) 1843, *etc.* 8°. **Tab.761.b.7.**

—— Hydraulic Engineering. *See* LAW (Henry) *Civil Engineer.* Civil Engineering, *etc.* 1869. 12°. **8703. cc. 25.**

—— [Another edition.] *See* LAW (Henry) *Civil Engineer.* The Rudiments of Civil Engineering, *etc.* 1881. 12°. **8767. b. 13.**

—— [Another edition.] *See* LAW (Henry) *Civil Engineer.* The Rudiments of Civil Engineering, *etc.* 1884. 8°. **08767. de. 60.**

—— Letter to . . . Viscount Palmerston . . . in reply to the Report of the General Board of Health, on the administration of the Public Health Act, and the Nuisances Removal and Diseases Prevention Act, from 1848 to 1854. pp. 15. [*J. Davy & Sons: London,* 1854.] 8°. **7305. c. 1. (13.)**

—— [Another copy.] **8776. ee. 13. (4.)**

—— New Public Health Bill. The privileges of Parliament endangered and the rights of the people violated. pp. 11. [*London,*] 1855. 8°. **7680. b. 8.**

—— Rudimentary Treatise on Limes, Cements, Mortars, Concretes, Mastics, Plastering, etc. pp. vii. 124. *John Weale: London,* 1850. 12°. **8703. a. 7.**

—— Fifth edition, with appendices. pp. vi. 136. *Virtue Bros. & Co.: London,* 1865. 8°. C.T. **261. (2.)**

—— The Rudiments of Hydraulic Engineering . . . With illustrations. 2 pt. pp. viii. 283. *John Weale: London,* 1858, 59. 12°. **8703. c. 48.**

BURNELL (HENRY) Landgartha. A tragie-comedy, as it was presented in the new Theater in Dublin, *etc.* [In verse.] *Dublin,* 1641. 4°. **644. b. 5.**

—— [Another copy.] **162. c. 27.**

—— [Another copy.] **G. 11220.**

BURNELL (HENRY BLOMFIELD) The London—City—Tithes Act, 1879, and the other Tithe Acts effecting the commutation and redemption of tithes in the City of London. With an introduction, notes, etc. pp. iv. 215. *Stevens & Sons: London,* 1880. 8°. **6426. df. 8.**

BURNELL (JOHN) Bombay in the Days of Queen Anne. Being an account of the settlement . . . With an introduction and notes by Samuel T. Sheppard . . . To which is added Burnell's narrative of his adventures in Bengal, *etc.* [With maps.] pp. xxx. 192. 1933. 8°. *See* LONDON.—III. *Hakluyt Society.* Ac. **6172/125.**

BURNELL (MAISIE) *See* DADSWELL (Herbert E.) Methods for the Identification of the Light-Coloured Woods of the Genus Eucalyptus . . . By H. E. Dadswell . . . M. Burnell, *etc.* 1934. 8°. [*Australia. Council for Scientific and Industrial Research. Bulletin.* no. 78.] **C.S.G.548.(2.)**

BURNELL (MAISIE)

—— *See* DADSWELL (Herbert E.) and BURNELL (M.) Methods for the Identification of the Coloured Woods of the Genus Eucalyptus, *etc.* 1932. 8°. [*Australia. Council for Scientific and Industrial Research. Bulletin.* no. 67.] **C.S.G.548.(2.)**

BURNELL (RICHARD DESBOROUGH)

—— *See* ENGLAND.—*Amateur Rowing Association.* The British Rowing Almanack . . . Edited by R. D. Burnell. 1948, *etc.* 8°. P.P. **2489. ic.**

—— The Oxford & Cambridge Boat Race, 1829–1953. [With plates.] pp. xii. 244. *Oxford University Press: London,* 1954. 8°. **7921. b. 49.**

—— Sculling. With notes on training and rigging. [With plates.] pp. xv. 110. *Oxford University Press: London,* 1955. 8°. **7922. bb. 27.**

—— Swing together. Thoughts on rowing. pp. xv. 192. pl. 16. *Oxford University Press: London,* 1952. 8°. **7921. aaa. 46.**

BURNELL (SIDNEY WILLIAM) The Arithmetic of the Triangle. pp. vii. 103. *London,* 1935. 8°. [*Macmillan's Senior School Series.* Arithmetic Terminal Book E.] **12207.aaa.4/6.**

—— [Another edition.] With answers and solutions. pp. vii. 103. xii. *London,* 1935. 8°. [*Macmillan's Senior School Series.* Arithmetic Terminal Book E.] **12207.aaa.4/6.**

BURNELL (SIDNEY WILLIAM) and **DICKS** (ARTHUR JAMES)

—— Inorganic Chemistry. pp. 372. *Ralph, Holland & Co.: London,* [1911.] 8°. **08909. aa. 43.**

BURNELL (THOMAS) Official Guide to Criccieth, North Wales. Written for the Urban District Council of Criccieth by the chairman, T. Burnell, and illustrated, *etc.* (Second edition.) pp. 67. 1905. 8°. *See* CRICCIETH. **010370. eee. 19.**

—— (Third edition.) pp. 73. 1909. 8°. *See* CRICCIETH. **10351. bbb. 35. (4.)**

BURNELL (THOMAS COKE) The Exhibition Dorking; with hints to exhibitors and poultry fanciers in general. With illustrations. pp. 46. *Journal of Horticulture & Cottage Gardener Office: London,* [1875.] 8°. **7295. aaa. 5.**

BÜRNER (   ) [For the German surname of this form:] *See* BUERNER.

BURNES, *Family of.* *See* BURNES (James) *Physician-General in India.* Notes on his Name and Family, *etc.* 1851. 8°. **1327. e. 21.**

—— *See* ROGERS (Charles) *D.D.* Genealogical Memoirs of the Family of Robert Burns, and of the Scottish House of Burnes. 1877. 8°. **9905. c. 44.**

BURNES (ALEJANDRO) *See* BURNES (*Sir* Alexander)

BURNES (*Sir* ALEXANDER) *See* BUIST (George) *LL.D.* Memoir of Sir Alexander Burnes, C.B. 1851. 8°. [*BURNES (James) Notes on his Name and Family.*] **1327. e. 21.**

BURNES (*Sir* ALEXANDER)

—— *See* DALPATRĀM PRĀṆJĪVAN KHAKHAR. Report on the Architectural and Archæological Remains in the Province of Kachh . . . With five papers by . . . Sir A. Burnes. 1879. 8°. [*Selections from the Records of the Bombay Government. New ser.* no. 152.] **I.S. BO. 127.**

—— Cabool: being a personal narrative of a journey to, and residence in that city, in the years 1836, 7, and 8. With numerous illustrations [including a portrait]. pp. xii. 398. *John Murray: London,* 1842. 8°. **2356. c. 5.**

—— A Memoir of a Map of the Eastern Branch of the Indus, giving an account of the alterations produced in it by the earthquake of 1819 and the bursting of the dams in 1826; also a theory of the Runns formation & some surmises on the route of Alexander the Great, *etc.* pp. 123. [*Bombay,* 1828?] 4°. **1298. h. 18.**
Lithographed.

—— Travels into Bokhara; being the account of a journey from India to Cabool, Tartary and Persia; also, Narrative of a voyage on the Indus . . . in the years 1831, 1832, and 1833. [With illustrations, including a portrait.] 3 vol. *John Murray: London,* 1834. 8°. **1046. c. 5–7.**

—— Second edition. 3 vol. *John Murray: London,* 1835. 16°. **G. 2240–42.**

—— New edition, with a map and illustrations. 3 vol. *John Murray: London,* 1839. 8°. **10056. de. 12.**

—— Alexander Burnes' Reisen in Indien und nach Bukhara. 2 Bd. *In:* WIDENMANN (E.) and HAUFF (W.) Reisen und Länderbeschreibungen der älteren und neuesten Zeit, *etc.* Lief. 3, 7. 1835, 36. 8°. **1294. c. 1, 2.**

—— Viaggi di Alessandro Burnes. Prima versione italiana. (Traduttore, D. Agostini.) 3 pt. *Prato,* 1842. 8°. [MARMOCCHI (*F. C.*) *Raccolta di viaggi, etc.* tom. 7–9.] **1424. i. 4.**

—— Cabul. [An abridged translation into Spanish of vol. 1. chap. 5 of "Travels into Bokhara."] 1860. *See* FERNANDEZ CUESTA (N.) Nuevo Viajero Universal, *etc.* tom. 2. 1859, *etc.* 8°. **10005. g. 14.**

BURNES (ELEANOR) "Success" on Getting Married. pp. 24. *Success Publishing Co.: London,* [1919.] 8°. **08415. ee. 40.**

BURNES (J. FRED) The Political and Social Condition and Relation of England and Ireland 400 years hence. The marriage of King Bull with Hibernia; or, How a lady won Home Rule. pp. 16. *Bowers Bros.: London,* [1884.] 8°. **12316. k. 11. (7.)**

BURNES (JAMES) *Physician-General of India.*

—— Memoir of James Burnes, *etc.* (Four speeches delivered by Dr Burnes.) [The preface is signed: W. A. L.] 1850. 8°. *See* L., W. A. **10863. de. 57.**

—— Narrative of a Visit to the Court of . . . the Ameers of Sinde, at Hyderabad . . . in the year 1827–28, compiled officially for the Government of Bombay, *etc.* [With a table.] pp. v. 166. **L.P.** 1829. 8°. *See* BOMBAY, *Presidency of.* [*Miscellaneous Public Documents, etc.*] **10057. dd. 24.**

—— [Another edition.] [With maps.] pp. 253. *John Stark: Edinburgh,* 1831. 8°. **1046. k. 13. (2.)**

BURNES (JAMES) *Physician-General of India.*

—— Notes on his Name and Family, by J. Burnes. [Followed by a memoir of Sir Alexander Burnes by George Buist, and a memoir of James Burnes by William Alexander Laurie.] 3 pt. *Printed for private circulation: Edinburgh,* 1851. 8°. **1327. e. 21.**

—— A Sketch of the History of Cutch from its first connexion with the British Government in India to the conclusion of the treaty of 1819. 2 pt. *Lithographed for the perusal of the author's private friends,* [1829.] fol. **9057. h. 4.**

—— A Sketch of the History of the Knights Templars. pp. ii. 59. x. *W. Blackwood & Sons: Edinburgh,* 1837. 4°. **4785. ccc. 29.**
The titlepage is engraved. One of an edition of 100 *copies.*

—— Second edition. Illustrated with plates. pp. ii. 74. lx. *W. Blackwood & Sons: Edinburgh,* 1840. 4°. **486. e. 27.**
With an additional titlepage, engraved.

—— [Another copy.] **G. 19609.**

BURNES (JAMES NELSON) James Nelson Burnes, late representative in Congress from Missouri. His life, with a concise reproduction of his speeches and debates in Congress . . . By E. W. De Knight. [With a portrait.] pp. lix. 480. *A. C. McClurg & Co.: Chicago,* 1889. 8°. **8176. ee. 6.**

BURNES (WILLIAM) A Manual of Religious Belief, composed by W. Burnes, the poet's father, for the instruction of his children; with biographical preface. Now first printed. [With a facsimile of a letter by W. Burnes.] pp. l. *M'Kie & Drennan: Kilmarnock,* 1875. 8°. **3560. bb. 1.**

BURNESIDE (MARGARET) The Delusion of Diana. pp. 319. *Edward Arnold: London,* 1898. 8°. **012643. ccc. 16.**

BURNESS (ALEXANDER GEORGE) and **MAVOR** (FREDERICK JOSEPH) The Specific Action of Drugs on the Healthy System; an index to their therapeutic value, as deduced from experiments on man and animals. pp. x. 184. *Baillière, Tindall & Cox: London,* 1874. 8°. **7461. cc. 11.**

BURNESS (D. M.)

—— *See* ALLEN (Charles F. H.) Six-membered Heterocyclic Nitrogen Compounds . . . In collaboration with D. M. Burness, *etc.* 1951. 8°. **W.P. 54/2.**

BURNESS (DAVID) Report of the Public Discussion on Church Establishments and Endowments, between the Rev. D. Burness . . . and the Rev. George Campbell . . . at Strathaven, on the 19th of March 1839. Reported by Mr. Simon Macgregor. pp. iv. 76. *Edinburgh Printing & Publishing Co.: Edinburgh,* 1839. 8°. **4175. df. 6. (4.)**

BURNESS (ELEANOR) The Romany Dream Book. pp. 96. *A. Rogers & Co.: London,* 1927. 8°. **8633. df. 53.**

—— [Another edition.] pp. 96. *A. Rogers & Co.: London,* [1931.] 8°. **8631. a. 53.**

BURNESS (JOHN) *See* LAWRANCE (Robert M.) John Burness, a forgotten genius. [1931.] 8°. **010825. ff. 18.**

BURNESS (John)

—— Adventures of Thrummy Cap. A tale in the broad Scottish dialect. Also, The Ghaist o' Garron Ha'; or, Imposture detected. [In verse. With an introduction by J. M. Bulloch.] pp. 38. *W. Jolly & Sons: Aberdeen,* [1887.] 8°. **11607. dd. 8. (1.)**

—— [Another edition.] pp. 15. *See* Fleeman (Jamie) The Life and Death of Jamie Fleeman, *etc.* 1893. 8°. **10827. a. 20.**

BURNESS (Robert) *See* Lermontov (M. Yu.) The Demon. Translated . . . by R. Burness. 1918. 8°. **011586. cc. 4.**

BURNESS (William) *See* Jarvis (Thomas) The Farmer's Harvest Companion . . . A new edition . . . By W. Burness. 1870. 8°. **8506. bbb. 26.**

—— *See* Nesbit (Anthony) Nesbit's Practical Land-Surveying . . . Edited by W. Burness. 1864. 8°. **8534. cc. 24.**

—— —— 1870. 8°. **8505. ee. 33.**

—— *See* Periodical Publications.—*Edinburgh.* The Parliament-House Book for 1871–72 [*etc.*]. Compiled by W. Burness, *etc.* 1871, *etc.* 8°. **P.P.2511.fe.& 2018.a.**

—— The Equipment of the Farm. By W. Burness, J. C. Morton, and Gilbert Murray. pp. vi. 142. *Bradbury, Agnew & Co.: London,* 1884. 8°. [*Handbook of the Farm Series.* no. 6.] **7078. bb.**

—— Essay on the Elements of British Industry; comprising remarks on the cause of our present depressed state, agricultural, commercial & manufacturing, English, Scotch and Irish: together with suggestions for its removal. pp. 160. *Longman & Co.: London,* 1848. 16°. **1391. b. 69.**

—— Practical River Reform, in drainage and navigation, in water power and irrigation, in warping land and storing water. pp. 31. *Bradbury, Agnew, & Co.; Office of "The Agricultural Gazette": London,* 1882. 8°. **8776. dd. 27.**

BURNESTON (Edna B.)

—— *See* Berkley (Earl E.) A Study of the Quality of Abaca Fiber. By E. E. Berkley . . . E. B. Burneston, *etc.* 1949. 8°. [*U.S. Department of Agriculture. Technical Bulletin.* no. 999.] A.S. **800/2.**

BURNET (Adam W.)

—— The Lord Reigneth. The Russell Lectures for 1944 on the Book of Revelation. pp. 134. *Hodder & Stoughton: London,* 1946. 8°. **3188. aa. 7.**

—— Pleading with Men. Being the Warrack lectures on preaching for 1935. pp. 189. *Hodder & Stoughton: London,* 1935. 8°. **20020. aa. 23.**

BURNET (Alexander) Achilles Dissected: being a compleat key of the political characters in that new ballad opera, written by the late Mr. Gay. An account of the plan on which it is founded. With remarks upon the whole. By Mr. Burnet. To which is added, the First Satire of the Second Book of Horace, imitated in a dialogue between Mr. Pope and the Ordinary of Newgate [signed: Guthry]. pp. 30. *W. Mears: London,* 1733. 8°. **641. e. 28. (6.)**

BURNET (Alexander) *Archbishop of Glasgow. See* Russell (Duncan K. C.) Archbishop Alexander Burnet, 1664/84. [1916.] fol. **1765. a. 28.**

BURNET (Alexander) *LL.D. See* Walpoole (George A.) The New British Traveller, *etc.* [The section describing Scotland written with the assistance of A. Burnet.] [1784?] fol. **10348. l. 3.**

BURNET (Amos) The Isles of the Western Sea. The story of Methodist missions in the West Indies and Central America. [With plates.] pp. 64. *Wesleyan Methodist Missionary Society: London,* [1924.] 8°. **4766. c. 20.**

—— A Mission to the Transvaal . . . With map. pp. 127. *Robert Culley: London,* [1908.] 8°. [*Methodist Missionary Library.*] **4907. a. 16/10.**

BURNET (Andrew) The Spiritual Anatomy of Man, *etc.* pp. 294. *John Lawrence: London,* 1693. 8°. **4407. aa. 4.**

BURNET (Annie Forbes) *See* Euripides. [*Ion.—Greek.*] Euripides' Ion. With introduction and notes by J. Thompson . . . and A. F. Burnet. [1891.] 8°. **12205. c. 39.**

—— *See* Homer. [*Odyssey.—English.*] Homer's Odyssey, Book iv. A translation. By A. F. Burnet . . . and J. Thompson. [1891.] 8°. **12205. c. 40.**

—— *See* Horatius Flaccus (Q.) [*Satirae.—Latin and English.*] Horace: the Satires. Edited . . . by F. G. Plaistowe . . . and A. F. Burnet. [1891.] 8°. **12205. c. 49.**

—— *See* Juvenalis (D. J.) [*Satirae Selectae.—Latin.*] Juvenal: Satires viii., x., xiii. Edited . . . by A. H. Allcroft . . . and A. F. Burnet. [1891.] 8°. **12205. c. 42.**

—— *See* Juvenalis (D. J.) [*Satirae Selectae.—English.*] Juvenal: Satires viii., x.–xiii. A translation, with test papers . . . By A. H. Allcroft . . . and A. F. Burnet. [1891.] 8°. **12205. c. 105.**

—— *See* Juvenalis (D. J.) [*Satirae Selectae.—English.*] Juvenal: Satires viii., x.–xvi. A translation . . . By A. H. Allcroft . . . and A. F. Burnet. [1897.] 8°. **12205. c. 333.**

—— *See* Terentius (Publius) *Afer.* [*Adelphi.—English.*] The Adelphi of Terence. A translation. By A. F. Burnet . . . and J. H. Haydon. [1890.] 8°. **12205. c. 200.**

—— *See* Xenophon, *the Historian.* [*Anabasis.—English.*] Xenophon's Anabasis. Book iv. A translation. By A. F. Burnet. [1891.] 8°. **12205. c. 28.**

BURNET (Augustinus Josephus) Dissertatio inauguralis juridica de formulis donationis inter vivos. pp. 24. *Leodii,* 1819. 4°. **498. f. 2. (7.)**

BURNET (C.) *Pharmacien sous-aide-major à l'Hôpital militaire de Strasbourg.* Considérations générales sur la pleurésie aiguë, *etc.* pp. 26. *Strasbourg,* 1835. 4°. [*Collection générale des dissertations de la Faculté de Médecine de Strasbourg.* vol. 50.] **7381.*c.**

BURNET (Constance) Stockton Manor; or, Every cloud has its silver lining. *See* Proverb Stories. Proverb Stories, *etc.* ser. 1. [1885.] 8°. **12811. d. 19.**

BURNET (Dana) The Boundary Line: a drama in three acts. pp. 118. *Longmans & Co.: New York,* 1931. 8°. **11791. de. 79.**

BURNET (DANA)

— Broken Horizons. pp. 318. *Thornton Butterworth: London*, 1922. 8°. NN. **7823.**

— It is a Strange House. [A play.] pp. 188. *Little, Brown & Co.: Boston*, 1925. 8°. **11791.** aaa. **31.**

— The Lark, *etc.* [A novel.] pp. 308. *Little, Brown & Co.: Boston*, 1921. 8°. NN. **7564.**

— Poems. pp. xi. 267. *Harper & Bros.: New York & London*, 1915. 8°. **11686.** dd. **30.**

BURNET (DAVID STAATS) *See* PERIODICAL PUBLICATIONS.—*Buffalo, Virginia.* The Christian Baptist . . . Revised by D. S. Burnet, *etc.* 1835. 8°. P.P. **908.**

— *See* PERIODICAL PUBLICATIONS.—*Buffalo, Virginia.* The Christian Baptist, edited by Alexander Campbell . . . Revised by D. S. Burnet, from the second edition, with Mr. Campbells last corrections, *etc.* 1848. 8°. Mic. A. **239.** (**1.**)

— The Good Confession. [A sermon. With a biographical notice and a portrait.] *See* MOORE (William T.) The Living Pulpit of the Christian Church, *etc.* 1868. 8°. **4478.** l. **1.**

BURNET (DUNCANUS) *See* PARCOVIUS (F.) Gratulatio ad Cl. V. D. Burnetum, *etc.* [1608.] 4°. **1179.** b. **2.** (**6.**)

— De virginum cachexia, *etc.* *Praes.* F. Parcovius. *Typis I. Lucij: Helmaestadii*, 1608. 4°. **1179.** b. **2.** (**5.**)

— Iatrochymicus, siue de præparatione et compositione medicamentorum chymicorum artificiosa tractatus D. Bornetti . . . Studio ac opera Ioannis Danielis Mylii . . . nunc primum in lucem editus. pp. 115. *Typis N. Hoffmanni sumptibus L. Iennis: Francofurti*, 1616. 4°. **1033.** h. **40.**

— Editio altera. Nunc secunda cura accuratiore reuisa, repurgata . . . studio ac opera Ioannis Danielis Mylii, *etc.* pp. 111. *Typis E. Kempfferi, sumptibus L. Jennis: Francofurti*, 1621. 4°. **1033.** l. **21.**

BURNET (ÉDOUARD LOUIS) Essai sur la chronologie en usage dans les chartes du diocèse de Genève au XIIme siècle, 1078–1206. 1908. *See* GENEVA.—*Société d'Histoire et d'Archéologie.* Mémoires et documents publiés par la Société. tom. 31. livr. 1. 1841, *etc.* 8°. Ac. **6941.**

— Le Premier tribunal révolutionnaire genevois, juillet–août 1794. Études critiques. pp. 454. *Genève*, 1925. 8°. [*Mémoires et documents publiés par la Société d'Histoire et d'Archéologie de Genève.* tom. 34.] Ac. **6941.**

BURNET (ELIZABETH) A Method of Devotion: or, Rules for holy & devout living, with prayers on several occasions, and advices and devotions for the Holy Sacrament. Written by Mrs. Burnet, late wife of . . . Gilbert Lord Bishop of Sarum. The second edition. To which is added, some account of her life, by T. Goodwyn. [With a portrait.] pp. xli. 395. *Joseph Downing: London*, 1709. 8°. **861.** l. **3.**

— The third edition, *etc.* pp. xli. 395. *Joseph Downing: London*, 1713. 8°. G. **19772.**

— The fifth edition, corrected, *etc.* pp. xliv. 331. *M. Downing: London*, 1738. 8°. **4380.** g. **24.**

BURNET (ÉTIENNE) Essences. Paul Valéry et l'unité de l'esprit. Montherlant et les mystères. Proust et le bergsonisme. [With portraits.] pp. 252. *Paris*, 1929. 8°. **11824.** p. **11.**

BURNET (ÉTIENNE)

— La Lèfre. Légende, histoire, actualité. pp. 185. *Paris*, 1932. 8°. **07688.** de. **29.**

— La Lutte contre les microbes. pp. ix. 318. *Paris*, 1908. 8°. **07561.** g. **33.**

— The Campaign against Microbes . . . Translated from the French by E. E. Austen. pp. xi. 248. *J. Bale, Sons & Danielsson: London*, 1909. 8°. **7561.** k. **1.**

— [Microbes et toxines.] Microbes & Toxins . . . With a preface by Élie Metchnikoff. Translated from the French by Dr. Charles Broquet and W. M. Scott . . . Illustrated. pp. xvi. 316. *William Heinemann: London*, 1912. 8°. **07561.** g. **46.**

— La Porte du Sauveur, *etc.* [A novel.] pp. 282. *Paris*, 1926. 8°. **12515.** r. **3.**

— The Saviour's Gate . . . Translated by Margaret Sinclair. pp. 319. *Hodder & Stoughton: London*, [1928.] 8°. **12515.** s. **19.**

— La Tour blanche. Armée d'Orient, 1916–1917. [Sketches.] pp. 247. *Paris*, 1921. 8°. **012547.** aaa. **81.**

BURNET (F.) Propositions et observations sur diverses maladies de l'encéphale, et principalement sur celles des enfans; thèse, *etc.* pp. 16. *Paris*, 1830. 4°. **1184.** d. **5.** (**16.**)

BURNET (*Sir* FRANK MACFARLANE)

— *See* BEVERIDGE (William I. B.) and BURNET (F. M.) The Cultivation of Viruses and Rickettsiae in the Chick Embryo. 1946. 8°. [*Medical Research Council. Special Report Series.* no. 256.] B.S. **25/8.**

— *See* MACKERRAS (Ian M.) and (M. J.) Experimental Studies of Ephemeral Fever in Australian Cattle . . . With a section in collaboration with F. M. Burnet. 1940. 8°. [*Commonwealth of Australia. Council for Scientific and Industrial Research. Bulletin.* no. 136.] **C.S.G.548.(2.)**

— Biological Aspects of Infectious Disease. pp. vii. 310. *University Press: Cambridge*, 1940. 8°. **07560.** g. **49.**

— [Biological Aspects of Infectious Disease.] Natural History of Infectious Disease . . . Second edition. pp. x. 356. *University Press: Cambridge*, 1953. 8°. **7564.** aaa. **30.**

— The Immunological Reactions of the Filterable Viruses. By F. M. Burnet, E. V. Keogh, and Dora Lush . . . Reprinted . . . from "The Australian Journal of Experimental Biology and Medical Science," *etc.* 1937. 4°. *See* ADELAIDE.—*University of Adelaide.* **07560.** i. **20.**

— The Production of Antibodies. A review and a theoretical discussion. By F. M. Burnet. With the collaboration of Mavis Freeman . . . A. V. Jackson . . . Dora Lush. pp. 75. *Melbourne*, 1941. 8°. [*Monographs from the Walter and Eliza Hall Institute of Research in Pathology and Medicine.* no. 1.] Ac. **3856.** cb.

— The Production of Antibodies. By F. M. Burnet . . . and Frank Fenner . . . Second edition. pp. viii. 142. *Macmillan & Co.: Melbourne*, 1949. 8°. [*Monograph of the Walter and Eliza Hall Institute.* no. 1.] Ac. **3856.** cb.

BURNET (*Sir* Frank Macfarlane)

—— [A reissue.] The Production of Antibodies, *etc.* *Melbourne*, 1953. 8°. [*Monograph of the Walter and Eliza Hall Institute, Melbourne.* no. 1a.] Ac. **3856**. cb.

—— The Use of the Developing Egg in Virus Research. pp. 58. *London*, 1936. 8°. [*Medical Research Council. Special Report Series.* no. 220.] B.S. **25/8**.

—— The Virus and the Cell, *etc.* pp. 20. *Washington*, 1953. 8°. [*R. E. Dyer Lecture.* 1952.] Ac. **3859**. m.

—— Virus as Organism. Evolutionary and ecological aspects of some human virus diseases. (The Edward K. Dunham Lectures for the Promotion of the Medical Sciences, 1944.) pp. 134. *Cambridge, Mass.*, 1945. 8°. [*Harvard University Monographs in Medicine and Public Health.* no. 8.] **Ac.2692/42.(8.)**

—— [A reissue.] Virus as Organism, *etc.* (Second printing.) *Cambridge, Mass.*, 1946. 8°. [*Harvard University Monographs in Medicine and Public Health.*] Ac. **2692/42**. (8a.)

—— Viruses and Man. [With plates.] pp. 197. *Penguin Books: London*, 1953. 8°. [*Pelican Books.* no. A 265.] **012209**. d. **4/265**.

BURNET (*Sir* Frank Macfarlane) and **CLARK** (Ellen)

—— Influenza. A survey of the last 50 years in the light of modern work on the virus of epidemic influenza. pp. 118. *Macmillan & Co.: Melbourne*, 1942. 4°. [*Monographs from the Walter and Eliza Hall Institute of Research in Pathology and Medicine.* no. 4.] Ac. **3856**. cb.

BURNET (G. B.) The Bishop: memories of John Angus, minister at Barr, Ayrshire 1888–1918. [With a portrait.] pp. 136. *Marshall Bros.: London*, 1924. 8°. **4956**. ee. **31**.

BURNET (George) *See* Burnett (G.) *of Balliol College, Oxford.*

BURNET (George Bain)

—— The Book of the Abiding Christ. An interpretation of the hymn " Abide with me " [by Henry F. Lyte]. pp. 124. *Saint Catherine Press: London*, 1955. 8°. **4384**. aa. **31**.

—— The Story of Quakerism in Scotland, 1650–1850 . . . With an epilogue on the period 1850–1950 by William H. Marwick. pp. 230. *James Clarke & Co.: London*, 1952. 8°. **04715**. f. **52**.

BURNET (Gibbie) *pseud.* An Address to the Revolution Club. [A satire on William iii.] *See* England.—*Proclamations.*—ii. George iii. His Majesty's Proclamation of the Twenty-first of May, *etc.* 1792. 8°. **8135**. cc. **26**.

BURNET (Gilbert) *Bishop of Salisbury.*

Arrangement.

BURNET (Gilbert) *Bishop of Salisbury.*

COLLECTIONS.

—— Six Papers containing i. Reasons against repealing th Acts of Parliament concerning the Test . . . ii. Reflec tions on His Majesties Proclamation for a Toleration i Scotland, together with the said proclamation. iii. Re flections on His Majesties Declaration for Liberty o Conscience. Dated the fourth of April, 1687. iv. A Answer to a Paper . . . entitled, A New Test of th Church of England's Loyalty. v. Remarks on the tw Papers, writ by His late Majesty King Charles ii. con cerning Religion. vi. The Citation, togethar with Thre Letters to the Earl of Midleton. pp. 1–60. 1687. 4°. **116**. c. **33**
Imperfect; wanting the second and third of the letters t the Earl of Midleton.

—— A Discourse concerning Transubstantiation and Idolatry Being an answer to the Bishop of Oxford's Plea [entitle " Reasons for Abrogating the Test "] relating to those tw points. [An edition of two tracts by G. Burnet entitle " A Second Part of the Enquiry into the Reasons offere by Sa. Oxon for Abrogating the Test " and " A Con tinuation of the Second Part of the Enquiry," *etc.*] pp. 36 1688. 4°. *See* Parker (Samuel) *Bishop of Oxford.* **859**. h. **16**

—— [Another copy.] **3936**. bbb. **2**. (4.

—— [Another copy.] T. **1867**. (8.

—— [Another copy.] **222**. e. **10**. (4.

—— A Collection of Eighteen Papers, relating to the Affair of Church & State, during the reign of King James th Second, *etc.* pp. 244. *For John Starkey & Richard Chiswell: London*, 1689. 4°. T. **1629**. (1.

—— [Another copy.] **698**. d. **7**
Imperfect; wanting the second leaf of the table of contents

—— [Another copy of pp. 119–244.] **699**. f. **6**. (13.

—— Six Papers . . . To which is added, i. An Apology fo the Church of England, &c. and ii. An Enquiry into th Measures of Submission to the Supream Authority, &c 3 pt. *London*, 1689. 4°. **699**. f. **6**. (11.
Previous edition 1687.

—— [Another copy.] T. **1669**. (12, 5.

—— [Another copy.] few ms. notes. T. **692**. (1.
In this copy the " Enquiry " bears the signature A.

—— Dr. G. Burnet's Tracts in two volumes. Vol. 1. con taining, i. His Travels . . . ii. Animadversions on th Reflections upon the Travels. iii. Three Letters of th Quietists, Inquisition, and State of Italy. Vol. 2. iv. Hi Translations of Lactantius of the Death of Persecutors v. His Answers to Mr. Varillas, *etc.* 2 vol. 6 pt. *For J. Robinson & A. Churchil: London*, 1689. 12°. **1019**. f. **3**

—— [A Collection of Several Tracts and Discourses writte in the year 1677, to 1704.] [Separate tracts bearing date ranging from 1678 to 1704 reissued together, with genera titlepages for each volume. With a portrait.] 3 vol. [*For Ri. Chiswell: London*, 1704, 03.] 4°. **699**. f. **1–3**
Imperfect; wanting the frontispiece, the general titlepag and three following leaves of vol. 1, *and the half-title to th tract* 6 *in vol.* 2.

—— [Another copy.] **225**. b. **15–17**.
In this copy tract 2 *of vol.* 2 *and tracts* 7 *and* 8 *of vol.* 3 *are of later editions than the corresponding tracts in the preceding. Imperfect; wanting the half-titles of tract* 3 *in vol.* 2 *and tract* 15 *in vol.* 3, *and many of the lists of books printed for Richard Chiswell.*

BURNET (GILBERT) *Bishop of Salisbury.* [COLLECTIONS.]

—— A Collection of Speeches, Prefaces, Letters, &c. with a description of Geneva and Holland: By Gilbert, Lord Bishop of Sarum. To which is added, his Citation to answer in Scotland for High-Treason, together with his answer, *etc.* pp. 110. *London,* 1713. 8°. T. **1583.** (7.)

—— The Last Will and Testament of Dr. Gilbert Burnet. Dr. Burnet's Solution of Two Cases of Conscience. (1. Is a woman's barrenness a just ground for divorce, or for polygamy?—2. Is polygamy, in any case, lawful under the Gospel?) *See* MACKY (John) Memoirs of the Secret Services of John Macky, *etc.* 1733. 8°. **808.** g. 26.

—— The Lives of Sir Matthew Hale . . . Wilmot, Earl of Rochester; and Queen Mary . . . To this edition are added, Richard Baxter's additional notes to the life of Sir Matthew Hale. And a sermon preached at the funeral of the Earl of Rochester, by the Rev. Mr. Parsons. 3 pt. *T. Davies: London,* 1774. 8°. **10817.** b. 18.

—— Lives, Characters, and a Sermon preached at the Funeral of the Hon. Robert Boyle . . . A new edition, with large additions. [With prefaces by Alexander Knox.] pp. xxiv. 319. *W. Watson: Dublin,* 1815. 8°. **4903.** e. 27.

—— A new edition, with large additions. pp. 312. *A. Watson: Dublin,* 1824. 12°. **4903.** bb. 26.

—— The Lives of Hale, Bedell, and Rochester . . . With Fell's life of Dr. Hammond. pp. 370. *J. F. Dove: London,* [1830?] 12°. **10804.** a. 8.
With an additional titlepage, engraved.

—— Lives, Characters, and an Address to Posterity . . . With the two prefaces to the Dublin editions . . . Edited, with an introduction and notes, by John Jebb. pp. lxx. 386. *James Duncan; J. Cochran: London,* 1833. 8°. **490.** c. 23.

—— Memorial of Mary, Princess of Orange, Queen-Consort to King William III . . . With an appendix. (Letters from Queen Mary to King William while in Ireland.—A Sermon preached before the Queen, at White-Hall, on the 16th day of July, 1690, *etc.*) pp. xvi. 85. l. 26. *Thomas Constable: Edinburgh,* 1842. 4°. **1452.** i. 12.

—— Deux nouveaux traitez concernant les affaires presentes d'Angleterre. Savoir, I. Reponse à un ecrit, intitulé le nouveau Test de fidelité de l'Eglise Anglicane. II. Lettre contenant quelques reflexions sur la declaration de sa Myesté pour la liberté de conscience. [By G. Burnet.] Traduit de l'anglois. pp. 77. 1687. 12°. [*Recueil de plusieurs pieces concernant les affaires presentes d'Angleterre, etc.* tom. 1.] *See* ENGLAND. [*Appendix.—History and Politics.*—II. 1687.] C. **65.** a. **24.**

—— Deux traitez concernans les affaires présentes d'Angleterre. Premiérement, Raisons contre la révocation des actes du Parlement d'Angleterre, touchant le Test. Secondement, Réflexions sur l'Edit de S. M. Britannique, touchant la tolérance des religions. Traduit de l'anglois. [By G. Burnet.] pp. 56. 1687. 24°. *See* ENGLAND. [*Appendix.—History and Politics.*—II. 1687.] **600.** a. **22.** (6.)

—— [Another copy.] **8410.** aaa. **6.** (2.)

—— [Another edition.] pp. 44. 1687. 12°. [*Recueil de plusieurs pieces concernant les affaires presentes d'Angleterre, etc.* tom. 1.] *See* ENGLAND. [*Appendix.—History and Politics.*—II. 1687.] C. **65.** a. **24.**

BURNET (GILBERT) *Bishop of Salisbury.*

LETTERS.

—— Four Letters which pass'd between the Right Reverend the Lord Bishop of Sarum and Mr. Henry Dodwell. [Edited by Robert Nelson.] pp. 39. *Richard Smith: London,* 1713. 8°. **698.** c. **15.** (2.)

—— Some Unpublished Letters of Gilbert Burnet the Historian. Edited . . . by Miss H. C. Foxcroft. 1907. *See* LONDON.—III. *Camden Society.* The Camden Miscellany. vol. 11. 1847, *etc.* 4°. Ac. **8113/39.**

SERMONS.

—— The Royal Martyr and the Dutiful Subject, in two sermons. [Entitled "The Royal Martyr Lamented" and "Subjection for Conscience-sake Asserted."] 2 pt. *For R. Royston: London,* 1675. 4°. **226.** i. **8.** (16.)

—— [Another edition.] 2 pt. *For Luke Meredith: London,* 1689. 4°. **699.** f. **4.** (8, 4.)

—— [Another copy of pt. 2.] **4473.** aaa. **45.** (4.)

—— [Another copy of pt. 2.] **226.** g. **7.** (14.)

—— [Another edition.] pp. 48. *J. Meredith: London,* 1710. 8°. **699.** f. **4.** (1, 2.)

—— [Another copy.] **225.** f. **8.** (2.)

—— Select Sermons on the following subjects, The love of God. The love of our neighbour. Swearing and perjury. The Sabbath. Chastity. Drunkenness. Death. 3 serm. And a sermon at the funeral of the Honourable Robert Boyle. pp. 213. *Robert Foulis: Glasgow,* 1742. 12°. **4453.** a. **9.**
The first seven sermons were published in 1713 *as "An Essay towards a New Book of Homilies," appended to "Some Sermons preach'd on Several Occasions."*

—— Because Iniquity shall abound, the Love of many shall wax cold. A sermon preach'd before the Right Honourable the Lord-Mayor . . . at S. Sepulchres Church, on Easter-Monday, 1706. Being one of the Anniversary Spittal-Sermons. pp. 28. *Ri. Chiswell: London,* 1706. 4°. **226.** i. **1.** (15.)

—— A Charge given at the Triennial Visitation of the Diocesse of Salisbury in October 1704. To which is added, a sermon preach'd at Salisbury, and some other places, in the said visitation. pp. 66. *For Ri. Chiswell: London,* 1704. 4°. **699.** f. **4.** (23.)

—— [Another copy, without the general titlepage.] MS. NOTES. **91.** h. **15, 15*.**

—— Charitable Reproof. A sermon preached . . . to the Societies for Reformation of Manners, the 25th of March 1700. pp. 28. *Ri. Chiswell: London,* 1700. 4°. **114.** f. **31.**

—— An Exhortation to Peace and Union. A sermon preached . . . at the election of the Lord-Mayor of London, on the 29th of September, 1681. pp. 35. *For Richard Chiswell: London,* 1681. 4°. **693.** f. **4.** (10.)

—— [Another copy.] **226.** i. **3.** (19.)

—— [Another copy.] G. **15501.** (3.)

—— [Another copy.] **226.** h. **8.** (8.)
Without the list of "Books lately printed by Richard Chiswel" on the verso of the last leaf.

—— An Exhortation to Peace and Union, in a sermon preached at St. Lawrence-Jury, on Tuesday the 26th of Novemb. 1689. pp. 30. *For Richard Chiswell: London,* 1689. 4°. **699. f. 4. (11.)**

—— [Another copy.] **226. h. 10. (14.)**

—— [Another copy.] **226. f. 13. (3.)**
Imperfect; wanting the half-title.

—— The second edition. pp. 49. *For Richard Chiswell: London,* 1690. 12°. **693. d. 7. (11.)**

—— Four Discourses delivered to the Clergy of the Diocess of Sarum, concerning I. The Truth of the Christian Religion. II. The Divinity and Death of Christ. III. The Infallibility and Authority of the Church. IV. The Obligations to continue in the Communion of the Church. pp. x. 110. *For Richard Chiswell: London,* 1694. 4°. **699. f. 4. (18.)**

—— [Another copy.] **226. h. 6. (16.)**

—— [Another edition.] pp. xl. 352. *For Richard Chiswell: London,* 1694. 8°. **1022. a. 16.**

—— *See* TRINITY. Considerations on the Explications of the Doctrine of the Trinity. Occasioned by . . . a Discourse by the Lord-Bishop of Salisbury [i.e. the second of the "Four Discourses"], *etc.* 1695. 4°. [*A Third Collection of Tracts, etc.*] no. 1. **4224. c. 1.**

—— *See* TEMPORA. Tempora Mutantur. Or, the great change from 73 to 93. In the travels of a Professor of Theology at Glasgow, *etc.* [A criticism of G. Burnet's "Four Discourses delivered to the Clergy of the Diocess of Sarum."] 1694. 4°. **8133. aaa. 11.**

—— —— 1703. 8°. **1103. f. 1.**

—— *See* TILLOTSON (John) *Archbishop of Canterbury.* The Charge of Socinianism against Dr. Tillotson, considered . . . To which is added Some Reflections upon the second of Dr. Burnet's Four Discourses, concerning the divinity and death of Christ, *etc.* 1695. 4°. **701. i. 10. (7.)**

—— Notes upon the Lord Bishop of Salisbury's Four late Discourses to the Clergy of his Diocess. Particularly upon the last, relating to the Dissenters. In a letter to a friend. [By John Chorlton.] pp. 34. *Printed in usum Sarum: London,* 1695. 4°. **4106. d. 11.**

—— [Another copy.] **699. f. 6. (16.)**
Imperfect; wanting the last leaf, which is supplied in MS.

—— Of the Propagation of the Gospel in Foreign Parts. A sermon preach'd at St. Mary-le-Bow, Feb. 18. 170¾, *etc.* pp. 29. *Joseph Downing: London,* 1704. 4°. **226. h. 13. (12.)**

—— [Another copy.] **226. h. 8. (4.)**

—— [Another copy, with a different titlepage.] *D. Brown & R. Sympson: London,* 1704. 4°. **226. h. 21. (18.)**

—— A Sermon preach'd, and a Charge given at the Triennial Visitation of the Diocese of Salisbury. pp. 68. *J. Churchill: London,* 1714. 4°. **693. f. 5. (2.)**

—— [Another copy.] **225. i. 15. (16.)**

—— [Another copy.] **698. h. 26. (7.)**
Imperfect; containing the Charge only.

—— *See* SALISBURY. More News from Salisbury: viz. I. An examination of some parts of the Bishop of Sarum's sermon and charge at his late triennial visitation, *etc.* 1714. 8°. **T. 1787. (5.)**

—— A Sermon preached at Bow-Church, before the Court of Aldermen, on March 12. 16$\frac{89}{90}$, *etc.* pp. 34. *For Richard Chiswell: London,* 1690. 4°. **226. i. 10. (25.)**

—— A Sermon preach'd at St. Brides before the Lord-Mayor and the Court of Aldermen: on Monday in Easter-Week. 1711. pp. 23. *John Churchill: London,* 1711. 8°. **4475. bb. 13.**

—— A Sermon preach'd at St. Bridget's-Church, on Monday in Easter-Week, March 29. 1714. before the Right Honourable the Lord Mayor, the Aldermen and Governours of the several hospitals of the City. pp. 32. *J. Churchill: London,* 1714. 8°. **693. d. 7. (5.)**

—— [Another copy.] **225. h. 9. (12.)**

—— [Another edition.] pp. 32. *William Brown: Edinburgh,* 1714. 12°. **4175. aa. 101. (9.)**

—— *See* SEWELL (George) The Reasons for writing against the Bishop of Salisbury. With remarks upon his Lordship's Spittal-Sermon preached on Easter Monday last. 1714. 8°. **T. 1787. (4.)**

—— *See* TORY. Some Few Obvious and Just Reflections on the Bishop of Sarum's Charity . . . Sermon: preached . . . March 29, 1714., *etc.* 1714. 8°. **8138. aa. 11.**

—— A Sermon preached at St. Dunstans in the West at the Funeral of Mrs. Anne Seile, the 18th of July 1678. pp. 29. *Printed by Mary Clark: London,* 1678. 4°. **1417. g. 54.**

—— A Sermon preach'd at St. James's Church, upon the reading the Brief for the persecuted exiles of the Principality of Orange. pp. 28. *Ri. Chiswell: London,* 1704. 4°. **693. f. 4. (18.)**

—— [Another copy.] **4452. bbb. 24. (1.)**

—— [Another copy.] **226. f. 17. (16.)**

—— A Sermon preach'd at the Cathedral Church of Salisbury on the xxvii[th] day of June MDCCVI. being the Day of Thanksgiving for the great successes God has given to the arms of Her Majesty and her allies in Flanders and Spain, &c. pp. 28. *Rich. Chiswell: London,* 1706. 4°. **693. f. 4. (20.)**

—— [Another copy.] **226. i. 1. (17.)**

—— The second edition. pp. 14. *Rich. Chiswell: London,* 1706. 8°. **225. h. 15. (1.)**

—— A Sermon preached at the Chappel of the Rolls, on the fifth of November, 1684. being Gun-powder-Treason-Day. pp. 30. *Printed for the Author; sold by R. Baldwin: London,* 1684. 4°. **694. f. 6. (6.)**

—— [Another copy.] **226. i. 2. (10.)**

—— A Sermon preached at the Coronation of William III. and Mary II. King and Queen of England, - - - - France, and Ireland . . . April 11. 1689. pp. 29. *For J. Starkey & Ric. Chiswell: London,* 1689. 4°. **693. f. 4. (13.)**

—— [Another copy.] **226. i. 7. (19.)**

—— [Another copy.] **694. g. 9. (3.)**
Imperfect; wanting the half-title.

— [Another copy.] **8122. aaa. 24.**
Imperfect; wanting the half-title.

— Sermon prononcé au Couronnement de Guillaume III. et Marie II. . . . Dans l'église de l'Abaïe de Westminster, le 11 d'avril 1689. pp. 42. *Veuve de P. Savouret: Amsterdam*, 1689. 12°. **8122. a. 56. (5.)**

— Krönungs-Predigt, so bey der Kröhnung Wilhelm des Dritten und Maria II. . . . in der Abtey-Kirchen von West Münster den 21 [*sic*] April 1689 . . . gehalten worden . . . ins Teutsches übersetzet [by E. G. Happel]. [With a folding plate.] [*T. von Wiering:*] *Hamburg*, 1689. 4°. **4473. h. 8.**

— [Another issue.] *See* Happel (E. G.) Fortuna Brittannica, *etc.* 1689. 4°. **9512. dd. 4.**

— A Sermon preached at the Funeral of Mr. James Houblon, who was buried at St. Mary Wolnoth Church in Lombard-street, June 28. 1682. pp. 38. *For Richard Chiswel: London*, 1682. 4°. **1416. i. 60.**

— [Another copy.] **1416. i. 59.**
In this copy the List of books printed for, and sold by Richard Chiswell, on sig. F 4, *contains six more entries than that in the preceding copy.*

— [Another edition.] pp. 48. *B. M. Pickering: London*, 1863. 8°. **4903. eee. 24. (2.)**

— A Sermon preached at the Funeral of the Honourable Robert Boyle; at St. Martins in the Fields, January 7. 169½. pp. 40. *For Ric. Chiswell & John Taylor: London*, 1692. 4°. **226. h. 11. (14.)**

— [Another edition.] pp. 40. *For Ric. Chiswell & John Taylor: London*, 1692. 4°. **1415. d. 56.**
Cropped.

— Exequialis dicta in funere illustris viri domini Roberti Boyle, *etc.* (In Latinum vertit Daniel Ernestus Jablonski.) *See* Bentley (Richard) *D.D., Master of Trinity College, Cambridge.* [*Two or more Works.*] Stultitia et Irrationabilitas Atheismi, *etc.* 1696. 8°. **847. h. 28.**

— Appendix relating to the Honourable Robert Boyle, Esq. [An extract from Burnet's funeral sermon.] *See* Budgell (Eustace) Memoirs of the Lives and Characters of the Illustrious Family of the Boyles, *etc.* 1737. 8°. **276. i. 15.**

— A Sermon preached at the Funeral of the Most Reverend Father in God John . . . Lord Archbishop of Canterbury . . . who died . . . the 22d. day of November . . . and was buried . . . on the 30th. of that month . . . 1694. pp. 36. *For Ri. Chiswell: London*, 1694. 4°. **1417. h. 56.**

— [Another edition.] pp. 34. *For Jacob Milner: Dublin*, 1694. 4°. **4903. c. 93.**

— [Another edition.] pp. 16. *Henry Hills: London*, 1709. 8°. **4903. c. 45.**

— [Short extracts from the funeral sermon on Tillotson.] *See* H., F., *M.A.* The Life of the Most Reverend Father in God John Tillotson, Arch-Bishop of Canterbury . . . With many curious memoirs, communicated by the late Right Reverend Gilbert, Lord Bishop of Sarum [or rather, extracted from his funeral sermon on Tillotson]. 1717. 8°. **203. b. 17.**

—— *See* Pitt (Moses) A Letter from Moses Pitt, to the authour [i.e. George Hickes] of a book, intituled, Some Discourses upon Dr Burnet . . . and Dr Tillotson . . . occasioned by the late funeral-sermon of the former upon the latter. 1695. 4°. **1417. f. 46.**

—— Some Discourses upon Dr. Burnet and Dr. Tillotson; occasioned by the late funeral sermon of the former upon the later. [By George Hickes.] pp. 88. *London*, 1695. 4°. **699. f. 7. (1.)**

—— A Sermon preached at the Funeral of the Right Honourable Anne, Lady-Dowager Brook. Who was buried at Breamor, the 19th day of February, 169⁰⁄₁. pp. 34. *For Ric. Chiswell: London*, 1691. 4°. **1416. d. 28.**

—— [Another copy.] **1416. d. 29.**

—— [Another copy.] **226. g. 21. (21.)**

—— A Sermon preached at White-Hall, on the 26th of Novemb. 1691. Being the Thanksgiving-Day for the preservation of the King, and the reduction of Ireland. pp. 35. *For Ric. Chiswell: London*, 1691. 4°. **226. f. 15. (1.)**

—— [Another edition.] pp. 24. *For Richard Chiswell: London*, 1691. 4°. **4475. cc. 21.**

—— A Sermon preach'd before His Majesty King George, at his Royal Chappel of St. James's; on Sunday, the 31st. of Octob. 1714. pp. 32. *J. Churchill: London*, 1714. 8°. **693. d. 7. (4.)**

—— [Another copy.] **225. h. 13. (15.)**

—— *See* Leslie (Charles) *M.A.* Mr. Lesley to the Lord Bishop of Sarum [in answer to his sermon on the 31st of October, 1714]. [1715.] 4°. **701. g. 21. (1.)**

—— —— [1715.] 4°. **E. 2007. (4*.)**

—— A Sermon preached before the Aldermen of the City of London, at St. Lawrence-Church, Jan. 30, 168⁰⁄₁, *etc.* pp. 30. *For Richard Chiswel: London*, 1681. 4°. **226. i. 4. (19.)**

—— The second edition. pp. 30. *For Richard Chiswel: London*, 1681. 4°. **4473. c. 1. (6.)**

—— A Sermon preached before the House of Commons, on the 31st of January, 1688. Being the Thanksgiving-Day for deliverance of this kingdom from popery, and arbitrary power, *etc.* pp. 35. *For John Starkey & Ric. Chiswell: London*, 1689. 4°. **225. h. 25. (16.)**
The half-title reads "A Thanksgiving-Sermon before the House of Commons."

—— [Another copy.] **226. i. 11. (25.)**
The half-title reads "Dr. Burnet's Thanksgiving-Sermon before the House of Commons." Imperfect; wanting pp. 29, 30. *Cropped. The last leaf is slightly mutilated.*

—— Predikatie, gedaan voor 't Lager-Huys van de Conventie, den 10. February, 1689 [31 Jan. 1688 o.s.], zynde de dankdag, voor de verlossinge van het koninkryk van 't pausdom en de arbitraire macht door middel van Zyn Hoogheyd de Prince van Orange . . . In 't Engelsch tot London gedrukt . . . en daar uyt vertaalt. pp. 19. *Weduwe van S. Swart: Amsterdam*, 1689. 4°. **8122. ee. 12. (10.)**

— Sermon prononcé devant la Chambre des Communes le trente uniéme de janvier $168\frac{8}{9}$. jour d'action de graces pour la delivrance de ce royaume de la papauté & du pouvoir absolu, par le moyen de Son Altesse Monseigneur le Prince d'Orange. Traduit de l'anglois, *etc.* pp. 35. *R. E. pour R. Chiswel: Londres,* 1689. 4°. **699. f. 4. (10.)**

— Sermon prononcé devant la Chambre des Communes d'Angleterre . . . le 31. de janvier 1688., *etc.* pp. 48. *P. Savouret: Amsterdam,* 1689. 12°. **8122. a. 56.** (3.) *Cropped. A different translation from the preceding.*

— A Sermon preached before the House of Peers . . . on the 5th. of November 1689. being Gun-powder Treason-Day, *etc.* pp. 32. *For Ric. Chiswel: London,* 1689. 4°. **226. i. 7. (20.)**

— A Sermon preached before the King & Queen, at White-Hall, on Christmas-Day, 1689. pp. 36. *For Richard Chiswell: London,* MDCLXC [1690]. 4°. **693. f. 4. (14.)**

— A Sermon preached before the King and Queen, at White-Hall, on the 19th day of October, 1690. being the Day of Thanksgiving, for His Majesties preservation and success in Ireland. pp. 36. *For Ric. Chiswell: London,* 1690. 4°. **226. i. 7. (21.)**

— [Another copy.] **699. f. 4. (16.)** *Imperfect; wanting the half-title.*

— A Sermon preach'd before the King, at St. James-Chapel, on the 10th. of February $169\frac{4}{5}$, *etc.* pp. 32. *For Ri. Chiswell: London,* 1695. 4°. **693. f. 4. (16.)** *The half-title reads "The Bishop of Sarum's Lent-Sermon before the King, $169\frac{4}{5}$."*

— [Another copy.] **226. f. 20. (11.)**

— A Sermon preached before the King, at Whitehall, on Christmas-Day, 1696. pp. 28. *For Ri. Chiswell: London,* 1697. 4°. **693. f. 4. (17.)**

— A Sermon preached before the King, at Whitehall, on the second of December, 1697. Being the Day of Thanksgiving for the Peace. pp. 31. *For Ri. Chiswell: London,* 1698. 4°. **693. f. 4. (19.)**

— [Another copy.] **226. i. 11. (22.)** *Imperfect; wanting the half-title.*

— [Another edition.] pp. 15. *Re-printed by the Heirs & Successors of Andrew Anderson: Edinburgh,* 1697. 4°. **4473. aaa. 66.**

— A Sermon preach'd before the Queen, and the two Houses of Parliament, at St. Paul's, on the 31st of December, 1706, the Day of Thanksgiving for the wonderful successes of this year. pp. 32. *A. & J. Churchill: London,* 1707. 4°. **693. f. 5. (1.)**

— [Another edition.] pp. 16. *A. & J. Churchill: London,* 1707. 8°. **4475. b. 29.**

— [Another edition.] pp. 16. *A. & J. Churchill: London,* 1707. 8°. **699. f. 4. (24.)**

— [Another copy.] **225. h. 5. (2.)**

— [Another edition.] pp. 16. *Booksellers of London & Westminster: London,* [1707.] 8°. **4475 b. 30.**

— A Sermon preached before the Queen, at White-Hall, on the 16th day of July, 1690. Being the Monthly-Fast. pp. 34. *For Ric. Chiswell: London,* 1690. 4°. **693. f. 4. (15.)**

— A Sermon preach'd before the Queen, at White-Hall, o the 11th of March, $169\frac{3}{4}$, *etc.* pp. 33. *F. Ric. Chiswell: London,* 1694. 4°. **226. f. 21. (15**

— A Sermon preached before the Right-Honourable tl Lord-Mayor and Aldermen of the City of London, at Bo Church, September 2. 1680, *etc.* pp. 32. *F. Richard Chiswel: London,* 1680. 4°. **693. f. 4. (8**

— The second edition. pp. 32. *For Richard Chiswe. London,* 1681. 4°. **693. f. 4. (9**

— The second edition. pp. 24. *For Richard Chiswel London,* 1681. 4°. **4475. cc. 2**

— A Sermon preach'd in Lent, at the Chappel of James's, on the 10th day of March, $170\frac{5}{6}$. pp. 28. *Ri. Chiswell: London,* 1706. 4°. **226. i. 1. (1**

— A Sermon preach'd in the Cathedral-Church of Sal bury, on the 29th day of May, in the year 1710. pp. 16. *J. Churchill: London,* 1710. 8°. **4475. b. 3**

— A Sermon preached in the Chappel of St. James before His Highness the Prince of Orange, the 23d December, 1688. pp. 33. *For Richard Chiswell: Londo* 1689. 4°. **699. f. 4. (1**

— [Another issue.] *London,* 1689. 4°. **226. i. 11. (2**

— [Another copy.] **226. i. 7. (1**

— [Another edition.] pp. 16. *For Richard Chiswel London,* 1689. 4°. **693. f. 4. (1**

— [Another edition.] pp. 10. *Edinburgh,* 1689. 4°. **4475. bb. 2**

— Een Predikatie, gepredikt in de Capel van St James, vo Zijn Hoogheidt den Prins van Orangie, den 23 Decemb 1688, *etc.* [Translated by Jacobus Koelman.] pp. 15. *Wed: van S. Swart: Amsterdam,* 1689. 4°. **8122. ee. 12. (**

— Sermon prononcé dans la Chappelle de S. Jaques 23. de décembre, 1688 . . . Traduit de l'anglois. pp. 4 *P. Savouret: Amsterdam,* 1689. 12°. **8122. a. 56. (**

— Des berühmten englischen Theologi Dr. Gilbert Burn . . . Danck-Predigt, welche er . . . den 23. Decem 1688. in der Cappell zu St. James in Londen gehalt Anietzo . . . ins Hochdeutsche übersetzet. pp. 24. [*Hamburg?*] 1689. 4°. **3906. g.**

— A Sermon preached on the Fast-Day, Decemb. 1680, *etc.* pp. 42. *J. D. for Richard Chiswell: Lond* 1681. 4°. **226. i. 4. (1**

— [Another copy.] **226. i. 11. (2**

— [Another copy.] **226. i. 5. (** *Imperfect; wanting the leaf before the titlepage bearing recommendation of the House of Commons.*

— Some Sermons preach'd on Several Occasions; and Essay towards a new book of Homilies, in seven sermo prepar'd at the desire of Archbishop Tillotson and so other bishops. pp. xxv. 349. *John Churchill: Lond* 1713. 8°. **695. f. 36. (**

— A Sermon [preached at St. Clement's in 1683] concern Popery, with the preface to the volume in which it is c tained [entitled: "Some Sermons preach'd on Seve Occasions," 1713]; giving an account of the Glori Revolution. pp. xxiv. 24. *R. Fleming & Co.: Edinbur* 1746. 8°. **4473. e. 10. (**

—— *See* PHILOCLERUS, *pseud.* Speculum Sarisburianum . . . With a postscript containing some reflections on the preface introductory to his Lordship's Sermons, preached on several occasions, *etc.* 1714. 8°. **702**. f. **10**. (**3**.)

—— *See* SEWELL (George) A Second Letter to the Bishop of Salisbury, upon the publication of his new volume of Sermons. Wherein his Lordship's preface . . . and the case of Lord Russel, are examin'd. Also, some passages in the Sermons, and the Essay for a New Book of Homilies remark'd on. 1713. 8°. T. **1787**. (**2**.)

—— Subjection for Conscience-sake Asserted: in a sermon preached at Covent-Garden-Church, December the sixth, 1674. pp. 39. FEW MS. NOTES. *For R. Royston: London*, 1675. 4°. **699**. f. **4**. (**3**.)

—— Two Sermons, preached in the Cathedral Church of Salisbury: the first, on the fifth of November, Gun-powder-Treason Day; the second, on the seventh of November, being the Thanksgiving-Day: in the year 1710. pp. 32. MS. NOTES. *John Churchill: London*, 1710. 8°. **699**. f. **4**. (**25**.)

—— [Another copy.] T. **1747**. (**1**.)

—— [Another copy.] **225**. f. **8**. (**1**.)

—— [Another copy.] **694**. f. **7**. (**5**.)

—— The second edition. pp. 32. *John Churchill: London*, 1710. 8°. **4475**. a. **34**.

—— *See* BRETT (Thomas) *LL.D.* A Letter to the Author of Lay-Baptism Invalid [i.e. Roger Laurence]: wherein the Popish doctrine of lay-baptism, taught in a sermon, said to have been preach'd by the B— of S— [i.e. G. Burnet, Bishop of Salisbury], the 7th of November, 1710, is censur'd and condemn'd, *etc.* 1711. 8°. **4326**. c. **7**.

—— *See* LAURENCE (Roger) An Essay on Confession, Penance, and Absolution . . . occasioned by the publication of Two Sermons preached at Salisbury the 5th and 7th of November, 1710 [by G. Burnet]. 1852. 8°. **4071**. a. **38**.

—— *See* POWERS. Sacerdotal Powers . . . In an essay. Occasion'd by the publication of Two Sermons preach'd at Salisbury the 5th and 7th of November. 1710. By the author of Lay Baptism Invalid [i.e. Roger Laurence]. 1711. 8°. **4372**. df. **18**. (**1**.)

—— —— 1713. 8°. **4324**. i. **34**. (**2**.)

—— Remarks on Two Late Sermons, preach'd in the Cathedral-Church of Salisbury [by G. Burnet]: in a letter to a friend. To which is added a postscript, wherein the charge of uncharitableness against the Church for condemning lay-baptism as invalid, is more particularly consider'd and confuted. pp. 24. *J. Morphew: London*, 1711. 4°. **698**. i. **4**. (**15**.)

DISCOURSE OF THE PASTORAL CARE.

—— A Discourse of the Pastoral Care. pp. xxxiii [xvii]. 3–125. *For Richard Chiswell: London*, 1692. 4°. **698**. h. **22**. (**6**.)

—— [Another edition.] pp. xxxiv. 252. *R. R. for Ric. Chiswell: London*, 1692. 8°. **857**. b. **20**.

—— The third edition, with a new preface suited to the present time; and some other additions. pp. xxii. 244. *Dan. Midwinter, & Benj. Cowse: London*, 1713. 8°. **698**. c. **15**. (**4**.)

—— The fourth edition. pp. xxii. 244. *Dan. Midwinter, & Benj. Cowse: London*, 1713. 8°. **857**. b. **21**.

—— The fourth edition, with additions. pp. xxi. 226. *J. Hyde & R. Gunne: Dublin*, 1726. 12°. **4498**. aa. **7**. *Without the "new preface" first published in* 1713.

—— The fourth edition. With a new preface to the third edition, in 1713. Wrote by the author. pp. xliv. 244. *J. Walthoe, sen., etc.: London*, 1736. 8°. **857**. b. **22**.

—— [Another edition.] pp. xli. 208. *R. & A. Foulis: Glasgow*, 1762. 16°. **1120**. a. **4**.

—— The fifth edition, *etc.* pp. xliv. 244. *C. Bathurst, J. Rivington, etc.: London*, 1766. 8°. **4498**. a. **20**.

—— [Another edition.] A Discourse of the Pastoral Care. By the Right Reverend Father in God, Gilbert, Lord Bishop of Sarum; with his Advice to the Clergy. Published in the conclusion of the History of his own Time. To which is prefixed, his Character, by the Marquis of Halifax. pp. 202. *William Halhead: Dublin*, 1777. 12°. **4498**. a. **21**.

—— Twelfth edition. Including the new preface first published in the third edition. pp. 219. *W. Baynes: London*, 1805. 12°. **4499**. aaa. **40**.

—— [Another edition.] *See* CLERGYMAN. The Clergyman's Instructor, *etc.* 1807. 8°. **858**. d. **23**.

—— Thirteenth edition, *etc.* pp. 217. *W. Baynes: London*, 1818. 12°. **4498**. e. **10**.

—— [Another copy.] **4516**. aa. **21**.

—— Fourteenth edition, carefully corrected; to which is prefixed a life of the author. [With a portrait.] pp. viii. 252. *Rivingtons & Cochran: London*, 1821. 12°. **4498**. e. **11**.

—— [Another edition.] *See* CLERGYMAN. The Clergyman's Instructor, *etc.* 1824. 8°. **858**. d. **24**.

—— Out of Bishop Burnet's Pastoral Care. [A short extract on elocution.] *See* RULES. Some Rules for Speaking and Action, *etc.* 1732. 8°. **11805**. c. **13**.

—— The New Preface and Additional Chapter to the Third Edition of the Pastoral Care . . . Publish'd singly, for the use of those who have the former editions. pp. 40. *D. Midwinter, & B. Cowse: London*, 1713. 8°. **699**. f. **4**. (**27**.)

—— [Another copy.] **4109**. aa. **22**. (**2**.)

—— *See* ASG . . L, *Mr.* Mr. Asg . . l's Congratulatory Letter to the L . . d B . . . . p of S . . . m, upon the excellent modern preface just publish'd by his L . . . . . . p, *etc.* [A criticism of G. Burnet's preface to the third edition of his "Discourse of the Pastoral Care."] 1713. 8°. T. **1829**. (**6**.)

—— *See* SEWELL (George) Mr. Sewell's First Letter to the Bishop of Salisbury . . . Being a full answer to his Lordship's New Preface to his Pastoral Care, *etc.* [1713.] 8°. T. **1787**. (**1**.)

—— The Bishop of Salisbury's New Preface to his Pastoral Care, consider'd, with respect to the following heads, viz. I: The Qualifications of the Clergy. II. The Distinction of High and Low Churoh [*sic*]. III. The Present Posture of Affairs. pp. 43. *A. Baldwin: London,* 1713. 8°. **4106**. b. **27**.

—— The second edition. pp. 43. *A. Baldwin: London,* 1713. 8°. **702**. f. **10**. (**1**.)

—— The Bishop of Salisbury's New Preface to his Pastoral Care, consider'd . . . The second edition. [Erroneously described. Consisting in fact of G. Burnet's preface to his translation of the "De mortibus persecutorum" of Lactantius.] pp. 24. *J. Bradford: London,* [1713?] 8°. **4106**. b. **28**.

—— The Bishop of Salisbury's New Preface to his Pastoral Care, consider'd . . . The third edition corrected. pp. 43. *A. Baldwin: London,* 1713. 8°. **698**. c. **15**. (**3**.)

—— The Clergy and the Present Ministry Defended. Being a letter to the Bishop of Salisbury, occasion'd by his Lordship's New Preface to his Pastoral Care. [By George Sewell.] pp. 30. *J. Morphew: London,* 1713. 8°. **699**. f. **4**. (**28**.)

—— The Oxford-Scholar's Answer to the Bishop of Sarum's New Preface, in the third edition of his Pastoral Care. pp. 16. *G. G.: Dublin,* 1713. 8°. **4103**. aa. **54**.

EXPOSITION OF THE THIRTY-NINE ARTICLES.

—— An Exposition of the Thirty-nine Articles of the Church of England. [With the text.] pp. xxiv. 396. 1699. fol. *See* ENGLAND.—*Church of England.* [*Articles of Religion.—Editions with commentaries.—Burnet* 1699.] **695**. k. **12**.

—— [Another copy.] **10**. c. **10**.

—— The second edition corrected. pp. xxiv. 396. 1700. fol. *See* ENGLAND.—*Church of England.* [*Articles of Religion.—Editions with commentaries.—Burnet* 1699.] **3505**. g. **24**.

—— The third edition corrected. pp. xxiv. 396. 1705. fol. *See* ENGLAND.—*Church of England.* [*Articles of Religion.—Editions with commentaries.—Burnet* 1699.] **3557**. h. **6**.

—— The fourth edition corrected. pp. xxiv. 368. 1720. fol. *See* ENGLAND.—*Church of England.* [*Articles of Religion.—Editions with commentaries.—Burnet* 1699.] **3505**. g. **15**.

—— The fourth edition corrected. pp. xxiv. 396. 1737. fol. *See* ENGLAND.—*Church of England.* [*Articles of Religion.—Editions with commentaries.—Burnet* 1699.] **676**. g. **12**.

—— The sixth edition, corrected. pp. xlviii. 501. 1759. 8°. *See* ENGLAND.—*Church of England.* [*Articles of Religion.—Editions with commentaries.—Burnet* 1699.] **3506**. f. **20**.

—— [Another edition.] pp. xlvi. 505. 1796. 8°. *See* ENGLAND.—*Church of England.* [*Articles of Religion.—Editions with commentaries.—Burnet* 1699.] **692**. d. **13**.

—— [Another edition.] pp. xlviii. 542. 1805. 8°. *See* ENGLAND.—*Church of England.* [*Articles of Religion.—Editions with commentaries.—Burnet* 1699.] **3506**. d. **16**.

—— [Another edition.] Revised and corrected, with copio notes, and additional references, by the Rev. James Page. pp. 7*. xxxvii. 585. 1837. 8°. *See* ENGLAND. *Church of England.* [*Articles of Religion.—Editions w commentaries.—Burnet* 1699.] **2009**.

—— A Brief Exposition of the Thirty-nine Articles. Chie from Bishop Burnet. *See* SMITH (John Bainbridg A Manual of the Rudiments of Theology, *etc.* 1830. 1 **1115**. b. **1**

—— [Another edition.] *See* SMITH (John Bainbridge) Manual of the Rudiments of Theology, *etc.* 1846. 12°. **3559**. aaa. **1**

—— An Exposition of the Thirty-Nine Articles of the Chur of England . . . A new edition. pp. xl. 503. 1850. 8 *See* ENGLAND.—*Church of England.* [*Articles of Religion.- Editions with commentaries.—Burnet,* 1699.] **3408**. f. **4**

Appendix.

—— *See* BAPTISM. Lay-Baptism Invalid . . . With an a pendix wherein the boasted unanswerable objection of t B. of S. [i.e. G. Burnet, in his "Exposition of the Thirt nine Articles"] & other objections are answer'd . . . By Lay-Hand [i.e. Roger Laurence]. 1712, *etc.* 8°. **844**. m. **10**. (**1**,

—— *See* EDWARDS (John) *D.D.* A Free Discourse concer ing Truth and Error . . . Together with reflections several authors; but more particularly on the Lord Bish of Sarum's Exposition of the Thirty Nine Articles, *etc.* 1701. 8°. **1113**. i. **1**

—— *See* ENGLAND.—*Church of England.* [*Articles of I ligion.—Editions with commentaries.—Burnet* 1699.] Analysis of Bishop Burnet's Exposition of the Thirt nine Articles, with notes. By T. Newland. 1829. 12°. **692**. b.

—— *See* ENGLAND.—*Church of England.* [*Articles of I ligion.—Editions with commentaries.—Burnet* 1699.] Analytical Epitome of Bishop Burnet's Exposition of t Thirty-nine Articles, with notes . . . By R. Hobart. 1832. 12°. **1119**. a.

—— *See* ENGLAND.—*Church of England.* [*Articles of I ligion.—Editions with commentaries.—Burnet* 1699.] Defence of the Right Reverend the Lord Bishop of Saru In answer to a book [by W. Binckes], entituled, A Pre tory Discourse, *etc.* [By J. Hoadly.] 1703. 4°. **699**. f. **7**. (

—— *See* ENGLAND.—*Church of England.* [*Articles of I ligion.—Editions with commentaries.—Burnet* 1699.] F amination Questions and Answers, selected from Bur on the Thirty-nine Articles, *etc.* 1838. 8°. **693**. b.

—— —— 1847. 8°. **3504**. cc. **1**

—— *See* ENGLAND.—*Church of England.* [*Articles of I ligion.—Editions with commentaries.—Burnet* 1699.] T Exposition given by My Lord Bishop of Sarum, of t Second Article of our Religion, examined. [By Jonath Edwards.] 1702. 4°. **4224**. e.

—— *See* ENGLAND.—*Church of England.* [*Articles of Re gion.—Editions with commentaries.—Burnet* 1699.] M Lord Bishop of Sarum's Exposition of the Twenty Thi Article of the Church of England, defended and clear from the exceptions of a late book, entituled, The Vindic tion of the Twenty Third Article . . . from my Lo Bishop of Sarum's Exposition. 1703. 4°. **4106**. c.

BURNET (GILBERT) *Bishop of Salisbury.* [EXPOSITION OF THE THIRTY-NINE ARTICLES.]

—— *See* ENGLAND.—*Church of England.* [*Articles of Religion.—Editions with commentaries.—Burnet* 1699.] A Prefatory Discourse to an Examination of a late Book, entituled An Exposition of the Thirty Nine Articles . . . by Gilbert, Bishop of Sarum . . . By a Presbyter of the Church of England [i.e. W. Binckes]. 1702. 4°.
699. f. **7.** (**2.**)

—— *See* ENGLAND.—*Church of England.* [*Articles of Religion.—Editions with commentaries.—Burnet* 1699.] A Vindication of the Twenty Third Article of the Church of England, from a late exposition, ascribed to my Lord Bishop of Sarum. [By W. Thornton?] 1702. 4°.
3504. f. 4.

—— *See* KIMBERLEY (Jonathan) A Letter to the Reverend Mr. Jonathan Kimberly . . . concerning his late sermon before the Lower House of Convocation. And his reflections therein on the Lord Bishop of Sarum [i.e. on G. Burnet's exposition of the first of the Thirty-nine Articles]. 1702. 4°. **225.** i. **11.** (**14***.)

—— *See* LAURENCE (Roger) Lay-Baptism Invalid . . . With an appendix, wherein the boasted unanswerable objections of Dr. Burnet [in his "Exposition of the Thirty-nine Articles"] and other new objections are answer'd, *etc.* 1723. 8°. **4324.** i. 4.

—— *See* WARD (Thomas) *Roman Catholic Soldier.* The Controversy of Ordination truly stated . . . Especially, the attempt of Dr. Burnet . . . to clear that point [in his "Exposition of the Thirty-nine Articles"], is impartially consider'd, *etc.* 1719. 8°. **3935.** b. 4.

HISTORY OF MY OWN TIME.

—— Bishop Burnet's History of His Own Time. [vol. 1 edited by Gilbert Burnet, second son of the Bishop, and others; vol. 2 edited, with a life of the author, by Sir Thomas Burnet.] 2 vol. **L.P** *Thomas Ward: London,* 1724, 34. fol. **629.p.2.**
Vol. 2 bears the imprint "Printed for the editor, by Joseph Downing and Henry Woodfall."

—— [Another copy.] **672.** l. **9, 10.**
With many portraits inserted.

—— [Another copy.] **L.P.** MS. NOTES. **201.** i. **2, 3.**

—— [Another copy.] **L.P.** G. **7258, 59.**

—— [Another edition.] [With a portrait.] 2 vol. *J. Hyde: Dublin,* 1724, 34. fol. **806.** i. **8, 9.**

—— [Another edition.] [With portraits and maps.] 6 vol. *Printed for the Company of Booksellers: London,* 1725, 34. 8°. **9525.** cc. **10.**

—— [Another edition.] (A Chronological . . . Account of the Works of the Right Reverend . . . Dr. Gilbert Burnet . . . interspersed with some critical . . . observations. By R. F. [i.e. Roger Flexman, the editor of the whole.]) 4 vol. *A. Millar: London,* 1753. 8°. **599.** g. **16–19.**

—— [Another copy.] G. **4899–4902.**

—— [Another edition.] Carefully corrected and revised by the folio copy. 6 vol. *Hamilton, Balfour, & Neile: Edinburgh,* 1753. 12°. **9525.** a. **17.**

—— The third edition. 4 vol. *T. Davies: London,* 1766. 8°. **599.** g. **20–23.**
Slips bearing MS. *additions to Flexman's bibliography of Burnet are inserted in vol.* 4.

—— [Another edition.] 4 vol. **L.P.** *R. H. Evans, etc.: London,* 1809. 8°. **194.** b. **16–19.**

BURNET (GILBERT) *Bishop of Salisbury.* [HISTORY OF MY OWN TIME.]

—— [Another edition.] 4 vol. *Samuel Bagster: London,* 1815. 8°. **1326.** f. **5–8.**

—— [Another edition.] Bishop Burnet's History of his own Time: With the suppressed passages of the first volume, and notes, by the Earls of Dartmouth and Hardwicke, and Speaker Onslow, hitherto unpublished. To which are added the cursory remarks of Swift and other observations. [The editor's preface signed: M. J R., i.e. Martin Joseph Routh.] 6 vol. *Clarendon Press: Oxford,* 1823. 8°.
2084.a.

—— The Additional Annotations in the second edition of Bishop Burnet's History [i.e. the Oxford edition of 1833] . . . accommodated to the pages of the first edition. pp. 180. [*University Press: Oxford,* 1833.] 8°. **2084.a.**

—— [Another copy.] G. **4920–26.**

—— Second edition, enlarged. 6 vol. *University Press: Oxford,* 1833. 8°. **9512.** dd. **1.**

—— A new edition, with historical and biographical notes. pp. xx. xvi. 949. *William Smith: London,* 1838. 4°.
601. b. 2.

—— A new edition based on that of M. J. Routh . . . Part 1. The reign of Charles the Second edited by Osmund Airy. In two volumes. (A Supplement to Burnet's History of my own Time, derived from his original memoirs, his autobiography, his letters to Admiral Herbert and his private meditations; all hitherto unpublished. Edited by H. C. Foxcroft.) 3 vol. *Clarendon Press: Oxford,* 1897–1902.
2084.a.
No more published.

—— [Another copy.] **09504.** g. **19.**

—— Geschiedenis van Engeland, vervattende eerstelyk, een kort verhaal van de voornaamste gevallen sedert 't jaar 1600. tot 't jaar 1660. Ten tweeden: de gedenkwaardigste zaaken zo in kerk als in staat, seedert 't jaar 1660 tot 't jaar 1689, *etc.* 4 dl. *'s Gravenhage,* 1725. 12°.
9525. a. **16.**

—— Histoire de ce qui s'est passé de plus mémorable en Angleterre pendant la vie de Gilbert Burnet, *etc.* [tom. 1 translated by François de la Pillonnière.] 2 tom. *La Haye,* 1735. 4°. **9525.** ff. **1.**

—— Histoire de mon temps, par Burnet, évêque de Salisbury. [A translation of vol. 1. only.] 4 tom. *Paris, Rouen,* 1824. 8°. [*Collection des mémoires relatifs à la Révolution d'Angleterre.*] **12213.** h. **1/10.**

—— [A reissue.] Histoire de mon temps, *etc. Paris,* 1827. 8°. [*Collection des mémoires relatifs à la Révolution d'Angleterre.* tom 17–20.] **599.** d. **9–11.**

Abridgments and Extracts.

—— An Abridgment of Bishop Burnet's History of his own Times. By the Reverend Mr. Thomas Stackhouse. [An abridgment of vol. 1.] pp. xvi. 440. *J. Smith, etc.: London,* 1724. 8°. **9512.** b. **1.**

—— Bishop Burnet's Proofs of the Pretender's Illegitimacy; extracted from the History of his Own Times, and compared with the account given by other writers of the same fact, viz. Mr. Archdeacon Echard, F. Orleans, Mr. Salmon, and Bevil Higgons, Esq. By George Wilson. pp. viii. 56. *M. Smithson: London,* 1724. 8°. **702.** f. **10.** (**10.**)

—— [Another copy.] **111.** c. **57.**

—— An Impartial Examination of Bishop Burnet's History of his own Times. Containing an abridgment of that history, and suitable remarks on every material paragraph . . . By Mr. Salmon. 2 vol. pp. xii. 291–1068. *Charles Rivington; John Clarke: London,* 1724. 8°. **599.** e. **24, 25.**

The pagination and signatures continue those of T. Salmon's " A Review of the History of England," vol. 2.

—— The Conclusion of Bishop Burnett's History of his own Life and Times. pp. 46. *London,* 1734. 8°. **702.** f. **10.** (**11.**)

—— [Another issue.] pp. 48. *London,* 1734. 8°. T. **1618.** (**6.**)

—— [Another edition.] pp. vii. 98. *A. Millar: London,* 1751. 12°. **599.** a. **25.**

—— The second edition. To which are added, his . . . letter to King Charles II. and the . . . letter of the Earl of Rochester to Doctor J. Peirce. pp. vii. 110. *G. Keith: London,* 1760. 12°. **598.** a. **3.**

—— Bishop Burnet's Exhortation to all Mankind to become truly religious, who order'd it not to be published till after his decease, *etc.* [An extract from the conclusion of the " History of My Own Time."] pp. 8. *See* Goldney (Edward) Infallible Remedies, for the Perfect Cure of All Personal, and National Unhappiness, *etc.* [1770.] 8°. **4376.** bb. **32.**(7)

—— To the generous English Nobility . . . and the public in general this excellent treatise, intitled, Advice to Princes upon the Throne of England, by the learned Bishop Burnet, with its translation into French, is most humbly inscribed by . . . M. Hop of Chelsea. [An extract from the conclusion of Burnet's " History of My Own Time."] pp. 12. *W. Richardson: London,* 1781. 4°. **8006.** e. **2.**

—— Extracts from the Conclusion of Bishop Burnett's History of his own Times. pp. 19. *J. Brettell: London,* 1813. 12°. **4498.** a. **22.**

—— Bishop Burnet's History of the Reign of King James the Second. [Extracted from the " History of My Own Time."] Notes by the Earl of Dartmouth, Speaker Onslow, and Dean Swift. Additional observations now enlarged. [Edited by Martin Joseph Routh.] pp. iv. 509. *University Press: Oxford,* 1852. 8°. **10805.** d. **5.**

—— An Exhortation to the Practice of Religion. Written by Gilbert Burnet, Bishop of Sarum. [An extract from the conclusion of " The History of My Own Time."] To which is subjoined an appendix. pp. 12. *Tract Association of the Society of Friends: London,* 1856. 12°. [*General Series.* no. 35.] **4151.** b. **2.** (**6.**)

—— The History of his own Times. By the Right Rev. G. Burnet . . . Abridged by the author for the use of students. [Incorporating the abridgment of vol. 1 by Thomas Stackhouse.] New edition. pp. xviii. 414. *Virtue, Spalding & Daldy: London,* [1874.] 8°. **9525.** aa. **18.**

—— [Another edition.] pp. viii. 409. *J. M. Dent & Co.: London; E. P. Dutton & Co.: New York,* [1906.] 8°. [*Everyman's Library.*] **12206.p.1/96.**

BURNET (Gilbert) *Bishop of Salisbury.* [History of My Own Time.]

Appendix.

—— *See* Anne, *Queen of Great Britain and Ireland.* [*Biography.*] The Life and Reign of . . . Queen Anne . . . To which is annexed some political remarks on Bishop Burnet's history of the reign of Queen Anne. 1738. 8°. **9525.** b. **7.**

—— *See* Arscott (Alexander) Some Considerations relating to the Present State of the Christian Religion, *etc.* (pt. 3. With an appendix containing some remarks on a passage in the second volume of Bishop Burnet's History of his own Times.) 1732, *etc.* 8°. **873.** k. **33.**

—— *See* Braddon (Lawrence) Bishop Burnet's late History charg'd with great partiality and misrepresentations, to make the present, and future ages believe, that Arthur Earl of Essex, in 1683, murdered himself, *etc.* 1725. 8°. **9512.** b. **17.**

—— *See* Brand (*Sir* Alexander) A Second Specimen of the Candour and Integrity of Dr. Burnet, late Bishop of Salisbury. [A criticism of passages in his " History of My Own Time."] [1715.] 8°. **699.** f. **8.** (**7.**)

—— *See* Burnet (*Sir* Thomas) *One of the Justices of the Court of Common Pleas.* A Letter to Thomas Burnet, Esq; shewing that he hath used the same fidelity in printing a letter of Dr. Beach's in the Life of Bishop Burnet, as the editors of Bishop Burnet's History of his own Times have exemplified in the publication thereof; with a specimen of some of the castrations in that History, *etc.* 1736. 8°. **116.** h. **62.**

—— *See* Cockburn (John) *D.D.* A Specimen of some Free and Impartial Remarks on Publick Affairs and Particular Persons, especially relating to Scotland; occasion'd by Dr. Burnet's History of his own Times. [1724.] 8°. **699.** f. **8.** (**4.**)

—— *See* Cockburn (John) *D.D.* A Vindication of the late Bishop Burnet from the calumnies and aspersions of a libel, entitled, A Specimen of some Free and Impartial Remarks, &c. occasioned by Dr. Burnet's History of his own Times, by J. Cockburn. 1724. 8°. **702.** f. **10.** (**9.**)

—— *See* Elliot (Robert) *M.A.* A Specimen of the Bishop of Sarum's posthumous History of the Affairs of Church and State of Great-Britain, during his life. 1715. 8°. **9525.** aa. **20.**

—— —— [1715?] 8°. **699.** f. **8.** (**5.**)

—— —— [1715?] 8°. **699.** f. **8.** (**6.**)

—— *See* England. [*Appendix.—History and Politics.*—I.] The Critical History of England . . . To which are added remarks on some objections made to Bishop Burnet's History of his own Times. [By John Oldmixon.] 1724, *etc.* 8°. **195.** a. **9, 10.**

—— —— 1726. 8°. **598.** e. **11.**

—— —— 1728, *etc.* 8°. **598.** e. **13, 14.**

—— *See* Gentleman. A Review of Bishop Burnet's History of his own Times . . . shewing the partiality, inconsistency, and defects of that political history. 1724. 8°. **702.** f. **10.** (**7.**)

—— *See* Granville (George) *Baron Lansdowne.* Remarks upon the Right Honourable the Lord Lansdowne's Letter to the author of the Reflections historical and political, &c. [i.e. John Oldmixon] as far as relates to Bishop Burnet [i.e. to his " History of My Own Time "]. [By Sir Thomas Burnet.] 1732. 4°. **598.** h. **21.** (**3.**)

BURNET (Gilbert) *Bishop of Salisbury.* [History of My Own Time.]

—— *See* Higgons (Bevill) Historical and Critical Remarks on Bp. Burnet's History of his own Time. 1725. 8°. **599**. e. **26**.

—— —— 1727. 8°. **294**. h. **14**.

—— *See* Woodburn (Samuel) Woodburn's Gallery of Rare Portraits . . . illustrative of Granger's Biographical History of England . . . Burnet's History of his own Time, *etc.* 1816. fol. Dept. of Prints & Drawings.

—— Remarks on Bp. Burnet's History of his own Time. Containing, a detection of the partiality, absurdity, and falsity of it, in many particulars. With a vindication of the family of the Stuart's . . . By a True Briton [i.e. Hugh Tootell ?]. pp. 65. *A. Moore: London,* [1723.] 8°. **116**. i. **16**.

HISTORY OF THE REFORMATION OF THE CHURCH OF ENGLAND.

—— The History of the Reformation of the Church of England. (A Collection of Records and Original Papers . . . referred to in the . . . History.) 3 pt. *T. H. for Richard Chiswell: London,* 1679–1715. fol. **489**. k. **11–13**.
Pt. 3 bears the imprint "Printed for J. Churchill."

—— [Another copy.] G. **11936–38**.
Pt. 1 and 2 have additional titlepages, engraved, and engraved plates. In this copy the verso of the last leaf of pt. 1 bears an advertisement of the early publication of pt. 2.

—— [Another copy.] **F.P.** **205**. f. **5**.
Pt. 1 and 2 have additional titlepages, engraved, and engraved plates.

—— The second edition, corrected. 3 pt. *T. H. for Richard Chiswell: London,* 1681–1715. fol. **489**. k. **14–16**.
Pt. 3 is of the first edition.

—— [Another copy.] **673**. i. **1–3**.
Pt. 3 is of the first edition. With a portrait of Bishop Burnet pasted on the flyleaf of pt. 1.

—— The fourth edition, with additions, alterations, and amendments; communicated to the author by several hands. [With portraits.] 3 pt. *J. Walthoe & B. Tooke, etc.: London,* 1715. fol. **490**. k. **6–8**.
Pt. 3 is of the first edition.

—— [Another edition.] 3 pt. *R. Gunne; J. Smith & W. Bruce: Dublin,* 1730–33. fol. **4824**. k. **2**.

—— [Another edition of pt. 3.] pp. xxii. 770. x. *A. Millar: London,* 1753. fol. **4705**. h. **6**.

—— A new edition. 3 vol. *Clarendon Press: Oxford,* 1816. 8°. **1368**. k. **3**.

—— [Another copy.] **F.P.** **491**. h. **10–15**.

—— A new edition, embellished with twenty-two portraits, *etc.* 3 vol. *Richard Priestley: London,* 1820. 8°. **4705**. cc. **7**.

—— [Another edition.] [With a preface by E. Nares and a general index.] 3 vol. 7 pt. *University Press: Oxford,* 1829. 8°. **488**. d. **4–10**.

—— [Another copy.] **4705**. cc. **8**.
Without the preface by E. Nares.

—— [Another edition.] [With a portrait.] 2 vol. pp. xxii. vi. 864. dviii. *William Smith: London,* 1841. 8°. **20030**. d. **3**.

BURNET (Gilbert) *Bishop of Salisbury.* [History of the Reformation of the Church of England.]

—— A new edition carefully revised, and the records collated with the originals, by Nicholas Pocock. 7 vol. *Clarendon Press: Oxford,* 1865. 8°. **2011**. d.

—— Histoire de la réformation de l'église d'Angleterre, traduite . . . par M. de Rosemond . . . Nouvelle édition, corrigée & augmentée, avec les portraits de diverses personnes illustres. 4 tom. *S. de Tournes: Genève,* 1693. 12°. **4705**. aa. **22**.
Tom. 1. has an additional titlepage, engraved.

Introduction to the Third Volume.

—— An Introduction to the Third Volume of the History of the Reformation of the Church of England . . . The second edition. pp. 72. *John Churchill: London,* 1714. 8°. **702**. f. **10**. (**2**.)

—— *See* Misosarum (G.) *pseud.* A Preface to the B - - - - p of S - - r - - m's Introduction to the Third volume of the History of the Reformation of the Church of England. 1713. 8°. **4106**. a. **48**.

—— —— 1714. 8°. **488**. a. **27**.

—— *See* Philoclerus, *pseud.* Speculum Sarisburianum, in remarks on some passages in a pamphlet, entituled, An Introduction to the Third Volume of the History of the Reformation of the Church of England. By . . . Gilbert, Lord Bishop of Sarum . . . With a postscript containing some reflections on the preface introductory to his Lordship's Sermons, preach'd on several occasions, &c. lately published. 1714. 8°. **702**. f. **10**. (**3**.)

—— *See* S., G. An Introduction to the Life and Writings of G—t Lord Bishop of S—m. Being a third letter to his Lordship, occasioned by his Introduction to the Third Volume of the History of the Reformation, *etc.* [Signed: G. S., i.e. George Sewell.] 1714. 8°. T. **1787**. (**3**.)

Abridgments and Extracts.

—— The Abridgment of the History of the Reformation of the Church of England. 2 pt. *J. D. for Richard Chiswell: London,* 1682. 8°. **487**. b. **29**.
Imperfect; wanting the engraved portraits.

—— [A reissue.] *For R. C. [Richard Chiswell]: London,* 1682. 8°. **4650**. de. **1**.

—— [Another copy.] **295**. k. **10**.
Imperfect; wanting pp. 375–378 and the last leaf of pt. 2.

—— The second edition. 2 pt. *J. D. for Richard Chiswell: London,* 1683. 8°. **488**. b. **1**.

—— The fifth edition, with amendments from the last edition of the History published by the author. (An abridgment of the third volume . . . By Gilbert Burnet, M.A.) 3 vol. *J. Walthoe & B. Tooke, etc.: London,* 1718, 19. 12°. **4707**. a. **27**.
Vol. 3 is of the first edition.

—— The sixth edition, with amendments, *etc.* 3 vol. *J. Walthoe, etc.: London,* 1728. 12°. **4705**. a. **3**.
Vol. 3 is of the second edition.

—— The History of the Reformation of the Church of England. Taken from the writings of the Right Reverend Father in God, Gilbert, Lord Bishop of Sarum, and others. pp. 560. *J. Read: London,* 1737. fol. **489**. l. **20**.

BURNET (Gilbert) *Bishop of Salisbury.* [History of the Reformation of the Church of England.]

—— An Abridgment of Bishop Burnet's History of the Reformation of the Church of England . . . A new edition. pp. xxxi. 578. *Clarendon Press: Oxford,* 1808. 8°. **488. d. 11.**
Previous edition 1728.

—— The History of the Reformation of the Church of England, chiefly as abridged from the larger History, by Bishop Burnet and his son. Edited . . . by George Elwes Corrie. pp. xxvi. 524. *J. W. Parker: London,* 1847. 8°. **1367. e. 11.**

—— The History of the Reformation of the Church of England . . . New edition, with illustrations [of the abridgment of vol. 1 and 2 only]. pp. xix. 391. *Virtue & Co.: London,* 1872. 8°. **4705. aaa. 31.**
Previous edition 1808.

Appendix.

—— *See* C., W. A Letter written to Dr. Burnet, giving an account of Cardinal Pool's secret powers, *etc.* [Confirming statements in G. Burnet's "History of the Reformation."] 1685. 4°. **699. f. 1. (18.)**

—— *See* Collier (Jeremy) *the Nonjuror.* An Answer to some Exceptions in Bishop Burnet's third part of the History of the Reformation, &c. against Mr. Collier's Ecclesiastical History, *etc.* 1715. fol. **206. h. 10. (2.)**

—— *See* Collier (Jeremy) *the Nonjuror.* A Specimen of the Gross Errors in the second volume of Mr. Collier's Ecclesiastical History: being a vindication of . . . Dr. Gilbert Burnet . . . from the several reflections made on him and his History of the Reformation, *etc.* 1724. 8°. **702. f. 10. (8.)**

—— *See* Harmer (Anthony) *pseud.* A Specimen of some Defects and Errors in the History of the Reformation . . . wrote by G. Burnet, *etc.* 1693. 8°. **852. g. 18.**

—— *See* Le Grand (Joachim) Histoire du divorce de Henry viii . . . et de Catherine d'Arragon: avec . . . la Refutation des deux premiers livres de l'Histoire de la Reformation de M. Burnet, *etc.* 1688. 12°. **599. a. 12, 13.**

—— *See* Le Grand (Joachim) The History of the Divorce of Henry viii. and Katharine of Arragon . . . The refutation of the two first books of the History of the Reformation of Dr. Burnett, *etc.* [A review of Le Grand's works.] [1688.] 4°. **3938. cc. 29.**

—— *See* Le Grand (Joachim) Lettres de Mr Le Grand à Mr Burnet, touchant l'Histoire des variations [of Bossuet], l'Histoire de la Reformation [of Burnet], *etc.* 1691. 12°. **1123. b. 13.**

—— *See* Manby (Peter) *Dean of Derry.* A Reformed Catechism, in two dialogues concerning the English Reformation. Collected for the most part, word for word, out of Dr. Burnet [i.e. from his "History of the Reformation"], John Fox, and other Protestant historians, *etc.* 1687. 4°. **T. 1846. (7.)**

TRAVELS.

—— Some Letter[s] containing an account of what seemed most remarkable in Switzerland, Italy, &c. Written by G. Burnet . . . to T. H. R. B. pp. 307. *Abraham Acher: Rotterdam,* 1686. 8°. **10108. aa. 42.**
The titlepage is slightly mutilated.

BURNET (Gilbert) *Bishop of Salisbury.* [Travels.]

—— Some Letters. Containing an account of what seemed most remarkable in Switzerland, Italy, &c. Written by G. Burnet, D.D. to T. H. R. B. [i.e. the Honourable Robert Boyle.] To which is annexed his Answer to Mr. Varillas. 2 pt. *Amsterdam,* 1686 [1687]. 12°. **1050. d. 5. (1, 2.)**

—— [Another edition.] pp. 310 [300]. *Printed by Abraham Acher: Rotterdam,* 1686 [1687]. 12°. **10105. aa. 25.**
Without the "Answer to Mr. Varillas."

—— [Another edition.] Dr. Burnet's Travels, or, Letters containing an account of what seemed most remarkable in Switzerland, Italy, France, and Germany, *etc.* 3 pt. *For Peter Savouret & W. Fenner: Amsterdam,* 1687. 12°. **10107. a. 21.**

—— [Another edition.] Some Letters, containing an account of what seemed most remarkable in travelling through Switzerland, Italy, some parts of Germany, &c. in the years 1685. and 1686. . . . The second edition, corrected, and altered in some places by the author. To which is added, an appendix, containing some remarks on Switzerland and Italy, writ by a person of quality, and communicated to the author [or rather written by G. Burnet ?], *etc.* pp. 336. *For Abraham Acher: Rotterdam,* 1687. 8°. **1050. d. 4.**

—— The third edition, corrected, and altered in some places by the author, *etc.* pp. 321. *Printed by Abraham Acher: Rotterdam,* 1687. 12°. **10105. a. 24.**

—— The third edition, corrected and altered in some places by the author, *etc.* pp. 232. *For the Widow Swart: Amsterdam,* 1688. 12°. **10106. a. 12.**

—— [Another edition.] Together with some other additions, which were not in former editions [including "The History of the Divorce of Henry viii. and Katharine of Arragon . . . By Joachim le Grand. With Dr. Burnet's Answer" and "Animadversions on the Reflections upon Dr. B's Travels"]. pp. 400. *Sold by J. Robinson & Awnsham Churchill: London,* 1689. 12°. **1050. d. 6.**

—— [Another edition.] The third edition, corrected. pp. 322 [*London ?*] 1708. 8°. **10107. b. 12**

—— [Another edition.] pp. xxvi. 355. *J. Lacy: London,* 1724. 8°. **1048. h. 17.**

—— Burnet's Travels: or, a Collection of letters to the Hon. Robert Boyle, Esq. . . . A new edition. pp. xxiv. 264. *Ward & Chandler: London,* 1737. 12°. **10105. aa. 21.**

—— [Another edition.] Bishop Burnet's Travels, *etc.* pp. xxiv. 258. *Edinburgh; Thomas Glas: Dundee,* 1752. 12°. **10105. a. 25.**

—— Voyage de Suisse, d'Italie, et de quelques endroits d'Allemagne & de France, fait és années 1685, & 1686 . . . Avec des remarques d'une personne de qualité, touchant la Suisse & l'Italie. Seconde édition, reveuë, corrigée & augmentée. pp. 536. *A. Acher: Rotterdam,* 1688. 12°. **1050. d. 32.**

—— Dernière édition, revûë, corrigée, & augmentée d'un indice des principales matières. pp. 468. *A. Acher: Rotterdam,* 1690. 12°. **10107. a. 22.**

—— Des berühmten englischen Theologi, D. Gilberti Burnets, durch die Schweitz, Italien, auch einige Oerter Deutschlandes und Franckreichs im 1685. und 86. Jahre gethaner Reise, und derselben curieuse Beschreibung, worinnen die neuesten im Geist- und weltlichen Staat entstandene Revolutiones enthalten; anfänglich in Englisch . . . ietzo aber in deutscher Sprache beschrieben (von M. J. G. P. [i.e. Johann Georg Pritz]), und in dieser andern Edition . . . mit Fleiss übersehen und verbessert; nebenst beygefügter einer hochverständigen Person vollständigen Ausführung des Quietismi und Lebens-Beschreibung Molinos, wie auch vieler andern Italien betreffender merckwürdiger Begebenheiten. 2 pt. *J. F. Gleditsch: Leipzig,* 1688. 12°. **10106. a. 26.**

—— Supplement to Dr. Burnet's Letters relating to his Travels . . . Being further remarks on Switzerland, and Italy, &c. Written by a nobleman of Italy, and communicated to the author [or rather, written by G. Burnet?], *etc.* pp. 24. *Printed by Abraham Acher: Rotterdam,* 1687. 12°. **3939. aaa. 47. (1.)**

—— Three Letters concerning the Present State of Italy, written in the year 1687. I. Relating to the affair of Molinos, and the Quietists. II. Relating to the Inquisition, and the state and religion. III. Relating to the policy and interests of some of the States of Italy. Being a supplement to Dr. Burnet's Letters. [By G. Burnet.] pp. 192. 1688. 12°. *See* ITALY. [*Appendix.—Miscellaneous.*] **T. 1990. (1.)**

—— [Another copy.] **3939. aaa. 47. (2.)**

—— [Another copy.] **1050. d. 7.**

—— [Another copy.] **10136. a. 33.**

—— [Another edition.] pp. 191. 1688. 8°. *See* ITALY. [*Appendix.—Miscellaneous.*] **3902. de. 5.**

—— [Another copy.] **113. k. 64.**

—— Die eigentliche Beschreibung des gegenwärtigen Zustandes in Italien, insonderheit von dem Anfang und Fortgang des Quietismi, und Lebens-Lauffes des Molinos; der wider ihn angestellten Inquisition, und andern notabeln Sachen . . . Zu vollständiger Ausführung der Reise-Beschreibung des . . . Herrn D. Gilberti Burnets, von einer vornehmen und hochverständigen Person [i.e. G. Burnet] in englischer Sprache heraus gegeben und hierauf ins Frantzösische gebracht, jetzo aber aus dem Frantzösischen theils auch Italiänischen ins Teutsche übersetzet, und bey dieser neuen Auflage nach dem Englischen mit Fleiss übersehen von Jo. Georg. Pritio. pp. 364. 1693. 12°. *See* ITALY. [*Appendix.—Miscellaneous.*] **10129. a. 37.**

—— Reflexions on Dr. Gilbert Burnet's Travels . . . Written originally in Latin by Monsieur * * * [i.e. Antoine Varillas]. And now done into English. pp. 164. *Sold by Randal Tayler: London,* 1688. 8°. **1050. d. 5. (3.)**

MINOR WORKS.

—— Advice to Princes upon the Throne of England, *etc.* *See* supra: HISTORY OF MY OWN TIME.—*Appendix.*

—— Animadversions on the Reflections upon Dr. B's [i.e. Dr. Burnet's] Travels. [By G. Burnet.] pp. 57. 1688. 12°. *See* B., *Dr.* **1050. d. 5. (4.)**

—— An Answer to a Letter to Dr. Burnet [by Simon Lowth], occasioned by his Letter to Mr. Lowth. pp. 8. *For Richard Baldwin: London,* 1685. 4°. **699. f. 6. (5.)**

—— An Answer to a Paper printed with Allowance, entitled, A New Test of the Church of England's Loyalty. [By G. Burnet.] pp. 7. [1688.] 4°. *See* ENGLAND.—*Church of England.* [*Appendix.*] **4105. c. 20.**

—— [Another copy.] **116. d. 28.**

—— Antwoord op een geschrift, gedrukt met verlof. Genaamt Een Nieuwe Eed of Test wegens de getrouwigheyd der Kerk van Engeland. [By G. Burnet.] pp. 8. [1688.] 4°. *See* ENGLAND.—*Church of England.* [*Appendix.*] **8122. ee. 10. (43.)**

—— An Answer to Mr Henry Payne's Letter, concerning His Majesty's Declaration of Indulgence, *etc.* [Signed: T. T., i.e. G. Burnet.] pp. 4. [1687.] 4°. *See* T., T. **106. g. 67. (5.)**

—— An Answer to the Animadversions [by Thomas Comber] on the History of the Rights of Princes, &c. pp. 202. *For Richard Chiswell: London,* 1682. 4°. **699. f. 6. (2.)**

—— An Apology for the Church of England, with relation to the spirit of persecution for which she is accused. [By G. Burnet.] pp. 8. [1688?] 4°. *See* ENGLAND.—*Church of England.* [*Appendix.*] **4106. aaa. 21.**

—— [Another copy.] **699. f. 4. (30.)**

—— [Another edition.] An Apology for the Church of England, with relation to the spirit of persecution: for which she is accused. pp. 8. [1688.] 8°. *See* ENGLAND.—*Church of England.* [*Appendix.*] **1482. b. 14. (22.)**

—— [Another edition.] *See* SOMERS (John) *Baron Somers.* A Collection of Scarce and Valuable Tracts, *etc.* vol. 2. 1748. 4°. **184. a. 2.**

—— [Another edition.] 1813. *See* SOMERS (John) *Baron Somers.* A Collection of Scarce and Valuable Tracts, *etc.* vol. 9. 1809, *etc.* 4°. **750. g. 9.**

—— Een Apologie voor de Kerk van Engeland, ten opzigt van de geest der vervolginge waar over sy nu beschuldigt werd. [By G. Burnet.] pp. 15. 1688. 4°. *See* ENGLAND.—*Church of England.* [*Appendix.*] **8122. ee. 11. (2.)**

—— The Case of Compulsion in Matters of Religion stated. *See* infra: Preface to Lactantius.

—— Een Vervolgh van het Tweede deel van het Onderzoek over de redenen, die door Sa: Oxon, tot vernietiginge van den Test, zyn gepresenteert geweest; raakende de afgodery der Roomsche Kerk. [A translation of "A Continuation of the Second Part of the Enquiry into the Reasons offered by Sa. Oxon for Abrogating the Test." By G. Burnet.] pp. 16. [1688.] 4°. *See* PARKER (Samuel) *Bishop of Oxford.* **8122. ee. 10. (28**.)**

—— [Another copy.] **8122. ee. 10. (28***.)**

—— A Continuation of Reflections on Mr. Varillas's History of Heresies. Particularly on that which relates to English affairs. In his third and fourth tomes. pp. 152. *For J. S.: Amsterdam,* 1687. 12°. **1019. g. 19. (4.)**

—— The Conversion & Persecutions of Eve Cohan, now called Elizabeth Verboon, a person of quality of the Jewish religion, *etc.* [By G. Burnet.] pp. 27. 1680. 4°. *See* COHAN (Eve) afterwards VERBOON (Elizabeth) **482. b. 3. (13.)**

—— [Another copy.] **G. 15501. (4.)**

—— A Defence of the Reflections on the ninth book of the first volum of Mr. Varillas's History of Heresies. Being a reply to his Answer. [With a translation of J. Le Clerc's defence of the preface to his translation of the "Reflections."] pp. 144. *For J. S.: Amsterdam,* 1687. 12°. **4520. aaa. 7.**

—— [Another edition.] pp. 144. *For J. S.: Amsterdam,* 1687. 12°. **1019**. g. **19**. (**3**.)

—— A Discourse concerning Transubstantiation and Idolatry, *etc. See* infra: A Second Part of the Enquiry into the Reasons offered by Sa. Oxon for Abrogating the Test.

—— A Discourse on the Memory of that Rare and truely virtuous person Sir Robert Fletcher of Saltoun . . . Written by a Gentleman of his Acquaintance [i.e. G. Burnet]. pp. 180. 1665. 12°. *See* FLETCHER (*Sir* Robert) *of Saltoun.* **857**. h. **14**.

—— A Discourse wherein is held forth the Opposition of the Doctrine, Worship, and Practices of the Roman Church, to the Nature, Designs and Characters of the Christian Faith. *See* infra: The Mystery of Iniquity Unvailed.

—— An Enquiry into the Measures of Submission to the Supream Authority: and of the grounds upon which it may be lawful or necessary for subjects, to defend their religion, lives and liberties. [By G. Burnet.] pp. 8. [1688.] 4°. *See* ENQUIRY. **8122**. e. **32**.

—— [Another edition.] [Apparently extracted from a collected edition of Burnet's tracts.] pp. 14. [1688?] 4°. *See* ENQUIRY. **699**. f. **4**. (**29**.)

—— [Another edition.] 1693. fol. [*State Tracts.* pt. 2.] *See* ENQUIRY. **L.R.41.d.12.**

—— [Another edition.] With a preface. pp. 21. *For Ric. Chiswell: London,* 1693. 4°. **699**. f. **4**. (**17**.)

—— [Another copy.] **100**. i. **60**.

—— Een Ondersoek aangaande de maaten van onderwerpinge aan het opper-gesag, als ook van de gronden waar op het geoorloofd, of nodig sou konnen sijn voor onderdanen, om haar religie, leven en vryheden te defenderen. Uit het Engelsch vertaalt. [By G. Burnet.] pp. 15. [1688.] 4°. *See* ONDERZOEK. **8122**. ee. **11**. (**28**.)

—— Ondersoek over de manier van onderwerping aan de hoochste macht: en ontrent de gronden, op welke het den ondersaten geoorloft, of noodsakelik mach sijn haar religie, leven, en vrijheden te beschermen. Na de copye van Schotland, by James Warner, anno 1688. [By G. Burnet.] pp. 16. [1688.] 4°. *See* ONDERZOEK. **8122**. ee. **11**. (**27**.)

—— *See* ENQUIRY. Vindiciæ Juris Regii: or, Remarques upon a paper, entituled, An Enquiry into the Measures of Submission to the Supream Authority. [By Jeremy Collier.] 1689. 4°. **1103**. f. **28**.

—— An Enquiry into the Present State of Affairs: and in particular, whether we owe allegiance to the King in these circumstances? And whether we are bound to treat with him, and call him back again, or not? [By G. Burnet.] pp. 16. 1689. 4°. *See* JAMES II., *King of Great Britain and Ireland.* [*Appendix.*] **T. 1702**. (**11**.)

—— [Another copy.] **8122**. aaa. **21**. (**11**.)

—— [Another copy.] **E. 1966**. (**2***.)

—— [Another copy.] MS. NOTE. **100.h.69.**

—— [Another edition.] pp. 12. 1689. 4°. *See* JAMES II., *King of Great Britain and Ireland.* [*Appendix.*] **8138**. bb. **33**.

—— [Another edition.] *See* COLLECTION. A Collection of State Tracts, *etc.* vol. 1. 1705. fol. **2082.e.**

—— Een Naukeurigh ondersoeck nopende de tegenwoordige gesteltheyt van saken, en insonderheyt of we in dezes tyts omstandigheden eenige getrouwigheyt aen den Koning verschuldigt zyn, *etc.* [By G. Burnet.] pp. 14. 1689. 4°. *See* JAMES II., *King of Great Britain and Ireland.* [*Appendix.*] **8122**. ee. **12**. (**34**.)

—— Een Onderzoek ontrent de tegenwoordige staat der affairen . . . Uytgegeeven door authoriteyt. [By G. Burnet.] pp. 14. 1689. 4°. *See* JAMES II., *King of Great Britain and Ireland.* [*Appendix.*] **8122**. ee. **12**. (**33**.)

—— *See* JAMES II., *King of Great Britain and Ireland.* [*Appendix.*] A Word to the Wavering: or, an Answer to the Enquiry into the present state of affairs: whether we owe allegiance to the King in these circumstances? &c. With a postscript of Subjection to the Higher Powers; by Dr. G. B——. 1689. 4°. **E. 1965**. (**1**.)

—— An Enquiry into the Reasons for abrogating the Test imposed on all Members of Parliament. Offered by Sa. Oxon. [i.e. Samuel Parker, Bishop of Oxford.] [By G. Burnet.] pp. 8. [1688.] 4°. *See* PARKER (Samuel) *Bishop of Oxford.* **699**. f. **4**. (**14**.)

—— [Another copy.] **4105**. de. **4**. (**8**.)

—— [Another copy.] **T. 1701**. (**4**.)

—— [Another copy.] **T. 1867**. (**4**.)

—— [Another copy.] **222**. e. **9**. (**10**.)

—— [Another edition.] pp. 8. [1688.] 4°. *See* PARKER (Samuel) *Bishop of Oxford.* **702**. e. **11**. (**8**.)

—— [Another edition.] 1689. 4°. [*Fourteen Papers, etc.*] *See* PARKER (Samuel) *Bishop of Oxford.* **E. 1967**. (**13**.)

—— [Another edition.] 1813. *See* SOMERS (John) *Baron Somers.* A Collection of Scarce and Valuable Tracts, *etc.* vol. 9. 1809, *etc.* 4°. **750**. g. **9**.

—— Een Onderzoek over de redenen, die tot vernietiginge van den Test, welke alle de leden van 't Parlement word opgelegd, zijn gepresenteerd geweest door Sa. Oxon. [By G. Burnet.] pp. 16. [1688.] 4°. *See* PARKER (Samuel) *Bishop of Oxford.* **8122**. ee. **10**. (**28**.)

—— An Essay on the Memory of the late Queen. [With a portrait.] pp. 197. *For Ric. Chiswell: London,* 1695. 8°. **292**. d. **11**.

—— [Another copy.] **1200**. a. **1**. *Imperfect; wanting the portrait.*

—— The second edition. pp. 197. *For Ric. Chiswell: London,* 1696. 8°. **1448**. c. **10**.

—— [An Essay on the Memory of the Late Queen.] Discours sur la vie de la feuë reine de la Grande-Bretagne. pp. 183. *La Haye,* 1716. 12°. **10806**. a. **9**. *Imperfect; wanting sig.* A2.

—— Bishop Burnet's Exhortation to all Mankind to become Truly Religious, *etc. See* supra: HISTORY OF MY OWN TIME.—*Abridgments and Extracts.*

—— An Exposition of the Church Catechism, for the use of the Diocese of Sarum. [With the text.] pp. 342. 1710. 8°. *See* LITURGIES.—*Church of England,—Common Prayer.—Catechism.* [*English.*] **223**. d. **2**.

—— The History of the Rights of Princes in the disposing of Ecclesiastical Benefices and Church-Lands. Relating chiefly to the pretensions of the Crown of France to the Regale, and the late contests with the Court of Rome. To which is added, a Collection of letters written on that occasion: and of some other remarkable papers put in an appendix. 2 pt. *J. D. for Richard Chiswell: London,* 1682. 8°. **698.** d. **16.** **(1, 2.)**
Pt. 2 *bears the date* 1681.

—— Animadversions on Dr. Burnet's History of the Rights of Princes in the disposing of Ecclesiastical Benefices and Church-Lands. In a letter to a friend. [By Thomas Comber.] pp. 15. *London,* 1682. 4°. **699.** f. **6.** **(1.)**

—— The Infallibility of the Church of Rome examined and confuted. In a letter to a Roman priest. pp. 35. *Printed by M. Clark; sold by H. Browne & B. Tooke: London,* 1680. 4°. **873.** k. **6.** **(3.)**

—— A Letter, containing some Reflections on His Majesties Declaration for Liberty of Conscience, *etc.* [By G. Burnet.] pp. 8. [1687.] 4°. *See* ENGLAND.—*Proclamations.*—II. James II. [1685–1688.] **110.** g. **36.**

—— [Another copy.] **116.** c. **35.**

—— A Letter, containing some Remarks on the two Papers, writ by his late Majesty King Charles the Second, concerning religion. [By G. Burnet.] pp. 8. [1686.] 4°. *See* CHARLES II., *King of Great Britain and Ireland.* [*Letters and Speeches.*—II.] **116.** e. **35.**

—— [Another edition.] 1693. fol. [*State Tracts.* pt. 2.] *See* CHARLES II., *King of Great Britain and Ireland.* [*Letters and Speeches.*—II.] **L.R.41.d.12.**

—— Lettre d'un gentilhomme anglois à son ami touchant les deux écrits trouvez dans le cabinet du roi Charles II . . . [By G. Burnet.] Traduit de l'anglois. pp. 35. 1687. 12°. *See* CHARLES II., *King of Great Britain and Ireland.* [*Letters and Speeches.*—II.] **600.** a. **22.** **(4.)**

—— [Another issue.] 1687. 12°. [*Recueil de plusieurs pieces concernant les affaires presentes d'Angleterre, etc.* tom. 1.] *See* CHARLES II., *King of Great Britain and Ireland.* [*Letters and Speeches.*—II.] C. **65.** a. **24.**

—— Ein Brieff eines Englischen Edelmanns, betreffend die beyde Schreiben, welche nach des Königes Caroli II. Tode in seinem Cabinet gefunden, und auf Befehl Sr. Majest. des Königs Jacobi II. öffentlich heraus gegeben worden. [By G. Burnet.] *See* CHARLES II., *King of Great Britain and Ireland.* [*Doubtful or Supposititious Works.*—II.] Zwey Schreiben, *etc.* 1689. 4°. **8122.** b. **26.**

—— A Letter . . . to Mr. Simon Lowth . . . Occasioned, by his late book Of the subject of Church-Power. pp. 8. *For Richard Baldwin: London.* 1685. 4°. **699.** f. **6.** **(3.)**

—— A Letter to Dr. Burnet. Occasioned by his late Letter to Mr. Lowth. [By Simon Lowth.] pp. 7. *For Randal Taylor: London,* 1685. 4°. **699.** f. **6.** **(4.)**

—— A Letter from the Bishop of Salisbury, to the Clergy of his Diocese: to be read at the Triennial Visitation in April and May, 1708. pp. 8. [*London,* 1708.] 4°. **699.** f. **4.** **(26.)**

—— A Letter from the Bishop of Salisbury to the Clergy of his Diocese. To be read at the Triennial Visitation in May, 1711. pp. 8. [*London,* 1711.] 4°. **4473.** d. **5.** **(4.)**

—— A Letter occasioned by the second Letter to Dr. Burnet, written to a friend. pp. 8. *For Richard Baldwyn: London,* 1685. 4°. **699.** f. **6.** **(6.)**

—— A Letter to a Lord upon his happy Conversion from Popery to the Protestant Religion. pp. 4. [*Printed in Holland?*] 1688. 4°. **699.** f. **6.** **(8.)**

—— [Another copy.] T. **88*.** **(70.)**

—— A Letter to Mr. Thevenot. Containing a censure of Mr. Le Grand's History of King Henry the Eighth's Divorce. To which is added, a Censure of Mr. de Meaux's History of the Variations of the Protestant Churches. Together with some further reflections on Mr. Le Grand. pp. 57. *For John Starkey & Richard Chiswell: London,* 1689. 4°. **699.** f. **6.** **(12.)**

—— [Another copy.] **116.** e. **37.**

—— [Another edition.] A Letter to Monsieur Thevenot, being a full refutation of Mr. Le Grand's History of Henry VIII's divorcing Katharine of Arragon, *etc.* *See* LE GRAND (J.) The History of the Divorce of Henry VIII. and Katharine of Arragon, *etc.* [1690?] 4°. **3938.** cc. **29.**

—— Lettre de Mr. Burnet à Mr. Thevenot contenant une courte critique de l'Histoire du divorce de Henri VIII, écrite par Mr. Le Grand. pp. 27. [*The Hague,* 1688.] 12°. **1093.** b. **8.**

—— Nouvelle édition, augmentée d'un avertissement & des Remarques de M. L. G., qui servent de réponse à cette lettre. pp. 114. *La Veuve d'Edme Martin, J. Boudot, & Estienne Martin: Paris,* 1688. 12°. G. **1486.** **(1.)**

—— The Bishop of Sarum's Letter to the Reverend Doctor Williams. *See* WILLIAMS (John) *Bishop of Chichester.* A Vindication of the Sermons of His Grace John, Archbishop of Canterbury, *etc.* 1695. 4°. **479.** a. **19.** **(4, 5.)**

—— *See* UNITARIANS. The Agreement of the Unitarians with the Catholick Church, being a full answer to . . . the needless exceptions of My Lords the Bishops of Chichester, Worcester and Sarum [in John Williams's "A Vindication of the Sermons of His Grace John, Archbishop of Canterbury"]. 1697. 4°. **479.** b. **33.**

—— A Letter writ . . . to the Lord Bishop of Cov. and Litchfield [William Lloyd], concerning a book lately published, called, A Specimen of some Errors and Defects in the History of the Reformation of the Church of England, by Anthony Harmer. pp. 29. *For Ric. Chiswell: London,* 1693. 4°. **699.** f. **6.** **(15.)**

—— [Another copy.] A Letter writ by the Lord Bishop of Salisbury, to the Lord Bishop of Cov. and Litchfield, *etc.* *London,* 1693. 4°. **4481.** aaa. **37.** **(16.)**

—— [Another copy.] **698.** g. **20.** **(3.)**

—— *See* D., E. A Vindication of the Historiographer of the University of Oxford [i.e. Anthony à Wood] and his works, from the reproaches of the Lord Bishop of Salisbury, in his Letter to the Lord Bishop of Coventry and Litchfield, *etc.* 1693. 4°. **731.** k. **6.** **(17.)**

—— A Letter written upon the Discovery of the Late Plot. [By G. Burnet.] pp. 45. 1678. 4°. *See* LETTER. T. **1893.** **(10.)**

—— [Another copy.] E. **1959.** **(20.)**

—— [Another edition.] pp. 45. 1678. 4°. *See* LETTER. **108.** d. **58.**

—— The Libertine Overthrown, *etc.* *See* infra: Some Passages of the Life and Death of . . . John Earl of Rochester, *etc.*

—— The Life and Death of Sir Matthew Hale, Kt., sometime Lord Chief Justice of His Majesties Court of Kings Bench. [With a portrait.] pp. 218. MS. NOTES [by F. Hargrave]. *For William Shrowsbery: London,* 1682. 8º. **1418.** b. **29.**
In this copy the catch-word on p. 3 is "he."

—— [Another copy.] **1130.** a. **3.** (**1.**)

—— [Another copy.] MS. NOTES [by F. Hargrave]. **1130.** e. **15.**
In this copy the catch-word on p. 3 is "while."

—— [Another copy.] G. **14437.**
Imperfect; wanting the engraved frontispiece.

—— The Life and Death of Sir Matthew Hale, *etc.* pp. 102. *In:* HALE (*Sir* Matthew) Contemplations Moral and Divine. The third part, *etc.* 1696. 8º. **4382.** b. **14.**

—— [Another edition.] *See* HALE (*Sir* Matthew) The Works, moral and religious, of Sir Matthew Hale, *etc.* vol. 1. 1805. 8º **493.** b. **11.**

—— [Another edition.] Together with the Life of the Rev. H. Hammond, D.D. by John Fell . . . A new edition. pp. xv. 315. *Clarendon Press: Oxford,* 1806. 8º. **275.** d. **23.**

—— [Another copy.] G. **14672.**

—— The Life and Death of Sir Matthew Hale, *etc.* pp. ix. 114. *W. Povey: Wotton-Underedge,* [1810?] 8º. **10815.** aa. **5.**

—— [Another edition.] *See* WORDSWORTH (Christopher) *Master of Trinity College, Cambridge.* Ecclesiastical Biography, *etc.* vol. 6. 1818. 8º. **204.** c. **17.**

—— Memoirs of the Life and Character of Sir Matthew Hale. [An abridgment.] *See* BAXTER (Richard) [*Selections.*] Biographical Collections. vol. 2. 1766. 12º. **1112.** c. **2.**

—— The Life of William Bedell, D.D. Bishop of Kilmore in Ireland. [By G. Burnet.] (The Copies of certain Letters which have passed between Spain & England in matter of religion, concerning the general motives to the Roman obedience, between Mr. James Waddesworth, a late pensioner of the holy Inquisition in Sevil, and W. Bedell.) pp. 487. 1685. 8º. *See* BEDELL (William) *Bishop of Kilmore.* **295.** i. **4.**

—— [A reissue.] The Life of William Bedell, D.D., Lord Bishop of Killmore in Ireland . . . To which are subjoyned certain letters, *etc.* MS. NOTES. *Richard Chiswell: London,* 1692. 8º. **489.** a. **15.**
Sig. Ff 7 *is a cancel.*

—— The third edition, with additions. pp. 423. *William Williamson: Dublin,* 1758. 8º. **489.** e. **14.** (**1.**)
Pt. 2, *containing the letters, has a separate titlepage bearing the imprint of R. Gunne and the date* 1736.

—— The Life of Bishop Bedell. (Abridged from Burnet.) *See* BROWNE (George) *Archbishop of Dublin.* The Life of Archbishop Browne, *etc.* [1832.] 12º. **864.** f. **11/41.**

—— La Vie de Guilme Bedell eveque de Kilmore en Irlande. Traduite . . . par L. D. M. [i.e. Louis Dumesnil.] pp. 240. *P. Savouret: Amsterdam,* 1687. 12º. **1368.** a. **28.** (**1.**)
Imperfect; wanting pp. 147, 148.

—— The Memoires of the Lives and Actions of James and William, Dukes of Hamilton and Castleherald, &c. In which an account is given of the rise and progress of the civil wars of Scotland . . . from the year 1625, to the year 1652. Together with many letters, instructions, and other papers, written by King Charles the I., *etc.* pp. 436. *See* SPOTTISWOODE (John) successively *Archbishop of Glasgow* and *of Saint Andrews.* The History of the Church and State of Scotland, *etc.* pt. 2. 1677. fol. **194.** d. **8.**

—— [Another edition.] pp. xxxii. 555. *University Press: Oxford,* 1852. 8º. **10815.** e. **8.**

—— A Memorial drawn by King William's Special Direction, intended to be given in at the Treaty of Reswick: justifying the Revolution, and the course of his government, in answer to two memorials that were offer'd there in King James's name. [By G. Burnet.] pp. 23. 1705. 4º. *See* WILLIAM III., *King of Great Britain and Ireland.* **8122.** bb. **35.** (**15.**)

—— [Another copy.] **1093.** c. **89.**

—— [Another edition.] The Revolution and the Present Establishment Vindicated. In a Memorial drawn by King William's special direction, *etc.* pp. iv. 18. 1715. 8º. *See* WILLIAM III., *King of Great Britain and Ireland.* [*Appendix.*] **101.** e. **36.**

—— [Another edition.] A Memorial drawn by King William's special direction, *etc.* 1814. fol. [SOMERS (*John*) *Baron Somers. A Collection of Scarce and Valuable Tracts.* vol. 11.] *See* WILLIAM III., *King of Great Britain and Ireland.* [*Appendix.*] **750.** g. **11.**

—— A Modest and Free Conference betwixt a Conformist and a Non-conformist, about the present distempers of Scotland. In six dialogues. By a Lover of Peace [i.e. G. Burnet]. (A Pindarick Ode upon Contentions in matters of Religion, by a friend of the Authors, *etc.*) pp. 100. 1669. 8º. *See* SCOTLAND. [*Appendix.—Religion.*] **4175.** de. **42.**

—— *See* SCOTLAND. [*Appendix.—Religion.*] The True Non-Conformist. In answere to The Modest and Free Conference betwixt a Conformist and a Non-Conformist, about the present distempers of Scotland [by G. Burnet, Bishop of Salisbury]. By a lover of truth [i.e. R. MacWard], *etc.* 1671. 8º. **874.** d. **20.**

—— A Modest Survey of the Most Considerable Things in a Discourse [by Herbert Croft, Bishop of Hereford] lately published, entituled Naked Truth. Written in a letter to a friend. [By G. Burnet.] pp. 29. 1676. 4º. *See* TRUTH. **855.** e. **5.**

—— [Another copy.] **701.** g. **10.** (**12.**)

—— The Mystery of Iniquity Unvailed: in a discourse, wherein is held forth the opposition of the doctrine, worship, and practices of the Roman Church, to the nature, designs, and characters of the Christian faith. pp. 161. *Printed by W. Godbid; sold by M. Pitt: London,* 1673. 8º. **700.** f. **20.**

—— [Another edition.] A Discourse wherein is held forth the Opposition of the Doctrine, Worship, and Practices of the Roman Church, to the Nature, Designs, and Characters of the Christian Faith. pp. 71. *For J. Watts: London,* 1688. 4º. T. **1876.** (**4.**)

—— [Another copy.] A Discourse wherein is held forth the Opposition of the Doctrine . . . of the Roman Church, to the Nature . . . of the Christian Faith. *London,* 1688. 4°. **1482**. aaa. **26**. (**4**.)

—— [Another copy.] **222**. e. **19**. (**3**.)

—— The second edition. pp. 71. *For J. Watts: London,* 1688. 4°. **699**. f. **4**. (**7**.)

—— [Another edition.] *See* POPERY. A Preservative against Popery, *etc.* vol. 1. 1738. fol. **478**. f. **11**.

—— [Another edition.] 1837. *See* CARDWELL (Edward) *D.D.* Enchiridion Theologicum Anti-Romanum, *etc.* vol. 3. 1836, *etc.* 8°. **1119**. f. **26**.

—— [Another edition.] *See* GIBSON (Edmund) successively *Bishop of Lincoln* and *of London.* A Preservative against Popery, *etc.* vol. 1. 1848, *etc.* 8°. **3940**. k. **6/1**.

—— Anti-Haman; or, an Answer to M. G. Burnet's Mystery of Iniquiti [*sic*] Unvailed . . . By W. E. Student in Divinity [i.e. John Warner]. 1679. 8°. *See* E., W., *Student in Divinity.* **1019**. f. **25**.

—— News from France: in a letter giving a relation of the present state of the difference between the French King and the Court of Rome. To which is added, The Pope's Brief to the Assembly of the Clergy, and the Protestation made by them in Latin, together with an English translation of them. [By G. Burnet.] pp. 38. 1682. 4°. *See* FRANCE. [*Appendix.—History and Politics.—Miscellaneous.*] **4632**. b. **34**.

—— A Pastoral Letter writ by the Right Reverend Father in God Gilbert, Lord Bishop of Sarum, to the Clergy of his Diocess, concerning the Oaths of Allegiance and Supremacy to K. William and Q. Mary. pp. 29. *For J. Starkey & Ric. Chiswell: London,* 1689. 4°. **699**. f. **4**. (**12**.)

—— [Another copy.] **816**. m. **9**. (**89**.) *Imperfect; wanting the half-title.*

—— [Another copy.] **100**. h. **79**. *Imperfect; wanting the half-title and the last leaf.*

—— [Another edition.] pp. 8. *Edinburgh,* 1689. fol. **714**. i. **8**. (**20**.)

—— Een Pastorale brief . . . wegens de eeden van Allegiance en Supremacy of getrouwigheyd en opperhoofdigheyd, aan Koning William en Koninginne Maria. Uyt het Engelsch vertaald. pp. 16. *De Weduw van S. Swart: Amsterdam,* 1689. 4°. **8122**. ee. **12**. (**39**.)

—— *See* GALLAWAY (William) Reflections upon Mr. Johnson's Notes on the Pastoral Letter [of G. Burnet]. 1694. 4°. **T. 1881**. (**3**.)

—— *See* JOHNSON (Samuel) *Rector of Corringham.* Notes upon the Phœnix Edition of the Pastoral Letter [of G. Burnet]. 1694. 4°. **T. 1881**. (**2**.)

—— A Letter to the Bishop of Sarum: being an answer to his Lordship's Pastoral Letter. From a Minister in the Countrey [i.e. John Lowthorp]. pp. 41. MS. NOTES. [*London,*] 1690. 4°. **4445**. b. **15**.

—— [Preface to Lactantius.] The Bishop of Salisbury's New Preface to his Pastoral Care, consider'd . . . The second edition. [Consisting in fact of G. Burnet's preface to his translation of the "De mortibus persecutorum" of Lactantius.] pp. 24. [1713?] 8°. *See* supra: DISCOURSE OF THE PASTORAL CARE. **4106**. b. **28**.

—— The Case of Compulsion in matters of Religion Stated. By G. B. [i.e. G. Burnet], *etc.* [An extract from his preface to Lactantius.] pp. 15. 1688. 8°. *See* B., G. **698**. f. **26**.

—— The Celebrated Story of the Thebæan Legion no Fable. In answer to the objections of Doctor G. Burnet's preface to his translation of Lactantius de Mortibus Persecutorum. With some remarks on his Discourse of Persecution. Written in the year 1687, by a Dignify'd Clergy-Man of the Church of England [i.e. George Hickes], and now first publish'd from the author's own MS. 1714. 8°. *See* LACTANTIUS (L. C. F.) [*De Mortibus Persecutorum.*] **4505**. aa. **18**.

—— A Rational Method for proving the Truth of the Christian Religion, as it is professed in the Church of England. In answer to A Rational Compendious Way to convince without dispute all persons whatsoever dissenting from the true religion, by J. K. [i.e. John Keynes]. pp. 98. *For Richard Royston: London,* 1675. 8°. **699**. f. **5**. (**1**.)

—— Reflections on a Book [by Francis Atterbury, Bishop of Rochester], entituled, The Rights, Powers, and Privileges of an English Convocation, stated and vindicated. pp. 31. *Ri. Chiswell: London,* 1700. 4°. **698**. h. **21**. (**7**.)

—— [Another copy.] **T. 687**. (**1**.)

—— Reflections on a Late Pamphlet [by John Northleigh], entitled Parliamentum Pacificum, *etc.* [By G. Burnet.] pp. 8. 1688. 4°. *See* ENGLAND.—*Parliament.* [*Appendix.*] **100**. h. **33**.

—— [Another edition.] 1689. 4°. [*Fourteen Papers, etc.*] *See* ENGLAND.—*Parliament.* [*Appendix.*] **E. 1967**. (**13**.)

—— Aenmerkinge op het geschrift genaemt Parlamentum Pacificum . . . [By G. Burnet.] Uyt het Engels vertaelt. pp. 19. 1688. 4°. *See* ENGLAND.—*Parliament.* [*Appendix.*] **8122**. ee. **10**. (**23**.)

—— Reflectien op een schrift geintituleert Parliamentum Pacificum, *etc.* [By G. Burnet.] pp. 12. [1688?] 4°. *See* ENGLAND.—*Parliament.* [*Appendix.*] **8079**. e. **3**.

—— Dr. Burnett's Reflections upon a Book, entituled, Parliamentum Pacificum:—the first part—answered, by the author [i.e. John Northleigh]. pp. 147. *Printed & sold by Matthew Turner: London,* 1688. 4°. **8122**. d. **11**.

—— Reflections on a Paper, intituled, His Majesty's Reasons for withdrawing himself from Rochester. [By G. Burnet.] pp. 8. 1689. 4°. *See* JAMES II., *King of Great Britain and Ireland.* [*Letters, etc.*—II.] **693**. f. **4**. (**12**.)

—— [Another edition.] pp. 8. 1689. 4°. *See* JAMES II., *King of Great Britain and Ireland.* [*Letters, etc.*—II.] **T. 1675**. (**14**.)

—— [Another copy.] **T. 100***. (**213**.)

—— [Another copy.] **100**. h. **45**.

—— [Another edition.] *See* COLLECTION. A Collection of State Tracts, *etc.* vol. 1. 1705. fol. **2082.e.**

—— Reflection of aanmerkingen; op seker geschrift. Geintituleert: Redenen waaromme sijn Majesteit is vertrokken van Rochester, *etc.* [By G. Burnet.] pp. 8. 1689. 4°. *See* JAMES II., *King of Great Britain and Ireland.* [*Letters, etc.*—II.] **8122**. ee. **12**. (**4**.)

—— Reflections on Mr. Varillas's History of the Revolutions that hav[e] happned in Europe in matters of Religion. And more particularly on his ninth boo[k] that relates to England. pp. 203. *For P. Savouret: Amsterdam,* 1686. 12°. **1368**. a. **28**. (**2**.)
The titlepage is slightly cropped.

—— Reflections on Mr. Varillas's History of the Revolutions that have happned in Europe in matters of Religion, *etc.* pp. 203. *Printed for P. Savouret: Amsterdam,* 1686. 12°. **1483**. aa. **27**.
The imprint is probably false. Printed in London?

—— [Another edition.] pp. 106. *London,* 1689. 12°. **1019**. g. **19**. (**2**.)

—— Critique du neuvième livre de l'Histoire de M. Varillas, où il traite des révolutions arrivées en Angleterre en matière de religion. Traduite de l'anglois [by Jean Le Clerc]. pp. 135. *P. Savouret: Amsterdam,* 1686. 12°. **9512**. a. **24**.

—— *See* VARILLAS (A.) Réponse de Mr Varillas à la Critique de Mr Burnet sur les deux premiers tomes de l'histoire des revolutions arrivées dans l'Europe en matiére de réligion. 1687. 12°. **11858**. ee. **4**.

—— Reflections on the Relation of English Reformation, lately printed at Oxford [i.e. on Abraham Woodhead's "Church-Government Part v. A Relation of the English Reformation"]. By G. B. D.D. [i.e. G. Burnet.] pp. 64. 1688. 4°. *See* B., G., *D.D.* T. **1845**. (**3**.)

—— [Another edition.] pp. 96. 1688. 4°. *See* CHURCH GOVERNMENT. **699**. f. **6**. (**10**.)

—— [Another copy.] T. **1979**. (**10**.)

—— [Another copy.] **222**. e. **2**. (**1**.)

—— [A reissue.] *For Ric. Chiswell: London,* 1689. 4°. **699**. f. **4**. (**9**.)
The second part has a separate titlepage reading "Reflections on the Oxford Theses, relating to the English Reformation. Part II. Amsterdam: Printed for J. S. 1688."

—— Reflections upon a Pamphlet [by George Hickes], entituled, Some Discourses upon Dr. Burnet and Dr. Tillotson, occasioned by the late funeral-sermon of the former upon the later. pp. 166. *For Ri. Chiswell: London,* 1696. 8°. **699**. f. **33**.
The running title is "The Bishop of Sarum's Vindication."

—— A Relation of a Conference held about Religion, at London, the third of April, 1676. By Edw. Stillingfleet, D.D. and G. Burnet, with some gentlemen of the Church of Rome. [By G. Burnet.] pp. 58. 193. 1676. 8°. *See* STILLINGFLEET (Edward) *Bishop of Worcester.* **3936**. bb. **6**.

—— [Another edition.] pp. 64. 1687. 4°. *See* STILLINGFLEET (Edward) *Bishop of Worcester.* **699**. e. **11**. (**1**.)

—— A Relation of the Barbarous and Bloody Massacre of about an hundred thousand Protestants, begun at Paris . . . in the year 1572. Collected out of Mezeray, Thuanus, and other approved authors, *etc.* [By G. Burnet.] pp. 63. 1745. 8°. *See* PROTESTANTS. **4632**. b. **29**.

—— Remarks on the Examination [by Jonathan Edwards] of the Exposition of the Second Article of our Church. pp. 8. *Ri. Chiswell: London,* 1702. 4°. **699**. f. **3**. (**20**.)

—— [Another edition.] pp. 8. *John Ware: Dublin,* 1702. 4°. **4224**. e. **59**.

—— A Review of the Reflections on the Prince of Orange's Declaration. By the Prince of Orange's special command. [By G. Burnet.] pp. 4. 1688. fol. *See* WILLIAM III., *King of Great Britain and Ireland.* **816**. m. **3**. (**57**.)

—— A Discourse concerning Transubstantiation and Idolatry. Being an answer to the Bishop of Oxford's Plea relating to those two points. [A new edition of the work originally published as "A Second Part of the Enquiry into the Reasons offered by Sa. Oxon for Abrogating the Test." By G. Burnet.] pp. 36. 1688. 4°. *See* PARKER (Samuel) *Bishop of Oxford.* **859**. h. **16**.

—— [Another copy.] A Discourse concerning Transubstantiation, *etc.* 1688. 4°. *See* PARKER (Samuel) *Bishop of Oxford.* **1482**. aaa. **26**. (**2**.)

—— [Another copy.] **3936**. bbb. **2**. (**4**.)

—— [Another copy.] T. **1867**. (**8**.)

—— [Another copy.] **222**. a. **10**. (**4**.)

—— Tweede deel van het Onderzoek over de redenen die tot vernietiginge van den Test zijn gepresenteert geweest door Sa: Oxon. Of een antwoord op zyn pleytinge voor de transubstantiatie; en zyn verontschuldiging der Roomsche Kerk wegens afgodery. [A translation of "A Second Part of the Enquiry into the Reasons offered by Sa. Oxon for Abrogating the Test." By G. Burnet.] pp. 14. [1688.] 4°. *See* PARKER (Samuel) *Bishop of Oxford.* **8122**. ee. **10**. (**28***.)

—— Some Letters. Containing, an account of what seemed most remarkable in Switzerland, Italy, *etc. See* supra: TRAVELS.

—— Some Passages of the Life and Death of the Right Honourable John, Earl of Rochester . . . Written by his own direction on his death-bed, by Gilbert Burnet, D.D. [With a portrait.] pp. 182. *For Richard Chiswel: London,* 1680. 8°. **1418**. c. **43**.

—— The sixth edition. pp. 132. *J. Walthoe, etc.: London,* 1724. 8°. **490**. e. **6**. (**1**.)

—— [Another edition.] To which is subjoined, a further account of his conversion, and penitential sentiments by Robert Parsons. pp. 90. *R. & A. Foulis: Glasgow,* 1752. 8°. **4903**. c. **66**.

—— [Another edition.] With a sermon, preached, at the funeral of the said Earl by the Rev. Robert Parsons . . . To this edition is prefixed some account of the life and writings of the Earl of Rochester by Dr. Samuel Johnson [from his "Lives of the Poets"]. pp. xvi. 136. *T. Davies: London,* 1782. 8°. **275**. d. **33**.

—— [Another edition.] pp. 144. *W. Lowndes: London,* 1787. 12°. **10815**. de. **10**.

—— A new edition, *etc.* pp. 144. *W. Baynes: London,* 1805. 12°. **4903**. cc. **26**.

—— A new edition, *etc.* pp. 144. *W. Baynes: London,* 1810. 12°. **10817**. b. **5**.

—— [Another edition.] To which are prefixed two criticisms on the writings of the Earl of Rochester by the Honourable Horace Walpole and Dr. Samuel Johnson. pp. 143. *Ogle, Duncan & Co.: London,* 1819. 12°. **4903**. cc. **25**.

— [Another edition.] pp. 141. *W. Baynes & Son: London,* 1820. 12°. **10826.** aa. **5.**

— [Another edition.] pp. xii. 186. *T. Webster: Chedgrave,* [1820 ?] 12°. **4906.** de. **8.**

— [Another edition.] Reprinted in facsimile from the edition of 1680. With an introductory preface by Lord Ronald Gower. pp. vii. 182. *Elliot Stock: London,* 1875. 8°. **10817.** b. **13.**

— Bericht vom Leben und Ende des durch göttliche Gnade auff dem Todt-Bett bekehrten welt-bekandten Atheistens, Grafen Johns von Rochester . . . Deme beygefügt die bey ermeldten Grafens Leich-Begängniss . . . gehaltene Predigt von Robert Parsons, beydes ins Teutsche übersetzt, und zum andern mal heraus gegeben. pp. 282. *C. Henckel: Halle,* 1698. 12°. **1224.** d. **16.** (**6.**)

— The Libertine Overthrown: or, a Mirror for atheists . . . Containing a compendious account of the egregious vicious life, and eminently and sincerely penitent death of . . . John Earl of Rochester . . . Abstracted from the remarks of the Right Reverend Gilbert Burnet . . . and the Reverend Mr. Parsons. pp. 16. *J. Bradford: London,* [1700 ?] 8°. **1078.** k. **22.** (**2.**)

— [Another copy.] **491.** c. **13.** (**1.**)

— Some Reflections on his Majesty's Proclamation of the 12th of February 168$\frac{6}{7}$ for a Toleration in Scotland [by G. Burnet], together with the said Proclamation. pp. 8. [1687.] 4°. *See* Scotland.—*Proclamations.*—James ii., *King of Great Britain and Ireland.* **701.** d. **23.**

— [Another copy.] **4175.** bb. **12.**

— [Another copy.] **116.** c. **30.**

— [Another copy.] **111.** g. **44.**

— The Bishop of Salisbury, his Speech in the House of Lords, on the first article of the impeachment of Dr. Henry Sacheverell. pp. 16. *London,* 1710. 8°. E. **1989.** (**20.**)

— [Another copy.] **111.** a. **67.**

— [Another copy, with a different titlepage.] **518.** e. **4.** (**8.**)

— The Bishop of Salisbury's and the Bishop of Oxford's Speeches in the House of Lords on the first article of impeachment of Dr. Henry Sacheverell; and also, the Bishop of Lincoln's and Bishop of Norwich's speeches at the opening of the second article of the said impeachment. 2 pt. *John Morphew: London,* 1710. fol. **514.** l. **6.** (**4.**)

— [Another edition.] pp. 16. 16. 33–63. *John Morphew: London,* 1710. 8°. **518.** e. **3.** (**2.**)

— [Another copy.] **109.** c. **47.**

— [Another edition.] pp. 16. 16. 33–63. *John Morphew: London,* 1710. 8°. **518.** e. **2.** (**2.**)

— [Another edition.] pp. 16. 16. 33–63. *John Morphew: London,* 1710. 8°. **228.** g. **26.** (**2.**)

— Remarks on the Several Paragraphs of the Bishop of Salisbury's Speech in relation to the First Article of Dr. Sacheverell's Impeachment. In a letter to a friend. By a Presbyter of the Church of England. pp. 36. *William Ayscough: Nottingham,* 1710. 4°. **699.** f. **7.** (**6.**)

— [Another copy.] **111.** b. **28.**

— Some Considerations humbly offer'd to the Right Reverend the Ld. Bp. of Salisbury. Occasion'd by his Lordship's speech, upon the first article of Dr. Sacheverell's impeachment . . . By a Lay Hand [i.e. Edmund Curll]. pp. 38. *J. Morphew: London,* 1710. 8°. **698.** h. **13.** (**6.**)

— The second edition. pp. 40. *J. Morphew: London,* 1710. 8°. C. **28.** b. **11.** (**2.**)

— Some Queries propos'd to the Publisher of a certain Pamphlet called the Bishop of S - - - m's Speech, in the House of Lords, on the first article of the impeachment, of Dr. Henry Sacheverell, *etc.* pp. 16. *Sold by the Booksellers: London,* [1710.] 8°. **8138.** aa. **12.**

— A True Answer to the Bishop of Salisbury's Speech in the House of Lords on the first article of impeachment of Dr. Hen. Sacheverell, *etc.* [The dedication signed: L. H.] 1710. 8°. *See* H., L. **8138.** aa. **13.**

— A Vindication of the Bishop of Salisbury and Passive Obedience, with some remarks upon a speech which goes under his Lordship's name [entitled "The Bishop of Salisbury his Speech . . . on the first article of the impeachment of Dr. Henry Sacheverell"]. And a postscript in answer to a book [by Edmund Curll], just publish'd, entitul'd Some Considerations humbly offer'd to . . . the Lord Bishop of Salisbury, &c. pp. 16. 1710. 8°. **109.** c. **50.**

— The Bishop of Salisbury's Speech in the House of Lords, upon the Bill against Occasional Conformity. pp. 8. *Ri. Chiswell: London,* 1704. 4°. **698.** i. **35.**

— [Another copy.] **699.** f. **4.** (**21.**)

— *See* Layman. The Lay-man's Letter to the B — p of S — — y, in answer to his Speech for Occasional Conformity. 1704. 4°. **699.** f. **4.** (**22.**)

— The Bishop of Salisbury's Proper Defence from a Speech cry'd about the streets in his name, and said to have been spoken by him in the House of Lords, upon the Bill against Occasional Conformity. [By Charles Leslie.] pp. 58. *Sold by the Booksellers of London & Westminster,* 1704. 4°. **698.** i. **34.**

— [Another copy.] **701.** g. **21.** (**2.**)

— A Letter from a Country Justice of the Peace . . . concerning the Bishop of Salisbury's Speech in the House of Lords, upon the Bill against Occasional Conformity. [Signed: A. B. C.] 1704. 4°. *See* C., A. B. **4136.** b. **13.**

— The Orator Display'd: or, Remarks on the B - - - - - p of S - - - - bury's Speech upon the Bill against Occasional Conformity. [The dedication signed: H. E.] 1704. 4°. *See* E., H. **699.** f. **7.** (**4.**)

— [Another copy.] T. **704.** (**1.**)

— A Serious Answer, paragraph by paragraph, to the Bishop of Salisbury's Speech in the House of Lords upon the Bill against Occasional Conformity. pp. 40. *London,* 1704. 8°. **4106.** aaa. **4.**

— D. F. A.'s [i.e. Doctor Francis Atterbury's] Vindication of the Bp. of Sarum, from being the author of a late printed speech [on the Bill against Occasional Conformity,] *etc.* 1704. 4°. *See* A., D. F. **699.** f. **7.** (**5.**)

—— Thoughts on Education . . . Now first printed from an original manuscript. pp. xiii. 94. *D. Wilson: London,* 1761. 8°. **8305. b. 19.**

—— Bishop Gilbert Burnet as Educationist, being his Thoughts on Education with notes and life of the author. By John Clarke. pp. xi. 246. *Aberdeen,* 1914. 8°. [*Aberdeen University Studies.* no. 67.] Ac. **1482.**

—— [Another copy, with a different titlepage.] *D. Wyllie & Son: Aberdeen,* 1914. 8°. **8308. b. 11.**

—— Three Letters concerning the Present State of Italy, *etc. See* supra: TRAVELS.

—— A True Copy of the Last Will and Testament of the Right Reverend Father in God, Gilbert Lord Bishop of Sarum. (Containing, I. His profession of faith. II. His charitable benefactions.) *See* infra: APPENDIX. A Character of . . . Gilbert, Lord Bishop of Sarum, *etc.* 1715. 8°. **491. c. 10. (10.)**

—— [Another edition.] *See* infra: APPENDIX. A character of . . . Gilbert, Lord Bishop of Sarum, *etc.* [1715.] 8°. **491. c. 10. (11.)**

—— [Another edition.] To which is added, the inscription on the monument erected to his memory, in the parish church of St. James Clerkenwell. The fourth edition. pp. 24. *E. Curll: London,* 1717. 8°. **613. f. 20. (1.)**

—— The Lives and Last Wills and Testaments of the following eminent persons. I. Dr. Gilbert Burnet . . . II. Dr. Thomas Burnet . . . III. Dr. George Hickes . . . IV. Dr. Daniel Williams . . . V. Joseph Addison . . . VI. Mr. Mahomet . . . With several other valuable tracts, now first collected into a volume. 13 pt. *H. Curll: London,* 1728. 8°. G. **13773.**

—— [Another copy.] G. **13774.**

—— [Another edition.] [Two Dissertations. 1. A Defence of Polygamy . . . 2. That Sterility in Women is a sufficient cause of Divorce.] pp. 3–16. *See* CHAMBERS (John) *Esq., of Hereford.* Bibliotheca Recondita, *etc.* vol. 2. 1739. 12°. G. **13457. (1.)**

—— The Unreasonableness and Impiety of Popery: in a second letter written upon the discovery of the late plot. [By G. Burnet.] pp. 36. 1678. 4°. *See* POPERY. **3936. d. 42.**

—— [Another copy.] **108. d. 59.**

—— Dr. Burnet's Vindication of himself from the Calumnies with which he is aspersed, in a pamphlet, entitled, Parliamentum Pacificum [by John Northleigh], *etc.* pp. 8. 1688. 4°. **699. f. 6. (9.)**

—— Dr. Burnet's Vindicatie zijns selfs, van de lasteringen die op hem geworpen zijn, in een schrift, geintituleert Parliamentum Pacificum, *etc.* pp. 15. [1688.] 4°. **1103. f. 27. (9.)**

—— Verantwoordinge van Dr. Dilbert Burnet, van wegen de lasteringen tegenhem uitgestroid, in een geschrift genaamd Parlamentum Pacificum . . . Uit het Engels vertaald door E. W. [i.e. E. Walten.] pp. 20. 1688. 4°. **8122. ee. 10. (24.)**
A different translation from the preceding.

—— Défense de M. Burnet . . . composée en anglois par luy-même: pour réfuter les calomnies d'un livret intitulé, Parliamentum Pacificum, *etc.* pp. 38. 1688. 12°. **104. k. 29.**

—— A Vindication of the Authority, Constitution, and Laws of the Church and State of Scotland. In four conferences. Wherein the Answer to the Dialogues betwixt the Conformist and the Non-conformist, is examined. [With "Observations on the First and Second of the Canons, commonly ascribed to the Holy Apostles."] 2 pt. *By Robert Sanders: Glasgow,* 1673. 8°. **1019. d. 11.**

—— [Another edition.] 2 pt. *By Robert Sanders: Glasgow,* 1673. 8°. G. **5258.**

—— [Another copy of pt. 2.] **5063. a. 9.**
Imperfect; wanting all after sig. Kk 1.

—— A Vindication of the Ordinations of the Church of England. In which it is demonstrated that all the essentials of ordination, according to the practice of the primitive and Greek churches, are still retained in our church. In answer to a paper written by one of the Church of Rome to prove the nullity of our orders [entitled "Arguments to prove the Invalidity of the Orders of the Church of England"]. (An Appendix. About the forms of ordaining Priests and Bishops in the Latin Church.) pp. 181. *E. H. & T. H. for R. Chiswell: London,* 1677. 8°. **699. f. 30.**

—— The second edition. pp. xxviii. 94. 1688. 4°. *See* ENGLAND.—*Church of England.* [*Appendix.*] T. **1875. (2.)**

—— [Another edition.] *See* POPERY. A Preservative against Popery, *etc.* vol. 2. 1738. fol. **478. f. 12.**

—— [Another edition.] 1848. *See* GIBSON (Edmund) successively *Bishop of Lincoln* and *of London.* A Preservative against Popery, *etc.* vol. 2. 1848, *etc.* 8°. **3940. k. 6/2.**

WORKS EDITED, TRANSLATED, OR WITH CONTRIBUTIONS BY BURNET.

—— *See* CHRISTIAN RELIGION. The Life of God in the Soul of Man, *etc.* [With a preface by G. Burnet.] 1677. 8°. **4402. bbb. 39.**

—— —— 1707. 8°. **851. g. 16.**

—— —— 1739. 12°. **4405. ff. 12.**

—— —— 1742. 12°. **C.121.a.6.**

—— —— 1782. 12°. **4409. aaa. 13.**

—— —— 1807. 12°. **4403. cc. 24. (1.)**

—— —— 1819. 12°. **4404. ccc. 23**

—— *See* CHRISTIAN RELIGION. La Nature et l'excellence de la religion chrétienne. Avec une préface de Mr G. Burnet, *etc.* 1722. 8°. **4407. de. 25.**

—— *See* DRUMMOND (John) *Earl of Melfort.* The Earle of Melfort's Letter to the Presbyterian-Ministers in Scotland . . . together with some remarks upon it [by G. Burnet]. 1687. 4°. **111. g. 28.**

—— *See* DU MOULIN (L.) The Last Words of Lewis du Moulin: being his retractation of all the personal reflections he had made on the divines of the Church of England, *etc.* [Related by G. Burnet.] 1680. 4°. **699. f. 4. (6.)**

BURNET (GILBERT) *Bishop of Salisbury.* [WORKS EDITED, TRANSLATED, OR WITH CONTRIBUTIONS BY BURNET.]

— *See* FAGEL (G.) A Letter writ by Mijn Heer Fagel . . . to Mr. James Stewart . . . giving an account of the Prince and Princess of Orange's thoughts concerning the repeal of the Test and the Penal Laws. (Nov. 4, 1687.) [Translated by Bishop Burnet.] 1688. 4°. **T. 2230. (8.)**

— — 1688. 4°. **T. 1701. (3.)**

— — 1692. fol. **2082.e.**

— — 1748. 4°. **184. a. 2.**

— *See* FRANCE.—*Church of France.—Assemblée générale du Clergé.* The Letter writ by the last Assembly General of the Clergy of France to the Protestants, inviting them to return to their Communion . . . Translated . . . and examined by G. Burnet. 1683. 8°. **699. f. 32.**

— *See* GUIDE. A Discourse concerning a Guide in Controversies, in two letters, *etc.* [With a preface by G. Burnet.] 1728. 8°. **702. g. 5. (5.)**

— *See* LACTANTIUS (L. C. F.) A Relation of the Death of the Primitive Persecutors . . . English'd by G. Burnet, D.D. To which he hath made a large preface concerning persecution. 1687. 12°. **1019. g. 19. (1.)**

— — 1715. 8°. **3805. a. 43.**

— *See* PALLAVICINO (S.) *Cardinal.* The New Politick Lights of Modern Romes Church-Government . . . Englished out of French [by G. Burnet]. 1678. 8°. **5016. aa. 29.**

— *See* PALLAVICINO (S.) *Cardinal.* The Policy of Rome . . . Englished out of French. With a preface, by G. Burnet. 1681. 8°. **5016. aa. 29.**

— *See* ROME.—[*Emperors.*]—Justinian I., *Emperor of the East.* [527–565.] [*Digesta.—Single Titles.*] An Edict in the Roman Law: in the 25. Book of the Digests, Title 4. Section 10, *etc.* [Translated, with a commentary, by G. Burnet.] [1688.] 4°. **498. e. 23.**

— *See* ROME, *Church of.*—Innocent XI., *Pope.* A Decree made at Rome the second of March, 1679, condemning some opinions of the Jesuits and other casuists. [With an English preface and translation by G. Burnet.] 1679. 4°. **4091. e. 49.**

— *See* ROME, *Church of.* [*Appendix.*] Romes Glory; or, a Collection of divers miracles wrought by Popish saints . . . Together with a prefatory discourse, declaring the impossibility and folly of such vain impostures [by G. Burnet]. 1673. 8°. **1115. a. 30.**

— *See* SCOUGAL (Henry) The Works of the Rev. H. Scougal . . . Containing the Life of God in the Soul of Man . . . To which is added . . . a preface, by Bishop Burnet. 1818. 12°. **4423. a. 33.**

— *See* SCOUGAL (Henry) The Life of God in the Soul of Man . . . With a preface, by G. Burnet, *etc.* 1733. 8°. **4384. bb. 30.**

— *See* SCOUGAL (Henry) The Life of God in the Soul of Man . . . With recommendatory prefaces by Bishop Burnet and the late Dr. Wishart. 1791. 16°. **4408. aa. 29.**

BURNET (GILBERT) *Bishop of Salisbury.* [WORKS EDITED, TRANSLATED, OR WITH CONTRIBUTIONS BY BURNET.]

— *See* STERN (Johann) *Gent.* The Last Confession . . . of Lieuten. John Stern . . . with the last confession of George Borosky . . . With which an account is given of their deportment . . . in the prison . . . Written by G. Burnet, *etc.* 1682. fol. **669. d. 1. (8.)**

— — 1746. 4°. [*Harleian Miscellany.* vol. 8.] **185. a. 12.**

— — 1810. 8°. [*Harleian Miscellany.* vol. 9.] **1326. g. 9.**

— — 1811. 4°. [*Harleian Miscellany.* vol. 8.] **2072.g.**

— *See* STEWART (*Sir* James) *Bart., Lord Advocate of Scotland.* Some Extracts, out of Mr. James Stewart's Letters, which were communicated to Myn Heer Fagel . . . Together with some references to Mr. Stewart's printed letter. [Edited by G. Burnet.] [1688.] 4°. **699. f. 4. (15.)**

— — 1689. 4°. [*FAGEL (Gaspar) Their Highness the Prince & Princess of Orange's Opinion about a General Liberty of Conscience, etc.*] **3936. d. 54.**

— *See* TENISON (Thomas) successively *Bishop of Lincoln* and *Archbishop of Canterbury.* His Grace the Lord Archbishop of Canterbury's Letter to the Right Reverend the Lords Bishops of his Province. [With a letter from G. Burnet communicating it to the archdeacons of his diocese.] 1699. 4°. **699. f. 4. (19.)**

— *See* THOMAS [More] *Saint, Lord High Chancellor of England.* [*Utopia.—Burnet's translation.*] Utopia . . . Translated into English [by G. Burnet]. 1684. 8°. **714. b. 14.**

— — 1737. 12°. **6495. a. 38.**

— — 1743. 8°. **12350. d. 12.**

— — 1751. 12°. **12350. c. 29.**

— — 1753. 12°. **12350. c. 28.**

— — 1758. 8°. [*WARNER (Ferdinando) Memoirs of the Life of Sir Thomas More, etc.*] **1130. e. 8.**

— — 1762. 16°. **12331. d. 23.**

— — 1795. 8°. [*ROUSSEAU (J. J.) A Treatise on the Social Compact, etc.*] **8005. cc. 12.**

— — 1838. 8°. [*SAINT JOHN (James A.) Masterpieces of English Prose Literature.* vol. 4.] **1154. c. 8.**

— — 1850. 12°. **3605.a.12/6.**

— — 1885. 8°. [*MORLEY (Henry) Professor of English Literature, etc. Ideal Commonwealths.*] **12204.gg.1/23.**

— — 1889. 8°. **12208.bb.15/182.**

— — 1904. 8°. **012209. ff. 43.**

— — 1906. 8°. **012203. f. 33/14.**

— — [1908.] 8°. **12201. d. 31/229.**

DOUBTFUL OR SUPPOSITITIOUS WORKS.

— Animadversions on Mr. Hill's Book, entituled, A Vindication of the Primitive Fathers, against the Imputations of Gilbert, Lord Bishop of Sarum. In a letter to a person of quality. [By G. Burnet? Attributed also to Pierre Allix.] pp. 65. 1695. 4°. *See* HILL (Samuel) *Archdeacon of Wells.* **699. f. 6. (18.)**

—— *See* Holdsworth (Thomas) *Rector of Stoneham.* Impar conatui . . . With some account of the late scandalous Animadversions on Mr. Hill's book, intituled, A Vindication of the Primitive Fathers against the Imputations of Gilbert, Lord Bishop of Sarum, *etc.* 1695. 4°. **T. 688. (4.)**

—— The Court Sermon: 1674. Supposed to have been written by G. Burnet. [The editor's preface signed: R. C., i.e. Robert Clarke.] pp. viii. 54.
R. Clarke & Co.: Cincinnati, 1868. 8°. **4477. f. 78.**
The attribution to Burnet is false.

—— An Elegy on the Death of that illustrious Monarch William the Third, late King of England . . . Written by the Reverend Dr. Burnet. *E. Hawkins: London,* 1702. *s. sh.* fol. **C. 20. f. 2. (223.)**

—— The Ill Effects of Animosities among Protestants in England detected, *etc.* [By G. Burnet?] pp. 23. 1688. 4°. *See* England.—*Protestants.* [*Appendix.*] **698. i. 2. (7.)**

—— [Another copy.] **108. e. 54.**

—— Vertoog vande droevige uytwerckingen vande bitterheid, dieder is tusschen de Protestanten van Engeland . . . Uyt het Engelsch vertaalt. pp. 31. 1687. 4°. *See* England.—*Protestants.* [*Appendix.*] **8122. ee. 9. (44.)**

—— Les Funestes efets de l'animosité qui est entre les Protestans d'Angleterre mis en evidence . . . Traduit de l'anglois. pp. 90. ms. notes. 1687. 24°. *See* England.—*Protestants.* [*Appendix.*] **600. a. 22. (2.)**

—— [Another issue.] 1687. 12°. [*Recueil de plusieurs pieces concernant les affaires presentes d'Angleterre, etc.* tom. 2.] *See* England.—*Protestants.* [*Appendix.*] **C. 65. a. 24.**

—— A Letter from the Right Reverend G - - - - - lb - - - - - rt, late Lord Bishop of S - - - - - m, to the Right Reverend B - - - nj - - - - m - - - n, L - - d B - - - p of B - - ng - - r. [A satire.] pp. 21. 1717. 8°. *See* G - - - - - lb - - - - - rt, *Bishop of S - - - - - m.* **109. e. 64.**

—— The third edition. pp. 21. 1717. 8°. *See* G - - - - - lb - - - - - rt, *Bishop of S - - - - - m.* **4108. b. 7.**

—— A Letter to a Member of the House of Commons, concerning the proceedings against the Bishop of St. David's. [By G. Burnet?] pp. 11. [1699?] 4°. *See* Watson (Thomas) *Bishop of St. Davids.* **517. g. 38.**

—— Dr. Burnet's Letter to his Friend in London. Being an answer to a late scurrilous pamphlet entituled his Farewel. *G. C. for A. Gad: London,* 1683. *s. sh.* fol. **8133. g. 14.**
Cropped.

—— The Lives and Sufferings of the English Martyrs, who were executed and burnt for their religion, from the reign of Henry the ivth, to the end of the reign of Queen Mary i. and to the Reformation of the Church of England. Published by Bishop Burnet, for the use of all Christian families. [With plates.] pp. x. 427. *H. Owen & C. Sympson: London,* 1755. 8°. **1367. i. 19.**

—— A Memorial offered to her Royal Highness the Princess Sophia, Electoress and Duchess Dowager of Hanover. Containing a delineation of the constitution and policy of England . . . Now first published . . . [by J. G. H. Feder] according to the originals in the Royal Library at Hanover. By Gilbert Burnet [or rather, by George Smyth of North Nibley?] . . . To which are added, Letters from Burnet and Leibnitz, and fac similes of the handwriting, *etc.* pp. xiii. 125. *J. Mawman: London,* 1815. 8°. **195. b. 16.**

—— The Pious Instructor: or, the Heavenly warning piece. Being a token for youth . . . Written by Dr B—t, late Ld. Bishop of S—y, and found in his closet after his decease. [Purporting to be by G. Burnet.] pp. 8. [1715?] 8°. See B-t, Ld. Bishop of S-y. **4404. d. 3.**

—— The Protestant's Companion: or, an Impartial survey and comparison of the Protestant religion . . . With the main doctrines of Popery . . . By a true son of the Protestant Church of England [i.e. G. Burnet?], *etc.* pp. 45. 1685. 4°. *See* Protestant. **T. 1982. (10.)**

—— Samuel Lord Bishop of Oxon, his celebrated Reasons for abrogating the Test and Notion of Idolatry, answered by Samuel Archdeacon of Canterbury. [Here attributed to G. Burnet, but in fact written by John Phillips, Milton's nephew.] 1813. *See* Somers (John) *Baron Somers.* A Collection of Scarce and Valuable Tracts, *etc.* vol. 9. 1809, *etc.* 4°. **750. g. 9.**

—— Dr Burnet's Sermon of the Unpardonable Sin against the Holy Ghost; or, the Sin unto Death, *etc.* pp. 8.
H. Hills: London, 1707. 8°. **4474. bb. 8.**

Appendix.

—— *See* B——, *Mr., a North Wiltshire Clergyman.* A Letter to Mr. B—— . . . Wherein a character is given of the Bishop of Sarum, and an account of the clergy's behaviour towards him. 1710. 8°. **T. 1815. (6.)**

—— *See* B., A. Histrio Theologicus: or, an Historical-political-theological poetical account of the most remarkable passages . . . in the life of the late B—p of S—m [i.e. G. Burnet], *etc.* [A satire.] 1715. 8°. **G. 14173.**

—— *See* B - - - t, *Dr.* Dr. B - - - t's Farewell, Confessor to the late King of Poland; upon his translation to the Sey of Hungary. [A satire.] [1683.] *s. sh.* fol. **8133. g. 5.**

—— *See* Clarke (Thomas E. S.) A Life of Gilbert Burnet, Bishop of Salisbury. i. Scotland 1643–1674. By T. E. S. Clarke . . . ii. England 1674–1715. With bibliographical appendixes. By H. C. Foxcroft, *etc.* 1907. 8°. **4902. h. 7.**

—— *See* Conder (George W.) Bishop Burnet and the Times of the English Revolution and Protestant Settlement, *etc.* [1863.] 8°. **4461. d. 27.**

—— *See* England. [*Treaties, etc.*—ii. Charles ii.] Aenmerkinge op de Articulen raeckende de fugitiven en rebellen, zoo vanden Koninck van Engelandt, als van desen Staet, begrepen en het vi. en vii. articul van het Tractaet van Vreede . . . gesloten tot London 1662 . . . Met een bysondere reflexien op de Memorien van . . . den Marquis d'Albevylle, zoo raeckende den Doctor Burnet als 't oversenden vande ses Engelse en Schotse regimenten. 1688. 4°. **8122. d. 2. (3.)**

BURNET (Gilbert) *Bishop of Salisbury.* [Appendix.]

—— *See* England.—*Church of England.—Convocation.—Province of Canterbury.—Lower House.* The Humble Representation and Complaint of the Lower House of Convocation, against the Right Reverend the Bishop of Sarum, *etc.* 1705. 4°. **698**. h. **21**. **(15.)**

—— *See* Gilbertini, *Signor.* A Dialogue of the Dead; between the very eminent Signor Glibertini [*sic*] [i.e. G. Burnet], and Count Thomaso [i.e. Thomas Wharton] in the vales of Acheron. 1715. 8°. **12315**. g. **37**.

—— *See* Haddington, *Presbytery of.* Extracts from the Acts and Proceedings of the Presbytery of Haddington, relating to Dr. Gilbert Burnet and the library of the Kirk of Salton. MDCLXIV.–MDCLXIX. 1855. 4° [*Bannatyne Miscellany.* vol. 3.] Ac. **8248/19**.

—— *See* Horneck (Anthony) A Sermon preached at Fulham . . . at the consecration of . . . Gilbert, Lord Bishop of Sarum. 1689. 4°. **694**. d. **3**. **(11.)**

—— *See* Le Clerc (Jean) *of Amsterdam.* The Life of Dr. Burnet, late Lord Bishop of Sarum; with his character, and an account of his writings, *etc.* 1715. 8°. T. **1092**. **(4.)**

—— *See* Letter. Falshood detected in a defence of a Letter out of the Countrey to a Member of Parliament concerning the Bishops then under suspension. Against a late printed sheet falsely charging the Bishop of S - - - - ry, as the author of that letter, *etc.* 1690. 4°. **4103**. cc. **8**.

—— *See* Lowth (Simon) A Letter to Edw. Stillingfleet, D.D. &c. in answer to the epistle dedicatory before his sermon, preached . . . March 15. 168$\frac{4}{5}$ . . . With some reflections upon certain letters, which Dr. Burnet wrote on the same occasion. 1687. 4°. **699**. e. **11**. **(2.)**

—— *See* Miso-Dolos, *pseud.* The Good Old Cause; or, Lying in truth, being a second defence of the Lord Bishop of Sarum, from a second speech. [A criticism of G. Burnet's "Speech in the House of Lords, on the first article of the impeachment of Dr. Henry Sacheverell."] And also the dissection of a sermon it is said his Lordship preached . . . last 29th of May, *etc.* 1710. 4°. T. **704**. **(2, 3.)**

—— *See* Miso-Dolos, *pseud.* [i.e. Charles Leslie.] The Good Old Cause . . . being a second defence of the Lord Bishop of Sarum, *etc.* 1710. 4°. T. **1666**. **(14.)**

—— *See* Notes. Notes and Memorandums of the six days preceding the death of a late Right Reverend - - - - - - [i.e. G. Burnet], *etc.* [A satire.] 1715, *etc.* 8°. **4903**. c. **47**.

—— *See* Pearson (Samuel) Bishop Burnet and Contemporary Schemes of Church Comprehension. 1882. 8°. [*Congregational Union. Jubilee Lectures, etc.* vol. 2.] **4715**. c. **3**.

—— *See* Protestant Elm-Board. The Last Words and Sayings of the True-Protestant Elm-Board, which lately suffer'd martyrdom in Smithfield . . . Together with a true relation of a conference between Dr. B—— and the said Board. 1682. *s. sh.* fol. **816**. m. **19**. **(54.)**

—— *See* Protestant Elm-Board. More Last Words and Sayings of the True Protestant Elm-Board: or, a full answer to a late pretended sober vindication of the Dr. [i.e. G. Burnet] and the Board. 1682. *s. sh.* fol. **1881**. c. **3**. **(29.)**

—— *See* Sewell (George) An Essay towards a true Account of the Life and Character of the late Bishop of Salisbury; in remarks upon, and collections from his own writings. 1715. 8°. **702**. f. **10**. **(5.)**

—— *See* Tenison (Thomas) successively *Bishop of Lincoln* and *Archbishop of Canterbury.* A True Copy of the Arch-Bishop of Canterbury's Speech, in Jerusalem Chamber, on Thursday, February 19. 170$\frac{1}{2}$. [A reply to an address of Convocation complaining of a breach of its privileges by G. Burnet.] [1702.] 4°. **1897**. c. **19**. **(78.)**

—— *See* Ward (*Sir* Adolphus W.) Historical and Political Writers. I. Burnet, *etc.* 1912. 8°. [*Cambridge History of English Literature.* vol. 9.] **11870.g.1.**

—— An Answer to a Letter from a Citizen of New Sarum. being a true account of the affront offer'd the Bishop [G. Burnet] there: and a fresh proof of the mallice and injustice of his enemies. [By John Hoadly, successively Bishop of Leighlin and Ferns, Archbishop of Dublin and Archbishop of Armagh.] pp. 4. [1710.] fol. **1879**. cc. **15**. **(48.)**

—— Bibliotheca Burnetiana: or a Catalogue of the library of the late . . . Dr. Gilbert Burnet . . . which will begin to be sold by auction . . . the 19th of March, 17$\frac{15}{16}$, *etc.* pp. 68. *Thomas Ballard: London,* [1716.] 8°. S.C. **283**. **(1.)**

—— A Character of the Right Reverend Father in God Gilbert Lord Bishop of Sarum [by Sir Thomas Burnet]: with a true copy of his last will and testament . . . The second edition. pp. 32. *J. Roberts: London,* 1715. 8°. **491**. c. **10**. **(10.)**

—— [Another copy.] T. **1092**. **(4*.)**
Imperfect; wanting the titlepage.

—— [Another copy.] **1415**. b. **61**.
Imperfect; wanting the last leaf.

—— The third edition. pp. 32. *E. Curll: London,* [1715.] 8°. **491**. c. **10**. **(11.)**

—— The Citation of Gilbert Burnet D.D. . . . to answer in Scotland on the 27. June old stile, for High Treason: together with his answer; and three letters, writ by him, upon that subject, to the Right Honourable the Earl of Midletoune, his Majesties Secretary of State. pp. 4. [*The Hague?* 1687.] 4°. T. **1684**. **(7.)**

—— [Another copy.] T. **2029**. **(6.)**

—— [Another edition.] pp. 8. [*London?* 1687.] 4°. **113**. i. **62**.

—— De Citatie van Gilbert Burnet, Predikant. Om hem te komen verantwoorden in Schotland, den 27 Juny, oude stijl, wegens de beschuldiginge van hoog-verraat: met sijn antwoorde; en drie brieven door hem, dieshalven, geschreven aan den graaf van Midletoune . . . nu in Duyts vertaald. pp. 20. 1687. 4°. **8122**. ee. **9**. **(43.)**

—— [Another copy.] **8122**. b. **12**.

—— Lettres de citation à Mr Burnet . . . pour comparoître en Écosse le 27. juin, vieux stile. Avec la Réponse de ce Docteur, & trois lettres qu'il a écrites sur ce sujet, au Comte de Midletoune. pp. 24. 1687. 4°. **699**. f. **6**. **(7.)**

—— [Another edition.] pp. 48. *See* England. [*Appendix.—History and Politics.*—II. 1687.] Recueil de plusieurs pièces concernant les affaires presentes d'Angleterre. tom. 1. 1687. 12°. C. **65**. a. **24**.

BURNET (GILBERT) *Bishop of Salisbury.* [APPENDIX.]

—— The Life of the Right Rev. Gilbert Burnet, Bishop of Salisbury, *etc.* [Abridged by Edward Goldney from the life by Sir Thomas Burnet published in vol. 2 of G. Burnet's "History of My Own Time." With portraits.] pp. 16. *See* GOLDNEY (Edward) Infallible Remedies, for the Perfect Cure of all Personal, and National Unhappiness, *etc.* [1770.] 8°. **4376.bb.32.(8.)**

—— The Lives and Last Wills and Testaments of the following eminent persons. I. Dr. Gilbert Burnet, *etc. See* supra: MINOR WORKS. A True Copy of the Last Will and Testament of . . . Gilbert Lord Bishop of Sarum, *etc.*

—— Memoriæ Sacrum, Reverendi admodum in Christo Patris D. Gilberti Burnet, Salisburiensis Episcopi, *etc.* (Ejusdem Epitaphium.) [Latin verses.] [1715.] *s. sh.* fol. **835.** m. **8.** (**17.**)

—— A Short History and Vindication of the Revolution. Collected out of the writings of the learned Bishop Burnet and Dr. Kennet. [By John Lindsay.] pp. 8. *London,* 1716. 12°. **8122.** f. **10.**

—— [Another copy.] **4105.** a. **65.** (**2.**)

—— The White Crow: or, an Enquiry into some more new doctrines broach'd by the Bp. of Salisbury, in a pair of sermons utter'd in that Cathedral, on the V. and VII. of November, 1710. And his Lordship's last Restauration sermon. [By Edmund Curll.] pp. 36. [*London,*] 1710. 8°. **698.** h. **13.** (**7.**)

—— [Another copy.] **114.** b. **61.**
In this copy pp. 33 *and* 36 *are wrongly numbered* 25 *and* 32 *respectively.*

—— The second edition corrected. [By Edmund Curll.] pp. 36. [*London,* 1710.] 8°. **4106.** b. **26.**

BURNET (GILBERT) *Professor at Montauban.* G. Burnathi . . . Ethicæ dissertationes, quibus perfecta & solida philosophię moralis idea modo accuratissimo exhibetur, *etc.* pp. 1059. *Ex officinâ I. Maire: Lugduni Batavorum,* 1649. 8°. **8410.** c. **17.**

BURNET (GILBERT) *Son of the Bishop of Salisbury.* [For editions of Bishop Burnet's "History of My Own Time," of which the first volume was edited by his son Gilbert and others:] *See* BURNET (Gilbert) *Bishop of Salisbury.* [*History of My Own Time.*]

—— *See* BURNET (Gilbert) *Bishop of Salisbury.* [*History of the Reformation of the Church of England.—Abridgments and Extracts.*] The Abridgment of the History of the Reformation of the Church of England, *etc.* (An Abridgment of the third volume. By G. Burnet [the Younger], *etc.*) 1718, *etc.* 12°. **4707.a.27.**

—— —— 1728. 8°. **4705.** a. **3.**

—— —— 1808. 8°. **488.** d. **11.**

—— —— 1847. 8°. **1367.** e. **11.**

—— An Answer to Mr. Law's Letter to the Bishop of Bangor [on his sermon entitled "The Nature of the Kingdom, or Church of Christ"], in a letter to Mr. Law. pp. 48. *Timothy Childe: London,* 1717. 8°. T. **1862.** (**2.**)

—— [Another copy.] **701.** f. **15.** (**3.**)

—— [Another copy.] **109.** e. **10.**

BURNET (GILBERT) *Son of the Bishop of Salisbury.*

—— A Full Examination of Several Important Points relating to Church-Authority, the Christian Priesthood, the positive institutions of the Christian Religion, and Church-Communion. In answer to the notions and principles contained in Mr. Law's Second Letter to the Lord Bishop of Bangor. In a second letter to Mr. Law. With a postscript wherein his evasive answers to former objections are considered. pp. xi. 338. *Tim. Childe: London,* 1718. 8°. **701.** f. **15.** (**8.**)

—— [Another copy.] **109.** e. **15.**

—— [Another copy.] **225.** b. **30.**

—— The Generation of the Son of God, as taught in the Scriptures, consider'd; and the consequents of it, as to His unity of essence, and equality with the Father, examin'd. pp. 51. *John Clark: London,* 1720. 8°. **4224.** aaa. **5.**

—— A Letter to the Reverend Mr. Trapp, occasioned by his Sermon on the Real Nature of the Church or Kingdom of Christ, in answer to the Lord Bishop of Bangor's sermon on the same text; wherein the postscript also is considered. pp. 32. *Tim. Childe: London,* 1717. 8°. T. **1759.** (**21.**)

—— [Another copy.] **701.** f. **12.** (**5.**)

—— [Another copy.] B. **624.** (**3.**)

—— The second edition. pp. 32. *Tim. Childe: London,* 1717. 8°. **701.** f. **12.** (**4.**)

—— [Another copy.] **109.** f. **20.**

—— Letters between the late Mr. Gilbert Burnet and Mr. Hutchinson [or rather, Francis Hutcheson], concerning the true foundation of virtue or moral goodness . . . To which is added, a preface and a postscript, wrote by Mr. Burnet some time before his death. pp. viii. 85. *W. Wilkins: London,* 1735. 8°. **699.** f. **8.** (**1.**)

—— Reality without Existence: or, the Lecturer of St. Martin in the Fields' . . . and St. Martin Ironmonger-Lane's sermon, called The Real Nature of the Church and Kingdom of Christ; in answer to one preach'd by the Bishop of Bangor upon the same text, proved to be unnatural . . . By a Gentleman of Oxford, that understands Trapp [i.e. G. Burnet]. pp. 38. 1717. 8°. *See* TRAPP (Joseph) *D.D.* T. **1759.** (**20.**)

—— [Another copy.] **4474.** aaa. **58.**

—— [Another copy.] **109.** e. **11.**

—— [Another edition.] pp. 26. 1717. 8°. *See* TRAPP (Joseph) *D.D.* **4105.** aa. **89.** (**8.**)

—— A Sermon preach'd at St. Paul's Covent-Garden, on the first of August, 1725. Being the most happy inauguration of his Sacred Majesty, King George. pp. 27. *J. Roberts; A. Dodd: London,* 1725. 8°. **4474.** c. **42.**

—— The Son's Equality with the Father prov'd from his being the Object of Religious Worship. In a discourse on Hebrews, I. 6. pp. 38. *John Clark: London,* 1719. 8°. T. **1782.** (**2.**)

—— Le Chevalier de St. George, réhabilité dans sa qualité de Jacques III. par de nouvelles preuves. [A translation of "Some New Proofs by which it appears that the Pretender is truly James the Third" by Sir Thomas Burnet; here wrongly attributed to his brother, G. Burnet.] Avec la relation historique des suites de sa naissance, par Mr. Rousset. pp. 388. *Imprimerie du Cokpit: Whitehall* [*Amsterdam*], 1745. 8°. G. **1871.**

BURNET (Gilbert) *Surgeon.*

—— A.F.S. Urgent First Aid. pp. 76. *National Fire Brigades' Association: London,* 1939. 8°. **07481.** ff. **81.**

—— First Aid to the Injured . . . With forty illustrations. pp. xii. 153. *National Fire Brigades' Association: London,* [1927.] 8°. **07688.** ee. **3.**

BURNET (Gilbert) *Vicar of Coggeshall.* A Defence of Natural and Revealed Religion: being an abridgment of the sermons preached at the lecture founded by the Honble. Robert Boyle, Esq. By Dr. Bentley . . . Dr. Burnet [and others] . . . With a general index. By [i.e. edited by] G. Burnet. 4 vol. *A. Bettesworth & C. Hitch: London,* 1737. 8°. **695.** e. **17–20.**

—— Practical Sermons on Various Subjects, *etc.* [Edited by William George Barnes.] 2 vol. *C. Ackers: London,* 1747. 8°. **1021.** h. **16, 17.**

BURNET (Ian M.) *See* Claremont (Claude L. L.) and Burnet (I. M.) Some Common Domestic Pests, *etc.* [1932.] 8°. **07299.** ee. **37.**

BURNET (Jacob) *See* Fisher (Samuel W.) History—the Unfolding of God's Providence; a discourse occasioned by the death of Hon. J. Burnet, *etc.* 1853. 8°. **4986.** dd. **20.** (**14.**)

—— The Annual Address, delivered before the Cincinnati Astronomical Society, June 3, 1844 . . . Together with the Act of Incorporation, the Constitution of the Society, the annual reports, the officers, and a catalogue of the stockholders. pp. 46. 1844. 8°. *See* Cincinnati.—*Cincinnati Astronomical Society.* **8560.** b. **44.** (**1.**)

—— Notes on the Early Settlement of the North-Western Territory. [With a portrait.] pp. 501. *D. Appleton & Co.: New York; Derby, Bradley & Co.: Cincinnati,* 1847. 8°. **1196.** k. **16.**

—— Speech . . . in the Whig National Convention, giving a brief history of the life of Gen. William Henry Harrison. pp. 8. *Madisonian Office: Washington,* 1839. 8°. **10880.** d. **9.**

BURNET (James) *Lord Monboddo.* *See* Adams (John) *Rev., Master of the Academy at Putney.* Curious Thoughts on the History of Man; chiefly abridged or selected from the celebrated works of Lord Kaimes, Lord Monboddo, *etc.* 1789. 12°. **8405.** ee. **19.**

—— *See* Memmie Le Blanc (M. A.) An Account of a Savage Girl . . . With a preface [by Lord Monboddo] containing several particulars omitted in the original account. 1768. 12°. **957.** d. **22.**

—— Lord Monboddo and some of his Contemporaries. By William Knight. [A collection of letters. With "Observations on 'Ancient Metaphysics,' by Samuel Horsley, 1780." With a portrait.] pp. xv. 314. *John Murray: London,* 1900. 8°. **010817.** ee. **11.**

—— Antient Metaphysics; or, the Science of universals; with an appendix, containing an examination of the principles of Sir Isaac Newton's philosophy. [By Lord Monboddo.] 6 vol. 1779–99. 4°. *See* Metaphysics. **31.** c. **2–7.**

—— Of the Origin and Progress of Language. [By J. Burnet, Lord Monboddo.] 6 vol. 1773–92. 8°. *See* Origin. **623.** g. **14–19.**

—— [Another copy of vol. 2, 4–6.] **251.** l. **2, 4–6.**

—— [Another copy of vol. 2–4.] **440.** e. **14–16.**

BURNET (James) *Lord Monboddo.*

—— Second edition. With large additions and corrections. [With a portrait.] vol. 1, 3. 1774, 86. 8°. *See* Origin. **251.** l. **1, 3.**

—— [Another copy of vol. 1.] **440.** e. **13.**

—— Des Lord Monboddo Werk von dem Ursprunge und Fortgange der Sprache übersetzt von E. A. Schmid. Mit einer Vorrede des Herrn Generalsuperintendenten Herder. [An abridged translation of vol. 1–3.] 2 Tl. *Riga,* 1784, 85. 8°. **1331.** c. **6, 7.**

BURNET (James) *M.A., LL.B.* *See* Rome.—[*Emperors.*]—Justinian i., *Emperor of the East.* [527–565.] [*Institutiones.—Selections, etc.*] Aids to Justinian. [Extracts, with an English translation.] By J. Burnet. 1936. 8°. **20029.** eee. **14.**

BURNET (James) *M.D.* *See* Schultz (Frank) The X-Ray Treatment of Skin Diseases . . . Translated by J. Burnet, *etc.* 1912. 8°. **07640.** f. **13.**

—— Diseases of the Newborn. A textbook for students and practitioners. pp. xi. 275. *Oxford University Press: London,* 1927. 8°. [*Oxford Medical Publications.*] **20036.a.1/279.**

—— Handbook of Medical Treatment. A guide to therapeutics for students and practitioners. With an appendix on diet. pp. v. 168. *John Currie: Edinburgh,* 1911. 8°. **07306.** df. **39.**

—— [Another edition.] A Dictionary of Medical Treatment . . . Second edition revised. pp. 156. *London,* 1922. 8°. [*Black's Medical Series.*] W.P. **6085/3.**

—— Third edition. pp. 156. *London,* 1932. 8°. [*Black's Medical Series.*] W.P. **6085/11.**

—— Hints on Prescription-Writing . . . Second edition. pp. 31. *John Currie: Edinburgh,* 1910. 16°. **07306.** df. **38.** (**4.**)

—— Third edition, revised and enlarged. pp. 31. *Wm. Bryce: Edinburgh,* 1916. 16°. **07306.** df. **45.**

—— Fourth edition, revised and enlarged. pp. 32. *Wm. Bryce: Edinburgh,* [1920.] 8°. **07510.** de. **13.**

—— Manual of Diseases of Children. pp. ix. 406. *E. & S. Livingstone: Edinburgh,* 1905. 8°. **7580.** ff. **1.**

—— Second edition. pp. ix. 416. *E. & S. Livingstone: Edinburgh,* 1919. 8°. **07580.** e. **73.**

—— Materia Medica, with notes on prescription writing. pp. vii. 80. *J. & A. Churchill: London,* 1921. 8°. [*Students' Synopsis Series.*] **07306.b.6/6.**

—— The Nursing of Sick Children. pp. 66. *Scientific Press: London,* [1905.] 8°. **07686.** e. **41.**

—— Outlines of Industrial Medicine, Legislation, and Hygiene. pp. 87. *J. Wright & Sons: Bristol,* 1943. 8°. **6096.** aa. **2.**

—— Outlines of Industrial Medicine, Legislation, and Hygiene . . . Second edition. pp. 122. *John Wright & Sons: Bristol,* 1953. 8°. **6096.** aa. **13.**

—— The Pocket Clinical Guide. pp. viii. 141. *John Currie: Edinburgh,* 1910. 16°. **944.** c. **20.**

—— Third edition. pp. x. 150. *A. & C. Black: London,* 1921. 16°. **944.** bb. **5.**

BURNET (JAMES) *M.D.*

—— Fourth edition. pp. 154. *A. & C. Black: London*, 1932. 16°. **945**. e. **22**.

—— The Pocket Prescriber. pp. xi. 98. *John Currie: Edinburgh*, 1909. 16°. **7510**. dg. **21**.

—— Second edition. pp. xi. 98. *John Currie: Edinburgh*, 1909. 16°. **7510**. dg. **33**.

—— Third edition. pp. xi. 98. *John Currie: Edinburgh*, 1911. 16°. **7510**. dg. **40**.

—— Fourth edition. pp. xi. 98. *A. & C. Black: London*, 1915. 16°. **7510**. dg. **49**.

—— Fifth edition. pp. xi. 98. *A. & C. Black: London*, 1919. 16°. **7509**. de. **94**.

—— Sixth edition. pp. xi. 100. *A. & C. Black: London*, 1932. 16°. **945**. e. **21**.

BURNET (JEAN)

—— Next-Year Country. A study of rural social organization in Alberta. pp. xv. 188. *University of Toronto Press: Toronto*, 1951. 8°. [*Social Credit in Alberta*. no. 3.] W.P. **9973/3**.

BURNET (JOHN) *F.R.S. See* REYNOLDS (*Sir* Joshua) Sir Joshua Reynolds, and his Works. Gleanings from his diary, unpublished manuscripts, and from other sources . . . Edited by J. Burnet. 1856. 8°. **2263**. e. **12**.

—— *See* REYNOLDS (*Sir* Joshua) The Discourses of Sir Joshua Reynolds: illustrated by explanatory notes and plates, by J. Burnet. 1842. 4°. **786**. m. **10**.

—— A Practical Treatise on Painting . . . Consisting of hints on composition, chiaroscuro, and colouring. The whole illustrated by examples from the Italian, Venetian, Flemish and Dutch schools. [A reissue of "Practical Hints on Composition in Painting," "Practical Hints on Light and Shade in Painting" and "Practical Hints on Colour in Painting."] 3 pt. *J. Carpenter & Son: London*, 1827. 4°. **561***. d. **13**.
The several parts have separate titlepages, bearing the dates 1822, 1826 *and* 1827 *respectively.*

—— A Treatise on Painting . . . Consisting of an essay on the education of the eye with reference to painting, and practical hints on composition, chiaroscuro, and colour . . . New edition. 4 pt. *H. Sotheran & Co.: London*, 1880. 4°. **1763**. c. 5.

—— John Burnet's Principien der Malerkunst. Erläutert durch Beispiele nach den grössten Meistern der italienischen, niederländischen und andern Schulen. Aus dem Englischen von Adolph Görling. Mit einem Vorwort von Fr. Pecht. Zweite Auflage. (Abhandlung über die Bildung des Auges mit Rücksicht auf die Malerkunst.) 2 pt. *Reudnitz bei Leipzig*, [1885, 86.] 4°. **7857**. k. **13**.

—— Engravings from the Pictures of the National Gallery. [Engraved by J. Burnet and others; with descriptions in English and French by J. Burnet.] 1840. fol. *See* LONDON.—III. *National Gallery*. **746**. e. **8**.

—— An Essay on the Education of the Eye with reference to Painting. Illustrated by copper plates and wood cuts. pp. viii. 73. pl. 7. *James Carpenter: London*, 1837. 4°. **561***. e. **17**.

—— Landscape Painting in Oil Colours, explained in letters on the theory and practice of the art, and illustrated by examples from the several schools. pp. vi. 68. *David Bogue: London*, 1849. 4°. **1267**. g. **9**. **(1.)**

BURNET (JOHN) *F.R.S.*

—— [Another edition.] Re-edited, with an appendix, by Henry Murray. pp. vi. 70. *J. S. Virtue: London*, 1861. 4°. **1267**. g. **21**.

—— Practical Essays on various branches of the Fine Arts. To which is added, a Critical Inquiry into the principles and practice of the late Sir David Wilkie. pp. x. 200. *David Bogue: London*, 1848. 12°. **1401**. c. **35**.

—— Practical Hints on Composition in Pictures . . . Edited by Susan N. Carter. pp. v. 56. *G. P. Putnam's Sons: New York & London*, 1885. 8°. **7855**. b. **52**.

—— Practical Hints on Portrait Painting; illustrated by examples from the works of Vandyke and other masters. pp. iv. 54. pl. XII. *David Bogue: London*, 1850. 4°. **1267**. g. **9**. **(2.)**

—— [Another edition.] Re-edited, and with an appendix, by Henry Murray. pp. vi. 63. pl. XII. *J. S. Virtue: London*, 1860. 4°. **1267**. g. **20**.

—— The Progress of a Painter in the Nineteenth Century: containing conversations and remarks upon art. 2 vol. *David Bogue: London*, 1854. 8°. **1402**. e. **35**.

—— Rembrandt and his Works: comprising a short account of his life; with a critical examination into his principles and practice of design, light, shade, and colour. Illustrated by examples from the etchings of Rembrandt. pp. vi. 88. *David Bogue: London*, 1849. fol. **1268**. i. **5**.

—— [Another edition.] Re-edited by H. Murray. pp. viii. 91. *J. S. Virtue: London*, 1859. 8°. **1267**. g. **18**.

—— The School. Painted by Sir David Wilkie, R.A. Engraving . . . by J. Burnet, *etc.* [A description by J. Burnet.] pp. 8. *F. G. Moon: London*, [1844.] 12°. **1402**. b. **57**. **(5.)**

—— Turner and his Works: illustrated with examples from his pictures, and critical remarks on his principles of painting . . . The memoir by Peter Cunningham. [With a catalogue of pictures by J. M. W. Turner.] pp. 122. *David Bogue: London*, 1852. 4°. **1267**. i. **20**.

—— [Another edition.] Re-edited by Henry Murray. pp. 121. *J. S. Virtue: London*, 1859. 4°. **1267**. g. **19**.

BURNET (JOHN) *Independent Minister. See* ALEXANDER (William L.) Departed Saints with Christ: a sermon preached . . . on occasion of the death of the Rev. John Burnet. 1862. 8°. **4902**. d. **3**.

—— Authentic Report of the Discussion which took place between the Rev. John Burnet . . . and the Rev. T. M. M'Donnell . . . on the 7th. and 8th. of August, 1827, in Mount Zion Chapel, Birmingham, on the rule of faith as admitted among Catholics and Protestants respectively. Taken in short hand by Mr. William Oliver . . . Second edition. pp. 126. *B. Hudson: Birmingham*, 1827. 12°. **3939**. aa. **5**. **(4.)**

—— Third edition. pp. 123. *B. Hudson: Birmingham*, 1827. 8°. **3938**. cc. **52**. **(1.)**

—— The Best Methods of Understanding the Sacred Book. *See* BIBLE.—*Appendix*. [*Miscellaneous*.] A Course of Lectures to Young Men and Others, on the Vindication of the Bible, *etc.* [1839.] 8°. **4460**. dd. **11**. **(4.)**

BURNET (JOHN) *Independent Minister.*

—— The Call of Abraham, and subsequent separation of his descendants, as a peculiar people, established on the authority of ancient history. *See* BIBLE.—*Appendix.* [*Miscellaneous.*] A Course of Lectures on the Evidences of some Important Facts and Events recorded in the Bible, *etc.* [1838.] 8°. **4460**. dd. **11/1.**

—— The Church of England, and the Church of Christ; a lecture, *etc.* pp. 24. *J. Dinnis: London,* [1840.] 12°. [*Advocacy of the Voluntary Principle.* no. 1.] **701**. c. **34.**

—— [Another copy.] **4106**. aa. **12.**

—— [Another copy.] **4107**. a. **114**. **(4.)**

—— The Circumstances of the Birth of Christ announced by Ancient Predictions, *etc.* *See* JESUS CHRIST. Lectures on the Person, Life, and Ministry of the Lord Jesus, *etc.* [1839.] 8°. **4460**. dd. **11**. (3.)

—— Departed Friends in Heaven. *See* W., J. The Recognition of Friends in Heaven, *etc.* 1866. 8°. **4410**. ccc. **34.**

—— The Endowment of all Religious Sects. 1851. *See* LONDON.—III. *British Anti-State Church Association.* Tracts, *etc.* vol. 2. 1846, *etc.* 12°. **4107**. aa. **65.**

—— An Essay on the Deity of Christ viewed in connexion with the economy of redemption. pp. vii. 174. *J. Bolster: Cork,* 1821. 8°. **4224**. a. **36.**

—— The False Methods Adopted to Obtain Happiness. *See* LONDON.—III. *Albion Chapel.* A Course of Twelve Lectures on Human Happiness, *etc.* [1841.] 8°. **4460**. dd. **11**. **(8.)**

—— Observations on the Authority of Pastors in the Churches of Christ; together with remarks on the office of deacons. pp. 32. *B. L. Green: London,* 1848. 8°. **4135**. a. **18.**

—— The Reasonableness of the Doctrine of Future and Eternal Rewards and Punishments. *See* LONDON.—III. *Eagle Street Chapel.* A Course of Thirteen Lectures to Socialists, *etc.* [1840.] 8°. **4460**. dd. **11/7.**

—— A Renovation of Heart Essential to a State of Salvation, *etc.* *See* LONDON.—III. *Hoxton Academy.* Twelve Lectures, delivered at Hoxton-Academy Chapel, *etc.* [1840.] 8°. **4460**. dd. **11**. (5.)

—— The Separate Province of Divine and Human Governments, *etc.* [A sermon.] pp. 15. *W. M. Knight: [London,* 1835.] 8°. **908**. d. **4**. (15.)

—— Two Lectures on the Connexion between Church and State, in reply to the Rev. Hugh M'Neile, *etc.* pp. 64. *J. Dinnis: London,* [1840.] 12°. [*Advocacy of the Voluntary Principle.* no. 4.] **701**. c. **34.**

—— Voluntary Church Societies. The lecture delivered . . . in the Town Hall, Birmingham . . . on . . . February 23, 1836, *etc.* pp. 26. *J. W. Showell: Birmingham; Ward & Co.: London,* [1836.] 8°. **4372**. d. 3. (8.)

—— The Form and Order observed at the ordination of Mr. Burnet, at Woolwich, on Friday evening, March 15, 1811. *See* PIERCE (Samuel E.) On the Indwelling of Sin in Believers, *etc.* 1811. 8°. **4473**. c. **18**. (8.)

—— Services on occasion of the Death of the Rev. John Burnet . . . who died June 10th, 1862, *etc.* [By E. Miall and others.] *John Snow: London,* 1862. 8°. **4906**. bb. **51**. (4.)

BURNET (JOHN) *of Cork.* *See* BURNET (John) *Independent Minister.*

BURNET (JOHN) *Professor of Greek in the University of St. Andrews.* *See* ARISTOTLE. [*Ethica Nicomachea.—Greek.*] The Ethics of Aristotle. Edited with an introduction and notes by J. Burnet. 1900. 8°. **08461**. i. 5.

—— *See* ARISTOTLE. [*Selections.—English.*] Aristotle on Education: being extracts from the Ethics and Politics, translated and edited by J. Burnet. 1903. 8°. **012201**. e. 4/24.

—— *See* LORIMER (William L.) John Burnet, 1863–1928, *etc.* [With a bibliography.] [1930.] 8°. **10855**. f. **39.**

—— *See* PLATO. [*Works.—Greek.*] Platonis opera. Recognovit brevique adnotatione critica instruxit I. Burnet. [1900, *etc.*] 8°. **11305.dd.93/3.**

—— *See* PLATO. [*Works.—Greek.*] Platonis opera. Recognovit brevique adnotatione critica instruxit I. Burnet . . . Apologia, Meno. [1911.] 8° **11305.dd.93/18.**

—— *See* PLATO. [*Two or more Works.—Greek.*] Plato's Euthyphro, Apology of Socrates, and Crito. Edited with notes by J. Burnet. 1924. 8°. **08465**. df. **20.**

—— *See* PLATO. [*Phaedo.—Greek.*] Plato's Phædo. Edited with introduction and notes by J. Burnet. 1911. 8°. **8462**. eee. **31.**

—— *See* PLATO. [*Respublica.—Greek.*] Platonis Res publica. Recognovit brevique adnotatione critica instruxit I. Burnet. 1902. 8°. [*Scriptorum Classicorum Bibliotheca Oxoniensis.*] **11305.dd.93/9.**

—— Essays and Addresses . . . With a memoir by Lord Charnwood. [With a portrait.] pp. 299. *Chatto & Windus: London,* 1929. 8°. **012350**. ee. **53.**

—— Aristotle . . . From the Proceedings of the British Academy, *etc.* pp. 18. *Oxford University Press: London,* [1925.] 8°. [*British Academy. Annual Lecture on a Master-Mind, Henriette Hertz Trust.*] Ac. **1186**/9.

—— Early Greek Philosophy. pp. vi. 378. *A. & C. Black: London,* 1892. 8°. **8459.g.19.**

—— Second edition. pp. x. 433. *A. & C. Black: London,* 1908. 8°. **08486**. f. 2.

—— Third edition. pp. ix. 375. *A. & C. Black: London,* 1920. 8°. **08486**. f. **26.**

—— Fourth edition. pp. vii. 375. *A. & C. Black: London,* 1930. 8°. **2022.a.**

—— [Another copy.] **08486**. f. **27.**

—— Greek Philosophy. Part 1. Thales to Plato. pp. x. 360. *Macmillan & Co.: London,* 1914. 8°. [*The Schools of Philosophy.*] **08486**. c. 5/2.
No more published.

—— Greek Rudiments. pp. ix. 377. *Longmans & Co.: London,* 1896. 8°. **12923**. cc. **27.**

—— The Greek Strain in English Literature. An address, *etc.* pp. 8. [*London,*] 1920. 8°. [*English Association. Pamphlet.* no. 45.] Ac. **2664.**

—— Higher Education and the War. pp. x. 238. *Macmillan & Co.: London,* 1917. 8°. **08311**. de. 7.

BURNET (JOHN) *Professor of Greek in the University of St. Andrews.*

—— How Platonism Came to England. pp. 10. 1924. 8°. *See* LONDON.—III. *Classical Association.—Leeds and District Branch.* Ac. **1188**. d. (**2**.)

—— Ignorance, *etc.* (The Romanes Lectures, 1923.) pp. 20. *Clarendon Press: Oxford*, 1923. 8°. **8308**. dd. **35**.

—— Platonism. pp. 130. *University of California Press: Berkeley*, 1928. 8°. [*Sather Classical Lectures.* vol. 5.] Ac. **2689**. g/**17**.

—— The Socratic Doctrine of the Soul. pp. 27. *Oxford University Press: London*, 1916. 8°. [*British Academy. Annual Philosophical Lecture, Henriette Hertz Trust.* no. 2.] Ac. **1186/6**.

BURNET (JOHN) *Quaker.* *See* BURNYEAT.

BURNET (JOHN) *R.S.A.* The Hypotheneuse: an instrument for measuring the altitude of celestial objects. pp. 12. *Printed and published for the Author: [London,]* 1865. 12°. **8705**. aa. **24**.

BURNET (JOHN) *Secretary to Glasgow Corporation Water Works Commissioners.* History of the Water Supply of Glasgow, from the commencement of the present century. pp. viii. 184. *Bell & Bain: Glasgow*, 1869. 8°. **08776**. c. **14**.

BURNET (JOHN) *Vicar of Bradford.* An Address delivered in St. George's Church, Sutton . . . Dec. 23rd. 1842, *etc.* pp. 33. *Hamilton, Adams & Co.: London*, 1843. 12°. **4475**. de. **6**. (**8**.)

—— An Address, delivered to the Macclesfield Church Sunday School Teachers' Association . . . July 17th, 1845. pp. 19. *Longman & Co.: London*, [1845.] 12°. **8305**. aa. **21**. (**10**.)

—— A Lecture on the Acquittal of the seven Bishops, *etc.* pp. 36. *Thomas Agnew: Manchester*, 1848. 12°. **4705**. a. **27**.

—— Papal Supremacy. *See* D., W. A Course of Sermons on the Creed of Pope Pius IV., *etc.* 1841. 8°. **1352**. e. **10**.

—— Puseyism examined, in a course of lectures . . . Extracted from the Penny Pulpit. pp. 40. *James Paul: London*, [1842.] 8°. **4431**. bb. **23**.

—— A Sermon preached before the Church Pastoral-Aid Society . . . in the Parish Church of Saint Dunstan, Fleet-Street . . . May 8, 1848. 1848. *See* ENGLAND. —*Church of England.—Church Pastoral Aid Society.* Report of the Committee, *etc.* (Thirteenth annual meeting.) 1836, *etc.* 8°. P.P. **1025**.

—— A Sermon preached . . . in the Parish Church of St. Mary, Blackburn, on Ascension Day, 1836, *etc.* pp. 40. *W. H. Morrice: Blackburn*, 1836. 8°. [*Sermons preached before the Committee of the Association, in the Deanery of Blackburn, in aid of the S.P.G.*] **4473**. g. **16/11**.

BURNET (*Sir* JOHN) **TAIT AND LORNE.**

—— The Architects' Journal Library of Planned Information . . . Edited by Sir John Burnet, Tait and Lorne. vol. 1–5. *Architectural Press: London*, 1935–39. fol. P.P. **1667**. af. *No more published.*

BURNET (*Sir* JOHN) **TAIT AND LORNE.**

— Approximate Estimating. A reprint of fourteen information sheets from "The Architects' Journal Library of Planned Information" under the editorship of Sir John Burnet, Tait and Lorne, from information supplied by O. A. Davis. *Architectural Press: [London,]* 1937. fol. **8233**. d. **41**

—— The Information Book of Sir John Burnet, Tait and Lorne. [With plates.] pp. v. 57. *Architectural Press: London*, 1933. fol. **7817**. pp. **33**

—— The Information Book of Sir John Burnet, Tait and Lorne. (Fourth impression.) pp. v. 57. pl. 147. *Architectural Press: Westminster*, 1938. fol. **7822**. d. **8**

BURNET (LOUIS CHRISTIAN HEINRICH) *See* VORTISCH (L. C. H.) called BURNET.

BURNET (M. A.) Mountain Ways. The story of the Central Japan Pioneer Mission. [With illustrations.] pp. 14. [1931.] 8°. *See* LONDON.—III. *Central Japan Pioneer Mission.* **4763**. b. **38**

BURNET (*Lady* MARGARET) *See* KENNEDY, afterwards BURNET.

BURNET (MARGARETTA) A Laboratory Manual of Zoölogy. pp. 112. *American Book Co.: New York*, [1908.] 8°. **07207**. g. **3**

BURNET (MARY QUICK) Art and Artists of Indiana . . With illustrations, *etc.* pp. xvi. 448. *Century Co.: New York*, 1921. 8°. **7870.d.9.**

BURNET (MARY SCOTT) Marc-Antoine Legrand, acteur et auteur comique, 1673–1728. pp. 199. *Paris*, 1938. 8°. [*Bibliothèque de la Société des Historiens du Théâtre.* no. 14.] Ac. **6885**.

BURNET (MATTHIAS) An Election Sermon preached at Hartford . . . May 12, 1803. pp. 29. *Hudson & Goodwin: Hartford*, 1803. 8°. **4485**. f. **37**

—— The Evidences of a General Judgment from Scripture and Reason. 1791. *See* AUSTIN (David) The American Preacher, *etc.* vol. 3. no. 55. 1791, *etc.* 8°. **4487**. b. **9**

—— Moral Reflexions upon the Season of Harvest. 1791. *See* AUSTIN (David) The American Preacher, *etc.* vol. 2. no. 30. 1791, *etc.* 8°. **4487**. b. **9**

—— [Another edition.] *See* AMERICAN PREACHER. Select Discourses from the American Preacher, *etc.* pt. 1. no. 17. 1796, *etc.* 8°. **1025.k.12.(1.)**

BURNET (NELL) Buzz-Wuzz, Din-Din & Co. An illustrated book for children. pp. xi. 209. *A. H. Stockwell: London*, [1933.] 8°. **20052**. ee. **26**

BURNET (PERCY BENTLEY) *See* EDGREN (A. H.) and BURNET (P. B.) A French and English Dictionary, *etc.* 1901. 8°. **12956.b.10**

—— *See* EDGREN (A. H.) and BURNET (P. B.) The French and English Word Book, *etc.* 1902. 8°. **12950**. g. **11**

BURNET (PIERRE) *See* BEAU DE ROCHAS (A.) Cour impériale de Paris. Contrefaçon du Bateau-Burnet. Affaires Burnet contre Place et Consorts . . . Examen du rapport des experts suivi de notes, documents officiels et dessins concernant les Bateaux-Monoroue du système Burnet, *etc.* 1857. 4°. **7954**. e. **6**

BURNET (REGULA) *See* COOK (Ann) Ann Cook and Friend. With an introduction and notes by R. Burnet. 1936. 8°. **7941**. r. 6.

—— Green Ink. A play in one act. pp. 28. *Brown, Son & Ferguson: Glasgow*, [1939.] 8°. [*Scottish Plays*. no. 109.] W.P. **4554/109**.

—— Ladies Only. A play in one act. pp. 24. *J. B. Pinker & Son: London*, 1937. 8°. [*Eight One-Act Plays for Women's Institutes & Clubs*.] **11780**. aaa. **30/6**.

—— The New Baronet. A comedy in one act. pp. 22. *Brown, Son & Ferguson: Glasgow*, [1938.] 8°. [*Scottish Plays*. no. 105.] W.P. **4554/105**.

BURNET (RICHARD) *Chaplain to the Lewes Prisons*. The Christian Teacher. A sermon preached in St. Peter's Church, Brighton . . . September 14, 1848, being the day of the Eleventh Annual Meeting of the Chichester Diocesan Association. pp. 20. *Printed for the Association: Brighton*, [1848.] 8°. **4476**. c. **19**.

—— An Easy Catechism on the Creed, the Ten Commandments, and the Lord's Prayer . . . A new edition. pp. 36. *H. S. King: Brighton*, 1852. 18°. **3504**. de. 4. (4.)

—— A new edition. pp. 36. *W. F. King & Co.: Brighton*, 1854. 18°. **3504**. de. **9**. (**5**.)

BURNET (RICHARD) *Founder of the Devonport Mechanics' Institute*. To Her Majesty's Commissioners for the Exhibition, 1851. [Letters on the subject of exhibitions.] pp. 23. *Levey, Robson & Franklyn: London*, [1850.] 12°. **7955**. a. **48**.

—— A Word to the Members of the Mechanics' Institutes. pp. 145. *J. Johns: Devonport*, 1826. 8°. **C.109.d.14.**

BURNET (RICHARD) *Master of the Grammar School at Bungay, Suffolk*. Various English and Latin Poems, Translations, &c. preceded by an essay on the composition of Latin Verse, *etc*. pp. viii. 79. *R. M. Bacon: Norwich*, 1808. 8°. **625**. e. **21**.

BURNET (ROBERT) *Lord Crimond*.

—— *See* CRAIG (*Sir* Thomas) Jus Feudale tribus libris comprehensum, *etc*. [Edited by R. Burnet, afterwards Lord Crimond.] 1655. fol. **504**. g. **5**.

BURNET (ROBERT P.)

—— *See* MACBAIN (Alexander G.) and BURNET (R. P.) The Profits Tax, *etc*. 1948. 8°. **6429**. d. **18**.

BURNET (*Sir* ROBERT WILLIAM) *See* HOW. How to Keep Fit . . . By W. M. Eccles . . . Sir R. W. Burnet, *etc*. [1914.] 8°. **7404**. p. **11**.

—— Foods and Dietaries: a manual of clinical dietetics. pp. x. 196. *C. Griffin & Co.: London*, 1890. 8°. **7439**. aaa. 3.

—— Second edition. pp. x. 196. *C. Griffin & Co.: London*, 1892. 8°. **7404**. d. 10.

—— Fourth edition. pp. xii. 204. *C. Griffin & Co.: London*, 1905. 8°. **7391**. df. **40**.

BURNET (THOMAS) *Master of the Charter House*. T. Burnetii Telluris theoria sacra . . . Accedunt Archæologiæ philosophicæ, sive doctrina antiqua de rerum originibus. pp. 474. *J. Wolters: Amstelædami*, 1694. 4°. **4378**. e. 18.

BURNET (THOMAS) *Master of the Charter House*.

—— An Answer to the late Exceptions made by Mr. Erasmus Warren against the Theory of the Earth. [By T. Burnet.] pp. 85. 1690. fol. *See* WARREN (Erasmus) **1487.k.14.(3.)**

—— [Another copy.] **726**. l. **9**. (**1**.)

—— *See* WARREN (Erasmus) A Defence of the Discourse concerning the Earth before the Flood; being a full reply to a late answer to exceptions made against the theory of the earth, *etc*. 1691. 4°. **444**. b. **26**. (**2**.)

—— An Appeal to Common Sense: or, a Sober vindication of Dr. Woodward's State of Physick. By a Divine of the Church of England [i.e. T. Burnet]. pp. 17. 1719. 8°. *See* WOODWARD (John) *M.D.* **1172**. g. **7**. (**4**.)

—— Archæologiæ philosophicæ: sive Doctrina antiqua de rerum originibus. Libri duo. (Ad virum clariss. A.B. circa nuper editum de archæologiis philos. libellum authoris epistola.) pp. 358. *Typis R. N.* [*R. Norton*]*; impensis Gualt. Kettilby: Londini*, 1692. 4°. **725**. f. **3**.

—— Editio secunda. Accedunt . . . epistolæ duæ de archæologiis philosophicis. [With a portrait.] pp. xvi. 543. *Impensis J. Hooke: Londini*, 1728. 8°. **672**. d. **2**.

—— [Another copy.] **L.P.** **725**. f. **6**.

—— [A reissue.] **L.P.** *Impensis A. Bettesworth & C. Hitch: Londini*, 1733. 8°. **30**. i. **1**.

—— Archæologiæ philosophicæ: or, the Ancient doctrine concerning the originals of things . . . Faithfully translated into English, with remarks thereon, by Mr. Foxton. [With a preface, signed Philalethes; "A Letter to Mr. E. Curll, Bookseller," signed: C. B., i.e. C. Blount, being a new edition of "A Letter to my worthy friend Mr. Gildon in vindication of Dr. Burnet" from "Oracles of Reason"; "An Essay on the use of Reason in Religion" and a postscript by M. Earbery; "The Immobility of the Earth demonstrated," a treatise by E. Lécuyer de la Jonchère, with a prefatory letter by the translator, signed J. M., i.e. J. Morgan; and "An Appendix concerning the Modern Brachmans in the Indies," extracted from "Oracles of Reason" by C. Blount.] 2 pt. *E. Curll: London*, 1729. 8°. **725**. f. **7**.

—— [Another edition.] Doctrina antiqua de rerum originibus: or, an Inquiry into the doctrine of the philosophers of all nations, concerning the original of the world . . . Made English . . . by Mr. Mead and Mr. Foxton. [Preceded by a life of T. Burnet and a new edition of his "Relation of the Proceedings at the Charter-House upon occasion of King James's presenting a Papist to be admitted into that Hospital."] pp. 39. 275. *E. Curll: London*, 1736. 8°. **8706**. d. **14**.

—— Archæologiæ philosophicæ: or, the Ancient doctrine concerning the originals of things, *etc*. [A translation of bk. 2. ch. 7–10.] pp. x. 80. *J. Torbuck: London*, [1692.] 8°. **4373**. b. **12**.

—— *See* NICHOLLS (William) *D.D.* A Conference with a Theist; wherein . . . The Lapse of Mankind is defended, against the objections of Archæologiæ philosophicæ, *etc*. 1696. 8°. **857**. b. **23**.

—— —— 1698, *etc*. 8°. **222**. b. **11–14**.

—— —— 1723. 8°. **4015**. bb. **36**.

—— Moses vindicatus; sive asserta historiæ creationis mundi aliarumque, quales à Mose narrantur, veritas, adversus cl. v. T. Burnetii S.T.D. Archæologias philosophicas. pp. 221. *Apud G. Gallet: Amstelodami*, 1694. 12°. **1017**. a. **16**.

—— [Another copy.] **1411**. a. **27**.

—— De fide et officiis Christianorum. pp. 223. *Londini*, 1722. 4°. **695. h. 34.**

—— [Another copy.] **678. e. 14.**

—— [Another edition.] pp. 190. *Londini*, 1727. 8°. **1019. m. 9. (2.)**

—— [Another edition.] [The editor's preface signed: F. W., i.e. F. Wilkinson. With a portrait.] pp. 32. 216. **L.P.** *Impensis J. Hooke: Londini*, 1727. 8°. **227. e. 1.**

—— Editio secunda [of F. Wilkinson's edition]. (Appendix de futura Judæorum restauratione. Accedunt Epistolæ duæ de Archæologiis philosophicis.) pp. 32. 216. 112. **L.P.** *Impensis J. Hooke: Londini*, 1728. 8°. **474. b. 22. (1.)**

—— The Faith and Duties of Christians . . . Translated into English by Mr. Dennis. [With a portrait.] pp. xii. 276. *J. Hooke: London*, [1728.] 8°. **1019. l. 10.**

—— Des grossen englischen Schrifftgelehrten Thomas Burnets Buch von dem Glauben und den Pflichten der Christen . . . übersetzt und mit des Verfassers Leben und Kupfer-Bilde versehen. Als ein Anhang sind beygefüget zwo Abhandlungen [by J. Le Clerc]: 1. Dass niemand alle Religionen gleich viel gelten sollen. 2. Welchem unter den streitenden Theilen der Christenheit man seinen Beyfall geben müsse. pp. 302. 1737. 8°. **4403. f. 25. (1.)**

—— De fide & officiis Christianorum. Excerpta ex T. Burneti libello in usum juventutis christianæ. pp. vi. 90. *J. Potf [Pote]: Etonæ*, 1767. 12°. **3554. a. 9.**

—— De fide et officiis Christianorum. Excerpta ex T. Burnetii et Grotii libellis, in usum juventutis christianæ. Editio nova recognita. pp. 96. *Pote & Williams: Etonæ*, 1804. 12°. **3558. aa. 3.**

—— The Judgment of Dr. Thomas Burnet . . . concerning the doctrine of the Trinity [extracted from "De fide et officiis Christianorum."]: and the Judgment of Dr. Samuel Clarke . . . concerning 1. The satisfaction, 2. The merits, 3. The mediation and intercession of Christ. 4. The ordinary influence and assistance of the Holy Spirit. 5. The two Sacraments. With a preface concerning Mr. Lock, Sir Isaac Newton, and Mr. Wollaston. pp. xx. 43. *J. Roberts: London*, 1732. 8°. **4225. b. 13.**

—— *See* Roscius (G. G.) Georgii Gottfr. Roscii . . . De fide et officiis Christianorum ex Augustana Confessione dissertatio. Cui subjiciuntur in T. Burnetii De fide et officiis Christianorum librum, notæ et castigationes, *etc.* 1731. 4°. **854. g. 23.**

—— De statu mortuorum et resurgentium liber. Accessit epistola (ad virum clarissimum A. B.) circa libellum de Archæologiis philosophicis. pp. 308. 51. *Londini*, 1720. 4°. **4256. f. 2.**
One of an edition of a few copies printed for private distribution by Dr. Richard Mead.

—— [Another copy of sig. G–Y, Bb, Cc, Ee–Pp, Rr of De statu mortuorum, and sig. A–D of the Epistola.] **698. d. 10.**
Apparently printer's waste. In sig. G, I, K, M, Gg *the pages of the one forme are blank, those of the other mackled. Sig.* Bb *is mutilated. The blanks in sig.* K *and the mutilation of sig.* Bb *have been made good by the insertion of other leaves of a different imposition.*

—— [Another edition.] Accesserunt Epistolæ duæ circa libellum de Archæologiis philosophicis. pp. 327. 58. **L.P.** *Londini*, 1723. 4°. **678. e. 15.**

—— [Another copy.] **L.P.** **11. a. 7.**

—— [Another edition.] pp. 302. *Londini*, 1726. 8°. **1019. m. 9. (1.)**

—— [Another edition.] Adjicitur Appendix de futurâ Judæorum restauratione . . . Accedunt . . . Epistolæ duæ de Archæologiis philosophicis. [The editor's preface signed: F. W., i.e. F. Wilkinson. With a portrait.] pp. 316. 166. **L.P.** *Impensis J. Hooke: Londini*, 1727. 8°. **12. a. 20.**

—— [Another issue. Without the "Epistolæ duæ de Archæologiis philosophicis."] pp. 316. 112. **L.P.** *Londini*, 1727. 8°. **474. b. 22. (2.)**
The "Epistolæ duæ de Archæologiis philosophicis" though mentioned on the titlepage of the Appendix are not mentioned on the general titlepage.

—— Editio secunda [of F. Wilkinson's edition]. pp. viii. 432. *Impensis A. Bettesworth & C. Hitch: Londini*, 1733. 8°. **4257. cc. 10.**

—— Of the State of the Dead, and of those that are to rise. [A translation of chap. 1–3.] Translated . . . with remarks upon each chapter, and an answer to all the heresies therein, by Matthias Earbery. pp. 7. 102. *H. Curll: London*, 1727. 8°. **4374. c. 7.**

—— The second edition [containing the whole work]. 2 vol. *E. Curll: London*, 1728. 8°. **854. f. 16, 17. (1.)**

—— A Treatise concerning the State of Departed Souls, before, and at, and after the Resurection . . . Translated . . . by Mr. Dennis. pp. xi. 372. *A. Bettesworth & C. Hitch: London*, 1733. 8°. **226. a. 11.**

—— A Treatise concerning the State of the Dead, and of departed souls, at the Resurrection. To which is added an Appendix concerning the future restoration of the Jews, *etc.* pp. 408. *London*, 1737. 8°. **4255. aaaa. 10.**
Imperfect; wanting the Appendix.

—— A Treatise concerning the State of Departed Souls before, and at, and after the Resurrection . . . Translated into English by Mr. Dennis. The second edition, corrected. [With a portrait.] pp. iv. 372. *A. Bettesworth & C. Hitch: London*, 1739. 8°. **4257. cc. 26.**
Previous edition 1733.

—— Traité de l'état des morts et des résuscitans . . . Traduit du latin par Mr. Jean Bion. pp. 285. *Rotterdam*, 1731. 12°. **4372. b. 9.**

—— On the Separate State, extracted from no. iv of the Morning Watch, *etc.* [An extract from Burnet's "De statu mortuorum" translated by T. W. Chevalier.] pp. 26. *Ellerton & Henderson: London*, 1829. 8°. **4372. dd. 7. (3.)**

—— Dr. Burnet's Appendix to the Ninth Chapter of the State of the Dead. Concerning the two Resurrections, the New-Heavens and New-Earth; the Millenary-Reign of Christ, and of the Future Restauration of the Jews. Published from the author's Latin original by Francis Wilkinson, Esq; translated by Mr. Foxton. pp. 6. 119. *E. Curll: London*, 1729. 8°. **854. f. 17. (5.)**

—— *See* Muratori (L. A.) Opere, *etc.* (tom. 4. De Paradiso non expectata corporum resurrectione adversus Burnetum.) 1767, *etc.* 4°. **658. f. 4.**

—— *See* MURATORI (L. A.) De Paradiso Regnique Cælestis gloria, non exspectata corporum resurrectione justis a Deo conlata, adversus T. Burneti librum de statu mortuorum. 1738. 4°. **10. b. 14.**

—— The Last Will and Testament of Dr. Burnett, Master of the Charter-House. *See* PARTRIDGE (John) *M.D.* The Last Wills and Testaments of J. Partridge . . . and Dr. Burnett, *etc.* 1716. 8°. **518. k. 4. (1.)**

—— Reflections upon the Theory of the Earth occasioned by a late examination of it [by J. Keill]. In a letter to a friend. [By T. Burnet.] pp. 62. 1699. 4°. *See* THEORY. **444. c. 17. (6.)**

—— A Relation of the Proceedings at Charter-House, upon occasion of King James the IId his presenting a Papist to be admitted into that hospital. *See* infra: [Telluris theoria sacra.] The Sacred Theory of the Earth, *etc.* 1719. 8°. **970. f. 9.**

—— [Another edition.] *See* supra: [Archæologiæ philosophicæ.] Doctrina antiqua de rerum originibus, *etc.* 1736. 8°. **8706. d. 14.**

—— Remarks upon an Essay concerning Humane Understanding [by J. Locke] in a letter addressed to the author. [By T. Burnet.] pp. 15. 1697. 4°. *See* ESSAY. **699. e. 51. (1.)**

—— *See* LOCKE (John) *the Philosopher.* [*Essay concerning Human Understanding.—Controversy with Bishop Stillingfleet.*] Mr. Locke's Reply to the . . . Bishop of Worcester's Answer to his Letter, concerning some passages relating to Mr. Locke's Essay of Humane Understanding, *etc.* (An Answer to Remarks [by T. Burnet] upon an Essay concerning Humane Understanding.) 1697. 8°. **528. i. 24.**

—— Second Remarks upon an Essay concerning Humane Understanding in a letter address'd to the author [by T. Burnet]: being a vindication of the first Remarks against the answer of Mr. Lock, at the end of his Reply to the Bishop of Worcester. pp. 30. 1697. 4°. *See* LOCKE (John) *the Philosopher.* [*Essay concerning Human Understanding.—Appendix.*] **699. e. 51. (2.)**

—— Third Remarks upon an Essay concerning Humane Understanding: in a letter addressed to the author [by T. Burnet], *etc.* pp. 27. 1699. 4°. *See* ESSAY. **699. e. 51. (3.)**

—— *See* LOCKE (John) *the Philosopher.* [*Essay concerning Human Understanding.—Appendix.*] A Defence [by C. Cockburn] of the Essay of Human Understanding, written by Mr. Lock . . . In answer to some Remarks on that essay [i.e. the three pamphlets by Dr. Burnet]. 1702. 8°. **117. a. 31.**

—— A Review of the Theory of the Earth, and of its proofs: especially in reference to Scripture. [By T. Burnet.] pp. 52. *R. Norton, for Walter Kettilby: London,* 1690. fol. **1487.k.14.(2.)**

—— A Short Consideration of Mr. Erasmus Warren's Defence of his exceptions against the Theory of the Earth: in a letter to a friend. [By T. Burnet.] pp. 24 [42]. 1691. fol. *See* WARREN (Erasmus) **1487.k.4.(4.)**

—— [Another copy.] **726. l. 9. (2.)**

—— *See* W., E. Some Reflections upon the Short Consideration [by T. Burnet] of the Defence of the exceptions against the Theory of the Earth. By E. W. [i.e. E. Warren.] 1692. 4°. **444. b. 26. (3.)**

—— Telluris theoria sacra: orbis nostri originem & mutationes generales, quas aut jam subiit, aut olim subiturus est, complectens. 2 vol. *Typis R. N.* [*R. Norton*]; *impensis Gualt. Kettilby: Londini,* 1681, 89. 4°. **457. c. 5, 6.**

The titlepage to bk. 4 *bears the date* 1688.

—— [Another copy.] **233. g. 34.**

—— Editio secunda. 2 vol. *Typis R. N.* [*R. Norton*]; *impensis Gualt. Kettilby: Londini,* 1689. 4°. **1364. i. 23.**

Vol. 1 *only is of the second edition.*

—— Editio tertia recognita & contracta, *etc.* 4 bk. pp. 356. *Londini,* 1702. 4°. **7109. aaa. 32.**

—— The Theory of the Earth: containing an account of the original of the Earth, and of all the general changes which it hath already undergone, or is to undergo, till the consummation of all things. 2 vol. MS. NOTES. *R. Norton, for Walter Kettilby: London,* 1684, 90. fol. **459.a.15.& 1487.k.14.(2.)**

—— The Theory of the Earth: containing an account of the original of the Earth . . . The second edition. vol. 1 *R. Norton, for Walter Kettilby: London,* 1691. fol. **1487.k.14.(1.)**

No more of this edition published.

—— Third edition, review'd by the author. (A review of the Theory of the Earth, and of its proofs: especially in relation to Scripture.) 2 vol. *R. N.* [*R. Norton*] *for Walter Kettilby: London,* 1697. fol. **1144. k. 2.**

—— [Another copy.] **726. l. 1.**

—— [Another edition.] The Sacred Theory of the Earth . . . The fourth edition. In which is added, the author's defence of the work from the exceptions of Mr. Warren and an ode to the author by Mr. Addison. [With "A Relation of the proceedings at Charter-House, upon occasion of King James the IId his presenting a Papist to be admitted into that hospital," by T. Burnet.] 5 pt. *John Hooke: London,* 1719. 8°. **970. f. 8, 9.**

—— The fifth edition. To which is added the author's defence of the work from the exceptions of Mr. Warren, and the examination of Mr. Keil, *etc.* [With a portrait.] 2 vol. *J. Hooke: London,* 1722. 8°. **3125. cc. 25.**

—— The sixth edition, *etc.* 2 vol. *J. Hooke: London,* 1726. 8°. **970. f. 10, 11.**

—— [Another copy.] **674. b. 2, 3.**

—— The seventh edition. To which are now added, Memoirs of the author's life and writings, *etc.* 2 vol. *T. Osborn: London,* 1759. 8°. **233. h. 12, 13.**

—— [Another edition.] Together with copious notes on the wonders of nature, selected from the writings of the most learned divines. pp. v. 716. *J. M'Gowan & Son: London,* 1826. 4°. **8706. h. 12.**

—— Theoria sacra telluris. d. i. Heiliger Entwurff oder Biblische Betrachtung des Erdreichs, begreiffende, nebens dem Ursprung, die allgemeine Enderungen, welche unser Erd-Kreiss einseits allschon ausgestanden, und anderseits noch auszustehen hat . . . Ins Hochteutsche übersetzt . . . durch M. Joh. Jacob. Zimmermann. 4 bk. pp. 520. *Hamburg,* 1703. 4°. **4374. c. 6.**

The parts have separate titlepages bearing the date 1693.

BURNET (THOMAS) *Master of the Charter House.*

—— *See* BEAUMONT (John) *of Stony-Easton, Somersetshire.* Considerations on a Book, entituled The Theory of the Earth, publisht . . . by the learned Dr. Burnet. 1693. 4°. **B. 385. (4.)**

—— *See* BEAUMONT (John) *of Stony-Easton, Somersetshire.* A Postscript to a Book . . . entituled Considerations on Dr. Burnet's Theory of the Earth. 1694. 4°. **444.** c. **17. (4*.)**

—— *See* BUSSINGIUS (C.) C. Bussingii . . . De situ telluris paradisiacæ et chiliasticæ Burnetiano ad eclipticam recto, quem T. Burnetius in sua theoria Sacra telluris proposuit dissertatio mathematica, *etc.* 1695. 4°. **1014.** b. **60.**

—— *See* CROFT (Herbert) *Bishop of Hereford.* Some Animadversions upon a Book intituled " The Theory of the Earth." 1685. 8°. **990.** a. **8.**

—— *See* HALLER (E.) Die barocken Stilmerkmale in der englischen, lateinischen und deutschen Fassung von Dr. Thomas Burnets Theory of the Earth. [1940.] 8°. **W.P.1693/9.**

—— *See* KEILL (John) An Examination of Dr. Burnet's Theory of the Earth, *etc.* 1698. 8°. **970.** f. **12.**

—— —— 1734. 8°. **970.** f. **13.**

—— *See* KEILL (John) A Vindication of the New Theory of the Earth from the exceptions of Mr. Keill and others. With an historical preface of the occasions of the discoveries therein contain'd, *etc.* [By W. Whiston.] 1698. 8°. **970.** f. **37.**

—— *See* LEYDEKKER (Melchior) *Professor of Theology at Utrecht.* M. Leydeckeri de republica Hebræorum libri XII . . . subjicitur Archæologia sacra, qua historia creationis et diluvii Mosaica contra Burneti profanam telluris theoriam asseritur. 1704, *etc.* fol. **200.** g. **2, 3.**

—— *See* LOVELL (Archibald) A Summary of Material Heads which may be enlarged and improved into a compleat answer to Dr. Burnet's Theory of the Earth. 1696. 4°. **444.** c. **17. (5.)**

—— *See* MACKAILE (Matthew) Terræ prodromus theoricus. Containing . . . a new system, of the order and gradation, in the world's creation; by way of animadversions upon Mr. T. Burnet's thoery [*sic*] of his imaginary earth, &c. 1691. 4°. **531.** h. **29.**

—— *See* MIRACLES. Miracles, no Violations of the Laws of Nature. [A translation of the sixth chapter of Spinoza's " Tractatus theologicopoliticus," with extracts from T. Burnet's " Telluris theoria sacra."] 1683. 4°. **700.** e. **20. (1.)**

—— *See* WAGNER (Christianus) Animadversiones in . . . T. Burnetii Telluris theoriam sacram, *etc.* [1683.] 4°. **1326.** e. **11. (5.)**

—— *See* WARREN (Erasmus) Geologia: or a Discourse concerning the Earth before the Deluge. Wherein the form and properties ascribed to it, in a book intituled The Theory of the Earth, are excepted against. 1690. 4°. **457.** c. **7.**

BURNET (THOMAS) *Master of the Charter House.*

—— A Re-Survey of the Mosaic System of the Creation. With rules for the right judging and interpreting of Scripture . . . Translated from the Latin [i.e. from " Epistolae duae circa libellum de Archaeologiis philosophicis," of which the former was first published in " Archaeologiae philosophicae," the latter in " De statu mortuorum "] . . . by Mr. Foxton. [With " The Heathen Notions concerning the State of the Dead " by R. Simon, translated by J. Morgan, and " The Resurrection," a poem by J. Addison, translated by N. Amhurst.] pp. 48. 37. [*London*, 1728.] 8°. **854. f. 17. (2.)**

BURNET (THOMAS) *Professor of Philosophy in the Marischal College, Aberdeen.* Theses philosophicæ, quas . . . Abredoniæ, in . . . Academia Marischallana . . . sub præsidio T. Burnet publice propugnabunt; splendida laureæ corollâ hac vice condecorandi, *etc.* pp. 15. *Excudebat Ioannes Forbes: Abredoniæ,* 1686. 4°. **8464.** bb. **41.**

BURNET (THOMAS) *Rector of St. James's, Garlick-Hythe.* Art conducive to Religion. A sermon preached at St. James's, Garlick-Hythe . . . on Sunday, April 22, 1849 in recommendation of " The Iron, Hardware and Metal Trades' Pension Society." pp. 16. *W. E. Painter: London,* [1849.] 8°. **4475.** cc. **22.**

—— A Sermon on the Liturgy. pp. 16. *J. G. & F. Rivington: London,* 1835. 8°. T. **1912.** (8.)

BURNET (THOMAS) *Rector of West Kington, Wilts.* The Argument set forth in a late book [by Matthew Tindal], entitled, " Christianity as old as the Creation," reviewed and confuted. In several conferences. [With " An essay on the power of human reason, in answer to the question, how far Reason is sufficient for the happiness of mankind. With a short view of the nature and reason of the Christian revelation."] 4 pt. *A. Bettesworth & C. Hitch: London,* 1730–32. 8°. **109.** b. **18.**

—— [Another copy of Conference 1.] **699.** d. **13. (3.)**

—— The Demonstration of True Religion, in a Chain of consequences from certain and undeniable principles; wherein the necessity and certainty of natural and reveal'd religion, with the nature and reason of both, are proved and explain'd: and in particular, the authority of the Christian revelation is establish'd . . . in sixteen sermons preach'd . . . in the years 1724, and 1725; for the lecture founded by the Honourable Robert Boyle, Esq., *etc.* 2 vol. *Arthur Bettesworth: London,* 1726. 8°. **1021.** h. **18, 19.**

—— [Another edition.] *See* LETSOME (Sampson) and NICHOLL (I.) A Defence of Natural and Revealed Religion, *etc.* vol. 3. 1739. fol. **15.** d. **9.**

—— An Essay upon Government: or, the Natural notions of government demonstrated, *etc.* pp. 127. *J. Baker & T. Warner: London,* 1716. 8°. **523.** c. **10.**

—— The second edition, with additions. pp. 111. *A. Bettesworth: London,* 1726. 8°. **100.** k. **31.**

—— Love and Unity a necessary means of preserving our Religion and Liberties. A sermon, *etc.* pp. 31. *J. Peele: London,* 1722. 8°. **225.** g. **20. (10.)**

—— The Nature, Use and Efficacy of the Sacrament of the Lord's Supper, *etc.* pp. 31. *A. Bettesworth & C. Hitch: London,* 1731. 8°. **4326.** cc. **11.**

—— The Scripture Doctrine of the Redemption of the World by Christ, intelligibly explained to the capacity of mean people. Which may serve as an answer to a book, entitled, The Moral Philosopher, *etc.* pp. viii. 118. *A. Bettesworth & C. Hitch: London,* MCDDXXXVII [1737]. 8°. T. **1631.** (1.)

BURNET (Thomas) *Rector of West Kington, Wilts.*

— The Scripture-Trinity intelligibly explained: or, an Essay toward the demonstration of a Trinity in Unity, from Reason and Scripture . . . By a Divine of the Church of England [i.e. T. Burnet]. pp. ix. 198. FEW MS. NOTES. 1720. 8°. *See* SCRIPTURE-TRINITY. **1120**. d. 5.

— The Truth of the Christian Religion, with the falsehood of all other religions, prov'd, to the capacity of children and vulgar people. pp. 23. *A. Bettesworth: London,* 1730. 8°. **4016**. a. **12**.

BURNET (Thomas) *Verse-Writer.* The Sweets of Solitude, and other poems. pp. 88. *Printed for the Author: Birmingham; C. Law: London,* 1807. 8°. **11643**. c. **19**.

BURNET (*Sir* Thomas) *M.D.* *See* HIPPOCRATES. [*Works.—Latin.*] Hippocrates contractus. In quo . . . Hippocratis . . . opera omnia, in brevem epitomen . . . redacta habentur. Studio et opera T. Burnet. 1685. 12°. **539**. b. **8**.

— — 1765. 8°. **1174**. f. **42**.

— Currus iatrikus trumphalis. In quo conclusæ iacent ter trinæ principes difficultates medicæ, ad Apollinarem lauream consequendam, *etc.* pp. 12. [*D. Pech:*] *Monspelii,* [1659.] 4°. **1180.b.3.(8.)** *Cropped.*

— Disputatio de vomitu, *etc.* *A. Elzevier: Lugduni Batavorum,* 1691. 4°. **1185**. g. **20**. (9.)

— Quæstiones quatuor cardinales pro suprema Apollinari dapne consequenda, *etc.* *D. Pech: Monspelii,* 1659. 4°. **1185**. f. 3. (6.)

— Thomæ Burnet . . . Thesaurus medicinæ practicæ . . . A Daniele Puerario . . . auctus observationibus selectissimis. 2 tom. *J. H. Widerhold: Genevæ,* 1678. 12°. **773**. a. **18**.

— Editio novissima . . . auctior, *etc.* pp. 1012. *Lugduni,* 1702. 4°. **541**. f. **17**.

— Thesauri medicinæ practicæ breviarium; cum indice remediorum quæ inibi continentur. pp. 130. *Typis Georgii Mosman: Edinburgi,* 1703. 12°. **773**. a. **23**.

BURNET (*Sir* Thomas) *One of the Justices of the Court of Common Pleas.* *See* also DOGGREL (*Sir* Iliad) *pseud.* [i.e. Sir T. Burnet and G. Duckett.]

— *See* also TIMON, *pseud.* [i.e. *Sir* T. Burnet.]

— [For editions of Gilbert Burnet's "History of My Own Time," of which the second volume was edited with a biographical memoir by Sir T. Burnet:] *See* BURNET (Gilbert) *Bishop of Salisbury.* [*History of My Own Time.*]

— The Letters of Thomas Burnet to George Duckett 1712–1722. Edited by David Nichol Smith. [With a portrait of Burnet.] pp. xlii. 325. 1914. fol. *See* LONDON.—III. *Roxburghe Club.* C. **101**. g. **6**.

— An Answer to a Letter to the Bishop of Bangor, written by one Andrew Snap. [By Sir T. Burnet.] pp. 18. 1717. 8°. *See* SNAPE (Andrew) *D.D.* **701**. f. **12**. (1.)

— [Another copy.] **4473**. b. **7**. (2.)

— The second edition. pp. 24. 1717. 8°. *See* SNAPE (Andrew) *D.D.* **109**. e. **28**.

BURNET (*Sir* Thomas) *One of the Justices of the Court of Common Pleas.*

— The British Bulwark: being a collection of all the clauses . . . now in force against the Pretender, the Non-jurors and the Papists. With an appendix relating to the suspension of the Habeas Corpus Act. pp. 46. *J. Roberts: London,* 1715. 8°. **518**. a. **3**.

— [Another copy.] **112**. a. **57**.

— Burnet and Bradbury, or the Confederacy of the press and the pulpit for the blood of the last ministry. [By Daniel Defoe.] pp. 34. *S. Keimer: London,* 1715. 8°. **8140**. df. **12**.

— A Certain Information of a Certain Discourse, that happen'd at a certain gentleman's house, in a certain county. Written by a certain person then present, to a certain friend now at London. From whence you may collect the great certainty of the account. The second edition. [By Sir T. Burnet.] pp. 79. 1712. 8°. *See* INFORMATION. **104**. b. **8**.

— The History of Ingratitude: or, a Second part of Antient Precedents for Modern Facts. In answer to a Letter from a Noble Lord. [By Sir Thomas Burnet.] pp. 37. 1712. 8°. *See* HISTORY. **104**. b. **2**.

— A Letter to the People, to be left for them at the booksellers; with a word or two of the Bandbox Plot. [By Sir T. Burnet.] pp. 15. 1712. 8°. *See* LETTER. **1474**. b. **8**.

— The Life of the Right Rev. Gilbert Burnet Bishop of Salisbury, *etc.* [Abridged by Edward Goldney from the life by Sir T. Burnet published in vol. 2 of G. Burnet's "History of My Own Time." With portraits.] pp. 16. 1770. 8°. [GOLDNEY (*Edward*) *Infallible Remedies, for the Perfect Cure of all Personal, and National Unhappiness, etc.*] *See* BURNET (Gilbert) *Bishop of Salisbury.* [*Appendix.*] **4376**. bb. **32**. (8.)

— The Necessity of Impeaching the Late Ministry. In a letter to the Earl of Hallifax. pp. 37. *J. Roberts: London,* 1715. 8°. T. **2228**. (6.)

— The second edition. pp. 37. *J. Roberts: London,* 1715. 8°. T. **1108**. (4.)

— [Another copy.] E. **2005**. (7.)

— [Another copy.] E. **2006**. (3.)

— [Another copy.] **101**. e. **53**.

— The third edition. pp. 37. *J. Roberts: London,* 1715. 8°. E. **2006**. (4.)

— Schreiben . . . an den Grafen von Halifax, worinnen die Nohtwendigkeit, das letzte Ministerium in Rechten zu verfolgen, gezeiget wird; benebst unpartheyischen Bedencken von einem Liebhaber seines Vaterlandes, über dieselbe Materie; dem beygefügt Der entdeckte Verraht, in einer Antwort, auf die bosshaffte Schmäh-Schrifft, genandt: Engelländische Nachricht an die Einwohner von Engelland &c. Aus dem Englischen übersetzt. *See* ENGLAND. [*Appendix.—Descriptions, etc.*] Das vereinigte Gross-Britannien, *etc.* 1716. 4°. **796**. h. **19**.

— Britons Strike Home. The absolute necessity of impeaching somebody. In a letter to Tom. Burnet, Esquire. [A reply to "The Necessity of Impeaching the Late Ministry."] pp. 40. *E. Smith: London,* 1715. 8°. **8138**. aaa. **14**.

— The second edition. pp. 40. *E. Smith: London,* 1715. 8°. **101**. e. **52**.

BURNET (*Sir* Thomas) *One of the Justices of the Court of Common Pleas.*

—— A Letter to a Merry Young Gentleman, intituled, Tho. Burnet, Esq; in answer to one writ by him to . . . the . . . Earl of Halifax; by which it plainly appears, the said Squire was not awake when he writ the said letter. pp. 24. *J. Morphew: London*, 1715. 8°. **T. 2228. (7.)**

—— [Another copy.] **E. 1999. (4.)**

—— [Another copy.] **E. 2194. (1.)**

—— Schreiben des Msr: Leslei, eines vornehmen Tory, an den Ritter Thomas Burnet. (Schreiben an einen lustigen jungen Edelmann, genandt Thomas Burnet, Rittern.) Zur Antwort desselben, an den Grafen von Halifax geschriebenen, Briefes; nebst der Verthädigung des Ritters Burnet . . . [Signed: W. R.] Beyde aus dem Englischen übersetzt. [Translations of "A Letter to a Merry Young Gentleman, intituled, Tho. Burnet, Esq." and "Mr. Burnet's Defence," the former here wrongly ascribed to Charles Leslie.] pp. 52. 1716. 4°. [*Das vereinigte Gross-Britannien, etc.*] *See* Leslie (Charles) *M.A.* **796. h. 19.**

—— A Letter to the Bishop of Salisbury occasion'd by his son's Letter to the Earl of Hallifax. Containing a fair state of the case of the late ministry, and a full answer to all Mr. Burnet's arguments for an impeachment. By a good friend to the late ministers [i.e. Daniel Burgess, the younger]. pp. 33. *A. Dodd: London*, 1715. 8°. **8133. aaa. 13.**

—— Mr. Burnet's Defence: or, More reasons for an impeachment. In remarks on an infamous and trayterous libel . . . entitled, "A Letter to a Merry Young Gentleman." In a second letter to the Earl of Halifax. [The preface signed: W. R.] 1715. 8°. *See* R., W. **E. 2006. (5.)**

—— Our Ancestors as Wise as We: or, Ancient precedents for modern facts, in answer to a Letter from a Noble Lord. [By Sir Thomas Burnet.] pp. 34. 1712. 8°. *See* Ancestors. **8132. aaa. 1. (7.)**

—— A Protestant Index to Mr. Lock - - - - t's [i.e. George Lockhart's] Memoirs, concerning the Affairs of Scotland. [By Sir T. Burnet.] pp. 25. 1714. 8°. *See* Lock - - - - t ( ) *Mr.* **287. b. 19. (3.)**

—— [Another copy.] **116. h. 63.**

—— Remarks upon the Right Honourable the Lord Lansdowne's Letter to the author of the Reflections Historical and Political, &c. [i.e. John Oldmixon] as far as relates to Bishop Burnet. [By Sir T. Burnet.] pp. 34. 1732. 4°. *See* Granville (George) *Baron Lansdowne.* **598. h. 21. (3.)**

—— Some New Proofs, by which it appears that the Pretender is truly James the Third. The third edition. [By Sir T. Burnet.] pp. 28. 1713. 8°. *See* James Francis Edward [Stuart], *Prince of Wales*, called *the Pretender.* **111. c. 41.**

—— The fifth edition. pp. 28. 1714. 8°. *See* James Francis Edward [Stuart], *Prince of Wales*, called *the Pretender.* **8122. f. 36.**

—— Some New Proofs by which it appears that the Pretender is truly James the Third, *etc.* [By Sir T. Burnet.] pp. 31. 1745. 4°. *See* James Francis Edward [Stuart], *Prince of Wales*, called *the Pretender.* **1475. b. 61.**

BURNET (*Sir* Thomas) *One of the Justices of the Court* c *Common Pleas.*

—— [Another edition.] Some Farther Proofs, whereb it appears that the Pretender is truly James the Third . . Illustrated with notes and observations never befor publish'd. pp. 83. 1745. 8°. *See* James Franci Edward [Stuart], *Prince of Wales*, called *the Pretender.* **1093. e. 10**

—— Le Chevalier de St. George, réhabilité dans sa qualité d Jacques iii. par de nouvelles preuves. (Par Gilber Burnet.) [In fact a translation of "Some New Proofs by which it appears that the Pretender is truly James th Third," by Sir T. Burnet.] Avec la relation historiqu des suites de sa naissance, par Mr. Rousset. pp. 388. 1745. 8°. *See* Burnet (Gilbert) *Son of the Bishop* c *Salisbury.* **G. 187**

—— The True Church of Christ, which, and where to b found; according to the opinion of the late Judge Burnet With an introduction concerning divine worship. And caution to gospel-preachers, *etc.* pp. viii. 40. *Jonatha Scott; R. Baldwin: London*, 1753. 16°. **4402. i. 3**

—— Truth, if you can find it; or, a Character of the presen M - - - - - y and P - - - - - - t [i.e. Ministry and Parliament In a letter to a member of the March Club. [By Sir T Burnet.] pp. 37. 1712. 8°. *See* Truth. **T. 1990. (18**

—— Verses written on Several Occasions, between the year 1712 and 1721. [By Sir T. Burnet.] pp. iv. 71. 1777. 4°. *See* Verses. **643. k. 6. (9**

—— A Letter to Thomas Burnet, Esq; shewing that he ha used the same fidelity in printing a letter of Dr. Beach in the Life of Bishop Burnet, as the editors of Bish Burnet's History of his own Times have exemplified in t publication thereof, *etc.* [By Philip Beach.] pp. xii. 64. *Richard Reily: London*, 1736. 8°. **116. h. 6**

—— *See* Beach (Philip) A Second Letter to Thom Burnet, Esq; wherein the former Letter to him fully vindicated . . . By the author of the first Lett (Phil. Beach). 1736. 8°. **699. f. 8. (2**

—— *See* Sinclair (J.) Some Remarks on a Late Letter t Thomas Burnet, Esq; said to be written by a son o Dr. Beach. In a letter to the author of that pamphlet 1736. 8°. **699. f. 8. (3.**

—— A True Account of the Life and Writings of Thoma Burnett. The second edition. [A satire. By Georg Sewell.] pp. 26. *A. Dodd: London*, 1715. 8°. **T. 1787. (8.**

BURNET (*Sir* Thomas) *One of the Justices of the Court* *Common Pleas*, and **DUCKETT** (George)

—— A Second Tale of a Tub or, the History of Robert Powel the Puppet-Show-Mar [A satire on Robert Harley, Earl of Oxford. By T. Burne and G. Duckett.] pp. x. 219. 1715. 8°. *See* Powe (Robert) *the Puppet-Show-Man.* **1079. m. 14**

—— [Another copy.] **292. e. 1C**

—— A Summary of all the Religious Houses in England ar Wales, with their titles and valuations at the time of the dissolution. And a calculation of what they might b worth at this day. Together with an appendix concernir the several religious orders that prevail'd in this kingdor [By Sir T. Burnet and G. Duckett.] pp. xxiv. 100. 1717. 8°. *See* England. [*Appendix.—Religion.*] **4715. b. 1**

BURNET (*Sir* Thomas) *One of the Justices of the Court of Common Pleas*, and **DUCKETT** (George)

—— [Another copy.] **296.** l. **21.**

—— [Another copy.] G. **12016.**

BURNET (W. C.) *See* Bonwick (J.) Climate and Health in South Africa . . . Revised by W. C. Burnet. 1880. 8°. **7688.** a. **5.**

—— The Emigrants' Guide to South Africa . . . Seventh edition, *etc.* [The preface signed: W. C. B., i.e. W. C. Burnet.] pp. l. 139. 1891. 8°. *See* B., W. C. **10097.** ccc. **16.**

BURNET (W. Pickering) A Hand-Book of King's Lynn, or, a Visit to the Metropolis of Marshland. (A Directory of King's Lynn . . . for 1846.) 2 pt. *Whittaker & Co.: London*, 1846. 12°. **797.** d. **5.**

BURNET (Walter Desforges)

—— *See* Simons (Eric N.) Mechanics for the Home Student. By E. N. Simons . . . In association with W. D. Burnet, *etc.* 1950. 8°. **8764.** g. **8.**

BURNET (William) *Governor of Massachusetts and New Hampshire.* An Essay on Scripture Prophecy, wherein it is endeavoured to explain the three periods contain'd in the xii Chapter of the Prophet Daniel. With some arguments to make it probable, that the first of the periods did expire in the year 1715. [By W. Burnet.] pp. 167. 1724. 4°. *See* Bible.—*Appendix.—Daniel.* [*Miscellaneous.*] **3166.** bb. **51.**

—— A Poem presented to his Excellency William Burnet Esq; on his arrival at Boston. pp. 5. [*Boston*, 1728.] 8°. **11686.** d. **8.**

BURNET (William) *of Chertsey.* The Capital Principles of the People called Quakers, discovered and stated out of their own writings, *etc.* *London*, 1668. 4°. T. **370.** **(19.)** *Imperfect; wanting all after p.* 51.

—— *See* Whitehead (George) *Quaker.* The Light and Life of Christ Within . . . and the Quakers principles justified . . . from the false and blasphemous constructions put upon them by William Burnet, in his book, stiled, The Capital Principles of the People called Quakers, *etc.* 1668. 4°. **4151.** a. **2.** **(2.)**

BURNET (William) *Vicar of Childerditch.* The Catechetical Text-Book; or, First principles of Christian faith and practice, as taught in the Church Catechism, *etc.* pp. 31. *William Macintosh: London*, [1867.] 16°. **3504.** de. **12.** **(3.)**

—— The Church Catechism, simplified and proved from Holy Scripture. pp. 29. *Elliot Stock: London*, [1910.] 16°. **03504.** de. **11.**

—— George Lawrence Pilkington of Uganda. pp. 27. *Elliot Stock: London*, 1911. 8°. **4805.** bb. **28.** **(2.)**

—— Gleanings from a Parson's Diary, *etc.* pp. vi. 119. *Elliot Stock: London*, 1905. 8°. **4498.** bb. **4.**

—— Voices from Patmos. [Meditations on the second and third chapters of the Revelation of St. John.] pp. 136. *S. W. Partridge & Co.: London*, [1882.] 8°. **3186.** df. **2.**

BURNET (William) *Vicar of Childerditch*, and **WILLIAMS** (Arthur Lukyn)

—— The Jews in their Present Condition Witnesses to the Bible. pp. 44. *R.T.S.: London*, [1895.] 8°. [*Present Day Tracts.* no. 77.] **4018.** ee. **1/13.**

BURNET (*Sir* William) *K.C.B.* *See* Burnett.

BURNET (William Hodgson) Gullible's Travels in Little-Brit . . . Illustrated, *etc.* *W. Westall & Co.: London*, [1920.] 16°. **012330.** ee. **44.**

—— The M.P.'s Garden of Verses . . . Illustrated by T. C. Black. pp. 64. *A. L. Humphreys: London*, 1920. 4°. **11646.** i. **45.**

—— Quite so Stories . . . Illustrated by E. T. Reed, *etc.* pp. 96. *Cassell & Co.: London*, 1918. 8°. **012331.** f. **64.**

—— The Rubaiyat of Omar, M.P. . . . Illustrated by T. C. Black. pp. 45. *W. Collins, Sons & Co.: London*, [1921.] 8°. **012314.** k. **12.**

BURNETIUS (Thomas) *Master of the Charter House.* *See* Burnet.

BURNETT, *Family of, of Leys.* *See* Burnett (George) *Lyon King of Arms.* The Family of Burnett of Leys, *etc.* 1901. 4°. [*Aberdeen University Studies.* no. 4.] Ac. **1482.**

—— *See* Burnett (William K.) Genealogical Tree of the Family of Burnett of Leys, *etc.* [1893.] *s. sh.* fol. **09915.** bb. **25.**

BURNETT (Alexander) *Land Agent.* Tillage a Substitute for Manure, illustrated by the principles of modern agricultural science, and the precepts and practice of Jethro Tull, *etc.* pp. x. 212. xxiv. viii. *Whittaker & Co.: London*, 1859. 8°. **7077.** d. **13.**

BURNETT (Alexander) *M.D.* *See* Periodical Publications.—*London.* The Medical Adviser . . . Edited by A. Burnett. 1824, *etc.* 8°. P.P. **2785.**

BURNETT (Alexander George) France and the French: a lecture . . . Revised and enlarged by the author. [With a map.] pp. vii. 111. *Simpkin, Marshall & Co.: London*, 1868. 8°. **10169.** b. **38.**

—— France since the War: a lecture . . . Revised and enlarged by the author. pp. vii. 65. *Simpkin, Marshall & Co.: London*, 1872. 8°. **10171.** de. **25.**

BURNETT (Andrew) A Sermon preach'd at Barbican upon the sixteenth of April, 1696. Being a day of thanksgiving . . . for discovering and disappointing an horrid . . . conspiracy of Papists and other traiterous persons to assassinate his most Gracious Majesty's Royal Person, *etc.* pp. 23. *For Rich. Baldwin: London*, 1696. 4°. **4474.** cc. **15.**

BURNETT (Archibald) B.C. Politics. [Verses.] *Greenwood, B.C.*, 1908. *s. sh.* fol. **1879.** c. **12.** **(10*.)**

BURNETT (Arthur Wildman) Report on the Colombo Water Works. *See* Labugama. A Holiday Trip to Labugama, *etc.* 1891. 12°. **10057.** e. **34.** **(5.)**

BURNETT (Athole) *See* Elohta (Ttenrub) *pseud.* [i.e. A. Burnett.]

BURNETT (Beatrix)

—— Sign of the Pentagram. (Poems.) pp. 24. *Arthur H. Stockwell: Ilfracombe*, 1950. 8°. **11657.** cc. **118.**

BURNETT (Benjamin Lile) From Stable Boy to Merchant Prince. A Devonshire story. pp. 154. *Marshall Bros.: London*, [1888.] 8°. **12629.** a. **14.**

BURNETT (Bernard P.)
—— Reunion by Anticipation. pp. 23. *London*, [1949.] 8°. [*Council for the Defence of Church Principles. Pamphlet.* no. 12.] W.P. **9600/12.**

BURNETT (Bishop) A Reply to the "Report of the Commissioners of Inquiry at the Cape of Good Hope, upon the complaints addressed to the Colonial Government and to the Earl Bathurst by Mr. Bishop Burnett." [By B. Burnett.] pp. x. 296. 17. *Sherwood, Gilbert & Piper: London*, 1826. 8°. **8154. d. 27.**

BURNETT (C.) 50 Amusing Toys and how to make them, *etc.* pp. 89. *Universal Publications: London*, [1936.] 8°. **07908. de. 32.**

—— 171 Outdoor Games for Children, *etc.* pp. 89. *Universal Publications: London*, [1936.] 8°. **07908. de. 31.**

BURNETT (Charles) The 18th Hussars in South Africa. The records of a cavalry regiment during the Boer War, 1899–1902 . . . With maps and illustrations. pp. 319. *Warren & Son: Winchester*, 1905. 8°. **09061. cc. 29.**

—— The Memoirs of the 18th—Queen Mary's Own—Royal Hussars, 1906–1922, including operations in the Great War . . . With maps and illustrations. pp. 215. 1926. 8°. *See* England.—*Army.—Cavalry.—Eighteenth Hussars.* **08821. d. 15.**

BURNETT (Charles Henry) Hearing, and how to keep it. [By C. H. Burnett.] pp. 152. [1881.] 8°. [*Ward and Lock's "Long-Life" Series.* no. 10.] *See* Hearing. **7404. aaa. 65.**

—— [A reissue.] Edited by George Black. [1888.] 8°. *See* Hearing. **7404. cc. 38.**

—— System of Diseases of the Ear, Nose, and Throat. Edited by C. H. Burnett, *etc.* 2 vol. *H. K. Lewis: London; Philadelphia* [printed], 1893. 8°. **7615. cc. 14.**

BURNETT (Charles John) Burnt-in Photography on Porcelain Glass and Allied Vitreous and Ceramic Fabrics . . . Reprinted, with corrections, from the Edinburgh Advertiser, *etc.* pp. 4. *James Wood: Edinburgh*, [1857.] *s. sh.* 4°. **1701. b. 1. (2.)**

—— Photography in Colours: a fragment. By a member of the Edinburgh Photographic Society [i.e. C. J. Burnett]. pp. 8. 1857. 12°. *See* Photography. **787. d. 48.**

BURNETT (Charles Mountford) Crime and Insanity: their causes, connexion, and consequences; how distinguished, and how treated, by human legislation. pp. vii. 96. *Samuel Highley: London*, 1852. 12°. **6095. a. 26. (2.)**

—— The Philosophy of Spirits in relation to Matter, *etc.* pp. xx. 312. *Samuel Highley: London*, 1850. 8°. **8630. g. 11.**

—— The Power, Wisdom, and Goodness of God, as displayed in the Animal Creation, *etc.* pp. xv. 549. *James Burns: London*, 1838. 8°. **1114. g. 25.**

—— The Six Days' Creation and the Sabbath of Rest . . . Being the substance of a lecture, *etc.* pp. 52. *Benton Seeley: London*, 1856. 8°. **4377. g. 34. (6.)**

—— What shall we do with the Criminal Lunatics? A letter addressed to the Right Hon. Lord St. Leonard's, on the introduction of his new Lunacy Bills. pp. 30. *S. Highley & Son: London*, 1853. 8°. **6095. d. 4.**

BURNETT (Charles Philip Augustus) *See* Liturgies.—*Episcopal Church of America.—Common Prayer.—Separate Parts.—Communion Office.* The Ceremonies of the Mass, arranged conformably to the Rubrics of the Book of Common Prayer . . . The Ceremonies of High Mass. By the Rev. C. P. A. Burnett. 1905. 8°. **3406. df. 35.**

—— A Ritual and Ceremonial Commentary on the Occasional Offices of Holy Baptism, Matrimony, Penance, Communion of the Sick, and Extreme Unction. pp. xi. 288. *Longmans & Co.: New York*, 1907. 8°. **3477. dg. 27.**

BURNETT (Charles Theodore) Hyde of Bowdoin. A biography of William DeWitt Hyde, *etc.* [With plates, including portraits.] pp. xvii. 364. *Houghton Mifflin Co.: Boston & New York*, 1931. 8°. **10881. ppp. 10.**

—— Splitting the Mind: an experimental study of normal men. pp. 132. *Princeton & Albany*, 1925. 8°. [*Psychological Monographs.* vol. 34. no. 2.] **P.P. 1247. eb.**

BURNETT (Clifford William Furneaux)
—— *See* Stern (David M.) and Burnett (C. W. F.) A Modern Practice of Obstetrics, *etc.* 1952. 4°. **7582. dd. 2.**

—— The Anatomy and Physiology of Obstetrics. A short textbook for students and midwives, *etc.* pp. 168. *Faber & Faber: London*, 1953. 8°. **7583. b. 42.**

BURNETT (Constance Buel)
—— The Shoemaker's Son. The life of Hans Christian Andersen. [With plates, including portraits.] pp. 252. *G. G. Harrap & Co.: London*, 1943. 8°. **010760. g. 75.**

BURNETT (David) Recent Egyptian Discoveries concerning Joseph, Moses, and the Exodus. pp. 92. *Elliot Stock: London*, 1886. 8°. **7704. aaa. 35.**

BURNETT (E. E.) The Cause of Cancer & the "Cure." pp. 40. *C. W. Daniel Co.: London*, 1931. 8°. **7440. pp. 2.**

BURNETT (E. K.)
—— Inlaid Stone and Bone Artifacts from Southern California. pp. 60. pl. lxxi. *New York*, 1944. 8°. [*Contributions from the Museum of the American Indian Heye Foundation.* vol. 13.] **Ac. 1818.**

—— The Spiro Mound Collection in the Museum. By E. K. Burnett. Historical Sketch of the Spiro Mound. By Forrest E. Clements. pp. 68. pl. xciv. *New York*, 1945. 8°. [*Contributions from the Museum of the American Indian, Heye Foundation.* vol. 14.] **Ac. 1818.**

BURNETT (E. S.)
—— Temperature Entropy Chart of Thermodynamic Properties of Nitrogen. pp. 9. *Pittsburgh*, 1950. 8°. [*U.S. Bureau of Mines. Report of Investigations.* no. 4729.] **A.S. 229/8.**

BURNETT (Edmund Cody)
—— The Continental Congress. [The consultative assembly of the American colonies, 1774–1789.] pp. xvii. 757. *Macmillan Co.: New York*, 1941. 8°. **9551. l. 29.**

—— The Government of Federal Territories in Europe . . . Reprinted from the Annual Reports of the American Historical Association. *Providence*, 1898. 8°. [*Papers from the Historical Seminary of Brown University.* no. 9.] **Ac. 2692. r.**

URNETT (Edmund Cody)

— Letters of Members of the Continental Congress. Edited by E. C. Burnett. 8 vol. *Washington*, 1921–36. 8°. [*Carnegie Institute of Washington. Publication.* no. 299.] Ac. **1866**.

URNETT (Fincelius G.) *See* David (Robert B.) Finn Burnett, Frontiersman. The life and adventures of an Indian fighter, *etc.* [With a portrait.] 1937. 8°. **09555.n.1/1.**

URNETT (Frances Eliza Hodgson) *See* Browne (Frances) Granny's Wonderful Chair . . . With an introduction by F. H. Burnett entitled The Story of the Lost Fairy Book, *etc.* 1904. 8°. **012803**. cc. **15**.

— *See* Burnett (Vivian) The Romantick Lady, Frances Hodgson Burnett, *etc.* [With portraits.] 1927. 8°. **010855**. e. **10**.

— *See* Laski (Marghanita) Mrs. Ewing, Mrs. Molesworth and Mrs. Hodgson Burnett. [With a bibliography.] 1950. 8°. **11872.a.15/12.**

— *See* Stoddard (Richard H.) Frances Hodgson Burnett. 1882. 8°. [*Essays from "The Critic."*] **12296**. b. **2**.

— Louisiana, and That Lass o' Lowrie's. Two stories, *etc.* pp. viii. 332. *Macmillan & Co.: London*, 1880. 8°. **12619**. cc. **8**.

— The Captain's Youngest. *F. Warne & Co.: London*, [1894.] 8°. **012627**. m. **37**.
Registration copy, containing pp. 1–8 *only. The story was published in "The Captain's Youngest, Piccino, and other child stories,"* 1894.

— The Captain's Youngest. Piccino. And other child stories. [Illustrated by R. B. Birch.] pp. viii. 183. *F. Warne & Co.: London*, 1894. 4°. **12808**. m. **37**.

— Children I have Known, and Giovanni and the Other. pp. xii. 243. *J. R. Osgood, McIlvaine & Co.: London*, 1892 [1891]. 8°. **012803**. ee. **28**.

— [A reissue.] *London*, 1892. 8°. **012807**. ee. **31**.

— The Cozy Lion, as told by Queen Crosspatch . . . With illustrations by Harrison Cady. pp. 104. *Century Co.: New York*, 1907. 16°. **012806**. ee. **43**.

— The Dawn of a To-morrow . . . Illustrated by F. C. Yohn. pp. 159. *F. Warne & Co.: London*, 1907. 8°. **012625**. h. **46**.

— Dolly. A love story. pp. 219. *G. Routledge & Sons: London*, [1877.] 8°. **12638**. aa. **28**.

— [Another edition.] Vagabondia, *etc.* pp. 392. *J. R. Osgood & Co.: Boston*, 1884. 8°. **12706**. i. **8**.

— [Another edition.] Dolly . . . With illustrations by Hal Ludlow. pp. ix. 327. *F. Warne & Co.: London*, 1893. 8°. **012630**. g. **58**.

— A Fair Barbarian. pp. 184. *F. Warne & Co.: London*, [1881.] 8°. **12619**. aaaa. **26**.

— The Fortunes of Philippa Fairfax. pp. 124. *F. Warne & Co.: London*, 1888. 8°. **12627**. bb. **1**.

— "Haworth's." A novel. 2 vol. *Macmillan & Co.: London*, 1879. 8°. **12641**. h. **9**.

— [Another edition.] pp. viii. 374. *C. Scribner's Sons: New York*, 1879. 12°. **12618**. i. **18**.

BURNETT (Frances Eliza Hodgson)

— The Head of the House of Coombe. pp. 374. *William Heinemann: London*, 1922. 8°. NN. **7968**.

— [Another edition.] pp. 374. *McClelland & Stewart: Toronto*, [1922.] 8°. NN. **11011**.

— [A reissue of the London edition of 1922.] *London*, 1924. 8°. NN. **9831**.

— His Grace of Osmonde. Being the portion of the history of that nobleman's life omitted in . . . "A Lady of Quality." pp. 484. *F. Warne & Co.: London*, 1897. 8°. **012623**. ee. **46**.

— How Fauntleroy occurred, and a very real little boy became an ideal one. *F. Warne & Co.: London*, [1894.] 8°. **012627**. m. **36**.
Registration copy, containing pp. 1–8 *only. The story was published in "The Captain's Youngest, Piccino, and other child stories,"* 1894.

— In Connection with the De Willoughby Claim. [A novel.] pp. 477. *F. Warne & Co.: London*, 1899. 8°. **012643**. l. **28**.

— In the Closed Room . . . Illustrations by Jessie Willcox Smith. pp. iii. 129. *Hodder & Stoughton: London; printed in U.S.A.*, 1904. 8°. **012808**. m. **60**.

— Jarl's Daughter; and other stories . . . Reprinted from "Peterson's Magazine," *etc.* *T. B. Peterson & Bros.: Philadelphia*, [1879.] 8°. **12619**. aaaa. **13**.

— Kathleen. A love story. pp. 159. *G. Routledge & Sons: London*, 1878. 8°. **12638**. aa **26**.

— [Another edition.] Kathleen Mavourneen . . . Author's revised edition. pp. 147. *Chatto & Windus: London*, 1879. 8°. **12619**. aaaa. **10**.

— A Lady of Quality. Being a most curious, hitherto unknown history, *etc.* pp. x. 368. *F. Warne & Co.: London*, 1896. 8°. **012706**. m. **30**.

— The Land of the Blue Flower. pp. 62. *G. P. Putnam's Sons: London*, 1912. 8°. **012704**. a. **22**.

— Lindsay's Luck. pp. vi. 154. *C. Scribner's Sons: New York*, [1878.] 8°. **12638**. a. **5**.

— [Another edition.] pp. 128. *G. Routledge & Sons: London*, 1879. 8°. **12619**. bbb. **24**.

— Little Betty's Kitten tells her Story. *F. Warne & Co.: London*, [1894.] 8°. **012627**. m. **38**.
Registration copy, containing pp. 1–8 *only. The story was published in "The Captain's Youngest, Piccino, and other child stories,"* 1894.

— The Little Hunchback Zia . . . Illustrated by Charles Robinson. pp. 58. *William Heinemann: London*, 1916. 8°. **04419**. ee. **11**.

— [The Little Hunchback Zia.] The Hunchback Zia. pp. 59. *St. Hugh's Press: London*, [1949.] 16°. **4412**. f. **62**.

— Little Lord Fauntleroy . . . Eighth edition. pp. xi. 269. *F. Warne & Co.: London*, 1888. 8°. **12806**. t. **15**.

— [A reissue.] Little Lord Fauntleroy. *London*, 1908. 8°. **12828**. bb. **7**.

—— [Another edition.] Illustrated by C. E. Brock. pp. 310. *F. Warne & Co.: London*, 1925. 8°. **012803**. n. **31**.

—— [Another edition.] pp. 242. *F. Warne & Co.: London & New York*, [1937.] 8°. **20059**. e. **31**.

—— Le Petit lord—Little Lord Fauntleroy. Adapté de l'anglais . . . par Eudoxie Dupuis, *etc.* pp. vi. 292. *Paris ; Édimbourg* [printed], 1936. 8°. [*Bibliothèque Nelson illustrée.* no. 4.] **012209.d.2/4.**

—— Le Petit Lord Fauntleroy . . . Traduction nouvelle de Charlotte et Marie-Louise Pressoir . . . Illustrations de Marcel Bloch. pp. 213. *Nelson: Paris; Édimbourg* [printed], 1938. fol. **12812**. bb. **56**.

—— [Little Lord Fauntleroy.] Der kleine Lord . . . Autorisierte Übersetzung aus dem Englischen von E. Becher. pp. 152. *Stuttgart*, [1914.] 8°. **012803**. i. **51**.

—— [Little Lord Fauntleroy.] Der kleine Lord. Ins Deutsche übertragen von Richard Hummel. Mit vier farbigen Bildern, *etc.* pp. 124. *Stuttgart*, [1927.] 8°. **12650**. aa. **8**.

—— Der kleine Lord . . . Reich illustriert von Herta Boden. (Übersetzt aus dem Englischen von Eva Schumann.) pp. 320. *Potsdam*, [1937.] 8°. **012643**. p. **86**.

—— Little Lord Fauntleroy. A drama in three acts founded on the story of the same name. pp. 60. *Samuel French: London ; New York*, [1900.] 8°. [*Lacy's Acting Edition of Plays.*] **2304**. h. **38**.

—— Le Petit Lord. Comédie en trois actes. Par Jacques Lemaire, F. Burnett et Schurmann. [Adapted from F. E. H. Burnett's play, "Little Lord Fauntleroy."] pp. 115. 1895. 8°. *See* Lemaire (J.) **11740**. de. **1**.

—— The Little Princess. A play for children and grown-up children in three acts. [Based on the author's tale "Sara Crewe."] pp. 69. *London, New York*, [1921.] 8°. [*French's Acting Edition.*] **2304**. h. **101**. (**1**.)

—— A Little Princess. Being the whole story of Sara Crewe now told for the first time . . . With . . . illustrations . . . by Harold Piffard. pp. xi. 302. *F. Warne & Co.: London*, 1905. 8°. **12813**. s. **1**.

—— La Petite princesse . . . Traduit . . . par Valentine Leconte . . . Illustrations de Marcel Bloch. pp. 234. *Paris ; Édimbourg* [printed], 1934. 8°. **20054**. c. **6**.

—— [Another edition.] pp. v. 328. *Paris ; Édimbourg* printed, 1937. 8°. [*Bibliothèque Nelson illustrée.* no. 8.] **012209.d.2/8.**

—— Little Saint Elizabeth, and other stories . . . Illustrated . . . Second edition. pp. 160. *F. Warne & Co.: London*, 1890. 8°. **12806**. u. **35**.

—— The Lost Prince. pp. 320. *Hodder & Stoughton: London*, 1915. 8°. **NN. 3165**.

—— The Making of a Marchioness. pp. 346. *Smith, Elder & Co.: London*, 1901. 8°. **012639**. cc. **28**.

—— [Another edition.] pp. 286. [*London*, 1910.] 8°. [*Nelson's Library.*] **12202.y.1/252.**

—— [A reissue.] *London*, [1919.] 8°. **012625**. g. **4**.

—— Miss Crespigny. pp. 190. *G. Routledge & Sons: London*, [1878.] 8°. **12641**. aaa. **29**.

—— [Another edition.] pp. 190. *C. Scribner's Sons: New York*, [1879.] 8°. **12619**. aaaa. **11**.

—— My Robin . . . Illustrated by Alfred Brennan. pp. 42 *F. A. Stokes Co.: New York*, 1912. 8°. **7285**. cc. **33**

—— [Another edition.] pp. 60. *G. P. Putnam's Sons London*, 1913. 8°. **7285**. cc. **3**

—— Natalie, and other stories. *F. Warne & Co.: London* [1879.] 8°. **12600**. h.

—— The One I Knew the Best of All . . . With illustra-tions by Reginald Birch. pp. xv. 292. *F. Warne & Co London*, 1893. 8°. **012803**. f. **6**

—— Our Neighbour Opposite. [Tales.] pp. 183. *G. Routledge & Sons: London*, [1878.] 8°. **12638**. aaa. **2**

—— Pretty Polly Pemberton. A love story. pp. 19 *G. Routledge & Sons: London*, [1878.] 8°. **12638**. aa. **2**

—— [Another edition.] pp. vi. 213. *C. Scribner's Son New York*, [1878.] 8°. **12638**. a.

—— The Pretty Sister of José. A Spanish love stor pp. 127. *Spencer Blackett: London*, 1889. 8°. **12628**. bb.

—— Racketty-Packetty House. By Queen Crosspatc Spelled by F. H. Burnett. pp. 92. *F. Warne & Co London*, 1907. 16°. **012808**. k.

—— Racketty-Packetty House. A play, *etc.* [Based on t author's tale of the same name.] pp. 65. *Samuel Frenc New York, London*, [1927.] 8°. **11791**. ee. **34**. (

—— Robin. [A novel.] pp. xxii. 343. *William Heineman London*, 1922. 8°. **NN. 82**

—— Sara Crewe; or, What happened at Miss Minchin [The first instalment only, extracted from the periodi "St. Nicholas."] *T. Fisher Unwin: London*, 1887. 8° **12703**. i.

Imperfect ; wanting all after the first instalment.

—— Sara Crewe; or, What happened at Miss Minchin and Editha's Burglar. pp. 159. *F. Warne & C London*, 1888. 8°. **12806**. t.

—— Twentieth thousand. pp. 159. *F. Warne & C London*, 1891. 8°. **012803**. g.

—— The Secret Garden . . . Illustrated by Charles Robins pp. vii. 306. *William Heinemann: London*, 1911. 8° **012809**. aaa.

—— [Another edition.] pp. 375. *F. A. Stokes C New York*, 1911. 8°. **012704**. aa.

—— The Secret Garden, *etc.* pp. vi. 300. *William Heinemann: London*, 1950. 8°. [*New Windm Series.*] W.P. **6193**

—— The Secret Garden. pp. 253. *Penguin Books association with William Heinemann: Harmondswor* 1951. 8°. [*Puffin Story Books.* no. 69.] W.P. **13534/**

—— The Shuttle, *etc.* pp. vi. 512. *William Heineman London*, 1907. 8°. **012706**. bb.

—— The Spring Cleaning. As told by Queen Crosspat . . . With illustrations by Harrison Cady. pp. 99. *Century Co.: New York*, 1908. 8°. **012807**. h.

BURNETT (Frances Eliza Hodgson)

—— Surly Tim, and other stories. pp. 270. *Scribner, Armstrong & Co.: New York*, 1877. 8°. **12641. b. 2.**

—— [Another edition.] pp. 147. *Ward, Lock & Co.: London*, [1877.] 8°. **12638. aa. 22.**

—— [Another edition.] "Surly Tim," and other stories. By the author of "That Lass o' Lowrie's" [i.e. F. E. H. Burnett]. pp. 333. 1878. 8°. *See* Tim. C. **72. b. 8.**

—— T. Tembarom . . . Illustrated. pp. 527. *Hodder & Stoughton: London*, [1913.] 8°. NN. **1319.**

—— That Lass o' Lowrie's. A Lancashire story. pp. viii. 206. *F. Warne & Co.: London*, [1877.] 8°. **12619. bb. 1.**

—— [Another edition.] pp. vi. 269. *Scribner, Armstrong & Co.: New York*, 1877. 12°. **12641. b. 1.**

—— [Another edition.] pp. 181. *Ward, Lock & Co.: London*, [1877.] 12°. [*Lily Series.*] **12704. h. 3.**

—— [Another edition.] pp. 250. *G. Routledge & Sons: London*, [1878.] 8°. **12619. bbb. 25.**

—— *See* Hatton (Joseph) and Matthison (A.) Liz: a drama . . . founded upon the novel of "That Lass o' Lowrie's" [by F. E. H. Burnett], *etc.* [1879.] 12°. **2304. h. 5. (5.)**

—— "Theo." A love story. pp. 177. *Ward, Lock & Co.: London*, [1877.] 8°. **12638. aa. 32.**

—— [Another edition.] pp. 177. *F. Warne & Co.: London*, [1877.] 8°. **12600. h. 2.**

—— [Another edition.] pp. 183. *C. Scribner's Sons: New York*, [1879.] 8°. **12619. aaaa. 12.**

—— Through One Administration. 3 vol. *F. Warne & Co.: London*, 1883. 8°. **12643. d. 10.**

—— [Another edition.] pp. 564. *J. R. Osgood & Co.: Boston*, 1883. 8°. **12706. i. 6.**

—— [Another edition.] pp. 445. *F. Warne & Co.: London*, [1885.] 8°. **12619. aaaa. 37.**

—— [A reissue.] *London*, [1892.] 8°. [*Warne's Crown Library.* no. 20.] **12643. a. 55.**

—— The Tide on the Moaning Bar. (A Quiet Life.) [Two tales.] pp. 158. *G. Routledge & Sons: London*, [1879.] 8°. **12638. aa. 35.**

—— The Troubles of Queen Silver-Bell, *etc.* pp. 93. *F. Warne & Co.: London*, 1907. 16°. **012808. k. 59.**

—— Two Days in the Life of Piccino. *F. Warne & Co.: London*, [1894.] 8°. **012627. m. 39.**
Registration copy, containing pp. 1–8 *only. The story was published in "The Captain's Youngest, Piccino, and other child stories,"* 1894.

—— Two Little Pilgrims' Progress. A story of the City Beautiful, *etc.* pp. 215. *F. Warne & Co.: London*, 1895. 8°. **012808. eee. 18.**

—— Vagabondia. A love story. *See* supra: Dolly, *etc.*

—— The White People. pp. 111. *William Heinemann: London*, 1920. 8°. **012621. ee. 70.**

—— A Woman's Will; or, Miss Defarge. pp. 119. *F. Warne & Co.: London*, [1887.] 8°. **12600. h. 20.**

—— Ad ujævne Stier. Fortællinger. pp. 144. *Aarhus*, 1892. 8°. **012621. f. 4.**

BURNETT (Frank) *Rev.* The Enrichment of Life, and other sermons, *etc.* pp. 123. *A. H. Stockwell: London*, 1901. 8°. [*Baptist Pulpit.* no. 15.] **4479. k.**

BURNETT (Frank) *Traveller.* Summer Isles of Eden, *etc.* [With plates and a map.] pp. xvii. 213. *Sifton, Praed & Co.: London*, 1923. 8°. **10493. f. 12.**

—— Through Polynesia and Papua. Wanderings with a camera in southern seas . . . Illustrated. pp. xv. 197. *Francis Griffiths: London*, 1911. 8°. **10491. s. 12.**

—— Through Tropic Seas . . . Illustrated. pp. xvi. 173. *Francis Griffiths: London*, 1910. 8°. **10491. s. 7.**

—— The Wreck of the "Tropic Bird," and other South Sea stories. [With plates.] pp. 113. *Sifton, Praed & Co.: London*, 1926. 8°. **10496. a. 29.**

BURNETT (Frank Marsden) The Simplest Cure. Suggestions for a rational view of the prevention and treatment of disease. pp. 75. *Lawrence & Bullen: London*, 1905. 8°. **7461. de. 20.**

BURNETT (George) *Lyon King of Arms.* *See* Scotland.—*Court of Exchequer.* Rotuli scaccarii regum Scotorum. The Exchequer Rolls of Scotland. Edited by . . . J. Stuart . . . and G. Burnett. 1878, *etc.* 8°. **2073. (104.)**

—— *See* Woodward (John) *Incumbent of St. Mary's, Montrose*, and Burnett (G.) A Treatise on Heraldry, *etc.* 1892. 8°. **9904. f. 23.**

—— The Family of Burnett of Leys, with collateral branches. From the mss. of the late George Burnett . . . Edited by Colonel James Allardyce. [With a memoir of the author by Sir J. B. Paul, and plates.] pp. xxii. 367. *Aberdeen*, 1901. 8°. [*Aberdeen University Studies.* no. 4.] Ac. **1482.**

—— Popular Genealogists, or the Art of pedigree-making. [By G. Burnett.] pp. 108. 1865. 8°. *See* Genealogists. **9904. c. 12.**

—— The Red Book of Menteith reviewed, in reply to charges of literary discourtesy made against the reviewer, in a letter to the author of that work [i.e. Sir William Fraser]. pp. xvi. 67. *David Douglas: Edinburgh*, 1881. 4°. **9916. aa. 22.**

BURNETT (George) *of Balliol College, Oxford.* *See* Milton (John) [*Works.*] The Works of John Milton. (vol. 8. Joannis Miltoni Angli Pro populo anglicano defensio secunda. With the translation of G. Burnett.—vol. 9. Joannis Miltoni Angli Pro se defensio contra Alexandrum Morum ecclesiasten. With the translation of G. Burnett.) 1931, *etc.* 8°. **11603. l. 3.**

—— *See* Milton (John) [*Prose Works.*] The Prose Works of John Milton . . . With new translations, and an introduction. By G. Burnett. 1809. 12°. **12271. df. 5.**

—— *See* Milton (John) [*Prose Works.—Doctrine and Discipline of Divorce.*] John Milton's Abhandlung über Lehre und Wesen der Ehescheidung . . . Nach der abgekürzten Form des G. Burnett, *etc.* 1855. 8°. **5175. d. 85. (7.)**

—— Specimens of English Prose-Writers, from the earliest times to the close of the seventeenth century, with sketches biographical and literary, *etc.* 3 vol. *Longman & Co.: London*, 1807. 8°. **1162. d. 1–3.**

—— View of the Present State of Poland. pp. viii. 446. *Longman & Co.: London*, 1807. 12°. **10290. aa. 22.**

BURNETT (George) *of Newcastle upon Tyne.* Geo. Burnett's Improved Bill Book, for bills payable and receivable. 2 pt. *W. Fordyce: Newcastle upon Tyne,* [1835.] 4°. L.R. **111**. a. **24**.

BURNETT (George) *Public Relations Officer, B.B.C.* A Book of Border Verse. Selected . . . by G. Burnett. pp. xxxii. 192. *Blackie & Son: London,* 1926. 8°. **11607**. dd. **22**.

—— A Book of Scottish Verse. Chosen by G. Burnett, *etc.* pp. xiv. 208. *Methuen & Co.: London,* 1932. 8°. **11609**. pp. **1**.

—— Companion to Tweed . . . With sixteen plates. *London,* 1938. 8°. [*Methuen's Companion Books.*] W.P. **13538/4**.

—— Outside the Guest-House. Tales from North-West India. pp. 64. *W. & R. Chambers: London & Edinburgh,* 1935. 8°. [*Stories of Fact and Fancy.* set D. no. 140.] **012203.f.41.**

—— Scotland on the Air. (Descriptions of the working of various B.B.C. departments in Scotland by the officials in charge of them.) Compiled and edited by G. Burnett. [With plates.] pp. xi. 160. *Moray Press: Edinburgh & London,* 1938. 8°. **08757**. bb. **1**.

BURNETT (George) *Rev.*

—— The Third Testament; or, the Apocalypse. A brief exposition, *etc.* pp. ix. 115. *Northern Chronicle Office: Inverness,* 1937. 8°. **03185**. de. **28**.

BURNETT (George Murray)

—— Mechanism of Polymer Reactions. pp. xv. 493. *Interscience Publishers: New York, London; Cambridge* printed, 1954. 8°. [*High Polymers.* vol. 3.] W.P. **3840/3**.

BURNETT (Gilbert) *Bishop of Salisbury. See* Burnet.

BURNETT (Gilbert) *Son of the Bishop of Salisbury. See* Burnet.

BURNETT (Gilbert Thomas) *See* Burnett (M. A.) Plantæ utiliores: or, Illustrations of useful plants, *etc.* [With text selected by the artist, chiefly from the works of G. T. Burnett.] 1842. 4°. **1253**. h. **5**.

—— *See* Murray (Hugh) An Historical and Descriptive Account of China . . . By H. Murray . . . G. Burnett [and others], *etc.* 1836. 8°. [*Edinburgh Cabinet Library.* vol. 18–20.] **12203.t.1/18–20.**

—— —— 1843. 8°. **1158**. a. **5–7**.

—— *See* Periodical Publications.—*London.* The Medical and Physical Journal. (The London Medical and Physical Journal. New series. Edited by J. North, J. Whatley and G. T. Burnett.) 1799, *etc.* 8°. P.P. **2692**.

—— Amœnitates querneæ. (Botanical Diversions. I.) [By G. T. Burnett.] 1827. fol. [Burgess (*Henry W.*) *Eidodendron, etc.*] *See* Amoenitates. **1824**. e. **14**.

—— Inaugural Address, delivered at a meeting of the Medico-Botanical Society of London, *etc.* pp. 24. *J. & C. Adlard: London,* 1833. 8°. T. **1463**. **(20.)**

—— A Lecture delivered in King's College, London . . . being introductory to the first botanical course of the session opening the institution. pp. 37. *Adlard: London,* 1832. 8°. T. **1511**. **(9.)**

—— A Lecture delivered in King's College, London . . . Introductory to the second course. pp. 44. *Adlard: London,* 1832. 8°. T. **1511**. **(10.)**

—— Outlines of Botany, *etc.* 2 vol. pp. viii. vii. 1190. *John Churchill: London,* 1835. 8°. **443**. d. **24**.

BURNETT (Hallie Southgate)

—— This Heart, this Hunter. pp. 310. *Henry Holt & C*
New York, 1953. 8°. **12715**. d.

BURNETT (Hodgson) *See* Burnett (Frances E. H.)

BURNETT (Ian Alistair Kendall) *See* London.—I *British Museum.—Department of Printed Books.* List Catalogues of English Book Sales, 1676–1900, now the British Museum. [Compiled by H. Mattingly a I. A. K. Burnett, under the general editorship of A. Pollard.] 1915. 8°. **2713.c.2.**

BURNETT (Isabel) An Experimental Investigation in Repetitive Work. pp. iv. 26. *London,* 1925. 8 [*Industrial Fatigue Research Board. Report.* no. 30.] B.S. **25/**

BURNETT (Ivory) *pseud.* [i.e. Anna Augusta Whitta Ramsay.] *See* also Ramsay (A. A. W.)

—— The Ravens enter the House. pp. 333. *John Murra London,* 1931. 8°. NN. **1754**

BURNETT (Ivy Compton)

—— *See* Johnson (Pamela H.) I. Compton-Burnett. critical study. With a portrait.] 1951. 8°. W.P. **9502/**

—— *See* Liddell (John Robert) **The Novels of I. Compto Burnett. [With a portrait.]** 1955. 8°. **11871**. bb. **1**

—— Brothers and Sisters. pp. 23 *Heath Cranton: London,* 1929. 8°. NN. **1506**

—— Bullivant and the Lambs. *See* infra: Manservant a Maidservant.

—— Darkness and Day. pp. 235. *Victor Gollanc London,* 1951. 8°. NNN. **149**

—— Darkness and Day. pp. 298. *Alfred A. Knop New York,* 1951. 8°. NNN. **137**

—— Daughters and Sons. pp. 320. *Victor Gollanc London,* 1937. 8°. NN. **2709**

—— Dolores. pp. 330. *W. Blackwood & Son Edinburgh & London,* 1911. 8°. **012618**. bb. **1**

—— Elders and Betters. pp. 235. *Victor Gollancz: Londo* 1944. 8°. NN. **3438**

—— A Family and a Fortune. pp. 287. *Victor Gollancz London,* 1939. 8°. NN. **2988**

—— A Family and a Fortune. pp. 289. *Eyre Spottiswoode: London,* [1949.] 8°. NN. **3958**

—— A House and its Head. pp. 287. *William Heinemann London, Toronto,* 1935. 8°. NN. **24194**

—— A House and its Head. pp. 277. *Eyre & Spottiswood London,* 1951. 8°. NNN. **149**

—— Manservant and Maidservant. pp. 243. *Victor Gollancz: London,* 1947. 8°. NN. **36830**

—— [Manservant and Maidservant.] Bullivant and th Lambs. (Third printing.) pp. 299. *Alfred A. Knopf New York,* 1949. 8°. **012635**. c. **31**

—— Men and Wives. pp. 367. *William Heinemann: London* 1931. 8°. NN. **17535**

BURNETT (Ivy Compton)

—— Men and Wives. pp. 278. *Eyre & Spottiswoode: London*, 1948 [1949]. 8°. NN. **39268**.

—— More Women than Men. pp. 333. *William Heinemann: London*, 1933. 8°. NN. **20778**.

—— More Women than Men. pp. 228. *Eyre & Spottiswoode: London*, 1948. 8°. NN. **39195**.

—— Mother and Son. pp. 256. *Victor Gollancz: London*, 1955. 8°. NNN. **5793**.

—— Parents and Children. pp. 279. *Victor Gollancz: London*, 1941. 8°. NN. **32408**.

—— Pastors and Masters. A study. pp. 126. *Heath Cranton: London*, 1925. 8°. **012633**. e. **37**.

—— The Present and the Past. pp. 223. *Victor Gollancz: London*, 1953. 8°. NNN. **3944**.

—— Two Worlds and their Ways. pp. 285. *Victor Gollancz: London*, 1949. 8°. NN. **39579**.

BURNETT (Jacob) *See* Burnet.

BURNETT (James) *Botanist*. *See* Periodical Publications.—*London*. The Magazine of Botany and Gardening. (New series. Edited by J. Burnett and other eminent botanists.) 1833, *etc*. 4°. P.P. **2240**.

BURNETT (James) *Curate of Colerne*. Strictures on Various Passages of Scripture, which are by many considered favourable to the doctrine of Christ's personal reign on earth, with his risen saints, during the Millennium. pp. iv. 54. *A. E. Binns: Bath*, 1835. 8°. **3187**. d. **11**.

BURNETT (James) *of Craigend*. *See* Spottiswoode (John) *of Spottiswoode*. John Spottiswoode . . . Appellant. J. Burnett . . . Respondent. The appellants case. [1763.] fol. **516**. m. **19**. **(79.)**

—— *See* Spottiswoode (John) *of Spottiswoode*. John Spotswood . . . Appellant. J. Burnet . . . Respondent. The respondent's case. [1763.] fol. **516**. m. **19**. **(80.)**

BURNETT (James) *of Sunderland*. The History of the Town and Port of Sunderland, and the parishes of Bishopwearmouth and Monkwearmouth. pp. 152. *J. S. Burnett: Sunderland*, 1830. 12°. **10351**. bb. **20**.

BURNETT (James Compton) *See* Clarke (John H.) Life and Work of J. C. Burnett . . . With an account of the Burnett Memorial. [With a portrait.] 1904. 8°. **10827**. f. **16**.

—— Doctor Burnett's Essays, containing Ecce Medicus, Natrum Muriaticum, Gold, Causes of Cataract, *etc*. pp. 296. *Boericke & Tafel: New York, Philadelphia*, [1882.] 8°. **7509**. i. **8**.

—— Cataract: its nature, causes, prevention, and cure. pp. x. 219. *Homœopathic Publishing Co.: London*, 1889. 8°. **7611**. de. **33**.

—— The Change of Life in Women, and the ills and ailings incident thereto. pp. vi. 184. *Homœopathic Publishing Co.: London*, 1898. 8°. **07581**. f. **30**.

—— Curability of Cataract with Medicines. Its nature, causes, prevention & treatment. pp. 109. *Salzer & Co.: Calcutta*, [1938.] 8°. **7610**. dd. **27**.

BURNETT (James Compton)

—— Curability of Tumours by Medicines. pp. xiv. 332. *Homœopathic Publishing Co.: London*, 1893. 8°. **7630**. aa. **21**.

—— Second edition. pp. xiv. 332. *Homœopathic Publishing Co.: London*, 1898. 8°. **7630**. a. **40**.

—— Third revised edition. First Indian edition. pp. 384. *M. Bhattacharyya & Co.: Calcutta*, 1932. 8°. **07630**. de. **6**.

—— Delicate, Backward, Puny, and Stunted Children: their developmental defects, and physical, mental, and moral peculiarities considered as ailments amenable to treatment by medicines. pp. iv. 164. *Homœopathic Publishing Co.: London*, 1895. 8°. **07581**. de. **43**.

—— Diseases of the Skin, from the organismic standpoint. pp. xi. 100. *Homœopathic Publishing Co.: London; F. E. Boericke: New York & Philadelphia*, 1886. 8°. **7640**. a. **4**.

—— Second edition, revised and enlarged. pp. viii. 240. *Homœopathic Publishing Co.: London*, 1893. 8°. **7641**. a. **38**.

—— Third edition, revised and enlarged. pp. xii. 263. *Homœopathic Publishing Co.: London*, 1898. 8°. **7641**. a. **52**.

—— First Indian edition, from third edition, revised and enlarged. pp. x. 269. *M. Bhattacharyya & Co.: Calcutta*, 1933. 8°. **07641**. df. **23**.

—— Diseases of the Spleen, and their remedies clinically illustrated. pp. xi. 130. *J. Epps & Co.: London*, 1887. 8°. **7620**. a. **9**.

—— Ecce Medicus; or, Hahnemann as a man and as a physician, and the lessons of his life. Being the first Hahnemannian Lecture, 1880. pp. viii. 164. *Homœopathic Publishing Co.: London*, 1881. 8°. **7680**. a. **11**.

—— Enlarged Tonsils cured by Medicines. pp. 100. *Homœopathic Publishing Co.: London*, 1901 [1900]. 8°. **7616**. aaaa. **9**.

—— Fevers and Blood-Poisoning, and their Treatment, with special reference to the use of pyrogenium. pp. 56. *J. Epps & Co.: London*, [1888.] 8°. **07305**. f. **1**. **(3.)**

—— Fifty Reasons for Being a Homœopath. pp. xxiv. 175. *Homœopathic Publishing Co.: London*, 1888. 8°. **7321**. bb. **22**.

—— (Third edition.) pp. viii. 296. *Homœopathic Publishing Co.: London*, 1896. 8°. **7679**. de. **17**.

—— [Another edition.] To which is added some irrefutable, comparative, statistical proof thereof, by E. Petrie Hoyle. pp. 63. *Homœopathic Publishing Co.: London*, [1913.] 8°. **7307**. df. **7**. **(8.)**

—— [Another edition.] Introduced and edited by J. Ellis Barker. pp. 87. *Homœopathic Publishing Co.: London*, 1934. 8°. **07510**. ee. **40**.

—— Homœopathic Treatment; or, Fifty reasons for being a homœopath . . . Sixth edition. pp. 72. *Homœopathic Publishing Co.: London*, 1941. 8°. **7462**. pp. **47**.

—— Fifty Reasons for being a Homœopath . . . Popular edition. [An abridgment.] pp. 56. *Homœopathic Publishing Co.: London*, [1890?] 8°. **7462**. a. **56**.

—— Five Years' Experience in the New Cure of Consumption by its own virus. Presumably on a line with the method of Koch, *etc.* pp. viii. 116. *Homœopathic Publishing Co.: London*, 1890. 8°. **7616.** a. **31.**

—— [Another edition.] Eight Years' Experience in the Cure of Consumption by Bacillinum . . . Third edition, revised and enlarged. pp. xvi. 308. *Homœopathic Publishing Co.: London*, 1894. 8°. **7616.** a. **44.**

—— Gold as a Remedy in Disease . . . and as an antidote to the ill effects of mercury. pp. vi. 156. *Homœopathic Publishing Co.: London; Boericke & Tafel: New York & Philadelphia*, 1879. 8°. **7461.** aaa. **2**

—— Gout and its Cure . . . Second edition, revised and enlarged. pp. iv. 195. *J. Epps & Co.: London*, 1900. 8°. **7630.** a. **41.**

—— The Greater Diseases of the Liver: jaundice, gall-stones, enlargements, tumours and cancer: and their treatment. pp. xi. 186. *Homœopathic Publishing Co.: London*, 1891. 8°. **7620.** a. **15.**

—— [Another edition.] The Diseases of the Liver . . . Fourth edition. First Indian edition. pp. xiii. 232. *M. Bhattacharyya & Co.: Calcutta*, 1934. 8°. **07630.** de. **22.**

—— Homœopathic Treatment, *etc.* *See* supra: Fifty Reasons for being a Homœopath.

—— The Medicinal Treatment of Diseases of the Veins, *etc.* pp. vi. 166. *Homœopathic Publishing Co.: London*, 1881. 8°. **7630.** aa. **7.**

—— Diseases of the Veins . . . and their treatment by medicines. Second edition, revised and enlarged. pp. viii. 171. *J. Epps & Co.: London*, 1886. 8°. **7630.** a. **9.**

—— Natrum Muriaticum as Test of the Doctrine of Drug Dynamization. pp. 84. *E. Gould & Son: London*, 1878. 8°. **7509.** df. **5.**

—— [Another edition.] pp. 28. *Homœopathic Publishing Co.: London*, 1935. 8°. **07510.** ee. **45.**

—— On Fistula and its Radical Cure by Medicines. pp. vii. 141. *J. Epps & Co.: London*, 1889. 8°. **7630.** aa. **16.**

—— On Neuralgia: its causes and its remedies. pp. viii. 134. *Homœopathic Publishing Co.: London*, 1889. 8°. **7640.** aaa. **13.**

—— [Another edition.] With a chapter on angina pectoris . . . Second edition, enlarged. pp. viii. 172. *Homœopathic Publishing Co.: London*, 1894. 8°. **7630.** aa. **27.**

—— On the Prevention of Hare-Lip, Cleft-Palate, and other Congenital Defects, *etc.* pp. 18. *Homœopathic Publishing Co.: London*, [1880.] 8°. **07611.** e. **22.**

—— Organ Diseases of Women, notably enlargements and displacements of the uterus, and sterility, considered as curable by medicines. pp. vii. 156. *Homœopathic Publishing Co.: London*, 1896. 8°. **7581.** ccc. **14.**

—— Ringworm: its constitutional nature and cure. pp. 132. *Homœopathic Publishing Co.: London*, 1892. 8°. **7630.** aa. **18.**

—— Supersalinity of the Blood: an accelerator of senility, and a cause of cataract. pp. vi. 90. *Homœopathic Publishing Co.: London; Boericke & Tapel: New York & Philadelphia*, [1882.] 8°. **7441.** a. **15.**

—— Tumours of the Breast, and their treatment and cure by medicines. pp. viii. 213. *J. Epps & Co.: London*, 1888. 8°. **7581.** bbb. **27.**

—— Vaccinosis and its Cure by Thuja; with remarks on homœoprophylaxis. pp. viii. 129. *Homœopathic Publishing Co.: London*, 1884. 8°. **7641.** aa. **18.**

—— (Second edition.) pp. viii. 145. *Homœopathic Publishing Co.: London*, [1898.] 8°. **07561.** e. **1.**

—— Valvular Disease of the Heart from a New Standpoint. pp. 93. *Leath & Ross: London*, [1885.] 16°. **7616.** a. **30.**

BURNETT (James G.) *the Elder*, and **JEFFERSON** (Joseph) *Actor*. Blanche of Brandywine. An American patriotic spectacle. [A play. Adapted by J. G. Burnett and J. Jefferson from the novel of the same title by George Lippard.] pp. 40. [1868 ?] 12°. *See* Blanche, *of Brandywine*. **11791.** cc. **24.** **(1.)**

BURNETT (James G.) *the Younger*. Love and Laughter. Being a legacy of rhyme. [With a portrait.] pp. xii. 161. *G. P. Putnam's Sons: New York & London*, 1895. 8°. **11688.** g. **39.**

BURNETT (James Walton)

—— The Cathedrals of England & Wales from the water colour paintings by J. Walton Burnett. *Willmer Bros. & Co.: Birkenhead*, [1939– .] 8°. W.P. **12998.**

BURNETT (John) *Advocate*. Disputatio juridica, ad Tit v. Lib. xlvi. Digest. De Stipulationibus Praetoriis *etc.* pp. 20. *Balfour & Smellie: Edinburgi*, 1785. 4°. **6006.** ee. **6.** **(3.**

—— A Treatise on Various Branches of the Criminal Law o Scotland. [Edited by Robert Craigie.] pp. vii. 612. lxviii. xv. *A. Constable & Co.: Edinburgh*, *Longman & Co.: London*, 1811. 4°. **709.** h. **24**

BURNETT (John) *Colonial Secretary at Van Diemen's Land*. Appendix to a Narrative of the Case of John Burnett, Esq., *etc.* pp. 31. *James Ross: Hobart Town*, 1836. 8°. **8154.** c. **19**

—— Memorandum relative to the Case of John Burnett, Esq. *etc.* pp. 16. *James Ross: Hobart Town*, 1836. 8°. **8154.** c. **20**

—— The Sheriff's [J. Burnett's] claim to Compensation fo the damages, costs, and expenses, arising from the actio which William Turner brought against him in the Sup reme Court of Van Diemen's Land. pp. 58. *William Pratt: Hobart Town*, 1847. 8°. **1414.** i. **12**
"*Not published.*"

BURNETT (John) *Dissenting Minister at Hull*. A Sermon pp. ii. 29. *W. Savage: Hull*, 1798. 8°. **4475.** bb. **11**

BURNETT (John) *Quaker, of Friskney*. A Serious an Tender Exhortation . . . unto all sober and tender-hearted people, who are sincerely seeking after salvatio . . . to turn their minds inward unto the manifestatio of the light and spirit of Jesus Christ, *etc.* pp. 15. *T. Sowle: London*, 1704. 8°. **4152.** df. **2.** **(7.)**
Cropped.

BURNETT (John) *Secretary of the Amalgamated Society o Engineers*. Trades Unions as a Means of Improving th Conditions of Labour. *See* Oliphant (James) *of Charlott Square Institution*. The Claims of Labour, *etc.* 1886. 8°. **8207.** aa. **7**

BURNETT (JOHN) *Wesleyan Minister*. Bands of Hope in Town & Village ; how to start and work them. pp. viii. 70. *Elliot Stock: London*, 1877. 8°. **8436**. aaa. **9**. (**5**.)

BURNETT (JOHN CHAPLYN) Easy Methods for the Construction of Magic Squares. pp. 77. *Rider & Co.: London*, 1936. 8°. **7915**. ppp. **26**.

BURNETT (JOHN FREDERICK ROBERT) *See* GIBSON (Albert) and MACLEAN (R.) Gibson's Conveyancing. Fifteenth edition. By A. Weldon . . . J. F. R. Burnett. 1938. 8°. **6307.dd.1.**

—— Elements of Conveyancing, with precedents, for the use of students . . . Founded upon the fourth edition of Deane and Spurling's Elements of Conveyancing. By J. F. R. Burnett. pp. xxxii. 544. *Sweet & Maxwell: London*, 1932. 8°. **6305**. t. **9**.

—— Burnett's Elements of Conveyancing . . . Being a sixth edition of Deane and Burnett's Elements of Conveyancing. By J. F. R. Burnett. pp. xxxii. 501. *Sweet & Maxwell: London*, 1937. 8°. **6305**. r. **5**.

—— Elements of Conveyancing, with precedents. Seventh edition. pp. xxviii. 384. *Sweet & Maxwell: London*, 1944. 8°. **6307**. b. **9**.

—— The Elements of Conveyancing . . . Eighth edition. pp. xxxi. 508. *Sweet & Maxwell: London*, 1952. 8°. **6307**. e. **12**.

BURNETT (JOSEPH BERNARD) Plain and Short Instructions on the Sacrament of the Lord's Supper. With an address to different characters . . . Third edition. pp. 35. *L. B. Seeley ; Hatchard & Son: London*, 1822. 18°. **4422**. e. **6**. (**1**.)

—— [Another edition.] pp. 35. *L. & G. Seeley: London*, 1843. 18°. **4327**. a. **74**. (**1**.)

—— (Eleventh edition.) pp. 35. *Wertheim & Macintosh: London*, 1855. 18°. **4324**. aa. **54**.

BURNETT (JULIET COMPTON) *See* DUBACH-DONATH (A.) The Basic Principles of Eurhythmy . . . English translation by J. Compton-Burnett. 1937. 8°. **20031**. f. **11**.

—— *See* STEINER (Rudolf) *Philosophical Writer*. Eurhythmy as Visible Speech . . . English translation by V. and J. Compton-Burnett. 1931. 8°. **07911**. ee. **59**.

BURNETT (LAWSON) The Heart of Jesus. A study of the perfect man through illustrative examples of the Christlike in human character. pp. 316. *A. H. Stockwell: London*, [1916.] 8°. **4223**. i. **26**.

BURNETT (M. A.) Plantæ utiliores: or, Illustrations of useful plants, employed in the arts and medicine. [With text selected by the artist, chiefly from the works of Gilbert T. Burnett.] 4 vol. *Whittaker & Co.: London*, 1842 [1840–42]. 4°. **1253**. h. **5**.

BURNETT (M. E.) My First Book of Birds . . . Pictures by A. W. Seaby and others. pp. 63. *T. Nelson & Sons: London*, [1919.] 4°. **12800**. dd. **25**.

—— [A reissue.] *London*, [1920.] 4°. **12801**. d. **36**.

—— My First Book of Flowers. [With illustrations.] pp. 63. *T. Nelson & Sons: London*, [1920.] 8°. **7031**. i. **25**.

—— The Nursery Rhyme Primer . . . Pictures by Frank Adams. pp. 48. *T. Nelson & Sons: London*, [1917.] 8°. **12980**. de. **2**.

BURNETT (M. E.)

—— The Nursery Rhyme Reader. 2 no. *T. Nelson & Sons: London*, [1921, 22.] 8°. **12823**. a. **11**.

—— Teacher's Handbook to the Nursery Rhyme Alphabet, Reading Sheets, and Primer. pp. 56. *T. Nelson & Sons: London*, [1917.] 8°. **12980**. de. **1**.

BURNETT (MONICA DUNCAN) An Anthology of English Poetry for Foreign Students. Compiled and annotated by M. D. Burnett. pp. xiii. 217. *Longmans & Co.: London*, 1937. 8°. **20031**. aaa. **39**.

BURNETT (PETER HARDEMAN) The Path which Led a Protestant Lawyer to the Catholic Church. pp. xiv. 741. *D. Appleton & Co.: New York*, 1860. 8°. **3942**. e. **7**.

—— Recollections and Opinions of an Old Pioneer. pp. xiii. 448. *D. Appleton & Co.: New York*, 1880. 12°. **10881**. df. **18**.

BURNETT (PHILIP MASON)

—— Reparation at the Paris Peace Conference from the Standpoint of the American Delegation. 2 vol. *Columbia University Press: New York*, 1940. 8°. [*Paris Peace Conference History and Documents*.] Ac. **2297**. gb/**4**. (**3**).

—— Reparation at the Paris Peace Conference . . . Abridged edition without documents, *etc.* pp. xiv. 209. *Columbia University Press: New York*, 1940. 8°. [*Paris Peace Conference History and Documents*.] Ac. **2297**. gb/**4**. (**6**.)

BURNETT (RAYMOND WILL)

—— *See* VAN TIL (William) Democracy demands it . . . [By] W. Van Til . . . R. W. Burnett, *etc.* [1950.] 8°. **08385**. df. **24**.

—— The Opinions of Science Teachers on some Socially Significant Issues, *etc.* [A thesis.] pp. ii. 55. 8. *New York*, 1940. 8°. **08385**. d. **8**. *Reproduced from typewriting.*

BURNETT (RICHARD GEORGE)

—— *See* BUSS (Frederick H.) and BURNETT (R. G.) A Goodly Fellowship, *etc.* 1949. 8°. **4716**. aa. **22**.

—— *See* WISEMAN (Frederick L.) Frederick Luke Wiseman. A commemorative record by R. G. Burnett [and others], *etc.* 1954. 8°. **4909**. a. **28**.

—— Christ Down East. [An account of the East End Mission.] pp. 160. *Jarrolds: London*, [1931.] 8°. **04192**. aaa. **56**.

—— Chudleigh. A triumph of sacrifice. [With a portrait.] pp. 208. *Epworth Press: London*, 1932. 8°. **4909**. aa. **31**.

—— The Cinema for Christ. pp. 128. *R.T.S.: London*, 1934. 8°. **11795**. v. **9**.

—— London Lives On . . . Text by R. G. Burnett. Photography by E. W. Tattersall. pp. 198. *Phœnix House: London*, 1948. 4°. **010349**. dd. **44**.

—— London lives on. Text by R. G. Burnett. Photography by E. W. Tattersall. (Second edition.) pp. 206. *Phoenix House: London*, 1951. 8°. **010349**. tt. **6**.

—— Oxford and Cambridge in Pictures. Text by R. G. Burnett. Photography by E. W. Tattersall. pp. viii. 181. *Phoenix House: London*, 1950. 8°. **010368**. t. **8**

BURNETT (RICHARD GEORGE)

—— These My Brethren. The story of the London East End Mission. [With plates.] pp. 163. *Epworth Press: London*, 1946. 8°. **4194**. aa. **37**.

—— Through the Mill. (The life of Joseph Rank.) [With plates, including portraits.] pp. 226. *Epworth Press: London*, 1945. 8°. **10825**. eee. **44**.

BURNETT (RICHARD GEORGE) and **MARTELL** (E. D.)

—— The Devil's Camera. Menace of a film-ridden world. pp. 130. *Epworth Press: London*, 1932. 8°. **11796**. a. **9**.

BURNETT (ROBERT) *See* VERGER (P.) South Sea Islands. 48 photographic studies . . . With a foreword by R. Burnett. 1937. 8°. **Cup.804.1.1/13.**

—— The Life of Paul Gauguin. [With reproductions, including a portrait.] pp. xii. 294. *Cobden-Sanderson: London*, 1936. 8°. **010665**. f. **41**.

BURNETT (ROBERT) *Civil Service Tutor.* Aids and Exercises in French, for civil service and all student candidates. pp. iv. 152. *Civil Service Institute: Aberdeen*, [1900.] 8°. **12955**. a. **9**.

—— The Complete Spelling Book, for civil service, training college, and all student candidates . . . Second edition. pp. xvi. 148. *Civil Service Institute: Aberdeen*, 1896. 8°. **012986**. a. **3**.

—— The Complete Spelling Book, for civil service and all student candidates . . . Third edition. pp. xvi. 152. *Civil Service Institute: Aberdeen*, [1900.] 8°. **012986**. a. **4**.

—— Practical Guide to Civil Service History and Geography, *etc.* pp. vii. 176. *John Adam: Aberdeen*, 1892. 8°. **08367**. aa. **17**.

—— Practical Guide to the Geography of the British Isles, and General Geography, for civil service and all public examinations, *etc.* pp. vii. 132. *John Adam: Aberdeen*, 1893. 8°. **10003**. a. **35**.

BURNETT (SAMUEL HOWARD) The Clinical Pathology of the Blood of Domesticated Animals . . . Second edition, revised and enlarged, *etc.* pp. xvi. 166. pl. IV. *Macmillan Co.: New York*, 1917. 8°. **7441**. e. **44**.

—— Outline of Lectures in Special Pathology. ff. 65. *Carpenter & Co.: Ithaca*, 1916. 8°. **7440**. bb. **30**. *Printed on one side of the leaf only.*

BURNETT (SWAN MOSES) *See* LANDOLT (E.) The Introduction of the Metrical System into Ophthalmology . . . Translated by S. M. Burnett. 1876. 8°. **7306**. aa. **16**. **(17.)**

—— How we see. *See* WASHINGTON, *D.C.—Smithsonian Institution.—United States National Museum.* The Saturday Lectures, *etc.* 1882. 8°. **7004**. df. **2**.

—— Refraction in the Principal Meridians of a Triaxial Ellipsoid . . . With a communication on the monochromatic aberration of the human eye in aphakia by Prof. Wm. Harkness . . . Reprinted from the Archives of Ophthalmology, *etc.* pp. 21. *G. P. Putnam's Sons: New York*, 1883. 8°. **07305**. h. **19**. **(3.)**

BURNETT (THOMAS) *Master of the Charter House. See* BURNET.

BURNETT (THOMAS) *Rector of West Kington, Wilts. See* BURNET.

BURNETT (*Sir* THOMAS) *See* BURNET (*Sir* T.) *One of the Justices of the Court of Common Pleas.*

BURNETT (THOMAS J.) The Essentials of Teaching. A book for amateurs. pp. xv. 250. *Longmans & Co.: London*, 1916. 8°. **8304**. g. **25**.

BURNETT (THOMAS MOUNTFORD) The Wondrous Cross. A consideration . . . of the Seven Last Words in their sacramental aspect. pp. 89. *Skeffington & Son: London*, 1895. 8°. **4466**. d. **21**.

BURNETT (THOMAS PENDLETON) *See* SIMMONS (James) A Digest of Wisconsin Reports . . . Comprising all the published decisions of the Supreme Court of Wisconsin, presented in Burnett's, Chandler's and 20 vols. Wisconsin Reports. 1868. 8°. **6778**. c. **5**.

—— *See* WISCONSIN.—*Supreme Court.* Reports of the Supreme Court of the Territory of Wisconsin for 1842 and 1843. Reported by T. P. Burnett. 1844. 8°. **6622.p.7.**

BURNETT (V. COMPTON) *See* STEINER (Rudolf) *Philosophical Writer.* Eurhythmy as Visible Speech . . . English translation by V. and J. Compton-Burnett. 1931. 8°. **07911**. ee. **59**.

BURNETT (VERNE)

—— You and Your Public. A guide book to the new career —Public Relations . . . Revised edition. pp. x. 205. *Harper & Bros.: New York & London*, 1947. 8°. **08246**. f. **32**.

BURNETT (VIVIAN) The Romantick Lady, Frances Hodgson Burnett, *etc.* [With plates, including portraits.] pp. xvi. 423. *C. Scribner's Sons: New York, London*, 1927. 8°. **010855**. e. **10**.

BURNETT (WALDO I.) *See* SIEBOLD (C. T. E. von) [Lehrbuch der vergleichenden Anatomie.] Comparative Anatomy . . . Translated . . . and edited with notes and additions . . . by W. I. Burnett. 1854. 8°. **728**. h. **36**.

—— —— 1874. 8°. **7420**. b. **25**.

BURNETT (WHIT) *See* BURNETT (Whitney E.)

BURNETT (WHITNEY EWING)

—— *See* PERIODICAL PUBLICATIONS.—New York.—*Story.* A Story Anthology . . . Edited by W. Burnett and M. Foley. 1934. 8°. **012614**. dd. **38**.

—— *See* PERIODICAL PUBLICATIONS.—New York.—*Story.* Story in America 1933-1934 . . . Edited by W. Burnett and M. Foley. 1934. 8°. **12601**. tt. **25**.

—— The Literary Life and the Hell with it . . . With drawings by Bemelmans. pp. vii. 276. *Harper & Bros.: New York & London*, 1939. 8°. **010885**. ff. **62**.

—— The Maker of Signs. A variety. [Short stories.] pp. 320. *Jonathan Cape: London*, 1935. 8°. NN. **23550**.

BURNETT (WHITNEY EWING) and **FOLEY** (MARTHA)

—— The Flying Yorkshireman. Novellas. [By] Eric Knight [and others], *etc.* [Edited by W. Burnett and M. Foley. With portraits.] pp. 273. *Harper & Bros.: New York & London*, 1938. 8°. **12632**. ppp. **5**.

BURNETT (William) *Civil Engineer.*

—— *See* Dugdale (Thomas) England & Wales Delineated . . . By T. Dugdale . . . assisted by W. Burnett. [1845 ?] 8°. **010358.** r. **7.**

—— *See* Dugdale (Thomas) England & Wales Delineated . . . By T. Dugdale . . . Assisted by W. Burnett. [1850 ?] 8°. **010358.f.34.**

—— —— [1854, *etc.*] 8°. **10351.** g. **22.**

BURNETT (William) *General.* *See* Allardice (Robert B.) known as *Captain* Barclay. Letters from Captain Barclay, Mr. Farquharson, General Burnett, and Mr. Sturt; with a statement of facts, *etc.* 1814. 8°. **10815.** c. **33.** (**3.**)

BURNETT (William) *Wesleyan Minister.* Cruel Treatment of the Rev. William Burnett. [A letter reprinted from "The Wesleyan Times."] pp. 4. *John Kaye: London,* [1851.] 8°. **4135.** f. **15.** (**6.**)

BURNETT (*Sir* William) *K.C.B.* *See* Macloughlin (David) Copy of a Letter . . . relative to the Report on the Cholera which attacked the Fleet in the Black Sea, published by Sir W. Burnet, *etc.* 1855. 8°. **07561.** h. **30.**

—— *See* Pym (*Sir* William) *K.C.H.* Observations upon Bulam . . . or Yellow Fever, with a review of "A Report upon the Diseases of the African Coast, by Sir W. Burnett and Dr. Bryson," *etc.* 1848. 12°. **7560.** b. **59.**

—— *See* Reports. Reports on the Solution of Chloride of Zinc [invented by Sir W. Burnett], as employed for the purification of ships' holds; for the destruction of unwholesome . . . effluvia; and for the treatment of erysipelatous, ulcerative, and other diseases. 1851. 8°. **7945.** g. **1.** (**2.**)

—— *See* Rolleston (*Sir* Humphry D.) *Bart.* Sir William Burnett, *etc.* [With a portrait.] [1922.] 8°. **10816.** h. **21.**

—— An Account of a Contagious Fever, which occurred amongst the Danish and American prisoners of war at Chatham, in the years 1813, 1814. pp. 47. *Burgess & Hill: London,* 1831. 8°. **1168.** h. **29.**

—— Copy of a Report of the Proceedings and Evidence given upon oath before the Judicial Committee of the Privy Council, on the petition of Sir William Burnett . . . for an extension of his patent for the preservation of timber, *etc.* pp. 16. [*London,*] 1852. 8°. **6375.** b. **48.** (**10.**)

—— A Practical Account of the Mediterranean Fever, as it appeared in the ships and hospitals of His Majesty's Fleet on that station; with cases and dissections. To which are added facts and observations, illustrative of its causes, symptoms, and treatment; comprehending the history of the fever in the Fleet during the years 1810, 1811, 1812, 1813: and of the Gibraltar & Carthagena fevers. (Second edition.) pp. xvi. x–xv. 522. *J. Callow: London,* 1816. 8°. **1168.** h. **18.**

—— Reports and Testimonials respecting the Solution of Chloride of Zinc—Sir William Burnett's Disinfecting Fluid—as a means of destroying deleterious gases . . . First and second series. pp. v. 74. *S. Mills: London,* 1850. 8°. **07306.** g. **22.** (**2.**)

BURNETT (*Sir* William) *K.C.B.*

—— Reports on the Solution of Chloride of Zinc as an agent for the destruction of deleterious gases, or the effluvia arising from the decomposition of animal and vegetable substances, *etc.* [Compiled by Sir W. Burnett.] pp. 35. 1848. 8°. *See* England.—*Admiralty.* [*Miscellaneous Official Publications.*] C.T. **181.** (**11.**)

—— [Another copy.] C.T. **184.** (**8.**)

—— Sir William Burnett's Patent for the Preservation of Timber, Canvas, Cordage, Cotton, Woollen, etc., from dry rot, mildew, moth and premature decay. Prospectus and testimonials. pp. 18. *London,* 1843. 8°. **7953.** bbb. **29.** (**1.**)

—— [Another edition.] pp. 30. *London,* 1845. 8°. **7954.** c. **23.** (**2.**)

—— [Another edition.] Sir William Burnett's Patent Process, for the preservation of timber, *etc.* pt. 1, 2. [*London,* 1851.] 8°. **7945.** g. **1.** (**1.**)

BURNETT (William Brown)

—— Scotland laughing. The humour of the Scot . . . Illustrations by Graham. pp. 95. *Albyn Press: Edinburgh,* 1955. 8°. **12332.** eee. **90.**

BURNETT (William Hall) *See* Jackson (Edmund H.) The True Story of the Clitheroe Abduction . . . Edited by W. H. Burnett. 1891. 8°. **6145.** dd. **4.** (**5.**)

—— Broad Yorkshire, being poems and sketches from the writings of Castillo, Mrs. G. M. Tweddell, Reed, Brown, Lewis and others. Second edition. Edited by W. H. Burnett. pp. 70. *Hamilton, Adams & Co.: London; W. H. Burnett: Middlesbrough,* 1885. 8°. **12314.** ccc. **23.** (**3.**)

—— Old Cleveland, being a collection of papers compiled and written by W. H. Burnett. Local writers and local worthies. Section 1—complete. [With portraits.] pp. 152. *Hamilton, Adams & Co.: London; W. H. Burnett: Middlesbrough,* 1886. 4°. **10351.** k. **23.**

BURNETT (William Henry P.) *See* Ephemerides. The Original Midhurst Almanack, *etc.* [Edited by W. H. P. Burnett.] [1893.] 8°. P.P. **2508.** gi.

—— Bob and Jack. (Bob to Jack.) [Verses.] no. 29, 36, 37, 55. *W. H. Burnett: Midhurst,* [1899.] 8° & 12°. **1865.** c. **8.** (**78.**)

BURNETT (William Hickling) To His Most Excellent Majesty, William the Fourth, this work, containing fourteen views of Cintra, is . . . dedicated, by . . . W. H. Burnett. *C. Hullmandel:* [*London,* 1836 ?] fol. **744.** d. **14.**

BURNETT (William Kendall) Genealogical Tree of the Family of Burnett of Leys with the collateral branches. [1893.] *s. sh.* fol. **09915.** bb. **25.**

BURNETT (William Riley)

—— Adobe Walls. A novel of the last Apache rising. pp. 224. *Macdonald: London,* 1954. 8°. **12732.** aa. **24.**

—— The Asphalt Jungle. pp. 240. *Macdonald: London,* 1950. 8°. **12731.** b. **5.**

—— The Asphalt Jungle. pp. 254. *Transworld Publishers: London,* 1955. 8°. [*Corgi Books.* no. T 128.] W.P. **12745/256.**

BURNETT (William Riley)

—— Captain Lightfoot. pp. 240. *Macdonald: London,* 1955. 8°. NNN. **5944.**

—— The Dark Command. A Kansas Iliad. pp. 309. *William Heinemann: London, Toronto,* 1938. 8°. **12718.** cc. **17.**

—— Dark Hazard. pp. 282. *William Heinemann: London,* 1934. 8°. A.N. **1885.**

—— The Giant Swing. pp. 271. *William Heinemann: London,* 1933. 8°. NN. **19745.**

—— Good-bye to the Past. Scenes from the life of William Meadows. [A novel.] pp. 274. *William Heinemann: London, Toronto,* 1935. 8°. A.N. **2357.**

—— High Sierra. pp. 267. *William Heinemann: London, Toronto,* 1940. 8°. **12721.** cc. **11.**

—— Iron Man. pp. 312. *William Heinemann: London,* 1930. 8°. NN. **16826.**

—— King Cole. A novel. pp. 292. *Harper & Bros.: New York & London,* 1936. 8°. A.N. **3319.**

—— Little Caesar. pp. 288. *Jonathan Cape: London,* 1929. 8°. **12715.** d. **15.**

—— Little Men, Big World. pp. 256. *Macdonald: London,* 1952. 8°. **12701.** b. **37.**

—— Nobody lives Forever. pp. 164. *William Heinemann: London, Toronto,* 1944. 8°. **12727.** aa. **39.**

—— The Quick Brown Fox. pp. 252. *William Heinemann: London, Toronto,* 1943. 8°. **12725.** aaa. **8.**

—— Romelle. pp. 187. *William Heinemann: London, Toronto,* 1947. 8°. **12726.** a. **32.**

—— Saint Johnson. pp. 311. *William Heinemann: London,* 1931. 8°. NN. **18115.**

—— The Silver Eagle. pp. 310. *William Heinemann: London,* 1932. 8°. NN. **19398.**

—— Six Days' Grace. pp. 285. *William Heinemann: London, Toronto,* 1937. 8°. A.N. **3584.**

—— Stretch Dawson. pp. 172. *Frederick Muller, by arrangement with Fawcett Publications:* [London, 1953.] 8°. **12723.** b. **56.**

—— Tomorrow's another Day, *etc.* pp. 187. *William Heinemann: London, Toronto,* 1946. 8°. **12729.** aaa. **2.**

—— Vanity Row. pp. 222. *Macdonald: London,* 1953. 8°. **12731.** m. **5.**

BURNETT (Yelva) Richard Forrest's Folly. pp. 96. *Gramol Publications: London,* 1932. 8°. [*Regent Novels.* no. 4.] W.P. **10107/4.**

—— Wings of Wax. pp. viii. 334. *Methuen & Co.: London,* 1915. 8°. NN. **2411.**

BURNETTE (Harry Lascelles) Sons of Elohim. [A novel.] pp. 419. *Randolph, Sterling, & Van Ess: Chicago,* [1922.] 8°. **12702.** aa. **21.**

BURNETTE (William Anderson) *See* Clark (Neil M.) An Inside Story of Success. Life of William Burnette. 1929. 8°. **010884.** h. **28.**

BURNETT-HALL (Basil Graham) *See* Hall.

BURNETT-HURST (Alexander Robert) *See* Hurst.

BURNETT-SMITH (Annie S.) *See* Swan, afterwards Burnett Smith.

BURNETUS (Thomas) *See* Burnet (*Sir* Thomas) *M.D.*

BURNEY SCHOOL, *Greenwich. See* London.—iii.

BURNEY, *Family of. See* Hill (*Mary C.*) The House in St. Martin's Street. Being chronicles of the Burney family, *etc.* [With portraits.] 1907. 8°. **10854.** dd. **14.**

—— *See* Johnson (Reginald B.) Fanny Burney and the Burneys, *etc.* [With portraits.] 1926. 8°. **010855.** cc. **57.**

BURNEY (Beatrice) The Chance and the Beloved. [A tale.] pp. 84. *A. H. Stockwell: London,* [1920.] 4°. **04420.** i. **112.**

BURNEY (Carl) *See* Burney (Charles) *Mus.D.*

BURNEY (Charles) *B.A. See* Healey (*Sir* Charles E. H. C.) *Bart.* A Treatise on the Law . . . relating to Joint Stock Companies . . . By C. E. H. C. Healey . . . P. F. Wheeler . . . and C. Burney, *etc.* 1894. 8°. **6376.** g. **1.**

—— *See* Kerr (William W.) The Law and Practice as to Receivers . . . Fourth edition by P. F. Wheeler . . . assisted by C. Burney. 1900. 8°. **6376.** r. **10.**

—— *See* Wilson (Arthur) *Barrister-at-Law.* Wilson's Supreme Court of Judicature Acts, Rules and Forms . . . Sixth edition by C. Burney [and others], *etc.* 1887. 8°. **6281.** g. **15.**

—— —— 1888. 8°. **6281.** g. **25.**

—— Daniell's Chancery Forms—Fourth edition. Forms and Precedents of Proceedings in the Chancery Division, *etc.* pp. lxxxviii. 1172. *Stevens & Sons: London,* 1885. 8°. **6190.** h. **10.**
The third edition of this work is entered under Upjohn (*William H.*).

—— Fifth edition, *etc.* pp. xcii. 1432. *Stevens & Sons: London,* 1901. 8°. **6190.** ee. **3.**
The sixth edition of this work is entered under White (*Sir Richard*).

BURNEY (Charles) *D.D.*

WORKS WRITTEN, EDITED OR WITH CONTRIBUTIONS BY CHARLES BURNEY.

—— *See* Bentley (Richard) *D.D., Master of Trinity College, Cambridge.* [*Letters.*] Richardi Bentleii et doctorum virorum epistolæ, *etc.* [Edited by C. Burney.] 1807. 4°. **831.** i. **5.**

—— *See* England.—*Church of England.* [*Articles of Religion.* —1552.] Articles of Religion of the Church of England, in the reigns of King Edward vi. and Queen Elizabeth. [Edited by C. Burney?] 1811. 4°. **3506.** h. **2.**

—— *See* Euripides. [*Works.—Greek and Latin.*] *Εὐριπιδου ἁπαντα, etc.* [With notes by C. Burney and others.] 1821. 8°. **998.** k. **1–9.**

—— *See* Euripides. [*Electra.—Greek and Latin.*] *Εὐριπιδου Ἠλεκτρα* . . . Notis Porsoni, Burneii, Musgravii . . . illustrata. 1820. 8°. **998.** f. **22.**

—— *See* Euripides. [*Hercules Furens.—Greek and Latin.*] *Εὐριπιδου Ἡρακλης μαινομενος* . . . Notis Hermanni, Porsoni, Burneii . . . illustrata. 1820. 8°. **11705.** cc. **21.**

—— *See* Le Noir (Elizabeth A.) The Maid of La Vendée . . . With critical remarks by the late Dr. Burney, *etc.* 1819. 12°. **12612.** e. **13.**

BURNEY (Charles) *D.D.* [Works written, edited or with contributions by Charles Burney.]

—— *See* London.—iii. *Royal Institution of Great Britain.* A Catalogue of the Library . . . Including a complete list of all the Greek writers, by the late Rev. C. Burney, *etc.* 1821. 8°. **11903. h. 12.**

—— *See* Pearson (John) *Bishop of Chester*. The Exposition of the Creed, by J. Pearson . . . Abridged for the use of young persons by the Rev. C. Burney. 1810. 12°. **1018. e. 21.**

—— *See* Philemon. *Φιλημονος λεξικον τεχνολογικον, etc.* [Edited by C. Burney.] 1812. 8°. **624. e. 15. (1.)**

—— *See* Sophocles. [*Works.—Greek and Latin.*] Sophoclis quæ exstant omnia . . . Accedunt . . . notæ ineditæ C. Burneii, *etc.* 1824. 8°. **1348. f. 28–30*.**

—— [Proof-sheets with ms. notes and corrections by the author of a review by C. Burney of George H. Glasse's Greek translation of Mason's "Caractacus."] *See* Mason (William) *Poet. Καρακτακος ἐπι Μωνῃ, etc.* 1781. 8°. **1162. i. 16.**

—— [A Review, with ms. notes, by C. Burney of George I. Huntingford's "*Μετρικα τινα μονοστροφικα.*" Extracted from the "Monthly Review."] [1783.] 8°. *See* Huntingford (George I.) successively *Bishop of Gloucester* and *of Hereford.* **836. g. 8. (1.)**

—— [Another copy.] few ms. notes [by C. Burney]. **1087. c. 10. (1.)**

—— [A Review, with ms. notes, by C. Burney of George I. Huntingford's "An Apology for the Monostrophics." Extracted from the "Monthly Review."] [1785.] 8°. *See* Huntingford (George I.) successively *Bishop of Gloucester* and *of Hereford.* **836. g. 8. (2.)**

—— [Another copy.] few ms. notes [by C. Burney]. **1087. c. 10. (2.)**

—— [A Review by C. Burney of George H. Glasse's Greek and Latin translations of Milton's "Samson Agonistes." Extracted from the "Monthly Review."] [1789.] 8°. *See* Milton (J.) [*Samson Agonistes.—Greek and Latin.*] **1087. c. 10. (3.)**

—— [Another copy.] ms. notes [by C. Burney]. **833. h. 25.**

—— On the Threatened Invasion. 1803. [A poem. By C. Burney.] pp. 2. [1803.] *s. sh.* fol. *See* Invasion. **1881. a. 1. (69.)**

—— [Another edition.] pp. 3. ms. corrections [by the author]. [1804.] 4°. *See* Invasion. **1881. a. 1. (70.)**

—— To the People of Great Britain, on the threatened invasion 1803–4. [Another edition of the poem "On the Threatened Invasion," by C. Burney.] pp. 4. [1804.] 4°. *See* England. [*Appendix.—History and Politics.*—ii. 1804.] **11641. f. 30.**

—— Remarks on the Greek Verses of Milton. pp. 15. [*The Author: London,* 1790.] 8°. **1087. c. 10. (4.)**

—— [Another copy.] **79. c. 14.**
In this copy is inserted a ms. *letter from the author to Dr. Farmer.*

—— [Another edition.] *See* Milton (J.) [*Minor Poems.*] Poems upon Several Occasions, *etc.* 1791. 8°. **683. f. 27.**

—— [Another edition.] *See* Milton (J.) [*Poetical Works.*] The Poetical Works of John Milton, *etc.* vol. 6. 1801. 8°. **11623. i. 8.**

BURNEY (Charles) *D.D.* [Works written, edited or with contributions by Charles Burney.]

—— [Another edition.] *See* Milton (J.) [*Poetical Works.*] The Poetical Works of John Milton, *etc.* vol. 7. 1809. 8°. **11623. i. 9.**

—— [Another edition.] *See* Milton (J.) [*Poetical Works.*] The Poetical Works of John Milton, *etc.* vol. 6. 1826. 8°. **11607. f. 4.**

—— A Sermon preached at the Anniversary Meeting of the Stewards of the Sons of the Clergy . . . May 14, 1812. To which are added lists of the nobility, clergy, and gentry, who have been Stewards . . . and the sums collected at the anniversary meetings, since the year 1721. pp. xxiv. 39. *F. C. & J. Rivington: London,* 1813. 4°. **694. h. 7. (3.)**

—— Tentamen de metris, ab Æschylo in choricis cantibus adhibitis. *Typis ac sumptibus academicis: Cantabrigiæ,* 1809. 8°. **989. b. 22.**

—— [Another copy.] **623. f. 17.**

—— [Another copy.] ms. notes [by the author]. **834. l. 8**
Interleaved and bound in two volumes. A letter from J. Smith, University Press, Cambridge, is inserted in vol. 1.

—— [Another copy.] **G. 8616.**
One of six copies printed on large paper.

—— *See* Aeschylus. [*Single Works.—Choephori.—Greek and Latin.*] *Αἱ του Αἰσχυλου Χοηφοροι* . . . Adiecti sunt Choephorôn chorici cantus, sicut dispositi sunt in tentamine . . . C. Burneii. 1811. 12°. **998. a. 7.**

WORKS CONTAINING MS. NOTES BY CHARLES BURNEY.

—— *See* Aeschylus. [*Works.—Greek.*] *Αἰσχυλου τραγῳδιαι, etc.* copious ms. notes [by C. Burney and others]. 1557. 4°. **832. k. 26.**

—— *See* Aeschylus. [*Works.—Greek.*] *Αἰσχυλου τραγῳδιαι, etc.* ms. notes [transcribed from an edition of Aeschylus belonging to C. Burney]. 1580. 16°. **996. a. 9.**

—— *See* Aeschylus. [*Works.—Greek.*] Æschyli tragoediæ quæ supersunt, *etc.* copious ms. notes [by C. Burney]. 1782, *etc.* 8°. **997. d. 10–16.**

—— *See* Aeschylus. [*Works.—Greek.*] *Αἱ του Αἰσχυλου τραγῳδιαι, etc.* ms. notes [by C. Burney]. 1795. fol. **11707. i. 16.**

—— *See* Aeschylus. [*Works.—Greek and Latin.*] Æschyli tragoediae septem, *etc.* few ms. notes [by C. Burney]. 1800. 8°. **997. d. 17, 18.**

—— *See* Aeschylus. [*Works.—Greek and Latin.*] Aeschyli tragœdiæ, *etc.* ms. notes [by C. Burney]. 1806. 8°. **997. d. 1–7.**

—— *See* Aeschylus. [*Single Works.—Choephori.—Greek.*] *Τρεις τραγῳδιαι, Αἰσχυλου Χοηφοροι, Σοφοκλεους Ἠλεκταα, Εὐριπιδου Ἠλεκτρα, etc.* ms. notes [by C. Burney]. 1729. 8°. **997. e. 4.**

—— *See* Aeschylus. [*Single Works.—Prometheus Vinctus.—Greek and Latin.*] *Αἰσχυλου Προμηθευς Δεσμωτης, etc.* ms. notes [by C. Burney]. 1767. 8°. **832. e. 1.**

—— *See* Anacreon. [*Greek and Latin.*] Anacreontis Teii odæ et fragmenta, *etc.* few ms. notes [by C. Burney]. 1732. 4°. **997. f. 1.**

BURNEY (CHARLES) *D.D.* [WORKS CONTAINING MS. NOTES BY CHARLES BURNEY.]

—— *See* APOLLONIUS, *Rhodius.* [*Greek and Latin.*] Apollonii Rhodii Argonauticorum libri quatuor, *etc.* MS. NOTES [by C. Burney]. 1779. 8°. **997.** i. **12, 13.**

—— —— [Another copy.] MS. NOTES [by C. Burney]. 1779. 8°. **1348.** h. **16.**

—— *See* ARISTOPHANES, *the Poet.* [*Works.—Greek.*] Aristophanis comœdiæ, *etc.* MS. NOTES [by C. Burney]. 1783. 8°. **998.** h. **4–14.**

—— *See* ARISTOPHANES, *the Poet.* [*Works.—Greek and Latin.*] Aristophanis comœdiæ undecim, *etc.* MS. NOTES [by C. Burney]. 1710. fol. **11707.** i. **17.**

—— *See* ARISTOTLE. [*Single Works.—Poetica.—Greek, Latin and English.*] [The Poetica of Aristotle, made up from the editions of T. Tyrwhitt, T. Winstanley and T. Twining, interleaved and with MS. notes by C. Burney.] fol. **518.** m. **5–7.**

—— *See* ATHENAEUS, *Naucratita.* [*Deipnosophistae.—Greek and Latin.*] *Ἀθηναιου Δειπνοσοφιστων βιβλια πεντεκαιδεκα, etc.* COPIOUS MS. NOTES [by C. Burney]. 1612. fol. **832.** m. **5, 6.**

—— *See* ATHENAEUS, *Naucratita.* [*Deipnosophistae.—Greek and Latin.*] *Ἀθηναιου Δειπνοσοφιστων βιβλια πεντεκαιδεκα, etc.* FEW MS. NOTES [by C. Burney]. 1657. fol. **834.** bb. **1.** (**1.**)

—— *See* AURELIUS ANTONINUS (Marcus) called the *Philosopher, Emperor of Rome.* [*Meditations.—Greek and Latin.*] *Μαρκου Ἀντονινου . . . των εἰς ἑαυτον βιβλια ιβʹ, etc.* MS. NOTES [by C. Burney]. 1704. 8°. **720.** f. **24.**

—— *See* BELLENDENUS (G.) Gulielmi Bellendeni . . . De statu libri tres, *etc.* MS. NOTES [by C. Burney]. 1787. 8°. **1389.** d. **1.**

—— *See* BENTLEY (Richard) *D.D., Master of Trinity College, Cambridge.* [*Letters.*] Richardi Bentleii et doctorum virorum epistolæ, *etc.* MS. NOTES [by C. Burney]. 1807. 4°. **829.** m. **6.**

—— *See* BIBLE.—*Psalms.* [*Greek.*] *Ψαλτηριον.* FEW MS. NOTES [by C. Burney]. [1497?] 4°. IA. **24458.**

—— *See* BIBLE.—*New Testament.* [*Greek.*] [*Ἡ Καινη Διαθηκη, etc.*] COPIOUS MS. NOTES [by C. Burney]. [1698.] 8°. **691.** d. **2.**

—— *See* BIBLE.—*New Testament.* [*Greek.*] *Ἡ Καινη Διαθηκη, etc.* FEW MS. NOTES [by C. Burney]. 1768. 8°. **697.** l. **21.**

—— *See* BIBLE.—*New Testament.* [*Greek.*] Novum Testamentum græce, *etc.* MS. NOTES [by C. Burney]. 1809, *etc.* 8°. **1003.** c. **8–19.**

—— *See* BOECLER (J. H.) Jo. Henr. Boecleri De scriptoribus Græcis et Latinis, *etc.* MS. NOTES [by C. Burney]. 1674. 8°. **819.** b. **6.**

—— *See* BRUNCK (R. F. P.) Analecta veterum poetarum græcorum, *etc.* MS. NOTES [by C. Burney]. 1772, *etc.* 8°. **653.** a. **11–13.**

—— *See* BURTON (John) *D.D.* [*Πενταλογια, etc.*] COPIOUS MS. NOTES [by C. Burney]. [1779.] 8°. **995.** e. **18.**

—— *See* CALLIMACHUS. Callimachi hymni et epigrammata, *etc.* FEW MS. NOTES [by C. Burney]. 1741. 8°. **997.** h. **6.**

BURNEY (CHARLES) *D.D.* [WORKS CONTAINING MS. NOTES BY CHARLES BURNEY.]

—— *See* CALLIMACHUS. Callimachi hymni, epigrammata et fragmenta, *etc.* MS. NOTES [by C. Burney]. 1761. 8°. **997.** h. **7.**

—— *See* CEBES. [*Greek and Latin.*] *Κεβητος . . . Πιναξ, etc.* [With a few MS. notes by C. Burney on inserted leaves.] 1745. 8°. **715.** c. **1.**

—— *See* CLEMENS (T. F.) *Alexandrinus.* *Κλημεντος Ἀλεξανδρεως τα εὑρισκομενα, etc.* FEW MS. NOTES [by C. Burney]. 1715. fol. **L.19.d.6.**

—— *See* CONSTANTINE VII., *Emperor of Rome,* called *Porphyrogenitus.* [*Works edited by order of Constantine.*] Eclogæ legationum, *etc.* MS. NOTES [by C. Burney]. 1603. 4°. **585.** g. **18.** (**2.**)

—— *See* DAWES (Richard) *Master of the Grammar School, Newcastle upon Tyne.* Ricardi Dawes Miscellanea critica, *etc.* MS. NOTES [by C. Burney]. 1781. 8°. **1087.** k. **10.**

—— *See* DEMOSTHENES. [*Works.—Greek and Latin.*] Demosthenis et Æschinis, principum Græciæ oratorum, opera, *etc.* FEW MS. NOTES [by C. Burney]. 1604. fol. Cup. **652.** dd. **4.**

—— *See* DEMOSTHENES. [*Works.—Greek and Latin.*] Demosthenis et Æschinis quae supersunt omnia . . . edidit . . . A. Auger, *etc.* MS. NOTES [by C. Burney]. 1790. 4°. **832.** l. **11.**

—— *See* DEMOSTHENES. [*Smaller Collections.—Public Speeches.—Greek and Latin.*] *Δημοσθενους λογοι ἐκλεκτοι* . . . Recensuit . . . Ricardus Mounteney, *etc.* MS. NOTES [by C. Burney]. 1731. 8°. **834.** h. **20.**

—— *See* DEMOSTHENES. [*Smaller Collections.—Public Speeches.—Greek and Latin.*] *Δημοσθενους λογοι δημηγορικοι δωδεκα* . . . Edidit Guilielmus Allen. FEW MS. NOTES [by C. Burney]. 1755. 8°. **654.** a. **4, 5.**

—— *See* DEMOSTHENES. [*In Midiam.—Greek and Latin.*] Orationes duae. Vna Demosthenis contra Midiam, altera Lycurgi contra Leocratem, *etc.* MS. NOTES [by C. Burney]. 1743. 8°. **834.** h. **22.**

—— *See* DIONYSIUS, *of Halicarnassus.* [*De Rhetoribus Antiquis.*] *Διονυσιου Ἁλικαρνασσεως περι των ἀρχαιων ῥητορων ὑπομνηματισμοι, etc.* FEW MS. NOTES [by C. Burney]. 1781, *etc.* 8°. **1089.** l. **10.**

—— *See* DUFRESNOY (C. A.) The Art of Painting, *etc.* MS. POEM [on the death of Sir Joshua Reynolds, by C. Burney]. 1783. 4°. **77.** g. **7.**

—— *See* ENGLAND.—*Church of England.* [*Articles of Religion.—Editions with commentaries.—Welchman,* 1713.] The Thirty-nine Articles of the Church of England, illustrated with notes . . . by the Rev. Mr. . . . Welchman, and now translated, *etc.* MS. NOTES AND CORRECTIONS [by C. Burney]. 1805. 8°. **692.** d. **15.**

—— *See* ESTIENNE (Henri) le Grand. *Θησαυρος της ἑλληνικης γλωσσης, etc.* MS. NOTES [by C. Burney]. 1572. fol. **749.** b. **1.**

—— *See* EURIPIDES. [*Works.—Greek.*] *Εὐριπιδου τραγῳδιαι ιθʹ, etc.* FEW MS. NOTES [by C. Burney]. 1571. 16°. **996.** d. **6.**

—— *See* EURIPIDES. [*Works.—Greek and Latin.*] *Εὐριπιδης.* Euripidis tragœdiæ XIX, *etc.* COPIOUS MS. NOTES [by C. Burney and others]. 1597. 8°. **999.** a. **8.**

BURNEY (CHARLES) *D.D.* [WORKS CONTAINING MS. NOTES BY CHARLES BURNEY.]

—— *See* EURIPIDES. [*Works.—Greek and Latin.*] [*Εὐριπιδου τραγῳδιων ὁσα σωζονται, etc.*] MS. NOTES [by C. Burney]. [1602.] 4°. **998. f. 4–14.**

—— *See* EURIPIDES. [*Works.—Greek and Latin.*] *Εὐριπιδου τα σωζομενα, etc.* MS. NOTES [by C. Burney]. 1778. 4°. **653. d. 17. & 833. l. 13.**

—— *See* EURIPIDES. [*Two or more Works.—Greek.*] [*Τετραλογια, etc.*] FEW MS. NOTES [by C. Burney]. 1771. 8°. **998. f. 26.**

—— *See* EURIPIDES. [*Two or more Works.—Greek and Latin.*] [Euripidis Hecuba, Orestes, et Phœnissæ, *etc.*] MS. NOTES [by C. Burney]. [1726.] 8°. **995. f. 20.**

—— *See* EURIPIDES. [*Two or more Works.—Greek and Latin.*] *Εὐριπιδου Ἰφιγενεια ἡ ἐν Αὐλιδι και Ἰφιγενεια ἡ ἐν Ταυροις, etc.* MS. NOTES [by C. Burney]. 1771. 8°. **998. e. 13.**

—— *See* EURIPIDES. [*Electra.—Greek.*] *Εὐριπιδου Ἠλεκτρα.* MS. NOTES [by C. Burney]. [1780.] 8°. **998. f. 21.**

—— *See* EURIPIDES. [*Hecuba.—Greek.*] *Εὐριπιδου Ἑκαβη, etc.* MS. NOTES [by C. Burney]. 1797. 8°. **997. l. 1.**

—— *See* EURIPIDES. [*Hecuba.—Greek.*] *Εὐριπιδου Ἑκαβη, etc.* MS. NOTES [by C. Burney]. 1802. 8°. **998. e. 11.**

—— *See* EURIPIDES. [*Hippolytus.—Greek and Latin.*] *Εὐριπιδου Ἱππολυτος, etc.* FEW MS. NOTES [by C. Burney]. 1768, *etc.* 4°. **832. k. 25.**

—— *See* EURIPIDES. [*Hippolytus.—Greek and Latin.*] *Εὐριπιδου Ἱππολυτος στεφανηφορος, etc.* MS. NOTES [by C. Burney]. 1796. 4°. **832. l. 12.**

—— *See* EURIPIDES. [*Medea.—Greek.*] *Εὐριπιδου Μηδεια, etc.* FEW MS. NOTES [by C. Burney]. 1801. 8°. **998. e. 16.**

—— *See* EURIPIDES. [*Orestes.—Greek.*] *Εὐριπιδου Ὀρεστης, etc.* MS. NOTES [by C. Burney]. 1798. 8°. **998. e. 18.**

—— *See* EURIPIDES. [*Orestes.—Greek.*] *Εὐριπιδου Ὀρεστης, etc.* MS. NOTES [by C. Burney]. 1798. 8°. **674. c. 12. (1.)**

—— *See* EURIPIDES. [*Phoenissae.—Greek.*] *Εὐριπιδου Φοινισσαι, etc.* MS. NOTES [by C. Burney]. 1799. 8°. **998. e. 19, 20.**

—— *See* EURIPIDES. [*Phoenissae.—Greek and Latin.*] *Εὐριπιδου Φοινισσαι, etc.* FEW MS. NOTES [by C. Burney]. 1755. 4°. **832. e. 9.**

—— *See* EURIPIDES. [*Supplices.—Greek and Latin.*] *Εὐριπιδου Ἱκετιδες, etc.* MS. NOTES [by C. Burney]. 1763. 4°. **1348. k. 11.**

—— *See* EURIPIDES. [*Supplices.—Greek and Latin.*] *Εὐριπιδου Ἱκετιδες, etc.* MS. NOTES [by C. Burney]. 1775. 8°. **995. g. 19.**

—— *See* GROOT (H. de) [*Works translated, annotated or edited by H. de Groot.*] Excerpta ex tragœdiis et comœdiis Græcis, *etc.* FEW MS. NOTES [by C. Burney]. 1626. 8°. **999. k. 10.**

—— *See* GROOT (H. de) [*Works translated, annotated or edited by H. de Groot.*] Excerpta ex tragœdiis et comœdiis Græcis, *etc.* MS. NOTES [by C. Burney]. 1626. 8°. **999. k. 11.**

—— *See* HARPOCRATION (V.) *Οὐαλεριου Ἁρποκρατιωνος περι των λεξεων βιβλιον, etc.* MS. NOTES [by C. Burney]. 1696. 4°. **827. e. 23.**

BURNEY (CHARLES) *D.D.* [WORKS CONTAINING MS. NOTES BY CHARLES BURNEY.]

—— *See* HARPOCRATION (V.) *Ἁρποκρατιωνος λεξικον των δεκα ῥητορων, etc.* MS. NOTES [by C. Burney]. 1683. 4°. **748. c. 2.**

—— —— [Another copy.] COPIOUS MS. NOTES [by C. Burney]. 1683. 4°. **749. a. 7.**

—— *See* HEPHAESTION, *Grammarian.* *Ἑφαιστιωνως* [*sic*] *Ἀλεξανδρεως ἐγχειριδιον, etc.* COPIOUS MS. NOTES [by C. Burney]. 1553. 4°. **836. g. 2.**

—— *See* HERMANN (J. G. J.) Godofredi Hermanni De metris poetarum græcarum et romanorum libri III. FEW MS. NOTES [by C. Burney]. 1796. 8°. **623. f. 14.**

—— *See* HOMER. [*Works.—Greek.*] *Εὐσταθιου . . . παρεκβολαι εἰς την Ὁμηρου Ἰλιαδα και Ὀδυσσειαν, etc.* MS. NOTES [by C. Burney and others]. 1560, *etc.* fol. **652. g. 5, 6.**

—— *See* HOMER. [*Works.—Greek.*] *Ὁμηρου Ἰλιας, etc.* FEW MS. NOTES [by C. Burney]. [1780, *etc.*] 8°. **995. c. 10–13.**

—— *See* HOMER. [*Works.—Greek and Latin.*] *Ὁμηρου ἁπαντα, etc.* FEW MS. NOTES [by C. Burney]. 1759, *etc.* 8°. **995. h. 1–5.**

—— *See* HORATIUS FLACCUS (Q.) [*Works.—Latin.*] Q. Horatius Flaccus. Ex recensione . . . R. Bentleii, *etc.* MS. NOTES [by C. Burney]. 1713. 4°. **654. d. 14.**

—— *See* HORATIUS FLACCUS (Q.) [*Works.—Latin.*] Q. Horatii Flacci opera, *etc.* MS. NOTES [by C. Burney]. 1778, *etc.* 8°. **833. l. 4.**

—— *See* HORATIUS FLACCUS (Q.) [*Works.—Latin.*] Q. Horatii Flacci opera, *etc.* MS. NOTES [by C. Burney]. 1792, *etc.* 4°. **654. d. 15, 16.**

—— *See* HUNTINGFORD (George I.) successively *Bishop of Gloucester* and *of Hereford.* An Apology for the Monostrophics, *etc.* COPIOUS MS. NOTES [by C. Burney]. 1784. 8°. **749. a. 11. (2.)**

—— *See* HUNTINGFORD (George I.) successively *Bishop of Gloucester* and *of Hereford.* *Μετρικα τινα μονοστροφικα, etc.* COPIOUS MS. NOTES [by C. Burney]. 1782. 8°. **749. a. 11. (1.)**

—— *See* IAMBLICHUS, *of Chalcis.* *Ἰαμβλιχου . . . λογοι δυο, etc.* MS. NOTES [by C. Burney]. 1598. 4°. **714. f. 7.**

—— *See* IAMBLICHUS, *of Chalcis.* *Ἰαμβλιχου . . . περι βιου Πυθαγορικου λογος, etc.* MS. NOTES [by C. Burney]. 1707. 4°. **714. f. 8.**

—— *See* JOHN, *Stobaeus.* Dicta poetarum, *etc.* MS. NOTES [by C. Burney]. 1623. 4°. **832. i. 5.**

—— —— [Another copy.] MS. NOTES [by C. Burney]. 1623. 4°. **1348. g. 11.**

—— *See* JULIAN, *the Apostate, Emperor of Rome.* [*Works.—Greek and Latin.*] *Ἰουλιανου αὐτοκρατορος τα σωζομενα, και . . . Κυριλλου . . . προς τα του ἐν ἀθεοις Ἰουλιανου λογοι δεκα, etc.* MS. NOTES [by C. Burney]. 1696. fol. **475. g. 13.**

—— *See* KNIGHT (Richard P.) An Analytical Essay on the Greek Alphabet. MS. NOTES [by C. Burney]. 1791. 4°. **624. i. 8.**

—— *See* KUSTER (L.) Lud. Kusterus De vero usu verborum mediorum, *etc.* FEW MS. NOTES [by C. Burney]. 1793. 8°. **624. b. 26. (1.)**

BURNEY (CHARLES) *D.D.* [WORKS CONTAINING MS. NOTES BY CHARLES BURNEY.]

—— *See* LABBÉ (P.) Eruditæ pronuntiationis catholici indices, *etc.* FEW MS. NOTES [by C. Burney]. 1751. 8°. **1090**. f. **16**.

—— *See* LE PAULMIER DE GRENTEMESNIL (J.) Jacobi Palmerii . . . Exercitationes in optimos fere auctores græcos, *etc.* FEW MS. NOTES [by C. Burney]. 1668. 4°. **836**. e. **16**.

—— *See* LONGINUS (D. C.) [*De Sublimitate.—Greek and Latin.*] *Διονυσιου Λογγινου περι ὑψους ὑπομνημα, etc.* MS. NOTES [by C. Burney]. 1752. 8°. **1089**. m. **1**.

—— *See* LONGINUS (D. C.) [*De Sublimitate.—Greek and Latin.*] Dionysii Longini De sublimitate, *etc.* FEW MS. NOTES [by C. Burney]. 1769. 8°. **1089**. l. **22**.

—— *See* LONGINUS (D. C.) [*De Sublimitate.—Greek and Latin.*] Dionysii Longini quæ supersunt, *etc.* MS. NOTES [by C. Burney]. 1778. 8°. **1089**. l. **14**.

—— *See* LUCIAN, *of Samosata.* [*Two or more Works.—Greek and Latin.*] Excerpta quaedam ex Luciani . . . operibus, *etc.* MS. NOTES [by C. Burney]. 1730. 8°. **1069**. c. **3**.

—— *See* LYCOPHRON. [*Alexandra.—Greek and Latin.*] *Λυκοφρονος . . . 'Αλεξανδρα, etc.* FEW MS. NOTES [by C. Burney]. [1702.] fol. **653**. d. **6**.

—— *See* MAITTAIRE (M.) Annales typographici, *etc.* tom. 5. MS. NOTES [by C. Burney]. 1719, *etc.* 4°. **129**. a. **1**.

—— *See* MENANDER, *the Poet.* Menandri et Philemonis reliquiæ, *etc.* COPIOUS MS. NOTES [by C. Burney]. 1709. 8°. C. **61**. a. **11**.

—— —— [Another copy.] MS. NOTES [by C. Burney]. 1709. 8°. C. **61**. a. **13**.

—— *See* MILTON (J.) [*Samson Agonistes.—Greek and Latin.*] *Σαμψὼν 'Αγωνιστης* . . . Græco carmine redditus, *etc.* COPIOUS MS. NOTES AND INDEX [by C. Burney]. 1788. 8°. **1162**. g. **11**.

—— *See* MURPHY (Arthur) The Life of David Garrick. MS. NOTES [by C. Burney]. 1801. 8°. **840**. e. **2**.

—— *See* MUSURUS (M.) *Archbishop of Malvasia.* M. Musuri Carmen in Platonem: I. Casauboni in Josephum Scaligerum ode, *etc.* MS. NOTES [by C. Burney]. 1797. 8°. **1213**. m. **34**.

—— *See* NEPOS (C.) Cornelii Nepotis Vitae excellentium imperatorum, *etc.* MS. NOTES [by C. Burney]. 1707. 8°. **609**. f. **1**.

—— *See* NEPOS (C.) Cornelii Nepotis Vitae excellentium imperatorum, *etc.* MS. NOTES [by C. Burney]. 1773. 8°. **609**. g. **7**.

—— *See* PHAEDRUS. Phædri . . . fabularum . . . libri quinque, *etc.* MS. NOTES [by C. Burney]. 1758. 8°. **637**. g. **2**.

—— *See* PHILELEUTHERUS, *Lipsiensis, pseud.* Emendationes in Menandri . . . reliquias, *etc.* MS. NOTES [by C. Burney]. 1713. 8°. **998**. i. **22**.

—— *See* PHILOSTRATUS, *the Elder.* Philostrati Lemnii opera quæ exstant, *etc.* [With a copy of R. Bentley's manuscript collation, in the handwriting of C. Burney.] 1608. fol. C. **48**. l. **3**.

—— *See* PHILOSTRATUS, *the Elder.* *Τα των Φιλοστρατων λειπομενα ἁπαντα, etc.* FEW MS. NOTES [by C. Burney]. 1709. fol. **713**. l. **4**.

BURNEY (CHARLES) *D.D.* [WORKS CONTAINING MS. NOTES BY CHARLES BURNEY.]

—— *See* PHRYNICHUS, *of Bithynia, the Grammarian.* Phrynichi Eclogæ nominum et verborum atticorum, *etc.* FEW MS. NOTES [by C. Burney]. 1739. 4°. **624**. e. **21**.

—— *See* PIERSONUS (J.) Joannis Piersoni Verisimilium libri duo. FEW MS. NOTES [by C. Burney]. 1752. 8°. **1087**. i. **20**.

—— *See* PINDAR. [*Greek.*] Carminum Pindaricorum fragmenta, *etc.* MS. NOTES [by C. Burney]. 1776. 4°. **652**. b. **7**.

—— *See* PINDAR. [*Greek and Latin.*] *Πινδαρου 'Ολυμπια, etc.* FEW MS. NOTES [by C. Burney]. 1698. fol. **653**. g. **17**.

—— *See* PLATO. [*Works.—Greek and Latin.*] *Πλατωνος ἁπαντα τα σωζομενα, etc.* MS. NOTES [by C. Burney]. 1578. fol. **713**. l. **1–3**.

—— *See* PLATO. [*Two or more Works.—Greek and Latin.*] Platonis Euthydemus et Gorgias, *etc.* FEW MS. NOTES [by C. Burney]. 1784. 8°. **525**. h. **13**.

—— *See* PLATO. [*Doubtful and Supposititious Works.—Two or more Works.—Greek and Latin.*] *Πλατωνος διαλογοι γ', etc.* FEW MS. NOTES [by C. Burney]. 1771. 8°. **714**. e. **7**.

—— *See* PLAUTUS (T. M.) [*Rudens.—Latin.*] M. Accii Plauti Rudens, *etc.* FEW MS. NOTES [by C. Burney]. [1798.] 8°. **999**. g. **29**.

—— *See* QUINTILIANUS (M. F.) [*Institutiones Oratoriae.*] Marci Fabii Quintiliani Institutionum oratoriarum libri duodecim, *etc.* MS. NOTES [by C. Burney]. 1760. 12°. **749**. a. **12**.

—— *See* RIGAULT (N.) Funus parasiticum . . . Item Juliani Cæsaris epistola. MS. NOTES [to pt. 2, by C. Burney]. 1601. 4°. **1079**. m. **27**. (**1, 2**.)

—— *See* RUDDIMAN (Thomas) Anticrisis, *etc.* MS. NOTES [by C. Burney]. 1754. 8°. **1087**. c. **19**.

—— *See* RUDDIMAN (Thomas) A Vindication of Mr. George Buchanan's Paraphrase of the Book of Psalms, *etc.* COPIOUS MS. NOTES [by C. Burney]. 1745. 8°. **1111**. e. **5**.

—— *See* SCHOTTUS (A.) *Jesuit.* *Παροιμιαι ἑλληνικαι, etc.* MS. NOTES [by C. Burney]. 1612. 4°. **635**. k. **8**.

—— *See* SOPHOCLES. [*Works.—Greek and Latin.*] *Σοφοκλεους τραγῳδιαι ζ', etc.* MS. NOTES [by C. Burney]. 1665, *etc.* 8°. **998**. b. **6**.

—— *See* SOPHOCLES. [*Works.—Greek and Latin.*] [Sophoclis tragoediæ septem, *etc.*] MS. NOTES [by C. Burney]. [1746.] 8°. **999**. c. **24**. & **998**. c. **15**.

—— *See* SOPHOCLES. [*Works.—Greek and Latin.*] [Sophoclis tragoediæ septem, *etc.*] COPIOUS MS. NOTES [by C. Burney]. [1758.] 8°. **995**. e. **17**.

—— *See* SOPHOCLES. [*Works.—Greek and Latin.*] Sophoclis quæ exstant omnia, *etc.* MS. NOTES [by C. Burney]. 1786. 4°. **833**. l. **11, 12**.

—— *See* SOPHOCLES. [*Two or more Works.—Greek and Latin.*] Sophoclis tragoediæ, Antigone et Trachiniae, *etc.* MS. NOTES [by C. Burney]. 1708. 8°. **998**. c. **2**.

BURNEY (CHARLES) *D.D.* [WORKS CONTAINING MS. NOTES BY CHARLES BURNEY.]

—— *See* SOPHOCLES. [*Two or more Works.—Greek and Latin.*] Sophoclis tragoediae, Oedipus Tyrannus, Philoctetes et Oedipus Coloneus, *etc.* MS. NOTES [by C. Burney]. 1746. 8°. **998.** c. **3.**

—— *See* SOPHOCLES. [*Philoctetes.—Greek and Latin.*] *Σοφοκλεους Φιλοκτητης, etc.* MS. NOTES [by C. Burney]. 1777. 8°. **995.** e. **19.**

—— *See* STATIUS (P. P.) [*Works.—Latin.*] P. Papinii Statii opera, *etc.* MS. NOTES [by C. Burney]. 1618. 4°. **833.** i. **8.**

—— *See* STATIUS (P. P.) [*Works.—Latin.*] P. Papinii Statii Sylvarum lib. V. Thebaidos lib. XII. Achilleidos lib. II., *etc.* FEW MS. NOTES [by C. Burney]. 1671. 8°. **1001.** k. **12.**

—— *See* STEPHEN, *of Byzantium. Στεφανου Βυζαντιου ἐθνικα κατ' ἐπιτομην, etc.* FEW MS. NOTES [by C. Burney]. 1694, *etc.* fol. **793.m.12.**

—— *See* SUIDAS. *Σουιδας.* Suidæ Lexicon, græce & latine, *etc.* MS. NOTES [by C. Burney]. 1705. fol. **12924.** k. **4.**

—— *See* TERENTIANUS, *Maurus.* Terentiani Mauri . . . De literis, syllabis, pedibus et metris tractatus, *etc.* MS. NOTES [by P. Burmannus and C. Burney]. 1531. 4°. **C. 64.** h. **5.**

—— —— [Another copy.] MS. NOTES [by C. Burney]. 1531. 4°. **623.** i. **10, 11.**

—— *See* TERENTIANUS, *Maurus.* Terentiani Mauri De literis, syllabis, pedibus, et metris, *etc.* MS. NOTES [by C. Burney]. 1584. 8°. **625.** c. **7, 8.**

—— *See* THEOCRITUS. [*Greek.*] Theocriti Syracusii quæ supersunt, *etc.* FEW MS. NOTES [by C. Burney]. 1770, *etc.* 4°. **653.** d. **9, 10.**

—— *See* THEOCRITUS. [*Greek and Latin.*] *Θεοκριτου τα εὑρισκομενα, etc.* MS. NOTES [by C. Burney]. 1699. 8°. **1067.** m. **19.**

—— *See* THEOCRITUS. [*Greek and Latin.*] Theocriti, Moschi & Bionis idyllia. MS. NOTES [by C. Burney]. 1760. 8°. **997.** f. **17.**

—— *See* THEOCRITUS. [*Greek and Latin.*] Theocriti decem eidyllia, *etc.* FEW MS. NOTES [by C. Burney]. 1773. 8°. **997.** f. **11.**

—— *See* THEOCRITUS. [*Greek and Latin.*] Theocriti, Bionis et Moschi carmina bucolica, *etc.* FEW MS. NOTES [by C. Burney]. 1779. 8°. **997.** f. **18.**

—— *See* THOMAS, *Magister. Θωμα του Μαγιστρου ὀνοματων ἀττικων ἐκλογαι, etc.* COPIOUS MS. NOTES [by C. Burney and others]. 1532. 8°. **684.** c. **6.**

—— *See* TIMAEUS, *the Sophist. Τιμαιου Σοφιστου λεξικον περι των παρα Πλατωνι λεξεων, etc.* FEW MS. NOTES [by C. Burney]. 1754. 8°. **624.** e. **23.** **(1.)**

—— *See* TOUP (Jonathan) Curæ novissimæ sive appendicula notarum et emendationum in Suidam. MS. NOTES [by C. Burney]. 1775. 8°. **827.** e. **7.** **(3.)**

—— *See* TOUP (Jonathan) Emendationes in Suidam, *etc.* MS. NOTES [by C. Burney]. 1760, *etc.* 8°. **827.** e. **10.**

—— *See* TOUP (Jonathan) Epistola critica ad . . . Gulielmum, episcopum Glocestriensem. MS. NOTES [by C. Burney]. 1767. 8°. **827.** e. **20.** **(1.)**

BURNEY (CHARLES) *D.D.* [WORKS CONTAINING MS. NOTES BY CHARLES BURNEY.]

—— *See* VIRGILIUS MARO (P.) [*Works.*] P. Virgilii Maronis opera, *etc.* FEW MS. NOTES [by C. Burney]. 1695. 8°. **1000.** g. **4.**

—— *See* WAKEFIELD (Gilbert) In Euripidis Hecubam, Londini nuper publicatam diatribe extemporalis. MS. NOTES [by C. Burney]. 1797. 8°. **995.** g. **16.**

—— *See* WALPOLE (Robert) *Rev.* Comicorum græcorum fragmenta, *etc.* MS. NOTES [by C. Burney]. 1805. 8°. **997.** c. **8.**

—— *See* XENOPHON, *the Historian.* [*Anabasis.—Greek.*] *Ξενοφωντος Κυρου ἀναβασεως βιβλια ἑπτα.* FEW MS. NOTES [by C. Burney]. 1772. 8°. **586.** g. **4.**

—— *See* XENOPHON, *the Historian.* [*Anabasis.—Greek and Latin.*] *Ξενοφωντος Κυρου ἀναβασεως βιβλια ἑπτα, etc.* FEW MS. NOTES [by C. Burney]. 1785. 4°. **749.** a. **8.**

—— *See* XENOPHON, *the Historian.* [*Cyropaedia.—Greek and Latin.*] *Ξενοφωντος Κυρου παιδειας βιβλια ὀκτω, etc.* FEW MS. NOTES [by C. Burney]. 1727. 4°. **586.** h. **1.**

—— *See* XENOPHON, *the Historian.* [*Hellenica.—Greek and Latin.*] Xenophontis Historia graeca, *etc.* MS. NOTES [by C. Burney]. 1778. 8°. **586.** e. **24.**

—— *See* XENOPHON, *the Historian.* [*Memorabilia.—Greek and Latin.*] *Ξενοφωντος ἀπομνημονευματων βιβλια δ', etc.* FEW MS. NOTES [by C. Burney]. 1759. 8°. **525.** g. **21.**

—— *See* XENOPHON, *the Historian.* [*Memorabilia.—Greek and Latin.*] *Ξενοφωντος ἀπομνημονευματων βιβλια δ', etc.* MS. NOTES [by C. Burney]. 1780. 8°. **720.** g. **7.**

MISCELLANEOUS COLLECTIONS MADE BY CHARLES BURNEY.

A Manuscript Catalogue of the Burney Collection of Newspapers will be found in the Reading Room Centre.

—— [Burney Collection. A collection of notebooks, containing MS. material and cuttings from books and newspapers, dealing with the careers of British actors and actresses, 1560–1816.] 7 vol. 4°. **939.** b. **1.**

—— [Burney Collection. A collection of notebooks, containing MS. material and cuttings from books and newspapers, dealing with the history of the stage in England, 1538–1807.] 46 vol. 4°. **938.** e. f.

—— [Burney Collection. A collection of notebooks, containing MS. material and cuttings from books and newspapers, dealing with the life and work of David Garrick. The last volume contains a list of all the dramatic parts in which he appeared.] 48 vol. 4° & fol. 939.d,e. & 937 g.95-96.

—— [Burney Collection. A collection of playbills of the theatre at Brighton.] [1804–08.] fol. **937.** f. **1.**

—— [Burney Collection. A collection of playbills of the theatres at Ipswich, Norwich, Lynn, Wisbech, Yarmouth, Bury St. Edmunds, St. Neots, Beccles, Stamford, Boston, Leicester, Portsmouth and of a few other miscellaneous theatres.] 9 vol. [1773–1801.] 4°. **937.** f. **2.**

—— [Burney Collection. Press-cuttings and MS. notes dealing with the work of David Garrick and miscellaneous theatrical subjects.] 4°. **938.** d. **20.**

—— [Burney Collection. "Theatrical Register." A collection of notebooks, containing MS. material and cuttings from books and newspapers, dealing with the history of the stage in England, 1660–1801.] 84 vol. 4°. **938.** a–d.

BURNEY (CHARLES) *D.D.* [MISCELLANEOUS COLLECTIONS MADE BY CHARLES BURNEY.]

—— [Burney Collection. "Theatrical Register." A collection of playbills of London theatres, chiefly of Drury Lane, Covent Garden and the Haymarket.] 59 vol. [1768–1817.] 4°. **937**. b–e.

—— [Burney Collection. Two volumes of notes, chiefly in MS., on the history of the Theatre in Goodman's Fields, 1729–43.] [1807?] 4°. **939**. b. **2**.

—— [A collection of playbills, notices and press-cuttings dealing with private theatrical performances, 1750–1808. The collection is variously attributed to Charles Burney and to Miss S. S. Banks.] fol. *See* COLLECTION.
937.g.96.

APPENDIX.

—— *See* LONDON.—III. *British Museum.—Department of Manuscripts.* Catalogue of Manuscripts in the British Museum. New series. vol. 1. (pt. 2. The Burney Manuscripts.) 1834, *etc.* fol. Circ. **84**. b.

BURNEY (CHARLES) *Mus.D.* *See* BURNEY, afterwards D'ARBLAY (Frances) Memoirs of Doctor Burney, arranged from his own manuscripts, from family papers, and from personal recollections. 1832. 8°. **614**. e. **17–19**.

—— *See* COLLIER (Joel) *pseud.* Musical Travels through England. [A satire on Dr. Burney's accounts of his Continental Travels.] 1774. 8°. **7895**. b. **42**.
—— —— 1775. 8°. **7895**. aaa. **34**.
—— —— 1775. 8°. E. **2229**. (**2**.)
—— —— 1776. 8°. E. **2097***. (**1**.)

—— *See* HAWKINS (*Sir* John) *Miscellaneous Writer.* A General History of the Science and Practice of Music. [With an autograph letter by C. Burney.] MS. NOTES [by C. Burney and others]. 1776. 4°. C. **45**. f. **4–8**.

—— *See* HEGAR (E.) Die Anfänge der neueren Musikgeschichtsschreibung um 1770 bei . . . Burney, *etc.* [1932.] 8°. W.P. **9947/7**.

—— *See* PROJET. Projet concernant de nouveaux signes pour la musique, *etc.* (Lettre à M. Burney sur la musique.) [By J. J. Rousseau.] 1781. 8°. Hirsch I. **522**.

—— *See* RICCI (C.) Burney, Casanova e Farinelli in Bologna, *etc.* [1890.] 8°. **10603**. e. **16**. (**6**.)

—— *See* ROBERTS (William W.) Charles and Fanny Burney in the light of the new Thrale Correspondence in the John Rylands Library, *etc.* 1932. fol. **10823**. k. **22**.

—— *See* ROBERTS (William W.) The Trial of Midas the Second. An account of Burney's unpublished satire on Hawkins's "History of Music" in the John Rylands Library, *etc.* 1933. 8°. **7894**. i. **36**.

—— *See* ROUSSEAU (J. J.) [*Le Devin du Village.*] The Cunning-Man, *etc.* [Translated by C. Burney.] 1766. 8°. **11777**. c. **88**.

—— —— 1766. 8°. **643**. h. **3**. (**5**.)

—— ——1784. 12°. [*Supplement to Bell's British Theatre.* vol. 2.] **82**. b. **19**.

—— —— 1786. 12°. [*A Collection of the Most Esteemed Farces and Entertainments performed on the British Stage.* vol. 2.] **1344**. c. **7**.

BURNEY (CHARLES) *Mus.D.*

—— *See* SCHOLES (Percy A.) The Great Dr. Burney. His life—his travels—his works—his family and his friends. [With portraits.] 1948. 8°. **7889**. c. **23**.

—— *See* TARTINI (G.) A Letter from the late Signor Tartini to Signora Maddalena Lombardini . . . Translated by Dr. Burney. 1771. 4°. **785**. k. **41**.

—— —— 1913. 8°. **7897**. cc. **48**.

—— De l'état présent de la musique en France et en Italie, dans les Pays-Bas, en Hollande et en Allemagne . . . Traduit . . . par Ch. Brack. [A translation of "The Present State of Music in France and Italy" and "The Present State of Music in Germany, the Netherlands, and the United Provinces."] 3 tom. *Gênes*, 1809, 10. 8°. **1042**. g. **6**, **7**.

—— Carl Burney's . . . Tagebuch einer musikalischen Reise durch Frankreich und Italien . . . Übersetzt von C. D. Ebeling. (Bd. 2. Durch Flandern, die Nederlande und am Rhein bis Wien. Bd. 3. Durch Böhmen, Sachsen, Brandenburg, Hamburg und Holland. [Bd. 2 and 3 translated by J. J. C. Bode.]) 3 Bd. *Hamburg*, 1772, 73. 8°. **1042**. f. **16**, **17**.

—— [Another copy.] Carl Burney's . . . Tagebuch einer musikalischen Reise durch Frankreich und Italien, *etc.* *Hamburg*, 1772, 73. 8°. Hirsch I. **642**.

—— Account of an Infant Musician [William Crotch] . . . Read at the Royal Society, Feb. 18, 1779. pp. 26. *J. Nichols: London*, 1779. 4°. T. **1560**. (**8**.)

—— An Account of the Musical Performances in Westminster-Abbey and the Pantheon, May . . . and June . . . 1784. In commemoration of Handel. [With plates, including portraits.] pp. vii. xvi. 56. 139. *T. Payne & Son; G. Robinson: London*, 1785. 4°. **785**. l. **29**.

—— [Another copy.] **130**. f. **3**.

—— [Another copy.] G. **2664**.
Imperfect; wanting four of the plates.

—— [Another copy.] An Account of the Musical Performances in Westminster Abbey and the Pantheon . . . in commemoration of Handel. *London*, 1785. 4°. R.M. **5**. g. **2**.

With an errata slip.

—— [Another copy.] An Account of the Musical Performances in Westminster Abbey and the Pantheon . . . in commemoration of Handel. *London*, 1785. 4°. Hirsch I. **644**.
Three of the plates are in duplicate.

—— [Another copy.] Hirsch I. **644**a.
With an errata slip. Imperfect; wanting one of the plates.

—— [Another edition.] pp. vii. xvi. 74. 145. *Moncrieffe: Dublin*, 1785. 8°. **7895**. aaa. **35**.

—— Dr. Karl Burney's Nachricht von Georg Friedrich Händel's Lebensumständen und der ihm zu London im Mai und Jun. 1784 angestellten Gedächtnissfeyer . . . Übersetzt von Johann Joachim Eschenburg . . . Mit Kupfern. pp. lii. 102. *Berlin & Stettin*, 1785. 4°. **785**. k. **9**.

—— [Another copy.] Dr. Karl Burney's Nachricht von Georg Friedrich Händel's Lebensumständen, *etc.* *Berlin & Stettin*, 1785. 4°. Hirsch I. **645**.

—— An Account of the Musical Performances . . . in commemoration of Handel . . . [An abridgment, containing only Burney's preface and introduction, and the programmes of the concerts.] To which is added, a Notice of the forthcoming Royal Musical Festival of 1834. pp. xxxix. *Duff & Hodgson: London,* 1834. 8°. **577. k. 21. (13.)**

—— [Another copy.] An Account of the Musical Performances in Westminster Abbey and the Pantheon . . . 1784, in commemoration of Handel, *etc.* *London,* 1834. 8°. Hirsch **3192.**

—— An Essay towards a History of the Principal Comets that have appeared since the year 1742 . . . With remarks and reflections upon the present comet. [By C. Burney.] To which is prefixed . . . A Letter upon Comets. Addressed to a Lady, by the late M. de Maupertuis, *etc.* [Translated from the French by Esther Burney.] pp. 92. 1769. 8°. *See* ESSAY. **117. d. 9.**

—— [Another copy.] **B. 499. (3.)**

—— [Another edition.] pp. 112. 1770. 12°. *See* ESSAY. **531. e. 32.**

—— A General History of Music, from the earliest ages to the present period. To which is prefixed, a Dissertation on the music of the ancients. [With plates, including a portrait.] 4 vol. *Printed for the Author: London,* 1776–89. 4°. **557*. f. 12.**

—— [Another copy.] **130. f. 8–11.**

—— [Another copy.] **2034.e.**
Imperfect; wanting the plates.

—— [Another copy.] A General History of Music, *etc.* *London,* 1776–89. 4°. **R.M. 5. g. 1.**
Imperfect; wanting the plates.

—— Second edition. 4 vol. *Printed for the Author: London,* 1789, 82–89. 4°. **G. 2660–63.**
Vol. 1 only is of the second edition.

—— [Another copy.] General History of Music, *etc.* *London,* 1789, 82–89. 4°. Hirsch I. **646.**
Vol. 1 contains a leaf bearing "Directions to the bookbinder."

—— [Another edition.] With critical and historical notes by Frank Mercer. [With a portrait.] 2 vol. *G. T. Foulis & Co.: London,* 1935. 8°. **07899. ee. 61.**

—— Memoirs of the Life and Writings of the Abate Metastasio. In which are incorporated, translations of his principal letters. [With a list of Metastasio's works, and a portrait.] 3 vol. *G. G. & J. Robinson: London,* 1796. 8°. **276. k. 32–34.**

—— Extract from Memoirs of the Life and Writings of . . . Metastasio. *See* METASTASIO (P. A. D. B.) Didon abandonnée, *etc.* [1810?] 12°. **11737. aa. 36.**

—— The Present State of Music in France and Italy: or, the Journal of a tour through those countries, undertaken to collect materials for a General History of Music. pp. vii. 396. *T. Becket & Co.: London,* 1771. 8°. **1042. g. 5.**

—— [Another copy.] The Present State of Music in France and Italy: or, the Journal of a tour through those countries, *etc.* *London,* 1771. 8°. Hirsch **2824.**

—— The second edition, corrected. pp. viii. 409. *T. Becket & Co.: London,* 1773. 8°. **129. a. 28.**

—— [Another copy.] The Present State of Music in Germany, the Netherlands, and United Provinces, *etc.* *London,* 1773. 8°. Hirsch I. **643.**
With a leaf bearing "Proposals for printing by subscription a General History of Music."

—— Viaggio musicale in Italia, 1770. Traduzione di Virginia Attanasio. [A translation of part of "The Present State of Music in France and Italy," from the French translation of Charles Brack. With plates, including a portrait.] pp. xv. 262. [*Milan,*] 1921. 8°. [*Collezione settecentesca.* no. 14.] **012226.b.1/13.**

—— The Present State of Music in Germany, the Netherlands, and the United Provinces. Or, the Journal of a tour through those countries, undertaken to collect materials for a General History of Music. 2 vol. *T. Becket & Co.: London,* 1773. 8°. **129. a. 26, 27.**

—— Dr. Charles Burney's Continental Travels, 1770–1772. Compiled from his journals and other sources by Cedric Howard Glover. [Selections. With a portrait and a map.] pp. xxii. 264. *Blackie & Son: London & Glasgow,* 1927. 8°. **010107. h. 32.**

—— [Another copy.] Dr. Charles Burney's Continental Travels, 1770–1772. Compiled from his journals . . . by Cedric Howard Glover. *London & Glasgow,* 1927. 8°. Hirsch **2825.**

—— A Catalogue of the Miscellaneous Library of the late Charles Burney . . . which will be sold by auction . . . on Thursday, the 9th of June, 1814, and eight following days, *etc.* pp. 63. MS. NOTES OF PRICES. [*London,* 1814.] 8°. **S.C.Sotheby 86.(6.)**

—— The Late Dr. Burney's Musical Library. A catalogue of the . . . music, printed and MS., of the late C. Burney . . . which will be sold by auction . . . 8th of August, 1814, and following days, *etc.* pp. 41. MS. NOTES OF PRICES. [1814.] 4°. S.C. **1076. (1.)**

—— [Another copy.] The Late Dr. Burney's Musical Library, *etc.* MS. NOTES OF PRICES. [*London.* 1814.] 4°. **C.61.h.1.(12.)**

BURNEY (CHARLES) *Staff-Commander, R.N.* The Boy's Manual of Seamanship and Gunnery, compiled for the use of the Training Ships of the Royal Navy. pp. vi. 239. *C. Le Feuvre: Jersey,* 1869. 8°. **8805. aa. 21.**

—— Second edition. pp. viii. 304. *F. Warne & Co.: London,* [1871.] 8°. **8805. aaa. 23.**

—— Fifth edition. pp. xxxii. 352. *Trübner & Co.: London,* [1877.] 8°. **8807. aaa. 7.**

—— [Another edition.] The Young Seaman's Manual and Rigger's Guide . . . Tenth edition, revised, *etc.* pp. xxxviii. 591. *Trübner & Co.: London,* 1889. 8°. **8805. aaa. 32.**

—— [Another copy.] **8805. aaa. 33.**

BURNEY (*Sir* CHARLES DENNISTOUN) *Bart.* The World, the Air and the Future. [With plates.] pp. xxiii. 356. *A. A. Knopf: London,* 1929. 8°. **09081. d. 11.**

BURNEY (Charles Fox) *See* Bible. [*English.*] The Oxford Church Bible Commentary. (General editor of the Old Testament volume—the Rev. C. F. Burney.) 1913, *etc.* 8°. **2201**. c. 5.

—— *See* Bible.—*Judges.* [*English.*] The Book of Judges, with introduction and notes. Edited by the Rev. C. F. Burney. 1918. 8°. **2200**. d. 3.

—— *See* Driver (Samuel R.) Studies in the Psalms . . . Edited, with a preface, by C. F. Burney. 1915. 8°. **03089**. g. **27**.

—— *See* Sanday (William) The New Lessons Explained . . . By W. Sanday . . . C. F. Burney, *etc.* 1920. 8°. **3477**. dg. **45**.

—— *See* Sanday (William) and Emmet (C. W.) The Psalms explained . . . With contributions from Dr. C. F. Burney. 1918. 12°. **3089**. a. **60**.

—— The Aramaic Origin of the Fourth Gospel. pp. 176. *Clarendon Press: Oxford,* 1922. 8°. **03226**. eee. **15**.

—— The Gospel in the Old Testament. pp. xi. 256. *T. & T. Clark: Edinburgh,* 1921. 8°. ["*The Scholar as Preacher.*"] **4466**. l. **1/14**.

—— The Growth of the Doctrine of Immortality among the Jews. [A lecture.] *See* London.—iii. *Union of Jewish Literary Societies.* The Jews at the Close of the Bible Age, *etc.* 1926. 8°. **04515**. de. **13**.

—— Israel's Hope of Immortality. Four lectures. pp. 105. *Clarendon Press: Oxford,* 1909. 8°. **4256**. ee. **13**.

—— Israel's Settlement in Canaan. The Biblical tradition and its historical background. [With maps.] pp. x. 104. pl. vi. *Oxford University Press: London,* 1918. 8°. [*Schweich Lectures.* 1917.] Ac. **1186/2**.

—— Second edition. pp. x. 104. pl. vi. *Oxford University Press: London,* 1919. 8°. [*Schweich Lectures.* 1917.] Ac. **1186/2**.

—— Third edition. pp. x. 104. pl. vi. *Oxford University Press: London,* 1921. 8°. [*Schweich Lectures.* 1917.] Ac. **1186/2**.

—— Notes on the Hebrew Text of the Books of Kings, with an introduction and appendix. pp. xlviii. 384. *Clarendon Press: Oxford,* 1903. 8°. **01903**. b. **16**.

—— The Old Testament Conception of Atonement fulfilled by Christ. With a criticism of Dr. Rashdall's Bampton Lectures. A sermon, *etc.* pp. 20. *Oxford University Press: London,* 1920. 8°. **4478**. k. **25**.

—— Outlines of Old Testament Theology. pp. 132. *Rivingtons: London,* 1899. 8°. [*Oxford Church Text Books.*] **03605**. de. **1/10**.

—— Second edition. pp. 132. *Rivingtons: London,* 1903. 8°. [*Oxford Church Text Books.*] **03605**. de. **1/11**.

—— The Permanent Religious Value of the Old Testament. *See* Contentio. Contentio Veritatis, *etc.* 1902. 8°. **4371**. f. **27**.

—— [Another edition.] *See* Contentio. Contentio Veritatis, *etc.* 1907. 8°. **4373**. dd. **19**.

—— The Poetry of Our Lord. An examination of the formal elements of Hebrew poetry in the discourses of Jesus Christ. pp. 182. *Clarendon Press: Oxford,* 1925. 8°. **03226**. f. **9**.

BURNEY (Charles Fox)

—— The Writers of the Old Testament and their Message. pp. 8. *Society for Promoting Christian Knowledge: London,* 1908. 8°. [*Pan Anglican Papers.* S.B. 24.] **4108**. cc. **35**.

BURNEY (Charles Parr) A Charge, delivered to the Clergy of the Archdeaconry of St. Alban's, by C. P. Burney . . . at his Visitation, June 16, 1841, *etc.* pp. 42. *J. G. F. & J. Rivington: London,* 1841. 8°. T. **2480**. **(5.)**

—— The Love of Our Country, a prize essay, recited in the Theatre at Oxford . . . June 14, 1809. pp. 31. *S. Collingwood: Oxford,* [1809.] 8°. B. **495**. **(11.)**

—— [Another copy.] T. **981**. **(11.)**

—— [Another copy.] **732**. c. **3**. **(4.)**

—— [Another edition.] 1830. *See* Oxford.—*University of Oxford.* [*Prize Poems and Essays.*] The Oxford English Prize Essays. vol. 2. 1836, *etc.* 12°. **8364**. b. **40**.

—— A Sermon, preached, in the Chapel of Lambeth Palace, at the consecration of the Honourable . . . Edward Legge, LL.D., Lord Bishop of Oxford. pp. 32. *T. Payne & H. Foss: London,* 1816. 4°. **694**. k. **10**. **(3.)**

—— [Another copy.] **1200**. cc. **23**. **(10.)**

BURNEY (Charlotte Ann) *See* Burney, afterwards d'Arblay (Frances) The Early Diary of Frances Burney . . . With a selection . . . from the journals of her sisters Susan and Charlotte Burney, *etc.* 1889. 8°. **10859**. a. **1**.

—— —— 1907. 8°. **2504**. l. **9**.

BURNEY (Christopher)

—— The Dungeon Democracy. [On the author's experiences in the concentration camp at Buchenwald.] pp. ix. 100. *William Heinemann: London, Toronto,* 1945. 8°. **9100**. a. **92**.

—— Solitary Confinement . . . Foreword by Christopher Fry. pp. 152. *Clerke & Cockeran: London,* 1952. 8°. **10863**. b. **8**.

BURNEY (E.) Christian Revolution. An essay in reconstruction. pp. 156. *Andrew Melrose: London & New York,* [1921.] 8°. **04018**. e. **19**.

BURNEY (Edmund Ernest Norbet) Report on Education in Hong Kong. pp. 27. 1935. fol. *See* Hong Kong. C.S. d. **92**.

BURNEY (Edward Francis) *See* Cabinet. The Cabinet of the Arts. A series of engravings by English artists, from original designs by Stothard, Burney, *etc.* 1799. 8°. **1401**. i. **25**.

—— *See* Glover (Richard) *Author of "Leonidas."* Leonidas: a poem . . . Adorned with plates [from designs by E. F. Burney and others]. 1804. 8°. **11633**. bb. **18**.

—— *See* Sainte-Beuve (C. A.) Galerie de portraits littéraires . . . Illustrée de portraits gravés à l'eau-forte par MM. Abot, Burney, *etc.* 1893. 8°. **10659**. f. **16**.

BURNEY (Estelle) An Idyll of the Closing Century. Duologue. pp. 16. *London; New York,* [1898.] 12°. [*French's Acting Edition.*] **2304**. h. **31**. **(12.)**

BURNEY (ESTHER) *See* MOREAU DE MAUPERTUIS (P. L.) A Letter upon Comets. [Translated by E. Burney.] 1769. 8°. [*An Essay toward a History of the Principal Comets, etc.*] **117.** d. **9.**

—— —— 1770. 12°. [*An Essay toward a History of the Principal Comets, etc.*] **531.** e. **32.**

BURNEY (ETHEL W.)

—— *See* PORTER (Bertha) and MOSS (R. L. B.) Topographical Bibliography of Ancient Egyptian Hieroglyphic Texts, Reliefs and Paintings. (VII. By B. Porter and R. L. B. Moss assisted by E. W. Burney.) 1927, *etc.* 4°. **2761.cc.1.**

BURNEY (FANNY) *See* BURNEY, afterwards D'ARBLAY (Frances)

BURNEY, afterwards **WOOD** (FANNY ANNE) *See* WOOD.

BURNEY, afterwards **D'ARBLAY** (FRANCES) *See* DOBSON (Henry A.) Fanny Burney, *etc.* 1903. 8°. **2326.** b. **48.**

—— *See* EDWARDS (Averyl) Fanny Burney, *etc.* 1948. 8°. **10861.** h. **26.**

—— *See* HAHN (Emily) A Degree of Prudery. A biography of Fanny Burney. [With a portrait.] 1951. 8°. **10858.** b. **30.**

—— *See* HALE (Will T.) Madame D'Arblay's Place in the Development of the English Novel. 1916. 8°. [*Indiana University Studies.* no. 28.] Ac. **2692.** w.

—— *See* HEMLOW (Joyce) Fanny Burney: playwright. [1950.] 8°. **11860.** ff. **19.**

—— *See* HILL (Mary C.) Fanny Burney at the Court of Queen Charlotte, *etc.* 1912. 8°. **10826.** cc. **10.**

—— *See* JOHNSON (Reginald B.) Fanny Burney and the Burneys, *etc.* [With a portrait.] 1926. 8°. **010855.** cc. **57.**

—— *See* LLOYD (Christopher) Fanny Burney, *etc.* [With a portrait.] 1936. 8°. **010822.** g. **42.**

—— *See* MACAULAY (Thomas B.) [*Essays.—Frances Burney.*] Macaulay's Essay on Frances Burney, *etc.* [With extracts from Frances Burney's works.] 1919. 8°. **012273.** de. **68.**

—— *See* MASEFIELD (Muriel) The Story of Fanny Burney, *etc.* 1927. 8°. **010826.** f. **46.**

—— *See* MOORE (Frank F.) The Keeper of the Robes, *etc.* [A life of Frances Burney.] [1911.] 8°. **010827.** k. **8.**

—— *See* OVERMAN (Antoinette A.) An Investigation into the Character of Fanny Burney. [With a portrait.] 1933. 8°. **010825.** k. **6.**

—— *See* ROBERTS (William W.) Charles and Fanny Burney in the light of the new Thrale Correspondence in the John Rylands Library, *etc.* 1932. fol. **10823.** k. **22.**

—— *See* TOURTELLOT (Arthur B.) Be Loved No More. The life and environment of Fanny Burney, *etc.* 1938. 8°. **10857.** bb. **15.**

—— The Early Diary of Frances Burney, 1768–1778. With a selection from her correspondence, and from the journals of her sisters Susan and Charlotte Burney. Edited by Annie Raine Ellis. 2 vol. *G. Bell & Sons: London,* 1889. 8°. **10859.** a. **1.**

—— [Another edition.] 2 vol. *G. Bell & Sons: London,* 1907. 8°. [*Bohn's Standard Library.*] **2504.** l. **9.**

BURNEY, afterwards **D'ARBLAY** (FRANCES)

—— Diary and Letters of Madame d'Arblay. (1778–1840.) Edited by her niece [i.e. Charlotte Frances Barrett]. [With plates, including a portrait.] 7 vol. *Henry Colburn: London,* 1842–46. 8°. **010854.** df. **1.**

—— A new edition. [With a portrait.] 7 vol. *Hurst & Blackett: London,* 1854. 8°. **10824.** a. **29.**

—— [Another edition.] 4 vol. *G. Bell & Sons: London,* 1891. 8°. **10855.** e. **16.**

—— [Another edition.] With preface and notes by Austin Dobson. 6 vol. *Macmillan & Co.: London,* 1904, 05. 8°. **10863.ff.1.**

—— The Diary and Letters of Madame d'Arblay . . . [Selected from Mrs. Barrett's edition.] With notes by W. C. Ward, and prefaced by Lord Macaulay's Essay. [With a portrait.] 3 vol. *Vizetelly & Co.: London,* 1890, 91. 8°. [*Cream of the Diarists and Memoir Writers.*] **10856.** df. **20.**

—— The Diary and Letters of Madame D'Arblay . . . Edited and selected, with a preface and notes, by Muriel Masefield. [With plates, including a portrait.] pp. 336. *G. Routledge & Sons: London,* 1931. 8°. [*Broadway Diaries, Memoirs and Letters.*] **12211.ss.2/6.**

—— Queeney and Fanny Burney. (Fanny Burney's letters [to Hester Maria Thrale].) *See* FITZMAURICE (Henry W. E. P.) *Marquis of Lansdowne.* The Queeney Letters, *etc.* 1934. 8°. **10713.pp.25.**

—— The Diary of Fanny Burney. [Selected and edited by Lewis Gibbs.] pp. xv. 416. *J. M. Dent & Sons: London; E. P. Dutton & Co.: New York,* 1940. 8°. [*Everyman's Library.*] **12206.p.1/743.**

—— The Diary of Fanny Burney. Selected and edited by Christopher Lloyd. [With a portrait.] pp. 256. *Roger Ingram: London,* 1948. 8°. **10862.** a. **35.**

—— Brief Reflections relative to the Emigrant French Clergy: earnestly submitted to the humane consideration of the ladies of Great Britain. By the author of Evelina and Cecilia [i.e. F. Burney]. pp. v. 27. *London,* 1793. 8°. *See* FRANCE.—*Church of France.—Clergy.* [*Appendix.*] T. **1121.** (**6.**)

—— Camilla: or, a Picture of youth. By the author of Evelina and Cecilia (F. d'Arblay). 5 vol. *T. Payne; T. Cadell Jun. & W. Davies: London,* 1796. 12°. **1206.** b. **17–21.**

—— Camilla . . . By the author of Evelina and Cecilia (F. D'Arblay). 3 vol. *G. Burnett: Dublin,* 1796. 12°. **12650.** a. **100.**

—— [Another edition.] 3 vol. 1840. 32°. *See* CAMILLA. **1208.** a. **12–14.**

—— Kamilla oder ein Gemälde der Jugend; aus dem Englischen . . . Mit einer Vorrede von D. Johann Reinhold Forster. 4 Tl. *Berlin & Stettin,* 1798. 8°. **12612.** ccc. **7.**

—— Cecilia, or Memoirs of an Heiress. By the author of Evelina [i.e. F. Burney]. 5 vol. 1782. 12°. *See* CECILIA. **94.** a. **5–9.**

—— Cecilia: or Memoirs of an heiress. 3 vol. *Price, etc.: Dublin,* 1783. 12°. **012646.** c. **46.**

—— [Another edition.] 3 vol. *Price & Co.: Dublin*, 1784. 12°. **12619**. pp. 9.

—— The fourth edition. 5 vol. 1784. 12°. *See* CECILIA. **12611**. e. 12.

—— The fifth edition. 5 vol. 1786. 12°. *See* CECILIA. **12614**. aaa. 8.

—— [Another edition.] 3 vol. *P. Wogan: Dublin*, 1795. 12°. **12611**. h. 15.

—— [Another edition.] 3 vol. 1810. 12°. *See* CECILIA. **248**. a. 38–40.

—— A new edition. 2 vol. 1820. 8°. *See* CECILIA. **12614**. i. 3.

—— [Another edition.] 3 vol. *C. S. Arnold: London*, 1823. 16°. **012611**. de. 12.

—— [Another edition.] [With engravings by Charles Heath from drawings by Henry Corbould.] 2 vol. *J. F. Dove: London*, [1825?] 8°. **012613**. de. 25.

—— [Another edition.] With a preface and notes by Annie Raine Ellis. 2 vol. *G. Bell & Sons: London*, 1882. 8°. [*Bohn's Novelist's Library.*] **2502**. e. 10.

—— [Another edition.] Edited by R. Brimley Johnson. Illustrated by W. Cubitt Cooke. 3 vol. *J. M. Dent & Co.: London*, 1893. 8°. **012612**. ff. 4.

—— [Another edition.] (With a preface and notes by Annie Raine Ellis.) 2 vol. *G. Bell & Sons: London*, 1904. 8°. [*York Library.*] **012201**. i. 1/1.

—— Evelina, or a Young lady's entrance into the world. [By F. Burney, afterwards D'Arblay.] 3 vol. 1778. 12°. *See* EVELINA. C. **117**. b. **80**.

—— Evelina, or, a Young lady's entrance into the world . . . [By F. Burney, afterwards D'Arblay.] The second edition. 3 vol. 1779. 12°. *See* EVELINA. **12650**. a. 128.

—— Evelina, or the History of a young lady's entrance into the world. The third edition. [By F. Burney.] 3 vol. 1779. 12°. *See* EVELINA. **635**. c. 26.

—— A new edition. 3 vol. 1783. 12°. *See* EVELINA. **243**. i. 8–10.

—— Evelina . . . By Miss Burney. 3 vol. *Printed for C. & F. Walther: Dresden*, 1788. 16°. **012635**. de. 6.

—— A new edition. 2 vol. 1791. 12°. *See* EVELINA. **12613**. bbb. 13.

—— A new edition. 2 vol. 1808. 12°. *See* EVELINA. **12613**. aa. 12.

—— [Another edition.] 2 vol. *F. C. & J. Rivington: London*, 1810. 12°. [*The British Novelists.* vol. 38, 39.] **248**. a. 36, 37.

—— A new edition, embellished with engravings. pp. 522. *Edward Mason: London*, 1821. 8°. **12613**. gg. 4.

—— [A reissue.] Embellished and illustrated with a series of humorous colored engravings, by the first artists. pp. 522. 1822. 8°. *See* EVELINA. C. **71**. e. 27.

—— [Another edition.] pp. xii. 444. *Bernard Tauchnitz: Leipzig*, 1850. 8°. [*Collection of British Authors.* vol. 190.] **12267.a.1/43.**

—— New edition. pp. ix. 469. *Thomas Harrison: London*, 1854. 8°. **12613**. c. 31.

—— [A reissue.] *London*, 1861. 8°. **12613**. d. 13.

—— [Another edition.] pp. 379. *Ward, Lock, & Tyler: London*, [1874.] 8°. [*Library of Favourite Authors.*] **12602**. cc. 9.

—— [Another edition.] With an introduction and notes by Annie Raine Ellis. pp. lxiii. 427. *G. Bell & Sons: London*, 1881. 8°. [*Bohn's Novelist's Library.*] **2502**. e. 9.

—— [Another edition.] pp. 380. *London*, [1888.] 8°. [*Cassell's Red Library.*] **12600**. ccc. 10.

—— [Another edition.] Edited by R. Brimley Johnson. Illustrated by W. Cubitt Cooke. 2 vol. *J. M. Dent & Co.: London*, 1893. 8°. **012612**. ff. 1.

—— [Another edition.] Illustrated by Arthur Rackham. pp. xv. 416. *George Newnes: London*, 1898. 8°. [*New Library.* vol. 8.] **012208**. f. 19.

—— [Another edition.] With an introduction by Austin Dobson, and illustrations by Hugh Thomson. pp. xxxv. 477. *Macmillan & Co.: London*, [1903.] 8°. **012612**. g. 21.

—— [Another edition.] 2 vol. *J. M. Dent & Co.: London*, 1903. 8°. [*Temple Classics.*] **012200.de.8/88.**

—— [Another edition.] (With introduction and notes by Annie Raine Ellis.) pp. lxiii. 427. *G. Bell & Sons: London*, 1904. 8°. [*York Library.*] **012201**. i. 1/2.

—— [Another edition.] pp. xvi. 512. *J. M. Dent: London; E. P. Dutton: New York*, [1909.] 8°. [*Everyman's Library.*] **12206.p.1/161.**

—— [Another edition.] With notes, indexes, and illustrations from contemporary sources, edited by Sir Frank D. Mackinnon. pp. 590. *Clarendon Press: Oxford*, 1930. 8°. **012601**. l. 17.

—— Evelina; eene Engelsche geschiedenis. [By F. Burney, afterwards D'Arblay.] 3 dl. 1780–85. 8°. *See* EVELINA. **12651**. aa. 44.

—— Evelina, oder eines jungen Frauenzimmers Eintritt in die Welt . . . Aus dem Englischen. [By F. Burney.] 3 Tl. 1779. 8°. *See* EVELINA. **12614**. dd. 14.

—— Les Imprudences de la jeunesse, par l'auteur de Cécilia [i.e. F. Burney, or rather, a translation of "Juvenile Indiscretions" by Agnes Maria Bennett]. Traduit de l'angois par Madame la baronne de Vasse. 4 vol. 1788. 12°. *See* IMPRUDENCES. **12808**. s. 10.

—— Memoirs of Doctor Burney, arranged from his own manuscripts, from family papers, and from personal recollections. 3 vol. *Edward Moxon: London*, 1832. 8°. **614**. e. 17–19.

—— [Another copy.] Memoirs of Doctor Burney, arranged from his own manuscripts, *etc.* *London*, 1832. 8°. Hirsch **2823**.

Imperfect; wanting the half-title in vol. 1, 2.

—— The Wanderer; or, Female difficulties. By the author of Evelina (F. B. d'Arblay), *etc.* 5 vol. *Longman & Co.: London*, 1814. 12°. **248**. e. 36–40.

BURNEY, afterwards **D'ARBLAY** (FRANCES)

—— Fanny Burney and her Friends. Select passages from her diary and other writings. Edited by L. B. Seeley . . . With . . . illustrations [including a portrait], *etc.* pp. x. 331. *Seeley & Co.: London*, [1890.] 8°. **10854**. ff. **16**.

—— Fanny Burney and her Friends . . . Edited by L. B. Seeley . . . New edition. pp. viii. 331. *Seeley & Co.: London*, 1895. 8°. **10856**. m. **21**.

—— Dr. Johnson & Fanny Burney. Being the Johnsonian passages from the works of Mme. d'Arblay. With introduction and notes by Chauncey Brewster Tinker. [With plates, including portraits.] pp. xxxviii. 252. *Andrew Melrose: London*, 1912. 8°. **010854**. i. **9**.

BURNEY (FRANCES) *Niece of Madame d'Arblay.* Tragic Dramas; chiefly intended for representation in private families: to which is added, Aristodemus, a tragedy, from the Italian of Vincenzo Monti. pp. xiv. 191. *Printed for the Author: London*, 1818. 8°. **841**. h. **4**.

BURNEY (GEORGE) *Chairman of the Epping Forest Preservation Society.* Epping Forest. June 19 and July 21st and 22nd, 1879. Proceedings before the Arbitrator, Sir A. Hobhouse. Address of Mr. Burney, *etc.* pp. 16. *Thomas & Bouttell: London*, 1879. 8°. **6146**. b. **37**. (**9**.)

—— Epping Forest to be Saved without a Corn Tax! pp. 8. [*London*, 1872.] 12°. **10350**. aa. **51**.

BURNEY (GEORGE) *Colonel.* Burney vs. Eyre. Report of the evidence and judgment in the above action for slander and defamation of characte[r], *etc.* pp. 71. vi. *J. A. Monnier: Calcutta*, 1863. 8°. **6605**. f. **3**.

BURNEY (HENRY) The Burney Papers. [Papers relating to Captain Burney's mission to Siam in 1825.] vol. 1—vol. 5. pt. 1. 1910–14. 8°. *See* BANGKOK.—*Vajirañāṇa Public Library.* **08023**. d. **6**.

BURNEY (JAMES) *See* MANWARING (George E.) My Friend the Admiral. The life, letters, and journals of Rear-Admiral James Burney, *etc.* [With portraits.] 1931. 8°. **010815**. i. **25**.

—— A Chronological History of North-Eastern Voyages of Discovery; and of the early Eastern navigations of the Russians. [With maps.] pp. viii. 310. *Payne & Foss: London*, 1819. 8°. **303**. f. **8**.

—— [Another copy.] G. **16022**.

—— A Chronological History of the Discoveries in the South Sea or Pacific Ocean . . . Illustrated with charts, 5 vol. *G. & W. Nicol: London*, 1803–17. 4°. **455**. b. **17–21**.

—— [Another copy.] G. **7231, 32**.

—— [Another copy of vol. 1–4.] **213**. c. **7–10**.

—— History of the Buccaneers of America . . . Reprinted from the edition of 1816. [Vol. 4 of "A Chronological History of the Discoveries in the South Sea."] pp. xv. 382. *Swan Sonnenschein & Co.: London*, 1891. 8°. **9551**. i. **14**.

—— [Another edition.] pp. xvi. 296. *London & New York*, 1902. 8°. [*United Library.* no. 7.] **012209**. ee. **3/7**.

—— [Another edition.] pp. xvi. 293. *London*, 1907. 8°. [*Hutchinson's Popular Classics.*] **012203**. ff. **1/16**.

BURNEY (JAMES)

—— History of the Buccaneers of America . . . Reprinted from the edition of 1816. With a new introduction by Malcolm Barnes. (Second impression.) pp. xvi. 382. *George Allen & Unwin: London*, 1949 [1950]. 8°. **9551**. h. **2**.

—— A Commentary on the Systems which have been advanced for explaining the Planetary Motions. pp. 60. *L. Hansard & Sons: London*, 1819. 8°. B. **500**. (**11**.)

—— An Essay, by way of Lecture, on the Game of Whist. pp. 87. *Printed for the Author: London*, 1821. 8°. **785**. c. **35**.

—— [Another edition.] A Treatise on the Game of Whist . . . Second edition. pp. 87. *T. & W. Boone: London*, 1823. 8°. **7917.de.9.(2.)**

—— [Another edition.] A Concise Treatise on the Game of Whist . . . Third edition, with additions and corrections . . . by Francis Paget Watson. *See* WATSON (Francis P.) Short Whist, *etc.* 1842. 12°. **785**. a. **30**.

—— Fourth edition, with additions and corrections by F. P. Watson. *See* WATSON (Francis P.) Short Whist, *etc.* 1848. 12°. **785**. a. **59**.

—— Memoir, explanatory of a Chart, of the Coast of China, and the Sea Eastward, from the river of Canton, to the Southern Islands of Japan. [With the chart.] pp. 23. *G. & W. Nicol: London*, 1811. 4°. B. **475**. (**8**.)

—— [Another copy.] **793**. l. **17**.

—— A Memoir on the Voyage of d'Entrecasteaux, in search of La Pérouse. pp. 21. *L. Hansard & Sons: London*, 1820. 8°. **10492**. d. **23**. (**1**.)

—— Observations on the Progress of Bodies floating in a Stream, *etc.* (New Method proposed for measuring a Ship's Rate of Sailing.) pp. 13. MS. NOTES. *L. Hansard & Sons: London*, 1808. 8°. B. **498**. (**13**.)

—— [Another edition.] Experiments made in the River Thames, with a view to discover a method for ascertaining the direction of currents: also, a new method proposed for measuring a ship's rate of sailing. pp. 15. *L. Hansard & Sons: London*, 1809. 4°. B. **470**. (**14**.)

—— [Another copy.] B. **470**. (**15**.)

—— [Another copy.] **533**. l. **16**. (**15**.)

—— Plan of Defence against Invasion: proposed by Captain J. Burney, *etc.* pp. 11. *G. G. & J. Robinson: London*, 1797. 4°. B. **468**. (**19**.)

—— [Another edition.] Plan of Preparation against Invasion . . . Second edition; in which a material objection to the plan, as before printed, is considered and provided against. pp. 12. *G. G. & J. Robinson: London*, 1797. 4°. B. **468**. (**20**.)

BURNEY (KARL) *See* BURNEY (Charles) *Mus. D.*

BURNEY (MOHAMMED ELIAS) *See* MUḤAMMAD ILYAS BARNĪ.

BURNEY (RICHARD)

—— An Answer or Necessary Animadversions, upon some late Impostumate Observations [by Henry Parker] invective against his Sacred Majesty, bearing the face of

BURNEY (RICHARD)

the publick, but boldly pen'd and publish't by a privado. [By R. Burney.] pp. 31. 1642. 4°. *See* CHARLES I., *King of Great Britain and Ireland.* [*Appendix.—Biography.*—II. 1642. *Miscellaneous.*] **100.** b. **41.**

—— [Another copy.] E. **108.** (**39.**)

—— Κερδιστον δωρον. King Charles the Second . . . presented to the Right Honourable Houses of Parliament in their next Session, as the Strength, Honour and Peace of the Nations, in the Iewells of his Crown, and Iustice of his People. Delivered in eight distinct sermons, *etc.* [With a portrait.] pp. 133. *Printed by I. Redmayne, for the Authour: London,* [1660.] 4°. E. **1054.** (**2.**)

BURNEY (SARAH HARRIET) Clarentine. A novel. [By S. H. Burney.] 3 vol. 1796. 12°. *See* CLARENTINE. **12613.** g. **5.**

—— Clarentine . . . Traduit . . . par Mme Élisabeth de Bon. 4 tom. *Paris,* 1819. 12°. **12808.** s. **11.**

—— Geraldine Fauconberg. By the author of Clarentine [i.e. S. H. Burney]. 3 vol. 1808. 12°. *See* FAUCONBERG (Geraldine) N. **2346–48.**

—— The Romance of Private Life. 3 vol. *Henry Colburn: London,* 1839. 12°. N. **2156.**

—— Tales of Fancy. (vol. 1. The Shipwreck. vol. 2, 3. Country Neighbours; or, the Secret.) 3 vol. *Henry Colburn: London,* 1816, 20. 12°. N. **1824–26.**

—— Second edition. 3 vol. *H. Colburn & Co.: London,* 1820. 12°. **1152.** f. **2.**

—— Les Voisins de campagne, ou le Secret . . . [A translation of "Country Neighbours," from "Tales of Fancy."] Traduit par Madame d'E . . . . [i.e. —— d' Espinard]. 4 tom. *Paris,* 1820. 12°. **12808.** s. **6.**

—— Traits of Nature. [A novel.] 5 vol. *Henry Colburn: London,* 1812. 12°. **012618.** df. **20.**

—— Le Jeune Cleveland, ou Traits de nature . . . Traduit . . . par le traducteur de Rob-Roy [i.e. A. J. B. Defauconpret], *etc.* 4 tom. *Paris,* 1819. 12°. **12808.** s. **12.**

BURNEY (STANFORD GUTHRIE) Studies in Psychology. pp. xvi. 535. *Cumberland Presbyterian Publishing House: Nashville,* 1890. 8°. **8462.** b. **19.**

BURNEY (SUSAN) *See* BURNEY (Susanna E.)

BURNEY (SUSANNA ELIZABETH) *See* BURNEY, afterwards D'ARBLAY (F.) The Early Diary of Frances Burney . . . With a selection . . . from the journals of her sisters Susan and Charlotte Burney, *etc.* 1889. 8°. **10859.** a. **1.**

—— —— 1907. 8°. **2504.** l. **9.**

BURNEY (WILLIAM) *See* FALCONER (William) *Poet.* A New Universal Dictionary of the Marine . . . modernized and much enlarged by W. Burney. 1815. 4°. **719.** k. **34.**

—— —— 1830. 4°. **8803.dd.17.**

—— The British Neptune; or, a History of the achievements of the Royal Navy, from the earliest periods to the present time. [With a map.] pp. vi. 490. *Richard Phillips: London,* 1807. 8°. **8807.** aa. **1.**

BURNEY (WILLIAM)

—— The Naval Heroes of Great Britain; or, Accounts of the lives and actions of the distinguished admirals and commanders who have contributed to confer on Great-Britain the empire of the ocean. [With portraits and maps.] pp. vi. ii. xii. 435. xvi. *Richard Phillips: London,* 1806. 12°. **615.** b. **21.**

BURNFORD (PAUL)

—— Filming for Amateurs, *etc.* [With plates.] pp. xi. 107. *Sir I. Pitman & Sons: London,* 1940. 4°. **8910.** f. **15.**

BURNHAM, *Bucks.* The Official Guide to Burnham & Cippenham. (The Official Guide to Burnham, Lent Rise and District.) *E. J. Burrow & Co.: Cheltenham,* [1928– .] 8°. **10360.** s. **3.**
Various editions.

—— *Church of St. Peter.* *See* PETER, *Saint and Apostle, Church of, at Burnham.*

Nashdom Abbey.

—— Laudate. The magazine (The quarterly magazine) of the Benedictine Community of Pershore Abbey, *etc.* (The quarterly magazine of the Benedictine Community at Nashdom Abbey, Burnham, Buckinghamshire.) vol. 1. no. 1—vol. 31. no. 93. 1 March 1923—July 1953. *Pershore,* 1923–53. 8°. P.P. **370.** ed.

BURNHAM, EDWARD FREDERICK, *Baron.* [1890– .] *See* LAWSON.

—— EDWARD LEVY, *Baron.* [1833–1916.] *See* LAWSON.

——, HARRY LAWSON WEBSTER LEVY, *Viscount.* [1862–1933.] *See* LAWSON.

BURNHAM COMMITTEE.

—— Burnham Committee on Scales of Salaries for Teachers in Primary and Secondary Schools (England and Wales). *See* ENGLAND.—*Board of Education,* afterwards *Ministry of Education.*

—— Burnham Committee on Scales of Salaries for Teachers in Public Elementary Schools. *See* ENGLAND.—*Board of Education.*

—— Burnham Committee on Scales of Salaries for Teachers in Secondary Schools. *See* ENGLAND.—*Board of Education.*

—— Burnham Committee on Scales of Salaries for Teachers in Technical and Art Schools. *See* ENGLAND.—*Board of Education.*

—— Burnham Committee on Scales of Salaries for Teachers in Technical Colleges and Institutes, Art Colleges and Schools (England and Wales). *See* ENGLAND.—*Board of Education,* afterwards *Ministry of Education.*

BURNHAM ON CROUCH.

—— Burnham-on-Crouch, Essex. The official guide, *etc.* [With illustrations.] pp. 31. *Century Press: London,* [1947.] 8°. **10359.** aa. **90.**

—— Burnham-on-Crouch, Essex. With district map and nine illustrations. The official guide of the Burnham-on-Crouch Urban District Council. pp. 35. *Century Press: London,* [1949.] 8°. **010368.** k. **89.**

BURNHAM ON CROUCH.

—— Burnham on Crouch Parish Registers. [Transcribed by K. V. Elphinstone.] 3 vol. [1930.] fol. **09917**. g. 9.
Typewritten.

—— *Royal Corinthian Yacht Club.* A Book of Designs of Deep Sea Racing Craft, *etc.* [With an introduction by Malden Heckstall-Smith.] pp. viii. 116.
E. J. Day & Co.: London, [1933.] *obl.* fol.
Cup.1246.b.4.

—— A Book of the Constitution, Rules, Sailing Regulations and House Rules of the Club, together with a list of the members and their yachts, *etc.* (Sailing programme, tide table, 1939.) 3 pt. *Chelmsford*, [1939.] 8°.
7922. bb. **24**.

BURNHAM, PARRY, WILLIAMS AND CO. Baldwin Locomotive Works. Illustrated Catalogue of Locomotives . . . Second edition. [With a historical sketch of the works.] pp. 153. *J. B. Lippincott & Co.: Philadelphia*, 1881. 4°. **8766**. g. 7.

BURNHAM POTTERY. Burnham Pottery; or, the Old well. [A tale.] pp. 34. *Wertheim, Macintosh, & Hunt: London*, [1862.] 24°. **4409**. a. **11**.

BURNHAM, *Family of.* *See* BURNHAM (Roderick H.) The Burnham Family, *etc.* 1869. 8°. **9903**. d. **26**.

BURNHAM (A. A.) Fostina Woodman, the Wonderful Adventurer. pp. 60. *Boston Stereotype Foundry: Boston*, 1853. 8°. **12706**. cc. 3.

BURNHAM (ABRAHAM) Character and Prospects of the Real Christian. A sermon, preached at Pembroke, New-Hampshire . . . after the interment of Mrs. Mary B. S. Kittredge, *etc.* pp. 23. *George Hough: Concord*, 1828. 8°.
4985. b. **34**. (**20**.)

—— A Good Minister of Jesus Christ. A discourse . . . commemorative of the character and ministry of the late Rev. Walter Harris, *etc.* pp. 28. *Asa McFarland: Concord*, 1844. 8°. **4985**. cc. **46**. (**12**.)

—— Ministers of Christ, Labourers with God. A sermon, delivered at the ordination of the Rev. Amos Wood Burnham, *etc.* pp. 24. *George Hough: Concord*, 1821. 8°.
4486. c. **30**. (**8**.)

—— A Sermon, preached at the Installation of the Rev. Luke A. Spofford, *etc.* pp. 21. *J. B. Moore: Concord*, 1826. 8°.
4486. c. **32**. (**5**.)

BURNHAM (ANNA F.) The King of Picture Books. *D. Lothrop & Co.: Boston*, [1878.] 4°. **12807**. i. **20**.

BURNHAM (ATHEL CAMPBELL) The Community Health Problem. pp. 149. *Macmillan Co.: New York*, 1920. 8°.
7404. p. **54**.

BURNHAM (BARBARA) *See* GOULD (Gerald) and BURNHAM (B.) Falling Angel. A play, *etc.* 1936. 8°.
11780. c. **38**.

—— *See* HILTON (James) *Novelist*, and BURNHAM (B.) Good-bye, Mr. Chips, *etc.* 1938. 8°. **11782**. bb. **50**.

—— *See* WINSLOE (C.) *Baroness Hatvany.* [Gestern und heute.] Children in Uniform . . . English adaptation by B. Burnham. 1932. 8°. **11745**. aaa. **29**.

—— —— 1933. 8°. [*Famous Plays of* 1932–33.]
011781. h. **122**.

—— —— [1933.] 8°. **11791**. tt. **1/231**.

BURNHAM (BARBARA)

—— Actors—Let's Talk Shop. pp. 83. *G. Allen & Unwin: London*, 1945. 8°. **11797**. e. **28**.

BURNHAM (BENJAMIN FRANKLIN) *See* PERIODICAL PUBLICATIONS.—*Boston, Massachusetts.* United States Digest, *etc.* (1868. By B. F. Burnham.—1869. By H. W. Frost and B. F. Burnham.) 1850, *etc.* 8°. **6615**. f, g.

BURNHAM (BENJAMIN FRANKLIN) and **BURNHAM** (CELESTE S.)

—— The Life of Lives, being the records of Jesus reviewed by a throng of recent Biblical scholars . . . Second edition. With a map of Palestine and portraits of many representative religious writers. pp. xi. 372. *Cleaves, Macdonald & Co.: Boston*, 1885. 8°. **4227**. bb. **16**.

BURNHAM (CELESTE S.) *See* BURNHAM (Benjamin F.) and BURNHAM (C. S.) The Life of Lives, *etc.* 1885. 8°.
4227. bb. **16**.

BURNHAM (CHARLES G.) Mental Arithmetic. By C. G. Burnham . . . Being an introduction to his new system of arithmetic, *etc.* pp. 100. *D. Appleton & Co.: New York*, 1851. 12°. **8505**. a. **42**.

—— A New System of Arithmetic, on the cancelling plan . . . Second edition. pp. 312. *B. M. Mussey: Boston*, 1841. 12°. **1393**. b. **10**.

BURNHAM (CLARA LOUISE) Clever Betsy. A novel . . . With illustrations by Rose O'Neill. pp. v. 410.
Houghton Mifflin Co.: Boston & New York, 1910. 8°.
012705. bb. **48**.

—— Flutterfly. pp. 64. *Houghton Mifflin Co.: Boston & New York*, 1910. 8°. **012804**. b. **29**.

—— The Golden Dog . . . Illustrated by Frank Aveline. pp. 79. *Gay & Hancock: London*, 1913. 16°.
012804. c. **8**.

—— Hearts' Haven. A novel, *etc.* pp. viii. 342.
Constable & Co.: London; Cambridge, Mass. [printed], 1919. 8°. **12719**. d. 4.

—— The Inner Flame. A novel. pp. v. 500.
Constable & Co.: London; Cambridge, Mass. [printed], 1912. 8°. **012704**. d. **28**.

—— Jewel. A chapter in her life. pp. 340.
A. Constable & Co.: Westminster; Cambridge, Mass. [printed], 1904. 8°. **012629**. a. 2.

—— [Another edition.] pp. 125. *London*, [1910.] 8°. [*Constable's Sixpenny Series.*] **012604.g.1/61.**

—— [Another edition.] pp. viii. 328. *Constable & Co.: London*, 1915. 8°. **12622**. aaaa. **19**.

—— [A reissue.] *London*, 1925. 8°. **12719**. d. 5.

—— Jewel's Story Book . . . With illustrations. pp. 343.
Gay & Bird: London; Cambridge, Mass. [printed], 1905. 8°. **012803**. d. **18**.

—— Kate's Wise Woman. A novel. pp. 430. *Gay & Bird: London; Cambridge, Mass.* [printed], 1896. 8°.
012627. l. 7.

—— The Lavarons. A novel. pp. 287.
Houghton Mifflin Co.: Boston & New York, 1925. 8°.
12709. cc. 5.

BURNHAM (CLARA LOUISE)

—— The Leaven of Love: a novel. pp. vi. 330. *A. Constable & Co.: London; Cambridge, Mass.* [printed], 1908. 8°. **012627. cc. 10.**

—— [Another edition.] pp. 124. *London*, [1911.] 8°. [*Constable's Sixpenny Series.*] **012604.g.1/60.**

—— Miss Bagg's Secretary. A West Point romance. pp. 424. *Houghton Mifflin & Co.: Boston & New York*, 1892. 8°. **012706. g. 15.**

—— Next Door. pp. 371. *Ticknor & Co.: Boston*, 1886. 8°. **12707. l. 6.**

—— [Another copy, with a different titlepage.] *David Douglas: Edinburgh; Boston* printed, 1886. 8°. **12706. k. 11.**

—— [Another copy, with a different titlepage.] *Trübner & Co.: London;* [*Boston* printed, 1886.] 8°. **12706. h. 7.**

—— No Gentlemen. [By C. L. Burnham.] pp. 348. 1881. 8°. *See* GENTLEMEN. **12704. dd. 8.**

—— The Opened Shutters. A novel, *etc.* pp. viii. 344. *Houghton Mifflin & Co.: Boston & New York*, 1906. 8°. **012706. bbb. 44.**

—— [Another edition.] pp. 150. *London*, [1909.] 8°. [*Constable's Sixpenny Series.*] **012604.g.1/3.**

—— The Quest Flower . . . With illustrations in color by Anna Milo Upjohn. pp. 132. *A. F. Bird: London; Cambridge, Mass.* [printed], [1908.] 4°. **4420. n. 37.**

—— The Right Princess. pp. 361. *A. P. Watt & Son: London; Cambridge, Mass.* [printed], 1902. 8°. **012707. l. 45.**

—— The Right Track, *etc.* pp. v. 421. *Constable & Co.: London; Cambridge, Mass.* [printed], 1914. 8°. **12719. d. 3.**

—— Tobey's First Case. A novel. pp. 236. *Houghton Mifflin Co.: Boston & New York*, 1926. 8°. **12711. aa. 16.**

BURNHAM (D. H.) **AND CO.** *See* GRAHAM, ANDERSON, PROBST AND WHITE. The Architectural Work of Graham, Anderson, Probst & White, Chicago, and their Predecessors, D. H. Burnham & Co., *etc.* 1933. fol. **L.R. 252. d. 3.**

BURNHAM (DANIEL HUDSON) *See* MOORE (Charles) *of the Library of Congress.* Daniel H. Burnham, architect, planner of cities, *etc.* [With portraits.] 1921. 8°. **10883. i. 9.**

BURNHAM (DANIEL HUDSON) and **MILLET** (FRANK DAVIS)

—— Worlds Columbian Exposition. The Book of the Builders, being the chronicle of the origin and plan of the World's Fair; of the architecture of the buildings and landscape, *etc.* pp. 1–48. *Columbian Memorial Publication Society: Chicago & Springfield, Ohio*, 1894. fol. [*Columbian Serial.* vol. 1. no. 1–6.] **1736. b. 8.**
No more published. Pp. 41–48 of this copy are proof-sheets; proof-sheets of pp. 33–40 and proofs of some of the plates have also been inserted.

BURNHAM (DAVID) This Our Exile. pp. 423. *C. Scribner's Sons: New York*, 1931. 8°. **A.N. 768.**

—— [Another edition.] pp. 422. *Peter Davies: London*, 1931. 8°. **A.N. 944.**

BURNHAM (DAVID)

—— Wedding Song. pp. 376. *Viking Press: New York*, 1934. 8°. **12709. ff. 24.**

—— [Another edition.] pp. 380. *Peter Davies: London*, 1934. 8°. **12709. m. 10.**

—— Winter in the Sun. pp. 300. *C. Scribner's Sons: New York*, 1937. 8°. **A.N. 3449.**

BURNHAM (ERNEST) Rural-Teacher Preparation in State Normal Schools. pp. 77. *Washington*, 1918. 8°. [*U.S. Bureau of Education. Bulletin.* 1918. no. 27.] **A.S. 202.**

BURNHAM (ERNEST J.) A Guide to Seaton & District, including Axmouth, Colyford, Colyton, Beer, and Branscombe . . . With 26 illustrations and two maps. pp. 80. *E. J. Burnham: Seaton*, 1912. 8°. **010352. de. 21.**

—— A Guide to Seaton & District, including Axmouth, Colyford, Colyton, Beer and Branscombe . . . Third edition. Revised and enlarged, *etc.* [With plates and maps.] pp. 99. *Ernest J. Burnham: Seaton*, [c. 1920.] 8°. **10362. a. 65.**

BURNHAM (FREDERICK)

—— Vier vriende. pp. 31. *Stellenbosch*, 1946. 8°. **04413. i. 109.**

BURNHAM (FREDERICK RUSSELL) Scouting on Two Continents . . . [An autobiography.] Elicited and arranged by Mary Nixon Everett. [With plates.] pp. xxii. 370. *William Heinemann: London; printed in U.S.A.*, 1926. 8°. **010815. h. 30.**

BURNHAM (G. CHAMPNEYS) and **CARTER** (CONRAD C.)

—— Little Miss Muffet. A basic pantomime in two acts. pp. xv. 74. *Samuel French: London*, [1950.] 8°. [*French's Acting Edition.* no. 589.] **11791. t. 1/986.**

BURNHAM (GEORGE)

—— Billy Graham: a mission accomplished. [With a portrait.] pp. 144. *Marshall, Morgan & Scott: London, Edinburgh*, 1955. 8°. **4192. g. 30.**

BURNHAM (GEORGE HERBERT) The Combined Treatment in Diseases of the Eye. pp. viii. 92. *H. K. Lewis: London*, 1906. 8°. **07610. de. 32.**

BURNHAM (GEORGE P.) *See* DURIVAGE (Francis A.) Stray Subjects, Arrested and Bound Over. Being the fugitive offspring of the " Old 'Un " (F. A. Durivage) and the " Young 'Un " (G. P. Burnham), *etc.* 1848. 12°. **12703. d. 20. (2.)**

—— The History of the Hen Fever. A humorous record . . . Illustrated. pp. 326. *J. French & Co.: Boston*, 1855. 8°. **7294. e. 13.**

—— Memoirs of the United States Secret Service . . . With accurate portraits of prominent members of the detective force . . . and a brief account of the life of Col. H. C. Whitley, *etc.* pp. 436. *Lee & Shepard: Boston*, 1872. 8°. **6057. aaa. 4.**

BURNHAM (GORDON WEBSTER) *See* WEBSTER (Daniel) Proceedings at the Inauguration of the Statue of Daniel Webster . . . erected . . . by G. W. Burnham, *etc.* 1876. 4°. **1854. h. 5.**

BURNHAM (HELEN) The Murder of Lalla Lee. pp. 288. *Arrowsmith: London*, 1931. 8°. **A.N. 945.**

BURNHAM (HELEN A.)

—— Boys will be Men. (Revised.) [By] H. A. Burnham . . . Evelyn G. Jones . . . Helen D. Redford, *etc.* pp. x. 477. *J. B. Lippincott Company: Chicago,* [1949.] 8°. **08408.** h. **91.**

BURNHAM (I. G.) *See* DUMAS (A.) *the Elder.* [*Crimes célèbres.*] Celebrated Crimes. Translated by I. G. Burnham, *etc.* 1895, *etc.* 8°. K.T.C. **32.** a. **2.**

BURNHAM (J. H.) *Captain.* Bloomington Township.—Normal Township.—White Oak Township. *See* MACLEAN, *County of, Illinois.* The History of McLean County, *etc.* 1879. 8°. **10409.** i. **11.**

BURNHAM (J. HAMPDEN) Canadians in the Imperial, Naval and Military Service abroad. pp. 240. *Williamson & Co.: Toronto,* 1891. 8°. **10883.** b. **24.**

—— Jack Ralston, or the Outbreak of the Nauscopees. A tale of life in the far North-East of Canada. pp. 448. *T. Nelson & Sons: London,* 1901. 8°. **012809.** ee. **8.**

—— [A reissue.] *London,* [1914.] 8°. **012807.** b. **18.**

—— Marcelle. An historical novel. pp. 409. *William Briggs: Toronto,* 1905. 8°. **012624.** ee. **51.**

—— [Another copy.] **012622.** h. **34.**

BURNHAM (JAMES) *of Reading.*

—— Free Trade and Socialism versus Preference and Tariff Reform. pp. 24. *Jas. Burnham: Reading,* [1909.] 8°. **08226.** aaa. **60.** (6.)

—— [Another edition.] Tariff Reform versus Free Trade and Socialism fully explained . . . New and enlarged edition, *etc.* pp. 32. *Tariff Reform Crusade: Reading,* [1910.] 8°. **8138.** eee. **7.** (5.)

BURNHAM (JAMES) *of the University of New York.*

—— *See* PELLOUX (R.) Un Nouveau Machiavel: James Burnham et ses idées sur la domination du monde. 1949. 8°. [*Cahiers de la Fondation Nationale des Sciences Politiques.* no. 8.] W.P. **14427/8.**

—— The Coming Defeat of Communism. pp. 286. *Jonathan Cape: London,* 1950. 8°. **08004.** df. **13.**

—— Containment or Liberation? An inquiry into the aims of United States foreign policy. pp. 256. *John Day Co.: New York,* [1953.] 8°. **8178.** b. **7.**

—— The Machiavellians: defenders of freedom. pp. v. 202. *Putnam & Co.: London,* 1943. 8°. **8011.** e. **1.**

—— The Managerial Revolution. What is happening in the world. (Sixth impression.) pp. 285. *J. Day Co.: New York,* [1941.] 8°. **8011.** b. **19.**

—— The Managerial Revolution; or, What is happening in the world now. pp. 271. *Putnam: London,* 1942. 8°. **8287.** ee. **62.**

—— The Managerial Revolution, *etc.* [With a portrait.] pp. 238. *Penguin Books: Harmondsworth,* 1945. 8°. [*Pelican Books.* no. 140.] **012209.** d. **4/140.**

—— *See* ORWELL (George) pseud. [i.e. Eric Blair.] James Burnham and the Managerial Revolution. 1946. 8°. **8288.** f. **66.**

—— The People's Front: the new betrayal. pp. 64. *Pioneer Publishers: New York,* [1937.] 8°. **8010.** bb. **54.**

BURNHAM (JAMES) *of the University of New York.*

—— The Struggle for the World. pp. 253. *Jonathan Cape: London,* 1947. 8°. **8011.** ee. **32.**

—— The Web of Subversion. Underground networks in the U.S. government. pp. 248. *John Day Co.: New York,* [1954.] 8°. **9615.** tt. **21.**

BURNHAM (JOAN) The Everlasting Miracle. A nativity play in six scenes. pp. 24. *St. Christopher Press; S.P.C.K.: London,* [1935.] 8°. [*Saint Nicolas Plays.* no. 15.] W.P. **9693/15.**

—— For Our Salvation. A Passion play. pp. 31. *St. Christopher Press; S.P.C.K.: London,* [1936.] 8°. [*Saint Nicolas Plays.* no. 19.] W.P. **9693/19.**

BURNHAM (JOHN) *Major.* Personal Recollections of the Revolutionary War. (Recollections of the Revolutionary War from Bunker Hill to Yorktown. Narrative of Major John Burnham, *etc.*) pp. 19. *Tarrytown, N.Y.,* 1917. 4°. [*Magazine of History.* Extra number. no. 54.] P.P. **3437.** bab.

BURNHAM (JOHN) *of Brentford.* *See* MACRITCHIE, afterwards HAYCRAFT (Margaret S.) Those Merry Bells, and other stories. Edited by J. Burnham. 1904. 8°. **04429.** h. **35.**

—— Chips from my Log, *etc.* pp. 262. *Baptist Tract & Book Society: London,* [1896.] 8°. **4906.** df. **35.**

—— "Fernbank" Letter Leaflets. [In verse.] 10 pt. *The Author: Brentford,* [1892, 93.] 8°. **11648.** i. **51.**

—— The Triumph of Truth, and other stories. By Margaret S. Haycraft and others. Edited by J. Burnham. pp. 192. *R.T.S.: London,* 1904. 8°. **04429.** h. **48.**

BURNHAM (JOHN) *of Dartmouth University.* A Funeral Oration, pronounced on the death of Eliphalet Hardy, *etc.* pp. 12. *Moses Davis: Hanover* [*N.H.*], 1806. 8°. **4985.** cc. **3.**

BURNHAM (JOHN) *Writer on Economics.*

—— Total War. The economic theory of a war economy. pp. 339. *Meador Publishing Co.: Boston,* [1943.] 8°. **8204.** e. **9.**

BURNHAM (JOHN BIRD) The Rim of Mystery. A hunter's wanderings in unknown Siberian Asia . . . With 60 illustrations and a map, *etc.* pp. xv. 281. *G. P. Putnam's Sons: New York, London,* 1929. 8°. **010055.** d. **5.**

BURNHAM (JOSEPHINE MAY) Concessive Constructions in Old English Prose . . . A thesis, *etc.* pp. vi. 135. *H. Holt & Co.: New York,* 1911. 8°. [*Yale Studies in English.* no. 39.] Ac. **2692.** ma/3.

BURNHAM (LOUIS W.) Book-keeping; its rules and reasons. pp. 16. [*New York?* 1860?] 8°. **8505.** ee. **35.** (3.)

BURNHAM (M. HOWARD) Modern Mine Valuation . . . With 19 illustrations. pp. x. 160. *C. Griffin & Co.: London,* 1912. 8°. **07108.** h. **59.**

BURNHAM (MARGARET)

—— The Player's Library. The catalogue of the library of the British Drama League, *etc.* (Compiled by M. Burnham.) pp. xvi. 1115. 1950. 8°.

—— First [*etc.*] Supplement to the Players' Library. 1951– . 8°.

See LONDON.—III. *British Drama League.* B.B.G. a. **1.**

—— [Another copy.] **11925.** e. **22.**

BURNHAM (Mary)

—— *See* Periodical Publications.—New York.—*American Catalogue of Books.* The United States Catalog . . . 1928. [With supplements.] Edited by M. Burnham, *etc.* 1928, *etc.* fol. **Circ.92.a.-93.a.**

BURNHAM (Paul Sylvester)

—— *See* Crawford (Albert B.) and Burnham (P. S.) Forecasting College Achievement, *etc.* 1946, *etc.* 8º **Ac.2692.mhc.(12.)**

BURNHAM (R. E.)

—— Who are the Finns? A study in prehistory. [With maps.] pp. 90. *Faber & Faber: London,* 1946. 8º. **10009.** pp. **32.**

BURNHAM (Ralph) There are a Few. (Story for a film play.) ff. 8. *London,* [1935.] 4º. **11795.** t. **53.** *Typewritten.*

BURNHAM (Reuben Wesley)

—— *See* Ahlenstiel (H.) [Rotgrünblindheit als Erlebnis.] Red-Green Blindness as Personal Experience . . . Translated by R. W. Burnham. [1951.] 8º. **07612.** e. **13.**

—— Mathematics for Machinists. pp. viii. 229. *New York,* 1915. 8º. [*Wiley Technical Series.*] **8711.** a. **1/14.**

—— Mathematics for Machinists . . . Second edition. pp. xii. 253. *J. Wiley & Sons: New York,* [1943.] 8º. **08534.** df. **76.**

BURNHAM (Richard) *Baptist Minister, of Grafton Chapel, Soho.* *See* Foxwell (William) A Check for Lordly Pastors . . . To which is added, a fac-simile of the epitaph on Mr. Burnham's tomb stone. [1811?] 12º. **4372.** de. **19.** (**3.**)

—— The Covenant of the Baptist Church, meeting together in Union Chapel, Little Chapel-street, Soho. [By R. Burnham?] pp. 7. 1786. 32º. *See* London.—iii. *Union Chapel, Soho.* **3440.** a. **43.** (**3.**)

—— An Elegy on the Death of Lord Nelson. *W. Smith & Son: London,* 1806. *s. sh.* fol. **695.** l. **14.** (**66.**)

—— Hymns particularly designed for the use of the congregation, meeting together in Grafton Street, Soho. pp. vix [xiv]. 406. *J. Whiting: London,* 1803. 12º. **3436.** e. **14.**

—— New Hymns on Divine Love. Chiefly designed for love-feasts, *etc.* pp. 36. *W. Smith: London,* [1785?] 18º. **3440.** a. **43.** (**2.**)

—— New Hymns on Various Subjects. pp. viii. 208. *Printed for the Author: London,* 1785. 18º. **3437.** b. **28.**

—— [Another copy.] New Hymns on Various Subjects, *etc.* *London,* 1785. 18º. **3440.** a. **43.** (**1.**)

—— The Triumphs of Free-Grace; with letters upon important subjects. pp. iv. 128. *W. Smith: London,* 1787. 12º. **4377.** a. **12.**

BURNHAM (Richard) *Biographer.* Pious Memorials; or, the Power of religion upon the mind in sickness and at death: exemplified in the experience of many divines and other eminent persons . . . With a preface by the Rev. Mr. Hervey. pp. xiii. 436. *J. Oliver: London,* 1753. 8º. **4825.** aaa. **9.**

—— The second edition. pp. xiii. 376. *J. Buckland: London,* 1754. 8º. **1371.** g. **8.**

BURNHAM (Richard) *Biographer.*

—— A new edition, to which is now added a large appendix, containing many valuable lives of ministers of the Gospel, *etc.* pp. 556. *George Caldwell: Paisley,* 1788. 8º. **4805.** d. **9.**

—— Third edition, revised . . . by the Rev. George Burder. pp. xii. 511. *Francis Westley: London,* 1820. 8º. **4902.** g. **10.**

BURNHAM (Roderick Henry) The Burnham Family; or, Genealogical records of the descendants of the four emigrants of the name, who were among the early settlers in America. pp. 546. *Case, Lockwood & Brainard: Hartford,* 1869. 8º. **9903.** d. **26.**

BURNHAM (Roy)

—— B-P's Life in Pictures. The story of Lord Baden-Powell of Gilwell. Text by R. Burnham. Drawings by Kenneth Brookes. Edited by F. Haydn Dimmock. *Boy Scouts Association: London,* [1952.] 4º. **10860.** d. **10.**

BURNHAM (Samuel) *the Elder.* *See* Harris (Walter) *D.D., etc.* A Sermon preached . . . after the interment of Deacon S. Burnham. 1811. 8º. **4486.** aaa. **92.** (**2.**)

BURNHAM (Samuel) *the Younger.* *See* Boston, *Massachusetts.—Congregational Library Association, etc.* The Congregational Quarterly, *etc.* (New series . . . Editors . . . A. H. Quint . . . S. Burnham.) 1859, *etc.* 8º. P.P. **863.** d.

BURNHAM (Sarah Maria) The Roman's Story in the Time of Claudius i . . . Illustrated. pp. 311. *A. I. Bradley & Co.: Boston,* 1898. 8º. **4808.** g. **21.**

—— Struggles of the Nations: or, the Principal wars, battles, sieges and treaties of the world. 2 vol. *Lee & Shepard: Boston,* 1891. 8º. **9008.** bbb. **1.**

BURNHAM (Sherburne Wesley) *See* Louisiana. —*Convention for the Revision and Amendment of the Constitution of the State of Louisiana.* Debates in the Convention for the Revision and Amendment of the Constitution of the State of Louisiana . . . By . . . H. A. Gallup, S. W. Burnham, *etc.* 1864. 8º. **8175.** bb. **8.**

—— Double Star Observations made with the thirty-six-inch and twelve-inch refractors of the Lick Observatory, from August, 1888, to June, 1892. pp. 255. *Sacramento,* 1894. 4º. [*Publications of the Lick Observatory of the University of California.* vol. 2.] **8567.** i.

—— A General Catalogue of Double Stars within 121º of the North Pole. 2 pt. *Washington,* 1906. 4º. [*Carnegie Institution of Washington. Publication.* no. 5.] Ac. **1866.**

—— A General Catalogue of 1290 Double Stars discovered from 1871 to 1899 by S. W. Burnham. Arranged in order of right ascension with all micrometrical measures of each pair. pp. xxx. 296. *Chicago,* 1900. 4º. [*Publications of the Yerkes Observatory of the University of Chicago.* vol. 1.] Ac. **4186.** e.

—— Measures of Proper Motion Stars made with the 40-inch refractor of the Yerkes Observatory in the years 1907 to 1912. pp. iv. 311. *Washington,* 1913. 4º. [*Carnegie Institution. Publication.* no. 168.] Ac. **1866.**

—— Report to the Trustees of the "James Lick Trust" of Observations made on Mt. Hamilton with reference to the location of Lick Observatory. pp. 32. *Knight & Leonard: Chicago,* 1880. 4º. **8567.** e. **1.**

BURNHAM (SMITH) Our Beginnings in Europe and America. How civilization grew in the Old World and came to the New . . . With illustrations and maps. pp. xvi. 375. *J. C. Winston Co.: Philadelphia, Chicago,* [1918.] 8°. **9005**. bbb. **22**.

BURNHAM (SMITH) and **JACK** (THEODORE HENLEY)

—— America Our Country, *etc.* pp. xv. 628. *J. C. Winston Co.: Philadelphia,* [1934.] 8°. **9615**. e. **16**.

—— The Story of America for Young Americans. 2 vol. *J. C. Winston Co.: Philadelphia,* [1932, 33.] 8°. **9615**. cc. **21**.

BURNHAM (THOMAS) Cheap Books on Sale . . . Burnham's catalogue of a scarce and valuable collection of books, *etc.* 2 pt. *P. Mackenzie: Northampton,* 1808, 09. 8°. S.C. **747**. (**1**.) & S.C. **749**. (**4**.)

BURNHAM (THOMAS HALL) Engineering Economics. pp. xiii. 326. *Sir I. Pitman & Sons: London,* 1929. 8°. **08225**. ccc. **61**.

—— Second edition. pp. xv. 376. *Sir I. Pitman & Sons: London,* 1930. 8°. **08244**. f. **27**.

—— Engineering Economics . . . Third edition. 2 vol. *Sir I. Pitman & Sons: London,* 1935. 8°. [*Pitman's Engineering Degree Series.*] W.P. **14752/20**.

—— Engineering Economics . . . Fourth edition. 2 bk. *Sir I. Pitman & Sons: London,* 1938. 8°. [*Pitman's Engineering Degree Series.*] W.P. **14752/33**.
Later editions are entered under BURNHAM *(T. H.) and* HOSKINS *(G. O.)*

—— Modern Foremanship, *etc.* pp. xi. 175. *Sir I. Pitman & Sons: London,* 1937. 8°. **8234**. b. **43**.

—— Special Steels . . . Chiefly founded on the researches . . . of Sir Robert Hadfield . . . and with a foreword by him. pp. xxi. 193. *London,* 1923. 8°. [*Pitman's Technical Primers.*] **07943**. aaaa. **1/64**.

—— Second edition. pp. xviii. 233. *Sir I. Pitman & Sons: London,* 1933. 8°. [*Specialists' Series.*] **08709.h.1/64.**

—— Works Management Education. With special reference to the case system, *etc.* pp. xi. 91. *Sir I. Pitman & Sons: London,* 1933. 8°. **08206**. h. **42**.

BURNHAM (THOMAS HALL) and **HOSKINS** (GEORGE OWEN)

—— Engineering Economics . . . Fifth edition [of the work originally written by T. H. Burnham]. [bk. 2 by T. H. Burnham alone.] 2 pt. *Sir I. Pitman & Sons: London,* 1940. 8°. [*Pitman's Engineering Degree Series.*] W.P. **14752/42**.

—— Engineering Economics . . . Sixth edition. (bk. 2 by T. H. Burnham and D. H. Bramley.) 2 bk. *Sir Isaac Pitman & Sons: London,* 1958, 50. 8°. [*Engineering Degree Series.*] W.P. **14752/76**.
The seventh edition is entered under BURNHAM *(T. H.) alone.*

—— Iron and Steel in Britain, 1870–1930, *etc.* pp. 352. *G. Allen & Unwin: London,* 1943. 8°. **8231**. f. **64**.

BURNHAM (WALTER DEAN)

—— Presidential Ballots, 1836–1892. pp. xix. 956. *Johns Hopkins Press: Baltimore,* [1955.] 8°. **9617**. g. **1**.

BURNHAM (WILLIAM HENRY) Bibliographies on Experimental Pedagogy. Edited by W. H. Burnham. pp. iv. 49. *Worcester, Mass.,* 1912. 8°. [*Publications of the Clark University Library.* vol. 3. no. 3.] Ac. **9727**.

—— Essentials of Mental Health. pp. 15. *National Education Association: Washington,* [1947.] 32°. [*Personal Growth Leaflet.* no. 109.] W.P. **15575/71**.

—— Great Teachers and Mental Health. A study of seven educational hygienists. pp. xiii. 351. *D. Appleton & Co.: New York, London,* [1926.] 8°. **08311**. aaa. **41**.

—— The Normal Mind. An introduction to mental hygiene and the hygiene of school instruction. pp. xviii. 702. *D. Appleton & Co.: New York, London,* 1924. 8°. **08465**. ee. **27**.

—— The Wholesome Personality. A contribution to mental hygiene. pp. xv. 713. *D. Appleton & Co.: New York & London,* 1932. 8°. **08458**. aaa. **25**.

BURNHAM (WILLIAM POWER) Three Roads to a Commission in the United States Army. pp. x. 160. *D. Appleton & Co.: New York,* 1893. 8°. **8823**. b. **18**.

BURNHILL (J. H.)

—— The Imitation of Woods and Marbles. [With illustrations.] pp. 124. *Sutherland Publishing Co.: Manchester,* 1948. 8°. **7948**. bb. **22**.

BURNIAT (JOHN) *See* BURNYEAT (J.) *Quaker.*

BURNIAT (POL)

—— Recherches sur les surfaces de bigenre un. 1936. *See* LIÈGE, *City of.—Société Royale des Sciences de Liège.* Mémoires, *etc.* sér. 4. tom. 1. 1843, *etc.* 8°. Ac. **2961**.

BURNIAUS, *de Tors. See* BRUNEAU, *de Tours.*

BURNICHON ( ) Insecticide Burnichon. Notice sur la fleur de pyrèthre, *etc.* pp. 64. *Paris,* [1863.] 16°. **7943**. a. **49**.

BURNICHON (JOSEPH) Le Brésil d'aujourd'hui. (Ouvrage orné de huit gravures. Troisième édition.) pp. ix. 340. *Paris,* 1910. 8°. **010480**. de. **62**.

—— La Compagnie de Jésus en France. Histoire d'un siècle, 1814–1914. 4 tom. *Paris,* 1914–22. 8°. **4092.t.1.**

—— Vie du Père François Xavier Gautrelet . . . 1807–1886. pp. x. 346. *Paris,* 1889. 18°. **4867**. de. **35**.

BURNIE (JESSIE M.) Poetry of the Pansy, Viola, and Violet. *See* PANSIES. Pansies, Violas, and Violets, *etc.* 1898. 8°. **07031**. de. **68**.

BURNIE (MARY D.) and **HINDLE** (FANNY)

—— Teacher Training in the Sunday School. pp. 128. *National Sunday School Union: London,* 1939. 8°. **4256**. ff. **49**.

BURNIE (O.) *pseud.* [i.e. OLGA NOBLE-MATHEWS.] *See* also MATHEWS (O. N.)

—— Guide to the County of Worcestershire. [With illustrations and a map.] pp. 96. *County Associations: London,* [1953.] 8°. **10361**. c. **10**.
The cover bears the title "Come to Worcestershire County Guide."

BURNIE (ROBERT DONALD) Idle-Hour Flights. [Verses.] pp. xvi. 108. *Gay & Bird: London*, 1903. 8°. **011651. k. 69.**

BURNIE (ROBERT WILLIAM) The Catholic Brief against Sir William Harcourt and others. An argument to demonstrate that ancient ceremonial and Reservation of the Sacrament are lawful by statute in the Church of England. pp. xii. 162. *Gay & Bird: London*, 1899. 8°. **4109. f. 24.**

—— The Criminal Law Amendment Act, 1885. With introduction, commentary and forms of indictments. pp. 92. *Waterlow & Sons: London*, 1885. 8°. **6485. aaa. 6.**

—— A Critical Examination of the Opinion of the English Archbishops concerning incense and processional lights. pp. 62. *"Church Review": London*, 1899. 8°. **4108. i. 6. (2.)**

—— Intercommunion with the Eastern Orthodox Church: the schism between East and West and the possible healing. pp. 57. 1915. 8°. *See* ANGLICAN AND EASTERN CHURCHES ASSOCIATION. **3926. aaa. 57.**

—— Memoir and Letters of Sidney Gilchrist Thomas, *etc.* pp. ii. 314. *John Murray: London*, 1891. 8°. **10826. b. 25.**

—— The Russian Church . . . Its constitution. *See* RUSSIA. *Orthodox Church.* [*Appendix.*] The Russian Church, *etc.* 1915. 8°. **4695. de. 8.**

BURNIE (WILLIAM) *Minister of Oxnam.* Church Establishments Considered. With special reference to the principle of political equality. pp. 19. *W. Blackwood & Sons: Edinburgh*, 1871. 8°. **4175. c. 1. (7.)**

—— Disestablishment from a Churchman's Point of View. *See* LECTURES. Lectures on the Principle and Advantages of a National Church, *etc.* 1879. 8°. **4175. f. 1.**

BURNIE (WILLIAM) *of Twynholm.* Poems. "The Cruelty of Fate," and other miscellaneous poems reflecting on various phases of human life. pp. 152. *J. H. Maxwell: Castle-Douglas*, 1912. 8°. **011649. e. 5.**

BURNIE (WILLIAM BECKIT) The 'What to Be' Books. Penny guides to trades and handicrafts for youths and girls leaving school. Edited by W. B. Burnie. 12 pt. *G. Philip & Son: London; Philip, Son & Nephew: Liverpool*, [1912.] 16°. **08228. de. 25.**

BURNIE (WILLIAM BECKIT) and **JENNINGS** (ARTHUR OLDHAM)

—— Paper read at the Summer Meeting . . . 1914, on Legal Compulsion in connection with Continuation Classes. pp. 14. *Bolton*, [1914.] 8°. [*Association of Technical Institutions. Miscellaneous pamphlets.*] **W.P.4362/1.(4.)**

BURNIER (ALPHONSE) De l'esprit public. De son influence possible sur l'état de la fabrique lyonnaise. Conférence, *etc.* pp. 16. *Lyon*, 1869. 8°. **8246. ee. 46. (10.)**

BURNIER (ANDRÉ) Considérations sur les rapports et les combinaisons de l'état saburral avec le spasme. Tribut académique, *etc.* pp. 16. *Montpellier*, 1817. 4°. **1180. h. 10. (25.)**

BURNIER (CHARLES) La Vie vaudoise et la Révolution. De la servitude à la liberté. pp. 384. *Lausanne*, 1902. 8°. **9305. de. 4.**

BURNIER (ÉDOUARD)

—— La Théologie systématique protestante en Suisse romande, 1920–1940. Notes historiques et critiques. [With a bibliography.] pp. 100. *Lausanne*, 1940. 8°. **4381. f. 23.**

BURNIER (EUGÈNE) Histoire de l'abbaye de Tamié en Savoie. pp. xxxi. 312. *Chambéry*, 1865. 8°. **10169. f. 7.**

—— Histoire du sénat de Savoie et des autres compagnies judiciaires de la même province. 2 tom. *Paris*, 1864, 65. 8°. **5405. ccc. 7.**

BURNIER (LOUIS)

—— Esquisses évangéliques. pp. 494. *Lausanne*, 1858. 8°. **4382. a. 1.**

—— Instructions et exhortations pastorales . . . Seconde édition. pp. 552. *Paris*, 1844. 8°. **4375. cc. 13.**

—— Prédication de l'Évangile à Bérée. *See* VAUD. Recueil de sermons, *etc.* 1831. 8°. **4426. cc. 1. (6.)**

BURNIER (MICHEL HENRI) Habitual Constipation and its Treatment. An account of a new therapeutic method . . . Translation by Herbert Child. pp. ix. 71. *Baillière & Co.: London*, 1929. 8°. [*Minor Monograph Series.*] **07305.aaa.1/3.**

BURNIER (RAYMOND)

—— Hindu Medieval Sculpture. 79 original photographs. *La Palme: Paris*, 1950. fol. **L.R. 299. cc. 13.**

BURNIER FONTANEL (PIERRE MARIE) Quelques réflexions médico-philosophiques, suivies de considérations sur les hémorrhagies utérines avant, pendant, et après l'accouchement; thèse, *etc.* pp. 21. *Paris*, 1827. 4°. **1183. i. 12. (3.)**

BURNING BUSH. The Burning Bush. *See* PERIODICAL PUBLICATIONS.—*Eton.*

BURNING GLASS MISCELLANY.

—— The Burning Glass Miscellany no. 1 [*etc.*]. *Ridgeway House: Shorne*, [1947– .] 8°. **W.P. 1582.**

BURNING GLASS PAPERS.

—— Burning Glass Papers. no. 1 (2, 7, 8, 10). (Burning Glass Paper no. 12, 14, 16–21, 24–30.) *M. Chaning-Pearce: Shorne*, [1946– .] 8° **4384.aa.5.**

BURNING SAND.

—— The Book of Revelation. By "Burning Sand," through his medium Louie Hill. [With portraits.] pp. 196. *Louie Hill: Hendon*, 1953. 8°. **8635. a. 15.**

—— Man's Desires and Fulfilments. By "Burning Sand," through his medium, Mrs. Louie Hill, *etc.* [Written down by Charles W. Raffety. With portraits.] pp. 186. *E. D. Paine: Worthing*, 1948. 8°. **8634. df. 39.**

—— Man's Self and Man's Inheritance. By "Burning Sand," through his medium Mrs. Louie Hill. [Written down by Charles W. Raffety. With a portrait.] pp. 150. *Louie Hill: Hendon*, 1947. 8°. **8634. df. 20.**

BURNING (MICHAEL) and **GREY** (ALTHEA)

—— Dusty Death. [A novel.] pp. 254. *Herbert Jenkins: London*, [1949.] 8°. **NN. 39612.**

BURNIP (JULIET E.) Twenty Poems. pp. 24. [*The Author: Nottingham*, 1938.] 8°. **11655. ff. 68.**

BURNISH FAMILY. The Burnish Family. [A tale. By Clara Lucas Balfour.] pp. viii. 184. *Scottish Temperance League: Glasgow*, 1857. 8°. **8435. a. 12.**

BURNISTON (ASA) A Common-Sense Algebra. An elementary course, *etc.* pp. vi. 141. *William Heinemann: London*, 1914. 8°. **8503. gg. 31.**

—— Real Arithmetic. (Junior series.) [With teacher's books.] 10 pt. *Collins: Glasgow*, 1936. 4°. **08532. h. 3.**

—— Real Arithmetic. Senior series. [With teacher's books and mathematical tables.] 13 bk. *Collins: London & Glasgow*, 1937–40. 8°. **08535. c. 38.**

—— The Workmanship of English. A course in English composition and grammar, *etc.* 3 pt. *E. J. Arnold & Son: Leeds*, [1929.] 8°. **12980. ppp. 12.**

BURNISTON (CARINGTON) Poems. pp. 19. *The Author: [Ilkley ?]* 1930. 8°. **11644. k. 31.**

BURNISTON (CHRISTABEL)

—— *See* ELLIS (Oliver C. de C.) Christmas in Spring . . . Selected by C. Burniston. 1949. 8°. **11606. aa. 30.**

—— The Rendering of English Verse. *In:* Poetic Technique, *etc.* pp. 121–184. 1949. 8°. **11869. aaa. 30.**

—— Speech Exercises, *etc.* pp. 32. *Poetry Lovers' Fellowship: Manchester*, [1951] 8°. **11806.bb.19.**

—— Speech Exercises . . . Second edition. pp. 32. *Poetry Lovers' Fellowship: Manchester*, [1951] 8°. **11806.bb.20.**

BURNISTON (CHRISTABEL) and **ELLIS** (OLIVER COLIGNY DE CHAMPFLEUR)

—— Choral Speech for Schools, Colleges and Festivals . . . Collated and edited by C. Burniston and O. C. de C. Ellis, *etc.* pp. 120. *Poetry Lovers' Fellowship: London, Manchester*, 1952. 8°. **11798. bbb. 4.**

BURNITZ (CARL PETER) *See* LEVIS (L.) Peter Burnitz 1824–1886. Ein Beitrag zur Geschichte der Malerei des neunzehnten Jahrhunderts in Frankfurt am Main, *etc.* 1937. 8°. **10710. b. 33.**

BURNITZ (GUSTAV) and **VARRENTRAPP** (GEORG) Methode, bei jeder Art von Wahlen sowohl der Mehrheit als den Minderheiten die ihrer Stärke entsprechende Zahl von Vertretern zu sichern. pp. 16. *Frankfurt*, 1863. 8°. **8073. e. 65. (5.)**

BURNITZ (PETER) *See* BURNITZ (Carl P.)

BURNLEY. Burnley, Lancs. . . . The official guide. Second [*etc.*] edition, *etc.* *E. J. Burrow & Co.: Cheltenham*, [1931– .] 8°. **10360. s. 4.**

—— County Borough of Burnley. Ceremony of the Honouring of the East Lancashire Regiment, 6th June 1953. *Dixon & Sons: Burnley*, 1953. 8°. **9930. p. 11.**

—— County Borough of Burnley. A Historical and Detailed Description of the Sewage Disposal Works. By F. S. Button. [With plans.] pp. 38. *John Dixon: Burnley*, 1893. 4°. **8777. cc. 32.**

BURNLEY.

—— County Borough of Burnley. Municipal Diary, 1926-27 (-1932-33, 1945-46). [*Burnley*, 1926–45.] 32°. **P.P. 2507. uga.**

—— County Borough of Burnley. Municipal year book and diary, 1941-42(-1944-45, 1946-47 [*etc.*]). [*Burnley*, 1941– .] 32°. **P.P. 2507. ugb.**

—— **County Borough of Burnley. The Year Book for the use of members of the Council from 9th November, 1895 to 9th November, 1896(-1940-41, 1945-46, [1951]).** *Burnley*, [1895]–1950. 16°. **P.P. 2507. ug.**
Wanting the issue for **1916/17.**

—— The Registers of the Parish Church of Burnley . . . 1562 to 1653. Transcribed and edited by William Farrer. pp. vii. 371. 1899. 8°. *See* LANCASTER, *County of.—Lancashire Parish Register Society.* Ac. **8088/2.**

Burnley and District Cotton Industry Study Group.
—— Report on Marketing. pp. 51. *Sherratt & Hughes: Manchester*, 1937. 8°. **8234. a. 48.**

Burnley and District Incorporated Chamber of Commerce.
—— Monthly Journal of the Preston, Blackburn, Bolton, & Burnley Chambers of Commerce. *See* PRESTON.—*Preston and District Incorporated Chamber of Commerce.*

—— *Burnley Equitable Co-operative Society.* Burnley Co-operative Record. (Burnley Equitable Co-operative Society, Limited, Monthly Record.) *Burnley*, 1911– . 8°. **P.P. 1423. lkd.**

—— *Burnley Free Church Ministers' Fraternal.* Free Church Burial Service. pp. 14. *Burnley*, [1933.] 12°. **3476. a. 32.**

—— *Burnley Grammar School.* Guide to the Eclipse of June 29th, 1927. [With a map.] pp. 16. *Burnley*, [1927.] 8°. **8562. eee. 48.**

—— A History of Burnley and the Grammar School during the Sixteenth Century. [By] W. Bennett. [With plates and a chart.] pp. 32. *Burnley*, 1930. 8°. **08364. f. 71.**

—— *Burnley Literary and Scientific Club.* Transactions. vol. 1–4. *Burnley*, 1884–87. 8°. Ac. **1336.**

—— *Burnley Mechanics' Institution.* Forty-ninth (fifty-eighth) Annual Report . . . 1883 (1892). *Burnley*, 1883, 92. 8°. **8365. bb. 34.**

—— Burnley Mechanics' Institution. Science, Art and Technical School. Opening of the new technical school, *etc.* (Programme of classes.) pp. 63. *Burnley*, 1893. 8°. **08365. e. 3.**

Corporation.

—— The History of Burnley . . . By W. Bennett. [With plates.] 4 pt. *Burnley*, 1946–51. 8°. **10361. bb. 20.**

Corporation.—Public Library Committee.

—— Public Library. Second [*etc.*] annual report of the Public Library Committee April, 1915—March, 1916 [*etc.*]. *Burnley*, [1916– .] 8°. A.R. **481.**

—— *Public Libraries.* Burnley Library Journal. *Burnley*, 1927– . 8°. **P.P. 6490. fx.**

—— Select List of Books on English History contained in the Central and Branch Libraries. pp. 20. *Burnley*, [1933.] 8°. **011903. e. 60.**

BURNLEY.

—— *Towneley Hall.* Towneley Hall. Shall we have it? [By John Allen.] pp. 16. *Burnley*, 1896. 8°. **10347**. h. 2. (2.)

—— Official Guide to Towneley Hall. By John Allen. pp. 53. *Burnley*, 1927. 8°. **7957**. aaa. 5.

Towneley Hall.—Art Gallery and Museum.

—— Hon. Secretary's Report for the year ended March 31st, 1912 [*etc.*]. *Burnley*, 1912– . 4°. **A.R. 648.** *Wanting issues for years* 1914–19, 24.

—— Spring and Summer Exhibition . . . 1930. [A catalogue.] pp. 35. *Burnley*, [1930.] 8°. **7957**. aaa. 25.

BURNLEY, ALFRED, *Bishop of.* *See* PEARSON.

—— EDGAR PRIESTLEY, *Bishop of.* *See* SWAIN.

BURNLEY AND DISTRICT COTTON INDUSTRY STUDY GROUP. *See* BURNLEY.

BURNLEY BUILDING SOCIETY. A Home of Your Own. A practical guide to the choosing, the buying and the equipment of a modern house. pp. 68. [*Burnley*,] 1934. 8°. **7817**. a. 48.

BURNLEY CO-OPERATIVE RECORD. *See* BURNLEY.—*Burnley Equitable Co-operative Society.*

BURNLEY EQUITABLE CO-OPERATIVE SOCIETY. *See* BURNLEY.

BURNLEY FREE CHURCH MINISTERS' FRATERNAL. *See* BURNLEY.

BURNLEY LIBRARY JOURNAL. *See* BURNLEY.—*Public Libraries.*

BURNLEY LITERARY AND SCIENTIFIC CLUB. *See* BURNLEY.

BURNLEY (CYRIL PELHAM)

—— Civil—or Self and Collective—Defence. The Boat. To all civil defence personnel within No. 11 district, Epsom and Ewell. [*Epsom*, 1943.] 8°. **8837**. h. 13.

BURNLEY (JAMES) Colorado's Golden Glories. Stories of the famous gold mines of the "Mineral State." pp. 51. *E. Tann: London*, 1901. 8°. **7109**. aaa. 37.

—— Fetters. A comedy-drama, in a prologue and three acts. pp. 59. *Printed for the Author: Bradford*, 1876. 8°. **11781**. bbb. 4.

—— The History of Wool and Woolcombing . . . With . . . illustrations and portraits. pp. xvi. 487. *Sampson Low & Co.: London*, 1889. 8°. **2251**. d. 3.

—— Idonia, and other poems. pp. viii. 200. *Longmans & Co.: London*, 1869. 8°. **11648**. bbb. 19.

—— Looking for the Dawn. A tale of the West Riding. pp. 392. *Simpkin, Marshall & Co.: London*, 1874. 8°. **12638**. ccc. 5.

—— Phases of Bradford Life: a series of pen and ink sketches. pp. 227. *Simpkin, Marshall & Co.: London*, [1871.] 8°. **12350**. e. 16.

—— The Romance of Invention: vignettes from the annals of industry and science, *etc.* pp. viii. 376. *Cassell & Co.: London*, 1886. 8°. **8708**. i. 11.

BURNLEY (JAMES)

—— The Romance of Life Preservation. pp. xi. 473. *W. H. Allen & Co.: London*, 1888. 8°. **12355**. p. 1.

—— The Romance of Modern Industry. pp. viii. 372. *W. H. Allen & Co.: London*, 1889. 8°. **08229**. de. 27.

—— Sir Titus Salt, and George Moore. [With portraits.] pp. 128. *Cassell & Co.: London*, 1885. 8°. [*World's Workers.*] **10601**. bbb. 35.

—— The Story of British Trade and Industry. pp. 224. *George Newnes: London*, 1904. 8°. **08228**. de. 11.

—— Summits of Success. How they have been reached, with sketches of the careers of some notable climbers. pp. vii. 434. *Grant Richards: London*, 1901. 8°. **10600**. de. 22.

—— Two Sides of the Atlantic. pp. 325. *Simpkin, Marshall & Co.: London*, [1880.] 12°. **10411**. de. 7.

—— West Riding Sketches. pp. 408. *Hodder & Stoughton: London*, 1875. 8°. **12314**. ee. 27.

—— Yorkshire Stories Re-told. pp. 316. *Richard Jackson: Leeds*, [1885.] 8°. **12331**. e. 35.

BURNLEY (MARY) The Burnley Readers, *etc.* 3 pt. *Nelson:* [*London*, 1937.] 8°. **012986**. b. 9.

BURNLEY (SYDNEY)

—— Catechism of First Aid for Gas Casualties. pp. 53. *J. Bale & Co.: London*, 1940. 16°. **07481**. de. 52.

BURNLEY (WILLIAM EWART) *See* DAWSON (Sidney S.) The Accountant's Compendium. By S. S. Dawson . . . Assisted by . . . W. E. Burnley, *etc.* 1908. 8°. **8225**. p. 14.

—— —— 1911. 8°. **8226**. tt. 1.

BURNLEY (WILLIAM HARDIN) Observations on the Present Condition of the Island of Trinidad, and the actual state of the experiment of Negro emancipation. pp. 177. *Longman & Co.: London*, 1842. 8°. **798**. g. 20.

—— Opinions on Slavery & Emancipation in 1823; referred to in a recent debate in the House of Commons, by Thomas Fowell Buxton, Esq. With additional observations, applicable to the Right Hon. E. G. Stanley's plan for the extinction of slavery. pp. lv. 44. *James Ridgway: London*, 1833. 8°. **8156**. c. 23.

BURN-MURDOCH (HECTOR) *See* MURDOCH.

BURN-MURDOCH (JAMES HENRY) *See* MURDOCH.

BURNOD ( ) *General.* *See* NAPOLEON I., *Emperor of the French.* [*Notes, Extracts, etc.*] Maximes de guerre et pensées de Napoléon Ier, *etc.* [Edited by General Burnod.] 1900. 8°. **8824**. aaa. 18.

BURNOD (GABRIELLE MAURICE) *See* MAURICE-BURNOD.

BURNOD (H.) Pèlerinage aux tombeaux de saint François de Sales et de sainte de Chantal, et itinéraire du pèlerin aux divers lieux, à Annecy et dans les environs qui rappellent le souvenir de ces deux saints . . . Seconde édition. pp. 138. *Annecy*, 1867. 16°. **10169**. de. 39.

BURNOT (PH.) *See* AUDIN (M.) Le Beaujolais. Images gravées en bois par P. Burnot. 1926. 4°. **L.R. 260**. a. 1.

BURNOT (Walter) Bubbles . . . Consisting of new jokes, conundrums, *etc.* pp. 55. *London,* [1898.] 8°. [*Turner's Nigger Notions.* no. 4.] **012314.** h. **36.**

—— G. H. Chirgwin's Popular Parody on the Village Blacksmith . . . Words only. *Francis Bros. & Day: London,* [1889.] 8°. **1875.** d. **9.** (**28.**)

—— Good Old Crusted Jokes, re-bottled by W. Burnot. pp. 63. *London,* [1898.] 8°. [*Turner's Nigger Notions.* no. 7.] **012314.** h. **36.**

—— Negro "Goaks," and Roasted "Chestnuts," grown, cooked and dished up by W. Burnot. pp. 56. *London,* [1898.] 8°. [*Turner's Nigger Notions.* no. 5.] **012314.** h. **36.**

—— New Elephant & Castle Theatre . . . Christmas Pantomime. Entitled Old Mother Goose and the Golden Eggs. pp. 25. *Wilkes & Co.: London,* 1882. 8°. **11779.** aaa. **9.** (**2.**)

—— Old and New Jokes, Darkey Dramas, *etc.* pp. 64. *London,* [1898.] 8°. [*Turner's Nigger Notions.* no. 9.] **012314.** h. **36.**

—— Turner's Nigger Notions, compiled by W. Burnot. pp. 56. *London,* [1898.] 8°. [*Turner's Nigger Notions.* no. 10.] **012314.** h. **36.**

BURNOT-LABOULAY (Antoine François) De la simulation considérée au point de vue du recrutement . . . Thèse, *etc.* pp. 35. *Montpellier,* 1844. 4°. **1182.** d. **7.** (**8.**)

BURNOTT (Walter) *See* Burnot.

BURNOUD ( ) *Abbé.* *See* Déléon (I.) Lettres à M. l'abbé Burnoud . . . en réponse à sa lettre du 12 mai 1856, versée au procès de Mademoiselle Lamerlière contre MM. Déléon et Cartellier, *etc.* 1857. 12°. **4806.** c. **14.**

BURNOUF (Aemilius) *See* Burnouf (Émile L.)

BURNOUF (Émile) *See* Iwagaki. La Mythologie des Japonais d'après le Kokŭ-si-ryakŭ . . . Traduite . . . par E. Burnouf. 1875. 8°. **4503.** f. **1.** (**5.**)

—— *See* Paris.—*Société des Études Japonaises, Chinoises, Tartares et Indo-Chinoises.* Annuaire de la Société . . . Publié par E. Burnouf et I. Warau. 1873, *etc.* 8°. Ac. **8810.**

BURNOUF (Émile Louis) *See* Bacon (Francis) *Viscount St. Albans.* [*Novum Organum.*] Bacon. Extraits du Novum organum . . . Traduction nouvelle, précédée d'une introduction, d'une analyse développée et d'appréciations philosophiques et critiques, par E. Burnouf. 1850. 12°. **8705.** a. **32.** (**2.**)

—— *See* Bezoles (R.) Science des religions. Le baptême . . . Avec une préface par E. Burnouf. 1874. 8°. **4325.** c. **11.**

—— *See* Blastos (S. A.) 1453. Les derniers jours de Constantinople . . . Avec préface de M. E. Burnouf. 1883. 8°. **9135.** ee. **12.**

—— *See* Coulomb (E. J.) Le Secret de l'absolu . . . Préface de Mr. E. Burnouf. 1892. 12°. **8632.** ccc. **25.**

—— *See* Lafont (G. de) *Count.* Les Grandes religions. Le Mazdéisme . . . Préface d'E. Burnouf. 1897. 12°. **4503.** dd. **5.**

BURNOUF (Émile Louis)

—— *See* Leupol (L.) *pseud.* Selectae e sanscriticis scriptoribus paginae. Choix de morceaux sanscrits . . . par L. Leupol. Avec la collaboration de E. Burnouf, *etc.* 1867. 8°. **14085.** c. **12.**

—— *See* Mahābhārata.—*Bhagavadgītā.* श्रीभगवद्गीता ॥ La Bhagavad-Gitâ . . . traduit par E. Burnouf. 1861. 8°. **14060.** c. **11.**

—— *See* Potagos (P.) Dix années de voyages dans l'Asie centrale et l'Afrique équatoriale . . . avec des notes . . . par M. E. Burnouf. 1885, *etc.* 8°. **10028.** g. **8.**

—— *See* Schliemann (H.) Ilios, Stadt und Land der Trojaner, *etc.* [With maps by E. Burnouf.] 1881. 8°. **560.** c. **5.**

—— *See* Schliemann (H.) Ilios: the city and country of the Trojans, *etc.* [With maps by E. Burnouf.] 1880. 8°. **07703.** i. **12.**

—— *See* Waldteufel (E.) La Politique étrangère de Louis xiv . . . Avec une préface de M. E. Burnouf. 1898. 12°. **9076.** ccc. **33.**

—— Le Catholicisme contemporain. pp. 463. *Paris,* 1879. 12°. **3902.** bbb. **19.**

—— Les Chants de l'Église latine. Restitution de la mesure et du rythme selon la méthode naturelle. pp. x. 218. *Paris,* 1887. 8°. **7898.** k. **25.**

—— De la nécessité des études orientales. Discours, *etc.* pp. 26. *Nancy,* 1861. 8°. **8309.** cc. **39.** (**1.**)

—— De Neptuno, ejusque cultu, præsertim in Peloponneso. Thesim proponebat . . . Æ. Burnouf. pp. 80. *Paris,* 1850. 8°. **4505.** e. **19.**

—— Des principes de l'art, d'après la méthode et les doctrines de Platon. pp. viii. 156. *Paris,* 1860 [1850.] 8°. **7805.** d. **7.**

—— Dictionnaire classique sanscrit-français, où sont coordonnés, revisés et complétés les travaux de Wilson, Bopp, Westergaard, Johnson, etc. . . . par E. Burnouf . . . Avec la collaboration de L. Leupol. livr. 1, 2. pp. viii. 781. *Nancy; Paris,* 1865 [1863–65]. 8°. **12906.** dd. **35.**
Published in parts.

—— [Another issue of livr. 1, 2.] Dictionnaire classique sanscrit-français, *etc.* pp. viii. 256. *Nancy; Paris,* 1863, [64.] 8°. **12908.** a. **13.**
With a different preface.

—— Essai sur le Vêda, ou Études sur les religions, la littérature, et la constitution sociale de l'Inde, depuis les temps primitifs jusqu'aux temps brahmaniques, *etc.* pp. vi. 476. *Paris,* 1863. 8°. **4504.** cc. **28.**

—— Histoire de la littérature grecque. 2 tom. *Paris,* 1869. 12°. **11852.** bbb. **24.**

—— [Another copy.] **L.P.** **12230.** e. **15.**

—— La Légende athénienne. Étude de mythologie comparée. [With plans.] pp. 215. *Paris,* 1872. 8°. **4506.** h. **4.**

—— Mémoires sur l'antiquité. L'âge de bronze—Troie—Santorin—Délos—Mycènes—Le Parthénon—Les courbes—Les Propylées—Un faubourg d'Athènes. [With plates.] pp. 338. *Paris,* 1879. 8°. **7706.** bb. **2.**

BURNOUF (ÉMILE LOUIS)

—— La Science des religions. Quatrième édition revue et complétée. pp. 288. *Paris*, 1885. 8°. **4506. aaa. 34.**

—— The Science of Religions . . . Translated by Julie Liebe. With a preface by E. J. Rapson. pp. ix. 275. *Swan Sonnenschein, Lowrey & Co.: London*, 1888. 8°. **4506. f. 3.**

—— Le Vase sacré et ce qu'il contient dans l'Inde, la Perse, la Grèce et dans l'Église chrétienne. Avec un appendice sur le Saint-Graal. pp. vi. 189. *Paris*, 1896. 8°. **12411. d. 3.**

—— La Vie et la pensée. Éléments réels de philosophie. pp. viii. 452. *Paris*, 1886. 8°. **8461. ee. 28.**

—— La Ville et l'Acropole d'Athènes aux diverses époques. pp. 215. pl. XXI. *Paris*, 1877. 8°. **560. c. 4.**

BURNOUF (ÉMILE LOUIS) and **LEUPOL** (L.) *pseud.* [i.e. FRANÇOIS ÉTIENNE LELOUP DE CHERAY.]

—— Méthode pour étudier la langue sanscrite, ouvrage composé sur le plan de la méthode grecque et de la méthode latine de J.-L. Burnouf, d'après les idées d'Eugène Burnouf et les meilleurs traités de l'Angleterre et de l'Allemagne, notamment la Grammaire de Bopp. [With eight lithographed plates illustrating the Sanskrit alphabet.] pp. xi. 182. *Nancy; Paris*, 1859. 8°. **12907. c. 16.**

BURNOUF (EUGÈNE)

—— *See* AVESTA. Commentaire sur le Yaçna . . . Ouvrage contenant le texte zend . . . et la version sanscrite inédite de Nériosengh. Par E. Burnouf. 1833. 4°. **696. i. 9.**

—— *See* AVESTA. Vendidad Sadé . . . publié par E. Burnouf. 1829, *etc.* fol. **Or.70.e.4.**

—— *See* AVESTA. Extrait d'un commentaire et d'une traduction nouvelle du Vendidad Sadé, l'un des livres de Zoroastre; par M. E. Burnouf, *etc.* 1829. 8°. **14990. b. 20.**

—— *See* BARTHÉLEMY-SAINT-HILAIRE (J.) [Notice sur les travaux de M. Eugène Burnouf.] Eugène Burnouf, *etc.* [With Burnouf's preface to his "Introduction sur le Yasna."] 1901. 8°. **010663. i. 30.**

—— *See* BURNOUF (Émile L.) and LEUPOL (L.) *pseud.* Méthode pour étudier la langue sanscrite, ouvrage composé . . . d'après les idées d'Eugène Burnouf, *etc.* 1859. 8°. **12907. c. 16.**

—— *See* FEER (L.) Papiers d'Eugène Burnouf conservés a la Bibliothèque nationale. Catalogue, *etc.* 1899. 8°. **011904. h. 4.**

—— *See* GÉRINGER ( ) L'Inde française . . . accompagnée d'un texte explicatif rédigé par M. E. Burnouf et M. E. Jacquet. [1827, *etc.*] fol. **1265. g. 28, 29.**

—— *See* JOMARD (E. F.) Institut royal de France . . . Funérailles de M. le baron Silvestre de Sacy, *etc.* (Discours prononcés par MM. Jomard . . . E. Burnouf, *etc.*) [1838.] 4°. **733. h. 2. (33.)**

—— *See* LENORMANT (C.) Eugène Burnouf. [1852?] 8°. **10663. g. 20. (1.)**

BURNOUF (EUGÈNE)

—— *See* PARIS.—*Société Asiatique.* Journal asiatique. (Nouveau journal asiatique . . . rédigé par MM. Burnouf, Chézy [and others.]) 1822, *etc.* 8°. **Ac. 8808.**

—— *See* PURĀṆAS.—*Bhāgavatapurāṇa.* Le Bhâgavata Purâṇa ou Histoire poétique de Krïchṇa. Traduit et publié par M. E. Burnouf. 1840, *etc.* 4°. **14016. f. 3–5.**

—— —— 1840, *etc.* fol. **14773. m. 3.**

—— *See* SADDHARMA-PUṆḌARĪKA. Le Lotus de la bonne loi traduit du sanscrit, accompagné d'un commentaire et de vingt et un mémoires relatifs commentaire et de vingt et un mémoires relatifs au buddhisme, par M. E. Burnouf. 1852. 4°. **14028. e. 2.**

—— —— 1925. 8°. **14070. ed. 2.**

—— *See* SILVESTRE DE SACY (A. I.) *Baron.* Institut de France . . . Funérailles de M. Saint Martin, *etc.* (Discours de MM. Silvestre de Sacy et E. Burnouf.) [1832.] 4°. **733. g. 17. (138.)**

—— *See* SUTTA-PIṬAKA.—*Dīgha-nikāya.* Sept suttas pālis tirés du Dîgha-Nikâya, *etc.* (Traduction du Sâmañña-phala-sutta de M. E. Burnouf.) 1876. 8°. **14098. d. 12.**

—— Choix de lettres d'Eugène Burnouf, 1825–1852. Suivi d'une bibliographie. Avec portrait et fac-similé. [Edited by L. Burnouf, afterwards Delisle.] pp. xvi. 584. *Paris*, 1891. 8°. **010920. f. 18.**

—— Discours prononcé aux funérailles de M. Letronne. *See* LETRONNE (J. A.) Œuvres choisies, *etc.* tom. 1. 1881, *etc.* 8°. **7702. cc. 22.**

—— Études sur la langue et sur les textes zends. tom. 1. pp. iv. 429. *Paris*, [1850.] 8°. **12906. dd. 15.** *No more published.*

—— Introduction à l'histoire du buddhisme indien. tom. 1. pp. v. 647. *Paris*, 1844. 4°. **14028. e. 1.** *No more published.*

—— Deuxième édition . . . précédée d'une notice de M. Barthélemy Saint-Hilaire sur les travaux de M. E. Burnouf. pp. xxxviii. 586. *Paris*, 1876. 8°. **4504. h. 27.**

—— Legends of Indian Buddhism. Translated from "L'Introduction à l'histoire du buddhisme indien" . . . with introduction by Winifred Stephens. pp. 128. *John Murray: London*, 1911. 8°. [*Wisdom of the East Series.*] **14003. a. 37.**

—— Mémoire sur deux inscriptions cunéiformes trouvées près d'Hamadan, et qui font maintenant partie des papiers du Dr Schulz. pp. vii. 198. pl. III. *Paris*, 1836. 4°. **811. k. 46.**

—— Observations grammaticales sur quelques passages de l'Essai sur le pali, de MM. E. Burnouf et Lassen. Par E. Burnouf. pp. 30. *Paris*, 1827. 8°. **12907. d. 25. (1.)**

—— Catalogue des livres imprimés et manuscrits composant la bibliothèque de feu M. E. Burnouf . . . dont la vente aura lieu le . . . 18 avril 1854, *etc.* pp. 370. MS. NOTES OF PRICES. *Paris*, 1854. 8°. **11904. f. 30.**

BURNOUF (Eugène) and **LASSEN** (Christian)

—— Essai sur le pali, ou langue sacrée de la presqu'île au-delà du Gange. Avec six planches lithographiées et la notice des manuscrits palis de la Bibliothèque du Roi. pp. 222. 1826. 8°. *See* Paris.—*Société Asiatique.* **622.** k. **30.**

—— [Another copy.] **622.** f. **20.**

BURNOUF (Jean Louis) *See* Burnouf (Émile L.) and Leupol (L.) *pseud.* Méthode pour étudier la langue sanscrite, ouvrage composé sur le plan de la méthode grecque et de la méthode latine de J.-L. Burnouf, *etc.* 1859. 8°. **12907.** c. **16.**

—— *See* Cicero (M. T.) [*Works.—Latin and French.*] Œuvres complètes, *etc.* [Translated by J. L. Burnouf and others.] 1825, *etc.* 8°. **831.** c. **5–10.**

—— *See* Cicero (M. T.) [*Works.—Latin and French.*] Œuvres complètes . . . avec la traduction en français [by J. L. Burnouf and others]. 1852. 8°. **11306.** m. **7.**

—— *See* Cicero (M. T.) [*De Officiis.—Latin and French.*] Cicéron Des devoirs. Traduction nouvelle par J. L. Burnouf, *etc.* 1861. 12°. **8404.** bb. **1.**

—— *See* Plinius Caecilius Secundus (C.) [*Works.—Latin and French.*] Pline le Jeune. (Œuvres complètes, avec la traduction en français [by J. L. Burnouf].) 1853. 8°. **11306.** m. **12.**

—— *See* Plinius Caecilius Secundus (C.) [*Panegyricus.—Latin and French.*] Pline le Jeune. Panégyrique de Trajan. Traduction . . . par J. L. Burnouf, *etc.* 1845. 12°. **10605.** df. **2.**

—— *See* Sallustius Crispus (C.) [*Works.—Latin.*] Caius Crispus Sallustius . . . recensitus . . . item Julius Exsuperantius . . . emendatus, curante J. L. Burnouf. 1821. 8°. **11305.** k. **4.**

—— —— 1822. 16°. **834.** a. **8.**

—— *See* Tacitus (P. C.) [*Works.—French.*] Œuvres complètes . . . traduites . . . par J. L. Burnouf. 1869. 8°. **11305.** bbb. **2.**

—— *See* Tacitus (P. C.) [*Annales.—Latin and French.*] Annales. Texte établi et, d'après Burnouf, traduit par H. Bornecque. 1933. 8°. **9042.** a. **27.**

—— *See* Tacitus (P. C.) [*Historiae.—Latin and French.*] Tacite. Histoires. Texte établi et, d'après Burnouf, traduit par Henri Bornecque. 1933. 8°. **9042.** a. **23.**

—— *See* Vālmīki. Yajñadattabaḍa . . . suivi . . . d'une traduction littérale latine par J. L. Burnouf. 1826. 4°. **14060.** e. **6.**

—— De la traduction. Opuscule publié par Victor Develay. pp. 38. *Paris,* 1861. 8°. **11825.** dd. **43.** (4.)

—— Méthode pour étudier la langue grecque . . . Quarante-cinquième édition, *etc.* pp. xx. 336. *Paris,* 1847. 8°. **826.** e. **29.**

—— [A reissue.] *Paris,* 1869. 8°. **12924.** c. **6.**

—— [A reissue.] *Paris,* 1873. 8°. **12923.** bb. **1.**

—— [A reissue.] *Paris,* 1888. 8°. **12923.** c. **31.**

—— *See* Duebner (J. F.) Examen détaillé de la méthode grecque de M. Burnouf. 1857. 12°. **12923.** aa. **31.** (4.)

BURNOUF (Jean Louis)

—— *See* Duebner (J. F.) La Méthode grecque de M. Burnouf devant le nouveau règlement pour l'adoption de livres classiques. 1856. 12°. **12924.** aa. **50.** (3.)

—— *See* Longueville (E. P. M.) Cours complet de thèmes grecs gradués, adaptés à la méthode de M. Burnouf, *etc.* 1828, *etc.* 8°. **12923.** bb. **27.**

—— Méthode pour étudier la langue latine . . . Vingt-sixième édition, *etc.* pp. xvi. 352. *Paris,* [1875.] 8°. **12935.** e. **3.**

—— *See* Geoffroy (J. B.) *Professeur.* Cours complet et gradué de thèmes latins, adapté à la Grammaire de M. Burnouf, *etc.* 1845. 8°. **826.** g. **8.**

—— Souvenirs de jeunesse, 1792–1796. (Fragment de correpondance, comprenant six lettres.) [The preface signed: L. D. B., i.e. Laure Burnouf, afterwards Delisle.] pp. 45. *Nogent-le-Rotrou,* [1889.] 8°. **10602.** d. **24.** (4.)

BURNOUF, afterwards **DELISLE** (Laure) *See* Burnouf (Eugène) Choix de lettres d'E. Burnouf, *etc.* [Edited by L. Burnouf, afterwards Delisle.] 1891. 8°. **010920.** f. **18.**

—— *See* Burnouf (J. L.) Souvenirs de jeunesse, *etc.* [The preface signed: L. D. B., i.e. L. Burnouf, afterwards Delisle.] [1889.] 8°. **10602.** d. **24.** (4.)

—— *See* Feer (L.) Papiers d'Eugène Burnouf conservés à la Bibliothèque nationale. Catalogue . . . augmenté de renseignements et de correspondances [by L. Burnouf, afterwards Delisle], *etc.* 1899. 8°. **011904.** h. **4.**

BURNOUF (Michel) Le Chapelet des heures. [Poems.] Preface de Xavier Privas. pp. 155. *Paris,* 1914. 8°. **011483.** aa. **8.**

BURNS CHRONICLE. Burns Chronicle and Club Directory. *See* Kilmarnock.—*Burns Federation.* Annual Burns Chronicle, *etc.*

BURNS CLUB. Burns Club of Atlanta. *See* Atlanta, *Georgia.*

—— Burns Club of Dumfries. *See* Dumfries.

—— Burns Club of London. *See* London.—iii.

—— Burns Club of Saint Louis. *See* Saint Louis, *Missouri.*

—— Burns Club of the City of New York. *See* New York.

BURNS COTTAGE. *See* Alloway.

BURNS COTTAGE ASSOCIATION. *See* Saint Louis, *Missouri.—Louisiana Purchase Exposition,* 1904.

BURNS EXHIBITION, *Glasgow.* *See* Glasgow.—*Royal Glasgow Institute of the Fine Arts.*

BURNS FEDERATION. *See* Kilmarnock.

BURNS' HOUSE. *See* Dumfries.

BURNS MANTLE BEST PLAYS. *See* Periodical Publications.—*Boston, Mass.* The Best Plays.

BURNS MONUMENT. *See* Alloway.

BURNS MONUMENT TRUSTEES. *See* Alloway.

BURNS, OATES AND WASHBOURNE, LTD. Copyright Pictures of Burns, Oates & Washbourne, Ltd., *etc.* [32 plates.] *London,* [1934.] 8°. **7862.** ppp. **4.**

BURNS, *Family of.* *See* GUTHRIE (Charles J.) *Lord Guthrie.* Genealogy of the Descendants of . . . Mrs. Anne Burns or Guthrie . . . Also incidental references to the families of Guthrie and Burns, *etc.* 1902. 4°. **9917.** h. **27.**

BURNS ( ) *Major.* *See* CONWAY (A. B.) *pseud.* [i.e. — Burns.]

BURNS (A. E.) *Novelist.* The Grand Duchess Benedicta. A story, *etc.* pp. v. 216. *Longmans & Co.: London,* 1915. 8°. **012807.** c. **39.**

—— Peggy in Demand. pp. 282. *G. T. Foulis & Co.: London,* [1924.] 8°. **12708.** aaa. **10.**

BURNS (A. R.) *See* PERIODICAL PUBLICATIONS.—*Birmingham.* The Market and Fair Trades' Annual . . . Edited by A. R. Burns. [1906, *etc.*] 8°. **P.P. 2497.** i.

BURNS (AGNES ETHEL) *See* BURNS (Robert E.) and BURNS (A. E.) Easy Latin for Beginners. 1928. 8°. **012933.** aa. **49.**

—— *See* BURNS (Robert E.) and BURNS (A. E.) Latin for Juniors, *etc.* 1930. 8°. **012933.** a. **47.**

—— *See* BURNS (Robert E.) and BURNS (A. E.) Latin for School Certificate. 1938. 8°. **012933.** a. **117.**

BURNS (ALAN CHAMLEY) Investigations on Raw Cotton. Deterioration of cotton during damp storage. [With plates.] pp. vi. 92. *Cairo,* 1927. 8°. [*Egypt. Ministry of Agriculture. Technical and Scientific Service. Bulletin.* no. 71.] **S. 872.**

BURNS (*Sir* ALAN CUTHBERT MAXWELL) *G.C.M.G.*

—— *See* SEMPER (Dudley H.) and BURNS (*Sir* A. C. M.) *G.C.M.G.* Index of the Laws of the Federated Colony of the Leeward Islands, *etc.* 1911. 8°. **6606.** aa. **26.**

—— Colonial Civil Servant. [Autobiographical reminiscences.] pp. 339. *George Allen & Unwin: London,* 1949. 8°. **10862.** g. **4.**

—— Colour Prejudice, with particular reference to the relationship between whites and Negroes. pp. 164. *George Allen & Unwin: London,* 1948. 8°. **08157.** eee. **60.**

—— History of Nigeria. [With maps.] pp. 360. *G. Allen & Unwin: London,* 1929. 8°. **9059.** aa. **6.**

—— (Second edition.) pp. 360. *G. Allen & Unwin: London,* 1936. 8°. **9062.** bb. **17.**

—— History of Nigeria. (Third edition.) [With a map.] pp. 360. *G. Allen & Unwin: London,* 1942. 8°. **09062.** c. **15.**

—— History of Nigeria. (Fourth edition.) pp. 322. *George Allen & Unwin: London,* 1948. 8°. **10098.** b. **22.**

—— History of the British West Indies. [With maps.] pp. 821. *George Allen & Unwin: London,* 1954. 8° **2090.** a

—— [Another copy.] **09525.** i. **33.**

—— The Nigeria Handbook . . . Compiled by A. C. Burns . . . Third issue. pp. viii. 227. lvi. *Government Printer: Lagos,* 1921. 8°. **10094.** c. **11.**
The sixth and later editions, published by authority, are catalogued under Nigeria.

BURNS (*Sir* ALAN CUTHBERT MAXWELL) *G.C.M.G.*

—— Other People, Other Ways. Some suggestions to Africans and Europeans visiting one another's countries. By Alan Burns and Robert Gardiner. (Prepared by the Colonial Office and the Central Office of Information.) pp. 19. 1951. 8°. *See* ENGLAND.—*Colonial Office.* **B.S. 7/178.**

BURNS (ALEXANDER) *See* O'CONNOR (*Right Hon.* Thomas P.) and MACWADE (R.) Gladstone—Parnell, and the great Irish Struggle . . . Canadian introduction by A. Burns, *etc.* [1888.] 8°. **8146.** c. **12.**

BURNS (ALFRED)

—— *See* ENGLAND.—*Home Office.* Inquiry into certain matters arising subsequent to the conviction at Liverpool Assizes of . . . A. Burns, *etc.* 1952. 8°. **B.S. 18/40. (98.)**

BURNS (ALLEN TIBBALS) Americanization Studies. A. T. Burns, director. *Harper & Bros.: New York & London,* 1920– . 8°. 10 Vol. **10414.aa.13.**

BURNS (ANDREW) Two Lectures on the Use and Abuse of the Bible. By the Rev. A. Burns . . . in the course of which he replies to some unfair statements made by Joseph Pease . . . in a lecture entitled "The Book and its Story." 2 pt. *T. Richardson & Son: London,* 1856. 8°. **3127.** e. **33.**

BURNS (ANDREW NISBET)

—— Post-Primary Exercises in English, *etc.* pp. 118. *Whitcombe & Tombs: Christchurch,* [1940.] 8°. **12987.** a. **17.**

BURNS (ANNE)

—— Data on Flight Loads obtained with Miller Recording Equipment, with particular reference to test flights in Lancaster PD. 119. pp. 27. *London,* 1951. fol. [*Aeronautical Research Council. Current Papers.* no. 48.] **B.S. 62/32.**

BURNS (ANNE) and **FAIRCLOUGH** (A. J.)

—— The Dynamic Landing Loads of Flying Boats, with special reference to measurements made on Sunderland TX. 293. pp. 38. *London,* 1952. 4°. [*Aeronautical Research Council. Reports and Memoranda.* no. 2629.] **B.S. 2/2.**

BURNS, afterwards **GUTHRIE** (ANNE) *See* GUTHRIE (Charles J.) *Lord Guthrie.* Genealogy of the Descendants of . . . Mrs. Anne Burns or Guthrie, *etc.* 1902. 4°. **9917.** h. **27.**

BURNS (ANNIE JOHNSON) Stories of Shepherd Life. (A social science reader.) pp. 124. *American Book Co.: New York,* [1934.] 8°. **20053.** g. **18.**

BURNS (ANNIE WALKER) Record of Wills in Nicholas County, Kentucky. Compiled by A. W. Burns. pp. 83. *Seat Pleasant,* 1936. fol. **09915.** k. **14.**
Reproduced from typewriting.

BURNS (ANTHONY) *See* BOWDITCH (William T.) The Rendition of Anthony Burns. 1854. 8°. **8156.** bb. **20.**

—— *See* CLARKE (James F.) The Rendition of Anthony Burns. Its causes and consequences, *etc.* 1854. 8°. **4485.** g. **16.**

BURNS (ANTHONY)

—— *See* GRAY (E. H.) Assaults upon Freedom! . . . A discourse, occasioned by the rendition of A. Burns. 1854. 8°. **8156.** e. **37.**

—— *See* STEVENS (Charles E.) Anthony Burns. A history. 1856. 12°. **4986.** d. **21.**

—— *See* WILLSON (Edmund B.) The Bad Friday: a sermon preached . . . the Sunday after the return of A. Burns to slavery. 1854. 8°. **8156.** ee. **41.**

—— *See* YOUNG (Joshua) *of Burlington, Vermont.* God Greater than Man. A sermon preached . . . after the rendition of A. Burns. 1854. 8°. **8157.** c. **21.**

—— Boston Slave Riot, and Trial of Anthony Burns, *etc.* pp. 86. *Fetridge & Co.: Boston,* 1854. 8°. **8156.** c. **24.**

BURNS (ARCHIBALD) *See* BALLANTYNE (Robert M.) Photographs of Edinburgh [by A. Burns], *etc.* [1868.] 4°. **10369.** h. **6.**

—— *See* HENDERSON (Thomas) *Antiquarian.* Picturesque "Bits" from Old Edinburgh. A series of photographs by A. Burns, *etc.* 1868. 4°. **10370.** bbb. **30.**

BURNS (ARTHUR) *Quartermaster-Sergeant.* Corporal Astley's Temptation, and other stories. pp. 64. *H. M. Tyrer: Caterham,* [1912.] 8°. **04419.** i. **13.**

BURNS (ARTHUR) *Teacher of the Mathematics in Tarporley, Cheshire.* Geodæsia Improved; or, a New and correct method of surveying made exceeding easy, *etc.* pp. ii. x. 353. *Printed for the Author: Chester,* 1771. 8°. **530.** e. **14.**

—— [Another copy.] **52.** e. **4.**

—— [A reissue.] pp. x. 353. *T. Evans: London,* 1775. 8°. **1394.** d. **13.**

BURNS (ARTHUR EDWARD)

—— Modern Economics. Second edition. ([By] A. E. Burns, Alfred C. Neal, D. S. Watson. Under the general editorship of Albert Gailord Hart.) pp. xxxiv. 790. *Harcourt, Brace & Co.: New York,* [1953.] 8°. **8208.** cc. **16.**

BURNS (ARTHUR EDWARD) and **WILLIAMS** (EDWARD AINSWORTH)

—— Federal Work, Security, and Relief Programs. [With plates.] pp. xviii. 159. *Washington,* 1941. 8°. [*U.S. Work Projects Administration. Division of Research. Research Monograph.* no. 24.] A.S. **978/7.**

BURNS (ARTHUR FRANK)

—— The Frontiers of Economic Knowledge. Essays. pp. ix. 367. *Princeton University Press: Princeton,* 1954. 8°. [*National Bureau of Economic Research. General Series.* no. 57.] W.P. **651/57.**

—— Production Trends in the United States since 1870. [A thesis.] pp. xxxii. 363. *New York,* 1934. 8°. [*Publications of the National Bureau of Economic Research.* no. 23.] W.P. **651/23.**

BURNS (ARTHUR FRANK) and **MITCHELL** (WESLEY CLAIR)

—— Measuring Business Cycles. pp. xxvii. 560. 1946. fol. *See* UNITED STATES OF AMERICA.—*National Bureau of Economic Research.* **8204.** h. **8.**

BURNS (ARTHUR ROBERT)

—— Comparative Economic Organization. pp. xv. 766. *Prentice-Hall: New York,* 1955. 8°. **8208.** g. **12.**

—— The Decline of Competition. A study of the evolution of American industry. pp. xiv. 619. *McGraw-Hill Book Co.: New York & London,* 1936. 8°. **8232.** cc. **18.**

—— Money and Monetary Policy in Early Times, *etc.* pp. xiii. 517. pl. XVI. *Kegan Paul & Co.: London,* 1927. 8°. [*History of Civilization.*] **09009.** e. **1/34.**

BURNS (ARTHUR ROBERT) and **BURNS** (EVELINE MABEL)

—— The Economic World, *etc.* pp. xvi. 304. pl. v. *University of London Press: London,* 1927. 8°. **08206.** de. **13.**

BURNS (B. K.) The Jury Woman. A play [in] 3 acts. [By B. K. Burns.] pp. 52. [1923.] 8°. *See* JURY WOMAN. **11791.** e. **17.**

—— Tread of Men. [A play.] pp. 48. [1924.] 8°. **11791.** ff. **7.**

BURNS (BARNET) A Brief Narrative of the Remarkable History of Barnet Burns, an English sailor . . . With a faithful account of the way in which he became a chief of one of the tribes of the New Zealanders . . . Written by himself. pp. 32. *Printed for the Author: London,* 1835. 12°. T. **1895.** (**14.**)

—— [Another edition.] A Brief Narrative of a New Zealand Chief, being the remarkable history of Barnet Burns, *etc.* [With illustrations.] pp. 16. *Bull & Turner: Birmingham,* 1842. 8°. **1414.** c. **83.** (**4.**)

BURNS (BOBBY) Carte blanche. [A set of cards, for teaching French.] [*London,* 1920.] 16°. **12950.** aaaa. **16.**

BURNS (BRYAN HARTOP) and **ELLIS** (VALENTINE HERBERT) Recent Advances in Orthopædic Surgery, *etc.* pp. viii. 296. *J. & A. Churchill: London,* 1937. 8°. [*Recent Advances Series.*] **7442.** p. **1/72.**

BURNS (C. A.)

—— Henry Céard and his Relations with Flaubert and Zola. [1953.] 8°. **11870.** g. **2.**
Proof-sheets.

BURNS (C. H.) "Legs, Gentlemen, Legs!" Notes on the theory and practice of riding and keeping horses, with reasons . . . Illustrated, *etc.* pp. xii. 131. *Constable & Co.: London,* 1937. 8°. **07295.** f. **10.**

BURNS (CECIL) *Mrs.* *See* BURNS (Edward S.) Memorials of Edward Spenser Burns, *etc.* [Edited by J. D. and C. Burns.] 1886. 8°. **10827.** bbb. **13.**

—— Memorial Leaves. A selection from the papers of Cecil Burns—Mrs. Dawson Burns. With a biographical sketch. [Edited by J. Dawson Burns. With a portrait.] pp. 104. *Ideal Publishing Union: London,* 1898. 8°. **4907.** i. **1.**
Printed for private circulation.

BURNS (CECIL) *Professor of Philosophy at St. Edmund's College, Ware.* *See* BIBLE. [*English.*] St. Edmund's College Series of Scripture Handbooks. (The Holy Gospel according to Saint Mark. With introduction and notes by the Rev. C. Burns.) 1897, *etc.* 8°. **03127.** ee. **5/1.**

BURNS (Cecil Delisle) *See* Drews (Arthur) The Christ Myth . . . Translated . . . by C. D. Burns. [1910.] 8°. **4016. i. 3.**

—— After War—Peace? pp. 48. *Watts & Co.: London,* 1941. 8°. [*The Thinker's Forum.* no. 11.] W.P. **7169/11.**

—— The Challenge to Democracy. pp. 266. *G. Allen & Unwin: London,* 1934. 8°. **8004. e. 35.**

—— Civilisation: the next step. pp. 291. *Nicholson & Watson: London,* 1938. 8°. **8288. df. 6.**

—— The Contact between Minds. A metaphysical hypothesis. pp. x. 138. *Macmillan & Co.: London,* 1923. 8°. **8470. aaa. 10.**

—— Democracy. pp. 255. *Thornton Butterworth: London,* 1935. 8°. [*Home University Library.*] **12199. p. 1/195.**

—— Democracy: its defects and advantages. pp. 217. *G. Allen & Unwin: London,* 1929. 8°. **08007. h. 4.**

—— Difetti e vantaggi della democrazia. (Traduzione di Camillo Pellizzi.) pp. 277. *Milano,* 1951. 8°. **8012. aaa. 20.**

"*Il mondo nuovo.*" vol. 28.

—— The First Europe. A study of the establishment of Medieval Christendom, A.D. 400–800. [With maps.] pp. 684. pl. 9. *George Allen & Unwin: London,* 1947. 8°. **4536. c. 17.**

—— La Prima Europa, *etc.* (Traduzione e note di Henry Furst.) [With plates.] pp. 827. *Bologna,* 1950. 8°. **4517. aa. 16.**

I Cento libri. vol. 1.

—— Government and Industry. pp. 315. *G. Allen & Unwin: London,* 1921. 8°. **08285. bb. 87.**

—— Greek Ideals. A study of social life. pp. ix. 275. *G. Bell & Sons: London,* 1917. 8°. **11313. f. 7.**

—— The Growth of Modern Philosophy. pp. 269. *Sampson Low & Co.: London,* 1909. 8°. **8486. bb. 28.**

—— The Horizon of Experience. A study of the modern mind. pp. 372. *G. Allen & Unwin: London,* 1933. 8°. **08458. d. 51.**

—— Industry and Civilisation. pp. 278. *G. Allen & Unwin: London; Macmillan Co.: New York,* 1925. 8°. **08275. c. 69.**

—— International Affairs To-day. *See* Affairs. International Affairs, *etc.* [1924.] 8°. **08027. df. 108.**

—— La Mento internaciona. (Extraktita . . . de "The International Mind," en "The Standard.") Da C. D. Burns. La Bezono di mento internaciona. Da Profesoro R. D. Carmichael. (Extraktita . . . de "The Need of an International Mind," en "The Scientific Monthly.") [Translated by J. W. Marelius.] pp. 12. *Stockholm; Luxemburg* [printed], 1926. 8°. **08007. h. 29.**

—— International Politics. pp. x. 189. *Methuen & Co.: London,* 1920. 8°. [*Library of Social Studies.*] **8288. eee. 13/3.**

—— An Introduction to the Social Sciences. pp. 112. *G. Allen & Unwin: London,* 1930. 8°. **08286. aa. 15.**

—— The League and Labour. pp. 16. *British Periodicals: London,* 1920. 8°. **08023. aaa. 47. (3.)**

BURNS (Cecil Delisle)

—— Leisure in the Modern World. pp. 216. *G. Allen & Unwin: London,* 1932. 8°. **20016. eee. 28.**

—— Fritiden i det moderna samhället . . . Översättning av Thure Nyman. pp. viii. 211. *Stockholm,* 1936. 8°. **20009. bb. 8.**

—— Modern Civilization on Trial. pp. 296. *G. Allen & Unwin: London,* 1931. 8°. **8275. tt. 32.**

—— Den Moderna civilisationen inför provet. (Auktoriserad översättning av Leif Björk.) pp. 342. *Stockholm,* 1932. 8°. **8282. tt. 27.**

—— The Morality of Nations. An essay on the theory of politics. pp. xii. 254. *University of London Press: London,* 1915. 8°. **8006. k. 6.**

—— A New Faith for a New Age, *etc.* pp. 22. *Ethical Union: London,* [1934.] 8°. [*Horace Seal Memorial Lecture.* no. 6.] **8412.df.75/6.**

—— 1918–1928: a short history of the world. pp. 447. *Victor Gollancz: London,* 1928. 8°. **09007. cc. 14.**

—— Old Creeds and the New Faith. pp. 282. *Francis Griffiths: London,* 1911. 8°. **4014. de. 17.**

—— The Philosophy of Labour. pp. 126. *G. Allen & Unwin: London,* 1925. 8°. **08282. ee. 55.**

—— The Place of the Arts in Modern Civilisation, *etc.* pp. 22. *A. Reid & Co.: Newcastle upon Tyne,* 1933. 8°. [*William Henry Charlton Memorial Lecture.* 1933.] Ac. **2671. g/2.**

—— Political Ideals: their nature and development. An essay. pp. 311. *Oxford University Press: London,* 1915. 12°. **8009. ccc. 4.**

—— Third edition. pp. 357. *Oxford University Press: London,* 1919. 12°. **8006. aa. 48.**

—— Fourth edition. pp. 358. *Oxford University Press: London,* 1929. 12°. **8010. aa. 43.**

—— The Principles of Revolution. A study in ideals. pp. 154. *G. Allen & Unwin: London,* 1920. 8°. **08282. aa. 60.**

—— A Short History of Birkbeck College, University of London . . . With eight illustrations. pp. 169. *University of London Press: London,* 1924. 8°. **08364. f. 33.**

—— A Short History of International Intercourse. pp. 159. *G. Allen & Unwin: London,* 1924. 8°. **09007. aa. 22.**

—— Syllabus of a Course of Twelve Lectures on the History of International Relations and the League of Nations. (Second edition.) pp. 31. *League of Nations Union: [London,]* 1928. 8°. **8029. ee. 21.**

—— War and a Changing Civilisation. pp. ix. 154. *John Lane: London,* 1934. 8°. [*Twentieth Century Library.*] **012207. n. 1/6.**

—— What to Read on Philosophy. pp. 28. *Leeds Public Libraries: [Leeds,]* 1930. 8°. ["*What to Read.*"] **11900. a. 67/9.**

—— Whitehall. [A description of the functions of Government offices.] pp. 78. *Oxford University Press: London,* 1921. 8°. [*World of To-day.*] **012207. n. 2/14.**

BURNS (CECIL DELISLE)

—— The World of States. pp. 143. *Headley Bros.: London,* 1917. 8°. [*New Commonwealth Books.* no. 1.] **08286. a. 2/1.**

BURNS (CECIL LAURENCE) *See* SHEPPARD (Samuel T.) The Byculla Club . . . Illustrated by C. L. Burns. 1916. 8°. **10056. i. 25.**

—— Catalogue of the Collection of Maps, Prints and Photographs illustrating the History of the Island and City of Bombay. pp. 92. 1918. 8°. *See* BOMBAY.—*Victoria and Albert Museum.* **010056. g. 21.**

—— Longmans' Charts of Colour Drawing and Design. Elementary (Advanced) series. 2 pt. *Longmans & Co.: Bombay,* [1905.] fol. Cup. **649. d. 9.**

—— A Monograph on Gold and Silver Work in the Bombay Presidency. pp. 25. pl. XIII. 1904. fol. *See* BOMBAY, *Presidency of.* [*Miscellaneous Public Documents, etc.*] I.S. BO. **45/9.**

—— A Monograph on Ivory Carving. pp. 10. pl. 6. [1900.] fol. *See* BOMBAY, *Presidency of.* [*Miscellaneous Public Documents, etc.*] I.S. BO. **45/6.**

—— Teachers' Handbook for use with the Scheme of Colour Drawing and Design for schools. pp. 12. *Longmans & Co.: London,* 1905. 8°. **07808. c. 2. (2.)**

BURNS (CECIL LAURENCE) and **COLENSO** (ROBERT JOHN)

—— Living Anatomy. pl. XL. *Longmans & Co.: London,* 1900. 4°. K.T.C. **30. b. 17.**

BURNS (CHARLES LOUIS CRAWFORD)

—— Maladjusted Children. pp. x. 80. *Hollis & Carter: London,* 1955. 8°. **7583. de. 21.**

BURNS (CLARICE MARGARET)

—— Infant and Maternal Mortality in relation to size of family and rapidity of breeding. A study in human responsibility, *etc.* pp. viii. 247. 1942. 8°. *See* NEWCASTLE-UPON-TYNE.—*University of Durham College of Physical Science,* afterwards *Armstrong College,* afterwards *King's College.—Department of Physiology.* **07581. i. 33.**

BURNS (CLIFFORD G.)

—— Colour Diagnoses: prelude to colour therapy. *Clark's Printing Services: Bristol,* [1955.] 8°. **8716. m. 49.**

BURNS (DANIEL) *See* PEEL (Robert) *Mining Engineer.* An Elementary Text-book of Coal Mining . . . Revised and enlarged by D. Burns, *etc.* 1921. 8°. **07107. f. 18.**

—— Electrical Practice in Collieries, *etc.* pp. viii. 224. *C. Griffin & Co.: London,* 1903. 8°. **8758. de. 22.**

—— Second edition, revised and enlarged, *etc.* pp. x. 265. *C. Griffin & Co.: London,* 1905. 8°. **08755. de. 3.**

—— Third edition, revised and enlarged, *etc.* pp. x. 307. *C. Griffin & Co.: London,* 1909. 8°. **08755. f. 11.**

—— Fourth edition, revised and enlarged, *etc.* pp. x. 353. *C. Griffin & Co.: London,* 1914. 8°. **8755. de. 14.**

—— Fifth edition, revised and enlarged, *etc.* pp. x. 407. *C. Griffin & Co.: London,* 1920. 8°. **8753. b. 2.**

BURNS (DANIEL)

—— The Elements of Coal Mining, *etc.* pp. vii. 236. *Edward Arnold: London,* 1917. 8°. **07106. c. 26.**

—— Safety in Coal Mines. A textbook of fundamental principles for firemen and other workers in mines. pp. 158. *Blackie & Son: London,* 1912. 8°. **07108. c. 32.**

BURNS (DANIEL) and **KERR** (GEORGE L.)

—— The Modern Practice of Coal Mining, *etc.* pt. 1–4. pp. xi. 630. *Whittaker & Co.: London,* 1907–[10]. 8°. **07106. ee. 39.**
No more published.

—— [A reissue.] pt. 1, 2. *Sir I. Pitman & Sons: London,* [1919.] 8°. **07104. e. 62.**
Imperfect; wanting the remaining parts.

BURNS (DAVID) *Minister of Nithsdale United Presbyterian Church, Glasgow.* God's Poem: nature sermons. pp. 194. *J. Clarke & Co.: London,* [1921.] 8°. **04478. f. 33.**

—— Grace to You! pp. 16. *R. L. Sinclair: Montrose,* [1909.] *obl.* 16°. **4372. a. 32.**

—— Philippians. Expository sermons on the Epistle of St. Paul. pp. 296. *J. Clarke & Co.: London,* [1917.] 8°. **04478. f. 5.**

—— Ruth. pp. 116. *H. R. Allenson: London,* [1924.] 8°. **03166. de. 35.**

—— Sayings in Symbol. Essays suggested by Bible figures of speech. pp. 200. *Hodder & Stoughton: London,* 1894. 8°. **4371. b. 22.**

—— The Song of the Well, and other sermons. pp. 293. *J. Clarke & Co.: London,* 1913. 8°. **4461. ee. 16.**

BURNS (DAVID) *of Stanwix, near Carlisle.* The May Queen. A Thespis. [In verse.] pp. 90. *C. Thurnam & Sons: Carlisle; Simpkin, Marshall & Co.: London,* 1894. 8°. **11779. b. 18.**

BURNS (DAVID) *Professor of Physiology at Durham. See* PATON (Diarmid N.) A Practical Course of Chemical Physiology . . . By D. N. Paton . . . D. Burns, *etc.* 1918. 8°. **7407.** pp. **9.**

—— An Introduction to Biophysics, *etc.* pp. xiii. 435. *J. & A. Churchill: London,* 1921. 8°. **07001. h. 8.**

—— Second edition, *etc.* pp. xix. 580. *J. & A. Churchill: London,* 1929 [1928]. 8°. **07001. k. 19.**

BURNS (DAWSON) *See* BURNS (James D.)

BURNS (*Mrs.* DAWSON) *See* BURNS (Cecil) *Mrs.*

BURNS (DOROTHY H.) Autumn Leaves. [Poems.] pp. 19. *A. H. Stockwell: London,* [1923.] 8°. **011645. eee. 18.**

BURNS (E. V.) *See* SIEGFRIED (André) Democracy in New Zealand. Translated . . . by E. V. Burns, *etc.* 1914. 8°. **8155. aaa. 30.**

BURNS (EDWARD)

—— Catalogue of a Series of Coins and Medals, illustrative of Scottish numismatics and history, selected from the cabinet of Thomas Coats, Esq. . . . and exhibited at a meeting of the British Association . . . Sept., 1876. Described and annotated by E. Burns. **L.P.** pp. 44. 1876. 4°. *See* COATS (Thomas) Dept. of Coins & Medals.

BURNS (Edward)

—— Coinage of Scotland, illustrated from the cabinet of Thomas Coats, Esq., of Ferguslie, and other collections. [Edited and completed by George Sim.] 3 vol. *A. & C. Black: Edinburgh*, 1887. 4°. **2261**. c. **1**.

One of forty-five copies printed on large paper.

BURNS (Edward John)

—— Some Financial Trends of Commercial Banks of Philadelphia, Pennsylvania, 1915–1941 . . . A dissertation, *etc.* pp. x. 122. *Catholic University of America Press: Washington*, 1945. 8°. **Ac.2692.y/15.**
[*Catholic University of America. Studies in Economics.* vol. 16.]

BURNS (Edward MacNall)

—— David Starr Jordan: Prophet of Freedom. [With a portrait.] pp. viii. 243. *Stanford University Press: Stanford*, [1953.] 8°. **10889**. c. **22**.

—— James Madison, philosopher of the constitution. pp. x. 212. *New Brunswick*, 1938. 8°. [*Rutgers University Studies in History.* vol. 1.] Ac. **2686**. f/3.

—— Western Civilizations: their history & their culture . . . With illustrative maps by Liam Dunne [and with plates]. pp. xx. 926. *W. W. Norton & Co.: New York*, [1941.] 8°. **9010**. ee. **16**.

BURNS (Edward Spenser) *See* Periodical Publications.—*Allesley*. The Allesley Lark . . . Edited by . . . E. S. Burns, G. D. Hardman, *etc.* [1878, *etc.*] 8°. P.P. **6145**. bh.

—— Memorials of Edward Spenser Burns . . . With special reference to his work in the service of the International African Association. [Letters and other writings, edited by J. Dawson and Cecil Burns. With a portrait.] pp. 240. *For private circulation: London*, 1886. 8°. **10827**. bbb. **13**.

BURNS (Elinor) British Imperialism in China. pp. 64. *London*, 1926. 8°. [*Labour Research Department. Colonial Series.* no. 3.] **20030**. e. **114/3**.

—— British Imperialism in Egypt. pp. 64. *London*, 1928. 8°. [*Labour Research Department. Colonial Series.* no. 5.] **20030** e. **114/5**.

—— British Imperialism in Ireland. pp. 66. *Workers' Books: Dublin*, 1931. 8°. **9508**. b. **13**.

—— British Imperialism in West Africa. pp. 64. *London*, 1927. 8°. [*Labour Research Department. Colonial Series.* no. 4.] **20030**. e. **114/4**.

—— A Call to Co-operators. pp. 19. *Communist Party: London*, 1954. 8°. W.P. **6556/209**.

—— Education. *See* Gollancz (Victor) The Making of Women. Oxford essays, *etc.* 1917. 8°. **08415**. h. **49**.

BURNS (Eliza Boardman) *See* Burnz.

BURNS (Elizabeth Rollit) Little Canadians . . . [In verse.] Illustrations by Miss Mary M. Phillips. *Desbarats & Co.: [Montreal*, 1899.] 4°. **011651**. h. **10**.
Printed on one side of the leaf only.

BURNS (Ellen Evans) The Novel Princess. A romantic farce comedy in three acts. pp. 112. *Samuel French: New York*, [1934.] 8°. **20018**. aa. **15**.

BURNS (Elmer Ellsworth)

—— Physics. A basic science. By E. E. Burns . . . Frank L. Verwiebe . . . and Herbert C. Hazel . . . Second printing. pp. xii. 656. *Chapman & Hall: London; printed in U.S.A.*, 1943. 8°. **8713**. b. **20**.

—— The Story of Great Inventions . . . With many illustrations. pp. xii. 248. *Harper & Bros.: New York & London*, 1910. 8°. **08709**. aa. **5**.

BURNS (Emile) *See* Cecilia Augusta Mary, *Consort of Frederick William, Crown Prince of Germany.* The Memoirs of the Crown Princess Cecilie, *etc.* (Translated by E. Burns.) 1931. 8°. **010705**. k. **35**.

—— *See* Engels (F.) Herr Eugen Dühring's Revolution, in Science, *etc.* (Translated by E. Burns.) [1935.] 8°. **08458**. b. **61**.

—— *See* Engels (F.) [Herr Eugen Dührings Umwälzung der Wissenschaft.] Anti-Duhring . . . Translated by E. Burns. 1943. 8°. **08074**. a. **3**.

—— *See* Engels (F.) Herr Eugen Dühring's Revolution in Science, *etc.* (Translated by E. Burns.) 1943. 8°. **08207.m.2.**

—— *See* Erckner (S.) *pseud.* Hitler's Conspiracy against Peace . . . Translated by E. Burns. 1937. 8°. **08073**. aa. **69**.

—— *See* Karlin (A. M.) [Einsame Weltreise.] The Odyssey of a Lonely Woman. Translated by E. Burns. 1933. 8°. **010028**. h. **16**.

—— *See* Liepmann (H.) [Der Frieden brach aus.] Peace Broke Out. (Translated by E. Burns.) 1932. 8°. **12556**. tt. **21**.

—— *See* Liepmann (H.) Murder—Made in Germany . . . Translated by E. Burns. 1934. 8°. **12557**. p. **13**.

—— *See* Leipmann (H.) Wanderers in the Mist. (Translated by E. Burns.) 1932. 8°. **12556**. tt. **20**.

—— *See* Lincoln (Ignatius T. T.) afterwards Chao-Kung. [Der grösste Abenteuer des xx. Jahrhunderts!?] The Autobiography of an Adventurer. (Translated by E. Burns.) 1931. 8°. **010795**. ee. **64**.

—— *See* Marx (C.) Theories of Surplus Value . . . Translated . . . by G. A. Bonner and E. Burns. 1951. 8°. **8204**. f. **28**.

—— *See* Nazhivin (I. T.) A Certain Jesus: the Gospel according to Thomas, *etc.* (Translated by E. Burns.) 1930. 8°. **012591**. aaa. **39**.

—— *See* Pointing (Horace B.) and Burns (E.) Agriculture, *etc.* 1927. 8°. **8219**. df. **18/11**.

—— *See* Spain. [*Appendix.—History and Politics.*] The Nazi Conspiracy in Spain . . . Translated . . . by E. Burns. 1937. 8°. **08042**. aa. **28**.

—— *See* Thorez (M.) France To-day and the People's Front . . . Translated . . . by E. Burns. 1936. 8°. **08052**. aa. **34**.

—— *See* Tolstoi (A. N.) *Count.* [Хождение по мукам.] Darkness and Dawn . . . Translated by E. Bone and E. Burns. 1935. 8°. **12591**. w. **24**.

BURNS (EMILE)

—— *See* TOLSTOI (A. N.) *Count*. [Петръ I.] Peter the Great . . . Translated by E. Bone and E. Burns. 1936. 8°. **12593.m.2.**

—— *See* VINOGRADOV (A. K.) [Черный консулъ.] The Black Consul. (Translated by E. Burns.) 1935. 8°. **12591**. p. **29**.

—— Abyssinia and Italy. [With a map.] pp. 223. *Victor Gollancz: London*, 1935. 8°. **20020**. c. **35**.

—— Capitalism, Communism, and the Transition. pp. 287. *Victor Gollancz: London*, 1933. 8°. **20017**. b. **6**.

—— Finance. Second edition, *etc*. pp. 24. *Labour Research Dept.: London*, [1925.] 8°. [*Syllabus Series*. no. 3.] **8282**. c. **92/3**.

—— A Handbook of Marxism. Being a collection of extracts from the writings of Marx, Engels and the greatest of their followers [i.e. N. Lenin and I. V. Dzhugashvili-Stalin] . . . The passages being chosen by E. Burns, *etc*. pp. 1087. *Victor Gollancz: London*, 1935. 8°. **8287**. a. **4**.

—— Imperialism. An outline course, *etc*. pp. 32. *Labour Research Department: London*, 1927. 8°. [*Syllabus Series*. no. 19.] **8282**. c. **92/19**.

—— The Meaning of Socialism. pp. 16. *Communist Party: London*, 1950. 8°. W.P. **6556/152**.

—— Modern Finance. pp. 64. *Oxford University Press: London*, 1920. 8°. [*World of To-day*.] **012207**. n. **2/3**.

—— Second edition, revised. pp. 64. *Oxford University Press: London*, 1922. 8°. [*World of To-day*.] **012207**. n. **2/3a**.

—— Money. pp. 94. *Victor Gollancz: London*, 1937. 8°. [*New People's Library*. vol. 1.] W.P. **4841/1**.

—— The Only Way Out. [On the contemporary economic crisis.] pp. 84. *Martin Lawrence: London*, [1932.] 8°. **8224**. r. **45**.

—— The Soviet Transition from Socialism to Communism. pp. 15. *Communist Party: London*, 1950. 8°. W.P. **6556/150**.

—— Special edition for working-class organisations. pp. 84. *Martin Lawrence: London*, [1932.] 8°. **8224**. w. **2**.

—— Russia's Productive System. pp. 288. *Victor Gollancz: London*, 1930. 8°. **08227**. ee. **80**.

—— What is Marxism? pp. 94. *Victor Gollancz: London*, 1939. 8°. [*New People's Library*. vol. 24.] W.P. **4841/24**.

—— What is Marxism? pp. 67. *Victor Gollancz: London*, 1943. 8°. **8287**. aa. **76**.

—— [What is Marxism?] An Introduction to Marxism. (New and revised edition.) pp. 63. *Lawrence & Wishart*. *London*, 1952. 8°. **8289**. m. **2**.

BURNS (EMILE) and **ROY** (F. M.)

—— The Roosevelt Illusion, *etc*. [A criticism of President F. D. Roosevelt's economic policy.] pp. 57. *Martin Lawrence: London*, 1934. 8°. **08229**. k. **76**.

BURNS (EUGENE)

—— The Last King of Paradise. [A biography of Kalakaua, King of the Hawaiian Islands.] pp. xxv. 345. *Pellegrini & Cudahy: New York*, [1952.] 8°. **010604**. bb. **36**.

BURNS (EVELINE MABEL) *See* BURNS (Arthur R.) and BURNS (E. M.) The Economic World, *etc*. 1927. 8°. **08206**. de. **13**.

—— The American Social Security System. pp. xviii. 460. *Houghton Mifflin Co.: Boston*, [1949.] 8°. **8285**. w. **72**.

—— The Social Security Act Amendments of 1950. An appendix to The American Social Security System. pp. 447–481. *Houghton, Mifflin Co.: Boston*, [1951.] 8°. **8285**. **w**. **72**.

—— British Unemployment Programs, 1920–1938, *etc*. pp. xx. 385. 1941. 8°. *See* UNITED STATES OF AMERICA.—*Social Science Research Council.—Committee on Social Security*. **08286**. k. **51**.

—— Toward Social Security. An explanation of the Social Security Act and a survey of larger issues. pp. xiii. 269. *McGraw-Hill Book Co.: New York, London*, [1936.] 8°. **8287**. cc. **57**.

—— Wages and the State, *etc*. pp. ix. 443. *P. S. King & Son: London*, 1926. 8°. [*Studies in Economics and Political Science*. no. 86.] **08207**. i. **1/84**.

BURNS (GAVIN JAMES) Glossary of Technical Terms used in Architecture and the Building Trades. pp. vii. 136. *E. & F. N. Spon: London; Spon & Chamberlain: New York*, 1895. 8°. **7817**. b. **6**.

BURNS (GEORGE) *Comedian*.

—— "French Long Underwear Maker" . . . A dramatic composition. By George Burns, Gracie Allen, Paul Henning and Keith Fowler. [*Samuel French: London*;] *Long Island City* printed, [1947.] 8°. **11792**. bb. **30**.

—— "Gracie Discovers a Movie Star." A dramatic composition. By George Burns, Gracie Allen, Paul Henning and Keith Fowler. [*Samuel French: London*;] *Long Island City* printed, [1947.] 8°. **11792**. bb. **29**.

—— "Sugar Throat Sings Again." A dramatic composition. By George Burns, Gracie Allen, Paul Henning and Keith Fowler. [*Samuel French: London*;] *Long Island City* printed, [1947.] 8°. **11792**. bb. **27**.

—— "What Every Old Husband Should Know" . . . A dramatic composition. By G. Burns, Gracie Allen, Paul Henning and Keith Fowler. [*Samuel French: London*;] *Long Island City* printed, [1947.] 8°. **11792**. bb. **31**.

—— "What Every Young Bride Should Know" . . . A dramatic composition. By George Burns, Gracie Allen, Paul Henning and Keith Fowler. [*Samuel French: London*;] *Long Island City* printed, [1947.] 8°. **11792**. bb. **28**.

BURNS (GEORGE) *D.D.* The Jewish Law: how far superseded by the Gospel. pp. 24. *Johnstone, Hunter & Co.: Edinburgh*, 1865. 8°. **4255**. aaa. **17**.

—— The National Church a National Treasure; or the Excellencies of the Scottish ecclesiastical establishment delineated; being the substance of a sermon delivered . . . on the 11th November 1834, at the opening of the Synod of Lothian and Tweeddale. pp. 48. *W. Whyte & Co.: Edinburgh*, 1835. 8°. T. **1569**. **(8.)**

BURNS (George) *D.D.*

—— Prayers for the Closet and the Family; with introductory remarks on prayer as a Christian duty. pp. 206. *Johnstone, Hunter & Co.: Edinburgh*, 1862. 16°. **3456**. b. **59**.

BURNS (*Sir* George) *Bart. See* Hodder (Edwin) Sir George Burns, Bart. His times and friends . . . With . . . portrait, *etc.* 1890. 8°. **10827**. d. **2**.

—— —— 1892. 8°. **10826**. ee. **30**.

BURNS (George J.) Address . . . at the Funeral Services of Dr. Benjamin H. Hartwell, *etc.* [With a portrait.] pp. 11. *H. S. Turner: Ayer*, [1904.] 16°. **10600**. aaa. **5**. (**1**.)

BURNS (George S.) *S.J.*

—— Fatherhood and the Future. pp. 12. *John S. Burns: Glasgow*, [1951.] 16°. **4409**. c. **55**.

—— Gibbets and Gallows. The story of Edmund Arrowsmith, S.J. [With a portrait.] pp. 86. *Burns Oates: London*, 1944. 8°. **4910**. aa. **4**.

—— Looking for Charity? [On the work and teachings of Antoine Frédéric Ozanam.] pp. 29. *Burns Oates: London*, [1944.] 8°. **4193**. e. **105**.

—— My Leader in Life. [A religious booklet for children leaving school.] pp. 96. *Burns, Oates & Co.: London*, 1942. 16°. **4398**. a. **39**.

—— Saint under Sail. The story of Francis Xavier. pp. 54 *Burns Oates: London*, [1944.] 8°. **4831**. b. **2**.

—— Short and Sharp. Retreat reflections. pp. 96. *Burns Oates: London*, [1944.] 8°. **4398**. aa. **114**.

BURNS (George Stewart) *See* Macaulay (George) *Minister of Stockwell Free Church.* The Lord's Law and Day. A review of Dr. Macleod's speech, with criticisms on a sermon preached in the Cathedral by Rev. G. S. Burns, *etc.* 1866. 8°. **4355**. aaa. **46**.

—— Teutonic and Scandinavian Religion. *W. Blackwood & Sons: Edinburgh & London*, [1882.] 8°. [*Faiths of the World.* Lecture 8.] **4466**. dd. **10/2**.

BURNS (Gerald P.)

—— Program of the Modern Camp. [By] G. P. Burns [and others], *etc.* pp. xv. 320. *Prentice-Hall: New York*, 1954. 8°. **7949**. r. **1**.
Part of the "Prentice-Hall Physical Education Series."

BURNS (Gilbert) *See* Burns (Robert) *the Poet.* [*Works.*] The Works of Robert Burns . . . Eighth edition, to which are now added, some further particulars of the author's life, new notes . . . and many other additions, by G. Burns. 1820. 8°. **1465**. h. **23**.

—— *See* Burns (Robert) *the Poet.* [*Works.*] The Works of Robert Burns . . . With . . . notes by G. Burns [and others], *etc.* 1840. 8°. **11613**. c. **4**.

—— *See* Burns (Robert) *the Poet.* [*Smaller Collections.*] The Poetical Works of Robert Burns . . . To which are prefixed, a history of the poems, by . . . G. Burns, and a sketch of his life. 1822. 12°. **11643**. a. **36**.

BURNS (Harrison) See Indiana, State of. [Laws.-I, etc.] Burns' Annotated Indiana Statutes . . . Annotated by H. Burns. 1901. 8°. **6614**. ee. **2**.

BURNS (Harry)

—— Olympic Lifting . . . A detailed analysis of the three Olympic lifts—with training schedules. [With plates.] pp. 28. *H. Burns: London*, 1946. 8°. **7917**. c. **20**.

BURNS (Islay) Select Remains of Islay Burns . . . Edited by Rev. James C. Burns. With memoir by Rev. W. G. Blackie. pp. xlvii. 397. *J. Nisbet & Co.: London*, 1874. 8°. **3755**. df. **12**.

—— Catholicism and Sectarianism. *See* Hanna (William) *LL.D., D.D.* Essays by Ministers of the Free Church of Scotland, *etc.* 1858. 8°. **12273**. d. **4**.

—— [Another edition.] (Appendix. The Theology of the Book of Common Prayer. From an article in the British and Foreign Evangelical Review.) pp. 40. *Edmonston & Douglas: Edinburgh*, 1864. 8°. **4373**. bb. **48**. (**8**.)

—— The History of the Church of Christ: with a special view to the delineation of Christian faith and life. From A.D. 1 to A.D. 313. pp. xi. 330. *T. Nelson & Sons: London*, 1862. 8°. **4532**. b. **5**.

—— Memoir of the Rev. Wm. C. Burns . . . missionary to China from the English Presbyterian Church . . . Third edition. [With a portrait.] pp. viii. 595. *J. Nisbet & Co.: London*, 1870. 8°. **4955**. bb. **28**.

—— The Pastor of Kilsyth; or, Memorials of the life and times of the Rev. W. H. Burns D.D. pp. 288. *T. Nelson & Sons: London*, 1860. 8°. **4955**. b. **19**.

—— Praxis Primaria: progressive exercises in the writing of Latin, *etc.* [With a key.] 2 pt. *Blackie & Son: London*, [1870,] 71. 8°. **12935**. bb. **19**, **20**.

—— The Sanctity of Home: being words of counsel and incitement to Christian fathers and mothers. pp. 107. *W. P. Kennedy: Edinburgh*, 1853. 12°. **4406**. c. **44**.

BURNS, afterwards BEGG (Isobel) *See* Begg (Robert B.) Isobel Burns, Mrs. Begg. A memoir, *etc.* [With a portrait.] 1891. 8°. **10825**. g. **14**.

—— —— 1894. 8°. **10827**. bbb. **30**.

BURNS (J. C.) *See* Heuvel (J. van den) The Statesmanship of Benedict xv . . . Translated by J. C. Burns. 1923. 8°. **4856**. aa. **24**.

BURNS (J. E.)

—— Adventures in Wildest Africa . . . Illustrated with third dimension pictures, *etc.* pp. 23. *W. Walker & Sons: London*, [1949.] *obl.* 4°. **7918**. aa. **155**.

BURNS (J. G.) *of the Government Fruit Research Station, Chaubattia, U.P.* Notes on Fruit Culture in the Hills. pp. 5. *Allahabad*, 1935. 8°. [*United Provinces of Agra and Oudh. Department of Agriculture. Bulletin. Fruit Series.* no. 10.] I.S. u.p. **142/15**.

BURNS (J. H.) and **GRAEME** (D. Sutherland)

—— Scottish University. [On the University of Edinburgh.] pp. xi. 177. *Darien Press: Edinburgh*, 1944. 8°. **08366**. l. **18**.

BURNS (Jabez) *See* also Marvell (Andrew) *Jun., pseud.* [i.e. J. Burns.]

—— *See* Evans (John) *LL.D., of Islington.* Evans' Sketch of the Denominations of the Christian World . . . A new edition, corrected and enlarged, with an account of several new sects . . . with explanatory and statistical notes and observations. By J. Burns. 1839. 8°. **4520**. a. **2**.

—— *See* Periodical Publications.—*London*. The Preachers' Magazine, and Pastors' Monthly Journal, *etc.* [Edited by J. Burns.] 1839, *etc.* 8°. **P.P. 835.**

—— *See* Staples (George) Macedonia . . . With an introductory essay by J. Burns. 1847. 16°. **4375. a. 49.**

—— "The Accursed Thing in our midst." The thirty-first annual temperance sermon, delivered . . . by J. Burns. pp. 16. *W. Tweedie: London*, 1871. 8°. **8435. b. 20.**

—— Second issue. *London*, [1871.] 8°. **8435. b. 65. (10.)**

—— An Appeal to the Scriptures, on the Ordinance of Baptism . . . Second edition. To which is annexed a review of the Rev. Jacob Stanley's . . . pamphlet, in defence of infant sprinkling, in a letter to that gentleman. pp. 31. *Wightman & Co.: London*, 1831. 12°. **T. 1456. (1.)**

—— The Ban of God on those who came not to the help of the Lord against the mighty. The thirty-third annual temperance sermon, preached . . . by J. Burns. (Second edition.) pp. 16. *W. Tweedie: London*, [1873.] 8°. **4479. bbb. 1. (12.)**

—— Christian Exercises for every Lord's Day Morning and Evening in the Year . . . Second edition. [With a portrait.] pp. 344. *Houlston & Wright: London*, 1859. 8°. **3456. f. 35.**

—— Christian Philosophy: or, Materials for thought. By the author of "Sketches and Skeletons of Sermons" [i.e. J. Burns], *etc.* pp. 252. 1845. 12°. *See* Christian Philosophy. **1361. i. 19.**

—— Second edition, revised and enlarged. pp. 270. *Houlston & Wright: London*, [1849.] 12°. **4406. ccc. 45.**

—— The Christian Preachers' Pocket Companion, comprising select essays on the work of the ministry . . . anecdotes of eminent preachers, with original skeletons of sermons. pp. 324. *Houlston & Stoneman: London*, 1846. 12°. **4498. a. 23.**

—— Second edition. pp. 324. *Houlston & Stoneman: London*, 1846. 12°. **1358. a. 12.**

—— The Christian's Daily Portion. *See* infra: The Golden Pot of Manna.

—— The Christian's Sketch Book . . . With an appendix, containing brief outlines of sermons . . . principally selected from the discourses of modern evangelical authors . . . Second edition. pp. xii. 352. *Printed for the Author: London*, 1829. 12°. **1026. g. 5.**

—— The Christian's Sketch-Book, second series, *etc.* pp. 328. *G. Wightman: London*, 1835. 12°. **865. h. 8.**

—— Doctrinal Conversations on Predestination, Free Will [and other questions] . . . Designed to illustrate the universal love of God, and the responbsibility [*sic*] of man. pp. 68. *Houlston & Stoneman: London*, 1849. 24°. **1355. a. 34.**

—— The Universal Love of God and Responsibility of Man, illustrated in a series of doctrinal conversations . . . New edition, revised and enlarged, with a three-fold summary of the whole. pp. 108. *Houlston & Wright: London*, 1861. 12°. **4406. cc. 10.**

—— Four Hundred Sketches and Skeletons of Sermons . . . Twelfth edition. 4 vol. *Houlston & Wright: London*, 1861, 60, 62. 8°. **4463. bb. 14.**
Vol. 2 is of the 13th edition, vol. 3 of the 11th, and vol. 4 of the 9th.

—— The Golden Pot of Manna; or, Christian's portion; containing daily exercises on the person, offices, work, and glory of the Redeemer. 2 vol. *G. Wightman: London; Hull, Harvey & Co.: Leicester*, 1837. 8°. **694. c. 3, 4.**

—— The Christian's Daily Portion, or Golden Pot of Manna . . . Fifth edition. pp. 593. *Houlston & Stoneman: London*, 1848. 8°. **4408. aaa. 36.**

—— The Good Child's Gift Book of interesting poetry, important counsels, striking anecdotes. [With illustrations.] pp. viii. 154. *Houlston & Wright: London*, 1861. 12°. **12807. a. 62.**

—— Help-Book for Travellers to the East; including Egypt, Palestine, Turkey, Greece and Italy . . . With tourist arrangements by Thomas Cook. [With maps.] pp. vi. 224. *Cook's Tourist Office: London*, 1870. 8°. **10076. b. 16.**

—— Hints to Church Members on the Duties and Responsibilities of Christian Fellowship . . . New edition, enlarged. pp. 36. *Houlston & Wright: London*, 1860. 12°. **4409. c. 53. (1.)**

—— Light for the House of Mourning: a book for the bereaved. pp. 224. *Houlston & Stoneman: London*, 1850. 8°. **4406. d. 91.**

—— Light for the Sick Room: a book for the afflicted. pp. 224. *Houlston & Stoneman: London*, 1850. 8°. **4405. f. 63.**

—— The Marriage Gift Book and Bridal Token. pp. xii. 10–320. *Houlston & Wright: London*, 1863. 8°. **8415. cc. 21.**

—— Missionary Enterprises in Many Lands. With a brief account of the rise and progress of missions . . . Third edition, illustrated by engravings on wood. pp. 416. *Knight & Son: London*, [1854.] 16°. **1366. b. 9.**
With an additional titlepage.

—— The Mothers of the Wise and Good: with select essays on maternal duties and influence. pp. 304. *Houlston & Stoneman: London*, 1846. 8°. **1387. b. 40.**

—— None but Jesus: or, Christ all and in all. pp. 128. *Houlston & Stoneman: London*, 1849. 32°. **4405. b. 7.**

—— Sixth thousand. pp. 136. *Houlston & Wright: London*, [1863.] 32°. **4404. aa. 58.**

—— Notes of a Tour in the United States and Canada, in the summer and autumn of 1847. pp. 180. *Houlston & Stoneman: London*, 1848. 12°. **10411. b. 12.**

—— One Hundred and Fifty Original Sketches and Plans of Sermons, comprising various series on special and peculiar subjects, adapted for week evening services. pp. 327. *Rd. Dickinson: London*, 1866. 8°. **4498. bb. 8.**

—— One Hundred Sketches and Skeletons of Sermons. By a Dissenting Minister [i.e. J. Burns]. vol. 1, 2, 4. 1836, 39. 12°. *See* Sketches. **694. b. 12, 13, 15.**

—— The Pulpit Cyclopædia; and Christian Minister's Companion. By the author of "Sketches and Skeletons of Sermons" [i.e. J. Burns], *etc.* 4 vol. 1844. 8°. *See* Encyclopaedias. **1358. h. 1.**

—— A Retrospect of Forty-five Years' Christian Ministry . . . With papers on theological and other subjects in prose and verse. pp. 444. *Houlston & Co.: London*, 1875. 8°. **4955. de. 9.**

BURNS (JABEZ)

—— Sermons, chiefly designed for family reading, and village worship. pp. 358. *Houlston & Stoneman: London,* 1842. 12°. **1357. d. 2.**

—— Sermons designed for the Sick Room, Family Reading, and Village Worship. pp. 436. *Houlston & Stoneman: London,* 1854. 8°. **4462. e. 9.**
A different work from the preceding.

—— Sketches of Discourses for Sunday Schools and Village Preaching . . . New edition, revised and enlarged. pp. 284. *Houlston & Wright: London,* 1860. 12°. **4463. a. 11.**

—— Sketches of Sermons chiefly on Christian Missions, original and selected. pp. vi. 360. *Houlston & Stoneman: London,* 1851. 12°. **4463. bb. 11.**

—— Sketches of Sermons designed for Special Occasions . . . New and enlarged edition. With additional sketches on "Revivals of Religion," "Christian Catholicity," etc. etc. pp. 331. *Houlston & Wright: London,* 1860. 12°. **4463. bb. 13.**

—— Sketches of Sermons on Christian Missions. Original and selected. By the author of "Four Hundred Sketches and Skeletons of Sermons" [i.e. J. Burns], *etc.* pp. vi. 360. 1845. 12°. *See* CHRISTIAN MISSIONS. **4461. bb. 9.**

—— Sketches of Sermons on Scripture Characters and Incidents. pp. 364. *Houlston & Stoneman: London,* 1851. 12°. **4461. e. 7.**

—— Sketches of Sermons on the Parables and Miracles of Christ: the Essentials of Saving Religion, &c. pp. iv. 10–316. *Houlston & Stoneman: London,* 1847. 12°. **4460. b. 6.**

—— Sketches of Sermons on Types and Metaphors . . . Fourth thousand, enlarged. pp. viii. 315. *Houlston & Wright: London,* 1860. 8°. **4463. bb. 12.**

—— Two Hundred Sketches and Outlines of Sermons as preached . . . since 1866. [With a portrait.] pp. 424. *Dickinson & Higham: London,* 1875. 8°. **4499. bb. 3.**

—— The Universal Love of God and Responsibility of Man, illustrated in a series of doctrinal conversations. *See* supra: Doctrinal Conversations, *etc.*

—— The Various Forms of Religion. A series of Lord's-Day evening discourses, *etc.* pp. 156. *Houlston & Stoneman: London,* 1851. 12°. **4406. b. 23.**

—— The Youthful Christian: containing instructions, counsels, cautions, and examples. pp. viii. 172. *Houlston & Stoneman: London,* 1842. 12°. **1361. h. 21.**

—— Youthful Piety, exhibited in its principles, excellencies, and happy results . . . Second series. [With illustrations.] pp. 160. *Houlston & Stoneman: London,* 1849. 32°. **4903. b. 54.**

BURNS (JAMES) *Bailie of Glasgow.* Memoirs by James Burns . . . 1644–1661. (The Glorious and Miraculous Battel at York . . . 1644.—The Diary of Mr. Robert Douglas, when with the Scotish army in England. M.DC.XLIV.) [Edited by James Maidment.] pp. xii. 80. **L.P.** *Thomas Stevenson: Edinburgh,* 1832. 8°. G. **14788.**

—— [A reissue.] *See* SCOTLAND. [*Appendix.—History and Politics.*] Historical Fragments, relative to Scotish affairs, from 1635 to 1664. 1833. 8°. **1325. c. 3.**

BURNS (JAMES) *Minister of Stoke Newington Presbyterian Church.* *See* MEHARRY (John B.) Sermons. With memoir by the Rev. J. Burns. 1917. 8°. **04478. ee. 1.**

—— The Christ Face in Art . . . With sixty-two illustrations. pp. xxii. 252. *Duckworth & Co.: London,* 1907. 8°. **7856. h. 18.**

—— The Graves of the Fallen. pp. 15. *J. Clarke & Co.: London,* [1918.] 16°. **04376. de. 44.**

—— The Happy Warrior. An interpretation of G. F. Watts's picture. *J. Clarke & Co.: London,* [1915.] 8°. **7854. aaa. 40.**

—— Illustrations for Preachers and Teachers, taken from literature, poetry and art. pp. 253. *J. Clarke & Co.: London,* [1925.] 8°. **4499. eee. 4.**

—— Illustrations from Art for Pulpit and Platform. pp. 322. *J. Clarke & Co.: London,* 1912. 8°. **07806. f. 27.**

—— Laws of Life and Destiny. Addresses to men. pp. vii. 184. *Robert Scott: London,* 1913. 8°. **4464. ee. 13.**

—— Laws of the Upward Life. Addresses to men. pp. vi. 185. *Robert Scott: London,* 1914. 8°. **4464. ee. 20.**

—— A New Pulpit Manual, *etc.* pp. 207. *J. Clarke & Co.: London,* [1936.] 8°. **03456. eee. 104.**

—— Order of Memorial Service for those fallen in the War, *etc.* pp. 15. *J. Clarke & Co.: London,* [1917.] 8°. **3456. ccc. 53.**

—— A Pulpit Manual. Containing forms of prayers used in the conduct of public worship; suggestive summaries; orders of service, *etc.* pp. 201. *J. Clarke & Co.: London,* 1914. 8°. **3408. df. 26.**

—— Revivals, their Laws and Leaders. pp. xii. 312. *Hodder & Stoughton: London,* 1909. 8°. **4530. eee. 15.**

—— Sermons in Art by the Great Masters. [With plates.] pp. viii. 276. *Duckworth & Co.: London,* 1908. 8°. **7856. h. 22.**

—— Sir Galahad. A call to the heroic. [Thoughts suggested by G. F. Watts's picture.] pp. 31. *J. Clarke & Co.: London,* [1915.] 8°. **8411. l. 11.**

—— To Them That Mourn. God's food for the afflicted. pp. 30. *G. Stoneman: London,* [1896.] 16°. **4375. de. 13.**

BURNS (JAMES) *Proprietor of the Spiritual Institution, London.*

—— *See* BRADLAUGH (Charles) Human Immortality proved by Facts. Report of a two nights' debate on modern spiritualism, between . . . C. Bradlaugh . . . and . . . J. Burns, *etc.* [1873?] 8°. **8635. a. 13.**

—— *See* DODS (John B.) The Philosophy of Mesmerism and Electrical Psychology . . . Edited by J. Burns. 1876. 8°. **7410. dg. 29.**

—— *See* DODS (John B.) Six Lectures on the Philosophy of Mesmerism . . . English edition, thoroughly revised, with notes by J. Burns. 1876. 8°. **7306. aa. 10. (4.)**

—— *See* EDMONDS (John W.) Letters and Tracts on Spiritualism . . . Edited by J. Burns. [1875.] 8°. **8631. eee. 1.**

—— *See* WEAVER (George S.) Lectures on Mental Science . . . With supplementary chapter by J. Burns. 1876. 8°. **7410. dg. 30.**

BURNS (JAMES) *Proprietor of the Spiritual Institution, London.*

—— Spiritualism and the Gospel of Jesus. pp. 4. *Progressive Library: London,* [1873.] 8°. [*Seed Corn.* no. 2.] **8631.** aaa. **1.**

BURNS (JAMES) *Publisher.* Burns's Standard Reading-Books, adapted to the requirements of the revised code, and containing exercises in writing, spelling, and arithmetic. 5 bk. *Burns, Lambert & Oates: London,* [1867.] 8°. **12202.** de. **6.**

—— Burns's Standard Reading-Books, adapted to the requirements of the code of 1871, *etc.* 6 vol. *Burns & Oates: London,* [1879.] 8°. **12200.** aaa. **10.**

BURNS (JAMES) *Writer on Lawn Tennis.* How to Play Tennis. [With plates.] pp. 112. *Outing Publishing Co.: New York,* 1916. 8°. **7904.** aa. **38.**

BURNS (*Sir* JAMES) *K.C.M.G.*

—— *See* MACINTYRE (Ronald George) The Story of Burnside, *etc.* [On the children's homes founded by Sir J. Burns. With a portrait.] 1947. 8°. **08366.** o. **57.**

BURNS (JAMES ALEXANDER) Useful Engineer's Constants for the Slide Rule, and how they are obtained. pp. 23. *C. Combridge: Birmingham,* [1903.] 8°. **08533.** df. **48.** (**4.**)

—— Second edition. pp. 36. *J. A. Burns: Glasgow,* [1917.] 8°. **08532.** df. **14.**

—— Third edition. pp. 78. *P. Marshall & Co.: London,* [1921.] 8°. **08532.** de. **69.**

BURNS (JAMES ALOYSIUS) Catholic Education. A study of conditions. pp. ix. 205. *Longmans & Co.: New York,* 1917. 8°. **8385.** df. **25.**

BURNS (JAMES C.) *See* BURNS (Islay) Select Remains of Islay Burns . . . Edited by J. C. Burns, *etc.* 1874. 8°. **3755.** df. **12.**

—— The Encouragements which Christians have to undertake the Conversion of the Jews. *See* ENGLAND.—*British Society for the Propagation of the Gospel among the Jews.* Lectures on the Conversion of the Jews, *etc.* 1843. 8°. **1352.** b. **11.**

—— Memorial of the Late James Maitland Hog, Esq. of Newliston. pp. 71. *John Maclaran: Edinburgh,* 1858. 8°. **10860.** aa. **59.** (**3.**)

BURNS (JAMES DAWSON) *See* BURNS (Cecil) *Mrs.* Memorial Leaves, *etc.* [Edited by J. D. Burns.] 1898. 8°. **4907.** i. **1.**

—— *See* BURNS (Edward S.) Memorials of Edward Spenser Burns, *etc.* [Edited by J. D. and C. Burns.] 1886. 8°. **10827.** bbb. **13.**

—— *See* CAINE (William S.) Local Option. By Rev. D. Burns, W. S. Caine, *etc.* 1885. 8°. **8139.** bbb. **44/6.**

—— —— 1896. 8°. **8139.** bbb. **44/6a.**

—— *See* EPHEMERIDES. Graham's Temperance Guide and Handbook for 1866. (Graham's Temperance Guide, Hand-book, and Almanack for 1867[–1875]. Edited by the Rev. D. Burns.) 1866, *etc.* 8°. P.P. **2485.** ql.

—— *See* HODGSON (Evelyn G.) Scripture v. Total Abstinence. A public discussion between the Rev. E. G. Hodgson . . . and the Rev. D. Burns, *etc.* [1870.] 8°. **8435.** cc. **52.** (**10.**)

BURNS (JAMES DAWSON)

—— *See* LEES (Frederic R.) and BURNS (D.) The Temperance Bible-Commentary, *etc.* 1868. 8°. **3126.** bb. **21.**

—— —— 1868. 8°. **3128.** ff. **1.**

—— —— 1872. 8°. **3128.** ff. **2.**

—— —— 1876. 8°. **8435.** e. **3.**

—— —— 1880. 8°. **8435.** e. **5.**

—— —— 1894. 8°. **8435.** e. **23.**

—— The Alpha Beta of the Temperance Question . . . Reprinted from the "Good Templars' Watchword." pp. 8. *J. Kempster & Co.: London,* [1877.] 16°. **8436.** aa. **14.** (**8.**)

—— Baptists and the Temperance Reform. *See* CLIFFORD (John) The English Baptists, *etc.* 1881. 8°. **4136.** aaa. **12.**

—— The Bible and Temperance Reform, *etc.* pp. 48. *Lees & Rapier Memorial Trustees: London,* [1906.] 8°. [*Lees and Raper Memorial Lecture.* no. 7.] **8435.** de. **48/7.**

—— Bible Temperance and the Revised Version of the Old Testament. A statement and review. [Reprinted from the Temperance Record.] pp. 16. *National Temperance Publication Depôt; Alliance Offices: London,* 1885. 8°. **8436.** aaa. **49.** (**12.**)

—— Second edition. pp. 16. *National Temperance Publication Depot: London,* 1885. 8°. **8435.** a. **108.** (**7.**)

—— Christendom and the Drink Curse: an appeal to the Christian world for efficient action against the causes of intemperance. pp. xii. 333. *Partridge & Co.: London,* 1875. 8°. **8435.** bbb. **4.**

—— The Liquor Traffic and Legislative Action. From "Christendom and the Drink Curse." pp. 54. *J. & W. Rider: London,* [1880?] 8°. **8435.** cc. **58.** (**3.**)

—— Country Walks and Temperance Talks. Presenting in conversational form a full discussion and review of all the principal aspects of the temperance question. pp. 172. *Ideal Publishing Union: London,* 1901. 8°. **8436.** f. **20.**

—— The Drinking System our National Curse, *etc.* pp. 50. [1886.] *See* PERIODICAL PUBLICATIONS.—*Maidstone.* The Temperance Worker, *etc.* vol. 20. [1874, *etc.*] 8°. P.P. **1161.** e.

—— England and Madagascar. A letter to . . . Earl Granville, *etc.* pp. 8. *Kegan Paul & Co.: London,* [1883.] 8°. **8138.** df. **12.** (**9.**)

—— [Another copy.] **8028.** de. **23.** (**2.**)

—— The Juvenile Temperance Catechism, *etc.* pp. 31. *Curtice & Co.: London,* [1873.] 16°. **8435.** aa. **88.**

—— The Late Mrs. Clara Lucas Balfour. The memorial discourse, preached . . . by the Rev. D. Burns . . . With the address in Paddington Cemetery, delivered . . . by Rev. J. W. Todd. pp. 24. *S. W. Partridge & Co.: London,* [1878.] 8°. **4906.** df. **7.** (**8.**)

—— Local Option . . . A new standard edition [of the work by W. S. Caine, W. Hoyle and D. Burns]. pp. 133. *Swan Sonnenschein & Co.: London,* 1909. 8°. [*The Imperial Parliament.* vol. 6.] **8139.** bbb. **44/6b.**

—— Mormonism, Explained and Exposed. pp. 56. *Houlston & Stoneman: London,* 1853. 12°. **4139.** c. **22.**

BURNS (James Dawson)

—— National Sobriety discussed in a Dialogue between a Publican, a Clergyman, and a Physician. pp. 14. *W. Tweedie: London*, [1870.] 8°. **8435.** bb. **19.**

—— No Scripture Sanction for Intoxicating Drink, *etc.* pp. 32. [1886.] *See* Periodical Publications.—*Maidstone.* The Temperance Worker, *etc.* vol. 20. [1874, *etc.*] 8°. P.P. **1161.** e.

—— Objections to the Temperance Movement: a lecture, *etc.* pp. 22. *W. Tweedie: London; W. Bremner: Manchester*, [1853.] 12°. **8435.** c. **9.**

—— Oliver Cromwell, and other poems. pp. 104. *S. W. Partridge & Co.: London*, [1887.] 8°. **11653.** k. **48.**

—— The Other Side: an examination of an article in the "National Review" . . . entitled "Intemperance; its causes & cures." pp. 36. *United Kingdom Alliance: Manchester*, [1860.] 8°. **8435.** cc. **11.**

—— Pen-Pictures of some Temperance Notables. Five temperance Johns, and other sketches. pp. 160. *National Temperance Publication Depôt: London*, 1895. 8°. **8436.** f. **4.**

—— The Popedom defined and defended by the Pope. A dispassionate review of the Encyclical of Pope Leo xiii. [dated 29 June 1896] upon the unity of the Church—De unitate Ecclesiæ. pp. 64. *Ideal Publishing Union: London*, 1897. 8°. **3942.** c. **3.** (**6.**)

—— Rays of Sacred Song for the Church and the Home. pp. 171. *S. W. Partridge & Co.: London*, [1884.] 8°. **11653.** i. **40.**

—— Rev. Charles Lee's Objections to Total Abstinence answered . . . in a lecture . . . Also the correspondence between the Rev. C. Lee . . . and the Committee of the Camden Temperance Society. pp. 12. *Job Caudwell: London*, 1866. 8°. **8435.** bbb. **13.**

—— Sacramental Wines: a review of the declaration of the Pan-Anglican Episcopate on Communion Wine. The Temperance of Total Abstinence: showing the true relation of temperance to intoxicating liquors. [Two articles.] pp. 16. *National Temperance Publication Depôt: London*, [1889.] 8°. **8436.** bb. **27.** (**3.**)

—— Scripture Light on Intoxicating Liquors. A sermon, *etc.* pp. 16. *W. Tweedie: London*, [1859.] 8°. **4478.** a. **12.**

—— Statistics of the Liquor Traffic. An examination of Professor Levi's letters to M. T. Bass, Esq., M.P., and of a paper read by Professor Levi before the Statistical Society of London . . . upon "The Capital Invested in the Liquor Trades" . . . Re-printed from the "Alliance News," with additions. pp. 32. *United Kingdom Alliance: London*, 1872. 8°. **8435.** h. **4.** (**6.**)

—— Temperance Ballads, with other metrical compositions, for recitation by young teetotalers. Also hymns for temperance meetings. [With a portrait.] pp. 52. *National Temperance Depôt: London*, [1884.] 8°. **8436.** a. **33.** (**2.**)

—— [A reissue.] *London*, [1888.] 8°. **8436.** aa. **36.**

—— The Temperance Dictionary. no. 1–34. pp. 544. *Job Caudwell: London*, [1861–64.] 8°. **8435.** aa. **92.**
No more published.

BURNS (James Dawson)

—— Temperance History. A consecutive narrative of the rise, development, and extension of the Temperance Reform, *etc.* 2 vol. *National Temperance Publication Depôt: London*, [1889–91.] 8°. **2236.** c. **17.**
Published in parts. Imperfect; wanting the table of contents of vol. 1 *and the indexes to the whole work in vol.* 2.

—— Temperance in the Victorian Age, *etc.* pp. 208. *Ideal Publishing Union: London*, 1897. 8°. **8436.** ee. **4.**

—— Think! A reply to Lord Bramwell's plea for "Drink." pp. 28. *National Temperance Publication Depôt; Alliance Offices: London*, 1885. 8°. **8436.** aaa. **49.** (**13.**)

—— The Vital Statistics of Total Abstinence. pp. 16. *National Temperance Publication Depôt: London*, [1884.] 8°. **8436.** aaa. **49.** (**5.**)

—— Why should Moderate Drinkers become Abstainers? The question answered. pp. 16. *National Temperance Publication Depôt: London*, [1883.] 8°. **8435.** de. **11.** (**7.**)

BURNS (James Drummond) *See* Hamilton (James), *Minister of the National Scotch Church, Regent Square.* Memoir and Remains of the Rev. James D. Burns, *etc.* [With a portrait.] 1869. 8°. **3752.** aa. **14.**

—— The Climax; or, No condemnation and no separation. A sermon . . . With an illustration [in verse] by another hand. pp. 24. *George Hunt: London*, [1864.] 8°. **4478.** aa. **119.** (**16.**)

—— The Evening Hymn. [A collection of hymns and prayers. By J. D. Burns.] pp. 128. 1857. 8°. *See* Evening Hymn. **3437.** d. **13.**

—— The Heavenly Jerusalem; or, Glimpses within the gates. pp. 130. *T. Nelson & Sons: London*, 1856. 8°. **4407.** b. **63.**

—— The Vision of Prophecy, and other poems. pp. 313. *Johnstone & Hunter: Edinburgh*, 1854. 12°. **11648.** b. **1.**

—— Second edition. pp. x. 325. *Edmonston & Douglas: Edinburgh*, 1858. 8°. **11651.** b. **2.**

—— Poems . . . Second edition, re-issued [of "The Vision of Prophecy, and other poems"]. pp. x. x. 325. *Edmonston & Douglas: Edinburgh*, 1865. 8°. **11640.** de. **7.**

—— Reminiscences of the late Rev. James D. Burns . . . From the 'Weekly Review,' *etc.* pp. 20. [1864.] 8°. **4905.** aa. **30.**

BURNS (James Golder) The Chosen Twelve. [Sermons.] pp. 191. *J. Clarke & Co.: London*, [1915.] 8°. **4479.** k. **9.**

—— Through a Padre's Spectacles . . . Second impression. pp. 187. *J. Clarke & Co.: London*, 1917. 8°. **9083.** ee. **42.**

BURNS (James Henry Laurence)

—— Character-Building. A series of readings for moral instruction periods, *etc.* (Second impression.) pp. 61. *United Society for Christian Literature: London & Redhill*, 1941. 8°. **8412.** aa. **12.**

—— Okugunjulwa. Ebisomesebwa mu biseera eby'okuyigiriza eby' empisa . . . Kyakyusibwa S. Sessanga. pp. 51. *Lutterworth Press: London*, 1950. 8°. **08407.** ee. **68.**

BURNS (James Henry Laurence)

—— [Character Building.] Ujenzi wa tabia. Kitabu kimeandikwa na J. H. L. Burns. Kimefasiriwa na J. K. Lukindo. pp. 48. *United Society for Christian Literature: London,* 1950. 8°. **12912**. f. **43**.

BURNS (James Jesse)

—— How to Teach Reading and Composition. [With a portrait.] pp. 160. *American Book Co.: New York,* [1901.] 8°. **11805**. c. **38**.

BURNS (James Joseph)

—— The Colonial Agents of New England . . . A dissertation, *etc.* pp. v. 156. *Catholic University of America: Washington,* 1935. 8°. **9555**. pp. **26**.

BURNS (James MacGregor)

—— Congress on Trial. The legislative process and the administrative state. pp. xiv. 224. *Harper & Bros: New York,* [1949.] 8°. **8177**. l. **9**.

—— [Another copy.] Congress on Trial, *etc.* *New York,* [1949.] 8°. **08176**. c. **13**.

BURNS (James MacGregor) and **PELTASON** (Jack Walter)

—— Government by the People. Dynamics of American national, state, and local government. Second edition. (Third printing.) [With illustrations and a bibliography.] pp. xxiv. 1070. *Prentice-Hall: New York,* 1954. 8°. **8178**. cc. **7**.
The verso of the titlepage bears the date 1955.

BURNS (James Pennington) *See* Colton, *Lancashire.* The Registers of Colton Parish Church . . . Edited by . . . A. A. Williams . . . and J. P. Burns. 1891. 8°. **9914**. bb. **11**.

—— Colton Charities. *See* Cartmel. The Rural Deanery of Cartmel . . . its churches and endowments, *etc.* 1892. 8°. **4705**. cc. **12**.

BURNS (Jean) *See* Mauchline.—*Jean Armour Burns Houses.* Jean Armour Burns Houses, Mauchline. Historical note and catalogue of manuscripts, portraits and other relics, *etc.* 1936. 8°. **10858**. a. **17**.

—— Death and Character of Mrs. Burns. From "Dumfries and Galloway Courier," *etc.* *See* Lockhart (John G.) Life of Robert Burns, *etc.* 1871. 8°. **10856**. aa. **23**.

BURNS (Jean D.) *See* Hog (Harriet C.) Supposing that Lots of Things were True . . . With pictures by J. D. Burns. 1929. 8°. **11643**. n. **28**.

BURNS (John) *of Monaghan.* An Historical and Chronological Remembrancer of all remarkable occurrences, from the Creation to . . . 1775. The lives and actions of the greatest patriarchs, philosophers, heroes, heroines, monarchs, *etc.* pp. 504. *Printed for the Author: Dublin,* 1775. 8°. G. **16610**.

—— [Another copy.] **580**. d. **15**.
The titlepage is slightly mutilated.

BURNS (John) *Regius Professor of Surgery in Glasgow University.* The Anatomy of the Gravid Uterus, with practical inferences relative to pregnancy and labour. pp. xxi. 248. *University Press: Glasgow,* 1799. 8°. **1178**. h. **6**. (**7**.)

—— Christian Fragments; or, Remarks on the nature, precepts, and comforts of religion. pp. xii. 260. *Longman & Co.: London,* 1844. 8°. **1361**. d. 4.

BURNS (John) *Regius Professor of Surgery in Glasgow University.*

—— Dissertations on Inflammation. 2 vol. *John Murdoch: Glasgow,* 1800. 8°. **1165**. i. **13**.

—— Observations on Abortion . . . Second edition. pp. 173. *Longman, Hurst, Rees & Orme: London,* 1807. 8°. **7582**. aaa. **21**.

—— The Principles of Christian Philosophy . . . Third edition. pp. vii. 422. *Longman & Co.: London,* 1829. 12°. **4402**. cc. **17**.

—— Fifth edition. pp. ix. 452. *Longman & Co.: London,* 1836. 12°. **1119**. b. **28**.

—— The Principles of Midwifery; including the diseases of women and children . . . Third edition, greatly enlarged. pp. xvi. 619 [639]. *Longman & Co.: London,* 1814. 8°. **1177**. i. **4**.

—— Sixth edition, enlarged. pp. xx. 801. *Longman & Co.: London,* 1824. 8°. **1177**. i. **5**.

—— Eighth edition, revised and greatly enlarged. pp. xx. 806. *Longman & Co.: London,* 1832. 8°. **1177**. i. **6**.

—— Ninth edition, greatly enlarged. pp. xxiv. 845. *Longman & Co.: London,* 1837. 8°. **1177**. i. **7**.

—— Traité des accouchements, des maladies des femmes et des Enfants . . . Traduit de l'anglais, sur la neuvième édition, *etc.* pp. 536. *Paris,* 1840. 8°. [*Encyclopédie des sciences médicales.*] **07305**. cc. **3/7**.

—— The Principles of Surgery. 2 vol. *Longman & Co.: London,* 1831, 38. 8°. **782**. h. **12**, **13**.

BURNS (John) *Temperance Lecturer.* Good Company; the Commercial Room; and, the Bottle. pp. 40. *W. Tweedie; Horsell & Caudwell: London,* 1860. 8°. **8435**. c. **56**. (**9**.)

BURNS (John) *Writer to the Signet.* *See* Currie (James G.) The Confirmation of Executors in Scotland . . . Fourth edition, revised and in part rewritten by J. Burns. 1923. 8°. **06583**. i. **6**.

—— *See* Encyclopaedias. Encyclopædia of Scottish Legal Styles . . . Joint editors: J. Keith . . . J. Burns. 1935, *etc.* 8°. **06583.f.1.**

—— Burns's Income-Tax Guide. *See* infra: Chambers's Income-Tax Guide.

—— Chambers's Income-Tax Guide, *etc.* pp. 196. *W. & R. Chambers: London, Edinburgh,* 1917. 8°. **6427**. df. **21**.

—— Second edition, enlarged, *etc.* pp. 272. *W. & R. Chambers: London, Edinburgh,* 1918. 8°. **6427**. df. **26**.

—— Fourth edition . . . enlarged, *etc.* pp. 284. *W. & R. Chambers: London, Edinburgh,* 1920. 8°. **6427**. df. **44**.

—— Burns's Income Tax Guide. Fifth edition, covering 1923 budget, *etc.* pp. iv. 289. *W. Green & Son: Edinburgh,* 1923. 8°. **6427**. p. **1**.

—— Sixth edition, covering 1924 budget, *etc.* pp. ix. 289. *W. Green & Son: Edinburgh,* 1924. 8°. **6427**. p. **7**.

—— Income-Tax Guide . . . Seventh edition, covering 1928 budget. pp. 247. *Richards Press: London,* 1928. 8°. **6427**. b. **55**.

BURNS (JOHN) *Writer to the Signet.*

—— Seventh edition. With particulars of the changes under the 1930 budget. pp. 247. *Richards Press: London,* [1931.] 8°. **6425**. p. **12**.

—— Burns's Income Tax Guide . . . Eighth edition. pp. x. 220. *Sir I. Pitman & Sons: London,* 1933. 8°. **6425**. pp. **14**.

—— Income Tax Guide . . . Ninth edition. pp. x. 214. *Sir I. Pitman & Sons: London,* 1935. 8°. **6425**. t. **8**.

—— The Conveyancing Guide, being explanations and forms relative to practice under the Conveyancing—Scotland—Act, 1924. pp. xi. 116. *W. Green & Son: Edinburgh,* 1924. 8°. **6583**. aaa. **33**.

—— The Conveyancing Guide, *etc.* pp. xi. 116. *W. Green & Son: Edinburgh,* 1925. 8°. **6584**. c. **2**.

—— Conveyancing Practice according to the Law of Scotland. pp. xxxv. 765. *W. Green & Sons: Edinburgh,* 1899. 8°. **6573**. e. **6**.

—— Second edition. pp. xxiii. 976. *W. Green & Sons: Edinburgh,* 1904. 8°. **6573**. i. **13**.

—— Third edition. pp. xxiii. 998. *W. Green & Son: Edinburgh,* 1926. 8°. **6583**. ee. **6**.

—— The Extinction of Casualties: being a commentary on the Feudal Casualties—Scotland—Act, 1914. pp. xi. 132. *W. Green & Son: Edinburgh,* 1914. 8°. **6573**. g. **17**.

—— Second edition. pp. xii. 197. *W. Green & Son: Edinburgh,* 1916. 8°. **06583**. h. **2**.

—— Handbook of Conveyancing. Second edition. pp. viii. 494. *W. Green & Sons: Edinburgh & London,* 1900. 8°. **6306**. g. **13**.

—— Third edition. pp. iv. 375. *W. Green & Son: Edinburgh,* 1924. 8°. **6306**. ppp. **9**.

—— Fourth edition. pp. iv. 362. *W. Green & Son: Edinburgh,* 1932. 8°. **6305**. p. **18**.

—— Fifth edition. pp. iv. 400. *W. Green & Son: Edinburgh,* 1938. 8°. **6305**. ppp. **3**.

—— Income-Tax Guide. *See* supra: Chambers's Income-Tax Guide.

BURNS (*Right Hon.* JOHN)

—— *See* BURGESS (Joseph) *Socialist.* John Burns: the rise and progress of a Right Honourable. [With portraits.] 1911. 8°. **10862**. a. **61**.

—— *See* BURGESS (Joseph) *Socialist.* John Burns: the Rise and Progress of a Right Honourable, *etc.* [With portraits.] 1911. 8°. **10826**. de. **40**.

—— *See* COLE (George D. H.) John Burns. [With a portrait.] 1943. 8°. **10804.s.12/3.**

—— *See* GRUBB (Arthur P.) From Candle Factory to British Cabinet. The life story of the Right Hon. John Burns, *etc.* [With portraits.] 1908. 8°. **010826**. de. **28**.

—— *See* KENT (William R.G.) John Burns. Labour's lost leader. A biography, *etc.* [With portraits.] 1950. 8°. **10862**. c. **18**.

BURNS (*Right Hon.* JOHN)

—— *See* KNOTT (G. H.) *M.A.* Mr. John Burns, M.P. [With a portrait.] 1901. 32°. **10803**. a. **24/3**.

—— *See* MACCARTHY (Justin) British Political Portraits. (v. John Burns.) 1903. 8°. **10803**. h. **25**.

—— *See* PIMENOVA (E. K.) Джонъ Бёрнсъ вождь рабочей партіи въ Англіи. 1908. 8°. **10803**. d. **18**. **(2.)**

—— Address . . . delivered at the National Conference on Infantile Mortality held at the Caxton Hall, Westminster, on the 13th and 14th June, 1906. pp. 12. [1906.] 8°. **07305**. m. **8**. **(6.)**

—— Address given . . . at the Opening of the Tudor Barn and Art Gallery at the Well Hall Pleasaunce on Saturday, May 23rd, 1936. [1936.] 8°. *See* LONDON.—II. *Borough Councils.—Woolwich.* **012301**. ee. **56**.

—— Brains Better than Bets or Beer. (A speech.) pp. 16. *London,* 1902. 8°. [*Clarion Pamphlet.* no. 36.] **08275.m.44.**

—— Labour and Drink, *etc.* pp. 51. *London,* [1904.] 8°. [*Lees and Raper Memorial Lecture.* no. 5.] **8435**. de. **48/5**.

—— Labour and Free Trade. pp. 19. *Kent & Matthews: London,* [1903.] 8°. **08225**. k. **22**. **(3.)**

—— The Liberal Government and the Condition of the People. A speech delivered . . . at Bradford, on November 11th, 1912. pp. 11. *Liberal Publication Department: London,* 1912. 8°. **12302**. bb. **29**.

—— The Man with the Red Flag, being the speech delivered at the Old Bailey by J. Burns, when tried for seditious conspiracy on April 9th, 1886 . . . With portrait. pp. 24. *Modern Press: London,* [1886.] 8°. **08275**. ee. **22**. **(4.)**

—— Municipal Socialism. A reply by Mr. John Burns, M.P., to "The Times." pp. 15. *London,* 1902. 8°. [*Clarion Pamphlet.* no. 37.] **08275.m.44.**

—— Speech delivered . . . on "The Liverpool Congress," at a meeting held at . . . Battersea . . . September 21, 1890, *etc.* [With a portrait.] pp. 31. *Green, McAllan & Feilden: London,* 1890. 8°. **8139**. bb. **51**. **(5.)**

—— Tragedy of Toil. (Labour's death roll.) pp. 24. *London,* 1899. 8°. [*Clarion Pamphlet.* no. 29.] **08275.m.44.**

—— The Unemployed. (Reprinted, with additions, from "The Nineteenth Century.") pp. 18. *London,* 1893. 8°. [*Fabian Tracts.* no. 47.] **8275.dd.7/47.**

BURNS (JOHN ALAN) *Baron Inverclyde.* Porpoises and People. [Accounts of two yacht-cruises. With plates.] pp. 229. *Halton & Truscott Smith: London,* 1930. 8°. **10496**. aa. **66**.

BURNS (JOHN FRANCIS)

—— *See* O'SULLIVAN (Jeremiah F.) and BURNS (J. F.) Medieval Europe. 1943. 8°. **09073**. dd. **43**.

—— Controversies between Royal Governors and their Assemblies in the Northern American Colonies. pp. 447. *Privately printed: Boston,* 1923. 8°. **9551**. d. **19**.

BURNS (JOHN HENRY) *See* also RAY (X.) *pseud.* [i.e. J. H. Burns.]

—— Our Child. (Reprint of a chapter from "Love: an outspoken guide to happy marriage" [originally published under the pseudonym X-Ray].) pp. 20. *C. W. Daniel Co.: London,* 1935. 8°. **07580**. bbb. **27**.

BURNS (JOHN HENRY)

—— A Vision of Education. Being an imaginary verbatim report of the first interplanetary conference, *etc.* pp. 112. *Williams & Norgate: London,* 1929. 8°. **08311**. c. **17**.

BURNS (JOHN HORNE)

—— A Cry of Children. pp. v. 250. *Secker & Warburg: London,* 1952. 8°. **12731**. i. **11**.

—— The Gallery. [A novel.] pp. vii. 342. *Secker & Warburg: London,* 1948. 8°. **12715**. dd. **1**.

—— Lucifer with a Book, *etc.* pp. 329. *Secker & Warburg: London,* 1949. 8°. **12730**. ff. **6**.

BURNS (JOHN WILLIAM) *See* SPREULL (John) called BASS JOHN. Miscellaneous Writings, *etc.* [Edited by J. W. Burns.] 1882. 8°. **12272**. i. 5.

BURNS (LOUISA)

—— Studies in the Osteopathic Sciences. vol. 3, 4.

3. The Physiology of Consciousness. pp. 352. 1911.
4. Cells of the Blood. pp. 410. pl. XIV. 1931.

Monfort & Co.; A. T. Still Research Institute: Cincinnati, 1911, 31. 8°. **7308**. d. **9**.
Imperfect; wanting vol. 1, 2.

BURNS (M. J.) *See* BENJAMIN (Samuel G. W.) The Cruise of the Alice May in the Gulf of St. Lawrence . . . With numerous illustrations [by M. J. Burns], *etc.* 1885. 4°. **10470**. dd. **3**.

—— *See* PATON (William A.) Down the Islands . . . With illustrations from drawings by M. J. Burns. 1888. 8°. **10470**. h. **17**.

BURNS (MARCA)

—— The Genetics of the Dog. [With a bibliography.] pp. viii. 122. pl. XII. 1952. 8°. *See* ENGLAND.—*Commonwealth Agricultural Bureaux.—Commonwealth Bureau of Animal Breeding and Genetics.* **U.N.P.266/19.**

BURNS (MARGARET) *Cookery Expert.*

—— *See* YEO (Alfred W.) The Cook's A.B.C. . . . Editor: A. W. Yeo, consulting with M. Burns, *etc.* [1942.] 16°. **7946**. de. **5**.

—— *See* YEO (Alfred W.) The Penny Guide to the most profitable Cooking of Vegetables . . . Written by A. W. Yeo, consulting with M. Burns, *etc.* [1940.] 8°. **07943**. de. **23**.

BURNS (MARGARET) *Housekeeper.*

—— *See* ANGUS (Charles) The Trial of Charles Angus . . . for the wilful murder of M. Burns, *etc.* [1808.] 8°. **6495**. aaa. **41**.

—— —— 1808. 8°. **1132**. e. **59**. **(1.)**

—— *See* GERARD (James) *M.D.* A Vindication of the Opinions delivered in evidence by the Medical Witnesses for the Crown, on a late trial at Lancaster, for murder [of M. Burns]. 1808. 8°. **1132**. e. **59**. **(2.)**

BURNS (MARGERY)

—— The Nottingham Club System of Contract Bridge. pp. 47. *Nottingham Bridge Club: Nottingham,* [1954.] 8°. **7919**. f. **85**.

BURNS (MARY) Mary Burns' Bible. By the author of "The Rev. Jeremiah Watkins' Dream," etc., etc. pp. 32. *Houlston & Sons: London,* [1878.] 16°. [*Village Conversations.* no. 5.] **4109**. a. **78**.

BURNS (MARY) *Docteur de l'Université de Paris.* La Langue d'Alphonse Daudet. [With a bibliography.] pp. 384 [374]. *Paris,* 1916. 8°. **011852**. k. **42**.

BURNS (MARY) *Writer of Children's Tales.* Peter's Sparrow. *See* MARCHANT, afterwards COTTON (Bessie) Tommy's Trek, *etc.* [1937.] 8°. W.P. **12085/3**.

BURNS (MARY ALBANIA)

—— Saint John Chrysostom's Homilies on the Statues: a study of their rhetorical qualities and form. A dissertation, *etc.* pp. viii. 123. *Washington,* 1930. 8°. [*Catholic University of America. Patristic Studies.* vol. 22.] Ac. **2692**. y/**16**.

BURNS (MARY GRACE)

—— A Critical Study of the Methods for the Estimation of Creatine, *etc.* pp. 43. *Catholic University of America Press: Washington,* 1939. 8°. [*Catholic University of America. Biological Series.* no. 32.] Ac. **2692**. y/**22**.

BURNS (MARY R.)

—— Lists of Publications of Roy G. Blakey and Gladys E. Blakey. (Lists prepared by M. R. Burns. Supplemented by G. C. Blakey.) ff. 14. 1948. 4°. *See* MINNEAPOLIS.—*University of Minnesota.* **11925**. d. **14**.

BURNS (NAN H.) Keep on the Sunny Side. A comedy-drama in three acts. pp. 117. *Samuel French: New York,* [1938.] 8°. **11792**. aaa. **1**.

BURNS (NED J.)

—— Field Manual for Museums. pp. xii. 426. [1941.] 8°. *See* UNITED STATES OF AMERICA.—*National Park Service.* A.S. **194/23**.

BURNS (PETER FREDERICK) *See* STAINES (Percy G.) and INGRAM (T.) The Way of Arithmetic. Compiled . . . under the direction of P. F. Burns. [1926, *etc.*] 8°. **08534**. de. **1**.

—— Daily Life Mathematics . . . Illustrated by Paul B. Mann. 5 vol. *Ginn & Co.: London,* 1952–59. 8°. 8508. aa. 30.

—— Answers. *Ginn & Co.: London,* [1960– .] 8°. 8508. aa. 30. a.

—— First Steps in Astronomy without a Telescope. pp. ix. 214. *Ginn & Co.: London,* [1942.] 8°. **08560**. f. **30**.

—— Reason-Why Arithmetic Course. 6 bk. *Collins: London & Glasgow,* [1922–24.] 8°. **8506**. d. **31**.

—— The Way of Number. By P. F. Burns . . . assisted by P. G. Staines & T. Ingram. [With "Teacher's Manual."] 4 pt. *Collins: London, Glasgow,* [1931.] 4° & 8°. **08531**. g. **22**.

BURNS (R.) *Writer on Printing.*

—— Printing Inks. *Sir Isaac Pitman & Sons: London,* 1947. 8°. [*Printing Theory and Practice.* no. 9.] W.P. **2467/9**.

BURNS (R. C.) The Fantastic Battle. The story of an idea. [Reprinted from "The Radio Times."] pp. 35. *Friends' Book Centre: London,* 1928. 8°. **012603**. c. **42**.

BURNS (Raymond) Minstrels' Gallery. A novel. pp. xi. 308. *Constable & Co.: London,* 1935. 8°. NN. **23824**.

—— Turncoat. A political thriller. pp. 307. *Constable & Co.: London,* 1937. 8°. NN. **26775**.

BURNS (Rhoda) Rhoda Burns, and other stories. By H. L. E. [1872.] 16°. *See* E., H. L. **4413**. aa. **75**. (**6**.)

BURNS (Richard)

—— The Broadvlei Mystery. An adventure story for boys. pp. 64. *John Crowther: London & Bognor Regis,* [1943.] 8°. **012646**. b. **9**.

—— Highveld Mystery . . . Illustrated by Raymond Sheppard. pp. v. 48. *Blackie & Son: London & Glasgow,* 1952. 8°. [*Crusader Series.* no. 2.] W.P. **4024/2**.

—— Richard Burns Introduces Vivien Leigh and Laurence Olivier. [With illustrations, including portraits.] *Griffs: London,* 1947. 8°. [*Meet the Stars.* no. 1.] W.P. **2299/1**.

BURNS (Robert) *Limner.* The House that Jack Built. [A book for children.] *Grant & Murray: Edinburgh, London,* 1937. fol. **1871**. e. **33**.

—— Scots Ballads. [Edited and illustrated by Robert Burns.] *Seeley Service & Co.: London,* [1940.] fol. C. **103**. k. **2**.

BURNS (Robert) *Minister of St. George's, Paisley. See* Halyburton (Thomas) The Works of the Rev. T. Halyburton . . . With an essay on his life and writings, by the Rev. R. Burns. 1835. 8°. **3752**. c. **6**.

—— *See* Wodrow (Robert) The History of the Sufferings of the Church of Scotland from the Restoration to the Revolution . . . With an original memoir of the author, extracts from his correspondence, a preliminary dissertation, and notes by the Rev. R. Burns. 1829, *etc.* 8°. **2210**. d. **5**.

—— The Anti-Patronage Catechism, *etc.* [By R. Burns.] pp. 27. 1841. 12°. *See* Anti-Patronage Catechism. **4175**. de. **34**. (**1**.)

—— Application of the Doctrine of Christ's Headship to the Calling and Settlement of Ministers, as illustrated in the history of the Church from 1690 to the present times, *etc. See* Jesus Christ. Lectures on the Headship of Christ, *etc.* 1840. 12°. **1120**. c. **19**.

—— A Charge addressed to the Rev. James Reid Brown, in the Scots Church, Swallow Street, 24th November, 1831. [Published from the notes of John Leslie.] pp. 15. *A. Douglas: London,* 1832. 8°. T. **1386**. (**10**.)

—— The Church Revived without the aid of Unknown Tongues. A sermon, *etc.* pp. 41. *A. Douglas: London,* 1831. 8°. T. **1345**. (**2**.)

—— [Another copy.] **764**. g. **16**. (**6**.)

—— The Gairloch Heresy tried . . . Second edition. pp. 82. *Alex. Gardner: Paisley,* 1830. 12°. **764**. a. **40**. (**2**.)

—— *See* Anglicanus. Universal Redemption . . . defended from the misrepresentations and calumnies contained in a late pamphlet entitled "The Gareloch Heresy tried," *etc.* 1830. 12°. **764**. e. **17**. (**5**.)

BURNS (Robert) *Minister of St. George's, Paisley.*

—— Letter to the Rev. Robert Burns . . . and the Rev. William Hamilton . . . occasioned by their late publications entitled "The Gairloch Heresy tried" and "Remarks on Certain Opinions recently propagated respecting Universal Redemption," &c. By a Lay Member of the Church of Scotland [i.e. Thomas Carlyle, of the Scottish Bar]. pp. 12. *R. B. Lusk: Greenock,* 1830. 12°. **764**. i. **20**. (**5**.)

—— Historical Dissertations on the Law and Practice of Great Britain, and particularly of Scotland with regard to the poor . . . Second edition, enlarged. pp. xviii. 503. *Young, Gallie & Co.: Glasgow,* 1819. 8°. **1390**. g. **45**.

—— Illustrations of the Divine Government, particularly in reference to late events. A sermon preached on . . . Dec. 2, 1813 . . . and on . . . Jan. 13, 1814; being the day appointed . . . as a general thanksgiving for the late successes of Great Britain and her allies. pp. 55. *S. & A. Young: Paisley,* 1814. 8°. **4462**. dd. **2**. (**2**.)

—— The Jewish Society of New York, arraigned at the bar of public opinion. pp. 40. *Charles Fletcher: Toronto,* 1853. 8°. **4033**. aa. **51**. (**7**.)

—— A Letter to the Rev. Dr. Chalmers of Glasgow, on the distinctive characters of the Protestant and Roman Catholic religions, occasioned by the publication of his sermon for the benefit of the Hibernian Society. pp. iv. 98. *Stephen Young: Paisley,* 1818. 8°. **3940**. l. **6**. (**4**.)

—— Memoir of the Rev. Stevenson Macgill, *etc.* [With a portrait.] pp. viii. 358. *John Johnstone: Edinburgh,* 1842. 8°. **4955**. aa. **17**.

—— A Modest Visit to the King at Brighton, described by Dr. Burns of Paisley, in a letter to his wife, 1831. With the same travestied. pp. 29. [1831.] 8°. **11644**. h. **24**.

—— A Plea for the Poor of Scotland, and for an enquiry into their condition: being the substance of two lectures, *etc.* pp. 36. *Alex. Gardner: Paisley,* 1841. 8°. C.T. **211**. (**7**.)

—— Plurality of Offices in the Church of Scotland examined, with a particular reference to the case of . . . Dr. M'Farlane, *etc.* pp. viii. 298. *Chalmers & Collins: Glasgow,* 1824. 12°. **4175**. a. **12**.

—— Reply to the Lay Member of the Church of Scotland [i.e. Thomas Carlyle]; with a note for the Reverend James Russel, Minister of Gairloch. By the author of the "Gareloch Heresy tried." [Signed: R. B., i.e. Robert Burns.] pp. 60. 1830. 12°. *See* B., R. **764**. a. **40**. (**3**.)

—— Protestant Truths and Popish Errors: a letter to the author of "The Gareloch Heresy tried," occasioned by his Reply to the Lay Member of the Church of Scotland. With a postscript addressed to the Rev. Dr. Hamilton. [By Thomas Carlyle, of the Scottish Bar.] pp. 52. *R. B. Lusk: Greenock,* 1830. 12°. **764**. i. **20**. (**6**.)

—— Report of Speeches of the Rev. Dr. Burns, Rev. Robert S. Candlish, and Alexander Earle Monteith, Esq., in the General Assembly . . . May 22, 1839, in the Auchterarder Case. Revised by the speakers. With an appendix containing reasons of adherence to the Church of Scotland; and answers to the various reasons of dissent from the decision of the Assembly. pp. 51. *John Johnstone: Edinburgh,* 1839. 8°. **1354**. e. **7**. (**1**.)

BURNS (ROBERT) *Minister of St. George's, Paisley.*

—— Second edition. pp. 51. *John Johnstone: Edinburgh,* 1839. 8°. **4175**. d. **11**.

—— [Another copy.] **4380**. h. **3**. **(5.)**

—— Sober Mindedness; a discourse to young men, *etc.* pp. 36. *W. Whyte & Co.: Edinburgh, Alex. Gardner: Paisley,* 1828. 12°. **4478**. a. **123**. **(1.)**

—— Truth and Love versus Prelacy and the Prayer-Book: being a reply to Rev. W. M. Wade's pamphlet [i.e. "The Truth spoken in Love, relative to Episcopacy and the Anglican Liturgy"]. pp. 19. *Alex. Gardner: Paisley,* 1840. 8°. **4109**. b. **14**. **(7.)**

BURNS (ROBERT) *of Hamilton.* Address from the Genius of Caledonia to his Grace the Duke of Hamilton, on the supposition of a French invasion. To which are added, two songs. pp. 8. [1797?] *See* POETRY. Poetry; original and selected. vol. 3. [1796, *etc.*] 8°. **1474**. a. **14/3**.

—— Address to Clydesdale. To which is added, Kattie, a song. pp. 8. [1797?] *See* POETRY. Poetry; original and selected. vol. 3. [1796, *etc.*] 8°. **1474**. a. **14/3**.

—— Cadzow Castle, a ballad, *etc.* pp. 12. *The Author: Glasgow,* 1809. 12°. **11641**. b. **4**.

—— The Echo of Friars-Carse Hermitage; also, Avon's Stream, a dirge. By R. Burns . . . To which are added, Verses written in the High Church-Yard, Glasgow (by John Taylor). pp. 8. [1797.] *See* POETRY. Poetry; original and selected. vol. 2. [1796, *etc.*] 8°. **1474**. a. **14/2**.

—— [Another edition.] Two Original Poems. I. The Echo of Friars-Carse Hermitage. II. Avon's Stream: a dirge. By R. Burns . . . To which are added, Verses written in the High Church-Yard, Glasgow [by John Taylor]. (The World. [An epigram.]) pp. 8. *Brash & Reid: Glasgow,* [1797?] 8°. **11601**. aa. **43**. **(2.)**

—— Invocation to Melpomene. To which are added, Winter. A song. And a Prologue to the Gentle Shepherd. pp. 8. [1798.] *See* POETRY. Poetry; original and selected. vol. 4. [1796, *etc.*] 8°. **1474**. a. **14/4**.

—— Ode to Temperance. To which are added, two songs. pp. 8. [1797?] *See* POETRY. Poetry; original and selected. vol. 3. [1796, *etc.*] 8°. **1474**. a. **14/3**.

BURNS (ROBERT) *the Poet.*

ARRANGEMENT.

WORKS.

—— The Works of Robert Burns; with an account of his life, and a criticism on his writings. To which are prefixed, some observations on the character and condition of the Scottish peasantry. [By James Currie.] 4 vol. *Printed by J. M'Creery: Liverpool; for T. Cadell, Jun. & W. Davies: London,* 1800. 8°. **79**. i. **21–24**.

BURNS (ROBERT) *the Poet.* [WORKS.]

—— The second edition. 4 vol. *T. Cadell, Jun. & W. Davies: London,* 1801. 8°. **1465**. h. **24**.

—— The third edition. 4 vol. *T. Cadell, Jun. & W. Davies: London,* 1802. 8°. **11609**. h. **1, 2**.

—— The fourth edition. 4 vol. *T. Cadell & W. Davies: London,* 1803. 8°. **012272**. ee. **2**.

—— A new edition. 4 vol. *Simms & M'Intyre: Belfast,* 1808. 8°. **12274**. de. **1**.
Vol. 3 is dated 1807.

—— The eighth edition. To which are now added, the Reliques of Robert Burns. [The editor's preface to vol. 5 signed: R. H. C., i.e. R. H. Cromek. With woodcuts by Thomas Bewick.] 5 vol. *T. Cadell & W. Davies: London,* 1814. 12°. **11611**. aa. **3–7**.

—— The Works of Robert Burns; with an account of his life, and a criticism on his writings. To which are prefixed, some observations on the character and condition of the Scottish peasantry. [By James Currie.] 4 vol. *Gale & Fenner: London,* 1815. 12°. **11607**. a. **4**.

—— A new edition, with additional pieces. 4 vol. *Smith & Hill: Montrose,* 1816. 12°. **11609**. e. **1, 2**.

—— The eighth edition. To which are now added, some further particulars of the author's life, new notes . . . and many other additions, by Gilbert Burns. 4 vol. *T. Cadell & W. Davies: London,* 1820. 8°. **1465**. h. **23**.

—— The Works of Robert Burns: including his letters to Clarinda, and the whole of his suppressed poems: with an essay on his life, genius, and character. 4 vol. *Printed for the Editor by Richards & Co.: London,* 1821. 12°. **11607**. aa. **15**.

—— The Works of Robert Burns: including his letters to Clarinda, and the whole of his suppressed poems; with an essay on his life, genius and character [signed: J. B.]. pp. 480. *William Clark: London,* 1831. 8°. **11612**. de. **23**.
The publishers' binding is probably of a later date than 1831.

—— The Works of Robert Burns; with his life, by Allan Cunningham. 8 vol. *J. Cochrane & Co.: London,* 1834. 8°. **991**. b. **1–4**.
With an additional titlepage, engraved, and an engraved frontispiece to each volume. Vol. 1 *and* 2 *also have additional printed titlepages on which the work is described as being "in six volumes," and which bear the imprint "Cochrane & M'Crone: London."*

—— [Another copy.] MS. NOTES AND ADDITIONS. **C. 45**. a. **26**.
With a MS. *note by Robert Southey on the half-title of vol.* 1.

—— The Works of Robert Burns; containing his life; by John Lockhart, Esq. The poetry and correspondence of Dr. Currie's edition; biographical sketches of the poet by himself, Gilbert Burns, Professor Stewart, and others; Essay on Scottish Poetry, including the poetry of Burns, by Dr. Currie . . . select Scottish songs of the other poets . . . with Burns's remarks, *etc.* pp. xv. clxvi. 425. 13. *William Pearson: New-York,* 1835. 8°. **11611**. ee. **22**.

—— The Works of Robert Burns, with selected notes of Allan Cunningham, a biographical and critical introduction, and a comparative etymological glossary to the poet. By Dr Adolphus Wagner, *etc.* pp. xxviii. 610. *Frederick Fleischer: Leipsic,* 1835. 8°. **11609**. i. **13**.
With an additional titlepage, engraved.

—— The Entire Works of Robert Burns; with an account of his life, and a criticism on his writings . . . By James Currie . . . Fifth diamond edition. Embellished with fourteen illustrations from original designs by Mr. Stewart. pp. xii. 323. *A. Bell & Co.: London*, 1836. 16°. **11630**. a. **43**.
With an additional titlepage, engraved, reading "The Complete Works of Robert Burns. By James Currie."

—— The Poems, Letters, and Land of Robert Burns: illustrated by W. H. Bartlett, T. Allom, and other artists. With a new memoir of the poet, and notices, critical and biographical, of his works, by Allan Cunningham. 2 vol. *George Virtue: London*, [1840.] 4°. **11611**. h. **13**.
With an additional titlepage, engraved, to each volume, that of vol. 1 *bearing the date* 1838, *that of vol.* 2, 1840. *Some of the plates are dated* 1838, *others* 1839, *others* 1840.

—— The Works of Robert Burns. With life by Allan Cunningham, and notes by Gilbert Burns [and others], *etc.* [With a portrait and facsimiles.] pp. xxiv. 820. *Thomas Tegg; Charles Daly: London*, 1840. 8°. **11613**. c. **4**.
With an additional titlepage, engraved.

—— The Works of Robert Burns. Edited by the Ettrick Shepherd, and William Motherwell. [With engravings.] 5 vol. *Fullarton & Co.: Glasgow*, 1840, 41, 38, 39. 12°. **11612**. aaa. **13**.
Vol. 1 *is dated* 1840, *vol.* 2 1841, *vol.* 3 1838, *vol.* 4 *and* 5 1839. *With an additional titlepage to each volume, engraved.*

—— The Complete Works of Robert Burns: containing his poems, songs, and correspondence. Illustrated by W. H. Bartlett, T. Allom, and other artists. With a new life of the poet, and notices, critical and biographical, by Allan Cunningham. pp. l. 422. *George Virtue: London*, 1842. 8°. **840**. i. **16**.
With an additional titlepage, engraved. Previous edition 1840.

—— The Entire Works of Robert Burns; with an account of his life and a criticism on his writings . . . By James Currie . . . Seventh diamond edition, *etc.* pp. xii. 323. *Andrew Moffat: London*, 1842. 16°. **11607**. aa. **18**.
With an additional titlepage, engraved, reading "The Complete Works of Robert Burns," etc., and dated 1841. *Previous edition* 1836.

—— [Another copy.] **11607**. aaaa. **5**.
Imperfect; wanting the printed titlepage.

—— The Works of Robert Burns. With life by Allan Cunningham, and notes by Gilbert Burns [and others], *etc.* pp. xxiv. 820. *H. G. Bohn: London*, 1842. 8°. Ashley **2599**.
With an additional titlepage, engraved.
A reissue of the Tegg and Daily edition of 1840.

—— The Complete Works of Robert Burns: containing his poems, letters, songs, his letters to Clarinda, and the whole of his suppressed poems: with an essay on his life, genius, and character [signed: J. B.]. pp. 480. MS. NOTES. *James Cornish: London*, 1843. 8°. **11611**. aa. **8**.
A reissue of the edition published by William Clark in 1831.

—— The Works of Robert Burns; with Dr. Currie's memoir of the poet, and an essay on his genius and character, by Professor Wilson. Also numerous notes, annotations, and appendices. Embellished by eighty-one portraits and landscape illustrations. 2 vol. *Blackie & Son: Glasgow*, 1843, 44. 8°. **1465**. i. **2**.
With an additional titlepage to each volume, engraved.

—— The Works of Robert Burns. With life by Allan Cunningham, and notes . . . New edition. pp. xxiv. 820. *H. G. Bohn: London*, 1845. 8°. **012274**. e. **7**.

—— The Works of Robert Burns; containing his life by John Lockhart, Esq., the poetry and correspondence of Dr. Currie's edition; biographical sketches of the poet by himself, Gilbert Burns, Professor Stewart, and others; essay on Scottish poetry, including the poetry of Burns, by Dr. Currie; Burns' songs, *etc.* pp. xv. cxlvi. 425. 13. *Otis, Broaders & Co.: Boston*, 1846. 8°. **11611**. f. **4**.
A reissue of the edition published by William Pearson, New York, in 1835.

—— The Works of Robert Burns. With life by Allen Cunningham, and notes by Gilbert Burns [and others] . . . New edition. pp. xxiv. 820. *H. G. Bohn: London*, 1847. 8°. **11611**. h. **8**.
With the additional engraved titlepage of the 1842 *edition.*

—— [A reissue.] *London*, 1850. 8°. **11607**. ee. **2**.
With the additional engraved titlepage of the 1842 *edition.*

—— The Life and Works of Robert Burns. Edited by Robert Chambers. 4 vol. *Edinburgh*, 1851, 52. 8°. [*Chambers's Instructive and Entertaining Library.*] **1157**. f. **4, 5**.

—— The Works of Robert Burns; with a complete life of the poet [by James Currie], and an essay on his genius and character, by Professor Wilson, *etc.* [With plates, including portraits.] 2 vol. *Blackie & Son: Glasgow & London*, 1855, 54. 8°. **11612**. n. **3**.
With an additional titlepage to each volume, engraved.
***A reissue of the edition of* 1843, 44.**

—— Library edition. 4 vol. *W. & R. Chambers: Edinburgh & London*, 1856, 57. 8°. **10854**. e. **7**.
Published in parts.

—— The Poetical Works and Letters of Robert Burns. With life. Eight engravings on steel. (In this edition the more objectionable passages and pieces are omitted.) pp. xxxvi. 656. *Gall & Inglis: Edinburgh*, [1859.] 8°. **11611**. bb. **1**.
With an additional titlepage, engraved.

—— The Complete Works of Robert Burns. Including his correspondence, etc. With a memoir by William Gunnyon. The text carefully printed, and illustrated with notes. With portrait and illustrations on wood by eminent artists. pp. 12. lxxviii. 405. *W. P. Nimmo: Edinburgh*, 1865. 8°. **12271**. k. **5**.
With an additional titlepage.

—— The Works and Correspondence of Robert Burns, including his letters to Clarinda; remarks on Scottish songs and ballads, illustrated by historical and critical notes, biographical notices [by James Currie], &c. &c. With an extensive glossary of the Scottish language; a life of the author; and an essay on his genius and writings. pp. xiv. 520. 29. *William Mackenzie: Glasgow*, [1866.] 8°. **11609**. i. **3**.
Published in parts. With an additional titlepage, engraved.

—— Life and Works of Robert Burns. By P. Hately Waddell . . . Enriched with portraits, and numerous illustrations in colour, *etc.* 2 pt. *David Wilson: Glasgow*, 1867 [1867–69]. 4°. **11609**. i. **8**.
Published in parts.

—— Poems, Songs and Letters, being the complete works of Robert Burns. Edited from the best printed and manuscript authorities, with glossarial index and a biographical memoir by Alexander Smith. (The Globe edition.) pp. xlviii. 636. *Macmillan & Co.: London,* 1868. 8°. **2290**. b. 5.

—— The Poetical Works of Robert Burns. Complete. (Correspondence of Burns.) With numerous illustrations. pp. xxxvii. 218. ix. *John Dicks: London,* 1870. 8°. **11611**. cc. **3**.

—— The Works of Robert Burns, poetical and prose. The Household illustrated edition, specially prepared for reading. Arranged and edited by "Gertrude" [i.e. Mrs. Jane Cross Simpson]. 2 vol. *W. R. M'Phun & Son: Glasgow,* 1870. 8°. **11609**. i. **1, 2**.
With additional titlepages to each volume, engraved.

—— The Works of Robert Burns. [Edited by William Scott Douglas.] 6 vol. *William Paterson: Edinburgh,* 1877–79. 8°. **12271**. i. **8**.

—— [Another copy.] Ashley **4721**.

—— Burns. [Poems, letters and journals. With plates, including a portrait.] pp. xviii. lv. 468. *Virtue & Co.: London,* [1879.] 8°. [*CUNNINGHAM (Allan) Poet, and MACKAY (Charles) Burns, Ramsay and the Earlier Poets of Scotland, etc.* vol. 2.] **11609**. k. **6**.

—— The National Burns. Edited by Rev. George Gilfillan, including the airs of all the songs, and an original life of Burns by the editor. [With plates, including portraits.] 2 vol. *William Mackenzie: Glasgow,* [1879, 80.] 4°. **11611**. h. **10**.

—— The Poetical Works and Letters of Robert Burns, with copious marginal explanations of the Scotch words, and life. Engravings on steel. pp. xxxii. 642. *Gall & Inglis: Edinburgh, London,* [1881.] 8°. **11604**. df. **1**.
Part of "The Landscape Series of Poets."

—— The Complete Works of Robert Burns . . . With a new life and notes critical and biographical by Allan Cunningham. With illustrations on steel. pp. lv. 468. *J. S. Virtue & Co.: London,* [1886, 87.] 4°. **12271**. h. **8**.
Published in parts. With an additional titlepage, engraved. A reissue of the edition of 1879.

—— The Works of Robert Burns. With a series of authentic pictorial illustrations, marginal glossary, numerous notes, and appendixes; also the life of Burns, by J. G. Lockhart; and essays on the genius, character, and writings of Burns, by Thomas Carlyle and Professor Wilson. Edited by Charles Annandale. 5 vol. *Blackie & Son: London,* [1888, 89.] 8°. **12273**. h. **7**.

—— The Life and Works of Robert Burns. Edited by Robert Chambers. 4 vol. *W. & R. Chambers: Edinburgh,* 1891. 8°. **12271**. f. **9**.
A reissue of the edition of 1856, 57.

—— [Another edition.] Revised by William Wallace. [With plates.] 4 vol. **L.P.** *W. & R. Chambers: Edinburgh,* 1896, 97. 8°. **12272**. i. **11**.

—— [Another copy of vol. 1–3.] **12272**. cc. **15**.

—— The Complete Works of Robert Burns. Gebbie self-interpreting edition. [Edited by George Gebbie and James Hunter.] Illustrated. 6 vol. *Bigelow, Brown & Co.: New York,* [1909.] 8°. **12274**. m. **4**.

—— The Complete Writings of Robert Burns. [The letters edited by Francis H. Allen. With an introduction by John Buchan, a biography by W. E. Henley, notes on the poems by W. E. Henley and T. F. Henderson, and plates, including portraits.] 10 vol. **L.P.** *Waverley Book Co.: London; Cambridge, Mass.* printed, 1927. 8°. **12269**. eee. **4**.

—— Robert Burns. The Complete Works and Letters. Introduction by William Harvey . . . Oration by the Earl of Rosebery and Midlothian . . . A short life of Burns by Robert Ford. Introduction to the letters by R. W. Mackenna. (Masonic edition.) [With plates.] 2 pt. *Collins: London & Glasgow,* [1928.] 8°. **11632**. cc. **28**.

—— Robert Burns. The Complete Works . . . With special articles of interest to every student of Burns. [With plates.] pp. cxxvi. 639. *Collins: London & Glasgow,* [1937.] 8°. **2292**. g. **32**.

SMALLER COLLECTIONS.

—— Here awa, there awa, &c.—Behind yon Hills, &c. *See* SONGS. Six Favourite Songs, Scots and English, *etc.* [1796.] 8°. [*Poetry; original and selected.* vol. 1.] **1474**. a. **14/1**.

—— Braw Lads on Yarrow Braes.—Farewell to Eliza.—Auld Rob Morris. *See* SONGS. Seven Favourite Songs, Scots and English, *etc.* [1797.] 8°. [*Poetry; original and selected.* vol. 2.] **1474**. a. **14/2**.

—— O wat ye wha's in yon town? and Open the Door to me, oh! . . . By Robert Burns. With three other favourite songs. pp. 8. [1797.] *See* POETRY. Poetry; original and selected. [1796, *etc.*] 8°. **1474**. a. **14/2**.

—— Tam Glen, and Gin a Body meet a Body [by R. Burns] . . . To which are added, The Negro Boy, and the Vicar and Hour-Glass. pp. 8. [1798.] 8°. [*Poetry; original and selected.* vol. 4.] *See* GLEN (Tam) **1474**. a. **14/4**.

—— The Tooth-ache: a poem. By R. Burns . . . Ye Banks and Braes of Bonnie Doon: a song. By the same author. Another song, to the same tune. And The Washing Day: a poem. pp. 8. [1798.] *See* POETRY. Poetry; original and selected. vol. 4. [1796, *etc.*] 8°. **1474**. a. **14/4**.

—— Holy Willie's Prayer, Letter to John Goudie, Kilmarnock, and six favourite songs, *etc.* pp. 16. *Stewart & Meikle: Glasgow,* [1799.] 8°. **1482**. aa. **25**.

—— The Kirk's Alarm: a satire. A Letter to a Taylor, the Deil's awa' wi' the Exciseman, and an Unco Mournfu' Tale, &c. &c. pp. 15. *Stewart & Meikle: Glasgow,* [1799.] 8°. **1482**. aa. **26**.

—— The Poetical Works of Robert Burns. A new edition. Including the pieces published in his correspondence, with his songs and fragments. To which is prefixed, a sketch of his life [signed: A. C., i.e. Alexander Chalmers]. 3 vol. *T. Cadell & W. Davies: London,* 1804. 8°. **11609**. aa. **2–4**.

—— For a' that, and a' that. [By R. Burns.] To which are added, Saw ye Johnnie comin'. Corn Rigs are Bonny. [By R. Burns.] Burns' Farewell to the Tarbolton Lodge. My Heart with Love is beating. A Furnished Table. pp. 8. [1805?] 12°. *See* FOR. **11621**. c. **3**. **(61.)**

—— Twenty Songs. pp. 24. *Thomas Duncan: Glasgow,* [1805?] 12°. **11621**. b. **18**. **(3.)**
Imperfect; wanting pp. 11–14.

—— The Poetical Works of Robert Burns. pp. 260. *Oliver & Boyd: Edinburgh,* [1807.] 16°. **011652. h. 179.**
The titlepage is engraved.

—— The Poetical Works of Robert Burns. Collated with the best editions: by Thomas Park. 2 vol. *Charles Whittingham for J. Sharpe: London,* 1807. 16°. **11609. de. 27.**

—— [A reissue.] *London,* 1808. 16°. [PARK (*Thomas*) *F.S.A. The Works of the British Poets, etc.* vol. 40.] **1066. d. 8.**

—— The Poetical Works of Robert Burns; with his life. Ornamented with engravings on wood by Mr. Bewick, from original designs by Mr. Thurston. 2 vol. *Catnach & Davison: Alnwick,* 1808. 8°. **11630. aa. 2, 3.**

—— [Selected poems and songs.] *See* BURNS (Robert) *Son of Robert Burns the Poet.* The Caledonian Musical Museum, *etc.* 1809. 12°. **11622. cc. 2.**

—— Seventeen Songs. (Second edition, containing eight songs not in the first.) pp. 16. *Thomas Duncan: Glasgow,* 1809. 16°. **11621. b. 21. (3.)**

—— The Poetical Works of Robert Burns . . . With a complete glossary, and life of the author. 2 vol. *S. A. Oddy: London,* 1810. 12°. **11642. aa. 56.**
With an additional titlepage to each volume, engraved.

—— Poems by Robert Burns: with an account of his life [by Josiah Walker], and miscellaneous remarks on his writings. Containing also many poems and letters, not printed in Doctor Currie's edition. [With engravings.] 2 vol. *Trustees of the late James Morison: Edinburgh,* 1811. 8°. **1465. h. 10.**

—— The Poetical Works of Robert Burns, including the pieces published in his correspondence and reliques, with his songs and fragments. To which is prefixed a sketch of his life [signed: A. C., i.e. Alexander Chalmers]. pp. xxvii. 528. *I. Cadell & W. Davies: London; W. Creech: Edinburgh,* 1813. 24°. **11630. aa. 43.**
With an additional titlepage, engraved.

—— The Bony Lass, Whistle, and I'll come to you my lad, I'll awa' to Nannie, My Lady's Gown there's gairs upon 't. The Birks of Aberfeldy. [All by or slightly altered from Burns.] pp. 8. 1814. 12°. *See* LASS. **11621. b. 10. (46.)**

—— Highland Mary. [By R. Burns.] To which are added, Donald M'Donald, The Miller, O Willie brew'd a Peck o' Maut [by R. Burns]. pp. 8. [1815?] 12°. *See* MARY, *Highland.* **11621. b. 10. (10.)**

—— Seventeen Favourite Songs, by the celebrated Scottish poets, Burns & Tannahill, *etc.* pp. 16. *T. Duncan: Glasgow,* [1815?] 16°. **11621. b. 21. (4.)**

—— The Poetical Works of Robert Burns . . . With a complete glossary, and life of the author. 2 vol. *W. Lewis & Co.: London,* 1816. 12°. **11609. b. 1, 2.**
With an additional titlepage to each volume, engraved. Previous edition 1810.

—— The Poetical Works of Robert Burns, including the pieces published in his correspondence and reliques; with his songs and fragments. To which is prefixed a sketch of his life [signed: A. C., i.e. Alexander Chalmers]. pp. xii. xxvii. 528. *T. Cadell & W. Davies: London,* 1817. 24°. **11612. aa. 20.**
Imperfect; wanting the frontispiece and additional engraved titlepage. Previous edition 1813.

—— The Poems & Songs of Robert Burns, with a life of the author . . . To which is subjoined, an appendix, consisting of a panegyrical ode, and a demonstration of Burns' superiority to every other poet as a writer of songs, by the Rev. Hamilton Paul. pp. xii. xlviii. 312. *Wilson, M'Cormick & Carnie: Air,* 1819. 12°. **1465. b. 4.**
With an additional titlepage, engraved. The glossary is not paginated.

—— The Poetical Works of Robert Burns; including several pieces not inserted in Dr. Currie's edition; exhibited under a new plan of arrangement; and preceded by a life of the author, and a complete glossary. 2 vol. *James Thomson: London,* 1819. 8°. **11611. a. 3, 4.**

—— The Poetical Works of Robert Burns. 2 vol. *C. Whittingham: Chiswick,* 1821. 8°. **11609. a. 2, 3.**
With an additional titlepage to each volume, engraved.

—— The Poems of Robert Burns. 2 vol. *C. Whittingham: Chiswick,* 1822. 12°. [*The British Poets.* vol. 75, 76.] **11603. aa. 12.**

—— The Poetical Works of Robert Burns; including the pieces published in his correspondence and reliques; with his songs and fragments. To which are prefixed, a history of the poems, by his brother, Gilbert Burns, and a sketch of his life [by Alexander Chalmers]. 2 vol. *John Bumpus: London,* 1822. 12°. **11643. a. 36**

—— The Poetical Works of Robert Burns. To which is prefixed the author's life. pp. 240. *Printed for the Booksellers: London,* 1822. 12°. **11607. aa. 23.**
With an additional titlepage, engraved.

—— The Poetical Works of Robert Burns: with a life of the author. 1822. *See* SANFORD (Ezekiel) The Works of the British Poets. vol. 38, 39. 1819, *etc.* 12°. **11602. a. 19, 20.**

—— The Songs of Robert Burns, accurately copied from the originals, and the errors of former editions carefully corrected. (Improved edition.) pp. viii. 152. *T. Kerr: Liverpool,* 1822. 16°. **T. 892. (3.)**

—— The Poetical Works of the late Robert Burns. A new edition. Containing many excellent pieces of the author's that never made their appearance in the copy-right edition. pp. xii. 374. *Thomas Turnbull: Edinburgh,* 1823. 12°. **11612. c. 13.**

—— The Poetical Works of Robert Burns, including the pieces published in his correspondence and reliques; with his songs and fragments. To which is prefixed a sketch of his life [signed: A. C., i.e. Alexander Chalmers]. 3 vol. *T. Cadell: London,* 1823. 8°. **1346. c. 17–19.**

—— The Songs and Ballads of Robert Burns: including ten never before published; with a preliminary discourse, and illustrative prefaces. pp. 320. *William Clark: London,* 1823. 12°. **11632. b. 12**

—— Songs, chiefly in the Scottish dialect. [With engravings after designs by R. Westall.] pp. vii. 264. *John Sharpe: London,* 1824. 12°. **11622. aaa. 11.**
With an additional titlepage, engraved, reading "The Songs of Burns."

—— The Poetical Works of Robert Burns: carefully collated. With original explanatory notes. pp. xvi. 428. *J. F. Dove: London,* 1826. 24°. **11643. a. 19.**
With an additional titlepage, engraved. One of a series entitled "Dove's English Classics."

—— The Beauties of Burns, consisting of selections from his poems and letters. By Alfred Howard. pp. 212. *Thomas Tegg: London,* [1826.] 12°. **11603. de. 44.**
Vol. 8 *of a series entitled "Howard's Beauties of Literature."*

—— [Another copy.] The Beauties of Burns, *etc.* *London,* [1826.] 12°. **12299.** de. **36.** (**2.**)

—— The Poems and Songs of Robert Burns. With a life of the author, and a glossary. [With woodcuts by Thomas Bewick.] pp. 336. *W. Davison: Alnwick,* 1828. 24°. **11633.** a. **8.**

—— The Poetical Works of Robert Burns. [With a memoir of Burns by Sir Harris Nicolas.] 2 vol. *William Pickering: London,* 1830. 8°. [*Aldine Edition of the British Poets.*] **1066.** e. **2.**

—— The Poetical Works of Robert Burns, with his life, a critique, glossary, &c. 2 vol. *Joseph Smith: London,* 1830. 16°. **11612.** aa. **31.**

—— Songs, chiefly Scottish. pp. 108. *See* BRITISH POETRY. The Cabinet of British Poetry, *etc.* 1830. 12°. **11601.** aaa. **22.**

—— The Beauties of Burns. *See* BYRON (George G. N.) *Baron Byron.* [*Smaller Collections.*] The Beauties of Byron & Burns, *etc.* 1837. 32°. **11647.** a. **84.** (**1.**)

—— The Complete Poetical Works of Robert Burns: with explanatory and glossarial notes; and a life of the author, by James Currie, M.D., abridged. New edition. pp. xxiv. 60. 564. *Scott, Webster & Geary: London,* 1837. 12°. **11611.** bb. **28.**
With an additional titlepage, engraved.

—— The Poetical Works of Robert Burns. To which are now added, notes illustrating historical, personal, and local allusions. [The editor's preface signed: R. C., i.e. Robert Chambers.] pp. 148. *W. & R. Chambers: Edinburgh,* 1838. 8°. **1340.** m. **17.** (**3.**)

—— The Poetical Works of Robert Burns: with a life of the author, a copious glossary, and an index. (Standard library edition.) pp. viii. 128. *William Smith: London,* 1838. 8°. **1164.** g. **6.**

—— [Another copy.] **11607.** ff. **6.** (**7.**)
Imperfect; wanting the wrappers.

—— The Poetical Works of Robert Burns. [With a memoir of Burns by Sir Harris Nicolas.] 3 vol. *William Pickering: London,* 1839. 8°. **1066.** e. **1.**
Previous edition 1830.

—— [Another copy.] ON VELLUM. C. **30.** b. **10–12.**
Without the portrait.

—— The Poetical Works of Robert Burns, with a memoir of the author's life and a glossary. pp. 400. *Jones & Co.: London,* 1839. 16°. **11607.** eee. **9.**

—— The Poetical Works of Robert Burns, with a memoir of the author's life, and a glossary. pp. xvi. 368. *William Milner: Halifax,* 1840. 16°. **1465.** a. **27.**

—— The Poetical Works of Robert Burns; with a memoir of the author's life and a glossary. pp. 351. *W. & T. Fordyce: Newcastle,* 1841. 16°. **11607.** a. **40.**
With an additional titlepage, engraved.

—— Burn's [*sic*] Farewell. Together with The Voice of Labour. Highland Mary. pp. 8. *W. Kelly: Waterford,* [1845?] 16°. **11622.** b. **30.** (**14.**)

—— The Poetical Works of Robert Burns. With the life and portrait of the author. pp. xxiv. 366. *Bernhard Tauchnitz: Leipzig,* 1845. 8°. [*Collection of British Authors.* vol. 90.] **12267.a.1/44.**

—— The Poetical Works of Robert Burns. [With engravings.] pp. xxix. 393. *Chapman & Hall: London,* 1848. 8°. **11609.** aaa. **5.**
With an additional titlepage, engraved. No. 3 *of "The Cabinet Classics."*

—— Burns' Songster. pp. 24. *John Gilbert: Newcastle-upon-Tyne,* [1850?] 12°. **1077.** d. **68.** (**13.**)

—— The Poetical Works of Robert Burns, as collected and published by Dr. Currie. *See* BRITISH POETS. Cabinet Edition of the British Poets, *etc.* vol. 2. 1851. 8°. **2504.** o. **1.**

—— The Poetical Works of Robert Burns. pp. viii. 128. *Nathaniel Cooke: London,* [1853.] 8°. [*Universal Library.* Poetry. vol. 2.] **12204.e.5/26.**

—— The Scottish Keepsake, or Songs of the Ayrshire Bard. pp. ix. 133. *W. & A. Smith: Mauchline,* [1855?] 16°. **11646.** de. **12.**

—— The Poetical Works of Robert Burns. Edited by the Rev. Robert Aris Willmott . . . Illustrated by John Gilbert. pp. lxiii. 478. *London,* 1856. 8°. [*Routledge's British Poets.*] **11603.** e. **3.**

—— The Poetical Works of Robert Burns. With memoir, critical dissertation, and explanatory notes, by the Rev. George Gilfillan. 2 vol. *James Nichol: Edinburgh,* 1856. 8°. **11603.** g. **3, 4.**

—— Poems and Songs . . . Illustrated with numerous engravings. pp. xvi. 272. *Bell & Daldy: London,* 1858 [1857]. 4°. **1347.** h. **6.**

—— The Songs of Robert Burns, with music. Centenary edition. pp. 128. *David Jack: Glasgow,* 1859. 8°. **11633.** a. **7.**

—— Illustrated Songs of Robert Burns. With a portrait after the original by Nasmyth. [Five songs.] *Royal Association for the Promotion of the Fine Arts in Scotland:* [*Edinburgh,*] 1861. fol. **1875.** b. **27.**

—— The Poems of Robert Burns. pp. 416. *Bell & Daldy: London,* 1863. 16°. **11609.** a. **4.**
One of a series entitled "Bell and Daldy's Pocket Volumes."

—— The Songs of Robert Burns. pp. 319. *Bell & Daldy: London,* 1863. 16°. **11609.** a. **5.**
One of a series entitled "Bell and Daldy's Pocket Volumes."

—— The Ballads and Songs of Robert Burns. With a lecture on his character and genius by Thomas Carlyle. [With illustrations.] pp. xvi. 224. *C. Griffin & Co.: London,* 1864. 8°. **11609.** aa. **5.**

—— The Poems of Robert Burns. pp. 416. *Bell & Daldy: London,* 1864. 16°. **11609.** aa. **6.**
A reissue of the edition of 1863.

—— The Poetical Works of Robert Burns. Edited from the best printed and manuscript authorities, with glossarial index and a biographical memoir by Alexander Smith. 2 vol. *Macmillan & Co.: London & Cambridge,* 1865. 8°. **11609.** aa. **7, 8.**

Part of the "Golden Treasury Series."

—— The Complete Poetical Works of Robert Burns. Edited by John S. Roberts. With an original memoir by William Gunnyon. With portrait and illustrations on wood by eminent artists. Seventh thousand. pp. cxlviii. 523. *W. P. Nimmo: Edinburgh,* [1866.] 8°. **11609**. aaa. **6**.
With an additional titlepage.

—— The Complete Poetical Works of Robert Burns and Sir Walter Scott. Illustrated, with fine steel portraits, and a fac-simile of a characteristic letter of Burns' to Mrs. Riddell. New edition. pp. 423. *C. Griffin & Co.: London,* 1866. 8°. **11611**. g. **1**.

—— The Illustrated Family Burns, with an original memoir. [With engravings, including a portrait.] pp. xxxii. 463. 72. vi. *William Mackenzie: Glasgow,* [1866.] 4°. **11611**. h. **2**.
Published in parts.

—— The Poetical Works of Robert Burns. [With a memoir of Burns by Sir Harris Nicolas.] 3 vol. *Bell & Daldy: London,* 1866. 8°. [*Aldine Edition of the British Poets.*] **2288**. c. **5**.
Previous edition 1839.

—— The Poetical Works of Robert Burns. Edited by the Rev. Robert Aris Willmott. New edition. With numerous additions. [The preface signed: P. A. N.] pp. lv. 299. *G. Routledge & Sons: London,* 1866. 8°. **11609**. aa. **9**.
Previous edition 1856.

—— Poems & Songs by Robert Burns. With original illustrations by R. Herdman, R.S.A., Waller H. Paton, R.S.A., Samuel Bough, A.R.S.A., Gourlay Steell, R.S.A., D. O. Hill, R.S.A., John M'Whirter and other eminent Scottish artists. Engraved by R. Paterson. pp. xviii. 336 *W. P. Nimmo: Edinburgh,* 1868 [1867]. 4°. **11651**. i. **17**.

—— The Poetical Works of Robert Burns. With memoir, critical dissertation, and explanatory notes. The text edited by Charles Cowden Clarke. [With a portrait.] 2 vol. *William P. Nimmo; James Nichol: Edinburgh,* 1868, 66. 8°. **11612**. l. **13**.

—— [Kilmarnock Complete Edition of Burns' Poems and Songs.] [Edited by James M'Kie.] 4 vol.

Poems, chiefly in the Scottish dialect. (Reprint and fac-simile of the original Kilmarnock edition. American edition.) pp. 240. 1870.
Poems, chiefly in the Scottish dialect . . . Poems as they appeared in the early Edinburgh editions. pp. viii*. xlviii. 10–244. 1869.
Poems, chiefly in the Scottish dialect . . . Posthumous poems. pp. xii. 370. 1869.
Songs, chiefly in the Scottish dialect. pp. xxiii. 396. xxvi. 1869.

James M'Kie: Kilmarnock, 1870, 69. 8°. **11609**. h. **3–6**.

—— The Poetical Works of Robert Burns. Re-edited from the best editions. With explanatory glossarial notes, memoir, etc. etc. pp. xxvi. 614. *F. Warne & Co.: London,* [1870.] 8°. [*Chandos Classics.*] **12204.ff.1/20.**

—— The Complete Poetical Works of Robert Burns, arranged in the order of their earliest publication . . . With a memoir of the poet . . . and new annotations, introductory notices, &c., written expressly for the present work by William Scott Douglas. (Kilmarnock popular edition.) 2 vol. *James M'Kie: Kilmarnock,* 1871. 8°. **11609**. bbb. **2, 3**.

—— The Poetical Works of Robert Burns. Edited, with a critical memoir, by William Michael Rossetti. Illustrated by John Moyr Smith. pp. xxxii. 512. *E. Moxon, Son & Co.: London,* [1871.] 8°. **11611**. cc. **4**.
With an additional titlepage, engraved.

—— The Complete Poetical Works of Robert Burns and Sir Walter Scott. Illustrated with . . . portraits, and a fac-simile of a . . . letter of Burns to Mrs. Riddell. New edition. pp. 423. *London,* [1872.] 8°. [*Blackwood's Universal Library of Standard Authors.*] **012202**. ee. **3**.
A reissue of the edition of 1866.

—— The Poetical Works of Robert Burns, *etc.* 2 vol. *Cassell, Petter & Galpin: London,* [1872.] 8°. **11607**. e. **3**.
Part of "Cassell's Library Edition of the British Poets." A reissue of the edition of 1868.

—— The Complete Poetical Works of Robert Burns . . . Edited by William Scott Douglas. (Kilmarnock edition . . . revised and extended.) 2 vol. *M'Kie & Drennan: Kilmarnock,* 1876. 8°. **11662.f.24.**
Previous edition 1871.

—— Memorials of Robert Burns and of some of his contemporaries and their descendants, by the grandson of Robert Aiken (P. F. Aiken) . . . With a numerous selection of his best poems and songs, and engraved portrait and fac-similes. pp. viii. 422. *Sampson Low & Co.: London; M'Kie & Drennan: Kilmarnock,* 1876. 8°. **11612**. bb. **2**.

—— Poems selected from the Works of Robert Burns. Edited with life of the author, notes, and glossary, by Alexander M. Bell. pp. 174. *Rivingtons: London,* [1876.] 8°. [*English School-Classics.*] **12205**. aaa. **40/4**.

—— Favorite Poems . . . Illustrated. pp. 106. *J. R. Osgood & Co.: Boston,* 1877. 16°. **11644**. e. **10**.

—— [Selected poems and songs.] *See* SCOTLAND. [*Appendix.—Miscellaneous.*] Caledonia described by Scott, Burns and Ramsay. 1878. 4°. **11602**. h. **4**.

—— The Poetical Works of Robert Burns. pp. xvii. 512. *Ward, Lock & Co.: London,* [1878.] 8°. **11609**. d. **24**.
A reissue of the edition published by E. Moxon, Son & Co. in 1871, *without the memoir by W. M. Rossetti and the illustrations.*

—— The Poetical Works of Robert Burns. Edited, with introductory biography and notes, by Charles Kent . . . With illustrations. pp. xii. 500. *G. Routledge & Sons: London,* [1878.] 8°. **11609**. d. **23**.

—— The Poetical Works of Robert Burns. Edited from the best printed and manuscript authorities, with glossarial index and a biographical memoir, by Alexander Smith. 2 vol. *Macmillan & Co.: London,* 1879. 8°. **11609**. ccc. **4**.
A reissue of the edition of 1865.

—— The Poetical Works of Robert Burns. Edited, with a critical memoir, by William Michael Rosetti [*sic*]. Illustrated by John Moyr Smith. pp. xxxii. 512. *Ward, Lock & Co.: London,* [1879.] 8°. [*Moxon's Popular Poets.*] **11604.ee.29/10.**
With an additional titlepage, engraved. A reissue of the edition published by E. Moxon, Son & Co. in 1871.

—— The Poetical Works of Robert Burns, *etc.* [With a portrait.] 3 vol. *Houghton, Mifflin & Co.: Boston,* [1880?] 8°. [*British Poets.*] **11613. e. 1/10.**

—— The Poetical Works of Robert Burns. Edited by the Rev. Robert Aris Willmott. pp. lxiii. 478. *G. Routledge & Sons: London,* [1880.] 8°. **11609. e. 17.**
Part of the "Excelsior Series." A reissue of the edition of 1856.

—— Poems of Robert Burns. With a glossary. 2 vol. *W. Kent & Co.: London,* 1881. 32°. **11612. a. 28.**

—— The Poetical Works of Robert Burns. Edited, with a critical memoir, by William Michael Rossetti. Illustrated by John Moyr Smith. pp. xxxii. 512. *Ward, Lock & Co.: London,* [1881.] 8°. **11609. h. 15.**
A reissue of the edition of 1879.

—— The Cotter's Saturday Night and The Twa Dogs. (Auld Lang Syne.) With life, introduction, and notes. pp. 32. *London & Edinburgh,* 1883. 8°. [*Chambers's Reprints of English Classics.*] **12205. aa. 18/2.**

—— The Poetical Works of Robert Burns. Edited, with introductory biography and notes, by Charles Kent. pp. xii. 500. *G. Routledge & Sons: London,* 1883. 8°. **11607. f. 13.**
A reissue of the edition of 1878.

—— The Poetical Works of Robert Burns; with memoir, prefatory notes, and a complete marginal glossary. Edited by John & Angus Macpherson. With portrait and illustrations. pp. 596. *J. S. Marr & Sons: Glasgow,* [1883.] 8°. **11609. g. 25.**
With an additional titlepage.

—— The Select Songs of Burns and Tannahill chronologically arranged, with memoirs. pp. vi. 98. *See* Life. A Strange Life, *etc.* [1883.] 8°. **12618. bbb. 12.**

—— The Poetical Works of Robert Burns. (Pearl edition.) pp. 512. *D. Bryce & Son: Glasgow,* [1884.] 32°. **11607. a. 39.**

—— The Poetical Works of Robert Burns. Edited with introductory biography and notes by Charles Kent. pp. xii. 500. *G. Routledge & Sons: London,* 1885 [1884]. 8°. **11611. d. 14.**
A reissue of the edition of 1883.

—— The Poetical Works of Robert Burns . . . With a prefatory notice, biographical and critical. By Joseph Skipsey. 2 vol. *Walter Scott: London,* 1885. 8°. [*Canterbury Poets.*] **11604. aa. 15.**

—— The Poetical Works of Robert Burns, with photographic illustrations by G. W. Wilson. (Prefatory notice by W. M. Rossetti.) pp. xxxii. 512. *Suttaby & Co.: London,* [1885?] 8°. **11612. k. 9.**
A reissue of the edition published by Ward, Lock & Co. in 1881, *without the illustrations.*

—— Poems of Robert Burns. With a glossary. 2 vol. *Cassell & Co.: London,* [1886.] 32°. **11607. cc. 1.**
Part of "Cassell's Miniature Library of the Poets." A reissue of the edition published by W. Kent & Co. in 1881.

—— Burns Holograph Manuscripts in the Kilmarnock Monument Museum, with notes. Compiled and edited by David Sneddon. pp. viii. 147. *D. Brown & Co.: Kilmarnock,* 1889. 8°. **11645. bbb. 62.**

—— The Poetical Works of Robert Burns. (Pearl edition.) 6 vol. pp. 507. *D. Bryce & Son: Glasgow,* [1889.] 32°. **11612. aa. 30.**
A reissue of the edition of 1884, *with the addition of a glossary.*

—— The Poetical Works of Robert Burns. With explanatory glossary, notes, memoir, etc. (The "Albion" edition.) pp. xxvi. 614. *F. Warne & Co.: London & New York,* 1889. 8°. **11612. c. 29.**

—— Burns. Selected Poems. Edited, with introduction, notes and a glossary, by J. Logie Robertson. pp. xxxi. 292. *Oxford,* 1889. 8°. [*Clarendon Press Series.*] **12205. t. 5.**

—— [Selected songs.] *See* Scotland. [*Appendix.—Miscellaneous.*] Songs of Bonnie Scotland, *etc.* [1890.] 8°. **11602. ee. 27. (6.)**

—— The Poetical Works of Robert Burns; with memoir, prefatory notes, and a complete marginal glossary. Edited by John and Angus Macpherson. pp. 597. *Walter Scott: London,* [1891.] 8°. **11612. df. 19.**
A reissue of the edition published by J. S. Marr & Son in 1883.

—— Selected Poems . . . With an introduction by Andrew Lang. pp. l. 223. **L.P.** *Kegan Paul & Co.: London,* 1891. 8°. **12200. k. 30.**

—— Love-Songs of Robert Burns, selected by Sir George Douglas, Bart., with an introduction and notes. pp. 118. *T. Fisher Unwin: London,* 1892. 8°. [*Cameo Series.*] **12205. ee. 2/1.**

—— Poems & Songs by Robert Burns. With original illustrations by R. Herdman, *etc.* (The "Edina" edition.) pp. xviii. 336. *W. P. Nimmo, Hay & Mitchell: Edinburgh,* [1893.] 4°. **11611. f. 29.**
A reissue of the edition of 1868.

—— The Poetical Works of Robert Burns. Edited with a memoir by George A. Aitken. 3 vol. *G. Bell & Sons: London,* 1893. 8°. [*Aldine Edition of the British Poets.*] **11612. cc. 10.**

—— The Poetical Works of Robert Burns. Edited, with a prefatory memoir, notes and glossary, by J. R. Tutin. pp. xl. 708. *Griffith, Farran & Co.: London,* [1893.] 8°. [*Newbery Classics.*] **012202. f. 8/2.**

—— The Poetical Works of Robert Burns. Edited with introductory biography and notes by Charles Kent. pp. xii. 500. *G. Routledge & Sons: London,* 1893. 8°. [*Sir John Lubbock's Hundred Books.* no. 58.] **012207.1.1/58.**
A reissue of the edition of 1878, *without the illustrations.*

—— [Selected poems and songs.] *See* Murison (William) Shorter Poems of Burns, Byron and Campbell, *etc.* 1893. 8°. **12201. df. 1/4.**

—— The Lyric Poems of Robert Burns. Edited by Ernest Rhys. pp. xxiv. 243. *J. M. Dent & Co.: London,* [1895.] 8°. [*The Lyrical Poets.*] **11607. ccc. 6.**

—— The Poetical Works of Robert Burns. pp. xii. 42–500. *R. E. King: London,* [1895?] 8°. **11612. k. 11.**
A reissue of the edition published by G. Routledge & Sons in 1893 *without the introductory biography.*

—— Shorter Poems by Burns, *etc.* [A reissue of the edition of 1893.] *See* Murison (William) Shorter Poems by Burns, Byron, *etc.* 1895. 8°. **12201**. df. **1/5**.

—— The Complete Poetical Works of Robert Burns. With notes, glossary, index of first lines and chronological list. Edited by J. Logie Robertson. (The Oxford miniature edition.) 3 vol. *Henry Frowde: London,* 1896. 32°. **11612**. dg. **4**.

—— In Memory of Robert Burns. Selected poems and songs. With an introduction by Richard Le Gallienne. [With plates.] pp. 90. **F.P.** *M. Ward & Co.: London,* 1896. 8°. K.T.C. **26**. a. **10**.

—— Robert Burns. Poems and Songs complete. (Edinburgh illustrated edition . . . Chronologically arranged. Notes, glossaries, and index by W. Scott Douglas, and life by Professor Nichol. With twelve photogravures after drawings by Marshall Brown.) 4 vol. *James Thin: Edinburgh,* 1896. 8°. **11612**. bbb. **24**.

—— The Poems and Songs of Robert Burns. Edited with introduction, notes and glossary by Andrew Lang, assisted by W. A. Craigie. With a portrait. pp. xlvi. 668. *Methuen & Co.: London,* 1896. 8°. **11647**. e. **55**.

—— Robert Burns. The Poems, Epistles, Songs, Epigrams & Epitaphs. Edited by Jas. A. Manson. With notes, index, glossary, and biographical sketch. 2 vol. *Clement Wilson: London,* 1896. 8°. **11612**. bb. **27**.

—— The Poetical Works of Robert Burns. Edited by John Fawside, *etc.* pp. 556. *Bliss, Sands & Foster: London,* 1896. 8°. **11611**. ee. **28**.

—— The Poetical Works of Robert Burns. With brief memoir, complete index . . . glossary. Illustrations by Faed, Harvey, *etc.* pp. xxix. 409. *D. Bryce & Son: Glasgow,* 1896. 8°. **11621**. bbb. **32**.

—— The Poetry of Robert Burns. Edited by William Ernest Henley and Thomas F. Henderson. (The Centenary Burns.) [With facsimiles.] 4 vol. *T. C. & E. C. Jack: Edinburgh,* 1896, 97. 8°. Tab. **537**. a. **5**.
No. 22 *of twenty-four copies on Japanese vellum.*

—— [Selected poems and songs.] 1896. *See* Todd (George Eyre) Abbotsford Series of the Scottish Poets, *etc.* (Eighteenth century. vol. 2.) 1891, *etc.* 8°. **11622**. ee. **17**.

—— The Complete Poetical Works of Robert Burns, *etc.* [Edited, with an introduction, by W. E. Henley.] pp. lxvi. 397. *Houghton Mifflin Co.: Boston & New York,* [1897.] 8°. [*Cambridge Edition of the Poets.*] **011604**. ff. **13/14**.

—— Select Poems of Robert Burns. Arranged in chronological order, with introduction, notes and a glossary by Andrew J. George. pp. xxxviii. 370. *Isbister & Co.: London,* 1897. 8°. **11644**. eeee. **40**.

—— The Poems (The Songs) of Robert Burns. (Edited by W. A. Craigie.) 2 vol. *J. M. Dent & Co.: London,* 1898. 8°. [*Temple Classics.*] **012200.de.8/12.**

—— Selections from the Poems of Robert Burns. Edited with introduction, notes, and vocabulary by John G. Dow. pp. xcvi. 287. *Ginn & Co.: Boston,* 1898. 8°. **11611**. c. **35**.
Part of " The Athenæum Press Series."

—— Love Poems of Burns. pp. xi. 120. *John Lane: London & New York,* 1901. 12°. [*Lover's Library.* vol. 7.] **11607**. aaaa. **1/7**.

—— Burns' Poems. pp. xii. 500. *Oxford Library Co.: London,* 1901. 8°. **11613**. b. **16**.
Part of " The New Oxford Library."

—— Robert Burns. The Poems, Epistles, Songs, Epigrams & Epitaphs. Edited by Jas. A. Manson. With notes, index, glossary, and biographical sketch. pp. xlvi. 651. *A. & C. Black: London,* 1901. 8°. **11607**. b. **30**.
A reissue in one volume of the edition published by Clement Wilson in 1896.

—— The Poetical Works of Robert Burns. Edited by Alexander Smith. Vignette edition. Illustrated by Moore Smith. With glossarial index and biographical memoir. pp. xxxiii. 362. *J. Pott & Co.: New York,* 1901. 8°. **11644**. dd. **1**.
Previous edition 1879.

—— The Poetry of Robert Burns. Edited by William Ernest Henley and Thomas F. Henderson. 4 vol. *T. C. & E. C. Jack: Edinburgh,* 1901. 8°. **11609**. c. **36**.
A reissue of the edition of 1896, 97, *without the facsimiles and most of the portraits.*

—— [Another copy.] The Poetry of Robert Burns, *etc. Edinburgh,* 1901. 8°. **11613**. b. **11**.

—— Selections from the Poetry of Robert Burns for the use of schools. Edited by D. M'Naught. 2 pt. *Glasgow,* [1901.] 8°. [*Gibson's Selections of Poetry for use in Schools.* no. 2, 3.] **11604**. c.

—— Songs. pp. 63. *Astolat Press: London,* 1901. 32°. K.T.C. **12**. a. **9**.

—— Songs by Burns. pp. 99. *O. Schulze & Co.: Edinburgh,* 1901. 4°. **11647**. e. **56**.

—— The Complete Poetical Works of Robert Burns. With a glossary. pp. xxiv. 790. *T. Nelson & Sons: London,* 1902. 8°. [*New Century Library.*] **012209**. de. **4/1**.
With an additional titlepage reading " The Poetical Works of Robert Burns."

—— The Poems and Songs of Robert Burns. With notes and glossary (by Robert Ford). [With the essay on Burns by Thomas Carlyle.] pp. lxxii. 580. *George Newnes: London,* 1902. 8°. **11607**. b. **33**.

—— Poetical Works of Robert Burns, with life and notes by William Wallace, LL.D. With twenty-one illustrations, *etc.* pp. xxvi. 553. *W. & R. Chambers: London & Edinburgh,* 1902. 8°. **11607**. d. **19**.

—— The Poetical Works of Robert Burns. pp. xxiii. 607. *Grant Richards: London,* 1903. 8°. [*World's Classics.* vol. 34.] **012209**. df. **28**.

—— The Songs of Robert Burns. Now first printed with the melodies for which they were written. A study in tone-poetry. With bibliography, historical notes, and glossary, by James C. Dick. 2 pt. pp. xxiii. 536. *Henry Frowde: London,* 1903. 8°. **11607**. h. 9.
No. 23 *of twenty-five copies printed on handmade paper.*

—— The People's Penny Burns. Selected poems. pp. 48. *J. Leng & Co.: Dundee & London,* [1904.] 8°. **11601**. i. **21**. **(5.)**

—— Burns' Poems & Songs. [A selection.] pp. 64. *George Newnes: London,* [1904.] 8°. **11601**. i. **22**. **(2.)**

—— The Poems of Burns. A selection. With an introduction by Neil Munro. pp. 192. *London*, 1904. 8°. [*Cassell's National Library*. New ser. no. 20.] **012209.ff.1/20.**

—— The Poetical Works of Robert Burns. (Complete edition.) With notes, glossary, index of first lines, and biographical note. The "Edina" edition. pp. xvi. 560. *W. P. Nimmo, Hay & Mitchell: Edinburgh*, 1904. 8°. **11607. d. 24.**

—— The Poetical Works of Robert Burns. With notes, glossary, index of first lines and chronological list. Edited by J. Logie Robertson. (Oxford complete edition.) pp. xx. 635. *Henry Frowde: London*, 1904. 8°. **11609. d. 27.**

Previous edition 1896.

—— Selected Poems. Edited, with introduction, notes, and a glossary by J. Logie Robertson. pp. xxxi. 292. *Oxford*, 1904. 8°. [*Clarendon Press Series.*] **2319. a. 9.**
A reissue of the edition published in 1889.

—— The Beauties of Burns. Selections from the poems and letters of Robert Burns. pp. 174. *Library Press: London*, [1905.] 8°. [*Cameo Classics.* no. 13.] **012203. e. 14/14.**

—— Selected Poems of Robert Burns. With an introduction by Andrew Lang. pp. l. 223. *Kegan Paul & Co.: London*, 1905. 8°. [*Dryden Library.*] **11604. ccc.**
A reissue of the edition of 1891.

—— The Songs of Burns. pp. 47. *J. Leng & Co.: Dundee & London*, [1905.] 8°. **11601. i. 23. (3.)**

—— Robert Burns' Poems. Selected and edited with notes by T. F. Henderson. pp. xxxv. 170. *C. Winter's Universitätsbuchhandlung: Heidelberg*, 1906. 8°. [*Englische Textbibliothek.* no. 12.] **12273. c. 21/12.**

—— Poems . . . With an introduction by Neil Munro. pp. xvi. 245. *Blackie & Son: London*, 1906. 8°. [*Red Letter Library.*] **012209.fff.1/37.**

—— The Poems and Songs of Robert Burns. [The text revised by T. F. Henderson. With an introduction by Andrew Lang.] pp. lii. 500. *London*, 1906. 8°. [*Methuen's Standard Library.*] **012203. f. 33/20.**

—— The Poems and Songs of Robert Burns. (With an introduction by James Douglas.) pp. xxxii. 649. *J. M. Dent & Co.: London; E. P. Dutton & Co.: New York*, [1906.] 8°. **12206.p.1/97.**

—— Burns. Love songs and other poems. [Edited by A. S. Cody.] pp. 128. *Old Greek Press: Chicago*, [1907.] 16°. [*Nutshell Library.* vol. 5.] **012208. de. 10/5.**

—— The Selected Works of Robert Burns. Edited by Rhona Sutherland. [With plates.] pp. lxii. 368. *Alexander Gardner: Paisley*, 1907. 8°. **11609. i. 24.**

—— Songs . . . With biographical introduction by Hannaford Bennett. pp. 126. *London*, 1907. 8°. [*John Long's Carlton Classics.*] **12204. p. 11/19.**

—— Auld Lang Syne, and other poems [by Burns and others]. Illustrated by Gordon Browne. pp. 47. *Ernest Nister: London; E. P. Dutton & Co.: New York; printed in Bavaria*, [1908.] 16°. [*Laurel Wreath Series.*] **012201.de.6/6.**

—— The Poems and Songs of Robert Burns. pp. 546. *Cassell & Co.: London*, 1908. 8°. [*People's Library.* no. 46.] **012206.de.1/43.**

—— Some Love Songs. *See* infra: LETTERS. Letters to Clarinda. [1908.] 8°. **12203. r. 8/29.**

—— Tam o' Shanter, and other poems. Embellished with pictures by S. B. Pearse. pp. 72. *Sisley's: London*, [1908.] 16°. **011651. de. 36.**

—— The Cotter's Saturday Night, and other poems from Burns, *etc.* *See* CARLYLE (Thomas) [*Critical and Miscellaneous Essays.—Extracts.*] Carlyle's Essay on Burns, *etc.* 1909. 16°. **12199.a.1/6.**

—— The Poetical Works of Robert Burns. Edited with biographical introduction by Charles Annandale . . . Music harmonized by Harry Colin Miller . . . Pictures by Claude A. Shepperson. 4 vol. *Gresham Publishing Co.: London*, 1909. 8°. **11612. h. 9.**

—— Poems. Selections. pp. 255. *H. M. Caldwell Co.: New York & Boston*, [1910.] 8°. **11646. df. 25.**
A slip is pasted on the titlepage, reading "London: Siegle, Hill & Co."

—— The Poems and Songs of Robert Burns, *etc.* [With plates, including a portrait.] pp. 609. *P. F. Collier: New York*, [1910.] 8°. [*Harvard Classics.* vol. 6.] **12209. ppp. 9/6.**

—— The Poetical Works of Robert Burns . . . Edited by J. Logie Robertson. (Oxford edition.) pp. xx. 635. *Oxford University Press: London*, 1910. 8°. **11613. aaa. 1.**
A reissue of the edition published by Henry Frowde in 1904.

—— Moments with Robert Burns. *Henry Frowde: London*, [1911.] 32°. **945. aa. 7.**

—— Selected Poems. pp. 159. *G. G. Harrap & Co.: London*, [1911.] 16°. [*King's Treasury of Literary Masterpieces.*] **012208. de. 6/7.**

—— Songs. pp. 105. *Siegle, Hill & Co.: London*, [1911.] 32°. [*Langham Booklets.*] **944. b. 65.**

—— Songs and Lyrics . . . Selected and edited by William Macdonald, with illustrations by W. Russell Flint and R. Purves Flint. pp. xxviii. 220. *Philip Lee Warner: London*, 1911. 8°. **11645. ff. 45.**

—— The Songs & Poems of Robert Burns. With appreciation by the Right Hon. the Earl of Rosebery, K.T., and containing forty-six illustrations in colour, *etc.* pp. xxvi. 652. *T. N. Foulis: London & Edinburgh*, 1912. 8°. **11607. ff. 2.**

—— Select Poems by Robert Burns, arranged in kindred groups. pp. vi. 90. *Blackie & Son: London*, 1919. 8°. [*Plain-Text Poets.*] **011604. ee. 1/17.**

—— Burns' Poems. With illustrations. [With a memoir.] pp. xxiv. 256. *Andersons: Edinburgh*, [1920?] 32°. [*Thistle Library.* no. 1.] **L.R. 258. b. 1/1.**

—— [Another issue.] Burns' Poems, *etc.* *Valentine & Sons: Dundee*, [1920?] 32°. **11658. de. 30.**

—— Burns' Songs. With illustrations. pp. 240. *Andersons: Edinburgh*, [1920?] 32°. [*Thistle Library.* no. 2.] **L.R. 258. b. 1/2.**

—— Selections from Robert Burns. Edited by J. Hunter Craig. pp. 192. *J. M. Dent & Sons: London & Toronto; E. P. Dutton & Co.: New York,* [1920.] 8°. [*Kings Treasuries of Literature.*] **012207.aaa.1/150.**

—— Autograph Poems and Letters of Robert Burns in the collection of R. B. Adam. [Transcribed by R. B. Adam. With a portrait.] ff. 107. *Privately printed: Buffalo, N.Y.,* 1922. 4°. Ashley **5670.**
Printed on one side of the leaf only.

—— The Poems of Robert Burns . . . Edited by James L. Hughes. [With plates.] pp. 292. *Hodder & Stoughton: London; printed in U.S.A.,* [1922.] 8°. **11642.** ee. **25.**

—— Songs and Ballads . . . With illustrations by Nora, England. pp. x. 222. *Hodder & Stoughton: London,* [1923.] 8°. **11642.** g. **48.**

—— Burns' Poetical Works. With introduction by W. J. Davies [or rather, W. H. Davies]. [With a portrait.] pp. xx. 627. *Collins: London & Glasgow,* [1925?] 8°. **11612.** dd. **20.**

—— Scottish Poems of Robert Burns in his native dialect. By Sir James Wilson. [A phonetic transcript and a translation.] pp. 364. *Oxford University Press: London,* 1925. 8°. **11643.** k. **37.**

—— Songs from Robert Burns. Selected by A. E. Coppard, with wood engravings by Mabel M. Annesley. pp. xvi. 112. *Golden Cockerel Press: Waltham St. Lawrence,* 1925. 8°. C. **99.** d. **28.**

—— Robert Burns. [Selected poems.] pp. 31. *Ernest Benn: London,* [1926.] 8°. [*Augustan Books of Modern Poetry.*] **11605.cc.12/45.**

—— Robert Burns. (Selections.) Compiled by M. F. Dee. pp. 160. *John Hamilton: London,* [1926.] 8°. [*Wedgwood Series.*] **11607.** aaaa. **18/4.**

—— Robert Burns. The Poems, Epistles, Songs, Epigrams & Epitaphs. Edited by Charles S. Dougall, *etc.* pp. xxiv. 711. *A. & C. Black: London,* 1927. 8°. **11633.** df. **35.**

—— Robert Burns. A selection from his poetry. By Dr. Wilhelm Schallas. [With "Wörterbuch."] 2 pt. *Georg Westermann: Braunschweig,* [1927.] 8°. **11632.** de. **56.**

—— Robert Burns. Selected poems. Edited by G. D. H. & M. I. Cole. pp. 61. *Noel Douglas: London,* 1928. 8°. [*Ormond Poets.* no. 13.] **11655.** f. **14/13.**

—— Selections from the Poems of Robert Burns. *See* Carlyle (Thomas) [*Critical and Miscellaneous Essays.—Extracts.*] Essay on Burns, *etc.* [1928.] 8°. **11854.** p. **11.**

—— Burns. Poetry & Prose. With essays by Mackenzie, Jeffrey, Carlyle and others. With an introduction and notes by R. Dewar. pp. xx. 203. *Clarendon Press: Oxford,* 1929. 8°. **11632.** d. **52.**

—— Poems of Robert Burns. Selected by George Ogilvie. pp. 96. *W. & R. Chambers: London & Edinburgh,* 1932. 8°. **11633.** df. **47.**

—— The Poetical Works of Robert Burns. With numerous illustrations. pp. 648. *Collins: London & Glasgow,* [1936.] 8°. **11655.** e. **81.**

—— Twenty-Five Burns Gems. *See* Esslemont (Peter) Brithers A'. A minute a day with Burns, *etc.* 1939. 8°. **10859.** f. **2.**

—— Burns' Poetical Works. With an introduction by W. H. Davies. pp. xx. 624. *Collins: London & Glasgow,* [1942.] 8°. **11612.** k. **5.**

—— Sprigs o' Heather. Songs & poems. [With a portrait.] pp. xxxj. *Whitcombe & Tombs: Christchurch, N.Z.,* [1942.] 16°. **11656.** h. **52.**

—— Songs of Liberty. By Robert Burns. A selection by Sir Patrick Dollan. pp. xii. 100. *A. & C. Black: London,* 1943. 8°. **011641.** df. **122.**

—— Robert Burns, the Inspired Peasant. [Selected poems, edited, with a commentary, by James Crawford Milne.] pp. 94. *Eneas Mackay: Stirling,* 1944. 8°. **10859.** n. **27.**

—— Poems. Selected and introduced by Hugh Macdiarmid. pp. 64. *Grey Walls Press: London,* 1949. 8°. [*Crown Classics.*] W.P. **2809/20.**

—— Poems of Robert Burns. Selected and edited by Laurence Brander. pp. xxi. 333. *Oxford University Press: London,* 1950. 12°. [*World's Classics.* no. 515.] **012209.** df. **398.**

—— Robert Burns. Some Poems, Songs and Epistles. Edited by John McVie and illustrated by Mackay. pp. xvi. 196. *Oliver & Boyd: Edinburgh, London,* 1951. 8°. **11606.** bb. **11.**

—— Songs from Robert Burns, 1759–1796. A selection, with a foreword by G. F. Maine. [With a portrait.] pp. 160. *Collins: London & Glasgow,* [1954.] 8°. [*Fontana Series.*] W.P. c. **17/9.**

—— Poems and Songs of Robert Burns. A completely new edition, including over 60 poems appearing for the first time in a collected edition, of which some have never before been published. Edited and introduced by James Barke. [With plates, including portraits.] pp. 736. *Collins: London & Glasgow,* 1955. 8°. **11606.** b. **49.**

—— Burns in English. Select poems of Robert Burns. Translated from the Scottish dialect by Alexander Corbett, *etc.* pp. viii. 112. *William Corbett: Glasgow,* 1892. 8°. **11612.** e. **21.**

—— [Another copy.] **11612.** e. **23.**

—— Burns into English. Renderings of selected dialect poems of Robert Burns by William Kean Seymour. pp. 160. *Allan Wingate: London,* 1954. 8°. **11605.** bb. **47.**

—— Lieder von Robert Burns. In das Schweizerdeutsche übertragen von August Corrodi. [With the text of the originals.] pp. 103. *Winterthur,* 1870. 12°. **11643.** aa. 12.

—— Lieder. [A new edition of "Lieder von Robert Burns, in das Schweizerdeutsche übertragen von August Corrodi."] pp. 119. *Verona,* 1949. 8°. Cup. **510.** ee. **19.**
Previous edition 1870. *No.* 89 *of an edition of one hundred copies.*

—— The Principal Songs of Robert Burns, translated into mediæval Latin verse, with the Scottish version collated. By Alexander Leighton. pp. 111. *W. P. Nimmo: Edinburgh,* 1862. 8°. **11632.** cc. **5.**

—— Poésies complètes . . . Traduites de l'écossais, par M. Léon de Wailly; avec une introduction du même. pp. xl. 356. *Paris*, 1843. 12°. **11609.** bbb. **1.**

—— Poésies imitées de Robert Burns par Louis Demouceaux. pp. xii. 96. *Paris*, 1865. 8°. **11632.** aaa. **6.**

—— Burns. Traduit de l'écossais avec préface par Richard de la Madelaine, *etc.* pp. xlii. 96. *Rouen*, 1874. 8°. **11641.** bb. **14.**

—— [Selected poems and songs.] *Fr. See* BUISSON DU BERGER (A.) Poètes anglais contemporains. Robert Burns—John Keats . . . Traduction inédite par A. Buisson du Berger. [1890.] 8°. **11601.** ee. **34. (6.)**

—— Dain, is Luinneagan . . . Eadar-theangaichte do'n Ghaidhlig, Albannach. Songs and Poems . . . Translated into Scottish Gaelic by Charles Macphater. [With plates.] pp. viii. 355. *Alex. M'Laren & Son: Glasgow; R. G. Mann: Dumfries*, [1910.] 8°. **11644.** eeee. **59.**

—— Gedichte von Robert Burns. Uebersetzt von Philipp Kaufmann. pp. xx. 163. *Stuttgart & Tübingen*, 1839. 8°. **11646.** h. **34.**

—— Robert Burns' Gedichte deutsch von W. Gerhard. Mit des Dichters Leben und erläuternden Bemerkungen. pp. xlviii. 372. *Leipzig*, 1840. 8°. **11632.** bb. **7.**

—— Lieder und Balladen des Schotten Robert Burns. Uebertragen von Heinrich Julius Heintze. Mit dem Bildniss und einem kurzen Lebensabriss des Dichters, nebst erläuternden Anmerkungen. pp. xxviii. 284. *Braunschweig*, 1840. 12°. **1465.** h. **9.**

—— Robert Burns' Gedichte. Uebertragen von H. Julius Heintze. Mit erläuternden Anmerkungen. pp. xxx. 264. *Leipzig*, 1859. 16°. **11642.** a. **6.**

—— Lieder von Robert Burns. Uebertragen von Georg Pertz. Mit einer biographischen Skizze von Albert Traeger, *etc.* pp. lvi. 96. *Leipzig & Heidelberg*, 1859. 8°. **11633.** a. **9.**

—— Robert Burns' Lieder und Balladen. Deutsch von Karl Bartsch. 2 Tl. *Hildburghausen*, 1865. 8°. [*Bibliothek ausländischer Klassiker.* Bd. 6, 7.] **12209.** e. 1/51.

—— Lieder und Balladen von Robert Burns. Deutsch von Adolf Laun. pp. xxvii. 204. *Berlin*, 1869. 12°. **11643.** a. **2.**

—— Gedichte von Robert Burns. Übersetzt von Edmund Ruete. pp. xi. 183. *Bremen*, 1890. 8°. **11612.** df. **18.**

—— Vieruntwintig schöne Lere von Robert Burns'n, denn'n Schottlänner. Noah Coarl Bartsch'n . . . sien hochdütsch Oewersettung in't Mäkelbörg'sch Plattdütsch oewerdroagen von Berndin Prinz'n. pp. 53. *Leipzig*, 1869. 16°. **11652.** a. **71. (3.)**

—— [Twenty five poems, translated into Low German.] *See* EHLERS (J.) Mikrokosmos, *etc.* 1877. 8°. **11528.** b. **23.**

—— Robert Burns . . . (Übertragungen ins Niederdeutsche.) Eingerichtet von Friedrich Schult. pp. 20. *Hamburg*, 1937. 8°. [*Das Gedicht.* Dec. 1937.] P.P. **5126.** m.

—— Burns Róbert költeményei. Forditotta Lévay József. (A költő arczképével.) pp. 558. 1892. 8°. *See* PEST.—*Kisfaludy Társaság.* Ac. **8983/35.**

—— Poesie di Roberto Burns. Prima versione italiana di Ulisse Ortensi. [With a preface in English by John Muir.] pt. 1. pp. 161. *Modena*, 1893. 8°. **11612.** bbb. **22.**
No more published.

—— [Another copy.] **11612.** aaa. **35.**

—— Роберт Бернс в переводах С. Маршака. [With a portrait.] pp. 231. *Москва*, 1950. 8°. **11603.** i. **42.**

—— Sånger och ballader af Robert Burns . . . Ofversättning [by K. H. von Becker and C. R. Mannerheim], *etc.* pp. x. 70. *Helsingfors*, 1854. 8°. **11632.** bb. **2.**

LETTERS AND JOURNALS.

—— Letters addressed to Clarinda, &c. . . . Never before published. pp. 48. *T. Stewart: Glasgow*, 1802. 16°. **10920.** aa. **14.**

—— [Another copy.] G. **5357.**

—— A new edition. pp. 48. *L. Rae: Belfast*, 1816. 8°. **10909.** bb. **19. (2.)**

—— *See* EWING (James C.) Robert Burns's Letters addressed to Clarinda. A history of its publication and interdiction, with a bibliography. [With facsimiles.] 1921. 4°. **10922.** dd. **9.**

—— The Letters of Robert Burns, chronologically arranged from Dr. Currie's collection. 2 vol. *John Sharpe: London*, 1819. 12°. [*British Prose Writers.* vol. 23.] **12271.** de. **1.**
The titlepages are engraved.

—— The Prose Works of Robert Burns; containing his letters and correspondence, literary and critical; and amatory epistles, including letters to Clarinda, &c. &c. Embellished with nine . . . engravings. pp. xi. 610. *Mackenzie & Dent: Newcastle upon Tyne*, 1819. 8°. **12272.** e. **11.**
With an additional titlepage, engraved.

—— [Collected letters.] *See* CURRIE (James) *M.D., of Liverpool.* The Life of Robert Burns, *etc.* 1826. 24°. **10855.** dg. **10.**

—— The Letters of Robert Burns, chronologically arranged. Comprehending the whole of Dr Currie's collection, and the most valuable portion of Cromek's Reliques. pp. 376. *R. Griffin & Co.: Glasgow*, 1828. 8°. **10921.** aaa. **14.**

—— The Prose Works of Robert Burns, with the notes of Currie and Cromek, and many by the present editor. [The editor's preface signed: R. C., i.e. Robert Chambers.] pp. 134. *W. & R. Chambers: Edinburgh*, 1839. 8°. **1340.** m. **17. (2.)**

—— The Correspondence between Burns and Clarinda. With a memoir of Mrs. M'Lehose—Clarinda. Arranged and edited by her grandson, W. C. M'Lehose. pp. xi. 297. *William Tait: Edinburgh*, 1843. 12°. **1454.** h. **1.**
With an additional titlepage, lithographed.

—— The Complete Prose Works of Robert Burns. pp. x. 461. *W. P. Nimmo: Edinburgh*, [1867.] 8°. **10921.** aaa. **26.**

—— [Pp. 281–408 of a copy of "The Prose Works of Robert Burns," published by Mackenzie and Dent, Newcastle-upon-Tyne, 1819, containing the correspondence between Burns and George Thomson.] [1877?] 8°. C. **60.** i. **8.**
Partly interleaved. With copious MS. *corrections and additions in three hands, apparently transcribed from the original* MSS. *by persons preparing a new edition of the text.*

—— The Letters of Robert Burns, selected and arranged, with an introduction, by J. Logie Robertson. pp. xxi. 350. *Walter Scott: London*, 1887. 8°. [*Camelot Series.*] **12205**. ff. **8**.

—— Robert Burns and Mrs. Dunlop. Correspondence now published in full for the first time, with elucidations by William Wallace. [With a portrait of Mrs. Dunlop.] pp. xxxi. 434. *Hodder & Stoughton: London*, 1898. 8°. **010910**. c. **5**.

—— *See* EWING (James C.) Letter to the Editor of "The Bookman" on certain paragraphs which appeared in that journal relative to a correspondence in "The Scotsman" on "Robert Burns and Mrs. Dunlop: correspondence now published in full for the first time," *etc.* 1898. 8°. **10601**. df. **19**. **(1.)**

—— Letters to Clarinda. (Some Love Songs.) [With an introduction by M. Y. Bankart.] pp. 227. *London*, [1908.] 8°. [*Sisley Books.*] **12203**. r. **8/29**.

—— Journal of a Tour in the Highlands made in the year, 1787 . . . Reproduced in facsimile . . . With introduction and transcript, by J. C. Ewing. *Gowans & Gray: London & Glasgow*, 1927. 4°. **10369**. h. **31**.

—— The Letters of Robert Burns. Selected, with an introduction, by R. Brimley Johnson. pp. ix. 188. *John Lane: London; Dodd, Mead & Co.: New York*, 1928. 8°. [*Quill Library.*] **010920.a.71/3.**

—— Robert Burns. The Letters of the Poet. Introduction by R. W. Mackenna. pp. xvi. 281. *Collins: London & Glasgow*, [1928.] 8°. **10906**. e. **28**.
Another issue of the corresponding part of "The Complete Works and Letters" published in 1928.

—— The Letters of Robert Burns. Edited from the original manuscripts by J. De Lancey Ferguson. [With plates, including facsimiles.] 2 vol. *Clarendon Press: Oxford*, 1931. 8°. **2409**. b. **11**.

—— The Journal of the Border Tour. (Edited by DeLancey Ferguson.) *See* FITZHUGH (Robert T.) Robert Burns: his Associates and Contemporaries, *etc.* 1943. 8°. **10861**. ee. **7**.

—— Selected Letters of Robert Burns. Edited and with an introduction by DeLancey Ferguson. pp. xxvii. 371. *Oxford University Press: London*, 1953. 8°. [*World's Classics.* no. 529.] **012209**. df. **415**.

POEMS, CHIEFLY IN THE SCOTTISH DIALECT.

—— Poems, chiefly in the Scottish dialect. pp. viii. 240. *Printed by John Wilson: Kilmarnock*, 1786. 8°. C. **39**. e. **38**.

—— [Another copy.] MS. NOTES AND ADDITIONS. C. **28**. f. **2**.

—— [Another copy.] Ashley **2597**.

—— Poems, chiefly in the Scottish dialect. pp. xlviii. 368. *Printed for the Author, and sold by William Creech: Edinburgh*, 1787. 8°. C. **28**. k. **1**.
With the reading "stinking" on p. 263.

—— The third edition. pp. xlviii. 372. *A. Strahan; T. Cadell: London*, 1787. 8°. **1164**. g. **7**.

—— [Another edition.] pp. x. 274. *William Gilbert: Dublin*, 1787. 12°. **11622**. df. **25**.

—— [Another issue.] *James Magee: Belfast*, 1787. 12°. **11641**. bb. **13**.

—— [Another edition.] pp. 304. *Peter Stewart & George Hyde: Philadelphia*, 1788. 8°. C. **58**. b. **15**.

—— Poems, chiefly in the Scottish dialect . . . To which are added, Scots poems, selected from the works of Robert Ferguson. [With a portrait.] pp. 306. *J. & A. M'Lean: New-York*, 1788. 8°. **Cup.401.d.6.**

—— [Another edition.] pp. x. 274. *William Gilbert: Dublin*, 1790. 12°. **11632**. aaa. **57**. **(1.)**

—— The second edition considerably enlarged. 2 vol. *Edinburgh; printed for T. Cadell: London; & William Creech: Edinburgh*, 1793. 8°. **1465**. h. **5**.

—— [Another edition.] 2 vol. *William Magee: Belfast*, 1793. 12°. **1465**. b. **3**.
Imperfect; wanting the portrait.

—— [Another copy of vol. 2.] **11632**. aaa. **57**. **(2.)**

—— A new edition, considerably enlarged. 2 vol. *Edinburgh; printed for T. Cadell: London; & William Creech: Edinburgh*, 1794. 8°. **1465**. h. **7**.

—— A new edition, considerably enlarged. 2 vol. *Edinburgh; printed for T. Cadell, jun. & W. Davies: London; & William Creech: Edinburgh*, 1797. 8°. **11642**. c. **41**.

—— A new edition, considerably enlarged. 2 vol. *Edinburgh; printed for T. Cadell, jun. & W. Davies: London; & William Creech: Edinburgh*, 1798. 8°. **11633**. f. **2, 3**.

—— [Another edition.] 2 vol. *James Robertson: Edinburgh*, 1801. 32°. **11601**. a. **33, 34**.
The titlepages are engraved.

—— [Another edition.] To which are added, several other pieces, not contained in any former edition of his poems. pp. xii . 360. *William M'Lellan: Glasgow*, 1801. 12°. **11633**. aaa. **6**.

—— [Another edition.] 2 vol. *H. Richardson for J. Taylor: Berwick*, 1801. 12°. **11632**. aa. **9, 10**.
With an additional titlepage to each volume, engraved, bearing the imprint "Printed by H. Richardson: Berwick upon Tweed; sold by David Forbes: Edinburgh."

—— A new edition, which includes all the poems and songs in that printed at Edinburgh, in 1787, under the author's own inspection. pp. viii. 224. *A. Cleugh: London*, 1803. 12°. **11641**. aaa. **16**.

—— [Another edition.] pp. xii. 222. *Printed by John Turnbull: Edinburgh; for Cameron & Co.: Glasgow*, 1804. 12°. **993**. a. **57**.
Inserted in this copy is a newspaper cutting describing the unveiling of the Burns statue at Dumfries, 1882.

—— [Another edition.] pp. xii. 221. *Denham & Dick: Edinburgh*, 1805. 12°. **11609**. a. **1**.

—— [Another edition.] [With engravings after the designs of R. Westall.] pp. xii. 255. *John Sharpe: London*, 1824. 12°. **1066**. f. **41**.
With an additional titlepage, engraved.

—— [Another edition.] (Reprint and fac-simile of the original Kilmarnock edition.) [1870.] *See* supra: SMALLER COLLECTIONS. [Kilmarnock Complete Edition of Burns' Poems and Songs.] 1870, *etc.* 8°. **11609**. h. **3**.

BURNS (ROBERT) *the Poet.* [POEMS, CHIEFLY IN THE SCOTTISH DIALECT.]

— [A reduced facsimile of the first edition.] pp. 240. *D. Bryce & Son: Glasgow,* [1896.] 64°. **528.** m. **23/25.** *In a case, with a magnifying glass.*

— The Geddes Burns. [A facsimile of the copy of the Edinburgh edition of 1787 formerly in the possession of Dr. Alexander Geddes.] pp. 26. xlviii. 368. 1908. 8°. *See* BOSTON, *Mass.—Bibliophile Society.* Ac. **9719/17.**

— Burns. Poems published in 1786. [A reprint of the Kilmarnock edition.] pp. 240. *Henry Frowde: London,* 1911. 8°. **11647.** de. **44.**

— Poems published in 1786 (The Kilmarnock edition). With an introduction and notes by M. S. Cleghorn. pp. xxxii. 280. *Clarendon Press: Oxford,* 1913. 8°. **11611.** de. **21.**

— Poems, chiefly in the Scottish dialect. [A facsimile of the Kilmarnock edition.] pp. viii. 240. *T. Werner Laurie: London,* 1927. 8°. **11633.** cc. **20.**

— [Another copy.] Poems, chiefly in the Scottish dialect. *London,* 1927. 8°. **11656.** c. **47.**

— Verses to the memory of James Thomson . . . By R. Burns . . . To which is added, a Poem written in Carse Hermitage, by Nithside; by the same author. [Both extracted from the 1793 edition of " Poems, chiefly in the Scottish dialect."] And an Epitaph on Sir Isaac Newton. pp. 8. [1795?] 8°. C. **58.** cc. **36.** **(2.)**

— The Cotter's Saturday Night, and Tam o' Shanter. pp. 48. *T. Goode: London,* [1854?] 48°. **528.** m. **23/68.**

— Tam o' Shanter.—Address to the De'il. pp. 16. *See* MURRAY (Archibald K.) and (T.) *Publishers.* Murray's Railway Readings. pt. 1. [1867, *etc.*] 8°. **12603.** c. **29.**

— Tam o' Shanter . . . and Lament of Mary Queen of Scots . . . Photo-lithographed [from the original MSS.] by W. Griggs. With an introductory note by H. R. Sharman. *E. W. Allen: London,* [1869.] fol. [*Photo-lithograph Facsimiles.* no. 1.] **11642.** i. **1.**

— The Cotter's Saturday Night, and other poems . . . [All from " Poems, chiefly in the Scottish dialect."] With prefatory and explanatory notes. pp. 31. *London,* 1879. 8°. [*Blackie's School Classics.*] **12200.** c. **15/2.**

— To a Mouse.—To a Mountain Daisy. [With notes.] *See* COTTERILL (Henry B.) Selected Poems of Gray, Burns, *etc.* 1904. 8°. **11601.** ccc **1.**

Appendix.

— *See* DOGS. The Twa Dogs. • A new version [of the poem by R. Burns]. [1870?] 8°. **11645.** ee. **45.** **(6.)**

— *See* WOLF (Edwin) " Skinking " or " Stinking "? A bibliographical study of the 1787 Edinburgh edition of Burns' Poems. [1947.] 8°. **11867.** ff. **30.**

MISCELLANEOUS.

— Burns Manuscripts in the Honresfeld Collection of Sir Alfred James Law. By Davidson Cook. [The text, with notes.] (Reprinted from the " Burns Chronicle.") pp. 35. *Printed for private circulation: Glasgow,* 1928. 8°. **011900.** bb. **51.** *One of an edition of* 100 *copies.*

BURNS (ROBERT) *the Poet.* [MISCELLANEOUS.]

— Robert Burns' Common Place Book. Printed from the original manuscript in the possession of John Adam, Esq., Greenock. [The preface signed: C. D. L., i.e. Colin Daniel Lamont.] pp. vii. 54. *Privately printed: Edinburgh,* 1872. 8°. **10854.** f. **6.**

— Robert Burns's Commonplace Book, 1783–1785. Reproduced in facsimile from the poet's manuscript . . . With transcript, introduction and notes by James Cameron Ewing . . . and Davidson Cook. pp. xiv. 43. *Gowans & Gray: Glasgow,* 1938. fol. L.R. **39.** c. **12.**

— [For editions of Burns's Commonplace Book published with collections of letters:] *See* supra: LETTERS AND JOURNALS.

— Fac-Simile of the Hand Writing of Robert Burns, copied from his Family Bible, by Charles Mackie. *Published for C. Mackie: London,* 1847. *s. sh.* fol. **1880.** c. **1.** **(105.)**

— The Merry Muses of Caledonia; original edition. A collection of favourite Scots songs . . . [Collected, and some of them written, by R. Burns.] A vindication of Robert Burns in connection with the above publication and the spurious editions which succeeded it. (The Court of Equity; or, the Libel summons. By Robert Burns, complete version.) pp. 135. [*D. Brown & Co.: Kilmarnock*,] 1911. 8°. **Cup.1000.a.13.** *Privately printed.*

— Notes on Scottish Song. *See* infra: Reliques of Robert Burns.

— Poems and Letters in the Handwriting of Robert Burns. Reproduced in facsimile through the courtesy of William K. Bixby and Frederick W. Lehmann by the Burns Club of St. Louis. With an introduction and explanatory notes by Walter B. Stevens. [With a portrait.] pp. 104. 1908. fol. *See* SAINT LOUIS, *Missouri.—Burns Club of Saint Louis.* C. **103.** k. **3.**

— Poems ascribed to Robert Burns, the Ayrshire bard, not contained in any edition of his works hitherto published. pp. 93. *Thomas Stewart: Glasgow,* 1801. 8°. **1164.** g. **9.**

— Reliques of Robert Burns; consisting chiefly of original letters, poems, and critical observations on Scottish songs. Collected and published by R. H. Cromek. pp. xxiii. 453. *T. Cadell & W. Davies: London,* 1808. 8°. **1340.** i. **14.**

— [Notes on Scottish song, extracted from the " Reliques."] *See* CROMEK (Robert H.) Select Scotish Songs . . . With critical observations and biographical notices by R. Burns, *etc.* 1810. 8°. **992.** c. **33.**

— Notes on Scottish Song . . . Written in an interleaved copy of the Scots Musical Museum with additions by Robert Riddell and others. Edited by the late James C. Dick. pp. liii. 134. *Henry Frowde: London,* 1908. 8°. **11850.** pp. **17.**

— *See* COOK (Davidson) Annotations of Scottish Songs by Burns: an essential supplement to Cromek and Dick, *etc.* 1922. 8°. **011851.** h. **86.**

— The Robin's Yule Song. Extracted from Chambers' Popular Rhymes of Scotland. [A story for children, taken from the recitation of Mrs. Begg and believed by her to have been composed by Burns.] Illustrated by W. F. F. and E. C. F. [1859.] *obl.* 4°. *See* ROBIN. **12806.** f. **3.**

— Second edition. 1860. *obl.* 4°. *See* ROBIN. **1876.** a. **11**

—— The Scots Musical Museum. Humbly dedicated to the Catch Club . . . By James Johnson. [Containing numerous contributions by Burns.] [1787, *etc.*] 8°. *See* Johnson (J.) *Musicseller and Engraver.* **M.E. 201.**

—— *See* Stenhouse (William) Illustrations of the Lyric Poetry and Music of Scotland . . . Originally compiled to accompany the "Scots Musical Museum," *etc.* 1853. 8°. **1077. k. 63.**

—— A Select Collection of Original Scotch Airs for the Voice, *etc.* [Containing numerous contributions by Burns.] [1793, *etc.*] fol. *See* Thomson (George) *Principal Clerk of the Trustees' Office, Edinburgh.* **M.G. 370.**

SINGLE POEMS.

—— An Address to the Deil. By R. Burns. With the answer, by John Lauderdale. pp. 8. 1795. 12°. **1078. k. 19. (12.)**

—— An Address to the Deil . . . with explanatory notes. Illustrated by numerous engravings on wood, after designs by Thomas Landseer. pp. 23. *William Kidd: London,* 1830. 12°. **T. 1310. (4.)**

—— Address to the People of Scotland, respecting Francis Grose, Esq., the British Antiquarian. By R. Burns . . . To which are added, Verses on seeing the Ruins of an Ancient Magnificent Structure [signed: R. G.]. pp. 8. [1795?] 8°. **C. 58. cc. 36. (1.)**

—— Address to the People of Scotland. By R. Burns. To which are added, Mary of Castle-Cary, the maid with the dark rolling eye; and The Banks o' the Rhine, a new song. pp. 7. *Brash & Reid: Glasgow,* [1796?] 8°. **11601. aa. 43. (1.)**

—— [Another issue.] [1797.] *See* Poetry. Poetry; original and selected. vol. 2. [1796, *etc.*] 8°. **1474. a. 14/2.**

—— [For a' that and a' that.] An Honest Man the Best o' Men, a favourite new song by the celebrated Robert Burns, to which is added, The Character of a Good Wife delineated, in an epistle to a friend [in verse], by the Honourable Lord Gardenstone. pp. 8. *Brash & Reid: Glasgow,* [1796?] 8°. **11601. aa. 43. (3.)**

—— [Another issue.] [1797.] *See* Poetry. Poetry; original and selected. vol. 2. [1796, *etc.*] 8°. **1474. a. 14/2.**

—— Auld Lang Syne [by R. Burns], Parody on Sweet Home (by J. N. Maffit), and My Old Horse. [1835?] *s. sh.* 4°. *See* Auld Lang Syne. **11630. f. 7. (114.)**

—— Auld Lang Syne . . . Illustrated by George Harvey. *Royal Association for the Promotion of the Fine Arts in Scotland: Edinburgh,* 1859. fol. **1875. b. 28.**

—— [Another edition.] [With illustrations.] *Castell Bros.: London; printed in Bavaria,* [1890.] *obl.* 8°. **11651. a. 79.**

—— [Another edition.] [With illustrations.] *Ernest Nister: London; E. P. Dutton & Co.: New York; printed in Bavaria,* [1905.] 8°. **11647. cc. 51.**

—— A Page of Greek. 1. Auld Lang Syne [by R. Burns]. A rendering by Father Knox. [1929.] *s. sh.* 4°. *See* Auld Lang Syne. **C. 100. l. 6. (1.)**

—— The Ayrshire Garland. *See* infra: The Kirk's Alarm.

—— Banks of Doon. [By R. Burns.] (The Banks of the Clyde.) [Songs.] [1850?] *s. sh.* 4°. *See* Doon, *River.* **11621. k. 4. (142.)**

—— The Calf [a satire on the Rev. James Steven, by Burns]; the Unco Calf's Answer; Virtue - - - to a Mountain Bard; and the De'il's Answer to his vera worthy Frien' Robert Burns. [All in verse.] pp. 8. *Printed in the present year,* [1787.] 8°. **11630. aaa. 3. (2.)**

—— Burns' Calf turn'd a Bull: or, Some remarks on his mean and unprovoked attack of Mr. S * * * * * [i.e. James Steven] . . . To which is added, some observations on Dr. M'G—ll's [i.e. William MacGill's] Practical Essay. By a Rhymer. [In verse.] pp. 8. 1787. 8°. **11630. aaa. 3. (1.)**

—— The Cotter's Saturday Night . . . rendered intelligible, to those unacquainted with the Scottish phrases of the original, for the use of the poorer classes in England. pp. 11. *Crocker: Frome,* 1831. 8°. **11602. ff. 24. (11.)**

—— The Cotter's Saturday Night . . . Illustrated by F. A. Chapman. pp. 47. *C. Scribner & Co.: New York,* 1867. 8°. **11651. bbb. 4.**

—— The Cottar's Saturday Night . . . Illustrated by J. Stanley. *J. Nisbet & Co.: London; printed in Germany,* [1888.] 4°. **11649. eee. 33.**

—— The Cotter's Saturday Night. A poem, by R. Burns The Dream of Jubal. A poem . . . by Joseph Bennett . . . Book of words with analytical notes by Joseph Bennett. pp. 40. *London & New York,* [1892.] 8°. [*Novello's Series of the Words of Oratorios.*] **7896. de. 1/4.**

—— The Cottar's Saturday Night . . . Illustrated. With an introduction by Rev. John Hall. ff. 22. *M. Ward & Co.: London,* [1893.] *obl.* 4°. **11650. ee. 45.** *Lithographed.*

—— [Another edition.] Illustrated by A. S. Boyd. pp. 95. *Chatto & Windus: London,* 1905. 8°. **11644. h. 36.**

—— [Another edition.] Illustrated by Gordon Browne. pp. 47. *Ernest Nister: London; E. P. Dutton & Co.: New York; printed in Bavaria,* [1910.] 16°. [*Laurel Wreath Series.*] **012201.de.6/4.**

—— [Another edition.] [With engravings designed by Arthur N. Macdonald.] 1915. fol. *See* Boston, *Mass.—Boston Bibliophile Society.* **Ac. 9719. c.**

—— The Cottar's Saturday Night [by R. Burns] and H.M. Queen Elizabeth's Broadcast Address to the Women of the Empire, *etc.* [With illustrations, including a portrait of the Queen.] [1943.] *obl.* 8°. *See* Cottar. **11655. f. 100.**

—— The Cottager's Saturday Night. A poem, *etc.* [In an Anglicised version.] pp. 8. [1800?] 12°. *See* Cottager. **11641. aaa. 21.**

—— [Another edition.] pp. 8. [1810?] 12°. *See* Cottager. **11621. aaa. 4. (18.)**

—— An English Versification of the Cotter's Saturday Night . . . By William Austin. pp. 7. *A. King: Portsea,* 1859. 8°. **11633. c. 11.**

—— The Election. A new song. [By R. Burns.] pp. 4. [1795.] 8°. *See* Election. **11621. c. 44.**

—— For a' that, and a' that [by R. Burns], When Kate was Nineteen, Let Drunkards Sing, and Blythe and Happy. [Songs.] pp. 8. 1818. 16°. *See* For. **11621. aaa. 10. (9.)**

—— A Man's a Man for a' that. [By R. Burns.] (The Bold Bloodhound.) [Songs.] [1850?] *s. sh.* 4°. *See* MAN. **11621. k. 5. (9*.)**

—— The Fornicators Court. pp. 8. [1825?] 8°. **1325. d. 3. (11.)**

—— [A facsimile of the original edition.] pp. 8. *Metuchen*, 1928. 8°. **11633. d. 9.**

—— Green Grows the Rashes, O'. [By R. Burns.] (The Garden Gate.—My Beautiful Rhine.) [Songs.] [1850?] *s. sh.* 4°. *See* RUSHES. **11621. k. 5. (126.)**

—— [Halloween.] The Ceremony of Halloween displayed: to which is added First of April, Hunt the gowk! or All-Fools' day . . . Compiled from Burns's works, by Willie Smith. pp. 16. [*Edinburgh*,] 1825. 8°. **840. m. 33. (8.)**

—— Highland Mary. [By R. Burns.] *In:* Buy a Broom . . . and Highland Mary. [1835?] *s. sh.* 4°. **11630. f. 7. (3.)**

—— Highland Mary. [By R. Burns.] *In:* Jovial Fellows . . . and Highland Mary. [1835?] *s. sh.* 4°. **11630. f. 7. (8.)**

—— Highland Mary. [By R. Burns.] To which are added Buonaparte's Farewell to Paris; The Soldier Tir'd. pp. 8. [1840?] 16°. *See* MARY, *Highland.* **11621. aaa. 30. (14.)**

—— Highland Mary. [By R. Burns.] (Buffalo Girls.—Sandy Boy.) [Songs.] [1860?] *s. sh.* 4°. *See* MARY, *Highland.* **11621. k. 5. (27.)**

—— [Another copy.] **11621. k. 5. (28.)**

—— John Anderson, my Joe, improved. *See* COTTON (Nathaniel) *M.D.* Domestic Happiness exhibited, in I. The Fireside. A poem by Dr. Cotton, *etc.* [1796.] 8°. **11632. aa. 59.**

—— John Anderson, my Jo. [By R. Burns.] *In:* Bonny Breast-Knots, John Anderson, my Jo, *etc.* [1835?] *s. sh.* 4°. **11630. f. 7. (46.)**

—— Fac-simile of Burns' Celebrated Poem, entitled The Jolly Beggars. From the original manuscript. [The advertisement signed: W. W., i.e. William Weir.] *J. Lumsden & Son: Glasgow*, 1838. 4°. **11632. h. 5.**

—— [The Kirk's Alarm.] The Ayrshire Garland, *etc.* [By R. Burns.] [1789.] *s. sh.* fol. *See* AYRSHIRE GARLAND. **C. 59. f. 27.**

—— My Heart's in the Highlands [by R. Burns], Up amang yon craggy cliffs, Dainty Davie, Oh! had I a house, and a cantie wee fire, My Anna, and On Ettrick banks, on a summer night. [Six songs.] pp. 8. 1818. 16°. *See* SCOTLAND. [*Appendix.—Miscellaneous.*] **11621. aaa. 10. (22.)**

—— An Unpublished Poem by Robert Burns. (My lord, I would not fill your chair, *etc.*) From the "Leeds Licensed Trades' Monthly." *W. D. Ross & Son: Leeds*, [1914.] *s. sh.* 8°. **1879. c. 12. (46.)**

—— My Nannie, O [by R. Burns], The Coggie, Loudon's Woods and Braes, and The Lass of Netherlee. pp. 8. 1818. 16°. *See* NANNIE. **11621. aaa. 10. (23.)**

—— Relic of Burns, *etc.* [A facsimile of a manuscript beginning "The trout in yonder wimpling burn," being stanzas 2, 3 and 4 of "Now Spring has clad the groves in green." Edited by T. C. S. Corry.] *M. Ward & Co.: [London,]* 1867. *s. sh.* fol. **1865. c. 18. (54.)**

—— The Rigs of Barley. [By Burns.] To which are added, The Bush aboon Traquair. Charlie's my Darling. Oscar's Ghost. The Pitcher. pp. 8. 1820. 12°. *See* RIGS. **1078. k. 5. (9.)**

—— [Another copy.] **11621. c. 6. (32.)**

—— The Soldier's Return. A song. By R. Burns . . . To which is added, a Sonnet written on the sea shore, and an Epigram. pp. 8. *See* POETRY. Poetry; original and selected. vol. 1. [1796, *etc.*] 8°. **1474. a. 14/1.**

—— The Soldier's Return. [By R. Burns.] To which are added, Young Doctor Stafford, The Egyptian Wedding, The Happy Soldier. pp. 8. [1805?] 12°. *See* SOLDIER. **11621. b. 10. (11.)**

—— The Soldier's Return, with his kind reception. [By R. Burns.] To which are added, Saturday's Night at Sea. Buxom Nan of Dover. Jamie Gay on the River Tweed. Liberty much to be Desired. [Songs.] pp. 8. 1805. 12°. *See* SOLDIER. **11621. b. 7. (6)**

—— The Soldier's Return [by R. Burns], The Irish Smugglers, Loudon's bonny Woods and Braes, The Sailor's Epitaph, and The Slighted Lover. [Songs.] pp. 8. [1815?] 12°. *See* SOLDIER. **11621. b. 15. (37.)**

—— The Soldier's Return [by R. Burns] and Soldier's Bride. [Songs.] [1835?] *s. sh.* 4°. *See* SOLDIER. **11630. f. 7. (95.)**

—— The Soldier's Return . . . Illustrated by John Faed. ff. 4. *Royal Association for the Promotion of the Fine Arts in Scotland: Edinburgh*, 1857. fol. **1875. b. 29.**

—— The Speech of King Robert the Bruce to his Troops . . . at the ever memorable Battle of Bannockburn . . . By R. Burns . . . To which is added, The Two Lamps: a fable. pp. 8. [1798.] *See* POETRY. Poetry; original and selected. vol. 4. [1796, *etc.*] 8°. **1474. a. 14/4.**

—— A Parody on Bruce's Address, before the Battle of Bannockburn. [With other satirical verses.] [*Dublin*, 1830?] 8°. **11642. bb. 29.**
A fragment from an unidentified larger work.

—— [Tam o' Shanter.] Aloway Kirk; or, Tam o' Shanter. A tale. pp. 8. [1795?] 8°. **C. 58. cc. 36. (3.)**

—— [Another edition.] pp. 8. *See* POETRY. Poetry; original and selected. vol. 1. [1796, *etc.*] 8°. **1474. a. 14/1.**

—— Aloway Kirk; or, Tam o' Shanter. A tale. pp. 8. *G. Caldwell: Paisley*, 1808. 12°. **11606. aa. 22. (32.)**

—— The Surprising Adventures of Tam o' Shanter, giving a full and particular account of his battle with the witches, and how the witches pull'd away his mare's tail at Aloway-Kirk. pp. 8. [*Paisley*, 1808?] 12°. **11606. aa. 22. (30.)**

—— Tam o' Shanter. A tale. *See* infra: APPENDIX.—*Miscellaneous.* Burns' Monument. Account of the grand masonic procession, *etc.* 1820. 12°. **11621. aa. 16. (1.)**

—— Aloway Kirk; or, Tam o' Shanter, *etc.* pp. 8. *J. Neilson: Paisley*, 1822. 16°. **11621. aaa. 3. (1.)**

—— Tam o' Shanter. A tale. pp. 8. *G. Caldwell: Paisley,* 1825. 12°. **11601**. aa. **43**. **(10.)**

—— Tam o' Shanter; a tale. To which are added Observations on the statues [by James Thom] of Tam o' Shanter & Souter Johnny. Now exhibiting. pp. 16. [*London,* 1829.] 8°. **11643**. bbb. **12**. **(12.)**

—— Sculpture. Tam o' Shanter, Souter Johnny, the Landlord & Landlady, executed by Mr. James Thom; and illustrative of Tam o' Shanter; a tale by Robert Burns. [With the text of the poem.] pp. 32. *C. Handy: London,* 1830. 8°. **1422**. g. **29**.

—— Tam o'Shanter and Souter Johnny, a poem . . . Illustrated by Thomas Landseer. pp. 16. *Marsh & Miller: London,* 1830. 8°. **11657**. c. **62**.

—— Tam o' Shanter. (Illustrated by John Faed.) ff. 5. *Royal Association for the Promotion of the Fine Arts in Scotland:* [*Edinburgh,*] 1855. fol. **1875**. b. **26**.

—— [Another edition.] With illustrations by E. H. Miller, *etc.* pp. 20. *W. J. Widdleton: New York,* 1868. 4°. **11651**. k. **14**.

—— [Another edition.] With illustrations by George Cruikshank. pp. 48. *Griffith, Farran & Co.: London,* [1884.] 4°. **1876**. c. **31**.

—— [Another edition.] Illustrated by John C. Duncan. *J. Walker & Co.: London,* [1888.] 16°. **11630**. aaa. **14**.

—— [Another edition.] pp. 12. ON VELLUM. *Printed at the Essex House Press; Edward Arnold: London; S. Buckley & Co.: New York,* 1902. 8°. C. **99**. c. **8**.

—— [Another edition.] Illustrated by Monro S. Orr. pp. 32. *T. C. & E. C. Jack: London & Edinburgh,* [1906.] 16°. **11646**. de. **54**.

—— [Another issue.] Tam o' Shanter, *etc.* *London & Edinburgh,* [1906.] 16°. **11658**. de. **1**.

—— [Another edition.] *See* Bliss (Douglas P.) The Devil in Scotland, *etc.* 1934. 8°. C. **99**. d. **49**.

—— [Another edition.] With wood-engravings by Iain Macnab. pp. 13. *Samson Press: Warlingham,* 1934. 8°. **11654**. b. **52**.

—— Burns ac Ingoldsby yn Gymraeg. Tri darn gan John Jones, Talhaiarn. [A Welsh adaptation of Burns's "Tam o' Shanter" and of two of the "Ingoldsby Legends."] Wedi eu newid gan J. Glyn Davies. [With illustrations, including a portrait of John Jones.] pp. 71. *Hughes a'i Fab: Wrecsam,* 1931. 8°. **11633**. df. **46**.

—— Tam o' Shanter's Ride. [Extracts.] *Wood & Son: Perth,* [1924.] 8°. **11632**. f. **84**.

—— [Their Groves of Sweet Myrtle, etc.] Caledonia. A favourite song. By R. Burns. To which are added, Stanzas by Mrs. Robinson. Address to a Cottage. And Verses on General Washington. pp. 8. [1797 ?] *See* Poetry. Poetry; original and selected. vol. 3. [1796, *etc.*] 8°. **1474**. a. **14/3**.

—— To Mary in Heaven . . . With facsimile, and introduction by William K. Bixby. pp. 26. 1916. 8°. *See* Boston, *Mass.—Bibliophile Society.* Ac. **9719/33**.

—— [What would a Young Lassie do wi' an Auld Man ?] The Young Lasses' Song, or ,What wou'd a young lassie do wi' an auld man. [By R. Burns.] And Bonaparte o'er the Sea, Auld Gudeman Ye're a Drunken Body, Lord Nelson's Garland. pp. 8. [1815 ?] 12°. *See* Lasses. **11621**. b. **10**. **(25.)**

—— The Whistle, a poem. pp. 8. [1795 ?] 8°. C. **58**. cc. **36**. **(4.)**

—— A Suppressed Ballad by Robert Burns (Why should na Poor People mow ?). [With a foreword by Clement K. Shorter.] [1916.] 4°. Ashley **2598**.
No. 16 *of an edition of twenty-five copies printed for private circulation.*

EXTRACTS.

—— The Burns Birthday Book. [Edited by James Gibson.] pp. 277. *Arthur Guthrie: Ardrossan,* [1877.] 16°. **12274**. a. **9**.

—— Auld Acquaintance. A birthday book of the wise and tender words of Robert Burns. Compiled by James B. Begg. pp. 416. *W. P. Nimmo & Co.: Edinburgh,* 1879. 16°. **11601**. bbb. **23**.

—— The Burns Birthday Book, *etc.* (Edited by James Gibson.) pp. 292. *G. Routledge & Sons:* [*London,* 1879.] 16°. **11601**. bb. **31**.

—— [Another issue.] [*London,* 1879.] 16°. **11601**. bb. **34**.

—— Birthday Chimes. Selections from the poems, songs, and ballads of Burns. pp. 255. *W. P. Nimmo, Hay & Mitchell: Edinburgh,* 1887 [1886]. 16°. **11612**. a. **31**.

—— Birthday Wishes from Burns. *W. P. Nimmo, Hay & Mitchell: Edinburgh,* 1892. 16°. **11648**. de. **2**.

—— Selections from Burns. With illustrations. ff. 30. *M. Ward & Co.: London,* [1892.] *obl.* 4°. **11611**. ee. **24**.

—— The Burns Birthday Record. Selections from the poems, letters, lyrics and ballads of Robert Burns. Edited by Douglas R. Campbell. pp. 254. *H. J. Drane: Chant & Co.: London; printed in Holland,* [1895.] 16°. **11607**. aa. **29**.

—— Gems from Burns. Selections from the poems, letters, lyrics and ballads . . . by Gordon Garrett. pp. 126. *H. J. Drane, Chant & Co.: London; printed in Holland,* [1896.] 16°. **11622**. a. **24**.

—— Guid Bits frae Robert Burns, witty, humorous, serious, pathetic & pithy. Glossary. Twenty-five original illustrations by W. Fulton Brown. pp. 218. *D. Bryce & Son: Glasgow,* [1903.] 8°. **11632**. aa. **64**.

—— Burns Day by Day. Selected by Rev. Albert E. Sims. Designs by Margaret Tarrant. pp. 103. *G. G. Harrap & Co.: London,* [1911.] 8°. [*Poets Day by Day.* no. 12.] **11604**. eee. **40/12**.

—— The Burns Birthday Book. From the writings of Robert Burns. pp. 255. *Ward, Lock & Co.: London,* [1914.] 16°. **11609**. ee. **9**.

—— Burns Birthday Book. With illustrations. *Andersons: Edinburgh,* [1920 ?] 32°. [*Thistle Library.* no. 17.] L.R. **258**. b. **1/17**.

—— The Burns Birthday Book. With 4 illustrations, *etc.* [Compiled by Edric Vredenburg.] *R. Tuck & Sons: London,* [1921.] 8°. **012305**. f. **53**.

BURNS (ROBERT) *the Poet.* [EXTRACTS.]

—— Robert Burns. Chapters of self-revelation. [Selections in verse and prose, arranged by A. Bain Irvine.] pp. 32. *Printed for private circulation:* [*London,*] 1925. 8°. **10855. d. 32.**

—— Moments with Robert Burns. *See* BRAYBROOKE (Patrick) Moments with Burns, Scott and Stevenson, *etc.* 1933. 8°. **12298. de. 31.**

—— Burns—by himself. The poet-ploughman's life in his own words—pieced together from his diaries, letters & poems—with comments by his brothers & his sister & a few other contemporaries. Arbitrarily arranged to form a continuous story with 68 illustrations by Keith Henderson. pp. x. 258. *Methuen: London,* 1938. 8°. **10858. e. 2.**

APPENDIX.

Bibliography.

—— *See* ANGUS (William C.) The Printed Works of Robert Burns. A bibliography in outline. 1899. 8°. **011904. h. 17.**

—— *See* ANGUS (William C.) The Craibe Angus Burnsiana. List of special items in the library, *etc.* 1902. 8°. **011900. h. 39. (1.)**

—— *See* BIGMORE (Edward C.) Descriptive List of a Collection of Original Manuscript Poems by Robert Burns. 1861. 8°. **11633. bb. 4.**

—— *See* BRIGHT (Henry A.) Some Account of the Glenriddell MSS. of Burns's Poems: with several poems never before published, *etc.* 1874. 4°. **11633. e. 10.**

—— *See* CUTHBERTSON (David) Manuscripts of Robert Burns. The property of Edinburgh University, *etc.* 1921. 8°. **11902. aa. 65.**

—— *See* EWING (James C.) A Selected List of Editions of the Works of Robert Burns, and of books upon his life and writings, *etc.* 1899. 8°. **011907. i. 5. (16.)**

—— *See* EWING (James C.) Bibliography of Robert Burns, 1759–1796. [With facsimiles.] 1909. 4°. **11924. d. 20.**

—— *See* GLASGOW.—*Royal Glasgow Institute of the Fine Arts.* Memorial Catalogue of the Burns Exhibition . . . 1896. 1898. 4°. **K.T.C. 29. b. 12.**

—— *See* LONDON.—III. *British Museum.—Department of Printed Books.* Robert Burns. An excerpt from the General Catalogue of Printed Books in the British Museum. 1939. fol. **Cup. 1247. i. 49.**

—— *See* MACKIE (James) *of Kilmarnock.* Bibliotheca Burnsiana. Life and works of Burns: title pages and imprints of the various editions in the private library of James M'Kie, Kilmarnock, prior to 1866. 1866. 8°. **11902. c. 17.**

—— *See* MUIR (John) *Editor of "The Annual Burns Chronicle."* Sale Catalogue of Editions, Selections, and Translations of Burns, Burnsiana, Relics and Curios from the Collection of John Muir. 1899. 8°. **11904. bb. 60. (4.)**

—— *See* ROSS (John D.) The Story of the Kilmarnock Burns. 1933. 8°. **20017. bb. 25.**

—— *See* SNEDDON (David) Catalogue of the M'Kie Burnsiana Library, *etc.* 1909. 8°. **11926. aaa. 45.**

BURNS (ROBERT) *the Poet.* [APPENDIX.—*Bibliography.*]

—— The Bibliography of Robert Burns, with biographical and bibliographical notes, *etc.* [The preface signed: J. G., i.e. James Gibson.] 1881. 8°. *See* G., J. **011900. h. 38.**

—— The Burns Calendar: a manual of Burnsiana; relating events in the poet's history . . . a concise bibliography, *etc.* [Edited by James Gibson.] 1874. 4°. *See infra*: APPENDIX.—*Miscellaneous.* **10855. g. 2.**

Biography and Criticism.

—— *See* ANGELLIER (A. J.) Robert Burns. [With a bibliography.] 1893. 8°. **10855. f. 18.**

—— *See* BARNES (*Right Hon.* George N.) Robert Burns. [1909.] 8°. **8282. tt. 8. (1.)**

—— *See* BEGG (Ferdinand F.) Rosebery Burns Club . . . Speech by F. Faithfull Begg, M.P., in proposing the toast of Caledonia and Caledonia's Bard. 1898. 8°. **10856. d. 4.**

—— *See* BELFAST.—*Belfast Burns Club.* Annual Supper. [A report of the speeches.] [1894.] *s. sh.* fol. **1879. c. 2. (44.)**

—— *See* BLACKIE (John S.) Life of Robert Burns. [With a bibliography by J. P. Anderson.] 1888. 8°. **10601. de. 5.**

—— *See* BROOKE (Stopford A.) Theology in the English Poets. Cowper—Coleridge—Wordsworth and Burns. 1874. 8°. **4465. g. 20.**

—— —— 1874. 8°. **4465. g. 21.**

—— *See* BROWN (Charles H.) There was a Lad. An essay on Robert Burns. [With portraits.] 1949. 8°. **10862. g. 2.**

—— *See* BROWNE (*Sir* James Crichton) Burns, from a new point of view. [1926.] 8°. **010827. ff. 21.**

—— —— 1937. 8°. **010855. a. 57.**

—— *See* BRUCE (Wallace) Here's a Hand. [Lectures and poems on Robert Burns and other subjects.] 1893. 8°. **011850. f. 15.**

—— *See* BUTCHART (Stewart F.) Sind die Gedichte "Poem on Pastoral Poetry" und "Verses on the Destruction of Drumlanrig Woods" von Robert Burns? 1903. 8°. [*Marburger Studien zur englischen Philologie.* Hft. 6.] **12981. h. 13.**

—— [For editions of Thomas Carlyle's essay on Burns:] *See* CARLYLE (T.) [*Essays.*]

—— [For editions of Thomas Carlyle's lecture entitled "The Hero as Man of Letters. Johnson, Rousseau, Burns":] *See* CARLYLE (T.) [*On Heroes.*]

—— *See* CARSWELL (Catherine R.) The Life of Robert Burns. 1930. 8°. **10824. bbb. 20.**

—— *See* CARSWELL (Catherine R.) Robert Burns. 1933. 8°. **W.P. 6397/16.**

—— *See* CARSWELL (Catherine R.) The Life of Robert Burns. 1951. 8°. **10857. d. 19.**

—— *See* CHIARINI (G.) Studi e ritratti letterari. Burns—Shelley, *etc.* 1900. 8°. **11853. aaa. 21.**

—— *See* COLLIGAN (James H.) Robert Burns and the English Arians. [1912.] 8°. **010822. g. 4.**

BURNS (ROBERT) *the Poet.* [APPENDIX.—*Biography and Criticism.*]

—— *See* CORRODI (A.) Rob. Burns und Pet. Hebel. Eine literar-historische Parallele. 1873. 8°. [*Sammlung gemeinverständlicher wissenschaftlichcr Vorträge.* Hft. 182.] **12249**. l. **8**.

—— *See* COX (Robert) *of Edinburgh.* An Essay on the Character and Cerebral Development of Robert Burns, *etc.* 1859. 8°. **7306**. e. **21**. (**9**.)

—— *See* CRAIGIE (*Sir* William A.) A Primer of Burns. [With a bibliography.] 1896. 8°. **10856**. df. **15**.

—— *See* CRICHTON (A.) *of Collace.* The Land o' the Leal. Who wrote it, Lady Nairne or Burns? *etc.* 1903. 8°. **11852**. f. **13**. (**1**.)

—— *See* CURRIE (James) *M.D., of Liverpool.* The Life of Robert Burns . . . with his correspondence and fragments. 1826. 24°. **10855**. dg. **10**.

—— *See* CURRIE (James) *M.D., of Liverpool.* The Life of Robert Burns, with a criticism of his writings, *etc.* 1838. 8°. **1340**. m. **17**. (**1**.)

—— *See* CUTHBERTSON (John) *of Troon.* Complete Glossary to the Poetry and Prose of Robert Burns, *etc.* 1886. 8°. **2312**. c. **1**.

—— *See* DAICHES (David) Robert Burns. 1952. 8°. **W.P.B.655/1.**

—— *See* DAKERS (Andrew) Robert Burns. His life and genius. 1923. 8°. **010856**. bb. **32**.

—— *See* DEDINSZKY (G.) Petőfi és Burns, *etc.* 1932. 8°. **11867.ccc.36.**

—— *See* DELUSCAR (Horace) *pseud.* Flensing the Krang—cutting the refuse—off Poet Robert Burns. 1913. 8°. **011853**. c. **30**.

—— *See* DOUGLAS (*Sir* George B. S.) *Bart.* Scott and Burns. Speeches, *etc.* 1900. 8°. **11850**. c. **49**.

—— *See* DRINKWATER (John) *Poet.* Robert Burns. An address, *etc.* 1924. 8°. **011852**. h. **77**.

—— *See* DRUMMOND (Robert B.) The Religion of Robert Burns: a lecture. 1859. 8°. **10856**. c. **13**.

—— *See* DUNCAN (Robert) *Hon. Secretary, Edinburgh Burns Club.* The Story of the Edinburgh Burns Relics, with fresh facts about Burns and his family. 1910. 8°. **010854**. de. **7**.

—— *See* EDWARD (William A.) "The Immortal Memory." An address, *etc.* 1934. 8°. **010825**. e. **15**.

—— *See* ESSLEMONT (Peter) Brithers A'—Brothers All. A minute a day with Burns, *etc.* [1933.] 8°. **20017**. c. **38**.

—— *See* ESSLEMONT (Peter) Brithers A'. A minute a day with Burns . . . And twenty-five Burns gems. 1939. 8°. **10859**. f. **2**.

—— *See* EWING (James C.) Robert Burns's Tour in Galloway, and the myth of the composition on that occasion of "Scots wha hae." 1938. 8°. **10857**. bb. **14**.

—— *See* FERGUSON (John De L.) Pride and Passion: Robert Burns, 1759–1796. 1939. 8°. **10859**. bb. **16**.

—— *See* FINDLAY (Jessie P.) Footprints of Robert Burns. 1923. 8°. **010855**. cc. **34**.

BURNS (ROBERT) *the Poet.* [APPENDIX.—*Biography and Criticism.*]

—— *See* FINGER (Charles J.) A Man for A' That. The story of Robert Burns. [With a portrait.] [1929.] 8°. **10824**. d. **20**.

—— *See* FORD (Robert) The Heroines of Burns and their celebrating songs. 1906. 8°. **10827**. h. **25**.

—— *See* FORSTER (Joseph) *Author of "Four Great Teachers."* Great Teachers. Burns, Shelley, *etc.* 1898. 8°. **10600**. r. **6**.

—— *See* FRÖDING (G.) Folkskalden Robert Burns. En lefnadsteckning, *etc.* 1892. 8°. **08282**. c. **1/44**.

—— *See* FYFE (William T.) Robert Burns' Centenary Illustrated Memorial. [A biographical sketch.] [1896.] 8°. **10803**. h. **10**. (**3**.)

—— *See* GAIRDNER (M. S.) Robert Burns: an enquiry into certain aspects of his life and character, *etc.* 1887. 8°. **10856**. aa. **4**.

—— *See* GEMMILL (James F.) Natural History in the Poetry of Robert Burns, *etc.* 1928. 8°. **011840**. dd. **67**.

—— *See* GIBSON (James) *Draper.* Robert Burns and Masonry. 1873. 8°. **4785**. bb. **57**. (**7**.)

—— *See* GRAY (*Sir* Alexander) Robert Burns, Man and Poet, *etc.* [1944.] 8°. **10859**. m. **22**.

—— *See* GUNNING (John P.) Burns, Poet and Excise Officer. 1899. 8°. **10856**. c. **21**.

—— *See* GUTHRIE (David) Burns from Various Aspects, *etc.* 1936. 8°. **011852**. ee. **57**.

—— *See* HAHN (Odwart) Zur Verbal- und Nominal-Flexion bei Robert Burns, *etc.* 1887, *etc.* 4°. **12902**. g. **31**. (**1**.)

—— *See* HARTUNG (Gustav) Ueber Robert Burns' poetische Episteln . . . Kritik und Beispiele im Originaltext nebst metrischer Uebersetzung. [1868.] 4°. **11603**. h. **2**.

—— *See* HARVEY (William) *of Stirlingshire.* Robert Burns as a Freemason. 1921. 12°. **010855**. aa. **45**.

—— *See* HARVEY (William) *of Stirlingshire.* Robert Burns in Stirlingshire. 1899. 8°. **10856**. h. **7**.

—— [For editions of William Hazlitt's lecture "On Burns, and the Old English Ballads":] *See* HAZLITT (W.) *the Elder.* Lectures on the English Poets.

—— *See* HEAVISIDES (Henry) The Minstrelsy of Britain . . . including a dissertation on the genius and lyrics of Burns. 1860. 8°. **11826**. cc. **13**.

—— *See* HECHT (Hans) *Professor der englischen Philologie an der Universität Basel.* Robert Burns. Leben und Wirken, *etc.* 1919. 8°. **11853**. ss. **33**.

—— *See* HECHT (Hans) *Professor der englischen Philologie an der Universität Basel.* Robert Burns, *etc.* 1950. 8°. **10862**. e. **49**.

—— *See* HECHT (Hans) *Professor der englischen Philologie an der Universität Basel.* Robert Burns. The man and his work, *etc.* 1936. 8°. **010822**. f. **5**.

—— *See* HENDERSON (Thomas F.) Burns, *etc.* 1914. 8°. [*Cambridge History of English Literature.* vol. 11.] **11870.g.1.**

—— *See* HENDERSON (Thomas F.) Robert Burns, *etc.* 1904. 8°. **10600**. df. **19/1**.

BURNS (Robert) *the Poet.* [Appendix.—*Biography and Criticism.*]

—— *See* Heron (Robert) *Miscellaneous Writer.* A Memoir of the Life of the late Robert Burns. 1797. 8°. **1164**. g. **8**.

—— *See* Higgins (James C.) Life of Robert Burns. 1893. 8°. **10856**. bb. **17**.

—— —— 1928. 8°. **10824**. h. **1**.

—— *See* Hill (John C.) *Minister of Mure, Irvine.* The Life and Work of Robert Burns in Irvine. 1933. 8°. **10827**. f. **23**.

—— *See* Hilson (James L.) Burns' Border Tour, 5–31 May, 1787, *etc.* [1906.] 8°. **10803**. h. **13**. (**2**.)

—— *See* Holmes (Daniel T.) Lectures on Scottish Literature. Ballad Minstrelsy. Allan Ramsay. Robert Burns. 1904. 8°. **11826**. ccc. **35**.

—— *See* Hughes (James L.) The Real Robert Burns. 1922. 8°. **010855**. aa. **59**.

—— *See* Ingram (John) *F.S.A., Scot.* Interesting and Characteristic Anecdotes of Burns, *etc.* 1893. 8°. **10856**. f. **9**.

—— *See* Jamieson (A. B.) Burns and Religion. 1931. 8°. **010827**. ff. **45**.

—— *See* Jamieson (Robert) *Writer on Robert Burns.* Burns in his Youth, and how he grew to be a poet. Burns in his maturity, and how he spent it. Papers read before the Belfast Burns' Club, *etc.* 1878. 8°. **11868**. aa. **14**.

—— *See* Jolly (William) Burns at Mossgiel, *etc.* 1881. 16°. **10855**. aa. **23**.

—— *See* Keith (Alexander) *M.A.* Burns and Folk-Song. 1922. 8°. **011850**. aa. **12**.

—— *See* Kellow (Henry A.) Burns & his Poetry. 1911. 8°. **11863.a.11/8.**

—— *See* Kelly (John K.) Robert Burns. His admirers, his inspiration, his genius, his mission. [1905.] 8°. **10856**. a. **31**.

—— *See* Ker (William P.) Two Essays. 1. Don Quixote. 2. The Politics of Burns. 1918. 8°. **011853**. p. **46**.

—— *See* Lindsay (Maurice) Robert Burns . . . The man, his work, the legend. [With a portrait.] 1954. 8°. **11870**. ee. **25**.

—— *See* Lindsey (John) *pseud.* The Ranting Dog. The life of Robert Burns. 1938. 8°. **10857**. bb. **9**.

—— *See* Livingston (Peter) Poems and Songs; with lectures on the genius and works of Burns, *etc.* 1852. 8°. **11661.aa.25.**

—— *See* Livingston (Peter) Poems and Songs: with lectures on the genius and works of Burns, and the Rev. George Gilfillan, *etc.* 1855. 12°. **11643**. b. **21**.

—— —— 1863. 8°. **011648**. f. **121**.

—— —— 1881. 8°. **11655**. bbb. **52**.

—— *See* Lockhart (John G.) Life of Robert Burns. 1828. 8°. **10855**. ee. **12**.

—— —— 1830. 12°. **1157**. c. **17**.

BURNS (Robert) *the Poet.* [Appendix.—*Biography and Criticism.*]

—— *See* Lockhart (John G.) Life of Robert Burns, *etc.* [With a portrait.] 1838. 8°. **10864**. e. **26**.

—— *See* Lockhart (John G.) Life of Robert Burns, *etc.* 1847. 8°. **10857**. a. **29**.

—— —— [1871.] 8°. **10856.aa.23.**

—— —— 1882. 8°. **2504**. e. **10**.

—— —— 1890. 8°. **012207**. h. **29**.

—— —— 1904. 8°. **10602**. e. **25/2**.

—— —— [1907.] 8°. **12206.p.1/133.**

—— —— 1914. 8°. **010826**. i. **30**.

—— *See* Logan (Alexander S.) On Robert Burns. An address, *etc.* 1871. 8°. **12272**. aa. **12**.

—— *See* Lowe (David) Burns's Passionate Pilgrimage; or, Tait's indictment of the poet, *etc.* [With a text of S. Tait's poems on Burns.] 1904. 8°. **11868**. a. **5**.

—— *See* MacDowall (William) Burns in Dumfriesshire: a sketch of the last eight years of the poet's life. 1870. 8°. **10856**. b. **8**.

—— *See* Macintosh (John) *Antiquarian.* Life of Robert Burns, *etc.* 1906. 8°. **10855**. de. **7**.

—— *See* Macintosh (William) *Rev., Editor of "The Anglican Church Magazine."* Burns in Germany, *etc.* 1928. 8°. **011824**. cc. **38**.

—— *See* Mackellar (G. D.) The Loves of Burns. [1860 ?] 8°. **10856**. aaa. **34**.

—— *See* Mackenzie (James) *M.P.S., F.S.A.S.* A New Life and Vindication of Robert Burns, *etc.* 1924. 8°. **010856**. f. **26**.

—— *See* MacNaught (Duncan) The Truth about Burns. 1921. 8°. **010855**. aaa. **28**.

—— *See* Macrae (David) *of Glasgow.* Robert Burns. Three lectures. 1886. 8°. **10803**. c. **6**. (**4**.)

—— *See* MacVie (John) Burns and Stair. 1927. 8°. **10862**. b. **18**.

—— *See* Mason (John E.) Makers of Literature. (no. 2. Robert Burns.) 1937, *etc.* 8°. W.P. **12114/2**.

—— *See* Maxwell (James) *of Paisley.* Animadversions on some Poets and Poetasters of the Present Age, especially R——t B——s, *etc.* [In verse.] 1788. 12°. **11632**. b. **58**. (**10**.)

—— *See* Meyerfeld (M.) Robert Burns. Studien zu seiner dichterischen Entwicklung. 1899. 8° **011852**. i. **49**.

—— *See* Mitchell (John O.) Burns and his Times as gathered from his poems. 1897. 8°. **011851**. g. **16**.

—— *See* Mitchell (Richard) *Literary Critic.* Burns, Scotland's sweetest singer. A few notes. 1913. 8°. **11825**. aa. **27**. (**2**.)

—— *See* Molenaar (H.) Robert Burns' Beziehungen zur Litteratur. 1899. 8°. **11822**. r. **4/17**.

—— *See* Montgomerie (William) New Judgments. Robert Burns. Essays by six contemporary writers, *etc.* 1947. 8°. **11865**. aa. **41**.

BURNS (ROBERT) *the Poet.* [APPENDIX.—*Biography and Criticism.*]

— *See* MORRIS (James A.) "The Immortal Memory." An Ayrshire appreciation, *etc.* 1912. 8°. **11850. d. 43.**

— *See* MUIR (James) *Minister of Kirkoswald.* Robert Burns till his Seventeenth—Kirkoswald—Year, *etc.* [With portraits.] 1929. 8°. **10824. b. 11.**

— *See* MUIR (John) *Editor of "The Annual Burns Chronicle."* Burns at Galston and Ecclefechan. 1896. 8°. **10601. dg. 6. (7.)**

— — 1896. 8°. **10604. bbb. 25. (2.)**

— *See* MUIR (John) *Editor of "The Annual Burns Chronicle."* Carlyle on Burns. 1898. 8°. **10855. cc. 9.**

— *See* MUNRO (Archibald) The Story of Burns and Highland Mary. 1896. 8°. **10856. b. 17.**

— *See* MUNRO (John J.) The Poetry of Robert Burns, *etc.* 1923. 8°. **011850. d. 28.**

— *See* MURCHLAND (Charles) Burns in Edinburgh. His wanderings to and fro, *etc.* 1907. 8°. **10862. a. 26.**

— *See* MURDOCH (John M.) Familiar Links with Robert Burns, *etc.* 1933. 8°. **20017. ee. 4.**

— *See* NEAVES (Charles) *Lord Neaves.* A Lecture on Cheap and Accessible Pleasures. With a comparative sketch of the poetry of Burns and Wordsworth, *etc.* 1872. 8°. **8408. bbb. 36. (6.)**

— *See* NEILSON (William A.) Robert Burns. How to know him, *etc.* [1917.] 8°. **011853. ppp. 27.**

— *See* NEW YORK.—*Burns Club of the City of New York.* The Centennial Birthday of Robert Burns, as celebrated by the Burns Club of the City of New York, *etc.* 1860. 8°. **9930. e. 10.**

— *See* OFFICER (William) Burns Poet-Laureate of Canongate Kilwinning a Myth, *etc.* [1892.] 8°. **4785. cc. 35.**

— *See* PETERKIN (Alexander) *the Elder.* A Review of the Life of Robert Burns, and of various criticisms on his character and writings. 1815. 8°. **1164. g. 10.**

— *See* POWER (William) *Historical Writer.* Robert Burns, and other essays & sketches, *etc.* 1927. 8°. **011840. aaa. 55.**

— *See* PRIMROSE (Archibald P.) *Earl of Rosebery.* Addresses delivered at the Opening of the Burns Exhibition, Glasgow . . . and at the public meeting in commemoration of the centenary of the poet's death . . . by the Right Hon. the Earl of Rosebery . . . and others. 1896. 8°. **10855. bb. 27.**

— *See* PRIMROSE (Archibald P.) *Earl of Rosebery.* Robert Burns. Two addresses, *etc.* 1896. 8°. **10855. bb. 26.**

— *See* PRIMROSE (Archibald P.) *Earl of Rosebery.* Wallace, Burns, Stevenson. Appreciations. 1905. 8°. **10856. dd. 11.**

— *See* REID (John B.) A Complete Word and Phrase Concordance to the Poems and Songs of Robert Burns, *etc.* 1889. 8°. **2041.g.**

— *See* RITTER (Otto) *of Halle.* Neue Quellenfunde zu Robert Burns. 1903. 8°. **011853. gg. 51. (7.)**

BURNS (ROBERT) *the Poet.* [APPENDIX.—*Biography and Criticism.*]

— *See* RITTER (Otto) *of Halle.* Quellenstudien zu Robert Burns, 1773–1791. 1901. 8°. **12203. ff. 1/20.**

— *See* ROGERS (Charles) *D.D.* The Book of Robert Burns. Genealogical and historical memoirs of the poet, his associates and those celebrated in his writings. 1889, *etc.* 4°. **Ac. 8241/18.**

— *See* ROGERS (Charles) *D.D.* Genealogical Memoirs of the Family of Robert Burns, *etc.* 1877. 8°. **9905. c. 44.**

— *See* ROSS (John D.) A Burns Handbook. 1931. 8°. **010855. de. 61.**

— *See* ROSS (John D.) The Burns Rosary. Undying words of love and appreciation by admirers of the poet, *etc.* 1923. 8°. **011850. aa. 51.**

— *See* ROSS (John D.) Burnsiana: a collection of literary odds and ends relating to Robert Burns, *etc.* 1892, *etc.* 4°. **10856. i. 12.**

— *See* ROSS (John D.) Henley and Burns; or the Critic censured, being a collection of papers replying to an offensive critique, *etc.* 1901. 8°. **11853. aaa. 5.**

— *See* ROSS (John D.) The Memory of Burns. Brief addresses commemorating the genius of Scotland's illustrious bard. Edited by J. D. Ross. 1899. 8°. **11867. g. 8.**

— *See* ROSS (John D.) Robert Burns and his Rhyming Friends, *etc.* 1928. 8°. **011604. k. 46.**

— *See* ROSS (John D.) Who's Who in Burns. 1927. 8°. **010803. de. 14.**

— *See* SCHIPPER (J.) Gedenkrede auf Robert Burns, *etc.* 1896. 8°. **10803. d. 2. (15.)**

— *See* SCOTCHWOMAN. Robert Burns: an inquiry into certain aspects of his life and character, *etc.* 1886. 8°. **10855. aa. 21.**

— *See* SEMPLE (David) *F.S.A.* The Tree of Crocston: being a refutation of the fables of the courtship of Queen Marie and Lord Darnley, at Crocston Castle, under the yew tree; and of the poet, Robert Burns, carving his name on the yew tree. 1876. 4°. **10805. e. 4.**

— *See* SETOUN (Gabriel) *pseud.* Robert Burns. 1896. 8°. **10803. ccc. 6.**

— *See* SHAIRP (John C.) Robert Burns. 1879. 8°. **2326. b. 7.**

— *See* SHELLEY (Henry C.) A Nicht wi' Burns . . . With musical illustrations from the poet's songs. [1901.] 8°. **10604. bbb. 25. (6.)**

— *See* SHELLEY (Henry C.) Robert Burns: Scotland's national poet. [1901.] 8°. **10856. d. 12.**

— *See* SIEPER (E.) Robert Burns, der schottische Volkssänger . . . Vortrag, *etc.* 1901. 8°. **11853. f. 13. (5.)**

— *See* SINTON (John) Burns, Excise Officer & Poet. A vindication. [1895.] 8°. **10803. e. 23. (12.)**

— — [1896.] 8°. **10803. e. 22. (8.)**

— — [1896.] 8°. **10854. dd. 2.**

— — [1897.] 8°. **10854. dd. 3.**

— *See* SMITH (David Nichol) Some Observations on Eighteenth Century Poetry. (Lecture III. Thomson—Burns.) 1937. 8°. **11859. ee. 36.**

—— *See* Smith (Grant F. O.) The Man Robert Burns, *etc.* [With portraits.] [1940.] 8°. **10859.** dd. **21.**

—— *See* Snyder (Franklyn B.) The Life of Robert Burns. 1932. 8°. **10823.** h. **12.**

—— *See* Snyder (Franklyn B.) Robert Burns. His personality, his reputation and his art. 1936. 8°. **010822.** df. **49.**

—— *See* Stewart (*Sir* James Purves) *K.C.M.G.* The Immortal Memory of Robert Burns. A medical aspect, *etc.* [1935.] 16°. **10824.** de. **13.**

—— *See* Stewart (William) *of the Labour Party.* Robert Burns and the Common People. 1925. 8°. **010856.** aaa. **34.**

—— —— 1927. 8°. **010856.** aaa. **33.**

—— *See* Streissle (A.) Personifikation und poetische Beseelung bei Scott und Burns. 1911. 8°. **11852.** dd. **31.**

—— *See* Sulley (Philip) Robert Burns and Dumfries, *etc.* 1896. 8°. **10856.** bbb. **15.**

—— *See* Taylor (James) *of Vancouver.* Robert Burns, Patriot and Internationalist. 1926. 8°. **010822.** e. **36.**

—— *See* Thomson (Arthur A.M.) The Burns We Love, *etc.* 1931. 8°. **010855.** de. **56**.

—— *See* Tocher (James F.) Ancestry, Youth, and Environment of Robert Burns, *etc.* 1922. 8°. **10856.** bbb. **20.**

—— *See* Tocher (James F.) The Tour of the North-East in 1787. [On Burns's visit to north-east Scotland.] 1931. 8°. **010822.** f. **11.**

—— *See* Tomlinson (John) Three Household Poets: viz.—Milton, Cowper, Burns, *etc.* 1869. 8°. **10856.** aaa. **25.**

—— *See* Turnbull (William R.) The Heritage of Burns. 1896. 8°. **11852.** df. **40.**

—— *See* Watt (Lauchlan M.) Burns. [1914.] 8°. **012206.h.1/21.**

—— *See* Webster (Alexander) *Minister of the Unitarian Church, Aberdeen.* Burns and the Kirk: a review of what the poet did for the religious and social regeneration of the Scottish people. 1888. 8°. **10856.** aaa. **28.**

—— —— 1889. 8°. **4175.** aaa. **14.**

—— *See* White (James) *Rev., of Bonchurch.* Robert Burns and Sir Walter Scott: two lives. 1858. 8°. **10856.** a. **13.**

—— *See* Will (William) Robert Burns as a Volunteer, *etc.* 1919. 8°. **010826.** de. **60.**

—— *See* Wilson (*Sir* James) *K.C.S.I.* The Dialect of Robert Burns, *etc.* 1923. 8°. **12980.** bb. **23.**

—— *See* Wilson (Tom) Burns and Black Joan, *etc.* 1904. 8°. **10856.** a. **29.**

—— *See* Wood (John M.) Robert Burns and the Riddell Family. 1922. 8°. **10862.** aa. **10.**

—— *See* Wordsworth (William) *Poet Laureate.* A Letter to a Friend of Robert Burns [James Gray]: occasioned by an intended republication of the account of the life of Burns, by Dr. Currie, *etc.* 1816. 8°. **C.117.c.20.**

—— *See* Wotherspoon (James) Kirk Life and Kirk Folk. An interpretation of the clerical satires of Burns. 1909. 8°. **04413.** g. **7.**

—— *See* Wright (Dudley) Robert Burns and Freemasonry, *etc.* [1921.] 4°. **10825.** k. **20.**

—— *See* Wright (Dudley) Robert Burns and his Masonic Circle. 1929. 8°. **010827.** ff. **37.**

—— Burnomania: the celebrity of Robert Burns considered: in a discourse addressed to all real Christians of every denomination. To which are added Epistles in verse, respecting Peter Pindar, Burns, *etc.* [By William Peebles.] pp. 103. *J. Ogle: Edinburgh,* 1811. 8°. **11826.** bb. **15.**

—— Burns: an essay for the working classes of Scotland. Part I. His influence as a moral teacher and social reformer. By a Member of the Literary Institute. pp. 31. *Maclachlan & Stewart: Edinburgh,* 1872. 8°. **11825.** ee. **23.**

No more published.

—— A Critique on the Poems of Robert Burns. Illustrated by engravings. [By George Gleig.] pp. iv. 70. *Bell & Bradfute: Edinburgh,* 1812. 8°. **011840.** f. **60.**

—— [Another issue.] A Critique on the Poems of Robert Burns, *etc.* [By George Gleig.] *Edinburgh,* 1812. 8°. **11867.** g. **21.**

—— History of Robert Burns, the celebrated Ayrshire poet. [A chapbook.] pp. 24. *W. & T. Fordyce: Newcastle,* [1840 ?] 12°. **11621.** b. **24.** **(3.)**

—— An Interesting History of Robert Burns; the Ayrshire bard. [A chapbook.] pp. 24. *Printed for the Booksellers: Glasgow,* [1850 ?] 12°. **12269.** a. **23.** **(11.)**

—— Robert Burns and the Ayrshire Moderates. A correspondence. Reprinted from "The Scotsman," with remarks. [Three letters signed: Aliquanto Latior, i.e. John Gairdner; three signed: Alex. Taylor Innes.] pp. vi. 48. *Privately printed: Edinburgh,* 1883. 4°. **10854.** g. **18.**

—— A Winter with Robert Burns, being annals of his patrons and associates in Edinburgh during the year 1786–7, and details of his inauguration as Poet-Laureate of the Can: Kil: [The dedication signed: J. M., i.e. James Marshall.] 1846. 8°. *See* M., J. **10803.** aa. **18.**

Miscellaneous.

—— *See* Adams (James) *M.D., of Glasgow.* Burns's "Chloris." A reminiscence . . . With facsimile of poem "The Song of Death" in the poet's handwriting. 1893. 8°. **10855.** aaa. **31.**

—— *See* Ainslie (Hew) A Pilgrimage to the Land of Burns, *etc.* 1892. 8°. **12272.** f. **15.**

—— *See* Allan, *Junior, pseud.* Burns in Scottish Scene & Song. 1925. 8°. **010369.** h. **7.**

—— *See* Alloway.—*Burns Cottage.* The Burns Cottage, Alloway. Catalogue of manuscripts, portraits, and other relics, *etc.* 1937. 8°. **11900.** e. **61.**

—— *See* Alloway.—*Burns Monument.* Short History and Catalogue of Relics. 1939. 8°. **10858.** a. **19.**

—— *See* ANDERSON (George) *of Glasgow*, and FINLAY (J.) *of Glasgow?* The Burns Centenary Poems. A collection of fifty of the best . . . written on occasion of the centenary celebration. 1859. 8°. **11648**. f. **7**.

—— *See* BALLANTINE (James) *Artist and Song-Writer.* Chronicle of the Hundredth Birthday of Robert Burns. 1859. 8°. **10855**. h. **5**.

—— *See* BELL (Robert A.) and PAGET (H. M.) Burns Pictures, *etc.* [1891.] *obl.* 8°. **11647**. de. **9**.

—— *See* BOSTON, *Mass.—Boston Burns Club.* Celebration of the Hundredth Anniversary of the Birth of Robert Burns . . . January 25th, 1859. 1859. 8°. **10803**. de. **30**. **(1.)**

—— *See* BROWN (Robert) *of Underwood Park, Paisley.* Paisley Burns Clubs, 1805–1893, *etc.* 1893. 4°. **10856**. i. **13**.

—— *See* CAMPBELL (John W.) Burns in Song. [In verse.] [1902.] 4°. **1876**. dd. **4**.

—— *See* CARRICK (John C.) William Creech, Robert Burns' Best Friend. 1903. 8°. **10603**. de. **12**. **(7.)**

—— *See* COMBE (George) *Phrenologist.* Phrenological Development of Robert Burns, *etc.* 1859. 8°. **7410**. e. **24**.

—— *See* CROZIER (Eric) Rab the Rhymer. A play . . . on the life and songs of Robert Burns. [With a portrait.] 1953. 8°. **11783**. bb. **33**.

—— *See* DEWAR (James) *of Belfast.* A Tribute to the Memory of Burns, *etc.* [A list of monuments, portraits, etc.] [1894.] *obl.* 8°. **10856**. de. **12**.

—— *See* DOUGALL (Charles S.) The Burns Country, *etc.* 1904. 8°. **010347**. bb. **3**.

—— —— 1911. 8°. **2366**. c. **15**.

—— —— 1925. 8°. **010352**. de. **66**.

—— *See* DUMFRIES.—*Burns' House.* Official Handbook of Burns' House, Dumfries, and other memories of the national poet, *etc.* [1935?] *obl.* 8°. **10857**. a. **6**.

—— *See* DUNCAN (Robert) *Hon. Secretary, Edinburgh Burns Club.* The Story of the Edinburgh Burns Relics, with fresh facts about Burns and his family. 1910. 8°. **010854**. de. **7**.

—— *See* DUNFERMLINE.—*Carnegie Public Libraries.* The Murison Burns Collection, *etc.* 1953. 8°. **11927**. e. **5**.

—— *See* EDINBURGH.—*Corporation.—Public Libraries and Museums Committee.* Robert Burns Exhibition, *etc.* [With portraits.] 1953. 8°. **7960**. df. 58.

—— *See* EVANS (W. Downing) Ode composed for the Centenary Festival in honour of Robert Burns. 1859. 8°. **11650**. cc. **26**. **(4.)**

—— *See* EWING (James C.) and MACCALLUM (A.) Alexander Cunningham, Friend of Burns, *etc.* 1933. 8°. **10859**. bb. **27**.

—— *See* EWING (James C.) and MACCALLUM (A.) Robert Graham, Twelfth of Fintry, Patron of Robert Burns, *etc.* [With a facsimile.] 1931. 8°. **10859**. g. **26**

—— *See* FINDLAY (William) *M.D.* Robert Burns and the Medical Profession, *etc.* 1898. 8°. **10856**. ee. **17**.

—— *See* FITZHUGH (Robert T.) Robert Burns: his Associates and Contemporaries. The Train, Grierson, Young, and Hope manuscripts . . . With the Journal of the Border Tour, edited by De Lancey Ferguson. 1943. 8°. **10861**. ee. **7**.

—— *See* GIBB (John T.) The Land of Burns. Mauchline, town and district. [1911.] 8°. **010360**. g. **30**. **(3.)**

—— *See* GLASGOW. Glasgow and the Land of Burns, *etc.* [1902.] 32°. **944**. d. **12**.

—— *See* GLASGOW.—*Royal Glasgow Institute of the Fine Arts.* Catalogue of the Burns Exhibition, *etc.* 1896. 8°. **7956**. h. **7**.

—— *See* GLASGOW.—*Royal Glasgow Institute of the Fine Arts.* Memorial Catalogue of the Burns Exhibition . . . 1896. 1898. 4°. K.T.C. **29**. b. **12**.

—— *See* GLEN (Tam) Answer to the Favourite Scots Song, Tam Glen [by R. Burns]. To which are added, The Birks of Abergeldie, and Willifou fa' the Cat, *etc.* [1798.] 8°. [*Poetry; original and selected.* vol. 4.] **1474**. a. **14/4**.

—— *See* GOODWILLIE (Edward) The World's Memorials of Robert Burns, *etc.* [1911.] 8°. **010854**. f. **23**.

—— *See* HENDERSON (Thomas F.) The Auld Ayrshire of Robert Burns. 1906. 8°. **010370**. ee. **14**.

—— *See* JACKS (William) Robert Burns in other Tongues. A critical review of the translations of the songs & poems of Robert Burns. [With selections from various translations.] 1896. 8°. **11612**. d. **24**.

—— *See* KENT (Wyndham) Burns. [A commemorative poem.] 1859. 8°. **11651**. d. **26**. **(4.)**

—— *See* KIDD (William) *Artist.* Series of Twelve Illustrations of the Poems of Robert Burns, *etc.* 1832. 8°. **11633**. f. **4**.

—— *See* KILMARNOCK.—*Burns Federation.* Annual Burns Chronicle and Directory, *etc.* [1892, *etc.*] 8°. P.P. **6197**. kc.

—— *See* KILMARNOCK.—*Burns Federation.* Commemoration at Dumfries of the 150th Anniversary of the Death of Scotland's National Poet. 1946. 8°. **10859**. pp. **19**.

—— *See* LACY (Fanny E.) Centenary Tribute to Robert Burns. [In verse.] 1859. 12°. **11650**. a. **76**.

—— *See* LAWRANCE (Robert M.) Burns's School Reading-book [i.e. "A Collection of English Prose and Verse for the use of Schools," by Arthur Masson], *etc.* 1931. 8°. **11912**. b. **10**.

—— *See* MACBAIN (James) Burns' Cottage. The story of the birthplace of Robert Burns, *etc.* [1904.] 8°. **10855**. aa. **37**.

—— —— [1907.] 8°. **10856**. aa. **22**.

—— *See* MACKERROW (Mathew H.) Notes on Places, Memorials, Buildings and Tombstones interesting from their associations with Robert Burns in Dumfries and Galloway. 1936. 8°. **010369**. ee. **90**.

—— *See* MACPHAIL (Myles) Burns' Vision of the Future, a centenary poem. [1859.] 8°. **11651**. d. **29**. **(6.)**

—— *See* MASSEY (Gerald) Robert Burns: a centenary song, *etc.* 1859. 4°. **11626. h. 14. (6.)**

—— *See* MAUCHLINE.—*Jean Armour Burns Houses.* Jean Armour Burns Houses, Mauchline. Historical note and catalogue of manuscripts, portraits and other relics, *etc.* 1936. 8°. **10858. a. 17.**

—— *See* MORRIS (James A.) Alloway. The protection and preservation of its memorials of Robert Burns, *etc.* 1930. 8°. **010369. i. 22.**

—— *See* MUNRO AND CO. Munro's Tourist Guide. The Land of Burns, the Clyde, *etc.* 1939. 8°. **010369. l. 19.**

—— *See* MURDOCH (John M.) Familiar Links with Robert Burns, *etc.* 1933. 8°. **20017. ee. 4.**

—— *See* NASH (Edward B.) The Raeburn-Burns Controversy, *etc.* [On three alleged portraits of Burns, attributed to Raeburn.] 1925. 8°. **7854. cc. 52.**

—— *See* NORTON (Caroline E. S.) *Hon. Mrs. George Chapple Norton,* afterwards STIRLING-MAXWELL (C. E. S.) *Lady.* The Centenary Festival. [Verses on Robert Burns.] [1859.] 4°. **11647. e. 17.**

—— *See* PEACOCK (Hugh C.) Robert Burns, Poet-Laureate of Lodge Canongate Kilwinning. Facts substantiating his election and inauguration on 1st March 1787. Gleaned from the Lodge records and other authentic sources by H. C. Peacock, *etc.* [With a portrait.] 1894. 4°. **4786. k. 5.**

—— *See* REID (A. Fraser) and TAYLOR (J.) *of Vancouver.* Vancouver's Tribute to Burns, *etc.* 1928. 8°. **010470. f. 28.**

—— *See* ROSS (John D.) Burns's "Blue-Eyed Lassie," *etc.* 1924. 8°. **010855. a. 21.**

—— *See* ROSS (John D.) Highland Mary. Interesting papers on an interesting subject. Edited by J. D. Ross. 1894. 8°. **10827. bbb. 29.**

—— *See* ROSS (John D.) A Little Book of Burns Lore, *etc.* 1926. 8°. **010855. a. 28.**

—— *See* ROSS (John D.) Round Burns' Grave: the paeans and dirges of many bards, *etc.* 1891. 8°. **011653. k. 47.**

—— —— 1892. 8°. **011653. l. 28.**

—— *See* SAINT LOUIS, *Missouri.—Burns Cottage Association.* [Report of a project to erect an exact replica of Burns's Cottage at the Louisiana Purchase Exposition.] [1902.] 8°. **10854. bb. 31.**

—— *See* SHELLEY (Henry C.) The Ayrshire Homes and Haunts of Burns, *etc.* 1897. 8°. **11622. df. 35.**

—— *See* SMEATON (William H. O.) The Footsteps of Burns from Doonside to Dumfries, *etc.* [1920 ?] 32°. **L.R. 258. b. 1/11.**

—— *See* STEPHENS (George) *Professor at Copenhagen.* The Rescue of Robert Burns, February 1759. A centenary poem. [1859.] 8°. **11649. f. 15. (11.)**

—— *See* STORER (James S.) Views in North Britain, illustrative of the works of Robert Burns, *etc.* 1805. 8°. **10369. pp. 4.**

—— —— 1805. 4°. **78. g. 8.**

—— *See* STORY (Robert) *of Wark, Northumberland.* The Alloway Centenary Festival. An ode, *etc.* 1859. 8°. **11651. d. 28. (6.)**

—— *See* TROVATO (Ben) *pseud.* Rival Rhymes, in honour of Burns; with curious illustrative matter, *etc.* 1859. 8°. **11651. c. 43.**

—— *See* WILSON (John) *Professor of Moral Philosophy in the University of Edinburgh,* and CHAMBERS (R.) *Publisher.* The Land of Burns, a series of landscapes and portraits, illustrative of the life and writings of the Scottish poet, *etc.* 1840. 4°. **10370. f. 9.**

—— The Answer to Burns' Bonny Jean. To which are added, Bold Maginnes, from the County Tyrone, Blithe was She, and Sally and Robert's Courtship. [Four songs.] pp. 8. *T. Duncan: Glasgow,* [1810 ?] 12°. **11621. b. 22. (3.)**

—— At Robin's Grave. A hundred years after. A rough rhyme by a Brother Gauger. pp. 22. *Cheney & Sons: Bambury,* 1896. 8°. **11601. h. 13. (6.)**

—— The Burns Calendar: a manual of Burnsiana; relating events in the poet's history, names associated with his life and writings, a concise bibliography, and a record of Burns relics. [Edited by James Gibson.] *James M'Kie: Kilmarnock,* 1874. 4°. **10855. g. 2.**

—— The Burns Centenary: being an account of the proceedings and speeches at the various banquets and meetings throughout the kingdom. With a memoir and portrait of the poet. pp. iv. 156. *W. P. Nimmo: Edinburgh,* 1859. 8°. **10854. a. 9.**

—— Burns' Monument. Account of the grand masonic procession, which took place at laying the foundation-stone of a monument to the memory of Robert Burns, in the vicinity of Alloway Kirk, on the 25th of January, 1820 . . . To which is added, Tam o' Shanter, a tale. pp. 24. *D. Macarter & Co.: Ayr,* 1820. 12°. **11621. aa. 16. (1.)**

—— Burns' Souvenir. *W. B. Reid & Co.: Mauchline,* [1904.] 8°. **10856. a. 30.**

—— Burns's Statue, Dumfries. Poetical garland for the proposed monument. Reprinted from the Dumfries' Standard, *etc.* pp. 18. *Standard Office: Dumfries,* 1879. 12°. **11602. e. 18. (9.)**

—— Celebration of Burns's Birthday, at Mr. Hastie's. [An account of Burns's punch-bowl. Signed: P. C., i.e. Peter Cunningham ?] [1865 ?] 8°. *See* C., P. **10856. c. 18.**

—— Colin. A pastoral elegy to the memory of Robert Burns. pp. 8. [1797 ?] *See* POETRY. Poetry; original and selected. vol. 3. [1796, *etc.*] 8°. **1474. a. 14/3.**

—— The Contemporaries of Burns, and the more recent poets of Ayrshire, with selections from their writings. [By James Paterson.] pp. 416. 24. *Hugh Paton: Edinburgh,* 1840. 8°. **10854. g. 9.**

—— Crystal Palace. The Burns' Centenary. A rejected ode. pp. 8. *Marchant Singer & Co.: London,* 1859. 8°. **11650. f. 37.**

—— A Day with the Poet Burns. [With extracts and with coloured plates.] pp. 47. *Hodder & Stoughton: London,* [1909.] 8°. [*Days with the Poets.*] **10600. bbb. 2/1.**

—— Elegiac Stanzas, applicable to the untimely death of the celebrated poet, Robert Burns. To which are added, Verses on Time, and on the Shortness of Life [by Simon Wastell]. pp. 8. *See* POETRY. Poetry; original and selected. vol. 1. [1796, *etc.*] 8°. **1474. a. 14/1.**

BURNS (ROBERT) *the Poet.* [APPENDIX.—*Miscellaneous.*]

—— Festival in commemoration of Robert Burns, and to promote a subscription to erect a national monument to his memory at Edinburgh: held . . . in London . . . May 5, 1819, *etc.* [A list of toasts and words of songs sung at the dinner.] pp. 26. *B. McMillan: London,* 1819. 8°. **11622**. cc. **3**.

—— Liverpool Testimonials, to the departed genius of Robert Burns, *etc.* [Poems.] pp. 19. *Merrill & Wright: Liverpool,* [1800 ?] 8°. **1346**. f. **58**.

—— Mausoleum and Memorials of Burns. pp. 5. *John Menzies: Edinburgh,* 1842. 8°. **1465**. i. **8**.

—— Monody on the Death of Robert Burns. To which are prefixed, Observations on his character and genius. [By William Reid.] pp. 8. [1797.] *See* POETRY. Poetry; original and selected. vol. 2. [1796, *etc.*] 8°. **1474**. a. **14/2**.

—— One of the Six Hundred and Twenty-one: a Burns centenary poem. pp. 19. *W. Tweedie: London,* 1859. 12°. **11650**. a. **80**.

—— A Pilgrimage to the Land of Burns; containing anecdotes of the bard, and of the characters he immortalized, with numerous pieces of poetry, original and collected. [By Hew Ainslie.] pp. 271. *Printed for the Author: Deptford,* 1822. 8°. **1164**. g. **12**.

—— Rhymes read in the Queen's Drawing Room at Aston Hall, January 25, 1859, in Memory of the Birth of Robert Burns, *etc.* [By Sebastian Evans.] pp. 7. *Cornish Bros.: Birmingham,* [1859.] 12°. **011644**. de. **170**.

—— Robert Burns, 1759–1796. [*Privately printed,* 1896.] 8°. **11602**. ff. **27**. **(10.)**
Described in a MS. *note as " a monody, by A. H."*

—— Robert Burns's Literary Correspondents 1786–1796. A chronological list of letters addressed to the poet with précis of their contents. [Originally compiled at the request of James Currie in connection with his edition of Burns's works. Edited by J. C. Ewing. With a facsimile.] pp. xii. 48. 1938. 8°. *See* ALLOWAY.—*Burns Monument Trustees.* **011899**. k. **21**.

—— A Spirit Message from Robert Burns to the Author. [Poems.] pp. 47. *Kegan Paul & Co.: London,* 1907. 8°. **011652**. i. **50**.

—— Verses to the Memory of Robert Burns, with an account of his interment . . . Also, his epitaph, written by himself. pp. 8. [1797.] *See* POETRY. Poetry; original and selected. vol. 2. [1796, *etc.*] 8°. **1474**. a. **14/2**.

BURNS (ROBERT) *Son of Robert Burns the Poet.* The Caledonian Musical Museum, or Complete vocal library of the best Scotch songs, ancient and modern. Embellished with a portrait and fac-simile of the hand-writing of Burns, and containing upwards of two hundred songs by that immortal bard. The whole edited by his son [Robert Burns]. pp. 294. *J. Dick: London,* 1809. 12°. **11622**. cc. **2**.

BURNS (ROBERT EDWARD) and **BURNS** (AGNES ETHEL) Easy Latin for Beginners. pp. xii. 83. *Methuen & Co.: London,* 1928. 8°. **012933**. aa. **49**.

—— Latin for Juniors. A second year Latin book. pp. viii. 186. *Macmillan & Co.: London,* 1930. 8°. **012933**. a. **47**.

—— Latin for School Certificate. pp. x. 171. *Macmillan & Co.: London,* 1938. 8°. **012933**. a. **117**.

BURNS (ROBERT ELLIOTT)

—— Escape to Prison. The true story of " Killer " Martin . . . 3rd impression. pp. 256. *Hurst & Blackett: [London,* 1939.] 8°. **10887**. a. **7**.

—— I am a Fugitive . . . With an introduction by the Rev. Vincent G. Burns. pp. 287. *Stanley Paul & Co.: London,* 1932. 8°. **10881**. ppp. **1**.

BURNS (ROBERT FERRIER) *See* NORTON (Robert) *Rev., of St. Catherines, Canada West.* Maple Leaves from Canada, for the Grave of Abraham Lincoln: being a discourse delivered by Rev. Robert Norton . . . and address by Rev. R. F. Burns, *etc.* 1922. 4°. [*Magazine of History.* Extra number. no. 85.] P.P. **3437**. bab.

BURNS (ROBERT LEO) Measurement of the Need for Transporting Pupils. Basis for state equalization of transportation costs, *etc.* [A thesis.] pp. 61. *Teachers College, Columbia University: New York,* 1927. 8°. **8385**. ccc. **17**.

BURNS (ROBERT MARTIN) and **BRADLEY** (WILLIAM WHITNEY)

—— Protective Coatings for Metals . . . Second edition. pp. xiv. 643. *Reinhold Publishing Corporation: New York,* [1955.] 8°. [*American Chemical Society. Monograph Series.* no. 129.] Ac. **3934/5**.

BURNS (ROGER) Two Boys in Australia. pp. 130. *T. Nelson & Sons: London,* [1936.] 8°. [*Seeing the World Series.*] W.P. **11975/3**.

BURNS (SHEILA) *pseud.* [i.e. URSULA HARVEY BLOOM.] *See* also BLOOM (U. H.)

—— Adventure in Romance. pp. 199. *Hutchinson: London,* 1955. 8°. NNN. **5756**.

—— Adventurous Heart, *etc.* pp. 253. *Cassell & Co.: London,* 1940. 8°. NN. **31964**.

—— Air Liner. pp. 246. *Eldon Press: London,* [1948.] 8°. NN. **38500**.

—— Beloved and Unforgettable. pp. 192. *Hutchinson: London,* 1953. 8°. NNN. **4486**

—— Bridal Sweet. pp. 221. *Cassell & Co.: London,* 1942. 8°. NN. **33267**.

—— Bride—Maybe. pp. 220. *MacDonald & Co.: London,* 1946. 8°. NN. **36427**.

—— The Chance Romance. pp. 248. *Eldon Press: London,* [1948.] 8°. NN. **38536**.

—— The Cuckoo never weds, *etc.* pp. 222. *Eldon Press: London,* 1950. 8°. NNN. **387**.

—— Desire Is Not Dead. pp. 223. *MacDonald & Co.: London,* 1947. 8°. NN. **37236**.

—— Dream Awhile. pp. 282. *Cassell & Co.: London,* 1937. 8°. NN. **27758**.

—— Faint with Pursuit. pp. 222. *Eldon Press: London,* 1949. 8°. NN. **39685**.

—— Honeymoon Island. pp. 278. *Cassell & Co.: London,* 1938. 8°. NN. **29050**.

BURNS (SHEILA) *pseud.* [i.e. URSULA HARVEY BLOOM.]

—— How Dear is my Delight! pp. 199. *Hutchinson: London*, 1955. 8°. **NNN. 6766.**

—— Lady! This is Love! pp. 280. *Cassell & Co.: London*, 1938. 8°. **NN. 28480.**

—— Live happily—love long. pp. 223. *Eldon Press: London*, 1952. 8°. **NN. 12097.**

—— Love me to-morrow. pp. 222. *Eldon Press: London*, 1952. 8°. **NNN. 2613.**

—— Meet Love on Holiday. A novel. pp. 287. *Cassell & Co.: London*, 1940. 8°. **NN. 31298.**

—— No Trespassers in Love. pp. 223. *Macdonald & Co.: London*, 1949. 8°. **NN. 39095.**

—— Not Free to love. pp. 224. *Eldon Press: London*, 1950. 8°. **NNN. 1146.**

—— The Passionate Adventure. pp. viii. 311. *Cassell & Co.: London*, 1936. 8°. **NN. 26671.**

—— Please burn after reading. pp. 191. *Hutchinson London*, 1954. 8°. **NNN. 5089**

—— Romance is Mine. pp. 286. *Cassell & Co.: London*, 1941. 8°. **NN. 32379.**

—— Romance of Jenny W.R.E.N. pp. 202. *Cassell & Co.: London*, 1944. 8°. **NN. 34644.**

—— Romantic Fugitive. pp. 199. *Cassell & Co.: London*, 1943. 8°. **NN. 34159.**

—— Romantic Intruder. pp. 192. *Hutchinson: London*, 1952. 8°. **NNN. 3251.**

—— Rosebud and Stardust. pp. 238. *Eldon Press: London*, 1951. 8°. **NNN. 1874.**

—— The Stronger Passion. pp. 252. *Cassell & Co.: London*, 1941. 8°. **NN. 32845.**

—— Take a Chance. pp. v. 280. *Cassell & Co.: London*, 1937. 8°. **NN. 27297.**

—— Thy Bride Am I. pp. 217. *Cassell & Co.: London*, 1942. 8°. **NN. 33450.**

—— To-morrow is eternal. pp. 224. *Macdonald & Co.: London*, 1948. 8°. **NN. 38337.**

—— Tomorrow we marry. pp. 192. *Hutchinson: London*, 1953. 8°. **NNN. 4067.**

—— Vagrant Lover. pp. 191. *Macdonald & Co.: London* [1945.] 8°. **NN. 35172**

—— Week-End Bride. pp. 287. *Cassell & Co.: London*, 1939. 8°. **NN. 30512.**

—— Wonder Trip. pp. 282. *Cassell & Co.: London*, 1939. 8°. **NN. 29884.**

BURNS (TEX)

—— Hopalong Cassidy and the Riders of High Rock. pp. 192. *Hodder & Stoughton: London*, 1952. 8°. **12731. k. 13.**

—— Hopalong Cassidy and the Rustlers of West Fork. pp. 191. *Hodder & Stoughton: London*, 1951. 8°. **12731. bb. 45.**

BURNS (TEX)

—— Hopalong Cassidy and the Trail to Seven Pines. pp. 190. *Hodder & Stoughton: London*, 1952. 8°. **12701. de. 5.**

—— Hopalong Cassidy, Trouble-Shooter. pp. 192. *Hodder & Stoughton: London*, 1953. 8°. **12731. n. 19.**

BURNS (THOMAS) *F.R.S.E.* Old Scottish Communion Plate . . . With a preface by the Right Rev. James Macgregor . . . and chronological tables of Scottish hall-marks prepared by Alexander J. S. Brook. [With plates.] pp. xxxii. 651. *R. & R. Clark: Edinburgh*, 1892. 8°. **3478. l. 2.**

BURNS (THOMAS) *Rev., of Renfrew.* An Humble Attempt to make Men grateful to God for Mercies received, two sermons, *etc.* pp. 64. *Brash & Reid: Glasgow*, 1799. 8°. **4477. c. 14.**

BURNS (THOMAS) *School Board Officer, of Newcastle-upon-Tyne.* City Songs. [With a portrait.] pp. 140. *T. F. Downie: London*, 1901. 8°. **11654. bbb. 55.**

BURNS (THOMAS FERRIER)

—— *See* DAWSON (Christopher H.) and BURNS (T. F.) Essays in Order, *etc.* 1931, *etc.* 8°. **12212.aa.3.**

—— A Monument to Saint Augustine. Essays on some aspects of his thought written in commemoration of his 15th centenary. [By various authors. The compiler's note signed: T. F. B., i.e. T. F. Burns.] pp. 367. 1930. 8°. *See* B., T. F. **3675. g. 8.**

BURNS (THOMAS FERRIER) and **SHEED** (FRANCIS JOSEPH)

—— A Sheed & Ward Anthology. A publisher's choice of pages from fifty chosen books. [The preface signed: T. F. B., F. J. S., i.e. T. F. Burns and F. J. Sheed.] pp. xii. 401. 1931. 8°. *See* B., T. F., and S., F. J. **12298. df. 9.**

BURNS (TOM)

—— Raging Seas and Azure Skies. [Reminiscences.] pp. 223. *Arthur H. Stockwell: Ilfracombe*, 1950. 8°. **10862. de. 46.**

BURNS (TOMMY) Scientific Boxing and Self Defence. [With plates, including a portrait.] pp. 172. *"Health & Strength": London*, 1914. 8°. **7911. df. 9.**

—— (Third edition.) pp. 93. *Athletic Publications: London*, [1934.] 8°. **7916. ee. 20.**

BURNS (VINCENT GODFREY) *See* BURNS (Robert E.) I am a Fugitive . . . With an introduction by the Rev. V. G. Burns. 1932. 8°. **10881. ppp. 1.**

BURNS (W. G.) *See* HENRY (George W.) *Methodist Minister.* Demonstrations of the Spirit originally called Shouting, genuine and spurious . . . Re-christened and re-printed by W. G. Burns. 1908. 8°. **03558. de. 10.**

BURNS (WALTER) In Commemoration of the Visit of the Prince and Princess of Wales to Ireland, April, 1885. [Verses.] [*Belfast*, 1885.] *s. sh.* 8°. **1865. c. 8. (28.)**

BURNS (WALTER NOBLE) The One-Way Ride. The red trail of Chicago gangland from Prohibition to Jake Lingle. pp. 313. *Doubleday, Doran & Co.: Garden City, New York*, 1931. 8°. **06055. g. 9.**

—— [Another edition.] pp. 286. *Stanley Paul & Co.: London*, 1931. 8°. **06055. de. 66.**

BURNS (WALTER NOBLE)

—— The Saga of Billy the Kid [William Bonney]. pp. 322. *William Heinemann: London; printed in U.S.A.,* 1926. 8°. **12702. c. 15.**

—— [Another edition.] Billy the Kid. [With plates, including a portrait, and a map.] pp. xi. 288. *Geoffrey Bles: London,* [1926.] 8°. **12702. dd. 8.**

—— The Saga of Billy the Kid. pp. 255. *Macdonald & Co.: London,* 1951. 8°. **12701. a. 17.**

—— The Saga of Billy the Kid. pp. 285. *Transworld Publishers: London,* 1955. 8°. [*Corgi Books.* no. T 88.] W.P. **12745/205.**

—— Tombstone. An Iliad of the Southwest. pp. ix. 388. *William Heinemann: London; printed in U.S.A.,* 1927. 8°. **12702. dd. 14.**

—— [Another copy, with a different titlepage.] *Geoffrey Bles: London; printed in U.S.A.,* 1928. 8°. **12713. dd. 1.**

—— Tombstone. The toughest town of Arizona. pp. 285. *Quality Press: London,* 1939. 8°. **12720. aa. 11.**

BURNS (WILLIAM) *Civil Engineer.* Illuminating and Heating Gas. A manual of the manufacture of gas from tar, oil and other liquid hydrocarbons, *etc.* pp. 68. *E. & F. N. Spon: London,* 1887. 8°. **8716. aaa. 26.**

BURNS (WILLIAM) *D.Sc.* *See* FIRMINGER (T. A. C.) Firminger's Manual of Gardening for India . . . Revised and edited by W. Burns. 1918. 8°. **07030. f. 7.**

—— Grassland Problems in Western India. By W. Burns . . . L. B. Kulkarni . . . and S. R. Godbole. [With plates.] pp. 51. ii. *Bombay,* 1933. 8°. [*Department of Agriculture, Bombay.* Bulletin no. 171.] **I.S. BO. 126.**

—— Some Wild Fodder Plants of the Bombay Presidency. By W. Burns [and others], *etc.* pp. 2. 24. pl. XXXIV. *Poona,* 1916. 8°. [*Bombay Department of Agriculture. Bulletin.* no. 78.] **I.S. BO. 126.**

BURNS (WILLIAM) *D.Sc.,* and **SUBBA-RĀVA HANUMANTA-RĀVA PRAYĀGA.**

—— The Book of the Mango. [With plates.] pp. iii. 98. *Bombay,* 1921. 8°. [*Bombay Department of Agriculture. Bulletin.* no. 103.] **I.S. BO. 126.**

BURNS (WILLIAM) *Minister of Dun.* Moravian Missions illustrated and defended, in a sermon, *etc.* pp. 44. 1814. *See* SERMONS. Sermons preached on Various Occasions, *etc.* [1825?] 8°. **4452. d. 2. (1.)**

BURNS (WILLIAM) *of Glasgow.* Address by William Burns . . . A review of the correspondence . . . as to the misuse of the terms "England" & "English," *etc.* pp. 53. *Glasgow Saint Andrew's Society: Glasgow,* 1869. 8°. **8138. bb. 113.**

—— Scottish History . . . Being an address to the Glasgow Saint Andrew's Society. pp. 57. *T. Murray & Son: Glasgow,* [1863.] 8°. **9509. de. 8.**

—— The Scottish War of Independence. Its antecedents and effects. [With maps.] 2 vol. *James Maclehose: Glasgow,* 1874. 8°. **9510. g. 6.**

BURNS (WILLIAM) *of Glasgow.*

—— What's in a Name? [On the substitution of the name "England" for "Great Britain."] pp. 72. *W. G. Blackie & Co.: Glasgow,* 1860. 8°. **8138. cc. 7. (12.)**
Printed for private circulation.

—— [Another edition.] pp. 143. *T. Murray & Son: Glasgow,* 1861. 16°. **10348. b. 10.**

BURNS (WILLIAM) *Theological Writer.* *See* EWING (David) A Letter to W. Burns, wherein the errors of his writings are confuted, *etc.* 1813. 8°. **4372. f. 5. (10.)**

—— The Law of Christ vindicated from certain false glosses of the Rev. Edward Irving, contained in his argument on a judgment to come. pp. 50. *R. Hunter: London,* 1824. 8°. **701. h. 17. (4.)**
The half-title reads: "A Letter from William Burns to the Rev. E. Irving."

—— [Another copy.] **764. f. 17. (1.)**

—— The New Era of Christianity, or its influence on the moral regeneration of society. pp. 30. *Rowland Hunter: London,* 1831. 8°. **T. 1376. (16.)**

—— The Primitive Doctrine concerning the Person and Character of Jesus Christ, *etc.* pp. 400. *Glasgow; printed for G. & W. B. Whittaker; & J. Hatchard & Son: London,* 1822. 8°. **1120. e. 13.**

BURNS (WILLIAM ALOYSIUS)

—— Horses and their Ancestors. (Pictures by Paula Hutchison.) pp. 62. *Whittlesey House, McGraw-Hill Book Co.: New York,* [1954.] 4°. **07295. t. 6.**

—— A World full of Homes . . . Pictures by Paula Hutchinson. pp. 120. *McGraw-Hill Book Co.: New York,* [1953.] 8°. **7823. ff. 13.**

BURNS (WILLIAM CHALMERS) *See* BIBLE.—*Psalms.* [*Chinese.—Mandarin dialect.*] 舊約詩篇官話 [Translated, with notes, by W. C. Burns.] [1870.] 8°. **15117. c. 3.**

—— *See* BURNS (Islay) Memoir of the Rev. Wm. C. Burns, *etc.* [With a portrait.] 1870. 8°. **4955. bb. 28.**

—— *See* CHINA. China and the Missions at Amoy, with letters of the Rev. W. C. Burns, *etc.* 1854. 8°. **4765. a. 24.**

—— *See* MATTHEWMAN (Phyllis) William Chalmers Burns. [A biography for children.] 1953. 8°. **W.P.D.380/3.**

—— *See* WYLIE (William S. H.) William Chalmers Burns, *etc.* [1923.] 8°. **20040.a.2/13.**

—— The Knowledge of Sin . . . Twenty-third thousand. pp. 32. *W. Middleton: Dundee,* 1843. 16°. **4372. aa. 7. (5.)**

—— The Knowledge of Sin. "Eolas a Pheacaidh." *Gael.* pp. 20. *R.T.S.: London,* [1860?] 12°. **4420. bb. 1. (53.)**

—— Letter to Sinners seeking Salvation . . . Litir do Pheacaich ag iarraidh slainte. *Gael.* pp. 12. *W. Whyte & Co.: Edinburgh,* [1860?] 12°. **4420. bb. 1. (13.)**

—— Notes of Addresses by the late Rev. William C. Burns . . . Edited by M. F. Barbour. pp. xiv. 237. *J. Nisbet & Co.: London,* 1869. 8°. **4462. aa. 23.**

BURNS (WILLIAM H.) *Rev.* A Word for the Sabbath; being a letter on the religious observance of the Lord's Day. By a Clergyman . . . New edition. [Signed: W. H. Burns.] pp. 15. *James Burns: London,* 1835. 12°. **908.** c. 4. **(14.)**

BURNS (WILLIAM HAMILTON) *See* BURNS (Islay) The Pastor of Kilsyth; or, Memorials of the life and times of the Rev. W. H. Burns. 1860. 8°. **4955.** b. **19.**

—— Mode of Conducting a Revival. *See* H., W. M. Lectures on the Revival of Religion, *etc.* 1840. 12°. **1114.** c. **27.**

BURNS (WILLIAM JOHN) *See* HORNBLOW (Arthur) The Argyle Case . . . Written in coöperation with Detective W. J. Burns. 1913. 8°. **012704.** c. **39.**

—— —— [1929.] 8°. **012601.** bbb. **82.**

—— The Masked War. The story of a peril that threatened the United States by the man who uncovered the dynamite conspirators and sent them to jail. pp. 328. *Hodder & Stoughton: London,* [1914.] 8°. **6056.** tt. **20.**

BURNS (WILLIAM JOHN) and **OSTRANDER** (ISABEL EGENTON)

—— The Lawton Mystery. pp. 320. *Eveleigh Nash Co.: London,* 1917. 8°. NN. **4198.**

BURNSALL. The Churchwardens' Accounts of the Parish of Burnsall-in-Craven, 1704 1769. Edited by W. J. Stavert. pp. 79. *"Craven Herald": Skipton,* 1899. 8°. **010360.** ee. **16.**

—— The Parish Register of Burnsall-in-Craven . . . Edited by W. J. Stavert. 4 vol.

vol. 1. 1559–1700. pp. xv. 163. 1893.
vol. 2. 1701–1739, 1783–1812. pp. x. 151. 1893.
vol. 3. Missing Portions recovered from the Transcripts at York, *etc.* pp. xxii. 117. 1912.
vol. 4. 1813–1900. pp. 164. 1915.

"Craven Herald": Skipton, 1893–1915. 8°. **9906.** b. **27.**

BURNS-BEGG (ROBERT) *See* BEGG.

BURNSHAW (STANLEY)

—— *See* KRUSE (Alexander Z.) Two New Yorkers . . . Edited by S. Burnshaw. [1938.] 8°. **11688.** r. **5.**

—— André Spire and his Poetry . . . Two essays and forty translations, *etc.* [With a portrait.] pp. 144. *Centaur Press: [Philadelphia,]* 1933. 8°. **11856.** bbb. **12**

—— The Sunless Sea, *etc.* pp. 191. *Peter Davies: London* 1948. 8°. NN. **38376.**

BURNSIDE (AMBROSE EVERTS) *See* POORE (Benjamin P.) The Life and Public Services of Ambrose E. Burnside, *etc.* [With a portrait.] 1882. 8°. **10880.** h. **9.**

—— *See* WOODBURY (Augustus) Major General Ambrose E. Burnside and the Ninth Army Corps, *etc.* [With a portrait.] 1867. 8°. **9602.** dd. **13.**

—— Memorial Addresses on the Life and Character of Ambrose E. Burnside . . . delivered in the Senate and House of Representatives, *etc.* [With a portrait.] pp. 79. 1882. 4°. *See* UNITED STATES OF AMERICA. [*Miscellaneous Public Documents.*] **10880.** g. **22.**

BURNSIDE (ANDREW WILLIAM) A Catechism on the Common Prayer. To which is added a glossary. pp. 40. *Smith, Elder & Co.: London,* 1845. 16°. **1219.** b. **23.**

BURNSIDE (ESTELLE) and **STRONG** (W. M.) *M.A.*

—— A Comparison of Pig Production before and after the War, *etc.* pp. 27. *Newton Abbot,* 1955. 4°. [*University of Bristol. Department of Economics (Agricultural Economics). Report.* no. 88.] W.P. **846/88.**

—— An Economic and Financial Study of Pig Production in Cornwall, Devon and Dorset, 1953–54. pp. 40. *Newton Abbot,* 1955. 8°. [*University of Bristol. Department of Agriculture (Agricultural Economics). Report.* no. 83.] W.P. **846/83.**

BURNSIDE (FRANCIS RASHLEIGH) Tea Roses, and how to grow and exhibit them, *etc.* pp. 23. *Jakeman & Carver: Hereford,* 1893. 16°. **7055.** a. **74.**

BURNSIDE (FREDERICK) *See* SAINT ALBANS, *Diocese of.* St. Albans Diocesan Calendar, *etc.* [Edited by F. Burnside.] [1877, *etc.*] 8°. P.P. **2506.** ek.

—— The Official Parochial Register of Church Services. 1899. *obl.* fol. *See* ENGLAND.—*Church of England.—Society for Promoting Christian Knowledge.* **1887.** a. **8.**

—— Village Sermons. By the late Rev. F. Burnside . . . With a brief memoir by one of his sons. pp. viii. 98. *Skeffington & Son: London,* 1904. 8°. **4479.** i. **16.**

BURNSIDE (HELEN) Poems. [Edited by R. J. Burnside.] pp. vii. 117. *Hatchard & Co.: London,* 1864. 8°. **11651.** aa. **30.**

BURNSIDE (HELEN MARION) *See* ARABIAN NIGHTS. [*Abridgments, Selections, etc.—English.*] The Arabian Nights. Arranged by H. M. Burnside. [1893.] 4°. **12410.** g. **23.**

—— —— [1897.] 8°. **12809.** u. **67.**

—— *See* BOOK. My Own Book of Pets. With stories and verses by H. M. Burnside, *etc.* [1913.] 8°. **1871.** a. **38**

—— *See* CAREY (Rosa N.) The Rosa Nouchette Carey Birthday Book. Compiled by H. M. Burnside, *etc.* [1901.] 8°. **12274.** df. **1.**

—— *See* LADS. Lads and Lassies. By E. Nesbit, H. M. Burnside, *etc.* [1894.] 4°. **12806.** k. **70.**

—— *See* LISTEN. Listen long and Listen well. Stories by H. M. Burnside [and others], *etc.* [1893.] 4°. **012803.** i. **22.**

—— *See* TALES. We've Tales to tell. Written by H. M. Burnside [and others], *etc.* [1893.] 4°. **012803.** i. **18**

—— Buttercup Pictures, with verses by H. M. Burnside, and . . . illustrations by L. M. Glazier. *Ernest Nister: London; E. P. Dutton & Co.: New York; printed in Bavaria,* [1899.] 4°. **12801.** dd. **26.**

—— The Children's Wonderland. Verses by H. M. Burnside. Pen & ink illustrations by Florence Hardy. *Ernest Nister: London; E. P. Dutton & Co.: New York; printed in Bavaria,* [1900.] 4°. **12801.** dd. **24.**

—— Christmas Gems. [1908.] *s. sh.* 8°. **1897.** b. **33. (37.)**

—— Circling Surprises. Verses by H. M. Burnside . . . Illustrations by H. K. Robinson. *Ernest Nister: London; E. P. Dutton & Co.: New York; printed in Bavaria,* [1901.] 4°. **12813.** s. **45.**

BURNSIDE (Helen Marion)

—— A Day with the Sea Urchins, *etc.* [With musical notes.] pp. 99. *F. Warne & Co.: London,* 1893. 8°. **12807.** o. **37.**

—— Drift Weed. Verses & lyrics. pp. xvi. 274. *Hutchinson & Co.: London; Nimeguen* printed, [1897.] 8°. **11652.** d. **54.**

—— The Fairy Ring. Verses by H. M. Burnside and . . . illustrations by T. J. & E. A. Overnell. *Ernest Nister: London; E. P. Dutton & Co.: New York; printed in Bavaria,* [1900.] 4°. **12813.** s. **47.**

—— Happy Days in the Country. pp. 64. *Ernest Nister: London; E. P. Dutton & Co.: New York; printed in Bavaria,* [1900.] 8°. **12812.** aa. **16.**

—— A Happy Greeting. [Verses.] *Ernest Nister: London; E. P. Dutton & Co.: New York; printed in Bavaria,* [1898.] 12°. **11647.** dg. **31.**

—— Her Highland Laddie. pp. 32. [*R.T.S.*:] *London,* [1906.] 8°. [*Girl's Pleasant Hour Library of Penny Books.*] **4430.** ee. **21/3.**

—— The Last Letter; or, the Adventures of a postage stamp. A story of the relief of Lucknow. pp. 96. *T. Nelson & Sons: London,* 1898 [1897]. 8°. **012807.** h. **13.**

—— The Little V.C. pp. 96. *T. Nelson & Sons: London,* 1898 [1897]. 8°. **012807.** h. **12.**

—— Round Nature's Dial . . . With illustrations by A. W. Cooper. 4 pt. *G. Routledge & Sons: London,* [1887.] 4°. **12354.** k. **5.**

—— A Story of a Birthday, *etc.* [In verse.] pp. 44. *S.P.C.K.: London,* [1887.] 8°. **12806.** s. **8.**

—— The Three Angels . . . [Verses.] Illustrated by Alice Price and F. Corbyn Price. *R. Tuck & Sons: London; printed in Germany,* [1890.] 8°. **11647.** f. **56.**

—— Wonderland Pictures. With verses by H. M. Burnside. Decorations by "Gar." *Ernest Nister: London; E. P. Dutton & Co.: New York; printed in Bavaria,* [1899.] 4°. **12813.** s. **44.**

BURNSIDE (John) *See* Rawnsley (Robert D. B.) Comfort to Mourners. A sermon preached . . . on the 1st of January, 1865, being the Sunday after the funeral of the Rev. J. Burnside, *etc.* 1865. 8°. **4920.** d. **53. (20.)**

BURNSIDE (M'Gregore) Oration, delivered before the Officers and Members of Merrimack Lodge, Haverhill, on the festival of St. John the Evangelist, *etc.* pp. 16. *Francis Gould: Haverhill* [*Mass.*], 1807. 8°. **4784.** bb. **22.**

BURNSIDE (Robert) *See* Shenston (J. B.) A Small Tribute to the Memory of the late pious, learned, and Rev. Robert Burnside, *etc.* 1826. 8°. T. **1179.** (4.)

—— The Fruits of the Spirit, the Ornament of Christians. A sermon, *etc.* pp. 51. *M. Gurney; W. Button: London,* [1805.] 8°. **4477.** aaa. **119. (6.)**

—— The Religion of Mankind, in a series of essays. 2 vol. *Printed for the Author: London,* 1819. 8°. **1114.** d. **9, 10.**

—— Remarks on the Different Sentiments entertained in Christendom relative to the Weekly Sabbath. pp. viii. 354. *Printed for the Author: London,* 1825. 12°. **1115.** d. **9.**

BURNSIDE (Robert)

—— Tea Table Chat; or, Religious allegories told at the teatable in a seminary for ladies. vol. 1. pp. vi. 191. *Printed for the Author: London,* 1820. 12°. **1118.** c. **2.**

BURNSIDE (Robert John) *See* Burnside (Helen) Poems. [Edited by R. J. Burnside.] 1864. 8°. **11651.** aa. **30.**

BURNSIDE (Samuel M.) Oration, delivered at Worcester, on the thirtieth of April, A.D. 1813, before the Washington Benevolent Society . . . in commemoration of the first inauguration of General Washington as President of the United States, *etc.* pp. 20. *Isaac Sturtevant: Worcester* [*Mass.*], 1813. 8°. **10880.** d. **11.**

BURNSIDE (Walter Fletcher) *See* Bible.—*Luke.* [*Greek.*] The Gospel according to St. Luke . . . Edited . . . by W. F. Burnside. 1913. 8°. **03025.** f. **19.**

—— *See* Bible.—*Acts.* [*Greek.*] The Acts of the Apostles . . . Edited . . . by W. F. Burnside. 1916. 8°. **03025.** f. **21.**

—— Old Testament History for use in Schools . . . With three maps. pp. xii. 330. *Methuen & Co.: London,* 1904. 8°. **03166.** e. **48.**

—— Second edition, revised. pp. xxii. 330. *Methuen & Co.: London,* 1906. 8°. **03149.** f. **7.**

—— Tenth edition. pp. xxii. 330. *Methuen & Co.: London,* 1923. 8°. **03149.** e. **32.**

BURNSIDE (Walter Fletcher) and **OWEN** (Arthur Synge)

—— Short Lives of Great Men. pp. viii. 296. *Edward Arnold: London,* 1905. 8°. **10803.** k. **15.**

BURNSIDE (William) *A.M.I.C.E.* Bridge Foundations, *etc.* pp. viii. 139. *Scott, Greenwood & Son: London,* 1916. 8°. [*Broadway Series of Engineering Handbooks.* vol. 19.] **8763.** de. **1/19.**

BURNSIDE (William) *F.R.S.* Theory of Groups of Finite Order. pp. xvi. 388. *University Press: Cambridge,* 1897. 8°. **08533.** g. **13.**

—— Second edition. pp. xxiv. 512. *University Press: Cambridge,* 1911. 8°. **8507.** g. **9.**

—— Theory of Probability. [Edited, with a memoir, by A. R. Forsyth.] pp. xxx. 106. *University Press: Cambridge,* 1928. 8°. **8507.** ccc. **23.**

BURNSIDE (William Smyth) Church Education v. the National Board. A letter addressed to the Lord Bishop of Meath, in vindication of the conduct of the Irish clergy, in reference to national instruction, being a reply to his Lordship's Primary Charge, *etc.* pp. 27. *George Herbert: Dublin,* 1851. 8°. **4165.** e. **6. (7.)**

—— The Connemara Peasant; or, Barney Brannigan's reasons, in a discussion with the priest of his parish, for reading the Scriptures without asking the priest's leave. [By W. S. Burnside.] pp. 12. 1854. 12°. *See* Brannigan (Barney) **3939.** b. **37.**

—— The Lex Evangelica: or, Essays for the times, proving that Holy Scripture is the only infallible interpreter to reason, in search after religious truth. Being a reply to a recent publication entitled "Essays and Reviews." pp. vi. 423. *George Herbert: Dublin,* 1861. 8°. **4373.** f. **14.**

BURNSIDE (William Smyth)

—— A Reply from " The Bible, and the Bible alone," to the Bishop of Ossory's tract on Baptismal Regeneration, in a letter to his Lordship. pp. 19. *George Herbert: Dublin*, 1873. 8°. **4017.** h. **1.** (**4.**)

—— A Sermon preached in Castleblaney Church . . . on the recent execution . . . of Patrick Coomey, Brian Grant, and Neal Quin for the murder of Thomas D. Bateson. pp. 16. *George Herbert: Dublin*, 1854. 8°. **4477.** d. **20.**

—— The Testimony of Jesus, the Best Evidence for the Truth of the Gospel. An act sermon, *etc.* pp. 23. *George Herbert: Dublin*, 1861. 12°. **4477.** b. **14.**

BURNSIDE (William Snow) and **PANTON** (Arthur William) The Theory of Equations; with an introduction to the theory of binary algebraic forms. pp. xvi. 387. *Hodges, Figgis & Co.: Dublin; Longmans & Co.: London*, 1881. 8°. [*Dublin University Press Series.*] **12201.** i. **1/5.**

—— Second edition. pp. xvi. 448. *Hodges, Figgis & Co.: Dublin; Longmans & Co.: London*, 1886. 8°. [*Dublin University Press Series.*] **12201.** i. **1/10.**

—— Third edition. pp. xvi. 496. *Hodges, Figgis & Co.: Dublin; Longmans & Co.: London*, 1892. 8°. [*Dublin University Press Series.*] **12201.** i. **1/11.**

—— Fourth edition. 2 vol. *Hodges, Figgis & Co.: Dublin; Longmans & Co.: London*, 1899, 1901. [*Dublin University Press Series.*] **12201.** i. **1/12.**

—— Fifth edition. 2 vol. *Hodges, Figgis & Co.: Dublin; Longmans & Co.: London*, 1904. 8°. [*Dublin University Press Series.*] **2322.** f. **6.**

—— Seventh edition. (Edited by M. W. J. Fry.) vol. 2. pp. ix. 317. *Longmans & Co.: London*, 1928. 8°. [*Dublin University Press Series.*] **12201.** i. **1/13.**
Vol. 1 was not published in this edition.

—— An Introduction to Determinants. Being a chapter from the Theory of Equations. pp. 84. *Hodges, Figgis & Co.: Dublin; Longmans & Co.: London*, 1899. 8°. **08533.** g. **44.**

BURNSIDE (William Stanford) *See* Rawnsley (Robert D. B.) Life and Death. A sermon preached . . . the Sunday after the funeral of W. S. Burnside, *etc.* 1870. 8°. **4906.** dd. **29.** (**16.**)

BURNSTAN (Arthur Rowland) Special Assessment Procedure. A critical study of the methods and practices in improvement finance in twenty-one New York cities, *etc.* [A thesis.] pp. 272. *J. B. Lyon Co.: Albany*, 1929. 8°. **8230.** cc. **9.**

BURNSTINE (David) *See* Jacoby (Oswald) The Four Aces System of Contract Bridge. By O. Jacoby, D. Burnstine, *etc.* [1935.] 8°. **7916.** f. **33.**

—— The Four Horsemen's One over One Method of Contract Bidding. 2 pt. *Blue Ribbon Books: London; Cornwall, N.Y.* printed, [1932.] 8°. **7916.** c. **9.**
A " Pocket Summary " of the Method is enclosed in an envelope at the end of the book.

BURNTISLAND. Burntisland. Official guide, *etc.* [With a map.] *E. J. Burrow & Co.: Cheltenham & London*, [1922– .] 8°. **10360.** s. **5.**
Various editions.

BURNUP (Charles R. E.)

—— *See* Edmundson (Joseph) and Burnup (C. R. E.) Athletics for Boys & Girls. 1954. 8°. **7921.** aaa. **55.**

BURNUP (Henry) The Carriage Tax. A letter to the Right Hon. Sir Charles Wood, Bart. Chancellor of the Exchequer. pp. 15. *J. King: London*, 1851. 8°. **8226.** a. **4.**

BURNWORTH (Edward) An Account of the Lives of the most notorious Murderers and Robbers; Edward Burnworth alias Frazier, William Blewet, Emanuel Dickenson Thomas Berry alias Teague, John Higgs, and John Legee. . . . To which is added an account of their tryal and conviction . . . for the barbarous murder of Thomas Ball. pp. 62. *J. Roberts: London*, 1726. 8°. **6496.** aaa. **1.**

—— A True and Exact Account of the Lives of Edward Burnworth alias Frasier, William Blewitt, Thomas Berry, and Emanuel Dickenson, &c. . . . With a true relation of the several robberies committed by them. Together with the particular manner of their murdering Thomas Ball, *etc.* pp. 40. *John Applebee: London*, 1726. 8°. **6496.** aa. **20.** (**2.**)

BURNY (Frédéric) and **HAMANDE** (Louis) Les Caisses d'épargne en Belgique. [With maps.] pp. 677. *Bruxelles*, 1902. 8°. [*Mémoires couronnés et autres mémoires publiés par l'Académie Royale des Sciences, des Lettres et des Beaux-Arts de Belgique.* Collection in-8°. tom. 56.] **Ac. 985/4.**

BURNY (H. de) Exposition triennale des beaux-arts de Gand, 1871. Compte-rendu du Salon. (Extrait du Journal de Bruxelles.) pp. 42. *Bruxelles*, [1871.] 8°. **7807.** h. **19.** (**1.**)

BURNYEAT (John) *Curate of St. Nicholas' Parish Church, Warwick.* A Farewell Sermon, preached in the Parish Church of St. Nicholas . . . March 23d, 1817, *etc.* pp. 20. *Henry Sharpe: Warwick*, 1817. 8°. **1026.** f. **3.** (**10.**)

BURNYEAT (John) *Quaker.* *See* Fox (George) *Founder of the Society of Friends*, and Burnyeat (J.) A New-England-Fire-Brand quenched, *etc.* 1679, *etc.* 4°. **4152.** d. **26.**

—— *See* Williams (Roger) George Fox digg'd out of his Burrowes, Or an Offer of a Disputation on fourteen Proposalls made . . . unto G. Fox . . . by R. W. As also how . . . the disputation went on . . . between J. Stubs, J. Burnet, and W. Edmundson on the one part, and R. W. on the other, *etc.* 1676. 4°. **C. 25.** c. **2.**

—— The Truth Exalted in the Writings of that eminent and faithful servant of Christ John Burnyeat, *etc.* [With a preface by William Penn.] pp. 20. 264. *For Thomas Northcott: London*, 1691. 4°. **1372.** b. **30.**

—— [Another edition.] Journal of the Life and Gospel Labours of John Burnyeat, *etc.* *See* Caton (William) Journals of the Lives and Gospel Labours of William Caton, and John Burnyeat, *etc.* 1839. 12°. [Barclay (*John*) *A Select Series . . . chiefly the productions of early members of the Society of Friends, etc.* vol. 6.] **1372.** b. **3.**

—— [Another edition.] 1847. *See* Evans (William) and (T.) *Publishers, of Philadelphia.* The Friends' Library, *etc.* vol. 11. 1837, *etc.* 8°. **4152.** gg. **4.**

BURNYEAT (John) *Quaker*, and **WATSON** (John) *Quaker, of Dublin.*

—— The Holy Truth and its Professors defended, in an answer to a letter, writ by Lawrence Potts . . . unto Robert Lacky a parishioner . . . occasioned by his forsaking his ministry and embracing the blessed truth herein vindicated. pp. 28. [*London?*] 1688. 4°. **4152.** ee. **46.** (**6.**)
The last leaf is mutilated.

BURNZ (Eliza Boardman) The Anglo-American Primer. Deziend tu teech a proper speling and pronunsiashon ov the English langwej, and tu serv az a direct gied tu the reeding ov ordinery English print. pp. 31. *Burnz & Co.: New York*, [1877.] 8°. **12981**. bb. **11**.

—— Help for Young Reporters . . . Also containing an explanation of the proposed revision of English spelling. pp. 47. *Burnz & Co.: New York*, 1881. 8°. **11852**. b. **5**.

—— The Step-by-Step Primer in Burnz' Pronouncing Print. Correct pronunciation shown without new letters or change of spelling. pp. 94. *Burnz & Co.: New York*, 1892. 8°. **11824**. b. **43**.
In this copy are inserted newspaper cuttings and type specimens.

BURO. *See* Buero.

BUROLLEAU (S. L.) Dissertation sur l'emploi diététique et médical du sucre, *etc.* pp. 30. *Paris*, 1815. 4°. **1183**. c. **10**. (**13**.)

BÜRON. *See* Bueron.

BURON (Edmond J. P.) *See* Alliaco (P. de) *Cardinal*. [*Imago mundi*.] Ymago mundi . . . Texte latin et traduction française . . . Étude sur les sources de l'auteur [by E. J. P. Buron]. 1930, *etc.* 8°. **10003**. s. **2**.

—— *See* Periodical Publications.—*Paris*. Annuaire financier canadien. [Edited by E. J. P. Buron and J. Dubois.] 1907, *etc.* 8°. P.P. **2539**. te.

—— Les Richesses du Canada. Préface de M. G. Hanotaux. pp. xiii. 368. *Paris*, [1904.] 8°. **08226**. cc. **14**.

BURON (François Alfred) De la pharyngite chronique. pp. 46. *Paris*, 1851. 4°. [*Collection des thèses soutenues à la Faculté de Médecine de Paris*. An 1851. tom. 2.] **7372**. d. **9**

BURON (Hélie de) *See* Hélie, *de Borron*.

BURON (J.) Dissertation sur le scorbut, *etc.* pp. 27. *Paris*, 1812. 4°. **1182**. h. **15**. (**22**.)

BURON (Jean Pierre) Thèse sur la fièvre ataxique—maligne—continue simple, *etc.* pp. 23. *Paris*, 1813. 4°. **1182**. i. **12**. (**18**.)

BURON (Joseph Duarte) Ilustracion de el derecho que compete a la Santa Iglesia Cathedral Metropolitana de esta ciudad de Mexico, para la percepcion del diezmo, que causa el fruto del maguey, el que por medio de su fermentacion passa naturalmente a la especie de pulque, de cuya bebida usan los naturales de estos reynos, y no pocos de los Españoles, *etc.* pp. 45 [85]. *Mexico*, 1750. fol. **5175**. i. **3**. (**8**.)

—— [Another copy.] **5125**. g. **9**. (**2**.)

BURON (Léon Louis) La Bretagne catholique. Description historique et pittoresque; précédée d'une excursion dans le boccage vendéen, vies de saints . . . anecdotes et paysages . . . Illustrations par M. Devaux, *etc.* pp. 460. *Paris, Lyon*, 1856. 8°. **10172**. d. **10**.

—— Cours de style. Corrigés des matières de compositions françaises en tous genres, *etc.* pp. viii. 291. *Paris, Lyon*, 1853. 12°. **12237**. aaa. **2**.

—— Cours de style. Recueil de matières de compositions françaises . . . Seconde édition, *etc.* pp. viii. 130. *Paris, Lyon*, 1857. 12°. **12237**. aaa. **1**.

—— Histoire abrégée des principales littératures de l'Europe, *etc.* pp. 443. *Paris*, 1867. 12°. **11852**. bb. **14**.

—— [A reissue.] *Paris*, 1876. 12°. **11850**. cc. **7**.

BURON (Léon Louis)

—— Histoire de la littérature en France depuis la conquête des Gaules par Jules César jusqu'à nos jours. pp. vii. 606. *Paris, Lyon*, 1851. 8°. **816**. f. **35**.

BURON (Robert)

—— Les Obligations du trustee en droit anglais. pp. 136. *Paris*, 1938. 8°. **6378**. cc. **3**.

BURONI (Giuseppe) *See* Cornoldi (G. M.) Il Panteismo ontologico e le nozioni di ontologia del M. R. G. Buroni. [1878?] 8°. **8463**. c. **3**. (**6**.)

—— Antonio Rosmini e la "Civiltà cattolica" dinanzi alla S. Congregazione dell'Indice, ossia spiegazione del "Dimittantur Opera A. Rosmini-Serbati" secondo la Bolla "Sollicita" di Benedetto xiv . . . Edizione seconda cresciuta di molte aggiunte, *etc.* pp. 218. *Torino*, 1880. 8°. **3902**. g. **18**.

—— De intolerantia catholica seu de sententia "Extra ecclesiam nulla salus" dissertatio theologica. pp. x. 142. *Taurini*, 1868. 8°. **4051**. dd. **9**.

—— De Romanitate primatus apostolici, seu de nexu indissolubili quo primatus Sedi Romanae adhaeret iure divino. pp. 34. *Taurini*, 1867. 8°. **4051**. e. **7**.

—— Del nuovo progetto di legge Vigliani circa il matrimonio. Considerazioni, *etc.* pp. 38. *Torino*, 1874. 8°. **5176**. f. **18**.

—— Dell'essere e del conoscere. Studii su Parmenide, Platone, e Rosmini . . . Sunto dell'opera inserta nelle Memorie della Reale Accademia delle Scienze di Torino, *etc.* pp. 50. *Torino*, 1877. 8°. **8463**. d. **10**. (**14**.)

—— Di un equivoco circa l'infallibilità pontificia con due appendici, *etc.* pp. 87. *Torino*, 1872. 8°. **3902**. g. **28**.

—— Risposta alla Civiltà cattolica e alla Unità cattolica in difesa della dissertazione De intolerantia catholica. pp. 101. *Torino*, 1868. 8°. **3901**. g. **5**.

—— La Conversione dialettica della Civiltà cattolica e la pace della chiesa. Sette poscritte all'edizione prima del libro La Trinità e la creazione . . . Estratto dall'edizione 2ª La Trinità e la creazione. pp. 71. *Torino*, 1879. 8°. **3902**. h. **5**. (**1**.)

BURONI (Gottardo)

—— Le Diverse tesi sulla battaglia del Metauro. [With plates.] pp. 354. *Urbania*, [1953.] 8°. **9043**. dd. **1**.

BURONTIUS DEL SIGNORE (Carlo Luigi) successively *Bishop of Acqui, of Novara* and *Archbishop of Turin*. *See* Atto ii., *Bishop of Vercelli*. Attonis . . . opera . . . Præfatione et commentariis illustrata a D. C. Burontio del Signore, *etc.* 1768. fol. **691**. k. **25**.

BUROS (Oscar Krisen) Buros Spelling Workbook. pp. 37. *American Book Co.: New York*, [1931.] 4°. **12980**. bb. **45**.

—— Educational, Psychological and Personality Tests of 1936. Including a bibliography and book review digest of measurement books and monographs of 1933–36. pp. 141. 1937. 8°. *See* New Brunswick, *New Jersey*.—*Rutgers University*.—*School of Education*. **08385**. b. **3**.

—— **The Third [*etc.*] Mental Measurements Yearbook. Edited by O. K. Buros.** ***Rutgers University Press: New Brunswick, N.J.***, **[1949– .] 8°.** P.P. **2520**. r.

BUROS (OSCAR KRISEN)

—— Statistical Methodology Reviews, 1941–1950. Edited by O. K. Buros. [A bibliography.] pp. 434. *John Wiley & Sons: New York*, [1951.] 4°. **08535**. l. **30**.

BUROT (FERDINAND) *See* BUROT (Prosper F.)

BUROT (PROSPER FERDINAND) De la fièvre dite bilieuse inflammatoire à la Guyane. Application des découvertes de M. Pasteur à la pathologie des pays chauds. Avec tableaux, *etc.* pp. xii. 540. *Paris*, 1880. 8°. **07561**. h. **70**.

—— Des phénomènes réflexes considérés au point de vue du diagnostic, dans les maladies du système nerveux. pp. 40. *Paris*, 1872. 4°. [*Collection des thèses soutenues à la Faculté de Médecine de Paris.* An 1872. tom. 3.] **7373**. n. **9**.

BUROT (PROSPER FERDINAND) and **LEGRAND** (MAXIMILIEN ALBERT HENRI ANDRÉ)

—— Les Troupes coloniales. Statistique de la mortalité. pp. 140. *Paris*, 1897. 8°. **07686**. k. **18**

BUROV (ALEKSANDR) *pseud.* [i.e. ALEKSANDR PAVLOVICH BURD-VOSKHODOV.] *See* also BURD-VOSKHODOV (A. P.)

—— Была земля. [Short stories. With a portrait.] pp. 261. *Берлинъ*, [1932.] 8°. **12590**. tt. **28**.

—— В царстве тенеи. Au royaume des ombres. In the kingdom of shadows. [With portraits.] *Russ.* pp. 91. *Париж*, 1950. 8°. **11758**. tt. **24**.

—— " Господи... Твоя Россія..." Романъ-лѣтопись. pp. 176. *Парижъ; Tallinn* [printed], 1938. 8°. **012593**. df. **30**.
Приложеніе къ "Иллюстрированной Россіи."

—— Москва далекая.... Moscow, the wide.... Moscou, la lointaine.... [With plates.] pp. 219. [*Leiden*,] 1950. 8°. **11587**. bbb. **26**.

—— Пѣвецъ зарубежной печали. Книга священнаго гнѣва. Романъ-лѣтопись. pp. 196. *Парижъ; [printed in Esthonia,]* 1938. 8°. **012593**. ee. **9**.

—— Тяжко мне, тяжко без сталинградовой России—в трех балладах—и Плач вопиющего в пустыне—читается как роман. [With plates, including portraits.] pp. 192. *Leiden*, 1947. 8°. **12263**. d. **3**.

BUROV (ATHANASY) La Politique extérieure de la Bulgarie. Discours, *etc.* pp. 20. *Sofia*, 1929. 8°. **8027**. ee. **47**.

BUROV (HARALAMBY A.) *See* BUROV (Kharalampy A.)

BUROV (KHARALAMPY A.) Makédonia! [An account of the Macedonian insurrection. With illustrations.] pp. 168. *Bruxelles, Paris*, 1905. 8°. **9134**. e. **19**.

BUROV (M. Ts.) La Réforme agraire en Bulgarie, 1921–1924. pp. 134. *Paris*, [1926.] 8°. **08276**. k. **50**.

BUROV (N. A.)

—— Указатель изданий Средне-Азиатского Государственного Университета. 1. [Compiled by N. A. Burov.] pp. 31. 1930. 8°. *See* TASHKEND.—*Средне-Азіатскій Государственный Университетъ.* Ac. **1163/2**.

BUROV (YAKOV IOSIFOVICH)

—— Деревня на переломе. Год работы в деревне. pp. 278. *Москва, Ленинград*, 1926. 8°. **08286**. c. **69**.

BUROV (YAKOV IOSIFOVICH)

—— Дома крестьянина. Как их организовать и какие задачи им поставить. Под редакцией и с предисловием В. Карпинского. pp. 126. *Москва, Петроград*, 1923. 8°. **8289**. c. **46**.

—— Организуйте деревню! Примѣрная памятка—наставленіе для отъѣзжающихъ въ деревню тов.-солдатъ и крестьянъ-ходоновъ, *etc.* pp. 168. *Петроградъ*, 1918. 8°. **8094**. de. **30**.

—— Что означает закон о свободѣ совѣсти и отдѣленіи церкви от государства? Подробное, постатейное разсмотрѣніе декрета о свободѣ совѣсти с приложеніем самого декрета. pp. 16. *Москва*, 1918. 8°. **8095**. gg. **12**. (**1**.)

—— [Another edition.] pp. 16. *Москва*, 1921. 8°. [*Законы Рабоче-Крестьянского Государства.* но. 1.] **5755.b.1.**

BUROVA (G. K.)

—— *See* LEBEDEV (A. K.) and BUROVA (G. K.) В. В. Верещагин и В. В. Стасов, *etc.* 1953. 8°. **10798**. c. **13**.

—— *See* VERESHCHAGIN (V. V.) Переписка В. В. Верещагина и В. В. Стасова . . . Письма приготовлены к печати и примечания к ним составлены А. К. Лебедевым и Г. К. Буровой, *etc.* 1950, *etc.* 8°. **10923.ee.18.**

BUROW (ALBERT) Geschichte des Königl. Preussischen 18. Infanterie-Regiments von 1813 bis 1847. [By A. Burow. Edited by R. von Wedell. With plates.] pp. 271. 1848. 8°. *See* PRUSSIA.—*Army.—Infantry.—Infanterie Regiment Nr.* 18. **9385**. e. **5**.

—— Das Kriegstheater der Dänischen Halbinsel und die Festung Rendsburg, *etc.* [With maps.] pp. 131. *Altona*, 1854. 8°. **8826**. h. **34**.

—— Die Krim-Expedition militair-wissenschaftlich beleuchtet von A. Burow. pp. 99. *Berlin*, 1856. 8°. **9080**. f. **2**.

BUROW (AUGUST) *See* BUROW (Carl A.)

BUROW (AUGUSTUS EDUARDUS EHRENHOLDUS PAULUS) De dentium dolore. Dissertatio inauguralis medica, *etc.* pp. 31. *Berolini*, [1865.] 8°. **7385**. b. (**17**.)

BUROW (CARL AUGUST) Beiträge zur Physiologie und Physik des menschlichen Auges, *etc.* pp. viii. 184. pl. XII. *Berlin*, 1841. 8°. **7306**. aaa. **13**. (**4**.)

—— Beschreibung einer neuen Transplantations-Methode—Methode der seitlichen Dreiecke—zum Wiederersatz verloren gegangener Theile des Gesichts. pp. 39. *Berlin*, 1855. 4°. **7481**. h. **24**. (**2**.)

—— Ein neues Optometer . . . Mit 3 lithographirten Tafeln. pp. 36. *Berlin*, 1863. 8°. **7610**. bb. **48**. (**4**.)

—— Resultate der Beobachtung an 137 Schieloperationen. pp. 28. *Königsberg*, 1844. 4°. **1186**. k. **29**.

—— Ueber die Reihenfolge der Brillen-Brennweiten. Eine Gratulationsschrift Carl Ernst von Baer . . . überreicht. pp. 20. *Berlin*, 1864. 8°. **8715**. e. **31**. (**3**.)

BUROW (ERNST) Laryngoscopischer Atlas enthaltend 61 Figuren auf 10 Tafeln in Farbendruck . . . gemalt und erläutert von Dr. E. Burow. pp. iv. 130. *Stuttgart*, 1877. 8°. **7615**. f. **2**.

—— Mittheilungen aus der chirurgischen Privat-Klinik 1875–1877, *etc.* pp. 232. *Leipzig*, 1880. 8°. **7482**. bbb. **10**.

BURROW (ERNST)

—— Über Lepra taurica. *See* LEPRASTUDIEN. Leprastudien, *etc.* [1885.] 8°. [*Monatshefte für praktische Dermatologie.* Bd. 4. Ergänzungshft. 1.] P.P. **3015**. e.

BUROW (FRIDERICUS GULIELMUS) De erysipelate ejusque speciebus praecipuis dissertatio inauguralis medica, *etc.* pp. 32. *Berolini,* [1818.] 8°. **7385**.*a. (21.)

BUROW, afterwards PFANNENSCHMIDT (JULIE) An der polnischen Grenze. Ein Lebensbild. pp. 198. *Wien,* [1861.] 16°. **12551**. aa. **3**.

—— Ein Arzt in einer kleinen Stadt. Roman. 2 Bd. *Leipzig,* 1854. 16°. **12551**. a. **3**.

—— Aus der letzten polnischen Revolution. Ein Lebensbild. pp. 228. *Wien & Leipzig,* 1864. 16°. **12550**. aa. **2**.

—— Bilder aus dem Leben. pp. 356. *Leipzig,* 1854. 12°. **12553**. b. **27**.

—— Blumen und Früchte deutscher Dichtung. Ein Kranz gewunden für Frauen und Jungfrauen von Julie Burow . . Fünfte Auflage. pp. xvi. 416. *Berlin,* 1861. 16°. **11528**. e. **92**.

—— Ein Grab an der Kirchhofsmauer. 1887. *See* HEYSE (P. J. L.) and LAISTNER (L.) Neuer deutscher Novellenschatz, *etc.* Bd. 23. 1884, *etc.* 8°. **12555**. aa.

—— In stillen Stunden. Gedanken einer Frau über die höchsten Wahrheiten des Menschen-Daseins . . . Vierte Auflage. pp. 263. *Berlin,* 1862. 16°. **4403**. aaa. **38**.

—— Julie Burow. Versuch einer Selbstbiographie. pp. 84. *Prag & Leipzig,* 1857. 16°. **10706**. a. **35**. (2.)

—— Die Preussen in Prag. Historischer Roman aus dem letzen deutschen Bruderkriege, *etc.* pp. 383. *Forst i./L.,* 1867. 8°. **12551**. i. **3**.

BUROW (PAULUS) *See* BUROW (Augustus E. E. P.)

BUROWICK (CARLOS)

—— Poemas. pp. 90. *México,* 1948. 8°. **11453**. e. **31**.

BURPEE (CHARLES WINSLOW) A Century in Hartford. Being the history of the Hartford County Mutual Fire Insurance Company, *etc.* [With plates.] pp. xi. 363. *Case, Lockwood & Brainard Co.: Hartford,* 1931. 8°. **8230**. c. **30**.

BURPEE (LAWRENCE JOHNSTONE) *See* BROOKE (Frances) The History of Emily Montague . . . With introduction and notes by L. J. Burpee, *etc.* 1931. 8°. **12602**. pp. **17**.

—— *See* HORNING (Lewis E.) and BURPEE (L. J.) A Bibliography of Canadian Fiction, English. 1904. 8°. Ac. **2702**. b/2.

—— *See* KANE (Paul) Wanderings of an Artist among the Indians of North America, *etc.* (Introduction and notes by L. J. Burpee.) 1925. 8°. W.P. **8557/1**.

—— *See* LAROCQUE (F. A.) Journal of Larocque from the Assiniboine to the Yellowstone, 1805. Edited with notes by L. J. Burpee. 1910. 8°. [*Publications of the Canadian Archives.* no. 3.] **C.S.E.2/2.**

—— *See* MORGAN (Henry J.) and BURPEE (L. J.) Canadian Life in Town & Country, *etc.* 1905. 8°. **10470**. ppp. **4**.

BURPEE (LAWRENCE JOHNSTONE)

—— *See* MURRAY (Alexander H.) Journal of the Yukon, 1847–48 . . . Edited with notes by L. J. Burpee. 1910. 8°. [*Publications of the Canadian Archives.* no. 4.] **C.S.E.2/2.**

—— *See* VARENNES DE LA VÉRENDRYE (P. G. de) Journals and Letters of P. G. de Varennes de la Vérendrye and his sons . . . Edited . . . by L. J. Burpee. 1927. 8°. Ac. **8565/2**.

—— [An account of the first fifty years' work of the Royal Society of Canada. An offprint.] pp. 8. [1932.] 8°. **8710**. cc. **14**.

—— Among the Canadian Alps . . . With four illustrations in colour, forty-five reproductions from photographs, and five maps. pp. 239. *John Lane: London ; New York ; Norwood, Mass.* [printed], 1915. 8°. **10470**. d. **7**.

—— The Discovery of Canada. pp. 96. pl. XXIV. *Graphic Publishers: Ottawa,* [1929.] 8°. **09555**. b. **28**.

—— The Discovery of Canada, *etc.* pp. vi. 280. *Macmillan Co. of Canada: Toronto,* 1944. 8°. **010470**. aaa. **29**. *A different work from the preceding.*

—— The Fate of Henry Hudson . . . Reprinted from The Canadian Historical Review, *etc.* [1940.] 8°. **010886**. h. **25**.

—— Highways of the Fur Trade. (From the Transactions of the Royal Society of Canada.) *Ottawa,* 1914. 8°. **010470**. i. **67**.

—— Jungling in Jasper. [With plates.] pp. 200. *Graphic Publishers: Ottawa,* [1929.] 8°. **010470**. i. **43**.

—— On the Old Athabaska Trail . . . With nineteen illustrations. pp. 259. *Hurst & Blackett: London,* [1927.] 8°. **010410**. g. **13**.

—— The Opening of the West. 1930. *See* ROSE (John H.) The Cambridge History of the British Empire, *etc.* vol. 6. 1929, *etc.* 8°. **2090.a.**

—— The Oxford Encyclopædia of Canadian History. pp. vi. 699. 1926. 8°. *See* ENCYCLOPAEDIAS. **010880**. h. **12/12**.

—— Pathfinders of the Great Plains. A chronicle of La Vérendrye and his sons. [With plates and a map.] pp. vii. 116. *Glasgow, Brook & Co.: Toronto,* 1920. 8°. [*Chronicles of Canada.* vol. 18.] **09555**. a. **8/19**.

—— The Pathfinders of the Great West. *See* SHORTT (Adam) and DOUGHTY (A. G.) Canada and its Provinces, *etc.* vol. 1. 1913, *etc.* 4°. **9551**. t. **1/1**.

—— Sandford Fleming, Empire Builder. [With plates, including portraits.] pp. 288. *Oxford University Press: London,* 1915. 8°. **010826**. g. **25**.

—— The Search for the Western Sea. The story of the exploration of North-Western America. [With plates and maps.] pp. lx. 651. *Alston Rivers: London,* 1908. 8°. **9551**. i. **26**.

—— New and revised edition. 2 vol. pp. lxi. viii. 609. *Macmillan Co. of Canada: Toronto,* 1935. 8°. **010470**. ee. **49**.

—— La Vérendrye's 1738–9 Journal . . . Reprinted from The Canadian Historical Review, *etc.* [On a translation of the Journal made by H. E. Haxo.] [1942.] 8°. **9555**. f. **24**.

BURPEE (Lawrence Johnstone)

—— The Vicissitudes of Fort Montgomery. (From the Transactions of the Royal Society of Canada.) *Ottawa*, 1941. 8º. **010470**. i. **68**.

—— Western Exploration. 2 pt. 1913. *See* Shortt (Adam) and Doughty (A. G.) Canada and its Provinces, *etc.* vol 4, 5. 1913, *etc.* 4º. **9551**. t. **1/4**.

BURPEE (Royal Huddleston)

—— Seven quickly administered Tests of Physical Capacity, and their use in detecting physical incapacity for motor activity in men and boys, *etc.* [A thesis.] pp. vi. 151. *Teachers College, Columbia University: New York*, 1940. 8º. **7393**. b. **10**.

BURQ (Victor) De l'anesthésie et de l'amyosthésie, *etc.* pp. 62. *Paris*, 1851. 4º. [*Collection des thèses soutenues à la Faculté de Médecine de Paris.* An 1851. tom. 2.] **7372**. d. **9**.

—— Metallothérapie. Traitement des maladies nerveuses . . par les applications métalliques, *etc.* pp. 48. *Paris*, 1853. 8º. **7640**. e. **31**. (**3**.)

—— Metallotherapie. Behandlung der Nerven-Krankheiten . . . durch Application von Metallen, *etc.* [Translated from the French.] pp. 54. pl. II. *Leipzig*, 1854. 8º. **7461**. f. **61**. (**2**.)

BURQUE (François Xavier) Le Docteur Pierre Martial Bardy. Sa vie, ses œuvres et sa mémoire. [With a portrait.] pp. vii. 354. *Québec*, 1907. 8º. **010883**. k. **3**.

—— Élévations poétiques. 2 vol. *Québec*, 1906, 07. 8º. **11498**. l. **23**.

—— Pluralité des mondes habités considérée au point de vue négatif. pp. vii. 407. *Montréal*, 1898. 8º. **8560**. cc. **30**.

BURQUIZA (Ponciano) *See* Muñoz Ledo (O.) and Burquiza (P.) Verdadera idea sobre el impreso titulado: " Donativo de medio millon de pesos." 1845. 4º. **9770**. aaa. **10**. (**3**.)

BURR AND SONS, *Auctioneers, Chatham.*

—— Catalogue of a Choice Collection of Stuffed Birds and Animals, Reptiles . . . also the household furniture . . . which will be sold by auction, by Burr & Sons . . . March 14, 1821, *etc.* pp. 20. *C. & W. Townson: Chatham*, 1821. 8º. **10368**. e. **6**. (**6**.)

BURR, *Family of.* *See* Burr (Chauncey R.) Bures of Suffolk . . . and Burr of Massachusetts Bay Colony, *etc.* 1926. 8º. **9907**. ee. **44**.

—— *See* Hardon (Henry W.) Some of the Ancestors and the Children of Heman Merrick Burr. 1903. *s. sh.* fol. **1856**. d. **1**. (**140**.)

—— *See* Todd (Charles B.) A General History of the Burr Family in America, *etc.* [With portraits.] 1878. 8º. **9916**. a. **5**.

BURR (A.) The Last Will and Testament, an original poem, *etc.* pp. 27. *Printed for the Author: London*, [1818 ?] 8º. **992**. i. **23**. (**1**.)

BURR (Aaron) *President of the College of New Jersey.* *See* Livingston (William) *Governor of New Jersey.* A Funeral Elogium on the Reverend Mr. Aaron Burr, *etc.* 1758. 4º. **1360**. h. **4**.

BURR (Aaron) *President of the College of New Jersey.*

—— *See* Ross (Robert) *Grammarian.* The American Latin Grammar . . . revised and corrected . . . by the late Presidents Burr, Finley, *etc.* 1780. 8º. **12933**. aa. **34**.

—— A Discourse delivered at New-ark, in New Jersey. January 1, 1755. Being a day set apart for solemn fasting and prayer, on account of the late encroachments of the French, and their designs against the British colonies in America. pp. 41. *Hugh Gaine: New-York*, 1755. 4º. **4487**. g. **7**.

—— A Servant of God dismissed from Labour to Rest. A funeral sermon preached at the interment of Jonathan Belcher, *etc.* pp. iv. 23. *Edes & Gill: Boston*, 1758. 8º. **10881**. b. **21**.

—— The Supreme Deity of our Lord Jesus Christ, maintained. In a letter to the dedicator of Mr. Emlyn's Inquiry into the Scripture-account of Jesus Christ, *etc.* [By A. Burr.] pp. 92. 1757. 8º. *See* Emlyn (Thomas) **4224**. cc. **32**.

—— [Another edition.] pp. 61. *E. E. Powars: Boston*, 1791. 8º. **4224**. cc. **33**.

—— The Watchman's Answer to the Question, What of the night, &c. A sermon . . . Second edition. pp. 46. *S. Kneeland: Boston*, 1757. 8º. **4485**. a. **64**. (**2**.)

BURR (Aaron) *Vice-President of the United States of America.*

—— *See* Abernethy (Thomas P.) The Burr Conspiracy. [With a portrait.] 1954. 8º. **9617**. d. **12**.

—— *See* Alexander (Holmes) Aaron Burr, the Proud Pretender. [With portraits.] 1937. 8º. **010886**. f. **17**.

—— *See* Aristides, *pseud.* [i.e. W. P. Van Ness.] An Examination of the Various Charges exhibited against Aaron Burr, *etc.* 1804. 8º. **1104**. c. **18**. (**1**.)

—— *See* Carroll (Mary T.) The Man Who Would Not Wait. The story of Aaron Burr. 1941. 8º. **10888**. f. **23**.

—— *See* Cheetham (James) Nine Letters on the subject of Aaron Burr's Political Defection, *etc.* 1803. 8º. **1104**. c. **18**. (**3**.)

—— *See* Davis (Matthew L.) Memoirs of Aaron Burr. With miscellaneous selections from his correspondence. [With a portrait.] 1836. 8º. **1453**. d. **5**.

—— *See* Jenkinson (Isaac) Aaron Burr. His personal and political relations with Thomas Jefferson and Alexander Hamilton. 1902. 8º. **010883**. ee. **4**.

—— *See* Kerkhoff (Johnston D.) Aaron Burr. A romantic biography. [1931.] 8º. **10880**. w. **18**.

—— *See* Knapp (Samuel L.) The Life of Aaron Burr. 1835. 8º. **10880**. b. **21**.

—— *See* Lewis (Addison) The Gadfly. A portrait in action [of Aaron Burr]. [With a portrait.] [1948.] 8º. **10890**. f. **16**.

—— *See* Lewis (Alfred H.) An American Patrician; or, the Story of Aaron Burr, *etc.* [With portraits.] 1908. 8º. **010883**. f. **36**.

—— *See* MacCaleb (Walter F.) The Aaron Burr Conspiracy, *etc.* 1903. 8º. **09603**. c. **18**.

—— —— 1936. 8º. **9605**. ppp. **22**.

—— *See* Merwin (Henry C.) Aaron Burr. [1899.] 16º. **10883**. a. **37/12**.

— *See* ORTH (Samuel P.) Five American Politicians . . . Aaron Burr, *etc.* [With a portrait.] 1906. 8º. **10881. a. 38.**

— *See* PARTON (James) The Life and Times of Aaron Burr, *etc.* [With a portrait.] 1861. 8º. **10881. cc. 17.**

— *See* PHILANTHROPOS, *pseud.* A Letter to Aaron Burr . . . on the barbarous origin . . . of duels; occasioned by his late fatal interview with . . . General A. Hamilton. 1804. 8º. **1104. c. 21. (3.)**

— *See* SAFFORD (William H.) The Blennerhassett Papers, embodying . . . the hitherto unpublished correspondence of Burr . . . and others in developing the purposes and aims of those engaged in the attempted Wilkinson and Burr revolution, *etc.* 1864. 8º. **10882. dd. 10.**

— *See* SAFFORD (William H.) The Life of Harman Blennerhassett. Comprising an authentic narrative of the Burr expedition, *etc.* 1853. 8º. **10880. bb. 31.**

— *See* SALADO ÁLVAREZ (V.) La Conjura de Aaron Burr y las primeras tentativas de conquista de México por Americanos del oeste, *etc.* 1908. 8º. **9770. i. 17.**

— *See* SCHACHNER (N.) Aaron Burr, *etc.* [With portraits.] 1937. 8º. **10887. e. 15.**

— *See* TODD (Charles B.) The True Aaron Burr. A biographical sketch. [With a portrait.] 1902. 8º. **10880. aa. 46.**

— *See* TOMPKINS (Hamilton B.) Burr Bibliography, *etc.* 1892. 8º. **011900. ee. 10.**

— *See* WANDELL (Samuel H.) Aaron Burr in Literature . . . Books, pamphlets, periodicals, and miscellany relating to A. Burr . . . Illustrated by portraits, *etc.* 1936. 8º. **W.P. 8928/6.**

— *See* WANDELL (Samuel H.) and MINNIGERODE (M.) Aaron Burr. A biography, *etc.* [With portraits.] 1925. 8º. **010883. h. 44.**

— *See* WICKHAM (John) Speech of Mr. Wickham, on the Trial of Aaron Burr . . . for high treason. 1815. 8º. [CARPENTER (*S. C.*) *Select American Speeches.* vol. 2.] **1205. c. 6.**

— *See* WILKINSON (James) *General, U.S. Army.* Burr's Conspiracy exposed; and General Wilkinson vindicated, *etc.* 1811. 8º. **1447. e. 10.**

— *See* WIRT (William) Speech of Mr. Wirt, on the Trial of Aaron Burr . . . for high treason. In reply to Mr. Wickham. 1815. 8º. [CARPENTER (*S. C.*) *Select American Speeches.* vol. 2.] **1205. c. 6.**

— *See* WIRT (William) The Two Principal Arguments of William Wirt . . . on the trial of Aaron Burr, *etc.* 1808. 16º. **1247. a. 1.**

— *See* WOOD (John) *Classical Tutor at New York.* A Correct Statement of the various Sources from which the history of the administration of John Adams was compiled, and the motives for its suppression by Col. Burr, *etc.* 1802. 8º. **1104. c. 18. (5.)**

— — 1802. 8º. **1104. c. 21. (1.)**

— The Private Journal of Aaron Burr, during his residence of four years in Europe; with selections from his correspondence. Edited by Matthew L. Davis. 2 vol. *Harper & Bros.: New York,* 1838. 8º. **1453. d. 6.**

— The Private Journal of Aaron Burr. Reprinted in full from the original manuscript in the library of Mr. William K. Bixby . . . with an introduction, explanatory notes, *etc.* [With plates, including a portrait.] 2 vol. *Printed for private distribution: Rochester, N.Y.,* 1903. 8º. **010881. g. 19.**

— Correspondence of Aaron Burr and his daughter Theodosia. Edited with a preface by Mark Van Doren. [With a portrait.] pp. ix. 349. *Covici-Friede: New York,* 1929. 8º. **010920. dd. 15.**

— The Conspiracy of Col. Aaron Burr, a historical romance. pp. 311. *G. W. Simmons: New York,* 1854. 12º. **12704. b. 5.**

— A Narrative of the Suppression by Col. Burr, of the History of the Administration of John Adams . . . written by John Wood . . . By a Citizen of New-York [i.e. James Cheetham]. pp. 72. *Denniston & Cheetham: New-York,* 1802. 8º. **1104. c. 21. (5.)**

— [Another copy.] **1104. c. 18. (4.)**

— [Another copy.] **523. e. 2. (4.)**

— Particulars of the late Duel, fought at Hoboken, July 11, between Aaron Burr and Alexander Hamilton . . . containing all the papers relating to that event. Together with the will of Gen. Hamilton, and the letters of Bishop Moore and the Rev. I. M. Mason. pp. 32. *A. Forman: New York,* 1804. 8º. **10880. bb. 35. (3.)**

— Reports of the Trials of Colonel Aaron Burr . . . for treason, and for a misdemeanor, in preparing the means of a military expedition against Mexico . . . To which is added, an appendix, containing the arguments and evidence in support . . . of the motion afterwards made by the counsel for the United States, to commit A. Burr, H. Blennerhassett and I. Smith, to be sent for trial to the State of Kentucky, for treason or misdemeanor . . . Taken in short hand by David Robertson, *etc.* 2 vol. *Hopkins & Earle: Philadelphia,* 1808. 8º. **6615. b. 6.**

— The Trial of Aaron Burr for High Treason . . . 1807 . . . Compiled from authentic reports . . . To which is added an account of the subsequent proceedings against Burr, Blennerhassett, and Smith . . . Prefaced by a brief historical sketch of Burr's western expedition in 1806. By J. J. Coombs. pp. lii. 392. *W. H. & O. H. Morrison: Washington,* [1864.] 8º. **6617.bb.10.**

— The Trial of Col. Aaron Burr, on an indictment for treason, before the Circuit Court of the United States . . . May Term, 1807; including the arguments and decisions on all the motions made during the examination and trial, and on the motion for an attachment against Gen. Wilkinson. Taken in short-hand by T. Carpenter. 3 vol. *Westcott & Co.: Washington City,* 1807. 8º. **1246. b. 16.**

— A View of the Political Conduct of Aaron Burr . . . By the author of the "Narrative" [i.e. James Cheetham]. pp. 120. *Denniston & Cheetham: New York,* 1802. 8º. **1104. c. 21. (2.)**

— [Another copy.] **1104. c. 18. (2.)**

— [Another copy.] **523. e. 2. (7.)**

BURR (AGNES RUSH) Alaska . . . With a map and fifty-four plates, *etc.* (Second impression.) pp. xii. 428. *Page Co.: Boston,* 1920. 8º. [" *See America First*" *Series.*] **10409. t. 1/14.**

BURR (ALLSTON) Sir Walter Scott. An index, placing the short poems in his novels and in his long poems and dramas. Arranged by A. Burr. pp. vi. 130. *Harvard University Press: Cambridge, Mass.*, 1936. 8°. **11858**. aa. **39**.

BURR (AMELIA JOSEPHINE) A Dealer in Empire. A romance, *etc.* pp. 297. *Harper & Bros.: New York & London*, 1915. 8°. NN. **2619**.

—— The Three Fires. A story of Ceylon. pp. 288. *Hurst & Blackett: London*, [1923.] 8°. NN. **8930**.

BURR (ANNA ROBESON) *See* JAMES (Alice) *Sister of Henry James*. Alice James: her brothers—her journal. Edited, with an introduction, by A. R. Burr. 1934. 8°. **010885**. ee. **29**.

—— The Autobiography. A critical and comparative study. [With a bibliography.] pp. viii. 451. *Houghton Mifflin Co.: Boston & New York*, 1909. 8°. **11840**. ppp. **9**.

—— Palludia. pp. 288. *Andrew Melrose: London*, [1929.] 8°. NN. **15480**.

—— Religious Confessions and Confessants. With a chapter on the history of introspection. pp. viii. 562. *Houghton Mifflin Co.: Boston & New York*, 1914. 8°. **04376**. h. **5**.

—— St. Helios. pp. 353. *Brentano's: London*, [1926.] 8°. NN. **12476**.

—— Weir Mitchell. His life and letters. (Second edition.) [With plates, including portraits.] pp. xii. 424. *Duffield & Co.: New York*, 1930. 8°. **10880**. r. **3**.

—— West of the Moon, *etc.* pp. 287. *Andrew Melrose: London*, [1927.] 8°. NN. **13060**.

—— The Wrong Move. A romance. pp. 351. *Brentano's: London*, 1924. 8°. **12708**. aa. **22**.

BURR (BETTY) "The Better Way." [Verses.] pp. 44. *Whitcombe & Tombs: Christchurch* [*N.Z.*], [1918.] 16°. **011652**. h. **129**.

—— "The Infinite Light." [Verses.] pp. 45. *Whitcombe & Tombs:* [*Christchurch, N.Z.*, 1918.] 16°. **011652**. h. **131**.

BURR (CARLOS)

—— Cooperativas de vivienda. ff. 15. *Bogotá*, 1953. 8°. [*Centro Interamericano de Vivienda. Serie: Resúmenes de clase.* no. 2.] U.N. P. **90**. **(8.)**

BURR (CHARLES BARTON) The Appeal of Lieut. Colonel Charles Barton Burr . . . to . . . the Marquis of Hastings . . . against the conduct of Brigadier General Lionel Smith . . . with the autograph reply and decision of his Excellency thereon . . . With the subsequent correspondence with the Bombay government, *etc.* pp. xi. 106. *J. Hatchard & Son: London*, 1819. 4°. **583**. i. **23**.

BURR (CHARLES CHAUNCEY) *See* LIPPARD (George) Washington and his Generals . . . With a biographical sketch of the author, by the Rev. C. C. Burr. 1847. 8°. **12703**. g. **32**.

—— *See* PERIODICAL PUBLICATIONS.—*Philadelphia*. The Nineteenth Century. [Edited by C. C. Burr.] 1848. 8°. P.P. **6388**.

—— A Discourse on Revivals, *etc.* pp. 14. *S. H. Colesworthy: Portland* [*Me.*], 1840. 8°. **4485**. dd. **2**.

BURR (CHARLES CHAUNCEY)

—— The History of the Union, and of the Constitution. Being the substance of three lectures on . . . American history, with an appendix containing the Constitution of the United States, and the Virginia and Kentucky Resolutions of '98. Third edition. pp. 92. 4. *Van Evrie, Horton & Co.: New York*, 1863. 8°. **8177**. aa. **12**.

—— Lectures of Lola Montez, Countess of Landsfeld, including her autobiography. [By C. C. Burr.] pp. 192. 1858. 8°. *See* MONTEZ (Lola) *Countess von Landsfeld*. **10825**. a. **44**.

—— [Another edition.] Autobiography and Lectures of Lola Montez, *etc.* pp. 192. [1858.] 8°. *See* MONTEZ (Lola) *Countess von Landsfeld*. **10825**. a. **42**.

—— Notes on the Constitution of the United States, with expositions of the most eminent statesmen and jurists, *etc.* pp. 95. viii. *J. F. Feeks: New York*, [1864.] 8°. **8177**. a. **24**.

—— Substance of an Extemporaneous Oration, on Irish Repeal, *etc.* pp. 28. *Munsell & Tanner: Albany*, 1844. 8°. **8145**. dd. **6**.

BURR (CHARLES WALTS) Some Medical Words in Johnson's Dictionary. (Reprinted from "Annals of Medical History.") *P. B. Hoeber: New York*, [1927.] fol. **12984**. v. **3**.

BURR (CHAUNCEY REA) Bures of Suffolk, England, and Burr of Massachusetts Bay Colony, New England. [Edited by Henry W. Hardon. With portraits and genealogical tables.] pp. x. 120. *Privately printed: New York*, 1926. 8°. **9907**. ee. **44**.
No. 86 *of an edition of* 100 *copies.*

BURR (COLONEL BELL) A Primer of Psychology and Mental Disease . . . Second edition, thoroughly revised. pp. ix. 116. *F. A. Davis Co.: Philadelphia*, 1898. 8°. **07660**. ee. **17**.

—— Third edition, thoroughly revised. pp. viii. 183. *F. A. Davis Co.: Philadelphia*, 1906. 8°. **07660**. ee. **18**.

BURR (DANIEL) *See* HIGFORD (William) Institutions, *etc.* [With a preface by D. Burr.] 1818. 8°. **8405**. dd. **14**.

BURR (DAVID H.) An Atlas of the State of New York . . . Projected and drawn up from documents deposited in the public offices of the State . . . under the superintendence and direction of Simeon De Witt . . . And also the physical geography of the State . . . & statistical tables of the same. pp. 29. pl. 52. *D. H. Burr: New York*, 1829. fol. Maps **2**. d. **16**.
The titlepage is engraved.

—— [Another edition.] (Republished with corrections and improvements.) pp. 40. pl. 52. *Stone & Clark: Ithaca*, 1841. fol. Maps **32**. e. **19**.
The titlepage is engraved.

BURR (DOROTHY) Terra-cottas from Myrina in the Museum of Fine Arts, Boston. A dissertation, *etc.* pp. v. 86. pl. XLII. *Vienna*, 1934. 4°. **7876**. h. **27**.

BURR (EBENEZER) The Creation, and other original poems, sacred and secular. pp. 120. *Printed for the Author: London*, 1870. 8°. **11650**. e. **28**.

BURR (EDWARD) *of Dunstable.*

—— *See* GAITSKELL (W. S.) Dunstable Brewery. Correspondence between Mr. E. Burr . . . and W. S. Gaitskell, *etc.* 1845. 8°. **1414**. f. **39**.

BURR (EDWARD) *of Dunstable.*

—— *See* GAITSKELL (W. S.) Statement of Mr. Gaitskell respecting his bill of costs against Mr. E. Burr. 1846. 8°. **6191**. b. **6**.

BURR (EDWARD) *of the U.S. Army.*

—— Historical Sketch of the Corps of Engineers, U.S. Army. pp. iv. 53. *Washington*, 1939. 8°. [*Engineer School, U.S. Army. Occasional Papers.* no. 71.] A.S. **629/9**.

BURR (EDWARD EVERETT)

—— Show-Card Making Simplified. By E. E. Burr . . . Assisted by Margaret Burr. Edited by William Koelling . . . Illustrated. pp. 35. *American Technical Society: Chicago*, 1951. 4°. **8218**. h. **6**.
A slip bearing the imprint "Technical Press: London" has been pasted below the original imprint.

BURR (EMILY) Psychological Tests applied to Factory Workers. pp. 93. *New York*, 1922. 8°. [*Archives of Psychology.* no. 55.] P.P. **1247**. gb.

BURR (ENOCH FITCH) About Spiritualism. By the author of "Ecce Cœlum" [i.e. E. F. Burr]. pp. 44. [1872.] 16°. *See* SPIRITUALISM. **8631**. a. **31**.

—— Ad Fidem; or, Parish evidences of the Bible . . . Second edition. pp. vii. 353. *Noyes, Holmes & Co.: Boston*, 1871. 8°. **4017**. aaa. **15**.

—— Aleph, the Chaldean; or, the Messiah as seen from Alexandria. [A novel.] pp. 413. *W. S. Ketcham: New York*, [1891.] 8°. **012705**. g. **67**.

—— [A reissue.] *Oliphant, Anderson & Ferrier: Edinburgh & London*, 1896. 8°. **012705**. i. **64**.

—— Celestial Empires. pp. 302. *American Tract Society: New York*, [1885.] 8°. **8563**. aa. **5**.

—— Ecce Cœlum; or, Parish astronomy. In six lectures. By a Connecticut Pastor [i.e. E. F. Burr]. Eleventh edition. pp. 4. 198. *Noyes, Holmes & Co.: Boston*, 1870. 8°. **8560**. bbb. **20**.

—— Ecce Terra; or, the Hand of God in the earth. pp. 320. *Presbyterian Board of Publication: Philadelphia*, [1883.] 8°. **4372**. c. **18**.

—— Pater Mundi; or, Modern science testifying to the heavenly Father. Being in substance lectures delivered to senior classes in Amherst College . . . First series. Second edition. pp. 294. *Nichols & Noyes: Boston*, 1870. 8°. **4379**. cc. **10**.

—— Supreme Things, in their practical relations. pp. 430. *American Tract Society: New York*, [1889.] 8°. **4374**. l. **18**.

—— Tempted to Unbelief. pp. 224. *American Tract Society: New York*, [1882.] 8°. **4018**. g. **16**.

—— Toward the Strait Gate; or, Parish Christianity for the unconverted. pp. vi. 535. *Lockwood, Brooks & Co.: Boston*, 1875. 8°. **4401**. dd. **12**.

—— Universal Beliefs; or, the Great consensus. pp. 312. *American Tract Society: New York*, 1887. 8°. **4372**. e. **21**.

BURR (F. BONHAM) The Strummings of a Lyre. pp. 64. *A. C. Fifield: London*, 1912. 8°. **011650**. eee. **73**.

BURR (FEARING) The Field and Garden Vegetables of America . . . with directions for propagation, culture and use . . . Illustrated. pp. xv. 674. *Crosby & Nichols: Boston*, 1863. 8°. **7076**. bb. **5**.

—— [Another edition.] pp. xv. 667. *J. E. Tilton & Co.: Boston*, 1865. 8°. **7076**. aaa. **12**.

BURR (FREDERIC MARTIN) Life and Works of Alexander Anderson, M.D., the first American wood-engraver, *etc.* [With illustrations, including portraits.] pp. x. 210. *Burr Bros.: New York*, 1893. 8°. **10880**. dd. **24**.

BURR (FREDERICK) Introduction to the Study of Geology . . . Intended to accompany the geological map of England and Wales, and the southern part of Scotland, published by J. and C. Walker. pp. iv. 71. *Whittaker & Co.: London*, 1836. 8°. **7202**. aaa. **5**.

—— The Elements of Practical Geology, as applicable to mining, engineering, architecture, &c.; with notices of the mines and mineral productions of Great Britain . . . Being a second edition, greatly improved and enlarged, of the "Introduction to the Study of Geology." pp. v. 288. pl. 6. *Whittaker & Co.: London*, 1838. 8°. **725**. b. **42**.

—— Notes of an Overland Journey to India, through France and Egypt, *etc.* pp. 97. *For private circulation: Madras*, 1841. 8°. **10028**. ee. **12**.

—— Outline of a Course of Six Lectures, embracing the elementary principles of physical geography, mineralogy and geology, *etc.* pp. 16. *A. Macintosh: London*, 1835. 8°. **7107**. b. **53**. **(1.)**

BURR (G. GORDON) *See* MUNRO (Alexander M.) Old Landmarks of Aberdeen . . . Sketches . . . by G. G. Burr, *etc.* 1885. 4°. Maps **17**. c. **24**.

BURR (GEORGE DOMINICUS) Instructions in Practical Surveying, topographical plan drawing, and sketching ground without instruments . . . Second edition. pp. xiv. 223. pl. v. *John Murray: London*, 1847. 12°. **1397**. g. **8**.

—— Third edition, *etc.* pp. xiv. 223. pl. v. *John Murray: London*, 1858. 8°. **1397**. g. **11**.

—— A Short Essay on Sketching Ground without instruments . . . Intended as a supplement to the treatise on Practical Surveying and Topographical Plan-drawing. pp. 23. *John Murray: London*, 1830. 8°. **T. 1313. (12.)**

BURR (GEORGE LINCOLN)

—— *See* BAINTON (Roland H.) George Lincoln Burr. His life, *etc.* [With a portrait.] 1943. 8°. **10881**. eee. **29**.

—— *See* LEA (Henry C.) Materials toward a History of Witchcraft . . . With an introduction by G. L. Burr. 1939. 8°. **8634**. dd. **18**.

—— The Carlovingian Revolution, and Frankish Intervention in Italy. 1913, *etc. See* BURY (John B.) The Cambridge Medieval History, *etc.* vol. 2. 1911, *etc.* 8°. [Latest edition.] **2070**. **f**. [Earlier editions.] **09004**. g.

—— The Century Historical Series. G. L. Burr (William E. Lingelbach) . . . general editor. *Century Co.: New York*, 1914– . 8°. W.P. **2486**.

BURR (George Lincoln)

—— The Fate of Dietrich Flade. 1891. *See* United States of America.—*American Historical Association.* Papers, *etc.* vol. 5. 1885, *etc.* 8°. Ac. **8504**.

—— Narratives of the Witchcraft Cases, 1648–1706. Edited by G. L. Burr . . . With three facsimiles. pp. xviii. 467. *C. Scribner's Sons: New York,* 1914. 8°. [*Original Narratives of Early American History.*] **9551**. p. **15**.

—— The Witch-Persecutions. Edited by G. L. Burr. pp. 36. *Philadelphia,* 1897. 8°. [*Translations and Reprints from the Original Sources of European History.* vol. 3. no. 4.] Ac. **2692**. p/5.

—— Selected Writings. (Edited by L. O. Gibbons.) *See* Bainton (Roland H.) George Lincoln Burr, *etc.* 1943. 8°. **10881**. eee. **29**.

—— Persecution and Liberty. Essays in honor of George Lincoln Burr. [With plates, including a portrait.] pp. xviii. 482. *Century Co.: New York,* [1931.] 8°. **2350**. g. **17**.

BURR (George Oswald) *See* Evans (Herbert M.) and Burr (G. O.) The Antisterility of Vitamine Fat Soluble E, *etc.* 1927. 4°. [*Memoirs of the University of California.* no. 8.] Ac. **2689**. h.

—— *See* Harris (James A.) J. Arthur Harris, botanist and biometrician. Edited by C. O. Rosendahl . . . G. O. Burr. [1936.] 8°. **010886**. eee. **45**.

BURR (Gilbert Basil)

—— British Government Securities: Taxation of Interest, *etc.* pp. 7. *Jordan & Sons: London,* 1943. 4°. **8234**. d. **67**.

—— British Government Securities: Taxation of Interest. (Second edition.) pp. 11. *Jordan & Sons: London,* 1945. 8°. **8234**. eee. **63**.

—— E.P.T. Acts Collated and fully Indexed. With case law and practice annotation . . . Including provisions of the Finance Act, 1943. pp. xvi. 167. *Jordan & Sons: London,* 1943. 8°. **6429**. bb. **3**.

—— Income Tax for H.M. Forces, *etc.* (Second edition.) pp. 56. *Taxation Publishing Co.: London,* [1942.] 8°. **6429**. b. **16**.

—— Income Tax for H.M. Forces . . . Third edition. pp. 48. *Fiscal Press: London,* [1943.] 8°. **8231**. f. **51**.

—— Income Tax for H.M. Forces and demobilised personnel . . . 1944–45 edition. pp. 52. *Jordan & Sons: London,* 1945. 8°. **8231**. f. **77**.

—— Sur-Tax and Undistributed Income. Assessment and avoidance. pp. xii. 237. *Taxation Publishing Co.; Gee & Co.: London,* [1939.] 8°. **6428**. r. **21**.

—— "Taxation" Practitioners' Guide. By G. B. Burr . . . in collaboration with Ronald Staples. ff. 55. 1934. 4°. *See* Periodical Publications.—London.—*Taxation.* **6427**. i. **10**.

BURR (Gilbert Basil) and **HOWARD** (Charles Gordon)

—— Income Tax Act 1945, Indexed. With official Explanatory Memorandum, and interpretation index. pp. xxx. iii. 70. *Jordan & Sons: London,* 1946. 8°. **6429**. c. **26**.

BURR (Gilbert Basil) and **STAPLES** (Ronald)

—— Burr & Staples on the Land Tax. Law and practice. pp. xii. 55. *Gee & Co.: London,* 1935. 8°. **6425**. ppp. **30**.

BURR (Grace Hardendorff)

—— Hispanic Furniture, with examples in the collection of the Hispanic Society of America . . . With 175 illustrations. pp. xvi. 240. *New York,* 1941. 8°. [*Hispanic Notes and Monographs. Catalogue series.*] Ac. **9729/10**. (**77**.)

BURR (Graham) Night's Pilgrimage; or, the End of papist tyranny. [A poem.] pp. 79. *Unwin Bros.: London,* [1910.] 8°. **011650**. ccc. **27**.

—— Thoughts in Solitude. The Story of the Bramble, and other poems. pp. viii. 79. *Elliot Stock: London,* 1909. 8°. **11647**. eee. **40**.

BURR (Hans) Das württembergische Infanterie-Regiment Nr. 475 im Weltkrieg . . . Mit 67 Abbildungen, 1 Übersichtskarte und 11 Skizzen. pp. 84. *Stuttgart,* 1921. 8°. [*Die württembergischen Regimenter im Weltkrieg.* Bd. 13.] **9085**. aa. **1/13**.

BURR (Hilda V.) Field Hockey for Coaches and Players. pp. xiv. 194. *A. S. Barnes & Co.: New York,* 1930. 8°. [*Athletics for Women.*] W.P. **8303/4**.

BURR (Irving Wingate)

—— Engineering Statistics and Quality Control. pp. xi. 442. *McGraw-Hill Book Co.: New York,* 1953. 8°. **8774**. bb. **23**.

BURR (James Burgett)

—— Student Teaching in the Elementary School. By J. B. Burr, Lowry W. Harding, Leland B. Jacobs. pp. ix. 440. *Appleton-Century-Crofts: New York,* [1950.] 8°. **08385**. e. **133**.

BURR (James E.) *See* Thompson (George) *of Oberlin.* Prison Life and Reflections, or, a Narrative of the arrest, trial, conviction, imprisonment . . . of Work, Burr, *etc.* 1855. 8°. **8157**. bbb. **35**.

BURR (James Henry Scudamore) A Petition, presented to both Houses of Parliament, during the session of 1842. Also, a protest against the principles of the Tithe Commutation Act, delivered to Charles Pym . . . together with a schedule, showing its probable results. pp. 18. *Clarke & Son: Chepstow,* 1842. 8°. **4109**. h. **6**. (**13**.)

BURR (Jane) The Glorious Hope. pp. 318. *Duckworth & Co.: London,* 1921. 8°. NN. **7059**.

—— Kittens' Tale. pp. 252. *Cecil Palmer: London,* 1924. 8°. NN. **10169**.

—— The Passionate Spectator. pp. 241. *Duckworth & Co.: London,* 1920. 8°. NN. **6554**.

—— That Woman. pp. 317. *Duckworth & Co.: London,* 1922. 8°. NN. **8263**.

BURR (John) The Crown of Character. A study of the Beatitudes of Our Lord. pp. 126. *J. Clarke & Co.: London,* [1932.] 8°. **4227**. d. **21**.

—— The Forgiveness of Sins. pp. 32. *Edinburgh,* 1938. 8°. [*Church of Scotland Booklets.* no. 117.] **4431.bb.26/17.**

BURR (JOHN)

—— God's Arms and the Man. pp. 189. *Allenson & Co.: London*, 1938. 8°. **04400. g. 26.**

—— The Lordship of Love. Studies in First Corinthians, Chapter XIII. pp. 271. *J. Clarke & Co.: London*, [1932.] 8°. **03265. g. 37.**

—— The Prayer of Prayers. [On the Lord's Prayer.] pp. 128. *Allenson & Co.: London*, [1937.] 8°. **03456. f. 76.**

—— The Prodigal's Progress and the Professor's Practice. An analysis of the parable of the Prodigal Son and the Elder Brother. pp. 157. *J. Clarke & Co.: London*, [1933.] 8°. **3226. aa. 38.**

—— Studies on the Apostles' Creed, *etc.* pp. 255. *J. Clarke & Co.: London*, [1931.] 8°. **03504. ff. 70.**

—— Studies on the Ten Commandments. pp. viii. 154. *Allenson & Co.: London*, 1935. 8°. **03166. g. 74.**

BURR (JONATHAN) A Compendium of English Grammar, *etc.* pp. 72. *Samuel Hall: Boston*, 1797. 12°. **12983. a. 23.**

—— God's Presence removes the Fear of Death. A sermon, preached . . . at the interment of the Rev. Oakes Shaw, *etc.* pp. 28. *Manning & Loring: Boston*, 1807. 8°. **4985. b. 34. (10.)**

BURR (L. G.) My Silent Voice. Information for my wife, my heirs or my executors in the event of my death or disability. [Blank forms.] pp. 42. *B. F. Stevens & Brown: London; printed in U.S.A.*, 1911. *obl.* 16°. **6355. a. 59.**

BURR (MALCOLM)

—— *See* ARSEN'EV (V. K.) Dersu the Trapper. [An abridged translation of По Уссурійскому краю and Дерсу Узала]. (Translated by M. Burr.) 1939. 8°. **010058. n. 4.**

—— *See* KRUIMOV (V. L.) Fienka. Translated . . . by M. Burr. 1949. 8°. **12594. b. 20.**

—— *See* KRUIMOV (V. L.) [За миллионами. том. 1. Сидорово ученье.] Out for a Million. Translated . . . by M. Burr. 1935. 8°. **12591. r. 39.**

—— *See* KRUIMOV (V. L.) [За миллионами. том. 2. Хорошо жили в Петербурге.] He's Got a Million . . . Translated . . . by M. Burr. 1936. 8°. **12593.k.1.**

—— *See* KRUIMOV (V. L.) [За миллионами. том. 3. Дьяволенок под столом.] End of the Imp . . . Translated . . . by M. Burr. 1937. 8°. **012590. dd. 74.**

—— *See* NAZAROV (P. S.) Hunted through Central Asia . . . Rendered into English . . . by M. Burr, *etc.* 1932. 8°. **010055. aa. 50.**

—— *See* NAZAROV (P. S.) Moved On! . . . Rendered into English . . . by M. Burr, *etc.* 1935. 8°. **010055. bbb. 36.**

—— *See* SMIRNOVA (N. V.) Marfa. A Siberian novel translated . . . by M. Burr. 1932. 8°. **012591. k. 54.**

—— *See* ZİYAOĞLU (R.) Tourist's Guide to Istanbul . . Rendered into English by M. Burr, *etc.* 1953. 8°. **010077. f. 68.**

BURR (MALCOLM)

—— British Grasshoppers and their Allies. A stimulus to their study, *etc.* pp. xvi. 162. pl. VI. *P. Allan & Co.: London*, 1936. 8°. **7298. aa. 56.**

—— British Orthoptera. Earwigs, grasshoppers and crickets, *etc.* pp. iv. 68. pl. v. *Economic & Educational Museum: Huddersfield*, 1897. 8°. **2252. d. 3.**

—— Dermaptera—Earwigs. pp. xviii. 217. pl. x. *Taylor & Francis: London*, 1910. 8°. [*Fauna of British India.*] **2250. c. 8.**

—— A Fossicker in Angola, *etc.* [With plates.] pp. 199. *Figurehead: London*, [1933.] 8°. [*Pioneer Series.*] **10026.t.25/5.**

—— In Bolshevik Siberia. The land of ice and exile, *etc.* [With plates and a map.] pp. 224. *H. F. & G. Witherby: London*, 1931. 8°. **010055. bbb. 2.**

—— The Insect Legion. [With plates.] pp. xiv. 321. *J. Nisbet & Co.: London*, 1939. 8°. **07299. ee. 70.**

—— The Insect Legion. (Second edition.) pp. xvi. 336. *James Nisbet & Co.: London*, 1954. 8°. **07299. bb. 24.**

—— The Plague of Locusts. pp. 52. *Oxford University Press: London*, 1940. 8°. [*Simple Science in Simple English.*] W.P. **4838/5.**

—— Madhara ya nzige . . . The Plague of Locusts. *Swahili.* pp. 39. *Oxford University Press; Sheldon Press: London*, 1942. 8°. **12912. ee. 8.**

—— Quest and Conquest. [Accounts of discoveries and inventions. With illustrations.] pp. xi. 180. *Oxford University Press: London*, 1937. 8°. **20031. e. 10.**

—— Quest and Conquest. (Second edition.) pp. x. 137. *Oxford University Press: Bombay*, 1952. 8°. **010028. p. 15.**

—— Slouch Hat, *etc.* [Reminiscences of travel in the Balkans. With plates and maps.] pp. 365. *G. Allen & Unwin: London*, 1935. 8°. **10127. eee. 24.**

—— The Story of Gold. pp. 70. *Oxford University Press: London*, 1940. 8°. [*The Empire at Work.*] **08229.m.60/3.**

—— A Synopsis of the Orthoptera of Western Europe. pp. 160. *Oliver Janson: London*, 1910. 8°. **7299. c. 16.**

BURR (MARGARET)

—— *See* BURR (Edward E.) Show-Card Making Simplified. By E. E. Burr . . . Assisted by M. Burr, *etc.* 1951. 4°. **8218. h. 6.**

BURR (MARVIN YARD) A Study of Homogeneous Grouping, in terms of individual variations and the teaching problem, *etc.* [A thesis.] pp. ix. 69. *Teachers College, Columbia University: New York*, 1931. 8°. **08385. e. 17.**

BURR (MARY) The First Aid Card for Hæmorrhage and Burns. [1894.] *s. sh.* 8°. **1830. c. 1. (112.)**

—— [Another copy.] **1830. c. 1. (112.)**

—— What to do for Burns and Scalds. [1894.] *s. sh.* 8°. **1830. c. 1. (112.)**

BURR (May Sybil) *See* Gregory (Joshua C.) and Burr (M. S.) Beryllium and its Congeners, *etc.* 1926. 8°. [*Friend* (*J. A. N.*) *Text-Book of Inorganic Chemistry.* vol. 3. pt. 2.] W.P. **2754.**

—— The Alkaline Earth Metals, *etc.* pp. xxvi. 346. *C. Griffin & Co.: London,* 1925. 8°. [*Friend* (*J. A. N.*) *Text-Book of Inorganic Chemistry.* vol. 3. pt. 1.] W.P. **2754.**

BURR (Nelson Rollin)

—— *See* United States of America.—*Congress.—Library. —General Reference and Bibliography Division.* Biographical Sources for Foreign Countries. (II. Germany and Austria. IV. The Japanese Empire. Compiled by N. R. Burr.) 1946, *etc.* 4°. **2761.b.1.**

—— Education in New Jersey, 1630–1871. [With a bibliography.] pp. 355. *Princeton University Press: Princeton,* 1942. 8°. [*Princeton History of New Jersey.*] Ac. **1833.** e/**2.** (**4.**)

—— Safeguarding our Cultural Heritage. A bibliography on the protection of museums, works of art, monuments, archives and libraries in time of war. Compiled by N. R. Burr. pp. x. 117. 1952. 4°. *See* United States of America.—*Congress.—Library.—General Reference and Bibliography Division.* **11924.** f. **32.**

BURR (Pamela)

—— My Turkish Adventure. [Reminiscences.] pp. 219. *W. W. Norton & Co.: New York,* [1951.] 8°. **10888.** f. **29.**

BURR (Reginald Crabb)

—— Do You Believe? or, Aids to faith. pp. 29. *C. J. Thynne: London,* [1908.] 8°. [*Church of England Manuals.* no. 3.] **4107.** ff. **59**/**3.**

—— The Lord's Day, "the Rest Day of the Heart." pp. 36. *C. J. Thynne: London,* [1910?] 8°. [*Church of England Manuals.* no. 18.] **4107.** ff. **59**/**18.**

—— Socialism, or Social Reform? . . . Second edition, *etc.* pp. 36. *C. J. Thynne: London,* [1910?] 8°. [*Church of England Penny Manuals.* no. 10.] **4107.** ff. **59**/**10.**

—— The Song of the Shepherd King [i.e. Psalm 23]. pp. xv. 88. *C. J. Thynne: London,* 1911. 8°. **3089.** bbb. **5.**

BURR (Robert) Story of Robert Burr, the carpenter-minister, of . . . Horsmonden. [Signed: W. A. B. With a portrait.] [1919.] 8°. *See* B., W. A. **4920.** aaa. **57.**

BURR (S. De Vere) Bicycle Repairing. A manual compiled from articles in The Iron Age . . . Fourth edition, revised and enlarged. pp. 208. *D. Williams Co.: New York,* 1898. 8°. **8768.** e. **33.**

—— Tunneling under the Hudson River, *etc.* [With plates.] pp. 70. *J. Wiley & Sons: New York,* 1885. 8°. **8766.** g. **14.**

BURR (S. J.) The Vocal Parts of the Grand Fairy Opera of "The Peri," or, the Enchanted fountain. The subject taken from a story in Washington Irving's History of Columbus, *etc.* pp. 15. *Weed, Parsons & Co.: Albany,* 1850. 12°. **11781.** aaa. **28.**

BURR (Sidney) and **TURNER** (Dorothy Mabel) British Economic Grasses: their identification by the leaf anatomy. pp. 94. *E. Arnold & Co.: London,* 1933. 4°. **7078.** k. **25.**

BURR (Sybil Edith)

—— Lantern of the North . . . Illustrated by Sheila Rose. [A novel.] pp. xi. 259. *Routledge & Kegan Paul: [London,]* 1954. 8°. **12837.** e. **11.**

—— My Candle the Moon. Illustrated by Sheila Rose. pp. viii. 259. *Routledge & Kegan Paul: [London,]* 1955. 8°. NNN. **7298.**

BURR, afterwards **ALSTON** (Theodosia) *See* Minnigerode (M.) Lives and Times . . . Theodosia Burr, prodigy, *etc.* [With portraits.] 1925. 8°. **010880.** i. **45.**

—— [Letters to A. Burr.] *See* Burr (Aaron) *Vice-President of the United States of America.* Correspondence of Aaron Burr and his daughter Theodosia, *etc.* 1929. 8°. **010920.** dd. **15.**

BURR (Thomas) *Deputy Surveyor-General of the Northern Province of South Australia.* Remarks on the Geology and Mineralogy of South Australia. pp. 32. *Andrew Murray: Adelaide,* 1846. 12°. **1255.** a. **12.**

BURR (Thomas) *Quaker.* *See* Hookes (Ellis) Due Order of Law and Justice pleaded against Irregular & Arbitrary Proceedings: in the case and late imprisonment of G. Whitehead and T. Burr, *etc.* 1680. 4°. **518.** g. **12.** (**2.**)

BURR (Thomas Benge) The History of Tunbridge-Wells. pp. xii. 317. *M. Hingeston: London,* 1766. 8°. **578.** f. **28.**

—— [Another copy.] **290.** a. **12.**

—— [Another copy.] G. **3927.**

BURR (Victor)

—— *Νεων καταλογος.* Untersuchungen zum homerischen Schiffskatalog, *etc.* [With plates and maps.] pp. vi. 158. *Leipzig,* 1944. 8°. [*Klio. Beihefte.* no. 49.] P.P. **3548.** ha.

—— Nostrum Mare. Ursprung und Geschichte der Namen des Mittelmeeres und seiner Teilmeere im Altertum. [With plates.] pp. x. 141. *Stuttgart,* 1932. 8°. [*Würzburger Studien zur Altertumswissenschaft.* Hft. 4.] W.P. **7430**/**4.**

BURR (Viktor)

—— Tiberius Iulius Alexander . . . Mit 1 Tafel. pp. 112. *Bonn,* 1955. 8°. [*Antiquitas.* Reihe 1. Bd. 1] **9436.a.1a/1.**

BURR (Walter) Rural Organization. pp. xi. 250. *Macmillan Co.: New York,* 1921. 8°. **08282.** cc. **16.**

—— Small Towns. An estimate of their trade and culture. pp. x. 267. *Macmillan Co.: New York,* 1929. 8°. **8277.** pp. **20.**

BURR (William)

—— *See* Hobbs (Henry) Hymns for Christian Melody, *etc.* [The preface signed: Henry Hobbs, Samuel Beede, William Burr.] 1841. 32°. **03440.** de. **13.**

BURR (William Henry) *See* Tilton (Theodore) The American Board and American Slavery. Speech of T. Tilton . . . Reported by W. H. Burr. [1860.] 12°. **8156.** a. **61.**

—— *See* United States of America.—*Woman's Rights Convention, etc.* Proceedings of the Woman's Rights Convention . . . 1850. (Proceedings of the Seventh National Woman's Rights Convention . . . 1856. Reported by W. H. Burr.) 1851, *etc.* 8°. **8415.** g. **49.** (**2.**)

BURR (WILLIAM HENRY)

—— Abstract of Colenso on the Pentateuch . . . to which is appended an essay on the nation and country of the Jews. [By W. H. Burr.] pp. 48. 1871. 8°. *See* COLENSO (John W.) *Bishop of Natal.* **03166**. de. **40**.

—— The Bacon-Shakspere Identities Revealed by their Handwritings. (Proof that Shakspere could not write. By W. H. Burr.—An Analysis of Sir Francis Bacon's Personality based on various specimens of his handwriting. By Herry O. Teltscher.) By Johan Franco [i.e. edited by him. With plates.] *Russell F. Moore: New York,* [1947.] 8°. **11767**. g. **33**.

—— Bacon and Shakspere. Proof that William Shakspere . . . could not write. The Sonnets written by Francis Bacon to the Earl of Essex and his bride, A.D. 1590. Bacon identified as the concealed Poet Ignoto. A.D. 1589–1600. pp. 52. *Brentano Bros.: Washington,* 1885. 8°. **11763**. e. **14**. (**2**.)

—— [Another copy.] **011765**. f. **33**. (**1**.) *With a portrait of the author inserted.*

—— The Declaration of Independence a Masterpiece: but how it got mutilated! In reply to an article . . . in the Truth Seeker of May 21, 1881. [Signed: W. H. B., i.e. W. H. Burr.] pp. 11. [1881.] 8°. *See* B., W. H. **8176**. aaa. **41**. (**3**.)

—— Junius, Casca, Common Sense, and Thomas Paine. [An answer to a footnote in M. D. Conway's "Life of Thomas Paine."] pp. 15. [1892.] 8°. **10803**. bb. **29**. (**9**.)

—— Light on Freemasonry. Lord Bacon its founder. The mystery of his death. pp. 16. [1906 ?] 8°. **011765**. f. **33**. (**2**.)

—— Plagiarism. Three sermons, *etc.* [Accusing W. E. Coleman of plagiarism from his "Sunday not the Sabbath."] pp. 16. [1881.] 8°. **4182**. b. **15**. (**5**.)

—— Revelations of Antichrist, concerning Christ and Christianity. [By W. H. Burr. A circular with specimen extracts.] 1879. 8°. *See* ANTICHRIST. **4372**. df. **15**. (**2**.)

—— A Roman Catholic Canard. An examination of the Bishop Fenwick account of a scene at the deathbed of T. Paine. *See* INGERSOLL (Robert G.) Thomas Paine's Vindication, *etc.* [1887.] 8°. **4018**. aa. **35**.

—— Self-Contradictions of the Bible . . . [By W. H. Burr.] Third edition. pp. 48. 1860. 8°. *See* BIBLE.—*Appendix.* [*Miscellaneous.*] **4016**. b. **7**.

—— [Another edition.] pp. xxi. 43. [1866.] 8°. *See* BIBLE.—*Appendix.* [*Miscellaneous.*] **3128**. bb. **27**.

—— Self-Contradictions of the Bible. [By W. H. Burr.] pp. 64. [c. 1920.] 12°. *See* BIBLE.—*Appendix.* [*Miscellaneous.*] **3131**. de. **3**.

—— Thomas Paine: was he Junius? pp. 31. FEW MS. NOTES. [*Washington,* 1890.] 8°. **11851**. pp. **17**. (**1**.)

—— Thomas Paine was Junius. pp. 28. *Washington,* 1880. 8°. **11825**. df. **16**. (**2**.)

—— Paine was Junius. [An abridgment of "Thomas Paine was Junius."] pp. 10. [1880 ?] 16°. **8009**. bb. **11**. *With newspaper cuttings inserted.*

BURR (WILLIAM HUBERT) Ancient and Modern Engineering and the Isthmian Canal. pp. xv. 473. *J. Wiley & Sons: New York,* 1902. 8°. **08766**. d. **27**.

—— The Elasticity and Resistance of the Materials of Engineering. pp. xv. 753. *J. Wiley & Sons: New York,* 1883. 8°. **8768**. e. **17**.

—— Sixth edition, rewritten and enlarged, *etc.* pp. xv. 990. *J. Wiley & Sons: New York,* 1903. 8°. **08768**. c. **39**.

—— Seventh edition, thoroughly revised. pp. xix. 928. *J. Wiley & Sons: New York,* 1915. 8°. **2246**. d. **1**.

—— Good Roads a Necessity. pp. 51. [1893.] 8°. **8707**. h. **24**. (**2**.)

—— Suspension Bridges, Arch Ribs, and Cantilevers. pp. xi. 417. *J. Wiley & Sons: New York,* 1913. 8°. **08768**. d. **20**.

BURR (WILLIAM HUBERT) and **FALK** (MYRON SAMUEL)

—— The Design and Construction of Metallic Bridges. pp. xiii. 532. *J. Wiley & Sons: New York,* 1905. 8°. **08767**. d. **36**.

—— Third edition. pp. xiii. 532. *J. Wiley & Sons: New York,* 1912. 8°. **2246**. d. **4**.

—— The Graphic Method by Influence Lines for Bridge and Roof Computations. pp. ix. 253. *J. Wiley & Sons: New York,* 1905. 8°. **08767**. g. **10**.

—— Third edition. pp. xi. 253. *J. Wiley & Sons: New York,* 1912. 8°. **08767**. d. **37**.

BURRA (EDWARD JOHN)

—— *See* WOLFE (Humbert) ABC of the Theatre. [Illustrated by E. Burra.] [1932.] 4°. **012316**. h. **17**.

—— Edward Burra. [Reproductions, with introductory text by John Rothenstein.] pp. 15. pl. 32. *Penguin Books: Harmondsworth,* 1945. *obl.* 8°. [*Penguin Modern Painters.*] W.P. **516/6**.

BURRA (ELLA M.) Copper. The life of a theatrical dog star . . . Illustrated by G. M. Tucker. pp. 74. *Thomas Burleigh: London,* 1906. 8°. **012804**. h. **10**.

BURRA (LANCELOT TOKE) A Practical Manual of Tuberculosis for Nurses. pp. 135. x. *J. Bale & Co.: London,* 1915. 8°. **07561**. ee. **13**.

BURRA (PETER JAMES SALKELD)

—— *See* FORSTER (Edward M.) A Passage to India. [With an introductory essay on the novels of E. M. Forster, by P. Burra.] 1942. 8°. **12206**. p. **1/756**.

—— Baroque and Gothic Sentimentalism. An essay. [With plates.] pp. 35. *Duckworth: London,* 1931. 8°. **11823**. tt. **17**.

—— Van Gogh. pp. 142. *Duckworth: London,* 1934. 8°. [*Great Lives.* no. 29.] W.P. **6397/29**.

—— Wordsworth. pp. 160. *Duckworth: London,* 1936. 8°. [*Great Lives.* no. 55.] W.P. **6397/63**.

—— [A reissue.] Wordsworth. *London,* 1950. 8°. [*Great Lives.* no. 63.] W.P. **6397/63**. a.

BURRAGE (ALBERT CAMERON)

—— Burrage on Vegetables. [With plates.] pp. x. 208. *D. Van Nostrand Co.: New York*, [1954.] 8°. **7082**. b. **18**.

BURRAGE (ALFRED McLELLAND) Courtland's Crime. pp. 288. *John Long: London*, 1928. 8°. NN. **13723**.

—— Don't break the Seal. pp. 159. *Gerald G. Swan: London*, 1946. 8°. NN. **37154**.

—— The Golden Barrier. pp. 112. *J. Leng & Co.: London*, [1925.] 8°. [" *People's Friend " Library*. no. 132.] **12645**. dd. **1/132**.

—— [Another edition.] pp. 128. *Gramol Publications: London*, [1935.] 8°. **12603**. w. **42**.

—— Poor Dear Esme. pp. 247. *George Newnes: London*, [1925.] 8°. NN. **11221**.

—— Seeker to the Dead. pp. 188. *G. G. Swan: London*, 1942. 8°. NN. **33778**.

—— The Smokes of Spring. pp. 318. *John Long: London*, 1926. 8°. NN. **12313**.

—— Some Ghost Stories. pp. vii. 276. *Cecil Palmer: London*, 1927. 8°. NN. **13346**.

—— Someone in the Room. By Ex-Private X. [i.e. A. M. Burrage], *etc.* pp. 285. [1931.] 8°. *See* X., *Ex-Private*. NN. **18555**.

—— War is War. By Ex-Private X. [i.e. A. M. Burrage.] pp. 288. [1930.] 8°. *See* X., *Ex-Private*. NN. **16097**.

BURRAGE (ALFRED S.) The Robin Hood Library. no. 1–88. *Aldine Publishing Co.: London*, [1901–06.] 8°. **12602**. i. **3**.

No more published.

BURRAGE (ATHOL HARCOURT) Air Fiend. Air adventure story for boys. pp. v. 242. *Sampson Low & Co.: London*, [1938.] 8°. **12820**. e. **11**.

—— Bending the Sails. pp. 248. *Wells Gardner & Co.: London*, [1938.] 8°. **12816**. bb. **36**.

—— Bravo! A school story for boys. pp. 141. *Richard Lesley & Co.: [London*, 1948.] 8°. **12830**. f. **24**.

—— Bravo, Sea Scouts! *etc.* [With illustrations.] pp. 208. *Wells Gardner, Darton & Co.: Redhill*, 1952. 8°. **12829**. aa. **67**.

—— The Captain's Secret. A sea mystery story. pp. 248. *Ward, Lock & Co.: London & Melbourne*, 1939. 8°. **12824**. a. **20**.

—— Carry on Rippleton. A school story. [With plates.] pp. vii. 248. *Sampson Low, Marston & Co.: London*, [1947.] 8°. **12830**. c. **18**.

—— Chu Tafu, *etc.* pp. 213. *Wells Gardner, Darton & Co.: Redhill*, 1947. 8°. **12829**. c. **7**

—— Cock of the Walk. A school story. pp. 188. *J. F. Shaw & Co.: London*, [1935.] 8°. **20055**. e. **26**.

—— For House and School. A school story. pp. vi. 250. *Sampson Low & Co.: London*, [1937.] 8°. **20059**. ee. **25**.

—— Hoorah for Gawthorne! A school story. pp. 250. *Wells, Gardner & Co.: London*, [1934.] 8°. **20054**. g. **19**.

BURRAGE (ATHOL HARCOURT)

—— The House of Golden Windows, *etc.* [With plates.] pp. 251. *Rylee: London & Birmingham*, [1953.] 8°. **12844.m.5.**

—— Hurtlers through Space. pp. 255. *Frederick Warne & Co.: London & New York*, [1952.] 8°. **12832**. h. **57**.

—— The Idol of Saint Moncreeth. A school story, *etc.* pp. 319. *T. Nelson & Sons: London*, [1925.] 8°. **012807**. g. **30**.

—— Kop of the Secret Service, *etc.* pp. 192. *Wells Gardner, Darton & Co.: Redhill*, 1951 [1952]. 8°. **12833**. ee. **59**.

—— Mutiny. pp. 256. *Frederick Warne & Co.: London & New York*, [1950.] 8°. **12833**. b. **23**.

—— The Mysteries of Saddleworth, *etc.* pp. 247. *T. Nelson & Sons: London*, [1928.] 8°. **12811**. aaa. **13**.

—— Odds Against . . . With illustrations by Comerford Watson. pp. 240. *Evans Bros.: London*, 1947. 8°. **12830**. eee. **41**.

—— [A reissue.] Odds against, *etc.* *London*, 1949. 8°. **12832**. a. **15**.

—— Pirate of the Skies. pp. 248. *Sampson Low, Marston & Co.: London*, [1947.] 8°. **12830**. c. **8**.

—— Rebel of the House. A school story. pp. v. 250. *Sampson Low & Co.: London*, [1937.] 8°. **20059**. f. **3**.

—— Rival Fifteens. A school story. pp. 306. *Wells, Gardner & Co.: London*, [1933.] 8°. **12837.aa.3.**

—— Scoundrel of the Air. An air story for boys. pp. v. 250. *Sampson Low & Co.: London*, [1938.] 8°. **012803**. d. **60**.

—— The Secret Voyage. A sea-adventure story for boys. pp. 256. *Juvenile Productions: London*, 1937. 8°. [*Runnymede Series*.] **12822**. d. **1/6**.

—— Three Chums. pp. 250. *Sampson Low & Co.: London*, [1929.] 8°. **12815**. aa. **12**.

—— Well Played, Sir! pp. v. 250. *Sampson Low & Co.: London*, [1937.] 8°. **012807**. f. **73**.

BURRAGE (CHAMPLIN) *See* BROWNE (Robert) *the Separatist*. A " New Years Guift " . . . Edited with an introduction . . . by C. Burrage. 1904. 8°. **Ac.2067/2.(2.)**

—— *See* BROWNE (Robert) *the Separatist*. The ' Retractation ' of Robert Browne . . . Published with a brief account of its discovery by C. Burrage. 1907. 8°. **4136**. g. **11**.

—— *See* PORY (John) John Pory's Lost Description of Plymouth Colony . . . Edited with an introduction and notes by C. Burrage. 1918. 8°. C. **100**. i. **2**.

—— *See* ROBINSON (John) *Pastor of the English Congregation at Leyden*. An Answer to John Robinson of Leyden. By a Puritan Friend. Now first published from a manuscript of A.D. 1609. Edited by C. Burrage. 1920. 8°. Ac. **2692/24**.

—— The Church Covenant Idea. Its origin and its development. pp. 230. *American Baptist Publication Society: Philadelphia*, 1904. 8°. **4744**. dd. **25**.

—— The Early English Dissenters in the light of recent research—1550–1641 . . . Illustrated. 2 vol. *University Press: Cambridge*, 1912. 8°. **4715**. ee. **27**.

BURRAGE (CHAMPLIN)

—— The Fifth Monarchy Insurrections . . . Reprinted from The English Historical Review,' *etc.* *Spottiswoode & Co.: London,* 1910. 8°. **09008**. bb. **6**. (**3**.)

—— The Ithaca of the Odyssey. A new attempt to show that Thi'aki is the Ithaca of Homer, *etc.* pp. 42. pl. VI. *B. H. Blackwell: Oxford,* 1928. 8°. **11313**. h. **41**.

—— John Penry, the so-called martyr of Congregationalism, as revealed in the original record of his trial and in documents related thereto. pp. 43. *Henry Frowde: London,* 1913. 8°. **4804**. i. **38**. (**3**.)

—— Nazareth and the Beginnings of Christianity. A new view based upon philological evidence, with critical appendices, including unnoticed precanonical readings, *etc.* pp. 68. *Humphrey Milford: London,* 1914. 8°. **4530**. eee. **23**.

—— New Facts concerning John Robinson, pastor of the Pilgrim Fathers . . . With facsimile frontispiece. (A tercentenary memorial.) pp. 35. *Henry Frowde: London,* 1910. 8°. **4806**. ff. **10**. (**4**.)

—— The Restoration of Immersion by the English Anabaptists and Baptists, 1640–1700 . . . Reprinted for private circulation from the American Journal of Theology, *etc.* [1912.] 8°. **4530**. e. **22**. (**5**.)

—— The True Story of Robert Browne—1550 ?–1633—Father of Congregationalism, including various points hitherto unknown or misunderstood, with some account of the development of his religious views, and an extended and improved list of his writings. pp. vii. 75. *Henry Frowde: London,* 1906. 8°. **4902**. dd. **12**.

BURRAGE (CHARLES DANA) *See* BOSTON, *Mass.—Omar Khayyám Club of America.* Twenty Years of the Omar Khayyám Club of America. [Edited by C. D. Burrage.] 1921. 4°. **11855**. c. **31**.

BURRAGE (DWIGHT GRAFTON)

—— Educational Progress in Greece during the Minoan, Mycenaean, and Lyric Periods . . . A thesis, *etc.* pp. iii. 68. *Cockle Printing Co.: Omaha, Neb.,* 1920. 8°. **7702**. p. **21**.

BURRAGE (EDWIN HARCOURT) Bob Hardy, Agitator. A novel. pp. 155. *London,* [1895.] 8°. [*Aldine Masterpieces of Modern Fiction.*] **012612**. f. **35/23**.

—— Carbineer and Scout. A story of the great Boer War, *etc.* pp. 240. *Blackie & Son: London,* [1901.] 8°. **012806**. g. **42**.

—— The Fatal Nugget, *etc.* pp. 128. *S. W. Partridge & Co.: London,* [1900.] 8°. **04410**. ee. **57**.

—— Gerard Mastyn, the son of a genius, *etc.* pp. 232. *S. W. Partridge & Co.: London,* [1877.] 8°. **12641**. a. **21**.

—— [Another edition.] pp. 318. *S. W. Partridge & Co.: London,* [1895.] 8°. **012628**. e. **13**.

—— J. Passmore Edwards, Philanthropist . . . With portrait. pp. 160. *S. W. Partridge & Co.: London,* 1902. 8°. **10827**. e. **24**.

—— A Knowing Dog. The story of a poodle much loved & often lost . . . Illustrated by "Yorick." pp. v. 135. *Greening & Co.: London,* 1908. 4°. **1876**. a. **76**.

—— The Lambs of Littlecote. 39 no. *Aldine Publishing Co.: London,* [1894, 95.] 4°. **012803**. i. **27**.

BURRAGE (EDWIN HARCOURT)

—— The Man who found Klondyke. *See* BEVAN (Tom) White Ivory and Black, *etc.* [1899.] 8°. **012804**. ff. **34**.

—— Mate's Illustrated Reigate and Redhill . . . A pictorial and descriptive souvenir, *etc.* *Bournemouth,* [1906.] *obl.* 8°. [*Mate's Illustrated Guides.*] **10369**. p. **47**.

—— The Missing Million, *etc.* pp. 320. *S. W. Partridge & Co.: London,* 1897. 8°. **012625**. l. **10**.

—— Never Beaten! The story of a boy's adventures in Canada, *etc.* pp. 166. *S. W. Partridge & Co.: London,* [1908.] 8°. **012804**. a. **44**.

—— Out of the Deep. A story of the Brays of Beachtown. pp. 320. *S. W. Partridge & Co.: London,* 1898. 8°. **012643**. b. **19**.

—— The Slave Raiders of Zanzibar, *etc.* pp. 320. *S. W. Partridge & Co.: London,* [1896.] 8°. **012808**. f. **19**.

—— Tom Tartar at School; or, True friend and noble foe. pp. 384. "*Best for Boys*" *Publishing Co.: [London,* 1891.] 4°. **012803**. i. **7**.

—— The Twin Castaways. pp. 328. *T. Nelson & Sons: London,* 1900 [1899]. 8°. **012804**. f. **46**.

—— [A reissue.] *London,* [1911.] 8°. **012808**. cc. **20**.

—— The Vanished Yacht. pp. 358. *T. Nelson & Sons: London,* 1898 [1897]. 8°. **012626**. i. **69**.

—— [A reissue.] *London,* [1929.] 8°. **012603**. c. **25**.

—— The Wurra Wurra Boys, *etc.* pp. 132. *Collins: London & Glasgow,* [1903.] 8°. **012803**. b. **48**.

BURRAGE (HENRY SWEETSER) *See* ROSIER (James) Rosier's Relation of Waymouth's Voyage to the Coast of Maine, 1605. With an introduction and notes. By H. S. Burrage. 1887. 4°. Ac. **8391/3**.

—— Baptist Hymn Writers and their Hymns. pp. xi. 682. *Brown, Thurston & Co.: Portland, Me.,* [1888.] 8°. **4999**. d. **15**.

—— The Beginnings of Colonial Maine, 1602–1658. [With plates.] pp. xv. 412. *Printed for the State: Portland, Me.,* 1914. 8°. **9602**. s. **10**.

—— Civil War Record of Brown University. Compiled by . . . H. S. Burrage. pp. x. 69. 1920. 8°. *See* PROVIDENCE, *Rhode Island.—Brown University.* Ac. **2692**. r/**8**.

—— Early English and French Voyages, chiefly from Hakluyt, 1534–1608. Edited by H. S. Burrage with maps and a facsimile reproduction. pp. xxii. 451. *C. Scribner's Sons: New York,* 1906. 8°. [*Original Narratives of Early American History.*] **9551**. p. **2**.

—— Gettysburg and Lincoln. The battle, the cemetery, and the national park . . . Illustrated. pp. xii. 224. *G. P. Putnam's Sons: New York & London,* 1906. 8°. **09605**. aaa. **11**.

—— A History of the Anabaptists in Switzerland. pp. xvi. 231. *American Baptist Publication Society: Philadelphia,* 1882. 12°. **4661**. aaaa. **22**.

—— Maine in the Northeastern Boundary Controversy. [With plates and maps.] pp. xiv. 398. *Printed for the State: Portland, Me.,* 1919. 8°. **9605**. g. **18**.

BURRAGE (HENRY SWEETSER)

—— The Plymouth Colonists in Maine. pp. 31. [1904.] 8°. **09004. b. 11. (5.)**

—— True to the End. A story of the Swiss Reformation. pp. 192. *Baptist Tract & Book Society: London; Philadelphia* [printed], 1895. 8°. **4400. dd. 37.**

BURRAGE (JOSEPH PERRIN) *See* CADY (Daniel A.) Memorial of Lieut. Joseph P. Burrage, *etc.* 1864. 8°. **4985. aaa. 15.**

BURRAGE (PAT)

—— *See* DRAVNEEK (Henry) Wanna be a Model? Here's how by Pat Burrage, *etc.* [1950.] 8°. **07743. b. 24.**

BURRAGE (R.)

—— Catalogue de monnaies antiques grecques et romaines contenant les collections de R. Burrage . . . Du Dr. J. S. de Vienne . . . Ainsi que la collection très importante de monnaies romaines formée par Sir Arthur J. Evans, *etc.* [With reproductions.] pp. 142. pl. 65. *Genève*, 1934. 4°. **7756. pp. 24.**

BURRAGE (WALTER LINCOLN) *See* KELLY (Howard A.) and BURRAGE (W. L.) American Medical Biographies. 1920. 8°. **10884. g. 2.**

—— —— 1928. 4°. **010883. i. 10.**

—— Gynecological Diagnosis, *etc.* pp. xvi. 656. *D. Appleton & Co.: New York & London*, 1910. 8°. **07581. g. 29.**

—— A History of the Massachusetts Medical Society, with brief biographies of the founders and chief officers, 1781–1922 . . . Illustrated, *etc.* pp. xiii. 505. *Privately printed: Norwood, Mass.*, 1923. 8°. **7680. g. 19.**

BURRALL (F. A.) Asiatic Cholera. pp. 155. *W. Wood & Co.: New York*, 1866. 12°. **7561. bb. 22.**

BURRARD, *Family of.* *See* BURRARD (*Sir* Sidney G.) *Bart.* The Families of Borard and Burrard. A genealogical sketch. 1892. 8°. **9902. f. 39.**

BURRARD (CHARLES) Guide to the Obligatory Test in Marathi. 2 pt. *Jatva-vivechaka Press: Bombay*, 1899. 8°. **14140. i. 13.**
Pt. 2 is lithographed.

BURRARD (*Sir* GERALD) *Bart.*

—— Big Game Hunting in the Himalayas and Tibet, *etc.* [With plates.] pp. 320. *Herbert Jenkins: London*, 1925. 8°. **7904. e. 11.**

—— La Grande chasse dans l'Himalaya . . . Avec 8 croquis. pp. 213. *Paris*, 1939. 8°. **07907. g. 31.**

—— Cartridges for Sporting Rifles. pp. 35. *Imperial Chemical Industries: London*, [1936.] 8°. **07908. ff. 41.**

—— Fly Tying: Principles and Practice. pp. 216. *Herbert Jenkins: London*, 1940. 8°. **07907. ee. 11.**

—— Fly Tying: principles and practice. (Second edition, revised.) pp. 160. *Herbert Jenkins: London*, 1945. 8°. **7918. aa. 38.**

—— Fly Tying: Principles and Practice. (Third edition.) [With illustrations.] pp. 160. *Herbert Jenkins: London*, 1951. 8°. **7921. aaa. 26.**

BURRARD (*Sir* GERALD) *Bart.*

—— The Identification of Firearms and Forensic Ballistics. pp. 220. pl. XL. *Herbert Jenkins: London*, 1934. 8°. **08821. i. 52.**

—— The Identification of Firearms and Forensic Ballistics. (Revised edition.) pp. 217. pl. XLI. *Herbert Jenkins. London*, 1951. 8°. **8838. e. 14.**

—— In the Gunroom. [Answers to questions on rifles and shotguns reprinted from the " Field."] pp. 125. *Herbert Jenkins: London*, 1930. 8°. **7916. a. 24.**

—— In the Gunroom. (Revised and enlarged edition.) pp. 147. *Herbert Jenkins: London*, 1951. 8°. **7921. aaa. 6.**

—— The Modern Shotgun. [With plates.] 3 vol. *Herbert Jenkins: London*, 1931 [1930]–32. 8°. **8821. ff. 31.**

—— The Modern Shotgun, *etc.* (Second edition.) 3 vol. *Herbert Jenkins: London*, 1944–50. 8°. **8839.g.1.**

—— The Modern Shotgun. Volume I. The gun. (Second edition, revised.) pp. 242. *Herbert Jenkins: London*, 1950. 8°. **8839. g. 2.**

—— The Mystery of the Mekong. [A novel.] pp. 311. *Herbert Jenkins: London*, 1928. 8°. **NN. 13717.**

—— Notes on Sporting Rifles for use in India and elsewhere. pp. viii. 80. *Edward Arnold: London*, 1920. 8°. **7904. ee. 9.**

—— Second edition. pp. 96. *E. Arnold & Co.: London*, 1925. 8°. **7904. df. 44.**

—— Third edition, revised and enlarged. pp. 142. *E. Arnold & Co.: London*, 1932. 8°. **7916. cc. 26.**

—— Notes on Sporting Rifles . . . Fourth edition, revised and enlarged, *etc.* pp. 183. *Edward Arnold & Co.: London*, 1953. 8°. **7920. a. 61.**

—— The Tiger of Tibet. [A novel.] pp. 312. *Herbert Jenkins: London*, 1924. 8°. **NN. 10377.**

BURRARD (*Sir* HARRY) [Evidence before the Court of Enquiry upon the conduct of Sir Hew Dalrymple relative to the Convention of Cintra.] *See* DALRYMPLE (*Sir* Hew W.) *Bart.* The Whole Proceedings of the Court of Enquiry, *etc.* 1808. 8°. **1103. h. 95.**

BURRARD (SIDNEY) The Annals of Walhampton. pp. 207. *W. J. Johnson: London*, 1874. 8°. **10368. dd. 4.**

BURRARD (*Sir* SIDNEY GERALD) *Bart.* An Account of the Scientific Work of the Survey of India, and a comparison of its progress with that of foreign surveys, *etc.* pp. 23. *Calcutta*, 1905. 4°. [*Survey of India. Professional Paper.* no. 9.] **I.S. 170/6.**

—— The Attraction of the Himalaya Mountains upon the Plumb-Line in India. Considerations of recent data. [With plates.] pp. vii. 115. xi. *Dehra Dun*, 1901. 4°. [*Survey of India Department. Professional Paper.* no. 5.] **I.S. 170/6.**

—— The Families of Borard and Burrard. A genealogical sketch. pp. xxiv. 71. MS. NOTES [by the author]. *B. V. Hughes: Dehra Dun*, 1892. 8°. **9902. f. 39.**

BURRARD (*Sir* SIDNEY GERALD) *Bart.*

—— Investigations of Isostasy in Himalayan and Neighbouring Regions. [With a map.] pp. 38. pl. II. *Dehra Dun,* 1918. 4°. [*Survey of India. Professional Paper.* no. 17.] I.S. **170/6.**

—— Mount Everest and its Tibetan Names. A review of Sir Sven Hedin's book [i.e. "Mount Everest"]. pp. 18. *Dehra Dun,* 1931. 8°. [*Survey of India. Professional Paper.* no. 26.] I.S. **170/6.**

—— On the Origin of the Himalaya Mountains. A consideration of the geodetic evidence. pp. 26. pl. II. *Calcutta,* 1912. 4°. [*Survey of India. Professional Paper.* no. 12.] I.S. **170/6.**

—— The Reproduction of Maps, Plans, Photographs, Diagrams, and Line Illustrations by the Survey of India for other Departments. Prepared under the direction of Colonel S. G. Burrard. pp. 44. 1914. fol. *See* INDIA.—*Survey of India.* I.S. **170/11.**

BURRARD (*Sir* SIDNEY GERALD) *Bart.*, and **HAYDEN** (*Sir* HENRY HUBERT)

—— A Sketch of the Geography and Geology of the Himalaya Mountains and Tibet. pp. vi. ii. 308. pl. L. 1907, 08. fol. *See* INDIA. [*Miscellaneous Official Publications.*] **10056.** v. **11.**

—— (Second edition.) Revised by Colonel Sir S. Burrard . . . and A. M. Heron. pp. x. 359. xxxii. pl. LII. 1933. fol. *See* INDIA. [*Miscellaneous Official Publications.*] **10056.** v. **21.**

BURRARD (WILLIAM DUTTON) *See* also ARAMIS, *pseud.* [i.e. W. D. Burrard.]

—— *See* LOUIS-LATOUR (T.) Princesses, Ladies and Adventuresses of the reign of Louis XIV. (Translated . . . by W. D. Burrard.) 1924. 8°. **10656.** c. **27.**

—— Chronicles of an Eminent Fossil. pp. 214. *T. Fisher Unwin: London,* 1896. 8°. [*Autonym Library.*] **012600.** e. **52/6.**

—— A Great Platonic Friendship. 3 vol. *Hurst & Blackett: London,* 1887. 8°. **012639.** l. **18.**

—— Out of the Depths. Poems. pp. 94. *Kegan Paul & Co.: London,* 1892. 8°. **11653.** d. **51.**

—— A Weaver of Runes. pp. viii. 327. *John Long: London,* 1899. 8°. **012642.** aaa. **33.**

BURRASTON (VICTOR HAROLD) The "Ins and Outs" of British Commerce for Foreign Students. pp. 181. *Swiss Mercantile Society: London,* 1932. 8°. **20016.** g. **13.**

BURRAU (CARL) Undersøgelser over Instrumentkonstanter ved Kjøbenhavns Universitets astronomiske Observatoriums Maaleapparat for fotografiske Plader. Afhandling, *etc.* pp. 51. *Kjøbenhavn,* 1895. 4°. **8562.** ff. **41.**

BURRAU (ØYVIND)

—— On the Weight of a physically determined Quantity. pp. 9. *København,* 1954. 8°. [*Geodætisk Institut. Meddelelse.* no. 28.] S. B. **84.**

BURRAUT (ROBERT) *See* CATO (M. P.) *the Censor.* [*Supposititious Works.—Disticha de Moribus.—English.*] Preceptes of Cato, *etc.* [Translated by R. Burraut.] 1553. 16°. C. **59.** aa. **2.**

—— —— 1560. 16°. C. **17.** a. **3.**

BURRAUT (ROBERT)

—— *See* LINDSAY (*Sir* David) The Tragical Death of Dauid Beatō Bishoppe of sainct Andrewes, *etc.* [Edited, with an address to the reader, by R. Burraut.] [1548?] 8°. **288.** a. **49.**

BURRE (HERBERT)

—— Das Freundschaftsmotiv und seine Abwandlung in den Dramen Shakespeares. Inaugural-Dissertation, *etc.* pp. viii. 56. *Marburg,* 1938. 8°. **11765.** dd. **20.**

BURRE (OTTO) Das Oberoligozän und die Quarzitlagerstätten unmittelbar östlich des Siebengebirges . . . Mit Beiträgen von Ernst Zimmermann. Mit 4 Tafeln, *etc.* pp. 69. *Berlin,* 1930. 8°. [*Archiv für Lagerstättenforschung.* Hft. 47.] Ac. **3139/4.**

BURREL (JOHN) *See* BURRELL (John) *Rector of Euston.*

BURREL (WILLIAM) A Paper sent to the Quakers from W. B. Truth appearing with an open face, against Opposers and False Prophets. [Signed: William Burrel.] pp. 7. [*London?* 1676?] 4°. **855.** f. **7.** (**23.**)

BURRELL (ABRAM BOGERT)

—— Reminiscences of George La Bar, the centenarian of Monroe County, Pa. . . . and incidents in the early settlement of the Pennsylvania side of the river valley, from Easton to Bushkill . . . With a portrait. pp. 111. *Claxton, Remsen & Haffelfinger: Philadelphia,* 1870. 8°. **10882.** f. **29.**

BURRELL (ALEXANDER) The Great Duty of Justice inforced. A sermon preached . . . March the 2d 1724. at the Assizes held at Ailesbury, *etc.* pp. 26. *A. Bettesworth: London,* 1725. 8°. **225.** h. **7.** (**15.**)

BURRELL (ANDREW) מוסדי הדקדוק A New Method to obtain the Knowledge of the Hebrew Tongue speedily and without a Master . . . being a Key to a Critical Analysis of all the Hebrew and Chaldaic words in the Bible, a work . . . of which a specimen is added, and is an analytical praxis for this key. (Proposals for Printing . . . A Critical Analysis, *etc.*—A Specimen of the Critical Analysis.) 2 pt. *Printed for the Author: London,* 1739. 8°. **64.** a. **18.**
The "Proposals for Printing, etc." bear the date 1738.

—— [Another copy.] **12903.** c. **28.**
Imperfect; wanting the specimen of the "Critical Analysis" and a plate.

—— Proposals for Printing . . . a Critical Analysis of all the Hebrew and Chaldaic Words in the Old Testament, *etc.* (A Specimen of the Critical Analysis.) pp. 14. [*London,* 1738?] 8°. **1016.** f. **15.** (**1.**)

BURRELL (ANDREWES) *See* WHITE (Peter) *Master of Attendance in the Navy.* A Memorable Sea-Fight . . . Published . . . by A. Burrell, Gent., *etc.* 1649. 4°. E. **572.** (**19.**)

—— A Briefe Relation Discovering Plainely the true Causes why the great Levell of Fenns in the severall Counties of Norfolk, Suffolk, Cambridge, Huntington, Northampton, and Lincolne Shires; being three hundred and seven thousand acres . . . have been drowned and made unfruitfull for many yeares past. And . . . how they may be drained, and preserved from inundation in the times to come. Humbly presented to the Honourable House of Commons assembled in Parliament. pp. 22. *Printed for Francis Constable: London,* 1642. 4°. **725.** d. **30.**

—— [Another copy.] E. **148.** (**18.**)

BURRELL (ANDREWES)

—— A Cordjall for the Calenture and those other diseases which distempers the Seamen. Or, a Declaration discovering and advising how Englands sea honour may be regained, and maintained as in the happy raigne of Queene Elizabeth, *etc.* pp. 13. *London*, 1648. 4°. **E. 537. (10.)**

—— Exceptions against Sir Cornelius virmudens Discourse for the Draining of the great Fennes . . . which in Ianuary 1638. he presented to the King for his designe, *etc.* pp. 19. *Printed by T. H., and are to be sold by Robert Constable: London*, 1642. 4°. **E. 148. (22.)**

—— [Another copy.] **725.** c. **36.**
Slightly mutilated.

—— To the Right Honourable, the High Court of Parliament, the humble Remonstrance of A. Burrell . . . for a Reformation of Englands Navie. (Englands Out-Guard: or Englands Royall Navie, surveyed and lamented.—Particulars extracted out of Mr. A. Burrells Paper, to which the Committee of Lords and Commons for the Admiralty and Cinque-Ports desire his answer, *etc.* [With the answers.]) pp. 22. [*London ?* 1646 ?] 4°. **E. 335. (6.)**

—— *See* ENGLAND.—*Commissioners of the Navy.* The Answer of the Commissioners of the Navie, to a scandalous pamphlet [i.e. " To the Right Honourable the High Court of Parliament, the humble Remonstrance of A. Burrell "] published by Mr A. Burrell. 1646. 4°. **E. 340. (31.)**

BURRELL (ANGUS) *See* BURRELL (John A.)

BURRELL (ARTHUR) *See* BIBLE.—*Selections.* [*English.*] The Shorter Bible: being the Authorised Version of the Bible arranged & edited for the use of schools and for home reading [by A. Burrell]. 1909. 8°. **03051.** h. **9.**

—— *See* CHAUCER (G.) [*Canterbury Tales.—Modernised Versions.*] Chaucer's Canterbury Tales for the Modern Reader. Prepared & edited by A. Burrell. [1908.] 8°. **12206.p.1/270.**

—— *See* LANGLAND (William) Piers Plowman . . . A version for the modern reader by A. Burrell. [1912.] 8°. **12206.p.1/411.**

—— *See* MACAULAY (Thomas B.) *Baron Macaulay.* [*Essays.—Life and Writings of Addison.*] Macaulay's Essay on the Life and Writings of Addison . . . Edited and annotated by A. Burrell. 1901. 8°. **12274.g.14/2.**

—— A Book of Heroic Verse. Chosen by A. Burrell. pp. xii. 292. *J. M. Dent & Sons: London; E. P. Dutton & Co.: New York*, [1912.] 8°. [*Everyman's Library.*] **12206.p.1/770.**

—— Clear Speaking and Good Reading, *etc.* pp. xiii. 164. *Longmans & Co.: London*, 1898. 8°. **011824.** g. **70.**

—— Revised edition. pp. xii. 162. *Longmans & Co.: London*, 1909. 8°. **011805.** f. **34.**

—— New edition. pp. xii. 143. *Longmans & Co.: London*, 1928. 8°. **011805.** h. **61.**

—— English Literature for Schools. Edited by A. Burrell. 20 vol. *J. M. Dent & Sons: London*, [1913–16.] 8°. **012208.** a. 2.

—— English Lyrical Verse. Selected and edited by A. Burrell. pp. 192. *J. M. Dent & Sons: London & Toronto*, [1927.] 8°. [*Kings' Treasuries of Literature.*] **012207.** aaa. **1/23.**

BURRELL (ARTHUR)

—— English Poetry: Lyrical. (Heroic & Patriotic Verse.—Selections from Shakespeare.) Edited by A. Burrell. 3 vol. *J. M. Dent & Co.: London*, [1905.] 8°. [*Temple English Literature Series for Schools.*] **12204.** p. **4/19.**

—— Exercises in Speech and Simple Recitations for Standards I. II. and III. (for Standards IV. and V.—Exercises in Speech and Recitations for Standards IV. and V. and for higher classes.) 3 pt. *Griffith, Farran & Co.: London*, [1891.] 8°. **11824.** bb. **54.**

—— A Guide to Story Telling. pp. xiii. 336. *Sir I. Pitman & Sons: London*, 1926. 8°. **011824.** b. **3.**

—— The Man with Seven Hearts, and other stories. pp. 188 *Elliot Stock: London*, 1893 [1892]. 8°. **012706.** ee. **29**

—— The Piebald Horse, and other stories. pp. 181. *T. Fisher Unwin: London*, 1896. 8°. **012806.** h. **4.**

—— Recitation. A handbook for teachers in public elementary schools. pp. 239. *Griffith, Farran & Co.: London*, [1891.] 8°. **11824.** de. **43.**

—— Stephen Philip Unwin, 1836–1919. Address, *etc.* [*Shipley*, 1919.] 8°. **10824.** a. **25.**

BURRELL (ARTHUR BROTHERTON) *See* MACDANIELS (Laurence H.) and BURRELL (A. B.) The Effect of Sulphur Fungicides, applied during the bloom, on the set of apple fruits. [1934.] 8°. **07075.** h. **1.**

—— Boron Treatment for a Physiogenic Apple Disease. (Reprinted from Proceedings of the American Society for Horticultural Science.) [1937.] 8°. **7029.** pp. **15.** (**2.**)

—— The Effect of Irrigation on the Occurrence of a Form of the Cork Disease and on the Size of Apple Fruits. (Reprinted from Proceedings of the American Society for Horticultural Science.) [1933.] 8°. **07076.** cc. **42.**

—— Effectiveness and Safety of Fungicide-Arsenical Spray Combinations on Apple in the Champlain Valley of New York. (Reprinted from Proceedings of the American Society for Horticultural Science.) [1933.] 8°. **07076.** cc. **38.**

BURRELL (BENJAMIN ARTHUR) An Elementary Course on Food-Testing. pp. viii. 92. *Baillière & Co.: London*, 1910. 8°. **8909.** aa. **64.**

BURRELL (CAROLINE FRANCES) *See* BENTON (Caroline French) *pseud.* [i.e. C. F. Burrell.]

BURRELL (CHARLES) **AND SONS.** A Summary of the Road Locomotive Acts, 1861, 1865, & 1878, in force in England & Scotland, *etc.* pp. 24. *Simpkin, Marshall & Co.: London*, [1879.] 12°. **6426.** b. **40.**

BURRELL (*Sir* CHARLES MERRIK) *See* CAREW (John E.) Report of the Trial in the Cause J. E. Carew against Sir C. M. Burrell, Bart. and Col. George Wyndham, executors of the late Earl of Egremont; and Report of the proceedings in the Court for the Relief of Insolvent Debtors, in the matter of J. E. Carew . . . on the opposition entered by Sir C. Burrell, *etc.* 1840, *etc.* 8°. **1243.** i. **21.**

—— Report of the late Important Trial in the Court of King's Bench, in which Sir Charles Merrik Burrell, Bart. was plaintiff and Henry John Nicholson, the defendant; respecting the parochial rates claimed by the parish of St. Margaret, Westminster, from the inhabitants of Richmond Terrace. Tried . . . the 9th of December, 1833. Taken in short-hand by F. N. Walsh. pp. 191. *J. B. Nichols & Son: London*, 1834. 8°. **1245.** b. **17.**

BURRELL (DAVID JAMES) Christ and Men. pp. 288. *F. H. Revell Co.: New York*, [1905.] 8°. **4226. k. 11.**

—— Christ and Progress. A discussion of problems of our time. pp. 267. *F. H. Revell Co.: New York*, [1903.] 8°. **4379. ee. 2.**

—— The Golden Parable. Studies in the story of the Prodigal Son. pp. 159. *F. H. Revell Co.: New York*, [1926.] 8°. **03226. e. 48.**

—— The Gospel of Certainty. pp. 246. *Hodder & Stoughton: London*, 1899. 8°. **4372. dd. 16.**

—— In the Upper Room. A practical exposition of John XIII.–XVII., with related passages. pp. vii. 145. *T. & T. Clark: Edinburgh*, 1913. 8°. [*Short Course Series.*] **03107. ee. 8/10.**

—— The Laughter of God, and other sermons—expository. pp. 217. *F. H. Revell Co.: New York*, [1919.] 8°. **4487. ee. 26.**

—— The Old-Time Religion; or, the Foundations of our faith. [With a portrait.] pp. 349. *Oliphant, Anderson & Ferrier: Edinburgh & London; printed in U.S.A.*, 1913. 8°. **03558. df. 26.**

—— A Quiver of Arrows. Being characteristic sermons of David James Burrell . . . selected and epitomized by Thomas Douglas, *etc.* [With a portrait.] pp. xi. 380. *Funk & Wagnalls Co.: New York & London*, 1902. 8°. **4487. g. 36.**

—— The Religions of the World. An outline of the great religious systems. pp. 332. *Presbyterian Board of Publication: Philadelphia*, [1888.] 8°. **4503. bb. 20.**

—— The Sermon. Its construction and delivery. (The James Sprunt Lectures delivered at Union Theological Seminary in Virginia.) pp. 329. *F. H. Revell Co.: New York*, [1913.] 8°. **4498. ee. 10.**

—— Wayfarers of the Bible. pp. 222. *F. H. Revell Co.: New York*, [1907.] 8°. **03129. ff. 53.**

—— Why I Believe the Bible. pp. 199. *F. H. Revell Co.: New York*, [1917.] 8°. **03129. de. 58.**

BURRELL (EDWARD J.) Elementary Building Construction and Drawing. pp. viii. 248. *Longmans & Co.: London*, 1889. 8°. **7820. c. 14.**

—— Second edition. pp. viii. 252. *Longmans & Co.: London*, 1889. 8°. **7820. aaa. 29.**

—— New edition. With an appendix for fire insurance students by Maurice Butler . . . and E. G. Skinner. pp. viii. 280. *Longmans & Co.: London*, 1931. 8°. **7817. a. 10.**

BURRELL (EVERAN M.) The Wager. A comedy in one act. pp. 27. *H. F. W. Deane & Sons: London*, [1937.] 8°. [*Village Drama Society Plays.*] **W.P. 8829/91.**

BURRELL (GEORGE) *of Thetford.* An Account of the Gifts and Legacies that have been given and bequeathed to charitable and public uses in the Borough of Thetford, with their present state and management, also a chronological account of the most remarkable events which have occurred at Thetford from the earliest period to the present time. pp. xi. 89. *Samuel Mills: Thetford*, 1809. 8°. **10352. h. 33.**

BURRELL (GEORGE) *Principal Librarian of the Athenaeum, Liverpool.* A Catalogue of the Library of the Athenæum Liverpool; by G. Burrell. (Laws and Regulations of th Athenæum.) pp. xxix. 404. 1820. 8°. *See* LIVERPOOL —*Athenaeum.* **620. h. 13**

—— [Another copy.] **F.P.** **11900. f. 14**

BURRELL (GEORGE ARTHUR) An American Engineer look at Russia. pp. 324. *Stratford Co.: Boston*, [1932.] 8°. **010291. f. 18**

—— Chart of Properties of Mine Gases. [1919.] *s. sh.* fol *See* UNITED STATES OF AMERICA.—*Bureau of Mines.* **1820.h.8.(110.**

—— The Condensation of Gasoline from Natural Gas. By G. A. Burrell, Frank M. Seibert and G. G. Oberfell pp. vi. 106. *Washington*, 1915. 8°. [*U.S. Bureau of Mines. Bulletin.* no. 88.] **A.S. 229**

—— Gasoline and how to use it. pp. 281. *Oil Statistical Society: Boston*, [1916.] 16°. **8715. aa. 60**

BURRELL (GEORGE ARTHUR) and **SEIBERT** (FRANK MEYERS)

—— The Sampling and Examination of Mine Gases and Natural Gas. pp. 116. *Washington*, 1913. 8°. [*U.S. Bureau of Mines. Bulletin* no. 42.] **A.S. 229**

BURRELL (HARRY) *See* LE SOUEF (Albert S.) and BURRELL (H.) The Wild Animals of Australasia, *etc.* 1926. 8°. **7208. g. 33**

—— The Platypus: its discovery, zoological position, form and characteristics, habits, life history, *etc.* pp. 227. pl. 35. *Angus & Robertson: Sydney*, 1927. 8°. **07207. ee. 16**

BURRELL (*Mrs.* HENRY) *See* BURRELL (J.) *Mrs.*

BURRELL (HERBERT LESLIE) *See* BOSTON, *Mass.*—*Municipal Institutions.*—*City Hospital.* Medical and Surgical Reports, *etc.* [ser. 6–15 edited by H. L. Burrell and others.] 1882, *etc.* 8°. **07687. i. 53**

—— *See* BOSTON, *Mass.*—*Miscellaneous Institutions.*—*Children's Hospital.* Medical and Surgical Report of the Children's Hospital, 1869–1894. Edited by T. M. Rotch . . . and H. L. Burrell. 1895. 8°. **7687. eee. 45**

BURRELL (HERBERT LESLIE) and **LOVETT** (ROBERT WILLIAMSON)

—— Habitual or Recurrent Dislocation of the Shoulder. (Extracted from the American Journal of the Medical Sciences.) pp. 14. [1897.] 8°. **7306. h. 16. (5.**

BURRELL (J.) *Mrs.* Crochet Lace Edgings; also, elegant receipts for collars, round d'oyly, lace sleeves, *etc.* pp. 22 *Groombridge & Sons: London; Mrs. Veall: Wisbech* [1847.] 24°. **1042. a. 48. (5.**

—— Crochet Simplified; being a full explanation of the various stitches, *etc.* pp. 21. *Groombridge & Sons. London; Mrs. Veall: Wisbech*, [1847.] 24°. **1042. a. 45. (2.**

—— Knitted Lace Edgings. (The Second Series of Knitted Lace Edgings.—The Third Series of Knitted Lace Edgings. [By J. Burrell.] 3 pt. [1845, 46.] 24°. *See* LACE EDGINGS. **1042. a. 41. (1.**

BURRELL (J.) *Tutor.* Memoir of the Rev. Thomas Lewis, of Islington; with extracts from his diary and correspondence. pp. xi. 396. *Ward & Co.: London,* 1853. 8°. **4906. b. 70.**

BURRELL (JAMES) *of Colorado.* History of Gilpin County. *See* CLEAR CREEK VALLEY, *Colorado.* History of Clear Creek and Boulder Valleys, *etc.* 1880. 4°. **10409. l. 13.**

BURRELL (JAMES) *Rev.* "The Beloved Persis." A memoir of Mrs. Tarbett. By her pastor [i.e. James Burrell?]. pp. 96. 1855. 12°. *See* TARBETT (Mary) **4906. b. 11.**

BURRELL (JAMES L. A.) *See* VAJDA (E.) Fata Morgana . . . Translated by J. L. A. Burrell, and P. Moeller. 1924. 8°. **012208.aa.4/2.**

BURRELL (JOAN MARY)

—— *See* CRAIG (John) *M.B., F.R.C.P.E.*, and BURRELL (J.) Paediatrics in the North-Eastern, Aberdeen, Region of Scotland, *etc.* 1950. 8°. **07581. i. 55.**

BURRELL (JOHN) *Pilgrim.* [For editions of the work by Henry Timberlake entitled: "A True and strange discourse of the trauailes of two English Pilgrimes . . . Written by one of them on the behalf of himselfe and his fellowe Pilgrime (John Burrell)":] *See* TIMBERLAKE (H.)

BURRELL (JOHN) *Poet. See* BUREL.

BURRELL (JOHN) *Rector of Euston.* The Divine Right of Kings, proved from the Principles of the Church of England. In a sermon, *etc.* pp. 23. *John Hayes for Sam. Simpson: Cambridge,* 1683. 4°. **4473. aa. 41. (5.)**

BURRELL (JOHN ANGUS) *See* BREWSTER (Dorothy) and BURRELL (J. A.) Adventure or Experience, *etc.* 1930. 8°. **11823. tt. 5.**

—— *See* BREWSTER (Dorothy) and BURRELL (J. A.) Dead Reckonings in Fiction. 1924. 8°. **011850. cc. 3.**

—— *See* BREWSTER (Dorothy) and BURRELL (J. A.) Modern Fiction. 1934. 8°. **11855. d. 48.**

—— A History of Adult Education at Columbia University. University Extension and the School of General Studies. pp. x. 111. *Columbia University Press: New York,* 1954. 8°. [*Bicentennial History of Columbia University.*] Ac. **2688/56. (1.)**

BURRELL (JOHN ANGUS) and **CERF** (BENNETT ALFRED)

—— The Bedside Book of Famous American Stories. Edited by A. Burrell and B. A. Cerf. pp. xvii. 1273. *Random House: New York,* [1936.] 8°. **012600. dd. 25.**

BURRELL (JOHN GLYN) An Epitome of the Ninth Edition of Salmond on Torts. pp. vii. 244. *Sweet & Maxwell: London,* 1937. 8°. **20031. h. 11.**

BURRELL (JOHN H.) Private Telegraph Code, compiled by J. H. Burrell, for the exclusive use of John H. Burrell & Co. . . . and their correspondents. pp. 40. *W. H. Tyerman: Liverpool,* 1888. 4°. **8757. l. 5.**

BURRELL (JOHN HUGH)

—— *See* ENGLAND.—*Home Office.—Committee on Police Extraneous Duties.* Report of the Committee, *etc.* [Chairman, J. H. Burrell.] 1953. 8°. B.S. **18/40. (106.)**

BURRELL (JOHN PALFREY) Official Bulletins of the Battle of Waterloo, in the original languages, with translations into English. Edited by J. P. Burrell. pp. 99. *Parker, Furnivall & Parker: London,* 1849. 8°. **1435. i. 4.**

BURRELL (JOSEPH FRANCIS) The Mystery of God; or, the Arian monitor. By which . . . the . . . doctrine of the Trinity in Unity is invincibly defended, *etc.* 2 pt. *Eshcol Chapel: London,* 1817, 18. 8°. **701. i. 18. (3.)**

—— The Triumph of Christ, or the Brand plucked out of the fire. Being a faithful account of the free . . . grace of God, displayed in the author's conversion . . . from the abominations of the Church of Rome, *etc.* pp. 120. *Eshchol* [sic] *Chapel: London,* 1819. 8°. **613. k. 21. (9.)**

—— Water Baptism, Circumcision, and the Lord's Supper, dissected and analized . . . To which is added, a concise history of the Anabaptists or Baptists, *etc.* pp. vii. 161. *Eshcol Chapel: London,* 1816. 8°. **701. i. 18. (2.)**

—— The Will of God, a Mystery, proved to be Eternal, Immutable, and Absolute. Sin and the Fall, with all other events, demonstrated to be fixed from all eternity, *etc.* pp. 64. *Eshcol Chapel: London,* 1818. 8°. **702. h. 11. (5.)**

—— Zion's Way-Marks; or, Triumphs over Satan and unbelief; being an account of the author's call to the ministry, *etc.* pp. 118. *Eschol Chapel: London,* 1816. 8°. **701. i. 18. (1.)**

BURRELL (KATHLEEN JOAN)

—— *See* also ALLEYNE (Margaret) *pseud.* [i.e. K. J. Burrell.]

—— *See* FARJEON (Eleanor) The Perfect Zoo . . . Illustrated by K. Burrell. 1947. 8°. **12831. g. 5.**

BURRELL (LANCELOT STEPHEN TOPHAM)

—— *See* FENTON (William J.) and BURRELL (L. S. T.) Diseases of the Chest. 1930. 8°. **7616. bb. 18.**

—— Artificial Pneumothorax. [With plates.] pp. vii. 174. *William Heinemann: London,* 1932. 8°. [*Practitioner's Series.*] **07306.b.1/2.**

—— Recent Advances in Pulmonary Tuberculosis, *etc.* pp. vi. 217. pl. XXXII. *J. & A. Churchill: London,* 1929. 8°. [*Recent Advances Series.*] **7442. p. 1/19.**

—— Second edition. pp. ix. 240. pl. XXXII. *J. & A. Churchill: London,* 1931. 8°. [*Recent Advances Series.*] **7442. p. 1/32.**

—— Third edition, *etc.* pp. viii. 320. pl. XLVI. *J. & A. Churchill: London,* 1937. 8°. [*Recent Advances Series.*] **7442. p. 1/73.**

—— Recent Advances in Respiratory Tuberculosis. By Frederick Heaf and . . . N. Lloyd Rusby . . . Fourth edition, *etc.* pp. vi. 290. *J. & A. Churchill: London,* 1948. 8°. [*Recent Advances Series.*] **7442. p. 1/112.**

A later edition is entered under HEAF *(Frederick R. G.) and* RUSBY *(N. L.)*

BURRELL (LANCELOT STEPHEN TOPHAM) and **MAC NALTY** (*Sir* ARTHUR SALUSBURY) *K.C.B.*

—— Report on Artificial Pneumothorax. pp. 104. pl. XVII. *London,* 1922. 8°. [*Medical Research Council. Special Report Series.* no. 67.] B.S. **25/8.**

BURRELL (MARTIN) Betwixt Heaven and Charing Cross. (Articles on literature.) pp. x. 328. *Macmillan Co. of Canada: Toronto*, 1928. 8°. **012350. ee. 44.**

—— Crumbs are also Bread. [Essays, for the most part on English literature.] pp. ix. 340. *Macmillan Co. of Canada: Toronto*, 1934. 8°. **11856. bb. 39.**

—— Fruit Raising in British Columbia. *See* BRITTAIN (John) Elementary Agriculture and Nature Study, *etc.* [1909.] 8°. **7074. f. 32.**

BURRELL (MARY) *Hon. Mrs. Willoughby Burrell.* Richard Wagner: his life and works from 1813 to 1834. Compiled from original letters, manuscripts & other documents . . . Illustrated with portraits & facsimilies. pp. cxxix. *Allan Wyon: [London,]* 1898. fol. Cup. **645. b. 1.**
Engraved throughout. No. 11 *of an edition of* 100 *copies.*

—— [Another copy.] Richard Wagner: his life and works, from 1813 to 1834, *etc.* [*London,*] 1898. fol. Hirsch **5219.**
No. 54 *of an edition of* 100 *copies.*

—— Thoughts for Enthusiasts at Bayreuth. Collected in memory of 1882 and 1883. [With plates, including portraits, and maps.] 3 pt.

Chapter I. Historical and Antiquarian.
Chapter II. Frédérique Sophie Wilhelmine de Prusse, Margrave de Bareith, Sœur de Frédéric-le-Grand.
Chapter IV. Unpublished Journal "Voyage d'Italie" and sixty unpublished letters of the Margravine of Bayreuth to Frederick the Great, together with sixteen unpublished letters from the King to the Margravine.

Pickering & Chatto: London, 1888–91. fol. **L.R. 41. b. 11.**
Chapter III *was never issued. Chapter* IV *was privately printed at the Chiswick Press, London.*

—— Catalogue of the Burrell Collection of Wagner Documents, Letters, and other biographical material. [Compiled by Peter E. Wright.] pp. xi. 99. *Nonpareil Press: London*, 1929. 8°. **11907. c. 31.**

—— [Another copy.] Catalogue of the Burrell Collection of Wagner Documents, *etc.* [By Peter E. Wright.] *London*, 1929. 8°. Hirsch **427.**

BURRELL (*Sir* MERRIK RAYMOND) *Bart.*

—— Hints on the Breeding and Management of Light Horses. pp. vi. 43. *Horace Cox: London*, 1913. 8°. **7294. df. 40.**

—— [Another edition.] Light Horses: their breeding and management . . . Second edition. pp. 47. *Field Press: London*, [1927.] 8°. **07294. e. 72.**

—— [A reissue.] *London*, [1934.] 8°. **07295. a. 53.**

—— Light Horses: their breeding and management . . . Third edition. pp. 47. *National Horse Association of Great Britain: London*, 1946. 8°. **7295. aaa. 67.**

—— Light Horses . . . Fourth edition. pp. 48. *British Horse Society: London*, 1953. 8°. **07295. k. 81.**

BURRELL (OLIVE)

—— The Bottle Book . . . Illustrated by Rowland Lindup. pp. 16. *Hope Press: London*, [1953.] 8°. **8436. ee. 45.**

BURRELL (ORIN KAY)

—— An Experiment in Speculative Behavior. pp. 48. [*Eugene,*] 1950. 8°. [*University of Oregon. School of Business Administration. Bureau of Business Research Pamphlets.*] Ac. **1789. /16. (11.)**

BURRELL (ORIN KAY)

—— A Study in Investment Mortality. pp. 56. [*Eugene,*] 1947. 8°. [*University of Oregon. School of Business Administration. Bureau of Business Research. Pamphlets.*] Ac. **1789/16. (10.)**

BURRELL (PERCIVAL) Sutton's Synagogue, or, the English Centurion: shewing the vnparrallelled bounty of Protestant piety. pp. 25. *T. C. [Thomas Cotes] for Ralph Mabb: London*, 1629. 4°. **693. f. 5. (3.)**
The pagination is irregular, the last four numbered pages being pp. 24, 25, 24, 25.

—— [Another copy, with a different titlepage bearing no date.] **491. c. 38.**

BURRELL (PETER) *Baron Gwydyr.* A Catalogue of the . . . Collection of Italian, French, Flemish, Dutch, and English Pictures, and a few casts from the antique, of the late Right Hon. Lord Gwydir . . . which will be sold by auction, by Mr. Christie . . . May the 8th, 1829, *etc.* pp. 15. MS. NOTES OF PRICES. [*London*, 1829.] 4°. **7855. h. 41. (25.)**

BURRELL (PETER ROBERT DRUMMOND) *Baron Willoughby de Eresby.* Ploughing by Steam. [Plans, with an explanation.] *J. Ridgway: London*, 1850. 4°. **7028. f. 6.**

BURRELL (PHILIPPA)

—— He was like a Continent. Being the tragedy of Paul Fingen. A satire in three acts, *etc.* pp. 80. *Adam Press: [London,]* 1947. 8°. **11783. ff. 3.**

—— The Wind and the Mill. A play in three acts. pp. 62. *F. & P. Piggott: Cambridge*, [1935.] 8°. **11780. b. 23.**

BURRELL (RANDALL CLAYFORD) *See* TOWNELEY PLAYS. The Towneley Play. Adapted by R. C. Burrell, *etc.* 1928. 8°. [ROBINSON (*Donald F.*) *Harvard Dramatic Club Miracle Plays.*] **11771. ddd. 7.**

BURRELL (ROBIN CHARLES) Chemistry for Students of Agriculture and Home Economics. pp. xviii. 459. *McGraw-Hill Book Co.: New York & London*, 1931. 8°. [*International Chemical Series.*] **8711. c. 1/55.**

—— Organic Chemistry. pp. xii. 331. *New York & London*, 1936. 8°. [*McGraw-Hill Euthenics Series.*] **12213.gg.4/11.**

BURRELL (SOPHIA) *Lady.* *See* CORNEILLE (T.) Maximian; a tragedy: taken from Corneille [by Lady Burrell], *etc.* 1800. 8°. **164. g. 53.**

—— Poems. 2 vol. *Leigh & Sotheby: London*, 1793. 8°. **11642. e. 23**
Vol. 2 *only contains the author's name.*

—— A Search after Perfection. A comedy in five acts. [By Lady Burrell.] 1814. 8°. [*New British Theatre.* vol. 3.] *See* SEARCH. **642. i. 3.**

—— Telemachus. [A poem based on the work of Fénelon.] pp. 78. *Leigh & Sotheby: London*, 1794. 8°. **11642. e. 36. (2.)**

—— Theodora; or, the Spanish daughter: a tragedy. [By Lady Burrell.] pp. vii. 100. 1800. 8°. *See* THEODORA. **164. i. 19.**

—— [Another edition.] 1814. 8°. [*New British Theatre.* vol. 1.] *See* THEODORA. **642. i. 1.**

BURRELL (Sophia) *Lady.*

—— The Thymbriad, from Xenophon's Cyropoedia [*sic*]. [A poem.] pp. 154. *Leigh & Sotheby: London,* 1794. 8°. **11632**. f. 9.

—— [Another copy.] **11642**. e. **36**. (**1**.)

—— Villario; a play, in five acts. [By Lady Burrell.] 1814. 8°. [*New British Theatre.* vol. 2.] *See* Villario. **642**. i. **2**.

BURRELL (W. S.) and **CUTHELL** (Edith E.) Indian Memories. By W. S. Burrell and E. E. Cuthell [or rather, by E. E. Cuthell]. pp. viii. 304. *R. Bentley & Son: London,* 1893. 8°. **010057**. e. **23**.

BURRELL (Walter) [Electoral addresses.] *See* Sussex Election. An Account of the Sussex election, *etc.* [1820.] 8°. **8135**. f. **32**.

BURRELL (Walter) and **CURTEIS** (Edward Jeremiah)

—— [Joint electoral addresses.] *See* Sussex Elections. An Account of the Sussex Elections, *etc.* [1820.] 8°. **8135**. f. **32**.

BURRELL (*Sir* William) *Bart.* *See* England.—*Court of Admiralty.* Reports of Cases determined by the High Court of Admiralty and upon appeal therefrom . . . 1758–1774. By Sir W. Burrell, *etc.* 1885. 8°. **6835**. ee. **8**.

—— *See* Lamb (Edward B.) Studies of Ancient Domestic Architecture, principally selected from original drawings in the collection of the late Sir William Burrell, *etc.* 1846. fol. **7815**. e. **32**.

—— A Catalogue of the Town-Library of the late Sir William Burrell . . . Which will be sold by auction . . . May 2. 1796, and the four following days, *etc.* pp. 54. [*London,* 1796.] 8°. **269**. c. **5**.

BURRELL (*Sir* William) *Trustee of the National Gallery of Scotland.*

—— French Paintings of the Nineteenth Century from the Burrell Collection. [A catalogue. With reproductions.] pp. 27. pl. viii. *Arts Council of Great Britain: [London,]* 1950. 8°. W.P. **12368/154**.

—— Loan Exhibition of the Burrell Collection, 1924. pp. 16. 1924. 8°. *See* London.—iii. *Tate Gallery.* **7960**. b. **49**.

—— Sussex Views, selected from the Burrell Collections. Being the Jubilee volume of the Sussex Record Society. Edited by . . . Walter H. Godfrey . . . and L. F. Salzman. pp. xviii. pl. 191. 1951. 8°. *See* Lewes.—*Sussex Record Society.* Ac. **8093/3**.

BURREN (F.) and **GREGORY** (G. R.) Moulds for Cast Stone and Concrete. pp. 79. *Concrete Publications: London,* [1930.] *obl.* 8°. [*Concrete Series.*] W.P. **6685/4**.

BURRENCHOBAY (M.)

—— A Guide for use by Committees of Co-operative Credit Societies, of unlimited liability type. pp. 13. *Modern Printing: Port-Louis,* [1951.] 8°. **8232**. a. **114**.

—— A Short Account of the Co-operation Credit Societies Movement in Mauritius, and the legislation by which it is controlled. Compiled by M. Burrenchobay. pp. xii. 115. 1944. 8°. *See* Mauritius, *Island of.*—*Department of Agriculture.* **8289**. e. **2**.

BURRES (Lorentz) Ein new Wundtartzney Buchlein, *etc.* *See* Ociorus, otherwise Schnellenberg (T.) Artzneybuch, *etc.* 1556. 4°. **545**. e. **2**.

BURRESI (Pietro) *See* Periodical Publications.—*Florence.* Lo Sperimentale . . . Diretto e compilato da C. Ghinozzi, P. Burresi, *etc.* 1871. 8°. P.P. **2923**. ha.

—— Sulle virtù terapeutiche delle acque termominerali di Chianciano. Brevi cenni. pp. 21. *Siena,* 1874. 8°. **7462**. g. **5**. (**8**.)

BURRET (J. P.) Essai sur l'exomphale que les enfans portent en venant au monde, suivi de propositions sur l'affection typhoïde; thèse, *etc.* pp. 28. *Paris,* 1833. 4°. **1184**. e. **15**. (**14**.)

BURRET (M.) Palmae Cubenses et Domingenses a Cl. E. L. Ekman 1914–1928 lectae, *etc.* pp. 28. pl. 14. *Stockholm,* 1929. 4°. [*Kungl. Svenska Vetenskapsakademiens handlingar.* ser. 3. bd. 6. no. 7.] Ac. **1070**.

BURRHUS (Franciscus Josephus) *See* Borro (Giuseppe F.)

BURRHUS (Joannes) *See* Burroughs (*Sir* John)

BURRI (Adolf) Johann Rudolf Sinner von Ballaigues, 1730–1787. Ein Beitrag zur Kultur- und Geistesgeschichte des 18. Jahrhunderts . . . Mit einem Porträt, *etc.* pp. 200. *Bern,* 1913. 8°. **010706**. f. **34**.

BURRI (Angiolo) Dei diritti delle donne secondo il Codice civile del regno d'Italia. *Firenze,* 1869. 8°. **5357**. e. **2**. *Imperfect; wanting all after p.* 128.

BURRI (Antonio) Il Lavoro. Studio sociale. pp. 152. *Roma,* 1888. 8°. **8277**. g. **44**.

—— Le Teorie politiche di San Tommaso e il moderno diritto pubblico. pp. 157. *Roma,* 1884. 8°. **3832**. d. **4**.

BURRI (Friedrich) Die einstige Reichsfeste Grasburg. Geschichte, Rekonstruktion, Einkünfte. [With illustrations.] *Bern,* 1935. 8°. [*Archiv des Historischen Vereins des Kantons Bern.* Bd. 33. Hft. 1.] Ac. **6926**.

—— Grasburg unter savoyischer Herrschaft. (Die Grasburg. Ihre Baugeschichte und ihr einstiges Bild.) 3 pt. 1906, 12. *See* Berne.—*Historischer Verein des Kantons Bern.* Archiv, *etc.* Bd. 18. Hft. 2; Bd. 20. Hft. 1, 2. 1855, *etc.* 8°. Ac. **6926**.

BURRI (Giovanni Battista) Assalonne. Azione sacra da cantarsi nell'oratorio de' RR. padri della Congregazione dell'Oratorio di Roma. pp. 15. *Roma,* 1825. 8°. **11715**. ee. **2**. (**6**.)

BURRI (Romolo) Le Commissioni tecniche istituite in Roma dal Governo italiano. pp. 184. *Roma,* 1874. 8°. **8777**. d. **2**.

BURRIDGE (Arthur F.) Life Assurance—an Investment. A dialogue. pp. 7. [*London,* 1886.] 12°. **8248**. cc. **8**. (**5**.)

BURRIDGE (Brainerd Marc) Robert Browning as an exponent of a philosophy of life. [With an introductory letter by E. Berdoe.] pp. viii. 55. *Book Shop: Cleveland,* 1893. 8°. **011850**. i. **24**.

BURRIDGE (Ezekiel) Historia nuperæ rerum mutationis in Anglia: in quâ res à Jacobo Rege contra leges Angliæ, & Europæ libertatem, & ab ordinibus Angliæ contra regem patratæ . . . recensentur. pp. 316. *J. H. impensis A. & J. Churchill: Londini,* 1697. 8°. **808**. g. **6**.

—— [Another copy.] G. **15513**.

BURRIDGE (Ezekiel)

—— A Short View of the Present State of Ireland: with regard particularly to the difficultys a Chief Governor will meet with there in holding of a Parliament. Written in the year 1700. [With an anonymous introductory letter on the Irish situation.] pp. 24. [*London?*] 1708. 4°. **8146. b. 37.**

BURRIDGE (Florence) *See* New Car, *pseud.* [i.e. J. A. Burridge and F. Burridge.]

BURRIDGE (Frank H. A.)

—— Southern Locomotive Spotting Chart, *etc.* [Compiled by F. H. A. Burridge.] *Ian Allan: London,* [1947.] 4°. **8768. dd. 31.**

—— Streamlining the Southern Railway, *etc.* [With diagrams.] *F. H. A. Burridge: Boscombe,* 1945. 16°. **08766. a. 66.**

Reproduced from manuscript.

BURRIDGE (Frederick Vango) *See* Hutchinson (Henry N.) Primeval Scenes . . . Illustrated by J. Hassall and F. V. Burridge. 1899. *obl.* 4°. **12809. s. 11.**

—— Education in Art in relation to Handicraft and Manufacture. An address, *etc.* pp. 19. *L.C.C. Central School of Arts and Crafts:* [*London,*] 1914. 4°. **L.R.404.m.19.**

—— The Little Craft Books. Edited by F. V. Burridge. 4 vol *Oxford University Press: London,* 1929-37. 4°. **07941.w.15.**

BURRIDGE (Henry Alfred) An Introduction to Forensic Medicine, *etc.* pp. xvi. 455. *H. K. Lewis & Co.: London,* 1924. 8°. **6095. dh. 5.**

BURRIDGE (John) Britannia's Protest against the Destruction of old England's Wooden Walls, by the Naval Dry Rot . . . in circulars to the British Fleet, Navy Boards, *etc.* pp. 15. *Ridgway & Son: London,* 1824. 8°. **533. d. 29. (2.)**

—— The Budget of Truth: relative to the present aspect of affairs in the religious and the political world, especially to the existing state of Christendom. To which are added observations on the restoration of the Jews, and "the Holy Alliance," *etc.* pp. xxii. 208. *Printed for the Author: London,* 1830. 8°. **1114. g. 18. (3.)**

—— [Another issue.] *London,* [1830.] 8°. **3185. d. 2. (2.)**
Imperfect; wanting the titlepage.

—— Improvements in Civil Architecture; proving the necessity . . . of a perfect system of ventilation, to render wood equally durable as walls, by new, cheap and simple methods, *etc.* pp. 50. *Priestley & Weale: London,* 1825. 8°. **07815. aa. 40.**

—— Kingcraft and Priestcraft, or, "the Mystery of Iniquity," dethroned, defeated, and destroyed, in the grand battle of Armageddon; being a church and state oracle, exposing the . . . fate of Christendom . . . Also an exposé of the Bishop of Winchester's job of £16,800, for mudlands near Gosport . . . By the author of The Budget of Truth (J. Burridge). pp. 36. *John Chappell: London,* 1830. 8°. **4108. f. 18. (2.)**

—— The Naval Dry Rot. An address . . . containing most important discoveries, and an answer to Sir Robert Seppings, and Mr. John Knowles . . . With a treatise on the . . . naval dry rot; and various remedies, by native substitutes for oak bark, *etc.* pp. xxvi. 136. *Ridgway & the Author: London,* 1824. 8°. **533. d. 29. (1.)**

BURRIDGE (John)

—— The Tanner's Key to a New System of Tanning So Leather, or the Right use of oak bark, *etc.* pp. xxiii. 13 *C. F. Cock: London,* 1824. 12°. **1043. c. 1**

—— [Another copy.] **1043. c. 1**

BURRIDGE (John Arthur) *See* New Car, *pseud.* [i. J. A. Burridge and F. Burridge.]

BURRIDGE (John Doble) A Concise and Imparti Essay on the British Constitution, blended with the la relating to landed property and the personal liberty of t subject . . . With a few . . . remarks . . . touching election the close borough system, and right of petition, *et* pp. 129. *E. Peall: London,* 1819. 8°. **522. i. 1**

—— A Narrative of an Interesting Trial at Law (J. D. Bu ridge, Gent . . . Plaintiff versus John D-yton . . Defendant) . . . with hints to the Whigs on the clo borough system. Second edition. pp. 78. *Printed f the Author: Southampton,* 1821. 8°. **8132. ee. 8. (**

BURRIDGE (Joseph Henry) God's Prophetic Plan. comprehensive view of God's dealings with man fro creation to the new heavens and new earth, *etc.* pp. xxii. 300. *Old Gospel Press: Birmingham,* [1930.] 8 **03187. ee. 6**

—— Near Eastern Politics and the Bible. Science, creati and revelation. pp. 152. *Old Gospel Press: Birmingha* [1930.] 8°. **03187. g. 5**

BURRIDGE (L. W.) *See* Bonnell (David G. R.) a Burridge (L. W.) The Prevention of Pattern Staining Plasters. 1931. 8°. [*Building Research Board. Bullet* no. 10.] **B.S. 38. a**

—— Reinforced Brickwork. pp. 13. 1937. 4°. *See* Londc —iii. *Clay Products Technical Bureau of Great Britain.* **7943. w.**

BURRIDGE (Richard) *See* Locke (John) *the Philosoph* [*Essay concerning Human Understanding.*] De intelle humano . . . nunc primum Latine reddita [by R. B ridge]. 1701. fol. **8406. i.**

—— —— 1709. 8°. **8403. f.**

—— *See* Lorrain (Paul) Popery near a-Kin to Pagani and Atheism . . . Set forth in a sermon . . . upon extraordinary occasion, viz. that of the abjuration . of the errors of the Church of Rome . . . made by Roman-Catholick (R. Burridge), *etc.* 1712. 8°. **693. e. 2.**

—— The Apostate Prince: or, a Satyr against the King Poland. [In verse.] pp. 16. *London,* 1700. fol. **1346. m.**

—— The Consolation of Death. As it was presented to Highness, the Princess Ann of Denmark: on the immat loss of William, late Duke of Gloucester. pp. 30. *William Pinnocke: London,* 1700. 8°. **1418. b.**

—— Hell in an Uproar, occasioned by a scuffle that happe between the lawyers and the physicians, for superior A satyr. [In verse. By R. Burridge.] pp. 16. 1700. fol. *See* Hell. **777. k. 16. (**

—— [Another edition.] pp. 15. 1725. 8°. *See* Hell. **993. e. 49.**

—— A New Review of London. Being an exact survey . of every street, lane, court . . . and all places . . . wi the Cities . . . or suburbs of London, Westminster, the Borough of Southwark . . . With the rates of domes and foreign letters, *etc.* pp. 40. *J. Roberts: Lon* 1722. 8°. **10349. bb.**

BURRIDGE (RICHARD)

—— Religio Libertini: or, the Faith of a converted atheist. Occasionally set forth by Mr. R. Burridge, who was lately convicted of blasphemy . . . To which is prefixed a narration of his life . . . an account of what pass'd on his tryal . . . with an abjuration and recantation, *etc.* pp. 80. *Sam. Briscoe: London,* 1712. 8°. **4016.** aaa. **12.**

—— The Shoe-Maker beyond his Last: or, a Satyr upon scurrilous poets, especially Ned W - - - - d [i.e. N. Ward], author of a poem intituled, A Journey to Hell: or, a Visit paid to the Devil. [By R. Burridge.] pp. 16. 1700. fol. *See* SHOEMAKER. **1346.** m. **46.**

BURRIDGE (SEATON) Artie Neney: a fairy tale for young and old. pp. 71. *F. D. Biddle: Newport, Mon.,* 1909. 8°. **12411.** bbb. **16.**

BURRIDGE (WILLIAM) *Professor of Physiology at Lucknow University.*

—— Alcohol and Anaesthesia. pp. 65. *Williams & Norgate: London,* 1934. 8°. **7440.** p. **32.**

—— Excitability. A cardiac study. pp. ix. 208. *Oxford University Press: London,* 1932. 8°. [*Oxford Medical Publications.*] **20036.a.1/361.**

—— A New Physiological Psychology, *etc.* pp. vii. 158. *E. Arnold & Co.: London,* 1933. 8°. **08465.** de. **40**

—— A New Physiology of Sensation, based on a study of cardiac action. pp. vi. 70. *Oxford University Press: London,* 1932. 8°. [*Oxford Medical Publications.*] **20036.a.1/360.**

BURRIEL (ANDRÉS MARCOS) *See* FREIRE (F. J.) Elogio de . . . Don Francisco de Almeida Mascareñas . . . Traducido . . . por un singular venerador de su Excellencia [i.e. A. M. Burriel]. 1746. 4°. **272.** g. **26.** (**11.**)

—— *See* SAINZ Y RODRÍGUEZ (P.) El P. Burriel, paleógrafo. 1926. 8°. **10634.** a. **19.**

—— *See* VENEGAS (M.) Noticia de la California, y de su conquista . . . Sacada de la historia manuscrita . . . por el padre M. Venegas . . . y de otras noticias, y relaciones antiguas, y modernas. Añadida de algunos mapas, *etc.* [Edited by A. M. Burriel.] 1757. 4°. **978.** i. **23.**

—— *See* VENEGAS (M.) A Natural and Civil History of California . . . Translated from the original Spanish [edited by A. M. Burriel], *etc.* 1759. 8°. **978.** i. **26, 27.**

—— *See* VENEGAS (M.) Natuurlyke en burgerlyke historie van California . . . Uit het oorsprongkelyk Spaans [edited by A. M. Burriel] . . . vertaald, *etc.* 1777. 8°. **9605.** cc. **26.**

—— *See* VENEGAS (M.) Histoire naturelle et civile de la Californie, *etc.* [Translated into French from the English translation of "Noticia de la California," edited by A. M. Burriel.] 1767. 12°. **978.** a. **30.**

—— Cartas . . . escritas sobre diferentes asuntos literarios. [Edited by A. Valladares de Sotomayor.] 2 pt. *Madrid,* 1788. 4°. [*Semanario Erudito.* tom. 2.] **248.** k. **7.**
There have been substituted for pp. 71–128 *pp.* 3–222 *of tom.* 16 *and pp.* 231–238 *of tom.* 17, *containing a corrected text.*

—— [Another edition.] Cartas Eruditas y Críticas. pp. 288. [*Madrid,* 1790?] 4°. **1060.** i. **32.**
Pp. 3–222 *are duplicates of those in the preceding edition.*

BURRIEL (ANDRÉS MARCOS)

—— Correspondencia que tuvo . . . A. M. Burriel con varias personas sobre la comision que le dió el Gobierno de examinar los archivos de Toledo, junto con otros papeles en que se da noticia de igual exámen de diferentes archivos del reino. 1848. *See* FERNÁNDEZ DE NAVARRETE (M.) Colección de Documentos, *etc.* tom. 13. 1842, *etc.* 8°. **9195.** ccc.

—— Informe de la Imperial Ciudad de Toledo al Real y Supremo Consejo de Castilla, sobre igualacion de pesos y medidas en todos los reynos . . . de Su Magestad, *etc.* [By A. M. Burriel.] pp. 394. 1780. 4°. *See* TOLEDO. **812.** e. **27.**

BURRIEL (ANTONIO) *Ayudante General.* Batalla de la Albuhera (ganada sobre los Franceses mandados por Soult el dia 16 de mayo de 1811, por el exercito aliado español, ingles y portugues). [An account of the battle with reports from divisional commanders and casualty lists. Preceded by a letter from General Joaquin Blake.] pp. 49. pl. II. *Cadiz,* [1811.] 4°. **9180.** d. **28.** (**1.**)

BURRIEL (ANTONIO) *Jesuit.* Vita di Caterina Sforza Riario Contessa d'Imola e Signora di Forli, *etc.* [With a portrait.] 3 tom. pp. xxxii. 861. xci. *Bologna,* 1795. 4°. **1448.** k. **18.**

BURRIEL ALBEROLA (FÉLIX) Viajes Marítimos. Las costas de España y Portugal. pp. 182. *Zaragoza,* 1903. 8°. **10162.** g. **18.**

BURRILL, *Family of. See* BURRILL (Ellen M.) The Burrill Family of Lynn during the Colonial and Provincial Periods, with some of their descendants, *etc.* [1907.] 8°. **9906.** ee. **36.** (**1.**)

BURRILL (ALEXANDER MANSFIELD) A New Law Dictionary and Glossary: containing full definitions of the principal terms of the common and civil law, together with translations and explanations of the various technical phrases in different languages . . . embracing also all the principal common and civil law maxims. Compiled on the basis of Spelman's glossary, and adapted to the jurisprudence of the United States, *etc.* pp. xviii. 1099. *J. H. Voorhies: New York,* 1850, 51. 8°. **06616.** g. **1.**

—— Second edition. 2 vol. *J. S. Voorhies: New York,* 1859, 60. 8°. **1384.** i. **15.**

—— A Treatise on the Law and Practice of Voluntary Assignments for the benefit of creditors; with an appendix of forms . . . Second edition. pp. xxviii. 692. *J. S. Voorhies: New York,* 1858. 8°. **6617.** f. **13.**

—— Third edition. Revised and enlarged by James L. Bishop. pp. xl. 751. *Baker, Voorhis & Co.: New York,* 1877. 8°. **6625.** s. **6.**

—— A Treatise on the Nature, Principles and Rules of Circumstantial Evidence, especially that of the presumptive kind, in criminal cases. pp. xxi. 706. *J. S. Voorhies: New York,* 1856. 8°. **6625.** cc. **8.**

BURRILL (ELLEN MUDGE) The Burrill Family of Lynn during the Colonial and Provincial Periods, with some of their descendants . . . A paper read before the Lynn Historical Society, *etc.* pp. 54. *Lynn, Mass.,* [1907.] 8°. **9906.** ee. **36.** (**1.**)

—— Our Church and the People who made it. *See* LYNN, *Massachusetts.—First Universalist Parish.* The First Universalist Parish of Lynn, *etc.* 1908. 8°. **4745.** g. **6.** (**8.**)

—— The State House, Boston, Massachusetts. pp. 66. 1901. 16°. *See* MASSACHUSETTS. [*Miscellaneous Public Documents, etc.*] **10412.** aa. **36.**

BURRILL (ELLEN MUDGE)

—— Eighth edition. pp. 166. viii. 1924. 8°. *See* MASSACHUSETTS. [*Miscellaneous Public Documents, etc.*] **010409.** eee. **43.**

BURRILL (HARRY R.) Report on Trade Conditions in Australasia. pp. 48. *Washington,* 1908. 8°. [*Special Agents' Series.* no. 17.] A.S. **130.**

BURRILL (HARRY R.) and **CRIST** (RAYMOND FOWLER)

—— Report on Trade Conditions in China. pp. 130. *Washington,* 1906. 8°. [*Special Agents' Series.* no. 7.] A.S. **130.**

BURRILL (JAMES) *See* ARNOLD (Josias L.) Poems, *etc.* [Edited by J. Burrill.] 1797. 12°. **11633.** b. **3.**

BURRILL (KATHARINE) Corner Stones. [Essays.] pp. 227. *J. M. Dent & Co.: London,* 1904. 8°. **012356.** l. **49.**

—— Loose Beads. [Essays.] pp. 223. *J. M. Dent & Co.: London,* 1906. 8°. **12357.** df. **33.**

—— Little Foxes . . . Illustrated by H. C. Preston Macgoun. [An essay. Reprinted from "Loose Beads."] pp. viii. 22. *T. N. Foulis: London & Edinburgh,* 1907. 8°. **04410.** g. **72.**

—— Shell Gatherers. [Essays.] pp. vii. 219. *J. M. Dent & Co.: London,* 1905. 8°. **12355.** ee. **29.**

BURRILL (KATHARINE) and **BOOTH** (ANNIE M.)

—— The Amateur Cook . . . Illustrated by Mabel L. Attwell. pp. iv. 296. *W. & R. Chambers: London & Edinburgh,* [1905.] 8°. **07943.** f. **70.**

BURRILL (LENNARD CONSTANTINE)

—— Propeller Cavitation: the physical mechanism and effects on ship performance . . . Being the Watt Anniversary Lecture for 1955, *etc.* [With plates.] pp. 16. *Greenock,* 1955. 8°. [*Papers of the Greenock Philosophical Society.*] Ac. **1495.** **(34.)**

BURRILL (THOMAS JONATHAN) and **HANSEN** (ROY) Is Symbiosis possible between Legume Bacteria and Non-legume Plants? *Urbana,* 1917. 8°. [*University of Illinois Agricultural Experiment Station. Bulletin.* no. 202.] **A.S.i.22/2.**

BURRINGTON (EDWIN HENRY) Revelations of the Beautiful: and other poems. pp. xi. 222. *William Pickering: London,* 1848. 12°. **11645.** e. **25.**

BURRINGTON (GEORGE) *See* HAYWOOD (Marshall D.) Governor George Burrington, with an account of his official administration in the Colony of North Carolina, *etc.* 1896. 8°. **10880.** f. 24. **(8.)**

—— An Answer to Dr. William Brakenridge's Letter concerning the number of inhabitants, within the London bills of mortality. Wherein the doctor's letter is inserted . . . his arguments proved inconclusive, and the number of inhabitants increasing. pp. 40. *J. Scott: London,* 1757. 8°. **1137.** i. **27.** **(5.)**

—— [Another issue.] **796.** e. 8. **(1.)**

—— Seasonable Considerations on the Expediency of a War with France . . . To which are added a postscript, on the list of the French army, a short comparison, between the British and French Dominions; and a state of the French revenues, and forces in the year, 1701. pp. 60. *F. Cogan: London,* 1743. 8°. **101.** g. **64.**

BURRINGTON (GILBERT) An Arrangement of the Genealogies in the Old Testament and Apocrypha, to which are added . . . a selection of single names, and chronological tables of the kings of Egypt, Syria, and Assyria; with notes, *etc.* [With a portrait.] 2 vol. *C. & J. Rivington: London; W. Strong: Bristol & Exeter,* 1836. 4°. **3166.** g. **31.**

BURRINGTON (JOHN) The Case of Sir Bouchier Wrey Baronet, an Infant, by J. Burrington Esq; his guardian; and of Charles Allanson Esq.; John Evans and Hugh Evans gentlemen; lately referred to the Committee of Privileges . . . of the . . . House of Commons. [1696.] *s. sh.* fol. **1888.** c. **11.** **(26.)**

BURRIQUI (HORATIUS) Calhabeidos Liber. *See* LATIN-PORTUGUESE MACARONICS. Macarronea Latino-Portugueza, *etc.* 1765. 8°. C. **46.** b. **19.**

BURRIS (F. H.) The Trinity . . . With an introduction by Professor Joseph Haven. pp. xxvii. 216. *S. C. Griggs & Co.: Chicago,* 1874. 8°. **4224.** bb. **34.**

BURRIS (GEORGE P.) *See* NORIE (John W.) Norie's Nautical Tables . . . Rearranged and . . . extended under the direction of Captain G. P. Burris, *etc.* 1938. 8°. **8803.** cc. **2.**

—— *See* NORIE (John W.) Norie's Nautical Tables . . . Arranged under the direction of Captain G. P. Burris, *etc.* (Abridged edition.) 1938. 8°. **8803.** cc. **3.**

BURRIS (QUINCY GUY) Richard Doddridge Blackmore: his life and novels. pp. 219. *Urbana,* 1930. 8°. [*University of Illinois Studies in Language and Literature.* vol. 15. no. 4.] Ac. **2692.** u/**15.**

BURRISH (GEORGE) *See* PAGE (Henry) The Trials at Large . . . held upon H. Page, C. Davids . . . also upon Capt. G. Burrish, *etc.* 1745. 8°. **518.** e. **17.** **(6.)**

—— The Case of Capt. George Burrish, late Commander of His Majesty's Ship the Dorsetshire. [By G. Burrish.] pp. 48. *J. Shuckburgh: London,* 1747. 8°. **1416.** d. **54.**

—— Copies of all the Minutes and Proceedings taken . . upon the several tryals of Captain George Burrish, Captain Edmund Williams, Captain John Ambrose, Lieutenant H. Page, Lieutenant C. Davids, Lieutenant W. Griffiths; and Lieutenant C. Smelt, respectively: before the Court Martial lately held at Chatham, *etc.* 3 pt. [*London,*] 1746. fol. **516.** m. **14.**

BURRISH (ONSLOW) Batavia Illustrata, or a View of the policy and commerce of the United Provinces: particularly of Holland. With an enquiry into the alliances of the States General, with the Emperor, France, Spain, and Great Britain. 2 vol. pp. v. 580. *William Innys: London,* 1728. 8°. **572.** c. **7, 8.**

—— Second edition. 2 vol. pp. v. 580. *W. Innys: London,* 1731. 8°. **794.** e. **24.**

BURRIS-MEYER (ELIZABETH) *See* MEYER.

BURRIS-MEYER (HAROLD) *See* MEYER.

BURRISS (CHARLES WALKER) Panama. A guide to the Pacific coast from Panama to San Francisco in picture and word. pp. 144. *C. W. Burriss: Kansas City,* 1912. 8°. **10481.** r. **7.** **(3.)**

BURRISS (ELI EDWARD) Taboo, Magic, Spirits. A study of primitive elements in Roman religion. pp. x. 250. *Macmillan Co.: New York,* 1931. 8°. **04504.** ee. **63.**

BURRITT (Arthur Winfield) Profit Sharing: its principles and practice. A collaboration by A. W. Burritt . . . Henry S. Dennison [and others], *etc.* pp. x. 328. *Harper & Bros.: New York & London,* 1918. 8°. **08285.** bbb. **45.**

—— *See* James (Gorton) Profit Sharing and Stock Ownership for Employees. By G. James . . . A. W. Burritt. [Based upon "Profit Sharing: its principles and practice," by A. W. Burritt and others.] 1926. 8°. **08286.** aaa. **20.**

BURRITT (Bailey Barton) Professional Distribution of College and University Graduates. pp. 147. *Washington,* 1912. 8°. [*U.S. Bureau of Education. Bulletin.* 1912. no. 19.] A.S. **202.**

BURRITT (Charles H.) The Coal Measures of the Philippines. A rapid history of the discovery of coal in the archipelago and subsequent developments, *etc.* (Report to the U.S. Military Governor in the Philippines.) [With maps and plans.] pp. 269. 1901. 8°. *See* United States of America.—*Bureau of Insular Affairs.* A.S. **639/2.**

BURRITT (Edwin C.) *pseud.* [i.e. Ethel Claire Brill.] *See* also Brill (E. C.)

—— Cameron Island. Adventures in the South Seas, *etc.* pp. 255. *Oliphants: London, Edinburgh; printed in U.S.A.,* [1919.] 8°. **12802.** bb. **7.**

BURRITT (Elihu) *See* Bible.—*Selections.* [*English.*] The Children of the Bible. Compiled by E. Burritt. 1872. 16°. **4805.** aa. **6.**

—— *See* Bible.—*Psalms.—Selections.* [*English.*] Prayers and Devotional Meditations, collated from the Psalms . . . By E. Burritt. 1870. 8°. **3090.** bb. **42.**

—— *See* Dyer (Alfred S.) A Hero from the Forge: a biographical sketch of E. Burritt. [1879.] 8°. **10803.** aa. **2. (8.)**

—— —— [1882.] 8°. [*Six Men of the People.*] **10803.** aa. **6. (2.)**

—— *See* Hopkins (Jane E.) An English Woman's Work among Workingmen . . . With an introduction by E. Burritt. 1875. 12°. **4192.** bbb. **3.**

—— *See* Kirton (John W.) Dr. Guthrie . . . Elihu Burritt. *etc.* [With a portrait.] 1885. 8°. **10601.** bbb. **27.**

—— *See* Periodical Publications.—*London.* Bond of Brotherhood. Conducted by E. Burritt. (Fire-side Words, by E. Burritt.) 1854, *etc.* 8°. P.P. **1126.** b.

—— *See* Stowe (Harriet E. B.) Uncle Tom's Cabin . . . With an introduction by E. Burritt, *etc.* 1852. 8°. **12705.** k. **24.**

—— *See* Stowe (Harriet E. B.) Onkel Tom's Hütte . . . Mit . . . einer Vorrede von E. Burritt, *etc.* 1853. 8°. **12705.** c. **8.**

—— *See* United States of America.—*American Peace Society.* The Advocate of Peace. [vol. 6. no. 9–12: New series vol. 1. no. 1–8 edited by E. Burritt.] 1837, *etc.* 8°. P.P. **1127.** b.

—— *See* Washington (George) *President of the United States of America.* Washington's Words to intending English Emigrants to America. With introduction and appendix [containing a description of the various States] by E. Burritt. 1870. 8°. **8282.** aa. **37.**

—— The Learned Blacksmith. The letters and journals of Elihu Burritt. By Merle Curti. [With a portrait.] pp. ix. 241. *Wilson-Erickson: New York,* 1937. 8°. **10887.** f. **2.**

BURRITT (Elihu)

—— Adresses amicales du peuple anglais au peuple français. Avec un appendice [by E. Burritt] sur un congrès des nations. [Edited by E. Burritt.] pp. 47. *Paris,* 1848. 12°. **8425.** c. **57. (3.)**

—— Chips from Many Blocks. [Essays.] pp. 294. *Sampson Low & Co.: London,* 1878. 8°. **12356.** f. **18.**

—— Fireside Words, and talks on various topics. 2 pt. *Cassell, Petter & Galpin: London,* [1869.] 8°. **12352.** cc. **23.**

A reissue of "The Bond of Brotherhood" for 1867, *and its continuation, "Fire-side Words" for* 1868, *with a collective titlepage.*

—— Jacob and Joseph, and the lesson of their lives for the young . . . With . . . illustrations. pp. vii. 162. *Sampson Low & Co.: London,* 1870. 8°. **4413.** g. **8.**

—— A Journal of a Visit of Three Days to Skibbereen and its Neighbourhood. pp. 15. *Charles Gilpin: London; J. W. Showell: Birmingham,* 1847. 8°. **8275.** d. **6. (5.)**

—— Lectures and Speeches. pp. viii. 345. *Sampson Low & Co.: London,* 1869. 8°. **12301.** bb. **11.**

—— Elihu Burritt's Miscellaneous Writings. pt. 1. pp. 108. *Thomas Drew, Jr.: Worcester, Mass.,* 1850. 12°. **12296.** bb. **12.**

—— Second edition. [With a portrait.] pp. 120. *Thomas Drew, Jr.: Worcester, Mass.,* 1850. 12°. **12296.** bb. **13.**

—— The Mission of Great Sufferings. pp. xi. 248. *Sampson Low & Co.: London,* 1867. 8°. **8405.** bbb. **25.**

—— The Neighbors; or, a Short lay sermon to people about home. pp. 24. *S. D. Hastings: Philadelphia,* 1844. 12°. **4410.** g. **54. (1.)**

—— [Another edition.] "And Who is my Neighbour?" A lay sermon, *etc.* pp. 20. *Dyer Bros.: London,* [1878.] 8°. **4372.** de. **7. (13.)**

—— Ocean Penny Postage; its necessity shown and its feasibility demonstrated. pp. 32. *C. Gilpin: London,* [1849.] 16°. **8228.** aa. **9. (1.)**

—— Old Burchell's Pocket for the Children. [With plates.] pp. 218. *Cassell, Petter & Galpin: London,* [1868.] 16°. **12707.** bb. **5.**

—— Olive Leaves for the People. ser. 1. pp. 36. *Elihu Burritt: Worcester, Mass.,* 1850. 12°. **8410.** cc. **21. (1.)**

—— On the Divine Philosophy of Labour. A lecture. pp. 30. *H. Armour: Edinburgh,* 1851. 32°. **8282.** a. **46.**

—— Peace Papers for the People. pp. iv. 144. *Charles Gilpin: London,* [1851.] 12°. **8425.** c. **6.**

—— A Plan of Brotherly Copartnership of the North and South, for the peaceful extinction of slavery. pp. 48. *Dayton & Burdick: New York,* 1856. 12°. **8177.** a. **77. (1.)**

—— A Sanskrit Handbook for the Fireside. pp. viii. 96. *Longmans & Co.: London,* 1876. 8°. **12906.** d. **26.**

—— Seed-Lives; their sowing and reaping. pp. 35. *S. W. Partridge: London,* [1863.] 12°. **4405.** aaa. **13.**

—— Sister Voices for the Field, Factory, and Fire-Side. Edited by E. Burritt. pp. iv. 212. *W. & F. G. Cash: London,* 1853. 18°. **8415.** a. **29.**

BURRITT (Elihu)

—— Sixty Short Stories for Sixpence, for nursery, school or fireside; or, Leaflets of the law of kindness for children. Edited by E. Burritt. no. 1–22, 24–64. *S. W. Partridge: London*, [1862.] 24°. **4416. a. 14.**
Imperfect; wanting no. 23.

—— Sparks from the Anvil. pp. 96. *H. J. Howland: Worcester [Mass.]*, 1846. 32°. **8415. a. 52.**

—— [Another edition.] pp. xii. 127. *Charles Gilpin: London*, 1847. 12°. **8405. d. 1.**

—— (The tenth thousand, with considerable additions.) pp. xii. 106. *Charles Gilpin: London*, [1847.] 12°. **8405. d. 2.**

—— [A reissue.] *A. W. Bennett: London*, [1864.] 12°. **8405. aaa. 8.**

—— Ten-Minute Talks on all Sorts of Topics . . . With autobiography of the author. pp. 360. *Sampson Low & Co.: London*, 1874. 8°. **12350. e. 18.**

—— Thoughts and Notes at Home and Abroad. pp. xii. 308. *Cassell, Petter & Galpin: London*, 1868. 8°. **12354. aa. 21.**

—— Thoughts and Things at Home and Abroad . . . With a memoir by Mary Howitt. [With a portrait.] pp. vi. vi–xxvi. 10–364. *Phillips, Sampson & Co.: Boston*, 1856. 12°. **4373. d. 9.**
A different collection from the preceding.

—— A Voice from the Back Pews to the Pulpit and Front Seats, in answer to "What think ye of Christ?" By a Backpewman [i.e. E. Burritt]. pp. 450. 1872. 8°. *See* Backpewman. **4380. aa. 5.**

—— Voice from the Forge . . . Sixth thousand. pp. vi. 134. *Charles Gilpin: London*, [1848.] 12°. **12314. cc. 24.**

—— Seventh thousand. pp. vi. 134. *Charles Gilpin: London*, [1848.] 12°. **12352. bb. 4.**

—— A Walk from London to John o'Groats, with notes by the way. Illustrated with photographic portraits. pp. ix. 420. *Charles Scribner: New York; London* [printed], 1864. 8°. **10348. c. 14.**

—— Jonas Webb, his life, labours and worth . . . Reprinted from "A Walk from London to John o'Groats." pp. 48. *Sampson Low & Co.: London*, 1868. 16°. **10825. aa. 28.**

—— A Walk from London to Land's End and back, with notes by the way. With illustrations. pp. ix. 464. *Sampson Low & Co.: London*, 1865. 8°. **10348. cc. 11.**

—— Second edition. pp. vii. 350. *Sampson Low & Co.: London*, 1868. 8°. **10348. cc. 12.**

—— Walks in the Black Country and its Green Border-Land. pp. vi. 448. *Sampson Low & Co.: London*, 1868. 8°. **10360. c. 22.**

—— The Western and Eastern Questions of Europe . . . Reprinted from the N. Y. Times, World, *etc.* pp. 51. *Hamersly & Co.: Hartford*, 1871. 8°. **8028. ee. 17. (3.)**

—— The Eastern Question. [An extract from "The Western and Eastern Questions of Europe."] pp. 16. *Hodder & Stoughton: London*, 1878. 8°. **8027. de. 20. (5.)**

—— Why I Left the Anvil. And other papers. pp. 16. *Dyer Bros.: London*, [1877.] 8°. **10803. aa. 2. (1.)**

BURRITT (Elihu)

—— William Ladd, "the Apostle of Peace." (Taken from E. Burritt's introduction to Hemmenway's "Life of William Ladd.") pp. 16. *New Vienna, O.*, 1873. 8°. [*Peace Association of Friends in America. Tracts.* no. 17.] **8425. de. 21.**

—— The Year Book of the Nations, for 1855. pp. iv. 48. *Longman & Co.: London*, 1855. 8°. **8232. a. 56.**

—— The Year Book of the Nations for 1856. pp. iv. 50. *D. Appleton & Co.: New York*, 1856. 8°. **8232 a. 57.**

—— Elihu Burritt; a memorial volume containing a sketch of his life and labors, with selections from his writings and lectures, and extracts from his private journals . . . Edited by Chas. Northend. pp. 479. *D. Appleton & Co.: New York*, [1879.] 8°. **010883. ee. 33.**

—— [A reissue.] *Sampson Low & Co.: London*, 1880. 8°. **10881. bbb. 4.**

—— A Hero from the Forge. A biographical sketch of Elihu Burritt. [By Alfred Stace Dyer.] pp. 14. *Dyer Bros.: London*, [1877.] 8°. **10803. aa. 2. (2.)**

BURRITT (Elihu) and HEMMENWAY (John)

—— From Before the Mast to the Platform, a popular biography of William Ladd, the eminent American philanthropist, from an account of his life by E. Burritt and J. Hemmenway [or rather, by J. Hemmenway, with an introduction by E. Burritt]. pp. 16. 1877. 8°. *See* Hemmenway (John) **10880. aaa. 1. (4.)**

BURRITT (Elijah Hinsdale) Atlas designed to illustrate the Geography of the Heavens [i.e. the work of that title by E. H. Burritt] . . . New edition. pl. viii. *Huntington & Savage: New York*, [1845.] fol. **1262. i. 23**

—— Logarithmick Arithmetick, containing a new and correct table of logarithms . . . To which are added a number of astronomical tables, *etc.* pp. 251. *Ephraim Whitman: Williamsburgh*, 1818. 8°. **1394. c. 4**

BURRITT (Maurice Chase) Apple Growing. pp. 177. *Macmillan Co.: New York*, 1923. 8°. **07077. e. 48**

BURRI-WAGNER (Marianne)

—— Über Poliomyelitis anterior acuta bei alten Leuten. Inaugural-Dissertation, *etc.* pp. 16. *Lörrach-Stetten* 1952. 8°. **7564. c. 32**

BURROS. Os Burros, ou o Reinado da Sandice. Poema heroi-comico-satyrico en seis cantos. [By J. A. de Macedo. Edited and greatly altered by H. J. de Araujo Carneiro.] pp. iv. 136. *Paris*, 1827. 16°. **11450. a. 31**

BURROUGH (Charles James) Is Jesus God? Popular addresses on the Deity of Christ, *etc.* pp. 159. *Skeffington & Son: London*, [1927.] 8°. **4225. ff. 22**

BURROUGH (Christopher) Aduertisements and reports of the 6. voyage into the parts of Persia and Media, for the companie of English merchants for the discouerie of new trades, in the yeeres 1579. 1580. and 1581. gathered out of sundrie letters written by C. Burrough, *etc.* *See* Hakluyt (Richard) The Principal Nauigations, *etc.* vol. 1. 1598, *etc.* fol. **683. h. 5**

—— [Another edition.] *See* Hakluyt (Richard) Hakluyt's Collection of the Early Voyages, *etc.* vol. 1. 1809, *etc.* 4°. **208. h. 10**

BURROUGH (CHRISTOPHER)

—— [Another edition.] 1886. *See* HAKLUYT (Richard) The Principal Navigations, *etc.* vol. 4. 1884, *etc.* 8°. **10027.** dd. **4.**

—— [Another edition.] 1903. *See* HAKLUYT (Richard) The Principal Navigations, *etc.* vol. 3. 1903, *etc.* 8°. **2060.aa.**

—— [Another edition.] 1906. *See* PURCHAS (Samuel) *the Elder.* Hakluytus Posthumus, *etc.* vol. 12. 1905, *etc.* 8°. **2060.a.**

—— [Another edition.] [1907.] *See* HAKLUYT (Richard) The Principal Navigations, *etc.* vol. 2. [1907, *etc.*] 8°. **12206.p.1/217.**

—— [Another edition.] 1927. *See* HAKLUYT (Richard) The Principal Navigations, *etc.* vol. 2. 1927, *etc.* 8°. **010025.** ee. **28.**

—— Aduertisements and Reports of the sixth Voyage into the parts of Persia and Media, gathered out of sundry Letters written by C. Burrough; and more especially a voyage over the Caspian Sea, *etc.* [A shorter compilation.] *See* PURCHAS (Samuel) *the Elder.* Purchas his Pilgrimes, *etc.* pt. 3. 1625. fol. **679.** h. **13.**

BURROUGH (EDWARD) *Chairman of the New Jersey State Board of Agriculture.* State Aid to Road-Building in New Jersey. pp. 20. *Washington,* 1894. 8°. [*U.S. Department of Agriculture. Bureau of Public Roads. Bulletin.* no. 9.] A.S. **852.**

BURROUGH (EDWARD) *of the Society of Friends.* *See* ATKINSON (Christopher) *of the Society of Friends.* The Standard of the Lord lifted up, *etc.* [With an epistle to the reader by E. Burrough.] 1653. 4°. E. **715.** (**7.**)

—— *See* BROCKBANK (Elisabeth) Edward Burrough: a wrestler for truth, *etc.* 1949. 8°. **4910.** aa. **44.**

—— *See* COOK (Edward) *of the Society of Friends.* A Short Account of the Vniust proceedings of the Court of Kingstone upon Thames, in a tryal between Richard Mayo, Priest, and E. Burrough, *etc.* 1658. 4°. **4151.** a. **108.**

—— *See* COOK (Edward) *of the Society of Friends.* A Second Account in short, of the substance of the proceeding in the Court of Kingstone upon Thames upon the matter between R. Mayo . . . Plaintiffe, and E. Burrough Defendant, *etc.* [1658.] 4°. **855.** f. **3.** (**42.**)

—— *See* FOX (George) *Founder of the Society of Friends.* The Great Mistery of the Great Whore Unfolded, *etc.* [With an epistle to the reader by E. Burrough.] 1659. fol. **4152.** gg. **1.**

—— *See* H., R. The Rebukes of a Reviler fallen upon his own head, in an answer to a book put forth by one Iohn Stelham, *etc.* [The postscript signed: E. B., i.e. Edward Burrough?] 1657. 4°. E. **919.** (**17.**)

—— *See* HOWGILL (Francis) The Fiery Darts of the Divel quenched . . . Also something in answer to a booke called a voice from the Word of the Lord, by one John Griffith . . . By . . . E. Burrough. 1654. 4°. E. **817.** (**16.**)

—— *See* HOWGILL (Francis) A Testimony concerning the Life, Death, Trials, Travels and Labours of Edward Burroughs, *etc.* [With notices by George Whitehead, Josiah Coale and George Fox.] 1662. 4°. **113.** b. **57.**

—— —— 1663. 4°. **4151.** c. **65.**

—— *See* HOWGILL (Francis) and BURROUGH (E.) The Visitation of the Rebellious Nation of Ireland, *etc.* 1656. 4°. E. **880.** (**6.**)

BURROUGH (EDWARD) *of the Society of Friends.*

—— *See* HUBBERTHORN (Richard) A Collection of the Several Books and Writings of . . . Richard Hubberthorn, *etc.* [With a biographical sketch by E. Burrough.] 1663. 4°. **855.** f. **21.**

—— *See* NAYLER (James) Deceit brought to Day-Light, *etc.* [With an "Epistle to the Reader, and to Thomas Collier" by E. Burrough.] 1656. 4°. **855.** i. **19.** (**7.**)

—— *See* TAYLOR (Ernest E.) Edward Burrough. "Son of thunder and consolation." [1931.] 8°. [*Friends Ancient and Modern.* no. 22.] **4804.aa.48.**

—— *See* WHITEHEAD (George) *Quaker,* and BURROUGH (E.) The Son of Perdition Revealed, *etc.* 1661. 4°. **4152.** f. **18.** (**3.**)

—— *See* WILLIAMS (Roger) George Fox digg'd out of his Burrowes . . . In which many quotations out of G. Fox & E. Burrowes book in folio are alleadged, *etc.* [With special reference to "The Great Mistery of the Great Whore Unfolded," by G. Fox, which contains an epistle to the reader by E. Burrough.] 1676. 4°. C. **25.** c. **2.**

—— —— 1872. 4°. [*Publications of the Narragansett Club.* ser. 1. vol. 5.] Ac. **9510.**

—— *See* WILSON (Thomas) *Rector of Arrow, Warwickshire.* The Spirit of Delusion reproved . . . Being an answer to W. Penn . . . E. Burroughs, *etc.* 1678. 8°. **856.** g. **8.** (**2.**)

—— The Memorable Works of a Son of Thunder and Consolation: namely . . . Edward Burroughs, *etc.* (Francis Howgil's Testimony concerning the Life, Death . . . and Labours of E. Burrough, *etc.*—George Whitehead his Testimony and Account concerning E. Burroughs.—Josiah Coale his Testimony, *etc.*—A Testimony of George Fox, *etc.*) [Edited by Ellis Hookes.] pp. 896. [*London,*] 1672. fol. **4151.** h. **8.**

—— Three Early Quaker Writings, *etc.* (A Declaration of the Sad and Great Perfection and Martyrdom of the People of God, called Quakers, in New England.—To the Rulers and to such as are in Authority: A True and Faithful Testimony concerning Religion.—A Vindication of the People of God, called Quakers.) ff. 54. *San Francisco,* 1939. 4°. [*Sutro Branch, California State Library. Occasional Papers. Reprint Series.* no. 6.] W.P. **1879/6.** *Reproduced from typewriting.*

—— An Alarm to all Flesh: with an Invitation to the true Seeker, forthwith to flye for his Life—clearly—out of the short-lived Babylon, into the Life; out of words, into the Word; out of the many and changeable Likenesses, into Him, the same yesterday, to day, for ever and ever . . . By E. B. [i.e. Edward Billing? or E. Burrough?] pp. 10. 1660. 4°. *See* B., E. **224.** a. **42.** (**40.**)

—— Antichrist's Government Justly Detected of Unrighteousness, Injustice, Unreasonableness, Oppression, and Cruelty; throughout the Kingdomes of this World . . . Shewed and declared, first, in the case of imposing upon conscience in matters religious by force of outward violence . . . Secondly, in the case of heresie, *etc.* pp. 49. *For Robert Wilson: London,* 1661. 4°. **4151.** d. **5.**

—— [Another copy.] **224.** a. **42.** (**2.**) *Cropped.*

BURROUGH (Edward) *of the Society of Friends.*

—— The Case of Free Liberty of Conscience in the Exercise of Faith and Religion, presented unto the King and both Houses of Parliament. And also proved absolute needfull . . . for them to grant, *etc.* pp. 15. *For Thomas Simmons: London,* 1661. 4°. **4151**. a. **85**.

—— The Case of the people called Quakers—once more—stated, and published to the World: with the accusations charged upon them; and their answers. [Signed: E. B., i.e. E. Burrough.] pp. 14. [1661?] 4°. *See* B., E. **4151**. a. **124**.

—— The Crying Sinnes Reproved. Whereof the rulers and people of England, are highly guilty; with additions to their own confessions held forth by them in a declaration of their own, bearing date Septem. 23. wherein these three nations are called to a day of solemn fasting . . . By . . . E. B. [i.e. E. Burrough.] pp. 17. 1656. 4°. *See* B., E. **100**. f. **33**.

—— A Declaration from the People called Quakers, to the Present Distracted Nation of England, *etc.* (Given forth . . . through E. Burrough.) pp. 14. *London,* 1659. 4°. **855**. f. 3. **(57.)**

—— [Another copy.] E. **1011**. **(3.)**

—— [Another edition.] pp. 14. *For Thomas Simmons: London,* 1659. 4°. **4152**. f. **18**. **(2.)**

—— A Declaration of the sad and great Persecution and Martyrdom of the People of God, called Quakers, in New-England, for the worshipping of God . . . Also, some considerations, presented to the King, which is in answer to a Petition and Address, which was presented unto him by the General Court at Boston, *etc.* [Signed: E. B., i.e. E. Burrough?] pp. 32. [1661.] 4°. *See* B., E. E. **1086**. **(4.)**

—— A Declaration to all the World of our Faith, and what we Believe, *etc.* pp. 8. *For Thomas Simmons: London,* 1657. 4°. **855**. f. **3**. **(16.)**

—— [Another edition.] pp. 6. *For Thomas Simmons: London,* 1659. 4°. E. **984**. **(11.)**

—— [Another edition.] A Declaration to all the World of our Faith, and what we believe who are called Quakers [signed: E. B., i.e. E. Burrough] . . . Also, what Ministers and Magistrates we own, and what, and whom, we deny [signed: A. P., i.e. Alexander Parker]. pp. 12. [1660?] 4°. *See* B., E. **4151**. b. **7**.

—— [Another edition.] A Declaration to all the World of our faith, and what we believe, *etc.* *See* Principles. The Principles of Truth, *etc.* [1675?] 8°. **856**. g. **16**.

—— Een verklaeringh aen de geheele werelt, van ons geloof, ende wat wy geloven, die Quakers genaemt worden, *etc.* pp. 7. *Amsterdam,* 1669. 4°. **855**. i. **1**. **(12.)**

—— A Description of the State and Condition of all Mankinde upon the face of the whole Earth. And a discovery unto all; shewing what man was in his creation before transgression, and what he is in transgression . . . Also, the way of restoration . . . is here declared unto all the sons and daughters of Adam, *etc.* pp. 14. *For Giles Calvert: London,* [1657.] 4°. E. **912**. **(3.)**

—— Een Beschrijvinge van den staet ende de gelegentheyt van het geheele menschelijk-geslacht, *etc.* pp. 15. [1657.] 4°. **855**. i. **1**. **(4.)**

BURROUGH (Edward) *of the Society of Friends.*

—— A Discovery of Divine Mysteries; wherein is unfoulded secret things of the kingdom of God, *etc.* pp. 39. *For Robert Wilson: London,* 1661. 4°. **4375**. b. **8**.

—— Edward Burrough his Vision, 22d of the 8th Month, 1661. *See* Penington (Isaac) *the Younger.* The Testimony of Isaac Pennington, *etc.* 1681. 4°. **855**. f. **7**. **(6.)**

—— An Epistle to Friends of Truth in and about London, *etc.* pp. 7. *London,* 1667. 4°. **4151**. a. **133**.

—— The Everlasting Gospel of Repentance and Remission of Sins; held forth and declared . . . And this is a message of reconciliation to all people . . . but more particularly to the inhabitants of Ireland, *etc.* pp. 32. *For Robert Wilson: London,* [1660?] 4°. **4151**. bb. **9**.

—— For the Souldiers, and all the Officers of England, Scotland, and Ireland, a warning from the Lord, that they forget not his kindness, but call to mind his mercies, and their own promises. [*London,* 1654.] *s. sh.* fol. **669**. f. **19**. **(9.)**

—— A Generall Epistle, and Greeting of the Fathers Love, to all the Saints, called . . . to faithfulness in Christ Iesus, *etc.* pp. 41 [14]. *For Thomas Simmons: London,* 1657. 4°. **4103**. c. **10**.

—— A General Epistle to all the Saints; being a visitation of the Fathers love unto the whole Flock of God . . . To be read in all the assemblies, of them, that meet together to worship the Father, *etc.* pp. 16. *For Robert Wilson: London,* 1660. 4°. **4103**. c. **12**.
A different work from the preceding.

—— Good Counsel and Advice, Rejected; by Disobedient Men. And the dayes of Oliver Cromwells visitation passed over; and also of Richard Cromwel his son, late Protectors of these nations. And the many precious warnings neglected by them . . . which . . . the servants of the Lord [i.e. E. Burrough and G. Fox] gave unto them, as declared in these following letters, *etc.* pp. 68. *For Thomas Simmons: London,* 1659. 4°. **4103**. c. **11**.

—— *Begin.* Here follows the Testimony concerning the Estate of the True Church, *etc.* [Signed: E. B., i.e. E. Burrough.] 1658. 4°. [*Penington (Isaac) the Younger. The Way of Life and Death, etc.*] *See* B., E. **4151**. d. **17**.

—— A Hue and Cry after the false Prophets and Deceivers of our Age; and a discovery of them by their works, *etc.* [Signed: E. B., i.e. E. Burrough.] pp. 8. 1661. 4°. *See* B., E. **4151**. de. **2**.

—— A Just and Lawful Trial of the Teachers and professed Ministers of England, by a perfect proceeding against them . . . By a friend to England's Common-wealth . . . E. B. [i.e. E. Burrough.] pp. 25. 1657. 4°. *See* B., E. E. **925**. **(14.)**

—— [Another edition.] Whereunto is added, a short description of the true Ministry of Christ . . . By . . . E. B. [i.e. E. Burrough.] pp. 22. 1659. 4°. *See* B., E. **4152**. bb. **132**. **(19.)**

—— [Another edition.] pp. 22. *For Thomas Simmons: London,* 1660. 4°. **4103**. c. **13**.

—— A Just and Righteous Plea, presented unto the King of England, and his Council, &c. Being the true state of the present case of the people called Quakers, truly demonstrated, *etc.* pp. 34. *For Robert Wilson: London,* 1661. 4°. **4151**. aa. **57**. **(6.)**

—— [Another copy.] **1478**. aa. **24**. **(2.)**

—— A Lyar reproved; or, a few words to a book called, A looking-glass for the quakers, put forth by one Samuel Morris of Bristol, *etc.* [Signed: E. B., i.e. E. Burrough?] 1655. 4º. [*AUDLAND* (*John*) *The Innocent delivered out of the Snare, etc.*] *See* B., E. E. **831.** (**11.**)

—— Many Strong Reasons confounded, which would hinder any reasonable man from being a Quaker; and offences taken out of the way. But particularly, foure and twenty arguments overturned and confuted; put forth and sent into the world by Richard Baxter [in "One Sheet against the Quakers"] . . . and this is for the satisfaction of honest people by a friend, E. B. [i.e. E. Burrough.] pp. 21. 1657. 4º. *See* B., E. **4152.** b. **3.**

—— A Measure of the Times: and a full & clear description of the signes of the times, and of the changing of the times; and of the reign of Antichrist, *etc.* pp. 39. *For Thomas Simmons: London,* 1657. 4º. E. **919.** (**6.**)

—— A Message for Instruction, to all the Rulers, Judges, and Magistrates, to whom the Law is committed, shewing what just Government is, and how far the Magistrates power reacheth . . . By . . . E. B. [i.e. E. Burrough.] pp. 29. 1658. 4º. *See* B., E. **4152.** ee. **17.** (**1.**)

—— A Message Proclaimed. By divine authority, from the chosen Assembly of the redeemed people in England, To the Pope . . . and to his Cardinals . . . that they may appear, and come forth to triall . . . Written by . . . E. B. [Signed: Edward Burrough.] pp. 24. *For Thomas Simmons: London,* [1658.] 4º. **4152.** f. **18.** (**1.**)

—— A Message to all Kings and Rulers in Christendom. pp. 8. [1659.] 4º. **4152.** bb. **128.**

—— A Message to the Present Rulers of England. Whether Committee of Safety, so called, Councell of Officers, or others whatsoever, *etc.* pp. 16. *For Giles Calvert: London,* 1659. 4º. **1093.** c. **49.**

—— [Another copy.] **855.** f. **3.** (**56.**)
Imperfect; wanting the half-title.

—— A Mite of Affection, manifested in 31. Proposals, offered to all the sober and free-born people within this Commonwealth, *etc.* [Signed: E. B., i.e. Edward Billing? or E. Burrough?] pp. 12. 1659. 4º. *See* B., E. E. **1001.** (**5.**)

—— [Another edition.] pp. 12. 1659. 4º. *See* B., E. **855.** f. **3.** (**48.**)

—— Persecution Impeached, as a Traytor against God . . . and the cause of the antient martyrs vindicated, against the cruelty inflicted upon them by the Papists in former dayes. Being a brief answer to a book, called Semper iidem, *etc.* [By E. Burrough.] pp. 38. 1661. 4º. ~~*See*~~ See FANATICS. **4151.** c. **91.**

—— [Another copy.] **108.** d. **41.**

—— A Presentation of Wholesome Informations, unto the King of England, &c. Being a defence pleaded . . . in answer to a certain accusation, charged before him—in a printed book, called, The thrice happy Welcom of King Charles the Second, by one George Willington, of Bristol City—against us, whom in derision, the accuser calls Quakers, *etc.* pp. 29. *London; sold by Richard Moon: Bristol,* 1660. 4º. T. **347.** (**8.**)

—— [Another copy.] E. **1043.** (**8.**)

—— A Returne to the Ministers of London; by way of answer to their seasonable exhortation, so called, directed to their Congregations. With sober reproof sent unto them, because of their recent smitings against the despised people called Quakers . . . By E. B. [i.e. E. Burrough.] pp. 29. 1660. 4º. *See* B., E. **4152.** f. **4.** (**7.**)

—— [Another copy.] **4151.** aa. **57.** (**1.**)

—— Satans Designe defeated. In a short answer to a manuscript sent by a Priest [Thomas Jackson] out of Sussex, to a Member of this present Parliament . . . By a Friend to Righteousnesse, E. B. [i.e. E. Burrough.] pp. 20. 1659. 4º. *See* B., E. **4152.** bb. **132.** (**18.**)

—— A Seasonable Word of Advice unto all that are or may through the subtlety of the Enemy, backslide from the Truth. [1660?] *s. sh.* fol. **L.7.a.4.(3.)**

—— Something in answer to a Book called Choice Experiences, given forth by one J. Turner. Also the copy of a letter sent to the assembly of those that are called Anabaptists in Newcastle, *etc.* pp. 15. 1654. 4º. E. **816.** (**2.**)

—— Something of Truth made Manifest—in relation to a Dispute at Draton in the County of Middlesex . . . in opposition to the false account given of it by one Philip Taverner, in his book styled the Quakers-Rounds; or a Faithfull account, *etc.* pp. 22. *For Thomas Simmons: London,* 1658. 4º. **855.** f. **2.** (**22.**)

—— Stablishing against Quaking, thrown down and overturned, and no defence found against it; or, an Answer to a book, called Stablishing against Quaking, put forth by Giles Firmin, *etc.* pp. 31. *For Giles Calvert: London,* 1656. 4º. E. **884.** (**4.**)

—— A Standard lifted up, and an Ensigne held forth, to all Nations; shewing unto the whole world . . . what the testimony of God is, and of his people which they hold, *etc.* pp. 35. *For Giles Calvert: London,* 1657. 4º. E. **923.** (**6.**)

—— [Another edition.] pp. 32. *For Giles Calvert: London,* 1658. 4º. **4152.** f. **22.** (**13.**)

—— Een Standaert opgerecht, ende een baniere voorgehouden tot alle natien . . . Nu in't Nederlants voor de derdemael herdruckt. pp. 28. *Christoffel Cunradus: Amsterdam,* 1669. 4º. **855.** i. **1.** (**14.**)

—— A Tender Salutation of Perfect Love unto the Elect of God, *etc.* [Signed: E. B., i.e. E. Burrough. Edited by Ellis Hookes.] pp. 16. 1661. 4º. *See* B., E. **4151.** aa. **57.** (**5.**)

—— A Testimony against a great Idolatry committed: and a true mourning of the Lord's servant upon the many considerations of his heart, upon that occasion of the great stir about an image made and carryed from one place to another [i.e. the funeral of Oliver Cromwell], happening the 23. day of the ninth month [Nov. 1658]. By E. B. [i.e. E. Burrough]. pp. 8. 1658. 4º. *See* B., E. **4152.** ee. **17.** (**2.**)

—— A Testimony concerning the Book of Common-Prayer, *etc.* [Signed: E. B., i.e. E. Burrough.] 1660. 4º. [*F., G. Something in answer to the Old Common-Prayer-Book, etc.*] *See* B., E. **4151.** a. **59.**

—— The Testimony of the Lord concerning London. Witnessed in truth and faithfulnesse, to the consciences of all people in it . . . By a Lover of all your soules, E. B. [i.e. E. Burrough.] pp. 17. 1657. 4º. *See* B., E. E. **925.** (**9.**)

— To all dear Friends & Brethren in the Everlasting Truth & Covenant of the Almighty Jehovah, Blessed for evermore. [An address to the Society of Friends, written from Newgate Prison, and signed: E. B., J. C., J. P., i.e. E. Burrough, John Cook, and Isaac Penington. With a postscript by Francis Howgill.] pp. 8. 1662. 4°. *See* B., E. **4151.** b. **8.**

— [Another edition.] pp. 8. [1662.] 4°. *See* B., E. **4152.** c. **2.**

— [Another edition.] pp. 8. [1662.] 4°. *See* B., E. **1478.** aa. **24.** (**3.**)

— To all that believe in Christ. [An exhortation to the Quakers to meet together.] *See* COALES (Josiah) A Salutation to the Suffering-Seed of God, *etc.* 1663. 4°. **4152.** b. **16.**

— To Charles Fleetwood, Steward, Robert Hatton, Recorder: Sackford Gunstone, Henry Wilcock, Bailiffs. Being judges in the Court of Kingstone upon Thames. The state of the old controversie once more laid before you, depending in your court, between Richard Mayo, plaintiffe, and Edward Burrough, defendant. pp. 15. *For Thomas Simmons: London,* 1659. 4°. **855.** f. **3.** (**41.**)

— *Begin.* To the Beloved and Chosen of God in the Seed Elected, particularly in London and elsewhere, *etc.* [Signed: E. B., i.e. E. Burrough.] pp. 8. 1660. 4°. *See* B., E. **4151.** b. **9.**

— To the Camp of the Lord in England. [An address.] *See* HOWGILL (Francis) This is onely to goe amongst Friends. 1656. 4°. E. **868.** (**8.**)

— [To the] Parliament of the Commonwealth of England . . . A presentation . . . that you may take off oppression, and free the people from all their cruel bonds, *etc.* *London,* [1659.] *s. sh.* fol. **855.** f. **3.** (**47.**) *Mutilated.*

— To the Parliament of the Common-wealth of England, who are in place of Authority to do justice . . . Councel and advice unto you . . . that men of truth and sound judgement, may be set to judge the people in outward things, and the exercise of good conscience in faith and worship left unto God, *etc.* pp. 8. [1659.] 4°. **4152.** bb. **93.**

— To the present Assembly, Members of Parliament at Westminster. The Considerations of a servant of the Lord, upon the present state of affairs, *etc.* [Signed: E. B., i.e. E. Burrough.] [1659.] *s. sh.* fol. *See* B., E. **855.** f. **3.** (**62.**)

— To the Rulers and to such as are in Authority a True and faithful testimony concerning Religion, and the establishment thereof, and how it may be established in persons and in Nations. pp. 12. *For Thomas Simmons: London,* 1659. 4°. **4152.** f. **22.** (**16.**)

— [To the whole] English Army, and to every particular Member thereof . . . whether of England, Scotland, or Ireland; these are for them to read, and consider as wholesome animadversions in this day of distractions. *For Giles Calvert: London,* [1659.] *s. sh.* fol. **855.** f. **3.** (**60.**) *Mutilated.*

— A True Description of my Manner of Life, *etc.* *See* infra: A Warning from the Lord to the Inhabitants of Underbarrow, *etc.*

— The True Faith of the Gospel of Peace contended for, in the spirit of meekness; and the mystery of salvation—Christ within, the hope of glory—vindicated . . . against the secret opposition of John Bunyan . . . or, an answer to his book, called, Some Gospel Truths opened, &c. . . . By . . . E. B. [i.e. E. Burrough.] pp. 30. 1656. 4°. *See* B., E. E. **886.** (**8.**)

— A Trumpet of the Lord sounded out of Sion: which . . . is a true noyse of a fearfull earthquake at hand . . . With a salutation to the seed who are gathered into the fold, *etc.* pp. 41. *For Giles Calvert: London,* 1656. 4°. E. **875.** (**3.**)

— Truth Defended. Or, Certain accusations answered, cast upon us who are called Quakers, by the teachers of the world, and the people of this generation, *etc.* [With a preface by Francis Howgill.] pp. 23. [*London,* 1654.] 4°. E. **808.** (**3.**)

— Truth, the Strongest of all, Witnessed forth in the Spirit of Truth, against all Deceit: and pleading . . . its owne cause . . . against . . . lyes, slanders, perverting of the Scriptures, contradictions and false damnable doctrines, held forth by the Independants. And in particular by one John Bunian . . . in two severall bookes put forth by him, against the despised scattered people called Quakers. And is a reply unto his second book called A Vindication, *etc.* pp. 63. *For Giles Calvert: London,* 1657. 4°. E. **910.** (**3.**)

— Two General Epistles; or, the Breathings of love, uttered from the pure Life, to the whole flock of God in England, Scotland, and Ireland, *etc.* [Containing one of "Two Epistles to Friends in London" and the greater part of "A General Epistle and Greeting of the Fathers Love to all the Saints."] pp. 22. *For R. Wilson: London,* 1663. 4°. **4103.** c. **14.**

— A Vindication of the People of God, called Quakers . . . being an answer to a book (called "A brief relation of some remarkable passages of the Anabaptists in Germany") . . . by one George Pressick . . . By E. B. [i.e. E. Burrough.] pp. 24. [1660.] 4°. *See* B., E. **4151.** a. **77.**

— A Visitation & Warning Proclamed and an Alarm Sounded in the Pope's Borders . . . Being the account of a journey to Dunkirk, and the proceedings there among the Jesuites, and Friars, and Papists, *etc.* pp. 36. *For Thomas Simmons: London,* 1659. 4°. **855.** f. **3.** (**14.**)

— A Visitation of Love unto the King, and Those call'd Royallists; consisting I. Of an answer to several queries proposed to the people—called Quakers—from a . . . Royallist. II. Of an objection answered, concerning the King's supremacy. III. Of an epistle directed to the King, & . . . Royallists. IV. Of certain queries returned to them, *etc.* pp. 39. *Printed & sold by Robert Wilson: London,* 1660. 4°. **4151.** b. **104.**

— [Another copy.] T. **347.** (**10.**)

— [Another copy.] E. **1034.** (**7.**)

— [Another edition.] pp. 39. *Printed & sold by Robert Wilson: London,* 1660. 4°. **4152.** f. **2.** (**5.**)

— A Warning from the Lord to the Inhabitants of Underbarrow, and so to all the Inhabitants in England . . . Also, a word to my brethren, and companions in tribula-

BURROUGH (Edward) *of the Society of Friends.*

tion . . . who is [*sic*] by the world scornfully called Quakers, *etc.* (A true Declaration, and a discovery to all the World of my manner of life; what I have been, and what now I am at present.) pp. 38. *For Giles Calvert: London*, 1654. 4°. E. **733**. (**5**.)

—— A True Description of my Manner of Life, of what I have been in my profession of religion . . . and what I am at present, *etc.* [An extract from "A Warning from the Lord to the Inhabitants of Underbarrow."] pp. 11. *For Robert Wilson: London*, 1663. 4°. **224**. a. **42**. (**14**.)

—— The Wofull Cry of unjust Persecutions, and grievous oppressions of the people of God in England, through the injustice of some of her rulers . . . and this may serve for an answer in full to all such who have persecuted . . . the innocent people in scorn called Quakers. With a short addition, which shewes unto all, the ground of persecution . . . By a friend to the suffering seed of God, E. B. [i.e. E. Burrough.] pp. 25. [1657.] 4°. *See* B., E. E. **927**. (**1**.)

—— [Selected passages from the works of Burrough.] *See* Pennyman (John) This is for the People called Quakers, *etc.* 1675. 4°. **874**. k. **26**. (**7**.)

—— A Memoir of the Life and Religious Labours of . . . Edward Burrough, *etc.* 1850. *See* Evans (William) and (Thomas) *Publishers, of Philadelphia.* The Friends' Library, *etc.* vol. 14. 1837, *etc.* 8°. **4152**. gg. **4**.

BURROUGH (Edward) *of the Society of Friends*, and **HOWGILL** (Francis)

—— Answers to severall Queries put forth to the despised people called Quakers, by Philip Bennett . . . Also, Answers to severall other subtil queries put forth by one Iohn Reeve. pp. 18. *For Giles Calvert: London*, [1654.] 4°. E. **813**. (**4**.) *Cropped.*

BURROUGH (Edward Herbert)

—— *See* Storm (T.) Der Schimmelreiter . . . Edited with an introduction and notes by E. H. Burrough. 1953. 8°. W.P. **13506**/2.

BURROUGH (Edward James)

—— *See* Strong (Robert A.) Fuel Briquetting. By R. A. Strong . . . E. J. Burrough. 1937. 8°. [*Canada. Bureau of Mines. Reports.* no. 775.] C.S. e. **38**/7.

BURROUGH (Henry) Lectures on the Church Catechism, Confirmation and the Nature and Obligation of Religious Vows . . . The second edition. pp. iii. 172. *J. Woodyer: Cambridge*, 1773. 8°. **3504**. dd. **8**.

—— Sermons on Several Subjects and Occasions. pp. 364. [*Printed at the private press of the author:*] *Wisbich*, 1770. 8°. **4455**. ee. **7**.

BURROUGH (*Sir* James) *See* Battely (John) Joannis Battely . . . opera posthuma, *etc.* (Appendix ad Antiquitates S. Edmundi Burgi. [By Sir J. Burrough.]) 1745. 4°. **984**. e. **6**.

—— Numismata Collegii de Gonvile et Caius nuper Jacobi Burrough et Joannis Smith. The donors' catalogue, edited by the Rev. J. J. Smith. pp. xiii. 71. 1846. 4°. *See* Cambridge.—*University of Cambridge.—Gonville and Caius College.* **7755**. e. 2. (**6**.)

BURROUGH (James Walrond)

—— *See* Grand (Dalton) The Mathematics and Geometry of Craft Work . . . Edited by J. W. Burrough. [1943, *etc.*] 8°. W.P. **12323**.

BURROUGH (Jeremiah) *See* Burroughs (Jeremiah) *Puritan Divine.*

BURROUGH (John) Zeal and Moderation Reconcil'd, and shewn to be the peculiar Glory and Ornament of the Church of England. In a sermon preach'd at the visitation of the Reverend Mr. Edward Trelawny . . . 1718, *etc.* pp. iv. 32. *Phil. Yeo: Exon*, [1718.] 8°. T. **1548**. (**4**.)

—— The second edition. To which is added, a postscript, in answer to the author of the Visitor Revis'd. pp. iv. 32. 8. *Phil. Yeo: Exon; J. Morphew: London*, [1718.] 8°. **4372**. g. **9**. (**1**.)

BURROUGH (*Sir* John) A true report of the honourable seruice at Sea perfourmed by Sir Iohn Burrough . . . 1592. 1599. *See* Hakluyt (Richard) The Principal Nauigations, *etc.* vol. 2. 1598, *etc.* fol. **683**. h. **5**.

—— [Another edition.] 1810. *See* Hakluyt (Richard) Hakluyt's Collection of the Early Voyages, *etc.* vol. 3. 1809, *etc.* 4°. **208**. h. **12**.

—— [Another edition.] 1889. *See* Hakluyt (Richard) The Principal Navigations, *etc.* vol. 11. 1884, *etc.* 8°. **10027**. dd. **4**.

—— [Another edition.] 1896. *See* Arber (Edward) An English Garner, *etc.* vol. 8. 1877, *etc.* 8°. **12269**. cc. **12**.

—— [Another edition.] *See* Arber (Edward) An English Garner. (Voyages and Travels. vol. 2.) 1903. 8°. **2324**. e. **9**/**3**.

—— [Another edition.] 1904. *See* Hakluyt (Richard) The Principal Navigations, *etc.* vol. 7. 1903, *etc.* 8°. **2060.aa.**

—— [Another edition.] [1908.] *See* Hakluyt (Richard) The Principal Navigations, *etc.* vol. 5. [1907, *etc.*] 8°. **12206.p.1/217.**

—— [Another edition.] 1927. *See* Hakluyt (Richard) The Principal Navigations, *etc.* vol. 5. 1927, *etc.* 8°. **010025**. ee. **28**.

BURROUGH (John Allan Benedict) "Daughterhood," or, the English daughter church of Jerusalem, the mother of all. (New edition.) pp. 15. *W. B. Darley: Burton-on-Trent*, 1917. 8°. **4532**. b. **31**.

BURROUGH (Maurice William) Income Tax for Farmers, including the provisions of the Finance Act, 1918, *etc.* pp. 36. *Iliffe & Sons: London*, [1918.] 8°. **6426**. p. **13**.

BURROUGH (Paul) *Novelist.*

—— Lodeleigh. A novel. pp. 384. *Chatto & Windus: London*, 1947. 8°. NN. **38002**.

BURROUGH (Ruth J.) From Snow to Sun. A mystery story for boys. pp. 227. *Longmans & Co.: New York, Toronto*, 1938. 8°. **12821**. bb. **11**.

—— Mystery House, *etc.* pp. vii. 228. *Longmans & Co.: New York*, 1933. 8°. **12708**. f. **7**.

—— Smiley Adams, *etc.* pp. vii. 244. *Longmans & Co.: New York, Toronto*, 1931. 8°. A.N. **803**.

BURROUGH (Stephen)

—— The Nauigation and discouerie toward the Riuer of Ob, made by Master Stephen Burrowe, *etc.*—The voiage of the foresaid M. Stephen Burrough . . . from Colmogro to Wardhouse, *etc.* *See* Hakluyt (Richard) The Principall Nauigations, Voiages, *etc.* 1589. fol. C. **32**. m. **10**.

BURROUGH (Stephen)

—— The Nauigation and discouerie toward the riuer of Ob, made by Master Steuen Burrough . . . with diuers things worth the noting, passed in the yere 1556.—The voyage of the foresaid M. S. Burrough. An. 1557. from Colmogro to Wardhouse, *etc.* *See* Hakluyt (Richard) The Principal Nauigations, *etc.* vol. 1. 1598, *etc.* fol. **683. h. 5.**

—— [Another edition.] *See* Hakluyt (Richard) Hakluyt's Collection of the Early Voyages, *etc.* vol. 1. 1809, *etc.* 4°. **208. h. 10.**

—— [Another edition.] 1886. *See* Hakluyt (Richard) The Principal Navigations, *etc.* vol. 4. 1884, *etc.* 8°. **10027. dd. 4.**

—— [Another edition.] 1903. *See* Hakluyt (Richard) The Principal Navigations, *etc.* vol. 2. 1903, *etc.* 8°. **2060.aa.**

—— [Another edition.] *See* Hakluyt (Richard) The Principal Navigations, *etc.* vol. 1. [1907, *etc.*] 8°. **12206.p.1/217.**

—— [Another edition.] *See* Hakluyt (Richard) The Principal Navigations, *etc.* vol. 1. 1927, *etc.* 8°. **010025. ee. 28.**

BURROUGH (Thomas) Christ the Sts Advantage both in Life and Death. A sermon preached at the funerall of Ms Elizabeth Coke, *etc.* pp. 49. *T. R. & E. M. for John Bellamy: London,* 1646. 12°. **E. 1200. (3.)**

BURROUGH (Thomas) *Baron Burrough.* *See* Burgh (T.) *Baron Burgh.*

BURROUGH (Thomas Hedley Bruce)

—— An Approach to Planning. pp. x. 85. pl. viii. *Sir Isaac Pitman & Sons: London,* 1953. 8°. **7824. gg. 18.**
Part of "The Architects' Library."

BURROUGH (William) *See* Borough.

BURROUGHES AND WATTS. Rules of the game Sixes: Billiards and Snooker combined, *etc.* *London,* [1934.] 8°. **7911. d. 33.**
A folding card.

BURROUGHES (Dorothy) *See* Ephemerides. The Animal Lovers' Calendar . . . Illustrated by D. Burroughes, *etc.* [1930, *etc.*] 4°. **P.P. 2487. sd.**

—— *See* Fyleman (Rose) Fifty-one New Nursery Rhymes . . . Illustrated by D. Burroughes. 1931. *obl.* 4°. **Cup.1254.p.31.**

—— *See* James (Norah C.) Tinkle the Cat . . . Illustrated by D. Burroughes. 1932. 8°. **20052. f. 14.**

—— *See* Pallister (Minnie) Gardener's Frenzy . . . Illustrated by D. Burroughes. 1933. 8°. **7054. a. 36.**

—— The Amazing Adventures of Little Brown Bear. Written and illustrated by D. Burroughes. pp. viii. 102. *Methuen & Co.: London,* 1930. 8°. **12810. de. 8.**

—— Captain Seal's Treasure Hunt. Written and illustrated by D. Burroughes. pp. 142. *John Lane: London,* 1933. 8°. **012804. c. 35.**

—— The Conceited Frog. pp. 44. *Hutchinson's Books for Young People: London,* [1949.] *obl.* 8°. **12831. de. 48.**

—— Dorothy Burroughes Nature Series. *E. J. Burrow & Co.. London,* [1944– .] 4°. **W.P. 783.**

BURROUGHES (Dorothy)

—— Harris the Hare and his Own True Love. Written and illustrated by D. Burroughes. pp. 174. *John Lane: London,* 1933. 8°. **012804. c. 36.**

—— The House the Moles Built. Written and illustrated by D. Burroughes. pp. 47. *Hutchinson & Co.: London,* [1939.] *obl.* fol. **12819. g. 31.**

—— Jack Rabbit, Detective; or, the Great pearl mystery. Written and illustrated by D. Burroughes. pp. vii. 126. *Methuen & Co.: London,* 1931. 8°. **012807. de. 102.**

—— The Journeyings of Selina Squirrel and her Friends. Written and illustrated by D. Burroughes. pp. viii. 126. *Methuen & Co.: London,* 1931. 8°. **12804. ff. 52.**

—— The Little Pigs Who Sailed Away. Written and illustrated by D. Burroughes. pp. 46. *Hutchinson's Books for Young People: London,* [1944.] *obl.* 8°. **12828. a. 18.**

—— The Little White Elephant. Written and illustrated by D. Burroughs. pp. 38. *Hutchinson's Books for Young People: London,* [1953.] 8°. **12836. dd. 14.**

—— The Magic Herb. Written and illustrated by D. Burroughes. pp. 48. *Hutchinson's Books for Young People: London,* [1945.] *obl.* 8°. **12830. aa. 33.**

—— More Adventures of the Odd Little Girl. Written and illustrated by D. Burroughes. pp. 150. *John Lane: London,* 1933. 8°. **012804. c. 34.**

—— Niggs, the Little Black Rabbit. Written and illustrated by D. Burroughes. pp. 46. *Hutchinson & Co.: London,* [1940.] 4°. **12815. b. 10.**

—— The Odd-Little-Girl. Written and illustrated by D. Burroughes. pp. vi. 151. *Methuen & Co.: London,* 1932. 8°. **012804. c. 31.**

—— The Strange Adventures of Mary Jane Stubbs. Written and illustrated by D. Burroughes. pp. 124. *John Lane: London,* 1933. 8°. **012804. c. 33.**

—— Teddy, the Little Refugee Mouse. Written and illustrated by D. Burroughes. pp. 48. *Hutchinson & Co.: London,* [1942.] *obl.* 8°. **12825. h. 26.**

BURROUGHES (Jeremiah) *See* Burroughs (Jeremiah) *Puritan Divine.*

BURROUGHES (Thomas) *See* Burroughs.

BURROUGHS ADDING MACHINE LTD.

—— Total to Date. The evolution of the adding machine: the story of Burroughs. By Bryan Morgan. [With illustrations.] pp. 65. *London,* 1953. 8°. **08228. i. 93.**

BURROUGHS MEMORIAL LECTURES. *See* England.—*Church of England.—Anglican Evangelical Group Movement.*

BURROUGHS, WELLCOME AND CO. [Miscellaneous publications.] *Burroughs, Wellcome & Co.: London,* [1901– .] 8°. **12199. d. 2.**

—— The A.B.C. Excerpta Therapeutica. (The Excerpta Therapeutica.) 1893, 1895, 1896. *London,* [1893–96.] 8°.
[Continued as:]
Wellcome's Excerpta Therapeutica. 1923–1941. *London,* [1922–40.] 8°. **7511. i. 1.**

BURROUGHS, WELLCOME AND CO.

—— Agenda médical Wellcome. *See* EPHEMERIDES.

—— Compendium pharmaceutique et thérapeutique Wellcome. Avec comparaison systématique de toutes les préparations des pharmocopées française et britannique. pp. 7. cclxxxiv. 10–325. *Burroughs, Wellcome & Cie.: Londres,* [1912.] 8°. **07510.** ff. **36.**

—— Infringement of Trade Marks in Italy. Burroughs, Welcome & Co. versus Farmacia Centrale Dompé, *etc. London,* 1902. 4°. **5359.** eee. **15.**

—— Prontuario fotográfico Wellcome. *See* EPHEMERIDES. Wellcome's Photographic Diary, *etc.*

—— 'Tabloid' Monthly Memoranda. March 1947, *etc. London,* 1947– . 8°. P.P. **1506.** ad.

—— The Wellcome Consultant's Appointment Book. *See* EPHEMERIDES.

—— Wellcome Photographic Exposure Calculator, Handbook and Diary. *See* EPHEMERIDES. Wellcome's Photographic Diary and Exposure Record.

—— The 'Wellcome' . . . Photographic Exposure Guide, *etc.* [With plates.] pp. 20. *London,* [1943.] 8°. **8911.** a. **7.**

—— Wellcome Photographic Year Book. *See* EPHEMERIDES. Wellcome's Photographic Diary and Exposure Record.

—— Wellcome's Chemist's Diary. *See* EPHEMERIDES. Chemists' Vest Pocket Diary, *etc.*

—— Wellcome's Excerpta Therapeutica. (Canadian edition.) pp. 255. *Burroughs, Wellcome & Co.: London,* [1922.] 8°. **07510.** ff. **35.**

—— Wellcome's Excerpta Therapeutica. (U.S.A. edition.) pp. 323. *Burroughs, Wellcome & Co.: London,* [1916.] 8°. **7462.** aa. **65.**

—— Wellcome's Materia Therapeutica for Medical Students. 1911-12(–1913-14). 3 pt. *Burroughs, Wellcome & Co.: London,* [1911–13.] **07510.** ff. **33.**

—— Wellcome's Materia Therapeutica. *Ger.* pp. 324. *Burroughs, Wellcome & Co.: London,* [1914.] 8°. **07510.** ff. **34.**

—— Wellcome's Medical Diary and Visiting List. *See* EPHEMERIDES. The ABC Medical Diary, *etc.*

—— Wellcome's Pharmacist's Diary. *See* EPHEMERIDES.

—— Wellcome's Photographic Diary and Exposure Record. *See* EPHEMERIDES.

Wellcome Club and Institute.

—— Souvenir of the Inauguration of the Wellcome Club and Institute, Dartford . . . 1899. (Founded for the benefit of Burroughs Wellcome & Co's employees.) [With illustrations.] pp. 12. [1899.] 8°. **10348.** aaa. **59.** (**4.**)

BURROUGHS (   ) *Mrs.*

—— The Monitor of Youth, and Companion to Manhood: or, Selections to create a taste for composition. [By Mrs. — Burroughs.] pp. 7. 109. 1807. 12°. *See* MONITOR. **012305.** k. **60.**

BURROUGHS (   ) *of Killingly, U.S.* The Right Hand of Fellowship [given at the ordination of Joel Benedict]. *See* HART (Levi) *Rev.* The Christian Minister, *etc.* 1771. 8°. **4486.** b. **61.** (**4.**)

BURROUGHS (ADONIRAM J.) *See* HARRIS (Mary) *of Chicago.* Official Report of the Trial of Mary Harris, indicted for the murder of A. J. Burroughs, *etc.* 1865. 8°. **6622.cc.1.**

BURROUGHS (ALAN)

—— *See* MILLER (Kenneth H.) Kenneth Hayes Miller. By A. Burroughs. [Reproductions, with an introduction.] [1931.] 8°. Ac. **4713.** g/2. (**6.**)

—— Art Criticism from a Laboratory. [With plates.] pp. xxiii. 277. *G. Allen & Unwin: London; printed in U.S.A.,* [1939.] 4°. **7866.** r. **19.**

—— Limners and Likenesses. Three centuries of American painting. [With plates.] pp. ix. 246. *Harvard University Press: Cambridge, Mass.,* 1936. 4°. [*Harvard-Radcliffe Fine Arts Series.*] Ac. **2692/37.** (**2.**)

BURROUGHS (ARTHUR THOMAS) A Sermon preached . . . in St. Nicholas-Without Parish Church, Dublin, January 20th, 1828. *See* BURROUGHS (Henry C.) Autumn Readings on the Poetical Books of the Bible. 1878. 8°. **3155.** e. **9.**

BURROUGHS (BRYSON) *See* NEW YORK.—*Metropolitan Museum of Art.* Bryson Burroughs. Catalogue of a memorial exhibition of his works. [With reproductions.] 1935. 8°. **7864.** pp. **8.**

—— *See* NEW YORK.—*Metropolitan Museum of Art.* Catalogue of an Exhibition of Spanish Paintings from El Greco to Goya. [With an introduction by B. Burroughs.] 1928. 8°. **7859.** pp. **30.**

—— *See* NEW YORK.—*Metropolitan Museum of Art.* Handbook of the Benjamin Altman Collection, *etc.* [The paintings described by B. Burroughs.] 1928. 8°. **7853.** t. **2.**

—— *See* NEW YORK.—*Metropolitan Museum of Art.* Landscape Paintings. A catalogue of an exhibition, *etc.* [With an introduction by B. Burroughs.] 1934. 8°. **7864.** pp. **1.**

—— *See* RANDOLPH (Lewis V. F.) Survivals . . . Embellished by B. Burroughs. 1900. 8°. **11688.** dd. **11.**

—— The Metropolitan Museum of Art. Catalogue of Paintings. pp. xi. 317. 1914. 8°. *See* NEW YORK.—*Metropolitan Museum of Art.* **2263.** b. **2.**

—— Ninth edition. pp. xiv. 434. 1931. 8°. *See* NEW YORK.—*Metropolitan Museum of Art.* **7852.** pp. **9.**

BURROUGHS (CHARLES) Charity a Prominent Duty of the Christian Ministry. A discourse delivered in St. Thomas's Church, Dover, N.H. . . . at the institution of the Reverend William Horton, *etc.* pp. 35. *J. W. Foster: Portsmouth, N.H.,* 1841. 8°. **4485.** i. **45.**

—— A Discourse (on Pauperism) delivered in the Chapel of the New Alms-house, in Portsmouth, N.H. . . . on the occasion of its being first opened for religious services. pp. 108. *J. W. Foster: Portsmouth, N.H.,* 1835. 8°. **8275.** e. **8.**

—— A Funeral Discourse preached in St. Paul's Church, Newburyport . . . at the Interment of the Reverend James Morss, *etc.* pp. 29. *J. W. Foster: Portsmouth, N.H.,* 1842. 8°. **4985.** cc. **46.** (**8.**)

BURROUGHS (DWIGHT) Jack, the Giant Killer, Jr. Being the thrilling adventures, authentically told, of a worthy son of the celebrated Jack, the Giant Killer, *etc.* pp. 203. *G. W. Jacobs & Co.: Philadelphia,* 1907. 8°. **12804**. v. **5**.

—— [A reissue.] *Grant Richards: London; printed in U.S.A.,* [1909.] 8°. **012803**. h. **66**.

BURROUGHS (E. G.)

—— Who's Who in the Red Army, *etc.* [With plates.] pp. 20. *Russia Today Society: Watford,* 1944. 8°. **10797**. ff. **21**.

BURROUGHS (EDEN) The Charge [delivered at the ordination of S. Bascom]. *See* EASTMAN (Tilton) A Sermon, preached . . . at the Ordination of the Rev. S. Bascom. 1806. 8°. **4486**. b. **61**. (**16**.)

—— A Sincere Regard to Righteousness and Piety, the sole Measure of a true Principle, of Honor and Patriotism. Illustrated in a sermon, preached before his Excellency the Governor, the Honorable Council and House of Representatives, in the State of Vermont, October 8th, A.D. 1778. [Reprinted from the edition of 1778.] 1931. *See* PERIODICAL PUBLICATIONS.—*New York.* The Magazine of History, *etc.* Extra number. no. 172. 1905, *etc.* 4°. P.P. **3437**. bab.

BURROUGHS (EDGAR RICE)

—— The Tarzan Novels. 19 pt. *Mark Goulden: London,* [1949–51.] 8°. **012603**. ccc. **1**.

—— At the Earth's Core, *etc.* pp. 277. *A. C. McClurg & Co.: Chicago,* 1922. 8°. NN. **8225**.

—— [Another edition.] pp. xi. 209. *Methuen & Co.: London,* 1923. 8°. NN. **8432**.

—— The Bandit of Hell's Bend. pp. 316. *A. C. McClurg & Co.: Chicago,* 1925. 8°. **12709**. aaa. **17**.

—— [Another edition.] pp. 254. *Methuen & Co.: London,* 1926. 8°. **12710**. a. **18**.

—— The Beasts of Tarzan, *etc.* pp. 336. *C. F. Cazenove: London; A. C. McClurg & Co.: Chicago; Chicago* [printed], 1916. 8°. NN. **3341**.

—— [Another edition.] pp. viii. 247. *Methuen & Co.: London,* 1918. 8°. NN. **4960**.

—— The Cave Girl. pp. 323. *A. C. McClurg & Co.: Chicago,* 1925. 8°. **012707**. g. **59**.

—— [Another edition.] pp. vi. 250. *Methuen & Co.: London,* 1927. 8°. **12712**. a. **9**.

—— The Chessmen of Mars, *etc.* pp. 375. *A. C. McClurg & Co.: Chicago,* 1922. 8°. **012705**. cc. **53**.

—— [Another edition.] pp. vii. 243. *Methuen & Co.: London,* 1923. 8°. NN. **8756**.

—— The Eternal Lover. pp. 316. *A. C. McClurg & Co.: Chicago,* 1925. 8°. **12709**. aa. **25**.

—— [Another edition.] pp. 248. *Methuen & Co.: London,* 1927. 8°. **12712**. c. **26**.

—— A Fighting Man of Mars, *etc.* pp. 319. *Metropolitan Books: New York,* [1931.] 8°. A.N. **963**.

—— [Another edition.] pp. xiii. 304. *John Lane: London,* 1932. 8°. A.N. **1253**.

BURROUGHS (EDGAR RICE)

—— The Girl from Hollywood. pp. 320. *Methuen & Co.: London,* 1924. 8°. NN. **9526**.

—— The Gods of Mars, *etc.* pp. xi. 348. *A. C. McClurg & Co.: Chicago,* 1918. 8°. NN. **5094**.

—— [Another edition.] pp. xi. 233. *Methuen & Co.: London,* 1920. 8°. NN. **6042**.

—— Jungle Girl. pp. 248. *Odhams Press: London,* [1934.] 8°. A.N. **2003**.

—— Jungle Tales of Tarzan, *etc.* pp. 319. *A. C. McClurg & Co.: Chicago,* 1919. 8°. NN. **5385**.

—— [Another edition.] pp. 250. *Methuen & Co.: London,* 1919. 8°. NN. **5784**.

—— The Land that Time Forgot, *etc.* pp. 422. *A. C. McClurg & Co.: Chicago,* 1924. 8°. **12702**. cc. **17**.

—— [Another edition.] pp. v. 279. *Methuen & Co.: London,* 1925. 8°. **12708**. d. **26**.

—— Lost on Venus. pp. v. 274. *Methuen & Co.: London,* 1937. 8°. A.N. **3771**.

—— The Mad King. pp. 365. *A. C. McClurg & Co.: Chicago,* 1926. 8°. **12711**. aa. **24**.

—— The Man without a Soul. pp. vi. 209. *Methuen & Co.: London,* 1922. 8°. NN. **7548**.

—— The Master Mind of Mars, *etc.* pp. 312. *A. C. McClurg & Co.: Chicago,* 1928. 8°. **12713**. d. **1**.

—— The Master Mind of Mars. Being a tale of weird and wonderful happenings on the red planet. pp. 216. *Methuen & Co.: London,* 1939. 8°. NN. **30695**.

—— The Monster Men. pp. 304. *A. C. McClurg & Co.: Chicago,* 1929. 8°. **12715**. b. **21**.

—— The Moon Maid. pp. 412. *A. C. McClurg & Co.: Chicago,* 1926. 8°. **12710**. aa. **5**.

—— The Mucker, *etc.* pp. 414. *A. C. McClurg & Co.: Chicago,* 1921. 8°. NN. **7529**.

—— [Another edition.] pp. v. 201. *Methuen & Co.: London,* 1921. 8°. NN. **7347**.

—— The Outlaw of Torn. pp. 298. *A. C. McClurg & Co.: Chicago,* 1927. 8°. **12712**. aa. **23**.

—— [Another edition.] pp. 250. *Methuen & Co.: London,* 1927. 8°. NN. **13071**.

—— Pellucidar. A sequel to "At the Earth's Core," *etc.* pp. 322. *A. C. McClurg & Co.: Chicago,* 1923. 8°. **012704**. d. **50**.

—— [Another edition.] pp. 253. *Methuen & Co.: London,* 1924. 8°. **12707**. de. **52**.

—— Pirates of Venus. pp. v. 312. *John Lane: London,* 1935. 8°. NN. **24000**.

—— A Princess of Mars, *etc.* pp. xii. 326. *A. C. McClurg & Co.: Chicago,* 1917. 8°. NN. **4563**.

—— [Another edition.] pp. 252. *Methuen & Co.: London,* 1919. 8°. NN. **5371**.

—— Princino de Marso . . . Tradukis el la usona originalo K. R. C. Sturmer. pp. 189. *Esperanto Publishing Co.: Rickmansworth,* [1938.] 8°. ["*Epoko*" *Libro-Klubo.* vol. 5.] W.P. **1570/5**.

—— The Return of Tarzan, *etc.* pp. 365. *C. F. Cazenove: London; A. C. McClurg & Co.: Chicago; Chicago* [printed], 1915. 8°. NN. **2510.**

—— [Another edition.] pp. viii. 246. *Methuen & Co.: London,* 1918. 8°. NN. **4789.**

—— [Another edition.] pp. 128. *George Newnes: London,* [1929.] 8°. **012604.** bbb. **37.**

—— The Son of Tarzan, *etc.* pp. 394. *A. C. McClurg & Co.: Chicago,* 1917. 8°. NN. **4341.**

—— [Another edition.] pp. 245. *Methuen & Co.: London,* 1919. 8°. NN. **5304.**

—— [Another edition.] pp. 128. *George Newnes: London,* [1929.] 8°. **012604.** bbb. **16.**

—— Synthetic Men of Mars. pp. 251. *Methuen & Co.: London,* 1941. 8°. **12723.** aa. **15.**

—— Tanar of Pellucidar, *etc.* pp. 312. *Metropolitan Books: New York,* [1930.] 8°. A.N. **398.**

—— [Another edition.] pp. vii. 274. *Methuen & Co.: London,* 1939. 8°. **12719.** aaa. **5.**

—— Tarzan and the Ant Men. pp. 346. *A. C. McClurg & Co.: London,* 1924. 8°. **12708.** aa. **8.**

—— [Another edition.] pp. vi. 250. *Methuen & Co.: London,* 1925. 8°. NN. **10614.**

—— Tarzan and the City of Gold. pp. 269. *John Lane: London,* 1936. 8°. A.N. **2891.**

—— Tarzan and the City of Gold . . . Illustrated by Jesse Marsh. Authorized abridged edition. pp. 184. *Publicity Products: London,* [1954.] 8°. [*Venture Library.* no. 5.] W.P. c. **150/5.**

—— Tarzan and the Forbidden City . . . Illustrated by Jesse Marsh. Authorized abridged edition. pp. 184. *Publicity Products: London,* [1954.] 8°. [*Venture Library.* no. 4.] W.P. c. **150/4.**

—— Tarzan and "The Foreign Legion." pp. 239. *W. H. Allen: London,* [1949.] 8°. 12715.de.24.

—— Tarzan and the Golden Lion, *etc.* pp. 333. *A. C. McClurg & Co.: Chicago,* 1923. 8°. NN. **8710.**

—— [Another edition.] pp. v. 245. *Methuen & Co.: London,* 1924. 8°. NN. **9434.**

—— Tarzan and the Jewels of Opar, *etc.* pp. 350. *A. C. McClurg & Co.: Chicago,* 1918. 8°. NN. **4869.**

—— [Another edition.] pp. vi. 247. *Methuen & Co.: London,* 1919. 8°. NN. **5618.**

—— Tarzan and the Leopard Men, *etc.* pp. 332. *E. R. Burroughs: Tarzana, Cal.,* [1935.] 8°. A.N. **2621.**

—— [Another edition.] pp. v. 278. *John Lane: London,* 1936. 8°. A.N. **3270.**

—— Tarzan and the Lost Empire, *etc.* pp. 313. *Metropolitan Books: New York,* [1929.] 8°. A.N. **45.**

—— [Another edition.] pp. 297. *Cassell & Co.: London,* 1931. 8°. A.N. **770.**

—— Tarzan at the Earth's Core, *etc.* pp. vii. 301. *Metropolitan Books: New York,* 1930. 8°. A.N. **690.**

—— [Another edition.] pp. vii. 273. *Methuen & Co.: London,* 1938. 8°. **12718.** aa. **11.**

—— Tarzan, Lord of the Jungle, *etc.* pp. 377. *A. C. McClurg & Co.: Chicago,* 1928. 8°. **012707.** h. **22.**

—— [Another edition.] pp. 316. *Cassell & Co.: London,* 1928. 8°. **012706.** i. **8.**

—— Tarzan of the Apes, *etc.* pp. 400. *A. L. Burt Co.: New York,* 1914. 8°. **12654.** d. **23.**

—— Tarzan of the Apes. pp. viii. 269. *Methuen & Co.: London,* 1917. 8°. NN. **4426.**

—— [Another edition.] pp. 127. *George Newnes: London,* [1929.] 8°. **012604.** bbb. **13.**

—— The Illustrated Tarzan Books. no. 1. Picturized from the novel "Tarzan of the Apes" . . . 300 pictures by Harold Foster. [With a summary of the novel.] pp. 79. *Grosset & Dunlap: New York,* [1929.] 8°. **012643.** p. **32.**

—— Tarzan the Invincible. pp. v. 314. *John Lane: London,* 1933. 8°. A.N. **1777.**

—— Tarzan the Magnificent. pp. ix. 278. *Methuen & Co.: London,* 1940. 8°. **12722.** a. **1.**

—— Tarzan the Terrible, *etc.* pp. 408. *A. C. McClurg & Co.: Chicago,* 1921. 8°. NN. **7293.**

—— [Another issue.] *McClelland & Stewart: Toronto,* [1921.] 8°. **12710.** a. **2.**

—— [Another edition.] pp. 243. *Methuen & Co.: London,* 1921. 8°. NN. **7195.**

—— Tarzan the Untamed, *etc.* pp. 428. *A. C. McClurg & Co.: Chicago,* 1920. 8°. NN. **6360.**

—— [Another issue.] *McClelland & Stewart: Toronto,* [1920.] 8°. NN. **6910.**

—— [Another edition.] pp. v. 281. *Methuen & Co.: London,* 1920. 8°. NN. **6434.**

—— Tarzan Triumphant. pp. v. 311. *John Lane: London,* 1934. 8°. A.N. **1895.**

—— The Tarzan Twins, *etc.* pp. 126. *Collins: London & Glasgow,* [1930.] 8°. **12819.** bb. **15.**

—— [A reissue.] *London & Glasgow,* [1934.] 8°. **20053.** g. **19.**

—— Tarzan's Quest. pp. vi. 296. *Methuen & Co.: London,* 1938. 8°. **12716.** d. **19.**

—— Thuvia, Maid of Mars, *etc.* pp. 256. *A. C. McClurg & Co.: Chicago,* 1920. 8°. NN. **6755.**

—— [Another edition.] pp. v. 218. *Methuen & Co.: London,* 1921. 8°. NN. **6826.**

—— The War Chief. pp. 382. *A. C. McClurg & Co.: Chicago,* 1927. 8°. **12713.** b. **9.**

—— [Another edition.] pp. v. 250. *Methuen & Co.: London,* 1928. 8°. **12714.** bb. **20.**

—— The Warlord of Mars, *etc.* pp. 296. *A. C. McClurg & Co.: Chicago,* 1919. 8°. NN. **5873.**

—— [Another edition.] pp. 221. *Methuen & Co.: London,* 1920. 8°. NN. **6195.**

BURROUGHS (Edward) *See* Burrough.

BURROUGHS (Edward Arthur) *Bishop of Ripon.* *See* Hood (Jack) *pseud.* The Heart of a Schoolboy . . . With a preface by Rev. E. A. Burroughs. 1919. 8°. **08364.** e. **2.**

—— *See* Mulliner (Harold G.) Arthur Burroughs. A memoir, *etc.* [With portraits.] 1936. 8°. **20030.** h. **4.**

—— *See* Stirling (John) The Study Bible. (St. Matthew . . . With new studies by the Bishop of Ripon and J. A. Findlay.) 1926, *etc.* 8°. **03126.** h. **2/9.**

—— *See* Woods (Frank T.) successively *Bishop of Peterborough* and *of Winchester.* The Creed of a Churchman. By F. T. Woods . . . E. A. Burroughs, *etc.* 1916. 8°. **4105.** de. **38.**

—— The Christian Church and War. pp. 45. *J. Nisbet & Co.: London,* [1931.] 8°. [*Lambeth Series.*] **4139.g.54/7.**

—— The Delayed Decision. Plain words on present hopes and fears. pp. 16. *Longmans & Co.: London,* 1918. 8°. **04376.** h. **28.**

—— The Divine Mission of Man. (Reprinted from "The Student Movement.") pp. 8. *Parker & Son: Oxford,* 1920 [1919]. 8°. **04403.** f. **62.**

—— Education and Religion. A course of lectures given in Bristol Cathedral. Edited, with an introductory chapter, by E. A. Burroughs. pp. 253. *Hodder & Stoughton: London,* [1924.] 8°. **04018.** e. **64.**

—— The End of It All. Thoughts on war aims and their attainment. pp. 11. *The Challenge: London,* [1918.] 8°. **04376.** f. **67.**

—— The Eternal Goal. Three letters to "The Times" on the spiritual issues of the present situation. pp. 22. *Longmans & Co.: London,* 1915. 8°. **4378.** g. **36.**

—— Faith and Power. A sermon, *etc.* (Reprinted from the Record newspaper.) pp. 8. *B. H. Blackwell: Oxford,* 1914. 8°. **4477.** i. **12.**

—— A Faith for the Firing Line. Two addresses to officers of the British Expeditionary Force at Rouen, together with a sermon preached in the chapel of the British headquarters there, *etc.* pp. 62. *Nisbet & Co.: London,* 1915. 8°. **4463.** de. **5.**

—— The Faith of Friends. pp. ix. 103. *Nisbet & Co.: London,* 1918. 8°. **04376.** de. **48.**

—— The Fight for the Future. pp. 127. *Nisbet & Co.: London,* 1916. 8°. **04376.** de. **24.**

—— The Latin Culture. A brief study in national education. pp. 68. *Duckworth & Co.: London,* 1920. 8°. **8311.** de. **16.**

—— The Patience of God. Some thoughts in preparation for the National Mission of Repentance and Hope. pp. viii. 39. *Longmans & Co.: London,* 1916. 8°. **04376.** de. **26.**

—— Prayer as a Problem. pp. 15. *Hodder & Stoughton: London,* [1924.] 8°. [*Anglican Evangelical Group Movement Pamphlets.* no. 21.] **4107.** ff. **55/21.**

—— Prayer in Practice. pp. 15. *Hodder & Stoughton: London,* [1924.] 8°. [*Anglican Evangelical Group Movement Pamphlets.* no. 22.] **4107.** ff. **55/22.**

BURROUGHS (Edward Arthur) *Bishop of Ripon.*

—— Progressive Meanings of Spiritual Life. A sermon . . . Reprinted from "The Guardian." pp. 10. *B. H. Blackwell: Oxford,* 1914. 8°. **4463.** i. **9.**

—— The Re-assertion of the Moral Idea . . . An address to the Ripon Diocesan Conference, *etc.* pp. 16. *Jowett & Sowry: Leeds,* [1932.] 8°. **4105.** de. **63.**

—— The Valley of Decision. A plea for wholeness in thought and life. pp. xix. 391. *Longmans & Co.: London,* 1916. 8°. **04376.** ee. **50.**

—— The Way of Peace. A study of the earliest programme of Christian life, *etc.* pp. 160. *Longmans & Co.: London,* 1920. 8°. **04403.** f. **59.**

—— World-Builders All. The task of the rising generation. pp. xv. 99. *Longmans & Co.: London,* 1917. 8°. **4016.** ee. **25.**

—— World Crisis. First thoughts on the new outlook. pp. 10. *The Challenge: London,* [1918.] 12°. **08027.** h. **6.**

—— You. A word to such as have not stopped growing. pp. 23. *Lutterworth Press: London,* [1933.] 32°. [*Lutterworth Messages.* no. 1.] **4384.aa.22/1.**

—— You. A word to such as have not stopped growing. pp. 15. *United Society for Christian Literature: London,* [1940.] 16°. [*Lutterworth Messages.* no. 1.] **4384.aa.22/1a.**

BURROUGHS (Edward Hartson) A Tabular View of the Law relating to Judgments and Recognizances in Ireland. *E. J. Milliken: Dublin,* 1858. *s. sh.* fol. **1881.** c. **7.** **(98.)**

BURROUGHS (Edward Hartson) and **GRESSON** (Henry Barnes)

—— The Irish Equity Pleader: being a collection of forms of bills in equity suits in Ireland, with preliminary dissertations and practical notes. pp. xxxi. 925. *Hodges & Smith: Dublin,* 1850. 8°. **6503.** d. **5.**

BURROUGHS (Elizabeth) An Account of the late Trial at . . . Bury St. Edmund's . . . for the Murder of Mary Booty; of which Eliz. Burroughs was convicted, *etc.* pp. 38. *London; W. Green: Bury; Fletcher & Hodson: Cambridge,* 1766. 8°. **6146.** f. **3.** **(1.)**

BURROUGHS (Elizabeth Harding) Bibliography of Petroleum and Allied Substances, 1915(–1921). 5 pt. *Washington,* 1918–23. 8°. [*U.S. Bureau of Mines. Bulletin.* no. 149, 165, 180, 189, 216, 220.] A.S. **229.**

BURROUGHS (Francis) *of London.* A Poetical Epistle to James Barry, Esq., containing strictures upon some of the works of that . . . artist. With an appendix. pp. xi. 132. *J. Carpenter: London,* 1805. 8°. **C.116.e.4.**

BURROUGHS (Francis) *Rev.* *See* Periodical Publications.—Dublin.—*The Batchelor.* Select Essays from the Batchelor, *etc.* [By R. Jephson, J. Courtenay, F. Burroughs and others.] 1772. 12°. **712.** c. **36.**

—— —— 1773. 12°. **12352.** c. **46.**

BURROUGHS (George Frederick) A Narrative of the Retreat of the British Army from Burgos . . . With an introductory sketch of the campaign of 1812; and military character of the Duke of Wellington. pp. liv. 88. *Joseph Routh: Bristol*, 1814. 8°. **1060**. f. **2**.

BURROUGHS (Harry Ernest) Tale of a Vanished Land. Memories of a childhood in old Russia . . . Illustrated with woodcuts by Howard Simon. pp. 336. *G. Allen & Unwin: London ; Cambridge, Mass.* printed, 1930. 8°. **010290**. f. **26**.

BURROUGHS (Henry) An Address to the Public; but more especially to the inhabitants of the parish of St. Leonard, Shoreditch, relative to the master of their workhouse. pp. 10. [*London?* 1784.] 12°. **8285**. a. **7**.

BURROUGHS (Henry Colclough) Autumn Readings on the Poetical Books of the Bible. (A Sermon preached by the late Rev. Arthur Thomas Burroughs . . . January 20th, 1828.) pp. xviii. 509. *J. Nisbet & Co.: London*, 1878. 8°. **3155**. e. **9**.

—— The Household of Faith; or, Family prayers for a fortnight. pp. iv. 91. *Carson Bros.: Dublin ; Simpkin, Marshall & Co.: London*, 1895. 8°. **3456**. ee. **35**.

—— Short Daily Readings on the Historical Books of the New Testament. pp. 348. *George Herbert: Dublin*, 1872. 8°. **3227**. aa. **16**.

—— Short Evening Readings on the Epistles and Revelation. pp. 484. *George Herbert: Dublin*, 1872. 8°. **3265**. aa. **27**.

—— Short Morning Readings on some of the Historical Books of the Old Testament. pp. 229. *George Herbert: Dublin*, 1873. 8°. **3128**. bbb. **17**.

—— Short Private Morning Prayers for one month. pp. 90. *Carson Bros.: Dublin ; Simpkin, Marshall & Co.: London*, 1894. 8°. **3456**. dd. **45**.

—— Short Reflections on what the Scripture saith concerning Baptism. pp. 63. *George Herbert: Dublin*, 1878. 8°. **4372**. g. **6**. **(12.)**

—— Summer Readings on the Pentateuch. pp. xv. 592. *George Herbert: Dublin*, 1875. 8°. **3149**. de. **42**.

—— Sunday Readings on the Four Greater Prophets. 2 vol. *William Ridings: Dublin*, 1876, 77. 8°. **3185**. de. **59**.

—— Sunday Readings on the Twelve Minor Prophets. pp. x. 10–308. *George Herbert: Dublin*, 1873. 8°. **3166**. aa. **54**.

—— Vernal Readings on the Book of Psalms. (A Sermon preached, February, 1882 in Rathfarnham Church.) 3 vol. *George Herbert: Dublin*, 1884, 85. 8°. **3090**. k. **7**.

—— Winter Readings on the Historical Books of the Old Testament. pp. xv. 478. *George Herbert: Dublin*, 1874. 8°. **3149**. de. **43**.

BURROUGHS (Humphrey) The Case of Humphrey Burroughs and George Reynolds, Respondents; upon the appeal of Anthony Parker, Appellant. Touching an award made by Dr. Oates, and set aside in Chancery, *etc.* pp. 3. [*London*, 1702.] fol. **1855**. c. **4**. **(14.)**

BURROUGHS (J.) *Minister at Wisbech.* A Narrative of the Conversion of Thomas Mackernesse, late of March in the Isle of Ely. Who was condemn'd for robbery, &c. and executed at Wisbech, Aug. 19, 1694; with an account of his penitential behaviour, *etc.* pp. 30. *For John Dunton: London*, 1694. 8°. **1132**. b. **34**.

BURROUGHS (Jeremiah) *Presbyterian Minister at Blackfriars.* A Sermon preach'd at Blackfriars, to a Society of Young Men, on January 1. 1715. pp. 24. *Eman. Matthews: London*, 1715. 8°. **695**. f. **2**. **(5.)**

—— Heavenly-Mindedness Recommended: in a discourse on Colossians iii. 2 . . . The second edition [of " A Sermon preached at Blackfriars "]. pp. 22. *John Clark: London*, 1715. 8°. **4377**. b. **49**. **(4.)**

—— A Short View of Popery: in a sermon, preach'd . . . on November 5. 1715. pp. 21. *S. Cliff: London*, 1716. 8°. **4476**. aaa. **26**.

BURROUGHS (Jeremiah) *Puritan Divine.* *See* Edwards (Thomas) *Author of "Gangræna."* Antapologia: or, a Full answer to the Apologeticall Narration of Mr Goodwin . . . Mr Burroughs, *etc.* 1644. 4°. E. **1**. **(1.)**

—— *See* Goodwin (Thomas) *D.D.* An Apologeticall Narration . . . By T. Goodwin . . . J. Burroughes, *etc.* 1643. 4°. **1103**. f. **11**. **(1.)**

—— —— 1934. 8°. [*Haller (William) Tracts on Liberty in the Puritan Revolution.* vol. 2. pt. 1.] **Ac.2688/45.(18.)**

—— *See* Goodwin (Thomas) *D.D.* A Copy of a Remonstrance lately delivered in to the Assembly. By T. Goodwin, I. Burroughs, *etc.* 1645. 4°. E. **309**. **(4.)**

—— *See* Goodwin (Thomas) *D.D.* The Reasons of the Dissenting Brethren (T. Goodwin, J. Burroughs [and others]) against the Third Proposition concerning Presbyterial Government, *etc.* 1645. 4°. E. **27**. **(14.)**

—— *See* Sibbes (Richard) The Christian's Portion, *etc.* [With an epistle to the reader signed: J. B., i.e. J. Burroughs ?] 1638. 12°. **4403**. d. **12**.

—— A briefe Answer to Doctor Fernes Booke [entitled " The Resolving of Conscience," *etc.*] tending to resolve Conscience, about the Subjects taking up of arms. pp. 14. [*London*, 1643.] 4°. **4175.b.103.(14.)**

—— The Difference between the Spots of the Godly, and of the Wicked. [Four sermons.] pp. 112. [*Thomas Parkhurst*:] *London*, 1668. 8°. **4453**. aaa. **4**.

—— The Eighth Book of Mr Jeremiah Burroughs. Being a Treatise of the Evil of Evils, or the Exceeding Sinfulness of Sin . . . Published by Thomas Goodwyn, William Bridge, Sydrach Sympson, William Adderly, William Greenhil, Philip Nye, John Yates. pp. 537. *Peter Cole: London*, 1654. 4°. E. **819**.

—— The Excellency of a Gracious Spirit. Delivered in a treatise upon the 14. of Numbers, verse 24. [With an epistle to the reader signed: W. Gr., i.e. W. Greenhill.] pp. 431. *M. F. [Miles Flesher] for R. Dawlman & L. Fawne: London*, 1638. 8°. **4400**. k. **7**.

—— [Another edition.] pp. 431. *M. F. [Miles Flesher] for R. Dawlman & L. Fawne: London*, 1640. 8°. C. **48**. c. **1**.

—— [Another edition.] Together with Moses his Self-deniall. 2 pt. *G. Dawson for Francis Eglesfield: London*, 1649. 8°. **3149**. b. **21**.

—— [Another edition.] Together with Moses his Self-deniall. *A. Neile for Francis Eglesfield: London*, 1657. 8°. **4406**. aaa. **34**.
Imperfect; wanting " Moses his Self-deniall."

—— The Excellency of Holy Courage in Evil Times, *etc.* pp. 215. *Peter Cole & Edward Cole: London,* 1661. 4°. **874. k. 39.**

—— An Exposition of the Prophesie of Hosea. Begun in divers lectures upon the first three chapters, *etc.* [With the text and with a portrait.] pp. 750. 1643. 4°. *See* Bible.—*Hosea.—Selections.* [*English.*] **1005. b. 19.**

—— [Another copy.] **E. 98.**

—— An Exposition with practical observations continued upon the fourth, fifth, sixth, and seventh chapters of the Prophesy of Hosea. Being first delivered in several lectures, *etc.* [With the text.] pp. 700. 1650. 4°. *See* Bible.—*Hosea.—Selections.* [*English.*] **1005. b. 20.**

—— An Exposition with practical observations continued upon the eighth, ninth, tenth, eleventh, twelfth, and thirteenth chapters of the Prophesy of Hosea. Being first delivered in several lectures, *etc.* [With the text and with a portrait.] 2 pt. 1654, 51. 4°. *See* Bible.—*Hosea.—Selections.* [*English.*] **1005. b. 21.**

—— [Another copy of pt. 2.] **E. 588.**

—— Four Books on the Eleventh of Matthew: viz. i. Christ Inviting Sinners to Come to him for Rest. ii. Christ the Great Teacher of Souls that Come to him. To which is added a Treatise of Meekness and of Anger. iii. Christ the Humble Teacher of those that Come to him. iiii. The only Easie way to Heaven. [Edited by T. Goodwin, W. Greenhill, W. Bridge, S. Simpson, P. Nye, J. Yates and W. Adderly.] 3 vol. *Peter Cole: London,* 1659. 4°. **E. 963. (2.)–965. (1.)**
The pagination of vol. 2 & 3, which contain bk. 2–4, is continuous.

—— [Another copy.] Four Books on the Eleventh of Matthew, *etc. London,* 1659. 4°. **1470. b. 1.**
In this copy a portrait of Burroughs, engraved by Cross, has been inserted. The last leaf of bk. 4 is slightly mutilated.

—— Four Useful Discourses: viz. i. The Art of Improving a full and prosperous Condition, for the Glory of God; being an appendix to the Art of Contentment: in three sermons . . . ii. Christian Submission . . . iii. Christ a Christian's Life; and Death his Gain . . . iv. The Gospel of Peace sent to the Sons of Peace, in six sermons, *etc.* [The editor's address to the reader signed: M. M., i.e. Matthew Mead ?] pp. 276. *For Thomas Parkhurst: London,* 1675. 4°. **1022. g. 23.**

—— The glorious Name of God, the Lord of Hosts. Opened in two sermons . . . vindicating the commission from this Lord of Hosts, to subjects, in some case, to take up arms. With a postscript briefly answering a late treatise [entitled, "The Resolving of Conscience," *etc.*] by Henry Ferne. pp. 146. *For R. Dawlman: London,* 1643. 4°. **693. f. 5. (4.)**

—— [Another edition.] 2 pt. *For R. Dawlman: London,* 1643. 8°. **4452. d. 29. (1.)**

—— Gospel Conversation: wherein is shewed, how the conversation of believers must be above what could be by the light of nature, *etc.* (The Miserie of those Men that have their Portion in this Life discovered.) [Edited by T. Goodwin, W. Greenhill, S. Simpson, P. Nye, W. Bridge, J. Yates and W. Adderly. With a portrait.] 2 pt. pp. 372. *For Peter Cole: London,* 1648. 4°. **E. 444. (1, 2.)**

—— [Another edition.] Gospel-Conversation . . . Being the third book [of Burroughs's works], published by Thomas Goodwyn, William Greenhil, Sydrach Simpson, Philip Nye, William Bridge, John Yates, William Adderly. pp. 359. *Printed by Peter Cole: London,* 1653. 4°. **851. d. 15.**

—— Gospel-Fear: or the Heart trembling at the Word of God, evidenceth a blessed frame of spirit. Delivered in several sermons, *etc.* [Edited by Thomas Brookes.] pp. 166. *J. D. for B. Aylmer: London,* 1674. 8°. **1481. bb. 9.**

—— Gospel-Reconciliation: or, Christs trumpet of peace to the world . . . To which is added two sermons . . . Published . . . by Thomas Goodwin, William Bridge, William Greenhil, Sydrach Sympson, Philip Nye, John Yates, William Adderley. pp. 451. *Printed by Peter Cole: London,* 1657. 4°. **3266. c. 24.**

—— Gospel Remission, or a Treatise shewing that true blessedness consists in pardon of sin . . . Being several sermons preached immediately after those of The Evil of Sin, by the same author. And now published by Philip Nye, William Greenhill, William Bridge, William Adderly, Matth. Mead, C. Helmes. pp. 220. *For Dor. Newman: London,* 1668. 8°. **4452. d. 8.**

—— Gospel-Revelation in three Treatises; viz, 1. The Nature of God. 2. The Excellencies of Christ. And, 3. The Excellency of Mans Immortal Soul . . . Published by William Greenhill, William Bridge, Philip Nye, John Yates, Matthew Mead, William Adderly. pp. 370. *For Nath. Brook & Thomas Parkhurst: London,* 1660. 4°. **E. 1029. (1.)**

—— Gospel-Worship: or, the Right manner of sanctifying the name of God in generall. And particularly in these 3. great ordinances, viz. 1. Hearing the word. 2. Receiving the Lords Supper. 3. Prayer. [Edited by T. Goodwin, W. Greenhill, W. Bridge, S. Simpson, P. Nye, J. Yates and W. Adderly. The address to the reader signed by the first five editors.] pp. 297. *For Peter Cole & R. W.: London,* 1648. 4°. **E. 408. (1.)**

—— [Another edition.] Gospel Worship . . . Being the second of the seven volumns [of Burroughs' works], lately published by Thomas Goodwin, William Greenhil, Sydrach Sympson, Philip Nye, William Bridge, John Yates, William Adderly. pp. 297. *Printed by Peter Cole: London,* 1653. 4°. **851. d. 14.**

—— [Another edition.] pp. 297. *Printed by Peter Cole: London,* 1658. 4°. **4452. c. 5.**

—— Irenicum, to the Lovers of Truth and Peace. Heart-divisions opened in the causes and evils of them: with cautions that we may not be hurt by them, and endeavours to heal them. pp. 302. *For Robert Dawlman: London,* 1646. 4°. **E. 306. (9.)**
The running title reads "Heart-divisions the Evill of our Times."

—— [Another edition.] pp. 302. *For Robert Dawlman: London,* 1653. 4°. **4404. e. 51.**
The running title reads "Heart-divisions the Evill of our Times."

—— Jacobs Seed: or the Generation of seekers. And Davids Delight, or the Excellent on earth. [Two sermons.] pp. 156. *Printed by Roger Daniel: Cambridge,* 1648. 12°. **E. 1162. (1.)**

—— Jerusalems Glory breaking forth into the World, being a scripture-discovery of the New Testament Church in the latter days immediately before the Second Coming of Christ. [Three sermons. Edited by William Adderly.] pp. 114. *For Giles Calvert: [London,]* 1675. 8°. **4474.** a. **38.**

—— [Another edition.] [With a portrait.] pp. 120. *Printed by J. H.; sold by J. Sprint: London,* 1697. 8°. **3185.** a. **4.**

—— The Miserie of those Men that have their Portion in this Life discovered. *See* supra: Gospel Conversation.

—— Moses his Choice, with his eye fixed upon heaven: discovering the happy condition of a self-denying heart. Delivered in a treatise upon Heb. II. 25, 26. pp. 754. *M. F. [Miles Flesher] for R. D. [Robert Dawlman]: London,* 1641. 4°. **1006.** d. **8.**

—— [Another edition.] pp. 722. *Printed by John Field; sold by Thomas Eglesfield: London,* 1650. 4°. **3266.** c. **23.**
The titlepage is mounted. A portrait of the author has been inserted.

—— Moses his Self-denyall. Delivered in a treatise upon Hebrewes 11. the 24. verse. [With an address to the reader by W. Greenhill.] pp. 262. MS. NOTE. *Printed by T. Paine; sold by H. Overton & T. Nichols: London,* 1641. 8°. **3267.** b. **2.**

—— [Another edition.] pp. 248. *J. Dawson for Francis Eglesfeild: London,* 1649. 8°. **3266.** b. **19.**
A duplicate of pt. 2 *of the* 1649 *edition of "The Excellency of a Gracious Spirit."*

—— The Ninth, Tenth, and Eleventh Books of Mr Jeremiah Burroughs: containing three treatises: I. of Precious Faith. II. Of Hope. III. The Saints walk by faith on earth; by sight in Heaven. Being the last sermons that the author preached at Stepney . . . Published by Thomas Goodwyn, William Bridge, Sydrach Simpson, William Adderly, William Greenhil, Philip Nye, John Yates. [With a portrait.] pp. 436. *Printed by Peter Cole: London,* 1655. 4°. E. **827.** (**1.**)

—— The Rare Jewel of Christian Contentment, *etc.* [Eleven sermons. Edited by T. Goodwin, S. Simpson, W. Greenhill, P. Nye, W. Bridge, J. Yates and W. Adderly.] (The Saints Duty in times of extremity. Opened in a sermon, *etc.*) [With a portrait.] 2 pt. pp. 329. *For Peter Cole: London,* 1648. 4°. E. **424.** (**1, 2.**)
The pagination is irregular, p. 208 *being followed by p.* 299.

—— [Another edition.] The Rare Jewel of Christian Contentment . . . The first of the three volumes [of Burroughs's works] that are published by Thomas Goodwyn, William Greenhill, *etc.* (The Saints Duty in times of extremity.) pp. 329. *For Peter Cole: London,* 1649. 4°. **4403.** gg. **10.**
The pagination is irregular, p. 208 *being followed by p.* 299.

—— [Another edition.] pp. 329. *Printed by Peter Cole: London,* 1655. 4°. **851.** d. **16.**
The pagination is irregular, p. 208 *being followed by p.* 299.

—— [Another edition.] pp. 208. *Printed by John Streater; sold by Richard Chiswel: London,* 1670. 4°. **4404.** i. **2.**

—— [Another edition.] pp. 288. *R.T.S.: London,* 1831. 12°. **863.** g. **11.**

—— [Another edition.] With a sermon on the Saint's duty in times of extremity . . . Reprinted from the edition of 1655. pp. 96. *T. Ward & Co.: London,* [1840.] 8°. **1126.** k. **12.** (**6.**)

—— [Another edition.] pp. 288. *H. G. Bohn: London,* 1845. 12°. **4400.** l. **4.**
A reissue of the edition of 1831.

—— The Saints Duty in Times of Extremity. Opened in a sermon . . . occasioned upon the news of extraordinary loss to the Parliaments forces in the west. *See* supra: The Rare Jewel of Christian Contentment.

—— The Saints Happinesse. Together with the severall steps leading thereunto, delivered in divers lectures on the Beatitudes . . . By Jeremiah Burroughs . . . Being the last sermons that ever he preached. Now published by William Greenhill, William Bridge, Philip Nye, John Yates, William Aderly, Mathew Mead. pp. 662. *M. S. for Nathaniel Brook: London,* 1660. 4°. E. **1028.**

—— The Saints Treasury . . . Being sundry sermons, *etc.* [Edited by James Nalton and others.] pp. 131. *T. C. for John Wright: London,* 1654. 4°. **4460.** aaa. **2.**

—— The Sea-Mans Direction in Time of Storme. Delivered in a sermon upon occasion of a strong stormie wind lately happening. pp. 87. *Printed by T. Paine & M. Simmons: London,* 1640. 8°. **1481.** d. **31.**
The signatures are: *4, Aa–Ee8, Ff4.

—— A Sermon preached before the . . . House of Commons . . . at their late solemn Fast, August 26. 1646. in Margarets Westminster. pp. 38. *Matthew Simmons, for Hanna Allen: London,* 1646. 4°. E. **351.** (**11.**)

—— A Sermon preached before the . . . House of Peeres, in the Abbey at Westminster the 26. of Novemb. 1645. Being the day appointed for solemne and publique humiliation. pp. 38. *For R. Dawlman: London,* 1646. 4°. E. **310.** (**2.**)

—— Sions Joy. A sermon preached to the . . . House of Commons . . . at their publique thanksgiving, September 7. 1641. for the peace concluded between England and Scotland. pp. 64. *T. P. [Thomas Payne] & M. S. [Matthew Simmons] for R. Dawlman, and are to be sold by Ben. Alline: London,* 1641. 4°. E. **174.** (**3.**)

—— [Another copy, with a different titlepage.] *T. P. & M. S. for R. Dawlman: London,* 1641. 4°. **4452.** d. **29.** (**2.**)

—— Mr. Jeremiah Burroughes his speech in Guild-hall on . . . the sixt of October, 1643. *See* LONDON.—II. *Livery of the City.* Foure Speeches delivered in Guild-Hall, *etc.* 1646. 4°. **102.** a. **76.**

—— Two Treatises . . . The first of earthly mindedness . . . The second treatise of conversing in Heaven and walking with God . . . The fourth volumn [of Burroughs's works] published by Thomas Goodwyn, William Greenhil, Sydrach Simpson, Philip Nye, William Bridge, Iohn Yates, William Addeley. pp. 339. *For Peter Cole: London,* 1649. 4°. E. **581.** (**2.**)

—— [Another edition.] pp. 339. *For Peter Cole: London,* 1652. 4°. **4400.** aaa. **43.**
The lower edge of the leaf containing the preface is cropped.

BURROUGHS (Jeremiah) *Puritan Divine.*

—— A Vindication of Mr Burroughes, against Mr Edwards his foule aspersions, in his spreading Gangræna, and his angry Antiapologia. Concluding with a briefe declaration what the Independents would have. [By J. Burroughs.] pp. 32. *For H. Overton: London*, 1646. 4°. **E. 345. (14.)**

—— *See* Edwards (Thomas) *Author of "Gangræna."* The third Part of Gangræna . . . As also some few hints and briefe observations on . . . M. Burroughs Vindication, *etc.* 1646. 4°. **108.b.56.(3.)**

—— An Elegie offered up to the memory of . . . Mr. Jeremiah Burroughs, *etc.* [Signed: I. C.] 1646. *s. sh.* fol. *See* C., I. **669. f. 10. (100.)**

BURROUGHS (John) *Naturalist. See* Audubon (John J.) Life and Adventures of Audubon the Naturalist, *etc.* (With an introduction by J. Burroughs.) [1912.] 8°. **12206.p.1/448.**

—— *See* Barrus (Clara) John Burroughs, *etc.* [With portraits.] 1921. 8°. **10884. bb. 12.**

—— *See* Barrus (Clara) The Life and Letters of John Burroughs, *etc.* [With portraits.] 1925. 8°. **010883. h. 45.**

—— *See* Barrus (Clara) Our Friend John Burroughs . . . Including autobiographical sketches by Mr. Burroughs, *etc.* [With portraits.] 1914. 8°. **10889. e. 38.**

—— *See* Barrus (Clara) Whitman and Burroughs, Comrades, *etc.* [With a portrait.] 1931. 8°. **10881. v. 2.**

—— *See* Blanchan (Neltje) *pseud.* Bird Neighbors . . . With introduction by J. Burroughs, *etc.* 1897. 8°. **K.T.C. 27. a. 22.**

—— *See* Kennedy (William S.) The Real John Burroughs, *etc.* [With portraits.] 1924. 8°. **10884. cc. 1.**

—— *See* Mayfield (John S.) The Luck of an Autograph Collector, being also a note on the aversion of J. Burroughs to A. C. Swinburne. [With facsimiles of J. Burroughs' autographs.] 1950. 4°. **11917. d. 5.**

—— *See* Sharp (Dallas L.) The Boys' Life of John Burroughs, *etc.* [With portraits.] 1928. 8°. **010884. de. 59.**

—— *See* White (Gilbert) *of Selborne.* Natural History of Selborne . . . Introduction by J. Burroughs, *etc.* 1895. 8°. **7001. b. 13.**

—— *See* Whitman (Walt) Lafayette in Brooklyn . . . With an introduction by J. Burroughs. 1905. 8°. **010661. h. 17.**

—— The Writings of John Burroughs. Riverside edition. [With portraits.] vol. 1–14, 16–20. *J. M. Dent & Co.: London; Cambridge, Mass.* printed, 1895–1919. 8°. **012295. a. 6.**

Vol. 10–20 *were published by Houghton, Mifflin & Co.: Boston & New York. Imperfect; wanting vol.* 15.

—— Thoreau's Wildness.—Emerson and the Superlative.—Nature in Literature. *See* Periodical Publications.—New York.—*The Critic.* Essays from "The Critic," *etc.* 1882. 8°. **12296. b. 2.**

—— Accepting the Universe. Essays in naturalism. [With a portrait.] pp. ix. 327. *Constable & Co.: London; Cambridge, Mass.* printed, [1921.] 8°. **08463. de. 45.**

—— Bird and Bough. [Poems.] pp. x. 70. *A. Constable & Co.: London; Cambridge, Mass.* printed, 1906. 8°. **11688. dd. 42.**

BURROUGHS (John) *Naturalist.*

—— Birds and Poets, with other papers. pp. 263. *Hurd & Houghton: New York*, 1877. 8°. **12356. aa. 19.**

—— [Another edition.] pp. 313. *David Douglas: Edinburgh*, 1884. 16°. **12357. a. 24.**

—— The Breath of Life. [With a portrait.] pp. ix. 294. *Houghton Mifflin Co.: Boston & New York*, 1915. 8°. **7007. aa. 2.**

—— Camping & Tramping with Roosevelt . . . With illustrations [including portraits]. pp. xiv. 110. *Houghton, Mifflin & Co.: Boston & New York*, 1907. 8°. **010883. ee. 31.**

—— The Exhilarations of the Road. *See* Praise. In Praise of Walking. 1905. 8°. **012203. e. 7/20.**

—— Far and Near. (Papers dealing with open-air themes.) pp. v. 287. *A. Constable & Co.: London; Cambridge, Mass.* printed, 1904. 8°. **10408. bb. 40.**

—— Fresh Fields. pp. 298. *David Douglas: Edinburgh*, 1885 [1884]. 8°. **12357. e. 31.**

—— [Another edition.] pp. 376. *David Douglas: Edinburgh*, 1885. 16°. **12352. a. 55.**

—— Indoor Studies. pp. 256. *Houghton, Mifflin & Co.: Boston & New York*, 1889. 8°. **12356. d. 34.**

—— The Last Harvest. [Essays, chiefly on literature, with special reference to Emerson and Thoreau. With a portrait of the author.] pp. ix. 294. *Jonathan Cape: London; printed in U.S.A.*, 1923. 8°. **012352. g. 8.**

—— Leaf and Tendril. pp. v. 288. *A. Constable & Co.: London; Cambridge, Mass.* [printed], 1908. 8°. **12352. s. 19.**

—— Literary Values, and other papers. pp. 264. *Houghton, Mifflin & Co.: Boston & New York*, 1902. 8°. **011853. e. 29.**

—— [Another copy, with a different titlepage.] *Gay & Bird: London; Cambridge, Mass.* printed, 1903. 8°. **11853. aa. 37.**

—— Locusts and Wild Honey. pp. 253. *Houghton, Osgood & Co.: Boston*, 1879. 8°. **12356. bbb. 24.**

—— [Another edition.] pp. 316. *David Douglas: Edinburgh*, 1884. 16°. **12357. aaa. 17.**

—— Narrative of the Expedition [i.e. of the Harriman Expedition to Alaska]. *See* Harriman (Edward H.) Harriman Alaska Series. vol. 1. 1901, *etc.* 8°. Ac. **1875/8.**

—— Notes on Walt Whitman, as Poet and Person . . . Second edition. pp. 126. *J. S. Redfield: New York*, 1871. 8°. **011840. f. 59.**

—— Pepacton. [Essays.] pp. iv. 260. *Sampson Low & Co.: London*, 1881. 8°. **12357. f. 11.**

—— [Another edition.] pp. 319. *David Douglas: Edinburgh*, 1884. 16°. **12357. a. 23.**

—— Riverby. (Out-of-door papers.) pp. 319. *Houghton, Mifflin & Co.: Boston & New York*, 1894. 8°. **012356. e. 21.**

—— Signs and Seasons. pp. 289. *Houghton, Mifflin & Co.: Boston & New York*, 1886. 8°. **10412. aa. 19.**

BURROUGHS (JOHN) *Naturalist.*

—— [Another copy, with a different titlepage.] *David Douglas: Edinburgh; [Cambridge, Mass.* printed,] 1886. 8°. **12357.** bb. **40.**

—— Time and Change. [With a portrait.] pp. vi. 278. *Constable & Co.: London; Cambridge, Mass.* [printed], 1912. 8°. **012354.** e. **24.**

—— Wake-Robin. pp. 312. *David Douglas: Edinburgh,* 1884. 16°. **7284.** a. **6.**

—— Ways of Nature. pp. vi. 279. *Houghton, Mifflin & Co.: Boston & New York,* 1905. 8°. **7005.** de. **28.**

—— Whitman. A study. pp. 268. *A. P. Watt & Son: London; Cambridge, Mass.* printed, [1896.] 8°. **10881.** aa. **36.**

—— [Another copy, with a different titlepage.] *A. Constable & Co.: London; Cambridge, Mass.* printed, [1897.] 8°. **10881.** de. **21.**

—— Winter Sunshine. pp. 285. *David Douglas: Edinburgh,* 1883. 16°. **12357.** aa. **7.**

—— A Year in the Fields. Selections from the writings of John Burroughs: with illustrations from photographs [including portraits]. pp. ix. 220. *Smith, Elder & Co.: London; Cambridge, Mass.* printed, 1896. 8°. **7001.** aa. **37.**

—— Birds and Bees. Selected essays with introduction, notes and study equipment. Revised edition. [With a portrait.] pp. xii. 88. *Houghton Mifflin Co.: Boston,* [1926.] 8°. **7286.** aa. **36.**

—— John Burroughs at Troutbeck: being extracts from his writings, published and unpublished, *etc.* pp. 20. *Troutbeck Press: Amenia,* 1926. 8°. [*Troutbeck Leaflets.* no. 10.] **12211.w.2/10.**

—— Sharp Eyes, and other papers . . . With introduction, notes and study equipment. Revised edition. [With a portrait.] pp. xii. 103. *Houghton, Mifflin Co.: Boston,* [1926.] 8°. **7006.** de. **39.**

BURROUGHS (JOHN) *Rector of Trusham.* The Devout Psalmodist. II Sermons, *etc.* pp. 59. *J. Downing: London,* 1712. 12°. **4476.** a. **138.** **(2.)**

—— [Another copy.] **4474.** a. **68.** **(2.)**

—— [A reissue.] *London,* 1714. 12°. **4454.** b. **38.** **(2.)**

—— The third edition. pp. 59. *J. Downing: London,* 1730. 12°. **4474.** a. **4.**

BURROUGHS (*Sir* JOHN) [For Heraldic Visitations made by the deputies of Sir J. Burroughs:] *See* ENGLAND.—*College of Arms.* [*Visitations.*]

—— Burrhi Impetus Juveniles: et quædam sedatioris aliquantulúm animi epistolæ. pp. 144. *Excudebat Leonardus Lichfield: Oxoniæ,* 1643. 12°. **1085.** a. **29.**

—— [Another edition.] *See* GISLENIUS (A.) A. Gislenii Busbequii omnia quæ extant . . . Quibus accedunt epistolæ insignium virorum, *etc.* 1660. 16°. **1084.** a. **18.**

—— Notes on the Treaty carried on at Ripon between King Charles I. and the Covenanters of Scotland, A.D. 1640, taken by Sir J. Borough . . . Edited . . . by John Bruce. pp. xli. 82. 1869. 4°. *See* LONDON.—III. *Camden Society.* Ac. **8113/91.**

BURROUGHS (*Sir* JOHN)

—— The Soveraignty of the British Seas, proved by Records, History, and the municipall Lawes of this Kingdome. Written in the yeare 1633. pp. 165. *For Humphrey Moseley: London,* 1651. 12°. **1128.** a. **23.**

—— [Another edition.] *See* MALYNES (G. de) Consuetudo, vel Lex Mercatoria, *etc.* 1686. fol. **509.** h. **4.**

—— [Another edition.] pp. viii. 56. *J. Roberts: London,* 1739. 8°. G. **16216.**

—— [Another copy.] **227.** h. **13.**
Imperfect; wanting the titlepage.

—— [Another edition.] Edited with introductory essay & notes by Thomas Callander Wade. pp. viii. 115. *W. Green & Son: Edinburgh,* 1920. 8°. **6836.** e. **12.**

BURROUGHS (JOHN JOSEPH) *See* TAYLOR (John A.) *of the New York Bar.* Exonerative Insanity. Addresses delivered . . . in the cases of Burroughs and Fuchs, *etc.* 1882. 8°. **6095.** f. **8.**

BURROUGHS (JOSEPH) *See* NOBLE (Daniel) *Rev.* The Hope of Immortality a most powerful motive to fervent charity. A sermon preach'd . . . on occasion of the death of . . . J. Burroughs. 1761. 4°. **1416.** d. **55.**

—— The Blessedness of a Benevolent Temper. A sermon, preached . . . to the Society for relief of the Widows and Orphans of Protestant Dissenting Ministers. pp. 34. *M. Fenner: London,* 1743. 8°. **4474.** bbb. **18.**

—— A Defence of Two Discourses relating to Positive Institutions; against the reflections contained in the appendix [by Caleb Fleming] to the Plea for infants. pp. 76. *John Noon: London,* 1743. 8°. **4323.** b. **14.**

—— The Duty and Reward of a Christian Pastor. A sermon preached . . . at the ordination of the Reverend Mr. Richard Barron. pp. 44. *J. Noon: London,* 1753. 8°. **695.** f. **2.** **(4.)**

—— A Farther Defence of Two Discourses relating to Positive Institutions: in answer to . . . Caleb Fleming's Vindication of the appendix to the Plea for infants. pp. viii. 108. *John Noon & Aaron Ward: London,* 1746. 8°. **4323.** b. **15.**

—— The Popish Doctrine of Auricular Confession and Priestly Absolution considered. A sermon, *etc.* pp. 48. *J. Noon & J. Gray: London,* 1735. 8°. **693.** d. **7.** **(9.)**

—— The second edition. pp. 48. *J. Noon & J. Gray: London,* 1735. 8°. **4477.** aa. **136.** **(2.)**

—— Third edition. pp. 48. *J. Noon & J. Gray: London,* 1735. 8°. **4473.** g. **5.** **(1.)**

—— A Sermon occasioned by the death of the Reverend Mr. Joseph Morris, *etc.* pp. 35. *J. Whiston: London,* 1755. 8°. **1417.** e. **40.**

—— [Another copy.] **225.** h. **20.** **(9.)**

—— A Sermon occasion'd by the Total Eclipse of the Sun, upon April the 22d, 1715. pp. 23. *A. Bell: London,* 1715. 8°. **4476.** aaa. **27.**

—— The second edition. pp. 23. *A. Bell: London,* 1715. 8°. **4474.** c. **44.**

BURROUGHS (Joseph)

—— A Sermon preached at an Ordination of Deacons, *etc.* pp. 39. *J. Noon & J. Gray: London*, 1730. 8º. **693**. d. **7**. (**7**.)

—— [Another copy.] **225**. h. **14**. (**6**.)

—— A Sermon preached at Barbican in London . . . upon the death of Dr. John Gale. pp. 31. *John Darby: London*, 1722. 8º. **1416**. g. **51**.

—— [Another copy.] **1416**. g. **52**.

—— A Sermon preached at Pinners Hall in London . . . upon the death of the Reverend Mr. John Weatherly. pp. 40. *John Noon: London*, 1752. 8º. **1417**. i. **29**.

—— [Another copy.] **1417**. i. **30**.

—— A Sermon preached to the Societies for Reformation of Manners, *etc.* pp. 46. *E. Matthews: London*, 1731. 8º. **693**. d. **7**. (**6**.)

—— Some Memoirs [of the life of Joseph Morris]. *See* Morris (Joseph) *Baptist Minister.* Sermons, *etc.* 1757. 8º. **1023**. k. **14**.

—— Stedfastness not in vain, in the Service of Christ. A sermon preached at Barbican in London . . . on occasion of the death of the Reverend Mr. Isaac Kimber. pp. 28. *J. Noon: London*, 1755. 8º. **1416**. k. **31**.

—— [Another copy.] **1416**. k. **30**.

—— A Thanksgiving Sermon, *etc.* pp. 32. *J. Baker: London*, 1713. 8º. **4474**. c. **43**.

—— Two Discourses relating to Positive Institutions. I. Christ's judgment concerning the fitness of obeying every divine command; II. Baptism designed for all those in every age, who profess Christianity; and not confined to the first converts only. pp. iv. 63. *J. Noon & Joseph Collyer: London*, 1742. 8º. **491**. d. **27**. (**14**.)

—— *See* Fleming (Caleb) Tracts on Baptism . . . III. An appendix to the plea for infants, in which their right to baptism is vindicated against . . . Mr. J. Burroughs's attempt to exclude them, in his Two Discourses . . . VI. A defence of infant baptism, or a vindication of the appendix . . . against . . . Mr. J. Burroughs's defence. 1745. 8º. **699**. h. **11**. (**6, 1–5, 9**.)

—— Two Sermons: the one against the traditions of the Church of Rome; the other about the right manner of contending for the Christian Faith; preached . . . on occasion of collecting for the relief of the persecuted Protestants of Saltzburg. pp. 42. *J. Noon: London*, 1732. 8º. **693**. d. **7**. (**8**.)

—— A View of Popery, taken from the Creed of Pope Pius the IV, *etc.* pp. 159. *J. Noon: London*, 1735. 8º. **702**. g. **5**. (**7**.)

—— The second edition, corrected. pp. 159. *J. Noon: London*, 1737. 8º. **3938**. aaa. **16**.

—— [Another copy.] **3505**. dd. **43**.

BURROUGHS (Joseph B.) A Medical Substitute for Alcohol in cases of emergency [i.e. nitro-glycerine] . . . Reprinted from the "Lancet," *etc.* pp. 16. *National Temperance Publication Depôt: London*, [1890.] 8º. **8436**. f. **1**. (**5**.)

BURROUGHS (Marie) The Marie Burroughs Art Portfolio of Stage Celebrities. A collection of photographs of the leaders of dramatic and lyric art. [With brief biographical sketches.] *A. N. Marquis & Co.: Chicago*, 1894. 8º. **10604**. g. **14**.

BURROUGHS (Prince Emmanuel) Building a Successful Sunday School. pp. 192. *F. H. Revell Co.: New York*, [1921.] 8º. **4192**. eee. **30**.

BURROUGHS (Roy Judson)

—— [Economics of Rural Tropical Housing.] Economía de la vivienda rural tropical. (Traducido por Marta Cubas: revisado por Jorge Videla y Luis Florén.) pp. 25. *Bogotá*, 1954. 8º. [*Centro Interamericano de Vivienda. Serie: Traducciones, adaptaciones y reimpresiones.* no. 2.] **U.N.P.90.(5.)**

BURROUGHS (Samuel) *See* also Fleetwood (Everard) *pseud.* [i.e. S. Burroughs.]

—— The History of the Chancery; relating to the judicial power of that court, *etc.* [By S. Burroughs.] pp. 118. 1726. 12º. *See* England.—*Court of Chancery.* [*Appendix.*] **883**. g. **20**.

—— The Legal Judicature in Chancery stated. With remarks on a late book [by Philip Yorke, Earl of Hardwicke] intitled, A Discourse of the Judicial Authority belonging to the Master of the Rolls in the High Court of Chancery. [By S. Burroughs, assisted by Bishop Warburton.] pp. 282. MS. NOTES [by F. Hargrave]. 1727. 8º. *See* England.—*Court of Chancery.* [*Appendix.*] **510**. d. **19**. (**2**.)

—— [Another copy.] **510**. d. **20**.

—— *See* England.—*Court of Chancery.* [*Appendix.*] A Discourse on the Judicial Authority belonging to the office of Master of the Rolls in the High Court of Chancery . . . With a preface, occasioned by a book [by S. Burroughs] entitled "The Legal Judicature in Chancery stated." 1728. 8º. **884**. i. **15**.

BURROUGHS (Stephen) Memoirs of Stephen Burroughs. pp. 296. *Benjamin True: Hanover, N.H.*, 1798. 8º. **1453**. d. **17**.

—— Memoirs of the Notorious Stephen Burroughs . . . Stereotype edition, newly corrected and revised. 2 vol. pp. 356. *Charles Gaylord: Boston*, [1840.] 12º. **10881**. a. **25**.

—— [Another edition.] pp. xii. 367. *Jonathan Cape: London; printed in U.S.A.*, 1924. 8º. **10884**. d. **16**.

BURROUGHS (Thomas) A Soveraign Remedy for all Kindes of Grief: or an approved way for the quieting of the soul in the greatest affliction: opened and applyed in a sermon at the funeral of Mr. John Langham, *etc.* pp. 39. *S. G. for John Baker: London*, 1657. 4º. **1417**. c. **2**.

—— [Another copy.] E. **926**. (**4**.)

—— The second edition, *etc.* pp. 39. **L.P.** *T. R. for John Baker: London*, 1662. 4º. **4903**. gg. **3**.

—— The third edition. To which are added Directions about preparing for death. 2 pt. pp. 154. *For John Baker: London*, 1675. 12º. **4406**. aa. **72**.
The "Directions about preparing for Death" are of the second edition.

—— [Another edition.] 2 pt. pp. 154. *Dan. Brown: London*, 1697. 12º. **1418**. i. **21**.
Pt. 2 is a duplicate of pt. 2 of the preceding.

BURROUGHS (W.) *Government Official.* Homesteads for the Native Poor: an appeal . . . for help to enable suitable abodes being constructed for the labouring classes, *etc.* pp. 10. *I. C. Bose & Co.: Calcutta*, 1885. 8°. **8277. d. 15. (2.)**

BURROUGHS (W. H.) A Treatise on the Law of Taxation, as imposed by the States and their municipalities, or other subdivisions, and as exercised by the government of the United States, particularly in the customs and internal revenue. pp. liv. 751. *Baker, Voorhis & Co.: New York*, 1877. 8°. **6616. k. 6.**

BURROUGHS (Wilbur Greeley) Directory of Kentucky Mineral Operators, ~~etc.~~ pp. 186. 1930. 8°. [*Kentucky Geological Survey Publications.* ser. 6. *Bulletin.* vol. 32.] *See* Directories.—*Mining.* [*U.S.A.*] **A.S. K. 40.**

—— The Geography of the Western Kentucky Coal Field . . . Illustrated, *etc.* pp. x. 211. *Frankfort, Ky.*, 1924. 8°. [*Kentucky Geological Survey Publications.* ser. 6. *Bulletin.* vol. 24.] **A.S. K. 40.**

—— Mineral Resources of the Ashland, Kentucky, Region. *See* Twenhofel (William H.) The Building of Kentucky, *etc.* 1931. 8°. [*Kentucky Geological Survey Publications.* ser. 6. *Bulletin.* vol. 37.] **A.S. K. 40.**

BURROUGHS (William) A True and Exact Particular and Inventory of all and singular the lands, tenements and hereditaments . . . of William Burroughs, *etc.* pp. 71. *S. Buckley: London*, 1732. fol. **712. k. 1. (7.)**

—— [Another copy.] **713. k. 10. (4.)**

BURROUGHS (William Dwight) The Wonderland of Stamps . . . With two hundred illustrations. pp. xviii. 238. *F. A. Stokes Co.: New York*, 1910. 8°. **08247. ee. 13.**

—— Second edition. pp. xviii. 238. *T. Fisher Unwin: London, Leipsic; printed in U.S.A.*, 1911. 8°. **08247. ee. 15.**

BURROUGHS (William E.) *See* Daunt (Achilles) *the Elder.* The Morning of Life . . . Edited by M. Day . . . W. E. Burroughs. 1881. 8°. **4466. b. 31.**

—— Signs of Spiritual Life—its growth, its decline, or its absence in the Christian minister. A paper, *etc.* pp. 16. *George Herbert: Dublin*, 1882. 8°. **4165. e. 7. (4.)**

BURROUGHS (Wolfenden Kenny) An Apology for the Church in Ireland's upholding Scriptural Education in antagonism to Rome. In a letter to . . . the Earl of Derby. pp. 31. *Seeleys: London*, 1852. 8°. **8308. d. 18.**

—— [Another copy.] **3942. cc. 1. (13.)**

—— Lectures on the Book of Genesis. pp. viii. 321. *Printed for the Author: Dublin*, 1848. 8°. **3149. f. 11.**

BURROW (C. F. Severn)

—— A Little City set on a Hill. The story of Malvern. (Reprinted from "The Malvern Gazette.") pp. 98. [*The Author:*] *Malvern*, 1948. 8°. **010368. k. 6.**

BURROW (Charles Kennett) Asteck's Madonna, and other stories. pp. 197. *J. M. Dent & Co.: London*, 1896. 8°. **012600. i. 1.**

—— Carmina Varia. pp. 109. *Martin Secker: London* [1912.] 8°. **011650. de. 88.**

—— The Fire of Life. pp. viii. 328. *Duckworth & Co.: London*, 1898. 8°. **012623. g. 22.**

BURROW (Charles Kennett)

—— The Lifted Shadow. pp. vi. 232. *J. Bowden: London*, 1899. 8°. **012643. bb. 46.**

—— London Dead, and other verses. pp. 47. *Alston Rivers: London*, 1908. 8°. **11647. ee. 46.**

—— Patricia of the Hills. pp. viii. 330. *Lawrence & Bullen: London*, 1902. 8°. **012637. dd. 46.**

—— Poems, in time of war, in time of peace. pp. 99. *W. Collins, Sons & Co.: London*, 1919. 8°. **011649.ff.39.**

—— Tony Heron. pp. 322. *W. Collins, Sons & Co.: London*, [1918.] 8°. **NN. 4990.**

—— The Way of the Wind. pp. 242. *Kegan Paul & Co.: London*, 1897. 8°. **012626. k. 47.**

—— The Yeoman. pp. vi. 305. *John Lane: New York & London*, 1904. 8°. **012629. a. 25.**

—— [Another copy, with a different titlepage.] *John Lane: New York & London; London* [printed], 1904. 8°. **012629. aa. 27.**

BURROW (Ed. J.) **AND CO.**

—— [For "Official" local guides published by E. J. Burrow & Co.:] *See* the name of the place.

—— [Miscellaneous handbooks published by E. J. Burrow & Co. for clubs, associations, and commercial concerns.] *E. J. Burrow & Co.: Cheltenham & London*, [1921– .] 8° & *obl.* 8°. **10360. s.**

—— Burrow's Cathedral Guides. *See* infra: Burrow's Penny Guides.

—— Burrow's Glossary of Church Architecture, Furniture & Fittings, *etc.* *See* Beasley (E. A.)

—— Burrow's Guide to Aberdeen. [Various editions.] [1917– .] 8°. *See* Aberdeen, *City of.* [*Official Documents.*] **10354. a. 1.**

—— Burrow's Guide to Beddington and Wallington, Surrey, *etc.* (Beddington and Wallington, Surrey. The official guide). *E. J. Burrow & Co.: London & Cheltenham*, [1936– .] 8°. **10354. a. 83.**
Various editions.

—— Burrow's Guide to Bedford, Elstow & Olney. pp. 40. *E. J. Burrow & Co.: Cheltenham*, [1928.] 8°. **10354. a. 84.**

—— Burrow's Guide to Bournemouth and Neighbourhood. *See* Bournemouth. [*Appendix.*] Bournemouth and Neighbourhood.

—— Burrow's Guide to Broadway, Worcestershire . . . With illustrations and a route map, *etc.* pp. 32. *E. J. Burrow & Co.: Cheltenham*, [1932.] 8°. **10354. a. 154.**

—— Burrow's Pocket Guide to Budleigh Salterton, *etc.* pp. 40. *E. J. Burrow & Co.: Cheltenham*, [1919.] 8°. **10354. a. 159.**

—— Burrow's Guide to the Channel Islands. (The Channel Islands.) *E. J. Burrow & Co.: Cheltenham*, [1921– .] 8° & 4°. **10354. dd. 1.**
Various editions.

—— Burrow's Guide to Colwyn Bay, Rhos-on-Sea and Neighbourhood. *See* Colwyn Bay. Colwyn Bay and Neighbourhood.

—— Burrow's Guide to the Glorious South Hams of Devon (to the Picturesque Hams of Glorious South Devon), *etc.* *E. J. Burrow & Co.: Cheltenham*, [1928– .] 8°. **10354. a. 391.**

Various editions.

—— Burrow's Guide to Devon and Cornwall. With introduction to Cornish section by Sir Arthur Quiller-Couch. Illustrated from drawings by Margaret Holman & H. Powell, *etc.* [With maps.] pp. 158. *Ed. J. Burrow & Co.: Cheltenham & London*, [1920.] 8°. **10354. a. 343. (1.)**

—— [Another edition.] pp. 172. *Ed. J. Burrow & Co.: Cheltenham & London*, [1922.] 8°. **10354. a. 343. (2.)**

—— Enlarged and entirely rewritten by Alison D. Murray, *etc.* pp. 152. *Ed. J. Burrow & Co.: Cheltenham & London*, [1928.] 8°. **10354. a. 343. (3.)**

—— 4th edition revised, *etc.* pp. 160. *Ed. J. Burrow & Co.: Cheltenham & London*, [1934.] 8°. **10354. a. 343. (4.)**

—— Burrow's Guide to Fifeshire, *etc.* pp. 52. *E. J. Burrow & Co.: Cheltenham*, [1932.] 8°. **10354. a. 291.**

—— Burrow's Guide to Fowey. *See* Fowey. The "Borough" Pocket Guide to Fowey.

—— Burrow's Guide to the Isle of Man, *etc.* *E. J. Burrow & Co.: Cheltenham & London*, [1936– .] 8°. **10354. a. 466.**
Various editions.

—— Burrow's Guide to the Lake District. *See* Piggott (Percy J.)

—— Burrow's Guide to Loch Lomond, Gareloch & Loch Long, *etc.* pp. 48. *E. J. Burrow & Co.: Cheltenham*, [1939.] 8°. **10354. a. 541.**

—— Burrow's Guide to London. By E. V. Lucas, A. H. Blake [and others] . . . Maps and plans . . . illustrations. pp. 122. *E. J. Burrow & Co.: London*, [1922.] 8°. **10354. a. 542.**

—— Malvern. (Burrow's Sixpenny Guide.) (About and around Malvern.) *E. J. Burrow & Co.: London & Cheltenham*, [1919– .] 8°. **10354. a. 598.**
Various editions.

—— Burrow's Guide to North Wales. *See* Piggott (Percy J.)

—— Burrow's Guide to Picturesque Perthshire. *See* Perth, *County of*. Picturesque Perthshire, *etc.*

—— Burrow's Guide to Portstewart. pp. 20. *E. J. Burrow & Co.: Cheltenham & London*, [1937.] 8°. **10354. a. 737.**

—— Burrow's Guide to Salisbury (The "Borough" Guide to Salisbury), *etc.* *E. J. Burrow & Co.: Cheltenham & London*, [1920– .] 8°. **10354. a. 793.**
Various editions.

—— Burrow's Guide to Shrewsbury. (Shrewsbury and Neighbourhood.) *E. J. Burrow & Co.: Cheltenham*, [1917– .] 8°. **10354. a. 782.**
Various editions.

—— Burrow's Guide to the South Coast Resorts, with Excursions Inland. A practical handbook for holiday makers and tourists. pp. viii. 162. *E. J. Burrow & Co.: Cheltenham & London*, [1921.] 8°. **10354. a. 893.**

—— Burrow's Guide to Stockton-on-Tees. *See* Stockton-upon-Tees. Stockton-on-Tees, Durham.

—— Stonehenge. The riddle of the centuries. Burrow's Guide. *See* Stonehenge. Stonehenge, Past and Present, *etc.*

—— Burrow's Guide to the River Thames. *See* Murray (Alison D.)

—— Burrow's Guide to the Thames Valley, *etc.* pp. 136. *E. J. Burrow & Co.: Cheltenham & London*, [1920.] 8°. **10354. a. 858.**

—— Burrow's Guide to Wessex, the Hardy Country. *See* Murray (Alison D.)

—— Burrow's Guides. National Series of Holiday Guides. 8 vol.

1. Holidays in the West of England.
2. Holidays in the South of England.
3. Holidays in South-East England.
4. Holidays in East Anglia.
5. Holidays in the North-East of England.

E. J. Burrow & Co.: Cheltenham, [1923–28.] 8°. **010352. bbb. 3.**
This set includes two editions of vol. 1, 2 *and* 4.

—— Burrow's Handy Guide to Europe . . . 29 maps & plans. pp. viii. 410. *E. J. Burrow & Co.: Cheltenham*, [1926.] 8°. **10108. b. 14.**

—— Third edition, *etc.* pp. x. 426. *E. J. Burrow & Co.: Cheltenham*, [1931.] 12°. **010106. de. 4.**

—— Burrow's New Series of Grey Guides, *etc.* *E. J. Burrow & Co.: Cheltenham & London*, [1930– .] 8°.
Various editions. **010368.s.57.**

—— Burrow's New Series of Grey Guides, *etc.* 6 vol.

1. Devon, Cornwall and West Somerset.
2. South of England.
3. South East England.
4. South Midlands.
5. Central Scotland.

E. J. Burrow & Co.: Cheltenham & London, [1930–34.] 8°. **010368. s. 57.**
Imperfect; wanting vol. 6: *South and Mid-Wales. This set includes two editions of vol.* 1.

—— Burrow's Penny Guides. 44 pt. *E. J. Burrow: Cheltenham*, [1919–28.] 12°. **07815. a. 160.**
The guides are divided into four series: "The Abbeys of Old England," "The Cathedrals of Old England," otherwise called "Burrow's Cathedral Guides," "The Churches of Old England," otherwise called "Historical Churches of Old England," and "The Castles of Old England."

—— Burrow's 'R. A. C.' County Map and Gazetteer Series. *See* England.—*Royal Automobile Club.* The R.A.C. County Road Maps and Guide.

—— Burrow's "R.A.C." Guides. *See* Harper (Charles G.)

BURROW (Edward) A New and Compleat Book of Rates; comprehending the rates of merchandize . . . With . . . a law index . . . containing an abridgment of the several Acts of Parliament now in force relative to the customs, *etc.* vol. 1. pp. ix. 665. *R. & A. Foulis: Glasgow*, 1774. fol. **509. h. 22.**
No more published.

BURROW (Edward Broadley) *See* Bible.—*Psalms.—Selections.* [*English.*] Select Psalms in English Verse . . . By the Rev. E. B. Burrow. 1848. 12°. **3434.** d. **48.**

—— The Mendip Hills. A descriptive poem. pp. 23. *Longman & Co.: London,* 1849. 4°. **1347.** l. **29.**
Printed in blue ink on tinted paper.

—— Sketches of Astronomy ; or, What are stars ? pp. vi. 45. *Longman & Co.: London,* 1857. 8°. **8561.** a. **21.**

BURROW (Edward John) *D.D., F.R.S. See* Christianity. Hours of Devotion for the promotion of true Christianity and family worship. Translated from the original German [of J. H. D. Zschokke] by the Rev. E. J. Burrow. 1830. 8°. **844.** l. **17.**

—— *See* Mount Radford.—*College School.* A Statement of the manner in which the Rev. E. J. Burrow D.D. became connected with the Institution at Mount Radford, and of the circumstances which led to his removal, *etc.* 1828. 8°. **1414.** h. **10.** (**3.**)

—— Elements of Conchology, according to the Linnæan System, *etc.* pp. xv. 248. pl. xxviii. *The Author: London,* 1815. 8°. **976.** k. **15.**

—— Second edition. pp. xxiii. 248. pl. xxviii. *Ogles, Duncan & Cochran: London,* 1818. 8°. **7298.** c. **2.**

—— The Elgin Marbles: with an abridged historical and topographical account of Athens . . . Vol. i. Illustrated with forty plates drawn and etched by the author. pp. xvi. 253. *Ogles, Duncan & Cochran: London,* 1817. 8°. **1422.** g. **16.**
No more published.

—— [Another edition.] pp. xvi. 263. *James Duncan: London,* 1837. 8°. **7706.** bb. **29.**

—— A Letter addressed to the Rev. William Marsh [occasioned by his " Questions and Answers on the Catechism of the Church of England "] . . . on the nature and tendency of certain religious principles frequently, but improperly, denominated evangelical. pp. 80. *F. C. & J. Rivington: London,* 1819. 8°. **3505.** dd. **19.**

—— Second edition. pp. 80. *F. C. & J. Rivington: London,* 1819. 8°. **701.** h. **15.** (**1.**)

—— Third edition. pp. 80. *F. C. & J. Rivington: London,* 1819. 8°. **4109.** h. **6.** (**3.**)

—— [Another copy.] **4106.** f. **8.**
Imperfect; wanting the last leaf, containing the "Postscript."

—— *See* Stoney (Thomas U.) Remarks upon the Review . . . in the Christian Observer for March 1819 of the Rev. E. J. Burrow's First Letter to the Rev. W. Marsh, *etc.* 1819. 8°. **701.** h. **15.** (**3.**)

—— A Second Letter addressed to the Rev. William Marsh [occasioned by his " Questions and Answers on the Catechism "] . . . contrasting the doctrines of the Church of England . . . with those principles which have been . . . denominated evangelical; and containing some further remarks on the subject of innocent amusements. pp. 132. *F. C. & J. Rivington: London,* 1819. 8°. **3505.** dd. **7.**

—— Second edition. pp. 103. *F. C. & J. Rivington: London,* 1819. 8°. **701.** h. **15.** (**2.**)

BURROW (Edward John) *D.D., F.R.S.*

—— *See* Stoney (Thomas U.) A Reply to a Pamphlet . . . entitled, The Discipline, Morals, and Faith, of the Church of England . . . in a letter addressed to the Rev. E. J. Burrow . . . occasioned by his Second Letter to the Rev. Wm. Marsh, *etc.* 1820. 8°. **4107.** bb. **78.**

—— A Letter to His Grace the Archbishop of Canterbury, on the subject of certain doctrines of the Church of England termed evangelical: occasioned by the observations contained in two letters addressed by the Rev. E. J. Burrow . . . to the Rev. William Marsh . . . including a brief inquiry into the objects and constitution of the British and Foreign Bible Society. By a lay member of the established church. pp. 74. *Wm. Walker: London,* 1819. 8°. **4105.** d. **7.**

—— Questions on the Memorial Scripture Copies, composed for the use of national and other schools. pp. 64. *Roake & Varty: London,* 1829. 12°. **844.** g. **25.**

—— Third edition. pp. 64. *Thomas Varty: London,* [1854.] 12°. **3128.** e. **12.**

—— A School Companion to the Bible, containing an explanation of all the words in the Memorial Scripture Copies, *etc.* pp. 110. *Roake & Varty: London,* 1831. 12°. **844.** k. **19.**

—— [Another edition.] pp. 110. *Thomas Varty: London,* [1854 ?] 12°. **3128.** e. **11.**

—— A Summary of Christian Faith & Practice confirmed by references to the text of Holy Scripture; compared with the liturgy, articles, and homilies of the Church of England, *etc.* 3 vol. *F. C. & J. Rivington: London,* 1822. 12°. **1114.** c. **28–30.**

BURROW (Edward John) *F.R.G.S. See* Major (Albany F.) and Burrow (E. J.) The Mystery of Wansdyke, *etc.* 1926. 8°. **10360.** k. **35.**

—— Ancient Earthworks & Camps of Somerset. Being a collection of over one hundred drawings . . . with descriptions and plans [and a map]. pp. 165. *E. J. Burrow & Co.: Cheltenham & London,* 1924. 4°. **7706.** dd. **16.**

—— The Ancient Entrenchments and Camps of Gloucestershire. [With illustrations and a map.] pp. 176. *E. J. Burrow: Cheltenham & London,* 1919. 4°. **7705.** ee. **33.**

—— (New and abridged edition.) pp. viii. 132. *E. J. Burrow: Cheltenham & London,* [1924.] *obl.* 8°. **10352.** e. **49.**

—— The Dunlop Book. The motorist's guide, counsellor and friend . . . Compiled by E. J. Burrow, Ed. R. Cross & A. J. Wilson. pp. vii. 614. *A. J. Wilson & Co.: London,* [1919.] 4°. **10348.** i. **12.**

—— Second edition, *etc.* pp. 625. 110. *A. J. Wilson & Co.: London,* [1920.] 4°. **10348.** i. **13.**

—— From Cave Man to Roman in Britain. pp. 60. *Great Western Railway Co.: London,* [1926.] 8°. **07709.** a. **21.**

—— " On the Road." The Dunlop pictorial road plans. 7 vol. *E. J. Burrow & Co.: London,* [1924–26.] 8°. **010349.** aa. **31.**

—— [Another edition of vol 1.] pp. 132. *E. J. Burrow & Co.: London,* [1926.] 8°. **10353.** a. **39.**

BURROW (Francis Russell) Alexander in the Ark . . . Illustrated by Edith Hope. pp. viii. 199. *C. A. Pearson: London*, 1904 [1903]. 8°. **012803. aa. 31.**

—— The Centre Court and Others. Being a chronicle by an eye-witness of the principal events of the last fifty years, 1886–1936, of the Lawn Tennis Championships at Wimbledon, *etc.* [With plates, including portraits.] pp. ix. 312. *Eyre & Spottiswoode: London*, 1937. 8°. **07908. ff. 58.**

—— The "Last Eights" at Wimbledon, 1877 to 1926. pp. 80. "*Lawn Tennis & Badminton*": *London*, [1927.] 8°. **07912. e. 6.**

—— Lawn Tennis: how to succeed, *etc.* pp. 46. *Evans Bros.: London*, [1933.] 8°. **07912. i. 58.**

—— Lawn Tennis. Some hints, *etc.* pp. 28. "*Country Life*" *& George Newnes: London*, 1919. 8°. **7911. df. 38.**
The title on the wrapper reads: "Lawn Tennis Hints."

—— Third edition. pp. 36. "*Country Life*" *& George Newnes: London; C. Scribner's Sons: New York*, 1920. 8°. **7911. df. 47.**

—— Lawn Tennis. The world-game of to-day. [With plates.] pp. xiii. 271. *Hodder & Stoughton: London*, [1922.] 8°. **07911. gg. 4.**

—— Lawn Tennis of To-day: its strokes, strategy, and tactics. pp. 120. *C. A. Pearson: London*, 1920. 8°. **7911. df. 40.**

—— New and revised edition. pp. 121. *C. A. Pearson: London*, 1924. 8°. **7911. dd. 32.**

—— My Tournaments. [With portraits.] pp. viii. 311. *Hodder & Stoughton: London*, [1922.] 8°. **07911. gg. 6.**

BURROW (G. H. S.) *See* Waller (Alfred R.) and Burrow (G. H. S.) John Henry Cardinal Newman. [1901.] 8°. **10803.a.25/5.**

BURROW (Ida)

—— The Dark Blanket. The Dusty Miller. Sophonisba. Fairy stories. Drawings by John Bainbridge. pp. 137. *Peter Lunn: London*, 1946. 8°. **12829. aa. 19.**

—— Eiderdown Country . . . Illustrated by Marjorie Alice Green. pp. 39. *Pixie Press: London*, 1946. 8°. **12828. bbb. 68.**

BURROW (J. C.) 'Mongst Mines and Miners; or Underground scenes by flash-light: a series of photographs, with explanatory letterpress, illustrating methods of working in Cornish mines. Part I.—An account of the photographic experiences, by J. C. Burrow . . . Part II.—A description of the subjects photographed, by William Thomas. pp. 32. *Simpkin, Marshall & Co.: London; Camborne Printing & Stationery Co.: Camborne*, 1893. 4°. **7105. e. 21.**

BURROW (James) *Gent.* Serious Reflections on the Present State of Domestic and Foreign Affairs . . . together with some critical remarks on lotteries, *etc.* pp. 50. [*London*,] 1757. 8°. **T. 1113. (6.)**

—— [Another copy.] **104. c. 59.**

BURROW (*Sir* James) *See* Jacob (Giles) Every Man his own Lawyer . . . With . . . additions from the Reports of Sir J. Burrow, *etc.* 1788. 8°. **516. c. 54.**

BURROW (*Sir* James)

—— *See* Millar (Andrew) *Bookseller.* The Question concerning Literary Property, determined by the Court of King's Bench . . . in the cause between A. Millar, and R. Taylor, *etc.* [Edited by Sir J. Burrow.] 1773. 4°. **515. f. 16. (1.)**

—— De usu et ratione interpungendi: an essay on the use of pointing, and the facility of practising it. pp. 44. *J. Worrall & B. Tovey: London*, 1771. 4°. **626. k. 21. (1.)**

—— [Another copy.] **T. 10*. (4.)**
Imperfect; wanting the appendix.

—— [Another edition.] pp. 44. *B. Tovey: London*, 1772. 4°. **626. k. 21. (2.)**

—— A Few Anecdotes and Observations relating to Oliver Cromwell and his Family, serving to rectify several errors concerning him published by N. C. Papadopoli . . . By a Member of the Royal Society [i.e. Sir J. Burrow], *etc.* pp. 14. 1763. 4°. *See* Papadopoulos (N. K.) **1200. a. 38.**

—— [Another copy.] **1200. d. 12. (2.)**

—— [Another copy.] **113. c. 15.**

—— [Another copy.] **G. 1892.**

—— Reports of Cases adjudged in the Court of King's Bench, since the death of Lord Raymond; in four parts, *etc.* pt. 4. vol. 1–5. 1766–80. fol. *See* England.—*Court of King's Bench.* [*Reports.*] **19. c. 9–13.**

—— [Another copy.] **513. i. 11–15.**

—— Second edition. pt. 4. vol. 1–5. 1771–80. fol. *See* England.—*Court of King's Bench.* [*Reports.*] **1242. i. 1–5.**

—— Reports of Cases adjudged in the Court of King's Bench, since the death of Lord Raymond . . . By Sir J. Burrow, *etc.* pt. 4. vol. 1–5. 1785, 84. 8°. *See* England.—*Court of King's Bench.* [*Reports.*] **6128. bbb. 1.**

—— Reports of Cases argued and determined in the Court of King's Bench, during the time of Lord Mansfield's presiding in that court, from . . . 1756, to . . . 1772 . . . The fourth edition, corrected; with the addition of marginal notes, *etc.* 5 vol. 1790. 8°. *See* England.—*Court of King's Bench.* [*Reports.*] **1243. b. 4–8.**

—— A Series of the Decisions of the Court of King's Bench upon Settlement Cases from the death of Lord Raymond in March 1732. (A Second Continuation of the Decisions, *etc.*) 2 vol. pp. 864. 1768. 4°. *See* England.—*Court of King's Bench.* [*Reports.*] **518. l. 5.**

—— [A reissue of the "Second Continuation."] 1776. 4°. *See* England.—*Court of King's Bench.* [*Reports.*] **518. l. 9. (1.)**

—— A Few Thoughts upon Pointing and some other helps towards perspicuity of expression. By J. B., F.R.S. and F.S.A. [i.e. Sir J. Burrow.] [An extract from "A Series of Decisions of the Court of King's Bench upon Settlement Cases."] 1768. 4°. *See* B., J., *F.R.S. and F.S.A.* **12901. k. 13**

—— [Another copy.] **818. cc. 15**

BURROW (John Holme) Adventures of Alfan; or, the Magic amulet . . . With eight illustrations by J. D. Watson. pp. vii. 393. *Smith, Elder & Co.: London*, 1863. 8°. **12808. bbb. 15.**

BURROW (John Holme)

—— Stories for Weekdays and Sundays, *etc.* pp. 128. *Routledge & Co.: London,* 1860. 16°. **12805**. a. **31**.

BURROW (Nicholas Trigant)

—— Science and Man's Behavior. The contribution of phylobiology . . . Edited by William E. Galt. Including the complete text of: The Neurosis of Man. [With plates, including a portrait.] pp. xii. 564. *Philosophical Library: New York,* [1953.] 8°. **7662**. c. **25**.
A slip bearing the imprint "Routledge & Kegan Paul: London" has been pasted over the original imprint.

—— The Biology of Human Conflict. An anatomy of behavior, individual and social. pp. xl. 435. *Macmillan Co.: New York,* 1937. 8°. **08459**. f. **67**.

—— The Determination of the Position of a Momentary Impression in the temporal course of a moving visual impression, *etc.* pp. 63. *Baltimore,* 1909. 8°. [*Psychological Monographs.* vol. 11. no. 4.] P.P. **1247**. eb.

—— [Another copy, with a different titlepage.] *Williams & Wilkins Co.: Baltimore,* 1909. 8°. **8708**. l. **19**. **(5.)**

—— The Neurosis of Man. An introduction to a science of human behaviour. [With plates.] pp. xxvi. 428. *Routledge & Kegan Paul: London,* 1949. 8°. **8473**. b. **20**.

—— The Social Basis of Consciousness, *etc.* pp. xviii. 256. *Kegan Paul & Co.: London,* 1927. 8°. [*International Library of Psychology, Philosophy and Scientific Method.*] **08460**. h. **1/5**.

—— The Structure of Insanity. A study in phylopathology. pp. 80. *Kegan Paul & Co.: London,* 1932. 8°. [*Psyche Miniatures.* General series. no. 40.] **012206.a.1/54.**

BURROW (Reuben) *See* Ephemerides. The Lady's and Gentleman's Diary . . . By R. Burrow. [1775, *etc.*] 12°. P.P. **2465**. d.

—— A Restitution of the Geometrical Treatise of Apollonius Pergæus on Inclinations. Also the Theory of Gunnery; or the doctrine of projectiles in a non-resisting medium. pp. 39. pl. 2. *The Author: London,* 1779. 4°. **534**. k. **29**. **(5.)**

BURROW (Richard Foster) Burrow's System of Banking. pp. 94. *R. W. Lightup & Samuel Wheeler: London,* 1873. 8°. **8228**. c. **13**.

BURROW (Robert) Civil Society and Government vindicated from the charge of being founded on, and preserv'd by dishonest arts: in a sermon preached . . . the day of election of a Lord Mayor, *etc.* pp. 31. *J. & B. Clark: London,* 1723. 8°. **693**. d. **7**. **(10.)**

—— [Another copy.] **225**. g. **10**. **(6.)**

—— A Dissertation on the Happy Influences of Society merely civil, in relation to the improvement and ornaments of the mind, *etc.* pp. 36. *J. Clark & R. Hett: London,* 1726. 8°. **698**. e. **17**. (4.)

—— Meletemata Darringtoniana. An essay upon Divine Providence, *etc.* pp. xxiv. 184. 84. *John Clark & Richard Hett: London,* 1725. 8°. **854**. e. **19**.

—— A Sermon preach'd . . . July 20. 1729. at the Assizes held at York, *etc.* pp. 27. *R. Hett: London,* 1729. 8°. **693**. d. **7**. **(13.)**

—— [Another copy.] **225**. g. **6**. **(11.)**

BURROW (Rube) *See* Agee (G. W.) Rube Burrow, King of Outlaws, *etc.* [1893.] 8°. **6057**. aa. **42**.

BURROW (Samuel Edwin) "Blinks." From slumland to mission field. A story founded on fact. pp. 128. *Pickering & Inglis: London,* [1932.] 8°. [*Excelsior Library.*] **12830.aa.81/17.**

—— Brindlewood Farm. A west country tale, *etc.* pp. 134. *S. W. Partridge & Co.: London,* [1913.] 8°. **04419**. e. **12**.

—— [Another edition.] pp. 126. *Pickering & Inglis: London,* [1929.] 8°. **012601**. bb. **81**.

—— Friend or Foe! A tale of three soldiers . . . With four illustrations by Geo. Soper. pp. 134. *S. W. Partridge & Co.: London,* [1912.] 8°. **012808**. cc. **30**.

—— [Another edition.] pp. 128. *Pickering & Inglis: London, Glasgow,* [1928.] 8°. **04413**. ff. **48**.

—— Gleanings from Life's Harvest. [Religious essays.] pp. 157. *Marshall, Morgan & Scott: London & Edinburgh,* [1935.] 8°. **04400**. de. **89**.

—— Gospel Gleanings. Daily readings in the Gospels. With notes and outlines. pp. vi. 87. *Marshall Bros.: London,* [1904.] 16°. **3224**. a. **50**.

—— Jabez Welldon; or, From tragedy to triumph. pp. 159. *Pickering & Inglis: London,* [1939]. 8°. NN. **31077**.

—— "Noodle"; or, From barrack room to mission field, *etc.* pp. 134. *S. W. Partridge & Co.: London,* [1908.] 8°. **04413**. ee. **31**.

—— [Another edition.] pp. 32. *Pickering & Inglis: London,* [1924.] 8°. [*Lily Library.*] **W.P.1001.**

—— Penlune: life in a Cornish village . . . With four illustrations. pp. 134. *S. W. Partridge & Co.: London,* [1912.] 8°. **04413**. g. **54**.

—— [A reissue.] *London,* [1914.] 8°. **04419**. e. **22**.

—— [A reissue.] *Pickering & Inglis: London, Glasgow,* [1926.] 8°. **04419**. ee. **96**.

—— Tre, Pol and Pen. A Cornish story, *etc.* pp. 130. *Pickering & Inglis: London, Glasgow,* 1927. 8°. **012643**. c. **54**.

—— True as Steel. The story of a waif. pp. 132. *Pickering & Inglis: London, Glasgow,* [1925.] 8°. **12813**. a. **4**.

BURROW (Thomas)

—— *See* Kroraina. A Translation of the Kharoṣṭhi Documents from Chinese Turkestan. By T. Burrow. 1940. 8°. [*James G. Forlong Fund.* vol. 20.] Ac. **8820/7**.

—— The Language of the Kharoṣṭhi Documents from Chinese Turkestan. pp. ix. 134. *University Press: Cambridge,* 1937. 8°. **012903**. g. **8**.

—— The Sanskrit Language. pp. vii. 426. *Faber & Faber: London,* 1955. 8°. [*The Great Languages.*] W.P. **3434/10**.

BURROW (Trigant) *See* Burrow (Nicholas T.)

BURROW (Wilfrid G.) Selected Poems. pp. 24. *A. H. Stockwell: London,* [1920.] 8°. **011648**. ff. **159**.

BURROWDALE. Burrowdale; a tale. pp. 243. *Hamilton, Adams & Co.: London,* 1861. 8°. **12632.** cc. **4.**

BURROWE (Edward) *See* Burrough.

BURROWE (Stephen) *See* Burrough.

BURROWES (   ) *Picture Collector. See* Hadfield (   ) *Picture Collector,* and Burrowes (   ) A Descriptive Catalogue, of the first part of the large Collection of Pictures made by Messrs. Hadfield and Burrowes during their tour through Flanders, *etc.* [1785.] 4°. S.C. **1070. (17.)**

BURROWES (Amyas Deane) The Modern Encyclopædia: or General dictionary of arts, sciences and literature, *etc.* 11 vol. [1816–20 ?] 4°. *See* Encyclopaedias. **12217.** pp. **3.**

BURROWES (Arnold Robinson) The 1st Battalion the Faugh-a-Ballaghs in the Great War. [With plates and maps.] pp. 182. [1926.] 4°. *See* England.—*Army.—Infantry.—Princess Victoria's (Royal Irish Fusiliers), 1st Battalion.* **09084.** d. **19.**

BURROWES (Charles L.) A Commercial Handbook of Jamaica . . . Compiled by C. L. Burrowes. pp. 117. 1911. 8°. *See* Directories.—*Commerce.* [Jamaica.] P.P. **2585.** kb.

—— A Commercial Pocket-Book of Jamaica. pp. 55. *Gleaner Co.: Kingston, Jamaica,* [1910.] 16°. **10481.** a. **43.**

BURROWES (Edward Denies) "The Christian in Expectation." A sermon, *etc.* pp. 24. *Hatchard & Co.: London,* 1863. 12°. **4477.** bb. **76. (2.)**

—— The Sixpenny Guide to Swanage, *etc.* pp. 47. *Marchant, Singer & Co.: London,* 1879. 8°. **10347.** c. **13. (3.)**

—— Swanage and its Immediate Neighbourhood; with special chapters upon its geology and botany, *etc.* pp. iv. 97. *Marchant, Singer & Co.: London,* 1873. 8°. **10360.** aaa. **64.**

BURROWES (George) A Commentary on the Song of Solomon. By the Rev. G. Burrowes. [With the text.] pp. 527. 1853. 12°. *See* Bible.—*Song of Solomon. [English.]* **3166.** c. **11.**

BURROWES (Henry) A Hue and Cry after the Letter to the Lord-Mayor of the City of Dublin [i.e. H. Burrowes]. [Consisting of "A Letter from a Country Gentleman, to the . . . Lord Mayor," and "The Answer to the Letter." In verse.] *E. Waters: Dublin,* 1729. *s. sh.* fol. **C.121.g.8.(171.)**
Slightly cropped.

BURROWES (J.) Life in St. George's Fields, or, the Rambles and adventures of disconsolate William, Esq.—from St. James's—and his accomplished Surrey friend, the Hon. Flash Dick . . . Containing original songs . . . and a slang dictionary, *etc.* [With a plate.] pp. 27. *J. Smith: London,* 1821. 8°. **992.** i. **6. (8.)**

—— [Another copy.] **12352.** e. **4.**

BURROWES (John Freckleton) A Guide to Practice on the Piano Forte. pp. 48. *The Author: London,* 1841. 12°. **785.** c. **4.**

—— The Piano-forte Primer, containing the rudiments of music, *etc.* pp. ix. 55. *Chappell & Co.; Clementi & Co.: London,* 1818. 12°. **1042.** e. **26. (1.)**

—— Second edition. pp. ix. 56. *Chappell & Co.; Clementi & Co.: London,* 1819. 12°. **1042.** e. **26. (2.)**

—— Third edition, with an appendix. pp. viii. 70. *Clementi & Co.; Chappell & Co.: London,* 1821. 12°. **1042.** k. **32. (2.)**

—— Fourth edition, *etc.* pp. viii. 70. *Chappell & Co.; Clementi & Co.: London,* 1823. 12°. **1042.** k. **32. (3.)**

—— Fifth edition, *etc.* pp. viii. 57. 12. *Chappell & Co.; Clementi & Co.: London,* 1824. 12°. **1042.** e. **26. (3.)**

—— Sixth edition, with additions. pp. viii. 58. 16. *Clementi & Co.; Chapell* [sic] *& Co.: London,* 1825. 12°. **1042.** e. **26. (4.)**

—— Seventh edition, *etc.* pp. viii. 58. 16. *Chappell & Co.; Clementi & Co.: London,* 1826. 12°. **7897.** aaa. **27.**

—— Eighth edition, *etc.* pp. viii. 58. 16. *Chappell & Co.; Clementi & Co.: London,* 1829. 8°. **1042.** e. **53.**

—— Eleventh edition, *etc.* pp. viii. 58. 16. *S. Chappell: Clementi & Co.: London,* 1831. 12°. **7897.** aa. **41.**

—— [Another edition.] Revised and enlarged . . . by W. C. Peters. pp. 58. *Peters, Webb & Co.: Louisville,* 1849. 12°. **7896.** aa. **13.**

—— Forty-eighth edition, *etc.* pp. vi. 60. 16. *The Author: London,* 1862. 8°. **7898.** a. **49.**

—— Thirty-eighth edition, with additions. pp. vi. 60. 16. *J. F. Burrowes: London,* 1872. 12°. **7897.** aaa. **37.**

—— The Thorough-Base Primer: containing explanations and examples of the rudiments of harmony; with fifty exercises. pp. viii. 107. *Chappell & Co.; Clementi & Co.: London,* 1819. 12°. **1042.** k. **35. (2.)**

—— Second edition. pp. viii. 92. 36. *Chappell & Co.: Clementi & Co.: London,* 1819. 8°. **1042.** k. **32. (1.)**

—— The Thorough-Base Primer . . . Fifth edition, with additions. pp. viii. 93. 36. *Published for the Author by Chappell & Co.; Clementi & Co.: London,* 1829. 12°. **7900.** m. **32.**

—— Thirty-seventh edition, with additions. pp. viii. 95. 36. *J. F. Burrowes: London,* 1871. 8°. **7897.** aaa. **35.**

—— A new edition, carefully edited. pp. viii. 95. *J. B. Cramer & Co.: London,* 1873. 8°. **7897.** b. **27.**

—— [Another edition.] (Edited by Henry Parker.) pp. viii. 80. *J. B. Cramer & Co.: London,* 1881. 8°. **7898.** f. **40.**

BURROWES (Katharine) The Burrowes Course of Music Study. Teachers' manual. Third edition. 3 vol. *Katharine Burrowes: Detroit; Whaley, Royce & Co.: Toronto,* [1910.] 8°. **7896.** v. **9.**

—— Musical Kindergarten Songs. pp. 17. *Whaley, Royce & Co.: Toronto,* [1902.] 8°. **11602.** dd. **13. (2.)**

—— Musical Puzzle Stories, *etc.* pp. 19. *Katharine Burrowes: Detroit,* [1905.] 4°. **7898.** m. **18.**

—— Tales of the Great Composers: Bach, Handel, Haydn. pp. 46. *Katharine Burrowes: Detroit; Whaley, Royce & Co.: Toronto,* [1911.] 8°. **10600.** h. **17. (4.)**

BURROWES (Peter) Speech [at the trial of Dr. Edward Sheridan]. *See* Hamilton (W. H.) *of Dublin.* State of the Catholic Cause, *etc.* 1812. 8°. **8145.** d. **38.**

BURROWES (Peter)

—— Speeches . . . on the trials of Edward Sheridan, M.D. and Thomas Kirwan, Merchant, upon indictments under the Convention Act: including the proceedings and evidence relative to the alledged interference of Sir Charles Saxton, with the jury on Mr. Kirwan's trial; and the speech to evidence thereon. pp. vi. 111. *J. J. Nolan: Dublin*, 1812. 8°. **1131**. g. **18**.

BURROWES (Robert) *Dean of Cork.* Advice Religious and Political, delivered in four sermons, *etc.* pp. 54. *The Author: Dublin*, 1801. 8°. **4461**. bbb. **9**.

—— A Sermon preached before the Association for Discountenancing Vice and Promoting the Practice of Virtue and Religion, *etc.* pp. 63. *W. Watson & Son: Dublin*, 1795. 8°. **4475**. d. **1**. (**4**.)

—— [Another copy.] **4475**. b. **12**.

—— Sermons on the First Lessons of the Sunday Morning Service, from the first to the thirteenth Sunday after Trinity, *etc.* pp. xiii. 407. *The Author: London*, 1817. 8°. **1021**. h. **20**.

—— [Another edition.] pp. viii. 400. *John Taylor: London*, 1829. 8°. **1021**. h. **21**.

—— Twelve Discourses in Explanation of the Liturgy of the Church of England, *etc.* pp. vii. 243. *John Bolster: Cork*, 1834. 8°. **1219**. g. **9**.

—— [Another copy.] **1219**. i. **18**.

BURROWES (Rose) Little Magda. The story of a child. pp. 253. *J. Nisbet & Co.: London*, 1874. 8°. **12803**. de. **43**.

—— Love, strong as Death. A novel. pp. 334. *Remington & Co.: London*, 1877. 8°. **12638**. n. **27**.

BURROWES (Samuel) Good Instructions for all Young-men and Maids. Being the substance of an excellent sermon preached at St. Stevens Colman Street . . . at a solemne thanksgiving and celebration of a fast . . . Published for the generall good by me R. H. pp. 13. *For T. B.: London*, 1642. 4°. E. **141**. (**15**.)

BURROWES (Thomas Henry)

—— *See* Mohr (Robert L.) Thomas Henry Burrowes, 1805–1871. [With portraits.] 1946. 8°. **10891**. b. **13**.

—— Address delivered . . . before the Educational Society of Lancaster County, *etc.* pp. 16. *M. D. Holbrook: Lancaster* [*Pa.*], [1851.] 8°. **8305**. ee. **34**.

—— Draft of a Revised Common School Law, and of a law relative to the preparation of Common School teachers; with explanatory remarks and a set of district regulations. pp. 61. *E. Guyer: Harrisburg*, 1839. 8°. **8365**. b. **11**.

—— Pennsylvania School Architecture. A manual of directions and plans for grading, locating, constructing, heating, ventilating and furnishing Common School houses. pp. 276. *A. B. Hamilton: Harrisburg*, 1855. 4°. **7816**. b. **15**.

—— State-Book of Pennsylvania, containing an account of the geography, history, government, resources, and noted citizens of the state, *etc.* pp. 314. *A. Hunt & Son: Philadelphia*, 1847. 12°. **10410**. bbb. **29**.

BURROWES (*Sir* Walter Dixon) *Bart.* *See* Putland (J.) John Putland, a minor [and others] . . . Appellants. Sir Walter Burrowes, Bart. Respondent. The appellants' case. [1725.] fol. **19**. h. **2**. (**153**.)

BURROWES (*Sir* Walter Dixon) *Bart.*

—— *See* Putland (J.) John Putland, a minor [and others] . . . Appellants. Sir Walter Burrows, Bart. Respondent. The respondent's case. [1725.] fol. **19**. h. **2**. (**154**.)

BURROWES (William) *See* Borough.

BURROWS AND COLTON. Concise Instructions in the Art of Retouching, *etc.* pp. viii. 65. pl. 4. *Marion & Co.: London*, 1876. 8°. **8908**. b. **9**.

BURROWS' LEGAL CALENDAR. *See* Ephemerides.

BURROWS (   ) *Professor at the Royal College, Port Louis, Mauritius.* *See* Goethe (J. W. von) [*Faust.—Tl.* 1.] Goethe's Faust. Translation [by Sir G. F. Duckett, Bart., turned into verse by Professor Burrows] from part of the " Faust " of Goethe, *etc.* [1885 ?] *s. sh.* fol. **11527**. h. **6**.

BURROWS (Alfred J.) *Master at Bosbury Grammar School.* Notes and Abstracts, or Heads of Gallery Lessons; adapted to simultaneous and class teaching, *etc.* pt. 1. pp. 63. *Hamilton, Adams & Co.: London*, [1852.] 8°. **8307**. e. **60**.

BURROWS (Alfred Joe) The Agricultural Depression and how to meet it; hints to landowners and tenant farmers . . . Reprinted, with considerable additions, from " The Journal of Forestry and Estate Management." pp. 103. *W. Rider & Son: London*, 1882. 8°. **7078**. f. **36**.

BURROWS (Alvina Treut) *See* Treut, afterwards Burrows (A.)

BURROWS (Arthur Richard) The Story of Broadcasting . . . With . . . plates. pp. x. 182. *Cassell & Co.: London*, 1924. 8°. **08755**. f. **57**.

BURROWS (Bamford) Stories from the Canals. [A religious tract.] pp. 4. *Wesleyan Methodist Book-Room: London*, [1882.] 8°. **04419**. h. **16**.

BURROWS (Benjamin)

—— Definitions of Forms [in music] and terms used in form. *F. W. Smith & Lewis: Leicester*, [1939.] 8°. **7895**. s. **21**.

Reproduced from typewriting.

—— Graded Harmony Tests. *F. W. Smith & Lewis: Leicester*, [1940– .] 4°. W.P. **13632**.

—— List of British Composers and Publishers up to the year 1800. pp. 44. *F. W. Smith & Lewis: Leicester*, [1939.] 8°. **10804**. a. **53**.

—— Notes on the Repair of Micrometers. pp. 8. *F. W. Smith & Lewis: Leicester*, 1944. 8°. **7946**. b. **53**.

BURROWS (C. W.) *of Lee.* Scapa and a Camera. Pictorial impressions of five years spent at the Grand Fleet Base, *etc.* pp. xx. 144. *Country Life; George Newnes: London*, 1921. 4°. **9081**. h. **38**.

BURROWS (Charles Nicholi)

—— Criminal Statistics in Iowa. pp. 112. *Iowa City*, 1930. 8°. [*University of Iowa Studies in the Social Sciences.* vol. 9. no. 2.] Ac. **2692**. f/3.

BURROWS (Charles Russell)

—— Radio Propagation over Plane Earth, *etc.* [A thesis. Reprinted from " The Bell System Technical Journal " and " The Proceedings of the Institute of Radio Engineers."] 2 pt. [1938.] 8°. **8759**. df. **25**.

BURROWS (Charles William) The Best Method of Demagnetizing Iron in Magnetic Testing . . . From Bulletin of the Bureau of Standards, *etc.* *Washington*, 1908. 8°. **8758**. ee. **16**.

—— The Postal Laws of the United States as related to business interests. (Extract from "Construction.") pp. 24. *Pittaburg*, 1905. 12°. **8247**. a. **64**.

BURROWS (Clement Larcom) *See* Ingham (Ernest G.) *Bishop of Sierra Leone*, and Burrows (C. L.) Sketches in Western Canada. [1913.] 8°. **4764**. aa. **22**.

BURROWS (Donald) The Human Leopard Society of Sierra Leone . . . Reprinted from the Journal of the African Society. [*London*,] 1914. 8°. **10006**. p. **12**. **(1.)**

BURROWS (E.) *Mrs.* The Martyr Land; or, Tales of the Vaudois. By the author of "Sunlight through the Mist" [i.e. Mrs. E. Burrows], *etc.* pp. 245. 1856 [1855]. 8°. *See* Waldenses. **4417**. aa. **59**.

—— Meadow Lea; or, the Gipsy children . . . By the author of "The Triumphs of Steam" [i.e. Mrs. E. Burrows], *etc.* pp. vi. 329. 1862. 8°. *See* Meadow Lea. **12804**. g. **37**.

—— Might not Right; or Stories of the discovery and conquest of America. By the author of "Our Eastern Empire" [i.e. Mrs. E. Burrows], *etc.* pp. viii. 246. 1858. 8°. *See* Might. **12807**. b. **32**.

—— The Monastery and the Mountain Church . . . By the author of "Sunlight through the Mist" [i.e. Mrs. E. Burrows], *etc.* pp. 277. 1855. 8°. *See* Monastery. **4417**. b. **45**.

—— A Nation's Manhood; or, Stories of Washington and the American War of Independence. By the author of "Sunlight through the Mist" [i.e. Mrs. E. Burrows], *etc.* pp. viii. 358. 1861 [1860]. 8°. *See* Washington (George) *President of the United States of America*. **10881**. b. **41**.

—— Our Eastern Empire: or, Stories from the history of British India. By the author of "The Martyr Land" [i.e. Mrs. E. Burrows], *etc.* pp. xii. 236. 1857 [1856]. 8°. *See* India. **9056**. b. **14**.

—— Sunlight through the Mist: or, Practical lessons drawn from the lives of good men . . . By the author of "The Monastery and the Mountain Church" [i.e. Mrs. E. Burrows] . . . New edition. pp. iv. 231. 1855. 8°. *See* Sunlight. **4825**. a. **36**.

—— [Another edition.] pp. viii. 213. 1860. 8°. *See* Sunlight. **4886**. b. **64**.

—— Tiny Stories for Tiny Readers in Tiny Words. By the author of "Triumphs of Steam" [i.e. Mrs. E. Burrows], *etc.* pp. vii. 117. 1864. 8°. *See* Stories. **12808**. de. **25**.

—— The Triumphs of Steam; or, Stories from the lives of Watt, Arkwright and Stephenson. By the author of "Might not Right" [i.e. Mrs. E. Burrows], *etc.* pp. viii. 263. 1859 [1858]. 8°. *See* Triumphs. **10804**. a. **32**.

—— A new edition revised and partly re-written by Henry Frith, *etc.* pp. xii. 263. 1892. 8°. *See* Triumphs. **8768**. bb. **3**.

—— Trottie's Story Book; or, True tales in short words and large type. By the author of "Tiny Stories for Tiny Readers" [i.e. Mrs. E. Burrows] . . . Second edition. pp. iv. 124. 1866. 8°. *See* Trottie. **12807**. bb. **28**.

BURROWS (E.) *Mrs.*

—— Tuppy; or, the Autobiography of a donkey. By the author of "The Triumphs of Steam" [i.e. Mrs. E. Burrows], *etc.* pp. 100. 1860. 8°. *See* Tuppy. **12808**. a. **43**.

—— [Another edition.] pp. 51. 1896. 8°. *See* Tuppy. **7206**. aa. **16/13**.

BURROWS (Edith Maie) Anti-Aunts. Three-act comedy. pp. xxvii. *J. Fischer & Bro.: New York*, [1913.] 8°. **11774**. bb. **30**. **(1.)**

—— "Dear Cyril." [A play.] pp. xxvii. *J. Fischer & Bro.: New York*, [1913.] 8°. **11791**. bb. **29**. **(2.)**

—— In a Flower Garden. A cantata, *etc.* pp. xiv. *J. Fischer & Bro.: New York*, [1914.] fol. **11791**. i. **4**. **(1.)**

—— "Their Lordships." [A play.] pp. xxiii. *J. Fischer & Bro.: New York*, [1913.] 8°. **11791**. bb. **29**. **(3.)**

—— The Wild Rose . . . Operetta, *etc.* pp. xviii. *J. Fischer & Bro.: New York*, [1915.] fol. **11791**. i. **4**. **(4.)**

BURROWS (Edmund Hartford)

—— Overberg Outspan. A chronicle of people and places in the south western districts of the Cape. Illustrated by Deon Krige. pp. xviii. 310. pl. A–Y. *Maskew Miller: Cape Town*, 1952. 8°. **10098**. aa. **33**.

BURROWS (Edward) *See* Lister (Thomas) *4th Baron Ribblesdale*. The Queen's Hounds . . . With an introduction on the hereditary mastership by E. Burrows, *etc.* 1897. 4°. **7906**. i. **26**.

BURROWS (Edwin Grant)

—— Ethnology of Uvea, Wallis Island. pp. iii. 176. pl. 8. *Honolulu*, 1937. 8°. [*Bernice P. Bishop Museum. Bulletin.* no. 145. Ac. **6245/3**.

—— Hawaiian Americans. An account of the mingling of Japanese, Chinese, Polynesian, and American cultures. pp. 228. *Yale University Press: New Haven*, 1947. 8°. **10009**. ppp. **21**.

—— Western Polynesia. A study in cultural differentiation . . . A dissertation, *etc.* 1938. *See* Gothenburg.—*Göteborgs Museum.—Etnografiska Museet.* Ethnological Studies. no. 7. 1935, *etc.* 8°. Ac. **1064/3**.

—— [Another issue.] Western Polynesia. A study in cultural differentiation . . . Reprinted . . . from Ethnological Studies . . . Edited and published by Walter Kaudern. *Göteborg*, 1938. 8°. **010007**. i. **56**.

BURROWS (Elizabeth) Irene of Tundra Towers, *etc.* pp. 311. *Doubleday, Doran & Co.: Garden City, New York*, 1928. 8°. **12714**. bb. **23**.

—— Judy of the Whale Gates, *etc.* pp. 296. *Doubleday, Doran & Co.: Garden City, New York*, 1930. 8°. A.N. **395**.

BURROWS (Eric Norman Bromley) *See* Ur Excavations. Ur Excavations. [Reports.] (vol. 2. The Royal Cemetery. Chapter 16. Inscribed Material. By E. Burrows.) 1927, *etc.* fol. W.P. **8565/2**.

—— *See* Ur Excavations. Ur Excavations. Texts. (vol. 1. Royal Inscriptions. By C. J. Gadd . . . and L. Legrain . . . With contributions by . . . E. R. [sic] Burrows. vol. 2. Archaic Texts. By E. Burrows.) 1928, *etc.* fol. W.P. **8565**. a/1, **2**.

BURROWS (Eric Norman Bromley)

—— The Gospel of the Infancy, and other Biblical essays . . . Edited by Edmund F. Sutcliffe. pp. viii. 139. *Burns, Oates & Co.: London,* [1941.] 8°. [*Bellarmine Series.* no. 6.] W.P. **5125/6.**

—— The Oracles of Jacob and Balaam [in Gen. cap. 49 and Num. cap. 23, 24] . . . Edited by Edmund F. Sutcliffe. pp. x. 115. *Burns, Oates & Co.: London,* [1939.] 8°. [*Bellarmine Series.* vol. 3.] W.P. **5125/3.**

BURROWS (Eric R.) *See* Burrows (Eric N. B.)

BURROWS (Francis) The Green Knight, and other poems. pp. 80. *Frank Palmer: London,* 1910. 8°. **011650. i. 19.**

—— Marsyas, and a prologue. [A dramatic poem.] pp. 86. *New Age Press: London,* 1909. 8°. **011650. h. 10.**

BURROWS (Frank Robert) *See* Gibson (John) *M.A.*, and Burrows (F. R.) Specimen Essays, *etc.* 1881. 8°. **12981. c. 4.**

—— —— 1886. 8°. **11824. cc. 5.**

—— Geographical Gleanings, *etc.* pp. 75. *G. Philip & Son: London,* 1906. 8°. **10002. cc. 18.**

—— The New Science. [A paper on geography.] pp. 32. *G. Philip & Son: London,* [1916.] 8°. **10001. df. 36.**

—— On Some Methods of Teaching Geography . . . Reprinted from the "Parents' Review." pp. 19. *G. Philip & Son: London,* [1896.] 8°. **8304. d. 19. (9.)**

BURROWS (G. E.) Tales of the Church in England. Boescus—a tale of Roman Britain. "The Fury of the Heathen." "Pro Ecclesia Dei." pp. 230. *A. R. Mowbray & Co.: Oxford,* 1904. 8°. **04412. k. 40.**

BURROWS (*Sir* George) *Bart.* Case of Extensive Carcinoma of the Lungs, with some practical remarks. From . . . the Medico-Chirurgical Transactions, *etc.* pp. 15. *Richard Kinder: London,* 1844. 8°. **7306. bb. 14. (2.)**

—— On Disorders of the Cerebral Circulation; and on the connection between affections of the brain and diseases of the heart. pp. xvi. 220. pl. 6. *Longman & Co.: London,* 1846. 8°. **1186. c. 18.**

BURROWS (George Joseph) On the Hydrolysis of Urea Hydrochloride. (Reprinted from the Journal and Proceedings of the Royal Society of N.S. Wales.) [1919.] 8°. **8903. aaa. 25. (3.)**

—— Volume Changes in the Process of Solution. (Reprinted from the Journal and Proceedings of the Royal Society of N.S. Wales.) 1919. 8°. **8903. aaa. 25. (2.)**

BURROWS (George Man) *See* Periodical Publications.—*London.* The London, Medical, Surgical, and Pharmaceutical Repository. (The London Medical Repository . . . By G. M. Burrows, W. Royston and A. T. Thomson.) 1814, *etc.* 8°. P.P. **2695.**

—— An Account of Two Cases of Death from eating Mussels: with general observations on fish poison. pp. 39. *London,* 1815. 8°. **778. d. 23.**

—— [Another copy.] **990. k. 17.**

—— Commentaries on the Causes, Forms, Symptoms, & Treatment, moral & medical, of Insanity. pp. xv. 716. *T. & G. Underwood: London,* 1828. 8°. **1191. h. 16.**

BURROWS (George Man)

—— An Inquiry into Certain Errors relative to Insanity; and their consequences; physical, moral, and civil. pp. ix. 320. *T. & G. Underwood: London,* 1820. 8°. **956. i. 17.**

—— Untersuchungen über gewisse die Geisteszerrüttung betreffende Irrthümer und ihre Einflüsse auf die physischen, moralischen und bürgerlichen Verhältnisse des Menschen. Uebersetzt nebst einer Abhandlung über die Seelengesundheit von Dr. J. C. A. Heinroth. pp. 260. *Leipzig,* 1822. 8°. **1185. f. 23.**

—— A Letter to Sir Henry Halford . . . touching some points of the evidence, and observations of counsel, on a Commission of Lunacy on Mr Edward Davies. pp. 38. *T. & G. Underwood: London,* 1830. 8°. **7306. bb. 14. (1.)**

—— Observations on the Comparative Mortality of Paris and London . . . From the . . . London Medical Repository, *etc.* pp. 20. *D. N. Shury: London,* 1815. 9°. **796. e. 8. (5.)**

—— A Statement of Circumstances connected with the Apothecaries' Act and its administration. pp. 47. xxii. *J. Callow: London,* 1817. 8°. **7306. bb. 12. (2.)**

BURROWS (George T.) *Agricultural Correspondent.*

—— History of Dairy Shorthorn Cattle. [With plates.] pp. 176. *Vinton & Co.: [London,]* 1950. 8°. **07295. f. 67.**

BURROWS (George Thomas) All about Bowls, with hints for beginners . . . With contributions from past English champions, *etc.* pp. viii. 152. *Mills & Boon: London,* 1915. 8°. **7911. df. 11.**

—— All about Bowls. A manual for novice and expert player, *etc.* [With plates, including a portrait.] pp. 136. *Hutchinson's Library of Sports & Pastimes: London,* [1948.] 8°. **7917. bbb. 6.**

—— Bowling Guide, and how to play bowls. [With a portrait.] pp. 17–107. *British Sports Publishing Co.: London,* [1917 ?] 8°. [*Spalding's Athletic Library.* no. 57.] **07908. i. 14/57a.**

—— Bowls: how to excel at the game. pp. 47. *"Country Life" & George Newnes: London; C. Scribner's Sons: New York,* 1920. 8°. **7911. df. 44.**

—— (Revised edition.) pp. 80. *Country Life: London,* 1936. 8°. **07908. de. 44.**

—— Bowls: theory and practice, *etc.* [With plates.] pp. 83. *Vinton & Co.: London,* [1931.] 8°. **7911. f. 11.**

—— Cheshire Sports and Sportsmen. Including a history of the Chester Cup. pp. 188. *Phillipson & Golder: Chester,* [1925.] 8°. **7904. ee. 16.**

—— The Game of Bowls. pp. 56. *Athletic Publications: London,* [1924.] 8°. **07912. f. 6.**

—— Gentleman Charles. A history of foxhunting, *etc.* [With plates.] pp. 240. *Vinton & Co.: London,* 1951. 8°. **7919. f. 36.**

—— Modern Bowls. pp. 80. *Vinton & Co.: London,* [1938.] 8°. **07908. i. 20.**

—— Some Old English Inns . . . With 25 pictures, *etc.* pp. cxxxvi. *T. Werner Laurie: London,* [1907.] 16°. **07816. de. 7.**

BURROWS (Guy) The Land of the Pigmies . . . With introduction by H. M. Stanley, M.P. With illustrations . . . and maps. pp. xxx. 299. *C. A. Pearson: London,* 1898. 8°. **2358.** d. **6.**

BURROWS (H.) *of the School of Art, Huddersfield.* Twelve Examples. Model Drawing Copies for the Second Grade Art Examinations. *J. W. Bean & Son: Leeds,* [1892.] 8°. **7854.** e. **40.**

BURROWS (Harold) *F.R.C.S.* *See* Jackson (George V.) The Perilous Adventures and Vicissitudes of a Naval Officer . . . Edited by H. Burrows, *etc.* 1927. 8°. **010815.** ee. **18.**

—— Biological Actions of Sex Hormones. pp. x. 514. *University Press: Cambridge,* 1945. 8°. **7008.** bb. **8.**

—— Biological Actions of Sex Hormones . . . Second edition, entirely revised, *etc.* pp. xiii. 615. *University Press: Cambridge,* 1949. 8°. **7008.** bb. **28.**

—— The Cultivation of Sentiment. pp. 64. *Leonard Parsons: London,* 1923. 8°. **08463.** de. **76.**

—— A Manual for Nurses on Abdominal Surgery. pp. 142. *Scientific Press: London,* [1907.] 8°. **07481.** f. **21.**

—— Second edition, rewritten and enlarged. pp. 144. *Scientific Press: London,* [1923.] 8°. **7482.** aa. **14.**

—— Mistakes and Accidents of Surgery. pp. viii. 470. *Baillière & Co.: London,* 1923. 8°. **7481.** bb. **40.**

—— Pitfalls of Surgery . . . Second edition [of "Mistakes and Accidents of Surgery"]. pp. x. 525. *Baillière & Co.: London,* 1925. 8°. **07482.** c. **17.**

—— The Muscular System . . . Profusely illustrated. pp. viii. 157. *Scientific Press: London,* [1915.] 16°. **7421.** a. **45.**

—— (Second and revised edition.) pp. xi. 184. *Scientific Press: London,* 1926. 16°. [*Pocket Guide Series.*] **07305.a.1/26.**

—— Third edition. pp. xi. 184. *Faber & Faber: London,* 1936. 16°. **7419.** a. **15.**

—— The Muscular System . . . Fourth edition. pp. v. 184. *Faber & Faber: London,* 1942. 16°. **7423.** a. **3.**

—— Pitfalls of Surgery. *See* supra: Mistakes and Accidents of Surgery.

—— Some Factors in the Localisation of Disease in the Body. pp. xi. 299. pl. viii. *Baillière & Co.: London,* 1932. 8°. **7440.** p. **12.**

—— Surgical Instruments and Appliances used in Operations. An illustrated and classified list, with explanatory notes. pp. 96. *Scientific Press: London,* 1905. 8°. **07481.** f. **19.**

—— Third edition, revised and enlarged. pp. 100. *Scientific Press: London,* [1910.] 8°. **07481.** f. **24.**

—— Fourth edition, revised and enlarged. pp. 103. *Scientific Press: London,* [1912.] 8°. **07481.** f. **26.**

—— (Fifth edition.) pp. 127. *Faber & Gwyer: London,* 1927. 8°. **07481.** f. **60.**

—— Sixth edition. pp. 134. *Faber & Faber: London,* 1931. 8°. **07481.** ee. **41.**

—— Seventh edition. pp. 138. *Faber & Faber: London,* 1933. 8°. **07481.** ee. **40.**

BURROWS (Harold) *F.R.C.S.*

—— Eighth edition. pp. 142. *Faber & Faber: London,* 1936. 8°. **07481.** ee. **45.**

—— Ninth edition. pp. 142. *Faber & Faber: London,* 1937. 8°. **07481.** f. **76.**

—— Surgical Instruments and Appliances . . . Tenth edition. pp. 146. *Faber & Faber: London,* 1939. 8°. **07481.** aaa. **7.**

—— Surgical Instruments and Appliances . . . Eleventh edition. pp. 146. *Faber & Faber: London,* 1942. 8°. **7483.** aa. **2.**

—— Surgical Instruments and Appliances used in Operations . . . Twelfth edition. pp. 146. *Faber & Faber: London,* 1943. 8°. **7484.** aa. **6.**

BURROWS (Harold) *F.R.C.S.*, and **HORNING** (Eric Stephen Gurney)

—— Oestrogens and Neoplasia, *etc.* pp. xv. 189. *Blackwell Scientific Publications: Oxford,* [1952.] 8°. **7581.** s. **45.**

BURROWS (Harold) *F.R.C.S.*, and **RAVEN** (Ronald William)

—— Surgical Instruments and Appliances used in Operations, *etc.* (Fourteenth edition.) pp. 160. *Faber & Faber: London,* 1952. 8°. **7484.** aa. **31.**

BURROWS (Harold) *LL.B.* The Prelude. [Poems.] pp. vi. 81. *T. Fisher Unwin: London,* 1890. 12°. **011653.** e. **116.**

BURROWS (Harold Jackson) and **COLTART** (William Derrick)

—— Treatment by Manipulation. pp. xii. 36. *Eyre & Spottiswoode: London,* [1939.] 8°. [*"The Practitioner" Booklets.* no. 1.] **7307.f.17/1.**

—— Treatment by Manipulation . . . Second edition, fully revised. pp. 80. *Published on behalf of "The Practitioner" by Eyre & Spottiswoode: London,* 1951. 8°. **7471.** b. **18.**

BURROWS (Harry Raymond) *See* Crew (Albert) Economics for Commercial Students and Business Men . . . Eleventh . . . edition. [Revised by H. R. Burrows.] 1935. 8°. **8230.** aa. **17.**

—— —— 1936. 8°. **8233.** aa. **9.**

—— Indian Life and Labour in South Africa. Edited by Professor H. R. Burrows. pp. 36. *South African Institute of Race Relations: Johannesburg,* [1943.] 8°. **08157.** ee. **88.**

BURROWS (Hedley Robert)

—— *See* Liturgies.—*Church of England.—Occasional Offices.—Institution and Installation of Deans.—Hereford.* Form of Installation of the Venerable H. R. Burrows . . . as Dean of the Cathedral Church . . . in Hereford, *etc.* [1947.] 8°. **3409.** c. **3.**

BURROWS (Helen) *See* Ilse, *Princess.* Princess Ilse. A story . . . Translated from the German [of Marie Petersen] by H. Burrows. 1856. 8°. **12554.** dd. **27.**

BURROWS (Helen M.)

—— The Silent Years. [A tale.] pp. 52. *A. H. Stockwell: Ilfracombe,* [1944.] 8°. **012643.** tt. **4.**

BURROWS (Henry) *J.P., Councillor of Poulton-le-Fylde.*

—— Poulton-le-Fylde, Lancs. The official guide, *etc.* [Various editions.] [1929– .] 8°. *See* Poulton-le-Fylde. **10354**. a. **706**.

BURROWS (Henry) ***Lord Mayor of Dublin. See*** **Burrowes.**

BURROWS (Henry William) *A.R.I.B.A.* *See* Harris (George F.) and Burrows (H. W.) The Eocene and Oligocene Beds of the Paris Basin, *etc.* 1891. 8°. Ac. **3172/6**.

BURROWS (Henry William) *Canon of Rochester.* *See* Rossetti (Christina G.) Annus Domini: a prayer for each day of the year, *etc.* [Edited by H. W. Burrows.] 1874. 16°. **3457**. a. **59**.

—— *See* Wordsworth (Elizabeth) Henry William Burrows. Memorials, *etc.* 1894. 8°. **4906**. df. **23**.

—— Address to those who have little Spare Time, and perhaps few opportunities of reception. *See* Lord's Supper. Plain Instructive Sermons on Holy Communion, *etc.* 1887. 8°. **4479**. bb. **43**.

—— Christ in his Sacraments. A sermon, *etc.* pp. 13. *J. H. & J. Parker: Oxford & London,* 1860. 8°. **4477**. c. **110**. (**3**.)

—— A Christ-like Clergy. A sermon, *etc.* pp. 20. *William Skeffington: London,* 1872. 16°. **4479**. aa. **1**. (**10**.)

—— The Clergyman in three Aspects. *See* Life. The Spiritual Life: addresses, *etc.* 1886. 8°. **4405**. bb. **5**.

—— The Conflict with Impurity. *See* Wilberforce (Samuel) successively *Bishop of Oxford* and *of Winchester.* The Enduring Conflict of Christ . . . Sermons, *etc.* 1865. 8°. **4477**. bb. **66**.

—— The Conversion of St. Paul. 1 Tim. i. 16. 1846. *See* Watson (Alexander) *Vicar of St. Marychurch.* Practical Sermons, *etc.* vol. 3. 1845, *etc.* 8°. **1358**. g. **6**.

—— Domestic Service. [A sermon.] 1873. *See* Fowle (Edmund) Plain Preaching, *etc.* vol. 2. 1873, *etc.* 8°. **4463**. de. **2**.

—— The Eve of Ordination. pp. 62. *W. W. Gardner: London,* [1875.] 16°. **4499**. aa. **2**.

—— Four Short Addresses delivered at a . . . meeting of the Coventry Clerical Society, *etc.* pp. 31. *S.P.C.K.: London,* 1881. 8°. **4473**. f. **19**. (**26**.)

—— The Great Exhibition; a sermon, *etc.* pp. 22. *Skeffington & Southwell: London,* 1851. 12°. **4475**. a. **35**.

—— The Half-Century of Christ Church, St. Pancras, Albany Street. pp. 76. *Skeffington & Son: London,* 1887. 8°. **4531**. aaa. **26**. (**5**.)

—— Harvest Thanksgiving. [A sermon.] *William Skeffington: London,* [1871.] 8°. [*Penny Monthly Sermons.* ser. 3. no. 8.] **4479**. b. **40**.

—— [Another edition.] 1873. *See* Fowle (Edmund) Plain Preaching to Poor People. ser. 3. 1875, *etc.* 12°. **4462**. a. **26**.

—— Hymns for use in Church. Collected by the Rev. H. W. Burrows. *William Skeffington: London,* 1855. 12°. **3437**. c. **23**.

—— Fourth edition. *William Skeffington: London,* 1864. 12°. **3437**. a. **33**.

BURROWS (Henry William) *Canon of Rochester.*

—— The Incarnation. A sermon. *See* Warnings. The Warnings of Advent, *etc.* 1853. 8°. **4461**. g. **29**.

—— Lectures on the Acts of the Apostles, *etc.* pp. 104. *S.P.C.K.: London,* [1883.] 8°. **3227**. df. **30**.

—— Lenten and other Sermons. pp. viii. 177. *W. W. Gardner: London,* [1880.] 8°. **4466**. aa. **21**.

—— Life prolonged that Christ may be embraced. [A sermon.] *See* Fowle (Edmund) Plain Preaching, *etc.* vol. 1. 1873, *etc.* 12°. **4463**. de. **2**.

—— The London Season. [A sermon.] 1874. *See* Kempe (John E.) "The Use and Abuse of the World," *etc.* ser. 2. 1873, *etc.* 8°. **4465**. b. **18**.

—— [Another edition.] *See* Kempe (John E.) "The Use and Abuse of the World," *etc.* ser. 2. 1877. 8°. **4420**. c. **6**.

—— Parochial Mission-Women Association. A sermon, *etc.* pp. 12. *J. Parker & Co.: Oxford & London,* 1867. 12°. **4478**. a. **126**. (**19**.)

—— Parochial Sermons. 3 ser. *William Skeffington: London,* 1857–72. 8°. **4462**. b. **13**.

—— Personal Responsibility of Man, as to his Use of Intellect. *See* Wilberforce (Samuel) successively *Bishop of Oxford* and *of Winchester.* Personal Responsibility of Man. Sermons, *etc.* 1869. 8°. **4477**. bb. **69**.

—— The Power of God and the Wisdom of God. A sermon, *etc.* pp. 16. *J. H. & J. Parker: Oxford,* 1859. 12°. **4475**. a. **122**. (**10**.)

—— The Private Life of the Parish Priest. An address to candidates for ordination, *etc.* *William Skeffington: London,* 1870. 16°. **4478**. e. **7**.

—— Saving Grace. [A sermon.] *See* Fruits. The Kindly Fruits of the Earth, *etc.* 1889. 8°. **4479**. aa. **39**.

—— A Sermon preached at the consecration of the Lord Bishop of Bombay, *etc.* pp. 16. *J. Parker & Co.: Oxford & London,* 1869. 8°. **4478**. cc. **11**.

—— Thoughts on the Festival of St. Luke the Evangelist. pp. 46. *S.P.C.K.: London,* [1865.] 12°. **4410**. bb. **47**. (**3**.)

BURROWS (Herbert) *See* Besant (Annie) [*Works written in collaboration.*] A Short Glossary of Theosophical Terms. By A. Besant and H. Burrows. 1891. 8°. **8630**. f. **52**.

—— *See* Besant (Annie) [*Works written in collaboration.*] Petit glossaire de termes théosophiques. Par A. Besant et H. Burrows. 1894. 16°. **8632**. b. **45**.

—— *See* Clarke (William) *Editor of Mazzini's Essays, etc.* William Clarke. A collection of his writings. [Edited by H. Burrows and J. A. Hobson.] With a biographical sketch [by H. Burrows]. 1908. 8°. **012272**. ee. **8**.

—— Zola. pp. 58. *Swan Sonnenschein & Co.: London,* 1899. 12°. **11852**. b. **32**.

BURROWS (Hubert Lionel) *See* Wood (Leonard S.) and Burrows (H. L.) The Pleasant Land of England, *etc.* 1925. 16°. **012207**. aa. **1/18**.

—— *See* Wood (Leonard S.) and Burrows (H. L.) Sports and Pastimes in English Literature, *etc.* 1925. 8°. **012207**. aa. **1/44**.

BURROWS (HUBERT LIONEL)

—— *See* WOOD (Leonard S.) and BURROWS (H. L.) The Town in Literature, *etc.* 1925. 16°. **012207.** aa. **1/36.**

—— The Story of English Industry and Trade . . . Containing thirty-six illustrations. pp. viii. 208. *A. & C. Black: London,* 1914. 8°. **08228.** ff. **77.**

—— English Industry and Trade . . . Third edition, *etc.* pp. viii. 213. *A. & C. Black: London,* 1923. 8°. **08228.** bb. **55.**

—— Fourth edition, *etc.* pp. viii. 213. *A. & C. Black: London,* 1928. 8°. **08246.** e. **23.**

—— [A reissue.] *London,* 1929. 8°. **08246.** ff. **27.**

—— The Story of English Industry and Trade . . . Fifth edition, *etc.* pp. viii. 216. *A. & C. Black: London,* 1934. 8°. **08229.** m. **36.**

—— The Story of English Industry and Trade . . . Sixth edition, *etc.* pp. vi. 218. *A. & C. Black: London,* 1939. 8°. **08230.** a. **23.**

—— The Story of English Industry and Trade . . . Seventh edition, *etc.* pp. vi. 218. *A. & C. Black: London,* 1952 [1953]. 8°. **8224.** aa. **53.**

BURROWS (J. F.) *Artistic Entertainer.* The Lightning Artist. A treatise on the art of lightning sketches . . . With drawings by the author, *etc.* pp. viii. 82. *Hamley Bros.: London,* [1905.] 8°. **7856.** i. **4.**

—— Secrets of Stage Hypnotism: Stage Electricity: and Bloodless Surgery. (Introduction by Will Goldston.) pp. 71. *G. Routledge & Sons: London,* [1912.] 8°. **7911.** b. **27.**

BURROWS (JAMES) *See* BYRON (George G. N.) *Baron Byron.* [*Extracts.*] The Byron Birthday Book. Compiled . . . by J. Burrows, *etc.* [1880.] 16°. **11601.** bb. **37.**

—— —— 1879. 16°. **11601.** bb. **26.**

BURROWS (JAMES FREDERICK) Ely Cathedral and other places of interest . . . Illustrated. pp. 60. *J. F. Burrows: Ely,* [1910.] 16°. **4707.** a. **48.**

BURROWS (JESSIE WHARTON) What's for Dinner? A collection of original luncheon and dinner menus for every day in the year. Also breakfast menus for one month, sample menus for one week for the kitchen, and some recipes. pp. 239. *J. E. Cornish: Manchester,* 1909. 8°. **07942.** de. **5.**

BURROWS (JOAN)

—— His is the Victory. Poems. pp. 16. *A. H. Stockwell: Ilfracombe,* 1945. 8°. **11657.** ee. **73.**

BURROWS (JOHN) *M.D.* A Dissertation on the Nature and Effects of a Vegetable Remedy, an acknowledged specific in all venereal, scorbutic and scrophulous cases . . . Fourth edition. pp. 80. *The Author: London,* 1784. 8°. **7509.** c. **13.**

—— A New Practical Essay on Cancers . . . To which is also added, a new more safe and efficacious method of administring hemlock. pp. xvi. 76. *The Author: London,* 1767. 8°. **7630.** c. **10.**

—— Nouvel essai de médecine pratique sur les cancers, *etc.* pp. xxiv. 91. *Londres,* 1767. 12°. T. **839.** (**3.**)

BURROWS (JOHN) *of Christ Church, Oxford.* On National Prejudices; their good and bad effects. 1817. *See* PERIODICAL PUBLICATIONS.—*London.* The Pamphleteer, *etc.* vol. 9. 1813, *etc.* 8°. P.P. **3557.** w.

BURROWS (JOHN LANSING) *See* PERIODICAL PUBLICATIONS.—*Philadelphia.* American Baptist Register. J. L. Burrows, editor. 1852, *etc.* 8°. P.P. **866.** b.

BURROWS (JOHN NELSON) and **PLIMPTON** (WALTER) Ritual Notes. A complete guide to the rights and ceremonies of the English Church. By the editors of "The Order of Divine Service" (H.C., E.C.R.L. [i.e. Henry Cairncross, Edward C. R. Lamburn]). Seventh edition [of the work originally written by J. N. Burrows and W. Plimpton], revised, entirely re-written and enlarged. pp. xii. 203. *W. Knott & Son: London,* 1926. 8°. **3474.** aa. **2.**

—— Ritual Notes. A comprehensive guide to the rites and ceremonies of the Book of Common Prayer of the English Church . . . Compiled by: Henry Cairncross, the Rev. E. C. R. Lamburn, the Rev. C. A. C. Whatton . . . Eighth edition. An entirely new version, considerably enlarged. pp. xv. 310. *W. Knott & Son: London,* 1935. 8°. **3474.** aa. **34.**

A later edition is entered under RITUAL NOTES.

BURROWS (JOHN WILLIAM) Essex Units in the War, 1914–1919. [Edited and compiled by J. W. Burrows.] 6 vol. *J. H. Burrows & Sons: Southend-on-Sea,* [1923–35.] 8°. **09079.** c. **28.**

—— The Essex Regiment. 1st Battalion, *etc.* (Second edition [of vol. 1 of "Essex Units in the War, 1914–1919"].) [With plates and maps.] pp. xxxi. 293. 1931. 8°. *See* ENGLAND.—*Army.—Infantry.—Essex Regiment, 1st Battalion.* **09080.** b. **22.**

—— The Essex Regiment. 2nd Battalion (56th) (Pompadours). (Second edition [of vol. 2 of "Essex Units in the War, 1914–1919"].) pp. xxviii. 232. 1937. 8°. *See* ENGLAND.—*Army.—Infantry.—Essex Regiment, 2nd Battalion.* **09079.** bb. **56.**

—— The History of Prittlewell Priory . . . 3rd edition. [With plates.] pp. 46. *Southend-on-Sea,* [1927.] 8°. [*Southend-on-Sea Museum Handbooks.* no. 4.] W.P. **555/4.**

—— 4th edition. Revised, *etc.* [With plates.] pp. 70. *Southend-on-Sea,* 1933. 8°. [*Southend-on-Sea Museum Handbooks.* no. 4.] W.P. **555/4a.**

—— Southend-on-Sea and District: historical notes. pp. 323. viii. *J. H. Burrows & Sons: Southend-on-Sea,* 1909. 8°. **10351.** ccc. **32.**

—— Southend Pier and its Story, 1829–1835–1935. (Reprinted from The Southend Standard.) [With plates.] pp. 41. *J. H. Burrows & Sons: Southend-on-Sea,* 1936. 8°. **010360.** c. **65.**

—— "Standard" Guide to Southend-on-Sea, Westcliff, Leigh-on-Sea, Shoeburyness, and district. pp. 208. *J. H. Burrows & Sons: Southend-on-Sea,* [1910.] 8°. **010352.** g. **8.**

—— [Another edition.] pp. 139. *J. H. Burrows & Sons: Southend-on-Sea,* [1924.] 8°. **010358.** e. **98.**

—— [Another edition.] pp. 202. *J. H. Burrows & Sons: Southend-on-Sea,* [1930.] 8°. **010360.** aa. **85.**

—— [Another edition.] pp. 204. *J. H. Burrows & Sons: Southend-on-Sea,* [1931.] 8°. **010360.** a. **76.**

BURROWS (John William)

—— [Another edition.] pp. 191. *J. H. Burrows & Sons: Southend-on-Sea*, [1933.] 8°. **010352**. b. **78**.

—— "Standard" Guide to Southend-on-Sea, *etc.* pp. 115. *J. H. Burrows & Sons: Southend-on-Sea*, [1946.] 8°. **10359**. b. **20**.

BURROWS (Joseph) *See* Robinson (Thomas) *of West Kirby, Cheshire*, and Burrows (J.) The Next Revolution, *etc.* 1894. 8°. **8282**. ff. **10**. (**13**.)

BURROWS (Kathleen)

—— Will You be my Friend? Animal stories and pictures for children. *Brockhampton Press: Leicester; printed in Holland*, [1947.] 8°. **07209**. c. **23**.

BURROWS (Leo)

—— The Eighth Army Epic. The African phase. pp. 15. *Northumberland Press: Gateshead on Tyne*, [1944.] 12°. **11652**. a. **96**.

—— Moods and Fancies. [Verses.] pp. 94. *Northumberland Press: Newcastle-upon-Tyne*, 1928. 8°. **011644**. f. **19**.

—— The Unfinished C.M.F. Pot Pourri. The Italian phase. pp. 19. *Northumberland Press: Gateshead on Tyne*, [1945.] 12°. **11657**. e. **51**.

BURROWS (Lionel) Ho Grammar, with vocabulary. pp. vii. 194. *Calcutta*, 1915. 4°. **14178**. i. **6**.

BURROWS (Margaret Florence) Robert Stephen Hawker. A study of his thought and poetry. pp. xi. 191. *Basil Blackwell: Oxford*, 1926. 8°. **4920**. f. **30**.

BURROWS (Maria) Counsel & Comfort: letters of Maria, Mrs. Burrows. Edited by Honble Mrs. Oldfield. pp. 85. *Longmans & Co.: London*, 1911. 8°. **010910**. bb. **50**.

BURROWS, afterwards **TURNER** (Mary) The Lay of a Loyal Subject. [*Tunbridge Wells?* 1863.] *s. sh.* 4°. **11647**. e. **1**. (**175**.)

—— Sketches of our Village, and other rhymes of idle hours. pp. viii. 103. *Pawsey: Ipswich*, 1852. 8°. **11647**. b. **45**.

—— Sketches of our Village, and other rhymes of early and later years. pp. ix. 127. *Lewis Hepworth: Tunbridge Wells*, 1883. 8°. **11644**. bbb. **64**.
An augmented edition of the preceding.

BURROWS (Millar) *See* Bible.—*Old Testament.* [*English.*] The Student's Old Testament. [vol. 6 arranged and translated by C. F. Kent and M. Burrows.] 1904, *etc.* 8°. **3050**. cc. **14**.

—— *See* Dead Sea Scrolls. The Dead Sea Scrolls of St. Mark's Monastery . . . Edited . . . by M. Burrows, with the assistance of John C. Trever and William H. Brownlee. 1950, *etc.* 4°. W.P. **11802**.

—— The Basis of Israelite Marriage. pp. viii. 72. *New Haven*, 1938. 8°. [*American Oriental Series.* vol. 15.] **14005**. aa. **2**.

—— Founders of Great Religions. Being personal sketches of famous leaders. pp. x. 243. *C. Scribner's Sons: New York, London*, 1931. 8°. **04503**. h. **64**.

—— The Literary Relations of Ezekiel . . . A dissertation . . . Abridged. pp. xi. 105. *Jewish Publication Society Press: Philadelphia*, 1925. **03187**. f. **60**.

BURROWS (Millar)

—— What Mean these Stones? The significance of archeology for biblical studies. [With illustrations.] pp. xvi. 306. *American Schools of Oriental Research: New Haven, Conn.*, 1941. 8°. **3130**. b. **38**.

BURROWS (Monica E.)

—— Architectural Model Making. pp. 15. *National Association of Girls' Clubs and Mixed Clubs: London*, [1950.] *obl.* 8°. **07822**. p. **62**.

BURROWS (Montagu) *See* Linstead (Henry C.) The Marvellous House . . . With an introduction by Professor Burrows. [1879.] 8°. **12809**. f. **29**.

—— *See* Oxford.—*University of Oxford.* The Register of the Visitors of the University of Oxford, from a.d. 1647 to a.d. 1658. Edited, with some account of the state of the University during the Commonwealth, by M. Burrows. 1881. 4°. Ac. **8113/120**.

—— *See* Stubbs (William) successively *Bishop of Chester* and *of Oxford.* Biblical Criticism . . . With preface by Professor M. Burrows. 1905. 8°. **04429**. a. **43**.

—— Antiquarianism and History. A lecture, *etc.* pp. 30. *Parker & Co.: Oxford & London*, 1885. 8°. **7709**. bbb. **20**. (**12**.)

—— Autobiography of Montagu Burrows . . . Edited by his son Stephen Montagu Burrows. With a supplementary note by Professor Oman. pp. xxi. 260. *Macmillan & Co.: London*, 1908. 8°. **010827**. g. **12**.

—— Cinque Ports. pp. viii. 261. *Longmans & Co.: London*, 1888. 8°. [*Historic Towns.*] **2366**. aa. **10**.

—— Collectanea. Second (Third) series, edited by M. Burrows. 2 vol. *Oxford*, 1890–96. 8°. [*Oxford Historical Society. Publications.* vol. 16, 32.] Ac. **8126/5**.

—— Commentaries on the History of England from the earliest times to 1865. pp. xiv. 533. *W. Blackwood & Sons: Edinburgh & London*, 1893. 8°. **09506**. g. **22**.

—— Constitutional Progress. Seven lectures delivered before the University of Oxford. pp. viii. 295. *John Murray: London*, 1869. 8°. **8007**. aaa. **47**.

—— The Family of Brocas of Beaurepaire and Roche Court, hereditary Masters of the Royal Buckhounds, with some account of the English rule in Aquitaine. pp. xii. 496. *Longmans & Co.: London*, 1886. 8°. **9915**. de. **17**.

—— History of the Families of Larcom, Hollis, and McKinley. pp. 125. *E. Pickard Hall & J. H. Stacy: Oxford*, 1883. 8°. **09917**. ccc. **36**.
Printed for private circulation.

—— The History of the Foreign Policy of Great Britain. pp. xiv. 372. *W. Blackwood & Sons: Edinburgh & London*, 1895. 8°. **9073**. d. **13**.

—— New edition, revised. pp. xv. 303. *W. Blackwood & Sons: Edinburgh & London*, 1897. 8°. **9076**. d. **32**.

—— Imperial England. pp. v. 253. *Cassell & Co.: London*, [1880.] 8°. **9525**. cc. **3**.

—— King Alfred the Great. pp. 29. *S.P.C.K.: London*, 1898. 8°. **4430**. bbb. **22**. (**2**.)

BURROWS (MONTAGU)

—— King Henry VIII. and the Reformation. An address delivered at Oxford in connexion with the Church Defence Institution. pp. 32. *S.P.C.K.: London,* 1898. 8°. **4430**. bbb. **22**. (**3**.)

—— The Life of Edward, Lord Hawke . . . With some account of the origin of the English wars in the reign of George the Second, and the state of the Royal Navy at that period. pp. xii. 508. *W. H. Allen & Co.: London,* 1883. 8°. **10816**. cc. **5**.

—— New edition. Revised and condensed. pp. ix. 333. *W. H. Allen & Co.: London,* 1896. 8°. **10816**. bb. **35**.

—— Third and revised edition, *etc.* pp. vi. 333. *J. J. Keliher & Co.: London,* 1904. 8°. **10815**. de. **36**.

—— The Manchester Church Congress and its probable results. A lecture, *etc.* pp. 30. *J. H. & J. Parker: Oxford & London,* 1863. 12°. **4108**. aa. **90**. (**6**.)

—— Memoir of Admiral Sir Henry Ducie Chads, G.C.B. By an old follower. [The preface signed: M. B., i.e. M. Burrows. With a portrait.] pp. 45. 1869. 8°. *See* B., M. **10817**. aaa. **24**.

—— Parliament and the Church of England. pp. vii. 143. *Seeley, Jackson & Halliday: London,* 1875. 8°. **5155**. de. **40**.

—— [Another copy.] **4705**. aaa. **1**.

—— Pass and Class. An Oxford guide-book through the courses of literæ humaniores, mathematics, *etc.* pp. xii. 256. *J. H. & J. Parker: Oxford & London,* 1860. 8°. **8364**. aa. **25**.

—— Second edition, with some of the latest examination papers. pp. xii. 291. *J. H. & J. Parker: Oxford & London,* 1861. 8°. **8364**. aa. **26**.

—— Third edition, revised and enlarged; with appendices on the Indian Civil Service, *etc.* pp. xii. 308. *J. Parker & Co.: Oxford & London,* 1866. 8°. **8364**. aaaa. **3**.

—— The Place of the Laity in Church Government. *See* WEIR (Archibald) and MACLAGAN (W. D.) successively *Bishop of Lichfield* and *Archbishop of York.* The Church and the Age, *etc.* ser. 1. 1870, *etc.* 8°. **4108**. f. **10**.

—— The Relations of Church and State historically considered. Two public lectures, *etc.* pp. 75. *Parker & Co.: Oxford & London,* 1866. 8°. **4705**. aaa. **17**.

—— Wiclif's Place in History. Three lectures, *etc.* pp. vi. 129. *W. Isbister: London,* 1882. 8°. **4902**. bbb. **36**.

—— Revised edition. pp. vi. 135. *W. Isbister: London,* 1884. 8°. **4902**. c. **37**.

—— Worthies of All Souls: four centuries of English history illustrated from the College archives. pp. xiii. 452. *Macmillan & Co.: London,* 1874. 8°. **8364**. de. **22**.

BURROWS (*Sir* MONTAGU) *See* BURROWS (*Sir* Stephen M.)

BURROWS (RAYMOND)

—— Bancor, Unitas and the Sages of Bretton Woods. The international money schemes. By R. Burrows. pp. 40. 1944. 8°. *See* DURBAN.—*Natal University College.—Department of Economics. Report.* no. 35. **8218**. b. **32**.

BURROWS (RAYMOND)

—— The Problems and Practice of Economic Planning. pp. ix. 280. *P. S. King & Son: London,* 1937. 8°. **8234**. bb. **27**.

BURROWS (RICHARD MORELL) Canterbury . . . The Tonbridge School Prize Poem; 1921. *Ackworth,* 1922. 16°. **1865**. c. **8**. (**44**.)
One of an edition of thirty-four copies.

BURROWS (*Sir* ROLAND)

—— *See* ENGLAND. [*Laws and Statutes.*—IV. *Factories.*] Acts relating to Factories & Workshops, with explanatory notes. The present edition by R. Burrows. 1908. 8°. [*ABRAHAM, afterwards TENNANT* (*May E.*) *The Law relating to Factories and Workshops, etc.*] **2228**. b. **15**.

—— *See* ENGLAND. [*Laws and Statutes.*—II.] Halsbury's Statutes of England . . . Editor-in-Chief, Sir R. Burrows. 1948, *etc.* 8°. **2016**. b.

—— *See* FRASER (*Sir* Hugh) A Compendium of the Law of Torts . . . By H. Fraser [assisted by R. Burrows], *etc.* 1910. 8°. **6325**. i. **18**.

—— —— 1914. 8°. **6325**. p. **12**.

—— —— 1927. 8°. **6326**. df. **8**.

—— *See* ODGERS (William B.) and (Walter B.) Odgers on the Common Law of England . . . Third edition. By R. Burrows, *etc.* 1927. 8°. **2016.f.**

—— *See* PHIPSON (Sidney L.) The Law of Evidence . . Seventh edition, by R. Burrows, *etc.* 1930. 8°. **6282**. s. **1**.

—— *See* PHIPSON (Sidney L.) The Law of Evidence . . . Eighth edition. By R. Burrows. 1942. 8°. **6147**. c. **2**.

—— *See* PHIPSON (Sidney L.) Manual of the Law of Evidence . . . Fifth edition. By R. Burrows, *etc.* 1938. 8°. **6190**. dd. **25**.

—— *See* PHIPSON (Sidney L.) Phipson's Manual of the Law of Evidence . . . Sixth edition, by R. Burrows. 1943. 8°. **6147**. aa. **2**.

—— *See* PHIPSON (Sidney L.) Phipson's Manual of the Laws of Evidence . . . Seventh edition. By Sir R. Burrows. 1950. 8°. **6283**. bb. **22**.

—— *See* SMITH (Frederick E.) *Earl of Birkenhead.* Judgments . . . 1919–1922. Edited . . . by R. Burrows. 1923. 8°. **6120**. b. **3**.

—— *See* WHITE (Frederick T.) and TUDOR (O. D.) A Selection of Leading Cases in Equity . . . Eighth edition by W. J. Whittaker . . . assisted by . . . R. Burrows. 1910, *etc.* 8°. **6126**. h. **1**.

—— Encyclopædia of Commercial Law . . . Edited by R. Burrows, *etc.* 2 vol. *Educational Book Co.: London,* [1911.] 8°. [*Harmsworth Business Library.* vol. 9, 10.] **08225**. k. **26**.

—— Interpretation of Documents. pp. lvi. 102. 7. *Butterworth & Co.: London,* 1943. 8°. **6147**. aa. **5**.

—— Interpretation of Documents . . . Second edition. pp. xix. 121. 8. *Butterworth & Co.: London,* 1946. 8°. **6147**. aa. **10**.

BURROWS (*Sir* ROLAND)

—— The Law of Income Tax relating to Business Profits. pp. xviii. 139. *Sweet & Maxwell; Effingham Wilson: London*, 1914. 8°. **6426**. p. **1**.

—— Second impression, revised. pp. xviii. 139. *Sweet & Maxwell: London*, 1915. 8°. **6426**. c. **30**.

—— The New Income Tax in relation to War and Business. pp. 32. *Newberry & Pickering: London*, 1915. 8°. **6427**. f. **20**.

—— Words and Phrases judicially defined. Under the general editorship of R. Burrows. 5 vol. *Butterworth & Co.: London*, 1943–45. 8°. **6003**. cc. **3**.

—— Pocket Supplement, 1947 [etc.] *Butterworth & Co.: London*, 1947–. 8°. **6003**. cc. **3a**.

BURROWS (*Sir* ROLAND) and **CAHN** (CHARLES MONTAGUE)

—— The Evidence Act, 1938, *etc.* pp. 55. *Sweet & Maxwell: London*, 1938. 8°. **6282**. dg. **15**.

BURROWS (RONALD MONTAGU) *See* GLASGOW (George) Ronald Burrows, *etc.* [With portraits.] 1924. 8°. **010856**. i. **19**.

—— *See* KATAPODES (P. S.) Pseudophilhellenes; a letter to E. Venizelos on the duplicity of Principal Burrows, *etc.* 1917. 8°. **08026**. dd. **21**.

—— The Abdication of King Constantine, June 12, 1917. Being a reprint of articles. pp. 24. [*London*,] 1917. 8°. [*Publications of the Anglo-Hellenic League.* no. 34.] **8027.b.65/34.**

—— The Discoveries in Crete and their bearing on the history of ancient civilisation . . . With illustrations. pp. xvi. 244. *John Murray: London*, 1907. 8°. **07703**. f. **15**.

—— Reprinted, with addenda on the season's work of 1907. (Second edition.) pp. xviii. 252. *John Murray: London*, 1907. 8°. **2258**. c. **13**.

—— The New Greece. (Reprinted from the Quarterly Review.) pp. 18. [*London*, 1914.] 8°. [*Publications of the Anglo-Hellenic League.* no. 14.] **8027.b.65/14.**

—— Reprint of Review by R. M. Burrows. From 'The Athenæum' . . . Carnegie Endowment for International Peace: Report of the International Commission into the Causes and Conduct of the Balkan Wars, *etc.* pp. 7. [*London*, 1914.] 8°. [*Publications of the Anglo-Hellenic League.* no. 15.] **8027.b.65/15.**

BURROWS (RONALD MONTAGU) and **WALTERS** (WILLIAM CHARLES FLAMSTEAD)

—— Florilegium Tironis Graecum. Simple passages for Greek unseen translation chosen with a view to their literary interest. pp. ix. 271. *Macmillan & Co.: London*, 1904. 8°. **11313**. aaa. **1**.

—— [A reissue.] *London*, 1930. 8°. **11313**. f. **39**.

BURROWS (S.) The Open Door. A popular plea for the Catholic faith, *etc.* pp. xix. 505. *Burns, Oates & Co.: London*, 1926. 8°. **3942**. eee. **21**.

BURROWS (*Sir* STEPHEN MONTAGU) *See* BURROWS (M.) Autobiography of Montagu Burrows . . . Edited by his son S. M. Burrows, *etc.* 1908. 8°. **010827**. g. **12**.

—— The Buried Cities of Ceylon. A guide book to Anuradhapura and Polonnarua. With chapters on Dambulla, Kalawewa, Mihintale, and Sigiri . . . Second edition. 3 pt. *A. M. & J. Ferguson: Colombo*, 1894. 8°. **7706**. a. **54**.

—— The Conquest of Ceylon, 1795–1815. *See* DODWELL (Henry H.) British India, 1497–1858, *etc.* 1929. 8°. [*Cambridge History of the British Empire.* vol. 4.] **2090.a.**

—— Report on Archæological Work in Anuradhapura and Pollonnaruwa. [With plans.] pp. 13. *Colombo*, 1886 [1887]. fol. [*Papers laid before the Legislative Council of Ceylon.* 1886. *Sessional Paper.* no. 10.] C.S. B. **13**.

—— Scouts with a Handicap. Handbook of the special tests department. pp. 73. [1932.] 8°. *See* ENGLAND.—*Boy Scouts' Association.* **8820**. a. **31**.

—— The Visitor's Guide to Kandy and Nuwara Eliya . . . Fourth edition . . . enlarged. pp. xiii. 64. xviii. *A. M. & J. Ferguson: Colombo*, 1897. 8°. **10058**. df. **17**.

—— Third edition, revised and enlarged. pp. xii. 62. xx. *A. M. & J. Ferguson: Colombo*, 1894. 8°. **10057**. aaa. **8**.

BURROWS (SYDNEY MALCOLM)

—— A Tuberculosis Survey of the Dinkas in the Eastern District, Bahr-el-Ghazal Province—Southern Sudan. *See* ENGLAND.—*Medical Research Council.* Studies of Tuberculosis among African Natives, *etc.* 1935. 8°. [*Tubercle.* Supple. Jan. 1935.] P.P. **2707**. ega.

BURROWS (TOM W.)

—— Club Swinging, as applied to health, development, training & display. pp. xi. 76. *Gale & Polden: London*, 1906. 8°. **7404**. e. **36**.

—— Physical Training with Clubs and Dumbbells . . . With a series of 24 exercises specially revised by Lt.-Col. H. E. Deane . . . Second edition. [With portraits.] pp. 90. *Athletic Publications: London*, [1944.] 8°. **7917**. de. **41**.

—— The Text-Book of Club-Swinging. pp. 79. "*Health & Strength*": *London*, [1908.] 8°. **7911**. bbb. **18**.

—— Fourth edition. pp. 78. *Athletic Publications: London*, [1922.] 8°. **7911**. cc. **33**.

—— Fifth edition. pp. 78. *Athletic Publications: London*, [1935.] 8°. **7915**. p. **46**.

—— Sixth edition. pp. 78. *Athletic Publications: London*, [1935.] 8°. **7912**. b. **62**.

BURROWS (V. A.) *Elder of St. Paul's Church, Redhill.*

—— The Nature of the Authority of the Bible. pp. 23. [*London*,] 1946. 8°. [*Presbyterian Church of England. Committee on the Church's Doctrine, Standards and Witness to the Faith.* Occasional Paper. no. 3.] W.P. **746/3**.

BURROWS (VICTOR)

—— The Blue Plaque Guide to Historic London Houses and the Lives of their Famous Residents. Edited by V. Burrows. With . . . drawings by E. W. Fenton. pp. 102. *Newman Neame: London*, 1953. 8°. **010349**. u. **13**.

BURROWS (VICTOR ALBERT) *See* SMITH, afterwards SMITH-HARTLEY (*Sir* Percival H. H.) The Expectation of Survival in Pulmonary Tuberculosis . . . By Sir P. Horton Smith-Hartley . . . R. C. Wingfield . . . and V. A. Burrows. [1935.] 8°. **7616**. bb. **23**.

—— Valuation Tables for Friendly Societies. Based upon sickness experience of the I.O.O.F. Manchester Unity during the five years 1893–97—occupation group, A. H. J. Combined with mortality rates of (a) central counties rural districts, (b) eastern counties rural districts—1921 census, males,—at 3, 3½ and 4 per cent interest. Compiled by V. A. Burrows . . . and Guy Woodrow . . . and reprinted from the Journal of the Institute of Actuaries. pp. 49. 1933. 8°. *See* LONDON.—III. *Institute of Actuaries.* **08548**. e. **98**.

BURROWS (W. F.) *Cartoonist.* Obstinate Artist. [Drawings.] pp. 124. *Hutchinson & Co.: London,* 1938. 8°. **12332**. a. **37**.

BURROWS (W. F.) *M.D.* Government by Quinary Civic Councils. pp. 58. *W. F. Burrows: Sarasota,* 1934. 12°. **20020**. a. **64**.

BURROWS (W. J.) Burrows's Fluent Shorthand. [*London,* 1918.] 8°. **1879**. c. **11**. **(68.)**
A card.

BURROWS (*Sir* WALTER) *See* BURROWES.

BURROWS (WILLIAM) *District Commissioner, Fiji.*

—— A Report on the Fiji Census, 1936, *etc.* pp. viii. 89. 1936. fol. *See* FIJI.—*Legislative Council.* C.S. G. **722/2**.

BURROWS (WILLIAM) *Professor of Bacteriology in the University of Chicago.*

—— *See* JORDAN (Edwin O.) A Textbook of General Bacteriology . . . Revised by W. Burrows, *etc.* 1938. 8°. **07560**. ee. **56**.

—— *See* JORDAN (Edwin O.) and BURROWS (W.) Textbook of Bacteriology, *etc.* 1941. 8°. **07560**. i. **44**.

—— *See* JORDAN (Edwin O.) and BURROWS (W.) Textbook of Bacteriology, *etc.* 1945. 8°. **7563.d.11.**

—— *See* JORDAN (Edwin O.) and BURROWS (W.) Jordan-Burrows Textbook of Bacteriology, *etc.* 1949. 8°. **7564**. c. **11**.

—— Textbook of Microbiology. Sixteenth edition. By W. Burrows . . . With the collaboration of Francis Byron Gordon . . . Richard Janvier Porter . . . James William Moulder. pp. xix. 824. *W. B. Saunders Co.: Philadelphia & London,* 1954. 8°. **7564**. dd. **42**.
Earlier editions, entitled "Jordan-Burrows Textbook of Bacteriology," are entered under JORDAN *(Edwin O.) and* BURROWS *(W.)*

BURROWS (WILLIAM) *Rev., B.A.* A Homiletical Commentary on the Book of Esther. pp. 323. *R. D. Dickinson: London,* 1881. 8°. [*Preacher's Complete Homiletical Commentary on the Old Testament.*] **3165**. ee. **5**.

—— A Homiletical Commentary on the Epistle of St. Paul the Apostle to the Romans. pp. 593. *Funk & Wagnalls Co.: New York,* 1896. 8°. [*Preacher's Complete Homiletical Commentary on the New Testament.*] **03126**. g. **9**.

BURROWS (WILLIAM) *Trooper.* Adventures of a Mounted Trooper in the Australian Constabulary, *etc.* pp. xx. 196. *Routledge & Co.: London,* 1859. 8°. **10492**. a. **25**.

BURROWS (WILLIAM BAMFORD) Michael the Lion of Ergakuk. [In verse. With illustrations.] pp. 52. *C. D. Cazenove & Son: London; W. B. Burrows: New York; New York* printed, 1910. 4°. **12806**. i. **68**.

BURROWS (WILLIAM BRAMWELL)

—— Black into White: John Allen. pp. 15. *Salvationist Publishing & Supplies: London,* 1950. 8°. **4431**. a. **79**.

—— The Mercy Seat. pp. 30. *Salvationist Publishing & Supplies: London,* 1951. 8°. **4194**. bb. **15**.

BURROWS (WINFRID OLDFIELD) successively *Bishop of Truro* and *of Chichester.* *See* BIBLE. [*English.*] The Books of the Bible, *etc.* (The First—the Second—Book of Kings. With introduction, notes, and maps. Edited by the Rev. W. O. Burrows.) 1895, *etc.* 8°. **3105**. de. **14/1**.

—— *See* BIBLE. [*English.*] The Books of the Bible, *etc.* (Amos. With introduction, notes, and maps. Edited by the Rev. W. O. Burrows.) 1895, *etc.* 8°. **3105**. de. **14/2**.

—— *See* MOORE (Mary) *Daughter of Bishop Winfrid Oldfield Burrows.* Winfrid Burrows, 1858–1929, *etc.* [With a portrait.] 1932. 8°. **4909**. aaa. **2**.

—— An Address in Explanation of the Prayer Book Measure. Delivered . . . to a meeting of the Chichester Diocesan Council, *etc.* pp. 64. *S.P.C.K.: London,* 1927. 8°. **3477**. eee. **40**.

—— The Call of the World to the Church. Presidential address . . . to the Sacred Synod of the Diocese [of Chichester] . . . Reprinted from the "Chichester Diocesan Gazette." pp. 8. *Brighton,* [1926.] 8°. **03226**. eee. **37**.

—— The Case of the Rev. L. S. Wason. An open letter to the clergy & laity of the diocese of Truro, from their late bishop. pp. 23. *Netherton & Worth: Truro,* 1919. 8°. **4708**. bb. **28**.

—— The Church's Ministry. *Society for Promoting Christian Knowledge: London,* 1907. 8°. [*Pan-Anglican Papers.* no. 3.] **4108**. cc. **35**.

—— The Churchman's Attitude towards the Spiritualists. pp. 24. *S.P.C.K.: London,* 1900. 8°. **04429**. c. **6**. **(3.)**

—— The Mystery of the Cross. Eight addresses on the Atonement. pp. xii. 227. *Rivington & Co.: London,* 1896. 8°. **4462**. ee. **5**.

BURROWSTOWN. A True Account of a New and Strange Sect now practising . . . at Burrowstown, 15 miles from Edenburrough . . . who assemble . . . in the night-time. *J. Smith: London,* 1681. *s. sh.* fol. **1850**. c. **6**. **(96*.)**

BURRUS (CAESAR) Caesaris Burri S. Carolus triumphans, *etc.* [In verse.] pp. 45. *Apud M. T. Malatestam: Mediolani,* 1611. 8°. **11403**. aa. **17**.

BURRUS (ERNEST J.)

—— *See* KINO (E. F.) Kino reports to Headquarters . . . Original Spanish text . . . with English translation and notes by E. J. Burrus. 1954. 8°. **10414**. c. **49**.

—— Francisco Javier Alegre, historian of the Jesuits in New Spain, 1729–1788. *In:* Archivum historicum Societatis Iesu. anno 22. fasc. 43. pp. 438–509. 1953. 8°. Ac. **2002**. f.

—— [A reissue.] Francisco Javier Alegre, *etc.* *Roma,* [1953.] 8°. **10899**. b. **34**.

BURRUS (ERNEST J.)

—— An Introduction to Bibliographical Tools in Spanish Archives and Manuscript Collections relating to Hispanic America. *In:* The Hispanic American Historical Review. vol. 35. no. 4. pp. 443–483. 1955. 8°. P.P. **3437**. ah.

BURRUS (FRANCISCUS JOSEPHUS) Judicium . . . de lapide in stomacho cervi reperto. *J. Lasché: Hanoviæ,* 1662. 4°. **784**. d. **11**. (**7**.)

BURRUS (PETRUS) Moralium Magistri Petri Burri Carminū Libri nouem, cum argumentis & vocabulorum minus vulgariū compendiosa explanatione [by J. Badius]. ff. clxxiii. *Impressum aīaduersione Ascēsiana: Parrhisiis,* 1503. 4°. **11405**. e. 8.
With the device of the Brothers De Marnef on the titlepage.

—— Pęanes quinq3 festorū diuę virginis marię & quidā alii eiusdē hymni: a Magistro Petro Burro . . . editi. Et ab ascēsio . . . expositi, *etc.* G.L. ff. cvii. *Impressum in edibus ascensianis; venundarurq3* [sic] *in hospitio vindocineñ.* [address of Pierre Joulet]*: Parrhisijs,* [1505.] 4°. C. **111**. c. **5**.

BURRY (BESSIE PULLEN) Blotted Out. pp. 106. *Roxburghe Press: London,* [1897.] 8°. **012625**. ee. **21**.

—— Eleanor Lewknor. 2 vol. *Remington & Co.: London,* 1889. 8°. **012632**. i. **30**.

—— Ethiopia in Exile. Jamaica revisited. pp. 288. *T. Fisher Unwin: London,* 1905. 8°. **2398**. b. **4**.

—— From Halifax to Vancouver . . . Illustrated. pp. xv. 352. *Mills & Boon: London,* 1912. 8°. **010470**. ee. **24**.

—— In a German Colony; or, Four weeks in New Britain . . . With eight illustrations and two maps. pp. xi. 238. *Methuen & Co.: London,* 1909. 8°. **10492**. eee. **15**.

—— Jamaica as it is, 1903 . . . Illustrated. pp. xiv. 240. *T. Fisher Unwin: London,* 1903. 8°. **2374**. a. **13**.

—— Letters from Palestine, February–April, 1922. pp. 137. *Judaic Publishing Co.: London,* [1922.] 8°. **010905**. de. **40**.

—— Nobly Won. A novel. 2 vol. *Remington & Co.: London,* [1888.] 8°. **012633**. e. **21**.

BURRY (JOHN) *See* ROSEVEAR (W. T.) A Sermon preached . . . on the occasion of the death of Mr. John Burry. [1868.] 8°. **4902**. cc. **29**. (**16**.)

BURRY (VIOLET) Gods and Heroes. pp. 176. *London, Edinburgh,* [1925.] 8°. [*Chambers's Periodic Histories.* bk. 1.] **09506**. g. **18**.

—— Old-World Empires. pp. 218. *London, Edinburgh,* [1925.] 8°. [*Chambers's Periodic Histories.* bk. 2.] **09506**. g. **18**.

BURS (ABRAHAM PIETERSEN)

—— Dissertatio medica inauguralis, de nausea et vomitu, *etc.* pp. 16. *Lugduni Batavorum,* 1725. 4°. **1185**. i. **1**. (**14**.)

BURSA. *See* BRUSA.

BURSA ASARI ATIKA MÜZESI. *See* BRUSA.

BURSA HUNGARORUM. *See* CRACOW.—*Universytet Jagiellonski.*

BURSA (ADAM)

—— *See* BRAARUD (T.) and BURSA (A.) The Phytoplankton of the Oslo Fjord, 1933–1934, *etc.* 1939. 8°. [*Hvalrådets Skrifter.* no. 19.] Ac. **1054/17**.

BURSAUX (PAUL AUGUSTE) Les Chemins de fer militaires au Maroc. Conférence, *etc.* pp. 24. 1918. 8°. *See* FRANCE.—*Army.—Troupes d'occupation du Maroc.—État-major.* **8157**. k. **48**. (**1**.)

BURSAY (L.) *See* KOTZEBUE (A. F. F. von) [*Dramatic Works.*] [Die Indianer in England.] Les Indiens en Angleterre, comédie . . . traduite . . . par L. Bursay. 1792. 8°. **1474**. bb. **10**.

—— *See* KOTZEBUE (A. F. F. von) [*Dramatic Works.*] [Menschenhass und Reue.] Misantropie et repentir, drame . . . traduit par Bursay, *etc.* [1799.] 8°. **11738**. aa. **27**. (**6**.)

—— —— 1823. 8°. **11738**. aa. **15**. (**1**.)

—— *See* METASTASIO (P. A. D. B.) Artaxerce, tragédie . . . Imitée de l'italien de . . . Metastasio. Par M. Bursay. 1765. 8°. **11738**. aaa. **12**. (**3**.)

BURSCH. Des lustigen Burschen Vademecum. Ein Studentenliederbuch, zusammengestellt von einem bemoosten Haupt. pp. 190. *Wien,* 1862. 16°. **11526**. aaa. **14**.

BURSCH (CHARLES WESLEY) and **REID** (JOHN LYON)

—— You Want to Build a School? pp. 128. *Reinhold Publishing Corporation: New York,* [1947.] 8°. **7822**. aa. **61**.

BURSCH (JAC. GEORGE)

—— Mikropaläontologische Untersuchungen des Tertiärs von Gross Kei, *etc.* pp. 69. pl. 5. *Basel,* 1947. 4°. [*Schweizerische Paläontologische Gesellschaft. Abhandlungen.* Bd. 65.] Ac. **3122**.

BURSCH (JAMES FREDERICK) *See* ALMACK (John C.) and BURSCH (J. F.) The Administration of Consolidated and Village Schools. [1925.] 8°. **12199**. s. **1/34**.

BURSCHE (EDMUND)

—— *See* APOLOGETICUS. Apologeticus, to jest obrona konfederacyej. Przytym seditio albo bunt kapłański na ewanieliki w Wilnie z wolej a łaski miłego Boga przed harapem wynurzony. Wydał i wstępem zaopatrzył E. Bursche. 1932. 8°. [*Polska Akademja Umiejętności. Bibljoteka Pisarzów Polskich.* no. 84.] Ac. **750/45**.

—— Konkordaty. Studjum historyczne. pp. ii. 88. *Warszawa,* 1930. 8°. [*Prace Towarzystwa Naukowego Warszawskiego.* wydział 2. no. 21.] Ac. **1150/2**.

BURSCHENFAHRTEN. Burschenfahrten. Beiträge zur Geschichte des deutschen Studentenwesens. pp. iv. 313. *Jena,* 1845. 16°. **731**. a. **16**.

BURSCHENSCHAFT. Was will und soll die Burschenschaft? Ein Wort zur Aufklärung. pp. 19. *Breslau,* 1864. 8°. **8307**. ccc. **14**.

BURSCHENSCHAFTLICHE BLAETTER. *See* PERIODICAL PUBLICATIONS.—*Berlin.*

BURSCHENSCHAFTLICHE HISTORISCHE KOMMISSION.

—— *See* GERMANY.—*Gesellschaft für burschenschaftliche Geschichtsforschung.*

BURSCHER (Johann Friedrich) *See* Buenau (H. von) *Count.* Herrn Heinrich . . . Grafen v. Buenau Betrachtungen über die Religion . . . herausgegeben von J. F. Burschern. 1769. 8°. **223**. i. **27**.

—— *See* Schoenemann (F. L.) D. Johann Friedrich Burscher's . . . Leben und Todtenfeyer, *etc.* 1885. 8°. **4804**. g. **3**. (**1**.)

—— Ecclesiae Christianae post Apostolos scriptorum antiquissimorum doctrina publica de Deo Trinuno et de Iesu Christi persona, ex scriptis duntaxat optimorum omnium criticorum confessione genuinis ipsorumque scriptorum verbis proposita. Collatis diuersis editionibus verba auctorum accurate descripsit, lectionis varietatem notasque suas varias adiecit . . . D. I. F. Burscher. *Gr. & Lat.* pp. 60. *Lipsiae*, 1780. 8°. **4224**. aaa. **31**.

—— Index et argumentum epistolarum ad D. Erasmum Roterodamum autographarum, quas ab anno 1520 usque ad annum 1536, Cardinales, Episcopi . . . aliique homines Erasmo familiares exararunt, et quae . . . nunc cum nonnullis aliis ex bibliotheca Erasmi autographis adservantur Lipsiae in bibliotheca D. J. F. Burscheri. [Compiled by J. F. Burscher.] pp. vii. 80. *Lipsiae*, 1784. 8°. **1209**. k. **19**.

BURSCOUGH (Robert) *See* Mayne (Zachary) Sanctification by Faith vindicated . . . To which is prefixt a preface by R. Burscough. 1693. 4°. **694**. d. **10**. (**1**.)

—— A Discourse, i. Of the Unity of the Church. ii. Of the Separation of the Dissenters from the Church of England. iii. Of their setting up Churches against the Conforming Churches; and of the Ordination of their Teachers. Being an answer to a book, entituled, Dissenters no Schismaticks, *etc.* pp. 195. *For Tho. Bennet: London; Charles Yeo: Exon.*, 1704. 8°. **4106**. c. **5**.

—— A Discourse of Schism: address'd to those dissenters, who conform'd before the Toleration, and have since withdrawn themselves from the communion of the Church of England. pp. 231. *For Tho. Bennet: London*, 1699. 8°. **851**. d. **25**.

—— Dissenters no Schismaticks. A second letter to Mr. R. Burscough about his Discourse of Schism, *etc.* [Signed: S. S., i.e. Samuel Stoddon.] 1702. 8°. *See* S., S. **873**. g. **16**.

—— A Letter to Mr. Robert Burscough, in answer to his Discourse of Schism, *etc.* [By Samuel Stoddon.] pp. 115. *For J. Clark: London*, 1700. 8°. **4106**. b. **29**.

—— A Treatise of Church-Government: occasion'd by some letters [by Richard Burthogge] lately printed concerning the same subject [entitled "The Nature of Church-Government freely discussed and set out"]. pp. xxxvii. 270. *For Samuel Smith: London*, 1692. 8°. **858**. e. **19**.

—— A Vindication of a Discourse of Schism . . . in answer to a letter lately publish'd against it. pp. xv. 182. *Thomas Bennet: London; Charles Yeo: Exon.*, 1701. 8°. **4106**. b. **30**.

BURSCOUGH (William) *Bishop of Limerick.* The Abuse of Liberty. A sermon preach'd before the Honourable House of Commons, on the 5th of November, 1722. pp. 30. *J. Nicks: London*, 1722. 4°. **694**. k. **15**. (**6**.)

—— [Another copy.] **1413**. e. **12**. (**18**.)

—— [Another copy.] **225**. h. **16**. (**21**.)

BURSCOUGH (William) *Bishop of Limerick.*

—— The Duty of Praise and Thanksgiving. A sermon preach'd before the King . . . on Sunday May the 29th. 1715. Being the anniversary of the Restoration of the Royal Family. pp. 23. *Sam. Crouch; Tim. Childe: London*, 1715. 4°. **696**. f. **10**. (**7**.)

—— [Another edition.] pp. 24. *S. Crouch; T. Childe: London*, 1715. 8°. **4475**. a. **36**.

—— The Question about eating of Blood stated and examin'd; in answer to two dissertations in a book [by Patrick Delany, Dean of Down] entitl'd, Revelation examin'd with Candour. [By W. Burscough?] pp. 40. 1732. 8°. *See* Question. **T. 851**. (**1**.)

—— [Another copy.] The Question about eating of Blood stated and examin'd, *etc.* [By W. Burscough?] 1732. 8°. *See* Question. **109**. b. **45**.

—— *See* Enquiry. An Enquiry about the Lawfulness of eating Blood . . . With some remarks upon the Question about eating of Blood stated and examin'd [by W. Burscough?]. By a Prebendary of York [i.e. Thomas Sharp, Archdeacon of Northumberland]. 1733. 8°. **1019**. l. **24**. (**4**.)

—— The Apostolical Decree at Jerusalem proved to be still in force, both from scripture and tradition: in answer to the Question about eating of Blood stated, &c. . . . To which is added, an appendix containing the testimonies of Fathers, councils, &c. . . . Also remarks upon the Enquiry about the Lawfulness of eating Blood [by Thomas Sharp, Archdeacon of Northumberland]. [By W. Burscough?] pp. 83. 1734. 8°. *See* Jerusalem. **4374**. c. **47**. (**1**.)

—— The Revolution Recommended to Our Memories. A sermon preach'd at the Abby-Church of St. Peter's Westminster, on November the Fifth, 1715. pp. 24. *Sam. Crouch; Timothy Childe: London*, 1715. 8°. **694**. f. **7**. (**16**.)

—— [Another copy.] **225**. h. **1**. (**10**.)

—— The second edition. pp. 32. *John Nicks: London*, 1722. 4°. **694**. f. **7**. (**17**.)

—— A Sermon, preach'd at the consecration of the Right Reverend Father in God, Richard, Ld Bishop of Gloucester, *etc.* pp. 23. *Sam. Crouch; Tim. Childe: London*, 1715. 8°. **225**. g. **8**. (**11**.)

—— A Sermon preach'd at the funeral of Catherine, Duchess of Rutland, *etc.* pp. 32. *Sam. Crouch; Tim. Childe: London*, 1711. 4°. **695**. g. **1**. (**3**.)

—— [Another copy.] **225**. h. **3**. (**11**.)

—— A Sermon preach'd before the Honourable House of Commons . . on the 29th of May, 1716. being the anniversary of the Restoration of King Charles and the Royal Family. pp. 30. *Tim. Childe: London*, 1716. 4°. **4473**. aa. **53**. (**2**.)

—— [Another copy.] **225.h.25.(17.)**

BURSELIUS (Samuel) Disputatio philologico-philosophica de sermone, *etc.* *Praes.* P. Holm. *See* Crenius (Thomas) *pseud.* Analecta philologico-critico-historica, *etc.* 1705. 8°. **58**. a. **5**.

BURSELL (Bernhard Salomon) *See* Ovidius Naso (P.) [*Metamorphoses.—Swedish.*] Ordagrann öfversättning öfver valda stycken ur Ovidii Metamorfoser . . . af B. S. B. [i.e. B. S. Bursell.] 1870. 8°. **11352**. b. **26**.

BURSELL (SVANTE)

—— Therapeutical Investigations on Induced Cancer in Mice, *etc.* *Almqvist & Wiksells Boktryckeri AB: Uppsala,* 1948. 8°. **07206.** g. **26.**

BURSELLIS (HIERONYMUS DE) *See* ALBERTUCCIUS DE BURSELLIS (H.)

BURSELLUS (HIERONYMUS) *See* ALBERTUCCIUS DE BURSELLIS (H.)

BURSER (JOACHIMUS) *See* BURSERUS.

BURSERIUS (JOANNES BAPTISTA) *See* BORSIERI (Giambattista)

BURSERUS (JOACHIMUS) *See* JUEL (H. O.) Studien in Burser's Hortus Siccus, *etc.* 1923. 4°. [*Nova Acta Regiae Societatis Scientiarum Upsaliensis.* ser. 4. vol. 5. no. 7.] Ac. **1076.**

—— *See* LINNAEUS (C.) Caroli Linnaei determinationes in hortum siccum Joachimi Burseri, *etc.* 1937. 4°. [*Catalogue of the Manuscripts in the Library of the Linnaean Society.* pt. 2.] Ac. **3020/9.**

—— *See* STROBELBERGER (J. S.) Epistolaris concertatio super variis . . . quæstionibus, febrim . . . petechialem concernentibus, agitata inter D. J. S. Strobelbergerum . . . et D. J. Burserum . . . Annexa est & disceptatio de venenorum natura . . . habita inter eundem D. Burserum et M. V. Herlelium. 1625. 8°. **1166.d.29.(2.)**

—— De febri epidemia seu petechiali probè agnoscenda & curandâ . . . commentatio. pp. 109. *Impensis hæredum T. Schüreri: Lipsiæ,* 1621. 8° **1166.d.29.(1.)**

—— De fontium origine tractatus. pp. 136. *Typis Martzanianis, autore impensas faciente: Hafniæ,* 1639. 8°. **536.** a. **16.** (**2.**)

—— Introductio ad scientiam naturalem, *etc.* 2 vol. *Apud J. Janssonium: Amstelodami,* 1652. 8°. **536.** a. **15, 16.** (**1.**)

BURSETUS (JOANNES) Epitome Partitionum Oratoriarum M. T. Ciceronis, in duos libros distincta, *etc.* pp. 24. *Apud D. Vallensem: Parisiis,* 1574. 4°. **11350.** f. **3.** (**9.**)

BURSFELD.—*Congregatio Bursfeldensis.* [For liturgies used by the Benedictines of the Bursfeld Union:] *See* LITURGIES.—*Latin Rite.*

—— Ceremoniale Benedictinum. Siue antiquæ et germanæ pietatis Benedictinæ thesaurus absconditus. A V.V. PP. Congreg. Bursfeldensis ante annos centum compilatus, & nunquam hactenus typis excusus. Prodit ex vet. MS. Abbatiæ S. Germani Parisiensis. [Consisting of the Cerimoniae and the Ordinarius.] pp. 392. *H. Drouart: Parisiis,* 1610. 8°. **861.** h. **26.**

—— *Begin.* [fol. 1 *recto*:] Prologus cerimoniarũ nigrorũ monachorũ ordinis sancti Bñdicti de obseruancia Bursfeldensi. [fol. 3 *recto*:] Tabula capl'oꝝ prime distinctõis. [fol. 4 *verso*:] De electione noui abbatis. *End.* [fol. 112 *verso*:] Expliciũt cerimonie nigroꝝ mõchoꝝ ordĩs scĩ bñdcĩ de obſuãcia bursfeld'. **G.L.** [*Fratres vitae communis: Marienthal,* 1475 ?] 4°. IA. **9706.**
112 *leaves, without signatures.* 26 *lines to a page.*

—— [Another edition.] Cerimonie. [fol. 2 *recto*:] Prologus cerimoniarũ nigrorum Monachorum: ordinis sancti Benedicti de obseruancia Brusfeldensi. [1520 ?] 4°. **4071.** de. **15.** (**3.**)

BURSFELD.—*Congregatio Bursfeldensis.*

—— [Another edition.] Statuta Congregationis Bursfeldensis, sub regula Divi Benedicti. Secundum sacros canones, Romanorum Pontificum, et SS. Concil. Tridentini decreta renovata, secundum recessus capitulorum eiusdem congregationis aucta et emendata. pp. 330. MS. NOTES. *J. F. Buch: Paderbornae,* 1700. 8°. **4071.** a. **9.**

—— *Begin.* [fol. 1 *recto*:] Prolog⁹ ordinarij d'inoꝝ nigroꝝ mõchoꝝ ordĩs scĩ bñdicti de obſuãcia Bursfeldẽsi. [fol. 2 *recto*:] Sequitur tabula. [fol. 4 *recto*:] Qua disciplina quaue ſuerẽcia opus dei pagendũ sit, *etc.* *End.* [fol. 90 *recto*:] Explicit ordinarius diuinoꝝ nigroꝝ monachoꝝ de obſuãcia Bursfeldensi. **G.L.** [*Fratres vitae communis: Marienthal,* 1475 ?] 4°. IA. **9712.**
90 *leaves, without signatures.* 26 *lines to a page.*

—— [Another edition.] *Begin.* Prologus ordinarij diuinorum nigrorum monachorum ordinis sancti Benedicti de obseruantia Bursfeldensi. **G.L.** [1520 ?] 4°. **4071.** de. **15.** (**4.**)

—— Die erste Fassung des Bursfelder liber ordinarius. [The Latin text. Edited, with an introduction, by Paulus Volk.] 1942. *See* PERIODICAL PUBLICATIONS.—*Rome.* Ephemerides liturgicae, *etc.* anno 56. no. 1/4. 1887, *etc.* 8°. P.P. **22.** b.

BURSHTIN (MICHAEL) *See* BURSZTYN (M.)

BURSHTYN (SAMUEL) [Alte Menshen weren yung. Teater-shpiel, *etc.*] [With a portrait.] pp. 67. *New York,* 1929. 8°. **11746.** h. **32.**

—— [Felsen Kliangen.] [Poems. With a portrait.] pp. 49. *New York,* 1917. 8°. **011528.** l. **62.**

—— [In Garten fun Troim. Dichtung un Poezie.] pp. 40. *New York,* 1916. 8°. **011528.** m. **58.**

—— [Der Spektakel fun di Piramiden.] [Poems. With a portrait.] pp. 47. *New York,* 1922. 8°. **11528.** l. **59.**

—— [Der Thurm fun bloie Benkshaft.] [With a portrait.] pp. 31. *New York,* 1919. 8°. **011528.** l. **69.**

BURSIA (CATHARINA) *See* BURSIUS.

BURSIAN (VON) Der Aufstand in der Stadt Braunschweig am 6. und 7. September 1830, und der bevorstehende Anfall des Herzogthums Braunschweig an Hannover. (Ergänzungs-Kapitel.) [By — von Bursian.] 2 pt. 1858, 60. 8°. *See* BRUNSWICK. [*Appendix.*] **10231.** d. **15.**

BURSIAN (ALEXANDER) Die Häuser- und Hüttensteuer in Deutsch-Ostafrika. pp. 77. *Jena,* 1910. 8°. [*Abhandlungen des staatswissenschaftlichen Seminars zu Jena.* Bd. 8. Hft. 2.] Ac. **2230.**

BURSIAN (CONRAD) *See* EXSUPERANTIUS (J.) Juli Exuperanti opusculum a C. Bursian recognitum. 1868. 4°. [*Rector Universitatis litterarum Turicensis commilitonibus certamina eruditionis . . . in annos MDCCCLXV–LXVI indicit.*] **8358.** d. **64.**

—— *See* FIRMICUS MATERNUS (J.) Iulii Firmici Materni de errore profanarum religionum libellus ex recensione Conradi Bursian. 1856. 8°. **4505.** d. **28.** (**11.**)

—— *See* HYGINUS (C. J.) Ex Hygini Genealogiis excerpta (a C. Bursian restituta). [1868.] 4°. [*Inclutae Litterarum Universitati Fridericiae Guilelmiae Rhenanae natalicia quinquagesima . . . celebranti . . . congratulantur . . . Universitatis Litterarum Turicensis rector atque senatus, etc.*] **20011.** ee. **9.**

BURSIAN (CONRAD)

—— *See* MENANDER, *the Rhetorician.* Der Rhetor Menandros und seine Schriften. Von C. Bursian. [The text of the treatises "*Διαιρεσις των ἐπιδεικτικων*" and "*Περι ἐπιδεικτικων*" with an introduction.] 1882. 4°. [*Abhandlungen der Königlich Bayerischen Akademie der Wissenschaften.* Philos.-philol. Classe. Bd. 16.] **Ac. 713/6.**

—— *See* PERIODICAL PUBLICATIONS.—*Berlin.* Jahresbericht über die Fortschritte der classischen Allerthumswissenschaft, *etc.* (Jahrg. 1–9. Bd. 1–29. Herausgegeben von C. Bursian.) 1875, *etc.* 8°. **P.P. 1897. f.**

—— *See* SENECA (M. A.) Annaei Senecae Oratorum et Rhetorum sententiae, divisiones, colores. C. Bursian recensuit et emendavit. 1857. 8°. **11396. g. 10.**

—— *See* VIBIUS SEQUESTER. Vibi Sequestris De fluminibus etc. libellus a C. Bursian recognitus. 1867. 4°. [*Rector Universitatis Litterarum Turicensis commilitonibus certamina eruditionis in annos MDCCCLXVII–LXVIII . . . indicit.*] **8358. d. 61.**

—— Aventicum Helvetiorum. 4 Hft. pp. 60. pl. 32. *Zurich,* 1867–69. 4°. [*Mittheilungen der antiquarischen Gesellschaft.* Bd. 16. Abt. 1. Hft. 1–4.] **Ac. 5367.**

—— Conradi Bursian De foro Athenarum disputatio. pp. 17. 1865. *See* ZURICH.—*Universität Zürich.* Rector Universitatis Litterarum Turicensis commilitonibus certamina eruditionis . . . in annos MDCCCLXV–LXVI [*etc.*] indicit. 1865, *etc.* 4°. **8358. d. 60.**

—— Erophile. Vulgaergriechische Tragoedie von G. Chortatzes aus Kreta. Ein Beitrag zur Geschichte der neugriechischen und der italiänischen Litteratur. pp. 89. 1870. *See* LEIPZIG.—*Sächsische Akademie der Wissenschaften.* Abhandlungen. Phil.-hist. Classe. Bd. 5. 1850, *etc.* 8°. **Ac. 700/4.**

—— Geographie von Griechenland. [With maps.] 2 Bd. *Leipzig,* 1862. 8°. **10125. dd. 20.**

—— Geschichte der classischen Philologie in Deutschland, *etc.* pp. viii. 1271. *München & Leipzig,* 1883. 8°. [*Geschichte der Wissenschaften in Deutschland.* Bd. 19.] **Ac. 714/4.**

—— Mosaikbild von Orbe. [With a plate.] pp. 7. *Zürich,* 1868. 4°. [*Mittheilungen der antiquarischen Gesellschaft.* Bd. 16. Abt. 2. Hft. 1.] **Ac. 5367.**

—— Quaestionum Euboicarum capita selecta. pp. 50. *Lipsiae,* 1856. 8°. **7702. cc. 5. (6.)**

—— Schauspieler und Schauspielkunst im griechischen Alterthum. 1875. *See* PERIODICAL PUBLICATIONS.—*Leipsic.* Historisches Taschenbuch, *etc.* Folge 5. Jahrg. 5. 1830, *etc.* 8°. **P.P. 3625.**

—— Ueber den religiösen Charakter des griechischen Mythos. Festrede, *etc.* pp. 27. *München,* 1873. 4°. **732. i. 25. (3.)**

BURSIAN (ER.) *See* LACHMANN (C. C. F. W.) Gromatici veteres, *etc.* (Indices von E. Bursian.) 1848, *etc.* 8°. **8530. dd. 2.**

BURSICS (ZOLTÁN)

—— A magyar anyagi büntetőjog rövid összefoglalása. pp. xii. 408. *Budapest,* 1947. 8°. **05549. de. 8.**

—— A magyar bűnvádi eljárási jog vázlata . . . III. kiadás. pp. viii. 338. *Budapest,* 1947. 8°. **05549. de. 9.**

BURSILL (ARCHIBALD) The Principles and Practice of Electric Wiring for evening students, *etc.* pp. xv. 215. *London,* 1911. 8°. [*Longmans' Technical Handicraft Series.*] **7945.r.5/1.**

BURSILL (HENRY) Hand Shadows to be thrown upon the wall: a series of novel and amusing figures formed by the hand, from original designs by H. Bursill. (A second series of hand shadows.) 2 vol. *Griffith & Farran: London,* 1859, 60. 4°. **1266. e. 19.**

—— Twelfth thousand. pl. 32. *Griffith & Farran: London,* [1879.] 8°. **12807. k. 20.**

BURSILL (HILARY)

—— *See* FRANK (Douglas) Your Barnes . . . Prepared for the Barnes Labour Party by D. Frank, with the assistance of H. Bursill, *etc.* [1946.] 8°. **8288. eee. 74.**

BURSILL (JOHN FRANCIS) George Cruikshank. Artist—humorist—moralist, *etc.* [With a portrait.] pp. 16. *John Bursill: London,* [1878.] 8°. **10803. bb. 40.**

—— The Gold Stripe. A tribute to the British Columbia men who have been killed, crippled and wounded in the Great War. [Edited by J. F. Bursill. With plates.] pp. 160. *Pacific Printers: Vancouver, B.C.,* [1918.] 4°. **12355. k. 24.**

BURSILL (PHILIP CHARLES) *See* ERWOOD (Frank C. E.) Well Hall . . . Edited by P. C. Bursill. [1936.] 8°. **10349. ff. 48.**

BURSINCK (GERHARDUS WILHELMUS) Cerebri et nervorum distributionis expositio brevis, *etc.* pp. 99. *Duisburgi,* [1786.] 8°. **T. 521. (8.)**

BURSIUS (ADAM) *See* CICERO (M. T.) [*Selections.—Latin.*] Dialectica Ciceronis, quæ disperse in scriptis reliquit . . . cum commentariis . . . A. Bursius composuit. 1604. 4°. **G. 9264.**

—— Vita et obitus illustrissimi herois Joannis Samoscii, Regni Poloniæ Cancellarii Supremi, *etc.* *See* SZYMONOWICZ (S.) *Bendoński.* Simonis Simonidæ poemata aurea, *etc.* 1619. 8°. **11409. d. 33.**

—— [Another edition.] Oratio funebris in anniversario depositionis illustrissimi Ioannis Zamoscii regni Poloniae supremi Cancellarii . . . habita Junij 5 A.D. 1606. *See* DZIAŁYŃSKI (A. T.) *Count.* Collectanea vitam resque gestas Joannis Zamoyscii . . . illustrantia, *etc.* 1861. 4°. **9475. h. 6.**

BURSIUS (CATHARINA) *See* LEIPZIG.—*Academia Lipsiensis.* Rector Academiæ Lipsiensis ad exeqvias . . . Catharinæ Bursiæ . . . cives suos . . . invitat. [1670.] 4°. **1090. l. 18. (17.)**

BURSIUS (JACOBUS) *See* B., R. Lachrymæ crocodili abstersæ, hoc est, notæ et castigationes in Threnum Sabbathicum I. B. [i.e. of J. Bursius], *etc.* [1627.] 8°. **4380. a. 6. (1.)**

BURSIUS (PETRUS) *Resp.* *See* SCHOOCK (M.) M. Schoockii Disquisitio . . . de signaturis foetus, *etc.* 1659. 8°. **1173. b. 2.**

BURSK (EDWARD COLLINS)

—— Getting things done in Business. Edited by E. C. Bursk. pp. 152. *Harvard University Press: Cambridge, Mass.,* 1953. 8°. **08230. aaa. 66.**

—— How to increase Executive Effectiveness. [By various authors.] Edited by E. C. Bursk. pp. 163. *Harvard University Press: Cambridge, Mass.,* 1953. 8°. **8208. e. 17.**

BURSK (Edward Collins)

—— The Management Team. Edited by E. C. Bursk. [By various authors.] pp. 221. *Harvard University Press: Cambridge, Mass.*, 1954. 8°. **8231. aa. 85.**

—— Thinking ahead for Business. Edited by E. C. Bursk. pp. viii. 215. *Harvard University Press: Cambridge, Mass.*, 1952. 8°. **08229. p. 70.**

BURSKI (Hans Albrecht von) Kemāl Re'īs. Ein Beitrag zur Geschichte der türkischen Flotte. pp. 83. *Bonn*, 1928. 8°. **10607. f. 24.**

BURSKY (M. I.)

—— *See* Dobiash-Rozhdestvenskaya (O. A.) and Bursky (M. I.) Агрикультура в памятниках западного средневековья . . . Под редакцией . . . О. А. Добиаш-Рождественской и . . . М. И. Бурского. 1936. 8°. [*Академия Наук СССР. Труды Института Истории Науки и Техники.* сер. 5. вып. 1.] Ac. **1125.** in.

—— *See* Moscow.—*Всесоюзная Ассоціація Сельскохозяйственной Библіографіи.* Тематические реферативные сборники. Под общей редакцией М. И. Бурского и Е. И. Чистякова, *etc.* 1934. 8°. **11925.** aa. **11.**

BURSKY (P. D.) and **ROZENOER** (S. M.) От Урала до Великого Океана. Путеводитель по Уралу, Сибири и Дальнему Востоку, *etc.* [With illustrations and maps.] pp. 308. 1928. 8°. *See* Moscow.—*Общество Изученія Урала, Сибири, и Дальнего Востока.* Ac. **1166/2.**

BURSLEM. [For institutes, societies, etc. in the district of Burslem:] *See* Stoke-on-Trent.

—— Burslem Parish Register. [Edited by Percy W. L. Adams.] pp. xi. 816. cii. 1913. 8°. *See* Stafford, County of.—*Staffordshire Parish Register Society.* Ac. **8131.** n.

—— The Age of Wonders, or Miracles are not ceased. Being a true but strange relation of a child born at Burslem in Staffordshire who, before it was three quarters old spake and prophesied strange and wonderful things touching the King . . . With divers other remarkable predictions . . . in relation to monarchy, *etc.* pp. 8. *Nehemiah Chamberlain: London*, 1660. 4°. E. **1017. (37.)**

BURSLEM BULLETIN.

—— Burslem Bulletin. *See* Doulton and Co.

BURSLEM (Rollo) A peep into Toorkisthān. [With plates and a map.] pp. 238. *Pelham Richardson: London*, 1846. 8°. **1425.** d. **14.**

BURSLEM (Willoughby Marshall) Pulmonary Consumption and its Treatment. pp. viii. 160. *John Churchill: London*, 1852. 8°. **1187.** d. **19.**

BURSLEY (Joseph Aldrich) *See* Allen (John R.) and Bursley (J. A.) Heat Engines, *etc.* 1910. 8°. **08767.** h. **45.**

—— —— 1925. 8°. **8763.** ee. **22.**

—— —— 1931. 8°. **08769.** d. **34.**

—— *See* Allen (John R.) and Bursley (J. A.) Heat Engines, *etc.* 1941. 8°. **8772.** b. **11.**

BURSON (Caroline Maude)

—— The Stewardship of Don Esteban Miró, 1782–1792. A study of Louisiana based largely on the documents in New Orleans. [With a portrait and a bibliography.] pp. ix. 327. *American Printing Co.: New Orleans*, 1940. 8°. **10889.** c. 3.

BURSOTTI (Federico) Discorsi politici. pp. 152. *Napoli*, 1869. 8°. **8033.** aaa. **40. (5.)**

—— Della necessità d'una nuova constituzione dell'Italia. Discorso. pp. 56. *Napoli*, 1867. 8°. **8033.** aa. **53. (8.)**

—— Memoria intorno al P. Francesco Bursotti, *etc.* pp. 15. *Napoli*, 1845. 8°. **4865.** e. **11.**

BURSOTTI (Francesco) *See* Bursotti (Federico) Memoria intorno al P. Francesco Bursotti, *etc.* 1845. 8°. **4865.** e. **11.**

BURSOTTI (G.) *See* Periodical Publications.—*Naples.* Biblioteca di Commercio, compilata per cura di G. Bursotti. 1841, *etc.* 8°. P.P. **1424.** g.

BURSOV (Boris)

—— *See* Gitovich (A.) and Bursov (B.) Мы видели Корею. 1947. 8°. **10055.** t. **24.**

BURSOV (Boris Ivanovich)

—— *See* Gor'ky (M.) *pseud.* Статьи и памфлеты. (Вступительная статья и примечания Б. И. Бурсова.) 1948. 8°. **012264.** g. **29.**

—— Вопросы реализма в эстетике революционных демократов. pp. 384. *Москва*, 1953. 8°. **11870.** b. **3.**

—— "Мать" М. Горького и вопросы социалистического реализма. pp. 165. *Москва, Ленинград*, 1951. 8°. **11868.** dd. **46.**

—— Труды Первой и Второй Всесоюзных Пушкинских конференций. 25–27 апреля 1949 г. и 6–8 июня 1950 г. (Под редакцией Б. И. Бурсова.) pp. 29. 1952. 8°. *See* Russia.—*Академия Наук СССР.* —*Институт Русской Литературы (Пушкинский Дом).* **11870.** b. **27.**

—— Чернышевский как литературный критик. pp. 131. *Москва, Ленинград*, 1951. 8°. **11869.** ff **18.**
The titlepage headed: Академия Наук СССР. Институт Русской Литературы—Пушкинский Дом.

BURSSENS (A. F. S.) *See* Boek. Dat boeck vander voirsienicheit Godes. Ingeleid en uitgegeven door Dr. A. F. S. Burssens. 1930. 8°. **3851.** df. **9.**

BURSSENS (Amaat)

—— Introduction à l'étude des langues bantoues du Congo Belge. pp. xxii. 152. *Anvers*, 1954. 8°. [*Kongo-overzee bibliotheek.* no. 8.] **10099.g.7/8.**

—— Kongo-overzee bibliotheek. Onder leiding van Prof. Dr. A. Burssens. 9 pt. *Antwerpen*, 1938–56. 8°. **10099.** g. **7.**

—— Manuel de Tshiluba—Kasayi, Congo Belge. pp. 94. *Anvers*, 1946. 8°. [*Kongo-Overzee bibliotheek.* no. 3.] **10099.g.7/3.**

—— Tonologische schets van het Tshiluba—Kasayi, Belgisch Kongo. pp. xiv. 231. *Antwerpen*, 1939. 8°. [*Kongo-Overzee bibliotheek.* no. 2.] **10099.g.7/2.**

BURSSFELD. *See* Bursfeld.

BURSST, *Family of.* Anno Domini 1274. Die Burssten. [With a coat of arms, coloured by hand.] [1888.] 4°. **1860.** d. **1. (36.)**

BURSTAL (Edward) Hand-Book for Pilots and Coasters, navigating to and from the River Thames, through all the Channels, to Dungeness and Orfordness. 1851. 8°. *See* England.—*Admiralty.—Hydrographic Department.—Sailing Directions.* [*Thames, River.*] **10496.** b. **55.**

BURSTAL (EDWARD KYNASTON) Tabulated Abstract of Acts of Parliament relating to Water Undertakings, 1879 to 1887. pp. 71. *Henry Frowde: London*, 1888. 8º. **6426**. bb. **38**.

—— Second edition, with rules and regulations, *etc.* pp. xvi. 84. *Henry Frowde: London*, 1889. 8º. **6425**. cc. **9**.

BURSTALL, *Family of.*

—— *See* SHERWOOD (George F. T.) Pedigree of Burstall. 1935. *obl.* fol. **1856**. g. **6**. (**44**.)

BURSTALL ( ) and **CAMPBELL** ( ) *of Melbourne.* Steam Communication with England; as it has been, and as it ought to be. pp. 14. *"Punch" Printing Office: Melbourne*, 1862. 8º. **8244**. b. **71**. (**7**.)

BURSTALL (FRANCIS HEREWARD) *See* MORGAN (*Sir* Gilbert T.) and BURSTALL (F. H.) Inorganic Chemistry, *etc.* 1936. 8º. **8899**. h. **5**.

—— —— 1938. 8º. **8902**. f. **16**.

BURSTALL (HENRY FREDERIC WILLIAM) *See* DONKIN (Sydney B.) A Text-Book of Gas, Oil, and Air Engines . . . With revision by Prof. Burstall, *etc.* 1911. 8º. **08766**. cc. **42**.

—— Education in Applied Science. *See* HUMANISM. Humanism and Technology, *etc.* 1924. 8º. **8703**. df. **25**.

—— The Energy-Diagram for Gas. pp. 20. *Constable & Co.: London*, 1912. 8º. **8766**. c. **41**.

BURSTALL (HENRY FREDERIC WILLIAM) and BURTON (CECIL GEORGE)

—— Souvenir History of the Foundation & Development of the Mason Science College and of the University of Birmingham, 1880–1930, *etc.* pp. 83. [1930.] 4º. *See* BIRMINGHAM.—*University of Birmingham.* **8364**. k. **29**.

—— [Another copy.] **08311**. k. **3**. (**3**.)

BURSTALL (HENRY ROBERT JOHN) The Testing of Heat-Engines. pp. 17. *London*, 1927. 8º. [*Institution of Civil Engineers. Institution Lecture to Students.* Session 1926-27.] Ac. **4313/23**.

BURSTALL (LILIAN) With the Wingle Wangle in Fairyland. pp. 120. *Morland: Amersham*, 1915. 8º. **12800**. c. **2**.

BURSTALL (SARA ANNIE) 'Christianity and Womanhood' . . . being the twenty-first of a series of lectures on Is Christianity True? *etc.* pp. 22. *C. H. Kelly: London*, [1904.] 8º. **4018**. eee. **30**. (**6**.)

—— The Education of Girls in the United States. pp. xii. 204. *Swan Sonnenschein & Co.: London*, 1894. 8º. **8311**. aaa. **7**.

—— English High Schools for Girls. Their aims, organisation, and management. pp. xiv. 243. *Longmans & Co.: London*, 1907. 8º. **8306**. cc. **37**.

—— Frances Mary Buss, an Educational Pioneer, *etc.* [With a portrait.] pp. 94. *S.P.C.K.: London*, 1938. 8º. **10858**. a. **1**.

—— Impressions of American Education in 1908. pp. xii. 329. *Longmans & Co.: London*, 1909. 8º. **8304**. c. **31**.

—— The Old Testament. Its growth and message. A handbook, *etc.* pp. x. 144. *E. Arnold & Co.: London*, [1923.] 8º. **03149**. de. **62**.

BURSTALL (SARA ANNIE)

—— Retrospect & Prospect. Sixty years of women's education, *etc.* pp. xv. 286. *Longmans & Co.: London*, 1933. 8º. **8366**. dd. **50**.

—— The Story of the Manchester High School for Girls, 1871–1911. [With a preface by T. F. Tout.] pp. xx. 214. *Manchester*, 1911. 8º. [*Publications of the University of Manchester. Educational Series.* no. 6.] Ac. **2671/7**.

BURSTALL (SARA ANNIE) and DOUGLAS (MARY ALICE)

—— Public Schools for Girls. A series of papers on their history. By members of the Association of Head Mistresses. Edited by S. A. Burstall . . . and M. A. Douglas. pp. xv. 302. 1911. 8º. *See* ENGLAND.—*Association of Head Mistresses.* **8306**. eee. **20**.

BURSTEIN (ABRAHAM)

—— *See* LIEBERMAN (C.) The Christianity of Sholem Asch, *etc.* (From the Yiddish by A. Burstein.) [1953.] 8º. **4035**. bb. **63**.

BURSTEIN (CHARLES L.)

—— Fundamental Considerations in Anesthesia. Second edition. pp. xiii. 219. *Macmillan Co.: New York*, 1955. 8º. **7484**. m. **37**.

BURSTEIN (JOSEF)

—— Myocardial Infarction, *etc.* (Translated by Alice Eager.) pp. 83. *Helsingfors*, 1953. 8º. [*Acta medica scandinavica.* suppl. 285.] P.P. **3081**. b. (**2**.)

BURSTEIN (JULIUS) *See* BAINTON (Joseph H.) and BURSTEIN (J.) Illustrative Electrocardiography. [1935.] *obl.* 8º. **7462**. p. **7**.

—— *See* BAINTON (Joseph H.) and BURSTEIN (J.) Illustrative Electrocardiography, *etc.* [1940.] *obl.* 8º. **7462**. p. **42**.

BURSTEIN (JULIUS) and **BLOOM** (NATHAN)

—— Illustrative Electrocardiography . . . Third edition [of the work of J. H. Bainton and J. Burstein]. pp. xvi. 309. *D. Appleton-Century Co.: New York, London*, [1948.] 8º. **7471**. c. **13**.

BURSTEIN (MOSHÉ) Self-Government of the Jews in Palestine since 1900. pp. 298. [*The Author*:] *Tel-Aviv*, 1934. 8º. **04033**. h. **28**.

BURSTEIN (N. S.) Ideas and Ideals, *etc.* [With a portrait.] pp. xii. 210. *K. S. Bhat: London*, [1932.] 8º. **04033**. e. **66**.

BÜRSTENBINDER ( ) [For the German surname of this form:] *See* BUERSTENBINDER.

BÜRSTER ( ) [For the German surname of this form:] *See* BUERSTER.

BÜRSTNER ( ) [For the German surname of this form:] *See* BUERSTNER.

BURSTON (DANIEL) *Dean of Waterford.* *Ευαγγελιστης ἔτι εὐαγγελιζομενος·* or, the Evangelist yet evangelizing. Submitted to the judgment and censure of the Churches of England and Ireland. pp. 286. *Printed by John Crook; and are to be sold by Samuel Dancer: Dublin*, 1662. 4º. **4106**. c. **6**.

The pagination is irregular.

BURSTON (GEORGE) *Colonel.* The Case of Col. Burston, with respect to the dispute between him and Lieutenant General Wills. pp. v. 63. *London,* 1720. 8°. **1093.** d. **33.**

BURSTON (GEORGE) *of Dublin.* *See* DUBLIN.—*Royal Hospital of King Charles II., etc.* Charter of the Royal Hospital of King Charles II., &c. [Edited, with an account of the foundation, by G. Burston.] 1760. 12°. **780.** b. **22.**

—— *See* DUBLIN.—*Royal Hospital of King Charles II., etc.* Abstract of the By-laws . . . made by the Governors of the Royal Hospital of King Charles II., near Dublin, *etc.* [By G. Burston.] 1752. 8°. **1159.** g. **21.**

BURSTON (ROY) Records of the Anthropometric Measurements of one hundred and two Australian Aboriginals. [With tables.] pp. 3. *Melbourne,* 1913. 4°. [*Bulletin of the Northern Territory.* no. 7a.] **C.S.G.546.**

BURSTON (WYNDHAM HEDLEY)

—— Social Studies and the History Teacher. pp. 27. *George Philip & Son: [London,]* 1954. 8°. [*Teaching of History Leaflet.* no. 15.] Ac. **8116.** b/**11.**

BURSTOW (HENRY) Reminiscences of Horsham, being the recollections of Henry Burstow, the celebrated bell-ringer & songsinger, *etc.* [Set down by William Allery.] pp. 128. *Free Christian Church Book Society: Horsham,* 1911. 8°. **010854.** de. **35.**

The titlepage is engraved.

BURSTOW (JOHN) *Begin.* This is to be conveyed to the Priest that made a dead Sermon to the dead body of him that was called Justice Waterton; contrary to the example of any of the Apostles; or to any that mourneth in the same deceit with them. pp. 4. [*London?* 1660.] 4°. **855.** f. **3.** (**27***.)

BURSTRÖM (HANS GEORG)

—— *See* LUND.—*Regia Academia Carolina.* Inbjudning till hötidligheten (varmed F. F. Schmidt och professorn i botanik, särskilt fysiologi och anatomi H. G. Burström komma att i sina ämbeten installeras), *etc.* 1943, *etc.* 8°. Ac. **1067/5.** (**6.**)

BURSTYN (SAMUEL) *See* BURSHTYN.

BURSTYN-TAUBER (CAMILLA)

—— Betriebswirtschaftliche Auswirkungen und Persönlichkeitswert der Berufsausbildung "Junger Männer und Frauen" in den Bat'awerken in Zlín. pp. 143. *Bern, Leipzig,* 1939. 8°. **08286.** k. **33.**

BURSY (BERNHARDUS) De Aristotelis *Πολιτειας Ἀθηναιων* partis alterius fonte et auctoritate, *etc.* pp. viii. 148. *Jurjewi,* 1897. 8°. **8008.** g. **22.**

BURSY (CARL VON) *See* MITAU.—*Kurländische Gesellschaft für Literatur und Kunst.* Sendungen, *etc.* [Edited by C. von Bursy and others.] 1850, *etc.* 4°. Ac. **1100.**

—— Das künstliche Licht und die Brillen. Zwei Vorlesungen. pp. iv. 43. *Mitau & Leipzig,* 1846. 8°. **8715.** d. **48.** (**1.**)

BURSZTA (JÓZEF)

—— Społeczeństwo i karczma. Propinacja, karczma i sprawa alkoholizmu w społeczeństwie polskim XIX wieku. [With illustrations.] pp. 262. *Warszawa,* 1951. 8°. **8435.** i. **50.**

—— Wieś i karczma. Rola karczmy w życiu wsi pańszczyźnianej. pp. 228. *Warszawa,* 1950. 8°. **10292.** ppp. **30.**

BURSZTYN (I.)

—— Niektóre kierunki rozwoju techniki w Planie 6-letnim. Praca zbiorowa. (Pod redakcją I. Bursztyna.) pp. 194. *Warszawa,* 1952. 8°. [*Biblioteka Planu Sześcioletniego.*] **8208.** cc. **31/9.**

BURSZTYN (MICHAEL)

—— ביי די טייכן פון מאזאוויע. [Bai di taichn fun Mazovie.] [With a portrait.] pp. 157. *Warszawa,* 1951. 8°. **12557.** bbb. **20.**

BURT FRANKLIN BIBLIOGRAPHICAL SERIES. *See* FRANKLIN (Burt) *Bookseller and Publisher.*

BURT, *Family of.* *See* BURT (Henry M.) and BURT (S. W.) Early Days in New England. Life and times of Henry Burt of Springfield and some of his descendants, *etc.* 1893. 8°. **9903.** d. **8.**

BURT (A.) *B.A.* *See* PERIODICAL PUBLICATIONS.—*Grahamstown.* The African Monthly . . . Edited by A. Burt. 1907, *etc.* 8°. P.P. **6231.** g.

BURT (A. E.) Swahili Grammar and Vocabulary. Drawn up by Mrs. F. Burt. [With an introduction and a chapter on phonetics by the Rev. W. E. Taylor.] pp. 252. *S.P.C.K.: London,* 1910. 8°. **12906.** de. **34.**

—— Second edition. pp. vii. 263. *S.P.C.K.: London,* 1917. 8°. **12911.** e. **1.**

BURT (A. W.) A Manual of Elementary Phonetics. pp. v. 93. *Copp Clark Co.: Toronto,* 1898. 8°. **12991.** d. **44.**

BURT (AGNES SANXAY)

—— Bibliography of Genetic Neurology. Compiled and annotated by A. S. Burt, *etc.* pp. 131. 1952. 4°. [*National Research Council. Publication.* no. 237. suppl.] *See* WASHINGTON, *D.C.—National Academy of Sciences.—National Research Council.—Committee on Neurobiology.* Survey of Neurobiology. 1952. 8°. Ac. **3039.** da/**2.**

BURT (ALFRED) Life Assurance. An historical and statistical account of the population, the law of mortality, and the different systems of life assurance; including the validity and non-validity of life-policies: with observations on friendly societies and savings' banks, *etc.* pp. 211. *Effingham Wilson: London,* [1849.] 8°. **8225.** e. **83.**

—— Life Assurance. Validity and non-validity of life policies. Statement of facts shewing the defective system of life assurance as in practice by life offices in refusing the payment of a life policy of assurance at the death of the assured. pp. 46. *Effingham Wilson: London,* [1849.] 8°. **8225.** e. **82.**

BURT (ALFRED LEROY) *See* BRADLEY (Arthur G.) Lord Dorchester, *etc.* [Edited by A. L. Burt.] 1926. 8°. **010880.** h. **12/3**

—— *See* MACILWRAITH (Jean N.) Sir Frederick Haldimand, *etc.* [Edited by A. L. Burt.] 1926. 8°. **010880.** h. **12/3.**

—— Imperial Architects. Being an account of proposals in the direction of a closer imperial union, made previous to the opening of the first Colonial Conference of 1887 . . . With an introduction by H. E. Egerton. pp. vii. 228. *B. H. Blackwell: Oxford,* 1913. 8°. **8155.** aaa. **29.**

—— The Old Province of Quebec. [With plates and maps.] pp. xiii. 551. *University of Minnesota Press: Minneapolis,* 1933. 8°. **2370.** e. **16.**

BURT (ALFRED LEROY)

—— The Problem of Government [in Canada], 1760–1774. 1930. *See* ROSE (John H.) The Cambridge History of the British Empire, *etc.* vol. 6. 1929, *etc.* 8°. **2090.a.**

—— The Romance of the Prairie Provinces. [With illustrations, including portraits.] pp. xii. 262. *W. J. Gage & Co.: Toronto,* 1931. 8°. **010470. aa. 29.**

—— A Short History of Canada for Americans. [With plates.] pp. xvi. 279. *University of Minnesota Press: Minneapolis,* [1942.] 8°. **9555. p. 6.**

—— A Short History of Canada for Americans. (Second edition.) pp. xvi. 309. *University of Minnesota Press: Minneapolis,* [1944.] 8°. **9555. pp. 27.**

—— The United States, Great Britain and British North America, from the Revolution to the establishment of peace after the war of 1812. [With maps.] pp. vii. 448. *Yale University Press: New Haven,* 1940. 8°. [*The Relations of Canada and the United States.*] Ac. **2297.** gb/**6.** (**16.**)

BURT (ANDREW) *B.D.* Our Village, and other Sermons. pp. 77. *A. H. Stockwell: London,* [1932.] 8°. **04478.** i. **83.**

BURT (ANDREW) *Lawyer. See* ENGLAND.—*Court of Chancery.* [*Appendix.*] Real Cases in Chancery. [A statement of the misconduct of A. Burt, in respect of the trusteeship of estates belonging to the Earl of Strathmore.] 1830. 8°. **6190.** b. **21.**

BURT (ARMISTEAD) Speech . . . in favor of adopting a Rule to exclude Abolition Petitions. pp. 8. [*Washington,* 1844.] 8°. **8177.** cc. **51.** (**7.**)

BURT (ARTHUR) *pseud.* [i.e. HERBERT ARTHUR SHAPPIRO.] *See* also SHAPPIRO (H. A.)

BURT (AUGUSTUS A.) A Catalogue of Ancient and Modern Books . . . on sale . . . by A. A. Burt, *etc.* pp. 16. *London,* 1835. 8°. S.C. **703.** (**11.**)

BURT (BENJAMIN CHAPMAN) *See* ERDMANN (J. E.) [Grundriss der Logik und Metaphysik.] Outlines of Logic and Metaphysics . . . Translated . . . with prefatory essay by B. C. Burt. 1896. 8°. **8466.** b. **40.**

—— *See* MORELAND (William H.) and BURT (B. C.) Northern India as a Market for Agricultural Machinery. [1910.] 8°. **8219.** bb. **31.**

—— A Brief History of Greek Philosophy. pp. xiv. 296. *Ginn & Co.: Boston,* 1889. 8°. **8486.** bb. **12.**

—— A History of Modern Philosophy from the Renaissance to the present. 2 vol. *A. C. McClurg & Co.: Chicago,* 1892. 8°. **8485.** de. **14.**

—— Railway Station Service. pp. viii. 292. *J. Wiley & Sons: New York; Chapman & Hall: London,* 1911. 8°. **08235.** aa. **28.**

—— Some Relations between Philosophy and Literature. pp. 18. *See* SEWALL (Henry) Herbert Spencer as Biologist. 1886. 8°. [*University of Michigan Philosophical Papers.* ser. 1. no. 4.] Ac. **2685/7.**

BURT (BERNARD) Across the Silver Streak in the "Nautilus." [With a plate.] pp. 20. *Printed for private circulation: Worthing,* [1884.] 32°. **10108.** a. **33.**

BURT (BERNARD)

—— Log Book of the "Gensing," of Shoreham, on a voyage from . . . Shoreham to Shields, and from Shields to Shoreham . . . commencing May 14, 1879, ending June 7, 1879. pp. 8. *W. F. Churcher: Worthing,* 1880. *obl.* 8°. **1853.** a. **11.**

BURT (CHARLES) *Alderman of Richmond, Surrey.* The Richmond Vestry. Notes of its history and operations from 1614 to 1890. (Borough of Richmond. The charter of incorporation. [With a map.]) pp. 82. 21. *R. A. Darnill: Richmond,* 1890. 8°. **010358.** f. **22.**

BURT (CHARLES) *of Southampton. See* EVANS (*Sir* Frank H.) and BURT (C.) To the Electors of the Parliamentary Borough of Southampton, *etc.* [With a portrait.] 1892. 8°. **8139.** aa. **53.** (**12.**)

BURT (CHARLES EARLE)

—— A Study of the Teiid Lizards of the Genus Cnemidophorus with special reference to their phylogenetic relationships. [With a bibliography.] pp. viii. 286. *Washington,* 1931. 8°. [*U.S. National Museum. Bulletin.* no. 154.] Ac. **1875/13.**

BURT (CHARLES EARLE) and **MYERS** (GEORGE SPRAGUE)

—— Neotropical Lizards in the Collection of the Natural History Museum of Stanford University. pp. 52. *Stanford University Press:* [*Stanford,*] 1942. 8°. [*Stanford University Publications. University Series. Biological Sciences.* vol. 8. no. 2.] Ac. **2692.** n/**8.** (**2.**)

BURT (CHARLES H.) Martyrs and Martyrs, & other poems. pp. 82. *Jacob & Johnson: Winchester; Simpkin, Marshall & Co.: London,* 1870. 16°. **11649.** ee. **21.**

BURT (CHARLES THOMAS)

—— The Moon Society. A century of achievement, 1848–1948. [With illustrations, including a portrait.] pp. 16. *Moon Works: Brighton,* [1949.] 8°. **8288.** c. **6.**

BURT (CYRIL GEORGE EDWARD)

—— *See* HAYDEN (Arthur) Chats on Old Silver . . . Edited and revised by C. G. E. Bunt. 1949. 8°. **7813.** aa. **18.**

BURT (*Sir* CYRIL LODOWIC)

—— *See* HARTOG (*Sir* Philippe J.) *K.B.E.*, and RHODES (E. C.) The Marks of Examiners . . . With a memorandum by C. Burt. 1936. 8°. **08364.** i. **31.**

—— The Backward Child. *See* infra: The Sub-normal School Child. vol. 2.

—— The Causes and Treatment of Backwardness. (Second edition, revised and enlarged.) pp. 128. *University of London Press: London,* 1953. 8°. **08308.** cc. **32.**

—— The Causes and Treatment of Backwardness. pp. 144. *National Children's Home: London,* [1953.] 8°. [*Convocation Lecture of the National Children's Home.* 1952.] W.P. **3592/6.**

—— Contributions of Psychology to Social Problems, *etc.* pp. 76. *Oxford University Press: London,* 1953. 8°. [*L. T. Hobhouse Memorial Trust Lecture.* no. 22.] W.P. **3769/22**

—— The Distribution and Relations of Educational Abilities *etc.* pp. xiii. 93. 1917. 8°. *See* LONDON, *County of.—County Council.—Education Committee.* **L.C.C.94.**

—— The Factors of the Mind. An introduction to factor-analysis in psychology. pp. xiv. 509. *University of London Press: London*, 1940. 8°. **8472**. aa. **17**.

—— Handbook of Tests for Use in Schools. pp. xvi. 106. *P. S. King & Son: London*, 1923. 8°. **08311**. i. **18**.

—— Handbook of Tests for Use in Schools . . . Second edition. pp. xvi. 110. *Staples Press: London, New York; printed in Holland*, 1948. 8°. **8312**. cc. **9**.

—— Test 1 (5, 9–14). [Reprinted from "Handbook of Tests for use in Schools."] 5 pt. *Staples Press: London*, [1949.] 8° & 4°. **8312**. d. **13**.

—— How the Mind Works. [Essays.] By Cyril Burt . . . Ernest Jones . . . Emanuel Miller . . . William Moodie. Edited by C. Burt. pp. 336. *G. Allen & Unwin: London*, 1933. 8°. **08465**. de. **31**.

—— Intelligence and Fertility. The effect of the differential birthrate on inborn mental characteristics. pp. 43. *Eugenics Society; Hamish Hamilton Medical Books: London*, 1946. 8°. [*Occasional Papers on Eugenics*. no. 2.] W.P. **8159/2**.

—— Intelligence and Fertility, *etc.* (Second edition.) pp. 44. *Eugenics Society; Cassell & Co.: London*, 1952. 8°. [*Occasional Papers on Eugenics*. no. 2.] W.P. **8159/2a**.

—— The Measurement of Mental Capacities. A review of the psychology of individual differences. [With plates.] pp. 52. *Edinburgh*, 1927. 4°. [*Henderson Trust Lectures*. no. 7.] Ac. **3850**. e.

—— Mental and Scholastic Tests, *etc.* pp. xv. 432. 1921. 8°. *See* LONDON, *County of.—County Council.—Education Committee.* **L.C.C.95.**

—— (Second impression.) 1922. 8°. *See* LONDON, *County of.—County Council.—Education Committee.* **2021**. d.

—— (Third impression.) 1927. 8°. *See* LONDON, *County of.—County Council.—Education Committee.* **8311**. f. **8**.

—— Northumberland Standardised Tests. 1925 series. 5 pt. *University of London Press: London*, [1925.] 4°. **8309**. e. **43**.

—— Northumberland Standardised Tests. 1925 series. Prepared by Sir C. Burt. 4 pt. *University of London Press: London*, [1950.] 8°. **08366**. r. **28**.

—— *See* SHEPPARD (N. F.) Northumberland Standardised Tests. Record scales . . . for use with Northumberland Standardised Tests, 1925 series . . . prepared by C. Burt. [1938.] 4°. **8534**. h. **38**.

—— A Study in Vocational Guidance, *etc.* [By various authors.] (Under the general direction of Cyril Burt.) pp. viii. 106. *London*, 1926. 8°. [*Industrial Fatigue Research Board. Report*. no. 33.] B.S. **25/7**.

—— The Subnormal Mind. pp. vii. 368. *Oxford University Press: London*, 1935. 8°. [*University of London Heath Clark Lectures*. 1933.] W.P. **10520/3**.

—— Second edition. pp. ix. 372. *Oxford University Press: London*, 1937. 8°. [*University of London Heath Clark Lectures*. 1933.] W.P. **10520/6**.

—— The Subnormal Mind . . . Third edition. pp. xix. 391. *Oxford University Press: London*, 1955. 8°. [*University of London Heath Clark Lectures*. 1933.] W.P. **10520/14**.

—— The Sub-normal School-Child. [With plates.]

vol. 1. The Young Delinquent. pp. xx. 643. 1925.
vol. 2. The Backward Child. pp. xx. 694. 1937.

***University Press: London*, 1925, 37. 8°. 8313. de. 2.**
No more published.

—— The Sub-normal School-Child.

vol. 1. The Young Delinquent . . . Second edition. pp. xx. 645. 1927.
vol. 2. The Backward Child . . . Second and revised edition. pp. xx. 694. 1946.

University Press: London, 1927,46. 8°. **8313.de.4.**

—— The Sub-normal School Child.

vol. 1. The Young Delinquent . . . Third and revised edition. pp. xx. 645. 1938.
vol. 2. The Backward Child. (Third edition.) pp. xx. 704. 1950.

University of London Press: London, 1938, 50. 8°. **8313**. de. **3**.

—— The Young Delinquent . . . Fourth and revised edition. [With plates.] pp. xx. 662. *University of London Press: Bickley*, 1944. 8°. **6058**. pp. **17**.

—— The Young Delinquent. *See* supra: The Sub-normal School-Child. vol. 1.

BURT (DAVID) A Discourse delivered Thanksgiving Day, Nov. 30, 1854. pp. 19. *Jones, Cogswell & Co.: Concord*, 1855. 8°. **4486**. aaa. **93**. **(18.)**

BURT (DOROTHY M.) Two Views, and other poems. pp. 12. *A. H. Stockwell: London*, [1933.] 8°. **11640**. df. **73**.

BURT (EDWARD) *Author of "Letters from a Gentleman in the North of Scotland."* Letters from a Gentleman in the North of Scotland [i.e. E. Burt] to his friend in London, containing the description of a capital town in that northern country . . . likewise an account of the Highlands, with the customs and manners of the Highlanders, *etc.* 2 vol. 1754. 8°. *See* LETTERS. **10370**. bbb. **25**.

—— [Another copy.] **287**. c. **30**, **31**.

—— [Another edition.] 2 vol. pp. viii. 362. 1755. 12°. *See* LETTERS. **566**. b. **24**.

—— The second edition. 2 vol. 1759. 8°. *See* LETTERS. **797**. h. **2**, **3**.

—— [Another copy.] **1430**. e. **19**, **20**.

—— [Another copy.] G. **5239**, **40**.

—— A new edition, with notes, *etc.* 2 vol. 1815. 8°. *See* LETTERS. **567**. c. **7**.

—— The fifth edition, with a large appendix . . . with an introduction and notes, by the editor, R. Jamieson . . . and the history of Donald the Hammerer, from an authentic account of the family of Invernahyle; a MS. communicated by Walter Scott. 2 vol. 1818. 8°. *See* LETTERS. **287**. f. **21**, **22**.

—— [Another copy.] G. **14847**.

—— Brieven van een heer uyt Noord-Schotland [i.e. E. Burt] aan zynen vriend te London. Behelzende een bericht omtrent de Hoog-Landen . . . Met figuuren. Uyt het Engels vertaald door J. J. D. [i.e. J. J. Dusterhoop.] 2 dl. 1758. 8°. *See* BRIEVEN. **10370**. bbb. **24**.

BURT (Edward) *Author of "Letters from a Gentleman in the North of Scotland."*

—— Schottländische Briefe, oder merkwürdige Nachrichten von Schottland, und besonders von dem Schottischen Hochlande . . . Aus dem Englischen übersetzt. Mit Kupfertafeln. [A translation by Eobald Toze of "Letters from a Gentleman in the North of Scotland," by E. Burt.] 2 Tl. 1760. 8°. *See* Scotland. [*Appendix.—Topography and Travels.*] **566**. b. **27**.

BURT (Edward) *Commander, R.N.* The Hurricane: a poem, descriptive of the unparalleled perseverance and constancy of the seamen on board H.M. Ship Theseus . . . commanded by Captain—now Rear-Admiral—E. Hawker . . . during three days' and nights' hurricane . . . By an Eye-Witness . . . Also, Historical notices of St. Domingo . . . With illustrations. [The introduction signed: E. B., Commander, R.N., i.e. E. Burt.] pp. 75. 1844. 8°. *See* B., E., *Commander, R.N.* **11646**. h. **8**.

BURT (Edward Alexander P.) Guide to Improved Round-Timber Cubing Rule, Bark and Railway Measurement Weight Calculator. pp. xv. 45. *W. Rider & Son: London,* [1898.] 8°. **8548**. cc. **18**.

—— The Key to the British Imperial Measures. Viz.:—the Cubic Foot. The Cubic Foot in Cylindrical Form. The "Erroneous" Cubic Foot by 144 divisor, *etc.* pp. 11. *W. Rider & Son: London,* [1901.] fol. **8531**. g. **25**.

—— The Measurement of Irregular Round Trees and Timber. The "Ellipse," *etc.* pp. 9. *W. Rider & Son: London,* [1901.] fol. **8531**. g. **24**.

—— The Railway Rates Standard Timber Measurer and Calculator. A practical treatise on the cubic and superficial measurement of all descriptions of timber . . . Second edition. pp. 311. *W. Rider & Son: London,* [1888.] 8°. **8548**. c. **49**.

—— Third edition. pp. 323. *W. Rider & Son: London,* [1900.] 8°. **8548**. cc. **24**.

—— Round Timber Measurement Weight Tables for Railway Rates, *etc.* pp. 18. *W. Rider & Son: London,* [1898.] 8°. **8548**. bbb. **63**.

—— The Standard English and Foreign Corn Calculator, *etc.* pp. 134. *The Author: London,* 1889. 8°. **8548**. d. **52**.

—— The Standard Stave Measurer and Calculator. A practical treatise on the measurement, sorting and classification of every description of staves, *etc.* pp. xv. 112. *W. Rider & Son: London,* [1891.] 8°. **8548**. de. **18**.

—— The Standard Timber Measurer, a practical treatise on the cubic and superficial measurement of all descriptions of timber, *etc.* pp. 311. *W. Rider & Son: London,* [1888.] 8°. **8767**. aaa. **38**.

BURT (Emily Rose) Make your Bazar Pay. pp. 157. *Harper & Bros.: New York & London,* 1925. 8°. **07943**. l. **79**.

—— Planning your Party. pp. viii. 322. *Harper & Bros.: New York & London,* 1927. 8°. **07912**. ff. **4**.

—— The Shower Book. Seventy-seven showers for the engaged girl. pp. x. 165. *Harper & Bros.: New York & London,* 1928. 8°. **8403**. ee. **15**.

BURT (Emma J.) The Seen & Unseen in Browning. pp. 191. *Basil Blackwell: Oxford,* 1923. 8°. **011850**. b. **33**.

BURT (Enoch) Immersion after Believing not Necessary to constitute Christian Baptism; illustrated and established by the conclusive testimony of Scripture. pp. 38. *Printed for the Author: Hartford,* 1828. 8°. **4325**. bb. **21**.

BURT (Ernest Whitby)

—— After Sixty Years. The story of the Church founded by the Baptist Missionary Society in North China. pp. 148. *Carey Press: London,* [1937.] 8°. **20031**. a. **10**.

—— Alfred George Jones. [With a portrait.] pp. 14. *Carey Press: London,* [1943.] 8°. [*Brief Biographies of Leading Laymen.* no. 8.] **10804.m.34/8.**

—— Fifty Years in China. The story of the Baptist Mission in Shantung, Shansi and Shensi, 1875–1925. [With plates.] pp. 127. *Carey Press: London,* [1925.] 8°. **4767**. aaa. **36**.

BURT (Federal) An Address, delivered at Durham, N.H., September 4th, 1815. before the Old Hundred Sacred Musick Society, on occasion of their first annual meeting. pp. 16. 1815. 8°. *See* Durham, *New Hampshire.—Old Hundred Sacred Musick Society.* **3477**. c. **57**.

—— Sketches of the Civil and Ecclesiastical History of Durham, N.H. 1837. *See* Concord, *New Hampshire.—New Hampshire Historical Society.* Collections. vol. 5. 1824, *etc.* 8°. Ac. **8415**.

BURT (Frank Allen)

—— American Advertising Agencies. An inquiry into their origin, growth, functions and future. pp. x. 282. *Harper & Bros.: New York & London,* [1940.] 8°. **08230**. h. **47**.

—— Successful Advertisements and how to write them. pp. xi. 194. *Harper & Bros.: New York & London,* 1940. 8°. **8222**. b. **17**.

BURT (*Mrs.* Frederick) *See* Burt (A. E.)

BURT (Frederick A.) *See* Brigham (Albert P.) Geology . . . Revised and expanded by F. A. Burt. 1928. 8°. **07104**. e. **17**.

BURT (George) Notes of a Three Months' Trip to Egypt, Greece, Constantinople, and the Eastern Shores of the Mediterranean Sea. pp. 47. *M. Singer & Co.: London,* 1878. 4°. **10125**. ee. **24**.

BURT (Gulielmus) *See* Burt (William)

BURT (Henry Jackson) Steel Construction, *etc.* pp. 372. 9. *American Technical Society: Chicago,* 1920. 8°. **07816**. f. **26**.

—— [Another edition.] Revised by Herman Ritow, *etc.* pp. 434. *American Technical Society: Chicago,* 1931. 8°. **07815**. eee. **29**.

—— [Another edition.] Revised by C. H. Sandberg, *etc.* pp. 438. *American Technical Society: Chicago,* 1944. 8°. **07815**. bb. **48**.

BURT (Henry Martyn) Burt's Guide through the Connecticut Valley to the White Mountains and the River Saguenay. [With maps and illustrations.] pp. 298. *New England Publishing Co.: Springfield, Mass.,* 1874. 16°. **10411**. aa. **44**.

BURT (Henry Martyn)

—— Cornet Joseph Parsons, one of the founders of Springfield and Northampton, Massachusetts . . . An historical sketch from original sources . . . With supplementary chapters . . . by Albert Ross Parsons. [With portraits.] pp. 187. *A. R. Parsons: Garden City, N.Y.*, [1898.] 8°. **010881**. i. **15**.

—— The First Century of the History of Springfield. The official records from 1636 to 1736, with an historical review and biographical mention of the founders. 2 vol. *H. M. Burt: Springfield, Mass.*, 1898, 99. 8°. **10409**. p. **6**.

BURT (Henry Martyn) and **BURT** (Silas Wright)

—— Early Days in New England. Life and times of Henry Burt of Springfield and some of his descendants. Genealogical and biographical mention of James and Richard Burt of Taunton, Mass. and Thomas Burt, M.P., of England. [With portraits, maps and facsimiles.] pp. 617. *C. W. Bryan Co.: Springfield, Mass.*, 1893. 8°. **9903**. d. **8**.

BURT (Horatio Luckett) *See* Burt (Horatio S.)

BURT (Horatio Sebastian) "Jacqueline." [A tale.] pp. 4. [*Douai?* 1888.] 16°. **4412**. ee. **15**. (**3**.)

BURT (Isabel) The Portrait and Autograph Birthday Book. Arranged by I. Burt. *G. G. Harrap & Co.: London*, [1912.] 8°. **012354**. ee. **2**.

BURT (Isabella) Historical Notices of Chelsea, Kensington, Fulham, and Hammersmith. With some particulars of old families, *etc.* pp. xii. 140. *J. Saunders: [London,]* 1871. 8°. **10349**. h. **20**.

—— The Lord's Prayer familiarly explained, *etc.* [With the text.] pp. 47. *Partridge, Oakey & Co.: London*, 1854. 12°. **3225**. aa. **50**. (**5**.)

—— New edition. pp. 51. *J. Teulon: London*, 1859. 12°. **3455**. b. **75**.

—— Memorials of the Oak Tree; with notices of the classical and historical associations connected with it. pp. 82. *Printed for the Authoress: London*, 1860. 8°. **7073**. b. **7**.

BURT (J.) *Pastor of the Congregational Church in Canton, Conn.* The Law of Christian Rebuke. A plea for slaveholders. A sermon delivered at Middletown, Conn., before the Anti-slavery Convention of Ministers and other Christians, October 18, 1843. pp. 20. *N. W. Goodrich & Co.: Hartford*, 1843. 8°. **8156**. aaa. **84**. (**3**.)

—— Moral Responsibilities of Citizenship. A discourse, delivered the day before the quadrennial meeting for the choice of Electors of President and Vice President of the United States, in the Congregational Church, Canton, November 3d, 1844. pp. 15. *Burleigh & Goodrich: Hartford*, 1844. 8°. **4486**. h. **35**.

BURT (J. E.) **AND CO.**

—— Burt's Directory and Guide of Mayfair and District. *See* Directories.—*London*.

BURT (James Patchett) Old Proverbs Illustrated: or, Homely chats with homely people. pp. 106. *T. I. Burton & Sons: Louth*, [1895.] 8°. **012305**. ee. **3**.

BURT (Jessie E.) *See* Kalamos, *pseud.* [i.e. J. E. Burt.]

BURT (Jessie May)

—— Chance Inheritance. pp. 224. *Stanley Paul & Co.: London*, 1952. 8°. NNN. **3140**.

—— Daughter of Paradise. pp. 192. *Stanley Paul & Co.: London*, 1955. 8°. NNN. **6213**.

—— For Love of Annie. pp. 208. *Stanley Paul & Co.: London*, 1953. 8°. NNN. **4381**.

—— The Gay Gordons. pp. 176. *Denis Archer: London*, 1945. 8°. NN. **35551**.

—— The Glendinning Fortunes. pp. 223. *Denis Archer: London*, [1947.] 8°. NN. **37322**.

—— Mr. Duffy calls the Tune. pp. 256. *Denis Archer: London*, [1951.] 8°. NNN. **1544**.

—— The Price of Distinction. pp. 256. *Stanley Paul & Co.: London*, 1952. 8°. NNN. **2588**.

—— Seavacuee. pp. 274. *G. G. Harrap: London*, 1942. 8°. **012826**. e. **5**.

—— The Stepbrothers. pp. 287. *Denis Archer: London*, [1949.] 8°. NN. **39297**.

—— The Swing of the Pendulum. pp. 184. *Denis Archer: London*, [1946.] 8°. NN. **36680**.

—— Treason in Fitzroy Place. pp. 224. *Denis Archer: London*, [1948.] 8°. NN. **38112**.

—— Ursula Takes Over. pp. 178. *Denis Archer: London*, [1944.] 8°. NN. **34968**.

—— A Wife for Giles. pp. 221. *Denis Archer: London*, [1950.] 8°. NNN. **779**.

BURT (Joan)

—— Epilogues for Cubs and Others. pp. 35. *Epworth Press: London*, 1949. 8°. **4397**. bb. **21**.

BURT (Job) *See* Brine (John) Remarks upon a Pamphlet [by J. Burt], intitled, Some Doctrines in the Superlapsarian Scheme impartially examin'd by the Word of God, *etc.* 1736. 8°. **4255**. bb. **7**.

—— *See* Forster (Josiah) *of Durham*. The People called Quakers defended, and the Baptists confuted, being a reply to J. Burt's pretended Answer to R. B's [i.e. R. Barclay's] 12th Proposition, and to a book [by J. Burt?] intituled, A Vindication of the Doctrine of Baptism, *etc.* 1740. 8°. **4151**. d. **11**.

—— The Doctrine of Eternal Reprobation . . . refuted . . . To which are added twenty propositions advanced by some men . . . professing that doctrine . . . with short remarks on each of them . . . by the Rev. Mr. Samuel Acton . . . with a large preface . . . by Thomas Davy. pp. 74. *T. Davy: London*, 1741. 8°. **113**. g. **41**.

BURT (John) *of the Bristol Athenaeum Chess Club.* The Bristol Chess Club; its history, *etc.* pp. xi. 202. *J. Fawn & Son: Bristol*, 1883. 8°. **7913**. cc. **33**.

BURT (John) *Pastor, of Bristol, R.I.* The Mercy of God to his People, in the vengeance he renders to their adversaries, the occasion of their abundant joy. A sermon preached at Bristol, in the Colony of Rhode Island, October the 25th, 1759, upon a thanksgiving for the reduction of Quebeck, the capital of Canada, *etc.* pp. 14. *J. Franklin: Newport, R.-I.*, [1759.] 8°. **4486**. c. **3**.

BURT (John Graham Macdonald) Letter to Lord Viscount Palmerston on Medical Reform. pp. 18. *W. Blackwood & Sons: Edinburgh & London*, 1857. 8°. **7679**. c. **6**.

BURT (John Heyliger) *See* Munch (A.) William and Rachel Russell . . . Translated . . . by J. H. Burt. 1862. 12°. **11781**. c. **29**.

—— *See* Munch (A.) Lord William Russell . . . Übertragen von J. H. Burt. 1858. 8°. **11755**. b. **45**.

—— —— 1860. 8°. **08276**. df. **1**. **(2.)**

—— [En Stemme fra St. Croix.] A Voice from St. Croix, addressed to the approaching Danish Diet. Translated from the Danish by the author. pp. 45. *Baker, Godwin & Co.: New York*, 1852. 8°. **8156**. c. **2**. **(4.)**

BURT (John Marshall) Notes on Military Correspondence. pp. 16. *Eyre & Spottiswoode: London*, [1896.] 8°. **8832**. aa. **6**.

BURT (John Thomas) The Adaptation of Punishment to the Causes of Crime. (Reprinted from the Transactions of the National Association for the Promotion of Social Science.) pp. 16. *Longmans & Co.: London*, 1873. 8°. **6146**. b. **1**. **(6.)**

—— Convict Discipline in Ireland: being an examination of Sir Walter Crofton's answer to "Irish Facts and Wakefield Figures." pp. 42. *Longman & Co.: London*, [1865.] 8°. **6055**. aa. **25**.

—— Discharged Prisoners' Aid Societies, considered in their financial results. pp. 23. *Longmans & Co.: London*, 1876. 8°. **6146**. h. **4**. **(28.)**

—— Irish Facts and Wakefield Figures in relation to Convict Discipline in Ireland; investigated by J. T. Burt. [Two papers, the second a reply to "Observations on the Treatment of Convicts in Ireland. By four Visiting Justices of the West Riding Prison at Wakefield," i.e. E. B. Wheatley Balme and others.] pp. 74. *Longman & Co.: London*, [1863.] 8°. **6055**. aa. **24**.

—— *See* Balme (Edward B. W.) A Reply to Mr. Burt's 'Wakefield Figures in relation to Convict Discipline.' 1863. 8°. **6055**. a. **14**.

—— *See* Crofton (*Sir* Walter) A Few Observations on a pamphlet recently published by J. Burt on the Irish Convict System. 1863. 8°. **6055**. b. **11**.

—— Results of the System of Separate Confinement as administered at the Pentonville Prison. pp. xvi. 287. *Longman & Co.: London*, 1852. 8°. **6055**. d. **48**.

—— A Sermon in behalf of the Birmingham Discharged Prisoners' Aid Society. pp. 26. iv. *Longman & Co.: London; Napper & Wright: Birmingham*, 1859. 8°. **4478**. d. **6**.

BURT (Joseph Bell)

—— *See* Burlage (Henry M.) Fundamental Principles and Processes of Pharmacy. By H. M. Burlage . . . J. B. Burt, *etc.* 1944. 8°. **W.P. 9344/7**.

—— *See* Burlage (Henry M.) Fundamental Principles and Processes of Pharmacy. By H. M. Burlage . . . J. B. Burt, *etc.* 1949. 8°. **W.P. 9344/7a**.

—— *See* Burlage (Henry M.) Introduction to Pharmacy . . . [By] H. M. Burlage . . . J. B. Burt, *etc.* 1954. 8°. **7511**. e. **2**.

BURT (Joseph Bell)

—— *See* Burlage (Henry M.). Laboratory Manual for Principles and Processes of Pharmacy. H. M. Burlage, editor . . . J. B. Burt, *etc.* 1946. 8°. **7509**. k. **24**.

—— *See* Burlage (Henry M.) Laboratory Manual for Principles and Processes of Pharmacy. H. M. Burlage, editor . . . J. B. Burt, *etc.* 1949. 4°. **07509**. l. **34**.

BURT (Joseph F.)

—— *See* Way (Eugene I.) Motion Pictures in Argentina and Brazil. (Based on reports by J. F. Burt [and others].) 1929. 8°. [*U.S. Bureau of Foreign and Domestic Commerce. Trade Information Bulletin.* no. 630.] A.S. **128/3**.

BURT (Katharine Newlin) Body and Soul . . . Based on the motion picture story by K. N. Burt. pp. 128. *Jacobsen-Hodgkinson-Corporation: New York*, [1927.] 8°. **012640**. d. **53**.

—— The Branding Iron . . . With illustrations. pp. vi. 310. *Constable & Co.: London; Cambridge, Mass.* printed, 1919. 8°. NN. **5948**.

—— Cock's Feather. A novel. pp. 317. *William Heinemann: London*, 1929. 8°. **12715**. c. **21**.

—— The Grey Parrot. A novel. pp. 320. *Hutchinson & Co.: London*, [1926.] 8°. **12709**. dd. **10**.

—— Hidden Creek. pp. 315. *Constable & Co.: London*, 1921. 8°. NN. **7082**.

—— The Men of Moon Mountain. pp. 286. *Hutchinson & Co.: London*, [1930.] 8°. NN. **16184**.

—— "Q." pp. 296. *Hutchinson & Co.: London*, [1923.] 8°. NN. **9103**.

—— Quest. A novel. pp. 376. *Houghton, Mifflin Co.: Boston & New York*, 1925. 8°. **12709**. aa. **14**.

—— Rapture Beyond. pp. 284. *C. Scribner's Sons: New York, London*, 1935. 8°. A.N. **2587**.

—— The Red Lady. pp. 240. *Constable & Co.: London*, 1920. 8°. NN. **6728**.

—— Snow-Blind. pp. 186. *Constable & Co.: London; Cambridge, Mass.* printed, 1922. 8°. NN. **7941**.

—— Still Water. pp. 256. *J. Coker & Co.: London*, 1951. 8°. **12730**. ppp. **24**.

—— Strong Citadel. pp. 256. *Coker & Co.: London*, 1951. 8°. **12730**. ppp. **22**.

—— This Woman and This Man. pp. 301. *C. Scribner's Sons: New York*, 1934. 8°. A.N. **2082**.

BURT (Llewellyn Charles) A Summary of English History designed for the use of schools. pp. 58. *Simpkin, Marshall & Co.: London; George Bishop: Wellington College*, [1877.] 8°. **9503**. d. **4**.

—— Second edition. pp. 59. *Simpkin, Marshall & Co.: London; George Bishop: Wellington College*, [1879.] 8°. **9503**. bbb. **6**.

—— Third edition. pp. 60. *Simpkin, Marshall & Co.: London; George Bishop: Wellington College*, [1880.] 8°. **9503**. bb. **16**.

BURT (Llewellyn Charles)

—— A Synoptical History of England . . . Second edition. pp. viii. 146. *Lockwood & Co.: London*, 1874. *obl.* 4°. **9504**. e. **6**.

BURT (Mary Anne) The German Parnassus. Specimens of the choicest lyrical compositions of the most celebrated German poets. Translated in English verse by M. A. Burt. pp. 126. *Leonh. Hitz: Chur*, 1853. 16°. **11525**. bb. **16**.

The title on the wrapper reads " The German Parnassus in twelve different languages. English part . . . volume 1," *but no more was published.*

—— Specimens of the Choicest Lyrical Productions of the Most Celebrated German Poets. From Klopstock to the present time. Translated by M. A. Burt. 2 vol. pp. 266. *E. Kiesling: Zürich*, [1853.] 16°. **11522**. a. 5

Vol. 1 *is another copy with a different titlepage of " The German Parnassus."*

—— [Another edition.] With biographical and literary notes . . . Second edition. pp. viii. 503. *The Author: London; Zuric* printed, 1856 [1855]. 8°. **11525**. c. **13**.

BURT (Mary Elizabeth) *See* Kipling (Rudyard) [*Selections.*] Kipling Stories and Poems every child should know . . . Edited by M. E. Burt, *etc.* 1909. 8°. **12635**. de. **11**.

—— *See* Lorenzini (C.) Adventures every Child should know. The marvellous adventures of Pinocchio . . . Edited by M. E. Burt, *etc.* 1909. 8°. **12316**. tt. **7**.

—— *See* Virgilius Maro (P.) [*Georgica.—English.*] Bees. A study from Vergil. Revised & adapted from Davidson's translation . . . by M. E. Burt. [1889.] 8°. **7205**. de. **1**. **(2.)**

—— Browning's Women . . . With an introduction by Rev. Edward Everett Hale. pp. xi. 225. *C. H. Kerr & Co.: Chicago*, 1887. 12°. **11826**. p. **28**.

—— The Child-Life Primary Reading and Education Chart . . . Illustrated . . . A complete course of primary study, *etc.* 25 sheets. *Ginn & Co.: Boston*, [1896.] fol. Cup. **649**. d. **12**.

—— Literary Landmarks. A guide to good reading for young people, *etc.* pp. 152. *Houghton, Mifflin & Co.: Boston & New York*, 1889. 8°. **11851**. bbb. **19**.

—— Poems that every Child should know. A selection of the best poems of all times for young people. Edited by M. E. Burt. pp. xxv. 355. *Doubleday, Page & Co.: London; New York* printed, 1904. 8°. **11604**. c. **8**.

BURT (Mary Elizabeth) and MARKHAM (Edwin)

—— The Burt-Markham Primer. The nature method. pp. 119. *Ginn & Co.: Boston*, [1907.] 8°. **12984**. bb. **44**.

BURT (Maxwell Struthers)

—— Along These Streets. pp. 344. *Rich & Cowan: London*, 1943. 8°. **012634**. m. **84**.

—— The Delectable Mountains. pp. 383. *Hodder & Stoughton: London*, [1927.] 8°. **12713**. b. **6**.

—— The Diary of a Dude-Wrangler. pp. viii. 331. *C. Scribner's Sons: New York, London*, 1924. 8°. **10884**. cc. **9**.

—— Entertaining the Islanders. pp. 458. *C. Scribner's Sons: New York*, 1933. 8°. A.N. **1308**.

BURT (Maxwell Struthers)

—— [Another edition.] pp. 422. *Lovat Dickson: London*, 1934. 8°. **12709**. l. **24**.

—— Festival. pp. 374. *Peter Davies: London*, 1931. 8°. NN. **18595**.

—— The Interpreter's House. pp. 319. *Hodder & Stoughton: London*, [1924.] 8°. NN. **9858**.

—— The Other Side. pp. xx. 329. *C. Scribner's Sons: New York, London*, 1928. 8°. **012352**. b. **49**.

—— Philadelphia. Holy experiment, *etc.* [With plates.] pp. 299. *Rich & Cowan: London*, [1947.] 8°. **10413**. t. **12**.

—— The Scarlet Hunter. pp. 318. *Hodder & Stoughton: London*, [1925.] 8°. NN. **10505**.

BURT (Michael)

—— The Case of the Angels' Trumpets, *etc.* pp. 255. *Ward, Lock & Co.: London & Melbourne*, 1947. 8°. NN. **37121**.

—— The Case of the Fast Young Lady. pp. 384. *Ward, Lock & Co.: London & Melbourne*, 1942. 8°. NN. **33438**.

—— The Case of the Laughing Jesuit, *etc.* pp. 253. *Ward, Lock & Co.: London & Melbourne*, 1948. 8°. NN. **37881**.

—— Catch-'em-Alive-O! [A novel.] pp. 320. *W. & R. Chambers: London & Edinburgh*, 1938. 8°. **12643**. pp. **5**.

—— Catch-'em-Alive-O! . . . Revised version, *etc.* pp. 251. *Ward, Lock & Co.: London & Melbourne*, 1944. 8°. **012643**. tt. **2**.

—— The House of Sleep, *etc.* pp. 221. *Ward, Lock & Co.: London & Melbourne*, 1945. 8°. NN. **35675**.

—— Hill Quest. pp. 319. *Ward, Lock & Co.: London & Melbourne*, 1937. 8°. NN. **27002**.

—— Lean Brown Men, *etc.* pp. 317. *Ward, Lock & Co.: London & Melbourne*, 1940. 8°. **012634**. pp. **3**.

—— The Road to Roundabout. pp. 315. *Ward, Lock & Co.: London & Melbourne*, 1937. 8°. NN. **28132**.

—— Secret Orchards. A traveller's tales. pp. 318. *Ward, Lock & Co.: London & Melbourne*, 1938. 8°. NN. **16608**.

—— We'll Soldier no more. pp. 288. *Ward, Lock & Co.: London & Melbourne*, 1943. 8°. NN. **33962**.

BURT (Myrtle)

—— *See* Young (Miriam) Mother Wore Tights, *etc.* [An account of the author's mother, Myrtle Burt.] [1944.] 8°. **11797**. b. **23**.

BURT (N.) *of the Naval and Drawing Academy, Tottenham Court Road.* Delineation of Curious Foreign Beasts and Birds in their natural colours; which are to be seen alive at the great room over Exeter Change and at the Lyceum, in the Strand. [Plates, with explanatory text.] pp. 44. *Printed for the Author: London*, 1791. 8°. **956**. h. **12**.

BURT (NATHANAEL) Advice, sent in a Letter from an Elder Brother, to a Younger . . . Relating to remedying and reforming severall abuses in the Common Wealth, by severall practisers pretending equitie and conscience in the High Court of Chancery, and that unsetled, irregular unlimmited Court of Probates, *etc.* pp. 36. *Printed for the Author: London,* 1655. 4°. E. **838.** (**8.**)

—— An Appeal from Chancery, to the Lord General and his Counsel of Officers; also to the Councel of State, and to all free-born English men of honest hearts, *etc.* *For Will. Larnar: London,* 1653. 4°. E. **697.** (**21.**)

—— For every individuall Member of the Honourable House of Commons. Concerning the Major Magstracy, and Officers of Dover. [A letter.] [*London,* 1649.] 4°. E. **568.** (**19.**)

—— An Individuall Letter to every man that calls himselfe a Minister of Jesus Christ. Penned more particularly for Mr. Christopher Love, upon some observations from his sermon, preached Jan. 29. 1644. at Windsor, *etc.* pp. 8. *London,* 1651. 4°. E. **637.** (**7.**)

—— Militarie Instructions, or the Souldier tried, for the vse, of the Dragon, being a part of Cavalrie, for fierings, on horsback, as the Harquebusier, & on foote, as Infantry, very necessary for such as desier to be studious in the waye of the Art Militarie, *etc.* [*London,* 1644.] *s. sh.* fol. **669.** f. **10.** (**9.**)

The title is engraved.

—— A New-yeers Gift for England, and all her Cities, Ports, and Corporations, and all such therein who are fit for the same, and desire it. Or, a gift of God to the wise, this new yeer 1653, to make them a free Commonwealth, *etc.* pp. 11. *Sold by Will. Larnar: London,* 1653. 4°. E. **684.** (**19.**)

BURT (NATHANIEL) *Novelist.*

—— Scotland's burning. pp. 300. *Victor Gollancz: London,* [1954.] 8°. NNN. **5687.**

BURT (NATHANIEL) *of Philadelphia.*

—— Address . . . February 12, 1875, on the Washington Mansion in Philadelphia. pp. 35. 1875. 8°. *See* PHILADELPHIA.—*Historical Society of Pennsylvania.* Ac. **8430/4.** (**2.**)

BURT (NATHANIEL CLARK) The Far East; or, Letters from Egypt, Palestine, and other lands of the Orient. Illustrated, *etc.* pp. 396. *R. W. Carroll & Co.: Cincinnati,* 1868. 12°. **10076.** bbb. **25.**

BURT (OLIVE WOOLLEY)

—— Camel Express. A story of the Jeff Davis experiment . . . Illustrated by Joseph C. Camana. pp. xiii. 178. *John C. Winston Co.: Philadelphia, Toronto,* [1954.] 8°. [*Winston Adventure Books.*] W.P. A. **269/24.**

—— The Oak's Long Shadow . . . Illustrations by Frederick T. Chapman. (A story of the Basque sheepherders in Idaho.) pp. xiii. 240. *John C. Winston Co.: Philadelphia, Toronto,* [1952.] 8°. [*Land of the Free Series.*] W.P. **13266/15.**

—— Our Magic Growth . . . Illustrated by Lily Meldrum. pp. 138. *Caxton Printers: Caldwell, Idaho,* 1937. 4°. **012802.** d. **50.**

—— Peter turns Sheepman, *etc.* pp. 108. *Henry Holt & Co.: New York,* [1952.] 8°. **7295.** r. **26.**

BURT (PETER) Copies of Reports of Experiments made . . . for the purpose of ascertaining the superiority of Burt's Sounding Buoy & Knipper over Massey's Sounding Machine, *etc.* pp. 32. *T. Sotheran: London,* 1819. 8°. **8807.** b. **35.** (**1.**)

BURT (SILAS WRIGHT) *See* BURT (Henry M.) and BURT (S. W.) Early Days in New England, *etc.* 1893. 8°. **9903.** d. **8.**

—— My Memoirs of the Military History of the State of New York during the War for the Union, 1861–65 . . . Edited by the State Historian, *etc.* pp. 192. *Albany,* 1902. 8°. [*War of the Rebellion Series.* no. 1.] A.S. N. **192/3.**

BURT (STANLEY W.)

—— *See* KERCHO (Marvin R.) Use of Recording and Transcribing Equipment in loading Delivery Trucks of Produce Wholesalers. By M. R. Kercho . . . S. W. Burt. 1951. 4°. [*U.S. Department of Agriculture. Agriculture Information Bulletin.* no. 43.] A.S. **824/22.**

BURT (STEPHEN SMITH) Exploration of the Chest in Health and Disease. pp. xiii. 206. *H. K. Lewis: London; printed in America,* 1889. 8°. **7615.** aa. **4.**

BURT (STRUTHERS) *See* BURT (Maxwell S.)

BURT (SYLVESTER) A Funeral Sermon delivered at Belchertown, March 23d, 1809, at the interment of . . . Mrs. Eunice Phelps, *etc.* pp. 21. *William Butler: Northampton* [*Mass.*], 1809. 8°. **4985.** cc. **45.** (**5.**)

—— A History of the Town of Great Barrington. *See* FIELD (David D.) *Rev.* A History of the County of Berkshire, Massachusetts, *etc.* 1829. 12°. **798.** b. **10.**

—— The Solemnity of the Last Day, especially to Ministers and their People, considered in a sermon delivered at Western, January 5, 1812, *etc.* pp. 22. *Thomas Dickman: Springfield, Mass.,* 1812. 8°. **4486.** h. **36.**

BURT (THOMAS) *Preacher of the Word.* The Glory of the Godlie Graine. A most comfortable sermon preached . . . in Paules Church on Whitsunday 1605, *etc.* pp. 44. *N. O.* [*N. Okes*] *for Roger Jackson: London,* 1607. 8°. **696.** a. **41.**

BURT (*Right Hon.* THOMAS) *See* BURT (Henry M.) and BURT (S. W.) Early Days in New England . . . Genealogical and biographical mention of . . . Thomas Burt, M.P., of England. 1893. 8°. **9903.** d. **8.**

—— *See* GILBERT-BOUCHER (M.) Étude sur les "Trade Unions." Un député ouvrier anglais [T. Burt]. 1892. 8°. **08282.** c. **52.**

—— *See* MEECH (Thomas C.) From Mine to Ministry. The life and times of the Right Hon. Thomas Burt. [With portraits.] [1908.] 8°. **010855.** b. **28.**

—— *See* WATSON (Aaron) A Great Labour Leader. Being a life of the Right Hon. Thomas Burt, *etc.* [With a portrait.] 1908. 8°. **010817.** k. **25.**

—— Thomas Burt . . . Pitman & Privy Councillor. An autobiography. With supplementary chapters by Aaron Watson, *etc.* [With portrait.] pp. 319. *T. Fisher Unwin: London,* 1924. 8°. **010856.** f. **11.**

BURT (THOMAS SEYMOUR) *See* also KOI HAI, *pseud.* [i.e. T. S. Burt.]

BURT (Thomas Seymour)

—— *See* Burt (William) *of Plymouth.* Christianity; a poem . . . Edited together with a short memoir of the author by . . . Major T. S. Burt. 1835. 12°. **1116. c. 17.**

—— *See* Burt (William) *of Plymouth.* Observations on the Curiosities of Nature . . . Edited by . . . T. S. Burt. 1836. 12°. **723. g. 19.**

—— *See* Virgilius Maro (P.) [*Works.—Polyglott.*] The Æneid, Georgics, and Eclogues of Virgil rendered into English blank verse . . . By T. S. Burt. *Lat. & Eng.* 1883. 8°. **11355. ff. 9.**

—— A Metrical Epitome of the History of England, prior to the reign of George the First. pp. viii. 76. *Pelham Richardson: London,* 1852. 8°. **11645. ff. 12. (10.)**

—— Miscellaneous Papers on Scientific Subjects, written chiefly in India. 3 vol. *Printed for the Author: London,* 1837–68. 12°. **8703. d. 27.**
Imperfect; wanting vol. 3. pt. 2.

—— Monody on the Death of Her Royal Highness the Duchess of Kent. [Signed: T. S. B., i.e. T. S. Burt.] 1861. *s. sh.* 8°. *See* B., T. S. **11647. e. 1. (164.)**

—— Narrative of a Late Steam Voyage from England to India via the Mediterranean. (Part II. Account of a Late Palankeen Trip from Bombay to Mhow and Lahore.) pp. 125. *Medical Journal Press: Calcutta,* 1840. 8°. **10027. ccc. 2.**

—— [Another edition.] Account of a Voyage to India, via the Mediterranean. pp. viii. 206. *Printed for the Author: London,* 1859. 8°. **10055. aa. 7.**
Imperfect; wanting vol. 2, entitled "A Trip in search of Ancient Inscriptions and other relics in India."

—— Stanzas composed on viewing the Photographic Portrait of Her Royal Highness the Princess Alice. [Signed: T. S. B., i.e. T. S. Burt.] [1861.] *s. sh.* 8°. *See* B., T. S. **11647. e. 1. (165.)**

BURT (William) *of Plymouth. See* also Danmoniensis, *pseud.* [i.e. W. Burt.]

—— *See* Carrington (Nicholas T.) Dartmoor: a descriptive poem . . . with notes by the late W. Burt, *etc.* 1826. 8°. **994. i. 7.**

—— Christianity; a poem, in three books, with miscellaneous notes . . . Edited, together with a short memoir of the author, by . . . Major T. Seymour Burt. pp. xxxii. 435. *Cochrane & Co.: London,* 1835. 12°. **1116. c. 17.**

—— Observations on the Curiosities of Nature . . . Edited by . . . T. Seymour Burt. pp. xviii. 353. *W. H. Allen & Co.: London,* 1836. 12°. **723. g. 19.**

—— Review of the Mercantile, Trading, and Manufacturing State, Interests, and Capabilities of the Port of Plymouth, by W. Burt . . . With miscellaneous additions by other persons, and notes. pp. 270. *Nettleton & Son: Plymouth,* 1816. 8°. **578. f. 19.**

BURT (William) *Warden of Winchester College.* Concio Oxoniæ habita postridie comitiorum July 13. 1658. pro gradu doctoris. pp. 75. *Excudebat H. Hall, impensis Thomæ Robinson: Oxoniæ,* 1659. 12°. **E. 2110. (1.)**

BURT (William Austin) A Key to the Solar Compass, and Surveyor's Companion . . . Also, description of the surveys, and public land system of the United States; notes on the barometer, *etc.* pp. 84. 118. *Printed for the Author: Philadelphia,* 1855. 8°. **8504. aa. 15.**

BURT (William Austin)

—— Reports of W. A. Burt and Bela Hubbard, Esqs. on the geography, topography and geology of the U.S. surveys of the mineral region of the south shore of Lake Superior, for 1845; accompanied by . . . a correct map of the mineral region . . . and also, a chart of Lake Superior, reduced from the British Admiralty Survey. By J. Houghton, Jr. and T. W. Bristol. pp. 109. *Charles Willcox: Detroit,* 1846. 12°. **7105. a. 11.**
The half-title bears the imprint L. Danforth: Buffalo.

BURT (William H.) *M.D.*

—— Physiological Materia Medica . . . Second edition. pp. 979. *Gross & Delbridge: Chicago,* 1881. 8°. **7509. i. 7.**

—— Therapeutics of Tuberculosis; or, Pulmonary consumption. pp. 230. *Boericke & Tafel: New York & Philadelphia,* 1876. 8°. **7615. df. 10.**

BURT (Winifred Mary) *See* Jolley (Prudence F. D.) and Burt (W. M.) Laundrywork, *etc.* [1934.] 4°. **7949.bb.27/1.**

BURTAL (A.) *See* Goizet (J.) Dictionnaire universel du théâtre en France et du théâtre français à l'étranger . . . Avec biographies de tous les auteurs . . . par M. A. Burtal, *etc.* [1867, *etc.*] 8°. **11794. i. 2.**

BURTCHAELL (George Dames) *See* Shaw (William A.) The Knights of England . . . Incorporating a complete list of Knights Bachelors dubbed in Ireland, compiled by G. D. Burtchaell. 2 vol. 1906. 4°. **2102.c.**

—— *See* Wright (William B.) The Boyne Peerage Case . . . With observations on the case and a report of a search made in Ulster's Office by G. D. Burtchaell. 1912. 8°. **9914. w. 11. (5.)**

—— Genealogical Memoirs of the Members of Parliament for the county and city of Kilkenny from the earliest on record to the present time; and for the boroughs of Callan, Thomastown, Inistiogue, Gowran, St. Canice or Irishtown, and Knocktopher, from their enfranchisement to the Union. pp. viii. 276. *Sealy & Co.: Dublin,* 1888. 8°. **10803. e. 4.**

BURTCHAELL (George Dames) and RIGG (James MacMullen)

—— Report on Franciscan Manuscripts preserved at the Convent, Merchants' Quay, Dublin. [A calendar of the collection transferred in 1872 from the Collegio di Sant' Isidoro dei Padri Francescani Irlandesi at Rome.] pp. xii. 296. 1906. 8°. [*Historical Manuscripts Commission.* no. 65.] *See* Dublin.—*Franciscan Convent. Merchants' Quay.* **Bar.T.1.(65.)**

BURTCHAELL (George Dames) and SADLEIR (Thomas Ulick)

—— Alumni Dublinenses. A register of the students, graduates, professors, and provosts of Trinity College . . . Edited by the late G. D. Burtchaell . . . and T. U. Sadleir . . . Illustrated edition. pp. xxiii. 905. 1924. 8°. *See* Dublin.—*University of Dublin.—Trinity College.* **08364. i. 29.**

—— New edition, with supplement. 2 pt. 1935. 8°. *See* Dublin.—*University of Dublin.—Trinity College.* **2094.a.**

—— [Another copy.] **08366. ppp. 2.**

BURTCHAELL (Somerset Brafield) *See* Lignana (G.) Letter on Rome and the Slavs . . . Translated by Rev. S. B. Burtchaell. 1876. 8°. **08028**. h. **71**.

BURTCHETT (Floyd Franklin) Investments and Investment Policy. [With a bibliography.] pp. x. 821. *New York*, 1938. 8°. [*Longmans' Economics Series*.] **8219**.m.1/15.

—— Questions and Problems for Corporation Finance. pp. 55. *Harper & Bros.: New York, London*, 1935. 8°. **8231**. aa. **36**.

BURTÉ (Antoine) Pour la Convention nationale. Des moyens de rectifier l'organisation du Département des Contributions publiques, de la Caisse de l'Extraordinaire, & de la Trésorerie nationale. pp. 60. *Paris*, 1792. 8°. F. **202**. (**6**.)

—— Questions sur les récompenses nationales, soumises au gouvernement, par Burté. pp. 31. *Paris*, [1800.] 8°. F. **521**. (**10**.)

BURTE (Hermann) *pseud.* [i.e. Hermann Struebe.]

—— *See* Dufner-Greif (M.) Der Wiltfeberdeutsche Hermann Burte. [With a portrait.] 1939. 8°. **10709**. f. **37**.

—— *See* Voltaire (F. M. A. de) [*Collections.—Verse.*] Gedichte Voltaires in das Deutsche übertragen von H. Burte. [1934.] 8°. [*Schriften der Corona.* no. 10.] P.P. **4736**. hef.

—— Apollon und Kassandra. Dramatische Dichtung in Versen. pp. 114. *Loerrach*, 1926. 8°. **11748**. k. **39**.

—— Der besiegte Lurch. Ein Gleichnis des Kampfes gegen das Leiden . . . Mit einem Nachwort von Heinrich Berl. pp. 77. *Leipzig*, [1933.] 8°. **012554**. e. **62**.

—— Drei Einakter: Der kranke Koenig. Ein Koenigsdrama. —Donna Ines. Eine Liebes-Tragödie.—Das neue Haus. Lustspiel. In Versen. pp. 150. *Berlin*, 1907. 8°. **11747**. i. **33**.

—— Die Flügelspielerin und ihr Tod. Sonette. pp. 150. *Leipzig*, 1921. 8°. **011528**. k. **80**.

—— Herzog Utz. Ein Schauspiel. [In verse.] pp. 202. *Leipzig*, 1913. 8°. **11748**. de. **50**.

—— Katte. Ein Schauspiel in fünf Aufzügen. pp. 133. *Leipzig*, 1920. 8°. **11747**. bb. **134**.

—— Krist vor Gericht. Drama. pp. 57. *Leipzig*, 1930. 8°. **20003**. cc. **7**.

—— Der letzte Zeuge. Bühnenstück in drei Aufzügen. pp. 133. *Leipzig*, 1921. 8°. **11747**. bb. **107**.

—— Miszellen. 1. [A collection of reprints. With plates.] [*Lörrach*,] 1932. 8°. **12356**. t. **6**.

—— Mit Rathenau am Oberrhein. Fragment aus dem Buche "Weg und Wahl." pp. 30. *Loerrach*, 1925. 4°. **1765**. f. **7**.

One of an edition of fifty copies.

—— Patricia. Sonette. (Zweite Auflage.) pp. 166. *Leipzig*, 1918. 8°. **011528**. f. **103**.

—— Prometheus. Eine Dichtung für die Bühne. pp. 156. *Leipzig*, 1932. 8°. **20003**. cc. **9**.

BURTE (Hermann) *pseud.* [i.e. Hermann Struebe.]

—— Sieben Reden von Burte. pp. 188. *Strassburg*, 1943. 8°. **11865**. i. **23**.

—— Simson. Ein Schauspiel. pp. 277. *Leipzig*, 1917. 8°. **11748**. ff. **38**.

—— Über Spitteler den Dichter. *See* Spitteler (C.) Carl Spitteler. In Memoriam, *etc.* 1925. 8°. **010703**. ee. **9**.

—— Ursula. Gedichte. pp. 318. *Leipzig*, 1930. 8°. **20003**. cc. **8**.

—— Wiltfeber, der ewige Deutsche. Die Geschichte eines Heimatsuchers. pp. 352. *Leipzig*, 1918. 8°. **012554**. ff. **61**.

BURTÉ (Jean Baptiste) *See* Burté (Jean François)

BURTÉ (Jean François)

—— *See* Rome, *Church of.—Congregatio Rituum.* Ordinis fratrum minorum conventualium. Concessionis et approbationis officii et missae in honorem B. Joannis Francisci Burté, *etc.* 1927. fol. **5035**. aa. **57**.

BURTELL (J.) *See* Kenrick (W. S.) and Burtell (J.) A New Fox-hunting Song, *etc.* [1785.] *s. sh.* fol. Rox. iii. **757**.

BURTENBACH (Anton Eberhard Schertel von) *Baron.* *See* Schertel von Burtenbach.

BURTEZ (Alexandre) Catalogue des plantes constituant l'herbier de Louis Gérard [preserved in the Musée Municipal at Draguignan]. Précédé d'une analyse de l'œuvre de ce botaniste. (Extrait du Bulletin de la Société d'études scientifiques et archéologiques de la ville de Draguignan.) pp. 436. 1899. 8°. *See* Draguignan.—*Musée Municipal.* **07031**. i. **11**.

BURTEZ (J. B.) De la suette miliaire. Thèse, *etc.* pp. 36. *Strasbourg*, 1845. 4°. [*Collection générale des dissertations de la Faculté de Médecine de Strasbourg.* sér. 2. tom. 8. année 1845.] **7381**.* c.

BURTHALL (Raunce) *pseud.* An Old Bridle for a Wilde Asse-Colt. Or, the New mystery of iniquity unfolded . . . in a briefe commentary on the second of Peter, chap. 2., *etc.* pp. 16. *For Stephen Dagnall: London*, [1750.] 4°. E. **615**. (**9**.)

BURTHE (Léopold) *See* Longus. Les Pastorales de Longus. Daphnis et Chloé . . . 43 compositions au trait par L. Burthe, *etc.* 1863. fol. **1870**. b. **3**.

BURTHE D'ANNELET, *Family of.*

—— *See* Morant (G. de) *Count.* Notice généalogique sur la maison de Burthe d'Annelet de Rosenthal, *etc.* 1920. 4°. **9918**. k. **21**.

BURTHE D'ANNELET (Jules Louis Charles de) A travers l'Afrique Française. Du Cameroun à Alger, *etc.* [With illustrations.] 2 vol. *Paris*, 1932. 4°. **1791**. d. **12**.

—— À travers l'Afrique française. Du Sénégal au Cameroun par les confins libyens . . . et au Maroc 1935 par les confins sahariens . . . Carnets de route, *etc.* [With illustrations, including a portrait, and maps.] 2 vol. pp. 1549. *Paris*, 1939. 4°. L.R. **106**. b. **19**.

BURTHEN. *See* Burden.

BURTHENS. *See* Burdens.

BURTHOGG (RICHARD) *See* BURTHOGGE.

BURTHOGGE (RICHARD) *See* CARY (Philip) *Apothecary.* A Disputation between a Doctor and an Apothecary; or, a Reply to the new argument of Dr R. Burthogge for infants baptism, *etc.* 1684. 12°. **1018**. c. **13**. (2.)

—— *See* GRUENBAUM (J.) Die Philosophie Richard Burthogges, *etc.* 1939. 8°. **8471**. h. **39**.

—— The Philosophical Writings of Richard Burthogge. Edited with introduction and notes by Margaret W. Landes. pp. xxiv. 245. *Open Court Publishing Co.: Chicago, London,* 1921. 8°. **08463**. h. **17**.

—— Causa Dei, or, an Apology for God. Wherein the perpetuity of infernal torments is evinced, and divine both goodness and justice . . . defended. pp. 422. *For Lewis Punchard: London,* 1675. 8°. **853**. d. **10**. (2.)

—— Christianity a Revealed Mystery; or, the Gracious purpose of God toward the Gentiles, set in a clear light, in some reflections on Rom. VIII. 28, 29, 30 . . . To which is added a brief discourse concerning perseverance in grace, *etc.* pp. 94. *Dan. Brown: London,* 1702. 8°. **4256**. b. **7**.

—— Disputatio medica inauguralis, de lithiasi et calculo, *etc.* *P. de Cro-Y: Lugduni Batavorum,* 1662. 4°. **1185**. g. **5**. (**20**.)

—— An Essay upon Reason, and the Nature of Spirits. pp. 280. *For John Dunton: London,* 1694. 8°. **719**. e. **20**.

—— *See* KEILL (John) An Examination of Dr. Burnet's Theory of the Earth, *etc.* [Including reflections upon R. Burthogge's "Essay upon Reason."] 1698. 8°. **970**. f. **12**.

—— —— 1734. 8°. **970**. f. **13**.

—— The Nature of Church-Government, freely discussed and set out. In three letters. [By R. Burthogge.] pp. 52. [1690.] 4°. *See* NATURE. **4109**. c. **23**.

—— *See* BURSCOUGH (Robert) A Treatise of Church-Government: occasion'd by some letters [by R. Burthogge] lately printed concerning the same subject [entitled "The Nature of Church-Government, fieely discussed and set out"]. 1692. 8°. **858**. e. **19**.

—— Of the Soul of the World; and of particular souls. In a letter to Mr. Lock, occasioned by Mr. Keil's reflections [in his "Examination of Dr. Burnet's Theory of the Earth"] upon an essay lately published concerning reason. By the author of that essay (R. Burthogge). pp. 46. *For Daniel Brown: London,* 1699. 8°. **699**. e. **52**.

—— [Another edition.] 1748. *See* SOMERS (John) *Baron Somers.* A Collection of Scarce and Valuable Tracts, *etc.* vol. 2. 1748. 4°. **184**. a. **2**.

—— [Another edition.] 1814. *See* SOMERS (John) *Baron Somers.* A Collection of Scarce and Valuable Tracts, *etc.* vol. 12. 1809, *etc.* 4°. **750**. g. **12**.

—— Organum vetus & novum. Or, a Discourse of reason and truth. Wherein the natural logick common to mankinde is briefly and plainly described. pp. 73. *For Sam. Crouch: London,* 1678. 8°. **851**. h. **17**.

BURTHOGGE (RICHARD)

—— Prudential Reasons for repealing the Penal Laws against all Recusants, and for a general toleration, penn'd by a Protestant person of quality [i.e. R. Burthogge], *etc.* pp. 11. 1687. 4°. *See* REASONS. T. **763**. (**23**.)

—— Τἀγαθον, or Divine goodness explicated and vindicated from the exceptions of the atheist, *etc.* pp. 134. *S. & B. Griffin, for James Collins: London,* 1672. 8°. **853**. d. **10**. (**1**.)

BURTHOGIUS (RICHARDUS) *See* BURTHOGGE (Richard)

BURTIN (FRANÇOIS XAVIER DE) *See* RELATION. Rélation authentique de la maladie et du trèpas après confession, & des funérailles solemnelles de Messire * * [i.e. F. X. de Burtin]. 1788. 8°. **107**. d. **18**.

—— Epitome dissertationis coronatæ . . . D. Burtin. De aliquot plantarum exoticarum succedaneis in Belgio reperiundis; omnes ejusdem articulos pro parte medica summatim complectens; ex dicto opere, quod Gallicè conscriptum extat, concinnata & latinè recensita à P. E. Wauters. pp. 51. *Gandavi,* 1785. 8°. B. **122**. (**5**.)

—— Oryctographie de Bruxelles, ou Description des fossiles tant naturels qu'accidentels découverts jusqu'à ce jour dans les environs de cette ville. pp. 152. pl. XXXII. [*Bruxelles,*] 1784. fol. **459**. e. **20**.
The titlepage is engraved.

—— [Another copy.] **33**. i. **9**.

—— Réponse à la question physique . . . sur les revolutions générales, qu'a subies la surface de la terre, et sur l'ancienneté de notre globe. (Andwoord op de natuurkundige vraage . . . over de algemeene omkeeringen, welke de aarde aan haare oppervlakte ondergaan heeft, en over de oudheid van onzen aardkloot.) *Fr. & Dutch.* pp. 389. pl. II. *Haarlem,* 1790. 4°. [*Verhandelingen, uitgegeeven door Teyler's Tweede Genootschap.* stuk 8.] Ac. **942/2**.

—— Traité theorique et pratique des connoissances qui sont nécessaires à tout amateur de tableaux . . . suivi d'observations sur les collections publiques et particulières, et de la description des tableaux que possède . . . l'auteur. 2 tom. *Bruxelles,* 1808. 8°. **562***. a. **24**, **25**.

—— Treatise on the Knowledge Necessary to Amateurs in Pictures. Translated and abridged from the French . . . by Robert White. pp. x. 338. *Longman & Co.: London,* 1845. 8°. **562***. b. **28**.

—— Réponse de Messire François Xavier B - - n, à la lettre pastorale du curé de * * *. On y a joint les notes de l'éditeur. [A satire on F. X. de Burtin.] pp. 16. *Burtinopolis [Brussels ?],* 1787. 8°. **108**. a. 4.

BURTIN (MARIE PIERRE AUGUSTE) *See* RIOLS DE FONCLARE (J. E. de) Un Soldat. Le lieutenant Burtin, 1874–1905. Alpes—Vosges—Tunisie—Mandchourie. [With a portrait.] 1907. 8°. **10660**. s. **14**.

BURTIN (NICHOLAS VICTOR) Vie de Catherine Tekakwitha, vierge iroquoise, *etc.* pp. x. 93. *Québec,* 1894. 12°. **4985**. a. **47**.

BURTIN (NICOLAS) Le Baron d'Eckstein. (Un semeur d'idées au temps de la Restauration.) [With a portrait.] pp. xviii. 408. *Paris,* 1931. 8°. **010703**. h. **13**.

BURTIN (PAUL DENIS) *See* ARNAULD (H.) *Bishop of Angers.* Négociations à la cour de Rome et en différentes cours d'Italie, *etc.* [Edited by P. D. Burtin.] 1748. 12°. **1193**. e. **9–13**.

BURTIS (EDGAR L.)

—— *See* TAYLOR (George R.) Barriers to Internal Trade in Farm Products. By G. R. Taylor . . . E. L. Burtis, *etc.* 1939. 4°. A.S. **824/10.**

BURTIS (MARY PENELOPE) **Factors affecting the Accuracy of the Quantitative Determination of Vitamin A. Dissertation,** *etc.* pp. 26. *New York,* 1928. 8°. **7383.** e. **36.**

BURTIS (THOMAS) *See* BURTIS (Thomson)

BURTIS (THOMSON) Daredevils of the Air, *etc.* pp. 215. *Grosset & Dunlap: New York,* [1932.] 8°. A.N. **1394.**

—— Flying Blackbirds, *etc.* pp. v. 242. *Grosset & Dunlap: New York,* [1932.] 8°. A.N. **1239.**

—— Four Aces, *etc.* pp. 216. *Grosset & Dunlap: New York,* [1932.] 8°. A.N. **1413.**

—— Rex Lee, Ace of the Air Mail. pp. 212. *Grosset & Dunlap: New York,* [1929.] 8°. **12813.** m. **11.**

—— Rex Lee, Aerial Acrobat. pp. 279. *Grosset & Dunlap: New York,* [1930.] 8°. **12819.** bb. **18.**

—— Rex Lee, Flying Detective. pp. 277. *Grosset & Dunlap: New York,* [1932.] 8°. A.N. **1412.**

—— Rex Lee, Gypsy Flyer. pp. 248. *Grosset & Dunlap: New York,* [1928.] 8°. **012707.** h. **21.**

—— Rex Lee, Night Flyer. pp. 239. *Grosset & Dunlap: New York,* [1929.] 8°. A.N. **36.**

—— Rex Lee on the Border Patrol. pp. 280. *Grosset & Dunlap: New York,* [1928.] 8°. **12811.** d. **45.**

—— Rex Lee, Ranger of the Sky. pp. v. 212. *Grosset & Dunlap: New York,* [1928.] 8°. **12811.** d. **46.**

—— Rex Lee, Rough Rider of the Air. pp. v. 218. *Grosset & Dunlap: New York,* [1930.] 8°. A.N. **402.**

—— Rex Lee, Sky Trailer. pp. v. 244. *Grosset & Dunlap: New York,* [1929.] 8°. **12715.** bb. **9.**

—— Rex Lee trailing Air Bandits. pp. 215. *Grosset & Dunlap: New York,* [1931.] 8°. A.N. **771.**

—— Rex Lee's Mysterious Flight. pp. 247. *Grosset & Dunlap: New York,* [1930.] 8°. **12813.** d. **17.**

—— Russ Farrell, Airman. pp. 238. *William Heinemann: London; printed in U.S.A.,* 1924. 8°. **12708.** aaa. **23.**

—— Russ Farrell, Border Patrolman. pp. 228. *William Heinemann: London; printed in U.S.A.,* 1927. 8°. NN. **13064.**

—— Russ Farrell over Mexico, *etc.* pp. 221. *Doubleday, Doran & Co.: Garden City, New York,* 1929. 8°. A.N. **35.**

—— Russ Farrell, Test Pilot. pp. 253. *William Heinemann: London; printed in U.S.A.,* 1926. 8°. **12711.** a. **3.**

—— Straight Shooting. Adventures of a film flyer, *etc.* pp. 279. *Doubleday, Doran & Co.: Garden City, New York,* 1931. 8°. A.N. **960.**

—— The War of the Ghosts. A flying adventure story, *etc.* pp. 262. *Doubleday, Doran & Co.: Garden City, New York,* 1932. 8°. **20053.** ee. **8.**

—— Wing for Wing, *etc.* pp. 212. *Grosset & Dunlap: New York,* [1932.] 8°. A.N. **1407.**

BURTIUS (NICOLAUS) Bononia illustrata. [Followed by Latin poems.] *Ex officina Platonis de Benedictis: Bononiæ,* 1494. 4°. IA. **28922.**
38 leaves. Sig. a–d⁸ e⁶. *26 lines to a page.*

—— [Another copy.] MS. NOTES. IA. **28923.**

—— [Another edition.] Nicolai Burtii . . . Bononia illustrata a Johanne Bentivolo II. 1736. *See* MEUSCHEN (J. G.) Vitæ summorum dignitate et eruditione virorum, *etc.* tom. 2. 1735, *etc.* 4°. **1329.** b. **2.**

—— Nicolai Burtii Elogium Bononiæ, *etc.* [A poem.] 1738. *See* MEUSCHEN (J. G.) Vitæ summorum dignitate et eruditione virorum, *etc.* tom. 3. 1735, *etc.* 4°. **1329.** b. **2.**

—— Musarum: nympharumqꝫ: ac sūmorum Deorū epytomata. Liber Ad lectorem.

Scriptoris uitio fuerā mendosus; et a me
Errores: mendas: nunc noua lima leuat, *etc.*

Per Vincentium et fratres de Benedictis: Bononiæ, die xxi. Ianuari, 1498. 4°. IA. **29243.**
44 leaves. Sig. a–e⁸ f⁴. *26 lines to a page.*

—— *Begin.* [fol. 2 *recto*:] Nicolai Burtij parmensis: musices professoris: ac iuris pontificij studiosissimi: musices opusculuꝫ incipit: cum defensione Guidonis aretini: aduersus quendam hyspanum, *etc.* G.L. *Impēsis Bñdicti librarij bonoñ ac suma industria Vgonis de rugerijs: Bonōie,* die vltima aprilis, 1487. 4°. G. **8952.**
68 leaves, the first blank. Sig. a–h⁸ i⁴. 29, 30 *lines to a page. Without the blank leaf.*

—— [Another copy.] Nicolai Burtij parmensis: musices professoris . . . opusculuꝫ incipit, *etc.* *Bonōie,* 1487. 4°. Hirsch I. **94.**

—— [Selected lyrical poems.] 1719. *See* ITALIAN POETS. Carmina illustrium poetarum italorum. tom. 2. 1719, *etc.* 8°. **657.** a. **17.**

BURTON, *Cheshire.—Burton Manor College.*

—— The Burton Manor Supervisory Management Notebook. (General editor: Norman C. Rimmer.) pp. 93. *Newman Neame: London,* 1953. 4°. **08228.** i. **94.**

BURTON, *Herefordshire.* The Dæmon of Burton, *etc.* [Certified in a letter signed: J. A.] 1671. 4°. *See* A., J. **8630.** d. **18.**

BURTON, *Mrs.* Mrs. Burton's Best Bedroom. By the author of "Jessica's First Prayer" [i.e. Sarah Smith], and other readings for working men's homes. With . . . engravings, *etc.* 12 pt. *R.T.S.: London,* [1878.] 4°. **12805.** n. **12.**
A reissue of no. 1–12 *of the series "Books for the People," with a collective titlepage.*

BURTON ABBOTS. Burton Abbots: a woman's story, *etc.* 3 vol. *T. C. Newby: London,* 1863. 8°. **12629.** aaa. **7.**

BURTON DAILY MAIL. Burton Daily Mail's Annual Record. *See* PERIODICAL PUBLICATIONS.—Burton-upon-Trent.—*Burton Daily Mail.*

BURTON FLEMING. The Registers of the Parish Church of Burton Fleming, otherwise North Burton, co. York. 1538–1812. Edited by the Rev. G. E. Park . . . and G. D. Lumb. pp. 118. [*Leeds,*] 1899. 8°. [*Publications of the Yorkshire Parish Register Society.* vol. 2.] Ac. **8136.**

BURTON HISTORICAL COLLECTION LEAFLET.
See DETROIT.—*Public Library.*

BURTON LATIMER.

—— Burton Latimer, Northants. The official guide, *etc.* pp. 16. *Ed. J. Burrow & Co.: Cheltenham & London,* [1952.] 8°. **010360. p. 41.**

BURTON MANOR COLLEGE. *See* BURTON, *Cheshire.*

BURTON-ON-TRENT GOLF CLUB. *See* BURTON-UPON-TRENT.

BURTON-ON-TRENT LICENSED VICTUALLERS' FRIENDLY AND PROTECTION SOCIETY.
See BURTON-UPON-TRENT.

BURTON-ON-TRENT NATURAL HISTORY AND ARCHAEOLOGICAL SOCIETY. *See* BURTON-UPON-TRENT.

BURTON-ON-TRENT RED BOOK. *See* EPHEMERIDES.

BURTON-UPON-TRENT.

MUNICIPAL INSTITUTIONS.

CORPORATION.

Museum and Art Gallery Committee.

—— [For the Annual Reports and Bulletins of the Public Library, Museum and Art Gallery, and Subscription Library:] *See* infra: *Public Library Committee.*

Public Library Committee.

—— Third [*etc.*] Annual Report of Public Library, Museum and Art Gallery, and Subscription Library, *etc.* *Burton-on-Trent,* [1926– .] 8° & 4°. **A.R.622.**
From 1936 *onwards reproduced from typewriting.*

—— Burton-upon-Trent Public Library, Museum and Art Gallery Bulletin. no. 13–37. June 1929—Sept. 1934. *Burton,* 1929–34. 8°.
[Continued as:]
The Burton-upon-Trent Bulletin. New series. [vol. 1.] no. 1.—vol. 4. no. 8. Jan. 1935—Dec. 1938. [*Burton,*] 1935–38. 8°.
[Continued as:]
The Book Quarterly. (The journal of the Public Library, Museum and Art Gallery, Burton-upon-Trent.) vol. 1. no. 1(-8.) Jan. 1939(-Oct. 1940.) [*Burton,*] 1939, 40. 8°. P.P. **6490.** ft.

—— Burton-upon-Trent Public Library, Museum and Art Gallery Bulletin.
[Continued as:]
The Reader's Handbook. Jan. 1941, *etc.* [*Burton,*] 1941– . 8°. P.P. **6490.** ft.

County Borough Council.

—— **The Tenants' Handbook,** *etc.* **(Municipal Tenants' Handbook.)** ***Ed. J. Burrow & Co.: Cheltenham & London,*** [1953– .] 8°. **8288. b. 120.**
Various editions.

MUSEUM AND ART GALLERY.

—— [For the Annual Reports and Bulletins of the Public Library, Museum and Art Gallery, and Subscription Library:] *See* supra: CORPORATION.—*Public Library Committee.*

BURTON-UPON-TRENT.

PUBLIC LIBRARY.

—— [For the Annual Reports and Bulletins of the Public Library, Museum and Art Gallery, and Subscription Library:] *See* supra: CORPORATION.—*Public Library Committee.*

—— [Lists of books on special subjects in the Burton-upon-Trent Public Library.] [*Burton-upon-Trent,* 1938– .] 8°. W.P. **8530.**

—— Wartime Service. pp. 7. *Burton-upon-Trent,* [1939.] 8°. **11900.** cc. **87.**
Reproduced from typewriting.

MISCELLANEOUS INSTITUTIONS.

ABBATIA BURTONENSIS.

—— *See* infra: MONASTERIUM DE BURTONA SUPER TRENT.

ARTS AND CIVIC COUNCIL.

—— Festival 1951 . . . Edited by K. F. Stanesby. [With illustrations.] pp. 64. *Burton-upon-Trent,* 1951. 8°. **010368.** pp. **64.**

BURTON-ON-TRENT GOLF CLUB.

—— Burton-on-Trent Golf Club, Ltd., *etc.* (Official handbook.) pp. 16. *New Centurion Publishing & Publicity Co.: Derby & Cheltenham,* [1933.] 8°. **07912.** e. **130.**

BURTON-ON-TRENT LICENSED VICTUALLERS' FRIENDLY AND PROTECTION SOCIETY.

—— Licensed Victuallers' Association Annual Dinner. Extracted from the " Burton Chronicle," *etc.* pp. 15. *Arthur Stebbings: Lowestoft,* [1884.] 8°. **8435.** de. **13.** (2.)

BURTON-ON-TRENT NATURAL HISTORY AND ARCHAEOLOGICAL SOCIETY.

—— Transactions, *etc.* vol. 1–7. *London,* 1889–1914. 8°. Ac. **3007.** b.

COMMERCIAL DEVELOPMENT COMMITTEE.

—— Burton-on-Trent . . . The official handbook, 1921–22 [*etc.*]. [With plans.] *E. J. Burrow & Co.: Cheltenham & London,* [1921– .] 8°. **10360.** s. **8.**

HOLY TRINITY CHAPEL.

—— *See* TRINITY.—*Church of the Holy Trinity, Burton-upon-Trent.*

MONASTERIUM DE BURTONA SUPER TRENT.

—— Annales Monasterii Burtonensis. Ab anno M.IV. ad annum M.CC.LXIII. *See* ENGLAND. [*Appendix.—History and Politics.*—I.] Rerum anglicarum scriptorum veterum tom. I., *etc.* 1684. fol. **9502.h.13.**

—— Annales Monasterii de Burton, 1004–1263, from MS. Cotton. Vespas. E. iii. 1864. *See* ENGLAND. [*Appendix.—History and Politics.*—I.] Rerum britannicarum medii ævi scriptores, *etc.* (Annales monastici. vol. 1.) 1858, *etc.* 8°. **2073. (36.)**

—— The Burton Chartulary . . . (An abstract. By Major-General Hon. G. Wrottesley.) 1884. *See* STAFFORD.—*William Salt Archaeological Society, etc.* Collections, *etc.* vol. 5. pt. 1. 1880, *etc.* 8°. Ac. **5704.**

BURTON-UPON-TRENT.

—— The Burton Chartulary. Derbyshire portion. By General the Hon. George Wrottesley. 1885. *See* DERBY.—*Derbyshire Archaeological and Natural History Society.* Journal, *etc.* vol. 7. 1879, *etc.* 8°. Ac. **5633.**

—— Descriptive Catalogue of the Charters and Muniments (of Burton Abbey) belonging to the Marquis of Anglesea, sometime preserved at Beaudesert but now at Plas Newydd, Isle of Anglesey. Compiled with introduction and index by I. H. Jeayes. [With a preface by Margaret Deanesly.] pp. lxix. 219. 1937. 8°. [*Collections for a History of Staffordshire.* 1937.] *See* PAGET (Charles H. A.) *Marquis of Anglesey.* Ac. **5704.**

APPENDIX.

—— A Glass of Pale Ale and a Visit to Burton. [A description of Bass, Ratcliff & Gretton's brewery.] pp. 32. *Wyman & Sons: London,* 1880. 8°. **7945.** bb. **6.**

—— Symposium Burtonense, *etc.* [A skit on a Liberal Party meeting at Burton-on-Trent. Signed: J. B. S.] [1885?] *s. sh.* 8°. *See* S., J. B. **8052.** i. **1.** **(134.)**

BURTON'S YARMOUTH ALMANAC. *See* EPHEMERIDES.

BURTON, *Family of.* *See* HARRISON (Francis B.) Burton Chronicles of Colonial Virginia, *etc.* [With genealogical tables.] 1933. 8°. **09917.** ee. **35.**

BURTON (A. W.)

—— The Highlands of Kaffraria. A review of outstanding incidents in Kafirland and British Kaffraria leading up to the rise of King William's Town, Keiskama Hoek and East London, with special reference to the history and situation of Fort Stokes . . . Illustrated with maps and road routes. pp. 56. *King William's Town,* 1942. 8°. **10095.** s. **22.**

BURTON (AGNES) *See* MAPLES (Ellen) afterwards COOK (E. G.) Personal Service. Being a short memoir of Agnes Burton, *etc.* 1913. 8°. **4908.** d. **3.**

BURTON (ALAN CHADBURN) and **EDHOLM** (OTTO GUSTAF)

—— Man in a Cold Environment. Physiological and pathological effects of exposure to low temperatures. pp. xiv. 273. *Edward Arnold: London,* 1955. 8°. [*Monographs of the Physiological Society.* no. 2.] Ac. **3823.** c/**2.**

BURTON (ALBERT HAROLD GODWIN) The Tuberculosis Handbook for Health Visitors and Nurses, *etc.* pp. viii. 58. *Scientific Press: London,* [1914.] 8°. **07561.** g. **56.**

BURTON (ALBERTA N.) *See* CRAINE (Edith J.) and BURTON (A. N.) Happy Days out West for Littlebits. [1927.] 8°. **12809.** l. **21.**

—— *See* CRAINE (Edith J.) and BURTON (A. N.) Littlebits, *etc.* [1926.] 8°. **012808.** bb. **41.**

BURTON (ALEXANDER BRADLY) Agencies at work for the Amelioration of our Home Population. A lecture. *See* SIGNS. Signs of the Times, *etc.* pt. 1. 1854. 8°. **4461.** b. **38.**

BURTON (ALFRED) *Canon of Perth, Western Australia.*

—— *See* WOLLASTON (John R.) Wollaston's Picton Journal, 1841–1844 . . . (Wollaston's Albany Journals, 1848–1856.) Collected by . . . A. Burton, *etc.* 1948, *etc.* 8°. **9781.** b. **37.**

BURTON (ALFRED) *of Manchester.* Rush-bearing: an account of the old custom of strewing rushes; carrying rushes to church; the rush-cart; garlands in churches; morris-dancers; the wakes; the rush. [With plates.] pp. x. 189. *Brook & Chrystal: Manchester,* 1891. 4°. **10360.** g. **26.**

BURTON (ALFRED) *pseud.* [i.e. JOHN MITFORD.] The Adventures of Johnny Newcome in the Navy. A poem in four cantos: with plates by Rowlandson, from the author's designs. pp. 259. *W. Simpkin & R. Marshall: London,* 1818. 8°. **C.116.bb.9.**

—— A new edition. pp. 246. *Methuen & Co.: London,* 1904. 8°. [*Illustrated Pocket Library of Plain and Coloured Books.*] **012203.** f. **32/13.**

BURTON (ALFRED) *Vicar of Stetchworth.* A Handbook on Clerical Elocution, for the use of the clergy, students, &c. pp. 39. *Skeffington & Son: London,* [1904.] 8°. **4499.** de. **18.**

—— Hints on Elocution for the Clergy, *etc.* pp. 31. *Skeffington & Son: London,* [1925.] 8°. **011805.** e. **71.**

BURTON (ALFRED HENRY) *See* BIBLE.—*Appendix.* [*Miscellaneous.*] The Bible: is it a revelation from God? *etc.* [By J. N. Darby. Edited by A. H. Burton.] 1892. 8°. **3129.** ee. **30.**

—— *See* DARBY (John N.) The Irrationalism of Infidelity . . . Abridged. [Edited by A. H. Burton.] [1890.] 8°. **4017.** f. **13.**

—— *See* NEWMAN (John H.) *Cardinal.* Analysis of Cardinal Newman's "Apologia pro Vita Sua," *etc.* [Edited by A. H. Burton.] 1891. 8°. **3940.** c. **6.**

—— *See* PERIODICAL PUBLICATIONS.—*London.* Echoes of Mercy. [Edited by A. H. Burton.] 1891, *etc.* 8°. P.P. **718.** bab.

—— The Apocalypse Expounded. pp. 279. *Advent Witness Office: London,* 1932. 8°. **2204.aa.15.**

—— The Assyrian. *See* CACHEMAILLE (E. P.) The Warfare of the End, *etc.* 1920. 8°. W.P. **2834/19.**

—— A Call to Confession: being a few remarks on part of the mission held at St. Leonard's-on-Sea during November, 1891 . . . Second edition. pp. 22. *James Carter: London,* [1891.] 8°. **3942.** e. **1.** **(3.)**

—— The Christian's Library . . . Edited by A. H. Burton. 12 vol. *James Carter: London,* [1899]–1910. 8°. **03605.** de. **9.**

From vol. 2. onwards issued in monthly parts and numbered accordingly. No more published after vol. 12. *no.* 123, *March* 1910. *The wrappers of the monthly parts forming vol.* 2–5 *are wanting.*

—— Does "Eternal" mean "Eternal"? pp. 15. *James Carter: London,* [1900.] 32°. **04420.** de. **8.** **(2.)**

—— Echoes of Mercy Hymn Book. *See* infra: Hymns for Special Services.

—— Echoes of Mercy Hymn Sheet. *See* infra: Hymns for Special Services.

—— Echoes of Mercy Leaflets. [Tracts reprinted from "Echoes of Mercy." Signed for the most part: A. H. B., i.e. A. H. Burton.] 16 no. [1893.] 12°. *See* B., A. H. **4421.** de. **31.**

BURTON (ALFRED HENRY)

—— Echoes of Mercy Series. [Tracts by A. H. Burton and others. Reprinted from "Echoes of Mercy."] no. 1–8, 11–14, 17–19. *James Carter: London*, [1893.] 24°. **4418**. de. **1**.
Imperfect; wanting no. 9, 10, 15, 16.

—— Falling away: what is it? or, Can a real believer ever be lost? By A. H. B. (A. H. Burton.) pp. 23. *Clarendon Tract Depot: London*, [1893.] 12°. **4418**. cc. **50**. (**4**.)

—— The Free Action of the Spirit. pp. 32. *James Carter: London*, [1905.] 8°. **4373**. a. **50**. (**5**.)

—— The Future of Europe; politically and religiously, in the light of Holy Scripture. pp. 62. *James Carter: London*, [1896.] 8°. **3187**. a. **75**.

—— Second edition. pp. 62. *James Carter: London*, [1897.] 8°. **3187**. aaa. **28**.

—— Third edition. pp. 64. *James Carter: London*, 1904. 8°. **03129**. e. **15**. (**2**.)

—— Fifth edition. pp. 64. *Pickering & Inglis: Glasgow*, 1917. 8°. **3187**. aaa. **58**.

—— God Left Out. Remarks on the present national crisis. pp. 15. *S. W. Partridge & Co.: London*, [1900.] 8°. **4109**. ee. **16**. (**3**.)

—— The Great Coronation and the Coming of the King. [A religious tract.] pp. 8. *James Carter: London*, [1902.] 8°. **04420**. g. **49**. (**3**.)

—— Hints on the Book of Daniel. [Reprinted from "The Christian's Library."] pp. viii. 219. *James Carter: London*, [1903.] 8°. **03187**. h. **4**.

—— [A reissue.] *Pickering & Inglis: Glasgow*, [1917.] 8°. [*Every Christian's Library*.] **03560**. h. **1/17**.

—— Hymns for Special Services. (Echoes of Mercy Hymn Book.) Compiled by A. H. B. [i.e. A. H. Burton.] Third edition, revised. pp. 64. [1893.] 16°. *See* B., A. H. **3436**. de. **11**. (**2**.)

—— [Another edition.] Echoes of Mercy Hymn Book . . . Compiled by A. H. Burton. pp. 192. *James Carter: London*, [1900.] 32°. **3436**. aaaa. **6**.

—— [Another edition of no. 1–36.] The Echoes of Mercy Hymn Sheet. no. 1. Compiled by A. H. B. [i.e. A. H. Burton.] [1893.] fol. *See* B., A. H. **3433**. i. **21**.

—— The Man of Sin: how, when, and where will he be judged? pp. 46. *James Carter: London*, [1896.] 24°. **03128**. e. **4**. (**1**.)

—— Methodism and the Bible. A series outlook. pp. 16. *James Carter: London*, [1894.] 8°. **4139**. bbb. **23**. (**6**.)

—— (Third edition.) pp. 15. *James Carter: London*, [1898.] 8°. **4139**. bbb. **28**. (**3**.)

—— The Midnight Cry; or, the Hope of the Church of God. By A. H. B. (A. H. Burton.) pp. 30. *Clarendon Tract Depot: London*, [1893.] 8°. **4418**. cc. **50**. (**5**.)

—— The Order of Corporate Reunion. Reminiscences of one of its "Bishops" [i.e. T. W. Mossman]. pp. 31. *James Carter: London*, [1899.] 8°. **4109**. de. **6**. (**4**.)

—— Priestly Absolution. A letter to an inquirer. pp. 32. *James Carter: London*, [1899.] 8°. **4109**. de. **6**. (**3**.)

BURTON (ALFRED HENRY)

—— Prophetic Outlines. pp. 34. *James Carter: London*, [1897.] 12°. **4422**. dddd. **49**. (**4**.)

—— The Prospects of the World; or, the Day of the Lord. By A. H. B. (A. H. Burton.) pp. 23. *Clarendon Tract Depot: London*, [1893.] 12°. **4418**. cc. **50**. (**6**.)

—— Rationalism or Revelation; which shall it be? Being the editor's preface to The Bible, is it a revelation from God? *etc.* pp. 8. *James Carter: London*, [1893.] 12°. **4422**. d. **16**. (**5**.)

—— The Real Presence. Brief remarks on the Archbishop of Canterbury's Charge to his Clergy, October 1898 . . . Reprinted from "Echoes of Mercy." pp. 31. *James Carter: London*, [1899.] 8°. **4109**. de. **6**. (**2**.)

—— Ritualism and the Reformation. pp. 15. *James Carter: London*, [1900.] 8°. **4109**. ee. **16**. (**4**.)

—— Ritualism or Christianity. Which is true? Being the editor's preface to "An Analysis of the late Cardinal Newman's 'Apologia pro Vita Sua,'" &c. pp. 8. *James Carter: London*, [1893.] 12°. **3939**. aa. **42**. (**6**.)

—— Russia's Destiny in the Light of Prophecy. pp. 61. *James Carter: London*, [1897.] 8°. **3187**. aaa. **26**.

—— Fifth edition. pp. 64. *Pickering & Inglis: Glasgow*, 1917. 8°. **3187**. aaa. **59**.

—— Spiritualism: is it real? pp. 22. *James Carter: London*, [1897.] 12°. **08631**. f. **11**. (**4**.)

—— The Three Judgments. By A. H. B. (A. H. Burton.) pp. 24. *Clarendon Tract Depot: London*, [1893.] 12°. **4418**. cc. **50**. (**7**.)

—— The Two Resurrections. By A. H. B. (A. H. Burton.) pp. 23. *Clarendon Tract Depot: London*, [1893.] 12°. **4418**. cc. **50**. (**8**.)

—— What is Exclusivism? A review of Mr. Alex. Marshall's "Holding Fast the Faithful Word." pp. 16. *James Carter: London*, 1908. 8°. **4106**. ee. **2**. (**1**.)

—— "Words of Life" Hymn Sheet. 3 no. *James Carter: London*, [1893.] 8°. **3437**. i. **19**.

—— Windows on the World. A record of the life of A. H. Burton . . . With selections from his writings . . . Selected by . . . F. W. Pitt. [With a portrait.] pp. 162. *Pickering & Inglis: London*, [1938.] 8°. **20031**. g. **50**.

BURTON (ALFRED HENRY) and SAINT JOHN (HAROLD)

—— Songs of Grace and Glory. Compiled by A. H. Burton & Harold St. John. pp. 40. *James Carter: London*, [1905.] 16°. **3436**. ee. **44**.

BURTON (ALFRED RICHARD EDWARD) Cape Colony for the Settler. An account of its urban and rural industries, their probable future development and extension, *etc.* [With maps and illustrations.] pp. ix. 355. *P. S. King & Son: London; J. C. Juta & Co.: Cape Town*, 1903. 8°. **010095**. gg. **15**.

—— Cape Colony To-day . . . Illustrated. pp. viii. 315. *Townshend, Taylor & Snashall: Cape Town*, 1907. 4°. **10097**. h. **35**.

BURTON (Alfred W.)

—— Sparks from the Border Anvil. [A record of events in the border districts of Cape Province. With plates.] pp. xviii. 293. *Provincial Publishing Co.: [King William's Town,]* 1950. 8°. **9062**. bbb. **28**.

BURTON (Alice Elizabeth) ***Novelist. See* also Kerby (Susan A.) *pseud.* [i.e. A. E. Burton.]**

—— Cling to Her, Waiting. [A novel.] pp. 268. *Andrew Dakers: London,* 1939. 8°. NN. 30995.

BURTON (Asa) *See* Periodical Publications.—*Middlebury, Vermont.* The Adviser . . . The editors . . . A. Burton, G. C. Lyman, *etc.* 1809, *etc.* 8°. P.P. **864**. aa. (**1**.)

—— A Discourse delivered before . . . Thomas Chittenden, Esquire, Governor, the Honourable Council and House of Representatives of the State of Vermont . . . October 8th, 1795, being the day of general election. pp. 35. *Rutland, Vt.,* 1795. 8°. **4485**. c. **10**.

—— Essays on some of the First Principles of Metaphysicks, Ethicks, and Theology. pp. 414. *Mirror Office: Portland [Me.],* 1824. 8°. **8404**. dd. **24**.

—— A Sermon delivered at Montpelier, Vermont, at the ordination of the Rev. Chester Wright, *etc.* pp. 24. *Samuel Goss: Peacham, Vt.,* 1809. 8°. **4486**. g. **29**.

—— A Sermon delivered at the Installation of St. John's Lodge of Free and Accepted Masons, in Thetford, Vermont, *etc.* pp. 22. *George Hough: Concord,* 1816. 8°. **4486**. h. **39**.

—— A Sermon delivered at the Ordination of the Rev. Thomas Abbot Merrill . . . at Middlebury, *etc.* pp. 29. *J. D. Huntington: Middlebury, Vt.,* 1806. 8°. **4486**. h. **37**.

—— A Sermon, preached at the Ordination of the Rev. Caleb J. Tenney, to the pastoral care of the First Congregational Church of Christ, in Newport, *etc.* pp. 24. *Office of the Newport Mercury: Newport [R. I.],* 1804. 8°. **4487**. e. **8**. (**7**.)

—— A Sermon preached at the Ordination of the Rev. Timothy Clark to the pastoral care of the Church of Christ in Greenfield, *etc.* pp. 24. *Alden Spooner: Windsor, Vt.,* 1800. 8°. **4486**. g. **28**.

—— The Works of God, an important study. A sermon delivered . . . at the ordination of the Rev. Benjamin White, to the pastoral care of the First Church of Christ in Wells, *etc.* pp. 23. *J. K. Remich: Kennebunk, Me.,* 1811. 8°. **4486**. h. **38**.

BURTON (Barbara) *See* Burton (Frances B.)

BURTON (Bartin) Jesus Christ God and Man—and the Necessity, on Scripture principles, of his being so, for the effecting of the salvation of the believing world, asserted and proved: in a sermon preached at a late visitation of the Revd. John Taylor, *etc.* pp. 27. *E. Withers: London,* 1756. 8°. **225**. g. **9**. (**7**.)

BURTON (Basil)

—— *See* Hall (Norman) *Writer on Photography,* and Burton (B.) Great Photographs, *etc.* [1954, *etc.*] *obl.* 8°. W.P. d. 815.

BURTON, afterwards **MORGAN** (Beatrice Payne) Easy. pp. 306. *Grosset & Dunlap: New York,* [1930.] 8°. A.N. **261**.

BURTON, afterwards **MORGAN** (Beatrice Payne)

—— The Flapper Wife. pp. 344. *Grosset & Dunlap: New York,* [1925.] 8°. **12709**. cc. **8**.

—— Footloose. Sequel to "The Flapper Wife." pp. 241. *Grosset & Dunlap: New York,* [1926.] 8°. **12710**. aa. **3**.

—— Her Man. pp. 376. *Grosset & Dunlap: New York,* [1926.] 8°. **12710**. dd. **1**.

—— The Hollywood Girl. pp. 380. *Grosset & Dunlap: New York,* [1927.] 8°. **12712**. bbb. **18**.

—— Honey Lou, the love wrecker. pp. 303. *Grosset & Dunlap: New York,* [1927.] 8°. **12712**. bb. **14**.

—— The Little Yellow House. pp. 310. *Doubleday, Doran & Co.: Garden City, New York,* 1928. 8°. **12714**. bb. **24**.

—— [Another edition.] pp. 311. *Hodder & Stoughton: [London,* 1929.] 8°. **12715**. cc. **22**.

—— Love Bound. pp. 382. *Grosset & Dunlap: New York,* [1926.] 8°. **12710**. cc. **5**.

—— Lovejoy. pp. 320. *Hodder & Stoughton: London,* [1931.] 8°. NN. **17547**.

—— Money Love. pp. 372. *Grosset & Dunlap: New York,* 1928. 8°. **12714**. bb. **22**.

—— The Petter. pp. 353. *Grosset & Dunlap: New York,* 1927. 8°. **12712**. b. **10**.

—— Sally's Shoulders. pp. 343. *Grosset & Dunlap: New York,* [1928.] 8°. **12713**. c. **28**.

BURTON (Benjamin) Benjamin Burton, Esq.; and Richard Nutley, Esq.; Appellants. John Slattery, Gent. Respondent. The appellants case. pp. 3. *[London,* 1725.] fol. **19**. h. **2**. (**152**.)

BURTON (C.) A Miraculous Escape, and four other stories. pp. 47. *A. H. Stockwell: London,* [1918.] 8°. **12611**. f. **27**.

BURTON (C.) *F.B.P.S.* Drunkards, Moderate Drinkers, Teetotalers. The people classified, and analysed to show their relation to the subject of temperance, as shown by the teachings of psychology, phrenology, physiognomy, graphology, palmistry, facts and figures, *etc.* pp. 38. *L. N. Fowler & Co.: London,* 1902. 8°. **8436**. eee. **42**.

BURTON (C. D.) How to do without a Trial Balance . . . A manual for book-keepers. pp. 43. *Book-keeper Publishing Co.: Detroit,* [1900.] *obl.* 8°. **8231**. de. **12**.

BURTON (C. E.) Burton's Amateur Actor, a complete guide to private theatricals, *etc.* pp. 150. *Dick & Fitzgerald: New York,* [1876.] 8°. **11795**. bb. **5**.

BURTON (C. S.) Phyllis: a pastoral play in one act. pp. 24. *Bunny & Davies: Shrewsbury,* [1887.] 8°. **11779**. bb. **13**. (**3**.)

BURTON (Caroline) *See* Williams (John) *a Negro and Ship's Cook.* A Full Account of a most Diabolical Murder, of C. Burton, by J. Williams, a black man, also giving the particulars of the discovery of a . . . murder, committed by him on the bodies of two sisters, and a child. [1842.] 8°. **6056**. r. **7**. (**2**.)

—— *See* Williams (John) *a Negro and Ship's Cook.* A Full Account of a most revolting rape and murder committed by J. Williams . . . on the body of C. Burton, *etc.* [1842.] 16°. **6495**. bb. **3**. (**2**.)

BURTON (CATHARINE) *See* MARY XAVERIA, *of the Angels* [C. Burton].

BURTON (CECIL GEORGE) *See* BURSTALL (Frederic W.) and BURTON (C. G.) Souvenir History of the Foundation & Development of the Mason Science College and of the University of Birmingham, *etc.* [1930.] 4°. **8364.** k. **29.**

BURTON (CHARLES) *Barrister-at-Law.* *See* BRUCE (George Evans) *of Limerick.* An Authentic Report of the . . . Trial for a Libel contained in the . . . poem called "The Nosegay" . . . Containing the speeches of Messrs. Goold . . . Burton, *etc.* [1816.] 8°. **6495.** c. **5.** (**1.**)

BURTON (CHARLES) *Captain.* Journal of a Voyage from London to Madeira and thence to New Providence and back again to London in the snow Thames of London. pp. 56. *George Robinson: London,* 1805. 8°. **C.108.dd.4.**

BURTON (CHARLES) *Rector of All Saints, Manchester.* The Bardiad, a poem . . . Second edition. With copious critical notes, *etc.* pp. xiii. 286. ii. *Longman & Co.: London,* 1823. 8°. **994.** k. **7.**

—— The Church and Dissent. An appeal to Independents, Presbyterians, Methodists, and other sects, on the constitution of the Church of England, and the character and unreasonableness of schism and dissent. pp. 46. *Hatchard & Son: London,* 1840. 8°. **4135.** a. **19.**

—— "The Comet," a sermon, *etc.* pp. 16. *William Bremner: Manchester,* [1858.] 8°. **4475.** de. **5.** (**13.**)

—— Conversion of the Jews. A sermon, *etc.* pp. 20. *J. Gleave & Son: Manchester,* 1824. 8°. **4452.** cc. **7.** (**3.**)

—— A Demonstration of Catholic Truth, by a plain and final argument, against the Socinian heresy. A discourse, *etc.* pp. 27. *Beresford & Galt: Manchester,* 1853. 8°. **4224.** e. **57.** (**6.**)

—— A Discourse on Protestantism . . . delivered on . . . March 26, 1837 on the occasion of admitting two Roman Catholics to the Protestant communion. (Second edition.) pp. 72. *L. & G. Seeley: London,* [1837.] 12°. **908.** c. **4.** (**13.**)

—— Discourses suited to these Eventful and Critical Times. pp. 183. *Holdsworth & Ball: London,* 1832. 8°. **4473.** g. **6.** (**13.**)

—— Lectures on Popery, *etc.* pp. 60. *J. Galt & Co.: Manchester,* 1851. 12°. **3939.** f. **31.**

—— Lectures on the Deluge and the World after the Flood. [With appendices.] 2 pt. *Hamilton, Adams & Co.; Hatchard & Son: London,* 1845. 8°. **1354.** h. **11.** (**2.**)

—— Lectures on the Millennium, the new heavens and new earth, and the recognition and intercourse of beatified saints. pp. xxvi. 298. *Hamilton, Adams & Co: London,* 1841. 8°. **1115.** f. **16.**

—— Lectures on the World before the Flood. [With appendices.] 2 pt. *Hamilton, Adams & Co.: London,* 1844. 8°. **1354.** h. **11.** (**1.**)

—— Psalms and Hymns, selected and arranged for the use of All-Saints' Church, Grosvenor Square, Manchester . . . By the Rev. C. Burton. pp. 468. 1820. 8°. *See* BIBLE.—*Psalms.—Selections.* [*English.*] **3434.** bb. **29.**

BURTON (CHARLES) *Rector of All Saints, Manchester.*

—— Psalms and Hymns, selected and arranged for the use of All-Saints' Church . . . Manchester . . . Fifth edition. pp. 468. 1853. 12°. *See* BIBLE.—*Psalms.—Selections.* [*English.*] **3091.** df. **24.**

—— Sentiments appropriate to the Present Crisis of Unexampled Distress. A sermon, *etc.* pp. 18. *J. Gleave & Son: Manchester,* 1826. 8°. **4475.** cc. **112.** (**10.**)

—— A Sermon on the Parable of the Barren Fig-tree. pp. 53. *Longman & Co.: London,* 1823. 8°. **695.** g. **7.** (**19.**)

—— Solemn Warning to Youth. A sermon occasioned by the untimely death of Joseph Dale . . . who was executed at Chester . . . as accessory to the murder of Mr. William Wood of Eyam; containing striking passages extracted from a memoir . . . written by himself. pp. 21. *J. Pratt: Manchester,* [1824.] 8°. **4452.** cc. **7.** (**4.**)

—— The Watchman's Cry; or Protestant England roused from her slumber. A discourse addressed to the members of the Grand Protestant Confederation, in All Saints' Church, Manchester, 12th. July, 1840. pp. 24. *Joseph Pratt: Manchester,* 1840. 12°. **908.** c. **4.** (**15.**)

BURTON (CHARLES HENRY) "Concurrent Festivals." A letter addressed to the members of the congregation of St. Philip's Church, Liverpool. pp. 16. *Deighton & Laughton: Liverpool,* 1850. 8°. **4107.** c. **30.**

—— The Royal Supremacy. A sermon, *etc.* pp. 18. *Deighton & Laughton: Liverpool,* 1850. 8°. **4326.** f. **13.**

—— "Ye see the Distress that we are in." A sermon, *etc.* pp. iv. 14. *Deighton & Laughton: Liverpool; F. & J. Rivington: London,* [1847.] 8°. **4475.** c. **17.**

BURTON (*Mrs.* CHARLES HENRY) Abbots Thorpe; or, the Two wills. 2 vol. *A. Hall, Smart & Allen: London,* 1864. 8°. **12633.** l. **2.**

BURTON (CHARLES JAMES) The Apostolic Fathers. Part I. The Epistles of SS. Clement of Rome and Barnabas, and the Shepherd of Hermas. With an introduction comprising a history of the Christian Church in the first century, by the late Dr. Burton. (Part II. The Epistles of St. Ignatius and St Polycarp. With introductory preface comprising a history of the Christian Church in the second century, by the late Dr. Burton.) 2 vol. *Griffith, Farran & Co.: London,* [1888, 89.] 8°. [*Ancient & Modern Library of Theological Literature.*] **3605.** g. **3/7.**

—— [A reissue.] The Apostolic Fathers. Part II. The Epistles of St. Ignatius and St. Polycarp, *etc.* *London,* [1889.] 8°. [*Ancient and Modern Library of Theological Literature.*] **3605.** g. **3/42.**

—— Authority of an Oath: a charge delivered at the visitation of the diocese of Carlisle, May, 1882. pp. 15. *J. Parker & Co.: London; C. Thurnam & Sons: Carlisle,* 1882. 8°. **4445.** b. **1.** (**6.**)

—— The Burial Question: a charge delivered at the visitation of the diocese of Carlisle, in May, 1876. pp. 19. *C. Thurnam & Sons: Carlisle; J. Parker & Co.: London,* [1876.] 8°. **4109.** h. **5.** (**3.**)

—— The Character and Claims of the Universal Church: a charge delivered at the visitation of the diocese of Carlisle, May, 1886. pp. 12. *J. Parker & Sons: London; C. Thurnam & Sons: Carlisle,* 1886. 8°. **4446.** b. **6.** (**1.**)

BURTON (CHARLES JAMES)

—— A Charge to the Clergy of the Archdeaconry of Carlisle, delivered . . . in May 1863. pp. 16. *Bell & Daldy: London*, 1863. 8°. **4446**. b. **17**.

—— A Charge to the Clergy of the Diocese of Carlisle; delivered in May, 1865. pp. 19. *Whittaker & Co.: London*, 1865. 12°. **4446**. aaa. **13**.

—— The Church on the Sacrament of Baptism. Intended for the use of persons about to be confirmed. pp. 21. *Whittaker & Co.: London*, 1865. 12°. **4326.aa.18.**

—— The Church on the Sacrament of the Lord's Supper, or Holy Communion. Intended for the use of persons lately confirmed. pp. 23. *Whittaker & Co.: London*, [1865.] 12°. **4326**. aa. **19**.

—— Considerations on the Abolition of Compulsory Church Rates: a charge delivered at the visitation of the diocese of Carlisle in May & June, 1869. pp. 21. *Whittaker & Co.: London; C. Thurnam & Sons: Carlisle*, 1869. 12°. **4445**. aaa. **15**.

—— Considerations on the Ecclesiastical Courts and Clergy Discipline. pp. 69. *J. Parker & Co.: London; C. Thurnam & Sons: Carlisle*, 1875. 8°. **5157**. aaa. **67**. (**12**.)

—— The Creed of St. Athanasius justified: in four sermons. pp. 28. *J. Masters & Son: London; C. Thurnam & Sons: Carlisle*, 1872. 8°. **3504**. ccc. **29**. (**1**.)

—— [Another copy.] **3504**. ccc. **39**.

—— The Creeds, the Church's Rule of Faith: a charge delivered at the visitation of the diocese of Carlisle in May, 1873. pp. 24. *J. Parker & Co.: London; C. Thurnam & Sons: Carlisle*, 1873. 8°. **4446**. bb. **2**. (**9**.)

—— A Defensive Inquiry into the Scripture Doctrine of the Immortality of the Soul; and into the notion, under the Patriarchal and Mosaical dispensations, of a future life. pp. 71. *J. Hatchard & Son: London*, 1824. 8°. T. **1007**. (**4**.)

—— Equality in Christian Worship: a charge delivered at the visitation of the diocese of Carlisle, May, 1885. pp. 13. *J. Parker & Sons: London; C. Thurnam & Sons: Carlisle*, 1885. 8°. **4446**. bb. **6**. (**1**.)

—— In Memoriam: the Church lessons briefly reviewed. pp. 31. *Whittaker & Co.: London; C. Thurnam & Sons: Carlisle*, 1872. 8°. **3476**. f. **55**. (**4**.)

—— Increase of the Episcopate, considered in a letter to the Right Hon. the Earl of Derby. pp. 30. *Whittaker & Co.: London; C. Thurnam & Sons: Carlisle*, 1867. 8°. **4108**. bb. **77**. (**10**.)

—— An Increase of the Episcopate; and the Congé d'Élire; considered in two charges, delivered at the visitation of the diocese of Carlisle in May, 1877. pp. 23. 24. *J. Parker & Co.: London; C. Thurnam & Sons: Carlisle*, [1877.] 8°. **4107**. f. **2**. (**16**.)

—— The Priesthood: a charge, delivered at the visitation of the diocese of Carlisle, in May, 1874. pp. 26. *J. Parker & Co.: London; C. Thurnam & Co.: Carlisle*, 1874. 8°. **4446**. bb. **2**. (**14**.)

—— Revelation vindicated, in two sermons, *etc.* pp. 33. *F. C. & J. Rivington: London*, 1820. 8°. **1026**. f. **3**. (**11**.)

BURTON (CHARLES JAMES)

—— A Sermon suited to the Times, *etc.* pp. 16. *F. C. & J. Rivington: London*, 1819. 8°. **1026**. f. **3**. (**9**.)

—— Sermons on the Christian Faith, *etc.* 2 vol. *J. Parker & Co.: London; C. Thurnam & Sons: Carlisle*, 1875. 8°. **4465**. c. **4**.

—— Sermons on the Offices for the Visitation of the Sick, and the Burial of the Dead. pp. xi. 261. *J. Parker & Co.: London; C. Thurnam & Sons: Carlisle*, 1872. 8°. **3476**. e. **36**.

—— [Another copy.] **3476**. e. **37**.

—— A Short Inquiry into the Character and Designs of the British and Foreign Bible Society. pp. 39. *Rouse, Kirby & Lawrence: Canterbury*, [1817.] 8°. **490**. f. **28**. (**7**.)

—— "Sirs, ye are Brethren": a charge delivered at the visitation of the diocese of Carlisle in May, 1871. pp. 20. *Whittaker & Co.: London; C. Thurnam & Sons: Carlisle*, 1871. 8°. **4445**. f. **12**.

—— The Supremacy. A charge delivered to the clergy of the diocese of Carlisle . . . in September, 1866. pp. 20. *Whittaker & Co.: London; C. Thurnam & Sons: Carlisle*, 1866. 8°. **4445**. aaa. **13**.

—— Three Lectures on "Archbishop Cranmer," *etc.* pp. vi. 151. *Bell & Daldy: London*, 1861. 8°. **4902**. d. **24**.

—— A View of the Creation of the World, in illustration of the Mosaic record. pp. xvi. 300. *J. G. & F. Rivington: London*, 1836. 8°. **1117**. i. **13**.

—— The Voice of the Church, on some important points: a charge, delivered at the visitation of the diocese of Carlisle, in June, 1868. pp. 28. *Whittaker & Co.: London; C. Thurnam & Sons: Carlisle*, 1868. 8°. **4445**. aaa. **14**.

BURTON (CHARLES PIERCE) The Bob's Cave Boys. A sequel to "The Boys of Bob's Hill," *etc.* pp. 302. *H. Holt & Co.: New York*, 1909. 8°. **012804**. a. **22**.

BURTON (CHARLES VANDELEUR) *See* EBERT (C. H. R.) Magnetic Fields of Force . . . Translated by C. V. Burton. 1897, *etc.* 8°. **8758**. ccc. **19**.

—— An Introduction to Dynamics including kinematics, kinetics, and statics, *etc.* pp. xiii. 302. *Longmans & Co.: London*, 1890. 8°. **8767**. cc. **19**.

BURTON (CHARLIE) Charlie Burton, a tale. [By Jane A. Sargant.] pp. 108. *S.P.C.K.: London*, 1856. 12°. **4415**. c. **12**.

—— [Another edition.] pp. 127. *S.P.C.K.: London*, [1880.] 12°. **4421**. ff. **24**.

—— Charlie Burton: conte. Traduit par Aug. Mandrou. pp. 90. *S.P.C.K.: Londres*, [1857.] 12°. **4415**. c. **10**.

—— Charlie Burton. Eine Erzählung. pp. 93. *S.P.C.K.: London*, 1854. 12°. **4415**. c. **11**.

BURTON (CLARENCE MONROE) *See* PONTIAC, *Chief of the Ottowas*. Journal of Pontiac's Conspiracy . . . Published [with a preface] by C. M. Burton, *etc.* [1913.] 8°. Ac. **8404/3**.

—— The Boundary Lines of the United States under the Treaty of 1782. Address. *See* SPARKS (Edwin E.) "Pioneers and Patriots," *etc.* 1908. 8°. **9904**. r. **26**.

BURTON (Clarence Monroe)

—— The Building of Detroit. pp. 44. [*Detroit*,] 1912. 8°. **10410**. r. 5. (3.)

—— "Cadillac's Village," or "Detroit under Cadillac." With list of property owners and a history of the settlement, 1701 to 1710. pp. 43. *Detroit*, 1896. 8°. **10408**. f. **25**. (3.)

—— A Chapter in the History of Cleveland. pp. 31. [*Detroit*, 1895.] 8°. **10410**. ee. **31**. (2.)

—— Detroit in Earlier Days. A few notes on some of the old buildings in the city. pp. 36. *Burton Abstract & Title Co.: Detroit*, 1914. 8°. **10410**. w. **11**.

—— Early Detroit. A sketch of some of the interesting affairs of the olden time. pp. 52. [*Speaker-Hines Press: Detroit*, 1910.] 8°. **09008**. cc. **9**. (4.)

—— Historical Paper delivered before the Society of Colonial Wars of the State of Michigan. (La Salle and the Griffon.) pp. 17. *Winn & Hammond: Detroit*, 1903. 8°. **9551**. i. **27**.

—— In the Footsteps of Cadillac. *Wolverine Printing Co.: Detroit*, 1899. 8°. **10410**. ee. **31**. (1.)

—— Manuscripts from the Burton Historical Collection. Collected and published by C. M. Burton . . . Edited by M. Agnes Burton. 8 no. pp. 401. *Detroit*, 1916–18. 8°. **9551**. d. **22**.

BURTON (Claude E. C. H.) Fife and Drum. [Verses.] By Touchstone of "The Daily Mail" and C. E. B. of "The Evening News." Second edition. pp. 133. *Simpkin, Marshall & Co.: London*, 1915. 8°. **011652**. i. **118**.
The author's name is revealed in the preface.

BURTON (Clement) A Concise Manual of Statistics, *etc.* pp. ix. 164. *Gee & Co.: London*, 1937. 8°. **08535**. ee. **43**.

—— A Concise Manual of Statistics, *etc.* (Second edition.) pp. 182. *Gee & Co.: London*, 1946. 8°. **08535**. i. **22**.

BURTON (Clifford Earp) *See* Milne (Alan A.) Make-Believe. A children's play . . . The lyrics by C. E. Burton. 1925. 8°. **11791**. tt. **1/21**.

BURTON (Cyril J.)

—— Crime by Persuasion. A play in one act. pp. 20. *H. F. W. Deane & Sons: London*, [1946.] 8°. [*Year Book Press Series of Plays*.] W.P. **2236/177**.

BURTON (D. M.) Mrs. Tomkins grows Confidential! Sketches of a London landlady. pp. 51. *A. H. Stockwell: London*, [1926.] 8°. **12637**. f. **23**.

BURTON (Daniel V.) Dissertatio medica inauguralis de diabete mellito, *etc.* pp. 29. *P. Neill: Edinburgi*, 1819. 8°. **7440**. bb. **33**. (20.)

BURTON (Donald) *M.B.E., D.Sc., F.I.C.*, and **ROBERTSHAW** (George Frederick)

—— Sulphated Oils and Allied Products. Their chemistry and analysis, *etc.* pp. 163. iv. *A. Harvey: London*, 1939. 8°. **8898**. g. **17**.

BURTON (Donald) *Translator.*

—— *See* Abrahamsson (H.) The Origin of Death, *etc.* [Translated by D. Burton.] 1951. fol. W.P. **3760/3**.

BURTON (Donald) *Translator.*

—— *See* Anell (B.) Contribution to the History of Fishing in the Southern Seas. [Translated by D. Burton.] 1955. fol. W.P. **3760/9**.

—— *See* Arne (T. A. J.) Excavations at Shah Tepé, Iran. [Translated in part by D. Burton.] 1945. 4°. W.P. **12853/7**. (5.)

—— *See* Birath (G.) Lung Volume and Ventilation Efficiency, *etc.* [Translated by D. Burton.] 1944. 8°. [*Acta medica Scandinavica*. suppl. 154.] P.P. **3081**. b. (2.)

—— *See* Friberg (Lars) Health Hazards in the Manufacture of Alkaline Accumulators, *etc.* [Translated by D. Burton.] 1950. 8°. [*Acta medica Scandinavica*. Suppl. 240.] P.P. **3081**. b. (2.)

—— *See* Hedin (S. A.) *Asiatic Explorer*. History of the Expedition in Asia, 1927–1935, *etc.* [Translated by D. Burton.] 1943, *etc.* 4°. W.P. **12853**. (2.)

—— *See* Porat (B. T. D. von) Blood Volume Determinations with the Evans Blue Dye Method, *etc.* (Translated by D. Burton.) 1951. 8°. [*Acta medica Scandinavica*. suppl. 256.] P.P. **3081**. b. (2.)

—— *See* Sirén (Oswald) Gardens of China. [Translated by D. Burton.] [1949.] 4°. L.R. **294**. c. **14**.

—— *See* Ström (F.) On the Sacral Origin of the Germanic Death Penalties. [Translated by D. Burton.] 1942. 8°. [*Kungl. Vitterhets Historie och Antikvitets Akademiens handlingar*. dl. 52.] Ac. **7800**.

—— *See* Tomenius (J. H.) A Study on the Gastric Sediment. [Translated by D. Burton.] 1947. 8°. [*Acta medica Scandinavica*. suppl. 189.] P.P. **3081**. b. (2.)

BURTON (Dora) Poppies in the Corn, and other verse. pp. 19. *A. H. Stockwell: London*, [1924.] 8°. **011645**. de. **90**.

BURTON (Doris) *See* Boulton (*Sir* Harold E.) *Bart.* The Huntress Hag of the Blackwater . . . With illustrations by D. Burton. 1926. 4°. **11643**. cc. **35**.

—— *See* Rhys (Brian) A Book of Ballads . . . Illustrations by D. Burton. 1929. 8°. **12827.b.1/7.**

BURTON (Doris Eliza)

—— *See* also Lucis Amator, *pseud.* [i.e. D. E. Burton.]

—— The Angel Who Guarded the Toys, and other stories for children . . . Illustrations by R. de Souza. pp. 171. *Sands & Co.: London, Glasgow*, [1948.] 8°. **12829**. d. **22**.

—— By Courage and Faith . . . Illustrated by T. J. Bond. [Brief biographies of various famous Roman Catholics.] pp. 163. *Sands & Co.: [London,]* 1955. 8°. **4535**. h. **10**.

—— Daring to live. Heroic Christians of our day. pp. 176. *Burns & Oates: London*, 1955. 8°. **4921**. aa. **7**.

—— From Oxford Group to the Catholic Church. pp. 20. *Catholic Truth Society: London*, 1948. 8°. **3943**. aa. **454**.

—— Great Catholic Mothers of yesterday and to-day. pp. 132. *Paternoster Publications: London*, 1951. 8°. **4869**. a. **15**.

BURTON (Doris Eliza)

— Heroic Missionary Adventures . . . Illustrated by T. J. Bond. pp. 128. *Sands & Co.: [London,]* 1952. 8°. **4768.** bb. **52.**

— Heroic Tales from many Lands . . . Illustrated by T. J. Bond. pp. 160. *Sands & Co.: [London,]* 1953. 8°. **04422.** bb. **37.**

— The Incarnation, and other poems. pp. 47. *Arthur Stockwell: Ilfracombe,* 1946. 8°. **11657.** aaa. **101.**

— A Penny for a Candle and Other Stories. pp. 96. *Douglas Organ: London,* [1947.] 8°. **04413.** i. **116.**

— Saint Emilie de Rodat, Foundress of the Sisters of the 'Holy Family.' [A biography. With plates, including a portrait.] pp. 118. *Paternoster Publications: London,* 1951. 8°. **4889.** aa. **33.**

— Saints and Heroes for Boys . . . Illustrated by Rosemary de Souza. pp. 118. *Sands & Co.: London, Glasgow,* 1950. 8°. **4830.** g. **39.**

— Through a Convert's Window. pp. 135. *Duckett: London,* [1950.] 8°. **3943.** aa. **528.**

BURTON (Dorothy) The Fruitful Seed. How Tony learnt about the Oxford Movement, *etc.* pp. 56. *A. R. Mowbray & Co.: London & Oxford,* 1932. 8°. **04419.** e. **69.**

BURTON (E. Milby) Hayden & Gregg, Jewellers of Charleston. pp. 13. *Charleston,* 1938. 8°. [*Charleston Museum Leaflet.* no. 11.] W.P. **6189/11.**

— South Carolina Silversmiths, 1690–1860. [With plates.] pp. xvii. 311. 1942. 8°. *See* Charleston, *South Carolina.—Museum of South Carolina, etc.* **7801.** b. **2.**

BURTON (E. S.) *See* Fawcett (Elizabeth N.) and Burton (E. S.) Over the Seas. [1932.] 8°. **09007.** bb. **46/4.**

— — 1937. 8°. **09505.** g. **10.**

BURTON (Earl)

— By Sea and by Land. The story of our amphibious forces. [With plates.] pp. 218. *McGraw-Hill Book Co.: London, New York,* [1944.] 8°. **9100.** k. **2.**

BURTON (Earl) and **BURTON** (Linette)

— The Exciting Adventures of Waldo . . . Illustrated by Helen Stone. pp. 64. *McGraw-Hill Book Co.: [New York,* 1945.] 8°. **012826.** d. **40.**

— Taffy and Joe . . . Drawings by Helen Stone. pp. 60. *McGraw-Hill Book Co.: [New York,]* 1947. 8°. **12828.** dd. **26.**

BURTON (Edmund) *Fellow of Trinity College, Cambridge.* *See* Manilius (M.) M. Manilii Astronomicon . . . Opera et studio E. Burton. 1783. 8°. **1001.** k. **11.**

— *See* Persius Flaccus (A.) [*Latin and English.*] The Satyrs of Persius. Translated into English, with notes critical and explanatory, by E. Burton. 1752. 4°. **644.** k. **17.** (5.)

— Antient Characters deduced from Classical Remains. pp. xxix. 190. *S. Rowlands: London,* 1763. 8°. **1448.** c. **25.**

BURTON (Edmund) *Novelist.*

— England's Eden: Isle of Wight. [With illustrations.] pp. 77. *Littlebury & Co.: Worcester,* [1946.] 8°. **010368.** i. **75.**

— Fathoms Deep. A tale of submarine adventure in the Pacific. [With plates.] pp. viii. 215. *Burns, Oates & Co.: London,* 1933. 8°. **20053.** e. **8.**

— Mackinlay's Millions. A story of submarine research. pp. 184. *P. R. Gawthorn: London,* [1946.] 8°. **12816.** b. **67.**

— Mystery Trail. pp. 184. *P. R. Gawthorn: London,* [1946.] 8°. **12816.** b. **68.**

— The Royal Special, and other stories. pp. 208. *Century Press: London, New York,* [1947.] 8°. **12831.** a. **38.**

— South Devon. "Drake's Dreamland." [With illustrations.] pp. 131. *Littlebury & Co.: Worcester,* [1948.] 4°. **10358.** l. **54.**

— Under the Red Rose, *etc.* pp. 152. *P. R. Gawthorn: London,* [1946.] 8°. **12816.** b. **65.**

— Wolf of the Revolution. A tale of 1793. pp. 184. *P. R. Gawthorn: London,* [1946.] 8°. **12816.** b. **69.**

— Wonderland of the West, North Devon. [With plates.] pp. 75. *Littlebury & Co.: Worcester,* [1952.] 8°. **010360.** r. **9.**

— "A Yule You'll Remember!", *etc.* [A tale.] pp. 32. *Pendulum Publications: London,* [1945.] 8°. **12828.** a. **38.**

BURTON (Edmund Francis) An Indian Olio . . . With illustrations, *etc.* pp. xi. 388. *Spencer Blackett: London,* [1888.] 8°. **10056.** bbb. **17.**

— Reminiscences of Sport in India . . . With illustrations, *etc.* pp. ix. 419. *W. H. Allen & Co.: London,* 1885. 8°. **7906.** e. **38.**

— Trouting in Norway . . . With illustrations, *etc.* pp. 168. *C. Thurnam & Sons: Carlisle; Simpkin, Marshall & Co.: London,* 1897. 8°. **7907.** de. **49.**

BURTON (Édouard) *pseud.* [i.e. Édouard Le Normant des Varannes.] *See* also Le Normant des Varannes (E.)

— Le Dernier dauphin de France. pp. xxxvi. 118. *Orléans,* 1884. 8°. **10601.** bb. **20.** (4.)

BURTON (Edward) *Antiquary.* The Life of John Leland, the first English antiquary. With extensive notes and a bibliography of his works, including those in ms. Printed from a hitherto unpublished work, by the learned Edward Burton. pp. 31. *Alfred Cooper: London,* 1896. 8°. **10854.** bb. **29.**
The attribution to Burton is doubtful.

BURTON (Edward) *Land Agent.* "Plots." Valuable and practical hints for plot buyers. pp. 21. *The Author: Woking,* [1890.] 8°. **08227.** e. **9.** (4.)

BURTON (Edward) *Novelist.* The Robber Chief; or, Too good for his trade. [With plates.] pp. 224. *J. F. Shaw & Co.: London,* [1883]. 8°. **12624.** h. **9.**

BURTON (Edward) *of Stanton, Derbyshire.* The Fathers Legacy: or Burtons Collections. Containing many excellent instructions for age, and youth . . . First written for the instruction of his only son, *etc.* pp. 202. *John Clowes for Mathew Walbancke: London,* 1649. 12°. **8403.** aaa. **27.**

BURTON (Edward) *Regius Professor of Divinity, Oxford.* *See* also Verus, *pseud.* [i.e. E. Burton.]

—— *See* Bible.—*New Testament.* [*Greek.*] Ἡ Καινη Διαθηκη. The Greek Testament with English notes. By the Rev. E. Burton. 1831. 8°. **1003**. g. **14**.

—— —— 1835. 8°. **3015**. bb. **5**.

—— —— 1848. 8°. **1109**. g. **16**.

—— *See* Bull (George) *Bishop of St. David's.* The Works of George Ball collected and revised by the Rev. E. Burton, *etc.* 1827. 8°. **493**. b. **19–25**.

—— —— 1846. 8°. **3752**. d. **2**.

—— *See* Cranmer (Thomas) *Archbishop of Canterbury.* A Short Instruction into Christian Religion, being a catechism set forth by Archbishop Cranmer, *etc.* [Edited with a preface by E. Burton.] 1829. 8°. **475**. d. **6**.

—— *See* Eusebius, *Pamphili, Bishop of Caesarea in Palestine.* [*Historia Ecclesiastica.—Greek*]. Εὐσεβιου του Παμφιλου ἱστοριας ἐκκλησιαστικης λογοι δεκα. Ad codices manuscriptos recensuit E. Burton. 1838. 8°. **1364**. g. **9**.

—— —— 1856. 8°. **4531**. g. **7**.

—— —— 1872. 8°. **2208**. aa. **3**.

—— *See* Eusebius, *Pamphili, Bishop of Caesarea in Palestine.* [*Historia Ecclesiastica. — Appendix.*] Supplementa notarum ad Eusebii Historiam ecclesiasticam et excerpta ex editione Burtoniana cum eiusdem ac Schoedelii vindiciarum Flavianarum censura . . . edidit F. A. Heinichen. 1840. 8°. **1125**. e. **10**. **(2.)**

—— *See* Oxford.—*University of Oxford.—Convocation.* The Substance of two Speeches, delivered in Convocation . . . February 26, 1829. [The second by E. Burton.] 1829. 8°. **4109**. i. **3**. **(5.)**

—— *See* Pearson (John) *Bishop of Chester.* An Exposition of the Creed . . . Revised and corrected by the Rev. E. Burton, *etc.* 1857. 8°. **3506**. e. **35**.

—— —— 1864. 8°. **3506**. cc. **31**.

—— Advice for the Proper Observance of the Sunday. Intended principally for the labouring poor. pp. 20. *C. J. G. & F. Rivington: London,* 1831. 12°. T. **1357**. **(5.)**

—— Third edition. pp. 20. *J. G. & F. Rivington: London,* 1832. 12°. **4372**. df. **6**. **(4.)**

—— [Another copy.] **4422**. h. **17**. **(4.)**

—— New edition. pp. 20. *S.P.C.K.: London,* 1841. 12°. **4355**. aaa. **79**. **(4.)**

—— [Another edition.] pp. 20. *S.P.C.K.: London,* 1847. 12°. **4422**. h. **8**. **(6.)**

—— An Attempt to ascertain the Chronology of the Acts of the Apostles and of St. Paul's Epistles. pp. 105. *Printed for the Author: Oxford,* 1830. 8°. T. **1289**. **(5.)**

—— The Benefit of the Sacrament of the Lord's Supper explained. Intended principally for the labouring poor. pp. 27. *J. G. & F. Rivington: London,* 1832. 12°. T. **1362**. **(7.)**

—— New edition. pp. 27. *J. G. & F. Rivington: London,* 1834. 12°. **4372**. d. **8**. **(8.)**

—— New edition. pp. 27. *J. G. & F. Rivington: London,* 1837. 12°. **4422**. ddd. **24**. **(10.)**

—— New edition. pp. 27. *J. G. F. & J. Rivington: London,* 1843. 12°. **4327**. b. **72**. **(5.)**

—— Concio ad clerum in synodo provinciali Cantuariensis provinciæ; ad D. Pauli die xxvii° Octobris, A.D.MDCCCXXX habita, *etc.* pp. 19. *S. Collingwood: Oxonii,* 1830. 4°. **4473**. h. **20**.

—— The Danger of being offended in Christ. *See* Family Sermons. Original Family Sermons. vol. 1. 1833, *etc.* 8°. **694**. b. **1**.

—— A Description of the Antiquities and other Curiosities of Rome. pp. viii. 581. *Joseph Parker: Oxford,* 1821. 8°. **574**. h. **8**.

—— Second edition, with additions. 2 vol. *C. & J. Rivington: London,* 1828. 8°. **574**. h. **9**.

—— A Description of the Antiquities and other Curiosities of Rome, *etc.* [With plates.] 2 vol. *L. Molini: Florence,* 1830, 31. 12°. **07705**. n. **26**.

—— History of the Christian Church; from the ascension of Jesus Christ, to the conversion of Constantine, *etc.* pp. viii. 440. *J. W. Parker: London,* 1836. 8°. **864**. e. **4**.

—— The second edition. pp. viii. 416. *J. W. Parker: London,* 1837. 8°. **4532**. aa. **7**.

—— An Inquiry into the Heresies of the Apostolic Age, in eight sermons preached before the University of Oxford, in the year MDCCCXXIX. At the lecture founded by the Rev. John Bampton. pp. xxxii. 600. *Printed for the Author: Oxford,* 1829. 8°. **4453**. ee. **16**.

—— An Introduction to the Metres of the Greek Tragedians. By a Member of the University of Oxford [i.e. E. Burton]. pp. vi. 54. 1821. 8°. **11705**. b. **32**.

—— Second edition. pp. vi. 54. 1824. 8°. *See* Greek Tragedians. T. **1163**. **(9*.)**

—— An Introduction to the Metres of the Greek Tragedians. By a Member of the University of Oxford [i.e. E. Burton]. Third edition. pp. 52. 1826. 8°. *See* Greek Tragedians. C. **121**. c. **4**. **(2.)**

—— Lectures upon the Ecclesiastical History of the First Century (of the Second and Third Centuries). 2 vol. *Printed for the Author: Oxford,* 1831, 33. 8°. **4532**. dd. **5**, **6**.

—— Lectures upon the Ecclesiastical History of the First Three Centuries, from the Crucifixion of Jesus Christ, to the year 313 . . . Second edition. 2 vol. *J. H. Parker: Oxford,* 1839. 8°. **4533**. aaaa. **13**.

—— One Reason for not entering into Controversy with an anonymous author of Strictures [i.e. William Irons, the author of "Strictures on the Rev. Mr. Bulteel's Sermon and the Rev. Dr. Burton's Remarks"]. pp. 8. *W. Baxter: Oxford,* 1831. 8°. T. **1353**. **(14.)**

—— [Another copy.] **764**. g. **22**. **(5.)**

—— Remarks upon a Sermon, preached [by H. B. Bulteel] at St. Mary's on Sunday, February 6, 1831. pp. 29. *W. Baxter: Oxford,* 1831. 8°. T. **1376**. **(8.)**

—— [Another copy.] **764**. g. **22**. **(2.)**

—— *See* BULTEEL (Henry B.) A Reply to Dr. Burton's Remarks upon a Sermon preached at St. Mary's, *etc.* 1831. 8°. **4256**. c. **12**.

—— *See* OUDEIS, *pseud.* The Doctrine of the Church of England at the time of the Reformation . . . compared with the Remarks of the Regius Professor of Divinity [E. Burton], *etc.* 1831. 8°. **764**. g. **22**. **(7.)**

—— *See* OXONIENSIS, *pseud.* [i.e. W. Irons.] Strictures on the Rev. Mr. Bulteel's Sermon and the Rev. Dr. Burton's Remarks. 1831. 8°. **764**. g. **22**. (**4**.)

—— *See* WILSON (David) *Bishop of Calcutta.* The Character of the Good Man as a Christian Minister . . . To which are subjoined notes on the controversy between the Professor of Divinity at Oxford [E. Burton], and the Rev. Mr. Bulteel. 1831. 8°. **4905**. aaa. **39**.

—— Sequel to Remarks upon Church Reform, with observations upon the plan proposed by Lord Henley. pp. 76. *Roake & Varty: London,* 1832. 8°. T. **1399**. (**9**.)

—— Second edition. pp. iv. 80. *Roake & Varty: London,* 1832. 8°. **4107**. cc. **48**. (**3**.)

—— Sermon preached before the University of Oxford on the 21st of March, 1832, being the day appointed for a general humiliation . . . Second edition. pp. 27. *Printed for the Author: Oxford,* 1832. 8°. T. **1383**. (**24**.)

—— Sermons, preached before the University of Oxford. pp. xii. 451. *J. G. & F. Rivington: London,* 1832. 8°. **1021**. h. **22**.

—— Testimonies of the Ante-Nicene Fathers to the Divinity of Christ. pp. xvii. 453. *Clarendon Press: Oxford,* 1826. 8°. **1120**. e. **15**.

—— Second edition, with considerable additions. pp. xvii. 489. *University Press: Oxford,* 1829. 8°. **1120**. e. **16**.

—— Testimonies of the Ante-Nicene Fathers to the Doctrine of the Trinity and of the Divinity of the Holy Ghost. pp. xvii. 151. *University Press: Oxford,* 1831. 8°. **1120**. e. **17**.

—— Thoughts on the Separation of Church and State. pp. 87. *Roake & Varty: London,* 1834. 8°. T. **1495**. (**13**.)

—— [Another edition.] pp. 66. *J. Parker & Co.: Oxford & London,* 1868. 8°. **4107**. aaa. **13**.

—— Thoughts upon the Demand for Church Reform. pp. 41. *W. Baxter: Oxford,* 1831. 8°. T. **1399**. (**8**.)

—— Second edition. pp. 44. *W. Baxter: Oxford,* 1831. 8°. **4107**. cc. **48**. (**2**.)

—— *See* CHURCHMAN. Remarks on Lord Henley and Dr. Burton on Church-Reform, *etc.* 1833. 8°. **4105**. d. **12**.

—— *See* EDEN, afterwards HENLEY (Robert H.) *Baron Henley.* A Plan of Church Reform . . . Containing the Union of Dr. Burton's & Lord Henley's Plans for the Augmentation of small Livings. 1832. 8°. **4108**. bb. **81**.

—— —— 1833. 8°. **5155**. b. **20**.

—— *See* EDEN, afterwards HENLEY (Robert H.) *Baron Henley.* Union of Dr. Burton's and Lord Henley's Plans for the Augmentation of small Livings. 1832. 8°. T. **1418**. (**3**.)

—— *See* PERRY (Samuel) A Letter to the King . . . on the necessary preliminary to a sound and constitutional church reformation, including observations on Dr. Burton's and Lord Henley's pamphlets. [On Burton's "Thoughts upon the Demand for Church Reform" and Henley's "A Plan of Church Reform."] 1833. 8°. **4109**. f. **11**. (**1**.)

—— *See* PULLEN (William) An Address to the Clergy, on Church Reform, with remarks on the plans of Lord Henley and Doctor Burton. 1833. 8°. T. **1418**. (**12**.)

—— Three Primers put forth in the reign of Henry VIII. Viz. I. A Goodly Prymer 1535; II. The Manual of Prayers, or the Prymer in English 1539; III. King Henry's Primer 1545. [Edited by E. Burton.] pp. lxvii. 526. *University Press: Oxford,* 1834. 8°. **692**. d. **28**.

—— What must I do to be saved? 1835. *See* FAMILY SERMONS. Original Family Sermons. vol. 5. 1833, *etc.* 8°. **694**. b. **5**.

BURTON (EDWARD GASCOIGNE) A Hand Book and Companion to Ramsgate, Margate, Broadstairs, Kingsgate, Minster, *etc.* pp. 55. *G. Griggs: Ramsgate,* [1859.] 8°. **10351**. c. **46**. (**2**.)

—— The Wreck of the "Northern Belle" . . . being a descriptive poem . . . to which is added: Midnight on the Cliffs, *etc.* pp. 48. *Henry Hart: Ramsgate,* [1857.] 8°. **11602**. ff. **16**. (**5**.)

BURTON (EDWIN) Visitors' Guide to Sydney . . . with which is incorporated The Tourists' Handbook . . . Second edition. With plan, *etc.* pp. 136. *William Maddock: Sydney,* [1874.] 8°. **10491**. aa. **7**.

BURTON (EDWIN HUBERT) *See* DOUAI.—*English College.* The Douay College Diaries, Third, Fourth and Fifth. 1598–1654. With the Rheims Report, 1579–80 . . . Edited by E. H. Burton . . . and T. L. Williams. 1911. 8°. [*Publications of the Catholic Record Society.* vol. 10, 11.] Ac. **8108**. c/**2**.

—— *See* DOUAI.—*English College.* The Douay College Diaries. The Seventh Diary, 1715–1778 . . . Edited by the late E. H. Burton . . . and E. Nolan. 1928. 8°. [*Publications of the Catholic Record Society.* vol. 28.] Ac. **8108**. c/**2**.

—— *See* KIRK (John) *Roman Catholic Priest.* Biographies of English Catholics in the Eighteenth Century . . . Edited by J. H. Pollen, S.J., and E. Burton. 1909. 8°. **2012.d.**

—— Baylis House, Salt Hill, Slough. Catholic school and Catholic centre, 1830–1907. pp. 19. *Charles Luff: Slough,* [1923.] 8°. **8366**. c. **55**.

—— Catalogue of Books in the Libraries at St. Edmund's College, Old Hall, printed in England and of books written by Englishmen printed abroad to the year 1640. Compiled by E. Burton. pp. v. 94. 1902. 8°. *See* WARE.—*Saint Edmund's College.* **011907**. e. **6**.

—— Handlist of the Secular Clergy. *In:* Biographical Studies, 1534–1829. vol. 2. no. 1, *etc.* 1953– . 8°. P.P. **6490**. faa.

BURTON (EDWIN HUBERT)

—— The Life and Times of Bishop Challoner, 1691–1781. [With plates, including portraits.] 2 vol. *Longmans & Co.: London*, 1909. 8°. **4902**. df. **8**.

—— *See* LOMAX (Michael T.) Bishop Challoner. A biographical study derived from Dr. E. Burton's "The Life and Times of Bishop Challoner," *etc.* [1936.] 8°. **20029**. b. **3**.

—— London Streets and Catholic Memories. pp. ix. 170. *Burns, Oates & Co.: London*, 1925. 8°. **010348**. ff. **5**.

—— The Penal Laws and the Mass. pp. 27. *Catholic Truth Society: London*, 1912. 8°. **3943**. aa. **180**.

—— [Another issue.] *London*, 1912. 8°. [*Publications of the Catholic Truth Society*. vol. 90.] **3943**. aa. **411/9**.

—— St. Edmund's College, Old Hall . . . Reprint from the Catholic Historical Review, *etc.* pp. 20. [1924.] 8°. **08364**. g. **25**.

—— St. Edmund's College, Old Hall . . . (Paper read before St. Thomas's Historical Society . . . 1923.) Supplement to "The Edmundian," Spring, 1925. pp. 20. *Jennings & Bewley: Ware*, [1925.] 8°. **04785**. k. **61**.

—— Sermons preached in St. Edmund's College Chapel on various occasions . . . Collected and arranged by E. Burton. pp. xii. 249. *Burns & Oates: London*, 1904. 8°. **4479**. i. **19**.

—— "Thy People at War." (A sermon.) *See* WARD (Bernard) Thoughts in War Time, *etc.* 1915. 8°. **04376**. e. **37**.

BURTON (EDWIN HUBERT) and **MYERS** (EDWARD) successively *Bishop of Lamus* and *Archbishop of Berea*.

—— The New Psalter and its Use. pp. xii. 258. *Longmans & Co.: London*, 1912. 8°. [*Westminster Library*.] **2206**. a. **9/8**.

BURTON (EDWIN HUBERT) and **POLLEN** (JOHN HUNGERFORD) *the Younger*.

—— Lives of the English Martyrs. Second series. The Martyrs declared Venerable. Volume I. 1583–1588. Edited by E. H. Burton . . . and J. H. Pollen. pp. xxxvii. 583. *Longmans & Co.: London*, 1914. 8°. **2214**. c. **5**.

No more published. The First Series, edited by Bede Camm, is entered under his name.

BURTON (ELAINE FRANCES) *Baroness Burton of Coventry*.

—— The Battle of the Consumer. pp. 28. *Labour Party: London*, 1955. 8°. [*Viewpoint Pamphlet*. no. 1.] W.P. D. **166/1**.

—— Domestic Work. Britain's largest industry. pp. 15. *Frederick Muller: London*, 1944. 8°. **8288**. b. **74**.

—— What is she Worth? A study of the Report on Equal Pay. pp. 11. *Fitzroy Publications: [London*, 1947.] 8°. **08415**. i. **82**.

—— What of the Women? A study of women in wartime. pp. 224. *Frederick Muller: London*, 1941. 8°. **8417**. a. **37**.

—— Women and Politics. pp. 15. *London*, [1944?] 8°. [*Common Wealth Popular Library*. no. 9.] W.P. **839/9**.

BURTON (ELI FRANKLIN)

—— *See* LANGTON (Hugh H.) Sir John Cunningham McLennan . . . With a chapter on his scientific work by E. F. Burton. 1939. 8°. **10859**. cc. **23**.

—— On the Physical Aspect of Colloidal Solution. pp. 79. [*Toronto*,] 1910. 8°. [*University of Toronto Studies. Papers from the Physical Laboratories*. no. 36.] Ac. **2702/22**.

—— The Phenomenon of Superconductivity. Edited by E. F. Burton . . . assisted by . . . members of the Department [of Physics, University of Toronto], *etc.* pp. 112. 1934. 8°. *See* TORONTO.—*University of Toronto.—Department of Physics*. Ac. **2702**. ai.

—— The Physical Properties of Colloidal Solutions, *etc.* pp. vii. 200. *Longmans & Co.: London*, 1916. 8°. [*Monographs on Physics*.] W.P. **1994/6**.

—— Second edition. [With bibliographies.] pp. viii. 221. *Longmans & Co.: London*, 1921. 8°. [*Monographs on Physics*.] W.P. **1994/9**.

—— Third edition. Prepared with the assistance of May Annetts Smith. pp. viii. 235. *Longmans & Co.: London*, 1938. 8°. [*Monographs on Physics*.] W.P. **1994/15**.

BURTON (ELI FRANKLIN) and **KOHL** (WALTER HEINRICH)

—— The Electron Microscope, *etc.* pp. 233. *Reinhold Publishing Co.: New York*, 1942. 8°. **8716**. dd. **42**

—— The Electron Microscope. An introduction to its fundamental principles and applications . . . Drawings by Dorothy Stone. Second edition. pp. 325. *Reinold Publishing Corporation: New York*, 1946. 8°. **08757**. cc. **37**.

BURTON (ELIZABETH) Party Card Games. pp. 64. *London & New York*, 1929. 8°. [*Warne's "Recreation" Books*. no. 24.] W.P. **7651/24**.

—— Party Games. pp. 63. *London & New York*, [1928.] 8°. [*Warne's "Recreation" Books*. no. 18.] W.P. **7651/18**.

BURTON (ELIZABETH) *Novelist*. *See* BURTON (Alice E.)

BURTON, afterwards **RODGER** (ELLA HILL) Aberdeen Doctors at home and abroad. The narrative of a Medical School. pp. xv. 355. *W. Blackwood & Sons: Edinburgh*, 1893. 8°. **7679**. df. **37**.

—— Miss in the Kitchen. Or, a Week's misadventures in housekeeping. pp. 31. *Edinburgh Publishing Co.: [Edinburgh*,] 1877. 12°. **7944**. de. **11**. **(7.)**

BURTON (ERNEST DE WITT) *See* BIBLE.—*Acts*. [*English*.] The Records and Letters of the Apostolic Age . . . Arranged for historical study by E. de W. Burton, *etc.* [1895.] 8°. **3266**. d. **40**.

—— *See* BIBLE.—*Gospels.—Harmonies*. [*English*.] A Harmony of the Gospels . . . By W. A. Stevens . . . and E. de W. Burton. [1895.] 4°. **3226**. d. **33**.

—— —— 1905. 4°. **3225**. cc. **2**.

—— *See* BIBLE.—*Gospels.—Harmonies*. [*Karen.—Sgau dialect*.] Harmony of the Gospels. By Stevens and Burton, *etc.* 1905. 4°. **11103**. b. **16**.

BURTON (Ernest de Witt)

—— *See* Chicago.—*University of Chicago.* The University of Chicago Publications in Religious Education. Edited by E. D. Burton, *etc.* 1922, *etc.* 8°. Ac. **2691**. d/**27**.

—— *See* Goodspeed (Thomas W.) Ernest De Witt Burton. A biographical sketch. [With a portrait.] 1926. 8°. **010884**. ee. **26**.

—— Christianity in the Modern World. Papers and addresses . . . Edited by Harold R. Willoughby. [With a portrait.] pp. xv. 195. *University Press: Chicago,* 1927. 8°. **4374**. dd. **18**.

—— A Critical and Exegetical Commentary on the Epistle to the Galatians. pp. lxxxix. 541. *T. & T. Clark: Edinburgh,* 1921. 8°. [*International Critical Commentary.*] **2006.b.**

—— Education in a Democratic World . . . Edited by Harold R. Willoughby. [With a portrait.] pp. xix. 165. *University of Chicago Press: Chicago,* 1927. 8°. **8311**. ccc. **8**.

—— A Handbook of the Life of the Apostle Paul. An outline for class room and private study. [With a map.] pp. 100. *University of Chicago Press: Chicago,* 1906. 8°. **04808**. ee. **59**.

—— New Testament Word Studies . . . Edited by Harold R. Willoughby. pp. xv. 117. *University of Chicago Press: Chicago,* 1927. 8°. **03225**. i. **30**.

—— The Politarchs in Macedonia and elsewhere. (Reprinted from the American Journal of Theology.) pp. 35. [*Chicago,* 1898.] 8°. Dept. of Greek & Roman Antiquities.

—— Religion and Education . . . An address, *etc.* pp. 24. [*Chicago,* 1925.] 8°. **08311**. aa. **35**.

—— A Short Introduction to the Gospels . . . Revised by Harold R. Willoughby. pp. xi. 158. *University of Chicago Press: Chicago,* 1926. 8°. **03226**. g. **12**.

—— A Source Book for the Study of the Teaching of Jesus in its Historical Relationships. pp. x. 277. *Chicago,* 1923. 8°. [*University of Chicago Publications in Religious Education.*] Ac. **2691**. d/**27**. (**2**.)

—— Spirit, Soul, and Flesh. The usage of *Πνευμα, Ψυχη,* and *Σαρξ* in Greek writings and translated works from the earliest period to 180 A.D., and of their equivalents רוּחַ, נֶפֶשׁ, and בָּשָׂר in the Hebrew Old Testament . . . Reprinted, with additions and revision, from the American Journal of Theology, *etc.* pp. 214. *University of Chicago Press: Chicago,* 1918. 8°. [*Historical and Linguistic Studies in Literature related to the New Testament.* ser. 2. vol. 3.] Ac. **2691**. do.

—— Syntax of the Moods and Tenses in New Testament Greek . . . Second edition revised and enlarged. pp. xxii. 215. *Isbister & Co.: London,* 1893. 8°. **12923**. de. **18**.

—— Third edition. pp. xxii. 215. *T. & T. Clark: Edinburgh; Boston* [printed], 1898. 8°. **12924**. o. **7**.

—— Why I am Content to be a Christian. pp. 7. *Christian Literature Society: London; Madras* printed, 1909. 8°. [*Pice Pamphlets.* no. 8.] **4763**. a. **1/8**.

BURTON (Ernest de Witt) and **MATHEWS** (Shailer)

—— The Life of Christ . . . Revised edition. pp. xix. 390. *Chicago,* 1927. 8°. [*University of Chicago Publications in Religious Education. Constructive Studies.*] Ac. **2691**. d/**27**. (**23**.)

BURTON (Ernest de Witt) and **MATHEWS** (Shailer)

—— The Life of Christ. For the use of students of high-school age. Adapted from the life of Christ by E. D. Burton and S. Mathews by Isaac Bronson Burgess. Revised edition. pp. xxii. 282. *Chicago,* 1930. 8°. [*University of Chicago Publications in Religious Education. Constructive Studies.*] Ac. **2691**. d/**27**. (**35**.)

—— *See* Burgess (Isaac B.) A Teacher's Manual for the Life of Christ [i.e. for " The Life of Christ . . . Adapted from the life of Christ by E. D. Burton and S. Mathews, by I. B. Burgess "]. 1927. 8°. Ac. **2691**. d/**27**. (**24**.)

BURTON (Ernest James) Art, Poetry, and Religion. pp. 19. *Pen-in-Hand Publishing Co.: Oxford,* 1935. 8°. **07805**. ee. **94**.

—— Drama in Schools. Approaches, methods & activities, *etc.* pp. 96. *Herbert Jenkins: London,* 1955. 8°. [*Practical Stage Handbooks.*] W.P. B. **612/12**.

—— Teaching English through Self-Expression. A course in speech, mime and drama. pp. 232. *Evans Bros.: London,* [1950.] 8°. **11868**. cc. **37**.

BURTON (Ernest W.) After the Storm, and other poems. pp. 16. *A. H. Stockwell: London,* [1921.] 8°. **11646**. ee. **53**.

BURTON (Eva) A Natural Bridge to Cross. [On spiritualism.] pp. 288. *G. P. Putnam's Sons: New York, London,* 1935. 8°. **8634**. bbb. **22**.

—— Your Unseen Forces. pp. 295. *G. P. Putnam's Sons: New York, London,* 1936. 8°. **8634**. bbb. **5**.

BURTON (F.) *Writer on Angling.* How to Catch Salmon Bass. pp. 12. *" Gazette " Printing Works: Eastbourne,* [1907.] 8°. **7920.aa.58.**

BURTON (F. T.) The Artists' Arcanum; or, the Essence of a variety of useful and entertaining arts . . . Second edition. pp. viii. 232. *Printed for the Author: Stamford,* 1812. 8°. **7942**. aaa. **16**.

BURTON (Fanny) Fanny Burton; or, Rome was not built in a day. pp. 94. *T. Nelson & Sons: London,* 1860. 16°. **4415**. a. **21**.

—— [Another edition.] pp. 64. *T. Nelson & Sons: London,* 1872. 16°. **12803**. aaa. **31**.

BURTON (Frances Barbara) Distant Glimpses; or, Astronomical sketches. pp. 190. *W. Pickering: London,* 1837. 12°. **531**. f. **41**.

—— [Another edition.] Astronomy simplified; or, Distant glimpses of the celestial bodies, *etc.* pp. 138. *Simpkin, Marshall & Co.: London,* 1838. 12°. **717**. f. **45**.

—— Elective Polarity, the universal agent. pp. viii. 171. *Simpkin, Marshall & Co.: London,* 1845. 8°. **1393**. d. **13**.

—— Second edition, with an introductory address. pp. xlii. 171. *Simpkin, Marshall & Co.: London,* 1846. 8°. **1395**. e. **15**.

—— Thoughts on Physical Astronomy: with practical observations thereon. pp. 30. *Smith, Elder & Co.: London,* 1840. 8°. **1395**. e. **16**. (**4**.)

—— Second edition . . . With considerable additions, including important demonstrations of the agency of the planets upon the atmosphere, during the year 1841. pp. 30. *J. Rodwell: London,* 1842. 8°. **8562**. bbb. **31**. (**3**.)

BURTON (Frances Barbara)

BURTON (Francis) *M.P.* *See* Cole (Owen B.) Biographical Sketch of the late Francis Burton . . . with his memorable speech in the House of Commons in defence of . . . the Duke of York, *etc.* [With a portrait.] 1845. 8°. **10826**. c. **17**.

—— *See* Oxford. A Collection of the Handbills . . . relative to the election of members to represent the city of Oxford . . . Candidates. F. Burton, Henry Peters, *etc.* 1802. 8°. **100**. l. **52**.

BURTON (Francis) *Vicar of Theddlethorpe All-Saints.* A Sermon, preached . . . upon Friday the 27th of February, 1778: being . . . a General Fast, *etc.* pp. 20. *H. Baldwin: London,* [1778.] 8°. **4473**. b. **47**. (**4**.)

BURTON (Francis George) The Commercial Management of Engineering Works. pp. xi. 310. *Scientific Publishing Co.: Manchester,* 1899. 8°. **08228**. g. **42**.

—— Second edition, revised and greatly enlarged. pp. xv. 432. *Scientific Publishing Co.: Manchester,* [1905.] 8°. **8227**. d. **70**.

—— Engineering Estimates and Cost Accounts. pp. viii. 125. *Technical Publishing Co.: Manchester,* 1896. 8°. **8768**. bb. **17**.

—— Second edition. pp. viii. 136. *Technical Publishing Co.: Manchester,* 1900. 8°. **8225**. aaa. **60**.

—— Engineers' and Shipbuilders' Accounts. pp. v. 108. *Gee & Co.: London,* 1902. 8°. [*Accountants' Library.* vol. 14.] **8532**. cc. **14/1**.

—— Second edition. pp. vii. 108. *Gee & Co.: London,* 1911. 8°. [*Accountants' Library.* vol. 14.] **8532**. cc. **14/2**.

—— The Naval Engineer and the Command of the Sea. A story of naval administration. pp. viii. 231. *Technical Publishing Co.: Manchester,* 1896. 8°. **8808**. e. **1**.

BURTON (Frank) Frank Burton's Dream and its Consequences. A chapter in the history of his habits. pp. 72. *Book Society: London,* [1872.] 16°. **4418**. bbb. **48**.

—— [Another copy.] **12804**. ee. **15**.

BURTON (*Sir* Frederic William) *See* London.—iii. *National Gallery.* Descriptive and Historical Catalogue . . . Foreign Schools, *etc.* [Revised and rewritten with a preface by Sir F. W. Burton.] 1884. 8°. **7860**. pp. **23**.

—— —— 1890. 8°. **7856**. de. **15**.

BURTON (Frederick Merryweather) The Lincolnshire Keuper Escarpment. And its bearing on and relation to the county, *etc.* pp. 5. [*Lincoln,*] 1908. 8°. [*Lincoln City & County Museum Publications.* no. 1.] **7959**. ff. **15**.

—— The Shaping of Lindsey by the Trent. pp. xi. 59. *A. Brown & Sons: London,* [1912.] 8°. **07108**. ee. **42**.

—— The Witham and the Ancaster 'Gap.' A study of river action. pp. 31. *A. Brown & Sons: London,* [1910.] 8°. **7106**. aa. **56**.

BURTON (Frederick Nuthall) *See* England.—*Army.—Infantry.—Royal Welch Fusiliers, 10th Battalion.* The War Diary, 1914–1918, of 10th—Service—Battalion Royal Welch Fusiliers. Edited by Lieut.-Colonel F. N. Burton, *etc.* 1926. 8°. **9081**. c. **16**.

BURTON (Frederick Russell) American Primitive Music, with special attention to the songs of the Ojibways. (pt. 2. Twenty-eight Ojibway songs, harmonized and provided with English words.) 2 pt. *Moffat, Yard & Co.: New York,* 1909. 4°. **7899**. t. **9**.

—— The Mission of Poubalov. [A novel.] pp. 236. *James Henderson: London,* [1897.] 8°. **012704**. ee. **11**.

—— Redcloud of the Lakes. A novel . . . Illustrations by Elfrieda Burton. pp. 374 *T. Fisher Unwin: London ; New York* [printed], 1909. 8°. **012705**. c. **39**.

—— The Song and the Singer. [A novel.] pp. 383. *Shurmer Sibthorp: London,* [1902.] 8°. **012704**. g. **23**.

—— Strongheart. A novel . . . Founded on William C. de Mille's play. Illustrations by Clarence Rowe. pp. 393. *T. Fisher Unwin: London ; New York* [printed], 1908. 8°. **012706.bb.52.**

—— A Wedding, but rather late. [A novel.] pp. 236. *James Henderson: London,* [1897.] 8°. **012704**. h. **5**.

BURTON (George) *of Stamford.* Chronology of Stamford. Compiled from Peck, Butcher . . . parliamentary reports, and other important works. 2 pt. *Robert Bagley: Stamford ; Edwards & Hughes: London,* 1846. 12°. **797**. d. **8**.

BURTON (George) *Rector of Eldon, Suffolk.* The Analysis of Two Chronological Tables . . . The one being a table to associate, scripturally, the different chronologies of all ages and nations: the other, to settle the Paschal Feast, from the beginning, to the end of known time. pp. 25. *Logographic Press: London,* 1787. 4°. **216**. b. **17**.

—— An Essay towards Reconciling the Numbers of Daniel and St. John, determining the birth of our Saviour, and fixing a precise time for the continuance of the present desolation of the Jews, *etc.* pp. 387. *W. Chase: Norwich,* 1766. 8°. **1016**. h. **3**.

—— The second edition. With a postscript, *etc.* 2 pt. *W. Nicoll, etc.: London,* 1769, 68. 8°. **218**. e. **10**.
The first part only is of the second edition.

BURTON (George Ambrose) *R.C. Bishop of Clifton.* *See* Clarke (Charles Cowley) Handbook of the Divine Liturgy . . . With an introduction by the Right Reverend G. A. Burton. 1910. 8°. **3477**. de. **25**.

—— *See* Steele (Francesca M.) Monasteries and Religious Houses of Great Britain . . . Preface by the Bishop of Clifton. 1903. 8°. **4061**. ee. **8**.

—— Catholic Education and the Duties of Parents . . . Lenten pastoral, 1906. pp. 12. *Catholic Truth Society: London,* [1906.] 8°. **3943**. aa. **403**. (**10**.)

—— Weld Sermon, Downside Abbey, 1904. pp. 23. 1904. 8°. **4473**. h. **26**. (**10**.)

BURTON (George C.) Victoriæ Reginæ quinquagesimo exacto imperii anno Ratcliffia gratulatur. [Verses, signed G. C. B., i.e. G. C. Burton.] [1887.] *s. sh.* 8°. *See* B., G. C. **1871**. e. **1**. (**230**.)

BURTON (George Eric)

—— Madagascar looks ahead. Present and future in Madagascar. pp. 23. *Livingstone Press: London,* 1947. 8°. [*New Advanced Papers.* no. 5.] W.P. **636/5**.

—— The Waiting Isle. Madagascar and its Church. pp. 95. *Livingstone Press: London,* [1953.] 8°. [*Broadway Books* no. 6.] W.P. **177/6**.

BURTON (George F.) The Art of Chocolate Making. [With illustrations.] 13 pt. *G. Burton's School of Confectionery: Blackpool,* [1923.] 4°. **7943. f. 38.** *Reproduced from typewriting.*

—— Cake Making. A practical handbook, *etc.* pp. 113. *Blackpool Union Printers: Blackpool,* 1915. 4°. **7953. l. 32.**

—— (Fourth edition.) pp. 174. *Blackpool Union Printers: Blackpool,* 1922. 4°. **7943. g. 31.**

—— The " New Era " Chocolate Book. Home made chocolates, bon-bons, *etc.* pp. 149. *J. Robertson & Co.: St. Annes-on-the-Sea,* [1924.] 8°. **07942. dd. 31.**

BURTON (George Henry) *See* Periodical Publications. —*Stamford.* Old Lincolnshire . . . Edited by G. H. Burton. [1886, *etc.*] 4°. **P.P. 1925. ef.**

—— Rambles round Stamford: a handy guide for visitors. [With plates.] pp. vii. 72. *W. P. Dolby: Stamford; Simpkin, Marshall & Co.: London,* 1872. 8°. **10360. bb. 21.**

BURTON (George Lee) Tackling Matrimony. To the men and girls who love each other more than ease and show and sham . . . Illustrated. pp. 218. *Harper & Bros.: New York & London,* 1913. 8°. **012704. bbb. 35.**

BURTON (George Simon Merceron) Sudan Arabic Note-Book. pp. xi. 251. *McCorquodale & Co.: London,* 1934. 8°. **012903. e. 19.**

BURTON (Georgia Winifred) Effect of Hydrogen Ion Concentration upon the Destruction of Vitamin B by Heat . . . Dissertation, *etc.* pp. 30. *New York,* 1925. 8°. **8899. g. 42.**

BURTON (Gertrude Hitz) *See* Hitz, afterwards Burton.

BURTON (Gideon J.) *See* Drake (Thomas W.) Poems . . . With a memoir by the Rev. G. J. Burton. 1858. 8°. **11688. ccc. 29.**

BURTON (Gilbert) *See* Musgrave (*Sir* Philip) *2nd Bart.* The Life of Sir Philip Musgrave . . . published from an original MS. by the Rev. G. Burton. 1840. 8°. [*Carlisle Tracts.* no. 4.] **1303. b. 3.**

BURTON (H. E.) *Writer of Verse.* Lindah; or the Festival. A metrical romance of ancient Scinde. With minor poems . . . By the author of The White Rose Wreath (H. E. Burton), *etc.* pp. viii. 88. *Smith, Elder & Co.: London,* 1845. 8°. **1466. f. 32.**

BURTON (H. H.)

—— My Black Daughters. [With illustrations.] pp. 80. *Assemblies of God Publishing House: Luton,* 1949. 8°. **4768. a. 68.**

BURTON (H. M.) *Translator.*

—— *See* Bazé (W.) [Un Quart de siècle parmi les éléphants.] Just Elephants, *etc.* (Translated by H. M. Burton.) [1955.] 8°. **7211. c. 18.**

—— *See* Diolé (P.) [L'Exploration sous-marine.] Under-Water Exploration . . . Translated by H. M. Burton. 1954. 8°. **7919. a. 42.**

BURTON (H. V. T.) The Black Crinoline. A fantasy. pp. 74. *Hendersons: London,* [1923.] 16°. **011779. de. 29.**

—— Princess Pavona. A pastoral, *etc.* pp. 75. *Hendersons: London,* [1923.] 16°. **011779. de. 30.**

BURTON (H. V. T.)

—— Vanguard. The payment of a debt of honour. pp. xv. 316. *Methuen & Co.: London,* 1940. 8°. **NN. 31395.**

BURTON (Hal)

—— *See* Washington, *D.C.—Urban Land Institute.—Central Business District Council.* The City fights back . . . Narrated and edited by H. Burton, *etc.* [1954.] 8°. **10483. b. 5.**

BURTON (Harold) The Life of St. Francis de Sales. Adapted from the Abbé Hamon's Vie de S. François de Sales. [With a map.] 2 vol. *Burns, Oates & Co.: London,* 1925, 29. 8°. **4830. cc. 14.**

BURTON (Harry Edwin) *See* Livius (T.) *Patavinus.* Selections . . . Edited with notes and introduction by H. E. Burton. [1905.] 8°. **11304. c. 11/2.**

—— —— [1905.] 8°. **11304. c. 11/6.**

—— The Discovery of the Ancient World. pp. 130. *Harvard University Press: Cambridge, Mass.,* 1932. 8°. **010004. g. 46.**

BURTON (Harry McGuire) *See* Rossetti (Dante G.) Selections from Rossetti & Morris. Edited by H. M. Burton. 1929. 8°. **011644. eee. 153.**

—— *See* Swinburne (Algernon C.) [*Selections.*] Selections from Swinburne. Edited by H. M. Burton. 1927. 8°. **011644. df. 154.**

—— The Education of the Countryman. pp. xi. 251. *Kegan Paul & Co.: London,* 1943. 8°. [*International Library of Sociology and Social Reconstruction.*] **W.P. 8084/6.**

—— English Writers through the Ages. pp. 132. *London,* [1926.] 8°. [*Nisbets' " Through the Ages " Series.*] **W.P. 8206.**

—— Life and Leisure. General editor. H. M. Burton. *Paul Elek: London; printed in the Netherlands,* 1948– . 8°. **W.P. 9529.**

BURTON (Henrietta Kolshorn) The Re-establishment of the Indians in their Pueblo Life through the Revival of their Traditional Crafts. A study in home extension education, *etc.* [A thesis.] pp. vi. 96. *Teachers College, Columbia University: New York,* 1936. 8°. **8287. e. 14.**

BURTON (Henry) Henry Burton; or, the Reward of patience . . . By the author of " The Little Drummer " . . . With illustrations. pp. 188. *F. Warne & Co.: London,* [1878.] 8°. **12809. aaa. 11.**

BURTON (Henry) *M.D.* Tentamen physiologico-medicum, de usu et effectu aëris puri in corpus humanum, *etc.* pp. 55. *Balfour & Smellie: Edinburgi,* 1788. 12°. **7461. aa. 17.**

BURTON (Henry) *Methodist Minister.* Alice; or, the Early crown . . . Second edition. pp. 94. *Robert Culley: London,* 1903. 8°. **04412. de. 31.**

—— Britain to America. A war poem. pp. 27. *C. H. Kelly: London,* [1918.] *obl.* 8°. **11647. dg. 23.**

—— The Coming of the Kingdom, and other sermons. pp. 301. *C. H. Kelly: London,* 1911. 8°. **4465. l. 23.**

—— Gleanings in the Gospels. pp. 304. *C. H. Kelly: London,* 1896. 8°. **3227. ff. 4.**

BURTON (Henry) *Methodist Minister.*

—— The Gospel according to St. Luke. pp. vii. 415. *Hodder & Stoughton: London,* 1890. 8°. [*The Expositor's Bible.*] **2201. a. 14.**

—— Killed in Action, and other war poems. pp. 25. *C. H. Kelly: London,* [1918.] 8°. **011648. e. 71.**

—— Songs of the Highway. pp. xii. 267. *Morgan & Scott: London,* 1924. 8°. **011645. e. 129.**

—— Speaking to the Captain. [A religious poem.] [1922.] *s. sh.* 16°. **1865. c. 8. (18.)**
A card.

—— Wayside Songs, of the Inner and the Outer Life. pp. xii. 190. *T. Woolmer: London,* [1886.] 8°. **11653. dd. 6.**

—— Mosaics. Selections from the writings of H. Burton . . . Compiled by . . . Hilda Burton, *etc.* pp. xii. 82. *Morgan & Scott: London,* 1922. 16°. **04402. ff. 42.**

BURTON (Henry) *Rector of St. Matthew's, Friday Street.* *See* Bastwick (John) A Briefe Relation of certain . . . passages, and speeches in the Starre-Chamber . . . at the censure of . . . Dr Bastwicke, Mr Burton, *etc.* 1637. 4°. **8122. e. 8.**

—— —— 1638. 4°. **4106. a. 70. (2.)**

—— —— 1745. 4°. [*Harleian Miscellany.* vol. 4.] **185. a. 8.**

—— —— 1809. 4°. [*Harleian Miscellany.* vol. 4.] **2072.g.**

—— —— 1809. 8°. [*Harleian Miscellany.* vol. 4.] **1326. g. 4.**

—— *See* Brown (David) *Gent.* Two Conferences . . . one whereof, was appointed with Mr. Burton, and a number of his church, *etc.* 1650. 4°. **E. 601. (11.)**

—— *See* Busher (Leonard) Religions Peace, *etc.* [The editor's preface signed: H. B., i.e. H. Burton ?] 1646. 4°. **E. 334. (7.)**

—— *See* Calamy (Edmund) *B.D., Minister of St. Mary, Aldermanbury.* An Answer to the Articles against Master Calamy . . . Master Burton, *etc.* 1642. 4°. **E. 132. (7.)**

—— *See* Calamy (Edmund) *B.D., Minister of St. Mary, Aldermanbury.* A Conspiracie of the Twelve Bishops in the Tower, against Mr. Calamie, Mr. Burton, *etc.* 1641. 4°. **E. 181. (32.)**

—— *See* Laud (William) successively *Bishop of Saint David's, of Bath and Wells, etc.* A Speech delivered in the Starr-Chamber . . . at the censure, of J. Bastwick, H. Burton . . . concerning pretended innovations in the Church. 1637. 4°. **1130. b. 39.**

—— *See* Prynne (William) A New Discovery of the Prelates Tyranny in their late prosecution of Mr. W. Pryn . . . and Mr. H. Burton, *etc.* 1641. 4°. **E. 162. (1.)**

—— An Apology of an Appeale . . . Also, an epistle to the true-hearted nobility. pp. 32. [*London,*] 1636. 4°. **5155. a. 28.**

—— [Another edition.] pp. 32. [*Amsterdam ?*] 1636. 4°. **853. d. 3. (1.)**

BURTON (Henry) *Rector of St. Matthew's, Friday Street.*

—— *See* Dow (Christopher) Innovations unjustly charged upon the Present Church and State. Or an Answer to the most materiall passages of a libellous pamphlet made by Mr. H. Burton, and intituled An Apologie of an Appeale, &c. 1637. 4°. **700. g. 3.**

—— An Answer to Mr. Prynn's Twelve Questions concerning Church Government, *etc.* [By H. Burton.] pp. 28. [1644.] 4°. *See* Prynne (William) **E. 15. (5.)**

—— Babel no Bethel. That is, the Church of Rome no true visible Church of Christ. In answer to Hugh Cholmley's challenge, and R. Butterfields Maschil, two masculine champions for the Synagogue of Rome. pp. 131. *For M. S.* [*M. Sparke*]*:* [*London,*] 1629. 4°. **108. d. 30.**

—— The Baiting of the Popes Bull. Or an vnmasking of the mystery of iniquity folded vp in a . . . Breeue or Bull, sent from the Pope lately into England . . . By H. B. (H. Burton). [With the text of the brief dated 30 May 1626, in Latin and English.] pp. 95. 1627. 4°. *See* Rome, *Church of.*—[*Popes.*] Urban viii. [1623–44.] **697. e. 21.**

—— [Another copy.] The Baiting of the Popes Bull, *etc.* 1627. 4°. *See* Rome, *Church of.*—[*Popes.*]—Urban viii. [1623–44.] **3936. d. 47.**

—— [Another copy.] The Baiting of the Popes Bull, *etc.* 1627. 4°. *See* Rome, *Church of.*—[*Popes.*]—Urban viii. [1623–44.] **111. a. 6.**

—— A Censure of Simonie, or a Most important case of conscience concerning simonie briefly discussed, *etc.* pp. 128. *William Stansby, for Edmund Weauer and Iohn Smethwicke: London,* 1624. 4°. **517. h. 1.**

—— Conflicts and Comforts of Conscience . . . Collected from priuate proof, for publike profit. By H. B. (H. Burton.) pp. 16. 278. *For Michael Sparke: London,* 1628. 12°. **1019. a. 33.**

—— Conformitie's Deformity. In a dialogue between Conformity, and Conscience. Wherein the main head of all the controversies in these times, concerning Church-Government, is asserted and maintained, *etc.* pp. 27. *For Giles Calvert: London,* 1646. 4°. **E. 358. (20.)**

—— *See* Edwards (Thomas) *Author of "Gangræna."* The Third Part of Gangræna. (Animadversions on M. Burtons Conformities Deformity.) 1646. 4°. **108.b.56.(3.)**

—— A Divine Tragedie lately acted; or a Collection of sundrie memorable examples of God's judgements upon Sabbath-breakers, and other like libertines, in their unlawfull sports, hapning within the realme of England, in the compasse onely of few yeers last past . . . By that worthy Divine Mr. Henry Burton [or rather, by William Prynne]. pp. 38. *For John Wright junior, and for Tho. Bates: London,* 1641. 4°. **E. 176. (1.)**
The date in the colophon is 1642.

—— [Another copy.] **G. 19765.**

—— Divine Examples of God's severe Judgments upon Sabbath-Breakers, in their unlawful sports, collected out of several divine subjects, viz. Mr. H. B. [i.e. Henry Burton] Mr. Beard, and the Practice of Piety [by L. Bayly, Bishop of Bangor], *etc.* 1672. *s. sh.* fol. *See* B., H., *Mr.* **816. m. 22. (50.)**

—— Englands Bondage and Hope of deliverance. A sermon, *etc.* pp. 33. *London,* 1641. 4°. **E. 174. (2.)**

—— For God, and the King. The summe of two sermons preached on the fifth of November . . . 1636. pp. 166. [*London*,] 1636. 4°. **4106.** b. **31.**

—— [Another edition.] pp. 166. [*Amsterdam?*] 1636. 4°. **853.** d. **3.** (**2.**)

—— *See* Heylyn (Peter) A Briefe and Moderate Answer, to the Seditious and Scandalous Challenge of H. Burton . . . in the two sermons by him preached on the fifth of November, 1636. And in the Apologie prefixt before them. 1637. 4°. **699.** e. **5.** (**1.**)

—— *See* Stafford (Anthony) The Life of the Blessed Virgin, *etc.* (A Just Apology; or, a Vindication of a booke entituled The Female Glory, from ye false and malevolent aspersions cast uppon it by H. Burton [in " For God and the King "].) 1860. 8°. **4806.** b. **39.**

—— The Grand Impostor unmasked, or, a Detection of the notorious hypocrisie, and desperate impiety of the late Archbishop—so styled—of Canterbury, cunningly couched in that written copy, which he read on the scaffold at his execution . . . aliâs, called . . . his funerall sermon. pp. 20. *For Giles Calvert: London*, [1645.] 4°. **4105.** a. **8.**

—— [Another copy.] E. **26.** (**4.**)

—— [Another copy.] **112.** b. **36.**

—— [Another copy.] G. **1316.** (**3.**)

—— Grounds of Christian Religion. Laid downe briefely and plainely by way of question and answer. By H. B. (H. Burton.) pp. 45. *G. M.* [*G. Miller*] *for Robert Bird: London*, 1636. 8°. **03504.** e. **7.**

—— Israels Fast. Or, a Meditation vpon the Seuenth Chapter of Ioshuah; a faire precedent for these times. By By H. B. Rector of S. Mathews Fryday-Street (Henry Burton). pp. 38. [*Thomas Cotes?*] *London*, 1628. 4°. **1492.** fff. **37.** (**2.**)
With several errors in the pagination.

—— [Another copy.] Israel's Fast. Or, a Meditation vpon the seuenth chapter of Joshuah, *etc.* *London*, 1628. 4°. **4475.** i. **1.**
A variant. In this copy the pagination of p. 17 *is printed correctly.*

—— [Another copy.] **4474.** c. **106.** (**4.**)
Imperfect; wanting the dedicatory epistle.

—— Jesu-Worship Confuted; or, Certaine arguments against bowing at the name Jesus. With objections to the contrary, fully answered. By H. B. [i.e. H. Burton.] pp. 12. [1640.] 8°. *See* B., H. **874.** c. **17.**

—— [Another edition.] pp. 6. *T. Bates: London*, [1641.] 4°. **4103.** aaa. **21.**
The titlepage is cropped.

—— [Another edition.] pp. 8. 1660. 4°. *See* B., H. **698.** g. **14.** (**7.**)

—— The Law and the Gospell reconciled . . . In answere to a letter written by an Antinomian, *etc.* pp. 70. *I. N.* [*John Norton*] *for M. Sparkes: London*, 1631. 4°. **4103.** b. **6.**

—— Meditations upon 1 Sam. 26. 19. Humbly presented to the Common-Councel of London, for their serious rumination, *etc.* pp. 12. *For Giles Calvert: London*, 1647. 4°. E. **399.** (**24.**)

—— A Most Godly Sermon . . . shewing the necessity of selfe-denyall and humiliation, by prayer and fasting before the Lord in regard of the present plague we now lye under, *etc.* *Printed by B. Alsop: London*, 1641. 4°. E. **172.** (**36.**)

—— A Narration of the Life of Mr. Henry Burton . . . According to a copy written with his own hand. [With a portrait.] pp. 51. *London*, 1643. 4°. E. **94.** (**10.**)

—— [Another copy.] G. **1315.**

—— [Another copy.] **113.** a. **5.**
Imperfect; wanting the titlepage.

—— [Another copy.] G. **1316.** (**1.**)
Imperfect; wanting the portrait, but with a different one inserted.

—— [Another copy, with a different titlepage.] *For John Rothwell: London*, 1643. 4°. T. **1092.** (**2.**)

—— The Peace-maker: or, Solid Reasons, perswading to peace; grounded upon the late Solemn Covenant. By H. B. [i.e. H. Burton.] pp. 10. 1646. 4°. *See* B., H. **873.** e. **97.**

—— [Another copy.] E. **329.** (**5.**)

—— A Plea to an Appeale: trauersed dialogue wise. By H. B. (H. Burton.) pp. 93. *Printed by W. I.* [*William Jones*]*: London*, 1626. 4°. **4255.** aaaa. **9.**

—— The Protestation Protested: or, a Short remonstrance, shewing what is principally required of all those that have or doe take the last Parliamentary Protestation. [By H. Burton.] 1641. 4°. *See* England.—*Parliament.* [*Parliamentary Proceedings.*—ii.] **100.** c. **22.**

—— *See* England.—*Parliament.* [*Parliamentary Proceedings.*—ii.] A Survey of that Foolish . . . Libell: The Protestation Protested [by H. Burton]. 1641. 4°. E. **164.** (**8.**)

—— *See* Geree (John) *M.A., Puritan Divine.* Judahs Joy at the Oath . . . Hereunto is annexed a briefe and moderate answere to the Protestation Protested [by H. Burton], *etc.* 1641. 4°. E. **170.** (**8.**)

—— The Seven Vials; or, a Briefe and plaine exposition vpon the 15: and 16: chapters of the Revelation, *etc.* pp. 146. *Printed by William Jones: London*, 1628. 4°. **115.** d. **41.**

—— *See* Butterfield (Robert) Maschil . . . For the Vindication of . . . the L. Bishop of Exeter, from the cauills of H. B. [i.e. H. Burton] in his book intituled The Seuen Vialls. 1629. 8°. **857.** b. **7.**

—— *See* Cholmley (Hugh) The State of the Now-Romane Church. Discussed by way of vindication of the . . . Bishop of Exceter, from the weake cauills of H. Burton [in " The Seven Vials "]. 1629. 8°. **3936.** b. **2.**

—— The Sounding of the Two Last Trumpets . . . or, Meditations by way of paraphrase upon the 9th. 10th. and 11th. chapters of the Revelation, as containing a prophecie of these last times. Digested by H. Burton during his banishment, *etc.* pp. 93. *For Samuel Gellibrand: London*, 1641. 4°. E. **174.** (**1.**)

—— To the Honorable the Knights, Citizens, and Burgesses, of the Common House of Parliament. The humble petition of H. Burton, late exile, *etc.* *See* Bastwick (John) The Severall Humble Petitions, *etc.* 1641. 4°. **1416.** c. **43.**

—— Aen de Hoogh-achtbare de Ridders, Burgeren, ende Gedeputeerde . . . De demoedige requeste van H. Burton, *etc.* *See* Prynne (William) De Oodtmoedighe Requesten, *etc.* 1641. 4°. T. **1724.** (**42.**)

—— Truth Shut out of Doores: or, a Briefe and true narrative of the occasion and manner of proceeding of some of Alderman-bury parish, in shutting their church-doores against me, *etc.* *For Giles Calvert: London,* 1645. 4°. E. **311.** (**1.**)

—— The Door of Truth opened: or, a Brief and true narrative of the occasion how Mr. H. Burton came to shut himself out of the church-doors of Aldermanbury: published in answer to a paper, called, Truth shut out of doors, *etc.* [By Edmund Calamy.] pp. 18. *For Christopher Meredith: London,* 1645. 4°. E. **311.** (**13.**)

—— Truth, still Truth, though shut out of doores. Or, a Reply to a late pamphlet entituled The doore of truth opened . . . With some animadversions upon a late letter of the ministers of London to the reverend Assembly, against toleration. pp. 31. *For Giles Calvert: London,* 1645. 4°. E. **315.** (**6.**)

—— [Another copy.] **105.** d. **9.** (**1.**)

—— *See* Calamy (Edmund) *B.D., Minister of St. Mary, Aldermanbury.* A Just and Necessary Apology against an Unjust Invective, published by Mr. H. Burton, in a late book of his, entituled, Truth still truth, *etc.* 1646. 4°. E. **320.** (**9.**)

—— Truth's Triumph ouer Trent: or, the great gulfe between Sion and Babylon. That is, the vnreconcileable opposition betweene the Apostolicke Church of Christ, and the apostate synagogue of Antichrist, in the maine and fundamentall doctrine of iustification . . . By H. B. Rector of S. Mathews Friday-Street [i.e. H. Burton]. pp. 373. 1629. 4°. *See* B., H., *Rector of S. Matthew's, Friday-Street.* **3935.** c. **27.**

—— A Tryall of Priuate Devotions. Or, a Diall for the houres of prayer. *For M. S.* [*M. Sparke*]*: London,* 1628. 4°. **851.** e. **2.**

—— A Vindication of Churches, commonly called Independent: or a Briefe answer to two books; the one intituled, Twelve considerable serious questions, touching Church-government: the other, Independency examined, unmasked, refuted, &c. Both lately published by William Prinne. pp. 72. *For Henry Overton: London,* 1644. 4°. **698.** h. **22.** (**2.**)

—— [Another copy.] E. **17.** (**5.**)

—— [Another copy.] **105.** c. **55.**

—— *See* Prynne (William) Truth triumphing over Falshood . . . In refutation of . . . my deare brother Burton's Vindication of Churches, *etc.* 1645. 4°. **700.** g. **4.** (**3.**)

—— Vindiciæ Veritatis: Truth vindicated against Calumny. In a briefe answer to Dr. Bastwicks two late books, entituled, Independency not God's ordinance, *etc.* pp. 34. *M. S.* [*M. Sparke*] *for Giles Calvert: London,* 1645. 4°. E. **302.** (**13.**)

—— *See* S., B. Innocency Cleared . . . in a letter sent to Mr. H. Burton . . . in defence of Dr. Bastwick. [With reference to "Vindiciæ Veritatis."] 1645. 4°. E. **265.** (**7.**)

BURTON (Henry Bindon) The Battle of the Lords. A political drama. [In verse.] pp. 70. *Hodges, Figgis & Co.: Dublin; Simpkin, Marshall & Co.: London,* 1910. 8°. **11775.** ff. **35.**

—— Eölsyné, and other poems. pp. vi. 152. *Maunsel & Co.: Dublin & London,* 1914. 8°. **11646.** h. **35.**

—— Eula, and other poems. pp. xii. 284. *Bell & Daldy: London,* [1871.] 8°. **11650.** bbb. **8.**

—— Der Kaiser von Potsdam. [A satire, in verse.] *Eng.* pp. 42. *Hodges, Figgis & Co.: Dublin,* 1915. 8°. **011652.** i. **107.**

BURTON (Henry Darwin) *See* Hetherington (Helen F.) and Burton (H. D.) Led On. 1894. 8°. **012642.** l. **4.**

—— *See* Hetherington (Helen F.) and Burton (H. D.) No Compromise. 1892. 8°. **012637.** i. **6.**

—— —— [1893.] 8°. **012641.** l. **25.**

—— *See* Hetherington (Helen F.) and Burton (H. D.) Paul Nugent—Materialist, *etc.* [1890.] 8°. **012632.** h. **13.**

—— —— 1891. 8°. **012631.** m. **52.**

—— *See* Hetherington (Helen F.) and Burton (H. D.) Paul Nugent, de Materialist, *etc.* [1895.] 8°. **12603.** ff. **22.**

BURTON (Henry R.) The Breakfast Half-Hour; or, Addresses to working men. pp. 116. *London; "Advertiser" Office: Malvern,* 1872. 8°. **4402.** bb. **46.**

—— Third edition, *etc.* [With illustrations.] pp. 159. *Wesleyan Conference Office: London,* 1877. 16°. **4413.** ff. **16.**

—— A Manual of Methodism and of Wesleyan Polity. pp. 67. *Hodder & Stoughton: London,* 1881. 8°. **4135.** df. **8.**

BURTON (Herbert)

—— *See* Hancock (William K.) Two Centuries of Change . . . Third edition, revised, by H. Burton. 1947. 8°. **9010.** de. **26.**

—— *See* Scott (*Sir* Ernest) A Short History of Australia . . . Seventh edition revised by H. Burton . . . with additional chapter and an appendix. 1947. 8°. **9781.** aaa. **36.**

—— *See* Scott (*Sir* Ernest) A Short History of Australia . . . Eighth edition, revised by H. Burton. 1950. 8°. **9781.** aaa. **38.**

BURTON (Hester)

—— *See* Tennyson (Alfred) *Baron Tennyson.* [*Selections and Extracts.*] Tennyson. Selection and commentary by H. Burton. 1954. 8°. W.P. c. **100/3.**

—— Barbara Bodichon. 1827–1891. [With plates, including portraits.] pp. xii. 219. *John Murray: London,* 1949. 8°. **10862.** f. **24.**

—— Coleridge and the Wordsworths. Selection and commentary by H. Burton. pp. 192. *Oxford University Press: London,* 1953 [1954]. 8°. [*Sheldonian English Series.*] W.P. c. **100/1.**

BURTON (HEZEKIAH) Several Discourses: viz. I. Of purity and charity. II. Of repentance. III. Of seeking first the kingdom of God. [With a portrait.] pp. 547. *For Richard Chiswell: London*, 1684. 8°. **1021**. h. **23**.

—— A Second Volume of Discourses, *etc.* pp. 608. *For Richard Chiswell: London*, 1685. 8°. **1021**. h. **24**.

—— A Discourse concerning the Authority of Men in the Kingdom of Christ. Being a sermon . . . now republish'd, *etc.* pp. 32. *R. Burleigh: London*, 1718. 8°. **114**. f. **32**.

BURTON (HILDA) *See* BURTON (Henry) *Methodist Minister.* Mosaics. Selections . . . Compiled by . . . Hilda Burton, *etc.* 1922. 16°. **04402**. ff. **42**.

BURTON (HOWARD N.)

—— Break for Musing. [Sketches.] pp. 123. *J. Clarke & Co.: London*, [1946.] 8°. NN. **36008**.

BURTON (HUMPHREY PHILLIPPS WALCOT)

—— The Story of the Parish Church—St. James—of Louth . . . Third edition . . . Illustrated. pp. 28. *British Publishing Co.: Gloucester*, [1943.] 8°. **07822**. a. **9**.

—— The Story of the Parish Church—St. James—of Louth . . . Fifth edition. pp. 36. *British Publishing Co.: Gloucester*, [1947.] 8°. **07822**. a. **38**.

—— Weavers of Webs. [An autobiography.] pp. 127. *H. Monkton: London*, 1954. 8°. **4910**. c. **17**.

BURTON (I. D.) May. Poetic mosaic from ancient and modern authors. Selected, arranged, and edited by I. D. Burton. pt. 1. pp. 136. *Printed for the Author: Stockport*, 1898. 8°. **11602**. ccc. **34**.

BURTON (IDA ROBINSON) and **BURTON** (MYRON GARFIELD) School Sewing based on Home Problems. pp. 393. *Ginn & Co.: Boston*, [1921.] 8°. **07742**. cc. **7**.

BURTON (ISABEL) *Lady. See* ALENCAR (J. de) Iraçéma . . . Translated . . . by I. Burton. 1886. 8°. **12431**. e. **38**. **(1.)**

—— *See* ARABIAN NIGHTS. [*English.*] Lady Burton's edition of her husband's Arabian Nights, *etc.* 1886. 8°. **2348**. f. **4**.

—— *See* BAITĀL-PACHĪSĪ. Vikram and the Vampire . . . Edited by . . . I. Burton, *etc.* 1893. 8°. **14156**. i. **35**.

—— *See* BLANCH (Lesley) The Wilder Shores of Love. [Biographies of Lady Isabel Burton and others. With portraits.] 1954. 8°. **10604**. ppp. **17**.

—— *See* BURTON (Jean) Sir Richard Burton's Wife. [With a portrait.] 1942. 8°. **10859**. l. **22**.

—— *See* BURTON (*Sir* Richard F.) *K.C.M.G.* The Memorial Edition of the Works of Captain Sir Richard F. Burton. [Edited by Lady Burton.] 1893, *etc.* 8°. **12273**. k. **1**.

—— *See* BURTON (*Sir* Richard F.) *K.C.M.G.* Explorations of the Highlands of the Brazil, *etc.* [Edited by Lady Burton.] 1869. 8°. **2374**. f. **3**.

—— *See* BURTON (*Sir* Richard F.) *K.C.M.G.* The Gold-Mines of Midian, *etc.* [Edited by Lady Burton.] 1878. 8°. **2358**. f. **3**.

—— *See* BURTON (*Sir* Richard F.) *K.C.M.G.* The Kasîdah—Couplets—of Hâjî Abdû Al-Yazdi, *etc.* [With a preface by Lady Burton.] 1894. 4°. **11651**. l. **36**.

—— —— 1900. 4°. **11651**. l. **50**.

BURTON (ISABEL) *Lady.*

—— *See* BURTON (*Sir* Richard F.) *K.C.M.G.* Personal Narrative of a Pilgrimage to Al-Madinah and Meccah . . . Edited by . . . I. Burton, *etc.* 1898. 8°. **2504**. k. **15**.

—— —— 1906. 8°. **012201**. i. **1/22**.

—— *See* CAMOENS (L. de) [*Works.*] Os Lusiadas . . . Englished by R. F. Burton: edited by . . . I. Burton. 1880, *etc.* 8°. **011451**. f. **40**.

—— *See* CATULLUS (C. V.) [*Works.—Latin and English.*] The Carmina of Caius Valerius Catullus . . . Englished into verse and prose: the metrical part by Capt. Sir Richard F. Burton, *etc.* [With a prefatory letter by Lady Burton.] 1894. 8°. **11385**. g. **31**.

—— *See* HARRIS (George W.) *of Algiers.* The Practical Guide to Algiers, *etc.* [With a preface by Lady Burton.] 1894. 8°. **10097**. a. **38**.

—— *See* PEREIRA DA SILVA (J. M.) Manuel de Moraes . . . Translated by R. F. and I. Burton. 1886. 8°. **12431**. e. **38**. **(2.)**

—— A E I. Arabia, Egypt, India. A narrative of travel. With fifteen illustrations and two maps. pp. viii. 488. *W. Mullan & Son: London & Belfast*, 1879. 8°. **010058**. h. **37**.

—— Prevention of Cruelty, and Anti-Vivisection, *etc.* [Extracted from "A E I. Arabia, Egypt and India."] pp. 32. *W. Mullan & Son: London & Belfast*, 1879. 8°. **8425**. f. **5**. **(5.)**

—— The Inner Life of Syria, Palestine, and the Holy Land. From my private journal, by I. Burton. With map, photographs, and coloured plates. 2 vol. *H. S. King & Co.: London*, 1875. 8°. **10075**. dd. **12**.

—— New and cheaper edition, with photographs and coloured plates. pp. xi. 516. *Kegan Paul & Co.: London*, 1879. 8°. **10076**. cc. **12**.

—— The Life of Captain Sir Richd. F. Burton . . . With numerous portraits, illustrations, and maps. 2 vol. *Chapman & Hall: London*, 1893. 8°. **10816**. dd. **11**.

—— [Another copy.] **10817**. dd. **13**.

—— [Another edition.] Edited, with a preface, by W. H. Wilkins. pp. xx. 548. *Duckworth & Co.: London*, 1898. 8°. **2407**. g. **2**.

—— The Passion-Play at Ober-Ammergau . . . Edited, with a preface, by W. H. Wilkins. [With a portrait.] pp. 256 *Hutchinson & Co.: London*, 1900. 8°. **011805**. f. **29**

—— The Romance of Isabel Lady Burton. The story of her life. Told in part by herself, and in part by W. H. Wilkins With portraits and illustrations. 2 vol. *Hutchinson & Co.: London*, 1897. 8°. **10825**. h. **19**

BURTON (J.) *of Rochester?* Lectures on Female Education and Manners. 2 vol. *Gillman & Etherington: Rochester*, 1793. 12°. **1031**. e. **13**.

—— Lectures on Female Education . . . The second edition 2 vol. *J. Johnson: London*, 1793. 12°. **08416**. a. **13**

—— Third edition. pp. xii. 430. *J. Milliken: Dublin*, 1794. 12°. **8415**. d. **26**

—— The first American edition. pp. 334. *Samuel Campbell: New-York*, 1794. 12°. **8415**. aa. **32**

BURTON (J. E.) *See* CATHER (Willa S.) Mon ennemi mortel, *etc.* (Traduit par J. Balay et J. E. Burton.) 1935. 8°. [*Les Œuvres libres.* no. 173.] **12208.** ee. **173.**

BURTON (J. M.) *pseud.* [i.e. JOSEPH BURTON MASON.] Under Westminster Bridge: a tale of the London dynamiters & unemployed. pp. 100. *H. Vickers: London,* [1888.] 8°. **12623.** f. **15.**

BURTON (J. W.) *formerly of Doctors' Commons.* The Law of Wills and Intestates' Estates. pp. 31. *Andrews & Co.: London,* 1906. 8°. **6146.** aa. **51.** (**3.**)

BURTON (J. W.) *of Calgary, Alberta.*

—— Juniper Root Carving. pp. 16. *Macmillan: [Toronto,* 1945.] 8°. [*Craftsmen's Library.* no. 17.] W.P. **1819/17.**

BURTON, afterwards HALIBURTON (JAMES) Excerpta hieroglyphica. no. 1–4. pl. LXI. [*Cairo,* 1825–29.] *obl.* 4°. **745.** a. **9.**

—— [Another copy.] **745.** a. **8.**
Imperfect; wanting all after plate LV.

BURTON (JAMES) *Assistant Master in the High School of the Liverpool Institute.* The Beginners' Drill-Book of English Grammar. Adapted for middle-class and elementary schools. pp. 113. *Rivingtons: London,* 1878. 8°. **12981.** bbb. **7.**

BURTON (JAMES) *Prisoner in York Castle.* The Warning: a religious and divine poem upon the contageous distemper amongst the horned cattle of this kingdom: also touching the late rebellion, earthquakes, *etc.* pp. 24. *Thomas Gent: York,* 1752. 8°. **11631.** c. **7.**

BURTON (JAMES) *Tanner, of Portsburgh.* *See* MERRILIES (Andrew) The Declaration of Andrew Merrilies . . . To which is subjoin'd, the declaration of Messrs. Burton and Goodlet before the Lord Justice Clerk, *etc.* 1751. 8°. **6573.** a. **7.**

BURTON (JAMES DANIEL) A Guide for Youth, recommending to their serious consideration vital piety, as the only rational way to present happiness, and future glory. pp. viii. 168. *T. Blanshard: London,* 1814. 12°. **864.** d. **5.**

BURTON (JAMES RYDER) A Letter addressed to the Editor of the "Morning Herald," on the national defences. pp. 16. *J. Hatchard & Son: London,* 1848. 8°. **1397.** e. **49.** (**11.**)

—— On the Concentration of the Material, the Manual and Physical Force, in her Majesty's Vessels of War, and on the most effective method of manning the Royal Navy . . . Third edition. pp. 112. *J. Hatchard & Son: London,* 1847. 8°. **1397.** d. **23.**

BURTON (JEAN)

—— *See* FORTUNE (Jan) and BURTON (J.) Elisabet Ney, *etc.* 1943. 8°. **10861.** aa. **4.**

—— Heyday of a Wizard, Daniel Home the Medium. With a foreword by Harry Price, *etc.* [With portraits.] pp. 244. *George G. Harrap & Co.: London,* 1948. 8°. **10862.** aa. **7.**

—— Sir Richard Burton's Wife. [With a portrait.] pp. 229. *G. G. Harrap & Co.: London,* 1942. 8°. **10859.** l. **22.**

BURTON (JEAN FRANÇOIS HENRI) Qu'est ce que le denier de Saint-Pierre? pp. 35. *Bruxelles,* 1867. 16°. **3902.** a. **62.** (**3.**)

BURTON (JOHN) *Commissioner for Licensing Hawkers.* The Case of John Burton, Commissioner for Licensing Hawkers, Pedlars, etc. [A petition to Parliament.] [*London,* 1726.] *s. sh.* fol. (S.P.R.) **357.** b. **10.** (**52.**)

—— [Another copy.] (S.P.R.) **357.** b. **10.** (**111.**)

—— A Short State of the Case of John Burton. [*London?* 1726.] *s. sh.* fol. **816.** m. **6.** (**61.**)

BURTON (JOHN) *Convict.* *See* TAYLOR (John) *Convict.* A Narrow Escape from the Punishment of Death; or the Case of J. Taylor and J. Burton, *etc.* [1830?] 12°. **864.** e. **31.** (**19.**)

BURTON (JOHN) *Curate of Alston cum Garrigill.* The Church of England Primitive and Apostolical, Pure and Scriptural, Holy and Beloved. A sermon. pp. 24. *Edwards & Hughes: London,* 1849. 12°. **4107.** a. **19.**

—— The Tradition of Confirmation. A sermon. pp. 12. *Edwards & Hughes: London,* 1849. 12°. **4326.** f. **12.**

BURTON (JOHN) *D.D.* *See* also PHILELEUTHERUS, *Londinensis, pseud.* [i.e. J. Burton.]

—— *See* BENTHAM (Edward) De vita et moribus Johannis Burtoni, *etc.* 1771. 8°. **696.** f. **4.** (**2.**)

—— *See* BIBLE.—*Old Testament.—Selections.* [*Polyglott.*] Sacræ Scripturæ locorum quorundam versio metrica, *etc.* [Edited by J. Burton.] 1736. 8°. **11408.** c. **12.**

—— Epistola critica, græce conscripta, ad Joh. Gul. Thompson . . . Accedit Eulogium memoriæ sacrum Johan. Rogers . . . Item Epistola ad Edw. Bentham. 2 pt. *J. & J. Rivington: Londini,* 1750. 8°. **1087.** i. **14.** (**6.**)

—— Occasional Sermons preached before the University of Oxford, on publick days, *etc.* 2 vol. *Clarendon Press: Oxford,* 1764, 66. 8°. **227.** d. **27, 28.**

—— [Another copy.] **696.** f. **1, 2.**
Vol. 2 *of this copy is a duplicate of vol.* 1, *with the exception of the titlepage and preliminary matter.*

—— Opuscula miscellanea metrico-prosaica. pp. v. 332. *E Typographeo Clarendoniano: Oxonii,* 1771. 8°. **696.** f. **4.** (**1.**)

—— Opuscula miscellanea theologica. 5 pt. *E Typographeo Clarendoniano: Oxonii,* [1771?] 8°. **696.** f. **3.**

—— Johannis Burton ad amicum epistola: sive Commentariolus Thomæ Secker Archiep. Cantuar. memoriæ sacer. pp. 10. *E Typographeo Clarendoniano: Oxonii,* 1768. 8°. **1020.** m. **31.** (**1.**)

—— De fundamentalibus, dissertatio theologica sive concio ad clerum londinensem, *etc.* pp. 78. *Apud Jacobum Fletcher: Oxonii,* 1756. 8°. **694.** e. **17.** (**17.**)

—— The Duty and Reward of Propagating Principles of Religion and Virtue exemplified in the history of Abraham. A sermon, *etc.* pp. 31. *J. March: London,* 1733. 4°. **4475.** c. **14.**

—— Elogium sacrum memoriæ Johannis Rogers, *etc.* pp. 10. *G. Innis & R. Manby: Londini,* 1734. fol. **815.** m. **18.**

—— [Another edition.] *See* ROGERS (John) *Canon of Wells.* Nineteen Sermons, *etc.* 1735. 8°. **1024.** g. **1.**

—— [Another edition.] *See* ROGERS (John) *Canon of Wells.* Nineteen Sermons, *etc.* 1784. 8°. **4455.** cc. **22.**

—— [Another edition.] *See* ROGERS (John) *Canon of Wells.* Fifty-six Sermons, *etc.* 1819. 8°. **4460.** gg. **2.**

—— Epistola ad Edw. Bentham. [An attack on William King, LL.D. With a titlepage bearing the imprint: Londini, prostant apud J. & J. Rivington; & J. Fetcher [*sic*], Oxonii. 1750.] pp. 36. *See* supra: [*Collections.*] Epistola critica, *etc.* 1750. 8°. **1087**. i. **14**. (**6**.)

—— Epistolæ, altera peregrinantis, altera rusticantis. [By J. Burton.] pp. 32. 1748. 8°. *See* EPISTOLAE. **012356**. h. **73**. (**1**.)

—— The Expostulation and Advice of Samuel to the Men of Israel Applied. A sermon, *etc.* pp. 24. *James Fletcher: Oxford,* 1746. 8°. **225**. f. **16**. (**7***.)

—— The Extensive Propagation of Abraham's Religion Represented. A sermon, *etc.* pp. 67. *Clarendon Press: Oxford,* 1765. 8°. **4474**. bbb. **19**.

—— The Folly and Wickedness of Misplacing our Trust and Confidence. A sermon, *etc.* pp. 44. *James Fletcher: Oxford,* 1744. 8°. **693**. d. **7**. (**12**.)

—— [Another copy.] **225**. f. **13**. (**3**.)

—— The Genuineness of Ld. Clarendon's History of the Rebellion, printed at Oxford, vindicated. Mr. Oldmixon's slander confuted. The true state of the case represented. pp. 173. *James Fletcher: Oxford,* 1744. 8°. **808**. e. **21**.

—— [Another copy.] **599**. g. **14**.

—— [Another copy.] **599**. g. **15**.

—— [Another copy.] **292**. f. **42**.

—— [Another copy.] **L.P.** G. **4917**.

—— Heli: sive Exemplum magistratus intempestiva lenitate peccantis. Concio, *etc.* pp. 23. *Impensis Viduæ Fletcher: Oxoniæ,* 1729. 4°. T. **941**. (**7**.)

—— [Another copy.] **226**. h. **7**. (**9**.)

—— Editio secunda. pp. 41–68. *E Theatro Sheldoniano: Oxoniæ,* 1761. 8°. **4474**. e. **9**.
The signatures and pagination continue those of the second edition of Hophni & Phinees.

—— Hophni & Phinees, sive Impietas sacerdotum publicæ impietatis causa. Concio, *etc.* pp. 26. *Impensis Viduæ Fletcher: Oxoniæ,* 1729. 4°. T. **941**. (**6**.)

—— [Another copy.] **226**. h. **7**. (**8**.)

—— Editio secunda. [With an appendix.] pp. 31. 32. *E Theatro Sheldoniano: Oxoniæ,* 1761. 8°. **4475**. bb. **27**.

—— King David's Charge to Solomon, or the Religious prince. A sermon, *etc.* pp. 45. *Clarendon Press: Oxford,* 1765. 8°. **4474**. bbb. **20**.

—— *'Οδοιπορουντος μελετηματα.* Sive Iter surriense & sussexiense. Præmittitur de linguæ græcæ institutionibus quibusdam epistola critica. pp. lxiv. 66. *J. & J. Rivington: Londini,* 1752. 8°. **792**. h. **19**.

—— [Another copy.] **290**. b. **35**.

—— Papists and Pharisees Compared: or, Papists the corrupters of Christianity. In a discourse, *etc.* pp. xii. 64. *J. Rivington: London,* 1766. 8°. **3938**. c. **16**.

—— [Another copy.] **696**. f. **3**. (**2**.)

—— *Πενταλογια*; sive, Tragoediarum græcarum delectus. *Σοφοκλεους Οἰδιπους Τυραννος, Οἰδιπους ἐπι Κολωνῳ, 'Αντιγονη. Εὐριπιδου Φοινισσαι. Αἰσχυλου 'Επτα ἐπι Θηβαις.* (Editor J. Burton.) pp. 48. 391. xci. *Ex Typographeo Clarendoniano: Oxonii,* 1758. 8°. **999**. d. **3**.

—— [Another copy.] **999**. d. **4**.

—— [Another copy.] **999**. d. **5**.
Imperfect; wanting the titlepage and the editor's introduction, pp. 1–48.

—— Editio altera. Cui observationes, indicemque græcum longe auctiorem et emendatiorem, adjecit Thomas Burgess. 2 tom. **L.P.** *Oxonii,* 1779. 8°. **165**. i. **9**, **10**.
The "Observationes" have a separate pagination and titlepage bearing the date 1778.

—— [Another copy.] **L.P.** G. **8459**, **60**.

—— [Another copy.] **L.P.** **682**. f. **7**, **8**.
Imperfect; wanting pp. 49–52.

—— [Another copy.] COPIOUS MS. NOTES [by Charles Burney]. **995**. e. **18**.
Imperfect; containing only the plays of Sophocles, with the "Observationes" on each.

—— [Another copy.] MS. NOTES [by Charles Burney]. **997**. e. **10**.
Imperfect; containing only the 'Επτα ἐπι Θηβαις of Aeschylus, with the "Observationes" on it.

—— [Another copy.] **624**. e. **23**. (**2**, **3**.)
Imperfect; containing only the introductory matter, and the Lexicon græcum, which is interleaved.

—— [Another edition.] pp. 558. *E Typographeo Clarendoniano: Oxonii,* 1801. 8°. **999**. d. **6**.

—— The Present State of Navigation on the Thames considered; and certain regulations proposed. By a Commissioner [i.e. J. Burton]. pp. 46. 1764. 4°. *See* COMMISSIONER. **8220**. aa. **6**. (**12**.)

—— The Present State of Navigation on the Thames considered; and certain regulations proposed. By a Commissioner [i.e. J. Burton]. The second edition. To which is added an appendix, containing observations on mills, weirs, locks, &c. pp. 54. 1767. 4°. *See* COMMISSIONER. **599**. g. **15**. (**2**.)

—— The Principles of Christian Loyalty. A sermon, *etc.* pp. vii. 39. *Mary Fletcher: Oxford,* [1743.] 8°. **694**. e. **14**. (**12**.)

—— [Another copy.] **4479**. bbb. **33**.

—— Principles of Religion the Only Sufficient Restraint from Wickedness. A sermon, *etc.* pp. 40. *James Fletcher: Oxford,* 1746. 8°. **225**. f. **16**. (**7**.)

—— Religious Education of Poor Children Recommended: a sermon . . . To which is annexed, an Account of the Society for Promoting Christian Knowledge. 2 pt. *J. Oliver: London,* 1759. 4°. **4475**. cc. **23**.

—— Sacerdos parœcialis rusticus. [A poem.] pp. 31. *Jacob. Fletcher: Oxonii,* 1757. 8°. **1213**. m. **16**. (**5**.)

—— [Another copy.] **11409**. gg. **54**. (**1**.)

BURTON (JOHN) *D.D.*

—— The Parish Priest: a poem. (A translation, with several alterations, of a Latin poem, entitled Sacerdos parœcialis rusticus.) [Translated by Dawson Warren. In verse.] pp. 38. *C. Whittingham: London,* 1800. 4°. **642.** k. **24.** (**1.**)
With an additional titlepage, engraved.

—— [Another copy.] **77.** g. **28.**

—— Samuel triplici nomine laudatus, propheta, populi israelitici judex, scholarum propheticarum rector. Conciones duae, *etc.* pp. 114. *Ex Typographeo Clarendoniano: Oxonii,* 1759. 8°. **4474.** e. **123.** (**3.**)

—— A Sermon preached before the Sons of the Clergy . . . on Thursday the 7th of May, 1761, *etc.* pp. 22. *C. Bathurst: London,* 1761. 4°. **694.** i. **14.** (**1.**)

—— A Sermon preached before the University of Oxford . . . Febr. 4. 1740–1. Being the day appointed for a general fast on occasion of the present war. pp. 30. *Printed at the Theatre: Oxford,* [1741.] 8°. **225.** h. **6.** (**13.**)

—— Two Sermons preached at St. Mary's before the University of Oxford, Feb. 11, 1757, and Mar. 12, 1762, *etc.* 2 pt. *J. Fletcher: Oxford,* 1762. 8°. **4474.** d. **26.**

—— University-Politicks. Or, the Study of a Christian, Gentleman, Scholar, set forth in three sermons, *etc.* pp. 99. *J. Fletcher: Oxford,* 1760. 8°. **4474.** d. **115.** (**10.**)

—— Elogium famæ inserviens Jacci Etonensis, sive Gigantis; or, the Praises of Jack of Eton, commonly called Jack the Giant [i.e. J. Burton]: collected into Latin and English metre . . . To which is added a dissertation on the Burtonic style. By a Master of Arts [i.e. William King]. pp. viii. 96. *S. Parker: Oxford,* 1750. 8°. **1465.** d. **9.**

—— [Another copy.] **161.** m. **65.**

BURTON (JOHN) *Exile in Holland. See* AUSTIN (John) *Roman Catholic Writer.* A Zealous Sermon . . . by a Jew, whose name is Not-Rub, *etc.* [A satire on J. Burton.] 1642. 4°. E. **149.** (**18.**)

BURTON (JOHN) *Incumbent of Alyth and Meigle. See* MINES (Flavel S.) Looking for the Church. Being an abridgment [by J. Burton] of " A Presbyterian Minister looking for the Church," *etc.* 1892. 8°. **4175.** cc. **27.**

—— En Deus: an essay on some elements of Christian evidence. pp. 58. *R. Grant & Son: Edinburgh,* 1870. 8°. **4412.** bb. **10.**

—— Our Protest against Rome. pp. 26. *R. Grant & Son: Edinburgh,* 1869. 8°. **3942.** c. **7.**

BURTON (JOHN) *M.D., of Edinburgh. See* LORIMER (Robert) *M.D.,* and BURTON (J.) Observations on the History and Treatment of Cholera, Asphyxia, *etc.* 1832. 8°. **1168.** k. **21.** (**7.**)

BURTON (JOHN) *M.D., of Walsall.* The Midland Masonic Calendar . . . Compiled from special returns, by . . . J. Burton, *etc.* pp. 38. [1862.] 16°. *See* EPHEMERIDES. P.P. **2472.** q.

BURTON (JOHN) *M.D., of York. See* DORAN (Alban H. G.) Burton—" Dr. Slop ": his forceps and his foes. 1913. 8°. **7307.** bb. **9.** (**11.**)

—— An Essay towards a Complete New System of Midwifry, theoretical and practical, *etc.* pp. xix. 391. *James Hodges: London,* 1751. 8°. **1177.** h. **6.**

BURTON (JOHN) *M.D., of York.*

—— Systême nouveau et complet de l'art des accouchements . . . Traduit . . . par M. Le Moine, *etc.* (Traité des maladies des enfants, depuis leur naissance jusqu'à leur adolescence [by Antoine Le Moine].) 2 tom. *Paris,* 1771, 73. 8°. **1177.** h. **11, 12.**

—— A Genuine and True Journal of the most miraculous Escape of the Young Chevalier from the Battle of Culloden, to his landing in France . . . By an Englishman [i.e. J. Burton]. pp. iv. 79. 1749. 8°. *See* ENGLISHMAN. **10806.** b. **25.**

—— [Another edition.] pp. 80. 1749. 8°. *See* ENGLISHMAN. **1203.** a. **15.** (**1.**)

—— [Another edition.] pp. 113. *Privately printed: Edinburgh,* 1884. 8°. [*Bibliotheca Curiosa.*] **012202.** de. **12.**

—— A Letter to William Smellie, M.D., containing critical and practical remarks upon his treatise on the theory and practice of midwifery, *etc.* pp. xii. 250. *W. Owen: London,* 1753. 8°. **7580.** aaa. **12.**

—— *See* WATTS (Giles) Reflections on Slow and Painful Labours . . . Interspersed with remarks on Dr. Burton's letter to Dr. Smellie, *etc.* 1755. 8°. **1178.** i. **4.**

—— Monasticon Eboracense: and the Ecclesiastical history of Yorkshire. Containing an account of the first introduction and progress of Christianity in that diocese, untill the end of William the Conqueror's reign, *etc.* (The appendix: containing charters, grants, and other original writings, *etc.*) 2 pt. *Printed for the Author: London,* 1758, 59. fol. **206.** i. **7.**

—— [Another copy.] **2068.f.**
Imperfect; wanting the appendix.

—— [Another copy.] G. **7444.**
Imperfect; wanting the appendix.

—— A Treatise on the Non-Naturals . . . To which is subjoined a short essay on the chin-cough, *etc.* pp. xxiii. 367. *A. Staples: York,* 1738. 8°. **1039.** l. **11.**

BURTON (JOHN) *Master of the Free School at Norwich.* Antiquitates Capellæ D. Johannis Evangelistæ; hodie Scholæ Regiæ Norwicensis. pp. 64. *See* BROWNE (*Sir* Thomas) [*Two or more Works.*] Posthumous Works, *etc.* 1712. 8°. **702.** h. **15.**

—— The History of Eriander. The first part. [A romance.] pp. 208. *R. Davenport for John Williams: London,* 1661. 8°. E. **2264.**

BURTON (JOHN) *Musical Instrument Maker.* Burton's Copyright Diagrams illustrating and fingering the 7 different positions on the violin. *J. Wallis: London,* [1886.] *s. sh.* fol. **1801.** d. **1.** (**123.**)

BURTON (JOHN) *of Aston. See* CAPELL (David) Joint Possession of the Borough and County Franchise. A verbatim report of the cases of Capell and Burton, appellants, and the Overseers of Aston, respondents, *etc.* 1850. 8°. **1244.** b. **2.** (**1.**)

BURTON (JOHN) *Rector of St. John the Baptist's, Bedford. See* BUNYAN (John) [*Some Gospel Truths Opened.*] Some Gospel-truths Opened, *etc.* [With an address to the reader by J. Burton.] 1656. 12°. C. **37.** f. **22.**

BURTON (John) *Religious Writer.* Sermons on Christian Life and Truth. pp. iv. 450. *Hamilton, Adams & Co.: London,* 1883. 8°. **4466.** i. **9.**

BURTON (John) *Schoolmaster at Leicester.* Burton's Grammatical and Pronouncing Spelling-Book, *etc.* pp. 155. *John Offer ; Richard Baynes: London,* 1823. *obl.* 8°. **12984.** de. **14.**

BURTON (John) *Sunday School Teacher, of Hull. See* Scott (John) *Incumbent of St. Mary's Church, Hull.* The Nature and Blessedness of Preparation for Death. A sermon preach'd . . . on occasion of the death of Mr. J. Burton. [1841.] 12°. **4906.** aa. **14.**

BURTON (John) *Tinker.* The Last Awful Moments of Six Unfortunate Malefactors, who suffered the extreme sentence of the law this day, Sep. 12, 1827, at Ilchester, viz.—John Burton, William Kerslake, Thos. Wiltshire, William Latcham, Richard Lovell, and William Southwood, for various offences. *Mary Shepherd: Bristol,* [1827.] *s. sh.* fol. **1880.** c. **20.** **(370.)**

BURTON (John) *Wesleyan Minister. See* Bible.—*Psalms.* [*English.—Miscellaneous Metrical Versions.*] The Book of Psalms in English Verse . . . By J. Burton. 1871. 8°. **3089.** bb. **34.**

—— Christian Devotedness; or, the Glorious life of a Christian: a Christian in earnest, a Christian altogether. pp. viii. 319. *John Snow: London,* 1860. 12°. **4404.** ccc. **28.**

—— The Christian Sabbath. pp. 32. *R. Jaques: Stratford,* 1876. 16°. **4355.** g. **2.**

—— One Hundred Original Hymns for the Young, and for use in Sunday Schools. By J. B., Essex [i.e. J. Burton]. [1850 ?] 32°. *See* B., J., *Essex.* **3434.** a. **3.**

—— A Summer's Day Walk, *etc.* [In verse.] pp. 12. *Jaques: Stratford,* [1875.] 8°. **011645.** eee. **124.** **(8.)**

—— War Irreconcilable with Christianity: an essay; including a careful examination of the teaching of the New Testament on the subject. pp. 30. *John Snow: London,* 1863. 16°. **8425.** a. **51.** **(5.)**

BURTON (John Barlow) Lectures on Entomology. [With coloured plates.] pp. 48. *Simpkin & Marshall: London,* 1837. 8°. **729.** a. **11.**

BURTON (John Daniel)

—— The G.T.S. Compact Series. A fascinating never failing guide to the language. *Globe Translating Service: Hounslow & Birmingham,* 1950- . *obl.* 8°. W.P. **3881.**
From 1954 *onward published by Bailey Bros. & Swinfen: London.*

BURTON (John E.) *of Geneva, Wisconsin.* The Inspiration of Bibles. A lecture, *etc.* pp. 28. *Herald Steam Book & Job Print: Geneva, Wis.,* 1881. 8°. **03128.** i. **15.** **(4.)**

BURTON (John Earp) *See* Ebstein (W.) The Nature and Treatment of Gout . . . Authorised translation by J. E. Burton. 1886. 8°. **7620.** b. **4.**

—— *See* Litzmann (C. C. T.) Handbook of Midwifery for Midwives, *etc.* [Translated by J. E. Burton.] 1880. 8°. **7581.** de. **27.**

—— —— 1884. 8°. **7581.** de. **38.**

BURTON (John Edward Bloundelle)

—— Across the Salt Seas. A romance of war and adventure. pp. viii. 333. *Methuen & Co.: London,* 1898. 8°. **012623.** ff. **41.**

BURTON (John Edward Bloundelle)

—— A Bitter Heritage. A modern romance. pp. vii. 310. *Cassell & Co.: London,* 1899. 8°. **012643.** g. **5.**

—— A Branded Name. pp. vi. 312. *Methuen & Co.: London,* 1903. 8°. **012638.** bb. **2.**

—— The Clash of Arms. A romance. pp. viii. 319. *Methuen & Co.: London,* 1897. 8°. **012623.** eee. **3.**

—— A Dead Reckoning. pp. vi. 306. *F. V. White & Co.: London,* 1904. 8°. **012629.** aa. **12.**

—— Denounced. A romance of love and sorrow. pp. viii. 350. *Methuen & Co.: London,* 1896. 8°. **012626.** f. **32.**

—— The Desert Ship. A story of adventure . . . With illustrations, *etc.* pp. viii. 399. *Hutchinson & Co.: London ; Nimeguen* [printed], [1893.] 8°. **012803.** g. **43.**

—— Skattsökarna, eller Skeppet i öknen . . . Med 8 helsidesplanscher. pp. 171. *Stockholm,* 1896. 8°. [*Gossarnas äfventyrböcker.* no. 4.] **12813.** t. **22/4.**

—— A Fair Martyr. A romance. pp. 317. *Everett & Co.: London,* 1910. 8°. **012623.** b. **16.**

—— The Fate of Henry of Navarre. A true account of how he was slain, with a description of the Paris of the time and some of the leading personages. [With plates, including a portrait.] pp. 349. *Everett & Co.: London,* [1910.] 8°. **10660.** y. **3.**

—— The Fate of Valsec. pp. vi. 330. *Methuen & Co.: London,* 1902. 8°. **012637.** c. **35.**

—— Fortune's Frown. A romance of the Spanish fury. pp. 320. *Everett & Co.: London,* [1913.] 8°. NN. **1320.**

—— Fortune's My Foe. pp. viii. 287. *C. A. Pearson: London,* 1899. 8°. **012642.** b. **14.**

—— A Gentleman Adventurer. A story of Panama, 1698 . . . With illustrations by Maynard Brown. pp. 287. *Andrew Melrose: London,* [1895.] 8°. **012628.** i. **6.**

—— [Another edition.] pp. 94. *Andrew Melrose: London,* [1908.] 8°. **012625.** ee. **120.**

—— [Another edition.] pp. xii. 257. *Pilgrim Press: London,* [1930.] 8°. **12818.** c. **16.**

—— His Own Enemy. The story of a man of the world. 2 vol. *Swan Sonnenschein & Co.: London,* 1887. 8°. **12621.** ccc. **1.**

—— The Hispaniola Plate. 1683–1893. pp. xii. 352. *Cassell & Co.: London,* 1895. 8°. **012629.** g. **21.**

—— [Another edition.] pp. 135. *Cassell & Co.: London,* 1901. 8°. **012624.** k. **47.**

—— In the Day of Adversity. A romance. pp. viii. 372. *Methuen & Co.: London,* 1896. 8°. **012627.** f. **22.**

—— The Intriguers' Way, *etc.* pp. 308. *R.T.S.: London,* [1903.] 8°. **04429.** h. **19.**

—— [Another edition.] With four illustrations by Adolf Thiede. pp. 160. *R.T.S.: London,* [1908.] 8°. [*Leisure Hour Monthly Library.* no. 33.] **012604.h.1/31.**

—— The King's Mignon. pp. 316. *Everett & Co.: London,* 1909. 8°. **012623.** b. **15.**

—— [Another edition.] pp. 252. *London,* [1912.] 8°. [*Everett's Library.* no. 6.] **12209.k.1/6.**

BURTON (John Edward Bloundelle)

—— Knighthood's Flower. A romance. pp. 354. *Hurst & Blackett: London,* 1906. 8°. **012633.** bb. **3.**

—— The Land of Bondage. A romance. pp. 318. *F. V. White & Co.: London,* 1905 [1904]. 8°. **012630.** a. **41.**

—— The Last of her Race. pp. 399. *John Milne: London,* 1908. 8°. **012625.** aaa. **9.**

—— Love Lies Bleeding. A romance. pp. 316. *Everett & Co.: London,* [1915.] 8°. NN. **2620.**

—— The Right Hand. A romance. pp. 313. *Everett & Co.: London,* [1911.] 8°. **12619.** ee. **8.**

—— The Scourge of God. A romance of religious persecution. pp. 310. *J. Clarke & Co.: London,* 1898. 8°. **012643.** ccc. **5.**

—— The Sea Devils. A romance. pp. 310. *F. V. White & Co.: London,* 1912. 8°. NN. **103.**

—— The Seafarers. pp. viii. 272. *C. A. Pearson: London,* 1900. 8°. **012641.** aaa. **5.**

—— Servants of Sin. A romance. pp. viii. 307. *Methuen & Co.: London,* 1900. 8°. **012641.** cc. **21.**

—— The Silent Shore. A romance. pp. 158. *J. & R. Maxwell: London,* [1886.] 8°. **12637.** aaa. **2.**

—— The Sword of Gideon. pp. 347. *Cassell & Co.: London,* 1905. 8°. **012631.** dd. **4.**

—— Traitor and True. A romance. pp. 318. *John Long: London,* 1906. 8°. **012632.** dd. **27.**

—— New edition. pp. 122. *John Long: London,* [1914.] 8°. **012600.** b. **97.**

—— New edition. pp. 124. *John Long: London,* 1921. 8°. **012600.** c. **154.**

—— Under the Salamander. A romance. pp. 320. *Everett & Co.: London,* 1911. 8°. **012618.** bb. **21.**

—— A Vanished Rival. A story of to-day. pp. xii. 295. *Cassell & Co.: London,* 1901. 8°. **012640.** cc. **16.**

—— Within Four Walls. pp. vi. 352. *John Milne: London,* 1909. 8°. **012618.** bb. **20.**

—— A Woman from the Sea. A romance of '93. pp. 374. *Eveleigh Nash: London,* 1907. 8°. **012625.** aaa. **10.**

—— The Year One. A page of the French Revolution, *etc.* pp. viii. 309. *Methuen & Co.: London,* 1901. 8°. **012639.** aa. **16.**

BURTON (John Francis) The Quest of New Life; sonnets, lyrics, and ballads of war and peace. 1914–1917. pp. 55. *J. F. Burton: London,* [1917.] 8°. **011648.** e. **50.**

—— The Story of the Vaccination Crusade in Hackney & Stoke Newington, 1902–1904, and what came of it. The cases of John Polley, William Pitt, and others, with an account of the action-at-law Polley v. Fordham. pp. 40. *Hackney Union Branch of the National Anti-Vaccination League:* [*London,*] 1904. 8°. **07305.** m. **7.** **(4.)**

BURTON (John Frederick) and **OWEN** (Denis Frank)

—— Bird-Watching in Kent. pp. 7. *London,* 1955. 8°. [*Royal Society for the Protection of Birds. Occasional Publications.* no. 24.] W.P. **10059/24.**

BURTON (John H.) *Writer on Military Defence.* Suffrage and Service . . . Reprinted from the United Service Magazine, *etc.* pp. xii. 28. *W. Clowes & Sons: London,* 1910. 8°. **8822.** aa. **50.** **(3.)**

BURTON (John Henry)

—— The Auditor and Mechanised Accounting, embracing external and internal audits. pp. 140. *Jordan & Sons: London,* 1947. 8°. **8218.** ee. **17.**

—— The Auditor and Accountant and Mechanised Accounting . . . Second edition, revised and enlarged [of " The Auditor and Mechanised Accounting "]. pp. 227. *Jordan & Sons: London,* 1950. 8°. **8219.** b. **27.**

—— Authors' Records and Accounts, *etc.* pp. 80. *Gee & Co.: London,* 1948. 8°. **8236.** e. **46.**

—— Control through Accounts, *etc.* pp. 63. *Gee & Co.: London,* 1950. 8°. **8219.** b. **12.**

—— Correct Book-Keeping, simply explained. pp. 143. *London,* 1924. 12°. [*Foulsham's Shilling Series.*] **12209.** ppp. **8/16.**

—— Costing for Control. pp. 96. *Gee & Co.: London,* 1948. 8°. **8218.** e. **43.**

—— Costing Schemes for Local Authorities. pp. xii. 130. *Sir I. Pitman & Sons: London,* 1929. 8°. **8224.** aaa. **17.**

—— Second edition. pp. xii. 136. *Sir I. Pitman & Sons: London,* 1931. 8°. **8224.** v. **9.**

—— Don'ts for Taxpayers & Ratepayers. pp. viii. 87. *A. & C. Black: London,* 1929. 32°. **6427.** de. **7.**

—— The Finance of Local Government Authorities. pp. 289. *C. Griffin & Co.: London,* 1934. 8°. **08229.** r. **13.**

—— How to appeal against Tax Assessments. A handbook for tax practitioners and taxpayers. pp. xxi. 210. *Jordan & Sons: London,* 1950. 8°. **6283.** bb. **21.**

—— How to Study for Profit, *etc.* pp. 86. *George Roberts: London,* 1929. 8°. **08311.** aa. **54.**

—— How to Study for Profit, *etc.* pp. 84. *Vawser & Wiles: London,* [1946.] 8°. **08311.** ee. **64.**

—— Investigations, accountancy and financial. pp. x. 162. *Sir I. Pitman & Sons: London,* 1930. 8°. **8224.** cc. **3.**

—— Loans and Borrowing Powers of Local Authorities. pp. xii. 215. *Sir I. Pitman & Sons: London,* 1924. 8°. **08228.** cc. **82.**

—— Local Authority Finance, Accounts and Auditing. pp. viii. 369. *Gee & Co.: London,* 1923. 8°. **08229.** bb. **14.**

—— (Second and revised edition.) 2 vol. pp. xvi. viii. 1075. *Gee & Co.: London,* 1932. 8°. **8224.** w. **28.**

—— Local Authority Finance, Accounts and Auditing, *etc.* (Third and revised edition.) pp. 304. *Gee & Co.: London,* 1954. 8°. **08218.** c. **30.**

—— Local Government for Everyman. pp. 76. *Pen-in-Hand Publishing Co.: Oxford,* [1949.] 8°. [***Everyman's Guide Series.*** **no. 5.**] **W.P. 3636/5.**

—— Local Rates. pp. x. 90. *Stevens & Sons: London,* 1950. 8°. [*This is the Law.*] W.P. **4832/30.**

BURTON (John Henry)

—— Mechanising for Control. [On mechanical office equipment.] pp. 95. *Gee & Co.: London,* 1950. 8°. **8222. aaa. 78.**

—— Mechanizing the Legal Office for Efficiency and Economy. pp. 38. *Gee & Co.: London,* 1951. 8°. **8286. bb. 65.**

—— Municipal Finance. pp. xi. 88. *Tower Bridge Publications: Hadleigh,* 1952 [1953]. 8°. **8219. e. 18.**

—— The Municipal Office Mechanized. pp. 127. *Gee & Co.: London,* 1951. 8°. **8219. l. 7.**

—— Preparation for Professional Examinations. pp. 91. *Gee & Co.: London,* 1952. 8°. **08311. e. 93**

—— A Rapid Course in Costing. pp. 52. *Barkeley Book Co.: Stanmore,* 1949. 8°. **8231.b.96.**

—— Rates and Taxes. Why pay too much? pp. viii. 140. *P. S. King & Son: London,* 1935. 8°. **6427. v. 19.**

—— Sinking Funds, Reserve Funds, and Depreciation. pp. viii. 91. *Sir I. Pitman & Sons: London,* 1922. 8°. **08228. ccc. 77.**

—— Second edition. pp. x. 129. *Sir I. Pitman & Sons: London,* 1926. 8°. **08229. i. 52.**

—— Stores Accounts and Stores Control. pp. ix. 144. *Sir I. Pitman & Sons: London,* 1929. 8°. **08225. ccc. 72.**

—— Second edition. pp. ix. 148. *Sir I. Pitman & Sons: London,* 1930. 8°. **8224. b. 13.**

—— Third edition. pp. xv. 236. *Sir I. Pitman & Sons: London,* 1937. 8°. **8234. f. 28.**

—— Stores Accounts and Stores Control . . . Fourth edition. pp. xvi. 278. *Sir I. Pitman & Sons: London,* 1941. 8°. **8222. d. 6.**

—— Stores Accounts and Stores Control . . . Fifth edition. pp. xv. 293. *Sir Isaac Pitman & Sons: London,* 1953. 8°. **8230. bb. 56.**

—— Wages and Salaries Recording & Distributing Methods. pp. 48. *Gee & Co.: London,* 1950. 8°. **8219. b. 40.**

BURTON (John Henry) and **NEWPORT** (Cecil Archer)

—— Local Authorities: Income Tax and Excess Profits Tax. pp. 134. *English Universities Press: London,* 1941. 8°. **6429. b. 4.**

BURTON (John Hill) *See* Africa.—*Company of Scotland trading to Africa and the Indies.* The Darien Papers, *etc.* (Edited by J. H. Burton.) 1849. 4°. Ac. **8248/90.**

—— *See* Atholl, *House of.* Jacobite Correspondence of the Atholl Family, *etc.* [Edited by J. H. Burton and D. Laing.] 1840. 4°. Ac. **8247/17.**

—— *See* Bentham (Jeremy) [*Selections.*] Benthamiana . . . Edited by J. H. Burton. 1843. 12°. **1127. e. 33.**

—— *See* Carlyle (Alexander) *D.D.* Autobiography, *etc.* [Edited by J. H. Burton.] 1860. 8°. **10825. e. 22.**

—— —— 1910. 8°. **10827. g. 10.**

—— *See* De Quincey (Thomas) De Quincey's "English Mail Coach," & other writings. With an introduction by the author of "The Book-Hunter" (J. H. Burton). [1912.] 8°. **12206.p.1/440.**

BURTON (John Hill)

—— *See* Encyclopaedias. A Cyclopædia of Commerce, Mercantile Law, Finance, and Commercial Geography . . . By W. Waterston . . . The law articles contributed by J. H. Burton. 1843. 8°. **1391. g. 35.**

—— —— 1847. 8°. **8245. cc. 22.**

—— —— 1863. 8°. **12224. aaa. 4.**

—— *See* Scotland.—*Privy Council.* The Register of the Privy Council of Scotland. Edited and abridged by J. H. Burton [and others], *etc.* 1877, *etc.* 8°. **2073. (111.)**

—— *See* Tytler (Alexander F.) *Lord Woodhouselee.* Tytler's Elements of History . . . New edition, revised and continued to the present time by J. H. Burton. 1855. 8°. **09009. b. 4.**

—— The Book-Hunter, *etc.* pp. viii. 384. **L.P.** *W. Blackwood & Sons: Edinburgh & London,* 1862. 8°. **011903. e. 55.**

—— Second edition. pp. viii. 408. *W. Blackwood & Sons: Edinburgh & London,* 1863. 8°. **11901. aaa. 13.**

—— A new edition, with a memoir of the author [by Katharine Burton]. [With a portrait.] pp. x. civ. 427. *W. Blackwood & Sons: Edinburgh & London,* 1882. 8°. **2308. f. 8.**

—— [Another edition.] Edited by J. Herbert Slater. pp. viii. 259. *G. Routledge & Sons: London,* [1908.] 8°. [*London Library.*] **12207. pp. 2/13.**

—— The Cairngorm Mountains. pp. 120. *W. Blackwood & Sons: Edinburgh & London,* 1864. 8°. **10369. b. 6.**

—— Convicts. By a Practical Hand [i.e. J. H. Burton?]. pp. 32. 1865. 16°. [*Odds and Ends.* no. 2.] *See* Convicts. **12355. aa. 37.**

—— Emigration in its Practical Application to Individuals and Communities. (The Emigrant's Manual.) pp. 92. *Edinburgh,* 1851. 12°. [*Chambers's Instructive and Entertaining Library.*] **1157. f. 7. (3.)**

—— The History of Scotland, from Agricola's invasion to the Revolution of 1688. 7 vol. *W. Blackwood & Sons: Edinburgh & London,* 1867, 70. 8°. **9509. g. 6.**

—— Second edition. [With an index volume.] 9 vol. *W. Blackwood & Sons: Edinburgh & London,* 1873. 8°. **2085.d.**

—— History of Scotland, from the Revolution to the extinction of the last Jacobite insurrection. 1689–1748. 2 vol. *Longman & Co.: London,* 1853. 8°. **1325. c. 16–17.**

—— A History of the Reign of Queen Anne. 3 vol. *W. Blackwood & Sons: Edinburgh & London,* 1880. 8°. **2394. e. 5.**

—— Introduction to the Study of the Works of Jeremy Bentham. pp. 83. *See* Bentham (Jeremy) [*Works.*] The Works of Jeremy Bentham, *etc.* vol. 1. 1843, *etc.* 8°. **12274. d. 1.**

—— The Law of Bankruptcy, Insolvency, and Mercantile Sequestration, in Scotland. 2 pt. *William Tait: Edinburgh,* 1845. 8°. App. xxx. xxii. 789. **6573. dd. 7.**

—— Letters of Eminent Persons addressed to David Hume, *etc.* [Edited by J. H. Burton.] pp. xxxi. 334. *W. Blackwood & Sons: Edinburgh & London,* 1849. 8°. **10920. g. 6.**

BURTON (John Hill)

—— Life and Correspondence of David Hume, *etc.* [With portraits.] 2 vol. *William Tait: Edinburgh*, 1846. 8°. **2408**. e. **1**.

—— Life of Professor W. Spalding. *See* Spalding (William) *Professor of Logic in the University of St. Andrews.* A Letter on Shakspere's Authorship of The Two Noble Kinsmen, *etc.* 1876. 8°. Ac. **9488**. c/**8**.

—— Lives of Simon Lord Lovat, and Duncan Forbes, *etc.* pp. xvi. 388. *London*, 1847. 8°. [*Chapman and Hall's Series.*] **1153**. k. **7**.

—— The Local Taxes of Scotland. *See* Fry (Danby P.) The Local Taxes of the United Kingdom, *etc.* 1846. 8°. **1391**. e. **32**.

—— A Manual of the Law of Scotland, civil, municipal, criminal, and ecclesiastical; with a practical commentary on the mercantile law, and on the powers and duties of . . . magistrates. (Supplement containing alterations and additions.) 2 pt. *Oliver & Boyd: Edinburgh*, 1839, 44. 12°. **1130**. g. **30**.

—— Second edition, enlarged. pp. xiv. 437. *Oliver & Boyd: Edinburgh*, 1847. 12°. **1384**. d. **6**.

—— Manual of the Law of Scotland . . . The law of private rights and obligations. Second edition, enlarged. pp. xiv. 506. *Oliver & Boyd: Edinburgh*, 1847. 12°. **1384**. d. **7**.

—— Memorandum on the Collection and Arrangement of the Judicial Statistics of Scotland, *etc.* pp. 20. [1868.] 8°. *See* Scotland.—*Department of Judicial Statistics.* **6146**. g. **11**. (5.)

—— Narratives from Criminal Trials in Scotland. 2 vol. *Chapman & Hall: London*, 1852. 8°. **1132**. f. **23**.

—— Political and Social Economy: its practical applications. pp. 345. *Edinburgh*, 1849. 8°. [*Chambers's Instructive and Entertaining Library.*] **1157**. f. **6**. (**1**.)

—— The Scot Abroad. 2 vol. *W. Blackwood & Sons: Edinburgh & London*, 1864. 8°. **10804**. b. **1**.

—— New edition. pp. xi. 488. *W. Blackwood & Sons: Edinburgh & London*, 1881. 8°. **2396**. b. **1**.

BURTON (*Mrs.* John Hill) *See* Burton (Katharine)

BURTON (John Marvin) Honoré de Balzac and his Figures of Speech. pp. 98. *Princeton University Press: Princeton; Librairie Édouard Champion: Paris; Macon* [printed], 1921. 8°. [*Elliott Monographs.* no. 8.] W.P. **4150**/**8**.

BURTON (John Richard) *Head Master of the Junior Department in the Bedfordshire Middle-Class Public School.* *See* Sanders (Samuel J. W.) and Burton (J. R.) Facts and Figures, *etc.* [1860?] 8°. **8306**. e. **15**.

—— Roots and Derivatives. pp. 18. *Educational Trading Co.: London*, [1870.] 8°. **12935**. bb. **59**.

BURTON (John Richard) *Rector of Bitterley.* *See* Browne (Edith O.) and Burton (J. R.) Short Biographies of the Worthies of Worcestershire, *etc.* 1916. 8°. **10854**. i. **34**.

—— Bewdley Worthies. 13 no. 1878–84. *See* Periodical Publications.—*Bewdley.* Parish Magazine for Ribbesford, *etc.* 1878, *etc.* 8°. P.P. **343**. w.

—— A History of Bewdley; with concise accounts of some neighbouring parishes. [With plates.] pp. 96. liv. *William Reeves: London*, 1883. 8°. **10360**. ccc. **12**.

BURTON (John Richard) *Rector of Bitterley.*

—— A History of Kidderminster, with short accounts of some neighbouring parishes. pp. xii. 234. *Elliot Stock: London*, 1890. 4°. **10368**. h. **27**.

—— Some Collections towards the History of the Family of Walcot of Walcot, and afterwards of Bitterley Court, Shropshire, *etc.* [With plates, including portraits.] pp. vii. 123. *Printed for the Author: Shrewsbury*, 1930. 8°. **09915**. e. **22**.

BURTON (John Richard) *Rector of Bitterley*, and **PEARSON** (F. S.)

—— Bibliography of Worcestershire . . . Edited . . . by the Rev. J. R. Burton . . . and F. S. Pearson. 2 pt. 1898, 1903. 4°. *See* Worcester.—*Worcestershire Historical Society.* **BB.K.c.7.**

BURTON (John Wear) *the Elder.*

—— The Alternative. A dynamic approach to our relations with Asia. pp. 116. *Morgans Publications: Sydney*, [1954.] 8°. **08023**. dd. **97**.

—— The Call of the Pacific. pp. xiv. 286. *C. H. Kelly: London*, 1912. 8°. **4764**. a. **18**.

—— [Another edition. With plates, and a map.] pp. xi. 286. *C. H. Kelly: London*, [1914.] 8°. [*Every Age Library.*] **12207**. r. **8**.

—— The Fiji of To-day . . . With an introduction by the Rev. A. J. Small . . . With seventy-five illustrations. pp. 364. *C. H. Kelly: London*, 1910. 8°. **4767**. dd. **30**.

—— Missionary Survey of the Pacific Islands. [With maps.] pp. 124. *London*, 1930. 8°. [*World Dominion Survey Series.*] **4769.e.1/17.**

—— Modern Missions in the South Pacific. pp. 224. *Livingstone Press: London*, 1949. 8°. **4768**. aaa. **82**

—— Papua for Christ. [With plates.] pp. 124. *Epworth Press: London*, 1926. 8°. **4763**. bb. **24**.

—— Snapshots in India . . . With thirty-two illustrations. pp. xii. 170. *Elliot Stock: London*, 1912. 8°. **10058**. p. **8**.

BURTON (John Wear) *the Elder*, and **DEANE** (Wallace)

—— A Hundred Years in Fiji. [With plates.] pp. 144. *Epworth Press: London*, 1936. 8°. **4768.bbb.24.**

BURTON (Joseph) *Author of "Gold and Competition."* Gold and Competition; or, the Wailing of a commission man. A satire. [In verse. The dedication signed: J. B., i.e. J. Burton.] pp. 56. 1863. 8°. *See* B., J. **11649**. bb. 49.

BURTON (Joseph) *Dissenting Minister.*

—— The Assistance which Christians may render to their Ministers in the Service of God. The circular letter from the Ministers and Messengers of the Buckinghamshire Association of Baptist Churches, assembled at Chesham, May 10th & 11th, 1842, *etc.* pp. 20. 1842. *See* England.—*Churches and Religious Bodies.—Baptists.—Buckinghamshire Association.* [Circular letters, 1830–46.] 1830, *etc.* 8°. **4139**. e. **13**. (**12**.)

—— Election. A sermon, *etc.* pp. 12. *E. Johnson: Cambridge*, 1853. 12°. **4255**. b. **17**.

BURTON (JOSEPH) *of Manchester.* A Treatise on the Importance and Utility of Classical Learning. pp. ii. 116. *Whittaker, Treacher & Arnot: London; J. Stanfield: Bradford,* 1831. 12°. **1088**. k. **32**.

BURTON (JOSEPH CYRIL GEORGE)

—— We Believe in Liberal Christianity. pp. 16. *Lindsey Press: London,* [1947.] 8°. [*Unitarian Statements.* no. 4.] **4140**. aa. **15/4**.

BURTON (JOSHUA)

—— Experimental Religion. The circular letter, from the Baptist Ministers and Messengers, assembled at Spalding . . . May 29, 30, 31. 1798, *etc.* pp. 8. [1798.] *See* ENGLAND.—*Churches and Religious Bodies.—Baptists.—Northamptonshire Association.* [Circular letters, 1768–1891.] [1768, *etc.*] 8°. **4139**. g. 4. (**19**.)

BURTON (JUDSON N.)

—— Price List no. 6 of Judson N. Burton, Wholesale Dealer in Postage Stamps, *etc.* (Price List of U.S. & Foreign Stamps, 1895–1896.) 2 pt. *Madison, N.Y.,* [1895.] 12°. Crawford **243**. (**6**, **7**.)

BURTON (JULIA) and **GARLICK** (PHYLLIS LOUISA)

—— Bless this Roof. [A story of negro life in Western Nigeria. With plates.] pp. 77. *Highway Press: London,* [1953.] 8°. **010094**. ee. **87**.

BURTON (JULIETTE T.) The Five Jewels of the Orient. pp. 244. *Masonic Publishing Co.: New York,* 1872. 12°. **4417**. bbb. **14**.

BURTON (K. A.)

—— *See* WOLLASTON (John R.) Wollaston's Picton Journal, *etc.* (Wollaston's Albany Journals. Edited by P. U. Henn [and K. A. Burton].) 1948, *etc.* **9781**. b. **37**.

BURTON (KATHARINE) *See* BURTON (John H.) The Book-Hunter . . . With a memoir of the author [by K. Burton]. 1882. 8°. **2308**. f. **8**.

—— Memoir of Cosmo Innes. [By K. Burton.] pp. vii. 83. 1874. 4°. *See* INNES (Cosmo) *Antiquary.* **10856**. g. **4**.

—— A Memoir of Mrs. Crudelius. Edited by K. Burton. pp. ii. 346. *Privately printed: Edinburgh,* 1879. 8°. **4955**. f. **13**.

—— My Home Farm. pp. 128. *Longmans & Co.: London,* 1883. 8°. **7078**. bb. **24**.

—— Our Summer in the Harz Forest. By a Scotch Family. [By K. Burton.] pp. ix. 278. 1865. 8°. *See* HARTZ. **10260**. bb. **29**.

BURTON (KATHERINE) *See* BOAS (Ralph P.) and BURTON (K.) Social Backgrounds of American Literature, *etc.* 1933. 8°. **11856**. ee. **42**.

—— According to the Pattern. The story of Dr. Agnes McLaren and the Society of Catholic Medical Missionaries. pp. 252. *Longmans & Co.: New York, Toronto,* 1946. 8°. **4909**. bb. **14**.

—— Brother André of Mount Royal. [A biography.] pp. 197. *Clonmore & Reynolds: Dublin,* 1955. 8°. **4987**. ee. **11**.

—— Celestial Homespun. The life of Isaac Thomas Hecker. pp. 393. *Longmans & Co.: London; printed in U.S.A.,* 1943. 8°. **10881**. t. **32**.

—— Difficult Star. The life of Pauline Jaricot. [With a portrait.] pp. x. 239. *Longmans, Green & Co.: New York,* 1947. 8°. **4865**. i. **28**.

BURTON (KATHERINE)

—— The Great Mantle. The life of Giuseppe Melchiore Sarto, Pope Pius x. [With a portrait.] pp. xiv. 238. *Longmans, Green & Co.: New York,* 1950. 8°. **4857**. aa. **1**.

—— His Dear Persuasion. The life of Elizabeth Ann Seton. pp. xi. 304. *Longmans & Co.: New York,* 1940. 8°. **20033**. bb. **39**.

—— In No Strange Land. Some American catholic converts. pp. xix. 254. *Longmans & Co.: New York, Toronto,* 1942. 8°. **20046**. b. **21**.

—— Mother Butler of Marymount. [With a portrait.] pp. xi. 290. *Longmans & Co.: New York, Toronto,* 1944. 8°. **4910**. b. **5**.

—— The Next Thing. Autobiography & reminiscences. [With plates, including a portrait.] pp. vii. 246. *Longmans, Green & Co.: New York, Toronto,* 1949. 8°. **10890**. ff. **14**.

—— No Shadow of Turning. The life of James Kent Stone —Father Fidelis of the Cross. [With a portrait.] pp. 243. *Longmans & Co.: New York, Toronto,* 1944. 8°. **20048**. b. **25**.

—— Paradise Planters. The story of Brook Farm. pp. x. 336. *Longmans & Co.: London; printed in U.S.A.,* 1939. 8°. **010410**. d. **5**.

—— Sorrow Built a Bridge. A daughter of Hawthorne. [The life of Rose Hawthorne Lathrop. With a portrait.] pp. 288. *Longmans & Co.: London; printed in U.S.A.,* 1937. 8°. **10887**. b. **2**.

—— Three Generations: Maria Boyle Ewing, 1801–1864; Ellen Ewing Sherman, 1824–1888; Minnie Sherman Fitch, 1851–1913. [With portraits.] pp. viii. 312. *Longmans, Green & Co.: New York, Toronto,* 1947. 8°. **9918**. aaa. **14**

BURTON (KATHERINE) and **PERRY** (LOUISE SANBORN GIFFORD)

—— The Bibliolatrous Series. no. 3, 5–8. *Periwinkle Press: Norton, Mass.,* 1939. 16°. Cup. **501**. a. **1**.
Imperfect; wanting no. 1, 2, 4.

BURTON (KATHLEEN M. P.)

—— *See* STARKEY (Thomas) A Dialogue between Reginald Pole & Thomas Lupset . . . Edited by K. M. Burton, *etc.* 1948. 8°. **8012**. aa. **14**.

BURTON (KENNETH GEORGE)

—— *See* WATTS (John) *of Reading.* The Memorandums of John Watts, Esq . . . Edited by K. G. Burton. 1950. 8°. **010368**. p. **36**.

—— The Early Newspaper Press in Berkshire, 1723–1855. [With plates.] pp. x. 290. *K. G. Burton: Reading,* 1954. 4°. **11918**. d. **4**.
Reproduced from typewriting.

BURTON (KIRKBY) To-day, To-morrow and For Ever. [A novel.] pp. 228. *Digby, Long & Co.: London,* 1892. 8°. **012634**. g. **22**.

—— New and cheaper edition. pp. 228. *Digby, Long & Co.: London,* [1893.] 8°. **012634**. f. **106**.

BURTON (L.) *Secretary, Brighton Deep Sea Anglers,* and **BROWN** (HENRY ELLIS) Famous Brighton Fishing Marks. Where and what to fish for. [Plans.] ff. 16. *H. E. Brown: Brighton,* [1921.] 16°. **7913**. aaa. **51**.

BURTON (L. M.)

—— The Scholars' Own Guide in Arithmetic. 2 bk. *Macmillan & Co.: London*, 1939. 8°. **08535. aa. 51.**

BURTON (LENA DALKEITH) Everychild: morality play. By L. D. Burton in cooperation with Marian Katherine Brown. *C. W. Thompson & Co.: Boston*, 1911. 8°. **11775. i. 4.**

BURTON (LINETTE)

—— *See* BURTON (Earl) and (L.) The Exciting Adventures of Waldo, *etc.* [1945.] 8°. **012826. d. 40.**

—— *See* BURTON (Earl) and BURTON (L.) Taffy and Joe, *etc.* 1947. 8°. **12828. dd. 26.**

BURTON (LITTLETON)

—— *See* NORTHEY (*Sir* Edward) and BOX (HENRY) Littleton Burton clerk [and others], appellants. Henry Lord Bishop of London, and M. Hutchinson clerk, respondents. The respondents' case. [Signed: E. Northey, H. Box.] [1711.] fol. **816. m. 16. (13.)**

BURTON (LUCY)

—— *See* ARMITAGE (Ethel) Garden and Hedgerow . . . With plates by L. Burton. 1939. 8°. **07032. tt. 15.**

BURTON (M. E.) *Wife of W. S. Burton.* Annabel . . . Illustrations by W. S. Burton. pp. 367. *Griffith, Farran & Co.: London*, 1889. 8°. **12807. t. 8.**

BURTON (MADELINE)

—— The Great Event. A sketch for 7 women, *etc.* pp. 18. *Leonard's Plays: London*, [1955.] *obl.* 8°. **11784. g. 54.**
Reproduced from typewriting.

BURTON (MARGARET) *F.L.A.* *See* ENGLAND.—*Library Association of the United Kingdom.* A Bibliography of Librarianship . . . Selected by M. Burton . . . and M. E. Vosburgh. 1934. 8°. **BBE.g.11.**

—— Famous Libraries of the World: their history, collections and administrations. By M. Burton . . . under the direction of and with an introduction by Arundell Esdaile. pp. xix. 458. pl. XXXI. *Grafton & Co.: London*, 1937. 8°. **11914. e. 13.**
No. 2 of "The World's Great Libraries."

BURTON (MARGARET) *of Darlington.* *See* DUNGETT (John) Life and Correspondence of the late Mrs. M. Burton, *etc.* 1832. 12°. **4920. bb. 14.**

—— Poetical Effusions, on subjects religious, moral, and rural. pp. xvi. 149. *Printed for the Author: London*, 1816. 12°. **11642. aaa. 6.**

BURTON (MARGARET ERNESTINE)

—— The Assembly of the League of Nations. pp. xi. 441. *University of Chicago Press: Chicago*, 1941. 8°. **8425. w. 34.**

—— The Education of Women in China . . . Illustrated. pp. 232. *F. H. Revell Co.: New York*, [1911.] 8°. **4764. e. 19.**

—— The Education of Women in Japan . . . Illustrated pp. 268. *F. H. Revell Co.: New York*, 1914. 8°. **08355. ff. 11.**

—— Notable Women of Modern China. [With illustrations.] pp. 271. *F. H. Revell Co.: New York*, [1912.] 8°. **4764. bb. 7.**

BURTON (MARGARET ERNESTINE)

—— Women Workers of the Orient . . . British edition, revised and adapted by E. I. M. Boyd. pp. 192. *United Council for Missionary Education: London*, 1920. 8°. **08285. a. 67.**

BURTON (MARIA S. B.) Happy Days and Happy Work in Basutoland, *etc.* pp. 64. *S.P.C.K.: London*, 1902. 8°. **04429. c. 64.**

BURTON (MARION LE ROY) The Problem of Evil. A criticism of the Augustinian point of view. pp. 234. *Open Court Publishing Co.: Chicago*, 1909. 8°. **03558. ee. 17.**

BURTON (MARJORIE) *Teacher of Modern Languages.*

—— Les Grandes vacances, *etc.* pp. 96. *London*, 1947. 8°. [*Harrap's Modern Language Series.*] **12213. a. 1/476.**

—— Nos amis les Beauvallon . . . Illustrated by Douglas Relf. pp. 108. *George G. Harrap & Co.: London*, 1949. 8°. [*Harrap's Modern Languages Series.*] **12213. a. 1/499.**

—— Das Wandern ist der Jugend Lust . . . Illustrated by W. T. Mars. pp. 96. *George G. Harrap: London*, 1951. 8°. **12964. aa. 78.**

BURTON (MARJORIE A.) A Caravan in the Bush. pp. 8. [*London*, 1937.] 8°. [*S.P.G. World Wide Series.* no. 5.] **W.P. 6214/5.**

—— Chandra, Doulat and the others. Six story lessons . . . for children, *etc.* pp. 64. *S.P.G.: London*, 1930. 8°. **4406. de. 1.**

—— Far Away Hospitals. Seven story lessons for children aged 7–11 years on the work of medical missions . . . With one sheet of pictures. pp. 57. *S.P.G.: London*, 1932. 8°. **4765. g. 24.**

—— The Nursery of the Kingdom, *etc.* pp. 36. *S.P.G.: London*, 1932. 8°. **4192. ff. 22.**

BURTON (MARJORIE A.) and **FOX** (ELSIE)

—— The Middle Kingdom. Lessons on the work of the Church in China. [With a sheet of pictures.] pp. 82. *S.P.G.: London*, 1933. 8°. **4765. gg. 9.**

BURTON (MARY) Mary Burton, or, the Bright Halfpenny. By the author of "The Cottage on the Common," *etc.* pp. 31. *W. J. Cleaver: London*, 1848. 32°. **1359. a. 47. (2.)**

BURTON, afterwards **CRYER** (MARY) *See* BARRETT (Alfred) *Wesleyan Minister.* Holy Living: exemplified in the life of Mrs. Mary Cryer, *etc.* 1825. 8°. **1373. g. 14.**

—— The Devotional Remains of Mrs. Cryer. With an introduction by the Rev. Alfred Barrett. pp. 270. *Hamilton, Adams & Co.: London*, 1854. 12°. **4906. d. 48.**

—— Third edition. pp. iv. 270. *John Mason: London*, [1862.] 12°. **4407. aaa. 34.**

BURTON (MARY AGNES) *See* BURTON (Clarence M.) Manuscripts from the Burton Historical Collection . . . Edited by M. A. Burton. 1916, *etc.* 8°. **9551. d. 22.**

BURTON (Mary Agnes)

—— *See* Lees (John) *of Quebec.* Journal of J. L. [i.e. John Lees], of Quebec, Merchant. [Edited by M. A. Burton.] 1911. 8°. Ac. **8404/2.**

—— *See* Pontiac, *Chief of the Ottawas.* Journal of Pontiac's Conspiracy . . . Edited by M. A. Burton. [1913.] 8°. Ac. **8404/3.**

BURTON (Maurice) *See* Bolitho (Henry H.) The Glorious Oyster . . . With certain chapters edited by M. Burton. 1929. 8°. **07290.** e. **17.**

—— *See* Coward (Thomas A.) Birds of the Wayside and Woodland . . . With introductory chapters by M. Burton, *etc.* 1952. 8°. **7288.** a. **20.**

—— *See* England.—*Colonial Office.*—" *Discovery* " *Committee.* Discovery Reports. (vol. 6. Sponges. By M. Burton.) 1929, *etc.* 4°. W.P. **243/6.**

—— *See* London.—iii. *British Museum.* British Antarctic —" Terra Nova "—Expedition, 1910. Natural History Report. (Porifera. pt. 2.—Antarctic Sponges. By M. Burton.) 1914, *etc.* 4°. **7006.w.1/6.**

—— *See* Vlasák (J.) and Seget (J.) Snow White. The story of a polar bear cub . . . Edited by M. Burton. 1949. 4°. **07209.** cc. **35.**

—— Animal Courtship . . . Drawings by Jane Burton. [With plates.] pp. 267. *Hutchinson: London,* 1953. 8°. **7211.** aa. **5.**

Part of " Hutchinson's Nature Library."

—— Animal Legends . . . Illustrated by Jane Burton. pp. 215. *Frederick Muller: London,* 1955. 8°. **7211.** aa. **23.**

—— Animals and their Behaviour. [With illustrations.] pp. 144. *Edward Arnold & Co.: London,* 1950. 8°. [*Merlin Books.*] W.P. **13274/6.**

—— Curiosities of Animal Life . . . Illustrated by L. F. Savage. pp. 224. *Ward, Lock & Co.: London & Melbourne,* 1952. 8°. **7209.** bb. **49.**

—— Hexactinellida, *etc.* pp. 18. *H. Hagerup: Copenhagen,* 1928. fol. [*Danish Ingolf-Expedition.* vol. 6. pt. 4.] Ac. **3572.**

—— Living Fossils. With eighty-three drawings by Jane Burton. pp. xiv. 282. *Thames & Hudson: London, New York,* [1954.] 8°. [*The Past in the Present.*] **9027.k.44/4.**

—— Margins of the Sea. [With illustrations.] pp. x. 210. *Frederick Muller: London,* 1954. 8°. **07290.** k. **9.**

—— Sponges (brought home by the Great Barrier Reef Expedition). *London,* 1934. 4°. [*British Museum (Natural History). Great Barrier Reef Expedition. Scientific Reports.* vol. 4. no. 14.] W.P. **2344/4.**

—— The Story of Animal Life, *etc.* [With plates.] 2 vol. *Elesevier Publishing Co.: London; Nijmegen* printed, 1949. 4°. **7210.** dd. **8.**

—— Suberites Domuncula-Olivi: its synonymy, distribution and ecology. By M. Burton. Notes on Asteroids in the British Museum, Natural History, iii and iv. By A. M. Clark. Some Inter-tidal Mites from South-West England. By G. O. Evans and E. Browning. [With plates.] *London,* 1953. 8°. [*Bulletin of the British Museum (Natural History). Zoology.* vol. 1. no. 12.] Ac. **1325.** a. (**2.**)

BURTON (Maurice)

—— When Dumb Animals talk . . . Illustrated by Jane Burton. pp. 112. *Hutchinson & Co.: London,* 1955. 8°. **7211.** a. **22.**

—— Wild Life of the World. Illustrated. Advisory editor, Dr. Maurice Burton. pp. 384. *Odhams Press: London,* [1950.] 8°. **7209.** bb. **40.**

BURTON (May)

—— For Love's Sake. pp. 36. *William Stevens: London,* [1945.] 8°. [*New Moon Series.* no. 577.] **12633.** pp. **1/382.**

BURTON (Michael) *See* Bible.—*New Testament.* [*Greek.*] *Της Καινης Διαθηκης άπαντα, etc.* copious ms. notes [by M. Burton]. 1728. 8°. **1408.** i. **9–11.**

BURTON (Mildred Dennis) Mixed Pickles, *etc.* [Tales for children.] pp. 83. *Roffey & Clark: Croydon,* 1929. 4°. **012803.** l. **10.**

BURTON (Miles)

—— Beware your Neighbour. pp. 192. *Collins: London,* 1951. 8°. NNN. **1868.**

—— The Cat Jumps. pp. 192. *Collins: London,* 1946. 8°. NN. **35908.**

—— The Charabanc Mystery. pp. 252. *W. Collins, Sons & Co.: London,* [1934.] 8°. NN. **21897.**

—— A Crime in Time. pp. 255. *Collins: London,* 1955. 8°. NNN. **7182.**

—— Dead Stop. pp. 192. *Collins: London,* 1943. 8°. NN. **33799.**

—— Death at Low Tide. pp. 252. *Collins: London,* [1938.] 8°. NN. **28541.**

—— Death at the Club. pp. 284. *Collins: London,* [1937.] 8°. NN. **26896.**

—— Death at the Cross-Roads. pp. 252. *W. Collins, Sons & Co.: London,* [1933.] 8°. NN. **21466.**

—— Death in Shallow Water. pp. 192. *Collins: London,* 1948. 8°. NN. **38195.**

—— Death in the Tunnel. pp. 252. *Collins: London,* [1936.] 8°. NN. **25017.**

—— Death leaves no Card. pp. 252. *Collins: London,* [1939.] 8°. NN. **29859.**

—— Death of Mr. Gantley. pp. 252. *W. Collins, Sons & Co.: London,* [1932.] 8°. NN. **19450.**

—— Death of Two Brothers. pp. 252. *Collins: London,* 1941. 8°. NN. **32487.**

—— Death Takes a Flat. pp. 252. *Collins: London,* 1940. 8°. NN. **32091.**

—— Death Takes the Living. pp. 192. *Collins: London,* 1949. 8°. NN. **39205.**

—— The Devereux Court Mystery. pp. 252. *W. Collins, Sons & Co.: London,* [1935.] 8°. NN. **23709.**

—— Devil's Reckoning. pp. 191. *Collins: London,* 1948. 8°. NN. **38613.**

BURTON (MILES)

—— Early Morning Murder. pp. 191. *Collins: London*, 1945. 8°. **NN. 35509.**

—— Fate at the Fair. pp. 252. *W. Collins, Sons & Co.: London*, [1933.] 8°. **NN. 19627.**

—— Four-Ply Yarn. pp. 192. *Collins: London*, 1944. 8°. **NN. 34491.**

—— Ground for Suspicion. pp. 256. *Collins: London*, 1950. 8°. **NNN. 78.**

—— The Hardway Diamonds Mystery. pp. 255. *W. Collins, Sons & Co.: London*, [1930.] 8°. **NN. 16869.**

—— Heir to Lucifer. pp. 192. *Collins: London*, 1947. 8°. **NN. 36917.**

—— Heir to Murder. pp. 191. *Collins: London*, 1953. 8°. **NNN. 4063.**

—— Look Alive. pp. 192. *Collins: London*, 1949. 8°. **NN. 39802.**

—— The Menace on the Downs. pp. 251. *W. Collins, Sons & Co.: London*, [1931.] 8°. **NN. 18083.**

—— The Milk-Churn Murder. pp. 252. *Collins: London*, [1935.] 8°. **NN. 24643.**

—— Mr. Babbacombe Dies. pp. 252. *Collins: London*, [1939.] 8°. **NN. 30455.**

—— Mr. Westerby Missing. pp. 252. *Collins: London*, 1940. 8°. **NN. 31748.**

—— Murder at the Moorings. pp. 252. *W. Collins, Sons & Co.: London*, [1932.] 8°. **NN. 19556.**

—— Murder in Absence. pp. 192. *Collins: London*, 1954. 8°. **NNN. 5102.**

—— Murder in Crown Passage. pp. 251. *Collins: London*, [1937.] 8°. **NN. 27842.**

—— Murder in the Coalhole. pp. 251. *Collins: London*, 1940. 8°. **NN. 31125.**

—— Murder, M.D. pp. 192. *Collins: London*, 1943. 8°. **NN. 34147.**

—— Murder of a Chemist. pp. 280. *Collins: London*, [1936.] 8°. **NN. 25524.**

—— Murder on Duty. pp. 188. *Collins: London*, 1952. 8°. **NNN. 2943.**

—— Murder out of School. pp. 187. *Collins: London*, 1951. 8°. **NNN. 2263.**

—— Murder Unrecognised. pp. 256. *Collins: London*, 1955. 8°. **NNN. 5910.**

—— Not a Leg to Stand on. pp. 191. *Collins: London*, 1945. 8°. **NN. 35091.**

—— The Platinum Cat. pp. 252. *Collins: London*, [1938.] 8°. **NN. 29214.**

—— The Secret of High Eldersham. pp. 249. *W. Collins, Sons & Co.: London*, [1930.] 8°. **NN. 17330.**

BURTON (MILES)

—— The Mystery of High Eldersham, *etc.* (Fifth impression [of " The Secret of High Eldersham "].) pp. 249. *W. Collins, Sons & Co.: London*, 1933. 8°. **012600. aaa. 12.**

—— Situation Vacant. pp. 192. *Collins: London*, 1946. 8°. **NN. 36308.**

—— Something to hide. pp. 192. *Collins: London*, 1953. 8°. **NNN. 3940.**

—— This Undesirable Residence. pp. 192. *Collins: London*, 1942. 8°. **NN. 33198.**

—— The Three Corpse Trick. pp. 192. *Collins: London*, 1944. 8°. **NN. 34812.**

—— The Three Crimes. pp. 252. *W. Collins, Sons & Co.: London*, [1931.] 8°. **NN. 17528.**

—— To Catch a Thief. pp. 252. *W. Collins, Sons & Co.: London*, [1934.] 8°. **NN. 22822.**

—— Tragedy at the Thirteenth Hole. pp. 252. *W. Collins, Sons & Co.: London*, [1933.] 8°. **NN. 20234.**

—— Unwanted Corpse. pp. 256. *Collins: London*, 1954. 8°. **NNN. 5344.**

—— Up the Garden Path. pp. 252. *Collins: London*, 1941. 8°. **NN. 32789.**

—— A Village Afraid. pp. 256. *Collins: London*, 1950. 8°. **NNN. 1323.**

—— Where is Barbara Prentice? pp. 320. *Collins: London*, [1936.] 8°. **NN. 26438.**

—— A Will in the Way. pp. 192. *Collins: London*, 1947. 8°. **NN. 37668.**

BURTON (MINA E.) Ruling the Planets. [A novel.] 3 vol. *R. Bentley & Son: London*, 1891. 8°. **012640. h. 19.**

BURTON (MONTAGUE) *Limited.* Ideals in Industry. Being the impressions of social students and visitors to the Montague Burton workshops. Edited by Stewart Wilkinson, *etc.* [With illustrations.] pp. 139. *Montague Burton: [Leeds,]* 1933. 8°. **08282. f. 82.**

—— Ideals in Industry . . . Third edition. pp. 312. [*London*,] 1936. 8°. **8287. bb. 113.**

—— Ideals in Industry. Being the story of Montague Burton Ltd. 1900–1950. Golden Jubilee issue, compiled and edited by Ronald Redmayne. pp. xxviii. 481. [*Montague Burton: Leeds*,] 1951. 8°. **8289. e. 37.**

—— Suggestions, Instructions and Telegraph Code. February 1st, 1918. Montague Burton, Ltd., *etc.* pp. 24. [*Leeds?* 1918.] 16°. **8246. aa. 17.**

BURTON (*Sir* MONTAGUE) Globe Girdling . . . Being the impressions of an amateur observer. 2 vol. *Petty & Sons: Leeds & London*, 1936, 38. 8°. **10125. ccc. 37.**

—— The Middle Path. Talks on collective security, arbitration and other aspects of international and industrial relations. pp. 76. *Petty & Sons: Leeds*, 1943. 8°. **08286. g. 96.**

BURTON (MYRON GARFIELD) *See* BURTON (Ida R.) and BURTON (M. G.) School Sewing based on Home Problems. [1921.] 8°. **07742. cc. 7.**

—— Shop Projects based on Community Problems. pp. 382. *Ginn & Co.: Boston*, [1915.] 8°. **07942. cc. 7.**

BURTON (NATHANAEL) *See* LORIQUET (J. N.) Sacred History . . . Translated . . . by N. J. Burton, *etc.* 1872. 16°. **3127**. aa. **55**.

—— History of the Royal Hospital, Kilmainham, near Dublin, from the original foundation . . . A.D. 1174 to the present time, *etc.* [With illustrations.] pp. iv. 230. *W. Curry, Jun. & Co.: Dublin*, 1843. 8°. **1406**. g. **13**.

—— Narrative of a Voyage from Liverpool to Alexandria, touching at the Island of Malta, and from thence to Beirout in Syria; with a journey to Jerusalem, voyage from Jaffa to Cyprus and Constantinople, and a pedestrian journey from Constantinople . . . to the town of Hamburgh, in the years 1836–37. pp. viii. 335. MS. NOTES. *John Yates: Dublin*, 1838. 8°. **10026**. c. **27**.
With a newspaper cutting containing an obituary notice of Dr. Burton inserted.

BURTON (NATHANIEL) A Petition, with seasonable advice, to the members of the new Parliament. pp. 61. *James Ridgway: London*, 1827. 8°. T. **1171**. **(10.)**

BURTON (NICHOLAS) Figuræ grammaticæ et rhetoricæ latino carmine donatæ, et exemplis tam græcis quam latinis, illustratæ . . . in usum Regiæ Scholæ Dunelmensis. pp. 76. *T. Leigh & D. Midwinter: Londini*, 1702. 12°. **623**. d. **20**.

BURTON (NORMAN LEE)

—— *See* HATFIELD (Henry R.) Accounting Principles and Practices . . . By H. R. Hatfield . . . N. L. Burton. [1940.] 8°. **8222**. bb. **25**.

—— Introduction to Cost Accounting. (Teacher's Key.) 2 pt. *Longmans & Co.: New York*, 1936, 37. 8°. [*American Business Fundamentals.*] W.P. **6536/3**.

BURTON (OLGA P.)

—— Stories of Bird and Bush . . . Illustrated by . . . L. A. Daff. pp. 39. *Oswald-Sealy (New Zealand): Auckland*, [1948.] 8°. **7286**. pp. **43**.

—— Thanking God. Little stories for little people . . . Illustrated by Joan Gale Thomas. pp. 22. *A. R. Mowbray & Co.: London & Oxford*, 1949. 12°. **4412**. f. **61**.

BURTON (OLIVE)

—— *See* EDWARDS (Harry) A Guide to Spirit Healing. By H. Edwards with the close collaboration of O. Burton. 1950. 8°. **7410**. p. **24**.

BURTON (ORMOND EDWARD) The Auckland Regiment: being an account of the doings on active service of the First, Second and Third Battalions, *etc.* [With maps and portraits.] pp. 323. 1922. 8°. *See* NEW ZEALAND.—Military Forces.—*New Zealand Contingent, British Expeditionary Force.—Auckland Regiment.* **09084**. bb. **42**.

—— Bart: the story of a dog. pp. 64. *J. Clarke & Co.: London*, 1944. 8°. **7294**. pp. **7**.

—— The Conflict of the Cross. pp. 156. *J. Clarke & Co.: London*, [1939.] 8°. **04373**. df. **27**.

—— The Silent Division. New Zealanders at the front: 1914–1919, *etc.* pp. x. 326. *Angus & Robertson: Sydney*, 1935. 8°. **09081**. aa. **67**.

—— A Study in Creative History. The interaction of the Eastern and Western peoples to 500 B.C. pp. 320. *G. Allen & Unwin: London*, 1932. 8°. **09008**. bb. **30**.

BURTON (P. H.) Granton Street. A play in three acts. pp. 91. *F. S. Powell: Port Talbot*, [1934.] 8°. **11780**. aa. **71**.

—— White Collar. A play in three acts. pp. 114. *W. H. Smith & Son: Stafford*, [1938.] 8°. **11782**. b. **32**.

BURTON (PERCY) Adventures among Immortals. Percy Burton—Impresario. As told to Lowell Thomas. [Reminiscences of theatrical life.] pp. vi. 330. *Dodd, Mead & Co.: New York*, 1937. 8°. **11797**. d. **18**.

—— [Another edition.] [With plates, including portraits.] pp. 256. *Hutchinson & Co.: London*, 1938. 8°. **11797**. d. **15**.

—— A Day Dream in Japan. [A play.] pp. 63. *John W. Luce & Co.: Boston*, 1916. 8°. **11792**. b. **43**.

BURTON (PERCY C.)

—— *See* PERIODICAL PUBLICATIONS.—London.—*Photography.* The Story of Hertfordshire. Edited by Lt.-Col. P. C. Burton. 1942. 4°. **010358**. l. **73**.

BURTON (PERCY MERCERON) and **SCOTT** (GUY HARDEN GUILLUM) The Law relating to the Prevention of Cruelty to Animals and some kindred topics, including the Wild Birds Protection Acts. pp. xix. 170. *John Murray: London*, 1906. 8°. **6485**. aa. **36**.

BURTON (PETER) The Case of P. Burton [and others], Clerk-sitters of the Poultry and Woodstreet Compters, in the City of London, whose freeholds will be greatly prejudiced, if not entirely destroyed, in case the . . . Bill for the more easy and speedy recovery of small debts within the City of London should pass into a law. [*London*, 1736?] *s. sh.* fol. (S.P.R.) **357**. c. **3**. **(45.)**

BURTON (PETER J.) Police Court Pictures at Richmond, Virginia. pp. 84. *C. N. Williams: Richmond [Va.]*, 1892. 8°. **6616.a.13.**

BURTON (PHILIP) Annihilation no Punishment to the Wicked, after the Day of Judgment; or, the Curse of God on Adam's eating the forbidden fruit; as proved from Scripture. pp. 25. *R. Bassam: London*, [1792.] 4°. **4372**. g. **10**. **(6.)**

—— Cases, with opinions of Eminent Counsel, in matters of laws, equity, and conveyancing, *etc.* [Originally collected by P. Burton.] 2 vol. 1791. 8°. *See* CASES. **513**. d. **5, 6**.

—— The Practice in the Office of Pleas of the Court of Exchequer epitomized. pp. 26. *J. Worrall & B. Tovey: London*, 1770. 8°. **518**. i. **16**. **(5.)**

—— Second edition improved. pp. 25. *E. Brooke: London*, 1777. 8°. **513**. c. **30**. **(4.)**

—— Practice of the Office of Pleas, in the Court of Exchequer . . . with precedents of pleadings, reports of cases in points of practice, and the Rules of Court which now regulate the . . . practice of that office. 2 vol. *E. & R. Brooke: London*, 1791. 8°. **227**. i. **20, 21**.

—— Seven Prophetical Periods; or, a View of the different prophetical periods mentioned by Daniel and Saint John . . . By the author of Speculum Britannicum [i.e. P. Burton]. pp. viii. 264. 1790. 4°. *See* BIBLE.—*Appendix.—Daniel.* [*Miscellaneous.*] **3205**. f. **17**.

—— Speculum Britannicum: or, a View of the miseries . . . brought upon Great Britain by intestine divisions, in the last and present centuries. By an Englishman [i.e. P. Burton]. pp. 237. 1778. 8°. *See* ENGLISHMAN. **808**. g. **30**.

BURTON (PHILIP WARD)

—— Advertising Copywriting. By P. W. Burton . . . Bowman Kreer . . . John B. Gray, *etc.* pp. xvi. 496. *Nicholas Kaye: London,* 1950. 8°. **8219**. i. **38**.

A later edition is entered under* BURTON *(P. W.) and* KREER *(G. B.)

—— Retail Advertising for the Small Store. [With illustrations.] pp. vii. 408. *Prentice-Hall: New York,* 1951. 8°. **8234**. ff. **91**.

Part of the "Prentice-Hall Retailing Series."

BURTON, afterwards **HILL** (PHILIPPINA) Miscellaneous Poems, written by a Lady, being her first attempt. [Signed in MS.: P. Burton.] vol. 1. pp. vii. 4. iii. 91. 1768. 8°. *See* LADY. **994**. g. **21**.

—— Mr. Hill's Apology for having been induced, by particular desire, and the most specious allurements that could tempt female weakness, to appear in the character of Scrub, Beaux Stratagem . . . at Brighthelmstone, last year, 1786 . . . With an address to Mrs. Fitzherbert. Also, some of Mrs. Hill's Letters to His Royal Highness the Prince of Wales, Mrs. Fitzherbert, and others, *etc.* pp. 51. *Printed for the Authoress: London,* [1787.] 4°. **1417**. k. **19**.

—— Portraits, Characters, Pursuits and Amusements of the present fashionable world, interspersed with poetic flights of fancy. [Chiefly in verse.] pp. xi. 84. FEW MS. NOTES. [*London,* 1785?] 12°. **992**. g. **4**. (**1**.)

—— [Another edition.] pp. xi. 84. [*London,* 1795?] 12°. **11633**. aa. **7**.

BURTON (REGINALD GEORGE) A Book of Man-Eaters, *etc.* [With plates.] pp. 293. *Hutchinson & Co.: London,* 1931. 8°. **7209**. cc. **18**.

—— The Book of the Tiger. With a chapter on the lion in India. [With plates, including portraits.] pp. 287. *Hutchinson & Co.: London,* 1933. 8°. **7209**. cc. **27**.

—— From Boulogne to Austerlitz. Napoleon's campaign of 1805 . . . With eight maps and plans. pp. vi. 105. *G. Allen & Co.: London,* 1912. 8°. [*Special Campaign Series.* no. 17.] **09009**. a. **1/17**.

—— A History of the Hyderabad Contingent. [With maps.] pp. v. 320. xc. *Office of the Superintendent of Government Printing: Calcutta,* 1905. 8°. **8837**. e. **28**.

—— The Mahratta and Pindari War. Compiled for General Staff, India. [With a map and plans.] pp. iv. 126. **1910. 8°.** ***See* INDIA.—*Army.—Army Headquarters.—General Staff.*** **I.S. 304/5**.

—— Napoleon's Campaigns in Italy, 1796–1797 and 1800 . . . With six maps and plans. pp. x. 142. *G. Allen & Co.: London,* 1912. 8°. [*Special Campaign Series.* no. 15.] **09009**. a. **1/15**.

—— Napoleon's Invasion of Russia . . . With six maps and plans. pp. xiv. 231. *G. Allen & Co.: London,* 1914. 8°. [*Special Campaign Series.* no. 19.] **09009**. a. **1/19**.

—— Sport & Wild Life in the Deccan . . . With illustrations & map. pp. 282. *Seeley, Service & Co.: London,* 1928. 8°. **07906**. e. **37**.

—— The Tiger Hunters . . . With 16 illustrations. pp. 255. *Hutchinson & Co.: London,* 1936. 8°. **07908**. g. **4**.

BURTON (REGINALD GEORGE)

—— Tropics and Snows. A record of travel and adventure . . . Illustrated by Miss Clare Burton, *etc.* pp. xvi. 349. *Edward Arnold: London,* 1898. 8°. **10026**. k. **23**.

BURTON (RICHARD) *Baptist Missionary in India.* *See* SHEPPARD (John) *of Frome.* Two Discourses occasioned by the deaths of the Rev. E. C. Daniell . . . and the Rev. R. Burton, *etc.* 1829. 12°. **839**. c. **9**. (**2**.)

BURTON (RICHARD) *Dramatist.* Brothers. A sketch in one act. pp. 18. *Samuel French: New York, London,* [1922.] 8°. **011779**. e. **104**. (**4**.)

—— Tatters. A character sketch. pp. 16. *Samuel French: New York, London,* [1922.] 8°. **011779**. e. **104**. (**5**.)

BURTON (RICHARD) *Open Golf Champion.*

—— Length with Discretion. With 21 illustrations. pp. 190. *Hutchinson & Co.: London & Melbourne,* [1940.] 8°. **07907**. ee. **16**.

BURTON (RICHARD) *pseud.* [i.e. NATHANIEL CROUCH.] *See* also CROUCH (N.)

—— Admirable Curiosities, Rarities, & Wonders in Great-Britain, and Ireland . . . By Robert Burton. The tenth edition. pp. 192. *A. Bettesworth & C. Hitch; James Hodges: London,* 1737. 8°. **577**. a. **11**.

Earlier editions are entered under B., R.

—— [Another copy.] G. **13188**.

—— A new edition; with additional wood-cut portraits, and a copious index. [Edited by James Caulfield.] pp. 168. **L.P.** *Machell Stace: Westminster,* 1811. 4°. **190**. b. **4**.

—— [Another copy.] G. **5225**. (**1**.)

—— The Apprentices Companion, containing plain . . . directions for servants, *etc.* pp. 249. *For Thomas Mercer: London,* 1681. 12°. G. **13216**.

—— The English Acquisitions in Guinea and East-India . . . (With an account of the admirable voyage of Domingo Gonsales, the little Spaniard, to the world in the moon . . . An ingenious fancy, written by a late learned bishop.) By Robert Burton. pp. 184. *A. Bettesworth; J. Batley: London,* 1728. 12°. **280**. c. **39**.

Earlier editions are entered under B., R. The first edition is entitled "A View of the English Acquisitions in Guinea & the East Indies."

—— [Another copy]. G. **13178**.

—— The English Empire in America: or, a View of the dominions of the Crown of England in the West-Indies . . . By Robert Burton. The sixth edition. pp. 192. *A. Bettesworth; J. Batley: London,* 1728. 12°. G. **13194**.

Earlier editions are entered under B., R.

—— A Seventeenth Century Survey of America, *etc.* (The English Empire in America . . . By R. B. Third edition. London, 1698.) ff. 124. *San Francisco,* 1940. 4°. [*Sutro Branch, California State Library. Occasional Papers. Reprint Series.* no. 18.] W.P. **1879/18**.

Reproduced from typewriting.

—— Female Excellency: or, the Ladies glory. Illustrated in the . . . Lives and . . . actions of nine famous women . . . By Robert Burton. The third edition. pp. 182. *A. Bettesworth; J. Batley: London,* 1728. 12°. **10604**. a. **28**.

Earlier editions are entered under B., R.

—— [Another copy.] G. **13192**.

BURTON (Richard) *pseud.* [i.e. Nathaniel Crouch.]

—— Historical Remarques, and Observations of the Ancient and Present State of London and Westminster . . . With an account of the most remarkable accidents, as to wars, fires, plagues . . . till the year 1681. Illustrated with pictures, *etc.* 2 pt. *For Nath. Crouch: London,* 1681. 12°. G. **13203**.

—— [Another copy.] **291**. a. **43**.
Imperfect; wanting pp. 77–116 *of pt.* 1 *and pp.* 1–10 *of pt.* 2, *in place of which pp.* 73–120 *of another edition have been inserted.*

—— The third edition enlarged. 2 pt. pp. 233. *For Nath. Crouch: London,* 1684. 12°. **577**. a. **8**. (**2**.)
Pt. 2 *has a special titlepage, bearing the imprint: Tho. Snowden for Nath. Crouch.*

—— [Another copy.] **578**. a. **4**.

—— A new edition with additional wood-cut portraits, and a copious index. [Edited by James Caulfield.] pp. 178. *Machell Stace: Westminster,* 1810. 4°. 10349. cc. 14.

—— [Another copy.] **L.P.** **190**. b. **3**.

—— [Another copy.] G. **5225**. (**2**.)

—— Historical Remarques and Observations of the Ancient and Present State of London and Westminster . . . Illustrated with pictures . . . ingraven on copper plates . . . The fourth edition. pp. 233. *Nath. Crouch: London,* 1691. 12°. **1471**. de. **10**.
Imperfect; wanting the plates. Pp. 71–76 *are mutilated.*

—— [Another edition, considerably altered.] A New View, and Observations on the Ancient and Present State of London and Westminster . . . By Robert Burton . . . Continued by an able hand. pp. 1–312. 145–240. 385–468. *A. Bettesworth & C. Hitch; J. Batley: London,* 1730. 12°. **578**. b. **5**.

—— [Another copy.] G. **3680**.

—— The History of Oliver Cromwel . . . By Robert Burton. The sixth edition. pp. 188. *A. Bettesworth; J. Batley: London,* 1728. 12°. **10806**. a. **16**.
Earlier editions are entered under B., R.

—— The History of the House of Orange . . . together with the History of William and Mary, King and Queen of England . . . from their Majesty's happy Accession **. . . to this time, 1693 . . . A new edition. [Edited by James Caulfield.] pp. iv. 144. L.P. *Machell Stace: Westminster,* 1814. 4°. 9918. bbb. 39.**

—— [Another copy.] G. 5227. (2.)

—— [Another copy.] 153. g. 10.

—— A new edition, with woodcut portraits. [Edited by James Caulfield.] pp. 145. L.P. *Machell Stace: Westminster,* 1811. 4°. 186. c. 3.

—— [Another copy.] G. **5226**. (**1**.)

—— The History of the Nine Worthies of the World . . . By Robert Burton. pp. 189. *A. Bettesworth; J. Batley: London,* 1727. 12°. G. **13190**.
Earlier editions are entered under B., R.

—— The fourth edition. (By Robert Burton.) pp. 189. *A. Bettesworth & C. Hitch; J. Hodges: London,* 1738. 12°. **1198**. a. **1**.
The frontispiece is mutilated.

—— [Another edition.] By Robert Burton. pp. 192. *Thomas Browne: Dublin,* 1759. 12°. **10605**. aa. **18**.

BURTON (Richard) *pseud.* [i.e. Nathaniel Crouch.]

—— The History of the Principality of Wales . . . By Robert Burton. The second edition. pp. 186. *A. Bettesworth; J. Batley: London,* 1730. 12°. G. **13186**.
The first edition is entered under B., R.

—— The Kingdom of Darkness. Or, the History of dæmons, spectres . . . and other supernatural delusions . . . By Robert Burton. The fourth edition. pp. xii. 176. *A. Bettesworth: J. Batley: London,* 1728. 12°. G. **13201**.
An earlier edition is entered under B., R.

—— Martyrs in Flames: or, the History of Popery. Displaying the . . . cruelties exercised upon Protestants by the Papists . . . by Robert Burton. Third edition. pp. 188. *A. Bettesworth; J. Batley: London,* 1729. 12°. G. **13211**.

—— Memorable Remarks upon the Ancient and Modern State of Judæa, *etc. See* infra: Two Journeys to Jerusalem, *etc.*

—— A New View, and Observations on the Ancient and Present State of London and Westminster. *See* supra: Historical Remarques, *etc.*

—— The Surprizing Miracles of Nature and Art, *etc.* pp. 298. *D. Paterson: Edinburgh,* 1762. 12°. **8632**. aaa. **44**.
Earlier editions are entered under B., R. The first edition is entitled "Miracles of Art and Nature."

—— Two Journeys to Jerusalem, Containing, I. A strange and true account of the travels of 2 English pilgrims some years since (in a letter from H. T. [i.e. Henry Timberlake]) . . . II. The travels of fourteen Englishmen in 1669 . . . By T. B. To which are prefixed, Memorable remarks upon the antient and modern state of the state [*sic*] of the Jewish ntaion [*sic*] . . . Together with a relation of the great council of the Jews in the plains of Hungary in 1650 . . . By S. B. an Englishman there present [i.e. Samuel Brett] . . . The ninth edition. pp. 183. *A Bettesworth; J. Hodges: London,* 1738. 12°.
Earlier editions are entered under B., R. **1298**. a. **42**.

—— [Another edition.] Judæorum memorabilia, or, Memorable Remarks upon the Ancient and Modern State of Judea and the Jewish nation . . . The original compilation by Robert Burton, *etc.* pp. vi. 221. *W. Matthews: Bristol,* 1796. 12°. **4516**. a. **18**.

—— [Another copy.] **10368**. a. **68**. (**2**.)

—— The Unfortunate Court-Favourites of England . . . by Robert Burton. The sixth edition. pp. 191. *A. Bettesworth; J. Batley: London,* 1729. 12°. **10817**. a. **8**. (**1**.)
Earlier editions are entered under B., R.

—— Unparallel'd Varieties: or, the Matchless actions and passions of mankind . . . By Robert Burton. The fourth edition. pp. 181. *A. Bettesworth; J. Batley: London,* 1728. 12°. G. **13179**.
Earlier editions are entered under B., R.

—— The Vanity of the Life of Man. Representing the seven several stages thereof, from his birth to his death . . . To which are added, several other poems . . . By Robert Burton . . . The fifth edition. pp. 92. *A. Bettesworth; J. Batley: London,* 1729. 12°. **11660**. de. **5**.
Earlier editions are entered under B., R.

—— The Wars in England, Scotland, and Ireland. Or, an Impartial account of all the battels . . . from the beginning of the reign of King Charles I. in 1625, to his Majesties happy Restauration, 1660. Illustrated, *etc.* pp. 210. *For Nath. Crouch: London,* 1681. 12°. **9505**. a. **27**.

—— [Another copy.] **807**. a. **5**.
Imperfect; wanting the frontispiece.

BURTON (RICHARD) *pseud.* [i.e. NATHANIEL CROUCH.]

—— [Another edition.] pp. 210. *For Nath. Crouch & John How: London,* 1681. 12°. **600. b. 10.**
The last leaves are cropped.

—— The fourth edition, very much enlarged. pp. 231. *For Nat. Crouch: London,* 1683. 12°. **599. a. 34.**

—— [Another copy.] G. **13183.**

—— The fifth edition very much enlarged. pp. 231. *J. R. for Nat. Crouch: London,* 1684. 12°. **577. a. 8. (5.)**
Cropped.

—— [Another copy.] **292. d. 50.**

—— The tenth edition. (By Robert Burton.) pp. 192. *A. Bettesworth & C. Hitch; J. Hodges: London,* 1737. 12°. **9512. a. 32.**

—— A new edition, with additional wood-cut portraits, and a copious index. [Edited by James Caulfield.] pp. ii. 201. **L.P.** *Machell Stace: Westminster,* 1810. 4°. **193. d. 17.**

—— [Another copy.] G. **5227. (1.)**

—— Winter-Evening Entertainments; in two parts. Containing, I. Ten pleasant . . . relations . . . II. Fifty . . . riddles . . . by Robert Burton. Sixth edition. pp. 173. *A. Bettesworth & C. Hitch; J. Hodges: London,* 1737. 12°. G. **13215.**

—— Wonderful Prodigies of Judgment and Mercy: discovered in above three hundred memorable histories *etc.* pp. 253. *David Paterson: Edinburgh,* 1762. 12°. **1477. d. 4**
Earlier editions are entered under B., R.

—— Youth's Divine Pastime . . . Containing . . . Scripture histories . . . Turned into English verse . . . The sixth edition. pt. 2. *C. Hitch; James Hodges: London,* 1749. 12°. **11626. aa. 39.**
Imperfect; wanting pt. 1. Earlier editions are entered under B., R.

BURTON (RICHARD EUGENE) *See* BACHELLER (Irving A.) In the Days of Poor Richard. [With an introduction by R. E. Burton.] [1926.] 8°. **12711. bb. 15.**

—— *See* HOLMES (Oliver W.) *the Elder.* The Autocrat of the Breakfast-Table . . . With an introduction by R. Burton. 1903. 8°. **012356. e. 78.**

—— The Collected Poems of Richard Burton, *etc.* pp. 368. *Bobbs-Merrill Co.: Indianapolis,* [1931.] 8°. **011686. c. 35.**

—— Bernard Shaw. The man and the mask. pp. viii. 305. *H. Holt & Co.: New York,* 1916. 8°. **011853. tt. 6.**

—— The Carpenter Lad, & other poems. pp. 96. *Bobbs-Merrill Co.: Indianapolis,* [1930.] 8°. **011686. df. 52.**

—— Charles Dickens . . . With portrait. pp. 308. *Bobbs-Merrill Co.: Indianapolis,* [1919.] 8°. **011853. ppp. 60.**
The cover bears the title: "Dickens. How to know him."

—— The Contemporary Drama Series. [Critical monographs.] Edited by R. Burton. 5 vol. *Little, Brown & Co.: Boston,* 1917–24. 8°. **11796. bbb. 36.**

—— Forces in Fiction, and other essays. pp. 177. *B. F. Stevens & Brown: London,* 1902. 8°. **011853. g. 4.**

—— How to see a Play. pp. ix. 217. *Macmillan Co.: New York,* 1914. 8°. **011795. b. 18.**

BURTON (RICHARD EUGENE)

—— Literary Likings. [Essays.] pp. 384. *Copeland & Day: Boston,* 1898. 8°. **11852. bb. 36.**

—— Little Essays in Literature and Life. pp. 356. *Century Co.: New York,* 1914. 8°. **012354. ee. 52.**

—— Lyrics of Brotherhood. pp. 75. *Small, Maynard & Co.: Boston,* 1899. 8°. **11688. aa. 36.**

—— Masters of the English Novel. A study of principles and personalities. pp. ix. 357. *H. Holt & Co.: New York,* 1909. 8°. **11852. t. 24.**

—— Why do you Talk like That? *etc.* pp. 294. *Bobbs-Merrill Co.: Indianapolis,* [1929.] 8°. **12980. ee. 46.**

BURTON (*Sir* RICHARD FRANCIS) *K.C.M.G.*

WORKS.

—— The Memorial Edition of the Works of Captain Sir R. F. Burton. [Edited by Isabel Lady Burton and Leonard Smithers. With illustrations and maps.] vol. 1–7.

vol. 1, 2. Personal Narrative of a Pilgrimage to Al-Madinah & Meccah. 1893.
vol. 3, 4. A Mission to Gelele, King of Dahome. 1893.
vol. 5. Vikram and the Vampire. 1893.
vol. 6, 7. First Footsteps in East Africa. 1894.

Tylston & Edwards: London, 1893, 94. 8°. **12273. k. 1.**
No more published.

SINGLE WORKS.

—— Abeokuta and the Camaroons Mountains. An exploration. [With plates, including a portrait, and a map.] 2 vol. *Tinsley Bros.: London,* 1863. 8°. **2358. c. 3.**

—— [Another copy of vol. 1.] MS. NOTES [by the author]. C. **60. i. 6.**

—— The Book of the Sword . . . With . . . illustrations. pp. xxxix. 299. *Chatto & Windus: London,* 1884. 8°. **7704. dd. 15.**

—— Camoens: his life and his Lusiads. A commentary, *etc.* [With a postscript by Isabel Lady Burton, entitled: "The Reviewer Reviewed."] 2 vol. pp. 738. *Bernard Quaritch: London,* 1881. 8°. **011451. f. 91.**

—— Captain R. F. Burton's Experiences [of spiritualism]. *See* HARRISON (William H.) *Editor of "The Spiritualist."* Psychic Facts, *etc.* 1880. 8°. **8632. bbb. 23.**

—— The City of the Saints, and across the Rocky Mountains to California. [With plates and maps.] pp. x. 707. *Longmans & Co.: London,* 1861. 8°. **10412. cc. 6.**

—— A Complete System of Bayonet Exercise. pp. 36. *W. Clowes & Sons: London,* 1853. 12°. **8827. d. 39.**

—— Etruscan Bologna: a study. pp. xii. 275. *Smith, Elder & Co.: London,* 1876. 8°. **2258. b. 18.**

—— Explorations of the Highlands of the Brazil; with a full account of the gold and diamond mines. Also, Canoeing down 1500 miles of the great river São Francisco, from Sabará to the sea. [Edited by Isabel Lady Burton. With illustrations.] 2 vol. *Tinsley Bros.: London,* 1869. 8°. **2374. f. 3.**

—— Falconry in the Valley of the Indus. [With illustrations.] pp. xii. 107. *John Van Voorst: London,* 1852. 8°. **7905. c. 2.**

—— First Footsteps in East Africa; or, an Exploration of Harar. [With plates.] pp. xl. 648. *Longman & Co.: London,* 1856. 8°. **2358. e. 3.**

—— [Another edition.] (With introduction by Henry W. Nevinson.) pp. xx. 363. *J. M. Dent & Sons: London; E. P. Dutton & Co.: New York,* [1910.] 8°. [*Everyman's Library.*] **12206.p.1/348.**

—— A Glance at the "Passion-Play." pp. 168. *W. H. Harrison: London,* 1881. 8°. **11794.** b. **38.**

—— Goa and the Blue Mountains, or, Six months of sick leave. [With plates.] pp. viii. 368. *Richard Bentley: London,* 1851. 12°. **2354.** a. **8.**

—— The First Four Chapters of Goa and the Blue Mountains . . . With the articles which recently appeared in the Madras Mail and Madras Times on the coming Exposition at Goa, &c. pp. 117. *Higginbotham & Co.: Madras,* 1890. 12°. **10058.** aa. **40.**

—— The Gold-mines of Midian and the Mined Midianite Cities. A fortnight's tour in North-Western Arabia. [Edited by Isabel Lady Burton.] pp. xvi. 395. *C. Kegan Paul & Co.: London,* 1878. 8°. **2358.** f. 3.

—— The Jew, the Gypsy, and El Islam . . . Edited with a preface and brief notes by W. H. Wilkins. pp. xix. 351. *Hutchinson & Co.: London,* 1898. 8°. **10007.** l. 8.

—— The Kasîdah—couplets—of Hājî AbOû El-Yezdî: a lay of the Higher Law. Translated and annotated by . . . F. B. [i.e. Frank Baker, pseudonym of Sir R. F. Burton; or rather, written by Sir R. F. Burton.] pp. 33. 1880. 4°. *See* 'Abdū, *Yazdī, Ḥāji,* calling himself Hīchmakānī. **757.** i. **44.**

—— [Another edition.] [Edited with a preface by Isabel Lady Burton.] ff. 6. 42. *Nichols & Co.: London,* 1894. 4°. **11651.** l. **36.**
One of an edition of 100 *copies. Printed on one side of the leaf only.*

—— [A reissue.] *H. J. Cook: London,* 1900. 4°. **11651.** l. **50.**

—— [Another edition.] With a foreword by Roger Ingpen. pp. xvi. 110. *Hutchinson & Co.: London,* 1914. 8°. **11653.** f. **54.**

—— [Another edition.] With additional notes by George Roe. pp. 128. *Ball Publishing Company: Boston,* 1918. 16°. **011651.** de. **78.**

—— [Another edition.] Illustrated by John Kettelwell. [With a bibliographical note.] pp. xiii. 169. *P. Allan & Co.: London,* 1925. 4°. **11645.** h. **44.**
One of fifty copies printed on large paper.

—— [Another edition.] pp. viii. 152. *E. Mathews & Marrot: London,* 1927. 8°. [*Bodoni Series.*] W.P. **4939/1.**

—— [Another edition.] Illustrated by Willy Pogany. pp. xv. 129. *D. McKay Company: Philadelphia,* [1931.] 4°. **011653.** o. **9.**

—— The Kasidah of Haji Abdu El-Yezdi. [An adaptation in rubia verse by H. B. Lister.] *See* Lister (Henry B.) The Rubaiyat of Omar Khayyam, *etc.* [1929.] 8°. **11654.** b. **54.**

—— The Lake Regions of Central Africa. A picture of exploration. [With plates.] 2 vol. *Longman & Co.: London,* 1860. 8°. **10096.** f. **13.**

—— Voyage aux grands lacs de l'Afrique Orientale . . . Ouvrage traduit . . . par Mme H. Loreau, et illustré de 37 vignettes. pp. 719. *Paris,* 1862. 8°. **010096.** i. **25.**

—— The Lake Regions of Central Equatorial Africa, with notices of the Lunar Mountains and the sources of the White Nile; being the results of an expedition undertaken under the patronage of Her Majesty's Government and the Royal Geographical Society of London, in . . . 1857–1859. [With a map.] pp. 464. 1859. *See* London.—iii. *Royal Geographical Society of London.* Journal, *etc.* vol. 29. 1832, *etc.* 8°. Ac. **6170.**

—— *See* Cooley (William D.) The Memoir on the Lake Regions of East Africa, reviewed, in reply to Capt. R. Burton's letter in the "Athenæum." No. 1899. [A criticism of "The Lake Regions of Central Equatorial Africa."] 1864. 8°. **10095.** bb. **20.**

—— The Land of Midian, Revisited. With map and illustrations, *etc.* 2 vol. *C. Kegan Paul & Co.: London,* 1879. 8°. **2358.** e. **4.**

—— Letters from the Battle-Fields of Paraguay. With a map and illustrations. pp. xix. 491. *Tinsley Bros.: London,* 1870. 8°. **2374.** f. **4.**

—— Lord Beaconsfield. A sketch. pp. 12. [1882?] 8°. C. **59.** c. **15.**

—— A Mission to Gelele, King of Dahome. With notices of the so called "Amazons," the yearly customs, *etc.* 2 vol. *Tinsley Bros.: London,* 1864. 8°. **2358.** c. **16.**

—— A New System of Sword Exercise for Infantry. pp. 59. *W. Clowes & Sons: London,* 1876. 8°. **8824.** bb. **30.**

—— The Nile Basin. Part i. Showing Tanganyika to be Ptolemy's Western Lake Reservoir. A memoir read before the Royal Geographical Society . . . With prefatory remarks. By R. F. Burton, F.R.G.S. Part ii. Captain Speke's discovery of the source of the Nile. A review by James M'Queen . . . Reprinted . . . from the "Morning Advertiser." pp. 195. *Tinsley Bros.: London,* 1864. 8°. **10096.** bb. **24.**

—— Personal Narrative of a Pilgrimage to El-Medinah and Meccah. [The editor's preface signed: T. L. W., i.e. Thomas L. Wolley. With illustrations and maps.] 3 vol. *Longmans & Co.: London,* 1855, 56. 8°. **10076.** d. **17.**

—— Second edition. 2 vol. *Longmans & Co.: London,* 1857. 8°. **10076.** b. **1.**

—— Third edition revised. pp. xvi. 518. *W. Mullan & Son: London & Belfast,* 1879. 8°. **10077.** de. **34.**

—— [Another edition.] Edited by . . . Isabel Burton. With an introduction by S. Lane-Poole. 2 vol. *G. Bell & Sons: London,* 1898. 8°. [*Bohn's Standard Library.*] **2504.** k. **15.**

—— [Another edition.] 2 vol. *G. Bell & Sons: London,* 1906. 8°. [*York Library.*] **012201.** i. **1/22.**

—— [Another edition.] A Pilgrimage to Meccah and Medinah. pp. 357. *Herbert Joseph: London,* 1937. 8°. [*Great Explorations.*] **10025.ppp.2/1.**

—— Peregrinacion a la Meca y Medina. [An abridged translation.] 1860. *See* Fernández Cuesta (N.) Nuevo Viajero Universal, *etc.* tom. 2. 1859, *etc.* 8°. **10005.** g. **14.**

BURTON (*Sir* Richard Francis) *K.C.M.G.* [Single Works.]

—— The Guide Book. A pictorial pilgrimage to Mecca and Medina, *etc.* [A guide book to an exhibition of paintings, etc. arranged by the Royal Polytechnic Institution to illustrate the material contained in R. F. Burton's "Personal Narrative of a Pilgrimage to el-Medinah and Meccah." With a portrait.] pp. 58. *The Author: London,* 1865. 8°. **010076.** g. **47.**

—— Scinde; or, the Unhappy valley. 2 vol. *Richard Bentley: London,* 1851. 12°. **10055.** c. **34.**

—— The Sentiment of the Sword. A country-house dialogue . . . Edited, with notes, by A. Forbes Sieveking . . . and a preface by Theodore A. Cook. Reprinted from the "Field." pp. xv. 151. *Horace Cox: London,* 1911. 8°. **7908.** aaaa. **32.**

—— Sindh, and the Races that inhabit the Valley of the Indus; with notices of the topography and history of the Province. [With a map.] pp. viii. 422. *W. H. Allen & Co.: London,* 1851. 8°. **10055.** d. **11.**

—— Sind Revisited: with notices of the Anglo-Indian Army; railroads; past, present, and future, etc. 2 vol. *R. Bentley & Son: London,* 1877. 8°. **2356.** b. **15.**

—— Stone Talk—λιθοφωνημα: being some of the marvellous sayings of a petral portion of Fleet Street, London, to one Doctor Polyglott, Ph. D. [In verse.] By Frank Baker, D.O.N. [i.e. Sir R. F. Burton.] pp. 121. 1865. 8°. *See* Baker (Frank) *D.O.N., pseud.* **11651.** bb. **27.**

—— Stone Talk, *etc.* ff. 86. *San Francisco,* 1940. 4°. [*California State Library, Sutro Branch. Occasional Papers. Reprint Series.* no. 24.] W.P. **1879/24.**
Reproduced from typewriting.

—— Two Trips to Gorilla Land and the Cataracts of the Congo. [With illustrations and a map.] 2 vol. *Sampson Low & Co.: London,* 1876 [1875]. 8°. **010095.** gg. **8.**

—— Ultima Thule; or, a Summer in Iceland. With historical introduction, maps, and illustrations. 2 vol. *W. P. Nimmo: London & Edinburgh,* 1875. 8°. **2364.** f. **1.**

—— Wanderings in Three Continents . . . Edited, with a preface, by W. H. Wilkins . . . With a photogravure portrait and with illustrations by A. D. McCormick. pp. xiii. 313. *Hutchinson & Co.: London,* 1901. 8°. **2352.** e. **11.**

—— Wanderings in West Africa, from Liverpool to Fernando Po. By a F.R.G.S. [i.e. Sir R. F. Burton]. With map and illustrations. 2 vol. 1863. 8°. *See* Africa, *West.* **10096.** bb. **36.**

—— Wit and Wisdom from West Africa; or, a Book of proverbial philosophy, idioms, enigmas, and laconisms. Compiled by R. F. Burton, *etc.* pp. xxx. 455. *Tinsley Bros.: London,* 1865. 8°. **2348.** d. **3.**

—— Zanzibar; city, island, and coast. [With illustrations and a map.] 2 vol. *Tinsley Bros.: London,* 1872. 8°. **2358.** e. **6.**

SELECTIONS.

—— Selected Papers on Anthropology, Travel & Exploration . . . Edited with an introduction and occasional notes by N. M. Penzer. pp. 240. *A. M. Philpot: London,* 1924 [1923]. 8°. **010025.** f. **15.**

—— [Another copy.] **010028.** ee. **24.**
One of 100 *copies printed on fine paper.*

BURTON (*Sir* Richard Francis) *K.C.M.G.*

WORKS WRITTEN IN COLLABORATION.

—— To the Gold Coast for Gold. A personal narrative. By R. F. Burton and Verney Lovett Cameron. 2 vol. *Chatto & Windus: London,* 1883 [1882]. 8°. **2358.** c. **4.**

—— Unexplored Syria. Visits to the Libanus, the Tulúl el Safā, the Anti-Libanus, the Northern Libanus, and the Aláh. By R. F. Burton and Charles F. Tyrwhitt Drake. [With contributions by Isabel Lady Burton and others.] 2 vol. *Tinsley Bros.: London,* 1872. 8°. **10075.** ee. **16.**

WORKS EDITED OR TRANSLATED BY BURTON.

—— *See* Arabian Nights. [*English.*] A plain and literal translation of the Arabian Nights' Entertainments . . . With introduction . . . notes . . . and a terminal essay . . . by R. F. Burton. (Supplemental Nights to the Book of the Thousand Nights and a Night, with notes . . . by R. F. Burton.) 1885, *etc.* 8°. Tab. **501.** a. **12.**

—— *See* Arabian Nights. [*English.*] Lady Burton's edition of her husband's Arabian Nights, *etc.* 1886. 8°. **2348.** f. **4.**

—— *See* Arabian Nights. [*English.*] The Book of the Thousand Nights and a Night. Translated . . . by Captain Sir R. F. Burton . . . Reprinted from the original edition and edited by L. C. Smithers, *etc.* 1894. 8°. Tab. **444.** c. **1.**

—— *See* Arabian Nights. [*English.*] The Arabian Nights Entertainments . . . The . . . Burton translation, *etc.* 1954. 4°. C. **105.** e. **7.**

—— *See* Arabian Nights. [*German.*] Die Erzählungen aus den Tausend und ein Nächten. (Vollständige deutsche Ausgabe auf Grund der Burton'schen englischen Ausgabe.) 1907, *etc.* 8°. **14582.** cc. **1.**

—— *See* Arabian Nights. [*Abridgments, Selections, etc.—English.*] The Arabian Nights . . . A complete and unabridged selection arranged by B. A. Cerf from the famous literal translation of R. F. Burton, *etc.* [1933.] 8°. **12403.** ee. **28.**

—— *See* Arabian Nights. [*Abridgments, Selections, etc.—English.*] A Plain and Literal Translation of the Arabian Nights' Entertainments . . . By Sir R. Burton. A selection by P. H. Newby, *etc.* 1950. 8°. **12431.** f. **54.**

—— *See* Baitāl-Pachīsī. Vikram and the Vampire . . . Adapted by R. F. Burton, *etc.* 1870. 8°. **14156.** h. **58.**

—— —— 1893. 8°. **14156.** i. **35.**

—— *See* Basile (G. B.) *Count of Torone.* Il Pentamerone . . . Being a translation by . . . Sir R. Burton, *etc.* 1893. 8°. **12470.** h. **23.**

—— *See* Basile (G. B.) *Count di Torone.* The Pentameron of Giambattista Basile. Translated by Sir R. Burton, *etc.* 1952. 8°. **12472.** dd. **4.**

—— *See* Camoens (L. de) Camoens. The Lyricks . . . Englished by R. F. Burton, *etc.* 1884. 8°. **011451.** f. **92.**

—— *See* Camoens (L. de) Os Lusiadas . . . Englished by R. F. Burton, *etc.* 1880. 8°. **011451.** f. **40.**

—— *See* Catullus (C. V.) [*Works.—Latin and English.*] The Carmina of Caius Valerius Catullus. Now first completely Englished into verse . . . by Capt. Sir R. F. Burton, *etc.* 1894. 8°. **11385.** g. **31.**

BURTON (*Sir* RICHARD FRANCIS) *K.C.M.G.* [WORKS EDITED OR TRANSLATED BY BURTON.]

—— *See* LACERDA E ALMEIDA (F. J. M. de) The Lands of Cazembe. Lacerda's Journey to Cazembe in 1798. Translated and annotated by Captain R. F. Burton, *etc.* 1873. 8º. Ac. **6170/4.**

—— *See* LEARED (Arthur) Marocco and the Moors . . . Edited by Sir R. Burton, *etc.* 1891. 8º. **10095.** dd. **33.**

—— *See* MARCY (Randolph B.) The Prairie Traveller . . . Edited by R. F. Burton. 1863. 8º. **10007.** aaa. **8.**

—— *See* PEREIRA DA SILVA (J. M.) Manuel de Moraes . . . Translated by R. F. and I. B. [i.e. R. F. and Isabel Burton.] 1886. 8º. **12431.** e. **38.** (**2.**)

—— *See* SA'DI. [*Gulistān.—English.*] The Gulistân; or, Rose garden of Sa'di. Faithfully translated [by Sir R. F. Burton], *etc.* 1888. 8º. **14749.** c. **8.**

—— *See* SA'DI. [*Gulistān.—English.*] Tales from the Gulistân . . . Translated by Sir R. Burton, *etc.* 1928. 4º. **14783.** f. **21.**

—— *See* STADEN (Johann von) The Captivity of Hans Stade . . . among the wild tribes of Eastern Brazil . . . Annotated by R. F. Burton. 1874. 8º. Ac. **6172/46.**

APPENDIX.

—— *See* BURTON (Isabel) *Lady.* The Life of Captain Sir R. F. Burton, *etc.* [With portraits.] 1893. 8º. **10816.** dd. **11.**

—— —— 1898. 8º. **2407.** g. **2.**

—— *See* DEARDEN (Seton) The Arabian Knight. A study of Sir Richard Burton, *etc.* [With portraits.] 1936. 8º. **01082?.** f. **15.**

—— *See* DEARDEN (Seton) The Arabian Knight. A study of Sir Richard Burton. 1953. 8º. **10863.** ee. **12.**

—— *See* DODGE (Walter P.) The Real Sir Richard Burton . . . With a frontispiece. 1907. 8º. **10854.** de. **17.**

—— *See* DOWNEY (Fairfax) Burton, *etc.* [With portraits.] 1931. 8º. **10824.** aaa. **28.**

—— *See* HALE (Richard W.) the Elder. Sir Richard F. Burton. A foot-note to history. Being an account of his trip from St. Jo, August 7, 1860, to Salt Lake City, *etc.* [With a portrait.] 1930. 8º. **10823.** bb. **5.**

—— *See* HITCHMAN (Francis) Richard F. Burton, *etc.* 1887. 8º. **10817.** ee. **10.**

—— *See* PENZER (Norman M.) An Annotated Bibliography of Sir Richard Francis Burton, *etc.* [With a portrait.] 1923. 4º. **011903.** dd. **57.**

—— *See* RAINY (William) The Censor Censured: or, the Calumnies of Captain Burton . . . on the Africans of Sierra Leone refuted, and his conduct relative to the purchase money of the brig "Harriett" tested, *etc.* 1865. 8º. **6835.** b. **36.**

—— *See* SCHONFIELD (Hugh J.) Richard Burton, Explorer. [With a portrait.] 1936. 8º. **010822.** g. **44.**

—— *See* STISTED (Georgiana M.) The True Life of Capt. Sir Richard F. Burton, *etc.* 1896. 8º. **10816.** bb. **36.**

BURTON (*Sir* RICHARD FRANCIS) *K.C.M.G.* [APPENDIX.]

—— *See* WILSON (*Sir* Arnold T.) *K.C.I.E.* Richard Burton, *etc.* 1937. 8º. **010821.** i. **15.**

—— *See* WRIGHT (Thomas) *of Olney.* The Life of Sir Richard Burton, *etc.* [With portraits.] 1906. 8º. **010827.** i. **19.**

—— Farewell Dinner to Captain R. F. Burton, given by the Anthropological Society of London, April 4th, 1865, *etc.* [Reprinted from the "Anthropological Review."] pp. 16. *Trübner & Co.: London,* [1865.] 8º. **10826.** bbb. **28.** (**2.**)

—— A Sketch of the Career of Richard F. Burton . . . By Alfred Bates Richards, up to 1876: by Andrew Wilson, up to 1879: by St. Clair Baddeley, up to the present date, 1886. [With a portrait.] pp. 96. *Waterlow & Sons: London,* 1886. 8º. **10827.** a. **65.**

BURTON (RICHARD JOWETT) *See* CHURCH PREEN. The Register of Church Preen. [Transcribed and edited by R. J. Burton.] 1912, *etc.* 8º. [*Shropshire Parish Registers.* Diocese of Hereford. vol. 16.] Ac. **8132.**

—— *See* DALE ABBEY. A Literal Transcript of the Earliest Register of Dale Abbey, Derbyshire. 1900. 8º. [*Journal of the Derbyshire Archaeological and Natural History Society.* vol. 22.] Ac. **5633.**

—— *See* EATON CONSTANTINE. Eaton Constantine Registers, 1684–1800. [With a preface by R. J. Burton.] 1912. 8º. [*Shropshire Parish Registers.* Diocese of Lichfield. vol. 13. pt. 2.] Ac. **8132.**

—— *See* PHILLIMORE (William P. W.) Phillimore's Parish Register Series, *etc.* (Derbyshire Parish Registers. Edited by W. P. W. Phillimore and R. J. Burton.) 1897, *etc.* 8º. **9905.** p. **3.**

BURTON (ROBERT) *Author of "The Anatomy of Melancholy." See* also DEMOCRITUS, *Junior, pseud.* [i.e. R. Burton.] **40.** f. **15.**

—— *See* BENSLY (Edward) Robert Burton, *etc.* 1909. 8º. [*Cambridge History of English Literature.* vol. 4.] **11870.g.1.**

—— *See* DIECKOW (F. A. F.) John Florio's englische Übersetzung der Essais Montaigne's, und Lord Bacon's, Ben Jonson's und Robert Burton's Verhältnis zu Montaigne, *etc.* 1903. 8º. **11840.** r. **3.**

—— *See* EVANS (Bergen) The Psychiatry of Robert Burton, *etc.* [With a portrait and a bibliography.] 1944. 8º. **11866.** bb. **30.**

—— *See* EWING (S. B.) Burtonian Melancholy in the Plays of John Ford. 1940. 8º. [*Princeton Studies in English.* no. 19.] Ac. **1833/5.**

—— *See* GOTTLIEB (Hans J.) Robert Burton's Knowledge of English Poetry, *etc.* [1937.] 8º. **11858.** d. **88.**

—— *See* LAKE (Bernard) A General Introduction to Charles Lamb. Together with a special study of his relation to Robert Burton, *etc.* 1903. 8º. **011852.** c. **33.** (**1.**)

—— *See* MADAN (Falconer) Robert Burton and the Anatomy of Melancholy. Papers, *etc.* 1926. 4º. [*Oxford Bibliographical Society. Proceedings & Papers.* vol. 1. pt. 3.] **N.L.25.a.**

—— *See* MUELLER (William R.) The Anatomy of Robert Burton's England. [A study of "The Anatomy of Melancholy."] 1952. 8º. [*University of California Publications. English Studies.* no. 2.] Ac. **2689.** g. **65.**

BURTON (ROBERT) *Author of "The Anatomy of Melancholy."*

—— *See* SMITH (Paul J.) Bibliographia Burtoniana. A study of Robert Burton's The Anatomy of Melancholy. With a bibliography of Burton's writings. [With a portrait.] 1931. 8°. **011900**. c. **77**.

—— *See* TAEUSCH (Henry W.) Democritus Junior Anatomizes Melancholy. [An address on Robert Burton.] 1937. 8°. **11859**. aa. **11**.

—— Philosophaster. Comoedia, nunc primum in lucem producta. Poemata, antehac sparsim edita, nunc in unum collecta. [Edited by W. E. Buckley.] pp. xxxvi. 147. 1862. 4°. *See* LONDON.—III. *Roxburghe Club.* C. **101**. c. **9**.

—— Robert Burton's Philosophaster, with an English translation of the same. Together with his other minor writings in prose and verse. The translation, introductions, and notes by Paul Jordan-Smith. [With plates, including a portrait.] pp. xxi. 283. *Stanford University Press: Stanford University*, 1931. 8°. **11408**. g. **68**.

—— The Anatomy of Melancholy, what it is. With all the kindes, causes, symptomes, prognostickes, and severall cures of it . . . Philosophically, medicinally, historically, opened and cut up. By Democritus Iunior, *etc.* pp. 880. *Iohn Lichfield & Iames Short for Henry Cripps: Oxford,* 1621. 4°. C. **45**. c. **30**.
The first edition. The author's name occurs as the signature of "The couclusion [sic] *of the author to the reader."*

—— **The Anatomy of Melancholy: what it is. With all the kindes, causes, symptomes, prognosticks, and seuerall cures of it. In three maine partitions, with their seuerall sections, members and subsections. Philosophically, medicinally, historically opened and cut vp, by Democritus Iunior. With a satyricall preface, conducing to the following discourse. The second edition, corrected and augmented by the author. pp. 64. 557.** ***John Lichfield & James Short. for Henry Cripps: Oxford.*** **1624. fol.**
See DEMOCRITUS, *Junior, pseud.* [i.e. R. Burton.] **8408**. l. **10**.

—— **The thirde edition, corrected and augmented by the author. pp. 77. 646.** ***Iohn Lichfield, for Henry Cripps: Oxford.*** **1628. fol.**
See DEMOCRITUS, *Junior, pseud.* [i.e. R. Burton.] **8408**. l. **6**.
With a titlepage engraved by Christian Le Blon, which includes a portrait of the author. This titlepage occurs in modified form in the fourth, fifth, sixth, seventh, eighth and sixteenth editions, entered below.

—— **The fourth edition, corrected and augmented by the author. pp. 78. 722.** ***Iohn Lichfield for Henry Cripps: Oxford,*** **1632. fol.**
See DEMOCRITUS, *Junior, pseud.* [i.e. R. Burton.] **715**. i. **12**.

—— **The fifth edition, corrected and augmented by the author. pp. 78. 723.** ***Printed for Henry Cripps: Oxford,*** **1638. fol.**
See DEMOCRITUS, *Junior, pseud.* [i.e. R. Burton.] **8408**. l. **5**.

—— **The sixth edition, corrected and augmented by the author. pp. 78. 723.** ***Printed & are to be sould by Hen. Crips & Lodo: Lloyd: London,*** **1652. fol.**
See DEMOCRITUS, *Junior, pseud.* [i.e. R. Burton.] **715**. i. **13**.
The colophon reads "Printed by R. W. [Robert White] for Henry Cripps . . . and are to be sold by Andrew Crook . . . and by Henry Cripps and Lodowick Lloyd."

BURTON (ROBERT) *Author of "The Anatomy of Melancholy."*

—— **The seventh edition, corrected and augmented by the author. pp. 78. 723.** ***Henry Cripps; Elisha Wallis: London,*** **1660. fol.**
See DEMOCRITUS, *Junior, pseud.* [i.e. R. Burton.] **715**. i. **14**.

—— **[Another copy.]** **G. 19650.**

—— **The eighth edition, corrected and augmented by the author. pp. 46. 434.** ***R. W. for Peter Parker: London,*** **1676. fol.**
See DEMOCRITUS, *Junior, pseud.* [i.e. R. Burton.] **40**. f. **15**.

—— The ninth edition, corrected; to which is now first prefixed, an account of the author. 2 vol. *Vernor & Hood: London,* 1800. 8°. **8406**. gg. **13**.

—— The eleventh edition, corrected, *etc.* 2 vol. *Vernor, Hood & Sharpe: London,* 1806. 8°. **8406**. g. **22**.

—— The twelfth edition, corrected, *etc.* 2 vol. *J. Cuthell: London,* 1821. 8°. **8403**. k. **11**.

—— A new edition. To which is prefixed the life of the author. 2 vol. *Thomas M'Lean: London,* 1826. 8°. **8409**. l. **31**.
With an additional titlepage, engraved.

—— **The sixteenth edition. Printed from the authorized copy of 1651, with the author's last corrections, additions,** ***etc.*** **pp. viii. 743.** ***B. Blake & J. Chidley: London,*** **1838. 8°.**
See DEMOCRITUS, *Junior, pseud.* [i.e. R. Burton.] **8406**. ccc. **3**.

—— A new edition, corrected, and enriched by translations of the . . . classical extracts. By Democritus Minor, *etc.* pp. xviii. 748. *Thomas Tegg: London,* 1845. 8°. **2041.a.**

—— [Another copy.] The Anatomy of Melancholy . . . A new edition, corrected . . . by Democritus Minor, *etc. London,* 1845. 8°. **08460**. k. **11**.

—— [Another edition.] 3 vol. *Riverside Press: Cambridge [Mass.],* 1861. 8°. **8405**. i. **19**.

—— [Another edition.] Edited by the Rev. A. R. Shilleto . . . with an introduction by A. H. Bullen. 3 vol. **L.P.** *G. Bell & Sons: London,* 1893. 8°. K.T.C. **11**. a. **3**.

—— [Another edition.] (Edited by the Rev. A. R. Shilleto, with an introduction by A. H. Bullen.) 3 vol. *G. Bell & Sons: London,* 1904. 8°. [*York Library.*] **012201**. i. **1/16**.

—— New edition, corrected and enriched by translations of the numerous classical extracts. 3 vol. *Duckworth & Co.: London; Cambridge, U.S.A.* [printed], 1905. 8°. **08407**. f. **19**.

—— [Another edition.] 3 vol. *G. Bell & Sons: London,* 1923. 8°. [*Bohn's Popular Library.*] **20031**. a. **14/12**.
A reissue of the edition of 1904.

—— [Another edition.] Illustrated by E. McKnight Kauffer. pp. xv. 588. *Nonesuch Press: London,* 1925. fol. C. **99**. k. **21**.

—— [Another edition.] Now for the first time with the Latin completely given in translation and embodied in an all-English text. Edited by Floyd Dell and Paul Jordan-Smith. pp. xix. 1036. *G. Routledge & Sons: London; printed in U.S.A.,* 1930. 8°. **8404**. f. **30**.

BURTON (Robert) *Author of "The Anatomy of Melancholy."*

—— [Another edition.] [Edited by Holbrook Jackson.] 3 vol. *J. M. Dent & Sons: London & Toronto*, 1932. 8°. [*Everyman's Library.*] **12206.p.1/684.**

—— [A reissue, with the addition of an index.] *London*, 1936. 8°. [*Dent's Double Volumes.*] **12212. a. 1/30.**

—— Melancholy; as it proceeds from the disposition and habit, the passion of love, and the influence of religion. Drawn chiefly from . . . Burton's Anatomy of Melancholy, *etc.* pp. xii. 420. *Vernor & Hood: London*, 1801. 12°. **8406.** bbb. **26.**

—— The Anatomy of Melancholy . . . Being an abridgment of Burton's celebrated work. pp. xiii. 339. *N. Hailes: London*, 1824. 12°. **8403.** b. **19.**

—— New edition. pp. xiii. 339. *John Bumpus: London*, 1827. 12°. **8403.** ccc. **36.**

—— Melancholy Anatomized . . . With anecdotic illustrations drawn from ancient and modern sources, and principally founded on the larger work entitled, "Burton's Anatomy of Melancholy." pp. ix. 292. *William Tegg: London*, 1865. 8°. **8405.** bb. **15.**

—— A new edition. pp. ix. 292. *Chatto & Windus: London*, 1881. 8°. **12207.** f. **5.**

—— Burton the Anatomist. Being extracts from the "Anatomy of Melancholy" . . . Edited by G. C. F. Mead and Rupert C. Clift. With a preface by W. H. D. Rouse. pp. xxxv. 251. *Methuen & Co.: London*, 1925. 8°. **08408.** de. **37.**

—— A Cure for Melancholy from the Anatomy of Melancholy. pp. 6. *Grafton House: London*, 1927. 16°. **08407.** g. **39.**

—— Curious Fragments extracted from a common-place book, which belonged to Robert Burton, the famous author of The Anatomy of Melancholy. [By Charles Lamb.] *See* Lamb (Charles) John Woodvil, *etc.* 1802. 12°. C. **59.** b. **7**

BURTON (Robert) *pseud.* [i.e. Nathaniel Crouch] *See* Burton (Richard)

BURTON (Robert Christie) *See* Thornton (Thomas) *Colonel.* Calumny combated. A complete vindication of Col. Thornton's conduct in his transactions with Mr. Burton, *etc.* 1806. 8°. **1414.** g. **45.**

BURTON (Robert Clerke) The Irish Branch of the United Church of England and Ireland. A lecture . . . Third edition. pp. 30. *Samuel Miller: Norwich*, 1868. 8°. **4165.aa.24.**

BURTON (Robert Edward) *See* Burton (Robert W.) Memorial of Robert Edward Burton, *etc.* 1851. 12°. **4419.** g. **19.**

BURTON (Robert Lingen) The Wedding Garment. 1835. *See* Family Sermons. Original Family Sermons. vol. 5. 1833, *etc.* 8°. **694.** b. **5.**

BURTON (Robert William) Memorial of Robert Edward Burton; or, the Great end of life answered, *etc.* pp. 51. *R.T.S.: London*, 1851. 18°. **4419.** g. **19.**

—— Scripture Expositions on the Old Lines. pp. xii. 339. *George Herbert: Dublin*, 1882. 8°. **4466.** h. **19.**

BURTON (Robert William)

—— The War of God's Sending. A sermon, *etc.* pp. 20. *Thomas Hatchard: London*, 1854. 8°. **4476.** d. **23.**

BURTON (Rodney Stuart) Gone Gay. A romance of modern days. pp. 311. *Herbert Jenkins: London*, 1931. 8°. NN. **18082.**

BURTON (Roger Taylor) Contemplations on Israel's Exodus considered allegorically. pp. iv. 164. *Hatchard & Co.: London*, 1867. 8°. **3155.** bb. **43.**

BURTON (Samuel) *See* Hay (John) *of Dublin.* The Case of John Hay and the other Separate Creditors of S. Burton, Esq; deceased. 1740. 8°. E. **2091.** (**1***.)

—— A State of the Case of the Creditors of Burton's Bank. In which is contained a narrative of the proceedings relative to the demands of the said creditors against the estate of Francis Harrison, Esq; deceased. Together with a collection of the papers published both for and against the proposal lately made by Abraham Creichton . . . to the said creditors. [Edited by Robert Roberts.] pp. 53. *Dublin*, 1751. 8°. **8223.** a. **11.**

BURTON (Samuel Chatwood) Spain Poised. An etcher's record. [Plates, with letterpress.] *University of Minnesota Press: [Minneapolis*, 1937.] fol. **7861.** v. **29.**

BURTON (Samuel Holroyd)

—— *See* Masefield (John E.) Martin Hyde, *etc.* (Concise edition edited by S. H. Burton.) 1953. 8°. **012208.** cc. **1/93.**

—— The Coasts of Cornwall. pp. 216. pl. 16. *Werner Laurie: London*, 1955. 8°. **010368.** b. **75.**

—— Comprehension Practice. pp. xi. 114. *Longmans, Green & Co.: London*, 1951. 8°. **012987.** aa. **14.**

—— A Comprehensive English Course. pp. x. 228. *Longmans, Green & Co.: London*, 1954. 8°. **12983.** s. **27.**

—— The Criticism of Poetry. pp. xiii. 172. *Longmans, Green & Co.: London*, 1950. 8°. **11868.** de. **62.**

—— English Appreciation. pp. xii. 195. *Longmans, Green & Co.: London*, 1953. 8°. **012987.** aa. **38.**

—— English Appreciation. (Second edition.) pp. xiii. 195. *Longmans, Green & Co.: London*, 1954 [1955]. 8°. **012987.** aa. **61.**

—— English Study and Composition. pp. x. 102. *Longmans, Green & Co.: London*, 1952. 8°. **012986.** a. **65.**

—— Exmoor, *etc.* pp. 175. pl. 16. *Westaway: London*, [1952.] 8°. **010368.** df. **53.**

—— Modern Précis Practice. pp. vii. 103. *Longmans, Green & Co.: London*, 1955. 8°. **012987.** aa. **60.**

—— The North Devon Coast. A guide to its scenery & architecture, history & antiquities. pp. xv. 172. pl. 17. *Werner Laurie: London*, 1953. 8°. **010368.** b. **40.**

—— Official Guide to Porlock and District. [With illustrations.] pp. 28. *Gore Allen & Co.: [Tiverton*, 1953.] 8°. **010368.** aa. **33.**

—— The South Devon Coast. A guide to its scenery and architecture, history and antiquities. [With a map.] pp. 181. pl. 16. *Werner Laurie: London*, 1954. 8°. **10361.** bb. **30.**

BURTON (SAMUEL HOLROYD)

—— Tiverton to Exeter . . . 2nd edition. *Gore Allen & Co.: [Tiverton,* 1952.] 8°. **010368**. e. **130**.

—— Tiverton to Exmoor, *etc.* [With illustrations.] *Gore Allen & Co.: [Tiverton,* 1951.] 8°. **010368**. w. **80**.

BURTON (SAVILLE) Education maketh a Gentleman, and other essays. pp. 24. *A. H. Stockwell: London,* [1926.] 8°. **012352**. c. **45**.

BURTON (SINCLAIR)

—— Buying Up the Opportunities. A tract for the times on religion-in-education. pp. 47. *National Society's Office: London,* 1947. 8°. **08311**. c. **72**.

—— The Renewing of Catholicism. Evangelical essays towards religious renewal and unification, *etc.* pp. 129. *Robert Scott: London,* 1916. 8°. **4014**. dd. **40**.

BURTON (STEPHEN MERCERON)

—— The Art of Modern Navigation. *See* infra: A Manual of Modern Navigation.

—— A Manual of Modern Navigation, *etc.* pp. viii. 120. *Brown. Son & Ferguson: Glasgow,* 1930. 8°. **8804**. f. **16**.

—— A Manual of Modern Navigation, *etc.* (Second edition.) pp. viii. 120. *Brown, Son & Ferguson: Glasgow,* 1941. 8°. **8809**. aa. **11**.

—— [A Manual of Modern Navigation.] The Art of Modern Navigation. pp. vii. 146. *Burton's Navigational Publications: [Glasgow,]* 1955. 8°. **8565**. b. **66**.

—— A Set of Nautical Tables for General Navigational Purposes. [With a supplement.] 2 pt. *G. Philip & Son: London,* 1936 [1935]. 8°. **08548**. dd. **52**.

—— A Set of Nautical Tables for General Navigational Purposes . . . Third edition, *etc.* [With a supplement.] pp. 250. 39. *G. Philip & Son: London,* 1939. 8°. **08548**. dd. **61**.

—— A Set of Nautical Tables . . . By S. M. Burton . . . assisted by Gilbert F. Cunningham . . . Fourth edition. pp. 260. *Burton's Navigational Publications: Alva,* 1945. 8°.

—— Supplement, *etc.* pp. 41. *Burton's Navigational Publications: Alva,* 1945. 8°. **08548**. dd. **78**.

—— A Set of Nautical Tables . . . By S. M. Burton . . . assisted by Gilbert F. Cunningham . . . Fifth edition. pp. xvii. 345. *Burton's Navigational Publications: Alva,* 1951. 8°. **08548**. d. **41**.

BURTON (STEPHEN MERCERON) and **CUNNINGHAM** (GILBERT FARM)

—— Burton's Four-Figure Navigational Tables. pp. x. 119. *Burton's Navigational Publications: Alva,* 1944. 8°. **08548**. dd. **69**.

—— Burton's Four-Figure Navigation Tables . . . Third edition, *etc.* pp. x. 137. *Burton's Navigational Publications: Alva,* 1953. 8°. **08548**. d. **44**.

BURTON (SYDNEY) *See* WHEATON (A.) AND Co. Wheaton's Suggestive Geographies. (New edition.) [pt. 3 by C. B. Thurston and S. Burton.] [1922.] 4°. **10007**. l. **27**.

BURTON (THEODORE ELIJAH) *See* SCHOENRICH (O.) Former Senator Burton's Trip to South America, 1915. 1915. 8°. [*Carnegie Endowment for International Peace. Division of Intercourse and Education. Publication.* no. 9.] Ac. **2297**. gd.

BURTON (THEODORE ELIJAH)

—— The Constitution of the United States, *etc.* (Cutler lecture for 1922.) pp. 51. *Yale University Press: New Haven,* 1923. 8°. **08176**. a. **2**.

—— Corporations and the State. pp. xvi. 248. *D. Appleton & Co.: New York & London,* 1911. 8°. **8175**. h. **25**.

—— Financial Crises and Periods of Industrial and Commercial Depression . . . With diagrams, bibliography and index. pp. ix. 392. *D. Appleton & Co.: New York,* 1902. 8°. **8227**. aa. **58**.

—— [Another copy, with a different titlepage.] *Effingham Wilson: London; New York* printed, 1902. 8°. **08228**. ff. **22**.

—— Henry Clay. 1928. *See* BEMIS (S. F.) The American Secretaries of State, *etc.* vol. 4. 1927, *etc.* 8°. **10880**. s. **3/4**.

—— John Sherman. pp. vi. 449. *Houghton, Mifflin & Co.: Boston,* 1906. 8°. [*American Statesmen.* ser. 2.] **010880**. h. **2/2**.

—— Modern Political Tendencies, and the Effect of the War thereon. [With a portrait.] pp. 119. *Princeton University Press: Princeton,* 1919. 8°. **08175**. b. **30**.

BURTON (THEODORE ELIJAH) and **SELDEN** (GEORGE CHARLES)

—— A Century of Prices. An examination of economic and financial conditions as reflected in prices, *etc.* pp. 118. *Magazine of Wall Street: New York,* [1919.] 8°. **08228**. a. **32**.

BURTON (THOMAS) *M.P.* Diary of Thomas Burton, Esq. member in the Parliaments of Oliver and Richard Cromwell, from 1656 to 1659: now first published from the original autograph manuscript. With an introduction, containing an account of the parliament of 1654; from the journal of Guibon Goddard Esq. M.P. also now first printed. Edited and illustrated with . . . notes by John Towill Rutt. 4 vol. *Henry Colburn: London,* 1828. 8°. **2406**. f. **9**.

BURTON (THOMAS) *Novelist.*

—— Bloodbird, *etc.* pp. 357. *Constable: London,* 1942. 8°. NN. **33524**.

—— The Great Grab. An American novel. pp. xiii. 299. *Constable: London,* 1941. 8°. **12723**. aa. **24**.

BURTON (THOMAS) *of Turnham Hall.* The History and Antiquities of the Parish of Hemingbrough in the County of York . . . Edited and enlarged by J. Raine. pp. xii. 406. *Sampson Bros.: York,* 1888. 8°. **010358**. i. **33**.

BURTON (THOMAS) *Vicar of Halifax.* A Sermon preached in the Parish Church of Hallifax . . . the 7th of July, 1713. Being the day appointed . . . for a publick thanksgiving for the peace. pp. 16. *W. Bowyer: London; for Francis Hillyard: York,* 1713. 8°. **225**. h. **5**. (**3**.)

BURTON (THOMAS DE) *See* THOMAS, *de Burton.*

BURTON (THOMAS JONES) *See* RUSSELL (John F.) Obedience to the Church in Things Ritual. Two sermons. [By J. F. Russell and T. J. Burton respectively.] 1842. 12°. **1358**. c. **56**.

BURTON (THOMAS R.) *of Ludgate, London.* *See* BOURCART (E.) Insecticides . . . Revised and enlarged by T. R. Burton, *etc.* 1925. 8°. **07076**. h. **69**.

BURTON (THOMAS RUDALL) From a Balcony. In verse. pp. 80. *A. H. Stockwell: London*, [1930.] 8°. **011644**. h. **25**.

BURTON (TOM) Tom Burton; or, the Better way. By the author of "The Working Man's Way in the World" [i.e. Charles Manby Smith]. pp. 80. *S. W. Partridge: London*, [1863.] 8°. **12808**. bb. **16**.

BURTON (VIOLET) An Artist in the Great Beyond. Messages from a father (William Shakespeare Burton) . . . Transcribed by . . . V. Burton, *etc.* [With a portrait.] pp. xxxiii. 122. *Hutchinson & Co.: London*, [1925.] 8°. **8633**. eee. **33**.

—— My Larger Life. pp. 187. *Rider & Co.: London*, [1930.] 8°. **08632**. g. **54**.

BURTON (VIRGINIA LEE)

—— Calico the Wonder Horse; or, the Saga of Stewy Slinker. Story and pictures by V. L. Burton. *Faber & Faber: London*, 1942. *obl.* 8°. **12821**. a. **25**.

—— Choo Choo. The story of a little engine who ran away. *Faber & Faber: London*, 1944. 4°. **12823**. e. **24**.

—— Katy and the Big Snow. Story and pictures by V. L. Burton. *Faber & Faber: London*, 1947. *obl.* 4°. **12831**. ff. **2**.

—— The Little House. Story and pictures by V. L. Burton. pp. 40. *Faber & Faber: London*, 1946. *obl.* 8°. **12828**. d. **17**.

—— Mike Mulligan and his Steam Shovel. Story and pictures by V. L. Burton. *Faber & Faber: London*, 1941. *obl.* 4°. **12824**. c. **33**.

BURTON (VIRGINIA N.) *See* BURTON (William H.) *A.M.* and (V. N.) Burton Civics Test. [1928.] 8°. **8276**. r. **2**.

BURTON (W.) *Certificated Teacher, Leeds.* First Grade Freehand Drawing. Advanced . . . 24 examples on cards. *W. & R. Chambers: London & Edinburgh*, [1877.] 8°. **7854**. aaa. **3**.

—— First Grade Freehand Drawing. Elementary . . . 24 examples on cards. *W. & R. Chambers: London & Edinburgh*, [1877.] 8°. **7854**. aaa. **4**.

—— Second Grade Freehand Drawing . . . 24 examples on cards. *W. & R. Chambers: London & Edinburgh*, [1877.] 8°. **7854**. ccc. **2**.

BURTON (*Mrs.* W. DINZEY) Sister Ellen's Nursery Stories. The Little Oxleys: their sayings and doings, *etc.* pp. 160. *G. Routledge & Sons: London*, 1867. 8°. **12804**. e. **20**.

BURTON (W. J. P.) *See* SECRETS. Some Secrets of Nature . . . With an introduction by W. J. P. Burton, *etc.* 1913. 8°. **7001**. tt. **7**.

—— Schemes of Nature Study for Schools, adapted to in-door and out-door work. pp. 45. *Central Education Co.: Derby*, [1903.] 8°. **8310**. g. **2**.
Interleaved.

BURTON (*Mrs.* W. S.) Harold and Lily; or, the Birthdays. A little tale for little children. pp. 120. *W. Hunt & Co.: London*, [1868.] 12°. **12804**. aaa. **37**.

BURTON (WALTER ERVIN)

—— Engineering with Rubber. Edited by W. E. Burton, *etc.* pp. xi. 486. *McGraw-Hill Book Co.: New York*, 1949. 8°. **08766**. c. **62**.

—— The Story of Tire Beads and Tires, *etc.* [With illustrations.] pp. 196. *McGraw-Hill Book Co.: New York*, [1954.] 8°. **8774**. cc. **51**.

BURTON (WALTER HENRY) Dialogues on the First Principles of the Newtonian System. [With plates.] pp. 68. *University Press: Oxford*, 1828. 8°. **T. 1233. (6.)**

—— An Elementary Compendium of the Law of Real Property. pp. xvi. 548. *J. & W. T. Clarke: London*, 1828. 8°. **514**. d. **5**.

—— Fourth edition, corrected. pp. xxxi. 574. *J. & W. T. Clarke: London*, 1837. 8°. **514**. d. **6**.

—— [Another edition.] From the last London edition. pp. xx. 277. *J. S. Littell: Philadelphia*, 1839. 8°. **1384**. g. **14**.

—— The fifth edition, with notes, shewing the alterations in the law to the present time, by Edward Priestley Cooper. pp. xxxv. 641. *V. & R. Stevens & G. S. Norton: London*, 1841. 8°. **1130**. g. **17**.

—— The sixth edition . . . by Edward Priestley Cooper. pp. xxxv. 728. *V. & R. Stevens & G. S. Norton: London*, 1845. 8°. **1130**. g. **31**.

—— The seventh edition . . . To which is now prefixed an introductory chapter . . . By Edward Priestley Cooper. pp. xcviii. 582. *V. & R. Stevens & G. S. Norton: London*, 1850. 8°. **6305**. e. **2**.

—— The eighth edition . . . By Edward Priestley Cooper. pp. xcviii. 577. *V. & R. Stevens & G. S. Norton: London*, 1856 [1855]. 8°. **6305**. aaa. **16**.

BURTON (WARNEY) Oddities of a Zulu Campaign. pp. 79. *C. Brooks & Co.: London*, 1880. 8°. **12314**. k. **10**.

BURTON (WARREN) The Culture of the Observing Faculties in the Family and the School: or, Things about home, and how to make them instructive to the young. pp. 170. *Harper & Bros.: New York*, 1865. 8°. **8309**. aa. **14**.

—— The District School, as it was. By one who went to it. Revised edition. pp. 206. *Phillips, Sampson & Co.: Boston*, 1850. 12°. **8307**. b. **45**.

—— [Another edition.] Edited by Clifton Johnson. pp. 171. *Lee & Shepard: Boston*, 1897. 8°. **8311**. bb. **31**.

—— Helps to Education in the Homes of our Country. pp. viii. 368. *Crosby & Nichols: Boston*, 1863. 8°. **8305**. aa. **7**.

—— My Religious Experience at my Native Home. pp. 32. *Gray & Bowen: Boston*, 1832. 12°. **4986**. bb. **24**.

—— Report of the Ministry at Large in the City of Worcester, for one year, ending April 14, 1850. pp. 36. [1850.] 12°. *See* WORCESTER, *Mass.—Ministry at Large.* **4183**. aa. **9**.

—— The Scenery-Shower, with word paintings of the beautiful, the picturesque, and the grand in nature. pp. 119. *W. D. Ticknor & Co.: Boston*, 1844. 12°. **12352**. c. **39**.

BURTON (WILBUR) The French Strangle-Hold on Yunnan. A first-hand survey. [Reprinted from the "China Weekly Review."] pp. 46. *Shanghai*, [1933.] 4°. **20019**. d. **54**.

BURTON (William) afterwards **CONYNGHAM** (*Right Hon.* William) *See* Conyngham.

BURTON (William) *Bookseller.* Researches into the Phraseology, Manners, History and Religion of the Ancient Eastern Nations, as illustrative of the Sacred Scriptures, and into the accuracy of the English translation of the Bible. 2 vol. *W. Burton: London,* [1805.] 12°. **1159. k. 1.**

BURTON (William) *Calligrapher.* Business Handwriting. pp. vi. 85. *Sir I. Pitman & Sons: London,* 1932. *obl.* 8°. **7956. a. 61.**

BURTON (William) *Comedian.* A Pasquinade on the Performers of the York Company. pp. 24. *Printed for the Author: Leeds,* 1801. 8°. **11641. f. 9.**

—— [Another copy.] **641. h. 7. (3.)**

—— *See* Wilson (George) *Writer in Verse.* The Retort Courteous, *etc.* [An answer to "A Pasquinade on the Performers of the York Company," by W. Burton.] 1801. 8°. **10347. f. 8. (1.)**

BURTON (William) *D.D.* The Christian's God, his existence, nature, character, works, and gifts. pp. 190. *J. Clarke & Co.: London,* [1924.] 8°. **4016. de. 25.**

BURTON (William) *F.C.S.* *See* Auscher (E. S.) A History and Description of French Porcelain . . . Translated and edited by W. Burton, *etc.* 1905. 8°. **07807. k. 19.**

—— *See* Falkner (Frank) *of Bowdon.* Catalogue of a Collection of English Pottery Figures deposited on loan by Mr. F. Falkner. [With an introductory note by W. Burton.] 1911. 8°. [*General Guide to the Art Collections. National Museum, Dublin.*] **7959. e. 14.**

—— *See* Falkner (Frank) *of Bowdon.* The Wood Family of Burslem . . . With an introduction by W. Burton. 1912. 4°. **9916. gg. 13.**

—— *See* Solon (L. M. E.) A History and Description of Italian Majolica . . . With a preface by W. Burton, *etc.* 1907. 8°. **07808. h. 17.**

—— *See* Solon (L. M. E.) A History and Description of the old French Faïence . . . With a preface by W. Burton, *etc.* 1903. 8°. **K.T.C. 27. b. 17.**

—— An Analysis of the Regulations governing the Manufacture of Pottery in the British Isles. Compiled by W. Burton. pp. 86. *Pottery Gazette: London,* 1913. 8°. **06005. ee. 45. (4.)**

—— A General History of Porcelain . . . With thirty-two plates in colour and eighty in black-and-white. 2 vol. *Cassell & Co.: London,* 1921. 8°. **07807. l. 42.**

—— A History and Description of English Earthenware and Stoneware, to the beginning of the 19th century . . . Containing twenty-four plates in colours, together with reproductions of marks and numerous illustrations. pp. xv. 192. *Cassell & Co.: London,* 1904. 8°. **07807. l. 30.**

—— A History and Description of English Porcelain . . . Containing twenty-four plates in colours, together with eleven plates of marks printed in colours and gold, and numerous illustrations. pp. xii. 196. *Cassell & Co.: London,* 1902. 8°. **7921.cc.2.**

BURTON (William) *F.C.S.*

—— Josiah Wedgwood and his Pottery . . . With . . . plates. pp. xii. 195. *Cassell & Co.: London,* 1922. 8°. **L.R. 35. c. 2.**

—— Porcelain. Its nature, art and manufacture. pp. viii. 264. pl. l. *B. T. Batsford: London,* [1906?] 8°. **07808. g. 12.**

—— The Use of Lead Compounds in Pottery, from the potters' point of view. pp. 83. *Simpkin, Marshall & Co.: London,* 1899. 8°. **7953. cc. 38.**

BURTON (William) *F.C.S.,* and **HOBSON** (Robert Lockhart) *Keeper of Oriental Antiquities and Ethnography, British Museum.*

—— Handbook of Marks on Pottery & Porcelain. pp. x. 210. *Macmillan & Co.: London,* 1909. 8°. **07807. f. 25.**

—— [Another edition.] pp. x. 212. *Macmillan & Co: London,* 1912. 8°. **07805. aa. 19.**

—— [Another edition.] (Revised and enlarged.) pp. x. 213. *Macmillan & Co.: London,* 1928. 8°. **07805. ee. 34.**

BURTON (William) *Governor of the State of Delaware.* [For official documents issued by W. Burton as Governor of Delaware:] *See* Delaware, *State of.*—Burton (W.) *Governor, etc.* **A.S. d. 26.**

BURTON (William) *M.D., of Yarmouth.* An Account of the Life and Writings of Herman Boerhaave. With an appendix [containing letters and a bibliography]. [By W. Burton. With a portrait.] pp. viii. 226. 1743. 8°. *See* Boerhaave (H.) [*Appendix.*] **10760. bbb. 3.**

—— The second edition. pp. vii. 226. *Henry Lintot: London,* 1746. 8°. **277. d. 23.**

BURTON (William) *Master of the Free Grammar School at Kingston-upon-Thames.* *See* Alsted (J. H.) The Beloved City, or the Saints reign on earth . . . Englished [by W. Burton], *etc.* 1643. 4°. **E. 90. (9.)**

—— *See* Antoninus, *Augustus.* A Commentary on Antoninus his Itinerary . . . so far as it containeth Britain. By W. Burton, *etc.* 1658. fol. **455. a. 8.**

—— *See* Clement i., *Saint, Pope.* Clement . . . his first Epistle to the Corinthians . . . Translated, *etc.* [Translated, with "Certaine Annotations upon Clement," by W. Burton.] 1647. 4°. **E. 396. (24.)**

—— —— 1652. 4°. **108. c. 29.**

—— Græcæ linguæ historia, *etc.* (Veteris linguæ persicæ λειψανα, *etc.*) pp. 104. *Apud Thomam Roycroft: Londini,* 1657. 8°. **622. a. 21. (2.)**

—— [Another copy.] **672. a. 29. (1.)**

—— Gulielmi Burtoni Historia græcæ linguæ. 1715. *See* Libri. Nova librorum variorum conlectio, *etc.* fasc. 4. 1709, *etc.* 8°. **271. a. 1.**

—— In doctissimi, clarissimi, optimi senis, Thomæ Alleni, vltimo Septembris mdcxxxii Oxonijs demortui, exequiarum iustis ab Alma Academia postridiè solutis, orationes binæ, *etc.* [The first by W. Burton, the second by George Bathurst.] pp. 16. *Excudebat G. Stanesbeius: Londini,* 1632. 4°. **835. g. 30.**

—— [Another copy, with a different titlepage.] **731. k. 7. (1.)**

BURTON (WILLIAM) *Master of the Free Grammar School at Kingston-upon-Thames.*

—— Gulielmi Burtoni . . . λειψανα veteris linguae persicae, quae apud priscos scriptores, græcos et latinos, reperiri potuerunt. Accedit Marci Zuerii Boxhornii epistola . . . de persicis Curtio memoratis vocabulis, eorumque cum germanicis cognatione . . . Edita, praefatione, notis & additamentis instructa a Io. Henr. von Seelen. pp. 143. *Lubecae*, 1720. 8°. **1103**. b. **3**. (**2**.)

—— [Another copy.] **58**. a. **25**.

—— Nobilissimi herois Dn. Caroli Howardi comitis Nottinghamiæ . . . ἀποθεωσις. Ad illustrissimum V. Dn. C. Howardum, comitem Nottinghamiæ . . . fratrem superstitem. [*London*, 1643.] *s. sh.* fol. **669**. f. **8**. (**1**.)

—— [Another copy.] Lutt. I. **175**.

BURTON (WILLIAM) *Minister at Reading. See* ERASMUS (D.) [*Colloquia.—Selections.*] Seven Dialogues both pithie and profitable . . . By W. B. [A translation by W. Burton of selections from the " Colloquia " of Erasmus.] 1606. 4°. **C.122.c.3.**

—— Certaine Questions and Answeres concerning the Attributes of God, *etc.* (An Exposition of the Lordes Prayer, *etc.*—God wooing His Church.—Dauids Euidence, *etc.*—Conclusions of Peace betweene God and Man, *etc.*—A Caueat for Suerties, *etc.*—The Rowsing of the Sluggard, *etc.*—Ten Sermons vpon the first, second, third and fourth verses of the sixt of Mathew . . . Whereunto is annexed another treatise called the Anatomie of Belial.) 2 pt. *Felix Kyngston for Thomas Man*, [1602.] 4°. **1479**. b. **26**.

The second part, entitled " Ten Sermons, etc.," has the imprint " Richard Field for Thomas Man: London, 1602." *The first part has a mutilated titlepage, and lacks leaf* O 5, *which has been supplied by photostat from the copy in the Folger Shakespeare Library.*

—— The Christians heauenly Treasure. ff. 80. *T. E. for Thomas Man senior & Ionas Man: London*, 1608. 8°. **1018**. i. **39**.

—— Dauids Euidence. Or, The assurance of Gods loue: declared in seauen sermons vpon the three last verses of the 41. Psalme, *etc.* pp. 152. *For Iohn Hardie: London*, 1596. 8°. **4452**. b. **2**.

—— Dauids Thankes-giving for the Arraignement of the Man of Earth, set forth in two sermons . . . Wherevnto are newly adioyned two other Sermons of the tryall of faith, *etc.* pp. 55. *For George Potter: London*, 1602. 4°. **4474**. bbb. **138**.

—— The Rowsing of the Sluggard. Deliuered in seuen sermons, *etc.* pp. 309. *R. Raworth for I. Man; sold by T. Paine & M. Simmons: London*, 1634. 8°. **1480**. a. **7**

—— A Sermon preached in the Cathedrall Church in Norwich . . . 1589 . . . published for the satisfying of some which took offence thereat. [1590?] 8°. **4474**. a. **85**.

—— Ten Sermons vpon the first, second, third and fourth verses of the sixt of Mathew. Containing diuerse necessary and profitable treatises . . . Whereunto is annexed another treatise called the Anatomie of Belial: set foorth in ten sermons vpon the 12. 13. 14. and 15. verses of the 6. Chapter of the Prouerbes of Salomon. pp. 255. *Richard Field for Thomas Man: London*, 1602. 4°.
Also issued as the second part of the Author's Works, 1602. **1477**. aa. **7**.

BURTON (WILLIAM) *Murderer.* A True, Full, and Particular Account of the Last Awful Moments of William Burton, who was executed at Gloucester County Goal [*sic*], on Thhursday [*sic*], April 8, 1819, for the wilful murder of William Syms, *etc.* (A true, full, and particular account of the truly melancholy and fatal accident which befel Mrs. Wilkinson, gunsmith, in St. Thomas-Street, on Saturday last, April 10, 1819, who was shot by a pistol, *etc.*) *Harry Bonner: Bristol*, [1819.] *s. sh.* 4°. **1880**. c. **20**. (**369**.)

BURTON (WILLIAM) *of Bristol.* A Hudibrastic Address to Opposition. pp. 30. *Emery & Adams: Bristol*, 1800. 8°. **11642**. bbb. **15**.

BURTON (WILLIAM) *of Brunswick Row, Bloomsbury. See* WALKER (John) *Fellow of Trinity College, Dublin.* Essays and Correspondence . . . Collected and prepared for the press, by W. Burton. (A general index . . . by W. Burton.) 1838. 8°. **1124**. e. **24**, **25**.

BURTON (WILLIAM) *Topographer. See* ACHILLES TATIUS, *the Rhetorician.* The Loves of Clitophon and Leucippe. Translated . . . by W. Burton, *etc.* 1923. 4°. L.R. **37**. b. **5**.

—— The Description of Leicester Shire. Containing matters of antiquitye, historye, armorye, and genealogy. [With a portrait and a map.] pp. 320. **L.P.** *For Iohn White: London*, [1622.] fol. G. **3495**.

—— [Another copy.] **190**. b. **16**.
Imperfect; wanting the portrait.

—— [Another copy.] COPIOUS MS. NOTES [chiefly by P. Le Neve]. **578**. i. **15**.
Imperfect; wanting the portrait. In this copy the heraldic designs have been coloured by P. Le Neve, and a MS. *index has been inserted. Partly interleaved.*

—— The second edition, enlarged and corrected. [With a map.] pp. iv. 300. pl. II. *W. Whittingham: Lynn*, 1777. fol. **2066.c.**

—— [Another copy.] **L.P.** **189**. f. **13**.

—— *See* NICHOLS (John) *F.S.A., etc.* The History and Antiquities of the County of Leicester . . . Including . . . Mr. Burton's Description of the county, *etc.* 1795, *etc.* fol. **2065.e.**

—— *See* THROSBY (John) Select Views in Leicestershire, *etc.* (To which are added, in notes, the most valuable parts of Burton, Nichols, and other antecedent writers on Leicestershire.) 1790, *etc.* 4°. **191**. a. **6**, **7**.

BURTON (WILLIAM) *Writer of Fiction.* A Comedy of Life. [A tale.] pp. 15. *Worbon Press: London*, 1926. 8°. **012643**. h. **52**.

BURTON (WILLIAM DINZEY) Burton's Yarmouth Almanac, 1862. *See* EPHEMERIDES.

BURTON (WILLIAM EVANS) *See* KEESE (William L.) William E. Burton, Actor, Author, and Manager, *etc.* [With portraits.] 1885. 8°. **10826**. cc. 5.

—— The Court Fool: or, a King's amusement. A tragic drama, in three acts. [Based on Victor Hugo's " Le Roi s'amuse."] pp. 16. *London*, [1883?] 8°. [*Dicks' Standard Plays.* no. 341.] **11770**. bbb. **4**.

—— Cyclopedia of Wit and Humor, of America, Ireland, Scotland and England . . . Embellished with . . . engravings . . . and a portrait, *etc.* pt. 1–23. pp. 1–1108. *D. Appleton & Co.: New York*, [1857, 58.] 8°. **12355**. g. **25**.

Imperfect; wanting pt. 24.

BURTON (WILLIAM EVANS)

—— Ellen Wareham, a domestic drama, in three acts, *etc.* pp. 42. *London,* [1833.] 8°. [*Duncombe's Edition.* vol. 12.] **2304.** a. **6.**

—— [Another edition.] Ellen Wareham, the wife of two husbands, *etc.* pp. 36. *London,* [1858.] 8°. [*Lacy's Acting Edition of Plays.* vol. 34.] **2304.** e. **8.** (**1.**)

—— Waggeries and Vagaries. A series of sketches, humourous and descriptive. [With plates.] pp. 192. *Carey & Hart: Philadelphia,* 1848. 12°. **12703.** d. **14.** (**3.**)
With an additional titlepage, engraved.

—— Bibliotheca Dramatica. Catalogue of the theatrical and miscellaneous library of the late William E. Burton, *etc.* [With a portrait.] pp. vi. 463. [*New York,* 1860.] 8°. **011900.** k. **11.**

BURTON (WILLIAM FREDERICK PADWICK)

—— Congo Sketches . . . Illustrated by the author. [With plates.] pp. v. 177. *Victory Press: London,* [1950.] 8°. **10098.** bbb. **20.**

—— God Working with Them. Being eighteen years of Congo Evangelistic Mission history. [With plates, including portraits.] pp. xiv. 264. *Victory Press: London,* 1933. 8°. **4763.** c. **31.**

—— How They Live in Congoland. An account of the character and customs of this . . . race and efforts to win them for Christ. [With plates.] pp. 159. *Pickering & Inglis: London,* [1938.] 8°. **20031.** g. **39.**

—— Mafundijyo a ku mukanda wa Leza. pp. 100. *Elizabethville,* [1948.] 8°. **3110.** cc. **7.**

—— Mudishi, Congo Hunter. [With plates, including a portrait.] pp. 193. *Victory Press: London,* 1947. 8°. **4768.** aaa. **47.**

—— Signs following. (Second edition.) pp. viii. 40. *Assemblies of God Publishing House: Luton,* 1950. 8°. **7409.** aaaa. **38.**

—— What Mean Ye by These Stones? Bible talks on the Lord's Table. pp. 96. *Victory Press: London,* 1947. 8°. **3130.** aa. **52.**

—— When God Changes a Man. A true story of this great change in the life of a slave-raider (Shalumbo). [With plates, including portraits.] pp. viii. 124. *Victory Press: London,* 1929. 8°. **10607.** aaa. **18.**

—— When God Changes a Village. [An account of the work of the Congo Evangelistic Mission in Bunda. With plates.] pp. x. 162. *Victory Press: London,* 1933. 8°. **4765.** g. **47.**

—— When God Makes a Missionary. Being the life story of Edgar Mahon. [With plates, including a portrait.] pp. viii. 124. *Victory Press: London,* 1936. 8°. **20030.** aa. **13.**

—— When God Makes a Pastor. [A biography of Elias Letwaba. With plates, including portraits.] pp. xvi. 122. *Victory Press: London,* 1934. 8°. **20019.** a. **25.**

BURTON (WILLIAM GLYNN)

—— The Industrial Uses of the Potato. *See* SALAMAN (Redcliffe N.) The History and Social Influence of the Potato, *etc.* 1949. 8°. **07078.** k. **37.**

BURTON (WILLIAM GLYNN)

—— The Potato. A survey of its history and of factors influencing its yield, nutritive value and storage. pp. xiv. 319. *Chapman & Hall: London,* 1948. 8°. **7080.** aa. **43.**

BURTON (WILLIAM HENRY) *A.M.* *See* BARR (Arvil S.) and BURTON (W. H.) The Appleton Series in Supervision and Teaching, *etc.* [1925, *etc.*] 8°. **8314.b.1.**

—— *See* BARR (Arvil S.) and BURTON (W. H.) The Supervision of Instruction, *etc.* [1926.] 8°. **8314.b.1/2.**

—— *See* FREDERICK (Robert W.) How to Study Handbook. By R. W. Frederick . . . With the editorial assistance of W. H. Burton. [1938.] 8°. **8311.** eee. **40.**

—— *See* SUPERVISION. Supervision. Principles and practices in the improvement of instruction. By A. S. Barr . . . W. H. Burton, *etc.* [1938.] 8°. **8314.b.1/15.**

—— *See* SUPERVISION. Supervision . . . By A. S. Barr . . . W. H. Burton, *etc.* [1947.] 8°. **8314.b.1/18.**

—— Introduction to Education. pp. xiv. 833. *New York, London,* [1934.] 8°. [*Appleton Series in Supervision and Teaching.*] **8314.b.1/11.**

—— The Nature and Direction of Learning. pp. xviii. 595. *New York, London,* [1929.] 8°. [*Appleton Series in Supervision and Teaching.*] **8314.b.1/5.**

—— Supervision and the Improvement of Teaching. [With bibliographical notes.] pp. xx. 510. *D. Appleton & Co.: New York, London,* 1922. 8°. **08311.** bb. **19.**

—— The Supervision of Elementary Subjects. Edited by W. H. Burton, *etc.* pp. xix. 710. *New York, London,* [1929.] 8°. [*Appleton Series in Supervision and Teaching.*] **8314.b.1/6.**

BURTON (WILLIAM HENRY) *A.M.*, and **BURTON** (VIRGINIA N.)

—— Burton Civics Test. 4 pt. *World Book Co.: Yonkers-on-Hudson,* [1928.] 8°. **8276.** r. **2.**

BURTON (WILLIAM HENRY) *Baptist Minister.* "Out on the Ocean sailing." A sermon . . . preached in the Metropolitan Tabernacle, London. [1891.] *See* PERIODICAL PUBLICATIONS.—*London.* The People's Pulpit, *etc.* no. 36. 1887, *etc.* 8°. P.P. **790.** gc.

—— Symbols from the Sea; or, the Port, the pilot, and the passage. pp. viii. 248. *R. D. Dickinson: London,* 1874. 8°. **4409.** gg. **34.**

BURTON (WILLIAM KINNINMOND) *See* INNES (Cosmo) *C.E.*, and BURTON (W. K.) Sanitary Inspection of Dwelling Houses, *etc.* [1880.] 8°. **8777.** g. **21.** (**5.**)

—— *See* INOUYE (Jukichi) Wrestlers and Wrestling in Japan, *etc.* [With plates after photographs by W. K. Burton.] [1895.] fol. **7912.** k. **1.**

—— *See* MILNE (John) *F.R.S.*, and BURTON (W. K.) The Great Earthquake in Japan, 1891, *etc.* [1891.] *obl.* fol. **1824.** b. **5.**

—— *See* MURDOCH (James) *M.A.* Ayame-San, a Japanese romance . . . Illustrated from photographs by W. K. Burton, *etc.* 1892. 8°. **012622.** g. **11.**

BURTON (WILLIAM KINNINMOND)

—— The ABC of Modern Photography . . . Reprinted from the "Photographic News." pp. 84. *Piper & Carter: London*, 1882. 8°. **8908**. ee. **22**.

—— Third, and enlarged edition. pp. viii. 124. *Piper & Carter: London*, 1883. 8°. **8908**. e. **29**.

—— [Another copy.] The A B C of Modern Photography, *etc. London*, 1883. 8°. **8913**. d. **23**.

—— Burton's Modern Photography . . . Formerly published as the "ABC of Modern Photography" . . . Fifth, and enlarged edition, *etc.* pp. viii. 130. *Piper & Carter: London*, 1885. 8°. **8908**. e. **44**.

—— Sixth, and enlarged edition, *etc.* pp. iv. 172. *Piper & Carter: London*, 1886. 8°. **8908**. e. **47**.

—— Seventh, and enlarged edition, *etc.* pp. iv. 177. *Piper & Carter: London*, 1887. 8°. **8908**. e. **52**.

—— Ninth, and greatly enlarged edition. pp. viii. 208. *Piper & Carter: London*, 1890. 8°. **8908**. e. **56**.

—— Tenth edition. pp. vi. 208. *Piper & Carter: London*, 1892. 8°. **8909**. aaa. **40**.
Imperfect; wanting the wrapper.

—— Burton's Manual of Photography. pp. 184. *P. Lund & Co.: Bradford, London*, 1895. 16°. **8909**. f. **37**.

—— Optics for Photographers . . . Reprinted, with alterations and additions, from the Photographic News. pp. viii. 153. *Piper & Carter: London*, 1891. 8°. **8909**. aa. **14**.

—— Practical Guide to Photographic & Photo-Mechanical Printing. pp. xiv. 355. *Marion & Co.: London*, 1887. 8°. **8909**. cc. **8**.

—— The Water Supply of Towns and the Construction of Waterworks . . . To which is appended a paper on the effects of earthquakes on waterworks by Professor John Milne, *etc.* pp. xvi. 304. pl. XLIV. *C. Lockwood & Son: London*, 1894. 8°. **8777**. i. **7**.

—— Second edition, revised and extended. pp. xvi. 318. pl. XLV. *C. Lockwood & Son: London*, 1898. 8°. **8777**. h. **29**.

—— Third edition, revised. Edited by Allan Greenwell. pp. xvi. 318. pl. XLV. *C. Lockwood & Son: London*, 1907. 8°. **8776**. eee. **29**.

—— Fourth edition . . . By J. E. Dumbleton . . . With . . . plates, *etc.* 2 vol. *C. Lockwood & Son: London*, 1928. 8°. **08776**. dd. **17**.

BURTON (WILLIAM M.) The Atomic Weight of Zinc, as determined by the composition of the oxide. A dissertation, *etc.* [With plates.] pp. 33. *Isaac Friedenwald: Baltimore*, 1889. 8°. **8909**. ccc. **6**. **(3.)**

BURTON (WILLIAM SHAKESPEARE) *See* BURTON (Violet) An Artist in the Great Beyond. Messages from a father (W. S. Burton) . . . Transcribed by . . . V. Burton, *etc.* [With a portrait.] [1925.] 8°. **8633**. eee. **33**.

BURTON (*Sir* WILLIAM WESTBROOKE) *K.C.B.*

—— The Insolvent Law of New South Wales, with practical directions and forms. pp. viii. 202. MS. NOTES. *Wm. Moffitt: Sydney*, 1842. 8°. **1376**. h. **7**.

BURTON (*Sir* WILLIAM WESTBROOKE) *K.C.B.*

—— The State of Religion and Education in New South Wales. [With a map.] pp. vii. 321. cxxxvi. *J. Cross; Simpkin & Marshall: London*, 1840. 8°. **798**. e. **21**.

—— *See* ULLATHORNE (William B.) *R.C. Bishop of Birmingham.* A Reply to Judge Burton, of the Supreme Court of New South Wales, on "The State of Religion" in the colony. 1840. 8°. **1369**. h. **31**.

BURTON-ALEXANDER (J. T.) *See* ALEXANDER.

BURTON-BALDRY (WALTER BURTON) *See* BALDRY.

BURTON-BROWN (CHRISTOPHER) *See* BROWN.

BURTON-BROWN (E.) *See* BROWN.

BURTON-BROWN (THEODORE) *See* BROWN (T. B.)

BURTON-FANNING (FREDERICK WILLIAM) *See* FANNING.

BURTON-OPITZ (RUSSELL) *See* OPITZ.

BURTONUS (GULIELMUS) *See* BURTON (William) *Master of the Free Grammar School at Kingston-upon-Thames.*

BURTONUS (JOHANNES) *See* BURTON (John) *D.D.*

BURTONUS (ROBERTUS) *See* BURTON (Robert) *Author of "The Anatomy of Melancholy."*

BURTONWOOD.—*Burtonwood Chapel.*

—— [For "The Register of Burtonwood Chapel in the Parish of Warrington, 1668–1837":] *See* WARRINGTON.

BURTORFF (AUGUST JOHANN)

—— *See* LEXIKON. Neu vermehrtes historisch- und geographisches allgemeines Lexikon . . . Dritte Auflage. In welcher das von J. C. Beck . . . und A. J. Burtorff . . . verfertigte Supplement . . . eingerucket worden. 1742, *etc.* fol. **613**. dd. **1**.

BURTSCHEID, *Cistercian Abbey of.* Das älteste Burtscheider Nekrologium. Von F. X. Bosbach. 1898. *See* AIX-LA-CHAPELLE.—*Aachener Geschichtsverein.* Zeitschrift, *etc.* Bd. 20. 1879, *etc.* 8°. Ac. **7008**.

BURTSCHER (GUIDO) Die Kämpfe in den Felsen der Tofana. Geschichte der von Mai 1915 bis November 1917 heiss umstrittenen Kampfabschnitte Travenanzes und Lagazuoi . . . Mit 78 Bilddrucken . . . und mit einer . . . Landkarte. pp. 232. *Bregenz*, 1933. 8°. **9081**. dd. **2**.

BURTSEV (ALEKSANDR EVGENIEVICH)

—— Русскія книжныя рѣдкости. Библіографическій списокъ рѣдкихъ книгъ. Составилъ А. Бурцевъ. (Описаніе русскихъ рѣдкихъ книгъ находящихся въ моей библіотекѣ.) часть 1. pp. 258. 9. *С.-Петербургъ*, 1895. 8°. **011904**. f. **56**.
No. 45 of a privately printed edition of fifty copies. No more published.

BURTSEV (VLADIMIR L'VOVICH) *See* also VIKTOROV (N.) *pseud.* [i.e. V. L. Burtsev.]

—— *See* BAKAI (M. E.) О разоблачителяхъ и разоблачительствѣ. Письмо къ В. Бурцеву. (Письмо Бурцева къ Бакаю.—Отвѣтъ Бакая.) 1912. 8°. **8095**. de. **24**. **(6.)**

—— *See* DUMBADZE (E. V.) На службѣ Чека и Коминтерна . . . Со вступительной статьей В. Л. Бурцева, *etc.* 1930. 8°. **9454**. aaa. **37**.

BURTSEV (VLADIMIR L'VOVICH)

—— *See* GRIBOYEDOV (A. S.) Горе отъ Ума . . . Подъ редакціей В. Д. Бурцева. 1919. 4°. **20012.** b. **21.**

—— *See* GRIBOYEDOV (A. S.) Горе отъ Ума . . . Подъ редакціей, съ примѣчаніями и вступительной статьей В. Л. Вурцева. 1919. 4°. **20010.** cc. **45.**

—— *See* LONGUET (J.) and ZILBER (G.) Les Dessous de la police russe. Terroristes et policiers . . . Préface de W.-L. Bourtsev. [1909.] 8°. **6056.** pp. **4.**

—— *See* PERIODICAL PUBLICATIONS.—*Geneva.* Свободная Россія . . . Редакторы: В. Бурцевъ и В. Дебогорій-Мокріевичъ. 1889, *etc.* fol. P.P. **3554.** egb.

—— *See* PERIODICAL PUBLICATIONS.—*London.* Былое, *etc.* [Edited by V. Burtsev.] 1903, *etc.* 8°. P.P. **3554.** emi.

—— *See* PERIODICAL PUBLICATIONS.—*London.* Народоволецъ, *etc.* (V. Bourtzeff, editor) 1897, *etc.* 8°. P.P. **3554.** ec.

—— *See* PERIODICAL PUBLICATIONS.—Paris.—*Иллюстрованная Россія.* "Былое" . . . Новая серія . . . Под редакціей В. Л. Бурцева. 1933, *etc.* 8°. P.P. **3554.** emv.

—— *See* RADISHCHEV (Aleksandr N.) Путешествіе изъ Петербурга въ Москву . . . Подъ редакціей В. Л. Бурцева. 1921. 8°. **010290.** eee. **6.**

—— *See* VOLKENSHTEIN (L. A.) 13 лѣтъ въ Шлиссельбургской Крѣпости . . . Съ примѣчаніями В. Л. Бурцева. 1900. 8°. **10602.** e. **11.** (2.)

—— Азефъ и Ленинъ. pp. 6. [*Paris*, 1918.] 8°. **010795.** aaa. **12.**

—— Боритесь съ Г П У!, *etc.* pp. 47. 1932. 8°. *See* PERIODICAL PUBLICATIONS.—Paris.—*Общее Дѣло.* **06055.** e. **50.**

—— Борьба за свободную Россію. Мои воспоминанія. 1882–1922 г.г. томъ 1. pp. 381. *Берлинъ*, 1923. 8°. **20003.** c. **2.**
No more published. The date on the wrapper is 1924.

—— Въ борьбѣ съ большевиками и нѣмцами. Статьи изъ газеты "Общее Дѣло" 1917 г. pp. 79. *Парижъ*, 1919. 8°. **8095.** ff. **59.** (3.)

—— Въ защиту правды. Перестанутъ ли они клеветать? Дѣло ген. П. П. Дьяконова. Дѣло полк. А. Н. Попова и полк. Н. А. де-Роберти. Заговоръ молчанія. pp. 32. 1931. 8°. *See* PERIODICAL PUBLICATIONS.—Paris.—*Общее Дѣло.* **6055.** s. **14.**

—— Долой царя!, *etc.* (Къ вопросу—что дѣлать?) pp. 56. 56. *Лондонъ*, [1905?] 8°. **8094.** de. **12.**

—— За сто лѣтъ, 1800–1896. Сборникъ по исторіи политическихъ и общественныхъ движеній въ Россіи . . . Составилъ В. Бурцевъ при редакціонномъ участіи С. М. Кравчинскаго, степняка. 2 част. *Russian Free Press Fund: London*, 1897. 8°. **8093.** bb. **15.**

—— Какъ Пушкинъ хотѣлъ издать "Евгенія Онѣгина" и какъ издалъ. Нѣсколько страницъ изъ біографіи Пушкина, *etc.* pp. 61. *Paris*, 1934. 8°. **010795.** aa. **86.**

—— Календарь русской революціи. Издательства "Шиповникъ." Подъ общей редакціей В. Л. Бурцева. [With plates. Second edition.] pp. 343. *Петроградъ*, [1917.] 8°. **9457.** dd. **13.**
The first edition, 1907, *was confiscated before publication.*

BURTSEV (VLADIMIR L'VOVICH)

—— Преступленія и наказаніе большевиковъ. По поводу 20-лѣтняго юбилея предателей и убійцъ. [Articles reprinted from periodicals.] pp. 79. *Парижъ*, [1938.] 8°. **8095.** aaa. **8.**

—— Проклятіе вамъ, Большевики! Открытое письмо [dated May 1917] большевикамъ. pp. 13. *Стокгольмъ*, 1918. 8°. **8095.** h. **23.**

—— Шестое изданіе. pp. 15. *Paris*, 1919. 8°. **8095.** ff. **59.** (1.)

—— Cursed be the Bolcheviks! [A translation of "Проклятіе вамъ, Большевики!"] pp. 16. *Paris*, 1919. 8°. **8095.** ff. **58.** (2.)

—— Soyez maudits, bolcheviks! [A translation of "Проклятіе вамъ, Большевики!"] pp. 15. *Paris*, 1919. 8°. **8095.** ff. **58.** (3.)

—— "Протоколы сіонскихъ мудрецовъ" доказанный подлогъ. Рачковскій сфабриковалъ "Протоколы сіонскихъ мудрецовъ," а Гитлерь придалъ имъ міровую извѣстность. pp. 188. *Paris*, 1938. 8°. **4034.** h. **18.**

—— Russian Documents in the British Museum. pp. 17. *Eyre & Spottiswoode: London*, [1926.] 8°. **011904.** h. **42.**

—— Юбилей предателей и убійцъ. 1917–1927. pp. 39. *Paris*, 1927. 8°. **8095.** c. **2.**

BURTSOV-PROTOPOPOV (VASILY THEDOROV) [For editions of the Азбука sometimes ascribed to V. Th. Burtsov-Protopopov:] *See* AZBUKA.

BURTT BROTHERS. Burtt's Railway Time Tables and Tide Table for Hull and district. *See* PERIODICAL PUBLICATIONS.—*Hull.*

BURTT, *Family of.* *See* BURTT (Mary B.) The Burtts. A Lincolnshire Quaker family, 1500–1900, *etc.* [With portraits.] 1937. 8°. **9907.** r. **28.**

BURTT (BRIAN L.)

—— British Flowers in Colour. Advisory editor: B. L. Burtt. Contributors: R. A. Blakelock [and others] . . . Illustrated with numerous photographs, and 65 plates . . . drawn by A. W. Darnell and Dorothy Fitchew. pp. 192. *Odhams Press: London*, [1952.] 8°. **07031.** i. **51.**

BURTT (EDWIN ARTHUR) The Metaphysical Foundations of Modern Physical Science, *etc.* [With a bibliography.] pp. ix. 349. *Kegan Paul & Co.: London*, 1925. 8°. [*International Library of Psychology, Philosophy and Scientific Method.*] **08460.** g. **1/30.**

—— Principles and Problems of Right Thinking, *etc.* pp. xii. 590. *Harper & Bros.: New York & London*, 1928. 8°. **08463.** h. **41.**

—— Religion in an Age of Science. pp. xiii. 153. *Williams & Norgate: London; printed in Saxony*, 1930. 8°. [*Religion and the Modern Series.*] W.P. **9889/2.**

—— Right Thinking. A study of its principles and methods. pp. xi. 764. *Harper & Bros.: New York & London*, 1946. 8°. **8471.** f. **54.**

—— Types of Religious Philosophy. pp. ix. 512. *Harper & Bros.: New York & London*, [1939.] 8°. **04374.** k. **17.**

BURTT (EDWIN ARTHUR)

—— Types of Religious Philosophy. Revised edition. pp. xi. 468. *Harper & Bros.: New York*, [1951.] 8°. **8459**. ccc. **30**.

BURTT (FRANK) Cross-Channel and Coastal Paddle Steamers. [With plates.] pp. 440. *Richard Tilling: London*, 1934. 8°. **2248**. c. **19**.

—— L. & S.W.R. Locomotives. 1872–1923. pp. 96. *Ian Allan: London*, [1949.] 8°. **W.P.14062/35.** [*ABC Locomotive Series*.]

—— L B & S C R Locomotives. An up-to-date survey from 1870. pp. 55. *Ian Allan: Staines*, 1946. 8°. [*ABC Locomotive Series*.] **W.P.14062/37.**

—— The Locomotives of the London, Brighton & South Coast Railway, 1839–1903. Reprinted from "The Locomotive Magazine," *etc.* [By F. Burtt. With plates.] pp. 245. 1903. 8°. *See* LONDON, BRIGHTON AND SOUTH COAST RAILWAY. **08767**. a. **10**.

—— SE & CR Locomotives, 1874–1923. pp. 46. *Ian Allan: London*, 1947. 8° [*ABC Locomotive Series*.] **W.P.14062/36.**

—— Steamers of the Thames and Medway. [With plates.] pp. 192. *Richard Tilling: London*, 1949. 8°. **8803**. bbb. **18**.

BURTT (FRANK) and **BECKERLEGGE** (W.)

—— Pullman and Perfection. [With illustrations.] pp. 40. *Ian Allan: London*, 1948. 8°. [*ABC Locomotive Series*.] W.P. **14062/29**.

BURTT (HAROLD ERNEST) Principles of Employment Psychology. [With a bibliography.] pp. xi. 568. *Houghton, Mifflin Co.: Boston*, [1926.] 8°. **08245**. h. **68**.

—— Psychology and Industrial Efficiency. pp. xviii. 395. *D. Appleton & Co.: New York, London*, 1929. 8°. **08246**. eee. **22**.

—— Psychology of Advertising. pp. x. 473. *Houghton, Mifflin Co.: Boston*, [1938.] 8°. **8234**. eee. **31**.

BURTT (J. H.)

—— Samuel Adjai Crowther. Mtumwa aliyepata kuwa Askofu, 1806–1891. pp. 15. *Sheldon Press: London*, 1948. 8°. **10608**. df. **8**.

BURTT (JOHN ORMISTON)

—— *See* MAIDMENT (Kenneth J.) Minor Attic Orators, *etc.* (vol. 2. With an English translation by J. O. Burtt.) 1941, *etc.* 8°. **2282.d.156.**

BURTT (JOSEPH) *Assistant Keeper of the Public Records. See* JOHN II., *Duke of Brabant.* Account of the Expenses of John of Brabant and Thomas and Henry of Lancaster, A.D. 1292–3. Edited by J. Burtt. 1853. 4°. [*Camden Miscellany.* vol. 2.] Ac. **8113/39**.

—— On Some Discoveries in connection with the Ancient Treasury at Westminster. *See* SCOTT (*Sir* George G.) Gleanings from Westminster Abbey, *etc.* 1861. 8°. **7820**. e. **29**.

—— [Another edition.] *See* SCOTT (*Sir* George G.) Gleanings from Westminster Abbey, *etc.* 1863. 8°. **2261**. e. **7**.

BURTT (JOSEPH) *F.R.G.S.* A Deal in Diamonds, and other stories, *etc.* pp. 94. *Burtt Bros.: Hull*, 1902. 8°. **012629**. k. **67**.

—— The People of Ararat, *etc.* [With plates.] pp. 184. *L. & V. Woolf: London*, 1926. 8°. **010076**. g. **7**.

—— The Voice of the Forest. [A novel.] pp. 314. *T. Fisher Unwin: London*, 1911. 8°. **012618**. bb. **23**.

BURTT (LUCY M.)

—— Our Christian Witness . . . Reprinted . . . from the Friends' Quarterly, April, 1947. pp. 7. *Friends Home Service Committee: London*, [1947.] 8°. **4152**. g. **18**.

BURTT (MARY BOWEN) The Burtts. A Lincolnshire Quaker family, 1500–1900. Compiled by M. B. Burtt, *etc.* [With plates, including portraits, and genealogical tables.] pp. viii. 200. *Burtt Bros.: Hull*, 1937. 8°. **9907**. r. **28**.

BURTT (PHILIP) China Revisited . . . A lecture delivered before the China Society. With report of the annual dinner. pp. 18. *London*, 1930. 8°. [*China Society. Lectures.*] Ac. **8823**. d/2.

—— Control on the Railways. A study in methods. [With plates and diagrams.] pp. 255. *G. Allen & Unwin: London*, 1926. 8°. **08235**. k. **47**.

—— Pitman's Transport Library. General editor: P. Burtt. *Sir I. Pitman & Sons: London*, 1926. 8°. **8232**. e. **27**.

—— The Principal Factors in Freight Train Operating. pp. 208. *G. Allen & Unwin: London*, 1923. 8°. **08235**. bb. **60**.

—— (Second edition, revised.) pp. 208. *G. Allen & Unwin: London*, 1924. 8°. **08235**. cc. **60**.

—— Railway Electrification and Traffic Problems, *etc.* pp. xvi. 197. *London*, 1929. 8°. [*Pitman's Transport Library.*] **8232**. e. **27/9**.

—— Railway Rates: principles and problems. pp. vii. 167. *London*, 1926. 8°. [*Pitman's Transport Library.*] **8232**. e. **27/4**.

BURTT (THOMAS) Ode, composed for the occasion, recited . . . at the Anniversary Dinner in aid of the funds of the Westminster Jews' Free School . . . 1859. [Signed: T. B., i.e. Thomas Burtt.] [1859.] *s. sh.* fol. *See* B., T. **1872**. a. **1**. (**49**.)

BURTT-DAVY (JOSEPH) *See* DAVY.

BURTY (PHILIPPE) *See* DELACROIX (F. V. E.) Lettres de Eugène Lacroix . . . Recueillies et publiées par M. P. Burty, *etc.* 1878. 8°. **10909**. k. **7**.

—— —— 1880. 12°. **10910**. cc. **22**.

—— *See* EUDEL (P.) L'Hôtel Drouot en 1881, *etc.* (L'Hôtel Drouot et la curiosité en 1884–1885. Avec une préface par P. Burty.) 1882, *etc.* 12°. **7858**. a. **29**.

—— *See* LAURENT-RICHARD ( ) Catalogue des tableaux anciens et modernes . . . formant la collection de M. Laurent-Richard, *etc.* [With a preface by P. Burty.] 1886. fol. **7857**. k. **17**.

—— *See* PERIODICAL PUBLICATIONS.—*Paris.* L'Eau-forte en 1874, *etc.* (1874, 75, 78. Texte par P. Burty.) 1874, *etc.* fol. Dept. of Prints & Drawings.

—— *See* PERIODICAL PUBLICATIONS.—*Paris.* L'Exposition des beaux arts, *etc.* (Salon de 1882. Avec le concours littéraire de P. Burty [and others].—Salon de 1883. [Text by P. Burty.]) 1880, *etc.* 8°. P.P. **1932**. fa.

BURTY (PHILIPPE)

—— L'Âge du romantisme. (Série d'études sur les artistes, les littérateurs et les diverses célébrités de cette période. Directeur de la partie artistique: Ph. Burty. Directeur de la partie littéraire: Maurice Tourneux.) [With reproductions and portraits.] livr. 1–5.

livr. 1, 2. Célestin Nanteuil, graveur et peintre . . . Par P. Burty. 2 pt. pp. 24.
livr. 3. Gérard de Nerval, prosateur et poète . . . Par M. Tourneux. pp. 12.
livr. 4. Camille Rogier, vignettiste. Par P. Burty. pp. 12.
livr. 5. Prosper Mérimée, comédienne espagnole et chanteur illyrien. Par M. Tourneux. pp. 12.

Paris, 1887. 4°. **11765**. i. **7**.
No more published.

—— Bernard Palissy. [With reproductions.] pp. 56. *Paris*, 1886. 8°. [*Artistes célèbres.*] **2264**. d. **4**.

—— Catalogue de tableaux et dessins de l'école française, principalement du XVIIIe siècle, tirés de collections d'amateurs et exposés au profit de la Caisse de secours des artistes peintres, sculpteurs, architectes et dessinateurs. (Deuxième exposition.) Rédigé par M. P. Burty. Seconde édition. pp. 63. *Paris*, 1860. 8°. **7854**. e. **27**. (**7**.)

—— Catalogue de tableaux et dessins de l'école française, principalement du XVIIIe siècle . . . Deuxième supplément. pp. 66–93. *Paris*, 1860. 8°. **7855**. c. **40**. (**8**.)

—— [Charles Méryon et son œuvre.] Charles Méryon, Sailor, Engraver, and Etcher. A memoir and complete descriptive catalogue of his works. Translated . . . by Marcus B. Huish. pp. vii. 106. *Fine Art Society: London*, 1879. 8°. **7857**. g. **41**.

—— Chefs-d'œuvre des arts industriels . . . Céramique, verrerie et vitraux, émaux, métaux, orfévrerie et bijouterie, tapisserie . . . Deux cents gravures sur bois. pp. 598. *Paris*, [1866.] 8°. **7943**. g. **9**.

—— [Another copy.] **7953**. l. **23**.

—— Chefs-d'Œuvre of the Industrial Arts . . . Edited by W. Chaffers. [With plates.] pp. viii. 391. *Chapman & Hall: London*, 1869. 8°. **7953**. k. **9**.

—— Constant Troyon. [An article reprinted from "La Presse."] *See* SOULLIÉ (L.) Les Grands peintres aux ventes publiques. vol. 1. 1900. 4°. **7854**. k. **29**.

—— Eaux-fortes de Jules de Goncourt. Notice et catalogue de P. Burty. [With reproductions and portraits.] pp. xviii. 19. pl. 20. *Paris*, 1876. fol. **1758**. b. **4**.

—— Les Émaux cloisonnés, anciens et modernes. [With plates.] pp. 70. *Paris*, [1868.] 12°. **7942**. bbb. **16**.

—— Maîtres et petits maîtres. pp. 387. *Paris*, 1877. 8°. **7858**. a. **5**.

—— Pas de lendemain. [A tale.] pp. 34. *Paris*, 1869. 8°. **12350**. bb. **23**.

—— Paul Huet. Notice biographique et critique, suivie du catalogue de ses œuvres, *etc.* [With a plate.] pp. 135. *Paris*, [1870.] 8°. **10661**. g. **9**.

—— La Vie de Meissonier. *See* LARROUMET (G.) Meissonier, *etc.* [1895.] 4°. K.T.C. **33**. b. **3**.

BURTY (PHILIPPE)

—— [La Vie de Meissonier.] Jean Louis Ernest Meissonier. [Translated by Clara Bell. With reproductions and a portrait.] *Chapman & Hall: London*, 1884. fol. [*Modern Artists.*] **L.R.407.h.4.**

—— Vingt-cinq dessins de Eugène Fromentin, reproduits à l'eau-forte par E. L. Montefiore. Texte biographique et critique par P. Burty, avec fac-simile d'après des croquis du maître. pp. 23. *Paris, Londres*, 1877. fol. **1761**. d. **3**.

—— Collection Ph. Burty. Catalogue de peintures & estampes japonaises, de miniatures indopersanes et de livres relatifs à l'Orient et au Japon, *etc.* pp. xv. 223. *Paris*, 1891. 8°. **7855**. i. **20**.

BURUAGA (FRANCESCO SOLANO ASTA) *See* SOLANO ASTA-BURUAGA Y CIENFUEGOS.

BURUALDE (MARTIN AGUIRRE) *See* AGUIRRE BURUALDE.

BURUIKH (E. B.)

—— Памятные места Московской области. Краткий путеводитель. Составители: Е. Б. Бурых [and others. With illustrations and maps]. pp. 354. 1954. 8°. *See* MOSCOW.—*Московский Областной Краеведческий Музей.* **10292**. n. **47**.

BURUISHKIN (P. A.)

—— Москва купеческая. pp. 349. *Нью-Йорк*, 1954. 8°. **10293**. aaa. **35**.

BURUJI. *See* ENGLAND.—*Army.—East Africa Force.—O.C.T.U.*

BURUNDA (JOSEPH ERAZU DE) *See* ERAZU DE BURUNDA.

BURUSHASKI STUDIES.

—— A Triplet of Burushaski Studies. By Georg Morgenstierne, Hans Vogt and Carl Hj. Borgstrøm. *In:* Norsk tidsskrift for sprogvidenskap. bd. 13. pp. 59–147. 1945. 8°. P.P. **5044**. dd.

BURVASSER (F. G.)

—— Технічні способи визначення альфа-целюлози. (Alpha-cellulose.) [With summaries in Russian and English.] pp. 74. *Київ*, 1938. 8°. Ac. **1101**. hc/**6**.
The titlepage headed: Академія наук УРСР. Інститут хемічної технології.

BURVENICH (CONSTANT) English and French Conversations. Conversations en langue française et en langue anglaise. pp. 142. *Simpkin, Marshall & Co.: Londres*, 1873 [1872]. 8°. **12950**. b. **10**.

—— The Metric System of Weights and Measures. pp. 38. *G. Corby: Northampton*, 1864. 12°. **8534**. a. **49**.

—— Second edition, considerably improved and enlarged. pp. 96. *Simpkin, Marshall & Co.: London*, 1871. 8°. **8506**. bbb. **42**. (**7**.)

—— Answers to all the Questions ginen [*sic*] in C. Burvenich's Metric System of Weights and Measures. pp. 22. *Simpkin, Marshall & Co.: London*, 1871. 12°. **8503**. b. **55**. (**3**.)

BURVENICH (FREDERIK) *See* PERIODICAL PUBLICATIONS.—*Brussels.* Jaarboek voor hofbouwkunde, uitgegeven door . . . F. Burvenich [and others], *etc.* 1864, *etc.* 8°. P.P. **2335**. aa.

—— *See* PERIODICAL PUBLICATIONS.—*Ghent.* Annuaire de l'horticulture belge, rédigé par F. Burvenich [and others], *etc.* [1874, *etc.*] 8°. P.P. **2127**. e.

BURVENICH (FREDERIK)

—— See PERIODICAL PUBLICATIONS.—*Ghent*. Revue de l'horticulture belge et étrangère, rédigée & publiée par F. Burvenich [and others], *etc.* 1875, *etc.* 8°. **P.P. 2224.** cb.

—— Apriculture moderne. Flore mellifère arbustive. pp. 74. *Liége*, [1897.] 8°. **7073.** cc. **7.** (2.)

—— Aspersien overal en voor idereen. Beredeneerd cultuurstelsel, *etc.* pp. 68. *Gent*, 1870. 12°. **8023.** aa. **19.**

—— De Boomgaard, of de Fruitboomen in betrekking met den landbouw, *etc.* pp. 120. *Gendbrugge*, 1866. 8°. **1145.** d. **8.**

—— (Tweede uitgave.) pp. 146. *Gent*, 1873 [1872]. 8°. **7032.** b. **15.**

—— [De Boomgaard.] La Grande culture des arbres fruitiers, *etc.* [Translated by the author.] pp. viii. 150. *Gand*, 1876. 8°. **7078.** b. **5.**

—— Praktische aanwijzingen over den snoei der fruitboomen . . . Derde oplage, *etc.* pp. 235. pl. II. *Gendbrugge*, 1867. 8°. **1145.** d. **50.**

BURVILL (G. H.)

—— See BALDWIN (J. G.) *B.Agr.Sc.* A Soil Survey of Part of the Kerang Irrigation District, Victoria. By J. G. Baldwin . . . G. H. Burvill, *etc.* 1939. 8°. [*Council for Scientific and Industrial Research. Bulletin.* no. 125.] **C.S.G.548.(2.)**

—— See HOSKING (J. S.) and BURVILL (G. H.) A Soil Survey of Part of the Denmark Estate, *etc.* 1938. 8°. [*Commonwealth of Australia. Council for Scientific and Industrial Research. Bulletin.* no. 115.] **C.S.G.548.(2.)**

BURWASH (DOROTHY) See BURWASH (Hazel D.)

BURWASH (EDWARD MOORE JACKSON)

—— The Deposition and Alteration of Varved Clays . . . Reprinted from Transactions of the Royal Canadian Institute, *etc.* [1938.] 8°. **07109.** b. **28.**

BURWASH (HAZEL DOROTHY)

—— English Merchant Shipping, 1460–1540. pp. xii. 259. pl. v. *University of Toronto Press: [Toronto,]* 1947. 8°. **8808.** l. **15.**

—— [Another copy.] English Merchant Shipping, *etc.* [*Toronto*,] 1947. 8°. **08805.** b. **35.**

BURWASH (NATHANAEL) See LANCELEY (John E.) The Devil of Names, and other lectures and sermons . . . Rev. J. E. Lanceley . . . With . . . a biographical sketch by the Rev. N. Burwash. 1900. 8°. **4486.** de. **7.**

—— Egerton Ryerson, *etc.* [Chapters 1, 11 by A. H. Reynar.] pp. 303. *G. N. Morang & Co.: Toronto*, 1905. 8°. [*Makers of Canada.*] **010880.** ee. **21/3.**

—— [Another edition. Revised by C. B. Sissons. With plates, including portraits.] pp. viii. 345. *Oxford University Press: London & Toronto; printed in Canada*, 1926. 8°. [*Makers of Canada Series. Anniversary edition.* vol. 6.] **010880.** h. **12/6.**

—— Manual of Christian Theology on the Inductive Method. 2 vol. *H. Marshall & Son: London*, 1900. 8°. **03558.** ee. **2.**

BURWAY (MUKUND WAMANRAO) See MUKUNDA VĀMANARĀU BARVE.

BURWAY (RAMKRISHNA GANESH) See RĀMAKṚISHṆA GAṆEŚA BARVE.

BURWELL. The Poll for the Nomination of Two Clerks to the Vicarage of Burwell, *etc.* pp. 17. *Printed for private circulation: Cambridge*, 1854. 12°. **8364.** a. **25.** (4.)

BURWELL (A.) Dramshops, Industry, and Taxes. An address to the people of Mississippi. pp. 24. *National Temperance Society & Publication House: New York*, 1875. 12°. **8436.** aaa. **9.** (3.)

BURWELL (ADAM HOOD) Doctrine of the Holy Spirit; in its application to the wants and interests of corporate man under the providence and moral government of God, stated and defended . . . and in these days revived in Britain by the Rev. Edward Irving, *etc.* pp. 124. *Printed for the Author: Toronto*, 1835. 8°. **764.** g. **15.** (9.)

—— On the Philosophy of Human Perfection and Happiness. pp. 29. *Lovell & Gibson: Montreal*, 1849. 12°. **764.** i. **13.** (12.)

—— Summer Evening Contemplations. [Verses.] pp. 12. *Lovell & Gibson: Montreal*, 1849. 12°. **764.** i. **13.** (13.)

BURWELL (CORA G.) See MERRILL (Paul W.) Intensities and Displacements of Interstellar Lines. [By] P. W. Merrill . . . C. G. Burwell. [1937.] 8°. [*Contributions from the Mount Wilson Observatory.* no. 576.] Ac. **1867.**

BURWELL (LETITIA M.) A Girl's Life in Virginia before the War, *etc.* [With plates.] pp. 209. *F. A. Stokes Co.: New York*, [1895.] 8°. **10881.** de. **18.**

BURWELL (THOMAS) See GROENEVELT (John) Reasons . . . why Dr. Thomas Burwell . . . should not be excused from the penalty of the Act 25 Car. II., *etc.* [1700.] *s. sh.* fol. **816.** m. **12.** (28.)

—— Disputatio medica inauguralis, de anatomia sanguinis ad explicationem plethoræ & cacochimiæ, *etc.* *G. de Haez: Lugduni Batavorum*, 1652. 4°. **1185.** g. **4.** (3.)

BURWELL (WILLIAM M.) See PERIODICAL PUBLICATIONS. —*Richmond, Va.* The Age. W. M. Burwell & E. Lagarde, editors. 1864. 8°. **P.P. 6380.** b.

—— Address delivered before the Society of Alumni of the University of Virginia at their Annual Meeting, *etc.* (Proceedings of the Society of Alumni.) pp. 27. 7. 1847. 8°. See CHARLOTTESVILLE.—*University of Virginia.—Society of Alumni.* **8365.** e. **32.** (2.)

BURWELL-BEDFORD (W. N.) *pseud.* [i.e. WILLIAM NEVILLE BORTON.] See BEDFORD.

BURWELLUS (THOMAS) See BURWELL.

BURWOOD (THOMAS WESLEY) "After Forty Years—a retrospect:" being the presidential address delivered at the Annual Homoeopathic Congress . . . 1909. pp. 28. *J. Bale & Co.: London*, [1909.] 8°. **7680.** e. **45.**

BURY, *Lancashire.*

—— The "Borough" Guide to Bury, Lancashire. (Issued under the auspices of the Town Council.) pp. 40. *E. J. Burrow: Cheltenham*, [1911.] 8°. **10354.** a. **163.**

—— Bury. Pictures of Bury and neighbourhood, *etc.* *Bury Times Printing & Publishing Co.: Bury*, 1903. 8°. **010360.** i. **3.**

BURY, *Lancashire.*

—— The County Borough of Bury, Lancs, by A. H. Fewtrell . . . Official handbook, *etc.* (Second [*etc.*] edition.) [With a plan.] *E. J. Burrow & Co.: Cheltenham & London,* [1931– .] 8°. **10360** s. **10.**

—— The Registers of the Parish Church of Bury . . . Christenings, Burials, & Weddings. 1590 to 1616 (1617–1646, 1647 to 1698). Transcribed and edited by the Rev. W. J. Löwenberg . . . and Henry Brierley. (Episcopal Transcripts.—Christenings, Burials and Weddings 1647 to 1698 transcribed and edited by Archibald Sparke. The index by Fanny Wrigley.) 3 pt. 1898–1905. 8°. *See* LANCASTER, *County of.—Lancashire Parish Register Society.* Ac. **8088.**

—— *Bury District Co-operative Society.* Bury Co-operative Quarterly (Half-Yearly) Review and Balance Sheet no. 82, *etc.* July 1912, *etc.* *Bury,* 1912– . 4° & 8°. P.P. **1423.** lm.

Bury Grammar School.

—— The Clavian. The magazine of Bury Grammar School. vol. 5. no. 11, *etc.* July 1948, *etc.* [*Bury,*] 1948– . 8°. P.P. **6147.** aq.

—— *Bury Ratepayers' and Residents' Association.* The Watch-Dog. The journal of the Bury Ratepayers' and Residents' Association. *Bury,* 1938– . 4°. P.P. **3611.** acw.

Chesham Unitarian Congregation.

—— Chesham Unitarian Congregation and Sunday School . . . A Brief Historical Sketch, *etc.* pp. 19. *Roberts & Spencer: Bury,* 1902. 8°. **4716.** a. **60.**

County Borough Council.

—— Centenary of the Death of Sir Robert Peel. "The Life and Work of Sir Robert Peel." A spoken address by G. Kitson Clark . . . in the New Technical College, Bury . . . Presented to the Council, *etc.* pp. 14. *Bury,* [1951.] 8°. **10859.** bb. **34.**

Public Library, Art Gallery and Museum.

—— Sixth (—28th) Annual Report, 1906-7(—1928-1929) (Statistical Report for the year ended October 8th, 1930). 24 pt. *Bury,* 1907–31. 8°. A.R. **989.**

—— Classified Catalogue . . . of Books on Physical Science, including Music, in the Lending Library. pp. 60. [*Bury,*] 1912. 8°. **11926.** aaa. **27.**

BURY, *Lancashire,* WILLIAM COUTTS, *Viscount.* *See* KEPPEL (W. C.) *Earl of Albemarle.*

BURY, *Suffolk.* *See* BURY SAINT EDMUNDS.

BURY AND ROSSENDALE HISTORICAL REVIEW. *See* PERIODICAL PUBLICATIONS.—*Bury.* The Bury Historical Review.

BURY AND WEST SUFFOLK ARCHAEOLOGICAL INSTITUTE. *See* BURY SAINT EDMUNDS.—*Suffolk Institute of Archaeology and Natural History.*

BURY COMMERCIAL ALMANAC. *See* EPHEMERIDES.

BURY CO-OPERATIVE QUARTERLY REVIEW AND BALANCE SHEET. *See* BURY, *Lancashire.* —*Bury District Co-operative Society.*

BURY DISTRICT CO-OPERATIVE SOCIETY. *See* BURY, *Lancashire.*

BURY GRAMMAR SCHOOL. *See* BURY, *Lancashire.*

BURY HISTORICAL REVIEW. *See* PERIODICAL PUBLICATIONS.—*Bury.*

BURY MAGAZINE. *See* PERIODICAL PUBLICATIONS.—*Bury.*

BURY OBSERVER. *See* PERIODICAL PUBLICATIONS.—*Bury.*

BURY PHILOSOPHIC ALBUM. *See* PERIODICAL PUBLICATIONS.—*Bury Saint Edmunds.*

BURY PRESBYTERIAN CLASSIS. *See* ENGLAND.—*Presbyterians.—Second Classis of the County of Lancaster.*

BURY RATEPAYERS' AND RESIDENTS' ASSOCIATION. *See* BURY, *Lancashire.*

BURY SAINT EDMUNDS.

OFFICIAL DOCUMENTS.

—— The Account of Charitable Donations in the Borough of Bury St. Edmund's, delivered in according to the 27th George III. *J. Rackham: Bury,* [1788.] *s. sh.* fol. **5805.** d. **6.** (**32.**)

—— Bury St. Edmunds. St. James Parish Registers. Baptisms, 1558–1800. (Masriages, 1562–1800. With preface.—Burials 1562–1800.) 3 vol. *Bury St. Edmund's,* 1915, 16. 4°. [*Suffolk Green Books.* no. 17.] **9914.** p. **17.**

BURY SAINT EDMUNDS.

MUNICIPAL INSTITUTIONS.

CORPORATION.

—— The Annual Report on the Sanitary Condition of the Borough of Bury St. Edmunds, for the year 1892 (1895, 1897, 1903–1905, 1907–1909), *etc.* 9 pt. *Bury St. Edmund's,* [1893–1910.] 8°. A.R. **282.**

—— The Borough of Bury St. Edmunds. Official guide, 1951, 1952, *etc.* [With illustrations and a street plan.] pp. 80. *New Centurion Publishing & Publicity Co.: Derby, Cheltenham,* [1951.] 8°. **10362.** aa. **25.**

—— The Borough of Bury St. Edmunds. Official guide, 1953, 1954, by H. J. M. Maltby, *etc.* [With illustrations and a street plan.] pp. 96. *New Centurion Publishing & Publicity Co.: Derby & Cheltenham,* [1953.] 8°. **10361.** bb. **49.**

—— [Another copy.] The Borough of Bury St. Edmunds. Official guide, 1953, 1954, *etc.* *Derby & Cheltenham,* [1953.] 8°. **10362.** aa. **23.**

—— Borough of Bury St. Edmund's . . . Year Book of general information for the use of the Town Council, 1891-92 (1896-97). 2 pt. *Bury Post Co.: Bury St. Edmund's,* [1891, 96.] 12°. P.P. **2508.** ar.

—— The Manuscripts of the Corporation of Bury St. Edmunds. *See* LINCOLN. The Manuscripts of Lincoln, Bury St. Edmund's, and Great Grimsby Corporations, *etc.* 1895. 8°. [*Historical Manuscripts Commission.* 14th Report. Appendix. pt. 8.] **Bar.T.1.(37.)**

—— The Official Guide to Bury St. Edmunds, *etc.* pp. 56. *E. J. Burrow & Co.: Cheltenham & London,* [1921.] 8°. **10360.** s. **6.**

—— [Another edition.] pp. 60. *E. J. Burrow & Co.: Cheltenham & London,* [1924.] 8°. **10360.** s. **7.**

BURY SAINT EDMUNDS. [MUNICIPAL INSTITUTIONS.]

—— The Official Guide to the Borough of Bury St. Edmunds . . . Edited by R.A.N. Dixon, *etc.* [With illustrations and a map.] pp. 88. *East Anglian Magazine: Ipswich,* [1947.] 8°. **10359**. aa. **52**.

—— Report of the Finance Committee of the Town Council of Bury St. Edmund's, upon the charity in that borough, called the Guildhall Feoffment, *etc.* pp. iv. 124. *Bury St. Edmund's,* 1839. 8°. **8285**. bbb. **42**.

CHARITY SCHOOLS.

—— The State of the Accounts of the Charity Schools in Bury St. Edmund's, for the year 1788. *P. Gedge: Bury,* 1788. *s. sh.* fol. **5805**. d. **6**. **(31.)**

GUILDHALL FEOFFMENT.

—— Guild-Hall Feoffment Estates, as contained in the Decree of the twenty-second of July, 1771. [Indenture and schedule.] pp. 24. 5. MS. NOTES. [*Bury St. Edmunds,*] 1772. 4°. **1303**. l. **13**.
One of an edition of thirty-seven copies.

MISCELLANEOUS INSTITUTIONS AND SOCIETIES.

ABBEY OF SAINT EDMUND.

—— Feudal Documents from the Abbey of Bury St. Edmunds. Edited by D. C. Douglas. [With facsimiles.] pp. clxxi. 247. *Oxford University Press: London,* 1932. 8°. [*Records of the Social and Economic History of England and Wales.* vol. 8.] Ac. **1186/5**.

—— The Kalendar of Abbot Samson of Bury St. Edmunds and related documents. Edited . . . by R. H. C. Davis. 1954. 4°. [*Camden Third Series.* vol. 84.] *See* LONDON.—III. *Historical Society of Great Britain.* Ac. **8118/7**.

—— Memorials of St. Edmund's Abbey. Edited by Thomas Arnold. 3 vol. *London,* 1890–96. 8°. [*Rerum Britannicarum Medii Aevi Scriptores.*] **2073**. **(96.)**

—— [Another copy.] B.S. **33/21**. **(96.)**

—— The Pinchbeck Register (of the Abbey of S. Edmund, compiled by Walter . . . of Pinchbeck), etc. Edited by Lord Francis Hervey. 2 vol. *Farncombe's: Brighton,* 1925. 8°. **4782**. de. **16**.

BURY AND WEST SUFFOLK ARCHAEOLOGICAL INSTITUTE.

—— *See* infra: SUFFOLK INSTITUTE OF ARCHAEOLOGY AND NATURAL HISTORY.

BURY ST. EDMUNDS CONGREGATIONAL CHURCH.

—— Bury St. Edmunds Congregational Church, Whiting Street. 1646–1946. Tercentenary Brochure and Celebration Programme, March to August 1946. pp. 12. *Bury St. Edmunds,* [1946.] 8°. **4708**. c. **7**.

BURY SAINT EDMUND'S GRAND MUSICAL FESTIVAL.

—— [Programmes, librettos, etc., for the Bury Saint Edmunds Grand Musical Festival of 1828. With MS. notes by Sir G. T. Smart.] *Bury St. Edmond's,* [1828.] 4°. C. **61**. g. **5**.

—— Bury St. Edmund's Grand Musical Festival, *etc.* [The programmes for the Concerts of Tuesday evening, 7 October, 1828—Friday morning, 10th October, 1828.] 6 pt. *Bury St. Edmund's,* 1828. 4°. R.M. **26**. f. **9**.

BURY SAINT EDMUNDS. [MISCELLANEOUS INSTITUTIONS AND SOCIETIES.]

COMMITTEE APPOINTED TO PROMOTE THE MAKING A NAVIGABLE CANAL FROM BURY ST. EDMUND'S TO MISTLEY.

—— Proposals, offered to the consideration of the Public; by the Committee appointed to Promote the Making a Navigable Canal from Bury St. Edmund's to Mistley, for raising the money necessary for the said work. pp. 3. *J. Rackham: Bury,* [1791.] fol. **5805**. d. **6**. **(29.)**

COMMITTEE FOR THE RESTORATION OF THE NORMAN TOWER.

—— Restoration of the Norman Tower, Bury St. Edmunds. [Proceedings of the Committee, letter of appeal and list of subscribers.] [*Bury St. Edmunds,* 1845.] 8°. **7816**. a. **16**.

—— Restoration of the Norman Tower. [Report of the Committee upon the completion of the work of restoration.] [*Bury St. Edmunds,* 1849.] 4°. **10351**. g. **18**. **(20.)**

KING EDWARD VI.'S SCHOOL.

—— Biographical List of Boys educated at King Edward VI. Free Grammar School, Bury St. Edmunds. From 1550 to 1900. [The compiler's preface signed: S. H. A. H., i.e. S. H. A. Hervey.] pp. xx. 483. *Bury St. Edmunds,* 1908. 4°. [*Suffolk Green Books.* no. 13.] **9914**. p. **13**.

—— The Burian. April 1895[—Dec. 1897]. 6 no. *Bury St. Edmund's,* 1895[–97]. 8°. P.P. **6151**. cd.

—— Bury St. Edmund's Grammar School List, 1900–1925. ff. 35. pp. 36–43. *Bury St. Edmund's,* 1930. 4°. **08364**. ee. **84**.
Printed on one side of the leaf only.

—— Prize Exercises, 1849. pp. 24. *Cambridge,* [1849.] 8°. **8364**. e. **19**.

SAINT JOHN'S CHURCH.

—— *See* JOHN, *Saint, Church of, at Bury Saint Edmunds.*

SAINT MARY'S CHURCH.

—— A Description of St. Mary's Church, Bury St. Edmunds. *See* SANDFORD (John H.)

—— St Mary's Parish Church, Bury St. Edmunds. History of this Ancient Church. *Bury Post Co.: Bury,* [1920?] 8°. **10352**. dd. **31**.

SUFFOLK INSTITUTE OF ARCHAEOLOGY AND NATURAL HISTORY.

Bury and West Suffolk Archæological Institute, 1848–1853.
Suffolk Institute of Archæology, Statistics, and Natural History, 1854–1863.
Suffolk Institute of Archaeology and Natural History, 1864–

—— Proceedings, *etc.* *Bury St. Edmunds,* 1849– . 8°. Ac. **5710**.

—— Index of articles, contributions, papers published in the Proceedings . . . vols. I. to IX. inclusive. pp. 25. [*Ipswich,* 1900.] 8°. **BB.O.e.9.**

—— A Calendar of the Feet of Fines for Suffolk. By Walter Rye. pp. xvi. 393. *Ipswich,* 1900. 8°. Ac. **5710/3**.

—— Catalogue of Books in the Library at the Athenæum, Bury St. Edmund's. pp. 30. [*Bury St. Edmunds,*] 1933. 8°. Ac. **5710/5**.

BURY SAINT EDMUNDS. [Miscellaneous Institutions and Societies.]

—— The Corbould Genealogy. By George C. B. Poulter. [With portraits and maps.] pp. 168. *Ipswich*, 1935. 4°. **09915. l. 16.**

—— Hand Book of Ely Cathedral. pp. 12. *Bury St. Edmund's*, [1851.] 12°. **4715. b. 26.**

—— [Another edition.] Archæological Guide to Ely Cathedral, *etc.* pp. 12. **L.P.** *Bury St. Edmund's*, [1851.] 12°. **4715. e. 12.**

—— Hawsted and Hardwick. Papers read before the meeting of the Suffolk Institute of Archæology and Natural History, on the occasion of their visit to Hawsted and Hardwick, on Thursday, June 17, 1853. pp. 39. *Bury St. Edmund's*, 1854. 8°. **10351. f. 35.**

—— The Household Book of Dame Alice de Bryene, of Acton Hall, Suffolk, Sept. 1412—Sept. 1413. With appendices. Translated by Miss M. K. Dale . . . Edited by Vincent B. Redstone. [With plates.] pp. viii. 145. *Ipswich*, 1931. 8°. **10862. f. 48.**

—— The Ship-Money Returns for the County of Suffolk, 1639–40. Harl. MSS. 7,540–7,542. Transcribed and edited by Vincent B. Redstone. pp. xvi. 225. *Ipswich*, 1904. 8°. Ac. **5710/4.**

West Suffolk Agricultural Society.

—— Copy of a Correspondence between Sir James Affleck, Baronet, and the Board of Trade, *etc.* pp. 43. *W. B. Frost: Bury St. Edmund's*, 1830. 8°. **10348. d. 23. (4.)**

West Suffolk Friendly Society.

—— Rules of the West Suffolk Friendly Society. No. 4047, *etc.* pp. 6. *Bury St. Edmunds*, [1862.] 8°. **8277. c. 9.**

APPENDIX.

—— An Account of the Proceedings at the Election of Members for the Borough of Bury St. Edmund's, Dec. 13 and 14, 1832, *etc.* pp. 163. *W. B. Frost: Bury St. Edmund's*, 1833. 8°. **8135. d. 12.**

—— The Belles of Bury, a poem. pp. 25. *Printed for the Author: Bury*, 1779. 4°. **11632. g. 9.**

—— Bury, and its Environs, a poem, written in the year MDCCXLVI. [By Dr. John Winter.] pp. 6 [7]. *W. Owen: London*, 1747. fol. **1890. b. 2. (6.)**

—— Bury St. Edmund's and District illustrated. ("Bury & Norwich Post" illustrated handbook to Bury St. Edmunds & district.) pp. 46. *Bury & Norwich Post & Suffolk Standard Newspaper Co.: Bury St. Edmund's*, [1906.] 4°. **10368. f. 36.**

—— [Another edition.] pp. 49. *Bury & Norwich Post & Suffolk Standard Newspaper Co.: Bury St. Edmund's*, [1907.] 4°. **10369. t. 5.**

—— A Concise Description of Bury Saint Edmund's, and its environs, within the distance of ten miles, illustrated by engravings and wood-cuts, of upwards of forty churches. pp. iv. 367. *Longman & Co.: London*, 1827. 8°. **578. e. 14.**

—— A Description of Bury St. Edmund's, and its Environs, within the distance of ten miles, with illustrations of the churches, *etc.* pt. 1. pp. 124. *John Deck: Ipswich*, 1825. 4°. **10368. h. 35.**

BURY SAINT EDMUNDS. [Appendix.]

—— A Description of the Ancient and Present State of the Town and Abbey, of Bury St. Edmund's, in the County of Suffolk, *etc.* pp. 4. 68. *W. Green: Bury*, 1768. 8°. **10360. ccc. 28.**

—— The second edition, with corrections, *etc.* pp. 4. 82. *W. Green: Bury*, 1771. 8°. T. **881. (5.)**

—— The third edition, with considerable additions. pp. 112. *William Green: Bury St. Edmunds*, 1782. 8°. **579. c. 41. (3.)**

—— [Another copy.] **291. e. 1.**
Interleaved. Imperfect; wanting pp. 109–112.

—— The Fair Candidate. By an English gentleman . . . To . . . the Corporation of St. Edmund's Bury in Suffolk. pp. 4. [*Bury St. Edmunds*, 1730.] fol. **5805. d. 6. (28.)**

—— A Guide to the Main Objects of Interest in Bury St. Edmund's. pp. 15. *Paul & Mathew: Bury St. Edmund's*, [1930?] 16°. **010368. q. 10.**

—— A Guide to the Town, Abbey, and Antiquities, of Bury St. Edmund's; with brief notices of the villages, & country seats, within a circuit of eight miles. pp. v. 156. *J. Deck: Ipswich*, 1821. 12°. **578. e. 13.**

—— Second edition. pp. vi. 132. *J. Deck: Bury St. Edmund's*, 1836. 12°. **579. b. 39.**

—— New edition. [With a map.] pp. 72. *Jackson & Frost: Bury St. Edmund's*, [1867.] 8°. **10360. aaa. 40. (6.)**

—— An Historical and Architectural Notice of the Gate-Tower of the ancient Cemetery of St. Edmund, known as the Norman Tower, St. Edmund's Bury. [By S. Timms.] pp. 22. *Jackson & Frost: St. Edmund's Bury*, 1846. 8°. **7816. a. 17.**

—— *Begin.* [p. 3.] I have perused a pamphlet entitled, Some reasons why the Practice of Inoculation ought to be introduced into the town of Bury at present, *etc.* [A reply to that pamphlet; by Dr. Warren?] pp. 3–32. [*Bury St. Edmund's*, 1733.] 4°. **1166. h. 9. (6.)**
Imperfect; wanting the titlepage.

—— The Poll for Members of Parliament for the Borough of Bury St. Edmund's taken . . . the 13th. and 14th. days of December, 1832, *etc.* *W. B. Frost: Bury*, [1832.] *s. sh.* fol. **10351. i. 24. (75.)**

—— Proceedings at the Election of two Burgesses for the Borough of Bury St. Edmund's, and the poll, taken . . . January 6, 8, & 9, 1835. Candidates, the Right Hon. Earl Jermyn, the Right Hon. Lord C. Fitzroy, Charles Fox Bunbury Esq. pp. 38. *Gedge & Barker: Bury*, [1835.] 16°. **809. c. 34.**

—— Restoration of the Norman Tower, Bury St. Edmunds. [Proposals and a list of subscriptions.] [*Bury St. Edmunds*, 1843.] 8°. **10358. g. 45. (4.)**

—— A True Relation of the Araignment of eighteene Witches, that were tried, convicted, and condemned at a Sessions holden at St. Edmunds-bury, in Suffolke . . . and so were executed the 27. day of August 1645, *etc.* pp. 8. *Printed by I. H.: London*, 1645. 4°. E. **301. (3.)**

—— A Tryal of Witches, at the assizes held at Bury St. Edmonds for the County of Suffolk; on the tenth day of March, 1664 . . . Taken by a person then attending the court. pp. 59. *For William Shrewsbery: London*, 1682. 8°. **8630. d. 21.**

—— [Another copy.] **8632. cc. 25. (1.)**

BURY SAINT EDMUNDS. [APPENDIX.]

—— [Another edition.] pp. 77–104. *D. Brown, etc: London,* 1716. 8°. G. **2395.**

—— [Another edition.] pp. 42. *P. Deck: Bury,* 1771. 12°. **8630.** b. **18.**

—— A Visit to Bury St. Edmund's; or, an Old-fashioned week in the nineteenth century. pp. ii. 145. *T. Stevenson: Cambridge,* 1845. 12°. **796.** a. **34.**

—— The Woefull and Lamentable wast and spoile done by a suddaine fire in S. Edmonds-bury in Suffolke, on Munday the tenth of Aprill. 1608. 𝕭.𝕷. *For Henrie Gosson: London,* 1608. 4°. **8716.** bb. **37.**

—— [Another copy.] Eg. MS. **2373.** f. **329.**

—— [Another edition.] [With a reproduction of the original titlepage.] pp. 28. *F. Pawsey: Ipswich,* 1845. 4°. **010358.** l. **12.** (**1.**)

One of an edition of twelve copies.

BURY SAINT EDMUNDS AND IPSWICH, *Diocese of.* The Diocesan Magazine for the County of Suffolk. Diocese of S. Edmundsbury and Ipswich. *Ipswich,* 1914– . 8°. P.P. **343.** cbb.

Imperfect; wanting vol. 1. *no.* 5.

—— St. Edmundsbury and Ipswich Diocesan Calendar and Clergy List for 1915 [*etc.*]. *Bury St. Edmund's,* [1914– .] 8°. P.P. **2506.** efa.

—— [A survey of the ecclesiastical archives of the Diocese of St. Edmundsbury and Ipswich.] ff. 14. [*London,* 1952.] fol. [*Survey of Ecclesiastical Archives.*] C. **120.** h. **8.** (**5.**)

BURY SAINT EDMUNDS AND IPSWICH, ALBERT AUGUSTUS, *Bishop of.* [1921–23.] *See* DAVID.

BURY SAINT EDMUNDS ODDFELLOWS' CALENDAR. *See* ODD FELLOWS, *Independent Order of.*

BURY TIMES STREET GUIDE. "Bury Times" Street Guide and Business Directory for Bury. *See* DIRECTORIES.—*Bury.*

BURY TRANSIT GUIDE. Bury Transit Guide. L. & Y. Ry. [Compiled by Lee Thorpe.] pp. 19. *Fletcher & Speight: Bury,* [1912.] 16°. **08235.** l. **20.**

BURY (   ) *Architecte.* Modèles de serrurerie, choisis parmi ce que Paris offre de plus remarquable sous le rapport de la forme, de la décoration et de la sûreté . . . suivis d'un abrégé de l'art du serrurier (par Hoyau) . . . Le tout accompagné d'exemples gravés géométriquement . . . sur les dessins et d'après les descriptions de MM. Bury . . . et Hoyau. 2 pt. *Paris,* 1826. fol. **1811.** a. **24.**

BURY (   ) *Lieutenant Colonel.* A Briefe Relation of the Siege at Newark, as it was delivered to the Councel of State . . . by Lieutenant Col. Bury . . . Together with articles of agreement betwixt Prince Rupert and Sir John Meldrum, *etc.* pp. 8. *For Peter Cole: London,* 1644. 4°. E. **39.** (**8.**)

BURY (ADRIAN)

—— *See* ROWLANDSON (Thomas) *Artist.* Rowlandson Drawings. Edited . . . by A. Bury. 1949. 4°. **7869.** g. **7.**

BURY (ADRIAN)

—— The Art of Reginald G. Eves, *etc.* pp. 55. pl. 88. *F. Lewis: Leigh-on-Sea,* 1940. 4°. **7866.** r. **36.**

—— Battle with the Dark, and other poems. pp. 29. *Grant Richards: London,* 1942. 16°. **11656.** h. **48.**

—— The Black Cat. An elegy, *etc.* [With plates.] pp. 19. *Printed for the Author: London,* 1947. 8°. **11658.** c. **14.**

—— Dusk to Dawn. Letters by a Warden [i.e. A. Bury]. [On experiences during air-raids in London.] pp. xi. 216. 1941. 8°. *See* WARDEN. **9101.** a. **1.**

—— An Elizabethan Coronal. Twenty-six sonnets. pp. 30. *Falcon Press: London,* 1953. 8°. **11658.** aaa. **250.**

—— Eros Uncrowned. [Poems.] pp. 47. *London,* 1949. 8°. **11659.** aaa. **93.**

—— Happy Flame. A book of sonnets. pp. 59. *Grant Richards: London,* 1930. 8°. **011648.** de. **196.**

—— John Varley of the "Old Society." [With reproductions and portraits.] pp. 84. pl. 77. *F. Lewis: Leigh-on-Sea,* 1946. 4°. **7867.** c. **44.**

—— The Life and Art of Thomas Collier, R.I. . . . With a treatise on the English water-colour. [With a portrait.] pp. 83. pl. 84. *F. Lewis: Leigh-on-Sea,* 1944. 4°. **7868.** d. **1.**

—— Oil Painting of To-day. (Special Spring Number of The Studio, 1938. Edited by C. G. Holme.) pp. 136. [1938.] fol. *See* PERIODICAL PUBLICATIONS.—London.—*The Studio.* P.P. **1931.** pcu. (**118.**)

—— The Private Encounter. Wherein is related the rare story of Harlequin and Fiammetta, *etc.* pp. viii. 290. *Grant Richards: London,* 1931. 8°. NN. **18599.**

—— Richard Wilson, R.A. The grand classic. pp. 79. pl. 48. *F. Lewis: Leigh-on-Sea,* 1947. 4°. **7868.** c. **41.**

—— Shadow of Eros. A biographical and critical study of the life and works of Sir Alfred Gilbert, *etc.* [With a portrait.] pp. iv. 108. pl. XXIV. *Dropmore Press: London,* 1952 [1953]. 4°. C. **103.** c. **16.**

No. 14 of fifty-three copies specially bound and signed by the author.

—— Shadow of Eros. A biographical and critical study of the life and works of Sir Alfred Gilbert, *etc.* [With a portrait.] pp. iv. 108. pl. XXIV. *Macdonald & Evans: London,* 1954. 8°. **10857.** g. **62.**

—— Syon House . . . With ten original copper-plate engravings by John Buckland Wright and an appreciation of the engraver's work by Henry Rushbury. pp. x. 41. *Dropmore Press: London,* 1955. 4°. C. **98.** c. **14.**

—— The Tide, and other poems. pp. 35. *Grant Richards: London,* 1936. 16°. **11655.** f. **16.**

—— Two Centuries of British Water-Colour Painting . . . With introductory and biographical notes. pp. 227. *George Newnes: London,* 1950. 4°. **7868.** dd. **48.**

—— Water-Colour Painting of To-day. (Special Spring Number of The Studio, 1937. Edited by C. G. Holme.) pp. 32. 1937. fol. *See* PERIODICAL PUBLICATIONS.—London.—*The Studio.* P.P. **1931.** pcu. (**115.**)

BURY (ARTHUR) *See* COLMER (James) A Vindication of Mr. James Colmar . . . from the calumnies of three late pamphlets. 1. A Paper publish'd by Dr. Bury, 1689. 2. The Account examin'd. 3. The Case of Exeter College related and vindicated, *etc.* 1691. 4°. **731.** k. **6.** **(10.)**

—— *See* OXFORD.—*University of Oxford.—Exeter College.* A Defence [by J. Harrington] of the Proceedings of the Right Reverend the Visitor and Fellows of Exeter College in Oxford. With an answer to 1. The Case of Exeter College related and vindicated. 2. The Account examin'd. 1691. 4°. **731.** k. **6.** **(9.)**

—— *See* TRELAWNY (*Sir* Jonathan) *Bart.*, successively *Bishop of Bristol, of Exeter* and *of Winchester.* An Account [by J. Harrington] of the Proceedings of the Right Reverend Father in God Jonathan, Lord Bishop of Exeter in his late Visitation of Exeter College in Oxford [in connection with the conduct of A. Bury and his expulsion of J. Colmer]. 1690. 4°. **731.** k. **6.** **(7.)**

—— —— 1690. 4°. **127.** b. **15.**

—— The Bow: or, the Lamentations of David over Saul and Jonathan, applyed to the Royal and Blessed Martyr K. Charles the I. in a sermon preached the 30th January, at the Cathedral Church of S. Peter in Exon. pp. 50. *For Henry Brome: London,* 1662. 4°. **226.** i. **10.** **(7.)**

—— The Case of Exeter-Colledge, in the University of Oxford, related and vindicated. [By A. Bury; sometimes ascribed to Joseph Washington.] pp. 74. 1691. 4°. *See* OXFORD.—*University of Oxford.—Exeter College.* **731.** h. **5.** **(1.)**

—— [Another copy.] **124.** k. **20.**

—— [Another copy.] G. **3709.** **(2.)**

—— The Constant Communicant, a diatribe, proving that constancy in receiving the Lords Supper is the indispensible duty of every Christian. pp. 328. *Leon. Lichfield for Stephen Bolton: Oxford,* 1681. 8°. **4327.** d. **14.**

—— The Danger of delaying Repentance; set forth in a sermon preached . . . at St. Mary's Church in Oxford, on New-Years-Day, 169½. pp. 28. *For Nathanael Ranew: London,* 1692. 4°. **4474.** d. **27.**

—— Latitudinarius Orthodoxus. I. In genere, de fide in religione naturali, Mosaica & Christiana. II. In particulari, de Christianæ religionis mysteriis, Sancta Trinitate, Christi Incarnatione, corporis resurrectione, Cœna Dominica. [By A. Bury.] Accesserunt vindiciæ libertatis Christianæ, Ecclesiæ Anglicanæ, & A. Bury, S.T.P. contrà ineptias & calumnias P. Jurieu. pp. x. 238. 1697. 8°. *See* LATITUDINARIUS. **1016.** d. **25.**

—— The Naked Gospel. Discovering I. What was the Gospel which our Lord and His Apostles preached. II. What additions and alterations latter ages have made in it. III. What advantages and damages have thereupon ensued. Part I. Of Faith. By a true Son of the Church of England [i.e. A. Bury]. pp. 64. 1690. 4°. *See* GOSPEL. T. **690.** **(1.)**

—— [Another edition.] pp. 102. 1690. 4°. *See* GOSPEL. **4105.** de. **4.** **(9.)**

—— [Another edition.] pp. 105. *For Nathanael Ranew: London,* 1691. 4°. **701.** i. **10.** **(3.)**

—— [Another copy.] **113.** g. **9.**

BURY (ARTHUR)

—— *See* FELTON (Henry) *Principal of St. Edmund Hall.* The Resurrection of the same Numerical Body, and its Reunion to the same Soul; asserted in a sermon . . . In which . . . the author of the Naked Gospel [i.e. A. Bury] is answered. [1725.] 8°. **693.** d. **14.** **(1.)**

—— —— [1725.] 8°. **693.** d. **14.** **(3.)**

—— *See* GOSPEL. An Historical Vindication [by J. Le Clerc?] of the Naked Gospel [by A. Bury], recommended to the University of Oxford. 1690. 4°. T. **690.** **(2.)**

—— *See* LONG (Thomas) *Prebendary of Exeter.* An Answer to a Socinian Treatise [by A. Bury], call'd, The Naked Gospel . . . With a postscript, in answer to what is added by Dr. Bury, in the edition just published. 16[91]. 4°. T. **752.** **(1.)**

—— *See* NICHOLLS (William) *D.D.* An Answer to an Heretical Book, called the Naked Gospel . . . With some reflections on Dr. Bury's new edition of that book, *etc.* 1691. 4°. **701.** i. **10.** (4.)

—— *See* OXFORD.—*University of Oxford.—Convocation.* Judicium & decretum Universitatis Oxoniensis . . . Contra propositiones quasdam impias, & haereticas, exscriptas & citatas ex libello quodam . . . cui titulus est The Naked Gospel, *etc.* 1690. fol. **1471.** cc. **15.** **(3.)**

—— *See* OXFORD.—*University of Oxford.—Convocation.* Judicium & decretum Universitatis Oxoniensis . . . contra propositiones quasdam . . . exscriptas et citatas ex libello quodam . . . cui titulus est, The Naked Gospel [by A. Bury], *etc.* 1690. fol. **4225.** l. **13.**

—— *See* OXFORD.—*University of Oxford.—Convocation.* The Fire's continued at Oxford: or, the Decree of the Convocation for burning the Naked Gospel [of A. Bury] considered. In a letter to a person of honour. [By J. Parkinson.] [1690.] 4°. T. **690.** **(3.)**

—— The Rational Deist satisfy'd by a Just Account of the Gospel . . . The second edition. pp. 128. *James Round: London,* 1703. 8°. **480.** a. **37.**

—— A Discourse of the Satisfaction of Christ, from Rom. VIII. i, ii, iii, iv. Wherein the sentiments of Dr. Bury [expressed in "The Rational Deist satisfy'd"] concerning that subject are stated and consider'd. pp. 24. *Printed for the Author: Exon,* 1703. 8°. **4372.** de. **4.** **(1.)**

—— The Account examined: or, a Vindication of Dr. Arthur Bury, Rector of Exeter College, from the calumnies of a late pamphlet [by J. Harrington], entituled, An Account of the Proceedings of the Right Reverend Father in God Jonathan, Lord Bishop of Exon, in his late visitation of Exeter College in Oxon. pp. 32. *Sold by Randall Taylor: London,* 1690. 4°. **8365.** bb. **10.**

—— [Another copy.] **731.** k. **6.** **(8.)**

—— [Another copy.] **126.** i. **24.**

—— [Another copy.] T. **2031.** **(19.)** *Imperfect; wanting the leaf preceding the titlepage.*

BURY (AUGUSTE) *See* BURY (Eustache L. J. A.)

BURY (BAGNELL JÁNOS) *See* BURY (John B.)

BURY (Catharine Maria) *Countess of Charleville.* *See* Bond (Richard W.) The Marlay Letters, 1778–1820, *etc.* [Letters of Lady Charleville and others, from the collection bequeathed to R. W. Bond by Charles Brinsley Marlay. With a portrait.] 1937. 8°. **010921**. f. **10**.

—— *See* Voltaire (F. M. A. de) [*La Henriade.*] The Henriade, an epic poem . . . Translated [by C. M. Bury, Countess of Charleville] . . . into English rhyme, with large historical and critical notes. 1797. 4°. **640**. l. **5**.

—— *See* Voltaire (F. M. A. de) [*La Pucelle d'Orléans.*] La Pucelle; or, the Maid of Orleans . . . From the French of M. de Voltaire [by C. M. Bury, Countess of Charleville], *etc.* 1796, *etc.* 8°. **11474**. h. **32**.

—— *See* Voltaire (F. M. A. de) [*La Pucelle d'Orléans.*] La Pucelle . . . A new and complete translation . . . corrected and augmented from the earlier English translation of W. H. Ireland, and the one attributed to Lady Charleville, *etc.* 1899. 8°. **11474**. g. **31**.

BURY (Charles Alfred) The Church Association. [An account of its origins and activities.] pp. 43. *William Macintosh: London,* 1873. 8°. **4109**. aa. **12**. (**2**.)

BURY (Charles Kenneth Howard) Mount Everest. The Reconnaisance, 1921. By Lieut.-Col. C. K. Howard-Bury and other members of the Mount Everest Expedition. With illustrations and maps. pp. xi. 356. **L.P.** *E. Arnold & Co.: London,* 1922. 4°. L.R. **33**. c. **8**.

BURY (*Lady* Charlotte Susan Maria) *See* Campbell, afterwards Bury.

BURY (Dd.) and **BURY** (Jean) Les Deux Josèph, comédie en un acte, par DD. et Jean Bury, frères, et On manège d'orphilins, comédie en un acte, par J. Bury, *etc.* pp. 46. *Liége,* 1887. 8°. **11740**. aaa. **27**. (**3**.)

BURY (Edmund) A Looking-glass for the Unmarried. By E. Bury . . . Words on Wedlock from various authors. pp. 68. *L. B. Seeley & Sons: London; Arthur Foster: Kirkby Lonsdale,* [1830?] 12°. **8404**. a. **4**.

BURY (Edward) *Civil Engineer.* *See* Bury (P. S.) Recollections of Edward Bury, *etc.* [1860?] 8°. **10803**. e. **23**. (**4**.)

BURY (Edward) *Minister of Great Bolas.* Death improv'd, and Immoderate Sorrow for deceased friends and relations reprov'd, *etc.* [With a portrait.] pp. 272. *For Tho. Parkhurst: London,* 1693. 8°. **4412**. bbb. **11**.

—— England's Bane, or the Deadly danger of drunkenness described in a letter to a friend, *etc.* pp. 80. *For Tho. Parkhurst: London,* 1677. 8°. **8435**. a. **101**.

—— A Help to Holy Walking, or, a Guide to glory. Containing directions how to worship God, and to walk with him in the whole course of our lives. pp. 352. *F. L. for Nevil Simmons: London,* 1675. 8°. **873**. f. **30**.

—— The Husbandmans Companion: containing one hundred occasional meditations, reflections and ejaculations, especially suited to men of that employment, *etc.* pp. 472. *For Tho. Parkhurst: London,* 1677. 8°. **1019**. i. **31**.

—— Garden Meditations. (Taken from "The Husbandman's Companion.") pp. viii. 172. *R.T.S.: London,* 1838. 12°. **1113**. b. **22**.

BURY (*Mrs.* Edward) *See* Bury (P. S.)

BURY (Elizabeth) *See* Bury (Samuel) An Account of the Life and Death of Mrs. Elizabeth Bury . . . chiefly collected out of her own diary. Together with her funeral sermon . . . by the Reverend Mr. William Tong, and her Elegy by the Reverend Mr. J. Watts. 1720. 8°. **1373**. g. **20**.

—— —— 1721. 8°. **4903**. cc. **32**.

—— —— 1721. 8°. **1416**. a. **22**.

BURY (Ernest)

—— The Tendencies of Modern Coking Practice, *etc.* pp. 30. *Colliery Guardian: London,* [1910.] 8°. [*Coal Trade Pamphlets.* no. 12.] **8229**. a. **53/12**.

BURY (Eustache Lambert Joseph Auguste) Traité de la législation des mines, des minières, des usines et des carrières en Belgique et en France, ou commentaire théorique et pratique de la loi du 21 avril 1810, *etc.* 2 tom. *Liége,* 1859. 8°. **5695**. b. **12**.

BURY (*Mme.* F. Blaze de) *See* Blaze de Bury (*Mme.* F.)

BURY (Fenton Ernest) The Self-Witness of the Son of God. pp. 45. *A. H. Stockwell: London,* [1902.] 8°. **4419**. i. **42**.

BURY (George Wyman) Arabia Infelix; or, the Turks in Yamen . . . With illustrations & maps. pp. x. 213. *Macmillan & Co.: London,* 1915. 8°. **10075**. ee. **27**.

—— The Land of Uz . . . With illustrations [including portraits]. [With a preface signed: P. J. M., i.e. Pelham James Maitland.] pp. xxviii. 354. *Macmillan & Co.: London,* 1911. 8°. **010075**. f. **30**.

—— Pan-Islam. pp. 212. *Macmillan & Co.: London,* 1919. 8°. **04503**. de. **60**.

BURY (Henri Blaze de) *Baron.* *See* Blaze de Bury.

BURY (Henry) The Execution of Henry Bury, one of the murderers of Sir Edmund-Bury Godfrey . . . To which is premised an exact narrative of the proceedings at the sessions, Febr. 26 and 27, *etc.* pp. 8. *For L. C.* [*Lionel Curtis*]: *London,* 167$\frac{8}{9}$. 4°. **6495**. a. **59**.

BURY (Herbert) successively *Bishop of British Honduras and Central America* and *for North and Central Europe.* *See* Hine (Sophie M.) Bishop Bury, late Bishop of North and Central Europe. A memoir, *etc.* [With a portrait.] 1933. 8°. **4907**. dd. **33**.

—— A Bishop amongst Bananas. [Experiences in Central America.] pp. xvi. 236. *Wells Gardner & Co.: London,* 1911. 8°. **4764**. f. **17**.

—— "The Glorious Dead." (Sermon.) pp. 14. *United Press:* [*London,* 1919.] 8°. **04478**. de. **24**.

—— Here and There in the War Area . . . With thirty-two illustrations. pp. xii. 328. *A. R. Mowbray & Co.: London, Oxford,* 1916. 8°. **09082**. aa. **38**.

—— My Visit to Ruhleben . . . With twenty-five illustrations and a plan of the camp. pp. xi. 81. *A. R. Mowbray & Co.: London, Oxford,* 1917. 4°. **09082**. c. **4**.

—— Russia from Within, *etc.* [With plates.] pp. xvi. 231. *Churchman Publishing Co.: London,* [1927.] 8°. **010291**. ee. **10**.

—— Russian Life To-day. [With illustrations.] pp. viii. 270. *A. R. Mowbray & Co.: London, Oxford,* 1915. 8°. **10292**. c. **28**.

BURY (JACOB) Advice to the Commons within all His Majesties Realms and Dominions . . . Containing the perfect harmony . . . between divinity and law . . . And that kingly government is by divine right. pp. 62. *Henry Hills for Richard Northcott: London*, 1685. 4°. T. **1684**. (**2**.)

BURY (JACQUES) La Logicque Chirurgicalle. Contenant la facilité et difficulté de l'intelligence tant de la medecine que de la chirurgie. pp. 157. *A. Saugrain: Paris*, 1613. 8°. **782**. b. **5**.
The titlepage is engraved.

BURY (JACQUES EUGÈNE) Thèse pour le doctorat en médecine, *etc.* (Questions sur diverses branches des sciences médicales.) pp. 46. *Paris*, 1840. 4°. [*Collection des thèses soutenues à la Faculté de Médecine de Paris.* An 1840. tom. 3.] **7371**. b. **4**.

BURY (JAMES) *of Manchester.*

—— Little Bits for Working Men. By one who respects them (James Bury). pp. viii. 78. *John Heywood: Manchester*, [1874.] 8°. **8276**. bbb. **59**.

—— Pickings up in Ireland. By an Englishman (J. Bury). pp. 92. *W. H. Smith & Son: London & Dublin*, 1859. 8°. **10390**. b. **11**.

BURY (JAMES) *of Wallawalla.*
—— In Pensive Mood. [Verses.] pp. 20. [1950.] 8°. **11659**. c. **18**.

BURY (JEAN) *See* BURY (D.) and BURY (J.) Les Deux Josèph . . . par DD. et J. Bury, frères, *etc.* 1887. 8°. **11740**. aaa. **27**. (**3**.)

—— Ine Amour inte deux aiwes. Opèrette èn ine ake, et Jote po Jote, opèrette èn ine ake, *etc.* pp. 39. *Liége*, 1890. 8°. **11740**. aaa. **27**. (**8**.)

—— Les Campinaire. Comèdèie d'une ake avou chants. pp. 31. *Liége*, 1892. 8°. **11740**. c. **58**. (**8**.)

—— Ès Dièrin baguège. Comèdèye d'ine ake mahèye di chants. pp. 32. *Liége*, 1894. 8°. **11740**. e. **25**. (**10**.)

—— 2e édition. pp. 32. *Liége*, 1897. 8°. **11740**. e. **35**. (**4**.)

—— Fâbites et critions. Recueil d'œuvres wallonnes, *etc.* [With musical notes, and with a portrait.] pp. 104. 16. [*Liége*, 1893.] 8°. **11498**. d. **37**.

—— On Manège d'Orphilins. Comédie. 1887. 8°. *See* BURY (D.) and BURY (J.) Les Deux Josèph, *etc.* **11740**. aaa. **27**. (**3**.)

—— Petits abions. 100 rondais (sos totes sôres de tâv'lais). pp. 104. *Liége*, 1894. 16°. **11498**. aa. **40**.

—— Ramaïes et Mossai. Œuvres wallonnes. Chansons—musique—théâtre. [With a biographical note by O. Gilbart.] pp. 244. *Liége*, 1906. 8°. **11737**. ee. **42**.

—— Wèzin Wèzene. Opérette ès ine acte. pp. 32. *Liége*, 1886. 8°. **11740**. aaa. **28**. (**9**.)

BURY (JOHN) *Captain.* A True Narrative of the late Design of the Papists to charge their horrid plot upon the Protestants. By endeavouring to corrupt Captain Bury and Alderman Brooks of Dublin, and to take off the evidence of Mr. Oats and Mr. Bedlow, &c. as appears by the depositions [of Bury and Brooks], *etc.* pp. 16. *For Dorman Newman: London*, 1679. fol. T. **95***. (**14**.)

—— [Another copy.] T. **1***. (**50**.)

BURY (JOHN) *Captain.*

—— [Another edition.] pp. 16. *For Dorman Newman: London*, 1679. fol. **515**. l. **21**. (**1**.)

—— [Another copy.] **193**. d. **11**. (**15**.)
With a different leaf preceding the titlepage.

BURY (JOHN) *Fellow of Balliol College, Oxford.* The Moderate Christian. A sermon preached in Exeter at a triennial visitation . . . March 24. 1630. pp. 26. *William Stansby for Nathaniell Butter: London*, 1631. 4°. **4474**. c. **45**.

BURY (JOHN BAGNELL) *See* BAYNES (Norman H.) A Bibliography of the Works of J. B. Bury . . . With a memoir, *etc.* 1929. 8°. **011899**. b. **36**.

—— *See* BAYNES (Norman H.) John Bagnell Bury, 1861–1927, *etc.* [1929.] 8°. **010855**. i. **32**.

—— *See* CONSTANTINE VII., *Emperor of the East*, called *Porphyrogenitus.* The Early History of the Slavonic Settlements in Dalmatia, Croatia, & Serbia. Constantine Porphyrogennetos, De administrando imperio, chapters 29–36. Edited by J. B. Bury. 1920. 8°. W.P. **4683/18**.

—— *See* DARKÓ (J.) Bury Bagnell János k. tag emlékezete, *etc.* 1930. 8°. [*A Magyar Tudományos Akadémia elhúnyt tagjai fölött tartott emlékbeszédek.* köt. 20. sz. 18.] Ac. **825/131**.

—— *See* EURIPIDES. [*Hippolytus.—Greek.*] *Εὐριπίδου Ἱππολυτος* . . . Edited, with introduction, notes and appendix, by J. P. Mahaffy . . . and J. B. Bury. 1881. 8°. **11705**. aa. **34**.

—— *See* FREEMAN (Edward A.) The Historical Geography of Europe . . . Third edition. Edited by J. B. Bury. 1903. 8°. **2060**. b.

—— *See* FREEMAN (Edward A.) History of Federal Government in Greece and Italy . . . Edited by J. B. Bury, *etc.* 1893. 8°. **2238**. b. **3**.

—— *See* GIBBON (Edward) *the Historian.* The History of the Decline and Fall of the Roman Empire . . . Edited . . . with introduction, notes, appendices, and index by J. B. Bury. 1896, *etc.* 8°. **2071.e.**

—— —— 1905, *etc.* 8°. **012203**. f. **33/1**.

—— —— 1909, *etc.* 8°. **09039**. dd. **14**.

—— *See* GIBBON (Edward) *the Historian.* Autobiography of Edward Gibbon as originally edited by Lord Sheffield. With an introduction by J. B. Bury. [1907.] 8°. **012209**. df. **75**.

—— *See* HAY (John S.) The Amazing Emperor Heliogabalus . . . With introduction by Professor J. B. Bury. 1911. 8°. **10606**. ccc. **17**.

—— *See* ORTON (Charles W. P.) The Shorter Cambridge Medieval History. [An abridgment of the Cambridge Medieval History.] 1952. 8°. **09073**. g. **6**.

—— *See* PALEY (Frederick A.) Remarks on Aesch. Agam. 1172 in emendation of Mr. Bury's reading, *etc.* 1885. 8°. **11313**. ff. **21**. (**2**.)

—— *See* PINDAR. [*Greek.*] *Πινδαρου Ἐπινικοι Νεμεονικαις.* The Nemean Odes of Pindar. Edited, with introductions and commentary, by J. B. Bury. 1890. 8°. **2282**. c. **20**.

BURY (JOHN BAGNELL)

—— *See* PINDAR. [*Greek*.] *Πινδαρου Ἐπινικοι Ἰσθμιονικαις.* The Isthmian Odes of Pindar. Edited, with introduction and commentary, by J. B. Bury. 1892. 8°. **2282.** c. **21.**

—— *See* RUFFINI (F.) Religious Liberty . . . With a preface by J. B. Bury. 1912. 8°. **2206.** cc. **19.**

—— Selected Essays . . . Edited by Harold Temperley. [With a portrait.] pp. xxxi. 249. *University Press: Cambridge*, 1930. 8°. **2350.** f. **11.**

—— The Achaeans and the Trojan War. 1924, *etc. See* infra: The Cambridge Ancient History, *etc.* vol. 2. 1923, *etc.* 8°. [Latest edition.] **2070. e–f**
[Earlier editions.] **09004.** de.

—— The Age of Illumination. 1927, *etc. See* infra: The Cambridge Ancient History, *etc.* vol. 5. 1923, *etc.* 8° [Latest edition.] **2070.e–f.**
[Earlier editions.] **09004.** de.

—— L'Allemagne et la civilisation slave. pp. 17. *Eyre & Spottiswoode: London*, 1915. 8°. **09325.** i. **22.**

—— The Ancient Greek Historians. Harvard lectures. pp. x. 281. *Macmillan & Co.: London*, 1909. 8°. **2382.** e. **9.**

—— Byzantine Texts. Edited by J. B. Bury. 5 vol. *Methuen & Co.: London*, 1898–1904. 8°. **2071.f.**

—— The Cambridge Ancient History. Edited by J. B. Bury . . . S. A. Cook . . . F. E. Adcock (M. P. Charlesworth, N. H. Baynes).

1. Egypt and Babylonia. To 1580 B.C.
2. The Egyptian and Hittite Empires. To c. 1000 B.C.
3. The Assyrian Empire.
4. The Persian Empire and the West.
5. Athens. 478–401 B.C.
6. Macedon. 401–301 B.C.
7. The Hellenistic Monarchies and the Rise of Rome.
8. Rome and the Mediterranean. 218–133 B.C.
9. The Roman Republic. 133–44 B.C.
10. The Augustan Empire. 44 B.C.–A.D. 70.
11. The Imperial Peace. A.D. 70–192.
12. The Imperial Crisis and Recovery. A.D. 193–324.
Volume of Plates I(–V). Prepared by C. T. Seltman.

University Press: Cambridge, 1923– . 8°.
[Latest edition of each vol.] **2070.e-f.**
[Earlier editions.] **09004.** de.

—— [Another copy.] **09004.** ee.
Various editions.

—— The Cambridge Medieval History. Planned by J. B. Bury . . . Edited by H. M. Gwatkin . . . J. P. Whitney (J. R. Tanner, C. W. Previté-Orton, Z. N. Brooke). [With maps.]

1. The Christian Roman Empire and the foundation of the Teutonic Kingdoms.
2. The Rise of the Saracens and the foundation of the Western Empire.
3. Germany and the Western Empire.
4. The Eastern Roman Empire. 717–1453.
5. Contest of Empire and Papacy.
6. Victory of the Papacy.
7. Decline of Empire and Papacy.
8. The Close of the Middle Ages.

University Press: Cambridge, 1911– . 8°.
[Latest edition of each vol.] **2070. f.**
[Earlier editions.] **09004.** g.

—— [Another copy.] **9010.** c.
Various editions.

—— The Constitution of the Later Roman Empire. Creighton Memorial Lecture delivered at University College, London, 12 November 1909. pp. 49. *University Press: Cambridge*, 1910. 8°. **09039.** d. **5.**

—— Dionysius of Syracuse. 1927, *etc. See* supra: The Cambridge Ancient History, *etc.* vol. 6. 1923, *etc.* 8° [Latest edition.] **2070.e-f.**
[Earlier editions.] **09004.** de.

—— Foreign Statesmen. (Edited by J. B. Bury.) 11 vol. *Macmillan & Co.: London*, 1896–1903. 8°. **10600.** ee. **12.**

—— Greek Literature from the Eighth Century to the Persian Wars. 1926, *etc. See* supra: The Cambridge Ancient History, *etc.* vol. 4. 1923, *etc.* 8°. [Latest edition.] **2070.e-f.**
[Earlier editions.] **09004.** de.

—— The Hellenistic Age and the History of Civilization *See* HELLENISTIC AGE. The Hellenistic Age, *etc.* 1923. 8°. **11313.** aa. **11.**

—— A History of Freedom of Thought. pp. 256. *Williams & Norgate: London; H. Holt & Co.: New York*, [1913.] 8°. [*Home University Library of Modern Knowledge.*] **12199.** p. **1/81.**

—— A History of Freedom of Thought . . . With an epilogue by H. J. Blackham. Second edition. pp. 246. *Oxford University Press: London*, 1952. 8°. [*Home University Library of Modern Knowledge.*] **12199.** p. **1/277.**

—— *See* BELLOC (Joseph H. P.) Anti-Catholic History: how it is written. (An examination of Prof. Bury's A History of Freedom of Thought.) 1914. 8°. **3943.** aa. **153.**

—— *See* VANCE (John G.) Freedom of Thought and Christianity. A criticism of Professor Bury's "History of Freedom of Thought." 1914. 8°. **3943.** aa. **201.**

—— A History of Greece to the death of Alexander the Great . . . With maps and plans. pp. xxiii. 909. *Macmillan & Co.: London*, 1900. 8°. **9025.** bbb. **23.**

—— [Another edition.] 2 vol. *Macmillan & Co.: London*, 1902. 8°. **9026.** e. **25.**

—— (Second edition.) pp. xxv. 909. *Macmillan & Co.: London*, 1913. 8°. **9027.f.1.**

—— A History of Greece to the Death of Alexander the Great . . . Third edition. Revised by Russell Meiggs. pp. xxv. 925. *Macmillan & Co.: London*, 1951. 8°. **9025.** cc. **34.**

—— [A reissue.] A History of Greece to the death of Alexander the Great . . . Third edition, *etc.* *London*, 1952. 8°. **2071.c.**

—— [A History of Greece.] Stair na Gréige . . . An Monsignor ró-Oirṁidneaċ Pádraig de Brún . . . do ċuir Gaeilge ar A History of Greece. [With illustrations.] Oifig an tSoláṫair: Baile Áṫa Cliaṫ, 1954. 3 cuid. 8°. **9027.aa.28.**

—— History of Greece for Beginners. [An abridgment of "A History of Greece to the death of Alexander the Great."] pp. xv. 472. *Macmillan & Co.: London*, 1903. 8°. **9026.** aa. **45.**

BURY (JOHN BAGNELL)

—— A History of the Eastern Roman Empire, from the fall of Irene to the accession of Basil I. A.D. 802–867. pp. xv. 530. *Macmillan & Co.: London*, 1912. 8°. **2382.** d. **12.**

—— A History of the Later Roman Empire, from Arcadius to Irene, 395 A.D. to 800 A.D. 2 vol. *Macmillan & Co.: London & New York*, 1889. 8°. **2070.** e.

—— [Another copy.] **2382.** e. **7.**

—— History of the Later Roman Empire from the death of Theodosius I. to the death of Justinian, A.D. 395 to A.D. 565. [With a bibliography.] 2 vol. *Macmillan & Co.: London*, 1923. 8°. **2071.e**

—— [Another copy.] **9042.** c. **8.**

—— History of the Papacy in the 19th Century, 1864–1878 . . . Edited, with a memoir, by the Rev. R. H. Murray. pp. lxi. 175. *Macmillan & Co.: London*, 1930. 8°. **4571.** eee. **13.**

—— Homer. 1924, *etc. See* supra: The Cambridge Ancient History, *etc.* vol. 2. 1923, *etc.* 8°. [Latest edition.] **2070.e-f.** [Earlier editions.] **09004.** de.

—— The Idea of Progress. An inquiry into its origin and growth. pp. xv. 377. *Macmillan & Co.: London*, 1920. 8°. **09009.** b. **27.**

—— The Imperial Administrative System in the Ninth Century. With a revised text of the Kletorologion of Philotheos. pp. 179. *Oxford University Press: London*, 1911. 8°. [*British Academy. Supplemental Papers.* no. 1.] Ac. **1186/3.**

—— An Inaugural Lecture delivered in the Divinity School, Cambridge, on January 26, 1903. pp. 42. *University Press: Cambridge*, 1903. 8°. **09008.** ee. **11.**

—— The Invasion of Europe by the Barbarians. A series of lectures. pp. xii. 296. *Macmillan & Co.: London*, 1928. 8°. **09073.** b. **13.**

—— The Itinerary of Patrick in Connaught, according to Tírechán, *etc.* [1903.] *See* DUBLIN.—*Royal Irish Academy.* Proceedings, *etc.* vol. 24. sec. C. no. 10. 1837, *etc.* 8°. Ac. **1540/4.**

—— The Life of Saint Patrick, and his place in history. pp. xv. 404. *Macmillan & Co.: London*, 1905. 8°. **2214.** d. **3.**

—— The Ottoman Conquest. *See* ACTON (John E. E. D.) *Baron Acton.* The Cambridge Modern History, *etc.* (vol. 1. The Renaissance.) 1902, *etc.* 8°. **2070.g.**

—— Romances of Chivalry on Greek Soil, being the Romanes Lecture for 1911, *etc.* pp. 24. *Clarendon Press: Oxford*, 1911. 8°. **12450.** i. **31.** (5.)

—— Russia. 1908. *See* ACTON (John E. E. D.) *Baron Acton.* The Cambridge Modern History, *etc.* (vol. 5. The Age of Louis XIV.) 1902, *etc.* 8°. **2070.g.**

—— The Student's Roman Empire. A history of the Roman Empire from its foundation to the death of Marcus Aurelius. 27 B.C.–180 A.D. pp. viii. 638. *John Murray: London*, 1893. 8°. **09039.** d. **3.**

BURY (JOHN PATRICK TUER)

—— *See* GREATHEED (Bertie) An Englishman in Paris: 1803 . . . Edited by J. P. T. Bury and J. C. Barry. 1953. 8°. **10175.** ff. **39.**

BURY (JOHN PATRICK TUER)

—— The College of Corpus Christi and of the Blessed Virgin Mary. A history from 1822 to 1952. pp. x. 362. pl. 44. [*Corpus Christi College:*] *Cambridge*, 1952. 8°. **8368.** ff. **40.**

—— France, 1814–1940. [With maps.] pp. xii. 348. *Methuen & Co.: London*, 1949. 8°. **09226.** bb. **6.**

—— France, 1814–1940. (Second edition.) pp. xii. 348. *Methuen & Co.: London*, 1950. 8°. **9232.** a. **2.**

—— France, 1814–1940. (Third edition, revised.) pp. xii. 348. *Methuen & Co.: London*, 1954. 8°. **9232.** a. **14.**

—— Gambetta and the National Defence: a republican dictatorship in France . . . With illustrations [including a portrait] and a map. pp. xxiv. 341. *Longmans & Co.: London*, 1936. 8°. **09226.** ee. **32.**

BURY (JOSEPH DÉSIRÉ FULGENCE DE) *See* also FULGENCE, *pseud.* [i.e. J. D. F. de Bury.]

—— *See* LEDOUX (P.) Le Béarnais, ou la Jeunesse de Henri IV., comédie . . . par MM. P. Ledoux, Fulgence de Bury, *etc.* 1825. 8°. **11738.** c. **28.** (8.)

BURY (JUDITH) *See* RATEL (S.) [Coq-en-fer.] The Weathercock, *etc.* (Translated by J. Bury.) [1938.] 8°. **12824.** d. **2.**

BURY (JUDSON SYKES) *See* ROSS (James) *M.D.* On Peripheral Neuritis . . . By J. Ross . . . and J. S. Bury, *etc.* 1893. 8°. **7620.** e. **23.**

—— The Bradshaw Lecture on Prognosis in relation to Disease of the Nervous System. pp. 32. *Sherratt & Hughes: Manchester*, [1902.] 8°. **07640.** e. **5.**

—— Clinical Medicine: a manual for the use of students and junior practitioners, *etc.* pp. xx. 468. *C. Griffin & Co.: London*, 1894. 8°. **7442.** ee. **16.**

—— Second edition. pp. xx. 532. *C. Griffin & Co.: London*, 1899. 8°. **7442.** cc. **21.**

—— Third edition, edited by J. S. Bury and Albert Ramsbottom, *etc.* pp. xxi. 530. *C. Griffin & Co.: London*, 1912. 8°. **7440.** r. **4.**

—— Concerning Old Age. pp. 32 *Sherratt & Hughes: Manchester*, 1930. 8°. **012350.** ee. **58.**

—— Diseases of the Nervous System. pp. xx. 778. *University Press: Manchester*, 1912. 8°. [*Publications of the University of Manchester.* Medical series. no. 14.] Ac. **2671.**

—— Selected Addresses by Dr. Judson Sykes Bury. [With plates, including a portrait.] pp. 151. *R. Seed & Sons: Preston*, 1940. 8°. **12360.** df. **36.**

BURY (MARIE PAULINE ROSE BLAZE DE) *Baroness. See* BLAZE DE BURY.

BURY (MARY) In the New Forest with the Fairies. pp. 15. *B. H. Blackwell: Oxford*, 1917. 8°. **12800.** a. **13.**

BURY (P. S.) Figures of Remarkable Forms of Polycystins, or allied organisms, in the Barbados Chalk Deposit . . . Drawn by Mrs. Bury, as seen in her microscope, *etc.* [With descriptive letterpress.] pl. 12. *John Garnett: Windermere*, [1862.] 4°. **7203.** e. **5.**

BURY (P. S.)

—— Recollections of Edward Bury . . . By his widow. pp. 24. *John Garnett: Windermere,* [1860?] 8°. **10803**. e. **23**. (**4**.)

Printed for private circulation.

BURY (PATRICK) *See* BURY (John P. T.)

BURY (REGINALD VICTOR) Vinum Sacramenti. A critical examination of the nature of the wine of the Holy Communion. pp. vi. 214. *Hodges, Figgis & Co.: Dublin; Simpkin, Marshall & Co.: London,* 1904. 8°. **8436**. eee. **13**.

BURY (RICHARD) *See* LOVE (John) *Member of the Society of Friends, the Younger.* The Cry of the Oppressed for Justice: or, an Account of the exercise, tryal and suffering of John Love, *etc.* (Made publick by R. Bury.) 1704. 4°. **855**. f. **9**. (**19**.)

—— A Collection of sundry Messages and Warnings to the Inhabitants of the city of Bristol, *etc.* pp. 62. *Bristol,* 1728. 4°. **4151**. aa. **57**. (**13**.)

Pp. 1–16 *are a reissue of* " *A Collection of Warnings, etc.,*" *published in* 1712.

BURY (RICHARD DE) *Advocate. See* JOSEPH I., *King of Portugal.* Réponse [by L. A. le Paige] au Jésuite, auteur de la Lettre [in fact by R. de Bury] au sujet de la découverte de la conjuration formée contre le roi de Portugal. [1759.] 12°. **4091**. b. **41**. (**7**.)

—— Essai historique et moral sur l'éducation françoise. pp. xviii. 507. *Paris,* 1777. 12°. **232**. l. **22**.

—— Histoire abrégée des philosophes et des femmes célebres. 2 tom. *Paris,* 1773. 12°. **010603**. a. **2**.

—— Histoire de la vie de Henri IV, roi de France et de Navarre, *etc.* [With portraits.] 2 tom. *Paris,* 1765. 4°. **181**. c. **14**, **15**.

—— [Another edition.] 4 tom. *Paris,* 1766. 12°. **10658**. aa. **34**.

Tom. 3 *bears the date* 1756.

—— Troisième edition, revue, corrigée et augmentée. (Éloge de Henri IV, roi de France: par M. de la Harpe.—Éloge de Maximilien de Béthune, duc de Sully, par M. Thomas.) 4 tom. *Paris,* 1779. 12°. **10659**. aa. **2**.

—— Examen de la nouvelle histoire de Henri IV. de M. de Bury, par M. le marquis de B * * * [i.e. L. Angliviel de la Beaumelle] . . . avec des notes [by Voltaire]. 1769. 8°. [*L'Évangile du jour.*] *See* B * * *, *M. le Marquis de.* **12316**. g. **13**. (**3**.)

—— Histoire de la vie de Louis XIII, roi de France et de Navarre. 4 tom. *Paris,* 1768. 12°. **284**. a. **12–15**.

—— Histoire de Philippe, et d'Alexandre le Grand, rois de Macédoine, *etc.* pp. xviii. 587. *Paris,* 1760. 4°. **198**. d. **3**.

—— Histoire de saint Louis, roi de France, avec un abrégé de l'histoire des Croisades. 2 tom. *Paris,* 1775. 12°. **283**. b. **4**, **5**.

—— Lettre sur quelques ouvrages de M. de Voltaire. [By R. de Bury.] pp. 122. 1769. 8°. *See* VOLTAIRE (F. M. A. de) [*Appendix.—Biography and Criticism.*] **73**. d. **12**.

BURY (RICHARD DE) *Bishop of Durham. See* AUNGERVILLE (Ricardus d')

BURY (ROBERT GREGG) *See* PLATO. [*Works.—Greek and English.*] Plato. With an English translation, *etc.* (VII. Timaeus. IX. Laws. By R. G. Bury.) 1914, *etc.* 8°. **2282**. d. **19**.

—— *See* PLATO. [*Philebus.—Greek.*] The Philebus of Plato. Edited with introduction, notes and appendices by R. G. Bury. 1897. 8°. **8460**. dd. **34**.

—— *See* PLATO. [*Symposium.—Greek.*] The Symposium of Plato. Edited with introduction, critical notes and commentary by R. G. Bury. 1909. 8°. **08461**. f. **41**.

—— —— 1932. 8°. **08458**. bb. **54**.

—— *See* PLATO. [*Symposium.—English.*] Plato's Symposium . . . Translated by F. Birrell & S. Leslie. [Revised by R. G. Bury.] [1924.] 8°. C. **99**. b. **17**.

—— —— [1925.] 8°. **Cup.510.as.6.**

—— *See* SEXTUS, *Empiricus.* Sextus Empiricus. With an English translation by the Rev. R. G. Bury, *etc.* 1933, *etc.* 8°. **2282**. d. **130**.

—— The Fourth Gospel and the Logos-Doctrine. pp. vii. 81. *W. Heffer & Sons: Cambridge,* 1940. 8°. **03265**. ee. **57**.

BURY (SAMUEL) An Account of the Life and Death of Mrs. Elizabeth Bury . . . chiefly collected out of her own diary. Together with her funeral sermon . . . by the Reverend Mr. William Tong, and her elegy by the Reverend Mr. I. Watts. pp. 244. *J. Penn: Bristol,* 1720. 8°. **1373**. g. **20**.

—— The second edition, corrected. pp. 230. *J. Penn: Bristol,* 1721. 8°. **4903**. cc. **32**.

—— The third edition, corrected. pp. 230. *J. Penn: Bristol,* 1721. 8°. **1416**. a. **22**.

—— A Collection of Psalms, Hymns, and Spiritual Songs, fitted for morning and evening worship in a private family. By S. Bury. pp. 146. 1707. 24°. *See* BIBLE.—*Psalms.—Selections.* [*English.*] **3436**. aa. **11**.

—— The Final Destruction of the Great Destroyer: or, Death made easy by Christ's personal and general conquest over it. Discours'd in a funeral sermon on the much lamented death of Robert Baker, *etc.* pp. 40. *N. Cliff & D. Jackson: London,* 1714. 8°. **1416**. c. **19**.

—— A Funeral Sermon for the reverend and pious divine Mr. John Fairfax . . . preached at Barking, Aug. 15. 1700, *etc.* (A Funeral Sermon for the reverend and pious divine Mr. Timothy Wright . . . preached . . . Nov. 25. 1701, *etc.*) pp. 138. *Tho. Parkhurst: London,* 1702. 8°. **1417**. b. **45**.

—— A Funeral Sermon occasioned by the death of the late reverend Mr. Samuel Cradock . . . preached at Bansfield Oct. 18. 1706. pp. 54. *Tho. Parkhurst: London,* 1707. 8°. **1416**. b. **41**.

Imperfect; wanting pp. 51, 52.

—— A Sermon preach'd at the ordination of Mr. Thomas Fisher, at Castle-Hedingham, in the County of Essex, on June 23, 1713 . . . To which is annexed, Mr. Fisher's Confession of Faith, and Mr. Cook's exhortation. pp. 45. *N. Cliff & D. Jackson: London,* 1713. 8°. **4476**. aa. **10**.

BURY (*Right Hon. Sir* THOMAS) Catalogue of the Libraries of the Right Honourable Sir Thomas Bury, Knt. . . . and of Robert Cony, of Rochester . . . which will begin to be sold . . . on Tuesday the 8th of December, 1724. by Fletcher Gyles, *etc.* pp. iv. 103. [*London,* 1724.] 8°. **128**. i. **4**. (**2**.)

BURY (THOMAS TALBOT)

—— *See* DENHAM (Joshua F.) Views exhibiting the Exterior & Interior & Principal Monuments of the very Ancient and Remarkable Church of S[t] Dunstan in the West, in the City of London. [Lithographed by W. Gauci from drawings by Thomas T. Bury.] [1832.] fol. **557*. g. 17.**

—— Coloured Views on the Liverpool and Manchester Railway, with plates of the coaches, machines, &c., from drawings made on the spot by Mr. T. T. Bury. With descriptive particulars, *etc.* pp. 8. pl. 13. *R. Ackermann: London,* 1831. 4°. **10351. i. 12.**

—— Remains of Ecclesiastical Woodwork. [Engravings.] pl. 20. *John Weale: London,* 1847. fol. **1263. g. 26.**

—— Rudimentary Architecture: for the use of beginners. The history and description of the styles of architecture of various countries, from the earliest to the present period. pp. vii. 167. *John Weale: London,* 1849. 12°. **8703. a. 6.**

—— Third edition, with numerous additional illustrations. pp. vii. 201. *John Weale: London,* 1856. 12°. **8703. c. 21.**

BURY (TOSSAINT) *See* BURY (Toussaint)

BURY (TOUSSAINT) Â Bal masqué, comèdeie èn ine acte. pp. 31. *Liége,* [1897.] 8°. **11740. ee. 39. (2.)**

—— On Calmoussège. Comèdeie mèlaie di chants, èn ine acte. pp. 46. *Liége,* 1884. 8°. **11740. aaa. 26. (2.)**

—— Li Crapaute d'on pïotte. Tâvlai populaire èn ine acte, et L'Amour a l'campagne. Sceinnette, 2e édition. pp. 31. *Liége,* 1890. 8°. **11740. aaa. 26. (9.)**

—— Les Deux rivâls. Mèlodrame è deux actes. [In verse.] pp. 56. *Liège,* 1885. 8°. **11740. aaa. 26. (3.)**

—— Ès manège. Comèdeie èn ine acte, et Li Jalot et l'vîreus. Tâv'lai pôpulaire. pp. 36. *Liège,* 1886. 8°. **11740. aaa. 19. (1.)**

—— Li Grand vantrin sins cowettes. Comèdeie èn ine acte. Deuxinme èdition avou cang'mints. pp. 39. *Liège,* 1888. 8°. **11740. aaa. 26. (7.)**

—— Ma tante Jôjè, ou Mon-onke et Ma-tante. Bouffonn'reie èn ine acte et on tâvlai. pp. 54. *Liége,* 1891. 8°. **11740. c. 57. (10.)**

—— Magré-bongré. Comedeie èn ine acte. pp. 36. *Liège,* 1892. 8°. **11740. aaa. 26. (12.)**

—— On Novai gârchampette. Bouffonn'rèye èn ine acte. pp. 32. *Liége,* 1897. 8°. **11740. d. 14. (6.)**

—— Papa Bidon. Comèdeie èn ine acte. pp. 44. *Liége,* 1888. 8°. **11740. aaa. 26. (6.)**

—— Li Pauve honteus. Pièce en vers èn ine acte. pp. 30. *Liége,* 1887. 8°. **11740. aaa. 26. (4.)**

—— On R'moërd. Comèdeie èn ine acte. pp. 43. *Liége,* 1890. 8°. **11740. aaa. 26. (10.)**

—— Les Sceinnes di cabaret. Comèdeie mèlaie di chants, èn ine acte. pp. 43. *Liége,* 1884. 8°. **11740. aaa. 26. (1.)**

—— Li S'cret d'a Gètrou. Mélodrame èn ine acte. pp. 46. *Liége,* 1890. 8°. **11740. aaa. 26. (11.)**

—— Treus caractéres. Comèdeie èn in'acte, *etc.* [In verse.] pp. 28. *Liège,* 1887. 8°. **11740. aaa. 26. (5.)**

BURY (TOUSSAINT)

—— Les Trucs d'ine costîre. Comèdeie èn ine acte. pp. 31. *Liége,* 1889. 8°. **11740. aaa. 26. (8.)**

BURY, otherwise **HUTCHINSON** (WILLIAM) *See* HUTCHINSON, otherwise BURY.

BURY (WILLIAM) *M.I.M.E.* The Powér and Speed of Steam Vessels; calculated by rules adapted for vessels of all types. pp. 28. *E. & F. N. Spon: London, New York,* 1878. 4°. **8807. bb. 26.**

—— The Resistance and the Proportions of Screw Propellers. pp. vii. 91. *E. & F. N. Spon: London,* 1883. 8°. **8807. i. 12.**

BURY (WILLIAM) *Vicar of Radcliffe on Trent.* A Pastoral Letter . . . on . . . Separation from the Communion of the Church. By the Vicar of Radcliffe on Trent [i.e. W. Bury] . . . Second edition. pp. 24. 1838. 12°. *See* LETTER. **908. b. 3. (4.)**

—— *See* KAY (Stephen) The Clerical Fiction of Apostolical Succession and Episcopal Supremacy; being a reply to the pastoral letter of the Vicar of Radcliffe on Trent (W. Bury). 1838. 8°. **908. d. 17. (7.)**

BURYA. Буря жизни. [A religious tale.] pp. 72. *въ Москвѣ,* 1886. 12°. **012589. e. 23. (2.)**

BURYAKOV (H. VON MURAV'EV) *See* MURAV'EV BURYAKOV (Kh.)

BURYAKOVSKY (YU.)

—— Прага остается моей. Пьеса, *etc.* *In:* Украинская советская драматургия. pp. 311–381. 1951. 8°. **11758. h. 62.**

BUR'YANOV (VIKTOR) Прогулка съ дѣтьми по С. Петербургу и его окрестностямъ. (Прибавленіе къ третьему тому. Продолженіе второй поѣздки.) 3 част. *С. Петербургъ,* 1838. 8°. **1295. g. 16.**

BURYAT-MONGOLIA. *See* BURIAT-MONGOLIA.

BURYAT-MONGOLIAN STATE SCIENTIFIC RESEARCH INSTITUTE.

—— Buryat-Mongolian State Scientific Research Institute of Language, Literature and History. *See* BURIAT-MONGOL AUTONOMOUS SOVIET SOCIALIST REPUBLIC.—*Бурят-Монгольский Государственный Научно-Исследовательский Институт Языка, Литературы и Истории.*

BURYAT-MONGOL'SKY GOSUDARSTVENNUY NAUCHNO-ISSLEDOVATEL'SKY INSTITUT.

—— Бурят-Монгольский Государственный Научно-Исследовательский Институт Культуры. *See* BURIAT-MONGOL AUTONOMOUS SOVIET SOCIALIST REPUBLIC.

—— Бурят-Монгольский Государственный Научно-исследовательский Институт Языка, Литературы и Истории. *See* BURIAT-MONGOL AUTONOMOUS SOVIET SOCIALIST REPUBLIC.

BURYAT-MONGOL'SKY NAUCHNO-ISLLEDOVATEL'SKY INSTITUT.

—— Бурят-Монгольский Научно-исследовательский Институт Культуры. *See* BURIAT-MONGOL AUTONOMOUS SOVIET SOCIALIST REPUBLIC.

BURYAT-MONGOLUI. *See* BURIAT MONGOLS.

BURYATO-MONGOL'SKAYA AVTONOMNAYA SOVETSKAYA SOTSIALISTICHESKAYA RESPUBLIKA.

—— Бурято-Монгольская Автономная Совѣтская Соціалистическая Республика. *See* BURIAT-MONGOL AUTONOMOUS SOVIET SOCIALIST REPUBLIC.

BURYATY. *See* BURIATS.

BURZELBAEUME. Burzelbäume meines Satyrs. [By Gustav Teubner.] 2 Bdchn. *Berlin*, 1811. 8°. **12314.** d. **15.**

BURZI (B. F.) О новѣйшихъ трудахъ по греческой исторіографіи. Вступительная лекція, *etc.* pp. 16. [*Kiev*, 1897.] 8°. [*Университетъ Святаго Владиміра. Университетскія Извѣстія.* год 37. no. 12.] Ac. **1099.**

BURZI (LUIGI) *See* BERIA (A.) Una Sfida religiosa. [A controversial correspondence with L. Burzi.] 1868. 12°. **3902.** b. **49.** (**4.**)

BURZIO (CESARE) Nuovi appunti sugli oneri reali, *etc.* pp. 55. 1910. *See* TURIN.—*Accademia delle Scienze.* Memorie, *etc.* ser. 2. tom. 60. 1818, *etc.* 4°. Ac. **2816.**

BURZIO (FILIPPO) Ginevra. Vita nuova. pp. 209. *Milano*, 1920. 8°. **012352.** f. **27.**

—— Lagrange, *etc.* [With portraits.] pp. 275. pl. VIII. *Torino*, 1942. 8°. **010632.** bb. **10.**

BURZIO (GIUSEPPE) Delle acque minerali di Retorbido. Saggio chimico-medico, *etc.* pp. xxxii. 62. *Pavia*, [1830.] 8°. **7383*.** c. **10.** (**6.**)

BURZIO (HUMBERTO F.)

—— La Ceca de la Villa Imperial de Potosí y la Moneda Colonial . . . Advertencia de Emilio Ravignani. Publicación conmemorativa del IV centenario de Potosí. [With plates.] pp. c. 297. *Buenos Aires*, 1945. 8°. *Facultad de Filosofía y Letras de la Universidad Nacional de Buenos Aires. Publicaciones del Instituto de Investigaciones Históricas.* no. 88.] Ac. **2694.** ca/**3.**

BURZIO (NICOLÒ) *See* BURTIUS (Nicolaus)

BURZŌE.

—— *See* **HONEYMAN (Alexander M.) The Mission of Burzoe in the Arabic Kalilah and Dimnah,** *etc.* **1936. 8°. 20032. k. 30.**

—— Burzōes Einleitung zu dem Buche Kalīla wa Dimna, übersetzt und erläutert von Theodor Nöldeke. pp. 27. *Strassburg*, 1912. 8°. [*Schriften der Wissenschaftlichen Gesellschaft in Strassburg.* Hft. 12.] Ac. **548.**

BURZYNA (STANISŁAW BURZYNSKI z) *See* BURZYŃSKI (S.)

BURZYŃSKI (LUDWIK) Le Crépuscule d'une autocratie. Quelques crises en Allemagne, *etc.* (Souvenirs des dernières années des règnes de L. M. Nicholas II et Guillaume II.) pp. 159. 100. *Florence*, 1926. 8°. **09076.** c. **20.**

BURZYŃSKI (STANISŁAW) *See* POLAND. [*Collections of Laws, etc.*] Zebranie wszystkich Seymow, y Praw polskich ad statum ściągaiących się ktore od początku Seymowania aź do naszych czasow są postanowione. Przez S. z Burzyna Burzynskiego. [With a dedication signed: Tadeusz Burzyński.] 1765. 8°. **1436.** c. **18.**

BURZYŃSKI (TADEUSZ) *See* POLAND. [*Collections of Laws, etc.*] Zebranie wszystkich Seymow, y Praw polskich ad statum sciągaiących się, *etc.* [With a dedication signed: Tadeusz Burzynski.] 1765. 8°. **1436.** c. **18.**

BURZYŃSKI (WŁODZIMIERZ)

—— O niedomaganiach i koniecznych uzupełnieniach de Saint-Venantowskiej teorii prętów prostych. pp. 76. *Wrocław*, 1951. 8°. [*Prace Wrocławskiego Towarzystwa Naukowego.* ser. B. no. 42.] Ac. **868.** b/**2.**

BUS. A Historical Bus. Comprising Brave Dame Mary, Anon: The Carved Cartoon by Austin Clare: My Lady Venturesome by Dorothea Moore. 3 pt. *Sheldon Press: London*, [1936.] 8°. **012600.** d. **13.**

"Brave Dame Mary" and "My Lady Venturesome" are reissues of the editions of 1924 *and* 1926 *respectively.*

BÚS, *Vitéz, pseud.* [i.e. PÁL MATKOVICH.] *See* DICKENS (C.) [*Dombey and Son.*] Dombey és fia . . . Forditotta Bús Vitéz. 1874. 16°. **12604.** bbb. **7.**

—— *See* SIMONS (Theodor) [Aus altrömischer Zeit.] Az ős-római időkből korrajzok. Simons T. után Bús Vitéz. 1875. 16°. [*Kis Nemzeti Museum.* köt. 32.] **12209.** b. **31.**

BUS TRANSPORTATION. *See* PERIODICAL PUBLICATIONS.—*New York.*

BUS (CÉSAR DE) *See* CHAMOUX (J. J.) Vie du vénérable César de Bus, *etc.* 1864. 8°. **4865.** aaa. **15.**

—— *See* DU MAS (P.) La Vie du vénérable César de Bus, *etc.* [With a portrait.] 1703. 4°. **4865.** ff. **2.**

—— *See* GENTILE (L.) Vita del ven. Cesare de Bus, *etc.* [1918.] 16°. **4863.** b. **29.**

BUS (FRANÇOIS DE) La Politique devant l'histoire. 2 tom. *Paris*, 1879, 80. 8°. **9231.** i. **4.**

—— [Another edition.] La Politique contemporaine devant l'histoire. tom. 1. pt. 1. pp. xvi. 371. *Paris*, 1882. 12°. **8026.** aaa. **17.**

No more of this edition published.

BUŠ (NIKOLAJS) *See* BUSCH (Nicolaus)

BUSA (VALENTINO) In funere R.P.M. Francisci Xaverii Vasquii Peruntini . . . oratio, *etc.* pp. xxx. *Firmii*, 1786. 8°. **4867.** aaaa. **43.**

BUSACCA (ANTONINO) *See* PERIODICAL PUBLICATIONS.—*Messina.* Annuario della città di Messina, compilato dal prof. cav. A. Busacca. 1875, *etc.* 8°. P.P. **2385.** l.

—— Storia del dritto, dai primi tempi fino all'epoca nostra. pp. xv. 248. *Messina*, 1889. 8°. **6005.** ee. **24.**

—— Storia della legislazione italiana dai primi tempi fino all'epoca nostra. pp. 785. *Messina*, 1883. 8°. **5359.** bb. **8.**

BUSACCA (RAFFAELLO) *See* SAMPOLO (L.) Della vita e delle opere di Raffaello Busacca, *etc.* 1895. 4°. [*Atti della Reale Accademia di Scienze e Lettere di Palermo.* ser. 3. vol. 3.] Ac. **99.**

—— Delle banche di permute in occasione della banca commerciale e industriale di Livorno di F. Garelli e compagni memoria. pp. 40. *Firenze*, 1857. 8°. **8226.** b. **78.** (**4.**)

—— Memorie economiche sulla Toscana, *etc.* pp. 158. *Firenze*, 1855. 8°. **8205.** cc. **8.**

BUSACHI (GIUSEPPE) Brevi osservazioni intorno ad uno scritto del sig. Filippo Vivanet sul tracciamento d'una ferrovia nell' isola di Sardegna. pp. 14. *Cagliari*, [1861.] 8°. **8235**. aaa. **57**. (**1**.)

BUSACK (E.) *See* GILLMER (M.) Berichtigungen und Zusätze zu der . . . " Uebersicht der von Herrn E. Busack bei Schwerin und Waren gefangenen Grossschmetterlinge." 1905. 8°. [*Archiv des Vereins der Freunde der Naturgeschichte.* Jahr 59.] Ac. **2890**.

—— *See* GILLMER (M.) Uebersicht der von Herrn E. Busack bei Schwerin und Waren gefangenen Grossschmetterlinge. 1903, *etc.* 8°. [*Archiv des Vereins der Freunde der Naturgeschichte.* Jahr 57, 58.] Ac. **2890**.

BUSAEUS (JOANNES) *See* BRUNO (Vincenzo) *S.J.* [Delle meditationi sopra le sette festività principali della B. Vergine.] R.P. Vincentii Bruni . . . meditationes . . . Item Commune sanctorum . . . Nunc ex italico in latinum translata [by J. Busaeus or M. Putzius]. 1602. 12°. **4404**. bb. **55**. (**1**.)

—— *See* BRUNO (Vincenzo) *S.J.* [Trattato del sacramento della penitenza.] R.P. Vincentii Bruni . . . brevis tractatus . . . cum examine generali ad confessionem de tota vita . . . Ex italico in latinum translata [by J. Busaeus or M. Putzius]. 1601. 12°. **4404**. bb. **55**. (**2**.)

—— *Praes. See* EBINGSHAUSEN (H.) Disputatio theologica de baptismi necessitate. 1589. 4°. **4326**. e. **27**.

—— *See* HINCMARUS, *Archbishop of Rheims.* Hincmari Rhemensis Archiepiscopi . . . epistolæ, *etc.* [Edited by J. Busaeus.] 1602. 4°. **1084**. l. **10**.

—— *See* JESUITS. [*Letters from Missions.*] Recentissima de amplissimo regno Chinæ, *etc.* [Translated by J. Busaeus.] 1601. 8°. **867**. f. **22**. (**1**.)

—— *See* PETER, *of Blois, Archdeacon of Bath.* Opera Petri Blesensis . . . ope et studio I. Busæi . . . in lucem producta, *etc.* 1600. 4°. **860**. l. **7**.

—— *See* PETER, *of Blois, Archdeacon of Bath.* Paralipomena opusculorum Petri Blesensis . . . editorum a I. Busæo, *etc.* 1624, *etc.* 8°. **1008**. a. **21**.

—— *See* PIMENTA (N.) Exemplum epistolæ P. N. Pimentæ . . . de statu rei Christianæ in India orientali, *etc.* (Ex idiomate italico translatum à I. B. S. I. [i.e. I. Busaeus].) 1602. 8°. **867**. d. **27**. (**5**.)

—— —— 1605. 8°. *See* JESUITS. [*Letters from Missions.*] De rebus Japonicis, *etc.* **4767**. d. **7**.

—— *Praes. See* SCHNEID (J.) De jejunio et delectu ciborum disputatio, *etc.* 1581. 4°. **491**. b. **8**. (**1**.)

—— *See* TRITHEIM (J.) Ioannis Trithemii . . . opera pia . . . a J. Busæo in vnum volumen redacta. 1604. fol. **3676**. f. **7**.

—— Enchiridion piarum meditationum in omnes dominicas, sanctorum festa, Christi passionem & caetera, *etc.* pp. 653. *Typis B. Belleri: Duaci*, 1616. 24°. C. **20**. f. **17**.

—— [Another edition.] pp. 474. *Typis B. Belleri: Duaci*, 1623. 16°. **1019**. a. **16**.

—— Meditations sur les Evangiles des dimanches, des fetes et des principales octaves de toute l'année. Du carême, et des quatres-temps . . . Seconde partie. Traduction nouvelle. *I. B. Coignard: Paris*, 1669. 12°. **857**. a. **18**.
Imperfect; wanting pt. 1.

BUSAEUS (JOANNES)

—— Meditations pour les dimanches, les festes, et les feries principales de toute l'année . . . Ouvrage . . . augmenté de plusieurs . . . meditations; & notamment de celles de la retraite annuelle . . . suivant l'ordre du Breviaire romain & divisé en deux parties. Traduction nouvelle. pp. 612. *A. Pralard: Paris*, 1677. 12°. **4403**. cc. **22**.
A different translation from the preceding.

—— Manuale di pie meditazioni. Composto prima in latino . . . poi trasportato nell'idioma francese, e accresciuto di molte meditazioni da un ecclesiastico parigino, e dopo nella lingua toscana tradotto dal P. Francesco Maria da Coll' Amato . . . Hora nuouamente traslatato . . . con aggiunta d'alcune altre meditazioni. 2 pt. *Nella stamperia della Sacra Congreg. di Propaganda Fede: Roma*, 1684. 12°. **3457**. b. **14**.

—— *Παναριον*, hoc est, Arca medica variis diuinæ Scripturæ priscorumq; patrum antidotis aduersus animi morbos instructa, *etc.* pp. 596. *Apud I. Albinum: Moguntiæ*, 1608. 4°. **474**. c. **13**.
The titlepage is engraved.

—— [Another edition.] 2 tom. *E. Couterot: Parisiis*, 1682. 12°. **848**. d. **22**, **23**.
The titlepage of tom. 1 *is engraved.*

—— Viridarium christianarum virtutum, ex sacrosanctæ Scripturæ sanctorumq; patrum sententijs . . . constructum, et in gratiam concionatorum . . . editum a I. Busæo. pp. 709. *Apud I. Albinum: Moguntiæ*, 1610. 4°. **473**. b. **12**.
The titlepage is engraved. Imperfect; wanting the last leaf of the index. The date has been altered in MS. *to* 1612.

BUSAEUS (PETRUS) *See* PETER [Canisius], *Saint.* Authoritatum . . . quae in Summa doctrinę Christianę doctoris P. Canisii . . . citantur, & nunc primùm ex ipsis fontibus . . . collectę, ipsis Catechismi verbis subscriptæ sunt, pars prima, *etc.* [Compiled by P. Busaeus.] 1569, *etc.* 4°. **4406**. i. **22**.

—— *See* PETER [Canisius], *Saint.* Opus catechisticum . . . praeclaris Diuinæ Scripturæ testimonijs, Sanctorumque Patrum sententijs sedulò illustratum opera D. P. Busæi, *etc.* 1577. fol. **L.19.b.2.**

—— —— 1586. fol. C. **79**. g. **7**.

—— —— 1606. fol. **3559**. f. **4**.

BU SA'ĪD, *House of. See* RUETE (Rudolph S.) Dates and References of the History of the Al Bu Said Dynasty . . . 1741–1856. With genealogical table and bibliography. [1931.] 8°. **09917**. ccc. **14**.

—— *See* THOMAS (Bertram S.) Arab Rule under the Al Bu Sa'id Dynasty of Oman, *etc.* [1938.] 8°. [*Raleigh Lecture on History.* 1938.] Ac. **1186/12**.

BUSALOV (A. A.)

—— *See* SPASOKUKOTSKY (S. I.) Труды . . . Редколлегия: Проф. А. Н. Бакулев, Доц. А. А. Бусалов, *etc.* 1948, *etc.* 8°. W.P. **3228**.

BUSALOV (A. A.) and **OCHKIN** (ALEKSEI DMITRIEVICH)

—— Сборник научных работ—xxv—Лечебно-санитарного управления Кремля. Ответственные редакторы А. А. Бусалов и А. Д. Очкин. (Symposium of Research Works of the Kremlin Health Department.) [With summaries in English.] pp. 411. 1946. 8°. *See* MOSCOW.—*Кремль.—Лечебно-санитарное Управление.* **7393**. b. **18**.

BUSANCY, Charles Emmanuel de Savoie Carignan, *Viscount de.* *See* Savoie-Carignan (C. E. de) *Count de Soissons.*

BUSANICHE (José Luis)

—— *See* Parras (P. J. de) Diario de sus viajes, 1749–1753, *etc.* [Edited by J. L. Busaniche.] 1943. 8°. **010481.** ee. **10.**

—— Lecturas de Historia argentina. Relatos de contemporáneos 1527–1870. [By various authors. Edited by J. L. Busaniche.] pp. 585. *Buenos Aires,* 1938. 8°. **9770.** p. **20.**

—— El General José de San Martín. Sus últimos años y la noticia de su muerte. 17 de agosto de 1850. Homenaje de Yacimientos Petroliferos Fiscales, *etc.* [An extract from J. L. Busaniche's "San Martín visto por sus Contemporáneos," including an account of San Martín's death by F. Frías. With a portrait.] [1944.] 8°. **10891.** c. **3.**

BÛSAREE. *See* Muhammad ibn Sa'īd, *al-Būṣīrī.*

BUŠAS (Arnst) *See* Busch (Ernst)

BUSATI (Luigi) *See* Scialoja (V.) Dizionario pratico del diritto privato. Direttore . . . V. Scialoja . . . Coadiuvato dall'avv. L. Busati, *etc.* [1900, *etc.*] 4°. **5359.** f.

BUŠATLIJA (Mahmud) *Pasha of Scutari.* *See* Maḥmūd, *Bushatliya, etc.*

BUSATO (Luigi) Un Onesto grido in nome di Dante. [In verse.] Precedono alcuni cenni intorno alla edizione minima detta il Dantino, e segue una polemica, La Disonestà letteraria di certi illetterati [a reply to "Agostino Palesa e le sue opere. Discorso letto . . . dall'avvocato Jacopo Dr. Lenner"], con facsimile dell'edizione stessa. pp. viii. 70. *Verona,* 1878. 8°. **11421.** h. **5.**

BUSATTI (Luigi) *See* Busati.

BUSATTI (Tommaso Maria) Panegirico di s. Filippo Benizzi recitato nella Venerabile Compagnia del medesimo santo l'anno 1719, *etc.* pp. 22. *Firenze,* 1720. 4°. **4424.** dd. **4.** **(17.)**

BUSATTI (Vincenzo) Del diritto alla irrogazione delle pene; della loro applicazione ed effetti per la sicurezza sociale, *etc.* pp. 367. *Siena,* 1841. 8°. **5322.** d. **2.**

BUSBACH, afterwards **WILTHEIM** (Margaretha von) *See* Monica, *Sister.*

BÚSBACH (Péter) Az utolsó öt év. Tisza-Szapáry Wekerle. Parlamenti viaszaemlékezések. pp. 62. *Budapest,* 1895. 8°. **8074.** ff. **33.**

—— Egy viharos emberöltő. Korrajz. 2 köt. *Budapest,* 1898, 99. 8°. **010795.** k. **24.**

—— *See* Duka (T.) Kossuth and Görgei . . . An historical essay, based on the Hungarian work of Dr. P. Busbach, entitled "Egy viharos emberöltő," *etc.* 1898. 8°. **09315.** f. **11.**

BUSBECKIUS (Augerius) *See* Gislenius (A.) *Seigneur de Busbecq.*

BUSBECQ, Augier de Ghislen, *Seigneur de.* *See* Gislenius (A.) *Seigneur de Busbecq.*

BUSBECQ (Ogier Ghiselin de) *See* Gislenius (A.) *Seigneur de Busbecq.*

BUSBEE (Perrin)

—— *See* Carolina, *North.—Courts of Justice.—Supreme Court.* Reports of Cases in Equity argued and determined in the Supreme Court of North-Carolina . . . By P. Busbee. 1854. 8°. **6622.i.3.**

BUSBEKIUS (Augerius) *See* Gislenius (A.) *Seigneur de Busbecq.*

BUSBEQUIUS (Augerius Gislenius) *See* Gislenius (A.) *Seigneur de Busbecq.*

BUSBEY (Hamilton) The Trotting and the Pacing Horse in America. [With plates.] pp. x. 369. *Macmillan Co.: New York,* 1904. 8°. [*American Sportsman's Library.*] **7286.** aaa. **1/9.**

BUSBEY (Katherine Olive Graves) Home Life in America . . . With twelve illustrations. pp. x. 410. *Methuen & Co.: London,* 1910. 8°. **12352.** t. **17.**

BUSBEY (T. Addison) The Biographical Directory of the Railway Officials of America . . . Edited and compiled by T. A. Busbey. pp. 418. [1893.] 8°. *See* Directories. *—Railways. [America.]* **08235.** i. **8.**

BUSBIE ( ) *Major.*

—— *See* Boumphrey (Robert S.) Preliminary Derivations of some Falkland Islands Place-Names. By R. S. Boumphrey . . . Major . . . . . . Busbie. 1950. fol. **10005.** h. **21.**

BUSBOM (Johannes Jonas) Dissertatio inauguralis juridica, exhibens decadem controversiarum ex materia testamentaria, *etc.* pp. 40. *Gissæ,* [1711.] 4°. **500.** c. **5.** **(14.)**

BUSBRIDGE (E. M.) Letter Writing and Etiquette. pp. 190. *London & Glasgow,* [1909.] 8°. [*Collins' Useful Books.* no. 3.] **12203.** de. **5/3.**

BUSBRIDGE (Ida Winifred)

—— *See* Kourganoff (V.) Basic Methods in Transfer Problems . . . By V. Kourganoff with the collaboration of I. W. Busbridge. 1952. 8°. W.P. **2180/41.**

—— On the Solution of the Equation of Radiative Transfer. (Reprinted from the Monthly Notices of the Royal Astronomical Society.) [*Oxford,* 1941.] 8°. [*Communications from the University Observatory, Oxford.* no. 21.] W.P. **7200/21.**

BUSBY (A.) Exposition of a New Method of Writing Music scientifically; and theoretic and stenographic railway for composition . . . With examples. pp. 28. *W. Clowes & Sons: London,* 1850. 12°. **7895.** b. **3.**

BUSBY (C. A.) An Essay on the Propulsion of Navigable Bodies. Extracted from the American Monthly Magazine . . . with considerable additions. pp. 31. *B. G. Jansen: New York,* 1818. 8°. **8805.** b. **51.**

—— A Series of Designs for Villas and Country Houses . . . With plans and explanations to each. pp. 20. pl. 24. *J. Taylor: London,* 1808. 4°. **7816.** h. **3.**

BUSBY (C. E.) *See* Condra (George E.) and Busby (C. E.) The Grenola Formation. 1933. 8°. [*Nebraska Geological Survey. Paper.* no. 1.] A.S. n. **21/2.**

BUSBY (Evelyn Christina)

—— *See* Saint Albans, *Diocese of*. Labourers together. A record of the common purposes of the Diocese of St. Albans and of the celebration in 1952 of the seventy-fifth anniversary of its foundation. Editor: E. C. Busby. pp. 23. 1953. 8°. *See* Saint Albans, *Diocese of*. **4708**. d. **14**.

BUSBY (F. G. C.)

—— Some Notes compiled for the use of Assistant Superintendents and the Supervisory Staff of Rubber Estates on the Organization of Daily Tasks, *etc*. pp. 17. *H. W. Cave & Co.: Colombo*, [1954?] 4°. **8222**. g. **40**.

BUSBY (George) *See* Derby, *County of*. Great News from Derbyshire . . . together with an account of the taking of one Busby, *etc*. 1681. *s. sh.* fol. **1298**. m. **11**. (**15**.)

—— The Tryal and Condemnation of George Busby, for High-Treason, as a Romish Priest and Jesuite . . . As it was faithfully taken, by a person of quality. pp. 38. *For Randolph Taylor: London*, 1681. fol. **6495**. i. **2**.

BUSBY (James)

—— *See* Ramsden (Eric) Busby of Waitangi, *etc*. 1942. 8°. **10861**. b. **2**.

—— Authentic Information relative to New South Wales, and New Zealand. [With a map.] pp. vi. 71. xxviii. *Joseph Cross: London*, 1832. 8°. **798**. e. **10**.

—— Journal of a Tour through some of the Vineyards of Spain and France. pp. iv. 138. *Stephens & Stokes: Sydney*, 1833. 8°. **7078**. bbb. **49**.

—— [Another edition.] With observations relative to the introduction of the vine into New South Wales. pp. xiv. 177. *London*, 1834. 12°. **966**. h. **29**.

—— A Manual of Plain Directions for planting and cultivating vineyards, and for making wine, in New South Wales. pp. 96. *R. Mansfield: Sydney*, 1830. 8°. C. **58**. b. **37**. (**2**.)

—— Our Colonial Empire and the Case of New Zealand. pp. xii. 194. *Williams & Norgate: London*, [1865.] 8°. **8154**. b. **29**.

—— A Treatise on the Culture of the Vine, and the art of making wine; compiled from the works of Chaptal and other French writers; and from the notes of the compiler during a residence in some of the wine provinces of France. pp. xxxiv. 270. *R. Howe: [Sydney,]* 1825. 8°. C. **58**. b. **37**. (**1**.)

BUSBY (John) *F.R.S.* Proposals for Drying of Malt with Hot Air; invented, and brought to perfection, by J. Busby. pp. 3. [1725?] fol. **816**. m. **13**. (**68**.)

BUSBY (*Sir* John) An Epithalamium upon the happy nuptials of Sr John Busby . . . and the eminently virtuous Lady Mrs Mary Dormer, *etc*. [*London*, 1668?] *s. sh.* fol. C. **40**. m. **11**. (**59**.)

BUSBY (John H.) Harpenden Hall, Harpenden, Herts. A short history, *etc*. [With plates.] pp. 18. [*Harpenden?* 1933.] 8°. **010352**. bbb. **66**.

BUSBY (Nicholas) *See* Kingsbury (Anna C.) A Historical Sketch of Nicholas Busby, the Emigrant, *etc*. 1924. 8°. **010855**. ee. **46**.

BUSBY (Olive Mary) Studies in the Development of the Fool in the Elizabethan Drama. A thesis, *etc*. pp. 87. *Oxford University Press: London*, 1923. 8°. **011795**. dd. **29**.

BUSBY (Oxymel) *Esq.*, *pseud.* *See* Periodical Publications.—*London*. The Scourge. By O. Busby. 1752, *etc*. fol. P.P. **5349**. db.

BUSBY (Richard) *See* Bagshaw (Edward) *the Younger*. A True and Perfect Narrative of the Differences between Mr Busby and Mr Bagshawe, *etc*. 1659. 4°. **731**. h. **3**. (**2**.)

—— *See* Barker (George F. R.) Memoir of Richard Busby, *etc*. [With portraits.] 1895. 4°. **4905**. f. **24**.

—— *See* Westminster School. Commemoration of the bicentenary of the death of Richard Busby . . . Nov. 18. 1895. [1895.] 8°. **4905**. df. **25**. (**12**.)

—— Hebraicae grammatices rudimenta, in usum Scholæ Westmonasteriensis. [By R. Busby.] pp. 28. 1717. 8°. *See* Hebrew Grammar. **12904**. bb. **20**.

—— [Another edition.] pp. 28. 1750. 8°. *See* Hebrew Grammar. **12903**. c. **47**. (**1**.)

—— [Another edition.] pp. 28. 1778. 8°. *See* Hebrew Grammar. **674**. d. **16**. (**1**.)

—— [Another edition.] Curavit et edidit Thomas Abrahamus Salmon. pp. ii. 83. *Sumptibus editoris: Londini*, [1794.] 8°. **12904**. bbb. **3**. (**1**.)

—— Grammatica Busbeiana auctior & emendatior, i.e. Rudimentum grammaticæ græco-latinæ metricum in usum nobilium puerorum in Schola Regia Westmonasterii. 2 pt. *Eliz. Redmayne: Londini*, 1702. 8°. **624**. c. **23**.

—— [Another edition.] pp. 222. *J. Redmayne; B. Barker: Londini*, 1722. 8°. **625**. d. **2**.

—— [Another copy.] **624**. d. **3**. (**1**.)

—— [Another edition.] pp. 222. [*London*, 1723?] 8°. **624**. c. **28**. (**4**.)

Imperfect; wanting the titlepage.

—— [Another edition.] pp. 230. *G. Ginger: Londini*, 1789. 8°. **674**. d. **16**. (**3**.)

—— Excerpta ex Grammatica Busbeiana, sive rudimento grammaticæ græco-latinæ metrico, *etc*. pp. 68. *E typographeo Clarendoniano: Oxonii*, 1819. 8°. **624**. d. **24**. (**2**.)

—— *See* Lowe (Solomon) A Critique on the Etymology of the Westminster Grammar [by R. Busby]. 1723. 8°. **625**. c. **26**. (**8**.)

BUSBY (Stanhope) Lectures on English Poetry, to the time of Milton. pp. vi. 118. *Whittaker & Co.: London*, 1837. 12°. **1162**. e. **22**.

BUSBY (Thomas) *See* Lucretius Carus (T.) [*English*.] The Nature of Things . . . Translated . . . with commentaries . . . by T. Busby. 1813. 4°. **840**. m. **39**.

—— The Age of Genius! A satire on the times. In a poetical epistle to a friend. pp. 48. *Harrison & Co.: London*, 1786. 4°. **11602**. h. **21**. (**8**.)

—— Arguments and Facts demonstrating that the Letters of Junius were written by John Lewis De Lolme . . . accompanied with memoirs of that "most ingenious foreigner," *etc*. [With facsimiles.] pp. 228. *Sherwood & Co.; J. Ridgway: London*, 1816. 8°. **8006**. dd. **12**.

BUSBY (Thomas)

—— A Complete Dictionary of Music. To which is prefixed a familiar introduction to the first principles of that science. *R. Phillips: London,* [1801.] 12°. **785.** b. **59.**

—— A Complete Dictionary of Music . . . Second edition, with additions and improvements. *Richard Phillips: London,* 1806. 8°. **7889.** a. **64.**

—— Fourth edition, with additions and improvements. pp. xxxiv. 330. *Richard Phillips: London,* 1817. 8°. **785.** d. **56.**

—— Concert Room and Orchestra Anecdotes, of Music and Musicians, ancient and modern. [With plates.] 3 vol. *Clementi & Co.; Knight & Lacey: London,* 1825. 12°. **1087.** a. **18–20.**
The titlepages are engraved.

—— A General History of Music, from the earliest times to the present; comprising the lives of eminent composers and musical writers, *etc.* 2 vol. *G. & W. B. Whittaker; Simpkin & Marshall: London,* 1819. 8°. **1042.** g. **22, 23.**

—— [Another copy.] A General History of Music, *etc.* *London,* 1819. 8°. Hirsch **608.**

—— A Grammar of Music . . . Second edition. pp. xvi. 367. *G. B. Whittaker: London,* 1826. 12°. **1042.** f. **20.**

—— A Musical Manual, or Technical directory, *etc.* pp. xi. 187. *Goulding & D'Almaine: London,* 1828. 12°. **1042.** g. **26.** (**2.**)

—— A Dictionary of Three Thousand Musical Terms, *etc.* (Third edition, revised by J. A. Hamilton.) pp. viii. 187. *D'Almaine & Co.: London,* [1840.] 12°. **1042.** e. **31.**

BUSBY (Thomas Lord) Civil and Military Costume of the City of London. Painted and engraved by T. L. Busby. 4 pt. *Robert Jennings: London,* 1824, 25. fol. **650.** a. **2.**

—— Costume of the Lower Orders of London. Painted and engraved from nature by T. L. Busby. *Baldwin & Co.: London,* [1820.] 4°. **7742.** e. **19.** (**2.**)

—— The Fishing Costume and Local Scenery of Hartlepool . . . Painted and engraved from nature by T. L. Busby. *J. Nichols & Son, etc.: London,* 1819. 4°. **7742.** e. **19.** (**1.**)

BUSBY (William) Episcopacy. pp. 15. *A. H. Goose: Norwich,* [1905.] 8°. **4377.** de. **13.** (**5.**)

BUSBY (William H.)

—— Our Evacuees: a reminiscence. pp. 23. *A. H. Stockwell: Ilfracombe,* [1941.] 8°. **4398.** aa. **26.**

BUSCA-PIQUE. *See* Periodical Publications.—*Lima.*

BUSCA (Gabriello) L'Architettura militare, *etc.* [With plates.] pp. 240. *G. B. Bidelli: Milano,* 1619. 4°. **534.** i. **4.** (**2.**)

—— Della espugnatione, e difesa delle fortezze, Libri due. [With illustrations.] pp. 256. *Nella stamperia dell'herede di N. Beuilacqua: Turino,* 1585. 4°. **62.** b. **15.**

—— [Another edition.] Di nuouo dall'autore corretti, & ampliati . . . Aggiontoui nel fine l'instruttione de' bombardieri. 2 pt. *Appresso G. D. Tarino: Turino,* 1598. 4°. C. **77.** d. **11.**

BUSCA (Ignazio) *Cardinal.* [For official documents issued by Cardinal Busca as Governor of Rome:] *See* Rome.—*The City.* [*Official Documents issued by the Governors of the City.*]

BUSCA (Jean de) Journée finie. pp. 197. *Paris,* 1895. 12°. **012550.** i. **40.**

BUSCADINI (Giovanni) La Famosa locandiera. Contrasto redicoloso, *etc.* [By G. Buscadini?] pp. 29. [1750?] 12°. *See* Locandiera. **11715.** a. **85.** (**5.**)

—— La Finta Turca, overo il Fonte d'Elicona. Contrasto di giudiata, *etc.* [In verse.] pp. 24. *Ronciglione,* [1750?] 12°. **11715.** a. **85.** (**4.**)

—— La Finta zingarella con il finto marchese, overo li Due facchini simili. Contrasto di giudiata, *etc.* [In verse.] pp. 34. *Macerata,* 1751. 12°. **11715.** a. **85.** (**2.**)

—— Li Finti giardinieri con li sposi trionfanti. Contrasto redicoloso, *etc.* [In verse.] pp. 29. *Ronciglione,* [1753?] 12°. **11715.** a. **85.** (**3.**)

—— La Schiava liberata, overo il Finto Giove. Contrasto di giudiata, *etc.* [In verse.] pp. 33. *Ronciglione,* [1752?] 12°. **11715.** a. **85.** (**1.**)

BUSCAIL (Michel) Étude clinique de l'hydrocèle. Thèse, *etc.* pp. 70. *Montpellier,* 1877. 4°. **7379.** l. **5.** (**2.**)

BUSCAINO (Alberto) *See* Buscaino Campo.

BUSCAINO-CAMPO (Alberto) *See* Fanfani (P.) Un Opuscoletto edificante. Fervorino. [A refutation of a charge respecting the publication of the work of P. Fanfani "La Storia di Attila Flagellum Dei" brought against the author by A. Buscaino Campo in "Alcuni aneddoti di storia letteraria in proposito della Bibliobiografia di P. Fanfani."] 1874. 8°. **1414.** h. **9.** (**15.**)

—— Del 'piè fermo' di Dante Alighieri [Inf. i. 30] non inteso dalla comune degl'interpreti. Esposizione, *etc.* pp. 73. *Trapani,* 1865. 8°. **11422.** cc. **23.** (**3.**)

—— Due brevi scritti criticofilologici. pp. 27. *Trapani,* 1886. 8°. **12902.** b. **33.** (**2.**)

—— Quistioni di critica religiosa, proposte da un uomo di buona fede ai pastori della sua chiesa. Edizione riveduta. pp. 45. *Trapani,* 1880. 8°. **3900.** g. **5.** (**8.**)

—— Un Saggio della libertà in Italia sotto il ministero riparatore. Narrazione documentata. pp. 27. *Trapani,* 1877. 8°. **8033.** e. **6.** (**6.**)

—— Scritti di polemica religiosa. pp. 246. *Palermo,* 1889. 8°. **3900.** c. **9.**

—— Sopra un verso della Divina Commedia [Inferno I, 30] non inteso dalla commune degl'interpreti. Lettera all'egregio signore professore Gaetano Daita. pp. 27. *Palermo,* 1861. 8°. 11420. bb. 46.

—— Spigolature guicciardiniane. pp. 16. *Trapani,* 1892. 8°. **10601.** ee. **19.** (**5.**)

—— Studii danteschi. pp. 189. *Trapani,* 1892. 8°. **11420.** d. **11.**

—— Edizione completa. pp. 268. *Trapani,* 1894. 8°. **11421.** d. **24.** (**1.**)

—— Giunta agli Studii danteschi. pp. 11. *Trapani,* 1894. 8°. **11421.** d. **24.** (**2.**)

BUSCAINO-CAMPO (ALBERTO)

—— Studj di filologia italiana. pp. 598. *Palermo*, 1877. 8°. **12941. e. 3.**

—— Appendice agli Studj di filologia italiana. pp. 94. *Palermo*, 1889. 8°. **12942. e. 20.**

—— Studj varj . . . Riveduti ed ampliati. pp. 560. *Trapani*, 1867. 8°. **12225. bbb. 9.**

—— Sul clericalismo e il potere temporale dei papi. Lettera, *etc.* pp. 30. *Firenze*, 1887. 8°. **8033. g. 30. (2.)**

BUSCALIONI (CARLO MICHELE) *See* BILLIA (L. M.) La Lega filellenica e l'ideale politico di C. M. Buscalioni, Memorie, *etc.* 1885. 8°. **8032. bb. 33. (2.)**

BUSCALIONI (LUIGI) *See* BECCARI (O.) Nuova Guinea, Selebes e Molucche . . . Con introduzione e note del prof. L. Buscalioni, *etc.* 1924. 8°. **10492. ff. 31.**

—— *See* MATTIROLO (O.) and BUSCALIONI (L.) Ricerche anatomo-fisiologiche sui tegumenti seminali delle papilionacee. 1892. 4°. [*Memorie della Reale Accademia delle Scienze di Torino.* ser. 2. tom. 42. pt. 1.] **Ac. 2816.**

—— Osservazioni e ricerche sulla cellula vegetale, *etc.* [With plates.] 1898. *See* ROME.—*The City.—Regio Istituto Botanico.* Annuario, *etc.* anno 7. 1884, *etc.* 4°. **Ac. 3241.**

—— Sulla struttura e sullo sviluppo del seme della " veronica hederaefolia L.," *etc.* 1893. *See* TURIN.—*Accademia delle Scienze.* Memorie. ser. 2. tom. 43. pt. 1. 1839, *etc.* 4°. **Ac. 2816.**

BUSCALIONI (LUIGI) and **FERMI** (CLAUDIO)

—— Contributo allo studio degli enzimi proteolitici e peptonizzanti dei vegetali, *etc.* 1898. *See* ROME.—*The City.—Regio Istituto Botanico.* Annuario, *etc.* anno 7. 1884, *etc.* 4°. **Ac. 3241.**

BUSCALIONI (LUIGI) and **LOPRIORE** (GIUSEPPE)

—— Il Pleroma tubuloso, l'endodermide midollare, la frammentazione desmica e la schizorrizia nelle radici della phoenix dactylifera L. pp. 102. pl. XII. 1910. *See* CATANIA.—*Accademia Gioenia di Scienze Naturali.* Atti, *etc.* ser. 5. vol. 3. 1825, *etc.* 8°. **Ac. 2805.**

BUSCALIONI (LUIGI) and **PURGOTTI** (ATTILIO)

—— Sulla diffusione e sulla dissociazione dei joni. (Con 20 tavole litografate.) 1908. *See* PAVIA.—*Università di Pavia.—Istituto Botanico dell' Università e Laboratorio Crittogamico.* Atti dell'Istituto Botanico, *etc.* Ser. 2. vol. 11. 1888, *etc.* 8°. **Ac. 107.**

BUSCALIONI (LUIGI) and **TRAVERSO** (GIOVANNI BATTISTA)

—— La Evoluzione morfologica del fiore in rapporto colla evoluzione cromatica del perianzio. Studi biologici. (Con 13 tavole litogr.) 1907. *See* PAVIA.—*Università di Pavia.—Istituto Botanico dell' Università e Laboratorio Crittogamico.* Atti dell'Istituto Botanico. ser. 2. vol. 10. 1888, *etc.* 8°. **Ac. 107.**

BUSCALIONI (PIETRO) La Consolata nella storia di Torino, del Piemonte e della Augusta Dinastia Sabauda. pp. 566. *Torino*, 1938. 8°. **20010. bb. 47.**

BUSCARDINI (GIOVANNI) *See* BUSCADINI.

BUSCARINI (GIUSEPPE) Dialoghi politico-filosofici ai Bagni di Tabiano. pp. 185. *Bologna*, 1870. 8°. **8033. aa. 22.**

—— [Another copy.] **8032. aaa. 17.**

—— Discussioni di filosofia razionale . . . Seconda edizione ritoccata dall'autore. 2 vol. *Milano*, 1857. 8°. **8464. aaa. 41.**

—— Lettere pastorali, *etc.* pp. 270. *Bologna*, 1869. 8°. **3902. bb. 23.**

BUSCARLET (K.)

—— Four Lessons on the Call from Africa. (Junior grade.) pp. 16. *Church Missionary Society: London*, [1927.] 8°. **4768. c. 37.**

—— Four Lessons on West Africa. (Junior grade.) pp. 15. *Church Missionary Society: London*, [1931.] 8°. **4768. c. 42.**

BUSCAROLI (REZIO) Forlì, Predappio, Rocca delle Caminate, Fornò, Pieve Quinta, Pieve Acquedotto. Con 163 illustrazioni. pp. 156. *Bergamo*, 1938. 8°. [*Collezione di monografie illustrate.* ser. 1. no. 116.] **7814. ccc. 1/114.**

—— Melozzo da Forlì nei documenti, nelle testimonianze dei contemporanei e nella bibliografia. [With illustrations, including reproductions.] pp. 256. *Roma*, 1938. 8°. [*Architettura, pittura, scultura.* no. 3.] **Ac. 104. fc/10.**

—— La Pittura di paesaggio in Italia, *etc.* pp. xv. 547. pl. C. *Bologna*, 1935. 8°. **2263. a. 8.**

—— La Pittura romagnola del quattrocento. Con 136 illustrazioni nel testo. pp. xiv. 468. *Faenza*, 1931. 8°. **7852. t. 8.**

BUSCAYOLO, GASPARO SQUARZAFIGO, *Marquis de. See* SQUARZAFIGO.

BUSCELLI (NATALITIO) *Baron de Serra Valle.* Canzoni siciliane. *See* SANCLEMENTE (P. G.) Le Muse siciliane, *etc.* pt. 1. 1662. 12°. **1070. b. 30.**

BUSCEMI (NICCOLÒ) Appendix ad Tabularium Regiæ ac Imperialis Capellæ Divi Petri in Regio palatio Panhormitano curis N. Buscemi. pp. 48. *Panormi*, 1839. fol. **4605. i. 3. (2.)**

—— Notizie della basilica di San Pietro, detta la Cappella Regia, raccolte ed esposte dal S. N. Buscemi. [With a map.] pp. 64. 48. pl. XVII. *Palermo*, 1840. 4°. **7814. f. 17.**

The titlepage is engraved.

—— La Vita di Giovanni di Procida privata e pubblica. Saggio storico. pp. 188. lxiv. *Palermo*, 1836. 8°. **10631. bbb. 16.**

BÜSCH (   ) [For the German surname of this form:] *See* BUESCH.

BUSCH (ADOLF)

—— Concerto del trio Busch, *etc.* [A programme of a concert of works by Beethoven and Schubert, with analytical notes and with a facsimile of the " Autografo dei tre maestri," containing works by Beethoven and Schubert.] [1935.] 8°. **Hirsch 2334.**

BUSCH (ADOLPH) Die Organisation und Buchführung des Eisengiesserei- und Maschinenbau-Betriebes. Nebst einem Anhange der wichtigsten Hilfstabellen zur Berechnung der beim Giesserei- und Maschinenbau-Betriebe vorkommenden Gegenstände. pp. iv. 182. *Nordhausen*, 1854. 8°. **7954**. cc. **6**.

BUSCH (ALEXANDER VAN DEN) called LE SYLVAIN. *See* BUSCHE.

BUSCH (ANDREAS CASPAR FRIEDRICH) Ad audiendam orationem . . . d. VI. Dec. habendam qua diem Nicolai I. . . . sancto nomini dicatum concelebrabit Universitas Literarum Dorpatensis invitat Fridericus Busch . . . Inest librorum S. Aurelii Augustini, praeter epistolas et sermones, tum servatorum tum perditorum, recensus plane novus, methodo quadam adhibita systematico-chronologica. pp. 20. *Dorpati*, 1826. 4°. **11904**. a. **39**. (**2**.)

—— Der Fürst Karl Lieven und die kaiserliche Universität Dorpat unter seiner Oberleitung. Aus der Erinnerung und nach seinen Briefen und amtlichen Erlassen geschildert von Dr. F. Busch. [With plates, including a portrait.] pp. 178. *Dorpat & Leipzig*, 1846. 4°. **732**. l. **16**.

—— Predigt am 13. Sonntag nach Trinitatis. *See* KOCH (E. E.) Evangelische Hauskanzel, *etc.* 1866, *etc.* 8°. **4423**. k. **19**.

BUSCH (ARTHUR JOHN) *See* MARCH (Michael) *pseud.* [i.e. A. J. Busch.]

BUSCH (AUGUST) *of Frankfort.* Geschlechtskrankheiten in deutschen Grossstädten, *etc.* pp. 42. *Breslau*, 1918. 8°. [*Schriften des Verbandes deutscher Städtestatistiker.* Hft. 6.] P.P. **3874**. cc.

BUSCH (AUGUST) *of Reval.* Eesti raamatute nimekiri. pp. 47. *Ревель*, 1897. 8°. **011901**. h. **14**.

BUSCH (AUGUST LUDWIG) *See* KONIGSBERG, *East Prussia.—Academia Albertina.—Sternwarte.* Astronomische Beobachtungen, *etc.* [Abt. 22–26, 29 edited by A. L. Busch.] 1815, *etc.* fol. **8564**. h.

—— Beobachtungen und Wahrnehmungen, welche bei der totalen Sonnenfinsterniss am 28. Juli 1851. gemacht worden sind. Ein Vortrag, *etc.* [With a plate.] pp. 47. *Königsberg*, 1852. 8°. **8560**. aa. **51**. (**2**.)

—— Reduction of the Observations made by Bradley at Kew and Wansted, to determine the quantities of aberration and nutation. pp. 25. 56. *University Press: Oxford*, 1838. 4°. **716**. i. **24**.

—— Systematisches Verzeichniss der in der Bibliothek der Universitäts-Sternwarte zu Königsberg enthaltenen Bücher. Herausgegeben von Dr. A. L. Busch . . . Zu der 25sten Abtheilung der Königsberger Beobachtungen gehörig. pp. 102. 1852. 8°. *See* KONIGSBERG, *East Prussia.—Academia Albertina.—Sternwarte.* **11901**. bb. **12**.

—— Verzeichniss sämmtlicher Werke, Abhandlungen, Aufsätze und Bemerkungen von Friedr. Wilh. Bessel. Zusammengetragen, chronologisch geordnet und mit einem gedrängten Sachregister versehen von Dr. A. L. Busch . . . Aus der XXIV. Abtheil. der Königsberger Astron. Beobachtungen . . . abgedruckt. pp. 34. *Königsberg*, 1849. 4°. **10705**. h. **18**. (**2**.)

—— Vorschule der darstellenden Geometrie . . . Mit einem Vorwort von C. G. J. Jacobi. pp. xii. 108. *Berlin*, 1846. 8°. **8531**. d. **1**.

BUSCH (AXEL) *See* CHRISTLIEB (M. L.) Opad Bakke i Indien . . . Oversat af A. Busch, *etc.* 1932. 8°. **20003**. f. **17**.

BUSCH (B.) *See* ROSEN (J.) Halbe Dichter. Schwank . . . nach einer Idee des B. Busch. 1885. 8°. **11746**. f. **16**. (**2**.)

—— *See* ROSEN (J.) Half-Poets . . . Based upon an idea of B. Busch. [1885.] fol. **11747**. l. **5**.

BUSCH (B.) *Schuhmachermeister.* Deutsches Reichspatent. Zur Schuhreform-Frage. Die deutsche Form und die Herstellung naturgemässer Leisten. Referat gehalten in der 4ten allgemeinen deutschen Schuhmacher-Fachconferenz zu Dresden im August 1884 . . . Als Beilage: 3 Tafeln, *etc.* pp. ii. 6. *Erfurt*, 1884. 8°. **8309**. e. **35**. (**2**.)

BUSCH (BENEDICTUS)

—— De initiatione Christiana secundum Sanctum Augustinum. *In:* Ephemerides liturgicae. anno 52. no. 2. pp. 159–178. 1938. 8°. P.P. **22**. b.

—— De modo quo S. Augustinus descripserit initiationem Christianam. *In:* Ephemerides liturgicae. anno 52. no. 4. pp. 385–483. 1938. 8°. P.P. **22**. b.

BUSCH (CARL) *See* also BUSCH (Karl)

BUSCH (CARL) *Architekt in Alsfeld.* Die Bauführung. Hand- und Hülfsbuch für die Praxis der Bautechniker, *etc.* pp. viii. 256. *Leipzig*, 1871. 8°. [*Schule der Baukunst.* Bd. 4. Abt. 4.] **7814**. bb. **6**.

—— Die Baustyle . . . Zweite Auflage der "Säulenordnungen und Baustyle" von Dr. L. Bergmann in vollständiger Umgestaltung. 2 Tl. *Leipzig*, 1864, 68. 8°. [*Schule der Baukunst.* Bd. 1. Abt. 2.] **7814**. bb. **6**.

BUSCH (CARL WILHELM CHRISTIAN) Kurzgefasste Geschichte der christlichen Kirche . . . Dritte verbesserte und vermehrte Ausgabe . . . besorgt von F. C. Bestenbostel. pp. viii. 140. *Hannover*, 1838. 8°. **4531**. a. **8**.

BUSCH (CHRISTIAN) Lehren aus der Elementar-Mathematik . . . Mit 9 lithographirten Tafeln. pp. viii. 241. *Münster*, 1845. 8°. **8530**. b. **19**.

BUSCH (CHRISTOPHORUS FR. GULIELMUS) Dissertatio inauguralis medica exhibens noxas ex incauto vasorum aeneorum usu profluentes, exemplis atque experimentis quibusdam illustratas, *etc.* pp. 62. *Gottingae*, [1790.] 8°. **7386**.* b. (**2**.)

BUSCH (CLAMOR. JOH. VON DEM) De jure prohibendi extructionem molendini. 1745. *See* STRYKIUS (S.) Viri . . . illustris . . . S. Strykii . . . opera omnia. vol. 7. 1743, *etc.* fol. **498**. g. **9**.

BUSCH (CLEMENS AUGUST) Specimen doctrinae de copticae linguae praepositionibus ac particulis. Dissertatio inauguralis, *etc.* pp. 28. *Berolini*, [1859.] 8°. **8363**. a. **8**. (**1**.)

BUSCH (DIETRICH WILHELM HEINRICH) *See* GRAEFE (C. F. von) Encyclopädisches Wörterbuch der medicinischen Wissenschaften. Herausgegeben von C. F. v. Gräfe (D. W. H. Busch), *etc.* 1828, *etc.* 8°. **773**. d. **1–24** & e. **1–13**.

—— *See* PERIODICAL PUBLICATIONS.—*Leipzig.* Summarium des neuesten aus der gesammten Medicin . . . herausgegeben (in Vereinigung mit D. W. H. Busch) von L. H. Unger und F. A. Klose. 1828, *etc.* 8°. P.P. **3140**.

BUSCH (DIETRICH WILHELM HEINRICH)

—— *See* PERIODICAL PUBLICATIONS.—*Weimar*. Gemeinsame deutsche Zeitschrift für Geburtskunde. (Herausgegeben durch D. W. H. Busch.) 1827, *etc.* 8°. P.P. **3173.**

—— Atlas geburtshülflicher Abbildungen, mit Bezugnahme auf das Lehrbuch der Geburtskunde. pp. xiii. 147. pl. XXXXVIII. *Berlin*, 1841. 8°. **7581.** g. **3.**

—— Das Geschlechtsleben des Weibes in physiologischer, pathologischer und therapeutischer Hinsicht. 5 Bd. *Leipsig*, 1839–44. 8°. **1177.** c. **26–30.**

—— Lehrbuch der Geburtskunde . . . Vierte vermehrte und verbesserte Auflage, *etc.* pp. xvi. 560. *Berlin*, 1842. 8°. **7581.** ee. **21.**

—— Fünfte vermehrte und verbesserte Auflage, *etc.* pp. xvi. 568. *Berlin*, 1849. 8°. **7581.** cc. **11.**

—— Die theoretische und practische Geburtskunde durch Abbildungen erläutert. pp. xii. 569. *Berlin*, 1838. 8°. **778.** g. **27.**

—— Atlas, *etc.* pp. 8. pl. L. *Berlin*, 1838. fol. **789.** h. **33.**

BUSCH (DIETRICH WILHELM HEINRICH) and **MOSER** (ADOLPHUS)

—— An Essay on Uterine Hæmorrhage, translated from Busch and Moser's Handbuch der Geburtskunde. *See* COPEMAN (Edward) Records of Obstetric Consultation, *etc.* 1856. 8°. **1177.** c. **25.**

BUSCH (E. H. VON) Beiträge zur Geschichte und Statistik des Kirchen- und Schulwesens der ev.-augsburg. Gemeinden im Königreich Polen, *etc.* pp. ix. 266. *St. Petersburg, Leipzig ; Leipzig* [printed], 1867. 8°. **4695.** b. **23.**

—— Materialien zur Geschichte und Statistik des Kirchen- und Schulwesens der ev.-luth. Gemeinden in Russland . . . Gesammelt und herausgegeben von E. H. Busch . . . Mit 2 Karten in Farbendruck. pp. xxvi. 696. *St. Petersburg ; Leipzig* [printed], 1862. 8°. **4695.** cc. **32.**

—— Personalstatus der evangelisch-lutherischen und evangelisch-reformirten Kirche in Russland herausgegeben von E. H. von Busch. pp. 99. *St. Petersburg*, 1875. 8°. **3926.** aaa. **7.**

BUSCH (ERNST) and **CHOMSKAS** (TĒODORAS) Lietuviškai vokiškas žodynas . . . Litauisch-deutsches Wörterbuch, *etc.* dal. 1. pp. 305. *Berlin & Leipzig*, 1927. 8°. **12975.** c. **30.**

No more published.

BUSCH (ERNST) *of Bad Godesberg.*

—— Die Idee des Tragischen in der deutschen Klassik. pp. 165. *Halle*, 1942. 8°.

[*Deutsche Vierteljahrsschrift für Literaturwissenschaft und Geistesgeschichte. Buchreihe.* Bd. 26.] W.P. B. **263/26.**

BUSCH (ERNST) *of Remschied.* Der Irrtum von Karl Marx. Aus E. Busch's Nachlass herausgegeben von Dr. Arthur Mülberger. pp. 59. *Basel*, 1894. 8°. **8282.** cc. **47.** (**13.**)

BUSCH (F.) *Kanzleirath im Kriegsministerium*, and **PFLUG** (FERDINAND) Preussens Heer. Eine Geschichte der preussischen Regimenter, ihrer Kriegsthaten und ihrer Führer . . . Herausgegeben von F. Busch und F. Pflug. Bd. 1 ; Bd. 2. pp. 1–160. *Berlin*, [1856–60.] 8°. [*Militairische Unterhaltungsbibliothek.* Bdchn. 4–7.] **8823.** b. **6.**

No more published.

BUSCH (F. B.) *See* PERIODICAL PUBLICATIONS.—*Leipsic.* Archiv für Theorie und Praxis des allgemeinen deutschen Handelsrechts . . . Herausgegeben von F. B. Busch. 1863, *etc.* 8°. P.P. **1385.** d.

—— Die Bienenzucht in Strohwohnungen mit unbeweglichem Wabenbau, *etc.* pp. xiv. 204. *Leipzig*, 1862. 8°. **7295.** bbb. **14.**

—— Handbuch des heutigen in Deutschland geltenden Bienen-Rechtes, *etc.* pp. 154. *Arnstadt*, 1830. 8°. **5511.** cc. **8.**

—— Die neuen Criminalgesetzbücher des Königreichs Sachsen, des Grossherzogthums Sachsen-Weimar-Eisenach, der Herzogthümer Sachsen-Altenburg und Sachsen-Meiningen, sowie des Fürstenthums Schwarzburg-Sondershausen, mit literärischen, praktischen und kritischen Bemerkungen herausgegeben von F. B. Busch. pp. xxiv. 424. 1848. 8°. *See* SAXONY.—*The Kingdom.* [*Laws, etc.* —I.] **5605.** c. **7.**

—— Die Stimme der Praxis bei den höchsten deutschen Landestribunalen und anderen Spruchcollegien über verschiedene Streitfragen aus dem Gebiete des bürgerlichen Rechts und Processes. pp. x. 378. *Erlangen*, 1862. 8°. **5510.** bb. **9.**

—— Theoretische-praktische Darstellung der Rechte geschwächter Frauenspersonen gegen ihre Verführer und der unehelichen Kinder gegen ihre Erzeuger . . . Nebst einem Anhange, enthaltend die hierüber bestehenden Verordnungen der . . . oestreichischen . . . preussischen, baierschen und königl. sächsischen Gesetzgebungen, *etc.* pp. xxiv. 502. *Ilmenau*, 1828. 8°. **5176.** bbb. **14.**

—— Was ist von der Dzierzon'schen Bienenzucht-Methode zu halten, oder: Wie ist der Bienenzucht in Wahrheit aufzuhelfen besonders bei dem Landmanne? Nebst Grundzügen zu einem sichern Betriebe derselben in honigarmen Gegenden. pp. xii. 136. *Eisenach*, 1853. 8°. **7295.** b. **63.** (**2.**)

BUSCH (FRANZ) *See* BERGSØE (J. V.) Von der Piazza del Popolo . . . Deutsch von F. Busch. 1871. 8°. **12553.** df. **13.**

—— *See* BJØRNSON (B. M.) [*Single Works.*] [De Nygifte.] Die Neuvermählten . . . Deutsch von F. Busch. 1871. 16°. **11754.** a. **13.**

BUSCH (FRÉDÉRIC) Découvertes d'un bibliophile [i.e. F. Busch], ou Lettres sur différents points de morale enseignés dans quelques séminaires de France. pp. 30. 1843. 8°. *See* BIBLIOPHILE. 8356.e.24.(1.)

—— Deuxième édition. pp. 41. 1843. 8°. *See* BIBLIOPHILE. **1387.** i. **11.**

—— [Another copy.] **8355.** f. **5.**

—— Supplément aux découvertes d'un bibliophile, ou Réponse à l'écrit intitulé: Les Découvertes d'un bibliophile réduites à leur juste valeur. [By F. Busch.] pp. 154. 4. 1843. 8°. *See* BIBLIOPHILE. **1387.** i. **7.**

—— [Another copy.] **F.P.** **8355.** f. **32.** (**1.**)

BUSCH (Frédéric)

—— Réponse du bibliophile [i.e. F. Busch] à la consultation des quatre avocats du barreau de Strasbourg. pp. 78. *Paris*, 1844. 8°. **1356**. e. **37**.

—— Catalogue de la bibliothèque de feu M. F. Busch, *etc.* pp. 348. *Strasbourg*, 1856. 8°. **823**. g. **62**.

BUSCH (Frederick Carl) Laboratory Manual of Physiology . . . Illustrated. pp. ix. 206. *Baillière & Co.: London; New York* printed, 1906. 8°. **7405**. cc. **11**.

BUSCH (Fridericus) *See* Busch (Friedrich)

BUSCH (Frieda) Tribute und ihre Wirkungen untersucht am Beispiel der französischen Zahlungen nach dem Krieg 1870/71. Inaugural-Dissertation, *etc.* pp. 97. *Basel*, 1936. 8°. **8231**. g. **16**.

BUSCH (Friedrich) *Direktor der Stadtbibliothek zu Hannover.* Bibliographie der niedersächsischen Geschichte für die Jahre 1908–1932. pp. xix. 749. 1938. 8°. *See* Hanover.—*Historische Kommission für die Provinz Hannover, etc.* Ac. **7348/3**.

BUSCH (Friedrich) *Physicist*, and **JENSEN** (Christian Albrecht Theodor) Tatsachen und Theorien der atmosphärischen Polarisation nebst Anleitung zu Beobachtungen verschiedener Art, *etc.* pp. 532. *Hamburg*, 1911. 8°. [*Mitteilungen aus dem Physikalischen Staatslaboratorium in Hamburg.*] P.P. **1766**. f. (**11**.)

BUSCH (Friedrich) *Professor at Dorpat.* *See* Busch (Andreas C. F.)

BUSCH (Friedrich) *Professor für Chirurgie a. d. Universität zu Berlin.* Allgemeine Orthopädie, Gymnastik und Massage, *etc.* pp. 272. *Leipzig*, 1882. 8°. [*Handbuch der allgemeinen Therapie.* Bd. 2. Tl. 2.] **7441**. dd.

—— General Orthopædics, Gymnastics and Massage . . . Translation edited by Noble Smith. 1886. *See* Ziemssen (H. W. von) Von Ziemssen's Handbook of General Therapeutics. vol. 5. 1885, *etc.* 8°. **7439**. e. **10**.

—— De raro quodam exemplo monstrositatis humanae. Dissertatio inauguralis, *etc.* pp. 31. *Berolini*, [1866.] 8°. **7385**. b. (**16**.)

—— Regeneration und entzündliche Gewebebildung. pp. 24. *Leipzig*, [1880.] 8°. [*Sammlung klinischer Vorträge.* Chirurgie no. 53.] **7441**. g.

—— Ueber die Schädelbildung bei niederen Menschenrassen. 1894. *See* Berlin.—*Deutsche Odontologische Gesellschaft.* Verhandlungen, *etc.* Bd. 6. 1889, *etc.* 8°. Ac. **3774**.

—— Zur Physiologie und Pathologie der Zähne des Elefanten. 1890. *See* Berlin.—*Deutsche Odontologische Gesellschaft.* Verhandlungen, *etc.* Bd. 1. 1889, *etc.* 8°. Ac. **3774**.

BUSCH (Fritz)

—— Aus dem Leben eines Musikers, *etc.* [An autobiography. With plates, including portraits.] pp. 224. *Zürich*, [1952.] 8°. **10710**. k. **21**.

—— [Aus dem Leben eines Musikers.] Pages from a Musician's Life . . . Translated by Marjorie Strachey. [With plates, including portraits.] pp. 223. *Hogarth Press: London*, 1953. 8°. **10710**. cc. **29**.

BUSCH (Fritz Otto)

—— Das Buch von der Kriegsmarine. Herausgegeben von F. O. Busch . . . unter Mitarbeit von Admiral a. D. Gladisch [and others] . . . Dritte wesentlich erweiterte und verbesserte Auflage, *etc.* pp. 192. pl. 48. *Berlin*, [1939.] 8°. **8803**. bb. **5**.

—— Drei kleine Kreuzer: Karlsruhe I, Kolberg, Regensburg . . . Bilder und Kartenzeichnungen von Marinemaler Walter Zeeden. pp. 436. *Berlin*, [1936.] 4°. **9086**. b. **1**.

—— Flug nach England. Ein Beitrag zum gegenseitigen Verstehen, *etc.* [With plates.] pp. 106. *München, Berlin*, [1937.] 8°. **010351**. k. **53**.

—— Das Geheimnis der "Bismarck." Ein Tatsachenbericht, *etc.* [With plates.] pp. 131. *Hannover*, 1950. 8°. **9102**. fff. **15**.

—— Germanische Seefahrt. [On the Vikings.] Von . . . F. O. Busch und . . . Heinz Docter . . . Mit 6 Karten und 26 Plänen. pp. 322. *Berlin*, [1935.] 8°. **08805**. h. **35**.

—— Die Kriegsmarine, 1919–1939. Aufgaben, Wiederaufbau, Dienst, Laufbahnen und Schiffsliste. [With plates.] pp. 188. [1940.] 8°. *See* Germany.—*Navy.—Oberkommando.* **8803**. bbb. **2**.

—— Minen und Menschen . . . Mit 33 Bildern, *etc.* [On the recovery of mines in the North Sea in 1919 and 1920.] pp. 164. *Berlin*, [1933.] 8°. **8808**. de. **20**.

—— Narvik. Vom Heldenkampf deutscher Zerstörer. [With plates.] pp. 408. *Gütersloh*, [1940.] 8°. **09100**. a. **63**.

—— Niobe. Ein deutsches Schicksal. Bearbeitet von F. O. Busch. [The story of the training ship "Niobe." By various authors. With plates.] pp. 90. *Leipzig*, [1932.] 8°. **08805**. i. **45**.

—— "7 Uhr 30 seeklar." Mit der Flotte nach Norwegen, *etc.* pp. 108. pl. 54. *Leipzig*, 1934. 8°. **10498**. cc. **14**.

—— Traditionshandbuch der Kriegsmarine. Von Korvettenkapitän a. D. F. O. Busch unter Mitarbeit von Dr. Gerhard Ramlow, *etc.* [With illustrations.] pp. 282. *München, Berlin*, [1937.] 8°. **08805**. b. **4**.

—— Tragödie am Nordkap. Untergang des Schlachtschiffes "Scharnhorst." Ein Tatsachenbericht, *etc.* [With plates.] pp. 147. *Hannover*, [1952.] 8°. **9102**. e. **17**.

—— Unsere neuen Zerstörer. [With plates.] pp. 72. *Berlin*, [1937.] 8°. **8808**. k. **6**.

—— Unter der alten Flagge, 1914–1918. Von F. O. Busch . . . unter Mitarbeit von Hermann Lorey. [A photographic record of the German Navy in the European War.] pp. 368. *Berlin*, [1935.] 8°. **9086**. aa. **10**.

—— Das Volksbuch vom Skagerrak. Augenzeugenberichte deutscher und englischer Mitkämpfer. [With plates.] pp. xii. 323. *Berlin*, [1938.] 8°. **09079**. d. **36**.

—— Weisse Segel—weite Meere. Segelschulschiffe der Kriegsmarine. Nach Berichten, Tagebuchblättern und Unterlagen des Kommandanten des Segelschulschiffes "Albert Leo Schlageter" . . . Bernhard Rogge. [With plates.] pp. 187. *Berlin*, [1939.] 8°. **8803**. c. **8**.

BUSCH (Fritz Otto) and **RAMLOW** (Gerhard)

—— Deutsche Seekriegsgeschichte. Fahrten und Taten in zwei Jahrtausenden. Mit Textzeichnungen und Bildtafeln von Marinemaler Walter Zeeden. pp. 864. *Gütersloh*, [1940.] 8°. **8809**. cc. **10**.

BUSCH (Gabriel Christoph Benjamin) Handbuch der Erfindungen. Vierte, ganz umgearbeitete und sehr vermehrte, Auflage. 12 Tl. *Eisenach*, 1802–22. 8°. **1393**. e. **1–11**.

—— Versuch eines Handbuchs der Erfindungen. 8 Tl. *Eisenach*, 1790–98. 8°. **1137**. b. **13–20**.

BUSCH (Georg) Die andere Beschreibung von dem Cometen, welcher in dem vergangenen 1572. Jar erschienen, vnd noch jtziger zeit in diesem 73. Jar . . . sichtbarlichen vorhanden, etc. G. Baumann: *Erffurdt*, [1573.] 4°. **1395**. c. **23**.

BUSCH (Georg Friedrich) Eva von Lauenburg und Adelbert von Stecklenburg. Eine Rittergeschichte aus den Zeiten der Kreuzzüge. 2 Bd. *Leipzig*, 1863. 8°. **12548**. bbb. **2**.

BUSCH (Georgius Nicolaus) Observationum ad Euripidis Phœnissas specimen, *etc.* pp. 36. *Rostochii*, 1826. 4°. T. **1340**. (**10**.)

BUSCH (Gerda Natalie) Untersuchungen zum Wesen der τυχη in den Tragödien des Euripides. Inaugural-Dissertation, *etc.* pp. 72. *Heidelberg*, 1937. 8°. **11312**. t. **37**.

BUSCH (Gerhard von dem) *See* Berg (F. T.) [Om torsk hos barn.] Ueber die Schwämmchen bei Kindern . . . Übersetzt von G. von dem Busch. 1848. 8°. **1178**. d. **28**.

—— *See* Huss (M.) [Om Sveriges endemiska sjukdomar.] Ueber die endemischen Krankheiten Schwedens. Ein Vortrag . . . übersetzt und mit einigen Anmerkungen versehen von Dr. G. von dem Busch. 1854. 8°. **7686**. c. **57**. (**3**.)

—— *See* Huss (M.) [Om typhus och typhoidfeberns statistika förhållanden och behandling.] Statistik und Behandlung des Typhus und Typhoid-Fiebers . . . Übersetzt von Dr. G. von dem Busch. 1856. 8°. **7560**. a. **43**.

—— *See* Malmsten (P. H.) [Om bright'sker njursjukdomen.] Ueber die Bright'sche Nierenkrankheit . . . Übersetzt und mit einigen Anmerkungen versehen von G. von dem Busch. 1846. 8°. **7641**. g. **2**.

—— Mittheilungen über die Cholera-Epidemie im Königreiche Dänemark im Jahre 1853. pp. ix. 193. *Bremen*, 1858. 8°. **7561**. f. **16**.

BUSCH (Gerhardus von dem) Disputatio theologica inauguralis de incessu Dei in sanctuario, ex Psalmi LXVIII. verss. 23–28, ejusdemque Psalmi argumento et oeconomia, *etc. Praes.* P. Latané. pp. 136. *Franequeræ*, 1707. 4°. **1014**. b. **14**. (**13**.)

—— [Another copy.] T. **2172**. (**28**.)

BUSCH (Gisela)

—— *See* Rippel-Baldes (A.) and Busch (G.) Über den Gehalt von Involutionsformen der Mikroorganismen an Nucleinsäuren und Aminosäuren. [1954.] 8°. [*Nachrichten der Akademie der Wissenschaften in Göttingen.* Math.-phys. Klasse. Biologisch-physiologisch-chem. Abt. Jahrg. 1954. no. 4.] Ac. **670/8**. (**14**.)

BUSCH (Gulielmus) *See* Busch (Wilhelm) *Professor der Chirurgie an der Universität Bonn.*

BUSCH (Gustav Robert August)

—— Beitrag zur Physiologie der sensiblen Hautnerven . . . Inaugural-Dissertation, *etc.* pp. 58. *Halle*, 1872. 8°. **7386**. c. **16**. (**6**.)

BUSCH (H.) *Kreisgerichtsrat in Sondershausen. See* Periodical Publications.—*Berlin.* Zeitschrift für deutschen Civilprozess . . . herausgegeben von H. Busch (von H. Busch und F. Vierhaus). 1879, *etc.* 8°. P.P. **1294**. d.

—— *See* Periodical Publications.—*Leipzig.* Archiv für Theorie und Praxis des allgemeinen deutschen Handelsrechts, *etc.* (Neue Folge. Bd. 9–12. Fortgesetzt von H. Busch.) 1863, *etc.* 8°. P.P. **1385**. d.

BUSCH (H.) *of Calcutta.* H. Busch's Journal of a Cruise amongst the Nicobar Islands. [With plates and a map.] pp. 50. *For private circulation: Calcutta*, 1845. 8°. **10055**. df. **8**.

BUSCH (H.) *Stabsarzt.* Grösse, Gewicht und Brustumfang von Soldaten. Studien über ihre Entwickelung und ihren Einfluss auf die militairische Tauglichkeit . . . Mit 6 Holzschnitten. pp. iv. 85. *Berlin*, 1878. 8°. **8823**. m. **13**. (**9**.)

BUSCH (H. K.) Die Görbersdorfer Heilanstalt des Dr. H. Brehmer. Eine Klinik für chronische Lungenkranke, *etc.* [With a map.] pp. iv. 135. *Berlin*, 1875. 8°. **7470**. de. **3**.

BUSCH (Harald) *See* Sauerlandt (M.) Die Kunst der letzten 30 Jahre. Herausgegeben durch H. Busch, *etc.* [1935.] 8°. **07805**. f. **66**.

—— Alt-Hamburg. Bilder einer alten Stadt. Mit 72 Bildtafeln . . . Einleitung und Bildzusammenstellung von H. Busch. pp. xix. 78. *Hamburg*, [1939.] 4°. **10235**. f. **62**.

—— Meister des Nordens. Die altniederdeutsche Malerei, 1450–1550. [With reproductions.] pp. 352. *Hamburg*, 1940. 4°. L.R. **269**. b. **9**.

—— Meister Wolter und sein Kreis. I. Kirchliche Holzskulptur und Malerei des XVI. Jahrhunderts in Hildesheim vor der Einführung der Reformation, *etc.* pp. vii. 295. pl. XVI. *Strassburg*, 1931. 8°. [*Studien zur deutschen Kunstgeschichte.* Hft. 286.] **7805**. ss. **82**. *No more published.*

—— So war der U-Boot-Krieg. [With plates.] pp. 400. *Bielefeld*, [1952.] 8°. **9102**. bbb. **18**.

—— [So war der U-Boot-Krieg.] U-Boats at War . . . Translated . . . by L. P. R. Wilson. [With plates.] pp. 286. *Putnam: London*, 1955. 8°. **9102**. m. **29**.

BUSCH (Harald) and **BREIDENSTEIN** (H.)

—— Germany: the south, the west and the north. A volume of photographs . . . by Dr. Paul Wolff & Tritschler . . . and other leading photographers . . . Picture captions by Dr. H. Busch. (Editors: H. Busch and H. Breidenstein.) pp. 208. *B. T. Batsford: London; Frankfurt* printed, [1954.] 4°. **10250**. n. **18**.

BUSCH (Henricus) *Resp. See* Ames (William) *D.D.* Animadversiones in synodalia scripta Remonstrantium. disp. 9, 19, 28. 1629. 8°. **4255**. aa. **10**.

BUSCH (HENRICUS à) Disputatio medica inauguralis, de delirio, *Apud viduam & hæredes J. Elsevirii: Lugduni Batavorum*, 1668. 4°. **1185**. g. **8**. (**31**.)

—— Disputatio medica prima. De arte medica, *etc. Praes.* F. Schuyl. *Apud viduam & hæredes J. Elsevirii: Lugduni Batavorum*, 1665. 4°. **1185**. g. **6**. (**34**.)

—— Laurus Batava, in honorem . . . Henrici à Büsch, cum . . . de delirio habita disputatione summis in medicina honoribus efferretur, decantata ab amicis, *etc. Lat. & Dutch. Apud viduam & hæredes J. Elsevirii: Lugduni Batavorum*, 1668. 4°. **1185**. g. **8**. (**37**.)

BUSCH (HENRICUS VAN DEN) *See* BUSCH (Henricus à)

BUSCH (HENRICUS LUDOVICUS) Dissertatio inauguralis medica. De haemorrhagiis uteri, *etc.* pp. 74. *Marburgi Cattorum*, [1795.] 12°. T. **591**. (**23**.)

BUSCH (HENRY MILLER)

—— Conference Methods in Industry. A practical handbook of basic theory of group thinking and tested applications to industrial situations. pp. x. 107. *Harper & Bros.: [New York*, 1949.] 8°. **8222**. aa. **48**.

BUSCH (HUGO) Die ursprünglichen Lieder vom Ende der Nibelungen. Ein Beitrag zur Nibelungenfrage. pp. 73. *Halle*, 1882. 8°. **11840**. l. **31**. (**6**.)

BUSCH (I. ERNESTUS) Dissertatio inauguralis sistens experimenta quaedam circa mortem, *etc.* pp. 40. *Halae*, [1819.] 8°. **7386.c.7.(9.)**

BUSCH (ISIDOR) *See* EPHEMERIDES. Kalender und Jahrbuch für Israeliten, *etc.* (Herausgegeben von I. Busch.) 1842, *etc.* 12°. P.P. **2377**. g.

—— *See* PERIODICAL PUBLICATIONS.—*Vienna.* Oesterreichisches Central-Organ für Glaubensfreiheit, Cultur, Geschichte und Literatur der Juden . . . Redigirt von I. Busch und Dr. M. Letteris. 1848. 4°. P.P. **17**. b.

BUSCH (J. G.) Anweisung zur Anfertigung einer Universal-Hefe in flüssiger Form, in Form der Press- oder Pfundhefe, und als Hefenpulver, *etc.* pp. 7. *Wittenberg*, 1846. 8°. **1400**. i. **53**. (**3**.)

BUSCH (J. W.) Der Zimmerheiz-Koch-Sparofen. Eine neue Zugabe zu dem Werke: Die beste und wohlfeilste Feuerungsart nach einem neuen Systeme, *etc.* pp. 22. pl. IV. *Frankfurt*, 1866. 4°. **7943**. i. **16**.

BUSCH (JOANNES EBERHARDUS) De politia sive republica in specie sic dicta exercitatio politica, *etc. Praes.* H. Conringius. *Typis H. Mulleri: Helmestadii*, 1652. 4°. **897**. c. **3**. (**20**.)

BUSCH (JOANNES JACOBUS) *Praes. See* RIEDEL (A.) De spasmis, *etc.* [1784.] 4°. T. **572**. (**25**.)

BUSCH (JOH.) M. Joh. Busch dissertatio de odore quietis sacrificii Noachici ad Gen. VIII: 21. *See* MENTHEN (G.) Thesaurus theologico-philologicus, *etc.* tom. 1. 1701, *etc.* fol. **5**. g. **5**.

BUSCH (JOHANN) *See* BUSCHIUS (Joannes)

BUSCH (JOHANN CLAMER AUGUST VON DEM) *See* BUSSCH.

BUSCH (JOHANN DAVID) *See* PERIODICAL PUBLICATIONS.—*Marburg.* Teutsche Zeitschrift für die gesammte Thierheilkunde . . . herausgegeben von Dr. J. D. Busch. 1820, *etc.* 8°. P.P. **3284**. e.

—— *Praes. See* VOGLER (E. V.) De ictero, *etc.* [1786.] 4°. T. **561**. (**1**.)

BUSCH (JOHANN DAVID)

—— Dr. Johann David Busch . . . Beschreibung zweier merkwürdigen menschlichen Misgeburten, nebst einigen andern Beobachtungen aus der praktischen Entbindungskunst, *etc.* pp. xxii. 66. pl. 6. *Marburg*, 1803. 4°. **7580**. f. **4**.

—— Dr. Johann David Busch . . . kurzgefasste Hebammenkunst . . . Zweyte Auflage, *etc.* pp. viii. 112. *Marburg*, 1805. 8°. **1177**. e. **25**.

BUSCH (JOHANN DAVID) and **DAUM** (HEINRICH)

—— Archiv für Rossärzte und Pferdeliebhaber. 3 Bd. *Marburg*, 1788–93. 8°. **779**. b. **23**.

BUSCH (JOHANNES) *Augustinian Provost at Hildesheim. See* BUSCHIUS (Joannes)

BUSCH (JOHANNES) *of Dresden.* Ausserordentliche Eröffnungen über die natürliche und methaphysische oder geistige Beschaffenheit der Erde und ihres Mittelpunctes, *etc.* pp. viii. 263. *Meissen*, 1856. 8°. **8561**. c. **7**.

—— Ausserordentliche Eröffnungen über die natürliche und geistige Beschaffenheit des Planeten Saturnus nebst dessen 3-getheiltem Ring' und 7 Monden, *etc.* pp. xii. 164. *Meissen*, 1855. 8°. **8561**. c. **61**. (**3**.)

—— Ausserordentliche Kundgebungen und Eröffnungen über die naturmässige und geistige Beschaffenheit und Wesenhaftigkeit der Sonne, *etc.* 3 Abt. *Dresden*, 1864, 70. 8°. **8561**. bb. **31**.

—— Belehrungen der ewigen Liebe und Weisheit über das lebendige Wort, die Wiedergeburt des Geistes, den Geist und die Materie, *etc.* pp. 100. *Meissen*, 1856. 8°. **8470**. dd. **31**. (**2**.)

—— Geist-seelisch-wahres Licht-Wort über . . . Tischrücken . . . am 24. Februar 1854 vom Herrn Selbst dem . . . Schreiber . . . dictirt. Nebst Beifüge des " Schluessels zur Correspondenz mit seligen Geistern " &c. [by L. Haiela] . . . herausgegeben durch J. Busch. pp. 26. *Dresden*, 1869. 8°. **8631**. ff. **1**.

—— Psalmen und Gedichte in Dictaten vom Geiste der Wahrheit aus der Höhe der Höhen. Niedergeschrieben durch einen hierzu Erwählten, und herausgegeben in innerst vernommenem Beruf. pp. 114. *Dresden*, 1870. 8°. **11527**. f. **44**. (**5**.)

BUSCH (JOHANNES) *of the University of Copenhagen. Praes. See* WARBERGIUS (J. C.) Rhetorica sacra inchoata, *etc.* 1687. 4°. **491**. b. **17**. (**19**.)

BUSCH (JOHANNES JACOBUS) Dissertatio inauguralis medico-obstetrica de partu naturali difficili propter humerorum iniquum situm, *etc.* pp. 22. *Argentorati*, [1775.] 4°. T. **635**. (**3**.)

—— Recherches sur la nature et le traitement de la phthisie pulmonaire. pp. 144. *Strasbourg*, 1800. 8°. **1187**. e. **12**. (**2**.)

BUSCH (JOS. F.) *Writer on Philosophy.*

—— Bergson, of Betoomd élan als rhythme der schepping. pp. 251. *Amsterdam*, [1939.] 8°. **8471**. g. **20**.

BUSCH (JOSEF)

—— Die moralische und soziale Arithmetik Benthams. Inaugural-Dissertation, *etc.* pp. iii. 128. *Neisse*, [1937.] 8°. **8288**. aa. **7**.

BUSCH (JOSEF PAUL ZUM) *See* WEBER (Frederick P.) Endokrine Geschwülste, und andere Abhandlungen . . . Deutsche Übersetzung von Dr. J. P. zum Busch. 1936. 8°. **07641**. g. **39**.

—— *See* WEBER (Frederick P.) Gedanken eines Arztes über Seele, Natur und Gott . . . Deutsche Übersetzung von Dr. J. P. zum Busch. 1933. 8°. **012357**. l. **45**.

BUSCH (JOSEPH F.) The Art of Living with God. pp. 218. *Washbourne & Bogan: London; New York* printed, 1933. 8°. **4370**. i. **16**.

BUSCH (JULIUS) *See* EFFMANN (W.) Die St. Quirinus-Kirche zu Neuss. Unter Zugrundelegung der Restaurationspläne des Regierungsbaumeisters J. Busch, *etc.* 1890. 4°. **7807**. m. **6**. (4.)

BUSCH (JULIUS HERRMANN MORITZ) *See* ADELER (Max) *pseud.* Fern vom Weltgetümmel . . . übertragen von M. Busch. 1876. 8°. **12703**. dd. **28**.

—— *See* ALDRICH (Thomas B.) Die Geschichte eines bösen Buben und drei andere schöne Historien . . . Übertragen von M. Busch. 1875. 8°. **12703**. dd. **24**.

—— *See* ALDRICH (Thomas B.) Prudence Palfrey und andere Leute . . . Übertragen von M. Busch. 1874. 8°. **12703**. dd. **22**.

—— *See* ALDRICH (Thomas B.) Die Königin von Saba. Nebst anderen Erzählungen . . . Übertragen von M. Busch. 1877. 8°. **12703**. dd. **32**.

—— *See* BROWNE (Charles F.) Auswahl aus Artemus Wards Schriften . . . Übertragen von M. Busch. 1876. 8°. **12703**. dd. **29**.

—— *See* CLEMENS (Samuel L.) Jim Smiley's berühmter Springfrosch und dergleichen wunderliche Käuze mehr. Im Silberland Nevada . . . Übertragen von M. Busch. 1874. 8°. **12703**. dd. **23**.

—— *See* CLEMENS (Samuel L.) Die Abenteuer Tom Sawyers, . . . Übertragen von M. Busch. 1876. 8°. **12703**. dd. **30**.

—— *See* CLEMENS (Samuel L.) Die Arglosen auf Reisen . . . Übertragen von M. Busch. 1875. 8°. **12703**. dd. **25**.

—— *See* CLEMENS (Samuel L.) Die neue Pilgerfahrt . . . Übertragen von M. Busch. 1875. 8°. **12703**. dd. **26**.

—— *See* CLEMENS (Samuel L.) Skizzenbuch . . . Übertragen von M. Busch. 1877. 8°. **12703**. dd. **31**.

—— *See* CLEMENS (Samuel L.) and WARNER (C. D.) Das vergoldete Zeitalter . . . Übertragen von M. Busch. 1876. 8°. **12703**. dd. **27**.

—— *See* PERIODICAL PUBLICATIONS.—*Leipzig.* Die Grenzboten, *etc.* (Jahrg. 19. Semester 2—Jahrg. 29. Semester 1. Verantwortlicher Redacteur, M. Busch.) 1842, *etc.* 8°. P.P. **3668**. i.

—— Abriss der Urgeschichte des Orients bis zu den medischen Kriegen. Nach den neuesten Forschungen und vorzüglich nach Lenormants' Manuel d'histoire ancienne de l'Orient bearbeitet, *etc.* 2 Bd. *Leipzig,* [1868.] 8°. **9008**. bb. **6**.

—— Aegypten. Reisehandbuch für Aegypten und die angränzenden dem Pascha unterworfenen Länder . . . Mit vierzehn Ansichten, einer Reisekarte und einem Plane von Kairo. pp. xxxviii. 188. *Triest; Leipzig* [printed], 1858. 8°. [*Lloyd's illustrirte Reisebibliothek.* Bd. 3.] **10026**. b. **33**.

BUSCH (JULIUS HERRMANN MORITZ)

—— Hand-Book for Travellers in Egypt and adjacent countries subject to the Pascha. Translated . . . by W. C. Wrankmore. With fourteen illustrations, a travelling map and a plan of Cairo. pp. xl. 181. *Triest; Leipzig* [printed], 1858. 8°. **10096**. a. **15**.
The title on the spine reads: "The Austrian Lloyd's Handbook for Egypt."

—— Bilder aus dem Orient. Nach der Natur gezeichnet von A. Löffler und mit beschreibendem Text begleitet von Dr M. Busch. Mit 32 Stahlstichen. pp. 108. *Triest,* 1864 [1863, 64]. 4°. **1784**. a. **7**.
Published in parts.

—— L'Orient pittoresque. Publication artistique dessinée d'après nature par A. Löffler et accompagnée du texte descriptif du Dr M. Busch. Avec 32 gravures en acier. [Translated from the German.] pp. 108. *Trieste,* 1865. fol. **1784**. a. **8**.
Published in parts.

—— Bilder aus Griechenland. Nach der Natur gezeichnet von A. Löffler, mit beschreibendem Text begleitet von Dr M. Busch. Mit 18 Stahlstichen, *etc.* pp. 123. *Triest,* 1870 [1869]. fol. **1789**. b. **3**.
Published in parts.

—— La Grecia pittoresca. Quadri storico-geographici descrittivi. Disegnati dal vero da A. Löffler. Descritti da M. Busch. Versione italiana del professore Francesco Pastrello. Con 18 incisioni in acciaio, *etc.* pp. 124. *Trieste,* 1872. fol. **10125**. g. **6**.

—— Bismarck und sein Werk. Beiträge zur inneren Geschichte der letzten Jahre bis 1896. Nach Tagebuchsblättern . . . Fünftes bis sechstes Tausend. pp. iv. 120. *Leipzig,* 1898. 8°. **8074**. bbb. **25**.

—— Deutscher Volksglaube. pp. 377. *Leipzig,* 1877. 8°. **12431**. ccc. **3**.

—— Der gerechte und volkommene Austernesser. pp. 80. *Hannover,* 1868. 16°. **7943**. aa. **34**

—— Geschichte der Mormonen nebst einer Darstellung ihres Glaubens und ihrer gegenwärtigen socialen und politischen Verhältnisse. pp. 444. *Leipzig,* 1870. 8°. **4744**. dd. **3**.

—— Graf Bismarck und seine Leute während des Kriegs mit Franckreich. Nach Tagebuchsblättern von D. M. Busch. 2 Bd. *Leipzig,* 1878. 8°. **10703**. de. **12**.

—— [Another copy.] **10704**. bbb. **7**.

—— Bismarck in the Franco-German War 1870–71. Authorised translation, *etc.* 2 vol. *Macmillan & Co.: London,* 1879. 8°. **2402**. b. **12**.

—— Le Comte de Bismarck et sa suite, pendant la guerre de France, 1870–1871 . . . Traduit de l'allemand . . . Troisième édition. pp. 516. *Paris,* 1879. 8°. **010704**. de. **72**.

—— *See* BISMARCK-SCHOENHAUSEN (O. E. L. von) *Prince.* [*Writings.*] Bismarck als Zensor. Eigenhändige, bisher noch unveröffentlichte Randbemerkungen des ersten Reichskanzlers zu Moritz Buschs Werk "Graf Bismarck und seine Leute," *etc.* 1907. 8°. **11851**. tt. **19**.

—— *See* L***, A***, *Lieutenant.* Bismarck et le docteur Busch, *etc.* [A criticism of "Graf Bismarck und seine Leute während des Kriegs mit Frankreich."] [1897.] 8°. **10603**. cc. **18**. (7.)

BUSCH (Julius Herrmann Moritz)

—— Griechenland. Reisehandbuch für Griechenland . . . Mit zwölf Ansichten, einer Reisekarte und einem Plan von Athen. pp. xxxvi. 217. *Triest; Leipzig* [printed], 1859. 8°. [*Lloyd's illustrirte Reisebibliothek.* Bd. 4.] **10026. b. 35.**

—— Die gute alte Zeit. 2 Tl. *Leipzig*, 1878. 8°. **12356. i. 9.**

—— Die Mormonen. Ihr Prophet, ihr Staat und ihr Glaube. pp. 158. *Leipzig*, 1855. 8°. **4139. b. 21.**

—— Neue Tagebuchsblätter des Verfassers von "Graf Bismarck und seine Leute." pp. 44. *Leipzig*, 1879. 8°. **10704. bbb. 19.**
The author's name occurs only in the catchword on the first leaf of each gathering.

—— Schleswig-holsteinische Briefe. 2 Bd. *Leipzig*, 1856. 8°. **10281. b. 15.**

—— Tagebuchblätter, *etc.* [Memoirs of Prince Bismarck, 1870–1893.] 3 Bd. *Leipzig*, 1899. 8°. **10708. i. 6.**

—— [Tagebuchblätter.] Bismarck. Some secret pages of his history. Being a diary kept by Dr. M. Busch during twenty-five years' official and private intercourse with the great Chancellor. 3 vol. *Macmillan & Co.: London*, 1898. 8°. **10704. k. 12.**

—— Condensed edition. pp. ix. 576. *Macmillan & Co.: London*, 1899. 8°. **10703. ff. 40.**

—— Die Türkei. Reisehandbuch für Rumelien, die untere Donau, Anatolien, Syrien, Palästina, Rhodus und Cypern. [With plates.] pp. xxxv. 286. *Triest*, 1860. 8°. [*Lloyd's illustrirte Reisebibliothek.* Bd. 6.] **10026. b. 37.**

—— Dritte verbesserte Auflage. [With a map.] pp. vi. 232. *Triest; Wien; Wien* [printed], 1881. 8°. **10125. aa. 10.**

—— Das Uebergangsjahr in Hannover. pp. vi. 313. *Leipzig*, 1867. 8°. **9365. cc. 7.**

—— Unser Reichskanzler. Studien zu einem Charakterbilde. 2 Bd. *Leipzig*, 1884. 8°. **10704. bbb. 41.**

—— Our Chancellor . . . Translated . . . by William Beatty-Kingston. 2 vol. *Macmillan & Co.: London*, 1884. 8°. **2402. b. 5.**

—— Eine Wallfahrt nach Jerusalem. Bilder ohne Heiligenscheine. 2 Bd. *Leipzig*, 1861. 8°. **10075. bb. 25.**

—— Wanderungen zwischen Hudson und Mississippi 1851 und 1852. 2 Bd. *Stuttgart & Tübingen*, 1854. 8°. [*Reisen und Länderbeschreibungen aus der älteren und neuesten Zeit.* Lfg. 39, 40.] **1294. c. 10.**

—— Wunderliche Heilige. Religiöse und politische Geheimbünde und Secten. pp. v. 358. *Leipzig*, 1879. 8°. **4785. bbb. 11.**

BUSCH (Karl) *See* also Busch (Carl)

—— Raum- und Zeitgesetze deutscher Kunst. Eine allgemeine Einführung. pp. 96. pl. 16. *Berlin*, 1935. 8°. **07805. dd. 46.**

BUSCH (Karl August)

—— William James als Religionsphilosoph. pp. vii. 88. *Göttingen*, 1911. 8°. **8459. i. 14. (4.)**

BUSCH (Karl Matthias)

—— *See* Role, *pseud.* [i.e. C. M. Busch.]

BUSCH (Laurentius von den) Disputatio medico-chirurgica inauguralis de partu cæsareo, *etc.* pp. 40. *J. Gyzelaar: Franequeræ*, 1695. 4°. **T. 637. (7.)**

—— [Another copy.] **1185. i. 13. (26.)**

—— Disputatio physiologica de vita fœtus in utero materno, *etc.* pp. 50. *J. Gyzelaar: Franequeræ*, 1695. 4°. **1185. i. 13. (24.)**

—— Laurentii von den Busch . . . Oratio de incrementis medicinæ, seu præcipuis ac novissimis hujus sæculi in arte medica inventis, *etc.* pp. 23. *Typis H. Braueri: Bremæ*, 1699. 4°. **1185. b. 8. (12.)**

BUSCH (Lothar)

—— *See* Goulden (William O.) German-English Medical Dictionary. (Consultant editor for German text: L. Busch.) 1955. 8°. **12965. b. 21.**

BUSCH (Louis)

—— *See* Germany. [*Laws, etc.*—ii. *Civil Code.*] Das Bürgerliche Gesetzbuch . . . erläutert von Busch, Schaffeld, *etc.* 1922. 8°. **5607. c. 21.**

—— *See* Sydow (R.) Die deutsche Gebührenordnung für Rechtsanwälte . . . Fortgeführt von L. Busch . . . O. Krieg. 1922. 8°. **05656. e. 65.**

—— —— 1929. 8°. **2227. b. 17.**

—— *See* Sydow (R.) Neu bearbeitet . . . von Dr. L. Busch und O. Krieg. 1928. 8°. **2227. b. 15.**

—— *See* Sydow (R.) Gerichtsverfassungsgesetz mit Einführungsgesetz . . . Weiterbearbeitet durch L. Busch. 1905. 8°. **05656. e. 27.**

—— —— 1925. 8°. **2227. b. 14.**

—— *See* Sydow (R.) Konkursordnung und Anfechtungsgesetz . . . Fortgeführt von L. Busch. 1906. 8°. **05656. e. 26.**

—— —— 1926. 8°. **05656. e. 66.**

—— —— 1929. 8°. **05656. e. 83.**

—— —— 1932. 8°. **2227. b. 13.**

—— *See* Sydow (R.) Zivilprozessordnung und Gerichtsverfassungsgesetz . . . Fortgeführt von L. Busch. 1909. 8°. **05656. e. 4.**

BUSCH (Louis) and KRANTZ (Walter)

—— Änderungen der Zivilprozessordnung des Gerichtsverfassungsgesetzes und der Entlastungsverordnung durch die neuere Gesetzgebung. Nachtrag zur 17. Auflage der Zivilprozessordnung von Sydow—Busch—Krantz . . . Mit Erläuterungen herausgegeben von L. Busch . . . W. Krantz. pp. 100. *Berlin & Leipzig*, 1924. 8°. **5607. b. 19.**

BUSCH (Ludwig) *See* Liturgies.—*Latin Rite.* [*Rituals.*—i. *Abridgments and Extracts.*] Liturgischer Versuch oder Deutsches Ritual für katholische Kirchen. Von L. Busch. 1803. 8°. **1222. h. 15.**

BUSCH (Lydia) The Coon's Calendar of Courtship. By L. Busch, Reginald Rigby and Reginald Rivington. pp. 32. *T. S. Clark & Co.: London*, [1907.] 8°. **012804. h. 25.**

BUSCH (MANFRED VON)

—— Der Silberkrieg in Ostasien. pp. 143. *Berlin*, 1942. 8°. **8234. ff. 64.**

BUSCH (MARCUS) *Resp.* *See* VERBRUGGE (O.) Othonis Verbrugge . . . Disputatio philologico-theologica de voce גוים Gen. xxv. 23, *etc.* 1768. 4°. [OELRICHS (*J.*) *Collectio opusculorum, etc.* tom. 1.] **854. h. 25.**

—— Dissertatio de debilitate febrili, *etc.* pp. 19. *Lugduni Batavorum*, 1725. 4°. **1185. i. 1. (29.)**
The titlepage is engraved.

BUSCH (MARIE) *Dr.* Die Steuerverfassung Süderdithmarschens vom 16. bis zum 18. Jahrhundert. *Leipzig*, 1916. 8°. [*Quellen und Forschungen zur Geschichte Schleswig-Holsteins.* Bd. 4.] Ac. **7638/7.**

BUSCH (MARIE) *Translator.* *See* BANG (H. J.) [De uden Fædreland.] Denied a Country . . . Translated . . . by M. Busch, *etc.* 1927. 8°. **12582. ppp. 20.**

—— *See* BENECKE (Else C. M.) and BUSCH (M.) More Tales by Polish Authors. Translated by E. C. M. Benecke and M. Busch. 1916. 8°. **12589. r. 10.**

—— *See* BENECKE (Else C. M.) and BUSCH (M.) Selected Polish Tales, *etc.* 1921. 8°. **012209. df. 137.**

—— *See* DROGOSŁAW, *pseud.* Poland and the Polish Nation . . . Translated by M. Busch, *etc.* [1917.] 8°. **9475. aa. 37.**

—— *See* SCHUMANN (E.) Memoirs of Eugenie Schumann. Translated by M. Busch. 1927. 8°. **010703. eee. 21.**

—— Selected Austrian Short Stories. Translated by M. Busch. pp. vii. 290. *Oxford University Press: London*, 1928. 8°. [*World's Classics.*] **012209. df. 229.**

BUSCH (MARIE) *Translator*, and **PICK** (OTTO)

—— Selected Czech Tales. Translated by M. Busch and O. Pick. pp. xi. 258. *Oxford University Press: London*, 1925. 16°. [*World's Classics.*] **012209. df. 182.**

BUSCH (MAURICE) *See* BUSCH (Julius H. M.)

BUSCH (MICHAEL HEINRICH) *See* BUCH (Henry M.)

BUSCH (MORITZ) *See* BUSCH (Julius H. M.)

BUSCH (N.) *of Kiel.* *See* KRENKE (N. P.) Wundkompensation, Transplantation und Chimären bei Pflanzen . . . Übersetzt von Dr. N. Busch, *etc.* 1933. 8°. W.P. **5841/29.**

BUSCH (NICOLAUS) *See* LIVONIA. Livländische Güterurkunden (aus den Jahren 1207 bis 1500). Herausgegeben von H. von Bruiningk und N. Busch, *etc.* 1908. 8°. **10291. i. 14.**

—— Nachgelassene Schriften von Dr. . . . N. Busch, Stadtbibliothekar zu Riga. Im Auftrage . . . der Stadt Riga herausgegeben durch . . . L. Arbusow . . . Verzeichnis von Dr. N. Buschs Schriften . . . aus den Jahren 1889–1933, *etc.* 1934– . 8°. *See* RIGA. **20014.k.2.**

—— Die Geschichte der Rigaer Stadtbibliothek und deren Bücher. Redigiert von L. Arbusow. pp. 97. *Riga*, 1937. 8°. **11914. g. 20.**

BUSCH (NIKOLAI) *See* BUSH (N. A.)

BUSCH (NIVEN)

—— The Actor. pp. 239. *Frederick Muller: London*, 1955. 8°. NNN. **6700.**

—— The Carrington Incident. [A novel.] pp. 188. *Robert Hale: London*, 1942. 8°. NN. **33615.**

—— Duel in the Sun. pp. 256. *W. H. Allen: London*, 1947. 8°. **12728. bb. 30.**

—— The Hate Merchant. A novel. pp. 319. *W. H. Allen: London*, [1953.] 8°. **12701. h. 6.**

—— Twenty-one Americans. Being profiles of some people famous in our time, *etc.* pp. vi. 332. *Doubleday, Doran & Co.: Garden City, New York*, 1930. 8°. **010603. bb. 16.**

BUSCH (NOEL FAIRCHILD)

—— Adlai E. Stevenson. Portrait of a democrat. [With plates, including portraits.] pp. 240. *W. H. Allen: London*, 1952. 8°. **10889. aa. 43.**

BUSCH (OSCAR) Manual of German Conversation, *etc.* pp. x. 339. *F. A. Brockhaus: Leipzig*, 1855 [1854]. 8°. **12962. b. 40.**

BUSCH (OSCAR) and **SKELTON** (HENRY P.)

—— Handbuch der englischen Umgangsprache, *etc.* pp. x. 372. *Leipzig*, 1857. 8°. **12982. a. 25.**

BUSCH (OTTO) and **SCHERNITZKY** (ANTON)

—— Schwarz-Rot-Gold. Die Farben der Bundesrepublik Deutschland. Ihre Tradition und Bedeutung . . . Bearbeitet von Albert Franz. pp. 95. *Offenbach a.M.*, 1952. 8°. **08074. f. 1.**

BUSCH (OTTO) *Dr. Phil.*

—— Arthur Schopenhauer . . . Zweite, gänzlich umgearbeitete Auflage. pp. viii. 239. *München*, 1878. 8°. **8468. i. 12.**

—— Naturgeschichte der Kunst. pp. 205. *Heidelberg*, 1877. 8°. **7808. bb. 8.**

—— Zwanzig Schnurren und Märlein für die Klimperkleinen, mit einem Nachwort für die Ganzgrossen. pp. 40. *Einbeck*, 1868. 8°. **12804. b. 2.**

BUSCH (PAUL)

—— Friedrich Schlegel und das Judentum. Inaugural-Dissertation, *etc.* pp. 96. *Bottrop*, 1939. 8°. **04034. eee. 95.**

BUSCH (PETER) Ausführliche Historie und Erklärung des Helden-Liedes Lutheri, Eine feste Burg ist unser Gott! . . . Mit einer Vorrede von Lutheri Heldenmuthe und seiner Liebe zur Sing- und Dicht-Kunst, *etc.* pp. 238. *Hanover*, 1731. 8°. **3436. k. 2. (1.)**

—— Curieuse Nachricht von einer neuen Art Seide, welche von den Spinnen-Weben zubereitet wird, *etc.* [By P. Busch.] pp. 62. 1711. 8°. *See* NACHRICHT. **976. h. 28. (2.)**

—— [Another copy, with a different titlepage.] B. **640. (4.)**

—— Jubilæum cantionum ecclesiasticarum Lutheranarum, oder Evangelisch-lutherische Jubel-Freude über die öffentliche Reformation der Kirchen-Gesänge von D. Mart. Luthero Anno 1524 geschehen, *etc.* pp. 56. [*Hanover*,] 1724. 8°. **3436. k. 2. (2.)**

BUSCH (PHILIPPUS WILHELMUS VON DEM) *See* BUSCHE.

BUSCH (RICHARD) Grundfragen der strafrechtlichen Verantwortlichkeit der Verbände. pp. viii. 228. 1933. 8°. *See* LEIPZIG.—*Academia Lipsiensis.*—*Juristische Fakultät.* **06004.** i. **24.**

BUSCH (RUDOLF)

—— Der Dom zu Mainz. Kurzer Führer . . . Mit 20 Abbildungen und einem Domplan. pp. 30. 1929. 8°. *See* MAINZ.—*Cathedral Church.* **07822.** b. **75.**

BUSCH (TRISTAN)

—— Secret Service unmasked, *etc.* (Translated from the German by Anthony V. Ireland.) pp. 272. *Hutchinson & Co.: London,* [1950.] 8°. **9102.** c. **12.**

BUSCH (WERNER) Die Selbstbetrachtung und Selbstdeutung des jungen Schiller. pp. 116. *Würzburg,* 1937. 8°. **11860.** b. **1.**

BUSCH (WILHELM) *Artist.*

—— *See* ACKERKNECHT (Erwin. H.) Wilhelm Busch als Selbstbiograph. [With a portrait.] 1949. 8°. **10710.** g.**36**

—— *See* CREMER (H.) Die Bildergeschichten Wilhelm Buschs. 1937. 8°. **11855.** d. **60.**

—— *See* DAELEN (E.) Ueber Wilhelm Busch und seine Bedeutung . . . Mit bisher ungedruckten Dichtungen, Illustrationen und Briefen von W. Busch. 1886. 8°. **11824.** ff. **48.**

—— *See* DANGERS (R.) Wilhelm Busch, der Künstler, *etc.* [1937.] 4°. **7852.** t. **27.**

—— *See* HIRTH (G.) Franz von Seitz und Lorenz Gedon . . . mit den Gedichten von K. Hoff und W. Busch. 1884. 8°. **10601.** c. **9.** (**10.**)

—— *See* KOHUT (A.) Das Ewig-Weibliche bei Wilhelm Busch. [1904.] 8°. **010707.** ff. **51.**

—— *See* MORELL (H.) Europas Struwelpeter, nach Wilhelm Busch, *etc.* 1915. 8°. **011528.** m. **71.**

—— *See* VANSELOW (A.) Die Erstdrucke und Erstausgaben der Werke von Wilhelm Busch, *etc.* 1913. 8°. **11907.** bbb. **14.**

—— *See* VETH (C.) Wilhelm Busch. 1904. 8°. **10602.** de. **18.** (**4.**)

—— *See* WINTHER (F.) Wilhelm Busch als Dichter, Künstler, Psychologe und Philosoph. 1910. 8°. [*University of California. Publications in Modern Philology.* vol. 2. no. 1.] Ac. **2689.** g/**4.**

—— Wilhelm Busch-Album. Humoristischer Hausschatz. Sammlung der beliebtesten Schriften, mit 1500 Bildern, von W. Busch. Mit dem Portrait des Verfassers. Zweite Auflage, *etc.* pp. 358. *München,* [1887.] 4°. **12316.** w. **14.**

—— Bilderpossen: Katze und Maus—Der Eispeter—Krischan mit der Piepe—Hänsel und Gretel . . . In siebzig Bildern. [Edited by Arthur Rümann.] pp. 64. *Leipzig,* [1934.] *obl.* 8°. [*Insel-Bücherei.* no. 25.] **012213.** de. **1/25.**

—— A Bushel of Merry-Thoughts by Wilhelm Busch. Described and ornamented by Harry Rogers. (The Fearful Tragedy of Ice-Peter.—The Exciting Story of

BUSCH (WILHELM) *Artist.*

the Cat and Mouse.—The Disobedient Children who stole Sugar Bread.—The Terrible Punishment of the Naughty Boys of Corinth.) 4 pt. *Sampson Low & Co.: London,* 1868. *obl.* 8°. **1752.** a. **26.**
Printed on one side of the leaf only. Imperfect; wanting f. 13 *of pt.* 2.

—— Wilhelm Busch an Maria Anderson. Siebzig Briefe. 3. Auflage. [With a preface by Carl Herrmann, and an introductory note by Maria Anderson.] pp. viii. 116. *Rostock,* 1908. 8°. **10910.** ee. **19.**

—— Ist mir mein Leben geträumet? Briefe eines Einsiedlers, gesammelt und herausgegeben von Otto Nöldeke. [With plates, including portraits.] pp. 237. *Leipzig,* [1935.] 8° **010920.** d. **37.**

—— Abenteuer eines Junggesellen . . . Achte Auflage. pp. 88. *München,* 1881. 8°. **11525.** dd. **40.**

—— Allerlei Humor. Eine neue Sammlung von 75 Geschichten, Humoresken usw., mit 460 Bildern . . . Gesammelt und herausgegeben von Rudolf Will. [With a portrait.] 2 pt. *Leipzig,* [1912.] 4°. **12330.** m. **39.**
Printed on one side of the leaf only.

—— Antonius. Burlesk-Oratorium, *etc.* pp. 7. *Berlin,* 1888. 8°. **11748.** i. **33.** (**2.**)

—— Aus alter Zeit. Herausgegeben von Otto Nöldeke und Hans Balzer. Mit Handzeichnungen des Dichters. [Fairy tales, fables and ballads collected and rewritten by Wilhelm Busch.] pp. 203. *Leipzig,* [1936.] 8°. **20011.** f. **3.**

—— Balduin Bählamm, der verhinderte Dichter . . . Dritte Auflage. pp. 74. *München,* 1883. 8°. **11525.** dd. **34.**

—— Bilder zur Jobsiade [of C. A. Kortum]. [With verses.] pp. 67. *Heidelberg,* [1874.] 8°. **11525.** dd. **27.**

—— (Siebente Auflage.) pp. 67. *München,* 1880. 8°. **11525.** dd. **28.**

—— Dideldum! . . . Achte Auflage. pp. 64. *München,* 1880. 8°. **11525.** dd. **30.**

—— Diogenes and the two Naughty Young Corinthians. An English version of German comicalities [i.e. of " Diogenes und die bösen Buben von Korinth " by W. Busch] . . . By A. B. Westmacott. pp. 7. 1879. 4°. *See* DIOGENES, *the Cynic.* **12809.** n. **54.**

—— [Eduards Traum.] Edward's Dream. The philosophy of a humorist. Translated and edited by Dr. Paul Carus from the German of W. Busch. [With a portrait.] pp. 74. *Open Court Publishing Co.: Chicago,* 1909. 16°. **12352.** de. **20.**

—— Fipps, der Affe. pp. 89. *München,* 1879. 8°. **11525.** dd. **29.**

—— Die fromme Helene . . . Vierte Auflage. pp. 113. *Heidelberg,* 1872. 8°. **11525.** dd. **37.**

—— Naughty Jemima: a doleful tale. With . . . illustrations. [Translated from " Die fromme Helene " by John MacLush. In verse.] pp. 119. *Ward, Lock & Co.: London,* [1874.] 16°. **11652.** a. **65.**

—— Der Fuchs. Die Drachen. Zwei lustige Sachen. pp. 37. *München,* [1881.] 8°. **11528.** h. **25.**

BUSCH (Wilhelm) *Artist.*

—— Der Geburtstag, oder die Partikularisten. Schwank in 100 Bildern. Neunte Auflage. pp. 62. *München,* 1882. 8°. **11525. dd. 36.**

—— Die Haarbeutel. pp. 66. *Heidelberg,* 1878. 8°. **11525. dd. 31.**

—— Zweite Auflage. pp. 66. *Heildelberg,* 1878. 8°. **12315. dd. 3.**

—— [Hans Huckebein, der Unglücksrabe.] Hookeybeak the Raven, and other tales. With numerous comic pictures . . . The English version by H. W. Dulcken. pp. vi. 87. *G. Routledge & Sons: London,* [1878.] 8°. **12315. ccc. 11.**

—— Der Heilige Antonius von Padua. pp. 69. *Lahr,* [1870.] 8°. **11526. ff. 15.**

—— Légende de Saint Antoine. Imité de l'allemand de W. Busch. pp. 96. *Strasbourg,* [1873.] 8°. **012314. ee. 100.**

—— Le Grand Saint Antoine de Padoue . . . Badinage irrévérencieux par Ernest d'Hervilly. [A free translation of the verses of W. Busch.] 75 illustrations de W. Busch, *etc.* pp. 68. [1883.] 8°. *See* Hervilly (E. d') **11482. dd. 49.**

—— Hernach. [Sketches and verses. Edited by Otto Nöldecke.] pp. 52. *Leipzig,* [1937.] 8°. [*Insel-Bücherei.* no. 507.] **012213. de. 1/507.**

—— Herr und Frau Knopp . . . Siebente Auflage. pp. 72. *München,* 1882. 8°. **11525. dd. 39.**

—— Humoresker. ff. 133. *Kjøbenhavn,* 1876. 8°. **12331. h. 6.**
Printed on one side of the leaf only.

—— Julchen. (Neunte Auflage.) pp. 65. *München,* 1883. 8°. **11525. dd. 38.**

—— Kritik des Herzens . . . [In verse.] Zweite unveränderte Auflage. pp. 84. *Heidelberg,* 1875. 8°. **11528. aaa. 12.**

—— Kunterbunt. 2 Tl. ff. 59. *München,* [1872, 73.] 4°. **12350. l. 2.**
The titlepage is engraved. Printed on one side of the leaf only.

—— Maler Klecksel. [With illustrations.] pp. 68. *Basel,* 1947. 8°. **011528. m. 104.**

—— Max und Moritz. Eine Bubengeschichte in sieben Streichen. pp. 60. *München,* [1930.] 8°. **011528. m. 97.**

—— Max and Moritz. A story in seven tricks. ff. 53. *Braun & Schneider: Munich; A. N. Myers & Co.: London,* [1874.] 8°. **12803. g. 18.**
Printed on one side of the leaf only.

—— Max and Moritz . . . With the author's original illustrations. Freely translated by Arundell Esdaile. ff. 27. *G. Routledge & Sons: London,* [1913.] 8°. **11650. i. 43.**
Printed on one side of the leaf only.

—— Max et Moritz facinora puerilia septem dolis fraudibusque peracta ex inventione Gulielmi Busch, poetae pictorisque, in sermonem latinum conversa a versificatore sereno—Dr. G. Merten. Editio quinta. pp. 56. *Monachii,* 1932. 8°. **011388.d.22.**

BUSCH (Wilhelm) *Artist.*

—— Pater Filucius. pp. 40. *Heidelberg,* 1872. 8°. **11527. d. 65. (12.)**

—— [Another copy.] **11525. dd. 33.**

—— Siebente Auflage. pp. 40. *München,* 1882. 8°. **11525. dd. 32.**

—— Plisch und Plum . . . Dritte Auflage. pp. 65. *München,* 1882. 8°. **11525. dd. 35.**

—— Plish and Plum. From the German . . . by Charles T. Brooks. pp. 67. *Roberts Bros.: Boston,* 1883. 8°. **11528. h. 11.**

—— Schein und Sein. [Poems. Edited by Hans Balzer.] pp. 79. *Leipzig,* [1935.] 8°. [*Insel-Bücherei.* no. 478.] **012213. de. 1/478.**

—— Der Schmetterling. pp. 95. *München,* 1895. 16°. **012808. k. 2.**

—— Schnaken & Schnurren . . . Eine Sammlung humoristischer kleiner Erzählungen in Bildern . . . Dritte Auflage. 3 Tl. *München,* [1867–72.] 4°. **12806. l. 8.**
Printed on one side of the leaf only.

—— Schnurrdiburr, oder die Bienen . . . Sechste Auflage. [With illustrations.] ff. 72. *München,* [1890?] 8°. **20003. b. 52.**
Printed on one side of the leaf only.

—— Buzz a Buzz; or, the Bees. Done freely into English, by the author of My Bee Book [i.e. W. C. Cotton] from the German. pp. iv. ff. 72. *Griffith & Farran: London; Phillipson & Golder: Chester,* [1872.] 8°. **11649. eee. 20.**
Printed on one side of the leaf only.

—— [Another copy.] **11649. eee. 19.**
In this copy the illustrations are coloured.

—— Ein Skizzenbuch. Mit einem Geleitwort von Otto Nöldecke. [Plates.] pp. 7. *München,* 1924. *obl.* 8°. **7859. a. 14.**

—— Cousin Freddy's First and Last Donkey-ride . . . An English version of German comicalities [i.e. of "Vetter Franz auf dem Esel" by W. Busch] . . . By A. B. Westmacott. pp. 7. 1879. 4°. *See* Freddy, *Cousin.* **12809. n. 56.**

—— The Power of Sound; or, the Effect of music. With a moral . . . An English version of German comicalities [i.e. of "Der Virtuos" by W. Busch] . . . By A. B. Westmacott. pp. 8. 1879. 4°. *See* Power. **12809. n. 53.**

—— Zu guter Letzt . . . [Verses.] 26stes bis 30stes Tausend pp. 136. *München,* 1904. 8°. **011528. i. 35**

—— The Fool's Paradise, with the many wonderful adventures there, as seen in the strange, surpassing, Peep-Show of Professor Wolley Cobble. [The editor's preface signed: C. W. A selection from John Camden Hotten's extracts from W. Busch's contributions to "Münchener Bilderbogen."] pp. 72. *Griffith & Farran: London,* [1883.] 4°. **12805. s. 19.**

BUSCH (Wilhelm) *Dr. theol.* Der Weg des deutschen katholischen Katechismus von Deharbe bis zum Einheitskatechismus. Grundlegende Studien zur Katechismusreform. pp. xxv. 179. *Freiburg i. B.,* 1936. 8°. **03504. h. 18.**

BUSCH (Wilhelm) *Pfarrer in Essen.*

—— Die von Herzen dir nachwandeln. Gestalten des rheinisch-westfälischen Pietismus, *etc.* (3. Auflage.) pp. 166. *Gladbeck*, [1950.] 8°. **4889. aa. 42.**

BUSCH (Wilhelm) *Professor der Chirurgie an der Universität Bonn.* *See* Schwann (J. B.) Enarratur casus quidam de polypode laryngo-tracheali a professore . . . G. Busch operato, *etc.* [1865.] 8°. **7385.*d. (13.)**

—— Anleitung die Krankheiten der Feldhospitäler zu erkennen und zu heilen, *etc.* pp. x. 278. *Marburg*, 1812. 8°. **1168. e. 28.**

—— Beobachtungen über Anatomie und Entwickelung einiger wirbellosen Seethiere . . . Mit 17 Kupfertafeln. pp. viii. 143. *Berlin*, 1851. 4°. **7203. f. 13.**

—— Chirurgische Beobachtungen gesammelt in der königl. chirurgischen Universitäts-Klinik zu Berlin. pp. 296. *Berlin*, 1854. 8°. **7480. d. 7.**

—— Lehrbuch der Chirurgie. 2 Bd. *Berlin*, 1857–66. 8°. **7480. f. 15.**

Imperfect; wanting Bd. 2. Abt. 2. Hälfte 2.

—— Symbolae ad rhinoplasticen. [With plates.] *See* Bonn.—*Rheinische Friedrich-Wilhelms-Universität.* Sacram memoriam . . . Friderici Guilelmi III. . . . celebranda indicit M. I. Weber, *etc.* 1858. 4°. **8359. c. 3. (30.)**

BUSCH (Wilhelm) *Professor in the Faculty of Agricultural Economy of the University of Bonn.*

—— Raumordnung durch landwirtschaftliche Umsiedlung in der Rheinprovinz. Herausgegeben von der Reichsarbeitsgemeinschaft für Raumforschung in Verbindung mit dem Landeshauptmann der Rheinprovinz als stv. Vorsitzenden der Landesplanungsgemeinschaft Rheinland . . . Mit 24 Karten und 25 Plänen. pp. 155. 1943. 4°. *See* Germany.—*Reichsarbeitsgemeinschaft für Raumforschung.* **8235. t. 34.**

BUSCH (Wilhelm) *Professor of History at Tübingen.*

—— *See* Suckow (A. von) Rückschau . . . Herausgegeben und bearbeitet von Dr. W. Busch, *etc.* 1909. 8°. **10710. g. 21.**

—— Die Berliner Märztage von 1848. Die Ereignisse und ihre Überlieferung. pp. 74. *München & Leipzig*, 1899. 8°. [*Historische Bibliothek.* Bd. 7.] **09008. f. 1/7.**

—— Die Beziehungen Frankreichs zu Österreich und Italien zwischen den Kriegen von 1866 und 1870/71. *See* Tubingen.—*Eberhard-Karls-Universität.* Verzeichnis der Doktoren, *etc.* 1900. 4°. **9078. gg. 28.**

—— Bismarck und die politischen Anschauungen in Deutschland von 1847 bis 1862, *etc.* pp. 24. *Tübingen*, 1896. 8°. **8074. ff. 40. (5.)**

—— Cardinal Wolsey und die englisch-kaiserliche Allianz 1522–1525. pp. 97. *Bonn*, 1886. 8°. **9073. f. 11.**

—— Das deutsche Grosse Hauptquartier und die Bekämpfung von Paris im Feldzuge 1870–71. pp. 82. *Stuttgart & Berlin*, 1905. 8°. **09077. eee. 11.**

—— Drei Jahre englischer Vermittlungspolitik, 1518–1521. pp. xi. 194. *Bonn*, 1884. 8°. **8138. bb. 6.**

—— England unter den Tudors. (Bd. 1. König Heinrich VII. 1485–1509.) pp. xii. 434. *Stuttgart*, 1892. 8°. **9510. h. 21.**

No more published.

—— [Another copy.] **9510. h. 15.**

BUSCH (Wilhelm) *Professor of History at Tübingen.*

—— England under the Tudors. Vol. I.—King Henry VII . . . Translated, under the supervision of the Rev. A. H. Johnson . . . by Alice M. Todd. With an introduction and some comments by James Gairdner. pp. xvi. 445. *A. D. Innes & Co.: London*, 1895. 8°. **2394. g. 1.**

—— Die Kämpfe um Reichsverfassung und Kaisertum, 1870–1871. pp. 157. *Tübingen*, 1906. 8°. **9335. k. 15.**

—— Der Sturz des Cardinals Wolsey im Scheidungshandel König Heinrich's VIII. von England. 1890. *See* Periodical Publications.—*Leipsic.* Historisches Taschenbuch, *etc.* Folge 6. Jahrg. 9. 1830, *etc.* 8°. **P.P. 3675.**

—— Der Ursprung der Ehescheidung König Heinrich's VIII. von England. 1889. *See* Periodical Publications.—*Leipsic.* Historisches Taschenbuch, *etc.* Folge 6. Jahrg. 8. 1830, *etc.* 8°. **P.P. 3625.**

BUSCH (Wilhelm) *Writer on Philology.* Die deutsche Fachsprache der Mathematik. Ihre Entwicklung und ihre wichtigsten Erscheinungen mit besonderer Rücksicht auf Johann Heinrich Lambert. 1933. *See* Behaghel (O.) Giessener Beiträge zur deutschen Philologie, *etc.* Hft. 30. 1921, *etc.* 8°. **W.P. 7382/30.**

BUSCH (William) Some Miscellaneous Literary Berries, viz: novelettes, poems, pen sketches, *etc.* 4 pts. *St. Louis*, 1905. 8°. **012355. g. 16.**

BUSCH (Wolfgang)

—— *See* Levin (B. I.) [Пути реконструкции железнодорожного транспорта, *etc.*] Die Neugestaltung des Eisenbahnverkehrs im Rahmen des Stalinschen Nachkriegs-Fünfjahrplans . . . Übersetzt von W. Busch und G. Möchel. 1952. 12°. **8236. de. 36.**

—— *See* Luizlov (B. M.) [Основные вопросы технического нормирования.] Grundfragen der technischen Normung. Kollektivübersetzung von W. Busch [and others], *etc.* 1953. 8°. **8289. n. 7.**

—— *See* Punsky (J.) and Gal'tsov (A.) [Техническое нормирование в социалистической промышленности.] Die technische Arbeitsnormung in der sozialistischen Industrie. Kollektivübersetzung von W. Busch und G. Möchel, *etc.* 1953. 8°. [*Sowjetwissenschaft.* Beihft. 37.] **08285. g. 112.**

BUSCHAN (Georg Hermann Theodor) *See* Periodical Publications.—*Breslau.* Centralblatt für Anthropologie, Ethnologie und Urgeschichte. Herausgegeben von G. Buschan. 1896, *etc.* 8°. **P.P. 3863. c.**

—— *See* Periodical Publications.—*Stuttgart.* Ethnologischer Anzeiger . . . Herausgegeben von Dr. M. Heydrich und Dr. G. Buschan. 1926, *etc.* 8°. **P.P. 3863. dha.**

—— Altgermanische Überlieferungen in Kult und Brauchtum der Deutschen, *etc.* pp. 257. pl. XVI. *München*, [1936.] 8°. **10235. ee. 25.**

—— Die Basedow'sche Krankheit . . . Eine Monographie, *etc.* pp. 184. *Leipzig & Wien*, 1894. 8°. **7615. dd. 1.**

—— Geschlecht und Verbrechen . . . 3. Auflage. pp. 96. *Berlin & Leipzig*, [1908.] 8°. [*Grossstadt-Dokumente.* Bd. 48.] **12350. dd.**

—— Illustrierte Völkerkunde . . . Zweite, vollständig umgearbeitete und wesentlich vermehrte Auflage. 3 pt. *Stuttgart*, 1922–26. 8°. **010006. f. 7.**

BUSCHAN (Georg Hermann Theodor)

—— Im Anfang war das Weib. Neue Beiträge zur Menschen- und Völkerkunde, *etc.* [With plates.] 3 Bd. *Dresden,* 1927. 8°. **T.C.6.a.21.**

—— Kulturgeschichte Japans, *etc.* [With plates.] pp. 278. *Wien, Leipzig,* [1938.] 8°. **010056.** d. 2.

—— Leben und Treiben der deutschen Frau in der Urzeit. pp. 31. *Hamburg,* 1893. 8°. [*Sammlung gemeinverständlicher wissenschaftlicher Vorträge.* Neue Folge. Hft. 186.] **12249.** m. 8.

—— Studien und Forschungen zur Menschen- und Völkerkunde, unter wissenschaftlicher Leitung von G. Buschan. 15 vol. *Stuttgart,* 1907–1920. 8°. **10007.** dd. 16.

—— Ueber Myxödem und verwandte Zustände, zugleich ein Beitrag zur Schilddrüsenphysiologie und Schilddrüsentherapie, *etc.* pp. 181. *Leipzig,* 1896. 8°. **7615.** dd. 11.

—— Vorgeschichtliche Botanik der Cultur- und Nutzpflanzen der alten Welt, *etc.* pp. xii. 268. *Breslau,* 1895. 8°. **7030.** f. 17.

BUSCHARDT (Leo)

—— Vṛtra. Det rituelle Dæmondrab i den vediske Somakult. pp. 170. *København,* 1945. 8°. [*Kgl. Danske Videnskabernes Selskab. Historisk-filologiske meddelelser.* Bd. 30. no. 3.] Ac. **1023/14.**

BUSCHARDT (Leo) and **FABRITIUS** (Albert)

—— Besættelsestidens illegale blade og bøger. En bibliografi udarbejdet af L. Buschardt, A. Fabritius, Helge Tønnesen. (Illegale blade. [By L. Buschardt and A. Fabritius.] Illegale bøger. [By H. Tønnesen.]) pp. 201. 1954. 8°.

See Copenhagen.—*Kongelige Bibliotek.* **11927.** m. **22.**

—— Supplement og rettelser. pp. 80. [1960.] 8°. *See* Copenhagen.—*Kongelige Bibliotek.* **11927.** m. **22a.**

BUSCHBECK (A. E.) Die Einrichtung von Staats-Giro-Banken in der Preussischen Monarchie, *etc.* pp. 23. *Berlin,* 1845. 8°. **8225.** b. 24.

BUSCHBECK (Carl) Aus dem Kinderleben. Kleine Gedichte mit Bildern, *etc.* pp. 31. *Berlin,* [1870.] 8°. **11528.** k. 49.

BUSCHBECK (Erhard) *Evangelischer Pfarrer,* and **STEINACKER** (Gustav Wilhelm)

—— Verfassungsentwurf für die evang. Kirche Oesterreichs nach den, im Gutachten der österreichischen Superintendenten und Vertrauensmänner enthaltenen Grundlinien . . . Nebst dem Schematismus der evang. Gemeinden Oesterreichs und einem Unionsentwurf. pp. 111. *Triest,* 1850. 8°. **5125.** d. 24.

BUSCHBECK (Erhard) *Vicepresident of the Schutzverband deutscher Schriftsteller in Oesterreich.*

—— *See* Trakl (G.) Gesamtausgabe, *etc.* (Bd. 2. Aus goldenem Kelch. [Edited by E. Buschbeck.]) [1938, *etc.*] 8°. **11529.** aa. 1.

—— *See* Trakl (G.) Aus goldenem Kelch, *etc.* [Edited by E. Buschbeck.] [1939.] 8°. **11529.** a. 15.

—— Raoul Aslan und das Burgtheater. [With portraits.] pp. 161. *Wien,* 1946. 8°. **11797.** a. 74.

BUSCHBECK (Ernest Heinrich)

—— Austria. pp. xi. 251. *Oxford University Press: London,* 1949. 8°. **10215.** bbb. 21.

BUSCHBECK (Ernst Heinrich) Primitifs autrichiens. pp. 19. pl. 48. *Bruxelles; Paris,* 1937. 4°. **7861.** tt. **14.**

BUSCHBECK (F.) *Hauptmann.* Preussisches Feld-Taschenbuch für Offiziere aller Waffen zum Kriegs- und Friedens-Gebrauch, *etc.* 2 Tl. pp. xiv. 864. *Berlin,* 1853. 16°. **8828.** a. 10.

—— Buschbeck's Preussisches Feld-Taschenbuch . . . Zweite vollständig umgearbeitete Auflage. Herausgegeben von Karl von Helldorff. 2 Tl. *Berlin,* 1869, 70. 8°. **8832.** de. 1.

BUSCHBECK (Ferdinand Christian) Über Böhmens Schafwollhandel und Industrie, *etc.* pp. 24. *Prag,* 1843. 8°. **8244.bb.40.(3.)**

BUSCHBELL (Carl Gottfried Werner)

—— *See* Magnus (J.) *Bishop of Upsala.* Briefe von Johannes und Olaus Magnus . . . Gesammelt, erläutert und herausgegeben von G. Buschbell. 1932. 8°. [*Kungl. Samfundet för Utgifvande af Handskrifter rörande Skandinaviens Historia. Historiska handlingar.* dl. 28: 3.] **9425.** g. **1/28.**

—— *See* Meer (A. ter) Das Tagebuch des Abraham ter Meer . . . Bearbeitet von Dr. G. Buschbell. 1936. 8°. W.P. **11427/3.**

—— Reformation und Inquisition in Italien um die Mitte des xvi. Jahrhunderts. pp. xxiii. 344. *Paderborn,* 1910. 8°. [*Quellen und Forschungen aus dem Gebiete der Geschichte.* Bd. 13.] Ac. **2026/6.**

—— [Selbstbezeugungen des Kardinals Bellarmin.] Les "Confessions" du Cardinal Bellarmin. Contribution à l'histoire du nouveau saint. pp. 165. *Paris,* 1933. 8°. **20001.** g. **16.**

—— Das vatikanische Archiv und die Bedeutung seiner Erschliessung durch Papst Leo xiii. pp. 24. *Hamm,* 1903. 8°. [*Frankfurter zeitgemässe Broschüren.* Neue Folge. Bd. 22. Hft. 12.] **12209.** g.

BUSCHBELL (Gottfried) *See* Buschbell (Carl G. W.)

BUSCHE (Alexandre van den) called Le Sylvain. Cinquante ænigmes francoises, d'Alexandre Syluain, auec les expositions d'icelles. Ensemble quelques ænigmes espagnolles dudict autheur, & d'autres. 2 pt. *Chez G. Beys: Paris,* 1582. 8°. **11475.** bb. **36.**
The titlepage of pt. 2 reads: "*Quarenta ænigmas en lengua espannola.*"

—— Epitomes de cent histoires tragicques, partie extraittes des Actes des Romains & autres, de l'inuention de l'autheur, auecq' les demandes, accusations & deffences sur la matiere d'icelles. Ensemble quelques poëmes. ff. 295. *Par N. Bonfons: Paris,* 1581. 8°. G. **12417.**

—— [Another edition.] Histoires tragiques, redigees en epitome . . . Ensemble quelques poëmes. pp. 295. *Par N. Bonfons: Paris,* 1588. 8°. G. **2231.**

—— [Epitomes de cent histoires tragicques.] The Orator: handling a hundred seuerall discourses, in forme of declamations: some of the arguments being drawne from Titus Liuius and other ancient writers, the rest of the authors owne inuention . . . Englished by L. P. [The dedicatory epistle signed: Lazarus Piot.] pp. 436. *Printed by Adam Islip: London,* 1596. 4°. **11396.** aaa. **19.**

—— [Another copy.] **1091.** a. **22.**

—— [Another copy.] G. **10456.**

BUSCHE (ALEXANDRE VAN DEN) called LE SYLVAIN.

—— Declamation Ninety-Five. Of a Jew, who would for his debt have a pound of the flesh of a Christian. From the Orator of Alex. Silvayn, Englished by L. P. [i.e. Lazarus Piot.] [The translation here attributed to Anthony Munday.] *See* COLLIER (John P.) Shakespeare's Library, *etc.* vol. 2. [1843.] 8°. **1344. f. 3.**

—— Poemes et anagrames composez des lettres du nom du roy, et des roynes ensemble de plusieurs princes et gentilshommes et dames de France, *etc.* *Chez G. Iulian: Paris,* 1576. 4°. **11475. c. 5.**

—— Premier liure des proces tragiques, contenant cinquante cinq histoires . . . Ensemble quelque poësie morale. ff. 198. *Par G. le Niergue: Anuers,* 1579. 12°. **012330. de. 20.**

—— Le Recueil des dames illustres en vertu: ensemble vn dialogue de l'amour honneste: plus vn discours poëtique des miseres de ce monde. 2 pt. *Par B. Rigaud: Lyon,* 1581. 12°. **8415. a. 9.**

—— Œuvres choisies d'Alexandre Sylvain de Flandre . . . précédées d'une étude sur l'auteur et ses œuvres par Henri Helbig, et accompagnées d'une notice inédite par G. Colletet. pp. lxxxii. 121. *Liége,* 1861. 12°. **11475. bbb. 12.**

BUSCHE (CAROLUS) Observationes criticae in Euripidis Troades. pp. 47. *Lipsiae,* 1887. 8°. **11312. dd. 12. (9.)**

BUSCHE (H. C.) Untersuchungen über die Rentabilität einer Zuckerfabrik, mit Ausschluss des landwirthschaftlichen Antheils. pp. 33. *Hannover,* 1874. 4°. **7942. h. 16.**

BUSCHE (HERMANN VOM) *pseud.* [i.e. HERMANN BAUMSTARK.] *See* also BAUMSTARK (H.)

—— Die freie religiöse Aufklärung, ihre Geschichte und ihre Häupter . . . Eingeführt durch eine irenische Abhandlung über . . . Vereinigung zwischen Wissen und Glauben von Dr. H. E. G. Paulus. 2 Abt. *Darmstadt,* 1846. 8°. **3911. c. 107.**

—— Friedrich Carl Freiherr v. Moser. Aus seinen Schriften sein Geist an das neunzehnte Jahrhundert. pp. viii. 397. *Stuttgart,* 1846. 8°. **8072. c. 15.**

—— Populäres Staatslexicon in einem Bande. Staatswissenschaftliches Handbuch der politischen Aufklärung . . . herausgegeben durch Dr. H. vom Busche. coll. 2844. *Stuttgart,* 1846–52. 8°. **8007. f. 14.**
Published in parts.

BUSCHE (JULIUS VON DEM) Gefechts-Kalender der Hannoverschen Armee vom 30jährigen Kriege bis zur Schlacht bei Langensalza, *etc.* pp. 59. *Hannover,* 1877. 8°. **8823. h. 3.**

BUSCHE (PHILIPPUS WILHELMUS VON DEM) De foro principum et privatorum communi. 1745. *See* STRYKIUS (S.) Viri quondam illustris . . . S. Strykii . . . opera omnia, *etc.* vol. 7. 1743, *etc.* fol. **498. g. 9.**

BUSCHEK (WILHELM)

—— Die heutige Gefechtsweise der Infanterie. Vergleichende Reglements-Studie. pp. iv. 183. *Teschen,* 1898. 8°. **M.L. g. 25.**

—— Taktik. [With maps.] 2 vol. *Teschen,* 1894, 95. 8°. **8821. e. 1.**

BUSCHE-KESSEL (ELISE VON DEM) *See* BERNSTORFF (A. L. E. von) *Countess.* Gräfin Elise von Bernstorff, *etc.* [Edited by E. von dem Busche-Kessell.] 1896. 8°. **010707. h. 39.**

BÜSCHEL ( ) [For the German surname of this form:] *See* BUESCHEL.

BUSCHEN (ARTHUR VON) Aperçu statistique des forces productives de la Russie . . . Annexé au catalogue spécial de la section russe. pp. 268. 1867. 8°. *See* PARIS.—*Exposition Universelle de* 1867. [*Russia.*] **7959. c. 11.**

—— Bevölkerung des Russischen Kaiserreichs in den wichtigsten statistischen Verhältnissen dargestellt. pp. vi. 81. pl. 16. *Gotha,* 1862. 16°. **10291. aa. 42.**

—— Наличное населенiе имперiи за 1858 годъ. Съ картою населенности Европейской Россiи, *etc.* pp. x. 330. *Санктпетербургъ,* 1863. 8°. [*Статистическiя таблицы Россiйской имперiи.* вып. 2.] **S.N.168.**

BUSCHENAU UND THUMENBERG (GEORG FRIEDRICH KORDENBUSCH VON) *See* KORDENBUSCH (G. F.)

BUSCHENDORF (CARL FRIEDRICH) Gründlicher Unterricht von Thurmuhren welcher den Bau, die Einrichtung und Beschaffenheit, die Behandlung, Pflege und Stellung dieser Kunstwerke deutlich darstellt, erklärt, *etc.* pp. viii. 136. pl. VI. *Leipzig,* 1805. 4°. **8766. aaa. 7.**

BUSCHENDORF (KARL FRIEDRICH) *See* BUSCHENDORF (Carl F.)

BUSCHENHAGEN (FRITZ) and LUCKE (WALTER) Die Herbstschlacht in der Champagne und im Artois 1915 . . . Zweite Auflage. Mit 5 Kartenskizzen. pp. iv. 28. *Berlin,* 1916. 8°. **9083. bbb. 35.**

BÜSCHENTHAL ( ) [For the German surname of this form:] *See* BUESCHENTHAL.

BÜSCHER ( ) [For the German surname of this form:] *See* BUESCHER.

BUSCHER (HANS)

—— Der Basler Arzt Heinrich Pantaleon, 1522–1595. (Separat-Abdruck aus der Dissertation "Heinrich Pantaleon und sein Heldenbuch.") pp. xii. 76. 1947. 8°. *See* SWITZERLAND.—*Schweizerische Gesellschaft für Geschichte der Medizin und der Naturwissenschaften.* **10710. cc. 6.**

—— Heinrich Pantaleon und sein Heldenbuch. pp. ixx [xix]. 305. *Basel,* 1946. 8°. [*Basler Beiträge zur Geschichtswissenschaft.* Bd. 26.] **W.P. 9213/26.**

—— Die strafrechtliche Haftung des Kraftfahrzeughalters. pp. ix. 79. *Breslau,* 1931. 8°. [*Strafrechtliche Abhandlungen.* Hft. 289.] **6026.aa.1/289.**

BUSCHER (HEIZO) *See* BUSCHERUS.

BUSCHER (STATS) *See* NESMANN (J.) Jesuiter-Zunge in dem neulich zu Stade edirten Catechismo [of Martin Luther with notes by J. Gesenius], nach Anleitung . . . S. Buscheri, *etc.* 1724. 4°. **3506. f. 3. (7.)**

—— M. Stat. Buscheri . . . Paraenesis eximia. Monstrans egregiè quàm turpiter Christianismus cū ethnicismo in educatione juvenili commisceatur, *etc.* *See* WERDENHAGEN (J. A. von) Ioh. Angelii Werdenhagen I.C.C. Vniuersalis introductio in omnes respublicas, *etc.* 1632. 12°. **528. a. 7.**

BUSCHERBRUCK (CARL EMIL WILHELM) Die altfranzösischen Predigten des Heiligen Bernhard von Clairvaux. 1896. *See* PERIODICAL PUBLICATIONS.—*Erlangen.* Romanische Forschungen, *etc.* Bd. 9. Hft. 3. 1883, *etc.* 8°. **P.P. 5044.** ad.

BUSCHERBRUCK (KARL EMIL WILHELM) *See* BUSCHERBRUCK (Carl E. W.)

BUSCHERE (MARTINUS DE) Index divinorum operum ex augustissimo altaris sacramento erga Christianum populum symbolis latinis ac vernaculis quintupliciter partitus. Wyser vande goddelycke wercken in't hoogh-weerdigh Sacrament des Autaers. 3 pt. *L. Doppes: Brugghe,* 1686. 8°. **700.** b. **8.**

BUSCHERUS (ANTONIUS) *Resp. See* URSINUS (G.) Disputatio I. [*etc.*] quæstionum illustrium philosophicarum, *etc.* disp. 5. [1600?] 4°. **536.** e. **9.** (**4.**)

BUSCHERUS (CHRISTIANUS N.) De invidia exercitium academicum, *etc. Praes.* H. Forelius. pp. 38. *Upsalis,* [1704.] 8°. **1090.** e. **5.** (**1.**)

BUSCHERUS (HEIZO) *See* PISCATOR (Johann) *of Herborn.* Admonitio . . . de exercitationibus H. Buscheri. 1594. 8°. **1014.** aa. **12.** (**2.**)

—— Arithmeticæ logica methodo in vsum scholarum triuialium succincte conscriptæ libri duo . . . Editio tertia. pp. 46. *E Paltheniano Typographeo: Francofurti,* 1600. 8°. **C. 74.** a. **3.** (**2.**)

—— Editio quarta. pp. 46. *E Paltheniano Typographæo: Francofurti,* 1608. 8°. **536.** d. **24.** (**3.**)

—— [Another edition.] Arithmeticæ. Liber [*sic*] II. *See* SCHEIBLER (C.) Philosophia compendiosa, *etc.* 1623. 8°. **1478.** cc. **23.**

—— Trias sacra, virtutum, sapientiæ et pietatis doctrinam ex libris Salomonis R. & Siracidis methodice, neruose collectam et libris tribus ethicæ christianæ speculum exhibens. pp. 167. *Impensis & typis I. Bringeri: Francofurti,* 1615. 12°. **700.** b. **2.** (**2.**)

BUSCHERUS (STATIUS) *See* BUSCHER (Stats)

BUSCHEY (HENRI) Le Mystere de la saincte incarnation de nostre redempteur & sauueur Jesus-Christ: par personages, *etc.* [In verse.] (Action de graces, *etc.*) pp. 116. *De l'imprimerie de C. Plantin: Anuers,* 1587. 8°. **C. 39.** a. **28.**
A MS. *note on the titlepage reads "de la main de l'Autheur,* 1595."

BÜSCHGENS ( ) [For the German surname of this form:] *See* BUESCHGENS.

BUSCHHOFF (ADOLF) *See* LAIE. Der Antisemitismus . . . Unter besonderer Berücksichtigung des Prozesses Buschhoff. Culturhistorische Skizze von einem Laien. 1892. 8°. **4034.** m. **16.** (**7.**)

—— Der Fall Buschhoff. Aktenmässige Darstellung des Xantener Knabenmord-Prozesses, *etc.* pp. 56. *Frankfurt,* [1892.] 8°. [*Interessante Criminal-Faelle.* no. 2.] **5604.** d. **21.**

—— L'Infanticidio di Xanten e il processo di Cleve contro l'ebreo Wolf Buschoff. Dibattimento e osservazioni. Estratto dal Verona Fedele, *etc.* pp. 122. *Verona,* 1892. 8°. **5373.** de. **1.**

BUSCHHORN (CARL) Jugendstürme. Gesammelte Gedichte, *etc.* pp. 144. *Paderborn,* [1899.] 8°. **011528.** g. **82.**

BUSCHHORN (CARL)

—— Max Oberbreyer. Eine Würdigung seines litterarischen Schaffens. pp. 12. *Paderborn,* 1896. 16°. **10602.** e. **9.** (**4.**)

BUSCHI (AVERARDO) Averardo Buschi e le sue poesie. Con prefazione e disegni di Gaetano Crespi. pp. 126. *Milano,* 1886. 8°. **11436.** bbb. **35.**

BUSCHI (GIUSEPPE) A Cesena patria degli immortali pontefici Pio VI. e VII. già sede episcopale di Pio VIII. innalzato al trono li XXXI. marzo MDCCCXXIX. Giuseppe Buschi Cesenate . . . D.D.D. Sonetto. *Ancona,* 1829. *s. sh.* fol. **898.** i. **10.** (**10.**)

BUSCHI (NICOLAUS) *Bishop of Ferentino.* Nicolaus Buschi . . . episcopus Ferentinus . . . canonicis et capitulis clero et populo civitatis et diæcesis Ferentinatis salutem in Domino sempiternam. pp. viii. *Romæ,* 1800. 4°. **1356.** k. **1.** (**59.**)

BUSCHIAZZO (MARIO JOSÉ)

—— *See* ANGULO ÍÑIGUEZ (D.) Historia del arte hispano-americano, *etc.* [With chapters by E. Marco Dorta and M. J. Buschiazzo.] 1945, *etc.* 4°. **W.P. 11896.**

—— Estudios de arquitectura colonial hispano americana. [With plates.] pp. 153. *Buenos Aires,* 1944. 4°. **7823.** dd. **34.**

—— La Iglesia del Pilar. [The Church of Nuestra Señora del Pilar, Buenos Aires.] *Span., Eng. & Fr.* pp. 41. pl. CXV. *Buenos Aires,* 1945. 4°. [*Documentos de arte argentino.* cuaderno 21.] **W.P. 3787.**

BUSCHICK (RICHARD) Die Abhängigkeit der verschiedenen Bevölkerungsdichtigkeiten des Königreichs Sachsen von den geographischen Bedingungen. pp. 61. pl. 3. 1895. *See* LEIPZIG.—*Verein für Erdkunde, etc.* Wissenschaftliche Veröffentlichungen. Bd. 2. 1891, *etc.* 8°. **Ac. 6056/2.**

BÜSCHIN (SOPHIA) *See* BUESCHER (Sophie C.)

BÜSCHING ( ) [For the German surname of this form:] *See* BUESCHING.

BUSCHING (MARCO) *See* BOSCHINI.

BUSCHING (PAUL) Die Entwickelung der handelspolitischen Beziehungen zwischen England und seinen Kolonieen bis zum Jahre 1860. Mit Anhang: Tabellarische Uebersicht über den Kolonialhandel 1826–1900. pp. viii. 244. pl. v [IV]. *Stuttgart & Berlin,* 1902. 8°. [*Münchener volkswirtschaftliche Studien.* no. 48.] **08248.** f. **13.** (**3.**)

BUSCHIUS (GEORGIUS) Disputatio logica de prædicamentis, *etc. Praes.* A. Froelingius. *Typis H. Mulleri: Helmestadii,* 1661. 4°. **521.** d. **33.** (**4.**)

BUSCHIUS (HERMANNUS) *See* BIBLE.—*Hagiographa.—Selections.* [*Latin.*] Dictata quædam vtilissima ex Prouerbijs sacris & Ecclesiastico, ad studiosorum quorumꝗ vtilitatem, ab H. Buschio collecta. 1518. 4°. **3165.** bb. **8.**

—— *See* CLAUDIANUS (C.) Cl. Claudiani Proserpinae raptus: cũ H. Buschij Pasiphili . . . cõmentario, *etc.* 1514. 4°. **997.** l. **2.**

—— *See* HAMELMANN (H.) De Pœdobaptismo . . . Disputatio habita . . . ab H. Buschio aliisquè viris doctis, contra Bernhardum Rothmannum & eius complices, *etc.* 1572. 8°. **848.** d. **9.**

BUSCHIUS (Hermannus)

—— *See* Hamelmann (H.) Hermanni Hamelmanni De vita, studiis, itineribus, scriptis et laboribus H. Buschii . . . narratio. 1668. 4°. [*Goes* (*J.*) *Opuscula varia de Westphalia.*] 819. g. 10.

—— *See* Hamelmann (H.) De vita, studiis et laboribus v. cl. H. Buschii . . . narratio H. Hamelmanni. 1710. 8°. [*Rolle* (*R. H.*) *Memoriæ philosophorum . . . clarissimorum renovatæ.* decas 1.] 275. c. 16.

—— *See* Liessem (H. J.) De Hermanni Buschii vita et scriptis commentatio historica . . . Adiuncta sunt H. Buschii carmina quaedam. 1866. 8°. 10705. e. 32. (10.)

—— *See* Nuenare (H. à) *Count.* Epistolae trium illustrium viroꝝ [J. Reuchlin, H. Buschius and U. von Hutten] ad Hermannum comitem Nuenarium. Eiusdem responsoria una ad Io. Reuchlinum, & altera ad lectorem, *etc.* 1518. 4°. 10905. c. 28.

—— —— 1717. fol. [*Hardt* (*H. von der*) *Historia literaria reformationis, etc.* pt. 2.] 200. f. 5.

—— *See* Persius Flaccus (A.) [*Latin.*] A. Persii Flacci Satyræ . . . H. Buschii . . . epistola, qua Persiani prologi & primæ satyræ argumentum explicatur, *etc.* 1522. 4°. 833. f. 34.

—— —— 1531. 4°. 1001. h. 25.

—— —— 1534. 16°. 1001. a. 25.

—— —— 1546. 8°. 1002. d. 8. (4.)

—— *See* Persius Flaccus (A.) [*Latin.*] Auli Flacci Persii . . . satyræ sex, *etc.* (Hermanni Buschii docta & noua epistola.) 1551. fol. [*Iunii Iuuenalis et A. Persii Flacci, Satyræ.*] 655. d. 10.

—— *See* Silius Italicus (C.) Silii Italici De bello punico libri septemdecim. Cum argumentis H. Buschii, et scholiis in margine adiectis, *etc.* 1531. 8°. 237. a. 14.

—— In hoc opuscl'o hec ꝯtinent'. Hermãni Buschij Spicilegiũ .xxxv. illustriũ phõrum auctoritates vtilesqꝫ sententias continens. Eiusdem in laudẽ diue virginis Epigrãmata quedã. Epistole item et versus quorũdam doctorũ virorũ ad eundem. Oestrum in Tilmannũ Heuerlingũ eiusdem. G.L. ms. notes. [*J. Winter: Magdeburg,*] 1507. 4°. 8461. c. 29.

—— Hermanni Buschii Pasiphili Spicilegium .xxxv. illustriũ philosophorum Auctoritates vtilesqꝫ Sententias continens. Eiusdem de virtute Oda lyrica. G.L. *Venundantur in ędibus J. Ingersmytten: Embrice; excussum ꝑ me T. de Borne: Dauentrie,* [1515?] 4°. 8461. c. 13.

—— Hermanni Buschii Pasiphili ἐγκωμιον pacis . . . Eiusdem ode lyrica, quæ mõstrat omnem locum sibi inuisum, cui lr̃æ displiceant, *etc.* *See* Erasmus (D.) [*Two or more Works.*] D. Erasmi Roterodami liber bellissimus, cui titulũ prætulit, Querela pacis undiqꝫ gentium eiectæ profligatæqꝫ, *etc.* [1517?] 4°. 94. e. 8. (2.)

—— Carmen Saphicum de contemnendo mundo. *See* infra: Oda de contemnendo mundo, *etc.*

—— De saluberrimo fructuosissimoqꝫ diue virgĩs Marie Psalterio; triplex Hecatostichon Hermanni Buschij monasterieñ. [With a woodcut.] G.L. [*Retro Minores:*] *Cologne,* [1500?] 8°. IA. 5159.
12 *leaves.* *Sig.* a–c⁴. *The number of lines to a page varies.*

BUSCHIUS (Hermannus)

—— [Another edition.] Cum quibusdam alijs carminibus. Ma. Diui Cipriani . . . de ligno salutifere crucis carmen heroicũ Claudiani . . . inuocatio ad Christum pro Theodosio cesare Augusto. G.L. [*Heirs of H. Quentell: Cologne,* 1508?] 4°. 1070. m. 14.

—— De singulari auctoritate Veteris et Noui Instrumenti, Sacrorũ, Ecclesiasticorumq́; testimoniorum, Libri ii, *etc.* [*F. Rhode:*] *Marpurgi,* 1529. 8°. 845. a. 6.

—— De vita, miraculis, & passione Christi sertum rosaceum, *etc.* *See* infra: Sertum rosaceum diuæ virginis Mariæ de vita, miraculis, & passione Christi.

—— Her. Buschii Pasiphili. Decimationum Plautinarum πεμπτας siue quintana secunda. *Apud Helisabet viduam: Coloniæ,* 1518. 4°. 11707. d. 2.

—— Hermanni Buschij Pasiphili poete non incelebris humaniores litteras in famigeratissima: nominatissimaqꝫ Lipsensi Academia: publice docentis Epigrammatum Liber Tercius. G.L. *Impressum per M. Lantssberck: Lips,* 1504. 4°. 11408. b. 20.

—— Hermanni Buschii Pasiphili Hypanticon, illustrissimo principi . . . Georgio Comiti palatino Rheni, super solenni suo in Spirã urbem introitu, dicatum. pp. 57. *Apud Cratandrum: Basileæ,* 1520. 4°. 11408. d. 5.
The titlepage is engraved.

—— [Another edition.] *See* G., A. F. G. Delitiæ poetarum germanorum, *etc.* pt. 1. 1612. 16°. 238. i. 14.

—— In acerbum Joannis Murmellij Ruremũdensis . . . Obitum. H. Buschii Pasiphili funebre lessum. siue Epicedion. G.L. ms. notes. [*P. Quentell:*] *Colonie,* 1518. 4°. 11408. bb. 69.

—— Hermanni Buschij Pasiphili in artẽ Donati de octo ꝑtibus orõis cõmentarius ex Prisciano: Diomede: Seruio: Capro: Agretio: Phoca clarissimis grãmaticis: cura et labore nõ mediocri ad publicam iuuentutis vtilitatem institutionemqꝫ collectus. G.L. [*W. Stöckel:*] *Liptzk,* 1511. 4°. 12932. d. 8.

—— Hermanni Buschij Pasiphili in puellas Lipsenses Senarij. *See* Dati (A.) Epistola Augustini Dathi amoris leuitatem improbans, *etc.* [1510?] 8°. 10905. e. 28.

—— Inuitatio ad unum mediatorem Christum. *See* infra: Ode sapphica ad unum mediatorem inuitans Christum.

—— Hermanni Buschii Pasiphili poetæ celeberrimi Lipsica, cum Philippi Noueniani Hasfurtini scholiis. [With woodcuts.] *Ex officina M. Herbipolensis: Lipsię,* 1521. 4°. 11408. d. 6.

—— Hermãni Buschij Oda de cõtẽnẽdo mũdo, & amãda sola virtute & sciẽtia. *See* Spagnuoli (B.) *Mantuanus.* F. Baptiste Mantuani Bucolica, *etc.* 1503. 4°. IA. 5190. (5.)

—— [Another edition.] *See* Spagnuoli (B.) *Mantuanus.* F. Baptiste Mantuani Bucolica, *etc.* 1505. 4°. IA. 47689. (1.)

—— [Another edition.] *See* Spagnuoli (B.) *Mantuanus.* Baptiste Mantuani bucolica, *etc.* 1511. 4°. 1070. m. 12.

—— [Another edition.] *See* Spagnuoli (B.) *Mantuanus.* Baptiste Mantuani Bucolica, *etc.* 1517. 4°. 1213. l. 1.

—— Ode sapphica ad unum mediatorem inuitans Christum. *See* Melanchthon (P.) [*Separate Works.*] De unico seruatore et mediatore Christo, ex ipsius diuinae scripturae fontibus deprompta carmina, *etc.* 1544. 8°. 1477. bbb. 16.

BUSCHIUS (Hermannus)

—— Prestabili et rare eruditionis viro Martino Mellerstat alias Polichio ducali phisico et litteratorū oīm fauissori. [A letter.] G. L. [*Jacob Thanner: Leipsic,* 1504?] 4°. **3836.** b. **41.**

—— Sertum rosaceum diuæ virginis Mariæ de vita, miraculis, & passione Christi. *See* Mutius (M.) Triumphus Christi, *etc.* 1550. 4°. G. **9710.** (4.)

—— Succinctta [*sic*] & compendiaria Senece vita, *etc. See* Seneca (L. A.) [*Epistolae.*] Annei Senece moralissimi ad Lucillium Epistolarum opus, *etc.* [1510.] 4°. **1248.** e. **23.**

—— Hermanni Buschii Pasiphili Vallum humanitatis. *Per N. Cæsarem: Coloniæ,* 1518. 4°. **819.** f. **1.**

BUSCHIUS (Jacobus) *See* Plato. [*Works.—Greek.*] Ἅπαντα Πλάτωνος, *etc.* ms. notes [by J. Buschius and others]. 1534. fol. **722.** m. **11.**

BUSCHIUS (Joannes) *See* Grube (C. L.) Johannes Busch, Augustinerpropst zu Hildersheim, *etc.* 1881. 8°. **4867.** aa. **23.**

—— *See* Woude (Sape van der) Johannes Busch, Windesheimer kloosterreformator en kroniekschrijver, *etc.* 1947. 8°. **4888.** l. **21.**

—— Des Augustinerpropstes Johannes Busch Chronicon Windeshemense und Liber de reformatione monasteriorum . . . Bearbeitet von Dr. Karl Grube. pp. xxxxviii. 824. *Halle,* 1886. 8°. [*Geschichtsquellen der Provinz Sachsen.* Bd. 19.] Ac. **7161.**

—— Chronicon canonicorum regularium Ordinis S. Augustini Capituli Windesemensis auctore Ioanne Buschio . . . Accedit Chronicon Montis S. Agnetis auctore Thoma à Kempis . . . nunc primùm in lucem edita vna cum vindiciis Kempensibus Heriberti Ros-weydi . . . pro libro De imitatione Christi. 3 pt. *Apud P. & I. Belleros: Antuerpiæ,* 1621. 8°. **4660.** a. **1.**

—— Documenta historica ex Chronico Windeshemensi, Ordinis canonicorum regularium, authore Joanne Buschio, et ex Chronico Montis S. Agnetis auctore Thoma à Kempis. Quibus ostenditur, Thomam à Kempis libelli De imitatione Christi authorem dici non debere. pp. 104. *Ratisbonæ,* 1762. 8°. T. **483.** (2.)

—— M. Iohannis Buschii Liber reformationis monasteriorum quorundam Saxoniae, *etc.* 1710. *See* Leibnitz (G. W. von) *Baron.* Scriptores rerum Brunsvicensium, *etc.* tom. 2. 1707, *etc.* fol. **803.** l. **4.**

BUSCHIUS (Justus Henricus) *See* Stegmann (J.) Photinianismus. Hoc est, succincta refutatio errorum Photinianorum. Quinquaginta sex disputationibus breuiter comprehensa, *etc.* (disp. 27. De regno Christi.—disp. 47. De efficacitate baptismi. *Resp.* J. H. Buschius.) 1626. 8°. **1120.** a. **2.**

BUSCHKE (Abraham) Die Blastomykose. Nach den bisherigen Erfahrungen und eigenen Untersuchungen dargestellt, *etc.* pp. viii. 74. pl. ix. *Stuttgart,* 1902. 4°. [*Bibliotheca medica.* Abt. D[II]. Hft. 10.] **7391.** w. **1.**

—— Über Hefenmykosen bei Menschen und Thieren. pp. 20. *Leipzig,* 1898. 8°. [*Sammlung klinischer Vorträge.* Neue Folge. Chirurgie. no. 64.] **7441.** g.

BUSCHKE (Adolf) and **JACOBSOHN** (Friedrich) [Geschlechtsleben und sexuelle Hygiene.] Introduction to Sexual Hygiene . . . Translated . . . by Eden and Cedar Paul. pp. viii. 193. pl. xiii. *G. Routledge & Sons: London,* 1932. 8°. **07580.** bb. **39.**

BUSCHKE (Franz) *See* Buschke (Julius F.)

BUSCHKE (Julius Franz) *See* Cutler (Max) and Buschke (J. F.) Cancer, *etc.* 1938. 8°. **07620.** i. **30.**

—— *See* Schinz (H. R.) and Buschke (J. F.) Krebs und Vererbung, *etc.* 1935. 8°. **7440.** h. **7.**

—— Röntgenologische Skelettstudien an menschlichen Zwillingen und Mehrlingen. Ein Beitrag zu den Problemen der Konstitution und der Phylogenese, *etc.* pp. 47. pl. 50. *Leipzig,* 1934. 8°. [*Fortschritte auf dem Gebiete der Röntgenstrahlen.* Ergänzungsbd. 46.] **8901.** g. **1/46.**

BUSCHKENS (John Philip)

—— De Paradoxale apnoe. Experimentele studie over de invloed van koolzuur en narcose. The paradoxical apnœa, experimental study on the influence of carbondioxide and anæsthesia. With a summary in English. Proefschrift, *etc.* pp. 96. *Utrecht,* 1951. 8°. **08909.** t. **24.**

BUSCHKIEL (Alfred H.) Das Kassen- und Zahlungswesen der staatlichen und kommunalen Behörden im Königreich Sachsen und seine jüngste Entwicklung. Eine Untersuchung über die Wechselbeziehungen zwischen Banken und öffentlichen Kassen. pp. 95. *Stuttgart & Berlin,* 1909. 8°. [*Münchener volkswirtschaftliche Studien.* Stück 89.] **08248.** f. **27.** (4.)

BUSCHKIEL (Ludwig) Die deutschen Farben von ihren Anfängen bis zum Ende des zweiten Kaiserreiches. pp. xii. 103. *Weimar,* 1935. 8°. **9907.** r. **3.**

BUSCHKIEL (Reinhard) Die Rentabilität der Sächsischen Staatseisenbahnen. pp. 81. *Stuttgart & Berlin,* 1909. 8°. [*Münchener volkswirtschaftliche Studien.* Stück 93.] **08248.** f. **28.** (4.)

BUSCHLEN (John Preston) Behind the Wicket. Short stories relating to life in the Canadian banks. pp. 264. *William Briggs: Toronto,* 1914. 8°. NN. **1909.**

—— A Canadian Bankclerk. [A novel.] pp. 366. *William Briggs: Toronto,* 1913. 8°. NN. **1427.**

—— The Drummer. [A novel.] pp. 330. *Ansell Publishing Co.: Toronto,* 1915. 8°. NN. **4012.**

—— The War and our Banks. [With illustrations.] pp. 95. *Hollingsworth & Buschlen: Toronto,* [1914.] 8°. **8223.** de. **47.**

—— The World War. Poems. *Hollingsworth & Buschlen: Toronto,* [1914.] 8°. **11687.** f. **45.**
Printed on one side of the leaf only.

—— Poèmes de la guerre . . . Traduits par Marcel de Jonckheere. *Toronto,* 1915. 8°. **11687.** g. **46.**

BUSCHLINGER (Willi)

—— Entwicklungstendenzen in der Kreditpolitik der gewerblichen Kreditgenossenschaften seit der Stabilisierung. pp. 69. 1940. 8°. *See* Frankfort on the Main.—*Johann Wolfgang Goethe Universität.—Institut für Genossenschaftswesen.* **8219.** h. **15.**

BUSCHMAN (Alfred) Die Neuordnung des bundesstaatlichen Eisenbahndienstes in Österreich, *etc.* pp. ix. 138. *Wien,* 1925. 8°. **08235.** d. **65.**

BUSCHMAN (GOTTHARD VON) *Baron.* *See* EGINHARD, *pseud.* [i.e. *Baron* G. von Buschman.]

BUSCHMAN (JOSEPH OTTOKAR VON) *Baron.* Das Salz, dessen Vorkommen und Verwertung in sämtlichen Staaten der Erde. 2 Bd. *Leipzig*, 1909, 06. 4°. **7109.** dd. **26.**

BUSCHMAN (PETRUS) Disputatio medica inauguralis, de hæmoptoë; sive sanguinis sputo, *etc.* *Apud viduam & heredes J. Elsevirii: Lugduni Batavorum*, 1678. 4°. **1185.** g. **15.** (**1.**)

BUSCHMANN (ALOYS) Der alte Gott lebt noch. Volksstück in einem Akt. pp. 11. *Paderborn*, [1928.] 16°. [*Kleines Theater.* Hft. 467.] **11747.** d. **40.** (**11.**)

—— Schwiegervater. Schwank in einem Akt. pp. 38. *Paderborn*, [1914.] 8°. [*Kleines Theater.* Hft. 458.] **11747.** d. **40.** (**2.**)

BUSCHMANN (ARNT) *See* BOSMAN (Arent)

BUSCHMANN (CHRISTIAN FRIEDRICH LUDWIG)

—— *See* BUSCHMANN (H.) Christian Friedrich Ludwig Buschmann, der Erfinder der Mund- und der Handharmonika, *etc.* [With portraits.] 1938. 8°. **7893.** s. **9.**

BUSCHMANN (EDUARD) *See* BUSCHMANN (Johann C. E.)

BUSCHMANN (ERNEST) *See* BUSCHMANN (Joseph E.)

BUSCHMANN (HEINRICH)

—— Christian Friedrich Ludwig Buschmann, der Erfinder der Mund- und der Handharmonika. Ein Beitrag zur Geschichte dieser Musikinstrumente, *etc.* (Sonderbeilage der Hohner-Klänge.) [With portraits.] pp. 23. *Trossingen*, 1938. 8°. **7893.** s. **9.**

BUSCHMANN (HUGO) Charakteristik der griechischen Rhetoren beim Rhetor Seneca. pp. 22. *Parchim*, 1878. 4°. **11312.** m. **11.**

BUSCHMANN (J. E.) *Publisher, of Antwerp.* *See* PERIODICAL PUBLICATIONS.—*Antwerp.* De Vlaemsche school, *etc.* (Nieuwe reeks. jaerg. 1–14. Onze kunst. jaerg. 1–5. Uitgegeven door J. E. Buschmann.) 1855, *etc.* 4°. P.P. **4595.** ch.

—— *See* PERIODICAL PUBLICATIONS.—*London.* Art . . . Edited by J. E. Buschmann. 1903, *etc.* 4°. P.P. **1931.** ud.

BUSCHMANN (JEAN CHARLES ÉDOUARD) *See* BUSCHMANN (Johann C. E.)

BUSCHMANN (JOHANN CARL EDUARD) Das Apache als eine athapaskische Sprache erwiesen . . . In Verbindung mit einer systematischen Worttafel des athapaskischen Sprachstamms . . . (Abt. 2. Die Verwandtschafts-Verhältnisse der athapaskischen Sprachen.—Abt. 3. Systematische Worttafel des athapaskischen Sprachstamms.) Aus den Abhandlungen der Königl. Akademie der Wissenschaften zu Berlin, *etc.* 3 pt. *Berlin*, 1860, 63. 4°. **12911.** g. **18.**

—— Der athapaskische Sprachstamm . . . Aus den Abhandlungen der Königl. Akademie der Wissenschaften zu Berlin, *etc.* *Berlin*, 1856. 4°. **12907.** ff. **26.**

—— [Another copy, with a different titlepage.] **12906.** g. **3.**
A presentation copy from the author to Alexander von Humboldt.

BUSCHMANN (JOHANN CARL EDUARD)

—— Aperçu de la langue des îles Marquises et de la langue taïtienne, précédé d'une introduction sur l'histoire et la géographie de l'archipel des Marquises . . . Accompagné d'un vocabulaire inédit de la langue taïtienne par le baron Guillaume de Humboldt. pp. 197. *Berlin*, 1843. 8°. **1333.** f. **4.**

—— Grammatik der sonorischen Sprachen: vorzüglich der Tarahumara, Tepeguana, Cora und Cahita; als IXter Abschnitt der Spuren der aztekischen Sprache . . . Aus den Abhandlungen der Königl. Akademie der Wissenschaften zu Berlin. Abt. 1–3. *Berlin*, 1864, 69, 67. 4°. **12907.** ff. **21.**
No more published.

—— Die Lautveränderung aztekischer Wörter in den sonorischen Sprachen und die sonorische Endung *ame* . . . Aus den Abhandlungen der Königl. Akademie der Wissenschaften zu Berlin, *etc.* *Berlin*, 1857. 4°. **12907.** ff. **28.**

—— [Another copy, with a different titlepage.] **12906.** g. **4.**

—— Lehrbuch der englischen Aussprache. pp. xx. 112. *Berlin*, 1832. 8°. **12982.** c. **11.**

—— Die Pima-Sprache und die Sprache der Koloschen . . . Aus den Abhandlungen der Königl. Akademie der Wissenschaften zu Berlin, *etc.* *Berlin*, 1857. 4°. **12907.** ff. **27.**

—— [Another copy, with a different titlepage.] **12906.** g. **2.**

—— Die Sprachen Kizh und Netela von Neu-Californien. [Reprinted from the "Abhandlungen der phil.-hist. Klasse der Königlichen Akademie der Wissenschaften zu Berlin."] *Berlin*, 1856. 4°. **12906.** g. **1.**
A presentation copy from the author to Alexander von Humboldt.

—— Textes marquésans et taïtiens, publiés et analysés par J. Ch. Éd. Buschmann. pp. 40. *Berlin*, 1843. 8°. **1333.** f. **8.**

—— Über den Naturlaut. [Reprinted from the "Abhandlungen der Königlichen Akademie der Wissenschaften zu Berlin."] pp. 33. *Berlin*, 1853. 4°. **12901.** k. **12.**

—— On Natural Sounds . . . Translated by Campbell Clarke, *etc.* [Extracted from the "Proceedings of the Philological Society."] [*London*, 1855.] 8°. **12901.** ccc. **11.** (**1.**)

—— Über die Verwandtschaft der Kinai-Idiome des Russischen Nordamerika's mit dem grossen athapaskischen Sprachstamme. pp. 6. [*Berlin*, 1854.] 8°. **12907.** b. **2.**
A presentation copy from the author to Alexander von Humboldt.

BUSCHMANN (JOSEPH ERNEST) *See* BELGIANS. Les Belges illustres, etc. (pt. 2. Par MM. L. Alvin . . . E. Buschmann [and others]. 1844, *etc.* 8°. **1321.** f. **2, 3.**

—— *See* PAPENBROECK (D. van) Annales antverpienses . . . Ediderunt F. H. Mertens . . . et E. Buschmann. 1845, *etc.* 8°. **10270.** d. **1.**

—— L'Écuelle et la besace. Scènes historiques du XVIme siècle. [In verse.] pp. vii. 254. *Anvers*, 1839. 8°. **12512.** f. **7.**

—— Pierre Paul Rubens, *etc.* [With plates.] pp. 22. 1840. fol. *See* ANTWERP.—*Société Royale des Sciences, Lettres et Arts.* Tab. **1248.** c.

BUSCHMANN (P. J.) Offenes Sendschreiben an den Verfasser des Aufsatzes: "Clemens August und seine Gegner," in Nr. 18 des religiösen Blattes gleichen Namens. pp. 20. *Neuss*, [1848.] 8°. **3913**. c. **29**.

BUSCHMANN (Paul) *See* Antwerp.—*Koninklijk Museum van Schoone Kunsten.* Œuvres choisies de maîtres belges, *etc.* (Notice critique par M. P. Buschmann.) 1921. fol. **7859**. g. **28**.

—— *See* Cornette (A. H.) In Memoriam Dr. Paul Buschmann. [With a portrait.] [1924.] 8°. **010704**. i. **14**.

—— Études d'art contemporain, publiées sous la direction de M. P. Buschmann. 3 no. *Anvers*, [1914.] 4°. **7864**. s. **41**.

—— Exposition de l'œuvre de Antoine van Dyck, organisée par la ville d'Anvers à l'occasion du 300e anniversaire de la naissance du maître . . . Illustré de 30 héliogravures d'après les originaux. pp. 33. *Paris*, 1900. fol. Dept. of Prints & Drawings.

—— François Snyders . . . Extrait de la Biographie nationale, *etc.* pp. 15. *Bruxelles*, 1921. 8°. **7860**. ee. **59**.

—— Jacob Jordaens. Eene studie . . . naar aanleiding van de tentoonstelling zijner werken ingericht te Antwerpen in mcmv. Met 45 afbeeldingen buiten tekst. pp. viii. 140. *Amsterdam*, 1905. 8°. **7857**. v. **6**.

—— Jacques Jordaens et son œuvre . . . Étude publiée à l'occasion de l'Exposition Jordaens organisée à Anvers en mcmv. Traduite du néerlandais par Georges Eekhoud. Avec 45 reproductions hors texte. pp. viii. 141. *Bruxelles*, 1905. 8°. **7857**. t. **5**.

—— Het Oxaal van 's-Hertogenbosch thans in het Victoria-and-Albert Museum te Londen . . . Met 20 afbeeldingen. Overgedrukt uit "Onze kunst." pp. 36. *Nijmegen*, 1918. 4°. **7816**. e. **35**.

—— Rubens en Van Dyck in het Ashmolean Museum te Oxford . . . Met 27 afbeeldingen. Overgedrukt uit "Onze kunst." pp. 35. *Nijmegen*, 1916. 8°. **7859**. h. **18**.

BUSCHMANN (Roland)

—— Hinter der Maginot-Linie. pp. 95. *Berlin*, [1939.] 8°. **08052**. c. **51**.

BUSCHMANN-VAN RIJSWICK (Elsa)

—— *See* Antwerp.—*Koninklijk Museum van Schoone Kunsten.* Beschrijvende catalogus. (2. Moderne meesters. Door E. Buschmann-van Rijswijck.) 1948, *etc.* 8°. W.P. **12615**.

—— *See* Antwerp. — *Koninklijk Museum van Schoone Kunsten.* Catalogue descriptif. (1. Maîtres anciens. [By] A. J. J. Delen. Traduction par E. Buschmann-Van Rijswijck et G. Gepts-Buysaert.—2. Maîtres modernes. Par E. Buschmann-Van Rijswijck.) 1948, *etc.* 8°. **7960**. df. **46**.

BUSCH-MICHELL (Arthur Pitt) *See* Michell.

BUSCHOFF (Adolf) *See* Buschhoff.

BUSCHOFF (Wolf) *See* Buschhoff (Adolf)

BUSCHOR (Ernst)

—— Altsamische Standbilder. [With plates.] pt. 1-3. *Berlin*, 1934, 35. fol. [*Bilderhefte antiker Kunst.* Hft. 1–3.] **Ac.5388.aa/16.**

BUSCHOR (Ernst)

—— Bronzekanne aus Samos . . . Mit 3 Tafeln. pp. 33. *Berlin*, 1944. 4°. [*Abhandlungen der Preussischen Akademie der Wissenschaften.* Phil.-hist. Klasse. Jahrg. 1943. no. 17.] Ac. **855/6**.

—— Feldmäuse. [On apparitions from the earth in Greek vase-painting.] pp. 34. *München*, 1937. 8°. [*Sitzungsberichte der Bayerischen Akademie der Wissenschaften.* Phil.-hist. Abt. Jahrg. 1937. Hft. 1.] Ac. **713/8**.

—— Grab eines attischen Mädchens . . . Zweite Auflage. [With illustrations.] pp. 71. *München*, 1941. 8°. **7704**. p. **5**.

—— Griechische Vasen. Mit 282 Abbildungen. pp. 272. *München*, [1940.] 4°. **7802**. cc. **34**.

—— Griechische Vasenmalerei . . . Mit 150 Abbildungen. pp. 213. *München*, 1913. fol. Dept. of Greek & Roman Antiquities.

—— (Zweite Auflage.) pp. 229. *München*, 1925. fol. Dept. of Greek & Roman Antiquities.

—— Greek Vase-Painting . . . Translated by G. C. Richards, *etc.* pp. xii. 179. pl. xcvi. *Chatto & Windus: London*, 1921. 8°. **07703**. l. **33**.

—— Das hellenistische Bildnis, *etc.* [With plates.] pp. 70. *München*, [1949.] 8°. **7877**. b. **36**.

—— Maussollos und Alexander, *etc.* [A discussion of the sculptures of the Mausoleum at Halicarnassus. With plates.] pp. 55. *München*, [1950.] 8°. **7877**. i. **4**.

—— Pferde des Pheidias. pp. 34. pl. 12. *München*, [1948.] *obl.* 8°. Cup. **1246**. c. **4**.

—— Die Plastik der Griechen . . . Mit einhundert Abbildungen. pp. 123. *Berlin*, [1936.] 4°. **7876**. t. **1**.

—— Die Tyrannen-Mörder . . . Mit 16 Abbildungen, *etc.* pp. 31. *München*, 1940. 8°. [*Sitzungsberichte der Bayerischen Akademie der Wissenschaften.* Phil.-hist. Abt. Jahrg. 1940. Hft. 5.] Ac. **713/8**.

—— Vom Sinn der griechischen Standbilder. [With plates.] pp. 55. *Berlin*, 1942. 4°. **7877**. dd. **9**.

—— Zwei Niobiden-Meister . . . Mit 8 Abbildungen, *etc.* [Attributing the Niobid frieze from the throne of Zeus at Olympia to Phidias and Kolotes. With plates.] pp. 30. *München*, 1938. 8°. [*Sitzungsberichte der Bayerischen Akademie der Wissenschaften.* Phil.-hist. Abt. Jahrg. 1938. Hft. 3.] Ac. **713/8**.

BUSCHOW (Hans) Studien über die Entwicklung der Krypta im deutschen Sprachgebiet. [With illustrations.] pp. 59. *Würzburg*, 1934. 8°. **07815**. b. **36**.

BUSCH-ZANTNER (Richard)

—— Albanien. Neues Land im Imperium. pp. 217. *Leipzig*, [1939.] 8°. **10127**. e. **42**.

—— Bulgarien. [With illustrations.] pp. 238. *Leipzig*, 1943. 8°. **09136**. bb. **9**.

—— Faust-Stätten in Hellas. Topographie und Quellenfrage der griechischen Landschaften in Goethes "Faust." [With plates.] pp. 67. *Weimar*, 1932. 8°. **10108**. g. **29**.

BUSCIUS (Hermannus) *See* Buschius.

BUSCK (August) *See* Dyar (Harrison G.) A List of North American Lepidoptera . . . By H. G. Dyar . . . assisted by . . . A. Busck. 1902. 8°. [*Bulletin of the U.S. National Museum.* no. 52.] Ac. **1875/13.**

—— Descriptions of New Genera and Species of Microlepidoptera from Panama, *etc.* pp. 10. pl. 1. *Washington,* 1912. 8°. [*Smithsonian Miscellaneous Collections.* vol. 59. no. 4.] Ac. **1875/2.**

—— Notes on a Horn-feeding Lepidopterous Larva from Africa, *etc.* pp. 2. pl. 2. *Washington,* 1910. 8°. [*Smithsonian Miscellaneous Collections.* vol. 56. no. 8.] Ac. **1875/2.**

BUSCK (Frans)

—— **Bohuslänska folkmålsdikter från slutet av 1700-och början av 1800-talen, samlade af Frons Busck. [With a note on Busck, by Erik Rinman.] pp. 58. *Stockholm,* 1894. 8°. [*Bidrag till Kännedom om de svenska landsmålen ock svenskt folkliv.* bd. 13. no. 7.]** P.P. **5044.** g. **(1.)**

BUSCK (Gunni) Gunni Busck, et Levnetsløb i en Landsby-Præstegaard. Udgivet af Henr. Bech. [Busck's letters, with a sermon and a commentary on the First Epistle of John.] pp. 330. *Kjøbenhavn,* 1869. 8°. **4887.** aaa. **48.**

—— Om Biskop Martensens Grundtvigianisme. pp. 14. *Kjøbenhavn,* 1863. 8°. **3925.** bb. **19. (2.)**

BUSCO (Bernardino de') *See* Busti.

BUSCO (Gerardus de) *See* Trajecti (P.) and Busco (G. de) Vita Johannis Hatten, *etc.* 1719. 8°. [Dumbar (G.) *Gerhardi Dumbar . . . analecta, etc.* tom. 1.] **1193.** k. **18.**

BUSCO (J. de) *pseud.* [i.e. Joannes Cornelius Antonius Hezenmans.] *See* Hezenmans (J. C. A.)

BUSCO (Joannes de) *See* Buschius (J.)

BUSCO (Pierre) Les Cosmogonies modernes et la théorie de la connaissance. pp. 435. *Paris,* 1924. 8°. **8560.** dd. **34.**

BUSCODUCENSIS (Heinrich) *See* Zwerg (D. G.) Dithlef Gotthard Zwergs Nachrichten von . . . M. H. Buscoducensis Leben, *etc.* 1758. 8°. [Harboe (L.) *Zuverlässige Nachrichten von dem Schicksale des Johann a Lasco, etc.*] **4887.** a. **23.**

BUSCODUCENSIS (Nicolaus) *See* also Quadus (Nicolaus) *pseud.* [i.e. N. Buscoducensis.]

—— *See* Hugo, *de Sancto Victore.* Venerabilis patris Hugonis de Sancto Victore Questiones, *etc.* [Edited by N. Buscoducensis.] 1512. 4°. C. **64.** d. **10.**

—— *See* Lucian, *of Samosata.* [*Dialogues.—Collections.—Latin.*] Complures Luciani dialogi . . . à N. Buscoducensi illustrati, *etc.* 1528. 8°. C. **48.** b. **1.**

—— —— 1528. 8°. **720.** c. **14. (1*.)**

—— —— 1529. 8°. **836.** b. **36. (4.)**

—— —— 1530. 8°. **1474.** a. **7.**

—— —— 1533. 8°. **720.** c. **14. (2.)**

—— *See* Lucian, *of Samosata.* [*Dialogues.—Collections.—Latin.*] Luciani dialogi . . . Cum N. Buscoducensis succincta pariter & erudita explanatione, *etc.* 1548. 8°. **12316.** c. **26. (2.)**

BUSCOMARI (Isidorus a) S. Bonaventura Ordinis Fratrum Minorum minister generalis. pp. vii. 160. *Romae,* 1874. 8°. **4828.** df. **11.**

BUSCOMBE (William)

—— *See* MacKellar (Andrew) and Buscombe (W.) Intensities of Molecular Bands in the Spectra of three Early R-Type Stars. 1948. fol. [*Publications of the Dominion Astrophysical Observatory, Victoria, B.C.* vol. 7. no. 24.] C.S. e. **17/10.**

BUSCOT (Willibrord)

—— The History of Cotton College, at Sedgley Park, 1763–1873, at Cotton, 1873– . [With plates.] pp. xi. 308. *Burns, Oates & Co.: London,* 1940. 8°. **08366.** pp. **42.**

BUSDRAGHI (Vincenzo) *See* Busdrago (Vincentio)

BUSDRAGO (Vincentio)

—— *See* Coturri (E.) Una Rarissima edizione lucchese del Busdraghi. [On the oration entitled "Laudatio Ferdinandi Imp. Augusti" by Giovanni Francesco Graziani, published by Busdrago in 1564.] 1952. 8°. **11915.** b. **39.**

—— *See* Speroni degli Alvarotti (S.) Giuditio sopra la tragedia di Canace . . . con la tragedia appresso. [Edited by V. Busdrago.] 1550. 8°. **11715.** aa. **51.**

BUSDRAGUS (Gerardus) *Bishop of Argos.* Exemplum literarum R. D. G. Busdragi . . . ad . . . Franciscum Cardinalem Pisanum. In quibus agitur, quanam ratione præservari possit Italia, ne Lutherismo inficiatur. *See* Ursinus (J.) *pseud.* Hispanicæ inquisitionis & carnificinæ secretiora, *etc.* 1611. 8°. **866.** g. **2.**

—— Lectura super canone de Consecr. Dist. iii. De aqua benedicta . . . Denuò impressa vnà cum Antichoppino [by J. Hotman], Passauantio [by T. Beza], Matagone de Matagonibus [by F. Hotman], & Strigili Papirij Massoni [by F. Hotman]. 2 pt. *Wiliorbani,* 1594, 93. 8°. **1020.** d. **8. (1–5.)**

—— [Another copy.] **1020.** f. **8. (6, 2–5.)**

BUSDRAGUS (Gerhardus) *Bishop of Thessalonica.* [For editions of "Consilium quorundam episcoporum Bononiæ congregatorum" signed: Vincentius de Durantibus, Egidius Falceta, Gerhardus Busdragus:] *See* Rome, Church of. [Popes.]—Julius III. [1550–1555.]

BUSDRAGUS (Joannes Baptista) *See* Robortello (F.) Francisci Robortelli . . . de historica facultate disputatio . . . Explanationes in primum Aeneid. Virgilii librum . . . collectæ à I. B. Busdrago. 1548. 8°. **1088.** k. **16.**

BUSE (Adolph) *See* Anselm, *Saint, Archbishop of Canterbury.* [*Single Works.*] Sancti Anselmi . . . liber meditationum. Textum accurate recognovit . . . A. Buse. 1851. 16°. **3627.** a. **9.**

—— De nominibus Spiritus Sancti aeternis tractatum dogmaticum scripsit A. Buse. pp. iv. 72. *Moguntiae,* 1843. 8°. **1352.** h. **21. (1.)**

—— Paulin, Bischop von Nola und seine Zeit, 350–450. 2 Bd. *Regensburg,* 1856. 8°. **4827.** d. **9.**

BUSE (Gerhard Heinrich) Das Ganze der Handlung, oder vollständiges Handbuch der vorzüglichsten Handlungskenntnisse, *etc.*

Tl. 1. Vollständiges Handbuch der Waarenkunde, *etc.* 10 Bd. 1798–1820.
Tl. 2. Vollständiges Handbuch der Geldkunde, *etc.* 3 Bd. 1800–03.

BUSE (Gerhard Heinrich)

Tl. 3–5. Vollständiges Handbuch der Handlungs- Zahlungs- und Frachtkunde, *etc.* 2 Bd. 1807–08.
Tl. 6. Vollständiges Handbuch der Comtoirkunde, *etc.* Bd. 2–5. 1804–19.
Tl. 7. Geographisches Comptoir-Handbuch, *etc.* pp. 718. 1826.
Die Handlungsschule, *etc.* Abt. 1. Hft. 1. 1807.
Gründliches und vollständiges Hand- und Rechenbuch, *etc.* Bd. 3. 1821.

Erfurt; Erfurt & Gotha, 1798–1826. 8°. **8248.** ccc. **9.**
Imperfect; wanting Tl. 6. *Bd.* 1., *Bd.* 1, 2 *of the "Gründliches Hand- und Rechenbuch" and all after Tl.* 7.

BUSE (Heinrich)

—— St. Bonifatius. Leben und Wirken. pp. 19. *Fulda*, [1954?] 8°. **4831.** ee. **19.**
Lesebogen der Paedagogischen Gesellschaft, Fulda. Hft. 2.

BUSECK (Amandus von) *Bishop of Fulda.* *See* Kolbinger (J. C.) Der in dem Wege der Wahrheit geliebte des Herren Amandus; das ist, Der . . . Lebens-Wandel . . . Amandi, *etc.* 1757. fol. **4885.** f. **2.** (**17.**)

—— Monumentum mortis; in memoriam vitae et viventis post funera virtutis Amandi, primi episcopi, abbatis, & principis fuldensis, quando . . . Adalbertus, electus episcopus . . . antecessori suo . . . solemnibus exequiis parentavit, *etc.* [With plates.] pp. 48. [*Fulda*, 1757.] fol. **4885.** f. **2.** (**18.**)

—— Ordentlicher Leich-Conduct weyland des . . . Herrn Amandi, *etc.* (Lob- und Danck-Rede, welche . . . von dem . . . Cantzlar Weizell . . . abgelegt worden.) 2 pt. *Fulda*, [1757.] fol. **4885.** f. **2.** (**18*.**)

BUSÉE (Jean) *See* Busaeus (Joannes)

BUŠEK (Karel) *See* Kaminský (Bodhan) *pseud.* [i.e. K. Bušek.]

BUŠEK (Vratislav)

—— Náš socialism. Příspěvek k ideologii čs. strany národně socialistické. pp. 52. *v Praze*, 1947. 8°. **8095.** aaa. **43.**
Život. Praktická knižnice pro kulturní a politické otázky. no. 5.

—— Poválečné konkordáty. pp. 101. *v Bratislavě*, 1926. 8°. **08028.** cc. **50.**

BUSELLI (Remigio) *See* Ribetti (G.) La Fallibilità della Chiesa Romana chiaramente dimostrata dalle pie menzogne . . . dei molto reverendi padri Cherubino e Buselli . . . nella disputa livornese. 1868. 12°. **3902.** bb. **53.** (**1.**)

—— L'Emmaus evangelico dimostrato e difeso sessanta stadî distante da Gerusalemme . . . Risposta ad un anonimo. pp. 9. 189. *Livorno*, 1882. 8°. **10077.** g. **29.**

—— L'Emmaus evangelico dimostrato e difeso distante 60 stadi da Gerusalemme. Nuovi studi. 2 vol. *Milano*, [1885, 86.] 8°. **10077.** f. **30.**

—— Il Papa o la bibbia? Lettura cattolica, *etc.*—Risposta particulare . . . alle ingiurie, dette nel corso delle tre dispute dal Valdese Ribetti . . . contro alcuni papi e concilii. 2 pt. *See* Leghorn.—*Conferenze fra alcuni Sacerdoti Cattolici, etc.* L'Autorità in materia di fede, *etc.* 1868. 8°. **3901.** dd. **18.**

BUSEMANN (A.)

—— *See* Hilton (William F.) Limitations of Use of Busemann's Second-order Supersonic Aerofoil Theory. 1952. 8°. [*Aeronautical Research Council. Reports and Memoranda.* no. 2524.] B.S. **2/2.**

BUSEMANN (Adolf) Handbuch der pädagogischen Milieukunde . . . Herausgegeben von Adolf Busemann. Mit 8 Abbildungen. [With a bibliography.] pp. vi. 359. *Halle*, 1932. 8°. **8310.** dd. **31.**

—— Pädagogische Psychologie in Umrissen. pp. viii. 187. *Leipzig*, 1932. 8°. **8305.** g. **29.**

BUSEMANN (Carl) *See* Unruh (F. F. von) National-Sozialismus, *etc.* (Anhang: Dr. C. Busemann, Das Wirtschaftsprogramm.) 1931. 8°. **8074.** h. **42.**

BUSEMANN (Felix)

—— *See* Chervonenkis (Ya M.) Fundamental Problems of H.V. D.C. Transmission . . . Translated from "Elektrichestvo" . . . by Dr. Ing. F. Busemann. 1947. 4°. W.P. **9138/302.**

—— *See* Kaganov (I. L.) The D.C. System of Long Distance Power Transmission . . . Translated from "Electrichestvo" . . . by Dr.-Ing. F. Busemann. 1948. 4°. W.P. **9138/303.**

—— D.C. Power Transmission Development by the Siemens-Schuckert Concern in Germany, *etc.* pp. 20. pl. 21. [*London*,] 1947. 4°. [*British Electrical and Allied Industries Research Association. Technical Report.* Reference Z/T 67.] W.P. **9138/304.**
Reproduced from typewriting.

—— H.V. D.C. Inverter Stations: comparison of cost of supplying reactive volt-amperes by various methods. pp. 16. pl. 8. *Leatherhead*, 1954. 4°. [*British Electrical and Allied Industries Research Association. Technical Report.* no. B/T 118.] W.P. **9138/727.**

—— High Voltage D.C. Transmission, *etc.* 2 pt. *London*, 1947, 48. 4°. [*British Electrical and Allied Industries Research Association. Technical Report.* Reference Z/T68.] W.P. **9138/305.**
Reproduced from typewriting.

—— The Influence of Phase Number of a Convertor in Harmonics. pp. 12. pl. 5. *Leatherhead*, 1954. 4°. [*British Electrical and Allied Industries Research Association. Technical Report.* no. B/T 117.] W.P. **9138/759.**

—— The Magnetic Compass Error caused by D. C. Single-Core Sea Cables. pp. 12. pl. 4. *Leatherhead*, 1953. 4°. [*British Electrical and Allied Industries Research Association. Technical Report.* no. B/T 116.] W.P. **9138/690.**

BUSEMANN (L.) De Vriend der natuur door Dr. B. van der Meulen . . . en G. van Milligen . . . vrij bewerkt naar Busemann's Naturkundliche Volksbücher. 4 pt. *Zwolle*, 1888–90. 8°. **8705.** de. **24.**

BUSEMANN (M.) *See* Germany. [*Laws, etc.*—I.] Der Friedensvertrag mit der Ukraine vom 9. Februar 1918, der Zusatzvertrag und der deutsch-ukrainische Handelsvertrag . . . Herausgegeben von M. Busemann. 1918. 8°. **9081.** f. **18.**

BUSEMANN (Wilhelm) Reserve-Ersatz-Regiment Nr. 3, *etc.* [With plates.] pp. 137. *Oldenburg, Berlin*, 1925. 8°. [*Erinnerungsblätter deutscher Regimenter. Ehemals preussische Truppenteile.* Hft. 140.] **8836.** e. **1/140.**

BUSEMBAUM (Hermannus) *See* Busenbaum.

BUSEN. Der weibliche Busen, dessen Schönheit und Erhaltung, in seinen vier Epochen, als Kind, Jungfrau, Gattin und Mutter, physisch und moralisch dargestellt. Nebst einem Anhang von den Krankheiten desselben. pp. x. 83. *Hamburg & Altona*, [1810?] 16°. **1174.** c. **36.**

BUSENBARK (E. J.) *See* BIEGELEISEN (Jacob I.) and BUSENBARK (E. J.) The Silk Screen Printing Process. 1938. 8°. **7944.** s. **22.**

—— *See* BIEGELEISEN (Jacob I.) and BUSENBARK (E. J.) The Silk Screen Printing Process, *etc.* 1941. 8°. **07941.** t. **22.**

BUSENBAUM (HERMANN) Medulla theologiæ moralis . . . Accedunt propositiones ad hanc usque diem proscriptæ . . . Editio octava patavina. pp. 655. *Patavii,* 1729. 12°. **860.** c. **22.**

—— Theologia moralis antehac ex probatis auctoribus breviter concinnata à R.P. H. Busenbaum . . . Nunc pluribus partibus aucta à R.P. Claudio la Croix. (Index locupletissimus . . . Secundùm ordinem alphabeti digestus à R.P. Leonardo Colendall.) 9 tom. *Coloniæ Agrippinæ,* 1733, 24, 20. 8°. **850.** g. **1–9.**
A made-up set. Tom. 1, 2, 4 *and* 5 *are dated* 1733. *Tom.* 3, *which bears the description "Editio tertia correctior," and tom.* 6–8 *are dated* 1724. *The Supplement is dated* 1720.

—— R.P. Hermanni Busenbaum . . . Theologia moralis nunc pluribus partibus aucta à R.P.D. Alphonso de Ligorio . . . Editio quarta . . . Accedit etiam Francisci Antonii Zachariæ S. J. Dissertatio prolegomena de casuisticæ theologiæ originibus, locis, atque præstantia; necnon Joannis Dominici Mansi . . . Epitome doctrinæ moralis, et canonicæ ex operibus Benedicti XIV. 3 tom. *Romæ,* 1760. fol. **1227.** h. **2, 3.**

—— Theologia morum ab H. Busenbaum S.J. primum tradita, tum a Claudio La-Croix et Franc. Ant. Zacharia . . . aucta, nunc demum ab Angelo Franzoja . . . juxta saniores, ac præsertim angelicas D. Thomæ Aquinatis doctrinas ad trutinam revocata. Editio altera castigatior, in qua præter opportuna additamenta . . . accedunt disputationes duæ: altera de Summi Pontificis & œcum. conciliorum auctoritate; altera de prædestinatione & gratia. pp. xxiv. 680. *Bononiæ,* 1767. fol. **L.7.d.2.**

—— Medulla theologiæ moralis. (Ad medullam theologiæ moralis . . . appendix in qua præcipua quæ circa morum scientiam hactenus a Sancta Sede prodierunt et alia huc pertinentia continentur.) 2 tom. *Romæ,* 1844. 12°. **1351.** a. **3.**

—— [Another edition.] 2 tom. *Tornaci,* [1850?] 12°. **3557.** b. **1.**
Imperfect; wanting pp. 187–198, 605–616 *of tom.* 1, *and pp.* 394–396 *of tom.* 2.

—— P. Claudii Lacroix, S. J. Theologia moralis, seu ejusdem in H. Busembaum Medullam commentaria, a Zacharia, S. J. elucidata atque vindicata. Editio nova, annotante P. Dion. (Ad Tractatum v Mantissa seu Quæstio facti . . . Auctore Stephano de Champs.) 4 tom. *Parisiis,* 1874. 4°. **1215.** g. **13.**

—— Antonii Ballerini . . . Opus theologicum morale in Busembaum Medullam absolvit et edidit D. Palmieri. [With the text of the "Medulla."] 7 vol. 1889–94. 8°. *See* BALLERINI (A.) **4091.** h. **13.**

—— Propositiones damnatæ et damnandæ excerptæ ex libro cui titulus, Rev. Patris Busembaum . . . Theologia moralis, nunc pluribus partibus aucta à . . . Claudio Lacroix, *etc.* (Propositions condamnées et condamnables tirées du livre qui a pour titre Théologie morale du R.P. Busembaum, *etc.*) *Lat. & Fr.* pp. 22. [1757.] 4°. **5423.** h. **9.** (**29.**

BUSENBAUM (HERMANN)

—— *See* BRITTANY.—*Parlement.* Requisitoire de Monsieur le procureur général . . . Du 7 décembre 1761. [A request for permission to proceed against Jesuits disseminating the doctrines of Busenbaum's "Theologia moralis."] [1761.] 12°. **4091.** bb. **34.** (**2.**)

—— *See* HENN (P.) Das schwarze Buch. Beiträge zur Moral der Jesuiten, *etc.* (Otto Andreae und der Jesuit Busenbaum.) 1865. 8°. **4103.** bbb. **19.**

—— *See* PARIS.—*Parlement.* Arrest . . . qui condamne un imprimé ayant pour titre: Propositions condamnées & condamnables, tirées du livre intitulé, Théologie morale du R.P. Busembaum . . . à être lacéré & brûlé, *etc.* [1757.] 4°. **5423.** h. **9.** (**30.**)

—— *See* TOULOUSE.—*Parlement.* Arrest . . . qui condamne au feu le livre intitulé R.P. H. Busembaum . . . Theologia moralis, *etc.* [1757.] 4°. **5423.** h. **9.** (**28.**)

—— Ad reverendi patris Claudii La Croix Societatis Jesu Theologiam moralem alterius ex eadem societate theologi [i.e. F. A. Zaccaria] supplementum sive accessiones, in quibus de locorum theologicorum in morali scientia usu plurima disputantur; P. de Champs Quæstio facti animadversionibus aucta recuditur; Sacræ Congregationis Concilii resolutiones ac Benedicti XIV. Constitutiones, aliáque permulta vel ad emendandum vel ad vindicandum La Croixium adduntur. Editio post italicam in Germania prima. pp. 859. *Coloniæ Agrippinæ,* 1754. 8°. **850.** g. **10.**

—— Sincérité des Jésuites dans leurs désaveux sur Busembaum. Avec l'Arrêt du Parlement de Bretagne (du 12 janvier 1758) au sujet de ce livre, & d'autres faits récens . . . qui constatent de plus en plus les pervers sentimens desdits pères. pp. 24. [1759.] 12°. **4091.** aa. **18.**

BUSENBAUMIUS (IGNATIUS) In Ioannem Rongium Catilinaria prima. *See* POLES. Epistolae et orationes virorum obscurorum, *etc.* fasc. 1. 1845. 8°. **3910.** bb. **66.** (**6.**)

BUSENELLO (GIOVANNI FRANCESCO) *See* LIVINGSTON (Arthur) Gian Francesco Busenello e la polemica Stigliani-Marino. 1910. 8°. **011851.** f. **44.** (**5.**)

—— *See* LIVINGSTON (Arthur) Una Scappatella di Polo Vendramin e un sonetto di Gian Francesco Busenello. 1911. 8°. **011840.** k. **83.** (**6.**)

—— *See* LIVINGSTON (Arthur) La Vita veneziana nelle opere di Gian Francesco Busenello. 1913. 8°. **011852.** d. **33.**

—— I Sonetti morali ed amorosi di Gian Francesco Busenello, 1598–1659. Testo critico per cura di Arthur Livingston. pp. 144. *Venezia,* 1911. 8°. **11427.** h. **9.**

—— L'Incoronatione di Poppea . . . Opera musicale rappresentata nel Teatro Grimano l'anno 1642. pp. 61. *Andrea Giuliani: Venetia,* 1656. 12°. Hirsch IV. **1377**a.

—— [L'Incoronazione di Poppea.] The Coronation of Poppaea . . . Translated . . . by Robert Louis Stuart . . . With an explanatory introduction. pp. 40. *Holywell Press: Oxford,* 1927. 8°. **11714.** c. **43.**

—— Prospettiua del nauale trionfo riportato dalla Republica Serenissma contra il Turco, *etc.* [A poem.] *G. P. Pinelli: Venetia,* 1656. 4°. **1312.** f. **20.**

BUSENELLO (GIOVANNI FRANCESCO)

—— A Prospective of the Naval Triumph of the Venetians over the Turk, *etc.* [Translated by Sir Thomas Higgons.] pp. 62. *For Henry Herringham: London*, 1658. 8°. **1071**. m. **33**.

—— [Another copy.] E. **1826**. (**1**.)

—— *See* LIVINGSTON (Arthur) Una Poesia di Gian Francesco Busenello in Inghilterra, 1657–1667. [On Higgons's translation of Busenello's "Prospettiva del navale trionfo."] 1908. 8°. **011851**. f. **44**. (**2**.)

BUSENELLUS (PETRUS) De Joanna Papissa dissertatio . . . Editio altera. pp. xxxix. *Patavii*, 1767. 8°. T. **2289**. (**1**.)

—— De lapsu Marcellini Pontificis Maximi dissertatio. pp. xxxviii. *Patavii*, 1767. 8°. **296**. i. **28**.

—— De Summi Pontificis eligendi forma historica dissertatio. [By P. Busenellus.] pp. xl 1758. 8°. *See* POPE. T. **2288**. (**2**.)

BUSENNIUS (ANTONIUS) In Cl. Galeni . . . librum de inæquali intemperie commentarij, A. Busennii. [With the text.] ff. 108. 1553. 8°. *See* GALENUS (C.) [*De inaequali intemperie.—Latin.*] **774**. b. **10**. (**2**.)

BUSEO. *See* BUZĂU.

BUSEO (GIOVANNI) *See* BUSAEUS (Joannes)

BUSER (B.) Die Beziehungen der Mediceer zu Frankreich während der Jahre 1434–1494 in ihrem Zusammenhang mit den allgemeinen Verhältnissen Italiens. pp. viii. 562. *Leipzig*, 1879. 8°. **9073**. ff. **5**.

—— Lorenzo de' Medici als italienischer Staatsmann. Eine Skizze nach handschriftlichen Quellen. pp. vi. 198. *Leipzig*, 1879. 8°. **10629**. dd. **4**.

BUSER (ERNST ROLF)

—— Zur Entwicklung des Badewesens im Unterengadin. Ein Beitrag zur Geschichte der Balneologie der Schweiz. Inaugural-Dissertation, *etc.* pp. 51. *Basel*, 1954. 8°. **7471**. d. **35**.

BUSER (HANS) Johann Lukas Legrand, Direktor der helvetischen Republik. *See* BASLE. [*Appendix.*] Basler Biographien, *etc.* Bd. 1. 1900, *etc.* 8°. **010707**. ff. **80**.

BUSER (HIERONYMUS) Der rechte Dank für Gottes grosse Wohlthat, *etc.* *See* BASLE.—*Evangelische Missions-Gesellschaft.* Dein Reich komme. Eine Sammlung kirchlicher Zeugnisse, *etc.* 1865. 8°. **4426**. bb. **6**.

BÜSER (JACOB THEODOR) Klaroengalmen. Nationale liederen, *etc.* pp. 152. *Dordrecht*, 1867. 8°. **11557**. e. **25**.

—— Krijgslederen . . . Gedeeltelijk op muziek gebragt door H. Voorthuis. pp. 31. *Kampen*, 1859. 8°. **11556**. bbb. **69**. (**2**.)

—— Uit de dierenwereld; humoristische legenden, in rijmelende kreupelverzen, door een Ex-Schoolmeester (B . . . r [i.e. J. T. Buser]). pp. viii. 136. 1860. 12°. *See* B . . . R. **11556**. cc. **23**.

BUSER (PAUL)

—— Die Anwendbarkeit der allgemeinen Bestimmungen über die Verträge auf die einfache Gesellschaft im schweizerischen Obligationenrecht. Inaugural-Dissertation, *etc.* pp. viii. 118. *Olten*, 1935. 8°. **05549**. ff. **36**.

BUSER (PETER)

—— Bedeutung einzelner postoperativer Komplikationen nach gynaekologischen Operationen und Sectio caesarea vor und nach Durchfuehrung verschaerfter praeoperativer Massnahmen. Inauguraldissertation, *etc.* pp. 48. *Basel*, 1952. 8°. **7583**. e. **4**.

BUSER (ROBERT) *See* BOISSIER (P. E.) Flora orientalis, *etc.* (Supplementum, editore R. Buser.) 1867, *etc.* 8°. **7029**. f. **3**.

—— Kritische Beiträge zur Kenntnis der schweizerischen Weiden . . . Herausgegeben von W. Koch. 1940. *See* SWITZERLAND.—*Schweizerische Botanische Gesellschaft.* Bulletin, *etc.* Bd. 50. 1891, *etc.* 8°. Ac. **3256**.

BUSES.

—— Buses Illustrated. *See* PERIODICAL PUBLICATIONS.—*London.*

BUSET (GUGLIELMO)

—— *See* FRITZ (Georg) *Artist.* Strassen und Bauten Adolf Hitlers, *etc.* (Ins Italienische übersetzt von G. Buset.) 1939. 4°. L.R. **280**. b. **11**.

BUŠETIĆ (TODOR M.)

—— Левач. *In:* Српски етнографски зборник. књ. 5. Насеља српские земаља. књ. 2. pp. 459–511. 1903. 8°. Ac. **1131/4**.

—— Народна медицина срба сељака у Левчу. 1911. *See* BELGRADE.—*Српска Краљевска Академија.* Српски етнографски зборник. књ. 17. 1894, *etc.* 8°. Ac. **1131/4**.

—— Српске народне песме и игре с мелодијама из Левча. Прикупио Т. М. Бушетић. Музички приредио С. С. Мокрањац. pp. xxi. 110. *у Београду*, 1902. 8°. [*Српски етнографски зборник.* књ. 3.] Ac. **1131/4**.

BUSETTO (ANDREA) L'Italia e la sua guerra. [With plates.] pp. 211. *Milano*, 1931. fol. **9085**. cc. **15**.

BUSETTO (GIROLAMO) Il Maddaloni. Ultima impresa di Nino Bixio. pp. 111. *Bologna*, 1877. 8°. **10024**. bb. **1**.

—— Notizie del generale Nino Bixio. [With plates, including a portrait.] pp. 426. *Fano*, 1876. 8°. **10630**. ee. **4**.

BUSETTO (NATALE) Carlo de' Dottori, letterato padovano del secolo decimosettimo. Studio biografico-letterario. pp. viii. 397. *Città di Castello*, 1902. 8°. **10631**. dd. **15**.

—— La Genesi e la formazione dei Promessi Sposi [of Alessandro Manzoni]. pp. 411. *Bologna*, 1921. 8°. **011851**. d. **84**.

—— Giosuè Carducci nel suo tempo e nella sua poesia. pp. xii. 411. *Milano*, 1935. 8°. **11857**. a. **28**.

—— Le Idealità civili di Francesco Petrarca. *See* PETRARCA (F.) [*Appendix.—Miscellaneous.*] Treviso nel sesto centenario de la nascita di Francesco Petrarca. 1904. 8°. **10633**. i. **10**.

—— Saggi di varia psicologia dantesca. Contributo allo studio delle relazioni di Dante con Alberto Magno e con San Tommaso. pp. 170. *Prato*, 1905. 8°. **11421**. bb. **20**.

BUSETTO (Natale)

—— Saggi manzoniani. Contributo agli studi sulla formazione dei Promessi Sposi. pp. 44. *Napoli*, 1916. 4°. **011853**. t. **14**.

—— Studî e profili letterari. pp. 236. *Milano*, 1929. 8°. **11854**. s. **26**.

BUSEV (Aleksei Ivanovich)

—— Аналитическая химия висмута. pp. 380. *Москва*, 1953. 8°. **08909**. v. **41**.
The titlepage headed: *Академия Наук СССР. Институт Геохимии и Аналитической Химии им. В. И. Вернадского.*

BUŠEVICS (Ansis)

—— Mūsu politikas problemi. pp. 51. *Rīgā*, 1927. 8°. **8095**. a. **69**.

BUSEY (Garreta) The Windbreak. [A novel.] pp. 350. *Funk & Wagnalls Co.*: *New York & London*, 1938. 8°. **12718**. dd. **10**.

BUSEY (Samuel Clagett) Addresses by the President, Samuel C. Busey, M.D., at the celebration of the 75th anniversary of the Medical Society, D.C., *etc.* pp. 11. *Gibson Bros.*: *Washington*, 1894. 8°. **07305**. m. **2**. (**2**.)

—— Compulsory Reports of Zymotic Diseases; milk legislation; medical practice law; and society publication of its transactions. Annual address of the President of the Medical Society of the District of Columbia, *etc.* pp. 55. *Gibson Bros.*: *Washington*, 1895. 8°. **07305**. m. **2**. (**4**.)

—— The Conduct of Labor and the Management of the Puerperal State. *See* Mann (Matthew D.) A System of Gynecology, *etc.* (Obstetrics. vol. 1.) 1889. 8°. **7581**. d. **18**.

—— Congenital Occlusion and Dilatation of Lymph Channels. pp. xv. 187. *W. Wood & Co.*: *New York*, 1878. 8°. **7630**. h. **11**.

—— Immigration: its evils and consequences. pp. 162. *De Witt & Davenport*: *New York*, [1856.] 12°. **8177**. a. **25**.

—— The Medical Society of the District of Columbia in 1894 . . . Annual address of the President, *etc.* pp. 22. *Gibson Bros.*: *Washington*, 1894. 8°. **07305**. m. **2**. (**3**.)

—— The Organization, high esprit de corps, high standard of education and scientific attainments of the Army Medical Department. Address, *etc.* pp. 22. *Gibson Bros.*: *Washington*, 1897. 8°. **07305**. m. **2**. (**8**.)

—— Pictures of the City of Washington in the past. pp. viii. 17–384. *W. Ballantyne & Sons*: *Washington*, 1898. 8°. **10408**. ee. **30**.

—— The Year 1896: an epoch in the history of the Medical Society of the District of Columbia. Annual address of the President, *etc.* pp. 16. *Gibson Bros.*: *Washington*, 1896. 8°. **07305**. m. **2**. (**6**.)

BUSFEILD (Johnson Atkinson) *See* Baldwyn (Edward) Remarks on the Oath, Declarations, and Conduct of J. A. Busfield, *etc.* 1791. 8°. **10347**. ee. **10**. (**2**.)

—— Sermons . . . Sixth edition. (vol. 1, 2. Sermons on the most important Duties of the Christian Religion. vol. 3. Sermons on the Lord's Prayer, and on the great mystery.) 3 vol. *E. Lloyd & Son*: *London*, 1826. 8°. **1357**. d. **20**.
Vol. 2 is of the second, vol. 3 of the first edition.

BUSFEILD (Johnson Atkinson)

—— The Christian's Guide, in six progressive lectures, *etc.* pp. 157. *J. Fawcett*: *Halifax*, 1800. 8°. **4372**. h. **12**. (**1**.)

—— Sermons on the most important Duties of the Christian Religion. pp. lxv. 423. *B. E. Lloyd & Son*: *London*, 1819. 8°. **4454**. ff. **3**.

BUSFEILD (William) Life's Pilgrimage. A sermon, preached . . . on the Sunday immediately following the death of his Royal Highness the Duke of York. pp. 17. *C. & J. Rivington*: *London*, 1827. 8°. T. **1184**. (**13**.)

—— Second edition. pp. 17. *C. & J. Rivington*: *London*, 1827. 8°. **4906**. f. **27**. (**4**.)

BÚS FEKETE (László) Ruy Blas 38. Pièce en quatre actes d'après " Jean," de Bus-Fekete. [The adaptation by Pierre Chaine.] Précédée de Ruy Blas centenaire, avant-propos fantaisiste de Pierre Chaine. pp. 30. *Paris*, 1938. fol. [*La Petite Illustration.* Théâtre. no. 445.] P.P. **4283**. m. (**2**.)

—— [Szerelemből elégtelen.] Ladies in Love . . . Translated . . . by Victor Katona and Guy Bolton. pp. 354. *G. Allen & Unwin*: *London*, 1935. 8°. **12591**. tt. **24**.

—— Ladies And Gentlemen. A comedy in three acts . . . From a drama (" Twelve in a Box ") by L. Bus-Fekete. pp. 123. *New York*, [1941.] 8°. [*French's Standard Library Edition.*] **011781**. g. **1/476**.

—— The Lady Has a Heart. A comedy in three acts . . . Adapted by Edward Roberts. [With plates.] pp. 98. *New York*, [1939.] 8°. [*French's Standard Library Edition.*] **011781**. g. **1/461**.

BUSFIELD (Alfred)

—— The Salesmans Guide to Success, *etc.* ff. 30. *A. Busfield & Co.*: *Darlington*, 1952. 4°. **8219**. k. **22**.
Reproduced from typewriting.

BUSFIELD (Johnson Atkinson) *See* Busfeild.

BUSFIELD (Margaret) *See* Brine (John) The Covenant of Grace open'd: in a sermon occasioned by the death of Mrs. M. Busfield, *etc.* [1734.] 8°. **4903**. ccc. **36**. (**1**.)

BUSFIELD (T. L.)

—— The Chicago Drainage Canal. A review of the historical, technical, financial and international features. (Reprint from the Engineering Journal.) pp. 23. [1926.] 4°. **08777**. ff. **6**.

BUSH. The Burning Bush, not consumed. Wherein . . . one may judge, whether he be the Child of God, or not . . . Perused by I. D. [i.e. Jeremiah Dyke?] and divers other divines, *etc.* [With a preface signed: I. H., i.e. John Hart.] pp. 103. *Printed by Andrew Anderson*: *Edinburgh*, 1674. 12°. **4372**. a. **25**.

—— [Another edition.] pp. 103. *Printed by the Heir of Andrew Anderson*: *Edinburgh*, 1679. 12°. **4404**. aaa. **28**.

—— The Bush. (The St. Helena Command magazine.) *See* England.—*Army.*—*St. Helena Command.*

BUSH AND SON AND MEISSNER. Les Vignes américaines. Catalogue illustré et descriptif, avec de brèves indications sur leur culture . . . Ouvrage traduit de l'anglais par L. Bazille . . . Revue et annoté par J.-E. Planchon. pp. vi. 130. *Montpellier, Paris*, 1876. 4°. **7076**. i. **1**.

BUSH AND SON AND MEISSNER.

—— Le Viti americane. Catalogo illustrato e descrittivo con un breve cenno sopra la loro coltura . . . Opera tradotta dall'inglese da Farina e Comp. pp. 117. *Castellanza; Busto Arsizio*, 1881. 8°. **7078**. i. **3**.

BUSH'S BROMLEY BUDGET. Bush's Bromley Budget and Almanack, *etc.* *See* DIRECTORIES.—*Bromley, Kent.*

BUSH'S DIRECTORY. Bush's Directory of Bromley. *See* DIRECTORIES.—*Bromley, Kent.* Bush's Bromley Budget, *etc.*

BUSH (ADA LILLIAN)

—— Suggestions for Use in Making a City Survey, Industrial and Commercial, *etc.* pp. iv. 56. *Washington*, 1938. 8°. [*U.S. Department of Commerce. Bureau of Foreign and Domestic Commerce. Domestic Commerce Series.* no. 105.] A.S. **130/2**.

BUSH (ALAN DUDLEY)

—— *See* BELZA (I. F.) Handbook of Soviet Musicians . . . Edited by **A**. Bush. 1943. 8°. W.P. **8649/1**.

—— Music in the Soviet Union. (Two lectures.) pp. 30. *Workers' Music Association: London*, [1944.] 8°. **7891**. a. **60**.

—— Strict Counterpoint in Palestrina Style. A practical text-book, *etc.* [With musical illustrations.] pp. 27. *Joseph Williams: London*, [1948.] fol. **7891**. dd. **7**.

—— Tribute to Alan Bush on his Fiftieth Birthday, *etc.* [With a portrait and musical illustrations.] pp. 58. 1950. 8°. *See* LONDON.—III. *Workers' Music Association.* **7890**. cc. **37**.

BUSH (ARTHUR)

—— Portrait of London, *etc.* [With plates.] pp. 232. *Frederick Muller: London*, 1950. 8°. **010349**. n. **62**.

BUSH (BELLE) Voices of the Morning. [Poems.] pp. 270. *J. B. Lippincott & Co.: Philadelphia*, 1865. 12°. **11687**. aaa. **23**.

BUSH (BERTHA EVANGELINE) A Prairie Rose . . . With illustrations by Henry C. Pitz. pp. 305. *Little, Brown & Co.: Boston*, 1925. 8°. **12650**. dd. **9**.

BUSH (C. S.) Plain Facts, showing the falsehood and folly of the Rev. C. S. Bush . . . Being a reply to his tract against the Latter-Day Saints [entitled "Plain Facts, showing the falsehood and folly of the Mormonites"]. pp. 16. *W. R. Thomas: Manchester* [*N. H.*], [1840?] 12°. **4378**. e. **9**. (**4**.)

BUSH (C. W.) Table showing the Number of Days Accrued Interest on any one day during 1924(-1936) . . . Compiled by C. W. Bush. (14th, 15th year of issue. Compiled by J. A. Ruddiman.) 13 pt. *Edwards & Smith: London*, [1923-35.] fol. & 8°. **1879**. cc. **9**. (**28**.)
Imperfect; wanting the issues for 1922 *and* 1923.

BUSH (CHARLES) *Clerk of the Records in the Tower.* *See* CHRONICA. Chronica Juridicialia, *etc.* [With MS. notes and additions by C. Bush.] 1685. 8°. **1129**. a. **4**. (**1**.)

BUSH (CHARLES) *Secretary to the Board of Ordnance.* *See* POLLARD (Arthur) A Catalogue of the genuine Collection of scarce Greek and Roman Coins and Medals . . . of A. Pollard . . . and also the . . . collection of English coins and medals, of C. Bush, *etc.* [1757.] 8°. **603**. c. **4**. (**4**.)

BUSH (CHARLES G.) *See* SMITH (*Sir* Michael Angelo Raphael) *C.G.B., pseud.* [i.e. C. G. Bush.]

BUSH (CHARLES P.) Five Years in China; or, the Factory boy made a missionary. The life and observations of Rev. William Aitchison, *etc.* [With plates, including a portrait.] pp. 284. *Presbyterian Publication Committee: Philadelphia*, [1865.] 8°. **10057**. aa. **36**.

—— [Another edition.] The Martyr Missionary, *etc.* pp. viii. 198. *W. P. Nimmo: Edinburgh*, [1867.] 8°. **4955**. aa. **19**.

—— Work for all, and ways of working. pp. 128. *Presbyterian Publication Committee: Philadelphia*, [1868.] 12°. **4412**. aaa. **7**.

BUSH (CHILTON ROWLETTE) Editorial Thinking and Writing, *etc.* pp. xiii. 453. *D. Appleton & Co.: New York, London*, 1932. 8°. **20016**. bb. **7**.

—— Newspaper Reporting of Public Affairs. An advanced course in newspaper reporting, *etc.* pp. xix. 406. *D. Appleton & Co.: New York, London*, 1929. 8°. **011824**. aaa. **29**.

—— Newspaper Reporting of Public Affairs . . . New and enlarged edition. pp. xxiii. 455. *D. Appleton-Century Co.: New York, London*, [1940.] 8°. **11862**. bbb. **34**.

BUSH (CHRISTOPHER)

—— The Case of the Amateur Actor. pp. 205. *Macdonald: London*, 1955. 8°. NNN. **6998**.

—— The Case of the April Fools. pp. 316. *Cassell & Co.: London*, 1933. 8°. NN. **20043**.

—— The Case of the Benevolent Bookie. pp. 222. *Macdonald: London*, 1955. 8°. NNN. **5924**.

—— The Case of the Bonfire Body. pp. 279. *Cassell & Co.: London*, 1936. 8°. NN. **26601**.

—— The Case of the Burnt Bohemian. pp. 223. *Macdonald: London*, 1953. 8°. **012638**. m. **41**.

—— The Case of the Chinese Gong. pp. 316. *Cassell & Co.: London*, 1935. 8°. NN. **24163**.

—— The Case of the Climbing Rat, *etc.* pp. 280. *Cassell & Co.: London*, 1940. 8°. NN. **31304**.

—— The Case of the Corner Cottage. pp. 240. *Macdonald & Co.: London*, 1951. 8°. NNN. **1681**.

—— The Case of the Corporal's Leave. pp. 214. *Cassell & Co.: London*, 1945. 8°. NN. **35404**.

—— The Case of the Corporal's Leave. pp. 128. *Withy Grove Press: London & Manchester*, [1949.] 8°. [*Cherry Tree Book.* no. 262.] **12634**. p. **1/262**.

—— The Case of the Counterfeit Colonel. pp. 240. *Macdonald & Co.: London*, 1952. 8°. NNN. **3189**.

—— The Case of the Curious Client. pp. 223. *Macdonald & Co.: London*, 1947. 8°. NN. **37019**.

—— The Case of the Dead Shepherd. pp. 318. *Cassell & Co.: London*, 1934. 8°. NN. **22915**.

—— The Case of the Fighting Soldier. pp. 239. *Cassell & Co.: London*, 1942. 8°. NN. **33654**.

BUSH (CHRISTOPHER)

—— **The Case of the Flying Ass. A Ludovic Travers story. pp. 287.** ***Cassell & Co.: London,*** 1939. 8°. NN. **30460.**

—— The Case of the Fourth Detective. pp. 239. *Macdonald & Co.: London,* 1951. 8°. NNN. **2110.**

—— The Case of the Green Felt Hat. A Ludovic Travers story. pp. 281. *Cassell & Co.: London,* 1939. 8°. NN. **30003.**

—— The Case of the Hanging Rope. pp. 274. *Cassell & Co.: London,* 1937. 8°. NN. **27608.**

—— The Case of the Happy Medium. pp. 223. *Macdonald & Co.: London,* 1952. 8°. NNN. **2569.**

—— The Case of the Happy Warrior. pp. 240. *Macdonald & Co.: London,* 1950. 8°. NNN. **694.**

—— The Case of the Haven Hotel. pp. 240. *Macdonald & Co.: London,* 1948. 8°. NN. **37822.**

—— **The Case of the Housekeeper's Hair.** pp. 223. ***Macdonald & Co.: London,*** 1948. 8°. NN. **38531.**

—— The Case of the 100% Alibis. pp. 295. *Cassell & Co.: London,* 1934. 8°. NN. **22011.**

—— The Case of the Kidnapped Colonel. pp. 222. *Cassell & Co.: London,* 1942. 8°. NN. **11456.**

—— The Case of the Leaning Man, *etc.* pp. 287. *Cassell & Co.: London,* 1938. 8°. NN. **29105.**

—— The Case of the Magic Mirror. pp. 231. *Cassell & Co.: London,* 1943. 8°. NN. **33921.**

—— The Case of the Magic Mirror. pp. 160. *Mellifont Press: London; Dublin* printed, [1953.] 8°. **012638.** r. **6.**

—— The Case of the Missing Men. pp. 191. *Macdonald & Co.: London,* [1946.] 8°. NN. **35785.**

—— The Case of the Missing Minutes. pp. 296. *Cassell & Co.: London,* 1937. 8°. NN. **26893.**

—— The Case of the Monday Murders. pp. 281. *Cassell & Co.: London,* 1936. 8°. NN. **25252.**

—— The Case of the Murdered Major. pp. 255. *Cassell & Co.: London,* 1941. 8°. NN. **32579.**

—— The Case of the Platinum Blonde. pp. 191. *Cassell & Co.: London,* 1944. 8°. NN. **34859.**

—— The Case of the Purloined Picture. pp. 222. *Macdonald & Co.: London,* 1949. 8°. NN. **39949.**

—— The Case of the Red Brunette. pp. 222. *Macdonald: London,* 1954. 8°. NNN. **4851.**

—— The Case of the Running Mouse. pp. 219. *Cassell & Co.: London,* 1944. 8°. NN. **34686.**

—— The Case of the Second Chance, *etc.* pp. 250. *MacDonald & Co.: London,* 1946. 8°. NN. **36267.**

—— The Case of the Seven Bells. pp. 222. *Macdonald & Co.: London,* 1949. 8°. NN. **39141.**

—— [A reissue.] The Case of the Seven Bells. *London,* 1952. 8°. **12650.** a. **107.**

BUSH (CHRISTOPHER)

—— The Case of the Silken Petticoat. pp. 223. *Macdonald: London,* 1953. 8°. NNN. **4249.**

—— The Case of the Three Lost Letters. pp. 208. *Macdonald: London,* 1954. 8°. NNN. **5654.**

—— The Case of the Three Strange Faces. pp. 314. *Cassell & Co.: London,* 1933. 8°. NN. **20941.**

—— The Case of the Tudor Queen, *etc.* pp. 292. *Cassell & Co.: London,* 1938. 8°. NN. **28355.**

—— The Case of the Tudor Queen. pp. 187. *Penguin Books: London,* 1953. 8°. [*Penguin Books.* no. 849.] **12208.** a. **1/849.**

—— The Case of the Unfortunate Village. pp. 327. *Cassell & Co.: London,* 1932. 8°. NN. **3290.**

—— Cut Throat. pp. 316. *William Heinemann: London,* 1932. 8°. NN. **19461.**

—— Dancing Death. pp. 362. *William Heinemann: London,* 1931. 8°. NN. **18102.**

—— Dancing Death. pp. 362. *William Heinemann: London,* 1931. 8°. NN. **18102.**

—— Dancing Death. [An abridgment.] pp. 96. *Mellifont Press: London; Dublin* printed, [1944.] 8°. **012633.** p. **64.**

—— Dead Man Twice. pp. 307. *William Heinemann: London,* 1930. 8°. NN. **16834.**

—— Dead Man Twice. pp. 96. *Withy Grove Press: London & Manchester,* [1946.] 8°. [*Cherry Tree Book.* no. 222.] **12634.** p. **1/222.**

—— Dead Man's Music. pp. 304. *William Heinemann: London,* 1931. 8°. NN. **18585.**

—— Dead Man's Music. [An abridgment.] pp. 96. *Withy Grove Press: London & Manchester,* [1945.] 8°. [*Cherry Tree Books.* no. 210.] **12634.** p. **1/210.**

—— The Death of Cosmo Revere. pp. xii. 312. *William Heinemann: London; printed in U.S.A.,* 1930. 8°. NN. **16622.**

—— Murder at Fenwold. pp. 313. *William Heinemann: London,* 1930. 8°. NN. **17316.**

—— The Perfect Murder Case. pp. 312. *William Heinemann: London,* 1929. 8°. NN. **15151.**

—— The Perfect Murder Case. [An abridgment.] pp. 96. *Mellifont Press: London; Dublin* printed, [1943.] 8°. **012633.** p. **51.**

—— The Plumley Inheritance. pp. 282. *Jarrolds: London,* [1926.] 8°. NN. **12260.**

BUSH (CLARENCE A.) *See* BACHRACH (W.) The Outline of Swimming. By W. Bachrach . . . in collaboration with C. A. Bush. 1924. 8°. **2270.** b. **45.**

—— *See* WEISSMULLER (J.) Swimming the American Crawl. By J. Weissmuller, in collaboration with C. A. Bush. [1933.] 8°. **07911.** ee. **45.**

BUSH (DOUGLAS) *See* BUSH (John N. D.)

BUSH (E. ADOL'FOVICH) Список растений, собранных Е. А. и Н. А. Буш в Центральном Кавказе в 1911, 1913 и 1925 гг . . . С маршрутной картой. *Ленинград,* 1927. 8°. [*Труды Ботанического Музея.* no. 20.] Ac. **1125**. v.

BUSH (EDWARD) *Member of the Society for Psychical Research.* Spirit Photography Exposed. pp. 38. *John Fletcher: Wakefield,* [1920.] 8°. **8633**. df. **74**.

BUSH (EDWARD) *of Caerphilly. See* THOMAS (Cadwaladr T.) and BUSH (E.) Pebyll Seion, *etc.* 1904. 8°. **4715**. df. **16**.

BUSH (EDWARD) *Preacher.* A Sermon preached at Pauls Crosse on Trinity Sunday, 1571. By E. B. [i.e. Edward Bush.] **B.L.** 1576. 16°. *See* B., E. **4474**. a. **54**.

BUSH (ELIZA C.) My Pilgrimage to Eastern Shrines. pp. xii. 317. *Hurst & Blackett: London,* 1867 [1866]. 8°. **10075**. ee. **9**.

BUSH (ERIC WHELER)

—— How to become a Naval Officer—Special Entry. Being a detailed account of how a public school boy may become an officer in His Majesty's Navy, *etc.* [Revised by Robert L. B. Cunliffe. With plates.] pp. xix. 95. *Gieves: London,* 1935. 8°. **8809**. a. **31**.

BUSH (F. A.)

—— *See* JACKMAN (G. R.) and BUSH (F. A.) Shrubs and Trees for Everyman's Garden, *etc.* 1947. 8°. **7035**. b. **16**.

—— Gardens & Allotments in War Time. pp. 22. *Bath,* 1943. 8°. [*Bath and West & Southern Counties Society. Pamphlet.* no. 8.] **7080.de.42/8.**

BUSH (F. PERCY) and **FRICKER** (B. H.) Les Verbes anglais. A l'usage des étudiants français, *etc.* pp. vii. 51. *Hirschfeld Frères: Londres,* 1931 [1930]. 8°. **12981**. bbb. **74**.

BUSH (*Mrs.* FORBES) Memoirs of the Queens of France: with notices of the royal favourites. 2 vol. *Henry Colburn: London,* 1843. 8°. **1449**. h. **18**.

BUSH (FRANCIS ROBERT) *See* LEIGH (*Hon. Sir* Edward C.) *K.C.B.* Bar, Bat and Bit . . . Edited by F. R. Bush, *etc.* 1913. 8°. **010826**. i. **16**.

BUSH (FREDERICK GRANT) *See* DAY (Thomas A.) and BUSH (F. G.) Les Merveilles de Londres, *etc.* [1851.] 12°. **10350**. a. **39**.

BUSH (FREDERICK GRANT) and **DAY** (THOMAS ANTHONY)

—— The Excursionist's Guide; or, Three days in Paris. [By F. G. Bush and T. A. Day.] pp. 23. [1850.] 12°. *See* PARIS. [*Appendix.—Topography.—Guide Books.*] **1302**. a. **15**.

BUSH (G. A.) Obtaining Capital. ff. 47. [*Efficiency Publishing Co.: Harrow,* 1932.] fol. **1884**. b. **11**.
Reproduced from typewriting.

BUSH (GEOFFREY)

—— Musical Creation and the Listener. pp. 121. *Frederick Muller: London,* 1954. 8°. [*Man and Society Series.*] W.P. **5788/6**.

BUSH (GEORGE) *See* also CAMPAGINATOR, *pseud.* [i.e. G. Bush.]

BUSH (GEORGE)

—— *See* DYMOND (Jonathan) Essays on the Principles of Morality . . . With a preface by the Rev. G. Bush. 1834. 8°. **1388**. k. **5**.

—— *See* JUNG (J. H.) called STILLING. Theory of Pneumatology . . . Edited by Rev. G. Bush. 1851. 12°. **8465**. b. **22**.

—— *See* PERIODICAL PUBLICATIONS.—*New York.* The Hierophant . . . Conducted by G. Bush. 1844. 8°. P.P. **896**.

—— *See* PERIODICAL PUBLICATIONS.—*New York.* The New Church Repository . . . Conducted by G. Bush. 1848, *etc.* 8°. P.P. **868**.

—— *See* SWEDBERG, afterwards SWEDENBORG (E.) [*Diarium Spirituale.*] The Spiritual Diary of Emanuel Swedenborg . . . Translated by Professor G. Bush . . . and the Rev. J. H. Smithson. 1883, *etc.* 8°. **3716**. g. **3**.

—— Anastasis; or the Doctrine of the resurrection of the body, rationally and scripturally considered. pp. 396. *Wiley & Putnam: London,* 1845. 12°. **1355**. f. **12**.

—— *See* LANDIS (Robert W.) The Doctrine of the Resurrection of the Body asserted and defended; in answer to the exceptions recently presented [in "Anastasis"] by Rev. George Bush, *etc.* 1846. 12°. **1355**. f. **8**.

—— Gold for Brass and Silver for Iron; or, a Plea for the doctrines of the New Jerusalem. A sermon. pp. 16. *New-York,* 1853. 8°. **4486**. bb. **62**. (**9**.)

—— [Another edition.] A Plea for the Doctrines of the New Jerusalem. pp. 19. *J. S. Hodson: London,* [1856?] 12°. **3716**. d. **2**. (**4**.)

—— A Grammar of the Hebrew Language . . . Second edition, corrected and enlarged. pp. 276. *Gould, Newman & Saxton: New-York,* 1839. 8°. **825**. c. **26**.

—— Illustrations of the Holy Scriptures, derived principally from the manners, customs, rites, traditions, forms of speech, antiquities, climate, and works of art and literature of the Eastern nations; embodying all that is valuable in the works of Harmer, Burder, Paxton, and Roberts, and the most celebrated oriental travellers; embracing also the subject of the fulfilment of prophecy, as exhibited by Keith and others . . . Edited by Rev. G. Bush. [With plates.] pp. 656. *Brattleboro' Typographic Co.: Brattleboro',* 1839. fol. **3126**. i. **4**.
With an additional titlepage, engraved.

—— Letters to a Trinitarian; or, the Doctrine of the tri-personality of Jehovah inconsistent with the truth of the Incarnation. pp. 139. *Otis Clapp: Boston,* 1850. 8°. **4372**. h. **5**. (**4**.)

—— Life in its Origin, Gradations, Forms and Issues . . . Third edition. pp. 16. *J. S. Hodson: London,* 1851. 8°. **4422**. h. **19**. (**2**.)

—— The Life of Mohammed, founder of the religion of Islam, and of the Empire of the Saracens. pp. 261. *Harper & Bros.: New-York,* 1844. 12°. **12205**. b. **67**.

—— New Church Miscellanies; or, Essays ecclesiastical, doctrinal, and ethical . . . Republished from the New Church Repository. pp. 372. *Wm. McGeorge: New-York,* 1855. 8°. **3756**. b. **4**.

—— Notes, critical and practical, on the Book of Genesis . . . [With the text.] Reprinted from the American edition, 1838. pp. 495. *T. Ward & Co.: London,* [1841.] 8°. **1126**. k. **13**. (**4**.)

—— Seventh edition. 2 vol. *M. H. Newman: New York,* 1844. 12°. **3155**. f. **3**.

—— Notes, critical and practical, on the Books of Joshua and Judges . . . Reprinted from the American edition of 1838. [With the text.] pp. vi. 254. [1840.] 8°. *See* Bible.—*Historical Books.* [*English.*] **1126**. k. **11**. (**4**.)

—— Notes, critical and practical, on the Book of Joshua, *etc.* [With the text.] pp. 221. 1844. 12°. *See* Bible.—*Joshua.* [*English.*] **3165**. df. **18**.

—— Notes, critical and practical, on the Book of Judges, *etc.* [With the text.] pp. 257. 1844. 12°. *See* Bible.—*Judges.* [*English.*] **3165**. bb. **11**.

—— Notes, critical and practical, on the Book of Leviticus, *etc.* [With the text.] pp. 282. 1861. 8°. *See* Bible.—*Leviticus.* [*English.*] **3155**. f. **20**.

—— *See* Denham (Joshua F.) Marriage with a Deceased Wife's Sister not forbidden by the Law of Nature . . . Including an examination of Professor Bush's Notes on Leviticus. 1847. 8°. **5175**. b. **21**.

—— Notes, critical and practical, on the Book of Numbers, *etc.* (Specimen.) [With the text of chap. i. 1–46.] pp. 24. 1858. 12°. *See* Bible.—*Numbers.* [*English.*] **3155**. c. **15**.

—— The Origin of Priesthood and Clergy: or, Ecclesiastical rulers unknown to primitive Christianity. With scriptural arguments in favor of congregational church government, *etc.* pp. 168. *A. Colby's Sons: Portland, Me.,* [1857.] 8°. **4182**. b. **45**.
Imperfect; wanting pp. 5, 6.

—— The Christian Ministry, considered in relation to the priesthood of believers, and the free exercise of spiritual gifts. [An abridgment of "The Origin of Priesthood and Clergy" by G. Bush.] pp. vi. 119. 1867. 8°. *See* Christian Ministry. **4498**. aa. **9**.

—— The Past Required. A New Year's sermon. pp. 16. [*Brooklyn,* 1855.] 8°. **4486**. e. **51**. (**13**.)

—— The Prophecies of Daniel . . . By G. Bush. [With the text of chap. ii in Hebrew, Aramaic, Greek, Latin and English.] 2 pt. pp. 144. 1844. 8°. *See* Bible.—*Daniel.*—*Selections.* [*Polyglott.*] **3186**. dd. **16**.

—— Prof. Bush's Reply to Ralph Waldo Emerson on Swedenborg. A lecture, *etc.* pp. 32. *John Allen: New York,* 1846. 8°. **4885**. cc. **54**.

—— Reply to Rev. Dr. Woods' "Lectures on Swedenborgianism," *etc.* pp. 256. *John Allen: New York,* 1847. 8°. **4183**. cc. **12**.

—— The Resurrection of Christ; in answer to the question, whether He rose in a spiritual and celestial, or in a material and earthly body. pp. 92. *J. S. Redfield: New-York,* 1845. 12°. **4824**. bbb. **7**.

—— The Soul; or, an Inquiry into scriptural psychology, as developed by the use of the terms, soul, spirit, life, etc., viewed in its bearings on the doctrine of the Resurrection. pp. 141. *J. S. Redfield: New-York,* 1845. 12°. **1354**. h. **19**.

—— Statement of Reasons for Embracing the Doctrines and Disclosures of Emanuel Swedenborg. pp. 104. *J. S. Hodson: London,* 1847. 8°. **1355**. h. **15**.

—— [Another edition.] Sixth thousand. pp. 28. *Otis Clapp: Boston,* 1850. 8°. **3716**. dd. **8**.

—— [Another edition.] With a biographical sketch of the author [by Samuel Beswick]. [With a portrait.] pp. xxiv. 120. *E. H. Swinney: New York,* 1875. 12°. **4152**. aaaa. **5**.

—— [Another edition.] pp. xii. 121. *James Speirs: London,* 1885. 8°. **3716**. aa. **21**.

—— The Valley of Vision; or, the Dry bones of Israel revived. An attempted proof, from Ezekiel, chap. xxxvii. 1–14, of the restoration and conversion of the Jews. [With the text, in Hebrew, Greek, Latin and English.] pp. vii. 60. *Saxton & Miles: New-York,* 1844. 8°. **1352**. i. **22**. (**3**.)

BUSH (George) and **BARRETT** (Benjamin Fisk)

—— "Davis' Revelations" Revealed; being a critical examination of the character and claims of that work in its relations to the teachings of Swedenborg. pp. 43. *John Allen: New York,* 1847. 8°. **8465**. d. **11**.

BUSH (George F.)

—— Instruction Manual in Reading Engineering Drawings. With 711 questions and answers. pp. iii. 50. *J. Wiley & Sons: New York,* [1943.] 4°. **8769**. i. **28**.
Reproduced from typewriting.

—— Reading Engineering Drawings. [With blueprints.] pp. ix. 60. *J. Wiley & Sons: New York,* 1942. 4°. **8769**. i. **18**.

BUSH (George Gary) Harvard, the first American University. [With plates.] pp. 160. **L.P.** *Cupples, Upham & Co.: Boston,* [1886.] 16°. **8365**. f. **25**.

—— [A reissue.] *G. P. Putnam's Sons: London,* [1887.] 16°. **8365**. aa. **13**.

—— History of Education in New Hampshire. pp. 170. *Washington,* 1898. 8°. [*U.S. Bureau of Education. Circular of Information.* 1898. no. 3.] A.S. **203**.

—— History of Education in Florida. pp. 54. *Washington,* 1889. 8°. [*U.S. Bureau of Education. Circular of Information.* 1888. no. 7.] A.S. **203**.

—— History of Education in Vermont. [With plates.] pp. 216. *Washington,* 1900. 8°. [*U.S. Bureau of Education. Circular of Information.* 1900. no. 4.] A.S. **203**.

—— History of Higher Education in Massachusetts. [With plates.] pp. 445. *Washington,* 1891. 8°. [*U.S. Bureau of Education. Circular of Information.* 1891. no. 6.] A.S. **203**.

BUSH (George Leonard)

—— *See* Biddle (Harry C.) and Bush (G. L.) Dynamic Chemistry, *etc.* [1936.] 8°. **8901**. df. **24**.

—— —— [1937.] 8°. **8899**. e. **1**.

—— *See* Biddle (Harry C.) and Bush (G. L.) Laboratory Manual for Dynamic Chemistry, *etc.* [1936.] 4°. **8904**. h. **13**.

—— A Biology of Familiar Things. [By] G. L. Bush . . . Allan Dickie . . . Ronald C. Runkle. [With illustrations.] pp. 695. *American Book Co.: New York,* [1939.] 8°. **7006**. r. **7**.

BUSH (George Leonard)

—— Activities to accompany A Biology of Familiar Things. [By] G. L. Bush . . . Allan Dickie . . . Ronald C. Runkle. pp. iv. 252. *American Book Co.: New York,* [1939.] 4°. **7208.** b. **40.**

—— Guided Activities in Senior Science. [By] G. L. Bush . . . Theodore W. Ptacek . . . John Kovats, Jr. pp. iv. 251. *American Book Co.: New York,* [1937.] 4°. **8710.** ee. **45.**

—— Senior Science. Socialized for the high school. By G. L. Bush . . . Theodore W. Ptacek . . . and John Kovats, Jr. pp. vii. 835. *American Book Co.: New York,* [1937.] 8°. **8710.** ee. **24.**

—— Teachers' Manual and Key. Senior Science and Guided Activities in Senior Science. G. L. Bush . . . Theodore W. Ptacek . . . John Kovats, Jr. pp. iii. 144. *American Book Co.: New York,* [1939.] 8°. **08712.** aaa. **5.**

BUSH (George Leonard) and **THOMPSON** (Will Scroggs)

—— New Senior Science. [With illustrations.] pp. ix. 642. *American Book Co.: New York,* [1954.] 8°. **8713.** d. **22.**

—— Guided Activities for New Senior Science. [By] G. L. Bush. pp. 222. *American Book Co.: New York,* [1954.] 4°. **8713.** d. **22a.**

BUSH (H. Fulford) Foulsham's Physical Training Books . . . By H. F. Bush, in collaboration with E. J. Harrison, *etc.* 3 vol. *W. Foulsham & Co.: London,* [1935.] 8°. **07908.** de. **18.**

—— Foulsham's Physical Training Books. [vol. 2.] Physical Training for Women. By H. F. Bush in collaboration with E. J. Harrison, *etc.* [With plates.] pp. 90. *W. Foulsham & Co.: London,* [1940?] 8°. **7921.** a. **14.**

BUSH (H. W.) *See* Connan (Donald M.) and Bush (H. W.) Better than Cure, *etc.* [1927.] 8°. **7383.** c. **12.**

BUSH (Harold Richard) *See* Bath.—*Bath Proprietary College.* The Bath Propietary College Miscellany, *etc.* [Edited by H. R. Bush.] [1855, *etc.*] 8°. P.P. **6042.**

—— David's Choice of Three Evils . . . A sermon on the distress in the cotton districts. By a Layman [i.e. H. R. Bush]. pp. 8. 1862. 8°. *See* Layman. **4478.** c. **63.**

BUSH (Henry) Bristol Town Duties. A collection of original & interesting documents, intended to explain and elucidate the above important subject. pp. 134. *J. M. Gutch: Bristol,* 1828. 8°. **1302.** h. **18.**

BUSH (J. W.) *See* Dowsett (J. E.) and Bush (J. W.) Machine Woodworking. 1929. 8°. [*Greenhalgh (Richard) Joinery and Carpentry, etc.* vol. 1.] **07815.** e. **48.**

BUSH (James) The Choice: or, Lines on the Beatitudes. pp. 102. *R. Saywell: London,* 1841. *obl.* 8°. **11645.** de. **1.**

BUSH (James S.) The Atonement. A sermon, *etc.* pp. 32. *New York,* 1863. 8°. **4486.** aa. **69. (13.)**

—— More Words about the Bible. (Sermons.) pp. 83. *J. W. Lovell Co.: New York,* [1883.] 12°. **4487.** a. **31.**

BUSH (Jane) *See* Bush (Joseph) *Wesleyan Minister.* Joseph Bush. A memorial. Edited by his wife, *etc.* [1907.] 8°. **4908.** aa. **17.**

BUSH (John) *of Tunbridge Wells.* Hibernia Curiosa. A letter from a gentleman in Dublin, to his friend at Dover in Kent, giving a general view of the manners, customs, dispositions, &c. of the inhabitants of Ireland, *etc.* [With plans.] pp. xvi. 143. *W. Flexney: London,* [1767?] 8°. **797.** g. **20.**

—— [Another edition.] pp. xvi. 143. *W. Flexney: London,* 1769. 8°. T. **979. (3.)**

—— [Another copy.] **286.** b. **32.**

—— [Another copy.] G. **5619.**

BUSH (John) *Preacher.* The Necessity and Reward of a Willing Mind. A sermon, *etc.* pp. 32. *London; for Mich. Hyde: Exon,* 1693. 4°. **4462.** cc. **1. (2.)**

BUSH (John Dearden) and **MILLER** (E. T.) Five Years on a Training Ship . . . With illustrations by Savile Lumley. pp. viii. 267. *Pilgrim Press: London,* [1913.] 8°. **012809.** d. **35.**

BUSH (John Nash Douglas)

—— *See* Davenant (*Sir* William) Selected Poems . . With a prefatory note by D. Bush. 1943. 8°. **11656.** f. **6.**

—— *See* Spagnuoli (B.) *Mantuanus.* The Eclogues of Mantuan. Translated by G. Turbervile . . . Edited by D. Bush. 1937. 8°. W.P. **9530/11.**

—— Classical Influences in Renaissance Literature, *etc.* pp. 60. *Harvard University Press: Cambridge, Mass.,* 1952. 8°. [*Martin Classical Lectures.* no. 13.] Ac. **2691.** ra.

—— English Literature in the Earlier Seventeenth Century, 1600–1660. [With a bibliography.] pp. vi. 621. *Clarendon Press: Oxford,* 1945. 8°. [*Oxford History of English Literature.* vol. 5.] **W.P.12/5b.**

—— [A reissue.] English Literature in the Earlier Seventeenth Century, 1600–1660. *Oxford,* 1946. 8°. [*Oxford History of English Literature.* vol. 5.] **W.P.12/5b.**

—— English Poetry. The main currents from Chaucer to the present. pp. ix. 222. *Methuen & Co.: London,* 1952. 8°. [*Home Study Books.*] W.P. **6370/18.** *With an errata slip.*

—— Mythology and the Renaissance Tradition in English Poetry. pp. viii. 360. *University of Minnesota Press: Minneapolis,* 1932. 8°. **20016.** i. **2.**

—— Mythology and the Romantic Tradition in English Poetry. [With a bibliography.] pp. xvi. 647. *Cambridge, Mass.,* 1937. 8°. [*Harvard Studies in English.* vol. 18.] Ac. **2692/16.**

—— Paradise Lost in Our Time. Some comments. pp. ix. 117. *Cornell University Press: Ithaca, N.Y.,* 1945. 8°. **11826.** c. **47.**

—— The Renaissance and English Humanism. (The Alexander Lectures in English at the University of Toronto, 1939.) pp. 139. *University of Toronto Press: [Toronto,]* 1939. 8°. **11865.** b. **19.**

—— [A reissue.] The Renaissance and English Humanism. *Toronto,* 1941. 8°. **11826.** c. **46.**

BUSH (JOHN NASH DOUGLAS)

—— Science and English Poetry. A historical sketch, 1590–1950. pp. viii. 166. *Oxford University Press: New York*, 1950. 8º. [*Patten Lectures.* 1949.] **Ac.2692.w/14.**

BUSH (JOSEPH) *Vicar of Ormskirk.* The Soldier and Christian compared. A sermon, *etc.* pp. 16. *T. Hutton: Ormskirk*, [1860.] 8º. **4478.** d. **7.**

BUSH (JOSEPH) *Wesleyan Minister. See* BIBLE.—*Song of Solomon.* [*English.*] The Canticles of the Song of Solomon: a metrical paraphrase, with explanatory notes . . . By the Rev. J. Bush. [1867.] 8º. **3166.** aaa. **55.**

—— *See* DUNN (Lewis R.) The Mission of the Spirit . . . Edited by the Rev. J. Bush. 1872. 8º. **4379.** aa. **17.**

—— *See* WRAY (Samuel) W. O. Simpson, Methodist Minister . . . Edited by the Rev. J. Bush. 1886. 8º. **4907.** bbb. **32.**

—— Bread from Heaven. pp. 80. *John Mason: London*, 1859. 16º. **4376.** a. **69.** (**3.**)

—— Character: how it is made, and what it is worth. A sermon . . . Second edition. pp. 28. *Wesleyan Conference Office: London*, [1866.] 8º. **4478.** aa. **116.** (**15.**)

—— Courtship and Marriage. A lecture. pp. 56. *John Mason: London; Lawson & Groves: York*, 1863. 8º. **8415.** cc. **42.** (**4.**)

—— Friendly Counsels for Class Leaders. pp. 32. *C. H. Kelly: London*, [1902.] 12º. **4139.** bb. **19.**

—— How to Keep our Members. Practical counsels addressed to Class Leaders . . . Second edition. pp. 32. *T. Woolmer: London*, 1884. 8º. **4136.** aa. **18.** (**2.**)

—— The Intermediate State; or, the Condition of human souls between the hour of death and the day of judgment . . . Fifth edition. pp. 95. *C. H. Kelly: London*, 1896. 8º. **4256.** df. **5.**

—— Mary Bell Hodgson: a memorial. pp. 47. *William Parkhouse: Bolton*, 1865. 16º. **4906.** b. **71.** (**8.**)

—— Modern Thoughts on Ancient Stories. pp. 172. *C. H. Kelly: London*, [1897.] 8º. **3128.** d. **53.**

—— The Sabbath: whose day is it? A sermon. pp. 24. *John Mason: London*, 1856. 8º. **4355.** e. **24.**

—— Sermons, Addresses and Charges. [With a portrait.] pp. vi. 266. *Wesleyan Methodist Book Room: London*, 1889. 8º. **4479.** c. **41.**

—— The Witness of the Spirit; an exposition. pp. 32. *C. H. Kelly: London*, 1896. 16º. **04420.** de. **4.** (**3.**)

—— Joseph Bush. A memorial. Edited by his wife (Jane Bush). With a brief memoir by the Rev. Arthur Hoyle. [Sermons and obiter dicta. With portraits.] pp. 222. *Robert Culley: London*, [1907.] 8º. **4908.** aa. **17.**

BUSH (JOSEPH H.) *See* PRICE (Samuel W.) The Old Masters of the Bluegrass. Jouett, Bush, *etc.* [With a portrait.] 1902. 4º. [*Filson Club Publications.* no. 17.] Ac. **8423.**

BUSH (KATHARINE JEANNETTE) *See* VERRILL (Addison E.) and BUSH (K. J.) Revision of the Deep-Water Mollusca of the Atlantic Coast of North America, *etc.* 1898. 8º. [*Proceedings of the United States National Museum.* vol. 20.] Ac. **1875/12.**

BUSH (KATHARINE JEANNETTE)

—— Notes on the Family Pyramidellidœ [*sic*]. (From the American Journal of Science.) [*New Haven*, 1909.] 8º. **7006.** d. **14.** (**2.**)

—— Report on the Mollusca dredged by the "Blake" in 1880, including descriptions of several new species . . . With two plates. *Cambridge, Mass.*, 1893. 8º. [*Bulletin of the Museum of Comparative Zoology at Harvard College.* vol. 23. no. 6.] Ac. **1736/2.**

—— Tubicolous Annelids. 1904. *See* HARRIMAN (Edward H.) Harriman Alaska Series. vol. 12. 1901, *etc.* 8º. Ac. **1875/8.**

BUSH (LEWIS WILLIAM)

—— *See* HINO (Ashihei) War and Soldier . . . Translated from the Japanese by L. Bush. 1940. 8º. **11101.** c. **32.**

—— *See* KAGAMI (Y.) Handy Guide to Japan and the Orient . . . Revised by L. W. Bush. [1935.] 8º. **010056.** a. **35.**

BUSH (LEWIS WILLIAM) and **KAGAMI** (YOSHIYUKI)

—— Japanalia. Reference book to things Japanese. [With plates.] pp. xx. 193. *John Gifford: London; Tokyo* printed, 1938. 8º. **010058.** m. **1.**
A later edition, entitled "Japan Dictionary," is entered under BUSH (*Lewis W.*)

BUSH (LUCY PECK) *See* HANDLIRSCH (A.) Insects from the Tertiary Lake Deposits of the southern interior of British Columbia, collected by Mr. Lawrence M. Lambe, in 1906. (Translated by Miss L. P. Bush.) 1910. 8º. [*Geological Survey of Canada. Memoir.* no. 12.] C.S. E. **16/9.**

—— *See* ZITTEL (C. A. von) Text-book of Palaeontology. (vol. 3. Mammalia . . . Translated . . . by L. P. Bush and M. L. Engler.) 1900, *etc.* 8º. **7203.c.35.**

BUSH (M.) *Gentleman. See* BUSH (William)

BUSH (M.) *Writer on Art*, and **ZAMOSHKIN** (A.) Путь советской живописи, 1917–1932. [With illustrations.] pp. 158. *Москва*, 1933. 16º. **7857.** aa. **77.**

BUSH (MARION S.) Grannie's Patchwork Quilt. A story, *etc.* pp. 212. *James Lanham: St. Ives*, 1933. 8º. **012614.** aa. **10.**

BUSH (MAYBELL GRACE) *See* ANDERSON (Charles J.) Visiting the Teacher at Work . . . By C. J. Anderson . . . M. G. Bush. [1925.] 8º. **8314.b.1/1.**

BUSH (MILDRED) and **KOFOID** (CHARLES ATTWOOD)

—— Ciliates from the Sierra Nevada Bighorn, Ovis Canadensis Sierrae Grinnell. *Berkeley & Los Angeles*, 1948. 8º. [*University of California Publications in Zoölogy.* vol. 53. no. 6.] Ac. **2689.** g/**28.**
One of thirty copies printed on 100% *rag paper.*

BUSH (N. L.)

—— The Art and Science of Founding. A practical guide for those interested in foundry processes and practices. pp. 333. pl. 6. *Angus & Robertson: Sydney, London*, 1951. 8º. **8766.** de. **62.**

BUSH (NANCY)

—— The Great Bell of Burley. A children's opera, *etc.* pp. 33. *Novello & Co.: London*, 1952. 8º. **11784.** aa. **62.**

BUSH (NANCY)

—— The Spell unbound. An operetta for girls in an Elizabethan setting. Libretto by N. Bush, *etc.* pp. 25. *Novello & Co.: London,* 1954. 8°. **11782. dd. 54.**

BUSH (NIKOLAI ADOL'FOVICH) *See* BUSH (E. A.) Список растений, собранных Е. А. и Н. А. Буш в Центральном Кавказе, *etc.* 1927. 8°. [*Труды Ботанического Музея.* но. 20.] **Ac. 1125. v.**

—— *See* KUZNETSOV (N. I.) Delectus plantarum exsiccatarum quas anno 1898 permutationi offert Hortus Botanicus Universitatis Jurjevensis, *etc.* [By N. I. Kuznetsov, N. A. Busch and A. V. Thomin.] 1898. 8°. [*Ученыя Записки Императорскаго Юр'евскаго Университета.* год. 6.] **Ac. 1091.**

—— *See* PETRODVORETS.—*Петергофскій Біологическій Институтъ.* Travaux de l'Institut des Sciences Naturelles de Peterhof . . . Rédacteur en chef prof. N. Busch, *etc.* 1932, *etc.* 8°. **Ac. 1115.**

—— *See* RUSSIA.—*Академия Наук СССР.*—*Ботаническій Институтъ.* Флора СССР, *etc.* (Редактор VIII тома Н. А. Буш.) 1934, *etc.* 8°. **Ac. 3284/6.**

—— Ботанико-географический очерк России. Европейская Россия. [With a map.] pp. 87. *Петроград,* 1923. 8°. [*Естественные производительные силы России.* том. 5. отд. 1. вып. 1.] **Ac. 1125. i/3.**

—— Ботаническое путешествіе по западному Дагестану. [With a map.] 1905. *See* LENINGRAD.—*Императорскій Санктпетербургскій Ботаническій Садъ.* Труды, *etc.* том. 24. 1871, *etc.* 8°. **Ac. 3284.**

—— Ледники западнаго Кавказа. pp. ii. 134. pl. 12. *Санктпетербургъ,* 1905. 8°. [*Записки Императорскаго Русскаго Географическаго Общества по общей географіи.* том. 32. no. 4.] **Ac. 6130/2.**

—— Предварительный отчетъ о второмъ путешествіи по сѣверо-западному Кавказу въ 1897 году. 1898. *See* LENINGRAD.—*Императорское Русское Географическое Общество.* Извѣстія, *etc.* том. 34. 1888, *etc.* 8°. **Ac. 6130/5.**

—— Schedæ ad floram Caucasicam exsiccatam, *etc.* [By N. A. Bush, B. B. Markovich, G. N. Voronov.] fasc. 1–3, 5–14. 1905–09. *See* LENINGRAD.—*Императорскій Санктпетербургскій Ботаническій Садъ.* Труды, *etc.* том. 24, 26, 28. 1871, *etc.* 8°. **Ac. 3284.**

BUSH (P.) Remarks on the Unscriptural Union that has taken place amongst the different denominations of Dissenters, shewing the inconsistency of such conduct, *etc.* pp. 36. *Benj. Higman: Bath,* 1822. 8°. **4136. f. 2. (7.)**

BUSH (R. A.) *Writer of Tales.* Uncle Dick's Stories, *etc.* pp. 220. *Francis Griffiths: London,* 1926. 8°. **12801. h. 10.**

BUSH (R. E.) *Illustrator.*

—— *See* CULWICK (Arthur T.) and BUSH (R. E.) Hanahela, *etc.* 1943. 8°. **12912. f. 18.**

BUSH (R. E.) *of San Francisco.*

—— Legislation in California concerning Intoxicants. Compiled . . . by R. E. Bush. pp. 43. *Carruth & Carruth: Oakland,* 1890. 8°. **8436. i. 3. (2.)**

BUSH (RAYMOND GORDON WHELER)

—— *See* KIMBLE (George H. T.) and BUSH (R. G. W.) The Weather. 1943. 8°. **012209. d. 4/124.**

—— Frost and the Fruitgrower, *etc.* pp. viii. 119. pl. 23. *Cassell & Co.: London,* 1945. 8°. **7080. aaa. 31.**

—— Fruit Salad, *etc.* (Jottings from a fruitgrower's diary.) [With plates.] pp. ix. 156. *Cassell & Co.: London,* 1947. 8°. **7080. b. 33.**

—— A Fruit-Grower's Diary. [With plates.] pp. 248. *Faber & Faber: London,* 1950. 8°. **7080. de. 15**

—— Harvesting and Storing Garden Fruit. pp. 162. pl. 16. *Faber & Faber: London,* 1947. 8°. **7035. aaa. 34.**

—— Pruning for Amateurs. pp. 143. pl. 16. *Odhams Press: London,* 1955. 8°. [*Modern Living Series.*] **W.P. B. 437/8.**

—— Soft Fruit Growing for the Amateur . . . With a chapter on nuts and another on composting . . . Illustrated by the author. [With a portrait.] pp. 173. *Harmondsworth, New York,* 1942. 8°. [*Penguin Books.* Penguin Special. no. 119.] **12208.a.2/119.**

—— Fruit Growing Outdoors. (New and enlarged edition [of "Soft Fruit Growing for the Amateur" and "Tree Fruit Growing"].) [With plates.] pp. 518. *Faber & Faber: London,* 1946. 8°. **2251. c. 20.**

—— Soft Fruit Growing for the Amateur, *etc.* (Revised edition.) pp. 175. *Penguin Books: Harmondsworth,* 1944. 8°. [*Penguin Handbooks.* no. 1.] **W.P.4003/1.**

—— Soft Fruit Growing for the Amateur, *etc.* (Third revised edition.) pp. 200. pl. XIX. *Penguin Books: Harmondsworth,* 1948. 8°. [*Penguin Handbooks.* no. 1.] **W.P.4003/1a.**

—— Tree Fruit Growing. 2 vol. *Penguin Books: Harmondsworth, New York,* 1943. 8°. [*Penguin Handbook* no. 2, 3.] **W.P.4003/2,3.**

—— Tree Fruit Growing. (New revised edition.) 2 pt. *Penguin Books: Harmondsworth,* 1949. 8°. [*Penguin Handbook.* no. 2.] **W.P.4003/2a,3a.**

BUSH (REGINALD EDGAR JAMES)

—— *See* WALLS (Ernest) The Rivers of England. (With illustrations by R. E. J. Bush.) 1927, *etc.* 8°. **10359. c. 45/1.**

BUSH (RICHARD ARTHUR) Home Circles and the Cultivation of the Psychic Faculty, *etc.* pp. 15. *"Light": London,* [1921.] 16°. **8632. a. 40.**

—— Jesus Christ at Work. A selection from a series of communications . . . from the spirit-side of life, given through R. A. Bush. pp. xv. 304. *Two Worlds Publishing Co.: Manchester,* 1929. 8°. **08632. ff. 16.**

—— The Larger Spiritualism . . . Revised. pp. 32. *Spiritualists' National Union: Huddersfield,* 1919. 8°. **8633. c. 20.**

—— The Place of Jesus Christ in Spiritualism. An address to spiritualists, based on the logic of their own facts, *etc.* pp. 31. *Spiritualists' National Union: Huddersfield,* [1921.] 8°. **8633. c. 21.**

BUSH (Richard Arthur)

—— Spiritualism: its principles defined. pp. 7. *"Light": London*, [1921.] 16°. **8632.** b. **52.**

—— Sweet Corn from Heaven, *etc.* pp. ix. 106. *"The Greater World": London; Two Worlds Publishing Co.: Manchester*, 1930. 8°. **4403.** eee. **24.**

—— Whence have I come? A short treatise on the origin of individual being. pp. 108. *Garden City Press: Letchworth*, 1915. 8°. **8631.** h. **27.**

BUSH (Richard Harold) *See* Bush (Harold R.)

BUSH (Richard J.) Reindeer, Dogs, and Snow-Shoes: a journal of Siberian travel and explorations made in the years 1865, 1866, and 1867 . . . With illustrations [and a map]. pp. 529. *Harper & Bros.: New York*, 1871. 8°. **010058.** g. **46.**

—— [Another copy, with a different titlepage.] *Sampson Low & Co.: London*, 1871. 8°. **10056.** dd. **21.**

BUSH (Robert Nelson)

—— The Teacher-Pupil Relationship. pp. xvii. 252. *Prentice-Hall: New York*, 1954. 8°. **8313.** f. **20.**
Part of the "Prentice-Hall Education Series."

BUSH (Robert Ray) and **MOSTELLER** (Frederick)

—— Stochastic Models for Learning. pp. xvi. 365. *John Wiley & Sons: New York; Chapman & Hall: London*, [1955.] 8°. [*Wiley Publications in Statistics.*] W.P. **2440/29.**

BUSH (Robert Wheler) England's Two Great Military Captains, Marlborough & Wellington: a lecture, *etc.* pp. 61. *F. & J. Rivington: London*, 1853. 8°. **10815.** d. **5.**

—— The Life and Times of Chrysostom. pp. xvi. 344. *R.T.S.: London*, 1885. 8°. **4421.** aaa. **8.**

—— A Popular Introduction to the Books of Joshua, Judges, and Ruth. pp. 125. *R.T.S.: London*, [1883.] 8°. **3155.** e. **21.**

—— A Popular Introduction to the Pentateuch. pp. xi. 187. *R.T.S.: London*, [1883.] 8°. **3155.** f. **23.**

—— St. Athanasius: his life and times. pp. 252. *S.P.C.K.: London*, 1888. 8°. [*The Fathers for English Readers.*] **4421.** a. **45.**

—— St. Augustine: his life and times. pp. xii. 212. *R.T.S.: London*, [1883.] 8°. **4829.** aa. **28.**

—— Sanctification, or Growth in grace. A sermon. *See* Sermons. Twenty-seven Sermons, preached in 1863, *etc.* [1863.] 8°. **4464.** bb. **27.**

—— A Sermon, preached . . . on occasion of the death of the Rev. J. H. Spry, *etc.* pp. 16. *Rivingtons: London*, 1854. 8°. **4906.** e. **6.**

—— To Live is Christ: to die is gain. A sermon. *See* Wilson (Daniel) *Vicar of Islington.* Two Sermons, preached . . . on the occasion of the death of the Rev. Joseph Haslegrave, *etc.* [1875.] 16°. **4905.** a. **67.** (4.)

BUSH (Stephen Hayes) and **YOUNG** (Charles Edmund) Sixteenth Century French Anthology. Edited, with introduction, notes, and glossary by S. H. Bush and C. E. Young. pp. xxiii. 157. *Boston*, [1927.] 8°. [*Heath's Modern Language Series.*] **12213.** a. **1/229.**

BUSH (Sydney Frank) The Establishment and Well-being of Trout in Natal Waters; an ecological problem. (Reprinted from the South African Journal of Science.) [1933.] 8°. **07290.** ff. **19.**

—— Zoology in South Africa. An inaugural lecture. pp. 20. *Natal University College: Pietermaritzburg*, 1942. 8°. **7209.** aaa. **31.**

BUSH (Thomas) *Anti-Catholic Writer.* Popery Dissected, or the British Protestant's appeal to the senators of his country, against the claims of the Papists. A poem. pp. 26. *Printed for the Author: Boston* [*Lincs.*], 1819. 12°. **992.** g. **30.** (4.)

BUSH (Thomas) *of Bradford, Wilts.* *See* Bradford, *Wiltshire.* Parochial Regulations relative to the management of the poor, *etc.* [Edited by T. Bush and others.] 1801. 8°. **8275.** d. **2.** (1.)

BUSH (Thomas) *of Lamborne.* Christian Stewardship Exemplified, or a Memorial of Thomas Bush, Esq., late of Lamborne, Berks. pp. vi. 204. *Mason: London*, 1849. 12°. **4905.** c. **60.**

BUSH (Vannevar) *See* Timbie (William H.) and Bush (V.) Principles of Electrical Engineering. 1922. 8°. **8764.** de. **5.**

—— —— 1930. 8°. **08755.** aa. **39.**

—— *See* Timbie (William H.) and Bush (V.) Principles of Electrical Engineering, *etc.* [1951.] 8°. **8761.** de. **29.**

—— Biographical Memoir of John Ripley Freeman, 1855–1932. [With a bibliography and a portrait.] *Washington*, 1937. 8°. [*National Academy of Sciences. Biographical Memoirs.* vol. 17. no. 8.] A.S. **939/2.**

—— Endless Horizons, *etc.* [With a portrait.] pp. viii. 182. *Public Affairs Press: Washington*, [1946.] 8°. **12360.** ccc. **29.**

—— Modern Arms and Free Men. A discussion of the role of science in preserving democracy. pp. 116. *Simon & Schuster: New York*, 1949. 4°. **8426.** dd. **5.**

—— Modern Arms and Free Men. A discussion of the role of science in preserving democracy. pp. 300. *William Heinemann: London*, 1950. 8°. **8425.** v. **106.**

—— Operational Circuit Analysis . . . With an appendix by Norbert Wiener. pp. x. 392. *J. Wiley & Sons: New York*, 1929. 8°. **08755.** aa. **33.**

—— Science, the Endless Frontier. A report to the President . . . July 1945. pp. ix. 184. 1945. 8°. *See* United States of America.—*Office of Scientific Research and Development.* **08712.** a. **18.**

BUSH (Vladimir Vladimirovich) Очерки литературного народничества 70–80 гг. [With special reference to N. N. Zlatovratsky and A. I. Ertel'.] pp. 163. *Ленинград, Москва*, 1931. 8°. **11856.** bbb. **59.**

BUSH (W. J.) **AND CO.**

—— *See* Pocock (J.) The Brewing of Non-Excisable Beers . . . Revised and re-edited by W. J. Bush & Co., *etc.* 1900. 8°. **7950.** b. **7.**

—— *See* Skuse (E.) Skuse's Complete Confectioner. Revised and edited by W. J. Bush & Co., *etc.* 1921. 8°. **07942.** d. **67.**

—— —— 1928. 8°. **07943.** bb. **48.**

BUSH (W. J.) **AND CO**

—— Practical Recipes for the Manufacture of Aerated Beverages, cordials, non-alcoholic brewed beers, carbonated mineral waters, and other popular beverages . . . Seventh edition. pp. 183. *W. J. Bush & Co.: London,* 1909. 8°. **07944.** g. **77.**

BUSH (Wendell T.) *See* Periodical Publications.—*Lancaster, Pennsylvania.* The Journal of Philosophy, Psychology and Scientific Methods. [vol. 3, *etc.* Edited by F. J. E. Woodbridge and W. T. Bush.] 1904, *etc.* 8°. P.P. **1247.** g.

—— Avenarius and the Standpoint of Pure Experience. pp. iv. 79. 1905. *New York,* 1905. 8°. [*Archives of Philosophy, Psychology and Scientific Methods.* no. 2.] P.P. **1247.** ga.

BUSH (Wesley Amos)

—— Paradise to Leeward. Cruising the West coast of Mexico, *etc.* (Edited and designed by Eugene V. Connett.) [With plates, including a portrait.] pp. xix. 140. *D. Van Nostrand Co.: New York,* [1954.] 8°. **010493.** c. **12.**

BUSH (William) *Carpenter.*

—— A Brief Account of William Bush, late carpenter on board the " Henry Freeling " ; including his correspondence with Daniel Wheeler, a minister of the Society of Friends. pp. 20. *Tract Association of the Society of Friends: London,* 1856. 12°. [*General Series.* no. 106.] **4151.** b. **4.** (**11.**)

BUSH (William) *Gentleman.* A True Relation of the Trauels of M. Bush a Gentleman: who with his owne handes . . . made a Pynace, in which hee past by ayre, land, and water: from Lamborne, a place in Bark-shire, to the Custome-house Key in London. 1607. [The preface signed: A. N., i.e. Anthony Nixon.] 1608. 4°. *See* N., A. C. **32.** d. **16.**

BUSH (William) *Minister of the Gospel in Enfield.* An Earnest Invitation to the House of God, or the True Christian's love to God's publick worship: being the substance of two sermons, *etc.* pp. 37. *E. Matthews: London,* 1730. 8°. **695.** f. **32.** (**1.**)

—— The Inadvertencies and Indiscretions of Good Men, a great cause of general corruption in society. A sermon, *etc.* pp. 33. *R. Hett: London,* 1747. 8°. **4475.** a. **120.** (**5.**)

—— [Another edition.] *See* Protestant Writers. The Practical Preacher, *etc.* vol. 3. 1762. 8°. **4454.** f. **16.**

BUSH (William) *Minister of the Gospel in Wapping.* An Antidote against Excessive Sorrow. A funeral discourse preach'd on the decease of Mrs. Mary and Sarah Wilton. pp. 21. *Tho. Parkhurst: London,* 1706. 4°. **4476.** ee. **9.** (**10.**)

—— The Celestial Race. A discourse . . . Preached at the funeral of Mrs. Elizabeth Knock, *etc.* pp. 64. *For John Dunton: London,* MDCLXCII [1692]. 8°. **1418.** a. **10.**

BUSH (William) *of Chicago.* *See* also Prometheus, *pseud.* [i.e. W. Bush.]

—— *See* also Unicus, *pseud.* [i.e. W. Bush.]

—— Americanus; or, Empire against Republic. A drama in three acts, *etc.* [By W. Bush?] pp. 44. [1874.] 8°. *See* Americanus. **11778.** a. **7.** (**3.**)

BUSH (William) *of Chicago.*

—— The Ancient and the Modern Babel. A satirical comedy, in two acts. pp. 34. [*Chicago?* 1869?] 12°. **11791.** bb. **10.**

—— Claudius the Fickle, or, Fickleness, thy name is man—not woman. A comedy, in five acts. [By W. Bush.] pp. 52. 1869. 12°. *See* Claudius, *the Fickle.* **11791.** a. **2.**

—— The Maid of the Light House, or, All is well that ends well. An original idyllic drama . . . in three acts. By the author of " Men the Epitome of Good and Evil " [i.e. W. Bush], *etc.* pp. 34. [1869?] 12°. *See* Maid. **11791.** bb. **17.**

—— Ocean's Wave: a scientifical and practical survey of life's uses and abuses. pp. 126. *Missouri Democrat Book and Job Printing House: St. Louis,* 1868. 12°. **8416.** d. **44.**

—— Prometheus; or, Mephistopheles gets his fill. An . . . extravaganza in five acts. By the author of " Prometheus' Diary " [i.e. W. Bush], *etc.* pp. 57. 1869. 12°. *See* Prometheus. **11791.** bb. **20.**

BUSH (William Pope Duvall)

—— *See* Kentucky.—*Court of Appeals.* Reports of Selected Civil and Criminal Cases decided in the Court of Appeals of Kentucky. By W. P. D. Bush, *etc.* 1868, *etc.* 8°. **6686.bb.**

BUSHA, *pseud.* Practical Information on an occupation for young British manhood—that of an overseer on a plantation in the tropics. By " Busha." pp. 8. *C. E. Dainton: Westcliff-on-Sea,* [1925.] 8°. **08244.** ee. **17.**

BUSHAKRA (Mary Winifred)

—— I married an Arab. [Memoirs.] pp. 246. *Victor Gollancz: London,* 1952. 8°. **10889.** f. **41.**

BUSHATI (Hamdi) Shkurtorja e historis myslimane, e mârrun prej auktorvet të përmbendun. pp. 64. *Shkoder,* 1921. 12°. **9058.a.46.**

BUSHATLIYA (Maḥmūd) *Pasha of Scutari.* *See* Maḥmūd, *Bushatliya.*

BUSHBY (Anne S.) *See* Andersen (H. C.) *the Novelist.* [*Eventyr.—English.*] The Ice Maiden. (The Butterfly.—Psyche.—The Snail and the Rosebush.) Translated . . . by Mrs. Bushby, *etc.* 1863. 4°. **12808.** bbb. **8.**

—— —— 1875. 4°. **12803.** h. **28.**

—— *See* Andersen (H. C.) *the Novelist.* [*Eventyr.—English.*] A Poet's Day Dreams. [Translated by A. S. Bushby.] 1853. 8°. **12580.** c. **15.**

—— *See* Andersen (H. C.) *the Novelist.* [*Eventyr.—English.*] The Sand-hills of Jutland. [Translated by A. S. Bushby.] 1860. 12°. **12581.** d. **27.**

—— *See* Andersen (H. C.) *the Novelist.* [*Other Works.*] [At være eller ikke være.] To Be, or Not to Be? . . . Translated . . . by Mrs. Bushby. 1857. 8°. **12580.** f. **10.**

—— *See* Andersen (H. C.) *the Novelist.* [*Other Works.*] [I Spanien.] In Spain . . . Translated by Mrs. Bushby. 1864. 8°. **10160.** d. **26.**

BUSHBY (ANNE S.)

—— *See* GOLDSCHMIDT (M. A.) [En Jøde.] The Jew of Denmark. A tale . . . Translated . . . by Mrs. Bushby. 1852. 8°. **12601. b. 19.**

—— The Danes Sketched by Themselves. A series of popular stories by the best Danish authors. Translated by Mrs. Bushby. 3 vol. *Richard Bentley: London,* 1864. 8°. **12581. f. 42.**

—— Poems. pp. xi. 399. *R. Bentley & Son: London,* 1876. 8°. **11652. ee. 20.**

BUSHBY (AUDREY)

—— Deep Shadows. pp. 211. *Quality Press: London,* 1946. 8°. **NN. 36489.**

—— Ivycott Farm, *etc.* pp. 192. *Quality Press: London* 1952. 8°. **NN. 39052**

BUSHBY (BESSIE) The Bessie Bushby Postal Tuition Course of Beauty Treatment. 8 pt. [1928.] 4°. **7383. l. 5.**

Typewritten.

BUSHBY (DOROTHY) and **LE HARDY** (WILLIAM HENRY CLEMENT)

—— Wormley in Hertfordshire. [With plates.] pp. 176. *Staples Press: London,* 1954. 8°. **10361. f. 12.**

BUSHBY (DUDLEY CHARLES) The Royal Shepherdess, and other poems. pp. 44. *Digby & Long: London,* 1897. 8°. **11651. c. 61.**

BUSHBY (EDWARD) Essay on the Human Mind . . . Third edition. pp. xi. 106. *J. & J. J. Deighton & T. Stevenson: Cambridge,* 1834. 12°. **T. 2069. (3.)**

—— An Introduction to the Study of the Holy Scriptures. pp. 85. *John Smith: Cambridge,* 1825. 12°. **3129. ee. 13. (2.)**

—— [Another edition.] pp. 84. *John Smith: Cambridge,* 1829. 12°. **3128. df. 54.**

—— Third edition. pp. 84. *J. & J. J. Deighton: Cambridge,* 1834. 12°. **4372. de. 21. (6.)**

—— Fourth edition. pp. 84. *J. & J. J. Deighton: Cambridge,* 1839. 12°. **3103. aa. 39.**

—— Fifth edition. pp. 84. *Cambridge; Whittaker & Co.: London,* 1842. 12°. **3127. c. 21.**

—— Sixth edition. pp. 84. *Cambridge; Whittaker & Co.: London; Deighton: Cambridge,* 1848. 12°. **3128. c. 38.**

BUSHBY (*Lady* FRANCES) *See* RULES. Easie Rules on Earlie Rising, *etc.* (Illustrated by Lady F. Bushby.) [1867.] 4°. **1871. c. 39.**

—— Three Men of the Tudor Time. (Edward, first Lord North.—Roger, second Lord North.—Sir Thomas North.) [With portraits.] pp. ix. 198. *David Nutt: London,* 1911. 8°. **10804. h. 16.**

BUSHBY (HENRY JEFFREYS) *See* BUSHBY (Maud A.) Portrait of a Victorian. [A biography of H. J. Bushby. With portraits.] 1938. 8°. **10858. a. 3.**

—— Easie Rules on Earlie Rising, by a late philosopher [i.e. H. J. Bushby]. (Illustrated by Lady Frances Bushby.) [1867.] 4°. *See* RULES. **1871. c. 39.**

BUSHBY (HENRY JEFFREYS)

—— Echoes of Foreign Song. By the author of 'A Month in the Camp before Sebastopol' [i.e. H. J. Bushby]. pp. xiv. 94. 1877. 8°. *See* ECHOES. **11652. df. 31.**

—— A Manual of the Practice of Elections in the United Kingdom. With an appendix of statutes and forms. pp. xviii. 132. lxiii. *W. G. Benning & Co.: London,* 1857. 12°. **1380. d. 19.**

—— Second edition. pp. xvii. 136. lxiii. *Stevens & Haynes: London,* 1865. 12°. **6325. a. 11.**

—— Third edition. pp. xx. 150. cix. *Stevens & Haynes: London,* 1868. 12°. **6325. aa. 5.**

—— Fourth edition. By Henry Hardcastle. pp. xiii. 147. clxxxi. *Stevens & Haynes: London,* 1874. 8°. **6325. aa. 6.**

—— Fifth edition. By Henry Hardcastle. pp. xiv. 177. cxciv. *Stevens & Haynes: London,* 1880. 8°. **6325. eee. 8.**

—— A Month in the Camp before Sebastopol. By a non-combatant [i.e. H. J. Bushby]. pp. viii. 125. 1855. 8°. *See* NON-COMBATANT. **9077. d. 18.**

—— Second edition. pp. viii. 125. 1855. 8°. *See* NON-COMBATANT. **9077. d. 19.**

—— Third edition. pp. viii. 125. 1855. 8°. *See* NON-COMBATANT. **9077. d. 20.**

—— Widow-Burning: a narrative. pp. 62. *Longman & Co.: London,* 1855. 8°. **4504. c. 9.**

BUSHBY (MAUD ALICE) Portrait of a Victorian. [A biography of Henry J. Bushby. With portraits.] pp. 24. *Saint Catherine Press: London,* [1938.] 8°. **10858. a. 3.**

BUSHBY (ROBERT) Cosmetics, and how to make them. pp. vii. 103. *Sir I. Pitman & Sons: London,* 1936. 8°. **7943. v. 30.**

—— Cosmetics and how to make them . . . Second edition. pp. viii. 144. *Sir I. Pitman & Sons: London,* 1942. 8°. **7946. a. 47.**

—— Cosmetics and how to make them . . . Third edition. pp. x. 182. *Sir I. Pitman & Sons: London,* 1943. 8°. **7946. df. 50.**

BUSHE (AMYAS) Socrates, a dramatic poem. pp. vii. 98. *Printed for the Author: London,* 1758. 4°. **840. l. 14. (1.)**

—— [Another edition.] As it was corrected from the many errors of the London edition. pp. vi. 104. *E. Crofton & Co.: Kilkenny,* [1759?] 4°. **1346. b. 6.**

—— [Another edition.] pp. 104. *R. & A. Foulis: Glasgow,* 1762. 8°. **11777. a. 7. (1.)**

—— A Philosophical Dialogue between Socrates & Aristodemus; extracted from Mr. Bushe's dramatic poem, published in the Universal Magazine for 1758. [Edited by G. Thompson.] pp. 16. *G. Angus: Newcastle,* 1822. 8°. **11633. f. 5.**

BUSHE (C. T. A.) Quiet Havens and Stormy Seas. Three cards. Sketches of Irish scenery. [With scriptural texts.] *E. St. B. Holland: London; printed in Germany,* [1891.] *obl.* 8°. **1701. b. 1. (110.)**

BUSHE (*Right Hon.* CHARLES KENDAL) *See* SOMERVILLE (Edith Œ.) and ROSS (Martin) *pseud.* An Incorruptible Irishman. Being an account of Chief Justice C. K. Bushe, *etc.* [With a portrait.] 1932. 8°. **10823. k. 25.**

BUSHE (*Right Hon.* CHARLES KENDAL)

—— A Summary View of the Evidences of Christianity . . . With a preface and notes by the Rev. James Wills. pp. xi. 178. *W. Curry, Jun. & Co.: Dublin*, 1845. 8°. **1350**. b. **24**.

—— The Union. Cease Your Funning. (Or, the Rebel detected.) [By C. K. Bushe. In answer to a pamphlet by Edward Cooke, entitled "Arguments for and against an Union between Great Britain and Ireland, considered."] pp. 45. 1798. 8°. *See* UNION. **522**. d. **59**.

—— (Third edition.) pp. 45. 1798. 8°. *See* UNION. **1103**. g. **10**. (4.)

—— [Another edition.] pp. 45. 1799. 8°. *See* UNION. **117**. h. **32**.

—— [Another copy.] **111**. e. **1**.

—— [Another edition.] Cease Your Funning . . . Seventh edition, with a preface, and notes, by the author. pp. 48. 1799. 8°. *See* FUNNING. **8145**. d. **31**.

BUSHE (GEORGE) A Treatise on the Malformations, Injuries, and Diseases of the Rectum and Anus, *etc.* 2 pt. pp. 299. pl. IX. *French & Adlard: New-York*, 1837. 8° & 4°. **1188**. k. **36**. & **1167**. ccc. **6**.

BUSHE (GERVASE PARKER) *the Elder.* Case of Great Britain and America, addressed to the King, and both Houses of Parliament . . . The second edition. [By G. P. Bushe.] pp. 43. 1769. 8°. *See* ENGLAND. [*Appendix.—History and Politics.*—II. 1769.] **1103**. k. **30**.

—— [Another copy.] T. **1612**. (4.)

BUSHE (GERVASE PARKER) *the Younger.* Some Considerations on the Income Tax. pp. 35. *James Ridgway: London*, 1845. 8°. **1391**. e. **34**. (3.)

BUSHE (MARY C.) The Painted Bird and the Painted Text. A simple story, *etc.* pp. 198. *T. Nelson & Sons: London*, 1869. 8°. **12804**. f. **17**.

—— Rupert of the Rhine: the history of a brave prince, *etc.* pp. 191. *S.P.C.K.: London*, [1869.] 8°. **10805**. a. **20**.

BUSHE (NANCY) *See* CRAMPTON, afterwards BUSHE.

BUSHE (PAUL) *Bishop of Bristol.* A brefe exhortation set fourthe by the vnprofitable seruant of Iesu christ, Paule Bushe, late bishop of Brystowe, to one Margarete Burges wyfe to Ihon Burges, *etc.* B.L. *Imprinted by Ihon Cawodde: London*, [1556.] 8°. C. **53**. gg. **16**.

BUSHE (WILLIAM) *See* CARRICK-ON-SHANNON. An Authentic Report of the Discussion which took place by agreement at Carrick-on-Shannon . . . between three Roman Catholic priests and three clergymen of the Established Church [i.e. W. Bushe and others], *etc.* 1824. 8°. **3942**. b. **28**.

—— Introductory Lecture on the Doctrines of the Church of Rome, *etc.* pp. iii. 28. *R. M. Tims: Dublin*, 1824. 8°. T. **1183**. (3.)

—— Second edition. pp. 31. *R. M. Tims: Dublin*, 1824. 8°. **3938**. bb. **79**. (4.)

—— *See* BATTERSBY (William J.) The Methodists and Bible Societies, refuted . . . With remarks on the late fantastic lecture of the Rev. Mr. Bushe, *etc.* [1824?] 8°. **3940**. h. **7**. (1.)

BUSHE (WILLIAM)

—— A Sermon preached . . . before the Irish Auxiliary Society for Promoting Christianity amongst the Jews. pp. 40. *M. Goodwin: Dublin*, 1824. 8°. **4479**. ee. **2**.

—— Sermon, preached . . . before the London Society for Promoting Christianity amongst the Jews. 1821. *See* LONDON.—III. *London Society for Promoting Christianity amongst the Jews.* The First [*etc.*] Report of the Committee, *etc.* no. 13. 1810, *etc.* 8°. P.P. **1149**. a.

—— A Sermon, preached . . . on the death of His Majesty King George the IIId. pp. 34. *J. Jones: Dublin*, 1820. 8°. **10806**. b. **16**.

BUSHEA (ALEX. D.) Dr. Bushea's Phrenological Mirror. (Second edition.) *H. K. Causton: London*, [1851?] *s. sh.* fol. **1881**. c. **7**. (9.)

BUSHEE (ALICE HUNTINGTON) *See* ALEMÁN (M.) The Sucesos . . . Reprinted by A. H. Bushee, *etc.* 1911. 8°. **4867**. f. **35**.

—— *See* TÉLLEZ (G.) La Prudencia en la mujer . . . With introduction and notes by A. H. Bushee and L. L. Stafford. 1948. 8°. **11729**. e. **3**.

—— Three Centuries of Tirso de Molina. [With a portrait.] pp. x. 111. pl. 20. *University of Pennsylvania Press: Philadelphia*, 1939. 8°. **011850**. k. **70**.

BUSHEE (FREDERICK ALEXANDER) Ethnic Factors in the Population of Boston. [With a preface by W. Z. Ripley.] pp. vi. 171. *New York*, 1903. 8°. [*Publications of the American Economic Association.* ser. 3. vol. 4. no. 2.] Ac. **2388**.

BUSHE-FOX (JOSCELYN PLUNKET) *See* FOX.

BUSHEL (BROWN) *See* ENGLAND. [*Laws and Statutes.*—VIII. *Commonwealth*, 1649–1660.] An Act for the Tryal of Sir Iohn Stowel . . . B. Bushel [and others], *etc.* 1650. fol. **506**. d. **9**. (102.)

—— *See* HOTHAM (*Sir* John) A True and Exact Relation of all the proceedings of Sir Hugh Cholmleys revolt . . . with the regaining of Scarborough Castle by the courage and industry of Capt. Bushel, *etc.* 1643. 4°. C. **21**. b. **1**. (9.)

—— The Speech and Confession of Capt. Brown-Bushel, at the place of execution . . . Together with the manner of his tryall, and the articles and charge exhibited against him. Written by G. H. an eye-witnesse. [With a woodcut.] pp. 5. *Imprinted by R. W.: London*, 1651. 4°. **1132**. a. **48**.

—— [Another copy.] M.K. **1**. a. **8***. (14.)

BUSHEL (EDWARD) *See* BUSHELL.

BUSHEL (SETH) *See* BUSHELL.

BUSHEL (THOMAS) *See* BUSHELL.

BUSHELL (A. E.) The Housekeeper's Manual. Valuable recipes for making and preparing all kinds of ice creams, water ice, sherberts, cocktails, wines, *etc.* pp. vi. 39. *Mirror Printing Works: Port-of-Spain*, 1911. 8°. **07944**. de. **41**. (2.)

BUSHELL (BRIDGES) The Arraignment and Condemnation of Cap. Bridges Bushell; declaring the occasion and manner how a soldier was by him slain, about nine years since . . . Left behinde him in writing, *etc.* pp. 8. *For Marmaduke Boat: London*, 1657. 4°. E. **910**. (8.)

BUSHELL (CHARLES) The Rigger's Guide, containing practical instructions for completely rigging ships of war. pp. viii. 202. *H. Lewis: Portsmouth*, 1854. 8°.
8805. a. **38**.

—— Second edition, *etc.* pp. viii. 214. *H. Lewis: Portsmouth*, 1856. 8°. **8805**. a. **36**.

—— Third edition, with considerable additions, *etc.* pp. viii. 226. *H. Lewis: Portsmouth*, 1857. 8°.
8805. a. **37**.

—— Fifth edition. pp. 254. *Griffin & Co.: Portsmouth & London*, 1874 [1873]. 8°. **8805**. aa. **23**.

BUSHELL (EDWARD) *See* VAUGHAN (*Sir* John) *Lord Chief Justice of the Court of Common Pleas.* Bushell's Case. [A report.] 1707. 8°. [*The Phenix.* vol. 1.] **1103**. e. **1**.

—— *See* WHITEBROOK (John C.) Edward & John Bushell, puritans and merchants, *etc.* 1915. 8°.
9903. bbb. **17**.

BUSHELL (ERIC S.) *See* OUGHTRED (S. N.) and BUSHELL (E. S.) Truth from the Spirit World. [1921, *etc.*] 8°.
W.P. **7883**.

BUSHELL (H. S.)

—— *See* LONDON.—III. *Royal Society.* The Transliteration of Russian, Serbian and Bulgarian for Bibliographical Purposes. (Prepared by H. S. Bushell.) 1953. 8°.
11917. f. **14**.

BUSHELL (HERBERT HEDLEY)

—— The Look and Learn Geography Course. *E. Mathews & Marrot: London*, [1939.] 8°. [*Look and Learn Series.*] W.P. **649**.

BUSHELL (JOHN) *See* WHITEBROOK (John C.) Edward & John Bushell, puritans and merchants, *etc.* 1915. 8°.
9903. bbb. **17**.

BUSHELL (JOHN) and **BOND** (FRANCIS) *Merchant, of Bridge Town, Barbadoes.*

—— [A True and perfect] Narrative of the late dreadful fire which happened at Bridge-Town in the Barbadoes, April 18. 1668. as the same was communicated in two letters from Mr. John Bushel, and Mr. Francis Bond . . . to Mr. Edward Bushel, *etc.* pp. [6.] *Printed by Peter Lillicrap: London*, [1668.] 4°.
8715. a. **35**.

Cropped.

BUSHELL (JOHN JAMES) Bushell's Picturesque Bermuda Handbook . . . 1933 [*etc.*]. Twenty-fourth [*etc.*] edition. *J. J. Bushell: Hamilton, Bermuda; Glasgow* printed, [1933–]. 8°. P.P. **2587**. p.

BUSHELL (KEITH) *See* BUSHELL (N. Keith)

BUSHELL (L. P.)

—— The "H" Soundhead. pp. 11. [*The Author: East Croydon*, 1943.] 8°. **08715**. b. **91**.

BUSHELL (N. KEITH) Australia for the Emigrant . . . With seventeen illustrations from photographs. pp. x. 96. *Cassell & Co.: London*, 1913. 8°. **10481**. p. **5**.

—— Papuan Epic. [With plates.] pp. 318. *Seeley, Service & Co.: London*, [1936.] 8°. **10493**. d. **23**.

BUSHELL (SAMUEL HARLEY) A New Almanack, devoted exclusively to calculations on the wind and weather, for the year of Our Lord 1853. (A Weather Almanac . . . for 1854[–1864]). 1852–[63.] 12° & 16°. *See* EPHEMERIDES.
P.P. **2477**. ta.

BUSHELL (SETH) *See* TOWNE (Robert) A Re-Assertion of Grace, *etc.* [Edited by S. Bushell.] 1654. 4°.
4256. aaa. **43**.

—— The Believer's Groan for Heaven: in a sermon at the funeral of the Honorable Sir Richard Hoghton, *etc.* pp. 29. *For Tho. Sawbridg: London; Philip Burton: Preston*, 1678. 4°. **1416**. i. **24**.

—— [Another copy.] **1416**. i. **25**.

—— A Warning-Piece for the Unruly; in two sermons at the Metropolitical Visitation of . . . Richard, Lord Archbishop of York, *etc.* pp. 45. *For Will. Cademan; Tho. Passinger: London*, 1673. 4°. **696**. f. **9**. (**2**.)

—— [Another copy.] **226**. i. **8**. (**12**.)

BUSHELL (STEPHEN WOOTTON) *See* CHU (Yen) Description of Chinese Pottery and Porcelain. Being a translation of the T'ao Shuo . . . With introduction, notes and bibliography by S. W. Bushell. 1910. 8°.
15234. b. **25**.

—— *See* HSIANG (Yüan-pien) Chinese Porcelain. Sixteenth-century coloured illustrations, with Chinese MS. text . . . Translated and annotated by S. W. Bushell, *etc.* 1908. 4°. **15234**. a. **10**.

—— *See* MONKHOUSE (William C.) A History and Description of Chinese Porcelain . . . With notes by S. W. Bushell, *etc.* 1901. 8°. **2268**. d. **18**.

—— *See* MORGAN (John Pierpont) *the Elder.* Catalogue of the Morgan Collection of Chinese Porcelains. [By W. M. Laffan. With an historical introduction by S. W. Bushell.] 1904, *etc.* 8°. K.T.C. **37**. a. **17**.

—— *See* NEW YORK.-Metropolitan Museum of Art. Catalogue of the Morgan Collection of Chinese Porcelains. By S. W. Bushell and W. M. Laffan. [A second edition of vol. 1 of the catalogue by W. M. Laffan, revised, with an historical introduction, by S. W. Bushell.] 1907. 8°.
7813.e.37.

—— *See* T'ANG (Jung-tso) Jade in China. Introduction by S. W. Bushell. Yü shuo. A Discourse on Jade—Chinese text—by T'ang Jung-tso. With translation by S. W. Bushell. Yü tso t'ou. Illustrations of the Manufacture of Jade. By Li Shih-ch'üan. With Chinese manuscript notes, translated by S. W. Bushell. 1906. fol. [BISHOP (*Heber R.*) *The Bishop Collection, etc.* vol. 1.]
Tab. **741**. d. **1**.

—— *See* WATTERS (Thomas) On Yuan Chwang's Travels in India . . . Edited . . . by T. W. R. Davids . . . and S. W. Bushell. 1904, *etc.* 8°. **14003**. bb. **9**.

—— Chinese Art . . . With . . . illustrations. 2 vol. 1904, 06. 8°. *See* LONDON.—III. *South Kensington Museum, etc.* **07958**. ee. **41**.

—— Second edition, revised. 2 vol. 1909. 8°. *See* LONDON.—III. *South Kensington Museum, etc.* **07807**. g. **53**.

—— [A reissue.] 1910. 8°. *See* LONDON.—III. *South Kensington Museum, etc.* **07805**. g. **2**.

—— [A reissue.] 1921, 19. 8°. *See* LONDON.—III. *South Kensington Museum, etc.* **2270**. b. **39**.

—— Chinese Porcelain before the Present Dynasty . . . Extract from the Journal of the Peking Oriental Society. pp. 55. *Pai-t'ang Press: Peking*, 1886. 8°.
7704. g. **39**. (**5**.)

—— [Another copy.] **7942**. i. **43**. (**5**.)

BUSHELL (STEPHEN WOOTTON)

—— Notes of a Journey outside the Great Wall of China. ff. 17. [1874.] fol. **10057**. g. **15**. (**1**.)
Proof sheets.

—— Oriental Ceramic Art, illustrated by examples from the collection of W. T. Walters . . . Text and notes by S. W. Bushell. [With a preface by W. M. Laffan.] 10 pt. pp. viii. 429. pl. CXVI. *D. Appleton & Co.: New York*, 1897. fol. **1899.1.13.**

—— Text edition, to accompany the complete work. Text and notes by S. W. Bushell. pp. xiii. 942. *D. Appleton & Co.: New York*, 1899. 8°. **7812.bb.8.**

—— *See* PRANG (Louis) Prang's Progressive Proofs, *etc.* [A series of progressive proofs of one of the plates for S. W. Bushell's "Oriental Ceramic Art." Printed in colours by L. Prang.] [1897.] fol. **L.R.301.bb.5.**

BUSHELL (THOMAS) *See* DE LA PRYME (Abraham) Memoirs of Thomas Bushell, "the Recluse of the Calf," *etc.* 1878. 8°. [*Manx Society. Publications.* vol. 30.] Ac. **8130**.

—— *See* ENGLAND. [*Miscellaneous Public Documents, etc.* —III. Charles II.] His Majesties Gratious Order at Council Board, upon reading Mr. Bushels Grant of the Lead Customes, at the Court of White-hall, the 24th. of September 1662. [With other documents pertaining to the grant.] [1665?] 4°. C. **27**. f. **1**. (**7**.)

—— *See* GOUGH (John W.) The Superlative Prodigall. A life of Thomas Bushell. [With a portrait.] 1932. 8°. [*University of Bristol Studies.* no. 1.] Ac. **2676/3**.

—— Mr Bushell's Abridgment of the Lord Chancellor Bacon's Philosophical Theory in Mineral Prosecutions. (New Atlantis. A work unfinished. Written by . . . Francis, Lord Verulam, Viscount St. Alban.) *Printed by Tho: Newcomb: London*, 1659. 4°. G. **19405**.

—— [Another copy.] C. **27**. f. **1**. (**4**.)
Imperfect; wanting the "New Atlantis."

—— An Extract by Mr Bushell of his late Abridgment of the Lord Chancellor Bacons Philosophical Theory in Mineral Prosecutions. [With a portrait of Charles II.] *Printed by Tho. Leach: London*, 1660. 4°. C. **27**. f. **1**. (**6**.)

—— [Another copy.] **117**. k. **44**. (**1–3**.)
Imperfect; wanting the portrait.

—— The Apologie of Thomas Bushell . . . Esquire. By way of vindication from the supposed Treason, or Misprision of Treason laid to his charge, *etc.* pp. 6. *Antwerp*, 1650. 4°. **1245**. k. 2.

—— A Brief Declaration of the Severall Passages in the Treaty concerning the Surrender of the garrison of Lundy, now under the command of Tho: Bushell Esq; Governor thereof for His Maiestie. pp. 20. *London*, 1647. 4°. E. **401**. (**3**.)

—— [Another edition.] pp. 25. *London*, 1647. 4°. E. **433**. (**24**.)

—— The Case of Thomas Bushell . . . Esquire. Truly stated. Together with his progresse in minerals, and the desires of severall merchants and others that are willing and ready to advance so good a work . . . Humbly tendred to the serious consideration of the Honourable House of Commons, *etc.* pp. 16. *London*, 1649. 4°. C. **27**. f. **1**. (**3**.)

BUSHELL (THOMAS)

—— The Case of Thomas Bushell Esq; [*London*, 1660?] *s. sh.* fol. **516**. m. **18**. (**102**.)
A different work from the preceding.

—— A Iust and True Remonstrance of His Maiesties Mines-Royall in the Principality of Wales. [With the order of the House of Lords for the author's protection.] pp. 36. *Printed by E. G.* [*Edward Griffin*]*: London*, 1641. 4°. C. **27**. f. **17**.

—— [Another edition.] *Printed by E. G.* [*Edward Griffin*]*: London*, 1642. 4°. C. **27**. f. **1**. (**1**.)

—— [Another copy.] G. **4009**.

—— [Another edition.] *Printed by Robert Barker; and by the Assignes of John Bill: Shrewsbury*, 1642. 4°. C. **27**. f. **1**. (**2**.)

—— The Particular Services done by Tho. Bushell Esq; together with a late petition to His Majesty, and certificate of the nobility and gentry of Cornwall. pp. 7. [1667?] 4°. C. **27**. f. **1**. (**8**.)

—— Mr. Bushells Quæres. [Relating to the farming of the mines in Wales.] [1665?] *s. sh.* fol. **1244**. l. **12**.

—— *Begin.* To the Right Honourable the Lords assembled in Parliament. The Humble Petition of Thomas Bushell Esq. [*London*, 1659?] *s. sh.* fol. **516**. m. **18**. (**95**.)

—— The First Part of Youths Errors. pp. 173. *Imprinted at London*, 1628. 8°. **851**. f. **38**.

—— The Severall Speeches and Songs, at the presentment of Mr Bushells Rock to the Queenes Most Excellent Majesty. Aug. 23. 1636, *etc.* *Printed by Leonard Lichfield; sold by Thomas Allam: Oxford*, 1636. 4°. C. **33**. d. **13**.

BUSHELL (THOMAS ALEXANDER)

—— Eight Bells. Royal Mail Lines war story, 1939–1945, *etc.* [With plates.] pp. xv. 207. *Trade & Travel Publications: London*, [1950.] 8°. **9102**. f. 9.

—— "Royal Mail." A centenary history of the Royal Mail Line, 1839–1939. [With plates.] pp. xvi. 270. *Trade & Travel Publications: London*, [1939.] 8°. **08805**. cc. **48**.

BUSHELL (WARIN FOSTER)

—— School Sermons. pp. 145. *Churchman Publishing Co.: London*, [1950.] 8°. **4481**. aaa. **14**.

—— Teaching Boys to read. [A lecture.] pp. 20. [*Birkenhead Libraries, Museum & Arts Committee: Birkenhead*,] 1950. 8°. **8312**. de. **47**.

BUSHELL (WILLIAM) The Surveyor's and Builders' Perpetual Price Book, *etc.* pp. xviii. 243. *Printed for the Author: London*, 1816. *obl.* 8°. L.R. **111**. a. **17**.

BUSHELL (WILLIAM DONE) *the Elder.* Harrow Octocentenary Tracts. [With plates.] 14 pt. *Macmillan & Bowes: Cambridge*, 1893–1914. 8°. **010358**. g. **66**.

—— Introduction to the Architecture and History of the Parish Church of St. Mary, Harrow-on-the-Hill . . . Revised and reprinted, *etc.* pp. 32. *Bowes & Bowes: Cambridge*, 1912. 8°. **07816**. h. **40**. (**2**.)

—— St. Samson, Abbot of Caldey . . . Reprinted from "Archæologia Cambrensis," *etc.* pp. 22. 4. *Bedford Press: London*, 1911. 8°. **4804**. i. **41**. (**2**.)

BUSHELL (William Done) *the Elder.*

—— Strong in the Lord. A sermon, *etc.* pp. 18. *Rivingtons: London,* 1872. 16°. **4479. a. 66. (2.)**

—— The Teaching of the Holy Spirit and the Communion of Saints. Two sermons, *etc.* pp. 32. *Gilbert & Rivington: London,* [1867.] 8°. **4478. a. 122. (12.)**

—— William Done Bushell, of Harrow. [By various authors. With portraits.] pp. 74. *University Press: Cambridge,* 1919. 8°. **4908. e. 23.**

BUSHELL (William Done) *the Younger.*

—— The Church of St. Mary the Great, the University Church at Cambridge, *etc.* [With plates.] pp. xv. 223. *Bowes & Bowes: Cambridge,* 1948. 8°. **07822. e. 8.**

—— 'Finch's Walk,' and Messrs. Finch, Ironfounders, of Market Hill, Cambridge. (Reprinted from The Cambridge Public Library Record and Book-List.) pp. 4. *Cambridge,* [1934.] 8°. **010352. c. 18.**

—— Hobson's Conduit: the New River at Cambridge commonly called Hobson's River, *etc.* pp. xi. 140. pl. IX. *University Press: Cambridge,* 1938. 8°. **10353. aaa. 3.**

—— The Two Charles Lestourgeons, surgeons of Cambridge. Their Huguenot ancestors and their descendants. [With plates, including portraits. pp. viii. 66. *W. Heffer & Sons: Cambridge,* 1936. 8°. **010822. de. 83.**

BUSHEN (Artur Bogdanovich fon) *See* Buschen (Arthur von)

BUSHER (Charles William) The Tent and Awning Makers Guide. ff. 9. *C. W. Busher: Springfield, Ill.,* 1905. *obl.* 8°. **1879. a. 29.**
Printed on one side of the leaf only.

BUSHER (Leonard) Religions Peace: or, a Plea for liberty of conscience. Long since presented to King James, and the High Court of Parliament then sitting, by Leonard Busher . . . and printed in the yeare 1614, *etc.* [The editor's preface signed: H. B., i.e. Henry Burton?] pp. 38. *For John Sweeting: London,* 1646. 4°. **E. 334. (7.)**

—— [Another edition.] *See* Underhill (Edward B.) Tracts on Liberty of Conscience and Persecution, *etc.* 1846. 8°. **Ac. 2075.**

BUSHES. Among the Green Bushes. (The False Lover.—Jack Robinson.) [Songs.] [*London,* 1840?] *s. sh.* 4°. **C. 116. i. 1. (241.)**

—— Bushes and Briers. (Fair Phœbe.) [Songs.] *J. Catnach: London,* [1840?] *s. sh.* 4°. **C. 116. i. 1. (169.)**

—— The Green Bushes. (When First I Went to Sea.) [Songs.] *Hodges': London,* [1850?] *s. sh.* 4°. **11621. k. 4. (65.)**

—— The Green Bushes: or, a Hundred years ago. A romance. pp. 62. *E. Lloyd: London,* 1847. 8°. **12621. g. 15.**

BUSHETIĆ. [For the Serbocroatian surname in this form:] *See* Bušetić.

BUSHEY.—*Bushey Coronation Executive Committee.*

—— Coronation Souvenir Programme, 1953, *etc.* pp. 32. *Home Publishing Co.: Croydon,* [1953.] 8°. **9930. bb. 48.**

BUSHEY.—

Parish Church.

—— The Story of Bushey Parish Church. [With illustrations.] pp. 5. *British Publishing Co.: Gloucester,* [1955.] 8°. **010368. k. 263.**

—— -*Royal Caledonian Schools.* A Souvenir of the Royal Caledonian Schools, *etc.* *Bushey,* [1935.] *obl.* 8°. **8365. aaa. 41.**

BUSHEY CORONATION EXECUTIVE COMMITTEE. *See* Bushey.

BUSHEY DRAWING OFFICE.

—— [Trace-charts of screws, nuts and bolts.] *Bushey,* [1949– .] fol. **1856. g. 16. (41.)**

BUSHEY HEATH.—*Rosary Priory.* The Rosary Priory, Bushey Heath. Its history, development and present-day activities. [With illustrations.] pp. 24. *British Publishing Co.: Gloucester,* [1937.] *obl.* 8°. **8365. aaa. 58.**

BUSHEY PARISH CHURCH. *See* Bushey.—*Parish Church.*

BUSHEY (Joseph) The Beauty Spot. A comedy in three acts. pp. 30. *Burns & Harris: Dundee,* 1923. 8°. **011779. gg. 53.**

BUSHEYGRAMS. *See* Periodical Publications.—*Bushey.*

BUSHFIELD (C. F.) A Few Plain Directions how to Select and Settle on the Lands; with the Land Bill: and a summary of the Act, *etc.* (Second edition, revised and enlarged.) pp. 39. *W. H. Williams: Melbourne,* 1860. 8°. **8154. b. 30.**

BUSHIDO. Bushido. By foreign writers. pp. 68. *Tokyo Modern English Association: Tokyo,* 1905. 8°. **8410. h. 21.**

BUSHILL (John Herbert) *See* Bulloch (William) The Preparation of Catgut for Surgical Use. By W. Bulloch . . . J. H. Bushill. 1929. 8°. [*Medical Research Council. Special Report Series.* no. 138.] **B.S. 25/8.**

BUSHILL (Marian)

—— Seed Thought Series. By M. B. [i.e. Marian Bushill.] 6 pt.

1. Seed Thoughts for Daily Meditation.
2. The Evidence of Things Not Seen . . . Sixth edition.
3. For the Honour of the Family. Third edition.
4. The Riches of Our Inheritance . . . Second edition.
5. The Wings of Thought . . . Third edition.
6. In Quietness, Strength, *etc.*

[1920–40?] 8°. *See* B., M. **4398. de. 19.**

—— [Another edition of pt. 1.] Seed Thoughts for Daily Meditation. By M. B. [i.e. Marian Bushill.] (Seventeenth edition.) pp. 17. [1942?] 8°. *See* B., M. **4398. de. 20.**

BUSHILL (Percy Norman) The Best Story Book in the World. 366 Bible stories for young disciples. pp. 370. *Kingsgate Press: London,* [1935.] 8°. **03127. de. 89.**

—— Hosannas in the Temple. (Talks.) pp. 64. *Carey Press: London,* 1944. 8°. [*Furnival Library of Stories for Boys and Girls.*] **W.P. 10799/5.**

BUSHILL (Thomas William) Profit-Sharing and the Labour Question . . . With an introduction by Sedley Taylor. pp. 262. *Methuen & Co.: London,* 1893. 8°. **8277**. de. **22**.

BUSHINSKI (Edward A.)

—— *See* Vio (Thomas de) *Cardinal.* The Analogy of Names and the Concept of Being. Literally translated and annotated by E. A. Bushinski, *etc.* 1953. 8°. **8475**. h. 4.

BUSHINSKY (Vladimir Petrovich)

—— *See* Vil'yams (V. R.) Собрание сочинений, *etc.* (Редакционная коллегия: В. П. Бушинский, Т. Д. Лысенко, М. Г. Чижевский.) 1949, *etc.* 8°. **7011.h.1.**

—— Сборник памяти акад. В. Р. Вильямса. Под редакцией . . . В. П. Бушинского. [With plates, including portraits.] pp. 496. 1942. 8°. *See* Russia.—*Академия Наук СССР.—Почвенный Институт им. В. В. Докучаева.* **07078**. k. **20**.

BUSHINSKY (Vladimir Petrovich) and **ALEKSANDROV** (B. A.)

—— Василий Робертович Вильямс. [With portraits.] pp. 178. *Москва,* 1950. 8°. [*Московское Общество Испытателей Природы. Историческая сер.* no. 42.] Ac. **2988/15**.

BUSHIRE CONFERENCE.

—— Report of the Delegate for India, Bushire Conference. [On postal arrangements between India, Persia and Iraq.] pp. 27. 1923. fol. *See* India.—*Department of Posts and Telegraphs.* I.S. **84/3**.

BUSHLEN (John Preston) *See* Buschlen.

BUSHLEY. The Registers of Bushley, in the Deanery of Upton, 1538 to 1812. Transcribed by J. Rusling. [With an introduction by E. R. Dowdeswell.] 4 pt. 1913. 8°. *See* Worcester.—*Worcestershire Parish Register Society.* Ac. **8167/2**.

BUSHMAKIN (Nikolai D.) Лимфатическія железы подмышечной впадины и ихъ питаніе. Съ 7 рисунками въ краскахъ и 2 таблицами. pp. 221. ii. ii. *Казань,* 1911. 8°. [*Ученые Записки Императорскаго Казанскаго Университета.* год. 78. кн. 3, 4.] Ac. **1097**.

BUSHMAN. Hints and Tips for New-Comers to West Africa. By "Bushman." pp. 29. *J. Bale & Co.: London,* [1924.] 8°. **10094**. a. **5**.

— — A Love Story. By a Bushman [i.e. William Harvey Christie]. 2 vol. *G. W. Evans: Sydney,* 1841. 12°. **12612**. bb. **5**.

BUSHMAN (Jim) *pseud.* [i.e. Conrad H. Sayce.] In the Musgrave Ranges, *etc.* pp. 284. *Blackie & Son: London,* [1922.] 8°. **12800**. aaa. **30**.

—— [A reissue.] *London & Glasgow,* [1933.] 8°. **20052**. e. 4.

—— [A reissue.] In the Musgrave Ranges, *etc.* *London & Glasgow,* [1950.] 8°. **12827**. bbb. **17**.

BUSHMAN (John C.)

—— *See* Warfel (Harry R.) American College English . . . [By] H. R. Warfel . . . Ernst G. Mathews . . . J. C. Bushman. [1949.] 8°. **12986**. pp. **26**.

BUSHMEN. *Begin.* Now Exhibiting, at the Egyptian Hall, Piccadilly. The Bosjesmans, or Bush People, from the interior of South Africa, *etc.* pp. 4. *Chapman, Elcoate & Co.: [London,* 1847.] fol. Tab. **597**. c. (**95**.)

—— [Another copy.] **1856**. g. **15**. (**16**.)

BUSHMIN (A. S.)

—— *See* Russia.—*Академия Наук СССР.—Институт Русской Литературы (Пушкинский Дом).* Вопросы советской литературы, *etc.* [Edited by A. S. Bushmin and others.] 1953, *etc.* 8°. Ac. **1125**. o/**30**.

BUSHNAN (John Stevenson) *See* Dieffenbach (J. F.) Surgical Observations on the Restoration of the Nose . . . From the German . . . With the history and physiology of rhinoplastic operations, notes and additional cases, by J. S. Bushnan. 1833. 8°. **7615**. ee. **37**.

—— Address to the Medical Students of London. Session 1850–1. pp. 16. *John Churchill: London,* 1850. 8°. **7306**. ccc. 4. (4.)

—— Burton and its Bitter Beer. pp. 179. *W. S. Orr & Co.: London,* 1853. 8°. **1156**. e. **10**.

—— Cholera and its Cures: an historical sketch. [With a folding chart.] pp. viii. 169. *W. S. Orr & Co.: London,* 1850. 8°. **7560**. d. **24**.

—— Flowers and their Poetry. [Verses.] pp. 120. *W. S. Orr & Co.: London,* [1851.] 8°. **1347**. c. **13**.

—— The History of a Case in which Animals were found in blood drawn from the veins of a boy, with remarks. pp. 74. *S. Highley: London,* 1833. 8°. **783**. m. **23**.

—— Homœopathy and the Homœopaths. pp. ix. 214. *John Churchill: London,* 1852. 8°. **7390**. b. **10**.

—— Introduction to the Study of Nature; illustrative of the attributes of the Almighty, as displayed in the Creation. pp. vii. 310. *Longman & Co.: London,* 1834. 8°. **1115**. h. **22**.

—— Miss Martineau and Her Master. [A reply to "Letters on the Laws of Man's Nature and Development," by Henry G. Atkinson and H. Martineau.] pp. 173. *John Churchill: London,* 1851. 8°. **4015**. a. 5.

—— The Moral and Sanitary Aspects of the New Central Cattle Market, as proposed by the Corporation of the City of London. With plans. pp. 44. pl. 3. *W. S. Orr & Co.: London,* 1851. 8°. **8776**. b. **55**. (3.)

—— The Natural History of Fishes, particularly their structure and economical uses . . . With portrait and memoir of Salviani. pp. 219. pl. 31. *W. H. Lizars: Edinburgh,* 1840. 8°. [*Naturalist's Library.* vol. 28.] **1150**. a. **14**.

—— Observations on Hydropathy; with an account of the principal cold water establishments of Germany. pp. xii. 188. *J. Churchill: London; Frankfurt* [printed], 1846. 12°. **1171**. e. **34**.

—— Orr's Circle of the Sciences. A series of treatises on the principles of science, with their application to practical pursuits. [Edited by J. S. Bushnan.] 9 vol. 1854–56 [1853–56]. 8°. *See* Orr (Wm. S.) and Co. **8706**. b. **24–31**.

—— The Philosophy of Instinct and Reason. pp. xi. 316. pl. viii. *A. & C. Black: Edinburgh,* 1837. 8°. **1134**. b. **36**.

BUSHNAN (JOHN STEVENSON)

—— The Physiology of Animal and Vegetable Life. [By J. S. Bushnan.] 1854. 8°. [ORR (*Wm. S.*) AND *Co. Orr's Circle of the Sciences, etc.* vol. 1.] *See* PHYSIOLOGY. **8706**. b. **24**.

—— [A reissue.] *Houlston & Stoneman; W. S. Orr & Co.: London*, 1855. 8°. **8707**. d. **18**.

—— Religious Revivals in relation to Nervous and Mental Diseases. pp. x. 46. *John Churchill: London*, 1860. 8°. **4377**. e. **41**. (5.)

BUSHNAN (JOSEPH) *See* SWEET (Samuel W.) Two Letters to the Court of Directors of the Equitable Assurance Society . . . By four members of the Society [i.e. S. W. Sweat, J. Bushnan and others]. 1825. 8°. T. **1083**. (**13**.)

BUSHNEL (WALTER) *See* BUSHNELL.

BUSHNELL (ADELYN)

—— Pay the Piper. A novel. pp. 275. *Coward-McCann: New York*, [1950.] 8°. **12730**. ff. **10**.

—— Rock Haven. pp. 380. *Coward-McCann: New York*, 1948. 8°. **12729**. fff. **10**.

—— Strange Gift. pp. 309. *Coward-McCann: New York*, [1951.] 8°. **12701**. bb. **8**.

—— Tide-Rode. [A novel.] pp. 344. *Coward-McCann: New York*, [1947.] 8°. **12725**. cc. **4**.

BUSHNELL (ADELYN) and **BRADFORD** (MARSHALL)

—— Eight Radio Plays for classroom use and amateur broadcast. pp. 135. *Samuel French: New York, Los Angeles*, [1947.] 8°. **011791**. bb. **4**.

BUSHNELL (ARTHUR JOHN DE HAVILLAND) L'Anglais pour les Français. A manual for rapid self-tuition in English, *etc.* pp. 235. *Oxford University Press: London*, 1918. 8°. **12980**. c. **14**.

—— English Annals. Reign of George III . . . For army candidates. [Two folding sheets.] *Edward Stanford: London*, 1882. 8°. **9503**. ee. **5**.

—— Storied Windows. A traveller's introduction to the study of old church glass, from the twelfth century to the Renaissance, especially in France . . . With maps and illustrations. pp. xi. 338. *W. Blackwood & Sons: Edinburgh & London*, 1914. 8°. **07805**. cc. **10**.

BUSHNELL (CHARLES H.) Diesel Engine Operation, Maintenance and Repair. pp. viii. 285. *J. Wiley & Sons: New York*, 1930. 8°. **8769**. d. **26**.

BUSHNELL (CHARLES IRA) *See* HAWKINS (Christopher) *of North Providence, R.I.* The Adventures of Christopher Hawkins . . . With an introduction and notes by C. I. Bushnell. 1864. 8°. **10880**. dd. **11**.

—— *See* SMITH (Samuel) *of Smithfield, Rhode Island.* Memoirs of Samuel Smith . . . With a preface and notes, by C. I. Bushnell. 1860. 8°. **10880**. dd. **22**. (3.)

—— Crumbs for Antiquarians. [A collection of works written or edited by C. I. Bushell, bound together and reissued.] 2 vol. *Privately printed: New York*, 1864, 66. 8°. **10413**. k. **13**.
Imperfect; wanting no. 2 *of vol.* 1.

BUSHNELL (CHARLES IRA)

—— An Arrangement of Tradesmen's Cards, Political Tokens, also election medals, medalets, &c. current in the United States of America for the last sixty years, described from the originals, chiefly in the collection of the author. With engravings. pp. 118. pl. 4. *Printed for the Author: New York*, 1858. 8°. **7755**. c. **9**.

—— An Historical Account of the First Three Business Tokens issued in the City of New York. pp. 17. *Privately printed: New York*, 1859. 8°. **7755**. aaa. **16**.

—— A Memoir of Eli Bickford, a patriot of the Revolution. [Reprinted from the privately printed edition of 1865.] 1931. *See* PERIODICAL PUBLICATIONS.—*New York.* The Magazine of History, *etc.* Extra no. 166. 1905, *etc.* 4°. P.P. **3437**. bab.

BUSHNELL (DAVID)

—— The Santander Regime in Gran Colombia. pp. ix. 381. *University of Delaware Press: Newark*, 1954. 8°. [*University of Delaware Monograph Series.* no. 5.] Ac. **2690**. s.

BUSHNELL (DAVID IVES) *See* BATZ (A. de) Drawings by A. DeBatz in Louisiana . . . By D. I. Bushnell. 1927. 8°. [*Smithsonian Miscellaneous Collections.* vol. 80. no. 5.] Ac. **1875/2**.

—— *See* MAC KENNEY (Thomas L.) and HALL (James) The Indian Tribes of North America . . . Edited by F. W. Hodge (and D. I. Bushnell), *etc.* 1933, *etc.* 8°. **010410**. eee. **25**.

—— Burials of the Algonquian, Siouan and Caddoan Tribes West of the Mississippi. pp. x. 103. pl. 37. *Washington*, 1927. 8°. [*Bureau of American Ethnology. Bulletin.* no. 83.] A.S. **912**.

—— The Cahokia and Surrounding Mound Groups, *etc.* pp. 20. pl. v. *Cambridge, Mass.*, 1904. 8°. [*Papers of the Peabody Museum of American Archaeology and Ethnology, Harvard University.* vol. 3. no. 1.] Ac. **2692**. a.

—— The Choctaw of Bayou Lacomb, St. Tammany parish, Louisiana. pp. ix. 37. pl. 22. *Washington*, 1909. 8°. [*Bureau of American Ethnology. Bulletin.* no. 48.] A.S. **912**.

—— Evidence of Early Indian Occupancy near the Peaks of Otter, Bedford County, Virginia, *etc.* pp. 14. pl. 5. *Washington*, 1940. 8°. [*Smithsonian Miscellaneous Collections.* vol. 99. no. 15.] Ac. **1875/2**.

—— Indian Sites below the Falls of the Rappahannock, Virginia, *etc.* pp. v. 65. pl. 21. *Washington*, 1937. 8°. [*Smithsonian Miscellaneous Collections.* vol. 96. no. 4.] Ac. **1875/2**.

—— Native Cemeteries and Forms of Burial East of the Mississippi. pp. 160. pl. 17. *Washington*, 1920. 8°. [*Bureau of American Ethnology. Bulletin.* no. 71.] A.S. **912**.

—— Native Villages and Village Sites East of the Mississippi. pp. 111. pl. 17. *Washington*, 1919. 8°. [*Bureau of American Ethnology. Bulletin.* no. 69.] A.S. **912**.

—— Sketches by Paul Kane in the Indian Country, 1845–1848. [With illustrations, including a portrait.] pp. 25. *Washington*, 1940. 8°. [*Smithsonian Miscellaneous Collections.* vol. 99. no. 1.] Ac. **1875/2**.

—— Villages of the Algonquian, Siouan, and Caddoan Tribes West of the Mississippi. pp. x. 211. pl. 55. *Washington*, 1922. 8°. [*Bureau of American Ethnology. Bulletin.* no. 77.] A.S. **912**.

BUSHNELL (EDMUND) The Complete Ship-Wright. Plainly . . . teaching the proportion used by experienced ship-wrights . . . To which are added, certain propositions in geometry . . . Also, a way of rowing of ships by heaving at the capstane . . . The fourth edition, *etc.* pp. 48. *R. W. for William Fisher: London,* 1678. 4°. **8805.** a. **25.**

—— The fifth edition. pp. 56. *R. H. for William Fisher: London,* 1688. 4°. **533.** d. **36.**

BUSHNELL (EDWARD ROGERS) *See* MURPHY (Michael C.) Athletic Training . . . Edited by E. R. Bushnell, *etc.* 1914. 8°. **7904.** aaa. **23.**

BUSHNELL (F. L.) *See* CHENEY (Mary B.) Life and Letters of Horace Bushnell. (Closing years. By Miss F. L. Bushnell.) 1880. 8°. **10881.bbb.5.**

—— —— 1880. 8°. **4985.bbb.36.**

BUSHNELL (GEOFFREY HEXT SUTHERLAND)

—— The Archaeology of the Santa Elena Peninsula in South West Ecuador. pp. xiv. 154. pl. 5. *University Press: Cambridge,* 1951. 4°. [*Occasional Publications of the Cambridge University Museum of Archaeology and Ethnology.* no. 1.] Ac. **5626.** b/2.

BUSHNELL (GEOFFREY HEXT SUTHERLAND) and **DIGBY** (ADRIAN)

—— Ancient American Pottery. pp. xii. 51. pl. A-D. 80. *Faber & Faber: London,* 1955. 8°. [*Faber Monographs on Pottery and Porcelain.*] W.P. **2171/20.**

BUSHNELL (GEORGE ENSIGN) The Lungs. *See* PRATT (Joseph Hersey) Physical Diagnosis of Diseases of the Chest. By J. H. Pratt . . . and G. E. Bushnell, *etc.* 1925. 8°. **07616.** g. **12.**

—— A Study in the Epidemiology of Tuberculosis. With especial reference to tuberculosis of the tropics and of the negro race. pp. v. 221. *J. Bale & Co.: London; Albany, N.Y.* printed, 1920. 8°. **7616.** c. **25.**

BUSHNELL (GEORGE HERBERT)

—— *See* BAXTER (James H.) What to read about Poland . . . Revised and enlarged by G. H. Bushnell. 1942. 8°. **012213.b.9/3.**

—— *See* JOANNES, *de Hildesheim.* The Legend of the Three Wise Men. Retold with an introduction by G. H. Bushnell. [1935.] 8°. **4421.** de. **40.**

—— *See* LANG (Andrew) St. Andrews . . . Edited by G. H. Bushnell. 1951. 8°. **010370.** bb. **16.**

—— The Early History of the Libraries of St. Andrews University. *See* SALMOND (James B.) Henderson's Benefaction, *etc.* 1942. 4°. [*University of St. Andrews. Library Publications.* no. 2.] Ac. **1489/4.**

—— From Bricks to Books. A miscellany, *etc.* pp. 160. *Grafton & Co.: London,* 1949. 8°. **12360.** ccc. **32.**

—— From Papyrus to Print. A bibliographical miscellany. pp. 218. *Grafton & Co.: London,* 1947. 8°. **11913.** c. **18.**

—— A Handful of Ghosts. pp. 59. *University Press: St. Andrews,* 1945. 8°. **12650.** e. **54.**

BUSHNELL (GEORGE HERBERT)

—— Kościuszko. A short biography of the Polish patriot . . . With three portraits. pp. 54. *St. Andrews,* 1943. 8°. [*Scottish-Polish Society Publications.* no. 4.] **012213.b.9/4.**

—— The Life and Work of Edward Raban, St. Andrews' most famous printer. pp. 40. *J. & G. Innes: St. Andrews & Cupar,* 1928. 8°. **011903.** aa. **73.**

—— Scottish Engravers. A biographical dictionary of Scottish engravers and of engravers who worked in Scotland to the beginning of the nineteenth century. Compiled by G. H. Bushnell. With a chronological index. pp. xii. 60. *Oxford University Press: London,* 1949. 8°. **10804.** n. **5.**

—— Scottish Printers, Booksellers and Bookbinders, 1726–1775. *See* DICTIONARY. A Dictionary of the Printers and Booksellers who were at work in England, Scotland and Ireland from 1726 to 1775, *etc.* 1932. 4°. **2036.a.**

—— Sir Richard Grenville. The turbulent life and career of the hero of the little "Revenge." [With plates, including portraits.] pp. 341. *G. G. Harrap & Co.: London,* 1936. 8°. **10815.** h. **10.**

—— University Librarianship. pp. 219. *Grafton & Co.: London,* 1930. 8°. **011899.** aa. **10.**

—— The World's Earliest Libraries. pp. 58. *Grafton & Co.: London,* 1931. 8°. **011900.** c. **48.**

BUSHNELL (GUALTER) *See* BUSHNELL (Walter)

BUSHNELL (HORACE) *See* CHENEY (Mary B.) Life and Letters of Horace Bushnell. 1880. 8°. **10881.** bbb. **5.**

—— —— 1880. 8°. **4985.** bbb. **36.**

—— *See* DAVIS (Andrew J.) The Approaching Crisis: being a review of Dr. Bushnell's recent lectures on supernaturalism. 1852. 8°. **8631.** h. **2.**

—— *See* FAIRFIELD, *County of, Connecticut.—Association of Fairfield West.* Appeal of the Association of Fairfield West to the Associated Ministers connected with the General Association of Connecticut. [Praying the General Association to proceed against Dr. H. Bushnell, on account of the doctrines expounded by him in "God in Christ" and "Christ in Theology."] 1852. 8°. **4183.** d. **18.**

—— *See* MORISON (Walter) Passio Christi: three discourses . . . With notes on certain views of Mr. Maurice, Dr. Bushnell . . . and others. 1871. 8°. **4224.** bb. **41.**

—— *See* MUNGER (Theodore T.) Horace Bushnell, preacher and theologian. [1899.] 8°. **4985.** eee. **12.**

—— *See* MYERS (Alexander J. W.) Horace Bushnell and Religious Education. [With a portrait.] 1937. 8°. **20032.** ff. **45.**

—— *See* NEW HAVEN, *Connecticut.—Yale College, etc.* Addresses and Proceedings, including the Oration pronounced by Rev. Dr. Bushnell, at the Commemorative Celebration held . . . in honor of the alumni of Yale College who were in the military or naval service of the United States during the recent war, *etc.* 1866. 8°. **11903.** cc. **20.**

—— *See* POWELL (Lyman P.) Heavenly Heretics, *etc.* (H. Bushnell.) [With a portrait.] 1909. 8°. **4986.** ff. **37.**

—— *See* TYLER (Bennet) Letters to . . . H. Bushnell . . . containing strictures on his book intitled "Views of Christian Nurture, and subjects adjacent thereto." 1848. 8°. **4380**. k. **17**.

—— Views of Christian Nurture, and of subjects adjacent thereto . . . Second edition. [A republication of "Discourses on Christian Nurture" and "An Argument for Discourses on Christian Nurture," with other articles.] *Edwin Hunt: Hartford*, 1848. 12°. **4376**. b. **8**.

—— Literary Varieties. (I. Work and Play. II. Moral Uses of Dark Things. III. Building Eras in Religion.) 3 pt. *C. Scribner's Sons: New York*, 1881. 8°. **12274**. bb. **3**.

—— An Argument for "Discourses on Christian Nurture," addressed to the Publishing Committee of the Massachusetts Sabbath School Society. pp. 48. *Edwin Hunt: Hartford*, 1847. 8°. **4183**. cc. **41**. **(5.)**

—— Barbarism the First Danger. A discourse for Home Missions. pp. 32. *American Home Missionary Society: New-York*, 1847. 8°. **4486**. bb. **61**. **(19.)**

—— Pulpit Talent, Training for the Pulpit Manward, Building Eras in Religion, and Literary Varieties. [Nine articles, selected from the posthumous collection "Building Eras in Religion."] pp. 343. *R. D. Dickinson: London*, 1882. 8°. **4499**. c. **10**.

—— California: its characteristics and prospects . . . Published originally in the "New Englander." pp. 32. *Whitton, Towne & Co.: San Francisco*, 1858. 8°. **10410**. d. **36**. **(12.)**

—— The Character of Jesus. *See* infra: Nature and the Supernatural, *etc.*

—— Christ and His Salvation. In sermons variously related thereto. pp. viii. 412. *Alexander Strahan; Sampson Low & Co.: London*, [1865.] 8°. **4485**. aaa. **50**.

—— Christ in Theology; being the answer of the author, before the Hartford Central Association of Ministers, October, 1849, for the doctrines of the book entitled "God in Christ." pp. 348. *Brown & Parsons: Hartford*, 1851. 12°. **4225**. b. **14**.

—— Christian Nurture. *See* infra: Discourses on Christian Nurture.

—— Common Schools. A discourse on the modifications demanded by the Roman Catholics, *etc.* pp. 24. *Case, Tiffany & Co.: Hartford*, 1853. 8°. **4486**. bb. **63**. **(5.)**

—— Crisis of the Church. pp. 36. *D. Burgess & Co.: Hartford*, 1835. 8°. **4486**. bb. **61**. **(5.)**

—— A Discourse on the Moral Tendencies and Results of Human History, delivered before the Society of Alumni, in Yale College, *etc.* pp. 32. *M. Y. Beach: New York*, 1843. 8°. **1309**. d. **7**.

—— A Discourse on the Moral Uses of the Sea. Delivered on board the Packet-Ship Victoria, *etc.* pp. 20. *M. W. Dodd: New York*, 1845. 8°. **4486**. bb. **62**. **(5.)**

—— A Discourse on the Slavery Question, *etc.* pp. 32. *Case, Tiffany & Co.: Hartford*, 1839. 8°. **4485**. e. **13**.

—— Third edition. pp. 32. *Case, Tiffany & Co.: Hartford*, 1839. 8°. **8156**. bb. **24**.

—— *See* GILLETTE (Francis) A Review of the Rev. Horace Bushnell's Discourse on the Slavery Question, *etc.* 1839. 8°. **8156**. b. **28**.

—— [Discourses on Christian Nurture.] Christian Nurture. [Essays. Incorporating "Discourses on Christian Nurture."] pp. v. 264. *A. Strahan & Co.: Edinburgh*, 1861. 8°. **4409**. e. **12**.

—— [Another edition.] pp. 386. *T. Nelson & Sons: London*, 1861. 8°. **4377**. aa. **9**.

—— Christian Nurture, *etc.* pp. xl. 351. *Yale University Press: New Haven*, 1947. 8°. **4381**. c. **46**.

—— *See* TYLER (Bennet) Dr. Tyler's Letter to Dr. Bushnell on Christian Nurture. [In answer to his "Discourses on Christian Nurture."] [1847.] 8°. **8306**. h. **10**.

—— The Fathers of New England. An oration delivered before the New England Society of New-York, *etc.* pp. 44. *G. P. Putnam: New-York*, 1850. 12°. **9604**. aa. **32**.

—— Forgiveness and Law, grounded in principles interpreted by human analogies. pp. 256. *Hodder & Stoughton: London*, 1874. 8°. **4227**. aaa. **40**.

—— God in Christ. Three discourses, delivered at New Haven, Cambridge, and Andover, with a preliminary dissertation on language. pp. 356. *Brown & Parsons: Hartford*, 1849. 12°. **4225**. b. **15**.

—— [Another edition.] pp. 330. *John Chapman: London*, 1850. 12°. [*Catholic Series.*] **3605**. b. **11**.

—— [Another edition.] pp. vi. 356. *C. Scribner's Sons: New York*, [1876.] 8°. **4223**. i. **25**.

—— *See* CC. Contributions of CC., *etc.* [Remarks on the reviews and critical notices of H. Bushnell's "God in Christ."] 1849. 8°. **4183**. aaa. **87**. **(4.)**

—— *See* POND (Enoch) Review of Dr. Bushnell's "God in Christ." 1849. 12°. **4225**. b. **57**.

—— God's Thoughts Fit Bread for Children: a sermon, *etc.* pp. 38. *Nichols & Noyes: Boston*, 1869. 8°. **4485**. a. **4**.

—— A Letter to His Holiness Pope Gregory XVI. pp. 24. *Ward & Co.: London*, 1846. 8°. **3938**. c. **17**.

—— Lettera . . al Romano Pontifice. *See* TAPPARELLI D'AZEGLIO (M.) *Marquis*. Degli ultimi casi di Romagna, *etc.* 1864. 8°. **8032**. b. **71**.

—— Moral Uses of Dark Things. [Sixteen articles.] pp. 360. *C. Scribner & Co.: New York*, 1868. 8°. **4378**. f. **17**.

—— [Another edition.] pp. vi. 422. *Strahan & Co.; Sampson Low & Co.: London*, 1869. 8°. **4378**. f. **18**.

—— Nature and the Supernatural, as together constituting the one system of God . . . Fourth edition. pp. 528. *Charles Scribner: New York*, 1859. 8°. **4016**. e. **14**.

—— [Another edition.] pp. xii. 372. *A. Strahan & Co.: Edinburgh*, 1862. 8°. **4016**. b. **8**.

—— The Character of Jesus: forbidding his possible classification with men. [Chapter ten of "Nature and the Supernatural."] pp. vi. 157. *T. Nelson & Sons: London*, 1861. 32°. **4805**. a. **11**.

BUSHNELL (Horace)

—— [Another edition.] Ninth thousand. pp. 108. *A. Strahan & Co.: Edinburgh; Sampson Low & Co.: London*, 1861. 32°. **4805**. a. **12**.

—— The New Life. *See* infra: Sermons for the New Life.

—— An Oration delivered before the Society of Phi Beta Kappa, at Cambridge, *etc.* pp. 39. *George Nichols: Cambridge* [*Mass.*], 1848. 8°. **12301**. dd. **24**. **(6.)**

—— Third edition. pp. 39. *George Nichols: Cambridge* [*Mass.*], 1848. 8°. **8405**. g. **34**. **(11.)**

—— Parting Words. A discourse, *etc.* pp. 25. *L. E. Hunt: Hartford*, 1859. 8°. **4486**. e. **53**. **(19.)**

—— Politics Under the Law of God. A discourse, *etc.* pp. 19. *Edwin Hunt: Hartford*, 1844. 8°. **4486**. bb. **62**. (4.)

—— Second edition. pp. 19. *Edwin Hunt: Hartford*, 1844. 8°. **4485**. f. **38**.

—— Fourth edition. pp. 23. *Edwin Hunt: Hartford*, 1844. 8°. **4485**. f. **39**.

—— Prosperity Our Duty. A discourse, *etc.* pp. 24. *Case, Tiffany & Burnham: Hartford*, 1847. 8°. **4486**. bb. **61**. **(18.)**

—— Sermons for the New Life . . . Fifth edition. pp. 456. *Charles Scribner: New York*, 1859. 8°. **4485**. c. **74**.

—— [Another edition.] The New Life. pp. vi. 322. *A. Strahan & Co.: Edinburgh; Sampson Low & Co.: London*, 1860. 8°. **4485**. b. **28**.

—— [Another edition.] pp. 431. *T. Nelson & Sons: London*, 1861. 8°. **4485**. a. **56**.

—— New edition. pp. vi. 322. *R. D. Dickinson: London*, 1880. 8°. **4476**. k. **26**.

—— Sermons on Living Subjects. pp. 468. *Sampson Low & Co.: London*, 1872. 8°. **4487**. b. **31**.

—— Speech for Connecticut. Being an historical estimate of the State, delivered before the Legislature and other invited guests, at the Festival of the Normal School in New Britain, June 4, 1851. pp. 43. *Boswell & Faxon: Hartford*, 1851. 8°. **9604**. c. **22**. **(3.)**

—— Twentieth Anniversary. A commemorative discourse, delivered in the North Church, of Hartford, May 22, 1853. pp. 32. *Elihu Geer: Hartford*, 1853. 8°. **4486**. bb. **63**. **(6.)**

—— Unconscious Influence; a sermon, *etc.* pp. 16. *W. P. Kennedy: Edinburgh*, 1849. 8°. **4486**. c. **4**.

—— [Another edition.] pp. 34. *Partridge & Oakey: London*, 1852. 24°. **4406**. b. **81**. (5.)

—— [Another edition.] pp. 32. *Elliot Stock: London*, [1894.] 16°. **4422**. bbb. **65**. **(7.)**

—— The Vicarious Sacrifice, grounded on principles of universal obligation. pp. xxxvi. 476. *Alexander Strahan: London*, 1866. 8°. **4226**. bbb. **10**.

—— *See* Andrews (William W.) Remarks on Dr. Bushnell's "Vicarious Sacrifice." 1866. 12°. **4227**. aa. **27**.

BUSHNELL (Horace)

—— *See* Taylor (Oliver S.) Dr. Bushnell's Orthodoxy, or an Inquiry whether the factors of the atonement are recognized in his Vicarious Sacrifice; with a defense of the New England doctrine from his misinterpretation. 1867. 12°. **4226**. aaa. **60**.

—— Women's Suffrage; the reform against nature. pp. 184. *C. Scribner & Co.: New York*, 1869. 12°. **8415**. ccc. **21**.

—— Work and Play; or, Literary varieties. [Twelve articles.] pp. 464. *Charles Scribner: New York*, 1864. 12°. **12296**. bb. **19**.

—— [Another edition, containing eight articles only.] Work and Play. pp. vi. 310. *A. Strahan & Co.: London*, 1864. 8°. **12296**. bb. **18**.

BUSHNELL (John) A Sermon, preached at St. Mary's, Reading . . . at the Archdeacon's Visitation. pp. 20. *Cowslade & Co.: Reading*, 1816. 8°. **1026**. f. **3**. **(12.)**

BUSHNELL (Katharine C.) *See* Andrew (Elizabeth W.) and Bushnell (K. C.) The Queen's Daughters in India, *etc.* 1898. 8°. **8285**. de. **27**.

—— [A chart showing the incorrectness of certain renderings in the Authorised Version of the Bible.] *J. A. Thompson & Co.: Liverpool*, [1911.] *s. sh. obl.* fol. **1879**. cc. **8**. **(33.)**

—— Bible Interleaves. [A series of notes.] ff. 36. [*K. C. Bushnell: Oakland, Cal.*, 1920.] 8°. **03107**. ee. **3**.

—— God's Word to Women: one hundred Bible studies, *etc.* *The Author: Oakland, Cal.*, [1923.] 8°. **03127**. g. **27**.

—— God's Word to Women. 101 questions answered. A woman's catechism. pp. 69. *The Author: Southport*, [1910.] 16°. **08416**. e. **53**.

—— Third edition revised. pp. 69. *The Author: Southport*, [1914.] 16°. **08416.e.53.**

—— The Supreme Virtue: loyalty to God's Anointed King. (A historical exposition of the Song of Solomon.) [With an amended version of the text.] pp. 58. [1924.] 8°. *See* Bible.—*Song of Solomon.* [*English.*] **03187**. de. **109**.

—— The Women's Correspondence Bible Class. 3 ser. [1911, 12?] fol. **3129**. h. **13**.
Reproduced from typewriting.

—— [A revised edition of lessons 1–14, 19, of series 1, with additional lessons.] [1913?] fol. **L.17.f.4.**
Reproduced from typewriting.

—— [A revised edition.] 2 ser. [*K. C. Bushnell: Oakland, Cal.*, 1916, 18.] 8°. **3125**. df. **29**.

BUSHNELL (Nelson Sherwin) The Historical Background of English Literature. pp. ix. 360. *H. Holt & Co.: New York*, [1930.] 8°. **20016**. a. **17**.

—— A Walk after John Keats, *etc.* [The narrative of a walking tour in the North of England and Scotland following the route taken by John Keats and Charles Armitage Brown in 1818. With illustrations, including portraits.] pp. xii. 318. *Farrar & Rinehart: New York*, [1936.] 8°. **010352**. c. **40**.

BUSHNELL (Oliver Jackson) and **TURNBULL** (Albert Gilpin) Meter Testing and Electrical Measurements. A practical handbook covering the design and construction of measuring instruments, *etc.* pp. 180. 8. *American Technical Society: Chicago*, 1920. 8°. **08755**. aa. **14**.

BUSHNELL (Orazio) *See* Bushnell (Horace)

BUSHNELL (Paul Palmer) An Analytical Contrast of Oral with Written English, *etc.* [A thesis.] pp. v. 87. *Teachers College, Columbia University: New York,* 1930. 8º. **12982.** s. **6.**

BUSHNELL (Samuel C.) The Story of the Monitor and the Merrimac. pp. 12. [*The Author: New Haven,* 1925.] 8º. **9615.** dd. **24.**

BUSHNELL (Walter) A Narrative of the Proceedings of the Commissioners appointed by O. Cromwell, for ejecting scandalous and ignorant ministers, in the case of Walter Bushnell Clerk, Vicar of Box in the County of Wilts, *etc.* [By W. Bushnell.] pp. 256. *For R. Clavell: London,* 1660. 8º. E. **1837.** (**1.**)

—— *See* Chambers (Humphrey) An Answer of Humphrey Chambers . . . to the charge of Walter Bushnel . . . published in a book of his entituled: A Narrative of the Proceedings of the Commissioners, *etc.* 1660. 4º. E. **187.** (**5.**)

BUSHNELL (William) *Rev., of Boston, Massachusetts.* Sermon preached at the Funeral of Hon. William Jackson, *etc.* pp. 23. *S. Chism: Boston,* 1855. 8º. **4985.** cc. **47.** (**3.**)

BUSHNELL (William) *Rev., of Nailsworth, Gloucestershire.* *See* Hughes (Obadiah) The Saint Dismissed from Earth, and sent to rest. A sermon on occasion of the death of the late Reverend Mr. William Bushnell, *etc.* 1744. 8º. **1416.** d. **58.**

BUSHNELL (William H.) Ah-Meek, the Beaver; or, the Copper hunters of Lake Superior. pp. 104. *American News Co.: New York,* [1867.] 8º. **12706.** h. **53.**

—— The Hermit of the Colorado Hills. A story of the Texan Pampas. pp. 46. *Sinclair Tousey: New York,* [1864.] 8º. **12705.** g. **42.**

BUSHONG (Charles H.) Modern Gynecology, *etc.* pp. 380. *Henry Kimpton: London; printed in U.S.A.,* 1894. 8º. **7581.** b. **31.**

BUSHROD (W. T.) The Sunday School and its Story pp. 34. *Lindsey Press: London,* 1930. 8º. **04192.** aa. **59.**

BUSHTA, *al-Baghdādī.* Le Pacha-soldat. Vie du Pacha Si Mohammed el Baghdadi, *etc.* [By Bushta and Zaura al-Baghdādī and Christian Richard. With a portrait.] pp. 161. pl. ix. *Paris,* 1936. 8º. **20012.** ee. **69.**

BUSHTEDT (P. P.)

—— *See* Paton (E. O.) Альбом верстатів для автоматичного зварювання. *etc.* [By E. O. Paton, P. P. Bushtedt and others.] 1937. *obl.* fol. Ac. **1101.** cp/**2.**

—— *See* Paton (E. O.) Збірник присвячений сорокаліттю . . . Євгена Оскаровича Патона, *etc.* (Редакційна колегія: Ф. П. Белянкін, П. П. Буштедт, Б. М. Горбунов.) 1937. 8º. Ac. **1101.** b/**54.**

—— Автоматическая сварочная головка. Устройство, принцип работы и схемы управления. (Automatic welding head: arrangement, working principle, and scheme of management. Summary.) pp. 54. *Киев,* 1941. 8º. [*Институт Электросварки. Publications.*] Ac. **1101.** cp. (**45.**)

—— Механізація виробництва зварних бочок. (Die Mechanisation der Herstellung von geschweissten Fässern.) [With summaries in Russian and English.] pp. 11. *Київ,* 1937. 8º. [*Академія Наук УРСР. Інститут Електрозварювання. Publications.*] Ac. **1101.** cp. (**32.**)

BUSHTEDT (P. P.)

—— Работы Института электросварки Академии Наук УССР в области механизации дуговой сварки. (On the work of the Institute for Welding of the Ukrainian Academy of Sciences in the field of mechanizing arc welding. Summary.) pp. 80. *Киев,* 1936. 8º. [*Інститут Електрозварювання. Publications.*] Ac. **1101.** cp. (**14.**)

BUSHTEDT (P. P.) and **DYATLOV** (V. I.)

—— Автоматичне зварювання стрижневими електродами великого діаметра з якісним покриттям. (Automatic welding with heavily coated rod electrodes.) [With summaries in Russian and English.] pp. 46. *Київ,* 1938. 8º. [*Академія Наук УРСР. Інститут Електрозварювання. Publications.*] Ac. **1101.** cp. (**33.**)

—— Автоматичне зварювання якісних швів електродним дротом діаметром до 6 мм. (Automatic welding with tape-covered electrode wire.) [With summaries in Russian and English.] pp. 50. *Київ,* 1938. 8º. [*Академія Наук УРСР. Інститут Електрозварювання. Publications.*] Ac. **1101.** cp. (**28.**)

BUSHTEDT (P. P.) and **KUL'BERG** (L. M.)

—— Дослідження стабілізації зварної дуги і методи будування стабілізуючих обмазок . . . Research work on stabilizing the welding arc, *etc.* [With summaries in Russian and English.] pp. 72. *Київ,* 1936. 8º. [*Інститут Електрозварювання. Publications.*] Ac. **1101.** cp. (**10.**)

BUSHUEV (S. K.)

—— *See* Grekov (B. D.) Против исторической концепции М. Н. Покровского. Сборник статей. (Редакционная коллегия: Б. Греков, С. Бушуев [and others].) 1939, *etc.* 8º. Ac. **1125.** wb/**12.**

BUSHY PARK. The Tornado, Bushy Park. A souvenir. June 1st, 1908. [Signed: M. W., i.e. M. Warne.] [1908.] 12º. *See* W., M. **011651.** h. **81.** (**1.**)

BUSI (Clemente) La Logica soprannaturale, o i Misteri della ragione. pp. viii. 487. *Firenze,* 1868. 8º. **8467.** g. **25.**

BUSI (Leonida) Benedetto Marcello, musicista del secolo xviii. Sua vita e sue opere. pp. 127. *Bologna,* 1884. 8º. **10601.** bb. **20.** (**5.**)

—— Il padre G. B. Martini . . . Notizie raccolte da L. Busi. vol. 1. pp. xxviii. 521. *Bologna,* 1891. 8º. **4866.** i. **40.** *No more published.*

BUSIA (Kofi Abrefa)

—— Education for Citizenship. pp. 15. *London,* [1950.] 8º. [*West African Affairs.*] W.P. **13692/1.**

—— The Position of the Chief in the Modern Political System of Ashanti. A study of the influence of contemporary social changes on Ashanti political institutions. pp. xii. 233. 1951. 8º. *See* London.—iii. *International African Institute.* **010097.** m. **9.**

—— Report on a Social Survey of Sekondi-Takoradi. [With a map.] pp. 164. 1950. 8º. *See* Gold Coast. [*Miscellaneous Official Publications.*] C.S. c. **454/6.**

—— Self-Government for the Gold Coast. pp. 15. *Bureau of Current Affairs: London,* [1950.] 8º. [*West African Affairs.* no. 9.] W.P. **13692/9.**

—— West Africa and the Issues of the War. pp. 31. *London,* 1942. 8º. **8029.** a. **67.**

BUSIGNANO, CHARLES DE BRUC, *Count de.* *See* BRUC.

BÜSIN (PEIDAR) Beatæ memoriæ sacra. Epicedia, in decessum . . . Huldrici Albertini . . . Ex lacrymis Petri Busini, *etc.* *See* PARAVICINO (D.) La Conversatione, ò cittadinanza del cielo, *etc.* 1680. 4º. **4867.** bb. **21.**

—— Catechisem da chianter, in ilg quel vain cumprains la summa della vaira, vêglia, Prophetic-Apostolic-Evangelic-Catholica Religiun . . . In üss dalas baselgias d'Engiadina zura. pp. 44. *Turi,* 1674. 12º. **3504.** a. **27.**
Imperfect; wanting pp. 25, 26.

—— Ita illustrissimum . . . virum, Dominum Johannem à Salice . . . mœrens deplorabat Petrus Businus. [Obituary verses in Greek, Latin, German, French, Italian and Romansch.] [*Schuls,* 1680.] 8º. **885.** h. **30.** (2.)
The date is given in a chronogram on the titlepage.

—— Planctus super obitu . . . Dn. Lucæ Gernleri . . . effusus. [With other memorial poems in Greek, Latin and Hebrew, by various authors.] pp. 63. [*Basle,* 1675.] 4º. **489.** a. **9.** (4.)
The date is given in a chronogram on the titlepage.

BUSINELLI (ALBERTO) Gli Arditi del IX, *etc.* [Reminiscences of the author's experiences in the Italian Army, 1916–20. With plates.] pp. 199. *Roma,* 1934. 8º. **09081.** aaa. **45.**

BUSINELLO (GIOVANNI FRANCESCO) *See* BUSENELLO.

BUSINELLO (PIETRO) Historische Nachrichten von der Regierungsart, den Sitten und Gewohnheiten der osmanischen Monarchie. pp. viii. 222. 1778. *See* LUEDECKE (C. W.) Beschreibung des Türkischen Reiches, *etc.* Tl. 2. 1780, *etc.* 8º. **1053.** h. **16.**

BUSINESS.

—— Abroad on Business. (Radio talks.) pp. 47. [1939.] 12º. *See* LONDON.—III. *Institute of Export.* **8232.** ee. **5.**

—— Business. The journal for the man of affairs. *See* PERIODICAL PUBLICATIONS.—*London.*

—— *See* also PERIODICAL PUBLICATIONS.—*London.* System, *etc.*

—— Business Ahead. *See* PERIODICAL PUBLICATIONS.—*London.*

—— Business and the Public Welfare. pp. iv. 185. *New York,* 1912. 8º. [*Proceedings of the Academy of Political Science.* vol. 2. no. 2.] Ac. **2386.**

—— Business, Commerce and Finance. 8 vol. *Cree Publishing Co.: Minneapolis,* [1909, 10.] 8º. **08227.** dd. **9.**

—— The Business of Life. A book for everyone. By the author of "How to be Happy though Married" [i.e. Edward J. Hardy], *etc.* pp. 304. *T. Fisher Unwin: London,* 1891. 8º. **8411.** cc. **10.**

—— Business with Pleasure. (Supplement to "The Leave Book, 1947-48.") [With illustrations.] pp. 29. [1948.] 4º. *See* PERIODICAL PUBLICATIONS.—London.—*Leave Book.* **10368.** s. **14.**

—— How I Started Business without Capital. 1896. 8º. **08227.** g. **61.** (5.)

—— How to Develop and Expand a Retail Business, *etc.* pp. 155. xxviii. *A. W. Shaw Co.: Chicago,* [1920.] 8º. **08225.** k. **62.**

BUSINESS.

—— How to do Business: a pocket manual of practical affairs . . . and a dictionary of commercial terms. pp. 126. *J. S. Marr & Sons: Glasgow,* [1883.] 16º. **12357.** a. **16.** (1.)

—— How to do more Business. [The preface signed: G. C. M.] [1906.] 8º. *See* M., G. C. **08226.** e. **4.**

—— How to Finance a Business, *etc.* pp. 128. *A. W. Shaw Co.: Chicago, New York,* 1912. 8º. **08225.** ee. **70.**

—— How to make a Small Business pay. pp. 119. *Cassell & Co.: London,* 1913. 8º. **08226.** aa. **48.**

—— How to Organise a Business, *etc.* pp. 144. *A. W. Shaw Co.: London,* [1917.] 8º. **08228.** ff. **82.**

—— How to Purchase a Business. By "H. A. S." 1904. 16º. *See* S., H. A. **8228.** a. **59.**

—— How to Start and Run a Business of your own. *Business Service Institute: London,* [1936– .] 4º. W.P. **2502.**
Printed on one side of the leaf only.

—— How to Talk Business to Win, *etc.* pp. 128. *A. W. Shaw Co.: Chicago, New York,* 1913. 8º. **08225.** ee. **63.**

—— Mind your own Business. [A song.] *Paul: London,* [1850?] *s. sh.* 4º. **11621.** k. **4.** (**66.**)

—— [Another copy.] MS. CORRECTIONS. **11621.** k. **4.** (**67.**)

—— Mind your own Business. (The Heart bow'd down.) [Songs.] *E. Hodges: London,* [1860?] *s. sh.* 4º. **11621.** k. **4.** (**68.**)

—— Modern Business. *See* SCRANTON, *Pa.—International Correspondence Schools.*

—— Modern Business. A series of texts, *etc.* *See* DIBBLEE (George B.)

—— *See* also NEW YORK.—*Alexander Hamilton Institute.*

—— Of Business and Retirement. A poem. Address'd to the British Atticus. pp. 46. *John Watts: London,* 1635 [1735]. 4º. **11633.** f. **45.**

—— [Another copy.] **11630.** d. **12.** (**6.**)

—— [Another copy.] **11630.** c. **14.** (**20.**)

—— A Plain Answer to a late Pamphlet, intitled, "The Business of Pawnbroking stated and defended," *etc.* pp. 30. *George Woodfall; W. Bickerton: London,* 1745. 8º. **104.** g. **65.**

—— What's that to thee? and Mind your own Business. A sermon preach'd in London, June the 20th, 1708, *etc.* pp. 18. *John Lawrence: London,* 1708. 12º. **4474.** bb. **9.**

BUSINESS ADMINISTRATION. Practical Business Administration . . . Prepared by a staff of accountants, auditors, management engineers and specialists in business methods and administration, *etc.* 12 vol. *American Technical Society: Chicago,* 1934 [1933]. 8º. **8205.** t. **12.**

—— [Another edition.] 12 vol. *American Technical Society: Chicago,* 1935. 8º. **8230.** g. **33.**

—— Practical Business Administration . . . Revised edition. 12 vol. *American Technical Society: Chicago,* 1939. 8º. **08230.** aaa. **35.**

BUSINESS ADMINISTRATION.

—— The Cooperative System of Training in Practical Business Administration. Based on twelve volumes of text material [i.e. on "Practical Business Administration"], *etc.* *American Technical Society: Chicago*, 1935. 4°. **8230**. d. **27**.

—— *See* SYSTEM. The Cooperative System of Training in Practical Business Administration. Based on twelve volumes of text material [i.e. the series entitled "Practical Business Administration"], *etc.* 1939. 8°. **8230**. d. **61**.

—— The University Cooperative System of Training in Practical Business Administration. Based on the twelve-volume library [i.e. on "Practical Business Administration"], *etc.* *American Technical Society: Chicago*, [1933.] fol. **8225**. v. **28**.

BUSINESS ADVISER. The Business Adviser. An all-British business magazine for men and women. *See* PERIODICAL PUBLICATIONS.—*London.*

BUSINESS ADVISORY AND PLANNING COUNCIL. *See* UNITED STATES OF AMERICA.—*Department of Commerce.*

BUSINESS ARCHIVES COUNCIL. *See* ENGLAND.

BUSINESS BLUE BOOK. The Business Blue Book. A book for the progressive business men and all interested in commercial knowledge, *etc.* pp. xv. 281. *Curtis, Gardner & Co.: London*, [1906.] 8°. **08226**. c. **37**.

—— [A reissue.] *London*, [1907.] 8°. **8227**. dd. **34**.

—— [Another edition.] pp. xviii. 296. *Curtis, Gardner & Co.: London*, [1908 ?] 8°. **08227**. aaa. **46**.

—— (Tenth edition.) pp. xvii–xxvii. 317. *Curtis, Gardner & Co.: London*, [1911.] 8°. **08227**. aaa. **47**.

BUSINESS BUILDER. *See* PERIODICAL PUBLICATIONS. —*London.*

BUSINESS CHANCES. *See* PERIODICAL PUBLICATIONS. *Birmingham.*

BUSINESS CORRESPONDENCE. Business Correspondence. 3 vol. *A. W. Shaw Co.: Chicago*, 1917. 8°. **08227**. de. **56**.

—— Business Correspondence, *etc.* pp. vi. 202. *A. W. Shaw Co.: London*, [1921.] 8°. [*Efficiency Library.*] W.P. **5654/5**.
A different work from the preceding.

—— Business Correspondence and Office Management. By Edward A. Duddy . . . L. E. Frailey . . . and Raymond V. Cradit, *etc.* pp. 234. *American Technical Society: Chicago*, 1938. 8°. **8232**. e. **8**.

BUSINESS DESK BOOK. The Business Desk Book. pp. 42. *Curtis, Gardner & Co.: London*, [1907.] 8°. **8507**. f. **26**. (**5**.)

BUSINESS DIARY. The Business Diary and Trade Directory. *See* EPHEMERIDES.

BUSINESS DIRECTORY. Business Directory of Birmingham. *See* DIRECTORIES.—*Birmingham.*

—— The Business Directory of Ireland. *See* DIRECTORIES. —*Ireland.*

BUSINESS DIRECTORY.

—— The Business Directory of London. *See* DIRECTORIES.—*London.* The Business Directory of the Manufacturing and Commercial Cities of England. vol. 3. London.

—— The Business Directory of Manchester. *See* DIRECTORIES.—*Manchester.*

—— Business Directory of Sheffield, Rotherham, Masbro' and Attercliffe. *See* DIRECTORIES.—*Sheffield.*

—— The Business Directory of South Africa. *See* DIRECTORIES.—*Africa, South.* The General Directory of South Africa, *etc.*

—— The Business Directory of the Manufacturing and Commercial Cities of England. vol. 3. London. *See* DIRECTORIES.—*London.*

—— Business Directory of the principal Southern Cities [of the United States of America]. *See* DIRECTORIES.—*United States of America.*

BUSINESS ECONOMICS. Business Economics. *Newbery Press: London*, [1938– .] 8°. W.P. **12144**.

BUSINESS ENGLISH PROBLEMS. Business English Problems. [Loose sheets and blank forms.] *Harper & Bros.: [New York,]* 1921. 4°. **12983**. i. **11**.

BUSINESS ENTERPRISE. Business Enterprise. (The official organ of the Edinburgh City Business Club.) *See* EDINBURGH.—*Edinburgh City Business Club.*

—— Business Enterprise. The official organ of Scottish Business Clubs. *See* EDINBURGH.—*Central Committee of Scottish Business Clubs.*

BUSINESS EQUIPMENT TOPICS. *See* PERIODICAL PUBLICATIONS.—*New York.*

BUSINESS HANDWRITING COPY BOOK. Business Handwriting Copy Book. 3 pt. *Sir I. Pitman & Son: London*, 1936. 4°. **7941**. s. **16**.

BUSINESS HISTORICAL SOCIETY. *See* UNITED STATES OF AMERICA.

BUSINESS HISTORICAL STUDIES. *See* UNITED STATES OF AMERICA.—*Business Historical Society.*

BUSINESS HISTORY SERIES. *See* NEW YORK.—*University of the City of New York.—Graduate School of Business Administration.*

BUSINESS HOUSE HOLIDAY GUIDE. *See* DIRECTORIES.—*Hotels, Boarding Houses, etc.* [*Great Britain.*] Cutts' Holiday Apartments, *etc.*

BUSINESS LAW.

—— Business Law and Administration. *See* SCHMITTHOFF (Clive M.)

BUSINESS LAW REVIEW.

—— The Business Law Review. *See* PERIODICAL PUBLICATIONS.—*Ipswich.*

BUSINESS LIFE. Business Life. A journal for all preparing to enter the office, the civil service, and the professions. *See* PERIODICAL PUBLICATIONS.—*London.*

—— Business Life. The experiences of a London tradesman . . . Second edition. pp. xii. 236. *Houlston & Wright: London*, 1861. 8°. **8244**. a. **36**.

BUSINESS MAN.

—— The Business Man's Desk Book, *etc.* pp. 143. *Shaw Publishing Co.: London*, 1952. 8°. **12221.** l. **25.**
Pages 9–143 are another issue of those of vol. 6 of the "Executive's Practical Management Library."

—— The Business Man's Encyclopedia. *See* ENCYCLOPAEDIAS.

—— The Businessman's Guide to Britain. *See* PERIODICAL PUBLICATIONS.—London.—*The Economist.*

—— The Business Man's Library. 10 vol. *System Co.: Chicago*, 1907. 8°. **8226.** r. **1.**

—— The Business Man's Magazine. *See* PERIODICAL PUBLICATIONS.—*London.*

—— The Business Man's Note Book and Desk Directory. *See* PERIODICAL PUBLICATIONS.—*London.*

—— Tired Business Man's Library of Adventure, Detective and Mystery Novels. 9 vol. *D. Appleton-Century Co.: New York, London*, 1934, 35. 8°. **012631.** n. **1.**

—— What a Business Man ought to Know . . . By a Confidential Clerk. pp. 86. *Guilbert Pitman: London*, 1903. 8°. **08228.** f. **32.**

—— [Another edition.] pp. 110. *Guilbert Pitman: London*, 1904. 8°. **08228.** f. **38.**

BUSINESS MANAGEMENT SERIES. *See* QUAINTANCE (Hadly W.)

BUSINESS MEN. Business Men at Home and Abroad. *See* DIRECTORIES.—*Commerce.*

—— The Business Men of Texas. *See* DIRECTORIES.—*Texas.*

BUSINESS NEWS.

—— Business News. *See* PERIODICAL PUBLICATIONS.—*Johannesburg.* 'Εμπορικα νεα.

BUSINESS NEWS DIGEST. *See* PERIODICAL PUBLICATIONS.—*London.*

BUSINESS OPPORTUNITIES.

—— Business Opportunities. *See* PERIODICAL PUBLICATIONS.—*London.*

BUSINESS ORGANISATION. Business Organisation, *etc.* pp. 200. *A. W. Shaw Co.: London*, [1927.] 8°. **08244.** ee. **33.**

—— Business Organisation and Management. *See* PERIODICAL PUBLICATIONS.—*London.*

BUSINESS PRINTER. *See* PERIODICAL PUBLICATIONS.—*Salt Lake City.*

BUSINESS PROSPECTS YEAR BOOK. *See* PERIODICAL PUBLICATIONS.—*London.*

BUSINESS REGISTER. The Business Register, of Manufacturers, Merchants, and Professionals. *See* DIRECTORIES.—*Professions, Trades, etc.*

—— The Complete Business Register . . . arranged for a period of three years, *etc.* *Pamphilon & Co.: Congleton*, 1884. fol. **8228.** k. **11.**

BUSINESS REPORTS. Special Business Reports and Surveys. *See* PERIODICAL PUBLICATIONS.—Chicago.—*System.* System "How-Books."

BUSINESS RESEARCH BULLETIN. *See* LINCOLN, *Nebraska.—University of Nebraska.—College of Business Administration.*

BUSINESS RESEARCH INSTITUTE.

—— Business Research Institute at the Stockholm School of Economics. *See* STOCKHOLM.—*Handelshögskola.—Företagsekonomiska Forskningsinstitutet.*

BUSINESS SERVICE BULLETIN.

—— Business Service Bulletin. *See* UNITED STATES OF AMERICA.—*Department of Commerce.—Small Business Administration.*

BUSINESS SHORT CUTS. Business Short Cuts in Accounting, *etc.* *See* PERIODICAL PUBLICATIONS.—Detroit.—*The Book-keeper.*

BUSINESS STUDENT.

—— The Business Student. *See* PERIODICAL PUBLICATIONS. — London.

BUSINESS SYSTEMS.

—— Business Systems and Equipment. *Exhibitions of Business Systems: London*, 1931. 8°. **8234.** eee. **71.**

BUSINESS TELEGRAPH CODE. Business Telegraph Code. pp. vi. 298. *Business Code Co.: Chicago; E. & F. N. Spon: London*, [1907.] 8°. **08755.** de. **14.**

BUSINESS TERMS.

—— Business Terms and Phrases, with equivalents in French, German, and Spanish, and facsimile documents. pp. 164. *Sir Isaac Pitman & Sons: London*, 1900. 8°. **08225.** f. **8.**
Part of "Pitman's Commercial Series." Published in ten parts. The title on the wrappers reads "Pitman's Business Terms and Phrases."

—— [Another edition.] Business Terms, Phrases and Abbreviations, with equivalents in French, German, and Spanish, and facsimile documents. pp. 231. *Sir Isaac Pitman & Sons: London*, [1901.] 8°. **08228.** ff. **16.**
Part of "Pitman's Commercial Series."

—— [A reissue.] *London*, [1902.] 8°. **08225.** f. **10.**
Part of "Pitman's Commercial Series."

—— Fourth edition, revised and enlarged. pp. vi. 273. *Sir Isaac Pitman & Sons: London*, [1912.] 8°. **08228.** f. **52.**
Part of "Pitman's Commercial Series."

—— Fifth edition. pp. vi. 273. *Sir Isaac Pitman & Sons: London*, 1927. 8°. **08245.** e. **77**

—— Seventh edition. pp. viii. 273. *Sir Isaac Pitman & Sons: London*, 1932. 8°. **08226.** aaa. **72.**

—— Eighth edition. pp. viii. 271. *Sir Isaac Pitman & Sons: London*, 1935. 8°. **8230.** e. **51.**

—— Ninth edition. pp. viii. 277. *Sir Isaac Pitman & Sons: London*, 1937. 8°. **8233.** aa. **16**

—— Tenth edition. pp. viii. 287. *Sir Isaac Pitman & Sons: London*, 1939. 8°. **08230.** a. **35**

BUSINESS TERMS.

—— Eleventh edition. pp. iv. 283. *Sir Isaac Pitman & Sons: London*, 1947. 8°. **8233.** aa. **86.**

—— Twelfth edition. pp. v. 265. *Sir Isaac Pitman & Sons: London*, 1953. 8°. **012902.** dd. **1.**

BUSINESS TIMES. *See* PERIODICAL PUBLICATIONS.—*Manchester.*

BUSINESS TRIFLES. Business Trifles that Tell. By the Managing-Director of a well-known Business Organization. [A reissue of "100 Trifles that Tell in Business" by John M. Ouseley.] pp. 123. *Alexander Ouseley: London*, [1928.] 8°. [*New-Style Business Books.*] W.P. **6809/2.**

The half-title and running-title read: "100 Trifles that Tell in Business."

BUSINESS WORLD. The Business World. Men & methods of the new Georgian era . . . Illustrations. pp. 344. *Dod's Publications: London*, [1922.] 4°. **8232.** i. **14.**

—— [Another edition.] pp. 360. *Dod's Publications: London*, [1923.] 4°. **8232.** i. **15.**

—— [Another edition.] pp. 303. *Dod's Publications: London*, [1924.] 4°. **8232.** i. **16.**

—— [Another edition.] *Dod's Publications: London*, [1925.] 8°. **08230.** e. **6.**

—— [Another edition.] *Dod's Publications: London*, [1926.] 8°. **8234.** aa. **46.**

BÜSING ( ) [For the German surname of this form:] *See* BUESING.

BUSINGER (ALOYS) Der Kanton Unterwalden historisch, geographisch, statistisch geschildert, *etc.* pp. 199. *St. Gallen & Bern*, 1836. 8°. [*Historisch-geographisch-statistisches Gemälde der Schweiz.* Hft. 6.] **573.** d. **19.**

BUSINGER (JOOST ALOIS)

—— Some Aspects of the Influence of the Earth's Surface on the Atmosphere. [With a summary in Dutch.] pp. xii. 78. *Staatsdrukkerij- en Uitgeverijbedrijf: 's-Gravenhage*, 1954. 8°. [*Koninklijk Nederlands Meteorologisch Instituut. Mededelingen en verhandelingen.* no. 61.] Ac. **4074.**

—— [Another issue.] Some Aspects of the Influence of the Earth's Surface on the Atmosphere. *'s Gravenhage*, 1954. 8°. **8713.** ee. **39.**

BUSINGER (JOSEPH MARIA) Bruder Klaus und sein Zeitalter, oder die Lebens- und Zeitgeschichte des seligen Niklaus von Flüe aus Unterwalden, *etc.* [With a portrait.] pp. xvi. 148. *Luzern*, 1827. 8°. **4885.** cc. **5.**

—— Die Geschichten des Volkes von Unterwalden ob und nid dem Wald, von dessen frühester Abkunft an, bis auf unsere Zeiten, mit Hinsicht auf die Geschichten seiner Nachbarn von Ury und Schwyz. 2 Bd. *Luzern*, 1827, 28. 8°. **1437.** i. **10.**

—— Schweizer'sche Bilder Gallerie, oder Erklärung der vaterländischen Geschichten, in den Gemälden auf der Kapell-Brücke zu Luzern. 2 Bd. *Luzern*, 1820. 8°. **1437.** i. **9.**

—— Galerie des tableaux du Pont de la Chapelle à Lucerne . . . Traduit . . . par H. de Crousaz. pp. 184. *Lucerne*, 1821. 8°. **786.** e. **25.**

BUSINGER (JOSEPH MARIA)

—— Die Stadt Luzern, und ihre Umgebungen. In topographischer, geschichtlicher und statistischer Hinsicht. pp. xii. vii. 276. *Luzern*, 1811. 8°. **10196.** bbb. **9.**

The titlepage is engraved.

—— Luzern und seine Umgebungen . . . Neue Umarbeitung des frühern Werkes: "Die Stadt Luzern und ihre Umgebungen." pp. xii. 198. *Luzern*, [1836.] 12°. **10195.** aaa. **14.**

—— Itinéraire du Mont-Righi et du Lac des 4 Cantons, précédé de la description de la ville de Lucerne, et de ses environs. Traduit . . . par H. de C*** [i.e. H. de Crousaz]. pp. vi. 68. 90. *Lucerne*, 1815. 8°. **794.** f. **29.**

—— Lucerne, et ses environs, suivi d'un itinéraire au Mont-Righi, et autour du Lac des Quatre Cantons . . . Traduit . . . par Henri de Crousaz. Seconde édition, revue et augmentée. pp. ix. 163. *Lucerne*, 1821. 8°. **573.** e. **28.**

The titlepage is engraved.

BUSINGER (JOSEPH MARIA) and **ZELGER** (FRANZ NICOLAUS)

—— Kleiner Versuch einer besondern Geschichte des Freystaats Unterwalden, ob und nid dem Kernwalde. 2 Tl. *Luzern*, 1789, 91. 8°. **9305.** aaa. **25.**

BUSINGER (LUCAS CASPAR) [Das Leben unseres lieben Herrn und Heilandes Jesus Christus.] The Life of Christ. Adapted from the original . . . by Rev. John E. Mullett . . . Illustrated. pp. 439. *R. & T. Washbourne: London*, 1913. 8°. **4808.** ff. **21.**

BUSINGER (OTTO) Asthma. Aerodynamik und Therapie. pp. 68. *Bern*, [1936.] 8°. **07616.** f. **36.**

BUSINI (BATISTA) *See* BUSINI (Giovanni B.)

BUSINI (BENEDETTO) Polifila, comedia piacevole e nuoua nuouamente . . . stampata. [Attributed to B. Busini and to G. B. Gelli.] 1556. 8°. *See* POLIFILA. **1071.** i. **5. (3.)**

—— [Another copy.] **162.** e. **47.**

—— [Another copy.] G. **10388.**

—— [Another copy.] **1071.** h. **13. (2.)**

BUSINI (GIOVANNI BATTISTA) Lettere . . . a Benedetto Varchi sugli avvenimenti dell'assedio di Firenze, estratte da un codice della Biblioteca Palatina. pp. vii. 221. *Pisa*, 1822. 8°. **1440.** f. **11.**

—— [Another edition.] Corrette ed accresciute di alcune altre inedite, per cura di Gaetano Milanesi. pp. xii. 308. *Firenze*, 1860. 12°. **10910.** aaa. **29.**

BUSINK (TH. A.) Prothuron. Inleidende studie over het woonhuis in Oud-Griekenland. [With plates.] pp. xv. 160. [*Groningen*,] 1936. 8°. **7702.** t. **20.**

—— Sumerische en babylonische tempelbouw, *etc.* pp. 208. pl. XII. *Batavia*, 1940. 4°. **7700.** h. **18.**

BUSINUS (PETRUS) *See* BÜSIN (Peidar)

BUSIO (PAULO STIEVANO DE) De scorbuti natura dissertatio inauguralis, *etc.* pp. 19. *Patavii*, 1830. 8°. **7306.** b. **8. (37.)**

BUSIRI. Busiri, overo In van si fugge amore. Melodrama boschereccio di P. R., F.R.S. [i.e. Paolo Antonio Rolli.] *Ital. & Eng.* pp. 45. 1740. 8°. *See* R., P., *F.R.S.* **907**. i. **3**. (**8**.)

BŪṢĪRĪ. *See* MUḤAMMAD IBN SAʻĪD, *al-Būṣīrī.*

BUSIRI (GIULIO) *See* MOLZA (U.) Commentario della vita e della morte di G. Busiri. 1867. 32°. **10630**. aa. **26**.

BUSIRI-VICI (ANDREA) Il Celebre studio del mosaico della rev. fabbrica di S. Pietro . . . Memorie istoriche ed illustrazione di mosaici importanti, *etc.* pp. 122. pl. VI. *Roma,* 1901. 4°. **7858**. t. **16**.

—— La Musica dei colori, reminiscenze pittoriche nel III centenario del principe della musica, Giovanni Pierluigi da Palestrina. [With plates.] pp. 137. *Roma,* 1894. 8°. **7806**. dd. **19**.

—— Papyrus. Grato ricordo di Siracusa. [Essays.] pp. 74. pl. III. *Roma,* 1893. 8°. **10132**. l. **2**.

—— Quarantatrè anni di vita artistica. Memorie storiche di un architetto. pp. 503. *Roma,* 1892. 4°. **7820**. i. **10**.

—— Sessantacinque anni delle Scuole di belle arti della Insigne e Pontificia Accademia Romana denominata di S. Luca, *etc.* [Compiled by A. Busiri-Vici. With plates.] pp. 311. 1895. 4°. *See* ROME.—*Accademia Nazionale di San Luca.* **7808**. h. **9**.

—— Studii teorico-pratici con monografie sugli ospedali ed ospizii moderni. pp. 51. *Milano,* 1884. fol. **7815**. f. **11**.

—— I Tre celebri navigatori italiani del secolo decimosesto (Colombo, Vespucci, Andrea Doria). pp. 68. pl. VI. *Roma,* 1892. fol. **10630**. i. **9**.

BUSIUS (ABRAHAMUS) Decas quæstionum philosophicarum, *etc. Praes.* G. Jacchaeus. *Ex officina I. Margi: Lugduni Batavorum,* 1624. 4°. **534**. c. **36**. (**54**.)

BUSIUS (PAULUS) [Commentarius in universas Pandectas cum differentiis juris canonici et consuetudinum Germaniae.] pt. 2, 3. [*Zwolle & Franeker,* 1608–14.] 4°. **497**. d. **3**.

Imperfect; wanting pt. 1.

—— [Another edition.] Commentarius . . . in universas Pandectas Domini Justiniani, cum differentiis consuetudinum communium, et Germaniæ, Galliæ, Belgicæ, singularium juris canonici . . . Accessit Index omnium titulorum. (Tomi duo posteriores, quibus explicantur quatuor partes digestorum posteriores.) 3 tom. *Typis J. Columbii: Daventriæ,* 1656, 57. 4°. **5205**. aa. **13**.

—— De officio judicis liber, *etc. See* MASSA (A.) D. Antonii Massae Gallesii . . . De exercitatione jurisperitorum libri tres, *etc.* 1610. 8°. **5305**. a. **22**.

BUSIZ (ZUAN JOSEF) *See* VIRGILIUS MARO (P.) [*Georgica.—Italian.—Friulan Dialect.*] La Georgica . . . tradotta in viars furlans da Z. J. Busiz, *etc.* 1857. 4°. **11355**. aaa. **34**.

BUSK (DOUGLAS)

—— The Delectable Mountains . . . The sketches by Bridget Busk. [With a portrait.] pp. xi. 274. pl. XLVII. *Hodder & Stoughton: London,* 1946. 8°. **7918**. bb. **10**.

BUSK (EDWARD TESHMAKER) *See* BUSK (Mary) Edward Teshmaker Busk, *etc.* [With portraits.] 1917. 8°. **010856**. h. **8**.

—— —— 1925. 8°. **010826**. ee. **44**.

BUSK (GEORGE) *See* COHN (F. J.) On the Natural History of Protococcus Pluvialis. By F. Cohn. Abstracted . . . by G. Busk. 1853. 8°. [HENFREY (*Arthur*) *Botanical and Physiological Memoirs, etc.*] **Ac.3023/22.**

—— *See* CUVIER (G. L. C. F. D. de) *Baron.* [*Works written in collaboration.*] Notice of Ray, by Cuvier and Aubert Dupetit Thouars . . . Translated by G. Busk. 1846. 8°. [LANKESTER (*Edwin*) *Memorials of John Ray.*] Ac. **3023/17**.

—— *See* KOELLIKER (A. von) Manual of Human Histology . . . Translated and edited by G. Busk . . . and T. Huxley. 1853, *etc.* 8°. Ac. **3837/23**.

—— *See* LONDON.—III. *Ethnological Society.* Transactions, *etc.* (The Journal of the Ethnological Society. Edited by G. Busk [and others].) 1861, *etc.* 8°. Ac. **6234**.

—— *See* LONDON.—III. *Ray Society.* Reports and Papers on Botany. On the morphology of the coniferæ, by Dr. Zuccarini. Translated by G. Busk . . . On botanical geography, by Professor Grisebach. Translated by W. B. Macdonald . . . and G. Busk, *etc.* 1846. 8°. **Ac.3023/16.**

—— *See* LONDON.—III. *Ray Society.* Reports on Zoology for 1843, 1844. Translated from the German, by G. Busk . . . A. Tulk . . . and A. H. Haliday. 1847. 8°. **Ac.3023/10.**

—— *See* PERIODICAL PUBLICATIONS.—*London.* The Microscopic Journal . . . Edited by D. Cooper (G. Busk). [1841, *etc.*] 8°. P.P. **1990**.

—— *See* PERIODICAL PUBLICATIONS.—*London.* The Natural History Review . . . Edited by G. Busk, *etc.* 1861, *etc.* 8°. P.P. **1976**.

—— *See* PERIODICAL PUBLICATIONS.—*London.* Quarterly Journal of Microscopical Science. Edited by E. Lankester . . . and G. Busk. (New series. vol. 1–8 edited by E. Lankester and G. Busk.) 1853, *etc.* 8°. P.P. **1482**.

—— *See* STEENSTRUP (J. J. S.) On the Alternation of Generations; or, the Propagation and development of animals through alternate generations . . . Translated from the German version of C. H. Lorenzen, by G. Busk. 1845. 8°. **Ac.3023/14.**

—— *See* WEDL (C.) Rudiments of Pathological Histology . . . Translated and edited by G. Busk. 1855. 8°. Ac. **3837/25**.

—— Catalogue of Marine Polyzoa in the collection of the British Museum. [Edited by J. E. Gray.] 3 pt. 1852–75. 12°. *See* LONDON.—III. *British Museum.—Department of Zoology.* [*Polyzoa.*] **7207**. ccc. **10**.

—— A Monograph of the Fossil Polyzoa of the Crag. pp. xiii. 136. pl. XXII. *London,* 1859. 4°. [*Publications of the Palaeontographical Society.*] Ac. **3200**. (**2**.)

—— On Parasites, and the Diseases which they produce. 1864. *See* HOLMES (Timothy) A System of Surgery, *etc.* vol. 4. 1860, *etc.* 8°. **7480**. e. **30**.

—— [Another edition.] 1871. *See* HOLMES (Timothy) A System of Surgery, *etc.* vol. 5. 1870, *etc.* 8°. **7482**. bbb. **17**.

—— [Another edition.] *See* HOLMES (Timothy) A System of Surgery, *etc.* vol. 3. 1883. 8°. **07482**. k. **1**.

BUSK (George)

—— Report on the Polyzoa collected by H.M.S. Challenger during the years 1873–76. [With plates.] 2 pt. 1884, 86. *See* Thomson (*Sir* Charles W.) Report on the Scientific Results of the Voyage of H.M.S. Challenger, *etc.* Zoology. vol. 10, 17. 1880, *etc.* 4°. **1825.** aa.

—— Venomous Insects and Reptiles. 1864. *See* Holmes (Timothy) A System of Surgery, *etc.* vol. 4. 1860, *etc.* 4°. **7480.** e. **30.**

—— [Another edition.] 1871. *See* Holmes (Timothy) A System of Surgery, *etc.* vol. 5. 1870, *etc.* 8°. **7482.** bbb. **17.**

—— [Another edition.] *See* Holmes (Timothy) A System of Surgery, *etc.* vol. 3. 1883. 8°. **07482.** k. **1.**

BUSK (Hans) *the Elder.* *See* also Beaujolais ( ) *pseud.* [i.e. H. Busk.]

—— *See* Bible.—*Psalms.* [*English.—Miscellaneous Metrical Versions.*] Hebrew Lyrics. By an Octogenarian [i.e. H. Busk]. 1859. 8°. **3437.** g. **35.**

—— The Banquet: in three cantos. [By H. Busk.] pp. viii. 144. 57*–60*. 1819. 8°. *See* Banquet. **993.** i. **3.**

—— Second edition. pp. viii. 144. *Sherwood, Neely & Jones: London,* 1820. 8°. **11647.** e. **48.** (**1.**)
With an additional titlepage, engraved.

—— The Dessert, a poem, to which is added The Tea, by the author of "The Banquet" [i.e. H. Busk]. [With plates.] pp. x. 109. 1819. 8°. *See* Dessert. **992.** i. **22.** (**8.**)

—— Second edition. pp. x. 109. *Sherwood, Neely & Jones: London,* 1820. 8°. **11647.** e. **48.** (**2.**)

—— Fugitive Pieces in Verse. [With plates.] pp. vii. 272. *W. M. Thiselton: London,* 1814. 8°. **993.** l. **6.**
The titlepage is engraved.

—— The Lay of Life, a poem. pp. 246. *Simpkin & Marshall: London,* 1834. 8°. **994.** e. **8.**

—— The Vestriad, a poem. [With plates.] pp. xxi. 355. *Henry Colburn: London,* 1819. 8°. **991.** l. **4.**

BUSK (Hans) *the Younger.* *See* Hayes (*Sir* George) A Temple Elegy. Edited and illustrated by H. B. (H. Busk.) [1870?] 4°. **11641.** g. **57.**

—— Copies of the Testimonials of Hans Busk, M.A., *etc.* pp. 16. [1861?] fol. **9918.** k. **19.** (**12.**)

—— Hand-Book for Hythe [i.e. for the School of Musketry at Hythe]: comprising a familiar explanation of the laws of projectiles, and an introduction to the system of musketry, now adopted by all military powers, *etc.* pp. viii. 184. pl. 9. *Routledge, Warne & Routledge: London,* 1860. 8°. **8827.** b. **19.**

—— The Navies of the World; their present state, and future capabilities, *etc.* [With plates.] pp. xv. 312. 127. *Routledge, Warnes & Routledge: London,* 1859. 8°. **8806.** c. **33.**

—— A Reply to the Apology of the Right Hon. W. E. Gladstone, contained in his "Chapter of Autobiography," recently elicited by a handbill published at Berwick. [On the projected disestablishment of the Irish Church.] pp. 37. *Lock & Hadwen: London,* 1868. 8°. **8138.** bbb. **18.**

BUSK (Hans) *the Younger.*

—— Captain Hans Busk's Rifle Target Registers. Fourth edition. [Blank forms.] *Routledge, Warne & Routledge: London,* 1860. 8°. **8827.** e. **14.**

—— Rifle Volunteers: how to organize and drill them . . . With illustrations. pp. vi. 118. *Routledge, Warnes & Routledge: London,* 1859. 8°. **8828.** a. **21.**

—— Seventh edition, enlarged and improved. pp. 235. *Routledge, Warne & Routledge: London,* 1860. 8°. **8827.** c. **30.**

—— The Rifleman's Manual; or, Rifles, and how to use them . . . Second edition, *etc.* pp. xii. 10–129. *Charles Noble: London,* [1858.] 8°. **8828.** d. **32.**

—— The Rifle, and how to use it . . . Third edition [of "The Rifleman's Manual"], *etc.* pp. 181. *G. Routledge & Co.: London,* 1858. 8°. **8827.** b. **18.**

—— Seventh edition, considerably enlarged and improved, *etc.* [With a portrait.] pp. 255. *Routledge, Warne & Routledge: London,* 1860. 8°. **8827.** aaa. **23.**

—— The Substance of an Address on the Origin and Present State of the Laws of England, *etc.* pp. 25. *Jas. Wade: [London,* 1873.] 4°. **6145.** dd. **4.** (**2.**)

—— Tabular Arrangement of the Company Drill, *etc.* [A folding sheet.] *Savill & Edwards: London,* 1860. 8°. **8833.** f. **23.**

BUSK (Hans Acworth) *See* Busk (Mary) E. T. Busk . . . With a short memoir of H. A. Busk. [With portraits.] 1925. 8°. **010826.** ee. **44.**

BUSK (Henrietta) *See* London.—iii. *Bedford College.* Calendar, *etc.* [The 1888 and 1899 editions compiled by H. Busk.] 1888, *etc.* 8°. **P.P.2506.at.**

—— *See* Young (Ruth) *Biographical Writer.* The Life of an Educational Worker, Henrietta Busk, *etc.* [With portraits.] 1934. 8°. **010825.** de. **43.**

—— [For documents signed by H. Busk as Chairman of the General Committee, London Centre, Teachers' Guild of Great Britain and Ireland:] *See* London.—iii. *Teachers' Guild, etc.*

—— Geography as a School Subject. pp. 31. *Teachers' Guild of Great Britain & Ireland: London,* 1895. 8°. **010004.** g. **47.**

BUSK (Henry Gould) Earth Flexures: their geometry and their representation and analysis in geological section, with special reference to the problem of oil finding. pp. 106. *University Press: Cambridge,* 1929. 8°. [*Cambridge Geological Series.*] **8709.h.3/4.**

—— What will the Weather be? The amateur forecaster's vade mecum. [With charts.] pp. 27. *W. Heffer & Sons: Cambridge,* 1911. 8°. **08755.** e. **36.**

BUSK (M. M.) Biographical Sketches, European and Asiatic. pp. 380. *T. C. Newby: London,* 1847. 16°. **1448.** c. **13.**

—— The History of Spain and Portugal, from B.C. 1000 to A.D. 1814. pp. xvi. 364. *Baldwin & Cradock: London,* 1833. 8°. [*Library of Useful Knowledge.*] **737.** d. **5.**

—— Manners and Customs of the Japanese, in the Nineteenth Century. From recent Dutch visitors of Japan, and the German of Dr. Ph. Fr. von Siebold. [By M. M. Busk.] pp. xi. 423. 1841. 8°. *See* Japanese. **793.** g. **19.**

—— [Another edition.] pp. 298. 1845. 12°. *See* Japanese. **12205.** b. **21.**

BUSK (M. M.)

—— Mediæval Popes, Emperors, Kings, and Crusaders; or, Germany, Italy, and Palestine, from A.D. 1125 to A.D. 1268. [With maps.] 4 vol. *Hookham & Sons: London,* 1854–56. 12°. **9077. dd. 27.**

—— Plays and Poems. 2 vol. *Thomas Hookham: London,* 1837. 8°. **994. g. 6.**

—— Tales of Fault and Feeling . . . By the author of "Zeal and Experience" [i.e. M. M. Busk ?]. 3 vol. 1825. 12°. *See* TALES. **N. 330.**

BUSK (MARIAN) *Lady. See* KERNER VON MARILAUN (A.) The Natural History of Plants . . . From the German . . . by F. W. Oliver . . . with the assistance of M. Busk, *etc.* 1894, *etc.* 8°. **7029. k. 17.**

—— —— 1902. 8°. **7033.e.29.**

BUSK (MARY) Edward Teshmaker Busk. Born March 8th, 1886. Died November 5th, 1914. By M. B. (M. Busk.) [With plates, including portraits.] pp. 92. *R. Maclehose & Co.: Glasgow,* 1917. 8°. **010856. h. 8.**

—— [Another edition.] E. T. Busk, a Pioneer in Flight. With a short memoir of H. A. Busk. By M. Busk. [With a chapter by R. H. Mayo, and with portraits.] pp. xi. 167. *John Murray: London,* 1925. 8°. **010826. ee. 44.**

BUSK (RACHEL HARRIETTE) *See* BYRNE (Julia C.) Gossip of the Century, *etc.* (vol. 3, 4 edited by R. H. Busk.) 1892, *etc.* 8°. **012330. l. 1.**

—— Contemporary Annals of Rome: notes, political, archæological, and social. By the Roman Correspondent of the "Westminster Gazette" [i.e. R. H. Busk]. With preface by the Very Rev. Monsignor Capel. Series 1. March 1867 to March 1868. Centenary of St. Peter, Mentana Campaign. pp. xii. 438. 1870. 8°. *See* ROME.—*The City.* [*Appendix.—Miscellaneous.*] **10130. b. 33.**

[Another copy.]
—— Contemporary Annals of Rome: notes, political, archæological, and social. [By the] Roman correspondent of the "Westminster Review" [i.e. R. H. Busk]. With preface by the Very Rev. Monsignor Capel. Series I. March 1867 to March 1868. Centenary of St. Peter, Mentana campaign. pp. xii. 438. 1870. 8°. *See* ROME. —*The City.* [*Appendix.—Miscellaneous.*] **9166. ccc. 24.**

—— The Folk-Lore of Rome. Collected by word of mouth from the people. pp. xxiv. 439. *Longmans & Co.: London,* 1874. 8°. **2348. d. 4.**

—— The Folk-Songs of Italy. Specimens with translations and notes, from each province: and prefatory treatise. By Miss R. H. Busk. The specimens of the canzuni and ciuri of Sicily . . . selected expressly . . . by Dr. Giuseppe Pitrè. pp. 290. *Swan Sonnenschein & Co.: London,* 1887. 8°. **11431. de. 24.**

—— Household Stories from the Land of Hofer; or, Popular myths of Tirol, including the Rose-Garden of King Lareyn. By the author of "Patrañas; or, Spanish stories," etc. [i.e. R. H. Busk.] With illustrations by T. Green. pp. iv. 420. 1871 [1870]. 8°. *See* TYROL. **12431. e. 24.**

—— Patrañas; or Spanish Stories, legendary and traditional. By the author of "Traditions of Tirol" [i.e. R. H. Busk]. With illustrations by E. H. Corbould. pp. vii. 376. 1870. 8°. *See* SPANISH STORIES. **12431. df. 22.**

BUSK (RACHEL HARRIETTE)

—— Sagas from the Far East; or, Kalmouk and Mongolian traditionary tales. With historical preface and explanatory notes. By the author of "Patrañas" [i.e. R. H. Busk], *etc.* pp. xx. 420. 1873. 8°. *See* EAST. **2348. c. 8.**

—— The Valleys of Tirol. Their traditions and customs, and how to visit them . . . With frontispiece and three maps. pp. xxix. 453. *Longmans & Co.: London,* 1874. 8°. **10205. ccc. 24.**

BUSK (*Mrs.* WILLIAM) *See* BUSK (M. M.)

BUSKAGRIUS (PETRUS) Otium peregrinationis, seu De legione veterum Romanorum in genere, opusculum singulare. pp. 40. *Apud J. Janssonium, sumptibus authoris: Amstelodami,* 1662. 12°. **590. a. 11. (3.)**

BUSKE (MORRIS R.)

—— *See* ROEHM (A. W.) The Record of Mankind. [By] A. W. Roehm, M. R. Buske, *etc.* [1954.] 8°. **09007. d. 21.**

BUSKEN HUET (VAN DEVENTER) *Mevrouw. See* DEVENTER-BUSKEN HUET.

BUSKEN HUET (ANNE DOROTHEE) *See* HUET.

BUSKEN HUET (COENRAAD) *See* HUET.

BUSKEN HUET (GÉDÉON) *See* HUET.

BUSKES (J. J.)

—— Antwoord op het Herderlijk schrijven van de Generale Synode der Ned. Herv. Kerk betreffende het vraagstuk van oorlog en vrede. [With the text of the letter.] pp. 23. *Amsterdam,* [1953.] 8°. **8425. r. 45.**

BUSKETT (EVANS WALKER) Fire Assaying. A practical treatise on the fire assaying of gold, silver and lead, including description of the appliances used. pp. vii. 105. *D. Van Nostrand Co.: New York; E. & F. N. Spon: London,* 1907. 8°. **07109. i. 11.**

BUSKIN (ELIZABETH MAUD) *See* PERIODICAL PUBLICATIONS.—*Wincanton.* Questions. (Edited by E. M. Buskin.) 1909. *obl.* 8°. **1865. a. 10. (16.)**

—— "Billingshurst 'Coronation' Advertising Souvenir." pp. 28. [1911.] 16°. **7912. de. 51. (3.)**

—— (Second edition.) pp. 28. [1911.] 16°. **7912. de. 51. (4.)**
Imperfect; wanting pp. 1–4.

—— 'Crowned by Love.' June 22nd. 1911. Coronation poem. *C. Parsons: Bruton,* [1911.] 16°. **11601. cc. 23. (4.)**

—— Supplementary Verses to the Coronation Souvenir. By the Billingshurst Poet (E. M. Buskin). *Bracher: Wincanton,* [1911.] 16°. **7912. de. 51. (3*.)**

BUSKIN (SOCK) *Captain, pseud.* How to "get up" Theatricals in a Country House. *See* SORRELL (William J.) *Member of the Dramatic Authors' Society.* The Amateur's Hand-Book and Guide, *etc.* [1866.] 8°. **11795. bbb. 15.**

BUSLAEV (F. V.)

—— Корреспонденты Л. Н. Толстого. [An annotated catalogue of letters written to L. N. Tolstoi.] Составил Ф. В. Буслаев. Под редакцией Н. Н. Гусева. 1940– . 8°. *See* MOSCOW.—*Россiйская Публичная Библiотека, etc.* **Ac. 9658/14.**

BUSLAEV (Fedor Ivanovich) *See* Galakhov (A. D. and Buslaev (Th. I.) Конспектъ русскаго языка и словесности, *etc.* 1852. 8°. **12976. g. 11.**

—— *See* Lavrovsky (P. A.) Записка о второмъ изданiи первой части исторической грамматики Ѳ. И. Буслаева. 1865. 8°. [*Записки Императорской Академiи Наукъ.* том. 8. прил. no 3.] Ac. **1125/48.**

—— *See* Sheremetev (S. D.) *Count.* Памяти Ѳ. И. Буслаева и С. Д. Филипсонова. (Н. П. Кондаковъ. О научныхъ задачахъ исторiи древне-русскаго искусства, *etc.*) 1899. 8°. [*Общество Любителей древней письменности. Памятники древней письменности искусства.* 132. pt. 3.] Ac. **9086/6.**

—— Сочиненiя . . . Съ 40 рисунками въ текстѣ. [Edited by N. P. Kondakov. With a portrait.] том. 1, 2. 1908, 10. 8°. *See* Russia.—*Академия Наук СССР.—Отдѣленiе Русскаго Языка и Словесности.* Ac. **1125.** e/4.

—— [Another copy.] **12265. l. 10.**

—— Иванъ Михайловичъ Снегиревъ, 1793–1868 г. [Biographical sketch.] (Изъ Московскихъ Университетскихъ Извѣстiй, № 1-й, 1869 г.) pp. 7. [*Moscow,* 1869.] 8°. **10795. dd. 23.**

—— Изъ Праги. [Containing a sketch of a visit to the University at Berlin.] (Изъ № 6 Совр. Лѣт. 1864 г.) pp. 9. [*Moscow,* 1864.] 8°. **8355. f. 34. (11.)**

—— Испанскiй народный эпосъ о Сидѣ. pp. 98. *Санктпетербургъ,* 1864. 8°. [*Записки Императорской Академiи Наукъ.* том. 5. прил. no. 6.] Ac. **1125/48.**

—— [Another copy.] **11826. g. 9.**

—— Историческая грамматика русскаго языка. *See* infra: Опытъ исторической грамматики русскаго языка.

—— Историческая христоматiя церковно-славянскаго и древне-русскаго языковъ. Составлено . . . Ѳ. Буслаевымъ. pp. ii. col. 1632. pp. viii. *Москва,* 1861. 4°. **12265. i. 4.**

"Учебныя руководства и учебныя пособiя по преподаванiю Русскаго языка и словесности, издаваемыя одновременно Главнымъ Начальствомъ Военно-Учебныхъ Заведенiй" no. 5.

—— Историческiе очерки русской народной словесности и искусства. [With plates.] 2 том. *Санктпетербургъ,* 1861. 4°. **11850. i. 12.**

—— Лекцiи Ѳ. И. Буслаева Е. И. В. наслѣднику цесаревичу Николаю Александровичу 1859–1860 гг. 3 pt. 1904–07. *See* Leningrad.—*Общество Ревнителей Русскаго Историческаго Просвѣщенiя, etc.* Старина и Новизна, *etc.* кн. 8, 10, 12. 1897, *etc.* 8°. Ac. **7888.**

—— Мои досуги, собранныя изъ перiодическихъ изданiй. Мелкiя сочиненiя Ѳ. Буслаева, *etc.* 2 част. *Москва,* 1886. 8°. **12356. m. 3.**

—— Народная поэзiя. Историческiе очерки. pp. vi. 501. *Санктпетербургъ,* 1887. 8°. [*Сборникъ отдѣленiя русскаго языка и словесности.* том. 42. no. 2.] Ac. **1125/39.**

—— О народной поезiи въ древне-русской литературѣ. Рѣчь, произнесенная въ . . . Собранiи Императорскаго Московскаго Университета . . . Ѳ. Буслаевымъ. 2 pt. pp. 51. 32. [*Moscow,* 1859.] 4°. **11826. k. 5.**

BUSLAEV (Fedor Ivanovich)

—— Образцы письма и украшенiй изъ Псалтыри съ возслѣдованiемъ по рукописи XV вѣка хранящейся въ библiотекѣ Троицкой Сергiевой Лавры . . . со введенiемъ Ѳ. Буслаева. pp. 79. pl. 60. 1881. 4°. *See* Leningrad.—*Общество Любителей Древней Письменности.* Ac. **9086/44.**

—— Опытъ исторической грамматики Русскаго языка. Учебное пособiе для преподавателей. Составлено . . . Ѳ. Буслаевымъ. 2 част. *Москва,* 1858. 8°. **12976. i. 15.**

"Учебныя руководства и учебныя пособiя по преподаванiю Русскаго языка и словесности, издаваемыя одновременно Главнымъ Начальствомъ Военно-Учебныхъ Заведенiй" no. 2.

—— Историческая грамматика русскаго языка . . . Изданiе второе, передѣланное ("Опыта Исторической Грамматики Рускаго языка"). 2 част. *Москва,* 1863. 8°. **12976. h. 10.**

—— Палеографическiе и филологическiе матерiалы для исторiи письменъ славянскихъ, собранные изъ XV-ти рукописей Московской Сѵнодальной Библiотеки . . . Ѳ. Буслаевымъ, съ приложенiемъ 2-хъ снимковъ, литографированныхъ Iоною Шелковниковымъ. pp. 58. pl. к. *See* Moscow.—*Императорскiй Московскiй Университетъ.* Матерiалы для исторiи письменъ восточныхъ, *etc.* [1855.] fol. **1803. d. 8.**

—— Русская христоматiя. Памятники древне-русской литературы и народной словесности, съ историческими . . . и грамматическими объясненiями, съ словаремъ . . . Составилъ Ѳ. Буслаевъ. pp. xvi. 429. 1870. 8°. *See* Moscow.—*Общество распространенiя Полезныхъ Книгъ.* **12265. g. 7.**

—— Русскiй лицевой апокалипсисъ. Сводъ изображенiй изъ лицевыхъ апокалипсисовъ по русскимъ рукописямъ съ XVI-го вѣка по XIX-ый. Составилъ Ѳ. Буслаевъ. 2 vol. pp. xiv. 835. 8. pl. 285. 1884. 4° & fol. *See* Leningrad.—*Общество Любителей Древней Письменности.* Ac. **9086/48.**

—— Учебникъ русской грамматики, сближенной съ церковнославянскою, съ приложенiемъ образцовъ грамматическаго разбора. Для среднихъ учебныхъ заведенiй . . . Седьмое изданiе, исправленное и дополненное. pp. ii. 235. *Москва,* 1888. 8°. **12976. pp. 28.**

BUSLEY (Carl) Die Schiffsmaschine, ihre Construction, Wirkungsweise und Bedienung . . . Mit einem Atlas, *etc.* 3 Bd. *Kiel,* 1883, 86. 8°. **8804. d. 13.**

Bd. 2, and Bd. 3 containing the Atlas, are of the second edition.

—— Dritte vollständig umgearbeitete und bedeutend vermehrte Auflage. Bd. 1. pp. xi. 831. *Kiel & Leipzig,* 1901 [1891–1901]. 8°. **08805. ff. 30.**

Published in parts. No more of this edition published.

—— Atlas. Bd. 1. pl. 63. *Kiel & Leipzig,* 1901 [1891–1901]. *obl.* fol. **14001. b. 24.**

Published in parts. No more of this edition published.

—— The Marine Steam Engine, its Construction, Action, and Management . . . Third edition, thoroughly revised and enlarged. Translated by H. A. B. Cole. vol. 1. pp. xix. 736. *Lipsius & Tischer: Kiel & Leipzig; H. Grevel & Co.: London,* 1902 [1892–1902]. 8°. **14001. a. 44.**

Published in parts. No more published.

—— Atlas. vol. 1. pl. 63. *Lipsius & Tischer: Kiel & Leipzig; H. Grevel & Co.: London,* 1901 [1892–1901]. *obl.* fol. **14001. a. 44.**

Published in parts. No more published.

BUSLEY (Josef) *See* Bitterauf-Remy (M.) Die Kunstdenkmäler des Kreises Altenkirchen . . . Bearbeitet von M. Bitterauf-Remy in Verbindung mit J. Busley und H. Neu, *etc.* 1935. 4°. **20000**. i. **1/16**.

BUSLEYDEN (Jerome de)

—— Jerome de Busleyden, founder of the Louvain Collegium Trilingue. His life and writings. Edited . . . in their entirety . . . by Henry de Vocht, *etc.* [With a portrait.] pp. xi. 511. *Brepols Press: Turnhout,* 1950. 8°. [*Humanistica Lovaniensia.* no. 9.] W.P. **2413/9**.

BUSLIDIUS (Hieronymus) *See* Hardt (H. von der) Memoria Buslidii, Caroli v . . . consiliarii, Ariensis præpositi, aliorumque illustrium virorum, *etc.* 1717. 8°. **1010**. a. **22**. (**2**.)

BUSMAN (Georgius Conradus) Disputatio inauguralis medico-chirurgica de carcinomate, *etc.* pp. 22. *Lugduni Batavorum,* 1708. 4°. **1185**. h. **7**. (**36**.)

BUSMAN CORNELIUS (Ph. C.) *See* Cornelius.

BUSMANN (Cornelis Willem Star) *See* Hamaker (H. J.) Verspreide geschriften . . . Verzameld door Mr. W. L. P. A. Molengraaff en Mr. C. W. Star Busmann. 1911, *etc.* 8°. **6004**. k. **13**.

—— *See* Land (N. K. F.) Verklaring van het Burgerlijk Wetboek, etc. (dl. 1 ; dl. 5. stuk 1, 2 herzien door Mr. C. W. Star Busmann.) 1909, *etc.* 8°. **6060.h.1.**

BUSMANNUS (Dethmarus) Disputatio decima problematum ac controversiarum physicarum generalium. De qualitatis necessitate in corpore naturali, *etc.* *Praes.* Z. Flotwedelius. *Typis I. Matthæi: Wittebergæ,* 1615. 4°. **536**. f. **11**. (**3**.)

BUSMANNUS (Jo. Christianus) Collectio de professoribus eloquentiæ doctoribus Ecclesiæ celeberrimis priorum quatuor post C. N. sæculorum, *etc.* *Helmstadii,* [1710.] 4°. **488**. e. **7**.

BUSMANNUS (Joannes) *See* Salerno.—*Schola Salernitana.* Regimen sanitatis, Angliæ olim regi a Schola Salernitana vel Parisiensi scriptum . . . nunc germanicis rythmis illustratum, *etc.* [Edited by J. Busmannus.] 1546. 8°. **1039**. a. **8**.

—— Elegia cum nonnullis aliis contra obstinatos Papistas. *Impressum apud V. Creuzer: Vitebergæ,* 1546. 4°. **3902**. e. **15**.

BUSMANNUS (Johannes Eberhardus) Disputatio optico-astronomica de Veneris et Mercurii phasibus, *etc.* *Praes.* P. A. Colerus. [With a plate.] *Typis J. Borckardi: Wittebergæ,* [1664.] 4°. **531**. l. **4**. (**10**.)

BUSMANTI (Silvio) La Pineta. Idillio. pp. 33. *Ravenna,* 1888. 16°. **11427**. bb. **19**. (**4**.)
One of an edition of twenty-five copies.

—— Pomposa. Cenni storici . . . Terza edizione. pp. 30. *Imola,* 1881. 8°. **10107**. ff. **19**. (**3**.)

BUSNACH (William) *See* Bernard (Victor) *Dramatist,* and Busnach (W.) Un Fiancé à l'heure. Comédie-vaudeville, *etc.* 1872. 12°. **11739**. aaa. **22**. (**5**.)

—— *See* Cham, *pseud.*, and Busnach (W.) Le Myosotis. Aliénation mentale et musicale, *etc.* 1866. 12°. **11737**. bb. **67**. (**3**.)

—— *See* Clairville ( ) *pseud.* Ferblande, ou l'Abonné de Montmartre. Parodie . . . de MM. Clairville, O. Gastineau et W. Busnach, *etc.* 1870. 12°. **11740**. b. **2**. (**3**.)

BUSNACH (William)

—— *See* Clairville ( ) *pseud.* Paris—revue. Revue-ballet-féerie . . . par MM. Clairville, Siraudin et W. Busnach, *etc.* [1870.] fol. **11737**. i. **17**.

—— *See* Clairville ( ) *pseud.*, and Busnach (W.) Forte en gueule. Revue, *etc.* 1874. 12°. **11739**. ee. **77**.

—— *See* Clairville ( ) *pseud.*, and Busnach (W.) Héloïse et Abélard. Opéra comique, *etc.* 1872. 12°. **11739**. bb. **12**. (**7**.)

—— *See* Clairville ( ) *pseud.*, and Busnach (W.) La Malle des Indes. Revue, *etc.* [1875.] 8°. **11739**. k. **68**. (**14**.)

—— *See* Decourcelle (A.) and Busnach (W.) Le Premier tapis. Comédie, *etc.* 1876. 12°. **11740**. f. **5**. (**4**.)

—— *See* Duru (A.) Le Bas de laine. Comédie-vaudeville . . . par A. Duru, W. Busnach & O. Gastineau. 1879. 12°. **11740**. f. **14**. (**4**.)

—— *See* Flan (A.) and Busnach (W.) Bu qui s'avance. Revue, *etc.* [1865.] 8°. **11739**. k. **19**.

—— *See* Grangé (Eugène) *pseud.* L'Hirondelle. Comédie . . . par E. Grangé, V. Bernard, et W. Busnach. 1872. 12°. **11740**. b. **17**. (**5**.)

—— *See* Jaime (A.) and Busnach (W.) La Chambre nuptiale. Comédie-vaudeville, *etc.* 1882. 8°. **11740**. e. **12**. (**6**.)

—— *See* Jallais (A. de) and Busnach (W.) On lit dans l'Akhbar—. Vaudeville, *etc.* 1864. 12°. **11739**. bbb. **7**. (**7**.)

—— *See* Liorat (A.) La Fille de Fanchon la vielleuse. Opéra-comique . . . de A. Liorat, W. Busnach et A. Fonteny, *etc.* [1891.] 8°. **906**. h. **17**.

—— *See* Thiéry (H.) and Busnach (W.) Les Voyageurs pour l'Exposition. Revue fantaisie, *etc.* 1867. 4°. **11739**. k. **20**.

—— Trois pièces tirées des romans, et précédées chacune d'une préface, de Émile Zola. L'Assommoir. Nana. Pot-Bouille. pp. 482. *Paris,* 1884. 12°. **11740**. bb. **35**.
A previous edition of " L'Assommoir " is entered under Busnach (W.) *and* Gastineau (O.).

—— Cinq par jour ! Folie-vaudeville en un acte, *etc.* pp. 35. *Paris,* 1865. 12°. **11739**. bbb. **11**. (**1**.)

—— Les Esprits des Batignolles. A-propos-vaudeville en un acte. pp. 29. *Paris,* [1873.] 12°. **11739**. ee. **54**.

—— Le Petit gosse, *etc.* [A novel. With plates.] pp. 205. *Paris,* [1890.] 8°. **012547**. l. **24**.

—— Les Petits du premier. Opéra-bouffe en un acte, *etc.* pp. 36. *Paris,* 1865. 12°. **11739**. bbb. **11**. (**2**.)

—— Le Remplaçant. Comédie en trois actes. [By W. Busnach, G. Duval and M. Hennequin.] pp. 155. *Paris,* 1898. 12°. **11740**. eee. **15**.

—— Robinson Crusoé. Bouffonnerie-musicale en un acte, *etc.* pp. 29. *Paris,* [1866.] 8°. **11739**. aaa. **14**. (**11**.)

—— La Soucoupe. Comédie en un acte. pp. 32. *Paris,* 1881. 8°. **11740**. b. **18**. (**5**.)

—— Vain sacrifice. Roman. pp. 339. *Paris,* [1893.] 12°. **012550**. df. **17**.

BUSNACH (WILLIAM)

—— Les Virtuoses du pavé. Bouffonnerie musicale en un acte, *etc.* pp. 23. *Paris*, 1864. 12°. **11739**. bbb. **7**. (**1**.)

BUSNACH (WILLIAM) and **BLOCH** (FERDINAND)

—— Voleuse! Scènes de la vie populaire. pp. 31. *Paris*, 1900. 12°. **11739**. de. **45**. (**3**.)

BUSNACH (WILLIAM) and **BURANI** (PAUL)

—— Les Boniments de l'année. Revue en quatre actes et dix tableaux, *etc.* pp. 79. *Paris*, 1878. 12°. **11739**. f. **6**. (**6**.)

BUSNACH (WILLIAM) and **CHABRILLAT** (HENRI)

—— Dans le mouvement. Vaudeville en un acte, *etc.* pp. 34. *Paris*, 1872. 12°. **11739**. aaa. **9**. (**9**.)

—— [La Fille de M. Lecoq.] Lecoq, the Detective's Daughter. pp. 187. *Vizetelly & Co.: London*, 1888. 8°. [*Celebrated Sensational Novels*. no. 5.] **12511**. m. **1**.

BUSNACH (WILLIAM) and **DEBRIT** (HENRI)

—— Ma femme manque de chic. Comédie en trois actes. pp. 119. *Paris*, 1885. 12°. **11740**. b. **22**. (**5**.)

BUSNACH (WILLIAM) and **DECOURCELLE** (PIERRE)

—— Madame Cartouche. Opéra comique en trois actes. pp. 125. *Paris*, 1887. 8°. **11740**. c. **6**.

BUSNACH (WILLIAM) and **FLAN** (ALEXANDRE)

—— La Gazette des Parisiens. Journal-revue en un acte . . . Premier numéro, *etc.* pp. 48. *Paris*, [1866.] 8°. **11739**. d. **14**. (**10**.)

BUSNACH (WILLIAM) and **GASTINEAU** (OCTAVE)

—— L'Assommoir. Drame en cinq actes et neuf tableaux. [Adapted from the novel of the same title by Zola.] Avec une préface d'Émile Zola, *etc.* pp. 177. *Paris*, 1881. 12°. **11739**. e. **47**. (**8**.)

—— Mon mari est à Versailles. Comédie en un acte. pp. 37. *Paris*, 1876. 12°. **11739**. e. **52**. (**1**.)

BUSNACH (WILLIAM) and **LIORAT** (ARMAND) *pseud.* [i.e. GEORGES DEGAS.]

—— Kosiki. Opéra-comique en trois actes, *etc.* pp. 102. *Paris*, [1876.] 12°. **11740**. b. **7**. (**5**.)

The date on the wrapper is 1877.

—— [Another copy.] **11740**. b. **7**. (**2**.)

—— La Liqueur d'or. Opéra-comique en trois actes, *etc.* pp. 113. *Paris*, 1874. 12°. **11739**. ee. **63**.

—— Mariée depuis midi. Pièce en un acte, mêlée de chant. *etc.* pp. 17. *Paris*, 1874. 12°. **11739**. ee. **57**,

—— Le Truc du colonel. Pièce en un acte. pp. 27. *Paris*, 1876. 12°. **11740**. b. **7**. (**3**.)
The date on the wrapper is 1877.

BUSNACH (WILLIAM) and **MARQUET** ( ) *Dramatist.*

—— L'Ours et l'amateur des jardins. Bouffonnerie musicale en un acte, *etc.* pp. 35. *Paris*, 1869. 8°. **11739**. c. **15**. (**8**.)

BUSNEL (TH.) *See* DUFILHOL (L. A.) Guionvac'h . . . Avec frontispice et nombreuses illustrations de M. T. Busnel, *etc.* 1890. 4°. **12512**. k. **25**.

BUSNELLI (GIOVANNI) *See* DANTE ALIGHIERI. [*Works*.] Opere, *etc.* (vol. 4, 5. Il Convivio. Ridotto a miglior lezione e commentato da G. Busnelli e G. Vandelli.) 1934, *etc.* 8°. W.P. **12246**.

—— Il Concetto e l'ordine del ' Paradiso ' dantesco. Indagini e studii, preceduti da una lettera di Francesco Flamini. 2 pt. *Città di Castello*, 1911, 12. 8°. [*Collezione di opuscoli danteschi inediti o rari*. vol. 105–113.] **011420**. a. **1/53**.

—— Cosmogonia e antropogenesi secondo Dante Alighieri e le sue fonti. pp. 303. *Roma*, 1922. 8°. **011420**. c. **40**.

—— L'Etica Nicomachea e l'ordinamento morale dell' " Inferno " di Dante. Con un appendice, La Concezione dantesca del gran Veglio di Creta: contributo scientifico. pp. 195. *Bologna*, 1907. 8°. [*Biblioteca storico-critica della letteratura dantesca*. ser. 2. no. 4.] **11422**. dd. **27**.

BUSNELLI (MANLIO DUILIO) *See* PAOLO, *Servita*. Opere. (vol. 1, 2. Lettere ai Protestanti. Prima edizione critica a cura di M. D. Busnelli.) 1931, *etc.* 8°. **12227**. eee. **1/73**.

—— Stendhal traducteur de Goldoni. pp. 16. [*Paris*,] 1926. 8°. [*Éditions du Stendhal-Club*. no. 18.] **11868.g.27/18.**

BUSNELLI (VALERIO) Un Duello fra padre e figlio, ovvero un' Espiazione. Dramma in cinque atti. pp. 102. *Milano*, 1868. 16°. **11715**. df. **38**.

—— I Lituani. Memorie storiche del sesto secolo. pp. 95. *Milano*, [1874.] 16°. **12471**. a. **34**.

—— Processo del maresciallo Bazaine di Francia, colla descrizione dei fatti d'armi avvenuti nell'anno 1870. [With illustrations.] pp. 559. *Milano*, [1874?] 8°. **6875**. e. **14**.

—— Sua Santità Papa Leone XIII. Cenni storici e biografici. pp. 127. *Milano*, 1878. 8°. **4856**. aa. **3**.

BUSNOSARMAN. *See* VISHNUSARMAN.

BUSNOT (DOMINIQUE) [Histoire du règne de Mouley Ismael.] The History of the Reign of Muley Ismael, the present King of Morocco, Fez, Tafilet, Sous &c. . . . Translated from the French. pp. 250. *A. Bell; J. Baker: London*, 1715. 12°. **279**. b. **24**.

BUSNOT-LALANDE (A. CÉLESTE) Des abcès de l'avant-bras, suite de panaris et de plaies des doigts, spécialement du pouce et de l'auriculaire. pp. 27. *Paris*, 1856. 4°. [*Collection des thèses soutenues à la Faculté de Médecine de Paris*. An 1856. tom. 4.] **7372**. i. **4**.

BUSNOUT (CHARLES) Dissertation sur la rage, *etc.* pp. 45. *Paris*, 1814. 4°. **1182**. i. **14**. (**18**.)

BUSOLLI (GIUSEPPE) F. D. Guerrazzi. Ritratto, con appendice bibliografica. pp. 72. *Parma*, 1912. 8°. **10600**. ccc. **21**. (**5**.)

BUSOLLI (GIUSEPPE)

—— Gabriele d'Annunzio e sua evoluzione poetica. pp. 52. *Treviso*, 1902. 8°. **11853**. aa. **30**.

BUSOLT (GEORG) Forschungen zur griechischen Geschichte. Tl. 1. pp. 181. *Breslau*, 1880. 8°. **9026**. g. **3**.
No more published.

—— Griechische Geschichte bis zur Schlacht bei Chaironeia. Bd. 1, 2 ; Bd. 3. Tl. 1, 2. *Gotha*, 1885–1904. 8°. [*Handbücher der alten Geschichte*." Ser. 2. Abt. 1.] **9012**. ee. **1/7**.
No more published.

—— Zweite vermehrte und völlig umgearbeitete Auflage. Bd. 1, 2, Bd. 3. Tl. 1, 2. *Gotha*, 1893–1904. 8°. [*Handbücher der alten Geschichte*. ser. 2. Abt. 1.] **9012**. ee. **1/8**.
Bd. 1, 2 *only are of the second edition. Bd.* 3 *is another copy of Bd.* 3 *of the preceding. No more published.*

—— *See* SCHJOTT (P. O.) Det atheniensiske demokrati. [A review of G. Busolt's "Griechische Geschichte," Bd. 3. Tl. 1.] 1902. 8°. [*Christiania Videnskabs-Selskabs forhandlinger*. 1902. no. 5.] Ac. **1054**.

—— Staats- und Rechtsaltertümer. *See* GREEK-STATE ANTIQUITIES. Die griechischen Staats-, Kriegs- und Privataltertümer, *etc.* 1887. 8°. [*Handbuch der klassischen Altertums-Wissenschaft*. Bd. 4. Abt. 1.] **07702**. dd.

—— Die griechischen Staats- und Rechtsaltertümer . . . Zweite umgearbeitete und sehr vermehrte Auflage. pp. viii. 384. *München*, 1892. 8°. [*Handbuch der klassischen Altertums-Wissenschaft*. Bd. 4. Abt. 1. Hälfte 1.] **07702**. dd.

—— Griechische Staatskunde . . . Dritte, neugestaltete Auflage der Griechischen Staats- und Rechtsaltertümer. (Zweite Hälfte. Darstellung einzelner Staaten und der zwischenstaatlichen Beziehungen bearbeitet von Dr. Heinrich Swoboda.] 2 vol. *München*, 1920, 26. 8°. [*Handbuch der klassischen Altertumswissenschaft*. Bd. 4. Abt. 1.] **2071.c.**

—— Die Grundzüge der Erkenntnisstheorie und Metaphysik Spinozas, dargestellt, erläutert und gewürdigt von Dr. G. Busolt, *etc.* pp. 186. *Berlin*, 1875. 8°. **8469**. b. **16**.

—— Die Lakedaimonier und ihre Bundesgenossen. Erster Band. Bis zur Begründung der athenischen Seehegemonie. pp. viii. 486. *Leipzig*, 1878. 8°. **9026**. ff. **5**.
No more published.

—— Der zweite athenische Bund und die auf der Autonomie beruhende, hellenische Politik von der Schlacht bei Knidos bis zum Frieden des Eubulos. Mit einer Einleitung: Zur Bedeutung der Autonomie in hellenischen Bundesverfassungen. 1875. *See* PERIODICAL PUBLICATIONS.—*Leipsic*. Jahrbücher für Philologie und Pädagogik, *etc.* (Jahrbücher für classische Philologie. Bd. 7. Hft. 4.) 1826, *etc.* 8°. P.P. **4986**.

BUSONE [RAFFAELLI], *da Gubbio*. *See* RAFFAELLI (Bosone)

BUSONI (DEMETRIO) and **ZAMBELLI** (ANDREA) Sulla distribuzione nei motori a vapore ottenuta mediante un solo cassetto. Studj analitici e grafici. pp. 148. *Venezia*, 1871. 8°. **8530**. f. **6**.

BUSONI (FERRUCCIO BENVENUTO) *See* BREITKOPF UND HAERTEL. Ferruccio Busoni. Werk-Verzeichnis. Auf Grund der Aufzeichnungen Busonis zusammengestellt und herausgegeben von seinen Verlegern. [1924.] 8°. **11907**. aa. **30**.

—— *See* DENT (Edward J.) Ferruccio Busoni. A biography. [With portraits.] 1933. 8°. **10633**. v. **13**.

—— *See* GUERRINI (G.) Ferruccio Busoni, *etc.* [With a list of Busoni's compositions and with portraits.] 1944. 8°. **10630**. l. **16**.

—— *See* JELMOLI (H.) Ferruccio Busonis Zürcherjahre. [With a portrait.] [1929.] 4°. [*Hundertundsiebenzehntes Neujahrsblatt der Allgemeinen Musikgesellschaft in Zürich auf das Jahr* 1929.] Hirsch IV. **1135c**.

—— *See* LEICHTENTRITT (H.) Ferruccio Busoni . . . Mit einem Bildnis. [With a "Verzeichnis der veröffentlichten Kompositionen, der Bearbeitungen, Essays und anderer literarischen Arbeiten von F. Busoni."] 1916. 8°. Hirsch **2831**.

—— *See* LEICHTENTRITT (H.) Ferruccio Busoni . . . 1948. 8°. **7899**. bbb. **48**.

—— *See* NADEL (S. F.) Writer on Music. Ferruccio Busoni . . . Mit einem Bildnis und einem Faksimile. 1931. 8°. **10633**. b. **47**.

—— *See* PONNELLE (L.) A Munich . . . Ferruccio Busoni. 1913. 8°. **7896**. tt. **28**.

—— *See* SELDEN-GOTH (G.) Ferruccio Busoni, *etc.* [With a portrait.] 1922. 8°. **7894**. de. **31**.

—— *See* WASSERMANN (C. J.) In memoriam Ferruccio Busoni. (Mit einer Lichtdruckwiedergabe von Busonis Handschrift "Schlussmonolog der Dichtung Doktor Faust" [and with a portrait].) 1925. 8°. Hirsch **2833**.

—— Scritti e pensieri sulla musica. A cura di Luigi Dallapiccola e Guido M. Gatti, *etc.* [With plates, including portraits.] pp. xii. 142. *Firenze*, 1941. 8°. **7889**. c. **3**.

—— Busoni. Briefe an seine Frau. Herausgegeben von Friedrich Schnapp. Mit einem Vorwort von Willi Schuh. [With plates, including portraits.] pp. xxvi. 404. *Zürich, Leipzig*, [1935.] 8°. **010920**. c. **11**.

—— [Another copy.] Busoni. Briefe an seine Frau, *etc.* *Erlenbach-Zürich, Leipzig*, [1935.] 8°. Hirsch **2826**.

—— Fünfundzwanzig Busoni-Briefe. Eingeleitet und herausgegeben von Gisella Selden-Goth. [With plates.] pp. 77. *Wien*, 1937. 8°. **010921**. e. **3**.

—— [Another copy.] Fünfundzwanzig Busoni-Briefe, eingeleitet und herausgegeben von Gisella Selden-Goth. *Wien*, 1937. 8°. Hirsch **2827**.

—— Briefe Busonis au Hans Huber. Herausgegeben von Edgar Refardt. [With portraits.] pp. 48. *Zürich & Leipzig*, 1939. 8°. [*Hundertsiebenundzwanzigstes Neujahrsblatt der Allgemeinen Musikgesellschaft in Zürich auf das Jahr* 1939.] Hirsch IV. **1135c**.

—— [Another copy.] Briefe Busonis an Hans Huber. *Zürich, Leipzig*, 1939. 8°. [*Hundertsiebenundzwanzigstes Neujahrsblatt der Allgemeinen Musikgesellschaft in Zürich auf das Jahr* 1939.] Ac. **5132**.

BUSONI (Ferruccio Benvenuto)

—— Ferruccio Busoni: Letters to his Wife. Translated by Rosamond Ley. [With plates, including portraits.] pp. 319. *E. Arnold & Co.: London,* 1938. 8°. **10922.** c. **2.**

—— Arlecchino, oder Die Fenster. Ein theatralisches Capriccio, *etc.* pp. 25. *Leipzig,* [1917.] 12°. [*Breitkopf & Härtels Textbibliothek.* no. 413.] **11747.** ccc. **1/413.**

—— [A reissue.] Arlecchino, *etc.* *Leipzig,* [c. 1920.] 8°. Hirsch **5672.** (**3.**)

—— Die Brautwahl. Musikalisch-phantastische Komödie in drei Akten und einem Nachspiel nach E. T. A. Hoffmanns Erzählung, *etc.* pp. 86. *Leipzig & Berlin,* [1928.] 8°. [*Breitkopf & Härtels Textbibliothek.* no. 434.] **11747.** ccc. **1/434.**

—— Doktor Faust, *etc.* pp. 43. *Leipzig,* [1925.] 8°. [*Breitkopf & Härtels Textbibliothek.* no. 431.] **11747.** ccc. **1/431.**

—— Doktor Faust. Dichtung für Musik, *etc.* [The words only.] pp. 52. *Potsdam,* 1920. 8°. Hirsch **5683.** (**1.**)

—— [Another copy.] Doktor Faust, *etc.* *Leipzig,* [1925.] 8°. Hirsch **5672.** (**1.**)

—— Entwurf einer neuen Ästhetik der Tonkunst. Zweite, erweiterte Ausgabe. pp. 48. *Leipzig,* [1916.] 8°. [*Insel-Bücherei.* no. 202.] Hirsch **5386.**

—— [A reissue.] Entwurf einer neuen Ästhetik der Tonkunst, *etc.* (11.–20. Tausend.) *Leipzig,* [c. 1920.] 8°. [*Insel-Bücherei.* no. 202.] **012213.** de. **1/202.**

—— [Entwurf einer neuen Aesthetik der Tonkunst.] Sketch of a New Esthetic of Music . . . Translated from the German by Dr. Th. Baker. pp. 45. *G. Schirmer: New York,* 1911. 8°. **7896.** r. **24.**

—— *See* Pfitzner (H. E.) Futuristengefahr. Bei Gelegenheit von Busoni's Ästhetik [*sic*]. [On Busoni's "Entwurf einer neuen Ästhetik der Tonkunst."] 1917. 8°. Hirsch **4218.**

—— Turandot. Eine chinesische Fabel nach Gozzi in zwei Akten, *etc.* pp. 27. *Leipzig,* [1917.] 12°. [*Breitkopf & Härtels Textbibliothek.* no. 412.] **11747.** ccc. **1/412.**

—— [A reissue.] Turandot, *etc.* *Leipzig,* [c. 1920.] 8°. Hirsch **5672.** (**2.**)

—— Über die Möglichkeiten der Oper und über die Partitur des "Doktor Faust." [Two essays.] pp. 46. *Leipzig,* 1926. 8°. Hirsch **2828.**

—— Von der Einheit der Musik . . . Verstreute Aufzeichnungen von F. Busoni. Mit einem Verzeichnisse seiner Werke und vier Handzeichnungen. pp. vii. 376. *Berlin,* 1922. 8°. **07896.** de. **8.**

—— [Another copy.] Von der Einheit der Musik . . . Verstreute Aufzeichnungen, *etc.* *Berlin,* [1922.] 8°. Hirsch **2829.**

—— Das Wandbild. Eine Szene und eine Pantomime, *etc.* pp. 15. *Leipzig,* [1920.] 8°. [*Breitkopf & Härtels Textbibliothek.* no. 418.] **11747.** ccc. **1/418.**

BUSONI (Philippe) *Chef de division à la Préfecture de la Seine,* and **HUBERSON** (G.) Textes organiques de droit public administratif et civil, *etc.* (tom. 1. Recueillis, collationnés et mis en ordre par MM. P. Busoni, G. Huberson . . . Deuxième édition, revue et augmentée. —tom. 2–4. Recueillis et mis en ordre par M. G. Huberson.) 4 tom. *Paris,* 1883, 85. 8°. **5424.** de. **11.**
Tom. 1 *only is of the second edition.*

BUSONI (Philippe) *Miscellaneous Writer.* *See* Brizeux (J. A. P.) and Busoni (P.) Racine. Comédie, *etc.* 1828. 8°. **11738.** a. **36.** (**4.**)

—— Notice sur Charlotte-Élisabeth de Bavière, princesse palatine, duchesse d'Orléans. *See* Elizabeth Charlotte [of Bavaria], *Duchess d'Orléans.* Mémoires, *etc.* 1832. 8°. **10660.** dd. **18.**

BUSONI (Rafaello)

—— *See* Balzac (H. de) [*Single Works.*] Old Man Goriot . . . Illustrated by R. Busoni. [1949.] 8°. **12607.f.1/2.**

—— *See* Fish (Helen D.) Pegs of History . . . Drawings by R. Busoni, *etc.* 1943. 4°. **09009.** cc. **17.**

—— Lands and Peoples . . . Written and illustrated by R. Busoni. *Cassell & Co.: London,* 1939– . 8°. W.P. **10055.**

—— Somi builds a Church. A story from Lapland written and illustrated by R. Busoni. pp. 106. *Frederick Muller: London,* 1948. 8°. **04413.** i. **130.**

BUSOV (Konrad) *See* Bussow (Conrad)

BUSQUET (Alfred) *See* Ephemerides. [Almanach-album des célébrités contemporaines] po[ur] 1870. [Edited by A. Busquet.] [1869.] 8°. P.P. **2404.** o.

—— La Comédie du renard. Comédie en deux actes. pp. 154. *Paris,* 1885. 8°. **11740.** aaa. **3.**

—— La Nuit de Noël, poème. Christmas carol. pp. 64. *Paris,* 1861. 4°. **11481.** cc. **15.**
The wrapper bears the words: "*Première année.*"

BUSQUET (Bruno) Réflexions sur les pertes utérines qui surviennent vers le dernier temps de la grossesse pendant et après l'accouchement. Tribut académique, *etc.* pp. 27. *Montpellier,* 1815. 4°. **1180.** h. **2.** (**5.**)

BUSQUET (G. Paul) Les Êtres vivants. Organisation. Évolution. pp. 181. *Paris,* 1899. 8°. **7006.** f. **29.**

—— Étude morphologique d'un cryptogame nouveau trouvé dans une lésion circinée de la main. Thèse, *etc.* pp. 44. *Paris,* 1890. 4°. **07305.** l. **5.** (**2.**)

BUSQUET (Léon) Le Canal des Deux Mers et le chemin de fer à navires. pp. 6. *Bordeaux,* 1888. 8°. **08235.** h. **11.** (**3.**)

—— Études sur les Landes de la Gironde. pp. 64. *Bordeaux,* 1861. 8°. **10173.** bbb. **33.** (**1.**)

—— Manuel de hirudiculture ou de l'élève des sangsues. pp. 180. *Bordeaux,* 1854. 8°. **7461.** d. **3.**

—— La Triste fin du Canal des Deux Mers. pp. 2. *Bordeaux,* 1888. 8°. **08235.** h. **11.** (**2.**)

BUSQUET (Pierre Félix) De l'emploi de l'eau froide dans les maladies chirurgicales. pp. 35. *Paris,* 1849. 4°. [*Collection des thèses soutenues à la Faculté de Médecine de Paris.* An 1849. tom. 2.] **7372.** c. **2.**

BUSQUET (Raoul)

—— *See* Bouches-du-Rhône, *Department of the.* Les Fonds des Archives départementales des Bouches-du-Rhône, archives centrales de Provence, *etc.* (Vol. 1. Dépôt principal de Marseille. Séries anciennes A à F; Vol. 2. pt. 1. Dépôt annexe d'Aix-en-Provence. Série B. [By R. Busquet].) 1937, *etc.* 8°. **W.P. 1668.**

—— *See* Bouches-du-Rhône, *Department of the.* Inventaire des documents sur l'histoire religieuse de la Restauration . . . Par M. R. Busquet. 1913. 8°. [*Comité des Travaux Historiques. Notices, etc.* vol. 1.] **Ac. 437/7.**

—— *See* Bouches-du-Rhône, *Department of the.* Inventaire des archives départementales postérieures à 1789. (sér. L. Documents de la période révolutionnaire. tom. 3. Par M. R. Busquet . . . et M. J.-B. Riboulet.) 1889, *etc.* 4°. **S. 148. a. 14.**

—— *See* Bouches-du-Rhône, *Department of the.* Archives départementales des Bouches-du-Rhône. (Répertoire numérique de la série G . . . Dressé . . . sous la direction de M. R. Busquet.—Répertoire numérique de la série U. Justice. Dressé par M. R. Busquet.—Répertoire numérique de la série V. Cultes. Dressé par M. R. Busquet.) 1910, *etc.* 4°. **S. 148. a. 14.**

—— *See* Bouches-du-Rhône, *Department of the.—Conseil Général.* Les Bouches-du-Rhône, *etc.* (tom. 2. Antiquité et moyen âge. Par V. L. Bourrilly, R. Busquet, *etc.*—tom. 3. Les Temps modernes, 1482–1789. Par G. Arnaud d'Agnel . . . R. Busquet, *etc.*—tom. 5. La Vie politique et administrative. Par R. Busquet, J. Fournier.) 1932, *etc.* fol. **10167. r. 1/2, 3, 5.**

—— *See* Bourrilly (V. L.) and Busquet (R.) La Provence au moyen âge, *etc.* 1924. 8°. **9210. g. 9.**

—— *See* Richaud (Louis) *of Toulon.* Mémoires de Louis Richaud sur la révolte de Toulon et l'Émigration. Annotés et publiés par MM. R. Busquet . . . B. Roberty, *etc.* 1930. 8°. [*Bibliothèque de l'Institut Historique de Provence.* tom. 8.] **Ac. 6770.**

—— Le Commerce de Marseille dans l'antiquité. [With plates and maps.] *In:* Rambert (G.) Histoire du commerce de Marseille. vol. 1. pp. 1–105. 1949. 8°. **W.P. 3438.**

—— Étude historique sur le collège de Fortet, 1394–1764. 2 tom. 1906, 07. *See* Paris.—*Société de l'Histoire de Paris et de l'Île de France.* Mémoires, *etc.* tom. 33, 34. 1875, *etc.* 8°. **Ac. 6883/2.**

—— Études sur l'ancienne Provence. Institutions et points d'histoire. pp. 338. *Paris*, 1930. 8°. **010169. h. 32.**

—— [Another issue.] *Marseille*, 1930. 8°. [*Bibliothèque de l'Institut Historique de Provence.* vol. 9.] **Ac. 6770.**

—— Histoire de Marseille . . . VIe édition. [With plates.] pp. 476. *Paris*, 1945. 8°. **010171. pp. 16.**

—— La "Justice souveraine" de Marseille, 1593–1596, *etc.* [With plates.] pp. 30. *Marseille*, 1925. 8°. **10167. ee. 18.**

—— Légendes, traditions, et récits de la Provence d'autrefois. pp. 252. *Paris*, 1933. 8°. **010169. ee. 64.**

BUSQUET (Raymond) *See* Rodet (J.) and Busquet (R.) Les Courants polyphasés. 1894. 8°. [*Annales de la Société d'Agriculture, Sciences et Industrie de Lyon.* sér. 7. tom. 1.] **Ac. 362/3.**

BUSQUET (Raymond)

—— [Précis d'hydraulique.] A Manual of Hydraulics . . . Translated by A. H. Peake. pp. viii. 312. *Edward Arnold: London*, 1906. 8°. **08767. de. 36.**

—— Traité d'électricité industrielle. 2 tom. *Paris*, 1900. 8°. **8758. b. 39.**

BUSQUETS (Luis Vermell y) *See* Vermell y Busquets.

BUSQUETS Y PUNSET (Anton) *See* Verdaguer (J.) La Mellor Corona. Poesies . . . Aplegades y ordenades per N'A. Busquets y Punset, *etc.* 1902. 8°. **11452. cc. 10.**

BUSQUOY, Charles Bonaventure de Longueval, *Count de.* *See* Longueval (C. B. de) *Count de Bucquoy* and *de Gratzen.*

BUSRAI (Ebrahim Esoofally) *See* Ibrāhīm Yūsuf 'Alī Busrā'ī.

BUSS-PSALM. Buss-Psalm nach dem Feuer. Donnerstag den 7. Juli 1842. [1842.] 8°. **11528. cc. 20. (3.)**

BUSS (   ) *Naturarzt.* Frauenkrankheiten. Ihr Wesen und ihre operationslose Heilung. Vortrag, *etc.* pp. 16. *Im Selbstverlage des Verfassers: [London,]* 1905. 8°. **7307. df. 3. (2.)**

BUSS (Al.) Křivoklát. Průvodce po hradě a jeho okolí . . . K tisku upravil, doplnil a illustracemi opatřil P. Körber. pp. 36. *v Praze*, 1905. 8°. [*Körbrův illustrovaný průvodce.* seš. 3.] **10215. de. 1/3.**

BUSS (Arthur Herbert) The Real Object of Life. pp. xiv. 209. *Elliot Stock: London*, 1916. 8°. **04376. f. 41.**

BUSS (Carl Emil) Über Wesen und Behandlung des Fiebers. Klinisch-experimentelle Untersuchungen, *etc.* pp. vi. 246. pl. IX. *Stuttgart*, 1878. 8°. **7560. f. 12.**

BUSS (Claude Albert)

—— The Far East. A history of recent and contemporary international relations in East Asia. pp. viii. 738. *Macmillan Co.: New York*, [1955.] 8°. **09057. dd. 31.**

—— The Setting of American Economic Policy toward the Philippines. *In:* Jenkins (Shirley) American Economic Policy toward the Philippines, *etc.* pp. 1–24. [1954.] 8°. **08218. c. 9.**

—— War and Diplomacy in Eastern Asia. [With maps.] pp. xi. 570. *Macmillan Co.: New York*, 1941. 8°. **08023. d. 59.**

BUSS (Ernst) Der Bergsturz von Elm den 11. September 1881. Denkschrift von E. Buss . . . und Albert Heim, *etc.* [With plates and maps.] pp. 163. *Zürich*, 1881. 8°. **10196. f. 5.**

—— Die Bildung des Volkes im Kanton Bern. pp. 30. *Bern*, 1873. 8°. **10108. bb. 1. (4.)**

—— Die christliche Mission, ihre principielle Berechtigung und practische Durchführung, *etc.* pp. x. 352. *Leiden*, 1876. 8°. **4765. ee. 2.**

—— Die ersten 25 Jahre des Schweizer Alpenclub. Denkschrift, *etc.* [With tables.] pp. 240. 1889. 8°. *See* Switzerland.—*Schweizer Alpenclub.* **10196. b. 7.**

BUSS (Ernst)

—— [Glarnerland und Walensee.] Canton Glarus and the Lake of Wallenstadt, *etc.* [With plates.] pp. 143. *Orell Füssli & Co.: Zurich; C. Smith & Son: London,* [1887.] 8°. [*Illustrated Europe.* no. 69–72.] **10108.** de. **18.**

—— Der Volksaberglaube, *etc.* pp. 36. *Basel,* 1881. 8°. [*Oeffentliche Vorträge gehalten in der Schweiz.* Bd. 6. Hft. 8.] **12201.** e. **1.**

BUSS (Frances Mary) *See* Burstall (Sara A.) Frances Mary Buss, an Educational Pioneer, *etc.* [With a portrait.] 1938. 8°. **10858.** a. **1.**

—— *See* Holmes (Marion) Frances Mary Buss, *etc.* [With a portrait.] [1913.] 8°. **010803.** ee. **4.** (**7.**)

—— *See* London.—iii. *North London Collegiate School for Girls.* In Memoriam. Frances Mary Buss, obiit Christmas Eve, 1894. [With a portrait.] [1895.] 4°. **4804.** i. **20.** (**1.**)

—— *See* London.—iii. *North London Collegiate School for Girls.* The North London Collegiate School, 1850–1950 . . . Essays in honour of the centenary of the Frances Mary Buss Foundation. [With portraits.] 1950. 8°. **08368.** b. **35.**

—— *See* Ridley (Annie E.) Frances Mary Buss and her Work for Education . . . With portraits, *etc.* 1895. 8°. **4906.** de. **34.**

—— —— 1896. 8°. **4907.** f. **6.**

—— Leaves from the Note-Books of Frances M. Buss: being selections from her weekly addresses to the girls of the North London Collegiate School. Edited by Grace Toplis. pp. vi. 168. *Macmillan & Co.: London,* 1896. 8°. **8409.** d. **19.**

—— "Frances Mary Buss Memorial." [*London,* 1895.] 4°. **10604.** f. **18.** (**2.**)

BUSS (Franz Joseph von) *See* Gérando (J. M. de) *Baron.* System der gesammten Armenpflege. Nach den Werken des Herrn von Gérando und nach eigenen Ansichten von Dr. F. J. Buss. 1843, *etc.* 8°. **8285.** dd. **10.**

—— *See* Maciejowski (W. A.) Slavische Rechtsgeschichte . . . übersetzt von F. J. Buss, und von M. Nawrocki, *etc.* 1835, *etc.* 8°. **1378.** i. **2.**

—— *See* Rask (R. C.) [Frisisk Sproglære.] Frisische Sprachlehre . . . Aus dem Dänischen übersetzt, und mit einem Vorwort . . . begleitet von Dr. F. J. Buss. 1834. 8°. **829.** g. **22.**

—— *See* Story (Joseph) *One of the Justices of the Supreme Court of the United States.* Ueber die Verfassungs-Urkunde der Vereinigten Staaten von Nord-Amerika. Historischer Theil nach Story's Commentarien bearbeitet [by F. J. von Buss]. 1838. 8°. **8176.** b. **40.**

—— Ansprache der grossdeutschen Abgeordneten Westfalens im Erfurter Parlament an ihre Wähler. Herausgegeben von J. F. Buss . . . Mit einer gehaltenen und einer nicht gehaltenen Rede desselben. pp. xvi. 90. *Paderborn,* 1850. 8°. **8072.** ee. **18.**

—— Geschichte und System der Staatswissenschaft . . . Von Dr. F. J. Buss und G. Ph. Hepp. [With plates.] 3 Tl. *Freiburg* [*i. B.*], *Karlsruhe,* 1839. 8°. **8005.** e. **7.**

BUSS (Franz Joseph von)

—— Die Gesellschaft Jesu, ihr Zweck, ihre Satzungen, Geschichte, Aufgabe und Stellung in der Gegenwart. 2 Abt. pp. x. v [iv]–viii. 1726. *Mainz,* 1853. 8°. **4091.** f. **7.**

—— Der heilige Thomas, Erzbischof von Canterbury und Primas von ganz England, und sein Kampf für die Freiheit der Kirche. pp. xxviii. 720. *Mainz,* 1856. 8°. **4827.** d. **10.**

—— Die Methodologie des Kirchenrechts zur Feststellung einer richtigen Behandlungsweise dieser Wissenschaft, *etc.* pp. 184. *Freiburg i. B.,* 1842. 8°. **5125.** aa. **15.**

—— Österreich's Umbau in Kirche und Staat. Tl. 1. Abt. 1. pp. xxviii. 496. *Wien,* 1862. 8°. **3911.** cc. **47.** *No more published.*

—— Praktische Zeitschrift für die Freiheit und Entwicklung der katholischen Kirche in der oberrheinischen Kirchenprovinz. Jahrg. 1. Hft. 1. pp. 152. 1847. 8°. *See* Periodical Publications.—*Schaffhausen.* P.P. **86.** e.

—— Rechtfertigung des Anspruchs Tirols auf seine Glaubenseinheit. pp. xxvi. 198. *Innsbruck,* 1863. 8°. **5125.** aaa. **11.**

—— Ueber den Einfluss des Christenthums auf Recht und Staat . . . Ein Versuch in drei Büchern . . . 1. Theil. Von der Stiftung der Kirche bis zu den ersten Reformstrebungen in der abendländischen Kirche. pp. lxxxviii. 294. *Freiburg i. B.,* 1841. 8°. **3910.** ee. **1.** *No more published.*

—— Der Unterschied der katholischen und der protestantischen Universitäten Teutschlands, die Nothwendigkeit der Verstärkung der dortigen sechs katholischen Universitäten gegenüber den sechzehn protestantischen, insbesondere der Erhebung der ihrem katholischen Princip entrückten Universität Freiburg zu einer grossen rein katholischen Universität teutscher Nation. pp. vii. 528. *Freiburg i. B.,* 1846. 8°. **8355.** d. **25.**

—— Vergleichendes Bundesstaatsrecht von Nordamerika, Teutschland und der Schweiz. (Bd. 1. Das Bundesstaatsrecht der Vereinigten Staaten Nordamerika's. Nach J. Story's Commentaries on the Constitution of the United States.) pp. xxix. 833. *Karlsruhe,* 1844. 8°. **1389.** k. **16.**

No more published.

—— Winfrid-Bonifacius. Aus dem literarischen Nachlasse von Dr. F. J. von Buss . . . Herausgegeben von Dr. Rudolf Ritter von Scherer. pp. viii. 396. *Graz,* 1880. 8°. **4829.** aa. **12.**

BUSS (Frederick) A Practical Treatise on the Fuchsia . . . Illustrated. pp. 63. *E. W. Allen: London,* 1883. 8°. **1146.** f. **26.** (**2.**)

BUSS (Frederick Harold)

—— The Fruit of the Light. [Religious essays.] pp. 127. *Epworth Press: London,* 1949. 8°. **4397.** bb. **3.**

BUSS (Frederick Harold) and **BURNETT** (Richard George)

—— A Goodly Fellowship. A history of the hundred years of the Methodist Local Preachers Mutual Aid Association: 1849–1949. [With plates.] pp. 223. *Epworth Press: London,* 1949. 8°. **4716.** aa. **22.**

BUSS (Georg) Die Frau im Kunstgewerbe. *Berlin*, 1895. 8º. [*Der Existenzkampf der Frau im modernen Leben.* Hft. 4.] **8416**. g. **46**.

BUSS (Hans)

—— Aus der Entwicklung der Räder für Lastwagen und Omnibusse, *etc.* pp. xii. 176. *Schaffhausen*, [1952.] fol. **8764**. m. **1**.
Part of the "Schriftenreihe zum hundertfünfzigjährigen Bestehen der Georg Fischer-Werke."

BUSS (Hugh) *See* Wyld (Henry C.) The Universal Dictionary of the English Language . . With an appendix by H. Buss. 1936. 4º. **12984**. v. **15**.

BUSS (J. P.) *See* Germany. [*Laws, etc.*—I.] Amerikanische Menschlichkeit im Lichte des diplomatischen Notenwechsels. Erste Veröffentlichung und Bearbeitung des gesamten deutsch-amerikanischen Notenwechsels. Von J. P. Buss. [1917.] 8º. **08028**. i. **1/16**.

—— Die italienische Frage und die Zentralmächte im letzten Jahrhundert bis zur Gegenwart. pp. 75. *Diessen*, 1916. 8º. **09076**. cc. **2**.

BUSS (James Frederick) *See* New Jerusalem Church. Manual for Junior Members and Young People of the New Church . . . Edited by . . . J. F. Buss [and others], *etc.* 1903. 8º. **3716**. de. **12**.

—— *See* New Jerusalem Church.—*New-Church Home Reading Union.* Solutions of Questions and Difficulties presented by the Members during 1890, *etc.* (Writer of the solutions: J. F. Buss.) 1891, *etc.* 8º. **3716**. df. **22**.

—— *See* Periodical Publications.—*London.* The New-Church Quarterly. (Editor: J. F. Buss.) 1910, *etc.* 8º. P.P. **570**. aa.

—— *See* Swedenborg (E.) [*Two or more Works.*] The Coronis . . . then also "The Invitation to the New Church," *etc.* (J. F. Buss, editor and reviser.) 1931. 8º. **3716**. e. **21**.

—— *See* Swedenborg (E.) [*De Commercio Animae et Corporis.*] De commercio animæ et corporis, *etc.* [The editors' preface signed: F. B., L. G., i.e. J. F. Buss and L. Gilbey.] 1935. 8º. **3716**. ccc. **47**.

—— *See* Swedenborg (E.) [*De Equo Albo.*] De equo albo de quo in Apocalypsi, Cap: XIX, *etc.* [The editor's preface signed: F. B., i.e. J. F. Buss.] 1934. 8º. **3716**. ccc. **50**.

—— *See* Swedenborg (E.) [*De Scriptura Sacra, seu Verbo Domini, ab Experientia.*] De Verbo. The Sacred Scripture or Word of the Lord from Experience, *etc.* (A revision, by J. F. Buss, of the translation by J. Whitehead.) [1935?] 8º. **3716.ccc.56.**

—— *See* Swedenborg (E.) [*De Telluribus.*] De telluribus in mundo nostro solari, quæ vocantur planetæ, *etc.* [The editor's preface signed: F. B., i.e. J. F. Buss.] 1934. 8º. **3716**. ccc. **51**.

—— *See* Swedenborg (E.) [*Diarium Spirituale.*] The Spiritual Diary of Emanuel Swedenborg, *etc.* (vol. 4. Translated by G. Bush and J. F. Buss.—vol. 5. Translated by J. F. Buss.) 1883, *etc.* 8º. **3716**. g. **3**.

BUSS (James Frederick)

—— *See* Swedenborg (E.) [*Vera Christiana Religio.—Coronis.*] The Coronis . . . From the Latin of E. Swedenborg [by J. F. Buss]. 1893. 8º. **3716**. g. **14**.

—— *See* Swedenborg (E.) [*Selections.*] The Ten Commandments: their Christian Significance . . . Compiled by Rev. J. F. Buss. 1933. 8º. **3716**. ccc. **43**.

—— The Attitude of Modern Christendom towards Christ: a lecture. pp. 23. *James Speirs: London*, 1884. 8º. **3716**. aa. **23**. (**7**.)

—— The Criterion of Divine Authorship. pp. viii. 324. *New Church Press: London*, 1920. 8º. **03127**. h. **27**.

—— The Jewish Sacrifices in their relation to the Atonement. A study in two parts. pp. 36. *James Speirs: London*, 1902. 8º. **4373**. df. **6**. (**3**.)

—— Swedenborg: his life, character and mission. pp. 36. *James Speirs: London*, 1887. 8º. **3716**. aa. **28**. (**9**.)

—— Swedenborg's Solution of the Problems underlying Modern Biblical Criticism. A paper, *etc.* pp. 22. *Scottish New Church Evidence Society: Paisley*, 1903. 8º. **3716**. b. **23**.

—— The Uses and Benefits of the Holy Supper. pp. 16. *New-Church Press: London*, 1931. 8º. **4324**. f. **58**.

—— What the New Church Teaches. [Reprinted from "The New Church Magazine."] pp. vi. 190. *James Speirs: London*, 1897. 8º. **3716**. g. **18**.

BUSS (Joseph Franz) *See* Buss (Franz J. von)

BUSS (Kate) Studies in the Chinese Drama. [With plates.] pp. 77. *Four Seas Co.: Boston*, 1922. 8º. **011795**. d. **33**.

BUSS (Maria E.) Child-Drunkenness. [A letter by M. E. Buss, reprinted from the "Daily News"; with a commentary thereon, reprinted from the "Manchester Courier."] pp. 4. *Page & Pratt: London*, [1892.] 8º. **8435**. e. **24**. (**17**.)

—— Passing Thoughts. [In verse.] pp. vi. 55. *Elliot Stock: London*, 1900. 8º. **011651**. ee. **49**.

BUSS (Octavius) Hazard Whist. A new card game for 2, 3 or 4 players. Invented by O. Buss. *Geo. Wells: London*, [1906.] 8º. **7913**. de. **52**.

BUSS (Onko) Die Ganzheitspsychologie Felix Kruegers. Methodische Grundgedanken und grundlegende Ergebnisse. pp. viii. 60. *München*, 1934. 8º. **08466**. g. **66**.

BUSS (Robert William) *See* Dickens (Charles) [*Pickwick Papers.*] The Posthumous Papers of the Pickwick Club . . . With illustrations by . . . R. W. Buss [and others]. 1887. 8º. **012611**. l. **7**.

—— *See* Ephemerides. The Almanack of the Fine Arts . . . Edited by R. W. Buss. 1850, *etc.* 12º. P.P. **2495**. b.

—— *See* Marryat (Frederick) Jacob Faithful . . . With . . . plates . . . by R. W. Buss, *etc.* 1928. 8º. **012614**. i. **5**.

—— *See* Marryat (Frederick) Peter Simple . . . With . . . plates . . . by R. W. Buss, *etc.* 1929. 8º. **012601**. l. **8**.

BUSS (Robert William)

—— English Graphic Satire and its relation to different styles of painting, sculpture and engraving. A contribution to the history of the English school of art. The . . . illustrations selected and drawn from the originals by R. W. Buss, *etc.* pp. xx. 195. *Printed for the Author: London*, 1874. 4°. **7856**. eee. **16**.
For private circulation.

BUSS (Robert Woodward) The Ancestry of William Fleetwood, Bishop of St. Asaph and Ely. With a pedigree. pp. 7. *The Author: London*, 1926. 4°. **9907**. b. **13**.
No. 7 *of an edition of* 100 *copies.*

—— The Family of Fleetwood of Calwich, co. Stafford. With a pedigree and a discussion of the assumed failure of the male line. By R. W. B. [i.e. R. W. Buss.] 2 pt. 1908. 8° & fol. *See* B., R. W.
09915. dd. **4**. & Cup. **649**. d. **10**. **(20.)**

—— Fleetwood Family Records. Collected and edited by R. W. Buss. [With plates, including portraits, and with genealogical tables.] 7 pt. pp. vi. 62. *Privately printed:* [*London,*] 1920 [1914–20]. fol. **9902**. i. **29**.

—— Charles Fleetwood, Holder of the Drury Lane Theatre Patent . . . Reprinted from Fleetwood Family Records. pp. 5. *Privately printed:* [*London,*] 1915. fol.
10855. h. **15**.

—— List of Persons named Fleetwood who have served in the Naval and Military Forces. (Reprinted, with . . . alterations and additions, from Fleetwood Family Records.) pp. 5. *Privately printed:* [*London,*] 1920. 4°.
9914. l. **21**.

—— Life Assurance and the War. pp. 4. *Alfred Wilson: London*, [1915.] 8°. **08228**. f. **72**.

BUSS (Septimus) Roman Law and History in the New Testament. pp. viii. 480. *Rivingtons: London*, 1901. 8°.
3226. aaa. **32**.

—— Sir Christopher Wren's Church of St. Anne & St. Agnes, Gresham Street, City. A lecture. pp. 8. *F. E. Philp: Harlesden*, 1909. 8°. **07816**. h. **23**. **(8.)**

—— Text-Book for the Church Catechism in the Book of Common Prayer. pp. viii. 127. *Rivingtons: London*, 1900. 8°. **03504**. ff. **3**.

—— Text-Book for the Morning and Evening Prayer and the Litany in the Book of Common Prayer. pp. 96. *Rivingtons: London*, 1900. 8°. **3476**. b. **15**.

—— Text-Book for the Offices for Holy Communion, Baptism, and Confirmation in the Book of Common Prayer. pp. 97–188. *Rivingtons: London*, 1900. 8°. **3476**. b. **16**.
The pagination continues that of the preceding work.

—— Text-Book for the Three Creeds in the Book of Common Prayer. pp. 148. *Rivingtons: London*, 1900. 8°.
03504. ff. **2**.

—— The Trial of Jesus illustrated from Talmud and Roman Law. pp. 125. *S.P.C.K.: London*, 1906. 8°.
04429. c. **122**.

BUSS (*Mrs.* Septimus) *See* Buss (Maria E.)

BUSS (Truman C.)

—— *See* Burke (Arthur E.) Architectural Lettering for Plans and Ornamental Design. By A. E. Burke . . . with the collaboration of T. C. Buss. 1953. 4°.
7869. t. **22**.

BUSS (Truman C.)

—— Simplified Architectural Drawing. With examples and graded problems . . . Illustrated. pp. 258. *American Technical Society: Chicago*, 1946. 4°. **7822**. d. **23**.

BUSS (W. M.) Commercial Letter-Writing. pp. 96. *Longmans & Co.: London*, 1920. 8°. **010905**. de. **29**.

—— Letters are Important. pp. 93. *Juta & Co.: Cape Town & Johannesburg*, [1949.] 8°. **012987**. aa. **76**.

BUSSA (A. L.) *See* Boucheron (C.) De Clemente Damiano Priocca narratio . . . Volgarizzato da A. L. Bussa. 1818. 4°. **1440**. k. **3**.

BUSSA (Francesca) *See* Frances [Bussa], *of Rome, Saint.*

BUSSAC (A. T.) Moyens de conserver et d'améliorer les forêts nationales et d'en accroître le produit pour toutes les espèces de services particuliers et publics. [With a folding table.] pp. 36. *Paris*, an 5 [1797 ?]. 8°.
F. 531. **(10.)**

BUSSAEUS (Andreas) *See* Jonsson (A.) Arngrimi Jonæ Grönlandia . . . nu paa Dansk fortolket af A. B. (A. Bussæus.) 1732. 8°. **572**. b. **3**.

—— *See* Thorgilsson (A.) Arii Thorgilsis filii . . . Schedæ, seu libellus de Is-landia . . . brevibus notîs & chronologiâ . . . illustratus ab A. Bussæo. 1733. 4°.
590. e. **8**.

—— Historisk Dag-Register over den stormægtigste Monarks Kong Friderich den Fierdes . . . høylovligst Ihukommelse, fornemste høystpriselige Levnets og Regierings Begivenheder og Tilfælde . . . Hvorhos er tilføyet en Beskrivelse over de historiske Medailler, som ere slagne ved adskillige Leyligheder, *etc.* [With a portrait.] pp. 395. *Kiøbenhavn*, 1770. 8°. **10760**. c. **19**.

BUSSAGLI (Mario)

—— *See* Tucci (G.) In the Library. [Book reviews by G. Tucci and M. Bussagli.] [1951 ?] 4°.
1865. c. **3**. **(83.)**

—— L'Influsso classico ed iranico sull'arte dell'Asia centrale. Ricerche preliminari per uno studio sulla pittura e la scultura centro-asiatiche. [With illustrations.] *In:* Rivista dell'Istituto Nazionale d'Archeologia e Storia d'Arte. nuova serie. anno 2. pp. 171–262. 1953. 4°.
Ac. **5237**. **(2.)**

BUSSANI (Giacomo Francesco) Anacreonte Tiranno. Drama per musica nel famoso Teatro Vendramino di San Saluatore, l'anno M.DC.LXXVIII. pp. 72.
F. Nicolini: Venetia, 1678. 12°. **905**. m. **7**. **(4.)**

—— Cesare in Egitto. Drama du rappresentarsi nel pubblico Teatro di Pesaro nell'autunno dell'anno 1729, *etc.* [By G. F. Bussani.] pp. 56. 1729. 12°. *See* Caesar (C. J.) [*Appendix.—Miscellaneous.*] **905**. l. **4**. **(4.)**

—— Enea in Italia. Drama per musica nel famoso Teatro Grimani. [With a frontispiece.] pp. 69. *Nicolini: Venetia*, 1675. 12°. **11714**. a. **9**.

—— Enea in Italia . . . [A revised edition of the work by G. F. Bussani.] Rapresentato l'anno 1676 nel Teatro del Falcone. pp. 71. [1676.] 12°. *See* Aeneas, *the Trojan.* **906**. l. **8**. **(1.)**

BUSSANI (GIACOMO FRANCESCO)

—— Il Massenzio. Dramma per musica. Rappresentato in Roma nel nuovo Teatro di Tor di Nona nel presente anno 1674, *etc.* [By G. F. Bussani?] pp. 62. 1674. 12°. *See* MAXENTIUS, *Emperor of Rome.* **906**. b. **1**. (**2**.)

—— [Another copy.] **906**. l. **6**. (**4**.)

—— Il Ratto delle Sabine. Drama per musica nell'Augusto Teatro Grimani di S. Gio. Grisostomo, *etc.* pp. 66. *F. Nicolini: Venetia,* 1680. 12°. **638**. c. **28**. (**5**.)

—— La Terra maestra de Principi. Oratione politica, e morale, *etc.* pp. 19. *I. Paci: Lucca,* 1669. 4°. **4424**. dd. **2**. (**8**.)

BUSSANI (GIOVANNI FRANCESCO) *See* BUSSANI (Giacomo F.)

BUSSANI (GIUSEPPE GIACINTO) Ragionamento primo sopra la conservazione del vino. pp. xvi. 110. *Roma,* 1787. 8°. **7074**. g. **41**. (**3**.)

BUSSARD (LÉON) and **CORBLIN** (HENRI) L'Agriculture, comprenant l'agrologie, la météorologie agricole, les cultures spéciales, la zootechnie et l'économie rurale, *etc.* pp. vi. 504. *Paris,* [1892.] 8°. **7075**. de. **22**.

—— Deuxième édition revue et corrigée. pp. vi. 508. *Paris,* [1895.] 8°. **07077**. g. **4**.

BUSSARD (ODETTE) *See* GILBERT (Marion) *pseud.* [i.e. O. Bussard.]

BUSSARD (PAUL) The Living Source. [On the religious vocation.] pp. 65. *Sheed & Ward: London,* 1936. 12°. **4403**. de. **88**.

BUSSARD (VICTOR AMÉDÉE) Revue critique des diverses théories émises sur l'inflammation de la cornée. Anatomie pathologique. pp. 60. *Paris,* 1871. 4°. [*Collection des thèses soutenues à la Faculté de Médecine de Paris.* An 1871. tom. 2.] **7373**. m. **16**.

BUSSATO (MARCO) Giardino di Agricoltura . . . Nel quale con bellissimo ordine si tratta di tutto quello, che s'appartiene à sapere à vn perfetto giardiniero, *etc.* [With woodcuts.] ff. 53. *Appresso G. Fiorina: Venetia,* 1592. 4°. **7075**. d. **14**.

—— [Another copy.] **441**. b. **6**. (**2**.)

—— [Another edition.] Aggiontoui di nuouo molti capitoli, *etc.* ff. 71. *Appresso B. Carampello: Venetia,* 1593. 4°. **235**. g. **18**.

—— [Another edition.] ff. 82. *S. Combi: Venetia,* 1612. 4°. **441**. b. **20**. (**1**.)

—— [An extract from "Giardino di agricoltura."] *See* BIDET (N.) Trattato sopra la coltivazione della vite, *etc.* 1763. 8°. [TRINCI (C.) *L'Agricoltore sperimentato.*] **234**. d. **18**.

—— Prattica historiata . . . dell'inestare gli arbori in diuersi modi, *etc.* [With woodcuts.] pp. 42. *Appresso C. Cauazza: Rauenna,* 1578. 4°. **7078**. c. **16**.

BUSSATTI (MARCO) *See* BUSSATO.

BUSSAWA SIMHA. *See* STARKEY (Samuel C.) A Dictionary, English and Punjabee . . . by Captain Starkey, assisted by Bussawa Sing, *etc.* 1849. 8°. **12906**. df. **20**.

BUSSCH (JOHANN CLAMER AUGUST VON DEM) Plans de la maison de Son Excellence Monsieur de Bussch, ministre d'état de Sa Majesté le Roi de la Grande Bretagne et électeur de Brounswig-Lünebourg à Hannovre, *etc.* pl. 13. [*Gottingen,*] 1759. fol. **59**. d. **5**.

BUSSCHAERT (PIERRE GUILLAUME) De l'ischurie ou rétention d'urine complète. Thèse, *etc.* pp. 51. *Montpellier,* 1844. 4°. **1182**. d. **7**. (**12**.)

BUSSCHAU (WILLIAM JOHN)

—— The Measure of Gold. pp. xi. 164. *Central News Agency:* [*Johannesburg,*] 1949. 8°. **8231**. ee. **85**.

—— Report on the Development of Secondary Industries in Northern Rhodesia . . . 1945. pp. 91. 1945. 8°. *See* RHODESIA, *Northern.* C.S. D. **316/9**.

—— The Theory of Gold Supply. With special reference to the problems of the Witwatersrand. pp. x. 193. *Oxford University Press: London,* 1936. 8°. [*Oxford Studies in Economics.*] **8208.p.7/1.**

BUSSCHE, VON DEM, *Family of.* *See* BUSSCHE (G. von dem) *Baron.* Geschichte der von dem Bussche . . . Mit . . . Stammtafeln. [1887.] 8°. **1858**. b. **7**.

BUSSCHE (ALEXANDRE VAN DEN) called LE SYLVAIN. *See* BUSCHE.

BUSSCHE (ÉMILE VANDEN)

—— Inventaire des archives de l'État à Bruges. Section première. Franc de Bruges, ancien quatrième membre de Flandre, *etc.* 2 tom. 1881, 84. 4°. *See* BRUGES.—*Staatsarchief.* **11927**. dd. **12**.

BUSSCHE (EMMANUEL VAN DEN) *See* BUSSCHE (Jean E. van den)

BUSSCHE (GUSTAV VON DEM) *Baron.* Geschichte der von dem Bussche. Erster Theil: Regesten und Urkunden, mit 20 Stammtafeln. pp. viii. 242. 21. 7. *Hameln,* [1887.] 8°. **1858**. b. **7**.
No more published.

—— Stammtafeln der von dem Bussche. Zusammengestellt und herausgegeben von Freiherrn G. von dem Bussche . . . Anlage zur Geschichte der von dem Bussche, Theil 1, *etc.* pl. xx. *Hildesheim,* 1887. fol. **1858**. c. **29**.

BUSSCHE (JEAN EMMANUEL VAN DEN) *See* PERIODICAL PUBLICATIONS.—*Bruges.* La Flandre. Revue, *etc.* (1867–70. Publiée par E. van den Bussche [and others]. 1872–85. Directeur: E. van den Bussche.) 1867, *etc.* 8°. P.P. **3500**. d.

—— Fleurs de Noël par J. E. van den Bussche . . . Kersbloemen, door Desiderius Verest . . . Avec grav ıres, *etc.* pp. 79. *Antwerpen,* 1858. 4°. **12355**. aaa. **5**.

—— Le Monde artiste. livr. 1. pp. 26. *Anvers,* 1875. 8°. **10602**. i. **20**.
No more published.

BUSSCHE (PETRUS VAN DEN) Disputatio medica inauguralis de calculo renum & vesicæ, *etc.* *Apud viduam & hæredes J. Elsevirii: Lugduni Batavorum,* 1673. 4°. **1185**. g. **12**. (**34**.)

BUSSCHE-IPPENBURG (August Friedrich Philipp von dem) *Baron.*

—— *See* Schwertfeger (B. H.) Der Königlich Hannoversche Generalleutnant August Friedrich Freiherr v. d. Bussche-Ippenburg, *etc.* [With a portrait.] 1904. 8°. M.L. b. **102.**

BUSSCHE-IPPENBURG (Clamor von dem) *Baron.* Die Familien-Chronik der aus Niedersachsen stammenden Bacmeister. [With genealogical tables.] 2 Bd. *Osnabrück,* 1904, 03. 4° & fol. **9905.** f. **45.** & **9905.** k. **16.**

BÜSSCHER ( ) [For the German surname of this form:] *See* Buesscher.

BUSSCHER (Edmond de)

—— *See* Vigne (F. de) Album du cortége des comtes de Flandre, personnages et costumes dessinés par F. de Vigne . . . et texte . . . par E. de Busscher. 1852. 8°. **9916.** ee. **26.**

—— *See* Vigne (Félix de) Chars du cortége des comtes de Flandre, dessinés par F. de Vigne . . . avec texte . . . par E. de Busscher. 1853. 8°. **9916.** ee. **27.**

—— L'Abbaye de Saint Pierre à Gand . . . Nouvelle édition. [With plates.] pp. viii. 133. *Gand,* 1867. 8°. **04685.** f. **15.**

—— [Description du cortège historique des comtes de Flandre.] Beschryving van den historischen stoet der graven van Vlaenderen, naer het Fransch . . . Met eene plaet. pp. 87. *Gent,* 1849. 8°. **9914.** c. **16.**

—— Fresques du 14me siècle, découvertes à Gand. (Extrait des Bulletins de l'Académie royale de Belgique.) [With a folding plate.] pp. 20. *Bruxelles,* 1861. 8°. **7708.** d. **27.** (**3.**)

—— Notice sur l'abbaye de Saint Pierre à Gand. [With plates.] pp. 95. *Gand,* 1847. 8°. **07708.** bb. **11.** (**4.**)

—— Peinture murale à l'huile du 15me siècle à Gand. (Extrait des Bulletins de l'Académie royale de Belgique.) [With a plate.] pp. 67. *Bruxelles,* 1858. 8°. **7868.bbb.22.**

—— Recherches sur les peintres et sculpteurs à Gand, aux xvie, xviie, et xviiie siècles . . . xvie siècle. [With plates.] pp. 366. *Gand,* 1866. 8°. **10760.** dd. **11.**

—— Recherches sur les peintres gantois des xiv et xv siècles. Indices primordiaux de l'emploi de la peinture à l'huile à Gand. [With plates.] pp. 222. *Gand,* 1859. 8°. **7856.** ee. **13.**

—— Les Ruines de l'abbaye de Saint Bavon, à Gand . . . Troisième édition. [With plates.] pp. 55. *Gand,* 1854. 4°. **10271.** dd. **15.**

BUSSCHERE (Alphonse de) *See* Belgium. *Collections of Laws and Treaties.—*i.] Recueil des traités et conventions concernant le royaume de Belgique. (tom. 17–21 continué par A. de Busschere.) 1850, *etc.* 8°. **9415.** a. **1.**

—— Code de traités et arrangements internationaux intéressant la Belgique . . . annoté d'observations pratiques par A. de Busschere. 2 tom. 1896, 97. 8°. *See* Belgium. [*Collections of Laws and Treaties.—*i.] **8026.** i. **7.**

BUSSCHERE (Alphonse de)

—— La Législation de police sanitaire. (Décret-loi du 18 juillet 1831 . . . quelques dispositions éparses dans d'autres lois, et . . . une série d'arrêtés royaux et ministériels.) [Text with commentary.] Par D. de Busschere. pp. 235. 1901. 8°. *See* Belgium. [*Collections of Laws.* —iii. *Sanitation.*] **5695.** aa. **13.**

BUSSCHERE (Louis de) Le "Rapid Transit" de Londres. 1893. *See* Brussels.—*Société Royale Belge de Géographie.* Bulletin, *etc.* année 17. 1877, *etc.* 8°. Ac. **6098.**

BUSSCHOF (Bernard) Nieuwe lof-sangen en geestelijcke liedekens . . . Desen laetsten druck, op nieuws gecorrigeert en verbetert. pp. 155. *Amsterdam,* 1748. *obl.* 16°. **3425.** a. **9.**

—— Corte ende christelijcke aenmerckinghen op den schandeleusen loffsangh Bernardi Busschof . . . wiens beginsel is, Ghelooft sy Godt die my heeft uytvercoren. Neffens zijne uytlegginghe, vande doodelijcke sonden, *etc.* pp. 28. [*Utrecht?*] 1620. 4°. T. **2250.** (**7.**)

BUSSCHOF (Hermann) Two Treatises, the one medical, Of the Gout. By H. Busschof, Senior . . . The other partly chirurgical, partly medical, containing some Observations and Practices relating both to some extraordinary cases of women in travel; and to some other uncommon cases of diseases in both sexes. By Henry Van Roonhuyse . . . Englished out of Dutch by a careful hand. [With a folding plate.] 2 pt. *Printed by H. C.; sold by Moses Pitt: London,* 1676. 8°. **1188.** b. **4.**

With an additional titlepage, engraved, reading: "A New way of curing the Gout, etc."

BUSSE (Adolf) *Assistant Professor of German in the Ohio State University.* *See* Gerstaecker (F. W. C.) Germelshausen . . Edited with notes, exercises, and vocabulary by A. Busse. 1910. 8°. **012552.** a. **73.**

BUSSE (Adolf) *Direktor des Askan. Gymnasiums in Berlin.* *See* Aristotle. [*Appendix.—Criticism.*] Commentaria in Aristotelem graeca, *etc.* (vol. 4. pt. 1. Porphyrii Isagoge et in Aristotelis Categorias commentarium.—vol. 4. pt. 2. Dexippi in Aristotelis Categorias commentarium.—vol. 4. pt. 3. Ammonius in Porphyrii Isagogen sive v voces.—vol. 4. pt. 4. Ammonius in Aristotelis Categorias commentarius.—vol. 4. pt. 5. Ammonius in Aristotelis de interpretatione commentarius.—vol. 12. pt. 1. Olympiodori prolegomena et in Categorias commentarium.—vol. 13. pt. 1. Philoponi, olim Ammonii, in Aristotelis Categorias commentarium.—vol. 18. pt. 1. Eliae in Porphyrii Isagogen et Aristotelis Categorias commentaria.—vol. 18. pt. 2. Davidis prolegomena et in Porphyrii Isagogen commentarium. [Edited by A. Busse.]) 1882, *etc.* 8°. Ac. **855/9.**

—— Sokrates . . . Mit einem Bildnis. pp. x. 248. *Berlin,* 1914. 8°. [*Die grossen Erzieher.* Bd. 7.] **8304.** i. **2/7.**

BUSSE (Alvin Clayton)

—— *See* Borden (Richard C.) and Busse (A. C.) How to Win an Argument. [1926.] 8°. **011805.** g. **64.**

—— *See* Borden (Richard C.) and Busse (A. C.) The New Public Speaking. 1930. 8°. **011805.** g. **74.**

—— *See* Borden (Richard C.) and Busse (A. C.) Speech Correction. 1925. 8°. **12984.** ff. **17.**

BUSSE (ALVIN CLAYTON)

—— *See* SAWYER (W. E.) and BUSSE (A. C.) Sell as Customers like it, *etc.* [1951.] 8°. **08228.** aa. **66.**

BUSSE (ANNEMARIE) Die Verbreitung des Phytoplanktons im Sakrower See und seine Beziehungen zum Medium, *etc.* (Der Sakrower See. Tl. 4a.) pp. 59. *Berlin*, 1937. 8°. [*Veröffentlichungen des Instituts für Meereskunde an der Universität Berlin.* Neue Folge. Reihe A. Hft. 34.] Ac. **6076.**

BUSSE (ANTON WILHELM FERDINAND) De Dionysii Halicarnassensis vita et ingenio. Dissertatio inauguralis, *etc.* pp. 62. *Berolini*, [1841.] 4°. **10605.** f. **13.**

—— Ueber Kritik der Sprache. Abhandlung, *etc.* pp. 38. *Berlin*, 1844. 4°. [*Koellnisches Gymnasium. Programmes, etc.*] **8358.** cc. **35.**

BUSSE (ARTHUR)

—— *See* EVANS (Trevor) Bevin. (Übersetzung. Gemeinschaftsarbeit von Dr. A. Busse und dem Verlag.) [1947.] 8°. **10862.** aa. **12.**

BUSSE (BD.) **UND ROHRMANN.** Der Annalith als neuer Baumaterial, *etc.* pp. 22. *Leipzig*, 1860. 8°. **7816.** aa. **16.**

BUSSE (BRUNO) Sagengeschichtliches zum Hildebrandsliede. 1901. *See* PERIODICAL PUBLICATIONS.—*Halle.* Beiträge zur Geschichte der deutschen Sprache und Literatur, *etc.* Bd. 26. 1874, *etc.* 8°. **12964.f.1/26.**

BUSSE (CARL) *Architect.* Ausgeführte Bauwerke von C. Busse. [Plates with introductory text.] Hft. 1, 2. *Berlin*, [1855, 58.] fol. **1730.** b. **34.**

BUSSE (CARL) *Dr. phil.* *See* also DOERING (Fritz) *pseud.* [i.e. C. Buss.]

—— *See* PERIODICAL PUBLICATIONS.—*Cologne.* Literarisches Jahrbuch . . . Unter Mitarbeit von Dr. C. Busse [and others] . . . herausgegeben von P. Thiel. 1903. 8°. P.P. **2445.** h.

—— Deutsche Kriegslieder 1914/16. Herausgegeben und eingeleitet von C. Busse. Dritte, vollständig umgearbeitete und vermehrte Auflage. Mit 4 Bildnissen. pp. xxiii. 181. *Bielefeld & Leipzig*, 1916. 8°. [*Aus den Tagen des grossen Krieges.*] **9081.** b. **1/6.**

—— Gedichte. pp. viii. 162. *Grossenhain*, [1892.] 8°. **11526.** h. **9.**

—— Höhenfrost. Roman. 3 Bd. *Berlin*, 1897. 8°. **012552.** aaa. **44.**

—— Im polnischen Wind. Ostmärkische Geschichten. pp. 307. *Stuttgart & Berlin*, 1906. 8°. **12555.** r. **16.**

—— Neue Gedichte . . . Zweite Auflage. pp. viii. 151. *Stuttgart & Berlin*, 1901. 8°. **011528.** e. **121.**

—— Novalis' Lyrik. pp. viii. 156. *Oppeln*, 1898. 8°. **011851.** i. **28.**

—— Sturmvögel. Kriegsnovellen. pp. 250. *Leipzig*, 1917. 8°. **012553.** c. **65.**

BUSSE (CARL) *Novelist.* Die Hoermanns. Roman. pp. 287. *Berlin*, [1935.] 8°. **12557.** s. **19.**

BUSSE (CARL HEINRICH VON) Fürst Wladimir und dessen Tafelrunde. Alt-Russische Heldenlieder. [By C. H. von Busse.] pp. xvi. 160. 1819. 8°. *See* WLADIMIR, *Prince.* **1462.** b. **21.**

—— [Another copy.] **11517.** bb. **15**

—— Herzog Magnus, König von Livland. Ein fürstliches Lebensbild aus dem 16. Jahrhundert, von K. H. von Busse. Aus dessen nachgelassenen Papieren herausgegeben von Julius Freiherrn von Bohlen. pp. xvi. 160. *Leipzig*, 1871. 8°. **10708.** g. **15.**

BUSSE (CAROLUS JULIUS GUSTAVUS) De pulmonum oedemate. Dissertatio inauguralis medica, *etc.* pp. 32. *Berolini*, [1864.] 8°. **7385.** b. **(18.)**

BUSSE (CAROLUS OTTO) De legitimo judicio. Dissertatio inauguralis, *etc.* pp. 60. *Berolini*, [1835.] 8°. **6006.** e. **1. (1.)**

BUSSE (CHRISTIANUS) De jure præceptorum, *etc.* 1744. *See* STRYKIUS (S.) Viri quondam illustris . . . Samuelis Strykii . . . opera omnia, *etc.* vol. 5. 1743, *etc.* fol. **498.** g. **7.**

BUSSE (CURT) *Dr. phil.* Herbert Spencers Philosophie der Geschichte. Ein Beitrag zur Lösung sociologischer Probleme. pp. 114. *Leipzig*, 1894. 8°. **9008.** dd. **12.**

BUSSE (CURT) *of Berlin-Siemensstadt.* Hermann Sudermann. Sein Werk und sein Wesen. [With a portrait.] pp. 206. *Stuttgart & Berlin*, 1927. 8°. **011824.** aaa. **5.**

BUSSE (E.) *See* BUSSE (N. V.) Островъ Сахалинъ и экспедиция 1853–54 гг. Дневникъ, *etc.* [The editor's preface signed: Е. Б. i.e. E. Busse?] 1872. 8°. **10056.** e. **12.**

BUSSE (EBERHARD CURT) Ulrich von Türheim. pp. viii. 181. *Berlin*, 1913. 8°. [*Palaestra.* Bd. 121.] **12203.** ff. **1/121.**

BUSSE (FEDOR FEDORIVICH) Отвѣтъ гг. Невельскому и Рудановскому. *See* BUSSE (N. V.) Островъ Сахалинъ, *etc.* 1872. 8°. **10056.** e. **12.**

BUSSE (FRANCISCO PEDRO) Poemas Lyricos de hum Natural de Lisboa [i.e. F. P. Busse]. 2 tom. 1787, 89. 8°. *See* POEMAS. **11452.** aa. **29.**

—— [Another copy of tom. 1.] **1064.** b. **23.**

BUSSE (FRIEDRICH) *See* PERIODICAL PUBLICATIONS.—*Jena.* Journal der practischen Arzneykunde, *etc.* (Bd. 94–98. 1842–44. C. W. Hufeland's Journal der practischen Heilkunde. Fortgesetzt von F. Busse.) 1795, *etc.* 8°. P.P. **2985.**

BUSSE (FRIEDRICH GOTTLIEB) *See* ERLER (L. J. F.) Erler's . . . ausführliche Beschreibung des Pferdegöpels . . . Neue verbesserte Ausgabe mit Anmerkungen versehen von F. G. Busse, *etc.* 1811. 8°. **725.** a. **35.**

—— *See* METTLERKAMP (D. C.) Ueber Blitzableitungen gegen Busse's Theorie. [With special reference to F. G. Busse's "Beschreibung einer wohlfeilen und sichern Blitzableitung."] 1812. 8°. T. **963. (17.)**

—— Betrachtung der Winterschmidt- und Höll'schen Wassersäulenmaschine, nebst Vorschlägen zu ihrer Verbesserung . . . Mit einer Kupfertafel. pp. xxii. 294. *Freyberg*, 1804. 8°. **537.** g. **11.**

BUSSE (FRIEDRICH GOTTLIEB)

—— Kenntnisse und Betrachtungen des neueren Münzwesens für Deutsche. 2 Tl. *Leipzig*, 1795, 96. 8°. **603.** d. **9, 10.**

—— Kleine Beyträge zur Mathematik und Physik und deren Lehrmethode. Tl. 1. pp. x. xxxii. 159. *Leipzig*, 1786. 8°. **8532.** c. **1.**
No more published.

—— Neue Methode des Grössten und Kleinsten, nebst Beurtheilung und einiger Verbesserung des bisherigen Systemes, *etc.* 2 Hft. pp. 12. 220. pl. II. *Freyberg*, 1808, 09. 8°. **8533.** b. **11.**

BUSSE (GOTTLIEB CHRISTIANUS) Dissertatio inauguralis medica de actione cordis quatenus a nervis pendet, *etc.* *Praes.* A. E. Buechner. pp. 29. *Halae ad Salam*, [1769.] 4°. T. **521.** (**11.**)

BUSSE (GUSTAV FRIEDRICH) *See* HINZ (A.) Die Schatzkammer der Marienkirche zu Danzig . . . Mit 200 photographischen Abbildungen von G. F. Busse. 1870. 8°. **07709.** cc. **5.**

BUSSE (HANS) Aus der belagerten Feste Boyen. Feldzugsbriefe . . . Herausgegeben von Marie Busse. [With a portrait and maps.] pp. 150. *Berlin*, 1919. 8°. **9083.** bb. **27.**

BUSSE (HANS HEINRICH) *See* BOHN (E.) and BUSSE (H. H.) Geisterschriften und Drohbriefe, *etc.* 1902. 8°. **8632.** g. **41.**

—— *See* CRÉPIEUX-JAMIN (J.) Handschrift und Charakter . . . Unter Mitarbeit von H. Merckle in autorisierter Übersetzung . . . herausgegeben . . . von H. H. Busse, *etc.* [1905?] 8°. **7947.** aaa. **3.**

—— *See* CRÉPIEUX-JAMIN (J.) Praktisches Lehrbuch der Graphologie . . . Vierte neu bearbeitete Auflage, mit . . . einem Anhang herausgegeben von H. H. Busse. [1898.] 8°. **7947.** a. **12.**

—— Graphologie und gerichtl. Handschriften-Untersuchungen —Schrift-Expertise. Unter besonderer Rücksicht auf den Fall Dreyfus-Esterhazy. Mit . . . Facsimiles, *etc.* pp. 35. *Leipzig*, 1898. 8°. **07944.** k. **10.** (**9.**)

—— Grafologiens grunder. En kort redogörelse efter Hans Busse och Henry Frith [i.e. after H. H. Busse's " Graphologie und gerichtl. Handschriften-Untersuchungen," and H. Frith's " How to read Character in Handwriting "], *etc.* pp. 95. *Stockholm*, 1898. 8°. **05402.** eee. **4.**

—— Übersichtstafeln zur Geschichte der Graphologie. Auf Grund seiner " Bibliographie der Graphologie " entworfen von: H. H. Busse. 2. neubearbeitete Auflage. *München*, 1900. *s. sh.* fol. Cup. **651.** e. **4.** (**8.**)

—— Wie beurteile ich meine Handschrift? Populäres Lehrbuch der Graphologie . . . Mit 70 Handschriftenproben . . . 12.–14. Tausend. pp. 92. *Berlin*, [1909.] 8°. **7947.** b. **6.**

BUSSE (HERMANN ERIS) Alemannische Volksfasnacht . . . Mit 89 Bildern von E. von Pagenhardt. pp. 157. *Karlsruhe*, [1937.] 8°. [*Vom Bodensee zum Main.* no. 45.] W.P. **6677/45.**

—— Der Erdgeist. Saga vom Oberrhein. pp. 626. *Leipzig*, [1939.] 8°. **12557.** a. **16.**

BUSSE (HERMANN ERIS)

—— Hans Adolf Bühler, *etc.* [With reproductions, including a portrait.] pp. 180. *Karlsruhe*, 1931. 8°. [*Vom Bodensee zum Main.* no. 38.] W.P. **6677/38.**

—— Hans Thoma. Leben und Werk, *etc.* [With reproductions, including portraits.] pp. 119. *Berlin*, [1935.] 4°. **7863.** r. **27.**

—— Hermann Daur, *etc.* [With reproductions and a portrait.] pp. 80. *Karlsruhe*, 1924. 8°. [*Vom Bodensee zum Main.* no. 26.] W.P. **6677/26.**

BUSSE (J. E.) Gerold, erster Bischof von Lübeck, und die Kirche zu Ratekau. Zur Gedächtnissfeier des 700jährigen Bestehens dieser Kirche, *etc.* pp. 60. *Lübeck*, 1856. 8°. **4886.** d. **7.**

BUSSE (JOACHIMUS) בית לחם Patria Messiæ dissertatione historico-geographica descripta . . . Editio tertia. *Praes.* A. Strauch. *Typis C. Schrödteri: Wittenbergæ*, 1683. 4°. **479.** a. **23.** (**8.**)

—— [Another edition.] 1700. *See* CRENIUS (T.) *pseud.* Fascis I. [*etc.*] exercitationum philologico-historicarum, *etc.* fasc. 5. 1697, *etc.* 8°. **73.** b. **25**.**

—— Disputatio physica *κατασκευαστικη* quæstionis: An omnia agentia naturalia suos cognoscant fines? *etc.* *Praes.* C. Latzke. *M. Wendt: Wittebergæ*, [1660.] 4°. **525.** d. **3.** (**10.**)

BUSSE (JOHAN JOACHIM) Dissertatio juridica inauguralis de suggestionibus, earumque jure, *etc.* *Praes.* H. Coccejus. pp. 48. *Typis C. A. Zeitleri: Francofurti*, [1691.] 4°. **5510.** aa. **14.**

BUSSE (JOHANN BERNARD JOSEPH) Grundriss der christlichen Literatur, von ihrem Ursprunge an bis zur Erfindung und Ausbreitung der Buchdruckerei. Ein Handbuch für angehende Theologen. 2 Tl. *Münster*, 1828, 29. 8°. **1366.** f. **3.**

—— [Another copy.] **4999.** df. **18.**

BUSSE (JOHANN HEINRICH) *See* ARTEMY, *Araratsky.* Artemius von Wagarschapat . . . Leidensgeschichte seiner Jugend . . . Aus dem Russischen, begleitet mit einer Einleitung [by J. H. Busse], *etc.* 1821. 8°. **10790.** bb. **13.**

—— *See* RUSSIA.—[*Laws, etc.*—E. iii.]—Paul I., *Emperor.* [1796–1801.] Verordnungen Seiner Kaiserlichen Majestät Paul des Ersten . . . uebersezt auf allerhöchsten Befehl [by J. H. Busse]. [1797, *etc.*] 4°. **5758.** cc. **15.**

—— *See* SARUICHEV (G. A.) Gawrila Sarytschew's . . . achtjährige Reise im nordöstlichen Sibirien . . . aus dem Russischen übersetzt von J. H. Busse, *etc.* 1805, *etc.* 8°. **1425.** e. **21.**

BUSSE (JOHANN PHILIPP) Schreiben eines Bewohners des Himmels an einen Freund auf der Erde . . . Ein Trostgedicht für die leidende Menschheit. *Hannover*, 1809. 8°. **11521.** ee. **28.** (**76.**)

BUSSE (JOHANNES) Die Congruenz des Participii praeteriti in activer Verbalconstruction im Altfranzösischen bis zum Anfang des XIII. Jahrhunderts. pp. 70. *Göttingen*, 1882. 8°. **12924.** dd. **23.** (**1.**)

BUSSE (JOHN) *Biographer.* Mrs. Montagu, Queen of the Blues. pp. 83. *Gerald Howe: London*, 1928. 8°. [*Representative Women.*] **10602.** p. **3/11.**

BUSSE (JOHN) *of Dublin. Begin.* Tuesday the 7. Junii, 1642. Worthy Sir, *etc.* [A letter to a correspondent in London.] *See* BUCKINGHAM, *County of.* [*Appendix.*] The Humble Petition of the Captaines, Officers . . . and Voluntiers in the County of Buckingham, *etc.* [1642.] 4°. **E. 152. (12.)**

BUSSE (KARL HEINRICH VON) *See* BUSSE (Carl H. von)

BUSSE (KURT) *See* BUSSE (Curt)

BUSSE (LUDWIG) Beiträge zur Entwicklungsgeschichte Spinoza's. Inaugural-Dissertation, *etc.* pp. 88. *Berlin,* [1885.] 8°. **8468. k. 25. (1.)**

—— Geist und Körper, Seele und Leib. pp. x. 488. *Leipzig,* 1903. 8°. **08464. k. 19.**

—— Zweite Auflage. Mit einem ergänzenden . . . Anhang, von Ernest Dürr. [With a bibliography.] pp. x. 566. *Leipzig,* 1913. 8°. **08461. e. 25.**

—— Streifzüge durch die japanische ethische Litteratur der Gegenwart. 1892. *See* HAMBURG.—*Deutsche Gesellschaft für Natur- und Völkerkunde Ostasiens.* Mitteilungen, *etc.* Hft. 50. 1873, *etc.* fol. & 8°. **Ac. 1944.**

BUSSE (LYUDVIG FILIPPOVICH) *See* LENINGRAD.—*Verein der praktischen Thierärzte.* Memorabilien der Veterinair-Medizin in Russland . . . Redigirt von L. Busse. 1855, *etc.* 8°. **Ac. 3879.**

BUSSE (MARIE) *See* BUSSE (H.) Aus der belagerten Feste Boyen. Feldzugsbriefe . . . Herausgegeben von M. Busse. 1919. 8°. **9083. bb. 27.**

BUSSE (MARTIN) Hegels Phänomenologie des Geistes und der Staat. Ein Beitrag zur Auslegung der Phänomenologie und Rechtsphilosophie und zur Geschichte der Entwicklung des Hegelschen Systems. pp. vi. 141. *Berlin,* 1931. 8°. **8459. w. 17.**

BUSSE (MARTINUS) Dissertationem historicam . . . de doctoribus scholasticis Latinis . . . publicæ eruditorum διασκεψει . . . subjiciet . . . M. Busse. *Praes.* J. Thomasius. *Charactere Coleriano: Lipsiæ,* [1676.] 4°. **619. e. 29. (9.)**

BUSSE (MAX RUDOLPH VON) Geschichte des Königlich Preussischen Dreiundzwanzigsten Infanterie-Regiments von seiner Stiftung im Jahre 1813 und dem Ausmarsche in's Feld bis zu seiner Rückkehr im Jahre 1819 in die Friedens-Garnisonen: Neisse, Cosel und Frankenstein, *etc.* pp. 239. *Görlitz,* 1859. 8°. **8828. h. 37.**

BUSSE (NATALIYA)

—— Какво да четем във връзка с борбата за мир. Препоръчителна библиография. pp. 61. *София,* 1950. 16°. [*Поредица Препоръчителни списъци.* no. 10.] **Ac. 1137. e/5.**

—— Какво да четем върху Великата октомврийска революция. Препоръчителен списък. pp. 15. *София,* 1949. 8°. [*Поредица Препоръчителни списъци.* no. 1.] **Ac. 1137. e/5.**

BUSSE (NIKOLAI VASIL'EVICH) Островъ Сахалинъ и экспедиція 1853–54 гг. Дневникъ 25 августа 1853 г.—19 мая 1854 г. [The editor's preface signed: Е. Б., i.e. E. Busse?] Отвѣтъ Ѳ. Буссе гг-мъ Невельскому и Рудановскому. pp. 164. *Санктпетербургъ,* 1872. 8°. **10056. e. 12.**

BUSSE (OSCAR VON)

—— *See* CHANZY (A. E. A.) Feldzug von 1870–1871. Die zweite Loire-Armee . . . Uebersetzt von O. von Busse, *etc.* 1873. 8°. **M.L. df. 12.**

—— Die Heere der französischen Republik 1870–1871, mit einem Rückblick auf die letzte kaiserliche Armee und das französische neue Wehrgesetz. pp. 96. *Hannover,* 1874. 8°. **8825. cc. 33. (9.)**

BUSSE (OTTO) Ueber den Bau einer Locomotivbahn durch die Stadt Berlin. pp. 32. *Berlin,* [1873.] 8°. **8235. bbb. 48. (12.)**

BUSSE (RUDOLF) Luftrecht einschliesslich Luftverkehrsgesetz und Pariser Luftverkehrsabkommen, *etc.* pp. xviii. 448. *Berlin & Leipzig,* 1928. 8°. [*Guttentagsche Sammlung deutscher Reichsgesetze.* no. 170.] **2227. b. 170.**

BUSSE (WILFRED C.) The Blue Beyond. A romance of the early days in South-Eastern Australia. pp. 287. *Hutchinson & Co.: London,* [1930.] 8°. **NN. 16182.**

—— The Golden Plague. A romance of the roaring 'fifties. pp. 287. *Hutchinson & Co.: London,* [1930.] 8°. **A.N. 491.**

BUSSE (WILHELM) J. G. Fichte und seine Beziehung zur Gegenwart des deutschen Volkes. Erster Theil. Fichte der Philosoph. 2 Bd. *Halle,* 1848, 49. 8°. **1248. g. 20.** *No more published.*

BUSSE (WILHELM OSCAR) Der Zehntenstreit zwischen Hessen-Kassel und dem Fritzlarer St. Petersstift im Jahre 1606. pp. 198. *Berlin,* 1935. 8°. [*Historische Studien.* Hft. 266.] **09010. d. 1/266.**

BUSSE (WILHELM PAUL) Zur Lehre von den Krisen. Inaugural-Dissertation, *etc.* pp. 31. *Berlin,* [1870.] 8°. **7385.*c. (11.)**

BUSSECHE (ALEXANDRE VAN DEN) *See* BUSCHE.

BÜSSEL ( ) [For the German surname of this form:] *See* BUESSEL.

BÜSSELBERG ( ) [For the German surname of this form:] *See* BUESSELBERG.

BUSSELL, *Family of. See* SHANN (Edward O. G.) Cattle Chosen. The story of the first group settlement [by the Bussell family] in Western Australia, *etc.* 1926. 8°. **10493. de. 35.**

BUSSELL (DOROTHEA) Dunbarrow. pp. 344. *Herbert Jenkins: London,* 1926. 8°. **NN. 11535.**

—— Ghost and Chorus. Poems. pp. 40. *Basil Blackwell: Oxford,* 1937. 8°. **11655. g. 80.**

—— The New Wood Nymph. pp. 320. *Stanley Paul & Co.: London,* [1912.] 8°. **NN. 17.**

—— The Third Angel. pp. 286. *John Long: London,* 1929. 8°. **NN. 15050.**

—— Translate No Further. pp. 317. *Grayson & Grayson: London,* 1933. 8°. **NN. 20352.**

BUSSELL (EMILY) Epitaph for Harriet. [A novel.] pp. 336. *Stanley Paul & Co.: London,* [1936.] 8°. **NN. 25810.**

BUSSELL (EUPHEMIA E. G.) Miss Chatterbox; or, the Tenant of Dahlia Lodge and his opposite neighbours . . . Reprinted . . . from "New and Old." pp. 80. *J. T. Hayes; Swift & Co.: London,* [1884.] 8°. **4417. de. 35.**

BUSSELL (EUPHEMIA E. G.)

—— Self-Surrender; or, the Cruise of the yacht 'Ayacanora' . . . [A tale.] Edited by C. A. Jones. pp. 93. *J. T. Hayes: London*, [1876.] 16°. **4413.** bb. **1.**

—— The Wonderful Voice [by E. E. G. Bussell], and other stories. With . . . illustrations. 11 pt. *E. & J. B. Young & Co.: New York*, [1886.] 8°. **4418.** i. **11.**

BUSSELL (F. L.) *See* MAIS (Stuart P. B.) England of the Windmills . . . With drawings by F. L. Bussell. 1931. 8°. **010360.** aa. **79.**

BUSSELL (FREDERICK WILLIAM) *See* AUGUSTINE, *Saint, Bishop of Hippo.* [*De Civitate Dei.—English.*] The City of God, *etc.* [Edited by F. W. Bussell.] [1903.] 8°. **012200.de.8/93.**

—— —— 1931. 8°. **3805.** bbb. **28.**

—— A Brief Defence of the House of Lords, without technicalities. Arranged in question and answer. [By F. W. Bussell.] pp. 8. [1910.] 8°. *See* ENGLAND.—*Parliament.—House of Lords.* [*Appendix.*] **08138.** aa. **14.**

—— The Case of Breamore Curacy: presented by the Nominator and the Trustees, July, 1914. Drawn up by F. W. Bussell. pp. iv. 48. *Horace Hart: Oxford*, [1914.] fol. **Cup.1247.c.43.**

—— Christian Theology and Social Progress. The Bampton Lectures for 1905. pp. xl. 343. *Methuen & Co.: London*, 1907. 8°. **2206.** c. **5.**

—— Church Patronage Bill, 1894: a letter to Sir John Mowbray, Bart., M.P. for Oxford University. pp. 7. *Baxter's Press: Oxford*, 1894. 4°. **4108.** h. **4.** (4.)

—— De medietate hominis, ejusque desideriis. [By F. W. Bussell.] pp. 23. [1889.] 8°. *See* MEDIETAS. **8471.** aa. **51.**

—— Doctrine of the Office of Christ in the First Three Centuries. Being a dissertation, *etc.* pp. 64. *Printed for private circulation: London*, 1892. 8°. **20032.** f. **40.**

—— The Future of Ethics: Effort or Abstention? *See* STURT (Henry) *of Queen's College, Oxford.* Personal Idealism, *etc.* 1902. 8°. **8469.** k. **20.**

—— Itinerarium Rutilianum. F. G. Bucelii de exilio suo libri II. [In verse.] pp. 33. *Apud J. Parker & Socios: Oxonii*, 1886. 8°. **11403.** b. **23.**

—— Marcus Aurelius and the Later Stoics. pp. xi. 302. *T. & T. Clark: Edinburgh*, 1910. 8°. [*World's Epoch-Makers.*] **10600.** eee. **7/22.**

—— The National Church and the Social Crisis; or, the Churchman's attitude to political panaceas. pp. vi. 150. *Robert Scott: London*, 1918. 8°. **08285.** a. **39.**

—— A New Government for the British Empire. pp. xii. 108. *Longmans & Co.: London*, 1912. 8°. **8139.** f. **21.**

—— A Plea for Courtesy & Candour. An open letter addressed to the Bench of Bishops. pp. 24. *Parker & Co.: Oxford*, 1918. 8°. **4106.** f. **32.**

—— The Principle of Monarchy. Plain words to the British people. pp. 79. *Royal Martyr Church Union: Oxford*, 1918. 8°. **08139.** aaa. **14.**

—— Religious Thought and Heresy in the Middle Ages. pp. xiii. 873. *Robert Scott: London*, 1918. 8°. **04503.** h. **15.**

BUSSELL (FREDERICK WILLIAM)

—— The Roman Empire. Essays on the constitutional history from the accession of Domitian, 81 A.D., to the retirement of Nicephorus III., 1081 A.D. 2 vol. *Longmans & Co.: London*, 1910. 8°. **9042.** c. **6.**

—— The School of Plato. Its origin, development, and revival under the Roman Empire. pp. xvi. 346. *Methuen & Co.: London*, 1896. 8°. **2236.** d. **2.**

—— Vicarages, Perpetual Curacies and Donatives, *etc.* [By F. W. Bussell.] ff. 8. [1914?] 4°. *See* VICARAGES. **20046.bbb.8.**

BUSSELL (HENRY GEE) Bussell's Album of Ross and District. [Photographs.] [*H. G. Bussell: Ross*, 1896.] *obl.* 8°. **10360.** aa. **51.**

BUSSELL (JAN)

—— The Art of Television. [With "Sea Fever. A play for television."] [With plates.] pp. 163. *Faber & Faber: London*, 1952. 8°. **11798.** c. **31.**

—— The Model Theatre. pp. 31. *Dennis Dobson: London*, 1948. 8°. [*Theatre in Education Series.*] W.P. **3032/1.**

—— Plays for Puppets. Edited and introduced by J. Bussell. pp. 191. *Faber & Faber: London*, 1951. 8°. **11784.** aa. **47.**

—— The Puppet Theatre . . . Illustrated by Francis Gower. [With plates.] pp. 143. *Faber & Faber: London*, 1946. 8°. **11797.** g. **29.**

—— Puppet's Progress. [With portraits.] pp. 119. pl. 8. *Faber & Faber: London*, 1953. 8°. **11796.** bb. **51.**

—— The Puppets and I. An autobiographical account of the experience and travels of a puppet master. [With plates.] pp. 163. *Faber & Faber: London*, 1950. 8°. **011794.** bb. **23.**

BUSSELL (JAN) and **HOGARTH** (ANN) Marionettes. How to make them. pp. 27. *Pepler & Sewell: Ditchling*, 1934. 8°. **7943.** pp. **21.**

BUSSELL (PETER) The Diary of Peter Bussell, 1806–1814. Edited by his great-grandson (G. A. Turner) . . . With illustrations from original drawings by the author. pp. xiii. 232. *Peter Davies: London*, 1931. 8°. **9075.** b. **11.**

BUSSELL (WILLIAM) *See* EPHEMERIDES. The Civil Service Calendar . . . Edited by W. Bussell. 1886, *etc.* 8°. P.P. **2486.** kp.

—— Civil Service Tots; with answers. pp. iv. 35. *London*, [1887.] 8°. [*Stewart's Civil Service Text-Books.*] **12200.** f. **7/1.**

—— Digest of Returns and Tabular Statements. pp. 74. *London*, [1887.] 8°. [*Stewart's Civil Service Text-Books.*] **12200.** f. **7/3.**

—— Indexing and Précis-Writing. pp. 224. *London*, [1887.] 8°. [*Stewart's Civil Service Text-Books.*] **12200.** f. **7/4.**

—— Spelling-Book and Dictation Exercises, *etc.* pp. 143. *London*, [1887.] 8°. [*Stewart's Civil Service Text-Books.*] **12200.** f. **7/2.**

—— Stewart's Civil Service Arithmetic, *etc.* pp. 400. xlvii. *W. Stewart & Co.: London*, [1887.] 8°. **8533.** e. **23.**

BUSSELL (WILLIAM)

—— Stewart's Civil Service Book-Keeping by Double Entry, *etc.* pp. 214. *W. Stewart & Co.: London,* [1887.] 8°. **8535.** cc. **8.**

BUSSELLE (ALFRED)

—— *See* CAFFIN (Charles H.) How to Study Pictures . . . Edited by A. Busselle. 1941. 8°. **7866.** pp. **23.**

BUSSELS (M. C.) Inventaire des archives du Comité de l'Épizootie pour le Brabant et le Limbourg. 1937. 8° [*Archives générales du Royaume. Travaux du cours pratique d'archivéconomie.* 1936.] *See* BRABANT.—*Comité de l'Épizootie pour le Brabant et le Limbourg.* **011900.** aaa. **34.**

BUSSEMAKER (CAREL HENDRIK THEODOR) *See* BRINK (R. C. B. van den) Studien en karakterschetsen over vaderlandsche geschiedenis en letteren. [dl. 3 edited by S. Muller and C. H. T. Bussemaker.] 1911, *etc.* 8°. **9414.** e. **17.**

—— *See* MULLER (Pieter L.) Geschiedenis van onzen tijd, *etc.* (dl. 3 voortgezet door Dr. T. Bussemaker en J. S. Bartstra.) 1903, *etc.* 8°. **09077.** eee. **2.**

—— *See* PRINSTERER (G. G. van) Archives ou correspondance inédite de la maison d'Orange-Nassau, *etc.* (sér. 4. tom. 1–4 publiée par T. Bussemaker.) 1835, *etc.* 8°. **749.** c. **4.**

—— De Afscheiding der Waalsche gewesten van de Generale Unie, *etc.* 2 dl. 1895, 96. 8°. *See* HAARLEM.—*Teyler's Stichting.* Ac. **942/5.**

—— De Behandeling der algemeene geschiedenis. Rede, *etc.* pp. 37. *'s Gravenhage,* 1895. 8°. **9009.** dd. **5.** (**2.**)

—— Geschiedenis van Overijsel gedurende het eerste stadhouderlooze tijdperk. 2 dl. *'s-Gravenhage,* 1888, 89. 8°. **010271.** f. **2.**

—— Verslag van een voorloopig onderzoek te Lissabon, Sevilla, Madrid, Escorial, Simancas en Brussel naar archivalia belangrijk voor de geschiedenis van Nederland, *etc.* pp. viii. 207. *'s Gravenhage,* 1905. 8°. **11908.** e. **3.**

BUSSEMAKER (JAN BARLAGEN) Iets over het landbezit van den inlander in Nederlandsch Indië. Proefschrift, *etc.* pp. 165. *Leiden,* 1887. 8°. **5319.** de. **15.**

BUSSEMAKER (THEODOR) *See* BUSSEMAKER (Carel H. T.)

BUSSEMAKER (ULCO CATS) *See* NICANDER, *of Colophon.* Nicandrea . . . Accedunt . . . scholia in Alexipharmaca ex recognitione Bussemakeri, *etc.* 1856. 8°. **11335.** f. **35.**

—— *See* ORIBASIUS. Œuvres d'Oribase. Texte grec . . . traduit . . . en français . . . par . . . Bussemaker, *etc.* 1851, *etc.* 8°. **07305.** dd. **3.**

—— *See* ORIBASIUS. Dissertatio philologica-medica inauguralis, exhibens librum XLIV Collectaneorum medicinalium Oribasii . . . cum adjuncta versione latina adnotationibusque, quam . . . publico omnium examini offert U. C. Bussemaker. [1835.] 8°. **7320.** bb. **27.**

—— *See* THEOCRITUS. [*Scholia.*] Scholia in Theocritum, *etc.* (Scholia et Eutecnii paraphrasis in Nicandrum. Scholia et paraphrasis in Oppianum. Ex codicibus correxit, auxit et annotatione critica instruxit U. C. Bussemaker.) 1849. 8°. **011306.dd.3.**

BUSSEN. Der Bussen Meesterye. Hier begint een seer uytnemende . . . boecxkẽ, dickwils versocht eñ warachtich bevonden om alderhande gheschut te schieten, ende om salpeter, poeyer eñ alderhande vyerwerckẽ sonderlinghe te bereyden eñ is seer profytelijck voor allen busmeesters oft busschieters . . . nu eerst overgheset uyt den Hooghduytsche, *etc.* ff. 29. *Ghedruckt by C. Claesz.: Amstelredam,* 1593. 4°. **534.f.38.(4.)**
The colophon reads "Ghedruckt by E. Muller voor C. Claesz."

BUSSENIUS (AARNO) *See* HOLMBERG, afterwards HARVA (U. N. O.) Die Religion der Tscheremissen . . . Übersetzt von A. Bussenius. 1926. 8°. [*FF Communications.* no. 61.] Ac. **9883.** c.

—— *See* KROHN (K. L.) [Suomalaiset syntyloitsut.] Magische Ursprungsrunen der Finnen . . . Übersetzt von A. Bussenius. 1924. 8°. [*FF Communications.* no. 52.] Ac. **9883.** c.

—— *See* MALIN (A.) Der Heiligenkalender Finnlands, *etc.* [Translated from the Finnish by A. Bussenius.] 1925. 8°. [*Suomen Kirkkohistoriallisen Seuran toimituksia.* no. 20.] Ac. **2049.**

—— Zur ostseefinnischen Morphologie: Stammesalternation im Ostseefinnischen. pp. 116. *Berlin & Leipzig,* 1939. 8°. [*Ungarische Bibliothek.* Reihe 1. no. 24.] **Ac.856.h/2.(1.)**

BUSSENIUS (ADOLPH) Beiträge zur Kenntniss der liquiden Kohlenwasserstoffe. Inaugural-Dissertation, *etc.* pp. 38. *Göttingen,* 1858. 8°. **8906.** b. **11.**

BUSSENIUS (FRIEDRICH) Die Bleizucker-Fabrikation in ihrem ganzen Umfange und nach allen vorhandenen, Methoden, *etc.* pp. 64. pl. 3. *Quedlinburg & Leipzig,* 1848. 8°. **7955.** b. **35.** (**2.**)

BUSSE-PALMA (GEORG) Die singende Sünde. Neue Gedichte. pp. 105. *München,* [1904.] 8°. **011528.** g. **102.**

BÜSSER ( ) [For the German surname of this form:] *See* BUESSER.

BUSSER (BARTOLOMEO) *See* CACCIA (G. F.) *Count.* Testamento e codicillo del conte Giovanni Francesco Caccia . . . Testo originale con traduzione letterale per cura degli avvocati L. Bazzano . . . B. Busser. 1902. 4°. **10630.** h. **38.**

BUSSER (HENRI) *See* GUIRAUD (E.) Traité pratique d'instrumentation . . . Nouvelle édition complétée et révisée par H. Busser, *etc.* [1933.] 8°. **7894.** tt. **1.**

BUSSER (JOHAN BENEDICT) Utkast till beskrifning om Upsala. [With plates.] 2 vol. *Upsala,* 1773, 69. 8°. **152.** b. **23, 24.**

BUSSER (RALPH COX)

—— Southern Wales as a Market for Electrical Machinery and Supplies. pp. ii. 26. [*Washington,*] 1928. 8°. [*U.S. Bureau of Foreign and Domestic Commerce. Trade Information Bulletin.* no. 526.] A.S. **128/3.**

BUSSERO (GIUSEPPE LODOVICO) *See* GIUSEPPE ANGELO, *della Natività della B. V. Maria.*

BUSSERO (GOFFREDO DA) *See* GOFFREDO, *da Bussero.*

BUSSEROLLE (EUPHÉMIE CARRÉ DE) *See* CARRÉ DE BUSSEROLLE.

BUSSEROLLE (JACQUES XAVIER CARRÉ DE) *See* CARRÉ DE BUSSEROLLE.

BUSSERUS (Leonardus) *See* Garibus (J.) De phænomenis ostentis ab anno M.DC.XLI. ad M.DC.L. opusculum . . . Cum interpretationibus . . . L. Busseri, *etc.* 1651. 4°. **718**. g. **37**.

BUSSET (F. C.) M. Fétis mis à la portée de tout le monde. [Being an account of the author's litigation with F. J. Fétis and Maurice Schlesinger.] 2 pt. *Paris*, 1838. 8°. **1414**. f. **26**.

—— La Musique simplifiée dans sa théorie et dans son enseignement. pt. 1; pt. 2. sect. 1. *Paris*, 1836, [39.] 8°. **7895**. ff. **2**.
No more published?

BUSSET (Gabriel de Bourbon) *See* Bourbon-Busset.

BUSSET (Marie Louis Henri de Bourbon) *See* Bourbon-Busset.

BUSSET (Maurice) Gergovia, capitale des Gaules, et l'oppidum du plateau des Côtes. [With illustrations.] pp. 148. *Paris*, 1933. 8°. **07707**. i. **53**.

—— La Technique moderne du bois gravé et les procédés anciens des xylographes du XVIe siècle et des maîtres graveurs japonais . . . Édition ornée de bois gravés par l'auteur et de nombreuses reproductions de gravures de maîtres. pp. 172. *Paris*, [1925.] 8°. **7860**. cc. **25**.

—— La Technique moderne du tableau et les procédés secrets des grands coloristes des XVe, XVIe et XVIIe siècles recueillis et restitués . . . Édition ornée de dessins et de gravures de l'auteur, *etc.* pp. 192. *Paris*, 1929. 8°. **7859**. p. **25**.

—— Le Vieux pays d'Auvergne. Recueil des costumes, des types et des coutumes de Haute et Basse-Auvergne, *etc.* [With plates after designs by the author.] pp. 62. *Clermont-Ferrand*, 1924. fol. **10170**. l. **19**.
The date in the colophon is 1925.

BUSSETO (Ireneo di) Ricerche storico-canoniche . . . intorno la chiesa, il convento, e la fabbrica della Ss. Nunziata di Parma, dirette all'esame di una citazione con precetto inibitorio estorta dalla Curia Episcopale di Parma ad istanza dell'illustrissima Congregazione di detta fabbrica contro il guardiano, e i religiosi del prenominato convento. pp. 95. *Parma*, 1796. 4°. **703**. i. **21**.

BUSSETTI (Curzio) *See* Buzzetti.

BUSSEUIL (François Louis) Considérations particulières sur les fièvres bilieuses. Thèse, *etc.* pp. 28. *Paris*, 1815. 4°. **1183**. c. **8**. (**3**.)

BUSSEY INSTITUTION. *See* Cambridge, *Mass.—Harvard University.*

BUSSEY'S WOOD. Was it a Ghost? The murders in Bussey's Wood, *etc.* [The preface signed: J. B., i.e. H. J. Brent.] [1868.] 8°. *See* B., J. **8631**. bb. **5**.

BUSSEY (Alan) *See* West Wickham, *Kent.—New Renaissance Association.* Gloria. The official organ of the New Renaissance Association. Editor: A. Bussey. 1938, *etc.* 8°. P.P. **1556**. dao.

BUSSEY (Alec)

—— Onward Humanity. Life and endeavour on the heavenly spheres and on other planets. Set down by A. Bussey from dictation of Chas. Bussey, Robert Cook and other spirits of the "Band of the Golden Light," *etc.* (Volume 1.) pp. 109. *Wherry Press: Norwich*, 1938. 8°. **8634**. d. **17**.
Imperfect; wanting vol. 2.

BUSSEY (Alec)

—— Onward Humanity . . . Combination of volumes I, II & III. 3 pt. *Soman Wherry Press: Norwich*, 1948. 8°. **8634**. ff. **55**.

BUSSEY (Benjamin) *See* Gray (Thomas) *Minister at Roxbury, Mass.* A Tribute to the Memory of Benjamin Bussey, Esq., *etc.* 1842. 8°. **4986**. bbb. **38**. (**9**.)

BUSSEY (Claude de) Jésus enfant, modèle du jeune âge, ouvrage . . . revu et réédité dans le style naïf de l'original, par le père Benoît Valuy . . . Sixième édition. pp. xxviii. xviii. 420. *Lyon, Paris*, 1864. 24°. **4411**. aaa. **16**.

BUSSEY (Frank T.) Some Notes on West Hackney Church, 1824–1924, *etc.* pp. 51. *T. W. Childs & Sons: Teddington*, 1924. 8°. **04705**. cc. **10**.

BUSSEY (George Daniel) A Manual of Personal Hygiene. pp. x. 156. *Ginn & Co.: Boston*, [1917.] 8°. **7391**. aa. **14**.

BUSSEY (George G.) **AND CO.** A Popular Treatise . . . entitled The Bat of the Victorian Era, or the Evolution of the "Demon Driver," *etc.* pp. 32. *Sports Manufactory: London*, 1897. 8°. **7905**. d. **38**.

BUSSEY (George Moir) *See* Arabian Nights. [*English.*] The Arabian Nights' Entertainments . . . Carefully revised and corrected, with an explanatory and historical introduction, by G. M. Bussey, *etc.* 1839. 8°. **838**. k. **15**.

—— *See* Goldsmith (Oliver) *the Poet.* [*The Vicar of Wakefield.*] The Vicar of Wakefield . . . Prefatory memoir by G. M. Bussey, *etc.* [1845.] 8°. **12620**. e. **32**.

—— Bible Stories, from the Creation to the conquest of Canaan, *etc.* [With plates.] pp. iv. 204. *Joseph Thomas: London*, 1840. 16°. **1110**. a. **20**.

—— Fables, original and selected . . . Illustrated by . . . engravings, designed by J. J. Grandville. pp. xxxiv. 352. *Charles Tilt: London*, 1839. 8°. **12304**. g. **35**.

—— [Another edition.] pp. xxxiv. 352. *Willoughby & Co.: London*, 1842. 8°. **1461**. i. **2**.

—— [Another edition.] A Treasure House of Fables, *etc.* pp. 352. *Simpkin, Marshall & Co.: London; T. D. Morison: Glasgow*, [1892.] 8°. **12305**. k. **8**.

—— History of Napoleon. Illustrated by Horace Vernet. 2 vol. *Joseph Thomas: London*, 1840. 8°. **10659**. f. **2**.

—— Memoir of the Emperor Napoleon. (Chiefly abstracted by the author from his "History of Napoleon, illustrated by Horace Vernet.") pp. 12. *W. S. Orr & Co.: London; W. & R. Chambers: Edinburgh*, [1840?] fol. **1881**. a. **1**. (**103**.)

—— Tints of Talent, from many pencils . . . [An anthology of verse and prose.] Edited by G. M. Bussey. pp. 320. *Joseph Thomas; Simpkin & Marshall: London*, 1837. 8°. **12331**. bb. **27**.

BUSSEY (George Moir) **and GASPEY** (Thomas)

—— The Pictorial History of France and of the French People . . . Enriched with . . . designs by Jules David. 2 vol. *W. S. Orr & Co.: London*, 1843. 8°. **1442**. k. **4**.

BUSSEY (Harry Findlater) Sixty Years of Journalism. Anecdotes and reminiscences. pp. 303. *J. W. Arrowsmith: Bristol*, 1906. 8°. **10855**. de. **8**.

BUSSEY (Harry Findlater) and **REID** (Thomas Wilson)

—— The Newspaper Reader: the journals of the nineteenth century on events of the day. [Extracts, edited by H. F. Bussey and T. W. Reid.] pp. 288. *London*, 1879. 8º. [*Blackie's Comprehensive School Series.*] **12200**. bbb. **20/31**.

BUSSEY (Leslie D.) Song of the Seasons, and other poems. pp. 36. *A. H. Stockwell: London*, [1929.] 8º. **011644**. f. **82**.

BUSSEY (Peter) An Address to the Working Men of England, especially those from eighteen to thirty years of age, who are capable of serving in the standing army. pp. 15. *J. Ibbettson: Bradford*, 1838. 8º. **1389**. e. **38**. (**1**.)

BUSSHE (Thomas) *See* Rutton (William L.) The Penmanship of a Bookkeeper (Thomas Busshe), *etc.* [With facsimiles.] [1902.] 8º. **7702**. f. **43**. (**3**.)

BUSSI (Amedeo) *See* Nicodemi (M. A.) Storia di Tivoli . . . A cura di A. Bussi e V. Pacifici. 1926. 8º. [*Studi e fonti per la storia della regione tiburtina.* no. 4.] Ac. **6555**.

BUSSI (Corboli)

—— *See* Pirri (P.) La Missione di Mons. Corboli Bussi in Lombardia e la crisi della politica italiana di Pio ix. 1947. 8º. [*Rivista di storia della Chiesa in Italia.* anno. 1. no. 1.] P.P. **22**. da.

BUSSI (Emilio) La Donazione nel suo svolgimento storico. *See* Christianity. Cristianesimo e diritto romano. 1935. 8º. **5206.ee.50.**

—— Per la storia dei conflitti giurisdizionali dal Consiglio Legislativo al Consiglio di Stato, 1797–1815. 1940. *See* Periodical Publications.—*Rome.* Rivista di storia del diritto italiano. vol. 13. fasc. 2. 1928, *etc.* 8º. P.P. **1379**. k.

BUSSI (Feliciano) Istoria della città di Viterbo. [With plates.] pp. xx. 478. *Roma*, 1742. fol. **664**. g. **17**.

—— [Another copy.] **180**. g. **1**.

BUSSI (Giulio) *Count.* *See* Ovidius Naso (P.) [*Works.—Latin and Italian.*] [The Works of Ovid, *etc.*] (Le Epistole eroiche di P. Ovidio Nasone, tradotte in parte dal conte G. Bussi, ed in parte da Remigio Fiorentino.) 1731, *etc.* 4º. [*Malatesta* (*G. R.*) *Corpus omnium veterum poetarum latinorum, etc.* tom. 24.] **77**. c. **25**.

—— *See* Ovidius Naso (P.) [*Epistolae Heroidum.—Latin and Italian.*] L'Epistole eroiche di Ovidio tradotte in terza rima dal conte G. Bussi, *etc.* 1703. 12º. **11335**. aaa. **9**. (**3**.)

—— [Sonnets.] 1712. *See* Gobbi (A.) Scelta di sonetti, *etc.* pt. 4. 1709, *etc.* 8º. **240**. k. **17**.

BUSSI (Joannes Baptista) *Archbishop of Tarsus.* De Reverendissimi . . . Joannis Bussi, Nuntii Coloniensis, enormi agendi ratione, epistola historica. Cui inserta habentur edictum Serenissimi Electoris Coloniensis Archiepiscopi, Leodensis Episcopi &c. adversus eumdem [*sic*] Bussium, ut episcopalis juris violatorem, & mandatum quo idem Serenissimi Electoris edictum irritum declarare audet. pp. 8. [*Cologne?*] 1709. 4º. **490**. g. **29**. (**5**.)

—— De Reverendissimi . . . Joannis Bussi . . . enormi agendi ratione, epistola altera; sive . . . Comitis Palatini, S. R. I. Electoris & Illustriss. . . . Monasteriensis Episcopi ad Summum Pontificem Clementem xi. querimonia, contra

BUSSI (Joannes Baptista) *Archbishop of Tarsus.*

imprudentem . . . D. J. B. Bussi . . . protestationem, quâ compositioni inter Borussiæ regem & civitatem Coloniensem initæ intercessit. pp. 8. [*Cologne?*] 1709. 4º. **490**. g. **29**. (**5***.)

—— De Reverendissimi . . . Joannis Bussi . . . enormi agendi ratione, epistola tertia: sive ad S. R. I. Electorum et Principum Ecclesiasticorum Ministros in Comitiis Ratisbonensibus constitutos commonitorium, ut ordinariæ Dominorum suorum jurisdictioni sacræ solerter invigilent, adversùs consiliarios ejusdem Nuntii Pontificii, auctoritatis episcopalis invasores. pp. 32. [*Cologne?*] 1709. 4º. **490**. g. **29**. (**5****.)

—— Depulsio excommunicationis, per . . . D. Bussi . . . attentatæ in R.D. Matthiam Torkium: ubi eadem excommunicatio demonstratur planè nulla, evanida, cassa, irrita. pp. 16. [*Utrecht*, 1709.] 4º. **490**. g. **29**. (**5*****.)

BUSSI (Louis de) *See* Debussi.

BUSSI (Nicolás) *See* Escobar (F.) Esculturas de Bussi . . . en Lorca, *etc.* 1919. 8º. **7875**. df. **25**.

BUSSIANUS (Thomas) Epithalamion docti viri Christophori Trutenbuel, & virginis Claræ filiæ Consulis Marci Mulleri Ascaniensis. *Ex literaria officina Leucoreana: Wittembergæ*, 1544. 4º. **11409**. g. **34**.

BUSSIDON (Charles) Abyssinie et Angleterre—Théodoros [i.e. Theodore iii., Emperor of Abyssinia]. Perfidies et intrigues anglaises dévoilées. Souvenirs et preuves. pp. xxi. 322. *Paris*, 1888. 12º. **9061**. b. **23**.

BUSSIÈRE (de) *Mademoiselle.* *See* Hérault de Gourville (J.) Mémoires de Mons. de Gourville, *etc.* [Edited by Mademoiselle de Bussière.] 1724. 12º. **282**. a. **21**.

—— —— 1782. 8º. **679**. b. **15**.

BUSSIÈRE (E.) *See* Morellet (J. N.) Le Nivernais . . . publié par MM. Morellet, Barat, E. Bussière. 1838, *etc.* fol. **1300**. m. **10**.

BUSSIÈRE (François Auguste) Thèse pour le doctorat en médecine, *etc.* (Questions sur diverses branches des sciences médicales.) pp. 45. *Paris*, 1844. 4º. [*Collection des thèses soutenues à la Faculté de Médecine de Paris.* An 1844. tom. 3.] **7371**. e. **8**.

BUSSIÈRE (Gaston) *See* Vaughan (Bernard) Life Lessons from Blessed Joan of Arc . . . With illustrations by G. Bussière, *etc.* 1910. 8º. **4828**. ee. **7**.

BUSSIÈRE (Georges) Études historiques sur la Révolution en Périgord. 3 pt. *Bordeaux*, 1877–1903. 8º. **9225**. h. **28**.

—— Recherches inédites d'art et d'histoire sur l'abbaye de Brantôme. 6 pt. 1879–94. *See* Périgueux.—*Société Historique et Archéologique du Périgord.* Bulletin, *etc.* tom. 6, 7, 17, 19–21. 1874, *etc.* 8º. Ac. **6886**.

BUSSIÈRE (Georges) and **LEGOUIS** (Émile)

—— Le Général Michel Beaupuy. 1755–1796, *etc.* pp. viii. 246. *Paris, Périgueux*, 1891. 8º. **10661**. ee. **31**.

—— La Chemise sanglante du général Beaupuy, 25 octobre 1793. *See* Loir (M.) Au drapeau! Récits militaires extraits des mémoires de G. Bussière et E. Legouis, *etc.* 1897. 4º. **8821**. dd. **8**.

BUSSIÈRE (Joseph Antoine) Essai sur le spasme. Tribut académique, *etc.* pp. 27. *Montpellier*, 1831. 4°. **1181.** f. **6.** (**8.**)

BUSSIÈRE (Lucien) Propositions de pathologie et de thérapeutique; thèse, *etc.* pp. 13. *Paris*, 1835. 4°. **1184.** g. **5.** (**28.**)

BUSSIÈRE (Marie Théodore de) *Viscount. See* Renouard de Bussierre.

BUSSIÈRE (Teodoro di) *Baron. See* Renouard de Bussierre (Marie T.) *Viscount.*

BUSSIÈRES (Charles François Joseph Broquart de) *See* Broquart de Bussières.

BUSSIÈRES (Jean de) Joannis de Bussieres . . . Miscellanea poëtica. 2 pt. *Ex officina Anissoniana: Lugduni*, 1675. 8°. **11405.** aaa. **19.**
Imperfect; wanting the titlepage to pt. 1.

—— Ioannis de Bussieres . . . De Rhea liberata, poemation, *etc.* pp. 83. *I. B. Deuenet: Lugduni*, 1655. 12°. **1213.** b. **13.**

—— La Rhéade, ou l'Île de Rhé délivrée. Poème épique en trois chants écrit en latin au xviie siècle . . . Traduit en français en 1884 par le Dr Algier. pp. 106. *Angers*, 1898. 8°. **11409.** gg. **56.**

—— Chronologia principum, *etc.* [A fragment of an unidentified edition of J. de Bussières's " Flosculi ", consisting of pp. 1–18, 31–81 of the " Chronologia " only.] [*Lyons?* 1662?] 12°. **1433.** a. **11.**

—— Flosculi historici delibati . . . sive historia universalis . . . usque ad annum m.dc.lvi. Accessit . . . chronologia principum . . . Editio quinta. Cum appendice de rebus britannicis, *etc.* [By J. de Bussières.] 2 pt. 1663. 12°. *See* Flosculi. **9008.** a. **17.**

—— Editio sexta, auctior & emendatior. Cum appendice, *etc.* 2 pt. *W. Hall; impensis Joseph Godwin: Oxoniæ*, 1668. 12°. **800.** a. **11.**

—— [Another edition.] Ad annum hujus sæculi sexagesimum . . . Prodiere nunc primum in Germania continuati ad annum m.d.c.lxxx. Appenditur Chronologia, *etc.* 2 pt. *Sumptibus H. Demen: Coloniae Agrippinae*, 1688. 12°. C. **27.** c. **32.**
This copy is bound in silver, ornamented with a niello border surrounding open tracery. With an additional titlepage, engraved.

—— Johan de Bussieres Blümlein allerley Geschichten. Aus dem Lateinischen ins Hochteutsche übersetzet von einem unglückseeligen Fürsten, weil er die reine Warheit und Aufrichtigkeit liebet. pp. 308. *W. Schwendimann: Hannover*, 1673. 8°. **9004.** aaa. **15.**

—— Mémoires contenans ce qu'il y a de plus remarquable dans Villefranche, capitale du Beauiolois, *etc.* [By J. de Bussières. With plates.] pp. 187. 1671. 4°. *See* Villefranche. **576.** g. **11.** (**2.**)

—— Ioannis de Bussieres . . . Scanderbergus. Poema. Editio noua alterâ parte auctior. pp. 284. *Sumpt. L. Anisson & I. B. Deuenet: Lugduni*, 1658. 12°. **1213.** b. **14.**

—— Editio tertia longè emendatior. Cui accesserunt aliquot poemata. pp. 342. *Veronæ*, 1720. 8°. **11405.** aa. **12.**

BUSSIÈRES (Simon de) The Presence of God . . . Translated from the French of P. S. de Bussières, *etc.* pp. 40. *Burns & Oates: London*, 1879. 16°. [*Popular Franciscan Library.*] **4401.** cc. **55.**

BUSSIÈRES (Théodore Renouard de) *Baron. See* Renouard de Bussierre (Marie T.) *Viscount.*

BUSSIERRE (Alfred Renouard de) *Baron. See* Renouard de Bussierre.

BUSSIERRE (Léon Renouard de) *See* Renouard de Bussierre.

BUSSIERRE (Marie Théodore de) *Viscount. See* Renouard de Bussierre.

BUSSIERRE (Théodore de) *Viscount. See* Renouard de Bussierre (Marie T.)

BUSSIERRES (F.) Mélange d'observavations [*sic*] et de réflexions sur diverses maladies. pp. 36. *Paris*, 1820. 4°. **1183.** f. **8.** (**19.**)

BUSSILLET (Henri) Voyage à la capitale des microbes. pp. 228. *Niort*, 1936. 8°. **12512.** t. **1.**

BUSSILLET (Maurice) Beaux livres modernes . . . Première partie. (Vente des 26–27–28 octobre par le Ministère de Me Maurice Bussillet.) pp. 68. *Lyon*, 1937. 8°. **11900.** ee. **58.**

—— Bibliothèque d'un amateur forézien. Première partie, *etc.* (Vente des 30 novembre et 1er décembre 1934.) pp. 51. *Lyon*, 1934. 8°. **11912.** c. **34.**

—— Catalogues de livres anciens, romantiques et modernes. Dessins et gravures. (Vente du 1er avril, 1938 par le Ministère de Me Bussillet.) pp. 41. *Lyon*, 1938. 8°. **11900.** cc. **51.**

BUSSINESK (Zh.) *See* Boussinesq (J.)

BUSSING (Caspar) *See* Bussingius.

BUSSING (Irvin) Public Utility Regulation and the so-called Sliding Scale. A study of the sliding scale as a means of encouraging and rewarding efficiency in the management of regulated monopolies. pp. 174. *Columbia University Press: New York*, 1936. 8°. [*Studies in History, Economics and Public Law.* no. 415.] Ac. **2688/2.**

BUSSINGER (J. J.)

—— Ueber Felix Mendelssohn und seine Musik zur Antigone. Eine Vorlesung, *etc.* pp. 28. *Basel*, [c. 1880.] 8°. Hirsch **3660.**

BUSSINGIUS (Caspar) Conspectus heraldicæ, succincta, curiosa & perspicua ratione adornatæ . . . Insignia præcipuorum in cultiori Europa imperatorum, regum, principum ac statuum . . . exhibens, *etc.* (Conspectus heraldicæ pars secunda, potestatum extra Germaniam præcipua insignia sistens.) [With plates.] 2 pt. *Ex officina libraria Schultziana: Hamburgi*, [1693?] *obl.* 8°. **607.** a. **2.**

—— Einleitung zu der Herolds-Kunst, auff eine bequeme und deutliche Art verfasset, in zwey Theilen . . . in dieser Teutschen Übersetzung mit einem neuen Theil Von der Wapen-Kunst insgemein . . . vermehret von C. Bussingio. 3 pt. *In Schultzischen Buchladen: Hamburg*, 1694. *obl.* 8°. **9904.** a. **8.**

—— Casparis Bussingii . . . De situ telluris Paradisiacæ et Chiliasticæ Burnetiano, ad eclipticam recto, quem T. Burnetius in sua Theoria sacra telluris proposuit, dissertatio mathematica. Qua simul obliquitas eclipticæ a priori demonstratur. pp. 43. *Typis Zieglerianis: Hamburgi*, 1695. 4°. **1014.** b. **60.**

—— [Another copy.] **444.** c. **17.** (**3.**)
The titlepage is mutilated.

BUSSINGIUS (CASPAR)

—— Die die Lehrer sendende und entwendende Gnade Gottes, wie sie die rechtschaffenen Lehrer der Wahrheit ... erklähret für von Gott zum Heil gesandte ... Wunder. Als ... der hoch-ehrwürdige ... Herr, Herr Johannes Winckler ... erloschen zu seyn schiene ... an statt einer ... Leichen-Predigt ... fürgestellet ... von C. Bussingio. (Scripta Johannis Winckleri.—Elogium funebre ... dicatum a Georgio Eliezer Edzardo.—Memoria ... Dn Johannis Winckleri ... per Johannem Schultze ... recitata.) pp. 88. *Hamburg*, 1705. fol. **835. l. 9. (5.)**
Imperfect; wanting pp. 53–86 *and some matter at the end.*

—— C. Bussingii ... Mathemata universa in tabulas succinctas redacta. *Sumptibus autoris; typis Zieglerianis: Hamburgi*, [1695.] fol. **532. k. 17. (2.)**

—— Ratio lectionum publicarum in Lectorio Cathedrali, anno tertio, seculi XVIIIVI [i.e. 1703] habitarum, reddita a ... C. Bussingio ... labores ... simul intimans anni quarti. [*Hamburg*, 1704.] 4°. **473. a. 30.**

BÜSSING-NAG. *See* BUESSING-NAG.

BUSSI-RABUTIN (ROGER DE) *Count.* *See* RABUTIN (R. de) *Count de Bussy.*

BUSSIUS (   ) *Kreisdirector.* Agrarstatistisches [concerning the Duchy of Brunswick]. *See* BRUNSWICK, *Duchy of, etc.* [*Appendix.*] Die Landwirthschaft, *etc.* 1859. 8°. **7075. h. 2.**

BUSSIUS (AUGUSTUS FRIDERICUS) Disputatio medica inauguralis de passione hysterica. *A. Elzevier: Lugduni Batavorum*, 1692. 4°. **T. 559. (6.)**

BUSSIUS (FRIDERICUS AUGUSTUS) Dissertatione inaugurali medica observationes de cauto et præstantissimo vomitoriorum usu ... exponet auctor F. A. Bussius. *Praes.* F. Hoffmann. pp. 44. *Halæ Magdeburgicæ*, [1728.] 4°. **1179. e. 3. (25.)**

—— [Another copy.] **T. 603. (3.)**

BUSSIUS (JOANNES BAPTISTA) *Archbishop of Tarsus.* *See* BUSSI.

BUSSIUS (JOHANNES WILHELMUS) Disputatio inauguralis physiologico-medica qua astites viriles ... publico ... judicio tradit J. W. Bussius. *Erfordiae*, [1715.] 4°. **T. 520. (27.)**

—— [Another copy.] **1185. b. 21. (7.)**

BUSSIUS (THEODORUS) Disputatio inauguralis medica de epilepsia, *etc.* *Praes.* G. Moebius. pp. 83. *Literis C. Freyschmids: Jenæ*, 1659. 4°. **T. 547. (16.)**

—— [Another copy.] **1185. d. 2. (21.)**

BUSSLER (ERICH) Frauencharaktere aus den Tragödien des Euripides. pp. 43. *Hamburg*, 1892. 8°. [*Sammlung gemeinverständlicher wissenschaftlicher Vorträge.* Neue Folge. Hft. 158.] **12249. m. 7.**

—— Hiob und Prometheus, zwei Vorkämpfer der göttlichen Gerechtigkeit. Ein Vergleich. pp. 44. *Hamburg*, 1897. 8°. [*Sammlung gemeinverständlicher wissenschaftlicher Vorträge.* Neue Folge. Hft. 276.] **12249. m. 12.**

—— Religionsanschauungen des Euripides. pp. 44. *Hamburg*, 1894. 8°. [*Sammlung gemeinverständlicher wissenschaftlicher Vorträge.* Neue Folge. Hft. 192.] **12249. m. 8.**

BUSSLER (ERNST FRIEDRICH) Verzierungen aus dem Alterthume. [Plates.] Hft. 1–20. *Berlin*, [1805.] 4°. **7702. cc. 7.**
Imperfect; wanting Hft. 21.

BUSSLER (LUDWIG)

—— Musikalische Elementarlehre mit achtundfünfzig Aufgaben ... Fünfte verbesserte und vermehrte Auflage. pp. viii. 96. *Bielefeld & Leipzig*, 1890. 8°. Hirsch **5237.**

—— Musikalische Formenlehre ... Vierte Auflage, durchgesehen und erweitert von Dr. Hugo Leichtentritt. pp. xiii. 240. *Berlin*, 1920. 8°. **7899. dd. 31.**

—— Praktische Harmonielehre in vierundfünfzig Aufgaben ... Zweite verbesserte und vermehrte Auflage. pp. x. 224. *Berlin*, 1885. 8°. Hirsch **5238.**

—— Praktische Harmonielehre in vierundfünfzig Aufgaben ... Fünfte verbesserte Auflage, revidiert und mit erläuternden Anmerkungen versehen. pp. xv. 236. *Berlin*, 1903. 8°. **7898. i. 27.**

BUSSLER (ROBERT) Die Alba-Madonna, ein ächter Rafael in Berlin. Kunstgeschichtliche Notiz, *etc.* pp. 40. *Berlin*, 1868. 8°. **7855. aaa. 43. (7.)**

—— Der Rafael-Saal. Verzeichniss der im Königlichen Orangeriehause zu Sans-Souci ... aufgestellten Copien nach Gemälden von Rafael Sanzio. pp. 58. 1858. 8°. *See* SANS-SOUCI. **7854. c. 40.**

BUSSLER (WILHELM) Preussische Feldherren und Helden. Kurzgefasste Lebensbilder sämmtlicher Heerführer, deren Namen preussische Regimenter tragen, *etc.* 4 Bd. *Gotha*, 1890–96. 8°. **010707. h. 61.**

BUSSMANN (ALINE) *See* FOCK (Gorch) *pseud.* Nordsee ... Herausgegeben von A. Bussmann, *etc.* 1918. 8°. **012553. c. 62.**

—— *See* FOCK (Gorch) *pseud.* Sterne überm Meer ... Mit einer Lebensbeschreibung ... herausgegeben von A. Bussmann, *etc.* 1918. 8°. **010704. e. 31.**

BUSS-MANN (CHRISTIANUS) De officio boni præceptoris, disputatio politica, *etc.* *Praes.* J. Le Bleu. pp. 52. *Typis J. D. Hampelii: Giessæ Hassorum*, 1658. 4°. **526. k. 38. (2.)**

BUSSMANN (CONRADUS MAURITIUS CHRIST.) Observationes de ductu thoracico, *etc.* *Praes.* A. Haller. *See* HALLER (A. von) *Baron.* Disputationum anatomicarum selectarum volumen I [*etc.*]. vol. 1. 1746, *etc.* 4°. **45. e. 14.**

BUSSMANN (E. WILHELM) *See* GOUDSCHAAL (P. R.) and BUSSMANN (E. W.) Nieuw kortschrift, *etc.* 1885. 8°. **12991. g. 29.**

BUSSMANN (HANS) Untersuchungen über die Presse als Machtform. pp. 54. *Berlin*, 1933. 8°. **11854. w. 60.**

BUSSMANN (HANS B.)

—— *See* WICHMANN (K.) Wichmann's Pocket Dictionary of the German and English Languages ... Entirely revised by L. Borinski ... and H. B. Bussmann. 1952. 8°. **12964. a. 20.**

—— Hundert Meister der deutschen Sprache. Eine Sammlung grosser deutscher Prosa. Herausgegeben von H. B. Bussmann. pp. 526. *Berlin*, [1937.] 8°. **012253. s. 1.**

BUSSMANN (Otto) Der völkerrechtliche Garantievertrag insbesondere seit der Enstehung des Genfer Völkerbundes. pp. xii. 66. *Leipzig*, 1927. 8°. [*Frankfurter Abhandlungen zum Kriegsverhütungsrecht.* Hft. 3.]
06915.df.2/3.

BUSSMANN (Walter)

—— Treitschke. Sein Welt- und Geschichtsbild. [With a portrait.] pp. xv. 479. *Göttingen*, 1952. 8°. [*Göttinger Bausteine zur Geschichtswissenschaft.* Hft. 3/4.]
W.P. **13178/3–4.**

BUSSNANG, *Barons of.* *See* Brenner (C.) Geschichte der Freiherren von Bussnang, *etc.* 1870. 8°. [*Thurgauische Beiträge zur vaterländischen Geschichte.* Hft. 11.]
Ac. **6936.**

BUSSNANG (Conrad von) *Abbot of St. Gall.* *See* Brenner (C.) Geschichte der Freiherren von Bussnang, mit besonderer Beziehung auf Konrad von Bussnang, Abt von St. Gallen, *etc.* 1870. 8°. [*Thurgauische Beiträge zur vaterländischen Geschichte.* Hft. 11.] Ac. **6936.**

BUSSNANG (Conrad von) *Bishop of Strasburg.* *See* Brenner (C.) Geschichte der Freiherren von Bussnang, mit besonderer Beziehung auf . . . Konrad von Bussnang Bischof von Strassburg, *etc.* 1870. 8°. [*Thurgauische Beiträge zur vaterländischen Geschichte.* Hft. 11.]
Ac. **6936.**

BUSSOD (Antoine Julien) Précis sur la brûlure ; thèse, *etc.* pp. 20. *Paris*, 1830. 4°. **1184.** d. **8.** (**5.**)

BUSSOD (Claude Marie) Dissertation sur la saignée, considérée comme moyen thérapeutique, *etc.* pp. 15. *Paris*, 1815. 4°. **1183.** c. **12.** (**3.**)

BUSSOD (Jean) Sympathie réciproque de l'estomac et de la tête. Essai, *etc.* pp. 23. *Montpellier*, an vii [1799]. 4°.
1180. d. **5.** (**22.**)

BUSSOLA (Franciscus) De cantharidibus, dissertatio inauguralis, *etc.* *Ticini Regii*, [1828.] 8°.
7383*. c. **10.** (**26.**)

BUSSOLARI (Jacopo) *See* Migliazza (D.) Matteo Villani nel racconto delle gesta di Jacopo Bussolari. 1907. 8°.
11851. tt. **12.** (**4.**)

BUSSOLIN (Dominique)

—— Les Célèbres verreries de Venise et de Murano. Description historique, technologique et statistique de cette industrie divisée dans ses diverses branches, avec des notices sur le commerce en général des émaux et des conteries. pp. 88. *Venise*, 1847. 8°. **7950.** aa. **75.**

BUSSOLIN (Giovanni) Delle istituzioni di sanità marittima nel bacino del Mediterraneo. Studio comparativo . . . Con . . . tavole, *etc.* pp. 345. *Trieste*, 1881. 8°.
7687. f. **8.**

BUSSOLIN (Pietro) *See* Horatius Flaccus (Q.) [*Carmina and Epodi.—Selections.—Italian.*] Ventiquattro odi scelte di Orazio Flacco tradotte liberamente in verso e dialetto veneziano da P. Bussolin. 1832. 8°. [*Gamba (B.) Serie degli scritti impressi in dialetto veneziano, etc.*]
11451. b. **2.**

BUSSOLO (Francesco Orazio) Nel solenne ingresso alla Chiesa Episcopale di Feltre dell'illustrissimo . . . Andrea Benedetto Ganassoni, Arcivescovo . . . Orazione recitata . . . da F. O. Bussolo. pp. 22.
Feltre, 1780. 4°. **835.** l. **11.** (**5.**)

BUSSOM (Thomas Wainwright) The Life and Dramatic Works of Pradon. A dissertation, *etc.* pp. 194. *Édouard Champion : Paris*, 1922. 8°. **10657.** dd. **39.**

—— [Another issue.] A Rival of Racine. Pradon, his Life and Dramatic Works. *Pris*, 1922. 8°. **10657.** cc. **24.**
Without the last leaf, containing the author's "vita."

BUSSON (Arnold) Die Doppelwahl des Jahres 1257 und das römische Königthum Alfons x. von Castilien. Ein Beitrag zur Geschichte des grossen Interregnums. Mit bisher ungedruckten Briefen. pp. vi. 136.
Münster, 1866. 8°. **9340.** bbb. **18.**

—— Die florentinische Geschichte der Malespini und deren Benutzung durch Dante. pp. 89. *Innsbruck*, 1869. 8°.
11422. d. **28.** (**11.**)

—— Kleine Beiträge zur mittelalterlichen Münzkunde Tirols. 1889. *See* Periodical Publications.—*Vienna.* Numismatische Zeitschrift, *etc.* Jahrg. 21. 1869, *etc.* 8°.
P.P. **1889.** g.

—— Der Krieg von 1278 und die Schlacht bei Dürnkrut. Eine kritische Untersuchung. 1880. *See* Vienna.—Oesterreichische *Akademie der Wissenschaften.* Archiv für Kunde österreichischer Geschichts-Quellen. Bd. 62. 1848, *etc.* 8°. Ac. **810/8.**

—— Lykurgos und die Grosse Rhetra. Rede, *etc.* pp. 29. *Innsbruck*, 1887. 8°. **11312.** l. **37.** (**5.**)

—— Der Patinakrieg. Die Restaurirung des Maxdenkmals zu Innsbruck und der Streit für und wider dieselbe, aktenmæssig dargestellt. [By A. Busson, F. Disertori, and others.] pp. iv. 122. *Innsbruck*, 1883. 8°.
7875. bb. **11.**

—— Zur Geschichte des grossen Landfriedensbundes deutscher Städte. 1254. pp. 94. *Innsbruck*, 1874. 8°.
9325. bb. **5.**

BUSSON (Claude Ignace) *See* Feller (F. X. de) Biographie universelle . . . Édition revue et continuée . . . sous la direction de . . . M. l'abbé Busson. 1847, *etc.* 8°.
1329. g. **1–9.**

—— *See* Feller (F. X. de) Supplément général au Dictionnaire historique . . . sous la direction de M. C. Weiss et M. l'abbé Busson. 1851. 8°. **609*.** f. **13*.**

—— *See* Prémord (C. L.) Règles de la vie chrétienne . . . Traduites . . . par l'abbé C. I. Busson. 1838. 12°.
4403. bbb. **44.**

—— Premières lettres sur l'extatique de Niéderbronn (Elizabeth Eppinger), et sur ses révélations . . . Troisième édition. pp. vi. 160. *Besançon, Paris*, 1850. 12°.
4885. b. **15.**

BUSSON (Georges) *See* Rousselet (L.) Nos grandes écoles d'application . . . Ouvrage illustré . . . par G. Busson, *etc.* 1895. 8°. **8356.** i. **16.**

BUSSON (Gustave) *See* Mans.—*Cathedral Church.* Nécrologe-obituaire de la cathédrale du Mans. Publié par G. Busson et A. Ledru, *etc.* 1906. 8°. [*Archives historiques du Maine.* no. 7.] Ac. **5321.** b.

—— *See* Mans, *Diocese of.* Actus pontificium Cenomannis in urbe degentium. Publiés par l'abbé G. Busson et l'abbé A. Ledru, *etc.* 1901. 8°. [*Archives historiques du Maine.* vol. 2.] Ac. **5321.** b.

BUSSON (Henri) *Professeur à la Faculté des Lettres d'Alger.*

—— *See* La Fontaine (J. de) [*Minor Works.*] Discours à Madame de la Sablière . . . Commentaire littéraire et philosophique par H. Busson et F. Gohin. 1938. 8°. Ac. **9812/52.**

—— Charles d'Espinay, évêque de Dol, et son œuvre poétique, *etc.* [With " Les Sonnets " and with a portrait.] pp. iv. 201. *Paris*, 1923. 8°. [*Bibliothèque littéraire de la Renaissance.* sér. 2. tom. 6.] **2312.** h. **2/6.**

—— La Pensée religieuse française de Charron à Pascal. [With a bibliography.] pp. 664. *Paris*, 1933. 8°. **3901.** f. **51.**

—— La Religion des classiques, 1660–1685. pp. 476. *Paris*, 1948. 8°. **08467.** h. **41.**
Part of a series entitled " Bibliothèque de philosophie contemporaine."

BUSSON (Henri) *Professeur au Lycée Carnot, Paris. See* Stern (Alfred) La Vie de Mirabeau, *etc.* (II. Pendant la Révolution. Traduit . . . par M. H. Busson.) 1895, *etc.* 8°. **010664.** m. **11.**

—— La France d'aujourd'hui et ses colonies, *etc.* ([By] H. Busson, Joseph Fèvre, Henri Hauser.) [With bibliographies.] pp. ix. 692. *Paris*, 1920. 8°. **010169.** ee. **39.**

—— Notre Empire colonial. Par H. Busson . . . Joseph Fèvre . . . Henri Hauser . . . Avec 108 gravures et cartes dans le texte. pp. ii. 272. *Paris*, 1910. 8°. **8156.** d. **37.**

BUSSON (Jean)

—— Que passe le vent d'avril. Roman. pp. 339. *Paris*, 1950. 8°. **12519.** e. **19.**

BUSSON (Julianus) *Praes. See* Dienert (A. D.) Quæstio medico-chirurgica . . . An absque membranæ tympani apertura topica injici in concham possint. 1755. 4°. [*Haller (A. von) Baron. Disputationes chirurgicæ, etc.* tom. 2.] **7481.** ff. **20.**

—— *Praes. See* Poissonnier (P. J.) Quaestio medica, an ab origine monstra? 1760. 4°. [*Sigwart (G. F.) Quaestiones medicae Parisinae, etc.* fasc. 2.] **1179.** b. **18.**

—— Considérations philosophiques sur l'Histoire d'Éma. Seconde partie. *See* Thiard de Bissy (C. de) *Count.* Histoire d'Éma, *etc.* 1752. 8°. C. **108.** bb. **7.**

—— Quæstio medica . . . An redeunte vere citò redeat convalescenti sanitas? *Praes.* J. B. de Diest. pp. 4. [*Paris*,] 1741. 4°. **1182.** e. **6.** (**35.**)

—— Quæstio medica . . . An sanguis in fœtu à dextrâ in sinistram cordis auriculam per foramen ovale transeat, non secùs? *Praes.* L. Peaget. pp. 4. [*Paris*,] 1741. 4°. **1182.** e. **6.** (**17.**)

—— Quaestio medico-chirurgica, an ab ictu, lapsu, nisuve, quandoque vertebrarum caries? *Praes.* F. J. Hunauld. *See* Sigwart (G. F.) Quaestiones medicae Parisinae, *etc.* fasc. 1. 1759, *etc.* 4°. **1179.** b. **17.**

BUSSON (Paul) [Die Feuerbutze.] The Fire-Spirits . . . Translated . . . by J. Eglington. pp. 314. *William Heinemann: London*, 1929. 8°. **12554.** t. **26.**

—— Gedichte. pp. viii. 114. *Dresden & Leipzig*, 1901. 8°. **011528.** g. **95.**

BUSSON (Paul)

—— [Die Wiedergeburt des Melchior Dronte.] The Man who was born again . . . Translated by Prince Mirski and Thomas Moult. pp. ix. 302. *William Heinemann: London*, 1927. 8°. **012554.** b. **36.**

BUSSON BILLAULT (Julien) Deux ans de bâtonnat. Avec une préface de M. le comte d'Haussonville. pp. xi. 194. *Paris*, 1912. 8°. **012301.** f. **53.**

BUSSON-DESCARS (Pierre) Traité du nivellement. [With plates.] pp. viii. 71. 17. *Parme*, 1813. 4°. **1261.** c. **13.**

BUSSONE (Francesco) *Count Carmagnola. See* Battistella (A.) Il Conte Carmagnola, *etc.* 1889. 8°. **10630.** ff. **32.**

—— *See* Berlan (F.) Il Conte Francesco di Carmagnola. Memorie storico-critiche, *etc.* 1855. 8°. **10631.** c. **58.**

—— *See* Bustelli (G.) Sulla decollazione di Francesco Bussone, conte di Carmagnola, *etc.* 1887. 8°. **10630.** bb. **37.**

—— *See* Cibrario (G. A. L.) *Count.* La Morte del conte Carmagnola, *etc.* 1834. 8°. **1450.** e. **3.** (**1.**)

—— Carmagnola: an Italian tale of the fifteenth century. A poem in five cantos. pp. 114. *Saunders & Otley: London*, 1856. 8°. **11649.** c. **41.**

BUSSONI (Antonio)

—— Discurso de Padron Lisandro de la Regola fatto a la Gensola co Peppe er duro, Cremente Spacca, e Filicetto pe soprannome Trecciabella sull'aritrovato der cirusico romano Sor Angelo Comi pe impitrine, e conservane tal, e quale, tal, e quale le parte dell'ommini morti, l'uccelli, le bestie, le serpe, come fussino vivi vivi . . . tutto lavore, e opera de A. B. R. [i.e. A. Bussoni, romano]. pp. 88. 1840. 8°. *See* B., A., *R.* **1405.** h. **13.**

BUSSONNET (A.) *See* Nadal (V.) Blois, its Château and its Monuments . . . Translated by Mlle. A. Bussonnet, *etc.* [1910?] 8°. **10168.** aa. **6.**

BUSSOTTI (Dionigi) *Bishop of Borgo San Sepolcro. See* Soldus (J.) Antidotario per il tempo di peste . . . tradotto . . . da D. B. S. [i.e. D. Bussotti], *etc.* 1630. 4°. **1167.** g. **15.** (**3.**)

BUSSOTTI (Ferdinando) Miscellanea di scritti politici pubblicata per cura di F. Bussotti. pp. 264. *Firenze*, 1851. 8°. **8032.** g. **5.**

BUSSOTTO. Historia bellissima da ridere, di Bussotto, quale essendo pregato da vn monaro ad aiutarli a cauar vn' asino, esso gli spicò la coda. [In verse.] *G. Righettini: Treuigi*, 1636. 4°. **11426.** c. **11.**

BUSSOTTUS (Dionysius) *Bishop of Borgo San Sepolcro. See* Bussotti (Dionigi)

BUSSOVIUS (Conradus) *See* Bussow (Conrad)

BÜSSOW ( ) [For the German surname of this form:] *See* Buessow.

BUSSOW (Conrad) Relatio, das ist summarische Erzehlung vom eigentlichen Ursprung dieses itzigen blutigen Kriegs-Wesens in Moscowiter-Land oder Reussland. Und was sich innerhalb sechs und zwantzig Jahren

BUSSOW (CONRAD)

mit fünff regierenden Kaysern . . . daselbst allerseits begeben und zugetragen, *etc.* [1584–1612.] *See* LENINGRAD. —*Археографическая Коммиссия.* Rerum Rossicarum scriptores exteri, *etc.* tom. 1. 1851. 4°. Ac. **5581/3.**

BUSSUM. Gids voor Bussum en Naarden. pp. 65. [*Bussum*, 1925.] 8°. **010271.** ee. **18.**

BUSSWALD (MARIA ANNA) Das verlässliche und bewährte Grätzer-Kochbuch . . . Vierte . . . Ausgabe. [With tables.] pp. 336. *Grätz*, 1845. 8°. **1036.** c. **32.**

BUSSY, CHARLES JOSEPH PATISSIER, *Marquis de.* *See* PATISSIER (C. J.) *Marquis de Bussy-Castelnau.*

——, MICHEL CELSE ROGER DE RABUTIN, *Count de.* *See* RABUTIN (M. C. R. de) *Bishop of Luçon.*

——, ROGER DE RABUTIN, *Count de.* *See* RABUTIN (R. de) *Count de Bussy.*

BUSSY-CASTELNAU, CHARLES JOSEPH PATISSIER, *Marquis of.* *See* PATISSIER.

BUSSY (MARTIN DE) *See* MARTIN DE BUSSY.

BUSSY (MIGNOT DE) *See* MIGNOT DE BUSSY.

BUSSY (A. M. L. DE) *See* DEMOSTHENES. [*De Corona.—Greek.*] *Δημοσθενους περι στεφανου λογος* . . . Édition nouvelle, enrichie de notes . . . par A. M. L. de Bussy. 1869. 12°. **11391.** aa. **1.**

—— Histoire de la Petite Bretagne appelée aussi Bretagne Armorique. pp. xii. 304. *Paris*, 1843. 12°. **10170.** bb. **34.**

BUSSY (ANDRÉ) La Municipalisation des tramways. Ses résultats financiers à l'étranger. pp. xii. 343. *Paris*, 1908. 8°. **08235.** d. **5.**

BUSSY (ANTOINE ALEXANDRE BRUTUS) *See* FARADAY (Michael) Manipulations chimiques . . . revu pour la partie technique par M. Bussy, *etc.* 1827. 8°. **1035.** g. **23.**

—— Essai sur la pleurésie; thèse, *etc.* pp. 17. *Paris*, 1832. 4°. **1184.** e. **4.** (**2.**)

BUSSY (ANTOINE ALEXANDRE BRUTUS) and **BOUTRON-CHARLARD** (ANTOINE FRANÇOIS)

—— Traité des moyens de reconnaître les falsifications des drogues simples et composées, et d'en constater le degré de pureté. [With a plate.] pp. xii. 507. *Paris*, 1829. 8°. **7509.** ccc. **8.**

BUSSY (ANTOINE FRANÇOIS MARIE MIGNOT DE) *See* MIGNOT DE BUSSY.

BUSSY (ARTHUR LE COSQUINO DE)

—— *See* BRUGMANS (H.) Opkomst en bloei van Amsterdam . . . Herzien en bijgewerkt door Mr. A. Le C. de Bussy, *etc.* 1944. 8°. **9414.i.10/4a.**

—— Marken in Utrecht. [Text to accompany maps.] pp. xiv. 128. *'s-Gravenhage*, 1925. 8°. [*Geschiedkundige Atlas van Nederland.*] **Map.144.a.2.**

BUSSY (BERNARD F.) and **BLACKMORE** (W. T.) The Roundhead: an original drama in three acts. pp. 36. *London, New York*, [1885.] 12°. [*French's Acting Edition.* vol. 123.] **2304.** h. **14.** (**1.**)

BUSSY (CHARLES DE) *Chef de bataillon d'infanterie.* L'Église Saint-Nicaise de Rouen d'après les archives et des documents modernes. pp. 126. pl. VIII. *Rouen*, 1914. 8°. **4633.** cc. **3.**

BUSSY (CHARLES DE) *Directeur du Théâtre du "Journal."* Une Nuit de Musset. [A play.] Lettre-préface de M. Jules Claretie. pp. 69. *Paris*, [1910.] 8°. **11735.** f. **18.**

—— Rayonnements. Poésies diverses, *etc.* pp. vii. 344. *Paris*, 1906. 8°. **011483.** g. **23.**

BUSSY (CHARLES DE) *pseud.* [i.e. CHARLES MARCHAL.] Le Cas de M. Henri Rochefort. pp. 31. *Paris*, [1868.] 12°. **5423.** a. **16.**

—— Catéchisme politique à l'usage du peuple des villes et des campagnes. pp. 32. *Paris*, 1861. 16°. **8006.** a. **5.**

—— Les Conspirateurs en Angleterre 1848–1858. Étude historique. pp. 359. *Paris*, 1858. 8°. **8026.** aa. **3.**

—— Douzième édition. pp. 359. *Paris*, 1858. 12°. **8010.** a. **19.**

—— Les Courtisanes devenues saintes. Étude historique. pp. 192. *Paris*, 1859. 12°. **4807.** a. **9.**

—— Dictionnaire amusant. Recueil d'anecdotes drolatiques, *etc.* pp. vii. 320. *Paris*, 1859. 12°. **12355.** c. **1.**

—— Dictionnaire de l'art dramatique à l'usage des artistes et des gens du monde. pp. iii. 414. *Paris*, 1866. 8°. **11795.** ccc. **24.**

—— Dictionnaire de l'art vétérinaire à l'usage des cultivateurs, *etc.* pp. 340. *Paris*, 1865. 12°. **7294.** bbb. **23.**

—— Dictionnaire universel d'histoire, avec la biographie de tous les personnages célèbres et la mythologie. pp. 574. *Paris*, 1858. 12°. **10603.** bb. **2.**

—— [A reissue.] *Paris*, [1867.] 12°. **10603.** bb. **3.**

—— Dictionnaire universel de marine . . . avec la traduction des termes de la marine française en termes de la marine anglaise. pp. ii. 409. *Paris*, 1862. 12°. **8806.** b. **3.**

—— Dictionnaire universel des beaux-arts . . . suivi d'un dictionnaire d'iconologie. pp. 360. *Paris*, 1861. 12°. **7805.** aa. **9.**

—— Dictionnaire universel des sciences, des lettres et des arts. pp. 510. *Paris*, 1860. 12°. **814.** d. **3.**

—— [A reissue.] *Paris*, 1862. 12°. **814.** d. **4.**

—— [A reissue, with a supplement.] pp. 510. 576–78. *Paris*, 1867. 12°. **814.** d. **5.**

—— Dictionnaire usuel et pratique d'agriculture et d'horticulture. pp. 338 [838]. *Paris*, 1863. 8°. **7075.** aaa. **15.**

—— Histoire des excommuniés depuis les temps les plus reculés jusqu'à nos jours. pp. 192. *Paris*, 1860. 16°. **4807.** a. **10.**

—— Histoire et réfutation du socialisme depuis l'antiquité jusqu'à nos jours. pp. 323. *Paris*, 1859. 12°. **8206.** a. **25.**

—— Les Philosophes au pilori. Étude historique. pp. 223. *Paris*, 1858. 12°. **4014.** b. **10.**

BUSSY (CHARLES DE) *pseud.* [i.e. CHARLES MARCHAL.]

—— Les Philosophes convertis. Étude de mœurs au XIXe siècle. pp. 407. *Paris*, 1860. 12°. **3901.** bbb. **12.**

—— Poésies populaires. pp. 14. *Paris*, 1864. 16°. **11481.** a. **10.**

—— Les Régicides. Étude historique. pp. 351. *Paris*, 1858. 8°. **9007.** b. **24.**

—— Les Révoltés contre l'Église et l'ordre sociale. 2 tom. *Paris*, 1863. 12°. **4570.** bb. **6.**

—— Sauvons le Pape. [With Pius IX's Encyclical of 19 Jan. 1860.] pp. 71. *Paris*, 1860. 12°. **8033.** a. **42.** (**4.**)

—— La Science à la portée de tous. Encyclopédie universelle, répertoire classique, historique, géographique, scientifique, *etc.* sér. 1. 1862. 8°. *See* ENCYCLOPAEDIAS. **736.** e. **1.**

—— Les Toquades, illustrées par Gavarni. Étude de mœurs. pp. 160. *Paris*, [1858.] 4°. **12352.** g. **18.**

BUSSY (CHARLES DE) *S.J. See* HOANG (P.) Mélanges sur l'administration. [Translated from the Latin by Ch. de Bussy.] 1902. 8°. [*Variétés sinologiques.* no. 21.] **15235.** c.

BUSSY (CHARLES LE CLERC DE) *Count. See* LE CLERC DE BUSSY.

BUSSY (DOROTHY) *See* also OLIVIA, *pseud.* [i.e. D. Bussy.]

—— *See* BRÉAL (A.) Velazquez. (Translated . . . by Madame Simon Bussy.) [1905.] 16°. **7808.** de. **1/11.**

—— *See* GIDE (A. P. G.) Two Symphonies. (Isabelle, and, La Symphonie.) . . . Translated by D. Bussy. 1931. 8°. **12516.** s. **23.**

—— *See* GIDE (A. P. G.) Two Symphonies. Translated . . . by D. Bussy. 1949. 8°. **12240.** b. **22.**

—— *See* GIDE (A. P. G.) Fruits of the Earth. [A translation of "Les Nourritures terrestres" and "Les Nouvelles nourritures."] Translated . . . by D. Bussy. 1949. 8°. **12239.** df. **9.**

—— *See* GIDE (A. P. G.) The Return of the Prodigal . . . Saul . . . Translated by D. Bussy. 1953. 8°. **012551.** t. **19.**

—— *See* GIDE (A. P. G.) The School for Wives. Robert. Geneviève; or, the Unfinished confidence. Translated . . . by D. Bussy. 1953. 8°. **12519.** de. **41.**

—— *See* GIDE (A. P. G.) Lafcadio's Adventures—Les Caves du Vatican. Translated . . . by D. Bussy. 1928. 8°. **012548.** ccc. **63.**

—— *See* GIDE (A. P. G.) [Les Caves du Vatican.] The Vatican Cellars . . . Translated . . . by D. Bussy. 1952. 8°. **12519.** de. **40.**

—— *See* GIDE (A. P. G.) [L'École des femmes.] The School for Wives . . . Translated . . . by D. Bussy. 1930. 8°. **12516.** s. **10.**

—— *See* GIDE (A. P. G.) [Les Faux-Monnayeurs.] The Counterfeiters . . . Translated . . . by D. Bussy. 1928. 8°. **12547.** h. **20.**

—— *See* GIDE (A. P. G.) The Coiners. Translated by D. Bussy. 1950. 8°. **12549.** n. **17.**

BUSSY (DOROTHY)

—— *See* GIDE (A. P. G.) [L'Immoraliste.] The Immoralist. Translated . . . by D. Bussy. 1930. 8°. **12516.** s. **12.**

—— *See* GIDE (A. P. G.) The Immoralist. Translated . . . by D. Bussy. 1953. 8°. **12519.** ee. **7.**

—— *See* GIDE (A. P. G.) [La Porte étroite.] Strait is the Gate. Translated . . . by D. Bussy. 1924. 8°. **012547.** dd. **8.**

—— *See* GIDE (A. P. G.) Strait is the Gate. Translated . . . by D. Bussy. 1948. 8°. **012550.** a. **80.**

—— *See* GIDE (A. P. G.) [La Porte étroite.] Strait is the Gate . . . Translated . . . by D. Bussy. 1952. 8°. **12208.** a. **1/881.**

—— *See* GIDE (A. P. G.) [Retouches à mon Retour de l'U.R.S.S.] Afterthoughts, *etc.* (Translated by D. Bussy.) [1938.] 8°. **010291.** f. **43.**

—— *See* GIDE (A. P. G.) [Retour de l'U.R.S.S.] Back from the U.S.S.R. (Translated by D. Bussy.) 1937. 8°. **010291.e.48.**

—— *See* GIDE (A. P. G.) [Si le grain ne meurt.] If it die... Translated by D. Bussy. 1950. 8°. **10656.** m. **27.**

—— *See* GIDE (A. P. G.) [Si le grain ne meurt.] If it die . . . Translated by D. Bussy. 1951. 8°. **12519.** b. **32.**

—— *See* GIDE (A. P. G.) [Voyage au Congo.] Travels in the Congo. Translated . . . by D. Bussy. 1930. 8°. **10094.** d. **20.**

—— *See* HOGG (James) *the Ettrick Shepherd.* The Private Memoirs and Confessions of a Justified Sinner . . . With an introduction by André Gide (translated from the French by D. Bussy). 1947. 8°. W.P. **891/2.**

—— *See* MAUCLAIR (C.) Antoine Watteau, *etc.* (Translated . . . by Madame Simon Bussy.) [1906.] 16°. **7808.** de. **1/16.**

—— *See* MONTAIGNE (M. de) The Living Thoughts of Montaigne. Presented by A. Gide. (Translation of the introductory essay by D. Bussy.) 1939. 8°. **8473.p.1/3.**

—— *See* MONTAIGNE (M. de) The Living Thoughts of Montaigne. Presented by A. Gide. (Translation of the introductory essay by D. Bussy.) 1939. 8°. **8473.p.2/3.**

—— *See* SCHLUMBERGER (J.) [Saint-Saturnin.] The Seventh Age, or Saint Saturnin . . . Translated by Madame Bussy. 1933. 8°. **12514.** ppp. **14.**

—— *See* VALÉRY (P. A. T. J.) Dance and the Soul . . . With a translation by D. Bussy. 1951. 8°. **8459.** r. **35.**

—— Eugène Delacroix. [With plates.] pp. xix. 127. *Duckworth & Co.: London*, 1907. 8°. **010661.** aaa. **41.**

BUSSY (ERNEST) Poésies . . . Avec . . . une notice biographique . . . par P. Godet. pp. 288. *Lausanne*, 1888. 8°. **11483.** f. **30.**

BUSSY (ÉTIENNE G. MARION) *See* MARION BUSSY.

BUSSY (FRANÇOIS DE) *See* GRANT (William L.) La Mission de M. de Bussy à Londres en 1761, *etc.* 1901. 8°. **9008.** dd. **16.** (**6.**)

BUSSY (FREDERICK MOIR) Irish Conspiracies. Recollections of John Mallon, the great Irish detective, and other reminiscences. [With portraits.] pp. viii. 275. *Everett & Co.: London*, 1910. 8°. **010827.** h. **15.**

—— Mean Monopolists. Stricken soldiers condemned to avoidable suffering. A great science officially boycotted. [An attack on the attitude of the General Medical Council towards osteopathy.] pp. 32. *St. Clement's Press: London*, [1916.] 12°. **07481.** g. **24.**

—— [Another edition.] pp. 32. *F. M. Bussy: London*, [1917.] 12°. **07481.** ee. **8.**

—— Meccas for Americans. [With illustrations.] pp. 206. xxxv. *Everett & Co.: London*, 1912. 8°. **010347.** e. **9.**

—— Staggering Dogmatisms. Being the preface to a work entitled A Strangle-Hold on the Best, when orthodox medicine-healing fails. pp. 24. *J. J. Keliher & Co.: London*, [1922.] 8°. **7440.** de. **25.**

BUSSY (FREDERICK MOIR) and **CAINE** (GORDON RALPH HALL)

—— Gems of Oratory and notable passages from the lips of British and Irish statesmen and orators. Edited by F. M. Bussy . . . and G. R. H. Caine. pt. 1. pp. 108. *Collier & Co.: London*, [1909.] 8°. **012301.** e. **78.**
No more published.

BUSSY (GASTON) and **LÈBRE** (GASTON) Le Mahatma. [A novel.] pp. 357. *Paris*, [1888.] 12°. **012547.** k. **2.**

BUSSY (HONORÉE LE BEL DE) *See* LE BEL DE BUSSY.

BUSSY (IVONNE JEANNE LE COSQUINO DE)

—— Groei en bestrijding van algen in onoverdekte zwembaden . . . Rapport no. 1 . . . van de Commissie Zwembaden T.N.O. 2 dl. [1949.] fol. *See* NETHERLANDS. [Kingdom of the Netherlands.]—*Nederlandse Centrale Organisatie voor Toegepast Natuurwetenschappelijk Onderzoek.—Organisatiecommissie Gezondheitstechniek T.N.O.—Commissie Zwembaden T.N.O.* S. J. **310/41.**

BUSSY (IZAAK JAN LE COSQUINO DE) Ethisch idealisme. pp. 255. *Amsterdam*, 1875. 8°. **8466.** ff. **2.**

—— Inleiding tot de zedekunde. pp. 176. *Amsterdam*, 1898. 8°. **8470.** i. **2.**

—— De Maatstaf van het zedelijk oordeel en het voorwerp van het godsdienstig geloof. Beschouwingen naar aanleiding van Dr L. W. E. Rauwenhoff, " Wijsbegeerte van den godsdienst." pp. xi. 132. *Amsterdam*, 1889. 8°. **3925.** i. **45.**

BUSSY (J. H. DE) De Bussy's groene-serie. no. 1–6, 9. *Amsterdam, Pretoria*, 1913–17. 8°. **012203.** f. **58.**

—— De Bussy se historiese leesboeke. *Kaapstad, Pretoria*, 1927– . 8°. **W.P. 9980.**

—— Voorloopige lijst der houders van den Mercuur-Code. pp. 38. *Amsterdam*, 1892. 8°. **8756.** de. **47.**

BUSSY (JANE SIMONE) *See* GARNETT (David) La Femme changée en renard . . . Traduction de J.-S. Bussy, *etc.* 1924. 8°. **12237.** ppp. **1/43.**

BUSSY (JEAN MARC) Notes de J. M. Bussy, appointé voltigeur. Campagnes d'Espagne et de Russie. [Edited by Frédéric Barbey. With a portrait.] 1913. *See* SWISS SOLDIERS. Soldats suisses au service étranger, *etc.* tom. 5. 1908, *etc.* 8°. **08821.** e. **1/5.**

BUSSY (PAUL DE) *See* VOLTAIRE (F. M. A. de) [*Zaïre.*] Zaïre. Tagédie . . . With . . . notes by P. de Bussy. 1877. 8°. **11736.** dd. **1/35.**

—— *See* WITT (H. de) Derrière les haies . . . Edited by P. de Bussy, *etc.* 1876. 8°. **12954.** de. **43.**

—— Key to the Grammatical, Etymological and Scientific Questions, with the translation of idiomatic passages set in the French Examination Papers—C. Rühle's Collection . . . for the Royal Military College, Sandhurst ; direct commissions in the Army, *etc.* pp. 142. *Dulau & Co.; D. Nutt: London*, 1863. 8°. **12953.** f. **8.**

BUSSY (PIERRE GENTY DE) *See* GENTY DE BUSSY.

BUSSY (ROSA) *See* HEINE (H.) [*Buch der Lieder.*] Lose Blätter aus Heine's Buch der Lieder in Farbendruck nach Original-Aquarellen von R. Bussy. 1866. 4°. **11527.** i. **17.**

BUSSY (SIMON) Simon Bussy. Par François Fosca, *etc.* [Reproductions, with an introductory essay.] pp. 63. *Paris*, [1931.] 8°. [*Peintres nouveaux.* no. 43.] **7870.de.1/43.**

BUSSY (*Madame* SIMON) *See* BUSSY (Dorothy)

BUSSY (THÉODORE ROLAND DE) *See* ROLAND DE BUSSY.

BUSSY-DAGONEAU ( ) *Count.*

—— *See* DAGONEAU (E. M.) Pièces détachées, *etc.* [Concerning the detention of the Count de Bussy-Dagoneau.] [1790.] 8°. **R. 170.** (**18.**)

BUSSY D'AMBOISE (LOUIS DE CLERMONT DE) *See* CLERMONT DE BUSSY D'AMBOISE.

BUSSY D'AMBOISE (RENÉE DE) *See* MONTLUC DE BALAGNY (R. de) *Princess de Cambrai.*

BUSSY DE LAMET (ADRIEN AUGUSTIN DE) and **FROMAGEAU** (GERMAIN) Le Dictionnaire des cas de conscience, decidés suivant les principes de la morale, les usages de la discipline ecclesiastique, l'autorité des conciles et des canonistes, et la jurisprudence du royaume. [Edited by S. M. Treuvé.] 2 tom. *Paris*, 1733. fol. **504.** k. **4, 5.**

BUSSY-RABUTIN (MICHEL CELSE ROGER DE) *Bishop of Luçon.* *See* RABUTIN (M. C. R. de)

BUSSY-RABUTIN (ROGER DE) *Count.* *See* RABUTIN (R. de) *Count de Bussy.*

BUST (R. D.) New Zealand versus the World as a Long Wool producing Country, comprising a table of calculations, explanatory remarks, and data, by a practical sheep breeder (R. D. Bust), *etc.* pp. 28. *Waikouaiti*, 1863. 8°. **1146.** c. **17.**

BUSTAMANTE, *Family of.*

—— *See* BUSTAMANTE DE LA FUENTE (M. J.) Mis ascendientes, *etc.* 1955. 8°. **9906.** pp. **22.**

BUSTAMANTE (A. SÁNCHEZ DE) *Geographer.* *See* SÁNCHEZ DE BUSTAMANTE.

BUSTAMANTE (ANASTASIO) *President of the Republic of Mexico.* *See* ALPUCHE É INFANTE (J. M.) Primera (—5ª) Philípica. [Addressed to President A. Bustamante.] 1838, *etc.* 4°. **8179.** aaa. **76.** (**2.**)

—— *See* BUSTAMANTE (C. M. de) El Gabinete Mexicano durante el segundo periodo del . . . Presidente A. Bustamante, *etc.* 1842. 8°. **9771.** c. **21.**

—— *See* Cardonaleño. Hay [*sic*] pagará Bustamante, la sangre que ha derramado. [Signed: El Cardonaleño.] 1833. 4°. **9770. bb. 22. (25.)**

—— *See* Ibar (F.) Nuevo Clamor de Venganza ó Muerte, contra el intruso gobierno [of A. Bustamante], *etc.* 1831. 4°. **9770. aa. 1. (14.)**

—— *See* López de Santa-Anna (A.) *President of the Republic of Mexico.* Don Antonio el Arrogante (Santa-Anna) íntima la rendicion al general Bustamante. 1832. *s. sh.* fol. **9770. k. 10. (60.)**

—— [For official documents issued by A. Bustamante as President of the Mexican Republic:] *See* Mexico.—[*Laws, etc.*—ii.]—Bustamante (A.) *President.*

—— *See* San Luis Potosí, *State of.*—*Congreso.* Iniciativa a las Cámaras de la Union de la H. Legislatura de San Luis Potosí sobre el general Bustamante y sus ministros. 1833. 4°. L.A.S. **554/7.**

—— El Capitan general de Provincias Internas (A. Bustamante), á las de Guanajuato, S. Luis Potosí y Zacatecas. [On assuming charge of these provinces.] *México,* 1822. fol. **9770. k. 6. (66.)**

—— El Capitan general y Gefe superior político de provincias internas (A. Bustamante), á los habitantes del Nuevo Santander. [On certain disturbances in the province.] *México,* 1822. fol. **9770. k. 6. (65.)**

—— Convenio celebrado entre las divisiones al mando de . . . D. A. Bustamante y D. Antonio Lopez de Santa Anna. [Dated: Zavaleta, 23 Dec. 1832.] *México,* 1833. fol. **9770. k. 11. (23.)**

—— [Another copy.] **9770. k. 10. (73.)**

—— Discurso del Escmo. Sr. Vice-Presidente de la República, en la apertura de las sesiones estraordinarias del Congreso general, que se verificó hoy 28 de junio de 1830. [*Mexico,* 1830.] fol. **9770. k. 10. (8.)**

—— Discurso del Escmo. Sr. Vice-Presidente de la República, en la apertura de las sesiones ordinarias del Congreso general, que se verificó hoy 1° de enero de 1831. *México,* 1831. fol. **9770. k. 10. (39.)**

—— Discurso pronunciado por el Escmo. Sr. Vice-Presidente de la República . . . A. Bustamante, al abrirse las sesiones ordinarias del Congreso general en 1° de enero de 1830. [*Mexico?* 1830.] *s. sh.* fol. **9770. k. 10. (7.)**

—— Discurso que el Vice-Presidente de la República . . . pronunció en la clausura de las sesiones ordinarias del Congreso general el dia 21 de mayo de 1831. *México,* 1831. fol. **9770. k. 10. (40.)**

—— Discurso que el Vice-Presidente de la República . . . pronunció al abrirse las sesiones estraordinarias del Congreso general el dia 1° de agosto de 1831. *México,* 1831. fol. **9770. k. 10. (41.)**

—— Discurso que el Vice-Presidente de la República . . . pronunció en la clausura de las sesiones estraordinarias del Congreso general el dia 15 de diciembre de 1831. *México,* 1831. fol. **9770. k. 10. (42.)**

—— Discurso que el Vice-Presidente de la República . . . pronunció en la apertura de las sesiones ordinarias del Congreso general el dia 1° de enero de 1832. *México,* 1832. fol. **9770. k. 10. (78.)**

BUSTAMANTE (Anastasio) *President of the Republic of Mexico.*

—— Discurso que el Vice-Presidente de la República . . . pronunció en la clausura de las sesiones ordinarias del Congreso general el dia 23 de mayo de 1832. *México,* 1832. fol. **9770. k. 10. (79.)**

—— Ejército de Reserva, Protector de la Libertad y de las Leyes. [A letter from Bustamante to the Governor of the State of Mexico announcing his adoption of the revolutionary programme. With the governor's answer.] *México,* 1829. *s. sh.* fol. **9770. k. 9. (110.)**

—— *Begin.* Habitantes de las Provincias Internas de Oriente y Occidente. [On the proclamation of Agustin de Iturbide as Emperor. Dated: 19 May 1822.] [*Mexico,* 1822.] fol. **9770. k. 6. (110.)**

—— Manifiesto que el ciudadano A. Bustamante dírige á sus compatriotas como general en gefe del ejército de operaciones sobre Tamaulipas y demas Departamentos de Oriente. pp. 75. *México,* 1839. 8°. **8179. c. 10.**

—— Manifiesto que el Vicepresidente de la República Mexicana (A. Bustamante) dirige á la Nacion. pp. 20. *México,* 1830. 8°. **8180. aaa. 26.**

—— Noticia estraordinaria. [Military despatches from A. Bustamante. Dated: 30 Nov. 1832.] *México,* 1832. *s. sh.* fol. **9770. k. 10. (99.)**

—— Noticias de Guadalajara y Manifiesto del General Bustamante á la Nacion [dated: 29 Apr. 1824]. [*Mexico,*] 1824. 4°. **9770. bb. 15. (17.)**

—— Telegrafo estraordinario. Oficio del Escmo. Sr. General D. A. Bustamante participando estar en completa libertad el Escmo. Sr. Presidente . . . A. Lopez de Santa-Anna. [Dated: 12 June 1833.] *México,* 1833. *s. sh.* fol. **9770. k. 11. (264.)**

—— Agonías de la Usurpacion Bustamantina. [An extract from the "Demócrata mexicano."] pp. 11. *México,* 1832. 4°. **9770. aa. 1. (8.)**

—— *See* Agonias. Las Agonías de la Usurpacion, contestadas en Zacatecas. [A defence of F. García, Governor of Zacatecas, against a pamphlet entitled: "Agonías de la Usurpacion Bustamantina."] 1832. 4°. **9770. bb. 21. (28.)**

—— *Begin:* Al Escmo. Sr. General de Division D. A. Bustamante. [Accusing him of misgovernment.] pp. 20. *México,* 1832. 4°. **9770. aa. 1. (10.)**

—— Bustamante y Federacion: esto pide la Nacion. [Signed: Los Federalistas.] pp. 8. *México,* 1837. 4°. **9770. bb. 24. (20.)**

—— Cuanto mas amigos mas claros, ó sean reflecciones al Sr. Vice-Presidente (Bustamante) sobre las reformas que imperiosamente reclama el estado político del país. [Signed: P.] 1830. 4°. *See* P. **9770. bb. 20. (5.)**

—— Derrota del General Bustamante y su division. [Signed: J. M. B.] 1832. 4°. *See* B., J. M. **9770. aa. 1. (9.)**

—— Esta es la verdad pelada, tan pícaro es Bustamante como Pedraza y Santa-Anna. [An indictment of the three men.] 3 no. *México,* 1833. 4°. **9770. bb. 22. (21.)**

—— Estraordinaria. Traicion del General Bustamante al Presidente Santa-Anna. *México,* 1833. *s. sh.* fol. **9770. k. 11. (59.)**

BUSTAMANTE (Anastasio) *President of the Republic of Mexico.*

—— Grito de Venganza y Muerte, contra el intruso gobierno [of A. Bustamante]. 2 pt. *México*, 1831. 4°. **9770**. aa. **1**. (**13**.)

Severely cropped.

—— [Another copy of pt. 1.] **9770**. bb. **21**. (**12**.)

—— Segunda parte del Memorial de Justas Quejas al Escmo. Sr. Presidente [i.e. A. Bustamante]. [A federalist reply to the pamphlet: "Memorial de Justas Quejas," *etc.*] pp. 8. *México*, 1837. 8°. **9770**. bb. **24**. (**30**.)

—— Vindicacion del General Presidente, ó sea, proveído al Memorial de justas quejas (dirigido al Exmo. Sr. presidente D. A. Bustamante), *etc.* [Signed: E. E. D. L. L., i.e. L. Espino.] 1837. 4°. *See* L., E. E. D. L. **9770**. bb. **24**. (**39**.)

—— Observaciones al Exmo. Sr. Presidente de la República Megicana D. A. Bustamante. [On current politics.] pp. 8. *México*, 1837. 4°. **9770**. bb. **24**. (**31**.)

—— Prision de Bustamante por el asesino atroz [i.e. the contemplated assassination] del Presidente Santa-Anna. *México*, 1833. *s. sh.* fol. **9770**. k. **11**. (**234**.)

—— Tumba prócsima del Gobierno Usurpador [of A. Bustamante]. pp. 16. *México*, 1832. 4°. **9770**. aa. **1**. (**11**.)

BUSTAMANTE (Antonio de Estrada y) *See* Estrada y Bustamante.

BUSTAMANTE (Antonio Sánchez de) *See* Sánchez de Bustamante y Sirvén.

BUSTAMANTE (Benigno) Artículo sobre los fundamentos en que debe apoyarse el arreglo definitivo y general de los pesos y medidas mas convenientes en la República Mexicana. [Signed: B. Bustamante.] pp. 54. *México*, 1852. 12°. **8506**. aa. **57**. (**3**.)

BUSTAMANTE (Carlos María de) *See* Alegre (F. X.) Historia de la Compañía de Jesus en Nueva-España . . . Publícala . . . C. M. de Bustamante. 1841, *etc.* 8°. **4745**. c. **5**.

—— *See* Alva Ixtlilxuchitl (F. de) Horribles crueldades de los conquistadores de México . . . ó sea memoria escrita por D. F. de Alva Ixtlilxuchitl . . . Publícala por suplemento a la Historia del padre Sahagun, C. M. de Bustamante. 1829. 8°. **9771**. b. **10**. (**2**.)

—— —— 1838. 8°. [*Voyages, relations et mémoires originaux pour servir à l'histoire de la découverte de l'Amérique.* tom. 8.] **1196**. i. **6**.

—— *See* Alva Ixtlilxuchitl (F. de) Orribili crudeltà dei Conquistatori del Messico . . . Memoria . . . pubblicata . . . da C. M. de Bustamante, *etc.* 1843. 8°. [*Marmocchi (F. C.) Raccolta di viaggi, etc.* tom. 11.] **1424**. i. **5**.

—— *See* Badillo (M.) Vindicacion. Carta del que subscrive al S.L.D. Carlos Maria Bustamante. [Replying to an article entitled: "Examen crítico de la providencia dada por el S.P.E. sobre los generales Quintanar y Bustamante," published in the "Abeja de Chilpantzinco" of 6 July 1824.] [1824.] fol. **9770**. k. **8**. (**138**.)

—— *See* Bernardino [Ribeira], *de Sahagún, Franciscan.* La Aparicion de N[tra] Señora de Guadalupe de Mexico . . . Publícala, precediendo una disertacion sobre la aparicion Guadalupana, y con notas sobre la conquista de México C. M. de Bustamante. 1840. 8°. **9771**. b. **10**. (**1**.)

BUSTAMANTE (Carlos María de)

—— *See* Bernardino [Ribeira], *de Sahagún, Franciscan.* Historia de la Conquista de Mexico . . . Publícala por separado de sus demas obras C. M. de Bustamante. 1829. 8°. **9771**. b. **12**.

—— *See* Bernardino [Ribeira], *de Sahagún, Franciscan.* Historia General de las Cosas de Nueva España . . . Dala a luz con notas y suplementos C. M. de Bustamante, *etc.* 1829, *etc.* 8°. **9771**. b. **5**.

—— *See* Boturini Benaducci (L.) Crónica Mexicana, Teoamóxtli, ó libro que contiene todo lo interesante . . . de los antiguos Indios Tultecas y Mexicanos, redactado de un antiguo códice inédito del caballero Boturini, por el Lic. D. C. M. de Bustamante, *etc.* 1822. 4°. **604**. c. **32**. (**2**.)

—— *See* Boturini Benaducci (L.) Galería de Antiguos Príncipes Mejicanos, *etc.* (pt. 2. Galería de Príncipes Mejicanos . . . Redactada . . . por . . . D. C. M. de Bustamante.) 1821. 4°. **604**. c. **32**. (**1**.)

—— *See* Boturini Benaduci (L.) Tezcoco en los últimos tiempos de sus antiguos reyes, ó sea relacion tomada de los manuscritos inéditos de Boturini; redactados por el Lic. D. M. Veytia. Publícalos con notas y adiciones . . . C. M. de Bustamante. 1826. 8°. **9771**. b. **9**.

—— *See* Cavo (A.) Los Tres Siglos de Mexico durante el gobierno español hasta la entrada del ejército Trigarante . . . Publícala con notas y suplemento C. M. de Bustamante. 1836, *etc.* 8°. **9771**. b. **4**.

—— *See* Cosas. Cosas que jamás se han oido, *etc.* [An attack upon the public character of C. M. de Bustamante.] 1825. 4°. **9770**. bb. **15**. (**40**.)

—— *See* León y Gama (A. de) Descripcion histórica y cronológica de las dos piedras, que con ocasion del nuevo empedrado que se esta formando en la plaza principal de Mexico, se hallaron . . . el año de 1790 . . . Dala a luz, con notas, biografia de su autor . . . C. M. de Bustamante. 1832. 4°. **811**. g. **8**.

—— *See* López de Gomara (F.) Historia de las Conquistas de Hernando Cortés . . . Publícala . . . con varias notas y adiciones, C. M. de Bustamante. 1826. 8°. **9771**. b. **6**. (**1**.)

—— *See* Martínez de Navarrete (J. M.) Poemas Inéditos. Apuntes biográficos de D. C. M. de Bustamante. 1929. 8°. **011451**. h. **61**.

—— *See* Mexico. [*Appendix.*] Martirologio de algunos de los primeros insurgentes por la libertad e independencia de la America Mexicana . . . Publícalo C. M. de Bustamante. 1841. 4°. **9771**. c. **27**.

—— *See* Mexico, *City of.* [*Appendix.*] México por dentro y fuera bajo el Gobierno de los Vireyes . . . Manuscrito inédito que dá á luz . . . C. M. de Bustamante. 1831. 4°. [*Voz de la Patria.* tom. 4. supp. no. 1.] **9772**. c. **22**.

—— *See* Murguia y Galardi (J.) Memoria estadistica de Oaxaca . . . Publícala . . . C. M. de Bustamante . . . con una descripcion del antigüo palacio de Mictla, *etc.* 1821. 4°. **10480**. c. **20**. (**1**.)

—— *See* Ordoño (I. M.) Carta que dirige un Oajaqueño al Señor . . . C. M. Bustamante . . . 24 de junio de 1823. [A reply to a political pamphlet by Bustamante. With an autograph note by the latter.] 1823. fol. **9770**. k. **7**. (**30**.)

BUSTAMANTE (CARLOS MARÍA DE)

—— *See* PERIODICAL PUBLICATIONS.—*Mexico.* Voz de la Pátria. [Edited by C. M. de Bustamante.] 1830, *etc.* 4°. 9772. c. 22.

—— *See* PERIODICAL PUBLICATIONS.—Mexico.—*Voz de la Pátria.* Contestacion al artículo editorial [by C. M. de Bustamante] inserto en el suplemento número 7 de la Voz de la Pátria sobre el estanco del tabaco. 1831. 4°. 9770. bb. 21. (2.)

—— *See* SALADO ÁLVAREZ (V.) La Vida azarosa y romántica de Don Carlos María de Bustamante. [With a portrait.] 1933. 8°. 10633. ppp. 25.

—— *See* SANCHEZ (Francisco) called FLORALBO CORINTO. Principios de Retorica y Poética. [Edited by C. M. de Bustamante.] 1825. 12°. 11805. b. 35.

—— *See* SANTOYO (F.) Alla va ese temperante para D. C. Bustamante, ó ya sean reflecciones sobre el contenido de su Avispa [i.e. the periodical "La Abispa de Chilpancingo"] numero 6 en el tomo 2°. [1825.] 4°. 9770. bb. 15. (28.)

—— *See* SPAIN. [*Appendix.—History and Politics.*] Fastos militares de iniquidad, barbarie y despotismo del gobierno español, ejecutados en las villas de Orizava y Córdoba, *etc.* [Edited by C. M. de Bustemente.] 1843. 8°. 9771. c. 15.

—— *See* VEGA (Manuel de la) *Franciscan.* Historia del descubrimiento de la América Septentrional por Cristoval Colón escrita por M. de la Vega. Dala a luz con varias notas para mayor inteligencia de la historia de las conquistas de Hernan Cortes . . . C. M. de Bustamente. 1826. 8°. 9771. c. 24.

—— *See* VIRGILIUS MARO (P.) [*Aeneis.—Spanish.*] Los Cuatro primeros libros de la Eneida . . . traducidos del frances [of N. F. Le Blond de Saint Martin] al Castellano . . . por C. M. de Bustamante. 1830. 12°. 11355. b. 33.

—— La Aparicion Guadalupana de Mexico vindicada de los defectos que le atribuye el Dr. Juan Bautista Munoz en la disertacion que leyó en la Academia de la Historia de Madrid en 18 de abril de 1794, comprobada con nuevos descubrimientos. pp. 75. *México*, 1843. 4°. 4745. c. 16.

—— [Apuntes para la Historia] del General A. Lopez de Santa Anna hasta 6 de diciembre de 1844. pp. iii. 460. *México*, 1845. 4°. 9771. c. 18.
The titlepage is mutilated.

—— Campaña sin gloria y guerra como la de los cacomixtles, en las torres de las iglesias. Tenida en el recinto de México. Causada por haber persistido D. Valentin Gómez Farías, Vice-Presidente de la República Mexicana, en llevar adelante las leyes de 11 de enero y 4 de febrero de 1847, llamadas de Manos Muertas, que despojan al clero de sus propiedades, con oposicion casi general de la nacion. pp. 44. *México*, 1847. 8°. 9771. c. 28.

—— Campañas del General D. Felix Maria Calleja comandante en gefe del ejercito real de operaciones llamado del centro. 2 pt. *México*, 1828. 4°. 9771. c. 23.

—— Cuadro Histórico de la Revolucion Mexicana, comenzada en 15 de septiembre de 1810 por el ciudadano Miguel Hidalgo y Costilla . . . Segunda édicion . . . muy aumentada por el mismo autore. 5 tom. *México*, 1843–46. 8°. 9771. c. 22. (1.)

—— Resúmen Histórico de la Revolucion de los Estados Unidos Mejicanos; sacado del "Cuadro Historico," que en forma de cartas escribió . . . C. M. Bustamante, i ordenado en cuatro libros por D. Pablo de Mendibil. [With portraits.] pp. xxv. 423. *R. Ackermann: Londres*, 1828. 8°. 1061. c. 7.

—— Defensa de la Peticion hecha al Soberano Congreso . . . solicitando la restitucion de la Compañía de Jesus en la República Mexicana . . . Formóla el redactor de dicha peticion (C. M. B. [i.e. C. M. de Bustamante?]). pp. 28. 1841. 4°. *See* B., C. M. 4092. cc. 17. (1.)

—— Diario Histórico de México . . . Primera edición arreglada por Elías Amador. Tomo. I. 1822–1823. pp. v. 663. *Zacatecas*, 1896. 8°. 9772. p. 5.
No more published.

—— El Gabinete Mexicano durante el segundo periodo de la administracion del Exmo. Señor Presidente D. Anastasio Bustamante, hasta la entrega del Mando al Exmo. Señor Presidente interino D. Antonio Lopez de Santa-Anna, y continuacion del cuadro historico de la Revolucion Mexicana. (Apéndice.—Análisis crítico de la Constitucion de 1836.) 2 tom. *Mexico*, 1842. 8°. 9771. c. 21.

—— El General D. Felipe de la Garza vindicado de las notas de traidor é ingrato con que se le ofende en un papel intitulado: Catástrofe de D. Agustin de Iturbide [a translation of "Catastrophe de don Augustin de Yturbide," by N. Soulier], *etc.* pp. iv. 88. *Mexico*, 1826. 8°. 8180. aaa. 18. (1.)

—— Historia del Emperador D. Agustin de Iturbide hasta su muerte y sus consecuencias; y establecimiento de la Republica popular federal. (Continuacion del Cuadro Historico.) pp. 293. vii. *Mexico*, 1846. 8°. 9771. c. 22. (2.)

—— Historia Militar del General Don José Maria Morelos sacada en lo conducente a ella de sus declaraciones recibidas de orden del Virey de Mexico, cuando estuvo arrestado en la Ciudadela de esta Capital. (Suplemento al Cuadro Historico.) [With a portrait.] pp. 40. *Mexico*, 1825. 4°. 9771. b. 14.

—— Mañanas de la Alameda de México. Publícalas . . . C. M. de Bustamante. 2 tom. *México*, 1835, 36. 8°. 9771. b. 7.

—— Manifiesto de la Junta Guadalupana á los Mexicanos, y disertacion histórico-crítica sobre la aparicion de Nuestra Señora en Tepeyac: escrita por . . . C. M. de Bustamante, *etc.* [With other documents. The whole compiled by C. M. de Bustamante.] pp. 22. *México*, 1831. 8°. 8179. aaa. 35.

—— México por dentro y fuera bajo el gobierno de los Vireyes. Ó sea enfermidades políticas que padece la capital de la N. España en casi todos los cuerpos de que se compone, y remedios que se deben aplicar para su curacion, *etc.* pp. 173. *México*, 1831. 8°. 8179. aaa. 21.
Originally issued as supplement 1 to tom. 4 of the "Voz de la Pátria."

—— Necesidad de la union de todos los Mexicanos contra las asechanzas de la nacion española y liga europea, comprobada con la historia de la antigua república de Tlaxcallan. pp. 44. *México*, 1826. 8°. 9771. b. 6. (3.)

—— El Nuevo Bernal Diaz del Castillo, ó sea Historia de la invasion de los Anglo-Americanos en Mexico. 2 tom. *Mexico*, 1847. 8°. 9771. c. 4.

BUSTAMANTE (CARLOS MARÍA DE)

—— Suplemento á la historia de las conquistas de Hernan Cortés escrita por Chimalpain [or rather, translated by him into Mexican from the Spanish of F. López de Gomara], ó sea: memoria sobre la guerra del Mixtón en el Estado de Xalisco, cuya capital es Guadalaxara. pp. 39. *México*, 1827. 8°. **9771**. b. **6**. (**2**.)

—— Culebrina fulminante para el Señor Bustamante. [Against his article in Supplement 10 of the "Voz de la Pátria," defending the Spaniards. Signed: El Payo del Rosario, i.e. P. de Villavicencio.] pp. 8. [*Mexico*, 1831.] 4°. **9770**. bb. **21**. (**4**.)

—— Noticias biograficas del licenciado Don C. M. de Bustamante, y juicio crítico de sus obras. Escritas por un amigo de D. Cárlos y mas amigo de la verdad [i.e. Lúcas Alamán]. pp. 56. *Mexico*, 1849. 8°. **10882**. aaa. **32**.

BUSTAMANTE (CARLOS MARÍA DE) and **GUTIERREZ** (JOSÉ IGNACIO)

—— Voto particular de los diputados Lic. D. C. M. de Bustamante, y D. J. I. Gutierrez, individuos de la Comision nombrada por el Soberano Congreso Mexicano, en el expediente promovido por la Señora Doña Inez de Jauregui y Arostegui, viuda del General D. José de Iturrigaray, sobre devolucion de las cantidades que están impuestas en el tribunal de Minería, y que . . . la han condenado á perder. pp. 15. *México*, 1823. 8°. **9770**. aaa. **11**. (**9**.)

BUSTAMANTE (CIRIACO PÉREZ) *See* PÉREZ BUSTAMANTE.

BUSTAMANTE (DANIEL SÁNCHEZ) *See* SÁNCHEZ BUSTAMENTE.

BUSTAMANTE (DIEGO DE COSSIO Y) *See* COSSIO Y BUSTAMANTE.

BUSTAMANTE (F. CORONA) *See* CORONA BUSTAMANTE.

BUSTAMANTE (FERNANDO VELLO DE) *See* VELLO DE BUSTAMANTE.

BUSTAMANTE (FRANCISCO DÍEZ) *See* DÍEZ BUSTAMANTE.

BUSTAMANTE (FRANCISCO EUGENIO) Études sur le placenta, *etc.* pp. 166. *Paris*, 1868. 4°. [*Collection des thèses soutenues à la Faculté de Médecine de Paris.* An 1868. tom. 2.] **7373**. i. **6**.

BUSTAMANTE (GUILLERMO LÓPEZ) *See* LÓPEZ BUSTAMANTE.

BUSTAMANTE (GUTIERRE GUIDO DE HEVIA Y) *Marquis del Real Transporte.* *See* HEVIA Y BUSTAMANTE.

BUSTAMANTE (JAVIER AGUILAR DE) *See* AGUILAR DE BUSTAMANTE.

BUSTAMANTE (JORGE DE) *See* OVIDIUS NASO (P.) [*Metamorphoses.—Spanish.*] Libro del Metamorphoseos y fabulas del excelēte poeta y philosofo Ouidio . . . traduzido de latin ē romāce [by J. de Bustamante], *etc.* 1546. 4°. C. **63**. b. **3**.

—— *See* TROGUS POMPEIUS. [*Spanish.*] Justino clarissimo abreuiador de la historia general del famoso . . . historiador Trogo Pompeyo . . . traduzido en Castellano [by J. de Bustamante]. 1540. fol. C. **63**. m. **17**.

—— —— 1542. 8°. **584**. a. **22**.

—— —— 1586. 8°. **802**. b. **31**.

BUSTAMANTE (JOSÉ DE) [For official documents issued by J. de Bustamante as Governor of Guatemala:] *See* GUATEMALA.—Bustamante (J. de) *Governor.*

BUSTAMANTE (JOSÉ FERNÁNDEZ DE) *See* FERNÁNDEZ DE BUSTAMANTE.

BUSTAMANTE (JOSÉ LUIS) Biografía del Exmo. Señor Gobernador . . . Manuel Guillermo Pinto. Acompañada del fac-simile de su firma y rúbrica. [With a portrait.] pp. vii. 44. *Buenos Aires*, 1853. 8°. **10881**. d. **34**. (**6**.)

—— Bosquejo de la historia civil y política de Buenos Ayres desde la batalla Monte-Caseros. [With portraits.] pp. 358. *Buenos Ayres*, 1856. 8°. **9772**. c. **18**.

—— Los Cinco Errores Capitales de la Intervencion Anglo-Francesa en el Plata. pp. viii. 382. *Montevideo*, 1849. 8°. **8179**. aaa. **22**.

—— Ensayo historico de la defensa de Buenos Aires contra la rebellion del ex-coronel D. Hilario Lagos, apoyada y sostenida por el gobernador . . . Justo José de Urquiza, *etc.* pp. xii. 660. *Buenos-Aires*, 1854. 4°. **9772**. cc. **4**.

—— Memorias sobre la Revolucion del 11 del septiembre de 1852, *etc.* pp. 266. iv. *Buenos Ayres*, 1853. 4°. **9772**. e. **21**.

BUSTAMANTE (JOSÉ MARÍA AGUILAR DE) *See* AGUILAR DE BUSTAMANTE.

BUSTAMANTE (JOSÉ MARÍA DE OLOZAGA Y) *See* OLÓZAGA Y BUSTAMANTE.

BUSTAMANTE (JOSÉ S. DE) La Relijion y el Estado. Tésis, *etc.* pp. 49. *Buenos Aires*, 1871. 8°. **4183**. f. **9**.

BUSTAMANTE (JOSEPH IBÁÑEZ DE LA MADRIZ Y) *See* IBÁÑEZ DE LA MADRIZ Y BUSTAMANTE.

BUSTAMANTE (JUAN) Viaje al Viejo Mundo por el Peruano J. Bustamente, *etc.* pp. 168. *Lima*, 1845. 4°. **1426**. e. **17**.

BUSTAMANTE (JUAN RÚIZ DE) *See* RÚIZ DE BUSTAMANTE.

BUSTAMANTE (LEON VALENTIN DE) Discurso sobre la administracion y lo contencioso administrativo, pronunciado en el acto solemne de recibir la investidura de Doctor en jurisprudencia. pp. 16. *Madrid*, 1852. fol. **5385.ee.17.(2.)**

BUSTAMANTE (LUIS F.) De El Ebano a Torreón. Colección de reportazgos de guerra. pp. 129. *Monterrey, N.L.*, 1915. 8°. **9771**. df. **33**.

—— La Defensa de "El Ebano." Los Libertarios. (2ª edición ilustrada.) [With a plan.] pp. 254. *Tampico*, 1915. 8°. **9772**. ppp. **2**.

BUSTAMANTE (MANUEL GARCÍA) *See* GARCÍA BUSTAMANTE.

BUSTAMANTE (MANUEL PAYNO Y) *See* PAYNO Y BUSTAMANTE.

BUSTAMANTE (MIGUEL) *See* LOZANO (J. M.) Proyecto de Ley de Minería para . . . la Baja California, formado por . . . J. M. Lozano . . . é Ingeniero M. Bustamante, *etc.* 1874. 8°. **6784**. f. **2**. (**7**.)

—— *See* RAMIREZ (S.) Ligeras Observaciones al Proyecto de Ley de Minería para . . . la Baja California, formado . . . por . . . J. M. Lozano . . . é Ingeniero M. Bustamante. 1876. 8°. **6784**. f. **2**. (**8**.)

BUSTAMANTE (MIGUEL DE VALLE Y) *See* VALLE Y BUSTAMANTE.

BUSTAMANTE (MIGUEL LÚCIO Y) *See* LÚCIO Y BUSTAMANTE.

BUSTAMANTE (PAULO EMILIO)

—— *See* COLOMBIA. [Republic of Colombia, 1886– .] [*Laws.*—IV. *Separate Laws.*] El General Paulo Emilio Bustamante. (La ley ' por la cual se honra la memoria del General Paulo Emilio Bustamante '—25 de noviembre, *etc.*) [With a portrait.] 1937. 8°. L.A.S. **382/29.**

BUSTAMANTE (PEDRO) *See* PEDRO, *de Santa Teresa, Dominican* [P. Bustamante].

BUSTAMANTE (PERFECTO P.) Girón de Historia. Leyendas, tradiciones regionales y relatos históricos. pp. 278. *Buenos Aires,* 1922. 8°. **012403.** de. **7.**

BUSTAMANTE (RAMÓN) Cuba, *etc.* pp. 267. iv. *Foreign Publishing Co.: Saint Louis,* [1916.] 8°. **10482.** f. **3.**

BUSTAMANTE (RAMÓN SIERRA) *See* SIERRA BUSTAMANTE.

BUSTAMANTE (RAÚL MONTERO) *See* MONTERO BUSTAMANTE.

BUSTAMANTE (RICARDO JOSÉ) Hispano-América libertada. Canto epico. pp. 174. *Valparaiso,* 1883. 8°. **010882.** m. **30.**

BUSTAMANTE (SEBASTIÁN RODRÍGUEZ) *See* RODRÍGUEZ BUSTAMANTE.

BUSTAMANTE BUSTILLO (ANTONIO) *Begin.* Señor. El Doctor D. A. Bustamante Bustillo . . . representa á V.S. sus cortos literarios méritos, como opositor á la canongia doctoral vacante en esta Santa Iglesia, *etc.* pp. 4. [*Mexico,* 1766.] fol. **9770.** k. **2.** (**18.**)

BUSTAMANTE CARLOS, otherwise **CONCOLORCORVO** (CALIXTO) *See* CARRIÒ DE LA VANDERA (A.) El Lazarillo de ciegos caminantes desde Buenos-Ayres, hasta Sima con sus itinerarios . . . Sacado de las Memorias que hizo Don A. Carriò de la Vandera . . . por Don C. Bustamente Carlos, Inca, alias Concolorcorvo. 1773. 8°. **798.** c. **25.**

—— —— 1908. 8°. [*Biblioteca de la Junta de Historia y Numismática Americana.* tom. 4.] Ac. **8592/3.**

BUSTAMANTE DE LA CÁMARA (JUAN) Iohannis Busthamantini Camærensis . . . De animantibus Scripturæ Sacræ . . . De reptilibus vere animantibus Sacræ Scripturæ . . . Cum duplici locupletissimo indice, *etc.* ff. 375. 122. *Ex officina I. Graciani, apud viduam: Compluti,* 1595. 4°. **1012.** b. **16.**
In six books. Book 5 has a separate titlepage, and starts a fresh pagination.

—— [Another edition.] 2 tom. pp. 1382. *A. Pillehotte: Lugduni,* 1620. 8°. **987.** f. **31, 32.**

—— [Another copy.] **220.** d. **1.**

BUSTAMANTE DE LA FUENTE (MANUEL J.)

—— Mis ascendientes, *etc.* [With plates.] pp. 717. [*Lima,*] 1955. 8°. **9906.** pp. **22.**
Privately printed.

BUSTAMANTE DE SANTA TERESA (PEDRO) *See* PEDRO, *de Santa Teresa, Dominican* [P. Bustamante].

BUSTAMANTE PAZ (BENEDICTUS) Methodus in septem aphorismorum libris ab Hippocrate obseruata, quam & continuum librorum ordinem argumenta & schemata declarant, *etc.* ff. 67. *Apud Aldi filios: Venetiis,* 1550. 4°. **539.** g. **10.**

BUSTAMANTE Y BALLIVIÁN (ENRIQUE)

—— *See* XAMMAR (L. F.) La Poesía de Enrique Bustamante y Ballivián. 1945. 8°. **11868.** bb. **34.**

—— Obras completas. [With a portrait.]
I. Poesía. pp. 210. 1955. W.P. **8187/1.**
Lima, 1955– . 8°. W.P. **8187.**

—— Autóctonas. Odas americanas. pp. 165. *La Paz,* 1920. 8°. **11452.** ee. **48.**

BUSTAMANTE Y BUSTILLO Y RUEDA (FERNANDO)

—— Documentos relativos al Mariscal de Campo don Fernando Manuel Bustamante Bustillo y Rueda. *In:* DÍAZ DE VILLEGAS Y DE BUSTAMANTE (J.) Una Embajada española a Siam a principios del siglo XVIII. pp. 169–224. 1952. 8°. **09059.** k. **10.**

BUSTAMANTE Y CAMPUZANO (JUAN) Del Atlántico al Pacífico. Apuntes é impresiones de un viaje á través de los Estados Unidos. pp. 439. *Madrid,* 1885. 8°. **10409.** aaa. **32.**

BUSTAMANTE Y GUERRA (JOSÉ DE) *See* MALASPINA (A.) Viaje político-científico alrededor del mundo por las corbetas Descubierta y Atrevida al mando de los capitanes de navío D. Alejandro Malaspina y Don J. de Bustamante y Guerra, *etc.* 1885. 4°. **10003.** s. **6.**

BUSTAMANTE Y LOYOLA (SEBASTIÁN DE) *Begin.* Señor, El Licenciado Don S. de Bustamente [*sic*] y Loyola. [A memorial of the services of his ancestors in Peru and New Granada.] [1639.] *s. sh.* fol. **1324.** i. **2.** (**27.**)

BUSTAMANTE Y MEDRANO (JUAN MANUEL DE) Oracion funebre en la muerte de . . . Maria Luisa de Borbon, Reina de España. *See* MARY LOUISA, *Queen Consort of Charles II., King of Spain.* Succinta Descripcion de las Exequias, *etc.* 1689. 4°. **1060.** i. **17.** (**3.**)

BUSTAMANTE Y MONTORO (ANTONIO DE) Ironía y Generación. Ensayos. pp. 242. *La Habana,* 1937. 8°. **12358.** b. **2.**

BUSTAMANTE Y QUIJANO (RAMÓN)

—— A Bordo del " Alfonso Pérez." Escenas del cautiverio rojo en Santander. pp. 273. pl. 25. *Madrid,* [1940.] 8°. **9181.** pp. **33.**

BUSTAMANTE Y RIVERO (JOSÉ LUIS)

—— Panamericanismo e iberoamericanismo. *In:* Anuario de estudios americanos. tom. 8. pp. 323–397. 1951. 8°. Ac. **161** a/**2.**

BUSTAMANTE Y RUEDA (FERNANDO MANUEL DE BUSTILLO) *See* BUSTILLO BUSTAMANTE Y RUEDA.

BUSTAMANTE Y SIRVÉN (ANTONIO SÁNCHEZ DE) *See* SÁNCHEZ DE BUSTAMANTE Y SIRVÉN.

BUSTAMANTE Y URRUTIA (JOSÉ MARÍA DE)

—— Catálogos de la biblioteca universitaria [of Santiago de Compostela]. [With reproductions.] 4 pt. 1944-56. 8°. *See* SANTIAGO DE COMPOSTELA.—*Universidad de Santiago de Compostela.* **2721.c.1.**

BUSTAMANTINUS CAMAERENSIS (JOHANNES) *See* BUSTAMANTE DE LA CÁMARA (Juan)

BUSTAMENTE, *Family of.* *See* Asúa y Campos (M. de) El Valle de Ruiseñada . . . Los Brachos y los Bustamentes, *etc.* 1909. 8°. **10161.** f. **28.**

BUSTAMENTE (Joseph Angúlo y) *See* Angúlo y Bustamente (J.)

BUSTAMENTE Y LOYOLA (Sebastián de) *See* Bustamante y Loyola.

BUSTANI (Alfredo)

—— El Imamato en el Islam. El estado y la religión. pp. 46. [*Tetuan*,] 1954. 8°. **4508.** d. **9.**

BUSTĀNĪ (W. F.) The Palestine Mandate Invalid and Impracticable. A contribution of arguments and documents towards the solution of the Palestine problem, *etc.* pp. 168. *American Press: Beirut*, 1936. 8°. **20031.** bbb. **4.**

BUSTANOBY (Jacques Henri) Bustanoby's How to Mix Colors, *etc.* [With plates.] pp. 97. *J. S. Ogilvie Publishing Co.: New York*, 1929. 8°. **7941.** e. **32.**

—— Principles of Color and Color Mixing. pp. xi. 131. pl. 11. *McGraw-Hill Book Co.: New York, London*, 1947. 4°. **7947.** c. **39.**

BUSTARD (John) The Favourite Humbled and Exalted: a history of Joseph and his brethren: in verse. pp. 64. *John Mason: London*, 1834. 32°. **1017.** a. **31.**

—— A Memoir of Miss Mary Helen Bingham, who died on the 4th of June, 1825, in the seventeenth year of her age. [Based on her journal and letters.] pp. vi. 214. *John Kershaw: London*, 1827. 12°. **1124.** c. **28.**

—— Second edition. pp. vi. 208. *John Mason: London*, 1832. 12°. **1123.** f. **30.**

—— A Memoir of Mr. John Bingham, Jun., who died on the sixteenth of July, MDCCCXXVI., in the eighteenth year of his age. [With extracts from his diary and letters.] pp. 106. *John Mason: London*, 1832. 12°. **1123.** f. **29.**

—— Mildred: the Thanet Sunday-School teacher. pp. 88. *Printed for the Author: London*, 1838. 16°. **1121.** b. **36.**

—— The Thoughtful Child. A memoir of Mary Ann Bustard. pp. 52. *M. Nicholson: Stourport*, [1828?] 16°. **1210.** c. **19.** (**6.**)

—— L'Enfant réfléchi. Mémoire de Marie-Anne Bustard . . . Traduit de la seconde édition, *etc.* pp. 62. *Étienne Barbet: Guernesey*, 1836. 32°. T. **2076.** (**3.**)

—— The Young Miner: a memoir of John Lean, Jun., of Camborne in the county of Cornwall. pp. 75. *Printed for the Author: London*, 1838. 24°. **1121.** b. **37.**

BUSTARD (Mary Anne) *See* Bustard (John) The Thoughtful Child. A memoir of M. A. Bustard. [1828?] 16°. **1210.** c. **19.** (**6.**)

—— *See* Bustard (John) L'Enfant réfléchi. Mémoire de Marie-Anne Bustard, *etc.* 1836. 32°. T. **2076.** (**3.**)

BUSTEED (Henry Elmsley) Echoes from Old Calcutta, being chiefly reminiscences of the days of Warren Hastings, Francis, & Impey. pp. 304. *Thacker, Spink & Co.: Calcutta*, 1882. 8°. **9057.** a. **27.**

—— Second edition. Considerably enlarged and illustrated. pp. xi. 359. *Thacker, Spink & Co.: Calcutta; London* [printed], 1888. 8°. **9057.** a. **29.**

BUSTEED (Henry Elmsley)

—— Third edition. Considerably enlarged, *etc.* pp. xv. 343. *Thacker & Spink: Calcutta; London* [printed], 1897. 8°. **9056.** b. **36.**

—— Fourth edition, much enlarged, *etc.* pp. xvi. 431. *W. Thacker & Co.: London*, 1908. 8°. **09057.** bb. **35.**

BUSTEED (John) A Statistical Analysis of Irish Egg Production, Prices and Trade. pp. xi. 62. [*Cork*,] 1926. 4°. [*University College, Cork. Agricultural Bulletin.* no. 2.] Ac. **1526.**

BUSTEED (Michael) *See* Plato. [*Menexenus.—Greek and Latin.*] Orationes duæ funebres . . . Recensore M. Busteed. 1696. 12°. **524.** e. **10.**

BUSTEED (N. William) King Barnaby, or the Maidens of the forest. A romance of the Mickmacks. pp. 94. *Beadle & Co.: London*, [1862.] 8°. **12706.** a. **30.** (**3.**)

BUSTEED (Richard) Argument of Richard Busteed upon some of the Charges preferred by Henry Semple. pp. 12. [1869.] 8°. **010883.** k. **12.** (**1.**)

BUSTEED (Thomas M.) Trades' Unions, Combinations, and Strikes. pp. 41. *V. R. Stevens & Sons; W. Walker & Co.: London*, 1860. 8°. **8276.** c. **13.**

BUSTELLI (Francesco Antonio)

—— *See* Pechmann (G. von) Franz Anton Bustelli: die italienische Komödie in Porzellan. [1947.] 8°. **7812.** a. **5.**

—— *See* Simona (L.) F. A. Bustelli ritorna. [On the revival of interest in the work of F. A. Bustelli.] 1945. 8°. **7877.** b. **30.**

BUSTELLI (Giuseppe) *See* Mazzoni Toselli (O.) Racconti storici, *etc.* [With a biographical sketch by G. Bustelli.] 1866, *etc.* 8°. **6057.** aa. **29.**

—— *See* Redi (F.) Sei odi inedite. [Edited by G. Bustelli.] 1864. 8°. **12226.** bbb. **6.** (**4.**)

—— *See* Sappho. Vita e frammenti di Saffo . . . Discorso e versione . . . di G. Bustelli. 1863. 8°. **12226.** bbb. **5.** (**2.**)

—— L'Enigma di Ligny e di Waterloo, 15–18 giugno 1815, studiato e sciolto. 6 vol. *Cesena*, 1889–1900. 8°. **9080.** l. **1.**

Vol. 2–6 *were published at Viterbo.*

—— Le Imboscate nel Concorso di Firenze, giugno 1874, per l'assistenza di prima classe vacante in quella Biblioteca Nazionale. Narrazione apologetica. pp. 19. *Messina*, 1875. 8°. **1414.** h. **8.** (**16.**)

—— Sulla decollazione di Francesco Bussone conte di Carmagnola. Lettera, *etc.* pp. 157. *Cesena*, 1887. 8°. **10630.** bb. **37.**

BUSTELLI (Nicola) Dissertazione critica sulla complicità nei reati risguardata nei suoi politici e morali rapporti con il mandato criminoso. pp. 27. *Viterbo*, [1851.] 8°. **898.** d. **1.** (**9.**)

—— Sul mandato di arresto nei giudizj criminali. Ragionamento di economia politico-legale. pp. 21. *Civitavecchia*, 1853. 8°. **898.** d. **1.** (**8.**)

BUSTELLI-FOSCOLO (Giovanni de) *Duke.* Le Pape roi d'Italie. [Advocating the temporal supremacy of the Pope in Italy.] pp. 64. *Gilbert & Rivington: Londres*, 1878. 8°. **4050.** e. **1.** (**18.**)

BUSTELLI-FOSCOLO (GIOVANNI DE) *Duke.*

—— La Repubblica di Honduras, America centrale. Fondazione della Banca di Stato di detta repubblica, che favorirebbe possentemente lo stabilimento delle colonie italiane a sistema cooperativo con quel . . . paese. Studii. pp. 231. *Roma,* 1886. 8°. **10481**. aaa. **32**.

BUSTER. " Buster " and " Baby Jim." By the author of " The Blue Flag," *etc.* pp. 70. *Seeley, Jackson & Halliday: London,* [1871.] 4°. **12806**. ee. **5**.

BUSTETER (HANS) Ernstlicher Bericht, wie sich ain Frum̄e Oberkayt Vor, In, vnd Nach, den gefärlichsten Kriegssnöten, mit klugem vortayl, zu vngezweyfletem Sig, loblichen vben, vn̄ halten sol, an ain . . . Burgermayster, vnd Radt, des . . . Stat Augspurg . . . beschriben. [With a woodcut.] ff. xxvi. *Gedruckt durch H. Stayner: Augspurg,* 1532. 4°. **697**. h. **8**. (**5**.)

BUSTHAMANTINUS CAMAERENSIS (JOANNES) *See* BUSTAMANTE DE LA CÁMARA (Juan)

BUSTI (ANGELUS) Angeli Busti . . . Aduersus ea, quę disputationi suæ, de mellis conuenienti, atque legitima quantitate, ad theriacam componendam obiecta fuere, defensio, *etc.* [In answer to Fabius Ulmus.] pp. 90. *Ex Typographia A. Muschij: Venetiis,* 1617. 4°. **1038**. i. **30**. (**3**.)

—— De mellis conuenienti atque legitima quantitate ad theriacam componendam . . . disputatio, *etc.* pp. 35. *Muschius: Venetiis,* 1613. 4°. **1038**. i. **30**. (**1**.)

—— *See* ULMUS (F.) De mellis opportuna decentiue quantitate pro theriaca, mithridatoq; componendis . . . responsio, *etc.* [In answer to A. Busti's work on the same subject.] 1614. 4°. **1038**. i. **30**. (**2**.)

BUSTI (BERNARDINUS DE)

—— *See* CUCCHI (F.) La Mediazione universale della Santissima Vergine negli scritti di Bernardino de' Bustis, *etc.* 1942. 8°. **3834**. de. **15**.

—— *See* LITURGIES.—*Latin Rite.—Combined Offices.*—IV. *Officia Propria.—General. Begin.* [fol. 1 *recto*:] Beatissimo atq; Felicissimo dn̄o. d. Sixto 4°: sedis apl'ice sūmo pontifici sanctissimo Frater Bernardinus de busti . . . humilem ac debitam cōmendationem. [fol. 3 *recto*:] Incipit deuotissimū officiū īmaculate ꝯceptionis gl'ose v̇ginis marie: nuper editū ꝑ frēm Bernardinū de busti, *etc.* [1480.] 8°. IA. **26587**.

—— Defensorium montis pietatis contra figmenta omnia emule falsitatis. [With a woodcut and the printer's device.] G.L. [*Uldericus Scinzenzeler: Milan,* 1497.] 4°. IA. **26768**.
74 *leaves. Sig.* a–h⁸ i⁴ k⁶. *Double columns,* 47 *lines to a column. A few leaves slightly cropped.*

—— [Mariale.] *Begin.* [fol. 1 *recto*:] Beatissimo atq; felicissimo patri ac dn̄o. d. Innocentio octauo . . . frater Bernardinus de busti . . . humilē ac debitam cōmendationē, *etc.* [*ibid.* l. 39:] IN noīe domini nostri iesu xp̄i Incipit sermonariū de excellētijs gloriose uirginis genitricis dei marie: qd' mariale appellatur: atq; editū fuit ꝑ fratrē Bernardinū de busti, *etc.* [Nine sermons comprising pt. 1 of the Mariale, followed by the " Officium Immaculatae Conceptionis Beatae Virginis Mariae."] [With woodcuts.] G.L. *per Vldericuʒ scinzēzeler: Ml'i* [*Milan*], die septimo mensis Maij, 1492. 4°. IA. **26739**.
84 *leaves. Sig.* a–k⁸ l⁴. *Double columns,* 42 *lines to a column.*

BUSTI (BERNARDINUS DE)

—— Mariale de excellētiis Regine celi. [Pt. 1–12. With woodcuts.] G.L. *per Leonardum pachel: Mediolani,* die .xxi. Maij, 1493. 4°. IA. **26668**.
388 *leaves. Sig.* A⁸ B⁶; a–z⁸ ⁊⁸ ꝯ⁸ ꝵ⁸ A–V⁸ X⁶. *Double columns,* 58 *lines to a column.*

—— [Another edition.] Mariale eximii viri Bernardini de busti . . . de singulis festiuitatibus beate virginis per modū sermonū tractans, *etc.* G.L.
ꝑ *Martinū flach: Argētine,* Mēsis Iulii die vicesimosexto, 1496. fol. IB. **2197**.
378 *leaves. Sig.* A⁸ B⁶ a–d⁸ e–h⁶·⁸ i–q⁶·⁶·⁶·⁸ r–z aa–pp⁶·⁸ qq⁶ rr–yy⁶·⁸ zz⁶ AA–FF⁶ GG⁸. *Double columns,* 54 *lines to a column.*

—— [Another edition.] G.L.
ꝑ *Martinum flach: Argentine,* Mensis Augusti die decimoquinto, 1498. fol. IB. **2215**.
378 *leaves. Sig.* A⁸ B⁶ a–d⁸ e–h⁶·⁸ i–q⁶·⁶·⁶·⁸ r–z aa–pp⁶·⁸ qq⁶ rr–yy⁶·⁸ zz⁶ AA–FF⁶ GG⁸. *Double columns,* 54 *lines to a column.*

—— [Another edition.] ff. ccccviii. *I. Cleyn: Lugduni,* 1502. 4°. **851**. i. **7**.
Slightly mutilated.

—— [Another edition.] *Impensis J. rynman; in officina H. Gran: Hagenaw,* 1506. fol. **3834**. b. **16**.

—— [Another edition.] Nunc primum . . . in hanc emendatiorem, ac luculentiorem formam restitutum, *etc.* pp. 860. *Sumptibus A. Hierati: Coloniæ Agrippinæ,* 1607. 4°. **851**. i. **8**.
Tom. 3 *of the author's collected works.*

—— Rosarium sermonum predicabilium ad faciliorem predicantium cōmoditatem nouissime cōpilatum, *etc.* G.L. 2 pt. *per Georgium de Arriuabenis: Venetiis,* ꝑdie kalēdas Iunias [31 May], xvii. Kalen. Septembris [16 Aug.], 1498. 4°. IA. **22572**.
Pt. 1. 290 *leaves, the last blank, ff.* 32–289 *numbered* 2–261, *with errors. Sig.* (2–4)⁸ 3⁸ 4⁸ 5⁶; a–z⁸ ⁊⁸ ꝯ⁸ ꝵ⁸ aa–ff⁸ gg⁴. *Pt.* 2. 426 *leaves, the last blank, ff.* 19–425 *numbered* 1–409, *with errors. Sig.* ✠⁸ ✠✠¹⁰; A–Z⁸ AA–ZZ⁸ AAA–EEE⁸. *Double columns,* 52 *lines to a column.*

—— [Another edition.] G.L. 2 pt. *expēsis sūptibusqʒ Iohānis Rynman: per Heinricū Gran: Hagenaw,* xviij. die mensis Septembris, viij. die. mēſ decēbris, 1500. fol. IB. **13808**.
Pt. 1. 250 *leaves, the last blank, ff.* 28–249 *numbered* II–CCXXIII. *Sig.* aa⁸ bb⁸ cc¹⁰; a–z A–D⁸·⁸·⁶ E⁸ F⁸ G¹⁰. *Pt.* 2. 366 *leaves, ff.* 16 *and* 366 *blank,* 17–365 *numbered* I–CCCLIII, *with errors. Sig.* (ii–v)⁸ (1–5)⁸; aa–pp⁸·⁸·⁶ qq⁶ rr⁸ ss–zz AA–II⁸·⁸·⁶ KK⁸ LL⁶ MM–ZZ⁸·⁸·⁶ AAA⁶ BBB⁸. *Double columns,* 58 *lines to a column. Without the blank last leaf of pt.* 2.

—— [Another copy.] FEW MS. NOTES. IB. **13809**.
Without the blank last leaf in each part. The titlepage is mutilated.

—— [Another edition.] G.L. 2 pt. FEW MS. NOTES. *expēsis J. Rynmā; per H. Gran: Hagenaw,* 1503. fol. **473**. c. **13**.

—— [Another edition.] Nunc primum ex antiqua, in hanc emendatiorem, ac luculentiorem formam restitutum, *etc.* 2 tom. *Apud P. M. Marchettum: Brixiæ,* 1588. 4°. **3835**. b. **24**.

BUSTI (Carlo) Sopra alcune opere di scultura e di plastica di Antonio Canova. Poesie, *etc.* pp. 133. *Milano*, 1842. 4°. **7875**. c. **6**.

—— Storia dell'imagine di Maria Vergine, Madre della Salute, che si venera nella parochial chiesa di Santa Eufemia in Verona, e dell'incoronazione solenne che ne fu fatta il giorno 6 di maggio . . . 1857. pp. viii. 131. *Verona*, 1857. 8°. **4826**. cc. **4**.

BUSTI (Franciscus de) *See* Gregorius, *de Arimino. Begin.* [fol. 1 *verso*:] Magnifico ac generoso. d. Ambrosio Rosato . . . F. Busti . . . salutem dicit plurimam. [fol. 2 *recto*:] Gregorij ariminensis . . . in secundo sententiaꝝ admiranda expositio. Incipit, *etc.* [Edited by F. de Busti.] 1494. fol. IB. **26746**.

BUSTI (Vincenzo) Di Sarnico. Cenno illustrativo. pp. xv. 47. *Bergamo*, 1858. 16°. **10151**. a. **13**.

BUSTICO (Guido) *del R. Istituto Commerciale "Q. Sella" di Torino.* Dizionario del mare, *etc.* pp. xi. 320. *Torino*, [1932.] 8°. **8804**. e. **16**.

BUSTICO (Guido) *Professor. See* Brofferio (A.) *the Elder.* Il Carteggio Brofferio-Celesia. [Edited by G. Bustico.] 1910. 8°. **10905**. bbb. **24**.

—— Antonio Panizzi, il Passano e il Duca d'Aumale, con lettere inedite. pp. 16. *Genova*, 1913. 8°. **11825**. bbb. **44**. (**2**.)

—— Bibliografia di Giuseppe Parini. pp. viii. 180. *Firenze*, 1929. 8°. [*Biblioteca di bibliografia italiana.* no. 9.] P.P. **6476**. en.

—— Bibliografia di Vincenzo Monti. pp. viii. 218. *Firenze*, 1924. 8°. [*Biblioteca di bibliografia italiana.* no. 4.] P.P. **6476**. en.

—— Bibliografia di Vittorio Alfieri da Asti, con lettera del Prof. E. Bertana . . . Seconda edizione. pp. 149. *Salò*, 1907. 8°. **11904**. i. **22**.

—— 3ª edizione, interamente rifatta e continuata sino al 1926. pp. vii. 260. *Firenze*, 1927. 8°. [*Biblioteca di bibliografia italiana.* no. 6.] P.P. **6476**. en.

—— Dantisti e dantofili in Novara. [With a catalogue of the Dante collection in the Biblioteca Negroni.] *In:* Dante Alighieri. [*General Appendix—Biography and Criticism.*] Dante e Novara, *etc.* pp. 37–185. 1921. 8°. 011420. c. 33.

—— Il Romanzo italiano nel secolo xix. L'imitazione nell'arte—appunti. pp. 26. *Massa*, 1897. 8°. **11851**. ee. **21**. (**8**.)

One of an edition of fifty copies.

—— Vincenzo Monti. La vita. pp. 88. *Messina*, [1920.] 8°. **10634**. a. **8**.

—— La Vita e l'opera di Vincenzo Monti. [With plates, including portraits and facsimiles.] pp. 175. *Milano*, 1928. 8°. **10634**. bbb. **32**.

BUSTILLO (Antonio Bustamante) *See* Bustamante Bustillo.

BUSTILLO (Eduardo) *See* Lustonó (E. de) La Capa del Estudiante, *etc.* [With a preface by E. Bustillo.] 1880. 8°. **12357**. f. **20**.

—— Cartas Trascendentales. Comedia en un acto y en verso, *etc.* pp. 30. *Madrid*, 1877. 8°. **11728**. bbb. **7**. (**5**.)

BUSTILLO (Eduardo)

—— El Ciego de Buenavista. Romancero satírico de tipos y malas costumbres. pp. 231. *Madrid*, 1888. 8°. 11450. b. 24.

—— Cosas de la Vida. Cuentos y novelitas. pp. 267. *Madrid*, 1899. 8°. **12489**. ccc. **30**.

—— Las Cuatro Estaciones. Poesías. pp. 294. *Madrid*, 1877. 8°. **11450**. bbb. **5**.

—— Lazos de Amor y Amistad. Comedia en un acto y en verso . . . Segunda edicion. pp. 41. *Madrid*, 1865. 8°. **11726**. bbb. **22**. (**6**.)

—— El Libro Azul, novelitas y bocetos de costumbres. pp. 347. *Madrid*, 1879. 8°. **12491**. l. **13**.

—— El Libro de María. Cuadros de la vida de la Virgen. [In verse.] (Con cuatro láminas.) pp. 194. *Madrid*, 1865. 12°. **11450**. bbb. **29**.

—— Pájaros y Hombres, poema de un desconcierto. *See* Spanish Poetical Album. Album Poético Español, *etc.* 1874. 8°. **11450**. i. **1**.

—— Romancero de la Guerra de Africa, *etc.* [With plates.] pp. 187. *Madrid*, 1860. 4°. **11451**. h. **8**.

—— La Sal de María Santísima. Musa epigramática y cancionero festivo popular, con un prólogo de E. Bustillo. pp. xvi. 288. *Madrid*, 1882. 8°. **11450**. bb. **23**.

BUSTILLO (José) El Bufon de Su Alteza, zarzuela en dos actos y en verso, *etc.* pp. 37. *Madrid*, 1864. 8°. **11726**. e. **44**.

BUSTILLO (Lorenzo de Santayana y) *See* Santayana y Bustillo.

BUSTILLO (Miguel Oqueli) *See* Oqueli Bustillo.

BUSTILLO (Pedro J.)

—— El Derecho mercantil, de cambio, de quiebra y marítimo de Honduras. (Das Handelsrecht, Wechselrecht, Konkursrecht und Seerecht von Honduras.) Tratado y comentado por P. J. Bustillo . . . Übersetzt von Heinrich Hillebrand . . . und Karl Uerpmann. *Span. & Ger.* pp. 54. 54. [1910.] 8°. [*Borchardt* (*O.*) *Die Handelsgesetze des Erdballs.* Bd. 2.] *See* Honduras, *Republic of.* **6837**. f. **1/3**.

BUSTILLO BUSTAMANTE Y RUEDA (Fernando Manuel de) *See* Manila. Noticias de lo sucedido en la ciudad de Manila, *etc.* [An account of the actions of F. M. de Bustillo Bustamante y Rueda, Governor of the Philippine Islands, and of his death in a tumult.] [1720.] 4°. **1323**. c. **20**.

BUSTILLO ORO (Juan) Tres Dramas Mexicanos: Los que vuelven; Masas; Justicia, S. A. pp. 259. *Madrid*, 1933. 8°. **20001**. e. **1**.

BUSTILLOS (Victorino Márquez) *See* Márquez Bustillos.

BUSTIN (Hannah Charlotte) *See* Bustin (W.) Life Story of Madame Annie Ryall [Mrs. Bustin], Gospel soloist. By her husband, *etc.* [With portraits.] 1913. 8°. **4920**. h. **8**.

BUSTIN (Leonardus) Disputatio medica inauguralis de dysenteria, *etc.* pp. 22. *Harderovici*, 1719. 4°. **1185**. i. **17**. (**15**.)

BUSTIN (W.) Life Story of Madame Annie Ryall, Gospel soloist. By her husband, *etc.* [With portraits.] pp. xii. 98. *Morgan & Scott: London*, 1913. 8°. **4920**. h. **8**.

BUSTIN (WILLIAM RIDSDALE) A Militia; its relation to the Regular Army. The unjust, partial, and oppressive nature of the old system. A new system developed, and its tendencies, *etc.* pp. 36. *John Ollivier: London,* 1847. 8°. **1398.** f. **27.** (**2.**)

BUSTINZA (M. EVA G. L. DE) El Pintor Argentino Benito Quinquela Martín. [With reproductions.] pp. 45. 1937. 8°. *See* BUENOS AYRES.—*Asociación Euritmia.* Ac. **9197.**

BUSTIS (BERNARDINUS DE) *See* BUSTI.

BUSTIS (VINCENT DE) called RAVASCHIELLO. Arlequin deserteur devenû magicien, ou le Docteur mari ideal, ballet pantomime, *etc.* (Arlequin der Ausreisser, *etc.*) *Fr. & Ger. Bonn,* [1780?] 8°. **11740.** aa. **9.** (**1.**)

BUSTLE. The Bustle; a philosophical and moral poem. By the most extraordinary man of the age. pp. 82. *Bela Marsha: Boston,* 1845. 12°. **11687.** b. **51.** (**2.**)

BUSTO ARSIZIO. Storia della peste avvenuta nel borgo di Busto Arsizio 1630. Manuscrit original, appartenant autrefois à la Bibliothèque Belgiojosa à Milan. Publié par J. W. S. Johnsson. pp. 213. *Copenhague,* 1924. 4°. **7680.** ff. **24.**

BUSTO (AGUSTIN GODÍNEZ DEL) *See* GODÍNEZ DEL BUSTO.

BUSTO (ALEJO VANEGAS DE) *See* VANEGAS DE BUSTO.

BUSTO (ANDRÉS DEL) *Marquis. See* BUSTO Y LÓPEZ (A. del) *Marquis del Busto.*

BUSTO (ANTONIO RODRÍGUEZ DEL) *See* RODRÍGUEZ DEL BUSTO.

BUSTO (BERNABÉ) Introductiones grammaticas: breues ꝛ compēdiosas. G.L. *Salamanca,* 1533. 8°. **12941.** a. **25.** (**1.**)

BUSTO (BERNARDINUS DE) *See* BUSTI.

BUSTO (EMILIANO) La Administración Pública de Méjico. Breve estudio comparativo entre el sistema de administración de hacienda en Francia y el establecido en Méjico . . . Avec la traduction française. 2 pt. *Paris,* 1889. 4°. **8228.** l. **5.**

—— Estadística de la República Mexicana. Estado que guardan la agricultura, industria, minería y comercio. Resúmen y análisis de los informes rendidos à la Secretaría de Hacienda por los agricultores, mineros . . . de la República y los agentes de México en el exterior, *etc.* 3 tom. 1880. fol. *See* MEXICO.—*Ministerio de Hacienda.* **L.A.S.514/11.**

BUSTO (FRANCISCO IGNACIO DE AÑOA Y) successively *Bishop of Pampeluna* and *Archbishop of Saragossa. See* AÑOA Y BUSTO.

BUSTO (FRANCISCO RODRÍGUEZ DEL) *See* RODRÍGUEZ DEL BUSTO.

BUSTO (GONZALO) *See* ORTEGA (J. de) Tractado . . . d'arismetica y geometria . . . agora de nueuo emendado . . . por Juan Lagarto, y antes por G. Busto, *etc.* 1563. 4°. **529.** c. **6.**

BUSTO (HELIODORO DEL) Los Partidos en Cueros, ó Apuntes para escribir la historia de doce años, 1843–1855. pp. 80. *Madrid,* 1856. 8°. **8042.** d. **61.** (**3.**)

BUSTO (JOSÉ RODRIGUEZ) *See* RODRIGUEZ BUSTO.

BUSTO (JUAN CRUZ) *See* CRUZ BUSTO.

BUSTO (MARÍA VÉLEZ DEL) *See* VÉLEZ DEL BUSTO.

BUSTO (VALENTÍN GARCÍA DEL) *See* GARCÍA DEL BUSTO.

BUSTO DE VILLEGAS (SANCHO) Papel que Don Sancho Busto de Villegas . . . escribió al Rey Felipe II° á 15 de Agosto de 1574, sobre la venta de los vasallos de las Iglesias, y otras cosas, *etc. See* PERIODICAL PUBLICATIONS.—*Madrid.* Semanario Erudito, *etc.* tom. 6. 1788. 4°. **248.** k. **11.**

BU-STON. History of Buddhism, Chos-ḥbyung . . . Translated from Tibetan by Dr. E. Obermiller. 2 pt. *Carl Winter: Heidelberg,* 1931, 32. 8°. [*Materialien zur Kunde des Buddhismus.* Hft. 18, 19.] **14004.** f. **1.** (**18, 19.**)

BUSTORFF (A.) En Sammanställning af 342 starrextraktioner å senil starr. 1908. *See* HELSINKI.—*Finska Läkare-Sällskapet.* Finska Läkare Sällskapets handlingar. bd. 50. halfåret 1. no. 5. 1841, *etc.* 8°. Ac. **3810.**

BUSTOS (ABEL BAZÁN Y) *See* BAZÁN Y BUSTOS.

BUSTOS (ALFONSO DE BUSTOS Y) *Marquis de Corvera. See* BUSTOS Y BUSTOS.

BUSTOS (FRANCISCO GONZÁLEZ DE) *See* GONZÁLEZ DE BUSTOS.

BUSTOS (FRANCISCO VALLESPINOSA Y) *See* VALLESPINOSA Y BUSTOS.

BUSTOS (JULIO) *See* PRAST (A.) Arte Barroco de Madrid . . . Dibujos de J. Bustos. 1918. fol. **7817.** s. **7.**

BUSTOS (MARÍA JOSEFA)

—— *See* XUÁREZ (G.) Elogio de la Señora María Josefa Bustos, madre del Deán Funes, *etc.* 1949. 8°. [*Cuaderno de historia.* no. 15.] Ac. **2694.** gb/**3.**

BUSTOS (ROSENDO DE) El Cólera-Morbo y su Tratamiento, ó sea Método higiénico preservativo y curativo al alcance de todas las familias. pp. 30. *Madrid,* 1865. 16°. **7561.** a. **46.**

BUSTOS Y ANGULO (VENTURA DE) *See* VENTURA DE BUSTOS Y ANGULO.

BUSTOS Y BUSTOS (ALFONSO) *Marquis de Corvera.* La Patria de Cristóbal Colón. pp. 44. *Madrid,* [1928.] 8°. **10634.** d. **51.**

BUSTOS Y CASTILLA (RAFAEL) *Marquis de Corvera.* Discursos pronunciados el dia 19 de Diciembre de 1858, al ser legalmente constituida la Real Academia de Ciencias Morales y Políticas. (Discurso del . . . Marqués de Corvera.—Contestacion del . . . Marqués de Pidal.) pp. 32. 1858. 8°. *See* MADRID.—*Real Academia de Ciencias Morales y Políticas.* **8355.** ee. **13.**

BUSTOS Y MIGUEL (JOSÉ DE) Universidad de Salamanca. Discurso leído en la Solemne Apertura del Curso Académico de 1898 á 1899. [On the part taken by the University of Salamanca in the Gregorian correction of the calendar.] pp. 61. *Salamanca,* 1898. 8°. **8356.** l. **10.**

BUSTO VAEZA (JOSÉ)

—— Peumayén. Poemas del Sur. pp. 82. *Buenos Aires,* 1951. 8°. **11453.** d. **32.**

BUSTO VALDÉS (RAYMUNDUS DEL) Parva poemata latina, seu Ludicra litteraria . . . Editio II., amplificata et mendis expurgata. pp. 651. *Palentiæ,* 1895. 8° **11409.** gg. **50.**

BUSTO Y BLANCO (FERNANDO DEL) Topografía Médica de las Islas Canarias. [With a map.] pp. xi. 528. *Sevilla*, 1864. 8°. **7687**. aaa. **10**.

BUSTO Y LÓPEZ (ANDRÉS DEL) *Marquis del Busto.* *See* MADRID.—*Academia Quirurgica Matritense.* La Iberia Médica. Periodico . . . dirigido por el Doctor A. del Busto y López. 1857. 4°. P.P. **2710**. c.

—— De la Celulacion Primitiva. Memoria leída en la Sociedad Histológica de Madrid, *etc.* pp. 28. *Madrid*, 1875. 8°. **7306**. aaa. **11**. (**5**.)

—— Discurso pronunciado en la Real Academia de Medicina por D. Andrés del Busto, en su recepcion pública . . . El código de la naturaleza. Estudios acerca de las leyes de la materia y de la vida. 1877. *See* MADRID.—*Real Academia de Medicina de Madrid, etc.* Memorias, *etc.* tom. 4. 1797, *etc.* 4°. Ac. **3708/4**.

BUSTOS CERECEDO (MIGUEL)

—— *See* OTHON (M. J.) Manuel José Othon. Poemas y cuentos. Selección y prólogo de M. Bustos Cerecedo. 1945. 8°. **12214**. ee. **1/39**.

BUSTRON (FLORIO) *See* JERUSALEM, *Kingdom of.*—Godfrey [de Bouillon], *King.* L'Alta Corte. (La Bassa Corte.) Le assise . . . del reame de Hyerusalem. [Translated from the French by F. Bustron.] 1535. fol. **504**. k. **13**.

—— Chronique de l'île de Chypre . . . Publiée par M. René de Mas Latrie. *Ital.* 1886. 4°. *See* FRANCE. [*Appendix.* — *History and Politics, etc.* — *Miscellaneous.*] Collection de documents inédits, *etc.* (Mélanges historiques, *etc.* tom. 5.) 1835, *etc.* 4°, *etc.* **1885**. e. **8/5**.

BUSTUS (MATTHAEUS) *See* JOHN, *Archbishop of Euchaita.* Ioannis Metropolitani Euchaitensis Versus iambici . . . Nunc primum in lucem editi cura M. Busti. 1610. 4°. **3670**. bb. **26**. (**2**.)

BUSUIGIN (ALEKSANDR) Рабочее племя. [Short stories.] pp. 167. *Ростов на Дону*, 1932. 8°. **012590**. i. **13**.

BUSUIOCEANU (ALEXANDRU) *See* THEOTOKOPOULOS (D.) called EL GRECO. Les Tableaux du Greco de la Collection Royale de Roumanie. Avec une étude de A. Busuioceanu. [1937.] 4°. **7864**. w. **1**.

—— Andreescu. Cu 66 de reproduceri [including a portrait] afară din text. pp. 61. pl. 66. *București*, 1936. 8°. **7870**. b. **37**.
Part of a series entitled "Biblioteca artistica."

—— Iser. *Rum. & Fr.* pp. 29. pl. xxiv. *Craiova*, 1930. 8°. **7869**. r. **36**.
Part of the "Colecția Apollo."

—— Trois tableaux ignorés du Corrège. [With reproductions. Reprinted from the Gazette des Beaux-Arts.] *Paris*, [1938.] 4°. **7865** s. **15**.

BUSUTTIL (ALBERT)

—— Clarion-Call. [On Christianity, Nazism and Communism.] pp. 32. *Birkirkara*, [1948?] 8°. [*Fundamentals.* no. 2.] P.P. **716**. cc.

—— Notes on Elements of Physics. Fundamental measurements and hydrostatics. pp. 32. [*The Author: Birkirkara, Malta*, 1946.] 8°. **08710**. a. **43**.

BUSUTTIL (SALVATORE) *See* PISTOLESI (Erasmo) *Topographer.* La Colonna Trajana . . . disegnata da S. Busuttil, *etc.* 1846. fol. **1731**. c. **28**.

BUSUTTIL (VINCENZO) *See* PEARL FISHERS. The Pearl Fishers, *etc.* (I Pescatori di perle, *etc.*) [The English version by V. Busuttil.] [1899.] 16°. **11714**. c. **4**. (**2**.)

—— Holiday Customs in Malta, and sports, usages, ceremonies, omens & superstitions of the Maltese people. pp. 158. *L. Busuttil: Malta*, 1894. 16°. **12431**. a. **36**.

—— A Summary of the History of Malta, containing an abridged history of the Order of St. John of Jerusalem from its foundation to its establishment in Malta. pp. xv. 174. *G. Muscat: Malta*, 1890. 8°. **9055**. aaa. **16**.

—— A Summary of the History of Malta . . . Revised edition. pp. 185. *L. Busuttil: Malta*, 1894. 8°. **4782**. e. **34**.

BUSVINE (JAMES RONALD)

—— Insects and Hygiene. The biology and control of insect pests of medical and domestic importance in Britain . . . With 58 illustrations. pp. xiv. 482. *Methuen & Co.: London*, 1951. 8°. **07299**. b. **33**.

BUSVINE (KATHARINE)

—— *See* SAMIVEL. Here is the Story of Brown the Bear . . . Translated by K. Busvine and P. Quennell. 1940. fol. **12823**. e. **12**.

BUSVINE (RICHARD)

—— Gullible Travels. [An account of the author's experiences as a war correspondent.] pp. 349. *Constable: London*, 1945. 8°. **9101**. ee. **33**.

—— Rake's Harvest. [A novel.] pp. 255. *Francis Aldor: London*, [1947.] 8°. NN. **37955**.

BUSWELL (ARTHUR MOSES) *See* BORUFF (Clair S.) and BUSWELL (A. M.) Illinois River Studies, *etc.* 1929. 8°. [*Illinois State Water Survey. Bulletin.* no. 28.] A.S. I. **26/3**.

—— *See* MASON (William P.) Examination of Water . . . Revised by A. M. Buswell. 1931. 8°. **07560**. f. **30**.

BUSWELL (ARTHUR MOSES) and **NEAVE** (SIDNEY LIONEL)

—— Laboratory Studies of Sludge Digestion. pp. 84. *Urbana, Ill.*, 1930. 8°. [*Illinois State Water Survey. Bulletin.* no. 30.] A.S. I. **26/3**.

BUSWELL (ARTHUR MOSES) and **STRICKHOUSER** (SHERMAN ISRAEL)

—— The Depth of Sewage Filters and the Degree of Purification. By A. M. Buswell, S. I. Strickhouser, and others. pp. 100. *Urbana, Ill.*, [1930.] 8°. [*Illinois State Water Survey. Bulletin.* no. 26.] A.S. I. **26/3**.

BUSWELL (*Sir* GEORGE) *Bart.* A Copy of the Last Will and Testament of Sir George Buswell, Bar. of Clipston in the County of Northampton. To which is prefix'd an Epistle dedicatory to the . . . inhabitants of Clipston, Kelmarsh, etc. (Orders agreed upon by the trustees for the School and Hospital of Clipston, *etc.*) pp. 18. *London*, 1714. 8°. **1416**. d. **59**.

BUSWELL (GUY THOMAS) How People Look at Pictures. A study of the psychology of perception in art. [With illustrations.] pp. xv. 198. *University of Chicago Press: Chicago*, 1935. 8°. **7809**. r. **11**.

BUSWELL (GUY THOMAS)

—— A Laboratory Study of the Reading of Modern Foreign Languages. pp. xii. 100. *Macmillan Co.: New York,* 1927. 8°. [*Publications of the American and Canadian Committees on Modern Languages.* vol. 2.] **Ac.9957.b.**

—— Visual Outline of Educational Psychology. pp. iii. 106. *Longmans & Co.: New York,* [1939.] 8°. [*Students Outline Series.*] W.P. **10225/23.**

BUSWELL (HARRY) The Expiratory Groans of Wisbech Iron Bridge. [In verse.] *V. Cassell: Wisbech,* [1931.] 8°. **011641.** ee. **33.**

BUSWELL (HENRY FOSTER) The Civil Liability for Personal Injuries arising out of Negligence. pp. lxxxv. 463. *Little, Brown & Co.: Boston,* 1893. 8°. **06616.** k. **12.**

—— Ode. *See* THAYER (Christopher T.) Address delivered at the Dedication of Memorial Hall, Lancaster, *etc.* 1868. 8°. **10413.** h. **24.**

BUSWELL (HENRY FOSTER) and **WALCOTT** (CHARLES HOSMER)

—— Practice and Pleading in Personal Actions in the Courts of Massachusetts, *etc.* pp. xxii. 471. *G. B. Reed: Boston,* 1875. 8°. **6703.** aa. **8.**

BUSWELL (JOHN) *Gentleman of His Majesty's Chapel Royal.*

—— An Historical Account of the Knights of the Most Noble Order of the Garter, from its first institution, in the year MCCCL, to the present time. pp. xii. 318. *R. Griffiths: London,* 1757. 8°. **608.** i. **14.**

—— [Another copy.] MS. ADDITIONS. **608.** i. **15.**

—— [Another copy.] G. **1084.**

BUSWELL (JOHN) *Writer of Verse.*

—— Wayside Thoughts and other Poems. pp. 23. *Arthur H. Stockwell: Ilfracombe,* 1947. 8°. **11658.** ee. **10.**

BUSWELL (LESLIE) Ambulance no. 10. Personal letters from the front. [With plates.] pp. xxii. 155. *Constable & Co.: London; Cambridge, Mass.* [printed], 1917. 8°. **09082.** cc. **16.**

BUSWELL (WILLIAM) Plain Parochial Sermons on Important Subjects. pp. xii. 355. *J. Hatchard & Son: London,* 1842. 12°. **1357.** d. **7.**

BUSY BEE. *See* PERIODICAL PUBLICATIONS.—*Birmingham.*

BUSY-BEE, *Aunt.*

—— Aunt Busy Bee's New Series. 12 pt. *Dean & Son: London,* [1852.] 8°. [*Dean & Son's Colored Sixpenny Toy Books.*] **12824.** g. **54/2.**

BUSY BEES NEWS. *See* LONDON.—III. *People's Dispensary for Sick Animals.*

BUSY BEES SERIES.

—— Busy Bees Series. *Burgess & Bowes: London,* 1948– . 8°. W.P. **13200.**

BUSY BODY. *See* BUSYBODY.

BUSY HOUR NUMBER WORK BOOK.

—— Busy Hour Number Work Book. pp. 24. *Philip & Tacey: London,* [1954.] 8°. **8505.** de. **53.**

BUSYBODIES. The Busy-Bodies; a novel. By the authors of "The Odd Volume" [i.e. the Misses M. and — Corbett]. 3 vol. *Longman & Co.: London,* 1827. 12°. N. **465.**

BUSYBODY. The Busy Body. *See* PERIODICAL PUBLICATIONS.—*London.*

—— The Busy-Body. A novel. 3 vol. *Richard Bentley: London,* 1843. 12°. N. **2403.**

—— The Spirituall Courts epitomized, in a Dialogue betwixt two Proctors, Busie Body, and Scrape-all, and their discourse of the want of their former imployment. [With a woodcut.] pp. 6. [*London?*] 1641. 4°. E. **157.** (**15.**)

—— [Another edition.] 1744. *See* HARLEIAN MISCELLANY. The Harleian Miscellany, *etc.* vol. 2. 1744, *etc.* 4°. **185.** a. **6.**

—— [Another edition.] 1809. *See* HARLEIAN MISCELLANY. The Harleian Miscellany, *etc.* vol. 2. 1808, *etc.* 4°. **2072.g.**

—— [Another edition.] 1809. *See* HARLEIAN MISCELLANY. The Harleian Miscellany, *etc.* vol. 4. 1808, *etc.* 8°. **1326.** g. **4.**

BUSZ (CARL HEINRICH EMIL GEORG) Die Leucit-Phonolithe und deren Tuffe in dem Gebiete des Laacher Sees. 1891. *See* BONN.—*Naturhistorischer Verein der Preussischen Rheinlande.* Verhandlungen, *etc.* Jahrg. 48. Hälfte 2. 1844, *etc.* 8°. Ac. **2930.**

BUSZ (HENRICUS) *See* DEUSINGIUS (A.) Synopsis medicinæ universalis, *etc.* (pt. 1 sect. 1. disp. 3. De temperamentis.—sect. 2. disp. 1. De rebus non naturalibus.—pt. 2. sect. 2. disp. 1. De signis diagnosticis in genere.—sect. 3. disp. 2. De indicatione conservatoria ac curatoria. *Resp.* H. Busz.) 1649. 12°. **544.** a. **21.**

BUSZ (KARL HEINRICH EMIL GEORG) *See* BUSZ (Carl H. E. G.)

BUSZARD (F. W.)

—— The Jolly-Buszard Book of Fish Recipes, *etc.* pp. viii. 80. *Sir Isaac Pitman & Sons: London,* 1953. 8°. **7948.** a. **86.**

BUSZARD (LUDWIK ALEKSANDER) Geniusz Grecyi i tegoczesni malarze Francuzcy: Dawid, Ingres, Hippolit Flandrin, Eugeniusz Delacroix. Studyum krytyczne. pp. 71. *Warszawa,* 1868. 8°. **7854.** dd. **39.** (**11.**)

BUSZCZYŃSKI (BOLESŁAW)

—— Eine der neuesten Forschungen über Coppernicus. [On L. A. Birkenmajer's "Mikołaj Kopernik."] 2 pt. 1908, 09. *See* THORN.—*Coppernicus-Verein für Wissenschaft und Kunst.* Mitteilungen, *etc.* Hft. 16, 17. 1878, *etc.* 8°. Ac. **727.**

—— Ueber die Bahnen der am 11. Dezember 1852 und am 3. Dezember 1861 in Deutschland beobachteten hellen Meteore. pp. 32. *Halle,* 1886. 8°. **8756.** bbb. **34.** (**5.**)

BUSZCZYŃSKI (STEFAN) *See* also BEZSTRONNY (S.) *pseud.* [i.e. S. Buszczyński.]

—— *See* DAUDET (E.) Męczennik Miłości . . . Przekład S. Buszczyńskiego. 1880. 8°. **12518.** m. **3.**

—— *See* DEMBIŃSKI (H.) Pamiętnik H. Dembińskiego, Jenerała wojsk polskich. Z rękopismu wydał S. B. [i.e. S. Buszczyński.] 1860. 8°. **10795.** bb. **6.**

BUSZCZYŃSKI (Stefan)

—— *See* Kraszewski (J. I.) Wydanie jubileuszowe . . . Złote myśli z dzieł J. I. Kraszewskiego . . . Krytycznym przeglądem pism jubilata opatrzył S. Buszczyński. 1879. 8°. **12264.** c. **7.**

—— Zbiorowe wydanie pism Stefana Buszczyńskiego. tom 1–7. *Kraków,* 1894. 8°. **012265.** k. **11.**
Imperfect; wanting tom 8. *Tom* 9–12 *not published.*

—— La Décadence de l'Europe. [By S. Buszczyński.] pp. clxviii. 444. 1867. 12°. *See* Europe. **8404.** bb. **36.**

—— Deuxième édition. [With a preface signed: X., i.e. Michał Janik.] [With a portrait.] pp. clxxxiv. 480. *Berne,* 1916. 8°. **08026.** a. **1.**

—— Leliwa. Komedja we dwóch aktach dla amatorskiego teatru napisana. [Attributed alternatively to M. Walewski or S. Buszczyński.] pp. iv. 112. 1857. 12°. *See* Leliwa. **11758.** aaa. **70.**

—— Marzenia o pojednaniu się Polski z Moskwą przez S. B. [i.e. by S. Buszczyński.] (Odbitka z "Gazety Narodowej.") pp. 32. 1872. 8°. *See* B., S. **8094.** e. **17.** (**4.**)

—— Obrona spotwarzonego narodu. Powszechny ruch ludowy przed powstaniem. Styczniowe 1863 roku powstanie. Zasady w historycznych dziełach Krakowskiej Szkoły, z ostatniej ćwierci wieku od 1860 roku do dni dzisiejszych krytycznie rozebrał a . . . ocenił S. Buszczyński. 3 zesz. *Kraków,* 1888–90. 8°. **9476.** h. **28.**

—— Oświata w Polsce i u Niemców za czasów Kopernika i w dzisiejszych czasach. pp. 78. *Poznań,* 1873. 8°. **9004.** gg. **10.** (**1.**)

—— Pamięci Pułaskiego, Kościuszki, Niemcewicza w stuletnią rocznicę niepodległości Stanów Zjednoczonych. Ameryka i Europa, studium historyczne i finansowe z krytycznym na sprawy społeczne poglądem. 2 cz. *w Krakowie,* 1876. 8°. **8176.** bb. **10.**

—— Posłannicy. Obraz dramatyczny w pięciu odsłonach. [In verse. A revision of "Demokraci i arystokraci," originally written by Buszczyński under the pseudonym S. Busz.] pp. xxvii. 172. *we Lwowie,* 1876. 8°. **11758.** bb. **9.**

—— Freiheitshort. Deutung der Geschichte Polens, *etc.* (Aus dem polnischen Original von Friedrich Müller übertragen.) pp. xci. 324. *Krakau,* 1917. 8°. **09475.** f. **26.**

—— Die Wunden Europa's. Statistische Thatsachen mit ethnographischen und historischen Erläuterungen . . . Eintracht. Friede. Fortschritt. Analepsis. In voluntate libertas. In libertate salus. [By S. Buszczyński.] pp. 32. 1875. fol. *See* Europe. **8223.** df. **1.**

BUSZMA (Eugeniusz)

—— Drogownictwo w Planie Sześcioletnim. pp. 88. *Warszawa,* 1953. 8°. [*Biblioteka Planu Sześcioletniego.*] **8208.** cc. **31/16.**

BUSZYŃSKI (Maryan) *See* Poland. [*Collections of Laws, etc.*] Polskie ustawodawstwo wojskowe. W opracowaniu . . . M. Buszyńskiego . . . B. Matznera. 1930, *etc.* 8°. Ac. **4345.** b.

BUT. "But As For Me——." [A tract.] pp. 23. *R.T.S.: London,* [1878.] 24°. **4422.** aa. **16.** (**10.**)

—— But Once. [A tale. By Jane Alice Sargant.] pp. 176. *S.P.C.K.: London,* [1853.] 12°. **4416.** e. **11.**

BUT. Du but et de l'importance des humanités. (Par H. D. Nouvelle édition.) [The author's preface signed: C . . . . .] [1888.] 8°. *See* D., H. **8311.** aa. **3.**

BUT (A. I.)

—— Планирование в цветной металлургии. pp. 298. *Москва,* 1946. 8°. **07107.** tt. **3.**

BUT (Adrianus)

—— *See* Izelgrinus (J.) The Rethorica Nova attributed to Jacobus Izelgrinus, *etc.* (A redaction by A. de But of a series of lectures delivered by J. Izelgrinus.) 1947. 8°. **11804.** f. **3.**

—— Chronicon Flandriae. *See* Smet (J. J. de) Recueil des chroniques de Flandre, *etc.* tom. 1. 1837, *etc.* 4°. Ac. **986/4**

—— Chronique d'Adrien de But, complétée par les additions du même auteur. [A different work from the preceding, being a continuation of the chronicle of Aegidius de Roya, based partly on material collected by him.] *Lat. See* Kervyn de Lettenhove (J. M. B. C.) *Baron.* Chroniques relatives à l'histoire de la Belgique sous la domination des ducs de Bourgogne, *etc.* vol. 1. 1870. 4°. Ac. **986/14.**

—— Cronica abbatum monasterii de Dunis. (Appendix seu Auctarium compendii chronologici monasterii Dunensis . . . A R. P. Carolo de Visch . . . concinnatus.—Codex diplomaticus.) [With notes.] pp. xi. 181. *Brugis,* 1839. 4°. [*Recueil de chroniques . . . concernant l'histoire et les antiquités de la Flandre-Occidentale.* sér. 1.] Ac. **5517/4.** (**1.**)

—— [Another edition.] Cronica [by A. But] et cartularium monasterii de Dunis. [Edited by F. van de Putte. The chartulary transcribed and the indices compiled by Désiré van de Casteele.] pp. xix. 1054. *Brugis,* 1864. 4°. [*Recueil de chroniques . . . concernant l'histoire et les antiquités de la Flandre-Occidentale.* sér. 1.] Ac. **5517/4.** (**8.**)

BUT (Adrien de) *See* But (Adrianus)

BUTA (Nicolae)

—— *See* Rangoni (C.) *Bishop of Reggio-Emilia.* I Ragguagli di Claudio Rangoni, *etc.* [Edited with an introduction by N. Buta.] 1925. 4°. [*Diplomatarium italicum.* vol. 1.] Ac. **104.** f/2.

—— I Poesi romeni in una serie di "avvisi" del Settecento [*sic*], 1599–1603. [Documents selected from the Vatican archives. Edited by N. Buta.] *In:* Diplomatarium italicum. vol. 2. pp. 72–304. 1930. 4°. Ac. **104.** f/2.
The title corrected in an erratum slip as "I Paesi romeni in una serie di "avvisi" della fine del Cinquecento."

BUTADIENE COMMITTEE.

—— Butadiene Committee on Specifications and Methods of Analyses. *See* United States of America.—*Committee on Butadiene Specifications and Methods of Analyses.*

BUTAKOV (Aleksandr) Словарь морскихъ словъ и реченій, съ англійскаго на французскіі и русскій языки. Составилъ А. Бутаковъ. pp. 526. *С. Петербургъ,* 1837. 12°. **8805.** a. **16.**

BUTAKOV (Grigory Ivanovich) [Новыя соображенія пароходной тактики.] Nouvelles bases de tactique navale . . . Traduites du russe par H. de la Planche, *etc.* pp. xii. 203. pl. xxvi. *Paris,* [1864.] 8°. **8806.** ee. **13.**

BUTALOV (V. A.)

—— Заменители дефицитных металлов и сплавов. Издание второе, дополненное и переработанное. pp. 236. *Москва, Ленинград,* 1955. 8°. **7111.** b. **54.**

BUTARESCO (Marin) De l'hydropisie des villosités choriales. pp. 48. *Paris,* 1867. 4°. [*Collection des thèses soutenues à la Faculté de Médecine de Paris.* An 1867. tom. 2.] **7373.** h. **5.**

BUTASHEVICH (   ) *pseud.* [i.e. MIKHAIL VASIL'EVICH PETRASHEVSKY.] *See* PETRASHEVSKY.

BUTAT (HENRI) *See* MOORE (Thomas) *the Poet.* L'Épicurien. Traduit par H. Butat, *etc.* 1865. 8º. **12603. g. 6.**

BUTAT (PAUL) *See* AUZIAS-TURENNE (J. A.) Le Choléra et son traitement. [Retranslated by P. B., i.e. P. Butat, from the English version of the original, by Sir F. Bateman.] 1865. 8º. **7561. c. 7.**

BUTAUD (   ) *de Bourganeuf.* De la métrite chronique; thèse, *etc.* pp. 29. *Paris,* 1834. 4º. **1184. f. 14. (25.)**

BUTAUD (BERNARD JULES) Essai sur l'ovarite, et en particulier sur sa terminaison par hydropisie enkystée. Tribut académique, *etc.* pp. 20. *Montpellier,* 1832. 4º. **1181. f. 7. (27.)**

BUTAUD (MARC) De l'endocardite ulcéreuse. pp. 80. *Paris,* 1868. 4º. [*Collection des thèses soutenues à la Faculté de Médecine de Paris.* An 1868. tom. 2.] **7373. i. 6.**

BUTAVAND (F.) L'Enigme étrusque. Le foie de Plaisance. La tuile de Capoue. pp. vii. 45. *Paris,* 1936. 8º. **07702. bb. 65.**

—— L'Énigme ibère. Le plomb d'Alcoy, le bronze de Luzaga, le plomb de Puchol. pp. ix. 69. *Paris,* 1937. 8º. **07707. h. 31.**

—— L'Énigme lydienne. Les inscriptions de Sardes. pp. vii. 50. *Paris,* 1935. 8º. **7700. bb. 13.**

—— L'Épopée ligure. [On the origins and customs of the people inhabiting the region of Liguria.] pp. 79. *Paris,* 1935. 8º. **010151. de. 75.**

—— Études de linguistique africaine-asiatique comparée, *etc.* pp. ix. 109. *Paris,* 1933. 8º. **012903. i. 18.**

—— Glozel et ses inscriptions néolithiques. pp. xv. 31. *Paris,* 1928. 8º. **07707. h. 60.**

—— Le Secret du texte étrusque de la momie de Zagreb. [Maintaining that the text consists of fragments from the Odyssey.] pp. xv. 152. *Paris,* 1936. 8º. **07702. bb. 63.**

—— La Vérité sur Alésia. [Identifying Izernore, rather than Alise-Sainte-Reine, as the site of Alesia.] pp. 62. *Paris,* 1933. 8º. **07707. eee. 37.**

BUTAYE (ARTHUR) *See* VÉRON DE DEYNE (   ) and BUTAYE (A.) Ypres, *etc.* [1909.] 8º. **10171. ff. 23.**

BUTAYE (RENÉ) *See* BIBLE.—*Gospels.*—*Selections.* [*Kongo.*—*Kisantu dialect.*] E Kangu Diampa go mambu magangilu ye malongilu kwa mfumu eto Jizu Kristu masekulu mu kikongo kwa Tata R. Butaye. 1898. 8º. **3068. ee. 57.**

—— Dictionnaire kikongo-français, français-kikongo. [With Dutch-Kikongo and Kiswahili-French vocabularies.] 2 pt. *Roulers,* [1910.] 8º. **12906. n. 7.**

—— Leven van Pater Damiaan, apostel der melaatschen van Molokai . . . Zesde, herziene druk. [With portraits and maps.] pp. 246. *Brugge,* 1890. 8º. **4886. f. 1.**
The wrapper bears the words " Achtste, herziene druk."

BUTAYE (SÉVERIN BENOÎT AMAND) Méthode simplifiée, théorique et pratique, d'enseignement, d'instruction et d'éducation militaires, suivie de notions précises sur le cheval et l'équitation militaires, *etc.* pp. xii. 212. *Bruxelles,* 1874. 8º. **8830. aa. 17.**

BUTCHART (CHARLES BRUCE RIVERS)
—— Hampshire Castles. pp. ix. 29. pl. VIII. *Warren & Son: Winchester,* 1955. 8º. **010368. y. 29.**

BUTCHART (E. G.)
—— The Legend of Northgate Farm . . . With drawings by Wendy Koop. pp. 215. *Routledge & Kegan Paul: London,* 1951. 8º. **12832. i. 9.**

BUTCHART (ISABEL) Other People's Fires. [Essays.] pp. xii. 219. *Sidgwick & Jackson: London,* 1924. 8º. **012352. f. 50.**

—— Songs of a Day. pp. 76. *Country Life: London; G. Scribner's Sons: New York,* 1916. 8º. **011649. h. 109.**

BUTCHART (MONTGOMERY) *See* ORAGE (Alfred R.) Political and Economic Writings . . . Arranged by M. Butchart, *etc.* 1936. 8º. **8234. a. 36.**

—— Money. Selected passages presenting the concepts of money in the English tradition, 1640–1935. Compiled by M. Butchart. pp. 348. *Stanley Nott: London,* 1935. 8º. **08235. c. 64.**

—— To-morrow's Money. By seven of to-day's leading monetary heretics . . . Edited, with preface and concluding chapter, by M. Butchart. pp. 286. *Stanley Nott: London,* 1936 [1937]. 8º. **8234. aa. 18.**

BUTCHART (STEWART F.) Sind die Gedichte " Poem on Pastoral Poetry " und " Verses on the Destruction of Drumlanrig Woods " von Robert Burns? pp. 60. *Marburg,* 1903. 8º. [*Marburger Studien zur englischen Philologie.* Hft. 6.] **12981. h. 13.**

BUTCHENNA (BOLLAPRAGADA) *See* BUCHCHANNA, *Bollapragada.*

BUTCHER. The Butcher's Answer to the Taylors Poem: or, Their whole profession unmask'd. (The Tradesman's Hue and Cry after the Bumb-Bailiffs and Setters.) [In verse.] [*Dublin,* 1725.] *s. sh.* fol. **C.121.g.8.(91.)**

—— The Butcher's Daughter's Policy, or, Lustful Lord well fitted. [A ballad.] *John Evans: London,* [1812?] *s. sh. obl.* 4º. **1876. f. 1. (192.)**

—— [Another copy.] The Butcher's Daughter's Policy, *etc.* *London,* [1812?] *s. sh. obl.* 4º. **11623. m. 4. (16.)**

—— The Butcher's Frolic, or, the Affrighted tailor. To which is added, The Sailor Boy, and A New Touch on the Times. [Songs.] pp. 8. *T. Johnston: Falkirk,* [1820?] 12º. **11621. b. 10. (44.)**

—— [Another copy.] The Butcher's Frolic, *etc.* *Falkirk,* [1820?] 12º. **11606. aa. 24. (11.)**
Cropped.

—— Butcher's Overthrow. (The Oakham Poachers.) [Songs.] *Hodges: London,* [1850?] *s. sh.* 4º. **C. 116. i. 1. (167.)**

—— [Another issue.] *G. V. T. Wright: Shacklewell,* [1850?] *s. sh.* 4º. **C. 116. i. 1. (168.)**

—— The Experienced Butcher: shewing the respectability and usefulness of his calling, the religious considerations arising from it, the laws relating to it, and various profitable suggestions for the rightly carrying it on, *etc.* [By James Plumptre, assisted by Thomas Lantaffe.] pp. viii. 198. pl. 6. *Darton, Harvey & Darton & Baldwin, Cradock & Joy: London,* 1816. 12º. **1043. b. 38.**

BUTCHER.

—— The Jolly Butcher. [A ballad.] *L. Deming: Boston,* [1830?] *s. sh.* 4°. **11630.** f. **7. (103.)**

BUTCHER AND CO. Butcher & Co.'s Borough of Portsmouth Directory, *etc. See* DIRECTORIES.—*Portsmouth.*

BUTCHER (A. D.) The Calibration of Regulators. [With diagrams.] pp. 22. 1920. fol. *See* EGYPT.—*Ministry of Public Works.* S. **871.** gd. **4.**

BUTCHER (AGNES ANNIE) *See* SUMMERS (William H.) 'Gone Before.' A brief memorial of A. A. Butcher. 1885. 16°. **4906.** aaaa. **45.**

BUTCHER (ALICE MARY) *Lady.* Memories of George Meredith. With three illustrations [including a silhouette of Meredith]. pp. viii. 151. *Constable & Co.: London,* 1919. 8°. **010856.** de. **30.**

BUTCHER (ANDREW P.) Gip: a one-act dramatic sketch. *W. H. Western: Darwen,* 1915. 8°. **11774.** ccc. **11.**

BUTCHER (ANNA DEANE)

—— [Miscellaneous pamphlets concerning the system of phonetic signs known as Orthotype, and books marked according to this system.] 19 pt. [1910?–25?] 8°, *etc.* **12980.** dd. **6.**

BUTCHER (ARTHUR HERBERT) Materia Medica Tables. Designed for the use of students. pl. 20. *E. & S. Livingstone: Edinburgh,* [1896.] 8°. **7482.** ee. **19.**

BUTCHER (ARTHUR LEPINE)

—— Cave Survey. pp. x. 40. *Leamington Spa,* [1951.] 8°. [*Cave Research Group of Great Britain. Publication.* no. 3.] W.P. **2662/3.**
Reproduced from typewriting.

BUTCHER (ARTHUR LEPINE) and **GEMMELL** (ARTHUR)

—— A Key Plan of Gaping Gill. Skeleton surveys of the underground system related to a surface plane-table survey of the entrances and intervening shake-holes. [With a plan.] pp. 6. *Leamington Spa,* [1953.] 8°. [*Cave Research Group of Great Britain. Publication.* no. 5.] W.P. **2662/5.**
Reproduced from typewriting.

BUTCHER (BENJAMIN THOMAS) *See* BIBLE.—*Mark.* [*Kiwai.—Goaribari dialect.*] Pai mea Mareko titi naibaha riatiwa. [Translated by B. T. Butcher.] 1926. 8°. **03068.** ee. **98.**

—— James Chalmers. pp. 16. *London Missionary Society: London,* [1926.] 8°. [*Venturer Series.* no. 3.] **20041.a.21/3.**

BUTCHER (C. F.) How Milwaukee Stops Accidents. pp. ii. 25. 1936. 8°. *See* UNITED STATES OF AMERICA.—*Department of Commerce.—Accident Prevention Conference.* A.S. **94.**

BUTCHER (CHARLES H.) *Archaeologist.* Essex Bronze Implements and Weapons in the Colchester Museum . . . Reprinted from the Transactions of the Essex Arch. Soc. . . . With additions. [With plates.] pp. 12. *Colchester,* [1926.] 8°. [*Colchester Museum Publications.* no. 1.] Ac. **1234.**

BUTCHER (CHARLES HENRY) *Dean of Shanghai.* Armenosa of Egypt. A romance of the Arab conquest. pp. xv. 354. *W. Blackwood & Sons: Edinburgh & London,* 1897. 8°. **012626.** k. **16.**

BUTCHER (CHARLES HENRY) *Dean of Shanghai.*

—— The Oriflamme in Egypt. [A novel.] pp. viii. 320. *J. M. Dent & Co.: London,* 1904. 8°. **012630.** aaa. **47.**

—— Sermons preached in the East. pp. vi. 201. *Elliot Stock: London,* 1890. 8°. **4466.** b. **39.**

—— Sir Gilbert. A novel. [By C. H. Butcher.] pp. vii. 360. 1859. 8°. *See* GILBERT, *Sir.* **12632.** a. **19.**

—— The Sound of a Voice that is Still. A selection of sermons preached by the late Dean Butcher of Cairo. [Edited with an introductory memoir by Edith Louisa Butcher.] pp. viii. 216. *J. M. Dent & Co.: London,* 1908. 8°. **4477.** k. **18.**

BUTCHER (CYRIL) In Extremis . . . Worst moments in the lives of the famous, *etc.* [With portraits.] pp. 224. *Hutchinson & Co.: London,* [1934.] 8°. **010603.** h. **21.**

BUTCHER (D. G.) The A B C of Squash Rackets . . . Illustrated with sketches and 32 diagrams by the author. pp. 128. *I. Nicholson & Watson: London,* 1934. 8°. **7916.** eee. **19.**

—— Introducing Squash, *etc.* [With plates, including a portrait.] pp. 200. *Faber & Faber: London,* 1948. 8°. **7918.** aaa. **44.**

BUTCHER (D. S. St. A.)

—— The "NumeroLogic" Birth Path Calculator. [A card. With explanatory leaflet. By D. S. St. A. Butcher.] [1950.] *s. sh.* 8°. *See* NUMEROLOGIC BIRTH PATH CALCULATOR. **1856.** g. **14. (76.)**

BUTCHER (DEVEREUX)

—— Exploring our National Parks and Monuments. pp. 160. *Oxford University Press: New York,* 1947. 8°. **010410.** l. **33.**

BUTCHER (DONALD WILLIAM)

—— The Departmental Libraries of the University of Cambridge. [An offprint from the Journal of Documentation.] [1951.] 8°. **11916.** e. **12.**

BUTCHER (EDITH LOUISA) *See* FLOYER, afterwards BUTCHER.

BUTCHER (EDMUND) *See* BIBLE.—*Selections.* [*English.*] The Substance of the Holy Scriptures methodized . . . By the Rev. E. Butcher. 1801. 4°. **3053.** g. **8.**

—— An Excursion from Sidmouth to Chester, in the summer of 1803, in a series of letters to a Lady. Including sketches of the principal towns and villages in the Counties of Devon, Somerset, *etc.* 2 pt. pp. viii. 462. *H. D. Symonds: London,* 1805. 12°. **291.** b. **39.**

—— [Another copy.] G. **16074.**

—— The Heresy of St. Paul described, and applied to the Conduct of Modern Unitarians. A sermon, preached . . . before the members and supporters of the Unitarian Fund. pp. 48. *C. Stower: Hackney: D. Eaton: London; J. Wallis: Sidmouth,* 1813. 12°. **4226.** e. **57.** (4.)

—— A New Guide descriptive of the Beauties of Sidmouth . . . With an account of the environs . . . Fourth edition. [With plates.] *W. C. Pollard: Exeter; J. Wallis: Sidmouth,* [1830?] 12°. **10358.** aaa. **7.**

—— The Only Security for Peace. A sermon, preached at the Meeting House of the Protestant Dissenters in Sidmouth . . . on . . . June 1, 1802. Being the day appointed for a national thanksgiving on account of the peace between Great Britain, France, *etc.* pp. 23. *S. Woolmer: Exeter,* 1802. 8°. **4473.** f. **12.** (6.)

BUTCHER (Edmund)

—— Religious Education, recommended in a sermon preached . . . for the benefit of the Charity School, in Gravel Lane, Southwark. pp. 23. *C. Whittingham: London,* [1794.] 8°. **4474**. dd. **102**. **(4.)**

—— Sermons: to which are subjoined, suitable hymns. pp. viii. 472. *J. Johnson: London,* 1798. 8°. **4452**. f. **3**.

—— Unitarian Claims described, and vindicated. A discourse delivered . . . 1809 before the Society of Unitarian Christians, established in the West of England, etc. [With a list of members of the Society.] pp. 51. *P. Hedgeland: Exeter,* [1809.] 12°. **4478**. e. **90**. **(9.)**

—— [Another copy.] **1481**. d. **26**. **(13.)**

BUTCHER (Emily Elizabeth) *See* Bristol.—*Corporation of the Poor.* Bristol Corporation of the Poor. Selected records, 1696–1834. Edited by E. E. Butcher. 1932. 8°. [*Bristol Record Society's Publications.* vol. 3.] Ac. **8034**.

BUTCHER (Ernest H.) *See* Morgan (*Sir* Herbert E.) *K.B.E.*, and Butcher (E. H.) The Retailers' Compendium, *etc.* [1924.] 4°. **08229**. dd. **9**.

—— Success in Shopkeeping. Talks with retail traders. pp. 110. *London,* 1921. 8°. [*Cassell's "Business" Handbooks.*] **12827.aa.16/5.**

BUTCHER (F.) *Translator. See* Royova (K.) Martinko . . . Translated by F. and M. K. Butcher. [1920.] 8°. **12827.bb.61/7.**

—— *See* Royova (K.) Martinko . . . Translated by F. & M. K. Butcher. [1943.] 8°. **4414**. e. **46**.

BUTCHER (Frank) *See* Van Rennselaer (Alexander) and Butcher (F.) Yule Light, *etc.* [1930.] 8°. **11791**. de. **68**.

BUTCHER (G. B.) Butcher's Cardiff District Directory. *See* Directories.—*Cardiff.*

BUTCHER (Geoffrey E.)

—— *See* Bedwell (Stephen F.) A Glenn Miller Discography and Biography . . . Edited and with additional material by G. E. Butcher. 1955. 8°. **7901**. e. **22**.

BUTCHER (Gerald W.) *See* Farthing (Francis H.) Gardening . . . Including . . . a vegetable and fruit section by Mr. G. Butcher, *etc.* [1931.] 8°. **7054**. de. **31**.

—— Allotments for All. The story of a great movement. pp. 96. *G. Allen & Unwin: London,* 1918. 8°. **07078**. de. **13**.

—— Daily Express Vegetable Book, *etc.* pp. 94. *Lane Publications: London,* [1932.] 8°. **7054**. a. **21**.

—— Simplified Gardening. By G. W. Butcher, Edward Jackson and Richard Sudell. [With plates.] pp. 243. *Ernest Benn: London,* [1933.] 8°. **07028**. bb. **31**.

BUTCHER (Gerald W.) and **HARDING** (Cyril)

—— The Workers Garden. pp. 79. *Vacant Land Cultivation Society: London,* 1917. 8°. **07029**. g. **35**.

BUTCHER (H. G.)

—— An Extension of the Sum Theorem of Dimension Theory . . . Reprinted from Duke Mathematical Journal, *etc.* (A dissertation.) 1951. 8°. **08533**. k. **66**.

BUTCHER (Harry Cecil)

—— Three Years with Eisenhower. The personal diary of Captain H. C. Butcher . . . Naval Aide to General Eisenhower, 1942 to 1945. [With plates, including a portrait of General Eisenhower.] pp. xviii. 748. *William Heinemann: London, Toronto,* 1946. 8°. **9101**. cc. **40**.

BUTCHER (Henry William) Sermons preached at Margate by the late Rev. Henry W. Butcher. With brief memoir. [Edited by Kate F. Butcher. With a portrait.] pp. 152. *Hodder & Stoughton: London,* 1879. 8°. **4466**. bb. **17**.

—— In Memoriam. Rev. H. W. Butcher . . . i. Obituary notice. ii. The funeral, with address by the Rev. A. Turner. iii. Funeral services by the Revs. J. B. French and H. J. Bevis. [With a portrait.] pp. 30. *R. Robinson: Margate,* [1878.] 8°. **4907**. b. **3**.

BUTCHER (Herbert Borton) The Battle of Trenton, including its historical setting. pp. vii. 39. *Princeton University Press: Princeton,* 1934. 8°. **09603**. aa. **14**.

BUTCHER (Hugh Louis Montague) My Lane, and other poems. pp. 16. *A. H. Stockwell: London,* [1925.] 8°. **011645**. e. **160**.

—— **Report of the Commission of Inquiry into Allegations of Misconduct made against Chief Salami Agbaje, the Otun Balogun of Ibadan, and the Allegations of Inefficiency and Maladministration on the part of the Ibadan and District Native Authority.** pp. 58. 1951. 8°. *See* Nigeria. [*Miscellaneous Official Publications.*] C.S. c. **505/7**.

BUTCHER (James Williams) *See* Bonner (Carey) The New Series of Hymns for Anniversary Services. Joint editors: C. Bonner, J. W. Butcher, *etc.* [1924, *etc.*] 8°. W.P. **10979**.

—— *See* MacFarland (John T.) The Encyclopedia of Sunday Schools and Religious Education . . European editor Rev. J. W. Butcher. [1917.] 8°. **4193**. k. **11**.

—— *See* Nicoll (*Sir* William R.) and Butcher (J. W.) The Children for the Church, *etc.* 1913. 8°. **4136**. df. **12**.

—— Beware of Imitations! Talks to boys. pp. 176. *"Our Boys and Girls": London,* [1908.] 8°. **04403**. eee. **50**.

—— Boys' Brigade, and other talks. pp. 192. *C. H. Kelly: London,* [1903.] 8°. **04402**. e. **52**.

—— [Another copy.] **04402**. e. **55**.

—— The Camp on the Shore . . . Illustrated by J. D. Mills. pp. 118. *Henry Frowde; Hodder & Stoughton: London,* 1913. 8°. **012803**. h. **76**.

—— Crossing the Threshold. pp. 191. *Epworth Press: London,* 1918. 8°. **04376**. ee. **66**.

—— The Making of Treherne. pp. xiii. 264. *C. H. Kelly: London,* 1911. 8°. **012808**. dd. **17**.

—— Ray: the boy who lost and won. pp. 295. *Robert Culley: London,* [1908.] 8°. **12804**. tt. **19**.

—— The Senior Prefect, and other chronicles of Rossiter, *etc.* pp. 356. *C. H. Kelly: London,* 1913. 8°. **012808**. dd. **29**.

—— To Boys: talks on parade. pp. 205. *H. R. Allenson: London,* [1916.] 8°. **04403**. f. **28**.

—— The Work of the Sunday School. pp. 56. *Epworth Press; Wesleyan Methodist Sunday School Department: London,* 1925. 8°. [*Life and Work.* no. 2.] W.P. **7940/2**.

BUTCHER (Jesse) Old Chingford Church. [Verses.] [1888.] *s. sh.* 8°. **1871**. e. **1**. (**224**.)

BUTCHER (John) *of Nottingham.* Instructions in Etiquette, for the use of all; five letters on important subjects, exclusively for ladies; and conversational hints, to whom concerned . . . Third edition. pp. 120. *Simpkin, Marshall & Co.: London; Dearden: Nottingham,* 1847. 12°. **716**. b. **39**.

BUTCHER (John) *of the Society of Friends.* A Sermon preached . . . in Grace-Church-Street, March 11th, 1693. *See* Friends, *Society of.* Sermons preached by several of the people called Quakers, *etc.* 1775. 8°. **4151**. e. **3**.

—— [Another edition.] *See* Friends, *Society of.* Sermons or Declarations, *etc.* 1824. 8°. **4152**. c. **51**.

BUTCHER (John George) *See* Butcher (Samuel) *Bishop of Meath.* The Ecclesiastical Calendar, *etc.* [Edited by J. G. and S. H. Butcher.] 1877. 4°. **8565.dd.5.**

BUTCHER (John Henry) The Parish of Ashburton in the 15th and 16th Centuries; as it appears from extracts from the Churchwardens' accounts . . . With notes and comments. [By J. H. Butcher.] pp. 50. 1870. 8°. *See* Ashburton, *Devonshire.* **10368**. d. **26**. (**13**.)

BUTCHER (John Oliver) *See* Stocken (J.) Dental Materia Medica . . . Fourth edition. Revised by . . . J. O. Butcher. 1895. 8°. **7510**. df. **29**.

BUTCHER (Joseph) Sermons. 6 no. pp. 48. *T. Durley: Aylesbury,* [1866, 67.] 8°. **4462**. aaa. **12**.

BUTCHER (Kate F.) *See* Butcher (Henry W.) Sermons preached at Margate, *etc.* [Edited by K. F. Butcher.] 1879. 8°. **4466**. bb. **17**.

BUTCHER (M. J.) Notes on Details of Steamship Construction, *etc.* pp. 40. [*London,*] 1896. 8°. [*Shipmasters' Society. Papers, etc.* no. 47.] **08805**. bb. **1/47**.

BUTCHER (M. K.) *See* Royova (K.) Martinko . . . Translated by F. and M. K. Butcher. [1920.] 8°. **12821.bb.61/7.**

—— *See* Royova (K.) Martinko . . . Translated by F. & M. K. Butcher. [1943.] 8°. **4414**. e. **46**.

BUTCHER (Marcus Grigson) *See* Curling (William) A Sermon occasioned by the . . . death of the Rev. M. G. Butcher. 1835. 8°. **4905**. bb. **13**.

BUTCHER (Margaret)

—— Comet's Hair, *etc.* pp. 256. *Skeffington & Son: London,* [1939.] 8°. NN. **30396**.

—— Destiny on Demand. A novel. pp. 288. *Skeffington & Son: London,* [1938.] 8°. NN. **29219**.

—— Hogdown Farm Mystery. pp. 221. *Skeffington & Son: London,* [1950.] 8°. NNN. **786**.

—— Vacant Possession. A novel. pp. 256. *Skeffington & Son: London,* [1940.] 8°. NN. **31409**.

BUTCHER (Mary) The Lamentation of Mary Butcher, now confined in Worcester-City-Goal, on suspicion of murdering her male bastard child, *etc.* [1700?] *s. sh.* fol. **C.121.g.9.(120.)**

BUTCHER (Matthew) *See* Barrett (John) *Minister of Sutton in Ashfield, Nottinghamshire.* The Dying Christian's Triumph in a living Redeemer exemplified in a sermon . . . occasioned by the death of M. Butcher, *etc.* [1777.] 8°. **1416**. d. **60**.

BUTCHER (May)

—— *See* Cremona (A.) Vassalli and his Times . . . Translated by M. Butcher, *etc.* 1940. 8°. **10633**. s. **62**.

—— Elements of Maltese. A simple practical grammar. Pronunciation in English phonetics. pp. xi. 200. *Oxford University Press: London,* 1938. 8°. **012903**. e. **22**.

BUTCHER (Nellie Amelia)

—— Essentials for the New Age. pp. 62. *Arthur H. Stockwell: Ilfracombe,* [1952.] 8°. **04422**. aaa. **60**.

—— Golden Philosophy. [Poems.] pp. 32. *Simpson & Williams: Christchurch, N.Z.,* [1952.] 8°. **11652**. k. **72**.

—— Golden Philosophy, *etc.* [Poems.] pp. 48. *Simpson & Williams: Christchurch, N.Z.,* [1952.] 8°. **11652**. k. **73**.
Centennial Series. no. 2. *A different work from the preceding.*

—— Vital Truth for Parents and Children. pp. 41. *New Zealand Newspapers: Christchurch,* [1952.] 8°. **08416**. aaa. **95**.

BUTCHER (Orien L.)

—— Visual Identification. ff. 4. *O. L. Butcher: East Orange; Marks & Clerk: London,* [1939.] 4°. **6056**. h. **30**.
Typewritten.

BUTCHER (Richard) *of Bury, Lancs.* Week-Day Effort in its relation to Sunday School Labour. A paper, *etc.* pp. 23. *Sunday School Union: London,* 1872. 8°. **4192**. b. **1**. (**6**.)

BUTCHER (Richard) *Town Clerk of Stamford.* The Survey and Antiquitie of the Towne of Stamford, in the county of Lincolne; with its ancient foundation, grants, priviledges, *etc.* pp. 47. *Printed by Tho. Forcet: London,* 1646. 4°. E. **364**. (**12**.)

—— [Another copy.] G. **3395**.

—— The Survey and Antiquity of the Towns of Stamford in the County of Lincoln (by R. Butcher) and Tottenham-High-Cross in Middlesex (by Wilhelm Bedwell). Together with the Turnament of Tottenham: or the wooing, winning, and wedding of Tibbe the Reeu's daughter there. (Written . . . in verse by Mr. Gilbert Pilkington . . . Taken out of an ancient manuscript, and published . . . by W. Bedwell . . . 1631.) pp. 158. *W. Meares: London,* 1717, 18. 8°. **578**. e. **15**. (**1–3**.)

—— [Another copy.] **981**. a. **3**. (**1**, **2**.)

—— [Another copy.] **290**. a. **30**.

—— [Another copy.] G. **3394**.

—— [Another copy.] **578**. e. **16**.
Imperfect; wanting the collective titlepage.

—— [Another edition.] Continued by the author to 1660 & much enlarged, *etc.* *See* Peck (Francis) *Antiquary.* Academia tertia Anglicana, *etc.* 1727. fol. **2367**. dd. **3**.

BUTCHER (Richard George Herbert) An Account of the Opening of the "Admiral Butcher" Lifeboat Station . . . Fenit, on Tralee Bay, co. Kerry . . . Illustrated with photographs, *etc.* pp. 40. *Printed for the Author: Dublin,* 1881. 4°. **8808**. h. **18**.

—— Essays and Reports on Operative and Conservative Surgery. Illustrated by sixty-two lithographic plates, coloured and plain, *etc.* pp. viii. 933. *Fannin & Co.: Dublin,* 1865. 8°. **7482**. i. **24**.

BUTCHER (RICHARD GEORGE HERBERT)

—— On Excision of the Knee-joint . . . With coloured plates. From the Dublin Quarterly Journal of Medical Science, *etc.* pp. 60. *Hodges & Smith: Dublin,* 1855. 8°. **7480**. aaa. **6**.

—— Second Memoir on the Excision of the Knee-joint: to which is appended a remarkable example of the power of operative surgery in saving the same articulation . . . With illustrations. pp. 76. *M'Glashan & Gill: Dublin,* 1857. 8°. **7481**. d. **28**. (**3**.)

BUTCHER (ROBERT W.) The Orange-Blossom Tale. pp. 15. *Printed for private distribution: London,* 1917. 4°. C. **58**. g. **14**.

One of an edition of thirty copies.

—— The Sea-Mist. [A tale.] pp. 12. *Printed for private circulation: London,* 1909. 8°. **12626**. bb. **15**. (**1**.)

BUTCHER (ROGER WILLIAM) *See* COSTON (H. E. T.) River Management . . . [By] H. E. T. Coston . . . R. W. Butcher, *etc.* 1936. 8°. L.R. **256**. a. **1/24**.

—— *See* PENTELOW (Frederick T. K.) An Investigation of the Effects of Milk Wastes on the Bristol Avon. By F. T. K. Pentelow . . . R. W. Butcher, *etc.* 1938. 8°. [*Ministry of Agriculture and Fisheries. Fishery Investigations.* ser. 1. vol. 4. no. 1.] B.S. **3/20**.

—— *See* TEES, *River.* Survey of the River Tees. (Part III. The Non-Tidal Reaches—Chemical and Biological. [By] R. W. Butcher . . . J. Longwell . . . F. T. K. Pentelow.) 1931, *etc.* fol. [*Department of Scientific and Industrial Research. Water Pollution Research. Technical Paper.* no. 6.] B.S. **38**. m/3.

—— Further Illustrations of British Plants . . . Drawings by Florence E. Strudwick. [A companion volume to "Illustrations of the British Flora" by W. H. Fitch.] pp. iv. 476. *L. Reeve & Co.: Ashford,* 1930. 8°. **07028**. a. **16**.

—— [A reissue.] Further Illustrations of British Plants, *etc. Ashford,* 1946. 8°. **2028**. **d**.

—— An Investigation of the River Lark and the Effect of Beet Sugar Pollution. By R. W. Butcher . . . F. T. K. Pentelow . . . and J. W. A. Woodley. [With plates and a map.] pp. 112. *London,* 1931. 8°. [*Ministry of Agriculture and Fisheries. Fishery Investigations.* ser. 1. vol. 3. no. 3.] B.S. **3/20**.

—— Suffolk, East and West. *Geographical Publications: London,* 1941. 4°. [*The Land of Britain.* pt. 72–73.] W.P. **7867/72, 73**.

BUTCHER (SAMUEL) *Bishop of Meath. See* MACNEECE (Thomas) Sermons preached in the Chapel of Trinity College, Dublin . . . Edited by S. Butcher. 1863. 8°. **4463**. h. **14**.

—— *See* POLLOCK (Alexander M.) Sermons . . . Edited by S. Butcher. 1865. 8°. **4464**. bbb. **26**.

—— A Charge delivered to the Clergy of the Diocese of Meath, at the ordinary visitation, August 1869. pp. 70. *Hodges, Foster & Co.: Dublin,* 1869. 8°. **4445**. e. **1**. (**3**.)

—— The Claims of the Additional Curates' Fund Society. A sermon, *etc.* pp. 38. *Hodges, Smith & Co.: Dublin,* 1857. 8°. **4477**. d. **23**.

BUTCHER (SAMUEL) *Bishop of Meath.*

—— The Conservative Character of the English Reformation, viewed with reference to the present state of the Church. A sermon preached on the occasion of the consecration of the Right Rev. John, Lord Bishop of Cork, Cloyne, and Ross. pp. 44. *W. Curry & Co.: Dublin,* 1862. 8°. **4477**. f. **8**.

—— The Ecclesiastical Calendar: its theory and construction. [Edited by J. G. and S. H. Butcher.] pp. xii. 270. *Hodges, Foster & Figgis: Dublin,* 1877. 4°. **8565.dd.5.**

—— A Few Thoughts on the Supreme Authority of the Word of God: laid before the Morning Clerical Meeting held in the Rotunda, *etc.* pp. 20. *Hodges, Smith & Co.: Dublin,* 1864. 8°. **4379**. bbb. **13**.

—— General Proof of Gauss' Rule for finding Easter Day. pp. 20. *Hodges, Foster & Co.: Dublin,* 1876. 4°. **3477**. e. **34**.

—— An Introductory Lecture delivered in the Divinity School of Trinity College, Dublin . . . Michaelmas Term, 1854. pp. 56. *Hodges & Smith: Dublin,* 1855. 8°. **4372**. g. **21**. (**4**.)

—— On the Study of Ecclesiastical History. An introductory lecture. pp. 47. *Hodges & Smith: Dublin,* 1850. 8°. **4530**. d. **6**.

—— The Order of Baptism. Speeches delivered by the . . . Bishop of Meath and the . . . Bishop of Killaloe, in the General Synod of the Church of Ireland, 1873. (Reprinted, with additions from the Daily Express.) pp. 24. *William McGee: Dublin,* 1873. 8°. **4165**. e. **4**. (**9**.)

—— The Relative Value and Importance of Divine and Human Knowledge. A sermon, *etc.* pp. 31. *Hodges, Smith & Co.: Dublin,* 1857. 8°. **4477**. d. **22**.

—— Reunion with Rome, as advocated in the Eirenicon of Dr. Pusey. Two sermons, *etc.* pp. viii. 108. *Hodges, Smith & Co.: Dublin,* 1866. 8°. **3940**. cc. **76**.

—— The Victor on his Throne, the Mediator between God and man. *See* WILBERFORCE (Samuel) successively *Bishop of Oxford* and *of Winchester.* The Victor in the Conflict. Sermons, *etc.* 1868. 8°. **4477**. bb. **68**.

BUTCHER (SAMUEL HENRY) *See* ARISTOTLE. [*Poetica.—Greek and English.*] Aristotle's Theory of Poetry and Fine Art, with a critical text and a translation of the Poetics by S. H. Butcher. 1895. 8°. **11312**. q. **26**.

—— —— 1898. 8°. **11313.ff.23.**

—— —— 1898. 8°. **11312**. s. **14**.

—— —— 1902. 8°. **2236**. cc. **9**.

—— *See* BUTCHER (Samuel) *Bishop of Meath.* The Ecclesiastical Calendar, *etc.* [Edited by J. G. and S. H. Butcher.] 1877. 4°. **8565.dd.5.**

—— *See* CALDERWOOD (Henry) Speeches delivered at a meeting held in Queen Street Hall, Edinburgh . . . to uphold the legislative union between Great Britain and Ireland, by Professor Calderwood, LL.D., and Professor Butcher, LL.D. 1886. 8°. **8146**. d. **9**. (**18**.)

—— *See* DEMOSTHENES. [*Works.—Greek.*] Demosthenis Orationes. Recognovit brevique adnotatione critica instruxit S. H. Butcher. 1903, *etc.* 8°. **11305.dd.**

BUTCHER (SAMUEL HENRY)

—— *See* DEMOSTHENES. [*Works.—Greek.*] Demosthenis Orationes. Recognovit brevique adnotatione critica instruxit S. H. Butcher. [1938.] 8°. **11305.dd.93.**

—— *See* DEMOSTHENES. [*Olynthiacae.—English.*] The Olynthiacs of Demosthenes. Translated . . . by E. L. Hawkins, M.A., to correspond with the Oxford text of S. H. Butcher. 1905. 8°. **11391.** aaa. **31.**

—— *See* HOMER. [*Odyssey.—English.*] The Odyssey of Homer done into English prose by S. H. Butcher . . . and A. Lang, *etc.* 1879. 8°. **11315.** c. **33.**

—— —— 1887. 8°. **2280.** b. **14.**

—— —— 1924. 4°. **11315.** t. **1.**

—— —— 1930. 8°. **11340.** f. **22.**

—— *See* HOMER. [*Selections.—English.*] The Iliad and the Odyssey. Extracts from the translations by Lang, Leaf and Myers & Butcher and Lang, *etc.* 1935. 8°. **012209.d.1/44.**

—— Demosthenes. [An account of his life and works.] pp. 172. *Macmillan & Co.: London,* 1881. 8°. [*Classical Writers.*] **12207.** f. **24.**

—— Greek Idealism in the Common Things of Life . . . Reprinted from the "Journal of Education," *etc.* pp. 12. *C. F. Hodgson & Son: London,* [1901.] 8°. **11312.** g. **11.** (**1.**)

—— Harvard Lectures on Greek Subjects. pp. ix. 266. *Macmillan & Co.: London,* 1904. 8°. **11313.** ee. **3.**

—— [Another edition.] Harvard Lectures on the Originality of Greece. pp. viii. 266. *Macmillan & Co.: London,* 1911. 8°. **11312.** n. **38.**

—— Irish Land Acts and their Operation. An address delivered to the Liberal Unionist Association . . . Glasgow, *etc.* pp. 23. *J. Maclehose & Sons: Glasgow,* 1887. 8°. **8146.** c. **9.** (**5.**)

—— The Reign of Terror or the Rule of Law for Ireland. A speech. pp. 8. *Union Defence League: London,* [1908.] 8°. **8139.** cc. **9.** (**5.**)

—— Some Aspects of the Greek Genius. pp. xii. 396. *Macmillan & Co.: London,* 1891. 8°. **012357.** i. **12.**

—— [Another edition.] [With a new chapter on "The Dawn of Romanticism in Greek Poetry."] pp. vii. 321. *Macmillan & Co.: London,* 1893. 8°. **012357.** h. **53.**

—— Third edition. pp. vi. 324. *Macmillan & Co.: London,* 1904. 8°. **2312.** b. **13.**

—— What we owe to Greece. Inaugural address, *etc.* pp. 30. *W. Blackwood & Sons: Edinburgh,* 1882. 8°. **11312.** h. **43.** (**3.**)

—— Speeches at a Farewell Dinner given to Professor S. H. Butcher in Edinburgh, 20th Jan. 1904. pp. 54. *T. & A. Constable: Edinburgh,* 1904. 8°. **10827.** cc. **21.**

BUTCHER (SOLOMON D.) Pioneer History of Custer County, and short sketches of early days in Nebraska. pp. ii. 403. *S. D. Butcher & E. S. Finch: Broken Bow, Nebraska,* 1901. 8°. **10409.** i. **18.**

BUTCHER (*Mrs.* T. B.) A Peep at Jamaica and its People, *etc.* pp. x. 36. *C. H. Kelly: London,* [1902.] 8°. **10480.** de. **19.**

BUTCHER (THOMAS) "Mordichim." Recollections of cholera in Barbados, during the middle of the year 1854. pp. 57. *Partridge, Oakey & Co.: London,* 1855. 8°. **7560.** e. **29.**

BUTCHER (THOMAS) *Clerk of the Dry Stores at His Majesty's Victualling Office, Deptford.*

—— Facts explanatory of the Instrumental Cause of the Present High Prices of Provisions, *etc.* pp. vii. 48. *Printed for the Author: London,* 1801. 8°. **08218.** bb. **29.** (**10.**)

BUTCHER (W. HENRY) *See* KITE (Edward) Historical Notes . . . Edited by W. H. Butcher. [1880.] 8°. **10347.** c. **2.** (**9.**)

BUTCHER (W. HERBERT) Fallen Leaves. [A novel.] pp. 279. *Heath Cranton: London,* 1933. 8°. NN. **19772.**

BUTCHER (W. J.) *of Harlesden.* The Practical Veterinary or Farmers' Hand Book and Horse-Keepers' Guide, giving practical information for the treatment and cure of all diseases incidental to animal life. pp. 46. *W. Straker: London,* 1902. 16°. **7293.** a. **22.**

BUTCHER (WALTER ALFRED) The Faithfulness of God. A brief history of Rochester Baptist Church, 1888–1938. [With plates, including portraits.] pp. 51. *Hyde Press: [Rochester,]* 1938. 8°. **20032.** aa. **42.**

BUTCHER (WILLIAM) *Painter. See* SMITH (John) *Clockmaker.* Smith's Art of House-painting; improved by W. Butcher, *etc.* 1821. 8°. **1044.** h. **30.** (**4.**)

BUTCHER (WILLIAM) *Rector of Ropsley, Lincolnshire.* Plain Discourses delivered to a Country Congregation. 3 vol. *J. Hatchard: London,* 1814–16. 12°. **1022.** a. **17.**

—— Plain Discourses, delivered to a Country Congregation. pp. vi. 165. *S. Ridge: Grantham,* 1844. 16°. **1357.** c. **20.**

A different work from the preceding.

BUTCHER (WILLIAM DEANE) *See* BELOT (Joseph) *of the Hôpital Broca.* Radiotherapy in Skin Disease . . . Translated by W. D. Butcher, *etc.* 1905. 8°. **7462.** dd. **6.**

—— *See* GUILLEMINOT (W. H.) [Électricité médicale.] Handbook of Electricity in Medicine . . . Translated by W. D. Butcher, *etc.* 1906. 8°. **7462.** d. **13.**

—— *See* LEDUC (S. A. N.) [Études de biophysique. 1.] The Mechanism of Life . . . Translated by W. D. Butcher. 1911. 8°. **7006.** d. **17.**

BUTCHER (WILLIAM JAMES) and **WILSHAW** (ROBERT HEYWOOD) First Aid Notes. pp. 11. "*Mercury*": *Worthing,* [1914.] 16°. **07686.** f. **23.**

BUTCHERS. The Butchers' & Farmers' Ready Reckoner for calculating the weight and price of cattle by the score. *J. C. Fargher: Douglas, Isle of Man,* [1879.] 24°. **8507.** a. **12.**

—— Butchers Selling Price Guide. (Percentage Profit Ready Reckoner.) pp. 60. *E. E. Neale: Wembley,* [1934.] 12°. **08548.** b. **25.**

BUTCHERS (ARTHUR GORDON) *See* MULES (Mary) and BUTCHERS (A. G.) Bibliography of New Zealand Education. 1936. 8°. W.P. **10670/2.**

BUTCHERS (Arthur Gordon)

—— *See* Mules (Mary) and Butchers (A. G.) A Bibliography of New Zealand Education, *etc.* 1947. 8°. W.P. **10670/29.**

—— Education in New Zealand. An historical survey of educational progress amongst the Europeans and the Maoris since 1878; forming with "Young New Zealand" a complete history of education in New Zealand from the beginning of the nineteenth century. [With plates, including portraits.] pp. xxiii. 652. *Coulls, Somerville, Wilkie: Dunedin,* 1930. 8°. **8385.** h. **47.**

—— Young New Zealand. A history of the early contact of the Maori race with the European, and of the establishment of a national system of education for both races. (Second issue.) pp. xv. 380. *Coulls, Somerville, Wilkie: Dunedin,* 1929. 8°. **8385.** h. **48.**
The date on an inserted errata slip is 1930.

BUTCHERS (S. M.) A Waif on the Stream. [Verses.] pp. viii. 200. *Trübner & Co.: London,* 1866. 8°. **11648.** aa. **33.**

BUTCOMBE, *Somerset.* Marriages at Butcombe, Somersetshire, 1605–1835. Transcribed by Ethel Elizabeth Britten and Eric John Holmyard. pp. 11. *Alexander Moring: London,* 1913. 8°. **9904.** b. **37.** (**1.**)

BUTCULESCU (Dimitrie C.) Discursuri economice rostite in Camera, *etc.* pp. 221. *Bucuresci,* 1891. 8°. **08227.** f. **34.**

BUTE. The Kyles of Bute and Glendaruel in History, Poetry, and Folk-Lore. pp. 60. *"Oban Times": Oban,* 1904. 8°. **10369.** aa. **30.**

—— Walks and Drives in Bute. With maps . . . and views. pp. 24. *M. Mackenzie & Son: Rothesay,* [1930.] *obl.* 16°. **10369.** aa. **62.**

BUTE, John, *3rd Earl of.* [1712–92.] *See* Stuart.

BUTE, John Crichton, *Marquis of.* [1900–47.] *See* Stuart.

——, John Patrick Crichton, *Marquis of.* [1847–1900.] *See* Stuart.

——, Sophia Frederica Christina Rawdon Crichton, *Marchioness of.* [1809–59.] *See* Hastings (*Lady* S. F. C. R.) afterwards Stuart (S. F. C. R. C.) *Marchioness of Bute.*

BUTE COUNTY DIRECTORY. *See* Directories.—*Bute.*

BUTEAU ( ) *See* Brondex (Albert) *Ancien Directeur des Bacqs aux Messageries,* and Buteau ( ) Traité sur les postes aux lettres, *etc.* [1793.] 8°. F. **471.** (**14.**)

—— *See* France.—*Convention Nationale.—Comité de Salut Public.* Extrait du rapport fait à la Convention nationale au nom du Comité de salut public, le 23 ventôse de l'an 2e . . . Présenté à la Section des Amis de la Patrie par le citoyen Buteau. [1794.] 8°. F. **1243.** (**9.**)

BUTEAU (Félix) *See* Mailloux (A.) Promenade autour de l'Île-aux-Coudres. [With a biography of Mailloux by F. Buteau.] 1880. 8°. **10470.** ff. **28.**

BUTEAU (Henry) La Faute. [A novel.] pp. 311. *Paris,* 1904. 8°. **012548.** aaa. **2.**

—— L'Ordre des avocats. Ses rapports avec la magistrature, *etc.* pp. viii. 330. *Paris,* 1895. 8°. **06005.** f. **3.**

BUTEAU (Max) Le Droit de critique en matière littéraire, dramatique et artistique. Préface de M. Camille Le Senne. pp. iv. 180. *Paris,* 1910. 8°. **05402.** aaa. **24.**

—— Tenir. Récits de la vie de tranchées. pp. x. 294. *Paris,* 1918. 8°. **012352.** e. **63.**

BUTEL (Fernand) Les Congrégations religieuses et la loi Waldeck-Rousseau . . . Extrait du "Patriote des Pyrénées." pp. 28. *Pau,* 1901. 8°. **3900.** f. **14.**

—— L'Éducation des Jésuites autrefois et aujourd'hui. Un collège breton. [A history of the École libre Saint François-Xavier at Vannes.] pp. viii. 529. *Paris,* 1890. 8°. **8355.** df. **6.**

—— Le Péril de la séparation de l'Église et de l'État. pp. viii. 156. *Paris,* [1888.] 12°. **8005.** bbb. **20.**

—— La Vie de collège chez les Jésuites. Souvenirs d'un ancien élève. pp. 84. *Paris,* 1882. 8°. **8304.** d. **13.** (**3.**)

BUTEL (Pierre)

—— Géologie de l'Ile de Ré. Par P. Butel et Mireille Ters. pp. 37. *Paris & Liége,* 1953. 8°. [*Bulletin du service de la carte géologique de la France.* no. 234.] **7108.** g. **S.**

BUTEL-DUMONT (George Marie) *See* French. Conduite des François par rapport à la Nouvelle Écosse . . . Traduit de l'anglois [of Thomas Jefferys], avec des notes d'un François [i.e. G. M. Butel-Dumont], *etc.* 1755. 12°. **8154.** a. **5.**

—— Essai sur les causes principales qui ont contribué à détruire les deux premières races des rois de France . . . Par l'auteur de la Théorie du luxe [i.e. G. M. Butel-Dumont]. pp. 191. 1776. 8°. *See* France.—*Kings.* **286.** d. **25.**

—— Histoire et commerce des Antilles angloises, *etc.* [By G. M. Butel-Dumont. With a map.] pp. x. 284. 1758. 12°. *See* West Indies. **278.** c. **24.**

—— Histoire et commerce des colonies angloises, dans l'Amérique Septentrionale, *etc.* [By G. M. Butel-Dumont.] pp. xxiv. 336. 1755. 12°. *See* America, *North.* **278.** c. **21.**

—— Journées mogoles, opuscule décent d'un docteur chinois. [By G. M. Butel-Dumont?] 2 pt. 1772. 12°. *See* Mogul Days. **1073.** d. **53.**

—— Nouvelle édition. 2 pt. 1773. 12°. *See* Mogul Days. **1093.** a. **1.**

—— Mémoires historiques sur la Louisiane . . . Composés sur les mémoires de M. Dumont par M. L. L. M. [i.e. M. l'abbé Le Mascrier.] 2 tom. *Paris,* 1753. 12°. **1446.** b. **4.**

—— [Another copy.] **278.** a. **7, 8.**

—— History of Louisiana . . . from the Historical Memoirs of M. Dumont. 1853. *See* French (Benjamin F.) Historical Collections of Louisiana, *etc.* pt. 5. 1846, *etc.* 8°. **1444.** i. **5.**

—— Théorie du luxe; ou Traité dans laquelle on entreprend d'établir que le luxe est un ressort . . . nécessaire à la prospérité des états. [By G. M. Butel-Dumont.] 2 pt. 1771. 8°. *See* Théorie. **1248.** c. **21.** (**2.**)

—— [Another copy.] **32.** a **27.**

BÜTEMEISTER ( ) [For the German surname of this form:] *See* Buetemeister.

BUTENANDT (Adolf) Untersuchungen über das weibliche Sexualhormon—Follikel- oder Brunsthormon, *etc.* pp. vi. 93. pl. vii. *Berlin*, 1931. 8°. [*Abhandlungen der Gesellschaft der Wissenschaften zu Göttingen.* Math.-phys. Klasse. Folge 3. Hft. 2.] Ac. **670.** (2.)

BŪTĖNAS (Julius)

—— Žemaitė [i.e. J. Beniuševičiūtė-Žymantienė]. [A biography. With portraits and a bibliography.] pp. 227. [*Kaunas*, 1938.] 8°. **10796.** aa. **42.**

BUTENIUS (Cornelius) De usu Scripturæ Veteris Testamenti in Ecclesiâ christianâ, *etc.* 1643. *See* Spanheim (Friedrich) *the Elder.* Disputationum anti-anabaptisticarum prima generalis, *etc.* pt. 3. 1643, *etc.* 4°. **4323.** aaa. **37.**

BUTENOP (C. H.) Biographie des Kaiserl. Königl. Hof-Schauspielers Herrn Philipp Klingmann . . . aus Original-Documenten gesammelt, *etc.* pp. 52. [*Glogau?*] 1825. 8°. **10706.** *&c.* **46.** (2.)

BUTENPOST (Philippus) *Resp. See* Faber (Timaeus) Disputationes anniversariae ad quatuor libros Institutionum Imperial., *etc.* disp. 1. 1615. 4°. **5206.** c. **11.**

BUTENSCHOEN (Johann Friedrich) Caesar, Cato und Friedrich von Preussen, ein historisches Lesebuch. pp. 455. *Heidelberg*, 1789. 8°. **9004.** bb. **8.**

—— Petrarca. Ein Denkmal edler Liebe und Humanität. Bd. 1. pp. xvi. 322. *Leipzig*, 1796. 8°. **012554.** f. **41.** *No more published.*

BUTENSCHÖN (Andrea) *See* Upanishads. [*Kaṭha Upanishad.*] Upanishad. Öfversatt . . . af A. Butenschön. 1902. 8°. **14007.** b. **27.**

—— För länge sedan. Skådespel i tre akter, *etc.* pp. 99. *Stockholm*, 1909. 8°. **011755.** h. **8.**

—— The Life of a Mogul Princess. Jahānarā Begam, daughter of Shāhjahān, *etc.* [With plates.] pp. xiii. 221. *G. Routledge & Sons: London*, 1931. 8°. **10607.** ccc. **24.**

BUTENSCHØN (August Andresen)

—— Noget måtte hende. Betraktninger over Norges sosialpolitiske utvikling 1840–1940. pp. 133. *Oslo*, [1952.] 8°. **8081.** m. **6.**

BUTENSCHÖN (Hans Barthold Andresen) Symmetallism. An alternative to orthodox bimetallism, *etc.* pp. 195. *G. Allen & Unwin: London*, 1936. 8°. **8233.** b. **28.**

BUTENVAL (Charles Adrien His de) *Count. See* His de Butenval.

BUTEO (Joannes) *pseud.* [i.e. Jean Borrel.] Io. Buteonis Delphinatici opera geometrica, *etc.* [With woodcuts.] pp. 158. ms. notes. *Apud T. Bertellum: Lugduni*, 1554. 4°. **8530.** g. **42.**

—— [A reissue.] *Apud M. Ionium: Lugduni*, 1559. 4°. **530.** i. **2.**

—— De Arca Noe, cujus formæ capacitatisque fuerit, libellus. *See* Pearson (John) *Bishop of Chester.* Critici sacri, *etc.* tom. 8. 1660. fol. **C.80.k.8.**

—— [Another edition.] *See* Pearson (John) *Bishop of Chester.* Critici sacri. tom. 1. pt. 2. 1698. fol. **4.** f. **3.**

BUTEO (Joannes) *pseud.* [i.e. Jean Borrel.]

—— Io. Buteonis De fluentis aquæ mensura libellus. *See* Poleni (G.) *Marquis.* Joannis Poleni . . . Epistolarum mathematicarum fasciculus. 1729. 4°. **530.** l. **20.**

—— Della misura dell'acqua corrente libretto. 1766. *See* Raccolta. Nuova raccolta d'autori che trattano del moto dell'acque. vol. 3. 1766, *etc.* 4°. **8775.** d. **44.**

—— [Another edition.] 1767. *See* Raccolta. Raccolta d'autori che trattano del moto dell'acque. tom. 3. 1765, *etc.* 4°. **8775.** eee. **16.**

—— Ioan. Buteonis De quadratura circuli libri duo, vbi multorum quadraturæ confutantur, & ab omnium impugnatione defenditur Archimedes. Eiusdem annotationum opuscula in errores Campani, Zamberti . . . Io. Penæ interpretum Euclidis. pp. 283. *Apud G. Rouillium: Lugduni*, 1559. 8°. **714.** a. **29.**

—— Ioan. Buteonis Logistica, quæ & Arithmetica vulgò dicitur, in libros quinque digesta . . . Eiusdem, ad locum Vitruuij corruptum restitutio, qui est de proportione lapidum mittendorum ad balistæ foramen, libro decimo. pp. 396. *Apud G. Rouillium: Lugduni*, 1559. 8°. **530.** a. **16.**

—— [A reissue.] *Apud G. Rouillium: Lugduni*, 1560. 8°. **8503.** b. **7.**

—— Io. Buteonis Ad locum Vitruvii corruptum restitutio. Cui locus est de proportione inter lapides mittendos et balistae foramen. 1741. *See* Poleni (G.) *Marquis.* Exercitationes Vitruvianae primae (tertiae), *etc.* 1739, *etc.* 4°. **1261.** c. **20.**

—— [Another edition.] 1830. *See* Vitruvius Pollio (M.) M. Vitruvii Pollionis Architectura, *etc.* vol. 4. 1825, *etc.* 4°. **560.** d. **2.**

BUTEONE (Giovanni) *pseud.* [i.e. Jean Borrel.] *See* Buteo (Joannes)

BUTERA, Carlo Maria Carafa, *Prince di. See* Carafa.

—— Jane, *Princess di. See* Jane [of Austria], *Princess di Butera.*

BUTESHIRE NATURAL HISTORY SOCIETY. *See* Rothesay.

BUTET (Pierre Roland François) Abrégé d'un cours complet de léxicographie, *etc.* pp. lii. 191. *Paris*, 1801. 8°. **828.** e. **1.**

—— Cours pratique d'instruction élémentaire applicable à toute méthode d'enseignement . . . et spécialement à la méthode d'enseignement mutuel, *etc.* pp. 112. *Paris*, 1818. 8°. B. **698.** (7.)

—— Cours théorique d'instruction élémentaire, applicable spécialement à la méthode d'enseignement mutuel. 2 pt. *Paris*, 1818. 8°. B. **698.** (5, 6.)

BUTEUX (Charles Joseph) Esquisse géologique du département de la Somme. pp. 136. *Abbeville*, 1864. 8°. **7108.** cc. **12.**

—— Observations sur l'architecture ogivale et l'application de l'architecture grecque aux églises. pp. 103. *Paris*, 1862. 8°. **7814.** bbb. **36.** (5.) *Lithographed.*

BUTEUX (Petrus) Dissertatio medica inauguralis de morbis senectutis, *etc.* pp. 37. *Lugduni Batavorum*, 1726. 4°. **1185.** i. **2.** (7.)

BUTEUX (RAYMOND D.)

—— *See* FREY (George F.) and BUTEUX (R. D.) Current Readings in Marketing, *etc.* [1954.] fol. **8223.** df. **57.**

BUTH (FRANCISCUS) De ablativi casus formis Plautinis. (Beigabe zum Michaelis-Programm 1873 der Höheren Bürgerschule zu Lauenburg i. Pom.) pp. 27. *Leopoli Pomeranorum,* 1873. 8°. **12935.** cc. **25.**

BUTHENIUS (IMMANUEL) De testamento in itinere confecto. 1744. *See* STRYKIUS (S.) Viri quondam illustris . . . Samuelis Strykii . . . opera omnia. vol. 5. 1743, *etc.* fol. **498.** g. **7.**

BUTHILIERIUS DE RANCÉ (ARMANDUS) *See* LE BOUTHILLIER DE RANCÉ (Armand J.)

BUTHILLERIUS (DIONYSIUS) *See* BOUTILLIER (Denis)

BUTHMAN (WILLIAM CURT)

—— The Rise of Integral Nationalism in France. With special reference to the ideas and activities of Charles Maurras, *etc.* [A thesis.] pp. 355. *New York,* 1939. 8°. **08052.** cc. **40.**

BUTHMANN (JOACHIM MATTHIAS) Maurerische Vorträge . . . [In verse.] Zweite Auflage. pp. 120. *Hamburg,* 1865. 8°. **4784.** cc. **20.**

BÜTHNER ( ) [For the German surname of this form:] *See* BUETHNER.

BUTHNERUS (JOANNES ERNESTUS) *See* BUETHNER (Johann E.)

BUTHOULKAS (BASILIOS G.) *See* HORATIUS FLACCUS (Q.) [*Carmina and Carmen Saeculare.—Latin and Modern Greek.*] *Κοϊντου 'Ορατιου Φλακκου ᾠδαι, μετα κειμενου, εἰσαγωγης, μεταφρασεως . . . ὑπο Β. Γ. Βυθουλκα.* 1886. 8°. **11375.** bbb. **36.**

—— *See* ISOCRATES. [*Two or more Orations.—Greek.*] *Λογοι 'Ισοκρατους κατ' ἐκλογην . . . Μετα προλεγομενων, σχολιων . . . και . . . μεταφρασεως, ὑπο Β. Γ. Βυθουλκα.* 1875, *etc.* 8°. **11391.** i. **1.**

BUTHRED. Buthred; a tragedy, *etc.* [Attributed to Charles Johnston.] pp. [38]88. *F. Newbery: London,* 1779. 8°. **163.** k. **39.**

—— [Another edition.] pp. 72. *United Company of Booksellers: Dublin,* 1779. 12°. **640.** h. **34.** (**4.**)

BUTHROTUM. *See* BUTRINTO.

BUTHS (JULIUS) *See* ELGAR (*Sir* Edward W.) Die Apostel . . . Textbuch auf Grundlage des Bibeltextes für die deutsche Aufführung eingerichtet von J. Buths. [1904.] 8°. **11779.** dd. **8.** (**4.**)

—— *See* ELGAR (*Sir* Edward W.) Das Reich . . . Deutsche Übersetzung auf Grundlage des Bibeltextes von J. Buths. [1907.] 8°. **11778.** l. **5.** (**7.**)

—— *See* MEREDITH (Margaret) Sursum Corda . . . Deutsche Übersetzung von J. Buths. [1910.] 8°. **7896.** dd. **26.** (**1.**)

BUTI (CAMILLO)

—— [Picturæ parietinæ inter Esquilias et Viminalem collem superiori anno detectæ.] [12 coloured plates by Angelo Campanella, Petrus Vitali and Corratoni after drawings by A. R. Mengs and A. Maron.] [*Rome,* 1778–93.] *obl.* fol. Dept. of Prints & Drawings.
Without letterpress or titlepage. Imperfect; wanting pl. 5.

BUTI (DEIDAMIA) Applauso poetico per l'illustrissima Signora Deidamia Buti che veste l'abito religioso di S. Benedetto . . . col nome di Donna Maria Giuditta Deidamia Fortunata. *Pistoja,* 1737. 4°. **11431.** c. **59.** (**15.**)

BUTI (FRANCESCO DA) *See* BERNARDONI (Giuseppe) *Printer.* Lettera . . . al signor abate D. P. Zambelli . . . sopra varie lezioni tratte specialmente dal testo della Divina Commedia di Dante, spiegato da F. da Buti . . . nel suo commento a quel poema. 1842. 8°. **11420.** g. **5.**

—— *See* CENTOFANTI (S.) Al commento di Francesco da Buti sopra la Divina Commedia introduzione. 1858. 4°. **11420.** g. **19.** (**1.**)

—— *See* DANTE ALIGHIERI. [*Divina Commedia.—Italian.*] Commento di Francesco da Buti sopra la Divina Comedia, *etc.* 1858, *etc.* 8°. **2284.** f. **6.**

—— *See* DANTE ALIGHIERI. [*Divina Commedia.—Paradiso.—Selections and Extracts.—Italian.*] A Maria Vergine. [Paradiso, XXXIII. 1–39. With the "Commento" of F. da Buti.] 1858. 8°. **11420.** g. **19.** (**2.**)

—— Novella (di Romeo) . . . Testo di lingua. [A facsimile of the edition of 1565. Edited by Giovanni Papanti.] pp. iv. 11. *Livorno,* 1873. 8°. **12470.** h. **13.**

BUTI (GUIDO) Il Tempio crematorio di Trespiano. Appunti. pp. 16. *Firenze,* 1885. 8°. **7306.** de. **27.** (**4.**)

BUTI (LUIGI PIERI) *See* PIERI BUTI.

BUTI (MARIA BANDINI) *See* BANDINI BUTI.

BUTIAD. The Butiad, or Political Register; being a supplement to the British Antidote to Caledonian Poison. Containing . . . humorous political prints . . . with . . . songs, etc., calculated to . . . give . . . a concise view of . . . political affairs, during . . . 1762 and 1763. pp. 76. *E. Sumpter: London,* 1763. 8°. **11632.** df. **14.**

BUTIBAMBAS. *See* GUTIBAMBAS.

BUTIGELLA (HIERONYMUS) *Begin.* [fol. 1 *recto*:] Hieronymus Butigella. I. V. doctor Papiensis Magnifico: ⁊ clarissimo Artiuȝ doctori Io. Francisco Rosato salutem, *etc.* [fol. 2 *recto*:] Hieronymi Butigelle I. V. doc. ꝑ . . . Frācoꝝ Regis ꝯsiliario dignissimo Io. Phi. Gābaloita Oratio, *etc.* G.L. [*Pavia,* 1494?] 4°. IA. **31651.**
Six leaves. Sig. a⁶. 34, 35 *lines to a page.*

—— *Begin.* [fol. 1 *recto*:] Hieronymus Butigella I. V. doctor Reuerendo: & magnifico Artiū doctori Io. Frācisco Rosato. S. P. D. [fol. 2 *recto*:] Hieronymi Butigellæ. I. V. doc. pro . . . Frācoꝝ Regis cōsiliario dignissimo Io. Phi. Gambaloita Papiæ Prætore Oratio. [*Uldericus Scinzenzeler: Milan,* 1495?] 4°. IA. **26794.**
8 *leaves. Sig.* a⁸. 27 *lines to a page.*

—— Hieronymi Butigellæ . . . In primam partem C. [i.e. of the Justinian Codex] commentaria, ac repetitiones . . . additis summariis ac copioissimo [*sic*] repertorio, nunc primum in lucem edita. ff. 76. 1558. fol. *See* VENICE.—*Academia Veneta.* **5505.** e. **5.** (**3.**)

BUTIGNOT (MARIE FRANÇOIS XAVIER) Considérations sur la force vitale et médicatrice et sur les fièvres essentielles. Thèse, *etc.* pp. 56. *Montpellier,* 1837. 4°. **1181.** h. **7.** (**18.**)

—— Des applications de l'hygiène à la thérapeutique. Discours, *etc.* pp. 19. *Toulouse,* [1864.] 8°. **7460.** aa. **55.** (**9.**)

BUTIIS (Martinus de) Forma instrumentorum nouiter reperta. Itē taxa notariorū. 𝔊.𝔏. *Typis H. Soncini: Arimini*, 1526. 8°. 507. a. 38.

BÜTIKOFER ( ) [For the German surname of this form:] *See* Buetikofer.

BUTILLUS. Butillus, of de verrader des Ryks gestraft. Treurspel in drie bedryven. [In verse.] pp. 22. [*Amsterdam?*] 1784. 8°. 934. g. 12. (1.)

BUTIN, *Brothers*. Историческій очеркъ сношеній русскихъ съ Китаемъ и описаніе пути съ границы Нерчинскаго округа въ Тянь-дзинъ. Статья братьевъ Бутиныхъ. (Извлечено изъ № 4 и 5 Извѣстій Сибирскаго Отдѣла Императорскаго Русскаго Географическаго Общества за 1871 годъ.) (Маршрутъ . . . Экспедиціи Гг. Братьевъ Бутиныхъ съ 26 мая 1870 года.) [With a map.] pp. 99. 39. *Иркутскъ*, 1871. 8°. 10058. e. 12.

BUTIN (François Gabriel) Le Syndic Butin et la réunion de Genève à la France en 1798. Lettres de F.-G. Butin publiées par Marc Peter, avec une introduction, des notes, un portrait et trois autographes. pp. 226. *Genève*, 1914. 8°. 9305. f. 6.

BUTIN (Louis Joseph Marie) Dissertation sur la gastrite, *etc.* pp. 32. *Paris*, 1819. 4°. 1183. e. 15. (9.)

BUTIN (Romain François) The New Protosinaitic Inscriptions. *See* Starr (Richard F. S.) Excavations and Protosinaitic Inscriptions at Serabit el Khadem. 1936. 8°. W.P. 11331/6.

—— The Ten Nequdoth of the Torah; or, the Meaning and purpose of the extraordinary points of the Pentateuch—Massoretic text. A contribution to the history of textual criticism among the ancient Jews. pp. vi. 136. *J. H. Furst Co.: Baltimore*, 1906. 8°. 03166. k. 13.

BUTIÑA (Francisco Javier) [La Luz del Menestral.] Light from the Lowly; or, Lives of persons who sanctified themselves in humble positions . . . Translated from the Spanish by . . . W. McDonald, *etc.* 2 vol. *Gill & Son: Dublin*, 1884. 8°. 4825. aaa. 1.

BUTINI (Adolphus) De usu interno præparationum argenti. Dissertatio inauguralis, *etc.* pp. 27. *Montpellier*, 1815. 4°. 1180. h. 2. (6.)

BUTINI (Jean Antoine) *See* Newton (*Sir* Isaac) Abrégé de la chronologie des anciens royaumes . . . Traduit [by J. A. Butini], *etc.* 1743. 8°. 9005. cc. 8.

BUTINI (Pierre) Sermons sur divers textes de l'Écriture Sainte. 2 tom. *Genève*, 1708. 12°. 4428. a. 4.

BUTINUS (Joannes) *See* Hippocrates. [*Two or more Works.—Greek and Latin.*] Hippocratis Aphorismi . . . cum breui expositione ex Galeni commentariis desumpta. Eiusd. Hippocr. prænotionum libri tres, cum explicatione eodem ex fonte hausta per J. Butinum. 1580. 8°. 518. a. 42. (2.)

—— —— 1625. 8°. 539. a. 30.

—— *See* Hippocrates. [*Two or more Works.—Latin.*] Hippocratis Aphorismi . . . Eiusdem Hippocratis prænotionum libri tres, *etc.* [Edited by J. Butinus.] 1555. 8°. 539. a. 4.

BUTIO (Vincenzo) Vincentii Butii . . . De calido, frigido, ac temperato antiquorum potu, *etc.* pp. 69. *Ex typographia V. Mascardi: Romæ*, 1653. 4°. 1038. i. 3. (4.)

—— [Another edition.] 1699. *See* Graevius (J. G.) Thesaurus antiquitatum, *etc.* tom. 12. 1694, *etc.* fol. 144. i. 2.

—— Relazione dell'apparato fatto nell'Accademia de gli Humoristi per l'orazione funerale & altri componiment recitati da gli accademici in lode del cavalier Battista Guarini, *etc.* pp. 11. *G. Mascardi: Roma*, 1613. 4°. 10631. c. 46. (15.)

BUTIRONUS (Franciscus) *See* 'Abd Allāh ibn Aḥmad, called Ibn al-Baiṭār. Ebenbitar Arabs de Limonibus in lucem editus [by F. Butironus]. 1583. 8°. B. 226. (2.)

BUTIUS (Vincentius) *See* Butio (Vincenzo)

BUTKENS (Christophe)

—— *See* Dallemagne (C. G.) Le Manuscrit de l'écuyer Charles van Riedewijck. Source commune des travaux sigillographiques et archéologiques de Christophre Butkens et de Mgr. P. F. X. de Ram. 1943. 8°. [*Annales de la Société Royale d'Archéologie de Bruxelles.* tom. 46.] Ac. 5519.

—— Annales genealogiques de la maison de Lynden, diuisées en xv liures, *etc.* [With engravings and a table.] pp. 380. 143. *I. Cnobbart: Anuers*, 1626. fol. 608. k. 10.
The titlepage is engraved.

—— Trophées tant sacrés que prophanes . . . du duché de Brabant, contenant l'origine, succession & descendence des ducs & princes de cette maison, avec leurs actions les plus signalées . . . La Suite des ducs de Limbourg & Luxembourg, comtes de Dalhem, & sires de Fauquemont, *etc.* (Supplément aux Trophées, *etc.*) 4 tom. **L.P.** *La Haye*, 1724–26. fol. 156. k. 5–8.

BUTKĖRAITIS (Dom.) Keletas raštų apie Kražių atsitikimą. pp. 61. *Tilžėje*, 1895. 8°. 09004. aa. 10. (2.)

BUTKEVICH (Timothei Ivanovich) Зло, его сущность и происхожденіе. pp. xxii. 505. ii. *Харьковъ*, 1897. 8°. 8409. m. 11.

—— Обзоръ русскихъ сектъ и ихъ толковъ, съ изложеніемъ ихъ происхожденія, распространенія и вѣроученія и съ опроверженіемъ послѣдняго. Изданіе второе, *etc.* pp. 566. x. *Петроградъ*, 1915. 8°. 3925. l. 1.

—— Протестанство въ Россіи: изъ лекцій по церковному праву. pp. vi. 234. *Харьковъ*, 1913. 8°. 3926. h. 38.

BUTKEVICH (V. V.)

—— Стерилизация почвы. pp. 118. *Москва*, 1950. 8°. 7079. a. 65.

BUTKEVICH (Yu. V.)

—— *See* Glazunov (A. A.) Электрическая часть станций и подстанций, *etc.* [By Yu. V. Butkevich and others.] 1951. 8°. 8761. d. 12.

BUTKEVIČIUS (Filypas)

—— Elementarinis kokybinis analizis, *etc.* pp. viii. 467. *Kaunas*, 1929. 8°. [*Lietuvos Universiteto Matematikos-Gamtos Fakulteto leidinys.*] Ac. 1157. h. (6.)

BUTKEVIČIUS (Filypas)

—— Retųjų elementų kokybinis analizis, *etc.* pp. vi. 92. *Kaunas*, 1931. 8°. [*Vytauto Didžiojo Universiteto Matematikos-Gamtos Fakulteto leidinys.*] Ac. **1157**. h. (**9**.)

BUTKIEWICZÓWNA (Irena)

—— Powieści i nowele żydowskie Elizy Orzeszkowej, *etc.* [With a bibliography.] pp. 152. *Lublin*, 1937. 8°. **11858**. e. **9**.

BUTKIS (Cheslav) Совѣтская Россія въ сатирѣ. том. 1. pp. 93. *Берлинъ*, 1923. 8°. **20010**. h. **23**.

BUTKOV (Petr Grigor'evich) *See* Aleksandrov (A. V.) Современные историческіе труды въ Россіи . . . П. Г. Буткова, *etc.* 1845. 8°. **11826**. g. **11**.

—— Матеріалы для новой исторіи Кавказа съ 1722 по 1803 годъ. (част. 3, хронологический и алфавитный указатели, составленные Л. Броссе.) [Edited by L. Brosset.] 3 част. 1869. 8°. *See* Russia.—*Академия Наук СССР.* **9056**. gg. **9**.

—— Оборона лѣтописи русской, Несторовой, отъ навѣта скептиковъ. [The preface signed: П. Бутковъ.] pp. vi. 462. lxv. *Санктпетербургъ*, 1840. 8°. **1437**. k. **20**.

—— Списокъ литературнымъ трудамъ . . . П. Г. Буткова. (Въ видѣ особаго Прибавленія къ Извѣстіямъ II-го Отдѣленія и къ Спб. Вѣдомостямъ.) pp. 8. 1858. 4°. *See* Russia.—*Академия Наук СССР.* Ac. **1125/41**.

BUTKOV (Yakov Petrovich) Петербургскія вершины, описанныя Я. Бутковымъ. кн. 1, 2. *Санктпетербургъ*, 1845, 46. 8°. **12352**. f. **8**.

—— Степная Идиллія. Повѣсть Я. Буткова. (Подарокъ на новый годъ. Изъ записокъ бѣднаго Вильчирскаго священника. [Translated from J. H. D. Zschokke's "Blätter aus dem Tagebuche eines armen Pfarr-Vikars von Wiltshire," based by Zschokke on an article by O. Goldsmith in the British Magazine, entitled "The Journal of a Wiltshire Curate."]) 2 част. *С. Петербургъ*, 1856. 16°. **12550**. a. **1**.
Библіотека для дачъ, пароходовъ и желѣзныхъ дорогъ, pt. 67, 68.

BUTKOVSKAYA (R. Ya.) Карьеристка безъ карьеры. Романъ. pp. 133. *Варшава*, 1930. 8°. **12590**. ppp. **7**.

BUTKOVSKY (Aleksandr Petrovich) Весталки, римскія непорочныя дѣвы. Историческій очеркъ значенія и постепеннаго упадка ихъ въ древнемъ Римѣ, съ краткимъ извѣстіемъ о тождественныхъ съ весталками перувіанскихъ дѣвственницахъ . . . Съ рисунками. pp. 152. *Москва*, 1862. 18°. **7702**. a. **3**. (**3**.)

—— Нумизматика или исторія монетъ древнихъ, среднихъ и новыхъ вѣковъ . . . Съ III-мя таблицами, *etc.* [With chronological tables.] pp. 140. pl. III. *Москва*, 1861. 8°. **7755**. cc. **8**.

—— Dictionnaire numismatique pour servir de guide aux amateurs . . . des médailles romaines impériales & grecques coloniales avec indication de leur . . . prix actuel au XIXe siècle, *etc.* tom. 1, vol. 1, 2; tom. 2, vol. 1. coll. 1792. pp. lxii. *Leipzig*, 1884, 77–84. 8°. **7757**. d. **4**.

Published in parts.

BUTKOVSKY (Aleksandr Petrovich)

—— Petit Mionnet de poche, ou répertoire pratique à l'usage des numismatistes, en voyage et collectionneurs des monnaies grecques, *etc.* pp. 417. *Berlin*, 1889. 8°. **7756**. b. **12**.

—— Recherches historiques sur la ville de Tium en Bithynie, description d'une médaille inédite appartenant à cette ville. (Supplément.) 2 pt. *Paris, Heidelberg*, 1864, 67. 12°. **7755**. a. **4**.

—— Recueil spécial de grandes curiosités (Recueil de curiosités), inédites et peu connues, dans le champ de l'archéologie, de la numismatique et de l'épigraphie. 3 pt. *Saint-Pétersbourg; Genève; Paris*, 1868–92. 8°. **7756**. c. **12**.

BUTKOVSKY (E. I.) Половина жизни. Повѣсть Е. И. Бутковскаго [or rather by E. N. Butkovsky.] 2 част. *С. Петербургъ*, 1856. 16°. **12209**. a. **8**.
Библіотека для дачъ, пароходовъ и желѣзныхъ дорогъ, pt. 42, 43.

BUTKOVSKY (E. N.) Деревня. Повѣсть, *etc.* pp. 209. *С. Петербургъ*, 1856. 16°. **12209**. a. **9**.
Библіотека для дачъ, пароходовъ и желѣзныхъ дорогъ, pt. 26.

—— Половина жизни. Повѣсть Е. И. Бутковскаго [or rather by E. N. Butkovsky]. 2 част. 1856. 16°. *See* Butkovsky (E. I.) **12209**. a. **8**.

—— Сосѣдка. Разсказъ, *etc.* 2 част. *С. Петербургъ*, 1857. 16°. **12209**. a. **10**.
Библіотека для дачъ, пароходовъ и желѣзныхъ дорогъ, pt. 106, 107.

BUTKOVSKY (Georgy) Девятьсот тридцатый. Роман. Издание 2-е, исправленное. pp. 334. *Москва*, 1934. 8°. **12589**. t. **43**.

BUTKOVSKY (Yakov N.) Сто лѣтъ австрійской политики въ восточномъ вопросѣ. Составилъ Я. Н. Бутковскій. 2 том. *С.-Петербургъ*, 1888. 8°. **8028**. de. **24**.

BUTLAND (Ernest) Is Life Worth Living? *etc.* [With a portrait.] pp. 136. *Printers Ltd.: Montreal*, 1918. 8°. **12316**. l. **54**.

BUTLAND (Gilbert James)

—— Chile. An outline of its geography, economics, and politics. pp. vii. 128. 1951. 8°. *See* London.—III. *Royal Institute of International Affairs.* **010481**. cc. **39**.

—— Chile, *etc.* (Revised edition.) pp. vii. 128. *Royal Institute of International Affairs: London & New York*, 1953. 8°. **010480**. f. **74**.

BUTLAR (Stefan Congrat) *See* Congrat-Butlar (S.)

BUTLER. The Butler: by an Experienced Servant. The wine department by J. B. Davies. pp. 108. *Houlston & Stoneman: London*, [1855.] 12°. **787**. b. **76**.

—— The Butler's and Yacht Steward's Manual: with some receipts for new and celebrated beverages . . . Second edition. pp. 20. *Simpkin, Marshall & Co.: London; Wareing Webb: Liverpool*, [1851.] 8°. **7955**. b. **34**. (**3**.)

—— The Butler, the Wine-Dealer, and Private Brewer . . . By a Practical Man. pp. xvi. 136. *G. Biggs: London*, [1850.] 8°. **7955**. a. **32**.

BUTLER, *Father.* Father Butler. The Lough Dearg pilgrim. Being sketches of Irish manners. [By William Carleton.] pp. iv. 302. *W. Curry, Jun. & Co.: Dublin,* 1829. 12°. **4413.** f. **40.** (**3.**)

BUTLER, *Madam.* The Constant, but Unhappy Lovers. Being a full and true relation of one Madam Butler, *etc.* [A chapbook.] pp. 8. *E. B.: London,* 1707. 8°. **1076.** l. **22.** (**14.**)

BUTLER, *Prince, pseud.* Eleven Queries humbly tender'd, relating to the Bill for prohibiting the wearing of East-India Silks, and Printed and Dyed Calicoes. [By Prince Butler.] [1697?] *s. sh.* fol. *See* ENGLAND.—*Parliament.—Bills.—Appendix.* [*East India Wrought Silks.*] **816.** m. **13.** (**144.**)

—— Five Queries humbly tender'd, relating to the Bill for prohibiting the Consumption of East-India Silks, Bengals and Printed Callicoes. [By the writer who in other works used the pseudonym " Prince Butler."] [1696 ?] *s. sh.* fol. *See* ENGLAND.—*Parliament.* [*Bills.*—II.] [1696. Dec. 4.] **816.** m. **13.** (**133.**)

—— *Begin.* A Malicious Man makes Reasons. To the Honourable the Knights, Citizens, and Burgesses, in Parliament assembled. The Humble Petition of Prince Butler, *etc.* [With another short petition on the verso of the second leaf. Satires on James, 2nd Duke of Ormonde.] [*London,* 1700 ?] fol. T. **100*.** (**13.**)

—— [Another edition.] [*London ?* 1700 ?] *s. sh.* fol. **816.** m. **19.** (**28.**)

—— *Begin.* Pray Mony or no Mony, Right or Wrong, Irish or no Irish . . . To the Honourable Knights, Citizens, and Burgesses in Parliament assembled, the humble petition of Prince Butler, *etc.* [*London ?* 1700 ?] *s. sh.* fol. **816.** m. **19.** (**28*.**)
Cropped.

—— Querical Demonstrations, writ by Prince Butler, author of the Eleven Queries relating to the Bill for prohibiting East-India Silks and Printed Callicoes. [*London,* 1699 ?] *s. sh.* fol. **816.** m. **13.** (**129.**)

—— [Another copy.] MS. NOTES. **816.** m. **13.** (**130.**)

—— Prince Butler's Queries relating to the East-India Trade. *A. Baldwin: London,* 1699. *s. sh.* fol. **816.** m. **13.** (**128.**)

—— Prince Butler's Tale: representing the state of the Wooll-Case, or the East-India case truly stated. [In verse.] *A. Baldwin: London,* 1699. *s. sh.* fol. **816.** m. **13.** (**127.**)

BUTLER AND BROOKE. Butler and Brooke's National Directory of Victoria. *See* DIRECTORIES.—*Victoria, Australia.*

BUTLER AND STEVENS. Butler and Stevens' Sandhurst, Castlemaine and Echuca Directory. *See* DIRECTORIES.—*Sandhurst, Victoria.*

BUTLER AND TANNER.

—— A Hundred Years of Printing, 1795–1895. By John Rhode. [A history of the printing firm of Butler & Tanner. With plates.] pp. 82. *Butler & Tanner. Frome & London,* 1927. 8°. **11917.** e. **7.**
Printed for private circulation.

BUTLER BROTHERS.

—— Butler Bros.' Wholesale Price List of Foreign Postage Stamps, *etc.* [Sixty-nine catalogues.] *Butler Bros.: Nottingham,* 1887–[1905.] 8° & 4°. Crawford **117.** (**3.**)
Published successively in Nottingham, Brackley, Oxford and Clevedon. Imperfect; wanting various parts, including ten issued between 1901 *and* 1905.

BUTLER'S PHILATELIC OBSERVER. *See* PERIODICAL PUBLICATIONS.—*Canterbury.*

BUTLER, *Family of.* *See* BUTLER (James D.) Butleriana genealogica et biographica, *etc.* 1888. 8°. **9916.** aa. **39.**

—— *See* CLARE (Wallace) The Testamentary Records of the Butler Families in Ireland, *etc.* 1932. 8°. **09915.** l. **23.**

—— Some Account of the Family of the Butlers, but more particularly of the late Duke of Ormond, the Earl of Ossory his father, and James Duke of Ormond his grandfather. pp. 256. *John Morphew: London,* 1716. 8°. **606.** b. **20.**

—— [Another copy.] G. **5708.**

BUTLER, *Family of, of New England and Nova Scotia.*

—— *See* BUTLER (Elmer E.) Butlers and Kinsfolk: Butlers of New England and Nova Scotia, *etc.* 1944. 8°. **9906.** r. **2.**

BUTLER, *Messrs., Hardware Merchants.* Butler's Commercial List, or Price book of articles manufactured in London, Birmingham, Bristol . . . With . . . a table of stamp duties. pp. 112. *D. R. & W. Rees: Llandovery,* 1832. 8°. **712.** f. **45.**

BUTLER, *Messrs., of Dublin.* Butlers' Medicine Chest Directory and Family Catalogue of drugs, chemicals, miscellaneous articles &c. . . . Second edition, considerably enlarged and revised. pp. v. 112. *Dublin,* 1826. 12°. T. **894.** (**4.**)

BÜTLER (**)**

—— [For the German surname of this form:] *See* BUETLER.

BUTLER (**)** and **BREVITAS,** *pseud.* Auction Bridge in a Nut Shell. Royal Spades. pp. 67. *Simpkin, Marshall & Co.: London,* [1913.] 8°. **7911.** cc. **12.**

—— 3rd edition, revised and amplified, *etc.* pp. xxxiii. 90. *Simpkin, Marshall & Co.: London,* 1914. 8°. **7911.** aaa. **21.**

—— 5th edition, revised and amplified, *etc.* pp. v. 122. *Simpkin, Marshall & Co.: London,* 1919. 8°. **7911.** de. **36.**

—— 7th edition, revised and amplified, *etc.* pp. v. 126. *Simpkin, Marshall & Co.: London,* 1919. 8°. **7911.** de. **47.**

BUTLER (DE) *Mademoiselle.* Les Mémoires et avantures de Mademoiselle de Butler, remplis d'événemens très intéressans . . . Par Mr. de * * *. 2 pt. *Londres [Paris ?],* 1747. 12°. **244.** c. **35.**
The titlepages are engraved.

BUTLER (A.) *M.Sc.,* and **GODBERT** (A. L.)

—— The Colour Measurement of Mine Dusts as a Method of estimating their Contents of Inert Material. pp. 21. *London,* 1952. 8°. [*Ministry of Fuel and Power. Safety in Mines Research Establishment. Research Report.* no. 57.] B.S. **69**/**35.**

BUTLER (A.) *pseud.* [i.e. ARTHUR LE BOUTILLIER.] The Theory of Fifth Stave Accordion Bass Notation. [*Chingford*, 1936.] 8°. **07899. i. 67.**

BUTLER (A. G.) *Writer of Fiction.* Gracie; or, the History of a stair-carpet, *etc.* pp. 92. *Simpkin, Marshall & Co.: London*, 1898. 8°. **012804. f. 23.**

BUTLER (A. L.)

—— An Alphabet of Birds. Illustrated by A. L. Butler . . . Lettering by C. M. Bayly. *Perry Colour Books: [London*, 1955.] 32°. **7288. a. 34.**

BUTLER (AGNATA FRANCES) *See* HERODOTUS, *the Historian.* [*Greek.*] Ἡροδοτου Πολυμνια. Herodotus VII., with notes by A. F. Butler. 1891. 8°. **9026. a. 6.**

BUTLER (ALBAN) *See* BUTLER (Charles) *Barrister-at-Law.* An Account of the Life and Writings of the Rev. Alban Butler, *etc.* [With a portrait.] 1800. 8°. **10105. dd. 12. (1.)**

—— The Life of Sir Tobie Maethews [*sic*, for Matthews], *etc.* [With a portrait.] pp. 37. *J. P. Coghlan: London*, 1795. 8°. **4374. cc. 25. (1.)**

—— The Lives of the Fathers, Martyrs, and other principal Saints compiled from original monuments, and other authentick records; illustrated with the remarks of judicious modern criticks and historians. [By A. Butler.] 4 vol. 1756–59. 8°. *See* LIVES. **G. 19853–57.**

—— [Another copy.] **485. b. 5–9.**

—— The second edition, corrected and enlarged from the author's own manuscript, *etc.* 12 vol. *John Morris: Dublin*, 1779, 80. 8°. **677. c. 18–23.**

—— The third edition, *etc.* 12 vol. *Edinburgh; J. P. Coghlane: London*, 1798–1800. 8°. **4825. dd. 3.**

—— [Another edition.] 12 vol. *John Murphy: London*, 1812, 13. 8°. **485. c. 1–12.**

—— [Another copy.] **4823. f. 1.**

—— [Another edition. With plates.] 2 vol. *R. Coyne: Dublin*, [1833, 36.] 8°. **4831.d.20.**
The titlepages are engraved.

—— [Another copy, with different titlepages and plates.] *R. Coyne: Dublin; Joseph Hooker: London*, 1833, 36. 8°. **20032. bb. 26.**

—— [Another edition.] 12 vol. *James Duffy: Dublin*, 1847, 45. 8°. **4823. ee. 2.**
Vol. 2–7 *and* 9–12 *have each an additional titlepage, engraved.*

—— [Another edition. With a portrait.] 12 vol. *T. Richardson & Son: London & Derby*, [1850?] 16°. **4823. aaaa. 20.**
With an additional titlepage to each vol.

—— [Another edition.] Edited by the Rev. F. C. Husenbeth. (The History of the Blessed Virgin Mary. By the Abbé Orsini. Translated from the French by the Very Rev. F. C. Husenbeth.) 3 vol. *Henry & Co.: London*, [1857–60.] 8°. **4827. f. 12.**
Published in parts. Vol. 1 *and* 2 *have each an additional titlepage, engraved.*

—— [Another edition.] Edited by the Rev. F. C. Husenbeth, . . . Illuminated edition, *etc.* 2 vol. *Virtue & Co.: London & Dublin*, [1883–86.] 8°. **4828. g. 18.**
Published in parts.

BUTLER (ALBAN)

—— The Lives of the Saints . . . Edited, revised and copiously supplemented by H. Thurston (and Norah Leeson—H. Thurston and Donald Attwater). 12 vol. *Burns, Oates & Co.: London*, 1926–38. 8°. **20033. f. 1.**

—— The Lives of the Saints, Butler. First supplementary volume. By Donald Attwater. pp. xii. 200. *Burns, Oates & Washbourne: London*, 1949. 8°. **20033. f. 1a.**
No more published.

—— [Another edition.] Edited by the Rev. F. C. Husenbeth, *etc.* 3 vol. *Virtue & Co.: London*, [1936.] 8°. **20029. i. 14.**

—— [Another edition.] Edited, for daily use, by the Rev. Bernard Kelly. 5 vol. pp. xi. vii. vii. vii. vii. 1671. *Virtue & Co.: London*, [1937.] 4°. **20031. i. 6.**

—— The Lives of the Fathers, Martyrs and other principal Saints . . . Edited for daily use by the Rev. Bernard Kelly. [With plates.] 5 vol. *Virtue & Co.: London*, [1948.] 4°. **4831. c. 1.**

—— The Lives of the Fathers, Martyrs and other principal Saints . . . Edited . . . by the Rev. Bernard Kelly . . . Supplementary volume [i.e. vol. 5]. (Sixth edition.) pp. x. 507. *Virtue & Co.: London*, [1951.] 4°. **4832. bb. 3.**

—— Vies des Pères, martyrs, et autres principaux saints . . . Ouvrage traduit librement de l'anglais . . . par l'abbé Godescard . . . Nouvelle édition . . . revue et corrigée avec soin, et augmentée, *etc.* 10 tom. *Paris*, 1843. 8°. **1228. b. 1–5.**

—— Lives of Saints, selected and abridged from the original work of the Rev. Alban Butler, *etc.* [With "A Short View of the History of the Church" by R. Challoner, Bishop of Debra.] 2 vol. *Edward Walker: Newcastle*, 1799. 8°. **4824. cc. 5.**

—— The Life of Saint Bede, Confessor, Father of the Church. [From Butler's "Lives of the Fathers." *See* BEDE, *the Venerable, Saint.* [*Single Works.*] The History of the Primitive Church of England, *etc.* 1814. 8°. **210. b. 5.**

—— The Lives of the Irish Saints, extracted from the writings of the Rev. Alban Butler, and now placed in order, with a prefixed callender; to which is added, an Office and Litany in their honour, with a defence of the Monastic Institute. By a Cistercian Monk. pp. xviii. 217. *J. Coyne: Dublin*, 1823. 12°. **4825. a. 7.**

—— The Life of St. Ignatius of Loyola [from Butler's "Lives of the Fathers"] . . . To which is added the sixth book of his life written by the celebrated Bohours . . . which contains . . . the letter of Louis XIII, King of France, to Pope Gregory XV. [With a portrait.] pp. 108. *Richard Coyne: Dublin*, 1841. 12°. **4827. bbb. 26.**

—— One Hundred Pious Reflections, selected from Alban Butler's Lives of the Saints. [The editor's preface signed: M. T., i.e. Margaret T. Taunton.] pp. 202. *R. Washbourne: London*, 1870. 16°. **4412. aaa. 8.**

—— The People's Pictorial Lives of the Saints . . . Abridged, for the most part, from those of the late Rev. Alban Butler. *Catholic Publication Society: New York*, [1870?] 16°. **4806. aa. 13.**

—— Lives of the Saints. From Alban Butler. Selected and edited by the Right Rev. Mgr. Goddard. pp. 396. *R. Washbourne: London,* 1883. 8°. **4829.** aa. **27.**

—— Lives of Women Saints. From Alban Butler. Selected and edited by the Right Rev. Mgr. Goddard. pp. viii. 256. *St. Anselm's Society: London,* 1887. 8°. **4829.** cc. **4.**

—— Vies choisies des principaux saints, traduites de Butler par Godescard, *etc.* 6 tom. *Paris,* 1837. 12°. **4823.** aaa. **18.**

—— La Vita di Santa Caterina da Siena [from Butler's "Lives of the Fathers"], seguita da documenti e note varazzine. [Edited by D. Botta.] pp. 112. *Varazze,* 1875. 16°. **4827.** de. **13.**

—— *See* ATTWATER (Donald) A Dictionary of Saints. Being also an index to the revised edition of Alban Butler's 'Lives of the Saints.' 1938. 8°. **20032.** h. **15.**

—— *See* BUTLER (Charles) *Barrister-at-Law.* A Continuation of the Rev. Alban Butler's Lives of the Saints to the present time, *etc.* 1823. 8°. **1232.** d. **24.**

—— *See* KELLY (Bernard W.) Supplementary Volume to Butler's Lives of the Fathers, Martyrs and other principal Saints, *etc.* [1929.] 8°. **4828.** dd. **29.**

—— —— [1930.] 8°. **4828.** f. **20.**

—— —— 1936. 8°. **20029.** i. **15.**

—— *See* SHEA (John D.G.) Little Pictorial Lives of the Saints . . . Compiled from "Butler's Lives," *etc.* 1894. 8°. **4827.** df. **23.**

—— Complete General Index to the Lives of the Fathers, Martyrs, and other principal Saints. pp. 294. *T. Richardson & Son: London & Derby,* [1886.] 16°. **4824.** aa. **8.**

—— Meditations and Discourses on the Sublime Truths and Important Duties of Christianity, *etc.* [Edited by Charles Butler.] 3 vol. *J. P. Coghlan: London,* 1791–93. 8°. **4374.** cc. **25.** (**4.**)

—— New edition . . . revised and improved by the Rev. John Lanigan. [With a portrait.] pp. viii. 528. *James Duffy: Dublin,* 1840. 8°. **4374.** k. **1.**

—— The Moveable Feasts, Fasts, and other annual observances of the Catholic Church . . . With life of the author, by Charles Butler, Esqr. To which is added, a continuation of the Feasts and Fasts, by a Catholic Priest. [With a portrait.] pp. xlvii. 440. *James Duffy: Dublin,* 1839. 8°. **3477.** dd. **21.**

—— Remarks on the two first volumes of the late Lives of the Popes [by Archibald Bower]. In letters from a Gentleman to a Friend in the Country. [By A. Butler.] pp. 100. 1754. 8°. *See* GENTLEMAN. **113.** e. **55.**

—— Travels through France & Italy, and part of Austrian, French, & Dutch Netherlands, during the years 1745 and 1746. [Edited by Charles Butler.] pp. 272 [472]. *Edinburgh; Keating, Brown & Keating: London,* 1803. 8°. **10105.** dd. **12.** (**2.**)

—— An Account of the Life and Writings of the Rev. Alban Butler: interspersed with observations on some subjects of sacred and profane literature mentioned in his writings. [By Charles Butler. With a portrait.] pp. 158. *J. P. Coghlan: London,* 1799. 8°. **959.** d. **8.**

—— Indice cronologico delle cose principali contenute nelle Vite, nella Continuazione, nelle Feste mobili e negli opuscoli dell'ultimo tomo. [An index to "The Lives of the Fathers" by A. Butler, the Continuation thereof by Charles Butler, "The Moveable Feasts, Fasts and other annual observances of the Catholic Church" by A. Butler, "De Mortibus Persecutorum" by Lactantius and "An Account of the Life and Writings of the Rev. Alban Butler" by Charles Butler. Compiled by G. Brunati.] pp. 159. *Venezia,* 1826. 8°. **4826.** cc. **5.**
This is the index belonging to G. Brunati's Italian translation of these works. One of an edition of six copies.

BUTLER (ALBERT E.) Sectaphil Pole-lines System Competition Coupons Explained. *A. E. Butler: London,* 1931. 8°. **07912.** h. **32.**

BUTLER (ALEXANDER) *See* DEANE (Edmund) Spadacrene Anglica . . . With . . . biographical notes by A. Butler. 1922. 8°. **7470.** aa. **74.**

BUTLER (ALEXANDER HUME) Poems written in Barracks. pp. vii. 88. *Longmans & Co.: London,* 1868. 16°. **11647.** aa. **12.**

BUTLER (ALFRED) Elphinstone. [A novel.] 3 vol. *Richard Bentley: London,* 1841. 12°. **N. 2107.**

—— The Herberts. By the author of "Elphinstone" [i.e. Alfred Butler]. 3 vol. 1842. 12°. *See* HERBERTS. **N. 2272.**

—— Midsummer Eve; or, Days of Queen Mary. An historical tale, *etc.* 3 vol. *A. K. Newman & Co.: London,* 1844. 8°. **4411.** l. **3.**

BUTLER (ALFRED JOSHUA) *See* ABU ṢĀLIḤ, *al-Armanī.* The Churches and Monasteries of Egypt . . . With added notes by A. J. Butler. 1895. 4°. **12204.** f. **11/7.**

—— *See* GREEK ANTHOLOGY. Amaranth and Asphodel. Songs from the Greek Anthology. By A. J. Butler. 1881. 8°. **11340.** aa. **7.**

—— —— 1922. 8°. **11340.** de. **32.**

—— An Account of the Benefactions bestowed on the College.—The College Plate with a complete list of donors.—The College Estates and the Advowsons held by the College.—The College Pictures. *See* OXFORD.—*University of Oxford.—Brasenose College.* Brasenose College Quatercentenary Monographs. vol. 1. 1909, *etc.* 8°. . Ac. **8126/29.**

—— The Ancient Coptic Churches of Egypt. 2 vol. *Clarendon Press: Oxford,* 1884. 8°. **2202.** c. **8.**

—— [Another copy.] The Ancient Coptic Churches of Egypt. 2 vol. *Oxford,* 1884. 8°. **07705.** b. **18.**

—— The Arab Conquest of Egypt and the last thirty years of the Roman dominion. [With maps.] pp. xxxiv. 563. *Clarendon Press: Oxford,* 1902. 8°. **2386.** b. **7.**

—— Babylon of Egypt. A study in the history of old Cairo. pp. 63. *Clarendon Press: Oxford,* 1914. 8°. **07704.aaa.21.**

—— Court Life in Egypt . . . With illustrations. pp. vii. 298. *Chapman & Hall: London,* 1887. 8°. **10097.** e. **5.**

—— Islamic Pottery. A study mainly historical. pp. xxv. 179. pl. XCII. *Ernest Benn: London,* 1926. fol. L.R. **261.** c. **6.**

—— [Another copy.] L.R. **261.** c. **7.**
No. 10 *of fifteen copies printed on hand-made paper.*

BUTLER (Alfred Joshua)

—— Sport in Classic Times. [With plates.] pp. 213. *Ernest Benn: London,* 1930. 8°. **11312**. t. **16**.

—— The Treaty of Miṣr in Ṭabarī. An essay in historical criticism. pp. 87. *Clarendon Press: Oxford,* 1913. 8°. **09008**. cc. **21**. (**5**.)

BUTLER (Alfred Trego)

—— *See* England.—*College of Arms.* [*Visitations.—Worcestershire.*] The Visitation of Worcestershire, 1634. Edited by A. T. Butler. 1938. 8°. [*Publications of the Harleian Society.* vol. 90.] **2099**. c.

—— *See* Staples (Leslie C.) The Dickens Ancestry . . . Being notes on the unpublished work of the late A. T. Butler . . . and the late Arthur Campling, *etc.* 1951. 8°. **9918**. a. **42**.

BUTLER (Amos W.) Biological Survey of Indiana. (Bibliography of Indiana Ornithology. By A. W. Butler.—Bibliography of Indiana Mammals. By B. W. Evermann and A. W. Butler.) (From Proceedings of the Indiana Academy of Science.) 1894. 8°. **011904**. ee. **5**. (**1**.)

BUTLER (Andrew Pickens) *See* Douglas (Stephen A.) The Clayton Bulwer Treaty. Speeches of Senator Douglas in reply to Senators Clayton and Butler, on the Central American Treaty, *etc.* 1853. 8°. **8177**. df. **35**.

BUTLER (Andrew S. G.) *See* Butler (Arthur S. G.)

BUTLER (Ann) *of Benson.*

—— Fragments in Verse; chiefly on religious subjects. pp. 155. *Bartlett & Hinton: Oxford,* 1826. 12°. **1164**. i. **11**.

BUTLER (Ann) *of Castlemalgwyn.* *See* Butler (Anne)

BUTLER (Anna) Stories for Young Servants . . . Second edition, with an additional story. pp. 222. *J. Masters & Co.: London,* 1876. 12°. **4413**. ff. **7**.

BUTLER (Anna Maria) The Choristers' Own Book. pp. 95. *F. H. Morland: London,* 1908. 16°. **7898**. e. **45**.

—— Conversational Lectures on the Lord's Prayer. pp. 41. *E. B. Sargeant: Peterborough; William Macintosh: London,* [1870.] 8°. **3224**. a. **43**.

—— Steyning, Sussex. The history of Steyning and its church from 700–1913 . . . With illustrations and portraits. pp. 136. *W. D. Hayward: Croydon,* [1913.] 8°. **010360**. i. **17**.

—— Suicide or Murder. pp. 7. *F. H. Morland: London,* [1906.] 8°. **8425**. de. **44**. (**3**.)

BUTLER (Anne)

—— A Selection of Sacred Poems, . . . Edited by G. S. [identified in a ms. note as G. Smith.] pp. vii. 67. *Bemrose & Sons: London & Derby,* 1878. 8°. **03440**. h. **42**.

BUTLER (Annie Robina) By the Rivers of Africa, from Cape Town to Uganda . . . With a map and sixty illustrations. pp. 154. *R.T.S.: London,* [1901.] 8°. **4430**. g. **11**.

—— [A reissue.] *London,* [1914.] 8°. **4430**. ee. **14**.

BUTLER (Annie Robina)

—— The Children's King. The life of Jesus retold for young readers . . . With five coloured plates from pictures by J. J. Tissot, *etc.* pp. 192. *R.T.S.: London,* 1900. 4°. **4430**. g. **6**.

—— Third edition. pp. 192. *R.T.S.: London,* [1923.] 4°. **4427**. h. **19**.

—— Children's Medical Mission Stories. no. 1–10; New series. no. 1. *W. Mack: Bristol; Book Society: London,* [1876–87.] 32°. **4192**. a. **12**.
No. 5 is anonymous.

—— A Gift for a Pet . . . With verses by F. H. Butler, *etc.* pp. 254. *R.T.S.: London,* [1896.] 4°. **4430**. i. **1**.

—— Glimpses of Maori Land. pp. x. 260. *R.T.S.: London,* 1886. 8°. **10492**. b. **3**.

—— 'In the Beginning'; or, Stories from the Book of Genesis . . . With . . . illustrations. pp. 320. *R.T.S.: London,* 1889. 8°. [*Stepping Stones to Bible History.* no. 1.] **4420**. g. **4/1**.

—— Little Kathleen: or, Sunny memories of a child-worker (Kathleen A. Webber). [With a portrait.] pp. 88. *Morgan & Scott: London,* [1890.] 16°. **4906**. a. **58**.

—— Little Sufferers, and Little Workers; or, Stories about medical missions. pp. 57. *W. Mack: Bristol; Book Society: London,* [1877]. 16°. **4422**. bb. **4**.

—— Second edition. pp. 62. *W. Mack: Bristol; Book Society: London,* [1878.] 16°. **4412**. ee. **4**.

—— The London Medical Mission. What is it doing? pp. 47. *S. W. Partridge & Co.: London; C. Caswell: Birmingham,* 1877. 24°. **4192**. a. **67**.
No. 3 of an unnamed series of tracts.

—— Nearly a Hundred Years Ago. [An account of the life of Thomas Butler.] pp. 150. *S. W. Partridge & Co.: London,* [1907.] 8°. **4902**. aaaa. **4**.

—— The Promised King, or the Story of the children's Saviour. With thirty-eight illustrations. pp. 320. *R.T.S.: London,* 1890. 8°. [*Stepping Stones to Bible History.* no. 2.] **4420**. g. **4/2**.

—— Stories about China. pp. 48. *T. O. Smith: London,* [1887.] 16°. **4766**. a. **16**. (**1**.)

—— Stories about Japan. pp. 128. *R.T.S.: London,* [1888.] 8°. **4421**. aaaa. **12**.

—— W. Thomson Crabbe, F.R.C.S.E., medical missionary. pp. 79. *S. W. Partridge & Co.: London,* 1899. 8°. **4955**. df. **13**.

BUTLER (Archer) *See* Butler (William A.)

BUTLER (Arthur) A Dictionary of Philosophical Terms. pp. 114. *G. Routledge & Sons: London,* [1909.] 32°. **012216**. hh. **40**.

BUTLER (Arthur Gardiner) *See* London.—iii. *British Museum.—Department of Zoology.* [*Arthropoda.*] Illustrations of Typical Specimens of Lepidoptera Heterocera, in the collection of the British Museum. (pt. 1–3, 5–7 by A. G. Butler.) 1877, *etc.* 4°. **7296**. h. **9**.

—— Birds' Eggs of the British Isles . . . With 24 coloured plates . . . by F. W. Frohawk. pp. vii. 105. pl. xxiv. *L. U. Gill: London; C. Scribner's Sons: New York,* 1904. 4°. **7284**. f. **18**.

—— [A reissue.] *Brumby & Clarke: London,* [1910.] 4°. **7286**. h. **2**.

BUTLER (ARTHUR GARDINER)

—— British Birds' Eggs: a handbook of British oölogy . . . Illustrated by the author, in chromo-lithography. pp. 219. pl. XXXVII. *E. W. Janson: London,* 1886. 8°. **7285. aa. 8.**

Published in parts.

—— [Another copy.] **7285. aaa. 3.**

—— Canaries and other Cage-Birds. *See* HOME PETS. Home Pets, *etc.* [1907.] 8°. **07293. g. 77.**

—— Catalogue of Diurnal Lepidoptera described by Fabricius in the collection of the British Museum. [Edited by J. E. Gray.] pp. iv. 303. pl. III. 1869. 8°. *See* LONDON.—III. *British Museum.—Department of Zoology.* [*Arthropoda.*] **7207. g. 13.**

—— Catalogue of Diurnal Lepidoptera of the family Satyridæ in the collection of the British Museum. [Edited by J. E. Gray.] pp. vi. 211. pl. v. 1868. 8°. *See* LONDON.—III. *British Museum.—Department of Zoology.* [*Arthropoda.*] **7207. g. 21.**

—— Foreign Finches in Captivity . . . Illustrated with sixty plates by F. W. Frohawk . . . coloured by hand. pp. viii. 332. *L. Reeve & Co.: London,* 1894–[96.] 4°. **K.T.C. 26. b. 13.**

—— Hints on Cage Birds—British and foreign . . . Revised by G. F. Crawford . . . Second edition, *etc.* pp. 96. *Cage Bird Fancy: London,* [1936.] 8°. **7286. aa. 62.**

—— How to sex Cage Birds, British and foreign . . . With over fifty illustrations and four coloured plates. pp. 176. *"Feathered World": London,* [1907.] 8°. **7285. de. 6.**

—— Lepidoptera. *See* LONDON.—III. *British Museum.—Department of Zoology.* Report on the Zoological Collections made in the Indo-Pacific Ocean during the voyage of H.M.S. "Alert," 1881-2. 1884. 8°. **7208. d. 2.**

—— Lepidoptera Exotica, or, Descriptions and illustrations of exotic lepidoptera. pp. iv. 190. pl. LXIV. *E. W. Janson: London,* 1874 [1869–74]. 4°. **7297. h. 19.**

—— Order Passeres . . . Illustrated by F. W. Frohawk. 2 vol. *Brumby & Clarke: Hull & London,* [1896, 97.] 4°. [*British Birds, with their nests and eggs.* vol. 1, 2.] **7284. i. 14.**

—— Order Picariæ. [1897.] *See* BRITISH BIRDS. British Birds, with their nests and eggs, *etc.* vol. 3. [1896, *etc.*] 4°. **7284. i. 14.**

—— The Second Covenant: a tract on Baptism. pp. 16. *William Macintosh: London,* 1875. 8°. **4325. aa. 1. (13.)**

—— Tropical Butterflies and Moths. With descriptions by A. G. Butler. *S.P.C.K.: London,* [1873.] 8°. **7296. a. 16.**

—— The World Without End; or, Eternity by the light of the Old Testament. pp. 24. *William Macintosh: London,* 1875. 8°. **4422. h. 1. (20.)**

BUTLER (ARTHUR GARDINER) and BUTLER (MONTAGU RUSSELL)

—— The Two Spirits; or, Truth and error. Being a comparison of the teachings of Rome with the words of Jehovah. pp. 57. *Elliot Stock: London,* [1877.] 8°. **3939. bb. 2.**

BUTLER (ARTHUR GRAHAM)

—— The Digger, *etc.* [On the history and use of the term "Digger" as applied to members of the Australian Forces. With plates.] pp. 51. *Angus & Robertson: Sydney, London,* 1945. 8°. **10493. ff. 56.**

BUTLER (ARTHUR GRAHAM)

—— The Official History of the Australian Army Medical Services in the War of 1914–1918. [Edited by A. G. Butler.] 1930– . 8°. *See* AUSTRALIA.—*Military Forces.—Australian Contingent, British Expeditionary Force.—Medical Services.* **C.S.G.566/3.**

—— The Official History of the Australian Army Medical Services in the War of 1914–1918. (Second edition.) [Edited by A. G. Butler.] 1938– . 8°. *See* AUSTRALIA.—*Military Forces.—Australian Contingent, British Expeditionary Force.—Medical Services.* **W.P. 10187.**

BUTLER (ARTHUR GRAY) Charles I. A tragedy in five acts. [In prose and in verse.] pp. xix. 139. *Longmans & Co.: London,* 1874. 8°. **11781. cc. 23.**

—— Second edition, revised. pp. xvi. 124. *Henry Frowde: London,* 1907. 8°. **11778. i. 25.**

—— The Choice of Achilles, and other poems. pp. viii. 93. *Henry Frowde: London,* 1900. 8°. **011651. l. 24.**

—— Harold. A drama in four acts; and other poems. pp. viii. 226. *Henry Frowde: London,* 1892. 8°. **011653. m. 18.**

—— Second edition. pp. 118. *Henry Frowde: London,* 1906. 8°. **11779. ff. 48.**

—— Hodge and the Land. [Poems.] pp. 36. *B. H. Blackwell: Oxford,* 1907. 8°. **11603. dd. 11. (2.)**

—— The Three Friends. A story of Rugby in the forties. pp. vi. 127. *Henry Frowde: London,* 1900. 8°. **012804. g. 48.**

BUTLER (ARTHUR JOHN) *See* BISMARCK-SCHOENHAUSEN (O. E. L. von) *Prince.* [*Writings.*] Bismarck, the Man and the Statesman . . . Translated . . . under the supervision of A. J. Butler, *etc.* 1898. 8°. **2402. f. 9.**

—— *See* BUTLER (William J.) *Dean of Lincoln.* Life and Letters of William John Butler, *etc.* [The editor's preface signed: A. J. B., i.e. A. J. Butler.] 1897. 8°. **4905. dd. 29.**

—— *See* CAVOUR (C. B. di) *Count.* Count Cavour and Madame de Circourt. Some unpublished correspondence . . . Translated by A. J. Butler. 1894. 8°. **010920. k. 1.**

—— *See* COUCH (*Sir* Arthur T. Q.) Memoir of Arthur John Butler . . . With portraits. 1917. 8°. **010826. h. 28.**

—— *See* DANTE ALIGHIERI. [*Divina Commedia.—Italian.*] La Commedia di Dante Alighieri. [Edited by A. J. Butler.] 1890. 8°. **11420. cc. 1.**

—— *See* DANTE ALIGHIERI. [*Divina Commedia.—Italian and English.—Inferno.*] The Hell of Dante Alighieri. Edited with translation and notes by A. J. Butler. 1892. 8°. **2284. e. 4.**

—— *See* DANTE ALIGHIERI. [*Divina Commedia.—Italian and English.—Purgatorio.*] The Purgatory of Dante Alighieri. Edited with translation and notes by A. J. Butler. 1880. 8°. **2284. e. 12.**

—— *See* DANTE ALIGHIERI. [*Divina Commedia.—Italian and English.—Paradiso.*] The Paradise of Dante Alighieri. Edited with translation and notes by A. J. Butler. 1885. 8°. **2284. e. 14.**

BUTLER (ARTHUR JOHN)

—— *See* DANTE ALIGHIERI. [*Divina Commedia.—English.*] The Vision of Hell (the Vision of Purgatory and of Paradise) . . . Translated by the Rev. H. F. Cary, *etc.* [The editor's preface signed: A. J. B., i.e. A. J. Butler.] 1892, *etc.* 8°. **11421.** h. **12.**

—— *See* ENGLAND.—*Public Record Office.* Calendar of State Papers, Foreign Series, of the reign of Elizabeth, *etc.* (1577–1582, edited by A. J. Butler.—January–June, 1583, edited by A. J. Butler and S. C. Lomas.) 1863, *etc.* 8°. **2073.** (**152.**)

—— *See* FEDERN (C.) Dante & his Time . . . With an introduction by A. J. Butler, *etc.* 1902. 8°. **11421.** d. **30.**

—— *See* LONDON.—III. *Alpine Club.* The Alpine Journal, *etc.* (vol. 15, 16 edited by A. J. Butler.) 1863, *etc.* 8°. P.P. **3909.**

—— *See* MARBOT (J. B. A. M. de) *Baron.* The Memoirs of Baron de Marbot . . . Translated . . . by A. J. Butler, *etc.* 1892. 8°. **010661.** f. **53.**

—— —— 1893. 8°. **010662.** f. **8.**

—— —— 1897. 8°. **010664.** f. **5.**

—— *See* MARBOT (J. B. A. M. de) *Baron.* The Memoirs of Baron de Marbot . . . Translated . . . by A. J. Butler. [Abridged.] 1929. 8°. **012213.n.1/7.**

—— *See* PLUMPTRE (Edward H.) *Dean of Wells.* The Life of Dante . . . Edited by A. J. Butler. 1900. 8°. **11420.** b. **41.**

—— —— 1903. 8°. **11421.** bb. **15.**

—— *See* RATZEL (F.) The History of Mankind . . . Translated . . . by A. J. Butler, *etc.* 1896, *etc.* 8°. **7006.s.8.**

—— *See* SAINTE-BEUVE (C. A.) Select Essays . . . chiefly bearing on English literature. Translated by A. J. Butler. [1895.] 8°. **011850.** eee. **33**

—— *See* SCARTAZZINI (G. A.) A Companion to Dante. From the German of G. A. Scartazzini by A. J. Butler. 1893. 8°. **2284.** e. **1.**

—— *See* THIÉBAULT (D. A. P. F. C. H.) *Baron.* The Memoirs of Baron Thiébault . . . Translated and condensed by A. J. Butler. 1896. 8°. **10661.** r. **2.**

—— Dante; his times and his work. pp. ix. 201. *A. D. Innes & Co.: London,* 1895. 8°. **11420.** ccc. **15.**

—— The End of the Italian Renaissance. 1904. *See* ACTON (John E. E. D.) *Baron Acton.* The Cambridge Modern History, *etc.* vol. 3. 1902, *etc.* 8°. **2070.g.**

—— The Forerunners of Dante. A selection from Italian poetry before 1300. Edited by A. J. Butler. pp. xxxv. 262. *Clarendon Press: Oxford,* 1910. 8°. **11427.** c. **37.**

—— The Wars of Religion in France. 1904. *See* ACTON (John E. E. D.) *Baron Acton.* The Cambridge Modern History, *etc.* vol. 3. 1902, *etc.* 8°. **2070.g.**

BUTLER (ARTHUR STANLEY GEORGE)

—— The Architecture of Sir Edwin Lutyens. [By] A. S. G. Butler. With the collaboration of George Stewart & Christopher Hussey. [With a portrait.] 3 vol. *Country Life: London; Charles Scribner's Sons: New York,* 1950. fol. [*Lutyens Memorial Volumes.*] L.R. **301.** b. **4.**

BUTLER (ARTHUR STANLEY GEORGE)

—— Plain Impressions. pp. xii. 95. *Aeroplane & General Publishing Co.: London,* 1919. 8°. **9083.** a. **42.**

—— Portrait of Josephine Butler. [With plates, including portraits.] pp. 222. *Faber & Faber: London,* 1954. 8°. **10863.** f. **69.**

—— The Substance of Architecture. pp. xvii. 319. pl. VIII. *Constable & Co.: London,* 1926. 8°. **07815.** f. **23.**

—— Recording Ruin . . . [An account of the author's experiences whilst reporting on war damage for the Chelsea Borough Council.] Drawings by H. Russell Hall. pp. 146. *Constable & Co.: London,* 1942. 8°. **010349.** n. **3.**

—— [Recording Ruin.] Décombres et souvenirs . . . Dessins par H. Russell Hall. pp. 123. *Constable & Co.: Londres,* 1944. 8°. **010349.** n. **16.**

BUTLER (B. A.) Important Things. [Verses.] *E. J. Burrow & Co.: London,* [1930.] 8°. **11646.** d. **71.**

BUTLER (B. E.)

—— Soil Survey of Part of County Moira, Victoria . . . By B. E. Butler . . . J. G. Baldwin . . . F. Penman . . . R. G. Downes. [With maps.] pp. 48. *Melbourne,* 1942. 8°. [*Australia. Council for Scientific and Industrial Research. Bulletin.* no. 152.] **C.S.G.548(2.)**

BUTLER (B. W.) and **HALL** (E. J.) Die and Press-Tool Work, *etc.* pp. viii. 263. *London,* [1921.] 8°. [*Cassell's Workshop Series.*] W.P. **5728/5.**

BUTLER (BASIL CHRISTOPHER)

—— The Church and Infallibility. A reply to the abridged "Salmon" [i.e. to the abridged edition of "The Infallibility of the Church" by George Salmon]. pp. ix. 230. *Sheed & Ward: London & New York,* 1954. 8°. **3943.** de. **9.**

—— The Originality of St. Matthew. A critique of the two-document hypothesis. pp. vii. 178. *University Press: Cambridge,* 1951. 8°. **3228.** bb. **21.**

BUTLER (BEN) *pseud.* Laboratory
aboratory
boratory
oratory
ratory
atory
tory
ory
ry
y. A tale of Tories. [In verse.] By Ben Butler . . . The illustrations by Seymour. pp. 68. *Effingham Wilson: London,* 1832. 12°. T. **1368.** (**5.**)

BUTLER (BENJAMIN FRANKLIN) *Attorney General of the United States. See* also MARCUS, *pseud.* [i.e. B. F. Butler.]

—— *See* MACKENZIE (William Lyon) *Mayor of Toronto.* The Lives and Opinions of Benj'n Franklin Butler . . . and Jesse Hoyt, *etc.* 1845. 8°. **10880.** e. **43.** (**1.**)

—— *See* NEW YORK, *State of.* [*Collections of Laws.*—I.] The Revised Statutes of the State of New York, passed during the years one thousand eight hundred and twenty-seven, and one thousand eight hundred and twenty-eight . . . Printed and published under the direction of the revisers [i.e. B. F. Butler and others], *etc.* 1829. 8°. A.S. N. **228.**

BUTLER (Benjamin Franklin) *Attorney General of the United States.*

—— *See* New York, *State of.* [*Collections of Laws.*—i.] The Revised Statutes of the State of New York, passed from 1828 to 1835 inclusive . . . Prepared by and published under the superintendence of the late revisers [i.e. B. F. Butler and others], *etc.* 1836. 8°. A.S. n. **228/2.**

—— *See* New York, *State of.* [*Collections of Laws.*—i.] The Revised Statutes of the State of New York . . . passed between the years 1828 and 1845 inclusive . . . Prepared by J. Duer, B. F. Butler, *etc.* 1846, *etc.* 8°. A.S. n. **228/3.**

—— Anniversary Discourse, delivered before the Albany Institute, *etc.* pp. 88. *Webster & Skinners: Albany,* 1830. 8°. **8365.** bb. **11.**

—— Christian Missions: an introductory lecture, delivered before the Boston Young Men's Society for Diffusing Missionary Knowledge, *etc.* pp. 24. *T. R. Marvin: Boston,* 1842. 8°. **4745.** d. **31.** (**1.**)

—— Eulogy [of President Jackson] delivered at New York City, June 24, 1845. *See* Dusenbery (B. M.) Monument to the Memory of General Andrew Jackson, *etc.* 1846. 12°. **10880.** c. **33.**

—— The Military Profession in the United States, and the means of promoting its usefulness and honour; an address, *etc.* pp. 46. *Samuel Colman: New York,* 1839. 8°. **8827.** g. **19.**

—— Representative Democracy in the United States: an address, *etc.* pp. 43. *C. Van Benthuysen: Albany,* 1841. 8°. **8175.** bb. **61.** (**5.**)

BUTLER (Benjamin Franklin) *Major General of Volunteers.* *See* Bland (T. A.) Life of Benjamin F. Butler. 1879. 8°. **10882.** bb. **12.**

—— *See* Parton (James) General Butler in New Orleans. History of the administration of the department of the Gulf in . . . 1862: with . . . a sketch of the previous career of the General, civil and military, *etc.* 1864. 8°. **10881.** bb. **19.**

—— *See* Pierpont (Francis H.) Letter of Governor Peirpoint to . . . the President and the . . . Congress of the United States, on the subject of abuse of military power in the command of General Butler in Virginia and North Carolina. 1864. 8°. **9602.** cc. **32.** (**6.**)

—— *See* Robinson (William S.) The Salary Grab: a history of the passage of the Act increasing the salaries of members of Congress . . . With special reference to the responsibility of Gen. B. F. Butler, *etc.* 1873. 8°. **8176.** a. **30.** (**4.**)

—— [General Orders issued by Major-General B. F. Butler, in command of the United States Army in New Orleans, from 20 March to 15 Dec. 1862.] no. 1–106. [1862.] 8°. *See* United States of America.—*Army.* **9605.** bb. **25.**

—— Argument of Gen. Benj. F. Butler [in defence of T. C. A. Dexter]. *See* Dexter (Thomas C. A.) Before the President of the United States. Case of Thomas C. A. Dexter, *etc.* 1867. 8°. **6616.** d. **2.** (**5.**)

—— Butler's Book . . . A review of his legal, political, and military career . . . (Autobiography and Personal Reminiscences of Major-General Benj. F. Butler.) Illustrated with 125 engravings, maps, photogravures, *etc.* [With portraits.] pp. 1154. *A. M. Thayer & Co.: Boston,* 1892. 8°. **010882.** f. 22.

BUTLER (Benjamin Franklin) *Major General of Volunteers.*

—— Character and Results of the War. How to prosecute and how to end it. A thrilling and eloquent speech. pp. 32. *Printed for gratuitous distribution: Philadelphia,* 1863. 8°. **8175.** bb. **61.** (**14.**)

—— [Another copy, with a different wrapper.] **8175.** aaa. **73.** (**6.**)

—— Letter . . . to Hon. E. R. Hoar. Gives his official and political biography, with a reply to the Judge's imputations upon the General. pp. 32. *Published by request:* [*Lowell?*] 1876. 8°. **8176.** bbb. **3.** (**10.**)

—— Speech . . . at the Hebrew Fair in Boston. *See* Eaton (Herbert N.) An Hour with the American Hebrew, *etc.* 1879. 16°. **4033.** de. **1.**

—— The Five-twenty Bonds. General Butler's speech. [A letter signed: W. E.] [1867.] *s. sh.* fol. *See* E., W. **1879.** c. **10.** (**16.**)

—— Life and Public Services of Major-General Butler . . . the hero of New Orleans, *etc.* pp. 108. *T. B. Peterson & Bros.: Philadelphia,* [1864.] 8°. **10881.** bb. **27.** (**2.**)

—— The Record of Benjamin F. Butler. Compiled from the original sources. pp. iv. 95. *Boston,* 1883. 8°. **10601.** bb. **22.** (**3.**)

BUTLER (Bert Sylvenus)

—— *See* Calkins (Frank C.) and Butler (B. S.) Geology and Ore Deposits of the Cottonwood-American Fork Area, Utah, *etc.* 1943. 4°. [*U.S. Geological Survey. Professional Paper.* no. 201.] A.S. **209/6.**

—— *See* Gardner (Eugene D.) Copper Mining in North America. By E. D. Gardner, C. H. Johnson and B. S. Butler. 1938. 8°. [*U.S. Bureau of Mines. Bulletin.* no. 405.] A.S. **229.**

—— *See* Singewald (Quentin D.) and Butler (B. S.) Ore Deposits in the Vicinity of the London Fault of Colorado, *etc.* 1941. 8°. [*U.S. Geological Survey. Bulletin.* no. 911.] A.S. **212/2.**

—— *See* Tarr (Ralph S.) The Yakutat Bay Region, Alaska . . . A real geology by R. S. Tarr and B. S. Butler. 1909. 4°. [*U.S. Geological Survey. Professional Paper.* no. 64.] A.S. **209/6.**

—— The Ore Deposits of Utah. By B. S. Butler . . . and others. [With maps.] pp. 672. pl. lvii. *Washington,* 1920. 4°. [*U. S. Geological Survey. Professional Paper.* no. 111.] A.S. **209/6.**

BUTLER (Bert Sylvenus) and **BURBANK** (Wilbur Swett)

—— The Copper Deposits of Michigan, *etc.* [With plates, a portfolio of maps, and a bibliography.] pp. xii. 238. *Washington,* 1929. 4°. [*U.S. Geological Survey. Professional Paper.* no. 144.] A.S. **209/6.** & Maps **26.** a. **2.**

BUTLER (Bert Sylvenus) and **GALE** (Hoyt Stoddard)

—— Alunite. A newly discovered deposit near Marysvale, Utah. pp. 64. pl. iii. *Washington,* 1912. 8°. [*U.S. Geological Survey. Bulletin.* no. 511.] A.S. **212/2.**

BUTLER (Bert Sylvenus) and **VANDERWILT** (John W.)

—— The Climax Molybdenum Deposit, Colorado . . . With a Section on history, production, metallurgy, and development, by Charles W. Henderson. *Washington*, 1933. 8°. [*U.S. Geological Survey. Bulletin.* no. 846-c.] A.S. **212/2.**

BUTLER (Blanche)

—— Puppy Dog Number Book for Tiny Tots. Rhymes by B. Butler. Pictures by Grace Mallon. *Saalfield Publishing Co.: Akron*, [1939.] fol. **12807.** i. **85.**

BUTLER (C.)

—— *See* Brulart de Genlis (S. F.) *Marchioness de Sillery.* [*Single Works.*] The Age of Chivalry . . . Abridged and selected from the Knights of the Swan . . . by C. Butler, *etc.* 1799. 12°. **12510.** bb. **6.**

BUTLER (C. D.)

—— Wheaton's Italic Writing Cards: chancery script, *etc.* [By C. D. Butler. With an advisory booklet.] [1954.] 8° & *obl.* 8°. *See* Wheaton (A.) and Co. **7949.** r. **15.**

BUTLER (C. H.) *Troop-Leader of Boy Scouts.* Points for Patrol Leaders, *etc.* [Reprinted from "The Scout."] 2 ser. *C. A. Pearson: London*, 1922, 25. 8°. **8832.** b. **26.**

BUTLER (C. N.) **AND CO.**

—— [Miscellaneous price lists of postage stamps, post cards, albums, *etc.*] 7 pt. *Maidenhead*, [1879]–81. 8°. Crawford **687.** (**2–8.**)

—— C. N. Butler & Co.'s Descriptive Catalogue and Price List of British, Foreign & Colonial Postage Stamps, Post Cards, Envelopes, &c. pp. 39. *C. N. Butler & Co.: Maidenhead*, 1880. 8°. Crawford **880.** (**8.**)

—— C. N. Butler & Co.'s Wholesale Price List of Foreign Postage Stamps, Post Cards, &c. 1 May 1880; 1 Jan., 1 March, 1 May 1881. *C. N. Butler & Co.: Maidenhead*, 1880, 81. 8° & 4°. Crawford **117.** (**1.**)
Later catalogues are entered under Nichols, Butler and Co.

BUTLER (C. S.) *Journalist.*

—— The Northern Epirotes. pp. 11. [*London*, 1914.] 8°. [*Publications of the Anglo-Hellenic League.* no. 16.] **8027.b.65/16.**

BUTLER (Caleb) *See* Nightingale (Crawford) A Discourse preached at the Funeral of Caleb Butler. 1855. 8°. **4985.** dd. **4.** (**16.**)

—— History of the Town of Groton, including Pepperell and Shirley, from the first grant of Groton Plantation in 1655. With appendices, containing family registers, town and state officers, populations, and other statistics. pp. xx. 499. *T. R. Marvin: Boston*, 1848. 8°. **10410.** e. **4.**

—— *See* Andrews (David) Truth and Character Vindicated: being a review of Hon. C. Butler's History of the Ecclesiastical Affairs of Pepperell, *etc.* 1849. 8°. **4745.** c. **34.** (**2.**)

—— An Oration delivered at Leominster, Mass. before the Trinity and Aurora Lodges, on the festival of St. John the Baptist, June 24, A.L. 5816. pp. 20. *William Manning: Worcester* [*Mass.*], 1816. 8°. **4784.** dd. **21.**

BUTLER (Caleb)

—— A Review reviewed in a letter to David Andrews [and others] . . . Committee of the church. [A reply to "Truth and Character Vindicated" by D. Andrews and others.] pp. 36. *B. H. Greene: Boston*, 1850. 8°. **4183.** bb. **82.** (**16.**)

BUTLER (Carl) *See* Warburton (Edward) "Disallowed" . . . By E. Warburton and C. Butler. 1935. 8°. **8286.** a. **64.**

BUTLER (Caroline H.) The Ice King and the Sweet South Wind. [With plates.] pp. 176. *Phillips, Sampson & Co.: Boston*, 1852. 16°. **12805.** h. **16.**

—— [Another edition.] pp. 138. *Addey & Co.: London*, 1854. 12°. **12806.** e. **38.**

—— New edition. pp. 138. *Sampson Low & Son: London*, 1855. 8°. **12805.** dd. **13.**

—— Life in Varied Phases: illustrated in a series of sketches. pp. 288. *Phillips, Sampson & Co.: Boston*, 1851. 12°. **12705.** f. **5.**

—— The Little Messenger Birds, or, the Chimes of the silver bells . . . Illustrated by A. F. Lydon. pp. 153. *Groombridge & Sons: London*, [1871]. 8°. **12808.** m. **30.**

BUTLER (Caroline Maude Blanche) *Baroness Dunboyne.* Essays for Girls. pp. vii. 93. *Wells Gardner, Darton & Co.: London*, 1914. 8°. **08415.** g. **7.**

—— Thoughts for Mothers. pp. 127. *S.P.C.K.: London*, 1923. 8°. **08415.** ee. **24.**

BUTLER (Carolus) *See* Butler (Charles) *Vicar of Wotton.*

BUTLER (Charles) *Author of "An Easy Guide to Geography."* An Easy Guide to Geography, and the use of the globes. pp. 200. *T. Dean & Co.: London*, [1846?] 12°. **793.** a. **45.**

—— [Another edition.] Charles Butler's Young Pupils' Easy Guide to Geography . . . Twentieth edition, revised, and arranged from Dr. Farr's Guide to Geography, by Robert Henry Mair. pp. iv. 278. *Dean & Son: London*, [1868.] 12°. **10004.** aa. **30.**

—— The Guide to Useful Knowledge: containing in the form of a familiar catechism, a variety of information connected with the arts, sciences, and the phenomena of nature . . . Third edition, corrected and enlarged. pp. 190. *G. A. H. Dean: London*, [1828.] 12°. **12203.** b. **8.**

—— Twenty-fourth edition, considerably enlarged and improved. pp. 205. *Dean & Sons: London*, [1872.] 12°. **12203.** aa. **37.**

BUTLER (Charles) *Barrister-at-Law.* *See* Bible.—*Psalms.* [*English.*] A New Translation of the Book of Psalms . . . By Alexander Geddes. [Edited by J. Disney and C. Butler.] 1807. 8°. **3050.** e. **10.**

—— *See* Blanco y Crespo (J. M.) afterwards Blanco White (J.) A Letter to Charles Butler, Esq., on his notice of the "Practical and Internal Evidence against Catholicism." [With special reference to C. Butler's "Vindication of the Book of the Roman Catholic Church."] 1826. 8°. C. **126.** h. **12.**

—— *See* Butler (Alban) Meditations and Discourses on the Sublime Truths and Important Duties of Christianity. [Edited by C. Butler.] 1791, *etc.* 8°. **4374.** cc. **25.** (**4.**)

BUTLER (CHARLES) *Barrister-at-Law.*

—— *See* BUTLER (Alban) The Moveable Feasts, Fasts and other annual observances of the Catholic Church . . . With life of the author, by C. Butler, *etc.* 1839. 8°. **3477.** dd. **21.**

—— *See* BUTLER (Alban) Travels through France & Italy, *etc.* [Edited by C. Butler.] 1803. 8°. **10105.** dd. **12.** (**2.**)

—— *See* ENCYCLOPAEDIAS. The Oxford Encyclopædia . . . By the Rev. W. Harris . . . C. Butler, *etc.* 1828, *etc.* 4°. **12220.** t. **1.**

—— *See* FEARNE (Charles) *the Younger.* An Essay on the Learning of Contingent Remainders and Executory Devises . . . The sixth edition, with notes, and an analytical index, by C. Butler. 1809. 8°. **514.** g. **3.**

—— —— 1820. 8°. **514.** g. **4.**

—— —— 1831. 8°. **1130.** i. **10.**

—— —— 1844. 8°. **1383.** i. **6.**

—— *See* JESUS CHRIST. [*De Imitatione Christi.—Latin.*] Thomæ a Kempis de Imitatione Christi, *etc.* [With a life of Thomas a Kempis by C. Butler.] 1827. 12°. IX. Lat. **271.**

—— *See* JESUS CHRIST. [*De Imitatione Christi.—English.*] The Following of Christ . . . Translated . . . by R. Challenor . . . A new edition, containing some account of the life and writings of Thomas a Kempis by C. Butler. 1852. 32°. IX. Eng. **50.**

—— *See* LITTLETON (*Sir* T.) *One of the Judges of the Court of Common Pleas.* [*Tenores Novelli.—Norman-Fr. & Eng.*] The first part of the Institutes of the Laws of England . . . revised and corrected by F. Hargrave. [From fol. 190 to the end, with the Preface and index to the notes by C. Butler], *etc.* 1775, *etc.* fol. **508.** k. **4**, **5.**

—— —— 1789. fol. **508.** k. **2**

—— —— 1794. 8°. **508.** e. **3–5.**

—— —— 1809. 8°. **508.** e. **8–10.**

—— *See* LITTLETON (*Sir* Thomas) [*Tenores Novelli.—English.*] The First Part of the Institutes of the Laws of England . . . Revised and corrected . . . by Francis Hargrave and Charles Butler, *etc.* 1817. 8°. **508.** f. **12**, **13.**

—— —— 1823. 8°. **506.** b. **23.**

—— The Philological and Biographical Works of Charles Butler. [With a portrait.] 5 vol.

vol. I. Horæ Biblicæ.
vol. II. Germanic Empire. Horæ Juridicæ Subsecivæ. Life of L'Hôpital. Life of Mansfield.
vol. III. Lives of Fenelon, Bossuet, Boudon, De Rancé, Kempis, Alban Butler.
vol. IV. Confessions of Faith. Essays.
vol. V. Church of France.

W. Clarke & Sons: London, 1817. 8°. **1122.** e. **22–26.**

—— [Another copy.] **93.** b. **2–6.**

—— An Account of the Life and Writings of the Rev. Alban Butler: interspersed with observations on some subjects of sacred and profane literature mentioned in his writings. [By C. Butler. With a portrait.] pp. 158. 1799. 8°. *See* BUTLER (Alban) **959.** d. **8.**

—— [Another edition.] pp. 60. *Edinburgh; Keating & Brown: London,* 1800. 8°. **10105.** dd. **12.** (**1.**)

—— [Another copy.] **4374.** cc. **25.** (**2.**) *Imperfect; wanting the portrait.*

BUTLER (CHARLES) *Barrister-at-Law.*

—— *See* BUTLER (Alban) Indice cronologico delle cose principali contenute nelle Vite . . . e negli opuscoli dell' ultimo tomo. [An index to "The Lives of the Fathers" by A. Butler, "De Mortibus Persecutorum" by Lactantius and "An Account of the Life and Writings of the Rev. Alban Butler" by C. Butler.] 1826. 8°. **4826.** cc. **5.**

—— An Address to the Protestants of Great Britain and Ireland . . . Second edition, with additions. pp. 23. *Booker: London,* 1813. 8°. **3938.** bb. **79.** (**2.**)

—— [Another edition.] *See* PERIODICAL PUBLICATIONS.—*London.* The Pamphleteer, *etc.* vol. 1. 1813, *etc.* 8°. P.P. **3557.** w.

—— Extracts from an Address to the Protestants of Great Britain and Ireland . . . With additions, respecting the Irish Catholics, and the opinions of eminent statesmen on the Catholic Question. pp. 27. *T. Besley: Exeter.* 1813. 8°. **8145.** e. **7**

—— *See* CLERK. Mr. Charles Butler, of Lincoln's Inn, his Address to the Protestants of Great Britain and Ireland considered . . . By a Clerk. 1813. 8°. **701.** e. **19.** (**2.**)

—— *See* HILL (Rowland) *Minister of Surrey Chapel, Blackfriars Road.* A Letter . . . to Mr. Butler on his late "Address to the Protestants of Great Britain and Ireland;" and Mr. Butler's Reply. 1813. 8°. **3938.** bb. **27.**

—— *See* LE MESURIER (Thomas) A Counter Address to the Protestants of Great Britain and Ireland, in answer to the Address of Charles Butler, Esq. 1813. 8°. **3942.** b. **35.**

—— —— 1813. 8°. [*The Pamphleteer.* vol. 2.] P.P. **3557.** w.

—— An Appeal to the Protestants of Great Britain and Ireland, on the subject of the Roman Catholic Question: first published in the papers of the Protestant Union, in reply to a late Address by Charles Butler, Esq. pp. xi. 92. *J. Hatchard: London,* 1813. 8°. **3938.** cc. **20.**

—— The Book of the Roman Catholic Church: in a series of letters addressed to Robt Southey . . . on his "Book of the Church." pp. xii. 347. *John Murray: London,* 1825. 8°. **3939.** g. **23.**

—— Second edition. pp. xii. 352. *John Murray: London,* 1825. 8°. **487.** c. **12.**

—— *See* BLANCO Y CRESPO (José M.) afterwards BLANCO WHITE (Joseph) Practical and Internal Evidence against Catholicism, with occasional strictures on Mr. Butler's Book of the Roman Catholic Church, *etc.* 1825. 8°. **1119.** f. **9.**

—— —— 1826. 8°. **1119.** f. **10.**

—— —— 1826. 12°. **3939.** b. **15.**

—— *See* BLOMFIELD (Charles J.) successively *Bishop of Chester* and *of London.* A Letter to Charles Butler, Esq. . . . in vindication of English Protestants from his attack upon their sincerity in the "Book of the Roman Catholic Church." 1825. 8°. **3938.** c. **11.**

—— —— 1825. 8°. **3938.** c. **10.**

BUTLER (CHARLES) *Barrister-at-Law.*

—— *See* BLOMFIELD (Charles J.) successively *Bishop of Chester* and *of London.* A Letter to Charles Butler . . . Third edition. To which is added, a postscript, in reply to Mr. Butler's letter to the author. 1825. 8°. **T. 1002. (17.)**

—— —— 1825. 8°. **3940. h. 5. (5.)**

—— *See* CRANMER (Thomas) *Archbishop of Canterbury.* A Defence of the True and Catholick Doctrine of the Sacrament of the Body and Blood of our Saviour Christ . . . To which is prefixed an introduction, historical and critical . . . in vindication of the character of the author, and therewith of the Reformation in England, against some of the allegations . . . made by . . . C. Butler [in his "Book of the Roman Catholic Church"] . . . By the Rev. H. J. Todd. 1825. 8°. **1119. f. 6.**

—— *See* JEWEL (John) *Bishop of Salisbury.* An Apology for the Church of England . . . Faithfully translated from the original Latin . . . by the Reverend S. Isaacson. To which is prefixed . . . a Preliminary Discourse on the Doctrine and Discipline of the Church of Rome; in reply to some observations of C. Butler, Esq., addressed to Dr. Southey, on his Book of the Church. 1825. 8°. **1120. f. 11.**

—— *See* JUNIOR, *pseud.* Two Letters addressed to the Author of the 'Book of the Roman Catholic Church,' upon certain passages in his book, *etc.* 1825. 8°. **T. 1002. (15.)**

—— *See* PHILLPOTTS (Henry) *Bishop of Exeter.* Letters to Charles Butler, Esq., on the theological parts of his Book of the Roman Catholic Church, *etc.* 1825. 8°. **1119. e. 13. (1.)**

—— —— 1866. 8°. **3939. bb. 36.**

—— *See* TOWNSEND (George) *Canon of Durham.* The Accusations of History against the Church of Rome examined, in remarks on many of the principal observations in the work of Mr. Charles Butler, entitled the "Book of the Roman Catholic Church." 1825. 8°. **1119. f. 7.**

—— —— 1826. 8°. **3938. cc. 42.**

—— A Letter to Charles Butler, Esq. . . . containing brief observations upon his question, What has England gained by the Reformation? By a True Catholic. [A criticism of "The Book of the Roman Catholic Church."] pp. 26. *Hatchard & Son: London,* 1825. 8°. **T. 1002. (13.)**

—— A Connected Series of Notes on the Chief Revolutions of the Principal States which composed the Empire of Charlemagne, from his coronation in 814, to its dissolution in 1806: on the genealogies of the imperial house of Habsburgh, and of the six secular Electors of Germany, *etc.* pp. xvi. 296. *J. White: London,* 1807. 8°. **981. g. 10.**

—— [Another copy.] **1055. k. 1.**

—— [Another copy.] FEW MS. NOTES AND CORRECTIONS [by F. Hargrave]. **591. d. 16.**

—— A Continuation of the Rev. Alban Butler's Lives of the Saints to the present time: with bibliographical accounts of the Holy Family, Pope Pius VI. . . . and historical minutes of the Society of Jesus. pp. xvi. 40. 232. cxxxix. *Keating & Brown: London,* 1823. 8°. **1232. d. 24.**

BUTLER (CHARLES) *Barrister-at-Law.*

—— *See* BUTLER (Alban) Indice cronologico delle cose principali contenute nelle Vite, nella Continuazione, *etc.* [An index to "The Lives of the Fathers" by A. Butler, and the Continuation thereof by C. Butler.] 1826. 8°. **4826. cc. 5.**

—— An Essay on the Legality of Impressing Seamen. [By C. Butler.] pp. 126. 1777. 8°. *See* ESSAY. **517. c. 8. (2.)**

—— The second edition with additions. pp. xi. 138. *T. Cadell: London,* 1778. 8°. **E. 2097*. (4.)**

—— [Another copy.] **517. c. 19. (2.)**

—— On the Legality of Impressing Seamen . . . The third edition; with additions, partly by Lord Sandwich. pp. 63. 1824. *See* PERIODICAL PUBLICATIONS.—*London.* The Pampleteer, *etc.* vol. 23. 1813, *etc.* 8°. **P.P.3557. w.**

—— Historical Account of the Laws respecting Roman Catholics, and of the laws passed for their relief; with observations on the laws remaining in force against them: being the last note in that part of the new edition upon Coke Littleton, which is executed by Mr. Butler. pp. 45. *J. P. Coghlan: London,* 1795. 8°. **115. f. 55.**

—— An Historical and Literary Account of the Formularies, Confessions of Faith, or Symbolic Books, of the Roman Catholic, Greek, and principal Protestant Churches. By the author of the Horæ Biblicæ, and intended as a supplement to that work . . . To which are added four essays. I. A succinct historical account of the religious orders of the Church of Rome. II. Observations on the restriction imposed by the Church of Rome on the general reading of the Bible in the vulgar tongue. III. The principles of Roman-catholics in regard to God and the King, first published in 1684 . . . IV. On the reunion of Christians. pp. xv. 200. *Longman & Co.: London,* 1816. 8°. **692. c. 15.**

—— Historical Memoirs respecting the English, Irish and Scottish Catholics from the Reformation to the present time. (Additions to the Historical Memoirs, *etc.*) 4 vol. *John Murray: London,* 1819–21. 8°. **487.c.13,14.**

—— [Another edition.] Historical Memoirs of the English, Irish, and Scottish Catholics since the Reformation; with a succinct account of the principal events in the ecclesiastical history of this country antecedent to that period, and in the histories of the Established Church, and the dissenting and evangelical congregations . . . Third edition, corrected, revised, and considerably augmented. 4 vol. *John Murray: London,* 1822. 8°. **2212. bb. 4.**

—— *See* M., J., *Rev., D.D., F.S.A.* Supplementary Memoirs of English Catholics, addressed to Charles Butler, Esq., author of the Historical Memoirs of the English Catholics. By the Rev. J. M., D.D., F.S.A. [i.e. John Milner, Bishop of Castabala.] 1820. 8°. **487. c. 17.**

—— Horæ Biblicæ. (Part the second, containing a connected series of notes on the Koran, Zend-Avesta, Vedas, Kings and Edda.) 2 pt. [*Printed for private circulation: London,*] 1797, 1802. 8°. **1004. i. 18.**

—— [Another copy of pt. 2.] **B. 706. (8.)**

—— (The second edition.) 2 pt. COPIOUS MS. NOTES [by R. Gough]. *Oxford; J. White: London,* 1799, 1807. 8°. **1412. d. 1, 2.**

The words "The second edition" are taken from the title-page of pt. 2.

—— [Another copy of pt. 1.] **1016. k. 10.**

— [Another copy of pt. 1.] **1016**. k. **11**.

— [Another copy of pt. 1.] **219**. g. **12**.

— Third edition, corrected [of pt. 1 only]. pp. viii. 168. *R. E. Mercier & Co.: Dublin*, 1799. 8°. **1009**. c. **35**.

— The fourth edition. 2 vol. *J. White: London*, 1807. 8°. G. **19880**.
Vol. 2 is of the second edition.

— Horæ Biblicæ, ou Recherches littéraires sur la Bible, son texte original, ses éditions & ses traductions les plus anciennes & les plus curieuses. Ouvrage traduit de l'anglois. [A translation of pt. 1 only by A. M. H. Boulard.] pp. ii. 310. *Paris*, 1810. 8°. **1007**. g. **18**.

— Appendix to part I. Two Dissertations. I. On the truth of the Narrative [by Samuel Brett] of a Great Council of the Jews in the plain of Ageda in Hungary . . . with the Narrative subjoined. II. A short historical outline of the disputes respecting the authenticity of the verse of the Three Heavenly Witnesses of 1 John, chap. v. ver. 7. [A separate issue of the Appendix printed in pt. 2 of the second edition of "Horae Biblicae."] [*London*, 1807.] 8°. **1016**. k. **12**.

— Historical Outline of the Controversy respecting the text of the Three Heavenly Witnesses. [Extracted from the Appendix of "Horæ Biblicæ."] 1823. *See* SPARKS (Jared) A Collection of Essays and Tracts in Theology, *etc.* vol. 2. 1823, *etc.* 12°. **1357**. a. **2**.

— Horæ Juridicæ Subsecivæ: a connected series of notes, respecting the geography, chronology, and literary history, of the principal codes, and original documents, of the Grecian, Roman, feudal and canon law. pp. xv. 136. *Brooke & Clarke: London*, 1804. 8°. **959**. b. **6**.

— [Another copy.] **508**. c. **28**. (**2**.)

— The second edition. pp. xvi. 238. *J. White: London*, 1807. 8°. G. **1277**.

— The Inaugural Oration, spoken on the 4th day of November 1815, at the ceremony of laying the first stone of the London Institution for the Diffusion of Science and Literature. pp. 42. *Longman & Co.: London*, 1816. 8°. T. **1166**. (**4**.)

— [Another copy.] **733**. d. **7**. (**3**.)

— [Another copy.] B. **727**. (**14**.)

— [Another copy.] **117**. e. **42**.

— [Another edition.] 1816. *See* PERIODICAL PUBLICATIONS.—*London*. The Pamphleteer, *etc.* vol. 7. 1813, *etc.* 8°. P.P. **3557**. w.

— A Letter on the Coronation Oath: second edition. With notice of the recently published letters of the late King to Lord Kenyon, and his Lordship's answers; and letters of the late Mr. Pitt to the late King, and the late King's answers. pp. 15. *John Murray: London*, 1827. 8°. T. **1190**. (**12**.)

— *See* PHILLPOTTS (Henry) *Bishop of Exeter.* A Letter to an English Layman, on the Coronation Oath . . . in which are considered the several opinions of Mr. Jeffrey . . . Mr. C. Butler, *etc.* 1828. 8°. **1119**. e. **14**.

— A Short Reply to Doctor Phillpotts' Answer—in his "Letter to a Layman"—to Mr. Butler's Letter on the Coronation Oath. With a third edition, I. of that letter; and II., of Mr. Butler's letter on the alleged divided allegiance of English Catholics to their King. pp. 41. *John Murray: London*, 1828. 8°. T. **1231**. (**15**.)

— A Letter to a Nobleman, on the proposed repeal of the penal laws which now remain in force against the Irish Roman Catholics. pp. 16. *Coghlan: London*, [1801.] 8°. B. **505**. (**11**.)

— [Another copy.] **108**. d. **9**.

— Second edition. pp. 14. 2. *John Shea: Dublin*, 1801. 8°. **3942**. d. **66**.

— A Letter to a Roman Catholic Gentleman of Ireland, on the Chief Consul Buonaparte's projected invasion. pp. 16. *J. White: London*, 1803. 8°. G. **4803**. (**4**.)

— A Letter to an Irish Catholic Gentleman on the Fifth Resolution entered into at the Meeting of the English Catholics, on the first of February 1810, and accompanying the Roman Catholic Petition. pp. 43. *J. Booker: London*, 1811. 8°. **3938**. bb. **6**.

— *See* MILNER (John) *Bishop of Castabala.* Letters to a Roman Catholic Prelate of Ireland, in refutation of Counsellor Charles Butler's Letter to an Irish Catholic Gentleman, *etc.* 1811. 8°. **3942**. b. **76**. (**3**.)

— A Letter to the Right Reverend C. J. Blomfield, D.D., Bishop of Chester: from Charles Butler, Esq., in vindication of a passage in his "Book of the Roman-Catholic Church," censured in a letter addressed to him by his lordship. pp. 26. *John Murray: London*, 1825. 8°. **3940**. h. **6**. (**3**.)

— Second edition, revised and enlarged. pp. 15. 1825. *See* PERIODICAL PUBLICATIONS.—*London.* The Pamphleteer, *etc.* vol. 25. 1813, *etc.* 8°. P.P. **3557**. w.

— Third edition, revised and enlarged. pp. 31. *John Murray: London*, 1825. 8°. T. **1002**. (**16**.)

— The Life of Erasmus: with historical remarks on the state of literature between the tenth and sixteenth centuries. pp. ix. 244. *John Murray: London*, 1825. 8°. **489**. g. **19**.

— The Life of Fenelon, Archbishop of Cambray. pp. 236. *P. H. Nicklin & Co.: Baltimore*, 1811. 12°. **862**. i. **26**.

— The third edition. To which are added, the lives of St. Vincent of Paul, and Henri-Marie de Boudon: a letter on antient and modern music; and historical minutes of the Society of Jesus. pp. 316. *John Murray: London*, 1819. 8°. **489**. g. **24**.

— The Life of Hugo Grotius: with brief minutes of the civil, ecclesiastical, and literary history of the Netherlands. pp. x. 259. *John Murray: London*, 1826. 8°. **612**. f. **4**.

— The Lives of Dom Armand-Jean Le Bouthillier de Rancé, Abbot Regular and reformer of the Monastery of La Trappe; and of Thomas à Kempis . . . With some account of the principal religious and military orders of the Roman Catholic Church. pp. 163. *Longman & Co.: London*, 1814. 8°. **487**. b. **26**.

— A Memoir of the Catholic Relief Bill, passed in 1829; a preliminary minute of all the divisions in each House of Parliament, on the Catholic Claims, subsequent to the year 1778, when they were first urged: being a sequel and conclusion of the "Historical Memoirs of the English, Irish, and Scottish Catholics." pp. 45. *John Murray: London*, 1829. 8°. T. **1260**. (**10**.)

BUTLER (Charles) *Barrister-at-Law.*

—— Memoir of the Life of Henry-Francis d'Aguesseau, Chancellor of France; and of his ordonnances for consolidating and amending certain portions of the French law: and an historical and literary account of the Roman and canon law. Fourth edition. pp. 207. *John Murray: London,* 1830. 8°. **1130**. e. **30**.

—— On the Legality of Impressing Seamen. *See* supra: An Essay on the Legality of Impressing Seamen.

—— Reminiscences of Charles Butler, Esq. 2 vol. *John Murray: London,* 1822, 27. 8°. **613**. g. **4**. & **613**. g. **5**. (**2**.)

—— [Another copy of vol. 2.] **10854**. bb. **5**. (**2**.)

—— Third edition, considerably augmented. pp. xi. 381. *John Murray: London,* 1822. 8°. **613**. g. **5**. (**1**.)
Vol. 2 was not published in this edition.

—— Fourth edition, with a Letter to a Lady on ancient and modern music. pp. xi. 404. *John Murray: London,* 1824. 8°. **10854**. bb. **5**. (**1**.)
Vol. 2 was not published in this edition.

—— Reply to the Article [by Robert Southey] in the Quarterly Review for March 1826 on the Revelations of La Sœur Nativité. pp. 23. *John Murray: London,* 1826. 8°. T. **1011**. (**18**.)

—— Undivided Allegiance of Roman Catholics to their Sovereigns. By C. B. [i.e. C. Butler.] [1825?] *s. sh.* fol. *See* B., C. 1879.cc.15.(133.)

—— Vindication of "The Book of the Roman Catholic Church," against the Reverend George Townsend's "Accusations of History against the Church of Rome": with notice of some charges brought against "The Book of the Roman Catholic Church," in the publications of Doctor Phillpotts, the Rev. John Todd . . . the Rev. Stephen Isaacson . . . the Rev. Joseph Blanco White . . . and in some anonymous publications . . . With copies of Doctor Phillpotts's Fourth Letter to Mr. Butler, containing a charge against Dr. Lingard; and of a Letter of Doctor Lingard to Mr. Butler, in reply to the charge. pp. lxxi. 248. *John Murray: London,* 1826. 8°. **1119**. f. **11**.

—— Appendix to Mr. Butler's Vindication of "The Book of the Roman Catholic Church," in reply to Dr. Southey's preface to his "Vindiciæ Ecclesiæ Anglicanæ." pp. 11. *John Murray: London,* 1826. 8°. T. **1004**. (**6**.)

—— *See* Southey (Robert) [*Book of the Church.*] Vindiciæ Ecclesiæ Anglicanæ. Letters to Charles Butler, Esq., comprising essays on the Romish religion and vindicating "The Book of the Church." 1826. 8°. **487**. c. **11**.

—— *See* Todd (Henry J.) A Vindication of . . . Thomas Cranmer . . . against some of the allegations which have been recently made by the Rev. Dr. Lingard . . . and C. Butler . . . With notices of . . . Mr. Butler's remarks [in his "Vindication"] on the first edition. 1826. 12°. **1124**. b. **18**.

—— *See* Townsend (George) *Canon of Durham.* Supplementary Letter to Charles Butler, Esq., in reply to his Vindication of the Book of the Roman Catholic Church, *etc.* 1826. 8°. T. **1192**. (**15**.)

—— "The Irish Catholic Board and Charles Butler, Esq." (Extract from the Kilkenny Chronicle.) pp. 3. *London,* [1813.] 8°. **3942**. b. **31**.

BUTLER (Charles) *LL.D. See* Prentiss (George L.) The Union Theological Seminary in the City of New York . . . With a sketch of the life and public services of C. Butler. [With a portrait.] 1899. 8°. **8366**. e. **45**.

BUTLER (Charles) *of Philadelphia.* The American Gentleman. pp. 288. *Hogan & Thompson: Philadelphia,* 1849. 8°. **8405**. b. **33**.
With an additional titlepage, engraved.

—— The American Lady. pp. 288. *Hogan & Thompson: Philadelphia,* 1849. 8°. **8415**. c. **35**.
With an additional titlepage, engraved.

BUTLER (Charles) *Teacher of the Mathematics at Cheam School.* An Easy Introduction to Algebra, with notes . . . To which is prefixed, an essay on the uses of the mathematics, *etc.* pp. xxix. 282. *S. Staunton: London,* 1799. 12°. **8506**. ccc. **4**.

—— An Easy Introduction to the Mathematics; in which the theory and practice are laid down and familiarly explained. To each subject are prefixed, a brief popular history of its rise and progress, concise memoirs of noted mathematical authors, ancient and modern, *etc.* 2 vol. *Bartlett & Newman: Oxford,* 1814. 8°. **529**. h. **24**.

BUTLER (Charles) *Vicar of Wotton. See* Eichler (A.) Schriftbild und Lautwert in Charles Butler's English Grammar, 1633, 1634, und Feminin' Monarchi', 1634. 1913. 8°. [*Neudrucke frühneuenglischer Grammatiken.* Bd. 4. Hft. 2.] **12985**. g. **26/4**.

—— *See* La Ramée (P. de) Rameæ Rhetoricæ libri duo. In vsum scholarum. [Edited by C. Butler.] 1597. 8°. **1090**. b. **18**. (**2**.)

—— *See* Money (Frank R.) Charles Butler, Vicar of Wootton, 1600–1647, *etc.* [1952.] 8°. **4909**. cc. **6**.

—— The English Grammar, or the Institution of Letters, Syllables, and Words, in the English tongue. Whereunto is annexed an Index of words like and unlike. pp. 63. *William Turner for the Authour: Oxford,* 1633. 4°. C. **40**. e. **3**.

—— [A reissue.] The English Grammar, or the Institution of letters, syllables, and woords in the English tung. Wher'unto is annexed an Index of woords lik' and unlik'. *William Turner for the Author: Oxford,* 1634. 4°. G. **7509**. (**1**.)
A duplicate of the preceding with a new titlepage, and with the prefatory matter printed in Butler's reformed spelling.

—— [Another edition.] Charles Butler's English Grammar, 1634. Herausgegeben von Dr. A. Eichler. pp. xix. 134. *Halle,* 1910. 8°. [*Neudrucke frühneuenglischer Grammatiken.* Bd. 4. Hft. 1.] **12985**. g. **26/4**.

—— The Feminine Monarchie. Or a Treatise concerning bees, and the due ordering of them, *etc. Printed by Ioseph Barnes: Oxford,* 1609. 8°. **730**. a. **38**.

—— [Another copy.] **972**. h. **36**.
Imperfect; wanting the titlepage, preface, and all before sig. b. *Cropped.*

—— [Another edition.] The Feminine Monarchie: or, the Historie of bees . . . Together with the right ordering of them from time to time: and the sweet profit arising thereof, *etc. Iohn Hauiland for Roger Iackson: London,* 1623. 4°. **967**. i. **4**. (**3**.)

—— [Another edition.] The Feminin' Monarchi', or the Histori of bee's, *etc.* pp. 182. *William Turner, for the Author: Oxford,* 1634. 4°. **453**. a. **40**.
This edition is printed in Butler's reformed spelling.

BUTLER (Charles) *Vicar of Wotton.*

—— [Another copy.] The Feminin' Monarchi', *etc. Oxford,* 1634. 4°. Hirsch I. **95.**

—— [Another copy.] C. **27.** h. **7.**

—— [Another copy.] **40.** b. **22.**

—— [Another copy.] G. **7509.** (**2.**)

—— [Another copy.] G. **19197.**

—— Monarchia Fœminina, sive Apum Historia, enarrans naturam ipsarum mirabilem & proprietates; generationem & colonias; politiam, fidem, artem, industriam; hostes, bella, magnanimitatem, &c. Unâ cum Legitimo earum cultu, fructuque dulcissimo. Nunc . . . Interprete R. Ricardi F. [i.e. R. Richardson] . . . Latinitate donata. pp. 199. *Typis A. C. Impensis Authoris: Londini,* 1673. 8°. **450.** b. **45.**

—— [Another edition.] The Feminine Monarchy; or, the History of bees . . . Written in Latin by Charles Butler, and now translated into English by W. S. [or rather, translated from the Latin version of R. Richardson.] To which is added some observations of silk worms, *etc.* pp. 150. *A. Baldwin: London,* 1704. 12°. **7296.** a. **6.**

—— The Principles of Musik, in Singing and Setting: with the two-fold use thereof, ecclesiasticall and civil. pp. 135. *Iohn Haviland for the Author: London,* 1636. 4°. G. **7509.** (**3.**)

—— [Another copy.] The Principles of Musik, *etc. London,* 1636. 4°. Hirsch I. **96.**

—— [Another copy.] **52.** d. **30.**
Imperfect; wanting the last leaf, which is supplied in MS.

—— Rhetoricæ libri duo . . . in vsum scholarum accuratius editi. *Excudebat Josephus Barnesius: Oxoniæ,* 1600. 8°. **1090.** b. **18.** (**1.**)

—— Rhetoricæ libri duo . . . jam quartò editi. *Excudebant Iohannes Lichfield & Iacobus Short: Oxoniæ,* 1618. 8°. **11805.** b. **48.**

—— [Another edition.] Quibus recens accesserunt de oratoria libri duo. *Excudebat Ioannes Haviland impensis Authoris: Londini,* 1629. 4°. **11805.** d. **3.**
Without the two additional books " De oratoria."

—— [Another edition.] pp. 153. *Excudebat R. H.: Londini,* 1642. 8°. **11825.** aa. **1.**
The titlepage is slightly mutilated.

—— [Another edition.] pp. 160. *T. D.: Lugduni Batavorum,* 1642. 12°. **1088.** d. **2.**

—— [Another edition.] pp. 160. *Ex officina Guilielmi Bentley, pro Johanne Williams: Londini,* 1649. 12°. **1089.** a. **14.**

—— [Another edition.] pp. 160. *Ex officina Guilielmi Bentley, pro Andr. Crook: Londini,* 1655. 12°. **1090.** a. **15.**

—— *Συγγενεια.* De Propinquitate Matrimonium impediente, Regula. Quæ vna omnes quæstionis huius difficultates facilè expediat. pp. 71. *Excudebant Iohannes Lichfield & Guilielmus Turner: Oxoniæ,* 1625. 4°. **498.** b. **25.** (**1.**)

—— [Another edition.] *See* Florens (F.) Francisci Florentis . . . Tractatus de nuptiis consobrinarum, *etc.* 1643. 8°. **5176.** aa. **38.**

BUTLER (Charles Edward)

—— Cut Is the Branch, *etc.* [Poems.] pp. 61. *Yale University Press: New Haven,* 1945. 8°. [*Yale Series of Younger Poets.*] W.P. **6198/43.**

—— Follow me ever. A novel. pp. 158. *Secker & Warburg: London,* 1952. 8°. **12730.** s. **49.**

BUTLER (Charles Ewart) Directory of Musical Education. Part I. Being a guide to choir schools and choral foundations for boys, university degrees in music, *etc.* pp. 74. *Novello & Co.: London,* [1903.] 8°. **7899.** g. **38.**

—— Sermons on Christian Life & Hope, principally preached in Llandaff Cathedral. pp. vi. 84. *Bemrose & Sons: London,* [1888.] 8°. **4479.** c. **38.**

BUTLER (Charles George) An Essay on Military Sketching. pp. 16. *Parker, Furnivall & Parker: London,* 1854. 4°. **8820.** g. **10.**

BUTLER (Charles Henry) *Mathematician,* and **WREN** (Frank Lynwood)

—— The Teaching of Secondary Mathematics. pp. xii. 514. *New York & London,* 1941. 8°. [*McGraw-Hill Series in Education.*] W.P. **12179/29.**

—— The Teaching of Secondary Mathematics . . . Second edition. pp. xiv. 550. *McGraw-Hill Book Co.: New York,* 1951. 8°. [*McGraw-Hill Series in Education.*] W.P. **12179/73.**

BUTLER (Charles Henry) *of the New York Bar.*

—— *See* United States of America. [*Treaties, etc.—Separate Treaties.*] Our Treaty with Spain . . . Annotated by C. H. Butler. 1898. 8°. **8176.** c. **4.** (**2.**)

—— *See* United States of America.—*Supreme Court.* Reports of Cases . . . in the Supreme Court, *etc.* (vol. 187–247. October Term, 1902—October Term, 1915. C. H. Butler, reporter.) 1804, *etc.* 8°. **6622.pp.1.**

—— Freedom of Private Property on the Sea from Capture during War. A compilation of documents in relation, and opinions in regard, thereto . . . Special advance sheets. pp. 45. *D. Taylor & Co.: New York,* 1898. 8°. **06955.** g. **24.** (**5.**)

—— A Letter addressed to Captain A. T. Mahan in regard to freedom of private property on the sea from capture during war. [In answer to a letter by Captain Mahan in the "New York Times."] pp. 7. *Washington,* 1898. 8°. **06755.** g. **24.** (**6.**)

—— Letter addressed to the Hon. Gustav H. Schwab . . . in regard to freedom of private property on the sea from capture during war. pp. 10. *Washington,* 1898. 8°. **06955.** g. **24.** (**7.**)

—— A Memorial to the President of the United States, urging him to convene an International Congress at Washington, to consider the question of making private property on the sea free from capture during war. pp. 9. 1898. 8°. **06955.** g. **24.** (**4.**)

—— The Treaty-Making Power of the United States. 2 vol. *Banks Law Publishing Co.: New York,* 1902. 8°. **06955.** g. **36.**

—— A Twelve Mile Phantasy. An epic of the " Berengaria," *etc.* [An account in verse of the visit of the American Bar Association to London, July 1924. With plates.] pp. 16. *G. P. Putnam's Sons: London & New York,* [1924.] 4°. **11686.** i. **42.**

BUTLER (Charles Henry) *of the New York Bar.*

—— The Voice of the Nation. The President is right. A series of papers on our past and present relations with Spain. pp. 124. *G. Munro's Sons: New York*, 1898. 8°. **8175**. ee. **37**.

BUTLER (Charles MacArthur) The Society of Architects, *etc.* [A history. With plates.] pp. 94. [1926.] 8°. *See* London.—iii. *Society of Architects.* **07815**. g. **22**.

BUTLER (Charles Pritchard)

—— *See* Lockyer (*Sir* Joseph N.) *K.C.B.* On the Origin of certain Lines in the Spectrum of ϵ Orionis (Alnitam). By Sir N. Lockyer . . . C. P. Butler. [1909.] 4°. **8561**. k. **22**. (**3**.)

—— The Large Eruptive Prominence of 1915 April 19, *etc.* (Reprinted from the Monthly Notices of the Royal Astronomical Society.) [With a plate.] *Edinburgh*, [1915.] 8°. **8562**. eee. **47**.

—— Systematic Distribution of Solar Calcium Flocculi. (i. Inclination of Elongated Groups. ii. Life History of bright Solar Calcium Flocculi. Reprinted from the Monthly Notices of the Royal Astronomical Society.) [With plates.] 2 pt. *Edinburgh*, [1922, 24.] 8°. **8562**. ee. **28**.

BUTLER (Charles Stokes) Antiquities of the Book of Common Prayer, a lecture . . . With preface by the Rev. C. F. S. Money. pp. 23. *Christian Book Society: London*, 1877. 16°. **3478**. aaa. **19**.

BUTLER (Charles William) The Garden Gate, and other poems. pp. 156. *H. L. Shepard & Co.: Boston*, 1874. 12°. **11687**. e. **24**.

BUTLER (Christina Violet) Domestic Service. An enquiry by the Women's Industrial Council. Report by C. V. Butler. With a supplementary chapter by Lady Willoughby de Broke. pp. 148. 1916. 8°. *See* London.—iii. *Women's Industrial Council.* **08282**. c. **44**.

—— Social Conditions in Oxford. pp. vii. 262. *Sidgwick & Jackson: London*, 1912. 8°. **08276**. aa. **66**.

BUTLER (Christopher)

—— Ante-Nicene Christianity. pp. 40. *Catholic Truth Society: London*, 1934. 8°. [*Studies in Comparative Religion.* no. 22.] **3943**. aa. **45/22**.

BUTLER (Clement Moore) *See* Brittan (S. B.) The Tables Turned: a brief review of Rev. C. M. Butler [i.e. of a sermon by him entitled "Modern Necromancy"]. 1854. 12°. **8631**. d. **42**. (**2**.)

—— Analogies between God's World and Word. *See* Potter (Alonzo) *Bishop of the Protestant Episcopal Church in Pennsylvania.* Lectures on the Evidences of Christianity, *etc.* 1855. 8°. **4016**. f. **42**.

—— The Book of Common Prayer interpreted by its history. pp. 299. *J. B. Dow: Boston*, 1845. 12°. **3475**. b. **33**.

—— An Ecclesiastical History from the first to the thirteenth century. pp. xv. 600. *Claxton, Remsen & Haffelfinger: Philadelphia*, 1868. 8°. **4530**. bb. **18**.

—— Inner Rome: political, religious, and social. pp. xvi. 9–351. *J. B. Lippincott & Co.: Philadelphia*, 1866. 8°. **010136**. df. **5**.

—— Mission of the Protestant Episcopal Church in Boston. A farewell sermon, delivered in Grace Church, Boston, *etc.* pp. 26. *J. R. Dow: Boston*, 1847. 8°. **4486**. h. **41**.

BUTLER (Clement Moore)

—— Our Union—God's Gift. A discourse, delivered in Trinity Church, Washington, D.C., on Thanksgiving Day, November 28, 1850. pp. 29. *J. T. Towers: Washington*, 1850. 8°, **4485**. i. **46**.

—— The Reformation in Sweden; its rise, progress, and crisis; and its triumph under Charles ix. pp. iv. 259. *A. D. F. Randolph & Co.: New York*, 1883. 8°. **4685**. bb. **11**.

—— The Ritualism of Law, in the Protestant Episcopal Church of the United States. pp. 180. *Mrs. J. Hamilton: Philadelphia*, 1867. 12°. **4183**. aa. **46**.

—— St. Paul in Rome: lectures delivered in the Legation of the United States of America, in Rome. pp. 295. *J. B. Lippincott & Co.: Philadelphia*, 1865. 12°. **4823**. c. **10**.

—— A Sermon delivered at the request of the Board of Missions of the Diocese of Massachusetts, in St. Paul's Church, Boston, *etc.* pp. 22. *Dutton & Wentworth: Boston*, 1844. 8°. **4486**. h. **40**.

—— A Sermon preached in the Senate Chamber April 2, 1850 at the funeral of the Hon. J. C. Calhoun, *etc.* *See* United States of America.—*Senate.* Obituary Addresses delivered on the occasion of the death of the Hon. J. C. Calhoun, *etc.* 1850. 8°. 10880. e. 4.

—— [Another edition.] *See* Foster (Thomas) *Publisher*, and Cochran (G.) Eulogies delivered in the Senate and House of Representatives of the United States, *etc.* 1853. 8°. **10880**. ee. **9**.

—— The Strong Staff broken and the Beautiful Rod. A sermon on the occasion of the funeral of Henry Clay. *See* United States of America.—*Congress.* Obituary Addresses on the occasion of the death of the Hon. H. Clay, *etc.* 1852. 8°. 10880. e. 38.

—— [Another edition.] *See* Foster (Thomas) *Publisher*, and Cochran (G.) Eulogies, delivered in the Senate and House of Representatives of the United States, *etc.* 1853. 8°. **10880**. ee. **9**.

—— "A Wise Man is Strong." A sermon on the death of Daniel Webster, delivered in Trinity Church, Washington, *etc.* pp. 32. *W. M. Morrison & Co.: Washington*, 1852. 8°. **10882**. d. **24**. (**11**.)

—— The Year of the Church: hymns and devotional verse for the Sundays and Holy Days of the ecclesiastical year; with brief explanations of their origin and design. pp. 166. *Eli Maynard: Utica*, 1839. 12°. **3440**. b. **43**.

BUTLER (Clementina) Pandita Ramabai Sarasvati, pioneer in the movement for the education of the child-widow of India. [With plates, including portraits.] pp. 96. *F. H. Revell Co.: New York*, [1922.] 8°. **10607**. ee. **10**.

BUTLER (Colin Gasking)

—— Bee-Hives. pp. ii. 19. pl. iv. *London*, 1949. 8°. [*Ministry of Agriculture and Fisheries. Bulletin.* no. 144.] B.S. **3/75**.

—— Bee-Hives. (Second edition.) pp. iv. 20. pl. iv. *London*, 1952. 8°. [*Ministry of Agriculture and Fisheries. Bulletin.* no. 144.] B.S. **3/75**.

—— Beekeeping. (Eighth edition.) pp. 27. *London*, 1951. 8°. [*Ministry of Agriculture and Fisheries. Bulletin.* no. 9.] B.S. **3/75**.

BUTLER (Colin Gasking)

—— The Honeybee. An introduction to her sense-physiology and behaviour. pp. vi. 139. pl. vi. *Clarendon Press: Oxford*, 1949. 8°. **7296**. aa. **40**.

—— An Introduction to Beekeeping . . . Fully illustrated, *etc.* pp. 23. *Daily Mail School-Aid Department: London*, [1948.] 8°. [*Young Britain Educational Series.*] W.P. **1352/12**.

—— The World of the Honeybee, *etc.* pp. xiv. 226. pl. ii. 40. *Collins: London*, 1954. 8°. [*New Naturalist.*] W.P. **463/34**.

BUTLER (Constance) Illyria, Lady. [A novel.] pp. 228. *L. & V. Woolf: London*, 1934. 8°. NN. **22986**.

—— Square Pegs. A study of non-combatants. pp. 222. *Jonathan Cape: London*, 1947. 8°. NN. **37459**.

BUTLER (*Lady* Constance Mary) *See* Jesus Christ.—*Abbey of St. Saviour, at Duiske, co. Kilkenny.* The Charters of the Cistercian Abbey of Duiske . . . Transcribed by C. M. Butler, *etc.* 1918. 8°. [*Proceedings of the Royal Irish Academy.* vol. 35. sect. C. no. 1.] Ac. **1540/4**.

BUTLER (Cornelius) Dissertatio medica inauguralis de angina. pp. 18. *Lugduni Batavorum*, 1726. 4°. **1185**. i. **2**. (**17**.)

BUTLER (Cuthbert) *See* Butler (Edward C.)

BUTLER (D.) *Minister of the Church of England.* A Sermon occasionally preach'd on the Funeral of Sir Cloudesly Shovel, *etc.* pp. 8. *Thomas Smith: London*, 1707. 8°. **225**. g. **17**. (**7**.)

BUTLER (D. H.)

—— Metallic Arc Welds in Alpha-Phase Aluminium Bronze. pp. 11. *London*, 1950. 4°. [*British Non-Ferrous Metals Research Association. Research Reports, Association Series.* no. 877.] W.P. **3939/11**.

—— Metallic Arc Welds in Complex, 80/10/5/5, Aluminium Bronze. pp. 7. *London*, 1950. 4°. [*British Non-Ferrous Metals Research Association. Research Reports, Association Series.* no. 876.] W.P. **3939/12**.

BUTLER (D. P.) Butler's System of Physical Training. The lifting cure: an original, scientific application of the laws of motion or mechanical action to physical culture and the cure of disease, *etc.* pp. 104. *D. P. Butler: Boston*, 1868. 8°. **7460**. f. **13**.

BUTLER (Daniel) The Gospel Harvest. *See* Watson (Alexander) *Vicar of St. Marychurch.* Sermons for Sundays, Festivals and Fasts. ser. 1. 1845, *etc.* 8°. **1358**. f. **21**.

—— The Minister's Parting Prayer for his People. A sermon, *etc.* pp. 20. *Rivingtons: London*, 1855. 8°. **4476**. c. **20**.

—— The Old Paths of the Church of England. A sermon, *etc.* pp. 15. *F. & J. Rivington: London*, 1850. 8°. **4326**. d. **15**.

BUTLER (David) *Captain.* Extract uyt den brief geschreven in de Stadt Ispahan, van D. Butler. Den 6 maert, 1671 *See* Struys (J.) Drie aanmerkelijke en seer rampspoedige reysen, *etc.* 1676. 4°. **10025**. d. **19**.

—— [Another edition.] *See* Struys (J.) Drie aanmerkelijke en seer rampspoedige reysen, *etc.* 1686. 4°. **790**. f. **1**.

BUTLER (David) *Captain.*

—— The Copy of a Narrativ, sent from Capt. D. Butler, dated at Ispahan, March 6th, 1671. *See* Struys (J.) The Voiages and Travels of John Struys, *etc.* 1684. 4°. **303**. k. **13**.

—— Copie d'une lettre de David Butler, écrite à Ispahan le 6 de mars 1671 touchant la prise d'Astracan. *See* Struys (J.) Les Voyages de Jean Struys, *etc.* 1681. 4°. **981**. e. **11**.

—— Copia oder Abschrifft eines Brieffes, geschrieben in . . . Ispahan von Capitayn David Butlern. Den 6. Martii, 1671. *See* Struys (J.) Joh. Jansz. Straussens sehr schwere, wiederwertige, und denckwürdige Reysen, *etc.* 1678. fol. **10025**. f. **17**.

BUTLER (David) *Governor of Nebraska.* Impeachment Trial of David Butler, Governor of Nebraska, at Lincoln. Messrs. Bell, Hall and Brown, official reporters. 6 pt. *Tribune Steam Book & Job Printing House: Omaha*, 1871. 8°. **6615**. df. **12**.

BUTLER (David Butler) *See* Faija (Henry) Portland Cement for Users . . . Fifth edition, revised and enlarged by D. B. Butler. 1904. 8°. **8703**. bbb. **20**.

—— British Standard Specification for Portland Cement. Revised edition, June, 1907. Diagram for ascertaining at a glance, from the analysis, the hydraulic modulus or ratio of lime to silica and alumina . . . Arranged by D. B. Butler . . . assisted by G. J. Fenwick. *J. J. Griffin & Sons: London*, 1907. *s. sh.* fol. **1802**. c. **16**.

—— Portland Cement: its manufacture, testing, and use. pp. vi. 360. *E. & F. N. Spon: London*, 1899. 8°. **7817**. h. **10**.

—— Second edition, revised and enlarged. pp. x. 396. *E. & F. N. Spon: London*, 1905. 8°. **7817**. ee. **9**.

—— Third edition, revised and enlarged, *etc.* pp. xi. 458. *E. & F. N. Spon: London; Spon & Chamberlain: New York*, 1913. 8°. **07816**. h. **39**.

BUTLER (David Henry Edgeworth)

—— *See* Nicholas (Herbert G.) The British General Election of 1950 . . . With an appendix by D. E. Butler. 1951. 8°. **08139**. ccc. **16**.

—— The British General Election of 1955. pp. 236. pl. viii. *Macmillan & Co.: London*, 1955. 8°. **8140**. ff. **23**.

—— The British General Election of 1951. pp. viii. 289. *Macmillan & Co.: London*, 1952. 8°. **8140**. aaa. **48**.

—— The Electoral System in Britain, 1918–1951. pp. xiv. 222. *Clarendon Press: Oxford*, 1953. 8°. **08139**. ccc. **21**.

BUTLER (Denis) *See* Boulenc.

BUTLER (Denis B.) Sunlight and Shadows. A book of verse. pp. 32. *A. H. Stockwell: London*, [1931.] 8°. **11640**. eee. **47**.

BUTLER (Diana) *pseud.* [i.e. Henrietta Euphemia Tindal.] The Heirs of Blackridge Manor. A tale of the past and present. 3 vol. *Chapman & Hall: London*, 1856. 8°. **12630**. d. **2**.

BUTLER (Dugald) *See* Leighton (Robert) successively *Bishop of Dunblane* and *Archbishop of Glasgow.* Archbishop Leighton's Practice of the Presence of God . . . With biographical introduction by D. Butler. 1911. 8°. **3755**. df. **19**.

BUTLER (DUGALD)

—— Address to Lady Missionaries on their Departure for the Foreign Mission Field, *etc.* pp. 7. *Church of Scotland Women's Association for Foreign Missions: Edinburgh,* [1903.] 8°. **4765**. de. **41**.

—— The Ancient Church and Parish of Abernethy. An historical study. [With plates.] pp. xiv. 524. *W. Blackwood & Sons: Edinburgh & London,* 1897. 4°. **10369**. k. **8**.

—— Eternal Elements in the Christian Faith. pp. 188. *Oliphant, Anderson & Ferrier: Edinburgh & London,* 1905. 8°. **4379**. ee. **22**.

—— George Fox in Scotland. An appreciation of the Society of Friends and its founder. pp. 132. *Oliphant, Anderson & Ferrier: Edinburgh & London,* 1913. 8°. **4920**. h. **6**.

—— Gothic Architecture: its Christian origin and inspiration. pp. 216. *Oliphant, Anderson & Ferrier: Edinburgh & London,* 1910. 8°. **07816**. aa. **3**.

—— Henry Scougal and the Oxford Methodists: or, the Influence of a religious teacher of the Scottish Church. pp. x. 151. *W. Blackwood & Sons: Edinburgh & London,* 1899. 8°. **4903**. de. **53**.

—— John Wesley and George Whitefield in Scotland: or, the Influence of the Oxford Methodists on Scottish religion. pp. vii. 318. *W. Blackwood & Sons: Edinburgh & London,* 1898. 8°. **4907**. i. **3**.

—— The Life and Letters of Robert Leighton, Restoration Bishop of Dunblane and Archbishop of Glasgow. pp. xv. 607. *Hodder & Stoughton: London,* 1903. 8°. **2216**. b. **7**.

—— Prayer in Experience; or, Prayer in the life, thought and work of Christendom. pp. 302. *Marshall Bros.: London,* [1922.] 8°. **03456**. eee. **16**.

—— Saint Cuthbert of Melrose, Lindisfarne, Farne, and Durham, Apostle of Northumbria. pp. 51. *T. N. Foulis: Edinburgh & London,* 1913. 8°. [*Iona Books.* no. 9.] **03558.de.50/9.**

—— Saint Giles, the patron saint of ancient Edinburgh. pp. 59. *T. N. Foulis: Edinburgh,* 1914. 8°. [*Iona Books.* no. 12.] **03558.de.50/13.**

—— Scottish Cathedrals and Abbeys . . . With introduction by the Very Rev. R. Herbert Story. pp. xv. 210. *A. & C. Black: London,* 1901. 8°. [*Guild Library.*] **3622**. g. **1/15**.

—— Thomas a Kempis. A religious study. pp. 192. *Oliphant, Anderson & Ferrier: Edinburgh & London,* 1908. 8°. **4888**. aaaa. **22**.

—— The Tron Kirk of Edinburgh, or Christ's Kirk at the Tron. A history. [With illustrations.] pp. 383. *Oliphant, Anderson & Ferrier: Edinburgh & London,* 1906. 4°. **4735**. eee. **25**.

—— Unity, Peace and Charity. A tercentenary lecture in St. Giles' Cathedral, Edinburgh, on Archbishop Leighton. pp. 69. *Oliphant, Anderson & Ferrier: Edinburgh & London,* 1911. 8°. **4902**. de. **25**.

BUTLER (*Mrs.* E. D.) Gardening for Amateurs in Malaya. [Articles by various authors.] Edited by Mrs. E. D. Butler. pp. 91. *Young Women's Christian Association: Singapore,* 1934. 8°. **07030**. g. **13**.

BUTLER (E. G.) Birthright of Towns Series. no. 1, 2. *E. G. Butler: Wells, Somerset,* 1930. 8°. **10351**. bbb. **55**. *No more published.*

BUTLER (EDMOND) *Captain.* An Essay on "Our Indian Question." pp. 49. *A. G. Sherwood & Co.: New York,* 1882. 8°. **8176**. e. **17**. (**2**.)

BUTLER (EDMOND) *of New York. See* SAINT-GERMAIN (J. T. de) *pseud.* The Art of Suffering . . . Translated from the French by E. Butler. 1860. 16°. **8408**. a. **42**.

BUTLER (EDMUND) *Architect. See* CROUCH (Joseph) and BUTLER (E.) The Apartments of the House, *etc.* 1900. 4°. **7817**. bbb. **19**.

—— *See* CROUCH (Joseph) and BUTLER (E.) Churches, Mission Halls and Schools for Nonconformists. 1901. 4°. **7822.e.29.**

BUTLER (EDMUND) *Process Server. See* KENNEDY (John) *of Ballygerda, Labourer.* Report of the Trial of John Kennedy, for the murder of Edmund Butler, *etc.* 1832. 8°. **1131**. d. **46**. (**3**.)

BUTLER (EDMUNDUS) Dissertatio medica inauguralis de diarrhœa. pp. 27. *Cum Typis Academicis: Edinburgi,* 1763. 8°. T. **392**. (**5**.)

BUTLER (EDWARD) *M.I.M.E. See* NORTH (Sydney H.) Oil Fuel . . . Revised throughout and greatly enlarged by E. Butler, *etc.* 1911. 8°. **08806**. aa. **9**.

—— Carburettors, Vaporisers, and Distributing Valves used in internal combustion engines, *etc.* pp. xi. 176. *C. Griffin & Co.: London,* 1909. 8°. **08767**. g. **39**.

—— Second edition, revised and enlarged, *etc.* pp. viii. 288. *C. Griffin & Co.: London,* 1919. 8°. **8763**. aaa. **4**.

—— Evolution of the Internal Combustion Engine, *etc.* pp. xiv. 237. *C. Griffin & Co.: London,* 1912. 8°. **08767**. f. **55**.

—— Internal Combustion Engine Design and Practice . . . Second edition [of "Evolution of the Internal Combustion Engine"], revised, *etc.* pp. xvi. 273. *C. Griffin & Co.: London,* 1920. 8°. **8763**. aaa. **28**.

—— Modern Pumping and Hydraulic Machinery . . . Being a practical handbook for engineers, designers, and others, *etc.* pp. xvi. 473. *C. Griffin & Co.: London,* 1913. 8°. **08767**. i. **58**.

—— Second edition, revised, *etc.* pp. xviii. 475. *C. Griffin & Co.: London,* 1922. 8°. **8777**. f. **14**.

—— Oil Fuel . . . Third edition [of the work originally written by Sydney H. North], greatly enlarged, *etc.* pp. xiv. 328. *C. Griffin & Co.: London,* 1914. 8°. **08806**. aa. **24**.

—— Fourth edition, revised and greatly enlarged, *etc.* pp. xvi. 310. *C. Griffin & Co.: London,* 1921. 8°. **08715**. a. **20**.

—— Transmission Gears, mechanical, electric, and hydraulic for land and marine purposes . . . With . . . folding plates. pp. xii. 164. *C. Griffin & Co.: London,* 1917. 8°. **08767**. c. **45**.

—— The Vaporizing of Paraffin for High Speed Motors, electric ignition type, *etc.* pp. vi. 120. *C. Griffin & Co.: London,* 1916. 8°. **08715**. aaa. **15**.

BUTLER (EDWARD) *Miscellaneous Writer.* A Consideration of Gentle Ways, and other essays. pp. 198. *Elliot Stock: London,* 1890. 8°. **12356**. d. **39**.

BUTLER (EDWARD) *Miscellaneous Writer.*

—— 'For Further Consideration.' [Essays.] pp. vi. 208. *Elliot Stock: London*, 1887. 8°. **12357.** cc. **36.**

—— 'For Good Consideration.' [Essays.] pp. 210. *Elliot Stock: London*, 1885. 8°. **8411.** aaa. **39.**

—— [Another edition.] pp. 210. *Elliot Stock: London*, 1889. 8°. **12357.** aaa. **39.**

BUTLER (EDWARD ALBERT) A Biology of the British Hemiptera—Heteroptera, *etc.* pp. vii. 682. pl. VII. *H. F. & G. Witherby: London*, 1923. 8°. **7298.** e. **47.**

—— Our Household Insects. An account of the insect-pests found in dwelling-houses. pp. vi. 344. *Longmans & Co.: London*, 1893. 8°. **7298.** aaa. **22.**

—— Pond Life: Insects. pp. 127. *Swan Sonnenschein & Co.: London*, 1886. 8°. [*Young Collector Series.*] **7001.** aaa.

—— Silkworms. pp. 100. *Swan Sonnenschein & Co.: London*, 1888. 8°. [*Young Collector Series.*] **7001.** aaa.

BUTLER (EDWARD ARTHUR) A Catalogue of the Birds of Sind, Cutch, Káthiáwár, North Gujarát, and Mount Aboo . . . With references (confined as much as possible to Jerdon's Birds of India, Mr. Hume's Raptores and Stray Feathers) showing where each species is described . . . Contributed to the Bombay Gazetteer. pp. 83. *Government Central Press: Bombay*, 1879. 8°. **7206.** k. **2.** (**3.**)

BUTLER (EDWARD CUTHBERT) *See* BENEDICT, *Saint, Abbot of Monte Cassino.* [*Regula.*] Sancti Benedicti Regula monachorum. Editionem critico-practicam adornavit D. C. Butler. 1912. 8°. **4783.** aaa. **52.**

—— —— 1930. 4°. **Cup.510.aab.5.**

—— *See* FRANCIS [de Sales], *Saint, Bishop of Geneva.* St. Francis de Sales in his Letters . . . Introduction by the Right Rev. Abbot Butler, *etc.* 1933. 8°. **2410.** d. **12.**

—— *See* FRANCIS [de Sales], *Saint, Bishop of Geneva.* St. Francis de Sales in his Letters . . . Introduction by the late Right Rev. Abbot C. Butler, *etc.* 1954. 8°. **4828.** ee. **28.**

—— *See* HEDLEY (John C.) *R.C. Bishop of Newport and Menevia.* Evolution and Faith . . . With an introduction by Dom C. Butler. 1931. 8°. **3939.** g. **48.**

—— *See* PALLADIUS, successively *Bishop of Helenopolis* and *of Aspona.* The Lausiac History of Palladius. A critical discussion, together with notes on early Egyptian monachism, by Dom C. Butler. (II. The Greek text edited with introduction and notes by Dom C. Butler.) 1898, *etc.* 8°. [*Texts and Studies.* vol. 6. no. 1, 2.] **03605.h.21/6.**

—— Authorship of the Dialogus de Vita Chrysostomi [here attributed to Palladius of Helenopolis]. Estratto dal volume unico stampato a cura del Comitato per i festeggiamenti del XV° centenario di San Giovanni Crisostomo. pp. 14. *Tipografia Poliglotta: Roma*, 1908. 8°. **4826.** f. **19.**

—— Benedictine Monachism. Studies in Benedictine life and rule. pp. viii. 387. *Longmans & Co.: London*, 1919. 8°. **4782.** g. **50.**

—— Second edition, with supplementary notes. pp. x. 424. *Longmans & Co.: London; Berlin* printed, 1924. 8°. **04782.** f. **33.**

BUTLER (EDWARD CUTHBERT)

—— The Catholic Church and Modern Civilization. 1937. *See* EYRE (Edward) European Civilization, *etc.* vol. 6. 1934, *etc.* 8°. **09075.bb.13/6.**

—— Daily Life at Old St. Gregory's, with an inventory of 1636 . . . Reprinted from the Downside Review. pp. 23. *Western Chronicle Co.: Yeovil*, 1892. 8°. **3477.** eeee. **22.** (**2.**)

—— The Life and Times of Bishop Ullathorne, 1806–1889. 2 vol. *Burns, Oates & Co.: London*, 1926. 8°. **4908.** i. **2.**

—— Monasticism. *See* BURY (John B.) The Cambridge Medieval History, *etc.* vol. 1. 1911, *etc.* 8°.
[Latest edition.] **2070.f.**
[Earlier editions.] **09084.** g.

—— Mystical Books and Books on Mysticism. (Reprinted from Downside Review.) *Thomas Baker: London*, [1911.] 8°. **04376.** h. **23.**

—— Notes on the Origin and Early Development of the restored English Benedictine Congregation, 1600–1661, *etc.* [By E. C. Butler. With an introduction by Bernard Murphy.] pp. 78. [1887.] 8°. *See* ENGLAND.—*Churches and Religious Bodies.—Benedictines.* **4782.** cc. **5.**

—— Palladiana . . . An examination of Dr. Richard Reitzenstein's monograph: 'Historia Monachorum und Historia Lausiaca' . . . Reprinted from the Journal of Theological Studies, vol. XXII. pp. 53. *University Press: Oxford*, 1921. 8°. **04530.** g. **6.**

—— Religions of Authority and the Religion of the Spirit. With other essays, *etc.* pp. 190. *Sheed & Ward: London*, 1930. 8°. **04376.** de. **117.**

—— The Vatican Council. The story told from inside in Bishop Ullathorne's letters . . . With portraits. 2 vol. *Longmans & Co.: London*, 1930. 8°. **4571.** eee. **12.**

—— Ways of Christian Life. Old spirituality for modern men. pp. ii [xii]. 256. *Sheed & Ward: London*, 1932. 8°. **04784.** de. **92.**

—— Western Mysticism. The teaching of SS. Augustine, Gregory and Bernard on contemplation, *etc.* pp. xiii. 344. *Constable & Co.: London*, 1922. 8°. **3805.** ee. **9.**

—— Second edition, with afterthoughts. pp. xci. 352. *Constable & Co.: London*, 1927. 8°. **3805.** ee. **13.**

BUTLER (EDWARD DUNDAS) *See* ARANY (J.) [*Single Works.*] The Legend of the Wondrous Hunt (Rege a csoda-szarvasról [from Buda halála]) . . . Translated . . . by E. D. Butler. *Hung. & Eng.* 1881. 8°. **11586.** ee. **48.**

—— *See* EBÉD. Az olcsó ebéd. The Cheap Dinner; translated from the German into Hungarian and English. With an allegory and a few fables, by Fáy; translated from the Hungarian into English and German. By E. D. Butler. [1876.] 16°. **12304.** aaa. **4.**

—— *See* GODENHJELM (B. F.) Handbook of the History of Finnish Literature . . . Translated from the Finnish, with notes, by E. D. Butler. 1896. 8°. **11840.** b. **62.**

—— *See* RACE. The Race between the Hedgehog and the Hare. Translated from the Plattdüdsch, by E. D. Butler. [1876.] 16°. **12305.** ccc. **16.**

BUTLER (Edward Dundas)

—— *See* Vasenius (G. V.) Outlines of the History of Printing in Finland . . . Translated from the Finnish, with notes, by E. D. Butler. 1898. 8°. **11899**. ee. **42**.

—— Hungarian Poems and Fables for English Readers. Selected and translated by E. D. Butler . . . With illustrations by A. G. Butler. pp. vi. 88. *Trübner & Co.: London*, 1877. 8°. **11586**. bb. **2**.

—— [Another issue.] **11586**. bb. **6**.
Without the illustrations.

—— *Κλεις των ἐν τῃ Ἑλληνικῃ Γραμματικῃ του Βλαχου Θεματων. Ὑπο Ε. Δ. Β.* [i.e. E. D. Butler.] pp. 16. 1874. 8°. *See* B., E. D. **12923**. aa. **31**. (**7**.)

—— [Another copy, with a different titlepage.] *Φραγκισκος Θιμμ: ἐν Λονδινῳ*, 1874. 8°. **12923**. aa. **1**.

BUTLER (Edward Harry)

—— An Introduction to Journalism. pp. 127. *George Allen & Unwin: London*, 1955. 8°. **11871**. p. **5**.

—— The Story of British Shorthand. pp. ix. 247. *Sir Isaac Pitman & Sons: London*, 1951. 8°. **012991**. df. **36**.

BUTLER (Edward Montagu) *See* Shakespeare (W.) [*Smaller Collections of Plays.—English.*] Arnold's School Shakespeare, *etc.* (Julius Cæsar: edited by E. M. Butler.) [1894, *etc.*] 8°. **011765**. ee. **15**.

BUTLER (Edward Thomas) The Life and Work of Henry Martyn, chaplain, missionary, and translator. [With a portrait.] pp. 36. *Christian Literature Society for India: Madras*, 1921. 8°. **20018**. f. **11**.

BUTLER (*Sir* Edwin John)

—— An Account of the Genus Pythium and some Chytridiaceæ. pp. 160. pl. x. *Calcutta*, 1906. 8°. [*Memoirs of the Department of Agriculture in India.* Botanical ser. vol. 1. no. 5.] I.S. **356**. (**2**.)

—— The Bud-Rot of Palms in India. pl. v. *Calcutta, London*, 1910. 4°. [*Memoirs of the Department of Agriculture in India.* Botanical series. vol. 3. no. 5.] I.S. **356**. (**2**.)

—— The Dissemination of Parasitic Fungi and International Legislation. pp. 73. *Thacker, Spink & Co.: Calcutta; W. Thacker & Co.: London*, 1917. 8°. [*Memoirs of the Department of Agriculture in India.* Botanical series. vol. 9. no. 1.] I.S. **356**. (**2**.)

—— Fungi and Disease in Plants. An introduction to the diseases of field and plantation crops, especially those of India and the East. [With plates.] pp. iv. 547. *Thacker, Spink & Co.: Calcutta & Simla*, 1918. 8°. **7031**. i. **23**.

—— Fungus Diseases of Sugar-Cane in Bengal. pp. 53. pl. xi. *Calcutta*, 1906. 8°. [*Memoirs of the Department of Agriculture in India.* Botanical ser. vol. 1. no. 3.] I.S. **356**. (**2**.)

BUTLER (*Sir* Edwin John) and **'ABD AL-ḤĀFIẒ KHĀN.**

—— Red Rot of Sugarcane. *Calcutta, London*, 1913. 4°. [*Memoirs of the Department of Agriculture in India.* Botanical series. vol. 6. no. 5.] I.S. **356**. (**2**.)

BUTLER (*Sir* Edwin John) and **'ABD AL-ḤĀFIẒ KHĀN.**

—— Some New Sugarcane Diseases. [With plates.] *Calcutta, London*, 1913. 4°. [*Memoirs of the Department of Agriculture in India.* Botanical series. vol. 6. no. 6.] I.S. **356**. (**2**.)

BUTLER (*Sir* Edwin John) and **HAYMAN** (J. M.)

—— Indian Wheat Rusts . . . With a note on the relation of weather to rust on cereals. By W. H. Moreland. pp. 58. pl. v. *Calcutta*, 1906. 8°. [*Memoirs of the Department of Agriculture in India.* Botanical ser. vol. 1. no. 2.] I.S. **356**. (**2**.)

BUTLER (*Sir* Edwin John) and **JONES** (Samuel Griffith)

—— Plant Pathology. pp. xii. 979. *Macmillan & Co.: London*, 1949. 8°. **7033**. e. **18**.

BUTLER (*Sir* Edwin John) and **KULAKARṆĪ**, *G.S.*

—— Studies in Peronosporaceæ. [With plates.] *Calcutta, London*, 1913. 4°. [*Memoirs of the Department of Agriculture in India.* Botanical series. vol. 5. no. 5.] I.S. **356**. (**2**.)

BUTLER (Eileen) *See* Butler (*Right Hon. Sir* William F.) *G.C.B.* Sir William Butler. An autobiography, *etc.* [Edited by E. Butler.] 1911. 8°. **010856**. g. 3.

—— —— 1913. 8°. **010815**. f. **16**.

BUTLER (*Lady* Eleanor) *See* Bell (Eva M.) The Hamwood Papers of the Ladies of Llangollen [Lady E. Butler and Sarah Ponsonby], *etc.* [With portraits.] 1930. 8°. **10824**. d. 4.

—— *See* Gordon (Mary L.) Chase of the Wild Goose. The story of Lady Eleanor Butler and Miss Sarah Ponsonby, *etc.* [With portraits.] 1936. 8°. **010822**. ee. **39**.

—— *See* Hicklin (John) *of Chester.* The "Ladies of Llangollen" [Lady E. Butler and Sarah Ponsonby], as sketched by many hands, *etc.* 1847. 8°. **1203**. i. **17**.

BUTLER (Elenor) The Geography of History, with special reference to Ireland, to the Eastern Mediterranean basin and to the growth of modern industrial centres. pp. ii. 165. *Educational Co. of Ireland: Dublin & Cork*, [1927.] 8°. **09007**. bb. **31**.

—— Introduction to Geography. pp. 143. *Educational Co.: [Dublin*, 1928.] 8°. **10003**. ee. **16**.

—— [The Irish Student's Geography.] Géograif don Ġaeḋeal Óg . . . Liam Ó Briain (Míċeál Breatnaċ) d'aistriġ, *etc.* Comluċt Oideaċais na hÉireann: Baile Áta Cliat ⁊ Corcaiġ, [1930– .] 8°. W.P. **9839**.

—— [Structural Geography of Ireland.] Bonn agus Forsgreaṁ na hÉireann . . . Ar n-a aistriú go Gaeḋilge ag Míċeal Breatnaċ, *etc.* pp. 140. Muinntir C. S. Ó Fallaṁáin: [*Dublin*,] 1930. 8°. **10005**. aa. 38.

BUTLER (Eliza Marian)

—— *See* Rilke (R. M.) Selected Letters of Rainer Maria Rilke, 1907–1926, *etc.* [With a biographical introduction by E. M. Butler.] 1946. 8°. **10922**. ee. **14**.

—— Daylight in a Dream. [A novel.] pp. 125. *Hogarth Press: London*, 1951. 8°. NNN. **1733**.

BUTLER (ELIZA MARIAN)

—— The Direct Method in German Poetry. An inaugural lecture, *etc.* pp. 31. *University Press: Cambridge,* 1946. 8°. **11866**. aa. **23**.

—— The Fortunes of Faust. [With plates.] pp. xvii. 365. *University Press: Cambridge,* 1952. 8°. **11867**. m. **6**.
With an errata slip.

—— Goethe and Byron. pp. 28. *University of Nottingham: Nottingham,* [1950.] 8°. [*Byron Foundation Lecture.* 1949–50.] Ac. **2673**. b/3.

—— The Myth of the Magus. pp. xi. 281. pl. x. *University Press: Cambridge,* 1948. 8°. **4506**. h. **29**.

—— Rainer Maria Rilke. [With a portrait.] pp. x. 437. *University Press: Cambridge,* 1941. 8°. **010703**. h. **75**.

—— Ritual Magic. pp. x. 328. pl. VIII. *Cambridge University Press: Cambridge,* 1949. 8°. **8634**. dd. **30**.

—— The Saint-Simonian Religion in Germany. A study of the Young German movement. pp. xii. 446. *University Press: Cambridge,* 1926. 8°. **08286**. bb. **7**.

—— Sheridan. A ghost story, *etc.* [A biographical study. With a portrait.] pp. xiii. 312. *Constable & Co.: London,* 1931. 8°. **10823**. aaa. **23**.

—— Silver Wings, *etc.* pp. 139. *Hogarth Press: London,* 1952. 8°. NNN. **2664**.

—— The Tempestuous Prince, Hermann Pückler-Muskau. [With plates, including portraits.] pp. xii. 307. *Longmans & Co.: London,* 1929. 8°. **010703**. f. **51**.

—— The Tyranny of Greece over Germany. A study of the influence exercised by Greek art and poetry over the great German writers of the eighteenth, nineteenth and twentieth centuries. [With plates.] pp. viii. 351. *University Press: Cambridge,* 1935. 8°. **11857**. aaa. **21**.

BUTLER (ELIZABETH) *Duchess of Ormonde.* A Pastoral upon the Death of Her Grace the Duchess of Ormond pp. 4. *Printed and sold by N. Thompson:* [*London,*] 1684. fol. **1870**. d. **1**. (**16***.)

BUTLER (ELIZABETH) *Lady.* *See* THOMPSON (Elizabeth) afterwards BUTLER (E.) *Lady.*

BUTLER (ELIZABETH) *Mrs.* *See* BARRETT (William G.) Two Discourses . . . the second preached . . . on the removal of Mrs. E. Butler, *etc.* [1849.] 16°. **4906**. a. **30**.

BUTLER (ELIZABETH BEARDSLEY) Women and the Trades. Pittsburgh, 1907–1908 . . . Edited by P. U. Kellogg. [With plates.] pp. 440. 1909. 8°. *See* NEW YORK.—*Russell Sage Foundation.* **08276**. d. **9**.

BUTLER (ELLIS PARKER) The Behind Legs of the 'Orse, and other stories. pp. 222. *Houghton Mifflin Co.: Boston & New York,* 1927. 8°. **12712**. bb. **8**.

—— The Confessions of a Daddy. pp. 96. *Hodder & Stoughton: London,* [1907.] 8°. **12804**. p. **27**.

—— The Jack-Knife Man . . . Illustrated by Hanson Booth. pp. 318. *Century Co.: New York,* 1913. 8°. **012704**. c. **33**.

BUTLER (ELLIS PARKER)

—— Jibby Jones and the Alligator, *etc.* pp. vii. 252. *Houghton Mifflin Co.: Boston & New York,* 1924. 8°. **12800**. f. **11**.

—— Kilo: being the love story of Eliph' Hewlitt, book agent. pp. vii. 267. *Hodder & Stoughton: London,* [1908.] 8°. **012705**. aa. **13**.

—— Many Happy Returns of the Day. pp. 49. *Houghton Mifflin Co.: Boston & New York,* 1925. 12°. **012316**. df. **19**.

—— Mike Flannery on Duty and off . . . Illustrations by Gustavus C. Widney. pp. 101. *Doubleday, Page & Co.: London; New York* printed, 1909. 8°. **012331**. m. **9**.

—— [Another copy, with a different titlepage.] *Hodder & Stoughton: London; printed in New York,* 1909. 8°. **012331**. m. **10**.

—— Mr. Perkins of Portland. pp. viii. 171. *Hodder & Stoughton: London,* 1907. 8°. **012634**. b. **6**.

—— The Adventure of the Lame and the Halt. [Reprinted from "Mr. Perkins of Portland."] pp. 54. *Hodder & Stoughton: London,* [1932.] 16°. **012602**. de. **6**.

—— Pigs is Pigs . . . Second edition. pp. v. 47. *Hodder & Stoughton: London,* 1906. 8°. **12316**. ff. **7**.

—— [Another edition.] pp. 73. *London,* [1917.] 8°. [*Newnes' Trench Library.*] **012643**. f. **46/13**.

—— Pigs is Pigs. pp. 59. *St. Hugh's Press: London,* [1949.] 16°. **12332**. e. **27**.

—— That Pup . . . Illustrated. pp. 61. *Hodder & Stoughton: London; New York* printed, 1909. 8°. **012804**. cc. **21**.

—— The Thin Santa Claus. The chicken yard that was a Christmas stocking. Illustrated by Mary Wilson Preston. pp. 35. *Doubleday, Page & Co.: London; New York* printed, 1909. 8°. **012705**. a. **32**.

—— The Water Goats, and other troubles, *etc.* [With plates.] *Doubleday, Page & Co.: New York,* 1910. 8°. **12730**. de. **38**. (**1.**)
Bound with "The Big Strike at Siwash" by George H. Fitch. The cover bears a printed label giving the titles of both works.

—— The Young Stamp Collector's Own Book . . . Illustrated. pp. 342. *Bobbs-Merrill Co.: Indianapolis,* [1933.] 8°. **08247**. g. **34**.

BUTLER (ELLYS THEODORA)

—— Studies in the Patellariaceae . . . Reprinted . . . from Mycologia, *etc.* [A thesis.] *New York,* 1940. 8°. **7032**. pp. **36**.

BUTLER (ELMER ELLSWORTH)

—— Butlers and Kinsfolk: Butlers of New England and Nova Scotia, *etc.* [With portraits.] pp. 326. *Cabinet Press: Milford, N.H.,* 1944. 8°. **9906**. r. **2**.

BUTLER (ERNEST JOHN) The New Education Arithmetic. 6 pt. *J. L. van Schaik: Pretoria,* 1925. 8°. **08531**. e. **54**.

BUTLER (Ernest John) and **THOMPSON** (Frederick Handel)

—— Great South Africans. A series of biographies of twelve eminent South Africans for use in the upper classes of schools, *etc.* [With plates.] pp. 94. *Juta & Co.: Cape Town & Johannesburg,* [1938.] 8°. **10604**. c. **34**.

BUTLER (Ewan)

—— City Divided: Berlin 1955. [With plates.] pp. 187. *Sidgwick & Jackson: London,* 1955. 8°. **10256**. g. **23**.

—— Conspiracy of Silence. pp. 254. *Hodder & Stoughton: London,* 1950. 8°. NNN. **209**.

—— Strange Sanctuary. [A novel.] pp. 254. *Hodder & Stoughton: London,* 1949. 8°. NN. **39635**.

—— "Talk of the Devil," *etc.* [A novel. With plates.] pp. 128. *Oliver Moxon: London,* 1948. 8°. NN. **39164**.

BUTLER (Ewan) and **BRADFORD** (J. Selby)

—— Keep the Memory Green. The first of the many. France, 1939–40. [With plates.] pp. 179. *Hutchinson & Co.: London,* [1950.] 8°. **9102**. c. **25**.

—— [Keep the Memory Green.] The Story of Dunkirk. pp. 192. pl. 16. *Hutchinson: London,* 1955. 8°. **9103**. a. **11**.

BUTLER (Ewan) and **YOUNG** (George Gordon Fussell)

—— Marshal without Glory. [A biography of Hermann Goering. With plates, including portraits.] pp. 287. *Hodder & Stoughton: London,* 1951. 8°. **010709**. m. **39**.

—— Maréchal sans gloire, ou la vie orageuse de Hermann Goering . . . Traduit . . . par A. Ravaut et Y. Massip. 2 pt. *Paris,* 1952. 8°. [*France Illustration. Supplément théâtral et littéraire.* no. 114, 115.] P.P. **4283**. m. (**1**.)

BUTLER (F.) *Religious Writer.* The Prayer Book's Compromise in danger. pp. 12. *Church Newspaper Co.: London,* [1902.] 8°. **4109**. i. **17**. (**3**.)

BUTLER (F. J.) *Novelist.* High Seas Over. [A novel.] pp. 274. *G. P. Putnam's Sons: London & New York,* 1929. 8°. NN. **15695**.

BUTLER (Fanny) *See* Butlerd.

BUTLER (Fanny Jane) *See* Tonge (E. M.) Fanny Jane Butler, pioneer medical missionary, *etc.* [1930.] 8°. **4909**. b. **1**.

BUTLER (Frances) *See* Leigh (F.) *Hon. Mrs. J. W. Leigh.*

BUTLER (Frances Anne) *See* Kemble, afterwards Butler.

BUTLER (Francis) *Teacher of Languages, New York.* Breeding, Training, Management, Diseases, &c. of Dogs: together with an easy and agreeable method of instructing all breeds of dogs in a great variety of amusing and useful performances . . . Beautifully illustrated by T. C. Carpendale. pp. 216. *Francis Butler: New York,* 1857. 12°. **7294**. c. **9**.

—— Dogo-graphy. The life and adventures of the celebrated dog Tiger, *etc.* pp. 111. *Francis Butler: New York,* 1856. 8°. **12316**. k. **49**.

BUTLER (Francis) *Teacher of Languages, New York.*

—— The Spanish Teacher and Colloquial Phrase-Book . . . Eighth edition, revised & corrected. pp. 293. *D. Appleton & Co.: New York,* 1857. 8°. **12943**. a. **31**.

—— [Another edition.] El Maestro de Inglés, *etc.* pp. xvi. 240. *Colville, Dawson y Cia.: Lima y Callao; Trübner & Co.: London,* 1870. 8°. **12985**. bb. **51**.

BUTLER (*Sir* Francis) *See* England.—*Parliament.—House of Commons.* [*Appendix.*] A True and Just Account of what was transacted in the Commons House . . . When that House voted David Jenkins . . . and Sir Francis Butler to be guilty of high treason, *etc.* 1719. 8°. **518**. f. **31**.

BUTLER (Francis Henry) *See* Butler (Annie R.) A Gift for a Pet . . . With verses by F. H. Butler, *etc.* [1896.] 4°. **4430**. i. **1**.

—— Quæ Scripsi: a book of verse. pp. xii. 163. *Sands & Co.: London,* 1902. 8°. **11650**. ff. **30**.

BUTLER (Francis Herbert Culverhouse)

—— Realms of Natural Science. General editor: F. H. C. Butler. *Oxford University Press: London,* 1942. 8°. W.P. **12697**.

BUTLER (Frank)

—— *See* Butler (James) *Boxing Commentator.* The Fight Game. By J. and F. Butler, *etc.* [With a portrait.] 1954. 8°. **7919**. aa. **105**.

—— Randolph Turpin . . . Sugar Ray Robinson. Their story in pictures. *Jarrold & Sons: Norwich,* [1951.] 8°. **7921**. aaa. **20**.

BUTLER (Frank Arthur)

—— The Improvement of Teaching in Secondary Schools. pp. x. 389. *University of Chicago Press: Chicago,* 1939. 8°. **08385**. b. **46**.

—— The Improvement of Teaching in Secondary Schools. Revised edition. pp. xii. 399. *University of Chicago Press: Chicago,* 1946. 8°. **08385**. i. **43**.

—— The Improvement of Teaching in Secondary Schools. Third edition, *etc.* pp. xii. 433. *University of Chicago Press: Chicago,* 1954. 8°. **08385**. f. **140**.

BUTLER (Frank Edwin)

—— Signpost to the Stars. [With charts.] pp. 32. *G. Philip & Son: London,* 1941. 8°. **08560**. f. **29**.

—— [A reissue.] Signpost to the Stars, *etc.* *London,* 1951. 8°. **8565**. aa. **15**.

BUTLER (Frank Hedges) Fifty Years of Travel by Land, Water, and Air . . . With 89 illustrations [including a portrait]. pp. 421. *T. Fisher Unwin: London,* 1920. 8°. **010025**. g. **16**.

—— 5,000 Miles in a Balloon. Illustrated, *etc.* pp. 42. *Horace Cox: London,* 1907. 8°. **8708**. c. **21**. (**5**.)

—— Round the World . . . Illustrated. pp. 269. *T. Fisher Unwin: London,* 1924. 8°. **010025**. g. **34**.

BUTLER (Frank Hedges)

—— Through Lapland with Skis & Reindeer, with some account of ancient Lapland and the Murman coast . . . With 4 maps and 65 illustrations [including portraits]. pp. xii. 286. *T. Fisher Unwin: London*, 1917. 8°. **010281.** f. **10.**

—— [A reissue.] *London*, 1919. 8°. **010281.** f. **13.**

—— Wine and the Wine Lands of the World . . . With 55 illustrations. pp. 271. *T. Fisher Unwin: London*, 1926. 8°. **07075.** f. **19.**

BUTLER (Franklin) Singleness of Purpose in the Ministry. A sermon, *etc.* pp. 32. *Chronicle Press: [Windsor, Vt.,]* 1848. 8°. **4486.** bb. **62.** **(7.)**

BUTLER (Fred Clayton) Community Americanization. A handbook for workers. pp. 82. *Washington*, 1920. 8°. [*U.S. Bureau of Education. Bulletin.* 1919. no. 76.] A.S. **202.**

—— State Americanization. The part of the state in the education and assimilation of the immigrant. pp. 26. *Washington*, 1920. 8°. [*U.S. Bureau of Education. Bulletin.* 1919. no. 77.] A.S. **202.**

BUTLER (Frédéric Dubourg) *Count.* *See* Dubourg-Butler.

BUTLER (Frederick) A Complete History of the United States of America, embracing the whole period from the discovery of North America, down to the year 1820. 3 vol. *Printed for the Author: Hartford*, 1821. 8°. **1446.** e. **3–5.**

BUTLER (Frederick Brisbane) *See* Caesar (C. J.) [*De Bello Gallico.—Selections.*] Cæsar . . . With notes by F. B. Butler. 1871. 16°. **12201.** cc. **4.**

—— Sermons, principally preached in Haileybury College Chapel, *etc.* pp. vii. 175. *Griffith, Farran & Co.: London*, 1887. 8°. **4479.** d. **23.**

BUTLER (Frederick Burdett)

—— Early Days, Taranaki. [With plates, including portraits.] pp. 122. *Printed for the Author: New Plymouth*, 1942. 8°. **10493.** df. **42.**

BUTLER (Frederick William James) Can we Dispense with Christianity? *etc.* pp. 208. *Student Christian Movement: London*, 1922. 8°. **04375.** e. **55.**

—— Christian Thought, a Grammar of Reinterpretation; or, Christianity and nature. pp. xii. 147. *S.P.C K.: London*, 1929. 8°. **04018.** ee. **57.**

—— Christianity and History. pp. 159. *S.P.C.K.: London*, 1925. 8°. **4017.** d. **30.**

—— The Grounds of Christian Belief. pp. 119. *Skeffington & Son: London*, [1918.] 8°. **4017.** e. **47.**

—— The Permanent Element in Christianity. An essay on Christian religion in relation to modern thought. pp. 347. *H. R. Allenson: London*, [1910.] 8°. **4017.** d. **17.**

—— Personality and Revelation. A statement of the grounds of Christian certainty. pp. 87. *W. Heffer & Sons: Cambridge*, 1914. 8°. **4014.** df. **28.**

BUTLER (G. V.)

—— An Eastertide Greeting Book. A miscellany of Easter poems and prose. Compiled by G. V. Butler. *Sands & Co.: London*, 1947. 8°. **3438.** g. **24.**

BUTLER (*Sir* Geoffrey Gilbert) *K.B.E.* *See* Butler (*Sir* George G. G.)

BUTLER (Geoffrey L.) Madeleine Smith. pp. 189. *Duckworth: London*, 1935. 8°. [*Rogues' Gallery.*] W.P. **11661/1.**

BUTLER (Geoffrey L.) and **STERN** (Paul) *Vice-President of the Austrian Bridge League.*

—— The Two-Club System of Bidding. pp. 300. *Faber & Faber: London*, 1940. 8°. **07907.** ee. **24.**

BUTLER (George) *Canon of Winchester.* *See* Butler (Josephine E.) Recollections of George Butler. [1892.] 8°. **4906.** i. **16.**

—— *See* Butler (Josephine E.) Souvenirs & pensées. [Compiled from "Recollections of George Butler" and other sources.] 1908. 8°. **010855.** h. **15.**

—— Abounding in the Work of the Lord. A farewell sermon, *etc.* pp. 23. *Bell & Daldy: London*, 1858. 12°. **4477.** b. **15.**

—— Codex Virgilianus qui nuper ex bibliotheca Abbatis Matt. Lud. Canonici Bodleianæ accessit, cum Wagneri textu collatus, studio et opera Georgii Butler. pp. 66. *J. Wright: Oxoniæ*, 1854. 8°. **11355.** f. **7.**

—— Concio ad Clerum in Ecclesia B. Mariae Virginis Oxoniae . . . habita. pp. 16. [*Printed for private circulation:*] *Londini*, 1878. 8°. **4446.** f. **50.**

—— Education considered as a Profession for Women. *See* Butler (Josephine E.) Woman's Work and Woman's Culture, *etc.* 1869. 8°. **8415.** h. **18.**

—— The End of the Perfect Man. A sermon preached . . . after the death of the Very Rev. Hugh M'Neile, *etc.* pp. 20. *Macmillan & Co.: London*, 1879. 8°. **4906.** dd. **31.** **(16.)**

—— The Gospel preached to the Poor a Sign of Christ's Presence on Earth. Two sermons, *etc.* pp. 29. *Bell & Daldy: London*, 1858. 8°. **4478.** a. **13.**

—— The Higher Education of Women: an inaugural lecture. pp. 36. *Thomas Brakell: Liverpool*, 1867. 8°. **08311.** h. **20.** **(5.)**

—— On the Death of President Garfield. A sermon. pp. 15. *Macmillan & Co.: London*, 1881. 8°. **4985.** df. **22.** **(7.)**

—— On the Raphael Drawings in the University Galleries, Oxford. 1856. *See* Oxford Essays. Oxford Essays, *etc.* [1855, *etc.*] 8°. **12356.** t. **16.**

—— Prayers based on Select Psalms, suited for family use during the present crisis. pp. 32. *Bell & Daldy: London*, 1857. 8°. **3456.** e. **19.**

—— Principles of Imitative Art: four lectures delivered before the Oxford Art Society, *etc.* pp. xvi. 231. *J. W. Parker & Son: London*, 1852. 12°. **7805.** c. **7.**

—— Sermons preached in Cheltenham College Chapel. pp. xii. 404. *Macmillan & Co.: Cambridge & London*, 1862. 8°. **4464.** e. **11.**

—— Village Sermons, preached on Tyneside . . . 1856. pp. viii. 127. *J. H. & J. Parker: Oxford*, 1857. 8°. **4462.** b. **14.**

—— Testimonials in favour of George Butler . . . candidate for the Greek Professorship in the University of Edinburgh. pp. 32. *William Macphail: Edinburgh*, 1852. 8°. **8366.** bb. **33.** **(2.)**

BUTLER (GEORGE) *Dean of Peterborough.* *See* HARROW.—*Harrow School.* Harrow. A selection of lists of the School between MDCCLXX. and MDCCCXXVI., by G. Butler, *etc.* 1849. 12°. **732. a. 15.**

—— *See* LITURGIES.—*Church of England.*—*Common Prayer.*—*Communion Office.* [*Selections.*] [Extracts from the Communion Service of the Church of England. By G. Butler.] [1839.] 8°. **1881. a. 1. (83.)**

—— —— [1842?] 8°. **1881. a. 1. (107*.)**

—— *See* PETERBOROUGH.—*Cathedral Church.* Statutes of Peterborough Cathedral, translated . . . by . . . G. Butler. 1853. 12°. **4705. aa. 11.**

—— A Sermon preached in All Saints' Church, Northampton . . . at the sixth anniversary meeting of the Northampton District Committees of the Societies for Promoting Christian Knowledge and for the Propagation of the Gospel, *etc.* pp. 28. *C. J. G. & F. Rivington: London,* 1830. 8°. **T. 1291. (11.)**

—— A Sermon, preached in the Cathedral Church of St. Paul, on Thursday, May XI, 1843, at the Festival of the Sons of the Clergy, *etc.* pp. 48. *J. G. F. & J. Rivington: London,* 1843. 8°. **1359.g.12.(2.)**

BUTLER (GEORGE) *of Bruton Street, Berkeley Square.* The Rosciad, a poem: dedicated to Mr. Kemble. pp. 61. *Robert Butler: London,* 1802. 4°. **11641. g. 7.**

BUTLER (GEORGE B.) *of the Union League Club.* The Suppression of Small Bills. pp. 31. [*Union League Club:*] *New York,* 1880. 8°. **8176. e. 13. (7.)**

BUTLER (GEORGE BERNARD) St. Joseph's Church, West Hartlepool. Account of opening ceremony with history of mission, &c. Illustrated. pp. 52. *B. T. Ord: Hartlepool,* 1895. 8°. **4707. aa. 46.**

BUTLER (GEORGE COOPER) A Hand Book on the Law of Property. pp. viii. 82. *Shaw & Sons: London,* 1866. 8°. **6305. aaa. 5.**

BUTLER (GEORGE D.)

—— Introduction to Community Recreation. pp. xiv. 547. 1940. 8°. *See* UNITED STATES OF AMERICA.—*National Recreation Association.* **8289. dd. 1.**

—— Introduction to Community Recreation . . . Second edition. [With a bibliography.] pp. xiv. 568. 1949. 8°. *See* UNITED STATES OF AMERICA.—*National Recreation Association.* **8289. c. 43.**

—— Municipal and County Parks in the United States, 1935. [A study made by the National Park Service in cooperation with the National Recreation Association.] Under the direction of G. D. Butler. pp. ix. 147. pl. XIII. 1937. 8°. *See* UNITED STATES OF AMERICA.—*National Park Service.* **A.S. 194/27.**

BUTLER (GEORGE FRANK) A Text-book of Materia Medica, Therapeutics and Pharmacology. pp. 858. *Rebman Publishing Co.: London; printed in America,* 1897. 8°. **07509. g. 4.**

—— Third edition, thoroughly revised. pp. 874. *W. B. Saunders & Co.: Philadelphia,* 1900. 8°. **07509. g. 14.**

—— Sixth edition, thoroughly revised and enlarged, *etc.* pp. 708. *W. B. Saunders Co.: Philadelphia & London,* 1908. 8°. **2255. d. 1.**

BUTLER (*Sir* GEORGE GEOFFREY GILBERT) *K.B.E.* *See* EDMONDES (*Sir* Thomas) The Edmondes Papers . . . Edited by G. G. Butler. 1913. 4°. **C. 101. e. 21.**

—— Guide to an Exhibition of Historical Authorities illustrative of British History, compiled from the manuscripts of Corpus Christi College, Cambridge. pp. 16. 1920. 8°. *See* CAMBRIDGE.—*University of Cambridge.*—*Corpus Christi College.* **09504. h. 21.**

—— A Handbook to the League of Nations, *etc.* pp. x. 80. *Longmans & Co.: London,* 1919. 8°. **8425. s. 21.**

—— Second edition, revised, *etc.* (Brought down to the end of the fifth Assembly. With an explanation [and the text] of the Protocol.) pp. xvi. 239. *Longmans & Co.: London,* 1925. 8°. **08425. g. 4.**

—— Reissue with additions. *London,* 1928. 8°. **08425. ff. 8.**

—— International Law and Autocracy. A public lecture, *etc.* pp. 15. *Hodder & Stoughton: London,* 1917. 8°. **06955. f. 37.**

—— Studies in Statecraft: being chapters, biographical and bibliographical, mainly on the sixteenth century. pp. vi. 138. *University Press: Cambridge,* 1920. 8°. **9075. bbb. 3.**

—— The Tory Tradition: Bolingbroke, Burke, Disraeli, Salisbury. pp. xiii. 143. *John Murray: London,* 1914. 8°. **8139. c. 26.**

BUTLER (*Sir* GEORGE GEOFFREY GILBERT) *K.B.E.*, and **MACCOBY** (SIMON)

—— The Development of International Law. pp. xxxv. 566. *Longmans & Co.: London,* 1928. 8°. [*Contributions to International Law and Diplomacy.*] **6957.e.1/7.**

BUTLER (GEORGE GREY) *See* LORD (Walter F.) The Counts of St. Paul. MS. NOTES [by G. G. Butler]. 1904. 8°. **9904. r. 4.**

—— *See* SAINT PAUL (Horace) A Journal of the First Two Campaigns of the Seven Years War . . . Edited by G. G. Butler. 1914. 8°. **9072. f. 19.**

—— Colonel St. Paul of Ewart, Soldier and Diplomat. Edited by G. G. Butler. Illustrated with photogravure plates. 2 vol. *St. Catherine Press; J. Nisbet & Co.: London,* 1911. 8°. **010815. e. 1.**

BUTLER (GEORGE MIDDLETON) *See* BUTLER (James) *Infant,* and BUTLER (G. M.) To the Hon. the Commons of Great Britain . . . the humble Petition of James Butler and G. M. Butler, *etc.* [1720?] fol. **816. m. 5. (30.)**

BUTLER (GEORGE PAUL)

—— Best Sermons. 1946 [*etc.*] edition. (Edited by G. Paul Butler.) *Harper & Bros.: New York & London,* 1946– . 8°. **X.0100/55.**

BUTLER (GEORGE SLADE) Topographica Sussexiana: an attempt towards forming a list of the various publications relating to the County of Sussex . . . Reprinted from . . . Sussex Archæological Collections. pp. 76. [*London,* 1866.] 4°. **BB.K.b.4.**

BUTLER (GEORGE WILLIAM) The Book of the Generation of Jesus Christ. An explanation of the difficulties connected with the genealogy of Our Lord. pp. 32. *William Macintosh: London,* 1875. 8°. **4372. de. 8. (4.)**

BUTLER (George William)

—— Here and Hereafter; or, Life, death, and eternity. An exposition of the first part of the narrative of the Rich Man and Lazarus. pp. vii. 103. *S. W. Partridge & Co.: London,* 1898. 8°. **4399. aaaa. 41.**

—— "Is it True?" A protest against the employment of fiction as a channel of Christian influence. pp. 33. *William Macintosh: London,* 1869. 8°. **4379.** d. **47.** (5.)

—— The Lord's Host; or, Lessons from the Book of Joshua. pp. xv. 380. *W. Oliphant & Co.: Edinburgh,* 1878. 8°. **3155.** f. **11.**

—— A Plain Paper on Preaching. pp. 16. *William Macintosh: London,* 1874. 8°. **4499.** cc. **1.** (10.)

—— A Plea for Jewish Converts. pp. 16. *Operative Jewish Converts' Institution: London,* 1872. 16°. **4034.** aa. **4.**

—— Rebekah. A narrative from Holy Scripture, told in hexameter verse. pp. 32. *S. W. Partridge & Co.: London,* 1899. *obl.* 8°. **11652.** dd. **12.**

—— The Rich Man's Brethren; or, Holy Scripture sufficient. An exposition of the latter part of the narrative of the Rich Man and Lazarus. pp. viii. 105. *S. W. Partridge & Co.: London,* 1903. 8°. **03225.** de. **22.**

—— The Surrender. [A religious tract.] pp. 31. *Operative Jewish Converts' Institution: London,* 1898. 32°. **4418.** aaa. **32.** (1.)

BUTLER (Gerald)

—— Blow hot, blow cold. pp. 249. *Rinehart & Co.: New York, Toronto,* [1951.] 8°. **12701.** b. **1.**

—— Choice of Two Women. pp. 183. *Jarrolds: London,* 1951. 8°. NNN. **2156.**

—— Kiss the Blood off my Hands. pp. 251. *Nicholson & Watson: London,* 1940. 8°. NN. **31516**

—— [A reissue.] Kiss the Blood off My Hands. *Jarrolds: London,* [1941.] 8°. NN. **32483.**

—— Kiss the Blood off my Hands. pp. 128. *Jarrolds: London,* [1945.] 8°. NN. **35340.**

—— Mad with much Heart. pp. 136. *Jarrolds: London,* 1945. 8°. NN. **35449.**

—— Slippery Hitch. pp. 159. *Jarrolds: London,* [1948.] 8°. NN. **38458.**

—— Their Rainbow had Black Edges. pp. 160. *Jarrolds: London,* 1943. 8°. NN. **34020.**

—— They Cracked Her Glass Slipper. pp. 192. *Jarrolds: London,* 1941. 8°. NN. **32954.**

—— They Cracked her Glass Slipper, *etc.* pp. 127. *Jarrolds: London,* [1944.] 8°. **012642.** n. **42.**

—— [A reissue.] They cracked her Glass Slipper . . . 53rd thousand. *London,* [1945.] 8°. **012642.** pp. **63.**

BUTLER (Giuseppina E.) *See* Butler (Josephine E.)

BUTLER (Glentworth Reeve) The Diagnostics of Internal Medicine. A clinical treatise upon the recognised principles of medical diagnosis, *etc.* pp. xxviii. 1059. pl. v. *Henry Kimpton: London,* 1901. 8°. **7442.** cc. **3.**

BUTLER (Glentworth Reeve)

—— [Another copy, with a different titlepage.] *D. Appleton & Co.: New York,* 1901. 8°. **7442.** cc. **2.** *Imperfect; wanting plates* 4 *and* 5.

—— Second revised edition. pp. xxxiv. 1168. *D. Appleton & Co.: New York & London,* 1905. 8°. **7439.** ee. **1.**

—— Third revised edition. pp. xxiv. 1180. *D. Appleton & Co.: New York & London,* 1909. 8°. **7439.** ee. **7.**

—— Fourth, revised edition. pp. xxxvi. 1380. *D. Appleton & Co.: New York & London,* 1922. 8°. **7460.** h. **8.**

—— Emergency Notes. What to do in accidents and sudden illness, until the doctor comes . . . With eighteen original illustrations. pp. 102. *Funk & Wagnalls: New York,* 1889. 8°. **7482.** e. **8.**

BUTLER (Graham Wesley)

—— Ion Uptake by Young Wheat Plants. (General summary.) [A thesis.] pp. 4. *Carl Bloms Boktryckeri: Lund,* 1953. 8°. **7082.** ee. **7.**

BUTLER (Gurdon Montague) Handbook of Mineralogy, Blowpipe Analysis and Geometrical Crystallography. 3 pt. *J. Wiley & Sons: New York; Chapman & Hall: London,* 1918. 8°. **07107.** f. **16.**
A reissue of the author's "A Pocket Handbook of Minerals," second edition, corrected [1911], *"Pocket Handbook of Blowpipe Analysis," first edition, second thousand, corrected,* 1916, *and "A Manual of Geometrical Crystallography,"* 1918, *with a collective titlepage.*

—— Pocket Handbook of Blowpipe Analysis, *etc.* pp. v. 80. *J. Wiley & Sons: New York; Chapman & Hall: London,* 1910. 8°. **8904.** a. **22.**

—— A Pocket Handbook of Minerals, *etc.* pp. ix. 298. *J. Wiley & Sons: New York; Chapman & Hall: London,* 1908. 8°. **07108.** e. **22.**

—— Second edition. pp. ix. 311. *J. Wiley & Sons: New York; Chapman & Hall: London,* 1912. 8°. **07108.** e. **28.**

—— Second edition . . . corrected. pp. ix. 311. *J. Wiley & Sons: New York; Chapman & Hall: London,* [1916.] 8°. **07107.** f. **13.**

BUTLER (Guy Montagu)

—— The Art of Pace-Judgment, *etc.* pp. 24. *Vail & Co.: London,* [1948.] 8°. **7917.** de. **97.**

—— Athletics and Training . . . With 12 illustrations, *etc.* pp. 247. *A. & C. Black: London,* 1938. 8°. [*Sportsman's Library.* vol. 26.] W.P. **2607/26.**

—— Modern Athletics, *etc.* pp. xvi. 152. pl. xv. *University Press: Cambridge,* 1929. 8°. **07905.** l. **46.**

—— Running & Runners. [With plates, including a portrait.] pp. 175. *Herbert Jenkins: London,* 1938. 8°. **7908.** eee. **7.**

—— Sydney Wooderson and some of his great rivals. (The story of his sixteen years running career with an analysis of his greatest races.) [With portraits.] pp. 39. *Vail & Co.: London,* [1948.] 8°. **7917.** de. **88.**

BUTLER (Hannah) Alcohol and Character, and other temperance essays. pp. 31. *A. H. Stockwell: London,* 1925. 8°. **8436**. eee. **37**.

BUTLER (*Sir* Harcourt) *G.C.S.I.* *See* Butler (*Sir* Spencer H.)

BUTLER (*Sir* Harold Beresford) *K.C.M.G.*

—— *See* Fletcher (Charles R. L.) Historical Portraits, *etc.* (1600–1700. The lives by H. B. Butler . . . and C. R. L. Fletcher.) 1909, *etc.* 4°. **2409**. d. **4**.

—— *See* Southey (Robert) [*Life of Nelson.*] Southey's Life of Nelson. Edited, with introduction and notes, by H. B. Butler, *etc.* 1911. 8°. **010815**. de. **1**.

—— The Confident Morning. [Reminiscences. With a portrait.] pp. 192. *Faber & Faber: London,* 1950. 8°. **10862**. cc. **33**.

—— The Economic Factor in International Affairs. A lecture, *etc.* pp. 36. *Manchester,* 1939. 8°. [*Manchester University Lectures.* no. 35.] **Ac.2671/4.(35.)**

—— Industrial Relations in the United States. pp. 135. *Geneva,* 1927. 8°. [*International Labour Office. Studies and Reports.* ser. A. no. 27.] **U.N.H.4.**

—— The International Labour Organization. pp. 38. *Oxford University Press: London,* 1939. 8°. **8288**. de. **27**.

—— The Lost Peace. A personal impression. pp. 224. *Faber & Faber: London,* 1941. 8°. **9100**. c. **28**.

—— Peace or Power. [With maps.] pp. 269. *Faber & Faber: London,* 1947. 8°. **8011**. eee. **19**.

—— Peace through Social Justice. A speech delivered . . . at the Trades Union Congress . . . 1938. Together with extracts from the Labour Section of the Treaty of Versailles and the Constitution of the International Labour Organisation. With an editorial note. pp. 13. *Peace Book Co.: London,* [1939.] 8°. [*Platform Pamphlet.* no. 3.] **8025.cc.46/3.**

—— Problems of Industry in the East. With special reference to India, French India, Ceylon, Malaya and the Netherlands Indies. pp. iv. 74. *Geneva,* 1938. 8°. [*International Labour Office. Studies and Reports.* ser. B. no. 29.] **U.N.H.5.**

—— Unemployment Problems in the United States. pp. 112. *Geneva,* 1931. 8°. [*International Labour Office. Studies and Reports.* ser. C. no. 17.] **U.N.H.6.**

BUTLER (Harold Edgeworth) *See* Apuleius (L.) *Madaurensis.* [*Two or more Works.—English.*] The Apologia and Florida . . . Translated by H. E. Butler. 1909. 8°. **8460**. bbb. **24**.

—— *See* Apuleius (L.) *Madaurensis.* [*Apologia.—Latin.*] Apulei Apologia . . . With introduction and commentary by H. E. Butler . . . and A. S. Owen. 1914. 8°. **8486**. bb. **26**.

—— *See* Apuleius (L.) *Madaurensis.* [*Asinus Aureus.—English.*] The Metamorphoses or Golden Ass . . . Translated by H. E. Butler. 1910. 8°. **11375**. aaa. **16**.

—— *See* Apuleius (L.) *Madaurensis.* [*Asinus Aureus.—Selections.—Latin.*] Cupid & Psyche . . . With notes and introduction by H. E. Butler. 1922. 8°. **12403**. e. **31**.

BUTLER (Harold Edgeworth)

—— *See* Cicero (M. T.) [*Orations.—De Provinciis Consularibus.—Latin.*] M. Tulli Ciceronis De Provinciis Consularibus Oratio . . . Edited, with introduction, notes, and appendices, by H. E. Butler . . . and M. Cary. 1924. 8°. **11396**. de. **6**

—— *See* Edgeworth (Maria) [*Selections and Extracts.*] Tour in Connemara and the Martins of Ballinahinch. Edited by H. E. Butler. 1950. 8°. **010390**. ee. **21**.

—— *See* Edgeworthstown. The Black Book of Edgeworthstown. Edited by H. J. Butler and H. E. Butler. 1927. 8°. **9907**. aa. **10**.

—— *See* Fitzstephen (William) A Description of London . . . Translated by H. E. Butler. 1934. 8°. [*Historical Association Leaflet.* no. 93, 94.] Ac. **8116**. b.

—— *See* Giraldus [de Barry], *Cambrensis, Archdeacon of St. David's.* The Autobiography of Giraldus Cambrensis. Edited and translated by H. E. Butler, *etc.* 1937. 8°. **20030**. i. **17**.

—— *See* Horatius Flaccus (Q.) [*Carmina.—Latin and English.*] The Odes of Horace . . . With translations by various hands chosen by H. E. Butler. 1929. 8°. **11375**. de. **33**.

—— *See* Joannes, *Saresberiensis, Bishop of Chartres.* The Letters of John of Salisbury. Edited by W. J. Millor . . . and H. E. Butler, *etc.* 1955, *etc.* 8°. W.P. **3189/10**.

—— *See* Jocelinus, *de Brakelonda, Monk of St. Edmundsbury.* The Chronicle of Jocelin of Brakelond . . . Translated . . . with introduction, notes and appendices by H. E. Butler. 1949. 8°. W.P. **3189/1**.

—— *See* Livius (Titus) *Patavinus.* Livy, Book xxx. Edited by H. E. Butler . . . and H. H. Scullard, *etc.* 1939. 8°. W.P. **3360/1**.

—— *See* Livius (T.) *Patavinus.* Livy, book xxx. Edited by H. E. Butler . . . and H. H. Scullard. 1953. 8°. W.P. **3360/12**.

—— *See* Livius (T.) *Patavinus.* [*Latin and English.*] The Close of the Second Punic War . . . Edited by H. E. Butler. 1925. 8°. W.P. **6801/17**.

—— *See* Propertius (S.) Sexti Properti opera omnia. With a commentary by H. E. Butler. 1905. 8°. **011388.a.30.**

—— *See* Propertius (S.) Propertius. With an English translation by H. E. Butler. 1912. 8°. **2282**. d. **7**.

—— *See* Propertius (S.) The Elegies of Propertius. Edited with an introduction and commentary by H. E. Butler . . . and E. A. Barber. 1933. 8°. **11352**. cc. **13**.

—— *See* Quintilianus (M. F.) The Institutio Oratoria . . . With an English translation by H. E. Butler. 1920, *etc.* 8°. **2282**. d. **59**.

—— *See* Sallustius Crispus (C.) [*Catilina.—Latin.*] The Catilinarian Conspiracy, from Sallust & Cicero . . . Edited by H. E. Butler. 1921. 8°. W.P. **6801/3**.

—— *See* Sallustius Crispus (C.) [*Jugurtha.—Latin.*] Sallust. The Jugurthine War . . . Edited by H. E. Butler. 1921. 8°. W.P. **6801/1**.

—— *See* Suetonius Tranquillus (C.) [*Vitae XII. Caesarum.*] C. Suetoni Tranquilli Divus Iulius. Edited . . . by H. E. Butler, *etc.* 1927. 8°. **10607**. b. **12**.

BUTLER (Harold Edgeworth)

—— *See* Virgilius Maro (P.) [*Aeneis.—Latin.*] The Shorter Aeneid . . . With a preface and introduction by H. E. Butler. 1914. 8°. **11352.** c. **18.**

—— *See* Virgilius Maro (P.) [*Aeneis.—Latin.*] The Fourth Book of Virgil's Aeneid. Edited by H. E. Butler. 1935. 8°. **20019.** ee. **23.**

—— *See* Virgilius Maro (P.) [*Aeneis.—Latin.*] The Sixth Book of the Aeneid. With introduction and notes by H. E. Butler. 1920. 8°. **11352.** df. **15.**

—— Arcadia. The Newdigate Prize Poem, 1899. pp. 11. *B. H. Blackwell: Oxford,* 1899. 8°. **11601.** d. **39.** (**3.**)

—— Post-Augustan Poetry from Seneca to Juvenal. pp. viii. 323. *Clarendon Press: Oxford,* 1909. 8°. **11313.** d. **29.**

—— War Songs of Britain. Selected by H. E. Butler. pp. 239. *A. Constable & Co.: Westminster,* 1903. 8°. **11603.** d. **40.**

BUTLER (Harold Edgeworth) and **SOLOMON** (Lawrence)

—— Easy Passages for Translation into Latin Prose. Selected by H. E. Butler . . . and L. Solomon. pp. 61. *University Press: London,* 1923. 4°. **012933.** a. **20.**

BUTLER (Harriet) *Mrs., of London.* Vensenshon; or Love's mazes. A novel. 3 vol. *Printed for the Author: London,* 1806. 12°. **12613.** bb. **15.**

BUTLER (Harriet) *Wife of the Dean of Clonmacnoise.* A Memoir of the Very Rev. Richard Butler, Dean of Clonmacnois, and Vicar of Trim. [With a portrait.] pp. 262. [*Printed for private circulation:*] *Edinburgh,* 1863. 4°. **4956.** h. **4.**

BUTLER (Harriet Allen) *See* Butler (William Allen) A Retrospect of Forty Years . . . Edited by . . . H. A. Butler, *etc.* 1911. 8°. **010883.** ff. **32.**

BUTLER (Harriet E.) A Course of Simple Paper Modelling without a ruler. For infants and standard 1. ff. xxxiv. *Philip, Son & Nephew: Liverpool; G. Philip & Son: London,* [1909.] *obl.* fol. **1889.** a. **26.**

BUTLER (Harriet Jessie) *See* Edgeworthstown. The Black Book of Edgeworthstown . . . Edited by H. J. Butler and H. E. Butler. 1927. 8°. **9907.** aa. **10.**

BUTLER (Harriette) Lays of the Heart. pp. 104. *J. Gleave: Manchester,* 1833. 12°. **11646.** cc. **40.**

BUTLER (*Lady* Harriot) Memoirs of Lady Harriot Butler: now first published from authentic papers, in the Lady's own hand-writing. 2 vol. *R. Freeman: London,* 1741 [1761], 62. 12°. **12612.** cc. **7.**

BUTLER (Henricus) Dissertatio medica inauguralis de apoplexia. pp. 17. *Lugduni Batavorum,* 1710. 4°. **1185.** h. **8.** (**21.**)

—— [Another copy.] **1185.** h. **8.** (**25.**)

BUTLER (Henry) *Captain.* South African Sketches: illustrative of the wild life of a hunter on the frontier of the Cape Colony. pp. 15. *Ackermann & Co.: London,* 1841. fol. **1788.** a. **8.**

BUTLER (Henry) *Dramatic Agent. See* Periodical Publications.—*London.* The Manager's Circular . . . Edited by H. Butler. 1851. fol. **1880.** c. **1.** (**155.**)

—— Henry Butler's Dramatic Almanac, *etc. See* Ephemerides.

—— Henry Butler's Theatrical Directory and Dramatic Almanack. *See* Ephemerides. Henry Butler's Dramatic Almanac, *etc.*

BUTLER (Henry) *Temperance Missionary.* Love Everybody, and Fear Nobody: a temperance tract. pp. 16. *John Beall: Newcastle-on-Tyne,* [1866.] 8°. **8435.** aaa. **22.**

BUTLER (Henry D.) The Family Aquarium; or Aqua Vivarium . . . Being a familiar and complete instructor upon the subject of the construction, fitting-up, stocking, and maintenance of the fluvial and marine aquaria, or "river and ocean gardens." pp. 121. *Dick & Fitzgerald: New York,* 1858. 12°. **7298.** aa. **15.**

BUTLER (Henry Edmund) *Viscount Mountgarrett.*

—— *See* Butler (*Hon.* Pierce S.) Butler against Mountgarrett, *etc.* [1859.] 8°. **6504.** b. **6.**

BUTLER (Henry Montagu) *See* Bible.—*Selections.* [*Polyglott.*] Six Translations from the Old and New Testaments into Homeric Verse. By H. M. B. [i.e. H. M. Butler.] 1876. 8°. **3109.** de. **9.**

—— *See* Butler (James R. M.) Henry Montagu Butler, *etc.* [With portraits.] 1925. 8°. **010856.** g. **33.**

—— *See* Denman (*Right Hon.* George) Intervalla. Verses Greek, Latin and English. [Selected by H. M. Butler and Sir J. E. Sandys.] 1898. 8°. **11408.** ee. **75.**

—— *See* Graham (Edward) *Assistant Master in Harrow School.* The Harrow Life of Henry Montagu Butler, *etc.* [With portraits.] 1920. 8°. **4908.** g. **15.**

—— *See* Hymnals. Hymns. For the Chapel of Harrow School, *etc.* [Edited by H. M. Butler.] 1857. 16°. **3434.** b. **22.**

—— *See* Hymnals. Hymns for the Chapel of Harrow School, *etc.* [Edited by H. M. Butler and others.] 1895. 8°. **3435.** gg. **12.**

—— The Attraction of the Cross. *See* Vaughan (Charles J.) *Dean of Llandaff.* The School of Life, *etc.* 1885. 8°. **4465.** b. **3.**

—— Belief in Christ, and other sermons, preached in the Chapel of Trinity College, Cambridge, *etc.* pp. xx. 302. *Macmillan & Bowes: Cambridge,* 1898. 8°. **4477.** eee. **28.**

—— The Character of Edmund Burke. An oration, delivered in the hall of Trinity College, *etc.* pp. 16. *Macmillan & Co.: Cambridge,* [1854.] 8°. **10803.** bb. **29.** (**1.**)

—— The Christian Ideal and the Christian Hope. *See* Swete (Henry B.) Essays on some Theological Questions of the Day, *etc.* 1905. 8°. **4379.** h. **33.**

—— "Crossing the Bar," and a few other translations. By H. M. B. [i.e. H. M. Butler.] pp. 67. 1890. 8°. *See* B., H. M. **11408.** d. **58.**

—— The Death of the Bishop of Calcutta [G. E. L. Cotton]. A sermon, *etc.* pp. 15. *Macmillan & Co.: London; Crossley & Clark: Harrow,* 1866. 8°. **4905.** b. **45.** (**7.**)

—— "Feed my Lambs." A sermon preached . . . at the consecration of . . . R. T. Davidson, D.D., Lord Bishop of Rochester, and . . . Mandell Creighton, D.D., Lord Bishop of Peterborough. pp. 11. *Macmillan & Bowes: Cambridge*, 1891. 8°. **4475. g. 39. (17.)**

—— "Gather up the Fragments." A sermon, *etc.* pp. 12. *Macmillan & Bowes: Cambridge*, 1898. 8°. **4475. f. 55. (17.)**

—— "God is Light." A sermon preached . . . in reference to the sudden death of . . . the Rev. L. J. Bernays. pp. 16. *Macmillan & Co.: London; J. C. Wilbee: Harrow*, 1882. 8°. **4920. de. 13. (3.)**

—— "He served his Generation." A sermon preached . . . the Sunday after the funeral of the Very Rev. C. J. Vaughan. pp. 16. *Macmillan & Bowes: Cambridge*, 1897. 8°. **4804. h. 10. (9.)**

—— Hymns, for the Chapel of Harrow School. Third edition, enlarged [of the work originally edited by C. J. Vaughan], *etc.* [Edited by H. M. Butler.] pp. iv. 284. 1866. 8°. *See* Hymnals. **3438. e. 70.**

—— Hymns for the Chapel of Harrow School. Fourth edition revised and enlarged [of the work originally edited by C. J. Vaughan], *etc.* [Edited by H. M. Butler.] pp. viii. 486. 1881. 8°. *See* Hymnals. **3438. ff. 14.**

—— "I was in Prison, and ye came unto Me." An address delivered . . . at a meeting of the Discharged Prisoners' Aid Society. pp. 12. *Bowes & Bowes: Cambridge*, 1910. 8°. **4466. ee. 32. (5.)**

—— "It is I; be not afraid." A sermon, *etc.* pp. 16. *J. C. Wilbee: Harrow*, [1894.] 8°. **4476. df. 6. (9.)**

—— "Lift up your Hearts"; or, Words of good cheer for the Holy Communion. pp. xvi. 112. *Macmillan & Bowes: Cambridge*, 1898. 8°. **4324. bbb. 20.**

—— Second edition, enlarged. pp. xvi. 153. *Bowes & Bowes: Cambridge*, 1914. 8°. **4324. e. 21.**

—— "Lord, and what shall this man do?" The future of friends. A sermon, *etc.* pp. 16. *Parker & Co.: London*, 1889. 8°. **4473. g. 30. (2.)**

—— "The Mind of Christ." A sermon preached in Guiseley Church . . . March 29th, 1908. pp. 15. *University Press: Cambridge*, [1908.] 8°. **4481. a. 67.**

—— *Μνημονευετε των ἡγουμενων.* A sermon . . . in reference to the death of Lord Tennyson. pp. 15. *Macmillan & Bowes: London*, 1892. 8°. **10803. cc. 11. (15.)**

—— Nevile's Court a Hospital. A sermon, *etc.* pp. 10. *Bowes & Bowes: Cambridge*, 1914. 8°. **4465. m. 25. (4.)**

—— Overcome Evil with Good. A sermon, *etc.* pp. 16. *R.T.S.: London*, [1888.] 8°. **4473. g. 24. (7.)**

—— Public School Sermons. pp. 271. *Isbister & Co.: London*, 1899. 8°. **4479. ee. 31.**

—— Public Schools: the conditions of their permanence. A sermon, *etc.* pp. 18. *Macmillan & Co.: London; Crossley & Clark: Harrow*, 1867. 8°. **4477. aa. 16.**

—— The Romanes Lecture, 1912. Lord Chatham as an orator, *etc.* pp. 40. *Clarendon Press: Oxford*, 1912. 8°. **010803. g. 1. (7.)**

—— St. Paul's Fourfold Charge. A sermon preached . . . at the consecration of . . . F. H. Chase, D.D., as Bishop of Ely . . . C. H. Gill, M.A., as Bishop of Travancore, *etc.* pp. 12. *Macmillan & Bowes: Cambridge*, 1905. 8°. **4475. f. 67. (2.)**

—— St. Paul's Summary. A sermon preached before the University of Cambridge, *etc.* pp. 12. *Fabb & Tyler: Cambridge*, [1913.] 8°. **4463. h. 25. (11.)**

—— [A Sermon preached after the death of F. W. Farrar.] *See* Farrar (Frederic W.) *Dean of Canterbury.* Three Sermons, *etc.* 1903. 8°. **4906. k. 22.**

—— A Sermon preached in the Cathedral Church of St. Paul at the two hundred and twenty-seventh Anniversary Festival of the Sons of the Clergy. pp. 14. *Rivingtons: London*, 1881. 8°. **4473. f. 20. (20.)**

—— A Sermon preached in the Chapel of Jesus College, Cambridge, May 8, 1910, on the occasion of the death of His Majesty King Edward vii. pp. 12. *Bowes & Bowes: Cambridge*, 1910. 8°. **4463. h. 23. (5.)**

—— Sermons preached in the Chapel of Harrow School. 2 ser. *Macmillan & Co.: Cambridge; Crossley & Clarke: Harrow*, 1861, 69. 8°. **4463. f. 8.**

—— Some Leisure Hours of a Long Life. Translations into Greek, Latin, and English verse from 1850 to 1914. pp. xv. 593. *Bowes & Bowes: Cambridge*, 1914. 8°. **11405. bb. 44.**

—— Specialization. The presidential address delivered to the Teachers' Guild, May 24, 1900 . . . Reprinted from the "Journal of Education." pp. 11. *London*, [1900.] 8°. **08311. h. 70.**

—— "Sudden Death." A sermon, *etc.* pp. 16. *Macmillan & Co.: London; J. C. Wilbee: Harrow*, 1882. 8°. **4473. aa. 43. (5.)**

—— Ten Great and Good Men. Lectures. pp. xii. 313. *Edward Arnold: London*, 1909. 8°. **4804. e. 17.**

—— New edition. pp. xii. 313. *Edward Arnold: London*, 1912. 8°. **4804. e. 29.**

—— To the Vice-Master and All the Fellows of Our Dear College who so kindly joined in the address on the occasion of my eightieth birthday, July 2, 1913, *etc.* [A poem, signed: H. M. B., i.e. H. M. Butler.] [1913.] 8°. *See* B., H. M. **11656. b. 82.**

—— University Extension. Universities. An inaugural address, *etc.* pp. 20. *Bowes & Bowes: Cambridge*, 1908. 8°. **8306. de. 32. (4.)**

—— War in a Christian Spirit. A sermon, *etc.* pp. 16. *Macmillan & Co.: London*, 1879. 8°. **4479. d. 3. (11.)** *"Not published."*

BUTLER (Henry Thomas) The Existence & Immortality of the Soul. pp. 143. *Lincoln Williams: London*, 1932. 8°. **4256. dd. 21.**

—— New revised edition. pp. vii. 109. *Lincoln Williams: London*, 1933. 8°. **4255. ff. 39.**

—— Fifth edition. pp. 180. *Technical Publications: London*, 1937. 8°. **4225. h. 75.**

BUTLER (Herbert E.) *See* Blades (William) The Enemies of Books . . . Illustrated by L. Gunnis and H. E. Butler. 1896. 4°. **11906. cc. 3.**

—— *See* MacGaffey (Ernest) Poems of Gun and Rod . . . Illustrated by H. E. Butler. 1892. 8°. **11687. ee. 9.**

BUTLER (Herbert E.)

—— *See* Paris.—*Exposition Universelle Internationale de* 1900. The Paris Exhibition, 1900. Edited by D. Croal Thomson, assisted by H. E. Butler, *etc.* 1901. fol. **P.P.1931.pc/5.**

BUTLER (Herbert James) Body Repair and Painting. 1933. *See* Stuart (J. R.) *Writer on Motor Engineering.* Garage Workers' Handbooks, *etc.* vol. 3. 1933, *etc.* 8°. W.P. **10410/3.**

—— Motor Bodies and Chassis. A text-book dealing with the complete car, for the use of owners, students, and others. Foreword by . . . Lord Montagu of Beaulieu. pp. xxiv. 328. *Harper & Bros.: London & New York,* 1912. 8°. **08767.** bb. **42.**

—— Motor Body Drawing, *etc.* pp. xi. 113. pl. 16. *W. R. Howell & Co.: London,* 1927. 4°. **8763.** dd. **18.**
The plates are in a separate portfolio.

—— Motor Bodywork. The design and construction of private, commercial, and passenger types, *etc.* pp. xxiii. 492. pl. L. *W. R. Howell & Co.: London,* 1924. 8°. **8763.** d. **14.**

—— Private and Commercial Motor Body Building. pp. ix. 248. *Sir I. Pitman & Sons: London,* 1932. 8°. **07945.** i. **68.**

BUTLER (Herbert James) and **BUTLER** (Hugh E. J.)

—— Electrical Equipment of the Car. Comprising the various systems fitted to British, French, Italian, German and other European cars, *etc.* 3 vol. *W. R. Howell & Co.: London,* 1926. 8°. **8759.** b. **23**

BUTLER (Hildred M.) Blood Cultures and their Significance, *etc.* pp. xiv. 327. pl. 3. 1937. 8°. *See* Melbourne.—*Alfred Hospital.—Baker Institute of Medical Research.* **07560.** e. **45.**

BUTLER (Hiram Erastus) *See* Periodical Publications.—*Applegate.* The Occult and Biological Journal . . . H. E. Butler, editor. 1900, *etc.* 4°. P.P. **598.** wb.

—— *See* Periodical Publications.—*Boston, Massachusetts.* The Esoteric, *etc.* [Edited by H. E. Butler and others.] 1888, *etc.* 8°. P.P. **598.** w.

—— The Goal of Life; or, Science and revelation. pp. xi. 363. *Esoteric Publishing Co.: Applegate, Cal.; L. N. Fowler & Co.: London,* 1908. 8°. **4017.** ee. **38.**

—— The Narrow Way of Attainment . . . With introductory paper translated from the German, by Prof. Wieland. pp. 30. *Esoteric Publishing Co.: Boston,* 1888. 8°. **8630.** ee. **30.** **(3.)**

—— The Narrow Way of Attainment, *etc.* pp. 140. *Esoteric Publishing Co.: Applegate,* 1901. 8°. **08408.** h. **97.**

—— Practical Methods to Insure Success . . . Twenty-fourth edition. pp. 129. *L. N. Fowler & Co.: London; Esoteric Publishing Co.: Applegate, Cal.,* 1910. 8°. **7410.** aaaa. **37.**

—— The Seven Creative Principles: being a series of seven lectures . . . With colored illustrations. pp. 170. *Esoteric Publishing Co.: Boston,* 1887. 8°. **8632.** cc. **16.**

BUTLER (Hiram Erastus)

—— Solar Biology: a scientific method of delineating character; diagnosing disease . . . With illustrations [including a portrait]. [Edited by John Latham.] pp. xxxix. 290. *Esoteric Publishing Co.: Boston,* 1887. 8°. **8610.** ee. **12.**

—— Seventeenth edition, *etc.* pp. xxxix. 288. *Esoteric Publishing Co.: Applegate, Cal.; L. N. Fowler & Co.: London,* [1914.] 8°. **8610.** g. **10.**

BUTLER (Howard Crosby)

—— *See* Princeton, *New Jersey.—Princeton University.* Syria. Publications of the Princeton University Archæological Expeditions to Syria in 1904–5 and 1909. (Division I. Geography and itinerary.—Section B. The Expedition of 1909. By H. C. Butler.) 1907, *etc.* 4°. Ac. **1833.** c.

—— **Ancient Architecture in Syria. 2 vol.** ***E. G. Brill: Leyden,*** **1907–21. 4°. [*Syria. Publications of the Princeton University Archaeological Expeditions to Syria, in* 1904–1905 *and* 1909. Division 2.] Ac. 1833. c.**
Published in parts.

—— Architecture and other Arts. (Northern Central Syria and the Djebel Haurân.) pp. xxv. 433. *Century Co.: New York; William Heinemann: London,* 1904. 4°. [*Publications of an American Archæological Expedition to Syria in* 1899–1900. pt. 2.] **7701.ccc.9/2.**

—— **Early Churches in Syria, fourth to seventh centuries . . . Edited and completed by E. Baldwin Smith. pp. xx. 274. *Princeton,* 1929. fol. [*Princeton Monographs in Art and Archaeology.* Folio series. no. 1.] Ac. 1833/3A.**

—— Sardis . . . The Excavations. [With plans and illustrations.] pp. xi. 213. pl. IV. *E. J. Brill: Leyden,* 1922. 4°. [*Sardis.* vol. 1. pt. 1.] Ac. **5210.**

—— Scotland's Ruined Abbeys . . . With illustrations by the author. pp. xx. 287. *Macmillan Co.: New York,* 1899. 4°. **10370.** e. **24.**

—— The Story of Athens. A record of the life and art of the City of the Violet Crown, read in its ruins and in the lives of great Athenians . . . With many illustrations, *etc.* pp. xvi. 532. *Century Co.: New York,* 1902. 8°. **9026.** c. **21.**

—— [A reissue.] *F. Warne & Co.: London & New York,* [1903.] 8°. **9026.** c. **22.**

—— The Temple of Artemis. pp. xii. 146. *E. J. Brill: Leyden,* 1925. 4°. [*Sardis.* vol. 2. pt. 1.] Ac. **5210.**

—— Atlas of plates. *obl.* fol. **1735.** f. **5.**

—— Howard Crosby Butler, 1872–1922. [Memorial exercises. With a portrait.] pp. 106. *University Press: Princeton,* 1923. 8°. **10884.** b. **21.**

BUTLER (Howard Russell) Painter and Space; or, the Third dimension in graphic art. [With plates.] pp. xv. 178. *C. Scribner's Sons: New York.* 1923. 4°. **7870.ff.17.**

BUTLER (Hubert)

—— *See* Chekhov (A. P.) [*Single Works.*] The Cherry Orchard . . . Translated . . . by H. Butler, *etc.* [1934.] 8°. W.P. **2236/84.**

BUTLER (HUBERT)

—— *See* LEONOV (Leonid) [Воръ.] The Thief. (Authorized translation . . . by H. Butler.) 1931. 8°. **12590**. p. **4**.

BUTLER (HUGH D.)

—— British Market for Electrical Machinery and Equipment. pp. ii. 38. [*Washington*, 1928.] 8°. [*U.S. Bureau of Foreign and Domestic Commerce. Trade Information Bulletin.* no. 558.] A.S. **128/3**.

—— Expenditures and Commitments by the United States Government in or for Latin America. Report by Hon. H. Butler . . . and the Reply to such report made by Hon. Kenneth McKellar, *etc.* pp. xi. 170. *Washington*, 1943. 8°. [*U.S. Senate Documents.* 78th Congress. 1st Session. no. 132.] A.S. **10/4**.

—— The Irish Free State. An economic survey, *etc.* pp. vi. 86. *Washington*, 1928. 8°. [*U.S. Department of Commerce. Trade Promotion Series.* no. 62.] A.S. **126/2**.

BUTLER (HUGH E. J.) *See* BUTLER (Herbert J.) and (H. E. J.) Electrical Equipment of the Car, *etc.* 1926. 8°. **8759**. b. **23**.

—— Electric Resistance Welding. A practical guide to spot, seam, projection and butt welding methods. pp. 182. *George Newnes: London*, 1950. 8°. **8754**. bb. **33**.

BUTLER (HUGH ERNEST)

—— The Equivalent Widths of Calcium and Hydrogen Absorption Lines in the near Infra-Red of Stellar Spectra. pp. 28. pl. I. [*Dublin*, 1951.] 8°. [*Contributions from the Dunsink Observatory.* no. 1.] Ac. **1541**. c.

BUTLER (HUGH MONTAGU) Shakespeare Plays in Schools. pp. viii. 57. *C. A. Ribeiro & Co.: Singapore & Penang*, 1922. 8°. **011765**. h. **40**.

—— [Another copy.] **11765**. e. **46**.

BUTLER (I.) *Dr., of Woolwich.* *See* FENNER (David) A Reply to a letter written by Dr. Butler, published by Mr. Matthews of Woolwich. 1825. 8°. **4920**. f. **25**. (**5**.)

BUTLER (*Lady* IRENE JUNE BEATRICE) The Death of Summer, and other verses. pp. 26. *Hodder & Stoughton: London*, [1921.] 12°. **11647**. aaa. **64**.

BUTLER (ISABEL) *See* ROLAND. The Song of Roland. Translated into English prose by I. Butler. [1904.] 8°. **11498**. bbb. **42**.

—— —— 1906. fol. C. **70**. i. **5**.

—— —— [1907.] 8°. **12206**. c. **64**.

—— Tales from the Old French. Translated by I. Butler. pp. 264. *Constable & Co.: London; Cambridge, Mass.* [printed], 1910. 8°. **12403**. d. **30**.

BUTLER (IVAN)

—— *See* CARY (Thomas F. L.) and BUTLER (I.) The Paper Chain, *etc.* [1953.] 8°. **11791**. t. **1/666**.

—— Columbine in Camberwell. A play in one act. pp. 29. *H. F. W. Deane & Sons: London*, [1953.] 8°. [" *Deane's*" *Series of Plays.*] W.P. **11466/141**.

—— Crime out of Mind. A play in three acts. [With plates.] pp. 83. *Rylee: London*, [1952.] 8°. **11784**. f. **5**.

BUTLER (IVAN)

—— Tranquil House. A play in three acts. pp. 78. *Stacey Publications: London*, 1954. 8°. **11784**. f. **38**.

—— The Wise Children. A play in three acts. pp. 80. *Stacey Publications: London*, 1953. 8°. **11784**. f. **29**.

BUTLER (J.) *pseud.* [i.e. JEAN CHARLES JACQUES FRANÇOIS HERVÉ.] *See* BRASSEY (Annie) *Baroness Brassey.* Voyage d'une famille autour du monde . . . Traduit . . . par J. Butler, *etc.* [1878.] 8°. **10025**. s. **1**.

—— *See* MURRAY (Eustace C. G.) La Cabale de boudoir. Roman traduit . . . par J. Butler. 1876. 8°. **12604**. df. **2**.

—— *See* MURRAY (Eustace C. G.) Les Russes chez les Russes . . . Roman traduit . . . par J. Butler. 1878. 8°. **10290**. bb. **9**.

—— *See* MURRAY (Eustace C. G.) Une Famille endettée. Roman traduit . . . par J. Butler. 1878. 8°. **12604**. df. **16**.

—— *See* MURRAY (Eustace C. G.) Veuve ou mariée? Roman traduit . . . par J. Butler. 1877. 8°. **12604**. df. **6**.

—— *See* MURRAY (Eustace C. G.) Le Jeune Brown. Roman traduit . . . par J. Butler. 1875. 12°. **12603**. e. **5**.

BUTLER (J.) *Rev.* *See* BIBLE.—*Leviticus.* [*Chinese.—Ningpo dialect.*] Gyiu-iah shii Li-vi kyi. [Translated by J. Butler.] 1880. 8°. **15117**. b. **1**.

BUTLER (JAMES) *A.M.I.Mech.E.*

—— *See* ELWELL (A. G.) and BUTLER (J.) Thermosetting Moulding Shop Problems. 1947. 8°. W.P. **3139/17a**.

—— Moulds and Moulding. Part 1. The 69 grenade. pp. 96. *Institute of the Plastics Industry: London*, 1945. 8°. [*Plastics Monograph.* no. 24.] W.P. **3139/24**.

—— Transfer and Injection Moulding—thermosetting materials. pp. 138. *Institute of the Plastics Industry: London*, 1949. 8°. [*Plastics Monograph.* no. 16.] W.P. **3139/16**.

BUTLER (JAMES) *Author of "The Conundrum."* The Conundrum. (The Conundrum, or Vivat justitia . . . The first rehearsal of an heterocli'tical farce, neat as imported from Persia by Sir G——e O*sl*y, modernized by Le Sage, Cervantes, and Sterne, and as translated from the Arabic manuscript of Von Bravura de Rifla Boro, by James Butler.) pp. 146. MS. NOTES [by the author?]. *Printed for the Author: London*, [1816?] 4°. **1346**. m. **12**.

Not published.

—— [Another copy.] MS. CORRECTIONS [by the author?]. **11630**. f. **6**.

BUTLER (JAMES) *Boxing Commentator.*

—— *See* TAYLOR (W. Buchanan) What do you Know about Boxing? . . . J. Butler collaborated. 1947. 8°. **7918**. bb. **17**.

—— The Fight Game. By James and Frank Butler, *etc.* [With plates, including portraits.] pp. 222. *The World's Work: Kingswood*, 1954. 8°. **7919**. aa. **105**.

BUTLER (JAMES) *Captain.* *See* MURRAY (Alexander) *of Broughton.* Alexander Murray, Appellant. Capt. James Butler and others, Resp[ts]. The appellant's case. [1724.] fol. **19**. h. **2**. (**70**.)

BUTLER (James) *Commander of H.M. Sloop "Vulture."* The Case of James Butler, Esq., late an officer in his Majesty's Navy, respecting his connexions with the House of Ormond. pp. iv. 54. *London,* 1770. 8°. **1414**. h. **22**. **(3.)**

BUTLER (James) *Deputy Commissioner, Mergui.* Gazetteer of the Mergui District, Tenasserim Division, British Burma. pp. 84. x. *Government Press: Rangoon,* 1884. 8°. **10058**. k. **20**. **(3.)**

BUTLER (James) 1*st Duke of Ormonde.* [For official documents issued by the Duke of Ormonde as Lord Lieutenant of Ireland:] *See* Ireland.—[*Lords Lieutenant, etc.*]—Butler (James) 1*st Duke of Ormonde, Lord Lieutenant.*

—— The Copie of the Lord of Ormond's Letter to the Bishop of Dromer. [Dated: Bruges, 20 Sept. 1656.] (His Highnesse [Oliver Cromwell's] Letter to his Eminencie Cardinall Mazarin.) [*London,* 1657.] 4°. E. **912**. **(8.)**

—— The Declaration of His Excellency the Lord Marquis of Ormond, Lord Deputy of Ireland . . . Together with the Lord Inchequeene, and all the rest of the Kingdome; Concerning the death of His Sacred Majesty, who was murdered at White-Hall, the 30. of Ianuary; by an usurped power of the Commons of England, as they call themselves. Likewise their intentions to crown Prince Charles King, and ingage in his quarrell against England, *etc.* pp. 6. *Printed at Corke in Ireland, and now reprinted,* 1648. 4°. E. **544**. **(13.)**

—— The Marquesse of Ormond's Declaration, proclaiming Charles the Second, King of England, Scotland, France, and Ireland, *etc.* pp. 24. *For F. Tyton & I. Playford: London,* 1649. 4°. **522**. d. **63**.

—— Harangue de Monseigneur le Marquis d'Ormond Vice-roy d'Irlande, dans l'assemblée des catholiques de ce royaume là, sur la conclusion de leur paix, & leur vnion pour venger la mort de leur défunt roy, & asseurer le nouueau dans ses estats. *See* Charles ii., *King of Great Britain and Ireland.* [*Biography.*—i.] Nouuelle extraordinaire, *etc.* 1649. 4°. **807**. d. **7**. **(3.)**

—— [Another issue.] pp. 4. [*F. Prevveray: Paris,* 1649.] 4°. **9512**. c. **2**. **(14.)**

—— [Another edition.] pp. 8. *F. Prevveray: Paris,* 1649. 4°. **8145**. ee. **4**.

—— [Another copy.] **807**. d. **7**. **(12.)**

—— A Letter from his Grace James Duke of Ormond, Lord Lieutenant of Ireland, in answer to . . . Arthur Earl of Anglesey, Lord Privy-Seal, his observations and reflections upon the Earl of Castlehaven's Memoires concerning the rebellion of Ireland . . . With an answer to it by . . . the Earl of Anglesey. 2 pt. *For R. Baldwin: London,* 1682. fol. T. **3***. **(12.)**
The titlepage of the Letter of the Earl of Anglesey bears the imprint "Printed for N. P."

—— [Another copy.] **522**. m. **5**. **(13.)**

—— [Another copy of pt. 1.] **115**. i. **59**. **(4.)**

—— [Another edition.] 2 pt. *Sold by R. Baldwin: London,* 1682. fol. **807**. g. **5**. **(22.)**

—— [Another copy.] G. **5211**. **(1.)**

—— *See* Annesley (Arthur) *Earl of Anglesey.* A Letter . . . in answer to the Duke of Ormond's letter about his Lordship's observations upon the Earl of Castle-Haven's Memoires, concerning the rebellion of Ireland. 1682. fol. **115**. i. **26**.

BUTLER (James) 1*st Duke of Ormonde.*

—— A Letter sent out of Ireland from the right Honorable Earle of Ormond and Ossory, to his much honored Uncle, Sr Robert Poyntz, shewing the true estate of the Kingdome of Ireland at this present time (10 June, 1642), *etc.* *For Thomas Whitaker: London,* [1642.] *s. sh.* fol. **669**. f. **6**. **(38.)**

—— [Another copy.] **190**. g. **13**. **(47.)**

—— [Another edition.] *See* Smith (Samuel) *Waggon-Master to the Regiment of Sir C. Coote.* June the 24, 1642. The last joyfull newes from Ireland, *etc.* 1642. 4°. E. **152**. **(8.)**

—— The Marquesse of Ormond's Letter to His Majestie (4 Aug. 1649), concerning the late fight betwixt the forces under his command, and the garrison of Dublin . . . Together with the most considerable occurrences in relation to the appeasing of that kingdome, and embracing the Princes interest. pp. 6. [*London,*] 1649. 4°. E. **571**. **(21.)**

—— The Marquesse of Ormond's Letter to His Majestie King Charles ii. Wherein is truly related the manner of Collonel Jones sallying out of Dublin, Aug. 2. 1649 . . . And the taking of the two strong castles of Ballishannon and Athy, Aug. 8. Whereunto is added His Majesties Answer to his Letter, Aug. 11. 1649. pp. 5. [*London,*] 1649. 4°. E. **571**. **(16.)**

—— A True Copy of two Letters, the first [dated: 9 March 1648 o.s.] sent from the Earle of Ormond to the Honourable Colonell Michael Jones, Commander in chiefe of the Parliaments Forces in Leinster . . . With Colonell Jones his Answere [dated: 14 March 1648 o.s.], *etc.* [With two further letters, dated: 27 and 31 March 1649.] pp. 16. *Printed by William Bladen: Dublin, and now re-printed,* 1649. 4°. **8145**. b. **19**.

—— [Another copy.] E. **529**. **(28.)**

APPENDIX.

—— *See* Ayscue (*Sir* George) A Letter from Sir George Ayskew . . . of a great and famous victory obtained by Col: Jones, in the utter routing and defeating of the Marquesse of Ormond and his whole Army. [1649.] *s. sh.* fol. **C.112.h.4.(112.)**

—— *See* Boyle (Richard) 1*st Earl of Cork.* A Famous Battel fought by the Earle of Corke, the Earle of Ormond, and the Lord Moore against the rebels in Ireland . . . Also a great and bloody battell betwixt the Earle of Ormond and Tyrone, *etc.* 1642. 4°. **601**. d. **54**.

—— *See* Boyle (Roger) *Earl of Orrery.* A Collection of the State Letters of . . . Roger Boyle, the first Earl of Orrery . . . Containing a series of correspondence between the Duke of Ormond and his Lordship, from the Restoration to the year 1668, *etc.* 1742. fol. **2082**. f.

—— —— 1743. 8°. **596**. e. **23, 24**.

—— *See* Carte (Thomas) An History of the Life of James Duke of Ormonde, *etc.* 1736, *etc.* fol. **806**. i. **10–12**.

—— —— 1851. 8°. **2406**. g. **8**.

—— *See* Coffey (Diarmid) O'Neill & Ormond, *etc.* 1914. 8°. **9508**. cc. **17**.

—— *See* England. [*Proclamations.*—ii. Charles ii.] By the King. A Proclamation [dated 7 Dec. 1670, for the discovery of the persons who attempted to murder the Duke of Ormonde]. 1670. *s. sh.* fol. **1851**. c. **9**. **(43.)**

—— *See* ENGLAND. [*Miscellaneous Public Documents, etc.*—III. Charles I.] The Kings Letter to the Marquesse of Ormond: and the Marquesse of Ormonds letter to Monroe. [Dated: 13 Oct. 1646.] Relating the King's whole design, concerning all the three Kingdoms. 1646. 4°. **E. 340. (5*.)**

—— *See* ENGLAND. [*Miscellaneous Public Documents, etc.*—III. Charles I.] His Majesties Declaration to the Marquesse of Ormond (Dec. 1646) . . . With the Marquesse of Ormond's proceedings against this Kingdome and his delivering up the City of Dublin to the Rebels, *etc.* 1646. 8°. **E. 367. (9.)**

—— *See* ENGLAND. [*Miscellaneous Public Documents, etc.*—III. Charles I.] His Majesties Declaration and Message to the Marquis of Ormond . . . With a dangerous declaration of the said Marquis, *etc.* 1648. 4°. **E. 475. (28.)**

—— *See* FITZGERALD (Brian) The Anglo-Irish. Three representative types: Cork, Ormonde, Swift, 1602–1745. [With a portrait.] 1952. 8°. **9508. eee. 10.**

—— *See* FOX. The Fox Unkennel'd; or, the Whiggs Idol, *etc.* [Complimentary verses on the Duke of Ormonde.] [1672?] *s. sh.* fol. **Lutt. II. 83.**

—— *See* GARDNER (Winifred A. H. C.) *Baroness Burghclere.* The Life of James, first Duke of Ormonde. 1610–1688, *etc.* 1912. 8°. **010854. e. 30.**

—— *See* JONES (Michael) *General.* Lieut: General Jones's Letter to the Council of State, of a great victory . . . against the Earl of Ormond's and the Lord Inchiquin's forces, *etc.* 1649. 4°. **E. 568. (21.)**

—— *See* MORRES (Hervey R.) *Viscount Mountmorres.* The History of the Principal Transactions in the Irish Parliament from 1634 to 1666 . . . during the administration of . . . the first Duke of Ormond: with a narrative of his Grace's life, *etc.* 1792. 8°. **601. g. 2.**

—— *See* OXFORD.—*University of Oxford.* [*Academic Addresses, etc.*] Comitia philologica habita Aug. 6, 1677, in gratulatione solenni ob adventum expectatissimum Jacobi Ormondiæ Ducis, *etc.* 1677. fol. **105. f. 40.**

—— *See* PETERS (Hugh) A Declaration . . . With a more full and exact relation of the severall victories obtained by the Marquesse of Ormond, the L. Inchiquin, *etc.* 1646. 4°. **E. 363. (10.)**

—— *See* TREVERS (*Sir* Robert) A Certaine Relation of the Earle of Ormond's Proceedings in Ireland, *etc.* 1642. 4°. **E. 149. (14.)**

—— *See* WILLIAMS (John) successively *Bishop of Lincoln* and *Archbishop of York.* The Unpublished Correspondence between Archbishop Williams and the Marquis of Ormond, *etc.* 1869. 8°. **4905. d. 56. (13.)**

—— *See* WILSON (John) *Writer of Verse.* To his Grace James Duke of Ormond, Lord Lieutenant of Ireland, on his return to that government. 1677. *s. sh.* fol. **Lutt. I. (112.)**

—— Anonymous Account of the Early Life and Marriage of James, first Duke of Ormonde: with an appendix. Edited by the Rev. James Graves. pp. 27. *University Press: Dublin,* 1864. 8°. **10816. f. 4.**
One of a privately printed edition of twenty-five copies.

—— A Bloudy Fight at Dublin in Ireland, between the Marquesse of Ormond, and Col. Jones, *etc.* pp. 6. *For R. Williamson: London,* 1649. 4°. **E. 563. (6.)**

—— A Certaine Relation of the Earle of Ormond's nine dayes passages at his last going into the Pale against the Rebels. And also setting forth what prisoners he hath taken, *etc.* [Signed: W. L.] 1642. 4°. *See* L., W. **E. 141. (26.)**

—— Full Satisfaction concerning the Affairs of Ireland as they relate to the Marquesse of Ormonds transactions with the Lord of Inchiquin, *etc.* 1648. 4°. **9508.a.10.**

—— [Another copy.] **E. 536. (14.)**

—— A Great and Bloudy Fight at Dublin in Ireland, between the King of Scots Army, commanded by the Marq. of Ormond, and the Lord Inchiquin; and the Parliaments Army under the conduct of Col. Jones . . . shewing the manner, how the L. Inchiquin with a select, stout and resolute party, fell into the trenches of the Parl. forces, with the number killed and taken; his letter to Col. Jones concerning the Lord Lieut. Cromwell; a new Standard, erected and set up, for Charles the II, and the proclaiming of him King of England, Scotland, and Ireland, with all his titles thereunto belonging, and Col. Jones his resolution. pp. 6. *For R. W.* [*Robert Williamson*]: *London,* 1649. 4°. **E. 566. (2.)**

—— A Great Fight neer the City of Dublin in Ireland, betweene the Princes forces commanded by the Marquesse of Ormond, and the Parliaments forces under the conduct of Col. Jones, *etc.* pp. 6. *For R. W.* [*Robert Williamson*]: *London,* 1649. 4°. **E. 552. (25.)**

—— A Great Victory obtained by the Marquesse of Ormond and the Lord Inchiqueen against the Parliament forces, with the manner of their surrounding of Dublin . . . Also, the Declaration of the Irish Army, *etc.* pp. 6. *For R. Williamson: London,* 1649. 4°. **E. 568. (16.)**

—— Joyfull Newes from the Marquesse of Ormond and the Prince's Army in Ireland concerning their late fight with the Parliaments forces . . . Also, the Scots declaration [signed: A. Ker] concerning their declared King, and all those who have broken the Covenant, *etc.* pp. 6. *For R. W.* [*Robert Williamson*]: *London,* 1649. 4°. **E. 569. (12.)**

—— The Last Great and Bloudy Fight in Ireland on . . . the 29 of August, 1649, between the Marq. of Ormonds forces, and the Lord Governour Cromwels . . . Also, the Lord Governour Cromwels letter to the Parliament of England, *etc.* pp. 6. *For Robert Williamson: London,* 1649. 4°. **E. 572. (21.)**

—— The Late Prosperous Proceedings of the Protestant Army against the Rebells in Ireland. Being a true and perfect relation of a great and happy victory obtained by the Marquesse of Ormond, the Lord Lile, *etc.* [Signed: E. E., Doctor in Physicke.] B.L. 1643. 4°. *See* E., E., *Doctor in Physicke.* **E. 96. (8.)**

—— Observations on the Articles of Peace between James, Earl of Ormond, for King Charles the First, on the one hand, and the Irish Rebels and Papists on the other hand; and on a Letter sent by Ormond to Col. Jones, Governor of Dublin, *etc.* *See* MILTON (J.) *the Poet.* [*Prose Works.*] The Works of John Milton, *etc.* vol. 1. 1753. 4°. **685. i. 12.**

—— [Another edition.] *See* MILTON (J.) *the Poet.* [*Prose Works.*] The Prose Works of John Milton, *etc.* vol. 2. 1806. 8°. **2041. e.**

BUTLER (JAMES) 1*st Duke of Ormonde.* [APPENDIX.]

—— Ormonds Curtain drawn: in a short discourse concerning Ireland; wherein his treasons, and the corruption of his instruments are laid bare to the stroke of justice. [By Sir John Temple.] pp. 1–32. [*London*, 1646.] 4°. **E. 513. (14.)**
Incomplete; ending with p. 32. *No more published?*

—— Papers from Ireland, of the Marquesse of Ormonds coming in to the Parliament . . . And the manner of taking of Mariborough Fort, and the Castle of Athlone, *etc. For E. E.: London*, 1646. 4°. **E. 356. (2.)**

—— A Renowned Victory obtained against the Rebels on the first day of June neere Burros, the Duke of Buckinghams castle, by the valour of these noble and valiant commanders, the Earle of Ormond, the Earle of Eastmeath, *etc. For T. Horton: London*, 1642. 4°. **E. 150. (8.)**

—— [Another copy.] **G. 4156. (18.)**

—— To his Grace James, Duke of Ormond, Lord Lieutenant of Ireland, on his return to that government. [In verse.] [1677?] fol. **807. g. 5. (13.)**

—— To his Grace the Duke of Ormond, upon his leaving the government and kingdom of Ireland. [In verse.] *For Ben. Tooke: London*, 1685. *s. sh.* fol. **C. 38. l. 6. (21.)**

—— A True Account of the Whole Proceedings betwixt his Grace James Duke of Ormond, and . . . Arthur Earl of Anglesey, late Lord Privy-Seal, before the King and Council, and the said Earls letter of the second of August to His Majesty on that occasion. With a letter of the now Lord Bishop of Winchester's to the said Earl, of the means to keep out Popery, *etc.* pp. 28. *For Thomas Fox: London*, 1682. fol. **807. g. 5. (21.)**

—— [Another copy.] **1418. k. 22.**

—— [Another copy.] **514. l. 3. (8.)**

—— [Another copy.] **522. m. 5. (12.)**

—— [Another copy.] **C. 71. g. 2. (1.)**

—— [Another copy.] **G. 5211. (2.)**

—— A True and perfect Account of the discovery of a barbarous and bloody Plot by the Jesuites in Ireland, for the destroying of the Duke of Ormond . . . Sent over in a letter from Dublin, *etc.* [Signed: N. A.] 1679. 4°. *See* A., N. **G. 5579.**

—— A True Relation of divers great Defeats given against the Rebells of Ireland, by the Earle of Ormond . . . With a map describing the order of a battell lately fought there, *etc.* pp. 13. *Printed by Robert Barker and the Assignes of John Bill: London*, 1642. 4°. **E. 146. (11.)**

—— [Another copy.] **115. g. 5.**
Imperfect; wanting the map.

—— [Another copy.] **G. 4156. (41.)**
Imperfect; wanting the lower half of the map.

—— A True Relation of the late Expedition of the Rt. Hon. the Earl of Ormond, and Sir Charles Coote . . . into the severall Counties of Kildare, Queens County, Kings County, and the County of Catherlagh, *etc.* 1642. 4°. *See* L., A. **E. 144. (27.)**

—— Two Great Fights in Ireland . . . between the Marq: of Ormonds forces and the Lord Lieut. Cromwels at the two strong garrisons of Tredah and Dundalke, *etc.* pp. 6. [*London*, 1649.] 4°. **E. 574. (3.)**

BUTLER (JAMES) 2*nd Duke of Ormonde.* [For official documents issued by the Duke of Ormonde as Lord Lieutenant of Ireland:] *See* IRELAND.—[*Lords Lieutenant, etc.*]—Butler (James) 2*nd Duke of Ormonde, Lord Lieutenant.*

—— Letters . . . to Joseph Keally, Esq., *etc. See* BERKELEY (George M.) Literary Relics, *etc.* 1789. 8°. **1454. g. 6.**

—— Intercepted Correspondence of the Duke of Ormonde, &c., 1736 to 1738, from the Weston papers. *See* UNDERWOOD (Charles F. W.) The Manuscripts of Charles Fleetwood Weston Underwood, Esq., *etc.* 1885. 8°. [*Historical Manuscripts Commission.* no. 10.] **Bar.T.1.(10.)**

—— The Jacobite Attempt of 1719. Letters of James Butler, second Duke of Ormonde, relating to Cardinal Alberoni's project for the invasion of Great Britain on behalf of the Stuarts . . . Edited, with an introduction, notes and an appendix of original documents, by William Kirk Dickson. [With a portrait.] pp. lix. 306. *Edinburgh*, 1895. 8°. [*Publications of the Scottish History Society.* vol. 19.] **Ac. 8256.**

—— The Duke of Or - - - - - d's [i.e. the Duke of Ormonde's] Speech in the House of Lords on the behalf of Dr. Henry Sacheverell, &c. 1710. *s. sh.* fol. *See* OR - - - - - D, *Duke of.* **1865. c. 19. (68.)**

—— His Grace the Duke of Ormond's speech to His Majesty. (His Majesty's Most Gracious Answer.) *London*, [1714?] *s. sh.* fol. **Lutt. III. 5.**

—— Mémoires de la vie de mylord Duc d'Ormond . . . Traduit de l'anglois. 2 tom. *La Haye*, 1737. 8°. **292. d. 46.**

—— Memoirs of the Life of His Grace, James, late Duke of Ormond . . . Extracted from his own private Memoirs, lately printed at the Hague, in French; and now first translated into English. [With a portrait.] pp. 384. *J. Stanton: London*, 1738. 8°. **G. 4351.**

—— Memoirs of the Life of the Late Duke of Ormond. Written by himself . . . Translated from the French. pp. 312. *E. Applebee: London*, 1741. 12°. **1203. b. 14.**
A different translation from the preceding.

APPENDIX.

—— *See* ANNE, *Queen of Great Britain and Ireland.* [*Appendix.*] The Queen's and the Duke of Ormond's New Toast. 1712. *s. sh.* fol. **11602. i. 12. (6.)**

—— *See* BOYER (J. B. de) *Marquis d'Argens.* [*Le Mentor cavalier.*] Memoirs of the Count du Beauval, including some curious particulars relating to the Dukes of Wharton and Ormond during their exiles, *etc.* 1754. 12°. **1417. b. 25.**

—— *See* BUTLER, *Prince, pseud. Begin.* A Malicious Man makes Reasons, *etc.* [Satires on James, 2nd Duke of Ormonde.] [1700?] fol. **T. 100*. (13.)**

—— *See* ENGLAND. [*Proclamations.*—II. George I.] By the King. A proclamation for apprehending James Butler, late Duke of Ormond, and other persons attainted of High Treason, *etc.* 1718. fol. **21. h. 4. (148.)**

—— *See* ENGLAND.—*Parliament.—House of Commons.* [*Proceedings.*—II.] Artikelen van beschuldiging tegens den Graaf van Oxford . . . Hertog van Ormond, *etc.* 1716. 8°. **E. 2008. (11.)**

—— *See* ENGLAND. [*Appendix.—History and Politics.*—II. 1702.] Na [*sic*] Impartial Account of All the Material Transactions [of the] Grand Fleet and Land Forces, from their first setting out from Spithead, June the 29. till . . . the Duke of Ormond's arrival at Deal, November the 7th. 1702, *etc.* 1703. 4°. **1093**. c. **74**.

—— *See* IRELAND.—*Lords Justices and Council.* By the Lords Justices . . . A proclamation [offering a reward for the apprehension of the Duke of Ormonde]. [1719.] *s. sh.* fol. **1890**. e. **5**. (**90**.)

—— *See* MACD. (F.) *Student in the Mathematicks.* Loyalty Honour'd, or a Welcome to . . . James, Duke of Ormonde, *etc.* 1711. 8°. **11631**. bb. **57**.

—— *See* TEAGUE. Poor Teague: or, the Faithful Irishman's joy for the Duke of Ormond's happy deliverance. [In verse.] [1715.] *s. sh.* fol. **1876**. f. **1**. (**72**.)

—— *See* VISSAC (M. de) *Baron.* Mylord duc d'Ormond et les derniers Stuart, 1665–1745. 1914. 8°. **10817**. k. **24**.

—— An Account of the Great and Generous Actions of James Butler, late Duke of Ormond. Dedicated to the famous University of Oxford. pp. 48. *J. Moore: London*, [1715?] 8°. [By Daniel Defoe.] **10804**. aaa. **2**. (**2**.)

—— Astrea triumphans. The temple of gratitude, and the trophies of Vigo; being a congratulatory poem to His Grace the Duke of Ormond, on his happy accession to the Lieutenancy of the Kingdom of Ireland. pp. 12. *A. Baldwin: London*, 1703. fol. **1482**. f. **4**.

—— The Case of the Creditors of the Late Duke of Ormond, humbly offer'd to the consideration of the Hon. House of Commons, *etc.* [*London*, 1715.] *s. sh.* fol. **816**. m. **5**. (**104**.)

—— The Clamour of the Whigs against the Conduct of the Duke of Ormonde Consider'd and Expos'd. pp. 23. *John Morphew: London*, 1715. 8°. **1418**. c. **14**.

—— The Conduct of His Grace the Duke of Ormonde in the Campagne of 1712. pp. 64. *John Morphew: London*, 1715. 4°. **1417**. k. **4**.

—— [Another copy.] E. **2008**. (**8**.)

—— [Another copy.] E. **2008**. (**9***.)

—— [Another copy.] **101**. e. **17**.

—— [Another edition.] To which is prefixed a prefatory epistle humbly addressed to the . . . Earl of Chesterfield, in which a parallel is drawn between the management of that war and the present, *etc.* pp. x. 46. *W. Webb: London*, 1748. 8°. **8132**. c. **12**.

—— [Another copy.] G. **15519**.

—— Het Gedrag van den Hertog van Ormond, geduurende de veld-togt van't jaer 1712 . . . Uyt het Engelsch vertaalt. pp. 156. *Amsterdam*, 1713. 8°. E. **2007**. (**2**.)

—— Die Aufführung des Hertzogs von Ormond, währenden Feldzugs des Jahrs 1712. in Flandern . . . Aus dem Englischen übersetzt. pp. 56. *See* ENGLAND. [*Appendix.—Descriptions, Travels and Topography.*] Das vereinigte Gross-Britannien, *etc.* 1716. 4°. **796**. h. **19**.

—— An Examination of a Book intituled, The Conduct of the Duke of Ormond, anno 1712. In a letter to a member of the Secret Committee. By an Officer who made the campaign with his Grace. pp. 39. *J. More: London*, 1715. 8°. E. **1999**. (**9**.)

—— [Another copy.] E. **2193**. (**1***.)

—— [Another copy.] **101**. e. **21**.

—— A Vindication of Her Late Majesty, Queen Anne, of glorious memory; of his Grace the Duke of Ormonde; and of the late Ministry; from the horrid reflections cast upon them in a late pamphlet, intitled, The Conduct of his Grace the Duke of Ormonde, *etc.* pp. 35. *R. Burleigh: London*, 1715. 8°. E. **1999**. (**10**.)

—— The Congratulation. Humbly inscribed to his Grace the Duke of Ormond. [In verse.] *London*, 1712. *s. sh.* fol. **1850**. c. **10**. (**25**.)

—— Faithful Memoirs of the Life and Actions of James Butler, late Duke of Ormonde, &c. pp. 47. *W. Shropshire: London*, 1732. 8°. **10817**. c. **22**. (**2**.)

—— The Life and Character of James Butler, late Duke, Marquis and Earl of Ormond, *etc.* [The dedication signed: T. B.] 1729. 8°. *See* B., T. **1415**. b. **62**.

—— [Another edition.] 1730. 8°. *See* B., T. **4106**. a. **71**. (**10**.)

—— The Life and Character, together with all the remarkable actions of James Butler, late Duke of Ormond. pp. 8. [A chapbook.] *Gilbert Wilson: London*, 1716. 4°. **11621**. e. **2**. (**24**)

—— The Life of James, late Duke of Ormonde, *etc.* [With a biographical notice of the Ormond family, in manuscript, and MS. notes in pencil by another hand. With a portrait.] pp. vi. 544. iv. *M. Cooper: London*, 1747. 8°. **1202**. d. **27**.

—— [Another copy.] G. **4378**.
With an additional portrait inserted.

—— A Relation of the Great and Glorious Success of the Fleet and Forces of Her Majesty and the States-General at Vigo, the land forces being under the command of the Duke of Ormond, and the Fleet commanded by Sir George Rooke. [*London*,] 1702. *s. sh.* fol. **816**. m. **23**. (**112**.)

—— A Seasonable Expostulation with, and friendly reproof unto James Butler, who, by the men of this world, is stil'd Duke of O - - - - - - d, relating to the tumults of the people. By the same Friend that wrote to Thomas Bradbury [i.e. Daniel Defoe] . . . The second edition. pp. 31. *S. Keimer: London*, 1715. 8°. G. **13526**.

—— A Speech made by a Gentleman of the House of Commons, upon exhibiting articles of high treason, against the Duke of Ormonde. pp. 8. [*Dublin?*] 1715. 4°. **8145**. bb. **11**.

—— The Vigo Victory; or, the Happy success of the Duke of Ormond, in the taking of several French men of war, *etc.* [In verse.] [1702.] *s. sh.* fol. **1871**. f. **3**. (**16**.)

BUTLER (JAMES) *Earl of Ormonde and Ossory.* *See* BUTLER (James) 1st *Duke of Ormonde.*

BUTLER (JAMES) *Infant*, and **BUTLER** (GEORGE MIDDLETON) To the Hon. the Commons of Great Britain . . . The humble Petition and Case of James Butler and George Middleton Butler, Infants. [Claiming the estate of Richard Butler, forfeited upon attainder in 1715.] [*London*, 1720?] *s. sh.* fol. **816**. m. **5**. (**30**.)

BUTLER (James) *Marquis of Ormonde. See* Butler (James) *1st Duke of Ormonde.*

BUTLER (James) *Novelist.* Fortune's Foot-Ball; or, the Adventures of Mercutio. Founded on matters of fact. A novel, *etc.* 2 vol. *John Wyeth: Harrisburgh, Pa.,* 1797, 98. 12°. **12706.** b. **38.**

BUTLER (James) *of Birmingham.* Outlines of Practical Education: or, a Brief statement of the course of elementary, mathematical, classical, and philosophical studies, pursued by his own pupils. pp. 169. *Hamilton, Adams & Co.: London,* 1828. 8°. **1030.** i. **17.**

BUTLER (James) *of Mifflin County, Pennsylvania.* American Bravery Displayed, in the capture of fourteen hundred vessels of war and commerce, since the declaration of war by the President. pp. 322. *Printed for the Author: Carlisle, Pa.,* 1816. 12°. **9602.** aaa. **22.**

BUTLER (James) *of Royston, Hertfordshire.* The Extent and Limits of the Subjection due to Princes. A sermon preached on . . . the anniversary of the martyrdom of King Charles I. By a Country Clergyman [i.e. J. Butler]. pp. 28. [1747.] 8°. *See* Charles I., *King of Great Britain and Ireland [Funeral and Commemoration Sermons.]* **694.** k. **13. (8.)**

BUTLER (James) *Prisoner in Newgate. See* Newman (Alan) Criminal Executions in England. With . . . a demonstration of the innocence of James Butler, lately executed for the alleged crime of firing the floor-cloth manufactory of Messrs. Downing, at Chelsea. 1830. 8°. **1127.** c. **17.**

BUTLER (James) *R.C. Archbishop of Cashel.* The Most Rev. Dr. James Butler's Catechism, revised, enlarged, approved, and recommended by Bishop Bray and the Four R.C. Arch-Bishops of Ireland as a general cathechism [*sic*] for the kingdom. Twentieth edition, corrected and improved. pp. 71. *William Gossin: Clonmel,* [1820 ?] 12°. **3504.** aa. **27.**

—— [Another edition.] pp. 72. *Richard Grace: Dublin,* 1826. 12°. **03504.** e. **39.**

—— [Another edition. [A Catechism for the Instruction of Children . . . The twenty-second edition, with the author's latest additions and amendments. pp. 54. *J. S. Cunnabell: Halifax* [*N.S.*], 1833. 16°. **3505.** aa. **65.**

—— The Most Rev. Dr. James Butler's Catechism, with some pious prayers. pp. 111. *Urban College: Rome,* 1838. 12°. **3505.** de. **1. (2.)**

—— Twenty-eighth edition. Carefully corrected and improved, with amendments. pp. 72. *Richard Coyne: Dublin,* 1845. 12°. **3505.** df. **40. (1.)**

—— [Another edition.] pp. 78. *B. X. Furtado & Bro.: Bombay,* [1894.] 16°. **03504.** e. **3. (5.)**

—— [Another edition.] Revised and supplemented. pp. 146. *W. E. Blake & Son: Toronto,* [1918.] 16°. **03504.** e. **38.**

—— [Another edition.] Revised by the Basilian Fathers. pp. 122. *D. & J. Sadlier: Montreal,* [1923.] 12°. **03504.** eee. **18.**

—— [Another edition.] Revised, enlarged, approved & recommended by the four R.C. Archbishops of Ireland as a general catechism for the kingdom. pp. 118. *Guy & Co.: Cork,* [1927.] 12°. **3506.** aaaa. **18.**

BUTLER (James) *R.C. Archbishop of Cashel.*

—— The Most Reverend Doctor James Butler's Catechism, *etc.* (Catecismo de la Doctrina Cristiana . . . traducido del inglés.) [Edited by L. Gutierrez Corral.] *Eng. & Span.* pp. 145. *Puebla,* 1847. 12°. **3505.** aaa. **7.**

—— Suim Athghar an Teagasg Criosduighe. [By J. Butler.] pp. 78. 1784. 12°. *See* Christian Doctrine. **3505.** a. **9. (2.)**

—— An Teagusg Créesdeegh, chun aós óg no Canavh do heagusg . . . Aisdrighe a Béurla, go Gaóilge, le Muirertach Bán O'Céiliochuir. pp. 56. *Thomas do Wheete & Sheumus O'Haly: a Gorcuig,* 1792. 8°. **3457.** ff. **39. (2.)**

—— An Teagusg Criosduighe do reir ceist agus treagradh. Aistrighioghe ogh leabair, teagusg Easpoig Bullair. pp. 48. *D. Mulcahy: Cork,* 1862. 16°. **3457.** ee. **34. (3.)**

—— An Abridgment of Christian Doctrine, in which each question and answer is taken, word for word, from J. Butler's Catechism, *etc.* pp. 24. *J. Smyth: Belfast,* 1824. 12°. **843.** d. **17.**

—— [Another edition.] The errors of the press . . . are corrected in this, by the Right Rev. Dr. Blake. pp. 36. *C. M. Warren: Dublin* [1840 ?] 12°. **4405.** aaa. **27.**

—— An Teagasg Christuy, agus ornihe an mainne agus na traithnona. [Adapted from the catechism compiled by J. Butler.] pp. 49. [1840 ?] 8°. *See* Christian Doctrine. **3457.** ee. **34. (2.)**

—— *See* Ferris (Daniel) Manual of Christian Doctrine . . . Compiled . . . on the text of Butler's Short Catechism. 1880. 16°. **3505.** bbb. **40.**

—— *See* Sharp (Granville) *Philanthropist.* Remarks on "The Most Rev. Dr. * *'s [i.e. J. Butler's] Catechism," *etc.* 1810. 8°. **3506.** cc. **10.**

—— A Letter from the Most Reverend Doctor Butler, titular Archbishop of Cashel, to . . . Lord Viscount Kenmare. [A criticism of a pamphlet, by Richard Woodward, Bishop of Cloyne, entitled: "The Present State of the Church of Ireland."] pp. 8. *C. Finn: Kilkenny,* 1787. 8°. **4165.** b. **106. (1.)**

—— *See* Clergyman. A Short Refutation of the Arguments contained in Doctor Butler's Letter to Lord Kenmare. 1787. 8°. **4165.** aa. **27.**

BUTLER (James) *Roman Catholic Priest.* Stories of the Great Feasts of Our Lord, taken from the Gospel narrative and tradition. pp. 94. *Sands & Co.: London & Edinburgh,* 1907. 4°. **4806.** g. **40.**

BUTLER (James) *Writer on Boxing.* Kings of the Ring, *etc.* [With portraits.] pp. 256. *Stanley Paul & Co.: London,* [1936.] 8°. **07908.** de. **74.**

BUTLER (James Davie) Addresses on the Battle of Bennington, and the life and services of Col. Seth Warner, delivered before the Legislature of Vermont, in Montpelier, October 20, 1848, by J. D. Butler and George Frederick Houghton. pp. 99. *"Free Press": Burlington,* 1849. 8°. **9602.** d. **25.**

—— Butleriana, genealogica et biographica; or, Genealogical notes concerning Mary Butler and her descendants, as well as the Bates, Harris, Sigourney and other families, with which they have intermarried. pp. 162. *J. Munsell's Sons: Albany,* 1888. 8°. **9916.** aa. **39.**

BUTLER (JAMES DAVIE)

—— Deficiences in our History. An address delivered before the Vermont Historical and Antiquarian Society, *etc.* pp. 36. *S. Eastman & Danforth: Montpelier [Vt.]*, 1846. 8°. **9603**. b. **3**.

—— Incentives to Mental Culture among Teachers. 1853. *See* UNITED STATES OF AMERICA.—*American Institute of Instruction.* The Introductory Discourse and Lectures . . . delivered before the convention of teachers, *etc.* 1852. 1831, *etc.* 8° & 12°. Ac. **2690**.

—— [Another edition.] pp. 33. *Ticknor, Reed & Fields: Boston*, 1852. 12°. **8305**. aaa. **16**.

—— The Once Used Words in Shakespeare. pp. 31. *New York*, 1886. 8°. [*Papers of the New York Shakespeare Society.* no. 6.] Ac. **9509**.

BUTLER (JAMES DAVIE) and **DURRIE** (DANIEL S.)

—— Catalogue of Coins and Medals, ancient and modern . . . from the collection of James L. Hill. pp. 18. 1874. 8°. *See* HILL (James L.) *Mayor of Madison.* **7756**. de. **7**. (**6**.)

BUTLER (JAMES DONALD)

—— Four Philosophies and their Practice in Education and Religion. [On Naturalism, Idealism, Realism and Pragmatism. With a bibliography.] pp. xiii. 551. *Harper & Bros.: New York*, [1951.] 8°. **08464**. df. **33**.

BUTLER (JAMES EDWARD WILLIAM THEOBALD) *Marquis of Ormonde.*

—— The Manuscripts of the Marquis of Ormonde, preserved at the Castle, Kilkenny. [A calendar of selected letters and papers, by Sir John Thomas Gilbert. With an "Index to volumes I. & II.", compiled by S. C. Ratcliff.] 3 vol. *London*, 1895–1909. 8°.

—— New series. [Vol. 1–5 calendared by C. L. Falkiner; vol. 6 by C. L. Falkiner and F. E. Ball; vol. 7, 8 by F. E. Ball.] 8 vol. *London*, 1902–20. 8°. [*Historical Manuscripts Commission.* no. 36.] **Bar.T.1.(36.)**

Vol. 1 of the original series forms pt. 7 of the Appendix to the 14th Report of the Commission.

—— The Manuscripts of the Most Honourable the Marquis of Ormonde at Kilkenny Castle. [Catalogues of letters and papers, and a calendar of petitions. By Sir John T. Gilbert.] 7 pt. 1872–85. *See* ENGLAND.—*Royal Commission on Historical Manuscripts.* First [*etc.*] Report. 3rd, 4th, 6th–10th Report. Appendix. 1870, *etc.* fol. *etc.* **Bar.T.1.(2,3,5,8,14.)**

—— [Another copy.] B.S. **33/1**. (**1**.)

BUTLER (JAMES GLENTWORTH) *See* BIBLE. [*English.*] The Bible-Work . . . The revised text . . . with comments . . . Prepared by J. G. Butler. 1887, *etc.* 8°. **3109**. ee. **2**.

—— *See* BIBLE.—*Gospels.—Harmonies.* [*English.*] The Fourfold Gospel. The four Gospels, consolidated . . . into a continuous narrative . . . By J. G. Butler. 1890. 8°. **3224**. de. **43**.

—— *See* BIBLE.—*Appendix.—Concordances.* [*English.*] Topical Analysis of the Bible, *etc.* 1897. 8°. **3107**. de. **18**.

BUTLER (JAMES GODDARD) *See* IRELAND. [*Laws, etc.*—I.] The Statutes at large, passed in the Parliaments held in Ireland . . . A.D. 1310 . . . to A.D. 1800 inclusive. With marginal notes, *etc.* [Re-edited by J. G. Butler from the 1765 edition by F. Vesey.] 1786, *etc.* fol. **750**. h. **1**.

BUTLER (*Sir* JAMES RAMSAY MONTAGU)

—— *See* ENGLAND. [*Miscellaneous Official Publications.*] History of the Second World War. (United Kingdom Military Series. Edited by J. R. M. Butler.) 1949, *etc.* 8°. B.S. **68/33**. b.

—— *See* ROSE (John H.) The Cambridge History of the British Empire, *etc.* (vol. 3. General editors: E. A. Benians, J. R. M. Butler [and others].) 1929, *etc.* 8°. **2090**. a.

—— Colonial Self-Government, 1838–1852. 1940. *See* ROSE (John H.) The Cambridge History of the British Empire, *etc.* vol. 2. 1929, *etc.* 8°. **2090.a.**

—— Henry Montagu Butler: Master of Trinity College, Cambridge, 1886–1918. A memoir . . . With some poems and three addresses . . . With . . . illustrations [including portraits]. pp. xiii. 305. *Longmans & Co.: London*, 1925. 8°. **010856**. g. **33**.

—— A History of England, 1815–1918. pp. 252. *Thornton Butterworth: London*, 1928. 8°. [*Home University Library.* no. 135.] **12199**. p. **1/143**.

—— The Passing of the Great Reform Bill . . . With illustrations. pp. xiii. 454. *Longmans & Co.: London*, 1914. 8°. **9525**. d. **13**.

—— The Present Need for History . . . An inaugural lecture, *etc.* pp. 38. *University Press: Cambridge*, 1949. 8°. **9010**. de. **29**.

BUTLER (JANE) The Little Green Man's Fairy Tales. pp. 79. *Drane's: London*, [1922.] 8°. **12801**. c. **47**.

BUTLER (JANE ISABELLA) *See* BIBLE.—*Hagiographa.—Selections.* [*English.*] The Book of Job compared with the Book of Psalms. [The preface signed: Jane I. Butler.] 1877. 16°. **4372**. b. **18**. (**9**.)

BUTLER (JEAN M.) Christopher M. Dawson, parochial schoolmaster. Reminiscences of his life and times . . . Opening chapter by the Rev. John Wallace . . . Preface by the Marquess of Linlithgow. [With plates, including a portrait.] pp. xi. 172. *R. W. Hunter: Edinburgh*, 1906. 8°. **4955**. eee. **6**.

BUTLER (JESSIE HAVER)

—— Time to Speak Up. A speaker's handbook for women, *etc.* pp. xii. 264. *Harper & Bros.: New York & London*, [1946.] 8°. **011805**. i. **100**.

—— Time to speak up . . . Revised edition. pp. xxii. 261. *Harper & Bros.: New York*, [1952.] 8°. **11806**. bbb. **22**.

BUTLER (JOAN) *A.L.A.*

—— *See* ENGLAND.—*Library Association of the United Kingdom.* Books for Young People, *etc.* (Group 3. Fourteen to seventeen. Revised under the editorship of J. Butler.) 1952, *etc.* 8°. **11928**. aa. **5/3**.

BUTLER (JOAN) *pseud.* [i.e. ROBERT WILLIAM ALEXANDER.] *See* also ALEXANDER (R. W.)

BUTLER (JOAN) *pseud.* [i.e. ROBERT WILLIAM ALEXANDER.]

—— All change. pp. 191. *Stanley Paul & Co.: London,* 1955. 8°. NNN. **6916.**

—— All Found. pp. 288. *Stanley Paul & Co.: London,* [1940.] 8°. NN. **31570.**

—— Bed and Breakfast. pp. 288. *Stanley Paul & Co.: London,* [1933.] 8°. NN. **20353.**

—— Cloudy Weather. pp. 286. *Stanley Paul & Co.: London,* [1940.] 8°. NN. **32172.**

—— Cloudy Weather, *etc.* pp. 192. *Stanley Paul & Co.: London,* [1948.] 8°. **12650.** aaa. **33.**

—— Deep Freeze. pp. 256. *Stanley Paul & Co.: London,* 1952 [1951]. 8°. NNN. **2468.**

—— Double Figures. pp. 200. *Stanley Paul & Co.: London,* [1946.] 8°. NN. **36202.**

—— Fresh Heir. pp. 191. *Stanley Paul & Co.: London,* [1944.] 8°. NN. **34513.**

—— Full House. pp. 240. *Stanley Paul & Co.: London,* [1947.] 8°. NN. **37951.**

—— Gilt Edged. pp. 224. *Stanley Paul & Co.: London,* 1953. 8°. NNN. **3981.**

—— Ground Bait. pp. 256. *Stanley Paul & Co.: London,* [1941.] 8°. **012643.** n. **124.**

—— Ground Bait, *etc.* pp. 192. *Stanley Paul & Co.: London,* [1948.] 8°. **12650.** aaa. **34.**

—— Half Holiday. pp. 288. *Stanley Paul & Co.: London,* [1938.] 8°. NN. **29434.**

—— Half Shot. pp. 319. *Stanley Paul & Co.: London,* [1937.] 8°. NN. **26769.**

—— Happy Christmas! pp. 287. *Stanley Paul & Co.: London,* [1939.] 8°. NN. **30928.**

—— Heat Haze. pp. 256. *Stanley Paul & Co.: London,* [1949.] 8°. NN. **40007.**

—— The Heavy Husband. pp. 288. *Stanley Paul & Co.: London,* [1930.] 8°. NN. **16623.**

—— High Pressure. pp. 288. *Stanley Paul & Co.: London,* [1934.] 8°. NN. **23191.**

—— Landed Gentry. pp. 192. *Stanley Paul & Co.: London,* 1954. 8°. NNN. **5327.**

—— The Light Lover. pp. 287. *Stanley Paul & Co.: London,* [1929.] 8°. NN. **15472.**

—— Lost Property. pp. 288. *Stanley Paul & Co.: London,* [1938.] 8°. NN. **28836.**

—— Loving Cup. pp. 256. *Stanley Paul: London,* [1948.] 8°. NN. **38459.**

—— Low Spirits. pp. 192. *Stanley Paul & Co.: London,* [1945.] 8° **012331.** m. **174.**

—— Lucky Dip. pp. 240. *Stanley Paul & Co.: London,* 1953. 8°. NNN. **3659.**

—— Mixed Pickle. pp. 288. *Stanley Paul & Co.: London,* [1934.] 8°. NN. **22338.**

BUTLER (JOAN) *pseud.* [i.e. ROBERT WILLIAM ALEXANDER.]

—— Monkey Business. pp. 288. *Stanley Paul & Co.: London,* [1932.] 8°. NN. **19065.**

—— The Old Firm. pp. 236. *Stanley Paul & Co.: London,* [1947.] 8°. NN. **37156.**

—— Paper Money. pp. 223. *Stanley Paul & Co.: London,* 1954. 8°. NNN. **5104.**

—— Rapid Fire. pp. 288. *Stanley Paul & Co.: London,* [1939.] 8°. NN. **30172.**

—— Rapid Fire . . . 45th thousand. [An abridgment.] pp. 191. *Stanley Paul & Co.: London,* [1945.] 8°. **012642.** pp. **59.**

—— Set Fair. pp. 239. *Stanley Paul & Co.: London,* 1952. 8°. NN. **38883.**

—— Sheet Lightning. pp. 223. *Stanley Paul & Co.: London,* [1950.] 8°. NNN. **572.**

—— Shirty Work. pp. 208. *Stanley Paul & Co.: London,* [1943.] 8°. NN. **34150.**

—— Something Rich. pp. 320. *Stanley Paul & Co.: London,* [1937.] 8°. NN. **27929.**

—— Soothing Syrup. pp. 253. *Stanley Paul & Co.: London,* 1951. 8°. NNN. **1838.**

—— Space to let. pp. 191. *Stanley Paul & Co.: London,* 1955. 8°. NNN. **6176.**

—— Sun Spots. pp. 199. *Stanley Paul & Co.: London,* 1942. 8°. NN. **33231.**

—— Strictly Speaking. pp. 262. *Stanley Paul & Co.: London,* [1950.] 8°. NNN. **1300.**

—— Team Work. pp. 288. *Stanley Paul & Co.: London,* [1936.] 8°. NN. **25113.**

—— Trouble Brewing. pp. 288. *Stanley Paul & Co.: London,* [1935.] 8°. NN. **23978.**

—— Trouble Brewing, *etc.* pp. 175. *Stanley Paul & Co.: London,* [1943.] 8°. NN. **34101.**

—— Unnatural Hazards. pp. 288. *Stanley Paul & Co.: London,* 1931. 8°. NN. **18128.**

BUTLER (JOAN) *Writer of Children's Books.*

—— Peter and Pamela . . . Illustrated by Blanche Whatley. *George G. Harrap & Co.: London,* 1954– . 8°. W.P. D. **160.**

BUTLER (JOAN) *Writer of Children's Books,* and **WHATLEY** (BLANCHE)

—— No. 5 Charles Street. [A series of elementary readers.] *A. Wheaton & Co.: Exeter,* 1953– . 8°. W.P. B. **215.**

BUTLER (JOHANNA) *See* BUTLER (Marie Joseph)

BUTLER (JOHN) John Butler; or, the Blind man's dog. And other tales. pp. 32. *Johnstone, Hunter & Co.: Edinburgh,* [1870.] 16°. **4413.** aa. **8.**

BUTLER (JOHN) *B.D. See* Zz —— (J ——) The Genuine and uncommon Will of a Clergyman lately deceas'd . . . containing his remarkable apology for adultery. [A satire on J. Butler.] 1750. fol. **1418.** k. **35.**

—— Ἁγιαστρολογια. Or, the Most sacred and divine science of astrology. I. Asserted, in three propositions . . . II. Vindicated, against the calumnies of the Revd. Dr. More in his Explanation of the Grand Mystery of Godliness. III. Excused, concerning pacts with evil spirits, as not guilty in humble considerations upon the . . . discourse upon that subject by . . . Joseph [Hall], sometime Lord Bishop of Norwich. By J. B. B. D. (J. Butler). 2 pt. *Printed for the Author; sold by William Bromwich: London,* 1680. 8°. **718. e. 26.**
Each part has an additional titlepage.

—— *See* MORE (Henry) *D.D., the Platonist.* Tetractys Anti-Astrologica . . . wherein the wondrous weaknesses of John Butler, B.D., his Answer, called A Vindication of Astrology, &c., are laid open, *etc.* 1681. 4°. **718. e. 27.**

—— Bellua Marina: or the Monstrous beast which arose out of the sea. Being an historical description of the Papal Empire, as it is originally copied out of the prophesies of Holy Writ. Together with an epitome of the lives of all the Popes, who have reigned in the Church Empire, for these last 900 years . . . By J. B. B.D. a Minister of the Church of England [i.e. J. Butler]. pp. 444. *Printed by George Croom; sold by Richard Baldwin: London,* 1690. 8°. **861. b. 23.**
The dedication is signed: "Butler."

—— Explanatory Notes upon a Mendacious Libel, called Concubinage and Poligamy disproved; written by a nameless author, in answer to a book writ by J. B. as being a scurrilous libel, as not fit to be stiled an answer . . . By J. B., B.D. [i.e. John Butler.] pp. 26. 1698. 8°. *See* B., J., *B.D.* **498. b. 25. (2.)**

—— God made Man: or, an Account of time. Stating the day, hour and minute of our Saviour's Nativity . . . By a learned and reverend divine of the Church of England (J. Butler). 2 pt. pp. 320. *Printed for the Author: London,* 1675. 8°. **857. b. 16.**
Each pt. has a separate titlepage reading "Χριστολογια," etc., and bearing the imprint "Printed by Joseph Moxon: London, 1671."

—— God's Judgments upon Regicides: a sermon preached in the Fleet-Prison, on the 30th day of January 168⅔, proving, that the bloud of that pious monarch . . . King Charles the First, is not yet expiated. pp. 38. *T. Moore & J. Ashburne for Awnsham Churchill: London,* 1683. 4°. **4474. d. 28.**

—— The True State of the Case of John Butler . . . in answer to the libel of Martha his sometimes wife. Treating of a marriage dissolved, and made null by desertion. And of a lawful concubinage in a case of necessity, *etc.* pp. 36. *Printed for the Author: London,* 1697. 8°. **499. aa. 15. (3.)**

—— [Another copy.] **499. a. 36.**
Cropped.

—— [Another edition.] pp. 34. *Printed for the Authot* [sic]*: London,* 1617 [1697]. 8°. **G. 19526. (1.)**

—— *See* TURNER (John) *D.D., Vicar of Greenwich.* A Discourse on Fornication: shewing the greatness of that sin . . . As also a remark on Mr. Butler's explication of Hebr. xiii, 4, in his late book on that subject. 1698. 4°. **8415. e. 25.**

—— Concubinage and Poligamy disprov'd: or the Divine institution of marriage betwixt one man, and one woman only, asserted. In answer to a book, writ by John Butler, B.D., for which he was presented as follows, *etc.* pp. 95. *For R. Baldwin: London,* 1698. 8°. **499. a. 35.**

—— [Another copy.] **G. 19526. (2.)**

BUTLER (JOHN) *Baptist Minister, Hanover, Mass.* A Sermon delivered April 28, 1817, before the Association for the suppression of Intemperance, and the promotion of Morality in the town of Hanover, Massachusetts. pp. 16. *Lincoln & Edmands: Boston,* 1817. 8°. **4486. bb. 70.**

BUTLER (JOHN) successively *Bishop of Oxford* and *of Hereford.* An Address to the Cocoa-Tree. From a Whig. [By J. Butler.] pp. 21. 1762. 4°. *See* WHIG. **T. 47*. (14.)**

—— [Another copy.] **E. 2054. (7.)**

—— [Another copy.] **103. i. 68.**

—— The second edition. pp. 21. 1762. 4°. *See* WHIG. **8132.f.12.**

—— The third edition. pp. 21. 1762. 4°. *See* WHIG. **T. 1554. (6.)**

—— The fourth edition. pp. 21. 1762. 4°. *See* WHIG. **454. e. 18. (5.)**

—— An Address to the Cocoa Tree, from a Whig. (The fifth edition.) And a consultation on the subject of a standing-army, held at the King's-Arms Tavern, on the twenty-eight day of February, 1763. (The second edition.) [By J. Butler.] pp. vii. 56. 1763. 8°. *See* WHIG. **8138. bb. 19.**

—— The Bishop of Hereford's Charge to the Clergy of his Diocese at his primary visitation in June 1789. pp. 27. *C. Badham; J. Allen: Hereford,* [1789.] 4°. **694. h. 10. (11.)**

—— The Bishop of Hereford's Charge to the Clergy of his Diocese, at his triennial visitation in the year 1792. pp. 15. *D. Walker: Hereford,* [1792.] 4°. **4445. g. 4. (1.)**

—— Concio ad Clerum in Synodo Provinciali Cantuariensis Provinciae . . . die 20 Jan. 1775 habita . . . Accedit Oratiuncula (qua ad Superiorem Domum Convocationis præsentatus est Inferioris Domus Prolocutor, Jeremiah Milles Jan. 23, 1775). pp. 24. *J. Dodsley: Londini,* 1775. 4°. **694. k. 20. (3.)**

—— [Another copy.] **114. b. 7.**

—— A Consultation on the subject of a Standing Army, held at the King's-Arms Tavern, on the twenty-eighth day of February 1763. [By J. Butler.] pp. 32. [1763.] 4°. *See* CONSULTATION. **T. 47*. (16.)**

—— A Letter to the Protestant Dissenting Ministers who lately solicited Parliament for further relief. [By J. Butler.] pp. 59. 1772. 8°. *See* PROTESTANT DISSENTING MINISTERS. **4136. f. 2. (2.)**

—— The Man without Guile. A sermon preached at St. Margaret's Church, Westminster, on Sunday, May 13, 1753. Occasioned by the death of the Reverend Scawen Kenrick, D.D., Sub-Dean of Westminster, *etc.* pp. 21. *J. & R. Tonson; S. Draper: London,* 1753. 4°. **225. i. 19. (15.)**

—— [Another copy.] **1416. k. 15.**
Imperfect; wanting the half-title.

BUTLER (John) successively *Bishop of Oxford* and *of Hereford.*

—— The Bishop of Hereford's Pastoral Letter to the Inhabitants of his Diocese, on occasion of the great victory obtained by His Majesty's Fleet, on the coast of Egypt. pp. 15. *D. Walker: Hereford,* 1798. 4°. **695.** h. **13.** (**16.**)

—— [Another copy.] **694.** h. **10.** (**12.**)

—— Select Sermons ; to which are added, two Charges to the Clergy of the Diocese. pp. 382. *J. Robson: London,* 1801. 8°. **224.** k. **18.**

—— Serious Considerations on the Measures of the Present Administration. [By J. Butler.] pp. 20. 1763. 4°. *See* Considerations. T. **1554.** (**7.**)

—— [Another copy.] E. **2055.** (**3.**)

—— A Sermon on the Liturgy of the Church of England, preached at the Church of St. Mary le Bow, on St. Mark's Day, 1763, in pursuance of the last will of Mr. John Hutchins. pp. 22. *J. & R. Tonson: London,* 1763. 4°. **694.** g. **3.** (**10.**)

—— [Another copy.] **693.** f. **5.** (**10.**)

—— A Sermon preached at St. Margaret's Church, Westminster, on Thursday, October 9, 1746, being the day appointed . . . for a General Thanksgiving . . . for the suppression of the late unnatural Rebellion. pp. 23. *M. Cooper: London,* 1746. 8°. **693.** d. **7.** (**14.**)

—— [Another copy.] **225.** f. **25.** (**10.**)

—— A Sermon preached at St. Margaret's Church, Westminster, on Thursday, April 4, 1754, on occasion of the anniversary meeting of the Trustees of the Public Infirmary in James Street, Westminster. pp. 30. *J. & R. Tonson ; S. Draper: London,* 1754. 4°. **693.** f. **5.** (**8.**)

—— [Another copy.] **225.** i. **7.** (**9.**)

—— A Sermon preached at St. Mary's Church in Oxford, on Thursday, July 2, 1778, on occasion of the anniversary meeting of the Governors of the Radcliffe Infirmary. pp. 24. *Clarendon Press: Oxford,* 1778. 4°. **694.** g. **31.**

—— A Sermon preached before the Honourable House of Commons at St. Margaret's, Westminster, on Friday, February 17, 1758 ; being the day appointed . . . for a General Fast. pp. 24. *J. & R. Tonson: London,* 1758. 4°. **693.** f. **5.** (**9.**)

—— [Another copy.] **694.** i. **1.** (**8.**)

—— A Sermon preached before the Honourable House of Commons, at the Church of St. Margaret's, Westminster, on Friday, December 13, 1776, being the day appointed . . . as a day of Solemn Fasting and Humiliation. pp. 16. *T. Cadell: London,* 1777. 4°. **694.** i. **8.** (**2.**)

—— [Another copy.] **91.** h. **16.**

—— A Sermon preached before the House of Lords, at the Abbey Church, Westminster, on Friday, February 27, 1778 ; being the day appointed . . . to be observed as a day of Solemn Fasting and Humiliation. pp. 15. *T. Cadell: London,* 1778. 4°. **694.** i. **8.** (**10.**)

—— [Another copy.] **91.** h. **17.**

BUTLER (John) successively *Bishop of Oxford* and *of Hereford.*

—— A Sermon preached before the House of Lords at the Abbey Church, Westminster, Tuesday, January 30, 1787 ; being the anniversary of the Martyrdom of King Charles I. pp. 15. *T. Cadell: London,* 1787. 4°. **694.i.20.(2.)**

—— [Another copy.] **114.** b. **62.**

—— A Sermon preached before the Incorporated Society for the Propagation of the Gospel in Foreign Parts . . . on Friday, February 20, 1784. [With an abstract of the Charter, and of the proceedings of the Society for 1783–84.] pp. 77. *T. Harrison & S. Brooke: London,* 1784. 4°. T. **2142.** (**8.**)

—— [Another copy.] **91.** h. **18.**

—— A Sermon preached before the Sons of the Clergy . . . May 9, 1754 . . . To which is annexed a list of the annual amount of the collection for this charity, from the year 1721. pp. 21. *J. & R. Tonson, etc. ; London,* 1754. 4°. **693.** f. **5.** (**11.**)

—— [Another copy.] **694.** g. **2.** (**13.**)

—— [Another copy.] **225.** i. **8.** (**20.**)

—— A Sermon preached in the Chapel of the Magdalen-Hospital, on occasion of the anniversary meeting . . . May 11, 1786. (General State of the Magdalen-Hospital.) pp. 16. 7. *J. F. & C. Rivington: London,* 1786. 4°. **694.** h. **3.** (**5.**)

—— [Another copy.] T. **35.** (**3.**)

—— A Sermon preached in the Parish-Church of Christ-Church, London: on Thursday, April the 27th 1780. Being the time of the yearly meeting of the children educated in the Charity-Schools, in and about the cities of London and Westminster . . . To which is annexed, an Account of the Society for promoting Christian Knowledge. pp. 23. 116. *J. F. & C. Rivington: London,* 1780. 4°. **4473.** g. **12.** (**2.**)

—— Some Account of the Character of the late Right Honourable Henry Bilson Legge. [By J. Butler.] pp. 19. 1764. 4°. *See* Legge (*Right Hon.* Henry B.) **454.** e. **18.** (**6.**)

—— [Another copy.] **1417.** k. **28.**

—— [Another copy.] **113.** c. **54.**

—— [Another copy.] **131.** b. **1.**

—— [Another copy.] G. **1444.** (**2.**)

—— [Another edition.] pp. 19. 1765. 4°. *See* Legge (*Right Hon.* Henry B.) T. **1090.** (**6.**)

—— Superficial Observations upon the Bishop of Gloucester's "Rational Account of the Sacrament of the Lord's Supper." [By J. Butler.] pp. 22. 1761. 8°. *See* Warburton (William) *Bishop of Gloucester.* **494.** f. **26.** (**2.**)

BUTLER (John) *Canon of Windsor.* Christian Liberty asserted in opposition to the Roman Yoke, delivered in a sermon preached in His Majesties Royal Chappel of Windsor. The 8th of Decemb. 1678. pp. 35. *M. C. for Walter Kettilby: London,* 1678. 4°. **226.** i. **9.** (**6.**)

BUTLER (JOHN) *Licentiate of the College of Physicians of Ireland.* A Plan of Improvements in the Construction and Use of Fire-Arms, great and small, *etc.* pp. iv. 22. MS. NOTES. [1795 ?] 8°. **8826**. dd. **41**. (**1**.)

BUTLER (JOHN) *M.D., of New York.* Electricity in Surgery. pp. 109. *Boericke & Tafel: New York,* 1882. 8°. **7481**. bb. **7**.

—— Hot Water as a Remedy. *See* M., J. Hot Water as a Remedy, *etc.* [1887.] 8°. **7306**. de. **28**. (**2**.)

BUTLER (JOHN) *Major.* A Sketch of Assam: with some account of the Hill Tribes. By an Officer in the Hon. East India Company's Bengal Native Infantry [i.e. J. Butler] . . . With illustrations from sketches by the author. [With a map.] pp. viii. 220. 1847. 8°. *See* ASSAM. **1298**. h. **20**.

—— Travels and Adventures in the Province of Assam, during a residence of fourteen years, *etc.* [With plates and maps.] pp. x. 268. *Smith, Elder & Co.: London,* 1855. 8°. **10056**. d. **1**.

BUTLER (JOHN) *Marquis of Ormonde.* *See* CANICE, *Saint.* Vita Sancti Kannechi, *etc.* [Edited, with an introduction, by the Marquis of Ormonde.] 1853. 4°. [*Royal Society of Antiquaries of Ireland.* Extra vol. 1853.] **Ac.5785/2.(1.)**

—— *See* GUIZOT (F. P. G.) Meditations and Moral Sketches . . . Translated . . . by John, Marquis of Ormonde. 1855. 8°. **8406**. e. **13**.

—— *See* DUMAS (A.) *the Elder.* [*Le Maître d'Armes.*] Memoirs of a Maître d'Armes . . . Translated . . . by the Marquis of Ormonde. 1855. 8°. [*Traveller's Library.* vol. 22.] **1156**. h. **28**.

—— An Autumn in Sicily, being an account of the principal remains of antiquity existing in that island, with short sketches of its ancient and modern history. With a map and illustrations. pp. xi. 260. *Hodges & Smith: Dublin,* 1850. 8°. **10131**. f. **3**.

BUTLER (JOHN) *of Royston.* *See* BARRETT (William G.) Two Discourses, the first occasioned by the death of John Butler, of Royston, *etc.* [1849.] 16°. **4906**. a. **30**.

BUTLER (JOHN) *Spiritualist.*

—— Exploring the Psychic World. pp. 190. *Oak Tree Books: London & Melbourne,* 1947. 8°. **8634**. df. **45**.

BUTLER (JOHN) *Writer on the Art of Riding.* The Horse; and how to ride him: a treatise on the art of riding and leaping, *etc.* pp. 93. *Baily Bros.: London,* 1861. 8°. **7907**. b. **8**.

BUTLER (JOHN ALFRED VALENTINE) The Chemical Elements and their Compounds, *etc.* pp. xi. 205. *Macmillan & Co.: London,* 1927. 8°. **8902**. aa. **20**.

—— Electrical Phenomena at Interfaces in Chemistry, Physics and Biology. Edited by J. A. V. Butler, *etc.* [By various authors.] pp. vii. 309. *Methuen & Co.: London,* 1951. 8°. **8761**. de. **32**.

—— Electrocapillarity. The chemistry and physics of electrodes and other charged surfaces, *etc.* pp. viii. 208. *Methuen & Co.: London,* 1940. 8°. **08757**. bb. **21**.

—— The Fundamentals of Chemical Thermodynamics. 2 pt. *Macmillan & Co.: London,* 1928, 34. 8°. **08715**. aa. **46**.

—— (Second edition.) *Macmillan & Co.: London,* 1935– . 8°. W.P. **8994**.

BUTLER (JOHN ALFRED VALENTINE)

—— The Fundamentals of Chemical Thermodynamics. (Third edition.) *Macmillan & Co.: London,* 1939. 8°. **8907. df. 17.**

***Imperfect; wanting pt.* 2.**

—— Chemical Thermodynamics. (Fourth edition [of "The Fundamentals of Chemical Thermodynamics"].) [With an appendix by W. J. C. Orr.] pp. xvi. 569. *Macmillan & Co.: London,* 1946. 8°. **08900**. aa. **28**.

—— Man is a Microcosm. pp. xii. 151. pl. VIII. *Macmillan & Co.: London,* 1950. 8°. **7008**. de. **7**.

BUTLER (JOHN ALFRED VALENTINE) and **RANDALL** (JOHN TURTON)

—— Progress in Biophysics and Biophysical Chemistry . . . Editors: J. A. V. Butler . . . J. T. Randall (B. Katz [and others.]) [With plates.] *Butterworth-Springer: London,* 1950– . 8°. [*Progress Series.*] W.P. **13822/2**.
From 1951 *onwards published by Pergamon Press: London.*

BUTLER (JOHN CHARLES)

—— Sheet Metal: theory and practice, *etc.* pp. v. 173. *John Wiley & Sons: New York,* [1944.] 4°. **8771**. d. **41**.

BUTLER (JOHN F.)

—— The French Lumber Market. pp. ii. 13. *Washington,* 1922. 8°. [*U.S. Bureau of Foreign and Domestic Commerce. Trade Information Bulletin.* no. 51.] A.S. **128/3**.

BUTLER (JOHN G.) Projectiles and Rifled Cannon. Systems of projectiles and rifling, with practical suggestions for their improvement, as embraced in a report to the Chief of Ordnance, U.S.A., *etc.* pp. 164. pl. XXXVI. *D. Van Nostrand: New York,* 1875. 4°. **8824**. h. **3**.

BUTLER (JOHN OCTAVIUS) *See* BEECROFT (George) Companion to the Iron Trade . . . By G. Beecroft . . . The third edition, carefully revised and considerably enlarged by his nephew (J. O. B. [i.e. J. O. Butler]). 1851. 12°. **7954**. b. **21**.

—— —— 1857. 12°. **7954**. a. **37**.

BUTLER (JOHN OLDING) *See* BUTLER (William) *Writing-Master.* Chronological, Biographical, Historical, and Miscellaneous Exercises, *etc,* [Edited by J. O. Butler.] 1823. 12°. **9007**. bbb. **7**.

—— *See* BUTLER (William) *Writing-Master.* Geographical and Biographical Exercises . . . Enlarged by . . . J. O. Butler. 1848. 12°. **10004**. b. **12**.

—— A Brief Memoir of Mr. William Butler . . . The second edition, enlarged. [With a portrait.] pp. 27. *Printed for the Author: London,* 1826. 8°. **10854**. cc. **8**.

—— The Geography of the Globe, containing a description of its several divisions of land and water, to which are added problems on the terrestrial and celestial globes, *etc.* pp. xii. 356. *Printed for the Author & Proprietors: London,* 1826. 12°. **571**. b. **10**.

—— The fifth edition, with alterations and additions, by J. Rowbotham. pp. vii. 349. *Simpkin, Marshall & Co.; Darton & Harvey: London,* 1841. 12°. **794**. d. **36**.

BUTLER (John Olding)

—— Eighth edition, corrected to the present time. pp. vii. 360. *Simpkin, Marshall & Co.: London,* 1850. 12°. **1296.** b. **34.**

—— Ninth edition, corrected, *etc.* pp. vii. 362. *Simpkin, Marshall & Co.: London,* 1852. 12°. **1295.** b. **11.**

—— Tenth edition, corrected, *etc.* pp. vii. 362. *Simpkin, Marshall & Co.: London,* 1855. 12°. **1295.** b. **12.**

—— Eleventh edition, corrected, *etc.* pp. vii. 367. *Simpkin, Marshall & Co.: London,* 1858. 12°. **10003.** c. **7.**

—— Twelfth edition, corrected, *etc.* pp. vii. 373. *Simpkin, Marshall & Co.: London,* 1864. 12°. **10004.** bb. **35.**

—— Thirteenth edition. Corrected, *etc.* pp. vii. 374. *Simpkin, Marshall & Co.: London,* 1870. 12°. **10004.** bbb. **26.**

—— A New Introduction to Geography . . . The seventeenth edition. With an appendix, containing problems on the globes, *etc.* pp. 185. *William Walker: London,* 1854. 8°. **10003.** c. **27.**

—— The eighteenth edition, *etc.* pp. iv. 185. *William Walker: London,* 1860 [1859]. 8°. **10004.** b. **24.**

—— Nineteenth edition, thoroughly revised. pp. vii. 192. *W. Walker & Co.: London,* 1866. 8°. **10004.** aaa. **27.**

BUTLER (John Simpkins) State Preventive Medicine . . . Address, *etc.* pp. 31. *Case & Co.: Hartford,* 1879. 8°. C.T. **256.** (**2.**)

BUTLER (John W.) *of Sandhurst, Victoria.* *See* Directories.—*Daylesford.* Birtchnell's Daylesford Directory . . . Compiled by J. W. Butler. [1865.] 8°. P.P. **2640.** h.

—— *See* Directories.—*Sandhurst, Victoria.* Butler and Stevens' Sandhurst, Castlemaine and Echuca Directory, 1865–6 . . . Compiled by J. W. Butler and George Stevens. 1865, *etc.* 8°. P.P. **2640.** i.

BUTLER (John Wesley) Sketches of Mexico in prehistoric, primitive, colonial and modern times. Lectures at the Ohio Wesleyan University on the Merrick Foundation . . . Fifth series. pp. ix. 316. *Hunt & Eaton: New York,* 1894. 8°. **9771.** aaa. **4.**

BUTLER (John Weston) Origin of the Emery Deposits near Peekskill, New York . . . Reprinted from the American Mineralogist, *etc.* [A thesis.] [*New York,* 1936.] 8°. **07108.** bb. **62.**

BUTLER (Jonathan) *See* Daniel (Azariah) The Grand Kidnapper at last taken; or, a Full . . . account of the . . . apprehending of Cap. A. Daniel, for conveying away the bodies of Richard Blagrave and Jonathan Butler, *etc.* [1690 ?] *s. sh.* fol. **515.** l. **2.** (**2.**)

BUTLER (Joseph) successively *Bishop of Bristol* and *of Durham.* The Works of Joseph Butler . . . To which is prefixed, a life of the author, by Dr. Kippis; with a preface, giving some account of his character and writings by Samuel Halifax, D.D., late Lord Bishop of Gloucester. [With a portrait.] 2 vol. *A. Constable & Co. Edinburgh,* 1804. 8°. **3755.** cc. **8**

—— A new edition. 2 vol. *Clarendon Press: Oxford,* 1807. 8°. **492.** e. **26, 27.**

—— [Another copy.] **226.** c. **2, 3.**

—— New edition. 2 vol. *University Press: Oxford,* 1836. 8°. G. **12895, 96.**

BUTLER (Joseph) successively *Bishop of Bristol* and *of Durham.*

—— The Works of Joseph Butler . . . Edited by the Right Hon. W. E. Gladstone. 3 vol.

vol. 1. The Analogy of Religion . . . To which are added two brief dissertations i. Of Personal Identity; ii. Of the Nature of Virtue, and a Correspondence with Dr. Samuel Clarke. pp. xxxvii. 461.
vol. 2. Sermons, *etc.* pp. x. 464.
vol. 3. Studies subsidiary to the Works of Bishop Butler. By the Right Hon. W. E. Gladstone. Additional volume uniform with the Works. pp. vii. 371.

Clarendon Press: Oxford, 1896. 8°. **3757.d.2.**

—— [Another edition of vol. 1, 2.] 2 vol. *Clarendon Press: Oxford,* 1897. 8°. **3752.** ccc. **8.**

—— The Works of Bishop Butler. A new edition with introduction and notes by J. H. Bernard. 2 vol.

vol. 1. Sermons, Charges, Fragments and Correspondence. pp. xxxii. 352.
vol. 2. The Analogy of Religion, *etc.* pp. xxi. 313.

Macmillan & Co.: London, 1900. 8°. [*English Theological Library.*] **2206.** c. **4.**

—— The Sermons and Remains of . . . Joseph Butler . . . Newly edited with a memoir and indices by the Rev. E. Steere. pp. xcii. 430. *Bell & Daldy: London,* 1862. 8°. **3753.** a. **6.**

—— The Analogy of Religion, Natural and Revealed, to the constitution and course of Nature. To which are added two brief dissertations: i. Of Personal Identity. ii. Of the Nature of Virtue. pp. 320. **L.P.** *J., J. & P. Knapton: London,* 1736. 4°. **689.** g. **7.**

—— [Another copy.] **L.P.** **8.** b. **15.**

—— [Another edition.] pp. 320. *George Ewing: Dublin,* 1736. 8°. **4018.** f. **5.**

—— The Analogy of Religion . . . The second edition, corrected. pp. xvi. 467. *J. & P. Knapton: London,* 1736. 8°. **851.** i. **17.**

—— [Another copy.] **679.** c. **2.**

—— The Analogy of Religion . . . Third edition. pp. 467. *John & Paul Knapton: London,* 1740. 8°. **04018.** k. **27.**

—— The Analogy of Religion Natural and Revealed . . . To which are added two brief dissertations. i. Of personal identity. ii. Of the nature of virtue . . . Sixth edition. pp. 467. *John Beecroft; Robert Horsfield: London,* 1771. 8°. **04018.** k. **19.**

—— The seventh edition. pp. 356. *John Boyle: Aberdeen,* 1775. 8°. **4017.** aa. **15.**

—— [Another edition.] Together with a Charge delivered to the Clergy of the Diocese of Durham, at the primary visitation, in the year mdccli. . . . A new edition, corrected. With a preface, giving some account of the character and writings of the author, by Samuel Lord Bishop of Gloucester. pp. lxvii. 477. *J. F. & C. Rivington: London,* 1788. 8°. **1016.** l. **17.**

—— A new edition, corrected, *etc.* pp. lxvii. 477. *J. F. & C. Rivington: London,* 1791. 8°. **4016.** c. **10.**

—— A new edition, corrected, *etc.* pp. liii. 408. *F. & C. Rivington: London,* 1802. 8°. **4015.** aaa. **14.**

—— A new edition, corrected, *etc.* pp. lv. 408. *F. C. & J. Rivington: London,* 1809. 8°. **1115.** g. **2.**

—— [Another edition.] [With a portrait.] pp. lxiii. 398. *T. Hamilton, etc.: London,* 1813. 8°. **4016.** f. **39.**

—— [Another edition.] To which is prefixed, a life of the author, by S. Halifax. pp. xvi. 414. MS. NOTES. *Brett Smith: Dublin,* 1817. 12°. **699. f. 34.**

—— [Another edition.] pp. viii. 307. *J. & T. Allman: London,* 1819. 8°. **4017. df. 48.**

—— A new edition, *etc.* pp. lxxix. 456. *Clarendon Press: Oxford,* 1820. 8°. **4016. e. 15.**

—— The fourth edition. With an introductory essay by the Rev. Daniel Wilson. pp. 539. *William Collins: Glasgow,* 1831. 12°. **1115. g. 4.**

—— [Another edition.] With a preface . . . by Samuel Halifax. pp. lxx. 384. *University Press: Oxford,* 1833. 8°. **4016. b. 9.**

—— [Another edition.] With a memoir of the author, by the Rev. George Croly. pp. xl. 352. *J. Hatchard & Son: London,* 1834. 8°. [*Sacred Classics.* vol. 8.] **496. ee. 4.**

—— [Another edition.] With a prefatory memoir of the author and his writings. pp. 76. *W. & R. Chambers: Edinburgh,* 1838. 8°. **4372. h. 11. (1.)**

—— [Another edition.] With a preface, giving some account of the character and writings of the author. By Samuel Halifax. New edition, with an index. pp. lxi. 368. *Oxford; Thomas Tegg: London,* 1844. 8°. **1115. g. 22.**

—— [Another edition.] With a life of the author, notes, and index, by William Fitzgerald. pp. cxii. 371. *James M'Glashlan: Dublin,* 1849. 8°. **4375. d. 10.**

—— The Analogy of Religion; and select sermons. [With a prefatory memoir of the author.] pp. 322. *Edinburgh,* 1850. 8°. [*Chambers's Instructive and Entertaining Library.*] **1157. f. 3. (2.)**

—— The Analogy of Religion . . . A new edition, with an introductory essay, by Rev. Albert Barnes; and a complete index. pp. xxiv. 251. *J. C. Bishop: London,* 1851. 8°. **4376. b. 9.**

—— [Another edition.] To which are added, two brief dissertations . . . and fifteen sermons . . . With a preface by Samuel Halifax . . . New edition, with analytical introductions, explanatory notes, and an index. By a member of the University of Oxford. [With a portrait.] pp. vi. 546. *London,* 1852. 8°. [*Bohn's Standard Library.*] **2504. a. 10.**

—— [Another edition.] Also fifteen sermons (on subjects chiefly ethical), preached in the Chapel of the Rolls Court . . . With a life of the author, a copious analysis, notes, and indexes. By Joseph Angus. pp. xxi. 551. *R.T.S.: London,* [1855.] 12°. **4429. eee. 37.**

—— The Analogy of Religion . . . With analytical index by Edward Steere. pp. xviii. 468. *Bell & Daldy: London,* 1857. 8°. **4015. e. 9.**

—— [Another edition.] pp. xxvi. 400. *Bell & Daldy: London,* 1858. 8°. **4016. b. 10.**

—— A new edition, with an introductory essay, by Rev. Albert Barnes, and an index. pp. cix. 230. *Routledge & Co.: London,* 1859. 12°. **4016. a. 13.**

—— [Another edition.] With a life of the author, copious notes, and index by . . . William FitzGerald, D.D., Lord Bishop of Cork . . . Second edition. pp. cviii. 371. *William Tegg: London; M'Glashlan & Gill: Dublin,* 1860. 8°. **4016. e. 16.**

—— New edition, with an introductory essay, by Rev. Albert Barnes, and an index. pp. cix. 230. *William Tegg: London,* 1867. 8°. **4016. aaa. 13.**

—— A new and improved edition, with a complete index, and questions for examination, by the Rev. G. B. Wheeler. pp. xxxii. 352. *William Tegg: London,* 1868. 12°. **4014. aaa. 6.**

—— The Analogy of Religion . . . With an introductory essay by Albert Barnes . . . Twentieth edition. pp. lxi. 271. *Ivison, Blakeman, Taylor & Co.: New York & Chicago,* 1875. 8°. **04018. h. 92. (1.)**

—— [Another edition.] With a life of the author, copious notes, and an ample index. The whole edited by Rev. Joseph Cummings. pp. 395. *Nelson & Phillips: New York,* 1875. 8°. **4017. f. 5.**

—— [Another edition.] With introduction, life, epitome and notes by the Rev. F. A. Malleson. pp. viii. 240. *Ward, Lock & Co.: London,* [1878.] 8°. **3605. bbb. 2.**

—— [Another edition.] Also fifteen sermons . . . With a life of the author, a copious analysis, notes and indexes, by Joseph Angus. pp. xxi. 551. *R.T.S.: London,* [1881.] 8°. **4017. bbb. 14.**

—— [Another edition.] Also, three sermons on human nature, *etc.* pp. xxi. 415. *R.T.S.: London,* [1881.] 8°. **4017. bbb. 13.**

—— The Analogy of Religion . . . With an introduction and an appendix by Henry Morley. pp. 312. *G. Routledge & Sons: London,* 1884. 8°. [*Morley's Universal Library.* no. 10.] **12204. gg. 1/10.**

—— [Another edition.] pp. 312. *G. Routledge & Sons: London,* 1894. 8°. [*Sir John Lubbock's Hundred Books.* no. 66.] **012207. l. 1/66.**

—— [Another edition.] [With an introduction by H. H. Williams.] pp. xxiv. 219. *London,* 1906. 8°. [*Methuen's Standard Library.*] **012203. f. 33/18.**

—— [Another edition.] [With an introduction by Ronald Bayne.] pp. xxxii. 280. *J. M. Dent: London; E. P. Dutton: New York,* [1906.] 8°. [*Everyman's Library.*] **12206. p. 1/111.**

—— [Another edition.] Edited by the Right Hon. W. E. Gladstone. pp. xxxv. 424. *Oxford University Press: London,* 1907. 8°. [*World's Classics.* vol. 136.] **012209. df. 73.**

—— Cyfatebiaeth Crefydd, naturiol a dadguddiedig, i gyfansoddiad a threfn natur . . . Gyda nodiadau wedi eu dethol o Chalmers, Syr W. Hamilton, Archesgob Whately, Fitzgerald, Dr. Angus, &c. Gan y Parch. John Hughes. pp. xxviii. 234. *Thomas Gee: Dinbych,* 1859. 8°. **4016. b. 12.**

—— The principal parts of Bishop Butler's 'Analogy of Religion' . . . abridged; by the Rev. Francis Wrangham. pp. 33. 1820. 8°. **T. 1494. (4.)**
One of an edition of fifty copies.

—— [Another issue.] *See* WRANGHAM (F.) The Pleiad, *etc.* 1820. 8°. **1350. h. 23.**

—— Hints to Medical Students upon the subject of a Future Life; extracted from . . . The Analogy of Religion . . . With corresponding notices from other publications of high authority, and with a preface by the editor. pp. xxxii. 51. *J. Wolstenholme: York,* 1823. 12°. **4374. aa. 6.**

BUTLER (Joseph) successively *Bishop of Bristol* and *of Durham.*

—— The Analogy of Religion, *etc.* [Abridged.] pp. 339. *John Smith: Cambridge,* 1829. 8°. **1115**. g. **3.**

—— Rewards and Punishments. On the Government of God by Rewards and Punishments; being the second chapter of Bishop Butler's Analogy. pp. 21. *S.P.C.K.: London,* 1852. 12°. **4406**. f. **44**. **(7.)**

—— *See* Allen (M.) *Rev.* Four Hundred Questions on Butler's Analogy. 1841. 12°. **4376**. a. **68**. **(1.)**

—— *See* Angus (Joseph) An Analysis of Butler's Analogy of Religion and Three Sermons on Human Nature. [1882.] 8°. **4018**. b. **15.**

—— *See* Bentham (Edward) An Index to the Analogy of Bishop Butler, *etc.* 1842. 8°. **1115**. g. **21.**

—— *See* Boyce (John C.) Are Brutes Immortal? An enquiry . . . into Bishop Butler's hypotheses and concessions on the subject, as given in . . . his "Analogy of Religion." 1861. 8°. **8466**. c. **12.**

—— *See* Chalmers (Thomas) *D.D.* Lectures on Butler's "Analogy of Religion." 1839. 8°. **4016**. d. **15.**

—— *See* Duke (Henry H.) A Systematic Analysis of Butler's treatise on the Analogy of Religion, *etc.* 1847. 8°. **1115**. g. **24.**

—— *See* Eagar (Alexander R.) Butler's "Analogy" and Modern Thought. 1893. 8°. **4429**. bb. **33.**

—— *See* Eaton (John R. T.) Bishop Butler and his Critics. Two public lectures, *etc.* [With reference to the "Analogy of Religion."] 1877. 8°. **8469**. f. **5**. **(12.)**

—— *See* Gillett (E. H.) The Moral System, with an . . . introduction having special reference to Bp. Butler's "Analogy," *etc.* 1874. 8°. **3560**. aaa. **2.**

—— *See* Gorle (J.) An Analysis of Butler's Analogy of Religion, *etc.* 1855. 18°. **4377**. b. **12.**

—— *See* Hammond (Thomas C.) Age-Long Questions. An examination of certain problems in the philosophy of religion. [With special reference to Butler's "Analogy of Religion."] [1942.] 8°. **4381**. aa. **32.**

—— *See* Harvey (Frederick B.) Butler's Analogy. Part i. The Introduction and A Future Life. An analysis attempted after the manner of Euclid. 1879. 8°. **4018**. a. **11.**

—— *See* Hennell (Sara S.) Essay on the Sceptical Character of Butler's "Analogy." 1859. 12°. **4016**. a. **41.**

—— *See* Hobart (Richard) An Analysis of Bishop Butler's "Analogy of Religion," *etc.* 1834. 8°. **1117**. a. **13.**

—— *See* Holland (Henry S.) The Romanes Lecture, 1908. The Optimism of Butler's 'Analogy,' *etc.* 1908. 8°. **4378**. h. **37.**

—— *See* Huckin (Henry R.) The Analogy of Religion. Dialogues founded upon Butler's Analogy of Religion. [1873.] 8°. **4017**. df. **8.**

—— *See* Hughes (Henry) *M.A.* A Critical Examination of Butler's 'Analogy.' 1898. 8°. **4018**. ff. **22.**

—— *See* Hughes (William) *B.D.* A Catechetical Analysis of Butler's Analogy, part i. 1888. 8°. **4018**. aa. **36.**

—— *See* Hulton (Campbell G.) A Catechetical Help to Bishop Butler's Analogy. 1854. 8°. **4376**. b. **10.**

—— —— 1859. 8°. **4016**. b. **11.**

—— *See* Koehne (John B.) Bishop Butler's Challenge to Modernism. Retribution from "The Analogy." An interpretation. [1929.] 8°. **4105**. f. **33.**

—— *See* Leigh (Chandos) *Baron Leigh.* A Short Discourse on Natural and Revealed Religion, partly abstracted from Bishop Butler's Analogy. 1821. 8°. **702.h.11.(14.)**

—— *See* Napier (*Right Hon. Sir* Joseph) *Bart.* Lectures on Butler's Analogy of Religion, *etc.* 1864. 8°. **4016**. bb. **21.**

—— *See* Napier (*Right Hon. Sir* Joseph) *Bart.* The Miracles. Butler's argument on miracles, explained and defended, *etc.* 1863. 8°. **4016**. aa. **45.**

—— *See* Norris (John P.) Lectures on Butler's Analogy. 1887. 8°. **4421**. aa. **40.**

—— *See* Perronet (V.) A Second Vindication of Mr. Locke, wherein his sentiments relating to Personal Identity are clear'd up from some mistakes of the Rev. Dr. Butler, in his dissertation on that subject, *etc.* 1738. 8°. **528**. i. **26.**

—— *See* Philanthropus, *pseud.* [i.e. Thomas Bott.] Remarks upon Dr. Butler's sixth chapter of the "Analogy of Religion," *etc.* 1737. 8°. **702**. g. **11**. **(1.)**

—— *See* Poyntz (N.) The Truth of Christianity. The argument of Butler's Analogy in a popular form. 1872. 8°. **4479**. d. **39**. (4.)

—— *See* Pynchon (Thomas R.) Bishop Butler, a religious philosopher for all time. A sketch of his life. With an examination of the "Analogy." 1889. 8°. **4903**. eee. **16.**

—— *See* Review. A Review of the Doctrine of Personal Identity: in which are considered and compared the opinions of Locke, Butler, Reid, Brown, and Stewart, upon that subject, *etc.* 1827. 8°. T. **1234**. (8.)

—— *See* Sleater (Charles) A Succinct Analysis of the Analogy of Religion, *etc.* 1826. 8°. **1115**. g. **5.**

—— *See* Smith (John Bainbridge) *D.D.* A Compendium of Rudiments in Theology; containing a digest of Bishop Butler's Analogy, *etc.* 1836. 12°. **1115**. b. **17.**

—— *See* Smith (Leonidas L.) Questions on Butler's Analogy. [1875.] 8°. **04018**. h. **92**. **(2.)**

—— *See* Swainson (Charles A.) A Hand-Book to Butler's Analogy, *etc.* 1856. 8°. **4374**. c. **40.**

—— *See* Syāma Rāva (John) Remarks on Butler's Analogy. 1854. 12°. **4017**. aa. **87**. **(8.)**

—— *See* Thomas (Robert O.) A Synopsis of Butler's Analogy of Religion, *etc.* [1881.] 8°. **4018.df.1.**

—— *See* Thoughts. Thoughts on Miracles in general, and as they relate to the establishment of Christianity in particular: interspersed with remarks on Bishop Butler's Analogy of Religion, *etc.* 1757. 12°. **4014**. bbb. **11.**

BUTLER (JOSEPH) successively *Bishop of Bristol* and *of Durham.*

—— *See* WILKINSON (John) *M.A., of Merton College, Oxford.* A Systematic Analysis of Bishop Butler's Analogy, *etc.* 1847. 8°. **1115.** g. **23.**

—— *See* WILSON, afterwards PARKINSON (John P.) An Analysis of Bp. Butler's " Analogy of Religion," *etc.* 1837. 12°. **1115.** a. 4.

—— —— 1850. 8°. **4376.** a. **12.**

—— *See* WILSON (Joseph) *Rev., A.B.* Letters on the Truth and Certainty of Natural and Revealed Religion . . . intended as an introduction to Bishop Butler's Analogy of Religion, *etc.* 1810. 12°. **1114.** f. **24.**

—— Butler's Analogy: a lay argument by a Lancashire Manufacturer [i.e. Henry Bleekley]. Inscribed to the Bishop of Manchester. pp. 46. *Williams & Norgate: London & Edinburgh,* 1876. 8°. **4016.** e. **4.** (**6.**)

—— Remarks on Butler's Analogy, *etc.* pp. 122. *T. Smith: Canterbury,* 1783. 8°. **1115.** b. 4.

—— A Charge deliver'd to the Clergy, at the primary visitation of the Diocese of Durham, in the year, MDCCLI. pp. 29. *I. Lane: Durham.* 1751. 4°. **694.** h. **10.** (**10.**)

—— The second edition. With a preface, giving some account of the character and writings of the author, by Samuel, Lord Bishop of Gloucester. pp. iv. lxxxvi. 46. *T. Cadell: London,* 1786. 8°. **114.** b. **8.**

—— *See* BLACKBURNE (Francis) *Archdeacon of Cleveland.* A Serious Enquiry into the use and importance of External Religion. Occasioned by some passages in the . . . Bisbip of Durham's Charge . . . at his . . . primary visitation in . . . MDCCLI. 1768. 12°. [*BARRON* (*R.*) *The Pillars of Priestcraft, etc.* vol. 4.] **4106.** a. **12.**

—— A Serious Enquiry into the use and importance of External Religion. Occasioned by some passages in . . . the Lord Bishop of Durham's Charge to the Clergy of that Diocese at his Lordship's primary visitation in the year MDCCLI. Humbly addressed to his Lordship. [By Francis Blackburne.] pp. viii. 71. *S. Bladon: London,* 1752. 8°. **4109.** c. **36.**

—— [For editions of " Fifteen Sermons preached at the Rolls Chapel " published with " The Analogy of Religion ":] *See* supra: The Analogy of Religion.

—— Fifteen Sermons preached at the Rolls Chapel, *etc.* pp. 312. *J. & J. Knapton: London,* 1726. 8°. **1021.** i. 2.

—— The third edition. pp. xxxiv. 318. *J., J. & P. Knapton: London,* 1736. 8°. **227.** d. **29.**

—— Fifteen Sermons . . . To which are added Six Sermons preached on public occasions. The fourth edition. pp. xxxiv. 480. *Knapton: London,* 1749. 8°. **1021.** i. 3.

—— The fifth edition. pp. xxxii. 318. 162. *Robert Horsfield: London,* 1765. 8°. **677.** c. **30.**

—— A new edition, corrected. 2 vol. *R. Urie: Glasgow,* 1769. 8°. **4454.** aa. **12.**

—— The sixth edition. pp. 395. *F. & C. Rivington: London,* 1792. 8°. **4461.** cc. **8.**

—— [Another edition.] Sermons. pp. xxiv. 396. *W. P. Grant: Cambridge,* 1835. 12°. **4454.** aa. **13.**

—— Fifteen Sermons, preached at the Rolls Chapel: to which is added, a Charge to the Clergy of Durham . . . With an introductory essay, by the Rev. R. Cattermole, B.D., and an appendix, containing an analysis of the author's moral and religious systems, &c., &c., by Bishop Halifax. pp. xxiv. 344. [With a portrait.] *J. Hatchard & Son: London,* 1836. 8°. [*Sacred Classics.* vol. 27.] **496.** ee. **13.**

—— [A reissue.] *Joseph Rickerby: London,* 1841. 8°. **4477.** de. **30.**

—— [Another edition.] Sermons. pp. 447. *J. J. Chidley: London,* 1844. 12°. **4461.** a. **10.**

—— Bishop Butler's Ethical Discourses [i.e. " Fifteen Sermons " with the addition of the " Dissertation on Virtue "]; to which are added some remains, hitherto unpublished. Prepared as a text book in moral philosophy; with a syllabus, by Dr. Whewell. Edited, with an introductory essay on the author's life and writings, by the Rev. Joseph C. Passmore. pp. 375. *Charles Desilver: Philadelphia,* 1855. 8°. **4453.** d. **8.**

—— Fifteen Sermons preached at the Rolls Chapel . . . With notes, analytical, explanatory, and illustrative; and observations in reply to Mackintosh, Wardlaw, and Maurice. By the Rev. Robert Carmichael. pp. xiii. 266. *Longman & Co.: London, Dublin,* 1856. 8°. **4455.** e. **14.**

—— [Another edition.] With introduction, analyses, and notes by W. R. Matthews. pp. xxvii. 257. *London,* 1914. 8°. [*Bohn's Standard Library.*] **2504.** m. **9.**

—— On the Character of Balaam. [Sermon 7.] 1773. *See* ENGLISH PREACHER. The English Preacher, *etc.* vol. 2. 1773, *etc.* 12°. **4461.** aaa. **10.**

—— On the Love of God. [Sermons 13, 14.] 1773. *See* ENGLISH PREACHER. The English Preacher, *etc.* vol. 4. 1773, *etc.* 12°. **4461.** aaa. **10.**

—— Sermons. [Sermons 4, 7, 10, 13, 14.] *See* FAMILY LECTURES. Family Lectures, *etc.* vol. 1. 1791, *etc.* 8°. **224.** k. **1.**

—— Three Sermons upon Human Nature, with a Dissertation on the Nature of Virtue. pp. xiii. 63. *J. & J. J. Deighton & T. Stevenson: Cambridge,* 1834. 8°. **8407.** f. **31.** (**1.**)

—— Dissertation of the Nature of Virtue; Preface to Sermons; and Sermons on Human Nature, Compassion, Resentment and Forgiveness of Injuries, and on the Love of God. *See* WORDSWORTH (Christopher) *Master of Trinity College, Cambridge.* Christian Institutes. vol. 1. 1837. 8°. **495.** f. **22.**

—— Butler's Three Sermons on Human Nature and Dissertation on Virtue. Edited by W. Whewell . . . With a preface and syllabus of the work. pp. lx. 69. *Deightons: Cambridge: J. W. Parker: London,* 1848. 12°. **4375.** b. **9.**

—— Two Sermons upon the Love of God [sermons 13, 14] . . . and two extracts from the " Analogy of Religion " . . . With a preface [signed: J. M., i.e. John Muir]. pp. xix. 36. *A. S. Robertson: Cape Town,* 1852. 12°. **4477.** aa. **134.** (**11.**)

BUTLER (JOSEPH) successively *Bishop of Bristol* and *of Durham.*

—— Principles of Moral Science. Containing Bishop Butler's Three Sermons on Human Nature, and Dissertation on Virtue, with an introduction, analysis, vocabulary, etc. by the Rev. Henry Bower. pp. xliii. 96. *South India Christian School Book Society: Madras,* 1857. 8°. **4461.** aaa. **6.**

—— Upon the Government of the Tongue. [Sermon 4.] pp. 35. *James Hogg: Edinburgh; R. Groombridge & Sons: London,* 1857. 8°. [*Leaven Leaves.*] **4403.** f. **9.** (**5.**)

—— Upon Resentment. [Sermon 8.] pp. 16. [*Groombridge & Sons: London,* 1858.] 8°. [*Bishops' Tracts.* no. 23.] **4452.** b. **4.**

—— Bishop Butler's Ethical Discourses [i.e. selections from the "Fifteen Sermons"], and Essay on Virtue. Arranged as a treatise on moral philosophy; and edited, with an analysis, by J. T. Champlin. pp. 206. *J. P. Jewitt & Co.: Boston,* 1859. 8°. **4454.** df. **1.**

—— Two Sermons upon the Love of God [sermons 13, 14] . . . Reprinted from the Oxford edition of 1835. With an abstract of the argument [by John Muir]. pp. 35. *Edmonston & Douglas: Edinburgh,* 1867. 8°. **4461.** bb. **7.**

—— The Gist of Butler: sermons I., II., III. [upon human nature.] To which is appended an epitome of the Analogy: chap. III. By V. K. Cooper. pp. 31. *Andrews & Co.: Durham,* 1883. 8°. **4018.** e. **4.**

—— Human Nature and other sermons. [Sermons 1–7, 11–14. With an introduction signed H. M., i.e. Henry Morley.] pp. 192. *London,* 1887. 8°. [*Cassell's National Library.* vol. 93.] **12208.bb.15/93.**

—— Sermons . . . I., II., III. Upon Human Nature, or man considered as a moral agent. Introduction and notes by the Rev. T. B. Kilpatrick. pp. 123. *T. & T. Clark: Edinburgh,* [1888.] 8°. [*Handbooks for Bible Classes and Private Students.*] **3104.** aa. **8/4.**

—— Three Sermons on Human Nature and a Dissertation upon the Nature of Virtue . . . With introduction, analyses, and notes by W. R. Matthews. pp. xxvii. 81. *London,* 1914. 8°. [*Bell's English Classics.*] **012272.** aaaa. **1/37.**

—— *See* ANGUS (Joseph) An Analysis of Butler's Analogy of Religion and Three Sermons on Human Nature. [1882.] 8°. **4018.** b. **15.**

—— A Sermon, preached before His Grace Charles Duke of Richmond . . . and the Governors of the London Infirmary . . . March 31, 1748. pp. 31. *H. Woodfall: London,* [1748.] 4°. **693.** f. **5.** (**7.**)

—— [Another copy.] **225.** i. **3.** (**14.**)

—— A Sermon preached before His Grace Charles Duke of Richmond . . . and the Governors of the London Infirmary. To which is prefixed, His Lordship's Letter to the Archdeacon of Northumberland on that subject. (Abstract of statutes, rules and orders . . . for the government of the Infirmary at Newcastle.) pp. v. 25. 19. *M. Bryson & Co; J. Fleming: Newcastle upon Tyne,* 1751. 8°. **4475.** aaa. **18.**

BUTLER (JOSEPH) successively *Bishop of Bristol* and *of Durham.*

—— A Sermon preached before the House of Lords, in the Abbey-Church of Westminster, on Friday, Jan. 30, 1740-41. Being the day appointed to be observed as the day of the martyrdom of King Charles I. pp. 23. *J. & P. Knapton: London,* 1741. 4°. **225.** i. **18.** (**10*.**)

—— A Sermon preached before the House of Lords in the Abbey Church of Westminster, on Thursday, June 11, 1747, being the anniversary of His Majesty's happy accession to the throne. pp. 27. *J. & P. Knapton: London,* 1747. 4°. **693.** f. **5.** (**6.**)

—— A Sermon preached before the Incorporated Society for the Propagation of the Gospel in Foreign Parts at their anniversary meeting in the Parish-Church of St. Mary-le-Bow . . . February 16, 1738–9. pp. 27. *J. & P. Knapton: London,* 1739. 4°. **694.** f. **14.** (**2.**)

—— [Another copy.] **225.** i. **21.** (**12.**)

—— [Another edition.] *See* B., T. Twelve Anniversary Sermons preached before the Society for the Propagation of the Gospel. 1845. 8°. **1358.** e. **22.** (**1.**)

—— A Sermon preached before the Right Honourable the Lord-Mayor . . . and the Governors of the several Hospitals of the City of London, at the Parish Church of St. Bridget, on Monday in Easter-Week, 1740. (A True Report of . . . the several Hospitals . . . of the City of London.) pp. 32. *J. & P. Knapton: London,* 1740. 4°. **693.** f. **5.** (**5.**)

—— [Another copy.] **226.** f. **6.** (**16.**)

—— [Another edition.] *See* SCHOOLMASTER. The Schoolmaster; essays on practical education, *etc.* vol. 1. 1836. 12°. **1031.** i. **10.**

—— A Sermon preached in the Parish-Church of Christ-Church, London . . . May the 9th, 1745. Being the time of the yearly meeting of the children educated in the Charity-Schools, in and about the cities of London and Westminster . . . To which is annexed, an account of the Society for promoting Christian Knowledge. pp. 101. *B. Dod: London,* 1745. 4°. **694.** f. **10.** (**5.**)

—— [Another issue of the Sermon only.] *London,* 1745. 4°. **225.** i. **10.** (**13.**)

—— Several Letters to the Reverend Dr. Clarke, from a Gentleman in Glocestershire [i.e. J. Butler], relating to the first volume of the Sermons preached at Mr. Boyle's Lecture; with the Dr.'s answers thereunto. pp. 42. 1716. 8°. *See* CLARKE (Samuel) *Rector of St. James's, Westminster.* **T. 1029.** (**14.**)

—— Butler's Six Sermons on Moral Subjects; a sequel to the Three Sermons on Human Nature. Edited by W. Whewell . . . With a preface and a syllabus of the work. pp. xxviii. 118. *John Deighton: Cambridge; J. W. Parker: London,* 1849. 8°. **4455.** a. **7.**
First published with the fourth edition of "Fifteen Sermons preached at the Rolls Chapel."

—— Some Remains, hitherto unpublished, of Joseph Butler. [Edited by Edward Steere.] pp. 32. *Rivingtons: London,* 1853. 8°. **3753.** b. **3.**

APPENDIX.

—— *See* BAKER (Albert E.) *Rev.* Bishop Butler. 1923. 8°. W.P. **7964/1.**

BUTLER (Joseph) successively *Bishop of Bristol* and *of Durham.*

—— *See* Bartlett (Thomas) *Rector of Kingstone, Kent.* Memoirs of the Life, Character, and Writings of Joseph Butler, *etc.* [With a portrait.] 1839. 8°. **1126.** g. **21.**

—— *See* Broad (Charles D.) Five Types of Ethical Theory. (Spinoza, Butler, Hume, Kant, and Sidgwick.) 1930. 8°. **08460.** h. **1/36.**

—— *See* Collins (William L.) Butler. [With a portrait.] 1881. 8°. **2326.** a. **8.**

—— *See* Cook (Webster) The Ethics of Bishop Butler and Immanuel Kant. 1888. 8°. [*University of Michigan. Philosophical Papers.* ser. 2. no. 4.] Ac. **2685/7.**

—— *See* Egglestone (William M.) Stanhope Memorials of Bishop Butler. 1878. 8°. **4905.** bbb. **24.**

—— *See* Farrar (Adam S.) Bishop Butler and the Religious Features of his Times. 1863. 8°. [*Lectures delivered before the Young Men's Christian Association.*] **4461.** d. **27.**

—— *See* Goulburn (Edward M.) *Dean of Norwich.* Butler. The ethical preacher. 1877. 8°. [*Kempe* (*J. E.*) *The Classic Preachers of the English Church, etc.* ser. 1.] **4464.** i. **12.**

—— *See* Jones (Austin E. D.) Butler's Moral Philosophy. 1952. 8°. **012209.** d. **4/244.**

—— *See* Kitchin (George W.) *Dean of Durham.* Seven Sages of Durham, *etc.* (Bishop Joseph Butler.) 1911. 8°. **4920.i.6.**

—— *See* Mossner (Ernest C.) Bishop Butler and the Age of Reason, *etc.* 1936. 8°. **08486.** eee. **46.**

—— *See* Norton (William J.) Bishop Butler: Moralist and Divine, *etc.* 1938. 8°. **20035.** c. **1.**

—— *See* Pynchon (Thomas R.) Bishop Butler . . . A sketch of his life. With an examination of the "Analogy." 1889. 8°. **4903.** eee. **16.**

—— *See* Selby (Francis G.) Butler's Method of Ethics. 1881. 8°. **8463.** bb. **21.** (**5.**)

—— *See* Spooner (William A.) Bishop Butler. [With a portrait.] 1901. 8°. **4907.** dd. **6.**

—— *See* Taylor (William Edington) The Ethical and Religious Theories of Bishop Butler. 1903. 8°. **8410.** h. **18.**

—— *See* Whyte (Alexander) *D.D.* Bishop Butler, an appreciation; with the best passages of his writings selected and arranged by A. Whyte. 1903. 8°. **3751.** de. **5.**

—— Bishop Butler an avowed Puseyite and suspected Catholic. [Signed: P., i.e. Thomas Forster?] [1842.] 8°. *See* P. **4406.** g. **1.** (**108.**)

—— Metacosmos: a study in Bishop Butler's writings. pp. 16. *J. Snow & Co.: London,* [1883.] 8°. **4372.** df. **17.** (**1.**)

BUTLER (Joseph) *Vicar of St. Albans.*

—— *See* Bible. [*English.*] The Christian's New and Complete Universal Family Bible . . . With copious notes and annotations . . . by J. Butler, *etc.* [c. 1790.] fol. **L.14.d.6.**

BUTLER (Joseph) *Vicar of St. Albans.*

—— *See* Bible. [*English.*] The Christian's New and Complete British Family Bible . . . illustrated with . . . notes . . . By P. Wright . . . assisted by J. Butler, *etc.* [*C. 1800.*] fol. **L.14.g.5.**

BUTLER (Joseph B.)

—— *See* Dixey (Roger N.) and Butler (J. B.) Grass-Drying on the Farm, *etc.* 1939. 8°. Ac. **2674.** b. (**22.**)

BUTLER (Joseph Green) Fifty Years of Iron and Steel . . . An address delivered at . . . The American Iron and Steel Institute in Cincinnati . . . 1917, *etc.* (Fifth edition.) [With a portrait of the author.] pp. 173. *Penton Press Co.: Cleveland,* 1922. 8°. **08245.** i. **5.**

—— A Catalogue of Indian Portraits in the collection of J. G. Butler. pp. 39. *Vindicator Press: Youngstown, O.,* [1908.] 8°. **7858.** aaa. **31.**

BUTLER (Joseph Henry) Sketches by the Way Side; in prose and verse . . . With an introduction by Alonzo Potter, D.D., Bishop of Pennsylvania, and a memoir of the author [written by himself], &c. pp. 159. *Longman & Co.: London,* 1849. 8°. **12357.** bb. **23.**

BUTLER (Joseph V.) *See* Catholic Veto. The Catholic Veto and the Irish Bishops. A reply to a lecture [by J. V. Butler], *etc.* 1911. 8°. **4136.** df. **11.** (**4.**)

BUTLER (Josephine Elizabeth)

—— *See* Butler (Arthur S. G.) Portrait of Josephine Butler. [With portraits.] 1954. 8°. **10863.** f. **69.**

—— *See* Cooper (L. H.) Josephine Butler and her work for social purity, *etc.* [With portraits.] 1922. 8°. **010855.** aaa. **32.**

—— *See* Crawford (Virginia M.) Josephine Butler. [With a portrait.] [1928.] 8°. **010855.** e. **46.**

—— *See* Holmes (Marion) Josephine Butler, *etc.* [1913.] 8°. **010803.** ee. **4.** (**6.**)

—— *See* Marchant (*Sir* James) *K.B.E.* A Record of a Great Moral Crusade in Chatham . . . With a special introductory letter from Mrs. J. Butler. [1904.] 8°. **8425.** g. **41.**

—— *See* Mestral Combremont (J. de) La Noble vie d'une femme. Joséphine Butler. [With portraits.] 1927. 8°. **010856.** aaa. **18.**

—— *See* Stead (William T.) Josephine Butler, a life sketch. [1888.] 8°. **10827.** aaa. **24.**

—— *See* Thomas (Henry E.) The Martyrs of Hell's Highway . . . with preface and appendix by Mrs. J. E. Butler. 1896. 8°. **04410.** ee. **49.**

—— *See* Turner (Ethel M.) The Josephine Butler Centenary, 1828–1928. Josephine Butler: an appreciation. [With a portrait.] [1927.] 8°. **010855.** b. **58.**

—— *See* Welhaven (I.) Mrs. Josephine Butler. Et korstog mod lasten, *etc.* 1893. 8°. **3605.** i. **1/46.**

—— Address delivered at Croydon, July 3rd, 1871. pp. 15. *National Association: London,* 1871. 8°. **8282.** dd. **34.** (**6.**)

—— Catharine of Siena. A biography. pp. xix. 338. *Dyer Bros.: London,* 1878. 8°. **4829.** a. **6.**

—— Second edition. pp. xix. 338. *Dyer Bros.: London,* 1879. 8°. **4828.** de. **4.**

—— Catharine of Siena . . . Third edition. pp. xix. 338. *Dyer Bros.: London,* 1881. 8°. **4823.a.77.**

—— Catharine of Siena . . . Third edition. pp. 338. *Horace Marshall & Son: London,* 1894. 8°. **4831.** aa. **40.**

—— The Constitution Violated. An essay. By the author of the "Memoir of John Grey of Dilston" [i.e. J. E. Butler]. pp. 181. 1871. 8°. *See* ENGLAND. [*Appendix.—History and Politics.*—II. 1871.] **7640.** bb. **20.**

—— The Education and Employment of Women. pp. 28. *Macmillan & Co.: London,* 1868. 8°. **8415.** dd. **29.** (**5.**)

—— Government by Police. pp. 64. *Dyer Bros.: London,* 1879. 8°. **6056.** df. **3.**

—— Second edition. pp. 66. *Dyer Bros.: London,* 1880. 8°. **6057.** aa. **10.**

—— [Another edition.] pp. 64. *T. Fisher Unwin: London,* 1888. 8°. **8138.** i. **19.**

—— A Grave Question (the system of officially organized prostitution) that needs answering by the Churches of Great Britain. pp. 7. *Dyer Bros.: London,* [1886.] 16°. **8285.** a. **75.** (**2.**)

—— The Hour before the Dawn. An appeal to men. [By J. E. Butler.] pp. iv. 111. 1876. 8°. *See* HOUR. **8285.** bbb. **2.**

—— In Memoriam Harriet Meuricoffre. [With a portrait.] pp. 308. *Marshall & Son: London,* [1901.] 8°. **4907.** k. **16.**

—— The Lady of Shunem. [Papers on religious subjects.] pp. 143. *H. Marshall & Son: London,* [1894.] 8°. **4371.** aaaa. **19.**

—— Legislative Restrictions on the Industry of Women, considered from the women's point of view. [Signed by J. E. Butler and others.] pp. 18. *Matthews & Sons: London,* [1874.] 8°. **6146.** h. **4.** (**3.**)

—— [Another copy.] **8415.** e. **49.** (**8.**)

—— The Life of Jean Frederic Oberlin, Pastor of the Ban de la Roche, *etc.* pp. iv. 201. *R.T.S.: London,* [1882.] 8°. **4888.** b. **23.**

—— [Another edition.] pp. 190. [*London,*] 1886. 16°. [*R.T.S. Library.*] **4419.** aa. **20/7.**

—— Memoir of John Grey of Dilston. pp. viii. 360. *Edmonston & Douglas: Edinburgh,* 1869. 8°. **10826.** bbb. **7.**

—— Revised edition. pp. viii. 310. *H. S. King & Co.: London,* 1874. 8°. **10826.** aaa. **39.**

—— Memorie di Giovanni Grey di Dilston. Con prefazione di Marco Minghetti. pp. viii. 264. *Firenze,* 1871. 8°. **10826.** aaa. **29.**

—— Our Christianity tested by the Irish question. pp. 62. *T. Fisher Unwin: London,* [1887.] 8°. **8146.** c. **9.** (**6.**)

—— The Rejection of Home Rule. Our Christianity defended. A reply to Mrs. Josephine Butler's "Our Christianity tested." By an Irish Christian. pp. 36. *J. Kensit: London,* [1887.] 8°. **8146.** aaa. **28.** (**7.**)

—— Personal Reminiscences of a Great Crusade. pp. 409. *H. Marshall & Son: London,* 1896. 8°. **08416.** g. **17.**

—— Souvenirs personnels d'une grande croisade . . . Précédés d'une préface par Yves Guyot, *etc.* pp. xxii. 366. *Paris,* 1900. 8°. **08277.** ff. **59.**

—— "Mój pochód Krzyżowy." Zarysy autobiograficzne żywota i pracy. Z przedmową S. Posnera. pp. 131. *Warszawa,* 1904. 8°. **08276.** d. **19.** (**3.**)

—— Index to "Personal Reminiscences of a Great Crusade," by Josephine E. Butler. ff. 28. [*London,* 1935.] 4°. **8416.** k. **24.**
Reproduced from typewriting.

—— The Present Aspect of the Abolitionist Cause in relation to British India, *etc.* pp. 31. *British, Continental, & General Federation: London,* [1893.] 8°. **8282.** dd. **23.** (**8.**)

—— The Principles of the Abolitionists. An address delivered at Exeter Hall, Feb. 20th, 1885. pp. 14. *Dyer Bros.: London,* [1885.] 16°. **8275.** aa. **25.** (**4.**)

—— Rebecca Jarrett. pp. 59. *Morgan & Scott: London,* [1885.] 8°. **10601.** aaa. **25.** (**4.**)

—— Recollections of George Butler. [With illustrations and a portrait.] pp. 487. *J. W. Arrowsmith: Bristol,* [1892.] 8°. **4906.** i. **16.**

—— Souvenirs & pensées. Illustré de six portraits hors texte. [Compiled from "Recollections of George Butler" and other sources by E. Pieczynska, R. and L. Bergner, and H. Minod.] pp. xiv. 272. *Saint-Blaise,* 1908. 8°. **010855.** h. **15.**

—— The Revival and Extension of the Abolitionist Cause. A letter, *etc.* pp. 55. *J. T. Doswell: Winchester,* 1887. 8°. **8285.** aaa. **39.** (**4.**)

—— The Salvation Army in Switzerland. pp. 304. *Dyer Bros.: London,* 1883. 8°. **4136.** g. **3.**

—— Simple Words for Simple Folk, about the Repeal of the Contagious Diseases Acts—Women, *etc.* pp. 7. *J. W. Arrowsmith: Bristol,* [1886.] 16°. **8285.** a. **75.** (**3.**)

—— Social Purity. (An address given at Cambridge, in May 1879.) pp. 48. *Morgan & Scott: London,* [1879.] 8°. **8416.** a. **23.**

—— Second edition. pp. 48. *Dyer Bros.: London,* 1881. 8°. **8277.** aa. **14.** (**5.**)

—— Third edition. pp. 48. *Dyer Bros.: London,* 1882. 8°. **8410.** cc. **22.** (**2.**)

—— Some Thoughts on the present aspect of the Crusade against the State Regulation of Vice. pp. 22. *T. Brakell: Liverpool,* 1874. 8°. **08416.** k. **62.**

—— Speech delivered . . . at the fourth annual meeting of the "Vigilance Association for the Defence of Personal Rights," held at Bristol, October 15th, 1874. pp. 10. *Vigilance Association for the Defence of Personal Rights: [London,* 1874.] 8°. **8277.** d. **4.** (**14.**)

—— Sursum Corda; annual address to the Ladies' National Association. pp. 48. *T. Brakell: Liverpool,* 1871. 8°. **8277.** d. **4.** (**11.**)

BUTLER (Josephine Elizabeth)

—— [Une Voix dans le désert.] The Voice of one crying in the Wilderness. By Josephine Butler. Being her first appeal, made in 1874-5, to continental nations against the system of regulated vice. Now first translated into English by Osmund Airy . . . With introduction by the Right Hon. James Stuart. pp. 78. *J. W. Arrowsmith: Bristol,* 1913. 8°. **08276**. df. **30**.

—— Woman's Work and Woman's Culture. A series of essays. Edited by J. E. Butler. pp. lxiv. 367. *Macmillan & Co.: London,* 1869. 8°. **8415**. h. **18**.

—— Josephine E. Butler. An autobiographical memoir (taken chiefly from her Recollections of George Butler, and from Personal Recollections of a Great Crusade). Edited by George W. and Lucy A. Johnson. With introduction by James Stuart. [With plates, including portraits.] pp. xi. 318. *J. W. Arrowsmith: Bristol,* 1909. 8°. **4908**. ccc. **2**.

—— Second edition. pp. xi. 322. *J. W. Arrowsmith: Bristol,* 1911. 8°. **4907**. e. **27**.

—— (Third edition, revised and enlarged.) pp. xii. 276. *J. W. Arrowsmith: Bristol, London,* 1928. 8°. **4908**. k. **1**.

BUTLER (Josephus) Disputatio medica inauguralis de nutritione, *etc.* *Apud viduam & hæredes J. Elsevirii: Lugduni Batavorum,* 1676. 4°. **1185**. g. **14**. (**1**.)

—— Oratio in laudem artis medicæ, *etc.* *S. à Lier: Amstelodami,* 1668. 4°. **1185**. i. **15**. (**24**.)

BUTLER (Judson Rea) and **KARWOSKI** (Theodore Francis) Human Psychology. pp. xvi. 447. *Sir I. Pitman & Sons: London,* 1937. 8°. **08459**. g. **63**.

BUTLER (Julia) Donner à chacun ce qui lui appartient. [A letter addressed " A Monseigneur le cardinal Wiseman et à son clergé de Jersey."] pp. 27. [*St. Helier ?*] 1851. 12°. **4071**. a. **10**.

BUTLER (June) *See* Butler (*Lady* Irene J. B.)

BUTLER (June Rainsford)

—— Floralia. Garden paths and by-paths of the eighteenth century. [With plates.] pp. xiii. 187. *University of North Carolina Press: Chapel Hill,* [1938.] 8°. **07032**. tt. **5**.

BUTLER (Katharine G.)

—— *See* Van Riper (Charles G.) and Butler (K. G.) Speech in the Elementary Classroom. [1955.] 8°. **011805**. h. **79**.

BUTLER (Kathleen Theresa Blake) *See* Guez (J. L.) *Sieur de Balzac.* Les Premières lettres de Guez de Balzac, 1618–1627. Édition critique, précédée d'une introduction par H. Bibas et K.-T. Butler. 1933, *etc.* 8°. . Ac. **9812/42**.

—— ' The Gentlest Art ' in Renaissance Italy. An anthology of Italian letters, 1459–1600. Compiled by the late K. T. Butler. pp. xxvi. 376. *University Press: Cambridge,* 1954. 8°. **10923**. ee. **16**.

—— A History of French Literature, *etc.* 2 vol. *Methuen & Co.: London,* 1923. 8°. **011850**. b. **26**.

BUTLER (Kathleen Theresa Blake) and **REYNOLDS** (Eva Mary Barbara)

—— Tredici novelle moderne. Selected & edited with introduction and notes by K. T. Butler . . . and B. Reynolds. pp. ix. 108. *University Press: Cambridge,* 1947. 8°. **12944**. aa. **26**.

BUTLER (Keble) Somerton's Folly. pp. 288. *John Long: London,* 1930. 8°. NN. **17311**.

BUTLER (Ladson) and **JOHNSON** (O. R.) Management Control through Business Forms. pp. viii. 213. *Harper & Bros.: New York & London,* 1930. 8°. **08245**. k. **47**.

BUTLER (Laurie Shaw)

—— Can the Coming of Christ be expedited ? *etc.* (Reprinted from " The Covenant Message.") pp. 15. *Destiny Publishers: Johannesburg,* [1950.] 8°. **04034**. v. **19**.

—— Water Baptism. A Scriptural statement. pp. 23. *Kingdom Publishing Co.: London,* [1940.] 8°. **4324**. ff. **21**.

BUTLER (Leslie)

—— *See* Reading (Bill) So You're a Father ! . . . With illustrations by L. Butler. 1947. 8°. W.P. **997/4**.

—— An Alphabet of Flowers. Illustrations by L. Butler . . . Lettering by Cecil M. Bayly. *Perry Colour Books: London,* [1954.] 32°. **7035**. h. **7**.

BUTLER (Leslie Illingworth) Church Teaching in Rhyme for Children. Based on the Church Catechism. *Jas. Golder: Reading,* [1929.] 32°. **03504**. de. **28**.

BUTLER (Lewis William George) Annals of the King's Royal Rifle Corps . . . With illustrations and maps. 5 vol.

vol. 1. " The Royal Americans." (By L. Butler.) pp. xxiv. 379. 1913.
vol. 2. " The Green Jacket." (By L. Butler.) pp. xxi. 348. 1923.
vol. 3. The 60th: the K.R.R.C. (By L. Butler.) pp. xxviii. 334. 1926.
vol. 4. The 60th: the K.R.R.C. (By Sir Stewart Hare.) pp. xxxix. 398. 1929.
vol. 5. The Great War. (By Sir Stewart Hare.) pp. xvii. 478. 1932.
Appendix, dealing with uniform, armament and equipment. By S. M. Milne and Major-General Astley Terry, *etc.* pp. viii. 52. 1913.

1913–32. 8°. *See* England.—*Army.*—*Infantry.*—*King's Royal Rifle Corps.* **8835**. e. **3**.

—— Sir Redvers Buller . . . Reprinted, with additions, from ' The King's Royal Rifle Corps Chronicle ' . . . With portraits and facsimile letter. pp. 120. *Smith, Elder & Co.: London,* 1909. 8°. **10817**. f. **20**.

—— Wellington's Operations in the Peninsula, 1808–1814. . . . With sketch maps. 2 vol. *T. Fisher Unwin: London,* 1904. 8°. **09077**. g. **20**.

BUTLER (Lilly) Eight sermons, preached at the Lecture founded by the Hon. Robert Boyle . . . 1709. Religion no matter of Shame. *See* Letsome (Sampson) and Nicholl (J.) A Defence of Natural and Revealed Religion, *etc.* vol. 2. 1739. fol. **15**. d. **8**.

—— Dr. Butler's Boyle's Lectures, abridg'd. *See* Burnet (Gilbert) *Vicar of Coggeshall.* A Defence of Natural and Revealed Religion, *etc.* vol. 2. 1737. 8°. **695**. e. **18**.

—— A Sermon preached at St. Mary-le-Bow, before the Lord Mayor . . . on Wednesday, the 16th of September, a day appointed . . . for a solemn Monthly Fast. pp. 26. *For R. Baldwin: London,* 1691. 4°. **4473**. e. **19**. (**3**.)

—— A Sermon preached at St. Mary-le-Bow before the Lord Mayor . . . on Friday the 26th of June : a day appointed . . . for a General and Publick Fast. pp. 29. *For B. Aylmer: London,* 1696. 4°. **4473**. e. **19**. (**4**.)

BUTLER (LILLY)

—— A Sermon preach'd at St. Mary-le-Bow, to the Societies for Reformation of Manners, April 5. 1697. pp. 36. *For B. Aylmer: London*, 1697. 8°. **111**. a. **22**.

—— A Sermon preached at St. Mary-le-Bow, before the Lord Mayor . . . on Wednesday the 28th of April, a day appointed . . . for a General and Publick Fast. pp. 30. *For Brabazon Aylmer: London*, 1697. 4°. **4473**. g. **18**. (**2**.)

—— A Sermon preach'd at the Anniversary Meeting of the Sons of Clergymen, in the Cathedral Church of St. Paul, on Thursday, Nov. 30. 1704. pp. 23. *Brabazon Aylmer: London*, 1704. 4°. **226**. f. **14**. (**14**.)

—— A Sermon preach'd at the Funeral of Clopton Havers, M.D., April 29, 1702, at Willingale-Doe in Essex. pp. 28. *Brabazon Aylmer: London*, 1702. 4°. **1415**. i. **39**.

—— [Another copy.] **1415**. i. **40**.

—— [Another copy.] **226**. g. **9**. (**17**.)

—— A Sermon preached at the Funeral of Mr James Lordel, who was buried at St Magnus Church, March 27. 1694. pp. 23. *For Brabazon Aylmer: London*, 1694. 4°. **1417**. d. **54**.

—— [Another copy.] **226**. g. **7**. (**12**.)

—— A Sermon preached before the Lord Mayor . . . at the Cathedral Church of St. Paul: on Friday the fourth of April, 1701. being the Fast-Day appointed by proclamation, *etc*. pp. 27. *Brab. Aylmer: London*, 1701. 4°. **694**. g. **16**. (**4**.)

—— [Another copy.] **226**. g. **4**. (**14**.)

—— A Sermon preach'd before the Lord-Mayor . . . at the Cathedral-Church of St. Paul, on the fifth of November, 1710. pp. 22. *B. Aylmer: London*, 1710. 8°. **225**. h. **11**. (**6**.)

—— A Sermon preached before the Right Honourable the Lord Mayor . . . at St. Lawrence Jewry, on the Feast of St. Michael, 1696, at the election of the Lord Mayor for the year ensuing. pp. 27. *For Brab. Aylmer: London*, 1696. 4°. **226**. h. **9**. (**14**.)

—— The Sin and Mischief of Inordinate Self-Love. A sermon preached before the King at St. James's, June 3. 1716. pp. 22. *John Wyat: London*, 1716. 8°. **695**. g. **7**. (**20**.)

BUTLER (LILY CLARKSON) A Student's Manual of Birth Control. pp. 39. *Noel Douglas: London*, 1933. 8°. Cup. **364**. c. **22**.

BUTLER (LORINE LETCHER) Birds around the Year . . . Illustrated. pp. xi. 242. *D. Appleton-Century Co: New York, London*, 1937. 8°. **7286**. p. **46**.

BUTLER (M. MARY) The Truth that Makes Free. Revealed unto this generation by "that disciple whom Jesus loved." [Spiritualistic communications.] pp. 62. *Rider & Co.: London*, 1932. 8°. **08632**. de. **79**.

BUTLER (MAIDA)

—— The History of a House. [On the Rippon and Sargood families. With genealogical tables.] 2 pt. pp. 217. [1953?] 8°. **9918**. ee. **9**.
Typewritten.

BUTLER (MANN) An Appeal from the Misrepresentations of James Hall, respecting the history of Kentucky and the West . . . To which is annexed, a chronology of the principal events . . . in the history of the Western country of the United States, from the earliest Spanish and French explorations to 1806. pp. 32. *A. G. Hodges: Frankfort, Ky.*, 1837. 8°. **9603**. cc. **17**.

—— A History of the Commonwealth of Kentucky. pp. xi. 396. *Wilcox, Dickerman & Co.: Lousville, Ky.*, 1834. 8°. **1447**. g. **9**.

—— Second edition, revised and enlarged by the author. pp. lxxii. 551. *J. A. James & Co.: Cincinnati*, 1836. 12°. **1447**. g. **10**.

BUTLER (MARGERY BAYLEY)

—— A Candle was lit. Life of Mother Mary Aikenhead. [With plates, including portraits.] pp. 183. *Clonmore & Reynolds: Dublin*, 1953. 8°. **4956**. k. **47**.

BUTLER (MARGUERITE L.) Hindu Women at Home. pp. 34. *London Missionary Society: London*, 1921. 8°. [*World Womanhood Series*. no. 5.] **08416**. aa. **36**.

BUTLER (MARIAN) Susie's Mistake, and other stories. pp. 216. *Presbyterian Board of Publication: Philadelphia*, [1864.] 12°. **4414**. bbb. **17**.

BUTLER (MARIE JOSEPH)

—— *See* BURTON (Katherine) Mother Butler of Marymount. [With a portrait.] 1944. 8°. **4910**. b. **5**.

—— Reflections for Every Day of the Month. From the writings of . . . M. J. Butler . . . With concluding prayers from John Henry Cardinal Newman. [With a portrait.] pp. 71. *Frederick Pustet Co.: New York & Cincinnati*, 1947. 12°. **4398**. a. **96**.

BUTLER (MARION CLIFFORD) *Baroness Dunboyne*. Alfendeane Rectory. A tale. pp. 92. *S.P.C.K.: London*, [1897.] 8°. **4430**. c. **12**.

—— Anchor and Cross, *etc*. pp. 158. *S.P.C.K.: London*, [1895.] 8°. **4430**. cc. **5**.

—— Aunt Lily's Motto. A tale, *etc*. pp. 156. *S.P.C.K.: London*, [1891.] 8°. **4429**. aaa. **21**.

—— The Black Sheep of the Parish. pp. 92. *J. Nisbet & Co.: London*, 1883 [1882]. 8°. **4422**. m. **3**.

—— The Breaking of the Clouds. A tale. pp. viii. 212. *J. Nisbet & Co.: London*, 1894 [1893]. 8°. **4399**. h. **36**.

—— Charity. A tale. pp. 152. *J. Nisbet & Co.: London*, 1892. 8°. **4399**. aaa. **8**.

—— Elmore. A novel. pp. 320. *T. C. Newby: London*, 1873. 8°. **12638**. e. **5**.

—— Fritz and his Friends. A tale, *etc*. pp. 223. *S.P.C.K.: London*, [1893.] 8°. **4429**. bb. **22**.

—— From the Bench to the Battle. pp. 127. *S.P.C.K.: London*, [1887.] 8°. **4421**. c. **2**.

—— George the Sweep. A sketch from life. pp. 32. *S.P.C.K.: London*, [1887.] 16°. **4412**. f. **13**. (**2**.)

—— Heather and Roses. A tale, *etc*. pp. 223. *S.P.C.K.: London*, [1890.] 8°. **4419**. ccc. **42**.

—— Her Life's Work. pp. vi. 227. *J. Nisbet & Co.: London*, 1888. 8°. **4414**. ee. **15**.

BUTLER (Marion Clifford) *Baroness Dunboyne.*

—— Letty's Mission. A tale. pp. iv. 117. *J. Masters & Co: London*, 1885. 8°. **4416**. i. **22**.

—— Little Elsie's Summer at Malvern. pp. 86. *J. Nisbet & Co.: London*, 1871. 8°. **12706**. c. 4.

—— Madcap Meg. A tale. pp. 94. *S.P.C.K.: London*, [1899.] 8°. **4429**. d. **22**.

—— The Maitlands' Money-Box. pp. 128. *J. Nisbet & Co.: London*, 1881. 16°. **12808**. ddd. **24**.

—— Master Molyneux. A tale, *etc.* pp. 158. *S.P.C.K.: London*, 1894. 8°. **4429**. c. **41**.

—— The Romance of a Lawn Tennis Tournament. pp. 128. *Trischler & Co.: London*, 1890. 8°. **012631**. e. **75**.

—— Some Great Thing. pp. 186. *National Society's Depository: London*, [1900.] 8°. **04410**. i. **60**.

—— Summerland Grange. pp. 160. *J. Nisbet & Co.: London*, 1884. 8°. **4416**. gg. **12**.

—— A Sunbeam's Influence; or, Eight years after, *etc.* pp. 177. *J. Nisbet & Co.: London*, 1871. 8°. **12808**. l. **21**.

—— A Tale of two old Songs . . . 1. The Bridge. 2. The Village Blacksmith. pp. 156. *J. Nisbet & Co.: London*, 1871. 8°. **12637**. aa. **18**.

—— A Thankful Heart, *etc.* pp. 160. *S.P.C.K.: London*, [1896.] 8°. **4430**. d. **8**.

—— Through Shine and Shower. 2 vol. *J. Blackwood & Co.: London*, [1884.] 8°. **12636**. r. **4**.

—— A True Knight. pp. 144. *National Society's Depository: London*, [1902.] 8°. **04412**. e. **18**.

—— Uncle Guy. A story for children, *etc.* pp. 159. *S.P.C.K.: London*, [1889.] 8°. **4420**. cc. **49**.

—— A Year with the Everards. A tale. By the author of "Little Elsie's Summer at Malvern" [i.e. M. C. Butler, Baroness Dunboyne]. pp. 211. 1874. 8°. *See* Everards. **12703**. bbb. **36**.

—— The Young Squire. A story for children, *etc.* pp. 157. *S.P.C.K.: London*, [1890.] 8°. **4429**. aaa. **1**.

BUTLER (Marion E.) *See* Roth (Henry L.) The Aborigines of Tasmania. By H. L. Roth. Assisted by M. E. Butler, *etc.* 1890. 8°. **2374**. c. **6**.

—— —— 1899. 8°. **10492**. ff. **24**.

BUTLER (Martha) *See* Butler (John) *B.D.* The True State of the Case of John Butler . . . in answer to the libel of Martha his sometimes wife. Treating of a marriage dissolved, *etc.* 1697. 8°. **499**. aa. **15**. (3.)

BUTLER, otherwise **STRICKLAND** (Mary) The Tryal and Conviction of Mary Butler, alias Strickland, at the Justice-Hall in the Old Baily . . . on the 10th day of October, 1699. For counterfeiting a bond of £40,000 as the bond of Sir Robert Clayton, Kt. pp. 28. *F. C.: London*, 1700. 4°. **518**. f. **26**.

BUTLER (Mary) *Duchess of Ormonde.* A Short Memorial, and Character, of that Most Noble and Illustrious Princess, Mary Dutchess of Ormonde. [With a portrait.] pp. 30. [*London*, 1733.] 8°. **1419**. e. **19**.

BUTLER (Mary) *Novelist.* The Ring of Day. pp. 360. *Hutchinson & Co.: London*, 1906. 8°. **012633**. a. **11**.

BUTLER (Mary) *Novelist.*

—— Bláṫa Bealtaine . . . Tomás Ua Conceanainn d'aistriġ go Gaeḋilg. pp. 23. Connraḋ na Gaeḋilge: i mBaile Áṫa Cliaṫ, 1902. 8°. [Leabairíni Gaeḋilge le hAgaiḋ an tSluaiġ. 7.] Ac. **9954**. d/**2**.

BUTLER (Mary) *of the University of Pennsylvania.* Piedras Negras Pottery. A dissertation . . . Reprint of "Piedras Negras, Preliminary Report No. 4." ff. iii. 69. pl. xiv. *University Museum, University of Pennsylvania: Philadelphia*, 1935. 4°. **7810**. r. **13**.
Reproduced from typewriting.

BUTLER (Matthew Calbraith) *See* Brooks (Ulysses R.) Butler and his Cavalry in the War of Secession, 1861–1865. 1909. 8°. **09555**. dd. **5**.

—— General Butler's Narrative. [An account of the retreat from Yorktown, 3 May 1862.] *See* Augusta, *Georgia.—Confederate Survivors' Association.* Address, *etc.* 1895. 8°. **9602**. bbb. **32**. (**7**.)

BUTLER (Maude Mary) Adèle's Love. The story of a faithful little heart. pp. 256. *Oliphant, Anderson & Ferrier: Edinburgh*, [1889.] 8°. **4410**. p. **1**.

—— Bob's Heroine. A story, *etc.* pp. 159. *W. P. Nimmo, Hay & Mitchell: Edinburgh*, 1890. 8°. **4412**. ccc. **27**.

—— Cecil; the boy who stood between. pp. 252. *W. P. Nimmo, Hay & Mitchell: Edinburgh*, 1891. 8°. **012803**. f. **43**.

—— Daffodil, a brave little lady. pp. 128. *T. Nelson & Sons: London*, 1893 [1892]. 8°. **4412**. h. **9**.

—— [A reissue.] *London*, 1903. 8°. **04412**. i. **69**.

—— Fairy Greatmind, *etc.* pp. 125. *Oliphant, Anderson & Ferrier: Edinburgh & London*, 1897. 8°. **012806**. l. **27**.

—— The Ghost of Reeder's Wood. What it was and who found it out. pp. 175. *W. P. Nimmo, Hay & Mitchell: Edinburgh*, [1894.] 8°. **012807**. g. **19**.

—— [A reissue.] Midnight Pluck; or, the Ghost of Reeder's Wood. *Sampson Low & Co.: London*, [1925.] 8°. **012807**. b. **51**.

—— Paul. A little mediator. pp. 96. *S. W. Partridge & Co.: London*, [1896.] 8°. **4413**. ff. **27**.

—— The Rightful Daughter; or the Two lights of Fernlytton. pp. 276. *Jarrold & Sons: London*, 1896 [1895]. 8°. **04410**. de. **40**.

—— The Story of Little Hal and the Golden Gate, *etc.* pp. 175. *J. F. Shaw & Co.: London*, [1887.] 8°. **12806**. r. **1**.

—— Waiting and Serving; or, the Major's little sentinel. pp. 139. *T. Nelson & Sons: London*, 1892 [1891]. 8°. **012803**. eee. **57**.

BUTLER (Maurice) *F.C.I.I.* *See* Burrell (Edward J.) Elementary Building Construction and Drawing . . . With an appendix for fire insurance students by M. Butler . . . and E. G. Skinner. 1931. 8°. **7817**. a. **10**.

—— *See* Williamson (James J.) *F.C.I.I.* Common Features of Fire Hazard . . . With chapters on lighting, heating and ventilation by M. Butler. 1935. 8°. **08715**. b. **71**.

—— Diagrams of Reinforced Concrete Construction and Fireproof Floors. pp. 20. *M. Butler: Watford*, [1927.] fol. **7814**. c. **48**.

BUTLER (MAURICE) *F.C.I.I.*

—— Hop Growing and Hop Curing from the fire insurance viewpoint, *etc.* [With illustrations.] pp. viii. 74. *Tudor Press: London,* [1932.] 8°. [*Insurance Record Handbooks.*] **07030.** f. **54/1.**

BUTLER (MAURICE) *Land-Waiter in the Port of London.* The Case and Conduct of M. Butler, Land-Waiter in the Port of London, humbly submitted to the Publick, especially the Legislature, &c. &c. pp. 60. FEW MS. NOTES. *T. Stone: London,* 1750. 8°. **1414.** b. **66.** (**1.**)

BUTLER (MAYNARD) The First Year of Responsibility: talks with a boy. pp. 141. *Thomas Burleigh: London,* 1899. 8°. **8410.** ccc. **44.**

—— Second edition, with an introduction by the Master of Trinity College, Cambridge [H. M. Butler]. pp. viii. 119. *Swan Sonnenschein & Co.: London,* 1903. 8°. **8410.** e. **29.**

—— [Another copy.] **08407.** ee. **7.**

—— The Little Afrikander and the Great Queen. pp. 71. *Swan Sonnenschein & Co.: London,* 1904. 8°. **012803.** h. **57.**

BUTLER (MIFF M.)

—— Geomath . . . Correlates heat, light, sound, electricity, atomic structure, and gravity, states of matter, chemical elements, sun and earth, mountains and ocean currents, source and oil, runs a motor and radio. pp. 29. *General Engineering Co.: Casper,* [1941.] 8°. **08712.** a. **19.**

BUTLER (MILDRED ALLEN) Here comes the Bride. A comedy in one act. pp. 21. *Samuel French: Toronto,* [1937.] 8°. **11792.** a. **35.**

BUTLER (MONTAGU CHRISTIE)

—— *See* DICKENS (C.) [*Life of Our Lord.*] La Vivo de nia Sinjoro Jesuo . . . Tradukita de M. C. Butler. 1934. 8°. **4224.k.6.**

—— *See* HAGGARD (*Sir* Henry R.) *K.B.E.* Luno de Izrael . . . Tradukis . . . E. S. Payson kaj M. C. Butler. 1928. 8°. **012901.** ff. **59.**

—— *See* HYDE (Herbert E.) Internacia Parlamento. Cu Britujo montros la vojon? . . . Tradukis M. C. Butler. [1918.] 8°. **06496.** a. **10.**

—— *See* SAMENHOF (L. L.) Proverbs in Esperanto and English, *etc.* (Translated by M. C. Butler.) 1926. 32°. **945.** e. **1/11.**

—— *See* STEPHEN (Caroline E.) Fundamentoj de la Koakerismo. Esperantigita de M. C. Butler. 1916. 8°. **875.** r. **3.**

—— First Steps in Esperanto, *etc.* pp. 79. *British Esperanto Association: London,* 1922. 8°. **012901.** ff. **55.**

—— Second edition, revised & enlarged. pp. 158. *British Esperanto Association: London,* 1924. 8°. **012901.** ff. **56.**

—— [Another edition.] Step by Step in Esperanto . . . Third edition, revised and enlarged. pp. 239. *British Esperanto Association: London,* [1929.] 8°. **012903.** e. **12.**

—— Fourth edition. pp. 243. *British Esperanto Association: London,* 1933. 8°. **12903.** bbb. **33.**

BUTLER (MONTAGU CHRISTIE)

—— Himnaro Esperanta. Kompilata de M. C. Butler . . . Dua eldono, *etc.* pp. viii. 145. *British Esperanto Association: London,* 1921. 8°. **012901.** e. **5.**

—— Himnaro Esperanta . . . Kvara eldono, reviziita kaj pligrandigita. pp. x. 161. *British Esperanto Association: London,* 1954. 8°. **3438.** g. **65.**

—— Linguaphone Conversational Course, Esperanto. The Esperanto text prepared by M. C. Butler . . . Third edition revised and corrected. pp. xiii. 144. *Linguaphone Institute: London,* [1935?] 8°. [*Linguaphone Conversational Courses.*] **W.P.13705/6.(1.)**

—— Linguaphone Rapid Esperanto Course. Thirty simple lessons, *etc.* pp. 41. *Linguaphone Institute:* [*London,* 1930?] 8°. **012902.** m. **10.**

—— The Pros and Cons of Esperanto. pp. 8. *Standard Press: Blackburn,* [1918.] 8°. **012901.** ff. **45.**

—— Raporta Stenografio: alfaro de la angla sistemo Pitmana al Esperanto . . . Kuina eldono. pp. 47. *P. J. Cameron: London,* [1920.] 8°. **12991.** gg. **50.**

—— Roston's Rapid Esperanto Course . . . Prepared by M. C. Butler, *etc.* pp. 41. *Linguaphone Institute: London,* 1927. 8°. **12902.** c. **26.**

—— Step by Step in Esperanto . . . Sixth edition. pp. 243. *Esperanto Publishing Co.: Rickmansworth,* 1943. 8°. **012902.** m. **13.**

—— Step by Step in Esperanto . . . Seventh edition. pp. 280. *Esperanto Publishing Co.:* [*London,*] 1948. 8°. **012902.** l. **30.**

—— First Steps in Esperanto, *etc.* [A reprint of pp. 11–34 of "Step by Step in Esperanto," seventh edition.] pp. 24. *Esperanto Publishing Co.:* [*London,*] 1948. 8°. **012902.** l. **29.**

BUTLER (MONTAGU CHRISTIE) and **MERRICK** (FRANK)

—— Muzika Terminaro. pp. 35. *Internacia Esperanto-Ligo: Rickmansworth,* 1944. 16°. **012902.** l. **15.**

BUTLER (MONTAGU RUSSELL) *See* BUTLER (Arthur G.) and BUTLER (M. R.) The Two Spirits, *etc.* [1877.] 8°. **3939.** bb. **2.**

—— *See* PALMER (Edmund S.) How are the Scriptures known to be the Word of God. [A correspondence between E. S. Palmer and M. R. Butler.] [1877.] 8°. **3940.** de. **5.** (**1.**)

—— *See* PERIODICAL PUBLICATIONS.—*London.* The West End Quarterly Magazine. Edited by M. R. Butler. [1878.] 4°. **1866.** b. **4.** (**1.**)

—— Abbé Chiniquy. A brief sketch of his life and labours, *etc.* pp. 19. *A. S. Mallett: London,* [1879.] 8°. **3939.** de. **21.** (**1.**)

—— A Brief Catechism on English Orders. pp. 29. *Church Printing Co.: London,* 1895. 16°. **3940.** a. **11.**

—— The Doctrine of the Real Absence: a tract for thinking men. pp. 12. *William Macintosh: London,* [1875.] 8°. **4324.** h. **1.** (**2.**)

—— God's Word and Man's Word; or, the Bible and tradition . . . Second edition, enlarged. pp. 12. *William Macintosh: London,* 1873. 8°. **3940.** aaa. **86.** (**6.**)

BUTLER (Montagu Russell)

—— The Mennonite Brethren: now commonly called "Baptists." A brief review of the history and tenets of the Sect . . . Reprinted after revision from the Indian Churchman, *etc.* pp. 31. *Oxford Mission Press: Calcutta*, [1889.] 8°. **4136**. b. **26**. (5.)

—— Protestant Recruits: a record of modern priests, monks, nuns, and theological students who have left the Church of Rome. pp. 20. *A. S. Mallett: London*, 1879. 8°. **3940**. bb. **16**.

—— The Reformation in Canada. A report of the "Père Chiniquy Aid Fund," 1876–1877. pp. 16. *Operative Jewish Converts' Institution: London*, [1877.] 8°. **4183**. de. 4. (10.)

—— Rome's Tribute to Anglican Orders. pp. 27. *Oxford Mission Press: Calcutta*, [1889.] 8°. **3943.k.3.(4.)**

—— Second edition, revised and enlarged. pp. 54. *Church Defence Institution: London*, 1893. 8°. **3939**. de. **20**. (6.)

—— The Secrets of the Heart. A report on the confessional. Compiled by M. R. Butler. pp. 39. *Elliott Stock: London*, 1877. 8°. **4108**. de. 2. (5.)

—— The Snare of the Fowler: a tract on confession. pp. 18. *William Macintosh: London*, 1874. 8°. **4108**. de. 2. (2.)

BUTLER (N. E. K.) Moon Fairies, and other poems. pp. 32. *A. H. Stockwell: London*, [1926.] 8°. **011645**. h. **97**.

BUTLER (Nancy) 't Engelsche weesmeisje, of de historie van Nenci Butler, door haar zelfs geschreven . . . Uit het Fransch vertaelt. pp. 238. *Rotterdam*, 1761. 8°. **12515**. ee. **39**.

BUTLER (Nathaniel) *Captain.* The Historye of the Bermudaes or Summer Islands. [Attributed in the introduction to John Smith, Governor of Virginia, but in fact written by N. Butler.] Edited, from a MS. in the Sloane Collection . . . by General Sir J. Henry Lefroy. pp. xii. 327. 1882. 8°. [*Works issued by the Hakluyt Society.* no. 65.] *See* Smith (John) *Governor of Virginia.* Ac. **6172/57**.

—— Six Dialogues about Sea-Services. Between an High-Admiral and a Captain at Sea, *etc.* pp. 404. *For Moses Pitt: London*, 1685. 8°. **534**. b. **20**.

—— [Another edition.] Boteler's Dialogues. Edited by W. G. Perrin. pp. xxxix. 341. [*London*,] 1929. 8°. [*Publications of the Navy Records Society.* vol. 65.] Ac. **8109**.

BUTLER (Nathaniel) *of Alton.* *See* Duncan (John) *LL.D., Minister of the Scotch Church, Soho.* The London Apprentice: a narrative of the life and death of Nathaniel Butler, who was executed . . . Sept. 1657 for the murder of John Knight, his fellow apprentice, *etc.* 1802. 12°. **10600**. de. 4. (6.)

—— *See* Yearwood (Randolph) The Penitent Murderer. Being an exact narrative of the life and death of Nathaniel Butler, *etc.* 1657. 8°. **1244**. a. 6.

—— —— 1657. 8°. **615**. a. **23**.

—— —— 1659. 8°. **1132**. a. 13.

BUTLER (Nathaniel) *of Alton.*

—— Blood washed away by Tears of Repentance: being an exact relation of the cause and manner of that horrid murther committed on the person of John Knight, an apprentice . . . by Nathaniel Butler: with his unfained repentance for the same. Together with his apprehension, examination, and conviction . . . Likewise an exact relation of his life . . . Written with owne hand. pp. 25. *W. G. for I. Pridmore & H. Marsh: London*, 1657. 4°. E. **925**. (2.)

—— A Full and the Truest Narrative of the most horrid, barbarous and unparalled [*sic*] Murder, committed on the person of John Knight, apprentice . . . by the desperate and bloody hand of Nathaniel Butler . . . Also, an account of the tryall, condemnation and sentence . . . And his last speech upon the ladder . . . With observations and reflections upon the whole, *etc.* pp. 15. *T. Mobb for J. Saywell: London*, 1657. 4°. E. **925**. (1.)

—— Heavens Cry against murder. Or, a true relation of the bloudy & unparallel'd murder of John Knight, apprentice to Mr. Arthur Worth . . . on Thursday morning, Aug. 6, 1657 by one Nath: Butler, an apprentice to Mr. Munday in Carter-lane, *etc.* pp. 24. *For Henry Brome: London*, 1657. 4°. E. **923**. (1.)

—— A Serious Advice to the Citizens of London, by some Ministers of the Gospel in the said city: upon occasion of the horrid murder and dreadful death of Nathaniel Butler, an high malefactor. [*London*, 1657.] 8°. **1244**. a. 5. *Imperfect; wanting all after sig.* **3.

BUTLER (Nathaniel) *of Chicago.* *See* Swift (Harold H.) and Butler (N.) The World's Columbian Exposition and the University of Chicago, *etc.* [1923.] 8°. **8366**. dd. **41**.

BUTLER (Nicholas Murray) *See* also Cosmos, *pseud.* [i.e. N. M. Butler.]

—— *See* Canfield (*Hon.* Gordon) Paterson Salutes Dr. Nicholas Murray Butler, *etc.* 1946. 8°. **012301**. h. **63**.

—— *See* Kant (I.) Perpetual Peace . . . With an introduction by N. M. Butler. 1939. 8°. **8425**. v. **75**.

—— *See* Paulsen (F.) The German Universities . . . With an introduction by N. M. Butler. 1895. 8°. **8357**. bb. **37**.

—— *See* Periodical Publications.—*New York.* Educational Review. Edited by N. M. Butler, *etc.* [1891, *etc.*] 8°. P.P. **1225**. ga.

—— *See* Spingarn (Joel E.) A Question of Academic Freedom: being the official correspondence between N. M. Butler . . . and J. E. Spingarn . . . 1910-1911, *etc.* 1911. 8°. **8306**. de. **37**. (4.)

—— *See* Thomas (Milton H.) Bibliography of Nicholas Murray Butler, 1872–1932, *etc.* [With a portrait.] 1934. 8°. **11911**. aa. **46**.

—— *See* Washington, *D.C.—Carnegie Endowment for International Peace.—Division of Intercourse and Education.* The Family of Nations. By N. M. Butler [and others], *etc.* 1939. 8°. Ac. **2297**. gd/4.

—— The Meaning of Education, and other essays and addresses. pp. xi. 230. *Macmillan Co.: New York*, 1898. 8°. **8311**. bb. **24**.

—— The International Mind. An argument for the judicial settlement of international disputes. [Five addresses delivered at Lake Mohonk Conferences on International Arbitration.] pp. x. 121. *C. Scribner's Sons: New York*, 1912. 8°. **06955. e. 14.**

—— The International Mind. An argument for the judicial settlement of international disputes. pp. x. 121. *Charles Scribner's Sons: New York*, 1919. 8°. **08004. ee. 75.**

A reissue of the edition of 1912.

—— Is America Worth Saving? Addresses on national problems and party policies. pp. xiii. 398. *C. Scribner's Sons: New York*, 1920. 8°. **08175. cc. 60.**

—— [Another copy, with a different titlepage.] *T. Fisher Unwin: London*, 1920. 8°. **08175. cc. 63.**

—— The Faith of a Liberal. Essays and addresses on political principles and public policies. pp. xiii. 369. *C. Scribner's Sons: New York, London*, 1924. 8°. **08007. ee. 26.**

—— The Path to Peace. Essays and addresses, *etc.* pp. xiii. 320. *C. Scribner's Sons: New York, London*, 1930. 8°. **08425. e. 40.**

—— [Another copy.] **08425. e. 41.**

—— Looking Forward. What will the American people do about it? Essays and addresses on matters national and international. pp. xiv. 418. *C. Scribner's Sons: New York, London*, 1932. 8°. **08176. aa. 35.**

—— Two Worlds.—The Age in which we live. Addresses. [Offprints from the "Columbia University Quarterly."] *New York*, 1933. 8°. **12302. d. 10. (6.)**

—— Between Two Worlds. Interpretations of the age in which we live. Essays and addresses. pp. xv. 450. *C. Scribner's Sons: New York, London*, 1934. 8°. **08176. a. 46.**

—— [Another copy.] **20020. f. 44.**

—— The Family of Nations, its Need and its Problems. Essays and addresses. pp. xiii. 400. *C. Scribner's Sons: New York, London*, 1938. 8°. **08008. d. 31.**

—— Why War? Essays and addresses on war and peace. pp. xii. 323. *C. Scribner's Sons: New York, London*, 1940. 8°. **8426.a.26.**

—— [Another copy.] **2350. b. 23.**

—— Liberty—Equality—Fraternity. Essays and addresses on the problems of today and tomorrow. pp. xiii. 240. *C. Scribner's Sons: New York*, 1942. 8°. **8287. i. 19.**

—— The World Today. Essays and addresses. pp. xi. 225. *Charles Scribner's Sons: New York*, 1946. 8°. **12302. aa. 30.**

—— Points de vue. [Translations of eight addresses by N. M. Butler.] pp. xi. 213. *Paris*, [1932.] 8°. [*Dotation Carnegie pour la Paix Internationale. Division des relations internationales et de l'éducation. Bulletin.* 1931. no. 7–9.] **Ac. 2297. i. (40.)**

—— El Significado de la Educación. (Traducido de la segunda edición inglesa [by Jesus Semprum].) [With a portrait.] pp. x. 333. *Nueva York*, 1933. 8°. [*Biblioteca Interamericana.* tom. 5.] **20020. aa. 2/5.**

—— [An address broadcast on Armistice Day 1934.] *See* Family. The Family of Nations, *etc.* 1934. 8°. **W.P.12997.**

—— [An address broadcast on Armistice Day 1936.] *See* Family. The Family of Nations, *etc.* 1936. 8°. **W.P.12997.**

—— The Abdication of Democracy . . . An address, *etc.* pp. 4. [1938.] 8°. **12302. d. 10. (16.)**

—— Across the Busy Years. Recollections and reflections. [With plates, including portraits.] *C. Scribner's Sons: New York; London*, 1939– . 8°. **10888.i.1.**

—— Address at the Dinner commemorating the Dedication of the Statue of Liberty, *etc.* pp. 7. [1936.] 8°. **12302. d. 10. (12.)**

—— The Age of the Americas. An address delivered at the Parrish Memorial Art Museum . . . September 6, 1942. pp. 13. *Carnegie Endowment for International Peace: New York*, [1942.] 8°. **12301.p.91.**

—— America and Europe. An address, *etc.* pp. 7. [1933.] 8°. **12302. d. 9. (13.)**

—— The American as he is. pp. x. 104. *Macmillan Co.: New York*, 1908. 8°. **12352. w. 28.**

—— L'Américain tel qu'il est. pp. 116. *Paris*, 1938. 8°. **12357. k. 44.**

—— The American Plan to prevent War . . . An address delivered . . . June 2, 1942. pp. 6. [*New York*, 1942.] 8°. **08425. h. 49.**

—— Andrew Carnegie 1835–1935. (Reprinted from the New York Herald Tribune.) pp. 19. [*New York*, 1935.] 8°. **010822. f. 45.**

—— The Background of the Labor Problem. An address, *etc.* pp. 8. [1937.] 8°. **12302. d. 10. (15.)**

—— Building the American Nation. An essay of interpretation. pp. xviii. 375. *Cambridge; New York*, 1923. 8°. [*Watson Chair Lectures.*] **Ac. 2274.**

—— [Building the American Nation.] Les États-Unis d'Amérique. Leur origine. Leur développement. Leur unité. pp. vi. 335. *Paris*, 1925. 8°. [*Conciliation Internationale. Bulletin.* 1925. no. 2.] **Ac. 2297. i. (25.)**

—— A Call to Action. An address, *etc.* pp. 7. *Carnegie Endowment for International Peace: New York*, [1933.] 8°. **08230. ee. 19. (2.)**

—— Colossal Debts and Heavy Taxes. An address, *etc.* pp. 11. *Carnegie Endowment for International Peace: New York*, [1932?] 8°. **08230. ee. 19. (4.)**

—— Columbia University Honorary Degrees awarded in the Years 1902–1932. Appreciations by N. M. Butler. pp. 193. 1933. 8°. *See* New York.—*Columbia University.* **Ac. 2688/44.**

—— Columbia University Honorary Degrees, awarded in the years 1902–1945. Appreciations by N. M. Butler. pp. 301. 1946. 8°. *See* New York.—*Columbia University.* **Ac. 2688/52.**

—— De senectute . . . An address, *etc.* pp. 3. [1937.] 8°. **12302. d. 10. (14.)**

—— The Decline and Fall of Morals . . . An address, *etc.* pp. 6. [1936.] 8°. **12302. d. 10. (11.)**

—— Democracy in Danger. An address, *etc.* pp. 18. [1938.] 8°. **12302. d. 10. (17.)**

—— The Depression. A letter written in response to the request to appear before the Committee on Finance of the United States. pp. 11. [1933.] 8°. **12302. d. 10. (5.)**

—— The Duty of the University to the Teaching Profession . . . An address, *etc.* pp. 8. [*New York*, 1890.] 8°. **8304. bb. 8. (4.)**

—— Education at the Paris Exposition. (Reprinted . . . from the Christian Union.) pp. 7. [1889.] 8°. *See* NEW YORK.—*College for the Training of Teachers.* **8304. c. 5. (1.)**

—— Education in the United States. *See* infra: Monographs on Education in the United States.

—— The Effect of the War of 1812 upon the Consolidation of the Union. pp. 30. *Baltimore*, 1887. 8°. [*Johns Hopkins University Studies in Historical and Political Science.* ser. 5. no. 7.] **Ac. 2689.**

—— [Another copy.] **9615. pp. 7.**

—— Elihu Root. Memorial address delivered at the annual meeting of the American Academy of Arts and Letters, New York, November 12, 1937. *New York*, [1937 ?] 8°. **10887. e. 1.**

—— The Everlasting Conflict . . . An address delivered at the 185th Commencement of Columbia University June 6, 1939. pp. 4. [*New York*, 1939.] 8°. **12301. p. 86.**

—— Faith and the War . . . Address, *etc.* [1918.] 8°. **12302. d. 9. (1.)**

—— Fifteen Years after. An address, *etc.* pp. 7. [1933.] 8°. **12302. d. 9. (14.)**

—— The Function of the Secondary School . . . Reprinted from the Academy. pp. 18. [*Boston*, 1890.] 8°. **8304. e. 23. (7.)**

—— The High Cost of Government. An address, *etc.* pp. 7. *Carnegie Endowment for International Peace: New York*, [1933.] 8°. **08230. ee. 19. (3.)**

—— How long must the War go on? An address, *etc.* pp. 9. [1932.] 8°. **12302.d.9.(9.)**

—— Imponderables . . . An address, *etc.* pp. 17. [1930.] 8°. **12302. d. 10. (1.)**

—— The International Mind. (Address. Reprint from Columbia University Quarterly.) pp. 13. [1932.] 8°. **12302. d. 9. (9.)**

—— [The International Mind.] Der internationale Geist. (Eröffnungsansprache von N. M. Butler als Vorsitzendem der Lake Mohonk Konferenz für internationale Schiedsgerichtsbarkeit gehalten am 15. Mai 1912.) pp. 13. *Berlin*, 1913. 8°. [*Veröffentlichungen des Verbandes für internationale Verständigung.* Hft. 1.] **08026. bb. 6. (1.)**

—— The International Problem. Statement written on the invitation of the Editor of The Houston—Texas—Chronicle, *etc.* pp. 4. [1935.] 8°. **12302. d. 10. (10.)**

—— Is Thomas Jefferson the Forgotten Man? An address, *etc.* pp. 16. [*New York*,] 1935. 8°. **08008. b. 40.**

—— Liberty, Equality, Fraternity. An address delivered at the Parrish Memorial Art Museum . . . August 31, 1941. pp. 15. *Carnegie Endowment for International Peace: New York*, [1941.] 8°. **012301. m. 12.**

—— Manifold Personality. [Strictures on remarks of F. W. H. Myers at a meeting of the Society for Psychical Research.] pp. 3. [*New York*, 1889 ?] 8°. **8632. g. 25. (3.)**

—— Manual Training: an address delivered before the American Institute of Instruction, *etc.* pp. 20. [1888.] 8°. **8304. aa. 17. (7.)**

—— The Manual Training Movement . . . Reprinted from Methodist Review, *etc.* [*New York*, 1889.] 8°. **8304. bb. 7. (2.)**

—— Monographs on Education in the United States. Edited by N. M. Butler. 2 vol. pp. xviii. 977. 1900. 8°. *See* UNITED STATES OF AMERICA.—*Commission to the Paris Universal Exhibition*, 1900. [*Department of Education.*] **8385. f. 13.**

—— [Another edition.] Education in the United States. A series of monographs. Edited by N. M. Butler. pp. xxiv. 1068. *American Book Co.: New York*, 1910. 8°. **8385. f. 14.**

—— A Much Needed Prayer . . . An address, *etc.* pp. 5. [1935.] 8°. **12302. d. 10. (7.)**

—— Nation-building and Beyond, *etc.* pp. 23. *Cobden-Sanderson: London*, 1930. 8°. [*Richard Cobden Lecture.* no. 2.] **W.P. 9785/2.**

—— [Another edition.] pp. 19. *Carnegie Endowment for International Peace: New York*, [1930.] 8°. **12301. p. 17.**

—— New Year's Message, January 1, 1941 [*etc.*]. *Carnegie Endowment for International Peace: New York*, [1941– .] 8°. **8011. c. 2.**

—— New York, Commerce and the War . . . Address, *etc.* [1918.] 8°. **12302. d. 9. (2.)**

—— Our Ship of State. An address, *etc.* pp. 25. [1933.] 8°. **12302. d. 9. (12.)**

—— Our Times. Abstract of an address delivered before the Economic Club of Chicago . . . on April 15, 1932. pp. 14. *Carnegie Endowment for International Peace: New York*, [1932.] 8°. **08230. ee. 19. (1.)**

—— Our United States in this Backward-Moving World. An address, *etc.* pp. 16. *Carnegie Endowment for International Peace: New York*, [1940.] 8°. **012301. f. 70.**

—— Philosophy. (A lecture delivered at Columbia University, March 4, 1908. Third printing.) pp. vi. 51. *Columbia University Press: New York*, 1938. 8°. **8471. a. 19.**

—— The Place of Comenius in the History of Education. pp. 20. *C. W. Bardeen: Syracuse, N.Y.*, 1892. 8°. **8304. aa. 26. (1.)**

—— A Planless World. An address, *etc.* pp. 10. [1931.] 8°. **12302. d. 9. (4.)**

BUTLER (Nicholas Murray)

—— The Preparedness of America. pp. 18. *Carnegie Endowment for International Peace: New York*, [1914.] 8°. **08175.** c. **15.**

—— President Roosevelt's Appeal for Peace. A letter printed in The New York Times, 20 May, 1933. [By N. M. Butler.] pp. 11. [1933.] 8°. *See* Roosevelt (Franklin D.) *President of the United States of America.* **12302.** d. **9.** (**10.**)

—— Public Confidence must be restored. An address, *etc.* pp. 10. [1935.] 8°. **12302.** d. **10.** (**8.**)

—— The Republican Form of Government. An address, *etc.* pp. 16. [1931.] 8°. **12302.** d. **9.** (**6.**)

—— Scholarship and Service. The policies and ideals of a national university in a modern democracy. pp. xii. 399. *C. Scribner's Sons: New York*, 1921. 8°. **08385.** df. **4.**

—— The Search for Security. Abstract of an address, *etc.* pp. 7. [1931.] 8°. **12302.** d. **9.** (**5.**)

—— Self-Disciplined Liberty or Compulsion. An address, *etc.* pp. 11. [1933.] 8°. **12302.** d. **9.** (**11.**)

—— Some Problems for our Government. An address, *etc.* pp. 22. [1936.] 8°. **12302.** d. **10.** (**13.**)

—— Some Problems of World Federation. Address, *etc.* pp. 24. 1937. 8°. *See* Geneva.—*International Club.* **08008.** aa. **70.**

—— Teachers' Professional Library. Edited by N. M. Butler. 10 pt. *Macmillan Co.: New York*, 1900–29. 8°. **8308.** i. **1.**

—— This Changing World. (An address.) pp. 11. [1931.] 8°. **12302.** d. **9.** (**7.**)

—— Toward a Federal World. An address delivered at the Parrish Art Museum, Southampton, Long Island, September 3, 1939. pp. 17. *Carnegie Endowment for International Peace: New York*, [1939.] 8°. **08004.** g. **19.**

—— True and False Democracy. pp. xiii. 111. *Macmillan Co.: New York & London*, 1907. 8°. **8007.** de. **26.**

—— [A reissue.] True and False Democracy. *C. Scribner's Sons: New York*, 1940. 8°. **8011.** a. **45.**

—— Undermining Foundations . . . An address, *etc.* pp. 5. [1934.] 8°. **12302.** d. **10.** (**4.**)

—— Unemployment. An address, *etc.* pp. 18. [1931.] 8°. **12302.** d. **9.** (**8.**)

—— The United States must lead. An address, *etc.* pp. 10. [1938.] 8°. **12302.** d. **10** (**18.**)

—— The University and the International Mind. Abstract of an address, *etc.* pp. 4. [1931.] 8°. **12302.** d. **10.** (**3.**)

—— The University in Action. From the annual reports, 1902–1935, of N. M. Butler, President of Columbia University. Edited, with an introduction, by Edward C. Elliott. [With a portrait.] pp. xv. 515. *See* New York.—*Columbia University.* The Rise of a University. vol. 2. 1937. 8°. **08385.** ee. **14.**

—— What Does Freedom Mean? An address, *etc.* pp. 11. *Carnegie Endowment for International Peace: New York*, [1943.] 8°. **012301.** h. **57.**

—— Why should we Change our Form of Government? Studies in practical politics. pp. xiv. 159. *C. Scribner's Sons: New York*, 1912. 8°. **08175.** aa. **31.**

—— A World in Ferment. Interpretations of the war for a new world. pp. viii. 254. *C. Scribner's Sons: New York*, 1918. 8°. **08007.** df. **52.**

—— World Peace today. (Reprinted from The Argonaut.) [1935.] 8°. **12302.** d. **10.** (**9.**)

—— The World's Debt to England, *etc.* [An address.] [1918.] 8°. **12302.** d. **9.** (**3.**)
Printed on one side of the leaf only.

—— The Year 1934. A statement, *etc.* pp. 4. [1934.] 8°. **12302.** d. **9.** (**15.**)

—— A Dinner tendered to Nicholas Murray Butler by the Faculties of the University, to mark the twenty-fifth anniversary of his inauguration as President of Columbia University. April the Nineteenth, MCMXXVII, *etc.* [A souvenir.] pp. 51. *Columbia University Press: New York*, [1927.] 8°. **10884.** g. **26.**

—— Dinner to Nicholas Murray Butler in celebration of the 30th anniversary of his presidency [of Columbia University], 50th anniversary of his graduation, 70th anniversary of his birth . . . February eleventh MCMXXXII. [With a portrait.] pp. 72. *Columbia University Press: [New York*, 1932.] 8°. **010885.** eee. **44.**

—— Nicholas Murray Butler: his quarter centenary. A tribute. Dinner by the Trustees, March third. [With a portrait.] pp. 24. *Columbia University Press: New York*, 1927. 8°. **10884.** g. **27.**

—— Le Voyage du P^t N. Murray Butler en Europe. Introduction de M. D'Estournelles de Constant. [With plates.] pp. 159. *La Flèche*, 1921. 8°. [*Conciliation Internationale. Bulletin trimestriel.* 1921. no. 3.] Ac. **2297.** i. (**5.**)

BUTLER (Nina)

—— Billy in Search of a Tail . . . Illustrated by Roberta Asseln. *G. G. Harrap & Co.: London*, 1939. 8°. **12823.** bb. **9.**

BUTLER (Noble) *See* Sallustius Crispus (C.) [*Works.—Latin.*] Sallust's Jugurtha and Catiline: with . . . notes and a vocabulary. By N. Butler and M. Sturgus. 1855. 8°. **1308.** c. **10.**

—— A Practical and Critical Grammar of the English Language. pp. 312. *J. P. Morton & Co.: Louisville*, [1874.] 12°. **12983.** bb. **2.**

BUTLER (Nora) Geraldine. A tale from real life. pp. 192. *Oliphant, Anderson & Ferrier: Edinburgh & London*, 1890. 8°. **4414.** i. **5.**

BUTLER (Orma Fitch) Studies in the Life of Heliogabalus. *See* Sanders (Henry A.) Roman History and Mythology, *etc.* 1910. 8°. [*University of Michigan Studies.* Humanistic series. vol. 4.] Ac. **2685/10.**

BUTLER (Pardee) Personal Recollections of Pardee Butler. With reminiscences by his daughter, Mrs. Rosetta B. Hastings, and additional chapters by Eld. John Boggs and Eld. J. B. McCleery. [With a portrait.] pp. 346. *Standard Publishing Co.: Cincinnati*, 1889. 8°. **4986.** ee. **33.**

BUTLER (Patrick Richard) A Galloper at Ypres, and some subsequent adventures . . . With a frontispiece in colours by Lady Butler. pp. 276. *T. Fisher Unwin: London*, 1920. 8°. **9082**. bbb. **40**.

BUTLER (Patrick Theobald Tower) *Baron Dunboyne*.

—— *See* Haigh (John G.) The Trial of John George Haigh . . . Edited by Lord Dunboyne. 1953. 8°. **6496**. d. **1/71**.

BUTLER (Paul) *See* Throckmorton (*Sir* Nicholas) The Legend of Sir Nicholas Throckmorton. Edited . . . by the late J. G. Nichols. [The edition completed by P. Butler.] 1874. 4°. C. **101**. f. **20**.

BUTLER (Philip)

—— Houses of Parliament. Text by Philip Butler. Photographs by Derrick L. Sayer, *etc.* pp. 46. *Lincolns-Prager: London*, [1948.] fol. [*My London Gallery*.] W.P. **14204/1**.

BUTLER (Phoebe Anne Oakley) *See* Oakley (Annie)

BUTLER (Pierce) *Associate Justice of the United States Supreme Court*.

—— *See* Brown (Francis J.) The Social and Economic Philosophy of P. Butler, *etc.* 1945. 8°. [*Catholic University of America Studies in Sociology*. vol. 13.] Ac. **2692**. y/**17**.

BUTLER (Pierce) *of Philadelphia*. *See* Schott (James) A Statement by James Schott Jr. [On his duel with P. Butler and including the correspondence of the parties.] [1844.] 8°. **10880**. d. **42**.

BUTLER (Pierce) *of the Newberry Library*.

—— *See* Chicago.—*University of Chicago.—Graduate Library School*. Librarians, Scholars and Booksellers at Mid-Century . . . Edited by P. Butler. 1953. 8°. Ac. **2691**. dia/2. (**37**.)

—— *See* Jenson (N.) The Last Will and Testament of the late Nicolas Jenson. (Turned into the English tongue by P. Butler.) 1928. fol. **11907**. v. **8**.

—— Books and Libraries in Wartime. (Edited by P. Butler.) pp. 159. *University of Chicago Press: Chicago*, 1945. 8°. [*Charles R. Walgreen Foundation Lectures*.] Ac. **2691**. dw. (**15**.)

—— Check List of Incunabula in the Newberry Library. pp. ix. 62. 1919. 8°. *See* Chicago.—*Newberry Library*. Ac. **9724/3**.

—— [Another edition.] Check List of Books printed during the Fifteenth Century. pp. xiv. 192. 1924. 8°. *See* Chicago.—*Newberry Library*. **11902**. t. **9**.

—— A Check List of Fifteenth Century Books in the Newberry Library, and in other libraries of Chicago. pp. xxiv. 362. 1933. 8°. *See* Chicago.—*Newberry Library*. Ac. **9724/4**.

—— An Introduction to Library Science. pp. xvi. 118. *Chicago*, 1933. 8°. [*University of Chicago Studies in Library Science*.] Ac. **2691**. dia/2. (**1**.)

—— The Origin of Printing in Europe. [With plates.] pp. xv. 154. *Chicago*, [1940.] 8°. [*University of Chicago Studies in Library Science*.] Ac. **2691**. dia/2. (**22**.)

BUTLER (Pierce) *of the Newberry Library*.

—— The Reference Function of the Library. Papers presented before the Library Institute at the University of Chicago, June 29 to July 10, 1942. Edited by P. Butler, *etc.* pp. x. 366. 1943. 8°. *See* Chicago.—*University of Chicago.—Graduate Library School.—Library Institute*. Ac. **2691**. dia/**2**. (**29**.)

BUTLER (Pierce) *of Tulane University*. *See* Ficklen (John R.) History of Reconstruction in Louisiana, through 1868. [Edited by P. Butler.] 1910. 8°. [*Johns Hopkins University Studies in Historical and Political Science*. ser. 28. no. 1.] Ac. **2689**.

—— Judah P. Benjamin. pp. 459. *G. W. Jacobs & Co.: Philadelphia*, 1907. 8°. [*American Crisis Biographies*.] **010883**. ee. **44/5**.

—— Legenda Aurea [of Jacobus de Voragine]—Légende dorée—Golden Legend . . . A study of Caxton's Golden Legend with special reference to its relations to the earlier English prose translation, *etc.* pp. vi. 154. *J. Murphy Co.: Baltimore*, 1899. 8°. **011852**. i. **19**.

—— Materials for the Life of Shakespeare. Compiled by P. Butler. pp. x. 200. *University of North Carolina Press: Chapel Hill*, 1930. 8°. **011761**. e. **42**.

—— The Unhurried Years. Memories of the Old Natchez Region. [With plates.] pp. xv. 198. *Louisiana State University Press: [Baton Rouge*, 1948.] 8°. **10890**. fff. **12**

BUTLER (Pierce) *Rector of Ulcombe, Kent*. *See* Öhlenschläger (A. G.) Axel and Valborg: . . . Translated . . . by P. Butler, *etc.* 1874. 8°. **11781**. aaaa. **34**.

BUTLER (Pierce) *Son of Pierce Butler of the Newberry Library*. *See* Bibescu (M. L.) *Princess*. Worlds Apart . . . Translated by P. Butler, Jr. 1935. 8°. **12514**. tt. **7**.

—— *See* Brandes (G. M. C.) [*Works*.] [François de Voltaire.]. Voltaire. (Translation by O. Kruger and P. Butler.) 1930. 8°. **10655**. dd. **20**.

BUTLER (Pierce Mason) Extracts from Reports made by P. M. Butler, United States Agent for the Cherokee Indians. pp. 38. [*Fort Gibson?* 1845.] 12°. **8175**. c. **21**.

BUTLER (*Hon.* Pierce Somerset)

—— Butler against Mountgarrett. Comment upon the judgment of the House of Lords, as reported. pp. 17. *John Chambers: Dublin*, [1859.] 8°. **6504**. b. **6**.

BUTLER (Piers Edmund) An Apology for Religious Freedom. pp. 22. *T. Ward & Co.: London*, 1838. 8°. T. **2347**. (**13**.)

—— Hymns, and other poems. pp. x. 133. *M. Keene & Son: Dublin*, 1828. 12°. **11603**. b. **35**.

—— A Letter to the Congregation who assemble for worship in the Unitarian Chapel, Ipswich, occasioned by an advertisement in the Suffolk Chronicle, addressed to the writer; and containing some account of his discussion with the Rev. Joseph Ketley, which ended in Mr. Ketley's renunciation of Unitarianism. pp. 22. *R. Deck: Ipswich*, 1836. 8°. **4225**. bb. **7**.

BUTLER (Piers Edmund)

—— The Essential Passages of a Letter, addressed by the Rev. P. E. Butler . . . to the Unitarians of Ipswich . . . on the occasion of the Rev. Joseph Ketley's renunciation of Unitarianism. *See* Layman. Unitarianism tried by Scripture, *etc.* 1840. 8°. **1120. a. 40.**

—— [Another edition.] pp. 24. *J. B. Dow: Boston,* 1842. 12°. **4225. aa. 13.**

—— *See* Eyre (Charles) *B.A., of Trinity College, Cambridge.* Remarks on perusing the Rev. P. E. Butler's Letter, addressed to the Unitarians of Ipswich, *etc.* 1836. 8°. **4225. e. 12.**

—— The Rationality of Revealed Religion, illustrated in a series of sermons; to which are added an essay on the merits of modern fiction, and a lecture on the diffusion of knowledge. pp. xvi. 367. *R. Deck: Ipswich,* 1835. 12°. **1021. i. 4.**

—— Songs of the Sanctuary; and other poems. pp. viii. 248. *Printed for the Author: London,* 1837. 16°. **1066. a. 4.**

—— Two Discourses on the Doctrine of Baptismal Regeneration. pp. 28. *R. Deck: Ipswich,* 1836. 8°. **T. 2053. (3.)**

BÜTLER (Placid) *See* Buetler.

BUTLER (Rachel Barton) Mamma's Affair. A comedy in three acts. pp. 103. *New York, London,* [1925.] 8°. [*French's Standard Library Edition.*] **011781. g. 1/70.**

—— Prudence in Particular. A comedy in three acts. pp. 94. *New York, London,* [1928.] 8°. [*French's Standard Library Edition.*] **011781. g. 1/191.**

BUTLER (*Lady* Rachel Evelyn) *See* Russell, afterwards Butler.

BUTLER (Ralph) *See* Frederick William, *Crown Prince of Germany.* I Seek the Truth . . . Translated . . . by R. Butler. 1926. 8°. **09084. cc. 44.**

—— *See* Schacht (H. G. H.) The Stabilization of the Mark. [Translated by R. Butler.] 1927. 8°. **08229. k. 36.**

—— The New Eastern Europe. pp. vii. 176. *Longmans & Co.: London,* 1919. 8°. **08026. bb. 28.**

BUTLER (Ralph Starr) Marketing and Merchandising. [Based on "Marketing Methods."] pp. xxii. 363. *Alexander Hamilton Institute: New York,* [1923.] 8°. [*Modern Business.* vol. 5.] **08246. e. 4/5.**

—— Marketing Methods. pp. xxi. 346. *Alexander Hamilton Institute: New York,* [1917.] 8°. [*Modern Business.* vol. 5.] **08223. g. 26/5.**

—— Selling and Buying. *See* Selling. Selling, Credit and Traffic. pt. 1. [1914.] 8°. **08223. g. 15/3.**

BUTLER (Ralph Starr) and **BURD** (Henry Alfred)

—— Commercial Correspondence, *etc.* pp. vii. 531. *D. Appleton & Co.: New York, London,* 1919. 8°. **08228. aa. 10.**

BUTLER (Raymond Renard)

—— Building Science for Junior Technical Schools of Building. pp. 204. *English Universities Press: London,* 1946. 8°. [*Junior Technical Series.*] W.P. **6211/3.**

BUTLER (Raymond Renard)

—— Eye Protection in Welding Operations. pp. 39. *London,* [1922.] 16°. [*British Acetylene & Welding Association. Pamphlet.* no. 6.] W.P. **6229/6.**

—— Paper read at the Summer Meeting . . . 1934 on "Apprenticeship and the Irish Apprenticeship Act." pp. 19. *Loughborough,* [1934.] 8°. [*Association of Technical Institutions. Miscellaneous pamphlets.*] **W.P.4362/9.(7.)**

—— Scientific Discovery. pp. 252. pl. 71. *English Universities Press: London,* 1947. 8°. [*County College Series.* vol. 1.] W.P. **6621/1.**

BUTLER (Rayne) A Fatal Impulse. pp. 64. *George Newnes: London,* [1900.] 8°. **012330. k. 18. (8.)**

—— In the Power of Two. The Spider and the Fly. pp. 241. *Simpkin, Marshall & Co.: London,* 1896. 8°. **012626. e. 11.**

BUTLER (Reg) *Journalist.*

—— At large in the Sun. [An account of a vagabonding journey through North Africa, Cyprus, Turkey, Greece, Crete and Yugoslavia.] pp. 207. *Herbert Jenkins: London,* 1953. 8°. **010028. p. 17.**

BUTLER (Reginald Arthur)

—— Income Tax for Everyman. pp. 64. *Pen-in-Hand: Oxford,* 1947. 8°. [*Everyman's Guide Series.* no. 1.] W.P. **3636/1.**

—— Income Tax for Everyman. (2nd edition.) pp. 72. *Pen-in-Hand: Oxford,* 1948. 8°. [*Everyman's Guide Series.* no. 1.] W.P. **3636/1a.**

—— Income Tax for Everyman. (3rd edition.) pp. 71. *Pen-in-Hand: Oxford,* 1949. 8°. **6429. ee. 1.**

—— Income Tax for Everyman. (4th edition.) pp. 72. *Pen-in-Hand: Oxford,* 1950. 8°. [*Everyman's Guide Series.* no. 5.] W.P. **3636/5a.**

—— Income Tax for Everyman . . . 5th edition. pp. 71. *Tower Bridge Publications: Hadleigh,* 1951. 8°. [*Everyman's Guide Series.*] W.P. **3636/5. b.**

BUTLER (Richard) *A.M.* The British Michael, an epistolary poem, to a friend in the country. pp. 39. *William Lewis: London,* 1710. fol. **11630. h. 55.**

BUTLER (Richard) *Dean of Clonmacnoise. See* All Saints, *Priory of, at Dublin.* Registrum Prioratus Omnium Sanctorum juxta Dublin. Edited . . . by the Rev. R. Butler. 1845. 4°. Ac. **5783/7.**

—— *See* Butler (Harriet) *Wife of the Dean of Clonmacnoise.* A Memoir of the Very Rev. Richard Butler, Dean of Clonmacnois, *etc.* [With a portrait.] 1863. 4°. **4956. h. 4.**

—— *See* Clyn (Joannes) The Annals of Ireland . . . Edited . . . with introductory remarks by the Very Rev. R. Butler. 1849. 4°. Ac. **5783/11.**

—— *See* Dymmok (John) A Treatise of Ireland . . . Now first published . . . with notes, by the Rev. R. Butler. 1843. 4°. [*Tracts relating to Ireland.* vol. 2.] Ac. **5783/2.**

—— *See* Grace (James) Jacobi Grace, Kilkenniensis, Annales Hiberniæ. Edited, with a translation and notes, by the Rev. R. Butler. 1842. 4°. Ac. **5783/4.**

BUTLER (Richard) *Dean of Clonmacnoise.*

—— Five Sermons on the Holy Communion, preached in the Parish Church of Trim. pp. 67. *T. Hatchard: London,* 1858. 8°. **4327. b. 13.**

—— Sermons on the Morning Service, preached in the Parish Church of Trim. pp. 168. *T. Hatchard: London,* 1858. 8°. **4463. b. 7.**

—— Six Sermons on Home Duties, preached in the Parish Church of Trim. pp. 73. *T. Hatchard: London,* 1858. 8°. **4463. b. 8.**

—— Some Notices of the Castle and of the Abbies and other religious houses at Trim. Collected from various authorities. [With a plate.] pp. 64. MS. NOTES. *Henry Griffith: Trim,* 1835. 12°. **10390. b. 4.**

—— Second edition enlarged. pp. 143. *H. Griffith: Trim,* 1840. 12°. **10390. bb. 19.**

—— Third edition. pp. 312. *W. H. Griffith: Trim,* 1854. 8°. **010390. f. 25.**

—— Some Notices of the Church of St. Patrick, Trim. Collected from various authorities [by R. Butler]. pp. 38. 1837. 12°. *See* Trim.—*Church of St. Patrick.* **4735. a. 60.**

BUTLER (Richard) *Dramatist.* *See* Richard-Henry, *pseud.* [i.e. R. Butler and H. C. Newton.]

BUTLER (Richard) *Earl of Arran.* [For public documents issued by the Earl of Arran as Lord Deputy of Ireland:] *See* Ireland.—Butler (R.) *Earl of Arran, Lord Deputy.*

—— An Elegy on the Death of the Right Honourabe [*sic*] Richard, Earl of Arran. *Dublin,* 1685 [1686]. fol. **807. g. 5. (32.)**

—— An Elegy upon the Right Ho[nou]rable Richard Earle of Arran, with remarks on his most noble family. *Printed by Andrew Crook & Samuel Helsham, to be sold by Samuel Helsham: Dublin,* [1686.] *s. sh. fol.* **807.g.5.(33.)**
A different work from the preceding. Slightly mutilated.

BUTLER (Richard) *Earl of Glengall.* The Follies of Fashion; a comedy, in five acts. pp. vii. 147. *H. Colburn & R. Bentley: London,* 1830. 8°. **841. g. 2. (4.)**

—— [Another edition.] pp. 26. *London,* [1886.] 8°. [*Dicks' Standard Plays.* no. 729.] **11770. bbb. 4.**

—— The Irish Tutor; or, New lights: a comic piece, in one act . . . Printed from the acting copy, with remarks, biographical and critical, by D——g, *etc.* pp. 24. *London,* [1830 ?] 12°. [*Cumberland's British Theatre.* vol. 21.] **642. a. 11.**

—— [Another edition.] The Irish Tutor . . . Adapted from the French, by Lord Glengall. pp. 20. *London,* 1859. 12°. [*Lacy's Acting Edition.* vol. 36.] **2304. e. 10.**

—— [A reissue.] The Irish Tutor, *etc.* *London,* [1861.] 12°. [*Lacy's Acting Edition.* no. 538.] **11791. t. 1/1225.**

—— [Another edition.] pp. 7. *London,* [1879 ?] 8°. [*Dicks' Standard Plays.* no. 286.] **11770. bbb. 4.**

BUTLER (Richard) *M.D.* An Essay concerning Blood-Letting. Shewing the various effects and peculiar advantages of bleeding in different parts of the human body, particularly in the foot, *etc.* pp. vi. 148. *W. Mears: London,* 1734. 8°. **1172. i. 14. (3.)**

—— [Another copy.] **T. 397. (1.)**

BUTLER (Richard) *Rector of St. Silas' Church, Ashton Road.* The Ministry of the Church of England. *See* A., B. Lent Lectures for 1859, *etc.* [1859.] 8°. **4108. a. 70.**

BUTLER (Richard) *Viscount Mountgarret.* *See* Ireland.—Butler (J.) 1*st Duke of Ormonde, Lord Lieutenant.* xxix. Articles of Peace concluded . . . by the Marquesse of Ormond . . . and the Lord Viscount Mountgarret, *etc.* 1646. 4°. **E. 351. (6.)**

—— *See* Ireland. [*Appendix.*—i. *History.* (B.)] The Demands of the Rebels in Ireland . . . the Lord Mount Garret, Delvin, *etc.* 1641. 4°. **115. g. 1.**

BUTLER (*Right Hon.* Richard Austen)

—— *See* England.—*National Union of Conservative and Constitutional Associations.—Conservative Political Centre.* Tradition and Change. [By] the Rt. Hon. R. A. Butler [and others], *etc.* 1954. 8°. **8140. ff. 34.**

—— Fundamental Issues. A statement on the future work of the Conservative Education Movement. pp. 15. *Conservative Political Centre: London,* [1946.] 8° **08139.d.70.**

—— R. A. Butler talks with you about the Industrial Charter. pp. 19. *Conservative Political Centre: [London,]* 1947. *obl.* 8°. [*What Do You Think ?*] W.P. **14028/7.**

BUTLER (Robert) *Colonel.* Colonell Butler's Letter to the Club-men, June 30, 1645. *See* England. [*Miscellaneous Public Documents, etc.*—iii.—*Charles I.*] The Kings Answer to the Propositions for Peace, *etc.* 1645. 4°. **E. 296. (12.)**

BUTLER (Robert) *of St. Mary of the Angels, Bayswater.* Guide to the Archconfraternity of the Servants of the Holy Ghost. Edited by the Rev. R. Butler. pp. 34. *Burns & Oates: London,* 1887. 12°. **4401. aa. 45.**

BUTLER (Robert) *Philomath.* Butler. 1630. A New Almanacke and Prognostication for the yeere of our Lord God, 1630, *etc.* [1629.] 16°. *See* Ephemerides. P.P. **2465.**

—— The Scale of Interest, or Proportionall Tables and Breviats shewing the forbearance and discompt of any sums of money for any time, from a day to 100 yeares, at the rate of 8 per centum, per annum, *etc.* pp. 92. *Printed by John Norton; to be sold by Robert Bird: London,* 1633. 8°. **1395. c. 41.**

BUTLER (Robert) *Serjeant.* The Christian's Pocket Companion . . . With a recommendatory preface, by John Brown, D.D. . . . Third edition. pp. 175. *Johnstone & Hunter: Edinburgh,* 1855. 16°. **4407. a. 65.**

—— Narrative of the Life and Travels of Serjeant B—— [i.e. R. Butler]. Written by himself. pp. 12. 301. 1823. 12°. *See* B——, *Serjeant.* **4903. bbb. 12.**

—— Narrative of the Life and Travels of Serjeant Butler . . . Third edition, carefully corrected, and considerably enlarged. pp. xvi. 11–353. *Johnstone & Hunter: Edinburgh,* 1854. 12°. **4955. a. 38.**

BUTLER (Robert Gordon) *See* Welch (Philip H.) Said in Fun, *etc.* [Edited by R. G. Butler.] 1889. 8°. **12315. k. 8.**

BUTLER (Rodney Fawcett)

—— The History of Kirkstall Forge through Seven Centuries, 1200–1954 A.D. The story of England's oldest ironworks. (Second edition, revised and enlarged.) [With plates, including portraits.] pp. xiii. 265. *William Sessions: York*, 1954. 4°. **8285**. s. **41**.

BUTLER (Rohan d'Olier)

—— *See* Woodward (Sir Ernest L.) Documents on British Foreign Policy, 1919–1939. Edited by E. L. Woodward . . . and R. Butler. (First series. [1919–1929. Edited by R. d'O. Butler.]) 1947, *etc.* 8°. **2084.g.**

—— *See* Woodward (Sir Ernest L.) Documents on British Foreign Policy, 1919–1939. (Third series). [1938, 39. Edited by E. L. Woodward and R. Butler.] 1947, *etc.* 8°. **2084.g.**

—— The Roots of National Socialism, 1783–1933. pp. 310. *Faber & Faber: London*, 1941. 8°. **20041**. b. **12**.

BUTLER (Rosa Kate) Missions as I Saw them. An account of a visit to the important centres of the United Methodist Missionary Society in China & Africa . . . With 24 illustrations [including portraits]. pp. 284. *Seeley, Service & Co.: London*, 1924. 8°. **4763**. eee. **31**.

BUTLER (Rosa M.) Pilgrim Songs. pp. 70. *A. H. Stockwell: London*, 1902. 8°. **11651**. c. **62**.

BUTLER (Ruth Lapham) *See* Lapham, afterwards Butler (R.)

BUTLER (S.) *of Bristol.* An Essay upon Education, intended to shew that the common method is defective, in religion, morality, our own language, history, geography: and that the custom of teaching dead languages, when little or no advantage can be expected from them, is absurd. With a plan of a new method . . . By a Gentleman of Bristol (S. Butler). pp. 115. *Owen, etc.: London*, [1750 ?] 8°. **116**. b. **50**.

BUTLER (S. H.) *Writer on Cricket.*

—— A Concise History of Cricket. pp. 40. *Cricket Book Society: Hunstanton*, [1946.] 8°. **7919**. aa. **10**.

BUTLER (Sally) The History of Sally Butler. (The Passionate Boy.) [Religious tracts.] pp. 16. *American Tract Society: New York*, [1820 ?] 32°. **4422**. aa. **49**. **(3.)**

BUTLER (Samuel) *Bishop of Lichfield and Coventry. See* Aeschylus. [*Works.—Greek and Latin.*] Æschyli Tragœdiæ quæ supersunt . . . Ex editione T. Stanleii: cum versione Latina . . . Accedunt varia lectiones et notæ . . . quibus suas passim intertexuit S. Butler. 1809, *etc.* 4°. **11705**. e. **4**.

—— *See* Aeschylus. [*Appendix.*] Apparatus criticus . . . in Æschyli tragoedias. (vol. 1. Thomae Stanleii Commentarius . . . ab S. Butlero editus, *etc.*) 1832. 8°. **997**. d. **29**.

—— *See* Bather (Edward) A Sermon preached . . . on occasion of the death of the Right Reverend Samuel Butler, *etc.* 1840. 8°. **4477**. e. **106**. **(9.)**

—— *See* Bonaparte (Lucien) *Prince di Canino.* Charlemagne; or, the Church delivered . . . Translated by the Rev. S. Butler . . . and the Rev. F. Hodgson. 1815. 4°. **640**. l. **10**, **11**.

—— —— 1815. 16°. **11481**. a. **7**.

BUTLER (Samuel) *Bishop of Lichfield and Coventry.*

—— *See* Butler (Samuel) *Philosophical Writer.* The Life and Letters of Dr. Samuel Butler, *etc.* [With a portrait and facsimiles.] 1896. 8°. **4905**. g. **13**.

—— *See* Colman (David S.) Sabrinae corolla: the classics at Shrewsbury School under Dr. Butler, *etc.* [1950.] 4°. **08366**. r. **24**.

—— *See* Evans (Robert W.) A Sermon preached . . . at the consecration of the Right Rev. Samuel Butler, D.D., Lord Bishop of Lichfield and Coventry. 1836. 8°. T. **2012**. **(16.)**

—— *See* Heitland (William E.) Dr. Butler of Shrewsbury School, *etc.* 1897. 8°. **4902**. d. **53**. **(1.)**

—— *See* Jackson (Miles) A Reply to the Rev. Richard Ward and the Rev. G. A. Poole's Answers to Oxford Tracts Unmasked. [With a ms. letter from S. Butler inserted.] [1838.] 8°. **4108**. cc. **26**. **(2.)**

—— *See* Moore (Henry) *Vicar of Eccleshall.* A Sermon on the Death of the Right Reverend Samuel Butler, *etc.* [1839.] 8°. **4804**. i. **12**. **(3.)**

—— *See* Musurus (M.) *Archbishop of Malvasia.* M. Musuri Carmen in Platonem. Isaaci Casauboni in Josephum Scaligerum Ode. Accedunt poemata et exercitationes utriusque linguæ. Auctore S. Butler . . . Conscripsit atque edidit S. Butler. 1797. 8°. **1213**. m. **34**.

—— *See* Tasso (T.) [*La Gerusalemme Liberata.—Italian.*] [La Gierusalemme liberata, *etc.*] [With a ms. note by S. Butler.] [1581.] 4°. C. **45**. e. **22**.

—— Atlas of Ancient & Classical Geography. (Revised and enlarged.) pp. x. 93. pl. 27. *J. M. Dent & Co.: London; E. P. Dutton & Co.: New York*, [1907.] 8°. [*Everyman's Library.*] **12206.p.1/216.**
Earlier editions of this Atlas are entered in the Catalogue of Maps.

—— A Charge, delivered to the Clergy of the Archdeaconry of Derby . . . June 22 and 23, 1825. pp. 15. *Longman & Co.: London*, 1826. 4°. T. **1246**. **(1.)**

—— A Charge, delivered to the Clergy of the Archdeaconry of Derby . . . June 15 and 16, 1826. pp. 16. *Longman & Co.: London*, 1826. 4°. T. **1246**. **(3.)**

—— A Charge delivered to the Clergy of the Archdeaconry of Derby . . . July 26 and 27, 1827. pp. 19. *Longman & Co.: London*, 1827. 4°. T. **1246**. **(11.)**

—— A Charge delivered to the Clergy of the Archdeaconry of Derby . . . June 18 and 19, 1829. pp. 16. *Longman & Co.: London*, 1829. 4°. T. **1342**. **(8.)**

—— A Charge delivered to the Clergy of the Archdeaconry of Derby . . . June 24 and 25, 1830. pp. 20. *Longman & Co.: London*, 1830. 4°. T. **1342**. **(12.)**

—— A Charge delivered to the Clergy of the Archdeaconry of Derby . . . June 20 and 21, 1833. pp. 24. *Longman & Co.: London*, 1833. 4°. T. **2150**. **(3.)**

—— A Charge delivered to the Clergy of the Archdeaconry of Derby . . . June 26 and 27, 1834. pp. 20. *Longman & Co.: London*, 1834. 4°. T. **2150**. **(6.)**

—— A Charge delivered to the Clergy of the Archdeaconry of Derby . . . June 25 and 26, 1835. pp. 20. *Longman & Co.: London*, 1835. 4°. T. **2150**. **(11.)**

—— Christian Liberty. A sermon preached at St. Mary's, before . . . the Duke of Gloucester, Chancellor of the University, and the University of Cambridge, at the Installation, June 30, 1811. pp. 129. *W. Eddowes: Shrewsbury*, 1811. 8°. **4475**. c. **110**.

—— Considerations on the Holy Catholic Church. A charge delivered to the clergy of the Archdeaconry of Derby . . . June 24 and 25, 1831. pp. 18. *Longman & Co.: London*, 1831. 4°. T. **1342**. (**19**.)

—— The Genuine and Apocryphal Gospels compared. A charge delivered to the clergy of the Archdeaconry of Derby at the visitations, June 6 & 7, 1822. pp. 37. *William Eddowes: Shrewsbury*, 1822. 4°. T. **945**. (**15**.)

—— A Letter to Henry Brougham, Esq., M.P., on certain clauses in the Education Bills now before Parliament. pp. 24. *W. Eddowes: Shrewsbury*, 1820. 8°. **1031**. g. **11**. (**8**.)

—— A Letter to Philograntus [i.e. J. H. Monk], by Eubulus [i.e. S. Butler]: being a sequel to a pamphlet, entitled Thoughts on the Present System of Academic Education in the University of Cambridge. pp. 27. 1822. 8°. *See* EUBULUS, *pseud.* T. **711**. (**13**.)

—— [Another edition.] pp. 13. 1822. 8°. [*The Pamphleteer*. vol. 20.] *See* EUBULUS, *pseud.* P.P. **3557**. w.

—— A Letter to the Rev. C. J. Blomfield . . . containing remarks on the Edinburgh Review of the Cambridge Æschylus, and incidental observations on that of the Oxford Strabo. pp. 78. *W. Eddowes: Shrewsbury*, 1810. 8°. **1087**. c. **21**. (**3**.)

—— *See* MONK (James H.) *Bishop of Gloucester and Bristol.* A Letter to the Rev. Samuel Butler [in answer to his "Letter to the Rev. C. J. Blomfield"] . . . With Mr. Butler's answer. 1810. 8°. **1414**. d. **25**.

—— Memoir [of John Johnstone]. *See* JOHNSTONE (John) *M.D., F.R.S.* An Harveian Oration, and other remains of John Johnstone, *etc.* 1837. 8°. **7298**. eee. **16**.

—— The Mercy of God; especially considered with reference to our present situation. A sermon preached at St. Julian's, Shrewsbury. Sept. 14, 1800. pp. 24. *J. & W. Eddowes: Shrewsbury*, [1800.] 12°. **4401**. bbb. **9**. (**2**.)

—— A Praxis on the Latin Prepositions, being an attempt to illustrate their origin, signification, and government, in the way of exercise. pp. 259. *Longman & Co.: London*, 1823. 8°. **827**. g. **19**. (**1**.)

—— Second edition. pp. 261. FEW MS. NOTES. *Longman & Co.: London*, 1825. 8°. **12934**. bbb. **9**.

—— [A reissue.] *London*, 1831. 8°. **12933**. c. **20**.

—— A Key to Dr. Butler's Praxis on the Latin Prepositions. pp. 158. *Longman & Co.: London*, 1831. 8°. **827**. g. **19**. (**2**.)

—— Security in the Divine Protection. A sermon, *etc.* pp. 24. *J. & W. Eddowes: Shrewsbury*, [1805.] 12°. **3479**. a. **59**. (**3**.)

—— A Sermon preached at the Consecration of St. Michael's Church in Shrewsbury, August 24, 1830. pp. 15. *Longman & Co.: London*, 1830. 4°. T. **1342**. (**15**.)

—— A Sermon preached in the Church of Hatton, near Warwick, at the funeral of the Rev. Samuel Parr, LL.D., in obedience to his own request, March 14, 1825, *etc.* pp. 16. *Longman & Co.: London*, 1825. 4°. T. **912**. (**26**.)

—— Sidneiana, being a collection of fragments relative to Sir Philip Sidney, Knt., and his immediate connections. (Now first collected and partly first published.) [Edited by S. Butler.] pp. xi. 105. 1837. 4°. *See* LONDON.—III. *Roxburghe Club.* C. **101**. b. **7**.

—— [Another copy.] G. **90**. (**3**.)

—— A Sketch of Modern and Antient Geography, for the use of schools. pp. xxix. 246. *W. Eddowes: Shrewsbury*, 1813. 8°. **571**. f. **7**.

—— Fourth edition, considerably enlarged and improved. pp. xxiv. 260. *Longman & Co.: London*, 1813. 8°. **571**. f. **6**.

—— The seventh edition. pp. xxii. 341. *Longman & Co.: London*, 1825. 8°. **10026**. dd. **12**.

—— The eighth edition. pp. xxii. 345. *Longman & Co.: London*, 1828. 8°. **10004**. i. **23**.

—— The ninth edition. pp. xxii. 345. *Longman & Co.: London*, 1830. 8°. **571**. f. **8**.

—— A new edition. pp. xxii. 364. *Longman & Co.: London*, [1838 ?] 8°. **10004**. dd. **13**.

—— A new edition revised by his son [Thomas Butler]. pp. xxii. 379. *Longman & Co.: London*, 1842. 8°. **571**. f. **28**.

—— A new edition revised by the Rev. Thomas Butler. pp. xxvi. 402. *Longman & Co.: London*, 1851. 8°. **10002**. e. **22**.

—— A Sketch of Modern Geography . . . A new edition, revised by the Rev. Thomas Butler. pp. xvi. 264. *Longman & Co.: London*, 1855. 12°. **10005**. b. **6**.

—— A new edition, revised by the Rev. Thomas Butler. pp. viii. 315. *Longman & Co.: London*, 1862. 12°. **10005**. b. **4**.

—— A new edition, revised by the Rev. Thomas Butler. pp. viii. 328. *Longmans & Co.: London*, 1872. 8°. **10003**. bbb. **39**.

—— A Sketch of Antient Geography . . . A new edition, revised by the Rev. Thomas Butler. pp. xxiv. 254. *Longman & Co.: London*, 1855. 12°. **10005**. b. **5**.

—— Geographia Classica; or the Application of ancient geography to the classics. Abridged from Rev. Dr. Butler's Sketch of Ancient Geography. pp. 22. *Richard Cruttwell: Bath*, 1825. 12°. **10003**. b. **59**.

—— Abridgment of Dr. Butler's Modern and Antient Geography . . . Arranged in the form of question and answer . . . By Mary Cunningham. pp. 124. *Longman & Co.: London*, 1836. 12°. **571**. a. **28**.

—— Thoughts on Church Dignities. pp. 22. *Longman & Co.: London*, 1833. 8°. T. **1419**. (**13**.)

—— Thoughts on the Present System of Academic Education in the University of Cambridge. By Eubulus [i.e. S. Butler]. pp. 20. 1822. 8°. *See* EUBULUS, *pseud.* T. **711**. (**12**.)

—— [Another edition.] pp. 10. 1822. 8°. [*The Pamphleteer*. vol. 20.] *See* EUBULUS, *pseud.* P.P. **3557**. w.

—— Three Sermons on Infidelity preached at St. Mary's, Shrewsbury, and at Kenilworth, Warwickshire, *etc.* pp. 48. *W. Eddowes: Shrewsbury*, 1820. 8°. **1026**. f. **3**. (**13**.)

BUTLER (Samuel) *Bishop of Lichfield and Coventry.*

—— Bibliotheca Butleriana. A catalogue of the library of the late Right Rev. Samuel Butler . . . which will be sold by auction by Messrs. Christie & Manson . . . March 23rd, 1840, *etc.* [With prices in MS.] 3 pt. [*London*, 1840.] 8°. **011900.** ee. **18.** (**2.**)

—— A Catalogue of the highly interesting assemblage of Classical Antiquities . . . of the Right Reverend Samuel Butler . . . which . . . will be sold by auction by Messrs. Christie & Manson . . . Feb. 12, 1840, *etc.* [With prices in MS.] pp. 16. [*London*, 1840.] 4°. **011900.** ee. **18.** (**1.**)

BUTLER (Samuel) *Philosophical Writer.* The Shrewsbury Edition of the Works of S. Butler. Edited by Henry Festing Jones and A. T. Bartholomew. 20 vol. *Jonathan Cape: London ; E. P. Dutton & Co.: New York*, 1923–26. 8°. L.R. **40.** a.

—— [A collection of articles by Samuel Butler and other writers, extracted from "Il Lambruschini," relating to Butler's theory of the Trapanese origin of the Odyssey.] MS. NOTES [by Samuel Butler]. *Trapani*, 1892–94. 8°. **11313.** g. **42.** (**1.**)

—— Essays on Life, Art and Science . . . Edited by R. A. Streatfeild. pp. xi. 339. *Grant Richards: London*, 1904. 8°. **012355.** de. **55.**

—— [A reissue.] *A. C. Fifield: London*, 1908. 8°. **12355.** p. **5.**

—— The Humour of Homer, and other essays . . . [Containing the "Lecture on the Humour of Homer" and "Essays on Life, Art and Science."] Edited by R. A. Streatfeild. With a biographical sketch of the author by Henry Festing Jones, and a portrait in photogravure from a photograph taken in 1889. pp. 313. *A. C. Fifield: London*, 1913. 8°. **012354.** ee. **23.**

—— A First Year in Canterbury Settlement. With other early essays . . . Edited by R. A. Streatfeild. pp. xi. 272. *A. C. Fifield: London*, 1914. 8°. **12354.** p. **21.**

—— Erewhon and Erewhon Revisited. pp. xv. 389. *J. M. Dent & Sons: London & Toronto ; E. P. Dutton & Co.: New York*, 1932. 8°. [*Everyman's Library.*] **12206.p.1/650.**

—— Letters between Samuel Butler and Miss E. M. A. Savage, 1871–1885. [Edited by Geoffrey Keynes and Brian Hill. With portraits.] pp. 380. *Jonathan Cape: London*, 1935. 8°. **010920.** bbb. **27.**

—— Samuele Butler e la Valle Sesia da sue lettere inedite a Giulio Avienta, Federico Tonetti e a Pietro Calderini. [Edited with an introduction by Alberto Durio. With a portrait.] pp. 131. *Varallo Sesia*, 1940. 8°. **10151.** ff. **30.**

—— Alps and Sanctuaries of Piedmont and the Canton Ticino. Op. 6 . . . Second edition. [With illustrations.] pp. viii. 376. *David Bogue: London*, 1882 [1881]. 8°. **10132.** cc. **36.**

—— New and enlarged edition, with author's revisions and index, and an introduction by R. A. Streatfeild. pp. 335. *A. C. Fifield: London*, 1913. 8°. **2360.** c. **8.**

—— Ancora sull'origine Siciliana dell'Odissea. (Estratto dalla "Rassegna della letteratura siciliana.") pp. 26. *Acireale*, 1894. 8°. **11825.** q. **23.** (**6.**)

—— [Another copy.] FEW MS. CORRECTIONS [by the author]. **11335.** dd. **14.** (**2.**)

BUTLER (Samuel) *Philosophical Writer.*

—— The Authoress of the Odyssey, where and when she wrote, who she was, the use she made of the Iliad, and how the poem grew under her hands. pp. xv. 275. *Longmans & Co.: London*, 1897. 8°. **11335.** cc. **29.**

—— Second edition, corrected. [With plates.] pp. xxvii. 277. *Jonathan Cape: London*, 1922. 8°. **11335.** d. **33.**

—— Darwin among the Machines, *etc.* [Signed: Cellarius, i.e. S. Butler. A cutting from "The Press" of Christchurch, N.Z.] *See* Cellarius, *pseud.* [1863.] *s. sh.* fol. **1856.** g. **14.** (**36.**)

—— [Another edition.] [Extracted from "The Press," Christchurch, N.Z., 25 May, 1911.] *See* infra: Appendix. Samuel Butler and "The Press," *etc.* [1911.] 4°. **7002.** h. **22.**

—— Darwin on the Origin of Species. A philosophic dialogue . . . originally published in the year 1862, and now reprinted with the corrrespondence relating thereto. [Cuttings from "The Press," Christchurch, N.Z., June 1, 8 and 15, 1912.] *Christchurch*, 1912. 4°. **7002.** bb. **11.**

—— Erewhon; or Over the range. [By Samuel Butler.] pp. viii. 246. 1872. 8°. *See* Erewhon. **12637.** g. **4.**

—— Erewhon . . . [By Samuel Butler.] Second edition, revised and corrected. pp. xii. 244. 1872. 8°. *See* Erewhon. **12654.** bb. **3.**

—— [Another copy.] Erewhon . . . Second edition, *etc.* MS. NOTES [by the author]. 1872. 8°. *See* Erewhon. C. **60.** k. **9.**

—— Sixth edition. Op. 1. pp. xii. 244. *David Bogue: London*, 1880. 8°. **12619.** e. **40.**

—— Eighth edition. Op. 1. pp. xii. 244. *Longmans & Co.: London & New York*, 1890. 8°. **12612.** d. **26.**

—— New and revised edition. pp. xviii. 324. *Grant Richards: London*, 1901. 8°. **012622.** ee. **44.**

—— [A reissue.] *A. C. Fifield: London*, 1908. 8°. **012613.** h. **13.**

—— [Another edition.] [With an introduction by Francis Byrne Hackett.] pp. xxvii. 320. *E. P. Dutton & Co.: New York*, 1917. 8°. **012611.** g. **34.**

—— [Another edition.] With woodcuts by Robert Gibbings. pp. 327. *Jonathan Cape: London*, 1923. 8°. **012603.** b. 2.

—— [Another edition.] The wood-engravings by Blair Hughes-Stanton. pp. 266. *Gregynog Press: Newtown*, 1932. 8°. C. **99.** h. **44.**

—— [Another edition.] pp. 256. *John Lane: London*, 1935. 8°. [*Penguin Books.* no. 20.] **12208.a.1/20.**

—— Erewhon, *etc.* pp. 286. *London*, 1940. 8°. [*Nelson Classics.*] **012207.** c. **58.**

—— Erewhon, of Over de bergen. [By S. Butler.] Uit het Engelsch van P. G. van Schermbeck. pp. 300. 1873. 8°. *See* Erewhon. **12621.** dd. **20.**

—— Erewhon, ou De l'autre côté des montagnes. Traduit . . . par Valéry Larbaud. [With an introductory essay.] pp. xxxii. 230. [*Paris*,] 1934. 8°. **12602.** v. **2.**

—— Ergindwon, oder Jenseits der Berge. Nach der fünften Auflage von Samuel Butler's Erewhon von J. D. pp. iv. 247. *Leipzig*, 1879. 8°. **12604.** df. **15.**

—— Erewhon . . . Prima traduzione dall'inglese di G. Titta Rosa. pp. viii. 295. *Milano*, 1928. 8°. **012635. c. 40.**

—— Erewhon ó Allende las Montañas. Traducción, prólogo y notas de Ogier Preteceilla. [With a portrait.] pp. 366. *Valencia*, 1926. 8°. **012640. c. 52.**

—— Erewhon Revisited twenty years later, both by the original discoverer of the country and by his son. pp. xi. 338. *Grant Richards: London*, 1901. 8°. **012622. ee. 45.**

—— Erewhon Revisited, *etc.* (Second edition.) pp. x. 337. *Grant Richards: London*, 1902. 8°. **12654. cc. 15.**

—— [A reissue.] *A. C. Fifield: London*, 1908. 8°. **012621. i. 53.**

—— [Erewhon revisited.] Nouveaux voyages en Erewhon accomplis, vingt ans après la découverte du pays, par le premier explorateur et par son fils. Traduit . . . par Valery Larbaud, *etc.* pp. xxix. 308. *Paris*, 1924. 8°. **012551. t. 30.**

—— The Evidence for the Resurrection of Jesus Christ, as given by the four Evangelists, critically examined. [By Samuel Butler.] pp. viii. 48. 1865. 8°. *See* BIBLE.—*Appendix.—Gospels.* [*Miscellaneous.*] **3128. ee. 17. (1.)**

—— [Another copy.] **03127. ee. 14. (1.)**

—— [Another copy.] **03127. ee. 14. (2.)**

—— [Another copy.] **03127. ee. 14. (3.)**

—— Evolution, old and new; or, the Theories of Buffon, Dr. Erasmus Darwin, and Lamarck, as compared with that of Mr. Charles Darwin . . . Op. 4. pp. xii. 384. *Hardwicke & Bogue: London*, 1879. 8°. **7006. bbb. 11.**

—— Second edition, with an appendix and index. pp. xii. 430. *David Bogue: London*, 1882. 8°. **7001. ppp. 12.**

—— New edition, with author's revisions, appendix, and index. [Edited by R. A. Streatfeild.] pp. xvi. 430. *A. C. Fifield: London*, 1911. 8°. **2252. b. 7.**

—— Ex Voto: an account of the Sacro Monte or New Jerusalem at Varallo-Sesia. With some notice of Tabachetti's remaining work at the Sanctuary of Crea. pp. xiv. 277. *Trübner & Co.: London*, 1888. 8°. **7875. aaa. 26.**

—— Ex Voto: an account of the Sacro Monte or New Jerusalem at Varallo-Sesia. With some notice of Tabachetti's remaining work at the Sanctuary of Crea. (Additions and corrections.) pp. xiv. iv. 277. *Longmans & Co.: London & New York*, 1890. 8°. **7867. a. 8.**

—— Ex Voto. Studio artistico sulle opere d'arte del S. Monte di Varallo e di Crea. Edizione italiana tradotta . . . per cura di Angelo Rizzetti. [With plates.] pp. xii. 116 [316]. *Novara*, 1894. 8°. **7875. a. 42.**

—— The Fair Haven. A work in defence of the miraculous element in our Lord's ministry upon earth, both as against rationalistic impugners and certain orthodox defenders. By the late John Pickard Owen, edited by William Bickersteth Owen, with a memoir of the author. [The whole written by S. Butler.] pp. 70. 248. 1873. 8°. *See* OWEN (John P.) *pseud.* **4017. h. 23.**

—— Second edition. pp. ix. 70. 248. *Trübner & Co.: London*, 1873. 8°. **4016. e. 3.**

—— [Another edition.] Now reset; and edited, with an introduction, by R. A. Streatfeild. pp. xx. 285. *A. C. Fifield: London*, 1913. 8°. **4014. df. 14.**

—— [A reissue.] pp. xxi. 285. *Jonathan Cape: London*, 1929. 8°. **04018. ee. 61.**

—— [Another edition.] pp. xv. 233. *Watts & Co.: London*, 1938. 8°. [*Thinker's Library.* no. 70.] **12211. aa. 1/70.**

—— A First Year in Canterbury Settlement. [With a map.] pp. x. 162. *Longman & Co.: London*, 1863. 8°. **10491. a. 9.**

—— God the Known and God the Unknown. [Edited by R. A. Streatfeild.] pp. 91. *A. C. Fifield: London*, 1909. 8°. **03558. ee. 11.**

—— Holbein's Dance. [Photographs of two drawings attributed to Holbein, with critical remarks.] *Trübner & Co.: London*, [1886.] *s. sh.* 4°. **1882. c. 2. (1.)**

—— A Lecture on the Humour of Homer. Delivered at the Working Men's College . . . Reprinted, with a preface and additional matter, from "The Eagle." pp. vii. 43. *Metcalfe & Co.: Cambridge*, 1892. 8°. **11315. d. 30. (5.)**

—— [Another copy.] MS. CORRECTIONS [by the author]. **11335. bbb. 43. (1.)**

—— Life and Habit. pp. 307. *Trübner & Co.: London*, 1878 [1877]. 8°. **7001. ppp. 5.**

—— New edition, with author's addenda. Op. 3. [Edited by R. A. Streatfeild.] pp. x. 310. *A. C. Fifield: London*, 1910. 8°. **2236. a. 6.**

—— [Life and Habit.] La Vie et l'habitude. Traduit . . . par Valery Larbaud. pp. 291. *Paris*, 1922. 8°. **7009. e. 3.**

—— The Life and Letters of Dr. Samuel Butler, Head-Master of Shrewsbury School 1798–1836, and afterwards Bishop of Lichfield, in so far as they illustrate the scholastic, religious, and social life of England, 1790–1840, *etc.* [With plates, including a portrait and facsimiles.] 2 vol. *John Murray: London*, 1896. 8°. **4905. g. 13.**

In this copy after p. 404 in vol. 2 are inserted eight leaves made up of proof sheets from the "Shrewsbury Chronicle" containing letters written to Samuel Butler by the Rev. Edgar Montagu.

—— [Another copy.] FEW MS. NOTES AND CORRECTIONS. **L.R. 33. b. 19.**

To this copy are added two quarto volumes of "Discarded and Duplicate letters" arranged by the author.

—— *See* HEITLAND (William E.) Dr. Butler of Shrewsbury School, *etc.* [A review of Samuel Butler's "Life and Letters of Dr. Samuel Butler."] 1897. 8°. **4902. d. 53. (1.)**

—— Luck, or Cunning, as the Main Means of Organic Modification? An attempt to throw additional light upon the late Mr. Charles Darwin's theory of natural selection . . . Op. 8. pp. ix. 328. *Trübner & Co.: London*, 1887 [1886]. 8°. **7005. d. 29.**

—— Second edition, re-set, with author's corrections and additions to index. pp. 282. *A. C. Fifield: London*, 1920. 8°. **2252. b. 16.**

—— Lucubratio Ebria. [Extracted from "The Press," Christchurch, N.Z.] *See* infra: APPENDIX. Samuel Butler and "The Press," *etc.* [1911.] 4°. **7002. h. 22.**

—— Note on "The Tempest." Act III, Scene 1. [By S. Butler.] 1864. 8°. [*Literary Foundlings: verse and prose collected in Canterbury, N.Z.*] *See* SHAKESPEARE (William) [*The Tempest.—Appendix.*] C. **57.** k. **23.**

—— The Note-Books of Samuel Butler, author of "Erewhon." Selections arranged and edited by Henry Festing Jones. With photogravure portrait by Emery Walker from a photograph taken by Alfred Cathie in 1898. pp. xii. 438. *A. C. Fifield: London,* 1912. 8°. **012354.** ee. **8.**

—— [Another copy.] MS. NOTES [by Henry Festing Jones]. **012354.** ee. **15.**

—— Carnets. Traduits . . . et préfacés par Valéry Larbaud, *etc.* pp. 408. *Paris,* 1936. 8°. **12357.** s. **30.**

—— Selections from the Note-Books of Samuel Butler. [Edited by A. T. Bartholomew.] pp. 221. *Jonathan Cape: London,* 1930. 8°. [*Travellers' Library.*] **012208.m.1/51.**

—— Butleriana. [Compiled, mainly from previously unpublished portions of Butler's "Note-Books," by A. T. Bartholomew.] pp. xvi. 172. *Nonesuch Press: London,* 1932. 8°. C. **99.** d. **40.**

—— Further Extracts from the Note-Books of Samuel Butler. Chosen and edited by A. T. Bartholomew. [With a portrait.] pp. 414. *Jonathan Cape: London,* 1934. 8°. **12356.** p. **13.**

—— Selections from the Note-Books of Samuel Butler. [*London,*] 1950. 8°. [*The Travellers' Library.*] **012208.** m. **1/94.**

A reissue of the edition of 1930.

—— Samuel Butler's Notebooks. Selections edited by Geoffrey Keynes and Brian Hill. pp. 327. *Jonathan Cape: London,* 1951. 8°. **12361.** aa. **16.**

—— Samuel Butler and his Note-Books, *etc.* [Signed: J. F. H., i.e. John F. Harris.] 1913. 8°. *See* H., J. F. **011853.** bb. **18.** (**6.**)

—— La Nuova quistione omerica. L'autore dell'Odissea è una donna? [Extracted from "Quo Vadis?"] MS. NOTES [by the author]. *Trapani,* 1901. fol. **11315.** i. **39.**

—— *See* CASSISA (G. S.) La Nuova quistione omerica. Un intervista con Pietro Sugameli. [A criticism of the article by S. Butler entitled "La Nuova quistione omerica," *etc.*] 1901. fol. [*Quo Vadis.* anno. 1. no. 9–10.] **11315.** i. **41.**

—— On the Trapanese Origin of the Odyssey. [Reprinted from "The Eagle," with a preface added.] pp. 24. 13. *Metcalfe & Co.: Cambridge,* 1893. 8°. **11315.** d. **30.** (**7.**)

—— [Another copy.] MS. CORRECTIONS [by the author]. **11335.** bbb. **43.** (**5.**)

—— L'Origine siciliana dell'Odissea. (Estratto dalla "Rassegna della letteratura siciliana.") pp. 22. *Acireale,* 1893. 8°. **11335.** dd. **9.** (**2.**)

—— [Another copy.] FEW MS. CORRECTIONS [by the author]. **11335.** dd. **14.** (**1.**)

—— Seven Sonnets and a Psalm of Montreal. [Edited by R. A. Streatfeild.] pp. 15. *Printed for private circulation: Cambridge,* 1904. 8°. **11603.** ccc. **21.** (**8.**)

—— To the Electors of the Slade Professor of Fine Art. [A letter by Samuel Butler, with a list of his works and testimonials in support of his candidature for the Slade Professorship of Fine Art at Cambridge.] pp. 4. [*London,* 1886.] 4°. **10827.** h. **15.**

—— Unconscious Memory; a comparison between the theory of Dr. Ewald Hering . . . and the "Philosophy of the Unconscious" of Dr. Edward von Hartmann; with translations from these authors, and preliminary chapters bearing on "Life and Habit," "Evolution, old and new," and Mr. Charles Darwin's edition of Dr. Krause's "Erasmus Darwin" . . . Op. 5. pp. viii. 288. *David Bogue: London,* 1880. 8°. **7005.** bb. **36.**

—— New edition, entirely reset, with an introduction by Marcus Hartog . . . Op. 5. [Edited by R. A. Streatfeild.] pp. xxxvii. 186. *A. C. Fifield: London,* 1910. 8°. **7005.** d. **25.**

—— Third edition . . . With an introduction and postscript by Marcus Hartog. pp. xxxix. 186. *A. C. Fifield: London,* 1920. 8°. **2252.** b. **15.**

—— The Way of All Flesh. [Edited by R. A. Streatfeild.] pp. 424. *Grant Richards: London,* 1903. 8°. **Cup.400.a.23.**

—— Second edition. pp. 420. *A. C. Fifield: London,* 1908. 8°. **012613.** h. **12.**

—— [Another edition.] With an introduction by William Lyon Phelps. pp. x. 464. *E. P. Dutton & Co.: New York,* 1916. 8°. **012626.** c. **44.**

—— [Another edition.] pp. xxiii. 360. *J. M. Dent & Sons: London & Toronto; E. P. Dutton & Co.: New York,* 1933. 8°. [*Everyman's Library.*] **12206.p.1/653.**

—— [Another edition.] Illustrated with wood engravings by John Farleigh. pp. 511. *Collins: London,* 1934. 8°. **12602.** tt. **31.**

—— [Another edition.] With an essay by Bernard Shaw. pp. xiii. 421. *Oxford University Press: London,* 1936. 8°. [*World's Classics.*] **012209.** df. **312.**

—— [Another edition.] With drawings by Donia Nachshen. pp. 381. *Jonathan Cape: London,* 1936. 8°. **012627.** m. **71.**

—— The Way of All Flesh. pp. 373. *Harmondsworth, New York,* 1947. 8°. [*Penguin Books.* no. 511.] **12208.** a. **1/511.**

—— The Way of all Flesh . . . With an introduction by A. C. Ward. pp. 416. *Collins: London & Glasgow,* 1953. 8°. **12652.** a. **8.**

—— The Way of all Flesh, *etc.* pp. xxi. 360. *J. M. Dent & Sons: London; E. P. Dutton & Co.: New York,* 1954. 8°. [*Everyman's Library.* no. 895.] **12206.** p. **1/938.**

A reissue of the edition of 1933.

—— [The Way of All Flesh.] Ainsi va toute chair. Traduit . . . par Valery Larbaud . . . Deuxième édition. [The second part, containing chapters 47–86.] pp. 232. *Paris,* 1921. 8°. **012551.** t. **29.**

Imperfect; wanting the first part, containing chapters 1–46.

—— [The Way of all Flesh.] Der Weg alles Fleisches. Roman. (Autorisierte Ubersetzung [*sic*] von Herberth E. Herlitschka.) 2 Bd. *Wien,* 1929. 8°. **12654.** f. **38.**

BUTLER (Samuel) *Philosophical Writer.*

—— Selections from Previous Works. With remarks on Mr. G. J. Romanes' "Mental Evolution in Animals," and a Psalm of Montreal. pp. viii. 325. *Trübner & Co.: London,* 1884. 8°. **12272.** bb. **7.**

—— The Essential Samuel Butler. Selected with an introduction by G. D. H. Cole. [With plates, including a portrait.] pp. 544. *Jonathan Cape: London,* 1950. 8°. **12275.** ee. **5.**

WORKS EDITED, TRANSLATED, OR WITH MS. ANNOTATIONS BY BUTLER.

—— *See* AMSTERDAM. — *Stedelijk Museum.* Rembrandt. Schilderijen bijeengebracht ter gelegenheid van de inhuldiging van . . . Koningin Wilhelmina, *etc.* COPIOUS MS. NOTES [by S. Butler]. [1898.] 8°. K.T.C. **1.** a. **15.**

—— *See* DICKENS (Charles) [*Martin Chuzzlewit.*] A Translation, attempted in consequence of a challenge. [A translation into Homeric verse of a passage from "Martin Chuzzlewit." By Samuel Butler.] [1894.] *s. sh.* 8°. **1882.** c. **2.** **(224.)**

—— *See* FOLEY (James) *of Montreal.* Extracts from letters sent by Mr. Foley to the foreman of the works of the Canada Tanning Extract Co'y, *etc.* MS. NOTES [by S. Butler]. [1875.] 8°. **08226.** k. **48.**

—— *See* HESIOD. [*Opera et Dies.—English.*] Works & Days. A translation . . . by S. Butler, *etc.* 1924. fol. C. **98.** h. **3.**

—— *See* HOMER. [*Iliad.—Greek.*] Homeri Ilias, *etc.* [With MS. references to Odyssean passages by Samuel Butler.] 1893, *etc.* 8°. T.C. **6.** a. **12.**

—— *See* HOMER. [*Iliad.—English.*] The Iliad of Homer, rendered into English prose . . . by S. Butler. 1898. 8°. **11335.** e. **26.**

—— *See* HOMER. [*Odyssey.—Greek.*] Homeri Odyssea, *etc.* [With MS. references to Iliadic passages by S. Butler.] 1894. 8°. T.C. **6.** a. **13.**

—— *See* HOMER. [*Odyssey.—English.*] The Odyssey, rendered into English prose . . . by S. Butler. 1900. 8°. **11335.** cc. **33.**

—— —— 1922. 8°. **11335.** b. **24.**

—— *See* HOMER. [*Odyssey.—English.*] Sample Passages from a new prose translation of the Odyssey by Mr. S. Butler. [1894.] 8°. **11315.** df. **24.** **(2.)**

—— *See* KRAUSE (Ernst) Erasmus Darwin, *etc.* MS. NOTES [by S. Butler]. 1879. 8°. **10854.** b. **2.**

—— *See* PERIODICAL PUBLICATIONS.—*Leipzig.* Kosmos . . . Gratulationsheft zum 70. Geburtstage Ch. Darwin's. MS. NOTES [by S. Butler, on the article by Ernst Krause on Erasmus Darwin]. [1879.] 8°. **7001.** g. 3.

—— *See* SHAKESPEARE (William) [*Sonnets.*] Shakespeare's Sonnets. Reconsidered, and in part rearranged, with introductory chapters . . . by S. Butler. 1899. 8°. **2300.** d. **2.**

—— —— 1927. 8°. **011761.** e. **12.**

—— *See* SHREWSBURY.—*Royal School.* [Sixth Form Examination Paper. Aug., 1836.] MS. NOTES [by S. Butler]. [1836.] 8°. **4902.** d. **53.** **(2.)**

BUTLER (Samuel) *Philosophical Writer.* [WORKS EDITED, TRANSLATED, OR WITH MS. ANNOTATIONS BY BUTLER.]

—— *See* SHREWSBURY.—*Royal School.* Speeches and Distribution of Prizes, June 7, 1836. MS. NOTES [by S. Butler]. [1836.] 8°. **8364.** bb. **73.**

APPENDIX.

—— *See* BEKKER (W. G.) An Historical and Critical Review of Samuel Butler's Literary Works, *etc.* [1925.] 8°. **11824.** s. 35.

—— *See* BLUM (Jean) *Docteur ès lettres.* Samuel Butler. [1910.] 8°. **011853.** i. **82.**

—— *See* BOETTGER (H.) Samuel Butlers satirische Romane und ihre literarische Bedeutung, *etc.* 1936. 8°. **11859.** aaa. **2.**

—— *See* CAMBRIDGE.—*University of Cambridge.—Saint John's College.* The Samuel Butler Collection at Saint John's College, Cambridge, *etc.* 1921. 8°. **010855.** d. **18.**

—— *See* CANNAN (Gilbert) Samuel Butler. A critical study. 1915. 8°. **011853.** d. **42.**

—— *See* CARLO SEREGNI (E. di) Samuel Butler, *etc.* [With a portrait.] 1933. 8°. **010822.** de. **44.**

—— *See* CHRISTCHURCH, *New Zealand.—Christchurch Classical Association.* Samuel Butler and the Authoress of the Odyssey, *etc.* [With Butler's self-portrait.] [1950.] 8°. Cup. **645.** b. **9.** **(4.)**

—— *See* COLE (George D. H.) Samuel Butler. [With a portrait.] 1952. 8°. W.P. **9502/30.**

—— *See* COLE (George D. H.) Samuel Butler and The Way of All Flesh. 1947. 8°. **11873.a.15/2.**

—— *See* DELATTRE (F.) Samuel Butler et le bergsonisme, *etc.* [1936.] 8°. **8471.** h. **53.**

—— *See* FARRINGTON (Benjamin) *Professor of Classics, University College of Swansea.* Samuel Butler and the Odyssey. 1929. 8°. **11313.** b. **32.**

—— *See* FORT (Joseph B.) Samuel Butler, l'écrivain. Étude d'un style. 1935. 8°. **11855.** dd. **49.**

—— *See* FORT (Joseph B.) Samuel Butler, 1835–1902. Étude d'un caractère et d'une intelligence. [With a portrait and a bibliography.] 1935. 8°. **10826.** i. **42.**

—— *See* FURBANK (Philip N.) Samuel Butler, 1835–1902. 1948. 8°. **10860.** aa. **43.**

—— *See* GARNETT (Martha) Samuel Butler and his Family Relations. [With portraits.] 1926. 8°. **010855.** cc. **38.**

—— *See* HARKNESS (Stanley B.) The Career of Samuel Butler . . . A bibliography. 1955. 8°. **11918.** de. **12.**

—— *See* HARRIS (John F.) Samuel Butler, author of Erewhon, the man and his work. 1916. 8°. **010826.** g. **32.**

—— *See* HARTOG (Marcus M.) Samuel Butler and recent mnemic biological theories, *etc.* 1914. 8°. **7002.** b. **14.** **(6.)**

—— *See* HEITLAND (William E.) A "Few Earnest Words" on Samuel Butler, *etc.* [1916.] 8°. **011853.** t. **7.**

—— *See* HENDERSON (Philip) Samuel Butler, the incarnate bachelor. [A biography. With portraits.] 1953. 8°. **10863.** f. **28.**

BUTLER (Samuel) *Philosophical Writer.* [Appendix.]

—— *See* Hoppé (Alfred J.) A Bibliography of the Writings of Samuel Butler . . . and of writings about him . . . With some letters from S. Butler to the Rev. F. G. Fleay, *etc.* [With facsimiles.] [1925.] 4°. **11903**. f. **49**.

—— *See* Joad (Cyril E. M.) Samuel Butler, *etc.* 1924. 8°. **010803**. eee. **1/6**.

—— *See* Jones (Henry Festing) Charles Darwin and Samuel Butler: a step towards reconciliation. 1911. 8°. **011852**. aaa. **35**. (**4**.)

—— *See* Jones (Henry Festing) Diary of a Journey . . . undertaken for the purpose of leaving the MSS. of three books by Samuel Butler at Varallo-Sesia, Aci-Reale and Trapani. 1904. 8°. **010107**. h. **8**. (**4**.)

—— *See* Jones (Henry Festing) Samuel Butler . . . A memoir, *etc.* [With a bibliography.] 1917. 8°. L.R. **23**. c. **1**.

—— —— [With portraits.] 1919. 8°. **010854**. i. **32**.

—— —— 1920. 8°. **2409**. b. **7**.

—— *See* Kingsmill (Hugh) After Puritanism, 1850–1900. [With special reference to S. Butler, Frank Harris and W. T. Stead.] 1929. 8°. **010803**. f. **48**.

—— *See* Lange (Petronella J. de) Samuel Butler: critic and philosopher, *etc.* [With a portrait.] 1925. 8°. **010856**. b. **14**.

—— *See* Larbaud (V.) Samuel Butler. Conférence, *etc.* 1920. 8°. **20012**. h. **3/6**.

—— *See* **Meissner (K. W. P.) Samuel Butler der Jüngere. Eine Studie zur Kultur des ausgehenden Viktorianismus. 1931. 8°. 11823. r. 37.**

—— *See* Muggeridge (Malcolm) The Earnest Atheist. A study of Samuel Butler. [With a portrait.] 1936. 8°. **010822**. i. **78**.

—— *See* Pestalozzi (G.) Samuel Butler, der Jüngere, 1835–1902. Versuch einer Darstellung seiner Gedankenwelt, *etc.* 1914. 8°. **8461**. d. **45**.

—— *See* Rattray (Robert F.) Samuel Butler: a chronicle and an introduction. 1935. 8°. **010825**. de. **66**.

—— *See* Salter (William H.) Essays on Two Moderns: Euripides, Samuel Butler. 1911. 8°. **11840**. v. **7**.

—— *See* Sella (A.) Un Inglese fervido amico dell'Italia. Samuele Butler. [With a portrait.] 1916. 8°. **010826**. f. **12**.

—— *See* Stillman (Clara G.) Samuel Butler: a mid-Victorian modern. [With portraits.] 1932. 8°. **20016**. dd. **22**.

—— *See* Stoff (R.) Die Philosophie des Organischen bei Samuel Butler . . . Mit einer biographischen Übersicht, *etc.* [With a portrait.] 1929. 8°. **8470**. bb. **21**.

—— *See* Streatfeild (Richard A.) Samuel Butler: a critical study, *etc.* 1902. 8°. **011852**. k. **25**.

—— *See* Streatfeild (Richard A.) Samuel Butler. Records and memorials. [With a portrait.] 1903. 8°. **10856**. h. **10**.

—— *See* Sugameli (P.) Origine Trapanese dell' "Odissea" secondo Samuel Butler. Dimostrazione critica. 1892. 8°. **11315**. d. **30**. (**6**.)

—— *See* Wilcox, afterwards Hamelius, afterwards Moore (Dora) Samuel Butler in Canterbury, New Zealand, *etc.* 1934. 16°. [*Australian English Association. Leaflet.* no. 18.] Ac. **2682**. b.

—— *See* Williamstown, *Massachusetts.—Williams College.—Chapin Library.* Catalogue of the Collection of Samuel Butler . . . in the Chapin Library, Williams College . . . With a . . . portrait, *etc.* 1945. 8°. **11898**. b. **15**.

—— *See* Young (William T.) George Meredith, Samuel Butler, *etc.* 1916. 8°. [*Cambridge History of English Literature.* vol. 13.] **11870.g.1.**

—— Samuel Butler. [A critical study by G. S. Cassisa, extracted from the periodical "Quo Vadis?" With a portrait.] *Ital. Trapani,* 1902. fol. **10855**. h. **8**.

—— Samuel Butler. Records and memorials. [Obituary notices from various reviews. With a portrait.] pp. 57. *Printed for private circulation: Cambridge,* 1903. 8°. **10863**. f. **11**.

—— Samuel Butler and "The Press." The Germ of "Erewhon." [An article extracted from "The Press," Christchurch, N.Z., containing reprints of two articles by Butler, entitled "Darwin among the Machines" and "Lucubratio ebria."] [*Christchurch, N.Z.,* 1911.] 4°. **7002**. h. **22**.

BUTLER (Samuel) *the Poet.*

WORKS.

—— The Poetical Works of Samuel Butler . . . From the texts of Dr. Grey and Mr. Thyer. With the life of the author, and notes. [With a portrait.] 3 vol. *Apollo Press: Edinburg,* 1777. 12°. [*Bell's Edition. The Poets of Great Britain, etc.* vol. 31–33.] **1066**. b. **16, 17**.
With additional titlepages, engraved, bearing the imprint: John Bell: London.

—— Poems. 2 vol. *C. Bathurst: London,* 1779. 8°. [*Johnson (Samuel) LL.D. The Works of the English Poets, etc.* vol. 6, 7.] **11601**. c. **4**.

—— The Poems of Samuel Butler. 2 vol. *J. Buckland: London,* 1790. 8°. [*Johnson (S.) LL.D. The Works of the English Poets, etc.* vol. 13, 14.] **237**. d. **13, 14**.

—— The Poetical Works of Samuel Butler. To which is prefixed the life of the author. 1792. *See* Anderson (Robert) *M.D.* A Complete Edition of the Poets of Great Britain. vol. 5. 1793, *etc.* 8°. **11607**. ff. **1/5**.

—— The Works of Samuel Butler . . . With a preface, biographical and critical, by Samuel Johnson . . . and remarks, by J. Aikin. 2 vol. *J. Heath; G. Kearsley: London,* 1803. 12°. **11612**. dg. **21**.
The works of the English Poets with prefaces, biographical and critical, by Samuel Johnson. vol. 10.

—— The Poetical Works of Samuel Butler . . . With the life of the author, by Dr. Johnson . . . Embellished with superb engravings. 2 vol. *C. Cooke: London,* [1804.] 18°. [*Cooke's Pocket Edition of Select British Poets.*] **11613.h.1/35.**
With an additional titlepage to each vol.

—— The Poetical Works of Samuel Butler . . . Collated with the best editions: by Thomas Park. 3 vol. *John Sharpe: London,* 1806. 8°. [*Park (Thomas) F.S.A. The Works of the British Poets, etc.* vol. 5, 6.] **1066**. c. **17, 18**.

BUTLER (Samuel) *the Poet.* [Works.]

—— The Works of Samuel Butler. With a preface, biographical and critical, by Samuel Johnson . . . Re-edited, with new biographical and critical matter, by J. Aikin. 2 vol. *G. Kearsley: London,* 1806. 12°. **11607.** aaa. **1.**

—— The Poems of Samuel Butler. [With the life by Samuel Johnson.] *See* Chalmers (Alexander) *F.S.A.* The Works of the English Poets, *etc.* vol. 8. 1810. 8°. 11613.c.1.

—— The Poetical Works of Samuel Butler . . . Collated with the best editions: by Thomas Park. 3 vol. *Suttaby, Evance & Fox: London,* 1812. 8°. **11607.** a. **3.**
A reissue of the 8° *edition of* 1806.

—— The Poetical Works of Samuel Butler. With a life of the author by Ezekiel Sanford. 2 vol. *Mitchell, Ames & White: Philadelphia,* 1819. 12°. [Sanford (*E.*) *The Works of the British Poets.* vol. 9, 10.] **11602.** a. **5.**

—— The Poems of Samuel Butler. (The life of Samuel Butler by Dr. Johnson.) 2 vol. *C. Whittingham: Chiswick,* 1822. 12°. [*The British Poets, etc.* vol. 21, 22.] **11603.** a. **11.**

—— The Poetical Works of Samuel Butler. (Life of Samuel Butler. By the Rev. John Mitford.) [With a portrait.] 2 vol. *William Pickering: London,* 1835. 8°. [*Aldine Edition of the British Poets.* vol. 33, 34.] **1066.** e. **15.**

—— The Poetical Works of Samuel Butler. Complete edition. 2 pt. ms. notes. *Thomas Johnson: Manchester,* 1848. 16°. **11607.** a. **6.**
With an additional titlepage, engraved.

—— The Poetical Works of Samuel Butler. With life, critical dissertation, and explanatory notes by the Rev. George Gilfillan. 2 vol. *James Nichol: Edinburgh,* 1854. 8°. **11603.** f. **5, 6.**

—— The Poetical Works of Samuel Butler. (Life of Samuel Butler. By the Rev. John Mitford.) 2 vol. *Little, Browne & Co.: Boston,* 1854. 8°. **11607.** bb. **1, 2.**

—— Poetical Works . . . Edited by Robert Bell. 3 vol. *J. W. Parker & Son: London,* 1855. 12°. **11604.** e. **3.**

—— The Poetical Works of Samuel Butler. (Life of Samuel Butler. By the Rev. John Mitford.) [With a portrait.] 2 vol. *Bell & Daldy: London,* 1866. 8°. [*Aldine Edition of the British Poets.*] **2288.** c. **6.**

—— Poetical Works . . . Edited by Robert Bell. 3 vol. *C. Griffin & Co.: London,* [1867.] 12°. **11604.** e. **17–19.**
A reissue of the edition of 1855.

—— The Poetical Works of Samuel Butler. With life and critical dissertation by the Rev. George Gilfillan. The text edited by Charles Cowden Clarke. 2 vol. *Cassell & Co.: London,* [1877, 78.] 8°. **11607.** e. **13.**
A reissue of the Edinburgh edition of 1854.

—— The Poetical Works of Samuel Butler. 2 vol. *Houghton, Mifflin & Co.: Boston,* [1880?] 8°. [*British Poets.*] **11613.** e. **1/8.**
A reissue of the edition of 1854.

—— The Poetical Works of Samuel Butler. A revised edition with memoir and notes by Reginald Brimley Johnson. [With a portrait.] 2 vol. *G. Bell & Sons: London,* 1893. 8°. [*Aldine Edition of the British Poets.*] **11612.** cc. **11.**

BUTLER (Samuel) *the Poet.*

SMALLER COLLECTIONS.

—— Posthumous Works in Prose and Verse . . . [Mainly spurious.] From original mss. and scarce and valuable pieces formerly printed. With a Key to Hudibras, by Sir Roger L'Estrange. [With a portrait.] pp. 279. *R. Smith & G. Strahan: London,* 1715. 12°. **12270.** a. **10.**
Nine of the works have special titlepages, dated 1714.

—— The second edition. (The Second Volume of the Posthumous Works . . . With a Key to the ii. and iii. Parts of Hudibras, by Sir Roger L'Estrange.—The Third and Last Volume of Posthumous Works . . . To which is added, The Coffin for the Good Old Cause. Publish'd just before the Restoration. By Sir Samuel Luke.) 3 vol. *Sam. Briscoe: London,* 1715, 19. 12°. **1066.** a. **5–7.**
Vol. 2 is of the first, vol. 3 of the third edition.

—— The third edition. 3 vol. *Sam. Briscoe: London,* 1715, 17. 12°. **629.** a. **24.**
Vol. 2 and 3 are of the first edition.

—— The fourth edition, with additions. 3 vol. *Sam. Briscoe: London,* 1716, 15, 17. 12°. **1078.** a. **1.**
Vol. 2 is of the third, vol. 3 of the second edition.

—— The sixth edition, with cuts. 3 vol. *Samuel Briscoe: London,* 1720, 19. 12°. **12270.** a. **11.**
Vol. 3 is of the third edition.

—— The fourth edition, corrected. Adorn'd with cuts. pp. 336. *Richard Baldwin: London,* 1732. 12°. **1078.** f. **5.**

—— The sixth edition, corrected. Adorned with cuts. pp. 312. 11. *Richard Baldwin: London,* 1754. 12°. **991.** a. **2.**

—— The Genuine Remains in Verse and Prose of Mr. Samuel Butler . . . Published from the original manuscripts, formerly in the possession of W. Longueville, Esq. With notes by R. Thyer, *etc.* 2 vol. *J. & R. Tonson: London,* 1759. 8°. **991.** l. **10.**

—— [Another copy.] **79.** c. **20, 21.**

—— [Another copy.] G. **19017, 18.**

—— The Genuine Poetical Remains of Samuel Butler. With notes by Robert Thyer . . . With a selection from the author's Characters in prose. Illustrated with humorous wood-cuts, and portraits of Butler and Thyer. pp. 301. **L.P.** *Joseph Booker: London,* 1827. fol. **11609.** l. **1.**

—— Characters and Passages from Note-Books. Edited by A. R. Waller. pp. xii. 490. *University Press: Cambridge,* 1908. 8°. [*Cambridge English Classics.*] **12270.** dd. **6.**

—— Satires, and Miscellaneous Poetry and Prose. Edited by René Lamar. pp. xxi. 503. *University Press: Cambridge,* 1928. 8°. [*Cambridge English Classics.*] **12270.** dd. **17.**

SINGLE WORKS.

—— [Characters.] [With a portrait.] *See* Book. A Book of Characters: selected from the writings of Overbury, Earle and Butler. 1865. 8°. **12354.** aaa. **32.**

—— [A reissue.] *See* Mirror. The Mirror of Character: selected from the writings of Overbury, Earle, and Butler. 1869. 8°. **8403.** ccc. **23.**

—— Cydippe her Answer to Acontius. *See* Ovidius Naso (P.) [*Epistolae Heroïdum.—English.*] Ovid's Epistles translated, *etc.* 1680. 8°. **11352**. df. 3.

—— [Another edition.] *See* Ovidius Naso (P.) [*Epistolae Heroïdum.—English.*] Ovid's Epistles translated, *etc.* 1683. 8°. **1001**. i. 1.

—— [Another edition.] *See* Ovidius Naso (P.) [*Epistolae Heroïdum.—English.*] Ovid's Epistles translated, *etc.* 1701. 8° **1001**. d. 5.

—— [Another edition.] *See* Ovidius Naso (P.) [*Epistolae Heroïdum.—English.*] Ovid's Epistles translated, *etc.* 1705. 8°. **1068**. m. 14.

—— [Another edition.] *See* Ovidius Naso (P.) [*Epistolae Heroïdum.—English.*] Ovid's Epistles translated, *etc.* 1712. 8°. **76**. e. 15.

—— [Another edition.] *See* Ovidius Naso (P.) [*Two or more Works.—English.*] Ovid's Epistles: with his Amours, *etc.* 1725. 12°. **11355**. b. 16.

—— [Another edition.] *See* Ovidius Naso (P.) [*Two or more Works.—English.*] Ovid's Epistles: with his Amours, *etc.* 1729. 12°. **11375**. e. 8.

—— [Another edition.] *See* Ovidius Naso (P.) [*Two or more Works.—English.*] Ovid's Epistles: with his Amours, *etc.* 1761. 12°. **11355**. b. 17.

—— The Elephant in the Moon. *See* Deverell (Robert) Discoveries in Hieroglyphics, *etc.* vol. 1. 1813. 8°. **012330**. h. 1.

—— [Another edition.] *See* Deverell (Robert) Hieroglyphics, and other antiquities, *etc.* vol. 1. 1816. 8°. **959**. f. 12.

—— The Hellish Mysteries of the old Republicans set forth in a Vindication of King Charles the First. *See* infra: The Plagiary exposed, *etc.*

—— Hudribras. The first part. Written in the time of the late Wars. pp. 268. *Printed by J. G. for Richard Marriot: London,* 1663 [1662]. 8°. **239**. f. 33.
Anonymous.

—— [Another edition.] pp. 128. *Printed by J. G. for Richard Marriot,* 1663. 12°. **1078**. f. 30.
Anonymous.

—— [Another edition.] pp. 128. *Printed by J. G. for Richard Marriot: London,* 1663. 12°. **1490**. cc. 45.
Anonymous. Imperfect; wanting the license leaf.

—— [Another edition, unauthorized.] pp. 125. *London,* 1663. 8°. **1078**. f. 15.
Anonymous. With a rose and thistle on the titlepage, and errata on p. 125.

—— [Another copy.] G. **11448**.

—— [Another edition, unauthorized.] pp. 125. *London,* 1663. 8°. **1490**. cc. 44.
Anonymous. With a pattern of type ornaments on the titlepage, 14 *in the top row.*

—— [Another edition, unauthorized.] pp. 125. *London,* 1663. 8°. **11626**. aa. 14. (1.)
Anonymous. With a pattern of fleur de lys type ornaments on the titlepage, 13 *in the top row.*

—— Hudibras. The second part. [A spurious continuation.] 1663. *See* Hudibras.

—— Hudibras. The second part. By the authour of the first. pp. 216. *Printed by T. R. for John Martyn, and James Allestry: London,* 1664 [1663]. 8°. **1077**. d. 62.
Anonymous.

—— [Another edition.] pp. 125. *Printed by T. R. for John Martyn, and James Allestry,* 1664. 8°. **11626**. aa. 14. (2.)
Anonymous.

—— [Another copy.] G. **11449**.
Imperfect; wanting the blank leaf and the license leaf at the beginning.

—— Hudibras. The first and second parts . . . Corrected & amended, with several additions and annotations. pp. 412. *Printed by T. N. for John Martyn & Henry Herringman: London,* 1674. 8°. **11623**. c. 23. (1.)
Anonymous.

—— [Another edition.] pp. 412. *Printed by T. N. for John Martyn and Henry Herringman: London,* 1678. 8°. **11623**. bbb. 4. (1.)
Anonymous.

—— Hudibras. The Third and last Part. Written by the Author of the first and second parts. pp. 285. *Printed for Simon Miller: London,* 1678. 8°. G. **11450**.
Anonymous. Imperfect; wanting the last leaf containing the errata.

—— [Another edition.] pp. 285. *Printed for Simon Miller: London,* 1678. 8°. **11623**. c. 23. (2.)
Anonymous. In this edition the errata have been corrected.

—— [Another edition.] pp. 254. *Printed for Robert Horne: London,* 1679. 8°. **11623**. bbb. 4. (2.)
Anonymous.

—— Hudribras. In three parts. Corrected, with several additions and annotations. pp. 412. 254. *Sold by W. Rogers: London,* 1684. 8°. **11623**. b. 8.
Anonymous. Each part has a separate titlepage. Pt. 1 *bears the imprint: T. N. for Henry Herringman; pt.* 2*: T. H. for T. Sawbridge; pt.* 3*: For Robert Horne.*

—— [Another edition.] Hudibras. The first part, *etc.* pp. 412. 254. *Printed for Henry Herringman, and are to be sold by Tho. Sawbridge: London,* 1689. 8°. **11623**. c. 24.
Anonymous. Pt. 2 *and* 3 *have separate titlepages bearing the imprints: For R. Chiswell, T. Sawbridge, R. Bentley & G. Wells, and For Thomas Horne respectively.*

—— [A reissue.] Hudibras. In three parts, *etc.* *Sold by Richard Parker: London,* 1689. 8°. **1490**. cc. 46.
Anonymous. With a collective titlepage substituted for the title of pt. 1.

—— [Another edition.] Hudibras. The first part, *etc.* pp. 412. 254. *Printed by T. Warren for Henry Herringman, and are to be sold by R. Bentley, J. Tonson, F. Saunders, and T. Bennet: London,* 1694. 8°. **1078**. f. 18.
Anonymous. Pt. 2 *&* 3 *have separate titlepages bearing the imprints: For R. Chiswell, T. Sawbridge, R. Bentley & G. Wells,* 1693 *& For Thomas Horne,* 1694 *respectively.*

—— [Another edition.] Hudibras. The first part, *etc.* pp. 350. 230. *Printed by Tho. Warren for Henry Herringman; sold by Jacob Tonson, and Thomas Bennet: London,* 1700. 8°. **11626**. c. 9.
Anonymous. Pt. 2 *&* 3 *have separate titlepages, bearing the imprints of R. Chiswell, G. Sawbridge, R. Wellington, & G. Wells, and of Thomas Horne respectively.*

—— [Another edition.] 3 pt. *Geo. Sawbridge: London,* 1704. 8°. **11626**. e. **11**.
Pt. 2 and 3 have separate titlepages bearing the imprints of R. Chiswel and Thomas Horne respectively.

—— [Another edition.] 3 pt. *Geo. Sawbridge: London,* 1709. 8°. **11623**. cc. **1**.
Pt. 2 and 3 have separate titlepages bearing the imprints of R. Chiswel and Thomas Horne respectively.

—— [Another edition.] Adorned with cuts. 3 pt. *John Baker: London,* 1710. 12°. **1078**. a. **10**.
The titlepage of pt. 2 bears the date 1709.

—— [Another edition.] To which is added, Annotations to the Third Part, with an exact index to the whole; never before printed. Adorn'd with cuts. pp. xiv. 408. *R. Chiswel: London,* 1710. 12°. **11626**. aa. **1**.

—— [Another edition.] Illustrated with eighteen historical copper cutts, besides the author's effigies, *etc.* 3 pt. *George Sawbridge: London,* 1712. 8°. G. **19016**.
Pt. 2 and 3 have separate titlepages bearing the imprints of R. C. [i.e. R. Chiswell] and Tho. Horne respectively. The text is a reissue of that of the edition of 1709.

—— [Another edition.] Adorn'd with cuts. pp. xiv. 408. *T. Horne: London,* 1716. 12°. **1066**. a. **8**.

—— [Another edition.] pp. xiv. 408. *D. Browne: London,* 1720. 12°. **238**. a. **1**.

—— [Another edition.] Adorn'd with a new set of cuts, design'd and engrav'd by Mr. Hogarth. pp. 424. *D. Browne: London,* 1726. 12°. **1078**. f. **8**.

—— [Another copy, with a different titlepage.] COPIOUS MS. NOTES [by W. Oldys]. *B. Motte: London,* 1726. 12°. **11626**. aaa. **3**.

—— [Another edition.] pp. 385. *R. Gunne & Co.: Dublin,* 1732. 12°. **1347**. c. **19**.

—— [Another copy.] [Hudibras . . . Corrected and amended: with additions, *etc.*] [*R. Gunne & Co.: Dublin,* 1732.] 12°. **11658**. e. **40**.
Imperfect; wanting the titlepage and several plates.

—— [Another edition.] Adorn'd with a new set of cuts, design'd and engrav'd by Mr. Hogarth. pp. 400. *B. Moote* [sic]*: London,* 1732. 12°. **1078**. f. **9**.

—— [Another copy, with a different titlepage.] *Richard Wellington: London,* 1733. 12°. **11623**. aa. **4**.

—— [Another edition.] pp. 400. *D. Midwinter: London,* 1739. 12°. **11626**. aaa. **4**.

—— [Another edition.] Corrected and amended. With large annotations and a preface by Zachary Grey. 2 vol. *Cambridge; W. Innys: London,* 1744. 8°. **991**. l. **5, 6**.

—— [Another copy.] **L.P.** **80**. i. **18**.

—— [Another copy.] **L.P.** **671**. f. **13, 14**.

—— [Another copy.] **L.P.** G. **11580, 81**.

—— Hudibras . . . A new edition, corrected. Adorned with cuts. pp. 431. *R. Urie & Co.: Glasgow,* 1747. 8°. **11630**. aaa. **47**.

—— [Another edition.] pp. 401. *Charles Bathurst: London,* 1750. 12°. **1162**. a. **1**.

—— A new edition, corrected. Adorned with cuts. pp. 431. *R. Urie: Glasgow,* 1753. 12°. **11626**. b. **9**.

—— [Another edition.] 2 vol. *R. & A. Foulis: Glasgow,* 1761. 12°. **11626**. a. **10**.

—— A new edition, adorned with cuts. pp. xi. 358. *Robert Urie: Glasgow,* 1763. 12°. **11623**. aaa. **4**.

—— [Another edition.] With large annotations, and a preface, by Zachary Grey . . . Adorn'd with a new set of cuts. The second edition. 2 vol. *C. Hitch: London,* 1764. 8°. **11631**. f. **48**.

—— [Another edition.] With annotations and a complete index. pp. xii. 357. *James Knox: Glasgow,* 1765. 12°. **11623**. b. **1**.

—— [Another edition.] 2 vol. pp. xiv. 444. *Boulter Grierson: Dublin,* 1766. 8°. **11623**. bb. **6**.

—— [Another edition.] With large annotations by Zachary Grey. 3 vol. *S. Crowder, C. Ware, & T. Payne: London,* 1770. 12°. **11623**. a. **6**.
Imperfect; wanting pp. 49–60 *of vol.* 2.

—— [Another edition.] With large annotations by Zachary Grey. 3 vol. *Martin & Wotherspoon: Edinburgh,* 1770. 12°. **11626**. aa. **2–4**.

—— An accurate edition. pp. 382. *B. Long & T. Pridden: London,* 1773. 12°. **11626**. aaa. **5**.

—— [Another edition.] With annotations. 2 vol. *A. Kincaid & W. Creech; J. Balfour: Edinburgh,* 1773. 8°. [*British Poets.* vol. 5, 6.] **11604**. a. **5, 6**.

—— [Another edition.] With annotations, and a compleat index. 2 vol. *R. & A. Foulis: Glasgow,* 1774. 12°. **238**. a. **21, 22**.

—— [Another edition.] Adorned with cuts, designed and engraved by Mr Hogarth. pp. 401. *C. Bathurst: London,* 1775. 12°. **11632**. de. **7**.

—— [Another edition.] With large annotations and a preface by Zachary Grey. 2 vol. *Bell & Murray: Edinburgh,* 1779. 12°. **11626**. bbb. **6, 7**.

—— [Another edition.] From the text of Zach. Grey. 3 vol *Joseph Wenman: London,* 1781. 12°. **11630**. a. **4**.

—— A new edition. Adorned with cuts. pp. x. 338. *R. Clark, P. Anderson & A. Brown: Edinburgh,* 1784. 12°. **11623**. b. **2**.

—— [Another edition.] [With notes by T. R. Nash and illustrations after Hogarth.] 2 vol. **L.P.** *T. Rickaby: London,* 1793. 4°. **77**. l. **9–11**.
One of an edition of a 100 *copies. The titlepage is engraved.*

—— [Another copy.] **L.P.** **673**. i. **15–17**.

—— [Another copy.] **L.P.** G. **11617–19**.

—— [Another edition.] pp. 304. *A. Wren, G. Hodges & J. Taylor: London,* 1796. 8°. **11632**. df. **32**.

—— Hudibras . . . With large annotations and a preface by Zachary Grey, *etc.* [With plates, including a portrait.] 2 vol. *Vernor & Hood, etc.: London,* 1799. 8°. **11659**. bb. **7**.

—— [A reissue.] Hudibras, *etc.* *London,* 1801. 8°. **991**. l. **7**.

—— [Another edition.] pp. viii. 384. *Vernor & Hood: London,* 1805. 12°. **11630. a. 27.**

—— [Another edition.] Corrected and amended. With large annotations, and preface, by Zachary Grey . . . Embellished with engravings, by T. Rowlandson [from designs by Hogarth]. 2 vol. *Thomas Tegg: London,* 1810. 8°. **C.116.b.26.**

—— [Another edition.] pp. viii. 386. *Vernor, Hood & Sharpe: London,* 1811. 12°. **11626. aaa. 7.**

—— A new edition, with a life of the author, a preliminary discourse on the Civil War, &c. & new notes & illustrations. 2 vol. *Suttaby, Evance & Fox; Crosby & Co.: London,* 1812. 12°. **12206. aa. 3, 4.**
The titlepages are engraved.

—— [Another edition.] *See* DEVERELL (Robert) Discoveries in Hieroglyphics, *etc.* vol. 1. 1813. 8°. **012330. h. 1.**

—— [Another edition.] *See* DEVERELL (Robert) Hieroglyphics, and other antiquities, *etc.* vol. 1. 1816. 8°. **959. f. 12.**

—— [Another edition.] 2 vol. *C. Whittingham: Chiswick,* 1818. 12°. **11640. f. 30.**

—— [Another edition.] With notes, selected from Grey and other authors: to which are prefixed, a life of the author, and a preliminary discourse on the Civil War, &c. . . . A new edition, embellished with engravings. 2 vol. *Thomas M'Lean: London,* 1819. 8°. **C. 72. c. 7.**
The illustrations are coloured.

—— [Another edition.] With Dr Grey's annotations. A new edition, corrected and enlarged. 3 vol. *C. & H. Baldwyn: London,* 1819. 8°. **11626. f. 33.**

—— [Another edition.] With historical, biographical, and explanatory notes, selected from Grey & other authors. To which are prefixed, a life of the author, and a preliminary discourse on the Civil War. A new edition, embellished with twelve engravings. 2 vol. *Akerman: London,* 1822. 8°. **11623. f. 1, 2.**
The illustrations are coloured.

—— [Another edition.] With a biographical sketch of the author. pp. viii. 261. *W. S. Orr & Co.: London,* [1825?] 32°. **11630. a. 52.**

—— [Another edition.] With a life of the author, annotations, and an index. MS. NOTES. *J. F. Dove: London,* 1826. 12°. **11623. a. 7.**

—— [Another edition.] pp. viii. 319. *Printed by C. & C. Whittingham; sold by Thomas Tegg: London,* 1828. 12°. **1066. a. 58.**

—— [Another edition.] With notes by the Rev. Treadway Russell Nash . . . A new edition. 2 vol. *John Murray: London,* 1835. 8°. **991. l. 9.**

—— Hudibras . . . With notes and a literary memoir by . . . Treadway Russel Nash, *etc.* [With portraits.] pp. 498. *D. Appleton: New York; G. S. Appleton: Philadelphia,* 1850. 8°. **11660. aa. 5.**

—— [Another edition.] pp. 72. *See* BRITISH POETS. Cabinet Edition of the British Poets. vol. 2. 1851. 8°. **2504. o. 1.**

—— [Another edition.] With biographical and critical notices, edited by Ludwig Gantter. pp. 360. *Stuttgart,* 1854. 8°. [GANTTER (L.) *The Standard Poets of Great Britain, etc.* no. 7, 9, 11.] **11602. b. 17.**

—— [Another edition.] With a biographical sketch of the author. pp. viii. 261. *T. Nelson & Sons: London,* 1855. 32°. **11601. a. 5.**

—— [Another edition.] With variorum notes, selected principally from Grey and Nash. Edited by Henry G. Bohn . . . With sixty-two additional portraits. 2 vol. pp. xxiv. 472. *London,* 1859. 8°. [*Bohn's Illustrated Library.*] **2502. b. 8.**

—— [Another edition.] With notes and life of the author. pp. 410. *William Tegg: London,* 1864. 16°. **11626. aa. 7.**

—— [A reissue.] *London,* 1866. 16°. **11631. a. 10.**

—— Reprint of edition of 1779. [Edited by Alexander Murray.] pp. 159. *A. Murray & Son: London,* 1869. 8°. **11626. bbb. 8.**

—— Hudibras . . . With notes and preface, by Zachary Grey. pp. 331. *F. Warne & Co.: London,* [1871.] 8°. [*Chandos Classics.*] **12204. ff. 1/60.**

—— [Another edition.] Edited by Alfred Milnes. 2 vol. *Macmillan & Co.: London,* 1881, 83. 8°. **11626. bbb. 18.**

—— [Another edition.] pp. 286. *G. Routledge & Sons: London,* 1885. 8°. [*Morley's Universal Library.* vol. 22.] **12204.gg.1/22.**

—— [Another edition.] With an introductory note by T. W. H. Crosland. pp. xi. 418. *Greening & Co.: London,* 1903. 8°. **11630. bb. 27.**

—— [Another edition.] The text edited by A. R. Waller. pp. viii. 335. *University Press: Cambridge,* 1905. 8°. [*Cambridge English Classics.*] **12270. dd. 7.**

—— Hudibras . . . Adorned with cuts. (Hudibras. Poëme . . . traduit en vers françois [by J. Townley], avec des remarques [by P. H. Larcher] & des figures [by Hogarth].) *Eng. & Fr.* 3 tom. *London* [*Paris*], 1757. 12°. **1078. f. 2–4.**

—— [Another copy.] **238. c. 5–7.**

—— [Another copy.] **G. 18928–30.**

—— Second edition. *Eng. & Fr.* 3 vol. *London* [*Paris*], 1819. 12°. **11626. aaa. 8–10.**

—— Samuel Butlers Hudibras, ein satyrisches Gedicht wider die Schwermer und Independenten zur zeit Carls des Ersten, in neun Gesängen . . . Mit historischen Anmerkungen und Kupfern versehen. [Translated by Johann Heinrich Waser.] pp. xix. 528. *Hamburg und Leipzig,* 1765. 8°. **11623. c. 7.**

—— Hudibras, frey verteutscht, dem Herrn Hofrath Wieland zugeeignet von D. W. S. [i.e. D. W. Soltau.] pp. 444. *Riga,* 1787. 8°. **1078. f. 25.**

—— Butlers Hudibras. Frey übersetzt von Dietrich Wilhelm Soltau. pp. viii. 464. *Königsberg,* 1798. 8°. **11642. g. 49**

—— Samuel Butlers Hudibras. Ein schalkhaftes Heldengedicht. Im Versmasse des Originals frei verdeutschet von Josua Eiselein. [With plates.] pp. 362. *Freiburg i. B.,* 1846. 8°. **1078. f. 27.**

—— The Priviledge of our Saints in the business of Perjury. Useful for Grand-Juries. By the author of Hudibras [i.e. S. Butler]. [An extract from "Hudibras."] 1681. *s. sh.* fol. *See* PRIVILEGE. **162. m. 70. (5.)**

—— Speak Truth and Shame the Devil. In a dialogue between his cloven-footed Highness, of Sulphurious Memory, and an Occasional Conformist, *etc.* [A passage from "Hudibras," part 3, canto 1.] pp. 4. 1708. 4°. *See* TRUTH. **164. m. 45.**

—— *See* BÜELER (S.) J. H. Waser . . . als Übersetzer des "Hudibras" von S. Butler, *etc.* [1936.] 8°. **11861. e. 48.**

—— *See* GREY (Zachary) Critical, Historical, and Explanatory Notes upon Hudibras, by way of supplement to the two editions published in 1744, and 1745 . . . To which is prefixed, a Dissertation upon burlesque poetry. By the late . . . Montagu Bacon . . . And an appendix added; in which is a translation of part of the first canto of the first book into Latin doggrel. 1752. 8°. **1077. k. 47.**

—— *See* HUDIBRAS. A Continuation of Hudibras in two cantos. Written in the time of the unhappy contest between Great Britain and America, in 1777 and 1778. [By Joseph Peart.] 1778. 8°. **1078. f. 23.**

—— *See* HUDIBRAS. Hudibras. The Second Part. [A spurious continuation.] 1663. 8°. **1078. a. 23.**

—— —— 1663. 8°. **11623. aa. 16.**

—— —— 1663. 8°. **G.11452.**

—— *See* HUDIBRAS. Hudibras in Ireland; a burlesque on the late holy wars in the sister kingdom. [1825?] 12°. **3942. a. 54. (1.)**

—— *See* HUDIBRAS. Hudibras Redivivus: or, a Burlesque poem on the times. [By Edward Ward.] 1705, *etc.* 4°. **G.18957.**

—— ——·1708. 4°. **11631. e. 31**

—— —— 1709. 4°. **11631 bb. 17.**

—— *See* HUDIBRAS. The Modern Hudibras, *etc.* 1831. 8°. **T. 1359. (5.)**

—— *See* HUDIBRAS. Vulgus Britannicus: or, the British Hudibrass. 1710. 8°. **11631. d. 28.**

—— *See* P., N. Weighley, alias Wild. A poem, in imitation of Hudibras, *etc.* 1725. 8°. **11716. aa. 30.**

—— *See* RICHARDS (Edward A.) Hudibras in the Burlesque Tradition. 1937. 8°. [*Columbia University Studies in English and Comparative Literature.* no. 127.] **Ac. 2688/16. (68.)**

—— *See* TRUE DE CASE. Hudibras Answered by True de Case, in his own poem and language. [1674.] *s. sh.* fol. **Lutt. II. 99.**

—— Butler's Ghost: or, Hudibras. The fourth part. With reflections upon these times. [The dedication signed: T. D., i.e. Thomas D'Urfey.] 1682. 8°. *See* D., T. **11623. c. 12.**

—— Illustrations of Hudibras: sixty portraits of celebrated political and literary characters, impostors, and enthusiasts, alluded to by Butler in his Hudibras. *C. & H. Baldwyn: London,* 1821. 8°. **1267. d. 8.**

—— King Charles's Case truly stated, *etc.* *See* infra: The Plagiary exposed, *etc.*

BUTLER (SAMUEL) *the Poet.* [SINGLE WORKS.]

—— Mercurius Menippeus. The Loyal Satyrist, or, Hudibras in prose. Written by an unknown hand in the time of the late Rebellion. But never till now published. [By S. Butler.] pp. 24. 1682. 4°. *See* MERCURIUS, *Menippeus.* **8122. d. 72.**

—— [Another edition.] 1812. 4°. [SOMERS (*John*) *Baron Somers. A Collection of Scarce and Valuable Tracts, etc.* vol. 7.] *See* MERCURIUS, *Menippeus.* **750.g.7.**

—— Mola Asinaria . . . By William Prynne . . . Wherein is demonstrated what slavery the Nation must subject itself to, by allowing the lawfulness and usurped authority of the pretended Long Parliament now unlawfully and violently held at Westminster. [A satire on Prynne. By S. Butler.] pp. 6. 1659. 4°. *See* PRYNNE (William) **E. 985. (4.)**

—— The Plagiary exposed: or an Old answer to a newly revived calumny against the memory of King Charles I. Being a reply to a book entitled King Charles's Case, formerly written by John Cook of Gray's Inn, Barrister; and since copied out under the title of Collonel Ludlow's Letter. pp. 20. *For Tho. Bennet: London,* 1691. 4°. **E. 1969. (9.)**

—— [Another edition.] A Vindication of the Royal Martyr King Charles I. Wherein are laid open, the Republican mysteries of Rebellion. Written in the time of the usurpation. *See* LONDON.—III. *Calves-Head Club.* The Secret History of the Calves-Head Club, *etc.* 1705. 8°. **1089. g. 30.**

—— [Another edition.] The Plagiary exposed, *etc.* *See* LONDON.—III. *Calves-Head Club.* The Secret History of the Calves-Head Club, *etc.* 1705. 4°. **110. d. 33. (2.)**

—— [Another edition.] *See* LONDON.—III. *Calves-Head Club.* The Secret History of the Calves-Head Club, *etc.* 1706. 8°. **8122. aaa. 14.**

—— [Another edition.] *See* LONDON.—III. *Calves-Head Club.* The Secret History of the Calves-Head Club, *etc.* 1707. 8°. **G. 4696.**

—— [Another edition.] *See* LONDON.—III. *Calves-Head Club.* The Secret History of the Calves-Head Club, *etc.* 1709. 8°. **808. d. 23.**

—— [Another edition.] *See* LONDON.—III. *Calves-Head Club.* The Whigs Unmasked: being the Secret History of the Calf's-Head-Club, *etc.* 1713. 8°. **G. 4695.**

—— [Another edition.] The Hellish Mysteries of the old Republicans, set forth in vindication of King Charles the First. *See* LONDON.—III. *Calves-Head Club.* The Whigs Unmask'd: or, the History of the Calf's-Head-Club further exposed, *etc.* 1714. 8°. **292. f. 17.**

—— [Another edition.] King Charles's Case truly stated: in answer to Mr Cook's pretended Case of that Blessed Martyr. *See* SOMERS (John) *Baron Somers.* A Collection of Scarce and Valuable Tracts, *etc.* vol. 4. 1748. 4°. **184. a. 4.**

—— [Another edition.] 1811. *See* SOMERS (John) *Baron Somers.* A Collection of Scarce and Valuable Tracts, *etc.* vol. 5. 1809, *etc.* 4°. **750. g. 5.**

—— To the Memory of the Most Renowned Du-Vall: a pindarick ode. By the Author of Hudibras [i.e. S. Butler]. pp. 13. 1671. 4°. *See* DUVAL (Claude) *Highwayman.* **993. e. 43**

BUTLER (Samuel) *the Poet.* [Single Works.]

—— A True and perfect copy of the Lord Roos His Answer to the Marquesse of Dorchester's Letter written the 25 of February 1659. [By S. Butler.] [1660.] *s. sh.* fol. *See* Manners (John) 1*st Duke of Rutland.* **669. f. 24. (22.)**

—— [Another copy.] **190. g. 13. (371.)**

—— [Another edition.] 1660. 4°. [*The Lord Marquesse of Dorchester's Letter to the Lord Roos, etc.*] *See* Manners (John) 1*st Duke of Rutland.* G. **2032.**

—— Two Letters, one from John Audland a Quaker, to William Prynne. The other, William Prynnes Answer. By the author of Hudibras [i.e. S. Butler]. pp. 12. 1672. fol. *See* Audland (J.) **4139.** h. **1.**

—— [Another copy.] **515.** l. **18. (20.)**

DOUBTFUL OR SUPPOSITITIOUS WORKS.

—— The Acts and Monuments of our late Parliament: or, a Collection of the Acts, Orders, Votes, and Resolves that have passed in the House. By S. Butler, author of Hudibras. 1745. *See* Harleian Miscellany. The Harleian Miscellany, *etc.* vol. 5. 1744, *etc.* 4°. **185. a. 9.**

—— [Another edition.] 1810. *See* Harleian Miscellany. The Harleian Miscellany, *etc.* vol. 5. 1808, *etc.* 4°. **2072.g.**

—— [Another edition.] 1810. *See* Harleian Miscellany. The Harleian Miscellany, *etc.* vol. 7. 1808, *etc.* 8°. **1326. g. 7.**

—— His Epitaph. By the celebrated Mr. Butler. [Wrongly attributed to Butler.] *See* Charles I., *King of Great Britain and Ireland.* [*Biography.*—I.] A Comprehensive, tho' Compendious Character of the late Royal Martyr, *etc.* [1670?] *s. sh.* fol. **105. f. 17. (30.)**

—— Hudibras on Calamy's Imprisonment, and Wild's Poetry. To the Bishops. [In verse. Wrongly attributed to S. Butler.] [1663.] *s. sh.* fol. *See* Hudibras. Lutt. ii. **28.**

—— [Another copy.] C **20. f. 2. (84.)**

—— [Another edition.] By Mr. Butler, author of Hudibras. An Epistle to the Bishops, on Calamy's being released from Imprisonment, and Wild's Poetry. *See* Villiers (George) 2*nd Duke of Buckingham.* Miscellaneous Works, *etc.* 1704. 8°. **1085. k. 28.**

—— *See* Ralpho. Your Servant Sir, or Ralpho to Hudibras descanting on Wild's Poetry. [1663.] *s. sh.* fol. Lutt. ii. **248.**

—— *See* Wild (Robert) *D.D.* On the Answer to Dr. Wild's Poem upon Mr. Calamy's Imprisonment. [A reply to "Hudibras on Calamy's Imprisonment, and Wild's Poetry." In verse.] 1663. *s. sh.* fol. Lutt. ii. **26.**

—— A Letter from Mercurius Civicus to Mercurius Rusticus: or, Londons confession but not repentance. Shewing. that the beginning and the obstinate pursuance of this accursed horrid rebellion is principally to be ascribed to that rebellious city. By S. Butler. [Wrongly attributed to Butler.] *See* Somers (John) *Baron Somers.* A Second Collection of Scarce and Valuable Tracts, *etc.* vol. 1. 1750. 4°. **184. a. 5.**

BUTLER (Samuel) *the Poet.* [Doubtful or Supposititious Works.]

—— [Another edition.] 1810. *See* Somers (John) *Baron Somers.* A Collection of Scarce and Valuable Tracts, *etc.* vol. 4. 1809, *etc.* 4°. **750. g. 4.**

—— The Morning's Salutation: or, a Friendly conference between a Puritan Preacher and a family of his flock, upon the 30th of January. By Mr. Butler, author of Hudibras. [Wrongly attributed to Butler.] pp. 8. *Daniel Tompson: Dublin,* 1714. 8°. **11631. a. 63. (11.)**

—— A Proposal humbly offered for the Farming of Liberty of Conscience . . . By the author of Hudibrass. [Wrongly attributed to Butler.] 1682. 4°. [*Wit and Loyalty reviv'd in a collection of some smart satyrs in verse and prose on the late times.*] *See* Proposal. **11626. ee. 31.**

—— [Another edition.] 1811. *See* Somers (John) *Baron Somers.* A Collection of Scarce and Valuable Tracts, *etc.* vol. 5. 1809, *etc.* 4°. **750. g. 5.**

—— A Satyr against Marriage. By Mr. Butler, the author of Hudibras. [Wrongly attributed to Butler.] *See* Grove. The Grove; or, a Collection of original poems, *etc.* 1721. 8°. **992. k. 9. (2.)**

APPENDIX.

—— *See* De Beer (Esmond S.) The Later Life of Samuel Butler, *etc.* [1928.] 8°. **10859. cc. 7.**

—— *See* Gibson (Dan) Samuel Butler. 1933. 8°. [*Shafer (Robert) Seventeenth Century Studies.*] **Ac. 2685. gc.**

—— *See* Ramsay (Alexander) *Miscellaneous Writer.* Samuel Butler and his Hudibras and other works. 1846. 12°. **1156. c. 25. (1.)**

—— *See* Smith (William Francis) *Fellow of St. John's College, Cambridge.* Samuel Butler. 1912. 8°. [*Cambridge History of English Literature.* vol. 8.] **11870.g.1.**

—— *See* Veldkamp (Jan) Samuel Butler, the Author of Hudibras, *etc.* [1924.] 8°. **011851. dd. 69.**

BUTLER (Samuel) *Printer.* Butler's Altrincham Business Guide, *etc.* *See* Ephemerides.

—— Butler's Illustrated Guide to Bowdon and its environs. (Second edition.) pp. viii. 24. *Samuel Butler: Altrincham,* [1901.] 8°. **010347. f. 9. (5.)**

—— (Third edition.) pp. 24. *Samuel Butler: Altrincham,* [1903.] 8°. **10369. ccc. 43.**

BUTLER (Samuel) *Settler in Australia.* A Complete Guide to Canada. The emigrant's hand-book of facts, with directions how to proceed in his arrangements . . . New edition. pp. 106. *W. R. M'Phun: Glasgow & London,* 1858. 16°. **10470. a. 29.**

—— The Emigrant's Hand-book of Facts, concerning Canada, New Zealand, Australia, Cape of Good Hope, &c.; with the relative advantages each of the colonies offers for emigration, and practical advice to intending emigrants. pp. xii. 240. *W. R. M'Phun: Glasgow,* 1843. 12°. **798. c. 24.**

—— The Gold Regions of Australia. Who ought to go to the diggings, and who ought to remain at home. A complete guide to the diggings of New South Wales, being a supplement to Butler's celebrated "Emigrant's Complete Guide to Australia." pp. vi. 66. *W. R. M'Phun: Glasgow,* 1858. 12°. **10491. a. 10.**

BUTLER (Samuel) *Settler in Australia.*

—— The Hand-Book for Australian Emigrants; being a descriptive history of Australia, and containing an account of the climate, soil and natural productions of New South Wales, South Australia, and Swan River Settlement, *etc.* pp. viii. 240. *W. R. M'Phun: Glasgow,* 1839. 12°. **798.** c. **7.**

—— [Another edition.] The Australian Emigrant's Complete Guide . . . New edition. *W. R. M'Phun: Glasgow,* 1849. 12°. **10492.** a. **6.**

—— New edition. *W. R. M'Phun: Glasgow,* 1858. 12°. **10491.** a. **41.**

BUTLER (Samuel Worcester) *See* Periodical Publications.—*Philadelphia.* The Medical and Surgical Reporter. Edited by S. W. Butler, *etc.* 1859, *etc.* 8°. P.P. **2894.** h.

BUTLER (*Hon.* Simon) *See* Ireland.—*Parliament.*—ii. *House of Lords.* House of Lords. Friday, March 1st, 1793. [Proceedings against the Hon. Simon Butler for a libel on the House of Lords.] [1793.] fol. **8223.** e. **1.** (**5.**)

BUTLER (Slade) *See* Egan (Charles) *Barrister-at-Law.* A Practical Treatise on the Law of Bills of Sale . . . Third edition, comprising the Bills of Sale Act, 1878, the latest cases, and additional precedents and forms. By S. Butler. 1879. 12°. **6325.** de. **8.**

—— —— 1882. 12°. **6405.** aaa. **35.**

—— The Weights and Measures Act, 1878, 41 & 42 Vict., chap. 49. Including a practical summary of the Act, with notes and cases . . . Also the Bread Act, 1836, 6 & 7 Will. 4, chap. 37, so far as it relates to weights and measures. By S. Butler. pp. iv. 178. *Shaw & Sons: London,* 1879. 12°. **6426.** aaa. **29.**

BUTLER (Smedley Darlington) *See* Thomas (Lowell J.) Old Gimlet Eye. The adventures of S. D. Butler, *etc.* [1933.] 8°. **010885.** eee. **29.**

BUTLER (*Sir* Spencer Harcourt) *G.C.S.I.* India Insistent. pp. viii. 117. *William Heinemann: London,* 1931. 8°. **20016.** a. **9.**

—— Speeches by Sir Spencer Harcourt Butler, Lieutenant-Governor, Burma, 1915–1917. pp. viii. 177. [*Rangoon,*] 1918. 8°. I.S. Bu. **119/23.**

BUTLER (Spencer Perceval) The Causes of the Turkish Invasion of Europe. An essay which obtained the Le Bas Prize for the year 1853. pp. 32. *John Deighton: Cambridge,* 1853. 8°. **8032.** f. **14.**

BUTLER (Stephen) A Practical Essay on the use of Salt as Manure; with the method of preparing it for that purpose and instructions for its application, either for agricultural or horticultural purposes, *etc.* pp. 84. *Hodgson & Co.: London,* 1823. 12°. **966.** h. **25.**

BUTLER (Suzanne Louise)

—— My Pride, my Folly. [A novel.] pp. 254. *Hodder & Stoughton: London,* 1953. 8°. NNN. **4500.**

—— Vale of Tyranny. pp. 252. *Hodder & Stoughton: London,* 1954. 8°. NNN. **5517.**

BUTLER (Sydney T.) Voice-Production for School-Teachers. pp. 36. *Vincent Music Co.: London,* [1907.] 8°. **7899.** aaaa. **26.**

BUTLER (T. C.)

—— *See* Peltier (M.) [Attaché naval á Moscou.] Soviet Encounter. (Translated by T. C. Butler.) 1955. 8°. **10666.** e. **10.**

BUTLER (Thaddeus J.) The Catholic Church in America. A lecture, *etc.* pp. 39. *W. B. Kelly: Dublin,* 1869. 8°. **4183.** aaa. **84.** (**5.**)

BUTLER (Theobald) *B.A., late Modern Language Lecturer in Germany.* Boche Land before and during the War. pp. 205. *William Heinemann: London,* 1916. 8°. **10255.** de. **16.**

BUTLER (Theobald) *of Galway.* Theobald Butler, Appell^nt^. Dame Penelope Prendergast, and others, Resp^ts^. The Appellants case. pp. 4. [*London,* 1720.] fol. **19.** h. **1.** (**168.**)

—— Theobald Butler, Appell^t^. Sir Thomas Prendergast et al', Resp^ts^. The Respondents case. pp. 4. [*London,* 1720.] fol. **19.** h. **1.** (**169.**)

BUTLER (Theobald Fitzwalter) *Baron Dunboyne.*

—— *See* England.—*Parliament.*—*House of Lords.* [*Proceedings.*—ii.] Minutes of Evidence taken before the Committee for Privileges to whom were referred the petition of . . . T. F. Butler, Lord Baron of Dunboyne . . . praying Her Majesty, that the said title . . . of Lord Baron of Dunboyne . . . may be declared . . . to be now vested in the petitioner, *etc.* [1860.] fol. **6497.** dd. **12.** (**6.**)

BUTLER (Theobald Richard Fitzwalter)

—— *See* Archbold (John F.) Archbold's Pleading, Evidence & Practice in Criminal Cases . . . The thirty-first edition. By T. R. F. Butler . . . and M. Garsia. 1943. 8°. **6283.** bb. **6.**

—— *See* Archbold (John F.) Archbold's Pleading, Evidence & Practice in Criminal Cases . . . Thirty-second edition. By T. R. F. Butler . . . and M. Garsia. 1949. 4°. **6283.aaa.2.**

—— *See* Archbold (John F.) Archbold's Pleading, Evidence & Practice in Criminal Cases. Thirty-third edition. By T. R. F. Butler . . . and M. Garsia. 1954. 8°. **6060.k.4.**

—— *See* Cohen (Herman J.) The Criminal Appeal Reports, *etc.* (vol. 23. Edited by H. Cohen and T. R. F. Butler. vol. 24, *etc.* Edited by T. R. F. Butler.) 1909, *etc.* 8°. **6495.** dd.

BUTLER (Theophilus) *Baron of Newtown-Butler.*

—— An Elegy on the much Lamented Death of My Lord New Town Butler, who departed this life the tenth of this instant March, 1724. [*Dublin,* 1724.] *s. sh.* fol. **1871.** e. **2.** (**72.**)

BUTLER (Thomas) *Baron Cahir.* Thomas Lord Baron of Caher in Ireland, Appellant. Catherine Nagle, and others, Respondents. The Appellants case. pp. 4. [*London,* 1717.] fol. **19.** h. **1.** (**59.**)

—— Lord Caher . . . Appellant. Nagle and others, Respondents. The Respondents case. pp. 3. [*London,* 1717.] fol. **19.** h. **1.** (**60.**)

BUTLER (Thomas) *Bookseller.* The Case of Thomas Butler, bookseller and stationer in Pall-Mall, London, who was most cruelly treated at New-Market, October 6, 1753. In a letter to the Honourable * * * * *, *etc.* pp. 32. *London,* 1754. 8°. **1132.** f. **36.**

BUTLER (Thomas) *Captain, Puritan.* The Little Bible of the Man, or the Book of God opened in man by the power of the Lamb. Wherein God is the Spirit or in-side of the Book, and Man the Letter or out-side of it, *etc.* pp. 298. *Giles Calvert: London,* 1649. 8°. E. **1260.** (**2.**)

BUTLER (Thomas) *Captain, Royalist.* The Apprehending of Captayne Butler at Portchmouth . . . and his followers, who were bound with bullets and ammunition for Ireland . . . As also the true relation of a terrible Sea fight by the States of Holland, against a Fleet of the Spannish being furnished with men and ammonition for assistance to the Rebels in Irland, *etc.* pp. 6. *Printed for F. C. & T. B.: London,* 1641. 4°. E. **137.** (**18.**)

—— [Another copy.] G. **4155.** (**28.**)

—— The Examination and Confession of Captain Butler before the Committee, the said Captain answering for them all. *See* Henrietta Maria, *Queen Consort of Charles I., etc.* The Queens Majesties Gracious Answer to the Lord Digbies Letter, *etc.* [1642.] 8°. E. **138.** (**8.**)

BUTLER (Thomas) *D.D.*

—— *See* Aliquis. The Knights of the Hermitage; or, the Fearful combat of Sir Dominic Ritual and Sir Paul Testbook . . . In answer to a letter . . . from a minister of the papal communion (T. Butler), *etc.* [1832.] 12°. **1116.** b. **15.**

—— *See* Baylee (Joseph) Lecture on Transubstantiation, in answer to Dr. Butler, *etc.* [1841.] 8°. **3939.** e. **2.** (**7.**

—— The Immaculate Conception. pp. 27. *J. Miller: London,* 1855. 8°. **3940.** de. **4.** (**10.**)

—— Practical and Doctrinal Scripture Truths. pp. 312. *J. F. Shaw: London,* 1860. 12°. **4464.** f. **9.**

—— The Truths of the Catholic Religion proved from Scripture alone. 2 vol. *Booker & Dolman: London,* 1838, 41. 12°. **1119.** e. **30.**
Vol. 2 is of the second edition.

BUTLER (Thomas) *10th Earl of Ormonde.* *See* MacCraith (Flann) Panegyric on Thomas Butler, the tenth Earl of Ormonde, *etc.* 1853. 8°. **11595.** e. **21.** (**5.**)

—— *See* Meara (D. de) Ormonius: siue, Illustrissimi herois ac domini, D. Thomæ Butleri, Ormoniæ & Osoriæ Comitis . . . prosapia, *etc.* 1615. 12°. **1213.** g. **14.**

BUTLER (Thomas) *Earl of Ossory, son of James, 1st Duke of Ormonde.* *See* Flatman (Thomas) On the Death of the Right Honourable Thomas Earl of Ossory. Pindariq' Ode. 1680. fol. **807.** g. **5.** (**11.**)

—— —— 1681. fol. **162.** m. **41.**

—— A Brief Compendium of the Birth, Education, Heroick Exploits and Victories of . . . Thomas Earl of Ossory . . . who died in the preparation of his voiag [*sic*] to the relief of Tangiers, on the 30th of July 1680., *etc.* pp. 4. [*London,* 1680.] fol. T. **3*.** (**53.**)

—— An Elegy to the Memory of the Right Houourable [*sic*] Thomas Earl of Ossory, who depated [*sic*] this Life, July the 30th, 1680. [*London,* 1680.] *s. sh.* fol. C. **20.** f. **2.** (**130.**)

—— [Another copy.] Lutt. I. **109.**

BUTLER (Thomas) *Earl of Ossory, son of James, 1st Duke of Ormonde.*

—— An Ode in imitation of Pindar on the Death of the Right Honourable Thomas Earl of Ossory. By K. C. 1681. *s. sh.* fol. *See* C., K. **163.** n. **46.**

—— To the Right Honourable Thomas Earl of Ossory, Rear Admiral of the Blew Squadron, on his unexampled courage and gallantry as well in former actions as in the late engagement of the 11th of August 1673. [In verse.] [*London,* 1673.] *s. sh.* fol. Lutt. I. **110.**

BUTLER (Thomas) *M.D.*

—— A Safe, Easy, and Expeditious Method of procuring any Quantity of Fresh Water at Sea; by a menstruum entirely innocent and inoffensive, *etc.* pp. 43. *Printed for the Author: London,* 1755. 8°. **7511.** ee. **7.** (**6.**)

BUTLER (Thomas) *of Frittenden, Kent.* Notes of a Sermon preached at Staplehurst . . . after Mr. I. Lewes' [*sic*] funeral. *See* Lewis (Isaac) *Baptist Minister of Staplehurst, Kent.* A Memorial of the late Mr. Isaac Lewis, *etc.* 1896. 8°. **4907.** eee. **18.**

BUTLER (Thomas) *of Sydney.* Memoir of Professor Badham. *See* Badham (Charles) *D.D., etc.* Speeches and Lectures delivered in Australia. 1890. 8°. **12301.** g. **67.**

BUTLER (Thomas) *of the British Museum.* *See* Butler (Annie R.) Nearly a Hundred Years ago . . . With . . . portraits. [A biography of T. Butler.] [1907.] 8°. **4902.** aaaa. **4.**

—— All Alone! (To my Brother.) [In verse.] [*London,* 1873.] *s. sh.* 8°. **806.** k. **16.** (**121.**)

—— The Rencontre. (On the death of a young lady.—Penitence.) [In verse.] [*London,* 1873.] *s. sh.* 8°. **806.** k. **16.** (**121*.**)

BUTLER (Thomas) *Rector of Langar.* *See* Butler (Samuel) *Bishop of Lichfield and Coventry.* A Sketch of Modern and Antient Geography . . . By S. Butler . . . A new edition, revised by his son [T. Butler]. 1842. 8°. **571.** f. **28.**

—— —— 1851. 8°. **10002.** e. **22.**

—— *See* Butler (Samuel) *Bishop of Lichfield and Coventry.* A Sketch of Antient Geography . . . A new edition, revised by the Rev. T. Butler. 1855. 12°. **10005.** b. **5.**

—— *See* Butler (Samuel) *Bishop of Lichfield and Coventry.* A Sketch of Modern Geography . . . A new edition, revised by the Rev. T. Butler. 1855. 12°. **10005.** b. **6.**

—— —— 1862. 12°. **10005.** b. **4.**

—— —— 1872. 8°. **10003.** bbb. **39.**

—— A Sermon preached in the Parish Church of Meole Brace . . . on occasion of the death of the Venerable Edward Bather . . . Archdeacon of Salop, *etc.* pp. 20. *Sandford & Howell: Shrewsbury,* [1847.] 8°. **4906.** f. **26.** (**3.**)

BUTLER (Thomas) *Rev., of Mary Street.* A Faint Ray of Glorious Liberty; or, a Feeble attempt to display the exalted privileges . . . in which the subjects of the Kingdom of Heaven are called to participate, under the charter of the Gospel. pp. vii. 170. *J. Hatchard: London,* 1819. 8°. **702.** h. **11.** (**7.**)

BUTLER (*Mrs.* THOMAS) *See* BUTLER (Rosa K.)

BUTLER (*Sir* THOMAS) Extracts from the Register of Sir Thomas Butler, Vicar of Much Wenlock, in Shropshire [1538–1562] . . . By the Rev. Charles Henry Hartshorne. Reprinted from the "Cambrian Journal," *etc.* pp. 20. *R. Mason: Tenby,* 1861. 8°. **9510. f. 21.**

BUTLER (THOMAS BELDEN) A Concise Analytical and Logical Development of the Atmospheric System, and of the Elements of Prognostication, by which the weather may be forecasted . . . Revised edition. pp. 403. *Andrew Selleck: Norwalk, Conn.,* 1870. 8°. **8755. bbb. 47.**

—— The Philosophy of the Weather, and a guide to its changes. pp. xviii. 414. *D. Appleton & Co.: New York,* 1856. 12°. **8755. b. 21.**

BUTLER (THOMAS HARRISON) Bubonic Plague. With special reference to the epidemic in South Africa in 1901. A thesis, *etc.* pp. 88. *Printed for private circulation: London,* 1902. 8°. **07561. h. 24.**

—— Cruising Yachts: design and performance. [With a portrait.] pp. 143. *R. Ross & Co.: London,* 1945. 8°. **8804. aaa. 18.**

—— An Illustrated Guide to the Slit-Lamp. pp. xiii. 144. pl. v. *Humphrey Milford: London,* 1927. 4°. [*Oxford Medical Publications.*] **20036.a 1/490**

BUTLER (THOMAS HOWARD)

—— The History of Wm. Butler & Co., Bristol, Ltd., 1843 to 1943. [With illustrations.] pp. 92. 1954. 4°. *See* BUTLER (William) AND Co. **8207. m. 15.**

—— An Oil Trade Calculator for easy conversion of weights to gallons at different specific gravities. pp. viii. 201. *Scott, Greenwood & Son: London,* 1921. 8°. **08548. aa. 1.**

BUTLER (THOMAS PAGE) Alphabetical Index to the Statutes passed by the Parliament of Canada since the date of the Consolidated Statutes, 1859. With an appendix, shewing the amendments to all the Consolidated Statutes. pp. 56. *G. E. Desbarats: Ottawa,* 1867. 8°. **6606. bb. 16.**

BUTLER (TIMOTHY) *See* ENGLAND.—*Proclamations.*—II. Charles II. By the King. A Proclamation for the Discovery and Apprehension of John Lockier, Timothy Butler, Thomas Blood . . . and others [for rescuing John Mason]. [8 Aug. 1667.] 1667. fol. **21. h. 2. (44.)**

BUTLER (TOM) Tom Butler's Trouble. A cottage story. By the author of "Tom Burton, or, the Better way" [i.e. Charles Manby Smith]. With illustrations. pp. 123. *F. Warne & Co.: London,* 1868. 8°. **4416. aa. 19.**

BUTLER (TONY) Tony Butler. [A novel. By Charles James Lever.] 3 vol. *W. Blackwood & Sons: Edinburgh & London,* 1865. 8°. **12635. aaa. 2.**

BUTLER (UNA) Dreams and Memories. Verse. pp. 20. *A. H. Stockwell: London,* [1923.] 8°. **011645. df. 139.**

BUTLER (VIVIAN)

—— Guy for Trouble. A mystery thriller for young people. pp. 106. *John Crowther: Bognor Regis & London,* 1945. 8°. **NN. 35562.**

BUTLER (W.) *Writer on Pompeii.* Pompeii descriptive and picturesque. pp. 127. *W. Blackwood & Sons: London,* 1886. 8°. **7705. aa. 34.**

BUTLER (W. C.) *Confectioner.* The Modern Cook and Practical Confectioner. pp. ix. 314. *J. Menzies & Co.: Edinburgh,* 1894. 8°. **07944. e. 38.**

—— Butler's Modern Practical Confectioner, *etc.* pp. 88. iv. *A. Heywood & Son: Manchester,* 1890. 8°. **7944. aaa. 63.**

—— [Another edition.] pp. 97. *A. Heywood & Son: Manchester,* [1898.] 8°. **07944. df. 19.**

BUTLER (W. MEREDITH) The Golfer's Manual. Illustrated . . . With an introduction by Dr. Macnamara. pp. xv. 171. *T. Werner Laurie: London,* [1907.] 8°. **07906. de. 12.**

BUTLER (WALTER) *American Loyalist. See* SWIGGETT (Howard) War out of Niagara. Walter Butler and the Tory Rangers. 1933. 8°. [*New York State Historical Association Series.* no. 2.] **Ac. 8428/2.**

BUTLER (WALTER) *Colonel.* The Case of Collonel Walter Butler, of Munphin, in the County of Wexford, *etc.* [A petition to Parliament relating to the disallowance by the Trustees of the Forfeited Estates in Ireland of proofs of debt brought by W. Butler against the estate of Viscount Galmoy.] pp. 3. [*London?* 1705?] fol. **816. m. 17. (27.)**

BUTLER (WALTER) *of Havant. See* BINGLEY (William) *Rev.* Topographical Account of the Hundred of Bosmere in Hampshire, *etc.* [Edited by W. Butler.] 1817. 4°. **578. h. 8.**

BUTLER (WALTER C.) Cross over Nine. [A novel.] pp. 255. *Macaulay Co.: New York,* [1935.] 8°. **A.N. 2975.**

—— The Night Flower. pp. 311. *Macaulay Co.: New York,* 1936. 8°. **A.N. 3191.**

—— [Another edition.] pp. 287. *Stanley Paul & Co.: London,* [1937.] 8°. **12716. b. 3.**

BUTLER (WALTER ERNEST)

—— Magic: its ritual, power and purpose. pp. 76. *Aquarian Press: London,* 1952. 8°. **8634. de. 50.**

BUTLER (WALTER GASKING) *See* NEPOS (C.) De ducibus . . . Edited . . . by W. G. Butler. 1914. 8°. **10606. de. 5.**

—— One Hundred Latin Passages, for prepared or unprepared translation. pp. viii. 159. *Methuen & Co.: London,* 1937. 8°. **012933. c. 54.**

BUTLER (WEEDEN) *the Elder.*

—— *See* INDIAN VOCABULARY. The Indian Vocabulary, *etc.* COPIOUS MS. NOTES [by W. Butler]. 1788. 12°. **12906. a. 33.**

—— *See* WILCOCKS (Joseph) *F.S.A.* Roman Conversations, *etc.* [Edited by W. Butler.] 1797. 8°. **688. f. 7.**

—— The Cheltenham Guide; or, Useful companion, in a journey of health and pleasure to the Cheltenham Spa, *etc.* [By W. Butler.] pp. vii. 110. 1781. 8°. *See* CHELTENHAM GUIDE. **578. d. 13.**

—— [Another copy.] **290. f. 14.**

—— A Discourse addressed to the Loyal Pimlico Volunteers, previous to receiving their colours from the hands of the Countess of Carlisle . . . To which are prefixed, the ceremonial, the address of the Countess of Carlisle, on presenting the colours, and Major Rolleston's reply. pp. xiv. 21. *J. Polwarth: London,* 1799. 8°. **T. 2351. (2.)**

BUTLER (Weeden) *the Elder.*

—— Memoirs of Mark Hildesley, D.D., Lord Bishop of Sodor and Mann, and Master of Sherburn Hospital; under whose auspices the Holy Scriptures were translated into the Manks language. pp. xii. 691. *J. Nichols: London,* 1799. 8º. **204.** c. 4.

—— [Another copy.] G. **14176.**

—— The Perpetuity of Brotherly Love, recommended in a sermon for the Royal Cumberland School, *etc.* pp. 22. *B. White & Son; T. Cadell: London,* 1791. 4º. **4474.** l. **9.**

—— Philanthropy, Religion, and Loyalty, the best Characteristicks of a Christian Soldier. A sermon; addressed to the Armed Association of the Parish of Saint Luke, Chelsea, *etc.* pp. vi. 19. [*London,*] 1798. 8º. **695.** g. **19.** (**8.**)

—— A Sermon Preached in the Royal Hospital Chapel, before the Chelsea Armed Association, on receiving their colours from Miss North . . . With a short account of the ceremony used upon the occasion. pp. xvi. 22. *Davenport & Faulkner: Chelsea,* 1799. 8º. **695.** g. **20.** (**1.**)

—— Some Account of the Life and Writings of the Reverend Dr. George Stanhope, Vicar of Lewisham and Deptford, and Dean of Canterbury. [By W. Butler.] pp. 80. 1797. 8º. *See* Stanhope (George) *Dean of Canterbury.* T. **2405.** (**1.**)

BUTLER (Weeden) *the Younger. See* Épître. Épître à mon père. [By T. J. Du Wicquet, Baron d'Ordre With an English metrical version by W. Butler.] 1797. 8º. **11632.** d. **13.**

—— *See* Unterwalden. The Wrongs of Unterwalden . . . Translated by Rev. W. Butler. 1799. 8º. **8073.** e. **58.** (**3.**)

—— *See* Weiss (François R. de) A Prospect of the Political Relations which subsist between the French Republic and the Helvetick Body . . . Translated by W. Butler. 1794. 8º. **8073.** e. **58.** (**1.**)

—— *See* Zimao. Zimao, the African. Translated by the Rev. W. Butler. 1800. 8º. **837.** b. **35.** (**1.**)

—— —— 1800. 12º. **12330.** aaa. **3.** (**5.**)

—— —— 1807. 8º. **837.** b. **35.** (**2.**)

—— Bagatelles. Or Miscellaneous productions; consisting of original poetry, and translations; principally by the editor, W. Butler. pp. viii. 112. *T. Cadell; W. Davies: London,* 1795. 8º. **12316.** i. **25.** (**2.**)

—— Euthanasia. A sermon preached at Charlotte Street Chapel, Pimlico, *etc.* [On the death of Queen Charlotte.] pp. 38. *Nichols, Son, & Bentley: London,* 1818. 8º. T. **2330.** (**1.**)

—— The Warning Voice. A sermon preached at Charlotte Street Chapel, Pimlico . . . November 19, 1817 (on occasion of the death of the Princess Charlotte). pp. 19. *Nichols, Son, & Bentley: London,* 1817. 8º. T. **2053.** (**1.**)

BUTLER (William) **AND CO.**

—— The History of Wm. Butler & Co., Bristol, Ltd., 1843 to 1943. By T. Howard Butler. [With illustrations.] pp. 92. *Bristol,* 1954. 4º. **8207.** m. **15.**

BUTLER (William) *Architect.* The Cathedral Church of the Holy Trinity, Dublin—Christ Church. A description of its fabric, and a brief history of the foundation, and subsequent changes . . . With 32 illustrations. pp. x. 91. *Elliot Stock: London,* 1901. 8º. **4735.** df. **8.**

—— Christ Church Cathedral, Dublin. Measured drawings of the building prior to restoration (and historical sketch), *etc. The Author: Dublin,* [1874.] fol. **7815.** r. **18.**

BUTLER (William) *Attorney.*

—— William Butler Appellant. John Bourke, and Frances his wife, Respondents. The appellant's case. (Upon an original and cross appeal from a decree of the Chancery in Ireland.) pp. 4. [*London,* 1719.] fol. **19.** h. **1.** (**122.**)

—— Wm Butler, Appel^nt^, John Burke Esq; and Frances his wife, Resp^nts^, et e con. Upon an original and cross appeal from a decree of the Chancery in Ireland. The case of the said John Burke and Frances his wife, respondents in the original appeal; and also appellants in the cross appeal. pp. 3. [*London,* 1719.] fol. **19.** h. **1.** (**123.**)

BUTLER (William) *General in the U.S. Army. See* Slider (T. P.) General William Butler. (1759–1821.) 1909. 8º. [Brooks (*Ulysses R.*) *Butler and his Cavalry in the War of Secession.*] **09555.** dd. **5.**

BUTLER (William) *M.B., C.M., D.P.M., R.A.M.C.*

—— The Thames Barrage from a Health Aspect. *See* Bunge (Julius H. O.) Tideless Thames in Future London, *etc.* 1944. 4º. **8803.** cc. **21.**

BUTLER (William) *Major. See* W., R. The Fourth Paper presented by Major Butler to the Honourable Committee of Parliament for the propagating the Gospel of Christ Jesus, *etc.* 1652. 4º. E. **658.** (**9.**)

BUTLER (William) *Methodist Minister, of Boston.* From Boston to Bareilly and Back. [With plates, including a portrait.] pp. 512. *Phillips & Hunt: New York; Cranston & Stowe: Cincinnati,* 1885. 8º. **4766.** cc. **27.**

—— Mexico in Transition from the Power of Political Romanism to Civil and Religious Liberty . . . Illustrated. pp. xvi. 325. *Hunt & Eaton: New York; Cranston & Curts: Cincinnati,* 1892. 8º. **4182.** cc. **26.**

BUTLER (William) *Physician.* A Hundred Notable Things, or Doctor Butler's last legacy . . . by J. P. [i.e. John Pike.] 1686. 8º. *See* Pike (John) *of London.* **7953.** a. **51.**

BUTLER (William) *Rector of Saint Anns within Aldersgate.* The Character of a Good Magistrate. A sermon preached before the Lord-Mayor, and Court of Aldermen, *etc.* pp. 16. *John March: London,* 1729. 4º. **4474.** e. **10.**

—— The Duty of the Subject with regard to his Oath. A Sermon preached at the Visitation held at Rumford, April 19, 1723, by the Arch-Deacon of Essex. pp. 19. *John March: London,* 1723. 4º. **4473.** e. **29.** (**3.**)

—— A Sermon preach'd before . . . Sir Robert Beachcroft, Kt., Lord-Mayor, the Aldermen and citizens of London, at the Cathedral Church of St. Paul, on Wednesday, January 16th, 17$\frac{11}{12}$, being the day appointed . . . for a publick fast. pp. 23. *Sam. Crouch: London,* 1712. 8º. **225.** h. **11.** (**7.**)

BUTLER (William) *Rector of Saint Anns within Aldersgate.*

—— A Sermon preached to the Societies for Reformation of Manners, *etc.* (The Seven and Twentieth Account of the progress made in the cities of London and Westminster . . . by the Societies for Promoting a Reformation of Manners.) pp. 28. 8. *J. Downing: London,* 1722. 8°. **695.** f. **2.** (**6.**)

—— [Another copy.] **226.** f. **11.** (**15.**)

—— Vice the Destruction of the Soul. A sermon, *etc.* pp. 18. *John March: London,* 1719. 4°. **693.** f. **5.** (**12.**)

BUTLER (William) *Tar Distiller.*

—— Notes of a Voyage in the Orient Steamship Company's S.S. "Garonne," in the early part of the year 1891. With illustrations. [The introduction signed: W. B., i.e. W. Butler.] pp. vi. 109. 1892. 8°. *See* B., W. **010077.** e. **98.**

BUTLER (William) *Writing-Master. See* Butler (John O.) A Brief Memoir of Mr. William Butler, *etc.* [With a portrait.] 1826. 8°. **10854.** cc. **8.**

—— Arithmetical Questions, on a new plan: designed as a supplement to the author's engraved Introduction to Arithmetic . . . The second edition, enlarged. pp. ix. 208. *Printed for the Author: London,* 1795. 8°. **8504.** ee. **13.**

—— The fifth edition, enlarged. pp. xxiv. 484. *Printed for the Author and Proprietors: London,* 1811. 12°. **8531.** aa. **41.**

—— The sixth edition. pp. xxiv. 485. *Printed for the Author and Proprietors: London,* 1814. 12°. **8467.** aaa. **23.**

—— [Another edition.] Edited by . . . Thomas Bourn. With additions by George Frost . . . Fourteenth edition. pp. xvi. 496. *Longman & Co.: London,* 1853. 12°. **8505.** c. **16.**

—— Exercises on the Globes; interspersed with some historical, biographical, chronological, mythological, and miscellaneous information on a new plan; designed for the use of young ladies . . . The third edition, with additions. pp. xxxii. 381. *Printed for the Author: London,* 1803. 8°. **8562.** a. **12.**

—— The fourth edition, with additions. pp. xxxii. 400. *Printed for the Author: London,* 1808. 12°. **8562.** a. **23.**

—— [Another edition.] Exercises on the Globes and Maps . . . The seventh edition, enlarged. [With a portrait.] pp. xxxv. 468. *Printed for the Author: London,* 1816. 12°. **8560.** aa. **45.**

—— The eighth edition. pp. xxxv. 468. *Printed for the Author: London,* 1818. 12°. **8562.** aaa. **21.**

—— [Another edition.] With an appendix, by which the constellations and fixed stars may be easily known. By Thomas Bourn. The thirteenth edition. pp. xx. 496. *Harris: London,* 1837. 12°. **8560.** aaa. **19.**

—— A Chronological Table, on a new plan comprising articles of an historical, biographical, and miscellaneous nature, for daily use . . . The second edition [of part of "Exercises on the Globes"], enlarged. pp. xvi. 322. *Printed for the Author: London,* 1799. 8°. **582.** a. **20.**

BUTLER (William) *Writing-Master.*

—— [Another edition.] Chronological, Biographical and Miscellaneous Exercises on a new plan . . . The third edition, greatly enlarged. pp. xv. 550. *Printed for the Author: London,* 1807. 8°. **800.** a. **32.**

—— [Another edition.] Chronological, Biographical, Historical, and Miscellaneous Exercises . . . The fourth edition, enlarged. pp. xx. 500. *Printed for the Author: London,* 1811. 12°. **9009.** aaa. **6.**

—— The fifth edition, enlarged. pp. xxiv. 552. *Printed for the Author: London,* 1815. 12°. **9005.** b. **11.**

—— The seventh edition, enlarged. [Edited by John Olding Butler.] pp. xxiv. 623. *Printed for the Proprietor: London,* 1823. 12°. **9007.** bbb. **7.**

—— A Collection of Easy Arithmetical Questions designed for the use of Young Ladies, *etc.* *Printed for the Author: London,* 1788. 8°. **8508.** a. **44.** (**2.**)

—— Geographical and Biographical Exercises, designed for the use of young ladies . . . The seventh edition. pp. x. 36. *Printed for the Author: London,* 1811. 12°. **12201.** b. **1.** (**3.**)

—— [Another edition.] Enlarged by . . . John Olding Butler . . . Twenty-seventh edition. pp. iv. 101. *Grant & Griffith: London,* 1848. 12°. **10004.** b. **12.**
Imperfect; wanting the maps.

—— Geographical Exercises in the New Testament: describing the principal places in Judea, and those visited by St. Paul . . . With maps, and a brief account of the principal religious sects among mankind. [With a portrait.] pp. xvi. 237. *Printed for the Author: London,* 1813. 12°. **10076.** aaa. **32.**
Imperfect; wanting the maps.

—— The second edition, enlarged. pp. xxii. 304. *Printed for the Author: London,* 1816. 12°. **855.** c. **15.**

—— An Introduction to Arithmetic, consisting of printed examples of the first four rules, with approved tables of weights and measures, *etc.* pp. iv. 107. MS. NOTES. *Printed for the Author: London,* 1784. 8°. **8534.** bbb. **3.**

—— [Another copy.] An Introduction to Arithmetic, *etc.* *London,* 1784. 8°. **8508.** a. **44.**

—— [Another edition.] (Exercises in the preceding rules.) 2 pt. *The Author: London,* 1788. 8°. **8505.** bb. **21.**
The "Introduction" is engraved throughout.

BUTLER (William Allen) Poems. pp. vi. 263. *J. R. Osgood & Co.: Boston,* 1871. 8°. **11688.** bb. **36.**

—— "Two Millions"; and "Nothing to Wear." Two poems. pp. 88. *Ward & Lock: London,* 1858. 8°. **11687.** b. **2.**

—— Nothing to Wear . . . and Two Millions . . . New edition. pp. vii. 143. *Sampson Low & Co.: London,* 1881. 8°. **12209.** cc. **6.** (**1.**)

—— The Animal Book . . . With . . . illustrations . . . by Elsie Dodge Pattee. pp. 42. *F. A. Stokes Co.: New York,* [1914.] 8°. **012807.** a. **5.**

—— Domesticus. A tale of the Imperial City. pp. vii. 281. *C. Scribner's Sons: New York,* 1886. 8°. **12705.** dd. **22.**

BUTLER (WILLIAM ALLEN)

—— Evert Augustus Duyckinck. A memorial sketch, *etc.* [With a portrait.] pp. 16. *Trow's Printing & Bookbinding Co.: New York*, 1879. 8°. **10882**. i. **10**. **(3.)**

—— Lawyer and Client: their relation, rights, and duties. pp. 76. *D. Appleton & Co.: New York*, 1871. 12°. **6625**. a. **3**.

—— Martin Van Buren: lawyer, statesman and man. pp. 47. *D. Appleton & Co.: New York*, 1862. 12°. **10880**. aa. **32**.

—— Nothing to Wear: an episode of city life. [In verse. By W. A. Butler.] From Harpers Weekly. Illustrated by Hoppin. pp. 68. 1857. 8°. *See* NOTHING. **11687**. b. **10**.

—— [Another edition.] pp. 58. *Sampson Low & Co.: London*, 1857. 8°. **11687**. a. **12**.

—— [Another edition.] pp. 32. *Simpkin, Marshall & Co.: London; David Kelly: Manchester*, 1858. 12°. **11687**. aaa. **35**. **(2.)**

—— Rien à mettre, ou Crinoline et misère. Poème . . . traduit par Albert Le Roy. [A prose version.] pp. 34. *Paris*, 1858. 12°. **11687**. a. **60**.

—— [Another edition.] pp. 34. *Paris*, 1865. 16°. **11687**. a. **6**.

—— Rien à mettre . . . D'après l'anglais . . . mis en vers français par Ada Marie Berger. pp. 55. *Gotham Press: New York*, 1926. 8°. **011644**. de. **50**.

—— [Another edition.] pp. 55. *Gotham Press: New York*, 1927. 8°. **011483**. a. **50**.

—— *See* KNOT-RAB, *pseud.* Nothing to You . . . In answer to "Nothings" in general, and "Nothing to Wear" [by W. A. Butler] in particular. 1857. 12°. **11686**. aaa. **28**.

—— Oberammergau, 1890. [Verses. With illustrations.] pp. 46. *Harper & Bros.: New York*, 1891. fol. **11686**. l. **9**.

—— A Retrospect of Forty Years, 1825–1865 . . . Edited by . . . Harriet Allen Butler. With portraits and illustrations. pp. xviii. 442. *C. Scribner's Sons: New York*, 1911. 8°. **010883**. ff. **32**.

—— The Revision of the Statutes of the State of New York and the Revisers. An address, *etc.* pp. iv. 100. *Banks & Bros.: New York*, 1889. 4°. **8176**. bb. **24**.

—— True Love versus Fashion; or, the Flirt's failure. Also Brown's Daughter, and Husband v. Wife. By the author of "Nothing to Wear" [i.e. W. A. Butler]. Illustrated. [In verse.] pp. 79. [1859.] 8°. *See* LOVE. **11686**. a. **5**.

—— Two Millions. [In verse.] pp. 93. *D. Appleton & Co.: New York*, 1858. 12°. **11688**. bbb. **9**.

—— [Another edition.] pp. 96. *Sampson Low & Co.: London*, [1858.] 8°. **11687**. b. **1**.

—— Second edition. pp. 96. *Sampson Low & Co.: London*, [1860?] 8°. **11688**. b. **32**.

BUTLER (WILLIAM ARCHER) Christ Sought and Found in the Old Testament Scriptures. *See* ATONEMENT. The Atonement, *etc.* [1857.] 8°. **4226**. c. **15**.

BUTLER (WILLIAM ARCHER)

—— The Eternal Life of Christ in Heaven. A festal sermon. *See* WATSON (Alexander) *Vicar of St. Marychurch.* Sermons for Sundays, Festivals, and Fasts, *etc.* ser. 1. 1845, *etc.* 8°. **1358**. f. **21**.

—— Lectures on the History of Ancient Philosophy . . . Edited from the author's MSS. with notes, by William Hepworth Thompson. 2 vol. *Macmillan & Co.: Cambridge*, 1856. 8°. **8486**. e. **18**.

—— Letters on the Development of Christian Doctrine, in reply to Mr. Newman's Essay [i.e. "An Essay on the Development of Christian Doctrine"] . . . Edited by the Rev. Thomas Woodward. pp. xxviii. 391. *Hodges & Smith: Dublin*, 1850. 8°. **1354**. i. **10**.

—— Primitive Church Principles not inconsistent with Universal Christian Sympathy. A sermon preached at the Visitation of the United Dioceses of Derry and Raphoe, *etc.* pp. 48. *J. G. F. & J. Rivington: London; W. Curry, Jun. & Co.: Dublin*, 1842. 8°. **1358**. h. **21**. **(4.)**

—— Sermons, Doctrinal and Practical . . . Edited, with a memoir of the author's life, by the Rev. Thomas Woodward. [With a portrait.] pp. lxxiii. 562. *Hodges & Smith: Dublin*, 1849. 8°. **4460**. d. **11**.

—— Second edition. pp. lxiv. 422. *Hodges & Smith: Dublin*, 1852. 8°. **4460**. d. **12**.

—— [Another edition.] First series edited . . . by the Rev. Thomas Woodward. (Second series. Edited from the author's MSS. by James Amiraux Jeremie.) Third edition. 2 vol. *Macmillan & Co.: Cambridge*, 1855. 8°. **4462**. g. **8**.

—— The Church's Seasons a Safeguard against Partial Views of Christianity. (Reprinted from the "English Churchman.") [An extract from Sermon 5, Series 1, of "Sermons, Doctrinal and Practical."] pp. 4. *J. H. Batty: London*, [1853.] 8°. **4406**. d. **70**.

BUTLER (WILLIAM C.) An Historical Sermon in connection with St. Barnabas Church, also known as "Brick Church," Queen Anne's Parish, at Leeland, Prince George's County, Maryland, *etc.* pp. 18. *R. Beresford: Washington*, 1907. 8°. **4533**. ff. **10**. **(6.)**

BUTLER (WILLIAM F.) *of Milwaukee.* *See* CORNARO (L.) The Art of Living Long, *etc.* [Edited by W. F. Butler.] 1903. 8°. **7391**. e. **28**.

BUTLER (WILLIAM F.) *of the Department of Economics, McGraw-Hill Publishing Company.*

—— *See* KEEZER (Dexter M.) Making Capitalism Work . . . [By] D. M. Keezer, W. F. Butler [and others]. [1950.] 8°. **8207**. t. **25**.

BUTLER (WILLIAM FIELD) *See* SHAEN (Richard) "The Uncertainty of Life." A sermon occasioned by the death of W. F. Butler, *etc.* [1864.] 12°. **4920**. b. **57**. **(19.)**

BUTLER (*Right Hon. Sir* WILLIAM FRANCIS) *G.C.B.* Akim-Foo: the history of a failure . . . With route map, etc. pp. 300. *Sampson Low & Co.: London*, 1875. 8°. **9061**. eee. **1**.

—— Third edition. pp. 300. *Sampson Low & Co.: London*, 1875. 8°. **9061**. b. **2**.

—— The Campaign of the Cataracts; being a personal narrative of the Great Nile Expedition of 1884–5 . . . With illustrations from drawings by Lady Butler; also a map of the Nile, *etc.* pp. vii. 389. *Sampson Low & Co.: London*, 1887. 8°. **9060**. ccc. **28**.

BUTLER (*Right Hon Sir* WILLIAM FRANCIS) *G.C.B.*

—— The Channel Tunnel. [*London*, 1907.] *s. sh.* fol. **1850**. d. **26**. **(86.)**

—— Charles George Gordon. [With a portrait.] pp. vi. 255. *Macmillan & Co.: London & New York*, 1889. 8°. [*English Men of Action.*] **10803**. bbb. **17**.

—— Far Out: rovings retold. pp. xxiv. 386. *Wm. Isbister: London*, 1880. 8°. **10024**. b. **10**.

—— From Naboth's Vineyard: being impressions formed during a fourth visit to South Africa undertaken at the request of the Tribune newspaper. pp. xii. 267. *Chapman & Hall: London*, 1907. 8°. **010095**. de. **57**.

—— The Great Lone Land: a narrative of travel and adventure in the North-West of America . . . With illustrations and route map. Second edition. pp. x. 388. *Sampson Low & Co.: London*, 1872. 8°. **10412**. ee. **15**.

—— Fourth and cheaper edition. pp. x. 386. *Sampson Low & Co.: London*, 1873. 8°. **10470**. df. **36**.

—— The Invasion of England: told twenty years after. By an old soldier [i.e. Sir William F. Butler]. pp. 190. 1882. 8°. *See* ENGLAND. [*Appendix.—Miscellaneous.*] **12357**. f. **17**.

—— [Another copy.] The Invasion of England . . . By an old soldier [i.e. Sir William F. Butler]. 1882. 8°. *See* ENGLAND. [*Appendix.—Miscellaneous.*] **12332**. ee. **5**.

—— The Life of Sir George Pomeroy-Colley . . . 1835–1881 . . . With portraits, maps, and illustrations. pp. vii. 430. *John Murray: London*, 1899. 8°. **010817**. f. **12**.

—— The Light of the West. With some other wayside thoughts, 1865–1908. pp. 246. *M. H. Gill & Son: Dublin & Waterford*, 1909. 8°. **12350**. p. **19**.

—— A Narrative of the Historical Events connected with the Sixty-ninth Regiment. pp. iii. 130. *W. Mitchell & Co.: London*, 1870. 8°. **8830**. g. **25**.

—— Oliver Cromwell in Ireland. *See* LONDON.—III. *Irish Literary Society.* Studies in Irish History, 1649–1775, *etc.* 1903. 8°. **9508**. aaa. **13**.

—— Red Cloud, the Solitary Sioux. A story of the great prairie. [With plates.] pp. x. 327. *Sampson Low & Co.: London*, 1882. 8°. **12810**. bb. **23**.

—— Néall Dearg . . . Niall Mac Suiḃne d'aistriġ, *etc.* pp. 405. Oifig Diolta Foillseaċáin Rialtais: Baile Áṫa Cliaṫ, 1935. 8°. **875**. n. **67**.

—— Sir Charles Napier. [With a portrait.] pp. vi. 216. *Macmillan & Co.: London & New York*, 1890. 8°. [*English Men of Action.*] **10803**. bbb. **25**.

—— Sir William Butler. An autobiography . . . With four portraits in photogravure. [Edited by Eileen Butler.] pp. xi. 476. *Constable & Co.: London*, 1911. 8°. **010815**. g. **3**.

—— Second edition. pp. viii. 476. *Constable & Co.: London*, 1913. 8°. **010815**. f. **16**.

—— The Wild North Land: being the story of a winter journey, with dogs, across northern North America . . . With illustrations [including a portrait] and route map. pp. x. 358. *Sampson Low & Co.: London*, 1873. 8°. **10470**. cc. **28**.

BUTLER (*Right Hon. Sir* WILLIAM FRANCIS) *G.C.B.*

—— [Another edition.] pp. xxii. 360. *A. S. Barnes & Co.: New York*, 1904. 8°. [*The Trail Makers.*] **9551**. b. **15/3**.

—— [Another edition.] pp. xiii. 364. *Musson Book Co.: Toronto; printed in Great Britain*, 1924. 8°. **010460**. f. **9**.

—— Críoċa Fiaḋaine an Tuaiseirt. Niall Mac Suiḃne a rinne an leagan Gaeḋilge. pp. 333. Oifig an tSoláṫair: Baile Áṫa Cliaṫ, 1938. 8°. **010460**. i. **11**.

BUTLER (WILLIAM FRANCIS THOMAS) Confiscation in Irish History. pp. vii. 270. *Talbot Press: Dublin*, 1917. 8°. **9508**. c. **10**.

—— Gleanings from Irish History . . . With 9 maps, *etc.* pp. xv. 335. *Longmans & Co.: London; Dublin* [printed], 1925. 8°. **9508**. ccc. **28**.

—— The Lombard Communes. A history of the republics of North Italy . . . Illustrated. pp. 495. *T. Fisher Unwin: London*, 1906. 8°. **9150**. f. **15**.

—— Two Kerry Baronies in the Sixteenth Century. [Reprinted from the Journal of the Cork Historical and Archaeological Society.] pp. 7. [1929.] 8°. **9907**. aa. **20**.

BUTLER (WILLIAM FREDERICK) Ventilation of Buildings. A paper read before the Society of Civil and Mechanical Engineers . . . With additions. pp. 30. *Kell Bros.: London*, 1873. 8°. **8775**. b. **51**. **(10.)**

BUTLER (WILLIAM H. G.) *See* SALLUSTIUS CRISPUS (C.) [*Works.—Latin.*] Sallust's Jugurtha and Catiline, *etc.* (The vocabulary prepared by W. H. G. Butler.) 1855. 8°. **1308**. c. **10**.

—— *See* WARD (Matthew F.) A Full and Authentic Report of the Testimony on the Trial of Matt. F. Ward [for the murder of W. H. G. Butler], *etc.* 1854. 8°. **6736**. h. **11**.

—— *See* WARD (Matthew F.) Trial of Matt. F. Ward for the murder of Prof. W. H. G. Butler, *etc.* 1854. 8°. **6615**. aaa. **22**.

BUTLER (WILLIAM HENRY) *See* CANADA, *Lower.* [*Laws and Statutes.*] The Civil Code of Lower Canada and the Bills of Exchange Act, 1906, with all statutory amendments verified, collated and indexed by W. H. Butler. 1910. 8°. **06606**. e. **1**.

—— William Shakespeare and his Latest Traducer. A letter to Sir Edwin Durning-Lawrence, Baronet, in answer to statements in his book, entitled "Bacon is Shakespeare." pp. 11. *J. A. Thompson & Co.: Liverpool*, [1911.] 8°. Lamb. **74**. **(2.)**

BUTLER (WILLIAM JOHN) *Dean of Lincoln.* *See* ELFFEN (N.) [Scintilla cordis.] Light in the Heart . . . Edited by the Rev. W. J. Butler. 1869. 16°. **4410**. e. **16**.

—— *See* GILES (M.) Strength from Quietness . . . Including addresses by . . . Dean Butler. 1911. 8°. **3457**. f. **49**.

—— *See* HEURTLEY (Charles A.) The Doctrine of the Church of England touching the Real Objective Presence, the Eucharistic Sacrifice, and the Adoration of Christ in the Sacrament, being remarks on a declaration of belief addressed by the Rev. W. Butler . . . and several other clergymen, to the Archbishop of Canterbury. 1867. 8°. [*Manchester Diocesan Church Association Lectures.* no. 1.] **4108**. aaa. **70**.

—— —— 1868. 8°. [*S., T. A. Lectures delivered in St. Ann's Church, Manchester, etc.*] **4463**. ddd. **26**.

BUTLER (William John) *Dean of Lincoln.*

—— *See* Mary, *the Blessed Virgin.—Churches and Institutions.*—Wantage.—*Community of St. Mary the Virgin.* Butler of Wantage. His inheritance and his legacy, *etc.* [With portraits.] [1948.] 8°. **4910**. aa. **34**.

—— *See* Wilberforce (Samuel) successively *Bishop of Oxford* and *of Winchester.* On Penitentiary Work . . . With a short preface on sisterhoods, by W. J. Butler. 1861. 8°. **4478**. a. **126**. (**13**.)

—— Life and Letters of William John Butler, late Dean of Lincoln . . . With portraits. [The editor's preface signed: A. J. B., i.e. Arthur John Butler.] pp. xi. 401. *Macmillan & Co.: London,* 1897. 8°. **4905**. dd. **29**.

—— Advent Offerings. *See* Advent. The Warnings of Advent. A course of sermons, *etc.* 1853. 8°. **4461**. g. **29**.

—— Christian Liberty. *See* Church Treasures. Church Treasures: five sermons, *etc.* [1874.] 8°. **4479**. aa. **7**.

—— Communicant Classes. A parish paper . . . Reprinted from "The Literary Churchman." pp. 11. *W. Skeffington & Son: London,* 1886. 8°. **4372**. aaa. **31**. (**5**.)

—— Confirmation. Notes and questions. (Second edition.) pp. 10. *C. A. Bartlett & Co.: London; H. N. Nichols: Wantage,* [1875.] 8°. **4324**. h. **1**. (**3**.)

—— [Another edition.] pp. 22. *W. Skeffington & Son: London,* 1883. 8°. **4422**. l. **32**. (**2**.)

—— The Conflict:—in a Money-getting Age. *See* Wilberforce (Samuel) successively *Bishop of Oxford* and *of Winchester.* The Enduring Conflict of Christ . . . Sermons, *etc.* 1865. 8°. **4477**. bb. **66**.

—— The Faith once delivered to the Saints. A sermon, *etc.* pp. 16. *A. R. Mowbray & Co.: Oxford, London,* [1884.] 8°. **4478**. aaa. **128**. (**2**.)

—— God the Reward of the Faithful. *See* L., H. R. Sermons preached during Lent, 1864, in Great St. Mary's Church, Cambridge, *etc.* 1864. 8°. **4464**. aaa. **20**.

—— Henry Parry Liddon; or, the Life of zeal. A sermon, *etc.* pp. 16. *Longmans & Co.: London,* 1890. 8°. **4906**. dd. **39**. (**12**.)

—— "Hold Fast," and "Farewell." Two sermons, *etc.* pp. 22. *J. Masters & Co.: London; H. N. Nichols: Wantage,* 1881. 8°. **4478**. h. **10**. (**9**.)

—— Ignorance the Danger of the Church. A sermon, *etc.* pp. 19. *Rivingtons: London,* 1890. 8°. **4473**. g. **30**. (**6**.)

—— Meditations for every Week in the Christian Year, by the compiler of 'Plain Prayers' [i.e. W. J. Butler], *etc.* pp. vii. 127. [1877.] 8°. *See* Christian Year. **4401**. bb. **9**.

—— [Another copy.] **4413**. ee. **6**.

—— Meditations on the Hundred and Nineteenth Psalm, *etc.* pp. xii. 181. *Skeffington & Son: London,* 1894. 8°. **3089**. e. **18**.

—— The Memory of the Righteous. The substance of a sermon preached . . . July 15th, 1877, on the occasion of the unveiling of the statue of King Alfred in the Market Place, Wantage. pp. 14. *C. A. Bartlett & Co.: London; H. N. Nichols: Wantage,* [1877.] 8°. **4479**. cc. **14**. (**6**.)

BUTLER (William John) *Dean of Lincoln.*

—— Notes of Addresses given to the Guild of S. Scholastica in two Easter-tide retreats. pp. 179. *Convent of S. Mary: Wantage,* 1905. 8°. **4475**. l. **10**.

—— Plain Prayers. [By W. J. Butler.] pp. 47. 1871. 16°. *See* Prayers. **3457**. a. **62**. (**5**.)

—— Plain Thoughts on Holy Communion . . . Sixth edition, revised. pp. 24. *Rivingtons: London,* 1885. 16°. **4372**. df. **29**. (**2**.)

—— Seventh edition, revised. pp. 24. *Rivingtons: London,* 1889. 16°. **4372**. aa. **31**. (**6**.)

—— The Responsibility of Hearing, *etc.* pp. 16. [*London,* 1859.] 8°. [*Westminster Abbey Sermons for the Working Classes.* ser. 2.] **4477**. a. **127**. (**2**.)

—— School Prayers for Morning and Evening. Compiled by W. J. B., M.A., Vicar of Wantage [i.e. W. J. Butler]. pp. 18. 1848. 12°. *See* B., W. J., *M.A., Vicar of Wantage.* **3455**. b. **71**. (**3**.)

—— [Another edition.] [With musical notes.] pp. 39. *J. H. Parker: Oxford,* 1852. 16°. **3455**. c. **43**. (**4**.)

—— Sermons for Working Men. pp. xvi. 416. *Joseph Masters: London,* 1847. 12°. **1357**. a. **12**.

—— [Another edition.] pp. xxiii. 298. *A. R. Mowbray & Co.: Oxford, London,* 1904. 8°. [*Oxford Sermon-Library.* vol. 2.] **4475**. i.

—— A Short Manual for Nurses, intended for those engaged in nursing the sick. Compiled by the author of "Meditations for the Christian Year," &c. [i.e. W. J. Butler.] Edited by W. J. Butler. pp. vii. 39. [1881.] 32°. *See* Manual. **4400**. e. **12**.

—— [Another edition.] pp. 32. [1886.] 32°. *See* Manual. **4400**. f. **22**.

—— Twelve Short and Simple Meditations on the Sufferings of Our Lord Jesus Christ. Edited by W. J. Butler. pp. vii. 146. *Joseph Masters: London,* 1865. 8°. **4226**. aa. **17**.

—— Westminster School, its Past and its Future. A sermon preached in Westminster Abbey at the Commemoration of Benefactors on November 17, 1890. pp. 20. *Longmans & Co.: London,* 1891. 8°. **4473**. cc. **23**. (**11**.)

—— What is our Present Danger? A sermon, *etc.* pp. 20. *Longmans & Co.: London,* 1891. 8°. **4473**. cc. **23**. (**12**.)

BUTLER (William Joseph) The History & Antiquities of Laughton-en-le-Morthen, the Castles of Tickhill & Conisbro', Roche Abbey, and other places in the same vicinity. pp. 32. *Rawson & Richards: Nottingham,* 1856. 8°. **010358**. f. **8**. (**2**.)

—— Roche Abbey, and other poems, with a few essays in prose, *etc.* pp. vi. 176. *J. Hicklin & Co.: Nottingham,* 1835. 12°. **11646**. bb. **43**.

—— The Testimony of History to the Divine Inspiration of the Holy Scriptures; or, a Comparison between the prophecies and their historical fulfilment. pp. viii. 300. *Hamilton, Adams & Co.: London,* [1838.] 12°. **1115**. c. **15**.

BUTLER (William L.) How to Make Grocery Windows Pay. Edited by W. L. Butler. pp. vii. 198. *Progressive Grocer: New York,* [1932.] 8°. **8224**. v. **27**.

BUTLER (William Mill) *See* Congresses.—*International Commercial Congress.* Official Proceedings . . . 1899. (Edited by W. M. Butler.) 1899. 4°. Ac. **2501.**

BUTLER (William Orlando) *See* Blair (Francis P.) *the Elder.* The Life and Public Services of Gen. William O. Butler . . . With his letters and speeches on various subjects. [With a portrait.] 1848. 8°. **10882.** g. **20.**

—— *See* Cass (Lewis) Life of General Lewis Cass . . . To which is appended, a sketch of the public and private history of Major-General W. O. Butler, *etc.* [With a portrait.] 1848. 12°. **10881.** c. **9**

—— Speech . . . on the Proposition to restore the fine to Gen. Jackson. Delivered in the House of Representatives, January 11, 1843. pp. 16. [*Washington,* 1843.] 8°. **8177.** d. **11.**

BUTLER (Wilson) The Customs and Tenant-Right Tenures of the Northern Counties, with particulars of those in the district of Furness in the county of Lancashire, with notes on their enfranchisement under the Law of Property Act, 1922 . . . Being a dissertation, *etc.* pp. 30. *P. C. Dickinson & Sons: Millom,* 1925. 8°. **6305.** pp. **9.**

BUTLER-BOWDON (William Erdeswick Ignatius) *See* Bowdon.

BUTLERD (Fanni) Lettres de Mistriss Fanni Butlerd, à Milord Charles Alfred, duc de Caitombridge, écrites en 1735; traduites de l'Anglois en 1756, *etc.* [By M. J. Riccoboni.] pp. viii. 292. *Paris,* 1759. 12°. **244.** d. **15.**

—— Nouvelle édition. pp. viii. 292. *Paris,* 1759. 12°. **12512.** ccc. **29.** (**2.**)

BUTLER-JOHNSTONE (Henry Alexander Munro) *See* Johnstone.

BUTLER-JONES (Frank) *See* Jones.

BUTLER-JOYCE (Joan) *See* Joyce.

BUTLEROV (Aleksandr Mikhailovich)

—— *See* Claus (Carl) *Professor in Dorpat.* Fragment einer Monographie des Platins, *etc.* [Edited by A. M. Butlerov.] [1948?] 8°. **07106.** e. **45.**

—— *See* Goryainov (V.) and Butlerov (A. M.) Sur la condensation des hydro-carbures de la série éthylénique et la transformation de l'éthyléne en alcool éthylique, *etc.* 1873. 4°. [*Bulletin de l'Académie Impériale des Sciences de St.-Pétersbourg.* tom. 18.] Ac. **1125/44.**

—— *See* Gumilevsky (L. I.) Александр Михайлович Бутлеров, *etc.* [With portraits.] 1951. 8°. **10798.** a. **11.**

—— Избранные работы по органической химии. Редакция, статьи и примечания . . . Б. А. Казанского . . . А. Д. Петрова и Г. В. Быкова. [With portraits.] pp. 688. *Москва,* 1951. 8°. [*Классики науки.*] Ac. **1125/223.** (**14.**)

—— Сочинения. [With a portrait.] *Издательство Академии Наук СССР: Москва,* 1953– . 8°. W.P. c. **137.**

—— Химическое строеніе и "теорія замѣщенія," *etc.* [A reply to N. A. Menshutkin's "Изомеры углеводородовъ по теоріи замѣщенія."] pp. 34. *Санктпетербургъ,* 1885. 8°. [*Academia Scientiarum Imperialis. Записки Императорской Академіи Наукъ.* том. 50. прил. no. 2.] Ac. **1125/48.**

BUTLEROV (Aleksandr Mikhailovich)

—— Condensation des hydrocarbures de la série éthylénique. 2. Sur l'isodibutylène, l'une des variétés isomériques de l'octylène, *etc.* pp. 35. *St.-Pétersbourg,* 1876. 4°. [*Mémoires de l'Académie Impériale des Sciences de St.-Pétersbourg.* sér. 7. tom. 23. no. 4.] Ac. **1125/3.**

—— Condensation des hydrocarbures de la série éthylénique. 3. Sur l'isotributylène, *etc.* pp. 22. *St.-Pétersbourg,* 1879. 4°. [*Mémoires de l'Académie Impériale des Sciences de St.-Pétersbourg.* sér. 7. tom. 27. no. 3.] Ac. **1125/3.**

—— Sur l'oxydation du triméthylcarbinol et des alcools tertiaires en général, *etc.* pp. 7. *St.-Pétersbourg,* 1871. 4°. [*Mémoires de l'Académie Impériale des Sciences de St.-Pétersbourg.* sér. 7. tom. 17. no. 9.] Ac. **1125/3.**

—— Sur la structure chimique de quelques hydrocarbures non-saturés, *etc.* pp. 16. *St.-Pétersbourg,* 1870. 4°. [*Mémoires de l'Académie Impériale des Sciences de St.-Pétersbourg.* sér. 7. tom. 15. no. 7.] Ac. **1125/3.**

—— Sur les propriétés de l'acide triméthylacétique et sur ses dérivés, *etc.* pp. 17. *St.-Pétersbourg,* 1874. 4°. [*Mémoires de l'Académie Impéraile des Sciences de St.-Pétersbourg.* sér. 7. tom. 21. no. 7.] Ac. **1125/3.**

—— А. М. Бутлеров, 1828–1928. [A collection of articles in honour of A. M. Butlerov. With a portrait.] pp. 215. *Ленинград,* 1929. 8°. [*Очерки по истории знаний.* no. 5.] Ac. **1125/119.**

—— Документы, относящиеся к казанскому периоду жизни и деятельности А. М. Бутлерова. [With an introductory article by N. A. Figurovsky. With a portrait.] *In:* Научное наследство. том 2. pp. 11–82. 1951. 8°. Ac. **1125.** wbk/**3.**

BUTLERSBRIDGE. An Exact Account of the Taking of the Pass of Butlers'-Bridge, and of the Demolishing of Cavan. With the particulars of defeating the Irish forces at those places. In a letter from an officer at Belturbet, to a person of quality in London. *G. Goodman: London,* 1690. *s. sh.* fol. **816.** m. **23.** (**72.**)

BUTLER-SMYTHE (Albert Charles) *See* Smythe.

BUTLER-STONEY (T.) *See* Stoney.

BUTLERUS (Carolus) *See* Butler (Charles)

BUTLERUS (Thomas) *See* Butler.

BUTLEY.—*Butley Priory.*

—— The Register or Chronicle of Butley Priory, Suffolk, 1510–1535. Edited by A. G. Dickens, *etc.* [With a plan.] pp. xvi. 90. pl. iv. *Warren & Son: Winchester,* 1951. 8°. **4708.** d. **11.**

BUTLEY PRIORY. *See* Butley.

BUTLEY (John) For Our Country. A sermon preached . . . the 15th of June, 1748. Being a general meeting of the several Laudable Associations of Antigallicans. pp. 18. *Tho. Henderson: Greenwich; J. Millan: London,* 1748. 4°. **225.** i. **2.** (**29.**)

—— A Sermon preached in the Church of Greenwich . . . the 29th of May, 1754, before the Laudable Association of Antigallicans, established at Greenwich. pp. 24. *M. Cooper: London,* [1754.] 4°. **225.** i. **14.** (**15.**)

BUTLIN HOLIDAY BOOK. *See* PERIODICAL PUBLICATIONS.—*London.*

BUTLIN'S LTD.

—— [Brochures.] *London,* [1953– .] fol. W.P. D. **909**.

—— The Butlin Holiday Book. *See* PERIODICAL PUBLICATIONS.—*London.*

BUTLIN (CLAUDE MARTIN) White Sails Crowding. [The narrative of a voyage from Australia to England. With plates.] pp. 255. *Jonathan Cape: London,* 1935. 8°. **10496**. bb. **10**.

BUTLIN (DOROTHY MONTAGUE) Songs of the New Day, and other verses. pp. 20. *A. H. Stockwell: London,* [1933.] 8°. **011641**. de. **29**.

BUTLIN (F. M.) *Miss, of Chalfont St. Peter.* How Friar Juniper one Christmas Eve gave the Silver Bells from the Altar to a Poor Woman for Love of God. [In verse.] *E. R. House & Co.: Chalfont St. Peter,* [1931.] 16°. **11647**. b. **113**.

BUTLIN (F. M.) *Writer on Denmark.* Among the Danes . . . With twelve illustrations in colour by Ellen Wilkinson, *etc.* pp. xi. 278. *Methuen & Co.: London,* 1909. 8°. **10281**. ee. **16**.

BUTLIN (FRANCES MARIANNE)

—— Le Bateau et la bicyclette . . . Illustrated by Rosemary Trew. pp. 80. *George G. Harrap & Co.: London,* 1954. 8°. **012955**. a. **40**.

—— Le Français par les images. pp. 96. *J. M. Dent & Sons: London & Toronto,* 1928. 8°. **12951**. bb. **13**.

—— La Grammaire par les images. Avec exercices. pp. 143. *J. M. Dent & Sons: London,* 1932. 8°. **12951**. ff. **9**.

BUTLIN (*Sir* HENRY TRENTHAM) *Bart.*

—— *See* COOTE (Holmes) Abscess . . . Rewritten by H. T. Butlin. 1883. 8°. [HOLMES (*Timothy*) *A System of Surgery, etc.* vol. 1.] **07482**. k. **1**.

—— Diseases of the Tongue, *etc.* [With a bibliography.] pp. viii. 451. *Cassell & Co.: London,* 1885. 8°. [*Clinical Manuals.*] **07306**. df. **1/3**.

—— (New enlarged edition.) By H. T. Butlin . . . and Walter G. Spencer, *etc.* pp. xii. 475. *Cassell & Co.: London,* 1900. 8°. **07611**. g. **48**.

—— [Another edition.] Diseases of the Tongue. By Walter G. Spencer . . . and Stanford Cade . . . Being the third edition of Butlin's "Diseases of the Tongue," *etc.* pp. xvi. 561. pl. xx. *H. K. Lewis & Co.: London,* 1931. 8°. **2256**. f. **18**.

—— The Hunterian Oration for the year 1907 . . . On the Objects of Hunter's Life and the Manner in which he accomplished them. pp. 39. *Adlard & Son: London,* 1907. 8°. **7681**. b. **25**.

—— On Cancer of the Scrotum in Chimney-Sweeps and others. Three lectures . . . Reprinted . . . from the British Medical Journal, *etc.* pp. 56. *British Medical Association: London,* 1892. 8°. **7641**. bbb. **15**.

—— On Malignant Disease—Sarcoma and Carcinoma—of the Larynx. pp. 64. *J. & A. Churchill: London,* 1883. 8°. **7616**. b. **4**.

BUTLIN (*Sir* HENRY TRENTHAM) *Bart.*

—— On the Operative Surgery of Malignant Disease. pp. viii. 408. *J. & A. Churchill: London,* 1887. 8°. **7480**. f. **8**.

—— (Second edition.) By H. T. Butlin . . . with the co-operation of James Berry . . . W. Bruce Clarke . . . Alban Doran . . . Percy Furnivall . . . Walter Jessop . . . H. J. Waring, *etc.* pp. xii. 426. *J. & A. Churchill: London,* 1900. 8°. **07481**. h. **13**.

—— Sarcoma and Carcinoma. Their pathology, diagnosis, and treatment, *etc.* pp. viii. 202. pl. 4. *J. & A. Churchill: London,* 1882. 8°. **7641**. f. **13**.

—— Three Lectures on Unicellula Cancri, the Parasite of Cancer . . . Edited by R. H. Paramore. pp. x. 98. *H. K. Lewis: London,* 1912. 8°. **7630**. de. **54**.

BUTLIN (JAMES THOMAS) *See* BIBLE.—*Galatians.* [*English.*] A Letter to the Churches of Galatia. [Translated by J. T. Butlin.] 1875. 8°. **3051**. aaa. **17**.

—— A Handbook of Divine Healing, *etc.* pp. 143. *Marshall Bros.: London,* [1920.] 8°. **7409**. aaaa. **8**.

BUTLIN (JOHN FRANCIS) New and Complete Examination Guide and Introduction to the Law for the use of articled clerks and those who contemplate entering the legal profession, *etc.* pp. xxv. 592. *Stevens & Sons: London,* 1877. 8°. **6146**. ff. **9**.

BUTLIN (JOHN ROSE) Men of Action and Men of Thought. A lecture, *etc.* pp. 22. *L. Booth: London,* 1861. 8°. **8407**. ee. **25**. (2.)

—— The Sabbath Made for Man; or, Defence of the Crystal Palace. pp. 16. *Saunders & Otley: London,* 1853. 8°. **4355**. e. **23**.

—— Strive and Wait; or, Passages in the life of Philip Marsham. pp. vi. 267. *William Freeman: London,* 1865. 8°. **12632**. g. **5**.

BUTLIN (KENNETH RUPERT) The Biochemical Activities of the Acetic Acid Bacteria. pp. iv. 47. *London,* 1936. 8°. [*Department of Scientific and Industrial Research. Chemistry Research. Special report.* no. 2.] B.S. **38**. **b/1**.

BUTLIN (NOEL G.)

—— Finding List of Canadian Railway Companies before 1915. Compiled by N. G. Butlin. pp. 31. *Library of the Bureau of Railway Economics: Washington; Baker Library: Boston,* 1953. 4°. **08235**. n. **28**.

BUTLIN (RAYMOND THOMAS)

—— *See* JAMES (Arthur L.) Linguaphone Conversational Course, English Phonetic transcription by A. Lloyd James and R. T. Butlin, *etc.* [1935?] 8°. **W.P.13705/5.(4.)**

BUTLIN (SYDNEY JAMES)

—— Australia Foots the Bill. War finance 1939–41. By S. J. Butlin . . . T. K. Critchley . . . R. B. McMillan . . . A. H. Tange. pp. xvi. 128. *Angus & Robertson: [Sydney,]* 1941. 8°. [*Economic Society, N.S.W., Library.* no. 1.] Ac. **2367**. b.

—— Foundations of the Australian Monetary System, 1788–1851. [With plates and a bibliography.] pp. xvi. 727. *Melbourne University Press: Carlton,* 1953. 8°. **08218**. bb. **11**.

BUTLIN (WILLIAM) Universal & Christian Brotherhood. A sermon preached on the anniversary of the Northampton Friendly Society, *etc.* pp. 16. *Cordeux & Sons: Northampton*, 1858. 8°. **4473.** f. **19.** (8.)
Not published.

BUTLIN (WILLIAM HEYGATE) £300 a Year from my Poultry. pp. 32. [1895.] 8°. **07291.** h. **7.** (7.)

BUTLLETÍ.

—— Butlletí de dialectología catalana. *See* BARCELONA.—*Institut d'Estudis Catalans.*

—— Butlletí de la Biblioteca de Catalunya. *See* BARCELONA.—*Institut d'Estudis Catalans.*—*Biblioteca de Catalunya.*

—— Butlletí dels Museus d'Art de Barcelona. *See* BARCELONA.—*Junta de Museus.*

BUTMAN (ARTHUR B.) Report on Trade Conditions in Mexico. pp. 23. *Washington*, 1908. 8°. [*U.S. Bureau of Manufactures. Special Agents Series.* no. 22.]
A.S. **130.**

—— Shoe and Leather Trade in Argentina, Chile, Peru, and Uruguay. pp. 72. *Washington*, 1910. 8°. [*U.S. Bureau of Manufactures. Special Agents Series.* no. 37.]
A.S. **130.**

—— Shoe and Leather Trade in Brazil, Venezuela, and Barbados. pp. 43. *Washington*, 1910. 8°. [*U.S. Bureau of Manufactures. Special Agents Series.* no. 41.]
A.S. **130.**

—— Shoe and Leather Trade in Cuba and Mexico. pp. 24. *Washington*, 1909. 8°. [*U.S. Bureau of Manufactures. Special Agents Series.* no. 33.] A.S. **130.**

BUTMI (GEORGY) *See* NILUS (S. A.) Les Protocols des Sages de Sion, *etc.* (Le texte adopté par Mgr Jouin dans l'édition des " Protocols " de Butmi.) 1934. 8°.
C.114.f.2.

BÜTNER (   ) [For the German surname of this form:] *See* BUETNER.

BUTNER (D. W.)

—— Mining Methods and Costs at the Highland Surprise Mine, Shoshone County, Idaho. pp. 11. [*Washington*,] 1950. 4°. [*U.S. Bureau of Mines. Information Circular.* no. 7560.] **A.S. 229/6.**

BÜTNERS (GEORGES) Lalweeſchu łauschu dseeſmas un singes . . . Latweeſchu tautai un wiņņas draugeem ſagahdatas no Latweeſchu draugu beedribas. pp. xii. 284. *Jelgawâ*, 1844. 8°. [*Lettisch-Literärische Gesellschaft. Magazin.* Bd. 8.] Ac. **9085.**

BUTNERUS (JOHANNES ERNESTUS) *See* BUETHNER (Johann E.)

BUTON (GIO.) **E COMPAGNIA.** Cenni sullo eucalyptus globulus, pubblicati per cura della ditta Gio. Buton e C°. Proprietà Rovinazzi in Bologna. pp. 7. *Bologna*, 1874. 8°. **7031.** h. **4.**

BUTOR (MICHEL)

—— *See* LUKÁCS (G. S.) Brève histoire de ~~la~~ littérature allemande, du XVIIIe siècle à nos jours. Traduit . . . par L. Goldmann et M. Butor. 1949. 8°. **11869.** d. **29.**

BUTORAC (PAVAO)

—— Boka Kotorska nakon pada mletačke republike do bečkoga kongresa, 1797–1815. 2 pt. pp. 230. 1938. *See* ZAGREB.—*Jugoslavenska Akademija Znanosti i Umjetnosti.* Rad, *etc.* knj. 264, 265. 1867, *etc.* 8°.
Ac. **741/2.**

BUTOT (   ) Plan d'une démocratie. Par M. P * *, Pasteur à * * [i.e. — Butot]. Seconde édition [of " Cours de morale fondé sur la nature de l'homme "]. Revue, corrigée et augmentée. 2 tom. 1793. 8°. *See* P * *, *M., Pasteur à* * *. **8009.** e. **13.**

BUTOT (ALFRED)

—— De la consommation et du commerce du vin en Normandie, particulièrement en Basse-Normandie et en Cotentin, pendant la guerre de Cent Ans, *etc.* pp. 115. *Paris*, [1938.] 8°. **08230.** a. **40.**

BUTOVICH (M.) *Illustrator.* *See* КОТОСНОК. А-а, коточок! Збірка пісень, казок і приповідок для маленьких дітей. З малюнками М. Бутовича. 1922. 8°.
20003. ff. **62.**

BUTOVICH (M. F.) Дядя Томъ или какъ жили негры-невольники въ Америкѣ. Повѣсть передѣланная съ англійскаго [of Mrs. H. E. B. Stowe] М. Ф. Бутовичемъ. pp. 96. *Санктпетербургъ*, 1867. 8°. **12705.** aaa. **23.**

BUTOVSKY (ALEKSANDR IVANOVICH) Опытъ о народномъ богатствѣ, или о началахъ политической экономіи. 3 том. *Санктпетербургъ*, 1847. 8°. **8207.** g. **18.**

BUTOVSKY (NIKOLAI DMITRIEVICH) Наши солдаты. Типы мирнаго и военнаго времени . . . Изданіе второе. Съ рисунками. pp. 347. *С.-Петербургъ*, 1901. 8°. **012589.** g. **82.**

—— Прежняя служба и настоящая. Очеркъ развитія солдатской школы. pp. 44. *С.-Петербургъ*, 1890. 8°.
08821. aa. **81.**

—— Сборникъ послѣднихъ статей. [On military subjects.] pp. 152. *С.-Петербургъ*, 1910. 8°. **012330.** h. **63.** (5.)

—— Статьи на современныя темы. pp. 91. *С.-Петербургъ*, 1907. 8°. **12352.** y. **1.**

BUTOVSKY (VIKTOR IVANOVICH) *See* MOSCOW.—*Художественно-Промышленный Музеумъ.* Histoire de l'Ornement Russe du Xe au XVIe siècle d'après les manuscrits. [With an introduction by V. I. Butovsky.] 1870. fol. **Tab.443.a.10.**

—— О приложеніи эстетическаго образованія въ промышлености въ Европѣ и въ Россіи въ особенности. pp. 55. *С.-Петербургъ*, 1870. 8°. **07807.** i. **7.** (4.)

BUTOVSKY (VLADIMIR DMITRIEVICH) *See* VORONOV (P.) and BUTOVSKY (V. D.) Исторія Лейбъ-Гвардіи Павловскаго полка, *etc.* 1875. 8°. **8833.** g. **6.**

BÜTOW. *See* BUETOW.

BÜTOW (   ) [For the German surname of this form:] *See* BUETOW.

BUTOW (ROBERT JOSEPH CHARLES)

—— Japan's Decision to surrender, *etc.* pp. xi. 259. *Stanford University Press: Stanford*, 1954. 8°. [*Hoover Library on War, Revolution, and Peace. Publication.* no. 24.]
Ac. **2692.** nf.

BUTRET (C. DE) *Baron.* Taille raisonnée des arbres fruitiers, et autres opérations relatives à leur culture . . . Vingtième édition, augmentée . . . Par un membre de la Société centrale d'Horticulture, *etc.* [The editor's preface signed: B. H.] pp. 148. pl. IV. *Paris,* [1860.] 12°. **7294. b. 12.**

BUTRICK (RICHARD P.)

—— *See* MARÍN (J.) [Orestes y Yo.] Orestes and I . . . Translated . . . by R. P. Butrick. 1940. 8°. **11729. aa. 4.**

BUTRIGARIIS (JACOBUS DE) *See* BUTRIGARIUS (J.)

BUTRIGARIUS (GALEATIUS) *See* EDEN (Richard) The Decades of the newe worlde or west India, *etc.* (A discourse . . . of the voyage to Cathay and East India by the north sea: and of certeyne secreates touchynge the same vyage, declared by the duke of Moscouie his ambassadoure to . . . Galeatius Butrigarius.) 1555. 4°. **C. 13. a. 8.**

—— —— 1577. 4°. **304. d. 10.**

—— —— 1861. 8°. [*HERBERSTEIN* (*S. von*) *Baron. Notes on Russia, etc.* vol. 2.] **Ac. 6172. (10.)**

—— —— 1885. 4°. [*ARBER* (*Edward*) *The First Three English Books on America, etc.*] **2374. h. 6.**

BUTRIGARIUS (HERCULES) *See* BOTTRIGARI (Ercole)

BUTRIGARIUS (JACOBUS) Iacobi Butrigarii De testibus. *See* TRACTATUS. Tractatus vniuersi juris, *etc.* tom. 4. 1584. fol. **499. f. 5.**

—— [Another edition.] Tractatus circa materiam testium. *See* GYMNICUS (J.) Tractatus de testibus, *etc.* 1596. 4°. **500. e. 2.**

—— Solennis tractatus de dote. *See* TRACTATUS. Primum (—decimum-septimum) volumen tractatuum ex variis iuris interpretibus collectorum, *etc.* vol. 6. 1549. fol. **5305. i.**

—— [Another edition.] *See* TRACTATUS. Tractatus vniuersi iuris, *etc.* tom. 9. 1584. fol. **499. g. 1.**

—— Tractatus breuissimus . . . de oppositione compromissi, ⁊ de eius forma. *See* TRACTATUS. Primum (—decimum-septimum) volumen tractatuum ex variis iuris interpretibus collectorum, *etc.* vol. 3. 1549. fol. **5305. i.**

—— [Another edition.] *See* TRACTATUS. Tractatus vniuersi iuris, *etc.* tom. 3. pt. 1. 1584. fol. **499. f. 3.**

—— Incipit tractatus . . . iacobi đ' butrigarijs sub cōpendio reductus ⁊ p aliquos positus in eius lectura. in. l. i. ff. si quis cautōbus de terminis sub diuerꝭ verboꝝ formis datis ⁊ assignatis .⁊c. *See* SOCINUS (Marianus) *the Elder. Begin.* [fol. 1 *recto:*] Aureus ⁊ solēpnis tractatus đ' instantia, *etc.* 1491. fol. **IC. 33025.**

—— Tractatus singularissimus renuntiationum iuris ciuilis que in contractibus appoponi [*sic*] solent. *See* TRACTATUS. Primum (—decimum-septimum) volumen tractatuum ex varii iuris interpretibus collectorum, *etc.* vol. 5. 1549. fol. **5305. i.**

—— [Another edition.] *See* TRACTATUS. Selecti tractatus iuris varii, *etc.* 1570. fol. **5306. f. 7.**

—— [Another edition.] *See* TRACTATUS. Tractatus vniuersi iuris, *etc.* tom. 6. pt. 2. 1584. fol. **499. f. 8.**

BUTRIGARIUS (JACOBUS)

—— [Another edition.] *See* FEYERABEND (S.) Corpus selectorum tractatuum de pignoribus et hypothecis, *etc.* 1586. fol. **5510. f. 5.**

—— [Another edition.] *See* MERCATURA. De mercatura decisiones, *etc.* 1621. fol. **499. c. 10.**

—— [Another edition.] *See* MERCATURA. Benevenuti Stracchæ . . . De mercatura . . . decisiones & tractatus varii, *etc.* pt. 1. 1669, *etc.* fol. **502. k. 11.**

BUTRIMOV (IVAN ALEKSANDROVICH) О шахматной игрѣ. [Част. 1 is preceded by: О происхожденіи игры въ шахматы. Сочиненіе Виланда, i.e. paraphrase of that part of Auszüge aus den Mélanges tirés d'une grande bibliothèque, *etc.* in Das Teutsche Merkur, 1781, Vierteljahr 1, founded on Fréret's' L'Origine du jeu des échecs.] (Frerets Abhandlung von Ursprunge des Schachspiels.) 2 част. *Санктпетербургъ,* 1821. 8°. **7915. d. 3.**

BUTRINTO, NICOLAUS, *Bishop of.* *See* NICOLAUS.

BUTRIO (ANTONIUS DE) *See* BELLINCINUS (B.) [fol. 2 *recto:*] De probationibus. ℞ica. *End.* [fol. 181 *recto:*] Finis apostillarū per dñm Bartholomeum de bellentzinis super dñi Abba. necnō dñi Anto. de bu. lecturas editarū, *etc.* 1477. fol. **IC. 20329. (2.)**

—— *See* ROME.—[*Emperors.*]—Justinian I., *Emperor of the East.* [527–565.] [*Corpus Juris Civilis.*] *Begin.* [fol. 2 *recto:*] Compendium ad omēs materias In Iure ciuili inueniendas, *etc.* [fol. 77 *verso:*] Incipiunt Textus et glose singulares et speciales domini bar. bal. ange. . . . antho. de butri. . . . Secundum ordinem librorum Iuris ciuilis, *etc.* [1480 ?] 4°. **IA. 42725.**

—— [Consilia.] *Begin.* [fol. 1 *recto* (table): De constitutionibus.] [fol. 8 *recto:*] De sepulturis. [C]Ichinus quidam subriga de parrochia sancte agnetis Ciuitatis Ferrarie, *etc.* *End.* [fol. 70 *recto:*] Finis Consiliorum eximii decretorum doctoris. domini Anthonii đ Butrio, *etc.* *Per Adā Rot: Rome,* xiii. mensis Augusti, 1472. fol. **IC. 17573.**

70 leaves, fol. 7 blank. Without signatures. Double columns, 50 lines to a column. Imperfect; wanting the first six leaves containing the table.

—— [Lectura super primo libro Decretalium.] *Begin.* [fol. 1 *recto:*] Incipit lectura excellentissimi vtriusq̧ iuris īterpretis dñi Anto. de butrio a titulo de tñsla prela. vsq̧ ad ti. de offi. dele. sup quibus titulis dñs Abbas nō scripsit. vel si scripsit reperire pōt nemo. [fol. 53 *recto:*] Secūda ps dñi Anthonij. sup ꝑmo decretaliū. Feliciter incipit. G.L. [*Johannes de Colonia & Johannes Manthen: Venice,* 1477 ?] fol. **IC. 20328.**

82 leaves, fol. 52 blank. Sig. a^{10} b^8 C^8 c^8 d^8 e^{10}; a–c^8 d^6. *Double columns, 58 lines to a column.*

—— [Another copy.] **IC. 20329.**

—— [Another edition.] *Begin.* [fol. 2 *recto:*] Incipit lectura excellētissimi vtriusq̧ iuris interp̄tis dñi Anto. de butrio a titulo de trāsla. prela. vsq̧. ad ti. de offi. dele., *etc.* G.L. *Antonij koberger labore:* [*Nuremberg,*] iij Kl's Februarij [30 Jan.], 1486. fol. **IC. 7339.**

68 leaves, the first and last blank. Without signatures. Double columns, 70 lines to a column. Without the blank first leaf.

—— [Another edition.] Sequit Rubrica de trāslatione ep̄i . . . inserta etiā lectura do. auto. d'butrio in Rubricis sequen. *See* TUDESCHIS (N. de) *Cardinal, etc. Begin.* [fol.1 *verso:*] Tituli primi libri. [fol. 2 *recto:*] gRegorius episcopus. Quoniaȝ omnis ratio, *etc.* lib. 1. 1488, *etc.* fol. **IB. 37303.**

BUTRIO (ANTONIUS DE)

—— [Another edition.] *See* TUDESCHIS (N. de) *Cardinal, etc.* Secunda pars cōmētariorum seu Lecture . . . in primum librū Decretaliū, *etc.* 1539. fol. **5051**. i. **6**.

—— [Lectura super quarto libro Decretalium.] *Begin.* [fol. 1 *recto*:] Tabula titulorum et capituloruȝ quarti libri decretaliuȝ sunt enim tituli .xxi. et capitula centum et .lxvi. [fol. 123 *verso*:] Finis lecture eximii domini Anthonii de butrio super quarto decretalium, *etc.* G.L. *per Iohannem reinardi & Paulum leenen: rome,* die ueneris uigesimasexta. mensis Augusti, 1474. fol. IC. **17713**.
124 leaves, without signatures. Double columns, 54 lines to a column.

—— [Repetitio capituli ' Vestri.'] *Begin.* [fol. 1 *recto*:] [V]Estra Hanc .al. repecii in studio florentīo, *etc. End.* [fol. 20 *verso*:] Explicit solemnis repetitio capituli Vestra Celeberimi [*sic*] iuris utriusq; doctoris Domini Antonii de butrio exemplata. ac sumpta de proprio exemplari originali ipsius d. Antonii, *etc.* *per Vgoneȝ Rugeriuȝ: Bononiae,* die decima quarta menssis [*sic*] Nouenb'is [*sic*], 1474. fol. IC. **28591**.
20 leaves, without signatures. Double columns, 56 lines to a column.

—— *Begin.* [fol. 2 *recto*:] Speculum de confessione. [C]Ompulsus equidem fui fratres carissimi, *etc.* FEW MS. NOTES. *per Hermannum Leuilapidem: Vincentie,* die mercurii ultima mensis ianuarii, 1476. 4°. C. **11**. a. **13**.
58 leaves, the first and last blank. Sig. a–e⁸ f–h⁶. *26 lines to a page. Without the blank leaves.*

—— *Begin.* [fol. 2 *recto*:] Speculum de confessione, *etc.* [fol. 27 *verso*:] Circa presens oppsculum [*sic*]. Speculū de confessione nuncupatum. quod cōpositum fuit per dominuȝ Anthoniū de Butrio . . . diligēter stude, *etc.* [fol. 29 *recto*:] Opusculū qd' speculū aureū aīe peccatricis inscribit˜. incipit feliciter. [fol. 44 *recto*:] Speculum aureum anime peccatricis. a quodaȝ cartusiense [i.e. Jacobus de Gruitroede] editum. finit feliciter, *etc.* [fol. 45 *recto*:] Incipit tractatus artis bñ moriendi perutilis. [fol. 55 *recto*:] Domini Hugonis primi cardinal' ordinis predicatoꝝ [i.e. Hugo de Sancto Charo] tractatus amantissimus qui speculum ecclesie inscribitur. Incipit feliciter. [fol. 63 *recto*:] Ad sanctissimum ⁊ beatissimū dominum. dominū Paulum secundum. pontificem maximū. liber incipit dictus speculū humane uite . . . editus a Rodorico zamorensi, *etc.* [fol. 155 *recto*:] Speculum conuersionis peccatorum magistri dionisii de leuwis alias rikel ordinis Cartusiensis. G.L. *per Ioannē de westfalia: Louanii,* [1480 ?] fol. IB. **49226**.
170 leaves, ff. 1, 28, 108, and 170 blank. Sig. a–c⁸ d⁴; e⁸ f⁸; g¹⁰; h⁸; i–n⁸ o⁶ p–t⁸ u⁶; x⁸ y⁸. *Double columns, 41 lines to a column. Without the last blank leaf.*

—— [Tractatus ad confitendum.] *Begin.* [fol. 2 *recto*:] Incipit tabula super tractatu seu directorio ad confitendum. Et primo de supbia et eius spetiebus, *etc.* [fol. 4 *recto*:] Incipit tractatus seu directorium ad fidenter et diligenter confitenda peccata compositus p dñm Antoniuȝ de butrio utriusq; iuris doctorē famosissimū. [*In domo Antonii et Raphaelis de Vulterris: Rome,* 1474 ?] 8°. IA. **17698**.
45 leaves, the first blank. Without signatures, 30 lines to a page. A different work from the " Speculum de confessione."

—— [Another edition.] Confessionale dñi Antonij de Butrio Vtriusq; Juris Doc. [fol. 2 *recto*:] Primo de supbia ⁊ eius spēbus effectibus, *etc.* G.L. *Per S. de Luere: in alma Venetiarum ciuitate,* 1508. 8°. **4061**. de. **5**.

BUTRIO (ANTONIUS DE)

—— Tractatus de notorio ex altissimis iurisprudentie adytis erutus, *etc.* *See* TRACTATUS. Primum (—decimum-septimum) volumen tractatuum ex variis iuris interpretibus collectorum. vol. 5. 1549. fol. **5305**. i.

—— [Another edition.] *See* TRACTATUS. Tractatus vniuersi iuris, *etc.* tom. 4. 1584. fol. **499**. f. **5**.

BUTRON (HERMENEGILDUS DE ROXAS JORDAN DE TORTOSA ET) *See* ROXAS JORDAN DE TORTOSA ET BUTRON.

BUTRÓN (JACINTO MORÁN DE) *See* MORÁN DE BUTRÓN.

BUTRÓN (JUAN DE) Discursos apologeticos, en que se defiende la ingenuidad del arte de la Pintura; que es liberal, de todos derechos, no inferior a las siete que comunmente se reciben. ff. 122. *L. Sanchez: Madrid,* 1626. 4°. **564**. a. **7**.
With an additional titlepage, engraved.

—— [Another copy.] **57**. c. **22**.
Imperfect ; wanting the engraved titlepage.

BUTRÓN MOXICA (CARLOS BENITO DE) *See* ORTEGA (J. A. de) Sermon Funeral, en las Exequias del M. R. P. Fr. Carlos Benito de Butron Moxica, *etc.* [1745.] 4°. **4985**. de. **3**. (**10**.)

BUTRÓN Y DE LA SERNA (EMILIO JOSÉ) La Gente de Mar. (Obra póstuma.) [Edited by A. Butrón y Linares.] pt. 1. pp. 347. *Cádiz,* 1900. 8°. **08805**. g. **60**.
No more published.

BUTRÓN Y LINARES (ANGEL) *See* BUTRÓN Y DE LA SERNA (E. J.) La Gente de Mar. [Edited by A. Butrón y Linares.] 1900. 8°. **08805**. g. **60**.

BUTRÓN Y MOXICA (JUAN ALONSO DE) *See* MOSCOSO Y CORDOVA (C. de) *Begin.* El Licenciado D. Christoual de Moscoso y Cordoua, Fiscal del Real Consejo de Indias. Con Don I. A. de Butron y Moxica, nieto y heredero del General Almirante Don Alonso de Moxica, y con los que haziendo confiança del truxeron su plata, oro . . . sin registro. 1634. fol. **1324**. i. **4**. (**19**.)

BUTRÓN Y MUXICA (JOSÉ ANTONIO) Harmonica Vida de Santa Teresa de Jesus, *etc.* [In verse.] pp. 672. *Madrid,* 1722. 4°. **011451**. eee. **8**.

BUTROTO. *See* BUTRINTO.

BUṬRUS 'ABD AL-MALIK.

—— *See* PRINCETON, *New Jersey.—Princeton University.—Library.* Descriptive Catalog of the Garrett Collection of Manuscripts in the Princeton University Library. By P. K. Hitti . . . Buṭrus 'Abd-al-Malik. 1938. 4°. **15017**. i. **2/5**.

BUTRUS GAALĪ (B. Y.)

—— The Arab League, 1945–1955. *Carnegie Endowment for International Peace: New York,* [1955.] 8°. [*International Conciliation.* no. 498.] Ac. **2297**. f.

BUṬRUS IBN MUHADDIB (ABU SHĀKIR) called IBN AL-RĀHIB. Chronicon orientale [originally written in Arabic by Buṭrus ibn al-Rāhib] nunc primùm Latinitate donatum ab Abrahamo Ecchellensi . . . Cui accessit eiusdem Supplementum historiæ orientalis. pp. 288. 1651. fol. *See* EASTERN CHRONICLE. **581**. l. **10**.

—— Nova editio. pp. 264. 1685. fol. [*Corpus byzantinæ historiæ.*] *See* EASTERN CHRONICLE. **197**. h. **8**.

—— [Another edition.] pp. 270. 1729. fol. [*Corpus byzantinæ historiæ.*] *See* EASTERN CHRONICLE. **804.i.2/11.**

—— [Another edition.] Chronicon Orientale edidit L. Cheikho. (Interpretationem olim ab Abrahamo Ecchellensi institutam tum a I. S. Assemanno revisam iterum ad fidem arabici textus recognovit P. L. Cheikho.) *Arab. & Lat.* 2 pt. *Beryti,* 1903. 8°. [*Corpus scriptorum christianorum orientalium.* Scriptores arabici. ser. 3. tom. 1.] **14005**. a.

BUṬRUS IBN MUHADDIB (ABU SHĀKIR) called IBN AL-RĀHIB.

—— The History of Alexander the Great. *Ethiop. & Eng. See* ALEXANDER, *the Great, King of Macedon. [Romances on the Life of Alexander.—English and Ethiopic.]* The Life and Exploits of Alexander the Great, *etc.* 1896. 8°. **754**. d. **1**.

BUṬRUS ṢUFAIYIR

—— *See* MARONITE CHURCH. Disciplina antiochena. Maroniti. (1.A. Textus iuris approbati. [Edited by Buṭrus Ṣufaiyir.]) 1933. 4°. *[Codificazione canonica orientale.* ser. 1. fasc. 12.] W.F. **5471**.

BUTRY (JUERGEN HAHN) *See* HAHN-BUTRY.

BUTRY (THEODORUS) De veteriore venaesectionis historia. Dissertatio inauguralis historico-medica, *etc.* pp. 32. *Berolini*, [1863.] 8°. **7385**. b. (**7**.)

BUTRYMOWICZ (BOGUSŁAW) Za słońcem. Poezye. pp. 182. *w Krakowie*, 1898. 16°. **011586**. ff. **39**.

BUTS (JOAN) An Account of the Tryal and Examination of Joan Buts, for being a Common Witch and Inchantress . . . at the Assizes holden for the Burrough of Southwark and County of Surrey, on Monday, March 27. 1682. *S. Gardener: London*, 1682. *s. sh.* fol. **515**. l. **2**. (**59**.)

BUTSCH (ALBERT FIDELIS) *See* KURZWEIL. Strassburger Räthselbuch . . . Neu herausgegeben von A. F. Butsch. 1876. 8°. **12201**. f. **2**.

—— *See* SCHALK. Die acht Schalkheiten . . . Herausgegeben von A. F. Butsch. 1873. 4°. **1853**. b. **5**.

—— Die Bücher-Ornamentik der Renaissance. Eine Auswahl stylvoller Titeleinfassungen, Initialen, Leisten, Vignetten und Druckerzeichen hervorragender italienischer, deutscher u. französischer Officinen aus der Zeit der Frührenaissance. (Die Bücherornamentik der Hoch- und Spätrenaissance.) Nach der eigenen Sammlung herausgegeben und erläutert von A. F. Butsch. 2 Tl. *Leipzig*, 1878, 81. 4°. K.T.C. **9**. b. **7**.

—— Ludwig Hohenwang kein Ulmer sondern ein Augsburger Buchdrucker . . . Mit einer Tafel. pp. 16. *München*, 1885. 8°. **11899**. h. **25**.

—— Waffenstücke, Rüstungen, Kunstwerke & Geräthschaften des Mittelalters und der Renaissance. In einer Auswahl der schönsten Stücke aus der . . . Sammlung des Particuliers J. M. Soyter. Mit fünfzig Original-Photographien und kurz erläuterndem Text. Herausgegeben von A. F. Butsch. pl. 50. *Augsburg*, 1871. fol. **1704**. c. **9**.

BUTSCH (FIDELIS) *Bookselling Firm.*

—— Catalog einer kostbaren Sammlung von Holztafeldrucken, Pergamentdrucken und anderen typographischen Seltenheiten, welche nebst einer namhaften Anzahl auserlesener Bücher aus allen Fächern am Montag den 3. Mai 1858 und folgende Tage bei Fidelis Butsch in Augsburg öffentlich versteigert werden. pp. 57. [*Augsburg*, 1858.] 8°. **011900**. h. **40**. (**2**.)

—— Catalog einer kostbaren Sammlung von xylographischen und typographischen Seltenheiten, welche in den Tagen von 3. bis 8. Mai 1858 bei Fidelis Butsch in Augsburg öffentlich versteigert worden sind. Preis-Liste. pp. 14. [*Augsburg*, 1858.] 8°. **011900**. h. **40**. (**3**.)

BUTSCHEK (WILHELM) Die Arbeitslosenversicherung. Probleme und Lösungen. Ihre Regelung in den einzelnen Staaten der Welt. pp. 116. *Brünn*, [1937.] 8°. **8288**. aaa. **8**.

BUTSCHKOW (HEINRICH) Die bandkeramischen Stilarten Mitteldeutschlands. [With plates.] pp. 218. *Halle*, 1935. 8°. [*Jahresschrift für die Vorgeschichte der sächsisch-thüringischen Länder.* Bd. 23.] **Ac.5470/2.**

BUTSCHKY (MATTHIAS) Collegii Adiaphoristici disputatio . . . de choreis et comœdiis, *etc.* *See* MEISNER (B.) Collegii Adiaphoristici . . . disputatio prima (—duodecima), *etc.* 1618. 4°. **697**. f. **29**.

—— [Another edition.] *See* MEISNER (B.) Collegii Adiaphoristici . . . disputatio prima (—duodecima), *etc.* 1620. 4°. **478**. b. **14**. (**22**.)

BUTSCHKY (SAMUEL) A—z! Sam: Butschky . . . Hóchdeutscher Schreiben und Réden, I. und II. Teil: mit der neuen Réchtsreibung; einem Anhange von Brifen . . . vermehrt, *etc.* 2 Tl. *In des Autoris Búchdrukkerey: Schweidniz*, 1654. 12°. **1207**. a. **30**.

—— Des 1630. Hunger- vnd Kummer-Jahrs Gedenckmahl. Das ist: Christliche Betrachtung, darinnen . . . gehandelt wird: I. Von dem täglichen Brod. II. Von Hunger vnd Hungersnoth in gemein. III. Von Armuth vnd Hunger frommer Christen vnd gottloser Armen. IV. Von der Theurung. Mit allerley denckwürdigen . . . Historien illustriret, *etc.* pp. 216. *In Verlegung des Authoris: Leipzig*, 1633. 4°. **3908**. e. **30**.

BÜTSCHLI ( ) [For the German surname of this form:] *See* BUETSCHLI.

BÜTSCHLY ( ) [For the German surname of this form:] *See* BUETSCHLY.

BUTSCHOWSKYJ (M.)

—— *See* BEDERLUNGER (J.) Investigaciones tecnológicas y roentgenográficas del hierro de Zapla. Por J. Bederlunger, M. Aznárez y M. Butschowskyj. 1954. 8°. [*Comunicaciones del Instituto Nacional de Investigación de las Ciencias Naturales.* Ciencias geológicas. tom. 1. no. 11.] Ac. **3084**. b/**5**.

BÜTSER (MATTHIAS) *Resp.* *See* REYHER (S.) Disputatio mathematica . . . de perpendiculo, cultellatione et chorobate, ac in specie de horologiis automatis, perpendiculo moderandis, *etc.* [1705.] 4°. **536**. e. **21**. (**6**.)

BUTSIUS (ADRIANUS) *See* BUT.

BUTSKOVSKY (NIKOLAI ANDREEVICH) О дѣятельности прокурорскаго надзора вслѣдствіе отдѣленія обвинительной власти отъ судебной. pp. 80. *Санктпетербургъ*, 1867. 8°. **5758**. bbb. **8**.

BUTSON (A. A. STRANGE) The Art of Washing. (Reprinted with additions from Cassell's Magazine.) pp. 87. *Griffith & Farran: London*, 1880. *obl.* 8°. **7944**. bb. **29**.

—— On the Leads, or, What the planets saw . . . With illustrations by the author. pp. 128. *Griffith & Farran: London*, 1880. 8°. **12809**. h. **7**.

BUTSON (CHRISTOPHER) **successively** ***Bishop of Clonfert* and *of Killaloe, Kilfenora, Clonfert and Kilmacduach.***

——] The Love of our Country, a prize poem, *etc.* *See* OXFORD.—*University of Oxford.* [*Prize Poems and Essays.*] Oxford Prize Poems, *etc.* 1807. 8°. **992**. f. **29**.

—— (Second edition.) *See* OXFORD.—*University of Oxford.* [*Prize Poems and Essays.*] Oxford Prize Poems, *etc.* 1807. 8°. **1347**. c. **23**.

—— (Fourth edition.) *See* OXFORD.—*University of Oxford.* [*Prize Poems and Essays.*] Oxford Prize Poems, *etc.* 1810. 8°. **8364.aa.67.(2.)**

—— (Sixth edition.) *See* OXFORD.—*University of Oxford.* [*Prize Poems and Essays.*] Oxford Prize Poems, *etc.* 1819. 8°. **1467**. c. **13**.

—— (Seventh edition.) *See* OXFORD.—*University of Oxford.* [*Prize Poems and Essays.*] Oxford Prize Poems, *etc.* 1826. 8°. **8364**. de. **6**.

—— [Another edition.] *See* OXFORD.—*University of Oxford.* [*Prize Poems and Essays.*] Oxford English Prize Poems. 1828. 12°. **11648**. cc. **7**.

—— [Another edition.] *See* OXFORD.—*University of Oxford.* [*Prize Poems and Essays.*] Oxford Prize Poems, *etc.* 1839. 8°. **732**. b. **4**.

—— A Sermon preached before . . . John, Duke of Bedford . . . President, and the members of the Association incorporated for discountenancing Vice and promoting the Knowledge and Practice of the Christian Religion . . . 9th April, 1807. pp. 58. *William Watson: Dublin*, 1807. 8°. **4475**. cc. **24**.